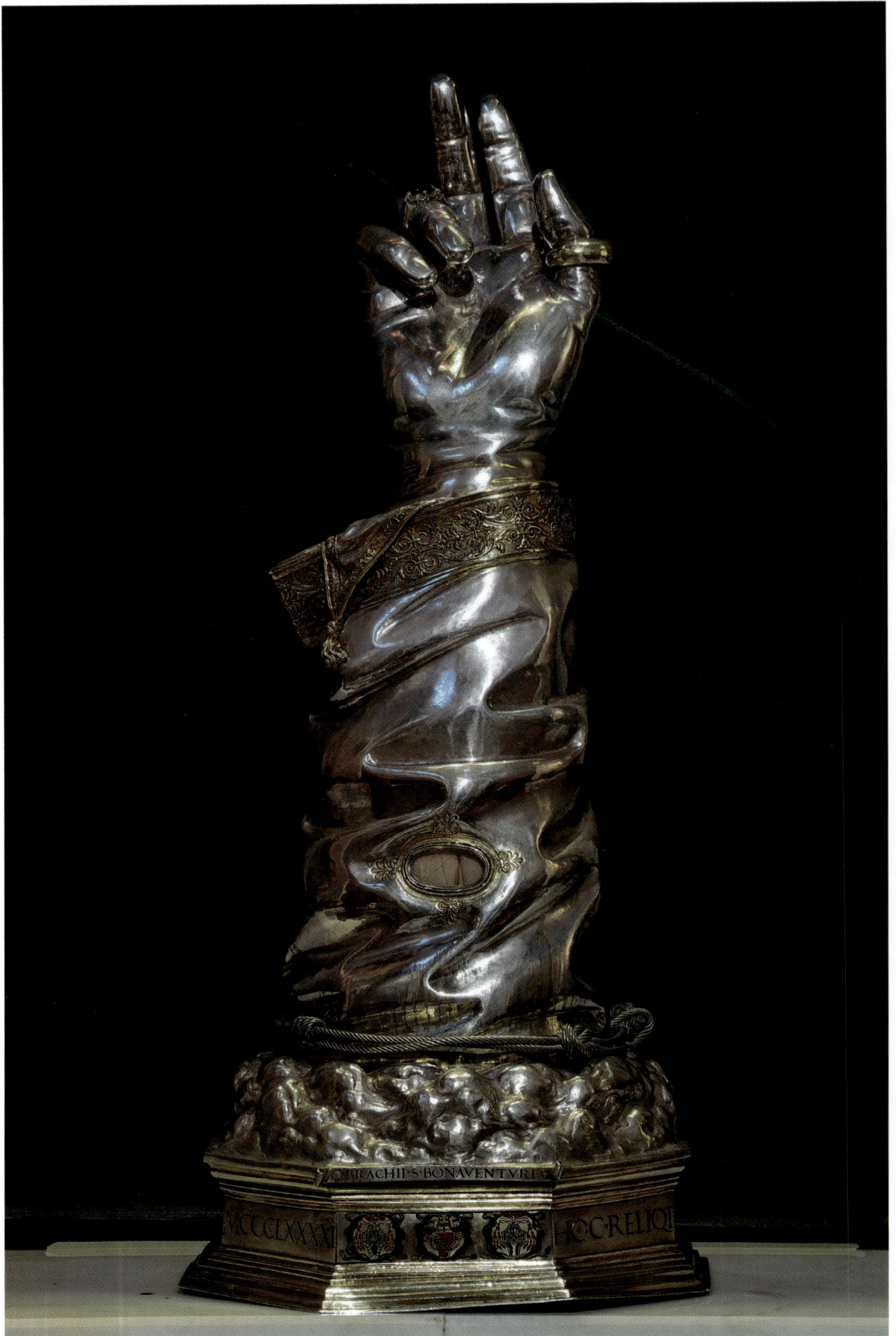

"IL SANTO BRACCHIO": the reliquary containing the bones of St. Bonaventure's right arm,
donated to the Convent of St. Francis of Assisi, Bagnoregio, by the Most. Rev. Francesco Sansone, Minister General,
May 1st, 1491 A. D.: Beaten Silver: conserved at the PARISH OF STS. NICHOLAS & BONAVENTURE, BAGNOREGIO, ITALY.

DOCTOR SERAPHICUS

ST. BONAVENTURE

CARDINAL BISHOP OF ALBANO

COMMENTARIES

ON THE FIRST BOOK OF SENTENCES

OF MASTER PETER LOMBARD

ARCHBISHOP OF PARIS

OPERA OMNIA: TOME I

ON THE ONE AND TRIUNE GOD

A Replica Translation, in English,
of the Critical Latin Edition, by the Quaracchi Fathers,
of 1882 A. D..

BY A FRANCISCAN BROTHER

With All accompanying Original
Prolegomena, Tabulae, Scholia and Footnotes,

Furnished with translations of
All the Variant Readings cited in the Original &

Enriched with *frequent* citation of
Scholastic terms in the Latin tongue

THE FRANCISCAN ARCHIVE
MANSFIELD, MASSACHUSETTS, USA

MMXIV

SERIES TITLE:	**Opera Omnia of St. Bonaventure**
VOL. NO.:	TOME I
FULL TITLE OF TOME 1:	**Commentaries on the First Book of Sentences**
SUBTITLE OF TOME 1:	ON THE ONE & TRIUNE GOD

AUTHOR: **Bonaventure of Bagnoregio, Saint (1217-1274).**
Minister General of the Friars Minor (1256-1273),
Master of the University of Paris (1257-1273),
Cardinal Bishop of Albano (1273-74),
Father of the Second Ecumenical Council of Lyons (1274),
Canonized by Pope Sixtus IV, on April 14, 1482,
Declared "Doctor of the Church", by Pope Sixtus V, on March 14, 1588.

ISBN: 978-0-9915269-0-1   FIRST EDITION: First Printing

TITLE OF ORIGINAL WORK: Doctoris Seraphici S. Bonaventurae S. R. E. Episcopi Cardinalis, Opera Omnia, iussu et auctoritate R.mi P. Bernardini a Portu Romatino, totius Ordinis Minorum S. P. Francisci Ministri Generalis, Edita studio et cura PP. Collegii a S. Bonaventura, ad plurimos codices mss. emendata, anecdotis aucta prolegomenis scholiis notisque illustrata, Tomus I, Ad Claras Aquas (Quaracchi), prope Florentiam, Ex Typographo Collegii S. Bonaventurae, MCCCLXXXII.

PUBLISHED BY:

The Franciscan Archive
A WWW Resource on St. Francis and Franciscanism
https://www.franciscan-archive.org

WORLD-WIDE DISTRIBUTION, MANAGED BY:

S.O.S.M., INC.   *For information on how to acquire a copy of this publication, go to:*
POB 123
Mansfield, MA 02048   https://www.franciscan-archive.org/bonaventure.html
USA

FRONT COVER OF JACKET (at Center): ST. BONAVENTURE GIVES COUNSEL TO POPE GREGORY X DURING THE SECOND ECU-MENICAL COUNCIL OF LYONS: *Bas relief* in metal: from the south side of the pedestal of the Statue of St. Bonaventure, Piazza di Sant'Agostino, Bagnoregio, Italy. (Photo by STUDIO GSG FOTO & VIDEO snc, Bagnoregio)

BACK COVER OF JACKET (in the Logo of the Publisher): A CONVENTUAL FRANCISCAN FRIAR COPIES A BOOK: An etching based upon a 15th century miniature: *La Croix*, Paris, France, c. 1880 A.D.; which appeared in William Blades, PENTATEUCH OF PRINTING WITH A CHAPTER ON JUDGES, A.C.M. McCLVRG & Co., Chicago, 1891.. Electronic image courtesy of http://www.fromoldbooks.org.

Printed in India by Saurabh Printers Pvt. Ltd. (www.thesakugroup.com)

TABLE OF CONTENTS

OPERA OMNIA OF ST. BONAVENTURE, TOME I

ON THE FIRST BOOK OF SENTENCES

Gloria Patri et Filio et Spiritui sancto,

sicut erat in principio et nunc et semper

et in saecula saeculorum. Amen.

INTRODUCTION

To the First Tome of St. Bonaventure's *Opera Omnia*

The most recent critical edition of St. Bonaventure's *Opera Omnia*, or collected works, was prepared and published by the Quaracchi Fathers of the *Collegio di San Bonaventura*, near Florence, Italy, from 1882 to 1902 A. D.. That edition was in 10 volumes or tomes, the first four of which contained the Seraphic Doctor's *opus maximum*: his *Commentaria in Quatuor Libros Sententiarum*. These were published in the years 1882, 1885, 1887 and 1889, respectively. For the utility of the edition, the Quaracchi Fathers also included, therein, a critical edition of Master Peter Lombard's, *Quatuor Libros Sententiarum*, distributing the text, Distinction by Distinction, among the Commentaries of the sage of Bagnoregio.

This present work, now, is a *replica translation* in English of the first tome of that OPERA OMNIA S. BONAVENTURAE.[1] By a *replica translation* there is intended to be signified a translation which presents in English everything which is contained in the Latin text of the original edition by the Quaracchi Fathers, such that every citation to the Latin edition corresponds exactly to the same page, column, paragraph and footnote of this English translation. This includes all the critical apparatus and the scholia by the Quaracchi editors.

This English translation has been undertaken to open up to a new generation of students and professors, the profound riches and treasures contained in Bonaventure's great summa of theology, which, heretofore, has never been translated in its entirety into any modern language.[2]

Written most likely from 1250 to 1252 A. D., at Paris, St. Bonaventure's COMMENTARIES ON THE FIRST BOOK OF THE SENTENCES of Master Peter Lombard was intended to be a complete commentary on Lombard's FIRST BOOK, which expounded the Mystery of the Most Holy Trinity according to the sentences of the Fathers of the Church. As such, St. Bonaventure wrote with the purpose of demonstrating his own theological preparation, in view of obtaining the academic degree of *magister sacrae doctrinae* at the University of Paris, which degree was officially conferred upon him on August 12, 1257.

Since the Quaracchi Fathers, in their *General Preface* to the *Opera Omnia* (see below, pp. I-XXXVIII) and in their *Prolegomena* to Bonaventure's COMMENTARIA (pp. LV to LXXV), have already said much regarding the Seraphic Doctor and his *opus*, let it suffice to say, here, something in general about St. Bonaventure and the work, which might serve to help the reader to better put in historical context what is presented, here, in English translation.

---

[1] The complete title of which can be found on the inside of the title page of the present work.

[2] The criteria employed in this translation are expounded in the Translator's Preface below (cf. pp. E-9 ff.). Members of the *Centro Studi Bonaventuriani*, in conjuction with the publisher, Città Nuova, have published Italian translations of nearly all the other works of the Seraphic Doctor (1990-present); a similar achievement has been accomplished over the years by scholars affiliated with the University of St. Bonaventure, Elmira, NY.

A Brief Biography of St. Bonaventure of Bagnoregio[3]

St. Bonaventure was born, most likely, in 1217 A. D. at *Balneo Regis*, a borgo in northernmost Latium, on the confines of Tuscany, about a day's walk south of Orvieto. His home town, today, is known by the name, *Cività di Bagnoregio*, and is situated on a lone rocky mount rising above a marvelous and ruggy valley of eroding volcanic tufa.[4] His parents were *Giovanni di Fidanza*, the town doctor, and Maria di Ritello. He grew up in a small home on the western side of the mount, about a stone's throw from the Cathedral. Today, there remains but the basement of the family home, the rest being lost to the inexorable erosion, which has chipped away at the city's mount since the Renaissance.

At his Baptism he was given the name of his father, *Giovanni*. He would have had his earliest education at the Cathedral School, though the brilliant clarity of his Latinity seems to indicate that he might have been privileged upon his father's purse to the services of private tutors. At the age of 17 or 18, Giovanni was sent by his father to the University of Paris to obtain the very best education that could be offered in that age. From his COMMENTARIES on Lombard one can infer that he may have seriously considered the study of Medicine as his profession, since he shows a very good familiarity with *Abu ali al-Husayn ibn Abd Alla ibn Sina's* (980-1037),[5] CANONS OF MEDICINE, and with the details of the state of medical science in his day.

We know, from his own testimony, however, that at Paris he studied under the English master, *Alexander of Hales*, who had returned to Paris in 1231; and that by the age of 26 he had already obtained the degree, *magister in artibus*. After Master Alexander and other famous Parisian masters, such as Adam of Marsh, William of York, and Richard Rufus, joined the Order of Friars Minor, the young Giovanni di Fidanza followed suit in 1243. On this occasion, he took the name, *Bonaventura*. He would later write, that he had done this out of gratitude to St. Francis of Assisi, to whose intercession his own miraculous cure from a deadly childhood disease, was attributed by his mother, Maria.[6] "Bonaventura", in Italian, means "good outcome".

He studied theology under Alexander of Hales up until 1245 A. D., when the latter passed from this life. He was ordained a priest, probably in 1244. After 1245, he studied under Odo Rigaud, the future Archbishop of Rouen, and then under William of Meliton.[7] During these years he familiarized himself with the teachings of other non-Franciscan masters, such as William of Auvergne, Phillip the Chancellor, William of Auxerre, Robert Grosseteste, and the Dominican Hugo of Saint-Cher. He also made the acquaintance of his fellow student, the future saint, Thomas Aquinas, who had become a son of St. Dominic in 1243 A. D..

In 1248, Bonaventure obtained the degree of *baccalaureatus biblicus* and began to teach biblical commentary, with the explicit and extraordinary permission of the

---

[3] The principal source of the information, contained in following short biography, is the article by Costanzo Cargnoni, *Vita e cronologia di san Bonaventura da Bagnoregio*, DIZIONARIO BONAVENTURIANO, a cura di Ernesto Caroli, Editrici Francescane, Padova, 2008, pages 67-87. Cf. also, Pietro Maranesi, *Opere di San Bonaventura*, ibid., pp. 89-107.

[4] Which he, perhaps, recalls to memory, when in Book I, d. 40, a. 2, q. 1, in reply to nn. 1-3, p. 707-8, he cited St. Severinus Boethius' observation about the advantages of a like situation.

[5] Known in the West, more commonly, by the name of *Avicenna*.

[6] Cf. St. Bonaventure's, OPERA OMNIA, tome VIII, *Legenda maior*, p. 505, n. 3 and *Legenda minor*, p. 579, lectio octava.

[7] On the name, William of Meliton, cf. the Translator's footnote, below, on p. LVIII.

Minister General of his order, Giovanni di Parma. In 1250-1251, as a *baccalaureatus sententiarius* he began to comment publically on the SENTENTIAE of Lombard, and did so in this order: Book I, Book IV, Book II, and Book III. His express intention in writing his COMMENTARIES was to follow in the footsteps of the Fathers and of his master, Alexander.[8] In doing so, he often opposed the nominalism of Richard of Cornwall.

In 1253, he completed the requirements for the degree of *magister sacrae doctrine* with the publication of his own, QUAESTIONES DISPUTATAE DE SCIENTIA CHRISTI.[9] Bonaventure was awarded this degree, however, only on August 12, 1257, on account of the opposition by the other masters of Paris, to the prospect of having, at once, two Franciscans among their number: William of Meliton and Bonaventure of Bagnoregio.

By reason of his celebrated defense of the Mendicants against the calumnies launched by those secular masters at the University who considered them a threat to their dominant role therein, Bonaventure was elected to the supreme office of his order, as *Minister general*, by the extraordinary General Chapter, celebrated at the Convent of Ara Coeli, at Rome, in the presence of Pope Alexander IV, on February 2, 1257.

As Minister general he worked for 17 years to extirpate the Joachimists from the Order, systemize the legislation of the community and clarify the significance of the evangelical life lived by their founder, St. Francis of Assisi. So lasting was the stability which he imparted to the fledgling and troubled order, that he was forever after named its co-founder. During his tenureship, he would travel from Italy to Oxford and back again, frequently visiting France, but not omitting Flanders, Germany and Spain.

In October of 1259, he wrote one of his most celebrated works, the ITINERARIUM MENTIS IN DEUM, while on retreat on Mount La Verna, in north-eastern Tuscany. In 1263, he completed his biography of St. Francis, the *Legenda maior*, called such because it was required reading for the formation of new members of the Order.

On February 5, 1265 he assisted at the coronation of Pope Clement IV, who so esteemed him for his talents, that on November 24 of the same year, he nominated Bonaventure as Archbishop of York, England; an honor which the future saint refused for humility sake, upon receiving the papal bull, at Paris.

From March 6, 1267 to April 17 of the same year, he gave his COLLATIONES DE DECEM PRAECEPTIS at Paris, and toward the end of that year publically criticized Averroism and the philosophical positions of Siger of Brabant. In the year which followed, he denounced several errors which would be listed in the famous denunciation made by the Bishop of Paris on December 10, 1270.

During the General Chapter of May, 12, 1269, held at Assisi, Italy, he recommanded the friars to participate in the Crusade organized by Pope Clement IV against Michael Paleologus and formally approved the Marian devotion of the daily recitation of the *Angelus* in honor of the Incarnation of Our Lord.

In 1270, Bonaventure published his most famous polemical work, the APOLOGIA PAUPERUM, a detailed theological exposition of the Scriptural doctrine of the evangelical counsels, as they were taught and lived by Our Lord Jesus Christ, observed by St. Francis of Assisi and contained in the Rule of St. Francis. He wrote this work to combat the calumnies advanced by Gerard of Abbéville and Nicolas of Lisieux.

---

[8] As St. Bonaventure testifies in the Preface to Book II: *Opera Omnia*, tome II, Praelocutio, n. 1, p. 1.

[9] An argument, which in St. Bonaventure's theology lies at the very heart of the reason for his affirmation of the abolute universality of Christ's Magisterium, and which is more fully developed in Sent., Bk. III, chiefly in dd. 13-14.

On May 16, 1271, he was present in conclave at Pisa for the election of Pope Gregory X, who charged him with assisting in the preparation of the Second Ecumenical Council of Lyons, for the reunion of the Greek schismatics.

From May 9, 1273 to the end of May of the same year, he preached at Paris his celebrated COLLATIONES IN HEXAËMERON, which contains the first systematic exposition of a theology of history, and which served as the matter of study of Fr. Joseph Ratzinger, the future Pope Benedict XVI. Yet, Bonaventure's work would remain unfinished, since on May 28, he received news that he had been named *Cardinal Bishop of Albano* by Pope Gregory X, by means of the bull, *A nostrae praemotionis*, which office he formally received, in Italy, at the castle of Santa Croce di Fagna al Mugello, near Florence, on July 15, 1273.

On September 14 of the same year, he set out, with Pope Gregory X, for Lyons, France, to prepare for the Ecumenical Council. On November 11 or 12, 1273, he was consecrated Bishop together with the dominican theologian, Bl. Peter of Tarentaise.

From November of that year, until May 7, 1274, he worked closely with Pope Gregory X for the preparation of the Council, who was so pleased with his efforts that he entrusted to him the presidency over the daily sessions. In the latter, he was assisted by two fellow Franciscans: Eudes Rigaud, Archbishop of Rouen, and Paolo di Segni, Bishop of Tripoli (Lebanon), and by the Dominicans, Bl. Peter of Tarentaise and St. Albertus Magnus.

On June 28, 1274, he had the joy to see the fourth session of the Council declare the reunion of the Greeks to the Catholic Church. During the papal mass on that day, he would give his final public sermon, for during the night of July 14-15, he passed from this life to the glory that he had so justly merited. Bl. Peter of Tarentaise preached the eulogy for his funeral, which was celebrated in the presence of the Pope. So moved was Gregory X at his passing, that he ordained that all Christendom should offer prayers for the repose of his soul. His mortal remains were interred at Lyons, and existed there, undisturbed, until 1562, when the Huguenots sacked his church and cast them into the Saône river.

Bonaventure of Bagnoregio was canonized by Pope Sixtus IV, on April 14, 1482, with the papal bull, *Superna caelestis patria*, and was named a co-primary doctor of the Church along with St. Thomas Aquinas, by Pope Sixtus V, on March 14, 1588, in the papal bull, *Triumphantis Hierusalem*. (Cf. here, below, pp. XXXIX et seq.).

His feast has been celebrated for centuries on July 14, on which night, still, at Bagnoregio, the reliquary containing bones of his right arm (see frontpiece) is borne in solemn procession through the city's streets.

The Importance of Bonaventure's COMMENTARIES on Lombard

Ever since their publication, the first copies of which date to the mid 13th century, St. Bonaventure's COMMENTARIA IN QUATUOR LIBROS SENTENTIARUM have been universally praised for their erudition, clarity, devotion and profundity. Since the Quaracchi editors in their Prolegomena, § 4, have already cited some of these, it remains useful, here, only to cite a few which are more important to our own age.

First, the importance of St. Bonaventure's contribution to Scholastic theology has been recognized by the highest authorities. Already, nearly a decade after the publi-

cation of Bonaventure's COMMENTARIA, Pope Clement IV, in his Apostolic Letters of Nov. 24, 1265 praised St. Bonaventure for the « eminentiam scientiae » contained in his Commentaries on the Third Book.[10] Popes Sixtus IV and Sixtus V[11] each praised him for his outstanding erudition; Popes Leo XIII,[12] John Paul II[13] and Benedict XVI[14] took occasion to recommend him as one of the primary Scholastic doctors. Pope Pius XII named him a « princeps » among theologians.[15] Sixtus V and Pius XI called him a great « luminary» for the Church.[16] So great was his authority, that his writings were employed at the Ecumenical Councils of Constance in 1417, of Florence in 1438, of Trent and of Vatican I in 1870.[17]

Composed as they were more than a decade before St. Thomas Aquinas would put pen to paper to begin his celebrated *Summa theologiae*, St. Bonaventure's COMMENTARIES hold, without doubt, the chief place among all works of Scholastic theology, after the *Summa theologiae* and *Scriptum super Sententias* of the Angelic Doctor. Yet, the importance of Bonaventure's COMMENTARIES lies in all that distinguishes them, in their own way, from the more famous work of the Angelic Doctor: their eloquence, their detail, their balance in theological reflection and their fidelity to theological tradition.

The Seraphic Doctor, who often cited the GRAMMATICAL INSTITUTIONS of Priscian, employed a very eloquent Latinity, which makes his COMMENTARIES eminently understandable and delightful in their theological expression; and, since, unlike the Angelic Doctor in his own *Summa theologiae*, St. Bonaventure did not intend them for beginners in theology, but for masters and students at the University of Paris, the profundity of their considerations and the exactness of their terminology serve to make them of perennial value for all who would acquire a detailed scientific and, yet, Scholastic understanding of theology. More importantly, however, unlike St. Thomas in his *Summa*, Bonaventure did not attempt in his COMMENTARIES an adequation or sub-positioning of theological discourse to the Aristotelian system, but holding to the teaching of the Fathers of the Church, he employed Aristotle only insofar as it assisted in resolving theological disputes, going so far as to show, on occasion, how the inadequate application of Aristotelian categories or distinctions lead to erroneous or not-so-apt theological conclusions. To this extent Bonaventure's methodology is more properly theological, as it does not constrain itself within a philosophical system born of a mind ignorant of those great revealed truths, which are at the foundations of Christian theology, but serves to demonstrate how the Scholastic method can be employed in a closer fidelity to and continuity with the Patristic tradition. Lastly, since Bonaventure's COMMENTARIES were written some years before St. Thomas' own two principal works, they are a very important testimony to the state of the question on a great number of theological problems which the Angelic Doctor would confront in each.

---

[10] Cf. *Opera Omnia*, tome X, p. 34, right column, 2nd paragraph.

[11] *Triumphantis Hierusalem*, March 14, 1588, §§ 3 & 10. The entire bull can be found below on pp. XLV ff..

[12] In his Encyclical letter, *Aeterni Paris*, August 4, 1879, n. 14, and in the audience he granted on Nov. 11, 1890, cited the *Opera Omnia*, tome X, p. 34, 4th paragraph.

[13] In his Encyclical letter, *Fides et Ratio*, September 14, 1988, n. 74.

[14] Cf. His discourse on the occasion of his pastoral visit to Bagnoregio, Sunday, September 6, 2009, which is available on the Vatican website.

[15] In his Encyclical letter, *Sacra Virginitas*, March 25, 1954, part I.

[16] The former in his Bull, *Triumphantis Hierusalem*, ibid., and the latter in his Encyclical Letter, *Rerum Orientalium*, Sept. 8, 1928, first paragraph.

[17] Cf. *Opera Omnia*, tome X, p. 37.

Finally, to have St. Bonaventure's COMMENTARIES, now, in English, will not only serve to help all better understand St. Bonaventure's genius and soberly appreciate the perennial validity of St. Thomas' work, but they will also serve to open to a new generation of theologians, in the English-speaking world, a large portal to that form of theological discourse which marks the classical age of the Scholastics at the University of Paris in the mid-13th century, an age in which Augustine and the Fathers reigned, and Aristotle and the philosophers merely assisted, in the elucidation and manifestation of the hidden treasures of Christian Faith. For this reason, this English translation will serve to renew Christian theology in the Patristic and Scholastic traditions, by assisting the voice of so eminent a Doctor to resound, once more, *in medio Ecclesiae*.

Thus, with the blessing and illumination of Christ Jesus, the Eternal Word, Light and Exemplar, may those who read these pages, profit therefrom for their own better understanding of the Faith and for the commencement, in the English-speaking world, of a new epoch in the academic science of Scholastic theology.

A Historical Note on the Quaracchi Edition of Bonaventure's OPERA OMNNIA

Seeing that the very existence of the study of Scholastic theology and philosophy according to the mind of St. Bonaventure was threatened to be extinguished from existence, on account of the confiscation and destruction of so many ecclesiastical institutions and libraries by the newly established KINGDOM OF ITALY, and in response to a desire in recent centuries for a critical edition of Bonaventure's works, the Most Reverend BERNARDINO DA PORTOGRUARO, Minister General of the FRATI MINORI RIFORMATI, shortly after 1874 A. D, commissioned Father FEDELE DA FANNA (baptized *Giorgio Maddalena*, b. 1838, d. 1881), to undertake the publication of such a work. To this purpose, after visiting more than 400 libraries throughout Europe, the latter founded the *Collegio di San Bonaventura*, in the old QUARACCHI Villa, outside Florence, to serve as an institute dedicated to the publication of the *Opera Omnia* of the Seraphic Doctor according to the exigencies of the new art of textual criticism.* The Fathers of this College, known collectively as the *Fathers* or *Editors Quaracchi*, represented the epitome of experts in Scholastic theology and philosophy in the Bonaventurian tradition of their day, and were highly skilled in the state of textual critique as it was then practiced. They employed a judicious set of critical rules, as they explain below in their *General Preface*, and produced a critical text of the Seraphic Doctor's authentic works which has lasting value today. While avoiding the vagaries and extremes of Rationalism which often plague such endeavors and stain them with untenable and unfounded conjectures, they strove to hold to the original sense and manner of expression with which the Seraphic Doctor had expressed himself in the entirety of his written works. After the great flood which inundated Florence and its environs at the beginning of the second half of the 20th century, the *Collegio* was moved to Grottaferrata, just outside of Rome. Today the *Collegio*, is located at Rome, at the Convent of Sant'Isidoro (Irish College). Those interested in acquiring a copy of the Quaracchi edition of Bonaventure's, *Commentaria in Quatuor Libros Sententiarum*, or of Lombard's, *Libri Sententiarum* should contact them through their website: www.fratiquaracchi.it.

---

* For a brief but illuminating introduction to this history, see Barbara Faes, *Padre Fedele da Fanna, OFM: Una vita di sacrificio e di lavoro per l'edizione dell'Opera Omnia di Bonaventura*, FRATE FRANCESCO, Anno 79-Nuova Serie: Aprile 2013, n. 1, pp. 139-149, which contains citations to original sources. For a copy of the Publication, write frate.francesco@iol.it.

PREFACE

TO THE ENGLISH TRANSLATION

I. Translator's Foreword

§ 1. *The Importance and Significance of this translation of Lombard's and Bonaventure's works.*

The publication of this English translation, is, I believe, of great import to the revival of the Return to the Texts Movement, which prevailed more than a century ago, and which at the present is rarely found in faculties of theology, dedicated, as many are, to the exclusive use of the historical method.

While the emphasis on a familiarity with the historical events and persons, significant to the development of the science of theology, is good, right and just for a proper understanding of the historical context of theological terms and questions; an all too exclusive use of the historical method in theology can lead to the degeneration of that science to such an extent, that its students become more worthy of a degree in the history of theology, than in the science of theology.

Yet, this august science, the queen of all other disciplines, as St. Thomas Aquinas teaches, is founded upon much more noble principles than those which historical methodologies can *ever* grasp or scrutinize, simply because they are intent, alone, upon temporal facts, events, and causes. For this reason, Bl. Pope Pius IX, in his Encyclical, *Qui Pluribus*, wisely pointed out that the very origin of the Christian Religion, placed it above the grasp of all methodologies which prescind from faith, when he said of It:

« *Our holy religion was not invented by human reason, but was most mercifully revealed by God: therefore, one can quite easily understand that the same religion acquires all its power from the authority of God who made the revelation, and that it can never be arrived at or perfected by human reason. In order not to be deceived and go astray in a matter of such great importance, human reason should indeed carefully investigate the fact of divine revelation. With this done, one would be definitely convinced that God has spoken and, therefore, would show Him rational obedience, as the Apostle wisely teaches* (Rom. 13:1).

« *For who can possibly not know, that all faith should be given to the words of God and that it is in the fullest agreement with reason itself to accept and strongly support doctrines which it has determined to have been revealed by God, Who can neither deceive nor be deceived?*

« *Moreover, how many wonderful and shining proofs are ready at hand to convince human reason in the clearest way, that the religion of Christ is divine and that "the whole principle of our doctrines has taken root from the Lord of the Heavens above" (St. John Chrysostom, Homily 1, "On Isaias"); therefore, nothing exists more definite, more settled or more holy than our Faith, which rests on the strongest foundations.*

« *This Faith which instructs for life and points towards salvation, which casts out all vices and is the fruitful mother and nurse of the virtues, has been established by the Birth, Life, Death, Resurrection, Wisdom, wonders and prophecies of Christ Jesus, its Divine Author and Perfecter!* ».

For this reason, an exclusive attention to historical questions, cannot but lead, among students of theology, to a woeful neglect of the formation of the rational faculties in the obedience of faith, and, as a result, to a much too frequent distancing in thought, between theologians of today and theologians of the past. This is but one of the sad consequences of the disintegration of Western culture, in which the notion of objective truth, especially in matters regarding religion, has faded, and this as a pragmatic effect of the religious schisms of the 16th century.

In contrast, the theology of Lombard and Bonaventure is an objective, rational science which studies God as He has revealed Himself through miracles and prophecies, testified to by human eye-witnesses, and explained by the holy Fathers and Doctors of the Church. Their theology is, therefore, in its very essence, a forensic science of analysis, which requires human testimony, and which builds upon this to lead the scientist-theologian to an objective and refined understanding of all that pertains to God and His creation. It is for this reason, that the return to the study of Master Peter Lombard's Four Book of Sentences is of

great importance for a renaissance in theology today, and under the guidance of such masters as St. Bonaventure of Bagnoregio, we can be sure of great profit, hailed as he has been by Popes Sixtus IV and Sixtus V as a most eminent theologian. (cf. below pp. XXXIX and XLV). In the writings of Lombard and Bonaventure, therefore, both theologian and student will find a rich mine of reasonings and an excellent gymnasium for the sanctification of reason by faith.

§ 2. *Recommendation to All Readers.*

For those reading St. Bonaventure's Commentary, I would offer this recommendation. Read first the corresponding Distinction from Lombard. This is especially helpful and necessary for modern readers, so as to put them in the context of the discussion which St. Bonaventure will undertake, which, to use a simile, is like a microscopic investigation of the details of Lombard's discussion.

§ 3. *Recommendation to All Instructors.*

For those teaching from St. Bonaventure's Commentary, I would not recommend the method to which I myself was subject: the mere summarization of the conclusions of the Seraphic Doctor. I would recommend rather, that the students have in hand, as a prerequisite, the great works of Scholastic theology, and that the manner of instructions require half the class to defend one side of each question, and the other half defend the other; wherein particular students would be assigned particular questions to lead the discussion, and the professor would sit as the judge and arbiter of the debate, using the texts of Thomas, Bonaventure and Lombard as their guide: vying among themselves to find and defend as much as is true and/or false in each opposing reasoning. I believe that such a method will teach the students to think in a most engaging manner, and result in a student who is fit to be a theologian of Holy Mother Church.

§ 4. *Translator's apologies.*

In conclusion: Since these English translations represent the work of myself only, all fault and deficiency in them is my own responsibility, and I ask your pardon. Like most large textual projects, despite the many hours of labor during the 12 years of their preparation, there may still be present various textual errors. I would cordially invite you to contact me directly, if you should find anything worthy of correction, addition, or emendation.

§ 5. *The Translator's gratitude.*

Finally, I wish to thank everyone who has helped me prepare and be able to prepare these translations in digitized and written form.

First, I wish to thank to Dr. Edward Dean Buckner, Ph.D. Philosophy, London, England, who through numerous correspondences encouraged and spurred me to write the *Rationale for the Translation of Peculiar Latin Terms*, which follows shortly. This is especially important for scholars, since in undertaking the work of the English translation, I have held more to the truth of the Scholastic terms than to the custom of philosophical terminology in the English speaking world, so that the thought of both Masters, Bonaventure and Lombard, might be opened up anew, apart from and without the baggage of the tradition of philosophical terminology in post-Reformation England. I have chosen this path, inspired by Dr. Etienne Gilson's remarks on the necessity of reading the great Scholastics in their own light, and of my own undergraduate training in Latin and Anthropology, which so emphasized the importance of conforming the mind of the researcher to the object of study, rather than to preconceptions.

Second, my gratitude to Drs. J. C. Klok, of Breda, Netherlands, who painstakingly read through the entire Latin text of Book I, and uncovered many hundreds of typographical errors, as well as transcriptional errors and errors of translation in the Latin and English texts.

Third, I wish also to thank in particular my benefactors in Italy, who enabled me to use a computer to begin the large part of this work; and Dr. Peter Felhner, O.F.M. Conv., former Rector of St. Anthony-on-the-Hudson Seminary, who first taught me the theology of the Seraphic Doctor, and whose exhortation to "*read Bonaventure*" was the guiding inspiration for me to undertake this work more than 12 years ago.

Fourth, I wish to thank Mrs. Helen Kansas, who, though a daughter of Israel, first taught me the tongue of the Romans at Satellite High School, Satellite Beach, Florida; and the faculty of the Department of Classical Studies at the University of Florida: Gainesville, my first alma mater.

Fifth, I owe a particular and important debt of gratitude to the Catholic philosopher, Dr. Peter Kreeft, and to the other faculty members of Our Lady of Grace Seminary, Boston, who taught me to think philosophically and who introduced me to Plato, Aristotle, and especially to the perennial doctor, St. Thomas Aquinas. It was among them, that I first read the works of Etienne Gilson and became convinced of the necessity "to return to the sources" for any authentic comprehension and restoration of Scholastic theology.

And, last, but not least, to my own family who have assisted me and housed me during much of the time of this work, at their own expense, and by whose charitable collaboration, this book was able to be, at last, published.

§ 3. *Translator's prayer for the reader.*

Finally, I pray, that your reading of these translations, be a rich source of intellectual light and a frequent occasion of prayer, so that with all the students of St. Bonaventure and Lombard, throughout the ages, you may attain to that Blessed Hope, to which they inspire.

THE TRANSLATOR

Rome
Vigil of St. Bonaventure, July 14, 2013 A. D.

II. The Ratio Interpretandi

Translatio autem fit propter duo: una ratio est propter similitudinem expressam, alia ratio est propter instructionem nostrum.[1]

God is Truth, and having created all according to His Eternal Word, He has fashioned all things in measure, number and reckoning. Thus has He made man capable of knowing the Truth and all truths contained in that Truth, with his own mind by the light of reason which He bestows upon him.

But since man, being composed of body and soul, is a rational creature which must communicate through sign and symbol, it is of necessity, both that he do so and that in doing so his very communication contain both an objective and subjective aspect, since no two men stand in the same shoes, no two men see the world from the same viewpoint and represent it exactly alike in the symbols of human expression, which are words.

For this reason, though human language can contain and attain to a proper and true expression of truth, nevertheless, the comprehension and expression of what another human has written or spoken is limited, especially when one can no longer speak or hold conversation with the author of the words.

Mindful of these truths, one must recognize that every translation is to some extent an interpretation; and at the same time no translation is of any value when that interpretation dominates. Indeed, the only utility of a translation is to make the author of the original text comprehensible to those who are not fluent in the language of the original. It is not and cannot be of any utility to anyone, if the translation attempts to obstruct that objective; just as no glass other than that which is crystal clear is of common value to human living.

Hence it is that, in this translation, it would be unauthentic if the English attempted to impose meaning upon the text, or impose more meaning upon the text than it contained, or subtract the meaning that was there. It would, furthermore, be incoherent if the English translation attempted to alter the linguistic context of the original, by attempting to interpret or replace the terms used by Lombard and Bonaventure with modern terms.

In this regard, though it is manifestly evident that English is another language, and that, since the time of the dissolution of the Catholic Church in England at the time of King Henry VIII, that English broke with the dominant Catholic culture of Europe of its day, and that subsequently there has been a long history in England of authors using terms in manners peculiar to spoken English, rather than Scholastic or Medieval Latin; nevertheless, it must remain the forum for scholars of history, philosophy and theology, to debate precisely the meaning of terms used by Lombard and Bonaventure, and, consequently, it must be recognized that a single translation, however, lengthy or precise according to its own rules, cannot resolve once and for all this debate.

For every author has the right to express himself in his own terms, and thus use words in his own peculiar manner, to a certain extent; and this is especially true and necessary in the recondite fields of philosophy and theology. More so, for authors such as Lombard and Bonaventure who lived more than 750 years ago, and who wrote and thought in a form of Latin which is no longer used, and barely understood, except

---

[1] St. Bonaventure, I. Sent, d. 27, p. II, a. sole, q. 4, in resp., pp. 489: Moreover, a translation is done for the sake of two (things): one reason is for the sake of an expressed similitude, the other reason is for the sake of our instruction. — Note, however, that in this passage, which I have accommodated for use here, the Seraphic Doctor is speaking of the transferal of analogical terms, in theology, to the Divinity. Yet, it's accommodation serves well, for a philosophy of translation, my own of which, I expound in this present essay.

in certain recondite circles of Catholic Theology and Philosophy.

The English reader, then, must take note. For in reading the present translations he must be disposed to leave aside, to a certain extent, his own preconceptions about what English terms should mean, and be ready and willing to accept what to him might seem to be new or novel meanings for some terms, which in fact are rather the non-vulgar senses of the English words which have now become obsolete for many English speakers, but which were drawn from the etymological roots of the same words and/or their cognates in Latin.

This English translation, therefore, is in this sense revolutionary. For just as Lombard and Bonaventure viewed all reality in the light of the Catholic Faith, which is the light of Christ Jesus, so they used their words and terms in the light of the way they were used by the authors of Sacred Scripture, by the Fathers of the Church, and by saintly and learned men who had lived before them. While admitting words can be used in differing and disparate senses, they nevertheless strove earnestly and zealously to bring to light the correct and proper understanding of things and terms by these lights, rather than by having the meaning of words imposed by those who, having been Catholic, had rejected Christ or His Church.

In a world that is at once post-Modern and post-Reformational, any attempt at the use of the English Language in this same manner will be at once, to some — and to many outside the centers of Catholic Thought, even if they be Catholic — both somewhat incomprehensible and somewhat reckless at best. Indeed, it is not a little obvious today, that there is as much a war for language, a war for words, as there is a war, but not only of words, against Christ and His Church, especially in the West. This war which began with the decline of Scholasticism and the rise of Nominalism, and was advanced by the Reformation, and which has been and is supported so intimately by Freemasonry today, is something for which the English translations of these two greatest of theologians, Master Peter Lombard, Archbishop of Paris (c. A. D. 1150), and St. Bonaventure of Bagnoregio, Master of the University of Paris (c. A.D. 1254), can be an effective tool in combating the enemies of Christ Jesus, which are also those of all that is humane and civil in the entire Western Civilization.

III. RATIONALE

FOR THE TRANSLATION OF PECULIAR LATIN TERMS

§ 1. *The necessity of this Rationale.*

Since English is manifestly very different from Latin, and since the modern reader has been formed, intellectually, to use words or terms differently than these two writers used them, I have prepared this *Rationale* for the sake of the added comprehension and appreciation of the Scholastic texts published here.

§ 2. *The utility of this Rationale.*

The utility of this Rationale, consists chiefly, in arranging in alphabetical order, various English expressions or terms, which I have employed to render various Latin expressions or terms. This is especially useful, to understand, why, so often in the text of the translations, I will cite the Latin within square brackets, immediately after the English employed for its translation. This was done for two reasons: (1) because, each author does not always use the same sense for each word, and hence, the English translation had to often use different words to render the same Latin term, since in English, the alternate senses of those Latin terms, are only expressed in different English words. And (2), when different Latin words are rendered in English, by the same English word, which just happens to embrace the senses of each Latin term.

§ 3. *The general rule for choice of English terms.*

I have used Cassel's (Funk and Collier editions) and Du Cange's (Favre, 1882-87) dictionaries, and on rare occasions, the online resources of the Perseus Project.

In choice of words, I have followed common usage; for technical terms of Scholastic theology and philosophy, I have preferred the use of the English cognates of the Latin terms, unless these were apt to lead to the implication of another sense. Otherwise, I rendered them into English according to their etymological meaning, since I found that this nearly always clarified and conveyed the precise sense of the Latin term(s).

For these reasons, the reader is due an explanation of the *Rationale* for the choices I employed in translating the texts. Which *Rationale*, though only partial, now follows:

Letter	English Term	Latin	Rationale for use of English term	Special Phrases
A			*Latin* in bold italics — **English** in bold	*Latin* in Italics, **English** Bold
	abstraction, **in the abstract,** **abstract(ed),** **withdrawn** **to remove,** **to withdraw,** **to abstract**	abstractio, in abstracto, abstractus abstrahere	**Abstraction** is a technical term of Medieval Logic for that form of expression which is composed in abstract terms, as in the saying: « Deity is superior to humanity » and « Generation presupposes existence ». It is opposed to **Concretion** (q. v.) In its root meaning *abstraho, -ere* means "to draw away", "to withdraw" "to remove", "to abstract". The sense must be rendered according to the context, "**to abstract**" in reference to logical acts, "**to withdraw**" or "**to remove**" or "**to draw away**" in reference to the alteration of meaning, signification, of propositions, or in other general senses, such as physical motion. — Likewise *abstractus, -a,-um* is rendered variously as "**abstract**", "**abstracted**", "**withdrawn**", "**removed**" etc., according to context: e.g. use "**abstracted**" rather than "**abstract**", when the noun modified is followed by a prepositional phrase such as « from its general sense » [*de sensu generali*].	*in abstracto:* **in the abstract**, when referring to the general manner of formulating a verbal or logical statement; **in an abstract (statement)**, when it refers to the use in an actual statement. *in abstractione:* **in abstraction**
	to accede *or* **befall** **to approach** *or* **accede** **accident**	accidere accedere accidens	The Latin verb, *accido, -ere*, means "to fall" or "to befall", from it there is derived the substantive, neuter participle, *accidens*, which is used for the ontological category, termed in English, as the "**accident**". Though the English language has a perfect cognate (i. e. "**accede**") for the Latin verb *accedere*, which means "to approach", it lacks one for the Latin verb *accidere*. However, since Master Peter Lombard equates the two verbs, in the context of a discussion of the accident, in Book III, d. 6, ch. 5, in this English translation, for fluency sake, the Latin verb *accidere* will be rendered in English, as "**to accede**" or "**to befall**", the Latin verb *accedere*, as "to approach" or "to accede", since in truth what *accidit* does in fact *accedit*, though the former Latin verb signifies, in addition, a certain lack of intentionality in the approach.	
	affection **affect**	affectio affectus	The Latin terms, *affectio* and *affectus*, are used equivocally by St. Bonaventure: either as the faculty of the soul, or its act or movement, though the Saint prefers the usage *affectus* to *affectio*, which properly is an act of the faculty. While English has the cognate, "**affect**", its usage is so rare, that it is often confused for a misspelling of "effect"; for that reason both Latin terms are to be translated as "**affection**", and only when necessary is the latter to be rendered "**affect**" when it is used as a technical term for the movement; in each case the Latin term will appear in brackets to indicate how the Seraphic Doctor is changing his usage. St. Bonaventure explains his usage of *affectus* in Sent., Bk. III, d. 29, a. sole, q. 6, in corp., thus: However, for the evidence of the reasons, which are adduced unto the contrary, it must be noted, that it happens that our "affection" [affectum] is accepted in a multiple manner... For sometimes "affection" is accepted for the passion, but sometimes for the movement, such that the affection-passion is said (to be) a certain fiery complacency [mulcebris complacentia], but the "affect" [affectus] as a movement is said (to be) a certain rational choice [rationalis eligentia]. — Moreover, the "affect" as a movement is accepted still in a twofold manner. For a certain one is the one elicited by charity, but a certain one the one commanded. The "affect" as elicited by charity is that by which one chooses for the other the Most High Good; but the "affect" as commanded, is that by which one chooses for another some temporal good, which has been ordered to the conservation of (his) nature.	
	assignation, **impression** **to assign,** **to impress**	assignatio assignare	The Latin term, *assignare*, can be rendered into English either in respect to a formative act or a logical act: It thus has two senses: 1) "**to impress**" something upon something else: e.g. « On the second impression of the image » [*De secunda assignatione imaginis*]. This sense is taken from the literal sense of the Latin verb, which means "to set a seal upon". In this manner it is be used to refer to the divinely determined location of the image, which is the thing created on account of the likeness with which God ordained it to be and have. 2) "**to assign**" something to something else, e.g. « In St. Augustine's theology, the image of God is assigned to the soul according to the reckoning of its three powers » [*In theologia S. Augustino imago Dei assignatur animae ratione potentiarum trium.*] In this manner it is used in regard to the rational determination by some human author of the locus of the image of the Trinity in a created thing.	

Letter	English Term	Latin	Rationale for use of English term	Special Phrases
B			*Latin* in bold italics — **English** in bold	*Latin* in Italics, **English** Bold
	'to be', 'being'; a being, being; of being, to be, of the act of being	esse ens, essendi	The Latin verb, **sum**, means "I am". Its present infinite is *esse* ("to be"), its present participle in medieval Latin is *ens, entis* ("being"). However, whereas in Latin the present infinite is also the gerund; in English the gerund is also the present participle. Finally, in Latin the gerundive is *essendus, -a, -um*. When the verb **sum** or any of its forms are used without reference to the category of being, ideally or really, they will be rendered into English with their normal equivalents without any special notation. **The ontological signification of *esse* and *ens*.** However, in medieval Scholastic philosophy the very act by which a thing exists, its **'to be'**, is rendered **esse**, and the general notion whereby a thing is what it is, is likewise its **esse**; but a individual thing which is, **a being**, is an **ens**; and yet, this present participle is also used as a supposit for the notion: **being**. Thus in respect to the terminology, there is an inherent equivocation in both languages; and in addition in medieval Scholasticism there is a further inherent equivocation regarding the terms for **being**. To make it quite clear to the reader, and to leave it to scholars to determine more exactly the meaning of the texts in Latin, the following method is employed throughout, to render these two Latin terms, in each of their senses into English, in an unequivocal manner: For clarity sake the real thing, which is always signified in Latin through the word **ens**, in the singular or plural, will be rendered in English as, **a/the being**, without quotes of any kind, in the singular with an article, or in the plural as **beings**; the act, **esse**, whereby a thing exists, will be rendered in English as **'to be'**, within single quotes; the general notion of being, when represented in Latin by **esse**, wherein it is used as a gerund, will be rendered in English as **'being'**, within single quotation marks, with or without the article, and rarely in the plural (cf. Sent. I, d. 23, a. 2, q. 2, 4. arg. ad opp. and ad 4.); and the general notion of being, when represented in Latin by **ens**, in the neuter single, will be rendered in English as **being**, without any article, and always in the singular. However, it must be noted that there is not always intended a notional distinction in the English translation by the diverse terms 'to be' and 'being', for some stylistic requirements of the English translation may at times require switching between these, as is done with other infinitives, used as gerunds. The gerundive **essendi**, which in Latin always is used in these texts for the act whereby a thing exists will be rendered **of being**, **for being** or **to be** according to the grammatical context. Finally, since it is the custom of this translation to indicate words used as terms, within double quotes; and since to do this, with the above English terms would make it difficult to discern 'being' or 'to be', when bracketed additionally with double quotes, when **esse** or **ens** are used in this manner they will not normally, be rendered into English, but will appear in the English text in their Latin forms, without quotes, but underlined, as is the custom in English for quoting Latin words.	*ratio essendi*: **reason to be, reason for being** or **reckoning of being**, in the sense of the act of being *ratio entis*: **reckoning of a being**, or **reason for the being**, or **reckoning of being**, in the general sense of being *esse primum*: **the first act of being** *esse secundum*: **the second act of being** *bene esse*: **'well-being'** *quid entis*: **something of a being** (a circumlocution generally used for substance) *non esse*: **'not being'** (in the sense of non-existing) *non-esse*: **'not-being'** (in the sense of the general notion of what is privative of being: the hyphenation of the Quaracchi Edition is to be retained) or **'not-to-be'** (in the sense of not existing) *non ens*: **a non-being** or **one not being** (in the sense of a 'being which is not') *non-ens*: **a non-being** (in the general notional sense: the hyphenation of the Quaracchi edition is to be retained) *in essendo*: **in being** (in the sense of the act) *privatio essendi*: **a privation of the act of being**

Letter	English Term	Latin	Rationale for use of English term	Special Phrases
C			*Latin* in bold italics — **English** in bold	*Latin* in Italics, **English** Bold
	the contents of a phrase **chance**	casuale casualis, -e	***Casuale*** is a technical term of Medieval Latin grammar for those words which follow a preposition, which, with the preposition, form the phrase which it introduces: e. g. in the sentence, « God The Father works through God the Son » [Deus Pater operator per Deum Filium], "through God the Son" [per Deum Filium] is a prepositional phrase, begun by the preposition "through" [per], in which phrase ***Deum Filium*** is the casuale of the phrase, that is, that word or name which is in the case [casus, -us] introduced by the preposition. In Latin ***casuale*** is the neuter singular of the adjective **casualis, -e,** (chance) because it is used as a substantive for ***nomen casuale*** (noun in the phrase) or ***verbum casuale*** [word in the phrase] which follows the preposition.	*circum suum casuale:* **about what accompanies it in its phrase** *suum casuale:* **the contents of its phrase**

	to cognize, cognition, cognizable, etc.	cognoscere, cognition, cognoscibilis etc.	The Latin verb, ***cognoscere,*** and its derivatives, which is very often translated into English by "to know", has the specific meaning among Scholastics of « to know in that manner in which a knower knows not through another but by means of its own power to know ».
			    It is therefore, a form of knowing distinct from scientific knowledge [scire, scientia], general knowledge [noscere, notitia],and thought [cogitare, cogitatio]; capable of being had by non-intellective powers, such as the senses [cf. St. Bonaventure's, Itinerarium mentis in Deum] and which does not preclude these other forms of knowing, so long as they originate through the power of the knower knowing the object known; though presupposing the presence of the object known to the knowing power, but not its being comprehended.
			    Since ***cognoscere*** has many cognates in English, to retain the standard usage of the Latin term(s), even the rarer forms of these such as **cognizable, cognizability, cognizant, cognizance, cognizing, cognition, cognitive** etc. must be employed.
			    Only rarely, outside of the context of manners of knowing, that is in passing remarks or idiomatic expressions, such as "to know" a person [cognoscere personam] can it be rendered as "**to know**", "**to recognize.**" The British English forms which use an -s- for the -z- are not used in this translation.
				cognoscere: **to cognize,** or **to recognize,** or **to know**
				
				cognoscibilis: **cognizable**
				
				cognoscibilitas: **cognizability**
				
				cognoscens: **cognizant** or **the one cognizing**
				
				cognitivus, -a, –um: **cognitive**
				
				cognoscitivus, -a, -um: **cognoscitive**
				
				cognitio: **the cognition,** or **the (act of) cognition,** or **the knowing**
				
				ad cognoscendum: **to cognize, know**

	concretion, in the concrete, **concrete, co-created**	concretio, in concreto concretus	**Concretion** is a technical term of Medieval Logic, in which a proposition is composed from concrete terms, as in the saying: « God generates a Son » or « Paul is a man from London » . It is opposed to **Abstraction** (q.v.).	*in concreto:* **in the concrete,** when it refers to the general manner of formulating a verbal or logical statement; **in a concrete (statement),** when it refers to the use in an actual statement. *in concretione:* **in concretion** *concretus, -a, -um:* **concrete** — in all senses; however, rarely as **co-created.**

Letter	English Term	Latin	Rationale for use of English term	Special Phrases
D			*Latin* in bold italics — **English** in bold	*Latin* in Italics, **English** Bold
	to define, to delimit	definire	The Latin verb, **definire**, in nearly all its forms is to be rendered in English normally by its cognate "to define". However, in the sense that a thing is defined by a place or in a place, the sense of the Latin **de-finire**, is that a thing bounds another, by confining it by boundaries, and thus in this usage **definire** in all its forms an derivatives is to be rendered by the English "**to delimit**" in all its forms and derivatives, even those which are not normally used in English.	*definitive*: **definitively** or in regard to dimensions and places **delimitively**
	to deign, to consider worthy **consideration of worthiness**	dignari, dignatio	The Latin verb, *dignari*, means "**to deign**", that is, "to consider another worthy". The Latin participle *dignatio* means properly the "act whereby the object is considered worthy", or "the act whereby the subject considers the object worthy", but that would be cumbersome to insert in every passage. It seems best rendered as a "**consideration of worthiness**" (cf. Sent., Bk. III, d. 2, a. 1, q. 2, 2nd opposed argument; compare, ibid., d. 6, a. 2, q. 3, in corp. p. 163). Hence *dignativus*, is to be rendered as "**considerative of the worthiness**", by a simple transferal of the -tive ending, transforming "consideration" to "considerative", if the reader will permit the neologism, "considerative", that is, "derived from or conducive of the consideration of something". Otherwise, it can be rendered as "born (out) of the consideration of" the recipient's "worth".	*dignativus, -a, -um*: **considerative of the worthiness**, *or* **born of the consideration of the worthiness**; only for brevity sake as **dignative**.
	deordination, act of being disordered, **disordering act of disordering**	deordinatio	Due to the use of the Latin participle form *-tio*, the verbal noun *deordinatio* must be rendered into English in a variety of verbal forms according to the context. As a technical term for that act whereby a thing is removed from its proper order, *deordinatio* will be rendered with its English cognate, **deordination**. Otherwise, when used for that relation of disorder, it will be rendered simply as **disorder**; when used in reference to the act whereby this disorder arises, **the (act of) disordering** or simply **disordering** in the active sense, and **the (act of) being disordered** in the passive sense; 'being disordered', when used in reference to this latter act, is an ontological state.	*ratio deordinandi*: **reason for being disordered** *ratio deordinationis*: **reckoning of disorder** *deordinare* (as transitive verb): **to disorder**; as intransitive verb **to cause disorder** *deordinatus, -a, -um*: **disordered**
	discretion	discretio	**Discretion**, in the common sense of the word, has the same sense in Latin and English. However the Latin *discretio*, has another sense, that is, "a division made by means of a dividing line" [*discrimen*]. In technical Scholastic terms, this second sense of discretion is distinguished from a **separation** and a **distinction**. A **distinction**, from the Latin *distinguere*, "to mark off", is any difference that does not suppose a division, nor a disparity. A **discretion** is a difference which supposes a division, but not necessarily a disparity. A **separation** is a difference which supposes a division and some disparity, at least in quality. Thus properly speaking the Divine Persons are distinct, not discrete nor separated; men are distinct and discrete and separate persons; and the members of the human body are distinct and discrete, but not separate according to their existence (Cf. especially Sent. Bk. I, d. 25, a. 1, q. 1, Scholium I, 1). In this regard it is useful to review what St. Bonaventure says regarding **separation**, **discretion** and **distinction**, in Sent. Bk. I, d. 24, notes on the text of Master Peter: Moreover, the reason for this is, that separation supposes a division, division a multiplicity, multiplicity a diversity, but diversity posits a distinction of form and/or of nature. And because among the divine there is an omnimodal unity of Nature, for that reason, since a diversity (of Nature) is not received, neither (are) any of those four. On the contrary discretion presupposes a distinction, distinction a plurality, plurality an otherness. But otherness is not only attained as much as regards form, but also as much as regards supposit; and because the Hypostases are many, for that reason the aforesaid four are received among the divine.	

Letter	English Term	Latin	Rationale for use of English term	Special Phrases
I			*Latin* in bold italics — **English** in bold	*Latin* in Italics, **English** Bold
	intellect, understand-ing, to understand, intelligence, understanding	intellectus, intelligere, intelligentia	The Latin term, ***intellectus***, can be two different words: a supine of the verb ***intelligere***, "to under-stand", i. e., **intellectus, -us**; and the adjective, meaning "**understood**": i. e., ***intellectus, -a, -um***. The adjective is easily translated, and will not be dis-cussed here. The supine has two different senses in English. 1) « the intellect »: the intellectual faculty of a rational being. The supine should be rendered by **intellect** only when there is an explicit reference to the intellectual faculty of a rational being. 2) « understanding »: an act of the intellect, or that which results from this act, namely the comprehen-sion of an intelligible being. In the former sense it can be rendered as **understanding**, or as **(act of) un-derstanding** » with or without an article; in the latter sense, that of the consequence of the act of the intellect, it is rendered always as **understanding**. However, the Latin verb **intelligere** is often used in as a gerund for the act of the intellectual faculty; thus it is it is rendered as **understanding**, or **(act of) understanding**. And the Latin noun, ***intelligentia***, is used in a twofold sense: for the intellectual faculty, **the intelligence**, and for the consequence of an act of this faculty, when reck-oned as something had, rather than a having, that is as knowledge; and thus is ren-dered as **understanding**. It is not always easy to understand the precise sense in which the supine is being used; whether as regards the faculty, or an act of the faculty or the result of an act of the faculty. A good example of this ambiguity in the use of the supine is found in St. Bonaven-ture's Commentary on Book I, d. 28.. There in Question 3, St. Bonaventure speaks of ***intellectu apprehendente***, and he explains this further in Dubium 1 of the same Dis-tinction. In that Dubium, it is not until the fourth paragraph of the Response, wherein St. Bonaventure writes: « ***Secundum hunc triplicem intellectum de comparatione Patris et Ingeniti*** » etc.. that it becomes clear that he is speaking not of the faculty, nor of its act, but of the consequence of an act of this faculty, namely an "**understanding**" of the terms in question.	*intellectus termini*: **the un-derstanding of a term** *intellectu*: frequently **as by understanding**, in the sense of a supine. *ad intelligentiam*: **for an un-derstanding**. *ad intelligendum*: **to under-stand**, or in the introduction to questions, **for an under-standing**.
	intention	intentio	The Latin term, ***intentio***, has two senses, based on its classical meaning of a "stretch-ing out or towards", or the "straining or stretching" of the mind. It has two technical senses which will both be rendered by its English cognate, **in-tention**: 1) the Logical: in this sense, intention is a technical term of Medieval Logic for the meaning of any term. 2) the Intellectual: in this sense, intention is a proposal of the mind to undertake or posit some act.	
	interemption	interemptio, interimere	**Interemption** is a technical term of Medieval Logic for that form of rebuttal which disproves the major and minor of the opposing argument: the use of the Latin term, ***interemptio***, is taken from St. Sev-erinus Boethius' translation of Aristotle's ELENCHAE. The Quaracchi Editors give this definition of **in-teremption**, tom. I, p. 87, footnote 4: Peter of Spain, SUMMULA., tract "*On sophistic Syl-logisms or on Fallacies*", at the end of the (discussion on) the fallacy of equivocation says: The right solu-tion is a manifestation of the false syllogism and that on account of which it is false. And this happens in a two fold manner, that is by distinguishing and/or by interemption; and in this second manner one must respond to everything sinning in the matter (i. e. the false propositions). Aristotle, ELENCHAE., Bk. II, ch. 3 (ch. 18), when proposing this twofold species of solution used the words *diairein* and *anairein*, which (St. Severinus) Boethius rendered in the Latin tongue by the words ***distinguere*** and ***interimere*** (i.e. to take away by negating).	*interimendo*: **by interemp-tion**, when referring to this form of rebuttal; **by denying**, when followed by a term for an argument or some part of an argument, as is *interimendo conclusionem*: **by denying the conclusion**. Nota Bene: in some uses *inter-imere* in any form of the verb, may retain its normal, non technical use, even speaking about forms or argument or classification; in such in-stances it is to be rendered as **to take away (by negating)** or **to deny**.

Letter	English Term	Latin	Rationale for use of English term	Special Phrases
J			*Latin* in bold italics — **English** in bold	*Latin* in Italics, **English** Bold
	judgement, decision	arbitrium	The Latin term, ***arbitrium***, means that whereby a thing is chosen, judged or decided. As such it can be rendered as choice, judgement or decision. Though, Neil Lewis in his article on Grosseteste, says: "Like most medieval thinkers Grosseteste typically uses the term 'free decision' (Liberum arbitrium) rather than 'free will' (libera voluntas). This notion involves a duality, the term 'free' pointing to the will and 'decision' to some kind of rational judgement."	*liberum arbitrium*: **free will** *libertas arbitrii*: **the liberty of judgement**, or **the liberty of decision** *arbitraria potestas*: **arbitrary power** *arbitratio*: **arbitration**

The proper distinction appears in this, that ***arbitrium*** refers to that whereby a thing is chosen, judged or decided, in deed, where as choice, judgement and decision, per se, are acts of the intellect distinguishing in an intellectual act between two or more beings or acts.

In addition, in English there is a long tradition of rendering ***liberum arbitrium*** as "**free will**" rather than as "free judgement", "free decision" or "free choice". This is seemingly because in Latin **libera voluntas** signifies properly in the real order ("a free will") rather than in the genus of qualities of power ("free will").

This tradition runs seemingly counter to that of the Scholastics, who as Master Peter Lombard indicates (Sent. II, d. 25, ch. 1) understood ***liberum arbitrium*** as the "**free judgement of the will**" [liberum de voluntate iudicium].

Yet, the tradition in English has its roots in Medieval Scholasticism, as is evidenced by what St. Bonaventure writes in Sent, Bk. I, d. 11, Doubt 4, p. 218:

Is likewise asked of this which he says: "not without Me and without My **judgement** [arbitrio] and (that) of the Father" etc.. It seems that he speaks badly, because he who has **judgement** [arbitrium] over anyone has dominion over him: therefore, it seems according to this, that the Holy Spirit is inferior to the Son. If you say, that "**judgement**" (here) means "**will**" [voluntatem]; this is nothing, because, similarly, since the one Will belongs to the Three, similarly the Son does not speak without the judgement of the Holy Spirit, and the Father similarly; because (the Will) is not said properly (of any one Person).

The Seraphic Doctor also uses the term **liberum arbitrium** in Sent. Bk. I, d. 17, p. II. a. sole, q. 3, in reply to nn. 1 and 2, p. 315, as a supposit for a free will (***libera voluntas***). This is seemingly because, being that the will is an active power, any genus of its acts is the same according to substance with the power itself.

Finally, that **arbitrium** pertains to the will, rather than the intellect, is taught by St. Augustine himself, as the Quaracchi Editors themselves note in Sent. Bk. II, d. 42, a. sole, q. 2, p. 748, footnote 8, where having cited Augustine's DE LIBERO ARBITRIO they write:

For speaking of sinful souls, (St.) Augustine says there (Bk. III, ch. 5, n. 16): "since such are still better than those, which, since they have no rational and free judgement of will, they cannot sin."

Indeed, according to St. Bonaventure, ***liberum arbitrium*** is properly not of the will alone, but, following St. Bernard, is a faculty of reason and will (Sent. II, d. 25, q. 4) and a habit of each (ibid., qq. 4 and 5.), though it is principally in the will (ibid., q. 5). Yet, according to the Seraphic Doctor, it ought rather be termed the "free judgement" than the "free will" (q. v., ibid, q. 6, in the body of the Response, at the end).

Thus, to walk along in the common tradition of Latin and English Scholasticism, ***liberum arbitrium*** will be rendered as "**free will**"; and to distinguish this from ***libera voluntas***, the latter will always be rendered with a definite or indefinite article ("a free will", "the free wills", etc.); even though this presents a small obstruction to the authentic understanding of thought of St. Bonaventure, if one does not keep these distinctions in mind.

Indeed, each expression, that in Latin and that in English, can be understood as a short hand for **the free judgement of the will**, in that the Latin **liberum arbitrium** can be understood as **liberum arbitrium (de voluntate)** and the English **free will** can be understood as **the free (judgement of the) will**.

Finally, by itself the term **arbitrium** will be rendered according to context, as either "**judgement**" or "**decision**"; "choice" being omitted because of its unduly generic signification in modern English.

Letter	English Term	Latin	Rationale for use of English term	Special Phrases
L			*Latin* in bold italics — **English** in bold	*Latin* in Italics, **English** Bold
	liable, liability	reus, -a, um reatus	While *reus* and *reatus* is often inaccurately translated in English as **guilty** and **guilt**, respectively, this English translation follows the precision of Master Peter Lombard, who in Book II, d. XXX, ch. 6 specifies that it is rather to be rendered **liable** and **liability**:	

While *reus* and *reatus* is often inaccurately translated in English as **guilty** and **guilt**, respectively, this English translation follows the precision of Master Peter Lombard, who in Book II, d. XXX, ch. 6 specifies that it is rather to be rendered **liable** and **liability**:

> For certain ones think, that original sin is the **liability for punishment** [reatum poenae] for the first sin of man, that is the debt and/or **liability** [obnoxietatem], by which we are **liable** [obnoxii] and doomed [addicti] to temporal and eternal punishment for the actual sin of the first man: because for that, as they say, eternal punishment is owed to all, unless they are liberated through grace.

Great difficulties and problems of interpretation have resulted in theology by rendering them thus, not the least of which is that of explaining how an infinitely just God can hold someone guilty of punishment, when he is only liable on account of the sin of Adam.

This interpretation of **reatus**, is supported by what Du Cange says in his Glossarium Mediae et Infimiae Latinitatis:

> ¶ 2. REATUS, *Crime*, according to Christian writers and more recent experts in law. These Budaeus castigates, with the approval of Vossius, De Vitiis sermonis, Bk. I, ch. 32, where he expounds *Reatus* through *the obligation for punishment*, so that between the crime and the punishment there is an intermediary *reatus*. According to the ancients, it was properly a habit and condition of the *reorum* or *accused*, as is rightly said De Lingua Latina Observationum, Bk. II, on this term.

This is confirmed by what the Quaracchi Editors say in on Sent., Bk. II, d. 35, a. 1, q. 1, Scholium II, n. 3, p. 824:

> But this fault more recent theologians, together with St. Augustine, call **the crime of the fault** [reatum culpae], to distinguish it from the actual fault. But the ancient Scholastics expressed each with the name of "fault" [culpae], but reserved the term *reatus* for **the liability for punishment** [reatu poenae] or **the obligation to sustain the punishment** (cf. below d. 42, Doubt 1).

On the other hand, guilt or the state of being guilty [**sons**, or **sceleratus**] or at fault, is a habitual quality in the moral order, respecting the sinner's deviation from order of justice, which quality arises from the fault and is distinguished from the deformity in the will, resulting from such a fault. Consequent to which quality, is an obligation or liability to sustain punishment on the part of the sinner. The knowledge that one has this quality, is called "remorse" by St. Bonaventure (cf. Sent., Bk. II, d. 36, a. 2, q. 1, in corp.).

This distinction becomes clearer when one considers that he who commits a mortal sin is both guilty and liable for eternal and temporal punishments; but he who is forgiven such a sin, is no longer guilty nor is he liable for the eternal punishment; yet, on account of an imperfect habit of charity, he might still be liable for some temporal punishment, even though he is no longer guilty of the sin itself. Likewise, he who does that, which he in no way knows to be a sin, inflicts upon himself the same moral deformity, formally speaking, according to habit, as if he did know this, and to some extent is liable for temporal punishment on that account; but he is not guilty of the sin and, consequently, senses no remorse.

| | **local, to/of a place** **placed, in a place** | localis, -e locatum, in loco | This Latin adjective, *localis*, *–e*, has the meaning of "*local*", "*of a place*"; thus, in constructions when combined with forms of the verb "to be" [esse], it has the sense of "belonging to a place" [esse locale; est localis]. | *localitas:* **quality of belonging to a place** *locabilitas:* **ability to belong to a place** *illocalitas:* **quality of not belonging to a place** |

This Latin adjective, *localis*, *–e*, has the meaning of "*local*", "*of a place*"; thus, in constructions when combined with forms of the verb "to be" [esse], it has the sense of "belonging to a place" [esse locale; est localis].

Thus does it seem best to render the adjective in regard to things being in a place; because in English to say that something is **local**, does not signify that it is in a place, per se, but rather that it pertains to a place or is native to a place; whereas to say "it belongs to a place" is to say both that it is "circumscribable to or by a place"; which sense *esse locale* has according to the Quaracchi Editors on Bonaventure's Commentary, Bk. I, d. 37, p. II, a. 1. q. 1, p. 652, fn. 2; and to say that it is under the laws of a place, that is governed by the conditions of a place, as St. Bonaventure says *esse locale* means loc. cit., p. 653, in the body of the Response.

Thus to distinguish the differing terms: *esse locale*, *locatum*, *in loco*, in English these are to be rendered respectively, with or without demonstrative adjectives, as « **to belong to a place** », « **the one placed** », and « **in a place** ».

Letter	English Term	Latin	Rationale for use of English term	Special Phrases
O			*Latin* in bold italics — **English** in bold	*Latin* in Italics, **English** Bold
	to order, to ordain **ordered, ordained, ordinate**	ordinare ordinatus	The Latin verb, *ordinare*, means "**to order**", "to put in order". Consequently its perfect passive participle or adjective *ordinatus* means properly "that which has been ordered" that is "placed in order"; and because in English we can also say that something has been "**ordained**" to another, that is "**or-dered**" to it, the Latin participle can also be rendered in this manner, and the verb likewise, that is as "**to ordain**". But since what has been ordered to another, is no longer out of an order, nor disordered, it is consequently, something "**ordinate**" [*ordina-tus*]. St. Bonaventure himself uses these allied	*ordinate*: **ordinately** or **in an ordinate manner**, when used in reference to the quality of the manner in which a thing is done or is; **in an ordered man-ner**, when referring to the order in which things are placed. *ordinate ad finem*: **in a manner ordained to (an/the) end**

senses of the term in Sent. Bk. I, d. 43, dubium 7, p. 778, where he speaks, first, of God's **ordained power** [potentia ordinata], and then contradistinguishes its manner of acting against what is done **inordinately** [inordinate]:

> I RESPOND: Some distinguish here God's Power in a twofold man-ner, saying, that God can either from (His) absolute Power, and thus He can save Judas and damn (St.) Peter; or (that He can) from (His) **or-dained** Power, and thus He cannot. — But this distinction does not seem to be fitting, because God can (do) nothing, which He cannot do **ordinately**. For to be able to do (something) **inordinately** is not a 'to be able', just as 'to be able to sin' and 'to be able to lie'. Wherefore, nei-ther by (His) absolute nor (His) **ordinate** Power can He lie.

Hence according to context, *ordinatus* must be rendered as "**ordained**" or "**ordinate**"; for clarity sake it will not normally be rendered "**ordered**", since in English this can be confounded with "ordered" [mandatum], that is "**com-manded**".

It thus will be rendered "**ordained**" when it refers to the application of one thing to another; and "**ordinate**" when it refers to the consequent quality of that which has been thus ordained (cf. Sent., Bk. I, d. 17, dubium 2, p. 1318: « and in a similar manner does (St.) Bernard accept (it), when he says, that virtue is an **or-dinate affection** [et similiter accipit Bernardus, cum dicit, quod virtus est *af-fectio ordinata*.] ».

Letter	English Term	Latin	Rationale for use of English term	Special Phrases
P			*Latin* in bold italics — **English** in bold	
	by means of presence **the quality of being present** **of presence or according to presence**	praesentialiter, praesentialitas, praesentialis	This adverb, *praesentialiter*, derived from the Latin adjective, *praesentialis*, *-e*, meaning **of or belong to a presence**, has the peculiar meaning of **in a man-ner of being present to**. This same adjective is the root of the archaic English cognate **presentiality**, which is the quality of being present. Since the concept is not easily conveyed except with an awkward circumlocution, the cognates **pre-sentially, presentiality,** and **presential** will be replaced with their logical equivalents, respectively, as **by means of presence, the quality of being pres-ent,** and **of presence** or **according to presence**. Regarding the specific context, these will have definite or indefinite articles and implied possessive adjectives, as in the phrases: "by means of His presence", "the quality of their being present", "according to His presence". In English we commonly say "presently", but this is more often understood of time, than of place, and so "presently" will not be employed to avoid confound-ing these terms. **Nota bene**: when *praesentialiter* is followed by other adverbs, such as *es-sentialiter* or *potentialiter* these are similarly translated in the same way, as part of the same construction, as in the phrase: « God is everywhere in all crea-tures by means of His Essence, presence, and power » [Deus ubique in omni crea-tura essentialiter, praesentialiter, potentialiter est.]: Master Peter Lombard, First Book of Sentences, D. XXXVII, ch. 1, at the end. Similarly: when **praesentialitas** is used in conjunction with terms connot-ing temporal relations it will be translated as « **being present** », as in the sen-tence: « since the same thing is now truly cognized under a **reckoning of being future** [ratione futuritionis], now under a **reckoning of being past** [ratione praeteritionis], now under a **reckoning of being present** [ratione praesential-itatis] » (St. Bonaventure, Sent., Bk. I, d. 41, a. 2, q. 1, 4 arg. ad opp.).	

Letter	English Term	Latin	Rationale for use of English term	Special Phrases
P			*Latin* in bold italics — **English** in bold	*Latin* in Italics, **English** Bold

	through the prior, through (a consideration of what is) prior
	
	 through the posterior, through (a consideration of what is) posterior
		per prius
		
		 per posterius
			The pithy Latin phrase, **per prius**, composed from the preposition, **per** ("through"), and the neuter form of the adjective, **prius** ("before"), is used when speaking of anything under the consideration or according to a reckoning of a before vis-à-vis an after.
			     In some usages it is used simply, in the sense of "**through a before**", "**through (something) prior**", etc..
			     However, sometimes its use in the Commentaries of St. Bonaventure is idiomatic, and must therefore, be rendered according to its exact logical sense, rather than a more directly verbal equivalent, since in English there is none.
			     Therefore, this phrase will most often be translated thus: **through (a consideration of what is) prior**: which English translation must include all the words, even those within parentheses as well as the parentheses.
			     Here the *parentheses, which are used generally throughout the English Translation of both Lombard and Bonaventure, to signify words which must be added to clarify the context or which are implicit in the context,* are used to notify the reader that the sense of this Latin phrase is much more than its verbal equivalent, and yet at the same time to indicate that the English translation here is taking a liberty which it does not normally do, by rendering this prepositional Latin phrase with a more complex syntactical structure.
			     The sense in which this Latin phrase is understood by St. Bonaventure is most manifest in Sent., Bk. I, d. 29, Doubt 4, at the end, where he says:
			
			     And thus it is clear, concerning which acceptation this name "principle" is said *per prius* according to diverse comparisons.
			
			     For by saying "according to diverse comparisons", he shows that *per prius* is said according to the reckoning or consideration of a before *vis-à-vis* an after.
			     Similarly, the equivalent expression, **per posterius**, is to be rendered, **through (a consideration of what is) posterior**
			     Note: In philosophical texts these two phrases are often understood as "in a prior sense" and "in a posterior sense"; however, this manner of translation is apt to induce the reader to understand that it is only in the sense of the words which follow and not according to an objective reckoning, that that which is said is said. Hence, this manner of rendering the two phrases will not be employed.
			     See the right column, for how to render each phrase with **quam**. Also note, that after **prius** or **posterius**, there can be any number of comparative adjectives in the neuter singular, all of which would likewise join the construction; e.g. **through a consideration of what is prior, more noble, and more unchanging** [per prius, nobilius, et immobilius.]
				per prius ... quam ...: **through (a consideration of what is) prior ... rather than ...;**
				
				 or **through (a consideration of what is) prior to ...**

	principle, beginning	principium	The Latin noun, **principium**, means both a "**beginning**" and a "**principle**".
			     The manner in which this term is rendered into English will follow the rationale taught by St. Bonaventure in Sent., Bk. I, d. 29, a. 1, q. 1, ad 1.
			     Hence, when **principium** is used,
			 1) in reference to an origin, it will be rendered in English as **principle**, since every origin of something is its principle, but not necessarily its beginning.
			 2) in reference to that which has nothing before it, it will be rendered as a **beginning**, since everything which has nothing before it is a beginning, but not necessarily a principle. Yet, St. Bonaventure argues ibid. ad 4, that a Divine Person can be said to be the "beginning" of another, inasmuch as He is a co-equal. And so when **principium** means the negation of something anterior and something greater in goodness, it is to be rendered as **beginning**, since a "principle", contrariwise, can be both anterior and greater.
			     Accordingly, in reference to God, it is said that in the order of existence **God is the beginning of creatures**, and in the order of essence **their principle**, since existing has a point in time of initiation, but the essential cause of essences and their being caused in the essential order are atemporal.
			     Likewise, it is more common to say that « the Father is the principle of the Son and Holy Spirit », than « Their beginning », since the latter might imply to some that They are not eternal. Similarly, if God be said to be « the beginning of creatures », this might lead some to think that God, as a beginning, is part of creation.	

Letter	English Term	Latin	Rationale for use of English term
R			*Latin* in bold italics — **English** in bold
	reason, reckoning	ratio	This one Latin term is rendered by two similar English terms: **reason** and **reckoning**. The Latin term, *ratio*, is derived from the Latin deponent verb *reor, reri, ratus* (to think or judge): *ratus, -a, -um*, is defined by D. P. Simpson, CASSEL'S LATIN-ENGLISH DICTIONARY, as **determined** or **settled**; and the phrase *ratum facere* as **to ratify, confirm** or **make valid**. And hence a *ratio* is a **reckoning**, an account, a calculation, a consideration. It thus has the sense of an "explanation", as one says in English, "how do you reckon, he did that?", as in the sense of "to render account of". And, hence, *ratio* takes on the meaning of a **reason**, cause, motive or explanation by which a thing is understood or under which aspect it is recognized as having a certain formality. In Scholastic philosophy and theology, *ratio* takes on specific technical usages: 1) **the reason**: considered as an intellective power or act, whereby the mind gives an explanation of something. This usage is nearly always confined to discussions of theories of knowledge or the powers of the soul, and rendering ratio as the reason should only be done when the context explicitly requires this attribution. 2) **reckoning**: by far the most common translation to be employed for the term *ratio*, when it is used to show the explanation or cause for the attribution of another term, especially when followed by a genitive term, such as a gerundive, as in the phrases a **reckoning of understanding** [ratio intelligendi], a **reckoning of cognizing** [ratio cognoscendi], or in phrases in which it is followed by a noun, in the genitive case, a **reckoning of similitude** [ratio similitudinis]. **Note:** that when the phrase is used in a general sense, without reference to some previously mentioned *ratio*, then it is to be rendered into English with the indefinite article, "a", as is done, here above. But when it refers to some specific previous mentioned *ratio*, or, to an ideal standard, then it is to be rendered with the definite article, "the". When to use one or the other article must be determined by the entire sense of the context and argument, often by that of the entire Question or Article in which it is used, and the final determination must be based on a philosophical and theological consideration of its use, rather than on a merely linguistic one. 3) **reason**: considered as the motive or cause of something or of some attribution. Since *ratio* as all *–io* derivative nouns in Latin is normally considered an action, but is properly passive in sense, it can have the sense of **reckoning** (passive) or of the **reason** (active) for which or by which something is done or attributed. When it has this sense (which can often occur in the same phrases of the same passage where it has the sense of reckoning), it is rendered as **reason**, as for example when followed by gerundive in the genitive: « **the reason for understanding** [ratio intelligendi]», « **the reason for speaking** [ratio loquendi] », « **the reason for cognizing** [ratio cognoscendi] »; and when followed by nouns in the genitive, as in « **one reason for the similitude** » [una ratio similitudinis] etc.. These English translations of the second and third sense of **ratio** are confirmed by what the Quaracchi Editors say in Sent. Bk. I, d. 35, Scholium, II, second paragraph, regarding the two sense of ratio cognoscendi: However, it must be noted, that properly speaking a *ratio cognoscendi* is accepted rather on the part of the power as a disposition, by which it is rendered equipped for understanding, or is that according to which (the object) is cognized. For that disposition by which it is equipped for understanding is its "reason for understanding", and that according to which the object is cognized is the "reckoning of understanding".
	respect, looking-back	respectus	The Latin supine, **respectus**, means "**a looking-back**"; that is a "regard", or "backward glance". The Latin word has two senses, and has two grammatical structures for its use. In some senses, it refers to an active relation, and is to be rendered as "**looking-back**", as in the phrase: « It is in the Son's looking-back to the Father that there is found the whole reckoning of His Name [In Filii respectu ad Patrem invenitur tota ratio sui nominis] » In others senses it has a passive sense, as in the phrase: « In respect of which reckoning is He said to be a "son"? [In respectu qualis rationis dicatur filius].». Here there must be distinguished the two different grammatical structures which follows the Latin term **respectus**: 1) « **in respect of** » [v. g. *in respectu illius*]: when followed by a genitive, the precise signification is that of a relation emanating from a principle, as in the phrase: « In respect of a beginning the Father is said to be the Author of the Divine Nature [In respectu principii Pater dicitur auctorem divinae naturae] ». 2) « **in respect to** » [v. g. *in respectu ad illum*]: when followed by the preposition to [ad], the precise signification is that of a relation extended toward a terminus, as in the phrase: « In respect to the Father the Second Person of the Most Blessed Trinity is said to be the Son [In respectu ad Patrem secunda persona sanctae Trinitatis dicitur Filius] ». **Note:** the active sense of the Latin term can only belong to a 'principle of which' (usage # 1), yet it can be found in the second usage, when the 'principle to which' it belongs is implied.

Letter	English Term	Latin	Rationale for use of English term	Special Phrases
S			*Latin* in bold italics — **English** in bold	*Latin* in Italics, **English** Bold
	to set (oneself) off from (ones) surroundings, **to set (oneself) off in (a) place**	facere distantiam	The Latin idiom, ***facere distantiam***, expresses a view of measuring very different from that which is commonly used today. Literally, the Latin idiom says that something *causes distance*, or according to the root of ***distantia***, causes **a standing away or apart**. The idiom, therefore, means to say that something causes the surroundings to stand at a distance, that is, is a cause of such that the surroundings can be measured as distant or as standing separately. This concept of a cause of measure, is formal, that is it is according to the reckoning of distance, measured from two *termini*, the thing and the surroundings, but speaks of this distance only in reference to the surroundings. In English today, though we speak of distance to places as *so many feet, miles, kilometers, etc. from here or there*, we do not speak of things causing others to be distant, but of things being distant from other things. Therefore, it seems more clear today to express a logical equivalent of this idiom, rather than the metaphor it employs, and thus to translate it as: **to set (oneself) off from (ones) surroundings**, or **to set (oneself) off in (a) place**, since by being set off from one's surroundings, or by being set off according to place, a thing becomes a terminus from which the distance to its surroundings can be measured. "**Being set off from**" retains the notion of ***distantia***, while the active form of the verb, **to set off**, retains the active sense of **facere**. Cf. Master Peter Lombard's Book of Sentences, Bk. I, d. 37, p. II, throughout.	
	to substantify, substantified	substantificare, substantificatus	The term "**to substantify**" [*substantificare*] is used by St. Bonaventure to signify 'that whereby a thing which is not a substance finds its locus of being in a substance', even if it in itself, does not become a substance therein; thus a nature in a hypostasis, simples in themselves, evil in a good, irrational souls in matter, warmth in the body. The term is discussed but not defined by the Quaracchi Fathers in their Scholium to Bk. III, d. 5, a. 2, q. 2, part III, p. 135. In addition to the sense in which St. Bonaventure uses this term, as noted by the Quaracchi editors, it can be seen from other passages that he uses it in a more general sense, in regard to simples (Sent., Bk. I, d. 19, p. I, a. sole, q. 4, ad 2, p. 349), to the necessity of evil's existence by means of a good (Sent., Bk. I, d. 46, a. sole, q. 4, ad 2; especially, Bk. II, d. 34, a. 2, q. 2, in corp.; cf. also Sent., Bk. I, d. 39, a. 1, q. 2, Scholium, n. II), to sensible souls in matter (cf. Sent., Bk. II, d. 19, a. 1, q. 2, ad 3), to warmth in the radical humidity (cf. Sent., Bk. II, d. 30, a. 2, q. 2, in corp.). To be faithful to the Latin term, ***substantificare*** shall be rendered as "**to substantify**", rather than "to substantiate", though in English the latter term can be used in the same sense.	
	to suscept, to undertake, to take up **suscipient, the one suscepting**	suscipere suscipiens	The Latin verb, ***suscipere***, means "to take up" in the sense of "to receive", but is distinguished from this, in that the former is limited to something inferior in some sense to the being of the one receiving, whereas in the latter, what is received is not specified in respect of the one receiving. Thus, a soul is a suscipient of grace, not a recipient, because grace is an accident, but a recipient of being, inasmuch as it is created by God, since what it receives is not inferior to itself. In English there exists the cognates "to suscept", "susceptible", "susceptive", "susception", but not "suscipient". This latter neologism must be employed to render ***suscipiens*** in its substantive uses, so as to distinguish it from a recipient, the former will be employed for ***susceptibilis***, ***susceptivus***, ***susceptio*** respectively; whereas the verb in all its forms will be rendered, when used in the common, non-technical sense, as "**to take up**", "**to undertake**".	
	suppose, supposition, etc. **to place under, to substitute, to subject**	supponere, suppositio	The Latin ***supponere*** means "to place under", "to substitute", "to subject". The verb, and all its derivatives in Latin, has two senses: first, the normal or idiomatic, as in **to place something under something** [supponere aliquid sub aliquo], or as in the phrase: « with the nature of the soul **supposed**, one can understand why it is said to be immortal [natura animae supposita, etc.] » In this latter idiomatic sense, it is used as **supposed** is used in modern English, in that rare sense, in which it is equivalent to **presuppose**. Second, the technical Scholastic one, which is defined by the Quaracchi Editors in d. 4, a. 1, q. 1, in the Scholium, p. 98 ff. (This entry is continued in the Table on the following page)	*supponere pro*: **to suppose on behalf of**, or **to suppose for**. *supposito*: **having supposed**, or **with ... supposed** *supponere*: **to substitute**, only in the Scholia, when the concept of supposition is being explained in reference to the understanding of propositions; in all other cases, it is to be rendered as **to suppose**, except in normal usages, where it retains its original sense of **to place under**, etc..

Letter	English Term	Latin	Rationale for use of English term	Special Phrases
S			*Latin* in bold italics — **English** in bold	*Latin* in Italics, **English** Bold

	suppose, supposition, etc.
	
	to place under, to substitute, to subject
		supponere, suppositio	*(Continued from previous page)*
			
			1. **Signification** is one thing, the **supposition** of any term, another. **Signification** is the representation of a thing through the voice and it befits all words both substantive and otherwise, whether in a proposition, or outside a proposition.
			    Supposition, as Peter of Spain (SUMMULA) would have it in his "Tract on Supposition", « is the acceptance of a substantive term on behalf of something », concerning which and/or which (things) a term of this kind in any proposition is verified. Thus the term "man" can **substitute** [*supponere*] for man in common, as in the proposition: "man is a species"; and/or for his inferiors comprehended under this species, v. g. "a man runs". Of **suppositions** one is common, the other discrete; the former is done through a common term, such as "man is mortal"; the latter is through a discrete (concrete) term, such as "Socrates", and/or through a common one, but determined through the demonstrative pronoun, as (in) "that man" [iste homo].
			
			    The English cognate, **to suppose**, has this same technical sense only in a rare usage (cf. WEBSTER'S THIRD INTERNATIONAL DICTIONARY, 1964). For this reason rendering *supponere* and its derivatives with **suppose** and its derivative will give the English reader cause for misunderstanding, if he has not first read this Rationale. However, substituting another English term for *supponere* would greatly reduce the coherency of the Translation with the Scholastic terminology.
			    The other common translation of *supponere* in this technical sense, "to supposit for" will not be employed, because it confounds a **supposit** (q.v.), which is what is substituted, with the **subject** of the verb, which does the substitution.
			    When in the context of the interpretation of a term in a proposition it is rendered as **substitute**, as is done in the citation of the Scholium above, it is rightfully criticized as being able to be understood as transferring the context of the argument from one wherein a term stands for a real thing, to one in which a term is replaced by another term. For in the phrase from the Nicene Creed: "God from God" [Deo de Deo], the first instance of "God" is said to suppose God the Son [supponit Deum Filium], rather than to substitute for "God the Son", for properly speaking one word or term is substituted by another word or term, not by that which is meant by another word or term.
			    The technical Scholastic use of **supponere** is founded on the metaphor of its innate meaning of 'placing something under something else'. In English we have the same simile in the use of the verb "to understand", because in the phrase from the Nicene Creed: "God from God", the first instance of "God" is under-stood to be, according to that which it is intended to mean, God the Son. Likewise, this word "God" supposes the Son of God according to the same reckoning, that is, that which is intended to be meant by its usage in that phase from the Creed is the Son of God, so that when there is said that « "God" supposes God the Son », what is meant is, « the word "God" supposes, in the order of meaning, the same which is meant by the words "God the Son", that is, God the Son. Thus **supposition** is not an immediate form of reference, but a terminal or final or ultimate form of reference, in which a word stands for something (rather than for another word) other than that which the word in its normal sense would stand for.
			    Rendering **supponere** in this fashion (as "under-stood to be ") would perhaps be more metaphorically accurate in English; but would create problems of comprehension for non-native English speakers who would be reading the English Translation; it would also confound in English the senses of the Latin *intelligere* and *supponere*.
			    Conclusion: To preserve the understanding of the Scholastic logical term, *supponere*, will be translated with the English cognates of « to suppose », except where it is used in Latin for the normal sense of 'placing something under', 'substituting' or 'subjecting'. In the first such instance of this usage, the reader will be notified of its technical sense, by a reference in the Footnotes, according to the standard notion [Trans. note: ....], that he should refer to this Rationale for the proper understanding of the term.	

	supposit, supposed	suppositum	A *suppositum* is what has been **supposed** (q.v.).
			    It is most often used as the technical equivalent term for the Greek *hypostasis*, that is, as a singular instance of a species or a nature.
			    However, it can be used as a neuter singular form of the adjective, that is as a substantive, in the general sense of anything supposed, such as a supposed term, wherein the term is supposed not in the technical sense of **supposition** (q.v.), but in the general sense of **substitution**, as in the phrase: "Thomas is a man", one can suppose "rational animal" for "man" and say equivalently, "Thomas is a rational animal"; and thus "rational animal" would be the supposed term for "man".
			    While the Latin term can be used in English, « **supposit** » will be used as the standard English translation of the ontological term, equivalent to the Greek *hypostasis*; but in the general sense it is to be render as « **supposed** » when used as a substantive, e.g. referring to a term or noun, which substitutes for another.	

<u>Letter</u>	<u>**English Term**</u>	<u>**Latin**</u>	<u>**Rationale for use of English term**</u>	<u>**Special Phrases**</u>
T			*Latin* in bold italics — **English** in bold	*Latin* Italics, **English** Bold
	in a time, in time, **on account of time,** **seasons, times**	in tempore ex tempore tempora	The first two Latin phrases, listed to the left, are idiomatic: 1) *in tempore*: « **in (a) time** », that is, in a specific or non specific period of delimited time. To distinguish this from the second sense of *ex tempore*, the former can be rendered with the indefinite article. This sense is defined by the Quaracchi Editors in the Scholium of d. 18, a. sole, q. 2, where they say that being *in tempore* means "that something is measured by time, which properly is said of corruptibles" [aliquid mensuari tempore, quod proprie dicitur corruptibilibus]. Cf. Sent., Bk. I, d. 30, dubium II, in the response. 2) *ex tempore*: a) The proper sense of this Latin phrase is, « **on account of time** », that is on account of being temporal, originating in time, and hence coming forth from, or out of, time. This sense of **ex tempore** is confirmed by St. Bonaventure in Sent., Bk. I, d. 30, a. sole, q. 1, ad 4. 4. To that which is objected, that that which is *ex tempore*, begins to be something; it must be said, that that is not in God on account of any change made in Him, but in the creature: and that has been determined above, in the Eighth Distinction. For in saying that "it is not in God on account of any change made in him" [non est in Deo propter mutationem aliquam etc.], the Seraphic Doctor manifests that the sense of *ex tempore* is *propter temporem*, that is, "**on account of time**". b) And hence, in some senses, the Latin phrase must be rendered « **in time** », that is, constrained within that existence which has a temporal dimension, but not in any specific delimited period, as in n. 1 above. An example of both these usages, is found in Lombard's Book of Sentences, Bk. I, d. 30, ch. 1, paragraph 2. For in that passage Lombard shows, that if one were to read "which began on account of time", instead, it might be understood to mean that something can begin on account of time, yet not in time, which the Seraphic Doctor expressly denies by saying "because there was no time before it began". This sense is defined by the Quaracchi Editors in the Scholium of d. 18, a. sole, q. 2, where they say that *ex tempore* means that a thing's "being has a start, and is said of all created things" [ipsum esse habere initium, et dicitur de omnibus creatis]. Cf. Sent., Bk. I, d. 30, dubium II, in the response. This sense ("**in time**") is commonly used of the procession, generation or granting of a Divine Person in time, when it refers to the act of procession, etc., but the former sense ("**on account of time**"), when referring to the reason for the act. (For evidence that contemporaries of St. Bonaventure sometimes understood **ex tempore** as **in tempore**, see Sent., Bk. III, d. 8, Doubt 3). c) « **out of time** »: except in phrases with verbs of motion or the like, where it can be understood as "forth out of time", this sense is to be avoided, since in popular English it means rather that time available has expired. The plural form of the noun, **tempora**, refers to the periods of time as it is measured, and is rendered **seasons** or **times**.	*ad tempora*: **according to (the) seasons**, or **according to the times.** *extra tempus*: **outside of time** *cum tempore*: **with time**

Letter	English Term	Latin	Rationale for use of English term
T			*Latin* in bold italics — **English** in bold
	a transduction, **to traduce,** **transduction** *or* **traducing**	tradux, traducere, traductio	In Latin a *tradux*, in the sense employed here, is a **cutting** or **slip** from which one mature plant is ultimately propagated from the mature plant, from which the **slip** was cut. Thus **de traduce** is often rendered « **from (a) propagation** », and **ex traduce** as « **on account of (a) propagation** »; however, the concept is more precise in Latin, since the term refers to that manner of propagation in which something properly of the parent becomes properly the offspring; whereas natural propagation in animals is such that something accidental in the parents, conjoined, becomes properly the offspring. The verb associated with *tradux* is *traducere*, and it is used by St. Bonaventure to express the action where by this manner of propagation takes place. The concept of **transduction** is central to the Augustinian theology of the contraction of original sin, and appears commonly in St. Bonaventure's Commentary on the Second and Third Books of the Sentences. In Sent., Bk. II, d. 18, a. 2, q. 3, the Seraphic Doctor speaks of **transduction** in reference to theories on the origins of souls (pp. 451-454): There is also another manner of speaking, that the production of souls is through a **transduction** [per traductionem], so that a soul is transduced out of a soul, just as the flesh (is) out of flesh; and just as from one candle many are lit, so from one soul, through its multiplication, many bodies are vivified without (its) diminution. And for a time Catholic tract-writers doubted concerning this, and (St.) Augustine most of all, just as is clear in (his) book, ON A LITERAL EXPOSITION OF GENESIS, and in (his) book, ON FREE WILL, and in (his) BOOK OF RETRACTATIONS, where he also says, that he could not arrive at the certitude of this question. Moreover, the reason, which caused him to doubt most of all, was the transfusion of original sin. — Nevertheless, (St.) Augustine himself expressly reprehends this position in the book, ON ECCLESIASTICAL DOGMAS, the quote from which Master (Peter) puts in the text, and he himself disproves this same manner (of reasoning) ON A LITERAL EXPOSITION OF GENESIS: since, if for the sake (of explaining the transmission of) original sin (one must say that) a soul is transfused out of a soul, either the Soul of Christ would not be of the genus of other souls, or it would have had original sin, each of which is false and impious. Thus, *de traduce* and *ex traduce* will be rendered as « **from a transduction** », « **out of** (or on account of) **a transduction** », respectively. The verb, however, will be rendered as « **to traduce** », to conserve the technical Latin sense. — St. Bonaventure uses this verb in the more general sense of "to transfer while retaining completely the inherent qualities of the same" in Sent., Bk. II, d. 30, a. 3, q. 1, 3rd opposed argument (p. 727); and on account of the propagation of original sin from parent to offspring by means of the propagation of the same flesh from Adam to his posterity, he says that « original sin is thus traduced » ibid., d. 31, a. 1, q. 2, body of the Question. For St. Bonaventure's theology of **transduction**, cf. ibid., d. 31, throughout; d. 33, a. 1, q. 1; in regard to Christ's Flesh, Sent., Bk. III, d. 3, p. II, a. 2, q. 1. Cf. also Master Peter Lombard, Sent., Bk. II, d. 18, ch. 7, and d. 31, throughout.
U			
	one, **'one',** **one [unum]**	unum	The Latin *unus, -a, -um*, is the numeral adjective "one". However, it three different uses in the neuter form, unum. 1) The common usage, that is, as an adjective describing a neuter noun. In this sense, it can be rendered in English as **one**, without any specification. 2) The specific usage, that is, as the **number 1**. In this sense it will be rendered as **'one'**, within single quotes, to indicate that it represents there the number 1, or the concept conveyed by the number 1. In this sense, the term signifies a *unity of indivision*. 3) The idiomatic usage, that is, as representing the unity of two or more beings. In this sense, it shall be rendered as **one [unum]**, that is, followed by the Latin term within square brackets. In this sense the term signifies a *unity of conformity*. St. Bonaventure distinguishes the second and third usage of this term in Sent., Bk. I, d. 31, p. II, q. 2, in reply to n. 1: 1. To that which is objected concerning one in number, it must be said, that there is a twofold unity, namely, of indivision and of conformity. The unity of indivision is attained in one in number, and this is a unity simply (speaking); but the unity of conformity is not in one in number, but in those to whom it happens that they are conformed with others, as has been said. In this third sense, when the term *unum* is refered to as a verbal expression, it is written in English as **"one"** [unum].

Letter	English Term	Latin	Rationale for use of English term
V			*Latin* in bold italics — **English** in bold
	and/or, either	vel	Let the reader understand that the Latin conjunction, *vel*, can be understood in three different senses: 1) **and/or**, simply understood, that is as the possibility of being a simple conjunction with an equal possibility of a disjunction; 2) **or**, in the disjunctive sense; 3) and as **either** when introducing the phrase *vel ... vel*, in which case the first *vel* can be translated as **either** or simply omitted in translation. However, the signification of this Latin term, must be understood from the context. Throughout this English translation, I have translated it as **and/or** and **either**, so as to leave the habit of expression used St. Bonaventure intact, rather than to impose the stricter habit of usage which prevails in the English speaking world, wherein the value of a logically precise understanding is generally accorded the necessity of a similarly strict unambiguous verbal expression. However, understand that the Seraphic Doctor uses *vel* rather than *aut* because his usage is not only more frequently that *of the inclusive optional*, but even when he intends the *exclusive disjunction*, he wishes the reader to understand that the diverse options share a unity under the single choice which must decide between them. (cf. Translator's note to Sent., Bk. III, d. 30, a. sole, q. 2, p. 661).

AN IMPORTANT NOTICE TO THE READER

ON THE USE OF PARENTHESES IN THE TEXT

NOTA BENE: In reading this English translation, it is necessary that the reader first know, that in the text there are two kinds of parentheses used: round parentheses, i. e. (); and square parentheses, i. e. [].

Round parentheses are used both in the Text translated, in the footnotes written by the Quaracchi editors, and in their Scholia.

Square parentheses are used rarely by the Quaracchi editors in their footnotes and Scholia.

Square parentheses are used very often by the English translator, in the text, in the footnotes, and in the Scholia.

HOW ARE THESE PARENTHESES TO BE READ, OR UNDERSTOOD?

Round parentheses in the text, footnotes or Scholia are used in 4 manners:

(1) To set off a reference, of the common form, such as: (q. v.), or (i. e. ...), or (cf. ...), or (v. g. ...).

(2) To enclose a parenthetical statement, of the common form, such as:

« *John was walking to the store (not to the one to which his father sent him)* ».

(3) To indicate a word or words in another language, most commonly in Greek.

(4) **By the Translator, to indicate which words he has added to the translated text** for the sake of explicating the sense of the Latin, which words are necessary in English, since English lacks cases and genders, which in Latin are used to signify intra-contextual references; and since English often requires possessive pronouns to indicate similar intra-contextual references. In this usage alone, unlike the others, the reader should read the text *as if* the marks of the parentheses, but not their content, *were removed from the text.*

(5) By the Translator, in the text or footnotes, to add names, places & dates, for the edification of the reader.

Square parentheses are used in three manners:

(1) By the Quaracchi editors, on rare occasions, in their Scholia, in any one of the above 3 manners, in which the round parentheses are used.

(2) **By the Translator in the text, to indicate the Latin word(s) for which the immediately preceding English word(s) are the translation.** This is done to show how the same Latin word, when used in different senses, is rendered by different English words; and to show when the same English word renders the same one sense which two or more Latin synonyms signify.

(3) By the Translator, always, in the footnotes of the Quaracchi editors, to show the Latin for the diverse variant readings, or to explain the changed reading.

ABBREVIATIONS

Omitted here are those for proper names of days and months,
and those used in the Latin titles, incipits or desinits of manuscripts.

A. D.	Anno Domini		**n.** or **nn.**	number(s)
A. *or* **a.**	article		**O. F. M. Conv.**	Order of Friars Minor Conventual
aa.	articles		**O. F. M.**	Order of Friars Minor
ad 1	Reply to argument 1		**O. F. M. Cap.**	Order of Friars Minor Capuchins
ad opp.	argument(s) for the opposite		**Ord. Min.**	Order of Minors
arg. or **argg.**	argument(s)		**O. P.**	Order of Preachers
B. C.	Before Christ		**op. cit.**	in opere citato, i. e.
Bk. or **Bks.**	book(s)			In the cited work
Bl. or **Bls.**	Blessed(s)		**O. S. A.**	Order of St. Augustine
Bonav.	Bonaventure of Bagnoregio		**O. S. B.**	Order of St. Benedict
Br.	Brother		**p.** or **pp.**	page(s)
Breviloq.	Bonaventure's BREVILOQUIUM		**p. I** or **II**	part I, *or* part I
ch. or **c.**	chapter		**parag.**	paragraph
Cap.	Capuchin(s)		**passim**	'here or there'
ch. or **chs.**	chapter(s)		**parv.**	parvo (a small sized book)
chart.	cartulary		**plut.**	pluteus (a library display table)
col.	column		**Ph.D.**	Doctor Philosophiae
cod. or **codd.**	codex or codices.		**PP.**	Supreme Pontiff
conf.	conference		**prov.**	province
cf.	confer, or compare		**Q.** or **q.**	question
d. or **dd.**	distinction(s)		**Qq.** or **qq.**	questions
dext.	on the right side		**q. v.**	see the entry bearing this name
Dist. or **dist.**	distinction		**Report.**	The Reportatio of Scotus's
Dr.	Doctor			Commentary on the Sentences
Drs.	Doctoral student		**Rev.**	Reverend
Dom.	A title for Benedictine Monks		**r.**	recto, i. e. on the front of a page
ed. or **edd.**	edition(s).		**saec.**	saeculo, i. e. in the century
e. g.	exempli gratia, for example		**St.** or **Sts.**	Saint(s)
etc.	et cetera, i. e. and the rest		**Sent.**	the Book of Sentences
f. or **ff.**	and in the following one(s)			or a Commentary on the same
fn. or **fns.**	footnote(s)		**sign.**	the sign identifying a codex
Fr.	Father *or* Friar		**S. J.**	Society of Jesus
fund.	Fundament (arguments *pro*)		**Summa.**	A Summa of theology
ibid.	In the same place or passage		**text.**	text, a sectional division in the
i. e.	id est, or "that is"			works of Aristotle
in corp.	In the body of the Question		**tr.**	tract
in resp.	In the Response the Question.		**Trans.**	Translator's (note).
Itiner.	Bonaventure's ITINERARIUM		**v.** or **vv.**	verse(s)
loc. cit.	in loco citato, i. e.		**v.**	verso, i. e., on the back of the page
	In the cited place/passage		**v. gr.**	to give an example
m.	A subdivision of Alexander of		**4 vo.** or **8 vo.**	quarto or octavo ligatures
	Hales, SUMMA THEOLOGICA			
magn.	magnum, or large-sized			
membr.	A parchment			
miscell.	A book containing a collection of			
	materials from different sources			
ms. or **mss.**	manuscript(s)			

Abbreviations for Books of the Bible

According to the Vulgate edition

Gen.	Genesis	**Mich.**	Micheas
Exod.	Exodus	**Hab.**	Habacuc
Lev.	Leviticus	**Zach.**	Zacharias
Num.	Numbers	**Mach.**	Machabees
Deut.	Deuteronomy	**Malach.**	Malachias
Jos.	Josue	**Mt.**	Gospel of St. Matthew
Paralip.	Paralipomenon (Chronicles)	**Mk.**	Gospel of St. Mark
Tob.	Tobias	**Lk.**	Gospel of St. Luke
Jud.	Judith	**Jn.**	Gospel of St. John
Ps.	Psalm	**Acts**	Acts of the Apostles
Prov.	Proverbs	**Rom.**	Letter to the Romans
Eccl.	Ecclesiastes	**Cor.**	Letter to the Corinthians
Cant.	Canticle of Canticles	**Gal.**	Letter to the Galatians
Wis.	Wisdom	**Eph.**	Letter to the Ephesians
Eccli.	Ecclesiasticus	**Philip.**	Letter to the Philippians
Jer.	Jeremias	**Col.**	Letter to the Colossians
Lam.	Lamentations	**Thess.**	Letter to the Thessalonians
Ezech.	Ezechiel	**Tim.**	Letter to Timothy
Dan.	Daniel	**Phil.**	Letter to Philemon
		Hebr.	Letter to the Hebrews
		Pt.	Letter of St. Peter
		Apoc.	The Apocalypse of St. John

UNDERSTANDING A SCHOLASTIC ARGUMENT

or A Brief Note on how to read St. Bonaventure's Commentaries

St. Bonaventure's COMMENTARIES ON THE FOUR BOOKS OF SENTENCES, the first published work of its kind, followed the tradition of Scholastic disputation which prevailed at the University of Paris in the mid 13th Century. The form of theological experimentation of that day, began by reading the text book or set-book: Master Peter Lombard's FOUR BOOKS OF SENTENCES, each Book of which had, according to the textual tradition, already been divided into Distinctions.

For each DISTINCTION, St. Bonaventure opens his own Commentary, with an outline of the text of Lombard's Distinction: which outline is called the DIVISION OF THE TEXT.

IN THE DIVISION OF THE TEXT, the Seraphic Doctor will divide the text of Lombard into parts, describing briefly what is treated of by Lombard in each part. Divisions are proposed for each Book, for each part of each Book, for the Distinctions in each part, and for subparts of each Division. The Division of the Text was the first and simplest exercise proposed for the student, to show his mastery of Lombard's text. For St. Bonaventure, the Division of the Text serves as the basis for the TREATMENT OF THE QUESTIONS.

IN THE TREATMENT OF THE QUESTIONS, St. Bonaventure proposes the matters to be analyzed. These he calls the problems [problemata]. For each problem, there is proposed an Article, and for each Article, normally, two to six questions.

IN EACH ARTICLE, you will find a topic to be discussed, the consideration of which arises from Lombard's text.

IN EACH QUESTION, you will find a specific theological inquiry to be undertaken, the consideration of which was of interest to St. Bonaventure and/or his contemporaries. Each question has several parts: **The Question**, the arguments of **The Fundament**, the arguments for **The Opposite, The Conclusion, The Response**, and the **Replies to the Objections**. The Quaracchi Editors, also, often add their own **Scholium**, or student's notes, after the replies.

The Fundament of the Question are those arguments in favor of St. Bonaventure's Response. **The arguments for the Opposite** are against the same. In some Questions, the Fundament is first, in some, it is second. The second group of arguments is introduced with the words: **But, on the Contrary**, or **On the Contrary**, or rarely, some sort of variation.

The Body of the Question is the same thing as **The Response**. The Body is introduced by the words CONCLUSION, followed by a brief text which summarizes the Response. **The Response** is that part of each Question which can be attributed most authentically to St. Bonaventure. The arguments of the Fundament and for the Opposite are less so, each in their own manner, as some of the former and latter were taken from famous authors, even contemporaries, but others rewritten or summarized by Bonaventure for the purpose of spurring on a better understanding of the Question. Note, that not all Questions have each of these parts; but all do have a Question, Conclusion and Response.

It is important for the reader to read all the parts, for otherwise St. Bonaventure's Response will not be well comprehended. But, if the Reader simply wishes to skim through the Commentaries, it is sufficient to read the Question and Response. THE SCHOLIUM is to assist the student of theology to understand Bonaventure's Response in its theological and historical context, especially in comparison with the other great Scholastic Masters.

Pro oblatione perpetua:

ante sedem Reginae Augustae

Mariae Immaculatae regiam:

Quae cum tam mirabili amore

ad aium peccatorum miserabilem

Condescendere degnaverit:

ut gratitudinis et famulatus

Signaculum.

St. Bonaventure (Giovanni di Fidanza) *as a child, is miraculously healed by St. Francis of Assisi,*
while the Immaculate Virgin indicates his future glory to the Saint:
the work of Giuseppe Cades: Oil on Canvass, 1795 A. D.: CONVENTO DI SAN FRANCESCO, BAGNOREGIO, ITALY.

OF THE SERAPHIC DOCTOR

ST. BONAVENTURE

CARDINAL BISHOP OF THE HOLY ROMAN CHURCH

THE OPERA OMNIA

BY THE ORDER AND AUTHORITY OF

THE MOST REV. FR. BERNARDINO DI PORTU ROMANTINO

Minister General of the entire Order of Minors of St. Francis

PUBLISHED UNDER THE STUDY AND CARE
OF THE FATHERS OF THE COLLEGIO DI SAN BONAVENTURA

EMENDED ACCORDING TO VERY MANY MANUSCRIPT CODICES
AUGMENTED WITH YET UNPUBLISHED PROLEGOMENA & SCHOLIA
AND ILLUSTRATED WITH NOTES

TOME I.

AD CLARAS AQUAS (QUARACCHI)

NEAR FLORENCE

COLLEGE OF ST. BONAVENTURE PRESS

1882

IMPRIMATUR *

Granted at Florence, Italy, on August 18, 1883 A. D.

† Eugenio Cecconi, Archbiship of Florence

---

* *Trans. note*: This notice of Imprimatur appeared in the original on the second page following page 870, below; but is moved here in the Translation, to conform to more modern usage for such notices. It has canonical value for the Latin original.

TO THE SERAPHIC PATRIARCH

OUR FATHER & LAWGIVER

SAINT FRANCIS OF ASSISI

ON THE SEVENTH CENTENARY OF HIS BIRTH

THIS NEW EDITION

OF THE OPERA OMNIA

OF THE SERAPHIC DOCTOR ST. BONAVENTURE

WE INSCRIBE, OFFER & DEDICATE

AND TO HIS PATRONAGE AND PROVIDENCE

WE DO COMMEND

THESE SONS, HUMBLE & POOR, BUT DEVOUT WITH ALL THEIR HEARTS

FRIAR BERNARDINO DI PORTU ROMATINO

MINISTER GENERAL

AND THE FRIAR EDITORS

GENERAL PREFACE

aint Bonaventure, called "Giovanni Fidanza" by his family, Italian by nation, a native of Bagnoregio, disciple of Alexander of Hales, doctor of the University of Paris, friend of St. Thomas Aquinas and of St. Louis (IX), King of the Franks, for seventeen years Minister General of the Order of (Friars) Minor, Cardinal Bishop of the Holy Roman Church, duly inscribed in the catalogue of the Saints by (Pope) Sixtus IV and as Doctor of the Church by (Pope) Sixtus V, most celebrated throughout the world and centuries for the splendors of (his) virtues, (his) accomplished deeds, (and his) clearest writings, « was » by common suffrage « named » antonomastically, « the "Doctor Seraphicus" for the singularity of (his) wisdom ».[1] Though all the holy Doctors of the Church are lamps burning in charity and shining in the splendor of the truth, and (though) their writings contribute very much to illumine the reader's mind in knowledge and inflame (his) affection with devotion, yet, they do not immediately proffer each in the same manner and grade. *For there are divisions of graces, but the same Spirit dividing to each as He wills.*[2] Moreover, the Scholastic Doctors, and nearly all the other theologians after them, were versed only in illuminating the intellect. But Saint Bonaventure, who occupies a primary place among the Scholastics with the Angelic Doctor, as one conjoining each and excelling all the other doctors in a certain divine force to inflame souls, merited rightfully for himself from time immemorial the name — confirmed by the diplomas of the Supreme Pontiffs and by the consent of the ages — of "Seraphic Doctor". Marked praise is proffered by this unique title. For, as *St. Bernard*[3] testifies, « to only light is vain; to only burn, too little; to light and to burn, perfect ». Therefore, these talents, this praise of St. Bonaventure's doctrine, which is given to few others, because, that is, as *Trithemius*[4] testifies, « many proffer doctrine, many preach devotion; few, in writing books, have taught each. But St. Bonaventure has surpassed the many and the few, since his doctrine

---

[1] Thus John of Torquemada, O.P., in (his) tract, *de Veritate Conceptionis B. V. M.*, p. VI, ch. 30. This title, *Seraphicus*, is of a later origin, since, at first, in the century following his death, he was commonly called the *Doctor devotus*. Sbaralea (*Supplementum et castigatio ad Scriptores trium Ord. S. Francisci*, Rome 1806, p. 143) asserts, that the first to be found to have ornamented St. Bonaventure with that title was Rainiero Pisano, O. P., in his *Summa* or *Pantheologia*, which he began in A. D. 1333. But in this the learned author is deceived, because the Prologue to the *Pantheologia*, in which this title *Seraphici* is found, belongs not to Rainiero, but to the editor of the work, who lived in the 15th century.

[2] 1 Cor. 12:4,11.

[3] *Sermon on the Nativity of St. John the Baptist*, h. 3 (Venetian edition of 1765, tome II, col. 115).

[4] *De Scriptoribus eccles.*, fol. 101 verso, Parisian edition of 1512, and/or c. 464 (in Fabric. Bibl. eccles., p. 113).

builds up (one's) devotion, (his) devotion, (one's) doctrine ». « Therefore, though there be other doctors, who are called "Cherubic"; Bonaventure, however, is most truly (called) at once by the name *Seraphicus* and *Cherubicus,* because he inflames the affections and instructs the intellect, leads (it) back and unites (it) to God through excitative love ».[1]

For this reason very many erudite men already had it in mind, not so long ago, to publish the Opera Omnia of this most eminent and most holy man (in a form) examined, enriched, corrected and illustrated by the new studies and assistances of the critical art. Who did not see that the arduous province of preparing this edition pertained, by special title, to both the right and office of the Seraphic Order? Now, the thoroughly singular merits themselves of this Saint ought to promote certain valid *stimuli* to the Order of St. Francis to undertake this work. Rightfully urging (all) to this were the lucid words, by which *Father Bernardino da Porto Romatino* (Portogruaro), the Most Rev. Minister General of the Order of Minors, truly worthy of the whole Order, exhorted his subjects to celebrate solemn feasts on the occasion of sixth centenary of St. Bonaventure's (death): « Though the Seraphic Bonaventure, rightly claims for himself the veneration of all Christians as Saint and also as Doctor of the Church of God, as a truly worthy Bishop and Cardinal, there is another reason, why we, most beloved Fathers and Brothers, should accompany him with chief honors. For it could scarcely be believed, how with wonderful discretion and sweetness he himself, as Minister General of the entire Order of Our Seraphic Father, Francis, and as one cleaving more closely to the footsteps of the Seraphic Patriarch, ruled the whole Order for seventeen years, how wisely and strongly he refuted the most hostile detractors and haters of the life of the Rule, with what solicitude he augmented the Order with (his) published laws, visitations, writings and example, recalled (it) to a certain form, illustrated (it) with knowledge, fostered (it) with piety. In a word, we owe so much to him, after Our Seraphic Father Francis, that he is not unworthily regarded as the other Founder of our Order. Therefore, it is fair, that on the solemnity of the sixth centenary we render a due service of reverence, piety and grateful spirit to the glory of the Omnipotent God for our Seraphic Doctor ». — This reason urges more in the matter, of which we speak, because in past centuries, as was already observed by many, the golden doctrine of St. Bonaventure, though praised continually in words, has in itself, if you except a few, truly wise men, lain rather neglected and been quasi handed over to oblivion.

But another most grave reason also impelled the Seraphic Order to undertake the burden of adorning a new edition, namely so that there might be revived more easily in our schools the truly Seraphic doctrine of St. Bonaventure, for this reason, that it might put down deeper roots and bear more abundant fruits. For by nearly unanimous suffrage it had already been desired for a long time, many as there were in the Order of men outstanding in doctrine and piety. First of all, the same Most Reverend *Fr. Bernardino,* though occupied most worthily with the office of Provincial in the Venetian Province of the Reformati, and afterwards, when he was led forth to the arduous duty of ruling the entire Order, applied all his powers, as he says, « to revive in our Order that which we have in our upper most wishes: the pious study in our Order of our Seraphic and the Church's Doctor, St. Bonaventure; and having been instructed in his school, we have sought after his knowledge, eagerly followed (his) discipline, (and) experience the sweetness of (his) piety ».[3] Therefore by a pious and optimum coun-

---

[1] John Gerson, in a Letter sent to Lyons, to a certain friar minor, in the year A. D. 1426 (Antwerp edition of 1706, tome I, col. 119).

[2] In his encyclical letter written, March 10, 1874.

[3] Ibid. in the same letter.

sel it happened that, already in the year 1871, by the impulse and authority of the same Most Rev. Minister General, the preparation of this new Edition was decreed, and preparatory labors were undertaken.

It seems that we must refrain in this place to say more of the Seraphic Doctor, Bonaventure, and his works, since there will be discussed at length in an orderly manner, elsewhere (namely, at the end of the entire edition, once the Opera have been published), the life and writings of the same.[1] Therefore, let it suffice, to propose briefly in this place some things concerning the ratio itself of this Edition, so that one might have a perspective, both as regards what *has been borrowed from others* in preceding ages in gathering and publishing the works of the Seraphic Doctor, and what *has been left* by others *undone and still to be done*, and what we ourselves *have either already done, and/or have proposed to do in this Edition*. Moreover, since that which has already been treated by Father Fedele da Fanna — well deserved of mention, who was the forerunner in first publishing the works of St. Bonaventure — for the most part in an outstanding and lengthy manner in his singular book,[2] which can be truly called the program of our Edition, we judge it to be expedient, to cite here, not but a few things more briefly. But we warn the benevolent reader, that much of what is to be said in this Preface has been described according to the mind and word of the mentioned book of Father Fedele; that which we cite word for word, or nearly so, we have distinguished with the quotes used commonly for this.

---

[1] The chief reason, why we reserve this dissertation on the life and writings of St. Bonaventure to the last tome, is had in this, that this dissertation will be a quasi synthesis of everything, which has been scattered in the Prolegomena of each work, through the manner of an analytical exposition. — Yet, it seems to be opportune, now, to note here the grave chronological error concerning the life of the Seraphic (Doctor), into which writers, many and of great authority, have uncautiously fallen. Wadding himself (*Annales*, tome I, on the year 1243, n. 5), having followed more ancient authors, affirms, that St. Bonaventure entered the novitiate of the Order in the twenty-second year of his life, to which (fact) the authors of the *Actuum Sanctorum* (tome III, June 14th) and very many others, and even the Breviary of the Order consent. Oudin (*de Script. eccles.*, tome III, Leipzig edition, col. 134) admits this, who on account of a false chronological supposition introduces another error, writing: « It is established, that Bonaventure never had (Alexander) of Hales as (his) master nor that he ever studied under him, when he was at Paris ». Echardus (*Scriptores Ord. Praedic.*, tome I, p. 277 ff.) consents to the same error. But Father Hyacinthus Sbaralea (*Bullar. Franciscan.*, tome III, p. 12, notes; and *Supplem. ad scriptores.*) sufficiently proves, that St. Bonaventure took the habit of the Order at the end of the year 1238, at about the age of 17, and in the following year, when Haymo was Minister General, took sacred vows. According to the same author, after three years of philosophy, in 1242, he was sent to Paris, where he had Alexander of Hales as (his) master unto the death of the latter (Aug. 12, 1245). According to the testimony of a contemporary author of the Order, the Bl. Francesco of Fabriano, « under Master Alexander he took the licentiate ». This chronology is defended by Bonelli, *Prodromus*, Bk. I, c. 1, n 5; and the author of the egregious work: *Storia compendiosa di S. Francesco e dei Francescani*, by Father Panfilio da Magliano, M. O. R., Rome 1874, who adds to the testimonies of other authors, that of Bernard a Bessa, a companion of St. Bonaventure himself, in the *Catalogus Ministrorum Generalium*, which manuscript is extant in the library of Turin, Cod. sign. I. VI. 33. fol., 120. vers. col. 2. This Catalogue was also published in a very rare book: « Speculum vitae beati Francisci et Sociorum eius; in fine: Impressum metis per Iasparem Hochffeder. Anno dni 1509 » (in 12vo.), where it is found in fol. 209 verso. Since this edition has several variant readings, we have inserted the unique ones in brackets in the text which follows, which was transcribed by Father Fedele da Fanna from the Turin codex: « Seventh, there succeeded Bl. Francis, the brilliant Father Friar Bonaventure of Bagnoregio, who, since he had entered the Order as a youth, was strong in so great an honesty of good nature, that that great (Ed. *egregious*) master Alexander used to sometimes say of him, that in him Adam seemed not to have sinned. He was seen to make progress as much in the lights of the sciences and most of all in the Sacred Scriptures (Ed. Writings) with a wonderful capacity, that he also increased continually in the grace of devotion, because he continually (Ed. lacks *continually*) ruminated with affection over every truth, which he perceived with the intellect, reducing (it) to the form of a prayer and divine praise. Hence it came to pass, that in the seventh year after his entrance into the Order (to the Order), that he read the Sentences at Paris, and the tenth year received the title of "Master", and in the XII. (Ed. thirteenth) and/or XIII. was assumed to the government of the Order ». The final numbers contain a manifest error, as Sbaralea and Bonelli have already observed. From the carelessness of copyists regarding these Roman numerals, there has been omitted the V, whence there are to be read as "XVII and/or XVIII". — These words of Bernard a Bessa are repeated by St. Antoninus, *Chronica*, p. III, section 24, ch. 8; yet he adds after *read at Paris*: « And he published a notable and devout writing on the Four Books of Sentences and received there the title of "Master" ».

[2] Which work bears the title: *Ratio novae collectionis* operum omnium or editorum or anecdotorum Seraphici Eccl. Doctoris S. Bonaventurae proxime in lucem edendae, manuscriptorum bibliothecis totius Europae perlustratis, mandante Reverendissimo P. Bernardino a Portu Romantino, totius Ordinis S. Francisci Generali Ministro, studio ac labore P. Fidelis a Fanna, lectoris theologi et sociorum eiusdem Ordinis; Turin, Pontifical & Archiepiscopal Typography of Eq. Pietro Marietti, 1874.

I.

Immediately, from the birthplace of the art of typography very many works and/or opuscula of the Seraphic Doctor, whether each singly or several united, were undertaken to be printed. So often were editions of this kind repeated, that there is scarcely numbered many years throughout the centuries in which not at least one or another opuscule of the Seraphic Doctor, whether retaining the original Latin tongue or as translated into various languages, was sent to press. In the 15th Century itself, at least fifty editions of this kind are counted, not a few of which came to light without notes regarding place, time and typographer. Yet, it will be better to deal with these editions of each work in the Prolegomena to be prefaced to each one; which will also be done concerning the various collections of the small opuscula. Here we shall deal briefly only with the editions of the *Opera Omnia* of Saint Bonaventure.

« And so, the first[1] edition of the *Opera Omnia et Opusculorum S. Bonaventurae* came forth at Rome, at the Vatican presses, by order of *Pope Sixtus V*, begun in the year 1588, and brought to completion under Clement VIII, in 1599. It comprised seven tomes *in folio*, the sixth and seventh of which contain the opuscula, arranged in four parts, the rest (of the tomes) the Opera. Hardly any work, as *Casimirus Oudinus*[2] says, proceeded from the Vatican typography, which can be compared with these works on account of the brightness and purity of the paper, the elegance and emendation of the printing, all contributing to the splendor of this edition. Collaborating to adorn the outstanding work were several of the most learned and ingenious men, thoroughly celebrated with praise, exceedingly expert in the art of critique for the age in which they lived: *Constantius* Cardinal *Sarnanus*, Friar Minor Conventual, who passed from life before he saw the work completed; *Angelus Rocca* of the Order of Hermits of St. Augustine, Prefect of the Apostolic Sacrarium and Bishop of Tagesta; *Franciscus Lamata*, doctor of theology, and finally, *Petrus Galesinius*, Protonotary Apostolic, as they say.

These very erudite men contributed such a great authority to the edition adorned by them, that another came forth according to its example, namely the Mainz (edition) of 1609, undertaken by Antonius Hieratus, and the third at Lyons in 1678, at the expense of Philip Borde, Laurence Arnaud and Pier Borde, each consisting in seven volumes *in folio*, having changed nothing of the order of the Vatican edition regarding the distribution of the works ».

Nevertheless, there were already not lacking to that age erudite men, who brought to light the various defects of the Vatican edition, especially that not all the works received were genuine, and that not all the received were the legitimate offspring of the Seraphic genius. For as *Wadding*[3] says: « *Iulius Negronius*, S. J., an otherwise pious and learned man, somewhat more incautious than the learned and critical, who more easily deny others' works, than write their own, opened the widest gate to eliminate whatsoever opuscule of Bonaventure and those ascribed to him, since, as *Heribertus Rosweydus* reports, he suspected, that all the spiritual opuscula, which went about in the

---

[1] Sbaralea, *Supplem.*, p. 143, n. 5, says: « The *Opera Omnia* (S. Bonaventurae) was published at Paris in 7 folio tomes in 1517, in 4vo. by Berthold Remblat, which edition is extant at Rome in the library of the Convent of the Twelve Holy Apostles ». The learned man and/or editor of this work seems to have erred. Perhaps this edition contains only several opuscula.

[2] In (his) *Commentarius de Scriptoribus eccles.*, tome III, col. 380, Leipzig, 1722.

[3] *Scriptores Ord. Min.*, Rome, 1806, p. 51, col. 2.

Order of Friars Minor without an author('s name), collected by the pious man were brought to light under the name of St. Bonaventure. And even Rosweydus himself called six of the opuscula of the saintly man into controversy and attributed (them) as the supposed off-spring of other Fathers: namely *Alphabetum monachorum*, the *Collectiones octo*; the *Speculum disciplinae ad Novitios*; the de *Profectu religiosorum*, Bk. I; the de *Profectu religiosorum*, Bk. II; the de *Institutione novitiorum*, part I ». Then, Wadding proffers several (things), by which he also strives to vindicate these six opuscula of the Seraphic Doctor.

What his arguments are worth will have to be discussed elsewhere. In regard to the five opuscula, which were placed by the editors of the Vatican edition in the appendix as sup-posed and/or at least doubtful, Wadding nearly agrees with them. On the other hand, the same author rightly asserted, that several genuine works of St. Bonaventure were still unedited, which he promised he was going to publish in an new edition of the *Opera Omnia S. Bonaventurae*, which he set in motion. « We are preparing », says he, « a great addition to those which heretofore have been published in the Vatican edition, the most copious of all (editions), with many works transcribed even out of the Vatican storehouse, which have never been published ». But yet, the outstanding man, carried off by death, was not able to execute his proposal; grieving over which, *Philippus Labbé*, S. J. said: « Would that someone be chosen in Wadding's place, to guarantee each work », that is to publish the unpublished and separate the genuine from the spurius.

Meanwhile, from the adverse side there arose *Casimirus Oudinus*, first professed in the Order of Premonstratensian, then apostate from the Order and from the Faith, who in his famous work: *Commentarius de scriptoribus ecclesiasticis*, both detracted with a virulent spirit the doctrine of the two saintly Doctors, Thomas Aquinas and Bonaventure, and strove to prove with the assistance of critical parties, wanting in studies, that very many writings of each are supposed. He asserted that neither (was) worthy of the title "Doctor of the Church" and used not infrequently light and/or even false arguments, to cast very many writings, es-pecially of the Seraphic (Doctor), among the spurious and/or at least doubtful.

After the intemperate critique of Oudin, though several times concluding true even out of light arguments, two Fathers of the Order of St. Francis of the Observance, omitting their own names (though they were *Fr. Giovanni Mazzucato* and *Fr. Giovanni de Augustinis*), pre-pared a new and fourth edition, which came to light at Venice in 1751, from the typography of Stefano Orlando and Giovanni Battista Albriti, in 13 tomes 4vo..

These published all and only the works and opuscula of the Vatican edition, having added only a certain very short letter of St. Bonaventure; yet they changed the order entirely, by distinguishing the whole edition into three parts, one of which comprised the certain works, the other the doubtful ones, and the third those which were supposed according to their own sentence. To the first tome they prefaced a foreward, which, together with a life of St. Bonaventure, exhibited the *Diatriba historico-chronologico-critica in opera eiusdem*, in which they gave their own sentence concerning each work, whether it be genuine, or not. Indeed, these edi-tors promised a more ornate and more correct edition, of the kind which Wadding also prepared and Philippus Labbé desired. « The prayers of Labbé », they said, « do not seem to have been uttered in vain. For, behold, we, who are little able in both use and in-genuity, are unequal to survey this province, unanimous in the endeavor and concordant in

---

[1] In the notes adjoined to the book by (St.) Robert Bellarmine, *de Scriptor. eccles.*, Venice, 1728, p. 449, col. 2.

[2] *Dissert. de script. S. Thomae*, tome III, col. 254; *Dissert. de script. S. Bonav.*, col. 373.

[3] *Diatriba*, pp. 45 and 46.

in the darings, have weighed into this with every effort, so that which was promised by
Wadding, we might plainly fulfill ». But the execution of the matter did not stand entirely
in favor of these promises. For the text of the works, which they promised to exhibit more
corrected, abounded with more and graver mistakes and even lacunae than the three preceding, general editions. In regard to the critical dijudication among the genuine and spurious works they themselves seemed to hold to a middle way between Oudin (whose violent
reproaches against the Seraphic Doctor, were, indeed entirely reproved) and the Roman editors, together with Wadding; but yet they very often follow Oudin, (their) torch bearer, as
they themselves confess (him). In accord with their judgment, among the thirteen volumes
of this edition, there are, sanely, only five, which contain the certain works of the Seraphic
(Doctor), twenty-eight in number.

But this critique, more intemperate than fair, and laboring under a certain levity, could
not not solicit learned Catholic men, first of all within the Order of St. Francis, both to refute the false assertions of Oudin and the Venetian editors, and to adorn with new care a
truly corrected edition. The Very Reverend Minister General of the whole Order of St. Francis, *Petrus Ioannetius de Molina*, by letters dated at Madrid, May 23, 1763, gave a mandate to
Fr. Benedictus Bonelli a Cavallesio, member of the St. Vigilius' Province of Trent for the Reformati, a man first of all learned and versed very much in the study of the monuments of
antiquity, to adorn a new edition of the Opera S. Bonaventurae in accord with the rules of
sane criticism and to simultaneously take precautions against the abberations of the Venetian editors, whom he complained loudly to have been deceived by the more intemperate
criticism of Casimir Oudin, a heterodox man.[1] Fr. Benedictus, after he was elected by the Father General of the Order to undertake this province, approached the arduous work with
the greatest study and unwearied labor. First, having begged everywhere as many documents for the work as he was able to have, he published an outstanding work, which he entitled: *Prodromus ad opera omnia S. Bonaventurae* etc., at the typography of Bassano in 1767,
at the expense of the Remondini. This work he divided into eight books, and in Book I he
treated of the life or deeds of St. Bonaventure, in the II., of his doctrine, in the III., he exhibited animadversions about his writings, in the IV., canons for rightly forming a judgment about the same writings, in the V., indicula and catalogues illustrated by notes, in
the VI., he enumerates the editions both general, and singular, in the VII., the handwritten codices, in the VIII. and last, he institutes an examination of each of the published
works, whether true or verisimilar, whether uncertain and doubtful, or manifestly supposed, and finally of (those) unpublished. The whole and corrected edition of these works
had to except this Prodromus; but yet, since Fr. Benedictus Bonelli was already at an advanced age and his strength worn out by labor, he feared, not without cause,

---

[1] A copy of this sufficiently long Epistle exists, faithfully transcribed by Fr. Chrysostomus ab Avolano, colleague of Fr. Benedictus
Bonelli, and conserved in the archive of the Convent of St. Bernardine at Trent, a copy of which, transcribed by Fr. Fedele da Fanna,
is extant in the archive of our College. On account of the value of the word, we have judge to subjoin here some things from it: «
Hence it is that . . . stirred by the most sublime merits of so great a Doctor (St. Bonaventure), towards whom we have professed a special
affection of devotion from our youth, and (who) had already for a long time enkindled the most ardent desire of our spirit, to procure
a new and most exact edition of his works, according to the norm of the prudent counsel, which the most famous father of the Annales
Franciscanorum, Luke Wadding, had conceived, but which having been prevented by death could scarcely complete . . . Nor was it
hidden from us, that according to the judgment of many, the editions of the works of our Seraphic doctor heretofore have abounded,
by public judgment, in interpolations and mistakes, from the number of which we do not except the latest Venetian edition, which even
if erudite men have approved as more copious and more exact than all the rest, yet there are not lacking theologians of equal erudition
and doctrine, who in studies withdrawn from partisanship, recalling the said edition to the more rigid canons of criticism, tore to pieces
with critical remarks the Venetian editors, who being deceived by the more intemperate critique of the heterodox Casimir Oudin,
faultily asserted several vain and incoherent suppositions against the golden and germain works of the Divine Bonaventure; but, on
the other hand, they alleged (to be) among the spurious and illegitimate so many, which are to be vindicated by certain documents as
having a sincere and genuine origin from the most excellent Doctor. And so, to take measures against these abberations, there would
be, in a word, no other obvious remedy than to adorn a new edition » etc..

that the immense work, which he had undertaken, would be unfinished. Wherefore, he did this one (thing), so that he might at least bring to light the unpublished (works), which he had collected, which he proffered in three volumes in folio, under the title: *S. Bonaventurae* etc. *operum omnium Supplementum,* under the auspices of the Roman Pontiff, Clement XIV, at Trent, in 1772-1774. These volumes contain forty-five works and/or opuscula illustrated with the most copious notes, each of which will be enumerated below. — We judge to be pertinent, the words of the editor of the same at the beginning of the dedicatory epistle to the Supreme Pontiff Clement XIV, prefaced to the first tome: « It was, indeed, to be wondered at and grieved, that these golden monuments of our Seraphic Doctor have been, in part, pulled this way and that by the same judgment of a more severe and intemperate critique and have been deprived of the honor of their own author, in part, too, allowed to gather dust for a long time, as (things) entirely ignored and neglected in the corners and hidden-places of libraries. On which account we, the same, have very often complained loudly to ourselves, as ones enkindled by an innate and just shame, understanding well, that our (authority) ought, for a long time, have intervened most ably, to vindicate them from every injury, whether of ages or of men ».[1] — Truly, before Fr. Benedictus Bonelli, another most learned man from the family of Friars Minor Conventual, Master *Ioannes Hyacinthus Sbaralea,* who died in the year 1763, had solidly refuted Oudin in many (things) and restored not a few works of St. Bonaventure with more certain arguments, in his work: *Supplementum ad scriptores* trium Ordinum S. Francisci, first edited at Rome, in the year 1806 (i. e. in the forty-third year after his death), which work in manuscript Fr. Bonelli wisely made use of, as he himself frankly says in the preface to the Prodromus, p. XI.. — Finally, through the course of the nineteenth century,

---

[1] The thoroughly singular, and insufficiently recognized merits of Fr. Benedictus Bonelli toward the works of the Seraphic Doctor seen to require by right, that in this place there be inserted something about this most erudite man, which we have taken from the booklet: *Cenni intorno alla vita ed agli scritti del P. Benedetto Bonelli da Cavallese, de' Minori Riformati di S. Francesco,* Trent, Monaunus, 1861. Therefore, he was born on Dec. 26, 1704 of noble lineage to Giovanni Domenico Bonelli and Francesca Antonia Miorini, in the village of Cavallese, in the valle of the Fiemme, not far from Trent. He dedicated himself to humanistic studies at Trent in the schools of the Society of Jesus; he took the habit of St. Francis, with the name of Benedictus, among the Minori Reformati on May 26, 1721. Having completed the novitiate *cum laude,* he gave himself in earnest to philosophical and theological studies in the schools of his Province. Excelling all others in piety and doctrine, he was promoted to the priesthood in the month of December, 1728. From the year 1731 he discharged at first the office of lector in philosophy and then in theology in the schools of the Order. At the same time he dedicated himself unflaggingly to the continuation of (his) studies, to writing books and to preaching the word of God. He was elected a Definitor of his Province in 1745 and afterwards substituted for his Minister Provincial in the General Chapter of 1746, celebrated at Murcia in Spain, where he was elected Definitor General for the German nation, in the execution of which office he was present at the General Chapter of 1765, held at Mantua. He was ordered by the Chapter, to compose letters to Clement XIII against the laxities breaking forth in books of moral doctrine and even against Probabilism; which he completed with much erudition. At the same time, he accepted from the Minister General, Petrus Ioannetio de Molina the mandate, of which we have spoken above, of editing the works of St. Bonaventure. In the year 1778, on March 28, he was assumed again to the dignity of Definitor General, as a substitute of Fr. Leander Luegmayer, at the latter's death. Exerting himself unflaggingly in labors until the end of (his) life, he died piously in the Lord, on October 28, 1778, at Trent, in the Convent of St. Bernardine. By (his) love of solitude, (his) hatred for sloth, (his) assiduity in preaching the word of God, (his) excellence of eloquence and memory, (his) rare patience in studies, the abundance of (his) erudition, the gravity of (his) morals, (and his) piety for God, he won over all by his singular reverence and authority. He wrote 107 works and/or opuscula, not a few of which pertain to ascetics, but very many to ecclesiastical history and the knowledge of antiquities and to Christian ethics. Only thirty of his works have been brought to press, among which, besides the two we have already mentioned, there are some pertaining to ascetics and very many to things historical, such as the *Dissertazione apologetica sul martirio del B. Simone da Trento nell'anno 1475 dagli Ebrei ucciso,* Trent 1747; *Vindiciae Romani Martyrologii XIII Augusti, S. Cassiani Foro-Corneliensis martyris* etc., Verona 1751, together with other opuscula defending this work; *Dissertazione intorno alla santità e mertirio del B. Adalpreto, Vescovo di Trento, dedicata a S. Santità Benedetto XIV,* Trent, 1754; *Notizie storico-critiche intorno al B. M. Adalpreto ed intorno ad altri vescovi della Germania e dell'Italia ai tempi dello scismo di Federigo I.,* in 2 volumes in 4vo., Trent 1760-1761; *Notizie storico-critiche della chiesa di Trento,* Trent, 1762; *Monumenta ecclesiae Tridentinae,* Trent, 1765, in 4vo.; *Osservazione sulla giunta e critica fatta dal P. Zaccharia; Dell'indulgenza della Porziuncula.* The very many (works) which he wrote to vindicate a more severe ethic, are for the most part unedited, just as (is) also the work, which he completed a few days before (his) death, when for the first time, in the year 1778, with a fire having broken out by chance in his cell, he was nearly burnt alive, the title of which is: *De fide, moribus et disciplina adversus profanas opinionum novitates doctrina sacra et antiqua, ex operibus Doctoris Seraphici Bonaventurae ac aliorum Patrum atque Doctorum deducta, secundum ordinem locorum theologicorum digesta et in libros XIV ac 3 tomos distributa, pro rite instituenda iuventute ecclesiastica et religiosa.*

four new editions of the *Opera Omnia S. Bonaventurae* were announced by diverse editors in Italy, but none of them saw the light.

But the fifth edition of these works began to come forth at Paris, in 1864, at (the press) of Ludovicus Vivès, under the care and study of A. C. Peltier, canon of the Church of Riems. In regard to the art of (its) typography, the edition merits praise; even the system of punctuation and orthography was accommodated to modern usages. But in regard to the intrinsic value of the edition, there were many (things) to be desired, many which cannot be approved of. First of all, there are not exhibited but the works, which were extant in the Venetian edition, with the addition only of the short letter of St. Bonaventure to Fr. Laurentius, which was taken from Wadding. The text published was in accord with the worst edition of all, the Venetian one, yet with typographical errors corrected here and there, and very often with not a few words changed, which seemed to Dom Peltier (to be) false. The same did not consult (any) codices but one *super Sententias*, of which, as he himself says, he hopes often to make use of;[1] yet no where else does he say, where he made use of it. In the first tome, the Life of St. Bonaventure and the Diatriba historico-chronologico-critica of the Venetian edition were republished. Yet there are added in the notes not a few general observations in the Gallic tongue to mitigate their immoderate criticism.[2] In the said preface the editor says, that he has published the *Commentaria in libros Sententiarum* in the first place, mostly for this reason, that he might apprehend by degrees and steps St. Bonaventure's manner of speaking and style.[3] Yet, there must be added, that after Dom Peltier had edited the first three tomes, as he himself says in the preface to the fourth tome, he obtained from the most famous Dom Prospero Guéranger the *Prodromus ad opera omnia S. Bonaventurae*, edited by Fr. Benedictus Bonelli, and thereupon prefaced to each work very many (things) drawn from the Prodromus to refute Oudin and the Venetian (editors); but neither did he adhere always to the opinions of Fr. Bonelli, even though he adduced no authority and/or special reason for diluting the reasonings of the Prodromus. Of the works published by Fr. Bonelli in the three tomes of (his) Supplementum, he makes no mention, though he was admonished of their existence, and he neglected entirely to publish and add them to all the other works.

On which account, by optimum counsel, the Most Rev. Minister General, *Fr. Bernardinus a Portu Romantino*, in 1871 proposed to publish with new care and studies the most complete edition of the works of St. Bonaventure, which would contain besides the works published in the five aforesaid editions, the entire *Supplementum* of Fr. Bonelli and the other unpublished opuscula, with an emended text and illustrated with marginal notes. To accomplish which work, he chose the most suitable man, *Fr. Fedele da Fanna*, lector in theology from the Venetian Province. Who, after he had collected for ten years, by immense labors, all the monuments pertaining to this edition, and conceived the idea for preparing

---

[1] Tome I, prèface: . . . dont nous espérons faire souvent usage.

[2] The singular reason why he used the Gallic tongue, is explained by the editor therein: « Le lecteur ne sìffensera pas si, dans la plupart de ces notes, comme dans cette prèface, nous lui parlons en français, au lieu de le faire en latin. C'est que nous voulons exprimer clairement notre pensée, et la faire comprehendre à nos lecteurs, et que nous courrions risque de manquer ce double but, si nous adoptions une autre langue que nostre langue maternelle ».

[3] « En l'étudiant donc avant les autres, nous apprendrons insensiblement à connaitre la manière et le style de nostre auteur, et per ce moyen nous nous mettrons plus en état d'apprécier le just valeur des obiections que les éditeurs de Venise ont cru pouvoir élever contre une partie certainement trop considérable des autres écrits qui portent le nom de saint Bonaventure, en se fondant plus souvent sur une prétendue différence de style ».

this edition, having employed every assistance of the modern art of criticism, and opened the way putting it into execution with (his) strong spirit, ought to be judged the first and principle author of this whole edition. Therefore, it seems just to us, that, though it has pleased Almighty God to snatch him from this present age at the beginning of this year, we now offer, at this point, a faithful memorial to his life and labors.

Father Fedele was born on December 24, 1838 to the honest parents Oswaldo Maddalena and Augela Marusmattius in the small village of Fanna, in the Italian province of Friuli. Having learned his first letters in his own land, he was soon versed in the studies of humanities, at Venice, under the discipline of the pious and learned priest, *Giovanni Battista Piamonte*. Called by a divine inspiration to embrace the Seraphic Order, he received the religious habit on September 29, 1855, in the same place, in the Convent of San Michele in Insula, from *Fr. Bernardino a Portu Romantino*, at that time Minister Provincial of the Province of Venice for the Reformati and presently the Minister General of the whole Order of St. Francis; and he pronounced his solemn profession in the hands of the same on September 19, 1858.

Endowed with an outstanding genius, a singular diligence and a firm and constant spirit, he made marked progress in the studies of rhetoric, philosophy and theology. At the same time he was initiated in the doctrine of the truly Seraphic St. Bonaventure, under the guide of A. R. P. *Antonio Maria a Vicetia*, the present Minister Provincial of the mentioned Venetian Province and most noted editor of the *Breviloquium S. Bonaventurae*, illustrated with various additions. Promoted to the priesthood on December 26, 1862, he was apprized by his superiors as being so thoroughly prepared and mature in doctrine and morals, that they committed to him the office of lector. Nor was the hope put in him deceived, as he explained in an outstanding manner the philosophical disciplines and the Breviloquium of St. Bonaventure in the schools of his Province. Yet, on account of the vicissitudes of the times he was driven very often to move with his clerical students, teaching in 1866-1867 in the Convent of the Swabian Province of St. Leopold of Tyrol, and then in the Convent of Cimellas, near Nice. Twice gripped with tuberculosis, he was driven to retire from the office of teaching in 1869. However, being restored to health, on the occasion of the (First) Vatican Council he was summoned (Feb. 9, 1870) by the Most Rev. Minister General, to defend the genuine doctrine of St. Bonaventure concerning the prerogatives of the Supreme Pontiff; which he completed in the shortest time with the opuscule: *Seraphici Doctoris S. Bonaventurae Doctrina de Romani Pontificis primatu et infallibilitate*, Rome, 1870. A little afterwards, he wrote a treatise in the Italian tongue against pseudo-liberalism: *Urgente escursione contro una mano di ausiliari massonici*, Venice, 1871. However, he was then commissioned by the Most Rev. Minister General, on his own authority, to adorn a new edition of the works of St. Bonaventure. By the aforementioned, most diligent, preparatory studies, he soon saw, that it was not sufficient to subject once again to the press, the ancient editions, however recognized, but that better codices and manuscripts, whether they contained edited or unpublished works, would have to be sought out from the dust of libraries, consulted, compared exactly, so that this new edition might be both complete and correct according to the rules of the critical art. On which account, charged with the special diploma of the Most Rev. Minister General, he undertook to travel among the treasures of very many libraries, with felicitous success. With letters dated at Venice, July 14, 1871 and sent to the Prefects of the principal libraries of Europe, he was able to collect much information concerning the codices pertaining to St. Bonaventure. Nevertheless, he understood that neither did this suffice, but that he himself would have to travel to and accurately survey the libraries,

so as to be able to collect all the documents pertaining to it. Whence, he traveled outside Italy to all the lands of Europe, if you except Russia and Sweeden, and he yielded to no difficulty nor spared any labor in collecting from libraries, both public and private, even documents of minor moment, which could illustrate in some manner the works or life of St. Bonaventure. Of the very suitable method, which he follows in visiting the libraries, he himself rendered an account in his own book, soon to be mentioned. Having employed this diligence and this his own method, he uncovered in the recesses of libraries, several works of the Seraphic Doctor, lying in hiding, heretofore unpublished, and collected the better codices of the books already edited to emend their not rarely distorted and/or mutilated text, and made note of very many documents of literary history, which served to resolve more certainly so many of the questions (which) had arisen, but (which) were not yet sufficiently answered, concerning the genuine works of St. Bonaventure. With incredible study and equal diligence and outstanding expertise in the art of paleography, he traveled, in the space of eight years, to nearly forty libraries in France, England, Belgium, Switzerland, Germany, Denmark, Austria, Bavaria, Holland, Spain, Portugal (and) Italy, and supported by the assistance of several colleagues he described no less than fifty thousand codices, examined more accurately, in many volumes dug up by hand. In his own commentaries, besides those which pertain to St. Bonaventure, he diligently noted down very many handwritten codices of other authors worthy of mention, especially all those, which pertain to the authors of our Order, living before the 16th Century, and/or to the history of the Order. Which notes concerning the ancient authors of our Order were compiled for this reason, because the great part of these works were not yet published at press, and not a few were unknown to Wadding himself and to Sbaralea.

On the occasion of the sixth centenary of the passing of St. Bonaventure, occurring in the year 1874, ceasing briefly from visiting libraries, he composed the aforementioned book: *Ratio novae collectionis operum omnium Seraphici Doctoris S. Bonaventurae*, in which he spoke diffusely, in an orderly manner, of the causes and method for preparing the new edition, and treated of certain handwritten books of St. Bonaventure, exhibiting for that reason various specimens; and then he composed a catalogue of unedited works, which are extant under the name of St. Bonaventure in many libraries and which had not, till then, been uncovered. This book, though put to gether in the shortest time, was everywhere received with applause by men, learned and exercised in the critical art.[1] Having returned from Spain and Portugal, Fr. Fedele took himself to his home, which the Most Rev. Father General had begun to prepare near Florence in the village, which is popularly called *Quaracchi* (Clarae Aquae): the *College of St. Bonaventure*, so that there with the colleagues, which he had employed in traveling the libraries, and according to studies of this kind, he might be better at leisure to arrange the edition with a long and arduous study. However, often leaving from there, he went to several libraries

---

[1] The most famous Lord, Leopold Delisle, Prefect of Manuscripts for the National Library of Paris, in a public session of the Academy of Letters honored this book with praises (*Académie des inscriptions et belles-lettres*, bulletin for July-August-September 1874, pp. 301, 302. In the same sense, there wrote of it: Fr. D. Sommervogle, *Études religieuses, philosphiques, historique et littéraires*, tome VI, August 1874; Fr. D. Eugène Gardereau, O. S. B., *Monde*, 1874, N. 300 & 309; *Polybiblion*, revue bigliographique universelle, Series II, Paris 1875; *L'Univers*, February 20, 1875; *L'Union*, Sept. 28, 1874. Likewise in Italy, Fr. D. Cesare Guasti, *Revista universale*, March 1875; *La Scienza et la Fede*, Naples, vo. 94, fasc. 562, Aug. 1874; *Carità, revista religiosa, scientifica, letteraria*, Naples 1875, February. In Germany: Fr. Scneemann, S. J.: *Stimmen aus Maria-Laach*, 1876, Heft 9; *Der Katholik*, 1876, July; *Litterarischer Handwiser*, 1874. In England: *The Tablet*. In Spain: Fr. D. I. Orti y Lara, *La Sciencia Cristiana*, Vol. 2, N. 7, 1877, March & April; *El Siglo futuro*, 1877, April 11. On the occasion of the Royal Academy of history of Madrid (La Real Academia de la historia) in the gathering held on Dec. 3, 1877, decreed on it own initiative that Fr. Fedele be granted a diploma honoring (him) as an oversees member.

in the years 1878-1879, and undertook not a few cares and labors, so that he might prepare the library of the new College with the best works suited to this purpose. Following the feast of St. Bonaventure, on July 14, 1879, he applied himself with the seven colleagues gathered there, to the preparation of the same new edition, with all his forces.

But by the inscrutable counsel of Divine Providence it happened, that during Lent of the year 1880, while he traveled to not a few libraries of northern Italy with exceeding labor, he caught the germ of the deadly disease, by which he was overcome. Growing heavier with that disease at the end of the month of May of the same year, we was constrained from the same time to remain lying in bed for the rest of the year and beyond, which, however, gave a certain free scope to the alacrity of (his) genius, to the fortitude of (his) spirit, (and) to (his) solicitude for the matter at hand; meanwhile, consumed by a slow consumption, (and) duly fortified most frequently with the Eucharistic food and the other Sacraments of the Church, consoled on the last day of his life by the Apostolic Benediction of the Supreme Pontiff and by the presence of the Most Rev. Father General, his own father in Christ, and resigned entirely to the Divine Will, he rested piously in the Lord among the prayers of the Friars, on the feast of St. Clare, the 12th of August, in the year of 1881. *Consummatus in brevi explevit tempora multa* (Wis. 4:13), whose memory be in benediction.

II.

With these (things) narrated according to the order of material, let us briefly propose, what was left to us by preceeding editors to be done for the new edition.

Indeed, the *first* defect of those editions is, that the text was not corrected fully in any of the works, nay, in very many works it abounds with mistakes, lacunae and interpolations, which had crept into the Vatican edition and passed over into the following ones. Not a few works, already in the first editions, came to light only as ones mutilated and vitiated, such that they seem hardly worthy of a mediocre genius, let alone of the Seraphic Doctor. To not speak, in this place, of other books, the very *Commentarius in libros Sententiarum* was lacking, least of all, in the vices just mentioned. Of this *Petrus Trigosus*, O. S. F. Cap.,[1] had already complained loudly in these words: « All the copies, which I have seen (speaking of a certain passage in q. 1, of the Prologue), are full of mistakes, which I find frequently in this Seraphic Doctor. And I grieve very much, that so great a Doctor overflows with so many mistakes, that I know not whom to fault. Yet, his emended and augmented works are very much desired by the order of Pope Sixtus V, of happy memory ». Many of their specimens, which both in the *Commentary on the Sentences*, and in the *Commentary on Ecclesiastes* were omitted, are offered by the mentioned *Ratio novae collectionis* etc..[2] This first tome of our edition provides several other specimens on nearly every page, though we have, indeed, made no mention of very many (of their) typographical errors. This grave vice of the preceding editions manifestly corroborates that this new edition is opportune; nor is it established that a remedy can be employed against this, except after having consulted several and better codices. For all erudite (men) know, that very many codices have been corrupted with mistakes and lacunae by the yawnings and in-expertise of copyists. This happened most of all from the 13th to 15th Centuries; partly on account of the very abbreviated writing, with many signs or compendary notes, and for that reason one often very difficult to read; partly on account of the multitude of inexpert transcribers, who quested for

---

[1] *Summa theol. S. Bonaventurae*, Lugduni 1616, p. 18, col. 1.

[2] Part II, p. 200 ff..

books to transcribe. Either entirely inexpert in the Latin tongue, and/or not sufficiently expert, these were accustomed to admit so very many errors, which hindered the clarity of expression, not rarely change the sense and/or at least caused the latinity, not despised by the author, to reek with a certain barbarity in solecisms, transpositions and/or omissions of words. There is an old complaint of learned men concerning books written badly. To be silent of Cicero, *Ioannes Gerson*[1] speaks of books corrupted through the ineptitude of transcribers, thus: « our age has brought forth very many of such a kind, the volumes of which are so erroneous, that it would be more advised to employ none, than such ... Some estimate that this no small loss was attributed to the studies and universities of our stormy age, when anyone was admitted to write unproven, unrecognized. Examples are also given uncorrected » etc.. Nor were there lacking, chiefly in the 14th and 15th Centuries, interpolators, who when copying, inserted glosses in the work, in good and/or bad faith; nor did others rarely omit any part of the work as less useful to themselves. Hence, often the outstanding works, both editioned and unedited, seemed (to be) so incorrect, obscure, (and) bearing contradictory sentences, that they appear often unworthy of their own authors. To restore these to their native purity by the riches of the critical art is of so great a value, that those who will guarantee this can be regarded as another parent of the work. Lead by this reasoning, Father Fedele da Fanna spared no diligence and labor, to find suitable, rather than very many, codices to guarantee this; and we have employed and promise to employ all diligence, so that the original text of St. Bonaventure, as much as (our) means and forces allow, be restored to (its) pristine integrity.

In the *second* place, this also must be grieved, namely, that in the preceding editions such a great incertitude still subsists in discerning the doubtful and/or spurious from the genuine writings of the Seraphic Doctor. The chief censors treating of this matter disagree among themselves so much, that they contradict themselves about many works. Hence, great confusion could not be avoided, so long as readers disagree not only in according to the diverse judgments of the censors whom they consult in regard to judging the authenticity of the works, but also, by alleging sentences taken from these books, proclaim now St. Bonaventure, now another author, to be (their) author. So that the reader can discern with his own eyes how great (is) the variety of (their) dissenting judgments, we judge worthy of consideration, to adjoin here an overview of all the works of St. Bonaventure, according to the book by Fr. Fedele,[2] with the diversity of sentences arranged in a row, by which those four authors, whom we have named further above, judged the same works as either certain, spurius or doubtful. These (authors) are *Oudinus*, the *Venetian editors*, *Sbaralea* and *Fr. Benedictus Bonelli*, in the passages already cited. We subjoin also a catalogue of those works, which were edited by the same *Bonelli* in his *Supplementum*, along with the notes, by which the author distinguished each, in the *Prodromus* and in the same *Supplementum*, as certain or verisimile.

---

[1] *De Laude scriptorum consid.*, 6.
[2] Page 28 ff..

OVERVIEW

OF THE WORKS OF THE VATICAN EDITION

AND OF THE NOTES BY WHICH EACH IS DISTINGUISHED

BY THE CHIEF CRITICS,

NAMELY

CASIMIR OUDIN, THE VENETIAN EDITORS,

FR. IOANNES HYACINTHUS SBARALEA & FR. BENEDICTUS BONELLI

ORDER OF THE VATICAN EDITION	According to Casimir Oudin	According to the Venetian Editors	According to Fr. Io. Hyacinth. Sbaralea	According to Fr. Benedictus Bonelli
1. **Principium S. Scripturae.** Incipit: *Ostendit mihi Dominus... fructus duodecim.* Probatissimae perfectissimaque legis integritas.	spurius	spurius	spurius	certain
2. **Illuminationes Ecclesiae**, or **Expositio in Hexaëmeron.** Incipit: *In medio Ecclesiae aperuit os eius...* In verbis istis docet Sapiens.	spurius	spurius	spurius	certain
3. **Expositio in Psalterium.** Incipit: *Quisquis ad divinae pagine lectionem erudiendus accedit.*	certain	spurius	certain	certain
4. **Expositio in Psalm. 118.** Incipit: *Alleluia, Laus, honor... Beati immaculati.* Nota: Sacra Scriptura dicitur paradisus.	certain	spurius	spurius	spurius
5. **Expositio in Ecclesiasten.** Incipit: *Beatus vir, cuius est nomen Domini...* Cum sicut vult beatus Dionysius.	certain	spurius	certain	certain
6. **Expositio in Sapientiam.** Incipit: *Diligite lumen sapientiae...* Quoniam eodem habet res formari.	certain	certain	certain	certain
7. **Expositio in Lamentationes Hieremiae prophetae.** Incipit: *Tempus plangendi et tempus saltandi.* In verbo isto.	certain	certain	certain	certain

ORDER OF THE VATICAN EDITION	According to Casimir Oudin	According to the Venetian Editors	According to Fr. Io. Hyacinth. Sbaralea	According to Fr. Benedictus Bonelli
8. **Expositio in cap. VI. Sancti Matthaei.** Incipit: *Pater noster* etc. Oratio haec privilegiata est.	certain	doubtful	certain	certain
9. **Expositio in Evangelium Lucae.** Incipit: *Spiritus Domini super me...* Considerantibus nobis.	certain	doubtful	certain	certain
10. **Expositio in Evang. Ioan.** Incipit: *Numquid ad praeceptum tuum...* Cum inter quatuor sancta animalia.	spurious	doubtful	spurious	spurious
11. **Collationes in Ioannem.** Incipit: *In principio erat Verbum.* Supposita luminali expositione.	spurious	doubtful	spurious	spurious
12. **Sermones de tempore.** Incipit: *His autem fieri incipientibus...*Quoniam in Evangelio hodierno ponuntur presagia.	doubtful	spurious	not all genuine	some certain, w. not a few spurious
13. **Sermones de Sanctis.** Incipit: *Mihi absit gloriari nisi in cruce...* Narrat Valerius Maximus.	doubtful	spurious	not all genuine	some certain, w. not a few spurious
14. **Semones de communi Sanctorum.** Incipit: *Species caeli gloria stellarum.* Per caelum recte Ecclesia sancta inteligitur.	doubtful	spurious	not all genuine	some certain, w. not a few spurious
15. **In libr. primum Magistri Sententiarum.** Incipit: *Profunda fluviorum scrutatus est...*Verbum istud sumtum ex Iob.	certain	certain	certain	certain
16. **In libr. secundum Magistri Sententiarum.** Incipit: *Solummodo hoc inveni quod Deus...* Sollicite consideranti praesentis libri.	certain	certain	certain	certain
17. **In libr. tertium Magistri Sententiarum.** Incipit: *Deus autem qui dives est in misericordia...* Verbum istud scribitur ad Ephesios.	certain	certain	certain	certain
18. **In libr. quartum Magistri Sententiarum.** Incipit: *Unguentarious faciet pigmenta suavitatis...* Verbum istud scribitur in Ecclesiastico.	certain	certain	certain	certain

ORDER OF THE VATICAN EDITION	According to Casimir Oudin	According to the Venetian Editors	According to Fr. Io. Hyacinth. Sbaralea	According to Fr. Benedictus Bonelli
19. **De reductione artium ad theologiam.** Incipit: *Omne datum optimum...* In hoc verbo tangitur origo omnis illuminationis.	doubtful	doubtful	certain	certain
20. **Breviloquium.** Incipit: *Flecto genua mea ad Patrem... ut impleamini in omnem plenitudinem Dei..* Magnus doctor gentium	genuine	certain	certain	certain
21. **Centiloquium.** Incipit: *Ecce descripsi eam tibi tripliciter...* Informans Sapiens in his verbis.	certain	certain	certain	certain
22. **Pharetra.** Incipit: In conversionis mea primordio cum ob mentis recreationem auctoritates Sanctorum legerem.	spurious	spurious	certain	certain
23. **Declaratio terminorum theologiae.** Incipit: Omnipotens Deus Pater, Filius, Spiritus sanctus unus est Deus.	doubtful	doubtful	certain	certain
24. **Compendiosum principium in Libros Sententiarum.** Incipit: *Gyrnum caeli circuivi sola* etc. Quam sit libri Sententiarum inaccessibilis celsitudo.	spurious	spurious	spurious	verisimile
25. **Sententiae sententiarum carmine digestae.** Incipit: O fons splendoris, vas dulcoris.	spurious	spurious	spurious	certain
26. **De quatuor virtutibus cardinalibus.** Incipit: De quatuor virtutibus cardinalibus sunt virtues politicae.	not unworthy	doubtful	spurious	verisimile
27. **De septem donis Spiritus sancti.** Incipit: *Omne datum optimum...* Sanctus Iacobus apostolus.	doubtful	certain	spurious	spurious
28. **De resurrectione a peccato ad gratiam.** Incipit: Paulus apostolus videtur firmiter asserere.	not unworthy	certain	spurious	spurius
29. **De tribus ternarius peccatorum infamibus.** Incipit: Tres sunt ternarii peccatorum infames.	not unworthy	spurious	doubtful	certain

ORDER OF THE VATICAN EDITION	According to Casimir Oudin	According to the Venetian Editors	According to Fr. Io. Hyacinth. Sbaralea	According to Fr. Benedictus Bonelli
30. **Dieta salutis.** Incipit: *Haec est via, ambulate in ea...* Magnam misericordiam facit qui eranti viam ostendit.	spurious	spurious	spurious	spurious
31. **Meditationes vitae Christi.** Incipit: Inter alia virtutum et laudum praeconia.	spurious	spurious	spurious	spurious
32. **Lignum vitae.** Incipit: *Christo confixus sum cruxi.* Verus Dei cultor Christique discipulus.	not unworthy	certain	certain	certain
33. **De quinque festivitatibus pueri Iesu.** Incipit: Cum secundum virorum venerabilium.	spurious	spurious	spurious	certain
34. **Officium de passione dominica.** Incipit: Domine, labia mea aperies... *Invitator.* Christum captum et derisum, flagellatum et crucifixum, venite adoremus. *Hymn.* In passione Domini	spurious	spurious	certain	certain
35. **Opus contemplationis.** Incipit: Iesus ineffabilis persona Trinitatis.	spurious	spurious	spurious	certain
36. **Laudismus de sancta cruce.** Incipit: Recordare sanctae crucis, Qui perfectam vitam ducis.	spurious	spurious	certain	certain
37. **Philomena.** Incipit: Philomena praevia temporis amoeni.	spurious	spurious	spurious	verisimile
38. **De septem verbis Domini in cruce.** Incipit: Iesu salutis hostia, salutis sacrificium.	spurious	spurious	certain	certain
39. **Speculum B. M. Virginis.** Incipit: Quoniam, ut ait beatus Hieronymus, nulli dubium est.	spurious	spurious	spurious	spurious
40. **Officium de compassione B. M. Virginis.** Incipit: Domine, labia mea aperies... *Invitator.* Cum Maria Virgine ferbide ploremus, in sepulcro positum venite adoremus.	spurious	spurious	spurious	doubtful

ORDER OF THE VATICAN EDITION	According to Casimir Oudin	According to the Venetian Editors	According to Fr. Io. Hyacinth. Sbaralea	According to Fr. Benedictus Bonelli
41. **Corona B. M. Virginis.** Incipit: Cum iucunditate memoriam nominis Mariae celebremus.	spurious	spurious	certain	certain
42. **Carmina super canticum Salve Regina.** Incipit: Salve Virgo virginum, stella matutina.	spurious	spurious	spurious	certain
43. **Laus B. V. Mariae.** Incipit: Ave caeleste lilium, Ave rosa speciosa.	spurious	spurious	spurious	certain
44. **Psalterium minus B. M. Virginis.** Incipit: Ave Virgo, vitae lignum.	spurious	spurious	spurious	verisimile
45. **Psalterium maius B. M. V.** Incipit: *Arripe illam, et exaltabit te... Psalm.* Beatus vir, qui diligent nomen tuum, Maria virgo.	spurious	spurious	spurious	doubtful
46. **Sermones de decem praeceptis.** Incipit: *Si vis ad vitam ingredi...* Verba ista scripta sunt in Mattaeo, et sunt verba Salvatoris.	spurious	spurious	certain	certain
47. **Epistola vigintiquinque memorabilium.** Incipit: In Christo suo dilecto... qualicumque homine veteri iam exuto.	certain	doubtful	certain	certain
48. **De regimine animae.** Incipit: Primum omnium necesse habes, anima mea.	uncertain	doubtful	certain	certain
49. **Formula aurea de gradibus virtutum.** Incipit: *Accedite ad Dominum et illuminamini...* Ius hominis est ad Deum accedere.	spurious	spurious	certain	verisimile
50. **De pugna spirituali.** Incipit: Eia nunc milites Christi, bellum spirituale ingressuri.	spurious	doubtful	doubtful	certain
51. **Speculum animae.** Incipit: *Arbor mala fructus malos facit,* dicit Dominus. Secundum Glossam interlinearem.	spurious	spurious	certain	certain

ORDER OF THE VATICAN EDITION	According to Casimir Oudin	According to the Venetian Editors	According to Fr. Io. Hyacinth. Sbaralea	According to Fr. Benedictus Bonelli
52. **Confessionale.** Incipit: In Dei tabernaculo, id est in sancta Ecclesia.	spurious	spurious	spurious	spurious
53. **De praeparatione ad missam.** Incipit: Ad honorem gloriosae et individuae Trinitatis.	uncertain	doubtful	certain	certain
54. **De instructione sacerdotis ad se praeparandum ad celebrandam missam.** Incipit: Ad missam celebrandam sex consideranda sunt.	uncertain	doubtful	spurious	certain
55. **Expositio missae.** Incipit: *Christus assistens Pontifex.* Apostolus ad Hebraeos dicit illa verba de Domino Iesu.	spurious	spurious	spurious	certain
56. **De sex alis Seraphim.** Incipit: *Da occasionem sapienti...* Cum igitur ex levi saepe occasione.	genuine	certain	certain	certain
57. **Collatio de contemptu saeculi.** Septem sunt in mundo, quae si homo bene perpenderet.	worthy	doubtful	certain	certain
58. **De septem gradibus contemplationis.** Incipit: Contemplativorum aquilinos obtutus acui.	spurious	spurious	spurious	certain
59. **Exercitia quaedam spiritualia.** Incipit: Ut in virtutibus conserveris, oportet.	spurious	doubtful	doubtful	certain
60. **Fascicularii** pars prima incipit: *Scire debes, quod quamvis omnia.* Pars secunda incipit: *Fasciculus myrrhae dilectus meus...* loquitur anima devota.	spurious	doubtful	doubtful	certain
61. **Soliloquium.** Incipit: *Flecto genua mea ad Patrem... ut impleamini in omnem plenitudinem Dei.* Apostolus Paulus, vas aeternae electionis.	worthy	certain	certain	certain
62. **Itinerarium mentis in Deum.** Incipit: In principio primum principium... *Beatus vir...* Cum beatitudo.	genuine	certain	certain	certain

ORDER OF THE VATICAN EDITION	According to Casimir Oudin	According to the Venetian Editors	According to Fr. Io. Hyacinth. Sbaralea	According to Fr. Benedictus Bonelli
63. **De septem Itineribus aeternitatis.** Incipit: *Eum qui venit ad me non eiiciam foras,* inquit Salvator. S. Augustinus de cognitione.	spurious	spurious	spurious	spurious
64. **Incendium amoris.** Incipit: Evigilans vero... *Ecce descripsi eam tibi tripliciter.* Cum omnis scientia.	spurious	certain	certain	certain
65. **Stimulus amoris.** Incipit: *Ad te, Domine, levavi animam meam...* Currite gentes undique.	spurious	spurious	spurious	spurious
66. **Amatorium.** Incipit: Praesens opusculum qui legerit... Ad te sermo meus dirigitur, quisquis.	spurious	certain	doubtful	certain
67. **De Ecclesiastica Hierarchia.** Incipit: *Invisibilia Dei per ea quae facta sunt... A magnitudine enim speciei et creaturae...* Ex quo apparet manifeste, quod humanus intellectus.	certain	genuine	certain	certain
68. **Legenda S. Francisci.** Incipit: *Apparuit gratia Dei...* in servo suo Francisco omnibus vere humilibus.	genuine	certain	certain	certain
69. **Expositio in regulam fratum Minorum.** Incipit: *Quicumque hanc regulam secuti fuerint...* Hanc plane puto regulam.	certain	doubtful	certain	certain
70. **Determinationes quaetionum circa regulam S. Francisci.** Incipit: Cum inter alios ordines religiosorum.	certain	certain	certain	certain
71. **Quare fratres minores predicent et confessiones audiant.** Incipit: Quia plerisque dubitant et quaerant.	certain	certain	certain	certain
72. **Libellus apologeticus in eos qui Ordini fratrum Minorum adversantur.** Incipit: Prater hoc quod surripitis clericis eleemosynas.	certain	certain	certain	certain
73. **De tribus Quaestionibus ad magistrum innominatum.** Incipit: Innominato magistro... Proponis carissime.	certain	certain	certain	certain

ORDER OF THE VATICAN EDITION	According to Casimir Oudin	According to the Venetian Editors	According to Fr. Io. Hyacinth. Sbaralea	According to Fr. Benedictus Bonelli
74. **De paupertate Christi contra magistrum Gulielmum.** Incipit: Quaestio est de paupertate, et quaeruntur duo.	certain	certain	certain	certain
75. **Quod Christus et Apostoli et discipuli eius discalceati incesserunt, sive de sandaliis Apostolorum.** Incipit: Talis lector, tali lectori... Quoniam secundum Apostolum Ioannem.	certain	certain	certain	certain
76. **Apologia pauperum.** Incipit: Summi legislatoris inviolabili constat definitione sancitum.	certain	certain	certain	certain
77. **Epistola ad quendam Provincialem Ministrum.** Incipit: In Christo sibi carissimo frati... Quoniam ad hoc potissimum.	certain	certain	certain	certain
78. **Epistola ad Ministros Provinciales et Custodes.** Incipit: In Christo sibi carissimis... Licet insufficientiam meam.	genuine	certain	certain	certain
79. **Biblia pauperum.** Incipit: Tanta pollet excellentia... Creatio rerum fuit ita mirabilis.	spurious	spurious	spurious	spurious
80. **Alphabetum religiosorum.** Incipit: *Vias tuas, Domine, demonstra mihi...* Obsecro te, Deus meus.	spurious	spurious	doubtful	doubtful
81. **Alphabetum religiosorum incipientium.** Incipit: Ama paupertatem, sis vilibus contentus.	spurious	spurious	certain	verisimile
82. **Collationes octo.** Incipiunt: Vide, anima mea, innovata mirabilia veritatis.	spurious	spurious	spurious	spurious
83. **Speculum disciplinae ad Novitios.** Incipit: Ad honestatem tendentes in primis necessarium habent.	spurious	spurious	spurious	certain
84. **De profectu religiosorum liber primus.** Incipit: Collationes meas... In priori formula novitiorum.	spurious	spurious	spurious	verisimile

ORDER OF THE VATICAN EDITION	According to Casimirus Oudin	According to the Venetian Editors	According to Fr. Io. Hyacinth. Sbaralea	According to Fr. Benedictus Bonelli
85. **De profectu religiosorum liber secundus.** Incipit: Profectus religiosi septem processibus distinguuntur.	spurious	spurious	spurious	spurious
86. **De institutione novitiorum, pars I.** Incipit: Primo semper debes considerare, ad quid veneris. Pars II. Incipit: Si vis in spiritu proficere.	spurious	spurious	spurious	verisimile
87. **Regula novitiorum.** Incipit: *Renovamini in novitate sensus vestri...* Hoc dicit Apostolus ad Romanos.	spurious	spurious	certain	certain
88. **Remedium defectuum religiosi.** Incipit: Simplicissimo animo hesterna luce ad me accedebas, frater Roberte.	spurious	spurious	certain	certain
89. **De perfectione vitae ad Sorores.** Incipit: *Beatus homo, quem tu erudieris, Domine...* Neminem censeri sapientem fateor.	certain	certain	certain	certain
90. **Summa de essentia et invisibilitate et immensitate Dei.** Incipit: Omnipotens Deus Pater, Filius et Spiritus sanctus, unus est atque trinus.	doubtful	spurious	doubtful	doubtful
91. **De sex alis Cherubim.** Incipit: Prima ala est confessio.	doubtful	spurious	spurious	doubtful
92. **De modo confitendi et de puritate conscientiae.** Incipit: Quoniam fundamentum et ianua virtutum.	spurious	spurious	certain	verisimile
93. **Mystica theologia.** Incipit: *Via Sion lugent...* Licet Hieremias propheta dixerit hoc verbum.	doubtful	spurious	spurious	doubtful
94. **Compendium theologicae veritatis.** Incipit: Veritatis theologicae sublimitas.	spurious	spurious	spurious	spuriou

So that there be better made known the difference, which exists between the mentioned critics of the works of St. Bonaventure, we have compiled the aforementioned table as a compendium, containing all the works, distinguished by numbers, arranged in three classes,

the first of which reports the certain, worthy and verisimilar works, the second the doubtful, but the third, the spurious, in accord with the various sentences of the critics. Therefore,
the works are indicated according to following numbers:

	In Oudin	In the Venetian Editors	In Fr. Sbaralea	In Fr. Bonelli
I. CERTAIN	nns. 3, 4, 5 6, 7, 8, 9, 15, 16, 17, 18, 20, 21, 26* 28* 29* 32* 47, 56, 57* 61* 62, 67, 68, 69, 70, 71; 72, 73, 74, 75, 76, 77, 78, 89.	nns. 6, 7, 15, 16 17, 18, 20, 21, 27, 28, 32, 56, 61, 62, 64, 66, 67, 68, 70, 71, 72, 73, 74, 75, 76, 77, 78, 89.	nns. 3, 5, 6, 7, 8, 9, 12, 13, 14, 15, 16, 17, 18, 19, 20, 21, 22, 23, 32, 34, 36, 38, 41, 46, 47, 48, 49, 51, 53, 56, 57, 61, 62, 64, 67, 68, 69, 70, 71, 72, 73, 74, 75, 76, 77, 78, 81, 87, 88, 89, 92.	nns. 1, 2, 3, 5, 6, 7, 8, 9, 12, 13, 14, 15, 16, 17, 18, 19, 20, 21, 22, 23, 24, 25, 26, 29, 32, 33, 34, 35, 36, 37, 38, 41, 42, 43, 44, 46, 47, 48, 49, 50, 51, 53, 54, 55, 56, 57, 58, 59, 60, 61, 62, 64, 66, 67, 68, 69, 70, 71, 72, 73, 74, 75, 76, 77, 78, 81, 83, 84, 86, 87, 88, 89, 92.
II. DOUBTFUL	nns. 12, 13, 14, 19, 23, 27, 48, 53, 54, 90, 91, 93.	8, 9, 10, 11, 19, 23, 26, 47, 48, 50, 53, 54, 57, 59, 60, 69.	29, 50, 59, 60, 66, 80, 90.	40, 45, 80, 90, 94, 93.
III. SPURIOUS	nns. 1, 2, 10, 11, 22, 24, 25, 30, 31, 33, 34, 35, 36, 37, 38, 39, 40, 41, 42, 43, 44, 45, 46, 49, 50, 51, 52, 55, 58, 59, 60, 63, 64, 65, 66, 79, 80, 81, 82, 83, 84, 85, 86, 87, 88, 92, 94.	1, 2, 3, 4, 5, 12, 13, 14, 22, 24, 25, 29, 30, 31, 33, 34, 35, 36, 37, 38, 39, 40, 41, 42, 43, 44, 45, 46, 49, 51, 52, 55, 58, 63, 65, 79, 80, 81, 82, 83, 84, 85, 86, 87, 88, 90, 81, 92, 93, 94.	1, 2, 4, 10, 11, 24, 25, 26, 27, 28, 30, 31, 33, 35, 37, 39, 40, 42, 43, 44, 45, 52, 54, 55, 58, 63, 65, 79, 82, 83, 84, 85, 86, 91, 93, 94.	4, 10, 11, 27, 28, 30, 31, 39, 52, 63, 65, 79, 82, 85, 94.

From this it is clear, that the Venetian editors conjectured as spurious, more (works) than
all the others, and disagreed little with Oudin in the quantity of works which they took away
and/or concede to the Seraphic Doctor. For, those which occur under the first class, distinguished with an asterisked number, are neither entirely certain nor openly doubtful in Oudin,
but only worthy and/or not unworthy of Bonaventure. But Father Bonelli judges few to be
doubtful and spurious, and to the many works of the Vatican edition, which he ascribes to
St. Bonaventure, there are to be added those, which he himself in (his) Supplement popu-
larized or equally ascribed to the Seraphic (Doctor), a catalogue of which here follows:

CATALOGUE OF THE SUPPLEMENT OF WORKS

BY BENEDICTUS BONELLI, THE BEST OF ALL THE EDITORS

WITH THE NOTES BY WHICH THE THESE

ARE ADJUDICATED TO BELONG TO ST. BONAVENTURE

1. **In Genesis cap. II. Commentariolum de plantatione paradisi.** Incipit: *Plantaverat autem Dominus Deus...* Sicut in Christum pie intendentibus aspectum carnis.	certain
2. **Tractatus in Psal. 45. de studio divinarum litterarum seu de contemplatione et scientia Dei.** Incipit: *Vacate et videte, quoniam ego sum Deus.* Sicut inter omnia nihil Deo altius et melius.	certain
3. **Expositio in Canticum Canticorum.** Incipit: In speculo brevi et aperto contueri volentibus.	certain
4. **Tractatus in cap. I. Ezechielis de sacrae Scripturae mysterio.** Incipit: *Cum essem in medio captivorum...* Conscendere cum Paulo volentibus. a	certain
5. **Tractatus in cap. X. Ezechielis de s crae Scripturae materia.** Incipit: *Ingredere in medio rotarum...* Scripturarum sanctarum pelagus et abyssus.	certain
6. **Sermo de Seminante, seu Expositio parabolarum evangelicarum de regno caelorum.** Incipit: *Simile est regnum caelorum homini, qui seminavit bonum semen...* Detinebant illum, ne discederet.	certain
7. **Commentarius in Evangelium sancti Ioannis.** Incipit: *Ecce intelliget servus meus...* Quia commendatio auctoris redundat in opus.	certain
8. **Commentarius in Apocalypsim.** Incipit Prologus Gilbertis: *Omnes qui pie volunt vivere in Christo Iesu...* Iuxta illud: *Fili, accedens ad servitutem Dei...* Prologus auctoris incipit: Praemittitur huic libro prologus magistralis. Expositio incipit: *Apocalypsis Iesus Christi.* Iste liber in duas partes dividitur.	certain
9. **Commentarium in vers. 8. cap. IV. Apocalypsis, de Doctrina evangelica.** Incipit: *Quatuor animalia, singula eorum habebant alas senas...* Superineffabilis altitudo doctrinae Evangelistarum.	certain

10. **Commentarius in vers. 1. cap. V. Apocalypsis, de Scripturarum sanctarum dignitate et excellentia.** Incipit: *Vidi in dextera sedentis super thronum...* Consideranti mihi Scripturarum sanctarum pelagum infinitum.	certain
11. **Tractatus de Vite mystica, sive Planctus de Passione Domini.** Incipit: *Ego sum vitis vera.* Iesu benigne, vitis vera.	verisimile
12. **Arbores de vitiis et virtutibus.** Incipit: Superbia radix omnium vitiorum — Humilitas radix virtutum omnium.	certain
13. **Tractatus de humilitate.** Incipit: Ad altitudinem humilitatis videndam.	certain
14. **Tractatus brevior de tribus virtutibus, humilitate, patientia et caritate.** Incipit: Quae potavi de fontibus Salvatoris, effundam.	verisimile
15. **Orationes.** Incipiunt: O Domine Ieus Christi, qui propter me tibi non perpercisti.	certain
16. **Paraphrasis ascetica domincae orationis.** Incipit: *Pater noster.* O immensa clementia! O ineffabilis benignitas!	verisimile
17. **Expositio eiusdem brevior.** Incipit: *Pater noster* privilegio conditionis, sacrificio recreationis.	certain
18. **Meditatio super salutatione angelica.** Incipit: *Ave Maria gratia plena, Dominus tecum.* Tibi, Domine Deus, gratias offero.	verisimile
19. **Meditatio, sive de regimine animae.** Incipit: *Ave Maria gratia plena...* Primum omnium necesse habes, Christi ancilla.	certain
20. **De silentio ad quandam sanctimonialem.** Incipit: Attende, quod natura dedit homini unicum os.	certain
21. **Ordinarium vitae religiosae, sive de partibus domus religiosae.** Incipit: *Religio munda et immaculata...* Ut ait B. Augustinus de vera religione.	certain

22. **Sex mandata fratri cuidam iuveni tradita.** Incipit: Fili mi iuvenis, si vis sine macula.	certain
23. **Sex cautelae ad castitatem servandam.** Incipit: Prima, ut homo temperate comedat et bibat.	certain
24. **De human iudicio.** Incipit: Triplex distinguitur iudicium de proximo.	certain
25. **De decem praeceptis divinae Legis.** Incipit: *Si vis ad vitam ingredi...* In isto verbo, scripto Matth. XIX, describit Salvator noster.	certain
26. **Ars concionandi.** Incipit: Omnis tractatio Scripturarum, ut ait Augustinus.	certain
27. **Collationes de septem donis Spiritus sancti praedicatae, in sermones octo distributae.** Incipit: *Hortamur vos, ne in vacuum...* Hortatur nos Apostolus in his verbis.	certain
28. **Sermones de laude melliflui Nominis D. N. I. C.** Incipit: Mulier Chananaea precibus importuna.	certain
29. **Sermones de diversis.** Incipit: *Cum eiecta esset turba, intravit Iesus...* In his verbis quatuor consideranda occurunt.	certain
30. **Sermones triginta duo de Eucharistia...** Incipit: De sacrosancto Corporis Domini locuturi Sacramento.	certain
31. **Sermo singularia de Corpore Christi.** Incipit: *Confiteantur Domino misericordiae eius... vinctos in mendicitate et fero.* In hoc verbo David propheta excitat nos.	certain
32. **Legenda S. Clarae.** Incipit: Quasi veterani mundi senecta vergente.	verisimile
33. **Lectiones novem in festo S. Clarae.** Incipit: Venerabilis Christi sponsae Deoque dicatae Virginis Clarae.	verisimile

34. **Lectiones novem in translatione S. Clarae.** Incipit: Admirabilis et venerabililis virgo Clara.	certain
35. **Legenda minor S. Francisci.** Incipit: *Apparuit gratia Dei Salvatoris nostri...* in servo suo Francisco, quem Pater misericordiarum.	certain
36. **Novem lectiones de canonizatione et de translatione S. Francisci.** Incipit: Franciscus igitur servus et amicus Altissimi.	certain
37. **Epistola ad fratrem de imitatione Iesu Christi.** Incipit: Frater, loquitur B. Augustinus ad Dominum Iesum Christum.	certain
38. **Epistola ad fratrem Laurentium.** Incipit: In Christo sibi carissimo... Dignum est et consonum rationi.	certain
39. **Epistola ad fratres universae.** Incipit: Universis fratribus praesentes litteras inspecturis... Cum ego relatione perceperim.	certain
40. **Epistola ad fratres custodem et guardianum Pisarum.** Incipit: In Christo sibi carissimis fratribus... Sororibus monasterii de Pisis.	certain
41. **Epistola ad abbatum Beatae Mariae Blesensis.** Incipit: Venerabili et religioso viro... Desiderio multo desideravit.	certain
42. **Rhythmica et leonina carmina de arbore vitae...** Incipit: O crux frutex calvificus... Quam flos exornat.	certain
43. **Contemplatio duodecim fructuum arboris sanctae crucis.** Incipit: O crux frutex salvificus... Cuius flos aromaticus.	certain
44. **Meditationes carmine scriptae in septem verba, quae in cruce Christus Dominus protulit.** Incipit: Iesu salutis hostia, salutis sacrificium.	certain
45. **Leonina carmina de doctrina proficiendi.** Incipit: Laus, honor, o Chirste, tua gloria sit liber iste.	certain

« Therefore, as the (matters) related above confirm, since the erudite men, who either published the works of St. Bonaventure, and/or employed censorious comment upon the same, were divided into diverse sentences, such that the very many works, which some judged legitimate, were cast again by others among the spurious and/or doubtful, it is necessary (that) everyone propose this obvious question to himself, "Whence (has arisen) such great diversity of opinions among men, otherwise outstanding in erudition, in judging upon such a grave matter?" »

« As much as regards Oudin, it can be justly affirmed, that he (was) driven to deny the greater part of St. Bonaventure's works, since in study and spirit he was often hostile to the Catholic side of every argument. But, though he himself erred more frequently by far, than all others, in judging the works and deeds of St. Bonaventure, yet, he hardly ever denied the true works, or judged the same as spurious. Whence, even later critics agreed with him in some (things), and it shall be necessary for us to also agree. But, it is, indeed, to be wondered at, that censors later than Oudin, though Franciscans both erudite and the greatest lovers of truth, agreed among themselves least of all in judging several work, and, sometimes, the very same work, which Oudin admitted as legitimate, was rejected by others as not genuine. Which, indeed, sufficiently shows, that they conducted themselves in good faith and did not want on account of (their) love for Oudin, whose colleagues they were, and St. Bonaventure's too, to whom they were most devoted, to deceive themselves or others ».

« To confirm what we have now asserted, the *Epistola viginti quinque memorabilium*, judged above under n. 47, in the list of the works of the Vatican Edition, was acknowledged by Oudin as genuine; but the Venetian editors, who wanted it to be doubtful, did not think the same. The *Summa de essentia et invisibilitate et immensitate Dei*, listed in the same place under n. 90, is according to the former was doubtful, among the latter spurious. The *Opus de quatuor virtutibus cardinalibus*, n. 26, Oudin regards as not unworthy of Bonaventure, the Venetian editors as doubtful, Fr. Sbaralea as spurious, but Fr. Bonelli ascribes it to Bonaventure as verisimile. Behold, therefore, the work, according to which all those (opuscula) just mentioned are arranged, by whom the works (of St. Bonaventure) are distinguished, when compared to their author. Oudin does not deny, that the *Commentarius in Evangelium S. Lucae*, n. 9, is the legitimate offspring of St. Bonaventure; but the Venetian editors regard (it) as doubtful, Sbaralea and Bonelli hold it (to be) certain. Oudin doubts concerning the work, cited under n. 27, *a septem donis Spiritus Sancti*; but the Venetian editors estimate (it to be) certain; Sbaralea and Bonelli place (it) again among the spurious. According to the judgment of Sbaralea, the works which are contained under nn. 1, 2, 42, 43, 54 and 55 are illegitimate, but these same were to be regarded as genuine according to the sentence of Fr. Bonelli ».

« To passover Oudin and the Venetian editors, the reason, why Fr. Sbaralea restores many (works) to the Seraphic (Doctor) from (those) previously taken away, is to be reckoned in this, that in this matter he excelled in greater expertise and erudition and expounded all (of his) reasons more diligently. Next, that Fr. Bonelli vindicated for the Seraphic Doctor many more (works) than Sbaralea (had done), we judge to have happened, indeed, for this reason, that, after the critical art began to thrive, he alone explored, and caused to be explored, all the published works which he could (find), with incredible labor and the greatest diligence, and he also labored for many years to arrive at a just judgment concerning them ».

Nevertheless, the reason, on account of which the mentioned censors disagree so much among themselves in dijudicating the works, seems also to be sought elsewhere than from a defect of erudition, diligence and labor. The cause of this dissension and incertitude was twofold.

« The first, namely, is the defect of ancient nomenclators, who composed exceedingly succinct, never whole, indicula of the works of St. Bonaventure, as they indicated in them, exhibiting a few in a definite manner, not a few others in more general words, e. g., *et multa alia*.[1] But, in affirming and/or rejecting the works of authors, none knew how to construct an extrinsic argument from the authority of equal writers and/or of (those) immediately succeeding (them); with which lacking, those who judged only according to an intrinsic argument, namely from the similarity of style and phrase and doctrine with other genuine works of the same author, nearly always parted unto diverse sentences ».

« But, the other reason for the discrepant judgements consists in the lack of a good knowledge of the manuscript codices, by those who ought to give sentence as inspectors (of the same). For the manuscript codices, bearing in front the name of (their) author, to the extent that they are the more ancient and approach more closely to the age of the author, are of greater weight for this (reason), to assert the works of the same and to rightly supply the defect of the ancient nomenclators. And thus, whensoever these are silent, to put an end to the argument one had to recur to the authority of the manuscript codices. Which, indeed, neither Oudin nor the Venetian editors did, whence their exceedingly great disagreement. They did, indeed, consult the authors, who dealt with ecclesiastical writings and writers, and even the catalogues, which they were able to have at hand, of the manuscript codices; but it has been discovered, that in both the former and in the latter there occur many errors and very many (things) have been omitted ».

« On which account Benedictus Bonelli approached nearer to the truth, when he investigated very many manuscript codices of the works of St. Bonaventure, supported upon the authority of which he both asserted very many of (the works) published as so certainly (belonging) to Bonaventure, that they could never again be called into doubt, and discovered many unpublished ones, with which he filled and arranged the three mentioned volumes of (his) Supplement ».

These (things) have been said truly and justly in favor of the sentence of Fr. Bonelli; but, yet, it must be conceded that one must not always agree with the judgement of Bonelli, even when he has well refuted the arguments of those, who asserted that some work was not written by St. Bonaventure. For that great progress, which this our own age has made, in the knowledge of more ancient times, has brought many new historical documents to light, which if Fr. Bonelli had known, he would have arrived at another sentence. Fr. Fedele, himself, uncovered many documents, which entirely overturned the judgement of Fr. Bonelli concerning several works, which he had declared genuine.[2] Which Fr. Fedele, himself, proves by many examples.[3]

Thus, the *Expositio in Psalterium*, placed under n. 3 in the above Catalogue, declared spurious by the Venetian editors alone, is called a "certain" (work) of the Seraphic Doctor by Oudin, Sbaralea and Bonelli.

---

[1] With these and similar (words), namely *et multa alia, et alia, et quam plurima alia, et alia plura* etc., do the indicula of the works of St. Bonaventure (composed by) Martinus Monachus Fuldensis, Salimbene Parmensis, Bartholomaeus Prisanus, Ioannes Gerson, the anonymous Stronconiensis, Iabocus Oddo Persuinus, Gullielmus Eisengreinius, Antonius Eugubinus, Octavimus de Martinis, Robertus de Licio, Gulielmus Vorrilongus, Ludovicus Prutenus, Ioannes Franciscus de Pavinis, Ioannes Trithemius, Ludovicus Granatensis, Franciscus Gonzaga, Maritius Bressius, and Marianus Florentius etc., conclude.

[2] « For Bonelli, himself, visited only a very few of the libraries of Italy. Indeed, very many he caused to be visited by Fathers Theodorus de Gavatio and Florianus de Tridento, but likewise only in Italy. And, moreover, these inspected only the manuscript works which the catalogues attributed to St. Bonaventure. But, there are many libraries of Italy, to which these did not go, and they searched none of those outside of Italy. Therefore, rightly did Fr. Bonelli advise, that libraries were to be thoroughly searched to enrich a new edition with the unpublished (works) ».

[3] *Ratio.*, p. II, p. 107 f..

But, yet, though Bonelli refutes in an outstanding manner the light reasons of the Venetian editors; these, nevertheless, had concluded true, though not out of true reasons. For Fr. Fedele, in the cited work, evidently proves by the more ancient manuscripts of St. Bonaventure, that this Exposition is to be restored to *Michelis Meldensis*, Archbishop of Sens, who died in 1199 A. D..

The opuscule *de sex Alis Cherubim* (placed under n. 91, in the Catalogue above), which the Vatican editors, Wadding, Oudin and Bonelli adjudged as doubtfully Bonaventurian, is rightly rejected among the spurious by Sbaralea and the Venetian editors, since, as Fr. Fedele testifies, it is found written in codices confected before St. Bonaventure's birth.

One is to judge similarly concerning the *Summa de essentia et invisibilitate et immensitate Dei* (n. 90 in the Catalogue), classified by Oudin, Sbaralea et Bonelli as doubtful, by the Venetian (editors) as spurious. For, it is already found among two codices of the ninth and tenth centuries. Even other judgements made by Fr. Benedetto Bonelli concerning several opuscula, which he ascribes as certain and/or verisimilar writings of the Seraphic Doctor, cannot be sustained further, after the discovery of new documents. This is true, first of all, concerning not a few ascetical books and verses, concerning various sermons and even concerning that *Commentarius in Apocalypsim*, which fills the second tome of the mentioned *Supplement*. But, this is to be treated of, in its own placed, in the prolegomena to each work and in the dissertation on the life and writings of St. Bonaventure. Yet, these (things), we wish to now indicate, so that the benevolent reader may be more certain, that we in no way want to adorn Bonaventure with the works of others, since it is certain, that neither is he in need of such, nor do the holy Doctors of the Church want to be honored or decorated with the writings of others.

The *third* defect of the preceding general editions consists in this, that none of them exhibit all the works of St. Bonaventure, which are heretofore extant.

First, indeed, let us lament, that the works of *Fr. Bonelli* published in (his) *Supplement*, not a few of which are genuine, have remained heretofore unknown. For this *Supplement* is yet more rarely found than his Prodromus, « since, indeed, as Fr. Fedele says,[1] if I had found it in no public library of France, England, Belgium and Switzerland, and (if) it occurs rarely in the libraries of Italy, more rarely (will it be found) in (those) of Germany ».

We have already warned, that the works contained in this Supplement, have been omitted even in the latest Parisian edition.[2] It is manifest, from these works and/or opuscula, that there are those, at least certain and/or verisimile, distributed according to their natural qualities into various classes, that are to be added to these, which the Vatican edition comprises, such that both these and the others uncovered after the edition of the *Supplement* coalesce at once for an ordinate and distinct unity and aptly arrive at one formed corpus. Fr. Bonelli had already observed that this was to be done,[3] where he speaks of the matter, thus: « These I regard, wherever

---

[1] *Ratio*, p. 45.

[2] The Parisian editor, seems to have had at hand, not only the *Prodromus*, but also the *Supplement*. For in the eleventh tome of the edition prepared by them, p. 1, they attach to St. Bonaventure's *Postilla in S. Joannis Evangelium*, the following note: « This other Postilla, first published at Trent in the year 1772 by the Minister General of the Order of Friars Minor, Paschalis a Varisio, under the auspices of (Pope) Clement XIV, if God grants, it is in our vows to bring it to light sooner or later. But we are driven to confess that we are not able to do this, except after have completed the matter of the Vatican edition, or if you prefer, the Venetian, which remains ». It must be more truly said, that the whole *Supplement*, which comprises the aforementioned Postilla, had already been published by *Benedetto Bonelli*, dedicated, however, to (our) most holy lord, Clement XIV, by the Minister General of the Order of Friars Minor, Paschalis a Varisio.

[3] *Supplementum.*, tome III, p. VIII.

(they have) been carefully sought out, zealously gathered together, cleansed anew from the *menda* of copyists, howsoever very many (they be), and by that study, which is suitable, arranged according to my small measure of learning in this third volume to be published; which once added upon all the others published in the first and second volume, complete the Supplement of the Sixtine edition, and/or which, if at any time favored by (my) superiors, shall appear as the new edition of the works of the Seraphic Doctor, as I have understood, by many promises, shall be done, which (works) could have obtained (their) place with the rest, which are in truth his; and, then, the same shall be separated from the apocryphal, but also from those supposed, which shall return to their legitimate authors, most of all, (to those) of the Order of Minors, according to a quasi *postliminary right*, according to the manner which I have handed down in the Prodromus ».

Second, it is established, that neither was it allowed to *Fr. Benedetto Bonelli*, according to the reckoning of that age, to uncover and collect all the works of the Seraphic Doctor, which are attributed by the ancient nomenclators and/or by the library catalogues to him. On which account, from the indiculum of the unpublished (works), left by him in Bk. VIII, part IV, of the Prodromus, we have excerpted the (names of) the following (works), which he did not publish, and/or which he knew not where they lay, and/or because he was not able to explore with his own eyes in so widely scattered libraries. Hence, these are:

1. *Sermo habitus in Concilio generali Lugdunensi*, which begins: *Exsurge Ierusalem, sta in excelso et circumspice ad orientem, et inde collige filias tuas ab oriente usque ad occidentem.* — This, we have learned, (is) from a contemporary writer, among the Labbeana Collection of Councils, by Baptista de Iudicibus and Marcus Ulyssiponensis.

2. *Sermones ad clerum*, described by Friar Marco de Monte Feltre, who heard them himself. — By (his) contemporary Salimbene of Parma.

3. *Conciones ad fratres*, held at Bologna. — By the same Salimbene of Parma.

4. *Sermo de B. Francisco* during the General Chapter of Paris. — By Umbertino de Casale and St. Bernardine of Siena.

5. *Postillae in libros Salomonis.* — By the contemporary Ptolomaeus Lucensis, O. P., auditor and confessor to St. Thomas Aquinas, and by Martinus Fuldensis.

6. *Postillae in Job.* — By Ptolomaeus Lucensis, Martinus Fuldensis and Joannes Mahusius.

7. *Postillae in Epistolas Pauli.* — By the same, Ptolomaeus, Martinus and Mahusius.

8. *Sermo de B. Francisco*, given at St. Mary of the Portiuncula, Assisi. — By Bartholomaeus Pisanus.

9. *Compendium de adventu Antichristi.* — By Guglielmus Vorrilongus.

10. *Officium Corporis Christi*, diverse from that which St. Thomas composed. — By Franciscus Samson, Gabrielis Barleta et Anonymus Pistoriensis.

11. *Sophismata.* — By Ioannis Franciscus Pavinus.

12. *De quatuor operibus religiosorum.* — By the same Pavinus.

13. *Epistola ad Michaëlem Imperatorem Graecorum.* — By the same Pavinus and Petrus Rudulphius.

14. *De divisione rerum universi.* — By the same Pavinus and Rudulphius.

15. *Laudatorium.* — By Ludovicus Prutenus.

16. *Liber de imitatione Christi.* — By Bernardinus de Bustis.

17. *Commentaria in duodecim Prophetas minores.* — By Joannes Mahusius.

18. *Commentaria in Marcum.* — By the same Mahusius.

19. *Commentaria in Epistolas Canonicas.* — By the same Mahusius.

20. *Compendium metricum scholasticum utriusque Testamenti*, beginning: *Mundus fit in principio*. — By Sixtus Senensis.

21. *Sermo*, in which mention is made of the multiple doubts of the friars about those (things) which are contained in the Rule (of St. Francis), among whom (they had) arisen in the time of Friar John Parente, Minister General. — From the manuscript, *Chronicle of the XXIV Minister Generals*.

22. *Tractatus de signis universalibus*. — Extant in the *Tabularium*, Assisi, (Italy).

23. *Quaestiones super quatuor libros Topicorum*. — Ibid..

24. *Quaestiones super quatuor libros Metheororum*. — Ibid..

25. *Quaestiones super librum de Generatione*. — Ibid..

26. *Viridarium consolationis*. — In the library of Cassino, of Veneto-Vineana and of St. Martin, at Tours, (France).

27. *Regulae theologicae*. — In the Royal Library of Paris.

28. *De quatuor gradibus vitae spiritualis*. — Ibid..

29. *Summa poenitentialis*. — Ibid..

30. *Epistolae declarantes regulam S. Augustini*. — In the library of Utrecht (Netherlands).

31. *Dialogus de creatione mundi et eius redemptione*. — In the library of Utrecht (Netherlands) and Buxheim (Priory).*

32. *Dialogus de statu Ecclesiae Militantis*. — In the library of Wolfenbüttel (Germany).

33. *Tractatus physicus*. — In the library of Leipzig (University:) Paulina (collection).

34. *In octo libros* (or rather *Epistolas*) *Doctoris gentium*. — In the library of Merton College, (Oxford), in England.

Finally, it must be observed, that several works of this list are falsely enumerated in the catalogues as the unpublished and genuine works of St. Bonaventure; e. g. the last number, which exhibits the title: *In octo libros Doctoris gentium*, is nothing other than the *Breviloquium*, as Fr. Fedele discovered with his own eyes.[1] Similarly, that *Tractatus physicus* (under n. 33), which is noted in the ancient catalogue of the library of Leipzig, are only a few leafs of some anonymous (writer), written by another hand, which have been gathered among the works of St. Bonaventure.

Many other works, which are either truly and/or falsely attributed to St. Bonaventure in codices, have been uncovered and briefly described by Fr. Fedele.[2] No a few others were found by the same after 1874, or after the edition of his book. There will be an orderly discussion of all of these in their own place. Let it suffice in this place to say, that among many, nay, very many spurious and/or doubtful writings of this kind there are also to be had some works, genuine and of no small moment, of the Seraphic Doctor. Besides all the others worthy of mention there are not a few *Quaestiones* which are called *disputatas*, and besides the genuine *Commentarium in Ioannem*, already published by Fr. Bonelli, (there are) the unpublished *Collationes in Ioannem*. There are still other tracts, either certainly and/or probably genuine, pertaining to ascetical and mystical (theology), and also not a very few sermons, which have never been printed.

III.

What has been, heretofore, said, seems already sufficient to prove, that it is both *opportune* to adorn a new edition of the Opera Omnia of St. Bonaventure, that

---

[1] *Ratio*, p. 56.   [2] *Ratio*, pp. 248-318.   * *Trans. note*: Near Memmingen, Germany.

the cited defects, might be taken away, as much as this is possible; and that to obtain this scope it is *necessary* to sustain arduous and lengthy labors. And, indeed, it is first of all clear, that neither can the text be aptly purged from *vitia* and restored to its integrity, nor can a judgement be given concerning the authenticity of each of the works, nor can the unpublished ones be drawn forth from the dust of libraries, unless one has studious recourse to the authority of the ancient, manuscript codices. But this cannot be done, unless a diligent disquisition be first done about the manuscript codices and the other documents pertaining to this matter, which are as yet conserved in so many libraries. This did *Father Bonelli* already observe,[1] advising, « that, in the new edition to be undertaken, no investigation of those (works) which are lacking and (which) lie hidden in libraries and tabularia, and no diligence to enrich it with unpublished ones, is to be omitted ». But that this investigation of ancient monuments cannot be perfectly accomplished, unless the libraries themselves are visited and thoroughly searched, is sufficiently established among the experts of the critical art, and confirmed by Fr. Fedele with various reasons and examples.[2]

Holding this for certain, Fr. Fedele entered this, indeed, difficult province with incredible labor and diligence and so perfectly completed (it), that, heretofore, as much as we know, no single man had ever visited so many libraries in search of the writings of any single author. In this, the same Father left nearly nothing to his colleagues to be done except the arduous effort of sifting the immense forest of documents and notes and pondering (them) in their own place with the lance of the critical art. It must, indeed, be grieved, that he himself, who was endowed with no common genius regarding the critical art and with a singular expertise, was not able to execute this difficult labor, overtaken (as he was) by death.

But, lest the fruits of such a labor perish, if the first author, with (his) work unfinished, would had failed on account of (his) death — which so often it happens in other undertakings — and to also have the assistance of associates to complete the immense labor; he judged that there was to be instituted a College, in which several of the colleagues of his own Order, freed from all other cares, could apply themselves to accomplishing this work with their conjoined forces. « For, indeed, the life and forces, » he said, « of one man would scarcely be sufficient to adorn the edition of St. Bonaventure's works in that manner, in which we are now preparing. The preparation of an edition of this kind is absolutely necessary, and it cannot be promoted and completed except by the society of several men, whose members, failing by death or other causes, can be substituted by others at the word of the one presiding over the society and/or of the one who established it. To established societies of this kind and watch over them is very suitable for the regular Orders and Congregations of religious men, as several examples of past ages, and even of our own, abundantly testify. Nor is it to be judged, that that from this, that several men and through several years, freed from all other cares, apply themselves in a nearly united effort, to bring to light the unpublished monuments and works of the more celebrated authors, that effort is wasted or that there comes forth less utility for the Church or for the society of men, than if they took leisure in other studies. For the most famous Fr. François Combefis, O. P.,[3] optimally observes, « that they *nearly* merit more for Christendom and the world of letters, who publish the sedulously examined, ecclesiastical monuments of a superior age, in which some light of truth is kindled, and Faith and Tradition defended, than they who increase the harvest of the Church by their genius and skill with their own new (works).

---

[1] *Supplementum*, tome III, Preface, p. 8.
[2] *Ratio*, p. 55 f..
[3] *Biblioteca Graecorum Patrum*, Acutar. noviss., Paris, 1672, P. I, in the "Praemonitio ad Lectorem".

Though several aspired to the latter of the two, and, furthermore, grasped more eagerly for the praise, the first, as the harder work and the one not so prone to praise, the greater part of the erudite neglected and rejected ». — Thus, that he had wanted that a college be instituted, we have already mentioned above. Meanwhile, in the course of eleven years there were gathered by the alumni of this *Collegio di San Bonaventura* and by the other associates of Fr. Fedele, whether ordinary or extraordinary, very many manuscript codices, wherever acquired, together with the printed editions, for the purpose of collecting variant readings. Not of few (of these manuscripts) were described in their entirely, if one speaks of the unpublished works and/or those not unworthy of mention. This daring labor of comparing manuscripts has already been completed in part, especially as regards the first five Tomes to be published (for this present Edition). Rightfully do we call this labor *daring*, because, as well may happen, there is not only required great patience, but even a longer time for study. Nor do these suffice, but there is also required not small genius and learning. For the manuscripts of the Middle Ages are accustom to abound in abbreviated notes and sigla, which are often of a doubtful reading, nay deceptive, and to be determined by the nature of the matter to be described.

To reform the text, it is clear, that even the first editions had be compared with the Vatican (edition). « For, indeed, the first, which they call *incunabula*, have a value nearly equal to the manuscript codices of the 16th Century, if it cannot be proven, that they were copied according to the exemplary manuscripts of a more ancient age; for this, if it were proven, it would give them nearly an equal value to the codices of that age, according to the norm of which they were made. Later ones have greater and/or less value according to the quality of the manuscript and the diligence and skill of him, who used the manuscript codices to correct them ». We already have a manifest example of this matter in the collection of the most ancient edition for both the First and Second Book of the *Commentaria in Sententias*. For the more ancient edition very often exhibits the readings of the codices of the 13th Century; but the later editions are demonstrated to have receded from the primitive text more because of this, that they are younger. — Moreover, we have observed in regard to the reformation of the text and the notation of variant readings, how very many variant readings we have gathered and are to collect from the many codices and editions, whereby the text can be more securely and better corrected. « Nevertheless, we are scarcely to publish all of them, since all together would outweigh in mass the very work, to which they belong. For we do not approve of the reasoning of those, who collect all the variant readings, howsoever many (they be), whether the best or good or of no moment, and/or judge that the manifest errors of drooping copyists are to be placed before the eyes of the reader, as scarcely otherwise than if they were diamonds and emeralds. This we reckon superfluous, if we do not call it harmful; on account of this, that they distract the mind of the reader by their number and cause tediousness. And so, the very many variant readings of the manuscripts and editions of the work of St. Bonaventure are being collected, so that we may prevail to select the best from the better, either to be received into the text, when that seems to be in need of emendation, and/or to be placed in the footnotes. The Vatican edition is not rarely convicted of manifest error; more often, the reading of the same — considering the number, quality, antiquity, (and) consonance of the codices and editions reading in another manner — loses (its) probability either wholly and/or in part, in which case the reading of the codices is to be preferred and received into the text. However, when the codices disagree, and/or their reading labors under the suspicion of being corrupted, and/or authority and reason militate for different sides, the reading of the Vatican edition is not to be deprived of the right of possession, but is itself to be called into doubt. In this case the dissident reading of the codices and/or of the editions is placed back in the footnotes ».

However, so great a mash of variant readings grew from our collection of so many codices and editions, that very many of them could not, indeed, find a place in the footnotes. For the First Book of the Commentaries alone, the number of variant readings grew to nearly 20,000.

On which account, besides the manifest errors of copyists, we have entirely omitted to name (those) variant readings which are entirely improbable, since they are proffered by one or another manuscript and/or published (work) against very many others and codices of better note, unless they were able in some manner to serve to understand and/or illustrate more easily the sense of the author, of which kind are the very many glosses, which ordinarily only have a few words, (though) sometimes they are even somewhat longer. Not a few glosses of this latter kind have crept into the Vatican edition, which sometimes assist the easier understanding of the sense of the author, with his laconic brevity of speech. Nevertheless, we have relegated additions of this kind to the footnotes.

In regarding to the reading, very often the ancient codices agree, excepting a few passages, in the most ancient codices and editions, which seem to labor under some corruption or omission of words or acceptance of some gloss into the text, of which we shall also advise the reader in the footnotes. In these cases, we have abstained and shall abstain from changing the text with any attempt at an uncertain and often fallacious conjecture, but having retained the reading of the Vatican (edition), we shall manifest our own opinion in the footnotes placed at the bottom of the page. For example, in the passage on p. 212 of the First Tome, referred to by footnote 13: there, the words placed within the hyphenation, « *because the Church could (do) this without them* », belabor this passage in a sufficiently incongruous manner. Therefore, either they are a marginal gloss, which has crept into the text, and/or some words have fallen away, v. gr. « *it was not necessary*, because the Church could *determine* this without them », and/or one must say, that St. Bonaventure has left it to the ready to supply what is lacking. Lest we posit the uncertain as certain, we have given the reading of the codices. But, yet, as much as regards this First Tome, at one or another time the common error of the editions and codices was so manifest, and our correction had a great probability on account of the context, that we did not hesitate to thus reform the text. Otherwise, we trust that our edition shall sufficiently demonstrate, that we have been alien from an excessive effort at innovating and reforming the text according to our own arbitrary judgement.

Another effort, and, indeed, a hard and tedious one, had to be undertaken, namely, the discovery, comparison and judgement of the nearly innumerable passages taken from very many authors, which are cited in the writings of St. Bonaventure, with the sources, from which they were taken. For, though the other editors of the printed works of St. Bonaventure had labored no small amount at finding these passages, yet, often the passages, which were judged by them, either do not correspond entirely, and/or do not exhibit that, which he cites, but a similar passage, and/or are entirely wanting. Nor have the manuscript codices been of much assistance, because they (often) do not agree among themselves, or they err more often than the editions themselves where they cite a determinate passage, or, more frequently, they indicate only generally the author and/or work and/or book (cited). For there are few examples, in which those ancient Scholastics ascribed by common error an entire book and more often at least some testimony to an author other than the true one to whom it should have been attributed.

It happens, that St. Bonaventure himself, according to the custom of his own age, very often employed the testimonies of others, without making mention of (their) author. This occurs nearly continuously in the arguments formed *ex ratione*, since he has put to his own use a nearly innumerable quantity of axioms, principles, definitions and various sentences

(taken) from Aristotle and his commentators, from Boethius, Augustine and the authors of many *Summula* and Sentences. For all erudite (men) know well, that the philosophical and theological disciplines of the Middle Ages had not only a common treasury, and (that) commonly received, of technical terms, but also of definitions, distinctions and very many axioms, which as firm principles of science and or argumentation had been committed to memory by all the cultivators of those disciplines, and (which) had been approved by common estimation, just as we now see to be received into use in the mathematical and physical (disciplines) of our own day. We look with horror on the fact that such a precious patrimony, gathered together by the wise men of many ages, has been miserably dissipated by the unbridled thinkers of recent times. For, now that a rather new passion, and one heretofore unknown, has arisen to laboriously destroy the old with the new, rather than to augment and perfect: no principle, no definition received into constant use, has remained untouched, and with the very technical terms of science changed either according to words and/or according to sense, there has followed a disagreement of minds and even a confusion of tongues, such that the very overseers of the workmen employed in the field of philosophy do not understand one another.

No one doubts, that it is of no mean interest to the reader, to know the origin of the said authorities, so that he may perceive better the strength of the arguments and the doctrine of (their) author. Moreover, we have not spared, nor shall we spare labor and time, to uncover these passages. What we have proffered in this regard in the *Commentary on the Sentences*, will be discussed in the Prolegomena which shortly follows.

In the testimonies from Sacred Scripture and from those authors, employed by the Seraphic (Doctor), we shall retain that reading, which the codices, either together and/or in the agreement of the best, do exhibit, not the one, which is now included in the Vulgate and/or modern editions of (those) authors. However, if there is a difference of reading of any moment, we indicate (this) in the footnotes. For, since it is established, that these testimonies at the time of St. Bonaventure had not rarely a different manner of reading in the codices, they ought to be cited by us in that manner, in which they are found in the codices, which the Seraphic Doctor had in hand. This *ratio agendi*, approved by the consent of erudite men, is of no small moment for the use of the critical art in regards to (identifying) those writings, which are cited by the Seraphic (Doctor).

In those passages, which can cause difficulty for the reader not versed in the ancient Scholastics, on account of either the familiar laconic brevity of St. Bonaventure, and/or the manners of speech most known in his age, but now obsolete, and/or on account of the profundity of the doctrine, we have subjoined notes at the bottom of the page, for their citation, as seem to serve the illustration of the text. These notes have either been distilled from St. Bonaventure himself, and/or from the doctrines of philosophy and theology received in his age. Yet, we have done this with moderation, lest we be called commentators rather than editors.

Nevertheless, in the first work of St. Bonaventure to be published by us, which is (his) great *Commentary on the Sentences of Peter Lombard*, what had to be done, according to the estimation of Fr. Fedele, after he had founded the College, and to us, was judged according to the needs of those who are beginning to study the doctrine of the Seraphic Doctor. For we have judged opportune, to adjoin to the individual questions of this Commentary a brief scholium, by which there will be explained, what is obscure in the arguments and/or conclusions; and the difficulties of whatever nature be resolved, if there be any; and there is briefly indicated, what relation the doctrine, handed down by our

author, has with the other ancient Scholastic authors, first of all with Alexander of Hales and (John Duns) Scotus and (then) with Bl. Albertus (Magnus) and St. Thomas (Aquinas); then, finally, there will be indicated the passages of the chief Scholastics of that age, where they treat of the same matter. With the Commentary on the Sentences adorned with notes and scholia in this manner, little labor shall be left for the explanation of the other works of St. Bonaventure, and/or only a few and brief notes shall suffice, to indicate to the reader, in which passage of the Commentary he will be able to find more abundant light. For St. Bonaventure, nearly always (and) everywhere consistent with himself, employs the same doctrine and/or at least the same principles, which he has discussed in the Commentary in accord with the custom of the schools.

There have been adjoined, too, in the margins, brief notes, indicating the matter being treated of.* In the Vatican (edition) and the other editions following it, similar notes were placed in only a few passages and without a uniform reason. Moreover, the editors of the Vatican (edition) accepted the same notes from the Roman edition of 1569.

To the individual works there are prefaced introductions under the name of *Prolegomena*, in which there are chiefly proposed those (things), which pertain to the critical judgement of that work. « Several recensions, and (those) of diverse subjects, serve for the copious material of these prefaces: namely, (those) of the nomenclators and authors, who attributed a subsequent work to the Seraphic Doctor; (those) of the manuscript codices according to the ages, in which they were written, and/or sometimes according to the families, to which they pertain and the other qualities of (their) depositories; (those) of the many editions of the same book and even of the various versions of the same, whether they had already been sent to press, or not. Having mentioned all these (things), we have said what each of the monuments and authorities are worth and what faith they merit, and we deduce the legitimate corollaries which follow therefrom. Then there is subjoined the recension of those authors, who have commented on (that) work of (St.) Bonaventure or (who) have illustrated (it) with notes, and/or have used it chiefly for composing their own works, and/or (who) took from it the reason for writing another (work), and/or (who) employed not meager nor few excerpts (from it). Finally, the reason for the work written by (St.) Bonaventure, (its) occasion, excellence, use, and the new arrangements of (its) parts and chapters, if any were introduced, changes of titles, accretions or diminutions of (its) material, and very many other (things), which would be too long to mention here, shall be discussed in the Prolegomena, and out of all (of which) a judgement shall be given concerning the author of the work ».[1]

In the last tome, there shall be published a new life of St. Bonaventure, augmented from those notes, which were discovered by us and/or others in this our own age, in which even those (things), which were spoken of here and there in the Prolegomena concerning (his) writings and doctrine, will be gathered together into one synthesis. It is truly to be grieved, that no author of sufficient dignity has written of the deeds, virtues and books of this most eminent and most holy man according to the proposed historical method. Even in the centuries subsequent to the canonization of this Saint the same negligence is to be deplored, at which the editors of the *Acta Sanctorum*, in (their own) previous commentary on the life of St. Bonaventure, rightfully marvelled.[2]

---

[1] *Ratio.*, p. 74.

[2] *Acta Sanctorum*, 14 Iulii, n. 54. However, it must be said, that there was not lacking to St. Bonaventure's age an author, who handed down the memory of his life, namely the Spaniard, *Fr. Ioannes Aegidius Zamorra*, Ord. Min., in his work, *de Viris illustribus*, or *Historia canonica et civilis*, in which he also wrote of the deeds of the Seraphic Doctor. He himself gives testimony of this in another unpublished work of his own, according to Fr. Fedele. *Ioannes Aegidius* flourished before 1300, and besides many other works he wrote also of the matters pertaining especially to the history of Hispania, as can be seen in Sbaralea (*Supplementum*). We will only briefly relate, that we have been unable, up to now, to find the mentioned work of *Ioannes Aegidius*. If any learned man comes upon this book of his, we beg him kindly, to know what in it pertains to St. Bonaventure.

* *Trans. note*: These have been omitted in this English translation.

We have proposed to publish the works of the Seraphic (Doctor), divided into various classes, in the following order. The first class comprises the *Commentaria in quatuor libros Sententiarum*, which several unpublished, disputed Questions cite, the *Breviloquium*, and the other opuscula pertaining to Scholastic theology. It seems expeditious, that there be adjoined to these not a few of (his) Sermons, which could be rather called "theological tracts", such as the *Sermones in Hexaëmeron*, (those) *de septem Donis Spiritus sancti* and *de decem Praeceptis*. For they contain a most brilliant theological doctrine and serve much to illustrate and amplify the doctrine, which is contained in (his) Commentary on Lombard and in the Breviloquium.

The second class exhibits (his) exegetical works, especially (his) Commentaries on several books of Sacred Scripture, which are very useful in particular for preachers.

In the third class, we have placed (his) mystical and ascetical works.

The fourth class contains all the works and opuscula pertaining in some manner to religious life, especially (that) of the Friars Minor, whether they be apologetic, or doctrinal, or historical.

The fifth and last class comprises very many Sermons, the greatest part of which have not been published.

Several copious indices, both special, and general, will be placed in their proper places according to the custom of the better editions.

Though our intention has been, that the original text, as much as is possible, be restored to its ancient integrity, yet, in regard to the form and reckoning of the writing of words or the orthography and in regard to the punctuation, it is sufficiently manifest, that the use most received in our own age is the one to be followed by us. Wherefore, in our edition we shall write, v. gr. *definitio, definitive*, though the codices and many editions write *diffinitio, diffinitive*.

In each matter the Vatican edition very frequently failed and it had to be reformed in nearly every line. Moreover, so as to more easily obtain that in the entire edition a uniformity of orthography be employed by the many collaborators throughout the entire time (of its composition), we have chosen as the norm of writing, to be always used, that, which the most famous *Forcellini* follows or prefers in his *Lexicon totius latinitatis*, third edition, Padua, 1827.

In regard to the method of distinguishing the text by punctuation, since there is no little discrepancy among the various nations, but nearly even among individual authors, we have proposed to follow a certain middle way. But the very property of the style of (St.) Bonaventure, marked in a laconic and often elliptical brevity, requires a greater number of punctuation marks, so that it be more easily understood. We have proposed to ourselves to pursue this end rather than always rigidly follow the form conceived beforehand.

It remains, that to all, who have proffered to Fr. Fedele and ourselves, for any reason, favor and assistance, for the preparation and execution of the arduous work of this edition, whether by the benefices conferred upon us or by the helps regarding letters, that we express our grateful spirit and give them special mention. Moreover, of those, who have rightly merited the best (of praise), there is such a great number in nearly all of Europe, that after the death of the same Fr. Fedele individual mention can hardly be made. We grieve that not a few of these have already passed from this life. But, in the first place, let us give thanks to nearly all the Prefects of the libraries and Conservators of manuscript codices, who for their kindness and love of letters offered themselves as benevolent promoters of this edition. It displeases us, not to indicate the names of so many illustrious men, of whom we will be forever grateful;

but, though we were to mention *many*, yet we could scarcely be excused from fault for being silent concerning *very many others*. However, we can scarcely refrain, at least, from naming those libraries, of which it was allowed to us a more frequent and longer use of codices, for the sake of which kindness we are obliged by a grateful spirit to mention. Of *Italian* libraries, before (all) others there are to be commended the following: the (Biblioteche) Nazionale and (Medicea) Laurenziana at *Florence*; the (Biblioteche Apostolica) Vaticana and Burghesiana, at *Rome*, the (Biblioteca) Ambrosiana, at *Milan*; the (Biblioteca Nazionale) Marciana, at *Venice*; the (Biblioteca) Nazionale, at Naples; the Biblioteca Antoniana, at Padua; the ancient library of the Convent of St. Fortunatus, at *Todi* (now the Biblioteca Municipale); the library of the Sacro Convento, at *Assisi* (now the Biblioteca Comunale); finally, the outstanding library of the Monastery of *Monte Cassino*, of the Order of St. Benedict. — However, in *France*, the outstanding Bibliothèque *National*, at *Paris*. — In *England*, the British Museum, at *London*; the libraries of Lincoln and Balliol Colleges, *Oxford*. — In Germany, first of all, at *Munich* the state opened to us for many years the doors of the Royal Library; special assistances were offered to us also at the Paulina library, at *Leipzig* (now the University Library), at the University of *Berlin* and the Provincial library of Düsseldorf. In Austria, the libraries of *Vienna*, *Kraków** and of very many Monasteries, specially of the Order of St. Benedict, have merited the most concerning our edition.

Moreover, many Fathers of our Order, from nearly all the Provinces, for many reasons, proffered us help as collaborators, whether ordinary or extraordinary. Therefore, if anything of good will come of this edition, concerning which let others be the judge, for the sake of justice, the praise and glory is to be distributed among very many men, whether as workers or as helpers. But, however, *to the Father of lights, from Whom descends ever best given and every perfect gift, and Who disposes all sweetly and attains (all) powerfully,*[1] be alone the honor and glory!

Looking to which, let us repeat the saying nearly word for word, with which the Seraphic Doctor concludes the Second Book of his Commentaries:° *This we ask, that if anyone will have found anything in this edition worthy of approval, let him give thanks to God, the Bestower of (all) goods. But, in the other passages, where he will have found either the false and/or doubtful and/or obscure, let him kindly pardon the insufficiency of the editors, who, without a doubt, wanted to pursue the truth. Moreover, to indefatigably seek this truth, to infallibly find (it), to inamissibly apprehend and hold (it), let Him grant Who is the Way, the Truth and the Life!*

In the Collegio di San Bonaventura
The solemnity of Our Seraphic Father St. Francis, (Oct. 4th), 1882

THE EDITORS

---

[1] James 1:17; Wis. 8:1.
 * *Trans. notes*: In 1882, *Kraków* was part of the Austro-Hungarian Empire; now it belongs to Poland. In the names of the Libraries mentioned above, I have completed their full names, as they now bear them.
 ° Cf. Book II, d. 44, Doubt 3, p. 1016, final paragraph.

SUPERNA CAELESTIS

THE DIPLOMA

OF OUR MOST HOLY LORD, POPE SIXTUS IV

BY WHICH BL. BONAVENTURE, CARDINAL BISHOP OF ALBANO

IS PLACED IN THE CANON OF THE SAINTS

SIXTUS IV, BISHOP

SERVANT OF THE SERVANTS OF GOD

As a perpetual memorial

The supernal, celestial fatherland, the City of Jerusalem, whose own participation is in herself, so rejoices in the salvation of all the Elect, that she receives more abundant joy from the rewards of (those) whose merits are the more outstanding. Which, the Prophet Isaiah seems to have understood, when, having been placed in an ecstasy of his mind, he said (Isaiah 12:6), *"Exult and rejoice, dwelling of Sion, since great in your midst (is) the Saint."* Therefore, let the choirs of all the Angels exult, who, solicitous that (her) empty thrones be filled, strive in humility to conduct (souls) from virtue to virtue, to those blessed mansions, from which the proud spirits were hurled down. Let all the souls of the just exult, who have followed the footsteps of Christ, and let all the faithful friends of God from both the Old and the New Testament also (exult), who, having contemned the vanities of this age, rejoice together with the multitude of (her) fellow citizens. Let Heaven exult with praises, let the Earth resound with joys, since the generation of the Saints has brought gladness to very many. For mightily does the piety of the faith demand, that what is conducted for the salvation of the many, be celebrated everywhere with common joys. Let the High Priest of the company of the Blessed, in particular, and the sacred assembly of the Doctors exult, who shine in Heaven as stars for perpetual eternities, among whom Saint Bonaventure has shown forth, as a new luminary, migrating, at God's call, from this valley of tears to the celestial (City), which is Jerusalem on high.

§ 1. We, however, who exercise the care of the Christian flock after having been borne to the height of the Apostleship by God's arrangement, which (flock) on account of the pleasant debt of the pastoral office, We aspire with intense desire to conform, as We ought, to the college of the Saints, can, by no means, unsuitably say to the Church Militant, for whose edification and increment, We have caused the same Bonaventure to be registered in the catalogue of the Saints: "Exult today and praise, o dwelling of Sion !" — that is the Christian religion in which, as on Mount Sion, there dwells by means of the True Faith, the True God — "since great in your midst is the Saint !" Certainly: *"In the midst of the Church, He opened*

his mouth, and the Lord filled him with the spirit of wisdom and understanding and clothed him with the stole of glory," (Eccli. 15:5), and He crowned him at the Gates of Paradise, in which one with the Angels he rejoices in (their) glory and felicity.

§ 2. Let us, therefore, be glad and exult, since that celestial Curia has from us, him to whom the care for us pertains, who protects with his own merits us, whom he instructs with his examples, illumines with his doctrines and confirms with his miracles; whom God gave to all peoples as a glory and honor, whose memory is held in benediction.

§ 3. For he wrote such things concerning divine things, that it seemed the Holy Spirit spoke in him. So piously, religiously and holily did he live, that his life befitted (his) writings, and what he wrote he taught by example. In whom the virtue of morals and the clarity of signs have been so thoroughly proven, that, as befits the greatest merits and miracles, there is owed to him by the Church Militant the testimony of true sanctity.

§ 4. For, when in the green flower of youth, when human things are not valued as things to be thrown away, he dedicated himself to the divine service, having entered the religion of Blessed Francis, which strives through arduous deeds, he advanced so much in diligent reading and assiduous prayer, that one could deservedly say with the Wiseman: *I have desired, and understanding was given to me.* (Wis. 7:7)

§ 5. For, (he was) illumined by Him, Who illumines every sense, Who is the Light, the Way, the Truth and even Life, (and) obtained in the space of a few years incredible knowledge; and he did not bind up the talent entrusted to him by the Lord in a handkerchief, nor did he bury (it) in the earth, but as a most wise dispenser he exchanged it for the utility of all. For, in the frequented lecture halls of Paris he reigned from a *cathedra*, where explaining in detail the hidden things of the Scriptures, he not only by his own voice benefited many, but even left very many of the best of books, both in sacred letters and in the primary sciences, as monuments, which would be for the benefit of every age to come.

§ 6. Great in doctrine, no less in humility and in the merits of life, whom Alexander of Hales, the *Doctor Clarissimus*, to whom he handed himself over to be trained, experienced him to be of such innocence and dovelike simplicity, as he was accustomed to say, that it seemed to himself, that in him Adam had never sinned.

§ 7. Great, too, in the Order of Friars Minor, which he benefited as one of all the very many after blessed Francis. For, having been called to its helms and created Minister General, at God's inspiration, he showed himself to be such to his own subjects, that in him that word of the Lord was seen to be fulfilled: *"Whoever be the greater among you, let him be your minister."* (Mt. 20:26; 23:11).

§ 8. Greater, indeed, in wisdom and in the integrity of morals, he exercised the office of prelate with such charity, that willingly humble, his hands were filled ministering to his inferiors, as a good soldier of Christ, now with doctrine, now with admonishments, now with fraternal exhortation, now even with bodily service. Nor did he only guard those things which had been piously and holily instituted by Blessed Francis himself, but he even added many other arrangements, which, with the growing number of friars, were seen to be necessary. He also divided the same Order into provinces and custodies.

§ 9. Great was he also in dignity, in the Roman Church. For growing strong in the fame of his innocence, doctrine and prudence, he was called by Pope Gregory X, Our predecessor of happy memory, to the honor of the Cardinalate, so that he might employ his works in the greatest and most difficult things which were happening in those times, upon whom Gregory himself employed a new example on account of the vast merits of the man. For he immediately entrusted to him the Church of Albano, which was not accustomed to be committed to any but the older Cardinals.

§ 10. As a man, optimal and most beloved by God, he did not deceive the expectation

of the Supreme Pontiff and the Sacred College. But, presiding in the Council of Lyons and directing all to the praise of God, having allayed discords and borne away difficulties, he was as a great ornament for the use of the Church Herself.

§ 11. By which things there is openly recognized, that the Lord established him as a testament of peace and made him a prince, so that the dignity of his priesthood would be forever, whom inane glory did not puff up, nor riches drive to the left hand; but persevering in faith and leniency, faithful unto God, merciful unto the poor, just unto all, he so put off this corruptible body, that with the Apostle he can say: *"I have fought the good fight, I have run the race, I have kept the Faith, as to the rest a crown of justice has been set aside for me."* (2 Tim. 4:7).

§ 12. Who, even if from his perseverance alone he could have been believed to be a Saint, according to that (verse): *"Be faithful unto death, and I will give thee a crown of life"* (Apoc. 2:10), yet, there followed after his death many and very great miracles, which offer certain evidence of his sanctity and induce us to the veneration of him, whom God showed by his preceding merits (was) to be venerated. For the Omnipotent God Himself, to manifest the power of His own virtue and to disclose the cause of our salvation, often even honors in the world His faithful elect, whom He crows in Heaven, by working signs and prodigies in his memory, whereby heretical depravity is confounded, and the orthodox faith guarded.

§ 13. We give thanks, therefore, to God as much as We can, that He has considered Us worthy (to be the one), through whom this canonization is celebrated, which though, with the divine, extant monuments of letters and trembling miracles, could have already long ago (been) duly done, yet, never before this had it been sought with such diligence either by princes or by others. In Our own time, Our most dear sons in Christ, Frederick the forever august Emperor of the Romans, the illustrious kings: the most Christian Louis of the Franks, Ferdinand of Sicily and Matthew of Hungary; and also (Our) beloved sons, the noblemen Alphonsus of Calabria, John Mazencio of the Venetians, John Hacam (who in Italian is called *"Giovanni Galeazzo Sforza"*) of Milan, and John Bourbon, the distinguished dukes; moreover, the citizens of Florence, Siena, Lyons, Paris and, that which bore such a beaming light, Bagnoregio, requested this from Us with such earnestness and such perseverance, that We would think it hard and impious to resist them in a thing so pious, which they were seen to request by God's admonition. The assiduous prayers of our venerable brother Julian, Bishop of Sabina, Protector of the same Order were added, and also (those) of our beloved sons Francis Samson, the Minister General, and Peter of Rudolf, the Procurator of the said Order, a professor of Sacred Theology, who in the name of their General Chapter requested it as something just and due. We had read most studiously the divine writings of this Saint, by which, after We were permitted to understand something after a lifetime, We were always delighted. We had heard also from the more ancient friars of the aforesaid Religion and indeed from grave men, that even those of greater age had known that the fame of the sacredness of his life was constant; We were accustomed to know of the many and greatest miracles, nor was there on that account any doubt in our mind, but that he had triumphed in the Church Triumphant in Heaven and merited veneration upon earth.

§ 14. But mindful, that We had entered same Order of Minors by vow, in which, with divine grace assisting, We had progressed in both sacred letters and religious customs and had exercised the same offices of ministry, and thence to the dignity of the Cardinalate, so that We might recognize that through similar steps We had been elevated to the apex of the Pontificate, by the Lord's arrangement, through which Saint Bonaventure himself was carried up to the unwithering glory of the Church Triumphant, lest in this We seem more ably moved by our own affection than by due devotion, We applied that diligence

and gravity, which the magnitude of the matter demanded. For We committed to three of Our venerable brothers, Cardinals of the Holy Roman Church, to order an inquiry into the truth of the miracles. And, since one of these, with the process begun, as it pleased God, had passed from this life, We suggested another Cardinal in the place of the departed, in whose place, when he was already deceased, We substituted another.

§ 15. Nor content with this, when the process itself had already nearly been completed, and those who had been delegated had reported most faithfully; We, however, to whom it did not seem that in the proceeding such solemnity, as is required, was observed, ordered it to be begun anew.

§ 16. At last, when it had been thoroughly proven from more abundant reporting and from the faith of more worthy witnesses concerning this undertaking, that many and great miracles were worked by God through this Saint, which in the sight of the multitude had been determined, lest We seem to resist the Holy Spirit, Who through the mouth of the Prophet commands that God be praised in His Saints, We had, in a secret consistory of Ours, after it considered the case of this matter, the votes of Our venerable brothers, the Cardinals of the Holy Roman Church, concerning a canonization of this kind, examined. And since one and the same had been the opinion of all, namely, that he should be registered among the number of the Saints:

§ 17. We, thereupon, held a public consistory, in which, with a great multitude of by-standers, We publicly proclaimed a triduum of prayers and fasting, so that God Omnipotent might deign to manifest to us what would be the best course of action in this matter, nor suffer, that His Church Militant err, who strives to conform Herself to (that) Triumphant.

§ 18. Thereupon, with the triduum elapsed, We commanded all who were prelates in the Roman Curia to assemble, who to a man having been questioned, what seemed must be done, agreed upon one opinion, and determined that Blessed Bonaventure (was) to be canonized.

§ 19. We, therefore, following the command and will of God and attentive, that it be just and due, that (those) whom God honors in Heaven, We praise with a office of veneration and glorify on earth, since He Himself is more powerfully praised and glorified in them, Who is praiseworthy and glorious throughout the ages, did establish this day to be cele-brated for the canonization of the same Saint Bonaventure in the midst of the Basilica of the Prince of Apostles in the City, in which the greatest multitude of every kind and order streamed together. There, with all remaining things legitimately transacted, the aforesaid Procurator of the Order of the Minors, standing in the midst, proclaiming the saying of the blessed John the Apostle with a clear voice, namely: *There are three, who give witness in Heaven, the Father, the Word, and the Holy Spirit* (1 John 5:7), proved also, with the process concern-ing the aforementioned things having been held, that the very Persons of the Most Blessed Trinity had borne witness: namely the Father in the power of his miracles, the Son in the wisdom of his doctrine, and the Holy Spirit in the goodness of his life. And, on that ac-count, not only in the names of all, who begged that this canonization be accomplished, but even on the part of the each member of the Trinity, Father and Son and Holy Spirit, did he request urgently, more urgently, and most urgently, that We deign to pronounce the same Blessed Bonaventure a Saint. Confident, therefore, that in this canonization God would not permit Us to err, who required that all requisite things in this of whatever kind be ob-served superabundantly, and did observe such, having been assured from the unanimous consent of Our same brothers, the Cardinals of the Holy Roman Church, and the prelates in the Roman Curia who were present, and with the mature counsel of the omnipotent God and the authority of His blessed Apostles, Peter and Paul, We determined that Bonaventure of Bagnoregio, of blessed memory, professor of sacred theology, from the bosom of the sacred Order of Minors and called from the office of the Generalate to be a

Cardinal Bishop, should be a Saint and will be inscribed, added, and entered into the catalogue of God's other Saints, and faithfully and firmly considered (as such); and according to these present documents, We solemnly inscribe the same in the company of the holy Confessors, Pontiffs and Doctors, whom the Holy Church of God venerates, and according to these present letters We do aggregate him to their number.

§ 20. Establishing, also, and commanding Our venerable brothers, the Patriarchs, Archbishops, Bishops and the beloved sons of the same and, also, the Chapters of the patriarchal, metropolitan, and cathedral churches, and the professors of whatever Orders, as much of Mendicants as of non-Mendicants, not without whatever kind of ecclesiastical persons, to celebrate the feast of this same Saint Bonaventure solemnly and devoutly on the second Sunday of the month of July, each year, and resolving that (they celebrate) the divine office just as for a Confessor, Pontiff, and Doctor, as much in public as in private, as may happen.

§ 21. To our truly beloved sons, the friars of the aforesaid Order of Minors, in so far as in that manner in which the said members of the Order are accustomed to celebrate the feasts and octaves of the other Saints, We concede the faculty to celebrate an office of this kind as a feast of double class and with an octave.

§ 22. In addition, in the Lord We mercifully indulge and bestow with that same authority to all who are truly penitent and have confessed, who on the same Sunday would devoutly visit the church, in which his holy body rests, yearly seven years and as many forty-days; to those truly, who at other times on any Sunday, one hundred days; to those moreover, who are present for the divine offices at churches of the Friars Minor, wherever constituted, as much as on the very day of the feast, as during the octave, those similar indulgences and remissions of sins, which the Roman Pontiffs have conceded for each of the feasts of the Saints of the same Order, from the Apostolic indults commonly promulgated, concerning the enjoined penances.

§ 23. Considering besides, that there was undertaken by this very Saint Bonaventure so great a measure of growth in science, holiness of life and in the dignity of the Episcopacy and the Cardinalate of the Holy Roman Church, and how great a familiarity and spiritual companionship the same Saint observed in this life with blessed Thomas of Aquino, his contemporary, fellow student and teacher, that fraternal charity joined together in this age them, whom We believe have attained the same rewards in Heaven, (and whom) the present Church venerates with equal honor, We, receiving and enumerating the aforesaid feast among the feasts of the Sacred Apostolic Palace, do concede the same indulgence on the aforesaid feast in the Church of the Holy Apostles in the City, which is had on the feast of the same Saint Thomas of Aquino in the Church of the Blessed Virgin Mary in the City, commonly named "(sopra) Minerva"; and, likewise, We determine, that the Friars Minor in the dear University of Paris can and ought to enjoy and rejoice with the same privileges on account of the merits of the same St. Bonaventure, with which from apostolic indults the Friar Preachers, who in the same University are accustomed to posses and rejoice in, and do rejoice, by the insight and grace of the same St. Thomas, or in whatsoever manner they will be able to either posses or rejoice in the future.

§ 24. Wherefore, We require and warn each and every person constituted in dignity, in so far as Our present letters, being solemnly published, to exhort them by all the clergy and people of their cities, dioceses and parishes, that God Himself, from Whom all good things proceed, be beseeched humbly, that having been entreated by the prayers and merits of the same holy Doctor and Confessor, Bonaventure, He might guard the Church Militant, the Apostolic Faith and all the faithful of Christ from the incursions of pagans and other infi-

dels and heretics and always protect and defend Her from all dangers; and, having borne away the dread of every enemy, may He grant with firm tranquility that peace which the world cannot give us; so that after the military service of this life and after having laid down the ministry of the pastoral office, one with the flock He has entrusted to Us, We may yet, also, merit to arrive at sempiternal joys.

§ 25. Finally, since it might be difficult that the present, original letters be communicated as news to everyone, We desire and determine, that to those transcripts of these documents, marked, however, with the seal of the Minister General of the aforesaid Order and duly signed by the hands of two public notaries, there be exhibited an indubitable faith in all things and through all things, and in those places wherever it be posted, even if the original letters of this kind might be also exhibited and displayed.

To entirely no man, therefore, be it licit to infringe this page of Our constitution, inscription, aggregation, statute, command, concession, indulgence, grant, reception, enumeration, admonition or will, or by rash daring to contravene it. If, however, anyone might presume to attempt this, let him know that he will incur the indignation of the Omnipotent God and of His Apostles, Peter and Paul.

Given at Rome at St. Peter's, in the year of the Lord's Incarnation, one thousand four hundred and eight-two, on the eighteenth of the Calends of May in the eleventh year of Our pontificate.*

---

* *Trans. note*: i. e., on April 14, 1482 A. D..

OUR MOST HOLY LORD POPE SIXTUS V'S

DECRETAL LETTERS

BY WHICH ST. BONAVENTURE, THE SERAPHIC DOCTOR,

CARDINAL BISHOP OF ALBANO,
IS NUMBERED AMONG THE EXCEPTIONAL AND EXTRAORDINARY DOCTORS
OF THE HOLY CATHOLIC CHURCH

SIXTUS, BISHOP
SERVANT OF THE SERVANTS OF GOD

To all Our venerable brother Patriarchs, Primates, Archbishops, Bishops and beloved sons, and those constituted as Prelates of the other churches throughout the entire globe, greetings and Apostolic benediction.

Triumphant Jerusalem's sempiternal glory and the never withering crowns of the Saints, most happily reigning with Christ — as one admiring these with joy, Holy Mother Church, militant upon this earth, (and) truly hastening to the same crown of justice, does not cease to preach that God is *wonderful in His Saints.* However, neither do they alone celebrate with exceptional praises the distinguished victories and the very bright merits of the Saints, but the same Saints, whom God wonderfully honors, She Herself also piously venerates and cares for, established (as She is) upon their preaching and salutary doctrine, founded upon their blood, instructed by their illustrious works of charity and example, She is helped each day by their fervent prayers before God. Wherefore, She greatly studies those things due to that celestial Hierarchy, where all are ordered in perfect charity, to conform Herself to that norm and image, indeed, inasmuch as it is permitted Her in the exile of this passing world. For just as there are many mansions in that great House of the greatest Head of the household, heaping with all good things, and just as those blessed souls enjoy a certain wonderful variegated beatitude of one glory, so the Catholic Church, which is the effigy of that Celestial (Mansion), arranged (as She is) as a battle line in a military camp, (and) illumined by divine light, acknowledges and distinguishes those sacred Orders in the veneration that must be exhibited to the Saints of God. And so, while She praises the glorious chorus of Apostles, the laudable number of Prophets, the army of strongest Martyrs and offers honors to the other Saints in their place and order, with due ceremony, She exults manifoldly in one spirit of charity and in a similar pious affection of devotion. Truly, among those most blessed choirs of Saints, whose memory is celebrated by all the faithful with a merited religious cult, there shines forth in distinguished splendor the order of holy Doctors, eloquently enumerated by Paul the Apostle, when he said, *"And He gave some indeed as Apostles, others however, as Prophets, others truly as Evangelists, others, however, as Pastors and Doctors,"* whom He constituted vigorous and faithful cultivators and workers in His vineyard, *"for the work of ministry, for the edification of the Body of Christ."* (1 Cor. 12:28; Eph. 4:12) These are those, concerning whom the Divine Wisdom shouts: *"They who make Me shine forth will have life eternal."* (Eccli. 24:31). Concerning these, the Angel spoke in

the presence of Daniel: "*Moreover, they who are learned, will shine like the splendor of the firmament, and they who train many unto justice, will be as stars for perpetual eternities.*" (Dan. 12:13) Finally, these the Savior Himself, Christ the Lord, decorates with that distinguishing eulogy: "*He who does these things and teaches them, will be called great in the Kingdom of Heaven.*" (Mt. 5:19) Since, however, at all times the study and doctrine of the sacred Doctors has been useful and salutary in the Church of God, this fact itself demonstrates that it is greatly fruitful and plainly necessary, when, with the furor of the horrible name of Christian persecutors repressed, in the very peace of the Church there were roused up more vehemently the wars of heresy. For then, by the care and diligence of the Doctors, there (were) detected the deceits and fallacies of the heretics, who, at the Devil's instigation, did not cease to overseed tares in the field of the Lord, and (their) pestiferous and detestable errors were cut off by *the sword of the spirit*, and, with the holy Doctors as attendants, (their) falsehood was laid low by the strength of Catholic Truth. Wherefore, by every right are the holy Doctors designated in the Church with the name of the stars, the Hyades, who then, in the very frigid winter and with the long nights of infidelity completed and the storm of persecution calmed, shone more brightly upon Holy Church, after the sun of truth grew warm among the hearts of the faithful, and as the year opened in truth, more lucidly with new faith.

§ 1. Among those, whom the great Lord willed to fill with a spirit of intelligence, and who have sent forth the utterance of their wisdom like a shower upon the Church of God, St. Bonaventure is deservedly numbered as a Confessor, Pontiff, and exceptional Doctor in the same Catholic Church, whom Our predecessor, Pope Sixtus IV, of happy remembrance, on account of the admirable sanctity of his life and (his) very excellent doctrine inscribed among the number of the Saints.

§ 2. For born at Bagnoregio in Tuscany, to satisfy the pious vow of his mother, he entered as an adolescent into the Religion of St. Francis, by means of whose still recent footsteps the new soldier of Christ, by progressing humbly and constantly, drank the most healthful observance of regular norms with such ardor of spirit and avidity of heart, that there appeared in him the highest sanctity, and with innocence and chastity of life, holy humility, patience, meekness, a disdain of earthly things, (and) a desire for those heavenly, he was an example to and the admiration of all. Inflamed in such great sweetness and fervor of divine love, his spirit was so rapt in God, that already as one introduced into the wine cellar of the Spouse and drunk with the best wine of charity, he seemed to gaze everywhere upon Jesus Christ, Crucified and Suffering, and to dwell in His wounds. Truly, to this exceptional holiness of life did this man of God join the great praise of outstanding doctrine, with God so disposing, so that for His glory and the utility of the Church, he would not only make very great progress in example, but in word and erudition. And so, when in the study of Sacred Letters, the reading of the holy Fathers and in the very necessary discipline of Scholastic Theology, having been versed most diligently by Alexander of Hales, the distinguished theologian of that age, for a brief space of time, with the goodness of (his) surpassing genius, by (his) assiduous labor, and what is chief of all, with the grace of the Holy Spirit, who molded him on all sides as a golden vessel for a chosen honor, he made such progress and arrived at such perfection of doctrine, that decorated in solemn custom with the distinctions of a Master in Theology in the frequented lecture halls of Paris, he taught Sacred Theology publicly in the same place.

§ 3. Truly, did he attain such great praise in the gift of interpreting and in the science of all theology, that most learned men admired his doctrine and erudition. And, indeed, there are extant many, moving and very bright writings of this holy man, which still are of great

utility to the Church and are not mediocre, by the benefice of God, everyone of which both erudite men, of Our age and ages past, have read with much fruit and most entirely approved, so great was he in theology, that they declare him sufficient. For he left those monuments of his divine genius to those who would come after him, by which questions, very difficult and involuted with many obscurities, are explained methodically and in order, straightforwardly and lucidly, with a great abundance of the best arguments, the truth of the Catholic Faith is illustrated, pernicious errors and profane heresies are overthrown, and the pious minds of the faithful are admirably inflamed to the love of God and the desire of the celestial Fatherland. For there was in St. Bonaventure something preeminent and unique, so that he stood out not only in the subtlety of arguing, in the facility of teaching, in the cleverness of defining, but he excelled in a certain divine strength of thoroughly stirring up souls. For, in writing with the greatest erudition, he so conjoined an equal ardor of piety, that he would move the reader by teaching and it would sink into the recesses of the soul, and then he would prick the heart with certain seraphic stings and it would pour forth with a wonderful sweetness of devotion; sanely admiring which grace poured out upon his mouth and pen, Our predecessor Pope Sixtus IV, had no doubts in saying, that the Holy Spirit was seen to have spoken in him.

§ 4. When, therefore, to (this) faithful servant, so many and very bright talents have been entrusted by the Lord, that he increases these by exercising them for the utility of his brothers and by buying the treasures of heavenly grace, by divine counsel and with the greatest consent of his whole Order he was made, at Rome, the seventh Minister General after blessed Francis; in which duty of office he not only exhibited prudence, vigilance, and solicitude, but he was consumed with such ardor of fraternal charity and slaved for his brothers with such a self-abasement of Christian humility, that there was acknowledged in him that saying of the Lord: *"Let him who is greater among you, be as your servant."* (Mt. 20:26)

§ 5. Yea, even Our Predecessor of pious memory, Pope Clement IV, who loved this holy man intensively and was delighted by his wonderful doctrine, obtained for him the distinguished Archiepiscopate of York, so that so excelling in virtue and prudence he might run about in a broader field for the utility of the many. But, since he could not suffer to tear himself from the embrace of seraphic poverty, he modestly and humbly refused the offered dignity.

§ 6. Moreover, when the Supreme Pontiff, Gregory X, on account of the most grave situation of the Christian republic had proclaimed the General Council of Lyons, and searched eagerly for men outstanding in sanctity, doctrine and wisdom, whose strong and faithful works he might use for the managing and arranging of this greatest matter, he chose first of all two of the clearest lights of that age from the two most flourishing Orders, of Preachers and of Minors, Saints Thomas and Bonaventure, whom he commanded to come in person. But when the former of the two had fallen sick on his journey and had happily flown forth to the crown of glory, St. Bonaventure, arriving at Lyons, was greeted most courteously by the Roman Pontiff, Gregory, who was wont to acquiesce so much in regard to his virtue and wisdom, that he determined that the parts of directing and administering the Council were to be assigned chiefly to him. For which reason, from the public utility and necessity of the Church, so that he would not only take part in the things of the Council, but preside over them, (Our Predecessor) decided to place the burning and shining light upon the highest candlestick, so that it would greatly brighten the house of God.

§ 7. And so, he immediately elected St. Bonaventure — seeking no honors, but rather fleeing them, and indeed submitting to the Vicar of Christ and not refusing to undertake any labors for the Church — just as in the theatre of the whole world he had elected him to the Sacred College of Cardinals and to the

order of Bishops; for he appointed him to the Church of Albano, the honor of which was accustomed to be given to the older Cardinal presbyters. He, who bore the fullest dignity, contributed at once to the glory of God and to utility of the Church. For, indeed, in the most arduous matters of the Council he performed the most uncommon tasks, defended the Catholic Faith most constantly, refuted depraved opinions most sharply, and by whose patience, doctrine, sanctity, and orations, the pastoral solicitude of the Pontiff Gregory was so greatly aided, that with the disagreement of the schismatics removed by the mercy of God, Michael Palaeologus, Emperor of the Greeks, and the oriental nations returned to the obedience, unity, and communion of the Apostolic See; and in the end he was held to be worthy, to be called by name in Greek, "Eutychius".

§ 8. Therefore, deservedly, when a little before, during the same Council, the strongest athlete of Christ had migrated forth from the pilgrimage of this life to the celestial fatherland, all grieved over his death, all deplored the common loss, all decorated his burial with tears and praises, but one before all the others celebrated most truly the most holy man's life, conducted most uprightly, his most proven morals, his very many labors undertaken for the Church, and his doctrine, esteemed in that same Council with distinguished praise. This man was Cardinal Peter of Tarentaise, of pious memory, a man outstanding in erudition and Christian eloquence, who afterwards, when raised to the high rank of the Pontificate, was named Pope Innocent V. Truly, did the Supreme Pontiff Gregory X, himself, having lost a brother, (and) grieving in the deepest affection of heart for his most faithful helper and counselor, testify openly with graver words, that the Catholic Church, which had received from the piety and doctrine of such a man the richest fruits, had lost greatly at his death. But truly has it been said by the Holy Spirit: "*In eternal remembrance will the just man be.*" (Ps. 111: 6) For he, who in life was illustrious, was long after death made more illustrious, with God, Who is admirable and glorious in His Saints, much approving him with very many signs and prodigies and with the greatest distinguishing miracles.

§ 9. When the fame of whose miracles had gathered great strength among all men, the same Sixtus, Our predecessor, surveying them from the sublime watchtower of the Apostolic See, understood that the finger of the God, who alone works great wonders, was plainly there. And so, both on his own, and at the very many vehement requests of Frederick, Emperor of the Romans, of good memory, of kings, republics, dukes and cities, and of the urgent demanding consent of nearly all the faithful, the Roman Pontiff had the worthy idea of registering that most outstanding man, the Cardinal Bishop, Bonaventure, among the Saints. Therefore, with the greatest care and having examined both the exceptional sanctity of that diligent life and the truth of his miracles and having gathered these together, at last with all things, which pertained to this matter, duly and rightly accomplished, for the glory of God and the exaltation of the Catholic Church, in virtue of his own power and that bestowed upon him by God in blessed Peter, the Apostle, he registered the same blessed Bonaventure among the Saints, with the consent of his brothers, the Cardinals of the Holy Roman Church, and all the prelates, and he inscribed and aggregated him among the number of the Saintly Confessors, Pontiffs, and Doctors, and he commanded that his anniversary feast day be celebrated on the second Sunday of the month of July, and that an office be recited for him, just as for a Confessor, Pontiff, and Doctor throughout the universal Church, likewise with other decrees added, which are more fully contained in the letters of the same Sixtus.

§ 10. And, though this Doctor, St. Bonaventure, be glorious and most celebrated in the Catholic Church, and be greatly resplendent in Heaven, where he is crowned with that crown, which God keeps for those who love Him, and although no human thing is lacking to him, who enjoys the good things with Christ, which neither the eye sees, nor ascend into

the heart of man; nevertheless, the charity of Christ and a burning affection of a certain devotion, by which for him We have been perpetually consumed from nearly Our first years,
urges Us to consider how to rather propagate and explain his sanctity and to a greater extent his doctrine, as much as We are able with the help of the Lord. Indeed, We are moved,
that there is a part of Our seraphic Religion, in holy communion with him, in which We
have been educated and versed for many years, and for whom as a for a most worthy
mother, We should manifest every honor of piety and gratitude of heart; but much more do
the glory of God, the pastoral office which We bear, the so many labors undertaken by this
most holy man on behalf of the Church of God, and his so many illustrious merits urge Us,
so conjoined as they are with the Roman Church, in whose broadest ranks and Senate he sat
with the highest praise. Finally, the utility of the universal Church moves Us, which can be
always more and more richly captivated by the erudition of such a Doctor, especially when
the ambushes and the diabolical machinations of heretics, by which they oppose most vehemently in this sad age that sacred theology, which is called "Scholastic", admonish Us
greatly, that We should retain, explain, and propagate this same theology, as something
which nothing can be more fruitful for the Church of God. For with the divine gift of Him,
Who alone gives the spirit of knowledge and wisdom and understanding, and Who fur-
nishes His Church throughout the lifetimes of generations with new benefits, as is needed,
and Who provides Her with new supports, there has been discovered by Our ancestors,
most wise men, Scholastic Theology, which two Doctors glorious above all, the angelic Saint
Thomas, and the seraphic Saint Bonaventure, most brilliant professors in this capacity, and
first among those, who have been registered among the number of the Saints, with excellent
genius, assiduous study, great labors and vigils have refined and decorated, and have
passed on to those who would come after, optimally arranged and in many ways very
clearly explained. And, indeed, such a salutary understanding and practice of this science,
which spread abroad from the richest sources of divine letters, of the Roman Pontiffs, of
holy Fathers and Councils, could certainly always bring the greatest assistance to the
Church, either to understand and interpret, truly and sensibly, the Scriptures themselves, or
to read through and explain the Fathers more securely and usefully, or to detect and refute
the various errors and heresies. Truly in these last days, in which there has already arrived those dangerous times described by the Apostle, and the blasphemous, proud,
(and) seductive men who advance to what is worse still, erring and sending others
into error, this (kind of theology) is necessary to sensibly confirm the dogmas of the
Catholic Faith and to confute heresies. And the state of affairs is such, that the
judges are the very enemies themselves of the truth, by whom Scholastic Theology
has become dreadful to the greatest degree, who scarcely understand, by that apt
and inner-connected coherence of things and causes, in that order and arrangement,
as by the training of soldiers in fighting, with those lucid definitions and distinctions, by that firmness of arguments and the sharpest disputations, to light is distinguished from shadows, and the true from the false, and their mendacity,
involuted with many deceptions and fallacies, like a vestment borne away, is
brought to light and stripped bare. Therefore, inasmuch as these men undertake to fight
and overturn this most fortified citadel of Scholastic Theology, so much more does it befit
us to defend this unconquered bulwark of the Faith, both to conserve and keep safe the inheritance of Our fathers, and to embellish, as much as we can, the keenest defenders of the
truth with merited honors.

    § 11. On which account, so that the erudition of the Seraphic Doctor may be diffused
more broadly for the utility of the many, and so that from his books and works erudite and
studious men may daily seize more copious and more tasty fruit (which must not be

doubted will add to the glory of this same Saint, though he is most blessed in heaven), We establish, first, indeed, in Our kind City, in this basilica of the Twelve Holy Apostles, a college by the name of "Saint Bonaventure", in which Sacred Theology is to be publicly explained chiefly from the works and commentaries of this exceptional and devout Doctor.

§ 12. Then, too, all his works, which can be found, whose editions are partly not yet carefully sought out nor have even been evaluated in every respect under our authority, and partly already published, We are taking care to publish all in proper form, so that both what is most faultless be printed and that these be brought to light from Our Vatican press. However, because from the very beginning of Our pontificate, with God, as We piously believe, inspiring, We have proposed constantly, to celebrate the name and merits of this holy Doctor among and for the sake of all men and to increase and amplify the faithful's veneration of him, and (because) We have also been sensibly and not too little stirred to do this by the example of Our predecessor, Pope Pius V, of holy memory, most worthy of the Christian republic, and whom as a father We still revere and honor.

§ 13. For he having been thoroughly moved with religious piety and singular devotion, by which he was influenced in regard to Saint Thomas of Aquinas, the honor of his Order and the ornament of the Catholic Church, desiring in the same manner to adorn the same Saint with suitable honors on account of his most outstanding merits in the Catholic Church, besides these, ordered and decreed this, that his feast day be forever celebrated each year as a rite of double office according to the likeness of the four holy Doctors of the Church; which equal honor We, indeed, estimate should be allotted to St. Bonaventure, an exceptional Doctor, since among these such a fine conjunction and similitude of virtues, holiness, doctrine, and merits intervenes. For these *are the two olive trees and two candlesticks* (Apoc. 11: 4) lighting the house of God, who both with the fat of charity and the light of science entirely illumine the whole Church; these two came forth by the singular providence of God at the same time as two stars rising up from the brightest families of the Orders of regulars, which have always stood ready as things most useful to holy Church to defend the Catholic Religion, and to undertake all labors and dangers for the orthodox faith, from which, as from a fertile and well cultivated soil, there are daily procreated by the grace of God fecund and fruitful plants, by this there is meant those men outstanding in doctrine and sanctity, who energetically conduct the strong and faithful work of the Barque of Peter, driven about by so many waves, and of the Roman Pontiff, holding (as he does) his key not without the greatest solicitude. These two Saints, since they were contemporaries and given to the very same studies, students together, teachers at the same time, after they both had been summoned to the Council by Gregory X, the Supreme Pontiff, for similar reasons, honored, and in the pilgrimage of this life by fraternal charity, by spiritual familiarity, have been very much conjoined in a fellowship of holy works, and at last migrating onward together with equal pace to the celestial fatherland, equally happy and glorious they enjoy to the full that sempiternal beatitude, where with the same affection of charity, as We piously believe, they pray for Us laboring in this vale of tears and implore the divine power of assistance, so that deservedly did the same Sixtus IV, acknowledging that these two Saints where thoroughly alike and almost twin brothers in Christ, establish, that Saint Bonaventure and St. Thomas must be adorned with a like prerogative of veneration and honor.

§ 14. Therefore, because by Us both the charity of the seraphic Order, and the magnitude of the merits of Saint Bonaventure, and the utility and edification of the Catholic Church, whose helms have been committed by God to Us, though undeservedly, require, with the mature deliberation of Our venerable brothers, the Cardinals of the Holy Roman Church, having been heard, from the counsel and unanimous consent of the same and from Our certain knowledge

and the fullness of Apostolic power bestowed upon Us, by this Our perpetually valid constitution, We also greatly praise and commend in the Lord the doctrine of this very Saint Bonaventure, praised by Our abovesaid predecessors, Clement IV, Gregory X, and Sixtus IV, greatly approved in the Council of Lyons, employed also at the Council of Florence to explain difficult matters, testified to and commended by the authority of the gravest of men and worthy of an exceptional Doctor of the Church, and the letters, too, of the same Sixtus IV, which We want to be considered expressly at this moment, excepting the arrangement for celebrating the feast day of St. Bonaventure on the second Sunday of July, approving and renewing by the tenor of these (letters), We determine and declare, that the same St. Bonaventure, lawfully inscribed and enumerated together with the company of the holy Doctors by the same Sixtus IV, by Apostolic authority with the tenor of these present letters, must be held and venerated among the preeminent and primary (Doctors of the Church), who excel in the guidance of theological ability.

§ 15. And on account of this, We, hoping in the Lord, that the nightly study of the Seraphic Doctor in doctrine and devotion, which We greatly desire to shine and burn among the clergy and Christian people, be as the greatest help, determine and will that his books, commentaries, smaller works, and, in a word, all his works, be cited, published, and when it is demanded, employed, in the manner in which they have been most faultlessly published by Our Vatican press, as has been said above, just as are those of the other Doctors of the Church, who are exceptional, not only in private, but in public, in lecture halls, academies, schools, colleges, in lectures, disputations, interpretations, addresses, sermons and in all other ecclesiastical studies and Christian practices.

§ 16. And, nevertheless, so that a glorious remembrance of this wisest Doctor, if not for the sake of his own dignity, at least for the sake of human refinement, be refostered on account of his vast merits with more ardent study, We, induced by the example of Our predecessor, Pope Boniface VII, of happy remembrance, who gave instructions concerning the four holy Doctors, and that of Pope Pius V, concerning the aforesaid same St. Thomas, do precept, that his office be celebrated by all persons ecclesiastical, secular, and regular of whatever Orders as much in public as in private, on the day before the Ides of July (with the aforesaid arrangement of Sixtus IV, concerning the second Sunday of the said month, not withstanding) and so that this should be explained and printed in the Calendars, with the name of the Doctor and the addition of "festum duplex", even if in the reforms of the most recent breviaries and of the Roman Missal it had been arranged otherwise, and We determine that it cannot be judged nor interpreted otherwise than as had been ordained by Us above, by whomsoever endowed with whatever authority

§ 17. Exhorting all the faithful of Christ, of both sexes, in the City of Bagnoregio, which gave forth this most bright light, and those of the diocese, that they abstain on this same feast day from servile works, according to the custom of the Church: however, so that the devotion of Christ's faithful be enkindled to honor the feast day of this Doctor and to piously implore his power of assistance, more than it is, on which they might perceive themselves to be refreshed by this gift of celestial grace, by the mercy of the omnipotent God and entrusted with the authority of His Blessed Apostles, Peter and Paul, We mercifully concede and grant in the Lord a plenary indulgence and remission of all sins, to all Christ's faithful, of both sexes, who, gathered together either in the said City and diocese of Bagnoregio, as in the very bright City of Lyons, where he fought the good fight lawfully, where with the race finished, the faith kept, he happily migrated from this calamitous age to the reward and crown of his merits in Heaven, and in Our kind

city, where in that Basilica of the Twelve Holy Apostles, a college had been erected by Us, as We have already said, devoutly honoring his very feast, as other festivities are usually observed according to the precept of the Church, truly penitent and having made a sacramental confession of their sins, would on the same day receive the Most Holy Sacrament of the Eucharist. To those who would truly visit the churches of the Friars Minor of St. Francis on the very day of the feast, from the first vespers until sunset on the day proper, pouring forth prayers there to God, as their own devotion might suggest, We remit ten years and as many forty-days of those penances enjoined upon them, or owed in any other manner whatsoever, by means of these present letters that will endure perpetually, which We do not want to be included under whatever revocations or limitations of indulgences.

§ 18. Wherefore, We command your fraternity and discretion by means of these Apostolic writings, to procure that whatsoever is contained in them be published solemnly in whatever of your provinces, cities, churches, and dioceses, and that by all persons ecclesiastical, secular, and regular of whatever Order, of whatever place and nation, they be observed perpetually inviolable.

§ 19. Moreover, We will, that to the copies of these present letters, even those printed, signed by the hand of any public notary, and endowed with the seal of any person constituted in ecclesiastical dignity, there be exhibited everywhere that same straightforward faith, which would be exhibited to these present letters, if they were displayed or show to them.

§ 20. To entirely no man therefore, be it licit to infringe, or with rash daring to contravene, this page of Our approbation, renewal, decrees, declaration, determinations, precept, concession, grant, remission and command. If anyone however, would presume to attempt this, he will know himself to have incurred the indignation of the omnipotent God and of His Apostles, Peter and Paul.

Given at Rome in the Basilica of the Twelve Holy Apostles, in the year of the Incarnation of the Lord, one thousand five hundred and eighty-eighth, one the day before the Ides of March, in the third year of Our Pontificate.*

---

* *Trans. note*: i. e., on March 14, 1588 A. D..

COMMENTARY

ON THE FIRST BOOK OF SENTENCES

PROLEGOMENA

TO THE FIRST BOOK OF SENTENCES

We have placed the outstanding and, among theologians, the most celebrated *Commentarius in libros Sententiarum* in the first position in our edition, in which we have followed the example of the Venetian and Parisian editions. The reason, which moves us to this, most of all, is this, that in this *Commentary* the Seraphic Doctor has so copiously and profoundly explicated his own sentence in matters theological and even philosophical, that, those (things), which he has written in the other books, pertaining to the various disciplines of sacred theology in order to illumine the intellect and inflame the affection, can for the most part be reduced to this *Commentary* as to their chief and firm foundation. Therefore, with the text of this *Commentarius* restored to its integrity and illustrated with opportune notes, it seems to us that we have worked no little contribution to the publishing of the other works. On which account, we considered it necessary to devote a certain, singular effort toward this, so that, having employed so very many and best manuscripts and other helps, our edition of this great work might be as correct as possible. Meanwhile, what seems to us to be observed concerning this *Commentarius* and our edition of it, we have arranged in three chapters, treating, *first,* in general of the Four Books of this *Commentary*; *second,* of the First Book in particular, and of those (things) which we have guaranteed in publishing it; *third,* of the Book of the Sentences of Peter Lombard, published by us. To these there shall be added not a few tables for the convenience of the reader.

CHAPTER I
On the Four Books of this Commentary, in general

§ 1. *That the Four Books of this Commentary are authentic, is beyond all controversy.* The incipit of the First Book is: *Profunda fluviorum scrutatus est*; of the Second: *Solummodo hoc inveni, quod Deus fecit hominem rectum*; of the Third: *Deus, qui dives est in misericordia*; of the Fourth: *Unguentarius faciet pigmenta suavitatis.* Indeed, so many writers, even those contemporary and nearly so, so many editions, so many manuscript codices proclaim St. Bonaventure to be the author of this book, that Fr. Benedictus Bonelli can rightly assert (*Prodromus*, Bk. VIII, p. I, ch. 1, § 3, col. 516), that « not one of even the more morose critics, discovered, indeed, by myself has, heretofore, been found, who dared to

call Commentaries of this kind into doubt. Therefore, why spend time on a matter placed by the light of the noon-day sun outside of the risk of all doubt »? Therefore, let it suffice to briefly recall, besides the witnesses of the Order of Minors, whom (shall be dealt) with below, what *Henricus Gandaviensis* (*de Scriptoribus ecclesiasticis.* ch. 47, ed. Alb. Fabricii), who died in 1293 A. D., reported concerning St. Bonaventure: « He wrote on the four books of Peter ». The same is affirmed by *Ptolomaeus Lucensis*, a disciple and familiar of St. Thomas (*Eccles. histor. novae*, Bk. XXIII, ch. 2, in Muratori, *Scriptores rerum Italicarum*, tome XI, col. 1165).

The very author of this *Commentary*, as is observed in the *Prodromus* (loc. cit.), sufficiently indicates himself not only to be a Franciscan, a disciple of Alexander of Hales, but even Bonaventure, writing at Paris. A *Franciscan*, indeed, since he says in Sent., Bk. II, d. 44, a. 2, q. 2, near the end: In the Rule of St. Francis there is simply precepted, that the professors of this Rule have entirely nothing as their own upon earth etc. A *disciple of Alexander of Hales*, when in the same Second Book, d. 23, a. 2, q. 3, near the end, he eloquently names Friar Alexander of Hales "*our father and master*", and elsewhere in the same *Commentary* he calls (him) "*of good memory*". Then, too, that (he is) *Bonaventure*, since he says in Sent., Bk. IV, d. 8, p. II, a. 2, q. 2, ad 3: « If they had one institution, there would be one name, just as this name "Bonaventure" etc. ». That (he is) also *writing at Paris*; for, in Sent. IV, d. 20, p. I, a. 1, q. 6, seeking to determine the place of Purgatory, he says, among other (things): « If we will say, that (it is) where they sinned, it is entirely both incredible and impossible, that all the souls, which have sinned at Paris, be punished at Paris ».

§ 2. *Concerning the time and occasion for writing this Commentary, the contemporary writers of the Order are to be heard.* Their testimony is summed up by Fr. Bonelli in the *Prodromus* (Bk. I, ch. 3) and by Fr. Sbaralea (*Supplementum.*, p. 168) in this manner, that St. Bonaventure had already begun to lecture on the *Sentences* in 1245, after the death of Alexander, but only in the presence of the friars of his own Order and in their cloisters. But, then, with the license of the Minister General he taught publicly from the year 1248, as *licentiatus* in the proper sense. Fr. Bonelli says, « Before all others, Fr. *Salimbenus de Adam*, of Parma, the contemporary of Bonaventure,[1] is to be heard, reporting in his own

---

[1] In the same year, each had taken the Seraphic habit. His *Chronica* was printed at Parma in 1857. — The passage cited here from Friar Salimbene, occurs on p. 129 of that edition.

Trans. note: Latin terms, phrases, names of authors and titles of works have been italicized. The first occurrence of each personal name is retained in Latin, so that he might be more easily identified by those unfamiliar with the Anglicized version. — Let the reader be advised, that

after this Prolegomena was written, some of the historical presuppositions made by the Quaracchi editors regarding the chronology of St. Bonaventure's life, have been disproven. For a useful summary of current scholarship, cf. Costanzo Cargnoni, "Vita e Cronologia di San Bonaventura da Bagnoregio", DIZIONARIO BONAVENTURIANO, a cura di Ernesto Caroli. Editrici Francescane: Padova, Italy, 2008; pp. 67-87; and Johannes Freyer, "Opere di Bonaventura", op. cit., pp. 89-136.

manuscript Chronicles concerning John of Parma, the Minister General: This Friar *Ioannes de Parma* gave license to Friar *Bonaventura de Balneo Regis*, to lecture at Paris, which he had never done elsewhere, because he was a *bacellarius* and not yet a *cathedraticus*; and, then, he wrote a *Lectura super totum Evangelium Lucae*, which is beautiful and optimal, and he wrote *super Sententias quatuor libros*, which are regarded up until the present day as useful and serious. The year, 1248, had already begun, but now I deal with the year of the Lord, 1284. *Iordanus* agrees in (his) manuscript *Chronicum* (Vatican library, fol. 259), where he says of the Seraphic Doctor: « In the VIIth year, he was promoted to the *bazalariatum* at Paris, and in the Xth year after (his) entrance into religion, to the *magisterium* ».

« According to these, that which the *Chronicon XV Ministrorum Generalium*, written in the year 1305, says: « In the seventh year after (his) entrance into the Order, he read the Sentences at Paris, and in the tenth, he received the cathedra of a master », seems (is) to be understood thus, that in the seventh year, i. e. 1245, he was made *baccalaureatus* and judged suitable to teach the theological disciplines at Paris; but not, that he, thereupon, took to lecturing from the public bench, which as for example, according to the testimony of Salimbene, he began not but in the year 1248, which is the tenth year, in which our Bonaventure has borne the habit of the Minors. In the same manner, it seems allowable to interpret the *Chronicon XXIV Generalium Ministrorum, Bartholomaeus Pisanus, St. Anthony, Alexander Aristus* and the ancient *Catalogus Generalium Ministrorum* in the *Speculum vitae B. Francisci* etc. ». This far, the *Prodromus*, which then corrects the false chronology of the Venetian editors (*Diatriba*, p. 10) who thought, that in the seventh year, in which St. Bonaventure lectured in the cloisters of our Order, is to be understood as 1250, and the tenth year, in which he accepted the cathedra, the year 1253. Finally, the same Fr. Bonelli concludes: « Yet, I did not deny, that in the seventh year he could have lectured to our students in the cloisters of the Minors, so long as the seventh year is reckoned, not at 1250, but as 1245 ». This interpretation is confirmed by the testimony of Bl. *Franciscus a Fabriano*,[1] who asserts concerning our Seraphic Doctor: « *licentiatus* under master Alexander, the first master of the Order, whom, when he was in the world, the whole University of Paris followed, under whom seven of our friars were *licentiati* and made *magistri* in sacred theology. This said Friar Bonaventure was a most eloquent man, wonderful in the understanding of the Sacred Page and of the whole of sacred theology, a most beautiful speaker before the clergy and preacher to the people, in whose presence every tongue of earth was silent ». — Even *Bernardus a Bessa*, as was related above in the general Preface,[2] says similarly: « Hence it came to be, that in the seventh year after (his) entrance into the Order he read the Sentences at Paris and in the tenth received the *cathedra* ».

From these testimonies it is clear, that St. Bonaventure began at a young age to interpret the Sentences in the schools of the Order, and there is at once confirmed that which Salimbene says, that he wrote his own *Commentarius* in the year, 1248. Which, however, as is well observed in the *Pro-*

dromus (col. 516), « is to be accepted with a grain of salt, by leaving due time before and after for undertaking, prosecuting and perfecting such a great work; not that he conceived and gave birth to it within the straights of the one year of 1248 ». For, if he already explicated the Sentences to his own brothers in the year 1245, he, without a doubt, put down in writing his own lectures, which he, then, composed more accurately according to the custom of the authors of his own age and published. Moreover, it seems sufficiently certain, that this work had already been completed by 1256, since the Saint was elected Minister General on February 2, 1257.[3] It is manifest, that St. Bonaventure would have been impeded by this most grave office from the disputations of the schools.

Wherefore, if it is thus, then we can conclude, that among all the nearly innumerable commentaries explaining Lombard, at least (the ones) which were published *on presses*, this work of St. Bonaventure occupies either the first and/or second place in the order of time. I said: *and/or second place*, lest I take the right from Bl. *Albertus Magnus*, who since he was older (he is said to have been born in 1193, and died in 1280), perhaps wrote his own Commentary before and/or at the same time as St. Bonaventure. Concerning this, we dare to affirm or deny nothing, because concerning the chronology of this most eminent man, many things are still uncertain.[4] — St. Thomas, if we proffer faith to Father *Bernardus Maria De Rubeis* (*Dissert. criticae*, diss. 10, ch. 1; and 12, ch. 2), began his outstanding *Commentarius* in 1253 and completed it after having accepted the degree of *magister*. — Concerning Peter of Tarentaise it is entirely established, that he wrote his own *Commentarius* after St. Bonaventure, the doctrine of which he summarized in many passages, as Dionysius the Carthusian has already observed, just as in other passages he exhibits an abbreviation of St. Thomas' Commentary. On the testimony of *Echardus* (Tome I, p. 250) Peter began to lecture on the Sentences in 1259, which after a respite of some years, was continued after 1267.

Nor do we think that the other Commentaries, conserved only in *manuscript codices*, were written by *members of the Order of Minors* before St. Bonaventure and published by their own author. Indeed, it is established, that at the University of Paris from the time, in which the Mendicants were admitted to hold a *cathedra* in it, lecturing on the Book of the Sentences had been prescribed either by law and/or by custom for (those) aspiring to the dignity of a master. Nor is there a doubt, that the lectors and masters put their own lectures into writing and that their disciples *reported* (their) lectures, i. e. that, in regard to (their) principal parts, they excerpted (them) in short hand. An example is proffered in Scotus' work at Paris, which we have only as a *Reportatio*. *Reportationes* of this kind of Commentary are also still extant in libraries for not a few, other authors. Nor do we wish to deny *in general*, that some Commentaries on the Master, whether as *reportationes* or written by their own author, but not yet published, could be more ancient than St. Bonaventure's *Commentarius*.

Not a few writers think, that a Commentary on Lombard was written before St. Bonaventure and (that) by his

---

[1] In his *Chronica Frabrianenses*, mss. fol. 9, concerning which manuscript Fr. Bonelli says several (things) in (his) *Prodromus*, Bk. I, ch. 15, col. 63, 64, note f.   [2] Page III, footnote 1.

[3] (Luke) Wadding (1588-1657), (*Annales Minorum*), under the year 1256, n. 3, says among other following (things), that this election was on Feb. 2, 1256, which is false according to the ordinary computation, but, indeed, true according to the computation received by many in that age, which reckoned the new year from the day of the Incarnation, i. e. March 25, not from January 1. The *Chronica XXIV Generalium* resolves this difficulty thus: « This Fr. Ioannes (de Parma), having called the Chapter

General at Rome, in the year 1256, according to those who compute the years from the Incarnation of the Lord, but according to those, who compute the years from the Nativity, 1257, on the Feast of the Purification of Blessed Mary. Cf. *Prodromus*, ch. 17, footnote d.

[4] Echardus, (*Scriptores O. Praed.*, tome I, p. 165) holds for certain, that Bl. Albertus was sent to Paris in the year 1245 to read *pro forma et gradu*, as they say. But, yet, Heinrich Denifle, O. P., who is most trustworthy in things pertaining to the history of that age, has communicated to us, out of his friendship for us, that this assertion of (Jacques) Echard (1624-1744) lacks foundation; but it has been proven, that Bl. Albertus lectured at Paris in 1248.

master *Alexander of Hales*. This is asserted by the author of the book, *Firmamenta trium Ord. B. P. N. Francisci*, (Paris edition of 1512, fol. 42 recto), who after having spoken of (his) *Summa theologiae*, says this: « He also wrote, *the first among all the doctors*, an outstanding writing *super Magistrum Sententiarum ad litteram* ». But, yet, *Natalis Alexander, Oudin* and many after them, want, that this Commentary be not diverse than the *Summa theologiae* of the same Alexander. If this is true, he certainly did not publish a commentary on the Sentences. For this Summa can least of all be called a commentary on the Master, as is manifest to anyone inspecting the same, since it has nothing of the things according to both order and (its) entire arrangement, which is required for a commentary, no more than the Summa of St. Thomas, which congruently speaking, no one, certainly, calls a "commentary on the Master." On the contrary, Sbaralea (*Supplementum.*, p. 17) strives to vindicate for Alexander such a commentary, besides the Summa, by adducing the testimonies of many writers, among whom he names *Henricus Gandaviensis*, who (*de Scriptoribus eccles.*, ch. 45) says, that Alexander wrote upon the Four Books of the Sentences. Similarly speak *Raynerius Pisanus*, O. P., in his own *Pantheologia*, *Alphonsus Toletanus*, O. S. A., *St. John of Capistrano, Dionysius the Carthusian*, who distinguish the *Summa* and the *Commentarius* of the same, and other later (writers), who can be seen in the same Sbaralea. Sbaralea could have also adduced the many manuscript codices, conserved in the libraries (of Europe), which are inscribed with the name of Alexander with the titles *Commentarius in Sententias* and/or *In Sententias*.

But, yet, these same codices, to which Sbaralea appeals, for the most part destroy (his argument). For, if they are more accurately examined, it appears, that they do not contain Commentaries diverse from the mentioned *Summa*, but rather not but the *Summa* itself. This same did we observe in not a few ancient codices, namely:

At Assisi, in the Library of the Sacro Convento (now, the Municipal), Cod. membr. in fol. parv., saec. XIII, sign. XXXII. B. 268 fol. 1 in upper margin: *Alexander Halensis I. Sentent.* The *incipit* being: *Quoniam sicut dicit Boethius in libr. de Trinit.* The final words: *Finis primi et initium secundi.* The Second Book is inscribed: *in librum II. Sententiarum.*

At Florence, in the Biblioteca (Medicea) Laurenziana, plut. XXIV. ext. Cod. IV. membr. in fol., saec. XIII, on fol. 325, annotated by a second hand: *Alexander de Hales super secundum Sententiarum.* The *incipit* being: *Completes tractatibus de iis quae pertinent ad speculationem Dei.*

At Paris, in the Library of St. Victor (now, the National); Cod. 14530 membr. saec. XIII: *in librum IV. Sententiarum.*

Nor do we think that *Ioannes a Rupella*, the successor of Alexander in the cathedra of Paris, published a commentary. We know of no codex of such a work. Nor does it seem verisimilar that St. Bonaventure was commanded by (his) Superiors to write a new commentary, if these two most celebrated masters had already completed a like work, since he himself in the year 1248 was no older than 27.

It cannot be denied, that that age of youth seems rather immature and unequal to undertaking such tasks, that is, of teaching theology in the most celebrated halls of the metropolis and of writing an immense book on so arduous matters. But one must consider, that the natural and supernatural gifts of this Seraphic man exceeded even more the common and normal order, which (order his) paucity of years was lacking according to the ordinary rule, so much that (Pope) Sixtus IV was rightfully able to say, in the Bull of (his) canonization: « In the

space of a few years, he acquired an incredible knowledge ».*

Otherwise, St. Bonaventure, in virtue of his singular modesty and humility, would have never presumed willingly and on his own initiative to strive to so arduous (works) as a young man, unless the obedience, which he professed towards (his) superiors, and the fraternal love towards his brothers, insistently asking for this labor, had precluded his own choice in the matter. He testifies this very (thing) at the end of the Third Book on the Sentences, in these words: « I beg Jesus Christ, to make it turn out for me for the merit of obedience and for the progress of the friars, *on account of which two this labor was taken up from the beginning* »;+ and still more expressly in a certain, unpublished Prologue to the Second Book of the Sentences and/or, rather, in an epilogue to the First Book, which Fr. Fidelis was first to uncover and transcribe from Codex 193, membr. in fol., saec. XIV, fol. 164 verso, in the library of the city of Angers (France). We shall publish this in its entirely in its own place;# but here (is) its beginning: « By the Savior's helping grace, on account of which one has arrived at the completion of the First (Book) of the Sentences,[1] with the intervening insistence of the Fathers, one is bound to undertake the second. But just as in the First Book I adhered to the sentences[2] and common opinions of the masters (of theology), and most of all (to those) of our master and father of good memory, Friar Alexander (of Hales), so in the following books I will not retreat from their footprints. For I do not intend to defend new opinions, but to explain in detail the common and approved ones. Nor may anyone appraise, that I want to be the craftsman of a new writing; for this I think and admit, that I am a poor and feeble *compiler* » etc.. This was said by the Seraphic (Doctor) more after the custom of the Saints and according to the inspiration of humility, than according to the truth of the matter, as all confess. It could also be easily demonstrated, that he is not to be named a simple "*compiler*", but truly an "author", *and/or at least a "commentator"*, if we attend to those definitions, which he himself proposes thus: « It must be noted, that fourfold is the manner of making a book. For one writes another's (words), by adding and/or changing nothing; and that one is called merely a "writer". Another writes another's (words), by adding, but not from his own; and that one is called a "compiler". Another writes both his own words and another's, but the other's as the principal ones, and his own as those adjoined for evidence; and this one is called a "commentator", not an "author". Another writes both his own and another's, but his own as the principal ones, the other's as things adjoined for confirmation; and such ought to be called an "author" » (Sent., Bk. I, Foreword, q. 4).°

He speaks with the same modesty at the end of the Second Book of Sentences: « But if it seems otherwise to anyone, and perhaps better *in the determination of this question, nay in the explanation of the two preceding Books*, I do not envy (him); but I pray this, that if anyone ... will have found anything in this opuscule (of mine) worthy of approval, let him give thanks to God, the Bestower of good (gifts). But in other passages, where[3] he will have found either the false, and/or the doubtful, and/or the obscure, let him be kindly indulgent to the insufficiency of the writer, who without a doubt, as (his) conscience testifies, desired to say the true and the open and the common ».§ Then, at the end of Book III, he says, « I give immense thanks to Christ, who has helped me arrive at the consummation of the little work, having taken mercy upon the poverty of my knowledge and genius ».

§ 3. *On the relation which exists between the Summa of Alexander of Hales and the Commentary of St. Bonaventure, much needs to be said.* In deciding the Questions, the author of the *Commentarius* follows

---

[1] Here the reading is doubtful; for *of the Sentences* [Sententiarum] one can read *of the brothers* [fratrum].

[2] The Sentences of Peter Lombard seem to be understood; which corresponds better with the context of this whole Prologue.

[3] Contrary to the codices, the Vatican edition has *to have found* [ut invenerit] for *where he will have found* [ubi invenerit].

* *Trans. notes*: cf. the Bull, here above, on p. XL, § 5.

+ Sent., Bk. III, d. 40, Doubt 3, p. 893, final paragraph.

I. e, Sent., Bk. II, pp. 1-3.

° At the start of the Response, pp. 14-15.

§ Sent., Bk. III, d. 44, Doubt 3, p. 1016, final paragraph. The words in italics are wanting on p. 1016; similar words appear in the ellipsis.

very often his own master, Alexander, yet, not always; and he more often determines the latter's sentence more clearly and more accurately. It must also be conceded, that he adopted very many authorities or passages, both of the Fathers and of philosophers, many definitions and many other (things) pertaining to (his) doctrine from the *Summa* of Alexander, according to the sense, and sometimes quoted very small parts word-for-word, nay, once and again, he has adopted a little more. Some passages from the Second and Third Book are pertinent to this; but chiefly Sent., Bk. II, d. 23, a. 2, q. 3, where he deals with the cognition of God, which Adam had in the state of innocence. The Response to this Question agrees mostly with that, which is read in the *Summa* of Alexander in two Questions, namely, in *Summa., p. II, q. 92, a. 1 & 2*. But, yet, everywhere one can easily acknowledge by the strength of speech and style, as much as by the wonderful connection and sublimity of ideas, the mark proper to the genius of the Seraphic (Doctor), even in those passages, where a greater disciple has persisted in the footsteps of his own great master.

But there remains a certain difficulty, which is to be discussed by us more accurately for this, that, heretofore, it has been observed by no one, as we, indeed, know. In a very rare work, which was printed under the name of *Alexander Halensis* and with the title, « *Summa virtutum* », as part of (his) *Summa theologiae*, which has been vindicated by not a few learned men for the same Alexander, there are exhibited more than 70 Questions, which, with only a few (things) missing and/or omitted, are found in the same *Commentarius* (of Bonaventure). To elucidate this matter, it seems necessary to inquire at some time more at length both concerning the great *Summa* of Alexander, and concerning that other treatise on the virtues. This, we shall do more willingly for this (reason), that it touches upon the honor not only of the Seraphic Doctor, but also (upon that) of the Angelic, as we shall shortly see.

The *Summa theologiae* of Alexander of Hales, was sent to press, according to Sbaralea, at Venice in 1475, in 4 tomes, folio, by *Ioannes de Colonia et socium*; at Nürnberg in 1481 by *Antonius Koberger*; at Magdeburg in 1489 by *I. Antonius Birettum*; again at Nürnberg in 1502; at Lyons in 1515 (by Koberger); at Venice in 1576 by *Ioannes Baptista Balainum Ord. Min. Convent.*, on the presses of *Franciscus de Franciscis*; then at Cologne in 1622, in 4 tomes, folio. These *two last* editions divide the Questions into parts II, III and IV, in a new order or by different numbers. For they have as the second part, 171 qq., but Koberger's 114, which we shall indicate more particularly, below, for the convenience of the reader, in the list of the authors, which St. Bonaventure uses.

After the many small Summas of theology, composed by preceding authors, this *Summa* caused much admiration both for the immense breadth of (its) volumes, and on for the manifold praise of (its) excelling doctrine; that (its) author is Alexander, is most certainly established. Of this we have a peremptory testimony in the Apostolic Letters of (Pope) Alexander IV, in the year 1256, which *Echardus* was first to edit (*De Scriptor*. etc., tome I, p. 321) from the Parisian codex, sign. 15751, fol. ult.. In Wadding this document is wanting, but it was received by Sbaralea both in the *Bullarium*, tome I, p. 151, and in the *Supplementum*, p. 17. These Apostolic Letters, since they are the quasi foundation of our argumentation, are here transcribed in full:

« Alexander, Bishop, servant of the servants of God: to (Our) beloved son, Minister of the Order of Minors in France, health and Apostolic benediction.

« The river stepping forth from the fountains of Paradise, that is, the exuberant understanding of sacred scriptures has flowed forth, widely in Our times, from the mouth of Friar Alexander, of your Order, of cherished memory: a gladness upon the earth according to (his) force, for having brought the treasury of knowledge and saving wisdom more manifestly to light. If, indeed, the same friar, as we comprehend from that which he wrote and handed down, as one full of God (for no one but one speaking, in the spirit of God, the mysteries of eternal truth would have stretched to this endeavor of inquisition) accommodated his own studies for public utility, and by undertaking the holy proposal of a laborious work on theological questions, labored upon a more useful, than prolix *Summa*, profitable for (those) making progress in the law of the Lord for those wanting to study (it) more compendiously. In which there are ordered battle-lines of *irrefragable sentences* to crush the obstinacy of contentious falsehood with the weight of truth. Indeed, if the delicate reader abhors in the same Summa (its) prolixity, the continuous utility, in it, of its parts renders this so brief for you, the studious, that in such a marching-column of words, which seems to contain immense discourses of divine profundity, nothing can reasonably offend us, other than that, with God imposing an end to the labors of the same Friar, before he completed the task of the work undertaken, and producing the denarius according to the contract of the reckoned wage, of perfect piety imperfect is the labor, by which there seem both few and insufficient for the satisfaction of the soul all (the works), which were written, if the mass of each work does not allot a destined end to its own beginning, and to which (end) the exhibited portion supports the spirits of (those) reading (them). On which account, precepting thy discretion strictly in virtue of obedience, We, as One considering prudently, that which is unfittingly left over, if there is negligently omitted the unfinished work of God, which not but the celestial Wisdom began through the ministry of thy servant in the very clear beauty of the part already published, do command, concerning the counsel of the discrete friars striving for the perfection of the same *Summa*, (that) thou convoke at Paris the Friars necessary according to number and suitable according to merit, from whatever places of thy administration of thy Order, to whom, on Our part, thou art to enjoin for the remission of their sins and for the accumulation of merits, that as ones assiduously assisting (Our) beloved son, Friar *Gulielmus de Melitona*,* the one deputed to this solicitude, and mutually helping him and themselves, without allowing for delay, they finally execute the work of the aforesaid *Summa*, assisting to this by one and the same spirit of the Lord, Who freely distributes the wonderful gifts of the sciences. Given at Anagni, the fifth day before the Calends of August, in the second year of Our Pontificate ». That is, July 28, 1256, since (Pope) Alexander was elected on December 21, 1254.

Three (things) are established by this document: 1. Alexander (of Hales) is the author of the *Summa theologiae*, which is described by the Pope as of the greatest size and utility. 2. That he left this work unfinished. 3. That the Supreme Pontiff had deputed Friar *William of Meliton* to this, to complete that Summa and that « he had commanded by precepting strictly in virtue of obedience » that the Minister provincial of the Order of Minors in Gaul, give Friar William other suitable friars as colleagues in this work. This one testimony is already sufficient — even if there are not lacking others, especially from St. Bonaventure himself — for anyone to be able to pronounce sentence, what is to be judged concerning certain words, which were inconsiderately written by *Rogerius Bacon* in the years 1266-1268, in his immoderate disposition, concerning Alexander:[1] « From his entrance (into the Order), the friars exult-

---

[1] In a certain, heretofore, unedited work of Roger Bacon, Brewer's edition, London, tome I, p. 325.

* *Trans. note*: Hereafter, Friar *William of Meliton* († 1257-1260). The Prolegomena to Alexander of Hales', *Summa theologica*, tome IV, Bk. III, 1948, p. CCXL, cites manuscripts for other spellings: *Militona, Militone, Milletona, Milletoni, Milletonne, Milddithone, Mideltoun, Milton*; this last, a lector at Cambridge, whom the Quaracchi editors speculated might be the same, citing Eccleston, in *Analecta Francescana*, I, 272; cf. G. A. Little (*Mélanges Mandonnet*, II, Paris 1930, pp. 398-400). The other place names cannot be identified. In Anglo-

Saxon a *mel* is a mill, a *ton* is a fenced holding. In East Anglia, the only toponym of such an etymology in the Domesday Book (c. 1086 A. D.) *with a mill* is *Meltuna* (Malton, Suffolk); held in part by William of Sahuala. It seems more probable that a future Master of Paris came from an environment where literacy would be held to be a constant in the formation of a youth: and, hence, would have come from a town or from a propertied family. For his name, I follow Robert Royal's translation: Jean-Pierre Torrell, O. P., *Saint Thomas Aquinas*, Cath. Univ., 2005, vol. 1, p. 76, which is also the form preferred in the *Dictionary of National Biography*, 1885-1900, vol. 37, in the article: "William of Meliton".

-ed[1] unto heaven and gave him authority over the whole *studium* and ascribed to him that great *Summa*, which is more than the weight of one horse, which not he, but others made; and, yet, on account of reverence for him it was ascribed to him, and called, "*Summa fratris Alexandri*". And, *if he had made either a great part, yet, he did not read natural (philosophy) nor metaphysics* nor did he help them, because they were not the principal books of those sciences, nor translated Commentaries ... Moreover, his *Summa* has several falsehoods and vanities of philosophy, the sign of which is, that no one caused it to be written again, nay the exemplar among the friars is rotting and remains untouched and unseen by these times ». Just as what he has just said is manifestly false, as so many codices and editions of this *Summa* testify, so, too, the other (things), which he says, seem are to be restricted to this, namely, that Alexander (who, as Sbaralea would have, began this enormous work in 1234) had some assistants as associates in this work. Perhaps it can be conceded, that after his death William of Meliton redacted some writings, begun and left unfinished by Alexander, into completed form, and/or if one wants, added also a few (things) taken from elsewhere.

This last (interpretation) Sbaralea denies, who, indeed, in (his) *Bullarium* (loc. cit.) affirms: « All, as many as treated of this matter after Wadding and dealt with this William, write that he completed the *supplementum* of the Summa (of Alexander) of Hales; but I contend that nothing was done by him; or, if he did add something, that addition is never read alongside the *Summa* (of Alexander) of Hales. For in several ancient and recent editions, that *Summa* stops at the part of the *Sacrament of Penance* and does not proceed further. Nor does it respond to me, that he added at least some (things) up until the *Sacrament of Penance*; for in p. IV, q. 30, mem. 2, a. 2, which is near the end of the uncompleted *Summa*, the author asserts, that the Rule of St. Francis was approved and confirmed for the friars *by Innocent, Honorius and Gregory*, the Supreme Pontiffs; nor does he mention the confirmation of *Innocent IV and Alexander IV*, which the Pontiffs themselves list in their own Bulls, *Nimis iniqua* etc., published in the years 1245 and 1256; of which William did not keep silent, whether after those years he had made an addition to that Summa. Therefore, after the manner of the *Summa theologicae* of St. Thomas, which also itself finishes in the part of the *Sacrament of Penance*, no one has dared to add a supplement; so, too, for the Summa (of Alexander) of Hales. For, indeed, they think that the words of great and the most loft of men remain unfinished, than that they are supplied by the hands of unequal others, mindful that Pliny, *Hist.*, Bk. 35, ch. 40, had handed down in writing: *That the extremely rare and worthy of memory, even the supreme works of craftsmen and the unfinished tablets, as the Iris of Aristides, the Tyndaris of Nicomachus, the Medea of Timomachus and the Venus of Apellis are in greater admiration, than completed.* Otherwise, » etc..

The last argument posited by Sbaralea is of no value, especially since the Supreme Pontiff himself, Alexander IV, strictly precepted the contrary. But the first argument, taken from silence, namely, that he was silent regarding the Bulls of Innocent IV and Alexander IV, is not peremptory in itself and its strength is nearly derogated for this reason, that not only the *fourth* part of the Summa, but also the second and the third were unfinished, since they manifestly have great *lacunae*, as De Rubeis has already observed (*Dissert. crit.*, dissert. 15, ch. 3.). In the *fourth* part, only, there are found treatises on the Sacraments in general an on the first four Sacraments in par-

ticular. But there are lacking the treatises on the other three Sacraments and on the Last (Things). In the *second* part, in the prologue to Q. 171 (Cologne edition), which concerns scandal, the author promises that he will treat of homicide, dueling, usury, fraudulent contracts and rapine. Yet, nothing of these things is found in the editions of the Summa. Rather, even the *third* part after Q. 68 « has a patent lacuna and hiatus » (as the cited author observes), and the end is entirely wanting. For, there are lacking the treatises which were promised in the prologue to Qq. 26 and 69 on the virtues in general, on the gifts, the fruits and the beatitudes. But Question 78 begins thus: « After *the treatise on the virtues in general* one must inquire concerning the species of the virtues according to the *preassigned* difference, and first one deals with the theological virtues, which are virtues unto the end ... Consequently, however, of the virtues, which are for the end, such as prudence, justice, fortitude, temperance etc. ».

But in the editions, nothing at all is read before the virtues in general, nor does anything occur afterwards, except in the following Q. 69, certain *fragmenta* on faith, on the passions consequent to faith, on the articles of the Faith and on Creeds. All the others promised by the author are lacking.

From which it can be construed, that Alexander, if he did not write the whole Summa, such as it is in our editions (as Sbaralea says), did not always compose the materials to be treated in that order, in which he wanted to publish them in his book, since several treatises, posterior according to the order of things, were completed first, having omitted others according to the same order. Per consequens, it can neither be certainly concluded, that *all* the parts of the Summa before the aforesaid declarations of (Popes) Innocent and Alexander had already been completed by Alexander (of Hales), and that entirely nothing was added afterwards by William (of Meliton) and/or by anyone else.

But, let us pass over, at last, to that *Summa virtutum*, concerning which opuscule there has been such a great discrepancy of opinions. This book was published in the form *quarto parvo*, in two columns, in small typeface; it has 8 folios containing *tabluae*, and 374 folios or 748 pages. The title page, adorned with the insignia of *Ioannes Parvus* (Jean Petit), redacted with compendiary notes according to the common writing, reads thus: « Irrefragabilis doctoris alexandri de hales ordinis minorum opus de virtutibus excellentissimum: hactenus nusquam impressioni traditum: et est tertie partis sue summe continuativum: prout ab eodem doctore in eadem tertia parte dudum pluries impressa: quaestionibus XXVI. et LXIX. extiti compromissum ».* — « Offered for sale at Paris, in St. James's Quarter, under the sign of the Silver Lion: at the home of the honest man, Jean Petit, sworn book-seller, at the expenses of whom this, indeed, most worthy work comes forth into the open for the first time (and never before): in the year 1509 ».

On the last folio there is written: « Finis. The *Summa de Virtutibus* of the *Doctor Irrefragabilis*, Alexander of Hales, reaches (its) end, in which there are originally had (nearly all which Saint Thomas gathered in the *Secunda secundae*): first printed by the Friars minor of the Convent of Paris at the expenses: of the honest and famous bibliophile, Jean Petit: by whom it is offered for sale in the Ville de Saint Jacques under the Silver Lion. In the year of the Lord 1509, June 8th ». — The inscription on folio 1: « Here begins the summa on virtues disputed and composed by Friar Alexander of Halles, of the Order of Minors, the *Doctor Irrefragabilis* which can be called the (pars) *tertia tertiae* of the same doctor ».[+]

The initial text shows, that this tract is not a distinct

---

¹ Brewer's edition: *exalted (him) unto heaven* [exaltaverunt] for *exulted unto heaven* [exultaverunt].

* *Trans. note*: Which in English can be rendered thus: « The Most Excellent "Opus on the Virtues" by the Doctor Irrefragabilis, Alexander of Hales, of the Order of Minors: heretofore never put to press: and it is the third, continuative part of his Summa: insofar as by the same Doctor

in the same third part (it has been) very often published for a long time: it has in questions 26 and 69 been compromised ». — The Latin of which was left intact, for the utility of those searching for this work in libraries; but what follows, is translated, since it is of minor import.

⁺ Here, the final quotation mark was omitted in the original; I have placed it at the end, since the context appears to require that.

work, but, rather, a part of another great work. For, it begins thus: « Therefore, with (a treatment) had concerning the grace making (one) pleasing and the grace (freely) given. Consequently, one must speak of virtue.

« First in general.

« Second, in particular.

« Third, concerning certain consequent properties.

« Concerning virtue in general there are asked several (things).

« For, first, there is asked concerning its entity » etc..

The opuscule was printed with the worst typeface and many compendiary notes and abounds in typographical errors. The treatise itself is incomplete. It is divided into three parts, the last of which is utterly wanting, just as (is) also several (things) from the second part, which concerns the virtues in particular. For it treats only of three theological virtues and the two cardinal, that is, of prudence and temperance; there are lacking the questions on fortitude and justice. It is divided into 106 « collationes », each one of which has several Articles, and these are accustomed to have several Questions, thus, that about 480 Questions are set forth ».

Of this work, besides *Possevinus* and very many moderns, the ancient author of the *Firmamentum trium Ordinum* makes mention (fol. 42) in these words: « The same wrote a *Summa virtutum* as a continuative of the *pars tertia*, which can be called the *tertia tertiae* of Alexander. And this work, now last of all, that is, in the year of the Lord, 1509, (was) first brought to light and produced in print » etc.. Likewise, the authors of the Venetian edition of the *Opera S. Bonaventurae* often cite the work in the index of authors, Sent., Bk. III, d. 23 and ff. — Fr. *Matthias Hauzeur*, of whom we shall speak below under § 7, in (his) work, *Collatio totius theologiae*, tome II, from col. 77 up to col. 128 redacts this whole opuscule under the title, « *Supplementum Alensis* », in a compendium, from the edition of Jean Petit. The other edition of this work came forth at Toledo, by *Ioannes Ulhaquira*, as *Ioannes a S. Antonio* asserts in his *Biblioteca*.

Nevertheless, concerning this opuscule, whether it be a *forgery* or not, there has arise a great controversy, which we shall as willingly touch upon here, as occasion is given us, for repairing the grave error of Wadding, into which the man — otherwise ingenious and a lover of truth, according to the report of others — incautiously fell, as one seemingly deceived, and how, drawn away from the right path, said not a few (things), which derogate from the honor of the highest Doctor, St. Thomas Aquinas. Others, as *Ioannes de Haye* and *Petrus de Alva*, followed Wadding in this. Let us briefly relate the origin and progress of this unpleasant controversy, which, from what we are to say, can, in our opinion, be perfectly laid to rest.

Wadding (*Annales.*, tome I, on the year 1245, nn. 20-21) first brings forward certain words of Gerson, saying among other (things) these: « The writings of the same St. Thomas, most of all of the *Secunda Secundae*, testify, how intimate and familiar he made for himself the one whom he cites as *doctor Alexander* ». Then, Wadding subjoins: « Gerson understands that the *Summa virtutum* written by Hales was most likely the familiar of St. Thomas, such that the *Secunda secundae* fully[1] excerpts word-for-word an insert of the former ». The most famous Annalist would have been in no manner able to write this, if he himself had that Summa in hand. For a like insertion is shown to be false, *first*, indeed, because this opuscule is double and more ample, than that part of the Summa of the Angelic (Doctor), which treats the same questions, whence it cannot be excerpted from it word-for-word; *second*, because each work, just as it appears to us

after a certain comparison, agree with the other not more, but rather less, than the *Summa* of the Angelic (Doctor) agrees with the *Summa theologica* of Alexander.

It is not to be wondered at, that several sons of St. Dominic opposed themselves to Wadding, among whom there stands forth Echardus (*Scriptores Ord. Praed.*, tom I, p. 318 ff., Paris, 1721) and De Rubeis (*Dissert. criticae*, dissert. 16, chs. 3 & 4). Yet, in this, these most erudite men were drawn beyond the limits of truth, to affirm themselves, after *Natalis Alexander*, that this *Summa virtutum* was an entirely forged work. For Echardus says (loc. cit, p. 319, ch. 1): « Wherefore, as many experts in literary matters already agree, the work is purely a forgery ». Moreover, he asserts, that *Natalis Alexander* had proven indisputably, that Hales not only did not write that *Summa virtutum* as a supplement to (his own) *Summa theologica*, but that he neither *could have* written (it), « by this *inescapable argument*, that Hales did not complete the *Summa theologica*. Would that Hales have thought to add a supplement to his own Summa, who had not yet finished that Summa »? But this *inescapable argument* loses its force, if one supposes, either that this Summa of the Virtues was written *before* the other, and/or even, as this Summa is not a *distinct work*, but was written to this end, that it be inserted into the Summa itself as a part of the same. Moreover, this second supposition is congruent to the matter, just as it is.

The arguments of Echardus are repeated in other words by De Rubeis, who (loc. cit. ch. 4.) adds: « Which (work), finally, if it be found as a manuscript or published somewhere on presses, *we ask that it be brought to light*, so that it may be compared very carefully with the *Secunda Secundae* of the *Summa theologica* of St. Thomas. *It does not compare nor could it ever be exhibited*, unless, perhaps, one proceeded to this audacity, to describe the very *Secunda Secundae* of St. Thomas, word-for-word, and take care to bring it forth under the name of the doctor of Hales, entitling it the *Summa virtutum* ».

Moreover, as much as we are able, to sift the true from the false and attribute to each, what is his own, three questions have to be distinguished among themselves, namely, first, whether this work, named, "*de Virtutibus*", by Wadding was, in truth, written, and still is extant; second, whether Alexander of Hales be the author of the same; third, whether St. Thomas in his own *Secunda Secundae* used this book in the manner Wadding asserts.

About the *first* nothing remains in doubt, since several exemplars of the Parisian edition, which we have described above, are still extant. Three of these, we have seen with our own eyes: the two, indeed, of *Münich* in the Royal Library and the third in our convent in the Belgian city of St. Truiden, which we have examined more accurately. We do not doubt, that other examples of the same work may be found elsewhere. It seems sanely to be wondered at, that Echardus, first of all, a very erudite and sharp man, and after him De Rubeis, had wanted to demonstrate by light arguments that this work, concerning which there were so many books testifying, (was) plainly a forgery.

Moreover, even if they had erred in this *fact*, yet, in regard to the *third* question, whether St. Thomas transcribed this work, it must be conceded to these authors, in service of truth and justice, that the assertion of Wadding is an erroneous one. Nor do we doubt, that Wadding himself, if he examined this Summa of Virtues, would have sincerely retracted what he had written against the honor of St. Thomas and against the truth. For, if this work be examined only a little, there is found

---

[1] This *fully* [plene] seems to be an error for *nearly* [pene], as one reads at the end of the mentioned Summa.

both in the arrangement of matters to be treated, and in the single Questions, to differ much from the Summa of St. Thomas; nor does one detect a greater likeness among each work, than that which is accustomed to be found among Scholastic authors writing on the same question. Moreover, though the way, which the defenders of St. Thomas held, of denouncing, namely, that this work (be) a forgery, now must be abandoned, a disquisition on the same ought to be conducted, to set forth testimony on behalf of the honor of the Angelic (Doctor). To this end, we have subjoined a general *tabula* of the matters treated of in the first part of the opuscule, so that the very many, who cannot inspect this most rare work, can judge, how much the Summa of the Angelic (Doctor) differs from it.

On the virtues in general

I. On the entity of virtue in the state of nature: lapsed, whole, (and) glorified, containing Collation 1, with 3 Articles.

II. On the necessity of virtue, Col. 2, with 3 Aa..

III. On the excellence of virtue, Col. 3.

IV. On the causality of virtue, Col. 3.
  1. On the efficient cause:
    a. the first cause (God), Col. 4, in 3. Aa..
    b. the second (created) cause, Col. 5, in 3. Aa..
  2. On the formal cause, Col. 6, in 3. Aa..
  3. On the material cause *circa quam*:
    a. about delectations and sadnesses, Col. 7, in 5 Aa., and the last article has 4 Questions.
    b. about actions and passions, Col. 8, in 2. Aa..
    c. on good and evil, Col. 9, in 2. Aa..
  4. On the final cause:
    a. on the uncreated, final cause, Col. 10, in 4. Aa..
    b. on the created, final cause.
      α. on the final cause in the Fatherland, Col. 11, in 2. Aa., each of which has 2 Questions.
      β. on the final cause on the way, Col. 12, in 6 Aa..
  5. On delectation:
    a. what it be according to thing,
    b. what is be according to definition,
    c. in what subject it be, Col. 13, in 3 Aa., each of which has 3 Qq..

V. On the multiple effect or utility, Col. 14.

VI. On the quiddity of virtue:
  1. According to thing, Col. 15, in 10 Aa..
  2. According to definition, Col. 16, in 6 Aa.. He speaks of 16 definitions and treats of 29 Qq..

VII. On the subject of virtue:
  1. As much as regards (its) substance, Col. 17, in 8 Aa., together with 12 Qq..
  2. As much as regards (its) power, Col. 17, in 6. Aa., together with 9 Qq..

VIII. On the act of virtue in general:
  1. On the common act of virtue on the way, Col. 19, in 4 Aa..
  2. On the common act of virtue in the Fatherland, Col. 20, in 3 Aa..
  3. On the common act of virtue on the way and in the Fatherland, Col. 21, in 3 Aa..

IX. On the object of common virtue, Col. 22, in 3 Aa..

X. On the cognition of virtue, Col. 23, in 4 Aa..

XI. On the division of virtue, Col. 24, in 4 Aa., together with 8 Qq..

Therefore, it, yet, remains to examine the *second* question, whether, that is, the author of the mentioned work is Alexander of Hales, according to the manner Wadding thought. In favor of this sentence, besides the authority of the ancient edition, there can be mentioned first of all, that

these treatises on the virtues were manifestly written as a part of some great theological Summa — because in the editions of the *Summa* of Alexander, p. III, before Q. 68 (according to the Venetian and Cologne editions, or Q. 78 according to the Koberger edition) a huge lacuna appears, to fulfill which these treatises would fit perfectly, if they, themselves, were complete — finally, because the prologue itself to Q. 78 manifestly supposes, that that lacuna has already been filled, since it reads: « *After the treatise on virtue in general* one must inquire concerning the species of the virtue according to the *preassigned difference*; and first one deals with the theological virtues, which are virtues unto the end ... But, consequently, with the virtues, which are for the end, such as prudence, justice ».

Yet, these not withstanding, we think that it is certain, that Alexander, himself, least of all wrote these treatises. Otherwise, that which Wadding says falsely of the Angelic Doctor, would have to be affirmed of the Seraphic, namely, that he had copied the greater part of these treatises nearly verbatim into his own Commentary. For, if you except not a few Questions, all those, which St. Bonaventure has both concerning the three theological virtues (Sent., Bk. III, d. 23-30, and Sent., Bk. I, d. 17), and concerning the cardinal virtues in general (Sent., Bk. III, d. 33), i. e. 70 Questions, are also read in these treatises with only a few arguments either added and/or omitted and/or shortened. Since the matter holds itself thus, it must necessarily be concluded, that either St. Bonaventure transcribed all these, if Alexander is in truth the author of these treatises, and/or that someone else, not Alexander, took them from St. Bonaventure. However, this first conjecture is demonstrated by the gravest arguments as entirely improbable, while for the second there militates no contemnible presumption. Which is to be briefly explained.

1. If one posits, that these treatises were written by Alexander, no reason can be given, why such an outstanding part has been excluded from (his) *Summa theologica*, such that there arises in it a huge and manifest lacuna. And it must be noted, that not only do all the editions of the Summa have this lacuna, but even the ancient manuscript codices, two of which we have examined concerning this matter. For, at *Florence* in the *Biblioteca (Medicea) Laurenziana*, plut. XXIV. dext., cod. V. membr. in fol., saec. XIII, there is found this Summa, which has this inscription by a second hand: *Alexander, tertius in Sententiis*. This codex, besides the same lacuna, exhibits also the same words in the prologue of the following Question, which we have already mentioned. Moreover, in the *tabula quaestionum* on this passage (in cod. after Q. 39) ample space has been left empty, so that other titles of Questions may be inserted; by which there is shown, that this lacuna did not escape the attention of copyists. The numbers of the following Questions are by a later hand. Another codex is *at Florence* in the *Biblioteca Nazionale*, cod. membr. in fol., at the beginning of saec. XIV, sign. 25. F. 5., entitled: *Tertius Alexandri de Hales*. The incipit: *Tota christianae fidei disciplina*. In this codex, too, this lacuna is found and there is insinuated a space left empty among the mentioned two Questions. All these indicate, that this lacuna existed from the time of Alexander.

2. Another greater reason argues (for this). It cannot be explained, why the Seraphic (Doctor), who treats of as many other Questions, occurring likewise in the Summa of Alexander, *never* transcribes the whole Question in such a manner, with its arguments on each side, with (its) Response and solution of the arguments, but always sets forth the whole Question as the true author. Nor does it withstand, that St. Bonaventure, as we have already observed, follows very closely the doctrine of his master and borrowed not a few things out of that great forest of material,

such as is the Summa of Alexander. But this, other Scholastics, after Alexander, also did, as Dionysius the Carthusian notes, yet in such a manner, that they are true authors of their own work without any stain of plagiary. A few propositions, which Bonaventure, in Bks. II & III, took verbatim from Alexander, are also of the same kind. For, just as in all our books of theology there are found the words of other authors, cited and transcribed, so, too, was it done by the Seraphic (Doctor), with this difference alone, that he, according to the custom of his own age, was not accustomed to name the name of the contemporary author. But how great a diversity exists among such a use of another's book and that, from which whole Questions are transcribed, is clearer in every light.

3. The Questions themselves, which are common to the Commentary (of St. Bonaventure) and to these treatises, breathe the method and spirit of the Seraphic Doctor so much, that they fit perfectly the whole Commentary. But no one will deny, that St. Bonaventure, just as, even, St. Thomas, had some singular properties in writing, by which their works can more certainly be distinguished, here and there, from the offspring of other authors.

These seem already sufficient, to regard (it) as certain, that these were not transcribed by St. Bonaventure out of Alexander, but rather by another, whoever he was, from the Commentary of St. Bonaventure.

Moreover, this *is confirmed* by this, that, if we suppose, that these treatises were written after our Commentary, everything can be nearly tied up; whence there arises, already, a great presumption in favor of this sentence.

For, first, it is not verisimilar, that Friar William of Meliton, who, according to Wadding, lived until the year 1260, after having accepted the mandate from the Supreme Pontiff, did entirely nothing for four years to complete the Summa (of Alexander), especially, in regard to filling that greatest hiatus in the third book. Moreover, since neither was he able to bring that treatise on the virtues to an end, it is easily understood, that this defective supplement by another author was never inserted into the Summa. For, the matter is regarded in one way in regard to the unfinished work of the first author, in another in regard to the incomplete supplement of another.

Then, according to this supposition, nothing is to be wondered at, that William of Meliton, to whom the Supreme Pontiff wanted that there be colleagues in his labor, opportunely used the very clear writings of the most celebrated disciple of the same Alexander, with the consent and approbation of St. Bonaventure himself, who at that time held the office of Minister General.

Therefore, we think, that Sbaralea approached the truth, when he said, that even if William composed several (things) to complete the work of Alexander, these were never inserted into the Summa itself. But we restrict this to the greater or principal parts, nor do we wish to contend, that William never moved a hand on the passages left in an unfinished condition by Alexander. But, to be able to pronounce something more certain on this matter, very many (things) would have to be completely searched out, first of all, moreover, the codices to be consulted for this work.

But, as much as we can judge, these treatises on the virtues taste entirely of the ancient Franciscan school before Scotus and even before *Richardus a Mediavilla*,* in particular of the method and spirit of Alexander in regard to the general arrangement they bear, such that they can at least convene well with William, a disciple of Hales, or if you please, with any of his colleagues.

We have expounded this a little more accurately to take precaution beforehand, lest, from this opuscule on the virtues, anyone take occasion, to accuse St. Bonaventure of theft in matters pertaining to letters. But, that the Seraphic (Doctor) held the doctrine of his most eminent master in such great honor, that he cleaved very often to his sentence and converted many (things) therefrom, unto his own use according to the manner expounded by us, can in no manner derogate from his honor. For it befitted both the piety of a good disciple, and the spirit of the Catholic Church. For the glory of the Catholic theologian is to be placed least of all in this, that he either exclude the new from his own genius, and/or having neglected the labors of other authors, as one alone and by himself, scrape together his own from ancient sources, and/or, even, strive by himself without father or mother, without master and school, as a doctor, new and separated from the wisdom of preceding ages and from the help of contemporaries. Far be it. For, *the scribe learned in the Kingdom of Heaven brings forth from his own treasury* (which is the treasury of the Church and of Catholic science) *new and old* (Mt. 13:52), *testing everything, holding fast to what is good* (1 Thess. 5:21). In this manner did those great Scholastic doctors proceed, nor did they spurn to learn more in the school of each other, upon which (school) the Father of lights poured forth the rays of truth. Hence, in the philosophical disciplines they proclaimed *Aristotle*, though a pagan, their own master and converted very many (things) from him to their own use; how much those masters, first of all Bl. Albertus and St. Thomas, did this, has been explored among all. What is to be wondered at, if St. Bonaventure used the writings of his own master in the same manner, the theologian most famous among all in his own age?

§ 4. *The outstanding nature of this Commentary is celebrated by the common suffrage of theologians of ancient and modern times.* But, not to preoccupy ourselves with the matter of the dissertation promised by us on the life and writings of our Doctor, we direct the reader to *Wadding* (*de Scriptoribus Ordinis Minorum*, p. 19, col. 2) and to *Sbaralea* (*Supplementum*, p. 142 ff.) and chiefly to the *Prodromus*, Bk. II, where from chs. 1-12 there are gathered so very many testimonies of writers concerning the doctrine of St. Bonaventure in general and of the use of the same in General Councils. Let it suffice to have noted here that *Angelus Rocca de Camerino*, O. S. A., writes in the preface of *Aegidius Romanus' In II. Sent.*, that by common estimation it is proven, that *Scotus* excelled in (his) Commentary on the First (Book) of the Sentences, *Aegidius (Romanus)*[+] on the Second, *Bonaventura* on the Third, *Richard of Middleton* on the Fourth. Which, however, we do not wish to be understood to the prejudice of the Angelic Doctor. But, Gerson[1] exalted with special praise our Doctor on the Second Book of the Sentences.

It will be established for the reader, that this Commentary (of Bonaventure) also knows nothing but the highest moderation, sincere piety and a certain, singular devotion. Our author believed that it is the duty of a Catholic doctor to teach the truth in the charity and humility, and not to contemn the sentences of other sons of (their) one Mother, the Church, and to contentiously impugn and sow and/or foster strifes to the detriment of charity. « For it is, indeed, foul », as Gregory of Nazianzen (Oratio 26, n. 27) says, « in divine disputations, to usurp the principality and rule for oneself and never to submit (one's own) fasces to another ». Lead by a spirit of charity and humility, how greatly alien from the study of novelties, curious questions, (and) singular opinions was the Seraphic Doctor; yet, against the errors of heretics he strenuously defended both the Faith and the knowledge handed

---

[1] In an Epistle written to a certain friar Minor (Paris edition, 1521, tome I, fol. 107, col. I), and also in P. IV of *Concordia Metaphysicae cum logica*, fol. 56, ch. 4, according to the testimony of the *Prodromus*, col. 227.

* *Trans. note*: Hereafter, *Richard of Middleton*, who is claimed by the town of that name, which is a few kilometers to the east of Oxford, England.

[+] Hereafter, *Giles the Roman*.

down, ingeniously and subtly explaining (these), and forti-
fying (them) with valid reasons. On (this) matter, he himself
says at the end of Sent., Bk. III: « It is sufficient to know
among doubts, what the wise judged, nor is it useful to zealously serve contentions. We say many (things) and we fail in
words ». In this respect, he is praised by a Chancellor of the
University of Paris, Gerson:[1] « He withdraws from curiosity
as much as he can, not mixing (himself) up in extraneous
positions and/or the worldly doctrines of dialectics or
physics, sketchy theological terms, as many do, but when he
strives for the enlightenment of the intellect, he refers all to
the piety and religiosity of the affection ». Nor shall it be unuseful for our own times to meditate on the words which the
same subjoins: « Whence it happed, that from undevout
Scholastics, of whom, alas !, the number is greater, he has
stood forth as less frequented, since no teaching is more sublime, none more divine, none more salubrious and sweet for
theologians. Finally, by as much as I have been more diligently turned again in my old age to study him, by so much
has my own garrulousness been the more confounded ». —
The same Gerson, also, well observes (P. IV, de Concordia
metaphysicae et logicae): « Bonaventure stove to ever elicit
from various opinions that which appeared true, and with
great sobriety to lay aside that which seemed too much or
too little ». In him, there certainly glittered an admirable
wisdom and art, by which he was accustomed to conciliate
the dissenting opinions of the masters, not only disparate
ones, but even contrary in the appearance of words, without
detriment to the truth, and/or at least to draw (those) said in-
adequately to a sane sense, he himself stepping along the
middle way between opposed sentences. It will help to insert
here something from a certain unpublished Question,[2]
which would be profitable in the greatest manner to serve the
peace among the members of the Church, chiefly among the
followers of the diverse schools, and to promote the true
progress of the science of theology, if they would be united
in spirit and mind more frequently, as he was accustomed (to
do). « Therefore, from these there is gathered, » as he says,
« that many opinions seem to be contrary, which, however,
coincide in one truth. And on that account I have sustained
all of the aforesaid opinions in the preceding, and I believe
that they are to be sustained in some manner. For it is not decent that juniors despise, but rather to humbly venerate and
faithfully explicate, the sentences of the ancients; because
one must not believe, that great lovers of and inquirers into
truth uttered their celebrated positions without cause; but
in all (their) sayings the cause for (their) being said is to be
considered. For, what seems superficially false, is frequently
found (to be) true, when one grasps the intention of the ones
saying (them) ».

Nor is another outstanding custom, constantly retained
by the Saint, to be passed over in silence, in choosing opinions and/or manners of speaking, concerning which Catholic
masters in the schools are in disagreement. In him one discerns, that when the judgement of human reason seems to
stand for one side, but the piety of faith more for the other,
he inclines more readily to that sentence, which supports
more the honor of God and/or of Christ and/or of the Saints
and the exercise of Christian virtue. Thus, e. g., treating of
that sentence, that the reason for the Incarnation is chiefly
the reparation of the human race (Sent., Bk. III, d. 1, a. 2, q.

4), he concludes thus: « Therefore, since this manner of
speaking, even if it does not seem to be as subtle, as the preceding one, is more consonant with the piety of the Faith, in
this that it concords more with the authorities of the Saints,
and honors God more, (and) even commend the Mystery of
the Incarnation more, and inflames our affection more ardently: for that reason, » etc..

Therefore, just as in choosing doubtful opinions a
humble modestly inclined the mind of the Seraphic Doctor
unto the more trodden and common way, and wise moderation unto the via media, so charity for God and neighbor unto
the way more consonant with piety.

§ 5. In these Commentaries, there are found not a few obsolete sentences, but not properly singular ones. For those few
opinions, which are now attributed to St. Bonaventure by certain (authors) as singular ones and are noted as singular ones,
either were the more common ones, at that time, in the schools
at Paris, but afterwards have become obsolete with the progress
of time and of theological science, and/or do not exhibit his genuine sentence. Yet, there are some opinions, which he seems to
have retracted after the example of Sts. Augustine and Thomas.
To say nothing of the dogma of the Immaculate Conception of
the B. V. Mary, concerning which his sentence, after all the even
unpublished genuine opuscula of his have been examined, one
must inquire more particularly,[3] he himself in (his) Commentary[4] follows the opinion of St. John Chrysostom, asserting that
St. John the Baptist did not know Christ but in general, but not
in particular, before Christ approached to be baptized by him.
Yet, this solution in the genuine Commentarius in Ioannem,[5] ch.
I, v. 31, he reproves with eloquent words. — Likewise, in Sent.,
Bk. IV, d. 23, a. 1, q. 2; d. 7, a. 1, q. 2; d. 17, p. II, a. 1, q. 3, he adheres
to the false opinion of Master (Peter) as the more probable one,
namely, that the two Sacraments of Confirmation and of Ex-
tremunction « were », indeed, « insinuated » by Christ, « but afterwards (were) instituted by the Holy Spirit ». However, in the
Breviloquium[6] he resolves, better and more conformly to the doctrine of the Council of Trent,[7] thus: « It must be held, that Christ
instituted the seven Sacraments of the Law of grace ... Moreover,
He instituted the aforesaid Sacraments in diverse manners: certain ones, namely, by confirming, approving and consummating them, such as Matrimony and Penance; but certain ones by
insinuating and initiating (them), such as Confirmation and Ex-
tremunction; however, certain ones by initiating and consummating and suscepting (them) in His very Self, such as the
Sacrament of Baptism, of the Eucharist and of Orders » etc..

There are certain others, which now are unpleasant to
many; whether philosophical, such as what he teaches concerning matter and form, that (it is) to be attributed in a certain sense to all creatures,* or theological, v. gr., his doctrine
concerning original sin, and concerning the contrition required in the Sacrament of Penitence, and concerning the
licit and/or illicit use of matrimony. But these were commonly taught at Paris in that age, concerning which and certain others we shall same something, in their place, in our
Scholia.

That there did not thrive, nor could have thrived, in the
age of St. Bonaventure a critical art for discerning the genuine
and/or spurious works of ancient (authors), and/or for establishing historical facts, just as (there did) in the ages after
the invention of the art of typography, is conceded by

---

[1] In his De Examinat. doctrinar., according to the testimony of the
Prodromus, where in col. 98 the following passage is also cited.

[2] Which seems to have been written by St. Bonaventure, and which we
shall publish whole at Sent., Bk. I, d. 27, p. I, q. 2.

[3] Let it suffice, here, to say, that he deals with the Immaculate
Conception of the Virgin, in accord with the sentence of the schools, then
prevailing, in Sent., Bk. III, d. 3, p. I, a. 1, q. 1, where, among other
(things), he says: « The Church celebrates the solemnity of no conception
except (that) of the Son of God, on the (Feast of) the Annunciation of the
B. V. Mary. Yet, there are some, who out of special devotion celebrates

the Conception of the Bl. Virgin, whom I do not dare entirely to praise or
simply to reprehend ». But, afterwards, being better informed, in the
Chapter of Paris, celebrated on May 20th, 1263, he corrected this and
decreed with the Chapter, « that there was to be admitted in the Order
the new feast of the Conception of the Blessed Virgin Mary ».

[4] Sent., Bk. IV, d. 5, Doubt 3.

[5] In Bonelli's, Supplementum, tome I, col. 479.

[6] In P. VI, ch. 4.   [7] In Session VII, canon 1.

* Trans. note: Yet, not 'matter' in the sense of the particulate corporeal.
Cf. Sent., Bk. II, d. 3, p. I, a. 1, q. 2, in the Response.

all. Whence, it is not to be wondered at, that even St. Bonaventure received not a few apocryphal and/or spurious (works) together with other doctors of his own time, and/or, at least, adhered as one doubtful of them, and that he did not reject some pious and ancient, but false, traditions pertaining to history. Yet, very often he speaks of similar (things) only hypothetically. Thus, v. gr., in Sent., Bk. IV, d. 20, p. I, Doubt 3, he does not entirely reject that story, that the soul of Trajan was liberated from the lower regions by the prayers of St. Gregory. For he says: « If to anyone He has given grace after death, it must be understood, that he had not been damned by (His) sentence, just as is read concerning Trajan ». — In nearly the same manner, St. Thomas speaks of this history, but explaining (it) hypothetically.[1]

On (this) matter, Bonelli speaks well:[2] « It would be madness to require in that age of our Doctor that knowledge of things, which only after several centuries was only known after the daring labors of critics and after having brought innumerable monuments to light. Hence, the *Quicumque* Creed, he attributes to St. Athanasius, the *Opus imperfectum* on Matthew, to John Chrysostom, several books to Dionysius the Areopagite, the books, *de Vita contemplativa*, to St. Prosperus, the work, *de Ecclesiasticis dogmatibus*, and another *de Fide ad Petrum*, to St. Augustine ». Even the book, *de Causis,* he still attributed to Aristotle, and the opuscule, *de Hebdomadibus*, which is also entitled, *de Paradoxis*, to Boethius, which is also done by *Trithemius* himself, though it seems, rather, to be the same as Alan (of Lille)'s, *Maxima theologiae.*

Yet, least of all does St. Bonaventure show himself to be entirely ignorant of the critical art. Thus, the book *de Nativitate*, which St. Jerome was held to have translated, he did not receive, saying:[3] « Though it be apocryphal, yet, it contains many very true (sayings) ». He also doubted of the authenticity of the *Quaestionum novi et veteris Testamenti*, which Master Peter Lombard cited under the works of St. Augustine, and he asserts:[4] « There are many (sayings), which do not seem the words of Augustine ». The book, *de Anima et spiritu* he often cites under the name of St. Augustine, but in Sent., Bk. II, d. 24, p. I, a. 2, q. 1, ad 1, he says: « Whether it was Augustine, or another ». Finally, the book, *de Ecclesiasticis dogmatibus*, which in (his) Commentary he attributes to Augustine, in (his) *Apologia pauperum* (resp. III, ch. 1), however, he restores to its true author, *Gennadius Massiliensis.*

§ 6. *By many other authors, opuscula were written, to illustrate fully the Commentary of St. Bonaventure. Let us first deal with the unpublished ones.* — Very many codices, written from the very age of St. Bonaventure, are found in libraries, which contract into *compendia* in diverse manners the *Commentarius* of St. Bonaventure. So great is the multitude of similar works, that there is sufficiently proven therefrom, how precious this book of St. Bonaventure was regarded in that age. Not a few of these works are simple abridgements of the length Commentary, as can be more easily compared and studied. Some, besides the sentence expounded briefly by St. Bonaventure, exhibit their own and/or others' opinions. Some have only *tabluae* or indices. Those works, which were noted by Fr. Fidelis, we subjoin here, ordering these codices inasmuch as we are able. In the first place, we put the opera, the author of which is named in the codices, then the anonymous ones according to the alphabetical listing of the libraries, and in the last place some codices, which exhibit not a few *tabulae* and/or cited pas-

sages. However, we warn the reader, that the notes, which we have, are often not sufficient, to determine with certitude, whether diverse codices contained the same work, or a diverse one. For, often, in the codices these works have the same *incipits*, but end in a different manner, and/or *vice versa*; or the First Book of Sentences agrees with another first book, but the Second and/or the rest agree least of all. But, even if the codices begin with other words, yet, this does not certainly demonstrate, that these contain diverse works, since either the incipit can be omitted in one codex, and/or in another something (be) added. Which happens so often in codices of opuscula of minor import, as all experts know. Wherefore, we do not doubt, that by a more accurate examination of the codices, more would yet be known as pertaining to one and/or the same work, especially concerning the anonymous opuscula which follow.

1. *Alexander ab Alexandria*, or *Lombardus*, at first lector of the sacred Palace, then from the year 1313, the Minister General of the Order of Minors, the author of very many books, which can be seen in Wadding and Sbaralea; (which Alexander) died at Rome, in 1314.

He wrote a *Summa quaestionum S. Bonaventurae in quatuor libros Sententiarum*, an exemplar of which is found *at Milan*, in the Biblioteca Ambrosiana, cod. B. 5. sup. membr. in 12 vo., saec. XIV. The *incipit* of the first book: *Alta profunditas, quis invenit eam? Eccle. 7, 25. Hic innuitur quadruplex causa libri Senentiarum.* The *desinit*, on fol. 47. recto: *Possum velle voluntate pietatis. Per hoc patet solutio ad obiecta.* On fol. 48 recto, the *incipit* of the second book: *Fecit Deus hominem rectum, et ipse se immiscuit infinitis quaestionibus. Eccle. 7. In verbo proposito clauditur tota intentio secundi Sententiarum.* The *desinit* on fol. 122 verso: *dum non sunt contraria animae et regulae suae. Per haec solvuntur omnia, quia vera procedunt. Amen. Explicit.* — The third book begins on fol. 124 r.: *Cum venerit plenitudo temporis etc. Hic duo principaliter quaeruntur: Primum est de Incarnatione possibilitate.* The *desinit* on fol. 174 r.: *Sicut pennae in avibus, et rotae in curribus, et vela in navibus, quia sine illis multo graviores sunt.* — Fol. 175 r. begins the fourth book: *Altissimus creavit de terra medicinam. Eccli. 38. Altissimus Deus Pater ... De terra, id est utero Virginis ... q. 1. Hic quaeruntur sex, scilicet, si Sacramenta debuerint institui etc..* It finishes on fol. 238 v.: *Per propriam virtuem, ut supra dictum est in principio huius paginae ... prohibentur.* — Then, there follows a table of the individual books, which finishes on fol. 248. Thereafter, by a hand of the 15th century, having erased the previous letters, there is added: *Summa quaestionum sancti Bone venture super* (here, the ancient hand continues) *quatuor libros Sententiarum in hoc volumine breviter reducta per venerabilem fratrem Alexandrum de Alexandria Ordinis Minorum.*

The same work is found also *at Assisi*, in the library of the Sacro Convento (now the Municipal), cod. membr. in fol. saec. XIV., sign. B. IX. 1.. It contains, however, only *questions abbreviated* from Sent., Bks. I, II, & III. — Likewise, *at Naples*, in the Biblioteca Nazionale, Cod. membr. in fol., saec. XIV, sign. VII. C. 40.: *Quaestiones abbreviatae* from Sent., Bks. I & II. — Likewise, *at Florence*, in the Biblioteca Nazionale, cod. membr. in fol., saec. XIV, sign. V. D. 26. A *compendium* from Sent., Bks. II & IV. — Likewise, *at Paris*, at the Bibliothèque de l'Arsenal, cod. membr. in 8., saec. XV, entitled: *Breviloquium super IV. Sent.* — Likewise, *at Rome*, in the Biblioteca della Società di Gesù, cod. membr. in fol., saec. XIV,

---

[1] Cf. *Prodromus*, col. 522.
[2] *Prodromus*, Bk. II, ch. 12, col. 113.

[3] Sent., Bk. IV, d. 28, a. 1. q. 6. — Cf. *Prodromus*, col. 533 & 113.
[4] Sent., Bk. III, d. 3, p. I, a. 2, q. 3, ad 2.

containing: *Quaestiones abbreviatae* on Sent., Bk. I, I, & III.; lacking a number; but the preceding Parisian codex is signed, n. 3413.

2. Friar *Henricus*, of the Order of Minors, Lector at Zürich, Switzerland. Who this *Henricus* is, we have not dared to determine. He is certainly an author of the 13th century, as is established by the codex placed by us in the last place, which is from the end of the 13th and/or the beginning of the 14th century. But we conjecture, that the author could be that most celebrated preacher *Henricus Gökelmann de Jsny*, who was the confessor and counsellor to the Emperor Rudolph I of Hapsburg, Bishop of Basel from 1255-1286, then Archbishop of Mainz († 1288). That he was a Lector at Mainz and Guardian at Luzern, seems established. But, since there was a Convent of Minors at Zürich from at least 1247, nothing withstands, that he did not serve in the office of lector for some years also in the same place. According to the judgment of Fr. Fidelis, his work is sufficiently well done.

At Bergamo, in the Civic Library, cod. Δ VIII. 3, membr. fol., near the middle of saec. XIV, written in Germany, as it seems. On fol. 1 recto, col. 1, there is a *tabula*: *Incipiunt questiones et problemata primi libri. Quid sit subiectum in hoc libro.* On fol. 2. verso, col. 2: *Expliciunt questiones et problemata primi libri. Questiones in universo sunt 230.* Then fol. 3. r. col. 1: *Incipit excerptum questionum Bone venture. Veritates questionum ex opere Bonaventure super librum Sententiarum pro modico intelligentiae mec ad instatniam fratrum extrahere cupiens, brevitati studui in hunc modum.* The *desinit*: *voluntate conditionali non vult. Benedictus Deus. Explicit. Suscipe placatus, bone rex de virgine natus, Henrici munus, qui regnas trinus et unus.* There, then, follows a *tabula* for the Second Book and after that: *Secundus liber ... de rerum omnium creatione.* The *desinit*: *in multis locis utilis est.* — There follows a *tabula* for the Third Book, the *incipit* of which is: *Determinatum est* etc. The *desinit*: *Hec videtur sentire Augustinus et Hugo de S. Victore.* After the *tabula*, the *incipit* on the Fourth Book is: *Finitis per Dei gratiam tribus libris, in quorum primo* etc. *Desinit ut in S. Bonaventura.* At the end there is read: « These, have I, friar H. of the order of friars Minor, existing as a lector of the same Order in Zürich, completely written by abbreviating from the work of Bonaventure, desiring with desire to satisfy the man poor in scriptures, so that they who cannot have a copy of the whole volume, at least may have this abbreviation *pro memoriali*. Wherefore, I beg the same pious reader, that, if it seem to him that I have erred in any passage, to have recourse to the whole work, and perhaps he shall find there that I have not erred. But, if this does not suffice for him, it pleases me and I ask, that if he find what has been badly understood by me or certainly arranged incautiously, in the Name of the Lord he correct and emend (it), as one receiving the wage with me from Him, who lives and reigns unto the ages of ages. Amen. »*

The same work is found *at Berlin*, in the Royal Library, cod. membr. fol. magn. saec. XV, sign. M. L. Fo. 355: *Veritates questionum ex opere Bonav. sup. librum Sent.* — Likewise, *at Fribourg*, in Switzerland, in the library of the Minors Conventual, cod. chart., of the year 1478, sign. 72: *Veritates questionum super librum Sententiarum.* It embraces the four books of this work. — Likewise, *at Nürnberg*, in the Civic library, membr. in 8, of the end of the 13th century and of the beginning of the 14th, sign. Centur. IV. mss. VI. n. 48: *Veritates questionum ex opere Bonav. super libr. Sent.* It contains four books.

3. *Ioannes de Alzeya*, a priest of Ratisbon (now Regensburg, Germany). Whether he be the author, or only the writer of the following excerpts, we do not know. This writing is extant at *Colmar*, in Alsace (France), in the Civic library, cod. chart., saec. XV. It contains Sent., Bk. II. The *incipit*: *Solummodo hoc*

inveni ... Sollicite consideranti. The *desinit*: *Finiunt excerpta ex scriptis Bonaventure supra secundo Sent. per me Iohannem de Altzeya, presbyterum in Regensburg; Basileens. Dioces. 1471.*

4. *Ioannes de Erfordia*, of the Order of Minors, lector and doctor *utriusque* of the Province of Saxony, wrote the work: *Tabula originalium*, already mentioned in the *Summa Astesana*, which was completed in 1317; likewise, a *Glossarium, seu Vocabularium latinarum vocum, quae in Bibliis habentur*, and several others, as can be seen in *Trithemius* and Sbaralea, but especially the compendium of St. Bonaventure's Commentary.

This work is conserved at *Lüneburg* in Prussia (modern Germany), in the Civic library; among the codd. theolog. latinae n. 20, membr. in fol., of the end of the 13th century and/or of the beginning of the 14th. On the front cover there is written: *Ioannes Erphordiensis supr primum, secundum et tertium Sententiarum, minorum doctor probatus.* The *incipit* of the First Book: *Primo queritur, utrum theologia sit scientia.* Of the Second: *Utrum sint plura principia, sicut Manichei dicunt.* To the Third there is prefaced the prologue of St. Bonaventure, *Deus autem, qui dives est* etc. Then: *Queritur, utrum divina natura potuerit uniri cum humana natura.* At the end: *Expliciunt scripta super tertium Sententiarum.* — Likewise, *at Leipzig*, in Saxony, in the (University Library:) Paulina (collection), cod. membr. in fol. min., saec. XIV, sign. 556: *Quaestiones abbreviate super I. II. et III. Sent.* — Likewise, *at Copenhagen*, in Denmark, in the Royal Library, cod. chart. in fol., saec. XV, sign. 69: *Questiones devoti doctoris Bonaventure super II. Sent.* — Likewise, *at Padua*, in the Biblioteca Antoniana, cod. membr. in fol., saec. XIV. sign. 128: *Questiones abbreviate in III. Sent.* — Likewise, *at Paris*, in the Bibliothèque National, cod. membr. in fol., from the end of the 13th century, sign. 14308: *Questiones abbreviate super III. et IV. Sent.* The *incipit* to the Third (Book): *Cum venit plenitudo* etc. The *incipit* to the Fourth: *Deus, docuisti me a iuventute mea.* The *desinit*: *et sic continue rodit* etc.

5. Friar *Ioannes de Fonte*, of the Order of Minors, a Frenchman. Sbaralea (*Supplementum*.), together with *Possevinus*, says, that he flourished c. 1483; but it appears from the age of the codices, that he is to be assigned to the 14th century.

At Sietenstetten, in Austria, in the library of the Benedictine Fathers, cod. chart. in fol., of the beginning of the 15th century, sign. CXCI: *Conclusiones super quatuor libros Sent.* — The *incipit*: *Ad preces studentium, dum essem lector in Montepessulano ... ego frater Ioannes de Fonte Ordinis minorum ...* The *desinit*: *a principio facte, patent ex dictis. Deo gratias.*

Likewise, *at Colmar*, in Alsace (France), in the Civic library, cod. chart. in fol. min., from the end of the 14th century and the beginning of the 15th, sign. 451: *Conclusiones super quatuor* etc.. — Likewise, *at Kremsmünster*, in Austria, in the library of the Benedictine Fathers, cod. membr. in 4, saec. XV, sign. 117: *Conclusiones* etc.. — Likewise, *at the Monastery of Einsiedeln*, in Switzerland, in the Convent library, cod. chart. in fol., saec. XV, sign. 216: *Conclusiones* etc.. — Likewise, *at Würzburg* in Bavaria, in the University library, cod. sign. 182: *Conclusiones* etc.. — Likewise, *at Lübeck* in Germany, in the Civic library, cod. chart. in fol., saec. XIV: *Conclusiones* etc.. — Likewise, *at Bratislava* in Prussia (now Wrocław, Poland), in the University library, cod. chart. in fol., saec. XIV, sign. 1. Clas. 197: *Conclusiones* etc.. — According to Sbaralea, the same works existed under the title, *Conclusiones*, in the library of the Society of Jesus, *at Louvain* (in Belgium).

6. Friar *Kiliani*, of the Order of Minors. — *At Bratislava* (*Wrocław*), in the University library, cod. 1. Clas. 186. chart. in fol. saec. XV, contains a lecture on the III. & IV (Books) of the Sentences. On fol. 1 r.: *Liber tertius, distinctio I. Cum venerit plenitudo temporis. Hic incipit tertius liber sententiarum, in quo Magister tractat de Christo.* The *desinit*

---

* *Trans. note*: An important explanation for the existence of *abbreviationes*. For the original Latin of this *desinit*, see the Quaracchi edition.

on fol. 77 r., col. 2: *qui custodit legem, beatus est hic in spe et in patria in re. Amen. Explicit lectura venerabilis baccalarei formati in sacra pagina, fratris videlicet Kyliani Ordinis Minorum super tertium sententiarum anno Domini ... .* On fol. 78: *Liber quartus, distinctio I, Samaritanus. Hic incipit liber quartus, qui est de Sacramentis.* The *desinit* on fol. 166. col. 2: « by entering the gates of paradise, which may the Crucified concede to us, Who for us, with the Father and the Holy Spirit (is) eternally blessed. Amen. Moreover, I wish, that the ones reading these writings on the Sentences know, that as much as I was able and could understand, I have followed the footsteps of the doctor of my order, as (is) commonly (done). There are chiefly two of which: one in speculatives, that Master John Duns, Scotch by nation; another in positives, namely that most devout Lord and friar, Cardinal Bonaventura. The sayings of whom and of their followers, even if I have not placed them always word-for-word, yet from their sentence and/or at least of one of them according to ... my (ability) I have not deviated, by adding at any time and/or omitting, or summarizing the sentence, as it seemed to be expedient to meagerness of my own genius. Wherefore, let it not move thee, that I have not as often cited them by name as they occurred, because this was not done under the title of pride or elation, but to remove my tedium in reading other (works) and in writing. But, if, when my own voice has sounded out a little, it has not receded presumptuously from the indications of the aforesaid fathers ».*

7. *Richardus Rufus*, of the Order of Minors, an Englishman. On this author, writers are not in agreement. Sbaralea (*Supplementum.*, p. 635), citing *Rodulphius* and *Possevinus*, inclines unto the opinion, that *Richardus*, who wrote a *Compendium Commentarii S. Bonaventurae*, was other than *Richardus Ruys*, who according to *Possivinus* wrote a *Commentarius* on the books of Sentences and is said to have flourished c. 1270. But the *Commentarius* cited by *Rodulphius* and *Possevinus* begins in the same manner, just as the work described below; which cannot even be called a "Commentary", because, besides the doctrine of St. Bonaventure, it often cites even other opinions as probable ones, alongside which there is not rarely placed in the margin of the codex, the note: *calumniosum, calumniam patitur,* and/or even *insanissimum.* The sentence of Antony Wood (*Hist. Universitatis Oxoniens*, Bk. I, p. 72), cited by Sbaralea, is more pleasant: that each is the same Richard.

At Assisi, in the library of the Sacro Convento (now the Municipal), cod. membr. in fol. min., of the end of the 13th century, which contains Bks. I & II. The *incipit: Altissimus creavit de terra medicinam. Verbum istud scribitur Eccli. XXXVIII, quod etsi contineat verborum paucitatem* etc. The *desinit: et que sunt hec vel illa precise patet ex dictis.* The second book begins immediately: *Creationem rerum etc. In hoc secundo libro principaliter intenditur de homine.* The *desinit: sicut ipse, qui est in malo obstinatus, a quo sumsit exordium omne malum.* — These two books, which were in this library at the time of Sbaralea, are now not found there, but only Bks. III & IV, cod. membr. in fol. min., of the end of the 13th century, sign. 36. The *incipit: Deus autem qui dives est* etc. After the foreword: *Hic queritur, utrum divina natura potuerit uniri cum humana: et videtur quod non.* The Fourth book extends up to Distinction XXV and ends: *quia inseparabiliter est adiuctum exteriori Sacramento et quod potest per pecuniam.* — The same work is extant also *at Berlin*, in the Royal library, cod. chart. in 4, saec. XV, sign. M. L. th. 48: but it has only Sent., Bks. I & II.

Anonymi

8. *At Amiens*, in France, in the Civic library, cod. membr. in fol., from the end of the 13th century, sign. n. 234, contains a compendium on the first Book of the Sentences. The *incipit* is: *Altissimus de terra creavit medicinam* (Eccli.

38:4). *In his verbis singulariter expositis quatuor cause sacre Scripture connotantur.* The *desinit: quoniam hoc non est nature tantum, sed etiam rationis.* — The author, though he took all from the Commentary of St. Bonaventure and most often used the words of the same, proceeds, however, in an order slightly changed. At the beginning, there is prefaced a *tabula quaestionum.* It is similar to, and perhaps the same work as, that which is extant in the Civic library at *Dôle* (France), which, besides Sent., Bk. I, also contains Bk. II, and which is described more accurately below under n. 18.

9. *At Assisi*, in the library of the Sacro Convento (the Municipal), cod. membr. in fol., saec. XIV, sign. B. IX. 1: *Questiones abbreviate in I. II. et III. Sent.* The First begins: *In medio et in circuitu sedis.* The *desinit: quia possumus sancte et iuste velle oppositum.* Book II's *incipit: Creationem rerum ... iste secundus liber dividitur ... In prima agit de hominis conditione. In secunda.* The *desinit: et ipse infinitis se immiscuit questionibus peccatorum, secundum quod series manifestat duorum librorum precedentium. cui est honor et gloria, laus et imperium per infinita sec. secul. Amen.* Book III's *incipit,* without a title: *Cum igitur venit plenitudo temporis etc. Liber iste tertius dividitur in partes duas. In prima Magister determinat de vita.* For the *desinit*, there are the words of St. Bonaventure: *et mandata dedit secundum quod in hoc libro explanatum est. Sit omnis honor et gloria per infinita secula seculorum. Amen.*

10. *At Assisi*, in the library of the Sacro Convento (the Municipal), cod. membr. in fol., saec. XIV, sign. B. X. 12, a Compendium on Sent. Bk. IV. The *incipit: Samaritanus iste.* The *desinit: ad quam nos perducat qui vivit et regnat in secula seculorum. Amen.*

11. Likewise, *at Basel* in Switzerland, cod. miscell. from several centuries, i. e., XIII, XIV, and XV, sign. B. X. 26, a Compendium from Bk. IV of the Commentary. The *incipit: Utrum Sacramenta debuerint institui.* The *desinit: dolorem spiritualem requiruntur.*

12. Likewise, *at Bruges* in Belgium, in the Civic library, cod. membr. in 8, saec. XIII, sign. 174, Questions on Bk. IV of the Commentary. The *incipit* of Bk. III, on the upper margin: *Prima questio. Utrum divina natura potuerit uniri cum humana natura.* The *desinit: quanto aliquid durius comedit, magis debilitatur et gravatur. Responsio ad obieta patet.* Book IV's *incipit: Utrum Sacramenta debuerint institui. Desinit: non oblatione novi.*

13. Likewise, *at Cambridge*, England, library of St. Peter's Hall, cod. membr. in fol., saec. XIV, sign. 1. 2. 0: *Questiones super quatuor libros Sent.* Book I's *incipit: De uti primo queritur, cum sit actio.* Book II's *incipit: De creatione primo queritur.* Book III's *incipit: Utrum divina natura potuerit uniri cum humana.* Book IV's *incipit: Utrum Sacramenta debuerint institui.* The *desinit: melius patuit et in questione de igne infernali.*

14. *In the same place*, codex. sign. 1. 7. 9, contains four books, abbreviated and divided by chapters. The *incipit* of ch. 1: *Veteris ac nove Legis continentiam* etc. The *desinit* of Book IV: *a facie exorsus sedentis per media ad pedes usque via duce pervenit.*

15. *At Chartres*, in France, in the Civic library, cod. membr. in 8, from the beginning of the 14th century, sign. n. 259 G/2: *Conclusiones in quatuor libr. Sent.* The *incipit: Cupientes* etc. *Questio prima. Utrum preter doctrinas philosophicas sit necessaria* etc.. Its *desinit: ... per comparationem ad naturam patientis.* The second book's *incipit: Creationem rerum etc. Utrum sint plura prima principia.* Its *desinit: et in his Prelato obedire necesse est.* The third books' *incipit: Cum venit igitur* etc. *Questio prima. Utrum congruum fuerit, Deum

---

* *Trans. note*: An important exposition of the motives for *compilationes*. For the original Latin of this *desinit*, see the Quaracchi edition.

incarnari. The *desinit: per beneficia et speranda.* The fourth book's *incipit: Samaritanus interpretatur custos* etc. *Questio prima. Utrum sacramenta fuerint necessaria. Desinit: ignis ille est turbidus et fumosus et feculentus. Explicit.* Then there is added: *conclusiones fratris Bonaventure de ordine fratrum minorum super quatuor libros sententiarum, optimum opus.*

The same *conclusiones* are *at Florence,* in the Biblioteca Medicea Laurenziana, Cod. Aedil. LXIX. chart. in fol. grand., saec. XIV and XV. A second hand has prefaced: *Itinerarium S. Thome seu Bone venture.* At the bottom of the page of Bk. IV: *Explicit itinerarium S. Thome, secundum alios Bone venture ... Anno Domini 1442.*

15. *At Cesena* in Italy, at the Biblioteca (Comunale) Malatestiana, cod. membr. in fol., near the middle of the 14th century, sign. plut. XVIII. III., a Summa on Sent. Bks. I, II and III. The *incipit* of Bk. I: *Veteris ac nove* etc. *Queritur de subiecto theologie, et quod sit Deus...* Its *desinit: quia ordinavit eam ad redemptionem nostram, ut dictum est.* Book II's *incipit: Creationem rerum insinuans* etc. *Circa istam distictionem queritur primo, utrum mundus sit eternus.* Its *desinit: que non sunt contra animam et regulam suam.* Book III's *incipit: Primo quaeritur de possibilitate Incarnationis.* Its *desinit: et laboris presentis continuationem nobis concedat* etc..

17. *At Darmstadt* in Germany, in the Ducal library, cod. chart. in 8 vo., of the end of the 15th century, sign. 95, *Excerpta super II. III. et IV. Sent.* Its *incipit: De creationis statu et casu Angelorum. Utrum in primo instanti creationis sue Angelus.* Its *desinit: sed plus ascendet quam aqua diluvit.*

The same work is also extant at *Karlsburg* in Transylvania (now Alba Iulia, Romania), in the Cathedral library, cod. chart. in fol., of the end of the 14th century and the beginning of the 15th, sign. I. 5. III. 5., *Commentarium in II. III. et IV. Sent.* Book II's *incipit: Queritur, utrum Angelus in primo instanti creationis sue. Desinit: invidentia fraterne caritatis.* There follows Bk. III: *Queritur, que sit precipua causa Incarnationis. Resp.: Reparatio humani generis.* Its *desinit: ad agendum vel patiendum persone.* Then immediately: *Queritur, utrum Sacramenta debuerint instintui. Resp.: Institutio Sacramentorum.* Its *desinit: omnia peccata memorabuntur, ut continue simul torqueantur.* — Likewise, *at Lambach* in Upper Austria, in the library of the Benedictine Fathers, cod. membr. in 4, of the beginning of the 14th century, sign. 132, *Questiones ex II. III. et IV. Sent.* — Likewise, *at Münich* in Bavaria, in the Royal library, cod. membr. in fol. min., saec. XIV, sign. C. L. M. 4647, *Quaestiones sumtae de II. III. et IV. Sent.* — In the same (library), cod. chart. in fol., saec. XV, sign. C. L. M. 5861, *Questiones super II. III. et IV. Sent.* — In the same, cod. chart. in 4, saec. XV, sign. C. L. M. 8986, *Quaestiones abbreviatae in II. III. et IV. Sent.* — In the same, cod. chart. in 4, saec. XV, sign. C. L. M. 11740, *Quaestiones abbreviatae in II. et III. Sent.* — In the same, cod. chart. in 4, saec. XV, sign. C. L. M. 11751, *Quaestiones abbreviatae in II. Sent.* — In the same, cod. membr. in fol. min., saec. XIV, sign. C. L. M. 116090, *Quaestiones abbreviatae in II. III. et IV..* — In the same, cod. chart. in 4, saec. XIV, sign. C. L. M. 18728, *Quaestiones abbreviatae in II. Sent.* — At *Münich,* in the University library, cod. chart. in 4, saec. XV, sign. 33, *Quaestiones abbreviatae in II. Sent.* — Likewise, *at Innsbrück* in the Tyrol, in the library of the Premonstratensian Fathers in Wiltin, cod. chart. in fol., saec. XV, sign. XXXII. B. 4, *Quaestiones exerptae ex II. Sent.* — Likewise, *at Paris,* in the Bibliothèque National, cod.

membr. in fol. min., saec. XIII, sign. 13742: *Solutiones questionum ex IV. Sent..* — Likewise, *at Rome,* in the Biblioteca (Apostolica) Vaticana, cod. Palat. chart., saec. XV, sign. 438, *Questiones super II. III. et IV. Sent..* — Likewise, at *St. Florian* in Austria, in the library of the Monastery, cod. chart. in fol., of the end of the 14th century, sign. XI. 103: *Compendium in II. III. et IV. Sent..* — In the same place, cod. chart. in fol., of the end of the 14th century, sign. XI. 25. It contains Sent., Bks. II, III, and IV.. — *At Trier* in Prussia (now Germany), in the Public library, cod. membr. in fol., saec. XIV, sign. 435: *Excerpta ex II. III. IV. Sent..*

18. *At Dôle* in France, in the Civic library, cod. membr. in fol., of the end of the 13th century, sign. n. 56. The First Book of Bonaventure, abbreviated. The *incipit: Queritur de causa finali, et dictum est* etc.. Book II's *incipit: Creationem rerum* etc. *Queritur hic de exitu rerum in esse.* Its *desinit: sententia pastoris sive iusta sive iniusta teneda est.* All the others books are lacking in (this) codex.

19. *At Florence,* in the Biblioteca Nazionale, cod. membr. in fol., saec. XIV, sign. 218. D. 5, once in the Convento S. Croce of the Friars Minor as n. 288. It contains a compendium on Sent., Bk. III. The *incipit: Cum igitur plenitudo temporis* etc.. The *desinit: et multiplicat sibi meritum et consolamen. Explicit liber Sententiarum tertius fratris Bonaventure. Deo gratias. Amen.*

The same work is had *at Vienna* in Austria, in the Palatine library, cod. membr. in fol., before the middle of the 14th century, sign. 1573. The *incipit: Bonaventura super tertium Sententiarum ... Cum igitur plenitudo* etc.. The *desinit: expliciunt questiones principales tertii libri Bonaventure. Deo gratia. Amen.*

20. *At Florence,* in the Biblioteca Nazionale, cod. membr. in fol., saec. XIV, sign. 225, B. 9: *Veritates summarie librorum Bonaventure super Sententias.* On fol. 2 r. by the first had there is prefaced: *Veritates summarie librorum Bonaventure et aliorum super Sententias.* The *incipit: Que sit causa finalis, quia ut boni fiamus.* The *desinit: tenetur enim homo ad hoc etiam sine iudicio sacerdotis.*

21. *At Florence,* in the Biblioteca Nazionale, cod. membr. in fol., saec. XIII, sign. 360. B. 5. It contains St. Bonaventure's Sent., Bk. IV, abbreviated. Its *incipit: Samaritanus vulnerato* etc. *Dividitur iste liber in tuas partes, in quarum prima* etc. Its *desinit: post plenam punitionem, que erit post iudicium, a qua nos custodiat qui cum Patre* etc.

22. *At Florence,* in the Biblioteca Nazionale, cod. membr. in fol., saec. XIV, sign. 507. A. 2. It contains *Extractiones* from St. Bonaventure's, Sent., Bks. I & II. Its *incipit: Questio I. Queritur, quid sit subiectum in scientia.* Its *desinit: et sic non habent ideam in Deo.* Book II's *incipit: Questio I. Utrum res habeant principium causale.* Its *desinit: vel possint esse plures.*

23. *At Florence,* in the Biblioteca Nazionale, cod. membr. in fol., of the beginning of the 14th century, sign. 846. G. 3. Its *incipit: liber I. a pertissimo Parisius exceptatus. Quoniam sicut dicit Hugo de sancto Victore, natura hominum.* On fol. 16, the *incipit* of Book II: *Solummodo hoc inveni* etc. Books III & IV are lacking in this codex.

24. *At Copenhagen* in Denmark, in the Royal library, cod. 1363, membr. in fol., end of the 13th century, contains the *conclusiones* on Sent., Bk. IV. The *incipit: Queritur, quid sit Sacramentum. Resp. Augustinus de Civ. Dei et in littera.* Its *desinit: ipso ad suscipiendum nos disponente, qui est benedictus in secula. Amen.*

25. *At Karlsburg* in Transylvania (now Alba Iulia, Romania), cod. membr. in fol., from the beginning of the 14th century, sign. G. 5. VI. 31. On fol. 105 r., col. 2, there is read: *Incipiunt veritates questionum Bonaventure super quartum Sententiarum de Sacramentis et remuneratione finali.* Then the *incipit: quartus liber de Sacramentis, et primo de Sacramentis*

in genere. Queritur autem primo, quid sit signum, quia omne Sacramentum est signum. The *desinit*, on fol. 193: *et ideo remota illa actione remanent incorruptibiles.* The writer wrote, holding the plume in his palm. A *tabula quaestionum* follows.

26. *At London*, in the Royal Library, cod. membr. in fol., of the beginning of the 14th century, sign. 18322, once belonging to the Monastery of Mt. St. George, it contains *Questiones cum problematibus.* Its *incipit* on fol. 3: *Circa quartum librum Sententiarum primo queritur, quid sit Sacramentum. Dicendum, quod Sacramentum quatuor modis.* Its *desinit: qui ad gaudia nos secum trahit eterna, ad que nos perducat Iesus Christus. Amen. Expliciunt extractiones super quartum librum Sententiarum continentes veritatem.*

27. *At Melk* in Austria, in the library of the Benedictine Fathers, cod. chart. in 4, saec. XIV, sign. A. 6, on fol. 3 of which there is read: *Questiones breves per modum concludionsum domini Bonaventure super primo Sententiarum, quam tabellam seu registrum sui operis principalis super librum Sententiarum institulat, eo quod hic questionum titulos modo et ordine principalis operis sui portiones questionum annotavit. Questio prooemialis: Utrum docere sit solius Dei. Actus docendi ut ab.* Its *desinit* on fol. 48 v.: *eorundem revocatoria in te placide determinetur. Amen. Expliciunt questiones per modum tabule.* On fol. 49. r.: *Secundi libri distinctionis prime questio prima, utrum aliquid sit eviternum Deo. Primum imperante bonitate.* The *desinit* on fol. 98 v.: *simplici et solide innitantur veritati.* On fol. 99 r.: *Tabula per modum registri super tertium Sententiarum Domini Bonaventure. Distinctio prima. An natura divina sit unibilis humane. Veneranda est sacratissima unio.* Its *desinit* on fol. 136 r.: *et de vita gratie, quam nobis per viturem donorum et mandatorum observantiam impendit. Explicit tabella per modum registri super tertium Domini Bonaventure secundum titulos questionum in vero scripto suo super Sententiis positos per ordinem.* — On the same fol. v.: *Libri Bonaventure de Sacramentis. Queritur, utrum Sacramenta debuerint institui. Respondeo: Institutio Sacramentorum Deum decuit.* Its *desinit* on fol. 175 v.: *mali simul omnia peccata memorabuntur, ut continue torqueantur.*

28. *At Mainz*, in the Civic library, cod. membr. in fol., saec. XIV, sign: chart. 363. It contains abbreviated questions from St. Bonaventure's Commentary on the Four Books of Sentences. Its *incipit* near the end of the codex: *Queritur, utrum in Deo (sit ponere) essentie seu nature unitatem. Et quod sic, videtur ratione ostensiva* etc.. These questions comprise 35 1/2 folia. After, there follow partly abbreviated questions from other (authors).

29. *At München*, in the Royal library, cod. chart. in fol. min., saec. XIV, sign. C. L. M. 5959. It contains abbreviated questions on only Bonaventure's first book. The *incipit* on fol. 4 r.: *Cupienties aliquid de penuria* etc. *Huic operi Magister premittit prooemium.* The *desinit* on fol. 94 r.: *a quo omnia et finis, ad quem ordinantur omnia, cui est honor et gloria, decus et imperium in secula seculorum. Amen.* A *tabula quaestionum* follows, but (it is) incomplete.

The same work is had *at Todi* (Italy), in the Biblioteca Municipale, cod. membr. in fol. min., of the beginning of the 14th century, sign. 33. It has the Commentary of St. Bonaventure on the First Book of the Sentences, abbreviated here and there. The *incipit* on fol. 2 r.: *Cupientes aliquid* etc. *Premittit Magister huic totali libro* etc. The *desinit* on fol. 83 r.: *explicit hic primus Sententiarum. Explicit expliciat, ludere scriptor est.*

30. *At München*, in the Royal library, cod. chart. in fol., saec.

XV, sign. C. L. M. 11414. It contains Bonaventure's second (book) on the Sentences, abbreviated, on fol. 1 r. of which there is prefaced a *tabula quaestionum*, and on fol. 11 r., col. 2, the *incipit: Dominus sapientia fundavit terram.* The *desinit* on fol. 329 r.: *et ideo malum dicitur corruptio istorum aequaliter.*

31. *At Naples*, in the Biblioteca Nazionale, cod. membr. saec. XIV, sign. VII. D. 5.. Outside, on the vellum band affixed to the *tabula*, there is written: *Bonaventura super primum et secundum Sententiarum, et tertius et quartus Scotelli de Aquila.* The *incipit: Cupientes aliquid de penuria, videlicet, queritur de hoc quo dicit opus.* On fol. 66, the *incipit* of Book II: *Creationem rerum. Ad intellegentiam eorum, quae in hac parte* etc..

32. *At Paris*, in the Bibliothèque de l'Arsenal, cod. membr. in fol. saec. XIII, sign. 619. It contains a compendium excerpted from St. Bonaventure's Commentary on the Four Books of Sentences. The *incipit: Veteris ac nove Legis* etc. *Hic queruntur duo principaliter 1. de fruitione; 2. de uti.* The *desinit* of the fourth book are the words of Bonaventure: *et nos apparebimus cum ipso in gloria, ad quam nos perducat Iesus Christus, Filius Dei praecibus beate Marie et adiutricis nostre, cui est benedictio* etc.

33. *At Paris*, in the Bibliothèque National, cod. membr., saec. XIII, sign. 14307. It contains an abbreviated exposition on Sent., Bks. I & II, gathered from St. Bonaventure's Commentary. On fol. 1 r., col. 1, the *incipit: Deus, docuisti me a iuventute mea ... verba ista scripta sunt in Psalmo.* However, the *incipit* of the Commentary: *Antequam accedatur ad formam tractatus, quedam communia possunt dubitari.* On fol. 135, the *desinit: loquitur de peccatoribus adhuc existentibus in via, non in vie termino, id est in inferno.* Book II's *incipit* on fol. 136: *Mirabilia testimonia tua ... Questio I. Utrum res create* etc. On fol. 252, its *desinit: et in iis que nec contraria sunt anime nec sue regule.*

34. *At Paris*, in the same library, cod. membr. in fol. min., saec. XIII, sign. 16417. It contains abbreviated questions upon Bonaventure's Sent., Bk. IV. On fol. 1. r., the *incipit: Queritur de hoc quod dicit, in duobus consistit Sacramentum.* The *desinit* on fol. 22. r.: *illa tamen tentatio, que est carnis a nullo est appetenda.*

35. *At Paris*, in the same library, cod. membr. in fol. saec. XIII & XIV, sign. 3085. After St. Bonaventure's *Commentarius* on Sent., Bk. I, it contains doubts on the text, abbreviated from the same holy Doctor's *Commentarius* on Sent., Bk. IV. On fol. 140 r., col. 1, the *incipit: Incipiunt questiones litterales quarti libri cum divisione littere. Samaritanus* etc. *Liber iste habet duas partes.* It ends, or, rather, fails on fol. 143, at the words: *characteris impressione.*

36. *At Padua*, in the Biblioteca Antoniana, cod. membr. in fol., of the beginning of the 14th century, sign. 126. On fol. 1 r. on the upper margin, a hand of the 18th century has written: *S. Bonaventurae liber secundus Sent. abbreviatus.* Its *incipit: Creationem rerum insinuans* etc. *Surp egit Magister in primo libro.* Its *desinit: quos per perfectam paupertatem, continentiam et obedientiam ad celestem perducat gloriam in s. s. Amen.*

37. *At Prague*, in the University library, cod. IV. II. 14., chart. in 4, saec. XIV. Abbreviated questions from Sent., Bk. IV.

38. *At Prague*, in the library of the Metropolitan Chapter, cod. membr. in fol., saec. XIV, sign. A. LXXXVII. It contains many excerpts from St. Bonaventure's *Commentarius* and from others. Its *incipit: Gloria Dei celare verbum et gloria regum investigare sermonem. Prov. XXV. Verbum Dei Patris eternaliter a Patre* etc. Its *desinit: sua maiestate implevit et ornavit, qui est benedictus in secula seculorum. Amen. Explicit scriptum extractum de diversis ope-*

ribus magistrorum, scilicet Bonaventure, Thome et Petri cum magno labore et vigiliis et sollicitudinibus.

39. *At Rome*, in the Biblioteca (Apostolica) Vaticana, cod. membr. in 8 vo., from the beginning of the 14th century, sign. 919. It contains the four books on the Sentences, abbreviated, as the inscription placed on fol. 74, indicates: *Bonaventura super quatuor libros Sententiarum abbreviatus.* The *incipit* of the work: *Quod theologia est de rebus.* The *desinit* on fol. 189: *et sic patent ea quae queruntur circa quartum librum.*

40. *At Rome*, in the same library, cod. membr. in fol., saec. XIII, sign. 914. It contains St. Bonaventure on Sent., Bk. II & III, abbreviated. On fol. 138, the *desinit: ad vincitam malorum, laudem vero bonorum et gloriam Dei, qui est benedictus in secula seculorum. Amen. Finito libro sit alus et gloria Christo.*

41. *At Rome*, in the same library, cod. 928. It contains a compendium on Sent., Bk. II. The *incipit: Qui vivit in eternum creavit omnia simul. His verbis opus creationis sufficienter exprimitur.*

The same work seems to be at *Torino*, in the University library, cod. in fol., saec. XIV, sign. D. III. 28. It contains excerpts from St. Bonaventure on Sent., Bks. II. & III. On fol. 18 r., col. 1, the *incipit: primus liber Bonaventure. Qui vivit in eternum creavit omnia simul. Verbum istud scribitur* etc. *Queritur, utrum mundus fuerit ab eterno.* The *desinit: explicit secundus Bonaventure exceptatus.* Book III's *incipit: Deus autem, qui dives est* etc. Its *desinit: explicit tertius Bonaventure exceptatus.*

42. *At Rome*, in the Biblioteca Casanate, cod. membr. in 8 vo., saec. XIV, sign. A. V. 1. A work abbreviated from the Commentary on the four books of the Sentences. Its *incipit: Veteris ac nove legis* etc..

43. *At Torino*, in the University library, cod. membr. in 4, saec. XV, sign. E. V. 48, the *beginning* of which is: *Summa Bonaventure in I. Sententiarum. Commendat autem Dominus caritatem suam* etc.. Its *desinit: consentiendo et in actum progrediendo.*

44. *At Troyes* in France, in the Civic library, cod. membr. in fol. minore, sign. 829, contains a compendium on Sent., Bk. IV. It closes with the words of St. Bonaventure: *tunc videbimus, amabimus et laudabimus, cum apparebit Christus vita nostra, et nos apparebimus* etc..

Note. In the same library there is a cod. membr. in 8, sign. 1862, which under the name of St. Bonaventure reports a commentary on Sent., Bks. III & IV; but the author is *Odo Rigaldus*, of the Order of Minors, Archbishop of Rouen (France).

45. *At Todi* (Italy), in the Biblioteca Municipale, cod. membr. in 8 vo., from the beginning of the 14th century, sign. 137. It contains, among other abbreviations, the Commentary of St. Bonaventure on Sent., Bks. III & IV. Its *incipit* on fol. 83: *Natura divina potuit uniri cum humana* etc.. Its *desinit* on fol. 121. Then the Bk. IV begins: *Samaritanus* etc. *Queritur, utrum Sacramenta debuerint institui.* The *desinit* is on fol. 244 r..

46. *At Tours* in France, in the Civic library, cod. chart. in 8, saec. XV, sign. 409. On fol. 38 r., it reports excerpts from St. Bonaventure, Sent., Bk. II.

47. *At Venice*, in the Biblioteca (Nazionale) Marciana, cod. membr. in fol., saec. XIV, sign. clas. III. 93. At the beginning there is prefaced: *in isto volumine continentur II. et III. Bonaventure ordinis minorum Presbyteri Cardinalis, quorum principia mutata sunt ab aliquo invido.* Its *incipit: Sapiens mulier aedificat donum* etc. *Questio 1. Ad maiorem evidentiam eorum, que hic dicuntur de exitu rerum in esse.* The *desinit* on fol. 65 v.: *isti ergo beatissime Trinitati sit sempiterna laus et gloria pro fine huius libri. Amen.* A *tabula quaestionum* follows. Book III's *incipit* on fol. 68 r.: *Veritas de terra orta est* etc. *Questio I. Ad maiorem evidentiam ... utrum*

divina natura uniri potest cum humana. Its *desinit* on fol. 134 r.: *hoc autem in quarto libro plenius declarabitur, adiuvante gratia Iesus Christi, cui cum Patre et Spiritu sancto pro fine huius libri sit honor et gloria cum laude perenni. Amen.*

48. *At Vienna* in Austria, in the Palatine library, cod. chart. in fol., miscell. saec. XIV, XV & XVI, sign. 3872. On fol 209. r (in characters of the 16th century) it has: *Ex primo Sententiarum secundum Doctoris seraphici palestram ac subtilissimi Scoti annotatio compendiosa.* The *incipit: Fluvius egrediebatur de loco voluptatis.* This annotation also precedes Bks. II & IV.

49. *At Vienna* in Austria, in the same library, cod. chart. in fol., saec. XIV, sign. 4363. It contains: *Determinationes de Sacamento Eucharistiae ac poenitentiae* etc. from St. Bonaventure's Commentary on Sent., Bk. IV.

50. *At Vorau* in Styria (Austria), in the library of the Canons, cod. membr. in fol., saec. XIV, sign. CXCV., contains: *Questiones Bone Venture super IV. librum sententiarum.*

Indexes or *tabulae* on St. Bonaventure's Commentary

51. *Bonaventura a Cineribus*, Italian, wrote *tabulae* on St. Bonaventure's Commentary. *Rodulphus* (III, on the year 1586), Wadding and Sbaralea make mention of this. Wadding asserts, that besides the very copious *tabula*, he wrote on all works: an *Epitomen* of the works of Bonaventure. But this Bonaventura seems to have only written a double *tabula*, which is exhibited at Siena. The authors cited in the age, in which he flourished, are ignorant (of it); but it is established from the codices, that he lived at least not after the middle of the 14th century.

At Siena in Tuscany (Italy), in the Civic library, cod. membr. in fol., saec. XIV, sign. F. V. 19. It contains *tabulae* on the books of the Sentences composed by friar *Bonaventura a Cineribus*. On fol. 137, the *incipit: Incipit super primum fratris Bonaventure.* At the end of the *tabula* for Bk. III, there is read: *Explicit tabula edita a fratre Bonaventure de Cineribus ordinis Minorum super tertium fratris Bonaventure de Ordine supradicto.*

To the *tabula* for each book of St. Bonaventure there is prefaced an *index rerum*, which are discussed by doctors (of theology) both on the Sentences, and on theological *quodlibeticals*; and it was written by a hand of the 14th century, and, as it seems, published by the same author, *Bonaventura de Cineribus.* The *incipit* on fol. 1 r.: *Abstinentia (absolutio) a culpa. Utrum quilibet sacerdos possit quemlibet absolvere.* The *desinit* is on fol. 136 v..

The same work is found *at Todi* (Italy), in the library of St. Fortunatus (now the Municipal), cod. membr. in fol., saec. XIV, sign. 14. It contains an alphabetical *tabula rerum* and for each entry, several questions, at the signs for each there are cited authors, among whom is often Bonaventure and more often Thomas. The *incipit* begins with the word *absolutio.* The *desinit: verbo Xps.*

The same work is also had *at Seville* in Spain, in the Biblioteca Colombina y Capitular, cod. membr. in fol. minore, saec. XV, sign. tabl. 130. n. 35, in which there has been erased a *tabula*, arranged in alphabetical order, on the four books of the Sentences. At the bottom of the page there is read: *A. de Solucar manu propria.*

The same work is found *at München* in the Royal library, cod. L. chart. in fol., saec. XV, sign. 22110. It contains questions on Sent., Bks. II & III. On fol. 128 v.: *Incipiunt capitula et rubrice secundi libri questionum Bone venture Cardinalis minorum fratrum existens.* The *desinit* on fol. 173: *Expliciunt capitula et rubrice secundi et terti libri sententiarum questionem Bona-*

venture Cardinalis ordinis minorum frater existens per me Conradum Berhnhartt de Aicheberg, Plebanum in Oggar, licet indignum, anno Domini 1460, in die sancte Prisce virginis et martyris. Deo gratias.

A similar work is had in the same library, cod. membr. in fol., saec. XIV and XV, sign. n. 8005, written by many hands. On fol. 135 v., col. 2, up to fol. 157 it contains titles of questions on Sent., Bks. I, II & III, extracted from the work of St. Bonaventure, the *incipit* of which: *Incipiunt tituli primi libri Bonaventure.* The *desinit: Explicit tertius liber Bonaventure.*

Finally, we will make mention of the following opuscule, in which several excerpts, treating of a particular question from the Seraphic Doctor, are exhibited.

52. *At Charleville* in France, in the Civic library, cod. membr. in 4, saec. XIV, sign. n. 47, contains excerpts from Bk. IV of the Commentary. — Likewise, at *Liège* in Belgium, in the library of the Major Seminary, cod. chart. in 4, saec. XV, sign. 6, g. 23.

53. At Bratislava (Wrocław, Poland), in the University library, cod. chart., saec. XV, sign. 1. clas. oct. 13. On fol. 1 r., the incipit: *prologus Magistri Mathie de Ianaw super XXVIII doctores pro quotidiana seu creba communione corporis Christi a plebeis christianis.* Anno Domini 1460. On fol. 25 v.: *Determinatio Vener. Magistri Bonaventure.* — Likewise, in the same place, in the Civic library, cod. membr. in fol., saec. XV, sign. I. 9. — Likewise, in the same place, in the Cathedral library, cod. chart. in 4, saec. XV, sign. D. III. 1.. The incipit is on fol. 114 v.. — Likewise, at *Vienna*, in the Palatine library, cod. ms. chart. in fol., saec. XV, sign. 4363, under the one heading of determinations on the Sacrament of Penance from St. Bonaventure's, Bk. IV. — Likewise, at *Graz* in Styria (Austria), in the University library, cod. chart. in fol., saec. XV, sign. 347, after the middle, and cod. chart. in fol., saec XV, sign. 492, have similar *determinationes* from the same book of St. Bonaventure.

To these opuscula we subjoin an ancient Index of passages, in which Sts. Thomas and Bonaventure disagree. Though this document contains nothing, which has not been covered (in our Scholia), yet we trust that it will by no means be of interest to lovers of antiquity. It was found both *at Rome*, in the Biblioteca Borghesiana, cod. membr. in fol., of the end of the 13th Century and/or beginning of the 14th, sign. 19, and *at Lüneburg* in Germany, Civic library, cod. membr. in fol. of the 13th Century and/or at the beginning of the 14th, sign. Theol. 20. in fol.. We exhibit (here) the text of the Borghesiana codex, having added within parentheses variant readings of the other codex, which are of some moment:

These are the passages, in which friar Bonaventure and friar Thomas disagree in the First Book on the Sentences (In these there dissent Thomas and Bonaventure on the First).

1. Whether theology is a speculative, and/or a practical science, in the Prologue.

2. Whether it happens that one uses evil, first d.

3. Whether the powers of the soul are substantial, and/or accidental to it, d. 3.

4. Whether the "power of generating" means a *something* [quid], and/or a '*regarding something*' [ad aliquid], d. 7.

5. Whether the "power of generating" and "of creating" are said univocally, and/or (equivocally, and) which *per prius*, d. 7.

6. Whether the reckoning of the vestige is in accidentals (accidents) and/or only in substantials (and/or in substances), d. 3, in Bonaventure on the text, in Thomas d. 3.

7. Whether measure, beauty and order and all other such are essential in creatures and/or accidental, d. 3 in

Bonaventure, in the solution of this question (argument): *whether the powers of the soul are substantial to it* (lacking *to it*).

8. Whether the rational soul has been composed out of matter and form, d. 8. Bonaventure that it is so, Thomas that is not (words after d. 8, lacking).

9. Whether "generation" and "procession" are said of the Holy Spirit and not of the Son, d. 13.

10. Whether charity is increased through an addition and/or a purification, d. 17.

11. Whether the increase of charity has a terminus, d. 17.

12. Whether "gift" is said only personally.

13. On the difference between "essence", "subsistence" (substance), "hypostases" and "person", d. 23.

14. Whether this name "*one*" [unus] is said positively, and/or privatively, d. 24.

15. Whether this name "*person*" [persona] signifies the Substance, and/or a relation, d. 25 in Bonaventure, in Thomas, d. 23.

16. Whether "person" is a common name among the divine, a diversity in the measure of quantity, d. 25 in Bonaventure, d. 26 in Thomas.

17. Whether the Father is the Father because He generates, and/or whether he generates because He is the Father, d. 27 in Bonaventure, d. 26 in Thomas.

18. Whether "word" is always (lacking *always*) said personally, among the divine, d. 27.

19. Whether "equality" posits something among the divine, d. 31.

20. Whether the Father loves Himself by the Holy Spirit, d. 32.

21. Whether the Angels are in a place in a delimited manner (lacking *in a delimited manner*), and in what manner they are in a delimited manner, d. 37.

22. Whether an Angel by moving himself from place (lacking *place*) to place, passes (add *necessarily*) through an intermediary one, d. 37.

23. Whether an Angel passes through (places) suddenly, and/or successively, d. 37.

24. Whether the antecedent of this conditional: "*If God foreknew, therefore, it will be,*" is contingent and/or necessary, d. 39.

§ 7. *There are also not lacking books, sent to press, which dedicated to the Commentaries of St. Bonaventure, explicate the works and/or teach his doctrine.* Of which we shall exhibit here a list of those which are known to us.

1. *Gulielmus Vorilongus* (alias *Vurrilonis, Vorlion*), a doctor of Paris, wrote: *In quatuor libros Sententiarum iuxta doctrinam S. Bonaventurae et Scoti*, Lyons, 1484, fol.; again in 1489, fol. (by *Ioannes Trechsel*); at Paris in 1563; at Venice in 1496 and 1519 (by *Ioh. de Leucho*, at the expense of *Lazarus de Soardis*). His doctrine is held so highly, that when the controversy concerning the Blood of Christ was disputed before the Supreme Pontiff, Pius II, by the Friars Minor and Preachers, that he was called by the Minister General from France to Rome, to defend the sentence of the Minors. What he suffered from 1460, is related in a letter by *Petrus Chambon*, in the book, *Firmamenta trium Ordinum S. Francisci, P. IV*, (Paris edition of 1512), near the end. He died at Rome in 1464, buried at Ara Coeli. Yet, in this, he follows mostly the Commentary of Scotus.

2. *Stephanus Brulifer* (Brulever), of the Order of Minors, wrote a *Reportata in IV. libros S. Bonaventurae*. A doctor at Paris, from Saint-Malo in Brittany (France), the auditor for *Gulielmus Vorilongus* and for some years Rector of studies in the Convent of the Minors at Mainz, author of several books, which Wadding and Sbaralea enumerate. He died c. 1499. He elucidated Bonaventure's Sent., Bk. I, at Mainz in 1490; the more briefly, Bks. II, III & IV, at Metz. After his death certain disciples of his sent those (things), which were excerpted from his mouth in

to press at Basel, at *Iacobus de Pforzheim's*, in 1501, and again in 1507, in 4 vo.. This book also came forth at Venice, at *Lazarus de Soardis* in 1504, in 4 vo., and at Paris in 1521, in 8 vo., by *Franciscus Regnaut*, according to the testimony of *Ioannes a S. Antonio* (*Biblioteca Francescana*, p. 80), who, however, errs, in attributing these *Reporata* to a certain Fr. *Sanctovilla Mediolanensis*. Again, at Paris in 1570 the same work came forth, as Fr. Bonelli affirms (*Prodromus*, col. 308). At the bottom of this book there was printed another opuscule of the same Brülifer, *de Formalitatibus Scoti*, exhibiting the text of Scotus with « a very lucid comment ». — In these *Reportata* there are prefaced to each question various definitions and axioms according to the Scotistic school; then, the response of the Seraphic (Doctor) to the question is explained in detail according to (its) distinct propositions, while the solution to the objections is also briefly explained. The author is committed to the Scotistic doctrine, yet, very often he strives to draw the sense of St. Bonaventure to the norm of (his) preconceived system less than later commentators (did). It is to be grieved, that this *Reportata*, at least (its) first two editions, are full of *menda* and errors, which are to be attributed in part to those who excerpted the words of their own master, in part to the typographer.

3. *Nicholas de Tudeschis*, O. S. B, abbot, afterwards Archbishop of Palermo, very expert in canon law, wrote, among others, also on St. Bonaventure's Sent., Bk. II: Venice 1477. Thus *Antonio Orlando*, the Carmelite in *Origine e progressi della stampa*, according to Fr. Bonelli, *Prodromus*, col. 310.

4. *Nicolaus de Niise*, of the Order of Minors of the Observance, wrote a work on the Four Books of the Sentences, entitled, *Resolutio theologorum*, first printed at Rouen, then also at Venice, in 1574. He was first a canon and the vicar general of Konstanz (Germany), then a friar Minor; he died in 1509. In his book, conspicuous for (its) brevity and clarity, he often reports the sentences of St. Bonaventure, but follows very often Scotus.

5. *Pelbartus de Temesvar*, of the Order of Minors of the Observance: *Rosarium iuxta quatuor Sent. libros quadripartitum ex doctrina Doctoris subtilis, D. Thomae, D. Bonaventurae aliorumque sanctorum Doctorum*. — He compiled the things-treated-of in alphabetical order according to the Four Books of Lombard's Sentences. The fourth book was supplied, after *Pelbartus'* death, by Fr. *Oswaldus a Lasco*. There are very many editions of this work, such as Hagenau 1503, 1504, 1507, 1508, in fol.; Venice 1586, at *Franciscus Ziletti's*, and again in 1589; at Brixen in 1594. *Pelbartus*, too, is more committed to the school of Scotus, that of Bonaventure.

6. *Hugo de Sletstad* (Sélestadt, now in France), of the Order of Minors, of whom *Trithemius* (*de Scriptoribus eccles.*, ch. 702) says: A German by nation, a man studious in the divine Scriptures and erudite and learned in an outstanding manner in the disciplines of philosophers, subtle in genius and a marked disputationalist on scholastic questions. He wrote certain (works), *as they say*, outstanding volumes, by which he left a memory of his name to posterity, of which are extant *Quaestionum Sententiarum libri IV* and certain others. But he was a follower, in his own determinations, of (our) divine father Bonaventure, of the Order of Minors and an enlightening interpreter, explaining in detail those, which could seem obscure and more rarified to the simple, in regard to the singular philosophy of the same. — Following the authority of *Trithemius, Fabricus* (*Biblioth. Latina mediae et infimae aetatis*, tom. III, pag. 299, Padua,

1754) and after each, Bonelli and many others remembered him. But, we have not be able to yet find any trace of this book of his.

Authors of the Order of Friars Minor Conventual, illustrating the doctrine of St. Bonaventure

7. *Petrus Capuleus Cortonensis* († 1625), promoted to Bishop of the Church of Conversano (Apulia, Italy) by (Pope) Paul V, in 1605, wrote a *Commentarius in I. et II. Sent. D. Bonaventurae*, printed at Venice in 1622, 2 vols. in fol..

8. *Felix Gabrielli*, of the Order of Minors Conventual, Minister General from 1653, then Bishop of Norcia (Italy), 1659.1684: *Disputationes de praedestinatione et reprobatione ad mentem S. Bonaventurae et Scoti*, Rome 1653, in 4 vo..

9. *Matthaeus Ferchius*, a Dalmatian by race, master at Padua († 1669; at age of 87): *De Angelis tractatus theologicus ad mentem D. Bonaventurae*, Padua 1658, in 4 vo.: who is cited as having written also others on St. Bonaventure by *Bartholomaeo de Barberiis* (*Prefat. ad cursum theolog.*) as « the sole most faithful Bonaventurista among them all ».

10. *Bonifacius de Augustinis*: *Theologia S. Bonaventurae in summam redacta*, Rome on (the presses of) *Corbelletum*, 1696, in folio. It seems, that only the first tome of this work came to light.[1]

Authors from the Order of Minors Capuchin

11. *Peter Trigosus*, Spanish by nation, a disciple of *Petrus Sotus*, at first professed in the Society of Jesus, then passing do the Capuchin fathers († 1593, at age of 68). He published the outstanding work: *S. Bonaventurae etc. Summa theologica, wham ex eius in Magistrum Sententiarum scriptis accurate collegit et in hunc ordinem redegit copiosisque commentariis illustravit R. P. F. Petrus Trigosius O. S. F. C., tomus I. Partis I.*, Ad Clementem VIII. Pont. Max., Rome, 1593. — Another edition « purged from the *menda*, of which the previous one had abounded, and also elucidated », as it says in the title, came forth at Lyons in 1616. Only the first tome of the first part, *de Deo uno*, was sent to press, in which large volume in fol., besides the prologue, there are treated of not but 21 distinctions of Sent., Bk. I. Having changed the order of things and having added many other questions or, as he says, *dubia*, he interprets the Seraphic (Doctor), thus, that he nearly always understands him according to the mind of St. Thomas and his school. — That which was wanting in *Trigosus* for the explication of St. Bonaventure's Bk. I, was supplied by another colleague in the same Order, as follows:

12. *Theodorus Foresti*, of Bergamo, Definitor General of his Order and Visitator Apostolic, familiar of (Pope) Urban VIII († 1637), wrote: *Paraphrases, commentaria et disputationes de alma et sanctissima Trinitate iuxta mentem D. Bonaventurae, in quibus praeter diligentem textus et verborum exositionem divinarum litterarum locis ac SS. Patrum assertis perpetuo fere cum D. Thomae assensu Seraphica doctrina illustratur et sustinetur*, Rome at *Iabobus Mascardus'* in 1633, in folio. This, as far as we know, unique edition, abounds in innumerable typographical errors. Though its author is learned, it should cede place to *Trigosus*.

13. *Franciscus (Longus) a Coriolano*, a town of Calabria,*

---

[1] Several similar works, but in manuscripts never sent to press, are extant. Among others cited by Sbaralea in (his) *Supplementum.*, there is *Petrus Paulus Carnata*, of Navarre, (friar) Minor Conventual, whose *Commentaria in quatuor libros Sententiarum iuxta mentem S.*

Bonaventurae, written from 1605-1608, are conserved in the library of the Sacro Convento (now the Municipal), at Assisi.

* *Trans. note*: Now known as *Corigliano Càlabro*, to the west of Rossano, on the Ionian littoral.

Italy, († 1625): *Summa theologiae ad instar Summae D. Thomae ex operibus D. Bonaventurae compacta variisque annotationibus illustrata*, Rome 1622, on the Vatican presses and at the expenses of the Camera Apostolica. As is established by the Bull of Gregory XV, which was printed at the beginning of *Breviarium chronologicum*, written by the same author, this Summa, was arranged in seven tomes in folio, but only the first tome came forth.

14. *Ioannes Maria Zamorra*, from Udine (Italy), who passed away at Verona in 1622, published, besides very many opuscula on the B. V. M., eight tracts or theological commentaries, in which he strove to settle all the controversies between St. Thomas, St. Bonaventure and Scotus. They were printed at Venice by *Iacobus Sarzina* in 1626, in fol..

15. *Bonaventura Lignonensis*, a Frenchman, wrote: *Bonaventura Bonaventurae, scil. Bonaventura et Thomas, sive Summa theologica ex omnibus fere SS. Thomae et Bonaventurae placitis concinnata, inter quos si aliquando videatur esse dissensio, aut benigna explicatione componitur, aut problematica disputatione ventilatur, difficultatesque omnes in scholis purlimum agitari solitae de mente illorum Sanctorum resolvuntur*; at Lyons, at the expenses of *Laurentius Annisson*, 1653-1673, 3 tomes in fol..

The same also wrote a philosophical course according to the mind of St. Bonaventure, which whether it was ever printed, we know not.

16. *Marcellus Regiensis*, a Frenchman: *Summa Seraphica, in qua S. Bonaventurae Seraphica theologia, per eius in Magistrum Sent. Commentarii libros dispersa, dilucide est enodata et accurate redacta in scholae methodum*; Marseille, at *Carolus Brebion* and *Ioannem Penot*, 1669, 2 tomes in fol..

17. *Marcus a Baudunio*, a Frenchman: *Paradicus theologicus unius et trium doctorum, Angelici, Seraphici, Subtilis, horumque conciliatoris fonte irriguus*: Lyons, at *Ioannes Molin*, 1663. The author strives always to draw these three Scholastic authors to the same sentence, but not always felicitously.

The same also wrote a *Compendium theologiae, tam speculativae quam practicae*, Lyons, 1673, 4 tomes in 8 vo.; and a philosophical course of lesser moment, entitled: *Paradisus philosphicus unius ac trium doctorum Angelici, Seraphici et Subtilis horumque conciliatoris fonte irriguus*; Marseille, 1654, in fol., and again in 1664, in 4 vo..

18. *Gaudentius* (Bontempi), of Brixen († 1672, at age of 69), after whose death his disciple, Fr. *Ioannes Franciscus Durantis*, of Brixen, published Bontempi's monstrously weightly work: *Palladium theologicum, seu tota theologica scholastica, ad intimam mentem D. Bonaventurae*; Lyons, at the expenses of *Arnandus, Petrus Bordete* etc., 1667, 7 tomes in fol.. This work excels in erudition, orders the doctrine of St. Bonaventure according to the method of Aquinas' Summa and nearly always interprets (it) according to the mind of the same, as Fr. *Bartholomaeus a Barberiis* notes in the preface to his own *Cursus theologicus*.

19. *Bartholomaeus a Barberiis*, an Italian, from Castrovetro, a member of the Province of Lombardy, versed, as he himself says, more than all others, in daily reading of the works of St. Bonaventure for 15 years, and very often a more faithful interpreter of the Seraphic (Doctor), published: *Cursus theologicus ad mentem Seraph. Doct. Bonaventurae*, arranged in 2 tomes; Lyons

at the expenses of *Franciscus Comba*, 1687, in fol.. These two tomes are of light weight. This edition was besmirched with intolerable typographical errors, of which the author, « weeping with the greatest shame », begs (pardon) from the reader. We have not seen the other Parisian edition of the same year, cited by others.

He also wrote a philosophical course according to the mind of St. Bonaventure, entitled: *Flores et fructus Seraphici ex Seraphico paradiso excerpti*, Lyons, at the expenses of *Laurentius Arnaud* etc., 1681. This index appeared again, with not a few changes, in the Parisian edition of the Opera Omnia S. Bonav.. tome XV.

Likewise: *Glossa seu Summa, ex omnibus S. Bonaventurae ex positionibus in sacram Scripturam exacte collecta et secundum ordinem biblicum concinnata*; at Lyons, 1681, 4 tomes in fol.. — A work, very useful for preachers.

20. *Franciscus Maria a Bruxellis*: *Theologica Seraphica*, at Ghent, in 1715, 4 tomes in 4 vo.; mentioned as a juicy work and one accommodated to praxis.

Several other works, elaborated by Capuchin fathers to illustrate the doctrine of St. Bonaventure, were never sent to press. Among others, there are mentioned by Sbaralea in his own *Supplementum*, the *Commentaria in quatuor libros Sent. ad mentem S. Bonaventurae*, by Fr. *Marcus Antonius Galitius*, of the Order of Minors General († 1665), which is conserved at Brixen in the Convent of the Capuchin fathers. Likewise, Commentaries on the same books by Fr. *Mauritius Gamborinus* in their Convent of the Immaculate Conception, at Genoa.

Authors of the Order of Minors Recollect

21. *Matthias Hauzeur*, of Verviers (Belgium), twice Provincial of the Prov. of Flanders and author of many polemical works, very versed in the doctrine of St. Augustine, whose works he redacted into a compendium and explicated in the book: *Anatomia Augustiniana*, 2 tomes in fol., 1644. He wrote: *Collatio totius theologiae inter maiores nostros F. Alexandrum Alensem, patriacham theologorum, Doctorem irrefragabilem, S. Bonaventuram, Doctorem Seraphicum, F. Ioannem Duns Scotum, Doctorem Subtilem. Ad mentem S. Augustini: sub Magisterio Christi; interiore, per Gratiam; exteriore, per Ecclesiam*. On the presses of the same Province (of Flanders), in the Convents of Liège and Namur, in the years 1646-1652, 2 tomes in fol.. — In a laconic style, he contracted the Summa of Alexander and the Commentaries of St. Bonaventure and Scotus into a compendium and explicated very many questions, and strove to conciliate their sentences among themselves and with St. Augustine, not without some acumen. The defect of the order and method obscures somewhat the copiousness of the doctrine and genius.

Other theological books, by members of the Order of St. Francis of the Observance, written by its three families in these last three centuries, follow for the most part either Scotus, and/or none of the Scholastics, and only sometimes make mention of St. Bonaventure, among whom there merits mention, the *Theologia dogmatica-scholastica* published by Fr. Henno, of the Province of Flanders.

There also merit to be mentioned here, two books published for the Sixth Centenary of St. Bonaventure, though they deal with the doctrine of St. Bonaventure in general, not particularly with (his) Commentary, namely: *Seraphicus Doctor S. Bonaventura in oecumenicis Catholicae Ecclesiae Conciliis cum Patribus dogmata definiens, disquisitio historico-theologica*, by Fr. *Ludovicus a Castrophanio*, Ord. Min. Obs. — and a work written in Italian: Della vera filosofia e delle

dottrine filosofiche del Seraphico Dottore S. Bonaventura, Studi del P. Marcellino da Civezza M. O., Genoa, at the Tipografia della Gioventù, 1874.

§ 8. *A listing of the Editions of this Commentary, which were printed.* There are not a few editions of this kind, but the first are incomplete, not all exhibit the four books. Of these, we shall speak first in an orderly manner.

Incomplete Editions

1. The Second Book of the Commentary, in fol. parv., arranged in two columns, came forth at *Tarvisio* (Friuli prov., Italy) in the year 1477, by *Hermanum Lichtenstein.*

The *incipit* on fol. 1 r., with sign A at the bottom of the page:[1] *Solummodo || hoc inveni, quod Deus fe||cerit hominem rectum || et ipse se infinitis etc..* The *desinit* on fo. 333 v., col. II: *Religiosi patris Bonaventure ordinis minorum || veritatis theologice professoris eximii. sacreque || apostolice sedis cardinalis super secundum sen||tentiarum scriptum finit. Anno salutis nostre || MCCCCLXXVII, per magistrum Hermanum || lichtenstein Taruisii feliciter impressum.*

Then, there follows: *tabula eiusdem libri* (which fills 2 1/2 folios). This edition was compared by us with the Vatican (edition).

2. Likewise, the Second Book of the Commentary in fol. parv., in two columns, came forth *at Venice* in 1477 by *Theodoricum de Reynsburch et Reynaldum de Novimagio socios.*

The *incipit* on fol. 1, with the sign a 2: *Viri excellentissimi artium et sacre || theologie divi monarce summique pro||fessoris: super 2° sententiarum domini Bonaven||ture minorum ex ordine opus praeclarissi||mum feliciter incipit: Soulmmodo hoc inveni* etc. The *desinit* on fol. 335 v., col. 1: *Religiosi patris Bonaventure ordinis || Minorum veritatis theologie professoris || eximii: sacreque apostolice sedis Cardinalis || super secundum sententiarum scriptum finit. || Per eccellentissimum sacre theologie do||ctorum magistrum Thomam penketh angl-||cum ordinis fratum hermitarum sancti Au||gustini in famosissimo studio Patavi||no ordinarie legentem maxima cum diligentia || emendatum. Anno salutis nostre, MCCCC||LXXVII. per Theodoricum de Reynsburch || et Reynaldum de Novimagio socios || Venetiis feliciter impressum.* — Then, there follows a table to the same book (which fills 2 1/2 folios).

This edition was compared by us with the Vatican (edition).

3. 4. The First Book of the Commentary in 4 vo., in two columns, was published at Brixen in 1490 by Father *Farfengo.* On fol. 1 r.: *Prologus. Reverendissimi patris: et domini sancti Bo||naventure septimi generalis minorum cardi||nalis. et episcopi: catholicique Doctoris Pa||risiensis Theologi. super primo sententiarum opus || seraphicum feliciter incipit.* — *Profunda fluviorum* etc. There precedes a *tabula quaestionum* of 6 folios. The *desinit: Reverendissimi patris et domini sancti Bonaventure septimi generalis minorum cardina||lis et episcopi catholici doctoris parisiensis. Super primo sententiarum opus seraphi||cum. Accuratissime correctivum* (sic!) *atque emendacitum* (sic!). *Maximaque diligentia ac studio || Brixie per presbyterum Baptistam de farfengo Feliciter. Impressum. Anno domini || MCCCCLXXXX. die vero vigesimo menis Octobris.* — Then the crest of the printer.

This edition was compared by us with the Vatican (edition), but in our exemplar two folios on dd. 35, 36 & 37 were missing. Among all the editions of the First Book this, more than all, represents the same text, which the ancient codices have, with which it nearly always agrees. But it abounds in innumerable and great *menda*, which seem to have arisen partly from badly formed *sigla*, partly from the corruption of the codex, partly and chiefly from the negligence of the typographer.

Fr. Bonelli cites another Brixen edition of the Commentary for the First Book, printed in 1496, which is said to be conserved in the library of the University of Paris.

5. A First Book of the Commentary, without place or year (of printing). According to Panzer (VI. 99. 210.) and Hain (I. n. 3536.) this edition was printed by *Eustadio Reyser* and is described by Hain thus: « F. I. a: () Rofunda fluviorum scru||tatus est et abscodi||ta produxit in lucem. ver||bum istud quod sumptum || est ex iob. XXVIII. diligen|| etc. *Expl. f. 165. a. col. 2. 1. 12:* generationes seculi seculorum. Amen. *F. 164. a:* Sequuntur questiones seraphici doctoris || domini bonaventure cardinalis super primo li||bro sententiarum. Et primo quatuor questiones preambule secundum quadruplex genus cause. Terminat tab. 16 co. I. 1. 29. s. l. a. et typ. n. f. mal. g. ch. s. f. c. et pp. n. 2 col. 62. l. 165. ff (Eustadii Reyser.) ».

6. We have found another edition of the First Book, without place (of printing), but with the year 1480 in the Bibliothèque National at Paris (Inventaire D. 1284), noted down by one of our collaborators, thus: *Questiones super primum Sententiarum S. Domini Bonaventure*, in gothic letters; at the end of 1480. — We leave to others to discern, whether this edition differs from the preceding ones.

7. Likewise, another edition of the First Book, conserved at London (in the Library of the British Museum, 3833. f.), was noted thus: Eichstadt, 1478, in fol. of two columns of 62 lines. The *incipit: Profunda fluviorum scrutatus est* etc. At the end, there follows a *tabula: Questiones domini Bonaventure.*

Complete Editions of the Four Books of this Commentary

8. One complete, without place, year and name of typographer, in three tomes, in fol., is mentioned by *Ioannes a S. Antonio* in his *Bilbiotheca universa Franciscana*, tome I, p. 156, which is perhaps the same as that, of which Panzer (IV. 99. 210.) speaks.

9. Another is cited by Mazzuchello, *degli Scrittori d'Italia*, tome II, part 4, p. 2360, as published at Strasbourg (France) in 1489, of which Sbaralea speaks (*Supplementum.*, p. 146, ch. 2): « This work is first said to have come forth at Strasbourg in 1489 ». — Since the editions under nn. 8 and 9, have never come into our hands, we leave to others the judgement, whether they are truly extant.

10-13. Four editions from the celebrated typographic shop of Koberger and/or of his associates. All these have two tomes in folio with two columns (of text). The *first*, though it does not indicate the year of printing, seems to be from 1491, as seems can be argued from the reply-letter of *Nicolaus Tinctor* to *Ioannes Beckenhaub*,[2] of Mainz, dated from Bamberg, March 2, 1491, and from another by *Iacobus Wimpfling*, of Sélestadt (in the Alsace), likewise dated 1491. Though it was very accurately described by Hain (tom. I, n. 3540), let a few (of his words) on this edition suffice, here: *Perlustratio in lib. quatuor sententiarum.* On fol. 1 v.: *Ioannes Beckenhab, Moguntinus, evan-*

---

[1] We have not abbreviated the *sigla* nor the compendiary notes.

[2] He was a cleric, who labored very much to publish new books, first at Strasbourg, then as an assistant to *Ioannes Koberger.*

-gelice theolgie summo doctori domino Niccolao Tinctoris de Guntzenhau||sen imperialis ecclesie Bambergensis praedicatori salutem etc.. A song by the same, in praise of each author, excerpts this letter, in which (there are) these verses: *Quo libri impressor Nurnberge Antonius ipse || Koberger tendat post sua fata precor.*

There follows the response of *Tinctor* from Bamberg, March 2, 1491, on fol. 3 r.: *Celebratissimi patris domini bonaventure || ordinis minorum artis divine summi discusso||ris: et apostolice sedis episcopi cardinalis prolo||gus in primum librum sententiarum.* The *explicit* on fol. 198. recto, col. 2: *Amen.* Then there are six folios of a *tabula*. The other books begin similarly, but the Fourth Book, the *explicit* of which is on fol. 264 v., has at the end: *Concludit epilogando breviter que in hoc libro et || omnibus precedentibus determinata sunt || etc..* On fol. 265 r. there is the letter of *Iacobus Wimplfing Sletstatensis* to all studious in theology, dated from Nürnberg, 1491: *Tabula super libros senten||tiarum cum Bonavnetura.* On fol. 2. r.: *Ioannis bekenhaub moguntini in scripta divi || bonaventure cum textu sententiarum tabula, quam si || etc..* On fol. 92 v.: *tabula super textum sententiarum cum Bonaventura finis. || In quam sparsim viciola quaedam adnotavi in Bona||ventura et lombardo suis locis emendanda etc..* On fol. 93 r.: *Sequuntur varii articuli erronei omnium pe||ne facultatum. In anglia et parisius studiose et autori||tative condemnati cum revocationbius eorundem.* The *explicit* is on fo. 103 v.: *Deo gratias.*

The *second* edition, differing little from the first, at the end of the Fourth Book on the Sentences, has the year of printing thus: *quartus Liber Sententiarum cum disputatis Ce||lebratissimi patris domini Bonaventure ordinis || minorum. per Antonium Kobergere Nurnberge in||presus Anno domini Millesimo quingentesimo. fi||nit feliciter.* — It is accurately described by Hain I. N. 3543.

The *third*, which is, after a manner, similar to the second, was published in 1510 and the expense of *Antonius Koberger*, with the help of *Iacobus Sacon*. For at the end of the Fourth Book one reads thus: *Quarti divi Bonaventure sententiarum libri dilucidatio adest || qui veluti et praecedentes nunc ab infinitis ferme quibus scatuit er||roribus corruptis (?) secundum exemplaria dudum per pie memorie Re||verendum sacre theologie parisienem doctorem profundissimum fratrem Stephanum brulifer ordinis minorum methis pro tunc eiusdem sera||phici doctoris scripta legentem: edita. Et ad debitam correctionis li||mam summis cum laboribus redacta. Pro dicti sancti Bonaventu||re honore et omnium studiosorum utilitate novissime impressus est. ||, sumtibus (sic!) atque impensis Anthonii Kobergis civis et incole Nurenbergensis. Industria quoque Iacobi sacon artis impressorie magistri so||lertissimi in lugdunensi galle metropoli civitate auspici fini datus. || Anno millesimo quigentessimo decimo vigestina Augusti.* * — Of this *Iacobus Sacon*, the typographic mark or crest of whom is conspicuous at the end of each book, Fr. Bonelli[1] says, that he was a typographer of Lyons, « the works of whom the celebrated Cobergerus of Nuremberg used for this (reason) in (his) Emporium ». — This edition, in regard to the text (received), recedes more from the ancient codices than the edition of 1491.

The *fourth* edition, also differing very little from the former, namely only in the initial letters and the words arranged on the pages, is marked with the same typographic sign of *Iacobus Sacon*. The first tome of this edition, comprising the Commentary on Sent., Bks. I & II,

we have in hand, in which we detest the printing. Yet, as Fr. Fidelis testifies, who saw the entire thing, it came forth at Lyons in 1515 by the same *Iacobus Sacon*. Sbaralea testifies to the same in his own *Supplementum*..

The second, third, and fourth editions also exhibit the letter of *Ioannes Beckenhaub*, with those verses: « whither the printer of the book at Nürnberg, Anthonius Koberger himself, tends after his life, I pray », and also the response of *Nicolaus Tinctor de Guntzenhausen*, and also the letter of *Iacobus Wimpfling Sletstatensis* to all studious for theology, yet with the date changed, by which these letters are shown to be written. For the first edition exhibits the same letter of *Iacobus Wimpfling* as written at Nürnberg in 1491; the second, as given from Nürnberg in 1499. The third, at the end of the Fourth Book, thus: « from Lyons, the most noble city of Gaul, in the year 1490 ».

These four editions also contain the Sentences of Lombard, and the *dubia* of St. Bonaventure on the text of Master (Peter), removed from their place and abbreviated and changed, in regard to (their) titles, they place on the margin of the text of Lombard. — If faith is to be given to the rubric placed at the end of the Fourth Book in the third edition, Fr. Stephan Brülifer corrected the text of these editions. But since he had died before 1500, this cannot be understood, except of the first and/or, perhaps, the second edition. Nor is it improbable, that Johann Beckenhaub, when he cared for the first edition, used a *commentarius reportatus* in correcting the text, such that Brülifer was not at hand for adorning this edition. — Otherwise, the edition of the year 1491 responds more to the reading of the ancient codices than the following ones, which have been changed in some (things), and/or entirely without having consulted the manuscripts and/or employed the codices of the 15th century.

Other ancient editions, but after Koberger's, published in Germany, France and Venice, manifestly follow very often, in regard to the text, one and/or another of these editions, whether by simply reprinting it, or by arbitrarily changing the text in not a few passages.

14. The edition of *Kilianus Piscatoris*, at Freiburg (im Breisgau), as it seems, printed in 1493, in 2 tomes, in fol., with 2 columns, manifestly repeats the first edition of Koberger. The verses of Johann Beckenhaub indicating the printer, read thus: « whither the printer of the book at *Freiburg, Kilian the Fisherman* himself, tends after his life, I pray ». In this edition the name of *Beckenhaub* is written *Bekenhub*, and *Guntzenhausen* is written *Guntzenhusen*; the reply-letter of Nicolaus Tinctor is dated from Bamberg, May 2, 1493, from which it is licit to suspect, that the edition was printed in the same year of 1493. The inscription on fol. 1 is: *Perlustratio Sancti Bonaventure || in Primum librum Sententiarum.* On fol. 3 r.: *Celebratissimi patris domini bonaventure or||dinis minorum artis divine summi discussoris: et || apostolice sedis episcopi Cardinalis prologus in pri||mum librum sententiarum.* This (edition) is accurately described by Hain under n. 3541.

By many others, there is mentioned another edition of this year, 1493, printed at Bamberg. But this one does not seem to differ from the edition of *Kilianus Piscator*. And it seems that an error has arisen from this, that the letter of Tinctor, placed at the beginning, cites this place and year. — Likewise, fictitious, seems the edition made at Leipzig in 1498, in fol., of which Mich. Maittair speaks in (his), *Annal. typogr.*, tome I, p. 556, and many others, together with Fr. Bonelli. None of these described this edition, nor did Panzer or Hain see it. Herr Dr. Krehl, prefect

---

[1] *Prodromus*, col. 334.

* *Trans. note*: which can be rendered in English thus: « The delucidation of the fourth book of sentences of the divine Bonaventure is at hand which as also the preceding one (has) now, from firmly infinite corrupted (readings) by which it abounds with errors, been published according to the exemplars by the Reverend Parisian Doctor, of good memory, Stephan Brülifer of the Order of Minors now lecturing by the methods of the same

Seraphic Doctor. And redacted according to the due limit of correction with the greatest labors. For the honor of the said Saint Bonaventure and the utility of all the studious has been lately printed. at the costs and expenses of Anthony Koberg (sic) citizen and inhabitant of Nuremberg. By the industry, too, of Jacob Sacon, most adroit master of the art of printing in the metropolitan City of Gaul, Lyons, given an auspicious end. In the one thousand five-hundredth year, on the twentieth of August ».

of the library of the University of Leipzig, in virtue of his most frequently demonstrated kindness to us, has communicated to us, that, having employed all diligence, he could find no certain knowledge of this edition, and that it is scarcely doubtful, that it is fictitious.

15-16. The Parisian edition at *Franciscus Regnault's* (typography), in 1522, in 8 vo., follows the text of the Koberger edition. Another Parisian (edition) was published in 1688.

17. At Venice in 1562, by order of the Minister General of the whole Seraphic Order of St. Francis, Fr. *Franciscus Zamora*, and on the presses of *Franciscus Sansovinus*, 4 tomes in 4 vo.. To the first tome there has been affixed that large *tabula*, on the 4 books of the Sentences, made by *Ioannes Beckenhaub*, of Mainz. At its end, there is added: « this alphabetical *tabula* has been revised and corrected by the Rev. Fr. friar *Iulianus Urceanus*, Ord. min. of the Observance, of the province of Brixen ». — After the folio exhibiting the title, there follows the dedicatory letter of Fr. *Aloysius Puteus* to the Minister General *Franciscus Zamora*, written at Trent (where its author assisted at the Ecumenical Council), Sept. 8, 1562, in which not a few (things) worthy of mention occur. In this letter, the author grieves over the common disregard of that true Scholastic theology in the schools of the Order, the cause of the loss of which he attributes « both to the unattainable height of the understanding of the *doctor Subtilis*, and to negligence in the studies of the Sacred scriptures ». Then, he says: « On which account, from this, to us, grievingly seeking and considering (it) in mind, that there come as a remedy to so great a danger, behold you have come at an opportune (time), who ... yourself have published, as manysoever in the observantine family profess theology, to prefer for your scholastics the books of the seraphic father, Bonaventure, vulgarly called *sententiarii*, nevertheless, with the doctrine of the most incisive Scotus, meanwhile, commanded to be valued by no means the less » etc.. There follows: « The letter to the lector fr. *Bonifacius de Ragusio*, O. Min., Guardian of the Sacred Mont of Sion, which celebrates the praise of the doctrine of St. Bonaventure, and which is subscribed: "in Her ecumenical and general Council of Trent, under the eighth day of Sept., 1562" ». — Then, there is another preface to the reader concerning the same argument, dated at Venice in the same year. — In the title, there is read: « Purged from nearly innumerable *menda* and decorated, lately now, with annotations both of things memorable and of all the passages of Scripture and of the Doctors, in the margin ». — Yet, this edition exhibits the text of the first Koberger edition, with only a few passages changed and (that) not always felicitously; it also places the *dubia* in the margin of the text of the Master, with the same edition. But, it stood out in this, that in the margin it indicated the passages, whence many authorities were taken.

18. At Venice at *Georgius Angelerius'* (typography), in 1573, 4 tomes in 4 vo., with the recognition of friar *Ioannes Balainius Andrius*, Conventual Franciscan, who also adjoined a five-fold index and dedicated his edition to Cardinal Felici Peretto de Monte Alto, who, afterwards, was Pope Sixtus V.

19. At Venice, in 1580, without the name of the typographer, 4 tomes in 8 vo., with the recognition of master *Angelus Rocch.*, O. S. A.. This edition follows entirely the edition of *Balainius*; it again separates the same *dubia* from the text of Master (Peter), but does not put them, as the codices (do), after the Questions, but immediately after the Division of the Text, having changed their titles. In this very change, the preceding and following editions follow the Roman (edition) of 1569.

In regard to the recension of the text, both editions convene much with the Roman edition of 1569, of which we now shall speak.

20-22. At Rome in the years 1569, 1573, 1580, at (the typography) of the *haeredes Antonio Bladii*, 4 tomes in 4 parvo. The title of the 1569 edition is: *Scriptum d. Bonaventurae ... in quatuor libros Sententiarum P. Lombardi. Ex antiquissimis exemplaribus nunc primum studio F. Antonii Posii a Monteilcino ordin. Min. Conv. ab innumeris pene erroribus emendatum, singulis quaestionibus argumentis adiectis, collationeque locorum atque controversiarum d. Thom., Io. Scot. et S. Bonav. in albis apposita illustratum. Munificentia ... S. N. D. Pii V. nec non solertia congreg. Fr. Capuccinorum, praesertim fr. Hieronymi Pistoriensis novissime impressum.** — It begins with the dedicatory letters of *Antonius Posius* to St. Pius V; it also exhibits the *tabula* of *Ioannes Beckenhaub*.

This edition passed nearly whole into the Vatican (edition), both in regard to the recension of the text, and in regard to the summary and marginal notes, with only a few (things) added and/or changed in the Vatican (edition).

23. At Venice in the year 1611, 4 tomes in fol., on the presses of *H. Scotus*.

24-28. In five editions of the *Opera Omnia S. Bonaventurae*, namely the Vatican, the Lyonnaise, the Mainzer, the Venetian, (and) the Parisian.

CHAPTER II
On Our Edition of the First Book of St. Bonaventure's Commentaries

§ 1. *On the codices and editions, which we have used in reforming the text of the First Book of the Commentaries, and on the method, observed by us in this labor, we refer these (things):*

Very rarely were the four books of this Commentary written and united thus, that one whole work appears from them, but ordinarily the single books are found (to be) written one in hand and other in volume, and/or two books conjoined as one in one volume. Hence it came to be, that in many libraries very many exemplars of one and/or the other of the books of these Commentaries are found, but none of the other of the three, and/or such that the codex of one book be optimum and ancient, but the codices of the others mediocre. It also happens, that for each book the number and excellence of the codices differ. Whence, just as in reforming the text of the four books we have had to use diverse codices of diverse libraries, so too must we speak of each codex singly in the Prolegomena to each Book. Publishing here the list of codices comprising the *First* Book, which (codices) Fr. Fidelis inspected and annotated, we place in the first place, according to the alphabetical order of the libraries, the codices, from which, when compared with the Vatican (edition), we have gathered the variant readings, then all the others. But, since this edition was reprinted at diverse times and places by several associates, whether ordinary or extraordinary, and the already very many codices, before the variant readings of all were gathered, would have had to be designated with certain alphabetical letters, it would have been exceedingly difficult for us, to express in an alphabetical order of letters the affinity of single codices and/or families. Hence, we made no fixed choice of such signs. — All the codices, gathered, are whole ones, excepting those few, of which the contrary is noted in the list itself.

---

* *Trans. note*: which can be rendered into English thus: « The writing of the divine Bonaventure ... on the four books of Sentences of Peter Lombard. From the most ancient exemplars now emendated for the first time by the study of Fr. *Antonius Posius a Monteilcino*, ord. Min. Conv., from nearly innumerable errors, with arguments adjoined to each question, and illustrated with an apposite comparison of passages and controversies of the divine Thomas, John Scotus and St. Bonaventure. By the munificence ... of our holy lord Pius V and also the adroitness of the congregation of Capuchin Fathers, especially of Fr. *Hieronymus Pistoriensis*, just now published ».

SYLLABUS OF MANUSCRIPTS

WHICH CONTAIN

THE COMMENTARIES OF SAINT BONAVENTURE

ON THE FIRST BOOK OF THE SENTENCES

I.
Codices compared by us with the text of the Vatican edition

1. *At Assisi* in Umbria (Italy), in the library of the Convent of St. Francis (now the Municipal), cod. N. 42, membr. in fol., of the end of the 13th century. On fol. 1 v. an ancient hand has prefaced: *Primus fatris Bonaventure*. The *incipit*: *Profunda fluviorum scrutatus est*. The *desinit* as in the published versions: *in Christo Iesu, in omnes generationes seculi seculorum. Amen.* — Splendidly written, but not without many *menda*, because it was not proof-read, which was customarily done in that age after the codex (was) written. In our edition, (marked) with the sign (of) the letter **A**.

2. *At Bamberg* (Germany), in the Public library, cod. B. III. 42., chart., saec. XV, in fol.. At the beginning there is written: *Prooemium sancti Bonaventure*. Then: *Profunda fluviorum*. The *desinit* (is) on fol. 243 v.. — Though it be of a more recent date, yet, it convenes sufficiently with the older codices; nevertheless, it has especially in the more difficult passages many readings proper to itself and sometimes useful. (In our edition, marked) with the sign **Y**.

3. *At Bologna* (Italy), in the library of the Collegio degli Spagnoli, cod. 35, membr. in fol., of the end of the 13th century. At the beginning, another hand has prefaced: *Primus Bonaventure*; the *incipit* and *desinit* as in the the published versions. — It has been inspected by us only in the more difficult passages. (In our edition, marked) with the sign **kk**.

4. *At Kraków* (Poland), in the University library, cod. 1246. D. D. XIV. 4, chart. in fol., saec. XV. The *incipit* on fol. 1 r., in col. 1: *Profunda fluviorum*. The *desinit* on fol. 274. v, col. 2, as in the published versions; to which there is added: *Explicit scriptum Bonaventure super primum sententiarum per me Petrum de Novagora 1474*. — A good codex, which follows nearly always the more ancient codex related under the following number, such that they pertain to the same family; in the construction of propositions it often departs from other codices, so as to render the Latin speech more correct and/or elegant; besides, it does not rarely proffer readings, which are worthy of attention. (In our edition, marked with), the sign **aa**.

5. *At Kraków* (Poland), cod. 1252. A. A. XI. 16, membr. in 4 vo., of the end of the 13th century. The *incipit* is on fo. 1. r., in col. 1. The *desinit* on fo. 160 v., in col. 1: *Explicit liber primus.* Then there follows *tabulae distinctionum*, at the end of which another hand of the 14th century wrote: *Bonaventura super primum sententiarum.* — It convenes nearly entirely with the preceding (edition). (In our edition, marked) with the sign **bb**.

6. *At Florence*, in the Biblioteca Nazionale, cod. C. 6. 209., membr. in fol. parvo, written entirely in two columns. The *incipit* is on fol. 2 r.. After the end, there follows a *tabula quaestionum*, the end of which is: *utrum Spiritus sanctus*

procedat a Patre mediante Filio. Amen. Then another hand proceeds: *Finito libro referamus gratiam Christo.* — *Per gratiam Trini finiunt capitula libri.* — *Primus est certe Bonaventure doctus a Patre ... Anno Domini millesimo ducentesimo octuagesimo quinto, die luneXXXIII mensis septembris indictione XII.* — As Fr. Fidelis a Fanna says in his review, which he made of this codex, one could doubt, that this hand is of the 13th century; yet the codex is of the 13th century, whence one is not to argue over the hand. It is one of those codices, which are of better note. (In our edition, marked) with the sign. **F**.

7. In the same library, cod. D. 5. 206, membr. in fol., saec. XIII. On fol. 1 v. an ancient hand has written: *Primus Bonaventure completus et bonus commentarius.* The *incipit* is on fol. 3 r., in col. 1. The *desinit*, just as the editions. Thereafter, the first hand has added: *Explicit liber primus Bonaventure.* — It abounded in many *menda*, but was corrected very frequently by a later hand. It exhibits, together with codd. aa and bb a notable addition to d. 27, p. I, q. 2. (In our edition, marked) with sign **G**.

8. In the same library, cod. D. 5. 207, membr. in fol., of the end of the 14th century. The *incipit* on fol. 3. r., col. 1: *Profunda fluviorum* etc.. The *desinit*, just as the editions. — It is to be numbered among the good codices. (In our edition, marked) with the sign **H**.

9. In the same library, cod. I. 7. 45, membr. in fol. min., saec. XIV. The *incipit* on fol. 2. r., col. 1: *Profunda fluviorum* etc.. The *desinit*: *in omnes generationes seculi seculorum. Amen, Amen, Amen, Amen.* — The codex was written by many hands. It exhibits readings not rarely differing from other codices, which at one or another time have been received by us. (In our edition, it has been marked) with the sign **I**.

10. In the same library, cod. C. 6. 208, membr. in fol., saec. XIII. The *incipit* is on fol. 2. r. col. 1. The *desinit* on the 3rd fol. before the last, in col. 2: *Explicit liber primus.* There follows a *tabula quaestionum*, the last (words) of which (are): *utrum teneamur conformari in volito. Explicit totum.* — The codex is a sufficiently good one, corrected by various hands. (In our edition, marked) with the sign **ff**.

11. *At Florence*, in the Biblioteca Medicea Laurenziana, plut. XXV. dext. cod. 2, membr. in fol. saec. XIII. The *incipit* is on fol. 4. r., in col. 1. The *desinit* on fol. 186. There follows a copious *tabula* of things and questions, even on the text. — Very often it is discrepant with all the other codices, especially in adding glosses, which, however, sometimes are of no value. (In our edition, marked) with the sign **K**.

12. In the same library, cod. L XX. Mediceo-Fesulan., membr. in fol. near the middle of the 14th century. The *incipit* is on fol. 1 r., in col. 1. The *desinit* on fol. 136 v. in col. 2. Afterwards, there is added by the first hand: *Explicit primus*

liber fratris Bonaventue super primum librum sententiarum. Deo gratias. There follows a *tabula*, which runs up to fol. 141. v., arranged in 3 columns. — The correction of the codex was made by the *first* and/or a nearly contemporary hand, only in regard to the first part; but corrections by diverse hands of a more recent century, are found both in the first, and the second part. It excels in clear writing and is to be numbered among the codices of good note. Sign. **ee**.

13. *At Leipzig* (Germany), in the (University) library (Paulina collection), cod. 491, membr. in fol., from the beginning of the 14th century. The *incipit* on fol. 1 r., in col. 1: *Profunda fluriorum.* At the end: *Explicit primus liber sententiarum Bonaventure fratris minoris.* Afterwards, there follows a *tabula quaestionum,* at whose foot there is again repeated: *Explicit liber primus fratris Bonaventure de Ordine fratrum minorum, sed Magister Petrus Lombardus, Episcopus Parisiensis, erat auctor principalis.* — It is to be judged among the best codices. Peculiar to it is that in several additions etc. it agrees with the codices of Oxford, below. (In our edition, marked) with the sign. **Z**.

14. *At Milan* (Italy), in the Biblioteca Ambrosiana, cod. I. 95. infer., bequeathed by the *Bernardinus Ferrari*, on March 9, 1830, but once belonging to *Franciscus Petrarcha*, the most famous poet. The *incipit* on fol. 3 r., on the upper margin: *Sancti Spiritus adsit mihi gratia. Amen, Amen, Amen.* Then: *Profunda fluviorum* etc.. The *desinit* on fol. 194, v., col. 1: *Hec sunt scripta fratris Bonaventure supra primum sententiarum.* There follows an *indiculus quaestionum* confected by another hand of the 13th century. — The codex has been entirely written, during the life of Bonaventure. A good codex, it is distinguished by an effort to emend the not so Latin expressions and uses, and especially at the end of the questions, it very often uses other words for the conclusion. (In our edition, marked) with the sign **V**.

15. *At Münich* (Germany), in the Royal library, C. L. M. 8079, chart. in fol., saec. XV, comprises only the doubts on the text of the Lord Bonaventure on the four books of the Sentences, as is read on fol. 241, r., in upper margin. Then, the *incipit* in col. 1: *Cupientes aliquid de penuria* etc. *Sed queritur de hoc quod dicit: opus agere presumpsimus; sed presumptio est peccatum.* The *desinit* on fol. 279, r., col. 1: *in omnes generationes seculi seculorum. Amen. Deo gratias. Explicit conscriptum domini Bonaventure circa primum de dubitationibus litteralibus.* — It contains only doubts on the text of Master (Peter). (In our edition, marked) with the sign **dd**.

16. In the same library, cod. lat. 14086, membr. in fol., of the end of the 13th century. The *incipit* and *desinit* are as in the published versions. — Prescinding from the many omissions and *menda,* which are commonly found in codices not well corrected, it exhibits the genuine text. (In our edition, marked) with the sign. **W**.

17. In the same library, cod. lat. 18344., chart. in fol., saec. XV. It is prefaced with a *tabula distinctionum,* then the *incipit*: *Profunda fluviorum.* The *desinit* is on fol. 287 v., in col. 2. — It agrees very often with the ancient codices, but, glossing, it both adds several (things), and strives to emend slightly incongruous expressions. (In our edition, marked) with the sign **X**.

18. *At Monte Cassino* (Italy), in the Monastery library, cod. membr. in fol., saec. XIII, sign. 398. 00., alias 252. On fol. 1 r. a later hand as prefaced: *D. Bonaventura in primum librum sententiarum.* And a yet more recent hand has subjoined at the foot of the same folio: *Thomas in primo sententiarum.* The *incipit*: *Profunda fluviorum* etc.. The *desinit*: *Explicit liber primus.* There follows an index of questions. The codex (is) ancient and good. Sometimes it proffers more exquisite readings. Sign **M**.

19. *At Modena* (Italy), in the Biblioteca Atestina, cod. membr. in fol., saec. XIII, noted as num. 974. VII. I. 14. The *incipit* on fol. 1 r., to which a hand of the 15th century, has added: *Primus Bonaventure.* Hence in col. 1: *Profunda fluviorum* etc. At the end, there is read: *Explicit liber primus, qui*

scripsit est benedictus. Finally, there follows a *tabula,* which runs up to distinction XIV. — It has not been totally compared, but only inspected in a few more difficult passages. (In our edition, it is marked) with the sign **ii**.

20. *At Naples,* in the Biblioteca Nazionale, cod. in 4. membr., saec. XIV, written in two columns, sign. VII. D. 28. On fol 1. r., in the upper margin, there is written: *Primus liber sententiarum fratris Bonaventure.* Then in col. 1: *Profunda fluviorum.* The *desinit,* as in all the others. It convenes with the ancient codices. But the writer has omitted many (things), perhaps leaving for an opportune time the spaces in the text, which remain still empty, for things yet to be written. (In our edition, marked) with the sign. **N**.

21. *At Oxford,* in the library of Balliol College, cod. 133, in fol. membr., of the beginning of the 14th century. On fol. 2 v., by an ancient hand: *Bonaventura super primum et secundum.* To the Commentary there is prefaced a *tabula,* arranged in alphabetical order. — The codex (is) of good note, yet exhibits many brief additions proper to itself, which are generally elegant and good. (In our edition, marked) with the sign **O**.

22. *In the same place,* in the library of Lincoln College, cod. 25. membr. in fol., of the end of the 13th century. At the foot of fol. 1, there is read: *Bonaventura super primum et secundum sententiarum.* It has been illustrated with marginal notes. — Marked with many emendations by diverse hands, by reason of which in very many passages it concords with codex O, sometimes even with the Vatican edition. (In our edition, marked) with the sign. **L**.

23. *At Paris,* in the Bibliothèque National, cod. 3085, membr. in fol., of the beginning of the 14th century. From fol. 1 upt to fol. 39, it contains doubts on the text and a *tabula* for the First Book of the Sentences. Then, the *incipit: Profunda fluviorum* etc.. The *desinit,* on fol. 139 v., with the words: *Explicit liber primus de quaestionibus extra litteram.* — This ancient codex has peculiarities both in regard to (its) form, and in regard to (its) matter. In regard to form, because the doubts on the text are not found at the end of each distinction, but are gathered together at the beginning of the volume. The same separation, also distinguished in a double column, was observed by D. Pelitier (Preface to tom. I, Parisian edition, page II) in a certain ancient codex, which first belonged to the Chapter of the church of Reims (cf. below n. 53). In regard to matter, because it strives to promote the clarity of the text, either by adding or changing one or another expression. (In our edition, marked) with the sign **R**.

24. In the same library, cod. 15821, membr. in fol., saec. XIII. The *incipit* on fol. 1 r.: *Profunda fluviorum.* The *desinit* on fol. 113 v., in col. 2: *Explicit liber primus.* (It is) to be numbered among the good codices. (In our edition, marked) with the sign **S**.

25. In the same library, cod. 17480, in fol. membr., saec. XIII. The *incipit* is on fol. 1 r., in col. 1, and the *desinit* on fol. 149 v., in col. 2: *Explicit liber primus.* Then: *Capitula super primum sententiarum.* There is a *tabula* of distinctions and questions arranged by a later hand. — In many (things) it convenes with the just named codex S. (In our edition, marked) with the sign **C**.

26. *In the same place,* in the library of the University of Paris at the Sorbonne, cod. membr., of the end of the 13th century, sign. Th. II. 48. At the beginning there is prefaced a *tabula distinctionum,* then the Commentary, which runs up to fol. 135. The *desinit,* as in the editions. — It has been corrected by various hands of a more recent age. In 1877, it was compared with published versions by D. Messager, then Vicar of the church of St. Stephan, at Auxerre; of whom we make grateful mentioned here. (In our edition, marked) with the sign **U**.

27. *At Padua* (Italy), in the Biblioteca Antoniana, cod. membr. in fol., saec. XIII, sign. num. 120. The *incipit* on fol. 3, but numbered fol. 1, without a title: *Profunda fluviorum.* The *desinit* on fol. 153 r., in col. 1: *Explicit liber primus.* — An ancient and correct (codex). In several difficulties in the text it was useful, especially on account of (its) precision and position of words. (In our edition, marked) with the sign **P**.

28. In the same library, cod. membr. in fol., saec XIII, sign. 125. The first folio is absent. The *incipit* begins: *siccatus est fluvius*

et transierunt etc.. The *desinit* on fol. 139 r., in col. 1: *Explicit liber primus.* A hand of the 14th century has added: *Bonaventure.* — Corrected by diverse hands. The more ancient corrections convene with the readings of the previous codex. On fol. 127 there is read: *Iste liber datus est ad usum fratis Guidonis anno 1285.* (In our edition, marked) with the sign **Q**.

29. In the same library, cod. 123, membr., written at the beginning of the 14th century. The *incipit* on fol. 1 r., in the upper part which there was written in large letters: *L. 1. fratris Bonaventure.* Below: *Profunda fluviorum* etc.. The *desinit* on fol. 152 v., in col. 2: *Explicit liber primus fratris Bonavenure super sententias.* There follows a *tabula*, which extends up to dist. XV. — Not entirely compared, but inspected only in several difficult passages. (Marked) with the sign **gg**.

30. In the same library, cod. 124., membr. in fol., saec. XIII. The *incipit* on fol. 1, in col. 1: *Profunda* etc. The *desinit* on fol. 156 r.: *Explicit liber primus sententiarum.* Another hand has added: *d. Bonaventure.* — Used in the same manner as the previous codex. (In our edition, marked) with the sign **hh**.

31. *At Rome*, in the Biblioteca (Apostolica) Vaticana, cod. Vat. lat. 907, membr. in fol., of the end of the 13th century. The *incipit: Profunda fluviorum* etc.. It has 192 folios. At the end, the first hand has added: *Explicit liber primus Bonaventure.* — It convenes with the other more outstanding codices. (In our edition, marked) with the sign **B**.

32. In the same library, from the same collection, cod. 908, membr. in fol., saec. XIV. The *incipit: Profunda fluviorum* etc. The *desinit* as in the published versions. — The same judgement as the previous one. (In our edition, marked) with the sign **D**.

33. *At Rome*, in the Biblioteca Chisiana, cod. B. VIII. 128., membr. in fol., of the end of the 13th century. The *incipit* on fol. 1: *Profunda fluviorum* etc.. The *desinit* on fol. 145, as in the published versions. Then, by the first hand: *Explicit primus liber boni fortune.* Which rubric was written on a red line, to which was added: *Explicit primus domini fratris Bonaventure super sententias.* — It has many *lacunae* and *menda*; nevertheless, it proffers good readings. (In ours, marked with) the sign **E**.

34. *At Todi* in Umbria (Italy), in the ancient library of S. Fortunatus (now the Municipal), cod. 39., membr. in fol., saec. XIII. The *incipit* on fol. 4 r., in col. 1: *Profunda fluviorum* etc.. The *desinit* on fol. 139 r., in col. 2, as in published versions. On the following folio there is subjoined a *tabula* in three columns, listing the distinctions, questions and doubts on the text. The *desinit* on fol. 142 r., in col. 1. — It holds the primacy among all our codices, both on account of (its) antiquity, since it was written in the time of Bonaventure, and on account of the multiple correction of the text, now by the first hand, by a contemporary one, and by more recent hands, and on account of the readings sometimes proper to itself, which we not rarely received into the text. It must also be noted, that any *mendum*, written in the text by the writer of the codex, but then corrected in this one, by an ancient hand, is most frequently not corrected in any of our other *ancient* codices, and is corrected in another manner in the *younger ones*. It seems to be certain, that this codex is one of the two codices comprising Sent., Bk. I, which, together with many other books, was bequeathed in 1289 by Cardinal Bentivegna de Bentivegnis, to the Convent of St. Fortunatus, at Todi. Here he was Guardian in the Ord. Min, the from 1276 Bishop of Todi, then successor to St. Bonaventure in the See of Albano. In the ancient library of St. Fortunatus there are still extant several ancient inventories of books (codd. 184, 186, 187), reported by Bonelli (*Prodromus*, col. 479); the ancient one of which, which reports 2 copies of Sent., Bk. I, seems to have been complied a little after the death of the Cardinal, c. 1289. (In our edition, marked) with the sign **T**.

35. In *our Collegio* there is conserved a cod. chart. in 4 vo., saec. XV, written in small letters and abbreviations, which among all our codices departs most of all from the reading of the codices of the 13th century and approaches more to the text of the Vatican edition. (Marked) with the sign **cc**.

II.

Codices which we have not used.

36. *At Angers* in France, in the Civic library, there is conserved cod. 193, membr. in fol., of the end of the 13th century, once belonging to the monastery of St. Albinus of Angers. On fol. 1 r., by a recent hand there is prefaced: *Primus liber Magistri sententiarum expositus ab anonymo.* Then by the ancient hand, which wrote the codex: *In nomine Patris et Filii et Spiritus sancti, amen. Profunda fluviorum* etc.. At the end: *Explicit liber primus.*

37. *At Berlin*, in the Royal library, cod. 55, membr., saec. XV. On fol. 1, in col. 1: *Tabula Bonaventure ordinis minorum spuer primo sententiarum incipit feliciter.* At the foot of the page: *Finis. Tabula Bonaventure oridnis minorum exit feliciter.* Then: *Prologus Bonaventure super sententiis incipit feliciter. Profunda fluviorum.* The *desinit* on fol. 224 r., in col. 1: *Finis. Liber primus Bonaventure super sententiis ordinis minorum exit feliciter.*

38. *At Bruges* in Belgium, in the Civic library, cod. 173, membr. fol., saec XIII. On fol 1. r, in the upper margin a latter hand has written: *Sanctus Bonaventura in quator libros sententiarum.* But now the codex comprises only the Commentaries on the first and second book.

39. *At Kraków* (Poland), in the University library, cod. 1250. A. A. VI. 1, membr. in fol., from the end of the 13th and beginning of the 14th century. The *incipit* on fol. 1 r., prefaced by a second hand with: *Scriptum fratris Bonaventure super primo sententiarum. Profunda fluviorum* etc. At the end there is added: *Explicit liber primus. Deo gratias.*

40. *At Erfurt* in Germany, in the Royal library: Amploniana Collection, cod. 122., membr. in fol., from the end of the 13th century. On fol. 1 r.: *Bonaventura super primum et tertium.* Then in col. 1: *Profunda fluviorum.* The *desinit* about halfway through the volume: *Explicit primus liber sententiarum.*

41. *At Seville* in Spain, in the Biblioteca Colombina (y Capitular), cod. Y. Tab. 132. N. 5, membr. in fol. parv., saec. XIV. On fol. 3 r., there is prefaced to the Commentary a *tabula quaestionum*, which ends on fol. 5 v. with the words: *Expliciunt problemata primi libri sententiarum.* Then, on fol. 6 r., in col. 1, the *incipit: Profunda fluviorum.* The *desinit* on the last folio of the codex: *Explicit expliceat, ludere scriptor eat.*

42. *At Leipzig* (Germany), in the University library, cod. 492, in fol. membr., befor the middle of the 14th century. On the pergamena adjoined to the exterior cover, there is read: *Bonaventura super primum librum sententiarum in questionibus et lectura.* The *incipit* is on fol. 2 r., in col. 1. The *desinit*, on the last folio of the codex, as in the published versions.

43. *At Lübeck* in Germany, in the Civic library, cod. theol. n. 15, in fol., chart. saec. XV. The *incipit* on fol. 1 r., in col. 1: *Profunda fluviorum.* The *desinit* on the last folio of the codex: *et hac voluntate merebatur.*

41. *At Münich* (Germany), in the Royal library, Cod. Lat. ms. 5175, chart. in fol., saec. XV. On fol. 1 r., there is read: *Registrum super primum sententiarum Domini Bonaventure.* This *registrum* is a copious *tabula* of things, questions and doubts on the text, which ends on fol. 8. On the following folio r., in col. 1 the *incipit* of the Commentary: *Profunda fluviorum* etc.. The *desinit* is on fol. 259.

45. In the same library, cod. C. L. M. 6949, chart. in fol., saec. XV. The *incipit* on fol. 1 r., in col. 1: *Profunda fluviorum.* As in the preceding (codex), a copious *tabula* follows the Commentary, which (*tabula*) finishes on fol. 357. r..

46. In the same library, C. L. M. 8844, chart. in fol., saec. XV. On fol. 1 r., there is read: *Principium Prologi in primum scriptum Domini Bonaventure est profunda fluviorum.* There follows a *tabula* by another hand, but confected in the same age, which extends up to fol. 3 r.. Then, the Commentary: *Profunda fluviorum* etc.. The *desinit* on fol. 327 f., in col. 2, is as in the published versions.

47. In the same library, C. L. M. 8950, chart. in 4 vo., saec. XV. On fol. 233 v., there is the Prologue of St. Bonaventure on the first books of the Sentences. The *incipit* is as in the published versions. The *desinit* on fol. 239 r.: *quo beata sit, nisi Deus. Et sic finitur principium Bonaventure super Sententias.*

48. In the same library, C. L. M. 11413. a., chart. in fol., saec. XV. The *incipit* on fol. 1 r.: *Profunda fluviorum* etc.. The *desinit* on the last folio, is as in the published versions.

49. *At Oxford* (England), in the Bodleian Library, Codices Canoniciani, cod. 16, in 4 vo. min, folio r. 152, from the beginning of the 15th century. On fol. 1: *Profunda fluviorum* etc.. The *desinit*, as in the published versions. Then: *Expliciunt veritates primi fratris Bonaventure cum tribus argumentis ad utramque partem.* A *tabula* follows. From these words it can be argued, that in many questions several arguments are missing.

50. In the same place, in the library of Merton College, cod. O. I. 8., membr. in fol., from the end of the 13th century. On folio 1 r.: *Bonaventura super primum librum sententiarum.* The *incipit*: *Profunda fluviorum* etc. The *desinit*, as in the published versions. Then, there is added by the first hand: *Completus est liber primus Bonaventure.*

51. *At Paris*, in the library of the University of the Sorbonne, there is conserved a cod. miscell., sign. num. 3572, membr. in fol. min., saec XIII. On fol. 77, the *incipit* without title and name of author: *Profunda fluviorum* etc.. That is, the Prologue of St. Bonaventure on the first book of the Sentences, to which there follows the Commentary, which is mutilated.

52. *At Padua* (Italy), in the University library, cod. 1098, in fol. membr., of the end of the 13th century. The *incipit* on fol. 1 r., in col. 1: *Profunda fluviorum.* The *desinit* is on fol. 158 v.. Then, there follows a *tabula*, to which there is added: *Explicit hic primus auctoris in agmine simus.* And then: *collectiones errorum in Anglia Parisius condemnatorum,* written by another hand, but of the same age.

53. *At Reims* (France), once belonging to the Chapter of Reims, cod. E 369/297 membr. in fol., saec. XIII. On fol. 1, in the upper part there is written: *Ave maria: Sancte Martialis.* Below, in col. 1, the *incipit* to d. 1, a. 1: *Veteris ac nove legis* etc. *Ad evidentiam definitionum et aliorum, que Magister ponit* etc.. The *desinit* on fol. 94. On the following folio there is subjoined a *tabula quaestionum.* On fol. 97, in col. 1, again, the *incipit* with the words of Master (Peter): *Cupientes aliquid de penuria* etc.; and it proceeds to list the questions about the text for the whole book, which run up to fol. 127. The *desinit*: *quae operatur in nobis, ipsi gloria in Ecclesia et in Christo Iesu in omnes generationes seculi seculorum. Amen.*

54. *At Rome*, in the Biblioteca (Apostolica) Vaticana, cod. Palat. 364, chart. in fol., saec. XV. On fol 1, in the upper margin there is read: *Liber primus sive scriptum primi sententiarum Seraphici doctoris Bonaventure Cardinalis. Profunda fluviorum* etc.. The *desinit* on fol. 266: *Explicit liber primus.*

55. In the same library, cod. Urbinat. 141, in fol. membr., saec. XV. At the beginning there is prefaced: *In hoc codice continetur liber Bonaventure de Balneo regio Ordinis minorum super primo libro sententiarum.* On fol. 3: *Incipit liber Bonaventure Ordinis minorum super primo libro sententiarum. Profunda fluviorum* etc.. At the end: *Explicit liber primus Bonaventure Ordinis minorum.* Then, there follows a *tabula*, to which there is added: *Tituli quaes-*

tionum Bonaventure super primo sententiarum expliciunt feliciter.

56. *At Epinal* in France, cod. 61, membr. in 4 vo, saec. XIII. A hand of the 18th century has added the title: *Commentarius in Magistrum sententiarum,* but is silent concerning the name of the author. The *incipit*: *Profunda fluviorum scrutatus est.* The *desinit*, as in the published versions.

57. *At Torino* (in Italy), in the University library, cod. D. III. 23., membr. in fol., saec. XIII. On fol. 1 r., by the first had there has been prefaced in the superior part: *nota hic proprietates fluvii.* Thence, in col. 1: *Profunda fluviorum* etc.. The *desinit* on fol. 185 v., in col. 2. There is added: *Finis adest operis, mercedem posco laboris; si bene lectus ero, si non, veniam mihi quaero.*

58. *At Tours* in France, in the Public library, cod. 372, membr. in fol., saec. XIII, mutilated at the beginning; for the *incipit* is from dist. XVI, the last question: *minorem dicens, si totum* etc. A hand of the 15th century, has prefaced above: *Bonaventure super primo sententiarum.* The *desinit*, as in the published versions.

§ 2. *On the process or reason observed, in emending the text of the First Book of Commentaries, we note these (things):*

That great mix of variant readings, accumulated from the collection of so many manuscripts and editions, had to be gathered by a new and tedious labor and placed under one consideration, so that one might use apt discretion concerning them, in emending the text. Then it appeared, that the more ancient codices of the 13th century ordinarily agree among themselves, but against the Vatican edition. Very often they hardly differ except in those *menda*, which are found so often even in manuscripts of good note, chiefly in the omission of words, when the same or similar terms are repeated. It also appeared, that the younger codices are wont to correct the *menda*, common to the older ones, with often new and disparate readings. Next, it appeared, that a codex of more recent age, signed **cc** (in our edition), departed much from the ancient ones and was a prelude often to the readings of the Vatican edition. Finally, it appeared, that this younger codex did not wander from the ancient text as much as the Vatican edition differed from it, which (edition) followed very closely the preceding editions. Whence, it was manifest, that through those editions of the 15th and chiefly the 16th century the primitive text had been not a little changed by glosses and arbitrary corrections, even though those editors professed to have purged the text from innumerable vices and *menda.* But it was already clear, that the editors of the 16th century had changed not a little and/or rather corrupted the text according to their own judgement and/or the systems used at that time, not rarely without consulting the more ancient manuscripts and/or in entirely neglecting all the codices. For the passages, which seemed obscure to them, and/or the manner of speech of which offended them as obsolete, they strove to correct by their own style and not rarely with an infelicitous outcome, as a diligent reader can often observe from our footnotes (to the received text).

The principles and rules which we have followed in choosing variant readings and in reforming the text of the Vatican edition, have already been briefly spoken of in the General Preface. In this place, we only observe, that we had no reason to use the editions successive to the Vatican (edition), since they appeared thoroughly useless for our scope. We have already spoken of the more ancient editions above (in ch. 1, § 8). The edition of Brixen (signed 1) and after it, the first of Koberger (signed 2) served us very much.

When we began the work of emending the text, it did not rarely happen, that the better codices unanimously proffered a reading

discrepant from the Vatican one, which (reading) seemed to us false at first sight, and/or not intelligible, and/or at least abhorrent to Latin diction and for that reason to be rejected. But having instituted a more accurate investigation, it appeared, that the reading of the codices was the genuine one and was thoroughly explained and proven by the use of speech in that age, as used in the schools. For in the ancient versions of the works of Aristotle, whether made by Boethius according to the Greek text, or by others according to the Arabic, in the *Commentaria* of Averroës and/or of Avicenna expressed in a similar Latinity, in the contemporary *Summulae* of philosophers and/or of theologians (v. gr. of Peter of Spain), we have found the same, often barbarous forms of speech, which in subsequent centuries ceased to be used in the schools. Hence, in the younger codices, but chiefly in the editions, they were not rarely suppressed as obsolete, nay as vicious and absurd, so as to purge, namely, the text from infinite vices according to this reckoning. The benevolent reader can see an example (of this) in this First Tome, on p. 13, footnote 7, and on p. 357, in footnote 8 (which refers to the first words on the following page). We, however, have restored the primitive reading of the codices, though (it be) a less usual and elegant one and have subjoined an explanation for the same in the footnotes. We can rightly affirm, that we have not changed anything in the text of the Seraphic Doctor by our own judgement, but have exacted all according to the norm of the codices and editions, having employed the rules of the critical art, sincerely and moderately, as much as God granted (us to do).

In listing the variant readings, we have not adopted the system, recently introduced, of placing so very many variant readings, of whatever value, at the foot (of the page), such that the burden is left to the reader himself, to choose those which please him. Whatever be the utility of this method in books pertaining to history and philology, not a few (things) are certainly adverse to its use in editing the works of St. Bonaventure. In this matter, we have consulted very many men in Italy, France and Germany, erudite in the critical art, by whose counsel we have retained in substance the ancient system of the Maurini editors, yet, noting the several variant readings, as are wont, but with very brief words, and at least indicating, too, the reason for our choice in the passages of greater moment.

Nevertheless, since one must stand for the authority of the codices, it appeared very clearly, that we would have to make so many changes — though, according to sense, they are often of minor import — to the text and have to place so many variants at the foot (of the page), that the frequency of the notes would be tedious to the readers and the exceeding number of signs in the text indicating footnotes would offend their eyes. To provide in some manner a remedy to these evils, we have *first* conjoined (those) several critical notes, pertaining to several lines somewhat connected to one another, under one and the same number, yet, thus, that the diverse readings can be found without difficulty.

Second, since in the codices, very many variant readings are found to be received into the text, which are of lesser moment and nearly undifferentiated, and as much as they are minute, so much do they occur more frequently, it seems vain and annoying to the reader, to always make mention of them and the change made in the text. Of this kind are the very frequent *transpositions* of words, when they touch least of all upon the sense; likewise, the *repetitions* of the same particles: *et, vel, sive* etc. and the words *est* and/or *sunt* in the passages where they can easily be supplied, v. gr. after *notandum, intelligendum,* (and) *dicendum*; likewise, the *substitution* of certain particles of the same signification, v. gr. *vel, aut, ac, et, nec,* (and) *neque* and chiefly *ergo* and *igitur*. Indeed, the better codices observe some difference between *ergo*, which they place nearly constantly after the

premises before the conclusions, and *igitur*, but the editions very often disagree in this. The same is to be said concerning some words, which in the codices, written less accurately, are either of a doubtful reading, such as *contingit* and *convenit, significat* and *signat, significatum* and *signatum*, and/or are confused with a false written form, such as *hic, hanc, hoc*. The codices and editions nearly continuously disagree among themselves in these and similar (words). After we have several times made mention of these variants and changes made in the text, in the first Distinctions, we have thereafter said nothing more about them. But, yet, we have changed nothing without the authority of the codices.

Even in the manner of the citations, the Vatican (edition) very often differs from the codices, by placing, v. gr. *Per Augustinum* and/or *dicitur ab Augustino* for *dicit Augustinus*. The same is true in regard to the titles of the Questions, in which by omitting and/or adding the same words, it often differs from the codices; which (codices), however, we have followed, when in the progress of this work we make no mention of a change.

Moreover, we warn the reader, that we have constantly restored the primitive order of the parts of the Commentary. For, to every distinction of Lombard, the Commentary has three distinct parts, and, indeed, in this order. In the first place, there is placed a brief *Division of the Text*, by which the whole book of the Sentences and each distinction are divided into parts; then, there follows several *Questions* on this material, proposed and solved by the Seraphic Doctor, which *Treatment* very often is subdivided into two and/or even three *principal questions* (named by the editors *Articles*), which, again, ordinarily contain two and/or more special Questions. In the third and last place, there follows the *dubitationes* (as the author called them) or *Doubts* about the words and/or sentence of Master (Peter), which are solved by the Seraphic Doctor in a more lengthy manner than by other commentators on the same book. This third part, the codices ordinarily begin with these words: *In this part are the doubts on the text and first, indeed, there is doubted* (or *asked*) etc.. We have already observed, that the place and order of these Doubts was changed in the editions. Since, in the first Nürnberg edition of 1491, there was adjoined to the Commentaries, the book of Peter Lombard (omitted in the codices of the Commentaries and first published versions), these Doubts were placed in the margin of the text of Master (Peter) thus, that by certain signs there were indicated the words, to which the explication of the Doubts was referred, with the titles of the Doubts and the words of Master (Peter which were) repeated by St. Bonaventure being omitted. But, afterwards, the Roman edition of 1569, and after it, the other editions, freed the text of Master (Peter) from these marginal additions; yet, did not restore these Doubts to their first place, but placed (them) immediately after the Division of the Text, neither separating (them) from the same Division with any title, nor wholly restoring to them (their) original titles and/or inscriptions, but supplying (them) *ad libitum* with other words. By this alteration, very many errors broke out in the later editions, not rarely perturbing the sense, and/or at least falsely citing some sentence already mentioned *ut supra* (that is, as in the Questions), which (sentence), however, according to the order of these editions is read in the *following* Questions. Moreover, all the codices, and even the most ancient editions, have the abovesaid order, which we have restored with the entire titles of the Doubts. But, it would be superfluous, to note this consent of all the codices and the difference and vices of the more recent editions on every single Doubt.

Moreover, this explication of the text of the Sentences, which St. Bonaventure wrote, was esteemed so highly, that it was several times excerpted by not a few as a separate work, an example of which we have in the codex signed with the note **dd**. D. Peltier, who cared for the Parisian edition, mentions, as we have said, a certain codex, which also had the Doubts separate

and written in a distinct volume. Yet, it is a wonderful hypothesis, which the same editor professes in the preface to tome I of his edition, that, namely, the Commentaries of St. Bonaventure contain a double course in theology, one of which, for beginners, explains the text of Master (Peter) with these Doubts on the text, but the other, afterwards, for the advanced, propounds the more profound Questions. That this supposition lacks all fundament, the easy editor would have perceived, if he had inspected the Commentaries of other ancients, v. gr. of St. Thomas, Peter of Tarentaise, (and) Richard of Middleton, who after the long questions explicate very briefly some doubts on the text of Master (Peter). Hence it is clear, that those few words following the Questions cannot be called a "first" course on theology. In St. Bonaventure, these Doubts are, indeed, very often more lengthy, but they are not able to be a first course for beginners, both because in the codices the passages follow in order that, which this editor calls the *"second"* course, and because, in often citing the preceding questions and in supposing their doctrine, they presuppose them as having been read. Wherefore it happens, that these Doubts are more difficult to understand than the Questions themselves.

Moreover, so that in (our) edition the three parts of the Commentary, which we have mentioned, might better appear to the eyes of readers, we have adjoined titles written above (them): *Division of the Text, Treatment of the Questions, Doubts on the Text of Master (Peter)*.

§ 3. *Of the other aides illustrating our edition, we subjoin these (things):*

The Vatican edition, which, in this, followed very closely the preceding editions, ordinarily placed back in the margin the citations of Sacred Scripture and of the Fathers, which had been placed in the text itself. But we have placed back into the text all the passages, which according to the codices we found placed in the very text of St. Bonaventure. We have consumed a great deal of time and labor in discovering and conferring the authorities, which are either cited here and there by the Seraphic Doctor himself, and/or are supposed by him, and/or are cited in our Scholia and footnotes. We have cited no passage, which we have not personally inspected, except for a few passages, where, with the work not available, we have expressly cited the testimony of another. We trust that this work of ours will be most agreeable to the learned men, who with us grieve that they have been often deceived by the testimony of these citations, which passed from book to book throughout the ages. They will pardon us, too, if, we, having employed even great diligence, have sometimes erred, whether in noting or in understanding or in transcribing some passage. This more easily could have happened in the first Distinctions of this Book than in the later ones, wherein, in the pages already arranged in type, we inspected nearly all the passages in their own sources. We have found many passages, which heretofore have also been either entirely neglected by the editors of other commentaries on Lombard, and/or falsely cited; only a few have escaped all our diligence.

Though the Seraphic Doctor in treating philosophical questions is very sober, yet he supposes very many philosophical (things) in this Commentary, as we have already observed in the General Preface. In all the arguments taken *ex ratione* he brings forward their fundaments from the *definitions, axioms* (and) *distinctions* received in that age, not rarely indicates their source and origin. We think that it will be pleasing to the students of philosophy, that we have given much labor to searching out the origin and/or at least the first root of these authorities, which very often had to be sought in the writings of Aristotle and/or his commentators.

In regard to the *Scholia*, added by us to singular Ques-

tions, to that which we have said above in the General Preface, we subjoin these (things). First of all, we judged that we had to follow the *truth* and *genuine interpretation* of the Seraphic Doctor, as much as God gave (us to do), lest from the preconceived opinions of scholars we arbitrarily subjoin to our Doctor our own and/or another's thought. Rightfully did Fr. *Bartholomaeus a Barberiis*, of the Capucine Order, in the Preface of his own *cursus theologicus*, say that all the commentators — excepting the one, *Matthaeus Ferchius*, of the Order of Minors Conventual, « truly the most faithful Bonaventurista » — drew the Seraphic Doctor very often more or less « to the side of either the Thomists and/or the Scotists according to the propensity of each », and call them not commentators, but adversaries of the Seraphic (Doctor)'s doctrine. — Otherwise, it is manifest, that in interpreting the more difficult and obscure passages one can also fall unwillingly into such an error. And Fr. *Bartholomaeus a Barberiis*, though employed daily for fifteen years in the study of the writings of the Seraphic Doctor, as he himself testifies, as one busied and very versed in them and very studious for the truth, as is seen, does not seem to us to have entirely escaped from that precipice, so as to attribute to St. Bonaventure the opinions of his own age. Hence, that we might proceed more cautiously in this, we have thought it necessary to have recourse not only to St. Bonaventure himself, but also to his master, Alexander of Hales, and to other contemporary writers, so that we might more easily follow the true sentence of our author. Among these latter, there stands forth Peter of Tarentaise, the friend of St. Bonaventure, who in his own Commentary on Lombard, manifestly follows St. Bonaventure in very many passages; (then) Bl. Albertus Magnus, St. Thomas and, of our own (Order), besides Alexander, chiefly Richard of Middleton and Scotus. The work of Fr. Brülifer, as reported by his disciples, was also of much profit to us; and also in the questions concerning the *One* God, that Summa of Fr. *Trigosus*, and in other questions the work of Fr. *Forestus de Trinitate*. The book of Fr. *Bartholomaeus a Barberiis* we have not accepted, except after the Scholia had already been written to Book I; yet, we did sometimes use it.

Otherwise, in these, our Scholia, we have presumed least of all, to propose anything to men consummate in theological doctrine, which would be worthy of their attention. We have also abstained from clarifying controversies, thoroughly scrutinizing profound mysteries, (and) writing long apologies, leasing these for wiser (men). For we have intended nothing in spirit but to proffer those, which could be of use for *beginners* in the study of this Commentary.

Moreover, we have tried to explain some passages, even at the cost of a very difficult labor. But, sometimes, perhaps, we have been too loquacious in explaining the easier passages; in such a case we have sinned against the favor of the reader, whom it seemed less unsuitable to briefly instruct in things he already knows, than to neglect the same in things he knows not.

At the end of the Scholia we have placed the passages of the chief Scholastics, responding to the preceding Question of St. Bonaventure. The Vatican edition already had done the same, yet, the citations of which we have very often corrected and supplied by adding other authors. However, it is established, that those great masters of the 13th century very often explain one another, and that the one explains with a supplement what was lacking in the other. To this list of authors we have added, also, some Scholastics of a later age and of lesser authority, such as Durandus (of Saint-Pourçain) and Gabriel Biel. For these, by their own very, not more probable opinions and insufficient reasons, can contribute not a little for a more distinct understanding of the truth by the wide reader. However, Dionysius the Carthusian, a doctor of the 15th century, we have added for this reason, that he both transcribed at length the passages of nearly all the ancient masters of the 13th century, even the unpublished ones (v. g., from the Summa of Uldaricus), and because he himself emulated the spirit of those ancients. Yet, it must be noted,

the passages transcribed by him were very often somewhat contracted and/or changed. We have advisedly refrained from citing the authors of later ages and/or from reporting their opinions, lest we oppress ourselves with labor and the reader with tedium.

To say something, too, concerning our *ratio* and *mens* in explaining St. Bonaventure, we have striven to conciliate and benignly interpret the diverse sentences of those great men rather than laboriously insisting upon the apparent differences among them, in his we have follows the great example of our Seraphic Doctor (cf. above ch. 1, § 4), according to (our) abilities. Moreover, we think, that the Seraphic Doctor was moved to this by the true spirit of the Church, which wants unity in necessaries, concedes liberty in doubts and commends charity in all (things). It is, indeed, a good and useful (thing) for the progress of students, if they adhere chiefly to one doctor and to one book; it would also be preferred, if the catholic schools returned to the same ancient philosophical principles and (those) perfectly proposed by St. Thomas, after the manner wisely recommended by our most holy lord, Leo XIII, in his most celebrated Encyclical, *Aeterni Patris Unigenitus* (August 4, 1879) to all the Bishop of the Catholic world, so that the intellect of men find remedy from the infinite errors obscuring (it) in this, our own age. These obstruct least of all that liberty, which the Church concedes to Her own doctors and schools in things doubtful, nay (which) stands guard for the good of the universal Church. For it seems more fitting both to the Divine Providence and to the utility of the Church, that in the course of the ages the holy Doctors thought out various reasons and manners of speech, chiefly in the arduous mysteries of faith, to explicate and display the unlimited and ineffable see of divine truth to human minds in a human manner. Nor does this plurality of sentences and/or of words, when it is restricted within certain limits, hinder the purpose of divine revelation, nay it can even render the revealed mystery more savory and credible to men.

On this point, Fr. Matthias Hauzeur, whom we mentioned above in ch. 1, § 7, explains in an outstanding manner (*Collationes*, tome I, Bk. III, col. 255), in what manner in the one Faith, which captivates the understanding of all in service to Christ, there can stand a plurality of reckonings and of manners of speaking without detriment to the end intended by God the Revealer: « both because each contribute something to a more perfect manner (of speaking); and because not all men grasp the same in the same manner, but as they are different in visage, so, too, often in the grasp and affection of mind; hence, the various manners of explaining the same mystery have been accommodated to the grasp of the many; and because each doctor aims for the same truth through his own ray of natural light and/or of some special illumination, therefore, they do not contradict one another as much, as they allow themselves to appear ... For, as each has his own certain sphere of sight and/or of hearing, according to which they judge of very distant objects in various manners, so, too, each has a certain intellectual sphere, common, indeed, concerning (things) evident, but as differing as rays concerning the obscure ».

Hence, it already follows, that it doest not belong to the wise, to contentious impugn the sentences and/or reasons of preceding Catholic doctors as false and to recommend their own and/or the new as the only true ones, but (rather) to guarantee, if it be possible, that all the sentences posited by Catholic doctors, in a not entirely erroneous manner, return to a certain concord among themselves and to the same ineffable truth, that to chop up Catholic truth by giving diverse opinions *ad infinitum*. This, does the author (tome I, Appendix, col. 27) commend in very clear words, thus: « *Since neither God, nor any truth of His, according to (its) unity or simplicity is the cause*

and/or occasion of any dissension, but (rather) of peace (1 Cor. 14:55), and (since) the individual Catholic doctors studiously aim as if from the circumference of truth under the distinct and proper rays (of each), right to its center; they are not to be alienated from one another by contentious interpretations and opinions, but rather to be conciliated among themselves and to the same truth, at least when unevenly understood, so that as Rom. 12:5-6 (says): each one may abound in his own sense, i. e. not only according to (their) studious intention, but also according to (their) uneven participation in the same truth ».

Finally, we were driven, to reform for the most part those summaries, which were placed under the name of *conclusions,* both in the Vatican edition and in our own, before the Response to the question. These had passed from the Roman edition of 1569 into the Vatican (edition). But, very often, the former ancient summaries seemed to us to express the doctrine of the Seraphic Doctor less justly.

CHAPTER III

On our edition of Peter Lombard's Books of Sentences

With our labors in publishing this Commentary scarcely begun, it manifestly appeared, that the Books of the Sentences, at least in the Vatican edition, labored under several vices both in regard to the text, and in regard to the errors in the passages cited, out of which Peter Lombard confected nearly his whole book. Though the publishing of a new critical edition of Peter Lombard did not pertain to the program we published, yet, Fr. Fidelis, while he was still in life, judged that something was to be done to correct this four books, on account of the intimate nexus, which there is between the Books of the Sentences and the Commentary on them. For St. Bonaventure took the great part of those authorities, which he used, from Master (Peter), and recurred always to the same, especially in the Doubts on the text. — Acceding to the execution of the counsel of whom, we soon discovered, that this labor is both longer and more difficult, than we had thought.

First, indeed, a daring work was required, so that all the sentences of the Fathers, to which this work refers, be found in their true locations and be compared with (their) original. — Then, one had to take care, that the very many, which the author excerpted from others, be discerned from those few, which he wrote from his own genius. For, it is familiar to Master (Peter), that the words, which he accepted from elsewhere, he excerpted from wheresoever (he could), such that sometimes he weaves together the words of one and the same proposition out of the propositions of several chapters of their authors, and converts these to his own use, by inflecting (and) transposing them in different cases and by omitting and/or even interpolating others. We have already exhibited for the readers not a few examples of this, such as should suffice them, both as much as how much labor would have been consumed in separating these testimonies, with the typographical signs used for this, from the rest of the text of Master (Peter), and because it would be impossible, to always exhibit the differences, which occur between the passages as cited by Master (Peter) and the original, whence they were taken. If, indeed, one were to place in the footnotes all the many (things) from these sources, these would exceed the work of Master (Peter) two and/or three times by their own mass.

To correct the text of Master (Peter), we employed five manuscript codices from the Biblioteca Nazionale at Florence, of which we shall give an index below (on p. LXXXVIII), and, in addition, nine codices. Having conducted an accurate comparison of these with the Vatican edition, we have soberly corrected the text

from many *menda*, not a few of which are sufficiently grave. But, since on account of the paucity of codices, which we have consulted, this labor of ours has not been completed in every part, we have ordinarily changed nothing in the text on the authority alone of these codices, unless their reading seemed to be completely proven by one or another edition, whether of Master (Peter), or of that author, from whom he had taken the words. Whence, some variant readings, though they seemed to us more probable, we have placed in the footnotes. Moreover, we have noted there all the variant readings, which are of some moment, having omitted other unuseful ones, especially those nearly innumerable transposition of words, which seemed nearly indifferent in regard to the sense and/or style. However, we have chosen from these and have exhibited in the text (those) which were more proven to us, though concerning such minute things we have often made no mention in our footnotes, just as we have observed about in regard to the text of St. Bonaventure. We have collected and noted in the footnotes several variants also for this sake, that if one perhaps by new studies is going to publish another and entirely perfect edition of Peter Lombard, he can use the variant readings of our codices. Yet, we are of the opinion, that the text exhibited by us has been sufficiently corrected.

On the authority of our codices and of those ancient editions, which exhibit the work of Lombard separately, with no adjoined commentary, of which kind are (those) which are distinguished by our numbers 1, 2, 7 & 9, we have restored the titles of each of the chapters placed after the Prologue and omitted from the other editions in that place, though they were placed there, as he himself testifies at the end of the Prologue. These titles, the other editions also inserted in their places in their own work; but very mutated and mingled with very many other rubrics, which by their own form manifest, that they were not composed by Master (Peter). For, here and there, they speak of Master (Peter) in the third person (v. gr. when they say, *he returns to the same*). These marginal rubrics have been manifestly added for the use of scholars, and seem to have been placed alongside in the margins either by the innumerable commentators and interpreters on this book, or by the students of scholars, or by the rubricists themselves. Little by little, they were mixed up with the genuine titles of the chapters. But no titles can be original other than (those) which are exhibited at the beginning of the work by Master

(Peter) himself. For, who could doubt, that Master (Peter) wrote a list of titles and subjoined (them) to the Prologue for this end, that in their own place the titles be placed before the individual chapters in the same form? Therefore, that these genuine titles, exhibited after the Prologue by the codices and ancient editions, are to be inserted in their own place and entirely separated from the very many additions of the rubricists, was our judgement and that of Fr. Fidelis, who also, to restore these titles more securely to their sincere form, wanted to confer in this part with fifteen codices besides those five Florentine ones, and in accord with these codices he distributed the text itself into chapters. It is true, that the chapters cited by St. Bonaventure, sometimes suppose another distribution of the text. But this proves nothing else, but that around the middle of the 13th century this change and addition of rubrics has already begun. It also seems, that the codex, which the Seraphic Doctor was using, has some readings diverse from those, which our codices and better editions exhibit. For the words of Master (Peter), cited by him in the Division of the Text and in the Doubts, more often are discrepant, to some extent, from our edition in minor particles and in the position of words. Which difference seems to be explained not entirely from the involuntary errors, easily occurring in a transcription. Moreover, since neither is it licit to imprudently change the text of Master (Peter) in accord with the reading of *one* codex of Bonaventure's work, nor to reject many codices of the Commentary on account of the reading of the text of Master (Peter), we have advisedly given each (reading) according to the codices proper to it.

The more outstanding rubrics, added at a later time and printed in other editions, we have placed in the margin,* and, indeed, (have) very often contracted (them) in a briefer manner; we have omitted not a few as unuseful. — It is to be wondered at, that Master (Peter) says nothing in his own Prologue concerning that distribution of the text into *distinctions*, which (distribution) is found in our codices and in all published versions, though with some difference, as we have warned in our notes. But it seems more probable to us, that this division into *distinctions*, which lack all title, is of a later origin and (was) done for use in a school. Likewise, that distribution into *two parts*, which is found in not a few distinctions, does not have Master (Peter) as (its) author, but (some) commentator.

In conclusion, we adjoin the three *tabula*, which follow:

---

* *Trans. note*: Since these rubrics serve to guide the reader who is not fluent in Latin, and present only summary identification of the parts of the Question, which are obvious in an English translation, they have been entirely omitted.

INDEX OF AUTHORS AND BOOKS

WHICH SAINT BONAVENTURE CITES IN THE FOUR BOOKS
OF HIS OWN COMMENTARIES

This Index has been written after the text, which is in the Vatican edition, having taken no counsel with the codices, which, however, sometimes differ in citing authors and/or books. Therefore, if any defect be found in this Index, we correct it in the footnotes, and at the end of (our) edition (of the Opera Omnia of S. Bonaventure) we will ad-join those works, which are cited in other books of the Seraphic Doctor, but not (those) in (this) Commentary. We have also named together the editions, which we have used, in this Index.*

1. *Alan of Lille*. His book, *On the Rule of faith*, is often cited by St. Bonaventure without the name of (its) author. (His) Opera omnia are had in the *Patrologia latina*, edited by Migne, tom. 210. We have used this edition.

2. *Bl. Flaccus Albinus Alcuin*. (His) Opera omnia in Migne, *Patrologia*, tomes 100 & 101.

3. *(St.) Alexander I, Pope*. The Epistles, Decrees, Privi-leges, Diplomas etc., both of this and of other Supreme Pon-tiffs, the names of whom are mentioned below, seem to have been accepted by St. Bonaventure very often from canon law, especially from the *Decretum Gratiani*. We have found very many of these even in the most ample collection of Councils of *Ioannes Dominicus Mansi*, Bishop of Lucca (Italy), in the Florentine and Venetian editions of 1757, 31 tomes in fol..

4. *Alexander III, Pope*.

5. *Alexander of Hales*. (His) *Summa theologica*. On the editions of this Summa, cf. the Prolegomena above, ch. 1, § 3. We have used the editions of Cologne of 1622, and of Venice of 1576. Since the preceding editions, just as also the codices, in parts II, III & IV have other numbers for the ques-tions, we subjoin here the difference, by comparing our edi-tions with the edition of Lyons of 1516, which agrees with the Nürnberg (edition) of *Antonius Koberger* in 1482.

In part II of the Cologne edition, it has 174 questions, in the edition of Lyons, 189. — Q. 72 (72, 73, 74, 75); q. 87 (90, 81, 92); q. 91 (96-97); q. 94-96 (101-107); q. 100 (111-116); q. 143 (159-160); q. 158 (175-176).

In part III, the Cologne edition has 69 questions, the Lyons edition 82. — Qq. 15 & 16 (15); q. 18 (11-23); q. 55 (55-59); q. 59 (63-67); q. 61 (69-71).

In part IV, the Cologne edition has 35 questions, the Lyons edition 114. — Q. 2 (2-5); q. 8 (11-23); q. 9 (24-28); q. 10 (29-42); q. 11 (43-53); q. 21 (80-81); q. 24 (84-86); q. 26 (88-96); q. 28 (97-104); q. 33 (109-112).

6. *Algazel, the Arabic philosopher*. *Logica et philosophia Algazelis Arabis*, Venice, 1506.

7. *St. Ambrose, Bishop of Milan*. Opera omnia. We have used the Venetian edition of 1748, 4 tomes in fol..

8. *(St.) Anacletus, Pope*.*

9. *St. Anselm, Bishop of Canterbury*. Opera omnia, Venice 1744, 2 tomes in fol..

10. *Apparatus*.*

11. *Lucius Medaurensis Apuleius*, the philosopher. (His) works were published by *Henricus de sancto Urso*, Vicenza, 1488, 1 tome in fol..

12. *Aristotle, the Stagirite*. — We have used various edi-tions to find and select that text, which agrees more with the ci-tation of words from Aristotle, made by St. Bonaventure. In regard to *Logic*, the version of Boethius was sufficient (Migne edition, tome 64, with which, in respect of the division of chap-ters, the Venetian edition of 1584 agrees); in regard to *Physics*, however, we have used *Metaphys. libros de Generat. et corrup-tione, de Caelo et mundo, de Anima, Meteororum*, Venice 1489 (at the expense of *Bernardinus de Tridino*), in which there are contained two versions, i. e., the Greek-Latin and the Arabic-Latin (which St. Bonaventure often employed), together with the commentary of *Averroës*. In regard to *Ethics*, we have consulted the ancient version in the works of St. Thomas (the edition of *Petrus Fiaccadorus*, Parma, 1869). In cases of some moment we have always named the edition, which we have used. In regard to the citation of chapters, we follow the Venetian edition of 1584, named above; moreover, we always cite the Parisian edition of 1878, made by *Ambrosius Firmin-Didot*, and you will find the ci-tations from it, placed in parenthesis.[1]

13. *St. Athanasius, Bishop of Alexandria*. Opera omnia in Migne, *Patrologia Graeca*,[2] tomes 25-28.

14. *St. Augustine, Bishop of Hippo*. Among the very many editions of the works of this holy Doctor we have chiefly used the Venetian of 1729, 14 tomes in folio. To St. Augustine there are even falsely attributed by the Seraphic (Doctor) the books, *de Spiritu et anima* (of which, there is some doubt, cf. Prolegomena, ch. 1, § 5), *de Fide ad Petrum*, which belongs to (St.) Fulgentius of Ruspe, and not a few others.

15. *Averroës* (ibn Rushd),° the most celebrated of the Arabic philosophers. Besides the Venetian edition of *Bernardinus de Trino* of 1489, we have also consulted the Venetian (edition) of 1560.

16. *Avicenna* (ibn Sina), *likewise Arabic*.+ We have employed the Venetian edition of 1508 (on p. 408, n. 4, erroneously: *sine anno*).

17. *St. Basil, Bishop of Caesarea in Cappadocia*. (His) Opera omnia, Venice, 1750, 3 tomes in fol.

18. *(St.) Bede the Venerable*. In Migne, *Patrologia Latina*, tomes 90-95.

---

[1] For finding the passages pertaining to philosophy, we have not rarely used this book: *Auctoritates Aristotelis, omnium recte philosophantium facile principis, insuper et Platonis, Boethii, Senecae etc.*, printed (Cologne) by *Henricus Quentel* in 1500. There are contained in this book propositions gathered from the aforesaid authors and very often some other added ones, which as logical conclusions respect those propositions and are held in the schools as sayings of these authors. Cf., v. gr. in our edition, p. 101, footnote 5.

[2] Understand: in the Greek, with the Latin translation.

* *Trans. note*: The names of authors are rendered in the manner that will be used in the English translation. Those marked with * are not found in the Index of authors listed in tome X of the Quaracchi edition.

° His full name is Abu al-Walid Muhammad ibn Ahmad ibn Muhammad ibn Rushd (1126 -1198). He was known in medieval Europe by the Latinized name Averroës. While he and Avicenna wrote in Arabic, he was an Almohad, and Avicenna an Iranian.

+ His full name is Abu ali al-Husayn ibn Abd Alla ibn Sina (980-1037). He was known by the Latinized name Avicenna.

19. *St. Benedict, Patriarch of western Monks. Regula et opuscula, Patrologia Latina,* tome 66.

20. *St. Bernard, Abbot of Clairvaux* (His) Opera omnia, Venice 1765, 6 tomes (3 volumes).

21. *Manlius Severinus Boethius,* (His) Opera omnia, Migne, *Patrologia Latina,* tomes 63 & 64.

22. *(St.) Celestine (I), Pope.**

23. *Callistus, Pope.**

24. *Sacred canons.* See below under n. 53.

25. *Cassian,* (His) opera, *Patrologia Latina,* tomes 49 & 50.

26. *(Flavius) Magnus Aurelius Cassiodorus, Patrologia Latina,* tomes 69 & 70.

27. *De Causis,* a book still ascribed by St. Bonaventure to Aristotle, which, however, contains only excerpts, from a certain unknown Arab philosopher made from the book of the Neoplatonic philosopher, Proclus, στοιχείωσις θεολογιή, which contains elements of metaphysics. This *libellum,* Gerhardus of Cremona († 1187) translated into Latin under the title, *de Expositione bonitatis purae.* On these (books), cf. Dr. Otto Bardenhewer: *Die pseudo-aristotelische Schrift Ueber das rein Gute* (Liber de Causis), Freiburg, Herder (edition), 1882.

28. *Marcus Tullius Cicero.* Opera omnia, Turin, 1824, 16 tomes in 8 vo..

29. *St. Clement I, Pope.*

30. *Council of Caesarea.* In the collection of Councils (which) we have already named above in n. 3.°

31. *Council of Carthage.*

32. *Council of Chalcedon* (in 451; Mansi, VI, col. 531 ff.).

33. *Council of Compiègne* (in 757; Mansi, XII, col. 651-652).

34. *Council of Elvira* (in 300; Mansi, II, col.. 1 ff.).

35. *Council of Laodicea* (c. 343-381; Mansi, II, col. 563 ff.)

36. *Council of the Lateran IV* (in 1215; Mansi, XXII, col. 954 ff.).

37. *Council of Nicea I* (in 325 A. D.; Mansi, II, col. 635 ff.).

38. *Council of Reims* (1148 A. D.; Mansi, XXI, col. 711 ff.).

39. *Council of Toledo VI* (638 A. D.; Mansi X, col. 659 ff.).

40. *St. Cyprian, Bishop of Carthage,* Opera omnia, *Patrologia Latina,* tomes 3 & 4.

41. *Didymus, the Alexandrine* (the Blind). *Patrologia Graeca,* tom 38.

42. *Dionysius, under the title, "the Areopagite".* We have used the Venetian edition of 1756, 2 tomes in fol., translated by *Balthasar Corderius,* S. J.; but, sometimes, the translation of *Ioannes Scotus Erigena,* in Migne, *Patrologia Latina,* tome 122.

43. *(St.) Evaristus, Pope.**

44. *Euclid of Megara.* (His) works, printed at Venice in 1509.

45. *St. Eusebius, Bishop of Vercelli.* (His) works, *Patrologia Latina,* tome 12.

46. *St. Fabianus, Pope.**

47. *St. Francis of Assisi. Regula et opuscula,* Paris 1641, 1 tome in folio.

48. *St. Fulgentius, Bishop of Ruspe.* Opera omnia, *Patrologia Latina,* tome 65. St. Bonaventure attributes his book, *On faith to Peter,* to St. Augustine.

49. *Gelasius, Pope.**

50. *Gennadius of Marseilles.* (His) works, *Patrologia Latina,* tome 58. His work, *On Ecclesiastical Dogmas* is attributed by St. Bonaventure, in his Commentary, to St. Augustine; but in his, *Apologia Pauperum,* rightly to Gennadius (cf. above, the Prolegomena, ch. 1, § 5).

51. *Gilbert of Porretain.* He published commentaries on some of the books of Boethius. There is also attributed to him the book,

Sex principiorum, published among the works of Aristotle. (His) Opera omnia in Migne, *Patrologia Latina,* tome. 188.

52. *Glossa ordinaria* of Walafrid Strabo, and the *Glossa interlinearis* of Anselm of Laon. Each is found in the Commentary of Nicholas of Lyra, Ord. Min., the edition of which, printed at Venice in 1588, in 6 tomes, folio, was used by us.

53. *Gratian. Decretum seu Concordia discordantium canonum.* Of the very many editions, we name the Roman of 1582, 2 tomes in fol., and the Parisian, *Patrologia Latina,* tome 187, which (two) we have used.

54. *St. Gregory I, Pope* (the Great). Opera omnia, Venice 1744, 4 tomes in fol..

55. *St. Gregory VII, Pope.**

56. *St. Gregory, Bishop of Nazianzen.* Opera omnia, Venice 1753, 2 tomes in folio.

57. *William of Auxerre. Summa theologica.*

58. *William, Bishop of Paris.* Opera, Venice 1591, 1 tome in folio.

59. *Haymo* (of Faversham). Opera omnia, *Patrologia Latina,* tomes 116, 117 & 118.

60. *Hesychius, a priest of Jerusalem.* Migne, *Patrologia Graeca,* tome 93.

61. *Hermas.* (The Shepherd). *Patrologia Graeca,* tome 2.

62. *St. Jerome. Opera omnia,* Verona 1734, 11 tomes in folio.

63. *St. Hilary, Bishop of Poitiers.* Opera omnia, Venice 1750, 2 tomes in folio.

64. *Horatius Flaccus.* (His) *Carmina,* Turin 1830, 2 tomes in 8 vo..

65. *Hugo of St. Victor.* Opera Omnia, *Patrologia Latina,* tomes 175-177.

66. *Huguccio,* of Vercelli, published *Glossas in decretum Gratiani;* cited in the Roman edition, above in n. 53.

67. *St. Innocent I, Pope.*

68. *Innocent III, Pope. Patrologia Latina,* tomes 214-217.

69. *Abbot Joachim (of Fiore).* St. Bonaventure cites him in Sent., Bk. I, d. 5, Doubt 4, but confusing (him with another).

70. *St. John Chrysostom, Bishop of Constantinople.* Opera omnia, Venice 1734, 13 tomes in folio.

71. *St. John Damascene.* Opera omnia, *Patrologia Graeca,* tomes 94, 95 & 96.

72. *Josephus (Flavius). De Bello Iudaico,* Venice 1487, 1 tome in folio.

73. *Isaac Beimiram. Liber Definitionum & de Diaetis.*

74. *Isaac, Abbot of Stellen* (Germany). Opera, *Patrologia Latina,* tome 194.

75. *St. Isidore, Bishop of Seville.* Opera omnia, *Patrologia Latina,* tomes 82, 83 & 84.

76. *Isidore Mercator. Collectio decretalium, Patrologia Latina,* tome 130.

77. *(St.) Julius I, Pope.*

78. *Julius Caesar. Commentarius de Bello Gallico et civili,* Padua 1746, in 1 tome.

79. *Legenda of the Saints;* in particular, St. Bonaventure mentions the Legends of St. Genevieve (*Acta Sanctorum,* on Jan. 3rd), St. Lawrence (ibid., Aug. 10th), and Sts. Martin and Nicolas.

80. *St. Leo I, Pope.* Opera omnia, Lyons 1700, 2 tomes in fol. 81. *Liber Institutionum:* whether it belongs to Lactantius Firminianus (*Divinarum institutionum libri VII.*), we know not.

82. *Macrobius.* Opera, Lyons 1550, 1 tome in 4 vo..

---

* *Trans. note*: Those marked with * are not found in the Index of authors listed in tome X of the Quaracchi edition. For Pope Julius (n. 77) and Pelagius (n. 90), I have added their proper enumeration.

° For those Councils which are cited in the text, I have added their proper enumerations, such as *First,* I, *Fourth,* IV etc.; and given their citation from Mansi, *Conciliorum Nova, et Amplissima Collectio,* Antonio Zatta, Venice 1758-98. Though, it should be noted, that the Quaracchi editors occasionlly cite a Council from another source.

83. *St. Maximus, Bishop of Tours.* Opera omnia, *Patrologia Latina*, tome 57.

84. *St. Melchiades, Pope.*

85. *Mercurius Trismegistus, De Potestate et sapientia Dei*, Venice 1491, 1 tome in 4 vo.. The dialogues, the title of which (is) *Asclepias*, are found above in n. 11, among the works of Apuleius.

86. *(St.) Nicholas I, Pope.*

87. *Odo*, Chancellor (of the University) of Paris, whom Bonaventure mentions (Sent., Bk. II, d. 24, at the end), since under him some errors of William, the Bishop of Paris, were reproved in 1240, which decree can be seen in several editions of Master (Peter's) Sentences, such as that of Venice 1489, Basel 1523, and others.

88. *Origen (of Alexandria).* Opera omnia, *Patrologia Graeca*, tomes 11-17.

89. *Ovid.* Opera omnia, Turin 1822, 8 tomes in 8 vo..

90. *Pelagius II, Pope.*

91. *Peter Comestor.* Cited under the name "*Master in history*". *Historia Scholastica, Patrologia Latina*, tome. 198.

92. *St. Peter Chrysologus, Bishop of Ravenna.* Opera omnia, Venice 1742, 1 tome in folio.

93. *Peter of Poitiers. Liber V Sententiarum, Patrologia Latina*, tome 211.

94. *Peter Lombard, the Master of the Sentences.* Opera omnia, *Patrologia Latina*, tomes 191 & 192.

95. *Peter Praepositivus.* (His work) seems to be still unedited.

96. *Philip*, Chancellor (of the University) of Paris.

97. *(St.) Pius I, Pope.*

98. *Plato.* Opera, the edition of H. Stephanus, of 1578, 3 tomes in folio.

99. *Porphyry.* (His) *Isagogue* and certain commentaries on Aristotle.

100. *Priscianus Caesariensis, the Grammarian.* (His) works, edited by Aug. Krehl, Leipzig 1819, 2 tomes in 8 vo.. This edition contains the 18 books of Priscian; other ancient editions divide these works into two parts, the first of which contains 16 books on the 8 parts of speech, the second, 2 books, on (grammatical) construction.

101. *St. (Tiro) Prosper of Aquitaine.* Opera, Venice 1744, 2 tomes in folio.

102. *Prudentius, (Bishop of Troyes).* Various works, *Patrologia Latina*, tome 115.

103. *Ptolemaeus the Alexandrine. Geographia*, Venice 1562, 1 tome in 4 vo..

104. *(Bl.) Rabanus Maurus.* Opera omnia, *Patrologia Latina*, tomes 107-112.

105. *St. Remigius, Bishop of Auxerre. Patrologia Latina*, tome 131.

106. *Richard of St. Victor. Patrologia Latina*, tome 196.

107. *Gaius Crispus Sallutius.* Opera omnia, Turin 1827, 1 tome in 8 vo..

108. *Lucius Annaeus Seneca.* Opera omnia, Turin 1828, 5 tomes in 8 vo..

109. *Simon of Tournai.* He was a master at the University of Paris c. 1216 A. D.. His *Summa theologica* seems to be still unpublished.

110. *(St.) Soter, Pope.*

111. *Strabo. Rerum geographicarum libri XVII*, Paris 1620, 1 tome in folio. Likewise, *de Motu orbis*, Venice 1510, 1 tome in folio.

112. *Walafrid Strabo.* See above, under n. 52.

113. *Symbola Apostolorum* (Apostles' Creed), the Nicene (Creed) and the Athanasian (Creed).

114. *Theodore I, Pope.* *

115. *(Bl.) Urban II, Pope.* *

116. *Victor, Pope.* *

117. *Victorinus Afer.* Opera, *Patrologia Latina*, tome 8.

118. *(St.) Zachary, Pope.*

To this list we add the editions of the authors, which we have often used in the footnotes and Scholia, namely Bl. Albertus Magnus, *in Libros Sententiarum*, Basel 1506; *Summa*, ibid. 1507. — St. Thomas (Aquinas), Opera omnia, *Parma*, Fiaccadori. — Scotus, Opera Omnia, Lyons 1639. — Richard of Middleton, *Comment. in Sententias*, Venice 1509. — Giles the Roman, *Comment. in Sententias*, venice 1521. — Gabriel Biel, *Comment. in Sententias*, Tübingen 1501. — Peter of Spain, *Summulae sive Isagogae in Aristotelicos dialecticaae libros*, Basel, Michaelis Furter 1511; *Parva Logicalia* (the tract on Syncategoremata), Venice 1572.

To be noted , regarding the following Table.

In the following Table, there are placed in one view, the codices gathered by us according to the alphabetical order of (their) *signs*.[+] A few of these codices, consulted by us in only some more difficult passages, are distinguished with the sign *. Lest by enumerating each single codex, we afflict the reader with an exceedingly long, tedious series of codices, we have signified in general terms their number in this manner. By placing the words "ancient codices" [*antique codd.*] we have noted all and/or nearly all the codices collected by us, except codex cc. — "Nearly all" [*fere omnes*] is employed by us, to signify all, as much as we conjecture. For, if very few of our codices are missing in regard to any reading, it has rather been presumed, that this silence ought to be explained out of a certain involuntary omission of the (editor) consulting (the text), and not out of a different reading of the codex. How easily these omissions in small things may even accede to those diligently consulting codices, all experienced in this subject know. — Under the term "very many" [*plurimi*] there are understood (to be signified) at least 20 codices, noted from every family and nation (of origin). — "Many" [*multi*] are understood (to be) 15 or more. — "Several" / "A large number of" [*plures / plerique*]° are at least 8. — When the number of these is less than 8, we employ the term "not a few" [*nonnulli*] and, then, "few" [*pauci*]. It is scarcely necessary to say, that under the general term "codex" we do not understand only those, which have been gathered by us along with the Vatican edition.

Moreover, we note these: 1. In citing the distinctions from the very Book of Peter Lombard we use *Roman* numerals; however, in citing St. Bonaventure's or another's Commentary, (we use) *Arabic* numerals. When, in citing the Commentary of St. Bonaventure, in any Distinction, we have omitted "*Article*" (or *a.*), it is a sign that in that Distinction there is only one Article. 2. For the sake of brevity in the Scholia and notes, we have used the word "this" [*hic or hoc*], to signify, that that passage is in the Commentary on the Books of Sentences and indeed in the same (book) and in the same distinction, which is being dealt with. 3. We have not been able to quote the passages cited from the other books of St. Bonaventure, because we used the text of the editions and, indeed, of the Vatican edition, in which we have only sometimes corrected some of the errors.

---

* *Trans. notes*: Those authors marked above with an asterisk are not found in the Index of authors listed in tome X. To the names of Pope Theodore and Urban, I have added their proper enumeration.

+ In the footnotes of the main text, these signs (letters) will indicate which of these codices are cited; "many", "few", etc., how many have that reading.

° It has been the custom of the English Translation of the First Book to render *plures* and *plerique* as "very many", even though it would be more accurate to render them as "several" or "very many", as shall be done hereafter in Bk. II & ff..

Nota bene: In the Quaracchi edition, there were 2 *tabula* on the following page; since these were not so easily comprehended, I have converted them both to tables for easier inspection. I have added the column titles and the final columns, extracting this information from the text of the Prolegomena itself. The two original footnotes on the following page (regarding the meaning of the Prologue n., and corrigenda for the citation of codex ee), have been omitted, since the Trans. notes serve the former and since in the translation all the errors originally indicated, on pp. LXXXVII & 871 have been corrected.

TABLE

OF THE CODICES AND EDITIONS USED

FOR THE FIRST BOOK OF THE COMMENTARIES

CODICES

Sign	Location	Library	Library Sigla	Proleg. n.[?]	Age [α]
A	Assisi	Municipal	42.	1	13 -»
B	Vatican	Apostolica	907.	31	13 -»
C	Paris	National	17480.	25	13
D	Vatican	Apostolica	908.	32	14
E	Rome	Chisiana	B. VIII. 128.	33	13 -»
F	Florence I	Nazionale	C. VI. Nation. 209.	6	13
G	Florence II	Nazionale	D. V. 206.	7	13
H	Florence III	Nazionale	D. V. 207.	8	13 -»
I	Florence IV	Nazionale	I. VII. 7. 45.*	9	14
K	Florence V	Medicea Laurenziana	plut. dext. XXV. 2.	11	13
L	Oxford	Lincoln College	25.	22	13 -»
M	Cassino	Monastica	398.00.	18	13
N	Naples	Nazionale	VII. D. 28.	20	14
O	Oxford	Balliol College	133.	21	-» 14
P	Padua I	Antoniana	120.	27	13
Q	Padua II	Antoniana	125.	28	13
R	Paris II	National	3085.	23	-» 14
S	Paris III	National	15821.	24	13
T	Todi	Municipale°	39.	34	13
U	Paris IV	Sorbonne	Th. II. 48.	26	13 -»
V	Milan	Ambrosiana	I. 95. infer.	14	= 13 =
W	München I	Royal	C. L. M. 14086.	16	13 -»
X	München II	Royal	C. L. M. 18344	17	15
Y	Bamburg	Civic§	B. III. 42.	2	15
Z	Leipzig	University+	491.	13	-» 14
aa	Kraków I	University	1246. DD. XIV.	4	15
bb	Kraków II	University	1252. A. A. XI. 16.	5	13 -»
cc	Florence	Collegio S. Bonaventura	—	35	15
dd	München III	Royal	C. L. M. 8079.	15	15
ee	Florence VI	Medicea Laurenziana	LXX. Fes.□	12	= 14 =
ff	Florence VII	Nazionale	C. VI. 208.	10	13
gg	Padua III*	Antoniana	123.	29	-» 14
hh	Padua IV*	Antoniana	124.	30	13
ii	Modena*	Atestina	974. VII. I. 14.	19	13
kk	Bologna*	Collegio degli Spagnoli	35.	3	13 -»

EDITIONS

Sign	Place Printed	Year Printed	Proleg. n.
1	Brixen	1490	3 & 4
2	Nürnberg	1492	10-13
3	Venice I	1562	17
4	Venice II	1673 µ	18
5	Venice III	1580	19
6	Lyons	1570	24-28

---

* Cfr. the Editors' Note to this table, on previous page.

* *Trans. notes*: In the Prolegomena, this sigla is written: I. 7. 45.

[?] The Proleg. n., refers to the entry above on pp. LXXVI-LXXVIII, for the first table; on pp. LXXIII-LXXV, for the second.

[α] The century in which the Quaracchi editors held the manuscript to have originated: -» **13** means *of the beginning of the 13th century;* **13** -» means *of the end of the 13th century;* = **13** = means *of the middle of the 13th century*; **13** means *of the 13th century.*

° While the Quaracchi editors, in the Prolegomena above, have cited this library as the ancient library of the Conventual Convent of St. Fortunatus, yet, in the Srolegomena to Book IV, p. II, they identify this as the Municipal library of Todi. Note that the Municipal library at Assisi, holds the contents of the library of the Sacro Convento. The library indicates where the codex was conserved in 1882.

§ In the Prolegomena, this library is called the Public library.

+ In the Prolegomena, this library is called the Paulina; its contents now form the Paulina collection at the University library.

□ In the Prolegomena, this sigla is given as LXX. Mediceo-Fesulan..

µ Cf. Prolegomena, p. LXXV, n. 18: this date might be an error for 1573, though the Quaracchi Editors in their errata on p. 871 say nothing on this.

TABULA

OF CODICES AND EDITIONS USED
OF THE BOOK OF SENTENCES OF PETER LOMBARD*

CODICES AT FLORENCE (Biblioteca Nazionale)

A.   Codex VI. 27. S. Marci
B.   Codex VI. 28. S. Marci
C.   Codex VI. 32. S. Marci
D.   Codex 2599. B. 1., once of the Abbazia di Firenze
E.   Codex 3559. A. 4., once of the Abbazia di Firenze.[1]

EDITIONS OF THE BOOK OF SENTENCES CONSULTED BY US

1. The Venetian edition of 1486.
2. The Nürnberg edition (i.e. the Koberger, containing St. Bonav.'s Comment.), of 1499.
3. The Venetian edition of 1509 (with the Commentary of Richard of Middleton).
4. The Lyonnaise edition of 1540.
5. The Cologne edition of 1535 (with the Commentary of Dionysius the Carthusian).
6. The Lyonnaise edition of 1639 (with the Commentary of Scotus).
7. The Venetian edition of 1489.
8. The Parisian edition of 1659 (with the Commentary of St. Thomas).
9. The Basel edition of 1513.

For the chapters, placed after the Master's Prologue, we have used these codices from the Biblioteca Medicea Laurenziana at Florence:

F — plut. 21	cod. 24.	L — plut. 30. dext.	cod. 1. S. Crucis
G — plut. 21.	cod. 26.	M — plut. 25. dext.	cod. 1. S. Crucis
H — plut. 21.	cod. 27.	N — plut 31. dext.	cod. 1. S. Crucis
I — plut 28. dext.	cod. 2.	O — Gaddian.	cod. 59.
K — plut. 24. dext.	cod. 1. S. Crucis		

From the Biblioteca Antoniana, at Padua:

P	N. VIII. cod. 151	S	N. VIII. cod. 149.
Q	N. VIII. cod. 136.	T	N. VIII. cod. 150.
R	N. VIII. cod. 139		

---

[1] These codices are from before the middle of the 13th century, except Codex E, which is of the 15th and, though written in a most splendid manner, is of lesser value for critical use than the other four, among which codex D is the preponderant one.

* *Trans. note*: In the *tabulae* on this page, I have updated the names of libraries, by the addition of the word *Biblioteca* in the first title, *Medicea* in third title, and by rendering the name of the library in the fourth, *biblioth. Patavina Conv. S. Antonii* as *the Biblioteca Antoniana, at Padua*.

ST. BONAVENTURE'S
FOREWORD

TO THE FIRST BOOK OF SENTENCES

The depths of rivers He has scrutinized, and things hidden away He has brought to light.
JOB 28:11

hat word, which[1] is taken from the twenty-eighth chapter of Job, having been considered more diligently by us, opened the way to foreknow the fourfold kind of cause in the BOOK OF SENTENCES, namely, the *material*, the *formal*, the *efficient*, and the *final*. For the material cause is signified in the name, *"of rivers"*, the formal cause in the investigation [perscrutatione] of *"the depths"*, the final cause in the revelation of *"things hidden"*, but the efficient cause is understood in the addition of two phrases, namely *"He has scrutinized"* and *"He has brought to light."*

The[2] *material* cause is hinted at by the name, *"of rivers"*, in the plural, not the singular, to not only touch upon the matter and/or subject of the whole book in general, but even of the smaller parts of the books in detail. On account of which it must be noted, that just as there is a fourfold property of a material river, so there is a fourfold property of a spiritual river, concerning which, according to their fourfold difference, are the four BOOKS OF THE SENTENCES. For I consider[3] the material river in regard to (its) duration, and I find (its) *perenniality*. For as (St.) Isidore (of Seville) says:[4] « A river is a perennial flowing ». I consider it as much as regards (its) extension, and I find (its) *spaciousness*. For in this a river is distinguished from a rivulet. I consider it as much as regards (its) motion, and I find (its) *circulation*. For just

as is said in the first chapter of Ecclesiastes:[5] *To the place, whence streams go forth, they return* etc.. I consider[6] (its) effect, and I find (its) *cleansing*. For a river, on account of the abundance of (its) waters, cleanses the lands, through which it runs, such that it is not polluted.[7] And since everyone speaking figuratively [transferentes], speaks figuratively[8] according to some similitude, according to the metaphor taken from this fourfold condition, a river is found to be fourfold in spiritual things, as we can gather from the Scriptures.

First, on account of (its) *perenniality* the Emanation of the Persons is called "a river", since that Emanation alone is without beginning, without end.[9] Concerning this River (there is said) in the seventh chapter of Daniel:[10] *The Ancient of Days sat, and a fiery and swift river stepped forth from His face.* That "Ancient of Days" is the eternal Father, whose antiquity is eternity. That Ancient One *"sat"*, because not only is eternity in Him, but also immutability.[11] *From the face of that Ancient One a fiery and swift river stepped forth,* that is, from the loftiness of His Divinity there proceeded the fullness *of love* and the fullness *of virtue*: the fullness *of virtue* in the Son,[12] for that reason the river was swift; the fullness *of love* in the Holy Spirit, and for that reason the river was fiery.

---

[1] On the authority of the manuscripts and edition 1, we substitute in the proposition the relative construction, adding *which* [quod] and *is* [est], for a simpler participle; which the Vatican edition has. Then by placing *opened* [aperuit] in place of *opens* [aperit] we follow the more outstanding of our codices A B C E G K O R S T W X Y ff and others which we have especially consulted.

[2] The Vatican edition, with the manuscripts and even edition 1 opposing it, reads *For the* [enim]; codex Y reads *Moreover, the* [autem]; we prefer however, the reading of the other codices and edition 1, which however, omit either word.

[3] Many codices like A G I O T V W Y aa bb have *By considering* [Considerando], which also then on account of the changed construction omit *and* [et] after *duration* [durationem]. Likewise it occurs in the three subsequent propositions here below. This reading, inasmuch as it could be more elegant in itself, is not displeasing, if it is supported by a sufficient number of codices, and if the aforesaid codices agree with it; but in the last proposition very few codices return to this reading.

[4] THE ETYMOLOGIES, or OF ORIGINS, Bk. XIII, ch. 21: "A river [Fluvius] is a perennial down-running of waters [decursus aquarum], called such by (its) perpetual flowing [fluendo]."

[5] Verse 7 — The Vatican edition, against manuscripts and editions 1, 2, 3, 6, in the now active voice has *Ecclesiastes says* [dicit Ecclesiastes].

[6] Codices F M X, agreeing with themselves, add *as much as regards* [quantum ad].

[7] The Vatican edition has *they are polluted* [inquinantur], but wrongly, as is gathered from having made a comparison with what follows, and with the manuscripts and edition 1 opposing this.

[8] This proposition, taken from Aristotle's TOPICS, Bk. 6, ch. 2, is quoted in the same words in the edition of Aristotle's works printed at Venice by Gregorius de Gregoriis at the expense of Benedict Fontana, in 1496 A.D., and in the Parisian edition by Ambrosius Firmin-Didot, 1878 A. D.; in other editions it is rendered thus: For all, using a metaphor, use it according to some similitude. — A little after this, with the manuscripts and edition 1 opposing this, the Vatican edition badly omits *taken* [sumta], then places *in rivers* [fluviis] for *river* [fluvius].

[9] Codex Y exhibits the last part of the sentence thus: *in as much as it alone is without beginning and without end* [in quantum ipsa sola est sine principio et sine fine].

[10] This text is taken partly from v. 9, partly from v. 10.

[11] Edition 1 has *incommutability* [incommutabilitas].

[12] The Vatican edition *the Son* [Filium] and a little after *the Holy Spirit* [Spiritum Sanctum]; but we prefer, as the better reading, the one received in the text, which belongs to almost all the manuscripts and edition 1; for *"virtue"* [virtus] is appropriated to the very terminus of the first divine emanation or the Son (see below, d. 32 a. 2 q. 2 to the end.), indeed *"love"* [amor] is appropriated to the terminus of the second emanation or the Holy Spirit. (d. 10 a. 2 q. 1).

Second, on account of (its) *spaciousness* an extension of mundane things is called a "river", on account of which cause this world is called not only a "river", but "the sea" by the Prophet in the Psalm:[1] *This sea, great and spacious* etc. This river is spoken of in the twenty-ninth chapter of Ezechiel:[2] *Behold I (come) for you Pharaoh, king of Egypt, who recline in the midst of the streams and say: "Mine is the river, and I made it Myself." I will place a bridle upon your jaws* etc. That great dragon, to whom the Lord speaks and which He threatens in the figure and person of the Pharaoh, is the Devil, who is the King of Egypt,[3] since he reigns in those, whom he has thoroughly blinded with the darkness of error, as heretics are reckoned to be, to whom[4] he also says: *Mine is the river, and I made it Myself,* as if to say that he himself had made this world and he himself has no other beginning. He mentioned this error and suggested it[5] for the sake of the impious Manicheans, who contend that the entire machine of visible things was established by an evil god. The jaws of this dragon the Lord *shall crush,*[6] when with his power to suggest false things born away, He will show, that He is the Establisher of this river; whence in the same authority it follows: *Let all the inhabitants of Egypt know, that I am the Lord.*

Third, on account of (its) *circulation* the Incarnation of the Son of God is called a "river", since, just as in a circle the last is conjoined with the beginning, so in the Incarnation the highest is conjoined with the lowest, that is God to slime,[7] and the First to the last, as the eternal Son of God to the man established on the sixth day. Of this river the twenty-fourth chapter of Ecclesiastes (says):[8] *I, like the river Dorix, and as an aqueduct have gone forth from paradise.* "Dorix" is interpreted "medicament of generation", and this is a figurative way of speaking, to be understood conversely, that is, as a "generation of a medicament". For the Incarnation of the Son of God was nothing other than a generation of medicament:* *For truly has He born our weaknesses and carried our infirmities.*[9] Therefore, rightly is the Incarnation of the Son called the river Dorix. And Christ[10] Himself truly says of Himself: *I like the river Dorix,* that

is, a medicinal river, *and as an aqueduct I have gone forth from paradise.* The nature of water is this,[11] that as much as it ascends, it descends. Such was the going forth of the Incarnation, according to what is said in the Psalm:[12] *From the highest Heaven His stepping forth, and His meeting even unto His height.* And in the sixteenth chapter of John:[13] *I have gone forth from the Father and have come into the world; again I leave the world and I go to the Father,* and so He made a circle. Also concerning this river, as much as regards His stepping forth from His Mother, there can be expounded, that, which is said in the tenth chapter of Esther[14] in the dream of Mordechai: *A tiny rivulet sprung into the river, and was converted into light and into the sun.* Who, I beseech, is this tiny rivulet except the most humble Virgin? She sprang into the river, when She generated Christ, who was not only a river through[15] an abundance of grace, but also is called "the Light of wisdom" and "the Sun of justice", according to what John says of Him in his first[16] chapter: *He was the true light* etc..

Fourth, on account of (its) *cleansing,* the dispensation of the Sacraments is called a "river", which, without themselves being polluted, cleanse us from the contaminations [coninquinationibus] of sins. Concerning this river the twenty-second chapter of the Apocalypse (says):[17] *He showed me the river of living waters, splendid as crystal, proceeding (down) from the throne of God and of the Lamb.* The dispensation of the Sacraments is called a river, "*splendid as crystal*", on account of the clarity and brilliance, which it leaves in the souls, who are washed in this river. It is also called a river "*of living waters*" on account of (its) efficacy of grace, which vivifies the soul. This (river) also "*proceeds from the throne of God and of the Lamb*". For sacramental grace proceeds *from God* as from (its) Author[18] and (its) efficient cause, *from Christ* as from (its) Mediator and from the One who merited it. On account of which, all the Sacraments are said to have efficacious grace from the Passion of Christ, whence Augustine testifies:[19] « From the side of the sleeping Christ

---

[1] Psalm 103:25 — A little before this very many of the codices, such as A B C D G H I K M O P R S T W ee and edition 1 omit *reason* [causam]; the reading, not to be spurned, is much more genuine, in so far as the relative *which* [quam] refers to *spaciousness* [spatiositatem].
[2] Verse 3. The Vulgate in this passage reads *of your streams* [fluminum tuorum]; immediately afterward edition 4 and 6 have *who* [qui] for *and* [et].
[3] Trusting the manuscripts and edition 1, we have expunged the passage in the Vatican edition, which is added here: *which is interpreted darkness* [quae interpretatur tenebrae]. Immediately afterwards codex O has *who* [quia] in place of *since he* [quoniam].
[4] The Vatican edition has *who* [quem], but this is entirely false, as is clear from the context itself and repugnant to the mss. with edition 1.
[5] Codices K V and edition 1 add *and suggests it* [et suggerit], indeed the others, such as codices A and T for *he suggested it* [suggessit] read *he suggests it* [suggerit] in regard to the Manicheans living in the time of the Seraphic Doctor.
[6] Codex U reads *shall rein in* [refrenabit]. Then codices B C D G I O T W X Z bb have the not so good reading *since* [quoniam], codex A has *who* [qui] in place of *when* [quando]. A little afterwards by the words *in the same authority* [in eadem auctoritate] understand Ezech. 29:6 where even the Vulgate with edition 1 reads *because* [quia] for *since* [quoniam].
[7] We have added the words omitted in the Vatican edition *that is God to slime* [ut Deus limo] with the assistance of the manuscripts and edition 1. Cf. the book, ON THE SPIRIT AND THE SOUL, chapter 14. — A little before this codex ee with edition 1 reads *has been conjoined* [coniunctum est] in place of *is conjoined* [coniungitur]. At the end of the passage codices A C F I M S T etc. have *sixth* [sexto]; the Vatican edition has *sixth* [sexta].
[8] Verse 41 in the Vulgate reads *I like the Dioryx of the river and as* etc.

[Ego quasi fluvii Dioryx et sicut etc.] Likewise this recurs a little below. But see (Nicholas) of Lyra and Cardinal Hugo of St. Charo on this verse.°
[9] Isaias 53:4, in which passage the Vulgate reads *our sorrows* [dolores nostros] for *our infirmities* [infirmitates nostras].
[10] On account of our trust in the manuscripts and edition 1, *Christ* [Christus] is badly lacking in the Vatican edition.
[11] With the codices and edition 1 opposing it, the Vatican edition puts *The nature of this water is* [huius], but faultily, because what is subjoined is appropriate not only to this or that water, but all water.
[12] Psalm 18:7 (6).
[13] Verse 28.
[14] Verse 6, in which passage the Vatican edition has here and a little afterwards *small* [parvus] not *tiny* [parvulus], though the manuscripts and edition 1 disagree; the Vulgate however, has : *A little fountain, which sprung* etc. [Parvus fons, qui crevit etc.] A little before this codices I and T omit *which is said* [quod dicitur], for that which the Vatican edition with edition 1 and one other codex have as *which ... says* [quod dicit].
[15] Codices H and ee have *on account of* [propter]; then codex M has *superabundance* [superabundantiam].
[16] Verse 9.   [17] Verse 1.
[18] On the authority of very many codices, such as K R Y Z and ee we substitute *author* [auctore] for *agent* [actore], which the Vatican edition has. Each word is often written in codices in the same manner. Then edition 1 adds after *Christ* [Christo] the adversative *but* [vero].
[19] ON THE GOSPEL OF JOHN, ch. 2, tr. 9, n. 10: "From the sleeping Adam, Eve is made from his side; after Christ died His side was pierced with the lance, so that the Sacraments would flow forth, by which the Church is formed." See also the book of quotations taken from Augustine (which is by Prosper

---

* *Trans. note:* i. e. a medicinal preparation, mixture, or balm.
° Cf. also Cornelius a Lapidé, COMMENTARII IN SACRAM SCRIP-

TURAM, Tomus V, "In Ecclesiasticum", Pelagaud et Lesne, Lyons 1841 ed., pp. 574-6.

flowed the Sacraments, while blood and water flowed from there. ».

All these rivers are contained at once and in order in the second[1] chapter of Genesis, where it is said, that *the river stepped forth from the place of pleasure, which from there divided into four sources: the name of the first, "Phison", the name of the second, "Gehon", the name of the third, "Tigris", and the name of the fourth, "Euphrates"*. That river stepping forth form Paradise is the entire matter of this Book. The four rivers proceeding from that (river) are the special matters of the four books, as one can easily adapt, who wants to diligently explain[2] the interpretations of the aforesaid names. For "Phison" is interpreted "mouth of change", and in this there is signified the Emanation of the Persons. For as out of a material mouth there proceeds word and spirit, so, out of the mouth of the Father, the Son and Holy Spirit, (as is said) in the twenty-fourth chapter of Ecclesiasticus:[3] *I went forth out of the mouth of the Most High, first born before every creature.* This the Son Himself says, who is the Word and Wisdom of the Father. And in the Psalm:[4] *By the Word of the Lord the heavens have been made firm: and the Spirit of His mouth* etc.. "Gehon" is interpreted "sand", and in this there is signified the extension of mundane things. For as the universe of creatures is compared to the sea on account of (its) spaciousness, so the sands on account of their numerosity, (as is said) in the first chapter of Ecclesiasticus:[5] *Sand of the sea and drops of the rain, who can count them?* "Tigris" is interpreted "arrow", and in this there is signified the Incarnation of the Son of God. For as in an arrow iron has been conjoined with wood, so in Christ the fortitude of the Divinity has been conjoined to the pliability of humanity. And as an arrow flies from bow and wood to strike one's adversaries, so did Christ, springing (down) from the Cross, destroy the Adversary. This is that arrow, of which there is said in the thirteenth chapter of Kings:[6] *Arrow of the Lord's salvation, and arrow of salvation against Syria.* "Euphrates" is interpreted "fruit-bearing", in which there is signified the dispensation of the Sacraments, which not only purge the soul from fault, but even fecundate it in grace. Which has been signified in the last chapter of the Apocalypse,[7] where it is said, that along the crystalline river *there was a tree bearing fruit, whose leaves were for medicine.*

Therefore, since four are the rivers, four are the *depths* of the rivers corresponding to the aforesaid rivers.

The depth of the *Eternal Emanation* is the loftiness of Divine 'Being' [esse divini], concerning which there can be understood that (which is said) in the seventh chapter of Ecclesiasticus:[8] *High profundity, who will find it?* Truly, so high a profundity and so profound a height, that the Apostle exclaims in the eleventh chapter to the Romans[9] and says: *O height of the riches of the wisdom and the knowledge of God, how incomprehensible are His judgements, and unsearchable His ways!* Truly incomprehensible judgements, because profound. *For the judgements of God (are as) the many things of the abyss.*[10] and in the first chapter of Ecclesiasticus:[11] *Depth of the abyss, who has measured it?* This profundity is hinted at in the eleventh chapter of Job:[12] *Perhaps you comprehend the footprints of God and repair even to the perfect Omnipotent? He is more exalted than Heaven, and what will you make? more profound than Hell, and whence will you know* [cognosces] *?* as if he were to say: "You are not able of yourself": for that reason the Apostle counsels (us) in the third chapter to the Ephesians:[13] *Be rooted and founded upon charity, so that you may be able to comprehend* etc..

And this *depth* the Master thoroughly scrutinizes in the first book. For the loftiness of Divine 'Being' [esse] consists in two things, namely in the noblest *emanations*, which are generation and procession, and[14] in the noblest *conditions*, which are Most High Wisdom, Omnipotence and the perfect Will, of which is the first book. For in the first part he deals with the Most Sacred Unity and Trinity, but in the second[15] with a special tract, he deals with His above said threefold condition or property.

The depth of *creation* is the vanity of created 'being' [esse creati]. For the creature inasmuch as it is more vanishing, so much more does it tend into the depth, either vanishing through fault or through punishment. On account of this there is said through the Prophet in the person of a man, who vanished through fault, in the Psalm:[16] *I have been thrust into the slime of the deep, and there is no substance.* And again the Prophet praying, lest he vanish through punishment: *Do not let it submerge me,* he said, *the storm of water, nor let it swallow me the depth* etc..

This depth the Master scrutinizes in the second

---

of Aquitaine) n. 329 — A little before this on account of codices A C F G H I K P R S T U X Y aa bb ee and edition 1 we put *whence* [unde] in place of *as* [ut]. Then codices S aa bb with edition 1 have *with Augustine as witness* [teste Augustino] for *Augustine testifies* [testator Augustinus], among whose words codex M adds *of the Church* [ecclesiae] after *the Sacraments* [fluxerunt].

[1] Verses 10-14, where the Vulgate adds *to irrigate Paradise* [ad irrigandum Paradisum] after *of pleasure* [voluptatis] and enumerates the names of the rivers in this fashion: *The name of one, Phison,... and the name of the second river, Gehon,...indeed the name of the third river, Tigris,...moreover, the fourth river, is itself the Euphrates* [Nomen uni Phison... et nomen fluvii secundi Gehon... Nomen vero fluminis tertii, Tigris... Fluvius autem quartus, ipse est Euphrates]. Many codices A F G I S W Y etc. with editions 1, 2, 3, 6 spell the name of the second river thus *Gyon* [Gyon]. — A little before this codex M has *according to their order* [secundum] in place of *in order* [per].

[2] Codex ee and edition 1 have *consider* [considerare].

[3] V. 5, where the Vulgate has *prodivi* [went forth] for *prodii* [went forth.]

[4] Psalm 32:6.

[5] Verse 3, in which text the Vatican manuscript with the Vulgate adds *and the days of a generation* [et dies saeculi] after *rain* [guttas]. — A little before we have substituted from codices A C G H I O R S T U Y Z bb ee ff and edition 1 *numerosity* [numerositatem] for *un-numerableness* [innumerositatem], though each reading has the same meaning.

[6] Verse 17.

[7] Verse 2, where the Vulgate reads: *The tree of life bearing twelve fruits, bearing its own fruit throughout every month and the leaves of the wood were for the healing of the nations* [Lignum vitae afferens fructus duodecim, per menses singulos reddens fructum suum et folia ligni ad sanitatem gentium].

[8] Verse 25.

[9] Verse 33, in which text, trusting in the codices and edition 1, we have added *and how unsearchable are His ways* [et investigabiles eius], which the Vatican edition omits.

[10] Psalm 35:7, where the Vulgate reads: *Thy judgements are as the many things of the abyss* [Iudicia tua abyssus multa].

[11] Verse 2.

[12] Verse 7 and 8.　　　[13] Verses 17 and 18.

[14] The Vatican edition has a confused reading, in which the conjunction *and* [et] is replaced with a period, so that a new sentence begins with *in* [in]: we have emended this from the manuscripts and edition 1.

[15] There has been inserted here in the Vatican edition the following sentence: *which he begins in distinction 35: And since we observed above* etc. [quae incipit in distinct. 35: Cumque supra disserverimus], which we have removed, as an interpolation, on the authority of the codices and edition 1.

[16] Psalm 68:2. The text of Sacred Scripture which follows is found in the same Psalm 68:16.

book. For the vanity of the created 'being' consists in two things, viz. in change from 'not being' [non esse] into 'being' [esse] and, again, in the reversion into 'not being' [non esse]. And although no creature passes entirely into 'one not being' [non ens] through nature, nevertheless, as Augustine says,[1] the sinner tends 'to be not' [non esse] through fault. And of these two is the entire second (book). For in the first part he deals with the stepping-forth of things, but in the second part[2] he deals with the Fall, as it concerns temptation by the devil, original sin and actual sin, through unto the end of the book.

The depth of the Incarnation is the merit of the Humanity[3] of Christ, which was so great, so that it can truly be called a depth, as if one not having a terminus nor bottom. Of this there can be understood that (which is said) in the second chapter of Jonas:[4] *Thou has cast me forth into the depth in the heart of my mother, and the stream has surrounded me.* This can be said of Christ, who was so humiliated, that truly he could be said to be "*cast forth*" and "*abject*", (as is said) in the fifty-third chapter of Isaias:[5] *And we have seen him, and no attractiveness belonged to him, and we desired him: despised and the last of men etc.* Truly therefore, He calls himself "cast forth", but where? *in the depth of the sea and of the stream.* For the Passion of Christ is compared to *the sea* on account of the bitterness of (its) penalty, but also[6] to *a stream* on account of the sweetness of (its) charity. For the Most Sweet Heart of Jesus Christ was stirred with such great a tenderness of love for[7] us, that it did not seem heavy for Him to sustain on our behalf an extreme and most bitter kind of death.

And this depth the Master thoroughly scrutinizes in the third book. For the merit of Christ consists in two things, namely in His *Passion*, through which He redeemed us, and in His *action*, through which He formed [informavit] us, which consists in His works of virtue, of gifts, and of precepts, of which two things is the third book. For in the first part the Incarnation and Passion are dealt with, in which consists our redemption, in the second[8] the virtues, gifts, and precepts, in which consist our formation [informatio].

The depth of the *sacramental dispensation* is the efficacy of a perfect medicament. For so great is the efficacy of sacramental medicine, that it exceeds the human mind, so that it can truly be called a "depth". Of this (there is said) in the fifty-first chapter of Isaias:[9] *Thou has placed the depth of the sea as Thy way, so that they (who) have been freed might pass over.* That depth, in which the Egyptians are submerged and the sons of Israel,[10] having been freed, pass over and are saved, is the efficacy of the Sacraments, in which the works of darkness are destroyed and there are conferred the arms of light and the gifts of graces, through which man is transferred from the power of darkness into the Kingdom of the Son of God of charity. This efficacy of the Sacraments is a depth "*of a sea*" and "*of a stream*": "*of a sea*",[11] in as much as at first it frees from fault and introduces one into the bitterness of penitence; "*of a stream*", in as much as it frees from misery and introduces one into the sweetness of glory.[12] Which was pre-signified best of all in the sons of Israel, for whom, as they went forth from Egypt, the sea was dried up, and they passed over *through dry land in its midst*, as is said in the fifteenth chapter of Exodus;[13] and for those entering into the land of promise the river was dried up, and they passed over through its midst, as is said in the fourth chapter of Josue.[14]

This depth the Master thoroughly scrutinizes in the fourth book. For the efficacy of perfect medicament consists in two things, namely in (its) *healing* of a variety of depressing infirmities and in (its) *freeing* from the totality of worsening miseries; and of these two is the entire fourth book. For in the first part he deals with the manifold *healing*, which the seven Sacraments effect. In the second[15] he deals with *perfect healing*, to which they lead, as with *the glory of the resurrected*, who truly and faithfully perceived the Sacraments of the Church; and contrariwise with *the punishments of the wicked*, who contemned the Sacraments of the Church.

Moreover, from the thorough scrutiny of the four depths in the four books there is elicited their *end*, namely the revelation of *four hidden things*.

---

[1] The words cited from Augustine are not found literally in his works, but only in regard to (their) sense; concerning this see CONFESSIONS, Bk. VII, ch. 16; ON THE TRUE RELIGION, chapter 11 and ON THE CITY OF GOD, Bk. XIV, ch. 13. — (A little before this), codex X with edition 1 has *tends* [tendat] for *passes* [cedat], and codices F H and aa *into 'not being'* [in non esse] for *into a non-being* [in non ens]; in the following sentence after *second* many codices B E H K P V W X ff add *book* [liber].

[2] The Vatican edition, against the authority of the manuscripts and edition 1, adds here *which begins in distinction 24: Therefore, the devil seeing etc.* [quae incipit in distinctione 24: Videns igitur diabolus etc.] and then for *unto the end* [in finem] reads *to the end* [ad finem].

[3] Parting with the manuscripts and editions 1, 2, 3 the Vatican edition has *humility* [humilitatis]. Then codices F I T concluding the sentence with the word *terminus* [terminum], begin the next differently: *This is the depth of which etc.* [Hoc est profundum de quo etc.], which is a reading not to be spurned.   [4] Verse 4.

[5] Verse 2 & 3, where the Vulgate omits *in him* [ei] after *there was* [erat].

[6] We have emended this undue omission of the words *but also* [sed et] with the help of nearly all the codices and edition 1.

[7] Codex Y has *for* [erga].

[8] The sentence, which the Vatican edition inserts here is : which begins in distinction 23: *But since this is considered above etc.* [quae incipit in distinctione 23: Cum vero supra habitum sit etc.]; *are dealt with* [agitur], is lacking in the manuscripts and in edition 1.

[9] Verse 10, where the Vulgate omits *your* [tuam].

[10] We have supplied *Israel* [Israel] on the basis of many codices K F S T X Y EE etc. and edition 1.

[11] We restore the mutilated reading of the Vatican edition, in which *and of a stream: of a sea* [et fluminis: maris] is lacking on the basis of the manuscripts and edition 1.

[12] The Vatican edition with very many codices has *of grace* [gratiae] in place of *of glory* [gloriae] contrary to codices aa and bb, whose reading nevertheless we judge to be genuine, because not only in the second part of the fourth book of the Sentences is grace not dealt with, but rather glory, but also because in the following paragraph only glory is dealt with. — A little below, following very many codices such as A F G H M T etc. with edition 1, we have substituted *pre-signified* [praesignatum] for *prefigured* [praefiguratum].

[13] Verse 19, which the Vulgate puts thus: *However the sons of Israel walked through dry land in its midst* [Filii autem Israel ambulaverunt per siccum in medio eius]. In the codices cited, chapter 22, verse 22 reads: *And the sons of Israel entered in through the midst of a dry sea* [Et ingressi sunt filii Israel per medium sicci maris].

[14] Verse 22-24. — On the authority of the manuscripts and edition 1 we have corrected the corrupted reading of the Vatican edition *The water was divided from Egypt, and they passed over through the midst of a dry sea, just as is said: And entering into the land of promise through a dry streambed Israel passed over that Jordan, with the Lord Our God drying up its waters etc. This is said in a similar manner in Joshua* [ex Aegypto divisa est aqua, et transierunt per medium sicci maris, sicut dicitur: Et introeuntibus in terram promissionis per arentem alveum transivit Israel Iordanem istum, siccante Domino Deo nostro aquas eius etc. Simile dicitur in Iosue.].

[15] The sentence added here in the Vatican ed. *which begins in distinction 43: At last concerning the condition of the resurrection etc.* [quae incipit in distinctione 43: Postremo de conditione resurrectionis etc.], is not found in the mss. nor in ed. 1. Then, ed. 1 has *namely* [scilicet] for *as* [sicut], which is just as sufficient.

The First is *the magnitude of the Divine Substance,* of which (there is said) in the fourty-fifth[1] chapter of Isaias: *Truly Thou art a God hidden away, the God of Israel, the Savior.* Truly the magnitude of the Divine Substance is hidden away according to that (which is said) in the twenty-sixth[2] chapter of Job: *Since we have scarcely heard a tiny drop of His speech, who will be able to gaze at the magnitude of His thunder?* Certainly no one can gaze upon It, except him, with whom the wisdom of God dwells. On account of this, that lover of wisdom asked, in the ninth chapter of Wisdom:[3] *Send her from Thy holy heavens and from the throne of Thy magnitude.*

This hidden thing the Master, replete with wisdom from on high, brought to light through the thorough scrutiny of the first book. For with the noblest emanations and noblest properties seen and known, there is made known [innotescit] to us, according to what is possible for wayfarers, the magnitude of the Divine Substance.

The second hidden thing is *the order of Divine Wisdom,* of which in the twenty-eighth[4] chapter of Job (it is said): *Where is wisdom found? and what is the place of understanding? it is hidden away from the eyes of all the living.* Truly hidden away, because, as is said in the same place,[5] *wisdom is brought from hidden places*; thus, for her to become known [cognoscatur], there needs to be a thorough scrutiny not of the profundity in her, but (of that) in her works, in which she herself glitters. Whence it is said in the first[6] chapter of Ecclesiasticus, that *one is the Most High Creator, who pours her forth upon all His works.*

Therefore, the Master manifests this hidden thing in the thorough scrutiny of the second book. For having seen the order of good and evil things, it is clear to us, in what manner the Wisdom of God has been *ordained* from eternity and *from ancient times, before the earth was made.*[7]

The third hidden thing is *the fortitude of the Divine Power,* of which in the third chapter of Habacuc:[8] *Horns (are) in His hands; there His fortitude has been hidden away*; (the prophet) speaks of Christ hanging on the Cross, where the fortitude of virtue lay hidden beneath the pallium of infirmity. And *this is the sacrament hidden away from the ages,* of which in the third chapter to the Ephesians (there is said):[9] *To me the least of all the Saints has been given this grace: to preach among the Gentiles the good news of the unsearchable riches [evan-* gelizare investigablies divitiae] *of Christ and to illumine all (as to), what is the dispensation of the sacrament hidden away in God from the ages.* This is *the sacrament hidden away,* the sacred secret, because[10] the Mighty God, to conquer the enemy, put on the arms of our infirmity; which is a thing unheard of by the ages.

However,[11] in the thorough scrutiny of the third book, where it is shown, that Christ in His infirmity conquered the contrary power, there is manifested the fortitude of the Divine Power. For if He conquered through infirmity, what would He have done, if He had fought though virtue? And if *the weak thing of God is stronger than men,* the arm of God *who will be able to weaken it?*[12] Truly is it clear, that inexplicable [inenarrabilis] (is) the fortitude of Him, whose infirmity is so strong.

The fourth hidden thing is *the sweetness of the Divine Mercy,* of which in the Psalm (it is said):[13] *How great the multitude of Thy sweetness, Lord, which Thou has hidden away for those who fear Thee!* Truly hidden away and reserved for those who fear (Him is) the sweetness of mercy, because, as is said in the Psalm:[14] *The Mercy of the Lord (is) from eternity and unto eternity upon those who fear Him, and upon those, who hope upon His Mercy.*

This sweetness is manifested in the thorough scrutiny of the fourth book. For having seen, how God forgives sins in the present, and what[15] medicines [medicamina] He applies to our wounds, and what rewards He will give in the future, there is opened for us the sweetness of the Divine Mercy.

Therefore, the public-exhibition [propalatio] of hidden things is the general end of the book, to which the Master of the Sentences, wanting to be lead and to lead, *has thoroughly scrutinized the depths of the* previous *rivers* by the grace of the Holy Spirit. For He is the chief thorough-scrutinizer of secrets and depths, according to that which is said in the second chapter of the First (Letter) to the Corinthians:[16] *The Spirit thoroughly scrutinizes all things, even the depths of God.* Driven by the charity of this Spirit and enlightened by (His) light and clarity, the Master composed this work and scrutinized the depths of rivers; with this Spirit also helping, he has become the revealer of things hidden away. For he is that very one, of whom it is written in the second chapter of Daniel:[17] *He reveals depths and things hidden away; and he knows*

---

[1] Verse 15. — In the following sentence we have restored *is* after *substance* [substantiae]on the basis of the manuscripts and edition 1.

[2] Verse 14: trusting in the mss. and edition 1, we have changed *small* [parvam] into *tiny* [parvulam]. The Vulgate reads *small* [parvam] here and at the end has: *who will be able to gaze at the thunder of His magnitude?* [quis poterit tonitruum magnitudinis illius intueri?].

[3] Verse 10. — A little before this, we have substituted with the help of the codd. & edd. 1, 2 and 3 *On account of* [Propter] in place of *For* [Pro].

[4] Verse 12, 20 and 21, following which text the Vatican edition, departing from the other manuscripts, adds: *and the birds of heaven He also hides* [volucres quoque coeli latet].

[5] Job. 28: 18. — Then the Vatican edition, opposing the manuscripts and edition 1, in place of *thus, for her to be known* [ita] has less correctly: *so that if she chooses to be known* [quod si cognosci optatur].

[6] Verse 8 and 10, where the Vulgate has *and* [et] for *who* [qui]. — A little after this the codices with edition 1 have more rightly *therefore* [igitur] in place of *therefore* [ergo].

[7] This refers to Proverbs 8:23.

[8] Verse 4. — Then the codices do not agree among themselves; the majority along with the Vatican edition has *this is read* [hoc legitur]; codex R has *this is read* [hoc legitur]; codex O has *which is understood* [quod intelligitur]; we have followed codices S Y ff and edition 1, which have *(the prophet) speaks* [loquitur].

[9] Verses 8-9.

[10] We have substituted on the basis of nearly all the mss. & ed. 1, *because* [quod] for *by which* [quo]; which reading seems to be more to the point. Codex R quotes the preceding sentence thus: *For this is the sacrament hidden away, that is the sacred secret* [Hoc enim est sacramentum absconditum, id est sacrum secretum].

[11] Codices I M W have *Moreover* [autem].

[12] This refers to 1 Cor. 1:25 and to Isaias 14:27. — Then the Vatican edition has *Therefore, truly is His inexplicable fortitude revealed, whose ...* [Vere igitur patet inenarrabilis eius fortitudo, cuius est tam]; which is indeed more elegant, as in the text reconstructed, with edition 1 the codices, which are nevertheless not a few, that is A B C E F O T U V W cc, omit in addition *His* [eius], others indeed, that is P Q S Y, have *is* [est] in place of *His* [eius], codex R has instead *was* [fuit].

[13] Psalm 30:20. — Then, after *reserved* [reservata] codices P Q R add *is* [est: which the trans. has followed for greater clarity]. Then, codd. H and T, having transposed the words and added *Divine* [divinae], read *the sweetness of the Divine Mercy* [divinae misericordiae dulcedo].

[14] Psalms 102:17 and 146:11.

[15] Codices A B D F M R X have not so well *in what way* [qualiter]. Then cod. R has *medicaments* [medicamenta] in place of *medicines* [medicamina]; and a little after the Vatican ed. with cod. cc, contradicting however, the more ancient mss. & ed. 1, has *He gives* [dat] for *He will give* [dabit].

[16] Verse 10, where the Vulgate adds *For* [enim] after (in the English: before) *The Spirit* [Spiritus]. — A little below this, we have added the est to *scrutinized* [scrutatus est] on the basis of the mss. & ed. 1.

[17] Verse 22. — Then, after *Desiring* [lucernam] (on the next page) we have inserted *he said* [inquit] on the basis of the mss. and ed. 1, which is absent in the Vatican edition.

(the things) constituted in darkness. And this was the intention and purpose [finis] of the Master, according to what he himself says in the Prologue: "Desiring, he said, to exalt a light of truth upon a candlestick, we have compiled this volume in sweat and much labor, with God as our witness, from the testimonies of truth founded upon eternity." And a little before this he had said, that his proposal is "to lay open the concealed things of theological inquiries".

Therefore, it is clear in the word proposed (from Job) in the present book, (that) the material, formal, efficient and final cause (are hinted at).

QUESTIONS ON THE FOREWORD

For an understanding of those things which were first touched upon,[1] four (things) can be asked in accord with the four aforesaid (conditions).

First,[2] what is the matter and/or subject of this Book.

QUESTION 1

What is the matter or subject of this Book and/or of theology?

And[3] it seems that God is the subject:

1. For in a science, that is the subject, concerning which and concerning the properties of which the whole science is;[4] but that whole Book of his concerns God and His works, inasmuch as (it concerns) the Creation and the Reparation; ergo etc..

2. Likewise, it seems that the subject of that Book of his is *things and signs.* For in a science that is the subject, according to the division of which that science is divided, because « sciences are cut into things »,[5] that is, they are divided according to the division of their subjects; but this (subject) is thing and sign, as has been manifested; ergo etc..

3. Likewise, it seems that the *credible* is the subject of this Book. For in a book that is the subject, about which the intention and treatment of the author turns; but the credible is of this kind. Whence Master (Peter) says in his Prologue that his proposal is, « to wall our faith with the round-shields of the Tower of David », that is, to adduce reasons to prove faith, not, I say, the *faith-habit*, but (the faith) as *believed*.[6]

BUT ON THE CONTRARY: 1. The subject in a science ought to embrace everything, which is determined in it; but in this Book there is determined not only (the things) concerning God, but also (those) concerning creatures: therefore, God is not the whole subject of that[7] Book of his, but only of the First Book.

2. Likewise, the same thing is shown in another way thus. Though three causes coincide in one, nevertheless matter does not coincide at the same time with its end;[8] because "matter" means "something incomplete", but "end" means the "complement of the work"; but God is the end of that whole work, because (He is) the end of the whole of theology: therefore, He is not its subject and/or matter.

3. Likewise, it seems that *things and signs* are not the subject.[9] For every science concerns things and/or signs: therefore, if things and signs are the subject of this Book, that Book is general for all. And if[10] a special science and doctrine is handed down in this Book, it is clear that things and signs ought not to be assigned in it for its subject.

4. Likewise, it is agreed that one is the science of things and another that of signs, as it clear; for conversational science differs from natural science; therefore, the science handed down in this Book either[11] is not of one genus, or is not at the same time of things and of signs; but it is of one genus: ergo etc..

5. Likewise, it seems that the *credible* is not the subject, because science and virtue[12] are diverse habits: therefore, they have diverse objects; therefore, since the credible, inasmuch as (it is) of this kind [in quantum huiusmodi], if it be the object of a virtue, will not be the object of the science, inasmuch as (it is) of this kind: ergo etc..

6. Likewise, just as the consideration of this book revolves [consideratio huius libri versatur]

---

[1] That is: what is generally said in the Foreword concerning the four causes of the BOOK OF THE SENTENCES. Now, four special questions concerning the same causes are proposed.

[2] Codices F and bb with edition 1 add here *there is asked* [quaeritur].

[3] We have restored from the manuscripts and edition 1 the conjunction *And* [Et]. Codex M reads *And I prove, it seems, etc* [Et ... probo videtur].

[4] See Aristotle, POSTERIOR ANALYTICS, Bk. I, ch. 7 and 8. — Then we follow the codices and edition 1 by placing *and* [et] for *of* and then *inasmuch as (it concerns)* [utpote] in place of *as for example* [ut puta]. Codices F and S have *operations* [operationibus] for *works* [operibus].

[5] Aristotle, DE ANIMA, Bk. III, text. 38 (in the Parisian edition of Firmin-Didot ch. 8), where it is had thus: Therefore, science and sense is cut into things. With which words the more ancient codices and edition 1 are concordant, contrary to the Vatican edition and the more recent codex cc, which has *as things* [ut res] in place of *into things* [in res]. A little before this, the Vatican edition adds *from others* [ab aliis] after *science* [scientia]; but faultily (if it indeed deals with the division of a science *in itself*, as is gathered from the points that follow) and unsupported by the manuscripts and edition 1. Then, the Vatican edition with codex cc, in opposition however, to the more ancient manuscripts and edition 1, repeats the conjunction *because* [quia] after *are divided* [dividuntur], but badly, for the reason that the points that follow most closely are not but an explanation of the words *are cut into things* [secantur in res]. A little after this, by the demonstrative *this* [hoc] understand "such a subject, according to the division of which theology is divided". We have substituted from codices A G H I M Y etc. and edition 1. *this* [hoc] in place of *this* [haec], though many codices together with the Vatican manuscript have the latter, because in their reading the syllogism is confused.

[6] The sense is: not, I say, faith inasmuch as it is a habit infused into the soul by God, but inasmuch as it is the very thing believed, namely revealed truths; or in other words, if however, they are rightly understood: faith taken not subjectively, but objectively. — The Vatican edition has *but believed by faith* [sed fide creditur]; editions 2, 3, 4, 5 and 6 read: *faith believed according to habit, but according to what is believed* [fidem creditum secundum habitum, sed secundum creditum]; but all codices with edition 1 exhibit our text.

[7] The Vatican edition with the more recent codex cc has *of this* [huius] in contradiction to the more ancient manuscripts and edition 1.

[8] Aristotle, PHYSICS, Bk. II, text. 70. (in the Parisian edition of Firmin-Didot. ch. 7), where it read thus: Moreover the three (causes) come upon one, for the most part.

[9] Codex V has *matter or subject* [materia seu subiectum]. Then after *and/or* [vel] we have restored from nearly all the manuscripts and edition 1 the omitted word *concerns* [de].

[10] The reading of the Vatican edition, which is also that of many codices, is explained by the following codex L: *But it is established that a special* [Sed constat quod specialis]; codices A C F R and aa have *But a special* [Sed specialis]; codex G has *But if a special* [Sed si specialis]. Then codices S U and ff add *therefore* [igitur] after *it is clear* [patet]. Next trusting in the manuscripts and edition 1 we have put *ought not* [debent] in place of *do not have* [habent].

[11] The Vatican edition together with the more recent codex cc wrongly and against the more ancient manuscripts and edition 1 transposes the conjunction *either* [aut] after *therefore* [ergo]. Then codex V adjoins *determined* [determinati] to the word *of a kind* [generis].

[12] The mistake of the Vatican ed. of having *truth* [veritas] in place of *virtue* [virtus] and a little below this *of truth* [veritatis] for *of virtue* [virtutis] we have corrected on the authority of the manuscripts and edition 1.

around faith, so also[1] around hope and charity: there-fore, if (what is) to be hoped for and/or loved or (what is) lovable is not the subject of this Book, for equal rea-son neither is the credible the subject in it.

CONCLUSION

God is the radical subject of theology, Christ is the integral subject, things and signs are the universal subject or even the credible one, insofar as it passes into the reckoning of the intelligible.

I RESPOND: It must be said, that the "subject" in any science and/or doctrine can be interpreted in a three-fold manner. In one manner a "subject" in a science is said (to be that),[2] to which all things are reduced as to their *radical principle*; in another manner, (that) to which all things are reduced as to their *integral whole*; in a third manner, (that) to which all things are reduced as to their *universal whole*.

An example of this is manifestly clear in *grammar*. For in the first manner the subject, to which all things are reduced as to their elementary or radical principle,[3] is the letter, which for that reason Priscian[4] calls (it) "*the ele-ment*", because it is the smallest thing, upon which the res-olution of grammatical (structure) depends [in quo ... stat]. The subject (in grammar), to which all things are re-duced as to their integral whole, is congruous and perfect speaking. But the subject (in grammar), to which all things are reduced as to their universal whole, is the voice literate, articulate[5] and able to be ordained to signify any-thing in itself and/or in another.

It is through this standard of measure that one distinguishes among *(the sciences) of the quadrivium*. For the subject in geometry, to which all (things)

are resolved[6] as to their principle, is the point. The sub-ject, to which all things are reduced as to their integral whole, is the body, which contains in itself every genus of dimension. The subject, to which all things are re-duced as to their universal whole, is continuous, im-movable quantity.

It is also through this manner that one assigns, in this Book, a subject according to a threefold difference.

For the subject, to which all things[7] are reduced as to their *principle*, is *God* Himself.

Also the subject, to which all things, which are de-termined in this Book, are reduced as to their *entire whole*, is *Christ*, insofar He comprehends the Divine Na-ture and the human or the created and the uncreated,[8] of which are the first two Books; and as Head and members, of which are the two following. And I inter-pret broadly[9] "*the entire whole*", as that which embraces many things not only through composition, but through union and through order.

We can also name the subject, to which all things are reduced as to their *universal whole*, through a cir-cumlocution[10] or under a disjunction; and in this man-ner (the subject of the whole work) is the thing and/or the sign (of theology); and this *sign* is called the Sacra-ment. We can also name it with one word; and thus it is the *credible*, however, insofar as the credible does pass into the reason in a (certain) manner, properly speak-ing, it is[11] the subject in this Book.

Therefore, (these) proving reasons must be con-ceded, and that *God*, and *things* and *signs*, and the *credi-ble*, in diverse ways [diversimode], are the subject, as has been said.

1. Therefore, that it is objected unto the contrary, that not only is God[12] dealt with in this book; it must be said,

---

[1] In the Vatican edition and the more recent codex cc *also* [etiam] is lacking, which is had, however, in the more ancient manuscripts and edi-tion 1. Then, codex F has *as* [sicut] in place of *if* [si]. Next trusting in all the codices and edition 1 we have expunged *believable and/or* [sperabile vel], which the Vatican edition prefaces with the word *lovable* [diligibile].

[2] Codex U well enough adds here *that* [illud]. Then, applying nearly all the mss. & ed. 1, we have substituted *another* [alio] for *a second* [secundo].

[3] The Vatican edition has *prime elemental and/or radical* [primum etc.] for *elementary and/or radical principle* [primcipium etc.]. On the authority of codd. ee & ff and ed. 1, we have received into the text *prin-ciple* [principium], in that it seems to correspond more to the preceding and subsequent (sentences); many codices on account of abbreviation are ambiguous (here); all however, with ed. 1 read *elementary* [elementare].

[4] GRAMMATICAL INSTITUTIONS, Bk. I, ch. 2, (On the Letter).* — Not much after this, cod. X has *of grammar* [grammaticae] for *of gram-matical (structure)* [grammatici].

[5] The explanation of these words comes from Priscian, GRAM-MATICAL INSTITUTIONS, Bk. I, ch. 1: That has been articulated, which been compressed, that is, joined together with another sense of the mind of him, who is speaking, mentioning ... That is literate [litterata], which can be written. — One or the other codex, like aa, conjoins these two adjectives by the conjunction *and* [et].

[6] Codices H I and K have *are reduced* [reducuntur]. Then after *principle* [principium], codices P Q X and ff add, as has also been added above in the text, *radical* [radicale]. A little after this codices H and Q have *integral* [integrale] for *entire* [integrum].

[7] Here codex D adds, as is also a little afterwards repeated in the text, *which are determined in this Book* [quae determinantur in hoc libro]; but codd. D & K add *radical and/or initial* [radicale vel initiale] after *principle* [principium] and cod. ff adds *radical* [radicale] only, which adjectives cor-respond with the preceding ones and render the text more distinct. A little after this, codd. K & Q have *integral* [integrale] in place of *entire* [integrum].

[8] The reading of the Vatican edition *or created and uncreated* [sive creatum et increatum], which seems exceedingly brief, is corrected on the authority of the manuscripts and edition 1.

[9] He says *broadly* [large] deliberately, because he says that *the en-tire whole* [totum integrum] in the strict sense has been composed out of parts; but the two natures in Christ make an entire whole according to the Scholastics through the hypostatic union, not through strict compo-sition. — The Vatican edition prefaces this with the adverb *here* [hic] and, then, adds *also* [etiam] after *but* [sed], which here and elsewhere all the manuscripts often omit, though less fittingly.

[10] Against the authority of the codd. and ed. 1 in place of *through a circumlocution* [per circumlocutionem] the Vatican ed. puts *by a twofold naming* [dupla nominatione], perhaps on account of the greater opposition with the words which follow a little after this: *with one word* [unico vocabulo].

[11] Against the testimony of the manuscripts and edition 1, the Vat-ican edition here repeats *credible* [credibile], which certainly must be un-derstood (as being) implicitly in the text. Then, codices P and Q together with editions 4 and 5 add well enough *however* [tamen] after *in diverse manners* [diversimode].

[12] The Vatican edition has *that what concerns God is not dealt with entirely in this Book* [quod de Deo non agitur per totum in hoc libro]; the manuscripts, together with edition 1, agree against the Vatican edition in this, that they omit *entirely* [per totum]; but codices R T ee ff and edi-tion 1, with transposed words and by adding *only* [tantum], supply the reading, which we have received into the text, which is also in itself clearer and corresponds to the structure [ad amussim] of the minor propo-sition placed above in the objections. Then (on the next page), after *how-ever* [tamen] we have supplied *God ... with* [de Deo] from codices T and ee, which words certainly have to be understood. Next, codex F adds *and operation* [et operationem] after *substance* [substantiam]. Several codices, deceived from the repetition of *substance* [substantaim] exhibit a mutilated proposition. But codex K proposes the whole response more succinctly in this manner: *Therefore, that it is objected unto the con-trary, that God does not embrace all things, which are considered here, it must be said, that from this it does not follow, that God is not the sub-ject in this science, but it only* (thus the reading of the primitive text, af-terwards corrected to *however*) *follows, that He is not the subject*

---

* *Trans. note*: Priscianus Caesariensis (fl. c. 500 A. D.), a native of Caesarea (now, Cherchell, Algeria): St. Bonav. will often cite or draw examples from the INSTITUTIONES GRAMMATICAE. The chapter cited here by the Quaracchi editors, On the Letter [de littera], its incipit, is also known as *de litteris*.

that, although God is not dealt with only as much as regards His substance, however, God is dealt with as much as regards His substance, and/or as much as regards His works; and for that reason He is not the subject as the whole, but as the principle.

2. That it is objected, that matter does not coincide in one with its end; it must be said, that matter is spoken of in a threefold manner: namely "matter *out of which*" [materia ex qua], "matter *in which*" [materia in qua] and "matter *about which*" [materia circa quam]; and this last "matter" is called the "object" rather[1] than the "matter". Therefore, when it is said, that matter does not coincide with its end, it is true of "matter *out of which*", which properly is the matter[2] but (it is) not (true) of the "matter *about which*", which properly is the object; for the same thing can be object, habit and end; and in such a manner "matter" is interpreted in science as the object of the virtue[3] of the one cognizing it.

3. 4. That there is an objection concerning *things* and *signs*, because they are the subjects of all sciences; it must be said, that thing and sign[4] can be interpreted *in their generality*; and so they do not pertain to a special science nor to the Book nor to the same science. Again they can be interpreted according to which they put on a reckoning *of the credible*, and so, in accord with the manner that there is one *virtue*[5] and one habit concerning all credibles, whether they be things or signs, as is faith, so there is one special *science* concerning all things, inasmuch as they put on that reckoning,[6] whether they be things or signs.

In another manner, it can be said, that there is a speaking in a twofold manner concerning things and signs, either *absolutely*, or in *relation* to enjoyment or to that, by which a thing is to be enjoyed. Indeed in the first manner they look towards the special and diverse sciences; in the second manner towards one science or doctrine. Whence in accord with the manner which concerns all beings, inasmuch as they are reduced to one Prime Being, there is one science and[7] one Book, so concerning all things and signs, inasmuch as they are reduced to one thing, which is their alpha and omega, there is one science.

5. 6. That it is objected, that the *credible* is the object of virtue[8] etc.; it must be said, that in one manner the credible is the object of virtue, in another (an object) of science. For the credible, according to which it has in itself a reckoning *of prime truth*, to which faith assents on account of itself and above all things, pertains to the habit of faith; according to which it adds above the reckoning of truth, the reckoning *of authority*, it pertains to the doctrine of Sacred Scripture, of which Augustine says (in his), On a Literal Exposition of Genesis,[9] that « greater perspicacity belongs to its authority than to human ingenuity »; but according to which it adds above the reckoning of truth and authority, a reckoning *of probability*, it pertains to the consideration of the present Book, in which there are posited reasons to prove our faith. And so it is clear, how different *faith* is from the credible, and *books* from the canon of Sacred Scripture, even *the present writing*. And for that reason that[10] objection is not valid, since that Book is not so much for the defense of hope and charity, as it is of the Faith; and for that reason it is not similar.

SCHOLIUM

I. The Seraphic Doctor supposes in these questions on the foreword and elsewhere passim, that theology is a true science; nay rather in the Breviloquium, part I, ch. 1, he says: *It alone is the perfect science.* In what sense this is said, is explained in Sent., Bk. III, d. 23, a. 1, q.1, at n. 4, and ibid. , q. 4. — (Bl. John Duns) Scotus (Prolog., q. 4) together with the Nominalists denies, that theology in wayfarers is *properly* a science; but St. Thomas (Summa., I, q. 1, a. 2) affirms it.

II. There is no question here of the subject, *in which* the science is, which is the intellect, but concerning the subject *from which* science is and *about* which it immediately revolves. It is called a *subject*, because the things, which are dealt with in that science, are predicated of it. Though these terms: *subject, object* and *matter about which* [materia circa quam], are not rarely confounded by authors, nevertheless, in the strict sense the object of a science is that thing *which* is known, but its subject is that thing *of which* (its) conclusions are predicated. The Seraphic Doctor interprets "subject" here in the strict sense.

III. About the distinction, which he has made in the solution to n. 2, this must be noted. "Matter *in which*" [materia in qua] is called the "subject", either corporal or spiritual, in which some accident is received: so the intellect can be said to be the "matter", in which science is received. "Matter *from which*" [materia ex qua] is said to be that part of the thing composed, which together with the form makes the composite. "Matter *about which*" [materia circa quam] is said in science to be the subject itself, about

---

as the whole, but as the principle. [Quod ergo obiicitur in contrarium, quod Deus non complectitur omnia, quae hic considerantur, dicendum, quod ex hoc non sequitur, quod Deus non sit subiectum in hac scientia, sed tantum (sic primitus, postea correctum in tamen) sequitur, quod non est subiectum / ut totum, sed ut principium]. The Seraphic Doctor explains his mind on this matter in the Breviloquium, Bk. I, ch. 1, in this manner: Since Sacred Scripture or theology is a science giving sufficient knowledge [notitiam] of the First Principle according to the state of the way ... and since God is not only the First Principle of things and the effective Exemplar in creation, but also the refective One in redemption and the perfective One in retribution; for that reason not only does it deal with God the Creator, but also with the creation (thus the codices against the editions, which have *creator*) and the creature.

[1] Codex N adds *properly* [proprie].

[2] Codex aa adjoins *and similarly concerning matter in which* [et similiter de materia in qua], which reading seems must be received into the text, if it is supported by a sufficient number of codices; nevertheless it certainly must be understood as implicit.

[3] The false reading of the Vatican edition, which has *of truth* [veritatis] in place of *of virtue* [virtutis], is emended from the manuscripts and from the first six editions.

[4] Codex as has *signs* [signa] well enough. Then codices A T Y etc. do not repeat the preposition *to* [ad] before *Book* [librum], codex I puts *and/or the Book* [vel librum], codex X has *nor to a book* [ad librum unum].

[5] The Vatican edition, which falsely puts *truth* [veritas], is corrected from the manuscripts and the first six editions.

[6] The Vatican edition, together with the more recent codex cc, adds superfluously here *namely the credible* [scilicet credibilis], which is lacking in the more ancient manuscripts and edition 1.

[7] From codices A F G H I K P R S T V Y etc., together with edition 1, we have put *and* [et] in place of *or* [aut]. Then, codices I and T after *book* [liber] do well to add *namely metaphysics* [scilicet metaphysica]. Next, opposing nearly all the manuscripts and edition 1, the Vatican edition has *are ordered* [ordinantur] in place of *are reduced* [reducuntur]; but codex bb has *are reduced and/or ordered* [reducuntur vel ordinantur].

[8] The Vatican edition, against the mss. and ed. 1, twice in this proposition has faultily *of the truth* [veritatis] in place of *of virtue* [virtutis].

[9] Book II, ch. 5: Indeed greater is the authority of this Scripture than the capacity of all human ingenuity. — Then, the Vatican edition, not trusting in the codices prefaces *but* [sed] to the word *according*; edition 1 adds *but* [vero].

[10] It would be more pleasing, if it had *the other* [alia] in place of *that* [illa]. Moreover, the Vatican edition without any authority from the manuscripts adjoins *concerning the hopeable and/or lovable* [de serpabili vel diligibili] after *objection* [obiectio]. Near the end of the proposition, the codices do not agree among themselves; the Vatican ed. with codex cc has *whence* [unde] for *and for that reason* [et ideo]; many codices such as A C F G S V W X bb etc place no conjunction at this point; codex D has *neither* [nec] for *and for that reason ... not* [et ideo non]; but codices B D K Q R exhibit our reading *and for that reason* [et ideo]; codices I and T have instead *for that reason* [ideo].

which the science revolves. This last under diverse respects can be both *the object* of the habit and *the end*, as is clear among the theological virtues: e. g. the object and end of faith is Prime Truth; for the Most High True One is believed on account of being the Most High True One. Cf. Alexander of Hales, SUMMA., p. I, q. 1, m. 3.

IV. In the solution to 3. the question of *the unity of the science of theology* is touched upon. This the Nominalists impugn from their false principles; but they build next to it, as St. Bonaventure says in BREVILOQUIUM., p. 1, c. 1; and Alexander of Hales, p. I, q. 1, m. 3, at nn 4 and 5. — (Bl. John Duns) Scotus, REPORTATIO, Bk. I, Prologue, quaestiunc. 2. — St. Thomas, SENT., Bk. I, Prologue, q. 1, a. 2; SUMMA., Bk. I, q. 1, a. 3. — Bl. (now St.) Albert the Great, SUMMA., p. I, tr. 1, q. 3, m. 2; SENT., Bk. I, d. 1, a. 3. — (Bl.) Peter of Tarentaise, SENT., Bk. I, Prologue. a. 2. — Giles the Roman, SENT., Bk. I, Prologue, part 1, principal 2, q. 3. — Henry of Ghent, SUMMA., a. 6, q. 3. — Durandus (of Saint-Pourçain), SENT., Bk. I, Prologue, q. 4.

V. In the solution of the principal question the ancient scholastics dissented strongly at least in words. Not a few affirm, that God indeed is the subject of theology, not however, under the reckoning of Deity, but under some limitation, e. g. to the extent that He is the restorer and glorifier (thus Giles the Roman) and/or to the extend He is the most perfect (Bl. Dionysius the Carthusian). But this limitation on the part of the subject does not seem probable. — Alexander of Hales posits three subjects according to the three things, which are in any complete being [ente completo], namely according to substance, virtue (potency) and operation: in the first manner the subject is God, in the second manner it is Christ, who is the virtue of the Father, in the third manner they are the works of restoration wrought through Christ. — To Scotus is attributed the opinion, that God under the reckoning of an infinite being [entis infiniti] is the subject of theology; but nevertheless since he himself says (SENT., Bk. 1, Prolog., q. 3, n. 9.): "That God under the reckoning of an infinite or necessary being [entis] is not legitimately posited as the object of theology," his opinion is thus explained by Fr. Claude Frassen, O.F.M., 1620-1711 A.D., (SCOTUS ACADEMICUS, tom. I, disp. procœm., a. 2, q. 5.) and by Fr. Franciscus Lychetus de Brixia, O.F.M., 1465-1520 A.D., (on the same loc. cit.), that it agrees in substance with St. Thomas, who (SUMMA., I., q. 1, a. 7.) assigns one subject, namely God under the reckoning of Deity. However, the difference between both consists in this, that Scotus thinks, that this subject *God* is understood *materially*, as a thing and the cause of truths, which He contains virtually in Himself; but St. Thomas understands God in *formal* reckoning, that is as knowable and/or revealable, but not in Himself and subjectively. On this difference cf. Cajetan in his COMMENTARY and Macedo (COLLATIONES DOCTRINAE S.THOMAE ET SCOTI, Coll. 2, diff. 4, sect 4.).

The now more common and more accurate opinion distinguishes in any science three objects: the *material* object (which in theology is everything revealed by God) and the twofold *formal* object. The first of these is held on the part of the subject, concerning which the science is, and it is the thing itself, which is first cognized [cognoscitur]; this is called the obiectum formale quod; the other is held on the part of potency as the reckoning, under which we understand it, and it is called the obiectum formale quo. By this last reckoning, those sciences, which have the same material object, are properly distinguished and specified.

As from the text it is clear, St. Bonaventure distinguishes in another and threefold manner the subject of theology and according to this distinction he fittingly [convenienter] assigns a threefold subject of theology; thus he strives to reconcile the diverse opinions of theologians. And it must be noted, that *the entire whole* [totum integrale] has been composed from parts, which together with other things constitute the whole, whence the are called "integral parts". But *universal whole* [totum universale] is any superior substantial taken according to its own inferior in the line of a predicament, as animal is to man and man to Socrates. Thus Peter of Spain, a contemporary of St. Bonaventure, in his SUMMULA SUPER LIBRUM TOPICORUM, "On concomitant places". Nor does the opinion of the Seraphic Doctor contradict that of St. Thomas, by which only one thing is assigned as the subject, since here subject is taken precisely as the subiectum formale quod. However, St. Thomas does not deny, that under diverse respects even other things can be reasonably assigned as subjects of theology; nay rather this in both places cited below he sufficiently hints at. Moreover, St. Bonaventure himself says in the body of the question, both that *God* and *Christ*, and *thing* and *sign*, and *the credible* are the subject, however, in diverse manners. Whence he himself establishing in conclusion 1, says together with St. Thomas, that God is the subject of theology; but he explains this in another manner, namely that He is the *radical* subject, to which all things are reduced as to their principle. This Fr. (Petrus) Trigosus (de Catalayud, O.F.M. Cap., 1533-1593 A. D) understands of the *adequate formal* subject and thus draws the Seraphic Doctor entirely towards the opinion of St. Thomas. From the context it is clear however, that it must be understood rather of the *material* subject, to the extent that God is *the principle*, from which all things are derived or, as he says in the BREVILOQUIUM, p. I, c. 1: The subject, from which all things are, is God. In conclusion 2, under another respect he posits Christ as the adequate material subject, through which and concerning which nearly all things are known. In conclusion 3, he posits a twofold subject, in fact [nempe] *things* and *signs* but under a reckoning *of the credible*, and God Himself as *credible*, to the extent that revealed truths becomes intelligible and probable through reasons. In this last conclusion the phrase "*universal whole*" signifies the subiectum *formale et attributionis*. Trigosus, SUM. S. BONAV. q. 1, a. 2, dub. 2; Fr. (Mathias) Hauzeur, (O.F.M. 1589-1676 A.D.), COLLATIO TOTIUS THEOLOGIAE, tom. I, q. 1..

VI. The ancient authors treating of this question: BREVILOQUIUM. p. I . c. 1. — Alexander Hales, SUM.. p. I. q. 1. m. 3. — (Bl. John Duns) Scotus, SENT., Bk. 1, Prolog., q. 3; REPORT., Bk. 1, Prolog, q. 1. — St. Thomas, SENT., Bk. I, Prolog., q. 1, a. 4; SUMMA., I., q. 1, a. 7. — Bl. (now St.) Albert the Great, SUMMA., p. 1, tr. 1, q. 3, m. 1; SENT., Bk. I, d. 1, a. 2. — (Bl.) Peter of Tarentaise, SENT., Bk. I, Prolog., a. 3. — Richard of Middleton, SENT., Bk. I, Prolog., q. 6. — Giles the Roman, SENT., Bk. I, Prolog., p. 1, princip. q. 1. — Henry of Ghent, SUMMA., a. 19. q. 1. — Durandus (of Saint-Pourçain), SENT., Bk. I, Prolog., q. 5. — Gabriel Biel, SENT., Bk. I, Prolog., q. 9.

QUESTION II

What is the formal cause or the manner of proceeding in these books of the Sentences?

Second, there is asked[1] concerning the *formal* cause or the manner of treatment [modo agendi]. And it has been said, that (the manner of treatment) is one *thoroughly scrutatory* and inquisitive of secrets.

BUT ON THE CONTRARY: 1. In the fortieth (chapter) of Isaias (there is written):[2] *God causes the scrutinizers of secrets (to be) as if they were not.*

2. Likewise, in the twenty-fifth (chapter) of Proverbs (there is said):[3] *The thorough scrutinizer of (His) majesty will be oppressed by (His) glory.*

3. Likewise, in the third (chapter) of Ecclesiasticus (there is written):[4] *Lest you think of things higher than yourself, and scrutinize things stronger than yourself.* Therefore, if those things which Master (Peter) thoroughly scrutinizes, are secrets,

---

[1] Contrary to the testimony of the manuscripts and edition 1, having omitted *Second there is asked* [Secundo quaeritur], the Vatican edition then adds, *of this Book. — And it has been said* [huius libri. — Et dictum est], that is, in the Foreword; *thoroughly scrutatory* [perscrutatorius], that is *reasoning* [rationativus] or rational, which word St. Bonaventure takes from the passage in Job, quoted at the beginning of the Foreword. It is established, that, with the principles of the faith supposed, through the use of reason there is formed a theological science, whose object, as

the Seraphic Doctor has expounded above in q. 1, is the credible, in so far as it passes over into the reckoning of the intelligible, and this through the addition of reason.

[2] Verse 23.

[3] Verse 27; the Vulgate reads: *He who is a scrutinizer of (His) majesty* etc. [Qui scrutator est maiestatis etc.].

[4] Verse 22.

are great, are high and strong, (then) Master (Peter) proceeds badly.

4. Likewise, it is shown thus *by reason*: the manner of proceeding in a part of a science ought to be uniform with the *manner* of the whole science:[1] but the manner of proceeding in Sacred Scripture is typical [typicus] and through a manner of narration, not of inquisition: therefore, since that Book of his pertains to Sacred Scripture, it ought not proceed by inquiring.

5. Likewise, the manner of acting ought to be convenient to the *matter*, which it concerns; whence in the beginning of the old ETHICS[2] there is said: « The subject of a conversation [sermones] must be inquired into according to (its) matter »; but the matter of this doctrine is the credible; but the credible is above reason: therefore, the manner of proceeding through reasons is not convenient for this doctrine.

6. Likewise, the manner of acting ought to be convenient to the *end*, towards which the science is ordered; but this science, as Master (Peter) says in the text[3] is ordained to the promotion of the faith; but reasons do not promote the faith, but empty it; whence (St.) Gregory:[4] « The faith, for which human reason offers experiment, has not merit »; therefore, such a manner is contrary to the end, therefore, it is not convenient. Whence even (St.) Ambrose says:[5] « Take away the arguments, when one is dealing with the Faith. It was believed by fishermen, not dialecticians ». Therefore, this manner seems vain and useless.

BUT ON THE CONTRARY: 1. In the third (chapter) of First Peter:[6] *(Be) prepared, to render to everyone requesting a reason concerning that faith and hope which is in you.* Therefore, since there are many, who impugn our Faith, they not only request a reason concerning it; it seems useful and congruous to build it up [eam astruere] through reasons and to proceed by an inquisitive manner and by reasoning [ratiocinando]: ergo etc..

2. Likewise, Richard of St. Victor in (his) book, ON THE TRINITY:[7] « I believe without doubt, that for

the explanation of anything, what is necessary is that there be not only probable, but also that there be not lacking necessary arguments, though it may happen that our effort [industriam] be hidden. Therefore since our Faith believes necessaries, those also have hidden reasons, and such need a thorough scrutinization, to be unknotted [enodentur];[8] it is clear that a thoroughly scrutatory manner is most convenient to this science.

3. Likewise, the truth of our Faith is not of a worse condition than other truths; but in the other truths it is thus, that everyone, which can be impugned through reason, can be and ought to be defended through reason: therefore, by an equal reason also the truth of our Faith.

4. Likewise, our Faith is now not of a worse condition than in the beginning; but in the beginning, when it used to be impugned through the false miracles of the magicians, it used to be defended through the true ones of the Saints: therefore, when it is now impugned through the false arguments of heretics, it ought to be defended through the true arguments of teachers.

CONCLUSION

The thoroughly scrutatory or ratiocinative manner of proceeding is convenient to this doctrine, since it prevails to confound the adversaries of the Faith, to warm the infirm in faith, (and) to delight the perfect.

I RESPOND: It must be said, that the thoroughly scrutatory manner is convenient for this doctrine or Book. For since the end imposes a necessity for those thing which are for the end; because, as the Philosopher says:[9] « A saw is toothed, because it is for cutting »; so this Book of his, because it is for the promotion of the Faith, has an inquisitive manner (of proceeding). For the ratiocinative or inquisitive manner prevails for the promotion of the Faith, and this in a threefold manner according

---

[1] Codex R. exhibits the major (proposition of the argument) in this manner: *the manner of proceeding in science ought to be convenient to the science* [modus procedendi in scientia debet convenire scientiae].

[2] On the basis of the authority of none of the manuscripts, the Vatican edition reads *of the first Ethics*. The reading of the manuscripts is confirmed by codex lat. 6569 of the Royal Library of Paris, which contains Aristotle's ETHICS arranged in two parts. The first part comprehends the *first* book of the ETHICS and belongs to the Greco-Latin translation, as is gathered from the word *proheresis*, which found even at the beginning. This part is entitled NEW ETHICS. The second part comprises the *second and third* book of the ETHICS and is called the OLD ETHICS. See Jourdain's RECHERCHES CRITIQUES SUR L'ÂGE ET L'ORIGINE DES TRADUCTIONS LATINES D'ARISTOTE, p. 179, where concerning this OLD ETHICS there is added: It does not seem to me, that this translation is much older in age. In the same work there is cited another Greco-Latin translation of the ETHICS, which is found in the works of St. Thomas under the name, "*Old Translation*" [Translatio vetus], and in that (Bk. II, ch. 2) the passage alleged by St. Bonaventure is exhibited thus: "The subjects of conversations [sermones] are to be sought out according to (their) matter." Indeed a similar passage is found in the ETHICS, Bk. I, ch. 3, which is however, even in the ancient translation exhibited in other words: "But it is said at least in a sufficient manner, if it is manifested according to the subject matter." — Then the Vatican edition, breaking with the manuscripts and edition 1, has in place of *but the credible* [sed credibile], the not so well *and the credible* [et credibile], because it is the minor supposition. In this proposition there is perhaps a reference to that passage from Dionysius (the Areopagite), ON THE DIVINE NAMES, ch. 1: Indeed the science and contemplation of His (Divinity) is impassible to all things.

[3] Cf. the PROLOGUE.

[4] In his 26th Homily, ON THE GOSPELS.

[5] In regard to this text of (St.) Ambrose we note, that it is exhibited both in the manuscripts and in the Vatican edition under the name of (St.) *Jerome*, but falsely; for it is not found in the works of St. Jerome, but in (St.) Ambrose's book, ON THE FAITH, Bk. 1, ch. 13, n. 84 these words are cited: Bear off arguments, where faith is sought ... it is not believed by philosophers, it is believed by fishermen; it is not believed by dialecticians, it is believed by publicans. — In which text, the Vatican edition, not agreeing with the more ancient manuscripts and edition 1, places *shepherds and* [pastoribus et] before *fishermen* [piscatoribus].

[6] Verse 15, where the Vulgate reads: *Always prepared for the satisfaction of everyone requesting (from) you a reason concerning that hope which is in you* [Parati semper ad satisfactionem omni poscenti vos rationem de ea quae in vobis est spe]. — Then, the reading of the Vatican ed., having *at least* [utique] in place of *not only* [non tantum], in which both the construction of the proposition is perturbed and its sense is not rendered integrally, we have emended from nearly all the mss. (some as H and ff have falsely *not only* [non tantum]) and from ed. 1. But cod. B, well explaining the reading of the other codd., has *and not only* [et non tantum]. Then cod. R has not so well *instructing them* [eos instruere] in place of *building towards it* [eam astruere]; and immediately afterwards from codd. A F G H I R S T etc. with ed. 1 we have substituted *inquisitive* [inquisitivo] in place of *inquisitory* [inquisitorio].

[7] Book I, ch. 4. — The Vatican edition, with the manuscripts and edition 1 disagreeing, introduces the relative *which* [quae] and the verb *is* [est] around the beginning of this quote, which having been omitted entirely altered the sense (of the text).

[8] Very many codices, as M P and Z together with edition 1 have *be thoroughly explained* [enucleentur].

[9] Aristotle, PHYSICS, Bk. II at the end, text 92, where there is read: But this (dividing or cutting) will not be, unless the saw have such teeth. And ON THE PARTS OF ANIMALS, Bk. I, ch. 5: For the cutting has not been made for the sake of the saw, but the saw for sake of cutting.

to the three genera of men. For certain ones are *adversaries* of the Faith, certain ones are *infirm* in faith, but certain ones (have been) *perfected*.

The inquisitive manner prevails *first to confound adversaries*. Whence (St.) Augustine (says) in the first (book) ON THE TRINITY:[1] Against the garrulous ratiocinators, more elated than capable, one must use catholic reasons and congruous similitudes for the defense and assertion of the faith. *Second* it prevails *to warm the infirm*. For as God warms the charity of the infirm through temporal benefactions [beneficia], so does it warm[2] the faith of the infirm through probable arguments. For if the infirm saw, that the reasons for the faith were lacking probability and (those) for the opposite abounded, no one would persist (in the Faith). *Third* it prevails *to delight the perfect*. For in a wonderful manner the soul delights in understanding what it believes with a perfect faith. Whence (St.) Bernard (says):[3] « We understand nothing more freely, than what we already believe by faith. ».

1. 2. 3. Therefore, because it is objected unto the contrary, it must be said, that all those authorities are understood concerning a curious, thorough scrutinization, not concerning a studious, thorough scrutinization. For the Lord Himself said to the Jews, in the fifth (chapter of the Gospel) of St. John:[4] *Scrutinize the Scriptures* etc..

4. Because it is objected, that this[5] manner of his is not suited [competit] to Sacred Scripture; it must be said that in this regard, that his Book is reduced to Sacred Scripture through the manner of a certain subalternation, not of the principal part; similarly also the books of the doctors (of theology), which are for the defense of the Faith. Which is thus clear: because not *every* determination drawing unto one side [trahens in partem] causes a subalternation of a science, but (only) a determination *drawing apart* [distrahens] in a certain manner.[6] For the science of the straight line is not said to be subalternated to geometry, but the science of the visual line (is), since this determination in a certain manner draws towards

other principles. Therefore, since Sacred Scripture concerns the credible as credible,[7] this concerns the credible as made intelligible, and this determination *draws apart* — « for what we believe, we ought to for an authority, and what we understand, for a reason »[8] — hence it is, that just as there is one [alius] manner of certitude in superior and inferior science, so there is another [alius] manner of the certitude in Sacred Scripture and another in this Book, and for that reason (there is) another manner of proceeding. And just as a subalternated science, where it is deficient, returns to the certitude of the subalternating science, which is greater; so also, when there is lacking to Master (Peter) the certitude of reason, he has recourse to the certitude[9] of Sacred Scripture, which exceeds all the certitude of reason.

5. Because you object, that[10] it ought to be convenient to the *matter*, it must be said, that it is convenient. And because it is objected, that the credible is above reason; (it must be said that) it is true, that (it is) above reason as much as regards *acquired science*,[11] but (it is) not above reason *elevated through faith* and through the gift of knowledge [scientiae] and understanding. For faith elevates one to assent (to what is to be believed); (the gifts of) knowledge and understanding elevate one to understand what has been believed.

6. Because it is objected, that it[12] is not convenient to the *end*, because it empties merit; it must be said, that, when it is assented to on account of reason itself, then it bears off a place for faith, because in the soul of a man the violence of reason dominates. But when faith does not assent on account of reason, but on account of love of Him to whom it assents, it desires to have reasons; it then does not empty human reason of merits, but augments consolation [solatium]. And in the first manner[13] (St.) Jerome understands, that dialectical arguments must not be introduced, by which a man would be principally supported, because one must be more principally supported by authority than by reason.

---

[1] Chapter 2, where there is said: Those garrulous ratiocinators, more elated than capable and for that reason suffering with a more dangerous disease, let us serve so that they may perhaps find something, whence they cannot doubt. — In this quote, the Vatican edition against the manuscripts and edition 1 adds *rather* [magis] before *more elated* [ratiocinatoribus].

[2] Here codex K adds *who* [quis], but not well, as is seen.

[3] ON CONSIDERATIONS, Bk. V, ch. 3 at the end: But we prefer to know nothing, which we know already by faith.

[4] Verse 39.

[5] We have substituted from the more ancient manuscripts and from edition 1 *this ... of his* [iste] in place of *that* [ille].

[6] That is, which draws a thing towards another concept and/or to other special principles.

[7] Thus the more ancient manuscripts (some of which, as A F G P Q and ee together with edition 1 repeat *concerning* [de] before *credible*) against the Vatican edition, which has *credible* [credibile]. Next by the demonstrative *this* [hic] there is understood the BOOK OF SENTENCES. Codex B adds *but* before this [Trans. note: according to the English syntax], and codex O has *but this science* [haec autem scientia] in place of *this* [hic]. Then codex F puts *an intelligible reason* [ratione] in place of *made intelligible* [facto].

[8] (St.) Augustine, ON THE UTILITY OF BELIEVING, ch. 11, n. 25: That which we therefore, understand, we ought to by reason, what we believe, by authority. In which text very many of the codices as F G H T etc. together with the Vatican edition have *ought to be* [debetur] in place of *we ought to* [debemus].

[9] The Vatican edition, together with the more recent codex cc, by omitting *the certitude of* [certitudinem], reads *authorities* [auctoritates]; codices B L N O T and ee, following the Vatican reading, add *and to certitude* [et ad certitudinem]; but codices C D F M P Q U W X Z aa and bb exhibit the reading received in the text, which we prefer

for the reason that in it the two species of certitude, namely *of authority* [auctoritatis] and *of reason* [rationis], are exhibited in a more distinct manner.

[10] Supply *the manner* [modus] which only the Vatican texts adds. — Codex R has *it is objected* [obiicitur] in place of *you object* [tu obiicis].

[11] That is, a habit (acquired) by the investigation of natural reason and in a natural manner, which according to the Scholastics begins from the way of sense and experience. To this science is opposed scientia infusa, under which is contained the cognition of faith, inasmuch as it, both in respect of the object cognized, and in respect of the manner of cognizing, is offered immediately by God to man. Cf. SENT., Bk. III, d. 35, a. 2. — Here the Vatican edition without the authority of the manuscripts and edition 1 adds *through evident reason* [per rationem evidentem], which addition, however, we judge to be exceedingly strict; (this is) certain even if it is that reason, unless it be elevated by the gift of faith, cannot stretch to the cognition of credibles, strictly speaking, nor indeed to the *probable* (cognition of them). This is better had in codex K which places *reason is considered in itself* [ratio in se consideratur] in place of *regards acquired science* [ad scientiam acquisitam]. Next very many of the codices A B C D F G I L M P Q S T V X Y and ee have *of wisdom* [sapientiae] in place of *of knowledge* [scientiae], which however, is disproved from what follows.

[12] Supply: *his manner* [modus iste]. — Next to keep the same subject in the proposition, we have, on the testimony of manuscripts A F G I K R S T etc. and edition 1, preferred *empties* [evacuat] to the passive *is emptied* [evacuatur], which the Vatican edition has.

[13] Favoring the manuscripts and edition 1, we have removed the addition made by the Vatican edition, *similarly (St.) Gregory and* [Gregorius similiter et], which addition, as is stated, having omitted punctuation, is erroneous, because what follows does not refer to the words of (St.) Gregory, but only of (St.) Jerome, Codex D adds the particle *also* [et] before *understands* [intelligit].

SCHOLIUM

I. In the solution *to n. 4* the Seraphic Doctor touches another question, namely whether theology is *a subalternate science*, concerning which the school of Scotus and the divine Thomas disagree, to the extent that its *subalternation* is understood in respect of the *theology of the blessed*. For (Bl. John Duns) Scotus holds a negative opinion, taking *subalternation* in the strict sense with all the conditions, which Aristotle requires (*Posterior Analytics*, Bk. I, ch. 10); but St. Thomas (SUMMA., I, q. 1, a. 2) admits some subalternation. Moreover, here the Seraphic (Doctor) speaks only of subalternation related to *Sacred Scripture* and in this solution he entirely agrees with St. Thomas (ibid.), with Bl. John Duns Scotus (here in the Prologue, q. 4. and 5) and with other doctors. — On subalternation in respect of the theology of the *blessed*, cf. (Bl. John Duns) Scotus., REPORTATIO, Bk. I, Prolog., q. 3, a. 3, quaestiunc. 4; SENT., Bk. I, Prolog., q. 4 and 5. — St. Thomas, SUMMA., I., q. 4, a. 2 together with Cajetan's commentary. — Bl. (now St.) Albert the Great, SENT., Bk. I, d. 1, a. 4 to the end. — Richard of Middleton, SENT., Bk. I, Prolog., q. 1, and 5. — Giles the Roman, SENT., Bk. I, Prolog., p. 1, princ. 2, q. 1. — Henry of Ghent, SUMMA., a 7, q. 4 ff.. — Durandus (of Saint-Pourçain), SENT., Bk. I., Prolog., q. 7, et 8.

II. When it is said in solution *to n. 6*: When it is assented to on account of reason itself; the sense is: when a man does not have the will to believe anything except on account of a convincing reason. Cf. SENT., (Bk. I,) d. 24, a. 2, q. 1, at nn. 2 and 5. — The form of expression is notable: « In the soul of man *the violence of reason dominates* ». For human reason which by closing itself within its own narrow limits rejects the influx of prime truth and denies its dutiful service[obsequium] to its own legitimate Lord, is condemned by a just judgement, to duly serve under the yoke of error.

III. In the solution to the same question all the Doctors are in sufficient agreement, and very many of the things said here are confirmed by the Vatican Council, ON THE CATHOLIC FAITH, ch. IV. — St. Bonaventure, BREVILOQUIUM., Foreword; COMMENTARY ON THE GOSPEL OF ST. JOHN, Prologue, n. 10. (in the first volume of Supplementary Writings, by Bonelli). — Alexander Hales, SUMMA., p. I, q. 2, m. 3, a. 4. — (Bl. John Duns) Scotus, SENT., Bk. I, Prolog., q. 3. in fine; Bk. II, d. 1, q. 4. — St. Thomas, SENT., Bk. I, Prolog., q. 1, a. 5; SUMMA. I., q. 1, a 8. — Bl. (now St.) Albert the Great, SUMMA., p. I., tr. 1, q. 5; SENT., Bk. I, d. 1, a. 5. — (Bl.) Peter of Tarentaise, SENT., Bk. I, Prolog., a. 6. — Richard of Middleton, SENT., Bk. I, Prolog., q. 7. — Henry of Ghent, SUMMA., a. 14, q. 2 and a. 8, q. 1. — (Bl.) Dionysius the Carthusian, SENT., Bk. I, Prolog., q. 3. — Durandus (of Saint-Pourçain), SENT., Bk. I, Prolog. q. 1. — Gabriel Biel, SENT., Bk. I, Prolog. q. 7.

QUESTION III

*Whether this book or theology is for the sake of contemplation, or that we become good,
or whether it is a speculative or practical science?*

Third, there is asked[1] concerning the *final* cause. And since it has been said, that this book is for revealing things hidden away, it is asked, whether this work is for the sake of contemplation, and/or that we become good. And that it is, that we become good, it seems thus.

1. Every doctrine, which concerns these things, without the cognition of which one does not happened to live uprightly, is (for this), that we become good; but this book of his is for the cognition of the true[2] faith, without which *it is impossible to please God* and live uprightly, as is said in the eleventh (chapter) to the Hebrews:[3] therefore, that book of his is (for this), that we become good.

2. Likewise, every doctrine, which convenes with *virtue* in object, is (for this), that we become good; this is self-manifest [per se manifesta]; but this doctrine convenes with faith in object, because it concerns the credible, of which also, or in which, is faith; ergo etc..

3. Likewise, a particular doctrine convenes with the whole in (its) *end*; but the end of the whole of Sacred Scripture is not only, that we become good, but also that we become blessed; and beatitude is the best: therefore, the end of that science of his is (this), that we become good.

ON THE CONTRARY: 1. Master (Peter) says in (his) text,[4] that his end or intention « is to lay open those things withdrawn from theological inquiries » but this pertains to him, whose end is speculation: ergo etc..

2. Likewise, the science which is, that we become good, pertains to morals; but although theology concerns faith[5] and morals, that book of his, however, (concerns) these things which look towards faith, not these which look towards morals: therefore, this work is not, that we become good.

3. Likewise, every science, which is, that we become good, is practical; but every such (science) concerns these things which are by our work;[6] but this does not concern these things which are by our work, but by God: therefore, it is for the sake of contemplation, not that we become good.

---

[1] The Vatican edition omits *Third there is asked* [Tertio quaeritur].

[2] Thus very many of the codices as A I K T X etc. together with edition 1 against the Vatican ed., which has *our* [nostrae]; we prefer the reading of the codices, as it is more familiar to the style of the Seraphic Doctor and expresses more plainly the prerequisite for upright living.

[3] Verse 6.

[4] In the Prologue, see below.

[5] We have substituted the particle *and* [et] in place of *not* [non de]. Indeed doubt has not lightly entered into our own mind in this regard, because, since the time of the Scholastics theology, commonly speaking, is contained in an compendious manner in the BOOK OF SENTENCES, as if it were immediately the subject of this book, which concerns *these things which look to faith, not these which look to morals*, so that even of theology must be said, that *it concerns faith, not morals*. But with the consent of all the manuscripts and edition 1 we have changed the reading of the Vatican ed.; having supposed which change, *theology* must be accepted in the broader sense, to the extent that it comprises diverse disciplines. — Next, several codd., among whom are even cod. T with ed. 1, add *concerns* [est] after *that book of his* [iste].

[6] Aristotle has things similar to these two propositions in ETHICS, Bk. II, ch. 2: Since the present treatise (the ETHICS) is not for the sake of speculation, to the measure that it (belongs) to another; for it has not come into being, that we may cognize, what is virtue, but that we may be made good. And in the METAPHYSICS, Bk. II, text 3 (in the shorter version, Bk. 1, ch. 1): For speculative (science)'s end is also truth, but practical's (is) work. — Codex K exhibits the 2nd proposition of this arg., thus: *and every practical science concerns these things which are from our work, not from God: but that science of his does not* etc. [et omnis scientia practica est de his quae sunt ab opere nostro, non a Deo: sed ista scientia non est etc.].

CONCLUSION

Theological science is an affective habit and the mean between the speculative and practical, and for (its) end it has both contemplation, and that we become good, and indeed more principally, that we become good.

I RESPOND: For the understanding of the aforesaid it must be noted, that our intellect is a thing perfectible by science.[1] But one happens to consider this in a threefold manner, that is *in itself*, and/or as far as it is extended *to affection*, and/or as far as it is extended *to work*. But the intellect is extended through a manner of dictating and regulating. According to this threefold state, because[2] it can err, it has a threefold *directive habit*. For, if we were to consider the intellect *in itself*, it is thus properly speculative and is perfected by a habit, which is for the sake of contemplation, which[3] is called *speculative science*. But, if we were to consider it as born to be extended *to work*, it is thus perfected by a habit, which is, that we become good; and this is *practical science* or moral (science). But, if we were to consider (it) in a middle manner as born[4] to be extended

to affection, it is thus perfected by a middle habit, between the purely speculative and practical, which comprises both; and this habit is called *wisdom*, which he calls simultaneously cognition and affection: *For wisdom is of doctrine according to its name*, in the sixth (chapter) of Ecclesiasticus.[5] Whence, this (habit) is for the sake of contemplation, and that we become good, however, principally, that we become good.

Such is the cognition handed down in this book. For this cognition helps faith, and faith is so in the intellect, that, as much as it concerns it own reckoning, it has been born to move the affection.[6] And this is clear. For this cognition, that Christ died on our behalf, and the like, unless a man be a sinner and hard (of heart), moves towards love; not so those things: that the diameter is the asymmeter of the side.[7]

Therefore, it must be conceded, that it is (for this), that we become good.

1. Because it is objected, that[8] it is for laying open things hidden away; it must be said, that that [ibi] is not a state, because that revelation orders towards affection.

2. 3. Because it is objected, that it does not concern morals nor these things which are by our work; the reply to that is already clear,[9] because this is said of that which is properly, that we become good, as (is said) of a practical (science).

SCHOLIUM

I. This question is commonly proposed thus: whether theology is practical or speculative? But strictly speaking, however, there is a difference between this and that manner of speaking. For *properly practical* is the knowledge [notitia], which is per se ordainable to *operation*; and in this sense the Seraphic Doctor denies, that theology is practical (reply to n. 2 and 3). But that *we become good* through direction to *the last end* or through an enkindling of the affection, among the speculative sciences this most properly belongs to theology.

II. In the body there is touched upon the question debated among the scholastics, whether theology is *wisdom*, which is commonly affirmed, cf. Alexander of Hales, SUMMA., p. I., a. 1, m. 1. — (Bl.) John Duns Scotus, SENT., Bk. I, Prolog., q. 3. — St. Thomas., SENT., Bk. I, Prolog., a. 1, q. 3; SUMMA., I., q. 1, a. 6. — Bl. (now St.) Albert the Great, SENT., Bk. I, d. 1,

a. 4, ad 1. — Richard of Middleton, SENT., Bk. I, Prolog., q. 5, ad 3. — Giles the Roman, SENT., Bk. I, Prolog., p. 2, q. 1. — (Bl.) Peter of Tarentaise, SENT., Bk. I, Prolog., q. 1. — Henry of Ghent, SUMMA., a. 6. q. 2. — Durandus (of Saint-Pourçain), SENT., Bk. I, Prolog., q. 1. in fine.

III. in this solution of the question both in matter and in manner of speaking Alexander of Hales, Bl. (now St.) Albert the Great, (Bl.) Peter of Tarentaise, Giles the Roman and Thomas of Argentina agree with the Seraphic Doctor. St. Thomas in his COMMENTARY ON THE SENTENCES, in the passage cited below, says simply: Therefore, (sacred science) is not practical, but speculative; but in the SUMMA (says) : It comprehends beneath itself both, but it is more speculative than practical. This last solution is not far from the doctrine of the Seraphic Doctor, which is thus clear.

---

[1] That is, the intellect is an apt subject to be perfected by science. — The Vatican edition, breaking with the manuscripts and edition 1, has *perfectible* [perfectibilis] in place of *a thing perfectible* [perfectibile].

[2] The Vatican edition, not trusting in the manuscripts and edition 1, by replacing *because* [quia] with the prefixed particle *and* [et] at the beginning of this proposition, alters in some respect the point of the statement. — Next, codex X has *perfect* [perfectum] in place of *directive* [directivum], and very many of the codices as C F G L R S etc. have the corrupted reading *ductive* [ductivum].

[3] The Vatican edition has less well *which* [quae]. The same recurs in the following proposition, in which the Vatican edition has *this* [haec] in place of *this* [hic]. Both ways, however, are contrary to the greater part of the manuscripts as A C F G H K M P Q S T U W Z cc ee ff and ed. 1.

[4] Codices K and Z, as in the preceding, have *we were to consider it as born* [consideremus ut natum]. Next, from the manuscripts and editions 1, 2, 3, and 6 we have corrected the mistake in the reading of the Vatican ed. which has *effect* [effectum] in place of *affection* [affectum].

[5] Verse 23, where the Vulgate transposes *est* after *nomen* [Trans.: regards only the Latin syntax; *its* refers to *wisdom*.] — The sense is: wisdom is, according to received etymology at the time of the Seraphic Doctor, the same thing as *tasty knowledge* [sapida scientia], which gives *a taste* [saporem]. Cf. Alexander of Hales, SUMMA., p. I., q. 1, m. 1; St. Bonaventure, Commentary, Bk. III. d. 35, q. 1. — A little above this, before *simultaneously* [simul], the Vatican edition against nearly all the codices and edition one has *because* [quia] in place of *which* [quae]. In the beginning of the following proposition for the demonstrative *this* [hic] understand *habit* [habitus]; edition 1 has *this* [haec], which refers to *wisdom* [sapientia]. Next, codex K with edition 1 has *more principally* [principalius] in place of *principally* [princaliter] well enough.

[6] Codices I and T have *and faith though it is in the intellect, however, as much as concerns its own reckoning, has been born to move the affection* [et fides licet sit in intellectu, tamen quantum est de sui ratione, nata est movere affectum]; a reading which is not to be spurned. — Next, codex X puts *Which thus* [Quod sic] in place of *And this* [Et hoc]. Then, from nearly all the manuscripts and edition 1 we have here restored the particle *that* [quod], which was lacking in the Vatican edition, but is more agreeable to the manner of speaking of the Scholastics; and conversely a little after *love* [amorem] we have expunged on the testimony of the manuscripts and edition 1 the words added in the Vatican edition, *and devotion* [et devotionem].

[7] That is, the diameter of the square is incommensurable with the side, which sentence occurs in the fourth book of Aristotle's PHYSICS, where according to the ancient version printed at Venice in 1489, edited by Bernardino of Tridino, text. 120 (ch. 12 in the Parisian edition) there is read: And because that which is not, will not be in time, whatever they are, they do not happen to be otherwise, such as "a diameter is symmetrical to the side". And the same according to the Arabic-Latin translation: That which is impossible, to be otherwise, as "a diameter is symmetrical to a side." (τὴν διάμετρον εἶναι τῇ πλευρᾷ σύμμετρον). For which text there is had in the Vatican edition *a circle conquers a diameter* [circulus vincit diametrum], but the codices and edition 1 oppose this.

[8] Understand here in the beginning of the following response: that book of his, and/or the science of the present book.

[9] The Vatican edition against the manuscripts and the first six editions, having perturbed the construction of the proposition, has *the two last* [duo ultima] in place of *that* [illud]. Immediately afterwards, very many of the codices as C G H L O Q etc. have less well *that* [quod] in place of *because* [quia]. — Next after *that* [illa] supply with the Vatican ed. *science* [scientia].

1. Each admits besides speculative and practical science a third member, which simultaneously contains both. Though (Bl. John Duns) Scotus (Prolog. q. 4) thinks badly of this division, it is however, admitted by nearly all and that reasonably and it is well defended by Giles the Roman, loc. cit.. Thus the habit of theological science, since it belongs to a superior order, because it is founded on the principles of (the virtue of) faith, which is commanded by the will and involves an inclination into God, seems to be eminently speculative and in a certain manner practical; for it has virtue for both illumining the intellect and inflaming the affection. Whence at least in the broad sense this science can be named practical, though on the part of the *object* it does not immediately direct operation, because on the part of the *end* from its own reason it inclines to the love of God. For an explanation one can use (what is said in the Commentary), Bk. III, d. 23, a. 1, q. 2, in the body of the reply.

2. If St. Thomas says, that theology is more speculative than practical, this is true, if it is considered on the part of the *object*; and St. Bonaventure has sufficiently inclined to this reason, since in the solution to n. 2 and 3 he denies, that this science is practical in the strict sense. But if the Seraphic Doctor affirms, that it is « principally, that we become good », this is again most true, if one looks at its *end*, which it is certainly greater, (namely) that we become good, than that we only gaze upon divine things.

3. St. Bonaventure here expressly does not name theology an *affective* science; however, the third member of the division, that it comprises the speculative and practical in itself, cannot, together with Bl. (now St.) Albert the Great and the other ancient authors, be inaptly distinguished by this word, when attending to the principal end, which is charity in the affection. For from the principal end anything can be well named. — Of the twofold genus of cognition, namely, speculation and devotion, cf. the COMMENTARY, Bk. III., d. 35, q. 1.

IV. On this whole question: Alexander of Hales, SUMMA., p. I. q. 1, m. 1 et 2. — (Bl. John Duns) Scotus, SENT., Bk. I, Prolog., q. 4. — St. Thomas, SENT., Bk. I, Prolog., q. 1, a. 3; SUMMA. , I., q. 1, a. 4. — Bl. (now St.) Albert., SUMMA., p. I, tr. 1, a. 3, m. 3; SENT., Bk. I, d. 1, a. 4. — (Bl.) Peter of Tarentaise, SENT., Bk. I, Prolog., a. 4. — Richard of Middleton, Prolog., q. 4. — Henry of Ghent, SUMMA., a. 8. q. 3 ff. — (Bl.) Dionysius the Carthusian, SENT., Bk. I, prolog., q. 2. — Durandus (of Saint-Pourçain), SENT., Bk. I, Prolog., q. 6. — (Gabriel) Biel, SENT., Bk. I, Prolog., q. 12.

QUESTION IV

What is the efficient cause or author of this book?

Lastly, for greater evidence one can ask[1] concerning the *efficient* cause. And it is said that it was Master Peter Lombard, Bishop of Paris. But it seems that he ought not be called the "*author*" of this book.[2]

1. He alone is to be called the "author" of a book, who is a teacher or author of doctrine; but, as (St.) Augustine says in the book, ON THE TEACHER:[3] « Christ alone is Teacher » therefore, He alone ought to be called the "author" of this book.

2. Likewise, as the Philosopher says in the OLD ETHICS:[4] « Not everyone who makes (things) grammatical or musical, ought to be called a "grammarian" and/or "musician", as (is the case) if it happens on occasion, by fortune, and/or by another substituting or speaking »; but Master (Peter) composed this work from another's doctrine, as he himself says in (his) text,[5] that « in this work you will find the examples and doctrine of (our) elders » therefore, he ought not be called (its) "author".

If you say,[6] that this is not only the doctrine of the Saints, but also his own, by which reckoning he ought to be called the "author": *on the contrary*: « From the greater and more worthy ought a denomination come to be »;[7] but Master (Peter) says, that « his own voice sounded out a little while, and then did not depart from the limits of (our) fathers »: therefore, that book ought not be said to be Master (Peter)'s.

ON THE CONTRARY: It is established that God did not write this book with His finger, therefore, it had another, created author;[8] but no other is given except Master (Peter).

Likewise, if the authority of Master (Peter) is received in this case [causa], he himself says in (his) text:[9] « In much labor and sweat, with God as (our) surety, we have compiled this volume »: therefore, it seems, that he himself was the "author" of the present book.

CONCLUSION

Peter Lombard, the Bishop of Paris,
is the author of this book.

I RESPOND: For an understanding of the things said, it must be noted, that fourfold is the manner of making a book. For one writes another's (words),[10] by adding and/or changing nothing; and that one is called merely a "*writer*" [scriptor]. Another writes another's (words), by adding, but not from his own; and that one is called a "*compiler*" [compilator]. Another writes both his own words and another's, but the other's

---

[1] With no codex supporting, the Vatican edition, having omitted the preceding words, begins from: *of the efficient cause* [De causa].

[2] The Vatican edition adjoins *thus* [sic], which however is lacking in the manuscripts and the first six editions.

[3] This is taken from ch. 14. Cf. also THE EXPOSITION ON THE FIRST EPISTLE OF ST. JOHN, Tract 4.

[4] The words of Aristotle (ETHICS, Bk. II, ch. 4) according to the ancient translation among the works of St. Thomas (Parma 1867) are: And/or is (a thing) thus held neither in the arts? For does happen that a grammarian makes something by chance and with another substituting; therefore, (he is) then a grammarian, if as a grammarian he also makes something grammatical. — See above q. 2. argument 5 in reply. — The Vatican edition alone omits *Old* [veteri]. — Codices I L N O V and X have *and/or teaching* [vel docente] in place of *or speaking* [sive dicente].

[5] In the Prologue. — From the manuscripts and the first six editions we have substituted *as* [sicut] in place of *for* [nam] and next we have supplied the omitted *that* [quod].

[6] Very many codices A H I K T etc. have *you may say* [dicas].

[7] Aristotle, ON THE SOUL, Bk. II, text 49 (ch. 4): *From (their) end it is just that all things be named*. Moreover Aristotle in diverse places (PHYSICS, Bk. II, text 23 & METAPHYSICS, Bk. V, text 3) calls the end the *best (part) of a thing* [optimum rei]. — For the words of Master (Peter) cited next, see below

in the Prologue. The Vatican edition, against the testimony of the manuscripts and edition 1, in the first part of the words of Master (Peter) adds *if* [si] after *that* [quod] and exhibits the last part of them thus: *he does not, however, depart from the limits of the Fathers* [non tamen a paternis limitibus discessit]. But it must be noted, that the Seraphic Doctor much more often cites either the words of Master (Peter) or of the holy Fathers not word-for-word, but only according to (their) sense. — Next from very many of the codices C F G I K L R S and T etc. we have put *ought* [deberet] in place of *ought* [debet].

[8] The Vatican edition together with the more recent codex cc, having omitted *created* [creatam], has the not so well *teacher* [doctorem] in place of *author* [auctorem], in disagreement with the more ancient manuscripts and edition 1.

[9] In the Prologue; see below. — In the first proposition of this argument, after *Likewise* [Item], we have inserted *if* [si] from the more ancient manuscripts and edition 1 and then we have substituted *case* [causa] in place of *part* [parte], which reading now seems to be preferred, according to that adage: No one is a judge in his own case. — Next after *is received* [recipitur] in the Vatican edition there is added *for that reason since* [ideo cum], which is absent from the manuscripts and edition 1.

[10] The Vatican edition and the more recent codex cc, incoherently with what follows, have *another's matter* [alienam materiam], with the firm opposition of the more ancient manuscripts and edition 1.

as the principal ones, and his own as those adjoined [annexa] for evidence; and this one is called a "*commentator*", not an "author" [auctor].[1] Another writes both his own and another's, but his own as the principal ones, the other's as things adjoined for confirmation; and such ought to be called an "*author*". Such was Master (Peter), who[2] put (forth) his own sentences and confirms the sentences of the Fathers. Whence he truly ought to be called the "author" of this book.

1. Therefore, because it is objected, that Christ alone is Teacher and Author; it must be said, that as (St.) Augustine says in the book, ON CHRISTIAN DOCTRINE,[3] teaching is twofold, as anyone is said in a twofold manner "to cause seeing". For in one way he causes seeing who has restored sight, another way, he who shows the visible thing with (his) finger; and[4] God does the first, man the second. Similarly in one way he teaches, who offers and/or shows the science, which he has in (his) soul,[5] (to others) by word and/or writing, in another, he who impresses the habit of science; each, however, is called a "teacher" and "author", but God more principally; so[6] in the proposed (objection).

2. Because it is objected, that he made[7] the book, with another substituting; it must be said, that no one for that reason is said to make, with another substituting, because[8] he has learned from another — for then few would be teachers and/or grammarians — but, if his science depends entirely on another, so that he does not have the habit inside (himself), as those who write good Latin, because others have told them,[9] but themselves are ignorant of the art; in this manner Master (Peter) was not (the author). For by the science, which he had acquired over a long time and/or with labor, he composed this work and through the doctrines of the Fathers confirmed his own sentences.[10] And, because there are many things said there by others, this does not take away from the Master's authority, but rather confirms his authority[11] and commends (his) humility.

---

[1] We follow codices R T X and ee by adding *not an author* [non auctor], which reading is proved both from itself and from what follows, as is confirmed besides from the false reading of many of the codices as A B F H I M V W Y Z aa bb ee and ff together with edition 1, which have *also an author* [et auctor].

[2] Trusting in the manuscripts and edition 1 we have changed *since* [quoniam] into *who* [qui]. Next very many of the codices as F H I O T U aa and edition 1 have *through the sentences of the Fathers* [per Patrum sententias].

[3] In the Foreword, where this sentence of (St.) Augustine is found in regard to its sense.

[4] In the Vatican edition the particle *and* [et], present in the manuscripts and edition 1, is lacking.

[5] The false reading of the Vatican edition and codex cc, which have *in regard to another* [alium] in place of *in (his) soul* [anima], we emend with the help of the other manuscripts and edition 1.

[6] We have substituted from codices D F H R aa ee and edition 1 *so* [sic] in place of *as* [sicut]; which reading seems to us more sincere for this, that by the particle *so* [sic] an application of general principles in the preceding matters has not yet been made, but now a better way for it to be done is indicated.

[7] Understand here: Master (Peter).

[8] Codices B C D G H K O S U V ee and ff together with edition 1 have *who* [qui] in place of *because* [quia], codex A has *which* [quae], but this is not good on account of the above placed *for that reason ... not* [non ideo]. A little afterwards the Vatican edition, against the manuscripts and edition 1, has *depends* [dependeat] for *depends* [dependet] and *have* [habeat] for *have* [habet].

[9] The lapsus of the copyist in the Vatican edition, ei for eis, we have emended; a little afterwards we have replaced *was ... (author)* [fuit] instead of *made that book* [fecit librum istum] on the authority of the manuscripts and edition 1.

[10] Codices F O and X have *through the doctrines and sentences of the Fathers* [per doctrinas et Patrum sententias]; a reading not to be spurned, from which only codices H S V and edition 1 depart in this, that they omit the particle *and* [et]. Codex R has *through the catholic sentences of the Fathers* [per catholicas Patrum sententias].

[11] Not so well does the Vatican edition together with codex cc omit *confirms* [confirmat], which is, however, had in the more ancient manuscripts and edition 1.

THE PROLOGUE OF THE MASTER
TO THE BOOKS OF THE SENTENCES[1]

esiring with the poor woman to place something from our penury and meagerness into the guardhouse of the Lord's treasury,[2] (and) to scale (its) steep (steps), we have presumed to do a work beyond our strength, placing (our) trust in (its) consummation and recompense in the Samaritan's labors,[3] who, having offered two denarii* to care for the half-alive man, professed to render the rest to the one spending the more [supereroganti]. The truth of the One proffering delights us, but the immensity of the labor frightens: the desire of making progress exhorts, but the infirmity of failing discourages, which (infirmity) zeal for the house of God conquers. « Catching fire from this (zeal),[4] our faith against the errors of carnal and animal men » we have studied to wall with the round shields of the Tower of David and/or to show rather that (it is) walled and to open those things withdrawn from theological inquiries and also to put on display [traducere] the knowledge of ecclesiastical sacraments to the limited extent[5] of our understanding, « not prevailing to resist lawfully the resolute wishes [votis] of (our) studious brothers, to serve the laudable studies in Christ of those entreating (us) with tongue and stylus, which as a two-horsed chariot in us the charity of Christ puts in motion ».[6]

« Although[7] we do not dispute, that every sermon of human speech has always been obnoxious to the calumny and contradiction of rivals, because, with dissenting movements of wills, the sensing of spirits also becomes dissenting », « so that, although every saying of truth [dictum veri] is perfected by reason, however so long as different (things) appear or please different ones, the error of impiety strives against the truth (which is) either not understood and/or offending,[8] and there results envy of will », « which *the god of this age works* in those *sons of diffidence*,[9] who do not subject (their) will to reason nor expend (their) study on doctrine, but strive to adapt the words of wisdom with those (things) for which they are dreaming, seeking not a reason for truth, but for pleasure, whom an iniquitous will incites not towards the understanding

---

[1] The editions and codices, with which we have conferred, either omit this epigraph, or exhibit it differently; and since they are not consistent, there is no basis for us to make any change. The editors of the Vatican edition, having followed edition 2, divided this prologue into three parts, distinguishing each with its own title — having contracted the titles and left them in the margin — but (this they did) not trusting in all the codices nor in the other editions, by whose authority we have supported the division. St. Bonaventure himself separated this Prologue in (his own) COMMENTARY into two principal parts, as noted in the margin.

[2] A reference to Luke 21:2 and Mark 12:42. Immediately after the word *scale* [scandere], there is added in ed. 8 alone, the conjunction *and* [et].

[3] An allusion to Luke 10:35.

[4] These words, having been changed a little and/or transposed by Master (Peter), are thus read in Augustine's ON THE TRINITY, Bk. II, n. 1: « On behalf of the study, by which I am catching fire to wall our faith against the error of carnal and animal men, it is necessary that I suffer ». All the codices and editions together with the Vatican edition read *and also* [atque] for *and* [et]. But even edition 2 has *error* [error] in place of *errors* [errores] together with Augustine, which (edition), however, having contradicted all the codices and the other editions, is not licit to follow, since it was a thoroughly familiar thing to Master (Peter) to change the words, which he accepted from another, for his own use, by inflecting, transposing and lessening them through various cases, and/or interposing and adding others of his own. Which we shall give the readers occasion for observing more than once.

[5] Codex B with all the editions reads *to the small measure* [pro modulo], breaking with codices A C D and E with many others, which we have consulted at Florence and Padua. In codex D another hand in the 15th century wrote on the margin *to the small measure* [pro modulo]: a gloss, which perhaps crept into the text from the margin in other manuscripts and, thereafter, was retained in the editions.

[6] St. Augustine loc. cit.: « ... but I may not prevail in resisting the brothers, lawfully, from this that I have been made their servant, entreating (me as they do), to serve most of all their laudable studies in Christ with my tongue and stylus, which as a chariot in me charity puts in motion ».

[7] St. Hilary (of Poitiers), ON THE TRINITY, Bk. X, n. 1: « There is no dispute, that every sermon of human speech has always been obnoxious to contradiction: because with dissenting movements of wills, the sensing of spirits also becomes dissenting; since being pricked by the affection of adversaries, it contradicts those assertions, by which it is offended. For although every saying of truth is made perfect by reason, however so long as different (things) appear or please different ones, the sermon of the truth lies open to the response of adversaries: because against the truth, either not understood or offending, the error of the foolish and/or vicious will strives. For unmeasured is every pertinacity of the wills that have undertaken (such things); and by an undeflected movement a study to resist [adversandi] persists, where a will is not subjected to reason nor study spent on doctrine, but we seek out a reason for those (things) which we want, and we adapt doctrine with those (things) for which we strive [studemus]. And hence [iam] in name [nominis] rather than in reality [naturae] will be the doctrine, which is fashioned: and there will remain no longer a reason for truth, but for pleasure, which (reason) one's own will has adapted more for the defense of pleasant things, which the instinct of a will will not incite through the understanding of a reasonable truth ». Then after the words *pleasant things* [placentium incitat], having omitted as much as he quotes, Master (Peter) copies the passage up to *against the truth* [foedere bellant] from the same Hilary ibid. n. 2 ff.. Then returning to St. Hilary, n. 1, those few (words): *For between the assertion* [Inter veri namque] up to *guards itself* [tuetur], he accepts, everywhere as is his custom even in those things, which he accepts, he subtracts, changes and interpolates something.

[8] The Vatican edition, against both the codices and nearly all the editions, adds badly *and* [et] before *of impiety* [impietatis], and then has the indicative for *strives* [obnititur] and *results* [resultat].

[9] 2 Cor. 4:4 and Eph. 2:2. — The Vatican edition has *of age this* [saeculi huius] in place of *of this age* [huius saeculi], but all the manuscripts together with editions 1 and 8 and the Sacred Text itself oppose this, and then at *sons* [fillis] it adds *his own* [suis] against the codices and all the editions and the Vulgate itself, where there is read: *works in sons of diffidence* [operator in filios diffidentiae].

---

* *Trans. note*: According to the monetary reforms enacted by the Emperor Augustus, c. 23 B. C., a denarius, the standard pay for a day's wage of a manual laborer (Mt. 20:2), contained about 3.8 grams of silver, (about $2.20 USD worth). Inscriptions show that at Rome, in the first century B. C., an innkeeper would charge 3/4 of a denarius for a full meal of meat and wine. The one spending the more, is the innkeeper (cf. Lk. 10:35b).

of the truth, but to the defense[1] of pleasant (things), not desiring to be taught the truth, but *converting themselves away from it towards the hearing of fables.*[2] Whose profession is more a pleasantry [placita] than a seeking out of (things) to be taught, and not a desiring of (things) to be taught, but an adapting of doctrine with things desired. *They have a reason for (their) wisdom in superstition:*[3] because mendacious hypocrisy follows defection from the faith, so that even[4] in (their) words there is a piety, which has lost (its) conscience, and they render that simulated piety impious with every[5] mendacity of words, contriving to corrupt the sanctity of the Faith with the instructions of false doctrine and forcing upon others an itching of the ears under the novel dogma of their own desire, who as students of contention war without the restraint of treaties [sine foedere] against the truth ». « For, indeed, between the assertion of truth and the defense of pleasure there is a persistent battle, so long as both[6] the truth holds fast [se tenet] and the will for error guards itself ». Therefore, lest they be able to pour forth the venom of their iniquity upon others, to both[7] turn the Church into (something) hateful to God and to stop up mouths of these (Her sons), we willing[8] to exalt the light of the truth upon a candlestick, in much labor and sweat, with God as (our) surety, have compiled this volume distinguished in Four Books, from the testimonies of the truth, founded in eternity.

In which you shall, again, find[9] the examples and doctrine of (our) elders, (and) in which we have brought to light through a sincere profession of faith in the Lord [dominicae fidei] the fraudulence of the viper's doctrine, have embraced an approach for demonstrating the truth and have not inserted[10] the danger of an impious profession, using a temperate means of guidance among both. But if our voice has sounded out a little anywhere,[11] it has not departed from the limits of the Fathers. « Therefore, this labor ought not seem superfluous to anyone learned sluggishly or much, since for the many diligent and the many unlearned, among whom even for myself, it is necessary »,[12] that one compile the sentences of the Fathers in a brief volume, with their appropriate testimonies, so that it is not necessary for one to seek to unroll numerous books, for whom a brief collection [brevitas collecta][13] offers what is sought without the labor. « Moreover, in this tract I not only desire the pious reader, but also the free corrector, most of all where a profound question of the truth is dealt with, which, one would wish, would have as many discoverers, as it has contradictors ».[14] Moreover, so that what is sought may more easily come to meet (the reader), we have placed beforehand the titles, by which the chapters of each of the books are distinguished.

HERE FINISHES THE PROLOGUE.

HERE BEGIN THE CHAPTERS OF THE FIRST BOOK OF SENTENCES[15]

DISTINCTION I

CHAPTER I: Every doctrine concerns things and/or signs.

II: On the things, which one is to enjoy and/or to use, and on those who use and[16] enjoy.

III: What is it to use and/or[17] to enjoy?

DISTINCTION II

CHAPTER I: On the Trinity and Unity.

II: What was the intention of the ones writing[18] on the Trinity?

III: What order is to be observed, when dealing with the Trinity?

IV: On the testimonies of the Old Testament, by which the Mystery of the Trinity is declared.

V: On the testimonies of the New Testament, pertaining to the same.

DISTINCTION III

CHAPTER I: On the cognition of God through the creatures, in which the vestige of the Trinity appears.

II: On the image and similitude of the Trinity in the human soul.

III: On the similitude of the creating and created[19] trinity.

IV: On the unity of the Trinity.[20]

DISTINCTION IV

CHAPTER I: Whether God the Father begot Himself God?[21]

II: Whether the Trinity may be predicated of the one God, as the one God of[22] the Three Persons?

DISTINCTION V

CHAPTER I: Whether the Divine Essence begot the Son, and/or was

---

[1] Only codex E reads *of the things pleasant to themselves* [sibi placentium].　　　　[2] 2 Tim. 4:4.

[3] Col. 2:33; in the Vulgate: Which are indeed possessing a reason in superstition. The rest of the editions and all the codices suppress the relative *which* [quae] and in its place put a period after *desired* [coaptare], while the Vatican edition and edition 4 reads *desired, which have* [coaptare, quae habent].

[4] The Vatican edition omits the *even* [vel], which we have restored from St. Hilary, as quoted in all the codices and editions, excepting n. 4. Then for *has lost* [amiserit] codex D reads *has lost* [amisit] and edition 2 *had lost* [amiserat]. The rest of the codices and editions together with St. Hilary reject both of these readings.

[5] Codices A B and E and editions 1 and 8, have badly *with mendacity of all words* [omnium verborum mendacio] for *with every mendacity of words* [omni verborum mendacio].

[6] Codices D and E wrongly repeat *and* [et] at this point.

[7] Only codex D with editions 1, 2, 3, 5, 7, 8 and 9 omit *both* [et] here. Both readings are good, but it is easier to read without the *both* [et — *Trans. note*: since the parallel construction of et ... et normally does not use atque as a substitute, as is done here].

[8] A reference to Mt. 5:15. — Then *this* [hoc] is lacking in codices A B and C and in editions 1 and 8. Then codices D and F have *and by four books* [et quatuor libris] in place of *in four books* [in quatuor libris].

[9] Codex E has *come upon* [invenies] for *find* [reperies]

[10] Only the Vatican edition and edition 4 have *uncertain* [incerti] here in place of *inserted* [inserti].

[11] Editions 2, 9 and 10 have *will have sounded out* [insonuerit]. Then codex B does well to add *however* [tamen] after *not* [non]; finally,

codex A reads *thresholds* [liminibus] for *limits* [limitibus].

[12] From St. Augustine's ON THE TRINITY, Bk. III, n. 1, with certain words omitted and not a few added; in which text codices A B D and E together with editions 1, 4, 5, 6 and 7 superfluously, and contrary to the original, add *and* [etiam] before *even* [et].

[13] In the Vatican edition and editions 3, 4, 5, 6, 7, and 9 and also in codex A *collection* [collecta] is lacking. A little before this edition 1 has *revolve* [revolvere] in place of *unroll* [evolvere].

[14] In St. Augustine's text, ibid., n. 2, this appears slightly different: Since in all my letters I would reasonably desire not only the pious reader, but also the unrestrained corrector, most of all in those, where the very magnitude of the question, could, one would wish, have as many discoverers, as it has many contradictors.

[15] We exhibit this *tabula*, having employed 19 codex manuscripts, as we have indicated in the Prolegomena, ch. 3. Moreover, we have added the Distinctions, to which the chapters refer.

[16] Codices C F P Q R S and T have *and/or* [vel].

[17] Codex B reads *and* [et] for *and/or* [vel]. The latter was frequently used by writers of a fancier Latinity in the copulative sense.

[18] Cod. I has *of writing* [scribendi] for *of the ones writing* [scribentium].

[19] Codex E has *creature* [creaturae] for *created* [creatae] and codex L for *creating* [creantis] has *Creator* [creatoris].

[20] Codices A B G and L read: *On the Trinity and Unity* [De Trinitate et unitate] for *On the unity of the Trinity* [De Trinitatis unitate], but faultily, both because the chapter of the preceding Distinction is entitled the same, and becauase in the present chapter one deals chiefly with the unity of the Trinity.

[21] Codd. G H L & M add *or whether another God* [an alium Deum].

[22] Codex D, for *of* [de], has *in* [in], but badly.

begotten by the Father, and/or whether the Son was born from It, and/or the Holy Spirit (is)[1] the One proceeding from It?

II: That the Son is not from nothing, but from someone or thing, not however, from matter, so,[2] too, is the Holy Spirit.

II: Why the Word of the Father is called the Son of His Nature.[3]

DISTINCTION VI

Whether the Father begot the Son by will, or by necessity;[4] and whether God is willing and/or unwilling.

DISTINCTION VII

CHAPTER I: Whether the Father could[5] and/or willed to beget the Son.

II: Or whether[6] there is some power in the Father that can beget the Son, which is not in the Son.

DISTINCTION VIII

CHAPTER I: On the truth and property of the Divine Essence.

II On the incommutability of the same.

III: On the simplicity of the same.

IV: On the corporal and spiritual creature, in what manner it be multiple, and not simple.

V: That[7] God, though He be simple, yet, is spoken of in a multiple manner.

VI: That the simplicity of God is subjected to none of the predicaments.

VII: That God is abusively said (to be) a "substance".

VIII: That there is not in God anything, which is not God.

DISTINCTION IX

CHAPTER I: On the distinction of the Three Persons.

II: On the coeternity of the Father and of the Son.

III: On the ineffable and unintelligible[8] manner of the generation.

IV: Whether there ought to be said: "God always is begotten", and/or "always has been begotten".

V: On the objections of the heretics striving to prove, that the Son is not coeternal to the Father.

DISTINCTION X

CHAPTER I: On the Holy Spirit, that[9] He is properly called "the Love" of the Father and of the Son, though there be in the Trinity a Love, which is the Trinity, just as the Word is properly called "Wisdom", and, yet, the whole Trinity is called "Wisdom".

II: That the same names are properly and universally accepted.

III: That the Holy Spirit, just as He is common to the Father and to the Son, so has a common proper name.

DISTINCTION XI

CHAPTER I: That the Holy Spirit proceeds from the Father and the Son, whom, however, the Greeks disavow to proceed from the Son.

II: On the Agreement of the Latins and the Greeks[10] in sense, and their difference in words.

DISTINCTION XII

CHAPTER I: Whether the Holy Spirit proceeds before[11] and/or more fully from the Father than from the Son.

II: That the Holy Spirit is said principally and properly to proceed from the Father.

DISTINCTION XIII

CHAPTER I: Why[12] is the Holy Spirit, since he is from the Substance of the Father, not said (to be) "begotten", but only "proceeding"?

II: Why is the Son said "to proceed", when the Holy Spirit is not said "to be begotten"?

III: That a mortal cannot distinguish between the generation of the Son and the procession of the Holy Sprit.

IV: Whether the Holy Spirit ought to be said (to be) "unbegotten", since He is not begotten.

DISTINCTION XIV

CHAPTER I: On the twin procession of the Holy Spirit, the temporal and eternal.

II: That not only the gifts of the Holy Spirit, but also the Holy Spirit[13] Himself is given and sent to men.

III: Whether or not[14] holy men could give the Holy Spirit.

DISTINCTION XV

CHAPTER I: That the Holy Spirit is given by Himself, and the Son is sent by Himself

II: In what manner is the mission of Each to be understood.

III: That the Son has been sent also[15] by the Holy Spirit.

IV: That the Son has also been given[16] by Himself.

V: In what manner this[17] must be understood: "I have not come on My own."

VI: Whether the Son has been sent only once, or often.

VII: On the two manners of the Son's mission.

VIII: That according to one manner He has been sent once, according to the other often; and according to one manner He is said (to have been) sent into the world, according to the other He is not.

IX: For what reason is the Father not said to be sent.

X: That the Son and the Holy Spirit are not as[18] ones lesser than the Father, because They have been sent.

DISTINCTION XVI

CHAPTER I: On the Mission of the Holy Spirit, which comes to be in two manners, visibly and invisibly.[19]

II: That the Son, according to which He is Man, is not merely less than the Father, but also less than the Holy Spirit.

DISTINCTION XVII

CHAPTER I: That the Holy Spirit is the charity, by which we love God and neighbor.

---

[1] Supply: *is* [sit], and/or read, together with editions 7 and 9, *proceeded* [processerit] for *(is) the One proceeding* [procedens].

[2] Codices A and B have *just as* [sicut] for *so* [sic].

[3] Codices C K and L, for *of the Nature* [naturae], read *by nature* [natura], but badly.

[4] The codices other than, A B and D, place *by will* [voluntate] after *Father* [Pater]; afterwards, codices A E K M P R S and T, together with edition 1, omit *and* [et]; then codd. C & R for *and/or* [vel] have *or whether* [an].

[5] Edition one places an *either* [vel] before this.

[6] Codex H has *Whether* [Utrum] for *Or whether* [an].

[7] Codex E, here and hereafter, has *Likewise* [Item] for *That* [Quod].

[8] The codd., together with edd. 1 & 9, have *intelligible* [intelligibili], which though explicable, yet we have corrected with the aide of edd. 2 & 7.

[9] Codices D H and L read *Who* [qui] for *that He* [quod]. Next codices A C E I Q R S and T, after *He is* [Filii] add *also* [et].

[10] Codices B K and N read *of the Greeks and Latins* [Graecorum et Latinorum].

[11] Through the dozing of copyists many codices and edition 1 have *more properly* [proprius] for *before* [prius]; but codex H *through a prior consideration* [per prius].

[12] Codices A and L have *That the ..., is not* [Quod] for *Why is ..., not* [Quare].

[13] Codices F P R S and T and edition 1 add *God* [Deus], which codices C H and N also read, yet, with C & H omitting *Holy* [sanctus], N *the Holy Spirit* [Spiritus sanctus].

[14] Codices M and N have *Whether* [utrum] for *Whether or not* [An].

[15] Read *also* [etiam] with *the Holy Spirit* not with *has*; each have a similar meaning (sic!). In codex B *also* is missing.

[16] Codex C has *is also given* [datur] for *has also been given* [sit datus].

[17] In codices A E F K M P R and T, and edition 1, one reads *there* for *this* [illud].

[18] In codices C H P and R *as* [quasi] is omitted.

[19] In codex H, between the title of this chapter and the next, there is inserted this rubric: *Since the Son is less than the Father according to the created form in which He appeared, why (is) the Holy Spirit not similarly* [Cum sit Filius minor Patre secundum formam creatam, in qua apparuit, cur non Spiritus sanctus similiter]. The same is found in codices G & L, with this exception, that for *Since the Son* [Cum Filius sit] there is *Why is the Son* [Cur Filius sit] and *created, why* and *similarly* are omitted; in codex G, after *appeared, why* [apparuit] there is added *too* [et].

II: That fraternal[1] love is God, and not the Father and/or the Son, but only the Holy Spirit.

III: That this verse: 'God is charity', has not been said in the manner of a cause, as this verse: 'Thou art my patience and my hope.'

IV: In what manner the Holy Spirit is sent and/or given to us.

V: Whether the Holy Spirit is increased in a man, and/or is less and[2] more had and/or given, and whether He is given to one having and to one not having.

VI: That some say, that the charity of God and neighbor is not the Holy Spirit.

DISTINCTION XVIII

CHAPTER I: Whether it must be conceded, that gifts are given through a gift.

II: Whether the Holy Spirit is said to be 'a gift' for the same reason, that He is said to be given or granted.

III: That just as the Son by being born accepted not only, 'to be the Son', but also '(to be) the Essence',[3] so the Holy Spirit by proceeding accepted not only, 'to be a gift', but 'to be the Essence'.

IV: That the Holy Spirit is said to be a 'gift' and a 'granted' according to the two aforesaid manners of procession, Who,[4] according to which He is a gift, is referred to the Father and the Son, according to which a given, to Him who gives and to those to whom He is given.

V: Whether the Son, since He has been given to us, can be said to be 'ours', as the Holy Spirit is.

VI: Whether the Holy Spirit is referred to Himself.

DISTINCTION XIX

CHAPTER I: On the equality of the Three Persons.

II: That eternity and magnitude and power in God is[5] one, even if they seem (to be) diverse.

III: That none of the Persons exceeds the Other in magnitude, because one Person is not greater than the Other, nor are Two something more than One, nor Three than Two and/or One.

IV: In what manner is the Father said to be in the Son an the Son in the Father and the Holy Spirit in Each.

V: That None of the Persons is a part in the Trinity.

VI: For what reason are the Three Persons said to be most highly one.

VII: When we say, that the Three Persons are the one Essence, neither do we predicate It as a genus of species nor as a species of individuals, because it is not that the Essence is a genus and a Person a species, and/or the Essence a species and the Persons individuals.

VIII: That neither[6] according to a material cause are the Three Persons said to be the one Essence.

IX: Nor are the Three Persons thus said to be the one Essence, as three men are one in nature and/or of one nature.

X: Whether the Three Persons differ in number, who have been distinguished by properties.

XI: For what reason are the Three Persons together not something greater than One (Person).

XII: That God is not to be said to be "threefold", but "triune".

DISTINCTION XX

CHAPTER I: That None of the Persons exceeds Another in power.[7]

II: That the Son is no less able than the Father.

III: On the objections of heretics against this[8] and the response of Catholics.

DISTINCTION XXI

CHAPTER I: In what manner can there be said: 'the Father alone', and/or 'the Son alone' and/or 'the Holy Spirit alone', since They are inseparable.

II: Whether there ought to be said: 'the Father alone is God', and/or 'the Son alone is God', and/or 'the Holy Spirit alone is God'; or whether, 'the Father is the only God', 'the Son is the only God', 'the Holy Spirit is the only God'.

III: In what manner is the Trinity said (to be)[9] God alone, since He is with the spirits and the souls.

DISTINCTION XXII

CHAPTER I: On the difference[10] of the names, which we use speaking of God.

II: On those[11] which convene with God temporally and are said relatively.

III: On this name which is "Trinity".[12]

IV: On those[13] which properly pertain to the each Person, and on those which signify the Unity of the Essence.

DISTINCTION XXIII

CHAPTER I: On this name, which is "Person",[14] that, since it is said according to substance, it is accepted not singularly, but plurally in the Most High.

II: By what necessity has there been said[15] by the Latins "Three Persons", and by the Greeks "Three Hypostases and/or Substances".

III: For what reason do we not say that the Father and the Son and the Holy Spirit are "Three Gods", as (we say that they are) "Three Persons".

IV: Why do we not say "Three Essences", since (we do say) "Three Persons".

V: That in the Trinity there is not a diversity and/or singularity and/or solitude, but a Unity and a Trinity and distinction and identity.

---

[1] Codices B E N P and T have *supernal* [superna] for *fraternal* [fraterna], but breaking with the text of Master (Peter). Next, codices M and P have *not* [non] for *and not* [nec]; codices E & R *nor* [nec] for *and/or* [vel].

[2] Codices E and H, and editions 7 and 9, *whether less and/or* [vel] for *and/or less and* [et]; codices H & P put *more* [magis] first. Next ,codices A C E and S: *and/or to the one* [vel non habenti] for *and to the one* [et non habenti]; but badly.

[3] Understand, together with codex I, *but (also) to be the Essence* [sed ut essent essentia]. At the end, editions 7 & 9 read not badly: *but also 'to be* etc. [sed etiam ut].

[4] Codices A F I K P Q and S have *on which account ..., He is* [quod] for *Who, ..., is* [qui].

[5] Codex E has *are* [sunt] for *is* [est]. Next, in codices B & Q ther is added *to be* [esse] to the verb *seem* [videantur]. Next, after *is not greater* [persona], in codices B D G H and H, ad editions 7 & 9, there is read *than the Other* [alia] for *than the Other* [quam alia].

[6] Codices B D P Q R S and T have *not* [non] for *neither* [nec].

[7] Codices B and Q have *in power* [potestate] for *in power* [potentia].

[8] Codex D has *these* [haec] for *this* [hoc].

[9] Codices A C F O P and S add here *is* [est].

[10] Codices A C E F I M O P Q R and T, and edition 1, have *differences* [differentiis] for *difference* [differentia]; next codices B and E have *they use* [utuntur] for *we use* [utimur].

[11] Codices A F and R have *those* [illis] for *those* [his].

[12] Codices C E G H L and M and editions 7, 1 & 9, with a few (things) changed, add here: *On those (names) which convene temporally with God and are not said relatively* [De illis quae temporaliter Deo conveniunt et non dicuntur relative]; where codices H and M have *those* [his] for *those* [illis], and codices C and E, together with edition 1, omit *not* [non]. Codex T alone has: *and of those (name) which convene temporally with God* [et de illis quae temporaliter Deo conveniunt]. We follow the authority of the better and very many manuscripts, which entirely omit this part of the title, (which) perhaps (was) taken over by copyists from the text of Master (Peter) itself.

[13] Codex D has *those* [illis] for *those* [his].

[14] Codices D and H omit *which is* [quod est]. Next, for *that, since it is* [quod cum] in many codices and editions there is, inded, had *which (name) is* [quod], yet not in all, below, where this title is prefaced to the chapter; where editions 7 and 9 after *to substance* [dicatur] add *yet* [tamen].

[15] Codex D reads *have there been* [dictae sunt] for *has there been* [dictum sit], codex C *are there* [dicuntur], codices P R S and T *do we say* [dicamus]; next Codex D omits *are* [esse].

VI: That God ought not be said (to be) "manifold".

DISTINCTION XXIV

What is signified by these names: "one",[1] "two", "three", "tri-une" and/or "trinity", "many" and/or "plurality", "distinction" and/or "distinct", when we use them, speaking of God.

DISTINCTION XXV

CHAPTER I: What is signified by this name, "Person", in the plural number, that is, when there is said "Persons".[2]

II: On the threefold acceptance of this name, "Person", in the Trinity.

III: Out of which sense is there said, "One, the Person of the Father, Another, the Person of the Son";[3] or "the Father is one in person, the Son another.

DISTINCTION XXVI

CHAPTER I: On the properties of the Persons and on the names relative to these.*

II: That not all names are said of God according to substance; for certain ones are said according to relation, however, nothing is said according to accident.

III: For what reason is it said that it is proper to the Only-Begotten, to be the Son of God, since even men are the sons God.

IV: That a man is said to be a "son" of the Trinity, and the Trinity, the "father" of men.

V: That the Holy Spirit is said to be "the Gift" by the same property, by which He is said to be "the Holy Spirit", and in each manner relatively to the Father and[4] the Son.

VI: Whether the Father and/or the Trinity Itself and/or the Son[5] can be said to be a "Holy Spirit".

VII: That not all[6] (the names), which are said relatively, respond, according to their terms, to one another in reverse.

DISTINCTION XXVII

CHAPTER I: What are[7] those properties, by which the Persons are distinguished.

II: That it is not entirely the same to say: "that He is the Father" and "that He has begotten and/or has a Son."

III: That the properties determine the Hypostases, not the Substance, that is, the Nature.

IV: On the general rule for those (names) which regard themselves, and for those which are said relatively.

V: Or whether according to substance there is said "God from God", and (sayings) of this kind.

DISTINCTION XXVIII

CHAPTER I: That there are not only three properties of the Persons.

II: Whether the Father alone ought to be said (to be) "not-begotten" and/or "not a Son", just as He is said to be "unbegotten".

III: On the property, which "unbegotten" notes.

IV: The response of St. Ambrose against the Arians concerning the Unbegotten.

V: Whether 'to be a father' and 'to be a son' is diverse.

VI: Whether[8] wisdom is said to be "begotten" according to relation, and/or according to substance.

VII: On "image".

DISTINCTION XXIX

CHAPTER I: On principium.

II: That from eternity the Father is a principle and the Son, but[9] not the Holy Spirit.

III: In what manner the Father is the principle of the Son, and He[10] with the Son the principle of the Holy Spirit.

IV: Whether the Father and the Son are the principle of the Holy Spirit according to the same notion.[11]

DISTINCTION XXX

CHAPTER I: On those (names), which are said of God temporally and relatively according to an accident, which accedes not to God, but to creatures.

II: Whether the Holy Spirit is said (to have been) given and/or granted relatively to Himself, since He is given by Himself.

DISTINCTION XXXI

CHAPTER I: Whether the Son is said to be "equal" and/or "similar" to the Father according to substance.

II: On the sentence of Saint Hilary, by which he shows the (names) proper to the Persons in the Trinity.

III: For what reason "unity" is attributed to the Father.

IV: For what reason are the Father and the Son said to be[12] unum and/or unus Deus, but not unus.

V: Why there is said to be an equality in the Son.

VI: Why in the Holy Spirit there is said to be of Each[13] the concord and/or a connection.

DISTINCTION XXXII

CHAPTER I: Whether the Father and/or the Son loves[14] by that love, which proceeds from Each, that is, by the Holy Spirit.

II: Whether the Father is wise by the Wisdom, which He begot.[15]

III: Whether the Son is wise by Himself and/or through Himself.

IV: Whether there is only one Wisdom of the Father.[16]

V: Just as in the Trinity there is the Love, which is the Trinity, and yet the Holy Spirit is the Love, which is not the Trinity, and for that reason there are not two Loves; so also concerning Wisdom.

---

[1] Only codex B and editions 7 and 9 adjoin the female for *"one"* [vel una: *Trans.*: like for *"two"*, which forms in English are implicit.], which form is also had in the text of Master (Peter) below. Next, codices C F P S and T have *since we use* [cum utamur] for *when we use* [cum utimur].

[2] The final clause is omitted in codex D. Codices E and R have *"three Persons"* [tres personae].

[3] In codex M and editions 1, 2, 7 and 9 there is added *Another, (that) of the Holy Spirit* [alia Spiritus sancti], and at the end *the Holy Spirit another* [alius Spiritus sanctus].

[4] Seven codices and edition 1 have *and/or* [vel] as the copulative.

[5] Editions 2 and 7 transpose (the words) thus: *the Father and/or the Son and/or the Trinity itself* [Pater vel Filius vel Trinitas ipsa].

[6] Very many codices and edition 1 here have badly *entirely* [omnino] for *all (the names)* [omnia], though they read contrariwise in the text (below). Next codex C has *to one another* [suis ad invicem] for *to one another* [sui ad se vicissim], edition 1 *alternatively* [suis vicissim], where all the other codices have *from one another* [a se vicissim] instead of *to one another* [ad se vicissim], which codex M and editions 7 & 9 have.

[7] Not a few codices have the indicative *Which are* [sunt] for the subjunctive *What are* [sint].

[8] Codex K has *Or whether* [An] for *Whether* [Si].

[9] Codices A D F and S have *and* [et] for *but* [sed]. In the next, codices E and R read *but not the Holy Spirit with the Son* [sed non cum filio Spiritus S.].

[10] Codices E and R read *and the Son Himself, the principle of the Holy Spirit* [et ipse Filius principium Spiritus sancti].

[11] Codices E and R have *reason* [ratione] for *notion* [notione].

[12] The *to be* [esse] is lacking in codices B D and M.

[13] In codices G L N and M, clearly written, there is found *of Each the* [utriusque], which corresponds to the text; all the other codices and all the editions have *the virtue,* [virtus].

[14] Editions 2, 7 and 9 *love Themselves* [se diligant]; codex S adds *and/or is loved* [vel diligatur]. Next codices B C E and S read: *i. e. the Holy Spirit* [i. e. Spiritus sanctus], codex S, however, adds *and/or the Holy Spirit* [vel Spiritus sanctus].

[15] Codices G H L M adjoin here: *Whether the Son is wise by begotten and/or unbegotten wisdom* [Utrum Filius sit sapiens sapientia genita vel ingenita]. A little before this, codex C, together with 4 editions, has badly: *by the wisdom, by which He begot* [qua genuit].

[16] Codices A C and E, together with edition 1, join this title with the following one, in which codex B has *one is the Love* [una est] for *there is the Love* [est].

---

* *Trans. note*: Below on p. 447, this first chapter is entitled: *On this name, "hypostasis"*; the same chapters follow, as chs. II-VIII.

---

[1] Codices C H and O have *the Same* [eandem] for *It* [eam]; codex B has *the Same* [ipsam].

[2] Codices P Q R S and T have *presence* [praesentia], but badly.

[3] Codices P Q R S and T have *and/or* [vel].

[4] In codex D there is falsely had: *That God dwells wheresoever He is, but not the other way around* [Quod Deus ubicumque est habitat, sed non e converso].

[5] Codices B G L M and Q have *any* [aliqua] for *a*. At the end of the next (chapter) title codex O reads *with their sordid (things)* [earum] instead of *with sordid things* [rerum].

[6] Codices A E P and R, together with edition 1, have *or* [aut].

[7] Codices A B G L N and Q have (the subjunctive) *knows* [sciat].

[8] Codices A E P Q R and S have *what* [quid] for *what* [quis];

codex B has *which* [qui]. The same, together with codices Q and T, after *effect* [effectus] add *and/or manner* [modus].

[9] For the last two *and/or* [vel] very many codices and editions have *and* [et].

[10] Codices A M P Q R S and T have *when we can* [possumus]; next only codex D, together with, editions 2, 7 and 9, has (the indicative) *cannot* [potest] for (the subjunctive) *cannot* [possit].

[11] Codices E and Q, together with editions 2, 7 and 9, have *That the Omnipotence ... is considered* [consideratur]* for *On account of what is the Omnipotence ... considered* [consideretur].

[12] Codices C and S omit *and/or* [vel].

[13] Codex B has *to be as to will* [esse quod velle] and then omits *all* [omnia].

---

* Which is the reading found, employed for the chapter title in the text of Master Peter below, on p. 743.

III: On the understanding of these expressions: "God knows, and/or[1] God Wills", "God knows all and/or wills something".

IV: That God's most highly Good Will is the Cause of all which naturally are, the cause of Which is not to be sought, because It is the First and Most High Cause of all.

V: In what manners God's "will" is accepted.[2]

VI: That God's preception, prohibition, permission, counsel, and operation are sometimes[3] understood by the name of "will".

VII: That God wills that, by all, there be done those (things) which He precepts, and/or that there not be done (those)[4] which He prohibits.

DISTINCTION XLVI

CHAPTER I: That the Will of God, which He Himself is, can be cancelled in nothing.

II: In what manner is this to be understood: "I willed to gather thy children together, and thou wouldst not", and this: "Who wills all men to come to be saved".

III: Whether evils come to be with God being willing and/or unwilling.

IV: In what manner is this saying of St. Augustine to be understood: "It is good that evils come to be".

V: On the multiple acceptation of the "good".

VI: That evils have value for the university (of things).

VII: That the cause, that man is worse, is not in God.

DISTINCTION XLVII

CHAPTER I: In what manner[5] the Will of God concerning a man is fulfilled, whithersoever he turns himself.

II: In what sense certain (things) are said to be done "against" the Will of God.

III: For what reason did God precept to all to do good and avoid evil, even if[6] He does not will that this be fulfilled by all.

DISTINCTION XLVIII

CHAPTER I: That a man sometimes, with good will, wills something other than God wills, and, with bad will, sometimes wills the same which God wills.

II: That God's Will is fulfilled through the evil wills of men.

III: Whether it pleased holy men, that Christ would suffer and die.

IV: Whether we ought to will the sufferings of the Saints.

COMMENTARY ON THE MASTER'S PROLOGUE

THE DIVISION OF THE TEXT

To the entire Book, Master (Peter) prefaces a prologue, in which he touches upon the causes of undertaking this work. Moreover, it is divided into two parts. In the first part, he posits the reasons, which moved[1] him to undertake [aggrediendum] the present business or work; in the second, the reasons, which ought to move students to kindly listen, there[2] near the end: *In which you shall again find etc.*, where he begins to speak to (his) listeners.

The first part is divided again into two parts, because a twofold reason can move anyone to do a work, namely, the *love of the good* and the *hatred of evil*. First, therefore, he posits the reasons taken from the part of the *love of the good*, namely of Catholic truth. *Second* from the part of the *hatred of evil*, namely of heretical depravity, there (where he says): *Although we do not dispute* etc.. The first part has four subparts. In the first, he touches upon[3] the exciting cause; and this is the desire for recompense and hope for help after the example of the widow and the parable of the Samaritan. In the second, he posits the restraining cause, which is twofold, namely the immensity of the labor and his own infirmity, there (where he says): *The truth of the*

One etc.. In the third, he posits the cause propelling him,[4] and this is the zeal influencing [accedens] him, there (where he says): *Which zeal for the house* etc.. In the fourth, he posits the cause compelling and prevailing (upon him), there (where he says): *Not prevailing* etc., and this is the petition of (his) studious brothers, whom one cannot lawfully resist, but (to whom) in a certain, necessary manner it is proper to submit (one's) neck.

DOUBTS ABOUT THE FIRST PART OF THE MASTER'S PROLOGUE

DOUBT I

But (the first doubt) is asked concerning this which he says:[5] *we have presumed to do a work*; but presumption is a sin: therefore, he has sinned.

I RESPOND: A presumption of *confidence* concerns divine assistance, and a presumption of *pride* concerns one's own ingenuity . The first is not a sin, but is a virtue;[6] but the second is a sin; but Master (Peter) speaks of the first.

And/or otherwise: There is a presumption according to the *truth*, and a presumption according to *one's own estimation*. The first is reprehensible, because (it belongs) to pride,

---

[1] Codices B D GH I K and V omit *and/or* [vel]. Codex A omits the final clause.

[2] Codex D has *is God's "will" accepted* [accipiatur].

[3] Codices A B C E and Q omit *sometimes* [interdum]. For *understood* [intelliguntur] codex L has *accepted* [accipiuntur].

[4] Codices E and R adjoin *those* [ea].

[5] Codices B F L M and N have *That* [Quod] for *In what manner* [Quomodo].

[6] For *even if* [etsi] codd. B D G H I L N and Q, and edition 1, have *but* [sed], codices P and S *if* [si]. At the beginning of this title, codd. P Q R S and T, together with ed. 1, have *does* [praecipit] for *did* [praecepit].

NOTES ON THE COMMENTARY

[1] Codex I and edition 1 have *move* [movent].

[2] We have supplied *there* [ibi], just as also a little below, after *is divided* [dividitur] we have supplied *again* [iterum], from the manuscripts and edition 1.

[3] Codex W and X have *posits* [ponit]. Next some of the codices, as F G K ee and ff, together with edition 1, have *this is* [hoc est] in place of *this is* [haec est], which reading occurs twice more in what follows, but not so well.

[4] The Vatican edition unduly, and against the manuscripts and edition 1, omits *him* [ipsum].

[5] Not trusting in the manuscripts and edition 1, the Vatican edition in this doubt and in the following ones, omits these opening words. Then the Vatican edition exhibits the whole passage of Master (Peter), by adding *beyond our strength* [ultra vires nostra] after *work* [opus], which words however, are lacking in the manuscripts and edition 1. This omission and mutation of the opening words in nearly all the texts of the doubts of the whole Commentary occurs in the Vatican edition, as has already been observed in the Prolegomenon.

[6] Less well and with the manuscripts and edition 1 opposing, the Vatican edition has here *but is the indication of truth.* [indicium].

but the second laudable, because (it belongs) to humility, nor is it culpable in anything; for a humble man in all[1] his works reputes himself unworthy and, as it were, presumptuous.

DOUBT II

Likewise, (the second doubt) is asked of this which he says: *having offered two denarii to the one paying out more* [supereroganti]; what is that supererogation? *If you say,* that it is the masters' and Saints' addition upon [superadditio] Sacred Scripture; *against* (you is St. John) Damascene:[2] « That which has been handed down to us through the Law and the Prophets we venerate, inquiring nothing beyond these things ».

Likewise, the last (chapter) of the Apocalypse:[3] *If anyone adds upon these (words), the Lord will add to him the plagues.*

I RESPOND: It must be said, that there is a *distracting* addition and there is a *completing* addition. Adding in the first manner does not supererogate, but rather diminishes and subverts; and such are the heretics, for whom the malediction is given. Adding in the second manner does supererogate, because with the sense of Scripture preserved[4] it makes it shine forth [dilucidat]. Therefore, through the *two denarii* I understand two Testaments, through the *Samaritan,* Christ, through *the half-alive,* man despoiled [expoliatum] and wounded in (his) natural gifts [gratuitis], through[5] the *supererogation* I understand a teacher expounding (Scripture).

And/or it another way it must be said, that there is an addition, in which the thing added is *contrary,* and there is (one),[6] in which the thing added is *diverse,* and there is (one), in which the thing added is *consonant.* The first addition belongs to error, the second to presumption; because it is presumption to say that (there is) in Sacred Scripture anything entirely diverse from those things, which have been expressed in it; the third (belongs) to faithful instruction; because one explicates what is implicit.

DOUBT III

Likewise, (the third doubt) is asked of this which he says: *Which zeal for the house of the Lord conquers,* what is that zeal of his? And why is he by this zeal more ignited [accenditur] against *animal* and *carnal* (men), than against the proud and other sinners? And since zeal is a private love, it does not seem that, he ought to have been ignited by zeal.

Besides,[7] since pride is a greater sin, it seems that he ought to have been ignited more against the proud.

I RESPOND: To the first it must be said, that zeal is love [amor] not wanting to have a partnership in the beloved. Evil zeal avoids all partnership, but good zeal avoids only evil (partnership);[8] whence those truly zealous [zelatores] for the house of God cannot see vices in the Church, that they do not rise up against. Whence in the second (chapter) of (St.) John, the Gloss says:[9] « Good zeal is that, by which the spirit, having cast off human fear, is ignited and by which it is eaten up, by which it acts in a manner sufficient [satagit] to correct any depraved things, which it sees, and if it cannot, (it) tolerates (them) and groans ».

To the second it must be said, that Master (Peter) was especially zealous for faith in the Church; and for that reason he used to be enkindled[10] against corruptors of the faith. But anyone corrupts the faith in two manners: either a movement by perversity of the will and the affection; and this is called *carnal.* For carnal affection is called here "the flesh", according to that (which is said) in the fifth (chapter of the Letter) to the Galatians:[11] *The works of the flesh have been manifested* etc. » In another manner one corrupts (the faith), (who is) moved by perversity of *judgement;* and here it is called *animal,* in a fanciful manner [quasi phantasticus], because fantasies [phantasiae] pervert the judgement of reason.

DOUBT IV

Which as a chariot, the charity of Christ
puts in motion in us.

ON THE CONTRARY: In the ninth (chapter) of Ecclesiastes (there is written):[12] *No one knows, whether he is worthy of hatred or of love.*

I RESPOND: It must be said, that "charity" in one manner means [dicit] "gratuitous virtue", in another manner it means broadly "the love (which)

---

[1] The Vatican ed. together with the more recent codex cc has *is not culpable, who in all his* [nec est culpabilis, qui in omnibus], which reading, mutilated and hence distracting from the force of the things said, is mended from the more ancient mss. and ed. 1.

[2] ON THE ORTHODOX FAITH, Bk. I, ch. 1: All the things, which have been handed down to us as much as through the Law and Prophets, as through the Apostles and Evangelists, we embrace, acknowledge and venerate; nor do we inquire for anything beyond these. — In which passage the Vatican ed. omits *these things* [haec], which are had in nearly all the mss. and ed. 1.

[3] Verse 18, where the Vatican ed. together with the Vulgate, against the mss. and ed. 1, has *to these (words)* [ad haec] in place of *upon these (words)* [super haec]; then the Vulgate reads *God will add upon him the plagues* [apponete Deus super illum plagas].

[4] With the more ancient mss. and ed. 1 favoring it, and also the grammatical structure, we have substituted *with the sense of Scripture preserved* [Scripturae] in place of *with (its) sense preserved, ... it makes Scripture itself* [Scripturam], which the Vatican ed. together with the more recent codex cc has.

[5] Less clearly does the Vatican ed., together with codex cc, read *and* [et] in place of *through* [per], in opposition to the older mss. together with ed. 1.

[6] Codex N in place of (one) twice, repeats *an addition* [additio].

[7] The Vatican ed., not trusting in the mss. and six of the first ed.s, has *Likewise* [Item] instead.

[8] Supply: partnership [consortium]. — The reading received here, and more conformable with the preceding things, is provided from the more ancient mss. and ed. 1, in place of the reading of the Vatican ed. and codex cc, which is *only evil (partnerships)* [malos]. — Next the perturbed, rather faulty reading of the Vatican ed. and of a few of the codd., as A F K and cc, *which rise against Her* [quae insurgunt contra ipsam], we have emended with the assistance of the other mss. and ed. 1.

[9] The Gloss, quoted in (Nicolas) of Lyra, loc. cit., v. 19, has this: Good zeal is fervor of spirit, by which the mind, having cast off fear, is enkindled on behalf of the defense of truth. By this one is eaten up who acts in a sufficient manner to correct any depraved things, which he sees; (and) if he cannot, he tolerates (them) and groans. — In regard to the first proposition codex O more than all other codd., agrees with this reading, because after *fear* [timore] it has *on for the defense of the truth* [pro defensione veritatis]; in regard to the second proposition the Vatican ed., departing from the mss. and ed. 1, reads *one tends to* [tendit ut] in place of *is eaten up, by this* [comeditur quo] and on account of the diverse construction has at the end of the proposition, *act in a sufficient manner, tolerate, groan* [satagat, toleret, gemat].

[10] The Vatican ed. has *Master (Peter) used to be set on fire* [Magister accendebatur]. All the mss. have *used to be enkindled* [succendebatur]; but very many, as M aa bb and ee, have *more* [magis] in place of *Master (Peter)* [magister], which reading we prefer as the only true one, as it is conformable to the above, posited objection. The error of the other mss. is explained more easily from this, that those two words [magis & Magister] are abbreviated in the same manner.

[11] Verse 18, where the Vulgate has *But the works* [Manifesta ... autem]. — Next after *corrupts* [quis] supply *the faith* [fidem], as in ed. 1.

[12] Verse 1, in which we have restored from many mss., such as A F G I K T etc. and ed. 1, and from the Vulgate, *whether* [utrum] in place of *or* [an].

much appreciates the beloved": whence charity (is called),[1] *a dear love* [amor carus]. Having taken charity in the first manner, it is true, that one does not know with certitude [cerrtitudinaliter nescit];[2] one can, however, by some experience of the sweetness of the Divine Mercy conjecture this with probability [probabiliter]; in the second manner one can know it [scire]. And if Master (Peter) speaks in the first manner, he does not say (it) by asserting, but by conjecture; if in the second manner, then he can be understood (to do so) in an assertive manner; and thus this is clear.

THE DIVISION OF THE TEXT OF THE SECOND PART OF THE PROLOGUE

Although we do not dispute etc. Above, Master (Peter) posited the reasons moving from approbation of[3] the good; here he posits the reasons moving from hatred and detestation of evil; and this is the evil of heretical perversity. Moreover, this part has four subparts. In the *first* part he touches upon their perversity, which consists in calumniating the good and the true out of the blindness of error and the equal malignity of envy.[4] In the *second* he touches upon the root of this perversity, which is a diabolic suggestion and one's own pride, there (where he says): *Which the god of this age*. In the third he touches upon the diffusion of this error,[5] which is through false superstition and mendacious and contentious speech, there (where he says): *They have a reason for (their) wisdom in superstition*. In the fourth he infers the reason, which moves him to the compilation of the present work, there (where he says): *Therefore, lest they be able*. And this reason is the subversion of error.

DOUBTS CONCERNING THE TEXT OF THE SECOND PART OF THE PROLOGUE

DOUBT V

Is asked of this which he says: *the truth (that is) not understood*. For[6] it seems, that he speaks badly, because truth is intelligible light, just as corporal light (is) sensible; but the eye having sight cannot ignore the sensible light: therefore, for an equal reason, neither will the intellect be ignorant of the intelligible light. *If you say*, that it is not similar; there is asked, why it is not similar, and why does nature fail in understanding more than (it does) in sense?

I RESPOND: It must be said, that it is similar, if one attends. For threefold is the cause, whereby someone does not see the visible: for he either does not see, because *he does not want* to look upon it [respicere], or if he wants to, he is impeded on account of a *defect of the organ*, or on account of an *absence of light*. This is manifest. Similarly in spiritual things the intellect[7] frequently does not understand some things, because *it does not want* to consider (them); but sometimes it does not understand on account of an *impediment* on the part of the body, as is clear in the mad and the stupid; sometimes on account of an *absence of light*. For though uncreated light does not withdraw itself as much as regards (its) *essence* and/or as much as regards whatever kind of influence, it has withdrawn,[8] however, itself from a man, when he sins, as much as regards (its) *perfect* influence; whence it is said to have inflicted ignorance upon him. Wherefore as the eye errs in darkness, so today (does) the wretched human intellect. But when it[9] will be fully restored to the light, just as the eye will be able to see every visible thing, so the intellect every intelligible thing.

DOUBT VI

Likewise, is asked of this which he says: *the truth offending*. On the contrary: « All men by nature desire to know »,[10] just as (they) also (desire) to be blessed; but beatitude offends no one, because all desire it: therefore, neither does truth offend anyone.

I RESPOND: It must be said, that there is a speaking of the truth as much as regards (its) first effect, which is *to illumine*; and as much as regards that no one hates it: for all naturally desire to be illumined. Again there is a speaking (of it) as much as regards (its) consequent effect, which is *expressing* [arguere]; and one has this in evils. For by manifesting evils one refutes [redarguit] the doer of evils;[11] and hence it is, that evil (men) hate the truth, because as is said in the third (chapter of the Gospel) of (St.) John:[12] *He who acts in an evil manner [male], hates the light*.

DOUBT VII

Who as students of contention war without the restraint of treaties against the truth. On the contrary: in the fourth (chapter) of the Third (Book) of Esdras:[13] *Great is truth and stronger than all. Every land invokes the truth, and all tremble before it.*

---

[1] The Vatican edition here adds *is called, as it were* [dicitur quasi], but this is corrected from the manuscripts and edition 1.

[2] Opposing the mss. and ed. 1, by having transposed the words in this manner: *it is certainly true, that no one knows* [verum est certitudinaliter, quod nescit aliquis], the Vatican ed. distorts the sense of the Seraphic Doctor. Codex cc omits *that* [quod]. Next, after *however* [tamen] edition 1 adds well enough the preposition *from* [ex, which thus renders the English, *from some*], and cod. M has *someone* [aliquis] instead of *some* [rendering the English: *someone can, however, by experience*]. The Seraphic Doctor expounds the sentence, which is proposed here, more fully below in d. 18, p. I, a. 1, q. 2 and in his COMMENTARY ON THE GOSPEL OF ST. JOHN, ch. 14, n. 999 (Bonelli's SUPPLEMENT, tom. I).

[3] Edition 1 has *a seeking after* [appetitione].

[4] The codd. here read in diverse manners; cod. V omits *blindness* [caecitate, rendering the English: *out of the equal malignity of error and envy*.]; cod. S with ed. 1 omits *equal* [pari]; cod. O has *a depraved* [prava] in place of *an equal* [pari]; others in other ways, but corrupted; we have decided to change nothing.

[5] Wrongly and against the codices and edition 1, the Vatican edition reads *the defense of error* [defensionem].

[6] We have inserted *for* [enim] from the manuscripts and edition 1.

[7] Codex T inserts *for* [enim] here, having moved the period; even

if the period is moved, one has *This is manifest similarly in spiritual things. For the intellect ...* [hoc manifestum est similiter in spiritualibus]; this same punctuation very many of the other codices also exhibit; but not so well.

[8] Several codices, as F G H K Y Z and editions 2, 3, 4, 5 and 6, have less well *it withdraws* [subtrahit], some of which, however, contradicting themselves, have next *he has sinned* [peccavit].

[9] Codex N has *the intellect* [intellectus]. Near the end of the proposition, the Vatican edition has *it will understand* [intelliget] in place of *the intellect* [intellectus], in contradiction to very many manuscripts and edition 1.

[10] Aristotle, METAPHYSICS, Bk. I, text 1.

[11] The corrupted reading of the Vatican edition, *for the manifestation of evil refutes evil* [manifestatio enim mali redarguit facientem], we have emended from the manuscripts and edition 1.

[12] Verse 20.

[13] Verses 35 and 36, where the Vulgate reads: *And the truth, great and stronger than all* etc. [Et veritas magna et fortior prae omnibus etc.].

I Respond: It must be said, that[1] there is a speaking of the truth *in a simple manner*, and/or of the truth *in this regard* or in a special way. *In the first manner* the truth is inexpugnable, and for that reason it prevails; and thus is understood that (verse) of Esdras. Again there is a speaking of the truth *in the second manner*, and[2] so it happens that it is overshadowed through fantastic reasons and impugned through contention. Whence (St.) Ambrose (says) on the First (Letter) to the Romans:[3] « Contention is an impugning of the truth with the confidence of clamor ».

Doubt VIII

From the testimonies of the truth founded in eternity. On the contrary: in the thirteenth (chapter) of the First (Letter) to the Corinthians:[4] *knowledge shall be destroyed*: therefore, also testimonies.

I Respond: That the testimonies of truth have been founded in eternity [in aeternum], as is said in the Psalm:[5] *From the beginning I have known* [cognovi] *of Thy testimonies* etc.. Because it is objected, that knowledge [scientia] will be destroyed; it must be said, that it is true as much as regards the manner of teaching and considering, but not as much as regards the thing cognized and the reason for cognizing, as the Psalm (says):[6] *For ever, Lord, does Thy word remain* etc..

THE DIVISION OF THE LAST PART

In which you shall find again. This is the last part, in which Master (Peter) posits the reasons moving (his) disciples to listen. And this part is divided into four parts according to the four things, which move disciples to listen, two of which[7] are from the part of the work, namely authority and utility; but two on the part of the one teaching, that is, humility and facility. In the first (manner) he prepares (their) docility, that is in *authority*. In the second, that is[8] in *utility*, he stirs up (their) attention. But in the following two, that is with *humility and facility*, he captures (their) benevolence.

In the first part, therefore, he shows, that his work is authentic, in the second (that it is) compendious, there (where he says): *Therefore, this labor ought not*; in the third he shows, that (his) manner of teaching is humble, in this that he wants to be corrected, there (where he says): *But in this tract* etc.. In the fourth he shows, that it is easy for to find and remember, there (where he says): *Moreover so that what is sought may more easily come to meet*.

A DOUBT ON THE LAST PART

Doubt IX

Is asked* of this which he says: *a free corrector*, what does he want to say by this name *free*?

I Respond: It must be said, that one is called a free corrector, as a free man, who « is only for his own cause », as the Philosopher says;[9] so one is called a free corrector who corrects only for the sake of correcting, not (for the sake) of envy and/or of the appearance of a cure [subsannationis]. This (kind of corrector) Master (Peter) desires after the example of (St.) Augustine in the second (book), On the Trinity,[10] where he says: « I shall love to be inspected by the upright more than I will fear to be bitten by the perverse. For thankfully [gratanter] does most beautiful and most modest charity take up a dove's kiss; but the teeth of dogs [dentem caninum] either does most cautious humility avoid and/or most solid truth hammers down: and I will choose to be reprehended by anyone rather than to be praised either by the errant or the flatterer ».

---

[1] In the Vatican edition *that* [quod] is lacking, but contrary to the manuscripts and edition 1 we have substituted *in this regard* [in hoc] in place of *as much as regards this* [quandum ad hoc], because *in this regard* [in hoc] corresponds more to the subject matter and the words immediately subjoined and occurs more frequently in the works of the Seraphic Doctor.

[2] With nearly all the manuscripts and edition 1 favoring, we have added *and*.

[3] Verse 29. — The exposition, which by the Seraphic Doctor and even by St. Thomas (here in the exposition of the text) is attributed to St. Ambrose, is found in the ordinary Gloss of (Nicholas) of Lyra. — The Vatican edition, against the more ancient codices, by omitting the special citation puts it this way: *Ambrose on that word of the Apostle: By Contention, says:* [super illud verbum Apostoli: Contentione, dicit].

[4] Verse 8. — Next codices X and Z add *it must be said* [dicendum] after *I respond:* [respondeo].

[5] Psalm 118:152.

[6] Psalm 118:89. — Codex Y has *Whence the Psalmist* [Unde Psalmista] in place of *as the Psalm* [Psalmus]. A little before this very many of the codices have *and* [et] in place of *but* [sed], though less well.

[7] As demanded by the manuscripts and edition 1, we have changed *which* [quae] into *of which* [quorum].

[8] The Vatican edition has *In the first (part)* [In prima] and *In the second (part)* [In secunda]; which reading, being less coherent with what is subjoined, we emend with the assistance of nearly all the manuscripts and edition 1.

[9] Metaphysics, Bk. I, ch. 3, where in the ancient edition printed at Venice in 1489, there is read: But as we call a man free, who is for his very own cause and not another's. — In the Parisian edition, ch. 2: But according to the manner in which we call a man free from this, who is for the sake of himself and not another.

[10] In the Foreword. — In this passage the Vatican edition, contradicted by the more ancient manuscripts and edition 1 and even the edition of the Works of St. Augustine, has *most chaste* [castissima] in place of *most modest* [modestissima] and a little below this, after *of dogs* [caninum], it omits *either* [vel]. The manuscripts depart from the edition of the Works of St. Augustine only in this, that they read *kiss* [osculum] in place of *eye* [oculum], and a little below this, before *the teeth* [caninum], they have *but* [vero] in place of *but* [autem]. We have followed the manuscripts. — A little above this, on the authority of none of the codices and also contrary to editions 1, 2, 3 and 6, the Vatican has *Augustine desires after the example in the second* [exemplo Augustinus] for *Master (Peter) desires after the example of (St.) Augustine in the second* [Magister exemplo Augustini].

---

* *Trans. note*: It will be the habit of the Seraphic Doctor to begin his doubts, thus, with it pressupposed that the Doubt begins with the title of each Doubt, as here: *Doubt I is asked* etc., or in the Doubts following the Distinctions: *Doubt II, likewise, is asked* etc.; *Doubt III, likewise, is objected* etc..

THE FIRST BOOK OF SENTENCES

ON THE UNITY AND TRINITY OF GOD

DISTINCTION I

CHAPTER I

Every doctrine concerns things and/or signs.

While considering the contents of the Old and New Law again and again by diligent chase [indagine], the prevenient grace of God has hinted to us, that a treatise on the Sacred Page is versed chiefly about things and/or signs. For as (St.) Augustine, the outstanding Doctor, says in the book ON CHRISTIAN DOCTRINE:[1] « Every doctrine is either of things, and/or signs. But even things are learned through signs. But here (those) are properly named "things", which are not employed to signify anything; but "signs", those whose use is in signifying ». But of these there are some, whose every use is in signifying, not in justifying, that is,[2] which we do not use except for the sake of signifying something, as (are) some Sacraments of the Law [legalia]; others, which not only signify, but confer that which helps inwardly, as the evangelical Sacraments (do). « From which it is openly understood, what are here named "signs": those things namely, which are employed to signify something. Therefore, every sign is also some thing. For what it is no thing », as (St.) Augustine said in the same (book), « it is entirely nothing; but conversely[3] not every thing is a sign », because it is not employed to signify anything. And since the studious and modest speculation of theologians is intent upon these, it turns toward the Sacred Page to hold the form prescribed in doctrine. Of these, therefore, there is to be an orderly discussion [disserendum est] by us who want, with God as (our) leader, to open an approach to understand to some extent the things divine [res divinas]; and first we would discuss in an orderly manner things, afterwards signs.

CHAPTER II

On the things which one is to enjoy, and/or to use, and on those which enjoy and use.

« Among things, therefore, this must be considered », that as (St.) Augustine says in the same (book),[4] « that there are some things, which one is to enjoy, others, which one is to use, others, which enjoy and use. Those, which one is to enjoy, make us blessed; by those others, which one is to use, we, as ones tending towards beatitude, are helped and, as it were [quasi], propped up, so that we can arrive at those things, which make us blessed, and cleave to them. But between both the things, which are enjoyed and used, we have been constituted, as it were », as both Angels and Saints.[5] « Moreover, "*to enjoy*" is to cleave to any thing by love for its very own sake; but "*to use*" (is) to refer that which has come to be used to obtain that, which one is to enjoy; otherwise it is abusing, not using. For an illicit use ought to be named "abuse" [abusum] and/or an "abuse" [abusio] ».[6] « The things, therefore, which one is to enjoy, are the Father and the Son and the Holy Spirit. However, the same Trinity is a certain most high Thing and common (Property) to all enjoying It, if however, It ought to be called a "thing" and not "the Cause of all things", if however, even a "cause". For it is not easy to find a name, which convenes with so great an Excellence, which this Trinity is better said (to be) except "the One God" ». Moreover, the things, which one is to use, are the world and the created things in it. Whence (St.) Augustine in the same (book says):[7] « This world is to be used — not enjoyed — so that *the invisible things of God, understood through those things which have been made, may be perceived* [conspiciantur],[8] that is, so that eternal (things) may be grasped from temporal ones ».* Likewise in the same (book he says): « Among all the things, only those, which are eternal and incommutable, are (those), which one is to enjoy; but all others one is to use, so that one arrives at the thorough enjoyment[9] of the former ones ». Whence (St.) Augustine (says) in the tenth book, ON THE TRINITY:[10] « We enjoy (things) cognized, in which very (things) the delighted will completely rests for its own sake; but we use those (things) which we refer to the other, which one is to enjoy ».

CHAPTER III

What is it "to enjoy" and "to use"?

But it must be noted, that the same (St.) Augustine in the tenth book, ON THE TRINITY,[11] accepting "to use" and "to enjoy" in another way than above, speaks thus: « 'To use' is to assume something into

---

[1] Chapter 2, n. 2; here and in the next passage, but with many words omitted by Master (Peter) and not a few added or changed.

[2] The Vatican edition and edition 4, not so well, omit *that is* [id est].

[3] The Vatican edition and editions 4 and 6 have *diversely* [e diverso] in place of *conversely* [e converso].

[4] Book I, ch. 3, n. 1.

[5] All the codices together with editions 1, 6 and 8 have *holy Angels* [Angeli sancti]. Reasons favor each reading; whence we have changed nothing. The reading *holy Angels* [Angeli sancti] comprehends, under *we have*, all good men whether they are wayfarers, or in their Fatherland; and it adds *holy* to *Angels*, to exclude the demons, since the damned in no manner enjoy God. But the other reading in one way posits *us*, who have alone been constituted in the strict sense between things, which are enjoyed, that is God, and those to be used as means towards God; in another way (it posits) the blessed *Angels* and *Saints*, who properly enjoy

God and do not need to use means towards the last end, but however, in some manner use creatures towards other ends.

[6] (St.) Augustine, loc. cit., ch. 4 and the next passage, which begins: *The things, therefore*, etc. [Res igitur etc.], ibid., ch. 5.

[7] Bk, I, ch. 4 and the next passage ibid., ch. 5.

[8] Rom. 1:20.

[9] The Vatican edition and editions 1, 2 and 4 have *enjoyment* [fruitionem], in contradiction to (St.) Augustine's text and the codices, together with the other editions, which have *thorough enjoyment* [perfruitionem].

[10] Chapter 10, n. 3. — The Vatican edition with codex A and all the editions, except 8, has at the beginning of the proposition: *The same* [Idem] in place of *Whence (St.) Augustine* [Unde Augustinus].

[11] Chapter 11, n. 17. — At the end of the text codex B, edition 1 and the original, have *one desired* [appetivit] for *one desires* [appetit].

---

* The final quotation marks, here and on p. 27, absent in the text, are placed according to the 3rd ed. of Lombard's Sentences, Grottaferrata, 1971.

the faculty of the will; but 'to enjoy' is to use with a joy no longer of hope, but already of a thing; and for that reason everything, which is enjoyed, is used; for one assumes something into the faculty of the will for the purpose [cum fine] of delectation. Moreover, not everything, which is used, is also enjoyed; if that which is assumed into the faculty of the will, one desires [appetit] not for its own sake, but for the sake of another ».

And attend, that[1] (St.) Augustine seems to say, that those only enjoy, who rejoice in a thing, no more in hope; and thus in this life we do not seem to enjoy, but only to use, where we rejoice in hope, since it has been said above, that 'to enjoy' is to cleave to any thing by love for its own sake, in which manner many even here adhere to God.

Therefore, these (authorities), which seem to contradict themselves, we thus determine saying, that we both here and in the future enjoy, but there properly and perfectly and fully, where through sight [per speciem] we shall see, what we enjoy; but here, while we walk in hope, we indeed enjoy, but not fully to that extent. Whence (St.) Augustine (says) in the tenth book, ON THE TRINITY:[2] « We enjoy (the things) cognized, in which very (things) the delighted will rests completely for its own sake ». Likewise, in the book, ON CHRISTIAN DOCTRINE[3] he says: « The Angels, enjoying Him, are already blessed, Whom we also desire to enjoy; and as much as in this life we do enjoy (Him) through a mirror and/or in an enigma, by so much shall we both more tolerably sustain and more ardently desire to finish our pilgrimage ».

It can also be said, that he who enjoys even in this life, not only has the joy of hope, but also of a thing, because he already delights in that which he loves [diligit], and thus he already has the thing to a some extent. It is therefore, established, that[4] we ought to enjoy God, not use (Him). « For Him », as (St.) Augustine says,[5] « you enjoy, by Whom you shall be made blessed and in Whom you place (your) hope, to arrive at that ». Concerning this the same says in (his) book, ON CHRISTIAN DOCTRINE: « We say that we enjoy that thing, which we love for its own sake, and that thing alone is to be enjoyed by us, by which we are made blessed; but all others (are) to be used ». « Frequently,* however, one is said "to enjoy (a thing)" when it bears a delectation together with itself [secum]. If, however, you would pass over through this (delectation) and refer it to that, where one is to thoroughly remain, you are using it and you will be said "to enjoy" not properly, but in an abusive sense [abusive]. But, if you cleave (to it) and thoroughly remain (in it), placing the end of your gladness in it, then truly and properly you are said "to enjoy"; which is not to be done except in that Trinity, that is, in the Most High and Incommutable Good ».[6]

Moreover, since men, who enjoy and use other things, are (themselves) other things, it is asked, « whether they ought to enjoy, or use themselves, or both »? To which (St.) Augustine responds thus, in (his) book, ON CHRISTIAN DOCTRINE:[7] « If a man is to be loved [diligendus est] for his own sake, we enjoy him; if for the sake of another, we use him: but it seems to me that he (is) to be loved for the sake of another. For what is to be loved for its own sake, in this is constituted the blessed life, hope for which consoles us even at this time. But in man hope is not to be placed, because *accursed is he* who does this. Therefore, if you clearly advert, no one ought to enjoy his very self, because he ought not love himself for his own sake, but for the sake of that, which one is to enjoy ». But what the Apostles says, speaking to Philemon,[8] seems contrary to this: *Thus, brother, do I enjoy you in the Lord.* Which (St.) Augustine determines thus:[9] « If he has said only *I enjoy you*, and had not added *in the Lord*, it would seem that end or hope of delectation was constituted in him; but because he added that, he placed (his) end *in the Lord* and signified that he enjoys Him ». « For, when », as the same (St.) Augustine says, « you enjoy a man in God, you will enjoy God rather than man ».

But when God loves us, as Scripture frequently says, which commends His love toward us very much, (St.) Augustine asks,[10] in what manner does He love, whether as one using, or as one enjoying, and he proceeds thus: « If He enjoys us, He is in want of our good, which no sane (person) would say; for the Prophet says:[11] *Thou are not in want of my goods.* For He Himself, and/or from Him, is our every good: therefore, He does not enjoy, but uses us. For if He neither enjoys nor uses us, I do not find, in what manner He loves us ». « And He does not so use us, as we use other things. For we refer the things, which we use, for this, that we thoroughly enjoy the goodness of God; but God refers our use to His own Goodness: for He has mercy on us for the sake of His own Goodness, but we have mercy on one another [nobis invicem] for the sake of His Goodness; He has mercy on us, so that we may thoroughly enjoy Him, but we have mercy on one another, to enjoy Him. For, when we have mercy on anyone and look to the interests [consulimus] of anyone, we indeed work for his utility and look at it attentively [intuemur], but the consequence is also ours, since the mercy, which we spend upon others, God has not left without it recompense [mercede]. Moreover, this is the highest recompense, that we may thoroughly enjoy Him ».[12] Likewise: « Because He is good, we are, and inasmuch as we are, we are good. Furthermore, because He is also just, we are not without impunity evil, and inasmuch as we are evil, to that extent [in tantum] we also

---

[1] The Vatican edition, together with codices B C and the editions, excepting 6 and 8, has *that* [quod] for *that* [quia].

[2] Chapter 10, n. 13. — The whole text we have taken from codex D and edition 1. The Vatican edition, together with all the other editions and codices, has *we enjoy (the things) cognized, in which the will is* [fruimur cognitis, in quibus voluntas est]. But we suspect, that the reading of *is* [est] must be *etc.* [etc]. The name *Augustine* [Augustinus], which is lacking after *Whence* [Unde], is supplied from codex C and D and editions 1 and 8.

[3] Bk. I, ch. 30, n. 31. — The passage of Scripture, to which (St.) Augustine here refers, is 1 Cor. 13:12.

[4] Only the editions, excepting 1 and 8, read *that therefore* [igitur quod] for *that* [quia]. Then the Vatican text, against the codices and editions 1 and 8, after *to joy God* [frui] add *and* [et].

[5] ON CHRISTIAN DOCTRINE, Bk. I, ch. 33, n. 37; the next passage ibid., ch. 31, n. 34.

[6] Loc. cit., ch. 33. n. 37. At the end of this quote all the codices and editions 1 and 8, have *in* [in] before *the Most High* [summo]; but below, near the of the same passage from St. Augustine only codex B, with the same two editions has this. But since *in* [in] is lacking in the original, we have changed nothing.

[7] Bk. I, ch. 22, but very many words have be excerpted according to the sense. — Next, all the manuscripts and editions 1 and 8, badly and against the text of (St.) Augustine, omit *us* [nos] at *consoles* [consolatur].

[8] Verse 20. — Immediately before this, the Vatican edition, together with editions 4 and 7, against the codices and all other editions, has *ought not seem* [bideri non debet] in place of *seems* [videtur].

[9] ON CHRISTIAN DOCTRINE, ch. 33, n. 37, where there is had in the original: For that reason (St.) Paul (says) to Philemon: *Thus brother*, he said, *do I enjoy you in the Lord.* Which if he had not added *in the Lord*, and had only said *I enjoy you*, he would have constituted in him the hope of his beatitude. — At the end of this passage, codices A C and D have *and ... he enjoys the same* [eodemque se fuit]. — The next passage is had from the same place.

[10] ON CHRISTIAN DOCTRINE, ch. 31, n. 34. — Next the Vatican edition has *He loves* [diligat] in place of *does He love* [diligit], contrary to the text of (St.) Augustine, the codices, and nearly all the editions. After this, to the words *If He enjoys* [si fruitur], here and a little below after *if He neither enjoys* [nec fuitur], there has been added *us* [nobus] from codex D and editions 1 and 8.

[11] Psalm 15:2. — Manuscripts A B C and E, together with editions 1 and 8, have *does not need* [indiges] in place of *are ... in want of* [eges], but this is repugnant to (St.) Augustine and the Vulgate.

[12] Ibid., ch. 32, n. 35; in which text after *the mercy which* [misericordiam quam] codices A B E and editions 1 and 8 in place of *upon others* [aliis] reads *others* [alii]; codex D reads *on another* [alicui]; and then in place of *we may thoroughly enjoy* [perfruamur], the Vatican edition, together with a few of the editions, reads *we may enjoy* [fruamur].

are less. Therefore, that use, by which God uses us, is referred not to His, but to our utility, however, only to His Goodness ».[1]

Here one must consider, whether one is to use virtues, or enjoy (them). To certain ones it seems, that one is to use them and not to enjoy (them), and this they confirm with the authority of (St.) Augustine,[2] who, as has been discussed [praetaxatum], says, that one is not to enjoy (anything) except the Trinity, that is, the Most High and Incommutable Good. Likewise they say, that for that reason one is not to enjoy those things, because they are not to be loved [amandae] for their own sake, but for the sake of eternal beatitude. Moreover, that, which one is to enjoy, is to be loved for its own sake. But that the virtues are not to be loved for their own sake, not even for the sake of beatitude alone, they prove with the authority of (St.) Augustine, who in the thirteenth book of ON THE TRINITY[3] says against certain men: « Perhaps the virtues, which we love for the sake of beatitude alone, do dare to persuade us, so as not love beatitude itself; which if they do, we at any rate desist in loving them themselves, when that, for the sake of which we have loved them, we love not ». Behold with these words (St.) Augustine seems to show, that the virtues not for their own sake, but for the sake of beatitude alone are to be loved. Which if (this) is so, therefore, one is not to enjoy them. But to others the contrary has seemed, namely, that one is to enjoy them, because[4] they are to be sought [petendae] and loved for their own sake. And this they confirm with the authority of (St.) Ambrose,[5] who says on the passage from the Epistle to the Galatians: *But the fruit of the Spirit is charity, joy, peace, patience* etc.: « He does not name these "works", but "fruits", because they are to be sought for their own sake ». But if they are to be sought for their own sake, therefore, they (are) to be loved for their own sake. But desiring to remove from the middle of these the things that which seems[6] repugnant to (these) authorities, we say, that the virtues are to be sought and loved for their own sake, and, however, for the sake of beatitude alone. Indeed they are to be loved for their own sake, because they delight their possessors with sincere and holy delectation and beget in them a spiritual joy. Still however, one must not stop here, but step beyond. Not here does the step of dilection[7]

stand still [haereat], nor is here the terminus of dilection, but this is referred to that Most High Good, to Whom alone one must entirely cleave [inhaerendum], because It is to be loved only for Its own sake, and beyond It nothing is to be sought [quaerendum]; for It is the supreme End. For that reason (St.) Augustine says, that because we love [diligimus] them for the sake of beatitude alone, we are not[8] to love them for their own sake, but because we refer that very thing, that we love them, to that Most High Good, to whom alone one is to cleave, and[9] in whom one is to thoroughly remain, that He is to be placed as the end of (all our) gladness; wherefore one is not to enjoy the virtues. But someone says: To enjoy is to cleave to something by love [amore] for its very own sake, as has been said; if therefore, the virtues are to be loved for their own sake, one is to enjoy them. To which we say: in that description, where it is said *"for its own sake"*, it must be understood in only this manner, that, namely, it is to be loved for its own sake only so as not to be referred to another, but the end be placed there, as (St.) Augustine shows above saying:[10] « If you cleave (to it) and thoroughly remain (in it), placing the end of your gladness (in it), then you are truly and properly to be said "to enjoy (it)". Which is not to be done except in that Trinity, that is, the Most High and Incommutable Good ». One is to use, therefore, the virtues and through them to enjoy the Most High Good; thus we speak and from a good will. Whence (St.) Augustine says in the tenth book of ON THE TRINITY:[11] « The will is that through which we enjoy »; thus and through the virtues we enjoy; not them, unless perhaps some virtue be God, as (is) charity, of which we will treat afterwards.[12]

Of all the things, therefore, which have been said, of which we have especially treated of things, this is the highest: that there are some things, which one is to enjoy,[13] others, which one is to use, others, which enjoy and use; and among these, which one is to use, there are also those, through which we enjoy, as (are) the virtues and powers of the spirit [animi], which are natural goods. All of which, before we treat of signs, must be dealt with, and first with the things, which one is to enjoy, namely, the Holy and Undivided Trinity.

---

[1] Ibid.; in which passage the Vatican edition, having not so well inversed the order of the words, reads *Furthermore, also because* [Porro etiam quia], and a little afterwards the same text reads *Therefore, that* [Ille ergo] in place of *Therefore, that* [Ille igitur].

[2] Loc. cit., ch. 33, n. 37; see above in the middle of this chapter. — A little before this codex C has *is confirmed by the authority* [confirmatur auctoritate]; codex D has *the authorities ... confirm* [confirmant auctoritates] and a little below this *the authorities ... prove*.

[3] Chapter 8, n. 11. — A little before this, manuscripts B C and E have *are* [sunt] in place of *are* [sint].

[4] Only codex D has *and that* [et propter] for *because* [quia propter], but badly (since the second clause would require the subjunctive).

[5] ON THE EPISTLE TO THE GALATIANS, 5:22: « He did not say: "the works of the spirit are charity", but "the fruits" ». — The words, which follow: « because the are to be sought for their own sake », (Peter) Lombard likewise has in COLLECT. IN EPIST. PAULI AD GAL., PATROLOG. LAT., tom., CXCII, col. 160: « *But the fruit*: as if he says, these things which I have enumerated, are the works of the flesh; but those are the works of the spirit, which follow, which however, he does not name (them) *"works"*, but *"fruits"*, because the are to be sought for their own sake ». From these is confirmed the reading of the codices and edition 1: *these he does not name* [haec non nominat], while all the other editions read *here he does not name (them)* [hic non nominat]; the Vatican edition and edition 4 have *But here ...* . [At hic etc.] Then in place of *he names* [nominat], codex D has *are named* [nominantur]. Afterwards the Vat-

ican edition and editions 2, 4, 7 and 9 have *therefore, they also* [ergo et propter]; we have omitted *also* [et], at the request of the manuscripts and the other editions. Then editions 1, 3 and 8 adjoin *are to be loved* [amanda sunt].

[6] Codices A B E and editions 2, 3, 5, 7, and 9 have *which seem* [videntur] in place of *that which seems* [videtur].

[7] The Vatican edition has wrongly: *delectation* [delectationis].

[8] The Vatican edition has *that we love them ... that we may not love* [quod]; editions 5, 8 and 9 *that we love them ... (we) who do not love* [qui], but rightly do the codices and other editions read *that because we love them ..., we ought not love* [quin], because Master (Peter) here holds a middle position between those who deny and assert, that the virtues are to be loved for their own sake.

[9] The Vatican edition alone omits *and* [et].

[10] ON CHRISTIAN DOCTRINE, Bk. I, ch. 33, n. 37; in which passage, besides the Vatican edition, all other editions and codices omit *your* [tuae]; but we have retained this with the original, because above in the same passage all the texts read this.

[11] Chapter 10, n. 13.

[12] Below in distinction 17. Editions 1, 3 and 8 read *afterwards* [postea] in place of *afterwards* [post].

[13] All the codices omit *one is* [est], and after this, codices A B and C, together with editions 1 and 8, do the same at *one is to use* [utendum]. Then codex D reads *of the soul* [animae] in place of *of the spirit* [animi] and together with edition 1 *gifts* [dona] in place of *goods* [bona].

COMMENTARY ON DISTINCTION I

The Division of the Book of Sentences and the Disputation about *enjoying* and *using*.

While considering the contents of the Old and New Law etc..

THE DIVISION OF THE TEXT

In this part of his, he begins the text [tractatus] of the Book, which is divided into four partial books. The first part has two parts. In the *first* part, Master (Peter) hunts the matter of this book and consequently of the others. In the *second*, he seeks out his division, which he begins there in the second distinction:[1] *And thus in this manner the true and pious faith etc..*

Likewise, the *first* part, in which he hunts the matter (of the book), has two[2] parts. In the first part, he hunts the matter through divisions, and for that reason he *first* posits a division, through which the three books are distinguished from the fourth, that is through *things* and *signs*. Second,[3] he posits a division, through which the first book is distinguished from the other three, which is through *enjoying* and *using*, there (where he says): *Among things, therefore, it must be considered.*[4]

Likewise, the *first* part has three subparts. In the *first*, he proposes a division and confirms it by the authority of (St.) Augustine, which is, that the whole doctrine of theology concerns things, and/or signs, that is, the common subject of theology is divided into these two. In the *second*, he explains the members of the division, there (where he says): *But here (those) are properly named things*, showing, what a thing is and what a sign according to the members of the aforesaid division. But in the *third* subpart, he applies the division to the proposed (subject), there (where he says): *And since ... the speculation of theologians is intent upon these*, saying, that he is going to speak of things and signs[5], first, however, of things.

Likewise, that part, in which he posits a division through *enjoying* and *using*, through which the first book is distinguished from the other three, has two parts. In the *first* he posits the division and explains it.[6] In the *second*, he says in addition [epilogat] what they are, there (where he says): *Of all the things, therefore, which have been said etc..* Therefore, the *first* part has three parts: in the

first he posits a division among the things, which one is to enjoy, and the things which one (is) to use; in the second he assigns certain definitions for greater clarity [evidentiam], there (where he says): *Moreover, to enjoy is to cleave to any thing by love etc..* But, in the third, he proposes and determines certain doubts [dubitationes], there (where he says): *Moreover, since men, who enjoy and use etc..*

And in the first subpart, he first posits a division according to the authority of (St.) Augustine, second he exemplifies (it), there (where he says): *Those which one is to enjoy etc..*[7]

To enjoy is to cleave by love. This second[8] subpart of that part, in which he posits a division in which the first book is distinguished from the other three, which concerns certain observations [notificationes], has four subparts. For, he first posits observations regarding *to enjoy* and *to use*; second he applies these to the proposed (subject), that is to the things, which one is to enjoy[9] and use, there (where he says): *The things therefore, which one is to use*; third he compares it to other acceptations [assignationes], there (where he says): *But it must be noted, that the same (St.) Augustine*; fourth, because (these) things seem[10] to contradict themselves, he puts forward [movet] and determines a certain doubt, there (where he says): *And attend that (St.) Augustine seems to say etc..*

Moreover, since men, who enjoy and use. This third part, in which he puts forward and treats of certain doubts, has three parts according to the three doubts, of which[11] *the first* is, whether man ought to enjoy man, the *second*, whether God enjoys man, or uses (him), and this he puts forward there: *But since God loves etc.*; the *third* question[12] is, whether one is to enjoy virtues, or use (them), there (where he says): *Here it must be considered, whether one is to enjoy the virtues etc..* And in any of these three parts of his he first puts forward the question, second, he determines the (question) put forward, third, he confirms the determination through authority. And the subparts have been made manifest in their own place.

---

[1] The Vatican edition, by adding *and this* [et hoc] after *his division* [suam], transposes the words *in the second distinction* [dist. 2] before the relative *which* [quae], but against the manuscripts and edition 1.

[2] The Vatican edition a little below, contradicting the manuscripts and edition 1, by adjoining a third member of the subdivision, places *three* [tres] here in place of *two* [duas]; but falsely, as will be clear from what is to be said. The error of the editors of the Vatican edition arose from this, that they thought, that by the words immediately following *In the first part* [In prima parte] there was signified the first part of the subdivision, when, however, really there was nothing else to be signified by these, except the first principal part, i. e. the whole first Distinction.

[3] On the authority of the codices and edition 1 we have substituted *Second* [secundo] in place of *In the second* [in secunda], as demanded in the above context, since *Second* [secundo] refers to *he first posits* [primo].

[4] With no manuscripts supporting and without edition 1 favoring it, the Vatican edition adjoins *In the third he determines certain doubts risen from the aforesaid things, there (where he says): Moreover, since all men, who enjoy* [In tertia determinat dubitationes quasdam ex praemissis orbus, ibi: Cum autem homines, qui fruuntur]; but falsely, since this part is the third subpart of the subdivision of the first part, as is had expressly below.

[5] Against the more ancient codices and edition 1, and less well, the Vatican edition has *was going to speak* [fuerit] . Next codices C S and cc have *Again* [Iterum] in place of *Likewise* [Item].

[6] Trusting the manuscripts and edition 1, we have supplied *and he explains it* [et explanat ipsam] and next from nearly all the codices together with edition 1 we have added *Therefore* [igitur] to *the first part has three parts*: [Prima], whereas codices P and Q have *Again* [iterum].

[7] Thus the manuscripts, together with edition 1; but in the Vatican edition the subdivision, which begins from the words *And in the first subpart* [Et in prima particula] up to *But to enjoy* [Frui autem], is lacking.

[8] The Vatican edition, inserting the word *is* [est] here, because of the varied construction at the end of the proposition, has prefixed before *has four* [quatuor] the word *and (it)* [et]; moreover, in the middle of the proposition after *a division* [divisionem] has *through which* [per quam] in place of *in which* [in qua], but the manuscripts and edition 1 contradict this.

[9] Trusting the manuscripts and edition 1, we have added *one is* [est].

[10] Thus very many of the manuscripts, as A C F G I K R T V X W Z etc. and edition 1, and also the text of Master Peter, against the Vatican edition, which has *(this) would seem ... itself* [videretur], and some of the codices as H L O S, which read *(this) seems ... itself* [videtur].

[11] From the more ancient manuscripts and edition 1 we have supplied *of which* [quarum], just as also a little below, before *uses* [fruatur], we have substituted *and/or* [ve] for *and* [et].

[12] Not trusting in the manuscripts or edition 1, the Vatican edition omits *question* [quaestio].

TREATMENT OF THE QUESTIONS

For the greater clarity [evidentiam] of the definitions and other things, which Master (Peter) posits by these words *to enjoy* and *to use*, six things are asked in this part, three of which pertain to *using*, three to *enjoying*.

Concerning *to use*, three things are asked.
    First, there is asked, what is it *to use*, essentially?
    Second, whether one happens to use every created thing?

Third, whether one is to use only a created good.

Concerning *to enjoy*, three things are similarly asked.
    First, what is it *to enjoy*, essentially?
    Second, whether one is to enjoy the uncreated Good.
    Third, whether one is to enjoy only the uncreated Good Itself.

ARTICLE I

What is it 'to use'?, and On the usable

QUESTION I

Whether 'to use' is an act of the will, or of the reason, and/or of every power?

About the first (problem)[1] concerning *to use*, what is it essentially, whether it is an act of the will, or of the reason? it is advanced in this manner. That it is an act of the will is shown thus:

1. By an act of using every single good thing is denominated;[2] but none is called good except by an act of the will: therefore, the act of using pertains to the will.

2. Likewise, (St.) Augustine in the tenth (book) ON THE TRINITY:[3] « *To use* is to assume something into the faculty of the will »: therefore, *to use* is an act of the will.

3. Likewise, this seems through a division of *to use* itself against the others, because in the tenth (book) ON THE TRINITY[4] (St.) Augustine divides these three, *ingenuity*, *doctrine* and *use*, and says, that ingenuity respects, what a man can (do), doctrine, what a man knows [sciat], use, what[5] he wants: therefore, use is an act of the will.

4. Likewise, « Opposites are bound to come to be about the same thing »;[6] but '*to use*' and '*to abuse*' [abuti] are opposites, therefore, since *the act of abusing* [abuti] belongs to the will alone, because it belongs to it alone to sin: therefore, '*to use*' will also be an act of the will alone.

ON THE CONTRARY: 1. Use or 'becoming accustomed' [assuefactio] is a way to acquire a habit;[7] but every power is bound to acquire a habit: therefore, *to use* seems to belong to every power.

2. Likewise, every power by means of its operation is ordained unto an end;[8] but for this reason it is said that anything (is) *usable* or that one *uses* it, because it is ordainable unto an end; but to be ordained unto an end by means of its own operation belongs to every power: therefore, also *to use* similarly.

3. Likewise, as (St.) Augustine says and as is had in the text (of Master Peter),[9] *to use* is that which comes to be referred unto use etc.. But to refer belongs to that, to which to confer belongs; but to confer belongs to the reason alone, therefore also to refer: therefore, also *to use* by definition.

4. Likewise, art uses its own instruments;[10] but art is in the rational or cognitive power, since it is knowledge [scientia]: therefore, since habit and act belong to the same power, if art is in the rational power, use will also similarly be in the same.

CONCLUSION

"To use" can be understood in five manners: if it is taken in its most common and common sense, it is an act of every power; if it is taken in its proper, more proper, and most proper sense, it is an act of the will.

I RESPOND:[11] It must be said, that "*to use*" is accepted in five manners, and according to this it is diversified according to thing and according to definition.

For "use" or "to use" is accepted *in the most common sense* [communissime], according to which it is divided against leisure [otium] or leisure-time [otiositatem], in place of the natural operation due any thing, or

---

[1] With the consent of the manuscripts and edition 1, we have restored the words *About the first (problem)* [Circa primum] and next we have changed *or* [aut] into *or* [an], which is also better grammatically (in Latin).

[2] This perhaps refers to that passage of Aristotle, ETHICS, Bk. II, ch. 3 at the end: For he who uses these (pleasures and sorrows) well, (is) good; he who (does so) evilly, will be evil.

[3] Chapter 11, n. 17: see above in the text of Master (Peter), ch. 3 at the beginning.

[4] Ibid., a little before; and in ON THE CITY OF GOD, Bk. XI, ch. 25.

[5] Codex X again adds here *a man* [homo].

[6] Aristotle, ON THE PREDICAMENTS, ch. "On Opposites", near the end: But it is clear, that around either the same species or genus there are bound to come to be contraries [nata sunt fieri contraria].*

[7] The same Bl. (now St.) Albert, SUMMA., I tr. 2, q. 8, m. 1, expresses this with these words: Second "*to use*" is said (to be) the exercise of a thing to induce a habit, according to which Victorinus says in his RHETORICS (or COMMENTARY ON THE RHETORICS OF CICERO, I. chs. 1-4, 25 and II, ch. 59), that nature makes one able [habilem], art powerful, use

facile. — See Aristotle, ETHICS, Bk. II, ch. 1.

[8] See Aristotle, METAPHYSICS, Bk. IX, text 16, (Parisian edition, Bk. VIII, ch. 8). — Next codices C F G H K L O R S U and cc and edition 1 have *utile* [utile] in place of *usable* [utibile]; codex Z has *utile or usable which* etc. [utile sive utibile quo etc.]

[9] Here in ch. 2. — Favoring the manuscripts and editions 1, 2, 3 and 6, we have substituted *in the text (of Master Peter)* [in littera] for *below* [infra]. In the conclusion of this argument, the Vatican edition has *therefore, to refer and consequently to use* [ergo referre et per consequens uti]; we have preferred, however, the reading of nearly all the manuscripts and edition 1 as more distinct.

[10] Aristotle, ON THE SOUL, Bk. I, text 53 (ch. 3). — Near the end of the argument the mistake of the Vatican edition, of placing *so* [sic] for *if* [si], is corrected from the manuscripts and edition 1. — Next the Vatican edition adds *or "to use"* [sive uti] after *use* [usus]; which is lacking in the more ancient manuscripts and edition 1.

[11] Very many of the codices, as A I T etc. have *The Solution:* [Solutio] in place of *I respond:* [Respondeo].

---

* *Trans. note*: In this translation, natum est shall be rendered as *it is bound* (literally it means *has been born*), since this phrase is used to express innate necessity. — Note, St. Bonav. himself calls the theological matter to be investigated a "*problem*"; cf. SENT., Bk. I, d. 5, a. 1, q, 1, p. 111, first paragraph.

toward that which any single thing [unaquaeque res] is ordained, and according to this the Philosopher says:[1] « The use of which is good etc. ».

In the second manner it is said *in its common sense* [communiter]; and so use is divided against disuse [dissuetudinem]. And in this manner it is defined by Victorinus:[2] « Use is an act frequently elicited by a power », and in this manner it can be said, that it is an act of every power and that it does not add (anything) upon the act except frequency.

In the third manner "to use" is accepted *properly*; and so it is divided against the habit of memory and intelligence, that is[3] against ingenuity and doctrine. And thus it is divided by (St.) Augustine in the tenth (book) ON THE TRINITY: « To use is to assume something into the faculty of the will », and so he calls it an act of the will in the proper sense.

In the fourth manner it is accepted *in its more proper sense* [magis proprie]; and so it is divided against the quietative act, that is against *to enjoy*. And so it is defined by (St.) Augustine:[4] « To use is to assume something into the faculty of the will for the sake of another », and so it is an act of the will while (the will is) related to another.

In the fifth it is accepted *in its most proper sense* [propriissime]; and so it is divided against the inordinate act, that is against *to abuse*. And thus it is defined by (St.) Augustine in ON CHRISTIAN DOCTRINE:[5] « To use is to refer that which comes to be used for that, which one is to enjoy », and thus "to use" means an act of the will related and ordained unto an end.

Therefore, the reason for the diverse observations is the multiple acceptation of what it is *to use*; and the reason for the multiple acceptation is its opposition to diverse things.

If, therefore, there is asked, to which power does[6] the act belong; it must be said, that *in the most common sense* and *commonly* speaking, it is an act of every power; and (St.)

Augustine does not speak in this manner; but *properly*, *in a more proper sense* and *in the most proper sense* it is an act of the will itself.

1. And so (that which is) first objected in the contrary is clear, that is, that (to use)[7] belongs to every power.

2. Because it is objected second, that every power is referred unto an end through its own act; it must be said, that that power is said to use its own act, which is lord of its own act; and to such a power belongs *to refer* its own act, not only *to be referred* (by its own act). And since the will alone is lord of its own act and it alone is moving itself, for that reason it is that alone, to which it belongs to use actively. But it happens that it uses the other powers materially and passively, because they have *to be referred*, and do not have to *refer*. And this is, what is said by (St.) Augustine:[8] « To use is to assume something into the faculty of the will »; for a faculty is said (to be) the dominion of that, by which it is able easily to act on its own [in actum suum] as (the latter's) prince.

3. To that which is objected, that "*to refer*" belongs to reason; it must be said, that "to refer" is twofold, that is through *collation* and *illation*, just as premises are referred to a conclusion; and this belongs to reason, and this is not "to use". And (this) is "to refer" through[9] *inclination* and ordination to another; and this properly belongs to the will, because it can assume anything by resting there, and/or by intending it; and this is the "to refer",[10] through which "to use" is defined etc..

4. To that which is objected concerning art, it must be said, that "art" means what belongs to *operation*, and what belongs to *speculation*. According to which it means[11] 'what belongs to *speculation*', it does not have a '*to use*', and thus belongs to reason; but according to which it means 'what belongs to *operation*', thus it is extended to the will and regulates it in using.

---

[1] The sentence: « Of which (the use) is good, is also itself good », is found in (St. Anicius Manlius Torquatus Severinus) Boethius († 525 A.D.),* ON DIFFERENCES OF THE TOPICS, Bk. II, about the middle, in which book the author proposes the divisions of the places of the topics, which are arranged on one side, by Themistius, following Aristotle, and on the other by Cicero, and indicates their differences.

[2] Fabius Marius (Laurentius) Victorinus, the Rhetor († 370-382 A.D.), who besides his lesser theological works against the Arians, composed various philosophical and rhetorical books; thus he translated Porphyry's book, ON PREDICAMENTS into Latin (cf. Boethius, AGAINST PORPHYRY, Dialogue I) and he wrote a commentary on the Rhetorics and Topics of Cicero (cf. Boethius, COMMENTARY ON THE TOPICS OF CICERO; and the edition of the OPERA CICERONIS, by Orelli, where Victorinus' COMMENTARY ON THE RHETORICS is found). Though the definition of "*use*" [usus], which is dealt with here, is not explicitly found in the aforenoted works of Victorinus, however, it seems that it can be gathered from the above (in the argument in reply to obj. 1) mentioned words of his under the definition of *exercise* [exercitationis], which he proposes in the COMMENTARY ON THE RHETORICS OF CICERO, ch. 2: Exercise is the continuation of a work undertaken. Cf. also ibid., ch. 25, where the definition of habitus is dealt with, in which a *use* or *exercise* is posited.

[3] The confused reading of the Vatican edition, which has *and* [et] in place of *that is* [scilicet], we have emended with the help of the manuscripts and six of the first editions. See also above in n. 3, and likewise for the definition given by (St.) Augustine which follows, cf. n. 2.

[4] See the text of Master (Peter) here at the beginning of ch. 3. — At the end of the proposition the Vatican edition, badly and against the manuscripts and edition 1, has *in a relative manner* [relative] for *related* [relatae].

[5] See above in the text of Master (Peter), ch. 2, in which codices A F G H I K S X Y etc., disagreeing with themselves, have *comes* [venit] in place of *comes* [venerit].

[6] Codices S Y and Z has the subjunctive sit instead of the indicative. Next the Vatican edition, disagreeing with the manuscripts and editions 1, 2 and 3, adds after *that* [quod] the phrase: *in the first two manners it is an act of every power, but in the last three it is an act of the will itself* [duobus primis modis est actus omnis potentiae, tribus vero ultimis est actus ipsius voluntatis]; but superfluously, because by the immediately following words the same is said. Then many codices, as C F K L M O R S U V W X Y Z etc. together with editions 2 and 3, by omitting the words *and commonly* [et communiter] after *in the most common sense* [communissime], transpose them after *(St.) Augustine* [Augustinus], and at the same time omit *and in the most proper sense* [et propriissime], by reading: *But commonly and properly it is an act of the will itself* [Communiter vero et proprie actus est ipsius voluntatis]; which reading manifestly contradicts the preceding. Codices D P Q and T, after *in the most proper sense* [propriissime], add *speaking ... in the most proper sense, that is in the last three manners* [loquendo, id est tribus ultimis modis].

[7] Supply with codex bb *to use* [uti]; But the Vatican text, not trusting in the manuscripts and edition 1, adds here *to use, taken in the most common sense* [uti communissime sumtum], by which addition it obtains another, but not false, sense; indeed in the text of the manuscripts there is given, by the Seraphic Doctor, no explicit response to the first objection, but the objection is only briefly repeated; on the other hand in the Vatican edition there is.

[8] As demanded by the majority of the codices F G H I R S T etc. and edition 1, we have replaced the active voice, *(St.) Augustine says* [Augustinus dicit] with the passive.

[9] Codex D has *according to* [secundum].

[10] The Vatican edition, together with the more recent codex cc, adds *by which ... is also* [quod vel], which however, is absent from the more ancient manuscripts and edition 1.

[11] Edition 1, here and a little below, has *to that* [illud] in place of *to which it means* [quod dicit].

---

* *Trans. note*: For the reader's edification, I will insert (in parentheses) dates and the titles *Saint* or *St.*, *Blessed* or *Bl.*, which they now bear, and expand the full names of those writers, more frequently cited by Bonaventure.

SCHOLIUM

In this question the ancient scholastics sufficiently agree. (Bl. John Duns) Scotus, SENT., Bk. I, d. 1, q. 3 and 5, in fine. — St Thomas, here at q. 1; SUMMA., I. II., q. 16, a. 1. — Bl. (now St.) Albertus Magnus, here at a. 13, 16, and 17. — (Bl.) Peter of Tarentaise, here at q. 1, a. 1, who briefly repeats the doctrine of St. Bonaventure. — Richard of Middleton, here at a. 1. a. 1. — Giles. R., here at a. 1, principally q. 3. — Henry of Ghent, SUMMA. a. 8. q. 1. — Durandus (of Saint-Pourçain), here at q. 3. — (Bl.) Dionysius the Carthusian, here at q. 1. — (Gabriel) Biel, here at q. 1.

QUESTION II

Whether one is to use every created thing

Second, having seen what "to use" is, through (its) essence [per essentiam], there is asked concerning the usable, that is, whether one is to use every created (being). And that (this is) so, seems in this manner:

1. According to the sixteenth (chapter) of Proverbs:[1] *God hast wrought each and every (being)* [universa] *for His very own sake*: therefore, all [omnia] are ordainable unto God: but it is fitting [convenit]* that one ordain every ordainable unto God; but by ordaining the ordainable to God we use (it) in a upright manner: therefore, if it is fitting* that one ordain all (things unto God), one is to use all (things).

2. Likewise, being [ens] and the good are convertible [convertuntur], as Dionysius (the Areopagite) wants [vult];[2] but all (things) are beings: therefore, all are good. But every good (is) to be loved: therefore, every created (being) is to be loved; but it is not to be loved for its own sake [propter se]: therefore, for the sake of another; but this is to use (it): therefore, it is fitting* that one use every created (being).

3. Likewise, it happens that one uses every virtue in an upright manner:[3] therefore, the work of every virtue is an upright use; but the use of *one* virtue, such as patience, is in respect of the evil of *punishment*, of *another*, such as penance, (is) in respect of the evil of *fault*: therefore it happens that one use all evils, that is of fault and punishment, in an upright manner: therefore, much more strongly (all) goods: ergo etc..

4. Likewise, « Opposites are bound to come to be about the same (thing) »;[4] but it happens that one abuses all things: therefore, it happens that one uses all things in an upright manner [recte]: therefore, one is to use every created (thing).

ON THE CONTRARY: 1. Charity is (that), through which we use (a thing) in an upright manner, because all (things) are ordained unto the End through charity, whatsoever are ordained in an upright manner; but as (St.) Augustine says ON CHRISTIAN DOCTRINE:[5] « Only four (things) are to be loved out of charity and only three (are) created, that is [ut] ourselves, (our) neighbor and our own body »: therefore, only three are referred or are ordained unto (their) End through charity, since there is not using in an upright manner except through charity: therefore, one is to only use three (things), therefore, not every created (thing).

2. Likewise, all, which we use, are subject [subiacent] to our will; but there are certain (things), which are not subject to our will, such as (things) necessary and perpetual: therefore, one is not to use them.

3. Likewise, every that, which we use in an upright manner, we do for a good end; but there are certain (things), which can be done for no good end, such as lying and the such, « which as soon as named are conjoined with evil »:[6] therefore one is not to use such.

4. Likewise, it does not happen that one use virtue in an evil manner [male], just as is clear from its definition:[7] therefore, ab oppositis,° it does not happen that one uses the evil of fault or vices in an upright manner: therefore, one is not use all (things) other than God.

CONCLUSION

We cannot use every thing as an instrument nor as a habit nor as an act, yet we can use every thing as an object, but in a fourfold manner, either by working, and/or accepting, and/or tolerating, and/or rejecting.

I RESPOND: It must be said, that "*to use anything*" is said in four manners: either just as an *instrument*, by which we work, just as someone uses[8] an instrument or organ; and in this manner it does not happen that one uses all (things), as for example [utpote] the powers, which are purely natural, accepting "*to use*" properly, just as (St.) Augustine accepts it;[9] or just as the *habit*, by which we are regulated, as for example a virtue; and in this manner it happens that one does not use all (things) in an upright manner, such as a habit of vice, by which it happens that one is rather turned aside (from his End); or just as an *act*, by which we are moved; and in this manner it happens that one does not use every act well,[10] such as those (things)

---

[1] Verse 4, where the Vulgate reads *the Lord* [Dominus] instead of *God* [Deus]. — Next we have also very often in the following arguments placed *it happens that* [contingit] in place of *it is fitting that* [convenit]. We note here and throughout this work, that the codices, especially the more ancient ones, very often exhibit those two words in the same abbreviated manner, so that either *it happens* or *it is fitting* can be read (cf. fn., p. 33).*

[2] ON THE DIVINE NAMES, ch. 5, where according to the Greek text there is read: To be good does not mean one (thing) and (to be) a being, another. — Then codex cc reads *but if all (things)* [sed si omnia].

[3] This is elicited from the definition of virtue, which (St.) Augustine posits in ON FREE WILL, Bk. II, ch. 18 and 19: A good quality of mind, by which one lives in an upright manner and (which) no one uses in an evil manner. — Then many codices, as C G H K O P Q R S U etc. and editions 2, 3, 4, 5, and 6 omit *such as patience* [ut patientiae] after *of punishment* [of any virtue], which however, the aforesaid codices afterwards badly replace with *such as penance* [ut poenitentiae]; but the cited editions preface these words with *such as penance* [ut poenitentiae].

[4] Aristotle, ON THE PREDICAMENTS, ch. "On Opposites about an end". See above, q. 1, 4th argument of the fundament.

[5] Book I, ch. 23, n. 22: Therefore, since there are four (things) to be loved: one, which is above; another, which we are; the third, which is alongside us; the fourth, which is beneath us: of the second and the forth no precepts were to be given. — And ibid., ch. 26, n. 27: Which if you understand the whole you, that is your spirit and body, and your (whole) neighbor, that is his spirit and body. — Codex W adds *namely God* [scilicet Deus] after *out of charity* [caritate]. — A little before on the testimony of the codices and edition 1, we have added *just as* [sicut].

[6] Aristotle, ETHICS, Bk. II, ch. 6: For certain (things) immediately as (they are) named are entwined with wickedness (the Ancient Latin Transl. in the ed. of the OPERA S. THOMAE, by Fiaccadori, 1866, tome 21).

[7] (St.) Augustine, ON FREE WILL, Bk. II, ch. 18 and 19, n. 50. See a little above in the 3rd argument of the fundament..

[8] We have substituted from nearly all the manuscripts and edition 1 *anyone uses* [aliquis utitur] in place of *we use* [utimur]. Codex V reads *just as we use something* [sicut aliquo utimur]. Next from very many codices, together with edition 1, we have twice substituted *as for example* [utpote] in place of *considered as* [ut puta].

[9] To the extend that 'to use' is to assume something into the faculty of the will. See above, q. 1. Cf. also Aristotle, ETHICS, Bk. I, last chapter, where he deals with the powers, which are not subject to the command of reason or of will.

[10] The Vatican edition, together with codex cc, badly omits *well* [bene], which the more ancient manuscripts and edition 1 have, and we have changed *it is fitting* [convenit] into *it happens* [contingit].

which as soon as named are conjoined with evil; or just as an *object*, toward which we are inclined; and in this manner it happens that one *uses* and *abuses* all (things). For all (things) can be taken [sumi] into the faculty of the will to be approved and/or rejected; and this is clear through (St.) Augustine, in the book, OF EIGHTY THREE QUESTIONS:[1] « We use by assuming and/or rejecting (things) according to (their) value [ad valetudinem], by tolerating (them) according to (our) patience, (and) by ordaining (them) to justice ».

Likewise, (St.) Augustine (says) in the tenth (book) ON THE TRINITY:[2] « (My) will seizes (my) whole intelligence, while I am using every that which I understand »; but evils are understood: therefore, it happens that one uses evils.

Yet, in one manner we use goods, in another (we use) evils. For among goods the reason for (their) being ordained [ratio ordinationis] is not only on the part of the one ordaining, but also on the part of the one ordained, because good things are per se useable and ordainable, and (this they are) from their own nature; but among evils the reason for (their) being ordained is not on the part of the (things) ordained, but rather on the part of the one ordaining; and for that reason evils are not said (to be) "useable".

Whence note, that, since 'to use' is to assume something into the faculty of the will, this can be in a fourfold manner: either into the faculty of the will *working*,[3] just as concerns those (things) which properly pertain to human use; and/or into the faculty of the will *accepting*, just as is the love [dilectio] of (one's) neighbor and (things) of this kind [huiusmodi]; and/or into the faculty of the will *tolerating*, just as are the evils of punishment; and/or into the faculty of the will *rejecting*, and in this manner the evils of fault are assumed and ordained. In the first two manners is understood that (which is said): « The use of which is good etc. ».

1. To that, therefore, which is objected concerning charity, that only three created (things)[4] are to be loved; it must be said, that *that something be loved out of charity*, this is that it be ordained unto the Most High Good, which charity loves per se. Moreover, this happens in a twofold manner: for either one happens to ordain that which is bound [natum est] to arrive at the End; and thus only three created (things) are to be loved out of charity; or (one happens to ordain) that through which there is an arriving at the Most High Good; and because this can be through every creature in its own manner, every creature can be loved out of charity, and one happens to use every creature.

2. To that which is objected, that not all (things) are subject to the will, it must be said, that something[5] is said "to be subject" to the dominion of the will in a twofold manner: either as much as regards the *'being' of the thing itself* [esse ipsius rei]; and thus all (things) are not subject; or as much as regards the *act of the will*, which is in rejecting and/or approving the thing itself, and this[6] for its own sake and/or for the sake of another; and in such a manner all (things) are subject to our will, that is as much as regards (its) act of desiring [appetitionis] and/or of rejecting, though not in the first manner.

3. 4. To that which is objected, that certain (things) can be done for no good end, *similarly*, (that) we always abuse vices; it must be said, that (this) is objected according to the way, by which it happens that one uses something as an intermediary *act*; and in this manner it does not happen[7] that one uses sin; and/or just as a regulating *habit*, similarly; yet it does happen that one uses (sin) in an upright manner as an *object*, through the movement of contrition and detestation.

SCHOLIUM

I. This and the following question the ancient doctors are accustomed to treat under one question and less accurately. — It has already been shown above, that 'to use' in the *active* sense belongs to the will alone; in this second question there is inquired, to what *objects* does the use of the will extend itself, or which things it is suitable to use *passively*. In the Response the Seraphic Doctor *first* posits a fourfold distinction about the *objects* of the will to be ordained and resolves the question according to *genus*. As regards the first member of this distinction, it is clear that the will cannot assume all things into its faculty, to use them as an instrument. For some powers of the soul itself are not subject to the command [imperio] of the will; whence they are called *"purely natural"*, such as the vegetative powers. *Second*, by discussing a *special* question, that is, "In what sense one can use evils?", he again distinguishes in a fourfold manner the modes of the ordaining will, that is, *working*, *accepting*, *tolerating*, *rejecting*. This use of evil on the part of the one ordaining is a « use per accidens », as Richard (of Middleton) well says (here in q. 2 at the end), « for that which has been or-

dained to another, accepts (its) ordinability, namely from the will ». — About this question concerning the use of evil, St. Thomas (loc. cit. at this question) speaks in other words than St. Bonaventure, but there is no difference in thought [sententia], indeed in the SUMMA., II, II, q. 78, a. 4, the Angelic (Doctor) agrees also with him in (his) manner of speaking.

II. Alexander of Hales, SUMMA., p. III., q. 61, m. 1. — (Bl. John Duns) Scotus, here in qq. 3 and 5, and in his QUODLIBETALS., q. 17. — St. Thomas, here in q. 2, a. 3; SUMMA., I, II, q. 16, a. 3. — Bl. (now St.) Albertus Magnus, here in aa. 10 and 11. — (Bl.) Peter of Tarentaise, here in q. 1, a. 2, so closely follows the Seraphic Doctor, that (Bl.) Dionysius the Carthusian says of him: « Peter, who wrote after Bonaventure, seems to have taken his own response from Bonaventure himself ». — Richard of Middleton, here in a. 1, q. 2. — Giles the Roman, here in a. 2, the beginning of q. 3. — Henry of Ghent, SUMMA., a. 72, q. 3, n. 11. — Durandus (of Saint-Pourçain), here in q. 4. — (Bl.) Dionysius (the Carthusian), here in q. 2. — (Gabriel) Biel, here in q. 1.

---

[1] Question 30: For thus does one use one's own body: by assuming and/or rejecting certain things according to (their) value [valitudinem], by tolerating certain things according to (one's) patience, by ordaining certain things to justice, by considering certain things according to some teaching [documentum] of truth. — In which text very many codices, as A B C D F G H I K S T W Z etc. omit *assuming and/or* [assumendis vel], in place of which edition 1 has *conferring or* [conferendis].
[2] Chapter 11, n. 18: My will also seizes my whole intelligence, *my whole memory*, while I use whole, what I understand *and remember*.
[3] Opposing the manuscripts and editions 1, 2 and 3, the Vatican edition puts *commanding* [imperantis] in place of *working* [operantis], but faultily, because this member does not exclude the other members of the division. The same distinction (Bl.) Peter of Tarentaise thus briefly proposes here at q. 1, a. 2: One can assume something into the faculty of the will in a fourfold manner: of the working will, as our goods, and/or of the approving (will), as another's goods, and/or of the tolerating (will), as one's own evils of punishment and of another's fault, and/or of the rejecting (will), as the evils of one's own fault.

[4] The codices together with edition 1 omit *created (things)* [creata], which, as certainly must be understood, we have retained for the sake of clarity, especially when it is also found a little later in the manuscripts. Next the Vatican edition, after *out of charity* [carotate], having omitted *this* [hoc], exhibits that proposition in the active voice: *to love, is to ordain something out of charity* [diligere, aliquid ex caritate est ordinare], however, in opposition to the manuscripts and edition 1. The objection, which the Seraphic Doctor here solves, he treats in another respect below in d. 17, p. I., q. 2.
[5] With no supporting manuscript nor edition 1, the Vatican edition reads *someone* [aliquis].
[6] Codex Z adds not badly here *either* [vel].
[7] As demanded by nearly all the manuscripts and edition 1, we have substituted *in this manner* [hoc modo] with *thus* [sic], and twice *it happens* [contingit] in place of *it is fitting* [convenit]. Then we have corrected the fault of the Vatican edition, *(sin), as an upright object through the manner of contrition* [recto per modum] on the basis of the manuscripts and edition 1.

---

* *Trans. note*: In the first and second argg. on p. 32, I have read *it is fitting* [convenit], wherever the Editors read *it happens* [contingit]. There in fn. 1, the editors give their reason, which they have not applied well on that page, since those 2 arguments suppose a necessity, not merely a contingency. Cf. also here Sent., Bk. I, d. 1, a. 3, q. 1, fn. 1
° Cf. translator's footnote on p. 52, below, regarding the meaning of this expression.

QUESTION III

Whether one is to use created good alone.

Third, having show, whether one is to use every thing created and[1] everything else (that is) from God, there is the question, whether one is to use only the created good. And it seems that (this is) so.

1. « Every good either is an end, or for an end [ad finem] »;[2] but one is to use only the good, which is for an end, because the reason for the useful [ratio utilis] is to lead unto an end: therefore, since the created good alone is for an end, one is to use only the created good.

2. Likewise, every good either has been created, or is uncreated. But if it happens that one use the uncreated Good, it happens that one refers It to another: therefore, either to (something) created, or[3] uncreated; but not to (something) uncreated, because there is naught but one Uncreated: therefore, to (something) created. But in this manner the Terminus is referred to the way, and the Cause to the effect; but this is an abuse, not a use; therefore, one is to use the created good or creature alone.

3. Likewise, (St.) Augustine in the book, OF EIGHTY-THREE QUESTIONS[4] divides the honest against the useful: therefore, no useful is honest and/or vice versa; but God is honest through essence: therefore, one is not to use God.

4. Likewise, it seems that one is not only not to use God or the uncreated Good, but to use it is always a mortal sin, because (St.) Augustine in the book, OF EIGHTY-THREE QUESTIONS[5] says: « The highest perversity is enjoying what is to be used and using what is to be enjoyed »; but he who uses the uncreated Good, uses a good that is to be enjoyed: ergo etc.

ON THE CONTRARY: 1. It happens that one serves God in an upright manner in consideration of a wage [intuitu mercedis], because there are many good mercenaries, as (St.) Ambrose says;[6] but it does not happen that one serves God except by loving [amando] (Him): therefore, it happens that one loves God in an upright manner in consideration of a wage; but the one thus loving uses God, because he refers (Him) to (something) else: ergo etc..

2. Likewise, Most High Goodness so holds Itself to love, as[7] Most High Truth (does) to cognition; but it happens that one cognizes created truth more clearly without a pre-judgement [praeiudicio] of Most High Truth and without error: therefore, similarly it happens that one loves [diligere] another goodness more ardently than the Most High (Goodness) without a pre-judgement of Most High Goodness and without disorder [deordinatione]: therefore, it happens that another is loved with an ordinate love [amore] more than God: therefore, it happens that God is loved [diligi] in an ordinate manner for the sake of another and thus one uses Him.

3. Likewise, it seems that there is no sin, when one uses God for the sake of his own salvation, because « whose end (is) good, (is) itself good »;[8] but the use of Him is good, that is, for our salvation: therefore, the use of God (is) good: therefore, it will not be a sin.

4. Likewise, the use of God is either good; and thus one (is) to use God; or is evil; and thus God (is) evil, because « whose use (is) evil, (is) itself evil »;[9] wherefore, if God is good, the use of Him (is) also good: therefore, one is to use God.

CONCLUSION

One is to use only the created good, and to use the uncreated Good is to abuse (It).

I RESPOND: It must be said, that one is to use only the created good, because, if we use the uncreated Good, there is always an abuse, and such an abuse is a mortal sin on account of the perversity against the End[10] with delectation, and on account of the inordinacy [inordinationem] of the will, which loves less That *which* it uses, than (that) *for the sake of which* it uses.

---

[1] Codices R and W have *and/or* [vel] in place of *and* [et].

[2] Cf. Aristotle, ETHICS, Bk. I, ch. 1-7: MAGNA MORALIA, Bk. I, ch. 3 and TOPICS, Bk. III, ch. 1, where this division is hinted at in diverse manners.

[3] Codex A together with ed. 1 adds well enough *to* [ad]. Then the Vatican ed., disagreeing with the more ancient mss. and ed. 1, omits *Uncreated* [increatum] after *one* [unum].

[4] Question 30: What is to be sought out for its own sake is called honest, but what is to be referred to another thing (is called) useful. — Then from many codd., as A F G H I K T U V aa bb ee ff together with ed. 1, we have put *and/or* [vel] in place of *and* [et]. A little below (this) the Vatican ed. puts *something* [quid] before *honest* [honestum], because God is the Honest Itself through essence.

[5] Question 30: And thus every human perversion, which is also called a vice, is to want to use the things which are to be enjoyed [fruendis] and to enjoy the things which are to be used [utendis].

[6] IN THE GOSPEL OF ST. LUKE, ch. 15, where according to the Venetian ed. of 1748 (there is read): But in truth the son, who has the pledge of the Holy Spirit in (His) heart, does not seek the small profits of worldly pay, to which he is a slave. The heirs are also mercenaries, who are lead to the vineyard. The good mercenary Peter etc.. — But the Codex, (kept) under n. 507 in the Biblioteca (Medicea) Laurenziana at Florence, membr. in fol., saec. XI, folio 116 r., col. 2, thus exhibits the final part: he does not seek, who guards the right of an heir. There are those who are conducted to the vineyard. The good etc.. With this codex III. Plut. XIV, in fol. saec. XV, Bk. VIII, ch. 35, agrees. The reading of that ed. errs in its words and punctuation.

[7] The Vatican ed., against the mss. and ed. 1, by inverting the comparison, namely *as the Most High Good, so the Most High Truth* [sicut summa bonitas, sic summa veritas], confuses the argument, as is clear from the subjoined. Then codex X after *more clearly* [clarius] adds, well enough, *by uncreated Truth* [veritate increata]. Then, favoring the more ancient mss. and ed. 1, we have expunged *some* [aliquam], which the Vatican ed. together with the more recent codex cc has prefaced by the word *another* [aliam]. In the last proposition of this argument many of the codd., C F G K L R S U V W aa bb together with ed. 1, falsely repeat *more* [plus] after *is loved* [diligi].

[8] (St. Severinus) Boethius, ON THE DIFFERENCES OF THE TOPICS, Bk. II. A topic a fine: Whose end is good, is itself also good. See below q. 1 in the body. That proposition seems to be derived from that of Aristotle, Topics, Bk. III., ch. 1: *Whose end is better, (is) also itself better.* According to the norm of the codd. and ed. 1, we have omitted *is* [est] and *also* [quoque], which the Vatican text together with (St. Severinus) Boethius has.

[9] (St. Severinus) Boethius, ON THE DIFFERENCES OF THE TOPICS, Bk. II. — Codices F O and X add after *evil* [malus] the particle *and/also* [et]. Immediately after, from nearly all the mss. and ed. 1, we have substituted *wherefore* [quod] in place of *because* [quia], codex R however, has *therefore, if God* [ergo si Deus].

[10] On the authority of the mss. and ed. 1, we have rejected the reading of the Vatican ed. *aversion from (its) end* [aversionem a fine] as less right, because such an abuse does not mean only a simple aversion from (its) end, but also a direct perversion of its very end, namely to the extent that the end itself is converted into a means [medium]. Codex O after *perversity* [perversitatem] adds *of intention* [intentionis]. Codex R exhibits the whole proposition thus: *and such an abuse is always a mortal sin, not* (perhaps *only* has been omitted here) *on account of the per- / -versity against the End with delectation, but on account of the will* etc. [et abusus talis semper est mortale peccatum, non propter pe veritatem in finem cum delectione, sed propter volutnatis etc.]. Then having followed a greater pert of the codd., as A C G I K L U V X etc. and ed. 1, we have

1. To that, therefore, which is objected, that it does happen that God is served in an upright manner in consideration of a wage; it must be said, that that wage either is God Himself, as He said to Abraham in the fifteenth (chapter) of Genesis:[1] *I (am) thy wage*; and the one, thus considering a wage, does not use, because he does not refer to another; or that wage is *another*, and then one can consider it either as *a moving cause*; and thus one is an evil mercenary;[2] or as an *inducing reason*; and so (one is) good, and in this manner one does not use.

2. To that which is objected, that the more clearer cognition of a creature does not prejudge the Creator, ergo etc.; it must be said, that it is not similar, because the clarity of cognition is not in our power, but the ardor of affection is in our power; for that reason there is required from us, that we ordain this (love) of ours, not that (cognition).[3] However, there is some act of cogni-

tion in our power, as for example, the act of faith, whereby, if one assents to Prime Truth on account of another, he prejudges Truth in a good manner [bene], just as to love [amare] on account of another, (prejudges) goodness.

3. To that which is objected, that the end of the use of God is good; it must be said, that an end is called "good" in a twofold manner: either as much as regards (its) *substance*, or as much as regards the *intention to order (something) to (this) end* [finiendi]; and that proposition is understood as much as regards the *intention to order to the End*, and this (intention)[4] consists in an upright ordering.

4. To the last, it must be said, that that proposition[5] is understood of those having an ordination to an end, but not of the end itself. — And/or it is understood of the natural act of the things themselves and the proper (act), which frequently is elicited from the thing itself, but not of (its) ordination unto[6] an end; and so the proposition is not valid for the proposed.

SCHOLIUM

I. In the conclusion the Seraphic Doctor proves the proposition, that to use the uncreated Good is an *abuse* and a sin, with a twofold reason, which is taken both from the part of the *last end*, and from the part of the *will*. On the part of the *end* it is an abuse, because an aversion from the end is not done without contempt for it and an offense to God, as is proven in SENT., Bk. II, d. 42, a. 2, q. 1. and a. 3, q. 2; on the part of the will on account of its inordinate state, because the will, when it uses God, places its end in another; but the end is better that those which are for the end (below in d. 29, a. 1, q. 1 in the body of the reply) and « as much as it concerns itself, it means an excess of goodness in respect to that, which is for the end » (ibid., at n. 4). From which the inordinate state (spoken of) in the proposition is clear. For the will in using loves the means

[diligit medium] less than the end. To which one applies that most general of the principles of Aristotle, very often repeated by the Seraphic Doctor: That for the sake of which any single thing is (such), is greater. Cf. also here in doubt n. 6, where he says, that every thing is either an end, or a means to an end, or arriving at an end. — In regard to the solution to n.1, namely in which manner we can serve God in consideration of a wage, cf. SENT., Bk. II, d. 38, a. 1, q. 3, reply to n. 2, and SENT., Bk. III, d. 27, a. 2, q. 2. — In regard to the axiom: Whose end (is) good, (is) also itself good (reply to n. 3), cf. SENT., Bk. II, d. 38, a. 1. q. 1.

II. In regard to that question: Alexander of Hales, SUMMA., p. III, q. 60, m. 3, q. 1 and 2, and p. II, q. 142, m. 2. — See the other authors in the Scholium at the preceding Question.

ARTICLE II

What is it 'to enjoy'?

With (the question) of *to use* and *the useable* having been considered, there is consequently asked, concerning *to enjoy* and *the enjoyable*,

first, what it is "to enjoy" through essence, that is, whether it is an act of the will, or whether (it is an act) of the other forces (of the soul).

QUESTION SOLE

Whether "to enjoy" is an act of the will, or whether (it is an act) of the other powers (of the soul)?

1. That it is an act of the will, seems through the first definition, which is: To enjoy is to inhere by love etc.;[7] but love belongs to the will: therefore, also *to enjoy* similarly. *If you say*, that love is taken there in the common sense [communiter], accord-

ing to which it is in any force [vi] in respect to its act; *on the contrary*: in all other definitions the same is said. Whence there is said in the following:[8] « We enjoy things cognized, in which the delighted will rests completely [conquiescit] ». But resting

---

twice substituted *uses* [utitur] for *we use* [utimur], which is grammatically better; the other codd. have in the first place *uses* [utitur], in the second place *we use* [utimur]. This relative proposition adduced by the Seraphic Doctor, which is immediately referred to the substantive *of the will* [voluntatis], implicitly contains the reason for the inordinate state noted in willing this; for the sense is: the ordinate will loves less *that which it uses*, i.e. the means, which (is) *on account of that which it uses*, i.e. the end; but in fact the contrary is had in this case; therefore, the will is inordinate.

[1] Verse 1. — A little before this we have used the reading of codd. R V W X Y Z aa and bb; the other codd. however, having omitted *God* [Deus], put *the Lord* [Dominus] after *Abraham* [Abrahae], from which the Vatican ed. does not dissent much in its reading: *(is) also He, as the Lord said to Abram* [et ipse, sicut Dominus dixit ad Abraam]. Then on the testimony of the more ancient mss. and ed. 1, we have expunged *God* [Deo] after *does not use* [utitur].

[2] The Vatican ed., contrary to the testimony of the mss. and ed. 1, adds here *and thus one uses* [et sic utitur].

[3] The Vatican ed. adds *love* [amorem] after *this* [istum] and after *that* [illam] adjoins *cognition* [cognitionem], which however, on the au-

thority of the mss. and edd. 1, we have expunged as superfluous (though necessary for clarity in English).

[4] Codex cc together with ed. 1 reads *this* [hoc]. Then the more ancient codd. and ed. 1 omit the proposition, which is had in the Vatican ed. and codex cc after *ordering* [ordinatione], that is: *and in that manner it does not happen that one uses God, because it is not fitting that He be ordained (to an end)* [et illo modo non contingit uti Deo, quia non convenit ordinari]. — The Seraphic Doctor treats of this matter more extensively in SENT. Bk. II, d. 28. a. 1. q. 1.

[5] That is, whose use (is) good, (is) also itself good. — The Vatican ed. together with codex cc adds a little before this, after *to the last (objection)* [ultimum], against the testimony of the more ancient mss. and ed. 1, *that is, the use of God is either good or evil*, etc. [scilicet usus Dei aut est bonus aut malus etc.].

[6] From the mss. and ed. 1, we have substituted *unto* [in] in place of *to* [ad]. — Concerning this second member of the response, see above in q. 1, near the beginning of the conclusion.

[7] See the text of Master (Peter), ch. 2.

[8] Cf. the text of Master (Peter), ch. 2.

belongs to the will. And in the other (definition)[1] similarly: « 'To enjoy' is 'to use with joy' ». But joy pertains properly to the will.

2. Likewise, it is shown *by reason*, because we take delight in enjoying,[2] according to which the delectable is a difference [differentia] of the good, since it is an honest, profitable [conferens] and delectable good; but the good is the object of the will: therefore, *to enjoy* belongs only to the will.

3. Likewise, we enjoy that, by which we rest; but resting looks back to the reckoning of an end [rationem finis], « and an end (looks back to) the reckoning of a good »[3] and « the good is the object of the will »: therefore, the enjoying, which is ordered to it, (does so) similarly.

BUT ON THE CONTRARY: 1. Every virtue desires [appetit] to be united to its object, in which, when had, it takes delight, if it cognizes (it), and rests (in it): therefore, a movement with resting and delectation belongs to every force: therefore, since such is enjoying, enjoying will be in everything, not only in the will.

2. Likewise, the absence of the thing loved completely saddens the one loving more than it delights (him);[4] for what delights him, is this, that he sees and has it. If therefore, the movement of enjoying is with a delectation and/or is the delectation itself: therefore, this[5] is, because he sees that in which is the very delectation; but vision respects the cognitive: therefore, etc..

3. Likewise, (St.) Augustine (says) in (his) book, ON CHRISTIAN DOCTRINE:[6] « This is the highest wage, that we thoroughly enjoy Him ». But on this (verse) of the Psalm: *I shall show him salvation* etc., the Gloss says,[7] that « vision is the whole wage » [tota merces]: therefore, if enjoying is the wage, enjoying is, through (its) essence, vision; but vision is in the cognitive (part) or in the reason: therefore, etc..

4. Likewise, by faith and hope we tend unto God: therefore, either by enjoying, or by using; but not by using, since one must not use God: therefore, by enjoying: therefore, by faith and hope we enjoy; but faith is a habit of the cognitive reason; but to whom belongs the habit, to him belongs the act: therefore, the act of enjoying is an act[8] of the reason; it seems similarly concerning the irascible: therefore etc..

CONCLUSION

"To enjoy", taken essentially, is an act of the will; taken dispositively, it is an act also of the other powers

I RESPOND: According to some[9] 'to enjoy' pertains to all the forces (of the soul); and they say this, because all the forces will be remunerated; these also say, that[10] in glory it shall more properly belong to reason, because it holds itself more immediately to delectation.

But it seems that it must be said otherwise according to (St.) Augustine, namely that it is an act of the will itself. For though three definitions are given for *"to enjoy"* [de frui], they are all given from within [penes] the act of the will, the considering of which is threefold. *In the first* manner (it is said) *commonly*, insofar as it means [prout dicit] a movement with delectation; and thus does (St.) Augustine define (it):[11] « "To enjoy" is to use with joy ». *In the second* manner, insofar as it means a movement with rest; and in this manner it is defined by (St.) Augustine in ON CHRISTIAN DOCTRINE: « "To enjoy" is to inhere by love to another thing for its own sake » and in this manner it is accepted *properly*. *In the third* manner it is accepted, insofar as it embraces both, that is resting and delectation; and in this manner it is defined by (St.) Augustine in the tenth (book) of ON THE TRINITY: « "To enjoy" is to rest in things known, with the will having taken delight for its own sake », and thus it is accepted *most properly*.

Therefore, because *"to enjoy"* according to every acceptation means a delectation and/or a rest and/or both of these, and every such has a reckoning of the good, and this is the object of the will: for that reason, speaking *essentially* [essentialiter], "to enjoy" is an act of the will. But, because the will neither delights nor rests except in that, which it cognizes through faith and/or sight [speciem],[12] and in that, which it holds through faith and/or in reality, for that reason acts of the other forces dispose to this, (but) they are not, however, *enjoying* itself, essentially speaking.

From this the solution[13] to that which is commonly accustomed to be asked, why *to enjoy* is not defined by an act of cognition, as (is) of delectation. However[14] this que-

---

[1] In the Vatican ed. there is here added *definition the very same is proven* [definitione probatur idipsum], which however, is absent from the mss. and ed. 1. Concerning this definition, see the text of Master (Peter), ch. 3.

[2] The manuscripts together with the first six editions, by omitting here what has been added by the Vatican edition, *but the delectable* [sed delectabile], were edited more carefully.

[3] Aristotle, MAGNA MORALIA, Bk. I, ch. 2: For the absolute end is the Good nor (is) the non-end the Good. — And concerning the following proposition, he says in RHETORICS, Bk. I, ch. 10 (in the Stoer edition, ch. 25): But the will is indeed the aiming [appetitio] for the good together with a conjoined reason; for no one wants, except when he has thought something is good. See also ETHICS, Bk. I, ch. 1. Then codex 1 has *is ordered* [ordinatur] in place of *it orders* [ordinat].

[4] We follow the greater part of the codices, such as A C F G I K L O R S U V W X Y Z etc., and editions 1, 2, 3 and 6 by substituting *it delights (him)* [delectat] in place of *it may delight (him)* [delectet], and then (excepting editions 2, 3 and 6) *that* [quia] in place of *that* [quod].

[5] The confused reading of the Vatican ed., which adds at this point *delighting* [delectare], we have corrected from the mss. and ed. 1.

[6] Bk. I, ch. 32, n. 35.

[7] (St.) Augustine, EXPOSITION OF THE PSALMS, n. 90, 16.

[8] Very many of the codices, such as A G H I K M V W Y Z etc., together with edition 1 omit *act* [actus].

[9] This is thought to have been the opinion of (William) of Auxerre, as testified by (Bl.) Dionysius the Carthusian, here at q. 3.

[10] Codex X here adds, well enough, *to enjoy* [frui]. Then the Vatican edition, together with codex cc has, not so well, *immediately* [immediate] for *more immediately* [immediatius].

[11] Concerning the three following definitions of enjoying, taken from (St.) Augustine, see, here, the text of Master (Peter), chs. 2 and 3. — Then the Vatican edition together with codex cc omits *manner* [modo] after *In the second* [Secundo].

[12] The faulty reading of the Vatican ed., of putting *hope* [spem] in place of *appearance* [speciem], we have corrected with the help of codd. F H I ee gg hh and ii and ed. 1; the error of many codd., who together with the Vatican ed. have *hope*, comes from the very same manner of abbreviating these two words. This saying is taken from the words of the Apostle, 2 Cor. 5:7: *For we walk through faith, and not through sight* [Per fidem enim ambulamus, et non per speciem]. Cf. also SENT., Bk. III, d. 31, a. 2, q. 1, reply to n. 5. — Then codex R has *(but) these are not* [tamen ipsi] instead of *(but) they are not* [tamen].

[13] Against the manuscripts and the first six editions, the Vatican edition has *resolution* [resolutio], and a little after this against a greater part of the manuscripts, as A C F G H K L R S T U V etc. and edition 1, it has *is accustomed* [consuevit] for *is accustomed* [solet]. Then many codices together with edition 1 have *of love* [dilectionis] in place of *of delectation* [delectationis], but not well, as it clear from the body of the question.

[14] The Vatican edition together with codex cc, having changed the punctuation and put *since* [cum] in place of *however* [Tamen], reads *of delectation, since this question is founded upon a false (assertion)* [delectationis, cum haec quaestio fundata sit super falsum]; but lest aptly, because the response together with this question is incongruously conjoined against the custom of the Seraphic (Doctor); besides it is against all the more ancient manuscripts and edition 1.

-stion is founded upon a false (assertion). For (St.) Augustine puts in one note, what belongs to cognition, when he says: « To enjoy is to rest in things known » it is defined [cadit] there, however, as a disposition.

From this it is also clear, why it is not defined by faith and[1] hope, as by charity, because charity informs the concupiscible (force), to which it belongs *to enjoy*. However, this question is similarly founded upon a false (assertion), because the love [amor], by which *"to enjoy"* is defined, is common to love, chaste and libidinous,[2] by which the avaricious enjoys gold, (it is) not proper to charity itself.

1. To that, therefore, which is objected, that every virtue has to delight and take rest,[3] when it is united with its object; it must be said, that the will itself, as (St.) Augustine maintains,[4] loves itself and others. And as (St.) Anselm also says:[5] « The will inclines the other forces and merits by them », for that reason its resting and delectation redound in the other forces. Whence just as the will does not cognize itself, but reason cognizes itself and the will, so the will takes delight in itself and in reason and causes it to rest.

2. To that which is objected, that the lover does not enjoy, unless he sees and/or has; it must be said, that *seeing* and *having* are required for *enjoying*, similarly also *loving* [amare]. For if one sees and has anything, he never takes delight (in it), unless he loves it; however, vision is required in another manner than love. For vision disposes, similarly also holding, but love supplies delights. Whence (love) is like a penetrating acumen,[6] and for this reason it is most fitting for it to unite and, as a consequence, to take delight and rest: for this reason (love) is essentially, not dispositively, enjoying. On account of which one must understand, that the act of the will can be considered in a twofold manner, that is, in the manner of an *appetite* and[7] of a *complacence*. In the first manner it can go before [antecedere] the vision itself; but in the second it follows it, and in this is the perfect reckoning of enjoying itself, that is, in a complacence in the thing seen and had.

3. To that (which is objected): Vision is the whole wage; it must be said that that is not said properly, but through concomitance,[8] because vision and complacence, in which there is a perfect reckoning of enjoying, hold themselves inseparably.

4. To that which is objected, that by faith and hope we enjoy, it must be said, that that is not true per se, because each of these accepts a reason for holding[9] from charity; whence enjoying is not from these except through charity. For only charity considers the end in the reason for the end and the object. Whence one is not said to hope God, as (he is) to love (Him).

SCHOLIUM

I. In the solution of the principal part of the question, that is, that *to enjoy is an act of the will*, all the ancient doctors agree with the Seraphic (Doctor); but there were, however, already in those times questions of controversy about certain subtle points of this matter.

First as regards *the concept itself of enjoying*, St. Bonaventure teaches, that enjoying presupposes a certain cognition or vision as (its) disposition, however, essentially speaking, it itself is an act of the will, which imports both dilection and delectation, or is formally the action of the will, namely its amorous inhesion, according to which *there follows* inseparably the passion of delectation; cf. here in the reply to n. 2 and in doubt 12; SENT., Bk. III, d. 29, a. 1. q. 2, and ibid., d. 35, a. 1, q. 1 in the body; SENT., Bk. II, d. 38, a. 1, a. 2 in reply to n. 4; ON THE HEXA-ÉMERON, Sermon 12, at the end. Likewise (Bl. John Duns) Scotus, together with his (disciples), Richard of Middleton, Bl. (now St.) Albert the Great, (Bl.) Peter of Tarentaise, Henry of Ghent. — But other doctors hold, that enjoying is formally *delectation* itself, not indeed whatever kind, but *the last* (kind), or which has be conjoined with resting; but this is not *love* [amorem] except connotatively and causally; thus the disciples of St. Thomas, as *Cajetan* testifies (commenting on the SUMMA., I. II., q. 1, a. 1), (Bl.) Dionysius the Carthusian and others.

Second, as regards the *act*, in which enjoying formally consists, St. Bonaventure teaches, here in reply to n. 1 and 2; SENT., Bk. II, d. 24, p. I, a. 2, q. 1: that every spiritual delectation has its rise from the love of the will, presupposing the perception of something agreeable. Alexander of Hales, Henry of Ghent, and Richard of Middleton agree, who among others says: « An act of the cognitive (part) does not follow delectation except by means of an act of the appetitive (part). » This is denied by the authors of the second opinion.

Third, here rises the celebrated controversy, chiefly promoted among the followers of St. Thomas and (Bl. John Duns) Scotus, whether, that is, *beatitude* in our fatherland formally consists in an act of the *intellect* or in the vision, which has inseparably adjoined both love and delectation, nay rather « it virtually contains and causally goes forth » (Cajetan), or rather, as (Bl.) Scotus holds with many others, in an act of the *will*, which supposes vision and is completed by delectation. St. Bonaventure touches upon this question, here in reply to n. 3; see more in SENT., Bk. IV, d. 49, p. 1, a. 5. This controversy is chiefly founded upon the psychological doctrines concerning the relation among the intellect and the will.

II. On the question here proposed: Alexander of Hales, SENT., Bk. IV, q. 26, m. 4. — (Bl. John Duns) Scotus, here in q. 3, in the OXFORD LECTURES and the REPORTATIO. — St. Thomas, here in q. 1, a. 1; SUMMA., I. II., q. 11, a. 1 and 2. — Bl. (now St.) Albert the Great, here in a. 12 and 17. — (Bl.) Peter of Tarentaise, here in q. 2, a. 1. — Richard of Middleton, here in a. 2, q. 1. — Giles the Roman, here in Bk. I, beginning of q. 1. — Henry of Ghent, SUMMA., a. 49, q. 6, n. 26.; he also deals with delectation in SUMMA., a. 50, q. 2. — Durandus (of Saint-Pourçain), here in q. 1. — (Bl.) Dionysius the Carthusian, here in q. 3. — (Gabriel) Biel, here in q. 2.

---

[1] Codex W has *and/or* [vel].

[2] On the authority of the manuscripts and edition 1 we have removed the particle *and/or* [vel], which has been badly added by the Vatican text, because the word *libidinous* broadly accepted comprises even the concupiscence of the eyes. Codices P and Q add *it is* [est] before *not* [non]; but codex X reads: *for that reason it does not properly belong to charity itself* [ideo non est proprius ipsius caritatis].

[3] Though many manuscripts, such as A C G K L O S T U V W X Y Z, omit *and to take rest* [et quietari], we have however, decided to retain it, both because it js found in the other more ancient manuscripts, as F H I etc., and because it is exhibited above in the very objection.

[4] This is gathered from ON THE TRINITY, Bk. XV, ch. 22, where it is shown, that memory, intellect, and love or will are not their own nor for themselves, but do, whatever they do, for the subject. And in the preceding chapters, by comparing the trinity discovered in the soul with the divine Trinity, he says in ch. 17, "On the Holy Spirit": but He himself naught but loves [diligit] both Himself and them. — Very many of the codices have *as (St.) Augustine holds* [ut vult] for *as (St.) Augustine says* [ut dicit].

[5] ON THE HARMONY OF THE PRESCIENCE OF GOD WITH FREE WILL, ch. 11 and 12, where he says, that the will moves all instruments, which are in us, such as the hands, etc.; and that from it « descends a man's every merit ». — On the doctrine here proposed see SENT., Bk. II, d. 24, p. 1, a. 2, q. 1.

[6] Here the manner of speaking is taken from Hugo of St. Victor, EXPOSITION UPON THE CELESTIAL HIERARCHY OF DIONYSIUS, ch. 7.

[7] Codex X here repeats *in the manner* [modum].

[8] We have restored from the manuscripts and edition 1 the more common *concomitance* in place of *concomitation* [concomitationem].

[9] Codex X *of holding* [tendentis]. At the end of the response, codex R adds *an on account of this it is not valid* [propter hoc non valet].

ARTICLE II

On the enjoyable.

With it shown, what it is *to enjoy* through essence [per essentiam], the question (now) concerns the enjoyable, and,

first, whether it is fitting [convenit]* that one enjoy God;

second, whether one is to enjoy Him alone.

QUESTION SOLE

Whether one is to enjoy God?

About the first, that one is to enjoy God, is shown thus:

1. « One is to enjoy that, which makes us blessed »,[1] because in beatitude there is an upright enjoying; but we become blessed by God, because He is our beatitude: therefore one is to enjoy God.

2. Likewise, the good is lovable [amabile]; therefore, the greater the good, the greater (it is) lovable and the most highly Good (is) the most highly lovable;[2] but we enjoy that, which we love most highly: ergo etc..

3. Likewise, beauty delights and[3] the greater the beauty, the greater it delights, therefore, the most highly Beautiful most highly delights; but we enjoy that, in which we delight most highly: ergo etc..

ON THE CONTRARY: 1. Where there is enjoying, there is delectation; « but delectation is the conjunction of convenient with convenient »;[4] But there is no convening [nulla convenientiae] of God with the creature; nay rather a most high distance: therefore, neither a delectation, therefore, neither an enjoying.

2. Likewise, an excellent sensible corrupts the sense and/or at least saddens it, because delectation is in the means [mediis]:[5] therefore, for an equal reason the excellent intelligible corrupts and/or saddens the intellect. But God is the Most Excellent Light: therefore, He saddens, not delights, ergo etc.. *If you say*, that the sensible power [sensibilis potentia] is corruptible, not the intellect; this does not solve (the matter), because

the intellect, while it is in the flesh, is fatigued and impeded in act, with the body corrupted.

3. Likewise, where (there is) enjoying, there (is) resting; but in the infinite there is no resting, « because there is always something extra to accept »:[6] therefore, since God is infinite, in God there is no resting, therefore, neither enjoying.

CONCLUSION

Properly (speaking), one is to enjoy God.

I RESPOND: It must be said, that one is to enjoy God, for the reason that He alone perfectly finishes [finit][7] and *delights* the soul itself on His own account [propter se] and above all things.

1. To that, therefore, which is objected, that delectation is a conjunction of the convenient etc.; it must be said, that there is a convening through *a participation of one nature* and/or through *a common comparison*.[8] The first convening causes a community of *univocation*, the second a community of *analogy* or of proportion. And this is according to a threefold difference: either according to a *similar* comparison *of two things to two*, just as man[9] to animal, so whiteness holds itself to color; or according to a *dissimilar* comparison *of two things to one*, as of an animal and food to health; and/or

---

[1] (St.) Augustine, ON CHRISTIAN DOCTRINE, Bk. I, ch. 33, n. 37: For you enjoy Him, by whom you shall be made blessed. In which text, codex R adds *alone* [solo] after *Him* [Illo].

[2] A similar argument is found in Aristotle, ETHICS, Bk. I, ch. 7, where he speaks of the felicity, which is the best good, and for that reason both most greatly to be longed for [exoptandum] and loved [amandum]. Cf. TOPICS, Bk. II, ch. 1 ff..

[3] We have supplied from the more ancient manuscripts and edition 1 the particle *and* [et].

[4] This definition of *delectation* is the Seraphic Doctor's and akin to the other Scholastics, and it agrees with that, which Avicenna exhibits at the end of METAPHYSICS, Bk. VIII., ch. 7, near the end: There is no delectation unless (there is) apprehension of the convenient, according to what is convenient. — Which definition given by Avicenna seems to be founded upon that, which Aristotle, RHETORICS, Bk. I, ch. 11, hands down: But delectation is a certain movement of the soul and an entire settling at once, of the sensible, in the existent nature (this definition is explained by Henry of Ghent, SUMMA., A. 50, q. 2). The Parisian Edition of 1878 thus interprets Aristotle: It is therefore posited for us, that pleasure is a certain motion of the spirit and a sudden and perceived-by-the-sense settling in a state convenient to nature. Cf. also ETHICS, Bk. VII, ch. 11 ff. and chiefly ETHICS, Bk. X, ch. 1-5 and MAGNA MORALIA, Bk. II, ch. 7, where very many things pertaining to delectation (pleasure) are explained. Then, contradicting the more ancient manuscripts and edition 1, the Vatican edition together with the more recent codex cc has *facture* [facturam] for *creature* [creaturam]. A little afterwards codex R has *infinite* [infinita] in place of *a most high* [summa].

[5] Aristotle, ON THE SOUL, Bk. II, text. 123 (in the Parisian Edition of Firmin-Didot, Bk. III, ch. 2), where according to the Venetian edition of 1489 there is read: But (it is) manifest from these, and on account of

that excellent sensibles corrupt the sensitive (part) ... And the cause is manifest from this, on account of which intense sensibles corrupt the instruments of sense. And text 124 (Parisian Edition, <u>loc</u>. <u>cit</u>.): But the proportion is a symphony ... wherefore there are even certain delectables, while they are called sincere and mixed beings according to reason ... but (things) excelling sadden or corrupt. Finally, in Book III., text 29: And to be delighted or saddened is 'to set (oneself) in motion' [agere] by a sensitive mean [meditate] toward good and evil, inasmuch as (the latter are) such things. — The Vatican edition, against the manuscripts and edition 1, exhibits an additional reason: *because true delectation is not but in means* [quia vera delectatio non est nisi in mediis]. Codex X about the end of this argument puts *in the body* [in corpore] in place of *in the flesh* [in carne].

[6] Aristotle, PHYSICS, Bk. III, text 63, (ch. 6): Therefore, the Infinite is that, according to the quantity of which for those accepting there is always something extra to accept; but of which there is nothing extra, that is perfect and whole. — Then not trusting in the more ancient manuscripts and edition 1, the Vatican edition together with the more recent codex cc has, not so well, *therefore, no enjoying* [ergo non fruitio].

[7] That is, *rests*.

[8] The corrupted reading of the Vatican edition and the more recent codex cc, in which there is placed *and* [et] in place of *and/or* [vel] and there is omitted *common* [communem], we have restored from the more ancient manuscripts and edition 1. A little before this codex X has *it must be said, that convening is said either through* [dicendum, quod convenientia dicitur vel per]. — On convenience see Aristotle, ON THE PREDICAMENTS, ch. 1, and PHYSICS, Bk. VII, text 21-34, (ch. 4).

[9] Very many of the codices together with edition 1 omit *is related* [se habet], which the Vatican edition together with only some of the codices adds here.

---

* *Trans. Note.* Here in the division of the Article the Quaracchi editors have read: *primo, utrum Deo contingat frui*, reading *contingat* in place of *conveniat*, according to their explanation set forth on p. 32, SENT., I, a. 1, q. 2, footnote 1. For the same reason set forth in the trans. fn. on p. 33, the English translation takes the contrary sense and reads *it is fitting* [conveniat] in place of *it happens* [contingat], since as St. Bonaventure poses the Question with a passive periphrastic, he seeks to know more than whether the fact of enjoying God occurs; this reading also agrees with the Response.

according to a comparison of *two things to one another*, as, for example, when one thing is the imitation or similitude of the other. For a similitude does not convene with something very similar[1] in the third (manner), but with itself. So it is in the proposed, because the soul is the expressed similitude of God. This convening in one extreme posits inclination and indigence, in the other a resting and sufficiency, because the one has been made for the sake of the Other, whence (the one)[2] is ordered to the Other. And since at the resting of inclination and the supplementation of indigence, where there is sense,[3] there is delectation or (it soon) follows, for that reason the soul, when it rests in God [quitetatur a Deo] in such a manner, enjoys Him.

2. To that which is objected, that the excellence of the sensible corrupts sense: ergo etc., it must be said, that it is not similar concerning *understanding* [intelligere] and *sensing* [sentire]. And there is a threefold reason for this: one is on the part of apprehensive *virtue*, another on the part of the *apprehended* or the object, the third is on the part of *the manner* of apprehending.

On the part of apprehensive *virtue*, because sense can be corrupted, but not the intellect. The reason for this is, because sense depends upon an organ, in which there is a certain mean [medietas] and harmony, which is not only corrupted through a contrary, but (also)[4] by the excellent; but the intellect does not depend on an organ, because it is an immaterial power, for that reason it is not saddened in the excellent.[5]

On the part of *the object* it is not similar, because the excellent, intelligible object[6] helps and comforts, because the influence of such a cognizable proceeds from the most interior and enters the power itself, and for that reason it comforts and thoroughly strengthens itself. Just as if a great mountain would give the virtue of carrying itself, more easily would it be borne than a small one (that gave not such virtue); so it is in the Intelligible, which is God. But the sensible object only excites outside itself [extra], and for that reason it corrupts this, but He (does) not.

On the part of *the manner* of apprehending there is similarly a dissimilitude, because sense in the apprehension of its own object tends to the exterior, wherefore, by percieving[7] that, it disperses the exterior and does not fortify the interior, for that reason it is debilitated. But the object of the intellect, since it is most interior to the intellect itself, is not dispersed in the perception of its virtue, but is gathered together, and as much as the virtue is more united, so much more (is it) stronger.

3. To that which is objected concerning the infinite; it must be said, that the "infinite" is spoken in a twofold manner, that is, through a *privation of perfection*; and thus matter is said (to be) "infinite", and for such an infinite there is no finishing, but it rather needs to be finished, according to which[8] it is able [possibile]. In another manner the "infinite" is said through a *privation of limitation*; and what is thus "infinite", properly has (an ability) to end, since one does not happen to seek for anything beyond it, since there is nothing greater to think of. Whence such an "infinity", which[9] has the greatest reason to be finished [maxime finiendi rationem], is agreeable to the last End.

SCHOLIUM

I. This and the following question the other ancient commentators on (Peter) Lombard treat under one question. — About *analogy* and its differences, of which there is a discussion in the solution to n. 1, the Seraphic Doctor speaks more fully below in d. 14, q. 2; d. 29, a. 1, q. 2; d. 7, q. 4, in the body of the question.; d. 25, a. 2, q. 2. in the body of the question. — Concerning the comparison of two things to two etc, see below in d. 46, a. 1, q. 5, in the body of the question. — Concerning the analogy of proportion and proportionality cf. below in d. 48, a. 1, q. 1; d. 35, a. 1, a. 1; SENT., Bk. III, d. 1, a. 1, q. 1 at n. 4; and in d. 29, a. 1, q. 1 at n. 2; SENT., Bk. IV, d. 1, Doubt 3.

II. On this question: (Bl. John Duns) Scotus, here in q. 3. — St. Thomas, here in q. 2, a. 1; SUMMA. , I. II., q. 11, a. 3. — Bl. (now St.) Albert (the Great), here in q. 12 ff. — (Bl.) Peter of Tarentaise, here in q. 2, a. 2. — Richard of Middleton, here in a. 2, q. 3. — Henry of Ghent, SUMMA., a. 72, q. 3, n. 11. — Durandus (of Saint-Pourçain), here in q. 2. — (Bl.) Dionysius the Carthusian, here in q. 4. — (Gabriel) Biel, here in q. 4.

QUESTION II

Whether one is to enjoy God alone or the uncreated Good?

Finally, there is asked, whether one is to enjoy God, or the uncreated Good, alone; and it seems, that (it is) so.

1. One is to enjoy that alone, which is to be loved for its own sake; but that alone[10] is to be loved for its own sake, which is good on its own account [propter se bonum]; but that is good on its own account, which has the goodness, which it

---

[1] Very many of the manuscripts, as A F G H K S T Y etc, together with edition 1 have *similar* [simili] instead of *completely similar* [consimili]. Then the error of the Vatican edition, which adds *itself to itself* [se ipsa] after *the soul* [anima], we have corrected from the manuscripts and edition 1; codex X reads *but it is similar to itself* [sed se ipsa similis]. In the reading received in the text *similitude* [similitudo] is taken concretely and the sense is: by a similar reason of similitude it agrees immediately with something very similar. — A little afterward codex T has *man* [homo] in place of *soul* [animal]; but very many codices, as C L T S U, omit *the soul* [anima], but not well.

[2] Codex X here repeats *one* [unum].

[3] Codices W X and Z adjoin (explicitly) *there* [ibi], and then codex A repeats *delectation* [delectatio] before *follows* [sequitur].

[4] Codex X adds *also* [etiam]. A little afterwards codices aa and bb have *spiritual* [spritualis] in place of *immaterial* [immaterialis]. Then the codices do not agree among themselves; for codices A C G I L S T UV omit *in* [in] after *are saddened* [tristatur] (thus reading in English *are saddened by*]; codices R and FF have *are saddened by* [ab]; but codex bb has *from* [ex]; but very many as F H K etc. together with edition 1 have *are saddened in* [in].

[5] On this difference among sense and intellect see Aristotle, ON THE SOUL, Bk. II, text 123 and 143. A little above these, there is also Bk. III, text 4 (Parisian Edition, ch. 4): Therefore, it is necessary, that (the intellect) understands all things, to be intermixed; and text 7: But that there is no similar impassibility of the sensitive and intellective, is manifest from sensors and sense. For sense can not sense from the vehement sensible ... but the intellect when it understands anything very intelligible, does not understand inferiors less, but even more; for the sensitive is not without a body, this (intellect) however, is separable.

[6] On the authority of the more ancient manuscripts we have substituted *intelligible* [intelligibile] in place of *of the intelligence* [intelligentiae].

[7] Thus reads codices C H K O S TU Y aa bb and edition 1, but codices A F I L M R V W X Z read *by participating* [participando]; but the Vatican edition together with codex cc has *through* [per]. Then codices X and Y have *comfort* [confortatur] in place of *fortify* [fortificatur].

[8] Codex cc has *that is as much as* [scilicet quantum] in place of *according to which* [secundum quod].

[9] Codex F and I read *to the last End which* [qui etc.], well enough, and they agree according to sense with codex T, which has *the last End, because ...* [quia etc.].

[10] From the more ancient manuscripts and edition 1 we have inserted *alone* [solum], which is badly absent from the Vatican text and the more recent codex cc. — On this minor proposition of the argument, cf. Aristotle, ETHICS, Bk. VIII, ch. 5: For what is absolutely good and jocund, is lovable and eligible; but to each (it is) such as it is to each. Cf. also ETHICS, Bk. I, ch. 1, 2 and 8, where it concerns the last End; and MAGNA MORALIA, Bk. I, ch. 2, where it deals with the common good.

has, not *from another*, nor is that goodness *for another*, but this is God alone: ergo etc..

2. Likewise, one is to enjoy that alone, which rests [quietat] the appetite of the soul; but the appetite of the soul is not rested [quietatur] sufficiently except in that which is more perfect and a greater good than it (is); but this is God alone: ergo etc..

3. Likewise, the appetite is not sufficiently rested except through something, which fills the soul, because on its own part the soul is lacking in the rest, which it lacks in (its) fullness; but (the soul)[1] it is capable [capax] of God according to (its) appetite: therefore, if every created thing is less than Him unto an infinite (degree), none fulfils the appetite of the soul. And this is what (St.) Augustine says:[2] « The soul capable of the whole Trinity: nothing less than the Trinity can fill it ».

4. Likewise, the good, which can be thought, can be desired [appeti]: therefore, if a good greater than something can be thought of, it can be desired more than it; but the greater-than-every-finite can be thought of: therefore, it can be desired more: therefore, no finite thing terminates the appetite of the soul sufficiently: therefore, one is to enjoy only the infinite Good, which is God, Whom when had, nothing more [amplius] can be thought of or desired.

ON THE CONTRARY: 1. It seems, that one happens to enjoy the created good, because, although the appetite for matter be infinite, however, through the incorruptible[3] created form it is sufficiently ended [finitur]: therefore, it similarly seems, that there is some created good, which will sufficiently end the appetite of the soul; but one is to enjoy every such (thing): therefore, one is to enjoy some created good.

2. Likewise, the human appetite is of a finite capacity, therefore, it captures [capit] naught but the finite, and/or if it captures the infinite, it captures it finitely: therefore, if it is ended through something which it captures, it is ended through a finite good: therefore, it seems, that one is to enjoy some finite good.

3. Likewise, it especially seems, that one is to enjoy *man*, because one is to enjoy every that, which God enjoys; but God enjoys man, because He loves man; but by that love [amore], by which He loves Himself, He loves man, because there is in Him[4] no twofold love; but the first belongs to enjoying: therefore, also the second.

4. Likewise, it especially seems concerning *virtue*; because one is to enjoy every that, which is to be desired [appetendum] for its own sake; this is per se manifest; but every honest good is to be desired for its own sake, « because the honest is that which draws us by its own force and allures us by its own dignity »; as (Marcus) Tullius (Cicero) says,[5] and (St.) Augustine divides the honest against the useful; but virtue falls in the genus of the honest: therefore, one is to enjoy virtue.

5. Likewise, it especially seems concerning *beatitude*. One is to enjoy every that, by which when had the spirit rests [quiescit] and delights and can seek nothing beyond (it); but created beatitude is of this kind: therefore, etc..

CONCLUSION

Properly (speaking), one is to enjoy God alone; improperly (speaking) it is licit to enjoy the spiritual goods, which delight and have been conjoined to (one's) End.

I RESPOND: It must be said, that one is to enjoy God alone, in the *proper* acceptation of *"to enjoy"* [frui], insofar as it means [prout dicit] a movement with delectation and a 'going to rest' [quietatione]. But in the *common* acceptation of *"to enjoy"*, inasmuch as it means a movement with delectation only,[6] all things, which spiritually delight and have been conjoined with (one's) End, of which kind are the fruits, the gifts and beatitudes, a man can not-unduly enjoy; but in the first manner God alone (is to be enjoyed).

And the reason for this is, that nothing can sufficiently *finish* [finire] the soul except the good, for which it is.[7] But this is the Most High Good, which is higher than the soul, and the infinite Good, which exceeds the powers [vires] of the soul. For the soul's natural *cognition*[8] is an unconstrained [non arctata] cognition; whence it is born in a certain manner to cognize all things, whence its cognition is not filled with anything cognizable, unless because it has in itself all cognizables and with this cognized all things are cognized. Similarly, its *affection* [affectio] is bound to love [diligere] every good; therefore, by no good is (its) affection [affectus] sufficiently ended [finitur], unless (by that) which[9] is the Good of every good and the All in all. Of which

---

[1] Supply with codex I *the soul* [anima]. A little further below this on the testimony of the codices and edition 1 we have expunged *created* [creatum] after *no* [nullum]; codex W has *fills* [implet] in place of *fulfills* [supplet].

[2] Or rather the author of the book, ON THE SPIRIT AND SOUL, ch. 27, where it is put thus: However, the soul of man, that is the mind, no creature can fill according to substance, except the Trinity alone. And a little below this: For it belongs to the Trinity alone to enter and fill the nature or substance, which It created.

[3] The Vatican edition and codex K has *the created, corporal and incorruptible* [creatam corporalem et incorruptibilem]; nearly all the codices omit *corporal and* [corporalem et]; the codices of better note, as F G H T W aa bb ee ff and edition 1 retain only *incorruptible* [incorruptibilem]; others as A have only *incorporeal* [incorporalem]; V has only *corporal* [corporalem], X *corruptible* [corruptibilem]; editions 2, 3, 4, 5 and 6 have *incorporeal and incorruptible* [incorporelem et incorruptibilem]. Besides the authority of the codices, the agreement of our reading both with the solution of this objection, and with the doctrine of our Doctor, argues on its own behalf. For the assertion here posited can be understood both of the *empyrean heaven*, as codex aa understands it, by adding *as is clear in celestial bodies* [ut patet in corporibus caelestibus], and of the *soul* itself, which according to the Seraphic (Doctor), though it is spiritual and incorporeal, it is not entirely destitute [expers] of composition of form and matter; and in SENT., Bk. II, d. 19, a. 1. q. 1 in the body of the reply there is an explicit affirmation of the same, that the appetite for matter is perfectly satisfied and quieted. As regards the empyrean

heaven the Scholastics, following Aristotle, commonly asserted, that it is both incorruptible and immobile. Cf. SENT., Bk. II, d. 12, a. 2. q. 1, and d. 14, p. I, a. 3. q. 1 and SENT., Bk. III, d. 13, a. 1. q. 3 at n. 6. — Then codex T has *does ... end* [finat] in place of *will ... end* [finiet].

[4] Codex K has *God* [Deo] in place of *Him* [eo].

[5] RHETORICS, Bk. II, ch. 53 (Turin ed., 1823): For (the honest) is a certain thing, which allures us to itself by its own power, not capturing by any emolument, but drawing by its own dignity. — On the division of the good, which is cited from (St.) Augustine, see his own book, OF EIGHTY-THREE QUESTIONS, a. 30. — Immediately after this we have corrected the error of the Vatican edition, which has *is divided* [dividitur] in place of *divides* [dividit], from the manuscripts and the first editions.

[6] Codex K here adds *in this manner* [sic]. Then many of the codices as A F G H K W X Y Z ee etc. together with edition 1 have *enjoying* [frui] in place of *(one's) End* [fini].

[7] The Vatican edition adds at this point *created* [creata], which however, is lacking in the manuscripts and edition 1.

[8] *Natural* refers to *cognition*, so that the sense is: If you inspect the nature of cognition, which befits the soul, it is not constrained. — The Vatican edition, contradicting the manuscripts and edition 1, has *rational* [rationalis] in place of *natural* [naturalis], but not so well. — On the proposition, which then follows, see Aristotle, ON THE SOUL, Bk. III, text 4, cited in the previous question.

[9] Codex K adjoins *through that* [per illud: rendering the reading, *unless through that which is the Good*], which seems to have been adjoined, because one must supply *by Him* [eo] or *by that* [illo].

Good (there is said) in the thirty-third (chapter) of Exodus:[1] *I shall show you the All Good.* But this is the Most High Good: ergo etc..

Likewise,[2] nothing sufficiently *finishes* the soul except the *infinite* Good, because for this, that it be finished, it is necessary, that it be finished according to (its) estimation [aestimationem]; otherwise it would not be blessed, unless it considered [existimaret] itself (to be) blessed. But estimation oversteps every finite, because something greater than every finite can be thought of: therefore, since the affection can[3] extend itself where (there is) also estimation, the affection of the soul necessarily oversteps every finite; and if this (is so), (then) by no finite good is it sufficiently finished. Therefore, one is to enjoy God alone, because (He is) the Most High Good and the Infinite One.

And one (is) not only to enjoy God on account of 'being perfectly finished' [perfectam finitionem], but also on account of a perfect *delectation*. For, for delectation there concurrs[4] the *delectable* and its *conjunction* with that which *is delighted*. But everything, which delights the soul, delights it in the reckoning of good and beauty; and since God alone is Goodness and Beauty Itself[5], for that reason only in God is there perfect delectation.

Likewise, because there is a *conjunction*; but only God is the one who is most perfectly conjoined (to the soul). For He is conjoined according to[6] truth and the deepest interiority [intimitatem]. For only God according to (His) Most High Simplicity and Spirituality glides into the soul, so that He is, according to the truth, in the soul and more interior to the soul than it (is) to itself.

For[7] all these four reasons are reduced to one, that is to this: because the soul has been born [nata est] to perceive the infinite Good, which is God, for that reason it ought to rest in and enjoy Him alone.

1. But to that which is objected concerning the appetite for matter; it must be said, that the appetite for matter is ordered to form as to substantial perfection, out of which (form)[8] and matter there comes to be one (being) [unum]; and for that reason it is necessary that the form be of the same genus with the matter, nor is (the form) entirely above the matter: for that reason every such form is finite. But such, if it be incorruptible, on account of the necessary union of itself,[9] constrains (its) appetite for matter

and finishes (what has been) constrained; whence it is not ended in its fullness. But the appetite of the soul is not thus constrained on account of (its) union with a desirable [appetibili], nay, rather, it is dilated; and for that reason it is proper, that it be perfected by something entirely most high.

2. To that which is objected, that (the appetite of the soul)[10] does not capture except in a finite manner; it must be said, that it captures the infinite Good in a finite manner, since it itself is finite. But since that Good is Infinite, for that reason it is totally absorbed by It, so that its capacity is already terminated in every respect [undique]. Whence it not only rejoices, but as (St.) Anselm (of Canterbury) says,[11] *it shall enter into joy of the Lord.* Because, if it only captured and was not conquered nor was absorbed, the appetite could still rise up to capture something more. Therefore, it is clear, that for this, that the soul be completely filled [compleatur], although it has a finite capacity,[12] it is, however necessary, that the infinite Good be at hand [adesse].

3. To that, however, which is objected concerning man; it must be said, that God loves [diligit] man, and the love [amor] of God is a love of enjoying; however, He does not enjoy man, because by loving [diligendo] Himself He loves man, that is, by enjoying Himself He uses man. Which is thus clear: because the love [dilectio] of God for a creature is not an affection, but the communication of an effect.[13] But a communication according to the reckoning of the *habit* [secundum rationalem habitualem] is attained according to goodness; because the good is what is bound to communicate itself. However, according to the reckoning of the *act* [secundum rationem actualem] it is attained or respects the will; for because He wills, for that reason He does. Therefore, the reason for communicating comes from a will and a goodness, just as a reason for cognizing (comes) from an exemplar and intelligence. Therefore, because He[14] loves us from a conversion of (His) Will upon His own Goodness, for that reason, by enjoying Himself, He loves us.

4. To that which is objected concerning virtue, that virtue is an honest good; it must be said, that a "honest good" is said in a twofold manner: either what is *purely good*, or in that which the *similitude* of that glitters. In the first manner, one is to enjoy the honest, in the *proper* acceptation of "to enjoy", because this alone terminates and gives rest [quietat]. In the second manner, (one is) not, unless one accepts (the term) *commonly*, insofar as it means 'dele-

---

[1] Verse 19.

[2] The Vatican edition against nearly all the manuscripts: *Similarly* [Similiter] in place of *Likewise* [Item] and a little afterwards it has *consideration* [existimatio] in place of *estimation* [aestimatio].

[3] The Vatican edition against codices A T aa bb etc. has *could* [posset], but less aptly, because there one deals with natural consequence, which is always in a subject. From this point and immediately afterwards, the Vatican edition disagreeing with the greater part of the manuscripts as A G K L O T V W X Y Z etc. and edition 1, has less well *extend itself to that, where there is esteem* [extendere eo, ubi est existimatio]. Codex cc has *as also estimation* [ut et ...] in place of *where (there is)* [ubi et ...]. A little below this on the authority of very many of the codices, as A C F G H K L O S T U V W Z etc., together with edition 1 we have substituted *this* [hoc] in place of *this* [haec]. Codex K more plainly reads: *and if this (is so), therefore* [et si hoc, ergo].

[4] From the more ancient manuscripts and edition 1 we have substituted *concurs* [concurrit] in place of *combined* [concernitur] and a little after this we have corrected the error of the Vatican edition, which together with the more recent codex cc has *delights* [delectat] in place of *is delighted* [delectatur]. — Cf. above in a. 3, q. 1, 1st opposed argument.

[5] We have supplied from the manuscripts and edition 1 *Itself* [ipsa], which the Vatican edition unduly omits.

[6] Codex W has *through* [per].   [7] Codex R has *but* [autem].

[8] Supply here, just as a little below this, with codex T after *entirely* [omnino] *form* [forma].

[9] Many of the more ancient and better codices as A C F G L O R S T U X Y Z etc. have *to itself* [sibi] in place of *of itself* [sui]. Then codex T falsely omits *not* [non] after *whence* [unde]. — The sentence here posited by the Seraphic Doctor is briefly comprised in SENT., Bk. III, d. 13, a. 1. q. 3 at n. 6 with these words: Just as we say of the form of the sky, that it completes the appetite of matter, because its matter does not desire [appetit] to be under a further form, to that extent [adeo] the form establishes it in a completed actuality. Cf. (Bl. John Duns) Scotus, PHYSICS, Bk. II, q. 4, n. 4 and 15.

[10] Understand with codex X *the human soul* [Trans. more exactly *the appetite of the soul*]. Then codex A reads *the soul* [anima] before *captures the infinite Good in a finite manner* [bonum finite].

[11] PROSLOGION, ch. 26: « Therefore, that whole joy will not enter into those rejoicing, but the whole of those rejoicing will enter into joy ». He alludes to Mt. 25:21. — Immediately afterwards the Vatican edition, not trusting in the manuscripts and editions 1, 2 and 3, has *the whole* [totum] in place of *only* [tantum].

[12] Very many of the more ancient codices as A C G O S T U X bb ee ff together with edition 1, retaining the same sense, have *although it has a finitude in (its) capacity, it is necessary that* [quamvis capacitate habeat finitatem, necesse est].

[13] The Vatican edition, which has *of an affection* [affectus], is emended from the manuscripts and editions 1, 2, 3, and 6.

[14] Edition 1 has *God* [Deus], which certainly must be understood.

-ctation'. For (virtues)[1] of this kind on account of (their) assimilation to God have a beauty, by which they delight and allure us; however, one is not to rest [quiescendum] in them, because then they lose their beauty, because « the virtues, when they are referred to themselves, are proud and puffed up ».[2]

5. To that which is objected concerning beatitude; it must be said, that created beatitude does not end the appetite by itself, but through a conjunction with uncreated (Beatitude): whence the soul loves [diligit] itself[3] for God's sake [propter Deum], not for its own sake [propter se].

SCHOLIUM

I. All the ancient doctors, except Durandus (of Saint-Pourçain), agree in that sentence, that one is to enjoy only God *objectively* and *materially*, but created beatitude or beatitude taken *subjectively* (as the moderns speak), only *formally*. The Seraphic Doctor in his solution to n. 5 already reproved Durandus (of Saint-Pourçain)'s singular and false opinion (here at q. 2), that the act of the mind, by which God is immediately attained, it the immediate object of fruition, but God its remote object.

II. How anyone can improperly enjoy *virtues*, is explained at greater length in SENT., Bk. II, d. 38, a. 1, a. 2, in reply to n. 3, where

there is also expounded, how gifts, fruits and beatitudes *are conjoined with (their) End*, which according to Scripture is charity. — Well noted are the profound and copious arguments, by which the Seraphic (Doctor) proves, that in God alone is there a perfect delectation and 'going to rest', of which he also speaks in an outstanding manner in SENT., Bk. II, d. 16, a. 1. q. 1. Cf. also St. Thomas, SUMMA CONTRA GENTILES, Bk. I, ch. 43; Bk. III, ch. 48 and 50. — As regards God's gliding into the soul cf. SENT., Bk. II, p. II, a. 1. q. 2.

In regard to the principal question, see the authors (cited) in the preceding Scholium.

DOUBTS ON THE TEXT OF THE MASTER

DOUBT I

In this part of my (commentary), very many things are asked about the text (of Master Peter), and first concerning this which he says: *But of these there are* certain ones, *whose every use is in signifying, not in justifying*. On the contrary: All the Sacraments are medicines, because according to Hugo of St. Victor[4] the Sacraments were in every season [omni tempore] medicines; but every medicine has an effect in curing: therefore, also the Sacraments similarly; but this curing of theirs is justification: therefore, the Sacraments have to justify in every season.

I RESPOND: It must be said, that there is a twofold manner of considering the Sacraments of the old Law, that is *in themselves* [in se] or by reason of the work worked [ratione operis operati]; and in this manner they were only for signifying; and/or *by reason of the adjoined faith* or charity [ratione fidei annexae seu caritatis] or by reason of the work of the one working [ratione operis operantis]; and thus the Sacraments of the Law [Sacramenta legalia], in addition to [praeter] Circumcision, were for justifying.[5]

DOUBT II

Therefore every sign is ... some thing. There is opposed concerning this division of his. For Master (Peter) seems to have divided badly, because the superior is not divided against its inferior; but the thing is superior to the sign: ergo etc.

I RESPOND: It must be said, that it is true, that the "superior" accepted in its general sense [in sua general-

itate] is not divided against its inferior; but the contracted [contractum][6] can well be divided. But here "thing" [res][7] is contracted to stand for a 'thing not signifying' [re non significante].

DOUBT III

Likewise, is asked of this which Master (Peter) says: *But, conversely, not every thing (is) a sign.* For he seems to speak badly, because a sign is that which leads unto cognizing the other; but every thing leads unto an other, because every thing is a cause, and/or an effect. But a cause leads unto the cognition of the effect,[8] and conversely. *If you say*, that not everything, which leads, is a sign, but (only) that what leads unto the prior; then every creature is a sign, since it leads unto God.

I RESPOND: It must be said, that "sign" [signum] is twofold; that is *natural* and *instituted*. One does not intend (to speak) here of the first (kind), but of the second; whence the objection to the proposed is not valid, since here[9] one intends (to speak) of a sign from institution [signo ex institutione], such as are verbal and sacramental signs [signa vocalia et sacramentalia].

DOUBT IV

Likewise, Master (Peter) seems to speak badly in this which he says: *First. . . things, afterwards signs.* For he seems that he should have spoken,[10] rather, the other way around, because the sign leads unto the cognition of the thing: therefore, one should deal and/or speak of signs before things.

---

[1] Understand with codex R *virtues* [virtutes]. Then very many of the more ancient codices as A C F G K L O R S U T Z and ee have *because* [quia] in place of *by which* [qua].

[2] (St.) Augustine, THE CITY OF GOD, Bk. XIX, ch. 25: The virtues, when they are referred to themselves and are not sought out on account of another, are then also puffed up and proud.

[3] The lapsus of the compilers of the Vatican edition of placing *itself* [ipsa] in place of *itself* [ipsam] we have corrected with the help of the manuscripts and edition 1.

[4] ON THE SACRAMENTS, Bk. I, p. 8, ch. 12 (Paris: 1526): Therefore, if one asks the time for the institution of the Sacraments, let him know, that as long as the deadly disease lasts, it is the time for medicine.

[5] Codex Z adds: *supply, which not only was to signify by reason of the work worked, but (also) to justify* [supple, quae non tantum erat ad

significandum ratione operis operati, sed ad iustificandum].

[6] That is, if a genus is contracted, by a difference, to the species.

[7] Codices L and O have well enough: *So it is here, and " thing" is contracted ...* [Sic est hic, et res contrahitur etc.]

[8] Several of the codices such as A C L O R T W Z etc. unduly omit: *But a cause leads unto the cognition of the effect* [causa autem ducit in cognitionem effectus].

[9] Having falsely contradicted the codices and editions 1, 2 and 3, the Vatican edition has *this* [hoc] in place of *here* [hic] and after *sacramental signs* [sacramentalia] it superfluously adds *therefore every thing is not such a sign; though every thing is a sign in the first manner* [tale ergo signum non est omnis res; licet omnis res sit signum primo modo].

[10] Many of the codices as A C F G K L O U W X etc together with editions 1, 2, 3 and 6, have *that he should have said* [debuisse dixisse].

I Respond: It must be said, that the cognition of the sign is prior to (that) of the thing, in respect of which the sign is; but it is not necessary [non oportet], that (it be) of every thing. Whence, he first deals with the things, of which the sacraments are not the signs.

Doubt V

Likewise, it seems, that this division of things: *some things which one is to enjoy* etc., is badly assigned in respect of the *divided*, because the divided is more simple than the ones dividing and there is[1] something common to the ones dividing; but there is nothing more simple than God nor is there anything common to God and creature: ergo etc..

I Respond: It must be said, that there is a division of the one thing common according to *name only*; and thus there is a division of the equivocal; there is another division of the common according to *name* and *thing*; and this is the division of the univocal; there is also a third (division) *by a middle manner*, and that is of the analogue, where there is no commonality [communitas] according to unity of nature[2] but according to similitude of proportion; and this commonality belongs to reason.

Doubt VI

Likewise, the division seems bad as much as regards its *members*: for it seems, that the third member is superfluous. For every thing either is to be used, or to be enjoyed: therefore, the third is superfluous.

Likewise, as there is a thing, which enjoys and uses, so there is a thing, which one is to enjoy and to use, as (is) Christ: therefore, by the reason by which there is posited[3] a third member, there ought to be posited a fourth.

I Respond: Every thing, which is in someway a nature, either is an *end*; and thus is a thing, which (one is) to enjoy; or *leading toward an end*; and thus is a thing, which (one is) to use; or *arriving at an end*; and thus is a thing, which enjoys and uses, as (is) man: and in this manner the members are accepted. And that division is sufficiently convenient to this science, because since theology is of the Creator and of creatures, it is useful, that the theologian teach, in what manner a man tends through other things unto God.

Doubt VII

Likewise, there is an objection concerning this which he says: *The things therefore, which one is to enjoy*; because if[4] there are Three per se and not per accidens, and by a diversity of things there is a diversity or multiplicity of enjoying: therefore, as there are Three things, so there will be three fruitions.

Likewise, there are three articles, because[5] Three Persons: therefore, by a similar (reason) also three fruitions.

I Respond: That "*thing*" [res] is accepted here commonly as regards essence and person on account of its generality; and because this word, "thing", is taken[6] by an act of the soul, for that reason the *Three* are said (to be) "*things*", because (there are) Three Persons, but however, "*one Thing*", because there is one Goodness in Them. Therefore, because (there is) one Goodness, for that reason (there is) also one enjoying, although (there are) Three things. — And since an "*article*" [articulus] signifies a 'what' [dicit quid] on the part of the soul that distinguishes, that is the intellect, and (since) enjoying respects the very[7] divine Essence and Goodness and Union of the affection commonly (speaking), for that reason the enjoying is one.

Doubt VIII

Likewise, is objected concerning this which he says: *Everyone, who enjoys, uses*; because it seems false, since foolish[8] men and beasts similarly enjoy, because they delight for their own sake in the delectable, but they do not use it. *If you say*, that it is said in a transferred manner [translative]; why is the verb, "*to use*", not similarly transferred?

I Respond: "*To use*" conveys [importat] liberty in its general acceptation, in a special manner it conveys liberty with a relation to another; "*to enjoy*" conveys liberty with delectation; and though neither liberty nor conferring [collatio][9] belong [conveniat] to beasts, delectation however, does belong to them. For that reason "*to use*" in no manner belongs to beasts; but "*to enjoy*" does belong to them in some manner, though improperly.[10]

Doubt IX

Likewise, it seems he badly says, that *in man hope is not to be placed*, because[11] of the Blessed Virgin there is sung "*Our life, our sweetness and our hope*" by the Church, which does not err.

---

[1] We prefer the reading of the mss. and edd. 1, 2 and 3, to the reading of the Vatican ed.: i.e. *and there ought to be a common divided among the ones* [divisum debet esse] in place of *and there is something common to the ones* [aliquid est], as it is more conformable to what is subjoined.

[2] From nearly all the manuscripts and editions 1, 2, and 3, we have emended the interpolation of the Vatican edition: *the third (division) is by a middle manner, and that is of the analogue, as is that, where there is not a community of the creature and God according to a participation of nature, but* [est tertia medio modo, et ista est analogi, sicut ista est, ubi non est communitas creaturae et Creatori secundum naturae participationem, sed]. Then at the end of the response codices D I X Y and ee add *and through this the response is clear, because the objection proceeds from a division of the univocal; but this division is of the analogue* [et per hoc patet responsio, quia obiectio procedit de divisione univoci; haec autem divisio est analogi]. This addition is pleasing, as it contains an application of the principle. Cf. above in a. 3, q. 1, in reply to n. 1.

[3] Breaking again with the manuscripts and edition 1, the Vatican edition has *he posits* [ponit]. Codex dd omits *as (is) Christ* [ut Christus] and then reads *therefore, the third is superfluous, and/or by the reason* [ergo tertium superfluit, vel qua ratione].

[4] We have supplied from the manuscripts and edition 1 *if* [si]. A little afterwards codex R has *for a diversity* [ad diversitatem] in place of *by a diversity* [a diversitate].

[5] Against the codices the Vatican edition omits *because* [quia].

[6] The Vatican edition against the manuscripts and editions 1, 2, and 3 has *assumed* [assumtum] and a little below this after *however* it adds *equally well* [aeque bene].

[7] Trusting in nearly all the codices and editions 1, 2, and 3, we have supplied *the very* [ipsam] and a little below this we have put *the affection* [affectus] in place of *effect* [effectus].

[8] The codices do not agree among themselves; for some, as A C G K L O R S U V W X etc. together with edition 1 put *many* [multi] in place of *foolish* [stulti], and then nearly all of them omit *and beasts similarly* [similiter et bestiae], while on the other hand the others as F H (T as corrected by a second hand), having omitted *foolish men and ... similarly* [stulti hominess similiter], retain *beasts* [bestiase], (codices H T have *a brute* [bruta]); editions 4, 5 and 6 have *wicked* [mali] in place of *many* [multi]. The words of (St.) Augustine, upon which the objection is founded, are: And indeed to that extent they are not judged harshly to enjoy food any corporal pleasure; but none, except the animal, which is a sharer in reason, can use any thing. For to know, that to which anything is to be referred, is not given to the ones who have no share in reason [rationis expertibus], but neither to those rational fools (Of Eighty-Three Questions, q. 30).

[9] We have substituted from very many of the manuscripts as A C F G H I K O S T U V W X Z etc. and edition 1 *conferring* [collatio] in place of *relation* [relatio]; codex R reads *delight* [delectio]. A little above this, codex O after *relation* [relatione] adds *and/or conferring* [vel collatione].

[10] Cf. (St.) Augustine, loc. cit.; in addition Bl. (now St.) Albert (the Great), here in a. 17, in reply to n. 2. — (St.) Thomas, here in q. 1, a. 1, and in Summa., I, II, q. 11, a. 2. — (Bl. John Duns) Scotus, here in q. 5. — Richard (of Middleton), here in a. 2, q. 2. — (Bl.) Peter of Tarentaise, here q. 2, a. 3.

[11] With the help of the codices and edition 1 we have expunged the particle *also* [et], which the Vatican edition places after *because* [quia].

Likewise, (as there is said) in the first (chapter) of Jonas:[1] *There came to him the governor*, the Gloss (reads): « It is natural for a man in dangers to confide more in others than in himself ».

I RESPOND: It must be said, that to hope in something is (said) in a twofold manner, either as in a *helper*, or as in a *savior*. The first hope can be (placed) in a man, the second not. — There is hoping for a final reward; and this ought to be only in God; and/or for a temporal benefice; and this can be in a man. The first, if it is placed[2] in a man, merits a curse, but the second does not.

DOUBT X

Likewise, is asked, why he says of man: *And thus, brother do I enjoy you in the Lord*, more than of the ass and/or of another creature, since in all creatures there glitters the vestige of the Divine Goodness.

I RESPOND: That someone be said[3] to enjoy another in God, the cause is not [non facit] representation, but rather inhabitation. Whence the converse is proper, namely the (words): *I enjoy the Lord in you*, since through (your) works I know, that God dwells in you; and (this) is figurative speech.

DOUBT XI

Likewise, is asked of this solution of (St) Augustine, by which he resolves the aforesaid authority through that determination "*in the Lord*". But in the eighth (chapter) of Ecclesiasticus[4] there is simply said: *Enjoy the great*. Likewise, in the twenty-eighth (chapter) of Deuteronomy:[5] *Sons and daughters you shall beget, and you shall not enjoy them.*; from this there is implied, that, if they had not sinned, they would enjoy (them).

I RESPOND: It must be said, that the aforesaid solution is not a general one, but only for the proposed authority. And for that reason one must recur to the aforesaid solution outside the text in the questions,[6] because, though "*to enjoy*" is accepted commonly and properly, in the aforesaid expressions [locutionibus] it is accepted only commonly.

DOUBT XII

Likewise, what Master (Peter) says, does not seem valid: *For if one neither enjoys, nor uses* etc., because God loves Himself, he does not however, use (Himself), because He does not love

Himself for the sake of an other; nor does He enjoy (Himself), because where (there is) enjoying; there is inherence and indigence, as (St.) Augustine says;[7] but God lacks both etc..

I RESPOND: It must be said, that "*enjoying*" in its general reckoning means a union of love [amoris], that is of the enjoyable with the one enjoying. Therefore, since it happens that something is united to itself and to an other, it happens that it not only enjoys the other, but also its very self; but where there is union to the other, there is dependency, inherence and indigence; but where (there is union) to its very self, if it is the Most High Good, there[8] is no inherence nor dependency and/or indigence, but (rather) sufficiency in every manner [omnimoda]. But if that good is deficient, it is lacking; and hence it is, that only God perfectly enjoys His very self, but nothing other by itself can perfectly enjoy its very self. For God alone is the Most High Good and He loves Himself by enjoying Himself, (and) He also loves others by enjoying Himself: and thus neither the enjoying of God nor the use is with indigence, as our enjoying and use (are).

DOUBT XIII

Likewise, is objected concerning that which he says: *Because He is good, we are*: therefore, because He is good from eternity, we are good from eternity.

I RESPOND: It must be briefly said, that this is, because *good* means a cause.[9] But there is a *natural* and a necessary cause, and a *voluntary* cause. But the Divine Goodness is the Cause of our '*being*' [esse] and of (our) '*being good*' [boni esse] through the manner of a will, not of nature; but this (kind of) cause does not posit its effect immediately, when it is.

DOUBT XIV

Likewise, it is still objected, why it similarly does not follow; because He is just, are we just?[10] *If (you) say*, that justice is not a disposition for Him inasmuch as (He is) a cause; *on the contrary*: wisdom is the disposition of God inasmuch as (He is) a cause: therefore by an equal reason, because He is wise, we are wise. *If you say*, that it is not an immediate disposition, as (is) goodness; it is objected concerning the will, which is most immediate, and however, it does not follow: because He is willing, we are willing.

I RESPOND: It must be said, that the reason for this consequence is threefold. One is, because goodness is a condition of a cause inasmuch as (it is) a cause; the second is, because

---

[1] Verse 6. The text of the interlinear Gloss according to (Nicholas) of Lyra is: It is natural for each one in danger to hope more in another than in himself.

[2] The Vatican edition against many codices, as A F G K T W X etc. and the first six editions, has (the subjunctive) *it be placed* [ponatur].

[3] The Vatican edition against the manuscripts and edition 1 has (the indicative) *is said* [dicitur]. A little below this the Vatican text against the codices C I S T V W X Z etc. and edition 1 superfluously add *consequently* [per consequens] after *the converse is* [conversa]

[4] Verse 10. Thus the codices and edition 1 and (Cardinal) Hugo of St. Charo on this passage; but the Vulgate has *to serve the great* [servire magnatis]; but the Vatican edition by citing Ecclesiastes 7:15 reads *enjoy the good things* [fruere bonis].

[5] Verse 41 — Then after *they would enjoy* [fruerentur] in the Vatican edition there is added *them* [eis].

[6] Here, in a. 2. q. 1. in the body of the reply. — Then the Vatican ed. not trusting in all the codices and first six edd., after *because* omits *though* [cum] and after *aforesaid* [praedictis] against the more ancient mss. puts *authorities* [auctoritatibus] in place of *discourses* [locutionibus].

[7] ON CHRISTIAN DOCTRINE, Bk. I, ch. 31, n. 34: But if He enjoys, He is in want of our good, which no one sane would have said. From the more ancient codices together with edition 1 we have inserted *is* [est] before *inherence* [ibi].

[8] On the authority of the codices and edition 1 we have supplied *there* [ibi]. A little below this codex dd has *nor* [nec] in place of *and/or* [vel] after *dependence* [dependentia].

[9] The Vatican edition reads *that this (is) because "He is good" means a cause* [quod hoc quia bonus est dicit causam], but we have followed the authority of the manuscripts and edition 1. Then the reading of the Vatican edition, (which) less rightly has *but there is some natural, even necessary, cause and there is some voluntary cause* [sed est aliqua causa naturalis etiam necessaria et est aliqua causa voluntaria], is corrected from the codices and edition 1. A little below this the Vatican text, after *of nature* [naturae], contradicting the manuscripts and edition 1, adds *and necessity* [et necessitatis].

[10] With the help of the manuscripts and edition 1 we have expunged the words, which the Vatican edition here adds: *just as because He is good, we are good* [sicut quia bonus est, boni sumus].

it is proximate to the act;[1] the third, because (it is) a general disposition, in which consists the reason for the vestige: for it means [dicit] a looking-back [respectum] to the end. Whence as the one God impresses unity, so the good (God impresses) goodness.

Doubt XV

Likewise, is objected of this which is said: *that, namely, it is to be loved for its own sake only*, because as <u>per se</u> (is) to <u>per accidens</u>, so *for its own sake* (is) to *for the sake of another*. But nothing, which convenes with someone <u>per accidens</u>, convenes <u>per se</u>: therefore, nothing, which convenes someone for another's sake, convenes for its own sake. If therefore, the virtues are to be desired [appentendae] for another's sake, therefore, not for their own sake.

I Respond: As the Philosopher says,[2] « The same is the end and the *for the sake of which* ». But the end is twofold: in one manner (it is) the *last* end, which most properly is the End, in which there is a standing still [status]; in another manner (it is) *an end under the end*, which[3] is properly called the terminus. So also the *for the sake of which* is diversified; whence in one manner it excludes the end, in another manner (it does) not, as Master (Peter) says.

Therefore, what is objected concerning <u>per se</u>; I say, that, as <u>per se</u> in one manner is opposed to that which is *through an other* [per aliud] — and thus <u>per se</u> is also the same as *according to what it itself (is)* [secundum quod ipsum], or the prime universal[4] — in another

manner it is opposed to that which is <u>per accidens</u>: thus *for its own sake* is also accepted in a twofold manner. In one manner it is opposed to that which is *for the sake of an other*, in another manner to that which is <u>per accidens</u>, because[5] it is ordered to that accidentally. According to this Master (Peter) distinguishes *for its own sake*, and consequently the honest or enjoyable, and then enjoying itself.[6]

Doubt XVI

Likewise, is objected of this which he says: *And there are* certain things, *through which we enjoy, as (are) the virtues*. It seems that the soul can enjoy powers themselves [solis].[7] For without any virtue one can enjoy a created good; therefore, since the uncreated Good is more enjoyable, and the soul is more bound to (do) this, according to this [eo] it will be able to enjoy powers by themselves.

I Respond: It must be said, that the Most High Good is what is above us; therefore, for this, that we be united to It, a twofold medium necessarily intervenes: one medium, through which the soul is bound to be united to an other diverse from itself; and this is power; the other a special one[8] above this, which lifts it up; and this is virtue. What is objected is not similar, because power <u>per se</u> can fail and be inclined, but not <u>per se</u> be elevated.[9]

---

[1] Without any authority from the codices and edition 1 the Vatican edition here adds: *because since the good is communicative of itself, from its own reckoning it conveys communicability, it also conveys a will, which two things put an effect in act* [quia cum bonum sit sui communicativum, de sui ratione importat communicabilitatem, importat etiam voluntatem, quae duo ponunt effectum in actu]. A little before this (on the previous page), disagreeing with the manuscripts and edition 1, the Vatican edition puts *disposition* [dispositio] in place of *condition* [conditio] and a little below this before *it means* [dicit] it omits *for* [enim]. This and the previous Doubt is explained at length by Alexander of Hales, Summa., I, q. 17, m. 9. — On the reason for *the vestige* cf. below in d. 3, p. 1, q. 2 at the end and in Doubt 6.

[2] Physics, Bk. II, text 298, (ch. 3), where according to the Venetian edition of 1489 (there is read): (A cause) is also said according to the intended end, and this is a that-for-the-sake-of-which.

[3] The Vatican edition together with very many codices, F G K etc., has *and it* [et] in place of *which* [qui].

[4] This proposition, taken from Aristotle, Posterior Analytics, Bk. I, text 11 (ch. 4), according to the ancient version (Venice: Octavianus Scotus, 1538), is thus exhibited: But <u>per se</u> and 'that according to what it itself (is)' (is) the same thing, just as <u>per se</u> there is in a line (both) the point and straightness [rectum]: and indeed [etenim] according to which (it is) a line ». And a little before this: « But I call a "universal", what at least both concerns every, and (is) <u>per se</u> and 'that according to what it itself (is)' ... But there is then a universal, when it is shown [monstraretur] (to be) in any and in the first ». — St. Thomas observes in his Commentary at this point, that here « a universal is not accepted in this manner, insofar as everything which is predicated of very many is called a universal, according to what Porphyry determines of the five universals; but it a "universal" is said here according to a certain adaptation and/or adequation of the predicate to the subject, when, that is, neither is the predicate found outside the subject nor the subject without the predicate ... First he says, that the universal, that is the predicate, is also that which is from all, that is, it is universally predicated of the subject; and also <u>per se</u>, that is it is in it, it convenes with the subject, according to which itself is a subject. For many things are predicated universally of

somethings, which do not convene with it <u>per se</u> and 'that according to which it itself is'. As every stone is colored, not however, according to which (it is) a stone, but according to which it itself is a thing having a surface » (Parma: 1865). — It is called *"the first* universal", when the universal predicated is not only in anything, of which it is predicated, but also is demonstrated (to be) *first* in the 'being' [in esse] of that, of which it is predicated; thus, to keep the example by Aristotle, to have three angles equal to two right (angles) does not convene *first* to an isosceles (triangle), but (rather) to a triangle (simply speaking), because it convenes with an isosceles inasmuch as it is a triangle, and to that extent it is also the *first universal* of a triangle, not of an isosceles. See the very many things pertaining to this matter [plura vide eis] in St. Thomas, <u>loc</u>. <u>cit</u>., and in (Bl. John Duns) Scotus, Posterior Analytics, Bk. I, q. 15-39. — According to the norm of the edition of the works of Aristotle and the codices, not excepting edition 1, we have substituted in the aforesaid proposition after <u>per se</u> the particle *and* [et] in place of *what* [quod].

[5] Not trusting in the manuscripts and the first six editions the Vatican edition here adds *the other* [aliud].

[6] In the solution of this doubt Richard (of Middleton) agrees, here in a. 2, q. 3 in reply to n. 1.

[7] On the authority of the manuscripts and edition 1, we have deleted the words here inserted by the Vatican edition *without any virtue* [sine omni virtute], which are able to be already, sufficiently indicated by the exclusive *themselves* [solis].

[8] Here there is added by the Vatican edition *and/or spiritual one* [vel spirituale], which is lacking in nearly all the codices and edition 1; a few of the codices, as H R W and cc put, less rightly, *spiritual one* [spirituale] in place of *special one* [speciale]. A little before this codex R has *concurs* [concurrit] for *intervenes* [intervenit], and codex X reads, well enough, *a general medium* [generale] in place of *one medium* [unum].

[9] In which sense one is to enjoy the virtues, see above in a. 3. q. 2 and in Sent., d. 18, a. 1. q. 2. — Bl. (now St.) Albert (the Great), here in a. 21. — Giles the Roman, here at the beginning of n. 1, q. 2.

DISTINCTION II

CHAPTER I
On the Trinity and Unity.

And, thus,[1] one must hold by a true and pious faith, « that the Trinity is the One and Only, True God, as (St.) Augustine says in the first book of ON THE TRINITY,[2] that is the Father and the Son and the Holy Spirit; and this Trinity is said, believed and[3] understood of one and the same Substance and/or Essence , which is the most high Good, that is discerned [cernitur] by the most purified minds. For the weak insight [acies invalida] of the human mind is not fixed in such an excellent light, unless it be cleansed through the justice of faith ». The same (is said) in the first book of RETRACTATIONS:[4] « I do not approve what I have said in the prayer: *God, who has willed that none except the clean know the truth.* For it can be responded, that many not clean also know many true things. There-fore,[5] one must deal with this most high and most excellent matter with modesty and fear, and with most attentive and devout ears listen, when one seeks the unity of the Trinity, that is of the Father and of the Son and of the Holy Spirit, because nowhere more dangerously does one err, nothing more laboriously does one seek, and nothing more fruitful does one find. ».[6] Therefore, let everyone, who hears and reads those thing which are said of the ineffable and inac-cessible light of the Deity,[7] strive to imitate and to also ob-serve, what the venerable Doctor, (St.) Augustine, in the first book of ON THE TRINITY,[8] said of himself: « It will not disgust me, he said, if anywhere I hesitate, to ask, nor will it be a cause of shame, if anywhere I wander [error], to learn. Therefore, let anyone (who) hears and/or reads these things, where he is equally certain, let him proceed with me; where he equally hesitates, let him ask with me; where he recognizes his own error, let him return to me; where mine own, let him recall me. Thus let us step upon the way of charity together, tending to Him of whom it is said:[9] *Seek His Face always* ».

CHAPTER II

What was the intention of those writing of the Trinity?

« But all catholic writers [tractatores], as (St.) Au-gustine says in the same (work),[10] who have written of the Trinity, which is God, intended to teach this ac-cording to the Scriptures, that the Father and the Son and the Holy Spirit are[11] of one Substance and by an inseparable equality are the One God, so that there is a Unity in the Essence and a Plurality among the Persons; and for that reason there are not three gods, but One God, though the Father begot the Son, and for that reason the Son is not He who is the Father; and the Son is begotten by the Father, and[12] for that reason the Father is not He who is the Son; and the Holy Spirit is neither the Father nor the Son, but only the Father's and the Son's Spirit coequal to both and pertaining to the Unity of the Trinity ». « Therefore, let us hold, that the Father and the Son and the Holy Spirit are naturally one God, as (St.) Augustine says in the book, ON THE FAITH TO PETER[13] and that the Father is not, how-ever, He who the Son is; nor the Son Himself He who the Father is; nor the Holy Spirit Himself He who the Father or the Son is. For one is the Father's and the Son's and the Holy Spirit's essence, which the Greeks call the ousios,[14] in which there is no other Father, no other Son, no other Holy Spirit, al-though personally the Father is another, the Son is another, the Holy Spirit is another ».

CHAPTER III

What order is to be observed, when dealing with the Trinity?

Moreover, as (St.) Augustine teaches in the first book, ON THE TRINITY: « The first thing ac-cording to the authorities of the Holy Scriptures, to be demonstrated is, whether the Faith is thus to be regarded. Then against the garrulous reasoners, more elated[16] than capable, one must use catholic reasons and congruous similitudes for the defense and assertion of the Faith, so that satisfying their questionings, we may more fully instruct the meek, and so that they, if they have not found what they seek, may complain more of their own minds than of the truth itself and/or of our orderly discussion [dissertione] ».[17]

---

[1] Edition 4 has *also* [quoque], but mistakenly, since the discourse [sermo] here is not one of addition, but of continuation from the preceding. Then, by an inverse order of words, editions 1 and 8 have *is the Only One and True God* [sit unus solus et verus Deus]; the Vatican edition and edi-tion 9 have *is the One and the Only True God* [unus sit solus verus Deus].

[2] Chapter 2, n. 4: « That the Trinity is the One and Only True God, and which is rightly called, believed, understood (as) the Father and the Son and the Holy Spirit of the one and same Substance and/or Essence ... and to be that most high Good, which is discerned [cerni-tur] by the most purified minds ... because the weak insight [acies in-valida] of the human mind is not fixed in such an excellent light, unless having been nourished by the justice of faith it be stirred up [vegetetur] (to this) ».

[3] The Vatican edition omits *and* [et].

[4] Chapter 4, n. 2: « I do not approve what I said in the prayer: God, who has not willed (any) to know the true except the clean (of heart) ». These words of the one praying are read in SOLILOQUIES, Bk. 1, ch.1, n. 2. — A little before this the Vatican edition and codices B and E have *likewise (there is said)* [item] in place of *The same (is said)* [idem]. But below codex D has *unclean* [immundos]in place of *not clean* [non mundos].

[5] We follow codices A B D and E. Codex C has *Therefore* [re ig-itur] for *Therefore* [ergo re]; the Vatican edition, together with all the oth-ers, has *Therefore* [re ergo]. A little below this codex E has *most devout* [devotissimis] in place of *devout* [devotis].

[6] (St.) Augustine, ON THE TRINITY, Bk. I, ch. 3, n. 5, but near the beginning the *that is* [scilicet] has been added by Master (Peter).

[7] The Vatican edition and editions 1, 2, 3, 4, 7 and 9 have *of the Divinity* [divinitatis].

[8] Chapter 2, n. 4, in which text, in place of *hears ... these things* [audit haec], the Vatican edition with codices A B E and very many of the editions reads *hears ... this* [audit hoc], but contradicting the original.

[9] Psalm 104:4.

[10] Namely ON THE TRINITY, Bk. I, ch. 4, n. 7, but with not a few things adjoined and/or changed. The Vatican Edition together with the others, except edition 1, reads: *as in the same Book I ON THE TRINITY, ch. 4* [in eodem I. libro de Trinitate cap. 4]. From these (words) we have ex-punged those, which all the codices together with edition 1 omit.

[11] The Vatican edition alone and faultily reads *is* [sit] in place of *are* [sint].

[12] The Vatican edition alone omits *and* [et]; the same reads below: *Therefore, let us hold* [Teneamus ergo] in place of *therefore* [igitur].

[13] Chapter 1, n. 5. This work is now commonly attributed to (St. Fabius Claudius Gordianus) Fulgentius of Ruspe (462/7—533 A.D.).

[14] In Greek: οὐσίαν. Besides the Vatican ed. and ed. 6, all the codd. and edd., by a remarkable error, read *homoousion* (consubstantial).

[15] Chapter 2, n. 4. In the Vatican edition together with editions 4, 6, and 9, there is read *First ..., it must be demonstrated* [primo] in place of *The first thing ..., to be demonstrated* [primum].

[16] The Vatican edition against the testimony of the codices, edi-tions 1, 6 and 8, and the text of (St.) Augustine, adds *rather* [magis].

[17] Codices A C and D together with the Vatican edition and edi-tions 4, 5, 6 and 8 reads *of our assertion* [assertione], which however, agrees less with the original.

CHAPTER IV
On the testimonies of the Old Testament, by which the mystery of the Trinity is declared.

Therefore, let us put on display [proponamus] in the midst of the Old and New Testaments the authorities, by which the truth of the Divine Unity and Trinity are demonstrated. And first there occurs the very exordia of the Law, where Moses says:[1] *Hear, O Israel, the Lord God, your God, is one.* Likewise:[2] *I am the Lord thy God, who has lead thee out of the land of Egypt; thou shalt not have other gods besides Me.* Behold He here signified the unity of the Divine Nature. « For "God and Lord," as (St.) Ambrose says in the first book, ON THE TRINITY,[3] is a name of nature, is a name of power ». Likewise elsewhere God speaking to Moses says:[4] *I am Who am, and if they ask My Name, go and say to them: Who is, He has sent me to you.* For saying *I am*, not *We are*, and *Who is*, not *Who are*, He has most openly declared, that He is only one God. In the Canticle in Exodus[5] there is also read: *The Lord, Omnipotent (is) His Name*; it does not say *the Lords*, wanting (thereby) to signify the Unity. The Lord also showed at the same time the plurality of Persons and the Unity of the Nature saying in Genesis:[6] *Let us make man to Our image and similitude.* For saying *Let us make* and[7] *Our*, He showed the plurality of the Persons: but saying *image*, the Unity of the Essence. For as (St.) Augustine says in the book, ON THE FAITH TO PETER:[8] « If in that nature of the Father and of the Son and of the Holy Spirit there were only one Person, He would not say: *Let us make man to Our image and similitude.* For when He says *to ... image*, He shows, that the Nature is one, to which image man will be made; but when He says *Our*, He shows, that the same God is not one but many [plures] Persons ».

(St.) Hilary (of Poitiers) in the third book, ON THE TRINITY, also says, that by these words there is signified, that in the Trinity there is neither diversity, nor singularity and/or solitude, but (rather) similitude and plurality or distinction. For he says thus:[9] « He who said: *Let us make man to Our image and similitude*, shows that they are mutually similar to themselves in that which He says: *Our image and similitude* ». « For there is not a sole image, and there is no similitude of Him:[10] nor does similitude of one to another permit that diversity be mixed into two ». Likewise (he says) the same in the fourth book:[11] « He wanted it to be more absolutely understood, that this sig-

nification is not to be referred to Himself alone, by saying: *Let us make man to Our image and similitude*; for the profession of a sharing [consortii] supported the understanding of a singular,[12] because any sharing cannot belong to one (who is) himself a solitary, nor again does the solitude of the solitary receive a *Let us make*, nor does anyone say *Our* to one alien from himself. Each saying [sermo], that is *Let us make* and *Our*, as it does not suffer a 'solitary' and a 'same', thus does neither signifies one diverse and alien from onself. To a solitary there convenes a *Let me make* and a *My*; but it does not befit a solitary to say *Let us make* and *Our*. Each saying, as (it does not only signify) a solitary, so, too, it does not signify a different 'being' [esse] and/or By us, too, neither is a solitary nor a diverse to be confessed. Therefore, God is thus found to have wrought man to the image and same similitude common with God Himself: so that neither does the signification of the One effecting admit the understanding of a solitude, nor does the constituted working toward the same image and/or similitude endure a diversity of Divinity ».[13]

In these words (St.) Hilary wanted the plurality of Persons to be understood by the name of "a sharing" [consortii], and he did signify, by the name of "a sharing" and/or of "plurality" that nothing other be posited, but (rather) be removed. For when "a plurality" and/or "a sharing" of Persons is said, a solitude and[14] a singularity is denied; when we say, that there are many Persons, we signify, that there is not one alone. For that reason (St.) Hilary, wanting this (saying) of his to be subtlety and sanely understood, says: « The profession of a sharing supported the understanding of a singular »,[15] (and) he does not say: "*it posited something*". Thus, too, when we say "*Three Persons*", take away singularity and solitude, and we signify that the Father is not alone, nor is the Son alone, nor is the Holy Spirit alone, and[16] that neither is there only the Father and the Son, nor is there only the Father and the Holy Spirit, nor only the Son and the Holy Spirit. But of this matter more is discussed [agetur] in the following (text),[17] where there will also be shown according to what the Three Persons are said (to be) "similar", and whether in any manner there be a diversity and/or difference.

But now let us return to what has been proposed and let us introduce the other authorities of the Saints to show[18] the plurality of Persons and the Unity of the Divine Essence. Moses says:[19] *In the beginning God created heaven and*

---

[1] Deut. 6:4; in the Vulgate and among (the writings of St.) Augustine, *Hear, Israel, the Lord Our God is one Lord* [Audi Israel, Dominus Deus noster Dominus unus est], but among (the writings of St.) Ambrose, ON THE FAITH TO GRATIAN, Bk. I, *God, thy God, is one* [Deus tuus Deus unus est], as in the text of Master (Peter).

[2] Ex. 20:23; where the Vulgate after the word *of Egypt* [Aegypti] reads: *from the home of servitude you shall not have another's gods before Me* [de domo servitutis non habebis deos alienos coram me], and codices B D and E and editions 1 and 3 have *another's gods* [dii alieni] in place of *other gods* [alii dii].

[3] Or ON THE FAITH TO GRATIAN, ch. 1, n. 7, where (there is read): *For "God and Lord" is a name of magnificence, a name of power* [Deus enim et Dominus nomen magnificentiae, nomen est potestatis]. The Vatican edition together with editions 4, 5, 6, and 9 (reads): *For "God", as Ambrose says in the first book, ON THE TRINITY, is a name of nature, but Lord is a name of power* [Deus enim, ut ait Ambrosius in primo libro de Trinitate, nomen est naturae, Dominus vero nomen est potestatis] .

[4] Ex. 3:14: *I am who am. He says: thus you shall say to the sons of Israel: He who is, sent me to you* [Ego sum qui sum. Ait: sic dices filiis Israel: Qui est, misit me ad vos.].

[5] Ex. 15:3: *The Lord like a fighting man, the Omnipotent is His Name* [Dominus quasi vir pugnatur, omnipotens nomen eius] .

[6] Gen. 1:26.

[7] The Vatican edition and edition 4 faultily reads *to* [ad].

[8] Chapter 1, n. 5: « For if in that ... there was one person, it would not say *to our image*, but *to My image*, nor would it have said *let us make*, but *let Me make*. But if in those three persons three substances are to be understood and/or believed, it would not say to *Our image*, but *to Our images*; for there cannot be one image of three unequal natures. But, while

to the one image of the One God man is said "to have been made", the One Divinity of the Holy Trinity is essentially hinted at ».

[9] ON THE TRINITY, Bk. III, n. 3; but very many things have been added here.

[10] The Vatican edition together with editions 2, 4, 5, 6, 7 transpose the words thus: *a similitude of Him there is none* [sibi non est].

[11] ON THE TRINITY, n. 17.

[12] Against the codices and editions 1 and 8, the Vatican text together with the all the other editions has *of a singularity* [singularitatis], and a little after this it has, together with not a few of the editions, *can neither belong* [nec potest], and at the end of the proposition codex D has *would anyone say* [loqueretur]; all the other codices together with editions 1 and 8 have *will anyone say* [loquetur]. Immediately after this, the Vatican edition together with not a few of the editions has *Therefore* [ergo], editions 1, 3 and 8 have *For* [enim] instead of *Therefore* [igitur].

[13] These have been excerpted from (St.) Hilary loc. cit, n. 18ff.

[14] The Vatican edition and not a few of the editions has *and/or* [vel]. Then codex D has *And for that reason* [Ideoque] in place of *For that reason* [Ideo].

[15] The Vatican edition again with many of the editions has *of a singularity* [singularitatis].

[16] Editions 2 and 7 omit *and* [et]; codex C by a change in punctuation reads thus: *and that the Father is not ... the Holy Spirit alone. We also signify that* [solus. Significamus etiam quod].

[17] Distinctions XIX, XXIV, XXXI and XXXIV of this book. A little below this codex B has *which* [quod] in place of *what* [quid].

[18] The Vatican ed. together with edd. 1 & 3 has the gerund, instead of the gerundive, for *to show* [ostendum].

[19] Gen. 1:1.

earth, by *God* signifying the Father, by *the beginning* the Son. And for that which among us is called *God*, the Hebraic Truth has *Elohim*, which is the plural of the singular, which is *El*. Therefore, because *El*, which is *God*, was not said, but (rather) *Elohim*, which can be interpreted "*gods*" or "*judges*", it refers to the plurality of Persons. It also seems to allude [attinere] to that, which the Devil said through the serpent:[1] *You shall be as gods*, for which in the Hebrew there is had *Elohim*, as [ac] if to say: "You shall be as the Divine Persons (are)". Also that greatest of the Prophets and kings, David, who preferred his own understanding to all others' saying:[2] *Above old men have I understood*, showing the unity of the Divine Nature, says:[3] *the Lord is His Name*; he does not say "*the Lords*". Elsewhere showing at the same time the Unity and Eternity of the same One he also says of the person of God:[4] *Israel, if you listened to Me, there will not be among thee a new* [recens] *God, nor shall thou adore another's God*. « One of these, as (St.) Ambrose says in the first book, ON THE TRINITY,[5] signifies eternity, the other a unity of non-differing substance, so that we may believe that the Son and/or the Holy Spirit is neither posterior to the Father, nor of another divinity. For if the Son and/or the Holy Spirit is posterior to the Father, He is *new* [recens]; and if He is not of the one Divinity, He is *of another* [alienus]; but He is neither posterior, because He is not new, nor of another, because born from [ex] the Father » was the Son, the Holy Spirit proceeded[6] from [ex] the Father. Elsewhere hinting also at the distinction of Persons he says:[7] *By the word of the Lord the heavens have been made firm, and by the Spirit of His mouth their every virtue*. Elsewhere he also says:[8] *May He bless us, God, Our God, may He bless us, God, and let them fear Him all the ends of the earth*. For the triune confession of God expresses the Trinity of Persons; but he uncovers [aperit] the Unity of the Essence, when he subjoins in the singular "*Him*". Isaias also says,[9] that he heard the Seraphim shouting: *Holy, Holy, Holy, the Lord God*. By this

which he says three times "*the Holy*" [Sanctus], he signifies the Trinity: through that which he adds "*Lord God*", the Unity of the Essence. David also openly hints at the eternal generation of the Son saying of the person of the Son:[10] *The Lord said to Me: My Son are Thou, this day have I begotten Thee*. Of this ineffable generation Isaias says:[11] *His generation who shall tell of it?* Also in the Book of Wisdom the eternity of the Son with the Father is demonstrated, where Wisdom thus speaks:[12] *The Lord possessed Me at the start* [in initio] *of His ways, before He made anything from the beginning* [a principio]*: from eternity I have been ordained, before the earth was made; nor were the abysses yet, and I already have been conceived: neither yet the springs nor yet the mountains or hills, and I was being brought forth* [parturiebar]*: He had not yet made the earth and the hinges of the orb of the earth: when He was preparing the heavens, I was there: when He was weighing out the foundations of the earth, with Him was I composing all things, and I took delight (with Him) throughout each day, playing before Him*. Behold an open[13] testimony of the eternal begetting, by which Wisdom itself maintains [perhibet], that He has been conceived before the world and brought forth, that is, has been begotten, and exists eternally with [apud] the Father. Elsewhere she also says:[14] *I out of the mouth of the Most High have come forth, the firstborn before every creature*. Micah the Prophet also hinted at the same time at the eternal generation of the Word and the temporal from Mary saying:[15] *And thou, Bethlehem Ephrata, are a little one among the thousands of Judah; out of thee shall step forth one who is the ruler in Israel, and His stepping forth (is) from the start, from the days of eternity*.

Of the Holy Spirit we also have express proofs [documenta] in the Old Testament. For in Genesis[16] there is read: *The Spirit of the Lord was borne above the waters*. And David says: *Where shall I go from Thy Spirit?* And in the Book of Wisdom[17] there is said: *The Holy Spirit shall flee from the one (who has) feigned discipline, for kind is the spirit of wisdom*. Isaias[18] also says: *The Spirit of the Lord is upon me* etc..

---

[1] Gen. 3:3. — A little after this contrary to the codices and editions 1, 3 and 8, the Vatican edition together with all the other editions has *in the Hebraic (text)* [hebraico] in place of *in the Hebrew* [hebraeo].

[2] Ps. 118:110. — A little before this only editions 1, 3 and 8 adds *(who) preceded (him)* [praecedentibus] after *to all the others'* [ceteris].

[3] Ps. 67:5. — The Vulgate and codices D and E omit the *is* [est] in this text, which however, is included by (Sts.) Jerome, Augustine, and Bede in this position.

[4] Ps. 80:9,10.

[5] Or ON THE FAITH TO GRATIAN, ch. 11, n. 68.

[6] The Vatican edition and editions 2, 3, 4, 5, 7, and 9, reads *proceeds* [procedit], which corresponds less with the preceding *born ... was* [natus est].*

[7] Ps. 32:6.

[8] Ps. 66:7, 8. — The words immediately following: *For the triune confession* etc. [Trina enim confessio etc.] are attributed by Master (Peter) to St. Ambrose's EXPLANATION OF THE PSALMS (loc. cit.), among whose (writings) we could not find them; but they are read without their author's name among the (writings) of (Peter) Abelard, CHRISTIAN THEOLOGY. From whom Master (Peter) accepted not a few things. These are once an argument and an example, which we here transcribe from a praiseworthy work (PATROLOGIA LATINA, tome CLXXVII, col. 1227-28): That also seems to pertain [attinere] to this plurality of Divine Persons, which ... was said through the serpent: *You shall be as gods* (Gen. 3:5), because, as has be said above, in Hebrew the word is *Elohim*. And thus did that greatest of Prophets and kings, David, speak, who preferring his own intelligence to all others' says: *Above all those teaching me have I understood, above old men have I understood*; he speaks, I say, of the distinction of the Trinity openly hinting: *By the Word of the Lord have the heavens been made firm, and by the Spirit of His mouth all their virtue* (Ps. 31:6). Who also in another place hints at the Unity equally with the Trinity, saying: *May He bless us God, our God, may He bless us God,*

and let them fear Him all the ends of the earth (Ps. 36:7) ... Indeed the triune confession of God expresses the Trinity of Persons ... but the Psalmist reveals [aperit] the Unity of the Divine Substance in the same (passage), when after the triune mention of the Divine Name understanding only one God in the Three Persons, he does not subjoin "*them*" in the plural, but "*Him*" in the singular. With this that (word) of Isaias is consonant, who says, that he say the Seraphim and heard them shouting: *Holy, Holy, Holy, the Lord God Sabaoth* (Is. 6:3).

[9] Is. 6:3.

[10] Ps. 2:3. — Editions 1, 3 and 8 add after *saying* [dicens] the word *thus* [ita].

[11] Chapter 53:8.

[12] Prov. 8:22-30. — The Vatican edition and editions 4, 5, 7 and 9, by contradicting even the Vulgate, read *the Lord possessed me from the start* [... ab inito] in place of *at the start* [in initio].

[13] The Vatican edition and editions 4 and 7 read *an apt*. Then before *begotten* [genitam] on the authority of codex D and editions 1, 5, and 8, we have supplied *has been* [esse]. Then codices A and E and editions 1 and 3 have badly: *For she elsewhere* [Ipsa enim].

[14] Eccli. 24:5. — A little before this codex D reads the generation *of Christ* [Christi] in place of *of the Word* [Verbi].

[15] Micah 5:2, where the Vulgate prefaces *for Me* [mihi] to the word *shall step forth* [egreditur]. Codex D has *in the land of Judah* [terra Iuda] in place of *Ephrata* [Ephrata]; likewise together with codices A and E, it reads *a little village* [parvulus vicus], Which reading (St.) Jerome expounding that text [locum] of Micah cites [commemorat] and rejects; ed. cit., tom. VI, col. 488.

[16] Chapter 1:2; the following citation is from Ps. 138:7.

[17] Chapter 1:5, 6. — A little before this the Vatican edition omits *And* [Et] before *in the Book* [in libro] contrary to the codices and editions 1, 3, 5 and 8.   [18] Chapter 61:1.

---

* *Trans. note*: Here the original footnote read: *suffered ... was* [passus est] for *born ... was* [natus est], faultily.

CHAPTER V

*On the testimonies of the New Testament
pertaining to the same*

But now after the testimonies of the Old Testament concerning faith in the Holy Trinity and Unity, let us proceed [accedamus] to the authorities of the New Testament, so that *in the midst of the two animals* (that is the Testaments) the truth *may be recognized* [cognoscatur][1] and *there may be taken by forceps from the altar the coal* [calculus] by which the mouths of the faithful are to be touched. And so the Lord Christ openly hinted at the Unity of the Divine Essence and the Trinity of the Persons, saying to the Apostles:[2] *Go, baptize all the nations* [gentes] *in the Name of the Father and of the Son and of the Holy Spirit.* « At any rate He said "*In the Name*", as (St.) Ambrose says in the first book, ON THE TRINITY, not "in *the Names*" », that the Unity of the Essence may be shown; through the three names, which He listed [supposuit], He declared the Persons to be Three. « He also said: *I and the Father, we are one (thing)* [unum]. He said "*one (thing)*", as (St.) Ambrose says in the same book, lest there be a separation [discretio] of power and nature; and He added "*We are*", that you may recognize [cognoscas] the Father and the Son, that is, so that a perfect Father may be believed to have begotten a perfect Son, and that the Father and the Son are one (thing), not by a confusion of a person, but by a Unity of the Nature ». (St.) John also said in his canonical Epistle:[3] *There are Three, who give* [perhibent] *testimony in Heaven: the Father, the Word and the Holy Spirit, and these Three are one (thing).* He also says at the beginning of his Gospel: *In the beginning was the Word, and the Word was with God, and the Word was God*; where he openly shows, that the Son was always and eternally with [apud] the Father, as one with another. The Apostle also openly distinguishes the Trinity, saying:[4] *God sent the Spirit of His Son into our hearts.* And elsewhere:[5] *If His Spirit, who raised up Jesus, dwells in us* etc.. Likewise he elsewhere commends the Trinity and Unity in a most evident manner, saying: *Since from Him, and through Him, and in Him are all things; to Him (be) the glory.* « He says "*from Him*", as (St.) Augustine says in the book, ON THE TRINITY,[6] on account of the Father; he says "*through Him*" on account of the Son; "*in Him*" on account of the Holy Spirit ». But by this, that he does not say "*from Them, through Them* and *in Them*", nor does he say "*to Them (be) the glory*", but "*to Him*", he hints, that this Trinity is the One Lord[7] God. But because a singular syllable of the New Testament harmoniously hints at this truth of the ineffable Unity and Trinity, let us forebear [supersedeamus] the introduction [inductioni] of testimonies upon this matter and let us show by reasons and congruous similitudes, insofar as our infirmity prevails, that it is so.

COMMENTARY ON DISTINCTION II

On the Unity and Trinity, according to what is believed.

And, thus, one must hold by a true and pious faith etc..

THE DIVISION OF THE TEXT

This is the second part, in which, having tracked down [indagata] the matter of the first book, Master (Peter) begins to follow after it; moreover, this part[1] is divided into two parts, since twofold is the considering of things, which one is to enjoy, that is *in themselves*, and in comparison to *creatures*: *in themselves* by a reckoning of (their) trinity and unity; in comparison to *creatures* by a reckoning of (their) knowledge [scientiae], power, and will. Therefore, first he deals[2] with the Holy Trinity and Unity; second with knowledge and power and will, below in the thirty-fifth distinction (which begins): *And since we have orderly discussed above.*

Moreover, one happens to treat of this Most Sacred

---

[1] Hab. 3:2; according to the Septuagint version: *In the midst of two animals shall you know* [In medio duorum animalium cognosceris]; the Vulgate: *In the midst of the years you shall make it known* [In medio annorum notum facies]. However all the codices, except B, and the editions, except 8, use the poetic genitive plural duum instead of duorum. All the codices and edition 1 omit *that is the Testaments* [id est Testamentorum], which words seem to be a gloss. That application of this text is (St.) Augustine's in ON THE CITY OF GOD, Bk, XVIII, ch. 32. The words *by forceps from the altar* etc. [forcipes de altari etc.] allude to Isaias 6:6: *And there flew toward me one of the Seraphim, and in his hand a coal,* [calculus] *which he had taken with forceps from the altar.* — At the beginning of this proposition codices A B and C omit *But*.

[2] Mt. 28:19; the Vulgate reads: *Going, therefore, teach all nations: baptizing them in the Name of the Father* etc. [Euntes ergo docete omnes gentes: baptizantes eos in nominee Patris etc.]. But among (the writings) of (St.) Ambrose, ON THE TRINITY or ON THE FAITH TO GRATIAN, Bk. I, ch. 1, n. 8: « *Go, baptize the nations in the Name of the Father and of the Son and of the Holy Spirit. At any rate In the Name, not in the Names. He also says: I and the Father are one (thing)* [unum], Jn. 10:30; He says *one (thing)*, lest there be a separation [discretionem] of power and nature; He adds *We are*, that you may recognize [cognoscat] the Father and the Son, that a perfect Father may be believed to have begotten a perfect Son, and that the Father and the Son are one (thing), not by a confusion of a person, but by a unity of nature ». — The Vatican text together with codex C and not a few of the editions omits *book* [libro] in the phrase *in the same book* [in eodem libro]; in addition the Vatican edition and the other editions omit *and* [et] after *separation of power* [discretion potestatis]. Then codices A B and C and editions 1 and 8 badly omit *of a person* [personae] after *a confusion* [confusione].

[3] Chapter 5:7, where the Vulgate together with codex D and editions 1 and 8 has *give testimony* [testimonium dant] in place of *give testimony* [testimonium perhibent]; but this alternate reading is found even among Pope (St.) Hyginus (138-142 A. D.), EPISTOLA DE FIDE ET RELIQUIS CAUSIS, as related by Isidore Mercator, PATROLOGIA LATINA, tom. CXXX, col. 109 and (St.) Cyril of Alexandria († 444 A. D.), BOOK OF TREASURES, assertion XXXIV (PATROLOGIA GRAECA, tom. LXXV, col. 615).

[4] Gal. 4:6, where the Vulgate has *your hearts* [corda vestra] in place of *our hearts* [corda nostra], as Master (Peter) has here and elsewhere. *Our* [nostra] in place of *your* [vestra] is used also by (St.) Ambrose in this passage and by (St.) Augustine in Ps. 118, serm. 14, n. 2, ON THE WORDS OF ST. MATTHEW THE EVANGELIST, serm. 71, n. 29, and it is the old reading now dismissed on the reckoning of (St.) Jerome.

[5] Rom. 8:11 and then 11:36.

[6] Bk. I, ch. 6, n. 12: "*From Him*", from the Father; "*through Him*", through the Son; "*in Him*", in the Holy Spirit. Codices B C and D and editions 1 and 8 have "*From Him*" he says [ait], and understand by this *he means* [dicit]. They omit *he says* [dicit], because it follows afterwards, in editions 1 and 8. Then in codices D and E there is had not *by this* [per hoc], but *on this account* [propter hoc].

[7] The Vatican edition, contrary to the codices and editions 1 an 8, omits *Lord* [Dominum].

NOTES ON THE COMMENTARY

[1] Without an reliance upon the authority of the manuscripts and edition 1, the Vatican edition exhibits this distorted reading: *The second part of the First Book, in which the matter ... is divided especially into* [Secunda pars Primi Libri, in qua materia ... dividitur praesertim in].

[2] Codices V and W read *one deals with* [agitur].

Trinity in a threefold manner, since, first, one happens to *believe* It, second, to *understand* (what is) believed, third, to *say* or enunciate (what is) understood. But believing is through authority, understanding through reason, saying through Catholic and reasonable[1] speech [locutionem]. For that reason he *first* deals with the Trinity and Unity Itself, according to what *is believed*; *second*, with It, according to which the (Trinity) believed is *understood* through reason, there, in the third distinction (which begins): *For the Apostle says*; *third*, according to which the (Trinity) believed and understood is *expressed* in a reasonable and Catholic manner, below, in the twenty-second distinction (which begins): *After the aforesaid things it seems that there must be an orderly discussion by us of the diversity of the Names.* And (thus) the order is clear. For believing It is prior and truer than understanding (It); for many believe, who do not understand; and, similarly, understanding (It) is prior to expressing (It) in speech [sermone].

The *first* part, that is according to what is believed, contains the present distinction; and since the matter is most difficult, he *first* posits a manner of proceeding; but *second* he seeks it out, there (where he says): *Therefore, let us put on display in the midst.*

Likewise, the first part has three parts according to (its) three chapters[2]. In the first he touches upon the *manner of writing* [modum agendi], since (this) ought to be with modestly, fear and diligence, prefacing the matter, about which he intends to write [agere]. In the second he subjoins the *intention of those writing* of the Trinity, there, in the second chapter (which begins): *Moreover all the catholic writers* [tractatores]. Third he touches upon the *order*, there (where he says): *Moreover, as (St.) Augustine teaches in the first book.*

The *manner* of writing of the Trinity ought to be founded upon the understanding of the Faith and with modesty and fear on account of the danger. The *intention* of those writing

of the Trinity is to show,[3] that the Father and the Son and the Holy Spirit are Three Persons and the One God. The *order* of (Master Peter's) writing is, first to show the truth through authorities, then through reasons and congruous similitudes.

Therefore, let us put on display in the midst. This is the *second* part, in which Master (Peter) by the authorities of Sacred Scripture intends to show the Trinity and Unity; and since[4] Sacred Scripture has two parts, that is the New and the Old Testament, for that reason he first shows this through the authorities of the Old Testament, then through the authorities of the New, there (where he says): *But now after[5] the testimonies* etc.. And since the Old Testament has two parts, that is the Law and the Prophets, in which the faith is explained, for that reason he shows (this) first through the testimonies of the Law, second through the testimonies of the Prophets, there (where he says): *That greatest of the Prophets.* Again the first part, in which he proves through the testimonies of the Law, has two parts: for he *first* proves the unity of the Essence; *second* the Unity and the Trinity at the same time, there (where he says): *The Lord also showed at the same time.* Similarly that (part)[6] concerning the testimonies of the Prophets has two (parts): in the first he proves the Unity of the Essence and the plurality of the Persons in common; but in the second in particular [in speciali] he shows the generation of the Son and the procession of the Holy Spirit, there (where he says): *David also openly hints at the eternal generation.* Similarly that part, in which he proves through the authorities of the New Testament, has two parts: for first he proves through the authorities or through the authority of Jesus Christ; second through the authorities of the Apostles, there (where he says): *(St.) John also said in his canonical Epistle.* The authorities and the explanations, number and diversities of them are sufficiently clear in (Master Peter's) text.

TREATMENT OF THE QUESTIONS

For a clarification of the things which Master (Peter) says of the Sacred Trinity and Unity, four things can be asked about this part.

First it is asked, whether in God there is a positing of a unity of essence or nature.

Second, whether in God there is a positing of a plurality of persons.

Third, whether among the divine Persons there is a positing of an infinity.

Fourth and lastly, whether among the divine Persons there is a positing of a Trinity.

ARTICLE SOLE

On the Unity of the Divine Essence and the plurality of the Persons.

QUESTION I

Whether there is only one God?

About the first, that in God there is to be posited a unity of essence or nature, seems by demonstrative reason [ratione ostensiva], having considered the threefold supposition, which is proper to be posited, both on account of His *simplicity*, and on account of a *common*

conception of spirit, which is, that God is the one greater than whom (nothing) can be thought, and by reason of (His) *status*, which is not *but* in the highest and first (position).

The first supposition is, that God is the *most*

---

[1] Codices I and cc have *rational* [rationalem].

[2] Not trusting in all the codices and edition 1, the Vatican edition omits *according to (its) three chapters* [secundum tria capitula]; then after in the first [prima] it adds *premised by a foreword on the Mystery of the Trinity and the Unity* [praemisso prooemio de mysterio Trinitatis et Unitatis], and below after *of the Trinity, there* [Trinitate ibi] it omits *in the second chapter* [secundo capitulo].

[3] We have inserted from codex I *to show* [ostendere], which is sanely to be understood.

[4] The Vatican edition, favoring no codex nor edition 1, by omitting

the words of Master (Peter): *Therefore, let us put on display in the midst* [Proponamus ergo in medium], inverts the construction of the following proposition by putting *Similarly* [Similiter] in place of *This is* [Haec est] and *it has two parts according to which* [habet duas partes secundum quod] in place of *and since* [et quoniam].

[5] Codices aa bb and cc have *through* [per].

[6] Supply with the Vatican edition *part* [pars], which the Codices and edition 1 omit. A little below this the Vatican edition not trusting in the manuscripts and edition 1, after *in common* [communi], puts less correctly *But in the second he especially shows* [Secundo vero specialiter].

simple. From this it argued, that since a thing [aliquid] can communicate with no thing diverse (from itself),[1] because, if it does communicate, and it differs: therefore, (it does so) not according to the same (respect); therefore, there is a composition (of being). If it can communicate nothing, therefore, (it can communicate) neither deity nor entity; therefore, if there are two gods, since one is Being [ens], the other is not Being [non est ens], if one is God, the other is not God: therefore, if there are two gods, there are not two gods.[2]

2. Likewise, the second supposition is, that God is, because God is the *most Omnipotent*.[3] From this it is argued: therefore, He will be able to cause [facere], that every power other than His own can (do) nothing: therefore, if there are two gods diverse in nature, one of the two can bring it about, that the other can (do) nothing, and conversely. But the one whose power can be borne away, is not God: therefore, if there are two gods, none is God.

3. Likewise, the third supposition is, that God is simply *the Most High (Being)* [summum].[4] From this it is argued: therefore, all things are below Him: therefore, all others (are) from Him and for Him. If, therefore, there are two gods, one is below the other, and conversely; one is from the other according to a diverse nature, and conversely; one is for the other, and conversely; but what is below the other in nature and from the other and for the other, is not God: ergo etc..

4. Likewise, this can be proved through *deduction to the impossible*. If there are two gods, either one is where the other (is), or (it is) not.[5] If one (is) where the other (is): therefore, one is in the other, since they are by the same manner of being [eodem modo essendi]: therefore, one is material to the other: therefore, the other is not God. If one is not where the other (is): therefore, each are limited, therefore, neither (is) infinite.

5. Likewise, if there are several good gods,[6] either one understands the other, or (he does) not. If not;

therefore, each is ignorant. If he does understand: therefore, either (he does so) through a *prior-sensing* [praesentiam] or through *appearance* [species], or through *his very self* as through its exemplar.[7] If, through a *prior-sensing*: therefore, one (is) in the other, therefore, God is inserted into [illabitur] God and perfects God; if through *appearance*: therefore, (there is) a composition [compositus]; if through an *exemplar*: therefore, one is the exemplar of the other, therefore, (one is) also the beginning (of the other).

6. Likewise, if there are two diverse gods, of which each is the Most High Good; either one loves [diligit] the other, as he is to be loved, or (He does) not. If so, since each is the Most High Good, each is to be loved with the love of enjoying: therefore, each enjoys the other; but what enjoys a good other than itself, is in need of it [indiget]: therefore, one is in need of the other: therefore, Each is indigent, therefore, neither (is) God.

BUT ON THE CONTRARY: 1. God can do more things, than our intellect can think of. But the human intellect, as [utpote] it belongs to the nations,[8] understands (that there are) several omnipotent gods: therefore, God can do the same [hoc]. But whatever can be in the Divine Nature, is there, because (It is) eternal:[9] ergo etc.

2. Likewise, more good things are better than fewer; but more gods are more goods: therefore, two will be a better thing than one. But according to (St.) Anselm[10] everything, which is better, is to be posited about God: therefore, more gods are to be posited.

3. Likewise, whose operation is diverse, diverse is the virtue and diverse is the nature;[11] but the operation of the Three Persons is diverse, because the apparition in the dove was of the Holy Spirit alone, and the Son alone assumed human nature: therefore, they are diverse in substance: therefore, there are several Gods [plures deos].

4. Likewise, great is the power, which a great one can (exercise), and greater (the one), which the greater (can exercise), and greatest (of all is that), which

---

[1] This phrase: *a thing ... communicate with ... thing* [communicare aliquid cum aliquo], here and elsewhere signifies: 'to have something common with another', or: 'to convene with another in some matter'. — The Vatican ed. against the codd. and ed. 1 here omits *a thing* [aliquid] and then, by putting *they are* [sunt] in place of *according* [secundum], it shatters the force of the argument [by reading *therefore, they are not the same*]. Then codd. X Y and Z read *one (thing)* [unum] in place of *the same (respect)* [idem]. Cf. Aristotle, METAPHYSICS, Bk. X, text. 12 (Parisian ed.: Bk. IX, ch. 3).

[2] This argument exhibited by the Seraphic Doctor with a few words can be thus explained: First: if God is simple, he cannot have anything common with another god, who is supposed to exist [esse]. It is proven: if one God had anything common with another or if he would communicate in another, e. g. in deity, with another, he would also differ, so that he would be another God; since the same thing according to the same cannot at the same time communicate or convene with another and differ (with it): therefore, they would convene with another, and differ or be distinguished by another: therefore, each would be composed. Second: but if they had nothing common: therefore, neither (would they have) deity or entity; from which follows the absurdity noted in the text.

[3] Very many of the codices as A C G L O R S U etc. together with edd. 1, 2, 3 and 6 have *the most omnipotent (being)* [omnipotenissimum].

[4] According to the norm of many of the manuscripts as A C G L O R S T U W aa bb ee and ff and editions 1, 2, 3 and 6 we have put *the Most High (being)* [summum] in place of *the Most High* [summus].

[5] Trusting in the very many codices together with edition 1, we have expunged *it is* [est], which the Vatican edition adds here.

[6] Codices O Y and Z omit *good* [boni], which reading would be more pleasing, if it were supported by a greater number of codices.

[7] We have inserted from codex I *as through its exemplar* [ut per illius exemplar], which words express the last member of the disjunction

more clearly and render the form of the whole argument more perfect, because below all the manuscripts and editions 1, 3 and 6 have *if through an exemplar* [per exemplar] in place of *if through its very self* [per se ipsum], which the Vatican edition has. Codices T and cc also in the first case put *through an exemplar* [per exemplar] in place of *through its very self* [per se ipsum], but (this) written by a second hand.

[8] Codices F aa and bb have *it belongs to the gentiles* [gentilium].

[9] Aristotle, PHYSICS, Bk. III, text 32: For being able to be by Himself He does not differ throughout the perpetual (ages).

[10] MONOLOGION, ch. 15: Just as it is a wicked thing to think, that the substance of the Most High Nature be anything, than which a not-Itself is better in any manner: so it is necessary, that it be whatever is entirely better, than what (is) not-Itself. For it alone is, than which nothing is thoroughly better. Cf. also PROSLOGION, ch. 5. Aristotle agrees, METAPHYSICS, Bk. XII, text 39 (Parisian edition: Bk. XI, ch. 7): And so we say, that there is a living, sempiternal, best God, wherefore life and the continual and eternal aevum is in Him, for this is (what) God (means). Cf. also (St. Severinus) Boethius, ON THE CONSOLATION OF PHILOSOPHY, Bk. III, Prose 10.

[11] Averroës,* METAPHYSICS, Bk. XII, text 25: The active is diversified in power and act through a diversity of forms and matters. (St. Severinus) Boethius, ON THE CONSOLATION OF PHILOSOPHY, Bk. III, Prose 11, exhibits the converse of this proposition: For indeed the substance belongs to those, which naturally are not a diverse effect. Each proposition is founded upon this axiom: operating follows being [esse], or: the same is the principle of being and operating. — In the conclusion of this argument codex O has *nature* [natura] in place of *substance* [substantia]. — Bl. (now St.) Albert (the Great), SUMMA, I, tract. 6, q. 29, m. 1, a. 1, proffers the same argument, and then adds: And this was the stronger objection of the Arians and Nestorians and Eutychians and the followers of Paul of Samosata.

---

* *Trans. note*: Averroës is the Latin name for the famous Almohad scholar *Abu al-Walid Muhammad ibn Ahmad ibn Muhammad ibn Rushd* (1126 A. D. -1198 A. D.), whose principle work was TAHAFUT AL-TAHAFUT or THE INCOHERENCE OF INCOHERENCE.]

the greatest (can do); but God above all thing is most highly potent: therefore, he can produce the Most High (Being);[1] but this is God: therefore, since « in eternal (ages) it is the same "to be" and "to be able" », ergo etc..

CONCLUSION

That there are more gods is impossible, nay, rather, if there be rightly understood, what God is, it is not (even) intelligible.

I RESPOND: It must be said, that it is impossible that there be more gods, and if the thing signified by this name *God* be rightly accepted, it is not only impossible, but also not intelligible: for *God* means simply the Most High (Being) both *in reality* [in re] and in the opinion of the *one thinking*. Because (He is such) *in reality*, for that reason all things (are) from Him and in Him and for Him, and in Him entirely is (their) stability [status];[2] for that reason it is impossible to understand, without violation of the intellect, that anything makes another equal to itself [sibi parificetur] from itself. *Likewise,* nothing greater than God can *be thought* nor even (anything) equal, because (He is) the Most High (Being) in the opinion (of rational creatures). For that reason it is impossible and not intelligible to posit more gods.

1. To that, therefore, which is objected concerning the nations; it must be said, that it was not an understanding, but a fiction;[3] besides (at that time) they did not understand God according to the divine nobility: for that reason (the argument) is not valid.

And for that: God can do more etc.; it must be said, that twofold is the intellect, that is the rational and the fantastic. Of the first it is true, but of the second not (so); because we can thing many things according to (our) fantasy, which God cannot do, because it is not agreeable [non convenit] to Him, « in Whom the inconvenient is impossible ».[4]

2. To that which is objected, that more good things are better than few; it must be said, that (the argument) has truth in (the case of) a created and finite good, which by reason of its finiteness [finitatis] receives an augment of goodness through addition of another good; but it does not have truth in (the case of) a infinite good, because however much you add an infinite good to an infinite, I will always understand as much of goodness in the one, as you[5] (do) among the more.

3. To the other which is objected concerning the diversity of operations; it must be said, that the Father and the Son and the Holy Spirit convene in every operation, but differ in relation. Whence in the Incarnation there is an operation of the production of that nature and there is a union; in the first the Three Persons convene, in the second not (so). — Similarly in the dove there is the formation of a dove and its signification;[6] in the first they convene, in the second not (so). The example of (St.) Augustine[7] concerns the Trinity, which for the formation of this name *memory* there convenes memory, intelligence and will; however, this name *memory* signifies one of the powers; it is (so) in a similar manner in the proposed (argument).

4. To that which is objected, that a great power, etc.; it must be said, that to produce anyone[8] is (said) in a threefold manner: *from one's very self,* and/or *from another created (thing),* and/or *from nothing.* From His very self God can produce the most high (being) simply (speaking), but It will not be another in nature on account of the simplicity of (His) nature. From another and/or from nothing He cannot produce the most high (being) simply (speaking), but (He can) according to the genus [in genere] (of created things), not on account of a defect of the power of the agent, but on account of a defect of the creature, which of necessity [necesse est] is limited; and thus He cannot produce another God.

SCHOLIUM

I. The first argument at the bottom is proposed more diffusely by Alexander of Hales, SUMMA., p. I, q. 14, m. 2, and by Richard of Middleton, SENT., Bk. I, d. 2. a. 3. — Against the second argument, taken from omnipotence, (Bl. John Duns) Scotus (SENT., Bk. I, d. 2. a. 3) removes [movet] a difficulty, because he against the common sentence supposes, that the omnipotence of God cannot be known certainly except by faith.

II. Against the doctrine handed down in the solution to n. 2 Durandus (of Saint-Pourçain) opposes (SENT., Bk. I, d. 44, q. 3), that God and the world together are a greater good than God alone. But this assertion is deservedly reprobated by all the classical theologians as false; cf. below d. 43, q. 2 at the bottom of n. 5; ITINER-ARIUM MENTIS, ch. 5. — In the solution to n. 3 as regards the proposition: « In the first the Three Persons convene, in the second {that is in the union} not (so) », it must be noted, that *union* can be accepted in a twofold send, as a unitive *action*, and/or as a *relation* of union. That (last) is common to the Three Persons of the Trinity, but this (former) respects the Person of the Son alone; and of this the Seraphic Doctor speaks here.

III. The unity of God has been defined by the Fourth Lateran Council, in ch. 1 of *Firmiter*, and also by the Vatican (Council), in the Constitution *de Fide*, under the title *On God the Creator.*

St. Bonaventure teaches more things about this question below in d. 4, q. 3; d. 23, a. 2, q. 3; SENT., Bk. II, d. 1, p. I, a. 2, q. 1;

---

[1] The Vatican edition together with the more recent codex cc, contrary to all the more ancient codices and edition 1, unduly reads *the most high Good* [bonum].

[2] This respects Rom. 11:36: Since from Him and through Him and in Him are all things. The sense is: from God all things proceed, in God all things are conserved, to God all things are returned. Cf. below in d. 36, dub. 4. — *In Him entirely is (their) stability,* i. e. God is the *principle,* beyond which we can in no manner pass in resolving or seeking the causes (of things). A little below this edition 1 has *to Him* [ei] in place of *to Himself* [sibi].

[3] Codex U has not badly: *rather a fiction; for (at that time) they did not understand* [fictio potius; non enim intelligebant]. Codex T has *truth* [veritatem] in place of *nobility* [nobilitatem].

[4] (St.) Anselm, CUR DEUS HOMO, Bk. I, ch. 20: But this is a postulate [praestitutum], because however, small the inconvenient it is impossible in God. — The Vatican edition contrary to the manuscripts and editions 1, 2 and 3, to *the inconvenient* [inconveniens] adds *the least* [minimum]. A little before this codex I has *many fantastic things* [multa ... phantastica] in place of *many ... according to (our) fantasy* [multa ... secundum phantasiam].

[5] From very many of the more ancient manuscripts as A C F G H K L O P S T etc. we have inserted *you* [tu]. A little before this codices S and X before *good* [bonum] omit *infinite* [infinitum]; a reading not at all to be spurned.

[6] In this manner very many of the codices as K R X Y Z and ff together with edition 1 read; the others are of a doubtful reading; codices I and aa read *figuring* [figuratio]; but the Vatican edition together with the other codices has *indication* [signatio].

[7] ON THE TRINITY, Bk. IV, ch. 21, n. 30: Since in accord with the manner I name my memory and intellect and will, singular names indeed are referred to singular things, but, however, singulars are signified [facta] by all three etc.. The sense is: for the formation of the word *memory* all three of the powers of the soul actively concur, however, the signification of the same is referred to one power alone.

[8] Trusting in the very many manuscripts as A C F G H L O R S T U Z etc. and edition 1 we have substituted *anyone* [aliquem] in place of *anything* [aliquid]. For it deals here with the production of *God,* and in what follows the masculine gender of *It* [ille] is used, which refers to that *most high (being) simply (speaking)* [summum simpliciter] without doubt to be taken for the same genus, that is *anyone most high* etc. [suumum aliquem etc.]. Codex H has *God produce anyone* [Deum producere aliquem].

BREVILOQUIUM, p. I, ch. 2, 5, 6; ITINERARIUM MENTIS, ch. 5. — Alexander of Hales, SUMMA., p. I, q. 14, m. 2. — (Bl. John Duns) Scotus, here in q. 3; DE RERUM PRINCIPIO, q. 1. — St. Thomas, SENT., Bk. I, here at q. 1, a. 1; SUMMA., I, q. 11, a. 3; and chiefly SUMMA CONTRA GENTILES, I, ch. 42. — Bl. (now St.) Albert (the Great), here in a. 2, 21; SUMMA.,

p. I, tr. 6, q. 29, a. 1, m. 1. — (Bl.) Peter of Tarentaise, here in q. 1. a. 1. — Richard of Middleton, here in a. 1, q. 1. — Giles the Roman, here in (a. ?) 1, at the beginning of q. 1. — Durandus (of Saint-Pourçain), here in q. 1. — Henry of Ghent, SUMMA., a. 25, q. 2, 3. — (Bl.) Dionysius the Carthusian, here in q. 1.

QUESTION II

Whether in God there is to be posited a plurality of Persons?

Second, there is asked, whether there is to be posited in God a plurality of persons. And that (this is) so, is shown by supposing four things concerning God: the first is, that in Him there is a *most high beatitude*; the second is, (that in Him is) a *most high perfection*; the third is, (that in Him is) a *most high simplicity*; the fourth is, (that in Him is) a *most high primacy*.

1. From the first supposition it is thus argued: if[1] there is a most high *beatitude* there; but wherever there is a most high beatitude, there is a most high *goodness*, a most high *charity* and a most high *jocundity*. But if there is a most high *goodness*, since it belongs to goodness to communicate itself in a most high manner,[2] and this is most greatly in producing from itself an equal and in giving its own 'being' [esse]: ergo etc.. If a most high *charity*, since charity is not a private love [amore], but (a love) for another: therefore, it requires a plurality. Likewise, if a most high *jocundity*, since « there is no jocund possession of any good without company [sine socio] »,[3] therefore, for the most high jocundity there is required society and, thus, plurality.

2. Likewise, from the second supposition thus: if there is a most high *perfection* there; but « to perfection belongs producing such a thing, which is itself in nature »:[4] therefore, it is necessary, that there be a multiplication; but this cannot be according to another essence: therefore, it is proper, that it be according to another person or supposit.

3. Likewise, from the third supposition thus: if there is a most high *simplicity* there; but *simplicity* is, that any nature be in more [pluribus], as is clear in the universal, but it is from a defect of simplicity, that it is numbered among them:[5] therefore, if in God there is a simplicity deficient in no manner, the non-numbered Essence will be in more [pluribus]: ergo etc..

4. Likewise, from the fourth supposition: if there

is a most high *primacy* there; but as much anything is prior, so much is it more fecund and the principle of others:[6] therefore, as the Divine Essence, because (it is) first, is the principle of other essences, so the person of the Father, since He is first, because (He is) from no one, is the principle and has[7] a fecundity in respect of persons; but a fecundity in God in respect of God cannot be except conjoined to acting [actui]: therefore, it is necessary, that there be more persons.

ON THE CONTRARY: 1. It seems, that from the same suppositions the contrary could be argued, and thus are destroyed the reasons and the conclusion.[8] For if there is a most high beatitude there, since it is sufficient for beatitude (that God be) blessed through the Essence of Himself alone [sibi soli]: therefore, it is not necessary to posit another Person for beatitude or jocundity.

2. Likewise, against the second supposition it is thus objected:[9] if there is a most high perfection there: therefore, equally, fully and perfectly is the Essence in one Person and in more. If therefore, beyond perfection an addition is superfluous, a plurality is superfluous; and if this (is the case), since among divine things nothing is superfluous, there is no plurality[10] among the divine (Persons).

3. Likewise, against the third reason thus: if there is a most high simplicity there, since plurality is opposed to simplicity, and « opposites cannot be about the same thing »:[11] therefore, if God is one and in Him there is simplicity, therefore, not a plurality, since in all things [per omnia] He is simple.

4. Likewise, against the fourth supposition thus: if there is a most high *primacy*; therefore, since stability is in the first principle, and stability is in unity: therefore, primacy does not posit plurality, but unity: therefore, it seems, that there is only one Person.

---

[1] Against the testimony of the manuscripts and edition 1, the Vatican edition here and in the other three arguments has the particle *if* [si].

[2] The Vatican edition has *it belongs to most high Goodness to communicate itself* [bonitatis summae sit se communicare], but less aptly and against the authority of the manuscripts and editions 1, 2 and 3; it would be better, if the reading of the Vatican edition and the manuscripts was found conjoined, so that it read: it belongs to most high Goodness to communicate itself in a most high manner. — This reason is founded on that proposition taken from Dionysius (the Areopagite), ON THE CELESTIAL HIERARCHIES, ch. 4 and ON THE DIVINE NAMES, ch. 4: The Good is diffusive of itself.

[3] (Lucius Annaeus) Seneca (4 B. C. — 65 A. D.), EPISTLE TO LUCILIUS, Bk. I, letter 6.

[4] Aristotle, ON THE SOUL, Bk. II, text 34 (ch. 4). — In the beginning of this and of the following argument, the Vatican edition omits the particle *Likewise* [Item] and after *supposition* [suppositione] adds *it is argued* [arguitur]; but this opposes the manuscripts and edition 1.

[5] Aristotle, METAPHYSICS, Bk. VIII., text 45 (Bk. VI, ch. 13) says: For a universal means this, that it is bound to be in more (things). And in POSTERIOR ANALYTICS, Bk. I, ch. 20 (ch. 24) he says: At any rate as much as it is greater according to (its) parts (or particulars), it falls unto into (the genus of) the unbounded [in infinita]; but the universal (falls) into (the genus of) the simple and an end. — Then the Vatican edition against the more ancient codices and edition 1 has *nothing* [nihilo] in place of *no manner* [nullo] and *is* in place of *will be*.

[6] Cf. BOOK OF CAUSES, propositions 1 and 17. — Codex K has *more noble and/or more fecund* [nobilius vel fecundius].

[7] The Vatican edition against the manuscripts and edition 1, with a changed punctuation, has *is from no principle, He has* [a nullo st principio, habet]; which reading detracts from the force of what is said.

[8] A major part of the codices as A F G H L O T V W X Y Z etc. together with edition 1 oppose the Vatican reading *the conclusions already posited* [conclusiones iam positae], and indeed rightly, since only one of all the reasons posited is the conclusion. The other manuscripts as CS (AT by a first hand) etc. have *the conviction* [convictio] in place of *the conclusion* [conclusio]. Codex R omits *and the conclusion* [et conclusio]. A little after this on the authority of the manuscripts and the first six editions we have substituted *it is sufficient (that God be) blessed* [beatum ... sufficiat] in place of *the blessed ... is sufficient* [beatus ... sufficiat]; the same recurs below in the solution to this objection.

[9] Codex cc has *it is argued* [arguitur]. A little after this the Vatican edition, opposing the more ancient manuscripts and edition 1, has *there is an equally full and perfect essence in ... as in more. But if beyond* [aeque plena et perfecta ... ut in pluribus. Si autem ultra].

[10] From the manuscripts and the first six editions we have substituted *is* [est] for *will be* [erit].

[11] Aristotle, ELENCHAE, Bk. II, ch. 5 (ch. 25) and METAPHYSICS, Bk. XI, ch. 4 (Bk. X, ch. 5). — A little before this codex X self-consistently has *supposition* [suppositionem] in place of *reason* [rationem].

CONCLUSION

Both the Faith teaches and one is persuaded by arguments of congruence, that a plurality of Persons is to be posited in divine things.

I RESPOND: It must be said, that in divine things one is to posit a plurality of Persons, as the Faith teaches and (as) the aforesaid reasons show, if one considers (the matter) without contradiction. For by reason of *simplicity*, the Essence is communicable and able [potens] to be[1] in more. By reason of the *primacy*, the (first) Person is bound [nata est] to produce Another from Himself; and here I the primacy an "innascibility", by reason of which, as the ancient opinion says, there is a fontal plenitude in the Father towards every emanation; and this will be clear below.[2] By reason of *perfection*, He is apt and prompt for this; by reason of *beatitude and charity* (He is) willing [voluntaria]. Having posited these conditions, it is necessary to posit a plurality of Persons.

1. To that, therefore, which is objected in the Contrary, that it is sufficient (that God be) blessed through the Essence of Himself alone, therefore, He is not in need etc.; it must be said, that it is true, that He is not in need; nor is Another posited[3] on account of indigence nor as One beatifying, but (as) One communicating in beatitude.

2. Similarly to that which is objected, that the Deity is equally fully in one and in more;[4] it must be said, that even if (It is) equally fully, it is not, however so fully declared. And *besides*, by that very reason by which It is fully in the Father, there redounds unto the other Persons a redundancy of perfection.

3. To that which is objected, that a plurality is repugnant to simplicity; it must be said, that there is a certain plurality through *addition*; and this is repugnant; (and there is) a certain (plurality) through *origin*; and this does not add nor compose nor is repugnant to simplicity, but rather to solitude; and thus it is among divine things, as will be clear below.[5]

4. To that which is objected, that in the first there is stability [status]; it must be said, that as among essences there is a prime Essence, from which and for which the others are, so also[6] among the Persons there is one Person, from whom and for whom the Others are; and in That is the stability of (Their) origin, because That (is) from none, and this is the Person of the Father. Whence (St.) Augustine[7] appropriates unity to that Person, saying: « In the Father unity » etc..

SCHOLIUM

I. Below in d. 3, p. I, q. 4, the Seraphic Doctor teaches, that the Mystery of the Most Holy Trinity can only be known by faith. Hence it is clear, in what sense the arguments from reason in this question and those brought forward elsewhere are to be understood, that is not as strictly demonstrative, but only as persuasive or probable through a certain congruence resulting from the principles of the Faith. (Bl. John Duns) Scotus, here in q. 7, disputes at length the value of these arguments and among others strives to refute this argument placed in second place. — As regards the argument taken from the fourth supposition cf. below in d. 28, q. 1. — In how many manners Sacred Scripture teaches the plurality of the Persons, is briefly taught below, here in Doubt 8. — Nearly the same arguments are exhibited by Alexander of Hales (who treats of this matter at length, and from whom, as testifies (Bl.) Dionysius the Carthusian, very many of the arguments of latter doctors seem to have been taken), by St. Thomas, by Richard (of Middleton), who adds a fifth argument, and by others

II. St. Bonaventure, BREVILOQUIUM, p. 1, c. 2; ITINERARIUM MENTIS ch. 6; HEXAËMERON., Sermon 11 and 21. — Alexander of Hales, SUMMA., p. I, q. 14, m. 1, 5, 6. — (Bl. John Duns) Scotus, here in q. 4, 7; REPORTATIO. here in q. 5. — St. Thomas, here in q. 1, a. 4; SUMMA., I, q. 30, a. 1, 2; SUMMA CONTRA GENTILES, IV, ch. 26; QUODLIBETALS., 7, a. 6. — Bl. (now St.) Albert the Great, here in a. 20; SUMMA., p. I, tr. 6, q. 29, a. 2, m. 1. — (Bl.) Peter a Tarentaise, here in q. 2, a. 1. — Richard of Middleton, here in a. 2, q. 1. — Giles the Roman, here in n. 2. at the beginning of q. 1. — Henry of Ghent, SUMMA., a. 53, q. 8. — Durandus (of Saint-Pourçain), here in q. 4. — (Bl.) Dionysius (the Carthusian), here in q. 5. — (Gabriel) Biel, here q. 11.

QUESTION III

Whether the number of Divine Persons is infinite?

Consequently, in the third place there is asked, whether among the Divine Persons one is to posit an infinity. And that (this is) so, is shown in this manner.

1. Because the creature is[8] finite, also whatever is in it, is in act finite: therefore, <u>ab oppositis</u>,* because the Divine Essence is infinite, whatever is in It, is in an infinite manner [infinite]: therefore, since in God there is a number of persons, it will be infinite; and thus there will be infinite Persons.

2. Likewise, since infinity is twofold, *virtual* and *numeral*,[9] there is a *virtual* infinity in God: therefore, for an equal reason a *numeral* infinity: therefore, in God there are infinite Persons.

---

[1] Codex K has *and can be* [et potest ese]. Codex O has *as one able to be* [ut potens esse].

[2] Distinction 27, p. I, q. 2 in reply to n. 3. — Then after *and charity* [caritatis] there is added in the Vatican edition *the same divine Essence is* [eadem essentia divina est], which is absent from the manuscripts and edition 1. Codex R prefaces the word *beatitude* [beatitudinis] with *the goodness of* [bonitatis].

[3] We have restored the reading of nearly all the ancient manuscripts and edition 1 by substituting *is ... posited* [ponitur] in place of *is ... to be posited* [ponendus] and by adding *neither* [neque], which the Vatican edition together with the more recent codex cc omits unduly.

[4] The Vatican edition here, as above, against the more ancient codices and edition 1 has *there is equally a full and perfect (essence) in one and in more* [aeque plena et perfecta est in uno et in pluribus], though the same always exhibit in the following passages the adverb *fully* [plene].

[5] Distinction 8, p. II, a. 1, q. 1 and d. 23, a. 2, q. 1 and 2. — A little before this codex X has *solely* [solum] in place of *rather* [potius].

[6] In the Vatican edition and the more recent codex cc *also* [et] is lacking, which however, is had in the ancient manuscripts and edition 1, and indeed well so. A little after this codex X has *none* [nulla] in place of *none* [nullo].

[7] ON CHRISTIAN DOCTRINE, Bk. I, ch. 5, n. 5: In the Father unity, in the Son equality, in the Holy Spirit the concord of unity and equality.

[8] Thus the codices and edition 1, while the Vatican edition has *the creature since it is finite* [creatura cum sit finita]. A little after this codex cc has *infinite* [infinitum] in place of *infinitely* [infinite]; but the other codices as M T V X together with edition 1 have less aptly *they will be infinite* [erunt infinitae] in place of *it will be infinite* [erit infinitus]; but we have judged that nothing is to be changed.

[9] Cf. (St.) Augustine, ON THE QUANTITY OF THE SOUL, ch. 3 ff. — Codex R here adds *if* [si], not badly.

---

* *Trans. note*: A topic <u>ab oppositis</u> is a proposition which is true in virtue of the truth of another proposition, which has the opposite logical form. Here, the first proposition, "because the creature is finite ... act is finite", is converted (cf. p. 112, trans. fn.), and the quality affirmed ("finite") is replaced by the affirmation of its opposite ("infinite"). Cf. Peter of Spain, SUMMULAE, tracts I, "On categoric propositions" and V, "On <u>loci ab oppositis</u>".

3. Likewise, infinite virtue, when it emanates[1] according to its total infinity, it not only produces an infinite *intensively*, but also *extensively*; but the virtue of the Father in the production of the Persons emanates according to His own omnimodal power: therefore, He not only produces persons infinite in virtue, nay rather also[2] infinite in number.

4. Likewise, this same is thus shown: a multiplication of persons either belongs to *virtue*, or (it does) *not*. If *not*: therefore, it ought not be posited among the Divine; if it does belong to *virtue* per se: therefore, a greater multiplication will belong to greater virtue; and to the most high virtue an infinite multiplication: ergo etc..

On the Contrary, this is shown by a fourfold condition, which is taken from this, that to God there is always to be attributed what is more noble, wherefore it is necessary to posit a finitude [finitatem] of Persons. The first (condition) is *distinction*, the second *order*, the third *connection*, the fourth *most high completion*.[3]

1. From the first condition it is thus shown: if there is *distinction* there, therefore, (there is) not a confusion; but where there is infinity, there is confusion: ergo etc..

2. Likewise, from the second, thus: where there is *order*, there is termination, because where termination is lacking, there is also[4] lacking mediation and per consequens order; but where there is termination, there is not infinity: therefore, if among the divine Persons there is order, there is not infinity.

3. Likewise, from the third, thus: where there is *connection*, it is necessary, that all the persons proceed from one; for if one (is) from another and thus consequently, then there is an infinite distance between the first and the last; but[5] this is inconvenient: therefore, all (are) from one: therefore, either in the same manners, or in diverse ones. If in the same: therefore, no distinction; if in diverse, but diverse manners of emanating are finite: ergo etc..

4. Likewise, from the fourth, thus: if there is a *most high completion* there, therefore, the Divinity is bound [nata est] to complete others: therefore, since there is a completion of persons in beatitude, It is bound to beatify (them).[6] But if the persons were infinite, it would be impossible that anyone would be beatified by God; for cognition of whatever person concerns the substance of beatitude, since the whole goodness, which is the substantial reward [praemium], is in each of the persons; therefore, either the soul would cognize all (of them), or it would not be blessed; but it would be[7] impossible that it cognized all, since its virtue is finite: ergo etc..

CONCLUSION

That the number of divine Persons is finite, both faith holds and reason persuades.

I Respond: It must be said, that among the divine Persons as much as regards (their) number, one is not to posit an infinity but a finitude [finitatem].

But the reason for this is, that a *numeral* infinity is repugnant to perfection and order, because it is through a withdrawal [recessum] form unity or from its origin. Similarly also[8] an infinity of *mass*; and for that reason neither is in God. But an infinity of *virtue* is through an approach [accessum] to unity and origin; and for that reason, since it belongs to perfection, it is to be posited in God, the others not (so).

1. 2. To that, therefore, which is objected, that whatever is in God, is infinitely (so); it must be said, that the True [verum] is there infinitely, but not in any kind of[9] infinite manner [qualicumque infinite], rather [sed] by that which God is infinite; and this is the infinity of immensity, and in such a manner the Trinity is infinite, not by a numeral infinity, which is not congruent with God.[10]

3. To that which is objected, that infinite virtue, infinitely[11] emanating, produces infinites; it must be said, that no production, except of the perfect, agrees with divine virtue; and for that reason there agrees with it no production of any infinity except of that, which stands with most high perfection. But this is not a numeral infinity, and for that reason it is not in God.

4. To the last which is objected, that to power it belongs to multiply oneself; it must be said, that not in every manner[12] does (multiplying oneself) belong to power, but to multiply oneself perfectly does belong to power; and for that reason it does not follow: therefore, that it multiplies itself more is a greater perfection, if it be understood perfectly; but that it multiplies itself infinitely according to number is (to be understood) imperfectly; and for that reason it does not agree with God.

---

[1] From the sense and the manuscripts, together with edition 1, which exhibit it, we have altered the subjunctive *since it emanates* [cum emanet], which the Vatican edition has.

[2] Favoring the more ancient codices and edition 1, we have supplied *also* [etiam].   [3] That is, a plenitude of perfection.

[4] By authority of the more ancient manuscripts and edition 1, we have here inserted *also* [et] and a little below this the *persons* [personis], omitted less rightly by the Vatican edition and codex cc.

[5] The Vatican edition against the manuscripts and edition 1 here and near the end of the argument puts *and* [et] in place of *but* [sed] after the *if in diverse* [si diversis].

[6] The sense seems to be: God completes all things or makes them perfect; but persons, i. e. intellectual natures or supposits, He completes by beatifying, therefore, it is proper for God to beatify. — The Vatican edition has *to complete them* [illas complere] in place of *to beatify* [beatificare] and a little before this it has *to complete persons and* [personas complere] in place of *to complete others; therefore* [alia complere]; which reading is contrary to all the codices and edition 1 and destroys the sequence of the argument. A little after this codex A together with edition 1 has *any* [aliquam], i.e. *any person*, in place of *anyone* [aliquem].

[7] Very many codd. as T and Y have *is* [est] and perhaps this is better.

[8] There is wanting here in the Vatican edition *also* [et], which the manuscripts and edition 1 exhibit. A little after this from the codices and edition 1 we have inserted the words *and origin* [et originem] and *the*

others not (so) [ac alia non], which the Vatican erroneously omits. Likewise the codices and edition 1 have *neither (genus of infinity)* [neutrum] in place of *neither (infinity)* [neutra], which the Vatican edition has.

[9] Codices A and T and the others together with edition 1 in place of *in any* [qualibet], which is in the Vatican edition, exhibit the more distinct *in any kind of* [qualicumque].

[10] On the testimony of all the manuscripts and edition 1, we have expunged the following proposition: *And by this is clear the response to the second, that is why a numeral infinity is not to be posited in God, as (is) a virtual*, which is here added by the Vatican in order to resolve the phrase. But once and always it must be noted, that often a special response to an objection is more often omitted by the Seraphic Doctor, when it is already clearly contained in the preceding text, as is for example here in the body of the article.

[11] The Vatican edition, disagreeing with the manuscripts and edition 1, has *in infinity* [in infinitate] in place of *infinitely* [infinite].

[12] The codices together with editions 1, 2 3 omit here what is added in the Vatican edition, *multiplying oneself* [multiplicare se], which is easily supplied. A little below this the Vatican edition together with the more recent codex cc, contrary to the other manuscripts and edition 1, by a changed punctuation and having put *it agrees with God* [convenit Deo] in place of *for that reason* [ideo], has *and it agrees with God: therefore, it does not follow, that ... more* [et convenit Deo: non sequitur ergo, magis]. Then near the end of the response we have inserted from the manuscripts and edition 1 the particle *and* [et] before *therefore* [ideo].

SCHOLIUM

I. Commonly a threefold infinity is distinguished, namely a *numeral*, which in a discrete quantity, one of *mass* [molis], which is in a continuous quantity, and one of *virtue* or of *immensity*; cf. below in d. 19, p. I, q. 1, q. 1 and 2. — For an easier understanding of the four arguments in the fundament we note the following: Those four properties of the Divinity, at least the first three, have been so interconnected, that the second, *order*, supposes the first, *distinction*, and the third, *connection*, both of them. The first argument taken from *distinction* proceeds thus: if that He is more noble is to be attributed to God, and if there is distinction there, that distinction ought to be without confusion, since confusion belongs to imperfection; but where there is an infinite multitude, there is confusion: ergo etc.; cf. below in d. 43, a. 1. q. 3. The second argument proceeds from this axiom, that, where there is order, there is necessarily a first and last (terminus) and a middle. The third argument is sufficiently evident. In the fourth argument, that is taken from a most high

completion, i. e. from a plenitude of perfection, the Seraphic Doctor supposes with the common opinion, that « the cognition of any Person concerns the substance of beatitude ». Of this, however, (Bl. John Duns) Scotus (SENT., d. 1, q. 1) is doubtful and he opines, that it is not, absolutely speaking, impossible, that in Heaven one enjoys the Essence of God, but not a Person. Concerning which sentence one can see Macedo, COLLATIONES DOCTRINAE S.THOMAE ET SCOTI, conf. 3, diff. 3.

II. About the next question: Alexander of Hales, SUMMA. p. I, q. 45, m. 6, where fundament 1 and 2 is more broadly explained. — (Bl. John Duns) Scotus, here in q. 5 and 7. — St. Thomas, SUMMA., I, q. 30, a. 2. — Bl. (now St.) Albert (the Great), on this question and the following, SUMMA., p. I, tr. 9, q. 41, m. 3. — Peter of Tarentaise, here in q. 2, a. 2. — Richard of Middleton, here in a. 2, q. 2. — Henry of Ghent, SUMMA., a. 53, q. 9. — Durandus (of Saint-Pourçain), SENT., Bk. I, d. 10, q. 2. — (Gabriel) Biel, SENT., Bk. I, d. 10, q. 1.

QUESTION IV

Whether there are only three Divine Persons?

Fourth and last, there is asked, whether among the divine Persons one is to posit a trinity. And that (one is) not, nor what is more a duality, is thus shown.

1. The Father gives the whole, of what He can, to the Son;[1] but he who gives the whole of what he can, cannot give more: therefore, neither (can he) produce another person, since that is a giving [dare].

2. Likewise, the Father generates the Son as the Word through all things equal and through all things saying and expressing Him; but a multiplication of persons is for the declaration of the Truth: therefore, it seems, that it is superfluous to produce another.

3. Likewise, it is shown that there ought to be a *quaternity* there by reason of the emanation. For because the Son emanates through generation, not through procession, for that reason, the force [vis] which does not generate, does however, by spirating produce; for the same reason it seems, that the Holy Spirit, although He does not produce by spirating, can generate or may generate, since He is not generated.

4. Likewise, since among the divine there is a twofold manner of producing,[2] that is one through a manner of nature, another through a manner of will, and there ought to be a complete reckoning of production there, it seems also, that there ought to be there a manner of producing a third through a manner of art. And if so, one will posit there a fourth Person according to this manner of producing.

ON THE CONTRARY: That a trinity alone is there, is shown from the suppositions made above, because it is

necessary, in that Trinity there be *beatitude, perfection, simplicity,* (and)[3] *primacy*.

1. From the first supposition it is thus shown: if there is a most high *beatitude* there: therefore, a most high concord; therefore, there is a most high sharing-of-one-origin [germanitas], a most high charity. But if there were *more than three*, there would not be a most high sharing-of-one-origin there; if *less*, there would not be a most high charity there: therefore, there are only three. The proof of *the minor*. If there is a fourth person there, either He proceeds from one, or from two, or from three. If from one and/or[4] two only, then He does not perfectly and equally convene with all; but if from three, then the two intermediate persons convene more with one another than with the extremes, because they are produced and produce; and thus there is not a perfect nexus there. — *Likewise*, if there were *less than three*, there would not be a perfect charity there, because a perfect love [amor] both is *liberal* and is *common*: because (it is) *liberal*, for that reason it tends unto[5] the other; because (it is) *common*, for that reason it wants one [illum] to be loved [diligi] by the other and that (one) love the other as itself and by itself: therefore, there is a dilection and a condilection there; but this cannot be among less than three [minus quam in tribus].

2. From the second supposition thus: if there is a most high *perfection* there: therefore, the Person producing perfectly produces both as much as regards the manner of producing, and as much as regards Him who is produced. But naught but a twofold, noble manner of producing is found: « for everything acting acts by means of nature, or by means of will », as the Philosopher has it;[6] therefore, by these two

---

[1] John 16:15: All things whatsoever the Father has are Mine [Omnia quaecumque habet Pater mea sunt].

[2] Very many of the codices as A C G I K L M O R S Z etc. have less rightly and not self-consistently *of proceeding* [procedendi]. A little below this after *of art* [artis] we have restored from the manuscripts and editions 1, 2 and 3 the particle *And* [et].

[3] Codices X and cc and edition 1 here add *and* [et].

[4] Very many of the mss. together with edition 1 repeat *from* [a], here.

[5] The Vatican ed., opposing the mss. and ed. 1, has *to* [ad] in place of *unto* [in] and a little afterwards it has *the other* [aliud] in place of *the one* [illum]; then, contrary, moreover, to edd. 2, 3, 4, 5 and 6 after *by the other* [altero], by reading *as by itself and it wants to love* [diligere], it afterwards omits *and by itself* [et a se]; which reading is, indeed, more graceful, but it seems that the sense is exceedingly constrained, for the reason that it does not contain one member

of the division in respect to the threefold mutual dilection. The elliptical construction of our reading sufficiently indicates that member. For the sense of the proposition here is: for that reason the Father wants, that the Son be loved by the Holy Spirit, and that He love the Holy Spirit, just as He wants, that He, that is the Father, be loved by both of the two and that both of the two be loved by Himself.

[6] (Aristotle,) PHYSICS, Bk. II, text 49 (ch. 5), where he says, that of those things which are made on account of an end « some indeed are made according to a purpose [propositum], but others not ... but they are on account of this (i.e. the end) both whatsoever is at least done by the intellect and whatever by nature ». Cf. ETHICS, Bk. III, ch. On the Voluntary, and MAGNA MORALIA, Bk. I, ch. "On the Spontaneous," and in the following chapters.

manners and by these only does He produce; but a person produced by any of those two manners is the most perfect: therefore, if there is anything *beyond* perfection it is superfluous, and what is *on this side* (of perfection) is lacking, it is necessary, that there be only two persons emanating and not more nor fewer, and one, from whom they emanate: therefore, only three.

3. Likewise, thus from the third: if there is a most high *simplicity* there, the Father only gives to each: therefore those proceeding or emanating are not distinguished from within [penes] those things which they accept,[1] but from within (their) manner of accepting and/or emanating; but there are only two manners of emanating: therefore, there cannot but be two persons emanating and a third producing: ergo etc..

4. Likewise, thus from the fourth: if by reason of *primacy* there is a most high fecundity there, no person can produce by any genus of producing, whereby he is produced,[2] because in respect of that he is not prior: therefore, since two persons emanate according to two manners of emanating, it is impossible, that they produce by these two manners, and there are not other manners: therefore, they cannot produce another person: therefore, there are only three.

CONCLUSION

That there are only three divine Persons, both the Catholic Faith teaches, and reason persuades.

I RESPOND: It must be said, that, as the Catholic Faith says, one is to posit only three Persons, not more nor less. And for this there is employed [sumitur] a reason for (its) *necessity* and *congruity*.

At any rate[3] the reason for *the necessity*, why there cannot be *fewer* than three, is most high *beatitude* and most high *perfection*. For most high *beatitude* demands [exigit] dilection and co-dilection; most high *perfection* a twofold emanation, that is of nature and of liberality; and for this there is at least three persons demanded. — *Likewise*, the reason for *the necessity*, why there cannot be *more*, is most high *simplicity*, which does not suffer the persons to be distinguished, except according to the manners of emanating; and[4] again the *principal fecundity*, which does not permit a person to produce by any genus of ema-

nation, except according to the reckoning of understanding it be prior to it. Whence the first Person, because[5] He is innascible and inspirable, generates and spirates; the second, because (He is) inspirable, but generated, does not generate, but does spirate; but the third Person, because He is spirated and proceeds from one generating, neither generates nor spirates. And for this reason it is impossible, that there be more[6] than three.

The reason for (its) *congruity* is taken from the *sufficiency of the combinations* and from the *perfection of the number three* [numeri ternarii].

From the *sufficiency of the combinations*, because since « there is *love* [amor] among all the Persons », as Richard (of St. Victor) says,[7] and there is not but a threefold love, namely « gratuitous and due and a mingling from both », there are only three Persons: *One*, who only gives, in whom is gratuitous love: *the Other*, who only accepts, in whom is due love; and *a Middle*, who gives and accepts, in whom is a love mingled from both. — *Likewise*, they can be combined in another manner according to the reason of *origin*; and the sufficiency of this manner of combination consists in three things. For it happens [contingit] that one understands a person, who is the beginning [principium] of a person and is not begun [principatum], and *again* a person, who is begun and not a beginning of a person, and in a *third* manner a person, who is begun and a beginning. But the *fourth* manner,[8] because it is neither a beginning nor begun, is entirely impossible and non intelligible.

The reason for the congruity *on the part of number* is, that this number, that is "three", has in itself the *first* and *most high* perfection, considered *in itself*, or in (its) *continuous quantity*, or in the *creature*.[9]

In itself it has *first* perfection, since it is the first number, which is composed [constat] from all its parts, that is from unity and duality, which joined[10] together makes three. But six [senarius] is called the first of perfect (numbers), because it is composed from all of its several parts, that is from three, two, and one. — *Likewise*, there is a *most high* perfection in it, because unity, which is the principle and completion of every number, reflected upon itself by a perfect[11] reduplication, of the kind [qualis] (as is) in a solid quadrate, is tripled according to reason, remaining one according to truth; as if it were called: once one once. And that is very similar to the uncreated Trinity,

---

[1] With the sense saved, many codices, A C F G L O S U V W etc., have *are accepted* [accipiuntur]. A little below this after *of accepting* [accipiendi] we have substituted from the older manuscripts and edition 1 *and/or* [vel] in place of *and* [et]; codex O has *or* [sive].

[2] Codex I has *produce another by that genus, by which it is produced* [producere aliam illo genere, quo producitur], and a little below this *that they produce by these two manners of emanating* [quod his duobus modis emanandi producant].

[3] We have added from the mss. and edition 1 *At any rate* [utique].

[4] Favoring the codices and edition 1, we have substituted *and* [et] in place of *There is* [Est]. Immediately after this many of the codices as A C R S W put *of fecundity* [fecunditatis] in place of *fecundity* [fecunditas], but badly.

[5] We have restored with the help of very many of the ancient manuscripts as A G I K M R S T U W X Y etc. and edition 1 *because* [quia], which the Vatican edition together with the other codices has less congruously changed into *who* [quae]. Then the Vatican edition, disagreeing with the more ancient manuscripts, reads *but the second person* [secunda vero persona] and omits *but* [vero] at *the third* [tertia].

[6] The codices together with edition 1 omit the *persons* [personis] here, which is read in the Vatican edition. A little below this edition 1 inserts *both* [et] after *is taken* [sumitur].

[7] ON THE TRINITY, Bk. V, ch. 23: Therefore, as much as for the substance of dilection there will be one at the same love in all the persons. And ibid., ch. 16: Moreover, it is established, that true love can be either only gratuitous, or only due, or a mingling from both.

[8] Codex X has *In a fourth manner* [Quarto modo] and consequently *impossible and not intelligible* [impossibile nec intelligibile].

[9] Though only few of the codices B D T have *the creature* [creatura] in place of *nature* [natura], we, however, prefer their reading, because it is both more congruous, and all the codices together with the Vatican below (on p.58) in the explanation of this member (of the argument) read *the creature* [creatura].

[10] Many of the codices as A F G H K S T V W X Y etc. together with edition 1 have the neuter plural *joined* [iuncta].

[11] With the agreement of the manuscripts and edition 1, we have deleted *quadrate* [quadrata], which the Vatican edition adds here. A little below this, after *reason* [rationem], there is inserted in codex U *however* [tamen] and in very many of the other codices as A C G K R S V as also in edition 1 the word *the reason* [ratio]; codex ff after *reason* [rationem] inserts *with (its) reckoning* [ratione] by changing *remaining* [remanens] in to *remaining* [remanente].

in which in the unity of the substance there is a trinity of reasons;[1] however, it is not entirely similar, because there with the unity of substance there is a trinity of reasons and of things, that is of Persons; here only a trinity of reasons.

Similarly, if that number is considered in (its) *continuous quantity*, it has in itself a *first* and *most high* perfection: *first*, because every quantity has a principle,[2] middle and last; *most high*, because the most high perfection of continuous quantity consists in a triune dimension, that is in length, width and height. And this is what the Philosopher says in the beginning of ON HEAVEN AND THE WORLD:[3] « For we say everything perfect in threes, and by this number we invite [adhibuimus] our very selves to magnify the one God, the Creator of all things, eminent in the properties of those things which have been created ».

Similarly, if that number is considered in the *creature*, it has in itself a *first* and *most high* perfection: *first*, because one happens to find a trinity of the vestige in every creature, howsoever small, howsoever least: *most high*,[4] because according to the reformed and deiformed trinity of the image the most high and most noble perfection of a creature, that is (its) beatitude, is attained.

1. To that, therefore, which is objected, that the Father gives the Son the whole which He can; it must be said, that it is true, but He does not give[5] *in every manner*, in which He can. And for that reason there is a (fallacy of) accident in the illation: « He cannot give more, therefore,

neither (can) He produce another person », because this is not giving more, but in another manner.

2. Similarly the following[6] is clear, because the Son does not declare in every manner, because even if (He does) according to a reckoning of nature, (He does) not, however, according to a liberality of will, except inasmuch as the Spirit proceeds from the Word Himself.

3. To that which is objected, that the Holy Spirit ought to generate; it must be said, that it is not similar, because[7] the Person of the Son precedes spiration, for that reason He has a reason for primacy; the Person of the Holy Spirit follows generation, and for that reason He does generate, because He is not innascible.

4. To that which is objected concerning the third manner of emanating, that is concerning art: it must be said, that art does not have a fecundity for emanating or for producing except through the will; and for that reason that manner ought not be distinguished from the manner of producing[8] through the manner of liberality or of the will.

And/or in another manner and better. The manner of producing through art convenes with the manner of producing through nature in this, that both ways a like is produced. But it differs, because in the production of a natural (thing) there is produced (a thing) alike[9] in substance and nature, (but) an other in person; but in the production of art there is produced a like according to the reckoning of the exemplar form, an unlike in substance and nature. But such a manner of producing is not co-possible with the Divine Essence, Which is incompatible [non compatitur] with a diversity of essences.

SCHOLIUM

I. What is here said of the properties of numbers, occurs also in the HEXAËMERON, Sermon 4, and also in that EXPOSITION OF THE PSALMS, (Ps. 129), which has been included among the Opera of St. Bonaventure, but whose author has been proven to be Michael Meldensis, Archbishop of Siena († 1199 A. D.), by

Father Fidelis a Fanna (RATIO NOVAE COLLECTIONIS, p. 180 ff.). This ancient doctrine was exhibited by the Greek mathematicians, such as Euclid (ELEMENTALS, Bk. IX, ch. 36), whom St. Augustine (ON A LITERAL EXPOSITION OF GENESIS, Bk. IV, ch. 2), and St. Isidore (ETYMOLOGIES, Bk. III, ch. 3, n. 11;

---

[1] Codex Z adds *and/or reasons* [vel rationem]. For a greater understanding of these things there is noted these words of Bl. (now St.) Albert (the Great): Certain of the moderns say, that relation is a medium of one being and one not being, for this that it is a *reckoning* of the thing and not a thing etc. (SENT., Bk. I, d. 26, a. 10). — A little after this Codex R has *in the unity* [in unitate] in place of *with the unity* [cum unitate].

[2] Many codices as A C F G I K L O S T U Z etc. together with edition 1 have *a first* [primum] in place of *a principle* [principium].

[3] Book I, text 2, where according the Venetian edition of 1489 it is had in the Arabic-Latin translation thus: And this ("three") is the number of anything, and it demonstrates a trinity of things, and we do not find this number except from nature, and we sustain it as if (it were) a law for us; and according to this number we are bound to magnify God the creator remote from the manners of creatures. The Parisian edition has this text thus: For, as the Pythagoreans also say, that everything and all things have been defined by three: for the end, the middle and the principle of every thing has a number: but this (belongs to) a trinity. Wherefore I reckon [numero] this as taken from nature, in a like manner both for the certain law belonging to it [illius] and in celebrating the sacrifices of the gods, as we are accustomed.

[4] We prefer the reading of codex Z which has *most high* [summam] in place of *perfect* [perfectam] as corresponding to the preceding (points). Codex T has *from within* [penes] and Codex V *through* [per] in place of *according to* [secundum]; then with the help of all the manuscripts and editions 2 and 3, we have substituted *deiformed* [deformatam] for *deiform* [deiformem]. Codex R, having omitted the preposition *according to* [secundum], after *of the image* [deiformitatem] adds *in which* [in qua], so that *trinity of image* [trinitatem imaginis] is referred to the above placed *one happens to find* [contingit reperire]; very many of the other codices as A C G K O R S favor this reading inasmuch as they omit the preposition *according to* [secundum].

[5] Very many of the codices not so well omit *He gives* [dat]. A little after this when the Seraphic Doctor says *a fault* [accidens], understand a *fallacy of accident* [fallaciam accidentis], of which Aristotle, ELENCHAE, Bk. I, ch. 4 (ch. 5): From accident there are certain paralogisms, since anything whatsoever has been postulated equally to be in [inesse] thing and accident. For since many things accede to the same thing, it is not necessary, for every predicate and subject, of which they are predicated, that all these be in (it); for otherwise all things will be the same. — In this one concludes falsely from a *thing* [a re] to a *manner of thing* [ad modum rei].

[6] On the authority of the manuscripts and edition 1 we have removed here *objection through this* [obiectio per hoc], added by the Vatican edition. A little below this after *a reckoning* [rationem] codices Y and ee adds *of the origin and (according to) the perfection of (His)* [originis et perfectionem], with which codices G H N and X concord, diverging in this only, that codices H and N omit *and*, in which place codex G has *or* [seu], but codex X *He declares* [declaret]. — On the difference of the manner of proceeding of both cf. below d. 13, q. 3.

[7] Codex R prefaces this with *for* [enim]. Then very many of the more ancient codices as A B C L O T W etc. put *principle* [principium] in place of *reason* [rationem] and then before *the person of the Holy* [persona] the codices together with edition 1 suppress the *but* [autem], which the Vatican edition adds.

[8] We follow codex Y by putting *of producing* [producendi] in place of *of proceeding* [procedendi], which is more conforming to both the preceding and the following, though the sense is the same in both readings.

[9] Codex O has *a like* [similis], which also together with codd. C and Y inserts *and* [et] after *nature* [natura]. A little below this very many of the codd. such as A F G K T etc. together with ed. 1 have *(a thing) unlike* [dissimilis] in place of *an unlike*[dissimile]. Then from very many mss. such as A D F G H K N T etc. and ed. 1 we have substituted *not co-possible for* [incompossibilis] in place of *impossible for* [impossiblis].

ON ARITHMETIC, Bk. I, ch. 20) follow, and innumerable others together with Peter Bunghi (DE NUMERORUM MYSTERIIS., Paris 1617, p. 456) and Stephen Brülifer (in his Commentary on this question). From these authors have been excerpted the things that follow.

1. *Several* [aliquotae] parts or (parts) *of some size* of any number used to be called by the ancients those things, which summed several times rendered precisely their whole. Thus 5 and 2 are some parts of the number 10. A *non-several* part is that, which summed several times cannot render any whole number, as 3 (is) in respect to the number 10. The number 1 is indeed a several part of any number; however, by the ancient mathematicians it did not used to be counted properly among the numbers, but was called *the principle of number*, as (St.) Isidore says (loc. cit., ch. 1), one is the seed of numbers, not a number.

2. The number 6 is the first *perfect* number in the strict sense, because it is equal to all its own several parts aggregated together. For the several parts of this number are 1, 2, 3 = 6. In this sense few numbers are perfect, namely in the series of numbers up to 10,000, as Bunghi says, (there are) only these four: 6, 28, 496, 8128. And thus the number "three" is not perfect, because it has only one several part, that is unity, which properly is not a number.

3. In a less strict sense a number is said (to be) perfect, which consists of all its own parts both several, as non-several, summed together; and in this sense the number "three" is the first perfect, because it consists of a several part (a '1') and a non several (a '2'), which joined together make three. It is called the *first perfect number*, because "two", though it consists of its parts summed together, i. e. two unities, it is not said (to be) a perfect number, because one properly did not used to be called a number.

4. Any number can *be reflected in two manners* upon itself, *imperfectly*, when it is multiplied by itself [ducitur in se ipsum] a single time (as 2 x 2 = 4), and then the number becomes a *quadrate*, but not a *solid*; and/or *perfectly*, when it is multiplied by itself twice (as 2 x 2 x 2 = 8), and this perfect reduplication renders it a *solid quadrate*.

II. With these things presupposed, the threefold proposition of the Seraphic Doctor is clear.

1. The number "three" considered *in itself* has the *first* and *most high* perfection; *first* indeed, because it is the first number consisting [constans] of all of its parts summed together through addition; but *most high*, because *one* tripled remains one (1 x 1 x 1 = 1).

2. Considered as (it is) in a *continuous quantity*, i. e. inasmuch as it is applied to quantity, it has *first* perfection, « because every quantity has a principle, middle and last; but *most high*, because the perfection of continuous quantity consists in a triune dimension, that is, in length, width and height », as is had in the text.

3. Considered as (it is) in *any creature* it again has a *first* and *most high* perfection: *first* indeed, because in any, even the least, creature there is found a trinity of *vestige* (the one, the true, the good); but *most high*, because in the angelic and human nature there is found a trinity of *image*, especially when the most noble part of the soul is reformed imperfectly through the deiformity of *grace* and/or perfectly through the deiformity of *glory*. Concerning this cf. below in d. 3, p. I, a. 1, q. 2 and p. II throughout and in SENT., Bk. II, d. 16 throughout.

III. On this entire question: Alexander of Hales, SUMMA. p. I, q. 45, m. 7. — (Bl. John Duns) Scotus, here in q. 5 and 7, and in REPORTATIO, here in q. 8. — St. Thomas, SENT., Bk. I, d. 10, q. 1, a. 5; SUMMA., I., q. 30, a. 2. — Bl. (now St.) Albert (the Great), SENT., Bk. I, d. 10, a. 12. — Giles the Roman, SENT., Bk. I, d. 10, at the beginning of n. 2. in q. 3. — (Bl.) Dionysius the Carthusian, here in q. 6.

DOUBTS ON THE TEXT OF THE MASTER

DOUBT I

In this part there is, first, a doubt [dubitatio] about the text concerning this which Master (Peter) says, that *it is discerned* [cernitur] *by the most purified minds*. For he seems to speak badly, because no mind, while it is in the wayfarer's state [in via], is the most purified, but only in the Fatherland.

I RESPOND: It must be said, that the mind for this, that it contemplate God perfectly, needs to be purged in regard to (its) *intellect* and *affection* [affectum]; for that reason he says "*through the justice of faith*", that is through the "*faith*", which makes one just in work and by itself [per se] purges the intellect, but *justice* (purges) the affection. But there is a threefold grade of the purgation of both. For the *intellect* is purged, when it is abstracted from sensible species, more purged, when it is cleansed from images of the phantasm, most purged, when (clensed) by philosophical[1] reasons. The grades of the purgation of the affection are these:

the affection is purged, when it is cleansed from fault, more purged, when (cleansed) from (its) consequence [sequela], most purged, (when cleansed) from the occasion (of fault);[2] and in this state it is fit [idoneus] to contemplate.

DOUBT II

Likewise, there is opposed concerning this which he says: *the weak insight* [acies invalida] *of the human mind is not fixed in such an excellent light*, etc.. For it seems, that even[3] (when) cleansed it is not fixed there, because howsoever much it be cleansed, that light still improportionably [improportionabiliter] exceeds the insight of the mind: therefore, is on account of its excellence it cannot be seen by one not having the faith, neither also by one having (it).

I RESPOND: It is different thing [differt] to say: "*to consider*" and "*to be fixed*" and "*to be comprehended*". It can *be considered* by an unclean mind; but '*to be fixed* in It' none can but a pure mind; none can *comprehend* It but a immense (mind).[4] But the reason,

---

[1] Thus codices L and O against the Vatican edition, which has *physical* [physicis]; in many codices on account of the abbreviation the reading is doubtful. But that ours it to be preferred, is clear form the doctrine of the Seraphic Doctor handed down elsewhere. If indeed in perfect contemplation, according to the doctrine of the Seraphic Doctor, which is taken from Dionysius the Areopagite's ON MYSTICAL THEOLOGY, it is proper « to both desert the senses and the *intellectual operations*, both sensibles and invisibles » (ITINERARIUM MENTIS IN DEUM, about the end of ch. 7). These philosophical reasons the Seraphic Doctor enumerates in the book, THE FIRE OF LOVE, before the end of ch. 1., where he says, that He, whom the perfect contemplator loves [diligit], is not demonstrable, definable, opinable ». Cf. ibid., at the end of ch. 3; BREVILOQUIUM, p. V, ch. 6; SENT., Bk. II, d. 23, a. 2, q. 3, in reply to n. 6; HEXAËMERON, about the end of Sermon 2, and about the middle of Sermon 20; COMMENTARY ON LUKE, 9:28. — In regard to the solution of this doubt cf. Alexander of Hales, SUMMA., p. I, q. 2, m. 2, a. 2. — Bl. (now St.) Albert (the Great), here in a. 3. — Richard (of Middleton) and Peter of Tarentaise, here in the exposition of the text.

[2] Against the authority of the mss. and edd. 1, 2, and 6, the Vatican ed., by applying the aforesaid to the objection, adds *but this is possible to be done in the wayfarer's state; for that reason Master (Peter) says: By most purified minds* etc. [hoc autem possibile est fieri in via; ideo dicit Magister: Purgatissimis mentibus etc.]. A little before this very many of the codd. together with ed. 1 after *more purged* [purgatior] and all the codd. together with edd. 1, 3 and 6, after *most purged* [purgatissimus] omit the *when* [cum], added by the Vatican ed..

[3] From the ancient manuscripts and edition 1 we have inserted *even* [etiam], which the Vatican edition together with codex cc omits less well. A little below this codex I has *excels* [excellit] in place of *exceeds* [excedit]; at the end of the objection codex dd adds *it* [eam].

[4] The Vatican edition, against the manuscripts and edition 1, corrupts the text with various additions by reading thus: *The Divine Light can be considered by a mind not cleansed, as by Philosophers; but none can be fixed in It except a mind pure of vices, It cannot be comprehended except in the Fatherland* [Considerat potest lux divina a mente non munda, ut a Philosophis; sed figi non potest in illa nisi mens a vitiis pura, comprehendi non potest nisi in patria].

why it cannot be fixed, is twofold: one, because it is above the intellect, and for that reason the intellect is not fixed in it, unless it has the gluten [gluten] of affection, but immediately falls back;[1] the other reason, because a healthy eye is proportionable to that light qualitatively, even if not quantitatively; but the infirm or bleary [lippus] eye is improportionable in each manner, and for that reason it is not fixed (there).

Doubt III

Likewise, is objected concerning this word of (St.) Ambrose: *God and Lord is a name of nature and a name of power*, because (St. John) Damascene says,[2] that this name, "*God*", is imposed by operation, whence it is said from (the word) <u>aithein</u>, which is to burn, and/or from <u>theein</u>, which is to warm, and/or from <u>theasthai</u>, which is to see.

I Respond: It must be said, that concerning this name, and those exactly like it [consimilibus], there is a twofold manner of speaking: either as much as regard that upon which it is imposed; and thus it is a name of a nature, because it is imposed upon that which[3] is the Most High Nature; or as much as regards that by whom it is imposed; and thus it is a name of an operation, because it is imposed by an operation.

Doubt IV

Likewise, is asked of this circumlocution: *I am who am*, whether this name: "*I am etc.*", is a name of an essence, and/or of a person. And that (it is) of a person, it does seem, because a certain demonstrative pronoun signifies a person. *And again*, speaking is an act of a person. *If perhaps you say*, that "*I*", because it signifies origin, stands for the Person of the Father, "*am*", because it signifies an act of stepping forth, the Person of the Son, "*who*", the relative tying both, stands for the Person of the Holy Spirit; this is nothing, because the relative and antecedent stand for the same one.

I Respond: It must be said, that that name, "*who is*", and "*I am who am*", is properly a name of an essence: for this[4] is a certain circumlocution, signifying an entity in every manner of perfection and absoluteness [absolutione], and this is the proper Name of the Divine Substance. And what is objected, that a pronoun

signifies a certain person; it must be said, that a person is there said (to be) a certain supposit of the Word, and this is a substance and a nature.[5]

Doubt V

Likewise, is asked of this authority: *Let us make man to Our image and Our similitude*, whether "*image*" stands there for *the Essence* or for a *Person*.[6] If for *the Essence*, therefore, saying "*Our image*" is the same, as [quod] "*Our essence*"; if for a *Person*, there ought to be said not "*Our*", but "*My*"; if for the *created* image, it is nothing regarding the proposed, because through this the unity of the nature is not proven.

I Respond: It must be said, that, according to what the Saints here accept, "*image*" and "*similitude*" mean essence and relation.[7] For "*image*" conveys [importat] unity with distinction, and "*similitude*" similarly, on account of (its) intrinsic relation. And for that reason in this name, "*image*" and "*similitude*", as much as regards one of its significations [ad aliquid suae significationis] a unity of essence is noted, as much as regards the other [ad aliquid] a plurality of persons is noted. And for that reason (St.) Augustine expounds (it) in one manner, (St.) Hilary (of Poitiers) expounds (it) in another.[8] (St.) Augustine considers part of the (its) signified, that is the Unity of the Essence; but (St.) Hilary the whole. Whence he says, that by the name of image and similitude there is understood together [simul] the Unity (of the Essence) and the plurality (of Persons). Similarly (St.) Augustine in that which is, the "*let us make*" and "*our*", considers only the consignified; and for that reason the Plurality. But (St.) Hilary considers the signified and the consignified, and[9] for that reason he says that in each there is understood the plurality and the Unity.

Doubt VI

Likewise, (St.) Hilary says: *Neither does the similitude of one to the other permit the diversity to be mixed into the two.*

On the Contrary: A similitude is the same quality of differing things: therefore, similitude is compatible with difference with itself.

I Respond: It must be said, that there is a similitude according to *accident*, and a similitude according to *substance*. And this is twofold, according to the whole and ac-

---

[1] Following several of the codices, such as as A I S Y etc., together with edition 1, which have *falls back* [recidit] in place of *recedes* [recedit]. Then after *proportionable* [proportionabilis] the Vatican edition, not consenting with the manuscripts and edition 1, proceeds thus: *according to quality, even if not according to quantity; but if the eye is infirm or bleary, as in one not having the faith, in each manner it is improportionable* etc. [secundum qualitatem, etsi non secundum quantitatem; sed si oculus sit infirmus sive lippus, sicut est in non habente fidem, utroque etc.].

[2] On the Orthodox Faith, Bk. I, ch. 9, where he thus says (concerning God's names in Greek): According to name, He is θεός (that is God), which is derived from the word or verb θέειν, because He 'runs' and 'circum-obviates' all things, and/or from αἴθειν that is 'to burn': for God is a consuming fire, and/or lastly (from) ἀπὸ τοῦ θεᾶσθαι, that is, because He 'sees completely' [conspiciat] all things. — Favoring the manuscripts and edition 1, we have added *that* [quod] after *Damascene* [Damascenus].

[3] Codex R has *Him who* [ei qui]. At the end of the response with the help the codices and edition 1 we have substituted *operation* [operatione] in place of *work* [opere].

[4] The Greek construction, *this* [haec] in place of *this* [hoc], is exhibited by codices A C G I K S T U aa cc ff together with edition 1.

[5] Concerning this name of God, *Who is*, cf. below in d. 22, q. 3, and Alexander of Hales, Summa., p. I, q. 49, m. 4, a. 1.

[6] Codex K here adds *or for the created image* [aut pro imagine creata], but not so well, because he deals here only with the image, inasmuch as it concerns God; and if the Seraphic Doctor afterwards says *if for the created image*, he says this more by excluding, than by exhibiting it as a member of the disjunction, as is clear from his own words. A little below this after *person* [persona] codex K sufficiently well inserts *either (for) one or many; not (for) many, because he would ought to have said "images"; if for one* [aut una aut pluribus; non pluribus, quia deberet dicere imagines; si pro una].

[7] Although the manuscripts and editions 1, 2 and 3 do not favor it, we have, however, left *and relation* [et relationem], since the context and the doctrine of the Seraphic Doctor below in d. 31, p. II, a. 1, q. 1 and 2, having handed it down most openly, require it. A little before this the Vatican edition against the codices and edition 1 has *holy doctors* [sancti doctores]. Codex R reads *according to what is here accepted, "image" and "similitude" mean essence* [secundum quod hic accipiuntur, imago et similitudo dicunt essentiam].

[8] The words of (Sts.) Augustine and Hilary can be seen above in the text of Master (Peter), ch. 4. — A little after this with the help of the manuscripts and edition 1, we have changed *according* [secundum] into *that is* [scilicet].

[9] We have supplied from the manuscripts the particle *and* [et].

cording to part. A similitude according to *accident*, and/or according to *part* of the substance admits a diversity;[1] but not a similitude according to the *whole*. And since in the Divine Essence there is a Most High Simplicity, for that reason there cannot be a similitude according to accident nor according to a part: and for that reason a similitude is not compatible with a diversity of nature.[2]

DOUBT VII

Likewise, is objected concerning this which Master (Peter) says: *He did signify, by the name of "a sharing" and/or of "plurality" that nothing other be posited, but (rather) be removed*, because from this it seems, that the saying of every numeral according to this posits nothing, but only deprives [privat]; but this seems false. For since among the divine there is a true plurality of Persons, they seem[3] to be spoken of not only privatively, but also positively.

I RESPOND: This was the position of Master (Peter), which is not commonly held, because it does not have the truth, as will be seen better below.[4] However, Master (Peter) is excused, because he said, that numeral names do not posit anything, because they convey [important] number, which is not properly among the divine. For number is caused from unity by aggregation and distinction; and the distinction of unities is made in a threefold manner: by division of the continuous, by inequality [disparatione] of forms,[5] by grade or order. Therefore, since among the divine there is no aggregation nor such[6] a distinction, for that reason neither (is there) number properly (speaking).

DOUBT VIII

Likewise, there is asked of this which he says: *In the beginning God created*, "Why does this name, *"God"*, stand or suppose more for the Person of the Father than for the Person of the Son, and in what manner is the Trinity understood from this?"

I RESPOND: To this it must be said, that[7] in eight manners the plurality of the Persons is hinted to us in Scripture. In the first manner by *signification*; in the last (chapter) of (St.) Matthew:[8] *In the Name of the Father and of the Son and of the Holy Spirit*. In the second manner[9] by *consignification*; at the beginning of Genesis, where we have *"God"* [Deus], the Hebrews have *Elohim*, which is the nominative plural of this singular *El*. In the third manner by *supposition*, as when there is said: "God begot God"; in the eighth (chapter) of Proverbs:[10] *Before all the hills the Lord has generated Me*. In the fourth manner by *appropriation*, as there:[11] *In the beginning God created* etc. For there *"God"* is appropriated there to the Father and *The Beginning* to the Son. In the fifth manner by *iteration*, as in the sixth (chapter) of Isaias:[12] *Holy, Holy, Holy the Lord God Sabaoth*. In the sixth manner by the *order of words*; the Psalm:[13] *May He bless us God, our God, may He bless us God*. In the seventh manner by *connotation* in the act of mission, as when there is said in the fourth (chapter) to the Galatians:[14] *God sent* etc.. In the eighth manner by *apparition*, just as the three men appeared to Abraham; in the eighteenth (chapter) of Genesis.[15]

DOUBT IX

Likewise, is objected concerning this which he says: *Also that greatest of the Prophets and kings, David*, because on that (verse from) the seventeenth (chapter) of (St.) Matthew:[16] *There appeared to them Moses and Elijah*, the Gloss says: « Elijah was the greatest of the Prophets »: therefore, David (was) not.

I RESPOND: The spirit of prophecy, given in greater abundance, made him a more excellent prophet of the Lord. Therefore it can be given in a greater abundance in a twofold manner: either because (its is) for *more*, or because (it is) for *higher* ones. Elijah was given (it) for more, because (it was) for a prevision of future things and the working of miracles; but David for higher ones, because, as is clear from his prophecy, he saw more and[17] and more clearly, because (it was by) an intellectual prophecy.

DOUBT X

Likewise, is objected concerning this which he says: *The Lord possessed me*; because *possession* belongs to an inferior thing, *order*,

---

[1] Codex K adds *of substance* [substantiae].

[2] For more on this matter see d. 31, p. I, a. 1, q. 1 and 2.

[3] Codices F and X and editions 4 and 5 have *it seems* [videtur].

[4] On this sentence of Master (Peter) cf. below in d. 24, q. 2, q. 1.

[5] Many codices as A C F G K L O R S T X Z etc. together with editions 2, 3, 4, 5 and 6 have less congruently *dispersion* [dispersione], others *disposition* [dispositione]; the Vatican ed. has disperatione; codd. H P Q ee and ff and ed. 1 exhibit the reading received in the text (above).

[6] The Vatican edition, against the manuscripts, has *nor a distinction in such a manner* [taliter].

[7] From the manuscripts and edition 1 we have inserted *that* [quod].

[8] Verse 10.

[9] From the mss. we have inserted *manner* [modo]; then with the help of the manuscripts we have deleted *created* [creavit] after *at the beginning* [principio], so that *at the beginning* [in principio] is not itself a text of Sacred Scripture, but indicates a place in the text. Then in the Vatican edition there is lacking *have* [habent] and after *of this* [huius] there is added *nominative* [nominativi], but against the codices and edition 1. Codex X has *number* [mumerus] in place of *nominative* [nominativus].

[10] Verse 25, where the Vulgate reads: *Before the hills I was born* [Ante colles ego parturiebar], while the Brixen edition of Sacred Scripture (1496 A.D.) adds *all* [omnes], with which the Vatican edition agrees and adjoins: *that is, the Lord generated Me* [omnes colles generat me]. On behalf of the reading the codices and the translation from the Septuagint militate: *before all the hills He generates Me* [omnes colles generat me], and (St.) Augustine, ON THE TRINITY, Bk. I, ch. 12, n. 24: *before all the hills He generated Me* [ante omnes colles genuit me]; (St.) Cyprian, TESTIMONIES, Bk. II, ch.. 1; (St.) Hilary (of Poitiers), ON THE TRINITY, Bk. XII, n. 37 and (St.) Justin, DIALOGUE WITH TRYPHO, n. 61.

[11] Gen 1:1. — The Vatican ed. against the mss. omits *as* [ut]. A little after this the codd. together with ed. 1 in an exceedingly abbreviated manner have: *God for the Father and Beginning for the Son* [Deus Patri et Principium Filio].

[12] Verse 3.

[13] Psalm 66:6.

[14] Verse 4.

[15] Verse 2. — The Vatican edition disagreeing with the manuscripts and edition 1 has *had appeared* [apparuerant]. — Cf. on this doubt Alexander of Hales, SUMMA, p. I, q. 67, m. 4, who enumerates seven of these manners. Richard of Middleton nearly repeats the same, here in a. 2. q. 4.

[16] Verse 3.

[17] In the Vatican edition there is wanting the *and* [et], which the manuscripts and edition 1 exhibit. — On intellectual prophecy and vision cf. SENT., Bk. II, d. 10, a. 3, q. 2 in the body (of the quest ion); HEXAEMERON, Sermon 9; CENTILOQUIUM, p. III, section 46. — St. Augustine, ON THE LITERAL EXPOSITION OF GENESIS, Bk. XII, ch. 6 ff. and the book, AGAINST ADIMANTUS, a disciple of Manichee, ch. 28. — On the question: who was *simply the greatest* of the Prophets, see St. Thomas, SUMMA., II. II., q. 174, q. 4, where he says: that though as much as regards one of some other of the Prophets Moses was the greater, however simply (speaking) Moses was greater than all of them. (Nicholas) of Lyra in his preface to ON THE PSALMS strives to infringe upon the reasons of St. Thomas; (Bl.) Dionysius the Carthusian in the foreword to (his), EXPOSITION ON THE PSALMS, undertakes to reconciles the contrary opinions.

to a posterior thing, *conception* resounds similarly unto the fragility of the sex and similarly (unto the fragility) of *giving birth* [partus]; none of which[1] convene with divine things.

I Respond: Wisdom is described through a comparison to an *effect* and through a comparison to a *principle*. Since through a comparison to an *effect* it both has in itself a treasure infinite in numerosity, and has order in discretion,* for that reason it is described by the word for *being possessed* and for *being ordered*.[2] Through a comparison to its principle, it emanates by an intrinsic emanation in that which concerns the substance of the one emanating; for that reason it is described by the word for conception and parturition.

DISTINCTION III

Part I

Chapter I
On the cognition of the Creator through the creatures, in which the vestige of the Trinity appears

For the Apostle also says,[1] that *the invisible (things) of God by the creature of the world through those things which have been made, being understood, are perceived, (as are) also His sempiternal virtue and Divinity*. By *the creature of the world*° there is understood man « on account of the excellence, by which he excels among the other creatures, and/or on account of the encounter [convenientiam], which he has with every creature ». Therefore, man could by the understanding of (his) mind perceive the invisible things of God and/or did also perceive (them) *through those things which have been made*, that is, through creatures visible and/or[2] invisible. For from the two he is helped, that is from nature, which was rational, and from the works wrought [facit] by God, to manifest truth to man. For that reason the Apostle said:[3] *that God revealed to them*, that is while He wrought the works, in which the evidence of the Craftsman [aritificis] glittered to some extent.

For as (St.) Ambrose says:[4] « So that God, who is by nature invisible, might also be able to be known by visible (things), He wrought a work, which manifested the Worker by its own visibility, that the uncertain might be known through the certain, and that He might be believed to be the God of all, He who made this, which by man is impossible to be wrought ». Therefore, they could cognize or they did cognize, that beyond every creature is He who made those (things), which none of the creatures has the strength [valet] to do and/or destroy.[5] Let the creature, howsoever strong [quaecumque vis], approach and let it make such a heaven and such an earth, and I will say, that it is God. But because no creature has the strength [valet] to make such (things), it is established, that He who made them is above every creature; and through this (line of reasoning) the human mind could cognize, that He is God.

In another manner, by the lead of reason, they were able to and/or even did cognize the truth of God. For as (St.) Augustine says in the book, On the City of God:[6] « The highest philosophers saw that no body is God, and for that reason they transcended all other bodies, seeking God (as they did); they also says, that whatever is mutable is not the Most High God and principle of all (things), and for that reason they transcended every soul and the mutable spirits; then they saw, that everything, which is mutable, cannot be except by Him, who incommutably and simply is. Therefore, they understood, that He both had made all these (things) and that He could come to be [fieri] from none (of them) ».

« They also considered, that whatever is in substances is a body and/or a spirit, and that any spirit is better than a body, but better by far Him who made spirit and body ».

« They also understood, that the appearance [species] of a body is sensible and the appearance of a spirit is intelligible, and they preferred the intelligible appearance to the sensible. We call sensibles, what can [queunt] be sensed by the sight or touch of a body, intelligibles, what (can) be understood by the sight [conspectu] of the mind.[7] Therefore, since in their sight both the body and the human spirit [animus] were more and less apparent [speciosa]; but if they could lack every appearance, they would be entirely nothings [nulla]: they saw that there is a Something, by which those (things) are made apparent, where there is a first and incommutable Appearance, and for that reason incomparable; and that It is the principle of things they did most rightly believe, because It had not been made, and (because) all other (things) had been made from It ». Behold, in so many manners the truth of God could be cognized. Therefore, though [cum] God is the one and simple essence, which consists of no diversity of parts and/or of accidents, the Apostle says, however, in the plural: *the invisible (things) of God*, because the truth of God is cognized in very many manners through those (things) which have been made. For from the perpetuity of creatures the eternal Founder is understood; from the magnitude of creatures the Omnipotent One; from (their) order and disposition the Wise One; from (His) governance (of them) the Good One. Moreover, all these (things) tend ultimately [pertinent] to manifest the unity of the Deity.

---

[1] The Vatican edition against the more ancient codices together with edition 1 adds *all* [omnia].

[2] Not trusting in the mss. and ed. 1, having changed the construction, the Vatican ed. here proceeds thus: *It is described also through a comparison to its principle, from which it emanates* [Describitur etiam per comparationem ad suum principium, a quo emanat]. A little below this cod. R omits the preposition *in* [thus reading *for the reason that it concerns*] and very many of the codd., such as K M X Y and ee, after *of the one emanating* [emanantis] add *by a perfect emanation* [emanatione perfecta].

NOTES ON THE BOOK OF SENTENCES

[1] Rom. 1:20; the Vulgate reads: *For the invisible (things) of Him by the creature* [Invisibilia enim ipsius a creatura]. The ordinary Gloss, which Master (Peter), with a few words varied, uses next, interprets the word *by the creature* [a creatura], thus: *By man through excellence, because he excels among the other creatures, and/or on account of the encounter which he has with all creatures*. Then, the Vulgate has *His virtue* [eius virtus] in place of *the virtue of Him* [virtus eius], which our mss. and edd. exhibit in complete agreement.

[2] Codices C D and E have *and* [et].

[3] A reference to Rom. 1:19: *What is known of God, has been made manifest unto them. For God has manifested it to them* [Quod notus est Dei, manifestum est in illis. Deus enim illis manifestavit]. — The Vatican edition together with the other editions has *And therefore* [ideoque], against all the codices and editions 1 and 8.

[4] On the Epistle to the Romans, ch. 1, v. 19, with a few things changed and omitted by Master (Peter). At the end of this text before *it is impossible* [impossibile est] the Vatican edition alone superfluously repeats: *(St.) Ambrose said* [ait Ambrosius].

[5] Mss. B D & E have *can* [potest]. Then the Vatican ed. alone reads: *the creature, whatever ones you wish* [quaecumque vis creaturae], understanding vis as a form of velle and quaecumque as a neuter plural. Immediately after, the same Vatican ed. prefaces *earth* [terram] with *such* [talem], having left out the other many things, against the codd. and edd. 1, 6 & 8.

[6] Book VIII, ch.6, with not a few things transposed and omitted. Below, the 3rd and 4th reason likewise, ibid.. A little before this, only cod. D has *and they did* [potuerunt et] for *and/or even did* [potuerunt vel etiam].

[7] The editions against our codices and Augustine's edition, by putting a period before *intelligibles*, and adding *can* [possunt] has *Intelligibles, which can* [Intelligibilia quae ... possunt].

---

*   *Trans. note*: Regarding *discretion*, cf. above p. E-16.
°   The Vulgate's use of the future active participle (creatura), to render ἀπὸ κτίσεως κόσμου in Rom. 1:20 as a creatura mundi, mislead the medievals away from the sense of the original Greek: *from the creation of the world*.

Now there remains to show, whether through those (things) which have been made anything could be regarded a vestige or scanty [exiguum][1] evidence of the Trinity. On this (St.) Augustine in the sixth book, ON THE TRINITY says: « It is proper, that perceiving the Creator with (our) intellect [intellectu] through the (things) which have been made, we understand the Trinity. For the vestige of this Trinity appears [apparet] in creatures. For all these (things),[3] which have been made by the Divine Art, both show a certain unity in themselves and an outward-appearance [species] and an order. For each of these creators is also some *one* [unum aliquid], as are the natures of bodies and of souls, and (each) is formed by some *species* [species], as are the figures and/or qualities of bodies and the doctrines and/or arts of souls, and (each) seeks or holds some *order*, as are the weights and/or positions [collocationes] of bodies and the loves [amores] and/or delectations of souls; and thus does the vestige of the Trinity shine forth in creatures. For in that Trinity there is a Most High Origin of all things [omnium rerum] and a Most Perfect Beauty [pulcritudo] and a Most Blessed Delectation ». « But the Most High Origin », as (St.) Augustine shows in the book, ON THE TRUE RELIGION,[4] « is understood to be God the Father, from whom are all things [omnia], from whom (is) the Son and the Holy Spirit. The Most Perfect Beauty is understood (to be) the Son, that is the Truth of the Father, dissimilar to Him from no vantage point [nulla ex parte], which[5] we venerate with and in the Father Himself, which is the Form of all, which has been made from the One and are referred to the One, which all, however, would neither have come to be from the Father through the Son nor would have been safe in their confines [suis finibus], unless God was the most highly Good, who both envies no nature, which[6] is good

from Him, and grants that the one as much as it wants, the other as much as it can, remain in the Good itself; which goodness is understood (to be) the Holy Spirit, who is the Gift of the Father and the Son. On which account, it is fitting that the very Gift of God, equally incommutable with the Father and the Son, take care of us [colere] and hold us. And, thus, through the consideration of creatures we understand the Trinity (to be) of one substance, that is the one God the Father, from whom we are, and the Son, through whom we are, and the Holy Spirit, in whom we are, that is the Principle, back to which we run, and the Form which we follow, and the Grace by which we are reconciled: that is, the One, by Whom, as Author, we have been founded; and His Similitude, through Which we are reformed according to a unity, and the Peace, by which we adhere to the Unity: namely, to the God, who said:[7] *Let there be*; and the Word, through which there is made everything, which substantially and naturally is; and the Gift of His benignity, Who was pleased that what was wrought by Him through the Word and reconciled to the Author, might not perish ». Behold, it has been shown, how among creatures to some extent the image of the Trinity is indicated; for through the contemplation of creatures a sufficient knowledge [notitia] of the Trinity cannot be had nor could it without the revelation of doctrine and/or of interior inspiration. Whence those ancient philosophers, as if through a shadow and from afar, saw the truth, deficient (as they were) in the contuition of the Trinity, like [ut] the magi of the Pharaoh at the third sign.[8] We, however, are helped to believe invisible things [in fide invisibilium] through those (things), which have been made.

PART II

CHAPTER II

On the image and similitude of the Trinity in the human soul

But, now, « let us come presently [iam] to that disputation, where in the human mind, which knows God and/or can know (Him), we discover the image of the Trinity ». For as (St.) Augustine says in the fourteenth book, ON THE TRINITY:[9] « Though the human mind is not of that nature, of which God is, however, the image of Him, better than whom nothing is, is to be sought and found in that, better than which our nature has

nothing, that is, in the mind. For[10] in the mind itself, even before it is a partaker of God, His image is discovered; for even if, having lost (its) participation in God, it be deformed, the image of God, however, thoroughly remains. For the image of God is a mind for this very (reason), because it is capable of Him and can be a partaker of Him. Therefore, let us now search in it for the Trinity, which is God. Therefore[11] behold: the mind remembers itself, understands itself, loves [diligit] itself; if we discern this, we discern a trinity, not, yet, indeed the God, but the image of God. For here there appears a certain trinity of memory, intelligence and love [amoris] ». These three, therefore, let us treat with most of all: memory, intelligence, will ». « Therefore, these three », as (St.) Augustine says

---

[1] Codex A omits *scanty*[exiguum]; codices B C D and E and edition 1, having omitted *vestige* [vestigium]and transposed the words, reads well enough *evidence of the Trinity even a meager one* [vel exiguum], having read *and/or* [vel] for *at least* [saltem] or for *even* [etiam].

[2] Chapter 10, n. 12, but with a transposition of the propositions. — At the beginning of this text the Vatican edition and edition 4 read badly *which have been made understood* [intellecta] in place of *with (our) intellect* [intellectu]; Augustine's edition has *the Creator understood through those things* [intellectum].

[3] All the codices and editions, besides the Vatican edition, omit *all ... things* [omnia], which however, both Augustine's edition and St. Bonaventure, below in Doubt n. 3, have. — A little after this codices C and E together with the text of (St.) Augustine have *whatever of these* [quidquid horum] in place of *each of these* [quodque horum]. Then the Vatican edition and editions 4, 5, 6 and 7, together with the text of (St.) Augustine inserts *the natural qualities* [ingenia] before *of souls* [animarum], which is lacking in all the codices and other editions.

[4] Gathered from ch. 55, n. 113 passim. — In the first proposition of this text after *all (things)* [omnia] only cod. C adds the particle *and* [et].

[5] The Vatican ed. and the other edd. against ed. 6 and all the codd. has *whom* [quem] in place of *which* [quam] and the against the same codd. and edd. 1, 4, 5, 6, 7 & 8, have *who* [qui] in place of *which* [quae]. Our reading is confirmed by the text of (St.) Augustine, who has: *Wherefore that truth, dissimilar in no way*

[nulla ex parte] we also venerate in Him and with Him, (that truth) which is the Form of all (things), which have been made by the One. — A little after this codex C has *by Him* [ab ipso] and editions 5 and 6 *from the start* [ab initio] in place of *from the One*. Then codex D has *which would not at all have come to be* [quae omnino non fierent] in place of *which all, however, neither would have come to be* [quae tamen omnia nec fierent].

[6] Codices A B C and E have well enough *because it* [quod], but disagreeing with the editions and the text of (St.) Augustine. Immediately after this codices A and B and editions 9 and 10 have *from the Good itself* [ab ipso bono] in place of *good from Him* [ab ipso bona].

[7] Gen. 1:3. — The Vatican edition together with editions 4, 5, 6 and 8 and codices D and E adds *light* [lux] badly after *Let there be* [fiat], by disagreeing with the rest of the editions and codices and also the text of (St.) Augustine.

[8] Ex 8:18.

[9] Chapter 8, n. 11, whence there are also understood, what precedes (this), from the words: *But now* [Nunc vero], but as is usual with not a few things omitted and/or added.

[10] The Vatican edition and the other editions, except 1 and 8, have less well: *Even in that mind before* [In ipsa etiam mente antequam].

[11] The Vatican edition against the codices and editions 1 and 6 reads *for* [enim]; and a little after this editions 2, 3 and 7 before *if we discern* [si cernimus] have *these things* [haec] in place of *this* [hoc].

in the tenth book, ON THE TRINITY,[1] « there are not three lives, but one life, nor three minds, but one mind, one essence. But "memory" is said regarding something, and "intelligence" and "will" or "dilection" similarly is said regarding something; but "life" and "mind" and "essence" is said regarding itself. Therefore, these three for this reason are one, because (there is) one life, one mind, one essence; and whatever else those each [singula] are said (to be) regarding themselves, they are at the same time also said, not in the plural, but in the singular. But for this reason they are three, because they are referred to one another [se invicem] ».

« They are also equal not only each to each [singula singulis], but also each to all [singula omnibus]; otherwise they would not seize one another; but they do seize one another. For they are grasped[2] both each by each and all by each. For I remember, that I have a memory and intelligence and a will; and I understand, that I understand and will and remember; and I will, that I will and remember and understand ».

« And I remember at once my whole memory and intelligence and will. For what I do not remember of my memory, that is not in my memory; but nothing is so in the memory, as the memory itself: therefore[3] I remember the whole. Likewise, whatever I understand, I know [scio] that I understand, and I know, that I will whatever I will; but whatever I know I remember. Therefore I remember my whole intelligence and whole will ».

« Similarly, when I understand these three, I at once understand the whole. For neither is there anything belonging to intelligibles, which I do not understand, unless I am ignorant of it. But because I am ignorant, I neither remember nor will. Therefore[4] whatever of intelligibles I do not understand, I also consequently do not remember nor will. Therefore, whatever of intelligibles I remember and will, I consequently understand ».

« The will also seizes my whole intelligence and my whole memory, while I use the whole of what [toto eo quod] I understand and remember. And so since by each [a singulis] in turn there are seized both every one and each entirely [omnia et tota], each entirely [tota singula] is equal to each entirely and each entirely at the same time (is equal) to all entirely; and these three (are) one, one life, one mind, one essence ». « Behold of that Most High Unity and Trinity, where one is the Essence and three the Persons, the human mind is the image, though not the peer [impar] ».[5] But "mind" is here accepted for the human spirit [animo] itself, where that image of the Trinity is; « but properly the "mind" means », as (St.) Augustine says,[6] « not the soul itself, but what in it is the more excellent », in which manner it is often accepted. That also one must know, that the memory is not only of (things) absent and (things) past, but also of (things) present, as (St.) Augustine says in the fourteenth book, ON THE TRINITY,[7] otherwise it would not seize itself.

Here, there must be diligently attended, in [ex] which

sense there must be accepted what is said above, that the three, that is the memory, intelligence and the will, are "one" [unum], (are) "one mind", (and) "one essence". Because, at any rate, it does not seem to be true according to [iuxta] the propriety of speech [proprietatem sermonis]. For the mind, that is the rational spirit, is an essence, spiritual and incorporeal. But those three natural properties or strengths [vires] belong to the mind itself and differ from one another [a se invicem], because memory is not intelligence and/or will, nor intelligence will or love [amor].

« And these three also are referred to themselves », as (St.) Augustine says in the ninth book, ON THE TRINITY:[8] « For the mind cannot love and/or remember itself, unless it also knows [noverit] itself: for in what manner does it love and/or remember what it does not know [nescit] »? And so in a wonderful manner those three are inseparable from their very selves [semetipsis]; and yet [tamen] each of them and all together are one essence, since they are also said in a relative manner [relative] regarding one another.

But presently [iam] it must be seen, in what manner these three are said (to be) "one substance"; for that reason that is, because in the soul itself and/or in the mind they exist substantially, not as accidents in subjects, which can be present [adesse] and absent. Whence (St.) Augustine in the ninth book, ON THE TRINITY[9] says: « We are admonished, that (they are there) substantially, not as in a subject, as color in a body, because even if they are said[10] in a relative manner regarding one another, they are, however, each [singula] in their own substance ». Behold in what sense those three are said to be "one" [unum] and/or "one substance". « Which three », as (St.) Augustine says in the fifteenth book, ON THE TRINITY,[11] « having been divinely instituted in the mind naturally, anyone ascertains in a lively manner [vivaciter perspicit], and how there is among them (something) great, from which even the Sempiternal and Immutable Nature can be reflected upon [recoli], plainly seen, (and) completely desired [concupisci] (for It is called to mind through memory, intuited through intelligence, embraced through dilection), (and) in a word (how) one discovers the image of that Most High Trinity ».

CHAPTER III

On the similitude of the creating and created trinity.

« However, let one still beware, lest he compare the image made from the same Trinity so to himself, that he estimates himself entirely similar, but rather in that similitude however, great let him discern [cernat] also the dissimilitude ».[12]

« Which can briefly be shown. One man through those three remembers, understands, loves [diligit], he who is neither memory nor intelligence nor dilection, but (who) has them. Therefore one man is he, who has these three, he is not these three. But in the Most High Simplicity of that Nature, which is God, although God is one, however, there are three Persons,

---

[1] Chapter 11, nn. 17 and 18. From the same chapter are taken all those, which follow up to: *Behold of that Most High Unity* [Ecce illius summae Unitatis].

[2] The Vatican edition and edition 9, corrupted, have *they seize* [Capiunt]. Immediately before this codices D and E have *also* [etiam] in place of *for* [enim], but against the text of Augustine and the other codices and all the editions.

[3] The codices and the text of Augustine have *therefore* [igitur] instead of *therefore* [ergo]. A little after this against the context and the original very many codices and editions have *I remember I know* [memini scio] in place of *I remember I know* [scio memini].

[4] The editions have *therefore* [ergo] instead of *therefore* [igitur].

[5] ON THE TRINITY, Book X, ch. 12, n. 19: « of whom the human mind is the uneven [impar] image, but nevertheless an image »; but the first part of the proposition is from Book XV, ch. 7, n. 11. — Before this the Vatican edition omits *there is* [est] after *where*. A little after this codex D has *the soul itself* [anima ipsa] in place of *the human spirit itself* [animo ipso].

[6] ON THE TRINITY, Book XV, ch. 7, n. 11, according to its sense.

[7] Chapter 11, n. 14, where in a longer discourse he proves this sentence received by St. Bonaventure (cf. here in p. II, a. 1. q. 1. in reply to n. 3).

[8] Chapter 3, n. 3, but as he does, Master (Peter) has added those (words) which are referred to the memory, namely *and/or remember* [vel meminisse] and *and/or remember* [vel meminit].* The preceding words *And these three* [Et haec tria], already cited above, occur in Book X, ch. 11, where editions 1, 6 and 8 have *to one another* [ad se invicem] in place of *to themselves* [ad se ipsa].

[9] Chapter 4, n. 5. But much more fully in (St.) Augustine. A little before this in place of *and absent* [et abesse] the Vatican edition together with editions 2, 3, 4, 5 and 7 reads *and/or absent* [vel abesse].

[10] Codex B and ed. 2 have (the subjunctive) *they are said* [dicantur].

[11] Chapter 20, n. 39, where *for* [enim] is lacking before *It is called to mind* [reminiscitur], and it is absent also from manuscripts B C and D; the rest, having also omitted it, the words *It is called to mind through memory* [reminiscitur per memoriam] etc. seem to be a parenthesis.

[12] Ibid., but with not a few things adjoined.

---

* *Trans. note*: Here -(s) and -(er)- have been removed from the two Latin forms of memini, respectively, which are erroneously written in the original foonote.

the Father and the Son and the Holy Spirit »,[1] and these Three[2] (are) the One God. « And thus the one is the Thing [res] itself of the Trinity, the other the image of the Trinity in another thing [in re alia]; on account of which image even that in which these three are, is said (to be) an "image", that is man. As the image is said (to be) both a "tablet" [tabula] and a "picture", which is in it; but a tablet is called by the name, "image", on account of the picture, which is in it ».[3]

« Again, that image of Him, which is the man having those three, is one person. But that of the Trinity is not one person, but Three Persons, the Father of the Son and the Son of the Father and the Spirit of the Father and of the Son. And, thus, in this his image of the Trinity, these three are not the one man, but belong to the one man. But in that Most High Trinity, Whose image this is, those Three do not belong to the one God, but (are) the one God; and those are three, not one Person ».[4] « For those three are not one man, but are of a man and/or or in a man. But could we ever [nunquid] say, that the Trinity is so in God, that It is something of God, or that It is God »?[5] Far be it that we believe this! Therefore, let us say, that there is in our mind an image of the Trinity,[6] but (that it is) a scanty one and of some kind [qualemcumque], which so bears a similitude of the Most High Trinity [trinitatis], that for the most part [ex maxima parte] it is dissimilar. But it must be known, that « this Trinity of the mind », as (St.) Augustine says in the fourteenth book, ON THE TRINITY,[7] is not on that account only an image of God, that (as) a mind remembers itself and understands and loves itself, but that it can also remember and understand and love Him, by whom it was made ».

In the soul, there can also be distinguished, in another manner and by other names, the trinity, which is the image of that Most High and Ineffable Trinity. For as (St.) Augustine says in the ninth book, ON THE TRINITY:[8] « Mind and its knowledge [notitia] and love [amor] are a certain three. For mind knows [novit] itself and loves itself; nor can it love itself, unless it also knows itself. A certain two are the mind and its knowledge; likewise a certain two are the mind and its love ». Therefore, when the mind knows itself and loves itself, there remains a trinity, that is the mind, love and knowl-

edge ». « But the "mind" is here accepted not for the soul, but for that which is the more excellent in the soul ». But these three, though they be distinct from one another, are, however, said "to be one", because they exist substantially in the soul.[9]

And the mind itself is a quasi parent, and its knowledge the quasi offspring of it. « For the mind when it cognizes itself, begets knowledge [notitiam] of itself and is the only parent of its own knowledge. The third is the love [amor], which proceeds from the mind itself and (its) knowledge, while the mind cognizing itself loves [diligit] itself; for it cannot love itself, unless it cognizes itself. It also loves [amat] its pleasing offspring, that is its knowledge; and thus love is indeed a certain embrace [complexus] of parent and offspring ».[10]

« For is the offspring less than the parent, while the mind knows itself (to be) as great [tanta], as it is; nor is love less than the parent and the offspring, that is than mind and knowledge, while the mind loves itself as much [tantum], as it knows itself and as much as it is ».[11]

« These are also each [singula] in themselves, because the mind loving is also in love, and love in knowledge of the one loving, and knowledge is in the mind knowing ».[12] Behold among these three there appears a vestige, of some kind [qualecumque], of the Trinity.

And thus the rational mind, considering these three and that one essence, in which these of his [ista] are, extends itself to the contemplation of the Creator and sees unity in trinity and trinity in unity. For it understands, that there is one God, one Essence, one Principle. For it understands, that if there were two, each would be insufficient, and/or one of the two would be superfluous; that if anything were lacking to the one, which the other had, there would not be a most high perfection there; but if there were lacking to the one nothing, which the other had, since in the one would be all things [omnia], the other would be superfluous. Therefore, it understood, that there is one God, one[13] Author of all, and it sees, that He is not without wisdom, as if (He were) a foolish thing [res fatua]; and for that reason it understood, that He has a wisdom, which is begotten from Himself; and because He loves [diligit] His own wisdom, it also understood, that there is a Love [amorem] there.

---

[1] Loc. cit., ch. 22, n. 42, according to the sense. — In place of *through those three* [per illa tria] the Vatican edition and not a few of the editions has *through those three of his* [per ista tria], and below editions 1 and 8 after *not* [non] add *however* [tamen]. Then the Vatican edition and very many of the editions read *the simplicity of that Most High Nature* [summae simplicitate naturae].

[2] The Vatican ed. together with many edd. adds *persons are* [personae sunt] by way of explanation.   [3] Ibid., n. 43.

[4] Loc. cit.. — All the editions, except 1, at the end of the text after *those are three* [sunt illae] inserts *persons* [personae] against the codices and the original. A little before this the modern editions of (St.) Augustine, having omitted *not* [non], read *is, are of the one God* [est unius Dei sunt], but this reading conveys a false expression and it both does not corresponds to the context and removes the antithesis. For those three, that is the memory, the intellect, the will, through an appropriation taken for the three Persons, *strictly* cannot be said to be "*of the one God*", but are *God* and *the one God*, because among the Persons and the Essence there is [datur] no real distinction. And so rightly does (St.) Augustine deny the parity of the created and uncreated image. For those three *are* of one man, since the powers of a man *are not* a man, but *are had* by a man. But the three Persons in the strict sense *are* the one God. This (St.) Augustine himself in the following text. — See below in Doubt 10, where the Seraphic Doctor not only admits with Master (Peter) the negative particle, but shows that the proposition is simply false by its defect.

[5] Loc. cit., ch. 7, n. 11, but much more at length.

[6] Codices B C D E and A (by the primary hand) and edition 1 have *a trinity of image* [imaginis trinitatem], which reading is neither commended in itself nor well coherent with the words in the accusative *but a scanty one and of whatever a kind* [sed exiguam et qualemcumque]. The Vatican edition alone immediately adjoins *thus* [ita]. — This conclusion of Master (Peter) is found, according to its sense, in (St.) Augustine, loc. cit., ch. 22, n. 43.

[7] Chapter 12, n. 15. — Codex A B D and E and edition 1 omit *be* [est] in *It must ... known* [Sciendum vero]. Then in the same text of (St.) Augustine the codices, except D, and very many of the editions incongruously has the subjunctive form of *remembers* [meminerit] instead.

[8] Chapter 4, n. 4: « But just as there are a certain mind and its love, when it loves itself; so a certain two are the mind and its knowledge, when it knows itself. Therefore, the mind itself and the love and its knowledge are a certain three, and these three are one thing [unum], and when they have been perfected, they are equals ». Those which follow have been taken from ch. 5, n. 8; concerning the last text see above in footnote 6, on p. 64.

[9] The codd. and edd. 1, 3, 5, 6, 7 and 9 have *the human spirit* [animo].

[10] (St.) Augustine, ON THE TRINITY, Bk. IX, ch. 12, n. 18, where there is read, moreover, many things that have been adjoined and changed. In which text codex C has *its* [eius] before *knowledge* [procedit]. Then the Vatican edition together with a few other editions has *cognizes itself it also loves* [cognoscit se et diligit] in place of *cognizing itself loves* [cognoscens se diligit]. With a few things interjected, codices A D and E read *For it loves* [Amat enim] in place of *It also loves* [Amat etiam], but against the context, since a twofold love of the mind is being distinguished, that is "toward itself" and "toward its offspring".

[11] Loc. cit.   [12] (St.) Augustine, loc. cit, ch. 5, n. 9.

[13] Absent in the Vatican edition and a few other of the editions is *one* [unam]. And a little below this at *without wisdom* [absque sapientia] the Vatican edition against the authority of the codices and editions, having omitted the particle *not* and hence varied the sense, has *He is without wisdom like* [quasi] *a foolish thing*. In our and the true reading understand *He were* [esset] before *a foolish thing* [fatua: which order is reversed in the Latin]. At the end of the chapter codices A B and D have *it understood in this, that there is also* [intellexit ibi, etiam esse], which reading confirms the sense implied in our punctuation of the text.

CHAPTER IV

On the unity of the Trinity

« Wherefore, in accord with this consideration », as (St.) Augustine says in the ninth book, ON THE TRINITY,[1] « let us believe, that the Father and the Son and the Holy Spirit are one God, the Founder and Ruler of each and every [universae] creature; that the Father is not the Son, nor that the Holy Spirit is the Father and/or the Son, but that (there is) a Trinity of Persons related to one another ». For as he himself says in the book, ON THE FAITH TO PETER:[2] « One is the nature or essence of the Father and of the Son and of the Holy Spirit, not one the person. For if there were one Person thus, as there is one substance of the Father and of the Son and of the Holy Spirit, truly it would not be called a trinity. Again, it would be a true trinity indeed, but the one God would not be the Trinity itself, if in accord with the manner the Father and the Son and the Holy Spirit are distinct from one another by the property of the persons, they had also been thus separated [discreti] by a diversity of natures ». « But did not the Faith of the Patriarch, Prophets and Apostles preach that God is the Trinity »?[3] « Therefore, in that Holy Trinity one is God the Father, who essentially alone begot from Himself one Son; and one the Son, who from the one Father (is) alone born essentially; and one the Holy Spirit, who alone essentially proceeds from the Father and the Son. But this Whole cannot be one person, that is, begetting itself and being born from itself and proceeding from itself ». For as (St.) Augustine says in the first book, ON THE TRINITY:[4] « There is no thing, which begets itself, to be ».

COMMENTARY ON DISTINCTION III

PART I

On the cognition of God through distant similitudes.

For the Apostle also says, that the invisible (things) of God etc..

THE DIVISION OF THE TEXT

Above, Master (Peter) dealt with the Holy *Trinity* and *Unity*,[1] inasmuch as It is believed. In this second part he deals with It, inasmuch as It is understood. And this part is divided into three parts, in the first of which, to understand the Trinity, he adduces congruent similitudes and reasons. In the second, he solves emerging doubts, below in the fourth distinction at the beginning: *Here there rises the sufficiently necessary question. It is established* etc.. In the third, having solved those doubts, he determines the properties and conditions of the Trinity and Unity, below in the eighth distinction: *Now concerning the truth or property*[2] *etc..*

Likewise, the first part has two (parts). In *the first* he adduces distant similitudes; in *the second* near or expressed similitudes, which are attained in the image, there (where he says): *But now let us come presently to that disputation.*

Likewise, *the first* part has two parts. In the first, he shows the Unity, in the second the Trinity, there (where he says): *Now it remains to show, whether through those things which have been made* etc..

The first part has four smaller parts. In the first he proves by the authority of the Apostle in the first (chapter of the Letter) to the Romans,[3] that God is cognizable through a creature. But in the second he adduces various manners of cognizing and reasons, there (where he says): *For as (St.) Ambrose said.* In the third he says, that those manners are implied in the authority of the Apostle, there (where he says): *Behold in so many manners.* In the fourth he touches upon, what through the aforesaid reasons it can be proven, that is the unity of the essence, not the trinity, there (where he says): *Moreover, all these things tend ultimately to manifest the unity* etc..

Now[4] *it remains to show, whether* etc.. Above, Master (Peter) shows through reasons the Unity or Entity of the Divine Essence. In this second part, he shows the Trinity by the distant similitude, which is attained in the vestige, and this chapter has four subparts. In the first, Master (Peter) shows the reason for the vestige in the creature. In the second, he shows, what responds to the vestige in the Creator, since the trinity of appropriated (names), namely of origin, beauty and delectation, as singulars are rendered to singulars, there (where he says): *For in that Most High Trinity.*

---

[1] Chapter 1, n. 1.
[2] Chapter 1, n. 4. — The author if this book. St. Fulgentius (of Ruspe), treats of this much more broadly, in which text codices C D and E by adding *not* [non] and by changing *but* [sed] into *if* [si] thus read: *Again the Trinity would not indeed be a true one, if the one God were not the Trinity: if in accord with the manner ... the Father and the Son and the Holy Spirit are distinct from one another by the property of persons, they had also been thus separated from on another by a diversity of natures* [Rursus quidem Trinitas non esset vera, si unus Deus Trinitas non esset: si quemadmodum ... Pater et Filius et Spiritus sanctus personarum sunt ab invicem proprietate distincti, sic fuissent naturarum quoque diversitate discreti]. But this reading confounds a twofold supposition and argumentation. At the end of the text the Vatican edition has *they had also been ... of nature* [fuissent quoque naturae] for *they had also been ... of natures* [fuissent naturarum quoque].
[3] Loc. cit.; the following authority is ibid., n. 6.
[4] Chapter 1, n. 1.
NOTES ON THE COMMENTARY
[1] Without the authority of any manuscript or edition 1, the Vatican edition omits *and Unity* [et Unitate] .

[2] Here codex O adds: *Likewise the first part has two parts, in the first of which Master (Peter) shows, that God is triune and one; in the second, because the reasons and similitudes, which he adduces, are not sufficient to fully understand the Trinity and Unity in the divine, he concludes, that this is in doubt, at the end of that distinction of his: wherefore in accord with this consideration of his* [Item prima pars habet duas partes, in quarum prima ostendit Magister, quod Deus est trinus et unus; in secunda, quia rationes et similitudines, quas adducit non sunt sufficientes ad plene intelligendum Trinitatem et Unitatem in divinis, concludit, hoc esse in dubio, in fine istius distinctionis: quapropter iuxta istam considerationem].
[3] Verse 20.
[4] The Vatican edition against the testimony of the manuscripts and edition 1, having omitted the words *Now it remains ... entity* [Nunc restat ... entitatem] and having changed the construction, proceeds: *Similarly the second part, in which he shows the Trinity through a distant similitude, which is attained in the vestige, has four smaller parts* [Similiter secunda pars, in qua ostendit Trinitatem per similitudinem longinquam, quae attenditur in vestigio, habet quatuor particulas].

In the third he teaches one to contemplate the Trinity in God through a consideration of the vestige in the creature, there (where he says): *And so through a consideration of creatures* etc., where he shows the Trinity of Appropriators in God both as much as regards the act of condition, and as much as regards the act of reformation. But in the fourth smaller part he shows, that the consideration of the Trinity through the vestige is not sufficient, but distant, there (where he says): *Behold it has been shown, how among creatures.*

But now let us come presently to that disputation. This[1] is the second part of that distinction of his, in which Master (Peter) proves the Trinity and Unity through a *near* and expressed similitude, of which manner is *the image.* And this part is divided into two: in the first he shows the Trinity and Unity in the Creator through the trinity and unity considered among the powers of the soul; but in the second among (its) habits, there (where he says): *There can also be distinguished in another manner and by other names.*

Again, *the first* part has four[2] smaller parts. In the first of which he shows, where the image is to be sought in the soul, since (it is) in the superior part and in[3] its three powers, that is in the memory, intelligence, and will. But in the second, he touches upon the conditions of the image, which are trinity, unity and equality, there (where he says): *Therefore,*

these three, as (St.) Augustine says. But in the third, he moves and solves the doubt, which rises out of the aforesaid: that is whether the soul is its powers, there (where he says): *Here it must be attended to diligently.* But in the fourth, he teaches one to beware of the error, which can be caused and/or[4] rise from showing, that the created trinity [trinitatis creatae quod] is an omnimodal similitude to the uncreated (Trinity); where he shows, that there is the greatest dissimilitude of the image to God, there (where he says): *However, let one still beware.*

There can also be distinguished in another manner and in other etc.. This is *the second* part of the second part of this distinction,[5] in which Master (Peter) intends to investigate the image in the habits of the soul according to what is possible, and this part is divided into four smaller parts. For, *first*, he touches upon those things, among which the image of the Trinity is tended towards, which are the mind, knowledge [notitia] and love [amor]. *Second*, having already touched upon them [praetactis], he shows, that in these the image is attained on account of consubstantiality, order and equality, there (where he says): *But these three, though they be* etc. *Third*, he shows, in what manner the rational mind makes progress in the contemplation of the created trinity to see and cognize the uncreated Trinity in Unity, there (where he says): *And thus the rational mind, considering these three.* But *fourth* he briefly recollects those things which have been demonstrated above, there (where he says): *Wherefore in accord with that consideration of his.*

TREATMENT OF THE QUESTIONS

For an understanding of those things which are touched upon in this first part of the present distinction, four things are asked.

The first is, whether God is cognizable by a creature.

The second is, whether He is cognizable through a creature.

The third is, whether the manner of cognizing (Him) through a creature befits [conveniat] man as much as regards his every state, namely the state of innocence, the state of fallen nature and the state of glorified nature.

The fourth is, what concerning God is cognizable through a creature.

ARTICLE SOLE
On the cognizability of God.

QUESTION I
Whether God is cognizable by the creature?

About the first, that God is not cognizable by a creature, is shown:

1. Through *the authority* of Dionysius (the Areopagite), ON THE DIVINE NAMES:[6] « It is possible neither to say nor to understand (what) God (is) ».

2. Likewise, it is shown *by reason* through a fourfold supposition, which must necessarily be [quam necesse est esse] in cognition, that is *proportion, union* or reception,

judgement and[7] being informed [informationem]. For the intellect does not understand except what is proportionable to it, and what is united to it in some manner, and of which it judges, and by which the insight [acies] of the intelligence is informed.

From *the first* supposition it is argued thus: it is necessary, that there be a proportion of the one cognizing to the thing cognizable;[8] but there is no proportion of God to the intellect, because God

---

[1] The Vatican edition by separating the two parts of the present Distinction, transposes the following exposition of the text below in the beginning of the second part of this distinction, but contrary to the manuscripts. Immediately after this, the Vatican ed. against the testimony of the codd. and ed. 1 has *of this* [huius] in place of *of this ... of his* [istius].

[2] Codex O reads *has six subparts* [habet sex particulas] and enumerating them singly, where it deals with the third, it reads: *In the third he teaches to evidence what is said, how in the aforesaid assignment of the image the mind and memory are interpreted, there (where he says): But the mind is here accepted for the human spirit* [In tertia ad evidentiam dictorum docet, quomodo in dicta assignatione imaginis accipiatur mens et memoria, ibi: Mens autem hic pro animo], then under the fourth and fifth it exhibits the third and fourth points in the text, and finally adds: *In the sixth smaller part he teaches, in respect of which object the image is attained in the said powers, there (where he says): But it must be known, that this trinity of the mind* [In sexta particula docet, respectu cuius obiecti attenditur imago in dictis potentiis, ibi: Sciendum vero, quod haec trinitas mentis].

[3] The Vatican edition against the unanimous consensus of the manuscripts and edition 1 omits *in* and *its*.

[4] The Vatican edition, opposing the manuscripts and edition 1, in place of *and/or* [vel] has less well *and* [et].

[5] The Vatican edition, having omitted the words of Master (Peter) and varied the construction of the sentence, reads: *Similarly the second part, in which ... is possible, is divided into four* [Similiter secunda pars, in qua ... possibile est, dividitur in quatuor]; but this is against the manuscripts and edition 1.

[6] Chapter 1. about the middle of the text: Whom it is neither possible to understand nor speak of (Migne's ed., according to the translation of Scotus Erigena).

[7] In the Vatican edition, *and* [et] is omitted contrary to the codices and edition 1.

[8] Aristotle, ETHICS, Bk. VI, ch. 1: If, indeed, out of a certain similitude and affinity, a cognition exists for them (i. e. the powers of the soul). — A little below after *intellect* understand *of the creature* or *human.* Then

is infinite, and the intellect finite: ergo etc.. *Furthermore*, if there is any proportion, it seems that it is not sufficient, because the truly uncreated is more distant from the human intellect, than any created intelligible (is) from sense.[1] But sense, which is perceptive of the sensible, is never elevated to the cognition of the created intelligible: therefore, neither shall the intellect ever be elevated to the cognition of the uncreated intelligible.

3. Likewise, thus from *the second* supposition: it is necessary, that there be a union of the cognizable and the one cognizing, so that one is in the other;[2] but the one cognizing is not in the cognizable, but just the opposite [e converso]; but it is impossible, that the infinite be seized by the finite itself: therefore, it is impossible that it be in it: therefore that God is in the intellect is impossible, since He is infinite.

4. Likewise, from *the third* supposition thus: for cognition it is necessary, that there be in the one cognizing a judgement of the cognized; but everything judging has an ability [posse] over the thing judged;[3] but the finite does not have an ability over the infinite: therefore, it does not judge of it; but for cognition there was required judgement: therefore, the finite intellect does not cognize the infinite God, over whom it has no ability.

5. Likewise, from the *fourth* thus: it is necessary, that the cognizing intellect be informed by the cognized;[4] but everything which informs another, either informs through (its own) *essence*, or through a *similitude* (of it); but God does not inform (the intellect) through (His) essence, because as a form He is united to nothing, nor through an abstract similitude (of it), because an abstract similitude is more

spiritual than that from which it is abstracted; but nothing is more spiritual than God nor can it be: ergo etc..

ON THE CONTRARY: 1. The rational soul is (made) to the image of God. But as (St.) Augustine says in (his) book ON THE TRINITY, and (as) it is (quoted) in the text of the present distinction:[5] « For that reason the mind is the image of God, by which it is able to seize [capax] God and can be a partaker (in Him) ». But seizing [capere] is not (here said) according to substance and/or essence, because in this manner [sic] they are in all creatures: therefore, (it is said) through cognition and love [amorem]: therefore God can be cognized by a creature.

2. Likewise, it is shown by *reason* thus: every spiritual cognition comes into being [fit] by reason of light, and by reason of uncreated light, as (St.) Augustine says in the SOLILOQUIES;[6] but light is the most cognizable, and God is Most High Light: therefore He is most cognizable to the soul itself: ergo etc..

3. Likewise, since there is[7] cognition of some things through presence, (and) of some things through similitude, those are more truly cognized, which are cognized through presence, as (St.) Augustine says;[8] but God is united to the soul itself through presence: therefore, God is more truly cognized than others, which are cognized through similitude.

4. Likewise, as most high Goodness is related to [se habet ad] goodness, so most high Truth (is) to cognition; but most high Goodness is most highly lovable by the affection [affectu]: therefore[9] most high Truth is most highly cognizable by the intellect.

5. Likewise, anything whatsoever [unumquodque] can be more efficacious unto that toward which it is naturally ordered;[10] but our intellect is naturally ordered to cognition of the most high light: therefore, that (light) is most highly cognizable.

---

the codices and the editions disagree among themselves; many codices such as A F G K M S T W X Z bb and ee after *infinite* [infinitus] omit less well *and the finite intellect* [et intellectus finitus]; very many such as H Y ff together with editions 2, 3, 4, 5, and 6 put *but* [sed] in place of *and* [et]; codex R has *but* [vero] at this point; finally, codex ee reads *our intellect* [intellectus noster]; we judge that nothing is to be changed. — Aristotle, On the Heavens, Bk. I, text. 52 (ch. 6): But there is no reckoning of the infinite to the finite.

[1] From manuscripts I X and Z we have substituted in place of the *sensible* [sensibili], which the Vatican edition has along with very many of the manuscripts, *sense* [sensu], which more corresponds to the context and renders the form of the argument more complete, and is confirmed from Richard of Middleton's (text), here at a. 1. q. 1, and from (Bl.) Peter of Tarentaise, here at q. 1, who likewise expound the argument in the same manner. A little before this codex K has *created* [creato] place of *human* [humano]. — Concerning the minor proposition of this argument, cf. (St. Severinus) Boethius, ON THE CONSOLATION OF PHILOSOPHY, Bk. V., Discourse 4.

[2] It is gathered from this, that cognition is an *immanent act*, concerning which see Aristotle, METAPHYSICS, Bk. IX, text 16 (VIII. 8.); and it is supposed from Aristotle, ON THE SOUL, Bk. III, text 6 and 37-39. (c. 4 and 8), where he says, that the soul is *a place of forms*, by cognizing that *it is in a certain sense all things*, (and that) in it there are not *things themselves, but forms of them* and that the intellect is *the form of forms*.

[3] (St.) Augustine, ON THE TRUE RELIGION, c. 29, n. 53: To judge of the bodies not only of sentient life, but also of reasoning is ... But it is already very easy to see that, more present is the one judging, than is that thing, of which it is judged. — Codex X here adds *as (St.) Augustine says* [sicut dicit Augustinus].

[4] See the text of Aristotle on this matter above in the argument from the second supposition. — Concerning the twofold manner of informing, namely, *through essence* and *through similitude*, cf. below at the bottom of 3. — Then after *God does not inform* [Deus non informat] supply with codex R *the intellect* [intellectum].

[5] About the beginning of chapter 2. In the text itself of (St.) Augustine the manuscripts together with edition 1 have *and* [et] in place of *and ... of Him* [eiusque], which the Vatican edition together with the original has. — A little below, after *But* [autem] codex O adds *here* [hic].

[6] The sense, not the words of (St.) Augustine chosen from his SOLILOQUIES, Bk. I, ch. 8, where it is had thus: It must be believed, that those (intelligible considerations of the disciplines) cannot be understood, unless we be enlightened by something like our sun (which sun, as is clear from what follows here, *is God* Himself *most secret*). — The Vatican edition has this text in mutilated from, that is, by omitting in the major proposition *and by reason of the light* [et ratione lucis], and in the minor has *God is the most high Light, therefore, He is most cognizable* [Deus est summa lux, ergo maxime est cognoscibilis].

[7] We have substituted, as a support from the manuscripts and editions 1, 2, and 3, *is* [sit] in place of *becomes* [fiat].

[8] Perhaps these words refer to those which are hand in ON THE TRINITY, Bk. X, ch. 8-11, where it is shown, that the soul by itself, because it is present to itself, has a more certain cognition of itself than of exterior things, which it perceives through images or similitudes; and/or also to those which are had in ON THE TRINITY, Bk. VIII, ch. 8, n. 12: Behold one can already have God more known [notiorem] (to him), than a brother; plainly more known, because more present, more known, because more interior, more known, because more certain. Which words St. Bonaventure explains in this manner below in d. 17. p. I., dub. 2, as he illustrates the sense of this argument. Cf. also his book, ON THE TEACHER, ch. 12, n. 39 and 40 and ON SEEING GOD, ch. 16, n. 38, where there is also proposed (this) twofold manner of cognizing, namely through presence and through similitude. — Very many of the more ancient manuscripts, as C I M S T V Y etc. after *are cognized* [cognoscuntur], though not incorrectly, have, however, what is not as good on account of the form of the argument, placing *through essence* [per essentiam] for *through presence* [per praesentiam]; codices L and O have the better *through essence and/or presence* [per essentiam vel praesentiam]. A little after this codex Y has *those* [illa] in place of *others* [alia].

[9] Edition 1 adds *and* [et] well enough.

[10] Cf. (St. Severinus) Boethius, ON THE CONSOLATION OF PHILOSOPHY, Bk. III, Discourse 11. Codex C exhibits this proposition thus: *anything is more efficacious, when it can be unto that* [unumquodque est efficacius, quando potest in di]. At the end of the argument codex X adds *to the soul itself* [ipsi animae]; it would be more pleasing to say *to our intellect* [intellectui nostro].

CONCLUSION

God, most highly cognizable in Himself, would be also most highly cognizable to us, if it were not for a defect on the part of our intellect.

I Respond: It must be said, that God in Himself as the most high Light is most highly cognizable; both as the Light most highly completing our intellect,[1] and as much as it concerns Him [est de se], He would be most highly cognizable even to us, unless there were some defect on the part [a parte] of the virtue of the one cognizing; which indeed is not borne away perfectly except through the deiformity of glory. Therefore, the reasons must be conceded (which prove): [2] that God is cognizable by a creature and also most clearly cognizable, as much as it concerns Him, unless there was some impediment and/or deficient (thing) on part of the intellect, as will be clear afterwards.[3]

1. To the objections unto the contrary it must be said, that there is cognition through *comprehension* and through *apprehension*. Cognition through apprehension consists in the manifestation of the truth of the thing cognized; but cognition of comprehension consists in the inclusion of (its) totatilty.[4] For the *first* cognition there is required a proportion of convenience; and such is in the soul in respect of God, because « in a certain manner the soul is all things »,[5] through assimilation to all things, because it has been born [nata est] to cognize all things, and it is most able to seize [capax] God through assimilation, because it is the image and similitude of God. As much as regards the cognition of *comprehension*, there is required a proportion of equality and equiparancy [aequiparantiae]; and such is not in the soul in respect of God, because the soul is finite, but God is infinite; and for that reason it does not have this; and this is what Dionysius understands, and what the objection is speaking [currit] about,[6] but not about the other.

2. To that which is objected concerning the distance of the intelligible and the sensible; it must be said, that there is[7] distance according to the reckoning of *being* [rationem entis], and according to the reckoning of a *cognizable*. In the first manner there is greater distance; in the second manner not (so), because each is intelligible, namely,

God and the soul. It is not thus concerning the intellect and the sense; because the sense is a determinate potency,[8] but the intellect not (so).

3. To that, that the infinite cannot be seized by the finite; some say that to seize the infinite is (spoken of) in a twofold manner, that is as much as regards *essence*; and thus (the infinite) is seized; and as much as regards *virtue*;[9] and thus it is not seized, as a point as a whole is touched by a line according to substance, but not totally according to virtue. But that solution of theirs does not seem to solve (the matter), because in God that which is the virtue is the same as the essence, and each of the two is infinite.

For that reason it must be said, that twofold is the infinite: one, which has itself through opposition to the simple; and such is not seized by (that) finite, which is an infinite mass [molis]; the other is, what has infinity together with simplicity, as God (does); and such an infinite, because (it is) *simple*, is everywhere whole, because (as an) *infinite*, it is thus in nothing, which it is not outside of. So it must be understood in the cognition of God. And for that reason it does not follow, that if the whole is cognized, that it is comprehended, because the intellect does not include His totality, just as the creature (does) not (contain[10] His) immensity.

4. To that which is objected: The one judging has an ability etc.; it must be said, that to judge of anything is (spoken of) in a twofold manner: in the first[11] manner by *discerning*, whether it is and/or is not; and in this manner judgement befits every intellect cognizing in respect of every object; in another manner by *approving* and/or reproving, whether it ought to be thus [ita]; and so it does not judge of truth, but of other things according to it, as (St.) Augustine says, ON THE TRUE RELIGION,[12] that « a judge does not judge of the law, but judges of other things according to it ». And of this manner it is true what (St.) Augustine says, that « no one judges of that truth, no one, however, judges without it ». And of this second[13] manner it is true that it opposes (the thesis), that the one judging can (be) above the thing judged; but of the first it is not true, that it can be above; however, it can be directed as unto an object for its support.

5. To that which is lastly objected concerning informa-

---

[1] That is, perfecting by illumining. — Immediately after this the Vatican edition, disagreeing with the manuscripts and first six editions, omits *and* [et], but less well; and a little after this it substitutes *deiformation* [deiformationem] for *deiformity* [deiformitatem].

[2] Supply together with codd.s N and V *which prove* [which prove]. A little below this the Vatican ed. not trusting the manuscripts and edition 1 has *another thing* [aliud] in place of *something* [aliquid], but less aptly.

[3] In the two following qq. and in SENT., Bk. II. d. 23, a. 2, q. 3.

[4] (St.) Augustine, ON SEEING GOD, ch. 9, n. 21, says: For it is one thing to see, and another to comprehend the whole by seeing. Since when that, which is in whatever manner [utcumque] sensed as present, is seen: the whole, however, is comprehended by seeing, because it is seen to such a degree [ita], that nothing of it lies hidden (to) the one seeing it, or that the ends of it can be circumspected.

[5] Aristotle, ON THE SOUL, Bk. III, text 37, (ch. 8). [Trans. note: For the definition of *equiparancy* see d. 19, p. I, a. sole, q. 3, p. 347, footnote 5.]

[6] From the manuscripts and edition 1 we have substituted the idiomatic *is speaking* [currit] for *disputes* [certat].

[7] Not trusting in the manuscripts and edition 1, the Vatican edition adds here *a twofold* [duplex].

[8] That is, on account of its binding to an organ or on account of its materiality it is limited to perceiving one genus of objects. On this difference of sense and intellect see Aristotle, ON THE SOUL, Bk. III, text 3-6, (ch. 4).

[9] The Vatican edition, against the coddices and edition 1, has *virtuosity* [virtuositatem].

[10] Codex R adds here *His* [eius].

[11] Edition 1 has *one* [uno]. Then codex O after *is not* [non sit] adds *and what it is* [et quod hoc].

[12] Ch. 31, n. 58: As is those temporal laws of theirs, although men judge of them, when they have instituted them, however when they have been instituted and made firm, it will not be licit for a judge to judge of them, but according to them. — In the place cited there are also found the words, which the Seraphic Doctor quotes from (St.) Augustine immediately afterwards: For as we and all rational souls rightly judge, according to the truth, of inferior things, so of us, when we cleave to it, truth itself alone judges ... thus as much as it can also (be) a law, (the man who is spiritual and conjoined to God) also himself becomes (that), according to which he judges all things, of which (law) he can judge of nothing. — Very many codices as H W and Y, having omitted the particle *of* [de], read *And in this manner* [Et hoc modo].

[13] We have placed in the text *this second manner* [hoc secundo modo] and a little after this *of the first manner it is not true* [de primo modo non est verum], though other codices as D G H and Y etc. have *of this first manner* [de hoc primo modo] for *in his second manner* [hoc secundo modo] (sic), others as F T and bb have *of the first manner* [de primo modo], others as A together with the Vatican edition have *of this manner* [de hoc modo] and a little after this all the codices read *but of the second it is not true* [de secundo vero non est verum]. Even if from the context it is established, that the readings of the codices are erroneous; this is also confirmed from (St.) Augustine loc. cit., near the end, where in nearly the same words he proposes the same thing as St. Bonaventure. The writers seem to have been lead into error from this, that those two numbers have been placed in inverse order. — The codices aa and bb have in the last sentences of this paragraph *has an ability to* [posse habet] in place of *can* [potest], well enough. Near the end of this response after *be directed* [dirigi] we have supplied from the manuscripts and the first six editions *as* [ut].

information; it must be said, that God is present to the soul itself and to every intellect through truth; for that reason it is not necessary, that there be abstracted from Him a similitude, through which He is cognized; nevertheless, however,[1] while He is cognized by the intellect, the intellect is informed by a certain knowledge [quadam notitia], which is as a certain similitude, not abstracted, but impressed, inferior to God, because it is inferior in nature, superior, however, to the soul, because it makes it better. And this (St.) Augustine says in the ninth (book) ON THE TRINITY, in chapter eleven:[2] « In accord with the manner, when through the sensation [sensus] of bodies we learn about bodies, there comes into being [fit] some similitude of them in our soul: thus when we know [novimus] God, there comes into being some similitude of God; that knowledge [notitia], however, is inferior, because it is inferior in nature ».

SCHOLIUM

I. The words of the Seraphic Doctor at the bottom of On the Contrary, n. 2, that every spiritual cognition comes into being by reason of the uncreated light, and below in reply n. 5, that God is present to every intellect through truth, and the other, very many, similar (words) which are read chiefly in the ITINERARIUM MENTIS IN DEUM and the HEXAËMERON, have been understood by Malebranche and many others thus, that they thought St. Bonaventure was teaching with them, that the human intellect indeed sees intelligible things obscurely, but immediately in the Word or in eternal reasons. But this sentence, as one cannot reconcile it with the Decree of the Sacred Congregation of the Inquisition (Sept. 18, 1861), by which there is reproved the proposition: « The immediate cognition of God, at least habitually, is essential to the human intellect, so that without this it cannot cognize anything, even if it is the intellectual light itself »; (which) also so manifestly contradicts the established [exploratae] doctrine of our Doctor. For he himself teaches, that not man in the state of innocence, nor the Angels themselves by their own natural powers can have any *immediate* vision or cognition of God. In regard to the Angels cf. SENT., Bk. II, d. 3, p. II, a. 2, q. 2, where among other things he says: « The divine light on account of its own eminence is inaccessible to the powers of every creature »; in regard to men in the state of integrity cf. SENT., Bk. II, d. 23, a. 2, q. 3, which passage entirely refutes (the said proposition). For having rejected various opinions, there is taught there at great length, that only in the state of *glory* is God seen immediately and in His substance and without obscurity; « but in the state of innocence and of fallen nature God is seen *by means of a mirror*, but differently, because in the state of innocence God was seen *through a clear mirror*; for there was no cloud of sin in the soul; but in the state of misery He is seen through a mirror obscured through the sin of the first man; and for that reason He is now seen *through a mirror and in an enigma* [aenigmate] ». There is also reproved there the sentence of those, who think that there is at least conceded by God in this life to contemplative men a certain, exilic grade of seeing God immediately. He concludes with these words (which) must be strongly noted: « Whence, if there is found authorities which say this, that God is seen and distinguished [cernit] by man in the present (life), they are not to be understood, that He is seen *in His essence, but that He is cognized in some inferior effect* »* etc. — The same is taught in SENT., Bk. III, d. 14, a. 1, q. 3 and there is at the same time refuted the distinction, which certain ones make between the *clarity* of God and His *nature*, because « the very nature is the clarity and the clarity the nature » and « the essence of the light does not differ from the act of lighting ». And in q. 2 there is said, that God, if He is immediately cognized, « now not accord to a part, but the whole is cognized » Cf. also SENT., Bk. I, d. 17, p. I, Doubt n. 2, and other places passim. See the many things said in Cardinal Zigliara's, DELLA LUCE INTELLETTUALE, II. c. 14-18; Father Lepidus', EXAMEN. PHILOS. THEOL. DE Ontologismo, ch. 17; and among our own, Father Luigi of Castroplanio's, SERAPHICUS DOCTOR S. BONAVENTURAE, Rome 1874, p. 61 ff.

The Seraphic Doctor is also contrary to the error of the Averroists, who supported the unity of the agent intellect in all men. For he affirms, that « this error destroyed the whole order of living and acting » (Serm. de Dono intellectus, Supplem. Bonelli, t. III. col. 475.), and he most manifestly teaches, that in the human soul, which has been created to the image of God, there is essentially an intellectual potency, which has its own proper [propram] and active virtue to elicit various intellectual acts; whence

it can be aptly called a certain [quoddam] created light. This he teaches in SENT., Bk. II, d. 24, p. I, a. 2, q. 4; and p. II, a. 1, q. 1, where he says, that « the superior reason does not only have to judge according to eternal laws, but it also has to judge according to its own [proprium] light and according to the light acquired by itself from the lesser (intellect) ». Cf. d. 17, a. 1, q. 1, ad 6; HEXAËMERON. Serm. 12, ff; cf. also Alexander of Hales, SUMMA, p. III, q. 27, m. 1, a. 2 and p. II, q. 69, m. 2, a. 3.

Therefore, though the *immediate* and *proximate* principle of intellectual acts is the potency of the soul, or a created light naturally conferred by the mind, however, in accord with the common setneces of the scholastics, the *truth, certitude* and *infallibility* of human cognition ought to be traced [refundi] into the prime and uncreated Truth, which is the first efficient, exemplar, and final cause of all things and intellects. Whence it is rightly said, that the created intellect cognizes all truth things *in eternal reasons*, not as in *an object cognized beforehand*, but as in *the principle of cognition*, or in the words of Alexander of Hales (SUMMA, p. I, q. 2, m. 3, a. 1 reply to n. 1), not *in* reasons, but *through* them. Thus St. Thomas, SUMMA, I., q. 84, a. 5; q. 88, a. 3, reply to n.1; q. 12, a. 11. reply to n. 3; q. 16, a. 6, reply to n. 1; SENT., Bk. IV, d. 49, q. 2, a. 7, reply to n. 9 ; SUMMA CONTRA GENTILES III., ch. 47; DE VERITATE, q. 1, a. 4; q. 10, a. 11, reply to n. 12; QUODLIBETALS., n. 10, q. 4, a. 7, and elsewhere. — Alexander of Hales, SUMMA, III., q. 27, m. 1, a. 2, reply to n. 1. — (Bl. John Duns) Scotus, SENT., Bk. I, d. 3, a. 4, chiefly nn. 18-23. — Richard of Middleton, SENT., Bk. I, d. 24, a. 2, q. 4; and many others.

The *fundamental* reason for this doctrine, which is commonly proposed by the ancient scholastics, is this, that the light of the uncreated Truth according to a similitude glitters in *created truth*, either this is accepted in the objective sense, or in the subjective (sense). Of created truth in the objective sense St. Bonaventure says (HEXAËMERON, Sermon 12): « in every creature there is a refulgence of the divine exemplar, but thoroughly mixed together with shadows ». In the subjective sense created truth is the created light itself of the mind, which is a certain [quaedam] impression of prime truth, whose similitude glitters in our intellect, which as the image of God, « bears in itself from its origin the light of the divine countenance » (St. Bonaventure, SENT., Bk. II, d. 16, a. 1, q. 1; cf. St. Thomas, EXPOSITIO IN PSALMIS, ps. 34; SUMMA., I., q. 105, a. 3).

The second reason is, that God not only creates and conserves the light of the intellect according to the divine exemplar, but also concurs to its acting, while He immediately moves and directs it. Even by this reckoning, that the intellectual acts depend from God and ought in some manner be traced back [refundi] into Him, is the common sentence of the ancient scholastics; cf. St. Thomas, SUMMA., I., q. 105, a. 3; I. II., q. 10, a. 4. — (Bl. John Duns) Scotus, in the very many places, collected by Fr. Girolamo da Montefortino, O.F.M., 1662-1738 A.D., in SUMMA SCOTI, Rome, 1728, p. I. q. 105. a. 3-5. — That divine concursus can not unworthily be called a certain immediate illumination of God, as his Eminence Cardinal Zigliara teaches in the work: PHILOSOPHIE DER VORZEIT t. I. 1. Abth. n. 60; cf. also St Thomas, IN IOANNEM ch. 1, reading 3, n. 2; SUMMA., III., q. 5, a. 4, reply to 2; SUMMA., I., q. 79, a. 4; QUAEST. UNICA DE ANIMA, a. 5, reply to n. 9; OPUSCULA 73 on (St. Severinus) Boethius, q. 1. and elsewhere.

Both St. Augustine and the Seraphic Doctor, St. Bonaventure, greatly stress this divine cooperation or illumination. The mind of the Seraphic Doctor concerning

---

[1] From the manuscripts and edition 1, 2, 3 and 6 we have added *however* [tamen].

[2] Num. 16; in which text very many of the codices as A G I T Y Z aa bb together with editions 2, 3, 4, 5, and 6 have *we discuss* [discutimus]; codex F K and X have *we discern* [discernimus] in place of *we learn* [discimus], and just after this very many of the codices as A C F G H K L O R S T U V W Y aa ee and ff have *by some similitude* [aliqua similitudine] for *a similitude of God* [similitudo Dei].

---

* *Trans. note*: This is not universally valid; for Christ Jesus Himself enjoyed the beatific vision while still a wayfarer, by virtue of the grace of the hypostatic union; and again, it is an approved opinion that the Blessed Virgin Mary enjoyed the same on occasions during Her own mortal life (cf. Bl. Mary of Agreda, THE MYSTICAL CITY OF GOD). Indeed, it is not unreasonable to consider that this gift of the Head is also communicated at times during this life to the greatest of the saints as a gratuitous gift. Since it is momentary and cannot be retained except in its effects, it does not destroy the habit of faith, but raises the soul from desire for this life, in accord with the Scriptures, "*Eye has not seen, ear has not heard, nor has it even entered into the mind of man what God has prepared for those who love him*," and "*No man can see God and live*," and this fulfills eschatalogically the new life in Christ, for "*Eternal life is this, to cognize Thee the Only True God and Jesus Christ whom Thou has sent*."

this point, briefly expressed six hundred times, it is manifested at length by a certain unpublished, disputed question, reported by Father Fidele a Fanna, O.F.M., and in regard to its principal part, published by RATIO NOVA COLLECTIONIS etc., Turin, 1874, p. 222. This entire question, with the addition of other unedited documents both of (St.) Bonaventure himself and of his three disciples, namely Matthew of Aquasparta, John Peckham and a certain Eustasius, God willing, we will publish very soon in a special book, by which both the sentence of the Seraphic Doctor will be thoroughly manifested, and it will be demonstrated that, Bl. (now St.) Albertus Magnus and the other ancients consented entirely with the Seraphic (Doctor) himself, and that St. Thomas did not teach the contrary on the principal point.

II. Having presupposed these things, the words « God is present to every intellect through truth », cause no difficulty, chiefly when by the Seraphic Doctor himself the interpretation of the Ontologists is explicitly reproved (SENT., Bk. II, d. 10, a. 1, q. 1, reply to n. 1, and ibid. d. 3, p. II, a. 2, q. 2, reply to nn. 3 and 4). He excellently explains his own sincere sentence below in d. 17. p. I. q. 4 in the body, where with St. Augustine he distinguishes cognition through *species* from infused and/or innate (cognition) »; and he adds: « But both, which are so cognized, are said by Augustine *to be cognized in truth* » On the similitude and/or innate habit cf. SENT., Bk. II, d. 39, a. 1, q. 2.. Rightly does the Seraphic Doctor (at n. 5) deny, that God is cognized through a similitude abstracted from Him, because we have no concept of God but one (which is) analogous and formed from elsewhere. Even St. Thomas (SENT., Bk. I, d. 3, q. 1, a. 1, reply to n. 3) teaches: « We are not said to cognized those things (God and Angels) through abstraction, but through *impression* in our understanding ». (St.) Albertus (Magnus) (here in a. 2, in reply to n. 2) and (Bl.) Peter of Tarentaise (here in a. 1, in reply to n. 4) agree.

III. In the solution to n. 5 the words « Our intellect is informed by a certain *knowledge* [notitia], which is like a certain similitude, not abstracted, but impressed », can be explained from the species, either impressed or expressed, which the intellect forms from *truth created* and impressed essentially upon the soul, of which the Seraphic Doctor speaks in d. 17, p. II, q. 4. However, this does not exclude, that under the term *knowledge* [notitia] one can understand also that divine illumination, of which we have spoken above. Other places in St. Bonaventure's (writings) seem to insinuate this, first of all Sent., Bk. II, d. 3, p. II, a. 2, q. 2 in reply to n. 4,, where having spoken of the cognition of the Angels, he concludes thus: « There is still a third manner of cognizing, namely through visible effects and through spiritual substances and through *the influence of a light connatural to the cognizing power*, which (light) is a certain similitude of God, not abstracted, but infused, inferior to God, because in an inferior nature » etc.. Cf. also what he says of the knowledge [scientia] of Christ in SENT., Bk. III, d. 14, a. 2, q. 1, in reply to nn. 1 and 2. In this sense Fr. Eustasius, a disciple, a Doctor at Paris in the 13th century, understands that the same passage from St. Augustine is praised here by St. Bonaventure, as is gathered from a certain unpublished question of the same author, soon to be published by us in the above mentioned book.

IV. St. Bonaventure wonderfully illustrated this and the following question in the ITINERARIUM MENTIS IN DEUM, and in the HEXAËMERON, Sermon 5 and 10. —Alexander of Hales, SUMMA., p. I., q. 2, m. 1 ff.. — (Bl. John Duns) Scotus, here in q. 1. — St. Thomas, here in q. 1, a. 1; SUMMA., I., q. 12, a. 12. — Bl (now St.) Albertus (Magnus), SENT., Bk. I, d. 1, a. 15; SUMMA ., p. I, tr. 3, q. 13, m. 1, and a. 14, m . 1. — (Bl.) Peter of Tarentaise, here in q. 1, a. 1. — Richard of Middleton, here in p. I, a. 1, q. 1. — Giles the Roman, here principally in q. 1. — Henry of Ghent, SUMMA., a. 33. — (Bl.) Dionysius the Carthusian, here in q. 1. — (Gabriel) Biel, SENT., Bk. I, d. 2, q. 9, and d. 3, q. 2 and 3.

QUESTION II

Whether God is cognizable through creatures?

Second, there is asked, whether God is cognizable through creatures. And that (He is) not, it seems:

1. Because the way to error is not the way to cognition; but cognition through a creature is a way of error: ergo etc. Proof of the minor: in the fourteenth (chapter) of Wisdom (it is said):[1] *The creatures of God are as a deception and hatred and as a mousetrap for the feet of the unwise.* Furthermore, (St.) Augustine, ON FREE WILL, speaks of those, who are occupied in creatures: « Turning (their) back to Thee, they are fixed upon a corporal work as upon their own shadow ».

2. Likewise, the darkness and/or a shadowy thing is not the way to cognize the light or a luminous thing;[3] but a creature is shadowy, moreover, God is light: therefore, God is not cognizable through a creature.

3. Likewise, the medium, through which anything is cognized and/or proven from (its) extreme, ought to communicate in some thing with that for which it is cognized;[4] but the Creator and the creature have nothing common: therefore, God is not cognized through creatures.

4. Likewise, every medium, through which one ascends to an extreme, is distant from it by finite steps;[5] but every creature, howsoever noble, is distant from God by infinite steps, because howsoever it is doubled, it will never arrive at His nobility: therefore, through a creature, one does not ascend unto the cognition of God.

ON THE CONTRARY: in the thirteenth (chapter) of Wisdom (there is written):[6] *From the magnitude of the beauty* [speciei] *and creature the Creator of these will be able to be seen in a cognizable manner.* Whence (St.) Isidore, ON THE SUPREME GOOD (says):[7] « From the beauty of the circumscribed creature, God makes His own Beauty, which cannot be circumscribed, to be understood ».

2. Likewise, it is thus shown *by reason*: it happens that not only is an effect cognized through (its) cause, but also the cause

---

[1] Verse 11, where contrary to the manuscripts and edition 1, the Vulgate reads: Since the creatures of God have become as hatred and as a temptation for the souls of men and as a mousetrap etc.. With this reading the Vatican edition agrees, except in this, that it has *deception* [deceptionem] in place of *temptation* [tentationem].

[2] Book II, ch. 16, n. 43: For as they put (their) back to Thee they are fixed upon a carnal work as upon their own shadow.

[3] Aristotle, POSTERIOR ANALYTICS, Bk. I, ch. 21 (25): On one hand to privative (propositions) a negative, universal proposition is prior and more known, on the other to affirmative (propositions) the negative is prior and more known (for through the affirmative the negative is known) and the affirmative is prior, just as 'being' [esse] is prior to 'non being' [non esse]. And ON THE SOUL, Bk. III, text 25 (ch. 6), where he teaches, that privations are not cognized except through their contrary, that is through the cognition of their habit. Cf. also ON HEAVEN, Bk. II, text 18 (ch. 3).

[4] Aristotle, POSTERIOR ANALYTICS, Bk. I, ch. 7: For from the same genus it is proper that there be extremes and means [media]. He says in

the same in his METAPHYSICS, text 22 (Bk. IX, ch. 7). And in THE PARTS OF ANIMALS, Bk. III, ch. 1: For even the mean [medium] is a partaker of each extreme. — "*Extreme*" [Extremum] is a name in Logic signifying the subject or predicate of a conclusion, for cognizing the union of which the *medium* employed is called a *middle term* [terminus medius]. — The Vatican edition against the codices and edition 1 omits *for* [ad] after *with that* [cum eo].

[5] Cf. Aristotle, POSTERIOR ANALYTICS, Bk. I, ch. 15 ff. (ch. 19 ff.) where he shows (something) similar in respect to this demonstration of his. — A little below this with the help of the manuscripts, in place of *it may be doubled, one never arrives* [duplicetur, nunquam pervenitur] we have substituted *it is doubled, it will never arrive* [duplicatur, nunquam perveniet]; supply "creature" [creatura]. Codex I better exhibits the major proposition formally, *Likewise no medium ... by infinite steps* [Item nullum medium ... gradibus infinitis]. In the conclusion very many codices as K T etc. have *to* [ad] in place of *unto* [in].

[6] Verse 5.

[7] Or SENTENCES, Bk. I, ch. 4.

through the effect:[1] therefore, if God is a cause operating according to its nobility, and the creature the effect, God will be able to be cognized through the creature.

3. Likewise, the sensible is a way of knowing the intelligible:[2] but a creature (is) sensible, (and) God (is) intelligible: therefore, through a creature there is a departure [devenire] unto the cognition of the Creator.

4. Likewise, it happens that like is cognized through like;[3] but every creature is like to God as vestige, and/or as image: therefore, through every creature it happens that God is cognized.

Therefore, it is asked, what is the difference between the vestige and the image; and since in every creature there is a vestige, it is asked, why not similarly an image, and according to what the vestige is attained.[4]

CONCLUSION

God can be cognized through creatures by the natural light of reason.

I RESPOND: It must be said, that, because a cause glitters [relucet] in (its) effect, and the wisdom of a craftsman [artificis] is manifested in (his) works, for that reason God, who is the Craftsman and Cause of a creature, is cognized through it.

And, for this, there is a twofold reason, one is on account of *fittingness* [convenientiam], the other on account of *indigence*: on account of *fittingness*, because every creature leads more unto God than unto something else; on account of *indigence*, because, since God, as a light most highly spiritual, cannot be cognized in His spirituality by the quasi material intellect, the soul needs [indiget] to cognize Him through a creature.[5]

1. To that which is objected, that the cognition of a creature is a way unto error; it must be said, that cognizing a creature is (said) in a twofold manner: as much as regards (its) *special properties* and[6] those which belong to imperfection, and/or as much as regards (its) *general conditions*, which belong

to completion; but if as much as regards special conditions and (those belonging to) *imperfection*: either *by attributing* (them) to God, or *by removing*. By the first manner there is a way of error, by the second a way of cognition; and so God is cognized through *ablation*.

But if He is cognized in regard to (His) conditions of *perfection*, He can be thus in a twofold manner, as a picture is cognized in a twofold manner: either as *a picture*, or as *an image*; whence either (cognition) stands still [sistitur] in the beauty of the creature, or through this it tends unto another. If by the first manner, then it is a way of deviation; whence (St.) Augustine in (his) book, ON FREE WILL:[7] « Woe to those who love Thy noddings [nutus] in place of Thee and wander about [oberrant] among Thy footprints [vestigiis] and forsake Thee as (their) leader. ». If by *the second* manner, insofar as it is a way unto the other, in this manner [sic] there is a reason for cognizing through superexcellence, because every noble property in a creature is to be attributed to God in (its) highest degree [summo]; and thus this is clear.[8]

2. To that which is objected, that the shadowy medium is not a way of cognizing the light; it must be said that there is a well disposed eye and a bleary [lippus] eye. Of the well disposed eye it is true, but not of the bleary one, to which the medium for seeing the sun is a concealing cloud and/or the ground suscepting the clarity of the light; so (it is) for our intellect, which holds itself as the eye of an owl to the most manifest things of nature.[9]

3. To that which is objected concerning the defect of community, it must be said, that[10] there is no common thing through *univocation*, there is, however, a common thing through *analogy*, which means a habitude *of two to two*, as in a sailor and a doctor, and/or *of one to one*, as of the exemplar to the *example* [exemplatum].

4. To that which is objected, that there are always infinite steps; it must be said, that ascent [ascensus] into God can be in two manners: either as much as regards a *looking towards the Presence*; and thus every creature is bound to lead (one) unto God, and so there are not infinite steps; or as much as regards an *equality of equiparancy;** and so it is true, that they are infinite, because the created good, how-

---

[1] See Aristotle, POSTERIOR ANALYTICS, Bk. I, ch. 10 (ch. 13) and Bk. II, ch. 17 (ch. 14). — In this proposition [p.71], on the authority of the manuscripts and edition 1, we have added *also* [etiam].

[2] Cf. Aristotle, ON THE SOUL, Bk. III, text 39 (ch. 8): By sensible forms intelligibles are hinted at ... and on that account, he who senses nothing, can learn and/or comprehend nothing. — Then after *creature* [creatura] and after *God* [Deus] supply with the Vatican edition *is* [est].

[3] Aristotle, TOPICS, Bk. VI, ch. 1 (ch. 2) speaking of metaphor says: « For a metaphor in a certain manner makes known that which is signified, *on account of* (i.e. through) *the similitude* », In the same place you will also find this definition of an image, with which St. Bonaventure deals a little below: « For the image is that, of which the generation is through imitation ». Cf. also PRIOR ANALYTICS, Bk. II, ch. 27 and 28 (chs. 29 and 30), where Aristotle deals with icons (εἰκός, i. e. the similar, the very similar, the agreeable) and *signs*, which if they are the most certain, are named *evidences* [indicia] by him, (by the Commentators *vestiges* and/or *prodigies*); and Dionysius (the Areopagite), ON THE CELESTIAL HIERARCHY, ch. 1.

[4] The Vatican edition, not consistently against the manuscripts and edition 1, has the indicative *is attained* [attenditur].

[5] The Vatican edition's interpolated and not apt reading: *as if the soul needed the material light, to cognize Him, that is through a creature* [quasi materiali luce indiget anima, ut cognoscat ipsum, scilicet per creaturam], we have corrected from the manuscripts and edition 1. Codex O has *naturally* [naturaliter] in place of *material* [materiali].

[6] From nearly all the manuscripts and edition 1 we have added here and a little below this after *special conditions* [speciales conditiones] an *and* [et], in place of which codex I in the first place has *that it* [id est], in the second *which belong to* [quae sunt]. Then codices O and Z have *as much as regards general properties and those which are* [quantum ad proprietates generales et quae sunt]. Then the manuscripts together with edition 1, against the Vatican edition, insert *moreover* [autem] in *but if as much* [si autem] and after *imperfection* [imperfectionis] they omit *this is in a twofold manner* [hoc est dupliciter].

[7] Book II, ch. 16, n. 43.

[8] On the threefold way of cognizing God, that is by causality, removing and superexcellence, cf. Dionysius (the Areopagite), ON THE DIVINE NAMES, ch. 6, and below in Doubt 1.

[9] Supply: the dark thing (or creature) is a medium for cognizing the light or god. On the comparison [comparatione] of the intellect with the eye of an owl cf. Aristotle, METAPHYSICS, Bk. II, text 1 (Bk. I, ch. 1, in the shorter version): For as the eyes of the ravens of the night [nocticoraceum] hold themselves to the light of day, so also the intellect of our soul to those things which are the most manifest of nature (Venetian edition of 1489).

[10] The Vatican edition, not trusting in the testimony of the manuscripts and edition 1, adds *if* [si]. A little after this a few of the codices as X and Y together with editions 2, 3, 4, 5 and 6 have not well *leader* [ductore] in place of *doctor* [doctore]. Cf. d. 25, a. 2. q. 1, in the body of the article, where the same example is explained, and SENT., Bk. II, c. 16. a. 1. q. 1 in the body of the article, where the example of the *sailor and the charioteer* occurs.

---

* *Trans. note*: For the definition of *equiparancy* [aequiparantiae], see d. 19, p. I, a. sole, q. 3, p. 347, footnote 5.

soever doubled, is never compared [aequiparatur] to the uncreated (Good).

But *the first* step as much as (it) regards the ascent towards the sight [aspectum] of the Presence is in the consideration of visibles, *the second* in the consideration of invisibles, as (it belongs to) the soul and/or another spiritual substance; *the third* is from the soul unto God, because « the image is formed by the Truth Himself and is immediately conjoined to God ».[1]

To that which is lastly asked *concerning the difference of the vestige and the image*, certain ones assign,[2] the vestige among sensibles, the image among spirituals. But that distinction and position of theirs is not valid, because the vestige is also among spirituals. For the unity, truth, (and) goodness, in which the vestige consists, are the conditions most universal and intelligible.

Others[3] say, that "vestige" is said, because it represents according to a part, but "image" according to the whole. But again this difference is not valid, because, since God is simple, He does not have (something) representing (Him) according to a part; again, since He is infinite, by entirely no creature, nor even by the whole world can He be represented according to the whole.

And for that reason it must be understood, that since the creature leads unto the cognition of God through a *shadow*,[4] through a *vestige* and through an *image*, their *more knowable* [notior] difference, by which they are also denominated, is accepted from within [penes] (their) *manner of representing*. For it is called a *"shadow"*, inasmuch as it represents in a certain elon-

gation and confusion; a *"vestige"*, inasmuch as (it represents) in[5] an elongation, but in distinction; but an *"image"*, inasmuch as (it represents) in nearness and distinction.

From this difference there is gathered a *second*, which is from within [penes] the conditions, in which these are tended towards. For creatures are said (to be) *a shadow* as much as regards (their) properties, which respect God in some genus of cause according to an indeterminate reckoning;[6] *a vestige* as much as regards (their) property, which respects God under a reckoning of a triple cause, the efficient, the formal[7] and the final, as are the one, the true and the good; *an image* as much as regards (their) conditions, which respect God not only in the reckoning of a cause, but also of an object, which (conditions) are memory, intelligence and will.

From these there are concluded *two other* differences: as much as regards those things which *lead*; for the creature as a shadow leads to the cognition of things *common*, as *common*; the vestige unto cognition of things *common*, as *appropriated*; the image to cognition of things *proper* , as *proper*.[8]

The *other* difference is from within [penes] those things in which *they are discovered*. For since every creature is compared [comparatur] to God both[9] in the reckoning of cause and in the reckoning of a triple cause, for that reason every creature is a shadow and/or a vestige. But since only the rational creature is compared to God as an object, because it alone is able to seize [capax] God through cognition and love [amorem]: for that reason it alone is an image.

SCHOLIUM

I. That God is not cognized immediately in Himself nor a priori by wayfarers, but through those things which have been made by Him, no one after the (First) Vatican Council (*de Fide*, canon 1 on Revelation) can call into doubt. This canon: "If anyone has said, that God the one and true, Creator and Our Lord, through those things which have been made, cannot be certainly cognized by the natural light of human reason, anathema sit," entirely agrees with the doctrine of the Seraphic Doctor. — At the end of the conclusion, in accord with the text reformed by us, the human intellect is called *quasi material*, which must be understood in comparison to the pure, divine spirituality. In this sense St. Bonaventure (SENT., Bk. I, d. 37, p. I, a. 2, q. 1, at n. 4) says: For nothing is entirely spiritual, except God alone, as (St.) Augustine says ON THE CUSTOMS OF THE CHURCH (and/or rather Gennadius of Marseille (fl. 494 A.D.), ON THE DOGMA OF THE CHURCH, ch. 2): God alone is incorporeal, because He fills all things.

II. That the vestige of the Trinity is found in every creature, is the common sentence. For every creature to the extent that is has in itself *one* 'to be' [unum esse], distinct from any other, looks back to God as

its efficient cause; to the extent that it has a *true* 'being' [verum esse], looks back to Him as (its) exemplar cause; to the extent that it has a *good* 'being' [bonum esse], it looks back to the Same as (its) final cause. — Not all assign the difference between the *image* and the *vestige* in the same manner. The Seraphic Doctor, as he appears from the text, gives a fourfold difference, to which St. Thomas adjoins another (SUMMA., I. q. 45. a. 7). But (Bl. John Duns) Scotus brings forward some difficulties against the words of St. Thomas (here in q. 3). Of this doctrine cf. the Seraphic Doctor himself, here in Doubt 3; SENT., Bk. II, d. 35, a. 2, q. 1; BREVILOQUIUM, p. II, c. 1 and 12; HEXAËMERON, sermon 12. — Alexander of Hales, SUMMA., p. II, q. 8, throughout and q. 7, m. 7; p. I, q. 18, m. 1 and 5. — (Bl. John Duns) Scotus, here in qq. 5 and 9. — St Thomas, here in q. 2, a. 1, 2 and 3; SUMMA., I, q. 45, a. 7. — Bl. (now St.) Albert the Great, here in a. 14 and 18. — (Bl.) Peter of Tarentaise, here in q. 3, a. 1. — Richard of Middleton, here in a. 3, q. 2. — Durandus (of Saint-Pourçain), here in p. I, q. 4. — (Bl.) Dionysius the Carthusian, here in qq. 4 and 5. — (Gabriel) Biel, here in q. 9.

III. More on this question: St. Bonav., SENT., d. 3, p. II, a. 2, q. 2. — Alexander of Hales, SUMMA., p. I, q. 2, m. 3, a. 1 & 2. — (Bl.) Scotus, here in qq. 1, 2, & 3. — St. Thomas, here in q. 1, a. 3; SUMMA., I, q. 2, a. 2

---

[1] (St.) Augustine, 83 QUESTIONS, q. 51, n. 2 says: Wherefore since man can be a partaker according to the interior man, he is thus, according to him, as an image, so that he is formed by no interposed nature, and for that reason nothing is more conjoined to God. And the author of the book, ON THE SPIRIT AND THE SOUL, ch. 11: Which (mind) has been thus made to the image of God, so that it is formed by the Truth itself (and by) no interposed nature.

[2] The Vatican edition adds for the sake of clarity *such a difference* [talem differentiam], which words, however, are lacking in the manuscripts and edition 1.

[3] The Vatican ed. against the mss. and ed. 1 adds *But* [autem]. A little after this very many of the codd., such as S V X and bb, omit *difference* [differentia], in place of which ed. 1 has *distinction* [distinctio].

[4] The Vatican edition adds *and* [et], which is lacking in the mss..

[5] On the authority of the manuscripts and edition 1, we have here and immediately afterwards substituted *as much as in* [quantum in] for *certain things* [quadam]. Then codex A after *but* [sed] adds *with* [cum].

[6] With the help of the manuscripts and edition 1 we have expunged here what was added by the Vatican edition: *of cause* [causae].

[7] Understand this of the formal *extrinsic* cause or of the exemplar cause, not of the formal *intrinsic* cause. Cf. below in d. 8, p. I, a. 1, q. 1, in reply to n. 2.

[8] In accord with the common sentence, the divine attributes are distinguished into the common *as common* [communia ut communia] or the common ones simply speaking [communia simpliciter], which are the essentials, such as 'to be', 'to live', (and) 'to understand'; the common ones *as appropriated* [communia ut appropriata], which are those essentials, which we grant to one Person before the others, such as "power" to the Father, "wisdom" to the Son, "goodness" to the Holy Spirit; the *proper* ones [propria] are paternity, filiation and spiration.

[9] We have supplied from very many codices and edition 1 the particle *both* [et], by which a more distinct reading is rendered. A little after this codex Z in place of *and/or* put *and* [et].

and 3. — SUMMA CONTRA GENTILES, I, ch. 13. — Bl. (now St.) Albert (the Great), here in a. 2 and 3; SUMMA., p. I, tr. 3, q. 15, m. 1. — (Bl.) Peter of Tarentaise, here in q. 2, a. 1. — Richard of Middleton, here in a. 1, q. 1 and a. 2, q. 1. — Henry of Ghent,

SUMMA., a. 24, q. 6. — Durandus (of Saint-Pourçain), here in p. I, q. 1. — (Bl.) Dionysius the Carthusian, and (Gabriel) Biel as in the preceding question.

QUESTION III

Whether man in every state cognizes God through creatures?

Third, there is asked, whether the cognition of God through creatures belongs to man as much as regards (his) every state. That it does belong to man as regards (his) *first state*, is shown thus:

1. Man in the state of innocence did not use to cognize God face to face: therefore, if he used to cognize God, he used to cognize (Him) through an effect, therefore, through a vestige, therefore through a creature.

2. Likewise, in man in the state of innocence sensible cognition was not as [in] an impediment, but as a support [adminiculum] for intellective cognition; but intellective cognition, on account of which man was made, is a cognition of God: therefore, every sensible cognition in the first man was ordained for this; but cognition of God through a sensible support is cognition through a creature: ergo etc..

Likewise, that it belongs to man as much as regards (his) *state of beatitude*, it does seem:

1. Because the Blessed cognize a Creature [i.e. the Humanity of Christ], but they do not stand still in it, but refer (it) to God: therefore, they cognize God through a creature.

2. Likewise, the blessed[1] souls praise God through creatures; but to praise God through creatures is to cognize (Him) through creatures; ergo etc..

ON THE CONTRARY: that it did not belong to *man as instituted*, is shown thus:

1. Cognition through a vestige is cognition through a medium; « but the mind », as (St.) Augustine says,[2] « is immediately formed by the Truth itself »: therefore, such a cognition does not befit [convenit] human nature as much as regards that state, nor even as much as regards another (state).

2. Likewise, it is not a right order, which the nearer arrives at the end through a more distant medium; but man in the first state was nearer to God that the rest of other[3] creatures: therefore, it did not use to be agreeable to him to arrive unto the cognition of God through other creatures.

Likewise, that such a cognition did not belong to man as much as regards (his) state of *beatitude*, it does seem:

1. Because cognition through a vestige is cognition through a being-lead-by-hand [manuductionem]: therefore, it is not a perfect cognition, therefore, it is a partial one [ex parte]:[4] therefore,

it does not remain among the Blessed, because among them there shall be emptied out what is in part [ex parte].

2. Likewise, the vestige or creature is as a stair to ascend and/or as a way to arrive at God; but when one has arrived at the terminus, there is no use for an ulterior way:[5] therefore, similarly, when man is on high, he does not need a stair; but the cognition of the Blessed is immediately upon [in] God: therefore, it is not through creatures.

CONCLUSION

God is cognized in creatures perfectly by comprehensors, semi-fully by wayfarers; but through creatures He is properly cognized by wayfarers, but one way before, another way after the Fall.

I RESPOND: For an understanding[6] of the aforesaid things it must be noted, that cognizing God *in* a creature is one thing, *through* a creature another. To cognize God *in* a creature is to cognize His presence and influence in a creature.[7] And this indeed belongs to wayfarers in a semi-full manner [semiplene], but to comprehensors in a perfect one; whence (St.) Augustine says at the end of the book, ON THE CITY OF GOD,[8] that God shall then be expressly seen, when God shall be the All in all. But to cognize God *through* a creature is to be elevated by cognition of a creature to cognition of God as if through an intermediary stairway [scalam mediam]. And this properly belongs to wayfarers, as (St.) Bernard says (in his letter) to (Pope) Eugenius.[9]

It another manner, however, it agrees with man in the state of instituted nature, and (in that)[10] of fallen nature: because in the first state he did use to cognized God through a creature as through a *clear mirror*, but after the Fall he cognized (Him) as *through a mirror and an enigma*, as the Apostle says in the thirteenth (chapter) of the First (Letter) to the Corinthians,[11] on account of the beclouding of the intellect and a worsening of things.

To that, therefore, which is objected concerning the state of *beatitude*; it must be said, that, as has been said, it does not belong to the blessed to cognize *through* creatures, but rather *in*

---

[1] The Vatican edition alone prefaces this with *all* [omnes].

[2] See above, q. 2 at n. 4. — In which text codex Y after *by the* [ipsa] adds *first* [prima].

[3] Trusting in the very many codices as A C G H I K L N O S T U etc. and edition 1 we have added *other* [aliis], and then after *to arrive* [pervenire] we have substituted *at* [ad] with *unto* [in].

[4] We prefer the more succinct reading of the mss.s and ed. 1 to the reading of the Vatican ed., in which after *perfect cognition* [cognitio perfecta] there is added *and if there is not a perfect cognition* [et si non est cognitio perfecta] and after *partial one* [ex parte] there is adjoined *and if it is partial* [et si est ex parte]. The argument here hints at the words of the Apostle, 1 Cor. 13:10: *But when there has come what is perfect, there shall be emptied out what is in part* [Cum autem venerit quod perfectum est, evacuabitur quod ex parte est].

[5] The faulty reading of the Vatican ed., placing *alternative* [alterius] for *ulterior* [ulterius], we have corrected from the mss. and ed. 1, just as also a little afterwards we have substituted (the subjunctive) *is* [sit] for the indicative *is* [est] and *but* [sed] for *for*

[nam]. — In this argument there is an allusion to the words of (St.) Bernard, ON CONSIDERATIONS, Bk. V, ch. 1: This stairway, the citizens (of Heaven) sanely do not need, but exiles (do).

[6] The Vatican edition against the manuscripts has *understanding* [intellectum] instead of *an understanding* [intelligentiam].

[7] Codices L and O have *upon the creature* [in creaturam].

[8] Book 22, c. 30, n. 4: We shall vacation for ever, seeing that He is God, by Whom we shall be filled, when He will be the All in all. — In which text, very many of the manuscripts such as A I T etc., together with edition 1, have *in the manner* [quomodo] in place of *when* [quando].

[9] ON CONSIDERATIONS, Bk. V, ch. 1, n.1: This (is) the more sublime and more worthy use of present things, since in accord with the wisdom of (St.) Paul, *the invisible (things) of God, through those which have been made, being understood, are perceived*. This stairway, the citizens (of Heaven) etc. (Migne, tom. 182, col. 788) [Trans. note: citation added].

[10] Codex X has *(more) than* [quam] in place of *and (in that)* [et].

[11] Verse 12.

creatures. And the reasons, which seem to prove the contrary, do not prove (it), but rather, that He used to be cognized by them *in* creatures.

1. To that which is objected concerning the state of *innocence* that the mind is immediately formed etc.; it must be said, that twofold is the medium, that is *efficient* and *disposing*. Of the first medium there ought to be understood what (St.) Augustine said, but of the second not (so);[1] since God is an efficient medium and the object of the mind itself. Moreover, (St.) Augustine says that [illud verbum] against the philosophers, whose opinion was, that the mind is not conjoined to the first (principle)[2] immediately, but by means of [mediante] some intelligence.

2. To that which is objected, that there is not a right order; it must be said, that man can be considered in a twofold manner: as a being *in itself* [ens in se], and/or *outside itself* [extra se]. In the first manner he does not arrive at God through creatures by himself, but being outside himself through cognition of creatures he is recollected in himself and elevated above himself.[3]

And/or it must be said, that other creatures can be considered as things, and/or as signs. In *the first* manner they are inferior to man, in *the second* manner they are means of departure [in deveniendo] or on the way, not in the terminus, because they do not arrive (there), but through them man does arrive at God, having left those thing behind him [illis post se relictis].

SCHOLIUM

I. In regard to the distinction between cognizing God *in* a creature and *through* a creature, which is had in the body (of the question), cf. SENT., Bk. III, d. 31, a. 2, q. 1 ad n. 5; ITINERARIUM MENTIS, ch. 1. (Bl.) Peter of Tarentaise agrees, here in q. 4; and so does Richard of Middleton, here in q. 2. q. 3. — Likewise the words occurring at the end of the body (of the question): « a beclouding of the intellect and a worsening of things » are approved and explained more amply by St. Thomas, SUMMA., I, q. 94, a. 1 at n. 3 and by Alexander of Hales, SUMMA., p. I, q. 2, m. 2, q. 4.

On the twofold medium, that is the efficient and disposing (in the solution to n. 2), the Seraphic (Doctor) explains his mind more clearly in SENT., Bk. II, d. 3, p. II, a. 2, q. 2 at n. 6, with these words: « (St.) Augustine wants, that between the mind and God there not fall a medium, that is, in the reckoning of a efficient and/or influencing cause, however, a medium of a being-lead-by-hand [manuductionis] does fall, which, however, does not properly have the reckoning of a medium, because it is more subservient to the cognizing power, than presiding over it [praesit] ». You will find very many things concerning the threefold medium of seeding God in SENT., Bk. II, d. 23, a. 2, q. 3 at n. 7. St. Thomas, SUMMA., q. 94, a. 1 at n. 3, agrees and so does Alexander of Hales, SUMMA., p. I, q. 2, m. 3, a. 1 at n. 3.

II. In regard to the order of the arguments and (their) solution it must be noted, that the Seraphic Doctor does not here hold to the customary manner, because a threefold response is give for the threefold state, so that not a few of the arguments in respect of one state are true, in respect of the others false. The first affirmative arguments rightly prove that conclusion, that man in the state of innocence did cognize God through creatures; the two arguments following are reproved by the Seraphic Doctor himself in the first solution (to the question) in regard to the Blessed; likewise arguments 1 and 2 in the *Contrary* are refuted in the last solution. But the two last ones are true in regard to the Blessed.

III. On this whole question: Alexander of Hales, SUMMA., p. I, q. 2, m. 2, a. 4, and m. 3, a. 1, and p. II, q. 92, m. 2, a. 1 and 2. — St. Thomas, SUMMA., I, q. 12, a. 11, and q. 94, a. 1. — Bl. (now St.) Albert (the Great), here in a. 13. — (Bl.) Peter of Tarentaise, here in q. 3, a. 2. — Richard of Middleton, here in a. 2, q. 3 (concerning the Blessed); SENT., Bk. II, d. 23, a. 2, q. 1 (concerning the state of innocence); ibid., d. 24, a. 3, q. 5 (concerning our present state). — Giles. R., here in a. 2 at the beginning of the last question.

QUESTION IV

Whether the Trinity of Persons with a unity of essence can be naturally cognized through creatures?

Fourth and last, there is asked, what concerning God is cognizable through creatures. And the Apostle says,[4] that (it is His) *sempiternal virtue and divinity*. And it is asked, whether through creatures the plurality of the Persons can be cognized. And it seems that (it is) so:

1. Because the philosophers did not have cognition of God except through creatures, and (yet) they cognized the Trinity: ergo etc.. The *minor* is patent through

(St.) Augustine ON THE CITY OF GOD:[5] « Philosophers say that there is a tripartite philosophy », in which is a cognition of the Trinity.

2. Likewise, the magi failed at the *third sign*, in the eighth (chapter) of Exodus;[6] and (that verse) is expounded (thus), that they failed in the cognition of the Third Person; therefore, either as much as regards (God's) *proper (names)* or as much as regards (God's) *appropriated (names)*. Not as much as regards (God's)

---

[1] Thus codex F; but the Vatican edition, having transposed the words *disposing and efficient* [disponens et efficiens], consequently has *Of the first manner there ought not be understood what (St.) Augustine says, but of the second, that* [De primo medio non debet intelligi quod dicit Augustinus, sed de secundo, quoniam]. We prefer the reading of codex F, because all the other codices and editions 2, 3 and 5, together with F itself, read *Of the first manner ... of the second not (so)* [De primo medio debet ... de secundo non], though they do agree with the Vatican edition in the transposition of the words *disposing and efficient*; but in the reading of the codices the sense is false, as is gathered both from the subjoined words and from the other passages cited from the Seraphic Doctor (here) in the Scholium.

[2] Supply: principle [principio]. — The Vatican ed., disagreeing with the mss. and ed. 1, has *eternal truth* [aeternae veritati] for *first (principle)* [primo].

[3] The sense is: man considered as a 'being in himself' [ens in se], i. e. a substance, is immediately referred to God and his cognition (likewise), because, as has been said in the solution of the preceding objection and above in q. 2 at n. 4, no medium falls between the substance of the soul and God. Man considered as a 'being outside himself' [ens extra se], i. e. as one perceiving exterior things, *is recollected in himself*, i.e. by

perceiving exterior things he draws these within himself and is stirred to reflection, and through *his own* mental operations both in respect of himself and in respect of exterior, cognized things *he is elevated above himself*, i. e. toward the cognition of God.

[4] Romans 1:20.

[5] Book XI, ch 25: Hence philosophers wanted there to be a tripartite discipline of wisdom. — From codex U we adjoin this gloss explaining the words of (St.) Augustine: *to whom are these to be ascribed, unless to the creator of all creatures, to the giver of intelligence, to the inspirer of love?* (from (St.) Augustine, loc. cit.) *Whence he wants to say, that natural philosophy concerns these things which pertain to the condition of nature; the "rational" concerns those things which pertain to reason and intelligence; "moral" concerns those things which pertain to love. For that reason "natural" is ascribed to the Father as Author, "rational" to the Son as Wisdom, "moral" to the love or goodness of the Holy Spirit.*

[6] Verse 18. See the exposition of this passage in (the COMMENTARIUM IN SACRAM SCRIPTURAM, of Nicholas) of Lyra and in Master (Peter Lombard's, SENTENCES), here at the end of chapter 2.

appropriated (names), because for us goodness glitters in the greatest manner [maxime] in a creature: therefore, as much as regards (His) proper (names): therefore, they cognized at least two Persons.

3. Likewise, this same (argument)[1] appears through *reason*: because the vestige, when it means "distinction", is a reason for cognizing God distinctively or in distinction: but there is no distinction in God except (that) of the Persons: therefore through a vestige they could cognize the distinction of the Persons.

4. Likewise, through the image there is a cognition of the Trinity as much as regards order, distinction and equality; but cognition through an image is cognition through a creature: therefore through a creature they could cognize the Trinity.

5. Likewise, the cognition of the hidden properties of creatures is more difficult than the cognition of the plurality of the Persons, because the former [illa] is not seized except by the great and subtle, but the latter [haec] is seized even[2] by the rough [rudibus] and foolish: therefore, if they could through the visible properties of creatures arrive at the invisible ones, much more strongly (did they arrive) at cognizing, that there are more Persons. And this is what is said in the thirteenth (chapter) of Wisdom:[3] *For, if they could know so much, that they could appraise the world,* [saeculum aestimare] *why did they not more easily find its Lord?*

ON THE CONTRARY: 1. The cognition of the Trinity is a cognition of faith: but cognition of faith is[4] of those (things) which are above reason; and (those) which are above reason cannot be cognized through creatures: ergo etc..

2. Likewise, there is no cognizing of God[5] through a creature except in two manners, either by affirming what is in the creature and/or (its) like, or by removing; but the Trinity is not cognized through a removal, but through a positing; but in no creature is there found a plurality of supposits with a unity of essence: ergo etc..

3. Likewise, written law is above[6] the law of nature, or the book of Sacred Scripture above the book of created world [mundanae creaturae]; but no one lacking faith comes through Sacred Scripture unto the cognition of the plurality of the Persons: therefore, much less through the book of the created world.

CONCLUSION

The Trinity of Persons is not cognizable through creatures, but only the trinity of the appropriated (names is), that is, "unity", "truth", (and) "goodness".

I RESPOND: It must be said, that a plurality of persons with a unity of essence is proper to the Divine Nature alone, the like of which is not discovered [reperitur] in a creature, neither can it be discovered nor be rationally thought: for that reason in no manner is the Trinity of the Persons cognizable through a creature, by ascending rationally from the creature into[7] God. But although It does not have (anything) entirely like (It), It does have, however, in some manner what is *believed* (to be) its like in a creature. Whence I say, that the philosophers never through reason cognized the Trinity of the Persons nor even[8] (Their) plurality, unless they had some habit of faith, as some heretics have; whence what they said, either they spoke (as) ones not understanding, or (as) ones enlightened by a ray of faith.

There is another trinity of appropriated (names), that is, of "unity", of "truth" and of "goodness",[9] and this they did cognize, because it has a like.

1. To that, therefore, which is objected, that through a tripartite philosophy philosophers cognized the Trinity; it must be said, that it is true, that through that and through other things they came into[10] the cognition of the appropriated (names), but as ones believing in the cognition of each trinity.

2. To that which is objected concerning the *third sign*, it is also well said, that the wisemen for that reason are said to have failed at the third sign, because they failed in the cognition of the most powerful effect[11] of Goodness, that is, of the Redemption.

3. To the other it must be said, that "vestige" means 'a distinction of essential properties', and to this responds the trinity of appropriated (names), not of proper ones or of the Persons.

4. To that which is objected concerning the image, it must be said, that there is a cognizing of the soul according to that which *it is*; and that cognition belongs to reason; and/or according[12] to which (it is) *an image*; and that cognition belongs to faith alone.

---

[1] The Vatican edition, disagreeing with the manuscripts and the first six editions, omits *same (argument)* [idem], for which codex Z has *very (argument)* [ipsum].

[2] Favoring the manuscripts and edition 1, we have added *even* [etiam], which the Vatican edition not so well omits. Then codex R has *philosophers* [philosophi] after *if* [si] and very many of the codices as A F G H I K S T Y etc. add *things* [rerum] after *of creatures* [creaturarum], in which the reading *of creatures* has been falsely put in place of *of created* [creatarum].

[3] Verse 9, where the Vatican edition after *know so much* [tantum ... scire] puts *that they could measure the age, why* [quod poterant saeculum mensurare, quomodo].

[4] Edition 1 here repeats *a cognition* [cognitio]. — On this argument, cf. Dionysius (the Areopagite), ON THE DIVINE NAMES, ch. 1 § 2.

[5] Codex K, well enough, *cognizing of anything of God* [aliquid Deo], codex X puts *of God* [Deum] for *of God* [de Deo]. Then, very many codd. such as A C F G H I L O S T U X etc. have *and/or (its) like, and/or by removing* [vel simile vel removendo]; we follow the codd. in regard to the first part, by putting *and/or (its) like* [vel simile], and the Vatican edd. in regard to the second, by retaining *or by removing* [aut removendo], because in this reading the members of the division and subdivision are more clearly exhibited. Codex Y omits *and/or* [vel] and edition 1 in place of *and/or* puts *as* [ut] before *(its) like*

[simile]. — Concerning this argument see Dionysius (the Areopagite), ON THE CELESTIAL HIERARCHY, ch. 2.

[6] Very many of the codices as B S and bb and edition 1 have here and a little afterwards *above* [supra].

[7] Edition 1 has *to* [ad]. Codex R a little after, for *what* [quod] has *and* [et] and codex T has *is discerned* [cernitur] for *is believed* [creditur].

[8] There is wanting in the Vatican edition *even* [etiam], which, however, is had in the manuscripts and edition 1. A little after this the Vatican edition has *whence those who meant this Trinity, either* [unde qui dixerunt hanc Trinitatem aut]; all the codd., with edition 1, agree in omiting *this Trinity*, however, they disagree, because some with the Vatican edition have *those who said* [qui], codex I *those who said this* [qui hoc], others as O T etc. *what they said* [quae], which we follow; finally edition 1 reads *those who for that reason said anything* [qui aliquid inde].

[9] The Vatican edition not trusting in the manuscripts and edition 1 has less aptly *truth, unity and goodness* [veritas, unitas et bonitas] and a little after this *they have a like* [habent].

[10] The Vatican ed., contrary to the mss. and ed. 1 has *to* [ad].

[11] The Vatican edition, striving against the manuscripts and edition 1, has less well *of the effect of most powerful Goodness* [effectus potissimae bonitatis]. Then codex O prefaces *of the Redemption* [redemptionis] with *of the Incarnation and* [incarnationis et].

[12] The Vatican edition against very many codices adds less well *that which (is)* [id quod].

5. To that which lastly[2] is objected, that it is more difficult to cognize the world [mundum]; it must be said, that that is understood, with the Divine Assistance supposed [supposito divino adminiculo]; but simply speaking it is false. For more swiftly would a man be disposed to the Faith, than would he acquire[2] a cogni-

tion of philosophy. Our intellect, however, is more able in regard to the cognition of mundane things than (in regard to those) of the Trinity; because That is above reason, and (out intellect) sees Its contrary in sensing; and for that reason it needs a new elevation, as, for example, a cognition through infusion.

SCHOLIUM

I. In regard to the proposition in the body (of the Question), which attributes to heretics some habit of faith, it must be known, that there is distinguished a twofold habit of faith, that is, infused and acquired, and the latter belongs to the natural order. Thus, even formal heretics can have the acquired habit.

It is rightly said in the solution to n. 4, that cognition of the image belongs to the Faith alone. For the image, inasmuch as (it is) an image, means "a looking back" [respectum] to that of which it is the image. But no "looking back" can be cognized unless each extreme has been cognized. Therefore, although the foundation of the relation *in the soul* is

cognized, i. e. the image understood *in a material sense* [materialiter], however, (the soul) is not recognized *formally* as *an image*, so long as the other terminus of the relation is not cognized, namely the Three Divine Persons.

II. St. Bonaventure, BREVILOQUIUM, p. I, ch. 2. — Alexander of Hales, SUMMA., p. I, q. 2, m. 1, a. 3. — (Bl. John Duns) Scotus, QUODLIBETALS., q. 14. — St. Thomas, here in q. 1, a. 4; SUMMA., I, q. 32, a. 1. — Bl. (now St.) Albert (the Great), here in a. 18; SUMMA., p. I, tr. 3, q. 13, m. 3. — (Bl.) Peter of Tarentaise, here in q. 2, a. 2. — Richard of Middleton, here in a. 2, q. 2. — Giles the Roman, here in the first principle of q. 4. — Henry of Ghent, SUMMA., a. 22, q. 4, n. 25. — (Bl.) Dionysius the Carthusian, here in q. 4.

DOUBTS ON THE TEXT OF THE MASTER

DOUBT I

In that part of his (text) there are doubts [dubitationes] about the text concerning those reasons, which Master (Peter) posits as much as regards the reason for proving and the force[3] of inferring, because all seem to not be valid [non valere] and/or to suppose a doubt [dubium].

And, indeed, the first reason is of such a kind:[4] 'He who can (make) what no creature can (make), is above every creature; but the One who made this world of ours, made what no creature can (make): therefore, He is not a creature, but above every creature'. And this reason starts there (where he says): *For as (St.) Ambrose says, that God* etc. In that reason of his a twofold[5] doubt seems to be supposed, namely, that this world of ours has been made, and that a creature could not make it, each of which is very doubtful [valde dubium].

The second reason is this:[6] 'He who made corporal (things) and mutable spirits, is above all corporal and mutable (things): therefore, He is spiritual and immutable'. This similarly seems to suppose a doubt, that God made spirits. And again, it does not follow from this, that, if He made mutables, that[7] He is immutable, nay rather the opposite seems to follow, that is, that He is mutable.

The third reason is this: 'He who made the good and the better, is the best; but God made corporals, which are good,

and spiritual (things), which are better: therefore, God is the Best'. This reason, similarly, seems not to be apparent [nullam habere apparentiam], because, then, any craftsman, who makes (things) good and better, would[8] similarly be the best, which is false.

The fourth reason is this: 'He who made (things) beautiful [pulcra] and more beautiful, is Beauty [pucritudo] Itself or outward Beauty [species], and this One is most outwardly-beautiful [speciosissimum]; but we see, that corporal (things) are outwardly-beautiful, and spiritual (things) are more outwardly-beautiful:[9] therefore, He who made these, is most outwardly-beautiful'. Similarly it seems, that neither aforesaid reason is valid on account of the aforesaid example [instantia].

Likewise, there is asked concerning the difference of those reasons of his, and in what manner they are distinguished. *If you say*, as some say, that there are four from within [penes] the four genera of causes, this is nothing, because the genus of material cause does not fall in God. *If you say*, that (they are) from within [penes] the manners of cognizing; *on the contrary*: there are not but three, that is, in the reckoning of cause, of ablation and of excellence.[10]

I RESPOND: It must be said, that all those reasons of his suppose something certain for this (purpose),[11] to prove and infer (the conclusion). For the first reason supposes, that the production of a thing from nothing cannot be except from an infinite potency. With this supposed, since it is certain, that no creature has an infinite potency,[12] it follows that

---

[1] With the help of the mss. we have substituted *lastly* [ultimo] for *further* [ulterius] and immediately afterwards we have adjoined *that* [quod].

[2] Codex Y has *than to acquire* [quam ad acquirendam]; a reading by no means to be spurned.

[3] Some codices as X Y in place of *force* [vim] have less well *truth* [verum], codices G and I have *thence* [inde]. Then from the manuscripts and edition 1 we have supplied *and/or* [vel] after *valid* [omnes].

[4] The Vatican ed., contradicting the mss. and ed. 1, omits *And indeed* [namque] and *is of such a kind* [talis st]. A little below this after *no* [nulla], we have twice expunged, trusting in the text of Master (Peter), the word *other* [alia], as it is able to distort the sense, though in the first place it is also found in the mss. and ed. 1. Then the words *And this reason* up to *as God* [Et incipit ... Deus] are lacking in the Vatican ed., but extant in the mss. and ed. 1.

[5] From very many manuscripts and edition 1 we have substituted *twofold* [duplex] in place of *in a twofold manner* [dupliciter], which the Vatican edition has less well. Codex I has *(Master Peter) seems to suppose a twofold doubt* [videtur supponere etc.].

[6] The Vatican edition here and hereafter omits *is this* [est haec] after each *reason* [ratio]; likewise, disagreeing with the manuscripts and edition 1, it then, after *mutable (things)* [mutabilia] reads *God is of this kind: therefore, God is an immutable spiritual* [Deus est huiusmodi: ergo Deus est spirituale immutabile].

[7] The Vatican ed., not trusting in the mss. and ed. 1, has *that, because He made mutables, for that reason* etc. [quod, quia fecit mutabilia, ideo].

[8] The Vatican ed. has *is similarly the* [est], but the mss. & ed. 1 oppose this. A little before this, cod. I has *made* [fecit] in place of *makes* [facit].

[9] Thus the codd. together with edd. 1, 2 & 3, but the Vatican ed. reads: *But God made beautiful (things) or outwardly-beautiful (things) because (they are) corporal, and more outwardly-beautiful (things) because (they are) spiritual* [Sed Deus fecit pulcra sive speciosa quia corporalia, et speciosiora quia spiritualia]; and a little below this, contrary to the mss. and ed. 1, it has *that reason of his does not seem to be valid* [videtur ratio ista non valere].

[10] Dionysius (the Areopagite), ON THE DIVINE NAMES, ch. 7, § 3: By a way and order, in proportion to (our) strength, we ascend in being-borne-away [ablatione] and in being-borne-above all [superlatione omnium] and in the cause of all. Cf. Alexander of Hales, SUMMA., p. I, q. 48, m. 2, a. 1. — St. Thomas, SENT., Bk. I, d. 3, p. I. division of the text. — The Vatican edition here adds: *To the objections against the four reasons already stated there is responded* [Ad obiectiones contra quatuor rationes iam dictas respondetur], which is lacking in the mss. and ed. 1.

[11] We have restored from the manuscripts and edition 1 the words *for this* [ad hoc]. Immediately after this codices E and Y have *which* [quod] in place of *to* [ut], and a little below this very many codices as I R aa bb and ff have *third* [tertium] in place of *certain* [certum].

[12] Aristotle, PHYSICS, Bk. VIII, text 79 (last chapter) according to the Venetian edition of 1489: Therefore, not to the finite does the infinite potency belong. Perhaps codex X intends this proposition, though it falsely references *Physics, Bk. IV* [libr. IV. Phys.]. — Then

the act of the production of a thing belongs to Him, who[1] is above every creature. And thus from this act as from what is proper to Him [ex proprio] there is cognized God the Omnipotent, the Immense. — In the other three reasons there is [supposed a stability [status], just as in all of philosophy there is supposed a stability among causes; and for that reason every mutable is lead back [reducitur] to an immutable, because in the mutable there is not a stability in the genus of the efficient except in the non-moved mover: for everything which is moved, is moved by another.[2] Similarly the good and the better are lead back to the best, because stability is not in the genus of the end except in the best. Similarly the beautiful and more beautiful to the most beautiful, because stability is not in the genus of species and form, except in the one which is itself essentially [per essentiam] species.

To that which is asked concerning the distinction of the reasons, from what has been said the response is already clear. For they cannot be distinguished from within [penes] the genus of causes only, nor from within the manners of cognizing only, but (they can) from within both.[3] For the first reason is taken according the reckoning of the cause; the others are taken from within the reckoning of cause and excellence, because they consider the order and they are distinguished according to order in a threefold genus of cause,[4] the efficient or motive [moventis], the final [finientis] and the exemplar.

DOUBT II

Likewise, is asked concerning this which Master (Peter) says afterwards, that *from the perpetuity ... the eternal Founder is understood*. For it has no value (to say): the effect is perpetual,[5] therefore, the efficient (cause) is eternal.

Likewise, there is similarly[6] asked concerning this which he says: *From the magnitude ... the omnipotent*. For it has no value (to say): it made great (things), therefore it is omnipotent and/or it can make all (things).

I RESPOND: To this some say, that there is only a certain persuasion through a sign, not a necessary argumentation. For they say, that omnipotence and eter-

nity, since they are infinite, cannot be sufficiently proven through creatures, which are finite.[7] — However, in another way it can be said, that although it does not follow in every efficient, however, it necessarily follows in the efficient or first perpetuating. For it is impossible, that a creature have a being [esse] and a great being [magnum esse][8] and this whole from another, which cannot be in the whole; and by this reason in this whole, and in anything. Similarly, if there is a first perpetuating, it is entirely in act and none (of it is) in potency; and if this (is so), since it can make another endure unto the infinite, it is itself infinite in the duration of its act [actu duratione]: therefore, eternal.

DOUBT III

Likewise, is asked concerning this which he says: *all ... which have been founded[9] by the divine Art, show ... a certain unity in themselves and an outward-beauty and order*. For he seems to say, first, (that it is) false, because if this (is so), since these three have been founded, then they have a *unity*, an *outward-beauty* [species], and an *order*, and thus concerning the others: therefore, if it is to stand, then some have been founded, which do not have these.[10]

Likewise, he seems to badly enumerate, because (St.) Augustine[11] posits these three: *measure* [modum], *outward-beauty* and *order*, and these others: *unity, truth, goodness*. Therefore, it is asked concerning the diverse manners of enumerating, whence do they come?

I RESPOND: To this some say, that this is understood of perfect creatures, and/or if of all (things),[12] then those three are not called conditions in the created thing, but in the uncreated exemplar. — However, it can be said, that in the first and general intentions[13] there is reflection and for that reason stability [status], and one is not to proceed beyond (this).

To that which is asked concerning the enumeration of the other three, that it does not seem to be fitting [conveniens]; it must be said that a created thing has to be considered in a threefold manner: either in

---

after *nothing* [nihilo] codex K reads *cannot be except from an infinite potency, and that the act belongs to the One which is above nature and above every creature* [non potest esse nisi a potentia infinita, et quod sit actus eius quod est super naturam et super onem creaturam]; then it omits the rest up to *In the other* [In aliis].

[1] The Vatican ed., against the mss. & to ed. 1, reads *that (power), which* [eius, quae]. A little below this, ed. 1 has *the first* [primo] for *its own* [proprio].

[2] Aristotle, PHYSICS, Bk. VII, text 1 & 3. — Then codex R after *because* [quia] adds *in the good* [in bono] and a little below this codex Y after *more beautiful* [pulcrius] inserts *are lead back* [reducuntur].

[3] Trusting in the manuscripts and edition 1 we have substituted *from both* [utrumque] for *from both* [utraque] and immediately after this we have put *for* [enim] in place of *but* [autem].

[4] The Vatican edition here adds *(such) as* [ut], but the manuscripts and editions 1, 2, 3, 4 and 5 oppose this. — For more on these arguments see below in d. 8, p. I, a. 1, q. 2 and HEXAËMERON, Sermons 5 & 10.

[5] This is that, which, though it has a start, does not have an end. — The Vatican ed. without the authority of the mss. and ed. 1, by omitting *For it has no value (to say)* [Nihil enim valet], proposes the objection thus: *The effect is not perpetual: therefore, neither is the efficient (cause) eternal* [Effectus non est perpetuus: ergo neque efficiens est aeternus]; but this is less effective in clarifying the response of the Seraphic Doctor to the objection.

[6] We have restored from the mss. and ed. 1 *similarly* [similariter].

[7] (Bl. John Duns) Scotus defends this opinion in SENT., Bk. I, d. 2, q. 3, n. 6 and in d. 42, q. sole and in QUODLIBETALS, q. 7.

[8] The distorted reading of the Vatican edition, *have so great a being and be so disposed, and this* etc. [habeat ita magnum esse et ita dispositum, et hoc], we have emended from the manuscripts and edition 1.

[9] Many codices omit *divine* [divina], but all have *founded* [condita] contrary to the Vatican edition, which has *made* [facta].

[10] The confused reading of the Vatican edition: *false, because (those things) which have been founded or made, have those three, that is unity, outward beauty and order: because some have been founded which do not have these, such as the devil and the reprobate* [falsum, quod quae condita sunt sive facta, habeant ista tria, scilicet unitatem, speciem et ordinem: quia aliqua condita sunt quae haec non habent, sicut diabolus et reprobi], is corrected with the help of the codices and edition 1, which in regard to the substance of the reading agree in the text of the (passage) received, though in regard to accidentals diverge; thus codex A has *because similarly* [qui similiter] in place of *because if this (is so)* [quia si hoc], codex O into *some have been founded* [condita sunt] inserts well enough *(of) these* [haec]; codices I and K have *therefore* [ergo] in place of *then* [tunc], codex M has *would not have* [non haberent] in place of *do not have* [non habent].

[11] ON THE NATURE OF THE GOOD, ch. 3: *Therefore these three: manner, species, order as general goods are in the things made by God, either in spirit, or in body.* The similar si in, THE CITY OF GOD, Bk. V, ch. 11. On *unity, truth and goodness* see, ON THE TRUE RELIGION, ch. 11, nn. 36 and 55. — Assisted by the mss. and ed. 1 we have substituted *posits* [ponit] for *enumerates* [enumerat] and, a little below this, we have supplied *and* [et] after *truth* [veritatem].

[12] Codices V and W here add *and* [et].

[13] That is, among the transcendental reasons *of unity, of truth, and of goodness* each one can be predicated of itself and of the others, e. g. the truth is true, one and good; but among the other reasons or forms this reflection is *properly* not admitted; thus improperly is whiteness said to be white. Cf. below in d. 17, p. I, q. 2 at the end. — The difficulty proposed here by the Seraphic (Doctor) is touched upon also below in d. 33, q. 4, at nn. 1 and 2. Cf. also Alexander of Hales, SUMMA, p. I, q. 18, m. 1 at n. 1 and p. II, q. 7, m. 2 at n. 6. — Bl. (now St.) Albert (the Great), here in a. 15. — Richard of Middleton, here on the text (of Master Peter) and in d. 33, a. 3, q. 2.

itself, or in comparison to other creatures, or in comparison to the first cause. And according to all these manners it happens that one finds a twofold trinity.

For, if it is considered as much as (it is) in itself and/or as much as (it is) for itself, that this, either as much as regards *the substance of its principles*; and thus there is that trinity: matter, form, composition, which is posited in (that) book, ON THE RULE OF FAITH;[1] or as much as regards (its) *habitudes*; and thus it is that (trinity spoken of), in the eleventh (chapter) of Wisdom:[2] *Thou has disposed all thing in number, weight and measure*. For in *number* there is understood a distinction of principles, in *weight* their proper inclination, in *measure* their[3] proportion to one another.

Likewise, if one creature is considered *in comparison to other creatures*, this can be[4] either inasmuch as it acts by *natural* action; and thus is taken that trinity of Dionysius (the Areopagite),[5] *substance, virtue* and *operation*; or inasmuch as it acts by *spiritual* action; and thus that (trinity) of (St.) Augustine, from (his book,) OF EIGHTY-THREE QUESTIONS,[6] « *that whereby it is established; that to which it is suitable; that whereby it is distinguished* », and the last is referred to the soul.

But, if (creatures) are considered[7] in *comparison to God*, this can be in a twofold manner: either inasmuch as they are referred only; and thus is there is that (trinity of), *manner, species* and *order*, or inasmuch as they are referred and assimilated; and thus there is that (trinity of), *unity, truth* and[8] *goodness*.

Therefore, since the vestige is attained in comparison to God properly (speaking), for this reason in this last conditions the vestige is accepted properly. And because there is a great fittingness among those comparisons of his, for that reason Master (Peter) mingles these together [ad invicem] on account of much fittingness and correspondence;[9] because *unity* responds to the *manner*, which looks back to God as efficient cause; *truth*

to the species, which looks back to Him as exemplar; *goodness to the order*, which[10] looks back to God as end.

DOUBT IV

Likewise, is asked concerning that saying which appropriates the truth to the Son: *The most perfect beauty is understood* (to be) *the Son, that is the Truth of the Father*. But against (this speaks St.) Augustine in the SOLILOQUIES:[11] « The truth is that which is »; but being is appropriated to no Person: therefore neither truth.

Likewise, it seems that *order* is badly appropriated to the Holy Spirit, because in the preceding chapter he says, that from order the wise is understood;[12] but *wisdom* is appropriated to the Son: therefore, also *order*.

I RESPOND: It must be said, that truth can be considered in a twofold manner, just as also[13] color. For in one manner color is considered according to *that in which it is*; and thus it is defined in the book, ON SENSING AND THE SENSED:[14] « Color is the extremity of the evident in a bounded body ». In another manner in comparison *to the seeing*, which it moves; and thus is it defined in the book, ON THE SOUL:[15] « Color is a motive of seeing according to the act of the lucid thing ».

Similarly, *truth* can be considered in comparison to that *in which it is*; and thus the truth is[16] that which is; in another manner through a comparison *to the intellect*, which it moves; and thus truth, as the Philosopher says in the second (BOOK) OF METAPHYSICS,[17] « is the end of speculative intelligence ». According to the first manner (St.) Anselm says:[18] « The truth of the Father is the essence of the Father ». As much as regard the second manner (St.) Hilary says,[19] that « truth is declarative 'being' [declarativum esse] ». And since the Son[20] proceeds as the Word, to whom is appropriated the reckoning of the one decla-

---

[1] Alan of Lille (1128-1203 A. D.), ON THE ART or ARTICLES OF THE CATHOLIC FAITH, a. 24: Matter and form and their joining-together are three utterly diverse (things). — The Vatican edition against the manuscripts and edition 1 has less conveniently *are posited* [ponuntur]. Codex V has *composite* [compositum] in place of *composition* [compositio].

[2] Verse 21. — A little before this after *habitudes* [habitudines] the Vatican edition, contradicting the mss. and edition 1, omits *and* [et].

[3] Codex W has *their own their* [propria eorum].

[4] Codex X inserts *in a twofold manner* (,) [dupliciter].

[5] ON THE CELESTIAL HIERARCHIES, ch. 11: All divine intellects are divided into three (categories) according to themselves: into essence and virtue and operation.

[6] Question 18: One is that whereby it is established, another that whereby it is distinguished, another that for which it is suitable. — In which text many manuscripts, together with the first six editions, have *what* [quod] in place of *whereby / for which* [quo], but ineptly. Codex X by glossing (reads): *that which is established from its own principles, that which is suitable in an order with other creatures, that which is discerned by other creatures through a reckoning of image* [quod constat ex suis principiis, quod congruit in ordine cum creaturis aliis, quod discernitur ab aliis creaturis per rationem imaginis].

[7] Supply: *creatures* [creaturae].

[8] From the codices we have supplied *and* [et].

[9] The Vatican edition not trusting the manuscripts has *resemblance* [respondentiam].

[10] The faulty reading of the Vatican edition, *which (goodness)* [quae], we have corrected from the manuscripts. — Although in the principal proposition, that namely in every creature there is a vestige of the Trinity, all the Scholastics agree, however, in the enumeration and explanation of the parts of this vestige there is some

difference among them, as on may see with (Bl.) Dionysius the Carthusian, here in q. 4. Cf. also Bl. (now St.) Albert (the Great), SUMMA., I, tract 3, q. 15, m. 2 and here at a. 13 ff.; and St. Thomas, here at q. 2, a. 3; and in the SUMMA., I, q. 45, a. 7, and at q. 93, a. 6.

[11] Book II, ch. 5: The true seems to me to be that which is.

[12] Codex V and X together with editions 2 and 3 read *wisdom* [sapientia], but contrary to the text of Master (Peter).

[13] We have restored from the manuscripts together with edition 1 the undue omission of the particle *also* [et].

[14] Chapter 3: Wherefore color at least [utique] will be the extremity of the evident [perspicui] in a determinate body (Venetian edition of 1489).

[15] ON THE SOUL, Book II, text 67 (ch. 7): For its every color is something moving according to the act of the diaphanous (Venetian edition of 1489 A. D.).

[16] The Vatican edition, not trusting in the manuscripts and edition 1, adds here less aptly: *which (St.) Augustine says: The truth is that* [quod dicit Augustinus: Veritas est id].

[17] Text 4, according to the Venetian edition of 1489 A.D.: For the end of speculative science is truth.

[18] The words cited seem to be taken from the MONOLOGION, ch. 46, where he shows, that the Son is the Truth and the essence itself of the Substance of the Father.

[19] This is gathered from ON THE TRINITY, Bk. V, n. 3 ff., where he expounds, that « truth is from nature and from virtue », or as is had a little below this, that « the virtue of nature manifests [praestat] truth ».

[20] Trusting in the testimony of many codices and edition 1 we have expunged *is He who* [est qui], which the Vatican edition has added here.

ring, for that reason there is appropriated to Him the reckoning of the exemplar and consequently the reckoning of the truth, as much as it regards the second manner of truth; but He accepts it in the first manner.[1]

To that which is objected concerning *order*, it must be said, that there is an order of things in the universe; and this is appropriated to wisdom; and there is an order of things to the end; and this is appropriated to goodness; and thus it is clear, that there is no contrariety.

COMMENTARY ON DISTINCTION III

PART II

On the cognition of God through near similitudes or through the image.

But, now, let us come presently to that disputation etc..

SEE THE TEXT OF THE MASTER ABOVE ON P. 63, AND ITS DIVISION, ON P. 66.

TREATMENT OF THE QUESTIONS

ARTICLE I

On the first impression of the image.

Consequently, for the understanding of the second part of his present distinction, the Division of which has been put above,[2] as much as regards the first impression [assignationem] of the image, which is through memory, intelligence and will, three (things) are required.

The first is, whether in these three (powers) a reckoning of an image is attained.

The second concerns the comparison of these to the object.

The third concerns their comparison to the soul and/or subject.

QUESTION I

Whether the reckoning of the image is attained in the memory, the intelligence and the will?

On the one hand, it seems, that it is in all together:

1. For there is required for the reckoning of the image an expressed conformation in a distinction; but distinction among the divine is attained as much as regards the Three Persons: therefore, most of all [maxime][3] is it attained in the created image as much as regards the three powers (of the soul).

2. Likewise, the reckoning of the image consists in a perfect capacity, because according to (St.) Augustine[4] « the mind is an image by that, whereby it can be a grasper of and sharer in God [capax et particeps Dei] »; but God is not grasped by the soul fully unless He is loved, nor is He loved unless He is understood, nor is He understood unless He is held present to the soul; but the first is through the will, the second through the intelligence, the third through the memory: ergo etc..

3. Likewise, knowledge [notitia] or intelligence is appropriated to the Son, will to the Holy Spirit: therefore, either the impression of the image will be truncated or diminished, or it is necessary to posit a power responding to the Father.

BUT ON THE CONTRARY: 1. To be an image there is required a representation in a distinction of origin and of order; but in these powers (of the soul) there is no such distinction, because all have been co-created [concreatae] together with the soul, nor is one from another nor one[5] after another: therefore among these there is no finding of a reckoning of image.

2. Likewise, an image is a representation according to an exterior disposition, as is clear;[6] but those three powers (of the soul) are most interior to the soul itself: therefore, among them there is not a reckoning of an image.

3. Likewise, that the *memory* in particular does not concern the reckoning of the image, it seems, because the image, since it of an essential soul and according to (its) rational power is in (the same), but the memory, as the Philosopher says,[7] is of sensibles, because it is in brutes; whence it differs from reminiscence, because reminiscence is not in brutes: therefore, it seems that memory does not pertain to the image. *Moreover,* whether[8] the memory is of sensibles or of in

---

[1] Concerning truth, see more below at d. 8, p. I, a. 1, q. 1.

[2] The Vatican edition omits: *the Division of which has been put above*[cuius division posita est supra], which however, is extant in the manuscripts and edition 1; and a little below this after *in these three* [in his tribus] it has *that is the memory, the intelligence and the will* [scilicet memoria, intelligentia et voluntate].

[3] The Vatican edition, disagreeing with the manuscripts, has *necessarily* [necessario]. — On the various definitions of an image, upon which this argument and the many following are founded, cf. d. 31, p. II, q. 1 and 2, and ibid., doubt 2 and 3.

[4] ON THE TRINITY, Bk. XIV, ch. 8, n. 11. See the text of Master (Peter), d. 3, ch. 2 near the beginning. — A little below this after *present* [praesens] we have put *to* [ad] in place of *with* [apud], with the help of the manuscripts.

[5] Very many codices, as A B I P Q T X etc. here repeat *is* [est].

[6] Codices I X Y read *as is patent in the painted image of a man* [ut in imagine hominis picit patet]. Immediately after this codex I has *therefore, if* [igitur si] in place of *but* [sed].

[7] (Aristotle's) book, ON MEMORY AND REMINISCENCE, chs. 1 and 2 (in other editions chs. 2 & 4). — A little below this after *brutes* [brutis] the Vatican ed. without the authority of any manuscript nor of ed. 1 omits *whence it differs* up to *in brutes* [unde differt ... in brutis], and then it has the indicative for *pertain* [pertinet]. A little before this codd. N and Z have *connatural* [connaturalis] in place of *essential* [essentialis].

[8] The Vatican edition against the manuscripts and edition 1 has *since* [cum] in place of *whether* [sive] and at the end of the argument (on the next page) *and temporal conditions* [temporalibus] in place of *conditions and times* [temporibus].

telligibles, it concerns a difference of time, because there is a present acceptance of (things) past; but an image abstracts from sensible conditions and times.: ergo etc..

4. Likewise, the image is attained in those which are bound to receive an image of reformation or similitudes; but that image consists in the three theological virtues, none of which is in the memory: ergo etc..

5. Likewise, it seems that the *will* does not concern the integrity of the image, because there is said in the book, ON THE SPIRIT AND THE SOUL:[1] « The image is in the power of cognizing, the similitude is in the power of loving [diligendi] »; but the will does not pertain to the cognitive power: ergo etc..

6. Likewise, every power, which concerns the image, ought to be equal to the others, because for the reckoning of an image there is required equality; but the will is not equal to the others, because we understand many (things), which we do not will: ergo etc.. *If you say*, that equality is not attained in respect of objects, but in respect of acts, as is sensing: whatever[2] I understand, I want myself to understand, yet it is not true, because we remember many (things), which we would want not to remember.

CONCLUSION

The reckoning of the image is attained in these three powers, the memory, the intellect and the will, with a comparison to the unity of essence and the plurality of acts.

I RESPOND: It must be said, that, as (St.) Augustine says and Master (Peter) recites,[3] the image is attained in these three powers, however, (this is) in comparison to the unity of essence and the plurality of acts, in which there is distinction and order and origin of one from the other through a certain manner of disposing. For the retention of the species disposes to understanding and understanding to loving, if what is understood is good.[4]

1. And through this the solution to that which is objected is clear: in those powers (of the soul) there is not a distinction through origin: ergo etc..

2. To that[5] which is objected, that an image is attained according to an exterior disposition; it must be said,

that there is a *corporal* and a sensible image of a thing; and this, because it offers itself to cognition through exteriors, has an image representing according to an exterior disposition. And again there is a *spiritual* image of a thing, which is most interior [intima] to each thing, and which is cognized according to which (its) virtue is recovered at a most interior level [recolligitur ad intima]; and this[6] has an image representing as much as regards most interior dispositions.

3. To that[7] which is objected, that memory is of sensibles; it must be said, that memory is accepted in a threefold manner: in one manner insofar as it is receptive and retentive of sensibles and things past; in another manner insofar as it is retentive of things past, whether sensibles or intelligibles; and in the third manner insofar as it is retentive of species, by abstracting from every difference of time, as of innate species. And in this third manner there is a part of the image; but the objection depends upon [currit de] the other first two manners. In the first manner the memory follows sensing, in the second manner it follows the intelligence itself and the will, in the third manner it precedes and (thus) corresponds to the Father.

4. To that which is objected, that the memory is not reformed: it must be said, that nay rather the memory is reformed both as much as regards the state of way and the state of fatherland: in the *first* through *hope*; and this is clear through the exposition of (St.) Augustine on that verse in the twenty-second (chapter) of (St.) Matthew:[8] *You shall love the Lord thy God with (thy) whole heart*, « that is, with an intellect without error, *with (thy) whole soul*, that is, with a will without contradiction, *with (thy) whole mind*, that is, with a memory without forgetting ». In the *second* state it is reformed as much as regards (its) *grasp* [tentionem]; whence (St.) Bernard[9] says, that « God is going to be the fullness of light for the intelligence, the multitude of peace for the will, the continuation of eternity for the memory ». Nor is it[10] unfitting, that the memory, although it be first, be reformed through the last dowry-gift [dotem]; because the order of reformation and deformation begins from the *posterior* [a posteriori], but the order of information[11] begins from the *superior*: for that reason reformation begins from the will and tends even unto the memory.

5. To that which is objected, that the image is in the power of cognizing; it must be said, that the similitude (of the soul to God) means something gratuitous, and for that reason it is said to be through an ap-

---

[1] Chapter 39: The rational soul and the intellect have been made to the image and similitude of God, that one may cognize his Maker in virtue of (His) image [pro imagine], and love (Him) in virtue of His similitude [pro similitudine diligat]. For from the image of God it has reason and from (His) similitude charity.

[2] The Vatican edition contrary to many codices, as A C F G H I K T etc. and edition 1 reads *anything* [quidquid].

[3] Here in ch. 2. — A little after, the Vatican ed. has *with* [cum] for *however, in* [tamen in], but less clearly [signanter] & against the mss. and ed. 1.

[4] The corrupted reading of the Vatican edition, *love according to what is understood to be good* [amandum secundum quod intelligitur esse bonum], we have emended with the help of the mss. and edition 1.

[5] Very many codices, such as A T etc. & edition 1 have *the other* [aliud] in place of *that* [illud].

[6] We have restored from the manuscripts and edition 1 *this* [haec]. A little before this after *virtue* [virtus] there is added in codex A *in an intelligible manner* [intelligibiliter].

[7] With the help of the ancient manuscripts and edition 1 we have expunged from the Vatican edition the added *therefore* [ergo]. A little below this after *of sensibles* [sensibilium] codex O omits *and* [et] and then codex M puts *receptive* [receptiva] in place of *retentive* [retentiva].

[8] Verse 37. The exposition of this passage, ascribed to (St.) Augustine, not only by St. Bonaventure, but also by St. Thomas (SENT., Bk. III, d.

27, exposition of the text), we could not find among the former's works. St. Thomas in the CATENA AUREA, Mt. 22:37, attributes it to the GLOSSA INTERLINEARIS, in which it reads thus: With (thy) whole heart, that is with the intellect, so that you leave no place for error in (your) confession of (His) Divinity; in (thy) whole soul, that is with the will, so that you will nothing contrary to Him, in (thy) whole mind, reminiscing nothing whereby you may think [sentias] less of him. — Both in the book, ON THE SPIRIT AND THE SOUL, ch. 35, and in the book, ON LOVING GOD, ch. 2, which are reckoned among the works of St. Augustine, there is said simply: That is with thy whole intellect and with thy whole will and with thy whole memory.

[9] In his COMMENTARY ON THE SONG OF SONGS, Sermon 11, n. 5. — The Vatican edition contrary to the manuscripts and edition 1 has *that* [quia] in place of *that* [quod].

[10] With the help of the manuscripts and edition 1 we have deleted *also* [etiam]. A little after this codex T has *prior* [prior] in place of *first* [prima].

[11] The Vatican edition reads *formation* [formationis], but this is opposed to the authority of the manuscripts and edition 1, which a little after this also omit *reformation* [reformatio], which for the sake of clarity we have not expunged. See the many things below in the Scholium regarding this question.

propriation in the will or in dilection. But "the image" does not mean "the gratuitous", and[1] for that reason it is said to be in the power of cognizing.

And/or otherwise concerning the image: because in the Son there is a proper[2] image, and to the Son is appropriated intelligence, which is in the cognitive power; for that reason the image is said to be in the power of cognizing.

6. To that:[3] The will is not equal to the intelligence; it must be said, that the will, insofar as it is commonly accepted for 'willing' and 'not-willing', each of which is an act of the will, is well equated, according to which

"using" is said to be common to each, just as (St.) Augustine says and as is had in the text (of Master Peter),[4] that the will seizes the others, while it uses etc.. For anything we think of [recordamur] and/or understand, we accept into the faculty of the will to be chosen and/or rejected; and it is that, according to this, that it means a *common* act of the will;[5] but according to a *special* act, which is 'willing' only, it is not equated; and from that it is opposed, because[6] 'willing' *in this manner* does not comprehend the whole will, as forgetting (does not comprehend) the whole memory and understanding, the whole intelligence.

SCHOLIUM

I. In the response there is a twofold proposition. The *first* is the principal conclusion itself, which says, that the image of the Most High Trinity consists in the said three powers of the soul, to the extent that they include both unity of essence and plurality of second acts. The *second* proposition, which explicates and proves that, is this: just as among the Divine Persons there is both *distinction* and *order* and *origin*, so also among the acts of these powers are these three found. For their acts are really distinguished; further the act of memory or the retention of species *disposes* to understanding and understanding to loving. Whence from the memory there quasi proceeds the act of the intellect, and from the memory and the intellect love.

That threefold distinction of memory (in solution to n. 3) is found also in Alexander of Hales, SUMMA., p. II, q. 62, m. 5, a. 7 and in (Bl.) Peter of Tarentaise, here at q. 5, a. 1.

II. In the solution to n. 4 there is said with the, then, <u>sententia communis</u>, that the memory is reformed in the state of the way through *hope*, in the state of glory through *grasping*. The reason, why hope is attributed to the memory, the Seraphic Doctor exhibits in SENT., Bk. II, d. 16, a. 2, q. 3 in the body, that is « because they have a conformity in act, which is *holding* ». — The words posited in the same place: « The order of reformation and of deformation begins from the posterior » have this sense: the *deformation* of the image through fault and the *reformation* through grace begin from the will, which in the order of powers is the last or the posterior, because the *act* of the

will presupposes the act of the intellect, and here the act of the memory, if "memory" is taken in the third sense, has been explained immediately before this. In this sense the memory is prior and more innermost [intimior] and consequently *superior*. For « in the human soul the same is most interior and supreme » (SENT., Bk. II, d. 8, p. II, q. 2). But in the order of *formation* or *information* these three powers consist of the spiritual life itself as if through a manner of informing form; and so the memory is the first power, and in this sense information begins from it. For an explanation cf. SENT., Bk. II, d. 26, a. 1. q. 5 chiefly in n. 4. — To objection 5 a twofold response is given; concerning the first cf. SENT., Bk. II, d. 16, a. 2, q. 3.

III. In regard to the reckoning of the image see below in d. 31, p. II, a. 1, q. 1 and the Scholium. The other very many things, which occur in this and the following questions, are expounded and proven by the Seraphic Doctor himself in SENT., d. 16; BREVILOQUIUM, p. II, ch. 12; ITINERARIUM MENTIS, ch. 4. — St. Thomas, here in q. 3 & 4; SENT., Bk. II, d. 16; SUMMA., I, q. 93, chiefly in a. 5 & 6. — Alexander of Hales, SUMMA., p. II, q. 62, m. 5, a. 6 and 7. — (Bl. John Duns) Scotus, here in q. 9 and in the REPORTATIO, here in q. 7. — Bl. (now St.) Albertus (Magnus), here in a. 19; SUMMA., p. I, tr. 3, q. 15, m. 2, a. 2. supposition n. 2. — (Bl.) Peter of Tarentaise, here in q. 5, a. 1. — Richard of Middleton, here in p. II, a. 1, q. 1. — Giles the Roman, here in n. 2. at the beginning of q. 1. — Henry of Ghent, SUMMA., a. 40, q. 7, n. 16. — Durandus (of Saint-Pourçain), here in p. II, q. 1. — (Bl) Dionysius the Carthusian, here in q. 8. — (Gabriel) Biel, here in q. 10.

QUESTION II

Whether the image is attained in these powers through their comparison to God?

Second, there is asked concerning the powers in comparison to (their) object, whether, namely, the image in them through their comparison to God.[7] And it seems, that (this is) so.

1. « For this reason the soul is the image, whereby one can be able to seize God and be a partaker (in Him) », as (St.) Augustine says in the fourteenth (book), ON THE TRINITY;[8] but one is able to seize as much as regards one's superior part: ergo etc..

2. Likewise, in the same (book):[9] « The image of Him, than which nothing is better, is to be sought and found there, where our mind has nothing better »; but this is the superior part: ergo etc..

3. Likewise, this seems to be the same by *reason*, because "image" is said by this that it leads unto a prototype:[10] therefore, since That is God, there is not attained in these powers an image,

---

[1] Trusting in the mss. we have restored the particle *and* [et].

[2] The Vatican edition contrary to the manuscripts and edition 1 reads *the prime* [prima]. Codex R reads *for because in the Son properly there is an image* [quia enim in Filio proprie est imago]. Then codices P and Q have *the cognitive power* [potentia cognitiva] in place of *the power of cognizing* [potentia cognoscendi].

[3] Very many codices as X and Y here add *that* [quod], others as B I aa and bb *which is objected that* [quod obiicitur quod].

[4] Here in ch. 2, near the middle, according to which text and with the help of the more ancient manuscripts and edition 1 we have changed in this passage *that* [illam] into *the others* [alia], that is the intelligence and the memory. — Then many codices together with edition 1 omit the particle *for* [enim].

[5] Cf. above d. 1, a. 1, q. 1.

[6] Thus the mss. with ed. 1, though some in place of *because* [quia] have less well *because* [quod], but the Vatican ed.: *From that there is opposition, in what manner willing in this manner* [De isto est opposition, quo modo sic].[7] Codex X adds *only and/or also attained in them through conversion of the soul upon itself and/or also through conversion*

of itself upon inferiors. And it seems first through a comparison to God [tantum vel etiam attendatur in eis per conversionem animae supra se vel etiam per conversionem ipsius super inferiora. Et videtur primo per comparationem ad Deum]. Then after *it seems* [videtur] we have expunged *that* [quia] with the help of very many of the codices and edition 1.

[8] Chapter 8, n. 11; see the text of Master (Peter), here in chapter 2.

[9] ON THE TRINITY, Bk. XIV, ch. 8, n. 11: However, the image of His nature, than which no nature is better, is to be sought and found there in us, where even our nature has nothing better. — In these words the Vatican edition contrary to the manuscripts and edition 1 puts *to be found* [inquirenda] in place of *to be sought ... there* [ibi quaerenda]. Very many codices together with edition 1 have a little after this have *this* [haec] in place of *this* [hoc].

[10] (St.) John Damascene (676-749 A.D.), ON IMAGES, Oration 1, says: And so the image is a similitude expressing the exemplar (πρωτότυπον) in such a manner [ita], however, that it differs from it in some reckoning. And <u>ibid.</u>, Oration 3: And so the image is a similitude, example and effigy of something, in which that of which it is, is shown.

except according to which they lead into God; but through these powers man is lead into God, so long as through them he is converted unto Him: ergo etc..

4. Likewise, God is the object of the theological virtues, in which consist the image of reformation: therefore, since the same is the object of each image, because one is ductive[1] of the other and perfective, if God is the object of one, (He is) also of the other.

ON THE CONTRARY: 1. (St.) Augustine in the ninth (book) of ON THE TRINITY[2] assigns the image in mind, knowledge [notitia] and love, according to which the soul remembers itself, understands itself, loves itself: therefore, it seems, that the image is attained through conversion of itself upon itself.

2. Likewise, (St.) Augustine in the twelfth (book) of ON THE TRINITY, in the fourth chapter:[3] « Since we seek a trinity in the nature of the human mind, let us seek in the whole, not separating the action of temporals from the contemplation of eternals, so that we might still seek a third something »: therefore the trinity of the image is attained according to the action of temporals, and thus through a conversion toward inferiors.

3. Likewise, according to which the soul is converted upon inferiors and/or upon itself, in that[4] there is an equality and order and origin and all things, which concur for the reckoning of the image.

4. Likewise, the image is in sinners turned away from God, and in them also who in no manner can be turned back (to Him), as are the damned: therefore, the reckoning of the image is not attained from within [penes] conversion to God.

5. Likewise, it is necessary [necesse est], as much as regards the perfect reckoning of the image that there be equated [aequari] the one cognizing and the one cognized, or the one saying and the one said; for those two represent the Father and the Son; but in conversion to God there is no such equation [aequatio]: ergo etc..

CONCLUSION

The image, first and principally, is in the powers of the soul, to the extent that they are converted unto God; but secondarily in them, to the extent they are converted toward the soul itself; but to the extent they are converted to inferiors, there is not in them an image, but only a vestige of the Trinity.

I RESPOND: For an understanding of the aforesaid, it is necessary [oportet] to presuppose three (things) in the reckoning of an image: for, *first*, an image is attained according to an express conformity to the one imaged; *second*, that that which is conformed to the image, consequently is conformed[5] to the one imaged; whence he who sees the image of Peter, consequently sees also Peter; *third*, that the souls according to its powers is rendered conform [conformis] to these to which it is converted, either according to (its) cognition, or according to (its) love.

Therefore, since, when the soul is converted to God, it is conformed to itself, and the image is attained according to the conformity: for that reason the image of God consists in this powers, according to which[6] they have (as their) object God.

Again, since the soul is the image of God, and because it is converted and conformed to the image, and to the one imaged,[7] for that reason the soul, according to which it is converted upon itself, does not recede from conformity; and for that reason the image does consist in these powers, according to this that they have the soul for an object.

But when it is converted to inferior creatures, it is conformed to them, in which there is not an image of God, but (rather) a vestige. For that reason[8] the powers of the soul, according to which they have inferiors for objects, recede from the reckoning of the image, because they recede from (their) express conformity.

And, so, though in powers of this kind, according to which they are converted toward inferiors, there is a discovering of a trinity and some conformity, similarly also in the sensitive powers, as (St.) Augustine shows;[9] however, because they lack [deficiunt ab] an express conformity, the reckoning of the image is not found in them. Whence (St.) Augustine investigates among all the powers of the soul for a trinity, not because the image is in them, but to exclude (them) from the reckoning of the image. Whence seeking the whole[10] trinity in the whole soul, he seeks it in the superior and inferior part of the reason and in the sense. And this is what he says in that authority: « When in the nature of the human mind we seek a *trinity*, we seek it in the whole »; he does not say "we seek the *image*." Whence (St.) Augustine in the twelfth (book of) ON THE TRINITY, in the fourth chapter:[11] « Although in the inferior part of reason a trinity can be found, however, the image cannot be found ».

It must be conceded, therefore, that the image consists in these powers, according to which they are converted toward the soul, however, first and principally, as they show the first reasons, according to which they are converted toward God. Whence (St.) Augustine in these two manners assigns the image: first it is in mind, knowledge and love,

---

[1] Some codices as F M Y together with edition 1 have *directive* [directiva] in place of *ductive* [ductiva]. Codex K (by a second hand) has *ductive and/or directive in the cognition of the other* [ductiva vel directive in cognitionem alterius]. Then the Vatican edition not trusting in the manuscripts and edition 1 after *perfective* [perfectiva] adds *moreover* [praeterea] and after *of one* [unius] adjoins *therefore* [ergo].

[2] Chapter 4, n. 4, in the assignment of which image the Vatican ed. ,both contrary to the text of (St.) Augustine and contrary to the mss. and ed. 1, puts *understanding* [intellectu] in place of *knowledge* [notitia].

[3] Number 4, in which text in place of *action of temporals* [temporalium] there is read in the original *rational action among temporals* [rationalem in temporalibus].

[4] We follow codices D F T by adjoining the manifestly to be supplied *in that* [in ipsa].

[5] The Vatican edition has (the indicative) *conformed* [conformatur] and a little after this (the indicative) *rendered* [redditur].

[6] We have restored the better reading of the manuscripts and edition 1 by putting *according to which* [secundum quod] in place of *which* [quae]. A little before this in many codices, as A F G H K T etc. after *image* [imago] there is absent *of God* [Dei].

[7] Thus the greater part of the codices B D E H I K V W etc. together with edition 1; the others omit *converted and* and/or *and conformed* [convertitur et]. But the Vatican edition against all the codices has *and according to which it is conformed to the image* [et secundum quod conformatur imagini]; codices L O Y by filling the ellipsis after *to the image* [imagini] add *it is conformed* [conformatur].

[8] Some codices, such as A T bb, together with edition 1, add *therefore* [ergo].

[9] For (St.) Augustine's opinion concerning the trinity in the powers of the soul turned toward inferiors, see ON THE TRINITY, Bk. XII, and on the trinity in the sensitive powers ibid., Bk. XI. — A little before this after *similarly* [similiter] the particle *and* [et], unduly omitted from the Vatican edition, we have recalled from the manuscripts and edition 1.

[10] We have supplied from the manuscripts *the whole* [totam].

[11] Number 4: But in this that it has been derived in the action of temporals, even if there can be a trinity, the image of God, however, cannot be found.

according to which the mind knows and loves itself; the second is in the memory, intelligence and will. And at the end of the book he shows, that the most complete reckoning of the image is in (their) comparison to God.[1]

1. 2. 3. From these the response to the first and second and third is clear: because the first argument must be conceded, but the second concludes, that in the inferior part there is a trinity, and the third, that (there is) a conformity; but these have been explained [soluta], because it is not an expressed (image).

4. To that which is objected concerning the aversion of sinners, it must be explained [solvendum],[2] that we do not speak of an image in these powers according to (their) *actual* conversion, but (rather according to their) *aptitudinal* (conversion), which never leaves the powers: just as a man is also said (to be) 'able to take steps' [gressibilis], who has truncated feet, even though he does not take steps.

5. To that which is objected, that is it necessary [necesse est] in the image, that the one cognizing and the one cognized be adequated [adaequari]; it must be said, that it is not necessary [oportet], that the one cognized be adequated to the one cognizing by an adequation of *thing to thing* [rei ad rem], but (rather) under *the reckoning of the cognizable* [sub ratione cognoscibilis]. Whence, the cognized is only in the intelligence, as much as it is represented by the memory. But it is not necessary that it be simply adequated; however, it is adequated, according to which the soul is converted upon itself. Whence, the reckoning of the image, in regard to something, is more in the conversion of the soul upon itself. In the conversion toward God, it is more, because it has more of the reckoning of loveliness [venustatis] and of conformity; in conversion toward itself, it has more a reckoning of consubstantiality and equality.

SCHOLIUM

I. The distinction of reckoning among the superior and inferior part, in the body (of the Question), is accepted not on the part of the *power*, but on the part of the *object*, to the extent that the soul attains the exterior and inferior object, and/or the interior and superior, or as the Seraphic Doctor says: « There is no difference except according to (their) gaze [aspectum] », SENT., d. 24, p. I, a. 2, q. 2, cf. also ibid. p. II, a. 1, q. 1; BREVILOQUIUM., p. I. ch. 12; ITINERARIUM MENTIS, ch. 1. — Alexander of Hales, SUMMA., p. I. q. 2. m. 3, a. 3. — St. Thomas, SUMMA., I. q. 79, a. 9 and 10; DE VERITATE., q. 15, a. 1 and 2.

II. In regard to the question itself: Alexander of Hales, SUMMA., p. II, q. 62, m. 5, a. 5 §. 2. — Bl. (now St.) Albertus (Magnus), here in a. 22; SUMMA., p. I, tr. 3, q. 15, m. 2, a. 2 subp. — (Bl.) Peter of Tarentaise, here in q. 5, a. 4. — Richard of Middleton, here in a. 1. q. 2. — Giles the Roman, here at 2nd princ., q. 3. — See the others, in the Scholium to the preceding (Question).

QUESTION III

Whether the memory, the intelligence and the will are the same in essence as the soul?

In the third place, there is asked concerning the comparison of those powers (of the soul) to the soul or to[3] (their) subject, whether namely they are the same in essence as the soul. And it seems, that (it is) so.

1. (St.) Augustine says in the tenth (book of) ON THE TRINITY:[4] « These three, memory, intelligence and will are one mind, one life, one essence, and through this one substance ».

2. Likewise, (St.) Bernard in ON THE SONG OF SONGS:[5] « I intuit a certain three in the soul, memory, intelligence and will, and that these three (are the soul) itself ». *If you say*, that this is said by way of a cause [per causam]; this is nothing, because (St.) Augustine in ON THE SPIRIT AND THE SOUL[6] says, that the soul « is its own certain (thing), as the powers, and a certain (thing) not its own, as the virtues »; which, if it were said by way of a cause, each could be said.

3. Likewise, this very (thing) the Philosopher seems to want to say,[7] because he says the same is the principle of being [principium essendi] and of operating: therefore since the principle of being is the substantial form itself, the principle of operating [principium operandi] will be the same; but the principle of operating is a power: therefore, a power is the principle of being; but there is no principle of being in man except the substantial form: therefore, a power and the substantial form are the same in substance.

4. Likewise, it is shown *by reason*: 'Just as prime matter is bound to receive all through truth, so the soul according to similitude;[8] but the power of prime matter in respect of the forms to be received [suscipiendarum] does not differ through essence from it:[9] therefore, it seems similarly, that the power of the soul (also does not differ)'. *Proof*: for if it would differ through essence, either it would be a *substance*, or an *accident*. Not an accident, because it antecedes every form and every

---

[1] Concerning the first impression see ON THE TRINITY, Bk. IX throughout; concerning the second ibid., Bk. X, ch. 11 and 12; concerning the most complete reckoning of the image ibid., Bk. XIV, ch. 8 and 12 ff..

[2] The Vatican edition, contrary to the manuscripts, has *I respond* [respondeo] for *it must be explained* [solvendum].

[3] Codex O adds *their own* [suum].

[4] Chapter 11, n. 18. See also here in the text of Master (Peter), ch. 2 at the beginning.

[5] Sermon 11. At the end of the text cited, supply, together with the edition of Works of St. Bernard, *are the soul* [animam esse]. The Vatican edition, at the beginning of this text, omits *three* [Tria] and near the end reads *and it itself is these three* [haec tria ipsa est].

[6] Chapter 13: God is all His own, and the soul a certain its-own. If indeed it has natural (powers) and is itself all (things). For its powers and strengths [vires] are the same (as) what it itself (is). It has accidentals, and it itself is not (these). It is its own strengths, it is not its own virtues. — At the end of the argument the Vatican edition contrary to the manuscripts and edition 1 omits *said* [dictum].

[7] See Aristotle, PHYSICS, Bk. II, text 28 (ch. 3); METAPHYSICS, Bk. VII, text 59 & 60 (Bk. VI, ch. 17) and Bk. VIII, text 8 (Bk. VII, ch. 3) and ON THE SOUL, Bk. II, text 2, where he teaches, that the substantial form is the principle of being, inasmuch as, that is, by its own actuality it gives the 'being' of a thing [esse rei] and constitutes it in a certain species; PHYSICS, Bk. II, text 11 ff. (ch. 1), where he asserts, that the substantial form is the *nature*, i. e. the principle of moving and resting; ON THE SOUL, Bk. II, text 24 (ch. 2), where he describes the soul as the substantial form: that by which we live and sense and are first moved and understand.

[8] Cf. Aristotle, ON THE SOUL, Bk. III, text 17 and 37 ff. (chs. 5 & 8).

[9] Aristotle, PHYSICS, Bk. I, text 81 ff. (last ch.); METAPHYSICS, Bk. VIII, text 3 ff. and Bk. XII, text 26 (Bk. VII, ch. 1 and Bk. XI, ch. 5). Thus does Averroës teach, in his book, ON THE SUBSTANCE OF THE ORB. — Then after *that* [quod] we have substituted from the manuscripts and edition 1 *power* [potentia] in place of *of the power* [potentiae]. Then after *Proof* [Probatio] the Vatican edition, contrary to the more ancient codices and edition 1, adds *of the minor* [minoris].

accident; if a *substance*, therefore either matter, or form. Moreover, if it differed, (power) would be a capable matter for it.[1]

5. Likewise, the accidental form is not more simple than the substantial form; but the power of operating does not differ from the accidental form, as for example [utpote] the power of making warm does not differ through essence from warmth, nor the power of illumining from light itself: therefore, it similarly seems, that neither does the power of the soul from the soul itself.

6. Likewise, what is an accident, is substantial of no substance;[2] but its powers are substantial: therefore, they are not accidents of the soul:[3] therefore, they are substances; it is established that (they are) not other than the soul. *Proof of the minor*: because in man the "rational", "sensible", "vegetable" soul does not mean a diversity of substances, but of powers: therefore, it is established, that in man these differences: *vegetable, sensible, rational*, are accepted as powers; but[4] differences of this kind are substantial: therefore, also the powers: ergo etc..

ON THE CONTRARY: 1. (St.) Augustine in the fifteenth (book of) ON THE TRINITY[5] assigns the difference of the created image to that Trinity, that is the Uncreated One, because in that Trinity there is One having that which it had, but here there is not one having that which is had: therefore, if the soul has three powers, therefore, essentially it is not them.

2. Likewise, Dionysius (the Areopagite)[6] says, that in every created (being) these three differ: *substance, virtue* and *operation*: therefore, in the soul, too, substance and powers differ.

3. Likewise, (St. Severinus) Boethius (says):[7] « In every created (being) there differ '*that whereby it is*' and '*that which it is*', or '*what it is*' and (its) '*to be*' [esse] »: therefore, similarly, nay rather more strongly, '*that it can*' and '*that whereby it can*'.

4. Likewise, it is thus shown *by reasons*: what differs in genus, differs in essence, and one is not predicated of the other essentially;[8] but the powers and the soul are of this kind, because the soul is in the genus of substance, but its powers are in the second species of quality, that is of a natural power and/or impotence: ergo etc..

5. Likewise, those of which one is outside the other, differ essentially and substantially; but virtue steps forth from substance,[9] because it works on the object, which is outside; but it is impossible, that it works where it is not; if therefore virtue is where it works, it works outside the substance of each [cuiuslibet]: therefore, it steps forth from substance: ergo etc..

6. Likewise, for this there is another reason, because if by the same essence there were soul and powers, therefore[10] one would not be multiplied unless according to the multiplication of the other; and thus, since there is only one soul, it would have only one power; but this is false: ergo etc..

CONCLUSION

The powers of the soul are substantial and are in the same genus, through reduction, in which the soul is; however, they are not entirely the same as it through essence.

I RESPOND: For the understanding of the aforesaid things it must be noted, that "natural power" is meant in a twofold manner.[11] *In one manner*, insofar as it means the manner of existing of a natural power in a subject, according to which it means a subject easy and/or difficult to do something; and thus "natural power" means a manner of quality and is generally in the second species of quality, as is clear, when there is said "*runner*" [cursor] and "*fighter*" [pugillator], each of which means a faculty, which is consequent to[12] the manner of existing of the power of stepping forth and/or resisting or acting in the subject. *In another manner*, "natural power" is meant (as) a power naturally stepping forth from a subject.[13] And this can be in a twofold manner. For any power steps forth from a substance *with an accident*, as

---

[1] Edition 1 reads *it would be incapable of it* [illius esset incapax].

[2] It is simply the converse of this proposition: *What truly is* (i.e. a substance) *accedes to nothing*, which Aristotle posts in PHYSICS, Bk. I, text 27, (ch. 3).

[3] The interpolated reading of the Vatican edition *what is an accident of one, is a substance of none, but those powers (of the soul) are substantial to the soul itself, therefore, they are not accidental to it and consequently they are not accidents* [quod uni est accidens, nulli substantia est, sed istae potentiae sunt ipsi animae substantiales, ergo non sunt ei accidentales et per consequens non sunt accidentalis], we have corrected from the manuscripts and edition 1, which also at *it is established* [constat] omit the *but* [autem], added by the Vatican edition.

[4] The Vatican edition, disagreeing with the manuscripts and edition 1, has *and* [et] in place of *but* [sed]. A little before this codex M prefaces *powers* [potentiis] with *those* [istis].

[5] See the passage above, in the text of Master (Peter), ch. 3, at the beginning.

[6] ON THE CELESTIAL HIERARCHY, ch. 11. Cf. above in p. I of this distinction, Doubt 3. — Trusting in the codices and edition 1, a little after this we have inserted *also* [et] after *therefore* [ergo].

[7] In the book, HOW SUBSTANCES TO THE EXTENT THAT THEY ARE, ARE GOOD or ON THE SEVEN DAYS says: Diverse is the "to be" [esse] and "that which is". And a little after this: For every composite the "to be" [esse] is one part [aliud], "itself" is the other. In explanation of this proposition Gilbert of Porretain says: The one is *what it is*, the other *that whereby it is*. See also the book, ON THE TRINITY, ch. 2. — Very many codices as A E S V W X after *or* [sive] read *what its' to be' is* [quid est esse], codex Y has *whatever its 'to be' was* [quiquid erat esse].

[8] Aristotle, METAPHYSICS, Bk. X, text 12, (Bk. IX, ch. 3): In genus (they differ) indeed, of which there is not a common matter nor a generation for one another, to whichever of these (belongs) the other figure of the category (of

predication). — A little below this after *but ... powers* [sed potentiae] we have restored the reading of the manuscripts and edition 1 by adding *its* [eius] and a little after this *and/or impotence* [vel impotentiae]. A little before this codex X reads *but the powers of the soul and the soul* [sed potentiae animae animae et anima]. — Concerning the four species of quality see Aristotle, ON THE PREDICAMENTS, ch. on Qualities.

[9] That is, outside of substance; thus Tacitus very often says *to step forth from the boundaries* [terminos egredi]. — A little after this to the word *it works* [operetur] codex X adds *there* [ibi]. Then codex M in place of *of each* [cuiuslibet] has *to which it belongs* [cuius est], but codex T has *of anything* [cuiusque].

[10] Trusting in the mss. and ed. 1 we have supplied the *therefore* [ergo] and a little below this from codices B D H N P Q V W X aa ee we have substituted *one* [una] for *one (thing)* [unum]. Codex F has *just as the soul is only one* [sicut anima est una tantum], with which codd. I and O agree, with this exception, that for *one* [una] they read *one (thing)* [unum] and then after *only one (thing)* [tantum] they add *as (is) the soul* [sic anima]. — Alexander of Hales, SUMMA., p. II, q. 65, m. 1, refers to the same argument and adds the principles upon which it founded, that is: For whatever same are of one and of the same, are among themselves the same.

[11] The Vatican edition against nearly all the codices and editions 1, 2, and 3 has less correctly *in a threefold manner* [tripliciter]. Then, having questioned the manuscripts, we have substituted *In one* [Uno] and a little below *In another manner* [Alio modo] in place of *In the first* [Primo] and *In the second manner* [Secundo modo].

[12] The Vatican edition has *follows* [sequitur] and a little after this it has *and* [et] in place of *and/or* [vel], but the mss. and ed. 1 oppose this.

[13] The Vatican edition, less strictly exhibits opposition with the first member of the division by putting *from a substance* [a substantia] in place of *from a subject* [a subiecto], in disagreement with the mss. and edition 1; then in place of *For* [Nam] it has *In one manner* [Uno modo].

the power of making-warm (does). For fire through its own substance does not make (anything) warm without warmth; and this power does not belong to another genus than is the quality, from which it steps forth; whence the power[1] of making-warm is in the same genus as warmth. In another manner is meant the "natural power", which naturally steps forth from[2] a substance and (does so) *immediately*, as (is) the power of generating as much as regards the induction of the ultimate form; and this indeed does not belong to another genus than substance, but it is reduced to the genus of substance as a substantial difference.

Through this standard of measure [modum] it must be understood in the powers of the soul. For *in one manner* one happens to name the powers of the soul according to the first manner, as they mean the facility, which means the manner of the existing of the power in the subject, as (are) ingeniousness and tardiness (of mind); and these indeed are in the second species of quality. *In another manner* one happens to name the powers, insofar as they mean the order of substance to the act, which is *by means of* [mediante] some accidental property, as (is) the power of syllogizing, which is in the soul, when it has the habit of syllogizing; and this is in the same genus, in which the science of syllogizing is, as[3] in the first species of quality. *Again* it happens that one names the powers of the soul, as they step forth *immediately* from the substance, as (one does) through[4] these three: memory, intelligence and will. And this is clear, because with every accident excluded [circumscripto],[5] having understood that the soul is a spiritual substance, by this very (thing) that (the soul) is present to itself and has been conjoined with itself, it has power to remember and understand and love itself. Whence its powers are consubstantial[6] to the soul and are in the same genus through a reduction, in that which is the soul. But however, since they step forth from the soul — for power holds itself through the manner of one stepping forth — they are not entirely the same through essence, nor, however, do they differ to such an extent, as to belong to another genus, but they are in the same genus through reduction.

A sufficiently manifest example can be given in a *thing* and in *its similitude*. For a thing does not have as great an identity with its similitude, that they be one in number, nor so much diversity, that they differ in genus.[7] For the similitude of Martin does not stand so far from Martin, that it differs thoroughly from him. And thus the similitude of a thing is in the same genus through a reduction as that, of which it is the similitude. For because it steps forth, for that reason it differs, but it does not pass over into another genus. And I speak of "similitude" according to the reckoning of similitude, not (according to the reckoning) of intention, that is, insofar that it goes forth from a subject[8] and does not withdraw (from it), as brilliance [splendor] (does) from light. Therefore, the reasons proving, that the soul is not its powers through essence, are to be conceded.

1. 2. To that, therefore, which is objected unto the contrary concerning (Sts.) Augustine and Bernard, that the soul is its own powers; it must be said that, There, there is no predication of accident from a subject, nor of the same by essence, but of the substantial and/or essential.

On account of which it must be noted, that (something) is said (to be) "essential" in four manners. *In the first manner* the "essential" is said[9] (to be) that which means the whole essence of the thing, as the species of the singular. *In the second manner* the "essential" is said (to be) that which concerns the essence and the constitution of the thing, as matter and form. *In the third* manner the "essential" is said (to be that) without which the thing cannot be nor can it be understood to be, as are those in which the reckoning of the vestige is attained, as unity, truth, (and) goodness. *In the fourth* manner the "essential" is said (to be that) without which the thing cannot be thought to have been perfected, as are the powers in the soul, in which the image is attained; and this is in the least manner substantial or essential; however, it does not pass over into another genus: for that reason the soul is said (to be) its powers.[10]

3. To that which is objected, that the same is the principle of being and operating; it must be said, that it is true of a remote principle, but of a proximate it is impos-

---

[1] With the help of the manuscripts and edition 1 we have expunged here the badly added *which is* [quae est]. A little after this codex Y reads *In the second manner* [Secundo modo] in place of *In another manner* [Alio modo], for which many codices as A B D E I N S T etc. together with edition 1 have, less aptly, *In a third manner* [Tertio modo].

[2] The Vatican edition, disagreeing with the manuscripts and edition 1, has *from* [de] in place of *from* [a] and immediately after this omits, less well, *and* [et]. A little below this same authority, after *to another genus* [generis] we have put *than* [quam] in place of *with* [cum], as being better grammatically and more conformable to the preceding things.

[3] Editions 4 & 5 have *namely* [videlicet] in place of *as* [ut]. Then codex X has *Beyond the third manner one happens* [Ultra tertio modo contingit] in place of *Again one happens* [Contingit iterum].

[4] The Vatican edition contrary to the manuscripts and the first six editions omits *through* [per]. That the powers immediately step forth from the substance, St. Thomas also teaches, SUMMA., I, q. 77, a. 6. Cf. in addition (Bl.) Dionysius the Carthusian, here in q. 14.

[5] That is, having excluded or prescinded from it. — At the end of this proposition in the Vatican edition there is omitted *and love* [et diligendum], but in very many codices (there is omitted) *and to understand* [et intelligendum], but contrary to the context and to the other codices, as I T aa together with edition 1.

[6] On the authority of the manuscripts and edition 1 we have put *consubstantial* [consubstantiales] in place of *substantial* [substantiales].

[7] In very many manuscripts and the Vatican edition there is had in a manifestly false manner *in number* [numero] in place of *in genus* [genere], which however, codex Z exhibits. Then the greater part of the codices together with edition 1 faultily read *Peter differs* [Petrus differt] in place of *it differs thoroughly* [penitus differat]. (St.) John Damascene, ON IMAGES, Oration 3, says: For one is the image, and the other that which is represented by the image; and it is necessary, that *not-nothing* of a diving line between each be perceived; if indeed this one would not

be the other thing, nor that one the other. — A little below this, having reviewed the manuscripts, we have substituted *thus* [ita] for *for that reason* [ideo].

[8] Codex A *the substance*. At the end of the response codex aa adds these (words): *And/or it can be said, that the soul is considered either according to essence as an essence, or according to essence as a substance, or according to essence as a subject. If in the first manner, it thus consists from its own principles, and thus the soul is not the very thing [idipsum] which its powers (are), but consequently they are held for it, for this reason that they are founded upon the vigor of its existence according to its principles. If in the second manner, then the soul is also its powers, because the soul subsists in its powers. If in the third manner according to essence in the reckoning of a subject, thus the soul itself is subjected to its virtues, and thus it is not the same with its powers.* A gloss according to the mind of Alexander of Hales, SUMMA., p. II, q. 21, m. 1, in reply to n. 2 and q. 65, m. 1.

[9] From the manuscripts and editions 1, 2, 3 & 6, we have supplied *is said (to be)* [dicitur]. Then the manuscripts have a doubtful reading, which can be read *the whole* [tantum] and *only the* [tantum]; although edition 1 has *only the* [tantum], we however retain *the whole* on account of the context. And this is confirmed by Bl. (now St.) Albert (the Great), SUMMA., I, tract 3, q. 13, m. 5, saying: For (St. Severinus) Boethius says, that species is the whole being [totum esse] of individuals. (COMMENTARY ON PORPHYRY, Bk. III, dealing with species says: But man is the whole substance of Socrates or Cicero.) — Then after *species* [species] for the sake of clarity the Vatican edition adds *means the whole essence* [dicit totam essentiam], though this is lacking in the manuscripts.

[10] The Vatican edition not trusting in the manuscripts and edition 1 repeats here *because it does not pass over into another genus* [quia non transit in aliud genus].

sible. For if the same where entirely the proximate principle, then it would be the same in the thing 'to be' and 'to work'. *Similarly*, if the same were the proximate principle, since the thing always has a being [esse], it would always have a working [operari]. Therefore, since[1] *form* means the proximate and immediate principle of being, but *power* the proximate and immediate principle of working, it is clear that it is impossible to be entirely the same.

4. To that which is objected concerning the power of matter, it must be said, that matter is not its own power by essence, since it is not itself an ordination to form; however, there is a power itself of matter essential to matter itself, just as an active power (is) to the substance itself. And indeed the power of matter is less distanced [elongatur] from matter than an active power (is) from substance; since the power of matter is a passive power, which means an 'order to something with a privation', but an active power means an 'order with position'; and for that reason it adds less to the power of matter upon matter, than an active power upon[2] substance. And hence it is, that the diverse powers are not so distinguished in the same matter, as (they are) in the same substance.

5. To that which is objected concerning the accidental form, it must be said, that an accidental form is not its own power. For the power belongs to it, inasmuch as it inflows into another; but however, that power does not add as much as the power of the substantial form (does), since the power of the substantial form means an ordination to act, but not 'one sufficient through itself', but (rather) '(sufficient) by virtue of the substance'. For just as the accident *is* not through itself, so that it does not have the virtue of *operating* through itself, but by the virtue of the substance; and thus this (argument) it is clear.

6. To that which is objected lastly, it must be said,[3] that the powers of the soul are not accidental. However, the argument is not valid, because perhaps the *rational, sensible,* (and) *vegetable* are not accepted as powers, but as diverse natures discovered in the soul.

But that argument, that has been made to the opposite, that they do differ, because they are in diverse genera, must be explained through interemption,[4] because they are not in diverse genera, but (they are) in the same (genus) through reduction.

SCHOLIUM

I. About the principal question, in those times three sentences used to be defended, which St. Bonaventure (SENT., Bk. II, d. 24, p. I, a. 2, q. 1) accurately explains. *The first* sentence posited there does not admit between the essence of the soul and the powers (anything) except a distinction *of reason*. Thus William of Paris, Richard of Middleton (here in a. 2, q. 1), Henry of Ghent (QUODLIBETALS, Bk. IV, q. 7),* besides all the Nominalists. — *The second* teaches a *real* distinction, and indeed such, that the powers agree *neither in genus* with the substance, since they are drawn to the genus of accidents. Thus St. Thomas (here in q. 4, a. 2; SUMMA., I, q. 54, a. 3 and q. 77 a. 1 and 3; DE SPIRITU CREATURIS, a. 11; ON THE SOUL, q. 12); Bl. (now St.) Albertus (Magnus) (here in a. 34); (Bl.) Peter of Tarentaise (here in q. 5, a. 2). — *The third* sentence, which Alexander of Hales teaches (SUMMA., p. II, q. 65, m. 1, and q. 21, m . 1), nearly approaches the preceding one. St. Bonaventure also favors this one more; however, he says: « But each of the said positions has its own defenders, nor it is easy to disprove any of them with cogent reasons ». Therefore, this last sentence indeed admits among the substance of the soul and its connatural and consubstantial powers a certain [quandam] *real* distinction, which however, does not draw the powers to a diverse genus of predicament, namely of accident (however, the *acquired habits*, by which other (things) outside the soul are cognized and loved, certainly fall under the genus of accidents). Nay if the powers were not consubstantial with the soul, the soul would never know and love anything outside itself, because, as St. Augustine says, no accident exceeds a subject, that is its own virtue. F or an accident, just as *it is* not except by virtue of its substance, so neither can it *work* except by virtue of the substance, and unless something substantial is spread beneath it. Whence neither can the acquired habits act except by virtue of the habits and/or substantial powers, cf. here at n. 5 and article 2, q. 2. at n. 4 and St. Thomas, SUMMA., I, q. 77, a. 1 at n. 4. — But it seems, that St. Bonaventure and Alexander (of Hales) take the concept of the *accident* as a logical

accident, (and) St. Thomas as a metaphysical accident, so that in re they do agree. Behold the words of Alexander (of Hales) (SUMMA., p. II, q. 21, m. 1): « It must be said, that the soul is in a certain manner its own power, to make a distinction among the substantial powers or strengths on one part and the accidents on the other, as much as regards this, that the powers and strengths substantially inhere and are one with the soul as much as regards the substance, I do not say as much as regards the essence; for by the substantial powers does the soul subsist. But the accidents, as prudence, fortitude and the like, do not adhere substantially, because they are there accidentally. Whence the powers and substantial strengths are said (to be) the same that the soul (is) by reason of indivision and substantial adherence ». Nearly the same is what St. Thomas (SUMMA., I, q. 77, a. 1, at n. 5) teaches. For he distinguishes a twofold sense of the word *accident*, and in the second sense, or « according to which it is posited as one of the five universals », he concedes, that « something is the medium between the substance and the accident », and that « the powers of the soul cant be said to be the media between the substance and the accident, as if natural properties of the soul ».

The fourth sentence is added by (Bl. John Duns) Scotus (SENT., Bk. II, d. 16, q. sole, § "Therefore, I say", who here applies his formal distinction; but in the thing St. Bonaventure scarcely departs, as Brülifer would have it in his Commentary on this point.

On this question, cf. besides those cited above, Bl. (now St.) Albertus (Magnus), SUMMA., p. I, tr. 3. q. 15, m. 2, q. 2, subp. 1. — Giles the Roman, here in n. 3 at the beginning of q. 1, a. 2. — Durandus (of Saint-Pourçain), here in p. II, q. 2 and ff.. — (Bl.) Dionysius the Carthusian, here in q. 13. — (Gabriel) Biel, SENT., Bk. II, d. 24 and 25.

II. So that there may be more easily understood the Doctor's words placed at the end of the conclusion: « I speak of the similitude according to the reckoning of similitude, not of intention », we note these things. Besides the *accidental* similitude, which is for example in an exterior figure, and the *essential*,

---

[1] The Vatican ed. contrary to very many codd. and ed. 1 has *Therefore, because* [Quia ergo].   [2] Codex O adds *form or* [formam aut].
[3] From the codices and edition 1 we have added *must* [est]. Very many codices as A T etc. a little before this have *is asked* [quaeritur] in place of *is objected* [obiicitur].
[4] Peter of Spain, SUMMULA., tract "On sophistic Syllogisms or on Fallacies", at the end of the (treatment on) the fallacy of equivocation says: The right solution is a manifestation of the false syllogism and that on account of which it is false. And this happens in a two fold manner, that is *by distinguishing* and/or by the *interemption* [interimendo] of one

of the premises; and in this second manner one must respond to everything sinning in the matter (i. e. to the false propositions). Aristotle, ELENCHAE, Bk. II, ch. 3 (ch. 18), when proposing this twofold species of solution, used the words διαιρεῖν and ἀναιρεῖν, which (St. Severinus) Boethius rendered in the Latin tongue by the words distinguere and interimere (i.e. to take away by negating). — A little above this some codices, such as A G H K T etc., together with edition 1, have (the subjunctive) for *they differ* [differant].

---

* *Trans. note*: In the Scholium to Sent., Bk. II, d. 24, p. I, a. 2, q. 1, p. 563, this citation is corrected to Quodlibetals, 3, q. 14.

which is in fittingness in nature and species, the Seraphic Doctor distinguishes another twofold similitude, that is the similitude *according to reckoning*, by which some are similar in a certain essential reckoning, as brilliance (is) in respect to light, and the similitude *according to intention*, which is among some, one of which has been made for the imitation of the other. From this it is clear, that *brilliance*, which is a similitude of light, though it goes forth from light, does not however, recede from it, remaining in the same genus of light.

III. In the solution to nn. 1 and 2 the Seraphic Doctor distinguishes *a threefold predication*. A predication by *essence* [per essentiam] is made, when the predicate concerns the intrinsic reckoning of the subject. Again this is twofold, namely according to a twofold sense of the word, "*essential*", here distinguished by the Seraphic Doctor. For even both the *metaphysical* essence, as the moderns call it (that is the genus and difference), and the constitutive *physical* parts (that is the form and matter), concern the essence of the thing and are predicated essentially of the subject. To this is opposed *accidental* predication, when the predicate only accidentally convenes with the subject, such as in, "The man is wise". — About the *third* predication, which is here distinguished, it must be noted, that it is one thing « to be from the essence of any thing », another « to be the same in essence with something ». « For *what belongs* [proprium] to any thing does not concern the essence of the thing, but is caused from the essential principles of the species, whence there is a medium between essence and accident » (St. Thomas, SUMMA., I, q. 77, a. 1, at n. 5). Even the powers of the soul do not concern the essence of the soul, nor are they predicated of it in the first manner of meaning *per se*, as genus is predicated of species. Nevertheless, the powers do participate in the same nature with the essence of the soul, or are « the same in essence with it ». Concerning which cf. Alexander of Hales, SUMMA., p. I, q. 18, m. 2 and Bl. (now St.) Albertus (Magnus), here in q. 34.

It is worth noting the doctrine of the Seraphic (Doctor) in the solution to n. 4 on the power of matter. Alexander of Hales teaches the same thing, SUMMA., p. II, q. 65, m. 1. Cf. (Bl. John Duns) Scotus, PHYSICS, Bk. I, a. 20; ON THE FIRST PRINCIPLE OF THINGS, q. 8, a. 2; SENT., Bk. I, d. 12, q. 1. — Richard of Middleton, SENT., Bk. II, d. 12, q. 10. — St. Thomas, here in q. 4, q. 2, at n. 4. — Bl. (now St.) Albertus (Magnus), SENT., Bk. I, d. 26, a. 6, at n. 8.

ARTICLE II

On the second impression of the image.

Consequently there is the question concerning the *second* impression of the image through mind, knowledge [notitia] and love [amorem]. And[1] about this there are asked three (things).

The *first* concerns these absolutely, namely, whether the image is attained in these as in the powers, or in the habits, or in the powers and habits simultaneously, or in the substance and in the habits.

The *second* concerns these in comparison to one another.

The *third*, whether this trinity of image leads necessarily unto cognition of the Trinity as much as regards the Persons.

QUESTION I

Whether the image is attained in mind, knowledge and love as in powers, or as in habits,

or in both at once, or according to substance and habits?

About the first, (the argument) is advanced thus:

1. *First* it is shown, that the image is not attained in these as in the *powers*, because the aforesaid assignation[2] was in the powers: therefore, if this would also be in the powers, it would be naught but a flourish of words [inculcatio verborum].

Besides, "knowledge" and "love" do not mean a power, but a habit, though "mind" can mean a power: therefore, the aforesaid three cannot be posited under a reckoning of powers.

2. Likewise, it is shown, that they do not mean *habits*, because (St.) Augustine[3] says on the assignation and approbation of the image: « The mind knows [novit] itself, loves [diligit] itself »; but to no habit does it belong to know or love [amare] itself: ergo etc..

Likewise, if "mind" stands for "habit", I ask, for which habit? If for the habit of memory, concerning which it rather seems, that there is not another to give (it to); but the act of this habit is to remember, (there is) no other; but (St.) Augustine[4] assigns to the mind those acts, that is to know and to love: ergo etc..

3. Likewise it is shown, that (it is) not[5] in the *powers and the habits*. For since the powers are three, and the habits three, then there would not be a group of three [ternarius], but a group of six [senarius].

4. Likewise I ask, which power does "mind" stand for there? for either it stands for all (of them), or for two, or for one. If for all, then there is no trinity there; if for two, then there is a quaternity there, since there are two habits; if for one, it can not have those two acts (of the soul),[6] to know and to love: therefore, trinity is taken according to the habits and the powers simultaneously.

1. Likewise it is shown, that (it is) not according to the *substance* and *habits* of the soul.[7] For since the habits of cognizing and loving are consequent to the substance itself in time, and (since) the substance can be without these, but the reckoning of the image is perpetual and inseparable and co-created [concreata] with the soul itself: therefore, it is not in the habits and in the substance (of the soul) simultaneously.

2. Likewise, if substance is numbered with the habits, since[8] the habits are three, and the substance one: therefore, there will be

---

[1] The Vatican edition omits *And* [Et], but contrary to the manuscripts and edition 1. A little below this after *The third* [Tertium] edition 1 adds *is* [est].

[2] That is the memory, the intellect and the will, concerning which (see) above in a. 1. — Then we have substituted from the manuscripts *this (assignation)* [haec] in place of *here (in the powers)* [hic].

[3] See the text of (St.) Augustine above in the text of Master (Peter), ch. 3, about the middle. — The Vatican edition a little before this puts *as in the habits* [aut in habitibus] in place of *do ... mean habits* [dicunt habitus], and a little after this it omits *and approbation*, but contrary to the manuscripts and edition 1. — Then from codex X together with edition 1 we have supplied after *does it belong* [est], for the sake of exactness, *itself* [se].

[4] The words of (St.) Augustine are found above, in the text of Master (Peter), ch. 3 about the middle. — A little above this after *to remember* [meminisse], on the authority of the manuscripts and editions 1, 2, 3 and 6, we have expunged *and* [et], which the Vatican edition adds.

[5] The Vatican edition, disagreeing with the manuscripts and the first six editions, adds *as* [ut].

[6] Codices X and Y add *that is* [scilicet].

[7] Thus the codices and the first six editions against the Vatican edition, which has *On the Contrary. It is shown, that (it is) not in the substance and habits simultaneously* [Contra. Ostenditur, quod non ut in substantia et habitibus simul] and a little after this it has *follow* [sequantur] in place of *follow immediately* [consequantur].

[8] We have substituted with the help of the manuscripts and edition 1 at this point *since* [cum] in place of *and* [et] and a little below this (on p. 89) *of intelligence* [intelligentiae] in place of *of the intellective (part)* [intellectivae].

a quaternity there. *If you say*, that knowledge [notitia] does not differ, accord to which it is a habit of the intelligence and the memory; *on the contrary*: the habits are dispositions of the powers; therefore, since there are three powers, there will be three habits.

3. Likewise, Master (Peter) says in (his) text,[1] that "mind" is accepted not for the substance of the soul, but for that which is the more eminent in it.

CONCLUSION

In this second impression of the image, which is mind, knowledge, (and) love, a trinity is attained as much as regards the substance of the soul and as much as regards the two habits of knowledge and love.

I RESPOND: It must be said, that this impression does differ according to certain (aspects) from the preceding, because the prior was in the powers, this is in the habits. And (these) correspond to the objections through a distinction of "mind" [mens]. For "mind" is diversified according to a fourfold manner of being accepted. For it is said in *one* manner as a <u>mene</u>,* which is a moon or defect; and thus it is said of the whole substance of the soul on account of the transmutations, which it has.[2] In a *second* manner it is said as *one measuring* [metiendo]; and thus it stands for the judicative strength, and thus does (St. John) Damascene accept it,[3] placing it in the cognitive powers. In a *third* manner it is said as *one outstanding* [eminendo]; and thus it stands for the superior part of the reason, and thus does (St.) Augustine frequently accept it.[4] In a *fourth* manner it is said as *to remember* [meminisse]; and thus it stands for the memory both as much as it regards an act and as much as it regards a habit.[5] Therefore, they say, that in the assignation of this trinity the *mind* stands for the habit of memory; but by adaptation [in adaptatione], when (St.) Augustine says:[6] « The mind knows itself and loves », it stands for the power of calling to mind [memorandi].

But that does not seem to be fittingly said, because adaptation ought to correspond to impression. And moreover, since the proper act of the mind, as it stands for memory, is to remember, that[7] ought to be touched upon; but (St.) Augustine in this assignation never makes mention except of two acts, that is to know and to love, which do not belong to the memory, but to the other powers.

Therefore, it must be responded, that that trinity is not in the *powers*; because *love* and *knowledge* [amor et notitia] do not mean powers;[8] nor in the *habits*, because "mind" cannot stand for a habit, when it is accepted as an agent; nor can it be in *powers and habits*, because "mind" cannot stand for one power, since to it are assigned the acts of two powers; nor can it similarly[9] stand for *more powers*, because it would not be a trinity. Therefore, it remains [restat], that it is necessary to posit, that that trinity is attained as much as regards the *substance* of the soul, by reason of the mind knowing and loving itself; and as much as regards (its) *habits*, by reason of (its) knowledge and love; and in this manner there is a trinity, since there is one substance, and there are two habits.

Therefore, this impression differs from the preceding: because the preceding was through a uniformity in the powers through a comparison to habits and[10] acts, but this one is in substance and habits. It differs *again* in this, that the preceding was through the conversion of the soul towards God, and this one is through conversion of the soul upon itself; and the image is not attained in man in more manners, as had been said above.[11] It differs *also*, because the preceding impression of the image is more proper and fitting than this one. For properly speaking, the image consists in a unity of essence and a trinity of powers, according to which (powers) the soul has been born to be sealed by the Most High Trinity with the image of similitude, which consists in grace and[12] the theological virtues. Whence (St.) Augustine first posits this assignation by investigating, so that through this (second assignation) he may arrive at That, in which finishes his speculation.[13] Whence this (latter) impression is not a proper one, just as the other (is); whence Master (Peter) places it second as the non-principal one.

1. To that, therefore, which is objected, that the habits are not coeval etc.; it must be said, that habit is *threefold*. For the power of the soul has a certain habit from *acquisition*, a certain one from an innate *disposition*, a third it has from *its very own origin*. But this is clear, because the habit is (that) whereby a power is facile unto act [quo potentia facilis est in actum]; but in these three manners there is a facile habit, v. gr., our *affection* [affectus] has a facility to love [diligendum] another good through an acquired disposition,

---

[1] Chapter 3, about the middle, which text, however, very many manuscripts together with the first six editions change here, by putting *soul* [animae] in place of *whole substance of the soul* [animae substantia tota]; but codices T and X *substance of the soul* [animae substantiae], which we follow, because their reading corresponds to the sense of the objections. Cf. Scholium.

[2] On this acceptation of "mind" see the book, ON THE SPIRIT AND THE SOUL, ch. 11.

[3] ON THE ORTHODOX FAITH, Bk. II, ch. 22: « The strengths [vires] placed in cognition are mind, thinking [cogitatio], opinion, (and) sense ». And pondering singulars, he says concerning the *mind*: *what is true, it judges* (considers, discerns; or, as Alexander of Hales refers, SUMMA., p. II. q. 69 in princ.: "mind" is said as *one measuring* [a metiendo].).

[4] Cf. EXPOSITION ON THE PSALMS, Ps. 3, n. 3; ON THE TRINITY, Bk. XV, ch. 7, n. 11. See also the book, ON THE SPIRIT AND THE SOUL, chs. 11 and 34. (St.) Isidore agrees, ETYMOLOGIES, Bk. XI, ch. 1.

[5] Cf. (St.) Isidore, <u>loc</u>. <u>cit</u>., and the book, ON THE SPIRIT AND THE SOUL, ch. 34. — Concerning these four etymologies, which ought to be judged by the custom of that age, see Alexander of Hales, SUMMA., p. IV, q. 12, m. 1, a. 2, near the end (in other editions, q. 55).

[6] The codices are divided among themselves; very many indeed as G O T and bb have *(St.) Augustine* [Augustinus], which we follow, but

others as A C L S Z etc. have instead *behold* [ecce]; however, all, contrary to the Vatican edition, have *says* [dicit] in place of *it is said* [dicitur]. Edition 1 has *Master (Peter) and (St.) Augustine (say) behold the mind* [dicit Magister et Augustinus: esse mens].

[7] The Vatican edition not trusting in the manuscripts and edition 1 has *there (it)* [ibi] in place of *that* [ille].

[8] The Vatican edition contrary to the manuscripts and edition 1 has less well *are ... meant (as) powers* [dicuntur potentiae].

[9] Very many codices as A F G H K T Y bb have *simultaneously* [simul] for *similarly* [similiter].

[10] The Vatican edition, disagreeing with the manuscripts and edition 1, here repeats *to* [ad]. A little below this at *it differs* [Differt] from very many codices as H P Q X Z and ee we have put *Again* [iterum] in place of *Also* [etiam].

[11] Here in a. 1, q. 2 in the body.

[12] The Vatican edition without the authority of any manuscript nor of edition 1 unduly omits *grace and* [gratia et]. For sanctifying grace is distinguished from the virtues.

[13] See ON THE TRINITY, Bk. IX, ch. 2, n. 2 and Bk. X, ch. 11, n. 17; Bks. XIV and XV, ch. 3, n. 5 ff.. — Understand by the word *this* [hanc] the *second* assignation.

---

* *Trans. note*: Cf. Du Cagne, GLOSSARIUM MEDIAE ET INFIMIAE LATINITATIS, tom. V, p. 337, L. Favre, 1885, defines <u>Mena</u>, n. 2, as the name of the Moon goddess, *Luna*; typifying the inconstancy of defect; from the Greek for *month* [μήν], or *moon* [μήνη], the <u>luna</u>, which Bonaventure uses here.

as through a virtue; but to love [diligendum] its own[1] good through an innate disposition; and to love its own self through its own natural origin. For, since it is united to itself without separation [indistanter], it is always handy [habilis] for loving itself. *Similarly*, since our *intellect* is always present to itself, it is always handy for itself to cognize itself. And, thus, is clear that which is objected concerning coevity [coevitate]; for in regard to such habits there is rightly a coevity.

2. To that which is objected, that the habits ought[2] to be three according to the three powers; it must be said, that in this trinity the habit of memory neither falls nor has a place, because (a trinity)[3] is attained in the soul itself according to which it is converted upon itself: and for that reason the substance itself of the soul holds a place for the memory, and the presence itself and the oblation, by which the soul always offers itself to its own intelligence, hold a place for the habit and act of memory. And thus it is clear, that there only the habits of the two powers fall; and for that reason there is a trinity there.

3. To that which is last objected concerning the word of Master (Peter); it must be said, that it is understood not for the whole substance of the soul;[4] because if it is otherwise understood, the word of Master (Peter) has not truth. Because it is clear through (St.) Augustine, who on the occasion of this image shows throughout almost the whole tenth (book of) ON THE TRINITY, that the soul has an innate cognition of itself, which is the cognition[5] of its substance. And *moreover*, no one thing [nihil unum] in the soul cognizes and loves [diligit] except the substance: therefore, if "mind" would stand for one power, it would not have those two acts, that is "to know" and "to love" [nosse et amare].

SCHOLIUM

I. On this question must be heard the Seraphic Doctor, who in the unpublished Prologue to the Second Book of Sentences (the beginning of which we have already published in the Prolegomenon, ch. 1, § 2) says first: « But perhaps it will seem to someone, that I have departed from the positions of the Master of Sentences most of all on two (points): that is in this, that when Master (Peter) in the second part of the third distinction, on the second impression of the Trinity, which he says consists in *mind, knowledge* and *love*, says, that "*mind*" is to be accepted not for the soul, but for the superior portion (of it), one discovers what was said by myself, that "mind" there stands for the substance of the soul. Again, when Master (Peter) says in d. 7, that the power of generating is common to the three Persons, as [utpote] a name signifying the essence, I adhered more to that opinion, which says, that the power of generating is said on account of relation. But if anyone rightly inspects (the matter), in neither of the aforesaid shall he find me (standing) or that I have departed from the position of Master (Peter) or from the foot-path of truth. For when I said, that in that assignation of a trinity "mind" is accepted for the substance of the soul by reason of (its) superior part, for that reason this was said, because, if "mind" stood there fore the superior portion, since that is a power of the soul, and (since) it does not belong to one power *to know* and *to love*, as is seen below (cf. SENT., Bk. II, d. 24, p. I, a. 2, q. 1), there would not be a trinity there, but a quaternity. *Again*, to act does not belong properly to a power, but to a substance through a power; and for that reason, if (St.) Augustine is speaking properly and truly, when he says, *the mind knows* etc., *mind* there supposes the substance of the soul. And this again does (St.) Augustine hint at [innuit], when after the occasion of this trinity he shows throughout almost the whole tenth (book of) ON THE TRINITY, that the soul knows its very self. *Finally*, since those habits of knowledge and love are entirely consubstantial, they do not add a new essence upon (their) power, but are by themselves [se ipsis] handy for power, and thus they cannot be communicated to the powers themselves nor to the superior part of the reason. And moreover, Master (Peter) does not deny, that "mind" is accepted for the soul itself, but (he denies) that it is accepted for the *whole* (soul), that is, for the soul according to all (its) powers, but (it is thus accepted) for the substance (of the soul) itself by reason of (its) superior portion. In this, therefore, I have not contradicted Master (Peter), but rather have explained his word in accord with the rule of truth, as I estimate it. ».

II. The words in the second fundament, that « to no habit does it belong to know or love itself », are thus to be understood: to understand and love oneself are not acts of any acquired habit, but co-created and consubstantial powers of the soul, though for those acts even habits can dispositively concur. Whence even Bl. (now St.) Albertus (here in a. 36) concerning the same text of (St.) Augustine says: « It does not belong to a habit to know itself and love itself, but rather it belongs *to the one having* the habit to know oneself and to love oneself according to the habit itself and/or through the habit itself ». Likewise (Bl.) Peter of Tarentaise (here in q. 7, a. 1) says: « But to cognized its very self the mind uses no habit ». Cf. also (St.) Bonaventure, here in a. 2, at n. 4.

II. In the solution to n. 1 a *threefold habit* is distinguished, that is as an *acquisition*, as an *innate disposition*, as *its own very origin*. The difference of the second and the third consists in this, that the second "habit" is not properly co-created and coeval to the soul, though a disposition to this habit is co-created and coeval. Thus the soul cognizes and loves [diligit] from an innate disposition (its) proper (suitable) good. But the third habit, whereby the soul cognizes and loves [diligit] its very self, has been co-created in it properly, cf. SENT., Bk. II, d. 39, a. 1, q. 2. — In the same solution is touched upon the question, by which sense our intellect *always understands itself*. The doctrine of the Seraphic (Doctor) concerning this concords entirely with St. Thomas (here in q. 4, q. 5; SUMMA., I, q. 93, a. 7, at n. 4), with (Bl. John Duns) Scotus (SENT., Bk. II, d. 3. q. 8, n. 13) and with Richard of Middleton (here at q. 2. q. 2). These deny, that the soul has an actual intellection of itself, especially such as whereby it discerns itself from others; however, they do concede, that on account of the presence of the object « nothing is lacking to the first act ... to which there ought to follow the second act, which is intellection. And perhaps on account of this does (St.) Augustine frequently say, that the soul always knows itself, on account of that nearness (of the soul) to the act of knowing, where there is no imperfection in the first act. But in this manner the soul does not always know the stone » etc. (Scotus loc. cit.). However other doctors, as (Bl.) Peter of Tarentaise (here in q. 5. a. 3) and Henry of Ghent (QUODLIBETALS, 4, q. 7) teach, that the soul always knows and loves itself, not only habitually, but even actually, but, however, that it does not advert to those most interior acts. Cf. also (Bl.) Dionysius the Carthusian (here in q. 12), who on this question clings to a twofold (position).

IV. Concerning the conclusion itself: Alexander of Hales, SUMMA., p. II, q. 62, m. 5, a. 6, § 1. — (Bl. John Duns) Scotus, here in q. 9; REPORTATIO, q. 7. — St. Thomas, here in q. 5; SUMMA., I, q. 93, q. 6. — Bl. (now St.) Albertus (Magnus), here in a. 36; SUMMA., p. I, tr. 3, q. 15, m. 2, q. 2, p. 2. — (Bl.) Peter of Tarentaise, here in q. 6, a. 1 and q. 7, a. sole. — Giles the Roman, here in princ. 2 of q. 2. — Richard of Middleton, here in a. 3, q. 1. — (Gabriel) Biel, here in q. 10.

---

[1] Codices I and O have *the most high* [summum] in place of *its own* [suum]; but not well. Then, codex T at *to itself* [sibi] inserts *very* [sibi ipsi] and, a little below this, it omits incongruously *our intellect* [intellectus noster].

[2] With the help of the manuscripts and edition 1, we have substituted *there ought* [debent] in place of *there are said* [dicuntur].

[3] Supply: a trinity [trinitas].

[4] Codex Z adds *but for (its) superior part, that is* [sed parte superiori scilicet], but ed. 1: *but supply for the conversion of the soul toward God and/or the reflection regarding the consideration of itself toward God* [sed supple pro conversione animae ad Deum vel reflexione ad sui considerationem ad Deum].

[5] The Vatican edition, not trusting in the mss. and ed. 1, has *acknowledging* [agnitio]; and immediately after this *on account of (this)* [propterea] in place of *besides* [praeterea], but falsely, because in truth a new

QUESTION II

Whether mind, knowledge and love have an order, equality and consubstantiality?

Second, there is asked concerning these, in comparison to each other, according to the threefold comparison, which (St.) Augustine posits, namely of *order*, *equality* and *consubstantiality*, and (which) Master (Peter) quotes [recitat] in the text.[1] An *order* is among them, because the mind is a parent, knowledge is (its) offspring, the third is the love [amor] proceeding from both. An *equality* is also there, because as much as it is, so much does the mind know itself, and as much as it knows itself, so much does it love [diligit] itself.[2] A *consubstantiality*, too; whence (St.) Augustine in the ninth (book) ON THE TRINITY:[3] « We are admonished, if we can in whatever manner see, that this exists substantially in the soul, not as in a subject, as color in a body, or (as) any quality or quantity; for whatever is such, does not exceed the substance, in which it is. But the mind by the love [amore], by which it loves itself, can love also another »; and, thus, he would (have it), that love be consubstantial to the mind.

1. But there is objected against this: First it seems, that among these there is not an *order* nor[4] an origin. For either they are accepted as *innate* habits, or as *acquired* (ones). If as *innate* (habits), there is no order, because they are simultaneously with the soul itself; if as *acquired* (habits), thus love precedes knowledge; for no one acquires[5] and/or strives to learn anything, unless he love to know. Whence (St.) Augustine at the end of the ninth (book) ON THE TRINITY says:[6] « Part of the mind goes before [antecedit] the appetite, from which that which we want to know by seeking and finding, there is born an offspring, which is knowledge itself ». Therefore, either there is not an order, or there is not such an order.

2. Likewise, it seems that there is not an *equality* there. For either knowledge and love are accepted through a comparison to *inferior things*, or to *the soul*. If to *inferior things*, it is manifest, that there is not an equality there; for we know many (things), which we do not love; if in comparison[7] to *the soul*, either there is equality as much as regards *intensity* [intensionem], or as much as regards *extension*. As much as regards *extension*, not (so); that is established,

because there is only[8] one (thing) there: therefore, as much as regards *intensity*; but it seems that this is false, because though we know [sciamus] that the soul (is) less than God and greater than the body, it happens sometimes, that we love it more than God, and less than the body; and thus the quantity[9] of love does not follow the quantity of knowledge.

3. Likewise, it seems that there is not a *consubstantiality* there, because love and knowledge are habits and they are[10] qualities; therefore, it seems, that essentially they differ from the mind itself.

4. Likewise, (St.) Augustine's[11] reason is, that they are not in the soul as accidents, because they extend themselves outside; but this is nothing, because accidents do extend themselves outside, as heat by a thing-that-heats [calor calefaciendo] and color by a that-which-alters a the sight [color immutando visum]. *Moreover*, man cognizes some cognizables by acquired knowledge [scientia acquisita], which is an accident, and, thus, extends itself outside.

CONCLUSION

Mind, knowledge, (and) love have an order, an equality and a consubstantiality.

I RESPOND: It must be said, that as (St.) Augustine[12] assigns (them), there is among these an *order*, an *equality* and a *consubstantiality*

But the *order* is attained among these connatural habits of the soul in comparison to *acts*, just as there is posited an order among faith,[13] hope and charity, though they are infused simultaneously.

1. And thus is clear what is objected in the Contrary, that there is not an order among the habits themselves considered absolutely, but through a relation to (their) acts.

Similarly there is an *equality* there according to the soul's conversion upon itself and the perfection of the aforesaid habits. On which account, (St.) Augustine says in the ninth (book), ON THE

---

argument is had, sought from reason, not from authority. Then on the authority of the mss. and edd. 1, 2, 3 and 6 after *in the soul* we have expunged *both* [et]. Codex O after *no* [nihil] adds *other* [aliud].

[1] Chapter 3, near the end. — Then the Vatican edition contrary to very many codices and edition 1, at *Order* add *But* [autem] and contrary to the more ancient codices and edition 1 it puts *because* [quod] in place of *because* [quia] and *the last* [ultimus] in place of *the third* [tertius].

[2] Trusting in codices I and aa we have inserted *itself* [se] which must certainly be supplied.

[3] Chapter 4, n. 5: We are also at the same time admonished, if we can in any manner see, that these exist in the soul and as things involuted they are ex-voluted, to be judged [sentiantur] and counted substantially, and/or, as I say, essentially, not as in a subject, as color or figure in a body or any other quality or quantity. For whatever is such, does not exceed the subject, in which it is. For that color or figure of this body cannot be also of another body. But the mind by the love, by which it loves itself, can love also another besides itself. — In which text very many codices falsely have *each* [utrumque] in place of *in any manner* [utcumque] and the less well *spirit* [animo] in place of *soul* [anima]; but the Vatican edition puts *consist* [consistere] in place of *exist* [existere].

[4] The Vatican edition contrary to the manuscripts and edition 1 has incongruously *and/or* [vel] in place of *nor* [nec].

[5] Thus all the codices and editions. Here *inquires into* [inquirit] would be more pleasing, if this reading were supported by any codex.

[6] Chapter 12, n. 18, in which text at *appetite* [appetitus] the original adds *a certain* [quidam] and at the end omits the words *which is*; but the Vatican edition after *from which* [quo] adds *for* [ad] and it puts *to know* [noscere] in place of *to know* [nosse].

[7] The Vatican edition has *through a comparison* [per comparationem], but contrary to the manuscripts. Then codices V and X after *soul* [animam] add *then* [tunc], edition 1 adds *and then* [et tunc].

[8] Many codd., such as A F T V X Y etc., with ed. 1 omit *only* [tantum].

[9] Very many codd., such as A C L R S U aa bb, with ed. 1 have less aptly *the quality* [qualitas]; since it deals with a grade of intensity.

[10] From the mss. and edition 1 we have inserted *they are* [sunt].

[11] ON THE TRINITY, Bk. IX, ch. 4. n. 5; see above in the 1st fundament of this question. — A little after this the Vatican edition not trusting in the manuscripts has *for accidents* [accidentia enim] in place of *because accidents* [quia accidentia] and at the end of the argument *do they extend themselves* [se extendunt] in place of *extends* [se extendit].

[12] ON THE TRINITY, Bk. IX, ch. 12, n. 18; see the text of Master (Peter), ch. 3 near the end.

[13] With the help of the manuscripts and edition 1 we have removed here the added *and* [et]. A little before this very many codices as A C G K L S T and bb together with edition 1 have *often among* [crebro in] in place of *an order among* [ordo in].

THE TRINITY,[1] that there is not among these habits an equality, except according to which they have been perfected.

2. And, thus, is clear the solution to that which is objected concerning love,[2] because that love is not a perfect love, but a libidinous and inordinate (one). — And/or it must be said, that they are equal, according to which they are *connatural*; for as much as any are handy [habilis] and/or facile to cognize themselves, so much (are they) to love themselves; but concerning *acquired* habits, evil and/or good, it is not true; and of these it is not understood (in this manner).

Similarly, there is a third there, that is a *consubstantiality*, because according to what has been said above,[3] love and knowledge [notitia] are connatural to the soul, according to which it is converted upon itself; and, thus, they add nothing entirely upon the powers themselves. For through this, that the soul it present to itself, it has knowledge; through this, that it is a 'one' to itself [unum sibi], it has the habit of love; and for that reason, just as the powers are consubstantial to the soul, as has been seen above,[4] so also habits of this kind. Whence, even if they seem to mean a manner of habit and/or of quality, however, they really add nothing upon the powers.

3. And thus is clear the response to the objection [obiectum], that[5] they are not qualities in that manner.

4. To that which is objected concerning (St.) Augustine's reason, it must be said, that that reason does not conclude from a principle [principaliter], that love and/or knowledge are in the soul substantially; and this is,[6] because then for an equal reason it could be said and objected concerning every love; but it concludes from the consequence [ex consequenti], that it is thus clear. For when love *is extended* outside its own subject by loving another, this is through the virtue of the substance, just as it *is* not through itself, except[7] through the substance. If therefore, love and knowledge are extended through substantial virtue, and these are the intelligence and the will; and love, by which the soul loves itself, is the same with the will itself; and similarly[8] knowledge, by which it cognizes (itself), is not other than the intelligence: it therefore, remains, that love and knowledge in respect to themselves are consubstantial to the mind itself.

SCHOLIUM

I. For a easier understanding of the threefold conclusion it must be noted, that the reason for the *order*, which *mind* and *love* have, is not to be understood, to the extent that those three are to be considered absolutely and in themselves, but in respect to their own acts. Similarly, *equality* it not attained in regard to an equality in entity, but in regard to the acts reflected upon [super] the soul, while the soul understands its whole self and loves [diligit] itself, as much as it cognizes itself. In regard to the solution to the argument against equality cf. Alexander of Hales, SUMMA., p. II, q. 62, m. 5, a. 7. Next, *consubstantiality* is not to be understood as absolute with the exclusion of any distinction, but in the sense explained in the preceding question. — Besides it must be noted, that the consubstantiality, which knowledge and love have with the mind, is not to be accepted properly, to the extent that they are acts (because second acts and accidents cannot be really the same with the substance of the soul), but to the extent they are co-created habits. In this sense (Bl. John Duns) Scotus says (here in q. 9): « Those three on the part of the soul, as they are under their own three acts, in those three, I say, there is a consubstantiality ».

II. In the solution *to n. 4* it is supposed, that no accident can extend itself <u>ad extra</u> on its own virtue, but only by virtue of something substantial, as we have already said in the Scholium to q. 3 of the preceding article. This substantial is itself the twofold power of the intellect and of the will; and this is true of any act, either as it tends <u>ad extra</u>, or as it is reflected upon itself. But, if the *acts* of these powers are referred to the mind itself as a thing cognized and loved, they are not in the soul, as an accident (is) in a subject, but substantially. — In the same manner also does St. Thomas explain this sentence of St. Augustine, SUMMA., I, q. 77, a. 1, at n. 1 and at n. 5.

III. This question is explicitly treated by Alexander of Hales, SUMMA., p. II, q. 62, m. 5, a. 7. — (Bl. John Duns) Scotus, here in q. 9. — Bl. (now St.) Albertus (Magnus), here in a. 37 and ff.; SUMMA., p. I, tr. 3, q. 15, m. 2, a. 2, at n. 2. — (Bl.) Peter of Tarentaise, here in q. 6, a. 2. — Giles the Roman, here in the 3rd principle of q. 2, a. 1. — (Bl.) Dionysius the Carthusian, here in q. 11.

QUESTION III

Whether the trinity of the image, which consists in mind, knowledge and love,
necessarily leads unto the cognition of the Three Divine Persons?

Third and last, there is asked, whether this trinity of image, that is of mind, of knowledge and of love, leads necessarily unto cognition of the Trinity as much as regards the Persons. And it seems that (this is) so:

1. Because in this trinity of the image there is a relation; but in God there is no relation except in regard to the Persons: ergo etc..

2. Likewise, in this trinity there is a distinction, because knowledge is not love; but in God there is no distinction except of the Persons: ergo etc.

---

[1] Chapter 4, n. 4: Therefore, we have rightly said, that these three, when they have been perfected, are consequently equals.

[2] Codex Z adds *that it is not valid* [quod non valet]. A little before this very many codices, such as A G I T and cc, after *solution* [solutio] put a period, then codex cc after *to that which is objected concerning love* [obiicitur] adds *it must be said* [dicendum]; we have judged that nothing it to be altered.

[3] Here in a. 2, q. 1, in reply to n. 1: For the power of the soul has a certain habit from *acquisition*, a certain one from an innate *disposition*, a third it has from *its very own origin*.

[4] Article 1, q. 3.

[5] Supply: mind, knowledge and love [mens, notitia et amor]. — Then, the codices do not agree among themselves, some such as A G H K T etc., together with the Vatican edition, read *a quality* [qualitas], but others, such as B D E G H I X Z, together with edition 1, read *qualities* [qualitates], which we follow.

[6] The error of the Vatican ed. of putting *from this* [ex hoc] in place of *and this it* [et hoc est], and a little after this *concluded* [conclusit] in place of *concludes* [concludit], is corrected from the mss. and edd. 1, 2, 3 & 6.

[7] The Vatican edition contrary to the manuscripts and edition 1 has *but* [sed] in place of *except* [nisi]. A little before this codices P and Q have *beyond* [ultra] in place of *outside* [extra]; then not a few codices as D E F H K Y have *another (thing)* [aliud], codex T *the other* [alterum], codices L and O *anything* [aliquid] in place of *another (subject)* [alium]. Codices Q (T in the margin) after *of the substance* [substantiae] add *because by itself it does not act* [quia per se non agit]; a reading not to be spurned.

[8] Thus codices Q and T with ed. 1; many codices, such as A B E F G H K P X Y Z aa etc., have *and so* [et sic], the Vatican edition *so* [sic], which also, a little below this, after *the intelligence* [intelligentia] puts a period, by which the argument, which is explained in the Scholium, is disturbed. At the end the Vatican ediction, contrary to the manuscripts and edditions 1, 2, & 3, has *substantial* [substantiales].

3. Likewise, in this trinity there is an origin of one being born[1] from one and a third from both: therefore, since that is proper to the Persons, it is clear etc.

4. Likewise, in this trinity love is[2] third, which (love) is proper to the Holy Spirit and which (love) is for the other: therefore, it seems, that it does necessarily lead unto the Trinity of Persons.

ON THE CONTRARY: 1. This trinity is understood in the creature without personal distinction: therefore, it can be understood even in God; but this is false: ergo etc..

2. Likewise, knowledge and love are in any of the Persons; but through those which are in all, one does not come [non venitur] to the cognition of personal distinction: ergo etc..

3. Likewise, with it understood that there would only be one Person, it would still know and love itself: ergo etc..

4. Likewise, the philosophers cognized that trinity, and they did not, however, cognize the Trinity of Persons: therefore this does not necessarily[3] lead unto that.

CONCLUSION

The reckoning alone from this trinity of mind, of knowledge and of love, does not ascend to the cognition of the Trinity.

I RESPOND: It must be said, that through this trinity one happens to cognize the Trinity in God, and this is by attributing those which are in this trinity to that Most High Trinity. But this can be in a twofold manner. For either those three can be attributed to God according to substance, as through the *mind*[4] we understand the mind in God, and through *knowledge* [notitiam] in the soul, the knowledge in God, and thus concerning the third; and so it does not lead unto cognition of the Trinity except as much as regards (things) *appropriated*; and thus did the philosophers understand (it).

Those[5] can also be drawn to God by reason of (their) *properties*, which are order and origin, distinction and relation; and thus do they lead unto the cognition of the Trinity in regard to what is proper [propria] (to each).

But faith can posit and/or understand those in God, but[6] not reason; and thus a perfect cognition of the image is not had except by faith. Whence it must be well conceded, that the image, perfectly cognized as image, leads unto the cognition of the Trinity, but not simply (speaking). And by this each part is clear.

1. 2. To that which is objected concerning love, it must be said, that "love" can mean "a complacency", and thus it is common; and/or it can mean "a connection" or "a communion" and/or "a gift", and thus it has the reckoning of a person.

SCHOLIUM

I. This question, the other more ancient Scholastics besides Giles (here in the 3rd principle of q. 2, a. 4) do not treat *ex professo*. Its solution depends on the same principles, which have been posited above in p. I, q. 4. Concerning the properties of the Divine Persons, and to what extent they imply [important] order and origin, relation and distinction cf. below in dd. 26 and 33. — The Seraphic Doctor does not explicitly solve the first and last objection, because the principles of the solution are contained clearly in the body of the question; the second and the third he briefly solves, by speaking expressing only of the essential and personal *love*, because (the same argument) can be applied easily to *knowledge*.

DOUBTS ON THE TEXT OF PART II

DOUBT I

In this part is asked about the text (of Master Peter) concerning this which he says: *The image of God ... remains throughout* [permanet]. ON THE CONTRARY: The Psalm (says):[7] *Lord, in the city Thou shalt reduce their image to nothing.*

I RESPOND: An "image" is said in a twofold manner: as much as regards *substantial* 'being' [substantiale esse]; and *this*[8] respects the trinity of powers and (their) order and equality, and thus it always remains throughout; in another manner insofar as upon 'being' one adds '*well* being' [bene esse], as decor and honor; and this can be lost, *because man, when he would be in honor, has not understood.*[9]

DOUBT II

Likewise, is asked concerning this which he says: *But "memory" is said regarding something* etc.; therefore memory,[10] intelligence and will are in the predicament of relation.

Likewise, there is asked, why *mind* is said more regarding itself than memory and/or intelligence?

I RESPOND: It must be said, that *to be said regarding something* is[11] in a twofold manner: *properly* and *per se*, as a father and a son, and/or *by reason of something adjoined*, because it has an adjoined regard [respectum] and inclination; and thus "memory" is said *regarding something*, because it has an innate regard for the memorable [ad memoriale], and similarly "intelligence" for the in-

---

[1] Very many codices omit *of one* [unius]; but the Vatican edition omits *being born* [nascentis], for which, however, all the codices can be alleged, though on account of the abbreviation it is as much a doubtful reading, as one can read either *one being born* [nascentis] or *nativity* [nativitatis] or with edition 1 *nascibility* [nascibilitatis]. In accord with that rule of paleography, according to which in similar cases, unless the sense withstands it, the shorter word is to be chosen, we have read *being born* [nascentis], retaining moreover, with codices H I T and edition 1 the word *of one* [unius]. Cf. below d. 13, q. 3.

[2] The Vatican edition, not trusting in the manuscripts and editions 1, 2, 3 and 6, reads thus: *there is discovered a love for a third (one)* [tertio reperitur amor]. Codex X explicitly after *a third* adds *place* [loco]. Edition 1 has *a third love* [tertius ... amor] instead. Codex N after *trinity* [trinitate] has *there is a knowledge, which is appropriated to the Son, and a love, which is* [est notitia, quae appropriatur Filio, et amor, qui est].

[3] With the help of the manuscripts and edition 1 we have restored the unduly omitted *necessarily* [necessario].

[4] Codex I and Y here add *well*, and coherently with what is subjoined, *in the soul* [in anima].

[5] Codices M aa and bb do not ineptly insert *three* [tria].

[6] The Vatican edition has *and* [et], but this withstands very many codices together with edition 1.

[7] Psalm 72:20, where the Vulgate at *city* [civitate] adds *Thy* [tua] and in place of *their* [ipsorum] has together with the Vatican edition *their* [eorum].

[8] The Vatican edition here and a little below this has the neuter *this* [hoc], but less well and contrary to very many manuscripts and edition 1.

[9] Psalm 48:21.

[10] The codices omit *memory* [memoria], but not well, as is clear from what is subjoined.

[11] The corrupt reading of the Vatican edition, in which in place of *to be said* [dici] there is put *it is said* [dicitur] and the following *is* [est] is omitted, we have corrected with the help of the manuscripts and six of the first editions.

telligible and the will for the willable [volibile]; and these objects have a regard for one another.

To that which is asked concerning the *mind*, it must be said, that "mind" is said from an essential act. On that account it must be understood, that (the essential act)[2] *whereby it is* gives to the soul a *most general* 'being' [esse generalissimum], and in this manner "*essence*" is meant; and/or inasmuch as it gives a *general* 'being' [esse generale], and in this manner "*life*" is meant, because the soul is in the genus of living (things); or[3] inasmuch as it gives a *spiritual* 'being' [esse spirituale], and in this manner "*the mind*" (is meant). For "mind" is not said unless a thing [quod] lives by an intellective life. — And/or the soul *in itself* is said (to be) an essence, as life (is said to be) an *act* of a body, (and) as the mind (is said to be) *perfectible* by God.

DOUBT III

Likewise, is asked concerning this which he says, that *the Three Persons are not of the One God*; because he seems to say the false [falsum], because, if They are of the one Essence; but the Essence is[4] God; therefore, They are of the One God. *If you say*, that this does not follow; I ask, why it is not conceded, that the three Persons are of the One God? If[5] on account of this, that the oblique denotes [notat] diversity; therefore, since the Essence is not diverse from the Person, there cannot be said: "the Three Persons are of the One Essence".

I RESPOND: It must be said, that the genitive (case)[6] sometimes is construed in the reckoning of *possession*, as if there is said: "the bull of Peter and/or of John"; sometimes out of the force of a *declaration of essence*, as "a woman of egregious form"; sometimes *intransitively*, as "a creature of salt". *Intransitively* the general is construed together with the special; and so there can be said: "the Substance and/or Person of God"; *out of the force of declaration of essence*, a name[7] conveying a form through the manner of a *form*; and so the Three Persons are said (to be) of the One Essence. Therefore, because, when there is said: "the Three Persons are of the One God", "*God*" does not *signify*[8] through the manner of a *form* nor through the manner of *one specifying*, for that reason it is understood through a manner of *one possessing* or of *one beginning* [principiantis]: and for that reason it is simply false.

DOUBT IV

Likewise, is asked concerning this which he says, that *for the most part it is dissimilar*. For it seems false, be-

cause an image is an expressed similitude: therefore, if it is mostly dissimilar, it is not an image.

I RESPOND: It must be said, that there is expression[9] *simply* (speaking), and/or *in a genus* [in genere]. Therefore, if we speak of an expression simply, I thus say, that the rational soul is not very [valde] similar to God; but if we speak in the genus of the creature, because it approaches[10] (Him) as much as a created nature can, thus (the soul) is said (to be) a very much similar and expressed similitude of God.

DOUBT V

Likewise, is asked concerning this which he says: *If there were two, each would be insufficient, and/or one of the two would be superfluous*; because according to that way it could be demonstrated, that there is not but one Person.

I RESPOND: It must be said, that among the *Persons* there cannot be a *superfluity*, because among Them there is one sufficiency; whence if One were superfluous, (so) also All. But[11] there cannot be There any *insufficiency*, because the Three have nothing more than the One (has). But if there were two *essences*, the two would be sufficient, if[12] any were sufficient by themselves; but if one of the two (were insufficient) with the other, any would be insufficient: and thus it is clear, that it is not the same concerning two essences, as concerning two Persons.

DOUBT VI

Likewise, is asked concerning this which he says, that (the mind) *understood, that God has a wisdom, which has been begotten from Himself, because it understood, that He is not a foolish thing* [rem fatuam]; therefore, it seems according to this, that the Father is wise by a begotten wisdom.

I RESPOND: It must be said, that that consequence is not to be understood immediately, that is; that He is not a foolish thing, therefore, He has a begotten wisdom. But this is to be understood in this manner: God is a spiritual substance: therefore, He is bound to cognize: therefore, if He does not have a wisdom, He is a foolish thing; but He is not a foolish thing: therefore, He has a wisdom; but there is no wisdom without a word, and there is no word, unless it proceeds from a mind and is thus generated: therefore, from the first,[14] if He has a wisdom, it is necessary, that the wisdom be begotten. And it is proper that all those consequences of his be understood immediately.[15]

---

[1] Concerning this twofold species of relation, see below d. 30. q. 3.

[2] It seems there must be supplied: *the essential act as* (that whereby it is) [actus essentialis ut (quo est)]. And/or understand as the Vatican ed., which after *that whereby it is* [quo est] adds *can be understood inasmuch as* [potst intelligi in quantum]. In the same way codd. F and H add *is said in a threefold manner and/or inasmuch as* [dicitur tripliciter vel in quantum]. But other codd. with edd. 1, 2 & 3 exhibit our text.

[3] Codex Y has *and/or* [vel]. Then edition 1 has well enough *special* [speciale] in place of *spiritual* [spirituale]; codices V and W after *in this manner* [sic] add *is* [est]. Codex Z after *mind* [mens] adds *Whence those three acts are essential, from which they mean essence, life, mind, that is, to be, to live and to understand* [Unde isti tres actus sunt essentiales, a quibus dicuntur essentia, vita, mens, scilicet esse, vivere et intelligere]; and a little below this in place of *a thing* [quod] it puts *because* [quia] and in place of *intellective* [intellective] it has *intellectual* [intellectuali].

[4] The Vatican ed. has *since they are of the One Essence and the Essence is* [cum sint unius essentiae et essential sit]; but contrary to ed. 1 and the codd., which disagree only in this, that not a few omit the particle *if* [si], cod. A in place of *but* [sed] puts *if* [si] and cod. I in place of *but* [sed] has *and* [et]. The reading received in the tex seems to be the more familiar one.

[5] The Vatican ed. without the mss. and ed. 1 adds *you say that* [dicis quod].

[6] The fault of the Vatican ed., reading *generated* [generatus] in place of *genitive* [genetivus], we have emended with the help of the mss. and

edd. 1, 2, 3, and 6. A little below this from the mss. and ed. 1 we have inserted the unduly omitted *of essence* [essentiae]. — Concerning the various significations of the genitive see below, d. 34. dub. 5 and Priscian, GRAMMATICAL INSTITUTIONS, Bk. XVIII, ch. 2, Krehl's ed., Leipzig, 1820, t. 2, p. 112. Cf. also (Bl.) Scotus, ON SPECULATIVE GRAMMAR, chs. 46-53.

[7] The Vatican edition not trusting the manuscripts and edition 1 has *as one* [ut] in place of *a name* [nomen]. After *bearing a form* [formam] supply : *is construed* [cosntruitur].

[8] Some codices as D and T have *is not signified* [non significatur]; other as X and Y omit the first *neither* [nec].

[9] Very many codices together with the first six editions have *excess* [excessus] here and a little below this *excess* [excessu] in place of *expression* [expressione]; codices Y and cc have *approach* [accessus] here and a little below this *approach* [accessu].

[10] The Vatican ed. against the codd. & ed. 1 has *expresses* [exprimit].

[11] Codex R has *Similarly* [Similiter] in place of *But* [Sed].

[12] Thus nearly all the codices together with edition 1, against the Vatican edition, which has *and* [et], the placing of which bears off the force of the argument; codex I falsely has *but* [sed].

[13] See the very many things concerning this doubt in d. 2, q. 4.

[14] Codex Y adds *lastly* [ad ultimum].

[15] Edition 1 has *non immediately*. Cf. concerning this doubt, d. 32, a. 2, q. 1.

DISTINCTION IV

CHAPTER I
Whether God the Father begot Himself God.

Here, there arises a sufficiently necessary question. For it is established and is irrefragably true, that God the Father begot the Son. For that reason it is asked, whether it must be conceded, that God begot God. For if God begot God, it seems that either He begot Himself God [se Deum], or an other.[1] However, [vero] if He begot an other God, there is not only one God; moreover, [autem] if He begot His very self God [se ipsum Deum], some thing begot its very self [se ipsam].

Responding to which, we say, that sanely and[2] in a catholic manner it is conceded, that One begot One, and that God begot God, because God the Father begot God the Son. In the Symbol it has also been written: « Light from Light, true God from true God ». However, because there is added: therefore, He begot Himself God and/or an other God, we say, that neither must be conceded. That He did not beget an other God,[3] is manifest, because there is only one God. Moreover, that He did not beget His very self, (St.) Augustine shows in the first book, ON THE TRINITY[4] saying: « Those who think that (it belongs) to His power to be God, so that He Himself begot His very self, for this reason err the more, because not only is God not thus (in origin), but neither (is) a spiritual nor corporal creature. For there is no thing, which begets its very self, to be »; and for that reason it must not be believed or said, that God begot Himself.

But still do the garrulous reasoners oppose (this) saying: if God the Father begot God, either He begot the God, who is God the Father, or a God, who is not God the Father. If he begot the God, who is not God the Father: therefore, there is a God who is not God the Father: therefore, there is not only one God. However, if He begot the God, who is God the Father: therefore, He begot His very self.

To which we respond, determining that[5] proposition of theirs, which they propose, thus: "if God the Father begot God, either the God, who is God the Father, or a God, who is not God the Father". For this can be understood (both) sanely and in a depraved manner [prave]; and for that reason one must be respond thus: "God the Father begot the God, who is Himself the Father", this we say is false; and we concede the other (proposition),[6] namely, that "He begot a God, who is not the Father"; neither, however, did He beget an other God, nor is the One, who has been begotten, a God other than the Father, but (rather He is) one God with the Father. However, if there is added: "He begot a God, who is not God the Father", here[7] we distinguish, because it can be understood in a twofold manner: "He begot a God, who is not God the Father, that is God the Son, who

(as) Son is not the Father, who is God"; here the sense is true. However, if it is understood in this manner: "He begot a God, who is not God the Father, that is, who is not the God, who is the Father"; this sense is false. For one and the same God is the Father and[8] the Son and the Holy Spirit; and conversely the Father and the Son and the Holy Spirit is the One God.

CHAPTER II
Whether "the Trinity" is predicated of the one God, just as "the one God" (is) of the Three Persons.

However, certain adversaries of the truth concede, that the Father and the Son and the Holy Spirit or the Three Persons are one God, one Substance, but[9] do not want to concede, that the one God or one Substance is the Three Persons, saying, that the Divine Substance is predicated of the Three Persons, not the Three Persons of the Divine Substance. But the Catholic Faith holds and predicates, both that the Three Persons are the One God,[10] the one Substance or Essence or Divine Nature, and that the One God or Divine Essence is the Three Persons. Whence (St.) Augustine in the first book, ON THE TRINITY[11] thus says: « Rightly is God itself understood (to be) the Trinity, the blessed and only Powerful One ». Behold, how he expressly said *"God itself ... the Trinity"*, to show both that God itself is the Trinity and the Trinity God itself. Likewise in the same (book he says): « Dealing with those words », he says, « of the Apostle, which concern the advent of Christ he says:[12] *Whom He shall show, the blessed and only Powerful One, the King of kings and the Lord of lords, who alone has immortality* etc., neither has the Father nor the Son nor the Holy Spirit been properly named, but (rather) the blessed and only Powerful One, that is the One and Only True god, who is the Trinity itself ». Behold here also he openly says, that the One Only True God is the Trinity itself; and if the One God is the Trinity, therefore, the One God is the Three Persons. Likewise in the fifth book, ON THE TRINITY:[13] « Not three gods, but the One God we say is the most outstanding Trinity itself ». Likewise in the book, which is called the ENCHIRIDION TO LAWRENCE, in the ninth chapter: « It is enough for the Christian, to believe that the cause of created things, visible and invisible, is not but the goodness of the Creator, who is the One and True God, and that there is no nature, which is not either He, or from Him, and that He is the Trinity, that is the Father and the Son and the Holy Spirit ». Likewise (St.) Augustine in the sermon on Faith:[14] « We believe, that the One God is the One Trinity of the

---

[1] The Vatican edition here adds *God* [Deum].

[2] The Vatican edition badly omits *and* [et].

[3] Only codices B C D E have the subjunctive *begot* [genuerit], which seems must be posited, if a little below this the same codices had not put the indicative *begot* [genuit].

[4] Chapter 1, n. 1, where in place of *think* [putant] and *err* [errant] there are the singular forms of the verb, and codices B and C in place of *to His power* [eius potentiae] badly reads *to the Same's power* [eiusdem potentiae].

[5] All the codices read *that* [illam] instead of *that ... of theirs* [istam].

[6] Only the Vatican ed. reads badly *the other (one)* [alterum].

[7] Editions 2, 3, 7 and 8 have *this* [hoc].

[8] Codices B and C omit here and just after *the Father* [Pater] the particle *and* [et].

[9] Codices D and E and all the editions, except 1 & 8, add *however* [tamen].

[10] The Vatican ed. and ed. 4 add *and* [et]; then codices C and D read *one essence* [unam essentiam] for *or essence* [sive essentiam].

[11] Chapter 6, n. 10, where here and in the next quote not a few things have been omitted and changed.

[12] 1 Tim. 6:15: *Whom in His own time He shall show, the blessed* etc. [Quem suis temporibus ostendet beatus et.]. In (St.) Augustine's (writings it reads): *Whom at proper times the Father shall show, the blessed* etc. [Quem temporibus proriis ostendet Pater beatus]. Manuscripts D and E and editions 3, 4, 5, 7 and 9, have the erroneous *He shows* [ostendit] in place of *He shall show* [ostendet].

[13] Chapter 8, n. 9. The citation of the next quote in all the manuscripts and editions, excepting the Vatican edition and edition 4, is thus: *Likewise in the book On the Faith to Peter in the exposition of the Creed* [Item in libro de Fide ad Petrum in expositione Sumboli]; but faultily, since the following words are not read in that (work), but (rather in his) ENCHIRIDION.

[14] Sermon 233, "On the Catholic Faith", n. 1, but in a slightly different manner, namely: *We believe in one God ... That this one God and this one Trinity belong to the Divine Name* [Credimus in unum Deum ... Hunc unum Deum et hanc unam esse divini nominis Trinitatem].

Divine Name ». (He says) the same in the sixth book, ON THE TRINITY:[1] « We say, that the only God is the Trinity itself ». Behold, by these and very many other authorities there is evidently shown, that it must be said and believed, that the One God is the Trinity, and the One Substance the Three Persons; just as conversely the Trinity is said to be "the One God", and the Three Persons are said to be the "One Substance".

Now let us turn back to the aforementioned question, where there was asked, whether God the Father begot Himself God, or whether (He begot) an other God. To which we say, neither is to be conceded. However, (St.) Augustine says in the LETTER TO MAXIMUS,[2]

that God the Father begot Himself the other [se alterum], with these words: « The Father, so that He would have a Son from His very self, did not diminish His very self, but so begot from Himself the other-Himself [alterum se], so that He remains whole in Himself and is as much in the Son, as He also (is) alone ». Which can thus be understood, that is, that from Himself He begot the Other than [a] Himself, not indeed the other God, but the other Person; and/or *He begot Himself the other*, that is, He begot the Other, who is this which He Himself (is). For even if the Father is other than the Son, He is not, however, an other thing [aliud] than the Son, but one [unum] (with Him).

COMMENTARY ON DISTINCTION IV

Questions out of the comparison of generation to an essential concrete term.

Here, there arises a sufficiently necessary question etc.

THE DIVISION OF THE TEXT

In the preceding distinction, Master (Peter) proved the Trinity and Unity through congruous similitudes and reasons. In the present distinction, there is posited a second part, in which he solves occurring doubts [incidentes dubitationes]. And a doubt occurs from this, that among the divine there is a Trinity and Unity, and thus something distinguishing and distinct, something indistinct, such as [ut] the substantial terms. Therefore, a doubt occurs from the comparison of the property of the one distinguishing to the substantial term. Moreover, this part has two (parts). In the first, he brings forth [movet] a doubt from a comparison of the property of the one distinguishing to the Substance and/or Essence; in the second to His power, below in the sixth distinction (where he says): *Moreover one is accustomed to ask.*

Likewise, the first part has two (parts), because the Substance can be signified in *concretion*, as through this name, "*God*", and/or in *abstraction*, as through this name, "*essence*". Therefore, first he brings forth a question from the comparison of generation to this name, "*God*", second, to

this name, "*essence*", below in the Fifth Distinction (where he says): *After these there is asked, whether it must be conceded* etc..

Moreover, this distinction has four subparts and this according to the four, which are touched upon there. In the *first*, having supposed that these (words) are true: "God begot God", there is asked concerning this: "*He begot Himself and/or another*", regarding[1] which he solves by interemption. In the *second* there is asked concerning this: "*He begot the God, who is God the Father, or who is not God the Father*", and regarding this he solves by distinguishing on the part of the predicate, and this there (where he says): *But ... still oppose*. In the *third* he asks concerning this: "*God is the Trinity*", and he proves by many authorities, that it is true, and this by the occasion of the aforesaid, there (where he says): *However, certain adversaries of the truth*. In the *fourth* he returns to his proposal, that is to the thing first sought; regarding the first, namely[2] adding to the solution of the first, that although there must not be conceded: "*He begot Himself, and/or another*" disjunctively [divisim], however, it can be conceded conjunctively, there (where he says): *Now ... to the aforementioned question.*

TREATMENT OF THE QUESTIONS

For an understanding of those (things) which Master (Peter) touches upon in the present distinction, four (questions) are asked.

First, whether this saying must be conceded among the divine: "God begot God".

Second, whether the Unity of the Essence admits of this saying: "God begot another God, and/or there is a God other than God [alius a Deo]".

Third there is asked concerning the consignification[3] of this name, "*God*", whether, namely, we can say grammatically (that there are) more gods.

Fourth and last there is asked concerning the supposition of this His name, "*God*", whether it supposes for a Person and/or for an Essence.

---

[1] Chapter 7, n. 9. — Immediately before this the Vatican edition and editions 1 & 2 have *likewise* [item] in place of *the same* [idem]; then after *Behold* [Ecce] the Vatican edition and edition 1 add *also* [et]. Then codices A B C D and editions 1 & 8 have *conceded* [concedendum] in place of *believed* [credendum], but not well, nor congruous to the two testimonies of (St.) Augustine, who speaks both of interior faith (*We believe*) and of the confession of the faith (*We say*).

[2] Letter 170 to Maximus the doctor, n. 5. — A little below this in the explanation of the words of (St.) Augustine, the Vatican edition badly omits *by* [a] after *from Himself ... the Other* [de se alterum].

NOTES ON THE COMMENTARY

[1] The Vatican edition contrary to the manuscripts and edition 1 omits *regarding* [ad].

[2] The codices and edition 1, contrary to the Vatican edition, add *regarding the first, namely* [ad primum videlicet].

[3] On the authority of very many manuscripts, such as A F G K T etc., and edition 1 we have substituted *consignification* [consignificatione] for *signification* [significatione] and *God* [Deus] in place of *Gods* [Dii] and then *of this, His* [istius] in place of *of that* [illius].

ARTICLE SOLE

On the comparison of the name of "God" to generation and on its consignification and supposition.

QUESTION I

Whether this expression: "God begot God", is to be conceded?

About the first, that this saying: "God begot God", is to be conceded,

1. Seems through that which is said in the Creed [in Symbolo]: *"God from God"* [Deum de Deo]; but this is naught but through generation:[1] therefore, God is generated from God: therefore, that saying of his must be conceded: "God begot God".

2. Likewise, generation is in respect of one similar in nature, whence « man generates man »;[2] whence if among the divine there is generation, one Similar in nature is produced: therefore, since the Father is God, He generates naught but God: therefore, this (saying) is true: "God generates God".

3. Likewise, whatever the Son has, He either has from Himself, or from an other; but He has deity, and not from Himself, because He would thus be unbegotten: therefore, He has it from an other; but He has naught but through generation, and[3] He does not have deity except from One having deity, and the One having deity is God: ergo etc..

ON THE CONTRARY: 1. This name, *"God"*, signifies an essence or substance, since it is a substantial term;[4] but this is not conceded, nay rather it is false: "the Essence generates an essence": therefore, similarly also that (saying) of his: "God begot God".

2. Likewise, this name, *"God"*, either supposes [supponit] for every Person, or determinately for some one (Person). If determinately for Someone: therefore, its signification[5] is restricted by Someone, nor is it to be granted, that (it is) by an Other except by this verb, *"begot"* and/or *"generates"*. But the rule is, that the term, posited in the predicate, does not restrict the term on the part of the subject according to a reckoning of signification: therefore, it stands for every Person. Therefore the saying does not seem true, according to which it is accepted for the Person of the Son: ergo etc..

3. Likewise, that term *"God"*, as much as it concerns itself, supposes equally well for "the Son", as[6] for "the Father": therefore, since it belongs to the Son *not to generate*, just as it belongs to the Father *to generate*, if this is true: 'God generates', for the Father, by the same reason also (is) this: 'God does not generate', for the Son; if therefore, this is not conceded, neither (is) the first.

4. Likewise, in a contradictory manner opposites are true of anything [quolibet] under a distinction, because of anything (there can be) an affirmation and/or a negation:[7] therefore, if "God begot God", either (the latter is) the God who is the Father, or a God who is not the Father. If the God who is the Father, therefore, the One generating has been begotten; if the God who is not the Father; but what is implied happens to be inferred simply, as if there is said: "the man, who does not run", one reckons [disputat]: 'therefore, the man does not run': therefore, similarly, if He begot a God who is not the Father, God is not the Father; but if He is not the Father, He does not generate: ergo etc..[8]

---

[1] From the manuscripts and edition 1 we have put *generation* [generationem] in place of *begetting* [gignitionem].

[2] Aristotle, METAPHYSICS, Bk. VII, text 28 (Bk. VI, n. 8): For even in certain things it is also manifest, that such as is the one generating, so that which is generated . . . for man generates man. Cf. ON THE SOUL, Bk. II, text 34 (ch. 4).

[3] Many codices as A F G I K T etc. together with the first six editions have *but* [sed] in place of *and* [et]. Codex R exhibits this proposition thus: *through generation and/or by One having deity, but One having* [per generationem vela b habente deitatem, sed habens].

[4] On the signification and substitution of this name, *"God"* [Deus], in which this and the following objections are founded, see below q. 4. — At the end of the argument very many codices as A F G I K T etc. together with edition 1 have *generates* [generat] in place of *begot* [genuit].

[5] Codices D H O (T and ff in the margin) have *supposition* [suppositio], which also below in the response to this objection nearly all the codices and the first six editions have, in place of *signification* [significationis]; cod. I reads *signification and/or supposition* [signification vel suppositio]. But see the rule a little below taken from Peter of Spain. Then many codices and edition 1 have *not* [non] in place of *nor* [nec]; codex R has *but not* [sed non]. Then after *of the signification* [significationis] codex X adds *but of the consignification* [sed consignificationis], which agrees with the explanation of that rule proposed by Peter of Spain, SUM-MULA, tract "on Restriction": Nothing posited on the part of the predicate can restrict a common term posited on part of the subject in regard to its principal signification, such as "man is white" ... Moreover, I say, in regard to its principal signification, that the predicate restricts the subject in regard to the consignification, which is the gender, v. gr. the masculine.

[6] Some codices as T and Z together with edition 1 add *also* [et]. A little below this after *just as* [sicut] codices Y and Y omit *also* [et]. Then codex Y reads *therefore if this is true for the Father, so shall it be true for the Son, that is "God does not generate"; if therefore, this is not conceded for the Son, neither (is) the first* [ergo si haec est vera pro Patre, sic illa erit vera pro Filio, scilicet Deus non generat; si ergo haec non con-

ceditur pro Filio, nec prima.]. Codices aa and bb near the end of the argument read: *but this is not conceded, therefore, neither (is) the first* [sed haec non conceditur, ergo nec prima]; edition 1 has *neither ought the first be conceded* [nec prima debet concedi]; codex Z reads *if therefore, this is not conceded for the Son, equally neither is that conceded for the Father* [si ergo haec non conceditur pro Filio, pariter nec illa conceditur pro Patre.]. — Very many codices, such as A C G I L M R S U and ff, omit this third argument, but unduly, as is clear from the response put below; however, codex O near the end of the preceding argument after *every person* [omni persona] inserts it under this form: *Likewise, if this is true: "God generates God", for the person of the Father, much more strongly will there be true: "God does not generate God", for the person of the Son and of the Holy Spirit; therefore, by the destruction of the consequents, if this in no manner must be conceded, neither (is) that one. Therefore, the saying etc.* [Item, si haec est vera: Deus generat Deum, pro persona Patris, multo fortius erit vera: Deus non generat Deum, pro persona Filii et Spiritus sancti; ergo a destructione consequentis, si haec nullo modo est concedenda, nec ista. Non ergo]. Codex Z exhibits nearly the same words at the end of this third argument.

[7] Cf. Aristotle, ON INTERPRETATION, Bk. I, ch. 6 and Bk. II, ch. 3, where he deals with affirmation, negation and contradiction; and TOPICS, Bk. VI, ch. 3 near the middle (ch. 6), where he says: *For of everything either the affirmation, or the negation, is true* [Nam de omni aut affirmation, aut negation vera est]; and also METAPHYSICS, Bk. IV, text 15 (Bk. III, n. 4): *Of everything the affirmation, or negation* [Deo omni affirmation, aut negatio]. The codices and edition 1 seem to refer to this last text and to ON INTERPRETATION, Bk. II, ch. 3, though omitting *is true* [vera est], which the Vatican edition adjoins. A little below this the Vatican edition is lacking the words *If the God* up to *but because* [si Deum ... sed quod], which, however, are had in the manuscripts and edition 1.

[8] Codex O here adds a new argument: *Likewise, if God generates God, God is begotten by God: therefore, God is distinct from God; therefore, there are two gods* [Item, si Deus generat Deum, Deus est genitus a Deo: ergo Deus est distinctus a Deo; ergo sunt duo dii].

CONCLUSION

There is rightly said: that God begot God,
which is proven by the four rules.

I RESPOND: It must be said, that the aforesaid saying, saving the unity of the Essence, is received as much as by the masters (of theology) as by the Saints. For the understanding of which, four rules must be noted.

The *first* is, that an *abstract* name is imposed upon a form and by a form, as whiteness is imposed upon whiteness itself[1] and by the form of whiteness; however, a *concrete* name is imposed by a form, but not upon a form, rather [sed] upon a supposit: as white is imposed by the form of whiteness, but not upon a form, rather upon a supposit, as upon any white thing, man and/or swan.

The *second* rule is, that a term having a multitude of supposits, (and) accepted without distribution, stands for that, for which it renders the saying true, as when there is said: "man runs", the saying is true for the one running, if there is anyone running.

The *third* rule is, that placing a negation before and after a term having a non-multipliable form, makes no difference [non differt]. Whence it makes no difference to say: "Peter does not run", and "not Peter runs".

The *fourth* rule is this, that a relative refers to an antecedent under the same manner of supposing, under which the antecedent precedes the relative itself, unless it forms [faciat] a simple relation.

1. From the first rule the response to the first is clear. For since that term, "*God*", is concrete, even if[3] it was imposed by an essential form, that is by deity, it is, however, imposed upon a Person or Supposit, as white is imposed by whiteness upon a white thing; and for that reason it supposes (on behalf of one or the other) and renders the saying true for a Person, not for a form. Moreover, this name, "*essence*" and/or "*deity*", is abstract, and for that reason it is imposed upon a form and by a form,

as whiteness (is), and for that reason it signifies the Essence and supposes (for It). And for that reason this is false: "the Essence generates an essence", because generation does not belong to a form, but to a supposit;[4] but this is true: "God begot God", (because "God" supposes) for a Person.

2. From the second rule the response to the second is clear. For although the signification of the term is not constrained [arctetur], however, it stands for that, for which the saying is true, such as "*a man runs*" (stands) for Peter and/or John, if for the latter, the expression is true; and, yet, it is not restricted to him. And this is clear, because if there is added a distribution, it will confound[5] that term for all; but if it were restricted, it would not confound except for those, to which the restriction would extend itself. Whence that *the term is restricted to one* is one thing, that *it renders the saying true for one* is another.

3. From the third rule the solution[6] to the third is clear. For though this be true for the Father: "God generates God", however, this: "God does not generate God", is not true for the Son. For since that term "*God*" means an unmultipliable form, it makes no difference to place a negation before or [et] after it; and for that reason since a negation placed before (it)[7] entirely removes the predicate from the subject, so also a negation placed after (it) totally removes the predicate from this term "*God*", since there is said: "God does not generate", because it removes it from any Supposit. And for this reason it has another manner of supposing in the affirmative than in the negative, because in the affirmative the saying is true for the Father; however, in the negative there cannot be truth, because the negation totally removes that predicate.

4. From the fourth rule the fourth (solution) is clear. For since an entirely relative (term) is had as a substitute for the antecedent, and that term "God"[8] in the predicate supposes for "the begotten God", (and as) a relative refers to Him [pro illo]. And thus the sense is: "God begot the God, which begotten God is the Father, and/or is not the Father"; and this is true for the negative (part), nor is it licit to infer: "therefore, God is not the Father"; because the supposition is changed, nay rather there it is a figure of speech.[9]

SCHOLIUM

I. For the sake of the readers, who are less exercised in the ancient logic, it helps here to put an explanation of the ancient terms, which in this question and elsewhere in this work often occur. These and many others elsewhere in the notes are explanations taken mostly from the SUMMULAE of Peter of Spain, which in the time of St. Bonaventure were in the hands of scholars. Afterwards Peter (Giuliano) wrote much concerning things philosophical and medical, (and) in the year 1275 was elected as Supreme Pontiff and assumed the name John XXI. He died on

May 16, 1277 A. D.. More (information on these matters) can be seen in any book treating of scholastic logic.

1. *Signification* is one thing, the *supposition* of any term, another. Signification is the representation of a thing through the voice and it befits all words both substantive and otherwise, whether in a proposition, or outside a proposition.

Supposition, as Peter of Spain would have it in his "Tract on Supposition", « is the acceptance of a substantive term on behalf of something », concerning which

---

[1] Very many codices together with the first six editions omit *whiteness itself and* [ipsi albedini est], but badly, as is clear from the context.

[2] The first of the aforesaid rules is hinted at by Aristotle, METAPHYSICS, Bk. VII, texts 21 and 27, and Bk. IX, text 12 (Bk. VI, ch. 6 and 8, and Bk. VIII, ch. 7); the second is had in Peter of Spain's, SUMMULA, tract "on Supposition and Distribution"; the third in the smaller work, which is also attributed to Peter of Spain, namely, PARVORUM LOGICALIUM, tract "on Negation and Affirmation", ch. 4; the fourth in the SUMMULA, tract "on Relatives".

[3] From very many manuscripts and edition 1 we have substituted *even if* [etsi] in place of *et* [and]. Then codex X after *deity* [deitate] has *it is not, however, imposed upon a form, but rather upon a person* [non tamen imponitur formae, sed personae].

[4] From that general principle: Actions belong to supposits.

[5] That is, it causes it to suppose for. — A little before this Codex R has *subject* [subiectum] in place of *that* [illum].

[6] From the more ancient manuscripts and edition 1 we have changed *response* [responsio] into *solution* [solutio] and a little after this *non multipliable* [non multipclicabilem] into *unmultippliable* [immultiplicabilem].

[7] The Vatican edition against the more ancient codices and edition 1 adds here *totally and* [totatliter et].

[8] We have supplied from the manuscripts and edition 1 *God* [Deus]. A little before this codex K in a negative manner has *the relative may have a supposition other than its antecedent* [relativum non habeat suppositionem aliam a sui antecedente]

[9] Codex K adds *such as here: "The begotten God is not the Father: therefore, God is not the Father"* [sicut hic: Deus genitus non est Pater: ergo Deus non est Pater].

and/or which (things) a term of this kind in any proposition is verified. Thus the term "*man*" can substitute [supponere] for man in *common*, as in the proposition: "man is a species"; and/or for his *inferiors* comprehended under this species, v. g. "a man runs". Of suppositions one is *common*, the other *discrete*; the former is done through a common term, such as "man is mortal"; the latter is through a discrete (concrete) term, such as "*Socrates*", and/or through a common one, but determined through the demonstrative pronoun, as (in) "*that man*" [iste homo].

The other divisions of supposition occurring in St. Bonaventure's (writings) are: *simple* and *personal* (i.e. as a hypostasis). The former is the common acceptation of a term, as when there is said: "man is a species"; "animal is a genus". Here the term "man" substitutes for man in common, and for any inferior; whence it is not licit to make a *descent*, as they say, by arguing thus: 'man is a species: therefore, some man is a species'. However, *personal* supposition is the acceptance of a common term for its inferiors, as when there is said: "man runs"; here that term "*man*" substitutes for its inferiors. — Of personal suppositions one is *determinate*, the other is *confused*. Determinate (substitution) is the acceptance of a common term taken indefinitely, and/or with a *particular* sign, such as "*a man runs*", and/or "*some man runs*"; and it is called determinate, because though in each of those propositions that term "*man*" substitutes for every man, both the one running and the one not running, however, when only one man is running, the proposition is true; and because it is one thing *to substitute* and another that *a saying is true and/or false* for something, therefore, in the aforesaid that term "man" *substitutes* for "every man running and not running", though *it renders the saying true* for only one running ... A *confused* supposition is the acceptance of a common term for very many, by means of a *universal* sign, as when there is said: "every man is an animal"; because the term "man" substitutes for any of its supposits. Thus Peter of Spain; others in regard to *confused* and *determinate* supposition explain the matter a little otherwise.

2. *Distribution* is the acceptance of a *common* term for those it signifies [pro suis significatis], or it is the multiplication of a *common* term by virtue of any universal sign, v. g. in the proposition: "every man runs", the term "*man*" is distributed (or *confounded*) for every man by virtue of that word *every* which is called a *distributive sign*.

3. *Restriction* is the constraining [coarctatio] of a common term by a greater substitution or extension to a lesser; as "*white man*" [homo albus] does not signify all men, but a portion of them.

4. "*To render a saying true*" signifies, that in a proposition, in which the subject substitutes disjunctively for very many, the sense is rendered true through this, that in at least one supposit

it is verified; v. g. the proposition: "man runs", is rendered true, with any one (man) running. Whence "*to render a saying true*" differs from the *restriction* of the term to one, as St. Bonaventure well says, here at n. 2.

II. With these things supposed, the four logical rules posited in the body and their application in the solution of the objections are easily understood. Thus the words (at n. 2): « because if there is added a distribution, it will confound that term for all », has this sense: if there is added the sign "*every*" to the term "*man*", then it will confound, i. e. distribute, that term, so that it shall be verified for all men; however, if the term "*man*" is restricted by "*white*", then it will not « confound except for white men ». — For an understanding of the application of the fourth rule it must be noted, that there is a twofold relation of a relative pronoun to its noun, that is a *simple* and/or *personal* relation. Through a *simple* relation the relative pronoun ("who", "which", "what") is not referred to the same antecedent in number or to the same supposit, however, (it is) rightly (referred) through the *personal* relation. An example: « She has damned us, who has saved us: a woman! » [Mulier damnavit, quae salvavit]; this relative *who* [quae] has a simple relation, not a personal one, because one person among women damned, namely Eve, an other saved, that is the Most Holy Virgin Mary. Whence the Seraphic Doctor rightly concludes, that in the objection brought forth there is a *figure of speech*, i. e. a fallacy of a figure of speech, because the term is taken under a diverse supposition. Concerning this, see the very many (things said) here in Doubt 3, (and) in Alexander of Hales, SUMMA., p. I, q. 50, m. 3, q. 2, §. 4, (and) in Richard of Middleton, here in q. 1.

III. Against the application of the third rule to "God", Durandus (of Saint-Pourçain) (here in q. 2), Aureolus, Brülifer (at this point) and other later Scholastics bring forward a subtle difficulty. For they deny that "*God*" is properly a singular term, since in some manner it may also be a common term, which even St. Bonaventure (below in q. 4) concedes. Hence they conclude, that the proposition: "God does not generate God", can be conceded. However, more approved theologians, such as St. Thomas (SUMMA., I, q. 39, a. 4, at n. 3), Richard (here in q. 1) and others together with our Seraphic Doctor (here in q. 3) disapprove rightly of this saying. Cf. Cajetan's commentary on this passage of St. Thomas.

IV. In regard to the solution of the question all the ancients agree. Cf. St. Bonaventure, below in d. 9, q. 1. — Alexander of Hales, SUMMA., p. I, q. 50, m. 3, a. 2, §. 1. 4. — (Bl. John Duns) Scotus, here in q. 1, at n. 1. — St. Thomas, here in q. 1 & 2; SUMMA., I, q. 39, a. 4. — Bl. (now St.) Albertus (Magnus), here in a. 6 & 7.; on this and the following qq., SUMMA., p. I, tr. 13, q. 51. — (Bl.) Peter of Tarentaise, here in q. 2, a. 1 & 3. — Richard of Middleton, here in q. 1. — Giles the Roman, on this and the following q. here in the 2. princ. of the sole question. — Henry of Ghent, on this and the following qq., SUMMA., a. 54, q. 3. — Durandus (of Saint-Pourçain), on this and the following qq. here in q. 2. — (Bl.) Dionysius the Carthusian, on this and the following aa., here in q. 2. — (Gabriel) Biel, on this and the following question, here in q. 1.

QUESTION II

Whether this expression can be admitted: "God generates another God"?

Second, there is asked, whether the Unity of the Essence admits this: "God generates another God" [Deus generat alium Deum]. And it seems that (it does) not.

1. (St.) Anselm ON THE PROCESSION OF THE HOLY SPIRIT (says):[1] « When we say "God from God", we do not understand another God, but the Same from His very self ».

2. Likewise, if He begot another God; but where there is one and another, there are two: therefore, if He begot another, there are two gods.

3. Likewise, "another" [alius] means an 'otherness' [alietatem] in general: therefore, since the general is specified through an adjunct, this name,

"*God*", specifies Him; but if it specifies, it specifies by reason of a form: therefore, there is noted an otherness in form; therefore, such a saying must not be admitted, since an otherness in form is not there.

ON THE CONTRARY: Generation conveys a distinction;[2] but distinction (conveys) some 'anotherness': therefore, generation also (does); therefore, if this is true: "God begot God", these also (are true) consequently [per consequens]: "God is distinguished by God" and/or "He begot an other God". *If you say*, that it does not follow, because to generate conveys a distinction as *manner* but 'to be distinguished' and/or 'to be another' (conveys a distinction) as a *thing*; *on the contrary*: to

---

[1] Chapter 24: For when we say "God from God" [Deum de Deo], "Son from the Father" [Filium de Patre], we do not understand one God from an other God, but the same God Itself from the same God Itself. — The codices, together with the Vatican edition, falsely have *in the Proslogion* [in Prosologio].

[2] For as Aristotle says, ON THE SOUL, Bk. II, text 47 (ch. 4): More-

over, nothing itself generates its very self. — On the minor proposition, Aristotle, METAPHYSICS, Bk. XIV, ch. 3 (Bk. XIII, ch. 1), says: "The other" (is the contrary) to "the same", "another" to "this one" (αὐτῷ). — In this minor proposition, the Vatican edition has *and* [et] in place of *but* [sed], contrary to the manuscripts and edition 1.

the consequence [consequentiam] as *manner* there follows the consecution [consecutio] as *thing*; whence if this is true: 'if there is a man, there is an animal',[1] to man there follows animal. *And moreover*, it is established that the distinction of generation is not only on the part of the one understanding, but also on the part of the thing: therefore, to that distinction as exercised there responds a real distinction.

2. Likewise, the affirmative is false: 'The begotten God is the generating God'; therefore, the negative is true: 'The begotten God is not the generating God'. But just as the affirmative signifies an identity, so the negative a diversity: therefore, just as it happens that God generating and begotten are compared to One another by means of a negation, so by means of an anotherness: therefore, this is true: "God begot an other God".

3. Likewise, the Father or God begot another; this is true, it is established: therefore, either another God, or another not God; but not another not God: ergo etc..

4. Likewise, "*another*" [alius] is a term of the masculine genus; but a term of the masculine genus[2] stands for a person among partitive terms: therefore, "*another*" means a personal anotherness; but this is true: 'God begot the God other [alium] in person'; therefore, simply (speaking) this is true: 'God begot another God'.

CONCLUSION

*In the strict sense of the words, the saying:
"God begot an other God", is false.*

1. **I RESPOND**: It must be said, that this (saying): "God begot another God", is accustomed to be distinguished, because "*another*" can be held *adjectively*; and thus it posits an otherness [alietatem] about the form of that term "*God*", and thus the saying is false; it can also be held *substantively* [substantive], so as to[3] become a substantive [substantivetur]; and then there is an appositive construction, as "*the animal: man*", and the sense is in this manner: "God begot another God", that is, "He begot Another who is God"; and in this sense the saying is true.

But, though that distinction on account of a certain proper manner of speaking has a place among theological sayings, however, as much as it would concern the virtue[4] of the expression [sermonis], it should not be distinguished; because an adjective adjoined to a substantive [substantivo], as "white man", is not said to become a substantive, nor is an appositive construction said to be there, most of all when that (construction) is less common in respect of the more common.[5] Whence since this name, "*another*", is an adjective having a substantive conjoined, in

the aforesaid saying it posits an otherness about it by a reckoning of supposit and of form.

And on that account, if we wish to proceed in an technical manner [artificialiter],[6] such a saying is to be judged false. On account of this, for the understanding of the said saying, a common rule must be noted: 'distinction[7] has no place, where there is no union out of diverse causes', for example, the Father and the Son and the Holy Spirit are united in this name, "*God*", not out of diverse causes or by reason of diverse (things), but by reason of the one Deity or Essence. There is a union out of diverse causes, as (when) in "*man*" there is united Peter and John by reason of diverse humanities, because the one is the humanity of Peter, and the other (that) of John.

And in accord with this rule, ab oppositis,[8] there must be accepted *another* rule: 'an omnimodal union does not have a place, where there is a distinction together with the union', as the Father and the Son and the Holy Spirit are united in one Deity or Essence, but have a distinction by reason of the plurality of the Persons.

According to this, one must pay attention, that among the divine certain words convey only a distinction, certain ones an omnimodal union, certain ones in a middle manner. Since, therefore, the generating God and the begotten God, even if They are personally distinct, yet they are united in the Deity from the same cause, because (They are) one according to deity: for that reason nouns conveying a simple distinction are not received[9] (in God). For that reason this is not admitted: "God is distinguished from God", similarly: "God begot another God". *Likewise*, by reason of the distinction words conveying an omnimodal union in supposit and form are not received; wherefore, this is not received: "God begot Himself". But those which hold themselves in a middle manner, are received, such as is this verb, "*generates*", because it means a distinction in person with[10] a unity of essence. Similarly, this is conceded: "The Father generates the other-Himself [alterum se]". Whence (St.) Augustine (says in his letter) To MAXIMI-NUS:[11] « The Father begot the other-Himself »; and similarly ON JOHN: « The Father sending the Son sent the other-Himself ». And from this it is, that there does not follow after generation a word conveying simply a distinction; and thus the first (objection) is clear.

2. To that which is objected second concerning negation, I rightly concede, that there is an otherness; but, yet, it does not follow, that there can be meant an otherness in the *essence* or form of the Deity. Whence there does not follow: "the Begotten is other [alius] than the One generating, therefore, (He is)[12] another [alius] God", because the supposition of this term "*God*" is changed.

---

[1] On the authority of the mss. and ed. 1, we have expunged the *also* [etiam] added here; cod. I, moreover, adds *similarly this is true* [similiter haec est vera]. Cod. O after *there is a man* [homo est] adds *therefore* [ergo]. — See the very many things concerning this consequence in (St. Severinus) Boethius, ON THE HYPOTHETICAL SYLLOGISM.

[2] The Vatican edition, disagreeing with the more ancient manuscripts and edition 1, has the less well *which* [qui] in place of *but a term of the masculine genus* [sed terminus masculini generis]; and near the end of the argument *similarly* [similiter] in place of *simply (speaking)* [simpliciter]. [3] Edition 1 *so that* [sic ut].

[4] Some codices as R and cc have *truth* [veritate], and a little below this very many codices together with edition 1, against the Vatican edition, have *joined* [iunctum] in place of *adjoined* [adiunctum].

[5] The sense is: most of all when an appositive construction is made by a conjunction of a less common term with a more common one.

[6] That is, strictly according to the rules of the arts, that is, of grammar and of logic.

[7] The codices together with the first six editions omit *an omnimodal* [omnimoda], to which term the Vatican edition prefixes *distinction* [distinctio].

[8] The Vatican ed. not trusting the codd.& ed. 1 has ab opposito.*

[9] Trusting in the manuscripts and edition 1 we have substituted *they are ... received* [recipiuntur] in place of *they do ... receive* [recipiunt]. A little below this many codices omit *similarly* [similiter].

[10] Codex X has *a distinction of persons in* [distinctionem personarum in].

[11] See the text of Master (Peter), ch. 2, a the end; and ON JOHN, ch. 3, tract. 14, n. 11: The Father sending the Son sent Himself-the-other [Pater mittens Filium se alterum].

[12] Codices M and X add *He is* [est].

---

* *Trans. note*: A topic ab oppositis is a proposition which is true in virtue of the truth of another proposition, which has the opposite logical form. Here, the second rule, is formed by converting (cf. trans. note, p. 112) the first one, in which the particular denial ("no union"), is replaced by the affirmation of the opposite ("omnimodal union"). Cf. Peter of Spain, SUMMULAE, tracts I, "On categoric propositions" and V, "On loci ab oppositis".

3. To that which is objected third: either another God", or another not God; I say, that (this) does not sufficiently divide (the matter); because there is no contradiction, unless there is accepted a negation in respect of the whole. For in this (saying): "He begot another God", two (things) are said, that is, that *God* (begot)[1] a *God*, and that (He has begot) an *other in deity*: and for that reason, for this, that a contradiction be obtained [sumatur], it is necessary, that it be brought upon the whole. Whence just as it is not valid, that having demonstrated that 'black is the monk, who is white by nature', (to say): "that one is either a white monk, or a white non-monk", because each (is) false; similarly it must be understood in the proposed. Nor is it valid (to say): "There is a God and there is an Other: therefore, there is another

God", nay there is (a fallacy of) the accident there, as here: "There is a good (man) and there is a cithara-player [citharoedus]: therefore, there is a good cithara-player".[2]

4. That which is objected last, it must be said, that *another* [alius], although it belong to the masculine genus, however, because it posits a thing about a substantive,[3] it draws away from it a supposition; and for that reason it is not held personally, except according to which it becomes a substantive [substantivatur], just as also this name, "one", (does); whence, just as if there were said "*one God*", "*one*" means a substantial unity, so if there were said "another God", "*another*" means a substantial otherness. And the reason for this comes not only, because (it is) an *adjective*, but because (it is) a *general* one, which is specified through (its) adjunct.

SCHOLIUM

I. The distinction posited at the beginning of the response, that "*another*" [alius] here can be held as an adjective and/or a substantive (namely as an apposite), the Seraphic Doctor disproves, since there is a rule of grammarians, that an adjective, if it has a substantive immediately conjoined with itself, cannot be accepted as a substantive or as an apposite. If moreover, "*another*" is an adjective, then is valid the rule of logic, that "*another*", when it is placed immediately adjacent [ad] to its substantive, conveys an « otherness » about its substantive both by a reckoning of a sup-

posit, and by a reckoning of form. Consequently, in our case this term would introduce a diversity in the Deity.

II. In the conclusion and solution of the objections the principle doctors agree. Alexander of Hales, SUMMA., p. I, q. 50, m. 3, a. 2, §. 2. — (Bl. John Duns) Scotus, here in q. 1. — St. Thomas, here in a. 3; SUMMA., I, q. 31, a. 2. — Bl. (now St.) Albertus (Magnus), here in a. 5. — (Bl.) Peter of Tarentasia, here in q. 2, a. 2. — Richard of Middleton, here in q. 2.

QUESTION III

Whether, congruously in accord with the rules of grammer, there can be said: "several gods"?

Third, there is asked, whether this name, "*God*", grammatically signifies a plural number, or whether congruously there can be said: "*several gods*" [plures dii]. And that (it is) so, seems:

1. Because, according to the Philosopher[4] the understandings (of words) are the same among all, although the words spoken [voces] are diverse; but manners of signifying are consequent to manners of understanding: therefore, when among the Hebrews there is congruously said *Elohim*,* which is equivalent to that (word) which (in our tongue) is "*Gods*" [dii], therefore, also among us.

2. Likewise, as the Philosopher wants,[5] the true supposes the congruous; whence « 'It belongs to Cato, and/or it does not belong', signifies neither the true nor the false »; but this is true: 'there are not several gods': therefore, (so is) the congruous (equivalent): therefore, also this congruous (equivalent): 'there are several gods', because negation does not remove the incongruity.

3. Likewise, as "God" convenes with One alone, thus 'the principle[6] of creatures' (with) One alone; but, although

there are falsely said (to be) several principles, yet, congruously ("several principles") are said: therefore, by an equal reason we can say: "several gods".

4. Likewise, this name, "*phoenix*" [phoenix], has naught but one supposit;[7] however, there is congruously said: "more phoenixes" [plures phoenices]. *If you say*, that the supposit is plurified through a succession of time; I object to you concerning this name, "*Sun*" [sol], which at no time is plurified; and, however, there is congruously said: "many suns" [plures soles]: therefore, also "many gods" [plures dii].

ON THE CONTRARY: 1. Every noun [nomen], which has a plural, is an appellative name [nomen appellativum]; for proper names are not plurified, for there is not said: "many Peters" and/or "(many) Johns";[8] but this noun, "*God*", is not an appellative name, because it does not signify a multipliable form: ergo etc..

2. Likewise, this noun, "*God*", is properly (speaking)[9] proper to the Divine Nature; but nothing such is multiplied: ergo etc..

---

[1] Codex R adds *begot* [genuit].

[2] The example taken from Aristotle, ON INTERPRETATION, Bk. II, ch. 2 (ch. 11), where according to the translation of (St. Severinus) Boethius there is had *if the cithara-player is also good, he is also a good cithara-player* [si citharoedus est bonus, est et citharoedus bonus], though other translations have a *tanner* [coriarius] (σκυτεύς) in place of *cithara-player* [citharoedus]. — Concerning this fallacy of the accident see above d. 2, q. 4, at n. 1.

[3] Here the Vatican edition has *subject* [subiectum] in place of *substantive* [substantivum], and a little below this after *is substantiated* [substantiatur] it puts *Therefore, just as, when there is said "one God", this name, "one", means a unity* [Sicut ergo, cum dicitur unus Deus, hoc nomen unus dicit unitatem], but contrary to the more ancient codices and edition 1.

[4] ON INTERPRETATION, Bk. 1, ch. 1: And in accord with the manner that letters are neither the same for all (peoples), so, too, spoken words [voces] are not the same for all (men): to whom, however, these signs (i. e. letters) belong first, because there these passions of the soul are the same for all.

[5] ON INTERPRETATION, Bk. I, ch. 2, according to the translation of

(St. Severinus) Boethius: « However, "It is always the name of Cato, and/or it is not"; for it does not yet say anything true or false »; in which text the rest of the translations put *to Philo* [Philonis] in place of *to Cato* [Catonis]. Regarding which passage the author of the book, AUCTORITATUM ARISTOTELIS etc. (1500 A. D.) adds: « From which there is commonly drawn, that the true and the false presuppose the congruous ». The incongruity of this saying consists in a *discoherence of accidents*, as is said below in the solution; for the subject of the genitive is lacking.

[6] Codex S adds *of all* [omnium]. The codices together with edition 1 at the end of the argument have *that (there are) many gods* [plures deos] in place of *many gods* [plures dii].

[7] The Seraphic Doctor speaks of the fabulous opinion of the ancients, that this bird exists in only one individual, from whose ashes there arises another. (St. Severinus) Boethius adduces the same example, ON THE CATEGORIES OF ARISTOTLE, Bk. I, ch. "On Denominatives".

[8] Cf. Priscian, GRAMMATICAL INSTITUTIONS, Bk. II, ch. 5.

[9] Having examined the manuscripts and edition 1, we have added *properly (speaking)* [proprie]. A little below this some codices as H and ff after *is multiplied* [multiplicatur] add *and/or plurified* [vel plurificatur]; edition 1 has *nor is it plurified* [nec plurificatur].

---

* Trans. note: Here *Elohim* [Heloim] transliterates the Hebrew, אלהים, which though plural (cf. Exodus 32:4), is also used for the one God (Genesis 1:1).

CONCLUSION

*The noun "God", properly speaking,
does not have a plural.*

I Respond: For an understanding of the aforesaid there must be noted, that this noun, "*God*" [Deus], is said in a threefold manner, that is *as a name* [nuncupative], *adoptively* and *naturally*. In the first two manners it is plurified; whence the Apostle in the eight (chapter) of the First (Letter) to the Corinthians (says):[1] *If, indeed, there are many gods, and many lords*; but in the third manner, not (so), because, in this manner this noun, "*God*", signifies the Divine Nature with (its) conditions, the collection of which is impossible to be discovered in another; and for that reason just as a proper name does not have a plural, according to the art of speaking [secundum artem loquendo], so, neither this[2] noun "God".

1. To that therefore which is objected, that among the Hebrews there is had a plural which is *Elohim*; it must be said that manners of signifying do not only follow[3] diverse, general manners of understanding, but also manners of expressing. And since they have articles and diverse manners of expressing, which we do not have (in Latin), for that reason they can have (the plural), but we (can) not.

2. To that which is objected, that the true supposes the congruous; it must be said, that there is a twofold in-congruity: *one* is from a discoherence of accidents,[4] as "*It belongs to Cato*"; the *other* is from a discoherence of understandings, as when there is said: "*many Peters*". The first incongruity takes away truth and falsity; however, the second incongruity has a falsity conjoined: and for that reason, because through a negation falsity is removed, and the Saints preferred to speak in a true manner, (rather) than observe the propriety of speech and speak less truly, for that reason they denied that (there are) many gods. It could,[5] however, be said, that although this sound [vox] "*gods*" is not a significative sound according to the art (of speaking) and (its) imposition, however, it is a significative sound from an accommodation of use, such as "*those*" [olli] for "*those*" [illi]: and for that reason an affirmative generates a false understanding, and a negative a true one, although not grammatically.

3. 4. To that which is objected, that a principle convenes with one alone, similarly also the phoenix; it must be said, that 'to convene with one alone' is in a threefold manner. For either it is, because a noun is imposed by a non-multipliable form, as in proper names; and, thus, it takes away plurality in *thing* and in *consignification*. Or, it is imposed by a form, which is *bound to* be communicated, although it is not *communicated on account of a determination*, as when[6] there is said: "the principle of creatures". Or, on account of a *defect of matter*, such as the phoenix; and such takes away a plurality *according to thing*, not *according to consignification*, because such a form can be consignified, as it can be multiplied through supposits.

SCHOLIUM

I. The question, here, does not concern the fundamental dogma, that God is one (which has been proved above, in d. 2, q. 1), but rather this: whether the noun "*God*" [Deus] by reason of the Three Persons can be inflected in the plural. Concerning this argument, the Seraphic Doctor disputes twice, that is, here in regard to the *manner of speaking*; again, below, in d. 23, a. 2, q. 3 in regard to the *thing* or intrinsic truth. The question discussed here, which regards rather grammar, which it seems to have arisen from (this), that among the Hebrews in the word, "Elohim", a plural is employed (cf. 1 argument to the opposite). That this must be explained by the proper inherent quality [indole] of the Hebraic tongue, St. Bonaventure so asserts, to which St. Thomas, Summa., I. q. 39, q. 3, at n. 2, consents.

II. (The following) teach the same (opinion): Alexander of Hales, Summa., p. I. q. 50, m. 2; but the triple distinction, posited here in the body (of the Question), is had in m. 1. — (Bl. John Duns) Scotus, here in q. 1 and 2. — St. Thomas, here in q. 1, a. 2, at n. 3; Summa., I, q. 13, q. 2. — Henry of Ghent, Summa., a. 4, q. 2, n. 28.

QUESTION IV

Whether this name, "God", supposes for a person, and/or for a nature?

Fourth and last, there is asked concerning the supposition of this name, "*God*". And it is asked, whether this name, "*God*", of itself, supposes a person, and/or a nature. And it seems, that (it supposes) a person.

1. Through that (word) of (St.) Ambrose on: *May He bless us, God, Our God, may He bless us God.*[7] Ambrose (says): « The triune confession of God indicates the Trinity of Persons », therefore, since "God" is there without adjunct, it of itself [de se] supposes a person.

2. Likewise, by *reason* it is, thus, objected: This noun "*man*" properly (speaking)[8] supposes on behalf of every one, in whom there is humanity: therefore by a similar (reason) this noun "*God*" also (supposes) on behalf of every

---

[1] Verse 5.

[2] The Vatican edition not trusting in the manuscripts and edition 1 has less aptly *so neither the name of God* [sic nec nomen Dei].

[3] From very many manuscripts as A C G G J M N R S T V X Y Z etc. we have substituted *follow* [sequuntur] in place of *require* [requirunt]; other codices as I U ff together with edition 1 have *follow after* [consequuntur]. The reading of the manuscripts is certainly to be preferred to the reading of the Vatican edition. A little below this the Vatican edition contrary to very many codices as A C G H I K S T V W Y etc. and edition 1 has *therefore, since* [quoniam ergo] in place of *And since* [Et quoniam]. Finally near the end of the argument, by disagreeing with the manuscripts and edition 1, the Vatican edition puts *say* [dicere] in place of *have* [habere]; in reading the manuscripts supple: plural.

[4] Priscian, Grammatical Institutions, Bk. XVII, ch. 1 (On Construction): For, if (the reason for the context) is incongruous, it will cause a solecism, as if by an awkward concourse of the elements of discourse [quasi elementis orationis inconcinne coeuntibus], in the manner that the awkwardness of letters and/or of syllables and/or of the accidents in their individual pronunciation [singulis dictionibus] cause a barbarism. — The Vatican edition alone has *adjacents* [adiacentium] in place of *accidents* [accidentium], which text also a little above this, contrary to nearly all the codices and edition 1, has *presupposes* [praesupponit] in place of *supposes* [supponit].

[5] The Vatican edition has *it can* [potest], but the manuscripts and edition 1 oppose this. Near the end of this response some codices as A C L O R S V Y have *from the understanding* [ex intellectu] in place of *understanding* [intellectum].

[6] We have supplied from the manuscripts and the first six editions *when* [cum]. At the end of the response the more ancient codices together with edition 1 have *be signified* [significari] in place of *be consignified* [consignificari], and codex Q (in the margin) has *able* [potens] in place of *can* [potest].

[7] Psalm 66: 7, 8. — The words, which are here by the Seraphic Doctor attributed to St. Ambrose, are also ascribed by Master (Peter) above in d. 2, ch. 4, to the same (author). See p. 48, note 8. — Within these words the Vatican edition, not trusting in the manuscripts and edition 1, has *profession* [professio] in place of *confession* [confessio].

[8] From the mss. and ed. 1 we have supplied *properly (speaking)* [proprie]. A little before this very many codd., together with ed. 1, have *shown* [ostenditur] in place of *objected* [obiicitur]. Then, after *God* the Vatican ed. repeats *supposes* [supponit], contrary to the codd.

one, in whom the Deity is; but this is a Person: ergo etc..

3. Likewise, this noun, "*God*", signifies deity in concretion; but (it signifies) naught, unless in concretion towards a supposit, which is a Person; but a concrete term properly supposes on behalf of that, in respect of which it conveys a form, as "a white" [album], properly supposes on behalf of a white thing rather than on behalf of a form: ergo etc..

ON THE CONTRARY: 1. A pronoun refers to a thing on behalf of its own supposit;[1] but when there is said: *May God bless us, and let them fear Him*, this pronoun "*Him*" refers to the Nature, not to a Person: ergo etc..

2. Likewise, because that term, "*man*", properly supposes on behalf of an individual, that (saying) of his is false: "man is Socrates and Plato", because the same individual does not receive that predication; but this is true: "God is the Trinity", and/or: "God is the Father and the Son": therefore, since that predicate does not convene upon one Person, it is clear that etc..

3. Likewise, a term, which properly supposes a person, having a partitive term added to it, stands solely for one, as when there is said: "one man runs": therefore similarly, when there is said, "*one God*": therefore, this is simply false: "one God is the Father and the Son".

CONCLUSION

The noun "God", since it has the nature both of a common term and a singular term, can properly suppose both on behalf of a nature as on behalf of a person.

I RESPOND: It must be said, that here there is accustomed to be a twofold opinion.

One (opinion), indeed, is, that this noun,* "*God*",

signifies properly a nature and supposes a person, sometimes one, as when there is said: "God breathes"; sometimes three, as when there is said: "God is the Trinity". And the reason for this is, as they say, that since ("God") has many supposits, it has the nature of a common term; moreover, a common term properly supposes on behalf of an individual, however, on behalf of a nature and/or a form it does not suppose properly,[2] unless it be (logically) extended [trahatur], as if there is said: "man is a species". In this manner they speak in the proposed (objection). Furthermore, they say, that because all (the Persons) have been supposed in that (term) by a unique[3] supposition, for that reason it can simultaneously suppose on behalf of many Persons, though that term "*man*", and/or an other common term could not (do) that; and thus they solve the objections.

An *other* opinion is, that it properly supposes a nature, just as it signifies, and does not suppose a person, unless it be (logically) extended by an other (term), as when there is said: "God generates"; and these say, that when there is said: "God is the Trinity", it stands there for the Nature, not for a Person; and[4] "the one Nature is the Three Persons": for that reason the saying is true. And the reason for this position is, that this noun, "*God*", has the nature of a discrete term, since it does not have a plural; for that reason it signifies and properly supposes the same (thing); therefore, since it signifies a nature, it properly supposes that.

But it is better to say (that it supposes) *each* — because it has the nature of a *common* term and of a *discrete* term: of a *common* term on account of a plurality of supposits, of a *discrete* term by reason of an non-multipliable form — that[5] it properly supposes as much a Nature as a Person. However, the reasons for each part conclude truly in their own manner. Moreover, this (use) cannot be found in any other term, and for that reason neither (can there be found) a exactly similar [consimilis] manner of supposing.

SCHOLIUM

I. Concerning the difference between signification and supposition, cf. Scholium here at q. 1. The *discrete* term, of which St. Bonaventure speaks, is the same as the *singular* term and it signifies something incommunicable. Whence « a singular term signifies and supposes the same (thing) » (St. Thomas, SUMMA., I, q. 39, a. 4). However, it is not necessary [non oportet] that a *common* term suppose on behalf of that which it signifies per se, v. gr. in the proposition: "a man runs", "*man*" does not suppose on behalf of the common human nature, but on behalf of some indeterminate individual.

II. Though the ancient doctors speak of this question in diverse manners, however, they seem to dissent very little in the matter. St. Bonaventure prefers the third sentence, which holds a middle way, that is that "God" properly supposes as much for a Nature as for a Person. St. Thomas in his COMMENTARY (here at q. 1, a. 2) seems to teach the sentence posited in the first place, however, he rejects the second one completely there and in the SUMMA. However, he so explains that first opinion in the SUMMA (I, q. 39, a. 4), that it agrees with the third and middle-sentence of St. Bonaventure. This is clear, if the sentence of St. Bonaventure is proposed in

distinct propositions. Proposition 1: 'To the noun "*God*" there convenes this property, that it is partly a common term, partly a singular one. The reason is, that it signifies simultaneously as much a *non multipliable* form, as a *communicable* nature'. St. Thomas teaches the same (SUMMA., loc. cit., at n. 2). Proposition 2: 'Hence it is, that "*God*" sometimes supposes on behalf of a nature, other times for a person'. St. Thomas and Alexander of Hales assert this same (teaching); however, the Angelic (Doctor) adds, that « *per se* it supposes on behalf of the common nature » (at n. 3), but « from *a manner of signifying* » it has the ability [habet ut possit] to properly suppose on behalf of a person (cf. in the body of the question).

III. About the question itself cf. St. Bonaventure, below in d. 29, a. 1, q. 2; SENT., Bk. III, d. 7, a. 1, q. 1. — Alexander of Hales, SUMMA., p. I, q. 50, m. 3, a. 1 and 2. — St. Thomas, locis citt.. — (Bl. John Duns) Scotus, here in q. 2 at the end. — Bl. (now St.) Albertus (Magnus), here in a. 5 and 6 and d. 32, a. 8. — (Bl.) Peter of Tarentaise, here in q. 4, a. 1. — Richard of Middleton, here in q. 3. — Henry of Ghent, SUMMA., a. 54, q. 3, n. 40. — (Bl.) Dionysius the Carthusian, here in a. 2 in princ. — (Gabriel) Biel, here in q. 2.

---

[1] Priscian, GRAMMATICAL INSTITUTIONS, Bk. XVII, ch. 2: For a pronoun put in the place of a noun signifies a substance and it indicates a congruous person with a word adjoined to it.

[2] The Vatican edition here omits *properly* [proprie] and a little after this it has *we say* [dicamus] in place of *there is said* [dicatur], but the authority of the manuscripts and edition 1 oppose this.

[3] Very many codd., such as A C F G I K L O R X and Z, have *one* [una]. A little below this the Vatican ed., contrary to the mss. and ed. 1, has

they solved [solverunt], however, the other codices as K P Q X read *there are solved* [solvuntur]. [4] Codex H adds *because* [quia].

[5] Thus nearly all the codd., together with ed. 1, in which reading *that* [quod] is referred to what is posited a little above this, *to say (that it supposes) each* [dicere utrumque]. The Vatican ed. for *because* [quod] puts *for that reason* [ideo], the sense of which reading is explained by cod. Z *and for that reason I say that properly* [et ideo dico quod proprie]. A little below this, codd. O and bb have *Whence* [Unde] in place of *However* [Tamen].

---

* Trans. note: Throughout this Question, I have rendered the Latin term, <u>nomen</u> (which has the common meaning of *name*, but which is also used in Latin, as the technical grammatical term for the part of speech, which in English is called, a "noun"), liberally, according to the exigencies of the context.

DOUBTS ON THE TEXT OF THE MASTER

DOUBT I

About the text, in this part, is asked of this which (the Nicene Creed) says: *God from God, Light from Light*; because since the preposition "*from*" [de] notes transition and thus diversity and[1] distinction, it seems that, for an equal reason and ab aequipollenti,* these are also true: "There is another God than God", "God is distinguished from God".

I RESPOND: It must be said, that to introduce distinction or diversity is twofold, that is, as a *manner* (of being regarded)[2] and/or as a *thing*, and/or as (something) *exercised* and/or as *conceived*. Therefore, since prepositions introduce distinction as (something) *exercised*, and distinction is among the divine as much as regards the Supposits, "*from*" [de] causes a term to stand for diverse Supposits. Therefore, since it places a manner (of being regarded) about that, about which it exercises a distinction, and such are the Persons: for that reason (the first) is a true saying. However, because this noun, "*another*", conveys a distinction as (something) *conceived*, similarly this verb, "*to distinguish*": for that reason it simply posits a distinction about the term by reason of its form; for that reason (the second and third expressions) are false.

DOUBT II

Likewise, is asked concerning the response, which Master (Peter) puts, there: *However because there is added: therefore, He begot Himself God* etc., because Master (Peter) solves the conclusion by interemption and he seems not to solve it rightly. For since '*the same*' and '*the diverse*' sufficiently divide being [ens],[5] it seems that necessarily there follows: 'He begot God: therefore Himself, and/or another'.

I RESPOND: It must be said, that Master (Peter)

by sustaining the first and by denying [interimendo] the conclusion hints, that the conclusion does not follow from the premises; and that it does not follow, he shows by bringing forward [ferendo] an instance[6] against that disjunction [disiunctum].

However, to that which is objected, that '*the same*' and '*the diverse*' sufficiently divide[7] being [ens]; it must be said, that simply speaking it is false. For a part is neither entirely the same as the whole nor simply diverse. It has, however, truth according to which (it is) *the same*. Whence: « if it is not the same as the other, it is diverse », is true according to that (principle), according to which it is not the same.[8] Moreover, the Son is not the same as the Father in person, and for that reason in person (He is) Another; nor does there, however, follow: '(He is) *another God*', because (in this) there is signified anotherness in essence.[9]

DOUBT III

Likewise, is asked concerning this distinction, which Master (Peter) posits concerning this predicate "*God the Father*", because it can be an *appositive* and an *immediate* construction, and/or a *mediate* one.[10] For *first* it seems, that that distinction of his is not intelligible, since those which are intransitively constructed on the same side (of the copula), seem to be construed only immediately. *Likewise*, it seems, that he does not solve (the question), since the right solution belongs, to the proposed opposite [dantem oppositum] which he does not happen to solve;[11] but that remote distinction of his, still remains a sophism, if in that place that which is "*God the Father*", there placed only "*the Father*": ergo etc..

I RESPOND: It must be said, that Master (Peter)'s distinction is a good one and according to the art (of grammar). For, as Priscian wants,[12] between the adjective and the substantive there is under-

---

[1] Not trusting in the manuscripts and edition 1 the Vatican edition here repeats *thus* [ita].

[2] Supply: of being regarded. — On this distinction see below in d. 26, q. 1 [especially at n. 3 and in the Scholium, II, nn. 2 & 3] and 2.

[3] The particle *from* [de] has been left out of the manuscripts and the editions, thought he context requires it.

[4] For a greater understanding and explanation of this doubt cf. qq. 1 and 2 of this distinction. — In regard to this preposition *from* [de] see below d. 5, a. 1, q. 2.

[5] Aristotle, METAPHYSICS, text 12 (Bk. IX, ch. 3): For indeed every whatever is a being, either the same or diverse.

[6] See Aristotle, PRIOR ANALYTICS, Bk. II, ch. 26 (ch. 28) On Instances.

[7] Codex S has the subjunctive *divide* [dividant].

[8] Codices T aa and bb add well enough *not (so), according to that (principle), to the extent that it is the same* [non, secundum illud secundum quod est idem], from which codex A diverges in this alone, that it transposes the particle *not* [non], not so well, after *that it is* [quod est].

[9] Concerning this doubt cf. Alexander of Hales, SUMMA., p. I, q. 50. m. 3, a. 2, §. 1; St. Thomas, here in q. 1. a. 3, at n. 3.

[10] The Vatican edition after *appositive* [appositiva] omits *and an* [et], which the codices, however, have together with edition 1, of which not a few then unduly omit *and/or a mediate one* [vel mediata]; codices. V and X omit *and an immediate* [et immediata], which however on account of the subjoined is better retained, though, because it implies this [ad rem attinet], can be omitted, since here the *immediate* is the same as the *appositive*; St. Thomas, here in q. 1, a. 3, at n. 4, opposes *mediate* to *appositive* construction. — The distinction of Master (Peter), which is dealt with here, respects that proposition: *Genuit Deum, qui non est Deus Pater*. If these words *Deus Pater* are understood as immediately conjoined, indeed so that the term *Pater*, as determining the other term *Deus*, is the principal term, then the proposition is true. For the sense is: *He begot the God, who is not God the Father, but rather God*

the Son. However, if they are understood disjunctively, so that the principal term is *Deus*, to which there is then added, *who is the Father*, it will thus be false; for the sense is then: *He begot the God, who is not God, and God is the Father*.

[11] That manner of speaking, which occurs also below in d. 15, p. II, q. 1 in the body, and in d. 44, a. 2, q. sole in the body, has been taken from Aristotle, ELENCHAE, Bk. II, ch. 3, according to the translation of (St. Severinus) Boethius: For if this would be the solution, it would not be possible to solve the objection being given. But according to the translation had in the Parisian Edition (Firmin-Didot.), ch. 22, thus: For if this would be the solution, he who would give the contrary cannot solve that, which they bring forward. — A little below this codex X has *would remain* [maneret], codex Z *would remain* [remaneret] in place of *remains* [manet].

[12] GRAMMATICAL INSTITUTIONS, Bk. XVIII, c. 1, in the second half: For a participle [participium] of the substantive word *being* [ens] is understood, which is now not in use among us, in place of which we can say and/or understand *that which is* and/or *that which was*. Similarly, for the other cases following after the nominative, for the nominative it is necessary that there be understood the above said participle and/or those things which are accepted in its place. — After having posited this rule of Priscian, the Seraphic Doctor applies it, having added a further distinction in respect of that copula together with an adjoined term. For apposition, if it has been conjoined by the participle *being* or by the relative ("which is", "who is") with a substantive, it can, in respect of the same, be held *implicatively* and/or *non implicatively* or *in a certain distance* (or relative as a relative). If implicatively, then there is an appositive and an immediate construction, and this saying: *God, who is the Father* (God, i. e. the Father) is equivalent to this: *the God, who is the Father Himself*; if non implicatively, then it is had as a mediate construction, and this saying: *God, who is the Father* is equivalent to this: *God, and that God is the Father*, or even: *the God, the one which is the Father*.

---

* *Trans. note*: Ab aequipollenti indicates the relation between two propositions, such that they both share the same subject and predicate and the same signified, while differing in grammatical form. Cf. Pietro Ispano, TRATTATO DI LOGICA, trans. A. Ponzio, (Bompiani, Milano, 2004), p. 604, fn. 8.

stood an intermediate copula, "*being*" [ens], and/or "*that which is being*" [quod est ens].[1] And since "that which is *being*" or "(that) which is *the Father*" can be held *implicatively*; and, in this manner, it is restricted and holds the place of an appositive construction and is equivalent to one term: for that reason there is said, that it can be held or construed *immediately*; and thus "*God the Father*" is not other than He Himself and thus in a certain distance; and, then, it is not restricted, and the sense is: "*God the Father*", that is "the *God*, who is the Father"; because it means [valet] only, "*He is God*", and "He is the Father".

Moreover, this solution of Master (Peter) solves a certain[2] sophism as much as regards one deception, and for that reason it is good. But, there again falls another deception concerning the *relative*, and for that reason one must [oportet] solve it still, not as regards that deception, but as regards another. For that reason (Peter) Praepositivus[3] solves it in another manner regarding this argument: 'therefore, that (He is) the God who is the Father', and/or '... who is not the Father', and he says, that it does not follow, nor[4] are they contradictories, because the supposition of this relative is not the same. For, in an affirmative (proposition), it supposes on behalf of the begotten God, because (in this manner alone the term) is not confounded;[5] however, in a negative (proposition it supposes) simply. Whence just as these do not contradict, but are both false: 'No man is Peter', 'John is Peter', so, he says in the proposed (text), that a negation does confound (the terms). Whence those two are both false: 'God the Son is the Father', 'God is not the Father'. — But though the solution of (Peter) Praepositivus has a place in the proposed (problem), because to place a negation before and after this term, "*God*", does not differ (it), nevertheless [tamen], it has no place among other (propositions). For a negation placed after a relative does not confound it.

And for that reason the moderns solve it in another manner, by distinguishing, that[6] this relative "*who*" [qui], can cause a *simple* and/or a *personal* relation. If a *simple (relation)*, the affirmative is true, the negative false; if a *personal (relation)*, conversely, the negative (is) true, the affirmative false. Which is clear, because this is false: 'the Person of the Son is the Father', and this is true: « the Person of the Son is not the Father ».[7]

DOUBT IV

Likewise, is asked concerning this which he says, that "*the one God is the Three Persons*". But on the contrary: Whatever are predicated of one and the same, are predicated of each other [de se invicem]: therefore, if "the one God is 'the Father and the Son' ": therefore, "the Father is the Son". *If you say*, that it is true, when they are predicates of one singular (term), but it is not true, when they are predicates of one common (term); *on the contrary*: nothing is subjected to two in a unique[8] supposition, even though it be common to them. Whence this is false: 'a man is Socrates and Plato': therefore, similarly in the proposed.

I RESPOND: It must be said, that it concerns the supposition of this noun, "*God*", differently than (it does) the supposition of any other term. For,[9] because it has the nature of a common and a discrete term, for that reason it stands at once for several, just as for one: and for that reason there does not follow: "God is the Father and the Son": therefore, "God the Father is the Son", and/or conversely.[10] Similarly, neither is it licit to infer from this, that the Father is the Son. And it must be noted, that such predication is through identity:[11] for that reason a supposit is truly predicated of [de] a formal term.

DOUBT V

Likewise, is asked concerning this which Master (Peter) says: *that the One Only True God is the Trinity*; because it seems to be contrary to that which he says further down,[12] that is, that "*trinity*" [trinitas] is a collective name, "*one and only*" [unus et solus], a partitive and discretive [discretivum] name: therefore, just as this is false: 'the one only man is every man', so also this.

I RESPOND: It must be said, that this noun "*Trinity*" is the collective (name)[13] of the Persons; moreover, "*one*" and "*only*", added to this term "*God*", do not mean the discretion [discretionem] of a Person, but of the Nature from other (Natures). Whence, the One

---

[1] *A being* [ens] here seems to be superfluous in accord with the words of Priscian. — Then, from codices F T etc. we have added *And* [et]. A little after this not a few codices as H I P Q together with edition 1 have *and then* [et tunc] in place of *and in this manner* [et sic].

[2] Trusting in many codices as A F G H I R S T etc. and edition 1 we have substituted the masculine *a certain* [quidem] in place of the neuter *a certain* [quoddam]; a reading certainly better.

[3] Italian by nation, Chancellor of the University of Paris from the year 1206, he wrote A THEOLOGICAL SUMMA OF THE SAYINGS OF THE HOLY FATHERS, not rarely quoted by St. Bonaventure and St. Thomas, and as yet unedited. On the Sermons of the same, cf. Lecoy, LA CHAIRE FRANÇAISE AU MOYEN ÂGE, p. 80. — Then the Vatican edition, contrary to the manuscripts and the first six editions, omits *for* [ad]. A little after this the codices have *therefore, God* [ergo Deus], but this is less conformable to the text of Master (Peter).

[4] The Vatican edition not trusting in the manuscripts and editions 1, 2, 3 has *and that they are not* [et quod non sunt] in place of *and they are not* [nec sunt]. Then codex Z has *have they been opposed in a contradictory manner* [sunt contradictorie opposita] in place of *are they contradictories* [sunt contradictoriae]. A little below this after *relative* supply: "who" [qui]. — Then codices O and Z after *the same* [eadem] add, well enough, *in an affirmative and negative* [in affirmativa et negativa], supply: proposition [propositione].

[5] That is, it does not suppose in a confused manner nor indiscriminately for the Three Persons, but determinately only for the Person of the Son; and contrarily in a negative (proposition) it supposes simply, i. e. indiscriminately and in a confused manner for the Persons and also for the Essence. Cf. here q. 4. Hence it is clear, what he wants a little below *a negation does confound (the terms)* (the codices have *is confounded* [confunditur]), that is, a negation causes [efficit ut] the relative *who* to be able to substitute as much for the Three Persons as for the Essence.

[6] The Vatican edition, disagreeing with the manuscripts and edition 1, less aptly has *this relative "who"* which) [hoc relativum qui quod]. A little after this very many codices have *distinction* [distinctionem] in place of *relation* [relationem]; however, edition 1 has *distinction and/or relation* [distinctionem vel relationem]. We have retained *relation* [relationem], as it corresponds more with what is said above in q. 1 in the body (of the Question). In the same place the division of the relation into *the simple* and *the personal* also occurs.

[7] Concerning the solution of this doubt see Alexander of Hales, SUMMA., p. I, q. 50, m. 3, a. 2, § 4. St. Thomas, here in q. 1, a. 3, at n. 4, and SUMMA., I, q. 39, a. 4, at n. 5. — (Gabriel) Biel, here in q. 1.

[8] The Vatican edition not trusting in the manuscripts and edition 1 has *one* [una].

[9] The Vatican edition, contrary to the codices and editions 1, 2, and 3, has *When* [cum] in place of *For* [enim].

[10] The codices do not agree among themselves; codex T in regard to the sense agrees with the Vatican edition by putting *and/or the Son is the Father* [vel Filius est Pater] in place of *conversely* [e converso]. Very many codices as A G N S V W aa bb have *therefore, God the Father and/or the Son is the Father and/or the Son. Similarly* [ergo Deus Pater est vel Filius est Pater vel Filius. Similiter]; others as C and O have *therefore He is God the Father and/or He is the Son. Similarly* [ergo Deus Pater est vel Filius est. Similiter]; the others are otherwise corrupt; but we judge nothing to be changed.

[11] Concerning predication by *identity*, see below d. 5, a. 1, q. 1, at n. 2; d. 33, q. 3 and d. 34, q. 2. — Concerning this doubt, cf. above q. 4 and (Bl. John Duns) Scotus, here in q. 2.

[12] Distinction XXII, ch. 3 and dd. XXIV and XXV.

[13] Codex T adds *name* [nomen].

Only God is said (to be) only one nature; and since among the divine the same is the *nature* [natura] and the *thing of the Nature* [res naturae] or the supposit [suppositum], for that reason by an identity in predication *"the Trinity"* is predicated of God.[1] Nor is it similar from this that *every man* is also *one man only*. For that term *"man"* is a term, which can be confounded and multiplied, and for that reason this is true: "every man is a man", nor does it stand simultaneously for more (men),[2] unless it be confounded; and for that reason this is false: "man is every man", because (this proposition) is neither true according to (its) reckoning of supposing, nor by an identity (in predication), nor is *nature* and the *thing of the nature* the same in man.[3]

DOUBT VI

Likewise is asked of this which he says: *It is enough for the Christian ... the cause of created things* etc.. For it seems that he says the false, since either he says *"enough"* [satis] as much as regards *faith*; and thus it is false, because it is proper to believe many other (things); or *"enough"* according to *science*; and that similarly is false, because nothing is known sufficiently from this cause of a thing.

I RESPOND: It must be said, that *"enough"* is understood as much as regards knowledge [scientia], not any (kind), but (that which is) necessary for salvation.

DOUBT VII

Likewise, is asked concerning this which he says, that *the Father begot the other-Himself* [alterum se]. For it seems that those two are badly conjoined, because "himself" [se] means every manner of identity, and *"the other"* [alterum] a diversity, and thus they are opposites, and thus[4] they imply opposites. *If you say*, that he diminished one from the other, I ask: *"What* (is diminished) and *from what* (is it diminished)?"

I RESPOND: It must be said, that direct opposition is always understood about the same (thing). Therefore, since among the divine there is simultaneously identity in nature and anotherness in supposit, and this without opposition; for that reason the name for *identity* and for *anotherness* in discourse [sermone] are united[5] without opposition, nay rather for the expression of the singular manner (of Being).

DOUBT VIII

Likewise, is asked concerning this which he says: *The Father to have a Son, did not lessen Himself*, because it seems that he says the false; because that argument means [valet]: 'whoever generates one son, so that he is not able to generate more, is lessened in his potency'; but so it is in the Father: ergo etc..

I RESPOND: That that is true, if 'to generate the other' belongs to potency; but that, 'one having begotten one, can generate the other', means an imperfection of power in generating, because from this there is shown, that he has not given (his) whole (being) to one.

DOUBT IX

Likewise, is asked concerning this which he says: *From Himself He begot the other (than) Himself, but not the other God, but (rather) the other Person*, whether one says more properly *"the other"* [alterum], and/or *"an other"* [alium]; and[7] it seems that *"the other"* (is more proper), because it means less diversity, because "Socrates" means 'the other than [a] himself'; but among the divine there is the least diversity. *But on the contrary*: accidental differences cause *"the other"* to be said;[8] but among the divine there is no accident: therefore, there ought not be said *"the other"*.

Likewise, it seems, that neither is said well. For if substantial differences cause *"an other (thing)"* [aliud] to be said, and accidental ones *"the other (one)"* [alterum], since neither occurs [cadat] among the divine, it seems that neither is to be said.

I RESPOND: It must be said, that because the Father differs from the Son both in supposit and in property, for that reason there can be said *"an other (one)"* [alius], and there can be said *"the other (one)"* [alter]. But since that property does not accede to the Person, for that reason there is more properly said *"an other (one)"* [alius]. And because *"an other (one)"* respects a supposit, *"an other (thing)"* [aliud] an essence: for that reason, even if there were received[9] there *"an other (one)"* in the masculine, nevertheless [tamen] (there ought not be) *"an other (thing)"* in the neuter.

---

[1] The Vatican edition contrary to the manuscripts and editions 1, 2, 3 has *Him* [eo] in place of *Deo* [God].

[2] Codex W has *all* [omnibus]. A little below this not a few codices as F H T Y cc together with editions 2 and 3 have *reckoning of the supposit* [ratione suppositi] in place of *reckoning of supposing* [ratione supponendi].

[3] Concerning the "thing of nature" [res naturae] or the supposit, see below d. 23, a. 1, q. 2, and d. 34, q. 1. — In regard to this solution cf below d. 24, a. 3, q. 1. — Alexander of Hales, SUMMA., p. I, q. 50, m. 3, a. 2, § 7. — St. Thomas, SUMMA., I, q. 39, a. 6.

[4] The Vatican edition contrary to nearly all the manuscripts and edition 1 has *those opposites* [illa opposita] in place of *thus ... opposites* [ita opposita], which one and/or the other codices omit.

[5] Trusting in the mss. and ed. 1, 2 & 3 we have expunged the-here-added *in one (term)* [uno] and a little after this, from the mss. and ed. 1, we have supplied *nay rather* [immo], in place of which editions 2 and 3 have *in one (term)* [in uno]. — On this doubt, cf. here in q. 2. — Alexander of Hales, SUMMA., p. I, q. 50, m. 3, a. 2, § 3. — St. Thomas, SUMMA., I, q. 39, a. 4, at n. 4.

[6] Cf. above d. 2, q. 3, at the last n..

[7] We have supplied from the manuscripts and edition 1 the particle *and* [et].

[8] Cf. Porphyry, ON PREDICABLES, ch. "On Difference".

[9] Though very many codices and edition 1 have *if* [si], we prefer, however, the reading of codices L R etc. *even if* [etsi]. The codices cited and edition 1 then read *there were received* [recipiatur] (many codices falsely have *were respected* [respiciatur]) in place of (sic) *there is received* [recipitur]. Concerning the solution of this doubt cf. here q. 2, and below d. 9, doubt 1. — Alexander of Hales, SUMMA., p. I, q. 65, m. 2, a. 2, at the last n., and a. 4. — St. Thomas, SUMMA., I, q. 31, a. 2, and III, q. 17, a. 1, at n. 7, where concerning the difference between *an other (thing)* [alium] and *the other (one)* [alterum] the same opinion is proffered.

DISTINCTION V

Chapter I

Whether the Divine Essence begot the Son, and/or has been begotten by the Father, and/or (whether) the Son was born from It, and/or the Holy Spirit has proceeded (from It).

After this, there is asked, whether it must be conceded, that the Father begot[1] the Divine Essence, and/or that the Divine Essence begot the Son, and/or the Essence begot the Essence, or whether the Divine Essence entirely did not beget nor has been begotten.

Consenting to which, with catholic authors [catholicis tractatoribus] we say, that neither did the Father beget, nor did the Divine Essence beget the[2] Essence. Moreover, here by the name of "Essence" we understand the Divine Nature, which is common to the Three Persons and is whole in each of them [in singulis]. For that reason there must not be said, that the Father begot the Divine Essence; because if the Father were said "to have begotten" the Divine Essence, the Divine Essence would be said in a manner relative to [relative ad] the Father and/or would be put in place of a relative. Moreover, if it would be said in a manner relative (to) and/or (if) it would be put in place of a relative, it would not indicate the Essence. For as (St.) Augustine says in the fifth book, ON THE TRINITY:[3] « What is said in a relative manner, does not indicate a substance ».

Likewise, since God the Father is the Divine Essence, if He was Its begetter, He would certainly [utique] be the begetter of that Thing, which He is; and thus the same Thing would have begotten Its very self, which (St.) Augustine denies, as we have shown above.[4]

Likewise, if the Father is the begetter of the Divine Essence, since He by the Divine Essence is and is God, therefore[5] by that which He generates, He both is and is God. Thus, therefore, not that which is generated, is God by [a] the Father, but the Father by that which He generates, both is and is God. And if He is thus, the one begetting (is) not (the cause) for the begotten, but rather the begotten[6] is the cause for the one begetting, to both be and be God. By a similar reason (St.) Augustine proves (this) in the seventh book, ON THE TRINITY,[7] « that the Father is not wise by the Wisdom, which He has begotten, because if He is wise by That, He is by That; for, There, 'to be' [esse] is that which (it is) 'to know'. On which account, if, There, 'to be' is that which (it is) 'to know', (then) not through that Wisdom, which He has begotten, is the Father wise. For what other do we say, when we say: "for Him [illi], 'to be' is that which (it is) 'to know' ", except, "He is by that by which He is wise?" Therefore, the cause which is His [illi], 'to be wise', is also the same cause for Him, to be [ut sit]. If, therefore, the Wisdom, which He has begotten, is the cause for Him, to be wise, It is also the cause for Him, to be. But in no manner has anyone said that the cause for the Father, by which He is, (is) the Wisdom begot-

ten by the Father; for what is more insane? Thus, therefore, if the Father has begotten the Essence, by which He is, the Essence, which He has begotten, is the cause for Him, to be ». Therefore, He did not beget the Essence itself, by which[8] He is. « For in that Simplicity », says (St.) Augustine,[9] « because 'to know' is not other than 'to be', There, Wisdom is the same which Essence (is) »; and for that reason what is of [de] Wisdom, this we say of the Essence. Therefore, just as He did not beget the Wisdom, by which He is wise, so neither the Essence, by which He is. For just as Wisdom is wise and the Power powerful [potentia potens], so also the Essence itself, and Wisdom and the Power is the same which Essence (is). And so it is clear from the aforesaid, that[10] the Father did not beget the Divine Essence.

But to this, there seems contrary what (St.) Augustine says in his one book, ON THE FAITH AND THE CREED, in the third chapter:[11] « God, when He begot the Word, begot That which He is, neither from nothing nor from any already made or founded matter, but from His very self That which He is ». Likewise:[12] « God the Father, who has willed and has been able to indicate Himself in a most true manner to the souls (who) are to know (Him), to indicate His very self begot This, which He who begot is ». Behold he openly says by these words, that God the Father has begotten That which He is. But that which He is, is naught but the Divine Essence: therefore, it seems that He did beget the Divine Essence. To which we respond, saying that those words are to be understood, thus: The Father from His very self begot That which He is, that is the Son, who is That which the Father is. For *what* the Father is, the Son is also this (Thing), but *who* the Father is, the Son is not also this (One).

Thus, too, there must not be said, that the Divine Essence begot the Son, because since the Son is the Divine Essence, the Son would already be the thing, by which He is generated: and thus the same thing would generate its very self. Thus we also say, that the Divine Essence did not beget the Essence. For, since a one and a most high, certain thing is the Divine Essence, if the Divine Essence has begotten the Essence, the same thing has begotten its very self, which entirely cannot be; but rather the Father alone has begotten the Son, and from the Father and the Son the Holy Spirit proceeds.[13]

But, to the aforesaid there seems contrary what (St.) Augustine says in the seventh book, ON THE TRINITY:[14] « For, for God », he says, « 'to be' [esse] is that which (it is) 'to know' [sapere]; whence the Father and the Son together are the One Wisdom, because (They are) the one Essence: and Each (is) the Wisdom of the Wisdom [sapientia de sapientia], just as (Each is) the Essence of the Essence [essentia de essentia] ». Behold, by these words (St.) Augustine openly says, that Wisdom (is) from Wisdom [sapientia de sapientia] and Essence from Essence [essentia de essentia], where it seems that he signifies, that Wisdom has begotten Wisdom and Essence

---

[1] Only codex A has three times the subjunctive *has begotten* [genuerit] in place of the indicative *has begotten* [genuit].

[2] The Vatican edition and editions 4 and 9 superfluously adds *Divine* [divinam].

[3] Chapter 7, n. 8, where it has: *What, moreover, is pronounced in a relative manner* etc.. A little above this editions 1, and 8 after *would not indicate the* [indicaret] add *Divine* [divinam].

[4] Distinction IV, ch. 1.

[5] The Vatican edition and edition 4 omit *therefore* [ergo] not so well; a little before this codices A B C E and edition 1 by adding *both* [et] read: *by the Divine Essence both is and is God* [essentia divina et sit et Deus sit]; but codex D has *also* [etiam] in place of this *both* [et].

[6] Codex D and edition 1, 2, 3, 8, and 9 have less well *the (thing) begotten* [genitum]; at the beginning of this proposition codex C has *Whereas if* [Quodsi] in place of *And if* [Et si].

[7] Chapter 1, n. 2; in which text the Vatican edition and editions 2, 3, 4, 7 and 9 twice reads *His* [sibi] in place of *There* [ibi]; edition 5 twice has *for Him* [illi]; the codices twice have *There* [ibi], except for D and E, which have in the first position *for Him* [ei]; the edition of (St.) Augustine has sometimes *There* [ibi], sometimes *for Him* [illi].

[8] Only the Vatican has the faulty *which* [quae].

[9] Loc. cit.. — The Vatican edition and editions 4, 5, 6, and 9 add *as* [ut] before *(St.) Augustine says* [inquit].

[10] Codex D together with editions 1 and 8 has the more elegant *that* [quod].

[11] Number 4. — All the codices and editions, except the Vatican edition and editions 4 and 9, read falsely in this manner: in the book, ON THE FAITH TO PETER.

[12] Loc. cit., in which text codices B D and E has *Himself* [se] in place of *His very self* [se ipsum]; after *begot This* [indicandum genuit], edition 8 adds *that is,* [id est]; editions 1 and 3 omit *which He who begot is* [quod est ipse, qui genuit].

[13] This doctrine of Master (Peter) was opposed by Abbot Joachim (of Fiore), but approved by the Fourth Lateran Council; cf. below (what St.) Bonaventure (says) in regard to this distinction in a. 1, q. 1 and doubt 4.

[14] From chapter 1, n. 2, and ch. 2, n. 3, excerpted passim. — The Vatican edition omits *in the seventh book, On the Trinity* [in libro septimo de Trinitate].

Essence. He says the same in the book, ON THE FAITH TO PETER:[1] « So believe Christ the Son of God (to be) the true God, that is that (He is) A [unam] Person of the Trinity, that you may not doubt His Divinity to have been born from the Nature of the Father ». Here he seems to say, that the Nature of the son has been born from the Nature of the Father. He also says the same in the fifteenth book, ON THE TRINITY:[2] « The Son is said (to be) "Counsel from Counsel" and "Will from Will", just as (He is) "Substance from Substance", "Wisdom from Wisdom" ». And here he seems to say, that Substance has been begotten from Substance and Wisdom from Wisdom. But we determine this (text)[3] thus: « He is Wisdom from Wisdom, and Substance from Substance », that is the Son, who is the Wisdom, who is the Substance, is from the Father, who is the Divine Nature. And that we may speak more expressly, we say, that the Son (as) Wisdom is from the Father (as) Wisdom, and we say, that the Son (as) Substance has been begotten from the Father and by the Father (as) Substance. Moreover, that (St.) Augustine ought thus to be understood, he shows in the seventh book, ON THE TRINITY[4] saying: « The Father Himself is Wisdom; and the Son is said (to be) "the Wisdom of the Father", in that manner He is said (to be) "the Light of the Father", that is, just as Light (is) from Light and each of the two [uterque] the one Light, so He is understood (to be) Wisdom from Wisdom; and each of the Two the one Wisdom and the one Essence ». Likewise:[5] « For that reason Christ is said (to be) "the Virtue and Wisdom of God", because from the Father, the Virtue and Wisdom, He Himself is also the Virtue and Wisdom, just as He Himself is the Light from the Father, the Light, and He Himself is the Fount of Life with [apud] God the Father, the Fount of Life. The Son, therefore, is the Wisdom from the Father, the Wisdom, just as the Son (is) the Light from the Father, the Light, and the Son of God (is) from God the Father, as each One [singulus] is both the Light and each One the God and each One the Wisdom, and simultaneously the one Light, the one God, the one Wisdom ». Behold, by these words (St.) Augustine manifestly reveals [aperit], in [ex] what sense there are to be accepted the aforesaid words and those similar, that is when there is said: "Substance from Substance", and/or "the Substance begot the Substance".

However, to this there also seem contrary that, which (St.) Hilary (of Poitiers) says in the fourth book, ON THE TRINITY:[6] « Nothing », he says, « except the Son has been born; and admiration for the honor of the one Begotten belongs in honor to the one Generating ». Since, therefore, the Son has the Essence — for the whole Divine Essence is in Him — it seems that Divine Essence Itself has been born. Likewise, in the fifth book[7] he says: « The Nativity of God cannot not hold [tenere] the Nature out of which it has arisen [profecta est], for no other [non aliud]

than God subsists, because from no one other [non aliunde] than from God does (this Nativity) subsist ». Behold here he says that the Nativity of God (has) arisen from the Nature, and thus it seems from these words and also from the aforesaid that the Nature of God has both begotten and been begotten. Which he says more openly in the ninth book, ON THE TRINITY:[8] « We », he says, « profess that the Only-Begotten God, remaining [manentem] in the form of God, remained in the form of man, nor do we pour back [refundimus] the unity of the servile form into the nature of the Divine Unity, nor again do we preach that the Father (is) in the Son by a corporal insinuation, but rather from this [ex eo] that in begetting Itself the Nature has begotten naturally a Nature of the same genus, which remaining in the form of the Nature Begetting It, has accepted a form of nature and of corporal infirmity. For the Nature of God had not failed to be; but rather remaining in Itself the Nature of God, It had undertaken [susceperat] for Itself the humility of an earthly [terrenae] nativity, exercising the power of Its own genus [generis sui] in the habit of the assumed humility ». Behold here he openly says, both that the Nature has begotten, and the Nature (has been) begotten, and that the Nature has assumed a nature; which by very many is denied. Likewise, in the same (book he says):[9] « Is it contumely to the Only-Begotten God, that His own Father is the innascible God [innascibilem Deum], since from the innascible God there subsists an unbegotten nativity for [in] the Unbegotten Nature »? Behold here he also says (that there is) an "Unbegotten Nature".

But because he wants these words to be sanely understood, he himself says the same in the fourth book:[10] « The understanding of the things said is to be assumed from the causes for speaking [ex causis dicendi], because a thing is not subjected to discourse [sermoni], but discourse to a thing ». Therefore, these words can be thus understood: "nothing has the Son except that He has been born [nisi natum]", that is, He has nothing according to which He is God, except what by being born He has accepted, and He Himself by being born had the Nature of the Father subsisting in Himself. Whence (St.) Hilary adds the same in the fifth book:[11] « The Begotten has the same Nature, which He who begot (has), however, thus, that the One Born is not He who begot (for in what manner shall He be the Father Himself, since He has been begotten?), but among These Themselves there subsists He who has been begotten, among which the Whole is He who has begot; because from no other [non aliunde] is He who has been begotten. And for that reason there is not referred to an other what in One subsists out of One. And so in the generation of the Son even His own Nature, as thus I call (it), does the unalterable [indemutabilis] God begetting the unalterable God follow [sequitur], nor His own Nature does the perfect Nativity of the unalterable God out of the unalterable God forsake [deserit]. Therefore, let us understand that the Nature of God (is) subsisting in Him, since God is in God [in Deo Deus insit]; nor is there besides Him who is God, any other God, because He Himself (is) God,

---

[1] Chapter 2, n. 15.

[2] Chapter 19, n. 37. — Immediately before this the Vatican edition together with the other codices, except 1 and 8, omits *also* [etiam].

[3] All the codices, contrary to the editions, have the just as good *these (words)* [quae].

[4] Chapter 1, n. 2; where after *Wisdom from Wisdom* [sapientia de sapientia] editions 1 and 8 add *and Essence from Essence* [et essentia de essentia].

[5] Chapter 3, n. 4. — Near the end of this text the codices twice by adding *is* [sit] read *each is the God and each is the Wisdom* [singulus sit Deus et singulus sit sap.,], to which in the second place there accedes editions 1, 5, 6, and 8. In place of *each* [singulus] and *simultaneously* [simul] editions 2, 3 and 7 four times read badly *each of them* [singulis]; at the end (of the passage) editions 1 and 8 add *and* [et] after *the one God* [unus Deus].

[6] Number 10.

[7] Number 37, in which text and a little after this the Vatican edition and editions 4, 7 and 9, twice read *advanced* [provecta] in place of *arisen* [profecta], but faultily.

[8] Number 51, in which text codices A B C and editions 5 and 9 read: first *of a slave* [servi], then *of God* [Dei]. However, the Maurini Editors have: *of God* [Dei] both times. These (scholars) consider our reading, which besides codices D E and the rest of the editions of Master (Peter), even the ancient editions of (St.) Hilary, exhibit, distorted, since (St.) Hilary by the noun of *form* understood something other than *nature*

itself, namely the "habit", which Christ bore before Him. According to them the sense is, that Christ according to the form of God always remained in the nature, unity and glory of God, even if according to the form of a slave from the assumption itself of man He did not immediately arrive at [assecutus est] the glory of the Divine Nature, but only through (His) resurrection. Cf. ibid., n. 38. Though the text of the Maurinists seems to be more probable, we however, do judge that that which is contrary to the codices and editions of Master (Peter) is not to be accepted [obtrudendum]. — In the same text together with (St.) Hilary codices A and C have the subjunctive *accepted* [acceperit] in place of the indicative *accepted* [accepit] and at the end in place of *humility* [humilitatis] the Vatican edition and very many editions have *humanity* [humanitatis].

[9] Loc. cit., n. 53.

[10] Number 14; codex A and ed. 4 add ON THE TRINITY [de Trinitate].

[11] Number 37, but with many things changed and omitted by Master (Peter). — The Vatican edition and edition 4 omit *the same* [idem] before *in the* [Hilarius]. In the quote itself there is omitted by the codices, edition 1 and the text of (St.) Hilary, *the Father* [Pater] after *in what manner shall He be* [quomodo erit]. Then contrary to the original, to codices A B C E and to edition 1, the Vatican edition together with the rest of the editions, having changed the construction and rejected the parentheses, reads the indicative *subsists* [subsistit] in place of the indicative *subsists* [subsistat]. Then in the same (quote) the Vatican edition and editions 4, 5, 6 and 9, by adding *et* has (the ambiguous) *in One subsists also out of One* or *subsists in One and out of One* [in uno subsistit et ex uno].

and God (is) in Him ». Therefore, the truth of the Nature of God the Father is taught to be in God the Son, since "the God in Him" is understood[1] to be, "He who is God". For One is in One and One (is) by One.

It is also said, and frequently in Sacred Scripture it is read, that the Father from His own Substance has begotten the Son. Whence (St.) Augustine in the book, ON THE FAITH TO PETER[2] says: « God the Father, begotten from no God, from His own Nature without a beginning [initio], did once begot God the Son equal and coeternal to Himself by the same Divinity by which He Himself is naturally eternal ». Behold here (St.) Augustine says, that the Son (has been) begotten from the Nature of the Father. Moreover, there is one Nature of the Father and of the Son and of the Holy Spirit. If, therefore, He has been begotten from the Nature of the Father, He has been begotten from the Nature of the Son and of the Holy Spirit, nay rather from the Nature of the Three Persons. Likewise, (St.) Augustine in the fifteenth book, ON THE TRINITY,[3] also says, that Christ is the Son of the Substance of the Father and (has) been begotten from the Substance of the Father, thus treating that word of the Apostle speaking of God the Father: *Who has snatched us from the power of darkness and has transferred us into the kingdom of the Son of His charity.* « Because there has been said », he says, « of the Son of His Charity, let nothing other be understood[4] than "of His Beloved Son", than "of the Son of His Substance". Indeed [quippe] the Charity of the Father, which is in an ineffable manner in His simple Nature, is nothing other than the Nature Itself and [atque] the Substance, as we have often said and it is not an annoyance [piget] to reiterate it [iterare], and by this [per hoc] the Son of His Charity is no one other, than He who has been begotten from His Substance ». Behold here (St.) Augustine openly says, that the Son has been begotten from the Substance of the Father and that the Son (is) of the Substance of the Father. (St.) Augustine also says the same in the second book, AGAINST MAXIMINUS THE HERETIC,[5] that the Substance of God has begotten the Son, and he asserts that the Son (has been) begotten from the Substance of the Father saying: « Full of carnal thoughts, you do not think that the Substance of God begets the Son from Its very self, unless by this It suffers, what a substance of flesh suffers, when it begets. *You err not knowing the Scriptures nor the Virtue of God.*[6] For in no manner do you think (that there is) a true Son of God, if you deny that He has been born from the Substance of the Father. For there was not already a Son of man and by God granting He became Son of God, born out of God by grace, not by nature. Or, even if there was not a son of man, nevertheless [tamen] was there by chance some whatever-kind-of creature and, with God changing (it), it was converted into the Son of God? But neither of these exists [nihilo horum est]: therefore, either from nothing, or from some substance has He been born. But lest we would believe, that you think that the Son of God is from nothing, you have affirmed,[7] that you do not say that the Son of God is from nothing. Therefore, He is from some substance; and if not from the Substance of the Father, say, which He is from; but you shall not find (one). Therefore, it is already an annoyance [pigeat] that you do not confess with us that the Only-Begotten Son of God, Jesus Christ, is from the Substance of the Father ». Likewise, in the same (chapter):[8] « We both read, *that we may be in His true Son,* Jesus Christ.

Therefore, tell us, whether that true Son of God, different [discretus] in a certain property from those who are sons by grace, is from no substance, or whether (He is) from some (substance)? I do not say, you say, "from no (substance)", nor do I say "from nothing": therefore He is from some substance. I ask, "From which?" If He is not from the Substance of the Father, I seek an other. If you do not find an other, acknowledge the Substance of the Father, and confess that the Son is consubstantial [homoousion] with the Father ». Likewise, in the same (chapter):[9] « I confess, that God the Father in an entirely incorruptible manner has begotten, but that He has begotten what He Himself is. Likewise, I say that there must be often said: "the Son of God either has been born from some substance, or from none"; if from none: therefore, from nothing; which you do not now [iam] say; however if (He is) from some (substance), and not, however, from the Substance of the Father, He is not the true Son; however, if from the Substance of the Father, of one and the same Substance are the Father and the Son. Moreover neither do you want a Son[10] begotten from the Substance of the Father; and nevertheless [tamen] you concede that He is neither out of nothing nor out of some matter, but rather out of the Father; nor do you see, how necessary it is, that He who is not out of nothing nor out of some other thing, but out of God, cannot be except from the Substance of the Father, and that This is what God is, from What He is, that is God born from God; because there was no Other prior, but He is the coeternal Nature from God ».

By these aforesaid words there seems to be hinted, that the Divine Substance[11] begot the Son, and that the Son has been begotten from the Substance of the Father, and that He is the coeternal Nature from God, and that the Father begot that which He Himself is. Moreover, That which He Himself is, is the Divine Essence; and thus it can be thought, that the Divine Essence has begotten. Vehemently do these words, which are to be understood in this manner, move us, I would prefer to hear (them) from others than to betray (them).[12] However, that I may speak without prejudice and [atque] temerity, from this sense there can be accepted the sayings [dicta]: "He is the coeternal Nature from God", that is, the Son coeternal to the Father is from the Father, in such a manner [ita] that He is the same Nature with Him and/or of the same Nature. Which sense (St.) Augustine confirms, subjecting (himself) to the same (opinion)[13] and as if explaining what he had said. For to the saying: « He is the coeternal Nature from God », he added: « The Son is not an other (thing) [aliud] than That from whom He is, that is, He is of one and same Substance ». Then more openly reveals that such an understanding of [ex] the aforesaid words shall be held, saying in the same book, AGAINST MAXIMINUS: « This Trinity is of one and the same Substance, because not from some matter and/or from nothing is the Son, but from Whom He has been begotten. And likewise the Holy Spirit is not from some matter and/or from nothing, but is from That [inde], whence He proceeds ». Certainly [utique] by these words he openly shows, that for this reason the Son is said to be from the Substance of the Father, because He has been begotten from the Father, in such a manner [ita] that He is of the same Substance with Him: and[14] that the Holy Spirit is from the Substance of the Father and the Son, because He proceeds from both, in such a manner that He is of the same Substance.

---

[1] Thus codices A B and E; the rest of the codices and editions have *when ... is understood* [cum ... intelligitur].

[2] Chapter 2, n. 10. — A little before this at *Scripture* [Scriptura] the Vatican edition together with a few of the editions omits *Sacred* [sacra].

[3] Chapter 19, n. 37. — The quote from the Apostle is Col 1:13, in which text the Vulgate has *of the Son of His delight* [filii dilectionis].

[4] The Vatican edition and editions 4 and 9 have *is understood* [intelligitur].

[5] Chapter 14, n. 2.

[6] Mt. 22:29, where the Vulgate reads: *you err not knowing* [erratis nescientes], to which our codices and edition 1 and 8 agree; the Vatican edition together with the other editions has *not knowing* [non scientes].

[7] The Vatican edition together with editions 4, 5, 6, 8, and 9 has *you affirm* [affirmatis]; (St.) Augustine wrote: *you have affirmed* [affirmasti].

[8] Loc. cit., n. 3. — In place of *both* [utrique] codices A B D and editions 3, 7 and 8 have *certainly* [utique], but contrary to the original. — The verse of Sacred Scripture alluded to is 1 Jn. 5:20.

[9] Loc. cit., n. 4 and 2. — Immediately before this the Vatican edition has *(He says) the same (thing)* [idem], contrary to the codices and editions 1 and 8.

[10] The Vatican edition together with codex A and a few of the editions here adds *of God* [Dei].

[11] Codices C and D add *and/or Essence* [vel essentia] and then, after *begot* [genuerit], codd. D & E have *and/or* [vel] in place of *and* [et].

[12] The Vatican edition together with editions 4, 6, and 8 puts *myself* [ipse] before the verb.

[13] AGAINST MAXIMINUS, Bk. II, ch. 14, n. 2; those things which follow are found in the same place. — A little after this the Vatican edition has *he adds* [addit] in place of *he added* [addidit].

[14] Only the Vatican edition omits *and* [et]; at the beginning of this proposition in place of *certainly* [utique] codex D has *and thus* [itaque].

CHAPTER II

That the Son is not from nothing, but from some one or thing,* not however from matter, just as (is) also the Holy Spirit.

It is also shown from those words, that the Son and Holy Spirit are not from nothing, but from some one or thing [de aliquo], nor, however, from some matter. Whence even (St.) Hilary in the twelfth book, ON THE TRINITY,[1] says: « The Only-Begotten God, since He has been born, testifies that the Father (is His) Author; since He has been born from the One remaining [manente], He has not been born from nothing; and since He has been born before time, He has by being born come before [praevenit] every sense ». Here there is openly said, that the Son has not been born from nothing. Similarly, also the Holy Spirit is not to be said to be and/or to proceed "out of nothing" [ex nihilo], « because the Son has been born from the Substance of the Father »,[2] that is, He is by the Father, with whom He is of the same Substance and is the same Substance. From [ex] which sense there must also be accepted this: « The Father begot That which He Himself is », that is, the Son, who is This which the Father (is). And (St.) Augustine reveals that this ought to be thus understood, saying in the first book, AGAINST MAXIMINUS:[3] « The Father begot This which He is; otherwise He is not the true Son, if what the Father is, the Son is not ». Likewise: « the Substance of God begot the Son », that is, the Father, the Substance, begot the Son, who is the same Substance and of the same Substance. Which (St.) Augustine shows must be thus understood, saying to Maximinus:[4] « Just as you say, Spirit begot Spirit; say thus: the Spirit begot a spirit of the same nature and/or substance. Likewise, just as you say: "God begot God", say thus, "God begot God of the same Nature and/or Substance". If you believed and said that, you would be accused nothing further concerning this matter [re] ». For, by these words, he reveals, in what manner the aforesaid (words) ought to be understood. Similarly: « The Son has been born from the Substance of the Father, and/or the Father has begotten the Son from His own Nature or Essence », that is, from Himself, the Nature and Essence, He begot the Son of the same Essence[5]

and Nature, and Who is the same Essence and Nature. Similarly, expound this: « The Son of the Substance of the Father », that is[6] the Son of the Father's Substance, that is, He who is the Substance, with whom the Son is also the same Substance, because consubstantial to the Father is the Son. And here the sense is assisted from the words of (St.) Augustine, who in the seventh book, ON THE TRINITY[7] says: « "That the Three Persons (are) of the same Essence", and/or "that the Three Persons (are) the one Essence" we do say. But "that the Three Persons (are) out of the same Essence" we do not say, as if There what the Essence is were one thing [aliud], what a Person is another ». By these words he shows, that it must not be said, that a Person is out of the Essence, except in [ex] the aforesaid sense. The sense of which is confirmed also from that which the same (author) says in the fifteenth book ON THE TRINITY:[8] « Just as our knowledge [scientia] is dissimilar to God's knowledge, so also our word, which is born from our knowledge, to that Word of God, which has been born from the Father's Essence. Moreover, it is such, as if I would say: "from the Father's Knowledge", "from the Father's Wisdom", and/or what is more expressly, "from the Father, the Essence", "from the Father, the Knowledge", "from the Father, the Wisdom" ». And thus from this understanding the Word of God the Father, the Only-Begotten Son, in [per] all things the like and equal of the Father, is rightly called "God from God", "Light from Light", "Wisdom from Wisdom", "Essence from Essence"; because He is entirely That which the Father (is), not[9] however, the Father, because This One (is) the Son, That One the Father.

CHAPTER III

Why the Word of the Father is called the Son of (His) Nature.

Hence it is, that the Only-Begotten of God alone is called [dicitur] the Son by nature, because He is of the same Nature and is the same Nature with the Father. Whence (St.) Hilary in the fifth book, ON THE TRINITY,[10] speaking of Christ says: « By nature He is the Son, because He has the same Nature, which He who begot (Him has) ».

COMMENTARY ON DISTINCTION V

On the comparison of generation to (its) essential abstract term, which is "essence".

After this, there is asked, whether it must be conceded etc..

THE DIVISION OF THE TEXT

In the preceding Distinction, Master (Peter) moves a question concerning the comparison of generation to (its) essential *concrete* term, which is this noun, "*God*". In the present (Distinction), he brings forward a question concerning the comparison of generation to (its) essential *abstract* term, which is "*essence*". And this part is divided into two parts.

In the *first* part, he brings forward a question from the comparison of generation to essence in the reckoning of a *term*, namely whether the Essence is generated; in the *second* in the reckoning of a *principle*, whether the Essence generates etc., there (where he says): *Thus, too, it must not be said, that the Divine Essence begot the Son etc..*

---

[1] Number 25.

[2] (St.) Augustine, ON THE FAITH AND THE CREED, ch. 4, n. 6. The following words: The Father begot that which He Himself is, ibid., ch. 3, n. 4; cf. above ch. 1.

[3] Chapter 18. — That which follows is from Bk. II, ch. 14; see above ch. 1 in the second half. In the same chapter 14 there occurs other texts, from which the propositions, which are here explained, have been taken.

[4] Bk. II, ch. 15, n. 3. — Codices B and C at the beginning of the text read: *the Holy Spirit ... the Holy Spirit* [Spiritus sancuts, Spiritum sanctum]; then codex C continues: *begot ..., thus it is, as you say « God begot God »*, thus say.

[5] The Vatican edition and edd. 4 and 6 has *Substance* [substantiae].

[6] The editions, excepting 1 and 8 and the Vatican edition, read not well *and* [et] in place of *that is* [id est].

[7] Chapter 6, n. 11. — The Vatican edition together with very many editions inserts *these* [his] before *words of (St.) Augustine* [verbis Augus.]. — A little below this the codices and edition 1 have *he shows* [ostendit], and codex C specifies the subject by adding *(St.) Augustine* [Augustinus]. The rest of the editions have *there is shown* [ostenditur].

[8] Chapter 13, n. 22, in which text near the end Master (Peter) adjoined *"from the Father, the Essence"* [de Patre essentia].

[9] Codex B has *nor* [nec].

[10] Number 37; see above ch. 1 about the middle.

---

* *Trans. note*: Here the Latin <u>aliquo</u>, which can be either masculine or neuter in gender, can be translated as *someone* and/or *something*, the ambiguity of which is essential to the context of the discussion, throughout what follows, and hence <u>aliquo</u> will be rendered into English as *some one or thing*, to make this opposition of *not however, from matter* intelligible.

Likewise, the *first* part has four parts. In the *first* part he proposes the problem [problemata], namely whether the Essence generates and/or is generated. In the *second*, he adduces three reasons proving, that the Essence is not generated by the Father, there (where he says): *For that reason it must not be said, that the Father begot* etc.. In the *third*, he adduces reasons to the contrary, there (where he says): *Moreover, to this there seems contrary* etc.. In the *fourth* and last, he solves and expounds, there (where he says): *To which we respond.*

Thus, too, it must not be said.[1] This is the *second* part of that Distinction of his, in which Master (Peter) determines the second part of the question, which concerns the comparison of generation to the Essence in the reckoning of a *principle*, and this part has three parts. In the *first*, he determines that question saying, that the Essence does not generate; and this he[2] confirms through a reckoning that leads to the impossible. In the *second*, however, he adduces authorities, which are directly contrary to the aforesaid solution, there (where he says): *To the aforesaid there seems contrary.* In the *third*, however, he adduces authorities, from which there can be elicited contrarieties, there (where he says): *There is also said, and frequently* etc..

Likewise[3] the second part has four parts. In the first part, he adduces the authorities of (St.) Augustine (which are) contrary to the aforesaid solution. In the second, he expounds the adduced authorities, there (where he says): *But these we thus determine.* In the third, however, against the aforesaid expositions he adduces the other authorities of (St.) Hilary, in which there are noted more expressly the contrarieties, there (where he says): *However, to this there also seems to be contrary.* In the fourth, however, he explains the aforesaid authorities and confirms his own explanation[4] through the words of (St.) Hilary, there (where he says): *But, because he wants these words to be sanely* (etc.).

It is also said, and frequently in Sacred Scripture it is read. This is the *third* part, in which he objects against the solution by the authorities, out of which *there is elicited* the aforesaid contrarieties to the solution — because[5] among these there is not said, that the Essence generates and/or is generated, but that from the Essence and/or the Substance of the Father, the Son is generated — and this part has four smaller parts. In the first, he adduces[6] authorities to the contrary. In the second, however, he explains the adduced (authorities), there (where he says): *By these aforesaid words there is hinted*; where he resumes the aforesaid exposition. In the third, from the opinion of the aforesaid he elicits a certain corollary, there (where he says): *It is also shown from those words* etc.. In the fourth and last, he returns to the proposed (question) and he shows, that his exposition is good, through the authority of (St.) Augustine, there (where he says): *And that this ought to be thus understood* etc..

TREATMENT OF THE QUESTIONS

In this part, for the understanding of the two principal parts of this Distinction, two (questions) are principally asked.

First, there is asked concerning the comparison of generation to substance or essence in the reckoning of a *principle*.

Second, there is asked concerning the comparison of the same to essence in the reckoning of a *term*.

And, two (questions) are asked as much as regards the first (problem), two, on the other hand, as much as regards the second. As much as regards the *first*, there is asked:

First, whether the Substance and/or Essence generates.

Second, whether Someone is generated from the Substance.

ARTICLE I

On the comparison of generation to substance or essence in the reckoning of a principle.

QUESTION I

Whether the Substance or Essence generates?

About the first, that the Substance does not generate, it is shown thus:

1. 'To generate' means (that there is) a relation: therefore, 'to generate' befits [convenit] the one, whom 'to be referred' also[7] befits; but it does not befit the Essence to be referred: therefore, neither to generate.

2. Likewise, to generate conveys a distinction: therefore, 'to generate' befits the one, whom, by consequence,[8] 'to be distinguished' also (befits); but the Essence, since it is one, is not distinguished: ergo etc.. Or, if It generates, there are more Essences. And towards these two unfitting (conclusions) Master (Peter) leads (the reader).[9]

3. Likewise, 'to generate' means a personal action: therefore, it is said of that alone, which signifies a Person

---

[1] The Vatican edition not trusting in the mss. and ed. 1, by omitting *Thus, too, it must not be said* [Ita etiam non est dicendum], and by varying the construction places the particle *Similarly* [Similiter] before *the second.* Likewise, at the end of the proposition it reads *of a principle, has three parts* [principii, habet tres partes]. The same recurs below for the third part. In the middle of the proposition it has *is in the comparison* [est in comparatione] for *concerns the comparison* [est de comparatione], but badly.

[2] The Vatican edition, contrary to the manuscripts and edition 1, reads *but this he also* [sed et hoc] for *and this he* [et hoc].

[3] We have supplied from the manuscripts and edition 1 *Likewise* [Item], after which we have emended the Vatican edition and the manuscripts, by substituting together with edition 1 *second* [secunda] in place of *first* [prima], which is manifestly false.

[4] The Vatican editions has *exposition* [expositionem], but contrary to the manuscripts and edition 1.

[5] This parenthetical remark explains why *there is elicited* [elicitur] is said, namely because those authorities do not explicitly contain a contrary assertion.

[6] Very many manuscripts, together with edition 1, read *he induces* [inducit].

[7] The Vatican edition, having omitted *and* [et] not well, at the end of the argument after *neither* [nec] repeats *does it befit* [convenit], but contrary to the manuscripts and edition 1.

[8] Thus very many codices together with edition 1, against the Vatican edition, which has *also by consequence* [etiam per consequens].

[9] Here in ch. 1.

and/or supposes a Person; but "the Essence" does not signify[1] a Person, since It is common (to Each), nor does it suppose a Person, since It is entirely abstract: ergo etc..

4. Likewise, 'to generate' is a property of a Person, communicability[2] is (a property) of the Essence: therefore, just as communicability holds itself regarding [se habet ad] regarding a Person, so a personal property regarding the Essence; but communicability never belongs to a Person, because this is false: 'The Father is communicable'; therefore, neither will a personal property belong to the Essence: therefore, neither 'to generate', since it belongs to a Person.

ON THE CONTRARY: 1. Whatever hold themselves, thus, that one is the same as the other [alii], and do not have diverse properties, whatever is said of one, (is) also (said) of the other;[3] but "person" and "essence" are of this kind, because a person is an essence, nor do they have diverse properties, because property in the divine is a distinguishing relation; but, if the Essence had some property, then it would be distinguished and referred: ergo etc.. *If you say*, that although a Person and the Essence do not have diverse properties, however, they differ through *having* a property and *not having* (one); *on the contrary*: a most high opposition is contradiction;[4] but such a diversity is through a contradiction: therefore, the Essence and a Person are more different than a Person and a Person; but a Person is not predicated of [de] a Person: therefore, neither a Person of the Essence; but this is false: ergo etc..

2. Likewise, whatever hold themselves thus, that one is predicated of the other, one supposes for the other, because a subject is truly subjected to a predicate;[5] but the Essence is truly predicated of the Father; whence this is true: "The Father is the Essence": therefore, it also supposes: therefore, just as God the Father generates, so there can be said, "the Essence generates".

3. Likewise, of whatever there is predicated a subject, (there is) also (predicated) a proper passion;[6] but 'to generate' is as [sicut] the proper passion of the Father; but this is true: "the Divine Essence is the Father": therefore, also this, similarly: "the Divine Essence generates".

4. Likewise, of whatever there is predicated (something) definite, (there is) also (predicated its) definition;[7] but the definition of "*father*" is 'a *father of a son*'. Therefore, since this be true: "the Divine Essence is the Father", this also will be true: "the Divine Essence is the Father of the Son": therefore, a convertibili:* "The Son is the Son of the Essence".

CONCLUSION

This saying: "the Divine Essence generates", is entirely improper and to be denied, and/or at least to be piously expounded.

I Respond: For an understanding of the aforesaid it must be noted, that the True Faith[8] professes [dicit] as a foundation, that God is Triune and One, and so triune, that the Trinity is not confounded [confunditur], and so one, that the Unity is not multiplied. If, therefore, it was necessary [oportet] to signify what we believe, there have been opportunely found names among the divine, nay rather manifested to us by God, which signify the Trinity under a distinction and the Unity without any [sine omni] multiplication. Therefore, just as the names imposed upon a Person are entirely incommunicable both as much as regards the Supposit and as much as regards the signified; whence this statement [oratio][9] is false: "the Father is the Son", and/or "the Father is communicable"; thus, on the part of the Essence and/or Nature, it was necessary [oportet] to impose names, which were not distinguished neither as much as regards the signified nor as much as regards a Supposit.

Moreover, it must be noted, that threefold is the genus of Names signifying the Essence. For certain ones signify in *concretion* [in concretione], as (does) this noun, "*God*"; certain ones in *an omnimodal abstraction* [in omnimoda abstractione], as (does) this noun "*essence*"; certain ones *in a middle manner*, as (do) "*light*", "*wisdom*", "*will*" and those completely similar [consimilia]; and those are said to signify in a middle manner, because they do not concern a Supposit through a manner of inherence, but rather they concern a Supposit through the reckoning of this, that they mean some reckoning of act and/or origin, which belongs to the Supposits Themselves. Therefore, since there are three (kinds) of Names of difference, a *concrete* noun supposes on behalf of a Person properly; a *middle* noun supposes partly properly, partly improperly; an *abstract* and absolute noun does not suppose except in an entirely improper manner [omnino improprie].[10]

Wherefore, this is proper: "God generates", and it is to be put [adducenda] to use; but this: "Wisdom generates[11] from Wisdom", (is) partly proper, partly improper; for this reason it is to be sustained, but not to be extended; but this: "the Essence generates", (is) entirely *improper*, and for that reason it is to be denied, and if it is read anywhere, it is to be explained [exponenda]. For the Saints

---

[1] The Vatican ed., with cod. cc, with the order inversed, puts *suppose* [supponit] here in place of *signify* [significat] and then *signify* in place of *suppose*, but the more ancient codd., with ed. 1, withstand this.

[2] Many codd., such as A C F G I K L O S T U W X etc., have *community* [communitas] in place of *communicability* [communicabilitas] three times, but less well.

[3] Aristotle, TOPICS, Bk. VII, ch. 1. — Then, after *because* [quia], codex O adds *whatever is* [quidquid est].

[4] Aristotle, METAPHYSICS, Bk. X, text 15 (Bk. IX, ch. 4): Of these (opposites) the first (is) contradiction.

[5] Aristotle, METAPHYSICS, Bk. VII, text 7 (Bk. VI, ch. 3): Moreover, it is the subject, of which the rest are said. Cf. also, ON PREDICAMENTS, at the beginning. — A little before this, after *because one* [quod unum] cod. Z adjoins *truly and essentially* [vere et essentialiter]; but cod. O a little below this after *of the other* [de altero] adds *essentially* and at the end of the argument has *therefore, just as God generates, because the Father generates* [ergo sicut Deus generat, quia Pater generat].

[6] Aristotle, TOPICS, Bk. I, ch. 7 (ch. 6) says: For this was proper, because it is conversely predicated (of a thing or subject). — Cod. M adds here *of that subject* [illius subiecti]. At the end of the argument the Vatican ed., against the mss. and ed. 1, has *similarly that is true* [similiter illa est vera] for *this, similarly* [haec similiter].

[7] Cf. Aristotle, TOPICS, Bk. VI, ch. 1 (ch. 3), where he shows that for a

good definition there is required, that it be able to be conversely predicated of the (thing) defined; and Peter of Spain, SUMMULA., tract "On Syllogisms". The Vatican ed., against very many codd. and ed. 1, has *a definition, (there is) also (predicated something) definite* [definition et definitum]; but for the form of the argument, less well. Codd. O & Z add *and conversely* [et e converso]. A little below this, the codd. with ed. 1 after *and this* [et haec] omit *will be true:* [erit vera:]; cod. H has *therefore, also this: the Divine* etc. [ergo et haec: divina etc.].

[8] Ed. 1 reads *our* [nostra] in place of *the True* [vera]. A little below this, codd. V W & X have *and so one, that the Trinity is not confused, and so triune, that the Unity* [et ita unum, quod trinitas non confunditur, et ita trinum, quod unitas]; a reading certainly to be preferred according to its sense. Then cod. I with ed. 1 after *therefore* [ergo] has *this which* [hoc quod] for *what* [quod].

[9] Codices V X and Z have *is entirely* [omnino est] in place of *statement is* [oratio est]. A little below this codex T (corrected by the other hand) has *by which one would not distinguish* [quibus non distingueretur] in place of *which were not distinguished* [quae non distinguerentur].

[10] The Vatican ed., against the more ancient mss. and ed. 1, transposes this as *does not suppose entirely except improperly* [non supponit omnino nisi improprie], but not so well.

[11] Codices M Y & Z here add *and/or Wisdom* [vel sapientiae]. Then the Vatican ed., against the older codd. and ed. 1, omits *but not to be extended* [sed non extendenda]; cod. O has *therefore, it is to be distinguished and not extended* [ideo est istinguenda et non extendenda].

---

* *Trans. note*: A convertibili is the conversion of a proposition, by exchanging subject and predicate. Cf. Peter of Spain, SUMMULAE, tr. 1, n.15.

speak more expressly to confound heresies whenever the peculiarity of discourse gives them occasion [proprietas sermonis sustineat].

1. To that, therefore, which is first objected, that the Essence and a Person do not have diverse properties; it must be said, that there is a diversity of reckoning in a twofold manner[1] among the divine. *In one manner*, through *having diverse* properties; and that induces a distinction, and thus they differ by a reckoning and are not predicated of the same (thing), as (are) the Father and the Son; *in another manner*, (the diversity of reckoning) is through *having* and *not having* a property; and that does not induce a distinction nor causes (one), because one is not predicated of the other; it does, however, cause that something is said of one, which is not said of the other, as is clear in "*Peter*" and "*man*": Peter is an individual, man is not; and, nevertheless [tamen], "man" is truly predicated of "Peter".

To that, that a *most high* opposition belongs to affirmation and negation; it must be said, that (this) is true, where negation posits nothing, just as (it is) among something and nothing; but where it posits an extreme (opposition), there can be a *minimum* (opposition) and (this) rises from howsoever small a small difference, whether of thing [rei] or of reckoning [rationis]; whence (the difference) is not sufficient to distinguish (them).

2. To that which objected second, that a predicate substitutes for a subject; it can be said *in one manner*, that — just as among inferiors there is predication according to *substance*, as "man is an animal", there is also predication according to *a reckoning*, as "animal is a genus"; and a predicate[2] supposes on behalf of that of which it is predicated according to substance, but with a predication according to substance changed into a predication, which is according to a reckoning, there (the predicate) is an accident; whence it does not follow: 'animal is a genus, man is an animal, therefore, man is a genus' — *similarly* they say among divine (things), that since there is *thing* and *reckoning* There, there is predication according to substance There; and so long as that (predication) remains [illa salvata], whatever is said of the predicate, (is) also (said) of the subject; but with a predication according to substance changed into a predication according to a reckoning, there (the predicate) is an accident; and such is in this:[3] 'The Father generates; but the Divine Essence is the Father: therefore, the Divine Essence generates'.

But that similitude does not seem fitting [conveniens], because among the divine a *reckoning*[4] is predicated of the Essence, whence this is true: 'the Essence is the Paternity and the generation'; which indeed is not discovered among inferiors. And[5] on this account it

must be said in another manner, that among the divine there is a twofold manner of predicating: through *identity* and through *inherence*. Through *identity*, as when there is said: "the Essence is the Father"; through *inherence* or denomination, just as adjectives and verbs do [faciunt].[6] Predication through *identity* is among divine (things) by reason of the most high Simplicity, which does not suffer a Person to be less simple than the Essence; which (predication), because is not among creatures, for that reason among them there is not discovered a predication through *an omnimodal identity* unless the same is enunciated of itself, as when there is said: "humanity is humanity"; but every proper predication is[7] through *inherence*, because nothing is entirely simple; whence this is false: "humanity is animality". However, in predication through *inherence* a term[8] signifies one thing and supposes another, because it signifies a common form and supposes on behalf of an inferior, and in such (a case) it is true, that it supposes on behalf of that, which is predicated of the other. But in predication through *identity* it signifies and supposes the same (thing). Whence the sense, then, is, 'that which (has) been signified through this term *Father* is the same, (as) that which (has) been signified through this term *essence*', and for that reason the Paternity is the Essence; and because this noun "essence" does not signify a Person, for that reason it does not suppose on behalf of It, since in no manner is it predicated of It except by a predication through *identity*.

3. To that which is objected third concerning passion and subject and things completely similar, it must be said, that *certain* words [vocabula] among divine (things) are substantial, which enclose within themselves a thing, about which they posit the form conveyed by themselves, as this noun "Father" (does); and such can be predicated through *identity*, as when there is said: "the Essence is the Father", that is, "that One who is the Father". There are *certain* (words), which are entirely for [in] the (words) adjacent (to them), just as verbs and names used as adjectives [adiective retenta],[9] as (are) "*generates*" and "*begotten*" and "*born*"; and such posit their own meaning [rem suam] about those, of which they are predicated, for that reason they are predicated only through *inherence*. And for that reason "to generate" posits a distinction, which it conveys, about the Essence, when it speaks of these; and for that reason this is false: "the Essence generates"; this, however, true: "the Essence is the generation". And, when, from a predication through *identity*, one passes [itur][10] to a predication through *inherence*, there it can be an accident. That which is therefore, said: "of whatever there is predicated a subject, (there is) also (predicated) a proper

---

[1] Not a few codices, such as T V and Y, together with edition 1 read *twofold diversity of reckoning* [diversitas rationis duplex], and a little below this many codices, such as A C G K L R S T V X etc., after *and* [et] add *through* [per], but less aptly. Then with the sense unchanged codices D and T read *nor is one predicated of the other, as (are) Father* [nec praedicatur unum de altero, ut Pater]. Cf. on this d. 26, a. 1, q. 1, at n. 2. Codex X after *the same (thing)*, by glossing, reads *whence the one is the Person of the Father, the other (that) of the Son, the other (that) of the Holy Spirit; for that reason one is not predicated of the other, as "the Father is the Son"* [unde ait est persona Patris, alia Filii, alia Spiritus sancti; ideo una non praedicatur de alia, ut Pater est Filius.]

[2] Very many codices, such as A B C L R S U X and bb, together with edition 1 falsely have *the predication* [praedicatio] in place of *the predicate* [praedicatum], and a little below this after *with a predication* [praedicatione] many codd., such as A F G I K T aa etc., together with edition 1 omit *according to substance* [secundum substantiam], but not well.

[3] The Vatican edition and the codex cc, contrary to the ancient codices and edition 1 have *this* [haec]; codex X has *here* [ibi].

[4] Codex Y reads *relation* [relatio]. *A reckoning* [Ratio] here stands for *relation*, cf. above (d. 2, a. sole, q. 4, near the end of the body of the response), p. 58, fn. 1.

[5] The Vatican edition contrary to the manuscripts and edition 1 omits *And* [Et].

[6] Codices I and X add *just as "God is just", just as "the Father generates"* [sicut Deus est iustus, sicut Pater generat]. — Concerning the twofold relation of predicating see above d. 34, q. 2.

[7] Codex W here adds *that which is of the superior in respect of the inferior* [illa quae est superioris respectu inferioris]; codices aa and bb, however, read *of the superior concerns the inferior* [superioris de inferiore est]; codex H at the end adds *among creatures* [in creaturis].

[8] Codices L and O have *a common term* [terminus communis]. A little below this after *for the other* [pro altero] codex T continues the construction with *but not in predication through identity where (they are) the same* [sed non in praedicatione per identitatem ubi idem]. In regard to the explanation of the doctrine cf. above d. 4, q. 2 and 4.

[9] The Vatican edition not trusting in the more ancient manuscripts and edition 1 omits *just as verbs and nouns used as adjectives* [sicut verba et nomina adiective retenta]. A little before this very many codices such as A E Q V and X after *entirely* [omnino] omit *for* [in], in which reading *adjacent* [adjacentia] is taken as a predicate adjective.

[10] Codex R has *one infers* [infertur], codex W has *one proceeds* [proceditur].

passion",[1] that (principle) of his does have an instance, where a property is extraneous to that, of which the subject is predicated, such as this intention '*species*', although it be a property of man, and "man" is said of Peter, however, there is not said of him this, that he is a "*species*".

And, if you object, that[2] there does not occur among the divine a reckoning of the extraneous, because an accident does not occur There; it must be said, that, even if there is not an extraneousness nor a diversity as much as regards *thing*, there is, however, in regard to a *reckoning* or in regard to the *manner of predicating*, which is threefold among the divine, as will be clear below.[3] Whence, just as here there is (a fallacy of the) accident: 'the Essence is a Person; but a Person is distinguished: therefore, also the Essence'; thus it is in the proposed.

4. To that which is last objected concerning this: 'the Essence[4] is the Father of the Son'; there is distinguished by (Peter) Praepositivus, that "the Father" can posit its own thing or the looking-back [respectum], conveyed through it, about the subject itself, which is the Essence; and then the saying is false; for the sense is, that 'the Essence is referred to the Son'. *And/or* it can close within it[5] the meaning [rem] of its own substantive, so that the sense is: 'the Essence is the Father of the Son', that is, 'the Essence is that One who is referred to the Son'; and in this manner the saying is true, and the argument is not valid: 'therefore, the Son is the Son of the Essence', nay, rather, there is (a fallacy of the) *accident* there. For, just as there does not follow: 'the Son is referred to That which is the Father, and this One is the Essence: therefore, He is referred and/or distinguished by the Essence': so (it is) also in the proposed.

SCHOLIUM

I. This question is about the *principle which* [principium quod] of the divine productions, which according to the Catholic Faith are themselves the Divine *Persons* producing. The conclusions of this and of the first Question of the following Article are against Abbot Joachim (di Fiore), whose doctrine was censured in the Fourth Lateran Council, in the canon *de Fide catholica*, in the chapter "We damn": « Moreover, We, with the Sacred Council approving, believe and confess with Peter (Lombard), that one certain Thing is indeed the incomprehensible and ineffable ... and that Thing is not generating nor begotten nor proceeding ». — This Catholic Doctrine the Seraphic (Doctor) confirms with the most grave arguments.

In the solution to n. 1, the Seraphic Doctor distinguishes a twofold diversity of reckoning in divine (things) according to the difference, which there is between *having diverse* properties and *having and/or not having one* same property, concerning which, cf. here, doubt 4 and below distinction 19, p. II, a. 1, q. 2, at n. 4. He also affirms, that one of the two induces a real distinction, the other does not. For among the divine there are three personal properties, that is, the paternity, the filiation and the passive spiration, and *having* these distinct properties induces a real distinction of persons; whence, one cannot even be predicated of the other. But the diversity of reckoning, which rises forth from *having some* property and *not having* the same one, does not introduce a real distinction. For the Divine Essence does not have the property of generating, which the Father has; nevertheless the paternity and the Divine Essence are not really distinguished and they can be predicated of themselves. Neither is the argument (1. ad opp.) valid, that *to have* a property and *to not have* are contradictorily opposed, and that from this [exinde] they induce a greater difference between a Person and the Essence, than which is between each of the Persons themselves. For the Seraphic Doctor well distinguishes between contradiction, one extreme of which posits nothing (as among *something* and *nothing*) and that contradiction, the extreme of which posits something. If one extreme posits nothing, it cannot be verified of some positive term, however, it (can) well (be), if it posits something. In addition, the least distinction of *reckoning* is sufficient for this, that

contradictories be said of distinct (things). Thus. an *incommunicable* term is verified of the paternity and predicated of it, not of the Essence, though this is not really distinguished from the paternity. Cf. below d. 26, q. 1, at n. 2; d. 34, q. 1; d. 33, q. 2: and St. Thomas, here in q. 1, a. 1.

III. The first opinion posited in the solution to n. 2, which distinguishes between predication according to substance and according to reckoning, is said to have belonged to (Peter) Praepositivus. The second opinion distinguishes between the predication through *identity* and through *inherence*, or denomination, which is called "formal predication" by (Bl. John Duns) Scotus. Concerning this distinction, cf. below d. 33, q. 3 and d. 34, q. 2. *Identical* predication comes about [fit] through abstract (terms); predication through *inherence* comes about always in a concrete (term) and by reason of a supposit. These predications differ, both because an abstract (term) signifies and supposes the same thing, but the concrete (term) often signifies one (thing) and substitutes for an other (see above d. 4, q. 1); and because an abstract noun is imposed upon a form and is denominated by a form, but a concrete (noun) is not imposed upon a form, but upon a supposit; and also because identical (predication) comprises every manner of identity, but predication through inherence (comprises) some diversity. Whence, false is the reasoning, which passes from identical predication to the other and from an abstract (term) to a concrete one; and in this Abbot Joachim (of Fiore) erred, as St. Thomas testifies, (SUMMA., I, q. 39, a. 5). — That identical predication does not have a place among created things in a proper sense, is the common sentence, if you except Francis of Mayrone.

IV. In regard to the conclusion itself, cf. above d. 4, a. 1, in the body (of the Question). — Alexander of Hales, SUMMA., p. I, q. 49, m. 1, a. 4 (where he removes and solves 25 contrary argg.); q. 42, m. 3, a. 1. — (Bl. John Duns) Scotus, here in q. 1. — St. Thomas, here in q. 1, a. 1; SUMMA., I, q. 39, a. 5. — Bl. (now St.) Albertus (Ma gnus), SENT., Bk. I, d. 4, a. 2, at the first question; SUMMA., p. I, tr. 7, q. 30, m. 3, a. 1. — (Bl.) Peter of Tarentaise, here in q. 1, a. 1. — Richard of Middleton, here in q. 1. — Giles the Roman, here 1, princ., q. 2, a. 1 and 2. — Henry of Ghent, SUMMA., a. 39, q. 3, n. 13; q. 4, n. 12, and a. 54, q. 3, nn. 21 & 28. — Durandus (of Saint-Pourçain), here in q. 1. — (Bl.) Dionysius the Carthusian, here in q. 1. — (Gabriel) Biel, here in q. 1.

QUESTION II

Whether there is to be conceded the expression, that "the Son is generated from the Substance of the Father"?

Second, there is asked, whether it must be conceded, that Someone is generated from the Substance of the Father, such as the Son. And it seems, that it is so:

1. Through the many *authorities* (quoted) in the text (of Master Peter)[6] and most of all through that (which is said): *It is also said, and frequently in Scripture it is read: that Father from His own Substance has begotten the Son;*

---

[1] Codices O and Z add *that (principle), however, is true, where a subject is predicated through inherence, not where it is predicated through identity. That (principle)* etc. [illud tamen habet veritatem, ubi subiectum praedicatur per inhaerentiam, non ubi praedicatur per identitatem. Illud].

[2] We have restored from the manuscripts and edition 1 *that* [quod], and a little below this we have substituted *even if* [etsi] in place of *si* [if]. Then codex V inserts *There* [ibi] before *there is not* [non sit].

[3] Distinction 26, a. 1, q. 1 in the body. That threefold manner of speaking is: *the essential, the personal, the notional.* — A little below

this after *thus* [ita], trusting in the manuscripts and edition 1, we have supplied the not well omitted *also* [et].

[4] The Vatican edition, contrary to the codices and edition 1, has *the Divine Essence* [essentia divina]. A little below this codices T aa & bb have *His relation* [suam relationem] in place of *His thing* [suam rem]; but ed. 1 has *His thing, that is His relation and/or* [suam rem, id est suam relationem sive].

[5] Very many ancient codd., such as A I T aa & bb. together with edition 1 omit *Himself* [se].

[6] Here, after the middle of ch. 1.

but Scripture does not say except (what is) true nor does it do (anything) frequently except (what is) proper: therefore, the aforesaid discourse is true and proper.

2. Likewise, it is shown *by reason* thus: whosoever is by [ab] someone[1] and is consubstantial to him, is from [de] his substance; but the Son is by the Father and is consubstantial to Him: therefore, He is from His substance.

3. Likewise, the Father generates the Son: therefore, either from something [de aliquo], or from nothing; not from nothing, because then He would be a creature: therefore, from something;[2] not from something other than Himself; therefore, from His own substance.

4. Likewise, among inferiors a son, who has part of (his) substance by the father, is said to be from the substance of the father: therefore, much more strongly, he who has the whole substance, is said to be from the substance of the one generating: therefore, this is true: 'the Son is from the Substance of the Father'.

ON THE CONTRARY: 1. Prepositions* are transitive,[3] and where (there is) transition, there is distinction and diversity: therefore, when there is said: "the Son (is) from the Substance of the Father", this preposition *"from"* [de] notes distinction between the Substance of the Father and the Son: therefore, since there is no distinction, because the Son is the Substance of the Father, the aforesaid proposition is false. *If you say*, that this preposition *"from"* occurs from that which is generally signified by prepositions [a generali significato praepositionum], being used in a *special* sense [retinens speciale]: therefore, it is there a solecism,[4] just as if one said, "Sublime does it fly," for "Sublimely (does it fly)," which is a stupid (thing) to say.

2. Likewise, it is objected concerning (that which is) *specially* signified. This preposition *"from"* [de], insofar as it is accepted in a special manner, is sometimes held *materially*, as "a knife (made) from iron"; (and) is sometimes held *ordinally*, as "from morning midday is made", that is "after morning"; sometimes *originally*, as if one said, "a ray from the sun" and/or "the splendor from the fire." But in whatever of these manners it be accepted, the saying is false; if *materially*, it is false, because the Son lacks matter; if *ordinally*, (it is) false, because the sense is, that the Son is after the Father or after the substance of the Father; if *originally*, (it is) similarly false because then the sense is, that the Son has arisen away from [a] the Substance of the Father; but this (saying) is not admitted: "the Substance of the Father generates the Son": therefore, it is in every manner[5] false. *If you say*, that (it is held) in none of those manners, but rather it is held in a fourth manner *substantially*; it is asked, "Whence has arisen this signification and where is it accepted in a completely similar manner [consimiliter]?";[6] and it seems that this is nothing, because then this would be true: "the Father is from the Substance of the Son", which no one concedes.

3. Likewise, this same is shown thus: this preposition *"from"* [de] is different and (so is) *"by"* [a]: because *"by"* properly means the habitude of an active principle, but this preposition, *"from"*, means

the habitude of a passive principle; but to God and to His Substance the reckoning of an active principle it is more fitting [convenit] than of a passive one: therefore, this is more true: "the Son is *by* the Substance of the Father", than *"from"*; but this (saying) is not received: therefore, neither ought the other be received.

4. Likewise, *"from"* either means *identity* or *diversity*; if *identity*: therefore, since there is a most high identity in the Essence and/or Substance, this will be true: "Substance[7] from Substance", which Master (Peter) denies; if (it means) a diversity; but the Substance of the Father is not distinguished from the Son, because the Son is the Substance itself of the Father: therefore, it is entirely false.

CONCLUSION

It must be conceded, that the Son is generated from the Substance of the Father.

I RESPOND: that it must be said, that the aforesaid saying is to be conceded.

And for an understanding of the aforesaid[8] it must be noted, that besides the aforesaid three manners, by which this preposition *"from"* [de] is accepted, it can also be accepted in a fourth manner, that is *substantially*, to mean a substantial fittingness [substantialem convenientiam] between extremes; but it never purely means this, since it is a preposition and it conveys some habitude and regard [respectum] for the extremes. For, if it were only held substantially;[9] just as there is said: "a son (is) from the substance of a father", it would thus mean: 'a father of the substance of the son'; which sounds awry [absonum est].

Moreover, it must be noted, that it is accustomed to be accepted *substantially* in a threefold manner. *Sometimes*, it is accepted substantially and partially, as when it is said, that parts are from the whole or from the substance of the whole, as "a jug of wine from the cask". *Sometimes*, it is accepted substantially and ordinally, as when there is said: "from bread the Body of Christ is made", for in this [ibi] there is an *order*, because the substance of the bread does not remain [manet] in the Body of Christ, just as neither the morning in the midday; but, furthermore, *substantially*, because the substance of the bread passes over into the substance of the Body of Christ. *Sometimes*, it is accepted[10] substantially and originally, as when there is said: "the Son from the Substance of the Father"; by reason of the ablative ("from the Substance") it is held substantially, by reason of the genitive ("of the Father"), originally: and for that reason it conveys [importat] some distinction of the Son regarding the Father, not regarding His Substance, and thus the preposition holds there a general and special significance [significatum].

1. 2. And thus is clear the response to the first and second argument. However, because it is said, that

---

[1] From nearly all the codices and edition 1 we have substituted *something* [aliquo] for *an other* [alio].

[2] The Vatican edition, contrary to very many codices and edition 1, adds *and* [et], in place of which codex A has the better *but* [sed].

[3] Cf. Priscian, GRAMMATICAL INSTITUTIONS, Bk. XIV, ch. 1 ff.. — Then after *there* [ibi] the Vatican edition has *also is* in place of *and* [et]. A little below this edition 1 prefaces the word *no* [nulla] with *in the Substance* [in substantia], well enough.

[4] Priscian, GRAMMATICAL INSTITUTIONS, ch. 1: For if (the ordering of the parts of an oration) be incongruous, it causes a solecism, as if the elements of the oration were arranged [coeuntibus] in an awkward manner.

[5] Very many codices, such as A F H K T Y etc., together with edition 1 have *in every manner* [omni modo], the Vatican edition has *entirely* [omnino]. — Aristotle has similar (sayings), METAPHYSICS, Bk.

V, text 29 (Bk. IV, 24) concerning the preposition *out of* [ex]. — A little below this not a few codices, such as K V W and X, after *manners* [modorum] add *is it held* [tenetur].

[6] The Vatican edition contrary to the manuscripts and edition 1 has *is it accepted in a similar manner* [similiter accipitur].

[7] The Vatican edition not trusting in the manuscripts and edition 1 adds *is* [est]. See the text of Master (Peter) above in ch. 1 and 2, near the end.

[8] Some codices such as T and V have explicitly *it must be noted* [est notandum] for *it must be noted* [notandum].

[9] The Vatican edition, disagreeing with the manuscripts and edition 1, has the less well *is held* [tenetur].

[10] We have substituted from the codices and edition 1 *it is accepted* [accipitur] for *it is said* [dicitur]. A little below this after *the Son* [Filius] codex V adds *is* [est].

---

* *Trans. note*: Here the Quaracchi text has *The propositions* [Propositiones], however, it appears here from nn. 1 & 2 of the response, as well as from I. of the Scholium, that it should rather be read as *Prepositions* [Praepositiones]. This is confirmed by the citation from Priscian, in fn. 3.

prepositions are transitive, it is not understood, that from this they necessarily note a diversity; but just as it is said, that oblique (cases, i. e. the accusative and the ablative,)[1] are transitive as much as regards manner; because they are transitively constructed with words, as, "I see myself"; similarly this is said of prepositions, which[2] are constructed with the oblique (cases).

3. Clear also is the third, because "*from*" not only means the habitude of a passive principle nor only the

habitude of an active principle, but rather a consubstantial habitude together with the habitude of an origin; which this preposition "*by*" [a] does not do; and for that reason it is not similar.

4. To that which is objected last, the response is clear, because "from"[3] does not mean that (there is) a thorough [penitus] identity There and not a diversity, but rather a consubstantiality with a habitude of an origin.

SCHOLIUM

I. For an understanding of some of the terms occurring in the solution to n. 1 and elsewhere, we note these (points) of ancient (Latin) grammar.

1. A twofold *transitive* construction used to be distinguished, that is both *of acts* as well as *of persons*. In the first the dependent constructible signifies through a manner of acting, as in transitive words, e. g. "I read a book"; but the second is, in which the dependent constructible signifies through a manner of substance. This is accomplished through oblique cases (e.g. "the son of Socrates" [filius Socratis]; "a similar to Cicero" [similis Ciceroni]) and/or even through prepositions, which are thence called "transitive". See (Bl. John Duns) Scotus, SPECULATIVE GRAMMAR, ch. 46-51, who disputes this point subtly.

2. A *transitive* construction according to the ancient definition is that, in which the constructibles pertain to diverse (things) and/or seem to pertain to diverse (things); but an *intransitive* (construction) is that, in which the constructibles pertain to the same (thing) and/or at least seem to pertain to the same (thing).

3. In what manner grammatical cases are transitive as much as regards (their) manner of signifying, (Bl. John Duns) Scotus explains at length, <u>ibid.</u>, ch. 19.

4. St. Bonaventure himself below in d. 37, p. I, doubt 2, teaches, that prepositions do not necessarily note a diversity.

A more ample exposition and application of this solution is exhibited by Alexander of Hales, SUMMA., p. I, q. 42, m. 4, a. 2, at n. 3, and by Richard of Middleton, here in q. 3, in reply to n. 1.

II. The doctors agree on the conclusion. Cf. Alexander and Richard <u>locc</u>. <u>citt</u>.. — (Bl. John Duns) Scotus, here in q. 2. — St. Thomas, here in q. 2, a. 1; SUMMA., I, q. 41, a. 3. — Bl. (now St.) Albertus (Magnus), SENT., Bk. I, d. 4. a. 2, at n. 1; SUMMA., p. I, tr. 7, q. 30, m. 3, a. 2, p. 3. — (Bl.) Peter of Tarentaise, here in q. 3, a. 1. — Giles the Roman, here in the 2nd princ. of q. 1. — Henry of Ghent, SUMMA., a. 54, q. 3, n. 53 ff.. — Durandus (of Saint-Pourçain), here in q. 2. — (Bl.) Dionysius the Carthusian, here in q. 2. — (Gabriel) Biel, here in q. 2.

ARTICLE II

On the comparison of generation to essence in the reckoning of a terminus.

Consequently, about the second Article of this Question, which is through the comparison of generation to essence in the reckoning of a *terminus*, two (questions) are asked.

First, there is asked, whether the Substance or Essence is generated.

Second, whether It is communicated through generation.

QUESTION I

Whether the Substance or Essence is generated?

Moreover, that the Substance is generated, is objected in this manner.[4]

1. Generation among inferiors is a movement [motus] towards substance;[5] because what is *movement*, belongs to imperfection, what is *towards substance*, belongs to perfection; therefore, if what belongs to perfection must be transferred to the divine: therefore, even generation is terminated at an essence.

2. Likewise, generation among the divine is terminated: therefore, either at a substance, or at an accident, because every being [ens] is a substance, and/or an accident;[6] but among the divine it is not terminated at an accident, since (this) is not There: therefore, at a

substance. *If you say*, that among the divine, although there is not an accident, there is however, a relation, which is distinguished regarding the Substance; then it is argued thus: either generation will be terminated *at a substance*, or *at a relation*, because *at something* <u>per se</u> is not an origin, nor is the production terminated:[7] therefore, it is terminated at a substance: therefore, a substance is generated.

3. Likewise, as the Philosopher says:[8] « With us moved, there are moved those things which are in us, and with us corrupted, there are corrupted those thing which are in us »; and this is,

---

[1] Supply: cases [casus]. — A little below this very many codices, such as A C F G H K L O R S V X etc. ,together with editions 2, 3, 4, 5 and 6 read "*he sees me*" [videt me] in place of "*I see myself*" [video me], but not well.

[2] The Vatican edition not trusting the more ancient manuscripts and edition 1 adjoins *also* [etiam]. Codex H has *because they* [quia] in place of *which* [quae].

[3] The Vatican edition puts *that* [quod] in place of *because* [quia] and omits *from* [de], but contrary to the manuscripts and edition 1.

[4] Codex H reads *shown* [ostenditur].

[5] This proposition, according to its sense, is found in Aristotle, PHYSICS, Bk. V, text 7 (ch. 1): That (change), however, which is simply [simpliciter] from 'not being' [ex non esse] into a substance, is generation in the simple sense [simpliciter]. Cf. also ON GENERATION AND CORRUPTION, Bk. I, texts 11-18 (ch. 3).

[6] Cf. Aristotle, ON PREDICAMENTS, ch. "On Composites and on Substance"; PHYSICS, Bk. I, texts 26-30 (ch. 3); METAPHYSICS, Bk. V, text 13 ff. (Bk. IV, ch. 7).

[7] Aristotle, PHYSICS, Bk. V, text 10 (ch. 2): Nor (is) there even (a movement) unto "toward something". — A little before this some codices, such as A I T and bb, have *it would be argued* [arguetur] in place of *it is argued* [arguitur]. At the end of the argument after *at a substance* [substantiam] codex I adds *but that, at which generation is terminated, that is generated* [sed ilud, ad quod terminator generation, illud generatur].

[8] Aristotle, TOPICS, Bk. II, ch. 3 (ch. 7), in which text the manuscripts together with the first six editions have *being moved* [moventibus] in place of *moved* [motis] (κινουμένων); the same recurs below in d. 8, p. I, a. 2, q. 2, at n. 3, and in d. 37, p. II, a. 1, objection 3. You will find the other part of the proposition in Aristotle, ON THE LONGEVITY AND BREVITY OF LIFE, ch. 2, in these words: For with living things corrupted (φθειρομένων), there is corrupted both the knowledge and health, which (was) in the living things. — Aristotle hints at an additional reason for this proposition in TOPICS, Bk. II, loc. cit. and he proves it more fully in METAPHYSICS, Bk. VII, texts 35 and 45 ff (Bk. VI, 10 and 13). After *there are corrupted* [corrumpuntur] codices V and X adds *all* [omnia] and codex K after *to be the same* [idem esse: on the following page] adjoins *and the same essence* [et eandem essentiam].

because a universal has to be the same with the singular: therefore, since much more is the Substance the same with a Person, and the Substance is in a Person, if a Person is generated, (so) also the Substance.

4. Likewise, 'to generate' both among the divine and among creatures is 'to produce a (something) similar to one's self';[1] but there is not similitude in person, but in substance and in nature: therefore, since (generation) is terminated at (something) similar, inasmuch as it is (something) similar, therefore, at a substance, according to which the similitude is attained.

ON THE CONTRARY: 1. Everything which is generated is generated by an other, because nothing begets its very self;[2] but the Divine Substance does not have an Other, nor is there an other (being) among the divine: therefore, It is not generated.

2. Likewise, everything which is generated has a principle *from which*;[3] but everything which has a beginning [principium], has been begun [est principiatum]; but the beginning and the begun are distinguished: therefore, if a substance is generated, it is distinguished: therefore, either (it is distinguished) from [a] the Substance, or from a Person; but each is impossible: ergo etc..

3. Likewise, everything which is generated is from the substance of the one generating;[4] therefore, if a substance is generated, the substance and/or essence is from the substance of the one generating; but there is not but entirely one Substance: therefore, the Same is from its very Self, which is impossible.

4. Likewise, generation is a production;[5] but production is a certain action, and every action of a creature is terminated at singulars: therefore, since generation is a certain action, in divine (things) it will be terminated at a singular or at a supposit; but such is not the Substance; therefore, it will not be terminated at It.

CONCLUSION

Since generation among the divine is terminated solely at the first substance, which is a Person, not at the second substance or essence, it is not in the least received, that the Substance is generated.

I RESPOND: It must be said, that generation from its own common reckoning is terminated at a substance. But

it must be attended to, that "substance" [substantia] is said in a twofold manner: the *first*, (that) which is an individual and a hypostasis or person, and the *second*, (that) which is (something) common.[6] Therefore, I say, that it is to be said of the terminus of one generating in a twofold manner: either as much as regards the *production*, or as much as regards the *intention*. As much as regards the production, since it is about a singular, it is terminated at the first substance, and[7] as much as regards the intention (it is terminated) at a common nature, because the nature producing this man intends to give him a common form.

But since among creatures the common form is numbered among supposits, for that reason among those a common form is produced and corrupted; and for that reason among creatures generation not only according to intention, but also according to production, is terminated at a common substance; and for that reason a universal is generated in the singular, because it is numbered.[8] But since in the Divine Substance there is not numbered nor does something new come upon it [advenit ei novum esse]: for that reason generation according to production is terminated solely at the first substance, which is a Person, because "a person" according to (St. Severinus) Boethius[9] « is an individual substance of a rational nature ». And since that alone is said properly to be generated, generation according to a reckoning of producing is terminated at that. And for that reason this is not received: "the Essence is generated".

And thus is clear all the objections on each side; for they proceed[10] by diverse ways.

3. It is also clear, why among the divine it does not follow, that, with a Person generated, a substance is generated, just as among creatures. However, it can be otherwise said, that (something) common is not generated except *in this one*;[11] and not only among creatures is this true, but also among the divine. Moreover, (something) common as "*in this one*" is not signified in abstraction, but in concretion; and for that reason, because this noun "*God*" signifies a substance in concretion,[12] "God is generated" and "God generates God". However, because "substance" and/or "essence" signifies in abstraction, for that reason it neither generates nor is generated; and thus proceed the reasons on the opposite sides.

---

[1] Cf. Aristotle, ON THE SON, Bk. II, text 34 (ch. 4), where he says, that the most natural of the works of living (things) is *to make a "such as itself"* [facere quale ipsum], that is to generate; and text 49: The end is to generate a "such as itself", that is a similar. — Then very many codices, such as A C F G H I T etc., together with edition 1 have *at a similar one* [ad similem] in place of *at (something) similar* [ad simile] and then *one is similar* [est similis] in place of *it is (something) similar* [est simile].

[2] Aristotle, ON THE SOUL, Bk. II, text 47 (ch. 4): Moreover, nothing itself generates its very self. — A little below this after *an other (thing)* [aliud] some codices, such as A T V Z and cc, omit *is there* [est], in place of which codex X puts *by which it is generated* [a quo generetur].

[3] Aristotle, METAPHYSICS, Bk. IV, text 22 (Venetian edition, 1489), where according to the Arabic-Latin translation it is had thus: And if it is generated, it is necessary, that (its) 'being' have a "that out of which it is generated", a "that which is generated out of it", and "a that through which it is generated". According to the Parisian edition (Firmin-Didot), Bk. III, ch. 5: If it is made, it is necessary that there is, a "out of which it is made", and a "from which there is generated".

[4] Cf. Aristotle, ON THE SOUL, Bk. II, texts 34-50 (ch. 4), where he deals with nutrition and generation. — Near the end of the argument at *one* [una] the Vatican edition less well omits *entirely* [omnino] and after *the same* [idem] it omits *is* [est], but contrary to the manuscripts and edition 1.

[5] Under this respect Aristotle, ON THE SOUL, Bk. II, text 34 (ch. 4),

defining the act of generating of a living (thing) says: it is a "to make a such as itself". Concerning the term of action Aristotle says, METAPHYSICS, Bk. I, ch. 1: Moreover actions and generations are all about a singular (thing). — At the end of the argument some codices, such as A I and T, together with edition 1 read *is terminated* [terminatur] in place of *will be terminated* [terminabitur].

[6] See Aristotle, ON PREDICAMENTS, ch. "On Substance".

[7] The codices omit the *however* [vero], added by the Vatican ed., here, after *as much as* [quantum], in place of which to the word *as much as* very many codd., such as A F G I K S T V X and Z, which we follow, preface the particle *and* [et], others, such as H P Q and Y, have *but* [sed]. A little below this trusting in the mss. and ed. 1, we have expunged *this* [haec] after *because* [quia].

[8] Cf. Aristotle, METAPHYSICS, Bk. VII, text 28 (Bk. VI, ch. 8).

[9] The book, ON THE PERSON AND THE TWO NATURES. ch. 3 at the beginning (Migne's edition). — Immediately after this the Vatican edition, contrary to the manuscripts and edition 1, has *But because* [Sed quia] in place of *And since* [Et quoniam]. — Concerning the term of generation cf. Aristotle, METAPHYSICS, Bk. VII, text 26 ff (Bk. VI, ch. 8).

[10] Trusting the manuscripts we have expunged the *down from* [de] added by the Vatican edition.

[11] That is, in an individual or a supposit. Concerning which cf. Aristotle, METAPHYSICS, Bk. VII, loc. cit. — The Vatican edition not trusting in the manuscripts as *as in this* [ut in hoc].

[12] The Vatican ed. incongruously and against the more ancient codd. and ed. 1 adds *for that reason in concretion* [ideo in concretione].

SCHOLIUM

I. Again, this conclusion is against Abbot Joachim (cf. the Scholium, here at a. 4, q. 1). To understand the conclusion rightly, it must be noted, that it is not a discourse concerning the *subject* of generation, which in the generation of creatures is the prime matter, which is presupposed to generation, but rather concerning the *terminus* of generation, which begins to be.

Perfect generation is terminated at a substance, not at an accident; but the Seraphic Doctor with the common sentence distinguished a twofold substance: one of the two is called the *first* substance, which is *every individual* in the genus of substance; but the other of the two is the *second* (substance), which is anything « common » in the genus of substance. The first substance is the total terminus of the generation as much as regards *production*; but the second substance is the formal (but partial) terminus as much as regards *intention*. Among creatures each terminus begins to be from (something) new, but not (so) in God. « Whence divine generation is terminated at the first substance, not at an essence, nor at a relation, inasmuch as it is a *relation*, but rather as much as it is a subsistent Person ». Thus Richard of Middleton on this Distinction.

II. In the conclusion and the principle arguments the doctors agree. Alexander of Hales, SUMMA., p. I, q. 42, m. 3, a. 1; p. IV, q. 10, m. 1. — (Bl. John Duns) Scotus, here in q. 1. — St. Thomas, here in q. 3; SUMMA., I, q. 39, a. 5. — Bl. (now St.) Albertus (Magnus), here in a. 2; SUMMA., p. I, tr. 7, q. 30, m. 3, a. 1. — (Bl.) Peter of Tarentaise, here in q. 2, a. 1. — Richard of Middleton, here in q. 2. — Giles the Roman, here in the 1st princ. of q. 2, second quaest.. — Henry of Ghent, SUMMA., a. 59, q. 1, n. 4. — Durandus (of Saint-Pourçain), here in q. 1. — (Bl.) Dionysius the Carthusian, here in q. 2. — (Gabriel) Biel, here in q. 1.

QUESTION II

Whether the Divine Substance or Essence is communicated through generation?

Lastly, there is asked, whether the Substance is communicated through generation; and that (this is) so, is shown[1] in this manner.

1. A thing is communicated through that, through which it comes to be [fit], so that it may be among several; but the Substance is in several Persons and is not (there) but through generation and through procession: therefore, through generation It is communicated.

2. Likewise, a cause is (that), which when posited a thing is posited and which when removed (a thing) is removed;[2] but with emanation posited among the divine, there is posited a community and a distinction; with generation and/or emanation removed, the Essence is in One alone, just as a Hypostasis (is): therefore, generation is a reason for communicating the Essence.

3. Likewise, what is given to someone and does not cease to be had by the one giving, through that[3] through which it is given, through that it is communicated; but the Substance is given by the Father to the Son through generation and does not cease to be had by the Father, while It is given to the Son: therefore, through generation It is communicated.

4. Likewise, generation among these lesser (things) is the reason for communicating a substance or nature; but among the divine the Nature is much more communicable than these (are),[4] because (It is) simpler: therefore, among the divine the Substance and/or Essence is communicated through generation.

ON THE CONTRARY: 1. Generation is a principle of distinguishing;[5] but the principle of distinguishing and of communicating is not the same: therefore, through generation there is not a reason for communicating among the divine: therefore through generation nothing is communicated.

2. Likewise, what makes something to be *in this one*, is not a reason for communicating, but for appropriating and individuating; but generation makes the Substance to be in such a Person, as [utpote] in the Person of the Son: therefore, it is not a reason for communicating, but for appropriating.

3. Likewise, every 'that' which is communicated through generation, is common through generation.[6] If, therefore, the Substance is communicated through generation, with generation excluded [circumscripta], It will not be common: therefore, (It will be) proper; but the proper cannot be communicated through generation: therefore, neither (can) the Substance.

4. Likewise, what is communicated through generation, through generation is given and received, and everything such, if it is not accidental to generation, is generated; but the Substance does not accede [accidit] to generation: therefore, etc..

CONCLUSION

The Divine Essence is communicated through generation, because through generation it comes to be, so as to be the One among Several.

I RESPOND: For this to be understood it must be noted, that the *common* [commune], as much as it is from itself, holds itself indifferently toward act and potency. For the common can be said (to be) that which is "the *communicable*", even though [quamvis] it be not among several; just as is clear in many universals, as in the Sun and the Moon and (things) of this kind. "The common" is also said (to be) "the *communicated*", because it is by act among several.

Therefore, I say, that according to which manner a form (is) a universal, as much as it is of itself [quanto est de se], it is communicable; but, yet, it is communicated by an act through the propagation[7] of

---

[1] The Vatican edition, disagreeing with the manuscripts and edition 1, has *it seems* [videtur].

[2] Aristotle, PHYSICS, Bk. II, text 37 (ch. 3): Indeed working and singular (causes) simultaneously are and are not with those, of which they are the causes. Cf. St. Thomas, COMMENTARY on this passage.

[3] We have substituted from many of the manuscripts and edition 1 *that* [illud] in place of *the same* [idem].

[4] The sense is: nature is much more simpler than (it is) in those inferior (beings). — Perhaps it would be better to omit with codex T *than they (are)* [illis].

[5] Cf. above d. 4, q. 2, objection 1. — Then after the first *therefore* [ergo] the Vatican edition indeed more plainly has *generation* [generatio] in place of *through generation there* [per generationem], but contrary to the manuscripts and edition 1.

[6] The Vatican edition without the authority of the manuscripts and edition 1: *Likewise, through generation there is communicated every 'that' which is common through generation* [Item per generationem communicatur omne illud quod per generationem est commune], and a little below this after *is communicated through generation* [communicatur] it adds: *through generation It is common.* *If, therefore, the Substance is communicated through generation* [per generationem est communis. Si ergo substantia per generationem communicatur], by which transposition and addition the force of the argument is weakened.

[7] Thus the more ancient codices together with edition 1, while the Vatican edition and codex cc has *it is not communicated by an act except through propagation* [actu non communicator nisi per propagationem]. Then the Vatican edition, contrary to the manuscripts and edition 1 adds *and/or aggregation* [vel aggregationem]; but this is clearly false. A little below this very many codices, such as A F G K T etc., together with edition 1 have the indicative rather than the subjunctive for *is communicated* [communicetur].

several, so the Divine Nature and/or Essence is of It-self, indeed, communicable, but because It is communicated by an act, It is not except through that which multiplies and/or plurifies Its Supposits; but this is generation.[1]

Therefore, since through generation the Persons are plurified, and the Substance is not numbered among Them, hence it is, that the Substance and/or Essence is most truly communicated through generation, because through generation it comes, to be the One among the Several.

1. To that which is objected, that generation is a principle of distinguishing; it must be said, that generation per se is a principle for distinguishing a supposit from a supposit, because per se (generation) is terminated at the latter; it is also a principle for communicating a common nature[2], because (it makes) a similar from a similar. But since nature in inferiors is numbered in supposits, for that reason it is a principle for distinguishing even (what is) common, but per accidens; but in God (generation) is neither per se nor per accidens.

2. To that which is objected, that 'to make the common to be in this' is a reason for appropriating; it must be said, that that has (its) truth, when the common is appropriable and/or appropriated through 'to be in this' [esse in hoc]. But the Divine Essence is not thus appropriable, and/or appropriated through a 'to be in this', because it is not appropriable in regard to the signified nor in regard to the Supposit, because it signifies and supposes the Same, just as has been shown above;[3]

but its signified is distinguished by no addition. For this is true: "the Essence of the Father and the Essence, which is in the Father, is the Son".

And/or it can otherwise be said, that 'to cause (something) to be in this' is in a twofold manner: either absolutely; and thus it is a reason for appropriating; or in comparison, as that which was first in one, afterwards comes to be [fit] in another; and thus it is a reason for communicating a nature. But there is a certain nature, which is distinguished[4] in supposits, as for example [ut puta] that (nature) to which an addition is made, (and there is) a certain one (that is) not, as in the Divine (Nature); and in the first there is a reason for communicating and of distinguishing, in the Divine solely (a reason) for communicating.

3. To that which is objected, that if it is communicated through generation, generation makes the Substance to be common;[5] it must be said, that it is true, according to which "the common" is said according to an act [secundum actum], because (it is) among several, but not according to potency [secundum potentiam]. Whence, with generation excluded, the Substance is common, because (it is) communicable; but It is not common, because (it is) communicated.

4. To that which is objected, that that which is given through generation, is generated; it must be said, that it is false: because 'to be generated' [generari] means a production and a distinction, but a 'being given' [datio][6] means an authorship and communication; and since through generation the Substance is not distinguished, though It is communicated: ergo etc..

SCHOLIUM

I. (Bl. John Duns) Scotus (here in q. 2) observes, that it is one thing 'to communicate something through generation', another 'to produce something through generation': for production introduces [infert] a real distinction between the one producing and the product, however, communication (does) not. Therefore, the Divine Essence is neither generated nor produced nor multiplied, however, according to all theologians it is communicated. The terminus of the whole generation in God is the Son, and the relation between the One generating and the One generated is real with a real distinction. But between the One communicat-

ing and the One communicated, because (each) is the Divine Essence, there is not a real relation, nor any distinction except according to reckoning. Cf. below d. 19, p. II, q. 2, in body, and at n. 2; and d. 34, q. 2, at n. 7, and ibid., q. 1.

II. Among the ancient Scholastics we have not found any who explicitly treat of this question, except Bl. (now St.) Albertus (Magnus), here in a. 1. — Henry of Ghent, SUMMA., a. 60, q. 1, n. 57 ff.. — Peter Aureolus, here in q. 5. — (Bl. John Duns) Scotus touches upon it, here in q. 2.

DOUBTS ON THE TEXT OF THE MASTER

DOUBT I

In this part there occur [incidunt] the doubts about the text, and the first doubt concerns Master (Peter's) reasons. For his first reason leads to this unfitting (conclusion), that is, that, if the Essence were generated by the Father, the Essence would be posited for a relative (term); and this reason is posited there (where he says): For that reason it must not be said, that the Father begot

the Divine Essence. But this seems (to be) nothing unfitting [inconveniens]. For if the Essence convenes more with a Supposit, than a universal (does) with a singular; if it is not unfitting, that a universal be posited[7] for a singular, neither is it unfitting, that the Essence be posited for a relative.

I RESPOND: It must be said, that if the Essence were posited for a relative (term), it would be unfitting [inconveniens], not on the part of the

---

[1] Codex O adds and procession [et processio].

[2] From the more ancient manuscripts we have inserted also [etiam], just as also a little below this, trusting in the manuscripts and edition 1, we have substituted similar [similem] in place of an exactly-similar [consimilem].

[3] Here in a. 1, q. 1, at n. 2.

[4] The Vatican edition has is divided [dividitur], but without the authority of any manuscript or edition 1. A little after this codex I has a certain one which is not distinguished [quaedam quae non distinguitur] in place of a certain one (that does) not [quaedam non], and then codex W after solely [solum] repeats a reason [ratio].

[5] Thus many codices, such as C L O S V W X Y etc., together with edition 1; but others, such as A F G H I T Z etc., read that if generation communicates a substance, it makes (it) common [quod si genera-

tion communicat substantiam, facit communem]. The Vatican edition has is communicated as a substance, there comes to be through generation a common substance [communicator substantia, fit per generationem communis substantia].

[6] The faulty reading of the Vatican edition, a 'being reckoned' [ratio] for a 'being given' [datio], we have corrected from the manuscripts and a little below this, trusting in codices B D F H I P Q T and Y, we have substituted and since [et quoniam] in place of because [quia], though other ancient codices, such as A E G K S W X Z ee and ff, together with edition 1 have solely since [quoniam], but less well.

[7] The Vatican edition together with codex cc reads when a universal is posited [cum universale ponitur], but less well and contrary to the other codices, some of which, however, having retained the particle that [quod], read is posited [ponitur] in place of be posited [ponatur].

of the thing, but on the part of the expression of the Faith. For then there would seem (to be) and to[1] be noted the Unity of the Essence in a certain distinction. It would also be unfitting [inconveniens], because what is posited for a relative inasmuch as (it is) of this kind, does not indicate an essence. Therefore[2] if the Essence would be posited for a relative, the Essence would sometimes not indicate the Essence, which is contrary to every reckoning.

DOUBT II

Likewise, second, there is a doubt [dubitatur] concerning (his) *second* reason, in which he leads (the reader) to this unfitting (conclusion), that the same thing would beget its very self, and (this) is posited, there (where he says): *Likewise, since God the Father is the Divine Essence, if He were its begetter, He would certainly* [utique] *be the begetter of that which He Himself is,* because "the *Essence*" means what (is) common, just as this noun "*God*" (does); but if there be said: "the man[3] Peter generates a man and he himself is the man: therefore, he generates himself", that argument of his is worth [valet] nothing. Similarly, does it seem here: "the Father generates God: therefore, etc.", for an equal reason neither (is it valid) in the proposed.

I RESPOND: It must be said, that "the *common*"[commune] is said (to be that) which it is in many; but this can be *in a threefold manner. either* because it is plurified in many, both as much as regards form and as much as regards supposit, as this noun, "*man*", (is); and such has a unity of reckoning, which admits a distinction both as much as regards thing and as much as regards the manner (of being regarded).[4] Whence a man is rightly said "to be from a man", and: (it is rightly said) "that there are two men". In *another* manner (something) is "*common*" because it is plurified as much as regards supposit, not as much as regards form, as this noun "*God*" (is); and such has a unity of thing, according to which the "thing" names "a nature with a multiplication of supposits": and for that reason it receives (something) distinctive,[5] which conveys a distinction as a manner (of being regarded), not as a thing. Whence there is conceded: "God from God", but not: "God is an Other than God". In a *third* manner (something) is "*common*" according to (its) name, which is in many (things), and yet it is not plurified as much as regards *form*, because it is "the one in the many", nor as much as regards (its) *supposits*, because it does not suppose on their behalf, as this noun, "*essence*", (does). Of such a common (thing) it is true to say, that it does not receive a dis-

tinction neither as much as regards a manner (of being regarded), nor as much as regards thing; for then there would be noted that the same is distinguished by the itself. And thus the argument of Master (Peter) is a good one: "if the Father begot the Essence, the Father begot Himself"; and[6] he speaks of the common on the part of the signifying word [vocis], not on the part of the thing, because on the part of the Thing the same commonality [communitas] is in This because It is "*God*" and in This because It is the "*Essence*".

DOUBT III

Likewise, third, there is the objection [obiicitur] against (his) *third* reason: if the Father begot the Divine Essence, then the Begotten is the cause for the One Begetting, to be and to be God, and (this) is posited there (where he says): *And if He is thus, the one begetting (is) not the cause* etc.. But this reason seems to be worth nothing, because the reckoning of cause does not occur among the divine; « for a cause is (that) of which it follows, that another is »;[7] but among the divine there is not another [aliud]: ergo etc..

Likewise, (this) does not follow: "the Father begot Wisdom: therefore, He is wise by the Wisdom begotten": therefore, for an equal reason neither is the aforesaid saying[8] valid.

I RESPOND: It must be said, that, taking the name for a cause in a proper (sense), it does not occur among the divine,[9] nevertheless [tamen] there does occur and there is received a reckoning of one beginning [principiantis] and a reckoning of one informing, and for these there is accepted the name of "cause". Therefore, since a reckoning of being [essendi] is signified through this name, "*essence*": for that reason "essence" signifies[10] in a certain manner in the reckoning of a cause in respect of a being [entis]. Therefore, if the Essence were begotten by a Being, It would signify in the reckoning of the effect or of One begun, and the Same would then be beginning and the begun in respect of the Same, which is impossible; and upon this (recognition) is founded (that) reason of Master (Peter).

To that which is objected concerning Wisdom; it must be said, that this has been touched upon in questions outside of the text,[11] because a name so abstract, as "*essence*" (is), does not suppose on behalf of a relative, (and) *wisdom* does suppose well on behalf of a relative; and thus there is a (fallacy of the) accident there (when it is argued): "the Father is wise by Wisdom and He begot Wisdom: therefore, He is wise by the Wisdom which He begot, and/or by the begotten Wisdom". But in the name of "*essence*" there is no accident, since it signifies and supposes the same (thing).

---

[1] Edition 1 reads *seem that there would* [videretur quod]; other codd., such as G U & dd, have *connoted* [connotaretur] for *noted* [notaretur].

[2] We give the better reading of the manuscripts and edition 1, which put *therefore* [ergo] in place of *for* [enim].

[3] The Vatican ed. has *in this manner* [hoc modo] in place of *man* [homo], this has been corrected from the mss. and the first six eddd. A little below this, the Vatican ed., against many codd., such as A C F G H I S T W etc., has *that ... not* [illud non] in place of *that ... of his ... nothing* [istud nihil].

[4] Supply: "of being regarded" [se habendi]. See above d. 4, doubt 1. — A little after this some codices, such as A B D F G H K etc., together with the Vatican edition have "*a man is by a man*" [homo est ab homine]. Concerning what is *common* in God and creatures, cf. below d. 19, p. II, q. 2; d. 23, a. 1, q. 3 and a. 2, q. 2.

[5] Codex T adds *according to* [secundum] well enough; not a few codd., suich as F G H K ee & ff, have *distinction* [distinctionem] for *(something) distinctive* [distinctivum], in which reading *which* [quod] , with codex H, must be taken as *that* [quia]. A little below this the mss., with edition 1, read *God to be an Other* [Deus esse alius] for "*God is an Other*" [Deus est alius]; codex O after *than God* [a Deo] adds *and/or (is) two gods.*

[6] The Vatican edition, not trusting in the manuscripts and edition 1 has *because* [quia] in place of *and* [et].

[7] In this commonly received definition of a cause, which can be gathered from Aristotle, PHYSICS, Bk. II, text 28-38 (ch. 3), METAPHYSICS, Bk. II, text 6 ff. (Bk. I, of the shorter version, ch. 2), METAPHYSICS, Bk. V, text 2-4 (Bk. IV, ch. 2), the Vatican edition here and elsewhere, contrary to the codices and edition 1, has *for a cause is (that) to whose 'being' there follows another* [causa enim est ad cuius esse sequitur aliud].

[8] We have substituted from the more ancient manuscripts and edition 1 *saying* [locutio] in place of *solution* [solutio].

[9] Cf. d. 29, a. 1, q. 1. — A little before this codex K after *for a cause* [causae] adds *of itself* [de se].

[10] The Vatican edition, contrary to many codices, such as A C F G H K L O S T U Y etc., and edition 1 has the passive voice *is signified* [signatur].

[11] Here in q. 1. — For more on this proposition of his: "wise by the begotten Wisdom" [sapiens sapientia genita], see d. 32, a. 2, q. 1 and Doubt 1 and 2. — A little below this from codex W we have inserted *wisdom does suppose well on behalf of a relative,* which certainly must be supplied and perhaps was omitted in the other manuscripts on account of the similar ending [communem desinentiam] of this and the preceding proposition *on behalf of a relative* [pro relativo]; and then, from the same codex W, we have added *there* [ibi].

DOUBT IV

Thus there also must not be said, that the Divine Essence begot the Son. Against this (Abbot) Joachim (of Fiore) objects, both against the *position* and against the *reckoning*. Against the *position*, because if the Essence does not generate nor is generated nor proceeds: therefore among the divine there is a Thing generating and begotten and proceeding, and a Thing not generating nor begotten nor proceeding; and thus there is There[1] a quaternity, (as) if there are four things.

Likewise, he mocks Master (Peter's) *reckoning*: 'if the Essence generates an essence, and the Essence is one thing: therefore, one Thing generates Its very self'. Similarly, (Abbot) Joachim says, « You could say, Peter: "God generates God, and[2] there is one God: therefore, the same Thing generates Its very self." »

I RESPOND: It must be said, that (Abbot) Joachim does not argue rightly, and his reckoning is deficient [deficit], because "thing" [res] is not accepted uniformly, because when "thing" is said in the first manner, there "thing" is accepted for "*a thing of nature*" [re naturae]; but when it is said[3] in the second manner, it is accepted for the Divine *Nature Itself*. *Moreover*, it is deficient by an insufficient (reckoning), because it is not valid (to argue thus): 'if anything is said of something,[4] and is not said of an other, that on this account they make a number'. Whence it is not valid (to argue thus): 'Peter is an individual: man is not an individual: therefore, Peter and man are two (things)'. For to have a property and not have (one) does not suffice to distinguish (two things).

Regarding his *opposed example* [instantiam] it must be said, that he does not rightly argue against it [instat]; because *the Essence* is one thing as much as regards supposit and signified; for it does not suppose the Persons; but "*God*" is one thing as much as regards the signified, but more as much as regards a Supposit. And for that reason (Abbot) Joachim reprehends Master (Peter) in an ignorant manner, and because,[5] since he was a simpleton [simplex], he did not revere Master (Peter), for that reason by the just judgement of God his little book [libellus] was condemned in the (Fourth) Lateran Council, and the position of Master (Peter) approved.[6]

DOUBT V

Likewise is asked concerning this which (St.) Hilary (of Poitiers) says: *The Son has nothing, but what He has accepted by being born.* Therefore there is asked concerning this word, "*He has accepted*", whether it means "(He accepted) *a substance*" and/or "*a relation*". If *a substance*: therefore, the Father similarly accepted; if *a relation*: therefore[7] since the Son accepted the Essence, the Essence is accepted: therefore, the Essence is referred.

I RESPOND: It must be said, that '*to accept*' [accipere] means two (things), that is, '*to have*' [habere] and '*to be* by an other' [esse ab alio]; as much as regards '*to have*' it respects the Essence; as much as regards this which is '*to be* by another', it respects a Person: whence through the verb for *being accepted* [accipiendi] there is signified, that the Essence is had by a Person, who is from an Other.[8]

DOUBT VI

Likewise is asked concerning this which he says: *And for that reason there is not referred to an other, what in One subsists out of One*, because it seems (to be) false; since the Son subsists by the Father, (but) however, He is referred to the Holy Spirit.[9]

I RESPOND: This can be understood in a twofold manner: in *one* manner, that the Son does not have a looking-back [respectum] except to one *Person*; and this is understood inasmuch as the Son, because inasmuch as He is one spirating [spirans], is referred to an Other; *and/or* that the Person of the Son does not have a looking-back except to one *Nature*; and this is true, because the Son does not have (anything) in Himself except the Nature of the Father.

DOUBT VII

Likewise is asked concerning this which he says: *Even His own Nature, as I thus call (it), does the unalterable God follow.* For among the divine there is not a prior nor a posterior, and thus neither a 'to precede' nor a 'to follow'. *If you say*, that there is (such) according to a reckoning of understanding; this is nothing, because God begetting, neither according to thing, nor according to the intellect, follows anything.[10]

I RESPOND: It must be said, that (St.) Hilary speaks improperly, and for that reason He adds a determination: *as I thus call (it)*; and He wants to say "*to follow*" only as much, as (it means) "*to be inseparably accompanied*"[11] and "*to thoroughly associate*" [consociare] and "*to not recede from him* [illo]", and this is clear through (what) follows.

DOUBT VIII

Likewise, is asked concerning the authorities of (St.) Augustine, first concerning this which he says, that *God once begot the Son*. For he seems badly to say *once* [semel], because "*once*" means a vicissitude; but in eternal generation no vicissitude occurs [non cadit]: ergo etc..

I RESPOND: It must be said, that "*once*" [semel] can mean the *now* of time [nunc temporis], and/or the *now* of eternity [nunc aeternitatis]. And, if he means the *now* of time, since time has diverse *nows*,

---

[1] The Vatican edition, disagreeing with the manuscripts and edition 1, transposes *There* [ibi] after *if there are* [si sunt].

[2] We have restores from the older manuscripts and edition 1 the particle *and* [et].

[3] We have substituted, on the testimony of not a few codd., V X and Y, and ed. 1, *it is said* [dicitur] in place of *is is accepted* [accipitur].

[4] The Vatican edition less well and contrary to the ancient manuscripts and edition 1 has *the other* [altero] in place of *something* [aliquo].

[5] The Vatican edition, not trusting in the manuscripts and edition 1, here omits *because* [quia], and a little below this in place of *for that reason* [ideo] it puts *and so* [et sic].

[6] See above a. 1, q. 1, in the Scholium.

[7] We have supplied from the manuscripts and edition 1 *therefore* [ergo], which the Vatican omits less well.

[8] Concerning these words of (St.) Hilary, cf. Alexander of Hales, SUMMA., p. I, q. 42, m. 3, a. 1, at n. 8.

[9] Trusting in the manuscripts we have added *Holy* [sanctum].

[10] The Vatican edition, contrary to very many codices and edition 1, has *an other* [aliud], and a little below this, contrary to the same, omits *It must be said* [dicendum].

[11] The Vatican edition has *to communicate and to harmonize* [communicare et consonare]; very many of the codd. have *to be communicated and to harmonize* [communicari et consonare]. But these words, on account of having been written in an abbreviated form in the codd. are often doubtful in reading and/or confounded with words received in our text. The verb *to be accompanied* [comitari] we have received from ed.1 and *to thoroughly associate* [consociare] from cod. Z. Then the Vatican ed. without the authority of the mss. and the first six edd. has *and through this the following is clear* [et per hoc patet sequens], but less well.

he notes a cut-off [intercisionem]; but if (he means) the *now* of eternity, and[1] that *now* always is both invariable and one, (then) *"once"* means an omnimodal invariability, perfection and unity.

DOUBT IX

Likewise is asked concerning this which he says: *of the Son of His charity*, whether "charity" [caritas] is accepted there *essentially*, or *notionally*. If *essentially*: therefore, Christ is the Son of the Essence, which is not conceded. *If you say*, that the saying is improper, and the sense is: *"of the Son, the Essence"*, that is, "of Him who is the Essence"; then it seems (to be) nonsense [nullus sensus], and for nothing (that there has)[2] been added this (word) which is *"of charity"* [caritatis]. And *again* (St.) Augustine expounds, *"of the Son of (His) charity"*, that is *"of (His) beloved Son"* [Filii dilecti]; but the Father loves [diligit] the Son by the Holy Spirit: ergo etc.. If on account of this *you say*, that it is held *notionally*; then the Son of God is therefore, the Son of the Holy Spirit, which is entirely absurd.

I RESPOND: Regarding[3] this some say, that that genitive ("of") is held neither properly essentially nor properly notionally, but in a middle manner, that is *appropriately*. For though charity be common to All and proper to the Holy Spirit, however, in one manner it appropriately befits the Father, because charity is gratuitous Love [amor gratuitus]; and thus Richard (of St. Victor) says, that gratuitous love is, "that which only gives and accepts nothing",[4] and this is in the Person of the Father, for that reason it is appropriated to the Father. In another manner it can be said, that "charity" there is held *essentially*, just as (St.) Augustine says, that[5] to say *"of the Son of (His) charity"* is nothing other than (to say) *"of the Son of (His) Substance"*; but the genitive is not construed in the reckoning of a principle, but from [ex] the force of the declaration of an essence,[6] and (thus) the sense is: *"of the Son of (His) charity"*, that is "of His dear Son"; and *"of the Son of (His) Substance and/or Nature"*, this is (to say), "of (His) consubstantial and natural Son".

DOUBT X

Likewise is asked concerning this which he says, that *the Son is from the Substance of the Father, homoousion* because — since among these inferior (creatures), a nat-

ural son draws part of (his) substance from [a] (his) father, part from (his) mother, and in God draws (His) whole Substance from the Father — it seems that the Father ought not only be called "a father", but also "a mother", and much more strongly "a mother", because a mother gives more than a father. *Likewise*, the Son of God calls Himself *"Wisdom"*, and a "Wisdom", which *"is conceived"* and *"given birth"* [parturitur], (as is written in) the eighth (chapter) of Proverbs.[7] Therefore, since this is proper to a mother, it seems that the Father more properly ought to be called "a mother" than "a father".

I RESPOND: It must be said, that the name of "mother" is not transferred to the divine. And (St.) Anselm assigns one reason (for this) in (his) MONOLOGION:[8] because a maternal principle demands before it [praeexigit] an other prior principle. And the reason for this is, that a mother is a passive principle, and every such (principle) is moved by an other: therefore before it there is an other principle. Therefore, since the Principle of the generation of the Son is the First and is purely actual, for that reason in no manner is a maternal principle transferred (into the divine); however there is transferred the maternal act, such as "to conceive" and "to give birth", for the reason that *there* one Principle acts, whereas [quod][9] *here* two (do).

DOUBT XI

Likewise is asked concerning this which he says, that *the Son and the Holy Spirit is not from nothing*. For it seems (to be) false, because that which is from no prejacent [praeiacente] matter, is from [de] nothing; but the Son and the Holy Spirit are of this kind: ergo etc.. *If you say*, that the Son and the Holy Spirit are from someone, as from the Father; then it is asked, whether the Father is out of nothing; and it seems that (He is) so, because *not anything* and *nothing* are convertible [convertuntur]; but the Father is not out of[10] something: therefore, He is out of nothing. *Likewise*, because the Father does not have an effective principle, for that reason He is said to be *by none* [esse a nullo]: therefore[11] since He does not have a matter, He ought to be said (to be) *from nothing*. If (this) is conceded concerning the Father; *on the contrary*: everything which has (its) "to be" from nothing, has been created:[12] ergo etc..

I RESPOND: It must be said, that when anything is said to be from nothing [esse de nihilo], according to (St.) Anselm in the MONOLOGION[13] (this) can be understood in a threefold manner. In *one manner*, so that

---

[1] The Vatican edition reads more clearly *since* [cum], which reading do all the codd. and ed. 1 withstand, as the form of the indicative (is employed) in the verb *is* [est]. A little below this, on the authority of very many codd. and ed. 1, we have expunged the *is* [est] prefixed to *invariable* [invariabile], and trusting in the mss. and ed. 1 we have substituted *invariability* [invariabilitatem] for *invariety* [invarietate]; the reading of the mss. is certainly to be preferred.

[2] The Vatican edition adjoins *there has* [est], but contrary to the more ancient codices and editions 1, 2 and 3. Codices R and X read *there is added* [additur]. A little below this after *that is* [id est] the Vatican edition, contradicting the older codices, omits *Son* [Filii]. The words of (St.) Augustine, ON THE TRINITY, Bk. XV, ch. 19, n. 27, are: of "of the Son of His charity", nothing other is understood, than "of His beloved Son".

[3] The Vatican edition, contrary to the more ancient codd. and ed. 1, has *that on account of* [quod propter] in place of *Regarding* [Ad].

[4] Thus the ancient codd. with ed. 1, while the Vatican ed. with the more recent cod. cc after *charity* [caritas] omits *is* [est] and then reads *and, as Richard (of St. Victor) says, because gratuitous love* [et sic dicit Richardus quia amor gratuitus]; finally, it reads *and does not accept* [et non accipit]. — See the text of Richard above in d. 2, q. 4.

[5] The Vatican ed. with codex cc reads *that* [quia] instead of *that* [quod], but the more ancient manuscripts and edition 1 are opposed.

[6] Concerning the signification of the *genitive*, see above d. 3, p. II. doubt 3. — Then the Vatican edition together with codex cc after *the sense is* [est sensus] adds *both* [et] and after *and/or* [vel] it inserts *even* [etiam], which particles are absent from the older manuscripts and edition 1.

[7] Verses 24-25. — A little before this the Vatican edition, contrary to the manuscripts and edition 1 has *He is the Wisdom, which* [sapientia est, quae] in place of *a Wisdom, which* [sapientiam, quae].

[8] Chapter 42: Because the first and principal cause of an offspring is in the father. For if in any manner the paternal cause always precedes the maternal: it is exceedingly incongruous, that there be adapted to that parent the name of "mother", with which to beget an offspring no other cause either associates nor does it precede. — Concerning the next reason see Aristotle, ON THE GENERATION OF ANIMALS, Bk. I, chs. 19 & 20 and Bk. II, ch. 4. — Not a few codd. after *an other* [aliud] omit *prior* [prius], and then the Vatican ed. with not a few mss. omits *And*, which we, trusting in many of the manuscripts and edition 1, have prefixed to the word *the reason* [ratio].

[9] The Vatican edition together with codex cc has *and* [et] in place of *whereas* [quod], but less well and contrary to the more ancient codices. For *there* understand: "in the generation of the Son".

[10] Some codices, such as aa bb dd and ff, together with edition 1, here and immediately afterward, read *from* [de] in place of *out of* [ex].

[11] The Vatican edition together with codex cc reads *in a similar manner* [simili modo] in place of *ergo* [therefore], which, however, the other codices together with edition 1 exhibit.

[12] From the mss. and ed. 1 we have substituted *has been created* [est creatum] for *is a creature* [est creatura]. The Vatican ed. without the authority of the mss. and ed. 1 adjoins such an argument: *Likewise, what is out of nothing, is vertible into nothing, ergo* etc. [Item quod est ex nihilo, est vertibile in nihilum ergo etc.]. [13] Chapter 8.

"nothing" is accepted simply privatively and/or negatively, as when there is said of one being silent: "that one speaks of nothing"; in *another manner* positively, as if thus there be said and/or[1] understood that something is made out of nothing, as "a knife from (formless) iron"; in a *third manner* partly positively, partly privatively, as if it be said that anything is made out of[2] nothing, (so) that after nothing there is something, just as it is said: "from a poor man he became a rich man".

Moreover, the reason for this multiplicity is this. For first it must be distinguished, that[3] the negation of that which is "*nothing*", can stand still *within* (this word), and/or be borne to this verb, "*to be made*". If it be borne to the verb, then "*to be made from nothing*" is this[4] "*not to be made from something*", just as "to speak of nothing", on that account is "(to speak) of no thing". But if it be not borne to the verb, then the "*to be made*" is affirmed; and then (the sense) is twofold, because "*from*" [de] can be understood *materially*; and then there is signified, that "the matter of something is nothing", and (in this manner) is had the second sense. *Likewise*, it can be held *in an ordered manner*, and then there is[5] a third sense, just as a creature is said "to be made from nothing".

Therefore, it must be said, that according to the first sense God can be said "to be from nothing", whether as the Father or as the Divine Essence; however, this manner (of speaking) is not usual [usitatus].

As much as regards the second manner, entirely nothing is made out of nothing, because nothing is the matter of nothing.[6] As much as regards the third manner, according to which (manner) (St.) Augustine speaks,[7] because a creature alone is made from nothing or is from nothing, because there "*from*" [de] notes an order, so that it has a 'to be' [esse] after a 'not to be' [non esse], for this (reason) that which is "*from nothing*" lacks [privat] a prejacent matter. Therefore although the Father and the Son and the Holy Spirit do not have a prejacent matter, yet, because they do not have a 'to be' after a 'not to be', for that reason they are not said "to be out of nothing" [esse ex nihilo]: and for that reason the first argument is not valid, because it proceeds by an insufficient (reckoning).

However, the second and third argument, made *concerning the Father*, proceeds, according to which the negation of that which is nothing, is borne outside to the verb and makes a negative statement [orationem negativam] — for otherwise '*not to be*[8] *from something*' [non esse de aliquo] and '*to be from nothing*' [esse de nihilo] are not equipollent — and according to this sense, just as it is conceded, that 'the Father be by *none*', thus (is He) '*from nothing*'. However, just as has been said, that sense is not usual; for commonly we use this saying, according to which the negation "*from nothing*" stands still within (the verb), and that which is "*from*" is accepted there *ordinally*.[9]

DISTINCTION VI

CHAPTER SOLE

Whether the Father by will begot the Son, or whether by necessity; and whether God is willing and/or unwilling.

Moreover, there is accustomed to be asked, "Whether the Father begot the Son by will, or whether by necessity?" Concerning this (St. Paulus) Orosius says to (St.) Augustine:[1] « Did the Father beget the Son by will and/or by necessity? Neither by will, nor by necessity, because necessity is not in God, (nor) can Will go before Wisdom ». « About which », as (St.) Augustine says in the fifteenth book, ON THE TRINITY,[2] « the dialectic of Eunomius is to be laughed at, from whom the Eunomian heretics have originated, he who, since he could not understand nor did he will to believe, that the Only-Begotten of God, the Word, is the Son of God by nature, that is, begotten from the substance of the Father, said that the Son was not of the Nature and/or Substance, but the Son of the Will of God, willing to assert an accident [accedentem] will to God, by which He begot the Son, just as we sometimes will something, which afterwards we not do not will; on account of which our nature is understood (to be) mutable, which (defect) far be it, that we believe it to be in God ». Therefore, let us say, that the Word of God is the Son of God "by nature", not "by will", as (St.) Augustine teaches in the fifteenth book, ON THE TRINITY,[3] where he commends a certain catholic responding to a heretic, saying: « Indeed he in an acutely sane manner responds to the heretic most cunningly interrogating (him), whether God willing or not willing begot the Son, so that if (the catholic) would say "*not willing*" [nolens], there would follow a most absurd misery for God; but if "*willing*", there would conclude continually what He was intending, that is that the Son is not of the Nature, but of the Will. But that most vigilant (catholic) in turn asked him [ab eo], whether God the Father is a willing, or an unwilling God, so that if he would respond "*unwilling*", there would follow a great absurdity and misery, which to believe of God is a great insanity [insania]; but if he would say "*willing*", he would respond

---

[1] The Vatican edition together with codex cc reads *or* [aut], but the more ancient codices together with edition one oppose this.

[2] Not a few codd., such as aa & bb, with edition 1 have *from* [de].

[3] From the ancient manuscripts and edition 1 we have substituted *that* [quod] in place of *that* [quia]. A little below this the Vatican edition together with codex cc has *and/or be borne outside to the verb* [vel extra ad verbum ferri] in place of *an/or be borne to this verb, "to be made"* [vel ferri ad hoc verbum fieri], but contrary to edition 1 and the rest of the codices, which only disagree among themselves in this, that in place of *be borne* [ferri] some, such as C L S U V aa and pp, put *outdoors* [foras], but others as A and W have *outside* [extra], codex O has *be borne outdoors* [foras ferri], finally others, such as G H I K R T X Z dd ee and ff, together with edition 1 exhibit our text.

[4] Very many codices together with edition 1 have *is this* [hoc est] in place of *is* [est], which the Vatican edition has.

[5] The Vatican edition, disagreeing with the mss. and ed. 1, has *there is had* [habetur] in place of *there is* [est]. Then very many codd. with ed. 1 have *just as* [sicut] in place of the *and thus* [et sic] of the Vatican ed..

[6] In the Vatican edition and in codex cc there is wanting these words, *because nothing is the matter of nothing* [quia nihil nullius est materia], which are however, had in the other manuscripts and edition 1.

[7] AGAINST MAXIMINUS, Bk. II, ch. 14, n. 2, and ON ACTS WITH FELIX THE MANICHAEAN, Bk. II, ch. 18 and ON THE NATURE OF THE GOOD AGAINST THE MANICHEANS, ch. 26.

[8] The Vatican edition, disagreeing with the manuscripts and edition 1, transposes *to be* [esse] before *not* [non], and a little after this, contrary to the more ancient codices and edition 1, after *even* [et] omits *to be*. Then after *thus* [ita], the Vatican edition alone adds, for the sake of clarity, *(also) that He be* [quod sit].

[9] We have supplied from the manuscripts and edition 1 *there* [ibi]. — For more concerning this matter, see above a. 1, q. 2. — The same doctrine, has Alexander of Hales, SUMMA., p. I, q. 42, m. 4. a. 1. — St. Thomas, here in q. 2, a. 2; and SUMMA., I, q. 41, a. 3. — Bl. (now St.) Albertus (Magnus), here in a. 10. — (Bl.) Peter of Tarentaise, here in q. 3, a. 2. — (Bl.) Dionysius the Carthusian, here in q. 2, at the end.

NOTES ON THE BOOK OF SENTENCES

[1] THE DIALOGUE OF 65 QUESTIONS, q. 7, in which text the Vatican edition after the first *by necessity* [necessitate] adds *but* [sed], and at the end puts *could* [could] in place of *can* [potest], but contrary to the codices and editions 1 and 6 and the original of (St.) Augustine.

[2] Chapter 20, n. 38, but with not a few things added; in this text codex C has *antecedent* [antecedentem]; the edition of (St.) Augustine's works has *accident* [accidentem] in place of *accident* [accedentem].

[3] Ibid.. — A little before this the Vatican edition after *not by will* [non voluntate] alone adjoins *nor by necessity* [neque necessitate].

to him: "And therefore, He Himself[1] is God by His own will, not by nature". Therefore, what remained, except for [ut] him to become dumb, seeing himself tied up [obligatum] with an insoluble chain by his own interrogation »? From the aforesaid there is taught, that it must not be conceded, that God by will and/or by necessity, willing and/or unwilling, is God; likewise, that He by will and/or by necessity, willing and/or not willing, begot the Son.

But against this there is thus opposed: 'The Will of God is the Nature or the Essence of God, because for God the 'to be' is not one thing, 'to will' the other; and for that reason, just as there is one Essence of Three Persons, so also one Will. Therefore, if God by nature is God, He is also by will God; and if the Word of God by nature is the Son of God, He is also by will the Son of God.' But this is easy to refute [refellere]. For both the Foreknowledge [praescientia] or Knowledge [scientia] of God, by which He knows [scit] and/or foreknows [praescit] (things) good and evil, is the Divine Nature or Essence; and the His predestination or Will is the same Divine Essence, nor is 'to know' [scire] and/or[2] 'to will' for God other than 'to be'. And though one and the same (thing) be the Knowledge and/or Will of God, nevertheless [tamen], there is not said of the Will, whatever is said of the Knowledge, and conversely. Nor does God by His own Will will all those (things), which He knows by His own Knowledge, since by His own Knowledge He knows [noverit] good as much as evil (things), but by Will He does not will except the good (things). Indeed the Knowledge and Foreknowledge of God is of (things) good and evil, but the Will and predestination is only of (things) good; and, nevertheless [tamen], in God one and the same (thing) is the Knowledge and the Will, and the Foreknowledge and the predestination. Thus, though one be the Nature and Will of God, the Father is, nevertheless [tamen], said to have begotten the Son by nature, not by will, and that God is by nature, not by will.

The aforesaid words, however, by which it has been prudently said, that God the Father is neither a "willing" nor an "not willing God", neither as One willing nor as One not willing begot the Son, whether by will or[3] by necessity, seem to me (are) to be accepted in [ex] such a sense, that we do not understand a precedent and/or accedent Will, in the manner that [qualiter] Eunomius understood it. For He Himself is not God[4] by a precedent and/or efficient Will, and/or as One willing, before (He was) God; nor by a precedent and/or accedent will did He beget the Son, nor first willing then generating did He beget the Son,[5] nor first generating then willing did He beget the Son. However, as One willing He did beget, just as One able He begot and as One good He begot and as One wise He begot and (as One) of this kind. For, if the Father, wise and good, is said "to have begotten the Son", why not as One willing? since thus it is that for God it is the same (to be) willing, as it is to be God; just as it is the same to be wise, as to be God. Therefore, let us say, that the Father as one Wise, thus willing begot the Son, but not by a precedent and/or accedent will. Which sense (St.) Jerome manifests [aperit] and confirms, thus saying ON THE EPISTLE TO THE EPHESIANS:[6] « Concerning the Son of God, that is, Our Lord Jesus Christ, it was written, that "He was always" with the Father, and that never did the paternal Will precede Him, so that He would be; and He indeed is (His) Son by nature ».

Brief Note. (St.) Hilary in the book, ON SYNODS, (says):[7] « Those, who say, that the Son of God is from non-extant (things), similarly, (those) who say, that the Father neither by counsel nor by will begot the Son, the Holy Church anathematizes. Likewise, if anyone says that the Son (has) been born by a not-willing Father, anathema sit. For not with the Father not willing, did the Father, coerced [coactus] and/or lead by natural necessity, since He was not willing, beget the Son, but as soon as He willed, He, without time and in an impassible manner, showed forth [demonstravit] the Only-Begotten out of Himself ».

COMMENTARY ON DISTINCTION VI

On the comparison of the act of generating to the power.

Moreover, there is accustomed to be asked, "Whether the Father begot the Son by will etc.".

THE DIVISION OF THE TEXT

In this part of his (text), Master (Peter) posits doubts emerging from a comparison of the act of generating *to the power* (of generating). And, since he happens to compare[1] the act of generating to the power, and the power of generating to the Supposit, from each comparison there also occurs [incidit] a doubt about the Unity of the Essence: for that reason *first* he posits a doubt from the comparison of the act of generating to the power; second he posits a doubt from the comparison of the power of gener-

ating to the Person, below in the Seventh Distinction (where he says): *Here one is accustomed to be asked by certain (men), whether the Father etc.*.

Likewise, the *first* part, which contains the present distinction, has four smaller parts [particulas]. In the *first*, Master (Peter)[2] proposes the question, whether the power and/or virtue of generating is one producing by necessity, and/or by will, and he determines the truth of this question. *Second*, regarding that question of his, he responds to the man

---

[1] Codices A B C and D omit *and ... Himself* [et ipse], which however, is had in the edition of (St.) Augustine's works. A little below this the Vatican edition, contrary to all the codices and editions 1, 8 and the original has *indissoluble* [indissolubili] in place of *insoluble* [insolubili].

[2] The Vatican edition, disagreeing with the codices and editions 1 and 8, has *and* [et].

[3] Codices A B C and editions 1 and 8 have *and/or* [vel]. Next editions 2, 3, 5, 9 and 10 omit *to me* [mihi]. Then codex A has (a negative purpose clause) *so that ... neither* [ut nec] in place of (a clause of fearing) *ut* [lest]; in codex B there is read *so that ... not* [ut non], the sense of these is the same.

[4] The Vatican edition contrary to codices B C D E and editions 1 and 8, having transposed the words, has less well *He Himself is ... God* [ipse Deus est].

[5] Editions 1 and 8 omit *did He beget the Son* [genuit Filium]. A little below this after *good He begot* [bonus genuit] the Vatican edition contrary to the codices and editions 1 and 8 has *the Son* [Filium].

[6] (Commenting) on chapter 1, verse 5. — All the codices and editions read *(St.) Augustine* [Augustinus] in place of *(St.) Jerome* [Hieronymus]. In which text the Vatican alone, together with the original, after *that is* [id est] adds *concerning* [de] and then after *Christ* it adjoins *in another passage* [in alio loco], namely Ecclesiasticus 1:1.

[7] Number 39, I, and n. 58, XXV. — In codex A, in regard to this Brief Note there is added: *and for (the reason) that Master (Peter) had not proven, that the Father has begotten the Son by will, for that reason this note has been placed (here)* [et qua Magister non probaverat, Patrem genuisse Filium voluntate, ideo haec nota posita est]. This Brief Note has been placed in the Vatican edition and in the other editions on the margin, and in editions 5 and 6 in the body of the text.

NOTES ON THE COMMENTARY

[1] The Vatican edition together with some manuscripts reads *it happens that the act of generating is compared* [contingit comparari ...].

[2] From the manuscripts and edition 1 we have supplied *Master (Peter)* [Magister].

by arguing against (him),[1] there (where he says): *Therefore, let us say, that the Word of God is the Son of God. Third,* however, he opposes (reasons) against the aforesaid solution and responds, there (where he says): *But against this it is thus opposed: the Will of God* etc.. *Fourth* and last,

he returns to an explanation of the first solution, there (where he says): *However, the aforesaid words, by which it has been prudently said,* where he explains the afore-had solution.

TREATMENT OF THE QUESTIONS

ARTICLE I

On the generation of the Son according to its conditions.

For a clear indication [evidentiam] of this part, three (things) are principally asked.

First, there is asked, whether the generation of the Son is according to a condition of necessity.

Second, whether it is according to a reckoning of will.

Third, whether (it is) according to a condition of exemplarity.

QUESTION I

Whether the generation of the Son is according to a reckoning of necessity?

About the first, that generation is according to a condition of *necessity,* is shown thus:

1. More fecund and actual is the Nature in the Father to produce the Son, than is (the nature) in light to produce a ray; but it is necessary that (there is) light to produce a ray, so that production in it is according to a condition of necessity: therefore much more strongly (is such a condition) in the Father in respect of the Son.

2. Likewise, everything which emanates from an other,[2] emanates according to a condition of necessity, or of contingency; therefore, even the Son emanates by one [altero] of those two manners; but not according to a condition of contingency, because then it would be contingent that the Son is generated: ergo etc..

3. Likewise, to detract from an omnipotent the maximum '*to be able*' [posse] is impossible; but God the Father is the Omnipotent, whose maximum '*to be able*' is to generate the Son: therefore, to detract from him a '*to be able to generate the Son*' is impossible. But among eternals potency [potentia] has been conjoined to act:[3] therefore, for an equal reason it is impossible to bear away an *act* of generation: therefore, it is impossible that He not generate; but the '*impossible not to be*' and the '*to be necessary*' are convertible [convertuntur]: therefore, it is necessary that He generate.

ON THE CONTRARY: 1. (St.) Augustine (says) To Orosius, and (as) Master (Peter) says in the text:[4] « Neither by will nor by necessity did the Father beget the Son, because necessity is not in God »: ergo etc..

2. Likewise, (St.) Hilary in the book, ON SYNODS:[5]

« Not led by natural necessity did the Father beget the Son »: therefore, there was not There a the natural necessity nor an other necessity, as there seems (in the fundament); ergo etc..

3. Likewise, more nobly producing is that which dominates its own action, than that which is subject [subiacet] to the action; but one acting according to a reason of necessity is subject to the action, because whether it wants to or not, it must do it [quia velit nolit oportet ipsum facere]: therefore, if[6] the Father, who is the Most Noble Agent, in a most noble manner produces the Son, therefore not according to a condition of necessity.

4. Likewise, this same can be shown thus: that what is given freely [gratis], is not given from necessity; but Richard (of St. Victor)[7] says, that in the Father there is a gratuitous love, because He gives 'Being' [esse] to the Son and to the Holy Spirit: if therefore, He gives freely, (then) not in a necessary manner.

CONCLUSION

Generation among the divine is necessary by a necessity of immutability, not however, by an other species of necessity.

I RESPOND: For an understanding of the aforesaid it must be noted, that necessity is multiple. For there is a certain necessity provenient out of a *unfitting* principle [principio disconveniente], a certain one (is) out of a *deficient* principle [principio deficiente], a certain one out of a *fitting* and *sufficient* principle [principio conveniente et sufficiente].

That[8] which comes forth out of a *unfitting* principle,

---

[1] The Vatican edition reads *he responds to the heretical man by arguing* [ad haereticum hominum arguendo], but the manuscripts and edition 1 are opposed.

[2] Not a few codices as K W X Y and ee have *something* [aliquo] in place of *an other* [alio].

[3] Aristotle, PHYSICS, Bk. III, text 32 (ch. 4): For "to be able" differs nothing from "to be by itself" among perpetuals. — A little below this after *to bear away* [auferre] codex O adds *from it* [ei]. — Concerning the conversion of these propositions regarding the manners "*impossible not to be*" and "*to be necessary*" cf. Aristotle, ON INTERPRETATION, Bk. II, ch. 3 (ch. 13) and concerning the relation among omnipotence and the power of generating see below d. 7, q. 14.

[4] At the beginning of this distinction.

[5] Number 58, XXV: For not with the Father non-willing, did the Father, driven and/or lead by natural necessity, since He was not willing, beget the Son.

[6] The Vatican edition, disagreeing with the more ancient manuscripts and edition 1, has *simply* [simpliciter] in place of *if* [si]. A little before this at *action* [actioni] codex O adjoins *its own* [suae].

[7] ON THE TRINITY, Bk. V, ch. 17-19, in which under the first heading he says: Moreover, He shows that He regards Himself as gratuitous love, who to Those proceeding from Himself He pays out [impendit] an abundance of His plenitude broadly as much as liberally and gratis. — And under the last heading summarizing what has been said, he says: For it is established, that in One of the Three (Divine Persons) there is a most high and only gratuitous love; however, in the Other a most high etc.. — The Vatican edition next has *whereby* [quo] in place of *because* [quia], but contrary to the manuscripts and edition 1, and at the end of the argument at *(then) not* [non] it reads *(then) he does not give* [non dat].

[8] In the Vatican edition and codex cc there is added *Moreover* [autem].

is twofold: for either (the necessity) is out of (a principle) moving contrary to *nature*, and this is the necessity of *violence*; or contrary to the *will*, and that is the necessity of *coaction* (i.e. compulsion);[1] and concerning those two manners, which are very usual, the heretic asks.

Similarly, that, which is out of a *deficient* principle, is two fold: for either it is in respect of that, by which a thing is bound [est nata] to be completed; and this is the necessity of *indigence*, as (is) food and drink; concerning this there is said in the third (chapter) of the First (Letter) of (St.) John:[2] *He who sees his brother suffering a necessity* etc.; or in respect of that, which it incurs out of the defect itself; and this is the necessity of *inevitability*, which is in death and in first movements [primis motibus]; a man incurs this necessity out of a lack of original justice, (as) the Psalm (says):[3] *From my necessities snatch me.*

Similarly, the third, which is out of a *sufficient* and *fitting* principle, is twofold: for either it is out of a principle sufficient in *disposing*, and this is the necessity of disposed matter, which can be called the necessity of *exigency*; or in *completing*, and this is the necessity of immutability.[4]

And this last[5] necessity occurs [cadit] in God, and principally in God, because He Himself alone is (the One) who is entirely sufficient for Himself and who entirely convenes with Himself. Moreover, this necessity is not repugnant to liberty of the will, but only to the vertibility, of the kind that is not in God.

1. To that which is objected concerning the *text*, it must be said, that that is understood of the necessity of coaction, which in no manner occurs [cadit] in God,[6] and concerning this the heretic was asking.

2. Similarly, (St.) Hilary also understands concerning this same (necessity), whence he also adds [subdit][7] in (his) text: *not by a natural necessity, since He is not willing*; for then there would be coaction There, so long as the will is repugnant (to it).

3. To that which is objected, that one acting through necessity is subject to its own action; it must be said, that it is false, unless there is a necessity repugnant to the will. For when there is a repugnant necessity, it is necessary that the will be subjected, because it cannot prevail. But when there is a necessity most highly consonant, unable of being in discord [non potens discordare] from the will, then it induces no subjection, as is clear. For[8] God necessarily is blessed and necessarily wants to be blessed; and just as it is a necessary, that He Himself be blessed, so also that He want (to be such); so must it be understood in the generation of the Son.

4. To that which is last[9] objected concerning gratuitous love, it must be said, that there are two in gratuitous love: the *one* is, which gives out of undiluted [mera] liberality, so that there is no exigency or debit of merit and/or of nature; the *other*, which[10] gives without retribution, and as much it regards this the second is called gratuitous love in the Father, not as much as regards the first. For the natural fecundity of the Father necessarily is the reason for communicating the Nature to an Other.

SCHOLIUM

I. In regard to generation itself among the divine, cf. below d. 9 throughout. — The same distinctions of *necessity*, explained in another manner, the Seraphic Doctor has in a certain disputed question, heretofore unpublished: *"Whether the Divine 'Being' is the most highly Necessary?"*, from which we insert this these (words): « There is a threefold necessity: a certain one *entirely extrinsic*, a certain one *partly extrinsic, partly intrinsic*, and a certain one *entirely intrinsic*. A necessity entirely extrinsic is that which has arisen from a principle, which is outside, enduring nothing as a cooperator; and this has (an ability) to be in a twofold manner, either in respect of natural works, and/or in respect of voluntary works; and, thus, there is a twofold necessity, that is of *violence* and of *coercion* [coactionis]. However, the necessity partly within [intra], partly outside [extra] is, that which in some manner is by an intrinsic principle looking-back to something outside and/or through a manner of a moving principle, and/or through the manner of the terminus of one resting; and in this manner is the said twofold necessity, that is of *inevitability* and of *indigence*. However, there is a certain necessity entirely intrinsic, which is in a thing out of its own nature; and this is the necessity of *immutability* and of independence, and such a ne-

cessity is discovered in a creature 'according to something' [secundum quid], but simply (speaking) it cannot be discovered except in the creating Essence. For It alone is, That which does not admit any dependence; but all the rest, since they have been created, necessarily depend from [ab] It. Moreover, this necessity necessarily is posited in the Divine 'Being' [in esse divino], because It is in Its very self and by Its very self » etc..

That last species of necessity, which the Seraphic Doctor calls the necessity of *immutability*, is to be understood in the absolute sense, so that its opposite is simply impossible. This had to be noted for this reason, because some doctors accept the necessity of immutability in another manner, namely for that by which something, thus, has to be, so that the opposite also can be, but not simultaneously with its own opposite (cf. Brülifer on this passage). — Concerning the various divisions of necessity, cf. St. Bonaventure, SENT., Bk. II, d. 7, p. I, a. 2, q. 2, at n. 3; and ibid., d. 25, p. II, q. 2 in the body; SENT ., Bk. III, d. 12, a. 2, q. 1, at n. 5.

II. In regard to the conclusion itself cf. Alexander of Hales, SUMMA., p. I, q. 42, m. 5, a. 1. — (Bl. John Duns) Scotus, here in q. 1, and REPORTATIO, here in q. 3. — St. Thomas, here in q. 1, a. 1; SUMMA., I, q. 42, a. 2. — Bl. (now St.) Albertus (Magnus), here

---

[1] Concerning this twofold necessity cf. Aristotle, ETHICS, Bk. III, ch. 1 and MAGNA MORALIA, Bk. I, chs. 11-16 (chs. 12-17). — A little before this from the older manuscripts and edition 1 we have supplied *that* [ista]. — Concerning the heretic, whom the Seraphic Doctor introduces at this point, see the text of Master (Peter) at this point.

[2] Verse 17, in which text the Vulgate in place of *suffering* [patientem] reads *that your brother has a necessity* [fratrem suum necessitatem habere].

[3] Psalm 24:17.

[4] Cf. Aristotle, PHYSICS, Bk. I, text 81 (ch. 9), where he deals with the natural appetite for matter in respect of form; and METAPHYSICS, Bk. V, text 6 (Bk. IV, ch. 5), where besides the necessity of immutability he proposes the other species of necessity, which have been touched upon in the preceding (points).

[5] The Vatican edition together with codex cc, disagreeing with the more ancient manuscripts and edition 1, reads *And in this last manner* [Et hoc ultimo modo], and a little below this after *is (the One) who* [est qui] less

aptly repeats *principally* [principaliter]. At the end of the body (of the response) codex T together with very many others after *of the kind that* [qualis] omits *not* [non], which reading is explained by the reading of codex R *wherefore (this necessity) it is in God* [quare est in Deo].

[6] The Vatican ed. against the mss. and ed. 1 has *unto God* [in Deum].

[7] We have substituted from the mss. and ed. 1 *he also adds* [et subdit] in place of *he subjoins* [subiungit]. — The text of (St.) Hilary has been exhibited in its entirety above in the 2nd arg. to the *Contrary*.

[8] Trusting the manuscripts and ed. 1 we have inserted *For* [enim].

[9] The Vatican edition with codex cc omits *last* [ultimo] here, and a little below this, after *gives* [dat], has *by undiluted liberality* [mera liberalitate], but the more ancient codices with edition 1 are opposed.

[10] From very many mss. and edition 1 we have substituted *which* [quod] in place of *because* [quia]. Near the end of the solution the Vatican edition, not trusting in the more ancient mss. and ed. 1, omits *natural* [Naturalis], and at the end *to the Other* [alii]. Edd. 2, 3, 4, 5 & 6, with codex cc read *For the fecundity of the Father's Nature* [Naturae enim fecunditas Patris], and also omit *to the Other* [alii] at the end.

in a. 1; SUMMA., p. I, tr. 7, a. 30, m. 3, a. 2. — (Bl.) Peter of Tarentaise, here in q. 1, a. 1. — Richard of Middleton, here in q. 1. — Giles of Rome, here in the 1st princ. of q. 1 and 2. — Henry of Ghent, on this and the following q., SUMMA., a. 54, q. 3, n. 45 ff.. — Durandus (of Saint-Pourçain), here in q. 1. — (Bl.) Dionysius the Carthusian, on this and the following, here in q. 1. — (Gabriel) Biel, on this and the following, here in q. 1.

QUESTION II

Whether generation among the divine is according to a reckoning of will?

Second, there is asked, whether the generation of the Son is according to a reckoning of *will*. And that (it is) not, is shown[1] first through *authorities*, second through *reasons*.

First, it is shown through the *authority* of (St.) Hilary, who says in the book, ON SYNODS:[2] « To all creatures the Will of God brings substance, but to the Son the Nature (of God) gives (substance) ».

2. Likewise, (St.) Augustine in the fifteenth (book) ON THE TRINITY[3] reprehends Eunomius, who posited that the Son of God is a Son of the Will: therefore, if he rightly reprehended (him), (then) the generation of the Son is not according to the condition of the Will.

3. Likewise, *by reasons* it is thus shown: Generation, as much as it is from itself, is a natural going-forth [exitus] or (a going forth) through a manner of nature; but that (generation) of His[4] is a manner of producing other than through will: therefore, etc..

4. Likewise, the Son is the Wisdom of the Father: therefore, if He proceeds according to a reckoning of the Will, the Will is prior to Wisdom; but this is unfitting, because cognition according to the natural order[5] of understanding precedes affection or will: ergo etc..

BUT ON THE CONTRARY: 1. In every nature the ordinate natural power is subject to the will, and/or is at least conformed to the will, as is clear in the first man; but in God there is a most ordinate Nature: therefore, nothing is by the Nature and/or through the Nature, which is not through the Will: ergo etc..

2. Likewise, completely similar [consimilis] is the manner of proceeding in a created image[6] and in the uncreated Trinity; but in the image knowledge [notitia] arises by means of the will by the mind: therefore, also the Son by the Father by means of the Will or through the Will. The *minor* is clear through (St.) Augustine in the ninth (book) ON THE TRINITY:[7] « The mind's giving birth does the appetite precede, by which while we, (after) having sought it, are finding what we will to know [nosse], there is born the offspring, knowledge [notitia] itself ».

3. Likewise, where there is greater communication, there is greater liberality; but the Father communicates more to the Son than to all creatures: therefore, there is a greater liberality There: therefore, since creatures proceed through a manner of liberality, much more (does) the Son, and so etc..

4. Likewise, among[8] creatures, nature and will move simultaneously in the act of generation, and nothing of [ex] this derogates from a son: therefore, if the Father produces a Whole more according to Himself than a creature (does): therefore, much more strongly through the Nature and the Will.

5. Likewise, in this regard [ad hoc] there is the authority of (St.) Hilary in the third (book) ON THE TRINITY:[9] « The Father before all time procreated the Son, imparting all that is God through the charity of His nativity »; if through charity: therefore, through Will.

6. Likewise, Origen speaking of the Divine Mind says: « Proffering an offshoot [germen] of (His) Will He becomes Father of the Word »:[10] therefore, it seems, that the Son is generated by the Father through the Will and that He is a Son of the Will.

CONCLUSION

The generation of the Son is according to the Will as in the reckoning of one approving, not however, as in the reckoning of one producing, except to the extent that the Will is a principle conjoined to the Nature and, indeed, thus, that the Nature produces principally, with the concomitant Will.

I RESPOND: It must be said, that the Will can be considered in a twofold manner in respect of the willed [voliti], that is, as in the reckoning of *one approving* and loving [diligentis]; and thus it is in respect of every good, whether it be necessary or whether it be[11] contingent, whether created or uncreated or from an other

---

[1] Trusting in the older manuscripts and edition 1, we have put *is shown* [ostenditur] in place of *is seen* [videtur].

[2] Number 58, XXIV: To all creatures the Will of God has brought substance, but to the Son a perfect nativity has given a Nature out of the impassible and not-born Substance. From these words it is clear, that the latter part of the proposition, is cited alleged by St. Bonaventure only in regard to (its) sense.

[3] Chapter 20, n. 38. See his words here in the text of Master (Peter), near its beginning. — At the end of the argument the Vatican edition with codex cc has *reckoning* [rationem] in place of *condition* [conditionem], but the rest of the codices together with edition 1 are opposed.

[4] We have substituted with the help of the more ancient mss. and edition 1 *that (generation) of His* [iste] in place of *that (going-forth)* [ille].

[5] Thus the older codices together with edition 1, but the Vatican edition together with codex cc has *reckoning* [rationem] in place of *natural order* [naturalem ordinem].

[6] The Vatican edition with codex cc has *of producing in a created trinity* [producendi in trinitate creata] in place of *of proceeding in a created image* [procedendi in imagine creata], but contrary to the rest of the codices and ed. 1, and contrary also to the subjoined, which deals always with a *manner of proceeding*. A little below this after *therefore* [ergo] we have restored from the more ancient mss. and ed. 1 the particle *also* [et].

[7] Chapter 12. See above d. 3, p. II, a. 2, q. 2, 1st opposed argument.

[8] Trusting in the more ancient manuscripts and edition 1, we have expunged the *existing* [existentibus], which the Vatican edition, together with codex cc, had less aptly added here. A little below this, codex O has *the generation of a son* [generationi filii] in place of *a son* [filio].

[9] Number 3: Therefore, this Unbegotten before all time begot the Son out of Himself, not out of some underlying matter ... but incomprehensibly, ineffably, before all time and ages. The Only-Begotten, did He, out of those (things) which were unbegotten in Himself, procreate, imparting all that is God through the charity and virtue of His nativity.

[10] These words are reported by (St.) Pamphylus, Martyr, among the fragments of Origin's COMMENTARY ON ST. JOHN, tome II, under n. 30, in the edition of Migne (PATROLOGIA GRAECA, tome XIV, col. 184), according to which edition, in place of *becomes* [fit] there is had *has become* [factus est]. — The Vatican edition places this and the preceding argument immediately after the first one, but contrary to the manuscripts and less well on account of the confusion (this causes), that is, of the arguments from *reason* and *authority*.

[11] In very many manuscripts and edition 1 *it be* [sit] is lacking.

or not from an other, as is clear; for this is true: 'the Father wills, that He Himself is God'.[1] In *another manner* (the will) is considered as in the reckoning of *one producing*. And this in a twofold manner: either insofar as it is a principle *distinguished* [distinctum] against nature, according to which there is said, that some (things) are by[2] nature, some by will; or insofar as it is *conjoined* (to nature).

If, insofar as it is a *distinguished* principle, the will is distinguished in a twofold manner, that is, (as) *one acceding* and (as) *one anteceding*. An *accident* will is (that), by which someone from not willing becomes willing; this is not in God, neither in respect of God nor in respect of a creature.[3] For God does not have some new Will neither in respect of Himself nor in respect of the Other. An *antecedent* will precedes the effect by causality and duration; this indeed is in God, but not in respect of God, but solely in respect of the creature; for the Divine Persons are all simultaneous.

In *another manner*, insofar as the will is considered as a principle *conjoined* to nature, it can be in a twofold manner; because then nature and will are the principle; therefore either Nature is producing *principally*, with a concomitant Will,[4] or *conversely*; for both cannot be (producing) principally.

If the Will is the principle, with concomitant Nature, thus there is the procession of the Holy Spirit, who proceeds through a manner of love [amoris], yet however, [tamen] similar in nature. However, if Nature is the first[5] principle, with a concomitant Will, thus there is the generation of the Son, who is produced as One entirely similar and through a manner of nature, nevertheless as the Beloved [dilectus]; and for that reason it is said, that *the Father thoroughly pleases*[6] Himself in Him,

and in the first (chapter of St. Paul's Letter) to the Colossians there is said: *the Son of (His) charity*.

1. 5. 6. To that which is objected in the contrary, that generation is through a manner of will or according to a reckoning of will; it must be said, that this is understood either of an approving will, as the two authority of (St.) Hilary and Origin show, or of a concomitant will,[7] as the reason, which is posited first, (shows).

2. To that, however, which is objected concerning the similitude of the image; it must be said that in this the created image is dissimilar to the Trinity Itself,[8] because There there is not born a word through a search [inquisitionem], as it can be born in us; whence it is rather valid for the opposite than for the proposed.

3. To that which is objected, that greater is the communication in the generation of the Son etc.; it must be said, that a greater and/or lesser communication does not cause [facit] a manner of emanating to be according to liberality and/or according to a manner of will, but a manner or reason for communicating (does). And because the Father communicates *to creatures* through Will, so that His Will is the producing Cause, (and) *to the Son*[9] through a fecundity of Nature: for that reason the Son is not said to be produced through the Will in the same manner, as creatures.

4. To that which is objected,[10] that in the generation of man nature and will move simultaneously; it must be said, that this is on account of a defect rather than on account of a complement; because a father by himself [per se] cannot generate, but (he can) out of conjunction with a different other [alio distante], which comes to be at the command [imperium] of the will; but God does not need another helping (Him); and for that reason it is not similar.

SCHOLIUM

I. Concerning the diverse manners of *willing*, which are here touched upon, the Seraphic (Doctor) in the unpublished, disputed question: *Whether the Trinity and Most High Necessity stand together*, has this (to say): « There is an *accident* will, i. e. arriving from (something) new; and this is not in God, neither in respect of Himself nor in respect of (something) created, on account of the immutability and necessity of God. Again there is an *antecedent* will; and this is in God, but not in respect to Himself, but in respect to the created, which He (Himself) antecedes by Nature and eternity. Third, there is a *concomitant* and *accepting* will; and this is in God in respect of Himself and in respect of the created; for the Divine Will approves and accepts every good whether created or uncreated, whether contingent or necessary. Therefore, having spoken of necessity and will in a threefold manner, the each third manner is suitable [competit] to the Most High Trinity, namely *an acceptable will* and

a necessity of immutability*: I say an "acceptable will" on account of the most high clarity in the One producing and a most high goodness in the One produced, which two (qualities) necessarily close (with) in themselves a will of complacence » etc.

II. In regard to the procession of the Holy Spirit according to a reckoning of will, cf. below d. 10, a. 1, q. 1. — About the difference among generation and spiration, cf. below d. 26, q. 1, and there in the Scholium.

III. In the conclusion the doctors agree: Alexander of Hales, SUMMA., p. I, q. 42, m. 5, a. 1; and q. 43, m. 3, a. 2. — (Bl. John Duns) Scotus, here in q. 1; REPORTATIO., here at q. 1 and 2. — St. Thomas, here in q. 2; SUMMA., I, q. 41, a. 2. — Bl. (now St.) Albertus (Magnus), here in a. 1 and 3. — (Bl) Peter of Tarentaise, here at q. 1, a. 2. — Richard of Middleton, here in q. 2. — Giles the Roman, here in the 2nd principle of q. 2. — Durandus (of Saint-Pourçain), here in q. 2.

---

[1] The Vatican edition without the authority of the mss. and of the three first editions reads *God the Father wills to be* [Pater vult esse Deus].

[2] From the ancient manuscripts and edition 1 we have supplied *by* [a], which the Vatican edition together with codex cc here, and a little after this, less well omits. Then in place of *conjoined* [coniunctum] some codices, such as A B D E F G H I X and Z, have *communicating* [communicans], others, such as K L O P Q S T U W and Y, together with edition 1 have *concomitant* [concomitans], but falsely, as is clear from the subjoined, where this member (of the argument) is explained and where all the codices put *conjoined* [coniunctum]. Codices aa and bb add *to nature* [naturae].

[3] We follow codex I, which adds *nor in respect of a creature* [nec respectu creaturae], which is lacking in both the other manuscripts and the Vatican edition, but less well, as is gathered from the context. A little below this with the help of very many manuscripts such as G H Y aa bb ee and ff, and edition 1, we have substituted *some* [aliquam] in place of *an other* [aliam]; a reading certainly to be preferred.

[4] Trusting in very many manuscripts and edition 1, we have put here and a little below this *concomitant* [concomitante] twice in place of *communicating* [communicante], which is had less congruously in the Vatican edition.

[5] We have added from the older manuscripts and edition 1 *first* [primum], which has not well been omitted in the Vatican edition and in codex cc.

[6] Mt. 17:5 and 2 Pt. 1:17. — In the text of the Letter to the Colossians 1:13, taken from the Vulgate, the Vatican edition also has *of dilection* [dilectionis] in place of *of charity* [caritatis], but the manuscripts and edition 1 as well as (St.) Augustine, ON THE TRINITY, Bk. XV, ch. 19, n. 37, support our reading.

[7] The Vatican edition here also has *a will communicating with nature* [voluntate communicante cum natura] in place of *a concomitant will* [voluntate concomitante], but the authority of very many codices and edition 1 is opposed. A little before this very many codices omit *show* [ostendunt]; edition 1 in place of *the two ... show* [ostendunt duae] has *as the ... say* [dicunt]. — After *the reason* [ratio] supply *shows* [ostendit].

[8] Chapter 13, n. 22: However, our knowledge [scientia] in very many things, on this account, is both able to be lost and received [amissibilis est et receptibilis]... On account of this, just as our knowledge (is) to that knowledge of God, so also our word, which is born from our knowledge, is dissimilar to the Word of God, which has been born from the Essence of the Father.

[9] Codex R adds *however* [vero].

[10] We recall from the older manuscripts and edition 1 the *which is objected* [quod obiicitur] which has been omitted in the Vatican edition and in codex cc, and a little below this we have substituted *conjunction* [coniunctione] in place of *communication* [communicatione]. Near the end of the solution codex B has *another support* [alio adminiculo] in place of *another helping (Him)*.

QUESTION III

Whether the generation of the Son is according to a reckoning of exemplarity?

Last, there is asked, whether the generation of the Son by the Father is according to a reckoning of *exemplarity*. And that (it is) so, seems in this manner.

1. On that (verse) of the Psalm:[1] *Once has God spoken*, the Gloss (says): « that is, He begot the Son, in whom He has disposed all (things) »; but an "eternal disposition" means that (there is) a "reckoning of an exemplar": therefore, if the Son proceeds as Word, He proceeds through a manner of exemplarity.

2. Likewise, the generation of the Son by the Father is similar to the production of knowledge from [notitiae ex] the mind;[2] but knowledge proceeds from the mind according to a reckoning of an exemplar, because an exemplar is the reason for cognizing: ergo etc..

3. Likewise, (that) which is the image in the product, this is the exemplar in the one producing; for when the product represents in an expressed manner, it is said (to be) an image. Similarly, when[3] one producing represents in an expressed manner, it is said (to be) an exemplar: therefore, since the Son proceeds as Image, (He does so) for the same reason through a manner of exemplarity.

4. Likewise, every cognitive principle of a thing to be produced[4] produces according to a reason for exemplifying [exemplandi];* but the Father is the cognitive principle of the Son: therefore, He produces the Son according to a reckoning of an exemplar. *If you say*, that that does not suffice, nay rather it is necessary, that the exemplar and the exemplified [exemplatum] differ in form and nature; this is nothing, because if a man, while he generates a man, could generate such a one, which he cognizes, then that generation would not only be according to nature, but also according to an exemplar. But the Father has entirely produced a Son, as He knew and willed: ergo etc.. *If you say*, that neither is that sufficient, but it is necessary, that the exemplar precede (the act of generation); *it is objected*: (even) if God from eternity would have created a world through the impossible, nevertheless the world would be a product according to a reckoning of exemplarity.

ON THE CONTRARY: 1. In inferior (beings) one acting through *nature* and through *exemplar* are divided by opposition [ex opposito], just as (are) nature and intellect:[5] therefore, *he who* is produced according to nature, is not produced according to a reckoning of an

exemplar, but the Son is produced by the Father according to nature: ergo etc..

2. Likewise, everything producing something[6] according to a reckoning of exemplarity produces according to a reckoning of will; but the Father, as has been shown above,[7] does not produce the Son through the Will: ergo etc..

3. Likewise, of a form there is not a form,[8] therefore, neither of an exemplar an exemplar: but the Son is the Art and Exemplar of all (things): therefore, He does not have an exemplar in the Father: therefore, He does not proceed according to a reckoning of exemplarity.

4. Likewise, what is in an other according to truth, is not in that according to an exemplar;[9] but the Son is in the Father according to truth: therefore, not according to an exemplar; but what is not in another according to exemplar, does not proceed according to a reckoning of an exemplar: ergo etc..

CONCLUSION

The Son proceeds from [a] the Father as a reason for exemplifying, not as an exemplified from [a] an exemplar.

I RESPOND: It must be said, that, just as to proceed through a manner of *will* and liberality is in a twofold manner — for in one manner there proceeds through a manner of liberality that which is not liberality, but which becomes and/or is given out of liberality; and in this manner creatures proceed from [a] God; in another manner as that[10] which is a reason for liberality, as love is [ut amor]; and in this manner there proceeds the Holy Spirit as the Love, who is the Gift, in whom all gifts are given — so through a manner of *exemplarity* "to proceed" is in a twofold manner. In *one* manner as an *exemplified* properly; and[11] in this manner a creature proceeds *from* [a] *God* as an exemplified from [a] an exemplar, and in this manner an exemplar conveys a formal causality in respect of the exemplified. In *another* manner "to proceed" is said through a manner of exemplarity[12] as a *reason for exemplifying*. And in this manner the Son Himself seems to proceed, He who is said (to be) the Word of the Father,

---

[1] Ps. 61:12. — The Gloss in (Nicholas) of Lyra (reads): With Himself (He has spoken) once, because He begot one Word, through which all (things) have been made and in which all (things) have been made simultaneously. — The Vatican ed. with cod. cc has *disposes* [disponit] in place of *has disposed* [disposuit], but the rest of the codd. with ed. 1 oppose this.

[2] Cf. (St.) Basil (the Great), AGAINST EUNOMIUS, Bk. II, at the middle, and his sermon on the words "*In the beginning was the Word*", at the middle.

[3] The Vatican edition contrary to many codices and edition 1 has *when* [cum]. — Concerning the various acceptance of the *exemplar* and the *image* see below d. 31, p. II, a. 1, q. 1; if they are accepted *properly*, then they are correlative terms, since an image is in the *product* or is a produced similitude, but the exemplar is that, for the imitation of which something is produced; however, if they are accepted *improperly*, then one term is not infrequently employed in place of the other.

[4] The manuscripts and edition 1 here read *produced* [productae], but below in the response *to be produced* [producendae].*

[5] See above d. 2, q. 4, fundament 2. — Then the Vatican edition together with codex cc, but contrary to the more ancient codices and edi-

tion 1 reads *what* [quod] in place of *he who* [qui] and a little below this *of exemplarity* [exemplaritatis] in place of *of an exemplar* [exemplaris].

[6] From the more ancient manuscripts and edition 1 we have substituted *something* [aliquid] in place of *an other* [aliud].

[7] In the preceding Question.

[8] Cf. Alan of Lille, RULES OF THEOLOGY,° rule 16.

[9] Cf. above d. 2, q. 1, fundament 5. — Then, the mutilated reading of the Vatican ed. and cod. cc, omitting the words *therefore, not* up to *does not proceed* [ergo non ... non procedit], are restored from the other mss. and ed. 1.

[10] The Vatican ed., against very many codd. & ed. 1, reads *that* [id].

[11] We have supplied from mss. F G H K S T Y and ed. 1 *and* [et].

[12] We follow many codices as F G H I K S T Y etc. together with edition 1 by putting *of exemplarity* [exemplaritatis] in place of *of the one exemplifying* [exemplantis]; the reading received in the text corresponds more to the context. A little below this some manuscripts together with edition 1 have *is said* [dicitur] in place of *seems* [videtur]. Then with the help of the older manuscripts and edition 1 we have inserted *the Father* [Pater] after *by whom* [loquitur].

---

* *Trans. note*: A little after this, at *for exemplifying* [exemplandi], the English has no equivalent for this late-Latin verb exemplo, -are, which first appears in St. Augustine's 149th Epistle, with the sense of *to adduce as an example* (Lewis & Short); in this context St. Bonaventure uses it in the sense of *to cause in the manner that an exemplar causes*; the perfect past participle, here a little below this, exemplatum is accordingly

that which is thus caused by an exemplar. Hence the English *to exemplify* and its inflected forms will be employed to translate exemplo, -are, though this is clearly a sui generis use of the English verb.

° This work is cited with the title ON THE RULES OF THE FAITH in the Prolegomena, p. LXXXIV, n.1, of this volume of St. Bonaventure's OPERA OMNIA.

by whom the Father not only speaks Himself, but even disposes all other (things). Whence the Son, according to (St.) Augustine in the sixth (book) ON THE TRINITY, is said (to be) « the Art full of all the reasons for living (beings) ». And hence there has arisen that which is accustomed to be said, that he who denies that there are ideas, denies that there is a Son of God. And that manner of proceeding of His[2] according to exemplarity is not repugnant to a natural processing [processui naturali], nay rather it cannot be but natural. However, the other manner is repugnant to a natural processing; for it is according to the command [imperium] of the will, so that the one producing and the product differ as cause and caused, and the one according to truth is not in the other.

Whence the reasons induced for this side proceed according to this way, and according to this they truly conclude; according to the other one, however, none conclude, nay, rather regarding all (of them) the solution must be [solvendum est][3] through interemption.

Moreover, those (reasons), which are objected to the contrary, all proceed according to the other way, because they say, that (the Son)[4] proceeds through a manner of exemplarity, because He is a *reason for exemplifying*; which is clear, because they are taken from [a] a reckoning of the eternal disposition, cognition and image. However, the last reason does conclude, because it proceeds through a manner of exemplarity, as an *exemplified* (does), and on this account it is to be solved through interemption.

4. To that which is objected, that every principle

of a thing to be produced, if it has cognition, produces through an exemplar; it must be said, that that is false, unless a reason for cognition precedes, so that it has a precognition at least according to a reckoning of a cause to an effect; which ordination exacts [exigit] an essential or substantial diversity. For the exemplified, according to which (it is) an exemplified, is not in the one exemplifying according to truth, but through a similitude, which similitude, I say, since it is a reason for cognizing and exemplifying, is said (to be) an exemplar. Therefore, the Son proceeds according to a reckoning of exemplarity, not as an exemplified through an exemplar, but as the Exemplar Itself and/or the Reason for exemplifying all other (things). *And if you object*, that the Exemplar is common to the whole Trinity, (William) of Auxerre responds to this in (his) question[5] concerning the world-archetype [mundus archetypus] or concerning ideas, that an idea or world-archetype is not only appropriated to the Son Himself, but is also proper (to Him).

And/or it can otherwise be said, that[6] according to which an exemplar means a reason for cognizing, in this manner it is common to the whole Trinity and is appropriated to the Son, just as Wisdom (is); and so He is introduced [importatur] through this name, *"the Word"*, as will be better explained [melius patebit] below.[7]

SCHOLIUM

The sense of this question is, whether the Son is produced according to a manner of *exemplarity*, just as creatures (are). — We find few of the ancient Scholastics explicitly treating this questions, namely, (Bl.) Peter of Tarentaise, here in q. 1, a. 4. — Richard of Middleton, here in q. 4. — Giles the Roman, here in the 2nd princ. of q. 1. — (Bl.) Dionysius the Carthusian, here in q. 1.

DOUBTS ON THE TEXT OF THE MASTER

DOUBT I

In that part about the text, there is a doubt concerning the reason of (St.) Augustine, TO OROSIUS, that *neither by will nor by necessity, because necessity is not in God* etc.. For the division seems (to be) sufficient[8]. For everything which God makes,

He either makes *naturally*, and thus necessarily, or *voluntarily*: ergo etc.. *If you say*, that (the reason) itself responds to the heretic's understanding, and the heretic understand (it) of an antecedent will and of a necessity of inevitability; *it is objected*, that nevertheless the statement is in itself manifold. But he who responds to a manifold statement by simply affirming

---

[1] Chapter 10, n. 11: A certain Art of the Omnipotent and also of the Wisdom of God, full of all the reasons for incommutable living (beings). St. Thomas, DISPUTED QUESTIONS ON THE TRUTH, q. 3, a. 1 exhibits the next proposition that follows thus: (St.) Augustine says in the book, ON THE CITY OF GOD: He who denies that there are ideas is an infidel, because he denies that there is a Son.

[2] The Vatican edition, not trusting in the mss. and the first six edd., reads *that manner of producing* [ille modus producendi], but less well.

[3] The Vatican edition has *the response must be* [respondendum est], but the manuscripts together with editions 1, 2, 3 and 6 are opposed.

[4] Supply with codices I and Z *the Son* [Filius]. Then from the ancient manuscripts and edition 1 we have substituted *through* [per] for *according to* [secundum]. A little below this edition 1, well enough, has *insofar as it is* [prout est] in place of *because He is* [quod est]. Then many codices together with edition 1 have *are* [sunt] in place of *are taken* [sumuntur]. Then codices L and O after *image* [imaginis] adds *and these are the first reasons* [et hae sunt primae rationiones].

[5] We have inserted on the authority of the more ancient manuscripts and edition 1 *in (his) question* [in quaestione]. — That passage of his is found in the SUMMA of the said author, at the end of Bk. I, which SUMMA was publishing at Paris in 1500 A. D.. Many copies of this manuscript exist in the Biblioteca (Medicea) Laurenziana at Florence. There in the codex (11. plut. sin. VII.) under the rubric: "de Creatione mundi", there is read: « We say, that "exemplar" or "idea" is said of the Son of God

both *properly* and *appropriately* ... But because disposition pertains to wisdom, through *appropriation* (this) can be said of the Son, because He is the Exemplar and/or Idea of things. But according to which He Himself is said properly (to be) the Image of the Father for the same reason, by which He Himself is the Word, there also glitter in that Image through the said reason all (things): and according to this there He Himself *properly* called the Idea and/or Exemplar of things » etc.. A little after this there follows: « Second it is asked, whether the Son of God is the world-archetype »; to which he responds: « Whence the Son of God in a certain manner is the World-Archetype *in an appropriated manner* [appropriate], in a certain manner *properly*, as has been said concerning an exemplar ».

[6] The Vatican edition together with codex cc has *because* [quia: and hence the main clause should read *it can be said in another manner*], but less well and contrary to the other codices and edition 1.

[7] Distinction 27, p. II, chiefly q. 3.

[8] Many codices, such as D F K S T V W etc., together with the first six editions have *insufficient* [insufficiens], of which reading the sense can be: it seems, that the division contained in the *response* of (St.) Augustine (to the two-fold question of St. Paulus Orosius): *Did He beget by will and/or by necessity?*, in which, that is, there is added a third part, *neither by necessity nor by will*, is insufficient, i. e., *not a good one*, because (St. Paulus) Orosius' division, is sufficient, i. e. *adequate*.

and/or by denying, responds badly, according to what the Philosopher says:[1] ergo, etc..

I RESPOND: It must be said, that (St.) Augustine responds according to the heretic's understanding. Moreover, although the statement in itself is manifold, because the heretic, nevertheless [tamen], accepts it in one sense, still that multiplicity would not cause [faceret][2] it to be solved, because he does not proceed according to it. But the distinction of a manifold proposition, when deception according to that multiplicity does not occur [cadit], is rather for show [ostentationem] than for a true response.

DOUBT II

Likewise, is asked concerning this which is said: *let us say, that the Word of God is the Son of God by nature, not by will.* For he seems to speak well, because by the one the Father is God, by the other He is the Father, because by the Deity He is God, and by the Paternity He is the Father, as (St.) Augustine says.[3] But the Son is God by the Nature of the Deity: therefore, the Son will not meant by this, but by the filiation itself.

I RESPOND: It must be said, that that ablative can be construed formally; and in this manner it is false, because *formally* by the one He is God, that is by nature, and by the other (He is) the Son.[4] Again it can be construed *originally* and in the reckoning of a principle; and in this manner it is true, and the sense is, that the Son has arisen by [a] the Father naturally.

DOUBT III

Likewise, is asked concerning this which is said: *Indeed he in an acutely sane manner responds,* because (St.) Augustine commends that solution of his, which is not to be commended, because to multiply (something) unfitting is not to solve (it).[5]

I RESPOND: It must be said, that there is a solution *to the man* [ad hominem] and there is a solution *to the statement* [ad orationem];[6] and sometimes it is better and more useful to give a solution [solvere] to the man than to the statement, as for example [ut puta], when the one responding is a debater [discolus] and does not want to understand the truth, and when the listeners [attendentes] are simpletons [simplices] and cannot grasp truth

and subtlety. For that reason because the heretic was rejecting [respuebat] the truth and was adverse to it [adversabatur], on that account one had to be adverse to the adversary [adversanti erat adversandum], and in such a manner, by which he would be more deprived [privaretur] of glory and the listeners of fallacy. For that reason (St.) Augustine commends that response of (the catholic), because[7] he manifestly bound (his) opponent by his question. This manner of responding does the Lord teach in the twenty-first (chapter) of (St.) Matthew,[8] where he said: *Was the baptism of John from* [de] *heaven, or from* [ex] *men? etc..*

Likewise, it is asked, since it is not a response to the statement, how must one respond (to it)? For[9] it must seem that the heretic's division be through an immediate (reckoning), because *to want* and *to not want* are opposed in a contradictory manner, between which there does not fall a middle-ground [medium]. And for this it must be said, that the heretic asks this of the accident will or of the antecedent; and then neither part is true, nor are the members opposed in a contradictory manner, but rather in a contrary one. For "to not will" and "to will" mean contrary acts of the will, between which there does fall a middle-ground. For there is something, in respect of which the will neither[10] has a reckoning of cause nor of repugnance; and thus that is clear.

DOUBT IV

Likewise, is asked concerning the solution of Master (Peter). For he seems to say the false, when he says: *the knowledge and foreknowledge of God (is) of (things) good and evil.* For the Gloss says on that (verse) of the Psalm:[11] *Those whom I knew not, were interrogating Me* etc.: « Art does not know of vices »; but in God there is the Art of arts, ergo etc.. *If you say*, that He does not know through a practical manner, but knows through a manner of speculation;[12] *on the contrary*: solely that does He know in this manner, which glitters in Him; but in God evils do not glitter: ergo etc..

Likewise, Master (Peter) does not seem to give a solution [solvere] to the argument; for to multiply (something) unfitting it not to solve (it).

I RESPOND: It must be said, that, just as will be said below,[13] God cognizes evils through His very self, just as the straight judges what is slanted and light what is darkness [rectum iudicat de obliquo et lux de tenebra]; nor is it proper, that evil shine in God, but it does suffice, that there shine in Him the opposite of evil.

---

[1] (Aristotle), ELENCHAE, Bk. II, ch. 2 (ch. 17) according to the translation of (St. Severinus) Boethius: It is manifest, since to none of those which are equivocal, it is fitting to simply respond.

[2] Not a few codices as A R T and U have *was not there to solve it* [non fuerat ad solvendum].

[3] ON THE TRINITY, Bk. VII, ch. 1, n. 1 and ch. 6, n. 11 and ON PSALM 68, Sermon 1, n. 5, according to the thought. Cf. below Master (Peter), SENT., d. 33, at the end. — Trusting in the mss. and ed. 1 we have twice substituted *by the Deity* [deitate] for *of the Divinity* [divinitatis], which also corresponds more with the words of (St.) Augustine in loc. cit. and with the manner of speaking of the Seraphic (Doctor), concerning which see below d. 15, p. II, Doubt 6.

[4] Codex X adds *that is by (His) filiation* [scilicet filiatione], which words are added by cod. I not here, but a little below this after *and the sense is* [et est sensus]. Then, from many mss., such as A G H K S T Y Z etc., and edition 1, we have put *that* [quod] in place of *because* [quia]. — For more concerning this doubt, see above q. 2 and below d. 33, q. 2 and Doubt 4. — St. Thomas, here in q. 1. a. 3. — Richard (of Middleton) here in q. 3.

[5] Cf. Aristotle, TOPICS, Bk. VIII, ch. 4 (ch. 8). — A little before this very many codd., S V W X Y and dd, with ed. 1 have *does not seem to be a solution* [non videtur solvere] for *is not a solution* [non est solvere].

[6] The Vatican ed. without the authority of the mss.s and the first six edd., has three times, here and a little below this, *reason* [rationem] for *statement* [orationem]. Cf. Aristotle, ELENCHAE, Bk. II, ch. 3 (ch. 22), where according to

Boethius' translation, who always reads oratio for λόγος, it is thus had: All these give a solution [solvunt] not to the statement, but to the man.

[7] The Vatican edition, against very many codd. and ed. 1, has *that* [quod] for *because* [quia], and a little below this at *This manner* [Hunc modum] it badly adds *therefore* [ergo].

[8] Verse 25. — The Vatican ed. not trusting in the mss. has *when* [cum] for *where* [ubi].

[9] We have supplied from the manuscripts and editions 1 and 6 *For* [enim], and a little below this after *asks* we have added *this* [hoc].

[10] The Vatican edition together with one or the other codex has *has not* [non habet] in place of *neither has* [nec habet].

[11] Ps. 34:11. The interlinear Gloss from (St.) Augustine in (Nicholas) of Lyra: Just as art of vices, because one deviates through having known art. — See (St.) Augustine on this Psalm, Serm. 2, n. 2. — A little below this, after *of arts* cod. G adds *and the Science of sciences* [et scientia scientiarum].

[12] The corrupt reading of the Vatican ed. and the codd., *but (through a manner) of speculation* [sed speculationis] is restored from cod. X, which after *but* [sed] adds *knows through a manner* [scit per modum].

[13] Distinction 39, a. 1, q. 1 and 2. — The Vatican ed. here reads *is said* [dicitur] in place of *will be said* [dicetur], and a little below this after *cognizes* [cognoscit] it adds *good (things) in His very self and* [bona in se ipso et], indeed not falsely, but against the mss. and less to the point, because the whole objection concerns only the cognition of *evils*. — On the proposition immediately following, see Aristotle, ON THE SOUL, Bk. I, text 85 (the last

To that which is objected concerning the solution of Master (Peter), it must be said, that he does not posit a solution, but nods his head [innuit] against the one arguing, as if to say: "From that, the one[1] cannot be inferred from the other, because although they are the same in essence, yet diverse (things) are connoted".

DOUBT V

Likewise, is asked concerning this which he says[2] in the Brief Note [notula]: that *the Holy Church anathematizes those who say, that God has not generated by counsel.* For he seems to contradict (St. John) Damascene[3] who says [dicenti], that *counsel* is not in God, because counsel belongs to an ignorant nature.

I RESPOND: It must be said, that *counsel*[4] is said in a twofold manner: in one manner by "*to counsel*" [consulere] there is meant "*to accept counsel*"; and thus it means ignorance and similarly (does) "*counsel*", said in this sense [dictum ab hoc]: in another manner by "*to counsel*" there is meant 'to give counsel' [dare consilium], and in this manner it means knowledge [scientiam], and in this (sense)[5] it can be transferred to the divine. For God in no manner accepts counsel from elsewhere. Whence it must be noted, that in counsel there are two (things): there is *cognition* of the hidden thing, and there is a firm *disposition*. Therefore, since in God there is a most true cognition of (things) hidden and Invariability, for that reason it is rightly said, that in Him there is counsel. Whence (St.) Gregory (the Great says):[6] « God changes sentence, but not counsel ».

DISTINCTION VII

CHAPTER I

Whether the Father could and/or willed to beget the Son.

Here, one is accustomed to be asked by certain (men), whether the Father could* and/or willed to generate the Son. For, if, they say, He could [potuit] and[1] did will to generate the Son: therefore, He could and willed (to do) something, which the Son neither could nor willed (to do); for the Son neither could nor willed to generate the Son. To which craftiness [versutiae] we easily respond, saying: that 'to be able' [posse] and/or 'to will' (is) subject to the (Divine)[2] Will and/or Power [potentiae]. However, it is a power [aliqua potentia] and/or will, namely [scilicet], 'to be able' and/or 'to will' to beget the Son; and for that reason the understanding of the proposed word is to be distinguished: "to be able and/or to will to beget the Son" is[3] "to be able and/or to will (to do) something". For neither is the generation of the Son something belonging to those (things), which have been subjected to the Divine Power and Will, nor is it something among all and/or from all, but rather over all and before all. For not before He willed and/or could, did He beget; just as neither before He was, did He beget, because[4] from eternity He was and from eternity He begot. From a similar (reason) we can also see this. For the Father can be the Father and wills to be the Father; moreover, the Son neither[5] can nor wills to be the Father: therefore, the Father can and/or wills to be something, which the Son cannot and/or does not will to be. It does not follow, that 'to be the Father' is 'not to be something' [esse aliquid], but it is 'to be regarding something' [esse ad aliquid], as will be shown in the following.[6]

But there vehemently moves us, what (St.) Augustine

says in the second book, AGAINST MAXIMINUS,[7] who used to assert that the Father (is) more powerful [potentiorem] than the Son, for the reason that He begot the Son (to be) God the Creator, but the Son (did) not; and he used to say that the Father could beget, the Son (could) not; and for that reason He is more powerful than the Son. To which (St.) Augustine, responding, seems to say, that the Son also could beget, wanting to show, that the Father is not more powerful than the Son, with these words: « Far be it, that the Father be more powerful than the Son for the reason, just as you think, that the Father begot the Creator, but the Son did not beget the Creator; for neither could He not, but rather it was not proper (that He do so) ». See and diligently attend to these words: "for not could He not, but rather it was not proper" [non oportuit]. For he seems to say, that the Son could beget, but it was not proper (that He beget); and thus He could (do) what was not proper (to do). Moreover why it was not proper, He subjoins [subdit], saying: « For the divine generation would be immoderate, if the Begotten Son would not beget a descendent [nepotem] for the Father, because even a descendent himself, unless he begets a great-grandson for his own grandfather, would be called impotent according to your wonderful wisdom. Similarly, also that one, if he did not beget a descendent for his own grandfather and a great-grandson for his own great-grandfather, would not by you be named "omnipotent"; nor is the series of generation fulfilled, if one of the two is always born out of the other; nor would any thoroughly accomplish [perficeret] this, if one omnipotent was is not sufficient. And thus the Nature of the Father begot, not made, the Son Omnipotent ».

Moreover, this does not seem to certain (men) to be able to stand, that is, that the Son could beget. For if the Son could[8] beget, He could be a father; if He could be a father, therefore, He could be a father either of Himself, and/or of the Father, and/or of the Holy Spirit

---

chapter): « For by the straight we cognize both itself and the slanted. For a ruler is by (being) straight a judge of each ». The last words in the Arabic-Latin translation sound thus: For a rule judges each through its own rectitude (Venetian edition of 1489).

[1] The confused reading of the Vatican edition, *as if he says from this what is from that, the same* [quasi dicat ex eo quod est ex illo, idem], is restored with the help of the manuscripts and editions 1, 2 and 3.

[2] Not trusting in the manuscripts and edition 1 the Vatican edition here has *(St.) Hilary says* [dicit Hilarius] and after *Brief Note* [notula] it adjoins *about that § However, the aforesaid* [circa istam § Praedicta tamen], moreover, in the quote itself it puts *does not generate* [generare] in place of *has not generated* [generasse].

[3] ON THE ORTHODOX FAITH, Bk. II, ch. 22, near the middle: God indeed does not deliberate, because to the ignorant it belongs to go unto counsel. — The Vatican edition, contrary to the more ancient codices and edition 1 has *because* [quia] in place of *that* [quod]. Some codices as aa bb ff together with edition 1 have *to counsel* [consiliari] in place of *counsel* [consilium].

[4] Codex dd adds *or to counsel* [aut consulere]. A little below this not a few codices as C I S V aa cc together with the five first editions have *for this (purpose)* [ad hoc] in place of *in this (sense)* [ab hoc].

[5] In the Vatican ed. and codex cc *in this (sense)* [hoc] is wanting.

[6] MORALS ON THE BOOK OF JOB, Bk. XVI, ch. 10: God, even though He very frequently changes the sentence, never the counsel.

NOTES ON THE BOOK OF SENTENCES

[1] The Vatican edition reads *and/or* [vel], but contrary to the codices and editions 1, 6, and 8.

[2] Supply with codex A *Divine* [divinae].

[3] The Vatican edition, contrary to the codices and editions 1 and 8, reads *and* [et]. A little before this codices A B C E together with editions 1, 3, and 7 read *previously placed* [praepositi] in place of *proposed* [propositi].

[4] Editions 1, 2, and 8 add *even* [et].

[5] The Vatican edition together with editions 4 and 6 reads *cannot nor* [non potest nec].

[6] Distinction XXVIII, ch. 5. — A little before this codices A B C E and edition 1 omit the proposition *but it is 'to be toward something'* [sed est esse ad aliquid], which editions 2, 3, 5, 6, 9, 10 exhibit in this manner: *but it can be 'toward something'* [sed potest esse ad aliquid].

[7] Chapter 12, n. 2. — Then the Vatican edition, disagreeing with the codices and editions 1 and 8, at *more powerful* [potentiorem] adds *is* [esse]. Then codex C well has (the subjunctive) *He begot* [genuerit] in place of (the indicative) *He begot* [genuit].

[8] Editions 2, 3, 7, 9, 10 have (the subjunctive) *could* [potuerit].

---

* *Trans. note*: This question turns about the Latin terms posse, potens, potentia, impotentia, omnipotens, all of which cannot be translated into English with the same cognate. For the sake of utility the fol-

lowing English words will be used, respectively: *to be able* or forms of the helping verb *can, able, power, impotency, omnipotent*.]

and/or of anyone else [alicuius aliua]. But not (of any-one)[1] else, because no other always was; neither of the Father, because the Father is unbegotten and innascible; neither of Himself, « because no thing can beget its very self »; nor of the Holy Spirit, because He could not be born. For if He could be born, He could (also) be a son, and thus He could be mutable.

Therefore, in what manner shall[2] what has been said above be accepted: "for not (that) He could beget, but it was not proper (that He do so)", as if He could, but it was not proper (that He do it)? To uncover, in what manner this may be true, is not clear [perspicuum] to us, and for that reason (it is clear to us) that in silence it must rather be passed by, unless the insistence [instantia] of questioners would drive me to say something on it.

Therefore, it can be thus understood: "for not (that) He could not,[3] but it was not proper", that is, it was not out of His impotence [impotentia], that the Son did not beget, but it was not fitting [non conveniebat] for Him, in the same manner [sic] God the Son is not God the Father; nor, however, is this out of His impotence. For, even the Father similarly is not the Son, nor is this out of the Father's impotence. But Maximinus, the Bishop of the Arians, asks: "Whence, therefore, is it, that the Father cannot be the Son, and/or the Son the Father?" Certainly not out of an impotence, but rather the Father by[4] the property of generation is the Father, by which it is proper that He not be the Son, and the Son by the property of nativity is the Son, by which it is proper that He not be the Father. Concerning which properties there will be a fuller treatment [plenius tractabitur] afterwards.[5]

CHAPTER II

Or whether there is some power in the Father that can beget the Son, which is not in the Son.

Likewise, there is asked by certain (men), "If the Father is by nature able [potens] to beget the Son?", and "Whether this[6] is some power, which is in the Son?" To which we say, that the Father is not able except by nature; for His power is by nature and/or essence. But they say, "if He is able to beget, therefore, He has a power to beget; however, the Son does not

have a power to beget, if He cannot beget: therefore, the Father has some power, which the Son does not have." (But this is a) non sequitur. For the Son thoroughly has the same power which the Father also (has), by which the Father could beget, and the Son could be begotten. For the same power is in the Son, by which He could be begotten, which is in the Father, by which He could beget. But against this there is objected: "It is one (thing) to be able to beget, it is another to be able to be begotten; because it is one (thing) to beget,[7] an other to be begotten." Here one must distinguish [distinguendum est]. For, if, when there is said: "it is one (thing) to be able to beget, another to be able to be begotten," you signify[8] the one Power, by which the Father is able to beget, and the other, by which the Son is able to be begotten, (then) there is a false understanding. But, if you say, "that the Father can have one property or notion, by which He is the Begetter; and the Son another, by which He is the Begotten," there is a true understanding. For the Father has one property, by which He is the Father, the Son another, by which He is the Son.

Thus also, when there is said: "the Son does not have the power to generate, which the Father has," it can be understood in a twofold manner. For, if there be said: "the Son does not have the power to generate which the Father also (has)", that is,[9] "by which He is able regarding the one to be generated [ad generandum], that is, to generate [ut genuerit], and/or to have generated as the Father (does)", it is true. However, if it be understood thus: "He does not have the power, by which He can be begotten and/or have been begotten, by which same (power) the Father is able, to generate and/or to have generated," it is false; just as there is said: "the Father has a power, by which He can be the Father; however, the Son does not have a power, by which He can be the Father" and conversely, "the Son has a power, by which He can be the Son, however, the Father does not have a power, by which He can be the Son:[10] therefore, the Father has some (power), which the Son does not have" and conversely. Far be it; because the same is the power of the Father, by which He can be the Father, and of the Son, by which He can be the Son. Thus also the same is the Will, by which the Father wills to be the Father, not the Son, and the Son wills to be the Son, not the Father: and the same is the Will of the Son, by which He wills to be begotten, and that the Father to have begotten; and of the Father, by which He wills to be the Begetter, and that the Son has been the Begotten.[11]

COMMENTARY ON DISTINCTION VII

On the comparison of the power of generating to the Person.

Here, one is accustomed to be asked by certain (men), whether the Father could and/or willed etc..

THE DIVISION OF THE TEXT

In the present Distinction, Master (Peter) posits a doubt from the comparison of the power of generating to the Person, whether namely [scilicet], just as in the Person of the Father, it be thus in the Person of the Son. And this part has two (parts): in the *first* Master (Peter) asks and determines, whether

the Son can generate; in the *second*, whether the power of generating be in the Son, there (where he says): *Likewise, it is asked by certain (men) if the Father is by nature able* etc..

Likewise, the *first* part has four smaller parts. In the *first* (of these) he brings forward [movet] a question, whether to be able and to will

---

[1] The Vatican edition, contrary to the codices and editions 1, 3, 5, 6, 7, and 8, here repeats *of anyone* [alicuius].

[2] The Vatican edition together with editions 4, 5 and 6, reads *is ... accepted* [accipiatur].

[3] The fault of the Vatican edition of omitting *not* [non] is corrected from the codices and editions 1, 2, 3, 5, 6, 8, 9, and 10. A little before this codex D has *Moreover, it can* [Potest autem] in place of *Therefore, it can* [Potest ergo].

[4] The codices here have *out of* [ex]

[5] Distinction XXVI.

[6] The Vatican ed., contrary to edd. 2, 3, 5, 9 & 10 has *this (thing)* [hoc]. Then, after *which* [quae], trusting in the codd. and edd. 1, 3, 5, 6 & 8, we have expunged the added *not* [non] of the Vatican ed.. A little

below this, after *we say, that* [dicimus, quod] the codd. and edd. 1 & 8 omit *the Father* [Pater].

[7] The Vatican edition, disagreeing with the codices and editions 1, 2, 9, and 10, adds *and* [et].

[8] The Vatican edition together with editions 4, 6, and 8, has the indicative *you signify* [significas]. A little above this after *to be able to beget* [posse gignere] codices A D and E add *and* [et].

[9] The Vatican edition, contrary to the codices and editions 1, and 8, has *that is* [scilicet].

[10] The Vatican edition together with edition 4 unduly omits *however the Father does not have a power, by which He can be the Son* [Pater vero non habet potentiam, qua possit esse Filius].

[11] In codices B D E and edition 1 there is lacking *has* [esse].

to generate are similarly compared to the Person of the Father and the Son. *Second*, he opposes against the solution through the authority of (St.) Augustine, there (where he says)d: *But we are vehemently moved by what (St.) Augustine etc.*. *Third*, he objects against the aforesaid authority by means of [per] reason, there (where he says): *Moreover, this does not seem to certain (men)*. *Fourth*, he returns to the above authority, expounding it,[1] there (where he says): *Therefore, in what manner is what has been said above to be accepted*.

Likewise, it is asked by certain (men) if the Father etc.. This is[2] the *second* part of this distinction, in which Master (Peter) asks, whether the power of generating be in the Son, and this part has two smaller parts. *First*, he asks and determines this question, whether some power be in the Father, which is not in the Son. *For if the Father by nature is able to generate the Son, and the Son not, it is clear* etc.. And[3] to this question Master (Peter) responds, that entirely the same is the power in the Father and the Son. But because there was doubt on this, for that reason he objected against the aforesaid solution and determined (it) through distinction. *Second*, he responds to the first question by

distinguishing, whether, that is, the Son has a power of generating, there (where he says): *Thus also when there is said, "the Son does not have"* etc. For if it be understood actively, the understanding is false, that is, that the Son can generate. However, if it be understood[4] passively, that is, that He has a power, by which he can be generated, it is true. And that distinction of his is founded according to some upon this, that the Latin for *"of generating"* [generandi] can be understood in a passive signification, and/or as an active one. If in the passive, then it is true; and the sense is: 'The Son has the power of being generated', that is 'a power, by which He is generated'. If[5] in the active, this can be in a twofold manner, because it can be a gerund for a *personal verb*, and then it has a determinate subject [suppositum determinatum] and it is false; for the sense is: 'the Son has' etc., that is, 'the Son has a power, by which the Son Himself generates'; and/or (for) a *impersonal* (verb); and then it does not have a certain subject [certum suppositum] and the saying is true; for the sense is: 'the Son has a power of generating', that is, 'He has a power, by which someone generates',[6] however, Master (Peter) does not posit this sense.

TREATMENT OF THE QUESTIONS

For the evidence of those (things) which Master (Peter) says concerning the power of generating, four (things) are asked.

First, there is asked, whether among divine (things) "to be able to generate" means a *'what'* [quid], and/or a *'toward something'* [ad aliquid].*

Second, whether the Father communicates to the Son[7] a power of generating, that is, whether in the Son there is a power of generating.

Third, whether "to be able to generate" and "(to be able) to create" is a unique "to be able", and/or (whether it is) not.

Fourth, whether "to be able to be generated and to be created" is an univocal "to be able".

QUESTION I

Whether the "power to generate" means something absolute, and/or relative?

About the first, that "to be able to generate" [posse generare] means a *'what'*, is shown:

1. First through the *authority* of Master (Peter) in the text:[9] « The Father is not able except by nature, and His power is by nature and/or essence »; but nature and power mean a *'what'* [quid], not a *'toward something'* [ad aliquid]: therefore, a power of generating also (means the same).

2. Likewise, by *reason* it is thus shown: to generate

is to produce a similar in nature to itself; but according to the Philosopher[10] « nature is a force implanted in things procreating similars out of similars »; therefore, a force of generating respects the nature itself or the essence of itself [de se], not the person; but every such (term) means a *'what'*: ergo etc..

3. Likewise, « in perpetuals *'to be'* [esse]and *'to be able'* [posse] do not differ »: therefore, much more strongly in eternals; therefore, the same

---

[1] From the older mss. and edition 1 we have supplied *it* [ipsam].

[2] The Vatican edition without the authority of the manuscripts and edition 1, by omitting the words: *Likewise, there is asked by certain (men), if the Father etc.. This is* changes the construction, because it afterwards eliminates the words *and this part*. Then the codices together with edition 1 have *three* [tres] in place of *two* [duas], but falsely.

[3] From manuscripts X Y bb and edition 1 we have added *And* [Et], in place of which very many codices have not so well *But* [Sed]; codex Q, however, has *Second* [Secundo] and a little below this *third* [tertio] in place of *second* [secundo], but falsely, as is clear to the one inspecting the text of Master (Peter) and the words of (St.) Bonaventure.

[4] From the more ancient mss. and ed. 1 we have substituted (the subjunctive) *is understood* [intelligatur] for (the indicative) *is understood* [intelligitur] and then *He has* [habeat] for *He has* [habet] and a little below this *that ... of his* [ista] for *that* [illa] and *some* [aliquos] for *others* [alios].

[5] The Vatican edition reads *But* [Sed], and a little after this it omits *this* [hoc], contrary to the older codices and edition 1, which also put *gerundive* [gerundivum] in place of *gerund* [gerundium].

[6] Codex O by glossing adds: *that is the Father, because the same power is in the Father and in the Son for this that He be generated, nor, however, does it follow from this, that the Son generates, but it follows from this, that someone generates* [scilicet Pater, quia eadem est potentia in Patre et in Filio ad hoc ut generetur, nec tamen ex hoc sequitur, quod Filius generat, sed ex hoc sequitur, quod aliquis generat].

[7] With the help of the manuscripts and edition 1 we have restored the omitted *to the Son* [Filio].

[8] The fault of the Vatican edition, we have corrected, trusting in the manuscripts, by substituting *univocal* [univocum] for *unique* [unicum].

[9] Chapter 2, at the start. — The Vatican edition, contrary to many codices as A G H I S T V Y Z bb and ff and edition 1, has *because His* [quia eius] for *and His* [eiusque] and in the minor proposition, contrary to all the codices and edition 1, it has *and essence* [et essentia] in place of *and power* [et potentia].

[10] Aristotle, MAGNA MORALIA, Bk. I, ch. 10, says: Every nature is a procreatrix of the essence of that, which it is. Cf. METAPHYSICS, Bk. V, text 5 (Bk. IV, ch. 4). — The Vatican edition (to which Richard of Middleton consents, here in q. 1), contrary to the manuscripts and editions 1, 2, and 3 puts *Isaac* (though in his book on definitions these words are not found) in place of *the Philosopher*. — Bl. (now St.) Albert (the Great), SENT., Bk. I, d. 4. a. 2, and SUMMA., p. I, a. 30, m. 1, attributes this definition to Boethius, but the editors of (his) works to Henry of Ghent's GRAMMATICAL INSTITUTIONS. The author of the book, ON THE SPIRIT AND THE SOUL, ch. 42 says: Nature indeed is a certain force and power implanted divinely into things to be created, which bestows upon each thing its own 'being' [esse].

---

* *Trans. note*: Here, the expression ad aliquid can be translated as *regarding something* or *towards something* or even as *for something*. The first is merely passive, the third, equivocal; the second, emphasizing the vector of a power to its object, St. Bonaventure upholds here in his Response.

is "to be" [esse] and "to be able" [posse],[1] and power and essence; but "to be" and "essence" among the divine mean a 'what', not a *toward something*, whether one says (them) <u>per se</u>, or with an adjunct; whence the Essence of the Father means a 'what': therefore, for an equal reason, (His) a "power of generating".

4. Likewise, among the divine it is the same according to thing 'to be able to know' [posse scire] and '(to be able) to will'; but among the divine there is not a proper knowledge [scientia propria] or a 'toward something',[2] nay rather "knowledge" (there) means the *What* and it belongs to Three, similarly also "will": therefore, the "power of generating" means a 'what' or essence.

BUT ON THE CONTRARY: 1. Master (Peter) says in the text, and (as) it is had in the first chapter:[3] To be able to generate is not a 'to be able (to do) something' [posse aliquid], therefore, it does not mean a 'what'; and he says (it is) a 'what' and/or a 'toward something': ergo etc..

2. Likewise, by reason it is shown thus: powers are distinguished through acts:[4] therefore, if an *act* of a power means a 'what' and a *power*, and if it means a 'toward something', then, also power, similarly. But, it is established that "*to generate*" does not mean, among the divine, a 'what', but a 'toward something': therefore, neither does a 'to be able to generate'.

3. Likewise, although in creatures virtue and operation differ, however, in God they are the same, just as Dionysius (the Areopagite) wants [vult]:[5] therefore, in God the same is 'to be able to generate' and 'to generate'; but '*to generate*' means, among the divine, a 'toward something' and not a 'what': therefore, similarly a 'to be able'.

4. Likewise, the Father generates and can generate: therefore, either He can for the reason that [ideo ... quia] He generates; or He generates for the reason that He can. It is established that He can generate not for the reason that He generates: therefore, He generates for the reason that He can generate.[6] Therefore, if the reckoning of the proper ought to be proper [esse propria]; and nothing is proper among the divine, except what means a 'toward something': ergo etc..

5. Likewise, every active power, which is in [inest] a creature, is in (it) according to some conditions or[7] properties, as is clear. For a 'to be able to illumine' is in the luminous through light, 'to be able to warm' in the warm through warmth. Moreover, although the power of generating is not active, however, it is similar to an active (power): therefore, since it is in the Father, it is in (Him) through some property; moreover, that property either means a 'what', or a 'toward something'. If a 'what': therefore,[8] it is in every Person, and thus (is) a 'to be able to generate', which Master (Peter) manifestly denies: therefore, it

means a 'toward something': therefore, also (does) the power, which is within according to it: ergo etc..

CONCLUSION

Among the three opinions concerning this matter, that seems more probable which asserts, that the "power of generating" signifies as much a relation as a substance, but in a right (sense), a relation.

I RESPOND: It must be said, that about this problem there were three positions.

There were[9] certain (authors), who distinguished the "power of generating" [potentiam generandi], saying, that the power of generating can be meant as a *bare* [nuda] power, and/or as a *disposed* power. If it is meant as a *bare* power, so they wanted[10] to say, that it means a 'what' and it is in all the *Three* Persons, since this power, said in this manner, is consequent to the Nature [consequitur naturam]; whence, since the Nature is in each Person, similarly, too, this kind of power. Moreover, according to which it means a *disposed* power, because it has not a disposition nor fittingness, to go forth into an act of generation except in the Person of the Father alone, they wanted to say, that it means a 'toward something' [ad aliquid].

But the words of that position of theirs do not seem *true* nor *sane*. I say, "not *true*", since whose power is bare, is bound to be equally [pariter] a disposed (power); therefore, if to the Three[11] there belongs a power of generating, as it is a bare power, similarly also (as) a disposed (power); and thus Each could generate. Moreover, it does not seem *sane*; for to posit a bare power, which holds itself in the same manner regarding 'being' [ad esse] and 'not being' [non esse] in respect to a generation, which is entirely necessary to be [quam omnino necessarium est esse], does not seem to be sanely or properly said "to be".

There were also others, who said, that since among the divine the Same is "to be able" and "to be", (so) also the Power and the Essence, because, according to the manner in which power and essence mean a 'what', similarly "to be" and "to be able" (mean a 'what'). And in accord with the manner, when I say the "Essence of the Father" and the "Essence of the Son" and the "Essence of the Holy Spirit", or "that the Father is",[12] "that the Son is", "that the Holy Spirit is", I do not mean (that there is) another Essence nor that there is an Other, but (the Same is) of the One and of the Other [alterius et alterius]; thus when I say (that there is) a Power of the Father, or that the Father can generate and that the Son can

---

[1] The mutilated reading of the Vatican edition and of codex cc, in which there are omitted the words *therefore, much* up to *and power* [ergo multo ... et potentia: trans. note: which begin on p. 134], are restored from the more ancient mss. and edition 1. — Concerning the first proposition of this argument, see above d. 2, q. 1, 1st arg. for the opposite.

[2] The Vatican edition, together with very many codices as H I K S U X Y Z bb and ff and edition 1, after *proper knowledge* [propria] adds *and/or a proper will* and after *or* [sive] the Vatican edition alone adjoins *knowledge and will* [scientia et voluntas]; we prefer, however, the reading of the other manuscripts as A C F G L O R T etc., which is also proved by the context, because otherwise afterwards there would be superfluously placed *similarly also (does) the will* [similiter et voluntas].

[3] The Vatican edition, not trusting in the mss. and ed. 1, has *after the start* [post initium] in place of *and it is had in the first chapter* [et habetur primo capitulo]. Then the Vatican ed. badly, and contradicting the manuscripts, omits *and he says (it is) a 'what' and/or* [et didi quid vel]; a few codices as I and cc have well enough *but* [sed] in place of *and* [et].

[4] Concerning this matter, there is commonly alleged Aristotle, ON THE SOUL, Bk. II, text 33 (ch. 4): For acts (are) prior to powers and operations are according to a reckoning; moreover if (they are) thus, to these the opposed (i.e. objects) are prior still.. Then the mutilated reading of the

Vatican ed. and cod. cc, in which there is omitted *also (does) the power; and, if it means a "toward something", then* [et potentia; et si dicit ad aliquid, tunc] we have reintegrated with the help of the rest of the mss. and ed. 1.

[5] The book, ON THE CELESTIAL HIERARCHIES, ch. 11, and ON THE DIVINE NAMES, ch. 4, § 1.

[6] Having queried the mss. and edition 1, we have put *therefore, He generates for the reason that He can generate* [ergo ideo generat, quia potest generare] in place of *but rather conversely* [sed e converso].

[7] The Vatican edition together with codex cc has *and* [et] in place of *or* [sive], but contrary to the more ancient codices and edition 1.

[8] From the older mss and ed. 1 we have supplied *therefore* [ergo].

[9] Edition 1, with one or another of the codices, adds *for* [enim].

[10] With the ancient manuscripts and edition 1 in favor, we have expunged here the badly added *some* [aliqui] and then after *all* [omnibus] we have inserted *the Three* [tribus].

[11] Codex H well enough adds *Persons* [personarum].

[12] The Vatican edition here and after *Son* [Filium], contrary to very many codices and edition 1, adds *or* [sive] and a little below this, contrary to the more ancient codices and edition 1, it omits *and (the Same) of the One* [et alterius] and also the particle *and* [et] after *generate* [generare].

be begotten, I do not mean one and another 'to be able', but (that 'being able') of One of the Two (of Them). And to this position belonged Master (Peter), as evidently appears in the text.[1] Whence, those of this (position) used to say, that a 'to be able to generate' means a '*what*', but according to a regard *toward something* [secundum respectum ad aliquid], because it is (something) essential extended [tractum] towards a Person. For, since it does not belong to every manner of abstraction, it can be extended toward a Person.

And that position of Master (Peter) is probable enough and seems to be able to be sustained well enough.

There were also more modern (authors) of a third (opinion), who said, that a "power of generating" among the divine means of itself a '*toward something*'. And their reason is, that "power" means a habitude of an original beginning towards the (thing) begun. And since a habitude can be of a person toward a person, and then it is truly a habitude; and of an essence to a creature, and then (it is such) according to a manner of speaking or of understanding: hence it is, that a principle from its own reckoning is not only an essential[4] appropriated through addition, nay rather it also means (what is) proper to a person [proprium personae]. For an equal reason, since "power" means an original habit, not only an essential one, it is not said or extended [trahitur] solely[5] toward a person, so that it means the essence essentially, nay rather it means (what is) proper, and thus of itself a '*toward something*'.

And that position of theirs, without prejudice, seems more probable. For a "power of generating" seems to mean naught but a fecundity for an act of generation; and that is proper to a person, whence similarly also (is) the power.[6] Nor is it similar concerning "to be able" and "to be" except in one manner. For this verb, "*is*" [est], sometimes is predicated <u>per se</u>, (and) sometimes is a *third adjacent*. When it is said <u>per se</u>, then it means an absolute act, because it means an act of a being according to the reckoning of essence [actum entis ratione essentiae]; and then it is proper, that it be said absolutely and that it mean a '*what*'. However, when it is a *third adjacent*, as when there is said "the Father is God" [Pater est Deus],[7] the Father is the Father, (and) then this verb, "*is*", means a habitude of the predicate toward the subject. And, since this can mean a habitude toward an essential and/or personal predicate,

for that reason it can mean an essential 'to be' [esse essentiale] and a personal manner of being [modum essendi personalem]. Moreover, "*to be able*" [posse] from its own proper reckoning means a habitude according to an origin [habitudinem secundum originem]; and, hence, it is, that it is specified through an adjunct, so that it means a condition of the principle of the Essence, and/or of the Person. Therefore, sustaining this position, I respond[8] to the arguments proving, that it means a '*what*' [quid]:

1. For what is first objected, it is clear: for I concede, that Master (Peter) was of this position. Whence they said, that the Son can be begotten by the same power, by which the Father can beget; which would not be,[9] unless "power" [potentia] meant a '*what*'. Whence he said, that the power of generating is in the Son, but not for *generating*, but for *being generated*. Moreover, *this* position[10] means, that it is in the Father alone, because it does not respect the Nature, but a property of a Person.

2. To that which is objected, that[11] to generate is consequent to nature; it must be said, that among the divine it is not consequent to the Nature simply, but to the Nature as in a Person; because not in every Person is the Nature fecund, but only in the Person of the Father, and this is through some property, which belongs to that Person alone; it is not thus among inferior (things), just will now be clear:[12] for that reason it is clear that that (argument) is not valid.

3. To that which is objected, that in eternals the same is '*to be*' and '*to be able*'; it must be said, that it is true; but, nevertheless [tamen], the argument is worth nothing.[13] For although it is entirely the same, among the divine, '*to be*' and '*to be the Father*', it does not, however, follow, that, if '*to be the Father*' is proper, that '*to be*' is proper. Similarly, neither if '*to be*' is common, that on this account '*to be the Father*' (is common).[14] Similarly, must it be said in the proposed (objection).

4. To that which is objected concerning knowledge, that it means a '*what*', whether 'be said by itself [per se], or with an other [cum alio]; it must be said, that it is not similar concerning knowledge and power. For knowledge [scientia], as much as it is of itself, means an absolute quality, and for that reason, as much as it is of itself, it always means a '*what*', unless it be extended [trahatur]; but power means

---

[1] Chapter 1, near the beginning. — The Vatican edition, contrary to very many manuscripts and edition 1, has *to a position of this kind* [huiusmodi positionis] in place of *to this position* [huius positionis], and a little below this after *to generate* [generare], disagreeing with the codices and edition 1, it badly adds *not only* [non tantum]. Then from codex T and edition 1 after *but* [sed] we have put *according to* [secundum] in place of *also* [etiam]; the other codices omit *but* [sed] and/or *according to* [secundum] (this omission was very easy, for the reason that <u>sed</u> and <u>secundum</u> are abbreviated in nearly the same manner), but less well. Codex R reads *means a "what" and a looking-back or towards something* [dicit quid et respectum sive ad aliquid].

[2] From the more ancient manuscripts and edition 1 we have supplied *of Master (Peter)*. A little before this, not a few codices as K S Z ff have *thus the* [ita] in place of *this* [ista], codex X has *for that reason* [ideo].

[3] Some codices as V X and Y add *and* [et].

[4] Some codices as G aa and bb add *common* [commune].

[5] All the codices together with editions 1, 2, 4, 5 and 6 have *an essential one* [essentialem] instead of the *essentially* [essentialiter], which the Vatican edition, with changed punctuation, refers to those things which follow; but falsely, because it is contrasted with to the word *original* [originalem]. From manuscripts F H P Q T Y and ee we have inserted *not ... solely* [non solum].

[6] Codex bb adds *of generating* [generandi].

[7] From the more ancient manuscripts and edition 1 we have supplied *"the Father is God"* [Pater est Deus], which the Vatican edition together with codex cc omits. — Concerning the *third adjacent*, see Aristotle, On Interpretation, Bk. II, ch. 1, and the Commentary of St.

Thomas on this passage (Lect. 2), where the same distinction concerning the word, "is", is also proposed and explained: And it is not said to be a third, because it is a third predicate; but because it is a saying placed third in enunciation, which simultaneously with a predicated noun makes one predicate.

[8] The Vatican edition has *one responds* [respondetur], but contrary to the manuscripts and edition 1.

[9] Codex X adds *true* [verum]. — Cf. the text of Master (Peter), here in ch. 2.

[10] That is, the third opinion. — Very many codices together with the first six editions have *power* [potentia] in place of *position* [positio], the sense of which reading is: moreover, this power, that is of generating, in accord with the aforesaid means or names that which is in the Father alone, namely a fecundity for an act of generation. It would read better (as): moreover, this position means, that the power is in the Father alone.

[11] The more ancient manuscripts and edition 1, contrary to the Vatican edition and codex cc, have *in what manner* [quomodo] in place of *that* [quod].

[12] Here in q. 2, especially at n. 6 and Doubt 4. — A little before this codices aa and bb after *property* [proprietatem] add *,that is, innascibility,* [scilicet innascibilitatem].

[13] The Vatican edition, disagreeing with very many manuscripts and edition 1, has *is not valid* [non valet] in place of *is worth nothing* [nihil valet].

[14] Supply: is common [sit commune]. — The mutilated reading of the Vatican edition and codex cc, in which there are omitted the words *Similarly* up to *the Father* [Similiter ... Patrem], we have restored with the help of the other manuscripts and edition 1.

a habitude toward[1] an origin, and for that reason it can mean a proper habitude and of a person toward a person. Wherefore, that similar (opinion) of Master (Peter) is not valid according to this position, which (says that),[2] "just as one is the Will, by which the Father wills to be the Father and does not will to be the Son, and conversely, similarly one is the power", as is seen (at the end of his second chapter).

If anyone, moreover, wants to sustain the position of Master (Peter), he can easily [de facili] respond to all the reasons to the opposite.

1. For no reason proves, that power of itself means (something) proper, but (it does prove) that a power of generating said actively or a 'to be able to generate' means from [ex] its adjunct a respect toward a person, and thus it means a 'toward something'; and this is solely by reason of the added. Whence[3] it must be noted that there are four genera of names among the divine. For certain ones are *essential* (and) said *essentially*, as "the Deity" and "the Majesty"; certain ones (are) *essential* (and) said *personally*, as the "power of generating"; certain ones (are) *personal* (and) said *personally*, as "the One generating" and "the One begotten"; certain ones (are) *personal*

(and are) said *essentially*, as "the One sent" and "the One incarnate" and (names) of this kind,[4] which means a looking-back toward a Person, and for that reason (they are) personal (names), and in the creature (mean) an effect, and for that reason they are said *essentially*.

2. To the two following reasons it is easy to respond, because that does not have truth, except when the act embraces the whole power;[5] not so is it in the Power of God, because in God the power to beget and to be begotten is the same.

3. To that which is objected, that 'to be able to generate' and 'to generate' is the same; it must be said, that it is not valid. For although the same is[6] the Father and the Substance, it does not however, follow, that if the Father is said *regarding something* [ad aliquid], that the Substance (is) also, as will be clear in a better manner below.[7]

4. 5. To the last two reasons it is difficult to respond well; however, one can say, that those reasons do not conclude, that power means a 'toward something' of itself , but solely by reason of the adjoined, which is "to generate"; and thus the rest are clear.[8]

SCHOLIUM

I. In the production of the Divine Emanations one distinguishes the *principle which* [principium quod] and the *principle by which* [principium quo]. The Persons producing are themselves the *principle which*, since the actions belong to the supposits. The *principle by which* (or reason, by which the supposits act) of the Divine Productions is commonly asserted to be the power of generating and spirating. But *what* this power *is*, is disputed, and about this St. Bonaventure here inquires. In other words this question is thus expressed: whether the power of generating means and absolute what (an essence), or a relative one or relation. There is the same difficulty about the power of spirating, which is common to the Father and the Son, concerning which see below d. 29, a. 2, q. 1 and 2. Each question concerns a manner of speaking rather than some weighty difference on the matter. — Moreover, if one asks concerning the principle by which of each emanation, what it is *in itself*, and who the one differs from the other, it is now commonly responded, that there is a twofold fecundity, that is through a manner of *nature* or intellect and through a manner of *will*; concerning which see below d. 13, q. 3 and the Scholium. — In regard to the question treated in this passage (Bl. John Duns) Scotus rightly observes (REPORTATIO, here in q. 1), that « the diverse sentences perhaps can be reconciled, nor do they seem to be contrary except in words ». However, because the contrary manners of speaking, which the doctors employ in this question, do not little influence the solutions of the other questions concerning the Trinity, which are treated below, it helps here to say something concerning the various solutions of this question. — St. Thomas (SUMMA., I, q. 41, a. 5) favoring the second opinion posited here in the body (of the Question) asserts, that the power of generating signifies « in a right (sense) the Divine Nature, but in oblique (sense) a relation », and in his COMMENTARY ON THE BOOK OF SENTENCES (here on q. 1) he affirms together with Bl. (now St.) Albert (here in a. 2), that it « is a quasi-middle (power) between the essential and the personal ». This opinion St. Bonaventure says is « probable enough, and seems to be able to be sustained well enough », nay rather he himself at the send of the solution of the objections strives to solve the arguments against it. — To this position there is directly

opposed the sentence of William of Auxerre, whose name in Latin is more correctly <u>Autissiodorensis</u> than <u>Altissiodorensis</u>, since the Latin name for Auxerre is <u>Autissiodorum</u> and/or <u>Autessiodorum</u>, and that of Durandus (of Saint-Pourçain) (here in q. 1), who would have, this power mean *a relation alone*. (Bl.) Dionysius the Carthusian attributes this same sentence to St. Bonaventure and approves it with these words: « It seems more true, that a generative power means purely a 'toward something' ... for when "generative power" is said, this complex is taken in virtue of one saying or name; for that reason howsoever much a power according to itself would be said absolutely, however, from such a limitation and contraction it is taken respectively ». But the one who has attentively pondered the words of the Seraphic Doctor, written here and in the doubts 5, 6 and 7 about the text, will already see throughout, that he has chosen the a certain middle way. This, his sentence, appears more clearly from the Seraphic (Doctor's) unpublished prologue to the Second Book of Sentences, some of which we have already quoted above in d. 3, p. II, a. 2, q. 1 in the Scholium, and now continue: « Similarly, neither in the other, that in the power of generating, have I disagreed with him. Because the same Master (Peter) hints in d. VII, that the "power of generating" is said according to substance, and that other say, that it is said according to a relation and is (something) proper, there is no controversy, nay rather each is true, if one attends (to the matter). For if we speak *in a divided manner* [divisim] of the power of generating, according to which it is signified by these two nouns, so, though the noun for "power" is of itself essential and the noun for "generative virtue" is personal, it means an essence and/or nature as in a person. Moreover, if we speak of that which is signified by those two words, thus that *they are connected in the understanding of one word*, then, since the power of generating is nothing other than a fecundity of power, and a "fecundity in producing a Person" is said entirely according to relation nor is it common, but proper, thus without doubt a "*power of generating*" and/or a "*to be able to generate*" is said according to a relation. And thus it is clear that each of those opinions of theirs is true, nor is one repugnant to the other. But this sentence I have rather appro-

---

[1] Trusting in the manuscripts and edition 1, we have substituted *toward* [ad] for *and* [et], which perfectly corresponds to what is said at the end of the body (of the question).

[2] With the Vatican edition we have left *which (says that)* [quod], though very many codices have *because* [quia], but less well.

[3] The Vatican edition together with codex cc has *Likewise* [Item], and a little below this after *essentially, as* [essentialiter, ut] it adds *the Divinity* [divinitas], but contrary to the other codices and edition 1.

[4] Very many codices as A I S T V Y and aa omit *the One incarnate and (names) of this kind* [incarnatus et huiusmodi].

[5] Codex I adds *when, that is, the power holds itself determinately toward one act, so that (it is) not toward another* [quando scilicet potentia se habet determinate ad unum actum, ita quod non ad alium].

[6] The Vatican edition, not trusting in the manuscripts and edition 1, adds *both* [et].

[7] Distinction 9, q. 2, first of all in reply to nn. 3 and 6, and distinction 26, qq. 1 and 3.

[8] Codices P and Q have *all* [omnia] in place of *the rest* [cetera]; codex V has *is clear the solution to all the objections* [patet solutio ad omnia obiecta].

ed, because it attains more to the truth of the matter, though for a *full expression of the truth one must sustain each* (opinion). Therefore, adhering to these and the other words of Master (Peter), having observed the reverence due ... I both have proposed and do propose, in accord with the thinness of (my) genius and the poverty of (my) science in these (things), in which I shall be able, to sustain, with these things only excepted, in which more commonly it is not sustained, nay rather the common opinion holds the contrary. Moreover, these are eight, so that in each book there are two » etc..

According to this explanation, the Essence and property of a Person constitute the *total principle which* [principium quod] of the Productions, and indeed in this manner, that the Essence is a quasi-fundament and start, but the property a completive and a quasi-formal reason, or as Richard of Middleton (here in q. 1) says: « The "power of generating" among the divine means a '*what*' and a '*toward something*', however, it seems to signify more formally a '*toward something*' ». (Bl.) Peter of Tarentaise (here in q. 1, a. 2) and Alexander of Hales (SUMMA., p. I, q. 42, m. 3, a. 2, at the last n., agree. Nor does Henry of Ghent (SUMMA.,

a. 54, q. 8, n. 27, and QUODLIBETALS, 3, q. 14) and (Bl. John Duns) Scotus seem to think otherwise, though the latter makes a response under other distinctions. And since even St. Thomas teaches, that a power of generating conveys both an essence and a relation, let it be allowed, that the others do not dissent except in the question, "what ought to be understood through (a consideration of what is) prior" [quid per prius intelligi debeat]. St. Bonaventure's solution of the rest (of the objections) is coherent with the principles, which he defends at length below in d. 27, p. I, q. 2.

II. Very notable is the doctrine of the Seraphic Doctor (at n. 1) concerning the fourfold genus of divine names. These have been taken from Alexander of Hales (loc. cit., a. 1).

III. In the solution of the arguments there is a departure from the usually order. Namely, (St. Bonaventure) defends the opinion of Master (Peter). The Seraphic Doctor strives to solve the arguments adduced for his own sentence in the second place. The marginal notes indicate the order of the solution. To the authors already praised there are adds: Bl. (now St.) Albert (the Great), on this and the following question, SUMMA., p. I, tr. 7, q. 30, m. 4. — Giles the Roman, here in the 1st principle of q. 2. — (Gabriel) Biel, here in q. 1 and 2.

QUESTION II

Whether the power of generating is in the Son?

Second, there is asked, whether the power of generating is in the Son; and that (it is) so, seems from *authorities* and *reasons*.

1. First thus: (St.) Hilary (of Poitiers) in the ninth (book) ON THE TRINITY[1] says: « The Son has in Himself naturally a Nature being begotten »: therefore, the Nature in the Son has been born to generate.

2. Likewise, (St.) Augustine in the book, AGAINST MAXIMINUS (says):[2] « For neither could the Son not generate », but two negations are equivalent to one affirmation: therefore, He could generate.

3. Likewise, by *reasons* it is shown thus: "to generate" is ordained more to the power of generating, than to the power of spirating; but the Father generating the Son communicates to Him[3] the power of spirating: therefore, much more the power of generating.

4. Likewise, the Son is the most expressed image of the Father: therefore, He only imitates the Father, because He cannot be thought (to be) more similar; but if the Son is thought to (be) generating, He is thought to imitate (Him) more: therefore, if He imitates (Him) more amply, than one can think, therefore, also in the act of generating.

5. Likewise, *through (what is) similar* it seems thus: a greater communication and diffusion is in the Eternal Light than in the created light; but created light gives to splendor a power of producing an other, and thus to (what is) to proceed (from it); and[4] if it were of an infinite virtue, it would produce infinite splendors: ergo etc..

6. Likewise, in carnal generation a father is not said to generate a perfect son, unless he gives him the power of

generating: therefore, for an equal reason, nay rather much more strongly,[5] the Son will not be perfect, unless He has the power for that, for which the Father can (act): therefore, to generate. Or if it is not thus among the divine, then, therefore, I ask for the reason, why concerning the perfection of eternal generation there is not in this manner a communication of the power of generating, as (there is) in created generation.

BUT ON THE CONTRARY: 1. (St.) Augustine (in his book), AGAINST MAXIMINUS,[6] says, « that it was not proper [non oportuit] that the Son generate »; but if it was not proper [opportunum], neither (was it) fitting [conveniens]; therefore, it was impossible that the Son generate: therefore, the Son cannot generate: therefore, He does not have the power of generating, because by every power is able the one who has it: ergo etc..

2. Likewise, (St.) Anselm in the PROSLOGION[8] (says): « He who can (do) what is not fitting for him (to do), by as much as he is more able (to do) that, by so much can there be more adversity and perversity in regard to it »: therefore, since 'to generate' does not convene with the Son, if He could (generate), that power would be a misery in Him; but He has no misery: therefore, neither (does He have) the power of generating.

3. Likewise, by *reason* this same is proved thus:[9] every that, in which two somethings are necessarily distinguished, if it befits one necessarily, it is impossible that it ever befit the other, as is clear: if Peter and John necessarily differ in whiteness, and whiteness is fitting to Peter, it is impossible, that it be fitting to John; but the Father and the Son are personally distinct, so that it is necessary that They be distinct, and there is naught to be granted (in that) in which

---

[1] Number 51: Nor, again, do we preach that the Father (is) in the Son by a corporal insinuation, but that He had a Nature, naturally begetting in Itself a Nature begotten out of Him of the same genus.

[2] Book II, ch. 12, n. 3; see the text of Master (Peter) above, ch. 1, near the middle; in which text some codices have *not* [non] in place of *neither* [neque], others *Not (that) the Son could not generate* [non potuit Filius non generare].

[3] We have supplied from the more ancient mss. and ed. 1 *to Him* [ei], which the Vatican edition together with codex cc less well omits.

[4] The Vatican edition, disagreeing with the manuscripts and the first six editions, omits *and* [et].

[5] The Vatican edition, not trusting in the manuscripts and edition 1 has *for a much stronger (reason)* [multo fortiori], and a little below this, contrary to very many manuscripts and edition 1, after *for that* [ad id] it omits *for* [ad]. Then a few codices as I and ff together with edition 1 have *has* [habet] in place of *can* [potest].

[6] Book II, ch. 12, n. 3; see the text of Master (Peter) above, near the middle.

[7] Cf. d. 2, q. 1, at n. 1.

[8] Chapter 7: For he who can (do) this, which is not expedient for him (to do), and which he ought not (do), can (do), what as much as he can more, so much more can adversity and perversity (be) in him. — Under the noun *adversity* [adversitas] is here understood not 'tribulation' (which, as it is, is a good to the Saints), but 'the harmful' [nocivum]. — The Vatican edition, contrary to the ancient codices and edition 1, has *this is ... able* [hoc potest] in place of *that is ... able* [illud potest].

[9] The confused reading of the Vatican edition and codex cc, we have emended with the help of the other codices and edition 1, by putting *thus* [sic] in place of *just as* [sicut], and a little below this *just as is clear* [sicut patet] in place of *as is thus clear* [ut patet sic]. Very many codices have *someones* [aliqui] in place of *somethings* [aliqua].

they are distinguished[1] except in this, that the former is the Generating, that of His (is) the Begotten: therefore, since "to generate" befits the Father, it is impossible, that it befit the Son: therefore, the Son cannot generate: therefore, He does not have the power of generating.

4. Likewise, the generation of the Son from [a] the Father is expressly similar to the very[2] generation of a word from a mind; but the word begotten does not have the power of generating another word, nay rather it is proper, that every word be immediately from [a] the mind: therefore, if the uncreated Word is rightly similar, He does not have a power of generating, but the power of generating is in the Father alone.

5. Likewise, let (St.) Augustine's[3] argument leading to the impossible be (supposed). If the Son has a power or a 'to be able to generate' [posse generandi], let it be posited that He generated; I ask concerning the second (son) similarly; and if there is not a standing still [stare] in the First, it is proper to posit infinite sons, because according to the reckoning by which it does not stand still [statur] in the First, therefore, neither in any: therefore, if there is a standing still — because this (lack of stability)[4] is repugnant to divine completion — but according to the reckoning by which it stands still in any (son), it stands still in the First: therefore, the first (Son) does not have the power of generating.

6. Likewise, let Richard (of St. Victor)'s argumentation be (made):[5] if the Son would generate another son; therefore, since a begotten son attains to the father more than to the grandfather, according to this there would not be There a most high and equal connection: therefore, neither a most high and equal dilection:[6] therefore, neither a perfect beatitude: all of which a pious faith rejects [respuit] as most highly impossible.

CONCLUSION

The Father does not communicate the power of generating to the Son, which is proven by two reasons.

I RESPOND: The opinion of some is, that in the Son there is a power of generating, but He does not generate. Moreover this is not, because He cannot, but because it is not fitting for Him.[7] And they posit a similar in the production of creatures or (in) creation. God can produce infinite creatures;

but that He does not produce (them), this is not out of impotency, but because it is not fitting for Him; thus also in the proposed (objection).

BUT ON THE CONTRARY: Let it be then posited, that that power, which is in the Son for generating, is led into act; it is established that the Son will generate an eternal God: therefore something will be able[8] *to begin* [incipere] to have 'being' and *to be eternal*; but this is impossible and non-intelligible.

On that account[9] it must be said, that the Father does not communicate to the Son a 'to be able to generate' on account of two (reasons). *One* is, that He can not, the *other*, that He ought not.

Moreover, the reason, why He *can* not, is this: because the fecundity to generate is in the Father, because (He is) the principle, and the principle for the reason that (He is) the first. Moreover it is impossible, that the first[10] communicate primacy to an other. For this is oppositio in adiecto, that a person produced be first. Therefore, because the fecundity to generate was in the Father from [ex] a primacy, for that reason He cannot communicate it to the Son; and this I believe to be His own reason, just as shall be clear below in the Twenty-Seventh Distinction,[11] where one deals with, why the Father generates.

Similarly, He *ought* not communicate, since[12] in the emanation of the Divine Persons there ought to be attained an *original distinction* and a *most full communication*: an *original distinction*, because it is necessary, that those which communicate in nature be distinguished through *matter*,[13] and/or through *origin*. Through *matter* it is impossible to distinguish the Persons; because where there is such a manner of distinguishing, there is composition and variation and the multiplication of form, which are all repugnant to God, who is simple and invariable and truly one. And for that reason it is necessary that They be distinguished through *origin* or habitude: therefore, through generating and being generated: therefore, if the Son can generate, He also cannot be distinguished. *If you say*, that there is still a distinction, because one (is) only the Father, another only the Son, another the Father and the Son; then I oppose you, because a second son could generate for the same reason, for which the first (does); and then there would be two, each of which would be father and son.

Similarly, on account of a *most full communication*

---

[1] From very many codices and edition 1 we have substituted (the subjunctive) *they are distinguished* [distinguantur] for (the indicative) *they are distinguished* [distinguuntur].

[2] The Vatican edition, not trusting in the manuscripts and the first six editions, omits *the very* [ipsi].

[3] AGAINST MAXIMINUS, Bk. II, ch. 12, n. 3; see the text of Master (Peter), ch. 1, about the middle. — A little below this very many codices as A F G H I K W Y etc. together with edition 1 have *I will ask* [quaeram] in place of *I ask* [quaero].

[4] A difficult and perhaps corrupted passage. Understand: "to posit infinite sons", or rather: "not to stand still in any (son)"; and for that reason the particle *because* [quia] in this position does not indicate a direct reason, but rather a presupposition in respect of the conditional proposition, *if there is a standing still*, which appears better in this position: "therefore, — because this is repugnant to divine completion — if there is a standing still". — Codex Z reads *therefore it is necessary that it stand still* [ergo necesse est stare]. A little below this after *completion* [completioni], we have added from the manuscripts and edition 1 *but* [sed: trans. note: in opposition to the parenthetical comment].

[5] ON THE TRINITY, Bk. V, ch. 10 ff., and Bk. VI, ch. 2 ff.. — The Vatican edition, disagreeing with the manuscripts and edition 1, after *be (made)* [Richardi] adds *that* [ut] and a little below this, not trusting in the more ancient codices and edition 1, but in the works of Richard (ON THE TRINITY, Bk. VI, ch. 6) in place of *to a father, than to a grandfather* [patri quam avo] it puts *toward a father than (anyone) else* [ad patrem quam alius].

[6] We follow codex O, while the other codices and editions read

distinction [distinctio], which seems to correspond neither to the context nor to Richard's argument.

[7] Very many codices together with edition 1 omit *for Him* [ei], which they, however, do include, inconsistently, a little below, where the same proposition recurs. Then ed. 1 with one or another cod. has (the subjunctive) *produce* [producat] for (the indicative) *produce* [producit].

[8] The Vatican edition together with codex cc has *had been able* [poterat], but the more ancient mss. together with ed. 1 withstand this.

[9] We have substituted *On this account* [Propterea] for *On account of this* [Propter hoc], trusting in the more ancient mss. and ed. 1, however, other mss. then read *this must be said* [hoc dicendum] and/or *to this (objection)* [ad hoc]. Then, on the authority of the same mss. and ed. 1 we have put *a 'to be able to generate'* for *the power of generating* [potentiam generandi].

[10] Thus the older codd. with ed. 1, against the Vatican ed. and cod. cc, which have *a principle* [principium] for *the first* [primum], but less elegantly. Then the codd. dissent among themselves; for some as F G H I K cc and ee read *for this (saying) is an* [nam haec est], others, such as P and Q with eds. 4 & 5 read *for this is* [nam hoc est], others still with the Vatican ed. and ed. 1 read *for here there is* [nam hic est].

[11] Part I, a. 1, q. 2.

[12] With the manuscripts and edition 1 favoring it, we have substituted *since* [quoniam] for *because* [quia]. Codex R after *Similarly* adds *on account of emanation* [propter emanationem].

[13] Very many codices together with edition 1 here and immediately below have *nature* [naturam] in place of *matter* [materiam], but falsely, as is clear from the context.

He ought not communicate, because a multiplication of supposits according to a similar manner of stepping forth is not but either on account of a *defect of duration*, just as has been said,[1] in (regard to things) generable and corruptible, that (their) 'to be' is perpetuated through a successive generation, or on account of a *defect of perfect action*, so that there is done [fiat] through the more, what cannot (be done)[2] through the one. Just as more stars have been made, because one would not suffice for that which all do, so also (there are) more Angels and more souls to fill that City (of God) and to manifest the goodness of God, which neither one soul nor one Angel could sufficiently manifest. Therefore, since in the Son of God there is a most full communication, because the Father gives His own whole Infinity to Him, it was not fitting, that He communicate to the Son that power: and for that reason it was impossible, because in the divine anything unfitting is impossible.[3]

1. To that, therefore, which is objected in the contrary through the authority of (St.) Hilary, that the Son has in Himself a nature begetting; it must be said, that that word is improper, and one must not argue out of improper words, but rather their impropriety is to be expounded, as Master (Peter) above expounded (them). For the sense is: 'He has in Himself a Nature begetting, that is the Nature of the Father begetting'.

2. To that which is objected, that neither[4] could He not; it must be said, that Master (Peter) expounds (this) well, that is, (that) He was not impotent out of this. Whence according to the art (of Logic) one must distinguish, when there is said, "the Son could not generate": because "*not*" can be held *privatively*; and then the sense is, "*He could not*", that is, 'He was impotent'; and then power is denied, and aptitude is left behind, just as concerning an amputee [tuncatus] there is said, that he cannot take a step, because (as) one *apt* he has been born to take a step and he *cannot* take a step;[5] in this

manner there cannot be said of the Son, that He does not have an aptitude for this; and in this sense (St.) Augustine speaks. In another manner "*could not*" [non posse] is held *negatively*; and in this sense it must be conceded, that the Son cannot generate.

3. To that which is objected: that the Father communicates to the Son a spirative power; the response is clear: because since the Son would generate, He cannot have a primacy in respect of generation; but since He is not spirated, He is unable to be spirated [inspirabilis]; and for that reason He could have a primacy and a fecundity in respect of that: and thus it is clear that[6] the reason is not valid.

4. To that which is objected, that the Son is the most expressed image etc.; it must be said, that the Son is said[7] (to be) the most expressed image for the reason that He represents (the Father) in all (respects), in which an image is bound to represent; but thus an image is bound to represent, however so that it not be the (thing) imaged; otherwise it would not be an image. Moreover, if the Son would represent (the Father) in the act of generating, He would already be the Father: and for that reason it is neither intelligible nor possible, that the Son generate or that the Father in generation be imitated.

5. To that which is objected concerning light and splendor, it must be said, that it is not similar, because light does not perfectly multiply itself in the first splendor: for that reason it does in more what it cannot in one.

6. Similarly, also in a carnal son (this) must be understood; whence one father generates more sons.[8] However, this reason is not the principal one, but that which has been said above (is),[9] because in these inferiors there is not a fecundity through a reckoning of primacy, but through a reckoning of perfection. In God, moreover, because He is the Most Perfect and First, it is not only through a Nature of perfection; because then it would be in all the Persons, and (its) standing still[10] could not be; but (also) through a reckoning of primacy. Likewise, those reasons do not proceed through the similar, nay rather (they proceed) more through the dissimilar.

SCHOLIUM

I. This Question adheres [cohaeret] intimately with the preceding In the Response there is said: that the Persons are distinguished through origin or habitude. This ought not be understood disjunctively, but rather thus: through origin with the relations resulting from this, cf. below d. 26, q. 3 and the Scholium. — In the solution to n. 2 the words: « and then power is denied and aptitude is left behind » etc. are easily understood, if one attends, that the statement is expounded with a privative negation by two propositions, one of which denies the act, the other of the two posits a subject out of its nature *apt* for acting. Therefore, if the words: "*The Son can not*", are taken privatively, i. e. that (He is) *impotent*, then there is *first* supposed,

that from the Nature itself He is apt for this, and *then* there is asserted, that He cannot be in act. Cf. St. Thomas and Richard (of Middleton), here about the text (of Master Peter).

II. Cf. Alexander of Hales, SUMMA., p. I, q. 42, m. 3, a. 2. — (Bl. John Duns) Scotus, REPORTATIO, here in q. 2 (where he explicitly approves of the Seraphic Doctor's solution). — St. Thomas, here in q. 2, a. 1; SUMMA., I, q. 42, a. 6, at n. 3. — Bl. (now St.) Albert (the Great), here in a. 5, 10, and 11. — (Bl.) Peter of Tarentaise, here in q. 2 at the beginning. — Henry of Ghent, SUMMA., a. 54, q. 8 and a. 58, q. 1. — Durandus (of Saint-Pourçain), here in q. 3. — (Bl.) Dionysius the Carthusian, here in q. 3. — (Gabriel) Biel, here in q. 3.

---

[1] Distinction 5, a. 2, q. 1. — The Vatican edition has *just as there is* [sicut est], but nearly all the codices with edition 1 withstand this.

[2] Supply with codex Z *be done* [fieri], and or read with not a few codices as A S T V and edition 1 *one cannot* [non potest unum]. Then with the help of the older manuscripts and edition 1 we have substituted *have been made* [sunt factae] in place of *have been perfected* [sunt perfectae]. Codex M with edition 1 read *as* [sic] in place of *just as* [sicut].

[3] See above d. 2, q. 1. at n. 1. — Then, trusting in the more ancient mss. and ed. 1, we have substituted *therefore* [ergo] for *moreover* [autem].

[4] We have inserted the particle *neither* [neque], which is required from the context and for the objection, in place of which codex T puts *not* [non]; very many codices omits this particle, reading *that He could not* [quod non potuit], perhaps for the reason that, just as we have noted above in the objection, the words of (St.) Augustine are quoted in another manner, namely *not (that) the Son could not generate*; in which reading the words *not generate* [non generare] are to be supplied. Codex T a little below this, after *the Son*, has *not could not*; but a twofold negation here does not seem as necessary, as (it does) a little above.

[5] The Vatican edition together with codex cc omits the words *because (as) one apt* [quia aptus] upto *to take a step* [gradi], but the more ancient codices together with edition 1 withstand this.

[6] Not a few codices as bb and ff with edition 1 have *why* [quare].

[7] Trusting in the older manuscripts and edition 1 we have supplied *for the reason* [ideo] and in place of *is* [est] we have substituted *is said (to be)* [dicitur], and a little below this after *but* [sed] we have expunged *nevertheless* [tamen].

[8] The more ancient codices together with edition 1 omit here *carnal* [carnales], which the Vatican edition together with codex cc superfluously adds.

[9] That is, first in the body of this question. — Then at *but through a reckoning of perfection* [sed per rationem perfectionis] codices L and O add not badly *only* [tantum].

[10] Codex K has *being begun* [principatus] in place of *standing still* [status]. At the end of the response codices aa and bb add *because light and a father produce (something) diverse from themselves* [quia lux et pater producunt diversum a se].

QUESTION III

Whether the power to generate and the power to create are a unique power?

Third, there is asked, whether '*to be able to generate*' and '*(to be able) to create*' is[1] a unique '*to be able*'; and it seems that it is not a unique one.

1. (St.) Augustine (says):[2] « To one belongs the Father, to the other belongs God »: therefore, to one belongs the one generating, to the other the one creating; but the power of generating is the one generating, the power of creating is the one creating: therefore, etc..

2. Likewise, powers are distinguished through acts and acts through objects:[3] therefore, if generation is terminated at God and creation at the creature, and these are entirely diverse: ergo etc..

3. Likewise, powers are plurified through subjects, since in several [pluribus] potent (things)[4] there are more [plures] powers; but the power of creating is in the Son or the "to be able to create" (is), but in Him there is not a "to be able to generate": therefore, they are not one 'to be able'.

4. Likewise, whatever hold themselves thus, that one can be understood, with the other of the two not understood, and conversely, those are not one; but a "to be able to generate" can be understood, with the power of creating excluded [circumscripta]; and conversely a "to be able to create", with the power of generating excluded:[5] ergo etc.

ON THE CONTRARY: 1. To one entirely simple potent (thing) there is only one 'to be able'; but[6] the Father is an entirely simple potent: therefore, He has only a unique 'to be able'; but He has a 'to be able to generate' and a 'to be able to create': therefore, those two are a unique 'to be able'.

2. Likewise, if there is one 'to be able' and an other,[7] since 'to be able to generate' regards a Person, 'to be able to create' the Nature: therefore, Nature and Person are two: therefore, neither is Nature said of Person, nor conversely, which is entirely false.

3. Likewise, if there is a distinction between 'to be able to generate' and 'to be able to create': therefore, there is an *order* there. Therefore, I ask, which is prior[8] according to the reckoning of understanding. And it seems, that the power of generating (is), because it is in respect of the eternal, and the eternal (is) before the temporal. *But on the contrary*: an understanding of the common is before the understanding of the proper; but the power of

creating means (something) common to the Three, the power of generating (something) proper to the Father: ergo etc..

CONCLUSION

The power of generating and the power of creating differ not according to thing, but only according to the reckoning of understanding.

I RESPOND: It must be said, that '*to be able* to generate' and '*to be able* to create' is[9] a *unique "to be able"*, said, however, in a twofold manner. For, in regard to the thing [in re], 'to be the Father' and 'to be God' is one 'to be', but differing according to the reckoning of understanding; because the former[10] is absolute, when I say "*to be God*", the latter one related, when I say "*to be the Father*". Similarly, also in a 'to be able' it must (thus) be understood. Whence just as the Essence and Person are, in regard to the thing, One, nevertheless [tamen] there is[11] a difference of reckoning in (their) understanding and in (their) saying; similarly it must be said concerning the power of generating and of creating.

And[12] just as the *difference* there is not according to thing [non re], but according to reckoning [secundum rationem], thus the *order*, there, is according to the reckoning of understanding. Whence, according to diverse comparisons they have one order and an other. For, when comparing "to be able to create" and "to be able to generate" to that *to which* they belong; since "to be able to create" belongs to nature, "to be able to generate" belongs to person, and (since) the understanding of the common (is)[13] before understanding of the proper; so without calumny the power of creating is prior according to the reckoning of understanding. Moreover, when comparing (that) to that *toward which* it is terminated; since the power of creating regards the temporal, but the power of generating the eternal; the power of generating is prior according to the reckoning of understanding to the power of creating; and, thus, are clear the objections concerning *order*.

Therefore, to be conceded are the reasons showing, that 'to be able to generate' and 'to be able to create' do not differ by a difference according to thing or according to essence.

1. To that which is objected, that to one belongs

---

[1] The Vatican edition here a little after this, not trusting in the manuscripts and edition 1, has *are* [sint].

[2] ON THE TRINITY, Bk. II, ch. 1 and 6, and ON PSALM 68, Sermon 1, n. 5. — The Vatican edition, contrary to the more ancient codices, has *Through (St.) Augustine (there is said)*; edition 1 has *(St.) Augustine, you are said (to have said)* [dicere Augustinus].

[3] See the words of Aristotle on this, above in q. 1, fundament 2.

[4] Thus the more ancient codices together with edition 1, but the Vatican edition together with codex cc has *because in several subjects* [quia in pluribus subiectis].

[5] The mutilated reading of the Vatican edition and of codex cc, which omit the words *and conversely* up to *of generating excluded* [e converso ... generandi], we have restored with the help of the other manuscripts and edition 1.

[6] We have inserted, from the older mss. and ed. 1, the less well omitted *but* [sed].

[7] Codex bb has well enough *if "to be able to create" is one "to be able" and "to be able to generate" an other* [si posse creare et posse generare est aliud et aliud posse].

[8] Very many codices, not so well nor coherently with what is subjoined, read *more principal* [principalius].

[9] The Vatican edition, contrary to the manuscripts, has *are* [sunt].

[10] The Vatican edition, contrary to nearly all the codices and edition 1, has *what* [quod] in place of *the former* [hoc], and a little below this *the same is* [idem est] in place of *the latter* [illud].

[11] The codices do not agree among themselves; some, such as A F G H K M T and V, together with edition 1, have *with* [cum] in place of *nevertheless there is* [tamen est], others together with the Vatican edition exhibit our text, codex R reads *there differ in reckoning* [differunt ratione]. Then, after *of reckoning* [rationis], not a few codices, such as A T X etc., together with edition 1, add the particle *both* [et].

[12] Trusting in the manuscripts and the six of the first editions we have supplied *And* [Et]. Then, a few codices, such as H and K, have *a reckoning of understanding, thus* [rationem intelligendi].

[13] With very many codices and edition 1 favoring it, we have expunged the here-added *is* [est].

[14] From the older mss. and ed. 1, we have inserted *therefore* [ergo].

God, to the other the Father; it must be said, that (St.) Augustine speaks of the one and the other according to an anotherness of reckoning [alietate rationis], and not of thing. And an anotherness of reckoning is understood through that manner, by which it has been said above in the Fifth Distinction,[1] where there is asked, whether the Essence would generate.

2. To that which is objected, that[2] powers are distinguished through acts etc.; it must be said, that this is true concerning those acts, which have (their) completion from (their) objects; but not so are the divine acts. Whence although a creature and the Son differ entirely, however, generation and creation are but the same, just as essence and person. For God in acting is not completed by an object, because He acts by His very self [se ipso].

3. To that which is objected, that powers are plurified through subjects; it must be said, that that is true

concerning a proper subject; but the Son (is) not, inasmuch as He (is) *the Son*, a subject of a power of creating, but rather inasmuch (as He is) *God*. And it is established, that the Divine Nature is not numbered [non facit numerum] with the Father; thus neither (is) the power regarding the Nature (numbered) with the power of the Father.

4. To that which is objected last, that the one can be understood without the other of the two and conversely; it must be said, that either you are speaking as much as regards the[3] *signified*, or as much as regards the *connoted*. If as much as regards the *connoted*, you speak a truth, because a creature can be understood, the Person of the Son not understood, and conversely. If as much as regards the *principal signified*, you speak[4] falsely; for it is impossible, that the power of generating be understood without the power of creating, just as it is impossible to understand the Person without the Essence.

SCHOLIUM

I. On the difference between essence and person cf. below, d. 33, q. 2 and the Scholium. — Regarding the words in the solution to n. 3: « that is true concerning a proper subject », it must be noted, that a proximate subject is distinguished from an adequate (subject) of any power and a remote one. The proximate or primary subject of the Divine Creative Power is unique, namely, the Divine Essence. And the axiom: 'powers are plurified through their subjects', does not have to be true, when it concerns a remote subject, which is a Divine Person.

II. The other ancient Scholastics do not but briefly treat of this question. The same is touched upon by the Seraphic Doctor below in d. 20, a. 1, q. 1. — Alexander of Hales, SUMMA., p. I, q. 20, m. 1. and 2. — St. Thomas, here at q. 1, a. 3; DE POTENTIA, q. 2, a. 6. — (Bl.) Peter of Tarentaise, here at q. 3, a. 1. — Richard o f Middleton, hic. q. 4. — Giles the Roman, on this and the following question, here in 1. princ., q. 3. — (Bl.) Dionysius the Carthusian., hic q. 2.

QUESTION IV

Whether "to be abe to be generated" and "to be able to be created" are a univocal "to be able"?

Last, there is asked, whether "*to be able to be generated*" [posse generari] and "*to be able to be created*" [posse creari] are[5] a univocal "to be able" [posse]. And it seems that (they are) not:

1. Because, although it is the same "to generate" and "to create" as much as regards the principal signified, nevertheless it is (something) else [est aliud] "to be generated" and "to be created", just as Creator and creature (are): therefore, since Creator and creature do not have[6] a univocal "to be" [esse]: ergo etc..

2. Likewise, creation means an egress and a change [mutationem], generation, however, excludes every change: therefore, since "to be able to be created" conveys a potency to be transmuted [potentia transmutandi], (and) "to be able to be generated" (does) not, since the powers [potentiae] differ in their generality in regard to the potency to be transmutated,[7] and in this they do not convene: therefore, (they convene) in no (power).

3. Likewise, "*every*" [omne] distributes a term on behalf of all, which are univocally and/or analogically meant [univocantur vel analogantur] in it;[8] but, when I say "*omnipotent*", a distribution does not come to be on behalf of that, which can generate, because, then, the Son would not be omnipotent: therefore, it is manifest, that each "to be able" [posse] is neither a univocal nor an analogical (term): otherwise omnipotence would not convene with the Son.

BUT ON THE CONTRARY: 1. '*Thing*' [res] is common to the enjoyable and the usable: therefore, since the *possible* [possibile] belongs to an equal and/or greater ambit than the *thing*, and (since) there is not a greater difference between the generated and the created[9] than between the enjoyable and the usable, for an equal reason the possible or the "to be able" is common to each.

2. Likewise, in eternals there cannot be multiplicity

---

[1] Article 1, q. 1.

[2] The Vatican edition not trusting in the manuscripts and edition 1 omits *that* [quod]. — Next the following proposition is understood of those acts, which *are caused* in some manner by their objects, just as happens in our act of understanding [intellectione].

[3] Codex Z, on account of what is subjoined, does not incongruously adds *principal* [principale], that is, that which is first and *per se* signified, having excluded every connotation.

[4] The more ancient codices such as A F G H K S W etc. either omit *you say* [dicis], which then certainly is to be supplied, and/or with edition 1 put *is* [est] in its place.

[5] Very many mss., together with the first six editions, have *is* [sit].

[6] The Vatican edition, disagreeing with many codices as H I S T W Z aa etc. and edition 1, has less aptly *does not have* [habeat].

[7] Cf. Aristotle, METAPHYSICS, Bk. V, text 17 and Bk. IX, text 2 (Bl. IV, ch. 2, and Bk. VIII, ch. 1), where the species of power are recounted

and for their proximate genus, in which they all agree, there is assigned, that they are the principle of movement or transmutation.

[8] Aristotle, METAPHYSICS, Bk. V, text 34 (Bk. IV, ch. 26): Of those (terms), indeed, the positing (of which) does not cause a difference, "*every*" is said. Cf. Peter of Spain, SUMMULA, tract "On Distribution". — Then the more ancient codices together with edition 1 have *to generate* [generare]; the Vatican edition and codex cc have the not well said *to be generated*. Indeed one deals with passive generation, but the argumentation begins from active power, introduced under the word *omnipotent*, and rightly is it inferred, that if an *active* power of generating does not properly fall under omnipotence, then *passive* generation also does not fall under the *all* which it can (accomplish): ergo etc..

[9] Trusting in the older manuscripts and edition 1, we have substituted *the created* [creatum] for *the creature* [creaturam].

nor diversity: therefore, since there were a "to be able to be created" and a "to be able to be generated" from eternity before the foundation of creation [ante conditionem creaturae], therefore they do not[1] have a multiplication in power itself.

3. Likewise, when I say: "a creature can be created", I mean[2] nothing created; because that (verb) is truly said of that which is (yet) entirely nothing, just as (one presently speaks) of the soul of the Antichrist: therefore, I only mean the power of the agent; but the power of God is unique, not having any multiplicity: therefore, to Him there belongs a univocal "to be able" regarding "to be able to be created" and "to be able to be generated".

CONCLUSION

"To be able to be generated" and "to be able to be created" in regard to the principal signified are the same according to thing and are said univocally, however, in regard to the connoted (they are said) analogically.

I RESPOND: It must be said, that when I say *"to be able to be created"* and *"to be able to be generated"*, I mean the *principal (thing) signified* [principale significatum] and I mean the (thing) *connoted* [connotatum]. As much as regards the *principal (thing) signified*, I say, that "to be able to be created" means the same according to thing, which "to be able to create" (means), differing solely according to[3] the manner of speaking and/or meaning: because what is said through a manner of action by "to be able to create", means through a manner of passion "to be able to be created". However, as much as regards the *connoted,* it means an effect in the creature.

When,[4] therefore, "to be able to be created" and "to be able to be generated" are compared, if they are compared according to the reckoning of the *principal signified*, I say, that not only is it *univocal*, nay rather (it is) also *unique*, as has been seen,[5] however, (it is) in one

manner [aliter] and (is) understood and enunciated in another [aliter]. But, if they are compared according to the reckoning of the connoted, thus I do concede, that it is *analogous*, just as the noun *"thing"* [res] (is) regarding enjoyables and useables. For, although the Creator and the creature do not have a common univocal (term), nevertheless [tamen], they do have a (common) analogous one.

It must be noted, however, that analogy is twofold: a *certain*[6] (kind of analogy is) through a reduction toward a *unity of nature* according to a 'before and after' [secundum prius et posterius]; and this can be by comparing creature to creature, and in this the sign[7] distributes on behalf of all the contained, unless there is a distribution restricted out of an addition, and/or out of use or a manner of speaking, just as an apt [accommoda] distribution[8] is meant, such as if one says: "heaven covers all" [caelum tegit omnia]. The *other* is the analogy through reduction toward a *unity of proportional similitude,* not (toward a unity) of nature; and what is thus analogically said [analogatur] is not among others, but over others.[9] Whence the distribution properly on behalf of that, does not distribute, unless it has been extended. Whence God is not a being [ens] among all (beings), but over all.

And, hence it is, that "omnipotent" does not distribute on behalf of the 'power of generating' properly accepted as a distribution, unless a certain extension be made, and from that, *per consequens*, a certain appropriation be made about the subject [suppositum]. Whence, *properly*, "omnipotent" convenes with Three, because it does not distribute[10] on behalf of a power of generating; but, *appropriately*, according to which there is an amplification [fit ampliatio] on the part of the sign, it belongs to the Father alone.

From these all the objections are clear; for they proceed by diverse ways, as is clear to the one looking at them attentively [patet intuenti].

SCHOLIUM

I. To understand rightly this subtle question, which is treated by few of the ancient Scholastics, one must attend to the sense in which the Seraphic doctor accepts the saying: *"to be able to be created"*. It is not taken in the sense of a *passive* power (or potency), which is on the part of the creature, but in the sense of an *active* power, which is in God, as is clear from the last argument. The reason for this manner of speaking is explained below in d. 42, q. 4, where the Seraphic Doctor says among other things the following (at n. 2): « "(the power of) the world to be created" [mundum creari], although it means a power through a manner of passion (i. e. a potency), however, according to thing it does not mean but an active power, because before the creation of the world there is nothing but active power. » Likewise, (at n. 1): « The "possible" can be said denominatively by reason of [a] a passive and/or active power; and because in God there is properly an active power, for that reason the "possible" is meant simply according to that which is denominated by it, not according to what (is) from passive (power) ». He proves this sentence in the body (of the Response). Cf. also Alexander of Hales, SUMMA., p. I, q. 20, m. 2 and 3, and St. Thomas, SENT., Bk. I, d. 42, q. 2, a. 2.

Certainly a creatable thing before its own creation is entirely nothing nor has (anything), therefore, neither (does it have) a passive power; whence only in the manner of a extrinsic denomination, i. e. with regard to the prime cause, is there attributed to it a *'to be able to be created'*.

II. With these supposed, there are manifestly three propositions (in the argument) of the Seraphic Doctor: 1. "To be able *to be created*" and "to be able *to create*", though they differ grammatically, they do not differ in thing, if one attends to the principal (thing) signified, which is the Divine, Creative Essence. — 2. "To be able *to be created*" and "to be able *to be generated*" by reason of the principal signified are univocal, nay rather unique. « For the Divine Substance Itself under the reckoning, by which it is communicable through generation, is the Power, by which the Son could be generated », Richard of Middleton (here at q. 3). — 3. "To be able *to be generated*" and "to be able *to be created*" by reason of *the connoted* do not have anything common except an analogous (term, i. e. "to be able"), since the first connotes the eternal Son, but the second a creature.

---

[1] Codex W reads *neither do they* [nec].

[2] The Vatican edition together with codex cc, contrary to the rest of the codices and edition 1, has *it means* [dicit]; codex I reads *that the creature can be created, I say that nothing is created* [creaturam posse creari, nihil dico esse creatum]. A little below this after *just as* [sicut] codex M reads *as it is (presently) concerning the soul* [est de anima].

[3] Trusting the mss. and ed. 1, we have expunged the here added *in* [in] for *according to*. Then, the Vatican ed., disagreeing with the mss. and e. 1, has *is meant by "to be able to be created"* [dicitur per posse creari] in place of *"to be able to be created" means* [dicit posse creari].

[4] The faulty reading of the Vatican ed., *By that manner which* [Quo modo] instead of *When* [Quando], is corrected from the mss. and ed. 1.

[5] A little above this; see also the preceding Question.

[6] The Vatican edition together with codex cc has *a certain one is* [est quaedam], which *is* [est] is absent from the rest of the manuscripts and edition 1.

[7] That is *"every"*, which is for that reason called *the sign*, because through it there is indicated, how much the other term is worth.

[8] The Vatican edition, not trusting in the more ancient manuscripts and edition 1, has *an accommodated distribution* [accomodata distributio], and a little below this *of the similitude of proportion* [proportionis similitudinis] in place of *proportional similitude* [proportionalis similitudinis]. A few codices have *rules* [regit] in place of *covers* [tegit], but incongruously and contrary to Peter of Spain's, SUMMULA, tract "On Distribution". — Then after *of nature* [naturae], codices aa and bb add *as of the Creator to the creature* [ut Creatoris ad creaturam].

[9] From the older manuscripts and edition 1 we have supplied *but above others* [sed super alia], and a little below this, with the consent of all the manuscripts and editions 1, 2, 3 and 6, we have inserted *but over all* [sed super omnia].

[10] Codices M and X add *properly* [proprie].

III. In regard to *analogy in general*, cf. above d. 1, Doubt 5, and ibid., a. 3, q. 1 and the Scholium. The text distinguishes a twofold analogy: the first species is that which comes to be through a "leading back" [reductionem] toward the unity of nature; the second, through a leading back toward the unity of proportional similitude. About the first species we note these (things). In any one genus of created things there is one, which is thus the measure of the others, so that anyone (of them) has perfection of its nature only inasmuch as it approaches more or less this measure. In this first species of analogy « a distributive sign (e. g. "every") distributes on behalf of all those contained », i. e. it applies the concept of the term (it modifies) to all and each comprehended under it. But this is not valid in regard to the second species. The second species

or the analogy of proportionality is explained in the text. From this principle the Seraphic Doctor deduces, that the power of generating in God is not comprehended properly under "omnipotence" (in the body and in Doubts 1 and 2). Teaching the same are: Alexander of Hales, SUMMA., p. I, q. 21, m. 1, a. 3. — (Bl. John Duns) Scotus, REPORTATIO, on SENT., Bk. I, d. 20, q. 2. — Bl. (now St.) Albert (the Great), here in a. 3. — (Bl.) Peter of Tarentaise, here in q. 3. a. 2. — Giles the Roman, SENT., Bk. I, d. 20, principle 1, q. 1 and 2. — (Bl.) Dionysius the Carthusian, here in q. 3. — St. Thomas also agrees, SENT., Bk. I, d. 20, q. 1, a. 1; SUMMA., I, q. 42, a. 6, at n. 3; however, in ON POWER, q. 2, a. 5 he speaks otherwise. But it seems, that solely (his) manner of speaking is diverse.

IV. In regard to the conclusion, cf. Alexander of Hales, SUMMA., p. I, q. 20, m. 1 and 2. — Bl. (now St.) Albert, here in a. 4.

DOUBTS ON THE TEXT OF THE MASTER

DOUBT I

In this part of his (text), there occur doubts about the text, and the first concerns that solution of Master (Peter's), which says, that it does not follow (that if): *the Father can generate, what the Son (can) not:*[1] *therefore, He can (do) something, which the Son (can) not*; and he responds, that *"to be able to generate" is not 'to be able (to do) something subject to the divine power'*. But this does not seem to solve, but rather aggravate the argument. For then, since *'to be able to* generate'[2] is the maximum *'to be able'*, it seems that a more unfitting (conclusion) follows, and it derogates more from the power of the Son, if He is deficient in this, than if in (those acts) subject[3] to the Divine Power.

I RESPOND: It must be said, that Master (Peter) solves (it) well. For the power of the Father has (an ability) to be compared to the inferior and to the equal, but not to a superior, since He lacks [careat] a superior. When it is compared to an *inferior*, then it is an essential power and (is) essentially retained, because it connotes (His) looking-back in regard to the creature [respectum in creatura][4]; and in respect of such a power it would be unfitting, that the Father would be able (to do) something, which the Son would not be able (to do), because They would then differ by Essence. Moreover, when it is compared to an *equal*, as to a Person, then it is extended [trahitur]* toward a Person; and then there is nothing [nullus] unfitting, if there is some personal property in the Father, which is not in the Son. For that reason it does not follow, that there is some power in the Father, which is not in the Son.[5]

DOUBT II

Likewise, is doubted concerning this which is said, that *the generation of the Son does not concern all*. For Richard of St. Victor[6] seems to say the contrary, who says, that because He is omnipotent, it cannot be excluded [excusari],

that the Son generate: therefore, the generation of the Son is contained under omnipotence: therefore, the Son is contained and is among *all*.

I RESPOND: It must be said, that, just as Master (Peter) says, the generation of the Son is not contained under "omnipotence", unless "omnipotence" would be accepted through appropriation. And what Richard says is not understood,[7] as if the Son is *among all*, but as *before all*; whence he argues a posteriori. For if the emanation of the Nature according to the reckoning of understanding preceded the emanation according to the reckoning of the Will, God would never be able to produce a creature through (His) Will, unless He also produced a Son through (His) Nature.

DOUBT III

Likewise, he seems to speak badly, when he says, that *'to be the Father' is not a 'to be something'*; because, between *something* and *nothing* there falls no medium [non cadit medium], if He is not a 'to be something': therefore, He is a 'to be nothing'.[8]

I RESPOND: "*To be something*" [esse aliquid] is said in a twofold manner: *either* commonly regarding essence and person; and thus there falls no medium, and in this sense "*to be the Father*" is a "*to be something*"; *in another manner*, insofar as it is extended[9] to essence; and thus there does fall between a '*to be something*' and a '*to be nothing*' a medium, that is, a '*to be someone*'; for a person is predicated as a '*who*', not as a '*what*'.[10]

DOUBT IV

Likewise, is asked concerning that illation of Master (Peter's): 'the Holy Spirit could be the Son, therefore, He could be changed', and it is posited there (where he says): *For if He could be born, He could be the Son* etc.. That illation of his seems not to be valid, because in creatures, where

---

[1] Supply here and a little below this, with codd. X & dd, *can* [potest].

[2] The Vatican edition confusedly and contrary to the more ancient codices and edition 1 has *When* [Cum] in place of *Then* [Tunc], and then it proceeds to read: *for 'to be able to generate Him' is the greatest 'to be able'* etc. [enim generare eum possit sit posse etc.].

[3] The Vatican edition falsely, in place of *in (those acts) subject* [in subiectis], puts *'that He generate the Son' would be something subject* [eum generare Filium esse aliquid subiectum] and contrary to all the codices together with edition 1, which dissent only in this, that many of them as A C F G H M R S T etc. after *than* [quam] omit less well the *if* [si]. Codex O has *for if He is deficient in this, He is more deficient, than if He is deficient in (those acts) subject (to the Divine Power)* [si enim in hoc deficit, plus deficit, quam si deficit in subiectis].

[4] Not trusting in the manuscripts and editions 1, 2, and 3, the Vatican edition prefaces this with *an effect or* [effectum seu], and a little before this it puts *held* [tenta] in place of *retained* [retenta].

[5] Concerning this and the following doubt see here q. 3 and 4 together with the Scholia.

[6] ON THE TRINITY, Bk. III, ch. 4: But who without doubt is omnipotent, cannot be excluded through an impossibility.

[7] Some codices read *does not understand* [non intelligit]; codices H and O have *you may not understand* [non intelligas]. A little below this, from the more ancient manuscripts and edition 1, after *he argues* [arguit], we have substituted *a* [a] in place of *ex* [ex].

[8] Thus the manuscripts together with edition 1, but the Vatican edition reads *if the Father would not be something, therefore, He would be nothing. I respond: It must be said that to be* etc. [si Pater non esse aliquid, ergo esse nihil. Resp. Dicendum quod esse etc.].

[9] Very many codices, such as A F G K T U V Y etc., together with edition 1, read *it is contracted* [contrahitur] for *it is extended* [trahitur].*

[10] (For) more (on this), see above d. 23, a. 1, q. 3.

---

* Trans. note: Here the Latin <u>trahitur</u>, is rendered by the English *extended*, and is said in respect of the signification of terms, not in respect of Divine relations, since extended, simply speaking, puts what is extended outside of or away from that which is extending.

relation differs more from supposit, it can be said that the[1] similar can be dissimilar to the other without its own change [mutatione]: therefore, since filiation and spiration are relations, for an equal reason the Son will be able to be the Holy Spirit, and <u>vice versa</u>, without change. *Likewise*, every mutable is something besides that, according to which it is changed, so that if a *non-white* becomes *white*, it is other than whiteness: therefore, if the Holy Spirit is understood to be changed, if He would be generated, then, in this, the one would be the *generation*, the other the *That who is generated*; but this (is) false: ergo etc..

I RESPOND: It is otherwise in the relations of creature and God: since relations in creatures do not grant relatives to exist [existere]; whence a thing can be without them and with them; but among the divine they grant Persons 'to exist'; and for that reason, if there is understood in the Persons, what a property[2] is in [insit] a hypostasis, it is understood to belong to a Hypostasis, and similarly, if it is understood to not be in (a hypostasis), it is understood not to belong to a Hypostasis. Therefore, since the Holy Spirit could not simultaneously be spirated and generated — because although one Person could produce in two manners, yet, one Person cannot but be produced in one manner — it follows of necessity [de necessitate]: if the Holy Spirit can and/or could be the Son, He is able not be the Spirit or not be spirated; and, if He could be generated, He could be (the Son): and, thus, He could be made a 'not being' from a 'being' and a 'being' from a 'not being', and through this be changed.

And, thus,[3] the last (objection) is clear, because one is not said to be changed on account of a diversification of properties about the same supposit, just as is in natural mutation, but on account of the corruption and inception of the same. Nor is that similar: 'the Father can generate and spirate without His own mutation: therefore, the Holy Spirit (can)[4] be generated and spirated'; because it is not an unfitting (conclusion), that one principle produce by more manners, but that One begun be produced by more manners is impossible and co-impossible [incompossibile]; and for that reason that (objection) is clear.

DOUBT V

Likewise, it seems that he speaks a falsehood, when he says: *the Father is not able except by nature; for His power is by essence*, because according to this "*to generate, what in no manner is essential*", would in no manner belong to (His) Power.

I RESPOND: Although Power, absolutely considered, is the same (thing) which Essence (is), nevertheless [tamen], "power" [potentia], because it is not a noun so [adeo] abstract as "essence" [essentia], is extended to a Person. Whence "the power of generating" does not

mean 'the Divine Nature' simply, but 'the Nature as (it is) in such a Person', that is, (in) an Innascible One; for that reason the (case) is not similar concerning this noun, "*essence*", and concerning this noun, "*power*".[5]

DOUBT VI

Likewise, it seems that he speaks badly there (where he says): *You signify the one power, by which the Father is able to beget* etc.; because there is a sufficient division of power by *active* and *passive*;[6] but "*to be able to generate*" means an active power, "*to be able to be begotten*" a passive power: therefore, another power cannot be signified. *If you say*, that '*to generate*' is not to act properly, nor (is) '*to be generated*' similarly '*to suffer*'; *it is objected*, that powers are distinguished through acts;[7] but it is one (thing) 'to beget' and another 'to be begotten': therefore, there is one [alia] power belonging to the latter and (another) to the former.

I RESPOND: That distinction of his, which Master (Peter) posits concerning the power of begetting and of being begotten [potentia gignendi active et passive], is founded upon this, that power can be considered according to that *which it is*; and thus it means the Nature, and just as one Nature is in the One generating and the One begotten, but in the Other it is in another manner, so (it is) the same power. Again it can be considered according to that *toward which it is*; and thus it means the manner of existing that the Mature (has) in a Person in comparison to the Other, Who is the Beginning and/or the Begun. And thus, since there are diverse manners, the diverse properties are called the "*to be able to generate*" and the "*to be able to be generated*" and they are distinguished according to personal acts; but not (so) in the first manner.

DOUBT VII

Likewise, is asked concerning this which he says, that *the Son has a power, by which He can be the Son or by which He can be begotten*. For it seems dubious and/or false, because '*to be begotten*' is entirely from '*to beget*', and '*to beget*' is from [a] the power of the Father: therefore, also '*to be begotten*'.

I RESPOND: Just as in the Father the power of begetting means naught but the Nature in the Person as it is bound [natam] out of Itself to produce an Other, so in the Son the power of being begotten [potentia gignendi] means naught but the Nature[8] in the Person as it is bound to be lead from an Other; for just as 'to generate' is fitting to the Hypostasis of the Father, so 'to be generated' is fitting to the Hypostasis of the Son. Nor is what is objected unto the contrary, valid. For everything which the Son has, whether essential or personal, He has from [a] the Father. For that reason although 'that He is begotten' is from the power of the Father, yet,[9] it does not exclude, that the power of being begotten [potentia gignendi passiva] be in the Son. But that power is

---

[1] The Vatican edition not trusting in the manuscripts and edition 1 adds *same* [idem].

[2] Concerning the varying accepting of this noun *property* [proprietas], that is, to the extent that it convenes with relation and is distinguished from it, just as also concerning the relations in God, see below d. 26 throughout. — The codices in this passage do not agree among themselves; for some as X and cc after *for that reason if* [ideo si] omit *in the Persons* [in personis], on the contrary codex T together with edition 1 adds *Divine* [divinis]; then after *to belong* [esse] many codices together with editions 1, 2 and 3 omit *to a Hypostasis*, which codex cc, with changed punctuation, puts in place of the prior *a hypostasis* [hypostasi].

[3] Very many codices as A G H I K S T W X Z together with edition 1 omit *thus* [sic], and a little below this nearly all the codices to-

gether with edition 1, contrary to the Vatican edition, put *a diversification* [diversificationem] in place of *a diversity* [diversitatem].

[4] Codex dd adds *can* [potest].

[5] (For) more on this Doubt, just as on the two following, see here qq. 2 and 3, and in Richard (of Middleton's Commentary), here in q. 3.

[6] See Aristotle, METAPHYSICS, Bk. V, text 17, and ibid., Bk. IX, text 2, (Bk. IV, ch. 12, and Bk. VIII, ch. 1).

[7] See above, q. 1, fundament 2.

[8] Some codices as T and cc have in a positive manner *in the Son ... means the Nature* [in Filio dicit naturam]. Codex bb after *Person* [persona] adds *of the Son*.

[9] The codices omit *yet* [tamen].

not the principle of generation, rather [sed] (it is) the idoneity of the Person or Hypostasis together with its property to be generated. Whence, that He is said "to be able to be generated", can be under- stood according to power *originally*, and, thus, it is in the Father alone; and/or *formally*, and, thus, it is posited to be in the Son; but in another manner, not (so).

DISTINCTION VIII

PART I

CHAPTER I

On the truth and property of the Divine Essence.

Now, one must deal with the truth or property, and the incommutability and simplicity of the Divine Nature and/or[1] Substance or Essence. « And thus God is », as (St.) Augustine says in (his) fifth book, ON THE TRINITY,[2] « without doubt a substance and/or, if this be better named, an "essence", which the Greeks call an <u>ousios</u>. For just as from that which it is to be wise [sapere], "wisdom" [sapientia] has been said, and from that which it is to know [scire], "knowledge" [scientia] has been said; so from that which it is to be [esse], "essence" [essentia] has been said. And who *is* more than that One, who in the third (book) of Exodus[3] said to his household-servant Moses: *I am Who am. And you shall say to the sons of Israel: He, Who is, has sent me to you* ». He Himself is truly and properly said (to be) "the Essence", whose Essence knows [novit] no past and/or future. Whence (St.) Jerome writing to Marcella[4] says: « God alone, who has no starting-forth [exordium], held the name of a true essence, because in comparison to Him, who truly is, because He is incommutable, those which are mutable are as if they are not. For of that which there is said "*it was*", *there is* not; and of that which there is said "*it shall be*", *there is* not yet. But God is the only one, who knows no '*having been*' [fuisse] and/or a '*going to be*' [futurum esse]. Therefore, God alone truly is, to whose Essence our 'to be' [esse] is not compared ».

Here, one must diligently advert, in what manner those words of (St.) Jerome ought to be understood, namely: « God is the only one and He knows no 'having been' and/or a 'going to be' »,[5] as if there could not be said of God "*He was*", and/or "*He shall be*", but only "*He is*", though we frequently discover written concerning Him: "He was from eternity", "He always was", and "He will be unto the ages", and (words) of this kind; whence, it seems, that there must not only be said of God "*He was*", (but) also "*He is*", and/or "*He shall be*". For if there would be said only "*He was*", it would be thought, that He has ceased to be; if there would be said only "*He is*", it would be thought, that He was not always, but He undertook to be [esse coeperit]; if there would be said only "*He shall be*", it would be thought that He is not now. Therefore, let it be said, that He always was, is and shall be, so that there is understood, that He neither undertook nor ceased nor ceases[6] nor will cease to be. Concerning this (St.) Augustine ON JOHN[7] speaks thus: « Since of the sempiternal Thing there is properly said "*It is*", according to us there is well said "*It was*" and "*It shall be*" and "*It is*": "*It was*", because It never ceased; "*It shall be*", because It shall never be remiss [deerit]; "*It is*", because It always is: "It has not passed by", as if That which does not remain; "It shall not rise",[8] as if (It were) what was not. Therefore, since our speech is varied throughout times, of Him there are truly said words of every time, Who at no time was remiss and/or is remiss and/or shall be remiss; and for that reason it is not a wonder, if the Truth speaking of the Spirit of Truth has said by means of the future tense [per futurum]: *Whatever He will hear, He shall speak*;[9] *He will hear*, that is from Him from whom He proceeds. To hear of Him is to know [scire], the same also[10] (is) to be. From whom, therefore, is His Essence, from Him the hearing [audientia], that is the knowledge [scientia], which is not other than the Essence. Therefore, He said "*He will hear*" of Him who has heard, does hear, that is, who always knew, knows and will know ». Behold (St.) Augustine says here, that words of every time are said of God, but nevertheless [tamen][11] properly (speaking) *He is*. Therefore, that which (St.) Jerome says, must be understood thus: He knows not a '*having been*' and/or a '*going to be*', but only a '*being*' [esse], that is, when it is said of God, that He was and/or shall be, it must not be understood, that He is past [praeterierit] and/or that He is going to be,[12] but that He exists simply without any temporal movement. For though substantive verbs of diverse tenses are said of God, as "was", "shall be", "is", "used to be", nevertheless [tamen] they do not then[13] distinguish temporal movements, namely the past [praeteritum] and/or future and/or past imperfect and/or past perfect and/or past pluperfect, but rather they simply hint at the Essence or the existence of the Divinity. Therefore, God alone properly is said (to be) an "essence" and/or "to be"; whence (St.) Hilary (of Poitiers) in (his) seventh book, ON THE TRINITY,[14] says: « "To be" is not an accident for God, but a subsistent truth and a remaining cause and the property of (His) natural genus ».

---

[1] The Vatican ed., against the codd. & edd. 1, 3, & 8, has *or* [sive].

[2] Chapter 2, n. 3. Cf. also THE CITY OF GOD, Bk. XII, ch. 2.

[3] Verse 14, where the Vulgate reads: *I am who am. He said: Thus you shall say* etc. [Ego sum qui sum. Ait: Sic dices etc.]. — Immediately before this the Vatican edition, contrary to the codices and editions 1, 5, 6, and 8, omits *Moses* [Moysi].

[4] Editions 6, 7, and 8, read *To Damasus* [ad Damasum], but, nevertheless, in neither place is this sentence literally found, but rather among (St.) Isidore, ETYMOLOGIES, Bk. VII, ch. 1, n. 10-13, where in Migne (PATROLOGIA LATINA, tome 82) it is rightly observed, that that passage has rather been conflated from various passages of (Sts.) Augustine and Gregory, and the first part, that is up to *are not*, has been taken from (St.) Augustine, CITY OF GOD, Bk. VIII, ch. 11. — See also (Bl.) Rabanus (Maurus), COMMENTARY ON EXODUS, Bk. I, ch. 6. — In the quote itself the Vatican edition together with codex A and editions 4, 5, 6, 7, and 8, reads *holds* [tenet] in place of *held* [tenuit], and then together with editions 1, 4 and 7, it has *(it is) as if there were not* [quasi non sint] in place of *(it is) as if there are not* [quasi non sunt].

[5] The codices and edition 1 omit *and/or a 'going to be'* [vel futurum esse], and a little below this codex D together with editions 1 and 8,

puts *concerning God* [de Deo] in place of *concerning Him* [de eo].

[6] In the Vatican edition and codex D, and also in editions 4, 5, 6, and 7, the words *nor ceases* [nec desinit] are wanting.

[7] Tract 99, n. 45; with some difference, however, at the beginning.

[8] Trusting in the codd. and edd. 1, 2, 3, 8, 9 & 10, and with the original consenting, we have substituted *It shall ... rise* [orietur] in place of *It shall ... be* [erit]. A little above this, the codd. with edd. 1, 2, 3, 6, 8, 9 & 10, omit, contrary to the context, *and It is* [et est].   [9] John 16:13.

[10] Codices B C D and E have *is* [est] in place of *also* [etiam]; codex A reads *also is* [etiam est:]. [Trans. note: here the sense is: *to hear of Him is to know of Him and to know of Him is to be from Him.*]

[11] The codices together with edition 1 omit *nevertheless* [tamen].

[12] The Vatican ed., against codices B C D & E and nearly all the edd., reads *He is past by and/or that He is going to* [praeteriit vel futurum sit].

[13] The Vatican ed. with the edd., except ed. 1, has *distinguish that there are temporal* [temporales motus esse distinguunt] for *then distinguish temporal* [temporales motus tunc distinguunt]. A little below this, the Vatican ed. with the edd., excepting ed. 1, has *of His own Divinity* [suae divinitatis].

[14] Number 11. — A little before this the Vatican ed. and the other edd., except the first, add *His* [sua] after *the existence of* [existentiam].

CHAPTER II

On the incommutability of the same.

The Essence of God alone is also properly said (to be) "incommutable", because neither is it changed nor can it be changed. Whence (St.) Augustine in the fifth book, ON THE TRINITY[1] says: « Other essences and/or substances take accidents, by which there comes to be in them a great and/or howsoever great mutation; but to God something of this kind cannot happen [accidere]; and for that reason the Substance alone and/or Essence, which is God, is incommutable, for Which indeed [profecto] it is most greatly and most truly suitable [competit] *to be*. For what is changed does not keep the same *to be* [non servat ipsum esse]; and what can be changed, even if it is not changed, can (become) what is was not (able) to be; and for that reason that alone, which not only is not changed, but also cannot be entirely changed, is most truly said "to be" », that is the Substance of the Father and of the Son and of the Holy Spirit. And for that reason the Apostle (Paul) speaking of God says:[2] *Who alone has immortality.* For as (St.) Augustine says in the first book, ON THE TRINITY:[3] « Since the soul in a certain manner is said "to be immortal" and it is, the Apostle would not say: *God alone has immortality,* unless (is was) because true immortality is the incommutability, which no creature can have, since it belongs to God alone ». Whence (St.) James says:[4] *Among Whom there is not transmutation nor the overshadowing of vicissitude.* And (King) David (says): *Thou will change them, and they shall be changed; but Thou art the very Same.* For that reason (St.) Augustine ON GENESIS[5] says, that God is neither moved through places nor through times, but a creature (is), through times and places. And '*to be moved through times*' is '*to be commutable* [commutari] *through affections*'; but God cannot be changed, neither in place nor in affection, Who through the Prophet says:[6] *I (am) God, and I am not changed,* who alone is incommutable. Whence rightly is *He alone* said "*to have immortality*". « For in every mutable nature », as (St.) Augustine says AGAINST MAXIMINUS,[7] « not even death is itself a mutation, because it makes something in it not to be, which used to be. Whence even the human soul, which for that reason is said (to be) "immortal", because according to its own manner it never ceases to live, yet, it has its own certain (kind of) death; because if it used to live justly and sins, it dies for justice; if it used to be a sinner and is justified, it dies for sin, to pass over in silence [ut taceam] its other mutations, of which the disputation [disputare] is long in measure. And the nature of celestial creatures could die, because it could sin. For even the Angels sinned and were made demons, whose prince is the Devil; and those who did not sin, could sin; and to whatever rational creature it is assured [praestatur], that it cannot sin, this does not belong to its own nature [naturae propriae], but to the grace of God. And for that reason *God alone,* as the Apostle says, *has immortality,* Who not by the grace of anyone, but by His own Nature neither could nor can be changed by any conversion, nor was nor will be able to sin by any mutation ». « Hence », as (St.) Augustine says in the first book, ON THE TRINITY,[8] « it is proper, though it be difficult, to intuit and know [nosse] that Substance of God, making mutables without any commutation of Itself and creating temporals without any of Its own temporal movement ». Therefore, truly and properly incommutable is the Essence of God alone, which without Its own mutation has founded all other natures.

PART II

CHAPTER III

On the simplicity of the same.

And the Same alone is properly and truly simple, where there is neither of parts nor of accidents or[9] of whatever forms any diversity or variation and/or multitude. But so that you may know [scias], in what manner that Substance be simple, as (St.) Augustine teaches in the sixth book, ON THE TRINITY,[10] « turn your mind first to (this), why every creature is multiple and in no manner is truly simple, and first concerning the corporal creature, afterwards concerning the spiritual. Certainly [utique] the corporal creature is established by parts, such that there one part is lesser, another greater, and the whole is greater than any part; and in any one body the magnitude is one (thing), the color an other, the shape [figura] an other. For it can, even with a lessened [minuta] magnitude, remain the same color and the same shape; and with the color changed, remain the same shape and the same magnitude. And through this the nature of a body is conclusively proven [convincitur] to be multiple, (and to be) moreover, in no manner simple ».

CHAPTER IV

On the corporal and spiritual creature,
in what manner it be multiple, and not simple.

A spiritual creature too, as is the soul, in comparison to a body is indeed simple, but apart from [sine] a comparison to a body it is multiple, and not simple. Which (creature) is for that reason is said (to be) "simple" in respect of a body, because (its) mass [mole] is not diffused through the space of a place, but in any one body both the whole (of it) is in the whole (body) and the whole (of it) is in any part of it. And for that reason, when something is done[11] in however so tiny [exigua] a particle of a body, which the soul senses, although it is not done in the whole body, nevertheless [tamen] that whole senses, because it does not lay hidden from the whole. But, nevertheless [tamen], neither in the soul itself is there true simplicity.

---

[1] Chapter 2, n. 3. — In which text after *does not keep the same* [non servat ipsum] contrary to the original, to the codices and to edition 1, the Vatican edition together with the other editions adds *true* [verum].

[2] 1 Tim. 6:16; the same text occurs twice below.

[3] Chapter 1, n. 2.

[4] Chapter 1:17. Only the Vatican edition has *Among God* [Apud Deum]. — The following text is Psalm 101:28.

[5] ON THE LITERAL EXPOSITION OF GENESIS, Bk. VIII, ch. 20, n. 39, according to the sense; cf. also chs. 21, 22, 23, and 26.

[6] Malachias 3:6. The Vulgate reads: *I (am) the Lord* etc. [Ego Dominus etc.].

[7] Book II, ch. 12, n. 1.

[8] Chapter 1, n. 3.

[9] The editions, excepting 1 and 8, have *nor* [nec].

[10] Chapter 6, n. 8. — A little before this we have restored from the codices and edd. 1, 6 and 8 *as* [ut] before *(St.) Augustine teaches.* In which text before *concerning the corporal* the Vatican ed. with the other edd., except edd. 1 and 4, has *at first* [primum] in place of *first* [primo]. Then, before *parts* [partibus] the Vatican ed. with very many edd. and codex B adds *out of.* Then, after *there* [ibi] the Vatican ed. puts *some (part)* [aliqua] for *one* [alia]. A little below this, before *shape* [figura] the Vatican ed. with very many edd. inserts *is* [est], and immediately after the omitted particle *even* [et] it puts *unlessened* [imminuta] for *lessened* [minuta] against codices B C & D and nearly all the edd.; (St.) Augustine has *diminished* [diminuta].

[11] Codices A B D E and edd. 3, 5, 7, 8, 9 have badly *is* [sit] in place of *is done* [fit]. — Below the Vatican ed. with a few edd. inserts not so well *whole* [tota] by reading *in the whole soul itself (is there) true;* and immediately after this edd. 2, 3, & 7, read *truly* [vere] for *true simplicity* [vera simplicitas].

For, since it is one (thing) to be artificial, another inert, another sharp, another mindful [memorem], another cupidity, another fear, another gladness, another sadness, and (since) these and others of this kind can be found (to be) innumerable in the nature of the soul, both some without others and others more,[1] others less, it is manifest, that (its) nature is not simple, but multiple. For nothing simple is mutable; moreover, every creature is mutable »:[2] therefore, no creature is truly simple. « However, God, even if he be called multiple, is nevertheless [tamen] truly and most highly simple. For He is called "great", "good", "wise", "blessed", "true" and whatever other (name) seems to be said in a not unworthy manner, but to Him belongs the same greatness, which (is) wisdom. For not in mass is He great, but in virtue, and (He is) the same goodness, which (is) wisdom and greatness and truth; and There is not One that is Itself blessed There, and Another that is great or wise or true or is good or entirely (any of these) ».

CHAPTER V

That God, though He be simple,
yet, is spoken of in a multiple manner.

Here, it must be diligently noted, since (St.) Augustine says, that God alone is truly simple, why he says, that he speaks of the Same in a multiple manner. But this he does not say on account of a diversity of accidents and/or of parts, but on account of a diversity and multitude of names, which are said of God; which though they are multiple, nevertheless [tamen] signify the One, that is the Divine Nature. For these are not accepted thus, when they are said of that incommutable and eternal Substance incomparably more simple than the human spirit, to the extent that they are said of creatures. Whence (St.) Augustine in the sixth book, ON THE TRINITY:[3] « For God 'to be' is that, which it is 'to be strong' and/or 'to be wise' and/or 'to be just', and if you have said anything concerning that simple multiplicity and/or multiple simplicity, by this His substance is signified. Moreover, for the human spirit 'to be' is not that, which it is 'to be strong or prudent or just'; for the (human) spirit can be and have none of those virtues ».

CHAPTER VI

That the simplicity of God is subjected
to none of the predicaments.

Moreover, that in the Divine Nature there is no diversity of accidents and thoroughly [penitus] no mutability, but (rather) a perfect simplicity, (St.) Augustine shows in the fifth book, ON THE TRINITY[4] saying: « We understand that God, as much as we can, is the Good without quality [sine qualitate], the Great without quantity [sine quantitate], the Creator without need [sine indigentia], the

One Presiding without position [sine situ], the One containing all without having [sine habitu], the One whole everywhere without place [sine loco], the One Sempiternal without time [sin tempore], the One making mutables without any change of His own and the One suffering nothing. Whoever thus considers [cogitat] God, even if he cannot yet find entirely what He is, nevertheless [tamen] piously let him beware, as much as he can, of thinking [sentire] anything of Him, which He is not ». Behold, if you subtlety understand [intendas], from this and the aforesaid it appears, that those predicaments of the dialectic art convene least (of all) with the Divine Nature, which is subject to none of the accidents.

CHAPTER VII

That God is abusively said (to be) a "substance".

Whence, neither is He properly said (to be) a "substance", as (St.) Augustine shows in the seventh book, ON THE TRINITY:[5] « In the same manner as from that which it is 'to be' "essence" is named, so from that which is 'to subsist' we say "substance", if, however, [tamen], it is worthy, that God be said "to subsist". For this concerning these things rightly is understood, in which subjects there are those (things) which are said to be in another subject, just as color or form (is) in a body. For a body subsists, and for that reason it is a substance. Therefore, mutable things and not simple ones are properly said (to be) "substances". Moreover, God, if He subsists, so that he can properly be said (to be) a "substance", is in that something as in a subject, and is not simple. Moreover, it is wicked [nefas est] to say, that God subsists and is beneath [subsit] His own Goodness, and also that that Goodness is not a substance and/or rather an essence, and that God Himself is not His own Goodness, but (that That) is in Him as in a subject. Whence it is manifest, that God is abusively called a "substance", as He is by more usual noun understood (to be) an "essence", which truly and properly He is said (to be), to such an extent that perhaps it is proper [oporteat] that God alone be said (to be) an "essence". For He is truly Sole [solus], because He is incommutable ».

CHAPTER VIII

That there is not in God anything, which is not God.

Moreover, of this Essence there is so great a simplicity and sincerity, that there is not in It anything, which is not Itself; but the Same is the One having and What is had. Whence (St.) Hilary in the seventh book, ON THE TRINITY[6] says: « Not out of composites does God, who is Life, subsist, nor is He who is Virtue, contained out of infirm (things), nor is He who is Light, fitted together from obscure (things), nor is He who is Spirit, formal from disparate (things): the whole which is in Him, is one ». (He says) the same in the eighth book, ON THE TRINITY:[7] « Not in a human manner is God from composites so that in Him there is one (thing)

---

[1] Here the Vatican edition alone repeats *and* [et] and *less* [minus] after *it is manifest* [manifestum est]; the same text together with editions 2, 6 and 8, adds *of the soul* at the end; codex D, however, adds *its* [eius].

[2] ON THE TRINITY, Book VI, ch. 6, n. 8. Those things which follow have been taken from ch. 6 and ch. 7. Near the end of this text after *the same goodness* [eadem bonitas] the Vatican edition, contrary to the codices and editions 1, 2, 3, and 7, adds *is His* [eius est]. Then not a few editions read *Another wise, another* [aliud sapientem aliud] in place of *or wise or* [aut sapientem aut].

[3] Chapter 4, n. 6. — The Vatican edition and the rest of the editions at the beginning after *To God* [Deo] add , *he says,* [inquit].

[4] Chapter 1, n. 2. — At the beginning of this chapter in place of *divine* [divina] codices B C and D read *of the Deity* [deitatis], A and E read *of the Divinity* [divinitatis]. In the same text at *site* [situ] editions 1 and 8 read *the One Present* [praesentem] in place of *the One Presiding* [praesidentem]; near the end of the same the Vatican edition and editions 4, 5, 8, and 9, at *what He is* [quid sit] add *Himself* [ipse].

[5] Chapter 4. at the end and ch. 5 at the beginning. — In the text before *subjects* [subiectis] the Vatican edition and editions 4 and 9 add *as* [ut]; editions 4, 6, and 8 here and a little below before *subject* [subiecto] insert *as in* [ut in] contrary to the original, to the codices and to the rest of the editions. Then the editions, not trusting the codices and the original text, at *mutable things* [Res ... mutabiles] put *However* [vero] in place of *Therefore* [ergo].

[6] Num. 27. (The Text of St. Augustine reads): *For not from composites and inanimates is God ... is He contained from* infirm things [infirmibus] ... *is He* formable [formabilis] *from disparate things; where* codex A reads *is He formed by disparate things.* In place of *formal* [formalis] in the text of Master (Peter) *formable* [formabilis] seems to need to be read. St. Bonaventure explains this text, here in p. II. Doubt 6.

[7] Num. 43. — In this text the Vatican edition and editions 4, 8 and 8, and codex B, in place of *is life, ... nature* [vita est natura] read corruptly *is one nature* [una est natura], where (St.) Hilary more clearly says: *but the whole, which He is, is Life* [sed totum, quod est, vita est].

which is had from Him, and another is He Himself who has, but the whole is Life, a Nature namely perfect and infinite and not constituted out of disparates, but living Itself throughout the whole ». Of this Same, (St. Severinus) Boethius in the first book, ON THE TRINITY[1] says: « About which It is truly the One, in which (there is) no number, no other in Him besides that which He is; for neither can He be become a subject ». (St.) Augustine also says in (his) book, ON THE FAITH AND THE CREED:[2] « In the Substance of God there is not anything, which is not the Substance, as if There one thing is the substance, another (is that) which accedes to the substance. But whatever can be understood (to be) There, is the Substance. Truly these (things) can be easily said and believed, on the other hand [autem] they cannot be seen except by an entirely pure heart ». Likewise, (St.) Augustine in the fifteenth book, ON THE TRINITY[3] (says of the Divine Nature): « It is so had in the Nature of each of the Three, that He who has This is, what He has, just as an immutable and simple substance (does) ». Whence (St.) Isidore[4] says: « God is said (to be) "simple", either by not admitting that He has, or that there is one thing that is Himself, and another that is in Himself ». And though the Divine Nature is of so great a simplicity and sincerity, It is, nevertheless [tamen] in that Trinity of the Persons. Whence (St.) Augustine in the

eleventh book, ON THE CITY OF GOD[5] says: « We do not say that the nature of the Most High Good (is) "simple" on account of this, that the Father alone is in It, or the Son alone (is) in It, or the Holy Spirit alone (is) in It, or that Trinity of Names alone is without a subsistence* of persons, just as the Sabellians thought: but He is said (to be) "simple" for this reason, that He is this which He has, except that whatever Person is said relatively in regard to an Other, nor is it the very (Other). For certainly [utique] the Father has a Son, in regard to whom He is relatively said (to be "the Father"), nor, yet, is He Himself the Son; and the Son has a Father, nor however, is He Himself the Father. In which (sense) there is said in regard to His very self, not in regard to an Other, This is what He has, just as in regard to His very self He is said (to be) "living", by having life, and the same Life is Himself. And so[6] on account of this, the Nature is said (to be) "simple", because there is not one having, and another that which It has, just as it is among all other things. For a liquid [liquor] is not one having liquid, nor (is) color a body, nor is the soul wisdom ». Behold, how great is the Identity, how great is the Unity, the Immutability, the Simplicity, the Purity of the Divine Substance, (which) we according to the strength [valitudinem] of our infirmity have expressed with signs [assignavimus].

COMMENTARY ON DISTINCTION VIII

On the properties and essential conditions of the Trinity and Unity.

PART I

On the truth and immutability of God.

Now, one must deal with the truth or property, and the incommutability etc..

THE DIVISION OF THE TEXT

Having terminated the above two parts of that principal part of his (book), which concerns the Trinity according to what *it is understood* (to be), in which to prove the Trinity Master (Peter) brought forward reasons and removed doubts; in this *third* part Master (Peter) determines the properties and conditions of the Trinity and Unity Itself.[1] And since there are certain properties respecting the *Essence*, as truth, certain ones the *Persons*, as generation, certain ones *both*, as equality: for that reason this part has three parts. In the *first* part Master (Peter) deals with the essential properties; in the *second*, with the personal properties, below in the ninth distinction: *Now let us approach the distinction of persons.*; in the *third*,

with the properties and conditions (which are) in a certain manner essential and in a certain manner personal, as is the equality of the Persons in eternity, magnitude and virtue,[2] below in the nineteenth distinction: *Now after we have hinted at the coeternity of the Three Persons* etc..

The *first* part, which contains the present distinction, has three parts according to the three properties, which he assigns: and the *first* concerns *truth*; the *second* concerns *immutability*, and this is put in the third chapter:[3] *Also of God alone is the Essence properly said (to be) incommutable*; the *third* concerns *simplicity*, which is put in the forth chapter:[4] *And the Same alone is properly, and truly simple* etc..

---

[1] Chapter 2. — In which text the Vatican edition after *besides that which* [praeter id quod] adds *in Him* [in eo], contradicting all the codices, editions 1 and 6, and the original.

[2] Chapter 9, n. 20. — The manuscripts and editions 2, 3, 5 and 7, cite falsely the ON FAITH TO PETER. — In which text codices B and C together with all the other editions put not so well the indicative for *accedes* [accidit].

[3] Chapter 17, n. 28. — In which text, contrary to the original, to the codices and to editions 1, 6 and 8, the Vatican edition puts *that* [quod] in place of *that* [ut]. Then after *just as* [sicut] codex A adds *He is* [est] and then puts *nature* in place of *substance*.

[4] ETYMOLOGIES, Bk. VII, ch. 1; the same occurs in SENT., Bk. I, ch. 1. — (St.) Isidore himself, loc. cit., writes: *or because there is no other* [seu quia non aliud est]; however, editions 1, 3, 5, 7, and 9, read *or (that) no other has what He is not* [seu non aliud habet quod non est], and edition 2 moreover, adds *that* [quia] after *or* [seu].

[5] Chapter 10, n. 1 and 2. — The Vatican edition and editions 4 and 5, omit *says* [ait] after *City of God* [Civitate Dei]. In this text all the codices and edition 1 after *Holy Spirit* [Spiritus sanctus] omit *in It* [in ea]; and immediately after this the codices and editions 1, 2, 3, 7, and 8

put *that is* [id est] in place of *or* [aut], contradicting the original. Moreover, editions 2, 3, 4, 5, 7, 9 have *substance* [substantia] in place of *subsistence* [subsistentia],* and in place of *without* [sine] all the editions together with codices C and E exhibit *or* [sive], but falsely and contrary to the original and codices A B and D.

[6] The Vatican edition has *certainly* [utique] contrary to all the codices and editions 2 and 6.

NOTES ON THE COMMENTARY

[1] Not trusting in the manuscripts and edition 1, the Vatican edition, having omitted *Master (Peter)* [Magister] substitutes *of It* [istius] in place of *Itself* [ipsius] and a little below this *both* [utraque] in place of *each* [utrasque].

[2] The Vatican edition has *unity* [unitate] in place of *virtue* [virtute], but contrary to the text of Master (Peter) and the codices.

[3] Thus, the codices, together with edition 1, according to the norm of the other division of the chapters; in our (edition), see ch. 2. — The Vatican edition here and in the following (quote) *there (where he says)* [ibi].

[4] In our edition ch. 3. — The Vatican edition reads *and this* [et haec] in place of *which* [quae], but contrary to the manuscripts.

---

* Trans. note: Here fn. 5 assumes that the text reads contrariwise *subsistence* for *substance*; I have followed the presumption of the note, and have altered the text above, for otherwise one would affirm a trinity of names without a underlying substance, which is not what the Sabellians held.

Likewise, the *first* part has two parts, because he *first* attributes to God the property of the truth; *second* he removes the doubt having risen out of the aforesaid, in the second chapter:[1] *Here it must diligently be adverted*. Similarly, the *second* part has two (parts): in the first he assigns to God[2] the property of incommutability and proves (it) by the authority of (St.) Augustine; in the second he confirms (it) through the Apostle, there (where he says): *And for that reason the Apostle (Paul) speaking* etc.. The *third* (part), concerning simplicity, is subdivided below.

TREATMENT OF THE QUESTIONS

In that part (of his text),[3] to evidence the two first properties, which Master (Peter) assigns first, that is, (the property) *of truth* and *of incommutability*, two (questions) are principally asked:

First, there is asked (the question) concerning the truth itself.

Second, concerning immutability.

Concerning the truth, there is again asked two (questions):

First, whether the truth be a property of the Divine 'Being' [divini esse].

Second, whether the property belongs to Him in a most high manner, that is, to such an extent that it cannot be thought not to be.

ARTICLE I

On the truth of God.

QUESTION I

Whether truth is a property of the Divine 'Being'?

That truth is a property of the Divine 'Being' [divini esse], is shown by *authorities* and by *reasons*.

1. In the first manner thus: (St.) Jerome to Marcella, and he has it in the text:[5] « God alone truly is, to whose Essence our 'being' [esse] is not compared »; but what is fitting to someone alone, is proper to him: therefore, truth is proper to the Divine 'Being'.

2. Likewise, (St.) Augustine ON THE TRUE RELIGION:[6] « Falsity is from those things, which imitate that One, by whom anything is one, inasmuch as they cannot fulfill that ». Therefore, if no creature can fulfill that most high One, there is no truth in any creature, but (rather) falsity in all (things).

3. Likewise, (St.) Augustine in (his) SOLILOQUIES and ON THE TRUE RELIGION[7] says, that the uncreated Light is the reason for cognizing Itself and all cognizables: therefore, if truth is the reason for cognizing, and the uncreated Light alone is the Truth: therefore, truth is a property of God alone.

4. Likewise, (St.) Anselm in (his) book, ON THE TRUTH[8] says, that all (things) are true by the first Truth: therefore, either he understands (this) *effectively*, or *formally*; not effectively, because all (things) can similarly be said (to be) true[9] by the first Goodness: therefore, it is understood formally: therefore, there is no truth other than the uncreated Truth: therefore, if that is in God and (is) God, truth is a property of God alone.

5. Likewise, by *reasons* it is proven thus: truth and vanity are opposed; but every creature has vanity[10] and a 'being thoroughly mixed' with 'not being' [permixtionem cum non esse], since it is out of nothing, and God alone entirely lacks this (mixture): therefore, in God alone is truth.

6. Likewise, truth is opposed to shadows. For that which is a shadow of a thing, does not have truth;[11] but creatures are the shadows of that Most High 'Being': therefore, they do not have truth in regard to 'being' [veritatem in esse].

7. Likewise, the truth is, that by which something is true; but the truth is true, since it is cognizable; but it is established that (it is such) not by another than itself, because, otherwise,[12] there would be an infinite regression [abire in infinitum]; but what is true by its very self, is true through (its) essence: therefore, every truth is true through (its) essence; but only the uncreated Truth is true through (Its) Essence: therefore, truth is a property of God alone.

ON THE CONTRARY: 1. If truth is a property of God, therefore, either (this property) is a *complex* truth, or a *non-complex* [incomplexa]. Not *complex*; because such is with composition, but in God there is no composition. Not *non-complex*; because this is convertible with being [ente]:[13] therefore since entity is not a property of God, for an equal reason neither is truth.

---

[1] In our edition ch. 1, near the middle.

[2] The codices together with edition 1 omit *to God* [Deo] and *of incommutability* [incommutabilitatis].

[3] The Vatican edition contrary to the manuscripts and edition 1 has *this* [hac] for *that ... (of his text)* [ista]; then it reads *of the first (parts)* [primarum], because *simplicity* is enumerated by Master (Peter) as the *third* (part); however, *of the first (parts)* [primarum] is omitted by a few codices and edition 1.

[4] From the more ancient manuscripts and edition 1 we inserted *there is asked (the question)* [quaeritur].

[5] Chapter 1 near the beginning. — The Vatican edition not trusting in the manuscripts and edition 1 reads *by the authority of (St.) Jerome* [auctoritate Hieronomi] in place of *(St.) Jerome* [Hieronomus].

[6] Chapter 36, n. 66: For if falsity is from those (things), which imitate the One, not inasmuch as they imitate It, but inasmuch as they cannot fulfill (It). — And *ibid.*, a little before this, he says: But if bodies fail to this extent [in tantum], inasmuch as they do not fulfill that One which they are proven guilty (in) imitating, from which Principle, whatever is, is one. — The Vatican edition contrary to very many codices has *most highly* [summe] in place of *most high* [summum].

[7] SOLILOQUIES, Bk. I, ch. 8, n. 15. — ON THE TRUE RELIGION, ch. 34, n. 64 and ch. 36, n. 66. — The Vatican edition, without any authority

from the manuscripts and edition 1, omits the words *Itself and all* up to *for cognizing* [se et omnia ... cognoscendi].

[8] Chapter 13, where he proves that there is only one rectitude of all things, from which he concludes: therefore, there is one truth in all those (things).

[9] Thus, together with edition 1 the more ancient codices, of which indeed some read (the indicative) for *can* [possunt]; but the Vatican edition together with codex cc has *can be said (to be) good* [possunt dici bona], which posited destroys the argument; if indeed rightly all are said effectively and are *good* by the first goodness. Near the end of the argument the Vatican edition together with codex cc, after *if that is* [si illa est] repeats the word *is* [est], and immediately after this the Vatican edition alone puts *etc., therefore* [etc. ergo] in place of *and (is) God* [et Deus].

[10] Rom. 8:20: *For to vanity has the creature been subjected* [Vanitati enim creatura subiecta est]. Cf. also Ecclesiastes 3:19.

[11] See Aristotle, METAPHYSICS, Bk. V, text 34. (Bk. IV, ch. 29). — Then after *most high* [summi] we have supplied from the manuscripts and edition 1 the badly omitted *'Being'* [esse].

[12] The codices together with edition 1 have *then* [tunc] in place of *otherwise* [alias], but not so well.

[13] Aristotle, METAPHYSICS, Bk. II, text 4 (in the shorter version, Bk. I, ch. 1): Any one (thing) just as it holds itself so as to be, thus also (does it hold itself) to the truth.

2. Likewise, the true is as equally common as the good, and in a certain sense moreso;[1] but goodness is not a property of God: therefore, for an equal reason neither truth.

3. Likewise, truth is the reason for discerning the Creator from the creature and a creature from a creature;[2] but that which is the reason for discerning and distinguishing is diverse in diverse (things): therefore, truth in God is other than (it is) in a creature, and in one creature than in another: therefore, it is not proper to God alone.

4. Likewise, (St.) Augustine in (his) SOLILOQUIES:[3] « The true is that which is », therefore, truth is entity itself: therefore, it is not proper to an essence, because if so, by the reckoning by which there is said: "Truth is[4] a property of an essence", there could be said conversely ("Essence is a property of truth"), since they are entirely the same.

CONCLUSION

Truth, to the extent that it is opposed to falsity, is even found in creatures according to its threefold comparison to the subject which it informs, to the principle which it represents, to the intellect which it excites; however, to the extent that it is opposed to confusion, it is a property of God alone.

I RESPOND: It must be said, that truth has a threefold comparison. For it has (an ability) to be compared to the *subject* which it informs, to the *principle* which it represents, and to the *intellect* which it excites. In being compared [comparatione] to a *subject* of the truth, truth is meant as the act and the indivision of the power. In being compared to a *principle*, truth is meant as the representation or imitation of the Most High and First Unity.[5] In being compared to an *intellect* truth is meant as the reason for discerning.

And in all those comparisons [comparationibus] truth can be accepted in a twofold manner: in *one manner*, insofar as it is distinguished against *falsity*; in *another manner*, insofar as it is distinguished against *confusion* [permixtionem], according to which the true is said to be pure and thoroughly unmixed [impermixtum].

Insofar as the truth is divided against falsity, which is a privation of indivision and imitation and[6] expression, thus since in a creature there is in some manner to be found both indivision and imitation and expression, so truth is not only in the Creator, but also in the creature; and in this manner a property of God is not assigned.

In *another manner*, insofar as truth is divided against confusion [permixtionem] or impurity, thus it is in God alone. For in God alone there is pure *indivision*, not confused [non permixta] with any diversity; in God alone there is pure *imitation* and similitude, not confused with any dissimilitude; and in God alone there is the *expression of a light* [luminis], not confused with obscurity.[7] In the creature, on the other hand, there is indivision with diversity of act and power and imitation with dissimilitude; there is, furthermore, in it an expression with obscurity. And for that reason in this manner truth is a property of the Divine 'Being'; and thus do Master (Peter) and (St.) Augustine and (St.) Jerome accept it. For they call a "true 'being'" [verum esse], that which has nothing concerning possibility, has nothing concerning vanity, nothing concerning non-entity [non entitate]. And for that reason in God there does not fall a '*passing away*' [praeteritio] and a '*coming to be*' [futuritio], which in some manner are not beings.

1, 2, 5, 6. And thus proceed the first two authorities and reasons.

3. However, to that which is objected, that there is no other truth than the eternal One, because It Itself alone causes understanding; it must be said, that just as color is the object of seeing and the motive for seeing — however, not without the act of light — and (and just as) it differs from[8] the light itself; so it must be said, that created truth, although it cannot move without uncreated Truth, nevertheless, it is motive in its own manner and a truth other than that One.

4. and 7. To that which is objected concerning (St.) Anselm, that all (things) are true by the First Truth; it must be said, that the true from its own imposition means a comparison to an exemplary cause, just as the good (does) to a final cause. For, just as "the good" is said according to a reckoning of *order*, so "the true" according to a reckoning of *expression*; and a reckoning of expressing belongs to the exemplar itself. Therefore, just as, when there is said of created goods, that "they are good" by the uncreated Goodness" [sunt bona bonitate increata], "goodness" is said before the *end* (of the phrase) in the ablative, *not* (before the) *form* (i. e. "good"), because the goodness[9] of God is the form of no created (thing); similarly, when there is said, that "all (things) are true by the uncreated Truth" [omnia sunt vera veritate increata], the ablative ("by Truth") means the formal, *exemplary* cause.[10] For all (things) are true and are bound to express themselves through the expression of that Most High Light; which, if It would cease to shine upon them [influere], all others would cease to be true. For that reason no created truth is true through (its) essence, but (rather) through participation; and by this (reckoning) the last (objection) is clear.

To that, however, which is objected in the contrary, that it is not a property; the response is clear: since

---

[1] The reason commonly alleged is, that *the true* is nearer to being [enti propinquius] and *in itself* more abstract.

[2] (St.) Augustine, ON THE TRUE RELIGION, ch. 7, n. 13: For every thing and/or essence ... at once has these three (characteristics), that it is both one something [unum aliquid], and by its proper species is discerned from all the others, and it does not exceed the order of things.

[3] Book II, ch. 5, n. 8: The true seems to me to be that which *is* [Verum mihi videtur esse id quod est].

[4] Many codices as B D F I P Q T X Y Z together with edition 1 omit *is* [est].

[5] From nearly all the more ancient manuscripts and edition 1 we have here substituted *unity* [unitatis] for *truth* [veritatis], and a little below this we have put *for discerning* [discernendi] in place of *for distinguishing* [distinguendi], which reading is also corroborated by the second argument in the affirmative and the third argument in the negative, quoted above.

[6] From very many manuscripts and edition 1 we have supplied twice the particle *ant* [et].

[7] The Vatican edition with codex cc has (the masculine) *not confused* [non permixti])referring to *a light)* rather than (the feminine) *not thoroughly mixed* [non permixta] (referring to *expression)*, but contrary to the more ancient codd., not a few of which, however, have only *in obscurity* [obscuritate], but less well and contrary to what immediately precedes this.

[8] The Vatican edition not trusting in the manuscripts and editions 1, 2 and 3, has *itself from the light* [ipsa a luce], but incongruously, and at the end of the argument contrary to the more ancient manuscripts it reads *is another truth from that One* [alia veritas est ab illa].

[9] The Vatican edition, against the more ancient codd., reads *uncreated goodness* [bonitas increata] for *goodness of God* [Dei bonitas].

[10] Codices D and T more expressly read *the ablative does not mean that there is a formal cause embracing things, but (rather) exemplary (of them)* [ablativus non dicit causam formalem esse rerum complectivam, sed exemplarem]. A little below this the Vatican edition together with codex cc, but contrary to the others and edition 1, reads *by an expression* [expressione] in place of *through an expression* [per expressionem], and at the end the Vatican ed. alone has *the last (objections) are clear* [patet ultima] in place of *the last (objection) is clear* [patet ultimum], but falsely.

it objects concerning the truth, according to which it has an opposition to the defect of *falsity*, not to the confusion of possibility; for in the aforesaid manner it not only convenes with the Creator, but also with the creature.

4. To that which is objected, that truth is the same as the Divine Essence; it must be said, that these three concern the reckoning of *property* in a creature: the first is, that it convenes with the latter alone [soli]; the second is, that it is a reason for (it) becoming known [ratio innotescendi]; the third is, that it differs from that of which it is the property.[1] The first two belong to perfection, but the last to imperfection, because it excludes simplicity. And for that reason, truth is said (to be) a "property" of the Divine Essence, not because it differs from and/or is inherent to the Divine Essence, as an accident[2] to a subject, but because it convenes with the latter alone and is a reason for cognizing it. And this is the cause, why conversely the Essence is not a property of truth, because it is not a reason for coming to know it [ratio innotescendi eam], just as (the latter is) conversely.

Moreover, if *you ask*, since "essence" and "truth" signify the same (thing), why is the one a reason for cognizing the other, and not conversely; to this some have said, that although "essence" and "truth" signify the same (thing), however, one, namely the truth, is a greater reason for cognizing by reason of the (thing) connoted. But this cannot stand, because the truth connotes nothing. Therefore, it must

be said, that this (lack of reciprocity) is by reason of the manner of signifying and understanding.

And it must be noted, that there is a twofold manner in which one speaks [dupliciter est loqui] of these nouns; in *one* manner, by reason of that which they name or signify; in *another* manner, by reason of that, in which there is signified that there is posited what they name.[3] Whence it is different to say "*sense*" [sensum] and "the *sense of a man*" [sensum hominis]; because in the first manner it is meant commonly according to the sense of man and brute, in the second (according to what is) proper to a man. Therefore, if we accept nouns of this manner according to *themselves*, one is the reckoning of the essence, another of the truth, since the "essence" means the *what*, the "truth", the *condition of the being*. However, when we treat of essence and truth as regards God, although they are the same (Thing), however, by reason of the general signifieds one is accepted as the property of the other; and there is not a synonym nor are nouns synonymous There, but (rather) there remains a reckoning of subject and of property according to the manner of signifying, and it remains also according to the manner of understanding; because through the essence in a creature we understand the Essence in the Creator, and through the truth of a creature we understand the uncreated Truth. Whence, just as created truth is a property and a reason for cognizing a created essence, so the uncreated Truth, according to a reckoning of signifying and understanding, is a reason for cognizing and understanding the uncreated Essence.

SCHOLIUM

I. The sense of the Question is, whether *truth* pertains [competat] to God as (something) proper, or whether it concerns the essence of God and (is) a property of God alone. *Truth* is here accepted, not insofar as it is formally in the intellect, nor even on behalf of a thing, to the extent that it is an object of the intellect, but in order to the thing itself, of which it is the act, or to the extent that it means an indivision of a being [indivisionem entis] and (its) 'to be' [esse]. — For an understanding of the terms, which in the first reason occur on behalf of the negative side and often elsewhere, it must be noted, that the *complex* and the *non-complex* are the same as the composite and the non-composite. *Complex* truth is a passion or property of a proposition, which means a connection of the predicate with the subject, and (this) is had in the second operation of the mind, namely in judgement. But an *non-complex* truth is a simple passion of any being and is defined through this, that it is an adequation of a thing to the intellect, which cognizes the thing just as it is. This is had in any first operation of the mind, which is simple apprehension.

II. Elsewhere St. Bonaventure, together with the common opinion, distinguishes "truth" in a threefold manner, that is, taken *formally*, which is truth in the intellect, and/or *radically* or causally, which is the one in things, and/or insofar as it is in *a verbal expression* [in oratione] as *in a sign*. Cf. below d. 31, p. II, a. 1. q. 1; above d. 3, p. I, dub. 7; SENT., Bk. II, d. 30, a. 3, q. 2; HEXAËMERON, Sermon 5, "On the truth of a *sign*", below in d. 46, a. 1, q. 4. — St. Thomas, SENT., Bk. I, d. 19, q. 5; ON THE TRUTH, q. 1, a. 1, and ff.; SUMMA., I, q. 16, aa. 1-3, 5. — In this passage and in the Prologue to the COMMENTARY ON ECCLESIASTES near the end he only deals with truth in *things*, or insofar as truth is a property of a being. This truth in things can again be considered in a threefold manner: first of all in respect to *a sub-*

ject; and thus truth is the indivision of act and potency, and/or with Avicenna in METAPHYSICS, Bk. VIII, ch. 6: The truth of any thing is a property of its 'being', which when established belongs to the thing; or the truth is that thing, which is in act; and under this respect there is defined: the indivision of '*being*' and *that which is*. — Second it is considered in respect to its *principle*, which is the Divine Exemplar, to which the thing is assimilated; and under this respect it is defined according to (St.) Augustine in (his) book, ON THE TRUE RELIGION, ch. 36, n. 66: Truth is the most high similitude of the principle, which without any dissimilitude is, whence falsity arises. — In the third manner, it is considered in respect to the *consequent effect*, to the extent that the object in the intellect causes truth; and thus it is a reason for cognizing a thing and for distinguishing it, and under this respect it is defined by (St.) Augustine (loc. cit.): Truth is that which shows what is; and by (St.) Hilary (of Poitiers): Truth is declarative '*being*'. Cf. above d. 3, p. I, dub. 7; Alexander of Hales, p. I., q. 15, m. 3; St. Thomas, ON THE TRUTH, q. 1, a. 1. — The other distinction of truth against falsity and against confusion is clear from the text.

III. In regard to the order of the arguments *pro* and *contra*, it must be noted, that the first proposition, which deals with truth, to the extent that it is distinguished against falsity, is proven by the three prior arguments on the *negative* side. But the second, which concerns truth, to the extent that it is distinguished against confusion [permixtionem], is proven in the 5th and 6th argument on the affirmative side. All the other arguments are explained through a distinction in the right sense. — Worthy of attention are those, which are here said in the body (of the Response) and in the solution to nn. 1 and 2 and to the last concerning created truth, namely that no created truth is truth through (its) essence,

---

[1] Cf. Aristotle, TOPICS, Bk. V, chs. 1 and 2, and Porphyry, ON PREDICABLES, ch. "On the Proper".

[2] The error of the Vatican edition of putting *antecedent* [antecedens] in place of *accident* [accidens], we have corrected on the testimony of the mss.s and the first three edd.. A little below this, after *of truth* [veritatis], not a few codd. with ed. 1 add not aptly the particle *and* [et].

[3] Very many codices as A R S T Y etc. read *they denominate* ... *Whence it would be different* [denominant. Unde differret] for *they name. Whence it is different* [nominant. Unde differt], and a little below this they have *then* [deinde] in place of *second* [secondo] and (the subjunctive) *we accept* [accipiamus] in place of (the indicative) *we accept* [accipimus].

but (rather) through participation, and that, nevertheless, in its own manner it is a reason for cognizing (those) distinct from uncreated Truth. What has been said is contrary to the rigid Ontologists.

IV. In regard to the first and second conclusion, cf. Alexander of Hales, SUMMA., p. I, q. 15, m. 5; and q. 17, m . 4. — For an explication of the text taken from (St.) Anselm (4th fundament) cf. St. Thomas (SUMMA., I, q. 16, a. 6) and especially Richard of Middleton (here in q. 2, a. 4), who treats of the matter extensively and well, though he proceeds in the other way as St. Bonaventure does. — On the difference among *the Divine 'to be'* and *a created 'to be'*, cf. here in Doubt. 8.

On the whole question: St. Thomas, SUMMA CONTRA GENTILES., I, ch. 60; SUMMA., I, q. 16, a. 5. — Bl. (now St.) Albert (the Great), here in a. 1, and d. 46, a. 11 ff., where he solves many questions concerning this matter at length; SUMMA., p. I, tr. 4, q. 19, m. 1 and 3. — (Bl.) Peter of Tarentaise, here in q. 2, a. 1 and 2. — Richard of Middleton, here in q. 1 and 2. — Giles the Roman, here in 1st princ. q. 1, and d. 19, 2nd princ. q. 2 and 3. — Henry of Ghent, SUMMA., a. 34. throughout. — (Bl.) Dionysius the Carthusian, here in q. 1.

QUESTION II

Whether the Divine 'To Be' is so true, that it cannot be thought not to be?

Second, there is asked, whether this property convenes with God in the highest (manner), that is, whether the Divine '*To Be*' [esse] is so true, that it cannot be thought [cogitari] not to be.

1. And that (it is) so, seems through (St.) Anselm (of Canterbury)[1] who says, that God according to the common conception of spirit is He whom nothing greater can be thought; but what cannot be thought not to be is greater, than that which can (be so thought); therefore, since nothing can be thought greater than God, the Divine 'To Be' is such, that It cannot[2] be thought not to be.

2. Likewise, (St. John) Damascene[3] says, that the cognition of what it is to be [essendi] God is naturally impressed upon us; but natural impressions do not leave nor grow accustomed (to what is) to the contrary: therefore, the truth of God impressed upon the human mind is inseparable from it: therefore, He cannot be thought not to be.

3. Likewise, greater is the truth in the Divine 'To Be' than in any (other) dignity;[4] but any (other) dignity is so true, that there is no internal contradiction [non est ei contradicere corde], so that, every whole is greater than its part, and similar (things); whence it cannot be thought not to be: therefore, much more strongly will this be true to say of the first Truth.

4. Likewise, our intellect understands nothing except through the first Light and Truth,[5] therefore, every action of the intellect, which is in thinking something not to be, is through the first Light; but through the first Light one does not happen to think, that the first Light or Truth is not: therefore, in no manner does one happen to think, that the first Truth is not.

5. Likewise, that which happens to think happens to enunciate;[6] but one does not happen to think, that the first Truth is not: therefore, neither to think (it). *Proof of the middle*: every enunciative discourse [sermo enunciativus] asserts, that it is true; whence it follows: if a man is a donkey, that a man is a donkey is true; but everything which posits truth, posits the first Truth, because every truth infers It: therefore, every discourse asserts, that the first Truth is: ergo etc..

6. Likewise, every enunciative[7] discourse is either affirmative, or negative; but an affirmative affirms *this of this*; but it follows: if there is a being which is this, it is a being which is not this, because when I say "*this being*" [ens hoc], I mean a limited, finite, constrained [arctatum] being; and with such posited, there is posited the most high Being: therefore, every affirmative discourse about a creature infers God.

7. Likewise, the negative similarly, because no discourse is more negative than this one: there is no truth. But (St.) Augustine in (his) SOLILOQUIES[8] proves, that that discourse posits, that there is some truth; because if there is no truth, it is true, that there is no truth; and if this is true, something is true; and if something is true, there is some truth: ergo etc..

BUT ON THE CONTRARY: 1. (St. John) Damascene (says):[9] « The pernicious wickedness of men prevails to so great an extent [in tantum], that it says, that God is not, according to that (word) of the Psalm: *The fool said* etc.. »

2. Likewise, the idolater says, that there is no other God except an idol, and this he believes and thinks; but it is established that an idol is not God: ergo etc..

3. Likewise, every that, which when understood not to be, can be understood as something, can be thought not to be. But (St. Severinus) Boethius says in the book, ON THE SEVEN RULES,[10] that having un

---

[1] PROSLOGION, ch. 2 ff.

[2] Some codices have the subjunctive *can* [possit].

[3] ON THE ORTHODOX FAITH, Bk. I, ch. 1 and 3: Indeed, there is no one mortal [nemo ... mortalium], in whom this has not been implanted by Him, to cognize that God is.

[4] *Dignity*, in Greek αξίωμα [axioma], here and passim signifies a proposition known immediately or per se, which Aristotle defines in POSTERIOR ANALYTICS, Bk. I, ch. 2, which is an indemonstrable proposition, which anyone who is to be taught necessarily has; and which (St. Severinus) Boethius in ON THE SEVEN RULES (says) is an enunciation, which is proven by anyone who has heard it.

[5] Concerning this proposition, which is founded upon the doctrine of St. Augustine, see above q. 1. arg. 3 of the affirmative part, and d. 3, p. I, a. 1, q. 1, fundament 2, where also in the Scholium the sense of this is explained. — Next the Vatican edition after *something* [aliquid] omits *not* [non] and a little below this after *to think* [cogitare] together with codex cc it omits the words *that there is not a prime* up to *to think* [non esse primam ... cogitare], which mutilated reading is repaired with the help of the other codices and edition 1.

[6] The Vatican edition contrary to the codices and editions 1, 2, and

3, transposes the words and exhibits the proposition in a negative manner, thus: *that which is not agreeable to enunciate, this is not agreeable to think* [quod non convenit enuntiare, hoc non convenit cogitare].

[7] Concerning enunciation and its species see Aristotle, ON INTERPRETATION, Bk. I, ch. "On Enunciation". — Then the Vatican edition not trusting in the manuscripts and edition 1 has *because it follows* [quia sequitur] in place of *but it follows* [sed sequitur].

[8] Book II, ch. 2, n. 2 and ch. 15. n. 28. — The Vatican text together with codex cc after *posits* [ponit] reads *that there is some first Truth* [primam aliquam veritatem esse], but contrary to all the other codices and edition 1 and contrary to the edition of the works of (St.) Augustine.

[9] ON THE ORTHODOX FAITH, Bk. I, ch. 3: Since, however, the improbity of Satan has prevailed so much against human nature, that it has pulled certain ones down into a most stupid and worse-than-any-evil chasm of departure, such that they deny that God is, whose foolishness the interpreter of the divine words, David, making clear, said: The fool said in his heart (Ps. 13:1) etc..

[10] Or in the book: IN WHAT MANNER THE SUBSTANCES WHICH ARE IN IT, ARE GOOD, near the middle.

derstood <u>per impossibile</u>, that there is not a most high Good, something can still be understood (to be) round and white: therefore, similarly in the most high True, and thus It will be able to be thought not to be.

4. Likewise, that which lays most hidden from us [maxime nos latet], easily can be thought not to be; but the truth of the Divine 'To Be' is of this kind, because *God dwells (in) light inaccessible*:[1] ergo etc..

5. Likewise, I ask, what is it to say, that God cannot be thought not to be? If because He cannot in any manner be thought[2] *neither truly nor falsely*, that is manifestly false; if because He cannot (be thought not to be) *truly*, similarly neither the soul nor Heaven and (things) of this kind.

6. Likewise, that which one happens to express one happens[3] also to think; but it happens that (someone) expresses, that the Divine 'To Be' is not: therefore, also to think (this). That it may happen, this is clear, since there is said in particular cases [in speciali]: "God is not", and in general: "there is nothing"; and that neither of these infers, that God is, it is clear, because an opposite does not infer an opposite,[4] and what posits nothing infers nothing; moreover, any of these posits nothing.

CONCLUSION

So great is the truth of the Divine 'To Be', that it cannot with an assent (of the mind) be thought not to be except on account of a defect on the part of the one understanding, who is ignorant of, what God is; on the part of the intelligible, however, there cannot be a defect neither of presence nor of evidence, either in itself, or in being proven.

I **RESPOND**: It must be said, that *'that something is thought[5] not to be'* is in a twofold manner. *Either* in a *false* reckoning, just as I think of this: 'man is an ass'; and *to think* this is nothing other than to understand what is, that which is said. In this manner there can be thought not to be the truth of the Divine 'To Be'.

In the other manner it is to think *with an assent* (of the mind), just as[6] I think something not to be, and I believe it not to be: and in this manner *'that one thinks something not to be'*, which is, can come either out of a defect of *the one understanding*, or out of a defect of *the intelligible*.

Moreover, a defect of *the one understanding* is a blindness and/or ignorance, because of which, since [quia] one is ignorant of a thing, one thinks[7] that it is not. Moreover, that there is a thinking of some being happens in a twofold manner, namely *if it is* and *what it is*.[8]

Moreover, our intellect is deficient in thought [cogitatione] of the Divine Truth as much as regards the cognition, *what It is*, however, it is not deficient as much as regards the cognition, *if It is*. Whence, Hugh (of St. Victor says):[9] « God has so tempered His own cognition in man from the start, that just as *what He is* could never be comprehended, so *that He is* could never be ignored » [ignorari]. Therefore, because our intellect is never deficient in the cognition of God, *if He is*, for that reason neither can it be ignorant of, that He is simply,[10] nor think that He is not.

However, because it is deficient in the cognition, *what He is*, for that reason frequently it thinks, that God is what He is not, as an idol, and/or that He is not what He is, as the Just God.[11] And because he who thinks, that God is not what He is, such as the Just One, consequently think, that He is not: for that reason by reason of the defect of the intellect God or the most high Truth can be thought not to be; not however, simply or generally, but from the consequence, just as he who does not know, that beatitude is in God, does not know that it is He.[12]

Moreover, in this manner proceed the reasons proving, that some intellect does think and/or can think[13], that the Divine '*to be*' is not.

In another manner it can be thought, that something is not on account of a defect *on the part of the intelligible*, and a defect of this kind can be in a twofold manner: either a defect of *presence*, or a defect of *evidence*; a defect of *presence*, to the extent [utpote] that (it is) not *always*, not *everywhere*,[14] and not everywhere totally. What is not *always*, sometimes is, sometimes is not: and for that reason sometimes it can be truly thought not to be. Similarly, concerning that which is not *everywhere*, because by the same reckoning, by which it can be thought not to be here, it can be thought not to be elsewhere. Similarly, concerning that which is present [adest] *according to a part*, (for it is therefore) absent according to a part.

Moreover, God is always and everywhere and (is) whole always and everywhere: for that reason He cannot be thought not to be. (St.) Anselm assigns this reason in the book, AGAINST THE FOOL.[15]

---

[1] 1 Timothy 6:16; in the Vulgate: *dwells in light inaccessible* [lucem inhabitate inaccessibilem].

[2] Codex W reads *He can be thought in some manner not to be neither* [potest cogitari aliquod modo non esse nec].

[3] The greater part of the codices as A C S T V W etc. omit *happens*.

[4] Nay rather it destroys it, by including a negation of its opposite.

[5] Very many codices together with edition one have *be thought* [cogitari], but less coherently with what is subjoined.

[6] Codices aa and bb add *when* [cum] well enough.

[7] Trusting in the older codices and edition 1 we have expunged *for that reason* [ideo], which the Vatican edition together with codex cc prefixed to the word *one thinks* [cogitat]. Codex V after *a thing* [rem] adds *to be* [esse].

[8] Aristotle, POSTERIOR ANALYTICS, Bk. II, ch. 1.

[9] ON THE SACRAMENTS, Bk. I, p. III, ch. 1 at the end. The Vatican edition alone in this passage adds *by a man* [ab homine] after *could* [poterat].

[10] On the authority of the more ancient manuscripts and edition 1 we have substituted in place of *similarly not* [similiter non], *simply, nor* [simpliciter nec], which also occurs a little after this, which reading, with changed punctuation, the Vatican edition together with codex cc also has; but its reading is not so clear.

[11] The Vatican edition together with codex cc, disagreeing however, with the other codices and edition 1, here and a little below this substitutes for *the Just (One)* [iustum] the less well *the not Just (One)*; each reading has one sense; in the reading of the codices *the Just* is referred to the preceding *is not* [non esse].

[12] We prefer the reading of the very many manuscripts as H P T Y ee etc., *it is He* [eum esse] instead of *it is* [eam esse], as that which is more distinct.

[13] Thus the codices together with edition 1, the reading of which is here preferred to the reading of the Vatican edition *be thought* [cogitari]. A little after this one or an other of the codices also puts *think* [cogitare] in place of *be thought* [cogitari].

[14] The Vatican edition, after having adding *that* [quia] after *always* [semper], here adjoins *or that, although always and everywhere* [aut quia, quamvis semper et ubique]; but the authority of the manuscripts withstand this, very many of which as A C F K L R S T U V on account of the repetition of the words *not everywhere* [non ubique], omit these words the first time [semel], but incongruously, as is clear from what is subjoined. Edition 1 reads *not always or not everywhere or not everywhere totally* [non semper aut non ubique aut non ubique totaliter]. Immediately after this the Vatican edition together with codex cc, not trusting in all the other manuscripts and edition 1, has less well *Because* [Quia] in place of *What* [Quod], to which codices aa and bb adjoin *For* [enim].

[15] Chapter 1.

Not only on account of a defect of *presence* can it be thought that something is not, but also on account of a defect of *evidence*, because it is not evident *in itself*, nor is it evident *in being proven*. But the truth of the Divine 'to be' is evident *in itself* and *in being proven*. *In itself*, because just as we cognize principles inasmuch as (we cognize)[1] terms, and because a cause of a predicate is closed in a subject, for that reason these are by their very selves evident; so also in the proposed. For God or the most high Truth is Itself the 'To Be', than whom nothing better can be thought: therefore, He cannot not be nor be thought not to be. For the predicate is closed in the subject. Nor does it only have evidence out of[2] itself, but also *out of proof* [ex probatione], since every created *truth and nature* proves and concludes that there is a Divine Truth, because if there is a being through participation and from another, there is a being through essence and not from another. Every *right intelligence* also proves and concludes it, because upon every soul has its cognition been impressed, and every cognition is through it. Again, every *affirmative proposition* proves and concludes it; for every such posits something; and with something posited there is posited the true; and with the true posited there is posited the Truth, which is the cause of every true.[3] On the other hand [autem] a *negative* proposition does not infer it except in a sophistic manner, as they say. Whence from this that it is *that nothing is*, and/or *that there is no truth*, one does not happen to conclude nor infer, that there is truth. For this proposition: "*that nothing is*",[4] destroys every truth. And for that reason after it there does not follow any affirmation, and this is false: if nothing is, "that nothing is" is true. And if it be said, that every proposition infers what is said, it is true, and if nothing is, no proposition is nor (is) anything. (St.) Augustine, however [autem], does not make such an argument for approving it, but for inquiring (into it).

Therefore, it must be conceded, that so great is the truth of the Divine 'To Be', that with an assent (of the mind) it cannot be thought not to be except on account of the ignorance of the one thinking, who is ignorant, *what* It is which is mean by the name for God.[5] And the reasons for this are to be conceded, though some are sophistic.

1. To that, therefore, which is objected in the contrary: To so great an extent does ... prevail etc.; it must be said, that (St. John) Damascene speaks of the thinking, which comes from a complete blinding [ab excaecatione]; which is clear from his very word when he says "*wickedness*".

2. Likewise, regarding that concerning an idol, it must be said, that for that reason (the idolater) errs,[6] because he is ignorant of, *what* He is; whence he does not think, that three is not a God in the universal (sense).

3. To that which is objected, that with God understood not to be, other (things) can be understood;[7] it must be said, that (St. Severinus) Boethius speaks of an understanding, by which we think something per impossibile, but do not assent (to it).

4. To that which is objected, that It lies most hidden from us; the response is clear, because[8] *what He is* does lie most hidden from us, but nevertheless [tamen] *if He is* lies most openly [maxime patet].

5. To that which is objected, "What it is to say, that the Divine Truth cannot be thought not to be?", it must be said, that this is to say, that[9] someone cannot believe, that God is not, so long as he uses reason. Not so concerning creatures; because even if it is certain, that one creature is present to one, (it is) not, however, [tamen], to all (thus certain), because (a creature) is not of so great virtue, that it offers itself equally to all, as the first Truth (does).

6. To that which is objected, (that) that which one happens to express one happens also to think; it must be said, that "to think" [cogitare] can be accepted *generally* for an act of the mind whether errant or not, whether assenting or not; and then that is true; and/or for thinking *with an assent*; and thus it is false, because it happens that one contradicts axioms [dignitatibus] as regards exterior reckoning, not however, as much as regards interior, as the Philosopher says in the book, POSTERIOR ANALYTICS.[10]

SCHOLIUM

I. This question nearly coincides with that, which is commonly expressed thus, whether "that God is" is known through itself [per se notum]. Nevertheless, so that the mind of the Holy Doctor may be well understood, it helps to observe, that the status of the question, and consequently also the form of the solution differs to some extent from the question posited in the above said form and its solution. For the Saint speaks here directly of the truth of the Divine 'To Be' and only indirectly of our cognition of this Divine 'To Be'; however, that other question immediately concerns our co-

---

[1] Supply: *we cognize* [cognoscimus]. Aristotle, POSTERIOR ANALYTICS, Bk. I, ch. 3 (according to St. Severinus Boethius' translation): We say that there is a certain principle of a science, inasmuch as we cognize (its) terms.

[2] From the more ancient manuscripts and edition 1 we have substituted *out of* [ex] for *in* [in].

[3] In what manner this reckoning is to be understood, see fundaments 5 and 6 above.

[4] The Vatican edition together with codex cc, disagreeing with the other codices and edition 1, as *there is nothing* [nihil est]. The next following proposition, which is exhibited in a corrupt and mutilated manner by the Vatican edition, we have restored with the help of the manuscripts and edition 1 by putting *affirmation* [affirmatio] in place of *affirmative* [affirmativa], then *false* [falsa] in place of *true* [vera], and by adding the words *that nothing is* [nihil esse] upto *if nothing is* [si nihil est]. The codices disagree in this only, that some have *it be said* [dicatur], others together with edition 1 *one says* [dicat], others *you say* [dicas].

[5] Very many codices together with edition 1 omit *of God* [Dei].

[6] Supply: *the idolater* [idolatra].

[7] Trusting in the manuscripts and edition 1 we have expunged here the not aptly added *to be* [esse].

[8] The Vatican edition contrary to the manuscripts and edition 1 has *that* [quod].

[9] We have supplied from manuscripts D G H K T Y Z aa bb ee ff and edition 1 the words *this is to say that* [hoc est dicere quod]. Then codex X has *think* [cogitare] in place of *believe* [credere]. A little below this from codex T we have inserted *present* [praesentem]; then from the same codex in place of *of ... a truth* [veritatis] we have put *of ... virtue* [virtutis], which reading is both in itself more distinct and seems to be insinuated in the body of the article (from *defect of presence*.

[10] Book I, ch. 8 (ch. 10) according to the translation of (St. Severinus) Boethius: For there is always an insisting [instare] as regards exterior discourse, but as regards interior discourse not always (πρὸς τὸν ἔξω λόγον, πρός τον ἔξω λόγον). Cf. St. Thomas' Commentary on this passage, lect. 19, where both in the ancient translation and in his Commentary *reckoning* [rationem] is always had in place of *discourse* [orationem]. — The Vatican edition transposes *reckoning* [rationem] before *to contradict* [contradicere] contrary to the sense of Aristotle's words, and a little before this it has *then* [tunc] in place of *and thus* [et sic], and after *axioms* [dignitatibus] it has *that is propositions known through themselves* [id est propositionibus per se notis], but contrary to the testimony of the manuscripts and edition 1.

gnition. Moreover, the distinctions posited in the text must be well attended to.

II. About the question, whether the existence of God is known through itself [per se nota], the ancient Scholastics speak in a diverse manner. However, all concede, that existence concerns the essential concept of God. St. Anselm teaches, that for everyone apprehending the significance of the word *God*, His existence is known through itself; whence from the very concept of God as of a being, a better than which cannot be thought, he forms the argument to prove the existence of God. Concerning the value of this argument there is a dispute. In its favor are cited Giles the Roman, d. 3, p. I, 1st princ., q. 2, and (Bl.) Dionysius the Carthusian, here in q. 2. Perhaps these two also slightly depart from the common sentence of the Scholastics, who restrict the efficacy of the argument to those, who already have and admit *their own* reckoning of God as the first and necessary Being. Furthermore the Nominalists assert, that neither to us, nor to the Blessed is that proposition, 'that God is', known through itself. (Bl. John Duns) Scotus mentions certain difficulties about the distinction between a proposition known through itself *in itself* and one known through itself *in regard to us*; but he, however, does concede it in regard to the principal matter [rem], that the said proposition is known through itself to God and to the Blessed, not however, to us. St. Thomas simply teaches, that the said proposition is known through itself according to itself, not however, to us (SUMMA., I, q. 2, a. 1; SENT., Bk. I, d. 3, q. 1 and quaestiunc. 2; ON THE TRUTH, q. 10, a. 12; SUMMA AGAINST THE GENTILES , I, chs. 10, 11).

However, all the ancient Scholastics concede, that in some sense the existence of God is also known through itself to us, that is not under a proper reckoning, but under common reckonings, namely of being, the true, the good, beatitude; cf. St. Thomas, SUMMA., I, q. 2, a. 1, at nn. 1 and 3; SUMMA AGAINST THE GENTILES, I. ch. 11, at n. 4; SENT., Bk. I, d. 3, q. 2. — Alexander of Hales, SUMMA., p. I, q. 3, m. 2, at n. 3, explains the matter thus: « The cognition of anything can be in two manners: in a common reckoning and in a proper reckoning. Therefore, something can be cognized in common reckoning, and however, be ignored under a proper reckoning, just as when someone cognizes *honey* under a common reckoning, namely that it is a soft, ruby body [corpus molle, rubeum], but is ignorant of it under a proper reckoning; and therefore, when he sees, that *gall* is a soft, ruby body, being deceived he believes, it to be *honey*. Similarly, the cognition of beatitude and an appetite for it are innate to us in a common reckoning, that it is a state perfected by the aggregation of all goods; however, in a proper reckoning some are ignorant of

it. Whence diverse (things) in diverse manners are posited and estimated to be beatitude ... Similarly, it must be said, that because idolaters are not ignorant of God in the common reckoning, that He is the Being, the Principle, the Omnipotent, the Lord; however, under a proper reckoning they are ignorant » etc.. He affirms the same in the solution to n. 4, that God according to the cognition of *what* He is can be ignored, not according to the cognition of *that* He is. The same distinction and the same example of gall and honey is had in Bl. (now St.) Albert (the Great), SUMMA., tr. 3, q. 19, m. 2. Cf. also Richard (of Middleton), here in p. I, a. 1, q. 2. — (Bl.) Peter of Tarentaise, here in q. 1, a. 2. — With this posited, that doctrine is understood to be common, (which says) that God is implicitly cognized in every act of intellectual cognition. Thus St. Thomas, ON THE TRUTH, q. 22, a. 2, at n. 1: « It must be said, that all cognizing cognize implicitly God in everything cognized. For just as nothing has a reckoning of an appetible except through a similitude of the first Goodness, so nothing is cognizable except through a similitude of the first Truth »; St. Bonaventure DE REDUCTIONE ARTIUM AD DEUM: « In every thing, which is sensed or which is cognized, God lays interiorly lays hidden »; (Bl. John Duns) Scotus, SENT., Bk. I, d. 3, q. 2: « For by cognizing whichever being, as this being is, *God is most indistinctly conceived* ».

Therefore, it is clear, that St. Bonaventure has not departed from the common way by saying, that our intellect does not fail in regard to the question, if God is (i. e. under some common reckoning), but only in regard to the question, what God is (i. e. under a proper reckoning). Cf. on this matter Trigosus, SUMMA THEOLOGICA, q. 2, a. 2, dub. 1 (who however, does not sufficiently consider this distinction). But if the Seraphic (Doctor) seems to approve the noted argument of (St.) Anselm, it must be observed, that he speaks of the Divine 'To Be' in itself, and/or of one understanding, who cognizes God already under a proper reckoning. For to this one it ought to be evident, that the existence of God is included in His essence. However, having been blinded in understanding and ignorant of, what God is, there remains hidden that which is evident in itself, so that he presumes to deny in his stupidity the true and living God.

III. In regard to those conclusions, besides those things already cited, cf. St. Bonaventure, ITINERARIUM., ch. 5; HEXAÉMERON, Sermons 5 and 10. — (Bl. John Duns) Scotus, SENT., Bk. I, d. 2d q. 2. — Bl. (now St.) Albert (the Great), SUMMA., p. I, tr. 4, q. 19, m. 1 and 4. — Henry of Gent, SUMMA., a. 22 throughout, and a. 30, q. 3. — Durandus (of Saint-Pourçain), here in p. I, qq. 3 and 1. — (Bl.) Dionysius the Carthusian, here in q. 2. — (Gabriel) Biel, here in q. 4.

ARTICLE II

On the Immutability of God.

Consequently, in the second place is the question concerning the second property of the Divine 'Being' [esse], that is immutability. Concerning which, two (questions) are asked:

First there is asked, whether immutability is in God.

Second, whether it is a property of God.

QUESTION I

Whether God is immutable?

That immutability is in God, is shown in this manner:

1. Every change [mutation] either is according to substance, or according to accident;[1] but God is not changed [mutatur] according to *substance*, because every such (thing) is corruptible, but God or the Divine Substance, since it does not have a principle, is incorruptible: ergo etc..

2. Likewise, neither according to *accident*, because

in God there is not an accident: therefore, there is no change in Him.

3. Likewise, everything which is changed, is through the prior in potency rather than in act,[2] and in such (its) act differs from (its) potency; but God is pure act: therefore, in no manner is He changed.

4. Likewise, let Richard (of St. Victor)'s deduction be made.[3] « Every change

---

[1] See Aristotle, PHYSICS, Bk. V, text 1 ff., and METAPHYSICS, Bk. XI, ch. 10 (Bk. X, ch. 11).

[2] Aristotle, METAPHYSICS, Bk. XII, text 8 (Bk. XI, ch. 2): Everything is changed from a being (in) potency to a being in act.

[3] ON THE TRINITY, Bk. II, ch. 3: And so it must be known, that every change is either from a state into a better state, or from a state

into a lower state [statum deteriorem], or from a state into a state equal to the prior one; but where there can be nothing of these, there is true incommutability. — Then edition 1 has *best* [optima] in place of *most truly* [verissime], and codex K at the end of the argument has *with the Divine Essence* [divinae essentiae] in place of *with the Divine 'Being'* [divini esse].

change is either into a better or a worse or an equal [parem] state »; but in none of these manners is the Divine Nature changed, because not into a better, because It most truly is; not into a lower, because It is by Its very self; not into an equal, because It is perfect: therefore, in no manner does mutability convene with the Divine "Being".

ON THE CONTRARY: 1. In the seventh (chapter) of Wisdom:[1] *More mobile than all moveables is Wisdom*: ergo etc.. *If it be said*, that Wisdom is said to be mobile [mobilis] through (the manner of) a cause, for this that it causes others to be moved; *on the contrary*: nothing gives what it does not have; but God gives movement [motum][2] to all: therefore, movement and/or change is most greatly in God.

2. Likewise, everything which is now something, because (it was) not before, has been changed;[3] but the Son of God is a man, moreover, from eternity He was not a man: therefore, He has changed. *If you say*, that man is predicated of the Son of God not through inherence, but through union; and union is a relation, and a relation comes without a change, as a price comes to be from a coin, as (St.) Augustine says in the fifth (book) ON THE TRINITY:[4] *on the contrary*: (St.) Ambrose[5] thus argues against the heretic, who posited that the Son (was) begotten by the Father in time [ex tempore], because if (He would be) in this (manner), then the Father has become *the Father* from *a non-Father*, therefore, He has changed: therefore, similarly in the proposed.

3. Likewise, whatsoever from not-acting becomes acting, is changed by a change, which is from leisure [ab otio] into act;[6] but God from not-creating has become creating: therefore, He has been changed. *If you say*, that God from not-acting becomes acting, not on account of a change of Himself, but on account of the change of an produced effect, just as the sun from not-illumining becomes illumining (with the advent of dawn); *on the contrary*: not because there is a creature, does God for that reason create, but because God creates, a creature is made or is produced. Therefore, it is through (a consideration of what is) prior, that God acts, rather than that a creature is made: therefore, since the posterior is not a cause of the prior, not because a creature is made a being from a non-being, does God become creating from not-creating, but conversely; and thus the change is according to the reckoning of the agent,[7] not of the effect.

4. Likewise, God wills something, which He does not will before, because He has willed to create in time [ex tempore], what He has not willed (to create) from eternity; but whosoever wills something, which (he did) not (will) before, has been changed:[8] ergo etc.. *If you say*, that from eternity He willed to create the world in that instant,[9] just as I will to hear Mass tomorrow; *on the contrary*: the Will of God is the cause of things proximate and immediate; but having posited a proximate and immediate cause, the effect is posited: therefore, if from eternity He did will (it), from eternity the world came to be.

CONCLUSION

God is entirely immutable both according to place, because (He is) immense, and according to time, because (He is) eternal, and according to form, because (He is) simple; and because (He is) immutable, for that reason He moves all (things).

I RESPOND: It must be said, that just as (St. Severinus) Boethius says,[10] « God, remaining stable, grants that all other (things) to be moved ». Whence the Divine Essence is *immutable*. For It is not changed *according to place*, because It is everywhere; not *according to time*, because It is at once Eternity; not *according to form*, because It is purely act. Whence simplicity bears off mutation according to form, eternity bears its off according to time, immensity bears it off according to place.

And for that reason in God there is a most high Stability, and hence *the causality of* every *movement*; because, just as (St.) Augustine proves[11] and the Philosopher wants, every movement proceeds from the immoveable; as when the hand is moved, the elbow stands still, and the elbow is moved, with the shoulder standing still [stante humero]. Therefore, because the Wisdom of God is stable,[12] for that reason it moves all (things).

1. What is therefore, objected concerning Wisdom, that it is called mobile [mobilis]; it must be said, that "mobile" is said of it *actively*, because it causes (others) to be moved,[13] not *passively*, as just as "sensible" (is said) of an animal.

And to that which is objected, (that) nothing gives to the other what it does not have; it must be said, that to have something is in a threefold manner, that is *formally, exemplarily, causally*;[14] and in any of those manners one can give what he has. In the first manner, moreover, God does not have movement, but in the second and third He does [sic].

2. To that which is objected concerning relation,

---

[1] Verse 24.

[2] Ed. 1 has *to be moved* [moveri], by which there is an allusion to (St. Severinus) Boethius, ON THE CONSOLATION ON PHILOSOPHY, Bk. III, Metro 9: And remaining stable *Thou dost grant all (things) to be moved* [Stabilique manens *das cuncta moveri*].

[3] See Aristotle, PHYSICS, Bk. V, text. 7, and Bk. VI, texts 32 & 73 (chs. 3 & 8).

[4] Chapter 16, n. 17: Moreover, a coin [nummus] when it is said (to be) the price, is said relatively, nor, however, has it been changed, when it undertook to be the price. — Note however, that the relation of price to a coin is only accidental, but the relation, which is in the Hypostatic Union, is substantial. For an explanation of this example, see below d. 30, Doubt 3.

[5] ON THE FAITH, Bk. I, ch. 9: For if the Father undertook to be, therefore, first there was God, the Father was made afterwards. — The Vatican edition together with codex cc after *then* [tunc], contrary to the other codices and edition 1, omits *the Father* [Pater]. Edition 1 has *if He would be in this (manner)* [si hoc esset].

[6] A similar passage is had in Aristotle, PHYSICS, Bk. VIII, text 7, and ON THE SOUL, Bk. II, text 45 (ch. 4), where he (speaks) in this manner: But the worker is changed solely from idleness into act.

[7] Some codices as K and V have *of the one effecting* [efficientis].

[8] Averroës in the book, THE DESTRUCTION OF DESTRUCTIONS, disputation 1, Doubt 1, and in COMMENTARY ON THE PHYSICS, Bk. VIII, text 15, strives to deduce from this proposition the impossibility of creation.

— A little before this, after *He willed to create* [ex tempore voluit], codices aa and bb add sufficiently well *the world* [mundum].

[9] Codex W adds *in which it was created* [in quo creatus est].

[10] ON THE CONSOLATION OF PHILOSOPHY, Bk. III, Metro 9, after which text codex Z adds *Psalm (101,28): Thou shall change things and they shall be changed* etc. [Psalmus: mutabis res et mutabuntur etc.]. A little below this, along with very many codd., such as A S T V W etc. and ed. 1, we read *purely* [pure] for *pure* [purus], which the Vatican ed. has.

[11] A LITERAL EXPOSITION OF GENESIS, Bk. VIII, ch. 24. — The words of Aristotle in the book, ON THE MOVEMENT OF ANIMALS, ch. 1, are these: Nevertheless, a principle, in as much as (it is) a principle, rests, in respect to a moved particle, which is beneath it: just as if with an arm moved, the elbow (rests), but in respect to the whole member, the shoulder does (Venetian edition of 1584).

[12] Codex W adds *and immoveable* [et immobilis]. Next codex F has *To that, therefore, which is objected* [Ad illud ergo quod obiicitur].

[13] The Vatican edition together with codex cc has *movement* [motum], but contrary to all the other manuscripts and edition 1.

[14] Cf. Dionysius (the Areopagite),ON THE DIVINE NAMES, ch. 5. — Next the codd. disagree among themselves; some indeed have *any* [quodlibet] for *in any* [quolibet], others with ed. 1 have *be given* [dari] for *give* [dare], others, such as A T bb & cc, have both *any* and *be given*; though *and what one has in any of those manners, one can give* [et quod quolibet istorum modorum habet, dare potest.] would read better.

it must be said, that "relation", when it is said of (something) new,[1] of necessity posits a mutation in one of the two extremes, and it is not proper that (it be) in both. For that reason that relation, which is of a person to a person, posits a mutation in one of the two persons; and with one changed, the rest is also changed, because they are the same essence: for that reason of necessity, if[2] the Father came to be from a non-Father, He would be changed. Moreover, a relation of an essence to an essence does not of necessity posit a mutation, except in one of the two extremes, because when the essences are diverse, one can be changed, with the other of the two thoroughly unchanged [non permutato]:[3] and for that reason in a relation to a creature a mutation is always understood to have been caused in the creature, not in God. Nevertheless, [tamen] properly speaking, just as will be shown elsewhere,[4] God is not referred to a creature, except according to a meaning [dici] and a manner of speaking.

However, it could be otherwise said, just as has been touched upon above,[5] that it is not similar: because a personal relation grants a person to exist, not so, however, a relation to a creature; and for that reason it follows: if He began *to be the Father*, He began *to be*; moreover, it does not follow: if[6] God began *to be a man*, He began *to be*. And for that reason the argument of (St.) Ambrose is very valid [bene valet], that if the Father would have begun to beget, because He had been changed, that He would have begun to be, not that He would have been changed from one state into the other.

3. To that which is objected, when from non-acting etc.; it must be said, that there is an agent, which is its own action, and there is an agent, which is not its own action, but is an action by itself.[7] The agent, which is not its own action, so acts, that between itself and (its) effect there falls a medium, which disposes it; and such an agent never becomes acting from a non-acting, unless it be changed, because there becomes present (something) new[8] to itself [novum sibi advenit]. But an agent, which is its own action, acts by its very self; and for that reason between itself and (its) effect there does not fall any disposing medium; and for that reason since the agent comes to be from a non-agent, because nothing new accedes to itself, therefore, it is not changed. Such an agent is God.

4. To that which is objected concerning the will, it must be said, that a proximate and immediate cause is said in a threefold manner: either in respect of *substance*, or of *disposition*, or of *act*; in respect of the *substance*, between which[9] and (its) effect there does not fall another, middle causing substance; in respect of the *disposition*, to which there is not added a new disposition to produce the effect; in respect of the *act*, when it is conjoined to an act. Therefore, I say, that the Will of God was the proximate and immediate cause from eternity in respect of the substance and disposition (of the world), but[10] not in respect of the *act* (of creating); because the Will was not conjoined to the act except for the time, in which He willed to act, as is clear, when there is said: "I will to read tomorrow", the will is not conjoined to the act except for the time of tomorrow [pro tempore crastino].

SCHOLIUM

I. In regard to the diverse species of *mutation* [mutationis] and immutability, cf. the following question, and in regard to the solution to n. 1, St. Thomas, SUMMA., I, q. 9, a. 1 to n. 2.

II. The immutability of God has already been defined in the Council of Nicea. Cf. Alexander of Hales, SUMMA., p. I, q. 4, m. 1, a. 2. — (Bl. John Duns) Scotus, here in q. 5; REPORTATIO., here in q. 2 on the principle of things (and) q. 3. — St. Thomas, here in q. 3, a. 1; SUMMA., loc. cit.. — Bl. (now St.) Albert (the Great), here in a. 16 ff.; SUMMA., p. I, tr. 4, q. 21, m. 1 and 2. — (Bl.) Peter of Tarentaise, here in q. 4, a. 1. — Giles the Roman, here in 3rd princ. q. 1. — Henry of Ghent, on this and the following question; SUMMA., a. 30. — Durandus (of Saint-Pourçain), on this and the following question; here in q. 4. — (Gabriel) Biel, of this and the following question; here in q. 7.

QUESTION II

Whether God alone is immutable?

Second, there is asked, whether immutability is a property of the Divine Essence, so that it convenes with no creature. And that (it is) so, it seems:

1. In the last (chapter) of the First (Letter) to Timothy there is said of God, that *He alone has immortality*. And (St.) Augustine says AGAINST MAXIMINUS:[12] « In every changeable [mutabile] nature not every change [mutatio] is itself a death »: therefore if God alone has immortality, He alone has immutability.

2. Likewise, every vertible is changeable; but every creature is vertible; whence (St. John) Damascene (says):[13] « Everything which starts from being turned [a versione],* tends towards being turned [in versionem] »: therefore, etc..

---

[1] Very many codices as A C L R U V X omit *of (something) new* [de novo], but badly. Codex W has *of two (things)* [de duobus] and edition 1 has *of a Divine Person* [de persona divina] in place of *of (something) new* [de novo], but ineptly. Codex G reads *when it arrives from (something) new* [cum de novo advenit].

[2] Codices aa and bb add *God* [Deus].

[3] The Vatican edition, not trusting in the mss. and ed. 1, has *one (essence) can be ... unchanged* [una mutari, altera non permutata], and immediately after this it omits *and* [et]; the other codd., such as A aa & bb with ed. 1, have *unchanged* [non mutato] for *thoroughly unchanged* [non permutato].

[4] Below in d. 30, q. 3. — Then after *a meaning* [dici] ed. 1 has *and/or according to a manner of speaking* [vel secundum modum loquendi].

[5] Distinction 7, Doubt 4. See also below, d. 26, q. 3. — Immediately after this, the Vatican ed. omits *that it is not* [quod non est], which corrupt reading is repaired with the help of the mss. and edd. 1, 2 & 3.

[6] The Vatican edition together with codex cc has *this does not follow: God* [non sequitur hic: Deus], and after *man* it adds *therefore* [igitur], but the authority of the other manuscripts withstand this.

[7] The Vatican edition contrary to nearly all the codices and edition 1 omits, not well, *but is an action by itself* [sed actio est ab ipso], in place of which codex Q has *but an action is a something by itself* [sed actio est aliquid ab ipso]. A little before this after *is objected* [obiicitur], *when* [quando] is lacking in codex V and edition 1.

[8] On the authority of the manuscripts and edition 1 we have expunged the here added *something* [quid: which is however, necessary to be infer in English context].

[9] From the manuscripts and edition 1 we have here substituted *between which* [inter quam] in place of *when between it* [cum inter eam] and a little below this *to which* [cui] in place of *when* [cum].

[10] The Vatican edition together with codex cc, contrary to the other codices and edition 1, has less clearly *and* [et] in place of *but* [sed].

[11] Verse 16.

[12] Book II, ch. 12, n. 2.

[13] ON THE ORTHODOX FAITH, Book I, ch. 3: For of those which start to be by mutation, it is necessary also that they be subject [subsint] to that mutation.

---

* *Trans. note:* here *versio* is used as a technical term meaning "a change in the order of being": it is derived from that metaphor for creating, which has creatures "turned away from nothingness"; whence in English we say, "turned into", for "became": thus, what is "able to be turned" is "vertible".

3. Likewise, everything, which left to itself passes [cedit] into nothing,[1] is of itself mutable; but every creature is of this kind; whence (St.) Gregory (the Great says):[2] « All (things) would tend unto nothing, unless the Hand of the Founder retained them (in being) »: ergo etc..

4. Likewise, no accident from itself has stability; but 'to be' [esse] accedes to every creature, just as (St.) Hilary (of Poitiers) says and (as) it is had in the text,[3] that it comes from another: therefore, every creature as much as regards (its) "to be" is instable.

5. Likewise, everything vain is subject to variability; but every creature (is) vain, since it is out of nothing; whence, in the eighth (chapter) of (the Letter) to the Romans (there is said):[4] *Unto vanity is the creature subjected* etc.; therefore, if every creature (is) vain, none (is) immutable.

6. Likewise, everything changed [omne mutatum] has a mutability in itself; but every creature has been made: therefore, every creature (has) changed, therefore, none (is) immutable.

ON THE CONTRARY: "Immutability" is not said except in a threefold manner. For "immutability" means either *invariability*, or *incorruptibility*, or *invertibility*.

1. Moreover, it is shown, that *invariability* convenes with creatures, as *principles*. For (St.) Augustine shows in the twelfth (book of his) CONFESSIONS,[5] that formless *matter* [materia informis] is invariable; because what is without [caret] form, is without order, and what is without order, is without vicissitude, therefore, without variation. Moreover, the author of THE SIX PRINCIPLES[6] says this of *form*, « that it is consistent in a simple and invariable essence ».

2. Likewise, it seems, that invariability convenes with the *Blessed*, because where (there is) perfect beatitude, there is no loss [deperditio], and where (there is) this,[7] (there is) no variation.

3. Likewise, variation is attained, just as (St.) Augustine says in ON A LITERAL EXPOSITION OF GENESIS,[8] either according to place, or according to time; but some creature is without a determinate place and time, such as a universal,

which is always and everywhere,[9] and the empyrean Heaven, which is outside of time and place [extra tempus et locum]: therefore, etc..

4. Likewise, if "immutability" means *incorruptibility*, the same is shown. « For every natural corruption comes out of a contrariety », just as the Philosopher says in his book, ON DEATH AND LIFE;[10] but many creatures are without contrariety: therefore, also without corruptibility.

5. Likewise, every corruption is in something prior to itself, because natural corruption is in a something;[11] but principles, as matter, do not have something prior: therefore, they are incorruptible.

6. Likewise, every perpetual (is) incorruptible;[12] but some creature is naturally perpetual: ergo etc.. The *minor* can be proved in this manner: perpetuity concerns the reckoning of an image; whence (St.) Augustine (says):[13] « The soul would not be an image, if it were enclosed [clauderetur] by death's terminus »; therefore, since the soul is naturally an image, therefore it is naturally immortal or perpetual.

7. Likewise, it is shown, that a creature is *invertible*, in this manner: there is vertibility into 'being not' [in non esse]; but there is nothing, which can turn any creature into 'being not', because (the creature) is not turned *by itself* [a se], when nothing corrupts it;[14] not *by another*, because the action of a creature is terminated upon that, out of which it starts; but the action of no creature starts from '*being not*': ergo etc.. Besides, there is an infinite distance between the 'to be' of a creature and nothing; but between extremes infinite in distance [in infinitum distantia] there cannot come to be a mutation through a finite virtue: therefore, nothing can pass into nothing, except by God causing it.

8. Likewise, "vertibility" is said through a corruption entirely into '*being not*'; but nothing, which is corrupted, secedes entirely into a non being [non ens]:[15] therefore, no corruptible (is) vertible. *If you say*, that a creature does not have invertibility through (its) *nature*, but only through *grace*;[16] *on the contrary*: what is in all (things), is natural,

---

[1] Not a few codices as D F K X and ee together with edition 1 have *tends* [tendit].

[2] MORALS ON THE BOOK OF JOB, Book XVI, ch. 37: All things [cuncta] indeed have been made out of nothing, and their essence would again tend toward nothing, unless the Author of all things [omnium] retained it (in being) with the Hand of (His) governance [regiminis manu].

[3] Chapter 1, at the end.

[4] Verse 10. — Then at the end of the argument the codices together with edd. 1, 2, 3 & 6 omit the *is* [est] added by the Vatican edition.

[5] Chapter 9, n. 9. [Tr. note: here *invertibility* is inability to be turned, rather than ability to be turned upside down.]

[6] Gilbert of Porretain, ch. 1: Form is contingent to composition, consistent with a simple and invariable essence. — After which text codex O adds *and thus it is varied neither in form nor in matter* [et ita nec forma nec materia variatur].

[7] From the ancient manuscripts and edition 1 we have substituted the neuter *this* [hoc] for the feminine *this* [haec], which is demanded by the sense. A little before this very many codices together with edition 1 omit *there* [ibi], and also at the end of the argument put *mutation* [mutatio] in place of *variation* [variatio].

[8] Book VIII, ch. 20.

[9] Aristotle, POSTERIOR ANALYTICS, Bk. I, ch. 24 (ch. 31). — Then by the noun *empyrean Heaven* [caelum empyreum] understand the last sphere, which according to the opinion then commonly received is immobile and uniform, because its intrinsic principle, namely matter and form, are « goods so conjoined by conjunction, that there falls in no contrariety in it », as the Seraphic Doctor says below at objection n. 4. Cf. above d. 1, a, 3, q. 2, op. 1, and Aristotle, ON HEAVEN, Bk. I, text 100 (ch. 9).

[10] It would be better to put: in the book, ON THE LENGTH AND BREVITY OF LIFE. Aristotle did indeed write two small works, of which one title is: ON YOUTH AND OLD AGE, ON LIFE AND DEATH; the other: ON

THE LENGTH AND BREVITY OF LIFE. In the former work very few things occur on the matter, which the Seraphic Doctor here proposes; in the latter, however, in ch. 2 ff., this matter is more broadly treated, and among all the others there is found these words: Wherefore, to that to which there is not a contrary and where it is not, it will be at least impossible for it to be corrupted.

[11] Cf. Aristotle, PHYSICS, Bk. I, texts 42 and 82 (chs. 6 and 9 at the end), and ON GENERATION, Bk. I, text 11 ff. (ch. 3), where the minor of this proposition is also hinted at.

[12] See Aristotle, ON HEAVEN, Bk. I, text 110 ff. (chs. 11 & 12).

[13] ON THE TRINITY, Bk. XIV, chs. 2-4, nn. 4-6, from which text that proposition of his can be gathered, but it is literally found in the book, ON SPIRIT AND SOUL, ch. 18, and in M. Aurelius Cassiodorus' book, ON THE SOUL, ch. 2: For in accord with what manner could it have been an image or similitude of God, if the souls of men were enclosed by death's terminus? — A little below this after *therefore, when* [cum ergo], the Vatican edition together with codex cc, withstanding however, the other codices and edition 1, has *the natural soul is* [anima naturalis est] in place of *soul is naturally* [anima est naturaliter].

[14] Cf. Aristotle, PHYSICS, Bk. I, text 81 (ch. 9) and (St. Severinus) Boethius, ON THE CONSOLATION OF PHILOSOPHY, Bk. III, prose 11. — Then with the help of very many mss., such as H I L O S U etc., we have substituted *from 'being not'* [a non esse], i. e. from nothing, in place of *before (its) 'to be'* [ante esse], which the Vatican edition has and which does not correspond with the manner of speaking of the Scholastics; many codices on account of their abbreviated writing are of a doubtful reading.

[15] Hence Aristotle, ON GENERATION AND CORRUPTION, Bk. I, text 17 (ch. 3): The corruption of this is the generation of the other.

[16] The Vatican edition, together with many codices, here omits *only* [solum] and transposes, a little above this, by reading *therefore, no*

since it is by a special grace; but the natural is what is the same among all;[1] but nearly every creature is invertible, because none is driven back into nothing: therefore, this is (something) *natural*.

9. Likewise, it is shown, that neither (does a creature have invertibility) *through grace*; because grace is the perfection of nature: therefore, what is repugnant to nature, is not given through grace: therefore, if invertibility is contrary to the nature of a creature, therefore, it is not given through grace.

10. Likewise, it is objected concerning *that grace*, because if a creature is, it is[2] vertible; and therefore, if invertibility convenes with it, it is proper that (it be) through an other grace; and thus there will be an infinite regression [abire in infinitum]. Therefore, if it is proper that it stand still, it is clear that (it cannot be) through grace. *If you say*, that that grace is not meant as a habit, but as God conserving by graces; this is nothing, because without God operating[3] no creature operates: therefore, just as no creature operates except by grace: therefore, no operation is natural, which is a foolish (thing) to say.

CONCLUSION

"Immutability", accepted as invariability, is proper to God alone, accepted as incorruptibility or invertibility, it is communicated by God to some creatures through nature and/or through grace.

I RESPOND: It must be said, that immutability is said through a privation of mutability. Moreover, *"change"* [mutatio] is said in a threefold manner: in one manner from a being into a being; and this is change according to accident[4] and is called *"variation"*; in another manner from a being simply into a being by potency or according to *something* [secundum quid]; and this is change according to form and is called *"corruption"*; in another manner there is a change from a being into simply a non being; and this is according to the whole substance of a thing and is called *"version"* [versio]. According to this it must be understood, that *"immutability"* is said in a threefold manner: in one manner as *"invariability"*, in another manner as *"incorruptibility"*, and in a third manner as *"invertibility"*.

Therefore, if immutability be called *"invariability"*, thus I say, that it is entirely in no creature neither through nature nor through grace; for every created (thing) is either an accident, or has an accident, and is thus variable; and this (invariability)[5] is properly proper to God Himself.

Moreover, if immutability be called *"incorruptibility"*, thus I say, that it is in some creatures: in certain ones through nature, as for example [ut puta] in simple (things), in certain ones through grace, as for example in glorified bodies. Nor it is in this manner properly proper to the Divine Essence.

However, if immutability be said in the third manner,[6] it is thus in all creatures through *grace*, but in none through *nature* except God alone. For the invertible through *nature* is, that which out of its very self it has, so that it can stand; but it is this, in which there is no vanity[7] and in which (there is) no mutation of essence as regards (its) 'being' [esse], nor as regards (its) *'being not'* [non esse]; and this is the Eternal One alone. For that reason this invertibility is in God alone and is properly proper to Him. But invertibility through *grace* is in all and/or very many creatures, because God by His gratuitous goodness contains all other (things), lest they pass into nothing; and I am speaking of creatures, which they call "something completed and per se existing" [quid completum et per se existens].

Therefore, it must be conceded, that immutability, insofar as it frees from [privat] a variation according to accident, as much as regards act[8] and potency, belongs to God alone. *Similarly* insofar as it frees from a change into 'non being' according to act and potency, as much as it is from *nature*, belongs to God alone, though through *grace* it does convene with many creatures; and thus do the reasons for the first part proceed, whence they are to be conceded.

1. To that which, therefore, is objected in the contrary, that the *principles* of things are *invariable*; it must be said, that it is true, if they are considered according to abstract essence; but if they are considered according the 'being of their nature' [esse naturae], they thus from necessity have accidents conjoined and can be varied; moreover[9] accidental variation respects the 'being' (of a creature).

2. To that which is objected, that in *the Blessed* there cannot be variation; it must be said, that it is true as much as regards the substance of the reward or as much as regards the substantial reward; however, (the argument) fails [cadit] as much as regards conversion toward the inferior, both as much as regards affections, just as is clear among the Angels, and as much as regards actions. Whence the Blessed shall be agile and able to be moved.

3. To that which is objected concerning *the universal* and concerning the *empyrean (Heaven)*, it must be said, that each receives variation; but the universal by the reckoning of that *in which* it is; because, « with us moved,[10] there are moved those (things) which are in

---

corruptible (is) only vertible [ergo nullum corruptibile vertibile solum]; which reading is false, unless one makes a transposition of terms, v. g. *therefore, no solely corruptible (is) vertible* [ergo nullum solum corruptible vertibile]; and/or *therefore, no vertible is only corruptible* [ergo nullum vertibile corruptibile solum]. Codices E H Z and ii omit *only* [solum] in both places; codices P Q and ee, however, put it where we have put it. — *Grace* is here accepted in the broad sense, which (St.) John Damascene uses, ON THE ORTHODOX FAITH, Bk. II, ch. 3, "On the Angel", where he says: Indeed a nature is not immortal, but by the gift and grace of God.

[1] See Aristotle, ON INTERPRETATION, Bk. I, ch. 1. — At the end of the argument after *this* [hoc] we have supplied from the older manuscripts and edition 1 *is* [est].

[2] Codex T together with edition 1 has *therefore, (it is)* [ergo] in place of *it is* [est].

[3] Codex A has *cooperating* [cooperante].

[4] Many codices, such as A B C D E F G L R S T U etc., have *act* [actus] in place of *accident* [accidens], less well, as is clear from what is put a little below this concerning invariability. —

Concerning the first two species of mutation see Aristotle, PHYSICS, Bk. V, text 7 ff. (ch. 1), and ON GENERATION AND CORRUPTION, Bk. I, text 23 and 24 (ch. 4).

[5] Supply: invariability. The Vatican edition reads *Accepted in this manner immutability* [Sic accepta immutabilitas] in place of *and this (invariability)* [et haec], but contrary to very many codices, some of which, however, as A F T etc. together with edition 1 put *in this manner (invariability)* [hoc] in place of *this (invariability)* [haec], less well.

[6] Another hand, adds here in cod. T *(to be) invertibility* [invertibilitas].

[7] The Vatican edition contrary to very many codices as A F G H I S T Z etc. together with edition 1 adds here *and/or variety* [vel varietas], and then at *no* [nulla] the word *there is* [est].

[8] The Vatican edition has *nature* [naturam] in place of *act* [actum], but falsely and contrary to the manuscripts and edition 1.

[9] Edition 1 reads *for* [enim].

[10] We have substituted *moved* [motis] in place of *moving* [moventibus], for the reason above in d. 5, a. 2, q. 1, 3rd argument for the opposed side.

us »; but the empyrean by a reckoning of the *contained*. For after containing something, which it does not contain, and (after) not containing something, which it does contain (it receives variation).

4. 5. 6. To that which is objected concerning *incorruptibility*, it must be said, just as it has been touched upon before, that it does convene with creatures; for there are some creatures so simple and so conjoined by a good conjunction, that there falls in them no contrariety, nor is there in them a reckoning of corruption greater than in (their) principles. Whence just as principles are not resolvable into something, yet, they would pass into nothing, if they were left to themselves; thus it must be understood in some substances. Whence it must not be said, that it is true, that every composite is resolvable according to *thing*; but just as (St.) Anselm says,[1] « it is resolvable according to *thing*, and/or according to *understanding* ». Whence the reasons induced for this are to be conceded.

7. 8. To that, however, which is objected *concerning vertibility*, it must be said, that any creature is vertible through nature, if it is left to itself.

If one asks for [quaeritur] the cause of this, it must be said, that of this version, since it is a pure defect, (its) cause is not to be reckoned as an *efficient* one and/or as one reducing into 'non being', but only as *deficient* one. On account of which it must be noted, that nature is called a natural origin. Moreover, the origin of a creature is both from nothing and is from its principles: according to this something is said in a twofold manner to be natural to a creature itself, because it is in it out of that, which is *out of nothing*, and/or because it is in it out of that which is out of *its own principles*. And because *nothing* is the efficient cause of no thing [nullius], but (rather) the deficient (cause of it), for that reason the properties, which are in a creature by the reckoning of that, which is out of nothing, are not positions, but (rather) defects, nor are they by virtue, but by a defect of virtue, nor have they an efficient cause, but (rather) a deficient one: and such are *vanity, instability, vertibility*. If therefore it be asked, from what is the creature vertible,[2] I say, that (it is) not by something effecting, but through a defect in its very self. Moreover, according to which the "*natural*" is said (to be) what is in[3] a thing through (its) proper and intrinsic principles, thus not privations and/or defects, but abilities [habilitates], are said to be naturally in (a thing): and for this reason when accepting the "*natural*" in this manner, no

creature is *vertible* into 'non being'; nor, however, is it said (to be) *naturally invertible*, because the *natural* is in what nature can (do); but the principles of a thing cannot (be) the conservation in a thing nor the conservation of itself; and for that reason invertibility does not belong to this kind of natural. Nor however, is it *contrary* to nature, nay rather it is consonant with it; because every nature[4] seeks to be saved [appetit salvari], although it cannot out of itself (do this), and most of all [maxime] that creature, which seeks to be beatified, and this is that which has been made to the image of God. And because the desire of nature is not by a trick [frustra],[5] where nature is deficient, the gratuitous influence of God supplies. And thus it is clear, that vertibility is in (a creature) through nature, but invertibility through grace.

9. To that which is objected concerning the comparison of grace to nature, it must be understood, that grace is said to be a help [adiutorium], coming from the Superior, in respect of that which is above the ability of nature [posse naturae]. Moreover, this help is twofold: either in respect of '*being*' simply [esse simpliciter], or in respect of the '*being*' of the perfect [esse perfecti].

If in respect of '*being*' simply, as for example the 'being' of being-conserved [conservationis esse], because no principles, since they are vain,[6] can of themselves conserve their very selves, in this manner it is not by means of any infused and/or given habit. Because it respects the 'to be', and because[7] 'to be' is common to all (things), for that reason this grace is common to all (things). Whence this is a grace having the manner of nature, and this is the grace, by which all the others are called "invertible".[8]

In another manner, grace is said (to be) a "help" in respect of the '*being*' of the perfect, and because *the perfection of 'being'* [perfectio esse] is in those which are ordered toward beatitude, it respects '*well-being*' [bene esse] and[9] what does not belong to all. For that reason this is a special habit of some, not all, and this is a grace through a manner of grace. From these it is clear that it objects[10] of grace: for it objects according to which grace is a special habit divided against nature, because in this manner it means something created from (something) new; but grace in the aforesaid manner (does) not.

10. And from this is clear the last objection: because grace is called a help in respect of that which is above the ability of nature; and because the conservation of principles is above the ability of nature, but the egress of actions (is) not, nay rather (it is) below (it), for that reason it is clear etc..

---

[1] ON THE FAITH OF THE TRINITY, ch. 3: Since it is necessary that every composite be able either in act or in understanding to be disjoined. — Then the greater part of the codices as A G H S T X together with edition 1 have *adduced* [adductae] in place of *induced* [inductae].

[2] Codices P and Q do well to have *the vertibility of a creature* [vertibilitas creaturae].

[3] The Vatican edition less distinctly and contrary to the manuscripts and edition 1 has *to be in* [inesse] in place of *(to be) what is in* [quod inest].

[4] Codex Z together with edition 1 reads *creature* [creatura].

[5] See Aristotle, ON HEAVEN, Bk. I, text 32 (ch. 4 at the end), and ON THE SOUL, Bk. III, text 45 (ch. 9). — Codices V and X have *in vain* [in vanum] in place of *by a trick* [frustra].

[6] A greater part of the codices as F G H I K P Q S T etc. have less well *various* [varia]; codex X has *variables* [variabilia]. — A little below this at *thus it is not* [sic non est], understand *help and/or grace* [adiutorium vel gratia].

[7] The Vatican edition not trusting in the manuscript and edition 1

puts at the beginning of this proposition *And* [Et], then here in place of *and because* [et quia] it has *which* [quod], which reading weakens the force of the reasoning.

[8] The Vatican edition has incongruously *there are given all other vertibles* [dantur cetera vertibilia]; all the codd. with ed. 1 have *invertibles* [invertibilia]; codex cc has *there are given* [dantur], but the more ancient codd. have *are called* [dicuntur], though some on account of abbreviation are of a doubtful reading.

[9] The Vatican edition has *and/or the "being" which* [vel esse] in place of *and what* [et], which a greater part of the codices have; other codd., such as O and T, with ed. 1 omit, moreover, the particle *and* [et], in place of which codex cc has *and/or* [vel]. A little after this, some codd., such as A M T & aa, with ed. 1 twice has *here* [hic] in place of *this* [haec].

[10] The Vatican edition contrary to the more ancient codices and edition 1 has *it is objected* [obiicitur], but less well on account of what is subjoined. Then the Vatican edition together with codex cc has *and* [et] in place of *because* [quia], but less distinctly and contrary to the testimony of all the other manuscripts and edition 1.

SCHOLIUM

I. *That threefold distinction of change* [mutatio], to which corresponds a threefold immutability, has been taken from (St. John) Damascene, On the Orthodox Faith, Bk. I, ch. 3. The first change, which is called "*variation*" by the Seraphic Doctor, comes to be, when a subject is changed [mutatur] from some accident into another accident; this now is commonly called a "movement" or "*accidental mutation*". The second is a *corruption* or a mutation from the substantial 'being' of a form in matter towards the 'non being' of the same, the matter, however, remains in potency to act. The third is *annihilation*, called "*version*" [versio] by the Seraphic Doctor, by which there comes to be from a being simply, a non being; cf. Sent., Bk. II, d. 1, p. I, a. 3, q. 2, in the body. Aristotle, Physics, Bk. V., ch. 1, by omitting this last member, distinguishes the changes in this manner: 'out of a subject into a subject' (alteration, augmentation), 'out of a subject into a non-subject' (corruption), 'out of a non-subject into a subject' (generation).

II. The Seraphic Doctor does not contradict himself by asserting here, that in certain creatures, as Angels, incorruptibility is through their nature, and elsewhere by saying, that incorruptibility belongs to God alone. For in the first place the discourse concerns incorruption in respect of their own particular nature, not in respect of dependence from a first cause; in the second place he speaks of that property, which befits [competit] the First Cause alone, which can create and annihilate. Cf. St. Thomas, Summa., I, q. 9, a. 2 in the body. — To be noted is the egregious doctrine (of the Seraphic Doctor) expounded in the solution to n. 6, 7, and 8. About the efficient and deficient cause, cf. Sent., Bk. II, d. 34, a. 1, q. 2.

III. In regard to the conclusion: Alexander of Hales, Summa., p. I, a. 4, m. 3, and p. II, q. 13, m. 2, 3, 4. —(Bl. John Duns) Scotus, here in q. 5; and Reportatio., here in q. 3. — St. Thomas, q. 3, aa. 1 and 2; Summa., loc. cit.. Bl. (now St.) Albert (the Great), here in a. 16 ff.; Summa., p. I, tr. 4, q. 21, m. 3. — (Bl.) Peter of Tarentaise, here in q. 4, a. 2. — Richard of Middleton, here in a. 2, q. 2. — Giles the Roman, here in 3. princ., q. 2.

DOUBTS ON THE TEXT OF THE MASTER

Doubt I

In the first part of his (text) there are doubts concerning the text, and first there happens to be a doubt concerning this which Master (Peter) says: *Now one must deal with the truth or property of the Divine Essence* etc.. For it seems that he speaks badly, because, everything, which has (what is) proper [proprium], is distinguished: but the Divine Essence is not distinguishable: therefore, It does not have (what is) proper.

I Respond:[1] It must be said, that the Divine Essence is distinguishable in that manner, in which It has properties, and conversely; because although in Itself it is not distinguishable through a plurification of Itself nor from [a] a Person through a diversity, It is however, distinguishable in respect of a created essence, in respect of which It has properties.

Doubt II

Likewise, is asked concerning those three properties, which he posits, that is concerning *truth, immutability,* (and) *simplicity*, since there are many other conditions of the Divine Essence, why does he deal solely with these three?

I Respond: It must be said, that through these three properties there is sufficiently distinguished *uncreated 'being'* from *created* ('being'). For *created ('being')*,[2] for the reason that it (is) created, has 'being' after being not, and thus (its) 'being' (is) vain and possible: for that reason it has a 'being' thoroughly mixed [permixtum] with possibility, and on this account it is lacking [deficit] in truth, stability and simplicity. *Uncreated 'being'*, however, has contrary properties, and in these it is sufficiently distinguished. For truth respects *what is*, immutability *how it is*,[3] simplicity *both* (of these). For that reason the sufficiency and order (of the argument) is clear.

Doubt III

Likewise, is asked concerning this which he says, that "*wisdom*" [sapientia] *is said from "knowing"* [sapere], because it does not seem that he says the true [verum]. For just as "brightness" regards the "bright white" [albedo se habet ad album], so wisdom regards "knowing"; but "brightness" is not said from "bright white", nay rather on the contrary:[4] ergo etc..

I Respond: It must be said, that according to a *composing* intellect "knowing" [sapere] is said from "wisdom" [sapientia], because a composing intellect proceeds from the abstract to the concrete; however, according to a *resolving* intellect it is conversely; and as much as regards this (understanding St.) Augustine speaks. — And/or it could be said, that he speaks according to the consideration of a grammarian, not of a logician.[5]

Doubt IV

Likewise, is asked concerning this which he says: *And who is more than that One, who ... said to his household-servant.* For he seems to speak badly, because 'being' does not receive a 'more and less', most of all even in God.

I Respond: It must be said, that a 'more and less' [magis et minus] can be considered in a twofold manner, that is in comparison *to the same* (thing); and thus they[6] mean an intensification and relaxation [intentionsem et remissionem];

---

[1] The Vatican edition together with codex cc, disagreeing however, with all the other codices together with edition 1, adds *To which* [Ad quod]. Next more of the codices as A F G K S V W X have not well *one* in place of *that* [eo], but others as H T aa and bb have *that* [illo].

[2] Some codices as F T and dd here repeat *'being'* [esse].

[3] Very many codices omit *it is* [est].

[4] Very many manuscripts together with edition 1 have *conversely* [e converso].

[5] Concerning a resolving or analytic intellect, and a composing or synthetic one see below in d. 28, dub. 1, and Sent., Bk. IV, d. 50, p. II, a. 1, q. 1 at n. 4. — Thence the second solution is taken, because the grammarians deriver the abstract form of words from the concrete one, but the logicians or philosophers (Aristotle, On the Predicaments, ch. 1) in a contrary manner. Cf. below d. 33, q. 3.

[6] The Vatican edition, not trusting in nearly all the manuscripts and editions 1, 2 and 3, adds *do not* [non], but falsely, because according to all the Scholastics, an intensification and relaxation or remission are movements *of the same thing*, v. g. of heat from an more imperfect state toward a more perfect one and vice versa. See St. Thomas, who on the same text solves a doubt with the exactly same distinction, that is: Something can be said (to be) "more" or "less" as much as regards the participated nature itself, which is intensified according to itself and is relaxed according to access to and/or recess from a terminus; and this is not but in accidents; and/or as much as regards a manner of participating; and thus there is also said in essentials a "more" or "less" according to a diverse manner of participating, just as an Angel is said (to be) "more" intellectual than a man.

and/or in comparison to *diverse substances* and natures; and thus they mean a step and excess, and thus it is well[1] to posit a 'more and a less' in being [in ente] in respect of the Creator and of the creature, and in respect of creatures in regard to one another. But in a comparison of Creator to creature there is an improportionable and infinite excess; in respect of creatures in regard to one another it is proportionable.

Doubt V

Likewise, is asked concerning this which he says: *Whose essence knows not past nor future.* For that property of His seems also to belong to the Angels, because (St.) Augustine, On the City of God,[2] says, that « the immortality of the Angels is not past, as if it is not, nor future, as if it is not yet », but is always present: therefore, it is not proper to God alone.

I Respond: *Certain ones* say, that the duration of the <u>aevum</u> is simple and wholly simultaneous [tota simul], not having past and future; nevertheless an eviternal (being)[3] does itself have a past and future as much as regards (its) affections; and thus (the lack of these)[4] is proper to God alone.

Others say, that in every created duration, since it differs from (the thing) enduring and[5] has a possible 'being', there is a prior and a posterior; but they distinguish among the prior and the posterior. For a certain one is what one calls the "*succession of duration*" [durationis successionem], a certain one the "*duration of the succession*" [successionis durationem] with variation and innovation. The first is in the aevum, the second in time; and this (St.) Anselm[6] wants to express, and this I believe (is) more probable. And the response to the word of (St.) Augustine is clear; for he himself speaks of the prior and the posterior, which he does indeed call innovation and variation and corruption.[7]

Doubt VI

Likewise, is asked concerning this which he says, that *to the Divine Essence our 'being' is not compared.* For it seems false, because what is in anything substantially is not taken away by any comparison; but 'being' is substantial to any thing: ergo etc.. *Likewise* from a comparison to God the creature is made better [melioratur], as (St.) Augustine says,[8] therefore, it is more, than if it were not compared: ergo etc..

I Respond: To accept such a comparison is in a twofold manner. In *one* manner according to the reckoning of influence and reception; and thus a creature compared to God is more, than if it were not compared. In *another* manner it is compared according to a habitude of equiparancy [aequiparantiae] and proportion; and in this manner it is true, because no (creature)[9] is proportionable according to the condition of truth and nobility of Divine 'Being' [esse divini]; and for that reason it is as if nothing, not entirely in itself, but nothing as regards proportion, because there cannot be found any quantitative proportion (between them).

Doubt VII

Likewise, is asked concerning this which he says: *Therefore, let it be said, that He always was, is and shall be.* For these words seem not to be spoken[10] of God, because they mean diverse times; but in God there does not fall a diversity of times.

I Respond: *Certain ones* wanted to say, that those acts (of God) do not predicate of God diverse times according to essence, but according to concomitance; because the Divine 'To Be' [divinum esse], entirely unvaried, is concomitant to every time. But this position does not solve it fully. For it is truly said, that God was before every time; therefore, then,[11] it there cannot said (to be) a "concomitance". For that reason *others* say, that the "time" consignified is not a disposition of a thing accepted or understood, when it is said of God, but only a manner of understanding; but when (it is said) of a mobile thing, (it is said) in each manner. An example is clear from the masculinity[12] in (the word) "stone" [lapide] and in "man" [viro]: since in "man" it is as a disposition of the thing accepted (under the figure of the word), in "stone" only as a manner of understanding. But this position does not seem sufficient, because the intellect does not posit a past about its own understanding, when it understands that God was: therefore, it is proper, that it posit (such) about the thing (understood).

On account of this it must be noted, that words of diverse tenses are said in one manner of the eternal, in another manner of the eviternal, in another manner of the temporal. For in respect of the temporal they convey [important] mutability and succession and duration. But according to which they are said of eviternals, they only convey two, succession and duration, just as (Sts.) Jerome,[13] Augustine and Anselm want. But according to which they are said of God they convey only duration. Whence there is said: "*God was*", because His du-

---

[1] Codex T reads *true* [verum], codex W reads *there* [ibi] in place of *well* [bene].

[2] Book XII, ch. 15, n. 2.

[3] This is an eviternal thing or a subject of the aevum, e.g. an Angel. — The Vatican ed. without the authority of any manuscript and ed. 1 does not well add *or eternal* [seu aeternum], because it is not the same as eviternal.

[4] Supply: not knowing or not having a past and/or future.

[5] The Vatican, not trusting in the manuscripts and edition 1, reads *also* [etiam], and a little after this *with the prior and the posterior* [cum priori et posteriori], (not a few codices have indeed *with* [sum] in place of *is* [est], but only codex cc reads *with the prior and the posterior*). On behalf of our reading there also militates those things which the Seraphic Doctor says in Sent., Bk. II, d. 2, p. I, a. 1, q. 3 in the body, where thoroughly treating this question more fully, deduces from the possibility of a creature or from this, that *no creature is entirely an act*, that the duration of succession or a prior and a posterior is in the aevum. — Next the Vatican edition, disagreeing with all the manuscripts and the first six editions, has *concerning* [de] in place of *among* [in]. A little below this after *the succession of duration* [successionem] codex I adds sufficiently well *without variation and innovation* [sine variatione et innovatione].

[6] See his Monologion, ch. 28, and his Proslogion, chs. 20 & 22.

[7] Concerning this doubt, cf. Alexander of Hales, Summa., p. I, q. 12, m. 9, a. 3. — St. Thomas, Summa., I. q. 10, a. 5.

[8] On a Literal Exposition of Genesis, Book I, chs. 4-5, nn. 9-10 and his book, Against the Letter of Manichee, ch. 40, n. 46.

[9] Understand: creature. — The Vatican edition, moreover, together with codex cc, disagreeing with the other codices, however, and with edition 1, adds *reckoning* [ratio] and a little below this in place of *as regards proportion* [ad proportionem] it has *from proportion* [a proportione].

[10] Disagreeing with very many codices, the Vatican edition prefaces this with *to ought* [debere].

[11] From the mss. and edd. 1, 2 and 3, we have supplied *then* [tunc].

[12] We have substituted on the testimony of the ancient mss. and ed. 1 *masculinity* [masculinitate] for *the masculine genus* [masculino genere].

[13] Concerning (St.) Jerome see the note here in the text of Master (Peter), ch. 1. — The text of (Sts.) Augustine and Anselm is taken from Doubt 5. — Cf. (Bl. John Duns) Scotus, Sent., Bk. I, d. 9, q. sole at the end. — A little before this, after *they convey* [important], some codd., such as F aa & bb, with ed. 1 add *that is* [scilicet], others, such as G I and ff, *also* [et].

---

* *Trans. note*: For the definition of *equiparancy* see d. 19, p. I, a. sole, q. 3, p. 347, footnote 5.

ration did not begin; "*(God) is*", because His duration is not interrupted; "*(God) shall be*", because He does not stop nor is He corrupted. Therefore, properly speaking, they are not said of God, as (St.) Jerome says; however, broadly speaking, they are said, as Master (Peter) and (St.) Augustine says; and according to this (sense) does the opinion of Master (Peter) go.[1]

DOUBT VIII

Likewise, is asked concerning the word of (St.) Hilary: 'To be' [esse] *is not an accident for God* etc., because neither is it an accident for a creature — for to entirely no thing does a 'to be' accede [accidit] — therefore, in what manner through this (argument) is God noted to differ from a creature?

I RESPOND: It must be said, that an "accident" means what is bound *to be* in another, *to go forth* form another, and *to recede* from that.[2] For an "accident" is said (to be) what *is in* a subject and *draws its rise* from it, and on this account it can *be present* and *not be present* [adesse et abesse]. In these three properties the created 'to be' communicates, though not in entirely the same manner. For our 'to be' is dependent on [pendet ab] one sustaining, rises from another effecting, the creature too is bound to loose its own 'to be': for that reason its 'to be' is a quasi-accident, not, however, truly an accident, because since it is dependent on God, it is not dependent just as (one is) on a subject. It is contrariwise in God; and for that reason (St.) Hilary says, that 'to be' is not an accident for God; and this on account of (His) contrary properties: because an accident is bound *to be in* another [alii inesse], on this account he says: "*a subsisting truth*"; because it is bound to *go forth* from another, he says against this: "*a remaining cause*"; because it is bound *to recede* from another, he says against this: "*the property of (His) natural genus, which does not dismiss its 'to be'*".[3]

DOUBT IX

Likewise, is asked, how is "*immortality*" to be understood, when there is said: *He alone has immortality*, and

(St.) Augustine says,[4] that it is accepted on behalf of incommutability; but this does not seem convenient. For death does not mean every mutability, but solely the corruptibility[5] of the living: therefore, to say (this) is not the same thing.

I RESPOND: Just as "life" is accepted *commonly* and *properly*, thus also "death", thus also "immortality". For in *one* manner "life" is said (to be) a continuous and internal act,[6] which is from [a] the spiritual form; and thus it is said properly, and thus "immortality" means such a life with an impossibility for its privation. In *another* manner "life" is said (to be) a complete act of potency, which is according to the nature of a thing, just as water is said (to be) "living", which has an operation convenient to water; and in this manner it conveys repugnance to corruption. And for that reason[7] it ought to be said according to this *immortal* life which is such in complete act, that in no manner can it receive any worsening [peiorationem]; and thus does the Apostle accept and (St.) Augustine expound it.

DOUBT X

Likewise, is asked concerning this which blessed Jacob says and is in the text:[8] *nor the overshadowing of vicissitude*; what is the difference between *vicissitude* and *overshadowing*, and what is the convenience, by the reckoning of which there is said that "*a vicissitude overshadows*"?

And it must be said, that "*vicissitude*" conveys the number of a *turn* [vicis], and that is a number with interruption; but "*overshadowing*" is said through a privation of the act of light. Therefore, since light is an act of a form, its privation is rightly said (to be) an "*overshadowing*"; and because *vicissitude* by the reckoning of a number means an interruption, and by the reckoning of an interruption means privation, and by reckoning of privation (means) *overshadowing*, hence it is, that there is rightly said "*overshadowing of vicissitude*".

COMMENTARY ON DISTINCTION VIII

PART II

On the simplicity of God.

And the Same alone is properly and truly simple, etc..

SEE THE TEXT OF MASTER (PETER), ABOVE ON P. 147.

THE DIVISION OF THE TEXT [9]

Above, Master (Peter) puts on display [ostendi] the two properties of the Divine Essence, that is truth and incommutability; here he puts on display the simplicity of the Divine Essence and/or Nature. And this part has three parts. In the *first* he shows, that *properly (speaking)* He is simple; in the *second*, that (His is) *truly* (simple), there (where he says): *Here it must be diligently noted, since Augustine*

---

[1] See above in the text, ch. 1, where the words of (St.) Augustine are also brought forward.

[2] The Vatican edition together with codex cc, contrary to all the other codices together with edition 1, reads *another* [alio] in place of *that* [illo]. — Concerning *accident* see Porphyry, ON PREDICABLES; Aristotle, TOPICS, Bk. I, ch. 4, and METAPHYSICS, Bk. V, texts 13 and 45 (Bk. IV, chs. 7 and 30).

[3] For more on this matter see part II, q. 2, and SENT., Bk. II, d. 37, a. 1, q. 2.

[4] See the words of (St.) Augustine above in the text of Master (Peter), ch. 2.

[5] Edition 1 reads *the corruption* [corruptionem].

[6] (St.) Bernard (of Clairvaux), ON GRACE AND FREE WILL, ch. 2, says: For there is in any body a life, an internal and natural movement, vigorous as much as intrinsic.

[7] Some codices as I Z and cc have *that* [illud] in place of *for that reason* [ideo]; edition 1 together with one or the other codex as W reads *for that reason that* [illud ideo].

[8] Chapter 2.

[9] In this Distinction, the Division of the Text of part II is placed in this position in the codices, while in others it is conjoined with the division of part I. Cf. the final words in the division of part I., p. 150.

says etc.. In *the third*, that (He is) *most highly* (simple), there (where he says): *Moreover of this sincerity and simplicity* etc..

Again, the *first* part has three parts. First he proposes, that properly (speaking) He is simple; second he shows, that (simplicity) does not convene with corporal nature, there (where he says): *But so that you may know, in what manner that Substance be simple* etc.. In the third, that it does not convene with spiritual nature, there (where he says): *A spiritual creature too* etc..[1]

Similarly, the part, in which he shows, that He is *truly* simply, has three parts. In the first he shows, that in God there is purely a multiplicity of names; in the second he shows, that in Him there is not a diversity of predicaments, there (where he says): *Moreover that in the Nature of the Divinity there is no diversity of accidents* etc.. In the third he concludes, that the names of the predicaments among the divine cannot be spoken properly, and even the name of the first predicament, there (where he says): *Whence neither is He properly said (to be) a substance.*

Similarly, the part,[2] in which he shows, that He is *most highly* simple, has three (parts). For first he shows, that there is so great a simplicity There, that there is no diversity of things There; second, that with this simplicity there stands a plurality of Persons, there (where he says): *And though the Divine Nature is of so great a simplicity* etc.. However, third and lastly he concludes commenting [epilogat], that there has been shown in the Divine Essence a threefold property, there (where he says): *Behold how great is the identity.*

TREATMENT OF THE QUESTIONS

For an understanding of those things which Master (Peter says) in the text, four (questions) are asked in this part.[3]

First there is asked, whether in God there is a most high simplicity.

Second, whether simplicity is a property of God.

Third, on account of that which is said in the text concerning the rational soul, there is asked, whether the rational soul is in the whole body, so that (it be) in any part.

Fourth there is asked, whether God is in any determinate genus.

QUESTION I

Whether God is most highly simple?

About the first (problem), that in God there is a most high simplicity, it is thus proved:

1. Every first is the most simple, because by as much as something (is) first, by so much (is it) more simple;[4] but God is the First in the genus of beings [in genere entium], for the reason that neither is there nor can there be nor (can there) be thought one more first: therefore, He is so simple, that nothing more simple can be and/or be thought than He: therefore, He is the most simple.

2. Likewise, everything which is whatever it has, is most simple;[5] but God is whatever He has ergo etc.. The first is clear in itself. The *minor* is proven thus: God has potency, wisdom, and likewise concerning the other (perfections); therefore either He is His own potency, or not. If so, I have (proven) the proposed. If He is not His own potency, since He is potent in potency, He has to be able by another, therefore, God is by another; which if this is false; therefore (so also) that from which it follows.

3. Likewise, in the most noble 'being' [esse] every condition of nobility ought to be posited in the highest (manner) [in summo]; but God is the most noble Being [ens], and simplicity is the condition of nobility; therefore, it is to be posited in God in the highest (manner); therefore, God is most highly simple.

4. Likewise, by as much as something is more simple, by so much is it more potent in virtue, and conversely, because « virtue can be more united than multiplied »;[6] but God is infinite and immense in virtue; therefore, He is infinite in simplicity; therefore, in God there is a most high Simplicity.

ON THE CONTRARY: 1. Something is thought more simple, when it is thought as one abstracted from very many, rather than because[7] it is thought as one contained in very many; therefore since our Faith thinks of God as in very many, it does not think of Him as the most simple; therefore, if faith thinks truly, God is not the most simple.

2. Likewise, there is greater simplicity, where there is identity without diversity, than when with diversity; but in God there is identity with diversity of supposits: therefore, in God there is not a most high simplicity.

3. Likewise, there is a greater simplicity, where there is unity without plurality (than with plurality);[8] because number means in some manner a composition, in respect of which there is a simple unity: therefore, since in God there is unity with a plurality of Persons, it is clear that etc..

4. Likewise, there is a greater simplicity, where not only subject, but also property is the same with property (, than where they differ);[9] because, when property differs from property in one (manner), they are more according to difference: therefore, it is not simple; but among the Divine Persons, in the same Person

---

[1] Codex I adds: *And first by a common reckoning, and second by a proper one, there (where he says): For nothing simple* [Et primo per rationem communem, et secundo per propriam, ibi: Nihil enim simplex].

[2] The Vatican manuscript contrary to very many codices and to edition 1 prefixes *third* [tertiam].

[3] Trusting in all the manuscripts and edition 1 we have restored the words *in this part* [in parte ista].

[4] Cf. Aristotle, METAPHYSICS, Bk. XI, ch. 1 (Bk. X, ch. 1.) — A little below this after *more first* [prius] codex O adds *than He* [eo].

[5] (St. Severinus) Boethius, ON THE SEVEN RULES. — Then trusting in the more ancient manuscripts and edition 1 we have added *but* [sed]. — Concerning this argument see (St.) Augustine, THE CITY OF GOD, Bk. XI, ch. 10, and (St. Severinus) Boethius, ON THE TRINITY, ch. 2.

[6] The book, ON CAUSES, proposition 17. — In the beginning of this argument the Vatican edition with codex cc twice omits *is (it)* [est], which however, is found in the other codices and in edition 1. Codex M after *more simple* [simplicius] adds well *in essence* [in essentia].

[7] Other codices such as H ee and ff together with edition 1 read perhaps better *when* [cum] in place of *because* [quod]. Then a few codices such as H V and ee read *concretized* [concretum] for *contained* [contentum].

[8] Supply with codex Z *than with plurality* [quam cum pluralitate] and/or with codices I *than where there (is) not* [quam ubi non].

[9] Understand with codex Z: *, than where they differ* [quam ubi differunt] or with codices Q and bb: *than when property differs from property* [quam quando proprietas differt a proprietate].

property differs from property, wherefore innascibility differs from paternity: therefore, etc..

CONCLUSION

The highest simplicity is in God.

I RESPOND: It must be said, that just as the first reasons prove, there is to be posited in God the highest Simplicity.

1. To that, therefore, which is objected, that the Faith does not understand Him as the most Simple; it must be said, that the Faith[1] does understand Him as the most Simple, and who understands Him otherwise, does not understand Him as most highly simple. Which is clear in this manner: since there is an understanding of a one in one, and of a one multiplied into the very many, and of a one not multiplied in very many. Moreover, it is more simply understood that a one has been multiplied into very many, than that a one (is) in a one; which is clear, because the universal is more simple than the singular;[2] and still it is much more simply understood, that there is a one not multiplied in very many. In[3] this manner our Faith understands God. And for that reason God is more simple, because He is in All (the Persons)[4] the One not-multiplied, than if He were in One alone, and/or as One multiplied in the More. Hence it is, that God is the most Simple, and (that) our Faith understands Him as the most Simple.

And he who understands God[5] as plurified in essence, and/or as One in supposit, derogates from His *most high* Simplicity, derogates also from the *nobility* of His simplicity.[6] Since where there is understood (to be) a *most high* simplicity, it is proper that there be understood a most high actuality, if it is most highly *noble*. And where there is a most high actuality, there ought to be posited a most high diffusion and communication; and that cannot be except in the sempiternal production of a Thing [rei] entirely infinite and equal in virtue; and this cannot be in an anotherness[7] of essence; therefore, the Divine Essence cannot be understood as the most Simple, unless it be understood to be wholly in three Persons, One of Whom is from an Other [ab alio].

Therefore, when it is objected, that the more simple has been abstracted from [a] the very many rather than[8] in the very many; it is true, if it is plurified in those very many. If, however, it is not plurified, it is not true.

2. To that which is objected, that there is greater simplicity, where (there is) no diversity; it must be said, that diversity can come about [venire] in a twofold manner: out of *addition*, and/or out of *origin*. Out of *addition*, when there is diversity in absolute properties, which are diverse in diverse (things), as whiteness in Peter and blackness in[9] Paul; and this strips away [privat] simplicity, because it posits composition. There is another diversity coming out of an *sole origin*, as suppose, because one Person emanates[10] from an Other, He differs from the other; and this is not repugnant to simplicity, because it posits no composition, but only an order to and a regard for an Other; and this[11] is not properly said (to be) a diversity, but (rather) a distinction and discretion. And this is manifest, if we understand, that the Father by His very Self generates the Son, and understand, that He generates and does not generate again, (then) here there is no composition, because (there is) no addition.

3. To that which is objected, that there is greater simplicity, where (there is) no plurality; it must be said, that plurality is twofold. A *certain one*, in which more is in two than in one, as in two men there is more of goodness [plus de bonitate] than in one; and that plurality is repugnant to simplicity, because unity adds to unity. Moreover, there is a *certain* plurality, in which as much as is in the very many, so much (is) in the one; and this is among the divine, because there is as much of 'being' [tantum de esse] according to both goodness and virtue in one Person, as (there is) in More; and that plurality adds nothing to the Unity; and for that reason it posits entirely no composition nor does it strip away simplicity.

4. To that which is objected, that in the Father property differs from property; it must be said, that property differs from property in a threefold manner: either in respect of the subject, or in respect of itself, or in respect of the object. If in respect of the *subject*, because they are caused from diverse natures[12] discovered in Himself; thus it posits composition, because it posits that the subject is out of[13] very many. If in respect of *itself*, in the same manner as music and grammar differ in Peter; thus it also similarly posits composition, because it posits that the subject is under very many. If in respect of the *object*, it thus posits that the subject is compared to very many; and from this[14] there is not posited a composition, but (rather) a distinction. An example (of this) is in the point, which is the beginning and end in respect of diverse lines. In this manner there is a difference of properties among the Divine (Persons).

---

[1] The codices do not agree among themselves, for very many such as F H I N P Q R & U, with edition 1, for *the Faith* [fides] have *nay rather it* [immo], others, such as C L O & Z, *it well* [bene], others, such as A T & aa, read *because it understands Him as* [quod ipsum intelligit ut], finally others (read) just as the Vatican and our edition (as above).

[2] Cf. Aristotle, POSTERIOR ANALYTICS, Bk. I, ch. 20 (ch. 24).

[3] Very many codd., such as E I P Q X & Z, with ed. 1 add *Moreover* [autem].

[4] That is, in three Divine Persons; other codices such as H I and Z together with edition 1 have *More* [pluribus] for *all* [omnibus], which reading in itself seems to be preferred.

[5] Codex Y adds *vel* [trans. note: to introduce the pair *as plurified ... and/or as One...*etc.; in this usage the first *vel* is omitted in translation and the second is rendered *and/or*].

[6] We have supplied with the help of the older manuscripts and edition 1 less well omitted *simplicity* [simplicitatis].

[7] Codex Z reads *except in an identity* [nisi in identitate] in place of *in an anotherness* [in alietate].

[8] Supply: *contained* [contentum] or with codex H *contracted* [contractum].

[9] On the authority of many manuscripts such as E H K M P Q U V Z etc. and edition 1 we have added *and blackness in* [et nigredo in], which the context also seems to require. The Vatican manuscript together with codex. cc, contrary to the other codices and edition 1, adds *and Gregory* [et Gregorio] after *in Paul* [in Paulo].

[10] From the more ancient manuscripts and edition 1 we have substituted *emanates* [emanat] in place of *emanating* [emanans].

[11] With very many of the manuscripts, such as A I T etc, and edition 1, not without the context (favoring it), we have replaced *this* [hoc] with *this* [haec]. Codex V reads *in this manner* [hoc modo]. A little before this codex O reads *another (Person)* [aliam] in place of *an Other* [alium].

[12] Codices aa and bb add *and/or principles* [vel principiis].

[13] We prefer the reading of many of the manuscripts such as H I K L O T X Z aa and bb etc., *out of* [ex] in place of *in* [in], which is also confirmed by the context.

[14] The Vatican manuscript reads *in this manner* [hoc modo] for *from this* [ex hoc], but this withstands the authority of the more ancient manuscripts and edition 1.

SCHOLIUM

I. Simplicity means a certain, most noble manner of unity, and divine simplicity (means) a simultaneous most high actuality. Distinguished here and in the following question is that which is *simply* simple, and that which is *most highly* simple. The first is found also in creatures, and is that which is not resolvable into essential or constitutive parts; thus prime matter through a removal [ablationem] of all act and perfection is also said (to be) simple. However, *the highest* simplicity excludes whatever kind of composition, both *active* or composition *out of* others, as much as *passive* or composition *with* others. This most high simplicity certainly conveys not only a privation of composition, but also « a most noble manner of unity, which God communicates to no creature » (cf. following question, at n. 1).

II. In regard to the third argument in the fundament, it must be noted, that that axiom (which St. Thomas also uses, SUMMA CONTRA GENTILES, Bk. I, c. 18, and Richard of Middleton, here in a. 3. q. 1), that the more simple are the more noble, is valid only, if there be understood: *ceteris paribus*. For in corruptible things the whole composite, which embraces the perfection of itself and of its parts, can be more perfect than the simple part, just as man is more noble than (his) matter, and/or even than the soul alone. Cf. Richard (of Middleton), <u>loc. cit.</u>, q. 2.

III. The conclusion itself, by which the error of Gilbert of Porretain and Abbot Joachim (de Fiore) is cast out, had been first defined in the Council of Rheims, then at the Fourth Council of the Lateran, in the chapter FIRMITER, on the Holy Trinity: « God is ... one essence, substance or entirely simple nature ». Cf. below Doubt 6. — Alexander of Hales., SUMMA., p. I, q. 5. m. 1. and 2, and q. 14, m. 1. — (Bl. John Duns) Scotus, here at q. 1; REPORTATIO., here at q. 4. — St. Thomas, here at q. 1, a. 1 and at q. 4, a. 1; SUMMA., I, q. 3, aa. 3, 4, 5 and 8. ; SUMMA CONTRA GENTILES, I, c. 16 and 18. — Bl. (now St.) Albert (the Great), here at a. 22. — (Bl.) Peter of Tarentaise, here at q. 5, a. 1. — Richard of Middleton, here at a. 3. q. 1. — Giles the Roman, here in 1. princ, q. 4. — Henry of Gent, concerning this and the following, SUMMA., aa. 28 and 29. — Durandus (of Saint-Pourçain), here at q. 1.. — (Bl.) Dionysius the Carthusian, here at q. 5. — (Gabriel) Biel, here at q. 7, Doubt 2.

QUESTION II

Whether a most high simplicity convenes with God alone?

Second, there is asked, whether simplicity is a property of God. And that (it is) so, seems in this manner:

1. No creature is pure act, because in every creature, as (St. Severinus) Boethius says,[1] *that whereby it is* and *what it is* differ; therefore, in every creature there is an act with the possible; but every such has in itself multiformity and lacks simplicity: ergo etc..

2. Likewise, every creature has a finite and limited 'being' [esse]; therefore, it has a constrained 'being' [esse arctatum][2]; but wherever limited 'being' is, there is something which contracts, and something which is contracted, and in every such there is composition and difference: therefore, every creature is a composite: therefore, none (is) simple.

3. Likewise, every creature has a 'to be' [esse] given from elsewhere [aliunde], therefore, it has a 'to be' accepted from elsewhere, therefore, no creature is its own 'to be', therefore, in every creature there is dependence or difference; but no such (is) simply simple: ergo etc..

4. Likewise, everything, which is after the First Unity, defects from That, therefore, it immediately falls into duality, just as Dionysius (the Areopagite) says,[3] that after the Monad is the dyad: but every creature is from [a] the First Unity: therefore every creature is defecting from That: ergo etc..

ON THE CONTRARY: 1. « From one there does not proceed but one »[4] and from the true there does not proceed but the true; but unity and simplicity have the same reckoning in God: therefore, just as from one, one, so from the simple, the simple.

2. Likewise, it especially seems, that simplicity is in creatures, because the simple is that which does not have a part; but a point does not have a part, because it is defined thus: "a point is, that of which there is not a part":[5] ergo etc..

3. Likewise, every that, before which there is not an other, is simple; because if it was composed, it necessarily has an other before itself; but there is a First Being [ens primum], as the author (of the book) ON CAUSES says:[6] « The first of created things is 'being' [esse]: ergo etc..

4. Likewise, every that is simple, in which resolution stands still [stat]; but resolution stands still in the principles, which are matter and form, because matter is not further resolved, since there is a stability [status] in (its) causes, otherwise there would be an infinite regress [ire in infinitum]:[7] therefore, since resolution stands still in the created, something created is simple. *If you say*, that principles do not have an every-mannered simplicity, because although they are not composed out of others [ex aliis], nevertheless [tamen] they are composed by others [aliis]; *on the contrary*: this does not seem to make (a case) against simplicity, that they are composed of an other [alii]. For that something is not composeable of an other [alii], does not cause any simplicity, since that property[8] (of it) is in complete individuals, which are in the greatest manner composite: therefore, that I say this, *composeable by others* [aliis], does not take away simplicity from them, and thus etc..

---

[1] In his book, ON THE SEVEN RULES and ON THE TRINITY, ch. 2. See above d. 3, p. II, a. 1, q. 3, fundament 3.

[2] Codex X reads *contracted* [contractum].

[3] ON THE DIVINE NAMES, chs. 1 and 13. — Then the reading of the Vatican edition, *therefore* [ergo] in place of *but* [sed], is corrected from the manuscripts and edition 1.

[4] Thus Avicenna, METAPHYSICS, Bk. IX, ch. 2 ff..* Cf. also Averroës, COMMENTARY ON METAPHYSICS, Bk. XII, text 44. There is an allusion also to ON GENERATION AND CORRUPTION, Bk. II, text 56 (ch. 10), where Aristotle says: For the same also holding itself similarly is bound to cause always the same.

[5] Euclid, GEOMETRY, Bk. I, where according to the translation of (St. Severinus) Boethius there is had: A point is, that of which there is no part.

[6] Proposition 4. — The error of the Vatican edition, which after *On Causes* [de Causis] has *but the first* [sed primum], is corrected with the help of the manuscripts and edition 1.

[7] Cf. Aristotle, METAPHYSICS, Bk. II throughout (Bk. I, shorter version), where a processing unto the infinite in the genus of causes is reproved. Concerning matter and form, to the extent that they are principles, see Aristotle, PHYSICS, Bk. I, texts 42, 82 (chs. 5, 9); and Gilbert of Porretain, ON THE SIX PRINCIPLES., proposition 1. — Codex V reads *go off* [abire] in place of *to go* [ire].

[8] Namely: that something be not composeable. — A little before this codex cc has *they are composed* [componantur] in place of *is composed* [componatur], where the subject is understood to be: something [aliquid].

---

* *Trans. note*: Avicenna is the Latin name for the famous Iranian scholar, *Abu ali al-Husayn ibn Abd Alla ibn Sina* (980 - 1037 A. D.), whose most famous works were THE CANON OF MEDICINE (first trans. into Latin in 12th Century), and the KITAB ASH-SHIFA or *Book of Healing*, a collection of philosophical treatises.

CONCLUSION

That God alone is most highly simple,
is proven in a twofold manner.

I RESPOND: It must be said, that simplicity of
essence deprives [privat] (a thing) of composition
and deprives (it) of essential difference or multiplicity. Whence the simple is, 'that which does not
have composition of parts nor multiplicity of actions[1] or of forms'. But in God alone is there privation of composition and of difference or
multiplicity: for that reason simplicity is essentially in God alone.

Whence it must be noted, that *composition* is
manifold. One composition is out of *essential*
parts; and this is in all <u>per se</u> (created) beings;[2] another is out of *integrating* parts; and this is in all
bodies; the third is out of *dissimilar* or repugnant
parts; and this is in all animals and living (things).
Whence in every substance that is through itself
[substantia per se ente], which is properly[3] said
(to be) a creature, there is composition, because
every creature either is corporal, or spiritual, or
composed out of both.

Similarly, is it to consider the threefold *difference* in creatures. The first is of *substance, virtue,*
and *operation,*[4] or of substance and accident; the
second is the difference of *supposit* and *essence*; the
third is the difference of *a being* and (its) *'to be'*
[entis et esse].[5] The first difference is of a thing,
insofar as it is an agent; the second, insofar as it is
a being in general; the third, insofar as it is a being
in itself. The first difference is in every *subject*,
since every[6] subject has a mixed 'being' [esse mix-
tum]: for that reason it does not act out of its
whole self, and for that reason there is a difference
in that *whereby* it acts and *what* acts, and the *action*
or subject and the property[7] (differ). The second
difference is in every *individual*, because every individual has a limited *'being'* [esse limitatum]; and
for that reason in something it convenes, in something it differs with an other, and for that reason in
every individual *essence* and *supposit* differ; for
essence is multiplied in supposits. The third difference is in every *created* and *co-created (being):*[8] because for every (thing), which is besides God, it

accepts a 'to be' [esse] from elsewhere, whether it be
a beginning or a begun [principium sive principia-
tum]: for that reason nothing is its own 'to be', just
as light is not its own lighting.

Therefore, if simplicity is meant through a privation of *composition*, so it is proper to God alone in the
reckoning of a *substance*, because there is no other substance, which does not at least have[9] a composition out
of possible and actual.

But if simplicity means a privation of *essential difference and dependence*, so that in essence there is no diversity nor dependence,[10] it is proper to God in the
reckoning of *a being* [in ratione entis], because there is
no other being [ens], in which there does not fall a diversity and/or dependence.

Therefore, it must be conceded, that simplicity is
proper to God, as has been seen. Moreover, composite
creatures are neither truly simple, because they have a
'being' [esse] mixed out of act and potency, because the
have a *limited* 'being' [esse limitatum], and thus contracted in genus and species through addition, because
they have a 'to be' [esse] *given from elsewhere*, because
they have a 'to be' *after the One God*, from whom they
defect; and thus they fall into composition.

Otherwise it can also be said briefly,[12], that simple is
meant through a privation of composition. But it must
be noted, that composition is meant in a twofold manner: in *one* manner of something *out of somethings*; in *an
other* manner, by which (composition)[13] something is
said to be composed *of an other*. Therefore, if simplicity
deprives a thing of composition *out of others*, thus it befits even created (things), as the first principles,[14] which
are not composed out of others. But if it deprives a thing
of composition *with others* and *out of others*, it thus belongs to God alone. For every creature either is a being
through itself and *in itself* [ens per se et in se];[15] and thus
(is) composed *out of others*; or it is a being *with an other*
and *in an other* [ens cum alio et in alio]; and thus (is)
composed *of an other*. And again every created either is
a *principle*; and thus (is) composeable of an other; or (is)
'that which depends upon a principle'; and thus (is) composed out of others; and in this manner is simplicity accepted, insofar as it is a property of a thing, through
privation, namely of each (kind of) composition.

1. To that, therefore, which is objected, that from one
there is not but one etc.; it must be said, that the 'simple'
is not a general condition of a being as 'one' is. For

---

[1] Edition 1 has *of accidents* [accidentium] in place of *of actions* [actionum], with which reading the words of Master (Peter) are
in agreement, here in ch. 3 at the beginning, and their explanation
given below in Doubt 2. For the reading of the manuscripts there can
be alleged Alan of Lille, RULES OF THEOLOGY, rule 1, where besides
the plurality of parts and properties he brings forward a plurality of
effects [effectuum], which is attained in the properties; thus whiteness causes white, causes (a thing to be) colored, causes such. But
God is not diverse in various effects, because He is not a *formal*
cause. Each reading, however, refers to the same thing, as is clear
from those things, which are had a little before this.

[2] Or substances, supply *created* [creatis]. — Then codex W has
second [secunda] in place of *the other* [alia].

[3] The Vatican edition together with codex cc, disagreeing with the
other manuscripts and edition 1, badly omits *properly* [proprie].

[4] Dionysius (the Areopagite), ON THE CELESTIAL HIERARCHIES, ch.
11. Cf. above p. 79, footnote 5.

[5] See (St. Severinus) Boethius, ON THE TRINITY, ch. 2 ff. and ON
THE SEVEN RULES.

[6] The Vatican edition falsely and contrary to the manuscripts
and to edition 1 has *a subjected 'being'* [esse subiectum] in place of
every subject [omne subiectum]. — (St. Severinus) Boethius, ON THE
TRINITY, ch. 2 shows, that no simple 'being' can be a subject of accidents; see the explanation of this proposition in Alan of Lille,
RULES OF THEOLOGY, rule 12.

[7] The corrupted reading of the Vatican edition, *or property of a
subject* [sive subiecti proprietas] is repaired with the help of the manuscripts and edition 1.

[8] Substances or supposits are said *"to be created"* [creari]; accidents and their adjoined (properties), among which is creation itself, passively considered, are said *"to be cocreated"* [concreari]. Cf. SENT., Bk
II, d. 1, p. I, a. 3, q. 2. — Then trusting in the more ancient manuscripts
and edition 1 we have inserted *For* [enim].

[9] Some codices as H T together with editions 1, 4 and 5, have the
subjunctive form of *have* [habeat].

[10] Not a few codices as H I aa and bb add *in this manner* [sic].

[11] See (St. Severinus) Boethius, ON UNITY AND THE ONE.

[12] From the older mss. and ed. 1 we have substituted *more briefly* [bre-
vius] for *more truly* [verius] and a little below this *But* [Sed] for *And* [Et].

[13] Thus very many codices as A C F H K R S T U cc ee together
with editions 1, 2, and 3; the Vatican edition has *whereby* [quo]; *by which*
[qua] refers to *composition* [compositio].

[14] The Vatican edition together with codex cc, not trusting in all
the others and edition 1, omits less well *principles* [principiis]. A little
before this very many codices as E F H I K Q X and Z have *creatures*
[creaturis] in place of *created (things)* [creatis].

[15] That is a complete substance, to which an accident is opposed. —
A little below this, trusting in very many mss., such as H T aa bb & ee, and
ed.n 1, we have placed after *again* [iterum] *every* [omne] for *'being'* [esse];
codd. aa & bb have *every created being* [omne esse creatum].

simplicity means a most noble manner of unity, which God communicates to no creature; because a creature cannot receive (it), since its 'being' [esse] has been limited, has been[1] mixed, (and) is also a 'to be' [esse] dependent and given from elsewhere.

2. 3. 4. To that which is objected concerning the simplicity of a point and of a being [entis] and of a principle, it must be said, that there is a simplicity through a privation of composition out of others there, but not insofar as simplicity means an every-mannered indifference [indifferentiam omnimodam]. For in all (things), as has been said, there falls some difference and dependence: for although they have not been composed, nevertheless [tamen] their 'being' does depend from a composite, or from a composition.

Whence there must be well conceded that which was said last, that that derogates from the simplicity of a thing, which is composeable of the other (of the two), inasmuch as simplicity deprives a thing of *multiplicity* and *difference* in a simple thing, although it does derogate, inasmuch as it deprives a thing of[2] *composition out of others*. For every dependence causes that which depends to recede from most high simplicity and indifference. But God alone is independent. Moreover, all others are by a dependence, whether by comparison to the principles, out of which they are, or whether (their) one composing principle (be) complex regarding another [complicetur ad aliud], or whether (theirs be) a 'being' dependent [esse dependens][3] by a comparison to God or from God Himself. But nothing, which depends, is its own dependence: for that reason nothing such is most highly simple, because every most simple is most absolute.[4]

SCHOLIUM

I. In the response it is said, that composition out of essential parts, namely matter and form, is « in all per se beings [per se entibus] ». With these words St. Bonaventure touches upon that opinion, which (says that) even in the Angels there is in some manner a *spiritual* matter and form. This manner of speaking both before and after St. Thomas was received and approved of in the schools; now, however, it is obsolete, nay rather to many it is undeservedly an point of contention.* In what sense this saying by St. Bonaventure himself, Alexander of Hales and many others was understood, will be said in another place; cf. in the meantime to SENT., Bk. II, d. 3, p. I, a. 1, q. 1, and d. 17, a. 1, q. 2. — Alexander of Hales, SUMMA., p. II, q. 61, m. 1; ibid., q. 20, m. 2. § 1.

II. Two solutions to the question are exhibited. In the *first* there are enumerated five genera of composition; the other sixth genus, which is out of genus and difference, is below (q. 4 of this distinction) especially explained. — The *second* manner of speaking the Seraphic Doctor declares (to be) truer, to which St. Thomas consents, SUMMA., I, q. 3, aa. 7 and 8.

III. Celebrated is the distinction between *what* [quod] one is and *whereby* [quo] one is, or between essence and existence. This distinction is taken from (St. Severinus) Boethius' book, ON THE SEVEN RULES, and/or rather out of the commentary, which Gilbert of Porretain wrote on this short work. God indeed is both His own Essence and His own 'to be' [esse], as the common sentence says, but in a creature the 'to be' (existence) is not that *which* exists, but that *whereby* the essence exists. This distinction is admitted by all, but concerning the nature of the same there was and is a controversy. The Nominalists want, that this distinction belong to *a reckoning alone*; very many of the Thomists, that it be *real*; (Bl. John Duns) Scotus, however, in SENT., Bk. II, d. 1, q. 2 and d. 3, q. 3) holds his own *formal* distinction on this point. The Seraphic Doctor in these two questions does not explicitly determine the nature of this distinction, however, his words agree very much with the words of St. Thomas. Trigosus (SUMMA., q. 3, a. 2, Doubt 4) thinks, that St. Bonaventure taught that there is a real distinction between the 'to be' [esse] and the essence of a creature, but not as if between two things, but just as (there is) between a thing and act or the manner of the same; moreover, he asserts that St. Thomas himself and even Scotus agreed in nearly the same sentence. Cf. on this controversy, Alexander of Hales, SUMMA., p. II, q. 12, m. 2 and 3. — Richard of Middleton, QUODLIBETALS, 1, q. 8. — Giles the Roman, here in 1 princ. q. 2. — (Bl.) Dionysius the Carthusian, here in q. 7, where he retracts that which he had first written on behalf of a real distinction in the sense of many of the Thomists; Henry of Ghent, SUMMA., a. 28, q. 4. — Durandus (of Saint-Pourçain), here in q. 2.

IV. In this and the following question there is touched upon another celebrated controversy concerning the distinction, which is in God *between His essence and attributes, and among the attributes themselves,* whether, namely, this be in the manner alone of a *rational reckoning,* as the Nominalists say, or whether it be *formal* in the sense of (Bl. John Duns) Scotus, here in q. 4, or whether (it be) *virtual* or fundamental, as St. Thomas wants it in SENT., Bk. I, d. 2, q. sole, aa. 2 and 3; SUMMA., I, q. 13, a. 4. To the sentence of the Angelic (Doctor) St. Bonaventure entirely consents in regard to the distinction between the Divine *Essence* and (His) *absolute attributes.* For the *virtual* distinction, in the sense of St. Thomas, he *egregiously* explains below in d. 45, a. 2, q. 1 in the body; cf. also d. 22, a. 1, q. 2 in the body and at n. 3; d. 27, p. I, a. 1, q. 3; d. 34, q. 2 in the body; d. 35, q. 2 in the body; d. 7, q. 4, and in this current distinction, p. I, q. 1; p. II, qq. 1 and 2. — Also in that connected question, whether the *virtual* distinction already suffices to verify the contradictory (statements) on the matter, St. Bonaventure seems to stand rather on the side of the school of St. Thomas, which affirms this, than on that of (Bl. John Duns) Scotus, which denies this. For St. Bonaventure says, below in d. 34, a. 1, q. 1, at n. 5, that « howsoever small a difference of reckoning suffices for affirmation and negation », which must be noted on behalf of the doctrine of the Most Holy Trinity. Cf. also d. 5, a. 1, q. 1, at n. 1; d. 19, p. II, a. 1, q. 2, at n. 4; d. 28, a. 1, q. 1 in the body, d. 35, a. 1, q. 3; d. 43, q. 1, at n. 3.

On the other hand there is the other question concerning the distinction between the *relations* and the Divine *Essence,* which the Seraphic Doctor with express words does affirm to be greater than the former, which is between (His) *absolute* attributes and (His) *Essence,*

---

[1] The Vatican edition without the authority of the mss. and the five first edd. has *and* [et] for *has been* [sit]. Then codices A C G L O R S X aa and bb have *so also* [sicut etiam] in place of *(and) also is* [sit etiam].

[2] Favored by many manuscripts and edition 1, we have substituted *it deprives a thing* [privat] in place of *it may deprive a thing* [privet].

[3] Thus codd. H & K with the Vatican ed., in which reading the words *a 'being' dependent* [esse dependens] refer to the subject *all others are* [omnia alia sunt]; all the other codd. with ed. 1 have *every dependent* [omne dependens], but less congruously, even if you supply the word *is* [est], on account of the change of the subject; each reading does not lack a grammatical difficulty.°

[4] SENT., Book II, d. 3, p. I, a. 1, q. 1 in the body, the Seraphic Doctor says: Every dependent by this very fact falls into some composition, because (its) *whereby it is* and *what it is* differ. — Take Bl. (now St.) Albert (the Great)'s explanation of this, SUMMA., p. I, tract 4, q. 20, m. 2: In the principles of a substance there also cannot be simplicity, because though substances are not composed out of other principles, they do have, however, this one *what they are,* and an other *whereby* the principles of the substance are; for this *what they are,* are certain things and substances, because out of non-substances there is not made a substance, as the Philosopher says. Moreover, by that *whereby* the principles of a substance are, each of the principles has a dependence as regards the other. Matter ... to form as to act, and form to matter as to that in which it has a distinct "to be" ... Similarly, it must be said concerning components. — SENT., Bk. I, d. 8, a. 24, regarding this objection: the relation of a creature to the Creator is something extrinsic, and to this extent it does not cause a composition of a creature, he responds: It must be said, that solely the relation to the efficient cause does not cause a composition of them, but that which is left in them out of such a going forth into 'being' [in esse] ... out of this itself, that a thing goes forth into 'being' after nothing, there remains a potency of tending into nothing, unless it be contained by an other.

---

* *Trans. notes*: Because many misconstrue the scholastic term "matter" [materia] with the term of modern physics, and, hence, misconceive it as the 'particulate corporeal' rather than the more general absolute potency for entity, as St. Bonaventure uses it.

° Which difficulty is easily solved by supplying *their* [eorum] as is had in the translation, which assumption seems to be the simplest contextual interpretation.

SCHOLIUM

and between these attributes as regards one another, and he exhibits this as the third and middle member of the distinction, while he deals with the threefold division of those, which differ only by reckoning; see below d. 26, q. 1, at n. 2 and 3, and d. 22, q. 4. This second species distinguished by the Seraphic (Doctor), as Brülifer wants it, gave Scotus occasion to think out his own *formal* distinction. On the sentence of St. Bonaventure, cf. d. 13, q. 3, and the Scholium on d. 26, q. 1.

About the virtual distinction, cf. Alexander of Hales, SUMMA., p. I, q. 52, m. 1, and q. 56, m . 7, a. 2. — Bl. (now St.) Albert (the Great), SUMMA., p. I, d. 3, a. 4, and here in aa. 3, 4, 5. — (Bl.) Peter of Tarentaise, SENT., Bk. I, d. 2, q. 1, aa. 2, 3. —

Richard of Middleton, SENT., Bk. I, d. 2, a. 1. — Giles the Roman, SENT., Bk. I, d. 2, 1st. princ. q. 2, 3. — Henry of Ghent, SUMMA., a. 51; et QUODLIBETALS. 5, q. 1. — Durandus (of Saint-Pourçain), d. 2, qq. 2 and 3. — (Bl.) Dionysius the Carthusian, SENT., Bk. I, d. 2, q. 2.

V. In the principal conclusion all agree: Alexander of Hales, SUMMA., p. I, q. 5, m. 3; p. II, q. 12 throughout. — (Bl. John Duns) Scotus, here in q. 2. — St. Thomas, here in q. 5, aa. 1 and 2.; SUMMA., I, q. 3, aa. 7, 8. — Bl. (now St.) Albert (the Great), here in a. 24. — (Bl.) Peter of Tarentaise, here in q. 6, a. 1. — Richard of Middleton, here in a. 3, q. 2. — Giles the Roman, here in 2nd princ. q. 1. — (Bl.) Dionysius the Carthusian, here in q. 7. — (Gabriel) Biel, here in q. 7, Doubt 3.

QUESTION III

Whether the rational soul is whole in the whole body, and whole in any part of it?

Third, there is asked, whether the rational soul is in the whole body, so that (it is) in any part. And it seems that (it is) so.

1. (St.) Augustine[1] says, that just as God is in the macrocosm [maiori mundo], so the soul in the microcosm [minori]; but God is so in the greater, that (He is) whole in any part: therefore, in this manner the soul is in the lesser one, that is, in the body.

2. Likewise, what gives 'being' [esse] to the whole and to the parts is united to the whole and to the parts according to essence, because form through its own essence gives 'being' [esse], and this (is) not (given) except to that to which it is essentially united;[2] but the soul gives 'being' [esse] to the whole body and to all the parts: ergo etc..

3. Likewise, in the eye there is seeing, there is sensing, there is living.[3] Therefore, I ask, whether these are one act and/or different ones. Not one; this is established, because, deprived of sight, one still senses through touch, deprived of sensing, one still lives, just as (is clear)[4] in a paralytic; therefore, since living is by a substance, seeing by a power [a potentia], the soul is in the eye according to substance; for the same reason it can be proven, that it is also in all the parts.

4. Likewise, the soul operates in the whole body, therefore, in the whole body[5] it is through (its) power [per potentiam]; but the power of the soul is simple: therefore, if there is one power in hand and foot, the same is in diverse parts; but there is not a more simple power than a substance: ergo etc..

5. Likewise, the soul is in the body: therefore[6] either it is in *every* part, or it is in *one* determinate (part), or it is in a *point*. If in *every* part, I have (proven) the proposed. If in *one*, since that has more parts, and the soul is simple, it will be in more parts: therefore,

it is not inconvenient, that the soul be in more parts. But by the reason by which it is[7] in parts of a part, by the same reason it is in parts of the whole. If it is in a *point* of the body,[8] therefore, since a point does not have a proportion to the whole body, the soul is improportionable to the whole body: therefore, there cannot be perfection, since a proportion is of a perfection to the perfectible.[9] *Similarly* « a point is a posited substance » or one having a position, therefore, the soul has a site in the body; but no situated form [forma situalis] is a sufficient motor (of the whole): ergo etc..

BUT ON THE CONTRARY: 1. A form, which is one in the whole and in the parts, denominates the parts and the whole by exactly the same reckoning [ratione consimili].[10] Whence every part of fire is fire: therefore, if the soul is in every part, then every part of the animal is an animal just as the whole,[11] since every part is a sensible, animated substance.

2. Likewise, the existence of the rational soul does not depend from any part of the body, since it has been fixed in itself: therefore, it is not in any (part).[12]

3. Likewise, its operation does not depend from any part of the body nor is it communicated to any: therefore, it is in no part of the body, neither inasmuch as (it is) a perfection, nor inasmuch as (it is) a motor. Whence the Philosopher[13] says, that « the soul is an act of no body », that is (it belongs) to no part of the body, but in that which it is, it is just as an act.

4. Likewise, the organic[14] body belongs to diverse reckonings in the parts and (in) the whole, therefore it has a diverse perfection: therefore, since the soul perfects the whole as much as regards essence, it perfects the parts as much as regards power: therefore, the rational soul is not in the parts except only

---

[1] The book, ON SPIRIT AND THE SOUL, ch. 13 at the end. — Then in the minor proposition after *the greater* [maiori] the Vatican edition repeats *word* [mundo].

[2] Cf. Aristotle, METAPHYSICS, Bk. VIII, text 15 and 16. (Bk. VII, ch. 6). — On the next, following proposition, see ON THE SOUL, Bk. II, text 4 ff and text 24 (chs. 1 and 2), and ON THE PARTS OF ANIMALS, Bk. I, ch. 1.

[3] From very many manuscripts and edition 1 we have twice supplied *there is* [est].

[4] Supply together with codex V *is clear* [patet]. — At the end of the argument after *parts* [partibus] codex Y adds *of the body* [corporis].

[5] The Vatican edition without the authority of the manuscripts and editions 1, 2, 3, and 6, omits less well *in the whole body* [in toto corpore].

[6] Trusting in very many manuscripts as M T V W X Z etc. and edition 1 we have inserted *therefore* [ergo], and then *it is* [est] three times.

[7] Very many codices together with edition 1 here and a little after this less aptly omit *it is* [est].

[8] Codices aa and bb add *therefore, it is a point* [ergo est punctus].

[9] Gathered from the saying of Aristotle, ON THE SOUL, Bk. II, text 24 (ch. 2): For the act of acts seems to be within the patient and the disposed. — And in text 26 he says, that it does not seem that any (subject) receives any (form). — The following definition of a point is given by Aristotle, ON THE SOUL, Bk. I, text 68 (ch. 4) and METAPHYSICS, Bk. V, text 12, (Bk. IV, ch. 6).

[10] Aristotle, ON THE HISTORY OF ANIMALS, Bk. I, ch. 1.

[11] Thus the ancient codices together with edition 1, though very many of them after *part* [pars] omit *of the animal* [animalis]; the Vatican edition, moreover, together with codex cc, having omitted the particle *then* [tunc], in place of *is an animal just as the whole* [est animal sicut totum] pluts *is said (to be) an animal* [dicitur animal].

[12] Codices W and W add *part* [parte].

[13] ON THE SOUL, Bk. II, text 11 (ch. 1) and Bk. III, text 6 (ch. 4).

[14] Some codices as A I W and Y read *organized* [organizatum].

as much as regards the reckoning of a power and this the Philosopher also says:[1] « Just as the soul (is) to the body, so the parts of the soul to the parts of the body ».

5. Likewise, if the soul is whole in every part of the body, therefore, it is whole in the hand; but when any whole is in anything, it is moved in that manner:[2] therefore, with the hand moved, the soul is moved, and similarly, with the hand resting, it rests: therefore, since one hand can be moved, with the other existing at rest, one soul can be moved, with the other existing at rest, the soul, one and the same in number, simultaneously rests and is moved according to the same (thing).

6. Likewise, if the soul is whole in more parts,[3] by the reason by which it is in three, by the same reason (it is) in more, and thus in infinite (parts), and however, much the body be extended: therefore, the soul is bound to be everywhere, and thus it seems, that the soul is not a limited substance, but (rather) an immense one.

7. Likewise, if the whole soul is in the hand just as in the other parts: therefore, since life is by[4] the soul, the hand does not receive more movement and sense from the heart, than the other way around [e converso]. But this is contrary to all philosophers;[5] and there follows from this, such an inconvenient (conclusion), that, just as with the heart wounded, life perishes, so with the hand wounded.

CONCLUSION

The rational soul is whole in the whole body and whole in every part.

I RESPOND: It must be said, that some say, that the soul according to essence is in some determinate part, but according to power it is and inflows in the whole body, just as a spider in a web.[6] Whence they said, that it is in the heart, because the heart is the domicile of life, and its inhabitor is the soul. And the *proof of experience* [experimentum] together with a *defect of reason* moved them to posit this. *The proof of experience*, because it visibly appears, that by a wound in the heart the soul is separated, and (that) from this (organ)[7] sense and movement flow, and (that) it is the noble member existing in the middle, as the cen-

ter of the body. *A defect of reason*, because they could not understand, in what manner something limited is the one and the same whole in the more; and because (our) Faith did not coerce (them) to believe, and reason did not understand, for that reason they say, that it is not to be posited, that it is in the whole by reason of any part.

But the opinion of others is, as (St.) Augustine's,[8] that the soul in any part of the body is whole; and the *proof of experience*, *example* and a reasonable *argument* move to posit this. *Proof of experience*, because the soul in parts distant from the heart senses as [ita] swiftly, as (it does) even in near ones; likewise[9] at once as if in the twinkling of an eye [in ictu oculi] it senses a wound in distant parts, and when the soul is separated, there is pain in the individual [singulis] parts and a release [resolutio]. *Example* similarly moves, just as (St.) Augustine says:[10] « For we see that in one, perfect, healthy animal there is one health in the individual parts, neither greater in the greater nor lesser in the lesser ». Therefore, if this is in a corporal form, how much more, in the spiritual? An *argument* of reason moves, because the soul is a *simple form* and a *sufficient motor*. Because (it is) the *form* of the whole body, it is in the whole; but because (it is) *simple*, it is not (there) according to a part and a part of itself; because (it is) a *sufficient motor*, for that reason it does not have a site, and for that reason neither is it in a point nor in a determinate part.* And because more reasonable is the opinion, which is founded upon[11] reason, than that which is founded upon defects of reason, and because (St.) Augustine says this, this I approve as the better one.

1. 2. To that, therefore, which is objected unto the contrary: a form which is in the whole etc.; it must be said, that the genus of form is threefold. For there is a *certain* one, which *perfects* and *is extended* and *does depend*. And this one, because it perfects the whole, is in the whole; but because it is extended, it communicates the perfection of the whole to the parts; but because it depends, neither does it act through itself, (but) it communicates the operation of the whole to the parts, as is clear in the form of fire, because any part of the fire is fire and any heats. There is *another*[12] form, which *perfects* and *depends*, but *is not extended*; and su-

---

[1] ON THE SOUL, Bk. II, text 9 (ch. 1).

[2] See above, d. 5, a. 2, q. 1, ad opp. 3.

[3] The Vatican edition together with codex cc, but disagreeing with the other codices and edition 1, here omits *parts* [partibus] and at the end of the argument *substance* [substantia], and contrary to very many codices as F H Y V V etc. it puts *by that reason* [ea ratione] in place of *by the same reason* [eadem ratione].

[4] Some codices as A C G I R S omit *by* [ab]. Codex T reads *since the soul is one* [cum una sit anima]. Codices L and O read *is the soul and/or by the soul* [sit anima vel ab anima].

[5] See Aristotle, ON THE PARTS OF ANIMALS, Bk. III, chs. 3 and 4.

[6] Chalcidius, who lived at the start of the fourth century, ON THE TIMAEUS OF PLATO (ed. Leipzig, 1876, Dr. Johannes Wrobel, editor, p. 296, n. CCXX): Just as the spider in the midst of a web holds all the warp of filaments with its feet, so that when any little beastie runs into a trap it senses from nearby (what is) on every side, so the soul's principle placed in the middle seat of the heart recognizes from nearby that it retains the warp of the senses, when for example they announce anything. — The Vatican edition has *flows* [fluit] in place of *inflows* [influit]. Then after *because* [quia] codex K adds *just as is said in the book, ON THE MOVEMENT OF THE HEART*. See Alexander of Hales, SUMMA., p. II, q. 87, m. 2, a. 1, § 1 (in other editions q. 91). — On this opinion cf. St. Gregory of Nyssa, ON THE WORK OF MAN, ch. 12.

[7] From very many manuscripts and edition 1 we have substituted *flows* [fluit] in place of *inflows* [influit]. — On the principality of the heart see Aristotle, ON THE PARTS OF ANIMALS, Bk. III, ch. 4.

[8] ON THE TRINITY, Bk. VI, ch. 6, n. 8; and ON THE IMMORTALITY

OF THE SOUL, ch. 16, n. 25; and ON THE ORIGIN OF THE SOUL, homily (epistle 166), n. 4; and also AGAINST THE LETTER OF MANICHAEUS, ch. 16, n. 20. — Then not a few codices in an inversed manner read *posited (them) to move this* [ad hoc movendum ponit], codices L and O have *posited (them) to demonstrate and/or move this* [ad hoc monstrandum vel movendum]; but this reading is not coherent with the subjoined. Then very many codices as A F G I K T etc. together with editions 1, 2 and 3 read *rational* [rationale] in place of *reasonable* [rationabile]. On the difference of these, cf. Augustine, ON ORDER, Bk. II, ch. 11, n. 31 ff.

[9] The Vatican edition, disagreeing with the more ancient mss. and edd. 1 and 6, repeats here *because* [quia]. Codex W has *and thus* [et ita], codex X has *and* [et] in place of *likewise* [item], but some codices as F and T do not badly add the particle *and* [et] after *simultaneously* [simul].

[10] The book, ON THE PRESENCE OF GOD (Epistle 187), ch. 4, n. 13: However, the quality of a body, which is said (to be its) health, when the whole body is healthy, is as much in the greater, as it is in the lesser parts. For, (it is) not (that) those which are less great, are for that reason less healthy, or (that) those which are more ample, (are) for that reason more healthy. — From the more ancient mss. and ed. 1 we have supplied *one* [uno].

[11] Edition 1 here and a little after this has *above* [super]. Some codices as V and Y together with edition 1 have *a defect* [defectum] in place of *defects* [defectus]. Then trusting in very many manuscripts and six of the first editions after *of reason* [rationis] we have added the *and* [et], which the Vatican edition has less well omitted.

[12] Not a few of the codices as A B D E G P T Y and W have *moreover* [autem] in place of *another* [alia]; codex I has *moreover, another* [autem alia].

---

* *Trans. Note*: a logical corollary (a contradictorio) to this sentence would be: since the possessing spirits are not the sufficient motor nor the essential form of any body, for that reason a body under diabolical possession must be inhabited by them in one or more sites of the body.

ch a form, because it perfects the whole, is in the whole and in any part; but because it is not extended, for that reason it does not attribute the act[1] of the whole to the parts; but because it depends, it communicates the operation of the whole to the parts; and such is the vegetable and sensible soul, because no part of an animal is an animal, however, any part of an animal lives and senses. There is *again* a[2] *form*, which *perfects* the whole, however, *it is neither extended nor does it depend* as much as regards operation; and such a one, because it is the perfection (of the whole), is in the whole and the parts; but because it is not extended, it does not communicate the perfection of the whole to the parts; (and) because it does not depend, for that reason[3] neither does it communicate the operation; and such is the rational soul, because no part of a man is a man, and no part of a man understands. However, even if it does not communicate (to a part or parts)[4] the act of the whole *as to the whole*, it does communicate (it) *as to the parts*; because any part is a part of a man and is vivified by the perfection of the man; and for that reason the perfection of a man is in any part.

3. And thus is clear the response to that, that of no body is it the act; because to no part of the body[5] does it communicate its proper operation nor the perfection of the whole, however, it does perfect all the parts in the whole. *Similarly* to the other concerning form, because the form, which is in the parts, does not denominate in a similar manner[6] the whole and the parts, unless it be a dependent and extended form; and I speak of a substantial form only, not of an accidental one.

4. To that which is objected, that the whole and the parts (of an organic body) do not belong to the same reckoning; it must be said, that in the parts (of the body) there is a considering of (their) *organization* and (their) *complexion*. By reason of (their) complexion they are uniform to the whole and have been disposed to the same genus of life and are perfected by one; by reason of (their) organization they belong to a diverse (reckoning) and are perfected by the powers [a potentiis] (of the soul).

5. To that which is objected, that (the soul)[8] is moved, with the hand moved etc.; it must be said, that perfection can (be) over the whole perfectible both as much as regards the substance and as much as regards a power; and since the soul is the perfection of the whole body, it can be over the whole, and for no less a reason, than there is a whole body, it is defined by its substance and not by (its) power; moreover, it is defined by its own body, which it perfects, and for that reason with the body moved, it is consequently [per consequens] moved; moreover, by its parts it is not defined, because they are less than the whole, and thus there is in the one (soul), that which is outside it.[9] And for that reason, because it is in no part definitively, it is not moved according to [ad] the movement of any part, just as God is neither moved according to the movement of any creature.

6. And through this the following is clear, because the whole body is compared to the soul itself as one place; and for that reason it is not in more parts except inasmuch as (it is) in one place; whence if they be separated, it will not be in them. Nor does it follow from this, that (the soul) is infinite, because « of all constant things nature is the term and the reason for (their) magnitude and increase [augmenti] »,[10] and thus of the human body. Whence there can be thought a body so great, that it could not be vivified by the soul.

7. To that which is objected last, that then one part does not receive from an other; it must be said, that just as God in the macrocosm is immediately in every creature as the One containing it, however, through[11] the order of the universe something inflows by one creature into another; so it must be understood, that the soul through its own presence is immediately in any part, which it contains and conserves, not however, entirely, but it inflows in all parts through one; and for that reason with that part and its influence ceasing, the essential order of the body perishes, and thus the soul is separated.

SCHOLIUM

I. The proposition in argument 1 ad opp., that some form denominates the parts and the whole, is true, when one deals with things lacking organization, the parts of which are for that reason [proinde] entirely homogeneous; but in a most false manner it is applied to organized bodies, just as is done in that sophism of (Fr. Jean) Buridan (1300 - 1358 A. D.) to prove that the finger of a man is a man. With that threefold distinction of forms the Seraphic Doctor already solves that difficulty of his.

II. For an understanding of the solution to n. 5 this must be noted. The soul is called the perfection of the whole body and the perfectible body, because according to Aristotle the soul, as the substantial form, is the act of the body, whence « it can be above the whole », i. e. through its own substance it can vivify the whole body and move (it) through (its) power. However, this does not exclude, that it inflows more in the more principal organs, as is explained in the solution to n. 7. The words: « For no less a reason, that there is a whole body, it is defined by its substance », has the sense, that the soul is in the whole body in a *definitive* manner, which is now called, *non-circumscriptive*. To be in a place *circumscriptively* is said, when the located whole is in the whole place, and a part of the (thing) located (is) in a part of the place; however, when something is indeed determined as regards some place, that it naturally cannot simultaneously be in another,

---

[1] Some codices, such as D G T & ff, add *or perfection* [sive perfectionem].

[2] Codices P and Q insert *third* [tertia].

[3] Many codices as A C E G H I O R S T U V Y Z and ff together with edition 1 omit *for that reason* [ideo].

[4] Understand: to a part and/or parts. — Many codd., such as A C E G L R S U V Y Z cc & ff, after *even if* [etsi] falsely omit *not* [non]; nearly all the codd., however, contrary to the Vatican edd., have (the subjunctive) *communicate* [communicet] for *communicates* [communicat]. Then the Vatican ed. with codex cc, but disagreeing with the other codd. and edition 1, omits *is a part* [est pars] and after *of a man* [hominis] the particle *and* [et].

[5] From codices H and Y we have supplied *part of the body* [parti corporis], which certainly must be understood. Edition 1, however, a little before this, reads *of no part of a body* [nullius partis corporis]. The sense of the response is rendered easier, if one puts it: "because, even if to no part" etc.. Then trusting in the more ancient mss. and ed. 1 we have substituted *however* [tamen] for *since* [cum] and the indicative *it perfects* [perficit] for the subjunctive *it perfects* [perficiat].

[6] The Vatican edition not trusting in very many manuscripts and edition 1, has *simultaneously* [simul] for *similarly* [similiter]; codex I reads *similarly also* [similiter et].

[7] Codex V adds *however* [vero].

[8] Supply together with codex E: *the soul* [anima].

[9] The ancient reading of the manuscripts and edition 1 we have restored by putting *what is outside it* [quod est extra illam] for *what is not outside another* [quod non est extra aliam]. A little before this codex W prefaces the particle *thus* [ita] with *for that reason* [ideo]. — On this solution, cf. Aristotle, ON THE SOUL, Bk. I, text 64 (ch. 4).

[10] ON THE SOUL, Bk. II, text 41 (ch. 4). — Immediately after this, the corrupt and false reading of the Vatican edition and of codex cc, *and thus the human body cannot(be)* [et ita corpus humanum non potest], is repaired from the other manuscripts and edition 1. Then on the authority of many codices as A F G H K T etc. and edition 1, we have substituted *could* [posset] for *can* [possit].

[11] One or the other codex as I together with edition 1 reads not badly *according to* [secundum] for *through* [per].

and in addition, that it is whole in the whole and whole in every part of the place, then it is said to be *definitively* in the place.

III. On the conclusion, common to all, cf. Alexander of Hales, SUMMA., p. II. q. 64. — (Bl. John Duns) Scotus, ON THE PRINCIPLE OF THINGS, q. 12, a. 3. — St. Thomas, here in q. 5, a. 3; SUMMA., I, q. 76, a. 8; SUMMA AGAINST THE GENTILES, II, ch.

72. — Bl. (now St.) Albert (the Great), here in a. 26. — (Bl.) Peter of Tarentaise, here in q. 6, a. 2. — Richard of Middleton, here in a. 4, q. 1. — Giles the Roman, here in 2nd. princ., q. 3. — Durandus (of Saint-Pourçain), here in q. 3. — (Bl.) Dionysius the Carthusian, here in q. 7 after the middle. — (Gabriel) Biel, SENT., Bk. II, d. 16, q. sole, Doubt 4.

QUESTION IV

Whether God is in any determinate genus or predicament?

Fourth and last, there is asked, whether God is in any *determinate* genus. And that (it is) so, is shown in this manner:

1. What is distinguished from other beings, is some determinate nature; but God is of this kind, because He is distinguished from all creatures, because no created (thing) is God: therefore, He is a determinate nature; but what is a determinate nature is in a determinate genus:[1] ergo etc..

2. Likewise, what has a univocal and essential superior, has 'being' [esse] in a determinate genus; but God has a superior to Himself,[2] as the substance, which is said of God and creatures both essentially and univocally, because according to that reckoning of Him which is 'a thing existing through itself' [res per se existens]: ergo etc..

3. Likewise, it seems that He is in *any genus*. Because everything, which belongs to completion[3] in a creature, must be attributed to God; but every predicament has something of completion: therefore, the qualities [res] of all predicaments are in God; but whatever is in God is God, and conversely:[4] therefore God essentially is the subject [subiicitur] of the predicament of every thing [rei omnis]: therefore, He is in any (of them).

4. Likewise, there is nothing of goodness lacking to the Most High Good: therefore, (there is) nothing[5] of entity (lacking) to the Most High Being [summo enti]: therefore, in God there is every entity and every difference of entity: therefore, since there are ten predicaments of difference belonging to beings, all (predicaments) are in God.

ON THE CONTRARY: 1. (St.) Augustine (says) in the fifth book, ON THE TRINITY:[6] « God is good without quality, great without quantity »: therefore, the magnitude of God is not in the genus of quantity nor (is His) goodness in the genus of quality: therefore, neither (is His) substance in the genus of substance: therefore, He is[7] in no genus.

2. Likewise, it seems that He is not in a *determinate* genus; because everything, which is in a determinate genus, has a finite and limited 'being' [esse]; but God is infinite: ergo etc..

3. Likewise, it seems that He is not in *any* genus, because, what has in itself that which pertains to [res] more genera is a composite: but God is most simple: ergo etc..

CONCLUSION

God is neither in any determinate genus, nor in more.

I RESPOND: It must be said, that it is not fitting [convenit] for God to be in *one determinate genus*, because every such has a limited and constrained [arctatum] and composite 'being' [esse]. He cannot be in *several*[8] genera. For either something is in several on account of a *diversity* of natures and properties, as the "white", inasmuch as it means some subject or white thing, it is in the genus of substance, but inasmuch as it means the form, which is *whiteness*, it is in the predicament of quality; or (it is such) on account of a *generality*, just as the 'one' and being [unum et ens].[9]

On account of a *multiformity*[10] of natures God cannot be in several (genera), because every such is composite and in a multiform manner, but God (is) simple. Not on account of a *generality*, because such a being [ens] is as one having[11] nothing distinct from created things. But God is the One having in Himself a being distinct from things [ens distinctum a rebus], and the One having a simple and infinite 'being' [esse simplex et infinitum]; and, for that reason, He can be neither in one genus nor in several.

1. To that, therefore, which is objected, that what is distinguished from others, is a distinct nature etc.; it must be said, that it is true, if it is distinguished through something, which contracts and constrains it[12], just as through a difference falling in a genus; but God is not distinguished in this manner, but (rather) by His very Self.

2. To that which is objected, that God has a univocal superior; it must be said, that for God there is not a superior, because[13] there is not a more simple one (than He); nor a univocal (one),

---

[1] Cf. Aristotle, ON PREDICAMENTS, at the beginning, where the five conditions commonly received by the Scholastics for which reason something is posited in a determinate genus are assigned, namely,. that which is univocal, that which is an non-complex being or a being per se one, that which is a real being, that which is universal and/or particular, that which is a finite being or which is determinable according to a special manner of a being.

[2] Very many codices as A B D F G K S T etc. together with edition 1 have *as a thing* [re] in place of *to Himself* [se].

[3] That is, to perfection. — Cf. (St.) Anselm, MONOLOGION., ch. 15.

[4] Cf. (St. Severinus) Boethius, ON THE TRINITY, ch. 4, and Alan of Lille, RULES OF THEOLOGY, rule 9.

[5] Codex V and edition 1 here repeat *there is ... lacking* [deficit].

[6] Chapter 1, n. 2: That thus we may understand God ... without quality good, without quantity great.

[7] From the more ancient manuscripts and edition 1 we have supplied *He is* [est].

[8] The Vatican edition not trusting in the manuscripts and the first six editions adds *even* [etiam].

[9] Which, just as *thing* [res], *something* [aliquid], *the true* [verum], *the good* [bonum] on account of the greatest universality, by which they are implied in all genera, are called *transcendentals* [transcendentalia].

[10] The Vatican edition reads *multiplicity* [multiplicitatem], but contrary to the manuscripts and edition 1.

[11] One or the other codex as E and V omit *one having* [habens].

[12] Codex V has *the reckoning* [rationem] in place of *it* [ipsum].

[13] Trusting in the more ancient manuscripts and edition 1 we have expunged here the added *for that reason* [eo], and a little after this we have substituted *that* [illa] for *a substance's* [substantiae].

because that reckoning does not uniformly befit creature and Creator. For God is a *being through Himself* [ens per se], because (He is as one) needing nothing; a creature is a *being through itself*, because it is not in another as in a subject, however, it does need another for its own conservation.

3. To that which is objected, that everything, which belongs to perfection and goodness, must be posited in God; it must be said, that this can be in a twofold manner: through[1] *diversity*, and this causes it to be in diverse genera;

and/or according to an omnimodal *unity*, and this causes it to be outside every genus.

4. To that which is last objected, that God lacks nothing of goodness; it must be said, that God it not said (to be) deficient in goodness on account of this, that every difference of particular good is in God through *difference*, but because it is in Him through *equivalence*.[2] For because He is the Most High Good, He embraces in Himself every good; thus it must be understood concerning entity; and thus that (objection) is clear.

SCHOLIUM

I. The *determinate genus*, which this question concerns, is the logical genus or predicament, which is predicated of the very many things, differing in species, e.g. substance. — Some Nominalists, as Gregory of Rimini, affirmed against the common and true sentence, that God is in the genus of substance. The Seraphic Doctor solves this Question with a twofold conclusion by teaching, that God is neither in *one* determinate genus, nor is He simultaneously in *more*. That He is not in *more*, he proves through parts: for since in a twofold manner something can be in more predicaments, neither manner befits God. The first manner is clear from the text; the second manner is « *on account of generality*, just as 'one' and being [ens] ». Which to understand, it must be known, that *being* [ens], *the One, the True, the Good* are called transcendentals [transcendentia], because they are so posited in all predicaments, that they are indeed predicated of them, but are not any predicament. For these transcendentals do not have a 'being' [esse] distinct from the predicaments, in which they are posited, v. g. a *being* [ens] in the predicament of substance is a substance, in the predicament of quantity it is a quantity. Whence in this manner it least of all befits God, who has a 'being' [esse] entirely determinate and distinct from things. With this doctrine pantheism is refuted.

II. The solution to n. 1 is derived from the distinction between a nature determinate through *some difference* [determi-

natam per aliquam differentiam], and one determinate through *its very self* [determinatam per se ipsam]; in the first case the difference contracts the genus to some species, which is in some predicament; then even the nature itself, thus determinate, is in this predicament. Otherwise there must be said of God, who is the most pure Act, that (He is) determinate *through Himself* and for that reason (is) outside every predicament. Cf. Richard of Middleton, here in q. 2.

III. In regard to the principal matter the ancient doctors agree. On the sentence of St. Thomas, who in his COMMENTARIA, here in q. 4, a. 2, speaks in a manner slightly different that in the SUMMA., I, q. 3, aa. 5 and 7, cf. Cajetan on this passage. (Bl. John Duns) Scotus, here in q. 3, n. 20, opposes not the conclusion, but only that reason, which is derived by St. Thomas from this, that God contains in Himself the perfections of all genera. Scotus, however, loc. cit., n. 16, thinks, that the reckoning of *a being* [entis] befits God and creatures *univocally*, which, how this is coherent with the other doctrines of Scotus, is explained in various manners by the Scotists. — Alexander of Hales, SUMMA., p. I, q. 48, m. 4, aa. 2 and 3. Bl. (now St.) Albert (the Great), here in a. 32; SUMMA., tr. 4, q. 20, m. 3 at the end. — (Bl.) Peter of Tarentaise, here in q. 5, a. 2. — Richard of Middleton, here in a. 4, q. 2. — Giles the Roman, here in 1st. princ., q. 3. — Henry of Ghent, SUMMA., a. 26. — Durandus (of Saint-Pourçain), SENT., Bk. II, d. 3, q. 1. — (Bl.) Dionysius the Carthusian, here in q. 6. — (Gabriel) Biel, here in qq. 1 and 2.

DOUBTS ON THE TEXT OF THE MASTER

DOUBT I

I that part of his there occurs here[3] the question concerning the *order* of the text [circa litteram ... de ordine]. For since *composition* in a creature is the reason and cause for mutation, *simplicity* is the cause of immutability; because if affirmation is the cause of affirmation, and negation the cause of negation:[4] therefore, since cause is before effect, Master (Peter) ought first to posit the property of simplicity.

I RESPOND: It must be said, that in truth [revera] composition according to the reckoning of the thing to be understood [intelligendi] is more first than mutation; but since negations hold themselves contrariwise [e contrario] to affirmation, hence it is, that immutability is more first; thus do some want to say it.

However, it can be said in another manner and better, that He is more first and more known *to us*, and more first *simply*;[5] and because simplic-

ity is most hidden to us on account of this, that the simple, inasmuch as (it is) simple, has a reckoning of principle; and we come from cognition of the posterior unto the cognition of the prior: for that reason he deals with immutability in a manner more first than simplicity.

DOUBT II

Likewise, is asked concerning this which he says in the text: *And the same (is) properly and truly simple, because it has neither composition of parts* etc.. For it seems superfluous to say, that the simple is that of which there is not a part, just as the composite is said (to be) that which has parts.

I RESPOND: It must be said, that Master (Peter) here makes known the simple, according to which it is proper to God; and thus it is opposed to *composition* and to *multiplicity*. Therefore,

---

[1] Codices V and X read *according to* [secundum], and a little below this codex T has *uniformity* [uniformitatem] in place of *unity* [unitatem].

[2] That is, through eminence or eminently.

[3] The Vatican edition, not trusting in the manuscripts and edition 1, has *this* [haec] in place of *here the* [hic]. Then after *simplicity* codex V has *will be* [erit] in place of *is* [est].

[4] Aristotle, POSTERIOR ANALYTICS, Bk. I, ch. 10 (ch. 13): Moreover, similarly also, if affirmation is the cause its own 'being' [ipsius esse], and negation of its own 'being' [ipsius esse]. — Here the codices

do not agree among themselves; some as H K V Y etc. together with edition 1 have the *is* [est], which the others as A F G I T etc. omit and in place of which the Vatican edition does not well have *may be* [sit]; codex V prefixes to the word *cause of negation* [causa negationis] a *will be* [erit]. A little below this after *of simplicity* [simplicitatis] codices H and Y add *than of immutability* [quam immutabilitatis].

[5] Aristotle, POSTERIOR ANALYTICS, Bk. I, ch. 2; in which proposition, trusting in the manuscripts and edition 1, we have inserted first an *and* [et], and then after the second *more first* we have expunged the repeated *more known* [notius].

as much as regards privation of *composition*, he says, that He does not have a multitude of parts; but as much as regards privation of *extraneous multiplicity*, he says that He does not have a variety of accidents; but as much as regards privation of *intrinsic multiplicity*, he says that He does not have a variety of forms, as of genus, species and difference; and in this manner the simple is the simple truly and properly, which does belong to God alone.[1]

DOUBT III

Likewise, is asked concerning that reason of (St.) Augustine: *For since it is one (thing) to be artificial, another inert* etc.. For he proves, that the soul is composite on account of the multitude of (its) properties. *But on the contrary*: no substance is composed out of properties neither through itself nor with another: therefore, from this it is not proved, that the soul is composite.

I RESPOND: It must be said, that (St.) Augustine does not prove this except a posteriori. For the composition of an accident regards [ad] a subject and (their) diversity necessarily presupposes another composition, because, as (St. Severinus) Boethius says,[2] « that which is purely form cannot be a subject »: therefore, for this, that something be a subject of more accidents, it is proper that an intrinsic composition pre-exist in it; but the soul captures in itself a multitude of accidents: and for that reason there is necessarily inferred a posteriori, that it itself is composite, though not out of accidents.

DOUBT IV

Likewise, is asked concerning this which he says: *the One Good without quality, the One Great without quantity* etc.. For it seems that he speaks badly; because from whomsoever a superior is removed, (is) also an inferior:[3] therefore, if He does not have quality, neither (does He) goodness. *If you say*, that that Goodness is not a species of quality, it is asked, why is divine quality not similarly meant in divine (things), just as divine goodness (is)?

I RESPOND: Certain ones want to say, that the noun for *genus* is not transferred to divine (things), both because it does not mean a complement of a thing, just as species (does); and because it signifies in the concretion to a subject and in dependence.[4] But *special* nouns connote the effect in the creature; and for that reason there is said *the One Good without quality*.

But if one wants to look into (this matter),[5] he finds that this does not have truth. Therefore, if there is asked: how does magnitude and goodness differ in God? it must be said, that magnitude signifies the Divine Essence through the manner of quantity, goodness through the manner of quality: therefore, those manners do occur [cadunt] in God.[6] And *again*, if there is asked: *what kind is God?* there is responded: Good and Great.

And for that reason it must be said, that nouns for genera are discovered among the divine, but not insofar as they have a reckoning of a genus, because God is in no genus; and to signify this (St.) Augustine[7] removes the names of the nine genera, inasmuch as they are genera.

DOUBT V

Likewise, is asked concerning this which is said: *if, however, it is worthy, that God be said "to subsist"* [substare].* For it seems sufficiently worthy, that the Most High Nobility is One that subsists through itself.

I RESPOND: It must be said, that twofold is the property of substance itself, namely, '*to stand through itself*' [per se stare] and '*to be beneath another*' [alii subesse]; the first belongs to perfection, the second to imperfection; and for that reason by a reckoning of the first, (God) is said (to subsist) in a worthy manner,[8] not by a reckoning of the second.

DOUBT VI

Likewise, is asked concerning this which (St.) Hilary says: *Not out of composites does God, who is Life, subsist* etc.; what difference is there between those differences? Because if[9] there is none, it seems to cause a flourish of words [inculcationem verborum].

I RESPOND: It must be said, that certain ones want,[10]

---

[1] See this Distinction, q. 2.

[2] The book, ON THE TRINITY, ch. 2: However, the form, which is without matter, will not be able to be a subject.

[3] Cf. Aristotle, TOPICS. Bk. IV, ch. 2, and Peter of Spain, SUMMULA, tract "On Topical Syllogisms".

[4] The error of the Vatican edition, *substance and independence* [substantia et indipendentia], we have corrected on the authority of the manuscripts and edition 1; codex dd reads *in concretion just as regards a subject and dependence* [in concretione sicut ad subiectum et dependentiam]. — St. Thomas, here in q. 4, a. 3, explains this saying: Quantity has its own reckoning in comparison to a subject; for quantity is the measure of the substance, quality the disposition of the substance; whence by the same reckoning they are removed from divine predication according to the reckoning of a genus, just as they were removed through the reckoning of an accident.

[5] Codex V here adds *this (matter)* [haec], and a little after this *that* [illud] in place of *this* [hoc]. Next codex dd has the subjunctive *differ* [differat] in place of the indicative *differs* [differt].

[6] The Vatican edition, contrary to the mss. and ed. 1, has *unto God* [in Deum]. A little below this after *Good* [bonus] some codices as K cc ee and ff together with editions 2 and 3 have *not* [non] in place of *and* [et], which reading, even if it is not false, however, is less to the point, because in the previous question the term *what kind* [qualis] is taken in a broad sense, to the extent that it comprehends all the attributes of God.

[7] ON THE TRINITY, Bk. V, ch. 8, n. 9. — For an understanding of this Doubt it must be noted, that here one does not deal with the question, whether God is

in any genus, with which the Seraphic Doctor has already dealt above in q. 4, but with the translation of generic nouns to divine (things) or even with the manner of signifying, that which these nouns have in respect of God. Here the reasons posited in the first place for this opinion are put by St. Thomas, here in q. 4, a. 3, and more clearly in ON POTENCY, q. 7, a. 4, at n. 2; Alexander of Hales, SUMMA., p. I, q. 48, m. 4, a. 3, § 4, at n. 2; — Bl. (now St.) Albert (the Great), here in a. 31; — (Bl.) Peter of Tarentaise, here in q. 5; and others. The second opinion belongs to the Seraphic Doctor, which consists in two parts, that is, first in this, that the names of genera *inasmuch as they are genera* are not transferred; and the reasons adduced for the first opinion prove this; second in this, that the aforesaid names *in some manner* are transferred, if namely they are accepted commonly or *improperly*, cf. d. 23, a. 1, q. 1, at n. 2, and this the authors cited on behalf of the first sentence do not deny. From which it is clear, that the Seraphic Doctor does impugn those who contend, that the said nouns can *in no manner* be transferred.

[8] Edition 1 adds *substance* [substantia]. — On this twofold property of substance see below d. 23, a. 1, q. 2.

[9] The Vatican edition, contrary to very many codices, reads *Because if* [Quia si], and next, contrary to the older manuscripts and edition 1, it omits *of words* [verborum].

[10] Having searched the more ancient manuscripts and edition 1, we have substituted *want* [volunt] in place of *wanted* [voluerunt]. Then codex dd adds *to say* [dicere].

---

* *Trans. note*: Here the English text follows the Latin of Lombard, above in ch. 7, p. 148, in reading *"to subsist"* [subsistere]; the reading, here, substare (*"to stand under"*) contradicts what follows, and would merit comment by the Editors, if it were not a typographical error.

that through those four there be excluded the four *genera of compositions*. For the *first* is of essence out of essential principles, for which reason it is said, that *God is not out of composites*, that is (things) simultaneously posited. The *second* is of substance out of the natural principles, which are matter and form; for this reason there is said: *neither out of (things) infirm*, because matter is subject to a privation, which causes form to be unstable[1] and infirm, and similarly matter; for infirm (things) are said (to be) instable. The *third* is composition of the mixed out of mixables, for which reason he says: *neither out of (things) obscure*, because where (there is) mixing, there (is) a certain confusion of forms, and thus an obscuring [obscuratio]. The *fourth* is the composition of an animal out of disparate parts, namely out of soul and body; for which reason he says: *neither out of disparate parts, because He Himself is a spirit*.

However, it can be said in another manner, that he does exclude composition by a reckoning of *diverse conditions*. For, for this, that some[2] principles constitute something, it is proper, that the principles be *different*, be *dependent*, be *imperfect*, be also 'differing in form' [difformia]. For if they were entirely conformal and perfect, they could not constitute anything, because out of two beings in act nothing comes to be.[3] Therefore, because (they are) *different*, for that reason they are composite, as if with others posited; because (they are) *dependent*, for that reason (they are) infirm;[4] because *imperfect*, for that reason obscure; because *dissimilar*, for that reason disparate. But God cannot be out of (things) different[5] and diverse, because He is Life through (His) essence; He cannot be out of (things) dependent and infirm, because (He is) Virtue through (His) essence; He cannot be out of (things) imperfect and obscure, because He is Light; similarly He cannot be out of (things) disparate and dissimilar, because (He is) Spirit through (His) Essence. Therefore, a most high *Actuality*, a most high *Power*, a most high *Clarity*, (and) a Most high *Spirituality* do not permit that in God there is any composition. Whence out of these four conditions four reasons are elicited proving that God[6] (is) the Most Simple.

DISTINCTION IX

CHAPTER I

On the distinction of the Three Persons.

Now, let us proceed [accedamus] to the distinction of the Three Persons. « We are bound, therefore, », as (St.) Augustine teaches in the book, ON THE FAITH TO PETER,[1] « that the Father and the Son and the Holy Spirit are the One God naturally, nor, however, that the Father Himself is He who the Son is, nor that the Son is He Himself who the Father is, nor that the Holy Spirit is He Himself who the Father is, or the Son. For one [una] is the Essence of the Father and of the Son and of the Holy Spirit, in which one thing [aliud] is not the Father, another thing the Son, another thing the Holy Spirit, although personally One [alius] is the Father, another One the Son, another One the Holy Spirit ».[2]

CHAPTER II

On the coeternity of the Father and of the Son.

For the Son is begotten by [a] the Father, and for that reason Another, nor, however, was the Father before [ante quam] the Son; for the Three Persons are coeternal to Themselves. But against this the heretic says, as (St.) Ambrose reports in his first book, ON THE TRINITY:[3] « Everything which is born, has a principle; and for that reason, because He is the Son, He has a beginning and undertook to be; which by the mouth of heretics is said in this manner ». « For Arius himself, as (St.) Augustine remembered in his sixth book, ON THE TRINITY,[4] is reported to have said: "If He is the Son, He has been born; if He has been born, there was a 'when the Son was not'" ».

Who says this « does not understand, *that to have been born of* [de] *God* is also to be sempiternal, so that the Son is coeternal to the Father [Patri], just as the splendor, which is begotten by [a] fire and is diffused (with it), is coeval to it, and would be coeternal, if the fire is eternal ».[5]

Likewise: « If the Son of God », says (St.) Augustine, « is the Virtue and Wisdom of God, and God was not ever without virtue and wisdom, (then) coeternal to the God the Father is the Son. Moreover, the Apostles says:[6] that *Christ is the Virtue of God and the Wisdom of God*; therefore, either there was not a 'when there was not a Son', or at sometime God did not have virtue and wisdom, which belongs to the demented to say ». For it is established, that He always had wisdom, therefore, He always had the Son.

To the same Arian question (St.) Ambrose[7] also responds in this manner: « I, I say, do confess that the Son has been born; because the rest belongs to impiety, I am

---

[1] The Vatican edition together with codex cc, disagreeing, however, with the other codices and edition 1, have *mutable* [mutabilem] in place of *to be unstable* [esse instabilem].

[2] We have supplied *some* [aliqua] from the first edition and all the manuscripts, many of which, however, next omit *something* [aliquid].

[3] Aristotle, METAPHYSICS, Bk. VII, text 49 (Bk. VI, ch. 13): For with two thus in act, they are never one in act ... for acting separates (them).

[4] Many codices together with edition 1 read *informal* [informia], but falsely.

[5] The more ancient codices together with edition 1 omit *different and* [differentibus et], in place of which codex cc and editions 2, 3 and 6 have *dependent* [dependentibus]. A little after this the Vatican edition together with codex cc, but disagreeing with the other manuscripts and edition 1, omit *dependent and* [dependentibus et].

[6] Some codices as K V Y and ee add *is* [esse]. — Cf. Bl. (now St.) Albert (the Great), here in a. 33. — St. Thomas and Richard (of Middleton), here on the text.

NOTES ON THE BOOK OF SENTENCES

[1] Chapter 1, n. 5. — In the beginning of the distinction all the codices omit *three* [trium].

[2] The Vatican edition adds to this chapter the words of the following chapter, *For the Son is begotten* [Genitus est enim] upto *Another* [alius].

[3] Chapter 11, n. 73. — Only the Vatican edition and editions 4, 6 and 8 cite this book under the name ON THE FAITH TO GRATIAN; cf. above D. II, ch. 4. In the text, contrary to the ordinal and our codices, the Vatican edition with the rest of the editions read *If He was born the Son* [Si Filius natus est].

[4] Chapter 1, n. 1, whence also the two quotes, which follow, are taken. In the first text only the Vatican edition and edition 4 and 6, together with the original of (St.) Augustine, add *time* [tempus] before *when* [quando]. But the noted adage of Arius is: There was a 'when He was not' (ἦν ποτε, ὅτε οὐκ ἦν).

[5] The Vatican edition alone, wrongly, omits *eternal* [aeternus].

[6] 1 Cor. 1:24; but in the Vulgate and (St.) Augustine there is lacking the *is* [esse]. A little before this at *coeternal* [coaeternus] the Vatican edition and editions 4 and 9 add *therefore* [ergo].

[7] Loc. cit.. — From the same book ch. 8, n. 55, the next passage is taken from this chapter, the second and third from ch. 9, n. 58 and 59, the fourth from the same chapter n. 60.

horrified ». « For it was written in the Old Testament,[1] to speak even of one of many (passages): *Before Me there was no other God, and after Me there shall not be (another)*. Who therefore, says this? The Father, or the Son? If the Son, *before Me*, He says, *there shall not be (another)*. This One (has not) one before (him), That One has not one after. For mutually in Themselves, both the Father in the Son, and the Son in the Father are cognized.[2] For when you say *"the Father"*, you have also designated His Son, because no one is a father to himself; when you name the Son, you also say [fateris] the Father, because no one is a son to himself. And so neither can the Son be without the Father, nor the Father without the Son: therefore, Father (is) always, and the Son is always ».

Likewise: « Tell me, I say, (you) heretic, was there a, when God the Father omnipotent was not, and God was? For if the Father undertook to be, therefore, first there was God and afterwards the Father was made. In what manner, therefore, is God immutable? For if before there was God, afterwards the Father, He has certainly [utique] been changed by an accession of generation ». « But may God turn (us) from such mindlessness! »[3]

CHAPTER III

On the ineffable and intelligible manner of the generation.

« But you seek from me », says (St.) Ambrose,[4] « how, if He is the Son, does He not have a prior Father? I seek, likewise, from you, when and/or in what manner do you think the Son has been begotten? For to me it is impossible to know the secret of (that) generation. The mind fails, the voice is silent: not mine only, but even (those) of the Angels; it is above the powers (of man) and above Angels, and above the Cherubim and above the Seraphim and above every sense, because it has been written:[5] *The peace of Christ is above every sense*. And if the peace of Christ is above every sense, in what manner is so great a generation not above every sense? » « You, therefore, *put your hand upon your mouth*; it is not licit to scrutinize the supernal mysteries. It is licit to know [scire], that He has been born, it is not licit to discuss, in what manner He has been born. The former is not licit for me to deny, the latter I have feared to question ». For ineffable is that generation; whence Isaias (says):[6] *His generation, who shall tell it forth?*

Certain ones, however, presuming from their own ingenuity say, that that generation can be understood and other (things) of this kind, adhering [inhaerentes] to that authority from (St.) Jerome on Ecclesiastes:[7] « In the Sacred Scriptures *who* most often is not posited for the impossible, but for the difficult, as there (where it says): *His generation who can tell it forth* »? But by this (St.) Jerome did not say,[8] for this reason [ideo], that the eternal generation

of the Son can be *"fully* understood and/or explained" by any of mortals, but that of it [de ea] *something* can be understood and/or said. Certain ones, however, accept this saying of the temporal generation of Christ.

CHAPTER IV

Whether there ought to be said: God always is begotten, and/or always has been begotten.

Here it can be asked, since the generation of the Son by [a] the Father has neither a beginning nor an end, because it is eternal, "Whether there ought to be said: "the Son is always begotten", and/or "always has been begotten", and/or "always will be begotten"?" Concerning this (St.) Gregory on Job[9] says: « The Lord God, Jesus, in this, that He is the Virtue and the Wisdom of God, has been born of [de] the Father before (all) times, and/or rather, because He neither undertook to be born nor failed (to be), let us say more truly *"always born"*; moreover, we cannot say *"always is born"*, lest He seem to be imperfect. But, on the other hand [vero], that He prevail to be designated as eternal and perfect, let us say *"always"* and *"born"*, to the extent that both *"born"* pertains to perfection and *"always"* to eternity; although through this very (thing), because we call (Him) the *"Perfect One"*, we deviate much from the expression of that truth, because what is not *made* [factum], cannot properly said to be a *"perfect one"* »; but by stuttering, as we can, we echo the highest (things) of God. « And the Lord, condescending to our infirmity in words, said, *Be perfect, just as your heavenly Father is perfect* ».[10] Also, on this passage of the Psalm: *I today have begotten Thee*, (St.) Augustine speaks thus of this generation:[11] « And yet [quamquam], through this, that he says, *"today"* [hodie], there can also be understood that day, in which Christ according to man was begotten; however, because *"today"* signifies the present [praesentiam], and (because) in eternity there is nothing past, as if it had failed [desierit] to be, nor a future, as if it were not yet, but only a present [praesens], because whatever is eternal, always is; it is more divinely accepted of the sempiternal generation of the Wisdom of God ».[12] Behold, with these words (St.) Augustine shows, that the generation of the Son always is, and (that) it is not past, nor is it future, because it is eternal. For[13] for this reason [ideo] he said *"I have begotten"*, lest He be reputed new, that is, lest He seem to have commenced [incepisse]: he said *"today"*, lest the generation seem past. « From these words, therefore, of the Prophet », as (St.) John Chrysostom says,[14] « nothing other is manifested, except that from the Essence Itself of the Father the Son has always been begotten ».

---

[1] Isaias 43:10.

[2] A reference to John 14:9,10. — A little above this after *one before* [priorem] the Vatican edition, contrary to the original, the codices and editions 1 and 8, adds *and* [et].

[3] Codices C E and A (in the margin) together with editions 1 and 8 add: *because He always had wisdom, He always had the Son* [quia semper habuit sapientiam, semper habuit Filium], which words, because they carry not a light suspicion of being an interpolation, we have not received into the text.

[4] ON THE FAITH TO GRATIAN, Bk. I, ch. 10, nn. 64 and 65. — In the beginning of this passage the Vatican edition alone reads *has* [habet] in the indicative. Then in codices B C D E and edition 1 there is lacking *when and/or* [quando vel], which however, is in the original.

[5] Philippians 4:7. The words, which follow below this: *put your hand upon your mouth* and *it is not licit to scrutinize*, refer to Eccli. 5:14 and 3:22.

[6] Chapter 53:8.

[7] Chapter 2.

[8] The Vatican edition with a few edd. reads *does not say* [non dicit].

[9] MORALS ON THE BOOK OF JOB, Bk. 29, ch. 1 at the beginning. The

word, which follow after *we echo the highest (things) of God* [excelsa Dei resonamus], are also found in the same place. In the beginning of the first passage codices A B D E and editions 1 and 8 omit *Jesus* [Iesus].

[10] Mt. 5:48. — A little before this the Vatican edition and editions 3, 4, 7 and 9 reads *let us echo* [resonemus] for *we echo* [resonamus].

[11] EXPOSITIONS ON PSALMS, Ps. 2:6. — A little before this the Vatican edition wrongly reads *Psalmist* [Psalmista]. The same Vatican edition and edition 4 omitt *also* [etiam] before *be understood* [intelligi].

[12] Codices A C and E at the margin and editions 1, 5, and 9 in the text insert these words: *Whence even (St.) Augustine in the book, ON 83 QUESTIONS speaking in an orderly manner* [disserens] *of the always born (q. 37) says: it is better (to say) "born", than "He who is always being born"* [nascitur], *because He is is always being born is not yet born and never has been born or will be born* [natus erit], *if He is always being born. For it is one (thing) to be born, another to have been born, and through this (line of reasoning) the Son never is, if He never has been born; but the Son is, because He is born, and He always is the Son, because He is eternal, therefore, always born."*

[13] The Vatican edition, contrary to the codices and editions 1 and 8, omits *For* [enim].

[14] ON THE EPISTLE TO THE HEBREWS, Homily 2, n. 3.

On the other hand [vero], Origin ON JEREMIAS[1] says, that the Son is always generated from [a] the Father, with these words: « Our Savior is the Wisdom of God; however, the Wisdom is the Splendor of the eternal Light: therefore, Our Savior is the Splendor of the Clarity. Moreover, splendor is not born once and stops [desinit], but as many times a light has risen, from which splendor rises, so often does the splendor of its clarity rise: in the same manner, therefore, the Savior is always born. Whence it says in the book of the Wise Man:[2] *Before all the hills the Lord generates me*, not, as certain ones badly read it, *"generated"* ». With these words Origin openly shows that sanely it can and ought be said: *"The Son is always born* [nascitur]", which seems contrary to that aforesaid word of (St.) Gregory, namely, « we cannot say: *"He is always born"* ».

But lest such great authors seem to contradict themselves in such a great matter [re], let us interpret those[3] words of (St.) Gregory in a benign manner [benige]. « The Lord Jesus », he says, « has been born before (all) times of the Father, and/or rather [potius], because He neither undertook to be born nor failed (to be), let us say more truly: *"always born"* ». But in what manner can there be more truly said this, namely that the Son has been always born, than that, namely that of the Father before (all) times He has been born? For that does the sincere and catholic Faith hold and preach as its own [istud]. For what reason [quare], therefore, does he say: « Let us say more truly », since each be equally [pariter] true, except[4] that he wanted it to be understood, that this is aid for a greater evidence and expression of the truth than that (other saying)? For indeed by these words every access to the heretic, wilily (enough) to calumniate it, is obstructed, by which the generation of Christ according to (His) Deity is shown to be without a start and without an end, and perfect. Moreover, the truth is not manifested so [adeo] openly[5], when there is said: "The Son before (all) times has been begotten of the Father, and/or the Son is always born of the Father." And for that reason (St.) Gregory says, that « we cannot say, "He is always born" »; not, I say, in so fitting a manner [ita convenienter], not in so congruous a manner for the explanation of the truth; however, it can be said, if it is understood in a sane manner. « For the Son is always born of the Father », as Origin says; not that every day that generation is iterated, but that it always is. Therefore, He is always born, that is, His nativity is sempiternal.

(St.) Hilary also says, that the Son is born out of [ex] the Father, in the seventh book, ON THE TRINITY[6] with these words: « The living God is also the Power of an eternal living Nature; and because He is born of Him with the sacrament of His Knowledge [cum sacramento scientiae suae],* He could not be other than living. For when He says: *Just as the living Father sent Me, and I live on account of the Father*, He taught, that Life was in Himself [in se inesse] through the living Father ». Behold here

you have, that[7] the Son is born out of the Father. Likewise, in the same (passage):[8] « When Christ says: *Just as the Father has life in Himself, in the same manner too He gives to the Son to have life in His very self* [semetipso], He has testified that all things living in Himself are out of One living [omnia viva sua ex vivente]. Moreover, because a living thing [vivum] has been born out of a living thing; it has (something) perfect belonging to its nativity without a newness of nature. For (something) is not new, which is generated out of (something) alive into (something) alive, because neither is it out of nothing; and a life, which takes a nativity out of life, is necessary through a unity of nature and a sacrament of a perfect nativity, so that it too[9] lives in One living and has in Itself a living Life ». Behold here you also have, that the living Son is generated out of One alive [vivo]. Likewise, in the same(chapter):[10] « In God the whole which is lives; for God is Life, and out of Life no thing [non quidquam] can be except (something) alive; and the Nativity is not out of a derivation, but out of virtue. And in this manner, while the whole which is lives, and while the whole which is born out of Him is Virtue, the Son has a nativity, not a de-mutation ». And here he says, that He is born. Likewise, in the ninth book, ON THE TRINITY:[11] « The Father grants to the Son to be as much as [tantum quantum] He Himself is, to Whom He imparts [impertit] by the sacrament of a nativity to be the Image of (His own) innascibility, Whom He generates in His own form ». Here he says, that the Father generates the Son.

Let us say, therefore, that the Son (has) been born of the Father before (all) times and that He is always born of the Father, but more congruently that He always (has) been born; let us say [fateamur] that the Same is both from eternity [ab aeterno] and is coeternal to the Father, that is to (His) author. For the Father by generation is the author of the Son, as will be shown in the following (distinction).[12] Therefore, as the Father is eternal, so also the Son is eternal, but the Father without an author, the Son, on the other hand, non (so), because the Father (is) innascible, the Son born. And as (St.) Hilary says in the twelfth book, ON THE TRINITY:[13] « It is one thing [aliud] to be eternal always without an author, another thing [aliud] to be coeternal to the Father, that is to an author. Moreover, where the Father is author, there also is a nativity; because just as a nativity is from [ab] an author, so also from an eternal author there is an eternal nativity. Moreover, everything [omne], which always is, is also eternal; but, yet, not everything, which is eternal, is also unborn [innatum]; because what is born from eternity [ab aeterno] has an eternal 'to be', which has been born. Moreover, because it has not been born, on that account [id] it has not been born with eternity [cum aeternitate]; on the other hand [vero], because it has been born out of an eternal [ex aeterno], on that account, if there is not an eternal Born, then [iam] there is not even an eternal Father-Author. Therefore, if anything (pertaining) to Him, Who has been born by the eternal Father, was lacking in eternity [ex aeternitate defuerit], on that account there is no ambiguity that He was lacking to His Author [auctori], because

---

[1] Homily 6, in ch. 11, near the end, but with not a few changes.

[2] Prov. 8:25 according the Septuagint; the Vulgate reads: *before the hills I desire to be brought forth* [parturiebar]. — Some editions cite it thus: *in the book of Wisdom* for *of the Wise Man*, which error even the codices favor; edition 9 reads *whence in Prov. 8 Wisdom says*.

[3] The Vatican edition alone omits *that* [illa].

[4] Manuscripts B C and E add *perchance* [forte].

[5] The Vatican edition and editions 4, 5, 6 and 9 superfluously add *always* [semper]. Immediately before this codex D and editions 1 and 8 read *is shown* [monstratur] for *is manifested* [manifestatur].

[6] N. 27. — The text of Scripture, cited by (St.) Hilary, is John 6:58, in which (St.) Hilary puts *through the Father* [per Patrem] in place of *on account of the Father* [propter Patrem], as the Vulgate has it.

[7] The codices read *that* [quod] in place of *that* [quia]. After this codex B and editions 1 and 8 read *of the Father* [de Patre] in place of *out of the Father* [ex Patre].

[8] Ibid.. — The text of Scripture is John 5:26, in which the Vulgate and editions 1, 2, 5 and 9 read *in His very self* [semetipso] for *in Himself* [in se]. Then after the next *out of* [ex] codex D reads by glossing *the living Father* [vivente Patre], and codex A has *entirely His own life* [omnino vitam suam] for *all things living in Himself* [omnia viva sua].

[9] Editions 1 & 8 omit *too* [et], which our other authorities have with (St.) Hilary; then *also* [et] after *Behold* [Ecce] is omitted by cod. D and ed. 8.

[10] Loc. cit., n. 28. — Codices C D and E add *(St.) Hilary (says)* [Hilarius], and C and E proceed: *Attend that the whole* [Attende quod totum] for *In God the whole* [In Deo totum]. Then editions 1, 3, 4, 5, 7, and 9, contrary to the original and badly, read *it is ... ut of the virtue of the nativity* [ex virtute nativitatis] for *the nativity ... out of virtue* [ex virtute nativitas]. Immediately after this the Vatican edition, together with very many editions, reads faultily *if* for *in the same manner* [sic], which is had in the original and in editions 5, 6, 8, and 9.

[11] N. 54, where against to the codd., edd. 5 & 9 and the original, all the other editions have *imparts* [impartit] for *imparts* [impertit]. Then, the Maurini ed. of (St.) Hilary reads *unto His own* [in formam suam] for *in His own* [in forma sua].

[12] Immediately after this one, and in Distinction 15, near the end.

[13] N. 21. — In this text near the middle in place of *out of an eternal* [ex aeterno] edd. 1 & 8 have not so well *from eternity* [ab aeterno], and a little after this codd. D & E have *one who (is) an* [qui] for *even an* [et].

---

* *Trans. note*: Here, the Latin can be rendered in two manners, as St. Bonaventure does here in Doubt VIII: either as the translation has it above, or with <u>sacramento</u> rendered as an ablative of means or specification: *when (by or according to) the sacrament of His Knowledge He is born of Him*, following St. Hilary's similar use at the end of this paragraph.

if to the one begetting [gignenti] there is an infinite begetting [gignere], there is also to the one being born [nascenti] even an infinite being born [nasci]. For the medium which (is) between the nativity of the Son of God and the generation of God the Father admits neither *reckoning*[1] nor sensing, because both the nativity is in the generation, and the generation is in the nativity, because without each neither is: therefore, each [utrumque] is without an interval to the other [sui] ».

CHAPTER V

On the objections of the heretics striving to prove,
that the Son is not coeternal to the Father.

« But the heretic will say: "Everything which has been born was not always, because it was born unto something [in id], that it might be." No one is doubtful [ambigit], that those things [ea][2] which have been born in human affairs [rebus], were not at some time. But it is one thing [aliud] to be born out of that, which

was not always, another thing [aliud] to have been born out of that, which is always. In this [ibi] there was not always, one who is father, nor is he a father always; and who is not always a father, has not always begotten. Moreover, where there is always a father, there is always a son. Because if it is always proper to God the Father, that He is always the Father, it is necessary, that it is always proper to the Son, that He is always the Son. In what manner, therefore, does it fall unto our understanding, that there was not always the One to Whom it is proper, to be always that which has been born?[3] Therefore, we confess that the Only-Begotten God (has) been born, but born before (all) times, neither that He is before [ante quam] being born, nor that (He has) been born before being; because what was a 'to be born', is presently not a 'to be born', but a 'to de-mutate one's very self by being born'. Moreover, this exceeds human sense [sensus] and understanding. This the reckoning of human understanding does not grasp, but is it the profession of the foresight of faith [prudentiae fidelis] ».[4]

COMMENTARY ON DISTINCTION IX

On the properties, which respect the Persons, and, indeed, on the emanation of generation.

Now, let us proceed to the distinction of the Three Persons etc..

THE DIVISION OF THE TEXT

Above, Master (Peter) dealt with the properties, which respect the Essence. Here he deals with those, which respect the Persons; and this part has two parts. For, because the distinction of Persons is tended to according to a twofold emanation, that is, of generation and of procession, for that reason he *first* dealt with generation, but *second* with procession, below in the tenth distinction: *But now after the eternity of the Son, let us discuss in an orderly manner the Holy Spirit* etc..

Likewise, the first part has two parts: in the *first* he shows, what must be thought [sentiendum] of the generation of the Son; *second*, from a question that crops up [ex incidenti], in what (manner of) speech is it to be expressed, there (where he says): *Here it can be asked, since the generation of the Son by the Father* etc..

The First part, again, has four parts.[1] First he proposes the truth, which is to be retained by Catholics, that is, that the One generating and the One begotten are through generation distinct and coeternal, so that the generation is distinctive and eternal. In the second, against this, he opposes through the opposition of heretics, there (where he says): *But against this the heretic says*. In the third, he determines, by arguing against (them) through the reasons of the catholic Doctors, (Sts.) Augustine and Ambrose, there (where he says): *Who says this does not understand, even that to have been born* etc.. In the fourth and last, he responds, by restraining the inquiry [compescendo inquisitionem] of

heretics and even of proud Catholics, there (where he says): *But you seek from me, says (St.) Ambrose* , where he shows that the sacrament of the generation is incapable of being thoroughly scrutinized [imperscrutablie].[2]

Here it can be asked, since the generation of the Son by the Father etc.. This is the *second* part of this Distinction, in which Master (Peter) determines, in what (manner of) speech the eternity of the generation is more congruently expressed; and this part has four parts. In the first, he posits the apparent controversy of the Doctors. For indeed they say, that it ought to be expressed through verbs[3] of the past tense, others, through verbs of the present (tense). In the second, he reduces the aforesaid controversy to harmony [concordantiam], there (where he says): *But lest such great authors seem to contradict themselves in such a great matter*. In the third, he confirms through the words of (St.) Hilary his own answer [responsionem], lest it seem that it is supported by the sayings of Origen, there (where he says): *(St.) Hilary also says, that the Son is born out of the Father* etc.. In the fourth, he concludes in a summary manner [summatim], what must be[4] said of the eternal generation or in what manner it must be spoken of and in what manner also it must be considered, there (where he says): *Let us say, therefore, that the Son has been Born of the Father*, where he confirms the truth through the authority of (St.) Hilary, through which he also solves the objection of (Arius), the heretic.

---

[1] The codices and very many of the editions, contrary to the original and Vatican texts, omits *neither a reckoning* [nec ratio]; and then before *in the generation* [in generatione] the Vatican edition with a few of the editions omits *both* [et].

[2] In the codices and (St.) Hilary there is lacking *those things* [ea]. — A little after this, before *another thing* [aliud] the Vatican edition and a few other editions read *it is* [aliud est].

[3] In the text of (St.) Hilary, Maurini edition, there is *because He has been born* [quod natus est], where it is said in the footnotes, that very many codices exhibit the reading *that which has been born* [quod natum est], which our manuscripts and editions have. — Then codices C D and E after *already not* [iam non] add *only* [tantum].

[4] The whole of this chapter has been excerpted from (St.) Hilary loc. cit., nn. 22-26, but with very many things omitted.

NOTES ON THE COMMENTARY

[1] Edition 1 has *smaller parts* [particulas].

[2] Having compared the manuscripts and edition 1, we have substituted *incapable of being thoroughly scrutinized* [imperscrutabile] in place of *inscrutable*. Then the Vatican edition, contrary to the manuscripts and edition 1, having omitted the words of Master (Peter), *Here it can be asked* etc., puts *Similarly* [Similiter] in place of *This is* [Haec est], then on account of a changed construction it omits *and this part* [et haec pars].

[3] One or the other codex, such as 1, together with edition 1, has *verb* [verbum] here, but a little after this very many codices, inconsistent with themselves, have *a verb of the present (tense)* [verbum praesentis].

[4] Trusting in very many mss. and ed. 1, we here have here inserted *be* [sit], which the Vatican ed. puts below this at *considered* [sentiendum].

TREATMENT OF THE QUESTIONS

For an understanding of those (things) which Master (Peter) says of the eternal generation, in the present Distinction four (questions are principally asked:

First, there is asked, whether generation is to be posited among the divine [in divinis].

Second, granted that it is, whether generation among the divine is[1] distinctive of the Persons.

Third there is asked, whether that generation is eternal.

Fourth and last, there is asked, whether that generation has been terminated.

ARTICLE SOLE

On generation among the divine.

QUESTION I

Whether generation is to be posited among the divine?

About the first, that generation be among the divine, is shown:[2]

1. First, <u>a minori</u>.* Much more strongly ought there be generation in Him who grants generation to others, than in those which receive it; but generation is in creatures: therefore also in God who grants it. And this is what is said in the last (chapter) of Isaias:[3] *If I grant generation to others, shall I be sterile? says the Lord,* as if to say, "No".

2. Likewise, that same is shown *a posteriori*. For through a (consideration of what is) prior, paternity is in God rather than in a creature; but paternity and generation are truly in a creature: therefore, also in God. That it is prior There, the Apostle says in the third (chapter of the Letter) to the Ephesians:[4] *Out of Whom every paternity in heaven and earth are named.*

3. Likewise, this very same is shown <u>a simili</u>,° because everything [omne] which belongs to perfection, must be attributed to God, in whom there is the sum [summa] of all perfection; but generation belongs to perfection in a creature, as the Philosopher would have it [vult],[5] because « perfect is that which can generate that which it is »: ergo etc..

4. Likewise, that same is shown *by another reckoning* thus:[6] the Divine Nature is most highly good and most actual: therefore, most highly is it able and does It will to communicate Itself; but the first and most high reckoning of communicating is in generation: therefore, it is necessary to posit generation among the divine.

ON THE CONTRARY: 1. Generation in creatures either belongs to *perfection*, or to *imperfection*. If to *perfection*, then, therefore, since spiritual and incorporeal substances are the most noble, generation ought to be among them: therefore since it is not among them, it does not belong to nobility; but what does not belong to nobility is not in God: ergo etc..

2. Likewise, where there is generation, there is variation; for generation is a species of movement [motus], and among all the species of movement greater is the variation in movement according to substance, because it belongs to a being in potency, less in motion according to place:[7] therefore, since in God there is not a variation nor any species of movement, (so) also that which is the least, as a mutation of place: ergo neither generation.

3. Likewise, where there is generation, there is corruption, whence the Philosopher[8] says, that « on account of their standing-still [stare] far from their Principle, God completed their 'being' [esse] in the last manner [reliquo modo], making generation continuous among them »; and the sign of this manner is, that only corruptibles generate and are generated in creatures; but in God no corruption occurs [cadit]: therefore, neither generation.

4. Likewise, where there is generation, there is[9] nourishing [nutritio]; whence the nutritive force extends itself to all and more than the generative; but in God there not a nutritive force: therefore, neither a generative, therefore, neither nourishing, nor generation: therefore, generation is not among the divine.

---

[1] On the authority of very many manuscripts and edition 1 we have expunged here the added *to be posited* [ponenda].

[2] Codex W adds *thus* [sic].

[3] Verse 9, where the Vulgate in place of *to others* [aliis] puts *to all others* [ceteris] and for *says* [dicit] has *says* [ait].

[4] Verse 15, in which text the Vulgate has *in the heavens* [in caelis] in place of *in heaven* [in caelo]. — A little before this edition 1 reads *through (a consideration of what is) prior* [per prius] for *prior*.

[5] ON THE SOUL, Bk. II, text 34, (ch. 4) and METEOROLOGY, Bk. IV, text 19, (ch. 3).

[6] The Vatican edition together with codex cc omits *thus* [sic], and puts *by that reckoning* [illa ratio] for *by another reckoning* [alia ratione], but the authority of the other manuscripts and edition 1 opposes this.

[7] See Aristotle, PHYSICS, Bk. 5, text 7 ff. and Bk. VIII, text 55 ff (ch. 7).

[8] (Aristotle), ON GENERATION AND CORRUPTION, Bk. II, text 59, according to the Arabic-Latin translation. But in the edition of Paris, ch. 10, it is exhibited thus: But this (to be or to exist) is impossible to be in [inesse] all things, on account of this that they are far distant from the Principle Itself: in the last manner God Himself completed the universe, having made generation continuous. See also ON THE SOUL, Bk. II, text 35, (ch. 4). — The Vatican edition in place of *Philosopher* [Philosophus] puts *Author (of the BOOK) OF CAUSES* [Auctor de causis], but falsely and contrary to all the manuscripts, of which a few, such as H I and O, even indicate the passage by adding *in the book, ON GENERATION AND CORRUPTION* [in libro De Generat. et corruptione], and very many put *the first (being)* [primo] for *the Principle* [principio]. Then not a few codd., such as H T ee and ff, together with edition 1, have *that* [quia] for *that* [quod].

[9] Trusting in the more ancient manuscripts and edition 1 we have inserted *is* [est]. — See Aristotle, ON THE SOUL, Bk. II, text 42 ff., (ch. 4).

---

* *Trans. note*: Here, <u>a minori</u> is shorthand, for *an argument a minori*. Such is the topical syllogism, which arrives at an affirmative conclusion, by means of arguing from what the lesser could do or has, and concluding that the greater can or has likewise. Cf. Pietro Ispano, TRATTATO DI LOGICA, tract, "De locis", trans. A. Ponzio, (Bompiani, Milano, 2004), p. 172-175, n. 32.

° Next, <u>a simili</u>, is shorthand, for *an argument a simili* is a topical syllogism, which arrives at an affirmative conclusion, by means of arguing that, if something can or has such in something, its similar can or has such in the similar of that something. Cf. <u>loc</u>. <u>cit</u>., pp. 174-175, n. 33.

CONCLUSION

Generation is to be posited among the divine,
the congruity and manner of which is explained.

I RESPOND: It must be said, that generation is to
be posited in the Divine 'Being' [in divino esse].[1]

And the strongest [potissima] reason for this is,
as I believe, because every nature is communicable;
and because in God there is, on account of His own
nobility, an aptitude conjoined to action [actui], nay
Action itself, it is necessary [oportet] that the Nature
be communicated to many [pluribus]; but there cannot be many from one Nature, unless [quin] one be
from an other, and/or both from a third: therefore,
since before the Divine Persons there was nothing, it is
proper that One be from an Other. And since They are
conform in Nature, and generation is an emanation
according to the conformity of nature: for that reason
I believe, that it is necessary to posit generation among
the divine.

Moreover, to understand, through which manner,
it must be noted, that *'to generate'* from its own proper
reckoning is to produce (something) similar to one's self
in substance and nature.[2] However, a similar to one's
self happens to be produced in a threefold manner:[3] *ei-*
ther through the impression of its own similitude in an
other; and in this manner there is generated a character
by a seal [sigillo], a light by the luminous, the species
by the object; *in another manner* through drawing out
[eductionem] of a complete similar species from an
other; and in this manner there is generated element
from element; *in a third manner* through the production
of a similar from [de] a similar or from [de] one's very
self; and in this manner there is generated the animate
by the animate; and this third manner is more perfect,
whence it is not found except in substances having the
noble form, which is life.[4] And this manner of generation is according to birth [nascentiam] and is in God
and[5] creatures, but *differently*; because to produce an
other out of one's very self can be in a twofold manner,
out of one's whole self [ex se toto], and/or *out of part of*
oneself [ex parte sui].

Out of one's whole self no one [non] can produce except Him, whose essence can be in many One and
Whole. For, if it cannot be in many one and whole, if
the one generating gives his whole substance to the one
generated, then the whole substance passes over into the
one generated,[6] and the one generating looses [perdit]
(his) whole substance by generating, which cannot be.
For that reason for this it is necessary, that it have such

a substance, which is one and whole in many. Moreover,
there is no [non est] such substance except the Substance
having a most high simplicity; moreover, this is the Divine
Essence alone,[7] in which on account of (its) most high simplicity a Supposit does not add to the Essence, whence it
neither constricts [coartat] it, nor limits (It), nor multiplies
(Its) form. And for that reason in It[8] there can be a generation communicating the same whole Substance; and such
a generation belongs to an omnimodal perfection and is
found in God alone, for the reason just said.

In another manner, it happens that someone produces out of himself as much as regards *part of himself.*
In this manner a natural father generates a son, by trans-
mitting and by letting fall off [decidendo] part of (his)
substance.[9] And this generation is necessarily with a
transmutation; for because a part fallen off [decisa] does
not have the action [actus] of the whole, it is necessary,
that it acquire it through a mutation; but because it acquires what it does not have, it is varied; for that reason
this generation is a mutation and has a conjoined variation. It is also with an adjoined *corruption*; for because
some part of the one generating is lost from it [de-
perditur], there is one generating, from whom an ablation can come to be and thus a corruption. There is also
an adjoined *conservation*;[10] for because a loss [disperdi-
tio] is wrought, it is necessary that through nourishment
[nutrimentum] there be wrought a restoration. And for
that reason generation in a creature belongs both to perfection and to imperfection: to perfection on the part of
the virtue of the one producing, to imperfection on the
part of the divisible subject. And for that reason it is in
animate (creatures) alone, which have the form of perfection, namely[11] the soul itself, and the defectible and
restorable body.

On the other hand, generation among the divine
belongs to an omnimodal perfection. For because[12] it is
not *out of a part*, it is for this reason, that it has *species in*
act [actu speciem]. And for that reason there is in the
Nature neither *imperfection* nor *variation*, because nothing new is acquired; nor *corruption*, because nothing is
taken away [adimitur]; nor a *nourishing*, because nothing[13] is re-established [restituitur].

And, from this, the solution of the objections is
clear; because *generation*[14] *from* [de] *the whole* is of so
great a perfection, that it cannot be in any creature; but
generation out of a part has so great a conjoined imperfection,[15] that it cannot be about an invariable and incorruptible and simple substance, not only in the
uncreated Nature, but also in one created. The other
reasons prove concerning [de] the generation which is
out of a part.

---

[1] From the codices and ed. 1, we have substituted *in the Divine*
'Being' [divino esse] for *among the divine* [in divinis], then, we have supplied
the particle *And* [Et]. Next, after *I believe* codices H & I have *that in the di-*
vine [quia in divinis] and ed. 1 *that of God* [et Dei] for *that every* [quia omnis].

[2] See Aristotle, ON THE SOUL, Bk. II, text 34, (ch. 4); META-
PHYSICS, Bk. VII, texts 22 and 28, (Bk. VI, chs. 7 and 8).

[3] The Vatican edition with codex cc, but disagreeing with the more
ancient mss. and ed. 1, has *However, to produce a similar to one's self in*
nature is in a threefold manner [Sibi vero simili in natura producere tripliciter est] for *However, a similar to one's self happens to be produced in*
a threefold manner [Sibi vero simili contingit produci tripliciter].

[4] Hence generation is also commonly defined in this respect: an origin of a living by a living as by a principle conjoined in a similitude of nature.

[5] Some codices, such as X and Z, repeat here *in* [in].

[6] Codex R has *and is in the one generated* [et est in generato] for
in the one generated [in generatum]. A little after this the error of the Vatican edition, which has *still* [adhuc] in place of *for this* [ad hoc], we have
corrected from the manuscripts.

[7] Edition 1 has *Substance* [substantia]. Then after *Supposit* [sup-
positum] codex R has *adds nothing* [nihil addit] in place of *does not add*
[non addit], and a little below this codex V has *it* [ipsam] at *nor limits*.

[8] Trusting in very many manuscripts and edition 1 we have substituted *It* [ea] for *Him* [eo], which the Vatican edition has.

[9] With the help of very many manuscripts and edition 1 we exhibit
by letting fall off [decidendo] in place of *by cutting off* [descindendo],
which does not correspond so well with the following *fallen off* [decisa].
Then codex T has *on account of transmutability* [causa transmutabili-
tatis] for *with a transmutation*.

[10] Namely: by a conservation taken in the passive sense. — We
have restored the ancient reading of the many manuscripts and of the first
six editions by putting *conservation* [conservatione] in place of *conver-*
sion [conversione]; each reading has the same sense.

[11] Thus the manuscripts together with edition 1, while the Vatican
edition here has *that is* [id est] for *namely ... itself* [ipsam scilicet] and
then *namely ... itself* [ipsum scilicet] about the noun *a body* [corpus].

[12] Agreeing with the manuscripts and edition 1, in this proposition
we have changed *Because* [Quod] into *Because* [Quia] and then *that*
[quia] into *that* [quod].

[13] Edition 1 adds *is restored and/or* [restauratur vel].

[14] Codex bb inserts *which is* [quae est].

[15] The Vatican edition, striving against the manuscripts and edition
1, has *adjoined* [adiunctam].

SCHOLIUM

I. The objections have already been solved in the body (of the reply). In regard to the Angels it is clear, that they can have no generation: not the *imperfect* generation, which is out of *a part*, on account of the simplicity of the angelic substance; not the *perfect*, which is out of *the whole*, because their nature is finite. — In regard to the arguments of congruency, which are here brought forward, having supposed the dogma of the Faith, cf. above d. 2, q. 2; d. 5, q. 2; dub. 2 and 10 of this distinction; BREVILOQUIUM, p. I, ch. 3; HEXAËMERON, Sermon 11. — Alexander of Hales, SUMMA., p. I, q. 42, m. 1 and 2. — (Bl. John Duns) Scotus, SENT., Bk. I, d. 2,

q. 6 and 7. — St. Thomas, SENT., d. 4, q. 1, a. 1; SUMMA., I, q. 27, a. 1 and 2; SUMMA CONTRA GENTILES , Bk. IV, c. 10 and 11. — Bl. (now St.) Albert (the Great)., SENT., Bk. I, d. 4, a. 3; SUMMA., I, tr. 7, q. 30, m. 1. — (Bl.) Peter of Tarentaise, SENT., Bk. I, d. 4, q. 1. — Richard of Middleton, here at a. 1, q. 1. — Giles the Roman, SENT., Bk. I, d. 4, 1st princ., q. 1. — Henry of Ghent, SUMMA., a. 58, q. 1, nn. 8-24. — Durandus (of Saint-Pourçain), SENT., Bk. I, d. 4, q. 1. — (Bl.) Dionysius the Carthusian, SENT., Bk. I, d. 4, q. 1. — (Gabriel) Biel, here in q. 1; d. 10, q. 1, prop. 1.

QUESTION II

Whether generation, among the divine, distinguishes between the One begetting and the One begotten?

Second, there is asked, whether, among the divine, generation is distinctive of the Persons. And that it is, is shown in this manner.

1. (St.) Augustine (says) near the beginning of ON THE TRINITY:[1] « There is no thing, which begets its very self, to be »: if therefore, it does beget, it begets another; but between *one* and an *other* is a distinction: ergo etc.

2. Likewise, generation is an emanation; but where there is emanation, there is multiplication or plurification; moreover where (there is) multiplication, there[2] is distinction: therefore where (there is) generation, there necessarily is distinction.

3. Likewise, generation among the divine is a relation;[3] but relation conveys respect and order; but where (there is) respect and order, there (is) a distinction of supposits and of (things) related or ordered: and thus etc..

4. Likewise, greater[4] diversity is sustained by a supposit and/or in a composed and multiform supposit than in a simple and uniform subject; but opposites do not stand in a relative manner at the same time [insimul] in the same individual created (thing): therefore, neither in a simple hypostasis. *A proof of the middle.* Well does it follow: 'Socrates is the father of Plato: therefore, he is not his son, and/or he is distinct from [ab] him': therefore, much more strongly (does it follow) among the divine.

ON THE CONTRARY: 1. The Father by generating the Son gives to Him the whole (of what He has); but He has an essence and a person: therefore, He gives to Him an essence and a person: therefore just as the Son is not distinguished from [a] the Father essentially, so neither personally, as it seems.

2. Likewise, the Father communicates to the Son His own Essence on account of the[5] most high simplicity; but equally simple is (His) Person as (is His) Essence: therefore, by the reckoning by which He communicates the Essence, He communicates (His) Person.

3. Likewise, in the Father the same (thing) is the Nature and the Person: therefore, it is impossible, that He communicate the One, (and) that He not communicate the Other, therefore, if He gives the Nature, (He) also (gives) the Person.

4. Likewise, it seems that relation does not distinguish by any[7] reckoning, because one and the same point is the beginning and the end in regard to [in respectu] diverse lines: therefore, if those relations are not distinctive, it seems similarly, that neither (are) paternity and filiation. *If you say*, that not all relations distinguish, but only mutual ones, as 'the beginning and the begun', 'the end and the ended'; *on the contrary:*[8] the Father and the Son hold themselves, just as the one understanding and one understood (do), as (St.) Anselm says;[9] but the same can be understanding and understood: ergo etc.

5. Likewise, greater is the repugnance in contraries than in relatives;[10] but whiteness and blackness, which are contraries, do not cause [faciunt] a distinction in [circa] Peter, because the same can now be white, now black: therefore, much more strongly one, among the divine, will not be now Father, now Son.

6. Likewise, *it is asked*, why do relations cause a distinction of person rather than of essence, since there can equally well be more essences and/or natures in one person, as conversely?

---

[1] Book I, d. 1, n. 1. — Near the end of this argument, trusting in many mss. & ed. 1, we have expunged *thing* [rem] after *between one* [inter aliam].

[2] The Vatican edition adjoins an *also* [et].

[3] Codex Y adds *but in creatures action and/or mutation* [in creaturis vero actio vel mutatio].

[4] Many codices, such as A C G K O R S U V Y etc., with the first six edd., have *less* [minor], but faultily. A little below this, from the more ancient mss. and ed. 1, we have substituted *subject* [subiecto] for *substance* [substantia] and *in a relative manner* [relative] for *relative* [relativa]. — The sense of the argument is: A created and composite supposit is capable of sustaining *more* diversity, than the uncreated and simple one; but in a created supposit there is not a capacity to sustain *together* [simul] opposites in a relative manner; therefore, much less so in a simple supposit etc.

[5] In the manuscripts and edition 1 there is lacking the *His* [suam] which the Vatican edition adds here. Then the Vatican ed. with codex cc, contrary to the other codices and edition 1, has *and* [et] for *as* [ut].

[6] We follow the older codices together with edition 1 by putting *(and) that He not* [quod non] in place of *(and) that He not* [quin]. Codex Z more briefly has *the one without the other* [unum sine altero].

[7] Many codices, such as A C L O P Q R S T U V Y etc, together with edition 1 read *another* [alia] in place of *any* [aliqua], but, as is seen, less well, even if under *by another reckoning* [aliqua ratione] you understand the manner of distinguishing proper to relatives, because, as is clear from what follows, it concerns this, that relation does not distinguish simply. Codex Z has *except by a reckoning* [nisi ratione] for *by any reckoning* [aliqua ratione].

[8] Codex Y adds *it seems that neither (do) mutual ones, because* [videtur quod nec mutuae quia]. Then the Vatican edition, together with codex cc, with, however, the others disagreeing, has *as* [ut] for *just as* [sicut].

[9] MONOLOGION, ch. 32, where this is found according to its sense.

[10] Cf. Aristotle, ON PREDICAMENTS, ch. "On Opposites".

CONCLUSION

Against Sabellius it is proved, that generation among the divine causes a real distinction between the One generating and the One begotten; on the other hand against Arius, that this distinction is as much as regards the Person, not as much as regards the Essence.

I RESPOND: It must be said, that generation among the divine, just as has been shown,[1] causes a real distinction between the One generating and the One generated, not only a rational and/or intellectual one, as Sabellius has said; and[2] a real one 'as much as regards *person*', not 'as much as regards *essence*', as Arius has said.

Which is clear in this manner. Generation in creatures means an emanation through a manner of *action* [actionis] or of *mutation* [mutationis], in[3] God (it means) an emanation through a manner of *relation*.

Inasmuch as (it is) an *emanation*, it means *some* distinction; inasmuch as (it is) *such* an emanation, it means a distinction in *person*.[4] By reason of *emanation* there is a *distinction*; because, just as (St.) Anselm says,[5] « neither does understanding [intellectus] grasp, nor does nature permit, that that, which is from [ab] another, be that, from which it is », according to which something is positively said to be from another — for the Father is privatively said to be from Himself, that is, not from another. Inasmuch as (it is) *such* an emanation, it posits a distinction in *person*. For generation is a production of one convening [convenientis] in nature; by reason[6] of the *Nature* there cannot be a distinction: therefore, it shall be by reason of a *supposit*, and/or of a *property*. If of a *property*, either absolutely, or respectively; not *absolutely*, because then there would be a distinction in the Nature; nor[7] respectively, considered [puta] as (belonging) to a relation, because in a relation according to itself there is no movement [non est motus] in creatures[8] nor origin among the divine; whence filiation is not generated except in another. Therefore, it is necessary, that the distinction be in a *supposit*.

Similarly, by reason of *relation* there is a distinction, because nothing is referred or ordered to itself [ad se]. However, by reason of *such* a relation there is a *personal* distinction; because *to generate* and *to be generated*, since they mean relation through a manner of action and passion,[9] mean this [eam] in a supposit and in respect of a supposit. And for that reason, because a relation between extremes notes a distinction, it is clear that the distinction there

belongs to the supposits. With these things seen,[10] it is easy to solve for the objections [ad obiecta].

1. What therefore, is objected: 'the Father communicates to the Son the whole which He has'; is true, except [praeter] generation and the distinction of generation; for the *reckoning of communicating* itself gives one to understand a distinction, because no one communicates to himself, but to another; and for that reason that in which it distinguishes, (the Father)[11] does not communicate.

2. To that which is objected, that a Person is equally simple, as the Essence; it must be said, that there is a simplicity of essence, because it is in Many; but there is a simplicity of supposit, because it is not in[12] Many. For "supposit" or "individual", as much as it is of itself [de se], is said because it is in one alone; for that reason it is not similar.

3. To that which is objected, that the same thing [idem] is the Essence and the Person; it must be said, that although they are the same thing, they are not, however, *for the same thing* [ad idem]: because the Person is for an Other, for that reason (the Other) is generated[13] and is referred; the Essence, on the other hand, not (so), for that reason the Essence is communicated and the Person is distinguished. Just as, therefore, although the same thing in the Father is Essence and Person, however, the Person generates, the Essence (does) not; so conversely the Essence is communicated and the Person is not.

4. To that which is objected of the beginning and end in a point, the response is clear, that those are not *mutual* relations, which properly is required for a distinction; whence it is not valid. What *it objects*[14] concerning *One understanding and One understood*, I say that there is not a relation there according to '*being*' [secundum esse], but according to '*being said*' [secundum dici]. For this, moreover, that a relation distinguishes, it is proper that the relations be mutual, because otherwise they do not distinguish; it is proper also, that they mean a relation according to '*being*' [esse].

5. To that which is objected concerning whiteness and blackness, it must be said, that there is no opposition of forms, except (those) considered[15] in respect of the same time; and it is impossible, that the same subject at the same time be white and black; but relations among the divine are simultaneous [simul].

6. To that which is last *asked*, why relations cause[16] a distinction in persons rather than in an essence; the response is clear from what has already been said. Any relation can also be returned [reddi], because a plurality of natures impedes

---

[1] Here in the fundament (n. 1).

[2] The Vatican edition, contrary to the manuscripts and the first six editions, has *but* [sed] in place of *and* [et], and a little after this *says* [dicit] for *said* [dixit]. Codex M has *accidental* [accidentalem] in place of *intellectual* [intellectualem].

[3] Codex bb adds *but* [autem].

[4] This outstanding emendation we own to the more ancient manuscripts and edition 1, while the Vatican edition omits the words *inasmuch as* [in quantum] up to *By reason* [Ratione], having changed also the punctuation. Not a few codices have *but inasmuch as such* [in quantum autem talis].

[5] ON THE PROCESSION OF THE HOLY SPIRIT, ch. 3: Indeed neither does nature permit, nor does understanding [intellectus] grasp, that one existing from [de] anything be from that which it exists, or from that which exists that there be one existing from itself. — Cf. also MONOLOGION, ch. 38.

[6] The Vatican edition, contrary to the manuscripts and the first six editions adds *therefore* [igitur], for which codices aa and bb incongruously put *for* [enim].

[7] Edition 1 has *not* [non].

[8] See Aristotle, PHYSICS, Bk. V, text 10, (ch. 2).

[9] Very many codices together with edition 1 omit *and passion* [et

passionis], which also twice instead of the plural put the singular *mean* [dicat] and *mean* [dicit]. — Cf. Aristotle, METAPHYSICS, Bk. V, text 20, (Bk. IV, ch. 15), where there are brought forward three species of relation, among which is *action and passion*.

[10] The Vatican edition, together with a few of the codices, incongruously and contrary to the other codices and edition 1, here adds *it is clear* [patet], and then omits *is* [est]. Not a few codices have *respond* [respondere] for *solve* [solvere].

[11] Supply: Father. — Codex R and edition 1 have more clearly *is distinguished* [distinguitur] for *distinguishes* [distinguit]. A little before this codex N reads *to his very self* [sibi ipsi] for *to himself* [sibi].

[12] Many codices, such as B D E S V X Y Z aa bb together with edition 1, have *out of* [ex] in place of *in* [in], but falsely, as is clear from the context. Then after *is said* [dicitur], trusting in the more ancient manuscripts and edition 1 we have expunged *to be* [esse].

[13] The Vatican edition, without the authority of the manuscripts and of the first six edition has *generates* [generat].

[14] The Vatican edition, contrary to the testimony of [praeter fidem] the manuscripts and editions 1, 2, 3, 6 has *is objected* [obiicitur]. Codex Y prefaces *And* [Et] to the relative *What* [Quod].

[15] Codex R adjoins *according to the same thing* [secundum idem].

[16] Codex Y read in the subjunctive: *cause* [faciant].

the simplicity of a person, but not so conversely. Which is thus clear: if[1] there are many natures in one person, either, therefore, (they are) through grace, or through nature. If through the *grace of union*, thus — because the united nature follows after [consequitur] the unity of the Person — it does not impede (simplicity);[2] but if *naturally*, as in *Peter*, there is a plurality of essences or of natures, then

— since the understanding [intellectus] of nature precedes the person, and (since) a nature is not out of persons, but a person out of natures[3] — it is necessary, that the person be composite; and hence it is, that among the divine there is a unity of Nature with a plurality of Persons, rather than the other way around [magis quam e converso].

SCHOLIUM

I. The two heresies of Sabellius and Arius reproved by the Nicene Creed and the other decrees of the Church, are refuted by the twofold conclusion of the proposition.

In regard to the distinctions of relation in the solution to n. 4, it must be noted, that relatives according to a *being said* [secundum dici] are those, which in the principal (thing) signified, do not convey a relation, but something absolute, which, however, secondarily involve a relation to an other, as a science to its object, i. e. the knowable; thus Brülifer on this passage. And/or more clearly with (Pd. Antoine) Goudin (O.P. 1635-1695 A.D.), PHILOS. LOGICA MAIOR., p. I, disp. 2, q. 4: « A relation according to a *being said* [secundum dici] is not something purely relative, but a *certain absolute* thing, *to which is consequent a habitude toward an other* [habitudo ad aliam], to such an extent

that it cannot be expressed, and that habitude also be not expressed ... in the same manner as a part, even though it be something absolute, it, yet, includes a habitude toward the whole, as a science (does) to (its) object ». What is a *mutual* relation, does not need explaining. See more below at d. 30, q. 3, in the Scholium.

II. Cf. above in d. 5, throughout. — (Bl. John Duns) Scotus, d. 11, a. 2; d. 26, q. sole. — St. Thomas, here at q. 1, a. 1; SUMMA., I, q. 28, a. 1 and 3; SUMMA CONTRA GENTILES , IV, c. 14. — Bl. (now St.) Albert (the Great), SENT., Bk. I, d. 26, a. 7; d. 9, a. 4. — (Bl.) Peter of Tarentaise, here at q. 1, a. 1. — Richard of Middleton, here at a. 1, q. 2. — Giles the Roman, here at 1. princ., q. 1 and 2. — Durandus (of Saint-Pourçain), here at q. 1. — (Bl.) Dionysius the Carthusian, here at q. sole.

QUESTION III

Whether generation, among the divine, is eternal?

Third, there is asked, whether divine generation is eternal. And that it is [sic], is shown in this manner.

1. In creatures the one working naturally works as swiftly as it can, and it concerns [est de] the perfection of an agent, that it can work in the swiftest manner:[4] therefore, since the production of the Son by the Father is through (His) Nature and most high Potency, as soon as He *was*, the Father *begot*; but He was from eternity: ergo etc..

2. Likewise, it concerns the perfection of generation, that what is generated be equated to the one generated:[5] therefore, since divine generation is the most perfect, the Son will be equal to the Father in all things [per omnia]; but the Father is infinite in duration: therefore, also the Son.

3. Likewise, a coeternal self-understanding [intelligere se coaeternum] belongs to the Divine Mind; for never is it posited, that from One not understanding [de non intelligente] God became One understanding [intelligens]; but a word is coeternal to the mind understanding it; for from this, that the mind understands itself, it begets a word. If, therefore, the Son is most properly a word, He is coeternal to the Father; and this is what blessed John says:[6] *In the beginning was the Word*.

4. Likewise, this[7] same (thing) is shown *through the impossible*. Everything which begins to be [coepit esse], has been changed according to

substance; but everything which begins [incipit] to be generated, begins to be [incipit esse]: therefore, everything which begins to be generated, has been changed according to substance; but generation[8] concerns the substance of the one generating: therefore, where generation has begun to be, the substance of the one generating is changed; but the substance of God the Father according to 'being' [secundum esse] is immutable: therefore, generation does not begin among the divine.

ON THE CONTRARY: 1. Just as corruption holds itself to '*not*[9] *being*' [non esse] on part of its end, in the same manner generation on the part of its beginning [principii]; but everything which is corrupted, has ceased to be [desinit esse]: therefore everything which is generated, begins to be; but nothing such is eternal: ergo etc..

2. Likewise, whatever produces the Divine Essence is posterior in time, or in duration, to it[10]: therefore, by an equal reason whatever produces a Divine Person, since the Essence and the Person are the same (thing).

3. Likewise, in God the same (thing) is His own 'being' [esse] and His own duration; but the Son has a beginning of being [principium essendi]: therefore, He has a beginning of duration: but what has a beginning of enduring [durandi][11] begins to be: ergo etc..

---

[1] The Vatican edition omits *if* [si], which a few codices, such as E X Z well add, since the argument is from a supposition. Then, codex E has *the same* [eadem] for *one* [una].

[2] Codex X adds *simplicity* [simiplicitatem].

[3] Very many codices, having changed the punctuation, together with edition 1, have at the end of this clause *thus* [sic] for *is* [sit], codex Y has *is* [est]; a little above this very many codices have the indicative *when ... precedes* [cum ... praecedit] for *since ... precedes* [cum ... praecedat]. We, however, prefer the reading of cod. I and ed. 1 on account of the congruity of the grammatical construction. Cod. I after *persons* [personis] adds *is established* [constat]. The Vatican ed., contrary to the older codd. and ed. 1, wrongly has *a nature* [natura] for *natures* [naturis].

[4] See Aristotle, METAPHYSICS, Bk. IX, text 10 (Bk. VIII, ch. 5). — A little below this edition 1 repeats *through* [per] after *and* [et], and codex T after *begot* [genuit] adds *the Son* [Filium].

[5] Aristotle, METEOROLOGY, Bk. IV, text 19 (ch. 3) says: That it is perfect on account that it can produce such as it is itself. See also, ON THE SOUL, Bk. II, text 34 (ch. 4).

[6] Jn 1:1.

[7] From the more ancient manuscripts and edition 1 we have supplied *this* [hoc]. — On this and the following argument, see Aristotle, PHYSICS, Bk. V, text 7; ON GENERATION AND CORRUPTION, Bk. I, texts 11-23 (ch. 3), and ON THE SOUL, Bk. II, text 34 ff. (ch. 4).

[8] Codex T has *He has been generated from* [generatus est de] for *generation concerns* [generatio est de], and then *if* [si] for *where* [ubi].

[9] Codex O omits *not* [non].

[10] Trusting in many manuscripts, such as H K Y bb and edition 1, we have replaced the dative referring to the Divine Nature, *to it* [ipsi] with the ablative *to it* [ipsa].

[11] We prefer the reading of not a few manuscripts, such as M P Q, which put *of enduring* [durandi] in place of *of being* [essendi], because in this both the progress and the force of the argument is rendered more distinct. Codex H and edition 1 put *of duration* [durationis]; cod. O however, *of being and of duration* [essendi et durationis].

4. Likewise, the Father lacks a principle [principium] and lacks a beginning [initio]: therefore, by that reckoning by which He communicates to the Son not to have a beginning [initium], by the same reckoning He communicates to Him not to have a principle; or if not this, neither that.

CONCLUSION

Generation among the divine is eternal on account of the most high fecundity of the One generating and the most high equality of the One begotten, and the most high actuality of each.

I RESPOND: It must be said, that the generation of the Son is eternal both by reason of the *One generating*, and by reason of the *One begotten*: by reason of the *One generating* on account of (His) most high and perfect fecundity, by reason of the *One begotten* on account of (His) most high and perfect equality; each condition of which prevents [tollit], that the Son be in a posterior manner[1] to the Father, just as has been seen in the objection [in opponendo]. *Another* reason is on account of the most high actuality in *each*, in which act does not distance itself [distat] from potency, nor does 'to be able' antecede 'to be'.

1. To that which is objected, that corruption posits a final terminus; it must be said, that corruption always means a variation and mutation, and thus a conversion of a being [entis] into 'not being' [non esse]; and for that reason it posits a final terminus. But generation sometimes means a mutation,[2] as in creatures, and in this manner it does posit an initial terminus; but among the divine it does not mean a mutation out of a non-being [non-ente], but an emanation by a being [ab ente].

2. To that which is objected, that the Essence produces nothing except out of time; it must be said, that just as Person produces another Person, so the Essence another Essence.

But it does not produce another Essence[3] out of itself, since it is incapable of being multiplied [immultiplicabilis], nor out of an other, because similarly there would be the asking, whence it produces that other; and so it is necessary in the first production of a creature, that It produce it out of nothing [ex nihilo]; and everything produced in this manner has a 'to be' after a 'not to be', and thus a beginning [initium]. Moreover, a Person produces a Person not from nothing [non de nihilo]; and for that reason It does not make from One not being a Being [de non ente ens], and for that reason such a production posits no beginning [initium].

3. To that which is objected, that the Son has a beginning of being [principium essendi]; it must be said, that *principium* is said in a twofold manner,[4] namely an *original* one and an *initial* one. According to which *principium* is said *originally*, in this manner the Son both as much as regards 'being' [esse], as regards duration has a principle, because He has each from the Other. But if *principium* is said to be a "*beginning*" [initium],[5] in this manner I say, that He neither has a beginning of being nor of enduring [principium essendi nec durandi]. The first (sense of the word) *principium* does not take away the reckoning of the eternal, but the second one does.

4. To that which is objected[6] last, why does the Father communicate to the Son a lack of a beginning [carentiam initii], (but) not of a principle; the response is already clear: because the *temporal* and the *eternal* of necessity differ through essence, (but) a *principle* and '*that which depends upon a principle*' [principiatum] not so; for that reason of this and that (the argument) is not similar. Therefore, because what has a beginning [initium] is temporal, what lacks it[7] is eternal; for that reason since the Father and the Son are of the One Essence, it is clear etc.. *Again*, since 'to have a principle' and 'to not have one' mean[8] a difference of Person, and there is this (difference) between the Father and the Son; for that reason just as the Father does not communicate (His) Person to the Son, but only (His) Nature or Essence, so He communicates to Him '*to not have a beginning*', but He does not communicate '*to not have a principle*'.

SCHOLIUM

I. The conclusion is *de fide*, defined at Nicea against the Arians. — The reasons in favor of the conclusion, brought forward briefly in the Response, are explained in argument 1 and 2 in the fundament. — In regard to *eternity*, cf. below d. 31, a. 1, q. 3, and SENT. Bk. IV, d. 3, p. II, a. 3, q. 1, at n. 1; SENT., Bk. I, d. 40, q. 2, q. 1, at n. 4; d. 41, a. 2, q. 1, at n. 4.

II. In regard to the conclusion: (Bl. John Duns) Scotus, here (in his Commentary) and in (his) REPORTATIO, q. sole. —

St. Thomas, here at q. 2, a. 1; SUMMA., I, q. 42, a. 2; SUMMA CONTRA GENTILES, IV, c. 11. — Bl. (now St.) Albert (the Great), here at a. 5, 6 and 7. — (Bl.) Peter of Tarentaise, here at q. 3, a. 1. — Richard of Middleton, here at a. 2, q. 1. — Giles the Roman, here 2nd princ., q. 1. — Henry of Ghent, SUMMA., a. 58, q. 1, n. 22 and 23. — Durandus (of Saint-Pourçain), here at q. 2. — (Bl.) Dionysius the Carthusian, on this and the following, here at the question sole. — (Gabriel) Biel, here at q. 3.

QUESTION III

Whether generation, among the divine, is eternal?

Fourth and last, there is asked, whether of the Son has been terminated. And it seems that (it is) so:

1. (St.) Augustine (says) in the book, OF EIGHTY-

THREE QUESTIONS:[9] « Who is always being born [nascitur], has never been born, and through this there is never a son ». No one, therefore, through generation is to be called a son, until the generation

---

[1] Edition 1 reads *be posterior to the Father* [sit poterior Patre].

[2] Codex bb adds *out of one not being* [ex non ente], which corresponds with what is subjoined.

[3] We offer the reading of the more ancient manuscripts and ed. 1, which is more elegant than the reading of the Vatican ed., *But the Essence does not produce another Nature* [Aliam autem naturam essentia]. The Vatican ed., also a little below this, exhibits less distinctly *immutable* [immutabilis] in place of *incapable of being multiplied* [immultiplicabilis]; with the Vatican ed. codex cc consents, except for this, that for *nature* [Naturam] it puts *creature* [creaturam]. Then codex R has *do you produce even* [produce et] in place of *does it produce* [producit].

[4] The Vatican edition less well, contrary to the manuscripts and edition 1, has *a twofold principle is meant* [principium dicitur duplex]. — For more on the notion of *principle* see below in d. 29, a. 1, q. 1 and 2.

[5] Codex bb has *initially* [initialiter].

[6] Not a few codd., such as F H & K, together with edition 1, have *is asked* [quaeritur].

[7] Codex Y adds *it* [eo].

[8] The Vatican edition, not trusting in the manuscripts and the three first editions, has *means* [dicat].

[9] Question 37: Who is always being born, has not yet been born; and he never has been born or will have been born, if he is always being born. For it

has been terminated; but the Word of the Father is rightly said to be the perfect Son: therefore, His generation has been terminated.

2. Likewise, it is shown *by reason* thus: *"to be produced"* is terminated at the *"to have been produced"*, therefore, *"to be generated"* at the *"to have been generated"*; but the Son of God has been generated and born: therefore, His production or generation has been terminated.

3. Likewise, it is more noble *to have been generated* than *to be generated*, because "to be generated" is a way toward "to have been generated", and not conversely; but what is more noble must be attributed to God: therefore, "to have been generated" out to be attributed to Him rather than *"to be generated"*: therefore, the generation of the Son is meant in (its) termination.

4. Likewise, in[1] a generation, which is always in one to be generated [generando], something and/or someone is always being produced [producitur]; but that which has been produced is not produced, according to that which has been produced: therefore, it is proper, that it be repeated [iteretur], and/or that the one generated succeed in such a generation; but in the Son of God there is neither succession nor iteration:[2] therefore, neither a continuous generation: therefore, the generation of the Son of God has been terminated.

ON THE CONTRARY: 1. (St. John) Damascene (says):[3] « God, a being [ens] both infinitely and without time, infinitely and in a restless manner [inquiescibiliter] generates »: therefore, the generation is never terminated.

2. Likewise, it seems that this same (argument) can be shown by *reason*. The Eternal does not hold Himself, now, otherwise than before, but always in an entirely uniform manner [omnino uniformiter]: therefore, if the Father from the beginning [a principio] generates,[4] He is still generating [generat]; otherwise He would hold Himself, now, in another manner than before, and thus the eternal generation would be changed.

3. Likewise, the simple[5] and the infinite lack every terminus; but the generation of the Son is simple and infinite: therefore, the generation of the Son lacks every terminus. That it be infinite, it is clear, because the Son is infinite, and again that generation is eternal, and the eternal is infinite in duration.

4. Likewise, more perfect is the potency always conjoined to act, than that which is not always: therefore, more

perfect is the fecundity always conjoined to the act of generation, most of all since the fecundity of generating is not lost, but is accomplished [perficiatur]:[6] if therefore, in God there is a perfect fecundity, He therefore, always generates; but He does not generate an other except the Son: therefore, the Son is always being generated [generatur].

CONCLUSION

The Divine Generation must be said to be "terminated", insofar as this word excludes imperfection, but not terminated, insofar as it excludes duration.

I RESPOND: For an understanding of the aforesaid it must be noted, that there are *certain things* [quaedam], in which it is the same '*to be*' [esse] and '*to have been made*' [factum esse], and yet (in which) '*to be made*' [fieri] and '*to be*' differ, as are those, whose '*to be*' is permanent and does not depend entirely on a producing principle,[7] nay they have some reason to subsist within themselves, either through their own principles or (those) of (their) subject, such as substances and innate accidents. There are *certain things*, in which '*to be*' and '*to have been made*' differ, however, (in which) it is the same '*to be made*' and '*to be*', as are successives, whose '*to be*' depends entirely on a producing principle existing in its actuality, as are movements and changes. There are *certain things*, in which it is the same '*to be made*' and '*to be*' and '*to have been made*', as are those, which have a permanent '*to be*' and (which) totally depend on a producing principle, existing in its actuality through the same mode [modum], through which (it) in the beginning [in principio],[8] not only in itself, but also in respect of the product (existed), such that a completely similar mode of actuality is attained as much as regards both; and such are influences, either corporal or spiritual. Whence St. Augustine in the eighth (book) of ON A LITERAL EXPOSITION OF GENESIS[9] says, that a light is always born and, while it is being born, it is, whence the air has been illumined and always is being illumined. Similarly, he says[10] entirely (the same thing) of the spiritual light, which is grace.

If, therefore, the Son of God has a most permanent '*to be*'

---

is one (thing) to be born, another to have been born. And through this ever (would there be) a Son, if He (had) never been born. — Then codex I has *Never* [Nunquam] for *No one* [Nullus], and codex S *for* [enim] for *therefore* [ergo].

[1] Trusting in many codices, such as B F H P Q Y, and edition 1 we have supplied *in* [in]; which reading is confirmed also from this, that below in the solution of this objection all the codices together with the Vatican edition, exhibit the preposition *in* [in]. Very many codices, such as A G K S T V Y Z falsely have the nominative *a generation of a nature* [generatio naturae] in place of the ablative *a generation* [generatione]; a few, such as F X, together with edition 1 have the ablative *a generation of nature* [generatione naturae].

[2] The Vatican edition together with codex cc adjoins *there* [ibi], which is well lacking in the other manuscripts and edition.

[3] ON THE ORTHODOX FAITH, Bk. I, ch. 8: For God, as one who is not subject [subsit] to time or beginning [principium], is free from [vacat] passion and from every flowing [fluxione] and is incorporeal and alone free [liber] from destruction, thus also begets beyond time and beginning [principium] and passion and flowing and without any congress, and His incomprehensible generation has neither start [initium] for end.

[4] Codex M adds *the Son* [Filium]. Then one or the other codex together with edition 1 has *has generated* [generavit] in place of *generates* [generat].

[5] The reading of very many codices, such as H I P Q ee ff, and edition 1, in which here an a little below this there is put *simply* [simpliciter] for *simple and*, is good enough.

[6] The Vatican edition, disagreeing with the manuscripts and edition 1, reads in the indicative *lost, but is accomplished* [perditur, sed perficitur].

[7] In the Vatican edition and codex cc there is here added *and this as one proximate producing the ' to be' in the one made* [et hoc proximo producente in facto esse], which however, is absent in the other manuscripts and edition 1 and seems superfluous, because this member of the distinction is explained by means of the other two sufficiently and better. A little below this the Vatican edition together with codex cc, however, striving against the other codices and edition 1, after *their own principles* [principia propria] has *their own* [sui] in place of *either* [sive], but not well. Then from the manuscripts and edition 1 we have substituted *substances* [substantiae] in place of *substance* [substantia].

[8] Understand: at the beginning of the production. The sense is: the mode of actuality of the principle producing in such a manner is the same in the beginning or start and in the continuation of the production, both in itself as in regard to the product; just as, for the sake of example, is the actuality of the sun illumining and of a light and/or the air illumined. The Vatican edition falsely and contrary to the more ancient codices and edition 1 adds *they are* [sunt] after *through which* [per quem].

[9] Chapter 12, n. 26: For, as we were saying, and not just as a man works the earth ... does God thus work the just man, that is by justifying him, so that if He separated Himself, there remains in the one separated, what He wrought; but more ably just as the air, with a light present, has not been made lucid, but is being made such, because if it had been made lucid, it would not be made such, (and) also would remain lucid with the light absenting itself; thus man is illumined with God present to himself, but with Him absent is immediately put in the shadows [tenebratur].

[10] See the text just cited. — The Vatican edition together with codex cc, but with the others and edition 1 resisting, has *it must be said* [dicendum] for *he says* [dicit].

and a 'to be' most conjoined with His productive Principle, as in one existing in its actuality, because the Son Himself is the Pure[1] Act; it is entirely the same in Him 'to be born' and 'to have been born'; and for that reason He is always being born and always has been born and always is, nor does He ever desist nor cease to be generated, nor does the Father (cease) to generate (Him).

When, therefore, it is it asked, whether the generation of the Son be *terminated*, it must be distinguished, that *terminated* either excludes *imperfection*; and in this manner the generation of the Son has been terminated, because (it is) perfect, since they are simultaneous,[2] nay (for Him) it is the same '*to be generated*' and '*to have been generated*'. But if it excludes *duration*, it is false, because it always endures [durat].

I concede, therefore, that the generation of the Son has not been terminated [est interminata] by reason of desisting [desitionis], because He never desists from being generated, just as the reasons adduced for the second part prove.

1. To that[3] which is objected unto the contrary, that who is always being born never has been born; it must be said, that it is true in that generation, in which

'*to be born*' and '*to have been born*' differ; but the divine generation is not such. But yet, because divine generation is understood through created generation, and in creatures "*to be born*" is not said of a perfectly born, but "to have been born" (is): for that reason (St.) Augustine wants,[4] that the Son is said better "*to have been born*", because it is more intelligible, not because it is not fitting [conveniat] for Him "*to be born*".

2. 3. To that which is objected, that "to be produced" is terminated at "to have been produced", and *similarly*, (that) it is more noble 'to have been generated' than 'to be generated'; it must be said, that all these (reasons) only have a place there, where 'to be generated' and 'to have been generated' differ. But in that[5] generation they do not have a place.

4. To that which is last objected, in a generation, which is always in the one to be generated etc.; it must be solved through interemption; for it is not true, that a generation always-being [generation semper ens][6] always produces something anew [de novo], because a ray is always arising from the Sun, and yet it is not always being iterated [iteratur] nor does it succeed, but it continued in (its) 'being' [in esse] by its own origin.

SCHOLIUM

I. In the preceding question it was proved, that the generation of the Son does not have a *beginning* [initium]; here it is asked, whether it has a *terminus*, or whether it has been terminated. And since the word *terminated* has a twofold sense, insofar as it excludes either imperfection or duration, this question is resolved also with a twofold conclusion. — The threefold distinction in the beginning of the response is notable enough.

II. On this question cf. here Doubt 8. — Alexander of Hales, SUMMA., p. I, q. 42, m. 5, a. 2. — (Bl. John Duns) Scotus, here at q. sole, n. 3. — St. Thomas, here at q. 2, a. 2; SUMMA., I, q. 42, a. 2, n. 4. — Bl. (now St.) Albert (the Great), here at a. 19; SUMMA., p. I, tr. 7, q. 30, m. 4, part. 1. — (Bl.) Peter of Tarentaise, here at q. 4, a. 1 and 2. — Richard of Middleton, here at a. 2, q. 2; a. 3, q. 1 and 2. — Giles the Roman, here at 2nd princ., q. 3. — Henry of Ghent, SUMMA., a. 54, q. 3, n. 70. — Durandus (of Saint-Pourçain), here at q. 4.

DOUBTS ON THE TEXT OF THE MASTER

DOUBT I

In this part there occurs doubts concerning the text (of Master Peter), and first there is a doubt concerning this which he says: *One thing is not the Father, another thing the Son, another thing the Holy Spirit, although personally* etc.. For it seems that what is said (is) false, because there rightly [bene] follows: 'Peter is a white man, therefore, he is a white animal', because "white" [albus] and "white" [album] signifies the same (thing): therefore, for a equal reason, because *another one* [alius] and *another thing* [aliud] signifies[7] the same (thing), there follows: it is *another one* [alius], therefore, it is *another being* [aliud ens]. *If you say*, that it is not similar concerning this noun *another one* [alius] and concerning this noun *a being* [ens];[8] *on the contrary*: there rightly follows: he is another man, therefore, he is another animal: therefore, by similar (reasoning) it does follow.

I RESPOND: It must be said, that because in God there is a singular anotherness [singularis alietas], because *anotherness belongs to a supposit* with an omnimodal *unity of nature*: for that reason it is proper that it be expressed in a singular manner. And since the masculine genus conveys [importat] a certain distinction and/or discretion,[9] for that reason it respects a person; but the neuter on account of (its) indistinction respects the nature: and for that reason "*another one*" [alius] conveys *anotherness* in person, "*another thing*" [aliud] (an anotherness)[10] in nature, and for that reason among the divine they do not signify the same (thing).

It could also be said, that in creatures it signifies one thing,[11] when I say: this is *other* [alius] than that, and another, when I say: *it is another thing* [aliud]; and one follows after the other. Not so among the divine: and it is not similar concerning (something) white, because white is imposed by a special form, which is whiteness.

---

[1] Thus the older manuscripts and edition 1, while the Vatican edition together with codex cc has *He Himself is the Son and the Pure* [ipse est Filius et purus]. A little before this one or the other codices, such as P and Q, together with edition 1 has *its own* [sua] in place of *its* [sui].

[2] The reading of the Vatican edition, *similar* [simile] in place of *are simultaneous* [simul sint] is corrected from the mss. and edition 1.

[3] Edition 1 adds *therefore* [ergo].

[4] See words of (St.) Augustine above in the objection itself. — Then edition 1 has *be said* [dicatur] in place of *is said* [dicitur].

[5] The Vatican edition, contrary to the mss., has *that ... of His* [ista].

[6] That is, what is always. A little below this after *and yet it is not always* [nec tamen semper] the Vatican edition by explaining adds *its generation* [eius generatio], which is lacking in the mss. and edition 1.

[7] The Vatican edition, contrary to the manuscripts and edition 1, here and a little after this has *signify* [significant].

[8] The Vatican edition, not trusting in the testimony of the manuscripts and the first six editions, has *another being* [aliud ens].

[9] The more ancient codices do not agree among themselves; for some, such as T and W, together with edition 1, omit *distinction and/or* [distinctionem vel], but others, such as A F G H I K S V X Y Z etc. *and/or discretion* [vel discretionem].

[10] The Vatican edition repeats here *anotherness* [alietatem], which is lacking in the manuscripts and edition 1.

[11] Edition 1 has *is signified* [significatur] and a little after this *follows completely* [consequitur] in place of *follows* [sequitur]. — For more on this subject see above d. 4, q. 2.

DOUBT II

Likewise, there is a doubt, second, concerning this which he says: *Coeternal to Themselves are the Three Persons*. It seems false, because if coeternal, also[1] eternal: therefore three Eternals, which is contrary to the (Athanasian) *Creed*, where it says: *Not three eternals*; and again, (it is) contrary to *reason*, because a plural number multiplies form. Whence it is not truly said: The Three are gods.

I RESPOND: It must be said, that a noun [nomen] signifying *substance* is found among the divine in a threefold manner. For *a certain* (noun) signifies[2] substance and through the manner of a substance, as a substantive noun [nomen substantivum], such as "God"; and such is in no manner plurified nor is said in a plural manner, whether it is a substantive, or has been made a substantive [substantivatum], such as[3] this noun "*the Eternal One*" [aeternus]; thus it is accepted in the Creed. *Certain* (nouns) signify substance through a manner of adjacency, just as adjectival nouns retained in the manner of an adjective [adiective retenta];[4] and such, because they draw (their) number from substantives, are said in a plural manner, and of the genus of such are verbs and participles. There are *other* names, which convey [important] substance in adjacents, by connoting within a mutual relation, such are *coeternals*;[5] and such can be said in a plural manner from a twofold cause, both by a reckoning of *consignification* or of a manner of signifying, as by a reckoning of *connotation*. And in this manner it is clear, that there is no contradiction.

Moreover, what[6] is objected, that a plural number plurifies form; it must be said, that this is not true in adjectives.[7]

DOUBT III

Who says this, does not understand, that to have been born etc.. Here Master (Peter) posits four reasons demonstrating, that the Son is coeternal to the Father, and that thus (this) argument of Arius is not valid [non valere]:[8] 'The Son has been born, therefore, He is not eternal'.

The first has been taken a simili and is such: 'the splendor is of the same duration with the fire or equal (to it), and yet it has been generated by the fire: therefore, much more strongly, since the Son is the Splendor of the Father,[9] though He is generated by Him, He will be coeternal to Him': therefore, the conclusion of the aforesaid reckoning is false, and that consequence is to be overturned [est interimenda]: 'if He has been born, there was a when He was not'. *But on the contrary*: If an emanation proceeding from [a] God is coeternal to Him, just as an emanation proceeding from [a] a creature is equally-coeval [coaequaeva]:[10] therefore, since things have come forth from [a] God, it seems that (they have done so) from eternity.

I RESPOND: It must be said, that the egress of splendor[11] from light and/or fire is a connatural egress; and such is the egress of the Son from [a] the Father, but not the egress of a creature from [a] the Creator, nay (this latter) is voluntary; and the argument is good in regard to the proposed.

Likewise, "If the Son of God," says (St.) Augustine, *"(is) the virtue and wisdom"*. This is (St.) Augustine's second reason: the Son is God's virtue and wisdom: therefore, if He is not eternal, God was at some time without virtue and wisdom; and this is impossible; ergo etc.. *But contrary* to this reason it is objected thus: for if it followed: if the Father does not have a begotten wisdom, He is not wise, it seems that He is wise by a begotten wisdom, which (St.) Augustine expressly denies in the sixth (book) ON THE TRINITY.[12]

I RESPOND: (St.) Augustine disproves [redarguit] that reason in the sixth (book) ON THE TRINITY,[13] showing, that that (reason) proceeds from a bad understanding of the word; and yet, because Master (Peter) adduces it, it can be said, that that reason is valid, not because the Father is wise by the Son [Filio], who is begotten wisdom, but because the Same[14] is the Begotten Wisdom and the Unbegotten; and thus, if one begins [incipit], also the other.

Also to the same question of Arius. This is the third reason which he adduces, and it belongs to (St.) Ambrose, taken from the authority of Isaias: *Before me there is not a God, and after Me there shall not be (one)*: therefore, neither (is) the Father before the Son, nor the Son before the Father. *But on the contrary*: Among the Divine Persons there is an order; but an order is not but of prior to posterior: ergo etc.

I RESPOND: It must be said, that, must as shall be clear below,[15] there is There no order of duration, by which one is prior to the other [alter est prior altero], but an order of origin, by which one is out of the other [alter ex altero].

For in One Another, the Father in the Son and the Son

---

[1] One or another codex, such as P and Q, have *therefore* [ergo] in place of *also* [et].

[2] Thus very many of the more ancient codices, while the Vatican edition together with edition 1 and codex cc reads *For certain (names) signify* [Quaedam enim significant].

[3] The Vatican edition together with codex cc, with changed punctuation, put *and* [et] in place of *such as* [ut]. — By the word *has been made a substantive* [substantivatum] understand an adjective and/or another noun employed in place of a substantive.

[4] In place of the non-congruous term *held* [tenta], we have substituted, with the help of the manuscripts and edition 1, *retained* [retenta]; then with the more ancient manuscripts consenting with edition 1, we have corrected the distorted reading of the Vatican edition and of codex cc by putting *because* [quia] in place of *which* [quae].

[5] Not a few codices, such as H M Y ee, with edition 1, add *and of this kind* [et huiusmodi]. A little after this, trusting in the more ancient manuscripts and edition 1 we have substituted *of consignification* [consignificationis] for *of signification* [significationis], because it exhibits the first reckoning more clearly, that is to the extent that they are adjectives or convey (the notion of) substance in adjacents; the second reckoning is founded in a connotated, mutual relation.

[6] Edition 1 reads *To that which is objected* [Ad illud quod obiicitur]. Then codex dd has *multiplies* [multiplicat] for *plurifies* [plurificat].

[7] Concerning this solution see below d. 24, a. 1, q. 2. Cf. also Alexander of Hales, SUMMA., p. I, q. 49, m. 3. — St. Thomas , here at q. 1, a. 2, and

SUMMA., I, q. 39, a. 3. — Bl. (now St.) Albert (the Great), here at a. 7. — (Bl.) Peter of Tarentaise, here at q. 3, a. 2. — Richard of Middleton, here on the text.

[8] The Vatican edition here adds *which is such* [quod tale est], which words, however, are lacking in the codices and in edition 1. Not a few codices, such as E F I K W Y Z, have *and thus ... is not valid* [et ita ... non valet] for *and that thus ... is not valid* [et ita ... non valere]. then at *therefore, ... not* [ergo non] we have supplied from the manuscripts and edition 1 *He is* [est].

[9] Trusting in the manuscripts and edition 1 we have expunged here the superfluously added *and* [et], and on the contrary a little below this after *consequence* [consequentia] was have inserted *is* [est].

[10] The codices dissent among themselves, for some, such as E F I N U X Z have *coeval* [coaeva] in place of *equally coeval* [coaequaeva], others, such as A G K S T W dd ff, falsely add *coeternal* [coaeterna], just as edition 1 also falsely has *coeval and coeternal*.

[11] The Vatican edition, not trusting in the manuscripts and editions 1, 2, 3, here adds *from the sun* [a sole], and a little below this after *such is* [talis est], contrary to the older codices and edition 1, it has *egression* [egressio] for *egress* [egressus].

[12] Chapter 1, n. 1. See also ibid., Bk. VII, ch. 1, n. 2, and Bk. XV, ch. 7, n. 12.   [13] Chapter 1, n. 2.

[14] Edition 1 adds *wisdom* [sapientia].

[15] Distinction 20, a. 2, q. 1 and 2. — A little below this many codices, such as A F G H I K T V W X etc., have the neuter *prior* [prius] in place of the masculine *prior* [prior].

in the Father is cognized. This is the fourth reason and it is such: relatives are simultaneous by nature;[1] but Father and Son are relatives: therefore, simultaneous; but the Father is eternal: therefore, the Son coeternal. The *proof,* that the Father is eternal: because, if first He was God and afterwards the Father, He has been changed.[2] *But contrary* to this reason of his there can be argued by an equal reason: He was first *God* and afterwards *Lord:* therefore, He has been changed.

I RESPOND: *Some* want to say, that that reason of his is valid, because generation is from [est de] the substance of the one generating; and for that reason if He begins to generate, (His) Substance is changed. But this does not seem (so), because generation among the divine does not mean movement [motum]. *Others* say, that because the One begotten is consubstantial to the One begetting, if the One begotten is changed, also the One begetting; but the One begotten is changed, if He is generated anew [de novo]: therefore, also the One generating as a consequence [per consequens]. The *other* manner of speaking is, that "paternity" means a true habitude in the Father, non so creation and/or domination; and for that reason an adventive paternity [paternitas adveniens][3] does change, not so domination.

But none of the aforesaid reasons[4] gives vigor to this reckoning against the heretics, because the heretic (Arius) said, that the Son was not coeternal, and through this neither consubstantial, nor the same in substance. On this account it must be noted, that the aforesaid reason is good against the heretic, made on supposition of this: that the heretic said that the Father and the Son differed in substance and nature, just as in carnal generation. For an equal reason (St.) Ambrose says against him: since it is thus, that that Father of yours[5] is changed by the accession of generation, who generates an other in substance; similarly among the divine the Father also generates an other in substance: therefore, by the accession of generation He is changed, as[6] that One of yours.

However, in whatever manner it be said, there is no [non] great danger, because not all arguments, which are made for the truth, are necessary.[7]

DOUBT IV

Likewise, is asked concerning this which he says: *The voice is silent: not mine only, but also that of the Angels.* For it seems that he says *that of the Angels* badly, because the voice is not but of those having organs and respiration; but the Angels do not have these. *If you say,* that they have spiritual voices, unspoken [non prolatas], just as (St. John) Damascene says,[8] that they betray to themselves their own understandings spoken [prolatas] without a voice; I ask, what is the necessity of a spiritual voice, and what manner of speaking (is this), and what manner of hearing?

I RESPOND: It must be said here briefly — because as much as it regards this part, this is outside the principal proposed (doubt) — that there is a necessity of speaking [locutionis];[9] because just as to each rational nature there has been given a free will, so (also) a secret conscience. Whence just as no one [non aliquis] can turn the will of another unto (something) else, but only to induce it, if it does not yield itself [se inclinet], besides God alone, in whose Hand are the hearts of men: so no one [nemo] can cognize[10] the conceptions of another, but only conjecture (what they are), besides God, unless the intelligence itself expresses them; and that expression is termed speaking [locutio]. Moreover, the *reason* for this is, that God alone forms the mind both as much as regards the intellect and as much as regards the affection [affectum]; and the manner of speaking [modum loquendi] is similar to the manner of learning something new [modo addiscendi]. For, just as we learn something new through sense, so that the species arrives through the interior sense at the intellect, in the same manner we express; because the word of internal thought [cogitationis internae] is united to the voice[11] in excogitation and after the manner of the sensible voice in pronunciation, and out of this expression it comes to be in act [fit in actu]. But an Angel by a unique virtue does what we do by many. Whence an Angel, just as he cognizes himself as through the application of a species innate to the cognoscible itself, so by ordaining the innate species to another, cognizant Angel, he reveals [aperit] his own concept; similarly the other (Angel) receives a mutual conversion; and in this manner one speaks [loquitur], the other hears. It is similar concerning two mirrors (placed) opposite to one another, if they could voluntarily conceal and offer[12] to others, the things which they reflect in themselves.

DOUBT V

Likewise, is asked concerning this, which he says: *Therefore, let us say more truly, "always born"*; and this is his reckoning, so that the eternal and perfect God be validly designated [valeat designari]. *But against* this is, that among all the tenses [tempora] the present has a greater fittingness [convenientiam] with eternity; because more truly is "*is*" said of God, than "*was*" and "*will be*", just as (St.) Augustine expounds it, as is had [habitum est] in the preceding distinction.[13] And the reason for this is, that the present means a being in act [ens in actu], the other tenses not (so).

---

[1] Aristotle, ON THE PREDICAMENTS, ch. "On Relatives". — Then after *therefore, simultaneous* [ergo simul], trusting in the more ancient manuscripts and edition 1, we have substituted *but* [sed] in place of *if* [si] and *The proof* [Probatio] for *It is proved* [Probatur].

[2] This is the reckoning of (St.) Ambrose, which is had in the text of Master (Peter), ch. 2 at the end.

[3] Trusting in many manuscripts, such as H I K M etc., and edition 1 we have substituted *an adventive* [adveniens] for *a coming* [veniens].

[4] Codex D has *responses* [responsionum]. Then codex Y has *against the heretic* [contra haereticum] for *against the heretics* [contra haereticos]. A little below this in the Vatican edition, contrary to the more ancient codices and edition 1, after *coeternal* [coaeternus] there is added *to the Father* [Patri], and for *neither* [nec] there is had *not* [non], and after *the same* [idem] there is omitted *in* [in].

[5] On the authority of the manuscripts and edition 1, we have deleted here the superfluous *carnal* [carnalis].

[6] The Vatican edition, disagreeing with the manuscripts and editions 1, 2 and 3, has *also* [et] pro *as* [ut].

[7] This doubt is more fully explained here in q. 3.

[8] ON THE ORTHODOX FAITH, Bk. II, ch. 3: But without any spoken speech [prolati sermonis] with mutual help they communicate to themselves their own thoughts [sensa] and counsels.

[9] We follow codices Y and Z, while many together with edition 1 have, but not so well, *that the necessity of speech* [quia necessitas locutionis], but the Vatican edition joining itself with the preceding words reads: *to which the necessity of speaking in the Angels belongs* [quae sit in Angelis necessitas locutionis].

[10] Codex V adds *the thoughts or* [cogitationes seu].

[11] In cod. T, added by a second hand *intelligible* [intelligibili].

[12] Trusting in many manuscripts, such as F H P Q cc dd and ee, we have substituted a good reading *offer* [offerre] for *bear off* [aufferre], in place of which codex Y has *shown* [ostendere] and edition 1 *bring toward* [afferre]. — For more on the speaking of the Angels see SENT., Bk. II, d. 10, a. 3, q. 1.

[13] Part I of the text of Master (Peter), ch. 1 and Doubt 7. — Then from the more ancient manuscripts and edition 1 we have inserted the particle *And* [Et], which a little above this, after *was* [fuit] we have also substituted in place of *or* [aut].

I RESPOND: It must be said, that just as be touched upon above,[1] that verbs of diverse tenses, said of God, do not signify other temporal acts, but convey the duration of the Divine 'To Be' [divini esse] without a beginning, such as (is) the past; without an interval, such as (is) the present; without a terminus, such as (is) the future. And because all these are found in God in a equally true manner; for that reason are all said of Him[2] in an equally true manner.

But, however, because many erred in regard to [in] the Generation as much as regards its beginning [ad initium], few and/or none as much as regards its interval and/or terminus: for that reason the sacred Doctors, to block up the mouths of heretics, expressed it[3] through a verb of the past tense, which always signifies that (something is) past, and, thus, that it never had a beginning [principium].

The other reason is, that we do understand the Divine Generation by a certain being led-by-hand [manuductione] through the generation, which is around us; and because we see in this generation, that one begotten, while he is generated, is imperfect, lest anyone might [posset] believe, that the Son of God be always imperfect,[4] for that reason they decided that He be called the always born.

It must be therefore, said, that as much as it is on the part of the thing, one (thing) is in an equally true and proper manner said, just as the rest. On the other hand, what (St.) Gregory says, he says as much as regards the greater explanation of the Faith, lest error have a place; and in this manner Master (Peter) expounds it.[5] It is fitting, therefore, that one rather say: always born, than He is always generated. Nor is it similar concerning this verb is and was; because this verb is signifies through a manner of rest, and therefore 'being' [esse], while it is, is perfect; but this verb to be generated, in accord with the following determinations [penes haec inferiora], (signifies) through a manner of becoming [fieri]; and[6] because in many this is true, for that reason it is not similar according the reckoning of the intelligence.

DOUBT VI

Likewise, is asked concerning this which he says: I today have begotten Thee, because it can be understood of the day, on which He was born of His Mother [ex matre]; but in this nothing seems to be valid, because according to this generation He did not have a father, but only a mother.[7]

I RESPOND: It must be said, that that verse must be understood causally; for according to the generation from His mother [ex matre] He is said to have been begotten, because (the Father) caused Him to be generated.

The exposition on that (verse) of Matthew (chapter) three is similar:[8] He is able to raise up from those stones sons for Abraham; the Gloss (says): « In testimony of this statement [huius rei] God begot a son from [de] Sara, that is, caused him to be generated ».

DOUBT VII

Likewise, is asked concerning this which Origen says: Moreover, splendor is not born once and stops. On the contrary: if this simile is correct, it seems that the Son is not born once: therefore, it is asked, why is the generation of the Son likened to splendor rather than to other things, most of all since splendor is not generated from light except in the presence of the body of an object [ad praesentiam corporis obiecti]? And besides, the Son is said to be light;[9] therefore, not the splendor of the light.

I RESPOND: It must be said, that the generation of the Son has it itself a perfect conformity, coeternity and equality;[10] and because we cannot find these simultaneously in one creature, for that reason we take them from many, and for that reason we liken many to that one [illi]. Therefore, as much as regards conformity, it is similar to the generation of a word,[11] which is the offspring perfectly representing that, from which it is. As much as regards coeternity, it is similar to the egress of splendor from light [a luce], in which there is coevity,[12] on account of the actuality of light. As much as regards equality (it is) similar to the generation of a living out of a living, which generates an entirely equal[13] to itself; and in this manner it has been compared in various manners by the Saints. Therefore, Origin compares it to the egress of splendor, not as much as regards the likening of a repetition [iterationis assimilationem], but as much as regards the privation of an intermission or of an interpolation.

And note, that splendor, ray and a light [lumen] differ, though all mean an influence from (something) luminous: because ray means an emission according to the diametrical distance; a light [lumen], according to the circumference, each[14] however, into the depth of transparent (space); splendor means a repercussion upon a non-transparent body, cleaned and limited. But Origen, however, here calls splendor a light stepping forward from light [lumen progrediens a luce].

To that, therefore, which is objected, that the Son is light; it must be said, that light has in itself a nature of manifesting; and thus respects cognition and is appropriated to the Son; (and) it has in itself a force of multiplying or of generating splendor; and thus it is appropriated to the Father.[15]

---

[1] In the preceding distinction, in the passage a little above the one cited. Cf. also here q. 4. — Trusting in the older mss. and ed. 1, we have expunged after It must be said [Dicendum] the superfluously added that [quod].

[2] The Vatican edition, contrary to many codices, such as A G I S T V X Z etc. together with edition 1, has of God [de Deo].

[3] The manuscripts together with edition 1 omit

[4] We have restored from the mss. and edition 1 the not well omitted always [semper].

[5] Here in ch. 2.

[6] We have supplied with the help of the manuscripts and the first six editions the particle and [et].

[7] Codex X exhibits the last part of the proposition thus: the generation a father did not beget, but only a mother. Then after It must be said [Dicendum] trusting in the more ancient manuscripts and edition 1 we have inserted that [quod].

[8] Verse 9, in which text the Vulgate there is said God is able [Potens est Deus], and for those [illis] it has those ... of yours [istis].

[9] John 1:9. — In the Vatican edition before besides [praeterea] there is lacking And [Et], which, however, is had in the older mss. and ed. 1.

[10] Codex T has coequality [coaequalitatem].

[11] One or the other [alterque] codex, such as M and Y, add out of a mind [ex mente].

[12] We prefer the reading of a few manuscripts ee, ff and edition 1, coevity [coaevitas] for coeternity [coaeternitas], since it is truer in itself.

[13] Codex W has similar [simile]. A little below this codex V has of a termination [terminationis] in place of of a repetition [iterationis].

[14] In the Vatican edition, which disagrees with the manuscripts and edition 1, there is had on both sides [utrinque], and then of transferring (medium) [transferentis] in place of of transparent (space) [trasparentis]. A little below this, at body [corpus], lead by cod. O we have inserted non, which reading is both self evident and confirmed by the authority of the other authors; Richard of Middleton, SENT., Bk. II, d. 13, q. sole; (Bl.) Peter of Tarentaise, here in q. 4, a. 1, at n. 4 etc.. — On the difference between light, a light, color, cf. below d. 17, p. I, q. 1 in the body of the response.

[15] For more on this similitude taken from splendor see Alexander of Hales, SUMMA., p. I. q. 42, m. 5, a. 3, and all the other authors just cited, and Giles the Roman, here about the text (of Master Peter).

Doubt VIII

Likewise, is asked concerning this which (St.) Hilary says, that *when by the sacrament of His Knowledge He is born.* For it seems according to this, that the Father generates the Son according to a sacrament of knowledge: therefore, knowledge is the reason for generating.

I Respond: It must be said, that (St.) Hilary calls here[1] a *sacrament* a sacred secret; moreover, he says, that the Son is born with a sacrament of knowledge, because the generation of the Son is not only sacred, but also secrete, not, I say, secret to God, but to us, because we comprehend it not; but[2] He Himself perfectly knows it. For that reason he says *with the sacrament* etc..

Doubt IX

Likewise, is asked concerning this which he says: *because a living thing* [vivum] *has been born out of a living thing; it has (something) perfect belonging to its nativity without a newness of nature.* For it seems (to be) false, because a son is born of a living father and a mother, and yet it has each, namely imperfection and newness.

I Respond: The reason of (St.) Hilary, as is clear through text that followed [sequentem],[3] is to be understood of a thing living through (its) *essence;* for where there is one living through (its) essence, one living does not come to be [fit] out of a non-living, just as happens [fit] in one living through *participation,* where there is not generated a living thing out of a living thing, except through a non-living thing, as is clear, because a human is not generated out of a human except by means of semen.

Doubt X

Likewise, is asked concerning this which he says: *And the Nativity is not out of a derivation, but out of virtue.* It seems the contrary, because according to (St.) Dionysius (the Areopagite)[4] and (St.) Anselm, the Father holds Himself to the Son and the Holy Spirit, as a spring, and They (to Him) as rivers; but a river is from [a] a spring through a *derivation.*

I Respond: It must be said, that a nativity, which is through a derivation, is attained as much as regards some transmutation about that which is transmuted, and thus it means a certain passion, and through this infirmity;[5] but One living, because He is life, is pure Act, and thus pure Life, in which there is not infirmity, but pure Actuality; and for that reason (St.) Hilary wants to say, that the Father generating is whole[6] according to life [totus vita], and what He generates is not through the passion and/or demutation [demutationem], which is attained in derivation,

but through an omnimodal virtue: therefore, the Son has been begotten as virtue, not born through a demutation.

Doubt XI

Likewise, is asked concerning this which he says: *Where the Father is author, There, there is also a nativity.* It seems that he speaks improperly,[7] because *authority* means causality; but this is not received among divine things: ergo etc..

I Respond: It must be said, that *authority* means a certain principality or authority in person, which has nothing from another, but all from it; and this authority in the Father is innascibility; whence it does not mean causality, but privation of principle, and through this a most high principality.[8]

Doubt XII

Likewise, is asked concerning this which he says: *On the other hand, because it has been born out of an eternal, on that account, if there is not an eternal born* etc.; and (St.) Hilary hints here at such an argument: if the Son has not been generated or born from an eternal, His generation is not eternal; and if this,[9] (then) the Father does not generated from an eternal: therefore, the Father is not eternal: therefore, who derogates from the eternity of the Son, derogates from the eternity of the Father. *But* this reckoning of his does not seem to be valid, because I may similarly argue on the part of the Creator and creature: if[10] a creature is not eternal, God has not created it from an eternal, and thus there is not an eternal Creator.

I Respond: It must be said, that it is not similar, just as is clear from his following (argument)[11] which (St.) Hilary supposes, that to be the Father is properly proper to that Person: therefore, since such is always fitting [conveniat], either the thing does not otherwise have a perfect 'being' [esse perfectum], there follows from necessity: either the Son is eternal, or the Father from eternity [ab aeterno] does not have a perfect 'being' [esse perfectum]. On the other hand, to create, even if it belongs to God alone, nevertheless by a reckoning of what is connoted [connotati] it has imperfection conjoined (to it), according to which it is not only impossible, but also non-intelligible, that something be created from eternity [ab aeterno].[12]

Doubt XIII

Likewise, is asked concerning this which he says: *But to demutate one's very self by being born;* because according to this, since the Son of God was born before, and afterwards was born of the Virgin:[13] therefore, He would have changed [esset mutatus].

---

[1] The Vatican edition, contrary to very many codices and edition 1, less well has *this* [hoc].

[2] Some codices, such as A I T Z bb and cc, have *form* [enim]; edition 1 has *however* [vero].

[3] Which words of (St.) Hilary are found in the text of Master (Peter), ch. 4, after the middle. — Then very many codices, such as F H I T X Y Z etc., together with edition 1, have *is understood* [intelligitur] in place of *is to be understood* [intelligenda est].

[4] On the Divine Names, ch. 2, § 5: The Father, the Spring in the supersubstantial Deity. (St.) Anselm, On Faith in the Trinity, ch. 8, and On the Procession of the Holy Spirit, ch. 17, where this similitude is expounded at length.

[5] Many codices, such as A C F G H I K L R S T U V etc., have, not coherently with what is subjoined, *formlessness* [informitatem].

[6] The Vatican edition, contrary to the manuscripts and edition 1, has the less apt *all life* [tota vita]. Then codex M has *thus what* [ita quod] in place of *and what* [et quod]. A little below this after *demutation* there

is added in the Vatican edition *or diminution* [deminutionem], which is absent from the ancient manuscripts and editions 1, 2 and 3.

[7] The Vatican edition has the subjunctive *says* [dicat]. Then codex Y has *is found* [reperitur] in place of *is received* [recipitur].

[8] Codex Z adds *or authority* [seu auctoritatem].

[9] In codex M there is added *therefore* [ergo].

[10] Trusting in codices F T and Y we have substituted *if* [si] for *but* [sed]. Then to the words *God did not create from eternity* [ab aeterno creavit Deus] codices W X and Y together with ed. 1 add *therefore* [ergo], the Vatican edition with some of the manuscripts adds *for* [enim]; codex H as *because God did not create* etc. [quia non ab aeterno etc]; many codices, such as A F G T V etc. omit one particle or another.

[11] Codex W has *consequent (argument)* [consequenti].

[12] Concerning which see Sent., Bk. II, d. 1, p. I, a. 1, q. 2.

[13] The Vatican edition together with edition 1, having changed the punctuation, has *afterwards born of the Virgin in this manner* [postea ex Virgine natus sic], but codices A F G H I K T etc. exhibit our text.

I RESPOND: It must be said, that (St.) Hilary himself[1] understands (it) according to the *same* Nature, according to which He was before. For if according to the same Nature He was before and afterwards He was born, it is necessary, that according to that Nature He be changed; but if according to *the other*,[2] it is proper that a mutation come to be in that nature, but not in the Person, since that nature does not mean anything *in* the Person, but rather something *with* the Person. Whence no mutation comes to be in the other[3] Nature.

DISTINCTION X

CHAPTER I

On the Holy Spirit, that He is properly said (to be) "the Love of the Father and of the Son", though there is in the Trinity a Love, which is the Trinity, just as the Word is properly said (to be) "Wisdom", and, nevertheless, the whole Trinity is said (to be) "Wisdom".

Now, after the eternity of the Son, let us speak in an orderly manner [disseramus] of the Holy Spirit, as much as, with God giving, one is granted to see it [videre conceditur]. The Holy Spirit is the love [amor] or charity or dilection of the Father and of the Son. Whence (St.) Augustine in the fifteenth book of ON THE TRINITY[1] says: « The Holy Spirit is neither of the Father alone nor is He of the Son alone, but of both, and for that reason He insinuates to us the common charity by which the Father and the Son love one another ».

Moreover, (St.) John in (his) canonical Epistle[2] says: *God is charity*. « He does not say: "the Holy Spirit is charity"; which if he had said, more absolute would (his) speech be, and not a little free from questioning [non parva pars quaestionis decisa]; but because he said: "*God is charity*", it is uncertain, and for that reason it must be asked,[3] "Whether God the Father is charity, or whether the Son, or whether the Holy Spirit, or whether God the Trinity Itself'", because It Itself is not three gods, but God is one ». To which (St.) Augustine in the same book, thus, says: « I do not know, why, just as wisdom is said (to be) both the Father and the Son and the Holy Spirit, and All together [simul omnes] not three, but one Wisdom, charity is not thus also said (to be) the Father and the Son and the Holy Spirit, and[4] All together one Charity. Not for that reason, however, does anyone consider [aestimet] that we unfittingly [inconvenienter] name the Holy Spirit "Charity", because God the Father and God the Son can be named [nuncupari] "Charity", just as properly the Word of God is also said (to be) "the Wisdom of God", though (the Divine) Wisdom is also the Father and the Holy Spirit ».

« If, therefore, properly anyone of these Three ought to be named [nuncupari] "Charity", who more aptly than the Holy Spirit? so that, namely, in[5] that Most high and Simple Nature, one (thing) is not the Substance, and another the Nature, but the Substance itself is Charity, and Charity itself is the Substance, whether in the Father or in the Son or in the Holy Spirit, and, nevertheless, the Holy Spirit properly be named [nuncupetur] Charity ». Behold with these words (St.) Augustine openly shows,[6] that in the Trinity "Charity" is sometimes referred to the Substance, which is the common (property) of the three Persons and whole in each [tota in singulis], sometimes specially to the Person of the Holy Spirit; just as the "Wisdom of God" is sometimes accepted for the Divine Substance, sometimes properly for the Son; and this is found to occur in many (attributes).

CHAPTER II

That the same names are properly and universally accepted.

« For by more examples one can be taught, that many terms [vocabula] of things are also posited universally, and are properly employed for certain things, just as by the name of the Law there are sometimes simultaneously signified all the passages [eloquia] of the Old Instrument,[7] but sometimes the Law, which has been given through Moses, is called (this) in a proper manner ». « Many other examples are at hand [suppetunt], but in an open matter [in re aperta] length of speech is to be avoided. Therefore, just as we call the unique Word of God by the name of "Wisdom", though universally Wisdom Itself is also the Holy Spirit and the Father; so the Holy Spirit is properly named [nuncupatur] with the term of "*charity*",[8] though universally Charity is also the Father and the Son ».

« But the Word of God, that is the only-begotten Son of God, openly has been said (to be) "the Wisdom of God" by the mouth of the Apostle saying[9] *Christ the Virtue of God and the Wisdom of God*, but we shall find where the Holy Spirit has said (to be) "Charity", if we diligently scrutinize the passage [eloquium][10] of the Apostle John, where after he had said: *Let us love [diligamus] one another, because love is of God [ex Deo est]*, he added: *And everyone, who loves, has been born of God, because God is love [Deus dilectio est]*. Here he has manifested that he had said, that God is the love, which he said (is) of God. Therefore, the God of God is love [Deus ex Deo est dilectio]; but because both the Son is born of [ex] God the Father, and the Holy Spirit proceeds from [ex] God the Father, whom of these we ought rather here to accept to be said to be "love", is rightly asked. For the Father alone is God,

---

[1] In the Vatican edition there is wanting *himself* [ipse], which is had in the manuscripts and editions 1, 2, 3 and 6.

[2] The Vatican edition together with codex cc here repeats the *nature* [naturam], which is lacking in the more ancient manuscripts and edition 1. A little below this at *not in the Person* [non in persona] some codices, such as I and T, add *it is* [est].

[3] Trusting in many manuscripts and edition 1 in place of *that* [illa] we have put *the other* [aliam], by which one understands the Divine Nature.

NOTES ON THE BOOK OF SENTENCES

[1] Chapter 17, nn. 27 and 28. — At the beginning of the distinction after *Now* [Nunc] codices D and E add *however* [vero].

[2] 1 John 4:6. — All, which follows in this chapter, has been excerpted out of (St.) Augustine, *loc. cit.*, nn. 27-31.

[3] The editions together with codex A add the *must* [est]. Then before *(St.) Augustine* [Augustinus] the Vatican edition and edition 4 put *this* [hoc] for *which* [quod].

[4] The Vatican edition and edition 4 omit *and* [et]. — Below, before *the Son* [Filius], codex C and edition 8 omit *God* [Deus]; at the end of this text codices B C D and edition 1 and 8 read *though both the Father and the Holy Spirit are Wisdom* [et Pater et Spiritus Sanctus sint sapientia].

[5] The Vatican edition faultily omits *in* [in]. At the end of this text the Vatican edition and very many editions has *is named* [nuncupatur] for *be named* [nuncupetur], in disagreement with (St.) Augustine and codices A C E and edition 8.

[6] The Vatican edition reads *says* [dicit], against the manuscripts and editions 1 and 8. Then only editions 1 and 8 ad *is* [est] before *whole in each* [tota in singulis].

[7] The Vatican edition together with editions 1, 4, 6, and 8 reads *Testament* [Testamenti], but all the codices and the rest of the editions together with the original contradict this.

[8] The Vatican edition together with all the editions, except edition 1, against the codices and the original, read *with the proper term "charity"* [proprio vocabulo caritas]. Then the Vatican edition and the rest of the editions, except ed. 1 and 8, against codices B D and E, omit *also* [et] before *the Father* [Pater].   [9] 1 Cor. 1:24.

[10] 1 John 4:7. The Vulgate reads: *because charity is from God ... God is charity* [quia caritas ex Deo est ... Deus caritas est].

thus, that He is not of God [ex Deo]; and for that reason the love [dilectio], which is thus God, to be of God [ex Deo], is not the Father Himself, but either the Son, or the Holy Spirit. But in what follows [in consequentibus], since (St.) John had recalled [commemorasset] the love of God,[1] with which He *had loved us*, and hence had exhorted, that *we also love one another*, and thus that *God remain in us*, because he had at any rate said that God is love [dilectionem], immediately, wanting to say something more openly about this matter, said: *In this we recognize, that we remain in Him, and He in us, because He has given us of his spirit*. And thus the Holy Spirit, of whom He has given us, causes [facit] us to remain in God, and Him in us. But love [dilectionem] does this. Therefore, God Himself is love [dilectio].[2] Therefore, God the Holy Spirit, who proceeds from God [ex Deo], is signified here where there is written: *God is love*, and *love is of God* ».[3] Behold with these words (St.) Augustine openly says, that the Holy Spirit is the charity of the Father and of the Son; and inasmuch as He also brings forth speech, as he seems to have said, the Holy Spirit is not only the love [dilectionem] of the Father and of the Son, by which They love one another and us, but also the love [dilectionem], by which we love [diligimus] God. But whether He be the charity, by which we love God, shall be explained in the following.[4]

Now, however, let us take up [curemus] what we began to show, namely that the Holy Spirit is the dilection or love of the Father and of the Son, by which namely the Father loves [diliget] the Son and the Son the Father. Of this (St.) Jerome on the seventeenth Psalm[5] says: « The Holy Spirit is neither the Father nor the Son, but the love [dilectionem], which the Father has unto [in] the Son and the Son unto the Father » (St.) Augustine also in the sixth book of ON THE TRINITY[6] says: « In all (things) the Son is equal to the Father and is of one and the same substance (as the Father). For which reason the Holy Spirit too consists in the same unity and equality of substance ».

« For, whether He is the unity of both, or the sanctity, or the charity, it is manifest, that One belonging to Two is not that by which Both are conjoined, by which the One begotten be loved by the One begetting and love His own Begetter, and They be not by participation, but by Their own Essence, nor by the superior gift of another, but by Their own *preserving* [servantes] *the unity of spirit in the chain of peace* ».[7] Behold here we have that the Holy Spirit is that by which the Son is loved by the Father and the Father by the Son, and that by which those Two "*preserve the unity of peace*". « Therefore, the Holy Spirit », as (St.) Augustine says in the same (passage), « is something common be-

longing to the Father and the Son, whatever He is. But that communion is consubstantial and coeternal, which if it can conveniently be said (to be) "friendship", let it be (so) called, but is more aptly said (to be) "charity"; and this (is) also the Substance, because God is a substance, and *God is charity*.[8] Therefore there are Three and not more: One loving Him, who is from Him, and One loving Him from whom He is, and the Love [dilectio] Itself, which if it is nothing, how is God love? If He is not the Substance, how is God a substance? »

CHAPTER III

That the Holy Spirit, just as He is common to the Father and to the Son, so has a common proper name.

Here, it must be noted, that just as the Holy Spirit in the Trinity is especially said (to be) the "Charity", which is the Union of the Father and of the Son, so He also has a name properly, which is befitting [congruit] to the Father and to the Son commonly in a certain manner. Whence (St.) Augustine says in the fifteenth book, ON THE TRINITY:[9] « If the charity, by which the Father loves the Son, and the Son loves the Father, demonstrates the ineffable communion of Both, what more conveniently (does this), than that He properly be said (to be) the "Charity", which is the spirit common to them both? For this is more sanely believed and understood, that not only is the Holy Spirit the Charity in that Trinity, but that He is not in vain properly called [nuncupetur] "charity", on account of those things which have been said; just as there is not either only *a Spirit* and/or *a Holy One* in that Trinity, because both the Father (is) spirit and the Son (is) spirit, and the Father holy and the Son holy, and nevertheless He is not in vain said (to be) "The Holy Spirit." For He who is common to Them both, is Himself called properly, that which Both (are) commonly. Otherwise if in that Trinity only the Holy Spirit is charity, then [profecto] too the Son is found (to be) not only of the Father, but also the Son of the Holy Spirit. For the Apostle[10] says of God the Father: *He has transferred us into the kingdom of the Son of His charity*. If, therefore, there is not in that Trinity a charity of God except the Holy Spirit, (The Son) is also the Son of the Holy Spirit. But because this is most absurd, it remains [restat] that there not only the Holy Spirit is Charity, but on account of those things of which we have sufficiently spoken in order, is called thus properly ».

---

[1] Ibid., verses 11-13. — The Vatican text alone ineptly reads *that* [quia] for *with which* [qua].

[2] The Vatican edition together with the rest of the editions contrary to the original reads: *Therefore, God Himself is love* [Ipse ergo Deus est dilectio].

[3] Everything in this chapter is from (St.) Augustine, ON THE TRINITY, Bk. XV, ch. 17, nn. 30,31. — A little before the end of the text at *God is love* [Deus dilectio est] the Vatican edition with a few of the codices omits *is* [est].

[4] Below in Distinction XVII. — The Vatican edition contrary to the manuscripts and to editions 1, 5, and 8, omits *the love* [dilectionem] after *but also* [sed etiam], and here together with edition 4 it reads *is explained* [explicatur] for *shall be explained* [explicabitur].

[5] Verse 1. — Before this after *Now* [Nunc] editions 1 and 8 have *therefore* [ergo] in place of *however* [vero].

[6] Chapters 4 and 5, nn. 6 and 7; from the last chapter of which the following quotes in this chapter have also been excerpted. At the end of the first quote in place of *consists* [consistit] codex D and codices 1 and 8 have *subsist* [subsistit], which would be more pleasant, if (St.) Augustine had favored it.

[7] Eph. 4:8. — A little before this in place of *and they be* [sintque] manuscripts A C D and E have *and they are* [suntque], and perhaps this is better. Then codices A and C begin the following quote with the words: *The Holy Spirit too* [Spiritus quoque sanctus] in place of *Therefore, the Holy Spirit* [Spiritus ergo sanctus].

[8] 1 John 4:16. — The Vatican edition and edition 4 after *it is nothing* [nihil est] faultily omit: *how is God love? If He is not the Substance* [quomodo Deus dilectio est, si non est substantia].

[9] Chapter 19, n. 37. — Codex C reads more briefly: *The Son the Father* [Filius Patrem] in place of *The Son loves the Father* [Patrem diligit Filius]. Then codices B C D and editions 1 and 8 together with the original in place of *ineffable* [ineffabilem] read *ineffably* [ineffabiliter], and thus with this adverb seem to modify the prior *loves* [diligit]. Then at the end of this proposition codex E and edition 8 have *the common spirit of them both* [spiritus communis amborum] in place of *the spirit common to them both* [spiritus communis ambobus].

[10] Colossians. 1:13. — The Vatican edition together with very many editions at *Trinity* [Trinitate] puts *that ... of Them* [ista] in place of *that* [illa]; afterwards editions 3, 5 and 9 after *but on account* [sed propter] read *those things of Theirs* [ista] in place of *those* [illa].

COMMENTARY ON DISTINCTION X

On the eternal procession of the Holy Spirit, as much as regards the Person who proceeds.

Now, after the eternity of the Son, let us speak in an orderly manner of the Holy Spirit etc..

THE DIVISION OF THE TEXT

Above, Master (Peter) dealt with the generation of the Son, but here he deals with the procession of the Holy Spirit. And because there is a twin [genima] procession of the Holy Spirit,[1] the eternal and the temporal, first he deals with the eternal procession, second with the temporal, below, in the fourteenth distinction: *Moreover, it must be noted, that there is a twin procession of the Holy Spirit* etc.. And, since the procession of the Holy Spirit can be compared in a threefold manner, namely according [ad] to the *Person* to whom He is, and according to the *principle* from which He is, and according to the *generation* by which He differs, for that reason this part has three (parts); in the *first* of which, Master (Peter) deals with the procession of the Holy Spirit as much as regards the Person, who proceeds; in the *second*, as much as regards the Principle from whom (He proceeds), below, in the eleventh distinction: *Here it must be said, that the Holy Spirit is from the Father and Son*; in the *third*, however, he deals with the same by means of a comparison to the generation, by which He is dis-

tinguished, below, in the thirteenth distinction: *After these it must be considered, as much as by such, as we are.*

Likewise, the *first* part, which contains the present distinction, has four (parts). In the *first* he says, that the Holy Spirit proceeds as love or charity and/or dilection; and this he proves by the authority of (St.) Augustine. In the *second*, however, because there was this[2] doubt, that the Holy Spirit is charity, he moves [movet] the question and solves (it), there (where he says): *And for that reason it must be asked, whether God the Father.* In the *third*, however, he confirms the solution by means of authority, both as much as regards the distinction, which is through the common and proper acceptation, and also as much as regards the truth, there (where he says): *For by more examples one can be taught* etc. In the *fourth* and last, however, he assigns a reason for the aforesaid solution, showing that[3] the Holy Spirit properly is called charity, since charity is the common name, and this there (where he says): *Here it must be noted, that just as the Holy Spirit in the Trinity.*

TREATMENT OF THE QUESTIONS

For the evidence of those (things) which are said of the Holy Spirit, in this part two (questions) are principally asked.

First there is asked concerning the manner of the proceeding itself of the Holy Spirit.[4]

Second concerning His propriety.

About the first, three (questions) are asked.

The first is, whether among the divine it is necessary to posit a Person proceeding through a manner of liberality.

Second, whether it is necessary to posit a Person proceeding through a manner of love [amoris].

Third, if[5] it is necessary to posit that Person proceeds through a manner of mutual charity.

ARTICLE I

On the Holy Spirit's manner of proceeding.

QUESTION I

Whether, among the divine, there is to be posited a Person, proceeding through the manner of liberality?

About the first, that it is necessary to posit a Person proceeding through a manner of liberality, is shown in this manner:

1. More perfect is mutual dilection than re-

flexive (dilection),[6] and more perfect still the mutual (dilection) communicated than (the mutual dilection) not-communicated, because such, namely the (mutual dilection) not-communicated,

---

[1] Codex A and edition 1 add *namely* [scilicet].

[2] From the manuscripts and editions 1, 2 and 3, we have substituted *this* [hoc] for *here* [hic]. Then, after *Holy Spirit* [Spiritus sanctus], from very many codices, such as T Y and bb, together with edition 1, we have used (the imperfect subordinate subjunctive) *is* [esset] for *was* [erat].

[3] Edition 1 reads *why* [quare].

[4] The Vatican ed., against the mss. and ed. 1, omits *holy* [sancti].

[5] A few codices as X and Y read *whether* [utrum]. Then codex V has *a Person proceeding* [personam procedentem] in place of *that a Person proceeds* [personam procedere].

[6] That is, that which is reflected toward the very one loving, or by which one loves one's own nature, while mutual love tends unto the other, which love can be *communicated* and/or *not communicated* (private), just as some thus mutually love one another, because they also want that the beloved be loved by others and that he love others, and/or not. See (Bl. John Duns) Scotus, III. SENT., d. 28, and Aristotle, MAGNA MORALIA, Bk. II, ch. 17 (ch. 13). — Then after *still the mutual* [adhuc mutua] codex M adds *and the* [et].

seems to smell [sapere] of libidinous love [amorem]: therefore, if in God there is a most high dilection and a most high delectation and[1] beatitude, There, there is not a Person, who is not mutually loved, but (rather a Person) to whom a mutual love is communicated; but the communication of a mutual love is through liberality: ergo etc..

2. Likewise, in these inferiors a twofold manner of proceeding[2] is found, namely through a manner of nature and through a manner of will: in the first manner the Son emanates from the Father, in the second manner a gift from a giver; but everything which is of nobility in a creature, must be attributed to God: ergo etc..

3. Likewise, in God one is to posit [est ponere] a nature and a will, and just as fecundity perfects the Nature, so most high liberality the Will; but with a nature perfected by fecundity, a person produces another person: therefore, for equal reason, with a will perfected by liberality, a Person[3] produces another Person: and in this manner etc..

4. Likewise, all creatures proceed from God through (His) cognition and willing (of them); but before positing the production of creatures there was among the divine the emanation of the Word from eternity, in whom the Father arraigned [disposuit] all that are to be made:[4] therefore, for an equal reason it was necessary that a Person emanate, in whom He would will and grant all (things); but Such proceeds through a manner of liberality: ergo etc..

ON THE CONTRARY: 1. There is not a similar manner of proceeding or of going forth [exeundi][5] among creatures in respect of God and in the (Divine) Persons; for creatures are from without [extrinsecus], but the Persons One in Essence; but the going-forth of creatures from God is through a manner of liberality: therefore, one is not to posit that a Person proceeds in this manner.

2. Likewise, the one going forth through a manner of the will from someone is not assimilated in substance to the one producing, neither is it equated, nor necessarily produced; but a Person, if He proceeds among divine (Persons), is in substance similar and in power equal and He is not able to hold Himself otherwise: ergo etc.

3. Likewise, among these inferiors there are not only those noble principles, namely nature and will, but also reason or (that which) operates through art:[6] therefore, if there are posited two Persons proceeding in these two manners, one ought to posit a third, which proceeds in a third manner; but that is not posited: therefore neither will any be posited[7] through a manner of the will for an equal reason.

4. Likewise, as much as dilection is communicated to more, so much (is it) more perfect, because every good-deduced-in-common shines forth more beautifully: therefore, not only is one to posit a third Person, to whom love [amore] is communicated to the second,[8] but also a fourth, to whom love is communicated to the third, and thus unto infinity [in infinitum]; but this is impossible among the divine, as has been shown above:[9] therefore, (love) is to stand still in the first Person producing: therefore, there is not a Person proceeding through a manner of liberality.

CONCLUSION

Among the divine through a manner of liberality there proceeds the third Person, who is called "The Gift".

I RESPOND: It must be said, that, as has been proved,[10] among the divine one is to posit a Third Person proceeding through a manner of liberality, who is called "The Gift". And the reason for this is the perfection of *dilection*, the perfection of *emanation* and the perfection of the *Will*, by which existing[11] most liberal, cannot not produce a Person; just as the Nature, by existing most fecund, cannot not produce a Person; and this is the proper reason of this emanation.

1. To that which is objected unto the contrary, that creatures emanate through a manner of liberality; it must be said, that to emanate through a manner of liberality is twofold: either as a (thing) *willed* [volitum], or as *a reckoning of willing*, or either as a (thing) granted,[12] or as a reckoning of granting. In the first manner there emanates creatures, which are without [extra]; in the second manner there emanates the Third Person in the Trinity, because a reckoning of willing and of granting is intrinsic to the most perfect Will.

2. To that which is objected, that a will is not[13] a principle assimilating nor necessarily emanating; it must be said, that a will or liberality is a twofold principle: in *one* manner distinct in nature, and thus does not assimilate in substance; in *another* manner by a concomitant[14] nature, and thus in substance assimilates. Therefore, since a Person thus proceeds through a manner of liberality, to however, be concomitant in the Nature: for that reason (He is) similar in substance, although the manner of proceeding itself be not through a manner of the similar; and in this manner that is clear.

---

[1] The Vatican edition, opposing the more ancient manuscripts, repeats here *a most high* [summa]. Then a greater part of the manuscripts, as follows, A C D G K L O R S U V W X Y Z, in place of *nor (a Person) to whom a mutual love is not communicated* [nec cui amor mutuus non communicetur] we have substituted *but (rather a Person) to whom mutual love is communicated* [sed cui amor mutuus communicetur], by which the sentence of the Doctor is more distinctly expressed, if you supply after *but* [sed]: there is a Person, that is, the Holy Spirit. See below q. 3, and a. 2, q. 2. The other codices in place of *but* [sed] put *and* [et], as codices F H P Q and T do, and/or as codex ff, *or* [sive], and/or as codex cc *but also* [sed et], but edition 1 has *that is* [id est].

[2] In the Vatican edition and codex cc, disagreeing with the more ancient manuscripts and edition 1, has *producing* [producendi], but less coherently with what is subjoined. Then codex T has *proceeds* [procedit] in place of *emanates* [emanat].

[3] Trusting in the more ancient manuscripts and edition 1 we have restored the not-aptly omitted *Person* [persona].

[4] (St.) Augustine, ENARRATIONS ON THE PSALMS, Ps. 61, n. 18 ff.. See below, d. 27, p. II, q. 2. A little below codex O has *it was necessary to posit* [necesse fuit ponere] for *one was to posit* [ponere fuit].

[5] Thus nearly all codices together with edition 1, while the Vatican edition together with codex cc alone puts *producing* [producendi], having omitted *or of going-forth* [sive exeundi]. Then codices aa and bb after *liberality* [liberalitatis] add *and/or of the will* [voluntatis] and codex

Y at the end of the argument puts *a Person proceeding in this manner* [personam in hoc modo procedentem] in place of *that a Person proceeds in this manner* [personam in hoc modo producere].

[6] See Aristotle, METAPHYSICS, Bk. XI, text 10, and Bk. XII, text 13 (Bk. VIII, ch. 5, and Bk. XI, ch. 3).

[7] The Vatican edition, disagreeing with very many manuscripts and edition 1, reads *is ... posited* [ponitur].

[8] Edition 1 has *to the first and to the second* [primae et secundae].

[9] Distinction 7, q. 2, penultimate fundament, and d. 2, q. 3.

[10] Here in the fundament and d. 2, q. 4.

[11] Codex U *because by a will existing* [quia voluntate existente].

[12] The Vatican edition together with codex cc has *given* [datum], but against the more ancient codices and edition 1, which also first having omitted *either* [aut] for the second put *or* [sive]; but grammatically this is not good.

[13] Many codices as A B D I S T W Z etc. together with edition 1 have *does not have* [habet non], but less coherently with what is subjoined.

[14] We prefer the reading of very many manuscripts, such as R X Y and edition 1, which, in place of *with a communicant* [cum communicante], read *by a concomitant* [concomitante], while others, such as C L O T & U, have *by an accompanying* [comitante], others, such as F G H I etc., have *by a communicant* [communicate]. Concerning this manner, see above d. 6, q. 2 and 3. The same diversity of reading

3. To that which is objected, wherefore there proceeds no person through the manner of reason; it must be said, that every manner of noble producing is reduced to those two; because every agent either acts naturally, or through its will; — for an agent through violence, or through fortune is an imperfect agent, and (its) manner of producing less noble[1] — whence (its) reason is not distinguished against nature and will as much as regard the manner of acting; and for that reason there is no Person proceeding in such a manner.

But, nevertheless, this does not seem to solve (the matter) fully, because in these creatures we distinguish an "egress through a manner of *liberality*" from an "*egress through a manner of art*". And[2] on that account it must be said, that a processing [processus] through a manner of liberality is twofold, either as a *reckoning* of liberality or liberality itself, or as (a thing) *liberally made*; similarly also in *art*, either as the *art itself* or the reason for art-making [ratio artificiandi], or as the (thing) *artfully-made* [artificiatum]; and in the first manner it can occur [cadere] in a divine Person, in the second manner (it can) not. And in the first manner proceeds the Son, who is « the Word and the Art full of all living reasons ».[3] But that manner of His emanating is not distinguished from the manner of emanating through a manner of a nature, because He emanates as One entirely similar and through a manner of perfect similitude. But the other

manner cannot be,[4] because it is necessary to communicate two Persons in the same Nature, and because it is necessary, that every manner of emanating, which is among the divine, be through a manner of nature principally, and/or with that (nature) concomitant.[5] Whence since a processing through a manner of *will* could be from within [intrinsecus], just as[6] love [amor] proceeds from the lover; but through a manner of *art* it is always from without [extrinsecus], inasmuch as (it is) of this kind: for that reason it is impossible that it occur [cadat] in God in respect of a Person, but it does occur only in respect of a creature.

4. To that which is last objected: if one is to posit a third Person on account of a communication, for an equal reason also a forth; it must be said, that every reckoning and nature concord, because there does not come to be through more what can come to be most sufficiently through one; otherwise, there is (something) superfluous There.[7] If, therefore, a mutual dilection cannot be less than toward one, and the mutual communication of that (dilection) not less than toward one, and there is in one a mutual dilection, and in the other a mutual communication of dilection in a most perfect manner, since each of the Two[8] accepts the Whole infinitely; it is clear that one is not to proceed further (in positing other Persons), but is to stand still there (in the Three). Whence the very same reason, which posits a plurality of persons, bears off an infinity and posits a Trinity.

SCHOLIUM

I. The Holy Spirit has the name of "Gift", and indeed of the Gift, in which all things are given (cf. d. 18 throughout). But whatever is given, is given *through a manner of liberality*. In which sense the Seraphic (Doctor) may here accept this expression, seems to require explanation. *Liberality*, besides the special moral virtue, implicitly also conveys a reckoning of *liberty* or of will, as is taught in the solution to n. 3. Since, therefore, there is a twofold manner of emanating in God, namely, through the manner of the Nature and through the manner of the Will, and the procession of the Holy Spirit is through a manner of will, that intrinsic perfection of the Divine Will, which diffuses and expresses itself in the procession of the Holy Spirit, as of the Gift of all gifts, is called by the Saint *liberality*. Moreover, it must noted, that "will" in God can be accepted and/or, insofar (as it is) according to our manner of understanding, distinguished as a *potency* against the Nature, and/or insofar as it is concomitant to the same Nature and communicates It in the reckoning of an Object most highly lovable. In the first sense the Will is the fecund principle in the production of created things, but not in the production of the Holy Spirit; but in the second sense it is the principle of the Holy Spirit. Whence it is clear what he says ad 1 and 2; one also understands what has been said above in d. 6, q. 2, concerning the difference between the production of the Son and of the Holy Spirit. For the Son proceeds from the Father through a manner of *nature*, with the Will concomitant; and because He proceeds through a manner

of *nature*, He proceeds as one entirely similar to the Father and as His perfect Image (cf. below d. 31, a. 1, q. 2). But the Holy Spirit is produced through a manner of *will*, with the Nature concomitant, indeed similar, nay rather entirely the Same in Nature, nevertheless in this manner, that by the force of the procession the *reckoning of image* is more completely in the Son.

II. The last argument in the fundament, which is deduced from the emanation of creatures, is approved even by Alexander of Hales, St. Thomas (here in his COMMENTARY.), Richard (of Middleton) and others, but is (here) unmeritedly impugned by Giles (the Roman), concerning which one may see (Bl.) Dionysius the Carthusian (here at q. 1 about the middle).

III. Concerning the question itself see Alexander of Hales, SUMMA., p. I, q. 43, m. 1, who, as (Bl.) Dionysius the Carthusian says here, « he writes most fully of these things, nay rather, because it had already be overlooked by many teachers, he alone of the all expressed it in his writings, and many other things, which none of the others seemed to have written about. ». — (Bl. John Duns) Scotus, here at q. sole. — St. Thomas, here at q. 1, a. 1 ff.. — Bl. (now St.) Albert (the Great), SENT., Bk. I, d. 13, a. 4; concerning which and the following questions, SUMMA., p. I, tr. 7, q. 31, m. 2. — (Bl.) Peter of Tarentaise, concerning this question and the following here at q. 1, a. 2. — Richard of Middleton, here at a. 1, q. 1. — Giles the Roman, here in 1st. principle of q. 1. — Henry of Ghent, SUMMA., a. 61, q. 10. — (Bl.) Dionysius the Carthusian, concerning this and the following question, here at q. 1. — (Gabriel) Biel, here at q. 2, concl. 3.

---

is found a little below this in regard to the word *will be concomitant* [concomitetur], where the Vatican edition even omits the particle *nevertheless* [tamen].

[1] Concerning an agent through violence see Aristotle, ETHICS, Bk. III, ch. 1, and MAGNA MORALIA, Bk. II, ch. 8 and 9 (ch. 7 and 8). — Concerning an agent through fortune cf. METAPHYSICS, Bk. XII, text 13 (Bk. XI, ch. 3), and PHYSICS, Bk. II, text 39 ff. (ch. 4-6).

[2] We have supplied from very many of the manuscripts and edition 1 the particle *And* [et].

[3] (St.) Augustine, ON THE TRINITY, Bk. VI, ch. 10 and 11. — A little below this codex A has *One entirely (and) completely similar* [omnino consimilis] in place of *One entirely similar* [omnino similis].

[4] Supply with edition 1: *among the divine* [in divinis].

[5] In the same manner, as a little more above this, there occurs even here a variety of readings: the Vatican edition with v⸱⸱⸱⸱ ny codi⸱

has *communicant* [communicante], others as G T and U have *accompanying* [comitante], others as H R O X Y aa bb ff together with edition 1 exhibit our reading.

[6] The Vatican edition together with very many codices faultily reads *in the same manner as* [sic] rather than *just as* [sicut].

[7] See Aristotle and Averroës, PHYSICS, Bk. I, text 50 and 56 (ch. 6), and TOPICS, Bk. VIII, ch. 4 (ch. 9 near the end), where in regard to the syllogism there is said: Moreover, there is a certain and identical sin against syllogisms, when there is shown through longer (arguments), what is grasped through short ones. — In this proposition the Vatican edition has *would be* [esset] for *is* [est]. A little before this in codex M after *nature* [natura] there is sufficiently well added *in this* [in hoc].

[8] On the authority of very many manuscripts as A F G H I K R U Y etc. and edition 1 we have substituted *each of the Two* [uterque] for *both of the Two* [utrumque], by which the sense is rendered clearer.

QUESTION II

Whether, among the divine, there is to be posited a Person, proceeding through the manner of love or charity?

Second, there is asked, whether among the divine it is necessary to posit a Person proceeding through a manner of love [amoris] or charity. And that (it is) so, seems:

1. There is no[1] perfect cognition without dilection [dilectione], therefore, neither a perfect word without word [amoris]: therefore, neither a perfect emanation of the Word without an emanation of love [amoris]: therefore, it is necessary to posit an emanation through a manner of love: ergo etc..

2. Likewise, love [amor] is a gift, in which all[2] other gifts are given; for nothing properly is given except out of love; if therefore, a Person proceeds through a manner of liberality, since It proceeds not through (something) else, but through Itself; therefore, through a manner of love or charity.

3. Likewise, every and the most high perfection of plurality is in unity, therefore, (the perfection) also of distinction (is) in a union; but among all unions, which are among distant (beings), the most high and most jocund is the unity of charity; therefore, if there is a distinction There, there is union; and if a union, there is an emanation of charity.

4. Likewise, the Holy Spirit, dwelling and existing in us, causes [facit] us to be similar to that Most High Trinity, just as the Lord says, in the seventeenth (chapter of the Gospel) of (St.) John:[3] « That they might be one, just as We (are) also »; but the Holy Spirit, existing in us, produces first the love of charity, according to the fifth (chapter of St. Paul's Letter to) the Romans:[4] « The charity of God has been poured upon our hearts ». Therefore, it is necessary, that in that most high Trinity, through (a consideration of what is) prior, there be discovered an emanation of charity.

BUT ON THE CONTRARY: 1. The Divine Persons, such as the Father and the Son, are perfect hypostases; but no "love" [amor] means a hypostasis, but (rather) its property or habit: therefore, no Person among the divine proceeds through a manner of love.

2. Likewise, love belongs to the one in whom affection rests: therefore, it is always accepted as one tending unto the other; but every person is perfectly a being in himself and distinct: therefore, no person proceeds through a manner of love.

3. Likewise, among the divine, an emanation through a manner of love is not posited on account of anything (else), except because the Father loves the Son; therefore, since the Son loves the Holy Spirit, for an equal reason there will be a positing of a further person emanation through a manner of love, and thus unto infinity; and[5] this is unfitting: ergo etc..

4. Likewise, since in an intellectual nature on the part of the motive power there is an accepting of the irascible, which respects honor, just as the concupiscible, which respects love,[6] there is the question, wherefore among the divine is a person not accepted according to the act of the irascible, just as according to the act of the concupiscible?

5. Likewise, since there are other *affections* in the soul, such as joy, hope, and (things) of this kind, wherefore does there proceed only through a manner of love a Person among the divine? *If you say*, that love does not have a reckoning of affection, then I object, because just as divine[7] love is not an affection, so neither (is divine) joy.

6. Likewise, since there are other *habits* in the soul conveying (its) completion [importantes complementum], of which kind, namely, are the gifts of the Holy Spirit, such as intelligence[8] and wisdom; for what reason does there rather proceed a Person through a manner of love, than through the manner of another habit? Because if one ought not be posited, neither (ought) this one, as it seems.

CONCLUSION

The Holy Spirit proceeds through a manner of love, because He proceeds through a manner of the will and liberality.

I RESPOND: It must be said, that, just as has been proved above,[9] it is necessary that some Person among the divine proceed through a manner of liberality, and That One we call "the Holy Spirit" [Spiritum sanctum]. Moreover, it is necessary that This One proceed through a manner of love; because, if one posits among the divine an emanation[10] through a manner of the will, it is necessary, that among all (affections) it be *first* and *most noble*. But an emanation through a manner of love is of this kind, which is clear, if we look back, in the soul. For the affection of love is *first* among all the affections and the root of all others, just as (St.) Augustine shows in very many passages, most of all in the fourteenth (book) of THE CITY OF GOD.[11] And that affection is the *most noble* among (them) all, since it has

---

[1] As required by the Manuscripts and edition 1, we have expunged here from the Vatican edition the added *for* [enim]. Then after *cognition* [cognitio] codex W adds *of the good* [boni]. — Cf. on this argument (St.) Augustine, ON THE TRINITY, Bk. IX, ch. 10., n. 15 where he also says: The Word is ... knowledge with love.

[2] From the many manuscripts and edition 1 we have added *all* [omnia]. — See the very many other things regarding this proposition below in d. 18, q. 1.

[3] Verse 22.

[4] Verse 5. — Then codex U has *communication* [communicationem] in place of *emanation* [emanationem].

[5] Edition 1 has *but* [sed] in place of *and* [et].

[6] We prefer the more distinct reading of the more ancient mss. and edition 1 to the reading of the Vatican edition and of codex cc *just as the love of the concupiscible* [sic concupiscibilis amorem]. This division of the motive powers, received by the Scholastics, occurs in the book by Nemesius, Bishop of Emesa, ON THE NATURE OF MAN, ch. 16 ff.; and in (St.) Gregory of Nyssa's book, ON THE SOUL AND THE RESURRECTION, and in the same's canonical Letter to St. Letoius; and (St.) John Damascene's, ON THE ORTHODOX FAITH, Bk. II, ch. 22, where the passions or affections of the soul are enumerated. See also Aristotle, ON THE SOUL, Bk. III, texts 41 and 53 (ch. 9 ff.); ON THE MOVEMENT OF ANIMALS, ch. 3 (ch. 6); ETHICS, Bk. II, ch. 5, and MAGNA MORALIA, Bk. I, ch. 8 (chs. 7 and 8).

[7] Codices V and Y have *among the divine* [in divinis].

[8] Edition 1 has *understanding* [intellectus]. — A little below this, codices T and V read *Because if it is not the other, neither ought this one be posited etc.* [Quod si non est alius etc.]

[9] In the preceding question.

[10] Codices R and T and edition 1 have *procession* [processio].

[11] Chapters 7 to 9. The manuscripts and all of the editions falsely cite ON THE TRINITY, Bk. XIV. — A little before this from very many of the manuscripts and edition 1 we have substituted *shows* [ostendit] in place of *says* [dicit]. Then after *Whence* [Unde] (on p. 198) codex Y has *this (affection)* [haec] in place of *this* [hoc].

has more of the reckoning of liberality. Whence this is the gift, in which all other gifts are given, and in which all delights of intellectual substance consist. Whence there is nothing among creatures that (they) consider so delicious, as mutual love; and without love there are no delights.[1] On this account the Philosopher says,[2] that friendship is either beatitude, or not without beatitude. If, therefore, there is an emanation through a manner of liberality among the divine, it was necessary that it be[3] first and most high; and thus it was necessary that it be through a manner of love.

1. To that which is, therefore, objected, that "love" [amor] names a habit, not a substance; it must be said, that there is a speaking of "love" according to the reckoning of that *which it names*, and in this manner it does not mean a substance; and/or according to the reckoning of that *about which it is posited*; and because it is posited in God, in Whom (there is) no accident, but He is entirely[4] substance, for that reason it does not mean a habit and/or a property, but rather the Substance; and since (love) means an egress, it means (also) a Hypostasis or Person. A similar (argument) must be said concerning the Word.[5]

2. To that which is objected, that the love of charity always tends unto another [in alium], and thus proceeds unto another and does not stand in itself; it must be said, that "proceeding unto an other" is (said) in a twofold manner: either because it looks back to (something) else as (its) object, or because it tends unto (something) else and is received (in that). *In the first* manner it is very fitting for a Person among the divine, because it is very fitting (that One Person) have respect for another Person; whence the Holy Spirit is the Love, by which the Father loves the Son. But if (love) means a "tending" in the *second* manner, thus it has no place in the proposed, because, when I love an other, love does not go forth from me, so that it is received in another, but only proceeds from (my) will, and because it is an accident, for that reason it does not go back [recedit], but subsists in (my) will. But among the divine, because (love) is a Hypostasis, for that reason It subsists in Itself.

3. To that which is objected, that similarly the Son, loving the Holy Spirit, would produce an other Person; it must be said, that He does not do this only, because the Father and the Son produce an other Person, because (this Person)[6] is the Love, by which They love Themselves, but also, because in Them there is a most fecund Will. The reason for this will be said below,[7] and this is not in the Holy Spirit. Nevertheless, however, it can be said, that there is a standing-still [status] in the first love. For with the first Love produced, since He loves[8] by His very self and is loved, it is not necessary [non oportet], that there be produced another Love or another Person through a manner of love.

4. To that which is asked, for what reason is there no emanation as much as regards the act of the irascible (force)? Certain (authors) answer, that this force [vis] does not have a place in a purely spiritual substance; however, supposing, that it is in an intellectual substance, its act is still not competent for the production of a Person, both because it naturally follows the act of the concupiscible; « for wrath is the vindicator of a wounded concupiscence », as (St. John) Damascene says;[9] and also, because its act consists either in respect *of a superior*, and this cannot be where there is nothing superior; or in respect *of an inferior*, and this similarly (can) not (be), because there is no inferiority There; in respect *of an equal* it similarly cannot be in God, because in this manner there is (an irascible act) with a certain coming-apart [disconvenientia] and victorious repulsion;[10] but among the Divine Persons it is necessary that there be a most high Union and Coming-together [convenientiam]. *And if you object*, that not every irascible act is in respect of (something) inconvenient [disconvenientis], which is clear in hope, and because among the Blessed one will (still) have the irascible act; it must be said, that it consists in respect of conquering the *inconvenient*, and/or in respect of attacking the arduous [ardui aggrediendi], and thus means a stepping-toward [gradus] and/or a coming-apart; but neither can be among Divine Persons.

5. 6. To that which is objected concerning the other *affections* and *habits*, the response is already clear. Because love is the most interior, and first, and most noble affections, because (it is) the origin of all the others, for that reason, it embraces in itself the whole nobility of emanation through a manner of liberality: for that reason no person ought to emanate through the manner of another habit, since such a manner is not a principle.

SCHOLIUM

I. Love or charity among the divine is accepted in a threefold manner: *essentially*, and thus there is that *complacence*, by which any Person loves Himself and the other two Persons; *notionally*, and thus there is that active spiration or *concordance* in spirating, by which the Father and the Son spirate the Holy Spirit; *personally*, and thus there is that Person proceeding, i.e. the Holy Spirit (cf. below a. 2, q. 1). And it must be noted, that the Holy Spirit does not proceed as something which is given through love, but as the Love given or produced.

---

[1] Cf. above d. 1, a. 2, q. 1.

[2] ETHICS, Bk. IX, ch. 9, where the converse is proved, namely that beatitude is not without friendship. — In the following passages it is proven that friendship has been conjoined with jocundity: ETHICS, Bk. VIII, ch. 1; MAGNA MORALIA, Bk. II, ch. 12 (ch. 11) and EUDEMEAN ETHICS, Bk. VII, ch. 2 ff, and RHETORICS, Bk. 1, ch. "On Pleasantries".

[3] Codex O has *it is necessary that it be* [necesse est eam esse]. Then, agreeing with the manuscripts and edition 1, we have inserted after *was* [fuit], *that it be* [esse].

[4] Very many codices together with edition 1 have not so well *the whole* [tota]. The Vatican edition here, against the more ancient codices and edition 1, repeats *in God* [in Deo].

[5] In the Vatican edition there is here added *for although the word in us is an accident, (it is) in God, however, the Substance* [quamvis enim verbum in nobis sit accidens, et tamen substantia in Deo], but this is against the authority of the manuscripts and edition 1.

[6] Supply: this Person. We prefer this reading, in which agree the greater part of the codices, such as I L O R S T U W X Y etc., while the Vatican edition here has *which* [quae] in place of *because* [quia], and then *because* [quia] for *because* [quod]; but all the other codices either consent with the reading of the Vatican edition entirely, or only in part; thus codex K together with edition 1 has *which is the Love, by which* [quae est amor, quo].

[7] Distinction 11, q. 2, and d. 13, q. 3. — Then at *a standing-still* [status] trusting in very many of the more ancient manuscripts and edition 1 we have substituted *there is* [est] for *there may be* [sit].

[8] The Vatican edition together with codex cc adds *Another* [alium], which is lacking in the more ancient manuscripts and edition 1. Then many codices, such as A C F G H K L R S U V W X Y etc. have *that Love* [illum] for *another Love* [alium amorem].

[9] ON THE ORTHODOX FAITH, Bk. II, ch. 16: Furthermore, wrath is the attendant of reason, the vindicator of cupidity.

[10] The Vatican edition exhibits the preceding sentence thus: *there is no inferiority in the Person produced in respect of the Father, it cannot be similar in God in respect of one coming-apart, because in this manner there is a certain coming-apart in a victorious repulsion* [nulla est inferioritas in persona producta respectu Patris, non similiter potest esse in Deo respectu disconventientis, quia sic est cum quadam disconvenientia in victoriosa repulsione], which interpolated and distorted reading is corrected by the authority of the manuscripts, which, in regard to the substance of the reading, all agree among themselves and with edition 1.

II. Having touched upon the question in solution n. 4, whether the irascible power has a place in a spiritual substance, is resolved by St. Bonaventure in regard to God (Sent., Bk. I, d. 45, Doubt 10) with the common sentence in this manner: « The irascible power is not received in God except transumptively ». In regard to the Angels and the *rational* appetite of the human soul, Henry of Ghent (Quodlibetals, 8, q. 15) affirms, that in the rational appetite there must be distinguished the irascible and the concupiscible power; but his arguments are impugned by (Bl. John Duns) Scotus (Sent. Bk. III, d. 26, q. sole). Even St. Thomas (Summa., I, q. 59, a. 4) does not admit that distinction of Henry of Ghent, neither does Richard of Middleton (Sent., Bk. II, d. 24, q. 2. q. 3) ; even (Bl.) Peter of Tarentaise (Sent., Bk. III, d. 26, a. 7) reputes this negative sentence

as the more probable one. Scotus explains his own sentence elsewhere (Sent., Bk. III, d. 34, q. sole), by admitting some distinction on the part of the object, to which St. Bonaventure (Sent., Bk. II, d. 25, p. I, q. 6, ad 2, and d. 24, p. I, a. 2, q. 1; Sent., Bk. III, d. 33, a. 1, q. 3.) et Alexander of Hales (Summa., p. II, q. 29, m. 3) agree.

III. The question itself is not explicitly treated by all the ancient writers. Cf. Alexander of Hales, Summa., p. I, q. 43, m. 2, a. 2. — (Bl. John Duns) Scotus, here in his question sole, and below in d. 32, q. 1. — St. Thomas, here in q. 1, a. 1; Summa., I, q. 37, a. 1. — Bl. (now St.) Albert (Magnus), here in a. 2. — (Bl.) Peter of Tarentaise, here in q. 1, a. 2. — Richard of Middleton, here in a. 1, q. 2. — Henry of Ghent, Summa., a. 61, q. 5.

QUESTION III

Whether, among the divine, there is to be posited a third Person, proceeding through the manner of mutual charity?

Third, there is asked, whether it is necessary to posit a Third Person proceeding through a manner of mutual charity: And that (it is) so, seems:

1. From the seventeenth (chapter of the Gospel of St.) John:[1] *That they may be one, even as We*; the Lord prays and asks for the unity of (His) disciples, not of nature, but of a dilection through a conformity to that most high Unity; but the members of Christ are united through a mutual love: therefore, among the divine there is an exemplar of this: thus etc..[2]

2. Likewise, (St.) Jerome on the seventeenth Psalm (says):[3] « The Holy Spirit is the Love, which the Father has for [in] the Son, and the Son for [in] the Father »: therefore, He is a mutual love.

3. Likewise, *by reason* this very (thing) is shown, because dilection is more perfect, when it is mutual, because if it is not mutual, it is deflected [claudicat] on the part of the other; but in that dilection there is a most high perfection and no deflection: ergo etc..

4. Likewise, he who does not love in turn the one loving him rightly and liberally either is iniquitous [iniquus], or ungrateful; therefore, since among the divine there is no iniquity, no ingratitude, it is necessary that there be There a mutual love.

On the Contrary: 1. If He is a mutual love, therefore, of the Son for [in] the Father and of the Father for the Son: therefore, the Father receives something from the Son: which is absurd.

2. Likewise, he who loves one-loving (him) does what he ought [debet], because this is the debt [debitus], which must be repaid; therefore, if among the divine there is a mutual love, therefore, it is a debt [debitus]: therefore, it is not most liberal, which is absurd.

3. Likewise, no mutual love is a unique love; this is self-evident [per se nota] ; therefore, if the Holy Spirit is a mutual love, He is not the unique Love.

4. Likewise, if He is a mutual love, therefore, He is the love of the Father for [ad] the Son; but (as) that (love of His), as Richard (of St. Victor) says,[4] is a gratuitous love, similarly, (the love) of the Son shall be for the Father; and that (love of His), as the same says, is a owed love [amor debitus]: therefore, if the Third Person proceeds through a manner of gratuitous and

owed love, therefore, He is a love thoroughly mixed from each: therefore not a pure love. And *again*, since that love is the Son, it seems that the Son is the Holy Spirit, because as Richard (of St. Victor) says,[5] in the Son there is a love thoroughly mixed from each.

CONCLUSION

The Third Person proceeds through the manner of mutual charity.

I Respond: It must be said, that since love has the perfection of delectation[6] and union and rectitude out of a mutuality, either it is not that one posits a Person among the divine to proceed through a manner of love, or, if He does proceed, he proceeds through a manner of mutual charity.

1. To that which is, therefore, objected unto the contrary, that then the Son gives something to the Father; it must be said, that from this, that one loving tends through love unto the one loved, he gives nothing to him; otherwise we would give something to God, when we love Him.

2. To that which is objected, that mutual love is a debt; it must be said, that it is a debt, because it is upright; but love, however, does not consider (itself) a debt. Whence however, much it be owed, while yet the debit is not attended to, the reckoning of liberality is not diminished, nay the reckoning of rectitude is shown.

3. To that which is objected: if mutual, not unique:[7] it must be said, that it is true among lovers, whose affections are diverse; not so is it in God.

4. To that which is objected, that (mutual love) is not a pure love; it must be said, that on the part of each it is liberal, and for that reason entirely pure. And what[8] Richard (of St. Victor) says, that it is a love, owed and gratuitous; it must be said, that those conditions of his do not mean a manner of loving about love, but mean a manner of emanating or of origin about the Persons.

---

[1] Verse 22.
[2] A few codices, such as H I P and Q, have: *and thus it is clear etc.*[et sic patet etc.].
[3] See the text of Master (Peter), (here) in the second half of chapter 2.
[4] On the Trinity, Bk. V, ch. 17 ff. — Then, after *gratuitous love* [amor gratuitus], in the Vatican edition, not trusting in the manuscripts and edition 1, there is added *therefore,* [ergo], and, a little below this, contrary to many codices, such as A G K T Z etc., and edition 1, there is had *He* [ille] in place of *that (love of His)* [iste].

[5] From the more ancient mss. & ed. 1, we have supplied *Richard* [Richardus].
[6] Not a few codices, such as A F K U Z, together with edition 1 have *of dilection* [dilectionis].
[7] Codex X has *is objected: no mutual love is unique* [obiicitur: nullus amor mutuus est unicus].
[8] The Vatican edition in place of *what* [quod] has *when* [cum], then it omits *Richard* [Richardus], disagreeing with the older manuscripts and edition 1, just as also a little below this it faultily puts *of emanating* [emanandi] in place of *of loving* [amandi].

SCHOLIUM

I. In the solution to n. 4, the words expounding the passage of Richard of St. Victor: « They do not mean a manner of loving about love etc.» have this sense: 'The Father has a *gratuitous* love, because He is not from an other, the Son a *thoroughly mixed* love, because He proceeds from the Father and with Him produces the Holy Spirit, to whom is attributed an *owed* love, because He does not produce a Person, but is Himself produced'. But since the love among the Three Persons is the same and most pure, the saying of Richard is to be taken non in the proper sense, but metaphorically; whence the latter Scholastics did not prove it. Cf. Brülifer on this passage of St. Bonaventure.

II. In regard to the conclusion, cf. Alexander of Hales, Summa., p. I, q. 13, m. 5. — (Bl. John Duns) Scotus, Sent., Bk. I., d. 12, q. 1, and d. 32, q. 1. in reply to n. 3 and 4. — St. Thomas, here in q. 1. a. 2. — Bl. (now St.) Albertus (Magnus), here in a. 7. — (Bl.) Peter of Tarentaise, here in q. 2, a. 2. — Richard of Middleton, here in a. 1, q. 3. — Henry of Ghent, Summa., a. 61, q. 4, and a. 54, q. 6, n. 47. — (Gabriel) Biel., Sent., Bk. I., d. 12, q. 2, nota 3.

ARTICLE II

On the property of the Holy Spirit.

Second there is principally asked concerning the second part, namely, concerning the property of the Holy Spirit, and about this three (questions) are asked:

First there is asked, whether love [amor] or charity [caritas] is proper to the Holy Spirit.

Second, whether the Holy Spirit is properly a "nexus" [nexus].

Third, whether the Holy Spirit properly is a "spirit" [spiritus].

QUESTION I

Whether love or charity is proper to the Holy Spirit?

About the first, that charity is proper to the Holy Spirit, is shown in this manner:

1. (St.) Augustine in the fifteenth (book of) On the Trinity (says):[1] « Just as in that Trinity the Holy Spirit is not the only spirit, yet is properly called the Holy Spirit; so, although the Father is charity and the Son charity, yet properly charity is said (to be) that Person, just as properly He is said (to be) the Holy Spirit ».

2. Likewise, this same is shown through the same (author in his work) on the First Canonical (Letter of St.) John,[2] where he intends to find the property of the Holy Spirit, and arrives at this saying, that the Holy Spirit is charity.

3. Likewise, that same (argument) is shown *by reason*: that[3] that (name) is properly proper to a Person, which means His manner of emanating; but "love" is of this kind, as has been proven:[4] ergo etc..

4. Likewise, just as "the Word" is reserved [verbum se habet] to the Son, so "Love" to the Holy Spirit; but "the Word" is proper to the Son: therefore, "Love" (is) proper to the Holy Spirit.

On the Contrary: 1. (St.) Augustine in the fifteenth (book of) On the Trinity (says):[5] « The Father is charity, and the Son is charity, and the Holy Spirit is charity, and all at once (are) one charity »: therefore, charity is not said properly of the Holy Spirit.

2. Likewise, love does not proceed otherwise than by loving: therefore, since love of necessity is within the one loving, and the Father and the Son by loving produce the Holy Spirit, it seems impossible, that it befit Him properly. Therefore, either the Holy Spirit is not a Person, or He is not love properly or[6] does not proceed through a manner of love.

3. Likewise, just as "Wisdom" is reserved to the Son, so "Love" to the Holy Spirit; but "Wisdom" is not proper to the Son, nay only appropriated: therefore even[7] "Love" similarly (is not proper) to the Holy Spirit: ergo etc..

4. Likewise, everything[8] which is properly said, conveys some relation: therefore, if "love" is properly said, it conveys a relation. I ask: for what? either for *the one loving*, or for *the one loved*.[9] If for *the one loving*, therefore, the one loving is not love; similarly if for *the one loved*, therefore, the Holy Spirit then either would not love or would not be loved; but this is impossible.

---

[1] Chapter 19, n. 37 : Just as there is not only in that Trinity a spirit and/or a holy one ... and nevertheless not as a trick is He properly called "the Holy Spirit". And ibid., ch. 17, a. 31: Thus the Holy Spirit properly is indicated by the word, "charity", though universally both the Father and the Son are Charity. — A little before this, trusting in the manuscripts and edition 1, we have substituted *is shown* [ostenditur] in place of *shows* [ostendit].

[2] Treatise 7, n. 6. See also On the Trinity, Bk. XV, chs. 17-20. — A little before this the Vatican edition, against the manuscripts and edition 1, omits *first* [primam], and edition 1 in place of *the same (author)* [idem] has *he* [ipsum]. Then, some codices, such as G K T W and Y, together with edition 1, have *he produces* [producit] in place of *he arrives at* [perducit].

[3] With the assistance of very many manuscripts, such as F T Z and ff, and edition1, we have put *that* [quia] in place of *that* [quod].

[4] Here in a. 1, q. 2.

[5] Chapter 17, n. 28: Thus even both the Father and the Son and the Holy Spirit are called "charity" and all together (are) the One Charity. In which text edition 1 adds *Three* [tres] after *all* [omnes].

[6] Some codices, such as V X Z and bb, falsely have (the disjunctive) *or* [aut] in place of (the alternative) *or* [sive].

[7] We have supplied here *even* [et]; then, we have substituted the genitive (of object) *to the Holy Spirit* [Spiritus sancti] for the dative (*to the Holy Spirit* [Spiritui sancto]), with the assistance of the manuscripts and edition 1.

[8] As required by the more ancient manuscripts and edition 1, we have expunged here the *that* [illud] added by the Vatican edition.

[9] In the Vatican edition and codex cc, the words *I ask ... or for the one loved?* [Quaero ... amatum] are lacking, though they are had in the other manuscripts and in edition 1.

CONCLUSION

Charity, accepted personally, is proper to the Holy Spirit; accepted essentially it means a complacency; but notionally, a concord in spirating.

I RESPOND: It must be said, that dilection among the divine can be accepted and is necessarily accepted *essentially*, *notionally* and *personally*: *essentially*, because each loves Himself [quilibet diligent se];[1] but *notionally*, because the Father and the Son concord in spirating the Holy Spirit, which concord is love or dilection; but *personally*, because He who is produced through a manner of perfect liberality, cannot be but Love or Dilection.

Whence, essentially said it means a complacency, but notionally a 'concord in spirating', and personally 'the One Processing in[2] that concord'.

Moreover, an example of this[3] can be posited in the created love, by which a bridegroom and bride love [diligunt] themselves. For they love themselves with a *social* love to live together [ad convivendum]; they love themselves furthermore with a *conjugal* love to procreate offspring, and that (offspring),[4] if it were produced from the will alone of concord, would be *love* [amor]; but now (the offspring) is *one loved*, unless "love" is said through the emphatic manner of speaking. But among the divine there is truly and properly a love, having the reckoning *of love* and *of a hypostasis*: *of love* on account of this, that from a most liberal will He first proceeds through a manner of perfect liberality; *of a hypostasis*, because since He is distinguished from the One producing and cannot be distinguished essentially, He is distinguished personally; but not so is it in created love.

1. 2. From this is clear that which is objected in the *first* and *second* (place), when it is said, that ("love")[5] is a *property* of those loving or producing; because ("love") is accepted notionally; for, insofar as *He proceeds* from them, He cannot be a property, but a distinct Person. Whence, the processing of created love and of uncreated Love is not entirely similar,[6] because here it is a property, There a Hypostasis and the Substance.

3. To that which is objected concerning "wisdom", it must be said, that it is not similar; because "wisdom" does not mean a looking-back to an other, and for that reason it is always said of itself as regards itself and is essential, unless it be appropriated; but "love" means a looking-back to those, who are joined by love. Whence just as "the Word" is proper to the Son, not appropriated,[7] because it connotes a looking-back to the One speaking; so also "love" or "charity" not only is appropriated, but also proper to the Holy Spirit. And just as the Son proceeds from the Father through a manner of a word, so the Holy Spirit through a manner of love. And from this it is, as will be more clear below,[8] that this (saying) is admitted: "The Father and the Son love Themselves with the Holy Spirit"; not, however, that the Father be wise by the begotten Wisdom.

4. To that which is last objected: *to what does it mean a looking-back?* it must be said, that (it means this) to those loving, according to which that which is "those loving" is held notionally, just as has been touched upon before.[9] For in one manner *to love themselves* is the same (thing) which *to spirate concordantly* (is); in this manner the Holy Spirit is not "loving", because He does not spirate. But he objects this concerning the essential (manner of using the term "love"),[10] who does not mean the egress from one loving, but only means the complacency of the will, by which any (of them) loves and is loved.

SCHOLIUM

The doctrine (contained) in this question is the common sentence: Alexander of Hales, SUMMA., p. I, q. 43, m. 3, a. 1, and q. 67, m. 3, a. 3. — (Bl. John Duns) Scotus, here at q. sole, and in d. 32, q. 1. — St. Thomas, SENT., Bk. I, d. 27, a. 2, q. 2; SUMMA., I, q. 37, a. 1. — Bl. (now St.) Albertus (Magnus), here in a. 4. — (Bl.) Peter of Tarentaise, here in a. 2, q. 1. — Richard of Middleton, here in a. 2, q. 1. — Giles the Roman, here in 1. princ., q. 2. — Henry of Ghent, SUMMA., a. 38, q. 2, n. 8. — (Bl.) Dionysius the Carthusian., on this and the following question, here in q. 1.

---

[1] Codex O adds *(Book) XV, chapter 17 of ON THE TRINITY* [XV. c. 17. de Trin.].

[2] Some codices, such as H I aa and bb, have *out of* [ex]. Then after *concord* [concordia] codex H adds: *In the first manner it is common to the Three, in the second manner it is in the Father and in the Son, but in the third manner it is proper to the Holy Spirit* [Primo modo est communis tribus, secundo modo est in Patre et Filio, tertio autem modo est proprium Spiritus sancti].

[3] Codex I adds *processing* [processus].

[4] Very many codices incongruously read *he* [ille]. Then after *would be love* [amor esset] codex W adds *and the reason for loving* [et ratio amandi]; then codex Y has *is not love* in place of *one loved* [amatus], which you should understand in the manner of a substantive. A little after this by *emphatic manner of speaking* [emphaticum loquendi modum] understand: emphasis, namely that grammatical figure, which is employed to intimate a greater expression, v. g. as when the abstract is employed for the concrete, when there is said: "I beg your Excellency."

[5] Understand: "love". — A little below this, after *because* [quia] in codices I and Z there is added *there "love"* [amor ibi].

[6] Not a few codices, such as A F R T X together with edition 1, having omitted the particle *and* [et], put *to uncreated love* [amori increato] in place of *of uncreated love* [amoris increati]. Then the particle <u>hic</u> refers to *created* love, and *there* [ibi] to *uncreated* love.*

[7] The Vatican edition, contrary to nearly all the codices and to edition 1, has *and is not appropriated* [et non appropriatur].

[8] Distinction 32, a. 1, q. 1, and a. 2, q. 1. — A little before this edition 1 has *there follows* [sequitur] in place of *it is* [est], which same also then adds *well* [bene] to *is admitted* [admittitur].

[9] Here, in the body and in reply to n. 1. — A little above this, the Vatican edition has *but* [sed] in place of *according to which* [secundum quod], but faultily and against the manuscripts together with the first six editions, some of which, however, such as O and Z, have *according to this that "those loving"* [amantes]. Then, very many codices, such as A I S T V W X and Y, have *they love* [diligunt] in place of *to love* [diligere].

[10] Supply with codex I *love* [amor]. The Vatican edition has *which* [quod] in place of *who* [qui], but less clearly and contrary to very many codices together with edition 1; some codices, such as H X and Y, together with editions 2, 3, 4, 5 and 6, have *that* [quia].

---

* *Trans. note*: It is better to understand the <u>hic</u> ... ibi construction, as a parallel construction of adverbs, so that the former refers to the created world, and the latter to Heaven, the uncreated world; the English translation follows this reading.

QUESTION II

Whether the Holy Spirit is the Nexus or Unity of the Father and the Son?

Second, there is asked, whether the Holy Spirit properly is the Nexus and/or Unity of Both. And that (He is) so, seems in this manner:

1. (St.) Augustine in the sixth (book of) ON THE TRINITY (says):[1] « He is not one of the two, by whom Both are conjoined »; but one is conjoined by a nexus: therefore, a nexus is not something belonging to the Two: therefore, He is properly a third Person.

2. Likewise, love among creatures is a nexus; but just as has been proven,[2] the Holy Spirit is a most perfect love: ergo etc.. But that love is a nexus, is clear through Dionysius (the Areopagite):[3] « Love, whether divine or intellectual, we call a unitive virtue ».

3. Likewise, the Holy Spirit according to the Greeks proceeds from the Father unto[4] the Son, according to the Latins from the Father and the Son. But in whatever one of these manners He proceeds, there are united in the Spirit the Father and the Son; but He, in whom They are united, is the nexus of both: therefore, the Holy Spirit is a nexus.

4. Likewise, either the Spirit of the Father is the Spirit of the Son, or not. If not: therefore, since *no one knows, what is in a man except the spirit of him, who is in him*, just as the Apostle (says),[5] the Father does not know the will of the Son, nor the Son (that) of the Father: therefore, if the Same is the spirit of (them) both, in the Spirit They are united.

ON THE CONTRARY: 1. There is no nexus except of (things) separate, for those which have not been separated,[6] do not need something connecting (them); but the Father has not been separated from the Son, nor conversely, because the Son (is) in the Father and the Father in the Son: ergo etc..

2. Likewise, a nexus is (that) in which some two convene; but the Father and the Son do not convene in a Person: therefore, no Person is the nexus of the Father and Son.

3. Likewise, those are said to be joined [necti] which convene in something, in which they are united. Therefore, if the Son and the Holy Spirit originally convened in the Father, therefore, the Father

is the nexus of the Son and the Holy Spirit: therefore, the Holy Spirit is not a nexus.

4. Likewise, a "nexus" is said, because[7] it is joined, or because it joins; if, therefore, the Holy Spirit is a nexus, therefore, either (it is) that He is joined, or that He joins. (But it is) not that He is joined; because then similarly another Person would be the nexus, similarly the Father would be the nexus; if because He joins the Father and the Son: therefore, He gives something to the Father and the Son; but this is unfitting [inconveniens]: ergo etc..

CONCLUSION

The Holy Spirit properly is said (to be) the "Nexus" or "Unity" of the Father and the Son.

I RESPOND: It must be said, that a "nexus", or "unity" of both, is properly said of the Holy Spirit. Moreover, the reason for this is, that the Father and the Son communicate in the One[8] Spirit, and for that reason He is the unity of Both. *And again*, that Spirit is Love, and for that reason They communicate in Him as in one Love; and because love is most properly a nexus,[9] for that reason the Holy Spirit properly is the Nexus, because He is[10] (Their) mutual Love, He is the Unique and Substantifying Love.

1. To that which is, therefore, objected unto the contrary, that there is no nexus except of (things) separate; it must be said that "separation" is said in a threefold manner: according to *distance*, and thus one means a local separation; and according to *difference through essence*,[11] and thus one means a substantial separation; and according to *difference of relative property*, and thus one does not mean a separation properly, but a distinction. And[12] a nexus happens to be according to any of these manners. Therefore, because the Father and the Son are distinct, for that reason They are rightly said (to be) "connected".

2. To that which is objected, that a "nexus" is that in

---

[1] Chapter 5, n. 7 : ... it is manifest, that He is not one of the two, through whom Both are conjoined.

[2] Here, in a. 1, qq. 2 and 3.

[3] ON THE DIVINE NAMES, ch. 4, § 15: We understand love (to be) a certain unitive and concretive virtue.

[4] Consenting with to manuscripts and edition 1, we have substituted *unto* [in] in place of *through* [per], which corresponds more with the manner of speaking of the Seraphic Doctor, concerning which cf. the following distinction, q. 1, and d. 14, a. 1, q. 1 in the body. Then a few manuscripts, such as aa and bb have *manners He may proceed* [modorum procedat], and the other codices, such as I Y together with edition 1, add *Holy* [sancto] to *in the Spirit* [in Spiritu].

[5] 1 Cor. 2:11. The Vulgate reads: For who of men knows, what (thoughts) belong to a man, except the spirit of the man, which is in him? — The Vatican edition, striving against the manuscripts and the first six editions, adds *any* [aliquo] after *are in* [sunt in], and a little below this after *Apostle (says)* [Apostolus] adds *and* [et]. Codex O exhibits the conclusion to argument thus: *therefore, if He is a spirit, and the Spirit of both; and if this, Both are united in the Spirit* [ergo si est spiritus, et spiritus amborum; et si hoc, ambo in Spiritu uniuntur].

[6] Codex T has *for they who have not been separated* [qui enim non separate sunt].

[7] In the Vatican edition this is prefaced with an *either* [aut].

[8] Codex E has *the Same* [eodem] in the place of *One* [uno], which less well, the Vatican edition, in disagreement with all the other manuscripts and edition 1, omits.

[9] Very many codices, such as A C G K L S U V W and Y, faultily add here *of Him* [eius]. Then, after *for that reason* [ideo], edition 1 adds *even* [et].

[10] The Vatican edition omits *He is* [est], by reading: *because mutual love is a unique and substantifying love* [quia amor mutuus est amor unicus et substantificus]; thus also the other editions and very many codices, with this difference, that very many codices have *united* [unitus] in place of *unique* [unicus], a few others have *vivifying* [vivificus]. More probable to us, on account of the context, appears the reading of codices H I and M, in the text here received.

[11] Codices H and Y have *essential* [essentialem] and codex A *of essence* [essentiae], which many codices, such as A D F G K L O R S T U V etc. together with the first six editions, omit.

[12] Trusting in many manuscripts, such as A F G H I K T V X etc. and edition 1, we have substituted *And ... according to any of these manners* [Et] for *A nexus in any of these manners happens to be* [in].

which some two convene; it must be said, that there is an *essential* convenience, and there is a convenience *of origin*,[1] and in each manner there can be a nexus; and although the Father and the Son do not convene *formally* in one Person, they do, however, convene *originally*, because one Person arises from each One and in the same manner.

3. To that which is objected, that the Son and the Holy Spirit convene in the Father; it must be said, that a convenience of *origin* is said in a twofold manner: either because they arise from one, or because one arises from them. If because from one,[2] thus it is not said (to be) a nexus, because a nexus is a union *consequent* to distinction, but unity in origin *antecedes* distinction. But if because (they are) the origin of one,[3] most properly is there a nexus; and thus it is in the Father and the Son in respect to the Holy Spirit.

Yet, it can be said otherwise, that it is not similar,

because the Son and the Holy Spirit are not produced in the same manner from the Father, but the Father and the Son do in the same manner spirate the Holy Spirit. And *again*, there is a convenience of the Father and the Son in the Holy Spirit, as in love, to which it belongs to join; in this manner the Son and the Holy Spirit do convene in the Father.

4. To that which is objected, that one means a "nexus", either because it joins, etc.; it must be said, that there are *certain* words, which in the active voice signify a passion, as the words pertaining to sensing, such as "I see", "I hear" and the like;[4] *certain ones* in the active voice signify action, such as "I make" and "I strike", similarly in the passive (voice). Therefore, it must be said, that this (word) which is "to join", when the Spirit is said to join, because He proceeds from Both, rightly signifies in the active voice a passion and in the passive an action; and for that reason does not signify,[5] that He gives something to the Father and to the Son, but that rather He receives.

SCHOLIUM

If the Holy Spirit is said (to be) a nexus, the sense is, that He is the Love from both, namely, from the Father and the son, as One produces uniformly from one principle. Cf. solution to n. 2. In regard to that conclusion, cf. below, Doubt 4. — Alexander of Hales, SUMMA, p. I, q. 43, m. 3, a. 3. — St. Thomas, here in a. 1. q. 3; SUMMA, I, q. 37, a. 1 ad 3. — Bl. (now St.) Albertus (Magnus), here in aa. 8 and 9. — (Bl.) Peter of Tarentaise, here in a. 3. q. 1. — Richard of Middleton, here in a. 2, q. 2. — Giles the Roman, here in 1. princ. q. 3.

QUESTION III

Whether the Holy Spirit is properly a spirit?

Third and last, there is asked, whether the Holy Spirit is properly a spirit. And that (it is) so, seems in this manner:

1. Because the Person of the Holy Spirit is designated most properly by this name of His, wherefore [quod] He is said (to be) "the Holy Spirit";[6] but this noun "*holy*" does not constrain this (noun) which is "*spirit*", since it is equally common: therefore, that Person is properly said (to be) "the Spirit."

2. Likewise, He is said (to be) the Spirit, because[7] He is spirated; but what is spirated, is not generated, nor the other way around: therefore, since *to be spirated* does not convene with the Father nor with the Son: therefore, it convenes with the Holy Spirit.

3. Likewise, men concordant [concordes] in one evil are said (to be) *conspirators*, not because they think the same, but because they desire the same evil, and because one affection, binding to the same evil, belongs to all: therefore, since *con-*

spiracy[8] comes from *spiration*, naught is said to be spirated except love: therefore, neither is the Holy Spirit said (to be) but Love: ergo etc..

ON THE CONTRARY: 1. *God is a spirit, and those, who adore Him, must adore in spirit and truth*, according to the fourth (chapter of the Gospel of St.) John;[9] but the whole Trinity is to be adored: therefore, the whole Trinity is a spirit; this same (thing) does (St.) Augustine say.[10]

2. Likewise, this same is shown *by reason*, in this manner: "spirit" is divided against "body": therefore, what is not a "body", is a "spirit":[11] therefore, ("spirit") is an absolute noun, not a relative (one): therefore, (it convenes with the whole Trinity).

3. Likewise, "spirit" is said either from *spirituality*, or from *spiration*. If from *spirituality*, thus it is divided against "body", and it is established that it convenes with the whole[12] Trinity; if from *spiration*; on the contrary: *to spirate* actively said

---

[1] The Vatican edition, agreeing with no codex, has *an original convenience* [convenientia originalis], and then against the more ancient codd.s and ed. 1, after *there can* [potest] adds *be said to* [dici], then against many codd., such as I K M R T Z etc., and ed. 1, for *do not convene* [non conveniat] it puts *do not communicate* [non communicent].

[2] Codices L and O here add *thus the Son and the Holy Spirit convene originally in the Father, but* [sic Filius et Spiritus sanctus conveniunt originaliter in Patre, sed].

[3] Thus very many codices with editions 2 & 3; but the Vatican ed. reads *because the origin of one (is) from two* [quia a duobus unius origo]; codex R together with edition 1 has *because one arises* [quia oritur]; codex X has *because one arises from two* [quia unus oritur a duobus].

[4] Edition 1 has *(words) entirely similar* [consimilia], and then after *certain ones* [quaedam] adds *which* [quau].

[5] Codex X has *it does not signify* [non significat], codex H *it does not follow* [non sequitur].

[6] One or the other codex, such as Z, together with edtion 1 omits *Holy* [sanctus], in place of which phrase codex O puts *because He is pro-*

duced through spiration [quia per spirationem producitur]. A little before this codex Z has *by which* [quo] in place of *wherefore* [quod], in place of which some codices have *because* [quia]. Then codices aa and bb after *does not contrain this* [non coarctat hoc] add *noun* [nomen] and edition 1 adds *Holy* [sanctus] to *"the Spirit"*.

[7] Trusting in many manuscripts, such as A F G H I K M T V Y etc. we have substituted *because* [quia] in place of *because* [quod].

[8] We offer the true reading from many mss., such as A F G H I K M S T W etc. and ed. 1, putting *conspiracy* [conspiratio] for *spiration* [spiratio].

[9] Verse 24.

[10] ON THE TRINITY, Bk. V, ch. 11, n. 12, and ibid., Bk. XV, ch. 19, n. 37. See here the text of Master (Peter), ch. 3. — Edition 1 has *this very (thing)* [hoc ipsum] in place of *this same (thing)*.

[11] In codex O there is added *but the whole Trinity is not a body, therefore* etc. [sed tota Trinitas non est corpus, ergo]. At the end of the argument supply: *it convenes with the whole Trinity* [convenit toti Trinitati].

[12] From the more ancient manuscripts and edition 1, we have supplied the not so well omitted *whole* [toti].

convenes with the whole Trinity, because the whole Trinity is said to inspire: therefore actively said, it is not said relatively, therefore, neither passively.

4. Likewise, according to which it is said from *spiration*, it seems that it more properly convenes with the Son; and this is clear through authority, Job (chapter) thirty-two:[1] *The inspiration of the Omnipotent gives understanding*; but this is appropriated to the Son: ergo etc..

5. Likewise, spiration is a natural act;[2] but the Son alone proceeds through a manner of nature: therefore, the Son alone is spirated.

CONCLUSION

"Spirit", to the extent that it is said from "spirituality", convenes with the whole Trinity; but to the extent that it is said from "spiration", it is proper to the Holy Spirit.

I Respond: It must be said, that this noun "spirit" is found in *bodies*, in *rational*[3] substances and in God; and though in God it be most proper, because most properly is there in Him spirituality and spiration, however, the reckoning of cognizing and of speaking begins from corporal substance, as from the posterior.

Moreover, in a *corporal* substance "spirit" is said in a twofold manner: either from *spirituality* (divided) against "corpulence"; and thus it is said absolutely, and "spirit" is called *a subtle body*, just as it is accepted in the book, ON THE DIFFERENCE OF SPIRIT AND SOUL;[4] or from *spiration*; and thus "a spirit" is said (to be) "a breath", just as (St. John) Chrysostom accepts it, in the third (chapter of the Gospel of St.) John:[5] *The Spirit breathes where he will* etc. And in the Psalm:[6] *Fire, hail, spirit* etc..

According to this twofold manner it is accepted in a *spiritual* or rational substance, either from *spirituality* (divided) against *corporality*: and thus a rational substance and/or its interior power is said (to be) "a spirit", Ecclesiastes (chapter) three:[7] *Who knows, if the spirit of the children* etc.; or from *spiration*; and thus an affection and/or love is said (to be) "a spirit". And the reason for this is, that the act of spiration in a body is an *internal* act, a *continual* act,

(and) a *vivifying* act, having its origin from *heat*.[8] Therefore, because an egress of love, as love is, comes from *within*; and love is a *vivifying* act, because love is life; and against love is a *continual* act, because love ought to be continually returned, and then it is perfect, when a man loves in this manner; again it is a spiritual *heat*: for this reason love alone is said spiritually to be spirated; and thus is accepted that verse from the last (chapter of St. Paul's) First (Letter) to the Thessalonians:[9] *That your whole spirit* etc..

According to this twofold manner it is accepted among *the divine*. For according to which "spirit" is said from spirituality, thus it convenes with the whole Trinity; for the whole Trinity lacks corporality and materiality; and thus it is an absolute noun, in the fourth (chapter of the Gospel of St.) John:[10] *God is a spirit*. But according to which it is said from spiration, it thus convenes that Person alone, who proceeds[11] as Love, for the reason already said. For "to be spirated" among spirituals belongs to love alone; and since love can be rightly and ordinately spirated, and thus is pure; and/or in an indirect and filthy manner, and thus is libidinous: for that reason that Person, who is Love, is not only said (to be) "the Spirit", but "the Holy Spirit". Not so is the Son said (to be) "Holy",[12] because generation is a natural movement, about which sanctity and/or purity is attained, just as it is attained about the love of the will.

1. 2. 3. 4. To that which is objected, that "spirating" belongs to the whole Trinity; it must be said, that "*to spirate*" is said in a twofold manner. *in one manner* "to spirate" is the same (thing) which "to produce the Spirit"[13] (is); and in this manner it does not convene the whole Trinity; *in another* manner "to spirate" is the same (thing) which "to inspire" (is); and in this manner[14] it convenes with the whole Trinity, because "to inspire" means "an effect of the spirit", which is from the whole Trinity. For one is said to be inspired because there is spiritually sent into our spirit, either an affection or the cognition (of something).

5. To that which is objected, that[15] it is a natural movement; it must be said, that, thus, it is in the corporeals, which pant [spirant] on account of the indigence of nature; but not so among spiritual substances, which sigh [spirant] out of the liberality of the will. Whence it is not transferred according to a reckoning of the former,[16] but by the reckoning of other properties.

SCHOLIUM

In conclusion the ancient Scholastics agree with the Latin and Greek Fathers. Alexander of Hales, SUMMA, p. I. q. 43, m. 1, and q. 63, m . 1. — Scot., SENT., Bk. I, d. 18, q. sole, in either redaction. — St. Thomas, here in a. 1, q. 4; SUMMA., q. 36, a. 1. — Bl. (now St.) Albertus (Magnus), here in a. 13; SUMMA., p. I, tr. 8, q. 36, m. 1. — Peter of Tarentaise, here in a. 3. q. 2. — Richard of Middleton, here in a. 2, q. 3. — Giles the Roman, here in 1. princ., q. 4. — Henry of Ghent, SUMMA., a. 61, qq. 1 and 2. — Durandus (of Saint-Pourçain), here in a. 1. — (Bl.) Dionysius the Carthusian, here in q. 2.

---

[1] Verse 8, in which text the Vulgate together with editin 1 has *intelligence* [intelligentiam] in place of *understanding* [intellectum]. Then edition 1 has *this (i. e. intelligence)* [haec] in place of *this (i. e. understanding)* [hoc].

[2] Cf. Aristotle, ON RESPIRATION.

[3] We have substituted with the help of many manuscripts, such as A F G K T etc. and editions 1, 2, 3 *rational* [rationalibus] in place of *reckonable* [rationabilibus].

[4] This book is attributed by Richard of Middleton (here in a. 2. q. 3) to Constabulus; but, cf. BIBLIOTECA PHILOSPHORUM MEDIAE AETATIS, edited by Barach, Innsbruck, 1876-1878, fascicule 2, where it cites: Excerpts from Costa-Ben Luca, DE DIFFERENTIAE ANIMAE ET SPIRITUS. See also the book, ON THE SPIRIT, ch. 1 (among the works of Aristotle).

[5] Homily 26 (a.k.a. 36) on the Gospel of John 3:8.

[6] Psalm 148:8.

[7] Verse 21.

[8] On these actus of respiration see Aristotle, ON RESPIRATION; and Nemesius, ON THE NATURE OF MAN, ch. 28.

[9] Verse 23.

[10] Verse 24.

[11] Codex K inserts *through a manner of love and/or* [per modum amoris vel]. Then after *said* [dicta] the Vatican edition and codex cc, not coherently with what is subjoined, and against the testimony of the other codices and edition 1, has *"to spirate"* in place of *"to be spirated"*.

[12] On the authority of the manuscripts and the first six editions we have expunged here the faultily added *Spirit* [Spiritus].

[13] In the manuscripts and in editions 1, 2 and 3, there is not added the *Holy* [sanctum], which is had in the Vatican edition.

[14] The Vatican edition, against the more ancient manuscripts and edition 1, has *that* [ille] in place of *in this manner* [sic].

[15] Supply: spiration. A little below this we prefer the reading of the very many codices, such as F P X Y and edition 1, which have *sigh* [spirant] in place of *inspire* [inspirant]

[16] The Vatican edition together with codex cc has *are not transferred* [transferuntur], but falsely, because the subject is "spiration", and against the older codices and edition 1. Codex K adds, sufficiently well, *to the divine* [ad divina].

DOUBTS ON THE TEXT OF THE MASTER

DOUBT I

In this part there are doubts about the text (of Master Peter), and, first, concerning this which he says, that *the Holy Spirit is the love or charity or dilection of the Father*. Therefore, it is asked, whether charity and dilection differ; and that they do [quod sic], seems through (St.) Isidore,[1] saying: *Love* [amor] belongs to rationals and irrationals, *dilection* only to rationals. *But on the contrary*: Dionysius (the Areopagite), ON THE DIVINE NAMES, chapter four:[2] « Theologians seem to me to say that [quid] with the common name of dilection and love »: and in the same place[3] he reprehends those distinguishing (the two), saying, that they fabricate a meaning among delicate sounds, as if we could not signify "four" through "twice two", and "fatherland" through "land of our birth" [per natale].

I RESPOND: Some wanted to say, that they do differ, because that properly is said (to be) "dilection", which is out of an ordinate will, but "love" [amor] is a libidinous affection. But this distinction is against Dionysius[4] and against (St.) Augustine (in his work) ON THE GOSPEL OF JOHN[5] and against the Canon of Sacred Scripture, because the Lord first asked from Peter: Simon (son) of John, *lovest thou Me?* [diligis me] and afterwards said: *lovest thou Me?* [amas me] and thus they are accepted for the same (idea); and Dionysius reprehends this difference.[6]

However, some difference can, nevertheless, be assigned. For although they can be said of one and the same affection, however, for one reason and another. For *"love"* [amor] means the adhesion of affection in respect to the one loved; whence Dionysius (says):[7] « We mean "unitive love" [amorem unitivum] ». But *"dilection"* adds an election to this; whence dilection is an election out of diverse (things); whence the fifth (chapter of the Canticle) of Canticles:[8] *My beloved, chosen out of a thousand* [Dilectus meus electus ex millibus]. Moreover, *charity* adds a great appreciation to this. For (what is) "dear" [carum] is said (to be) that which is estimated (to be) of great price, according to that which the Apostle in his letters calls (his) *"dearly beloved faithful"* [fideles carissimos], 1 Cor. 4.[9]

DOUBT II

Likewise, is doubted about this which he says: *properly the Word of God is also said (to be) the Wisdom of God*, either because it is accepted *properly*, because it befits one alone, or *properly*, because it is appropriated: because if *to one alone*, this is false, because *wisdom* in no manner means a personal property; if properly, because *appropriated*, this does nothing for the proposed (argument), because Master (Peter) wants to inquire into the property of the Holy Spirit, not an appropriated (title). *And again*, charity seems to be appropriated more to the Father, according to which there is said in that phrase, « The Father is Charity »:[10] *Likewise*, the same [hoc] is seen through Richard (of St. Victor),[11] that « gratuitous love is in the Father, due (love) in the Holy Spirit, (love) thoroughly mixed out of each in the Son »: therefore, since "charity" means "gratuitous love", it ought, therefore, be appropriated to the Father.

I RESPOND: It must be said, that there is not a omnimodal similitude (between "wisdom" and "charity"),[12] but there is a similitude in this: for commonly ("charity") can *be appropriated*, by maintaining a unity of voice and/or of signification. Similarly, any noun can be at the same time said as a [per] *property* and as an essence, by maintaining a unity of voice and of signification, and yet of itself it is common; and such is the noun "charity".

In another manner it can be said, that *"charity"* is a common and proper and appropriated (name); and (St.) Augustine,[13] first shows, that it is an appropriated (name) through the similitude to *wisdom*, and after (this), shows, that it is truly[14] a proper (name), below (where it is written): *Now, however, let us take up what we began to show*, etc.. Whence from this authority there is not had, that "charity" is a proper (name), but only that it is an appropriated (name). But, yet, from other words of (St.) Augustine there is had, that "charity" not only is an appropriated (name), but (is) also one properly proper to the Holy Spirit.

To that which is objected, that charity is appropriated to the Father; it must be said, that "charity" has a twofold

---

[1] Which can be gathered from these words taken from (his), ETYMOLOGIES, Bk. VIII, ch. 2: Moreover, every carnal dilection is not dilection, but rather is accustomed to be called "love". But the noun "dilection" is accustomed to be accepted only among better things. He says the same in (his), DIFFERENCES, Bk. I, under the verb, "to love" [amare et diligere]: Some said that "to love" [amare] has been naturally placed in us, but "to love" [diligere] out of election.

[2] § 12.

[3] § 11.

[4] Loc. cit.

[5] Tract 123, n. 5, where in the exposition of these words: *Simon son of John, lovest thou Me* etc. (John 24:15-17), he says: Where there is also demonstrated that love [amorem] and love [dilectionem] are one and the same.

[6] Codex dd reads *distinction* [distinctionem].

[7] ON THE DIVINE NAMES, Ch. 4, § 15. See (below) a. 2, q. 2, 2nd. arg. of the fundament, in this Distinction. — In which text, many codices, together with the first six editions, have falsely *mutual* [mutuum] in place of *unitive* [unitivum].

[8] Verse 10.

[9] Verses 14 and 17. — See more on these terms, below in d. 17, p. I, Doubt 1. St. Thomas, SUMMA, p. I II, q. 26, a. 3, Bl. (now St.) Albertus (Magnus), here in a. 2, Richard (of St. Victor) and (Bl.) Peter (of Tarentaise), here on the text itself, agree.

[10] In the OFFICIUM SS. TRINITATIS, 1st Antiphon for the 3rd Nocturne (« The Father is Charity, the Son Grace, the Holy Spirit the Communication (of Both), o Blessed Trinity! »).

[11] ON THE TRINITY, Bk. V, ch. 17 ff. See above, a. 1. q. 3, opp. 4. — Then from the more ancient manuscripts and edition 1, we have substituted *that* [quia] in place of *that* [quod].

[12] Namely, between *wisdom* and *charity* in regard to the appropriation and sense of their own (signified), insofar as it clear a little below from the second solution.

[13] See the text of Master (Peter), ch. 2, and, for the following, ch. 3.

[14] Trusting in the manuscripts and edition 1, we have inserted here *truly* [vere], and then after *below* [infra] we have expunged the *in the same distinction* [eadem distinctione]. Not a few codices, such as A G H I T etc., together with edition 1, have *truly properly* [vere proprie], but not so congruously; codex cc has *truly and properly* [vere et proprie].

comparison to other virtues. For, it is compared as (their) *mother*, as (St.) Ambrose says,[1] it is compared as (their) *bond* [vinculum], as the Apostle (Paul) says to the Colossians, chapter three:[2] *Charity is the bond of perfection.* By the reckoning of the first it is appropriated to the Father, by the reckoning of the second to the Holy Spirit.

To that which is objected concerning Richard, it must be said, that *"gratuitous"* does not mean a property of love or of loving, but a property of the person, who gives and does not receive.

Doubt III

Is likewise asked of this which he says, that *the Holy Spirit is the dilection, by which the Father and the Son love* [diligunt] *love in turn themselves and us.* It is asked, whether the Father and the Son love [diligant] *us* with the Holy Spirit. For whether They love *Themselves* with the Holy Spirit, is asked[3] in the thirty-third distinction, where that question is especially moved. But the first seems entirely false and improper. For when it is said: 'The Father and the Son love us' etc., it is established that the verb of *"loving"* [diligendi] is held essentially: therefore, if They love [diligant][4] with the Holy Spirit, They are the Holy Spirit. And *again*, (St.) Augustine says,[5] that this is in no manner conceded: 'The Father loves Himself with the Holy Spirit, because "to love" is held essentially': therefore, similarly in the proposed.

I Respond: *Certain ones* say, that that ablative is expounded through this preposition, *per*, with the accusative, that is *per Spiritum sanctum*; and the rule[6] is, that this preposition, *per*, with transitive verbs means a prepositional clause [subauctoritatem], however, with intransitives [absolutis] an instrumental clause [auctoritatem]. Whence when "to love" [diligere] is transitive, the sense is, that the Father and the Son love us through the Holy Spirit, as if one were to say: 'The Father works through the Son'. — But this exposition does not seem fitting, because similarly there could[7] be said: 'The Father and the Son punish or hate us with the Holy Spirit'; which (is) not (what St.) Augustine wants to say.

Moreover, it must be noted, that *"to love"* [diligere] sometimes is held *in a purely essential manner* [pure essentialiter], as when there is said: 'The Father loves Himself';[8] other times *in a purely notional manner* [pure notionaliter], as when there is said: 'The Father and the Son love Themselves with the Holy Spirit', just as will be clear;[9] other times *partly in an essential manner, partly in a notional manner*, just as when there is said: 'They love us with the Holy Spirit'; and this[10] is clear, because 'that the Father and the Son love us with the Holy Spirit' is the same as 'that They send the Holy Spirit to us or to inspire us'. Moreover, "to send"

or "to inspire" conveys a notional and essential act, because the sense is that They produce the Spirit and confer the gift of Him on us; whence it means at once the production of the Holy Spirit and the conferral of grace. And although in respect to the essential act the habit of the ablative is not received, it is however, received by a reckoning of its notion, just as (it is) here: 'The Father speaks Himself by His Word, He also speaks creatures by the Word'; in a similar manner it is to be understood in the proposed.

Doubt IV

Is likewise asked of this which he says: *For whether He is the unity of both, or the sanctity*; what is said by this name *unity*? Because "unity" means either an *essential unity*, or a *notional one*, or a *personal one*. Not an essential one, because then it would not belong to Both, but to the Three; not a notional one, because the Holy Spirit is not the common "spiration"; not the personal one, because the Father and the Son are not one (thing) in a Person. *Likewise* it is asked, in which manner these[11] are distinguished, *unity, sanctity, charity*.

I Respond: It must be said, that "unity" is held (here) *in the personal sense* [personaliter]. But it must be attended to, that a "unity" of anything is said in a twofold manner: either for the reason that some are one (thing), and thus to the Father and the Son does not belong a *personal* unity; or for the reason that some have been united, and thus the Father and the Son are united in a unique person, such as the Person of the Holy Spirit, who is the Love and Chain binding (the Two).[12]

To that which is asked, in what do those three differ? It must be said, that one[13] adds upon the other. For *unity* means a condition of every love, since every love is a unitive force; *sanctity* means a condition of chaste love (divided) against libidinous (love), which is not pure; *charity* means an outstanding [praecipui] condition of love; for He is said (to be) Charity for this reason, because He is the Love having been dearly beloved in an inestimable manner [amor inaestimabiliter habens carum amatum].

Doubt V

Likewise is asked of this which he says: *not by participation, but by Their own Essence, ... preserving the unity of spirit.* For it seems that he does not speak well, because to "preserve the unity of spirit" is to "produce the Holy Spirit": therefore, according to this the Father and the Son produce the Holy Spirit with Their own Essence, and thus it seems

---

[1] Commentary on the First Letter to the Corinthians, ch. 8, v. 2: For while charity, which is the mother of all good (things), is not eagerly followed, they do not know (the virtues), as one ought. The rest of the Commentary here is not genuine. Concerning (its) author (commonly called "Ambrosiaster"), see distinction XIX, ch. 4, note on the text of Master (Peter). [2] Verse 14.

[3] The Vatican edition together with some of the codices has the indicative *is asked* [quaeritur]. A little below this before *moves* [movet], one or the other codex, such as I and Z, add *Master (Peter)*.

[4] Edition 1 has the indicative *they love* [diligunt]. then codex T reads *They are by the Holy Spirit* [sunt Spiritu sancto] for *They are the Holy Spirit* [sunt Spiritus sanctus].

[5] On the Trinity, Bk. IV, ch. 7, n. 12, and ch. 17, n. 28.

[6] Codex O has *and the reason for this* [et ratio huius] in place of *and the rule* [et regula]. Then, after *intransitives* [absolutis] from the ancient mss. and ed. 1, we have substituted *however* [vero] for *but* [autem].

[7] The Vatican edition together with codex cc, but with the other codices together with edition 1 objecting, has *it can* [potest].

[8] The codices do not agree amongst themselves; many, such as A F G H K S T X Y etc., together with edition 1, exhibit our reading; the Vatican edition together with codex cc has less distinctly *the Father and the Son love Themselves* [Pater et Filius diligunt se]; codex I has *the Father and the Son loves Themselves* [Pater et Filius diligit se].

[9] Distinction 32, a. 1, qq. 1 and 2.

[10] The faulty reading of the Vatican edition, which has *from this it* [ex hoc] for *this* [hic], and the little below *namely* [scilicet] in place of *that* [quod], are corrected from the manuscripts and edition 1.

[11] Codex dd has *here are these* [hic] in place of *these* [haec].

[12] For more on this see a. 2, q. 2 of this distinction.

[13] Edition 1 adds *of Them* [istorum].

that They spirate with (Their) Essence.[1] *Likewise* what is said also seems (to be) false, *not by participation*, because the Father and the Son by sharing in the spiration [participatione spirationis][2] preserve (Their) unity.

I RESPOND: It must be said, that (St.) Augustine[3] wants to show, that there is a twofold manner of unity among the Father and the Son, which is (also) among the members of Christ, namely (that) *of nature* and *of will*; but differently, because in us there is a unity *of nature* through a sharing in one common essence, but we are not the essence itself.[4] However, the Father and the Son do not share the Essence as (something) diverse, nay they are the Essence Itself. Similarly, among us there is a conformity *of will* through a gift of God, which unites us; but the Father and the Son are united not by having received a gift from another, but by Their own Spirit; and this is clear the response.[5]

Likewise, is asked concerning the reckoning of (St.) Augustine: *For He who is common to Them both, is Himself called properly, that which Both (are) commonly*; therefore according to this, for an equal reason, the Holy Spirit is said (to be) God properly, since (the noun) "God" is common to Both.

I RESPOND: It must be said, that there is an equivocation in (the term), "*community*" [communitate]. For (St.) Augustine does not call "*common*" [commune] what is *among more* and *concerns more*, but what (is) *from more*; and thus (what is) "common" is said rather from "*communion*" [communione], than from "*community*", so that they be comparable in meaning just as "union" [unio] and "unity" [unitas] are. And since "charity" does not only mean a *community*, because (this is) among more, but (also) a *communion* through a unity[6] of distinct (persons): for that reason, although it is said essentially, nevertheless, it can, yet, be said personally.

DISTINCTION XI

CHAPTER I

That the Holy Spirit proceeds from the Father and the Son, Whom, however, the Greeks disavow to proceed from the Son.

Here, it must be said, that the Holy Spirit is from [a] the Father and the Son and proceeds from the Father and the Son, which (dogma) many heretics deny. Moreover, that He proceeds from [de] Both, « by the many testimonies of divine utterance is completely proven ».[1] For the Apostle says: *God sent the Spirit of His Son into our hearts.* Behold here the Spirit is said (to be) of the Son. And elsewhere:[2] *But he who does not have the Spirit of Christ, this one does not belong to Him.* The Son Himself also says of the Holy Spirit in the Gospel:[3] *Whom I shall send to you from* [a] *the Father.* Moreover, the Spirit is said (to be) of the Father, where there is read:[4] *If the Spirit of Him, who raised up Jesus from the dead, dwells in you.* And Christ Himself says:[5] *For you are not the ones, who speak, but the Spirit of your Father, who speaks.* And in another place:[6] *Whom the Father will send in My Name.* And elsewhere the Son Himself says of the Holy Spirit: *He proceeds from* [de] *the Father.* By these and very many other authorities is shown, that the Holy Spirit proceeds from [a] the Father and the Son.

The Greeks, however, say, that the Holy Spirit pro-

ceeds only from the Father, and not from the Son. Wherefore, for that reason they say, that the Truth in the Gospel wholly containing the Faith, saying of the procession of the Holy Spirit, mentions [commemorat] only the Father, saying: *The Spirit, who proceeds from the Father*;[7] and also for this reason, that in the principle Councils, which were celebrated among them,[8] their Symbols (i.e. Creeds) were so sanctioned with subjoined anathemas, that it is licit for no one to teach (anything) else concerning the Faith in the Trinity [nulli de Trinitatis fide aliud] and/or to preach in another manner, than is contained there. Indeed in which Symbols, when the Holy Spirit is mentioned to proceed from the Father, and not from the Son, anyone whomsoever, they say, adds that He proceeds from the Son, incurs anathema; whence they also accuse us as liable [reos] to anathema. They also add to the assertion of their own opinion and in testimony of our own damnation concerning the Symbol of Faith, that following [secundum] the tradition of the aforesaid Councils, (Pope) Leo III of Rome, left for posterity [posteris] transcribed on tablets of silver in front of the altar of blessed (St.) Paul, for the love of — as he said — and as a defense [cautela] for the orthodox Faith. Indeed, in which Symbol, only the Father is mentioned in the procession of the Spirit, with these words: « And in the Holy Spirit, the Lord and Vivifier, proceeding out of the [ex] Father, with the Father and the Son to be co-adored and glorified »[9] etc.. That is the Symbol, which is sung at Mass, put forth

---

[1] Trusting in the more ancient mss. and ed. 1, we have substituted *with (Their) Essence* [essentia] in place of *essentially* [essentialiter].

[2] A few codices, such as K V X, read *in the Holy Spirit* [Spiritus sancti] in place of *in the spiration* [spirationis].

[3] See the words of (St.) Augustine, in the text of Master (Peter), ch. 2, near the end.

[4] Codices L and O add *but with something added* [nis cum aliquot addito], and then rightly put *However* [vero] in place of the *For* [enim], which the editions and very many codices have.

[5] Codd. V & X have *that (argument)* [illud] for *response* [responsio].

[6] Codices H M and N have *connection* [connexionem] in place of *unity* [unitatem]; codex Y has *through union and connection* [per unionem et connexionem]; cod. cc has *but community through union* [sed communitatem per unionem]. A little before this, trusting in the more ancient mss. and editions 1, 2, 3 and 6, we have inserted *yet* [tamen].

NOTES ON THE BOOK OF SENTENCES

[1] (St.) Augustine, ON THE TRINITY, Bk. XV, ch. 26, n. 45. — The many texts of Sacred Scripture, which follow, are found in the same place; but in another order and with many words interposed. The first text of the Apostle is Gal. 4:6, where the Vulgate with (St.) Augustine and editions 1, 2, 5, 7 & 8 has *your hearts* [corda vestra] for *our hearts* [corda nostra].

[2] Rom. 8:9. — The codices and edition 1 cite *there* [ibi] instead of *elsewhere* [alibi], but faultily.   [3] John 15:26.

[4] Rom. 8:11, where the editions, contrary to manuscripts A C and E, read *Christ* [Christum] for *Jesus* [Iesum].

[5] Mt. 10:20. — Codd. B & D add with the Vulgate *in you* [in vobis].

[6] John 14, 26 and the following passage ibid. 15:26, where the Vulgate has: *proceeds from the Father* [a Patre procedit]. — The codices omit *in* [in] before *another place* [alio loco].

[7] John 15:26. — A little before this, for *wholly containing the faith* [fidem integre continente] the Vatican ed. with not a few codd. has *containing the whole Faith* [fidem integram continente], but in disagreement with the codd. and the better edd.. Even (Peter) Abelard (THEOL. CHRIST., Bk. IV, col. 1300 ff.) reads *wholly* [integre], from which (book) Master (Peter Lombard) excerpts nearly word-for-word the things which follow, up to: *That is the Symbol* [Illud est Symbolum].

[8] These Councils are Nicea (A.D. 325), Constantinople I (A.D. 381), Ephesus (A.D. 430) and Chalcedon (A.D. 451).

[9] In these words of the Symbol, edition 1 reads: *Vivifying One* [vivificantem] for *Vivifier* [vivificatorem]; and edition 5 has *conglorified* [conglorificandum] for *glorified* [glorificandum]. — The text popularly received is: « the Lord and Vivifier (in the Greek: τὸ πνεῦμα τὸ ἅγιον, τὸ κύριον, τὸ ζωοποιόν) who proceeds from the Father (ἐκπορευόμενον), who together with the Father and the Son is adored and conglorified ». Master (Peter) erroneously calls this the Nicene Creed, since it belongs to (that) of the First Council of Constantinople.

in the Nicene Council, at the end of which there has been subjoined: « He who has taught (something) else [aliud] and/or preached in another manner, anathema sit ». And for that reason the Greeks say we (are) anathematized, because we say, that the Holy Spirit proceeds from [a] the Son, which is not contained there. For because according to us there is said there: « Qui a Patre Filioque procedit » the second of the two (words has) been added by the Latins, namely *Filioque*.

But we determine those words thus: « who has taught (something) else, and/or preached in another manner », that is 'has taught *the contrary* and/or preached *in a contrary manner*, anathema sit'. Therefore, it puts *"(something) else"* [aliud] in place of *"opposite"*, just as the Apostle (Paul) does in (his) Letter to the Galatians:[1] *If anyone has preached another Gospel* [aliud evangelizaverit], that is "a contrary one", *anathema sit*. He does not say: "if one has added anything" [quid]. « For if he would say that, he would, as (St.) Augustine says,[2] have prejudged his very self, he who desired to come to certain ones, to whom he wrote, just as to the Thessalonians, to *supply, those (things) which were lacking to their faith*. But he who supplies, adds what was less, he does not take away what was therein. Moreover, he who steps aside from the rule of faith, does not enter upon the way, but retreats from the way. » Moreover, to that, which they oppose from the Gospel, we respond thus: 'that when the Truth says in it, *that the Holy Spirit proceeds from the Father*, He does not add *only*, and for that reason He does not deny that He proceeds from Himself; but names the Father only for this reason, that He is accustomed to refer to Him even that which is His own, because He has it from Him.'

CHAPTER II

On the agreement of the Latins and the Greeks in sense, and (their) difference in words.

It must be known, that the Greeks confess, that the Holy Spirit is of the Son, just as also of the Father, because the Apostle says[3] *the Spirit of the Son*, and the Truth in the Gospel *the Spirit of truth*. But since 'that there is Holy Spirit of the Father and/or of the Son' is not other, than 'that He is from the Father and the Son', they also seem in this to agree [conveniunt] in the same sentence of faith with us, though they dissent in words.

Whence, also certain catholic Doctors, understanding, there to be one and the same sentence of the aforesaid words, by which the Holy Spirit is said *"to proceed from the Son* and *to be of the Son"*, have professed, that the Holy Spirit also proceeds from the Son. Whence (St.) Athanasius in (his) Symbol of Faith (says):[4] « The Holy Spirit (is) from the Father and the Son, not made nor created nor begotten, but proceeding ». Behold he said openly that the Holy Spirit proceeds from the Father and the Son. Even (St.) Didymus (the Blind), their greatest Doctor, in the book, ON THE HOLY SPIRIT[5] says that the Holy Spirit proceeds from the Son: « The Savior, he says, who (is) also the Truth, says: *He does not speak by Himself*, that is, not without Me and without My judgement [arbitrio] and (that) of the Father, because (He is) inseparable from Me and from the Father's Will, because He is not out of [ex] Himself, but is out of the Father and Me. For this very (Being), which subsists and speaks, is His from the Father and from Me ». Likewise:[6] « The Holy Spirit, who is the Spirit of truth and the Spirit of wisdom, cannot hear, from [a] the Son speaking, (things) which He does not know, since He is the very (Being), which is proffered by the Son, that is, God proceeding from [de] God, the Spirit of the Truth proceeding from [a] the Truth, the Consoler overflowing [manans] out of the [ex] Consoler ». Likewise, (St.) Cyril, the Bishop, in the Letter addressed to Nestorius, says:[7] « The Spirit is understood through Himself, according to which He is the Spirit, and not the Son; but yet He is not alien from [a] Him. For He is named the Spirit of the Truth and flows forth from Him, just as (He flows) out of [ex] God the Father ». Also (St.) John Chrysostom, in a certain homily ON THE EXPOSITION OF THE CREED,[8] speaks in this manner: « This is the Holy Spirit proceeding from [de] the Father and the Son, who *divides* His own gifts, *as He wills* ». (He says) the same in another homily: « It must be believed, that the Holy Spirit is of the Father and of the Son. We say that this Holy Spirit of Theirs (is) coequal to the Father and Son and proceeding from the Father and the Son. Believe this, lest *evil conversations corrupt good customs* ».[9] Behold from the Doctors of the Greeks we openly have the testimonies, by which the Holy Spirit is shown to proceed from [a] the Father and the Son. Therefore, *let every tongue confess* that the Holy Spirit proceeds from the Father and the Son.

---

[1] Gal. 1:8-9. — But the Vulgate with (St.) Augustine, in the passage soon to follow, does not read *(something) else* [aliud], but in v. 8 has *besides the one which* [praeter quam quod], and in v. 9 has *besides that which* [praeter id quod]; Augustine reads *besides that which* [praeter quod].

[2] Tract 98, ON THE GOSPEL OF JOHN, n. 7. — At the end of the text the Vatican and the other edd., except n. 1, read *walks upon* [incedit] for *enters upon* [accedit], in disagreement with all the editions and the text of (St.) Augustine; in our reading understand: *to the end* [ad terminum].

[3] Gal. 4:6, and then Jn. 16:13. — A little above this, before *of the Father* [Patris], the codd. and edd. 1, 2, 3, 7 & 8, omit *and* [et]; at the end of the following prop., codd. B C D & E read *with words* [verbis] for *in words* [in verbis].

[4] The Creed *Quicumque*, widely known under the name, "the Athanasian Creed". — Here the Vatican edition alone leaves out *nor begotten* [nec genitus] after *created* [creatus].

[5] PATROLOGIA GRAECA, Vol. 34, tom. 39, col. 1063. — The Vatican edition with very many edd., against the mss. and the original, before *the Truth* [Veritas] reads *is* [est] for *(is) also* [et]. We have added *says* [dicit] after *the Truth* [Veritas], on the authority of cod. B and the original, and as required by the context. — The text of Scripture is Jn. 16:13. — Immediately after, the Vatican ed. and edd. 4 & 9 have *inseparably* [inseparabiliter] for *inseparable* [inseparabilis], which (St.) Didymus also has; then it proceeds: Inseparable from *Mine* [mea] for *Me* [me].

[6] Loc. cit., n. 36. — At the end of this text all the manuscripts and the editions, except the Vatican, read *consolation* [consolatione] for *the Consoler* [consolatore]. But since the version of (St.) Jerome

has *the Consoler* [consolatore] and the Greek text has been lost, we have changed nothing.

[7] Epistle 17. — Immediately before this the Vatican edition alone has *For (St.) Cyril* [Nam Cyrillus] for *Likewise (St.) Cyril* [Item Cyrillus].

[8] These homilies are not found in the Maurini edition of Chrysostom. In the same manner the same words are cited in each text referred to by (Peter) Abelard, THEOL. CHRIST., Bk. V, (Migne's edition), col. 1322 and 1323. — Morover these homilies have been published in the Latin edition of the works of St. John Chrysostom, Antwerp, John Keeberg, 1614, tom. V, p. 287: "An Exposition of the Apostle's Creed", Homily I, with the incipit: Universalis gaudet etc., p. 288, col. 1, where there is read: « *I believe in the Holy Spirit*. That Spirit is everywhere whole, He breathes where He will. He Himself is the One who said: *Separate for Me Paul and Barnabas for the work, for which I have undertook them.* He Himself is the Spirit proceeding from [de] the Father and the Son, who divides His own gifts to each one, as He wills. Therefore, this Spirit of Theirs consecrates, sanctifies etc. ». Ibid., Homily II, with the incipit: Super fabricam totius etc.; where in about the middle there is read: « *Born of the Holy Spirit*. That Holy Spirit we say is the Coequal of the Father and the Son, and the One proceeding from the Father and the Son. Believe this, lest evil conversations corrupt your good customs. For there are heretics » etc. — The following passage of Scripture is 1 Cor. 12:11; the Vulgate has *dividing to each as He wills* [dividens singulis prout vult].

[9] A reference to 1 Cor. 15:33, and then at the words *every tongue* etc. to Philip. 2:11.

COMMENTARY ON DISTINCTION XI

On the eternal procession of the Holy Spirit, as much as regards the Principle, from which He proceeds.

Here, it must be said, that the Holy Spirit is from the Father and the Son etc..

THE DIVISION OF THE TEXT

Above, Master (Peter) deals with the procession of the Holy Spirit in comparison to the One proceeding; this is the second part, in which he deals[1] with the same in comparison to the principle *from which* (He proceeds) [a quo]. And this part is divided unto two (parts). In the *first* he shows, that the Holy Spirit proceeds from the Father and the Son [a Patre et Filio]. In the *second* he determines, in what manner He proceeds from Them, below in the Twelfth Distinction, (where he says): *Likewise there is asked, since the Holy Spirit proceeds from the Father and the Son* etc..

Again,[2] the *first* part has four (parts). In the first,

Master (Peter) shows through many authorities, that He proceeds from the Father and the Son. However, in the second, contrariwise [e contra], through the reasons of the Greeks he shows, that (they say He proceeds) from the Father alone, there (where he says): *However, the Greeks say, that the Holy Spirit proceeds only from the Father.* In the third, he solves the authorities and reasons of the Greeks and determines (them), there (where he says): *But we determine those words thus.* In the fourth, he shows, that the Greeks' confession of faith implicitly contains ours,[3] there (where he says): *It must be known, that the Greeks confess.*

TREATMENT OF THE QUESTIONS

For an understanding of this part two (things) are principally asked.

First, there is asked concerning the procession of the Holy Spirit, as much as regards (His) principle, and there is asked, whether the Holy Spirit proceeds from the Father and the Son [a Patre et Filio].*

Second, whether (the Holy Spirit) proceeds from the Father and the Son, inasmuch as They are one [in quantum sunt unum], or, inasmuch as They are different [in quantum sunt differentes].

ARTICLE SOLE

On the principle of the procession of the Holy Spirit.

QUESTION I

Whether the Holy Spirit proceeds from the Father and from the Son?

But, that He proceeds only from the Father [solum a Patre], the Greeks prove *by reason* and *authority*.

1. *By reason* in this manner: the emanation of the Holy Spirit is a procession; but a procession is a movement from one unto another [ab uno in alium]: if there is rightly a procession among the divine, the Holy Spirit proceeds by an eternal procession from One unto Another. If, therefore, He proceeds from the Son, either He proceeds unto the Father, or unto another Person; but not unto the Father, because the Father accepts nothing from the Son, nor unto another Person, since one is not to posit a fourth (Person): therefore, He does not proceed from the Son.

2. Likewise, by another reason, in this manner: because the Holy Spirit proceeds through the manner of a breathing [spriationis], just as the Word through a

manner of a speaking: but thus we shall see among creatures, that the going-forth of speech [exitus locutionis] does not proceed the breath [spriationem], nor is the stepping forth [egressus] of the breath from the word: therefore, among the divine neither (is)[4] the Holy Spirit from the Son.

3. Likewise, the Holy Spirit, as all say, proceeds through a manner of a connection [nexus], but a nexus holds a reckoning of a mean [medii]: but if He were to proceed from the Father and[5] the Son, He would have the reckoning of a third and of an extreme, not of a mean: therefore, He does not proceed from the Father and the Son, but rather from the Father unto the Son.

4. Likewise, the Holy Spirit proceeds from the Father either sufficiently, or not. If not sufficiently and fully, therefore, the Father is[6] imperfect in spirating; if sufficiently,

---

[1] We follow the very many codices, such as F H T W etc., together with edition 1, by putting *he deals* [agit] in place of *is dealt* [agitur].

[2] The Vatican edition, not trusting in the manuscripts and edition 1, omits *again* [iterum].

[3] The Vatican, without the authority of the manuscripts and edition 1, (taking the object of the subordinate clause as its subject) has *convenes with ours* [convenire cum nostra].

[4] In codex W there is added *is* [est].

[5] We have restored from the ancient manuscripts and edition 1 the words, less well omitted by the Vatican edition, *the Father and* [Patre et], and a little below this the *rather* [potius].

[6] In the Vatican edition and codex cc the *is* [est] is omitted, which is however, had in the other manuscripts and in edition 1.

---

* *Trans. note:* Here one must note, that the Seraphic Doctor, in his most eminent wisdom, has avoided using the Latin preposition, *out of* [ex], employed in the version of the Nicene-Constantinopolitan Creed by the Roman Church, during the rite of Mass; which preposition, on account of its likeness to the Greek preposition, εκ, is the principal or fundament, on the basis of terminology, of the argument of the Greeks against the Catholic Church, since in Greek, the preposition εκ, precludes (according to them) two origins, even if they be conceived as one principle.

therefore, it is superfluous that there comes to be through Two what can come to be sufficiently through One:[1] therefore, if He proceeds from the Son, since He proceeds fully from the Father, in that Most High Trinity there is a superfluity, which is absurd.

5. Likewise, the Greeks strive to show this very (thing) through *authority*; but they cannot by bringing in [per introductionem] Sacred Scripture,[2] for this reason they argue through what is lacking [per privationem] in the Gospels, and mostly in the Gospel of (St.) John and (his) Epistles, where our Faith is wholly handed down, but in no (passage) is there said, that the Holy Spirit "proceeds" except only "from the Father" [a Patre tantum]; according to the fifteenth (chapter of the Gospel of St.) John:[3] *The Spirit of Truth, who proceeds from the Father:* therefore either the Gospels insufficiently teach the Faith, or the Holy Spirit proceeds only from the Father.

6. Likewise, in the four Councils celebrated among the Greeks, where the Faith was sufficiently explained by the Fathers, it is said, that the Holy Spirit proceeds from [a] the Father and nothing is said of the Son: therefore, if God sufficiently revealed the Faith to them: ergo etc..

7. Likewise, they strive to fortify[4] this error through the Doctors, who are not only celebrated among them, but also among us.

And first through (St.) Gregory Nazianzen,[5] who is called "the Theologian": « The Son and the Holy Spirit, twin rays of the Father, have sent unto us Their own brightness »: therefore, They have gone forth from the Father, as two rays.

8. And Dionysius (the Areopagite) also says in (his) book, ON THE DIVINE NAMES:[6] « Out of the immaterial and impartible Good there have risen forth cordial lights », — he is speaking of the Father — therefore, lights have risen forth; but such so hold themselves, that one is not from the other one: ergo etc..

9. Likewise, (St. John) Damascene[7] more expressly (says): « We say that the Holy Spirit (is) "out of" [ex] the Father and we name Him 'the Spirit of the Father'; however, we do not say that the Holy Spirit (is) "out of" the Son, and yet we do name Him 'the Spirit of the Son' ».

10. Likewise, if the Latins knew this, when[8] the Greeks did not know it, either it was *by the authority of Scripture*, or *by preaching*, or *by reason*, or *by revelation*. Not *by the authority of Scripture*; because the Greeks have the same Scripture in everything [per omnia]; similarly not *by preaching*, because the same (is) the Doctor of the Greeks, who is of the Latins,

who perfectly handed down the Faith, namely (St.) Paul the Apostle; if *by reason*, but it does not suffice to affirm by reason in those (things) which belong to the Faith. Whence (Sts.) Dionysius and (John) Damascene say, that nothing is to be said nor thought concerning that Most High Trinity except that which the Sacred Utterances have taught us, and (St.) Jerome (says):[10] « Nothing is believed by me, except what I have confirmed through the New and Old Testament ». If *by revelation*, it is asked, to whom was it revealed and since God wants all men to be saved, why did He not reveal this[11] to the Greeks? *And again* in what manner is it established that this was from God?

THE CONTRARY[12] 1. is argued *by a demonstrative reckoning* in this manner: The Holy Spirit according to all the faithful proceeds as a gift, just as is proven from many passages [locis] of Scripture; and *again*, all, both Greeks and Latins, say, that the Holy Spirit is given to us by the Son: therefore, all concede, that He proceeds from Both, since *nothing is given*, except by that from which it proceeds.

2. Likewise, the Holy Spirit according to all, as just as has been shown above,[13] proceeds as love, but 'to love' belongs not only to the Father, but also to the Son, whence the Son even loves in all things [per omnia], just as even the Father (does): therefore, if Love proceeds from a loving Father, for the same reason from the Son.

3. Likewise, the Holy Spirit according to all proceeds as a nexus;[14] but the more perfect nexus is that, which proceeds from each extreme, than that which (does) from one of the two [ab altero]: therefore, if the Holy Spirit is the most perfect Nexus, He proceeds not only from the Father, but also from the Son.

4. Likewise, the same (argument) is shown *by a reckoning leading to the impossible* in this manner: every distinction of Persons among the divine is attained according to relation and origin: therefore, if the Holy Spirit does not proceed from the Son, nor the other way around [nec e converso], there is no origin there: therefore, there is no mutual relation there, therefore neither a distinction.

5. Likewise, there is greater kinship [germanitas] among two, when one proceeds from the other, and both from a third, than if one has nothing from the other; this is self-evident [per se nota]: therefore, if the Holy Spirit is not from the Son, nor the other way around, there is not[15] a perfect union: therefore, neither a most high nor a perfect beatitude.

6. Likewise, more perfect is the expression, when the one

---

[1] See the words of Aristotle, above in d. 10, a. 1, q. 1, reply to n. 4.

[2] As required by the manuscripts and the first six editions, we have substituted *bringing in* [introductionem] in place of *inducing of* [inductionem]. Then the words *through what is lacking in the Gospels* [privationem in Evangeliis] are equivalent to: from the silence of the Gospels.

[3] Verse 26.

[4] The Vatican edition, contrary to the older codices and edition 1, has *protect* [tutari] in place of *fortify* [munire].

[5] ORATION 45, "To King Evagrius on Divinity" (Venice, 1753): Also, Our Savior and the Holy Spirit, that twin ray of the Father, together and to us continually [usque] minister the light of truth and are united to the Father.

[6] It seems that the Seraphic Doctor refers to these words of Dionysius, which are alleged both by St. Thomas (here in a. 1) and Richard of St. Victor (here in q. 1): « Again, we have received from the Sacred Scriptures, that the Father indeed is the Origin among the Divine (Persons), but that Jesus and the Holy Spirit exist, as the offspring of God, and/or, if it is permitted to speak thus, as the divine Germs, or Flowers and supersubstantial Lights ». But our citation is not found word-for-word in the versions of Scotus and Corderius.

[7] ON THE ORTHODOX FAITH, Bk. I, ch. 8.

[8] Trusting in many manuscripts, such as A E G H I K M O T V Z, we have put *when* [cum] in place of *yet* [tamen].

[9] ON THE DIVINE NAMES, ch. 1, near the beginning. — (St. John) Damascene, ON THE ORTHODOX FAITH, Bk. I, ch. 2.

[10] These words are commonly attributed by the Scholastics to St. Jerome, in which only a similar sentence is read in his Epistle 41 "to Marcellus". But there are those of St. Cyril of Jerusalem, CATH. DE DECEM DOGMAT., n. 17 (PATROLOGIA GRAECA, tom. 33, col. 478), who says: « Indeed, believe me not, when I proffer these things on my own accord, but accept the demonstration, which I am telling you, of them from the divine Scriptures. »

[11] Codex Y *was this not revealed* [hoc non est revelatum]. A little below this cod. W for *this* [hoc] has *this* [haec], that is, "revelation".

[12] Some codd., such as T V & X, have *In the Contrary it* [In contrarium].

[13] Distinction 10, a. 1. q. 2. — A little after this codex W has *love* [amore] in place of *"to love"* [amare].

[14] Distinction 10, a. 2, q. 2.

[15] The Vatican edition, together with codex cc, has less distinction and contrary to the other codices and edition 1, *neither* [nec] for *not* [non]. A little before this edition 1 has *this is self-evident* in the neuter [in the sense of *this argument* rather than *this reckoning*].

begetting communicates to the one begotten not only (his) substance, but also (his) acting, which is not repugnant to the nature of the one begotten; but the act of spirating is not repugnant to the Son, because nothing inconvenient follows from this, if He spirates: therefore, if the Father does not communicate this act[1] to Him, the Son is not the perfect Image of the Father.

7. Likewise, this very (thing) is shown *by authorities*, and first by authority of the Apostle (Paul in his Letter) to the Galatians, (chapter) four:[2] *God sent the Spirit of His Son* etc.: therefore, since the Father does not send the Spirit, except of the Son, the Same is the Spirit of the Father and of the Son; but the Spirit belongs to Him, from whom He proceeds; therefore, the Holy Spirit proceeds from the Father and the Son. *If you say*, that it does not follow, because *"of the Son"* is not said, because He proceeds *"from"* the Son, but because He is *"in"* the Son: therefore, by the same reckoning, since the Son is in the Holy Spirit, the Son can be said (to be) the Son of the Holy Spirit.[3]

8. Likewise, (the Gospel of St.) John, (chapter) fifteen:[4] *Whom I will send you from the Father, the Spirit of Truth*. From this (verse) it is thus argued: no one sends another, unless he has authority over him: but no one has authority over another, unless he bestows something upon him: but no Person bestows upon Another,[5] except that He proceeds from Him: therefore, from the first, the Holy Spirit proceeds from the Son. *If you say*, that He is sent from the Son in [ex] time and in time proceeds (from Him): *on the contrary*: The Son does not, for this reason, have authority, because He sends, but for this reason He sends, because He has authority: therefore, He has authority before he sends temporally: therefore, before He sends temporally, it is necessary that the Holy Spirit proceeds from the Son: ergo etc..

9. Likewise, (the Gospel of St.) John, (chapter) six:[6] *He will glorify Me, because He shall receive from Mine own* [de meo]. From this (verse) it is thus argued: Anyone is everything [omne] which He has, is everything which He accepts; but the Holy Spirit, since He is God most highly simple, is everything which He has, therefore, everything which He accepts: therefore, if He accepts anything from Anyone, He accepts (His own) 'Being' [esse];[7] but from Whom He accepts 'being', from Him He proceeds: therefore, if He accepts anything from the Son, He proceeds from the Son. *If you say*, that that *"accepting"* is (meant) temporally; then it is objected from this, that everything which accepts anything temporally from anyone,[8] is changed, etc..

CONCLUSION

The Holy Spirit proceeds from the Father and the Son.

I RESPOND: It must be said, that, as has been shown from authorities and by reasons, it is a truth of the Faith, that the Holy Spirit proceeds from the Father and the Son [a Patre et Filio].

But to understand the controversy of the Latins and Greeks, there must also be noted its origin, wherefore about the procession of the Holy Spirit from the Son there are two (things) to consider, namely, the *cognition* of the article (of the Faith) and the *profession* of the same cognized. In the first has arisen[10] a difference, in the second a controversy.

Moreover, the *cognition* of this article has (its) foundation from Scripture, (its) progress [profectum] and/or increment from reason, but its consummation[11] from Revelation. The Greeks and Latins agree in the authority of Scripture, which says, that the Holy Spirit *is of the Son* [esse Filii] and *is sent by the Son* [mitti a Filio]; but in *reason* and *revelation* they differ.

In *the reckoning of what, indeed, is to be understood*. For since Scripture says,[12] that the Holy Spirit *proceeds*, the Greeks have used one manner and one similitude of procession to understand (it), the Latins another manner. For since "procession" [processio] among creatures is said (to be) a '*local* movement from one unto another' [ab uno in alium] and is said (to be) a '*causal* movement of one out of[13] an other' [unius ex alio], the Greeks have understood the Procession in the first manner, *from one unto another*; the Latins, however, in the second manner. And in this the Latins have understood (it) better than the Greeks, because they have compared the eternal Procession in a more spiritual manner; and for that reason they have compared it in a more similar manner,[14] and thus better.

Similarly, Scripture says,[15] that the Holy Spirit proceeds *through spiration*. And since spiration is twofold, namely *of the exterior breath* and *of interior love*, the Greeks have compared the Spirit to the spiration *of the exterior breath*, but the Latins to the spiration *of interior love*: and for that reason the Latins (have done so) better, because they have adapted (their speech) in a more spiritual manner and by a more similar similitude.

Similarly, since Scripture says, that the Holy Spirit proceeds as a *"nexus"* and "communion" (of the Father and the Son), and there can be a "nexus" in a twofold manner, either as a *medium* joining a one[16]

---

[1] Some codices, such as G X Z, either have *the Father has an act which He does not communicate to Him* [Pater habet actum quem etc.] or, as K and T, have *the Father has the act and He does not* etc. [Pater habet actum et etc.].   [2] Verse 6.

[3] The Vatican edition, together with some manuscripts, omits *the Son* [Filius] one time, but contrary to other codices, such as A F G H K M T V etc together with edition 1.

[4] Verse 26, in which text contrary to the Vulgate and the more ancient codices, the Vatican edition omits *from the Father* [a Patre], just as a little afterwards it twice has *above* [supra] in place of *over* [super].

[5] From the older manuscripts and edition 1 we have supplied the badly omitted *Another* [alii].

[6] Verse 14. — Then, consenting with the ancient mss. and ed. 1, we have put *this (verse)* [hoc] in place of *which (verse)* [quo].

[7] Codices aa and bb add *from the Other* [ab alio].

[8] One or the other of the codices, such as S, have *an other* [alio].

[9] Some codices, such as H P Q and Y, have *and its origin, it must be noted, that* [et originis eius ... quod].

[10] We have left, with the Vatican ed. and ed. 1, *has arisen a* [orta est], though the majority of the codd. with editions 2, 3, 4, 5 & 6 have *there is an entire* [tota est], which suits the context less.

[11] We follow the very many codd., such as F H I K P Q T etc., and ed. 1, by putting *consummation* [consummationem] for *conservation* [conservationem], which corresponds more with the gradation of the di-

vision of the members and with the subjoined. Codex X has *confirmation* [confirmationem]. A little below this, after *agree* [conveniunt] the codf. disagree amongst themselves; the greater part of them, such as A C F G I L O R S V W X Z etc., have *because* [quia] for *which (authority)* [quae]; very many, such as C I L O & R, then have *they say* [dicunt] for *says* [dicit].

[12] Not a few codices, such as A S T V X and aa, less congruously have *For Scripture says* [Nam Scriptura dicit]. A little below this many codices, together with edition 1, read *according a similitude* [similitudine] for *and one similitude* [et alia similitudine].

[13] Codices aa and bb have *from that* [ab illo].

[14] Codex K has *according to the truth* [secundum veritatem], codex V has *according to reasons* [secundum rationes], in place of *in a ... similar manner* [simili].

[15] The canonical Scriptures do not say this expressly, but implicitly and according to the interpretation of the holy Fathers. Cf. d. 10, a. 2, q. 3 and 2, and here in reply to n. 5. — Then trusting in the many mss., such as A F G H K S T W X Y Z etc., and ed. 1, we have substituted *But since* [Sed cum] with *And since* [Et cum], and, a little below this, *compare* [comparant] with *have compared*. On account of the repetition of the words *of the exterior breath and of interior love* [flatus exterioris et amoris interioris] some codd. have erred, either by omitting or a permutation.

[16] From very many manuscripts, such a H M N P Q aa (T ee and ff in the margin), we have inserted *one* [unum], in place of which edition 1 has *the other* [alterum].

to the other, and/or as an extreme, in which they are conjoined; the Greeks compared in the first manner, the Latins in the second, and for that reason in a more spiritual and more similar manner,[1] because that "nexus" has to a greater extent the similitude of a person.

Therefore, because they had a difference in reckoning, and (because) the Latins compared (it) in a more spiritual and more fitting manner; for that reason they were elevated by their reckoning, and through this disposed to understand the Scripture, and for that reason they were instructed [edocti sunt] *by manifest revelation* concerning the procession of the Holy Spirit. The Greeks, however, because they adapted different and less proper (manners of speech), for that reason they were depressed by their reckoning; and not prevailing to understand, that the Spirit proceeds from the Word, or that He does not proceed unto Another from eternity, constrained Scripture to be understood concerning the temporal procession, and for that reason closed the way to revelation off for themselves. This, therefore, is the reason for the diversity in the *cognition* of this article.

However, *the controversy* came from the *profession* of this article. But *the profession* of this[2] article came from the Church of the Latins from a threefold cause, namely, from *the truth of the Faith*, from *the necessity of danger*, and from *the authority of the Church*. The Faith dictated this, and the necessity of danger was imminent, lest perchance someone deny this, into which danger the Greeks fell; and the authority of the Church upheld it [aderat]: and for that reason it ought to have been expressed without delay.

But *the denial* of this article came from a threefold cause, that is, from *ignorance*, from *pride* and[4] *pertinacity*. From *ignorance*, because they neither understood Scripture nor had a fitting reason nor an open revelation. From *pride*, because, since they reputed themselves to be all-knowing [sciolos] and had not been called (to a Council),[5] they did not want to profess what had not been invented by them. From *pertinacity*, lest they be convinced and seem to be moved irrationally, they invented for themselves reasons against the truth: and for that reason dared to defend their own sentence and to obviate the authority of the Roman Church; and for that reason have become heretics, because they reject [denegant][6] a truth of the Faith, and schismatics, because they have withdrawn from the unity of the Church.

But, because it is the custom of heretics and schismatics, when they cannot completely defend themselves with reasons, to accuse the opposed party; for that reason, they accuse and rebuke us [redarguunt] as *curious men* and as *excommu-*

nicated and *schismatics*. *Curious men*,[7] because without the profession of this article there was salvation. Why, therefore, did the Latins permit themselves to thoroughly search into that, which was not necessary (for salvation)?

But to this the response is clear, that[8] it was opportune on account of the danger into which they themselves have fallen.

Similarly, they say that we (are) *excommunicated*, because we have corrupted the Symbols, in which this had been prohibited through the holy Fathers under the pain of excommunication.

And to this the response is clear through the aforesaid, because we do not corrupt, but rather perfect;[9] nor is there a sentence levied against perfecters, but rather against corruptors. *And/or* it can be said, as (St.) Anselm says,[10] that we have put forth something new; and this indeed we could do, because the Roman Church has accepted from (St.) Peter the Apostle the plenitude of power, in which[11] no sentence nor interdict of the Fathers could either restrain [arctare] nor prejudge Her nor bind Her regarding anything.

Similarly they say that we (are) *schismatics*, because the division began[12] from us; for when we wanted to assert this, we did not want to call them (to a Council).

And one can respond to this on behalf of the Latins, that it was not *opportune* to call them — because the Church could (do) this without them — and this,[13] because it was *laborious* on account of the distance, was not *unfruitful*, because there was no longer the great wisdom among the Greeks, as there had been, nay it had passed over to the Latins, nevertheless it was *dangerous*, because it was dangerous to put [ducere] into doubt what was to be held as certain [pro certo habendum erat].

And, thus, it is clear, that their *accusations* are frivolous. But to (their) *reasons*, having understood what has been said, it is easy to respond.

1. To that, therefore, which is objected, that a *procession* is from one unto another; it must be said, that that is true concerning *local* procession, but it is not true concerning *causal* procession, just as will be more clear below;[14] since 'to proceed unto another' is twofold, either because it tends unto another as[15] an *object*; and in this manner the Holy Spirit is the Love, by which the Son loves the Father, just as (is true) the other way around; but if He is said "to proceed unto another" in this manner, as "*to be received* by *Him*", the understanding is entirely foolish. For (this) is to say, that the Love,

---

[1] Many codices omit *manner* [modo], which the Vatican transposes after *the second* [secundo].

[2] Trusting the mss. and ed. 1, we have supplied *this* [huius]. Then some codd., such as I & Z, with edition 1, have *the Latin Church* [Ecclesia Latina] for *the Church of the Latins* [Ecclesia Latinorum], and a little below this, many codd., such as A F G H T etc., with edition 1, after *necessity of danger* [periculi necessitate] add with us the particle *and* [et].

[3] The Vatican ed., against the more ancient codd. and ed. 1, has *some deny this* [aliqui hoc negarent].   [4] Ed. 1 adds *from* [ex].

[5] Edition 1 has *having been called they were missing* [vocati defuerunt] for *they were not called* [vocati non fuerunt]. A little below this after *pertinacity* [pertinacia] codices P and Q add *because* [quia].

[6] The Vatican edition together with codex cc has *deny* [negant], but contrary to the other codices and edition 1.

[7] Codex V has *As curios men* [Tamquam curiosos].

[8] Not trusting in the mss. and the first six edd., there is omitted in the Vatican ed. the *that* [quia], just as a little below this contrary to the more ancient codd. and edd. 1, 4 & 5, it omits the preposition *into* [in].

[9] Some codices, such as K X & Z, have *we have not corrupted, but rather have perfected* [non corrumpimus, sec perfecimus]; others, such as G H I S together with edition 1, have *we do not corrupt, but rather have perfected* [non corrumpimus, sed perfecimus]; others, with the Vatican edition, exhibit our reading.

[10] On the Procession of the Holy Spirit, ch. 22: We reply, that we have not corrupted it, but rather have put out something new. — Then from very many codices, such as X Y and aa, together with edition 1, we have put *and this indeed* [et hoc quidem] in place of *which indeed* [quod quidem], which is confirmed from the incongruous reading of the other codices *and which indeed* [et quod quidem].

[11] The Vatican edition, contrary to many codd., such as A F G I L O T W etc., and edition 1, has *into which* [in quam], and not trusting in the mss. and edition 1, has *to be able* [ponere] in place of *could* [potuit]. Edition 1 has *to interdict* [interdicere] for *interdict* [interdictum].

[12] We prefer the reading of not a few manuscripts such as H I W etc., which have *began* [incepit] in place of *is beginning* [incipit].

[13] On the authority of very many manuscripts and edition 1, we have supplied from the Vatican edition the omitted *this* [hoc], by which we understand: it was not opportune. Then after *unfruitful* [infructuosum], with the consent of the manuscripts and edition 1, we have expunged the words *on account of (their) foolishness* [propter insipientiam].

[14] Distinction 14, a. 1, q. 1.

[15] One or the other of the codices, such as H (in a second hand), together with edition 1 have *unto* [in], after which codex X adds *either because it thus tends unto another, because it is received by it; if because unto another it tends as an object* [aut quia in alium tendit ita, quod ab eo recipiatur; si quia in alium tendit sicut obiectum].

which is the Holy Spirit, arises from the Father and subsists in the Son, just as a river rises from a spring [fonte] and rests in a deep lake.[1]

2. To that which is objected concerning *spiration*, that it precedes a word; it must be said that it is true concerning an exterior word, and not (true) concerning an interior one: and the exterior (word)[2] is not similar (to the divine Procession).

3. To that which is objected concerning a *nexus*, it must be said, that a nexus does not have the reckoning of a mean, but a reckoning of a third (member), regardless of what[3] some wanted to say, that it holds the place both of a mean and of a third (member); and they wanted to sustain the opinion of the Greeks and the Latins and they distinguish a twofold manner of proceeding, that is, *unto another*, and in this manner He proceeds from the Father; and/or *from another*, and in this manner He proceeds from the Father and the Son. Today that (argument) of theirs[4] must be discarded [exsufflandum], because it does not have a sane understanding; nay He proceeds in entirely the same manner from Each, and yet is the Nexus of Each, just as is depicted in the example [ponitur exemplum] of two pieces of wood, from which proceed one flame.

4. To that which is objected, that from the other sufficiently, ergo etc.; it must be said, that that would be true, if there were diverse principles of the Holy Spirit; which is not true, just as will be clear below.[5] Whence just as this argument is not valid: 'The Father creates, and the Son similarly; and the Father is sufficient in creating: therefore, the Son is superfluous'; — because there is one principle in creating — similarly it is to be solved in the proposed.

5. To that which is objected, that it is not found in *Scripture*; it must be said, that if the words are not found, yet the sense (of them) is found, just as has been demonstrated in the objection. However, the argument is not valid: 'it is not found in Scripture, therefore, it is not true'; because the custom of Scripture is, that it is silent regarding certain (things) on account of instilling [insinuandam] humility: wherefore the Lord, as one wanting to instruct us regarding humility, He attributes everything, which is His, to the Father, just as He says in (the Gospel of St.) John, (chapter) seven:[6] *My doctrine is not mine*. Similarly, He says in (the Gospel of St.) John, (chapter) ten:[7]

Who proceeds from the Father, speaking of the Holy Spirit, and yet He Himself subjoins:[8] *all, which the Father has, are Mine*: and for that reason the argument is not valid.

6. To that which is objected concerning *Councils*, it must be said, that neither in those Council were all (things) instituted, which pertain [spectant] to customs, nor even all (things) said, which pertain [pertinent] to the Faith, just as in the Creed [Symbolo], which is chanted at Mass, nothing is said of the descent (of Christ) to the lower regions. But did not[9] the procession of the Holy Spirit from the Son lie hidden from the holy Fathers? and if it did not lie hidden, why did they not speak (of it)? I believe that it did not lie hidden, just as is clear through the ancient Greek (Fathers), the authority of whom Master (Peter) adduces in the text;[10] but nevertheless [tamen] it was not expressed, because there was no need. For none used to deny nor waned to deny (it). But heretics by their importunity compelled (us) to explicate many (things), which had been implicit in our Faith; and, thus, that is clear.

7. 8. To that which is objected concerning the authority of (Sts.) *Dionysius* and *Gregory*, it must be said, that there is not a omnimodal similitude, but a greater dissimilitude. Moreover, the similitude is attained in this; that is, as much as regards the plenitude of fontality in the Father and in the division[11] of Persons emanating from Him, and in the reception of influence in the creature; yet there is not a omnimodal similitude as much as regards the manner of emanating; and, thus, that is clear.

9. To that which is objected from (St. John) *Damascene*, it must be said, that there is no agreement on their side regarding him, for as I understand, he himself lived [fuit] in the time, when contention has arisen. On which account, he (is) not to be sustained in this, simply because he was a Greek, however, he does speak cautiously. Whence he does not say, that the Spirit *"is not* from the Son" [non sit a Filio],* but he says, *"we do not say from the Son"*, because the Greeks did not use to confess (this), yet, they did not use to deny (it); but, now, a cursed progeny has added to their fathers' mindlessness and says, that "He does not proceed from the Son except temporally". And, for that reason, the Roman Church damns them as heretics and schismatics.

---

[1] How this similitude is to be understood, is aptly explained by St. Anselm, ON THE PROCESSION OF THE HOLY SPIRIT, ch. 17: It is established that one and the same is the water, which is called both "a spring" and "a river" and "a lake"; not three waters, although there be three, the spring, the river and the lake. We also discern among the spring, river and lake, and we see that each of these, though they are three, are understood as [in] one water. Indeed in the spring the water ascending from the deep bubbles up; in the river descending from the spring it flows; in the lake it is gathered and remains. Therefore, through "spring" there is understood "water bubbling up from the deep"; through "river", that it flows from the spring; through "lake", that it is united together. Moreover, we see that a river is not of that, whence water is called "a spring", but of that, which it is, that is of water; nor is the lake of that, whence water is called "a spring" or "a river", but of water itself, which is one and the same in spring and river. Therefore, not from that, whence spring and river differ, but of that, in which they are one, does a lake exist. If, therefore, that is not more a spring, whence the lake is, than a river, "a lake" cannot be understood to be more from a spring than from a river. So also, when there is said, 'God the Father or the Son or the Holy Spirit', there is understood one Essence among Three and one God ... but in the Father there is understood the One begetting, in the Son the One Begotten, and in the Holy Spirit in a certain singular and ineffable manner the One Proceeding.

[2] Trusting in the manuscripts and edition 1 we have substituted *exterior* [exterius] for *for that reason* [ideo], namely 'exterior word', then supply: divine procession; codex R has *for it is not similar concerning the interior and the external ones* [non enim est simile de interiori et externis]; cod. Z after *exterior* [exterius] adds *and interior* [interius].

[3] Disagreeing with very many manuscripts and edition 1, the Vatican edition has *although* [quamquam].

[4] The Vatican edition, contrary to the manuscripts and edition 1, has *But that (argument) of theirs* [Sed istud].

[5] See the following Question.

[6] Verse 16.   [7] Verse 26.

[8] Ibid., 16:15, in which text the Vulgate in place of *which* [quae] has *whatsoever* [qauecumque].

[9] The reading of very many codices, such as H I L O ee ff and edition 1, in which *not* [nunquid] is put in the place of *never* [numquam], has been chosen by us, because it corresponds more with what is subjoined.

[10] Chapter 2. — A little before this the Vatican edition, having been corrupted, and not trusting in the more ancient manuscripts and edition 1, omits *is clear* [patet] after *just as* [sicut].

[11] Codex Y has *in distinction* [in distinctione], which reading explains, in which sense the word *division* [divisione] is to be taken.

---

* *Trans. note*: Here, it would be more clear if the text had *"we do not say out of the Son"* [ex Filio], because in the original text of St. John Damascene, which is cited correctly above in the 9th contrary argument (see fn. 7, p. 219), the Damascene says "out of" [ex], that is εκ.

SCHOLIUM

I. This conclusion, which the schismatic Greeks reject, is had in the Creed of the 11th Council of Toledo (A.D. 675) and was defined as an article of faith by the decrees of very many Councils, namely of Bari (A.D. 1098), the Second Council of Lyons [A.D. 1274] and the Council of Florence [A. D. 1439] in its Decree of Union [incipit: "Cantate Domino"]. But the formula used also among the Greeks, namely, that the Father spirates the Holy Spirit through the Son [per Filium], was approved by the Council of Florence (Decree of Union) and is explained in this sense: « that through this there is signified, that the Son, according to the Greeks, is indeed a cause, according to the Latins, however, a principle of the substance of the Holy Spirit, just as even the Father. And since everything, which belongs to the Father, the Father Himself has given to His own Only-Begotten Son by begetting Him, besides the 'Being' [esse] of the Father, this very thing, that the Holy Spirit proceeds from [ex] the Son, the Son Himself has eternally from [a] the Father, from whom eternally He has also been begotten.

II. The Seraphic Doctor (p. 212, second paragraph) says, that « the Latins have been instructed by manifest revelation »; this, however, is not to be understood of a new revelation, which adds anything to the Deposit of Faith, but as is clear from the context, concerns a charism of truth, by which the Deposit of Faith has been rightly expounded, in which this dogma had already been at least implicitly revealed.

III. In reference to the solution to n. 3, (Bl.) Dionysius the Carthusian (here in q. 1 at the end) says: « Also the distinction of Alexander (of Hales), posited at the beginning of the response to this question, which affirms that the Holy Spirit proceeds in the same manner from the Father and the Son, in the manner which one flame steps forth from two logs, Bonaventure says is now to be disregarded ». But this most learned and holy man errs. For St. Bonaventure does not disregard that distinction *in itself*, but only its *use*, which not a few thinkers understood as, that the Holy Spirit proceeds from the Father in one manner, and from the Son in another manner. That the Seraphic Doctor fully consents with his teacher, the following passage of Alexander (Summa., p. I, q. 43, m. 4) proves, which for this reason we describe here more freely, because in the editions it labors under a grave error. For there are lacking among those italicized letters, the words distinguished by us: *because there would follow from this, that He proceeds from the Son*, and immediately after this the editions have *unfitting* [inconveniens] in place of *fitting* [conveniens]. By this reading the sense is entirely distorted. We have corrected this error from the manuscript codex of the Biblioteca Nazionale of Florence, in folio membr., 14th Century, sig. I. III. 9., folio 75 recto; there, it is in q. 15. m. 12. a. 5:

« It must be said, that "to proceed" is said in a twofold manner: in one manner "to proceed" is said in a local movement, which movement is from something unto something. In another manner "to proceed" is said in the going-forth of a caused from a cause and/or a moved from a mover. According to the first manner, "to proceed" requires a twofold terminus: *from which* [a quo] and *unto which* [in quem]. According to the second manner, it does not require but one, namely, *from which*. Whence also, according to those two manners the verb, "to proceed", can be transferred to the Procession of the Holy Spirit. On the other hand, the Greeks have transferred the verb, "to proceed", from local movement; whence they understood the eternal Procession of the Holy Spirit from Someone unto Someone; and for that reason according to this manner they did not concede, that the Holy Spirit proceeds from the Son, *because there would follow from this, that He proceeds from the Son* unto the Father, which is not fitting (the editions have "unfitting"), since in the Father Himself is the reckoning of a first principle, and the Father has nothing from the Son. Moreover, if one were to say, that He proceeds from the Son unto the Father, the Father would seem to have something from the Son. But they have conceded, that He proceeds unto the Son, and it is even hinted at (in Sacred Scripture), that the Son has His 'Being' [esse] from the Father. On the other hand, the Latins take the verb, "to proceed" [procedendi], in a transferred manner [transsumunt] from a going-forth or processing of a caused from a cause. Wherefore they say, that "to proceed" is "to go forth from something", although not "unto something", according to which love is said to proceed from a mind, thought it is not understood (to proceed), unto something. And according to this manner (of understanding) the Latins says, that the Holy Spirit proceeds from the Father and the Son, because He has gone forth from Each, as the Love from the Knowledge and the Mind ».

IV. St. John Damascene, whose doctrine St. Bonaventure (here in the last reply) asserts not to be sustained in this matter, is also accused by St. Thomas (Summa, I, q. 36, a. 2, ad 3) of error, but we might add, is excused by not a few. But (Bl. John Duns) Scotus (here in q. 1) better explains that holy Doctor here and vindicates his orthodoxy in the matter, which defense now-a-days is commonly accepted by theologians.

VI. The fourth argument in the fundament, that, having denied the procession of the Holy Spirit from the Son, the distinction of each (Person) ought also to be denied, is approved by very many theologians, such as Alexander of Hales, Bl. (now St.) Albertus (Magnus), St. Thomas, (Bl.) Peter of Tarentaise, Durandus (of Saint-Pourçain), and nearly commonly by the theologians which followed, outside the school of (Bl.) Scotus. However, the contrary is taught by Henry of Ghent (Quodlibetals, 5, q. 8), (Bl.) Scotus (here in q. sole, and in the Reportatio, here in q. 2), (Bl.) Dionysius the Carthusian (here in q. 2); but Richard of Middleton (here in q. 2) adheres to the former. The controversy over this matter among the school of Scotus and Thomas and other theologians, is famous. Concerning the arguments of the Scotists see Fr. Claude Frassen (Scotus Academicus, tome 3, tract 3, disputation 3, a 3, q. 2), Fr. Juan de Rada, O.F.M., 1545-1609 A.D., (I. controv. 15), and Fr. Francisco Macedo, S. J., 1596-1681 A.D., (Collationes doctrinae S.Thom. et Scot., coll. 6, diff. 4.).

VI. As regards the conclusion: cf. Alexander of Hales, Summa., p. I, q. 43, m. 4, and q. 46, m . 5. — (Bl. John Duns) Scotus, here in q. sole; and in Reportatio., here in q. 1. — St. Thomas, here in q. 1, a. 1; Summa., I, q. 36, a. 2; Summa contra Gentiles., IV, c. 24 and 25; Opuscle. 6. "Against the Errors of the Greeks". — Bl. (now St.) Albertus (Magnus), here in a. 6; Summa., p. I, tr. 7, q. 31, m. 1 and 2. — (Bl.) Peter of Tarentaise, here in q. 1, a. 1. — Richard of Middleton, here in a. 1 and 2. — Giles the Roman, here in 1. princ., q. 1. — Henry of Ghent, Summa., a. 54, q. 6. — Durandus (of Saint-Pourçain), here in q. 1. — (Bl.) Dionysius the Carthusian, here in q. 1. — (Gabriel) Biel, here in q. 1 and 2.

QUESTION II

Whether the Holy Spirit proceeds from the Father and the Son, as from one principle?

Second, there is asked, whether the Holy Spirit proceeds from the Father and the Son, inasmuch as They are one, or inasmuch as (They are) different.

1. And that (He proceeds from Them) inasmuch as (They are) one , seems through (St.) Anselm (of Canterbury) in (his) book, On the Procession of the Holy Spirit,[1] (where he says): « No intellect grasps, that the Holy Spirit is of the Father and of the Son, according to which One is the Father, Another the Son, but according to which Each is the same God ».

2. Likewise, *by reason* it is shown thus: a unity of effecting is from a unity of acting, and a unity of acting is from a unity of power [potentiae] and/or of subject; therefore, since One is the Person produced from the Father and the Son, therefore, He is produced through one Act and through one Power: therefore, They spirate, inasmuch as They are one.

3. Likewise, that which is from two, inasmuch as (it is) two, either is insufficiently from one [ab quolibet], or superfluously from one of the two [ab altero]: but the Holy Spirit is insufficiently or superfluously from no Person, because neither (manner) befits a perfect nature: ergo etc..

4. Likewise, that which is from two, inasmuch as (they are) two, is a composite [compositum], if it is from them consubstantially;[2] therefore,

---

[1] Chapter 21 : No sense grasps, that the Holy Spirit is of the Father or of the Son ... and Each is the One and Same God.

[2] Very many codices, together with edition 1, have *consubstantially* [consubstantialiter] in place of *substantially* [substantialiter]. In the following, next sentence, we exhibit the reading

if from two, inasmuch as (they are) two, there proceeds one (Person) [unus], it is necessary [oportet] that that One (Supposit) [unum] have a difference; but the Holy Spirit is not a composite: ergo etc..

5. Likewise, nothing proceeds as one from two completely similar[1] in nature [consimilibus in natura] inasmuch as (they are) two, except the one be as an active principle, the other as a passive principle, or the one as a father, the other as a mother, but this is not among the divine: ergo etc..

ON THE CONTRARY: 1. He who proceeds from two, such that (his is) from one more principally than from the other, proceeds[2] inasmuch as they are two; but the Holy Spirit principally proceeds from the Father, just as (St.) Augustine says and as is had in the following distinction:[3] ergo etc..

2. Likewise, he who proceeds from two, inasmuch as they are distinct, proceeds from two, inasmuch as they are two; but a nexus is not but of (things) distinct: therefore, He who proceeds as a nexus, proceeds from Them as from distinct (Persons), and thus as from different ones.

3. Likewise, from the unity of a subject is the unity of (its) acting [actus], and from the plurality of subjects a plurality of actings;[4] but the Father and the Son are two (Persons): therefore, They spirate by a twofold spiration: therefore, the Holy Spirit is spirated by Them, inasmuch as They are two: ergo etc..

4. Likewise, if They spirate the Holy Spirit, inasmuch as They are one, either[5] inasmuch as They are one in *substance*, or in *notion*, or in *person*. If inasmuch as They are one in *substance*: therefore, since the Holy Spirit is the Same in Substance, the Holy Spirit proceeds from Himself. If inasmuch as They are the same in *notion*; this is nothing, because They do not for that reason spirate, because They are spirators, but the other way around. Nor inasmuch as They are one in *person*, because in person They are not united.

CONCLUSION

The Holy Spirit proceeds from the Father and from the Son, not to the extent that They are distinct Persons, but to the extent that in Them there is one Fecundity of Will or one active Spiration.

I RESPOND: It must be said, that the Holy Spirit proceeds from the Father and the Son, inasmuch as They are one [unum] in the fecundity of Will. Moreover, there is in the Father and the Son one Will, because the Father and the Son are one Substance; if, therefore, there is in Them a fecundity of Will, there is one Fecundity in Them. Moreover, there is a fecundity of the Will in the Father and the Son, because Each (is)[6] the improcessible God. For just as had been said above concerning the number of Persons[7] and (as) shall be more clear below,[8] when (Their) innascibility is dealt with, which is the same (thing) in the Father as (His) primacy; since the first and the beginning are the same;[9] the reckoning of primacy is the reckoning of beginning, or of fecundity. Therefore, since the Father is prior to every emanation, that is, to procession and generation, because He is neither generated nor proceeds, hence it is, that in each manner He is the principle [principium]. On the other hand, because the Son is prior to the Emanation of the Procession, not of the Generation — because He is generated, yet He is unable to be spirated [inspirabilis] — hence it is, that He is a principle of spirating, not of generating. On the other hand, because the Holy Spirit is regarded in neither manner, He is a principle in neither manner. Hence it is, therefore, that although the Holy Spirit proceeds from two (Persons), because, however, He proceeds, not inasmuch as [ut] They are different, but inasmuch as [ut] there is in Them one fecundity of Will, that[10] the Holy Spirit proceeds from Them, inasmuch [in quantum] as They are one.

1. To that which is objected, that principally

---

which is found only in very many codices, such as A H P Q W etc.. Indeed the greater part of the codices together with edition 1 read there proceeds *one (Person)* [unus] in place of there proceeds *one (Supposit)* [unum], which the Vatican edition has, but in the rest the sentence agrees with the Vatican edition, by putting *because* [quia] in place of *therefore* [ergo] and by prefacing the particles *and thus* [et ita] to *it is necessary* [oportet]. It is clear to whoever looks into the manner, that in this proposition the reckoning of the major is not contained; even if together with codex T there is read *that from two, inasmuch as (They are) two, there proceeds one (Person)* [quia a duobus in quantum duo no procedit unus]; whence in this there is contained an application of the major to something special, which also is indicated sufficiently clearly through the term *one (Person)* [unus], that is, the Person of the Holy Spirit, who as a certain one individual [quid unum] ought to have in Himself a composition or difference. Some codices, such a H M bb and ee, after *have* [habeat] read *in Himself* [in se].

[1] From the manuscripts and edition 1, we have substituted *completely similar* [consimilibus] for *similar* [similibus].

[2] In codex O there is added *from them* [ab eis].

[3] See the text of Master (Peter), ch. 2, and (also here at) q. 2.

[4] We have supplied from codex T *and from the plurality of subjects a plurality of actings* [et a pluralitate subiectorum pluralitas actuum], because the context also requires those words, and at the beginning of the solution of this objection they are explicitly cited. — This reckoning is founded in that axiom: 'Acts [actus] are of supposits; therefore, of two supposits there is not a unique action [actio].'

[5] Codex W non male addit *therefore* [ergo].

[6] Codex Y adds *is* [est]; but codex Z has *Each is improcessible* [uterque est improcessibilis] in place of *Each (is) the improcessible God* [uterque Deus improcessibilis].

[7] Distinction 2, q. 2 and 4.

[8] Distinction 28, throughout.

[9] Aristotle, POSTERIOR ANALYTICS, Bk. I, ch. 2: For I say that 'the first' and 'the beginning' are the same. — The Vatican edition, having varied the construction, not trusting in the manuscripts and in edition 1, has *both the first and the beginning are the same, and the reckoning* [et primum et principium sunt idem, et ratio] but less distinctly, which edition also a little below, together with codex cc, but against the more ancient codices and edition 1, has *is prior in* [prior est in] in place of *is prior to* [prior est].

[10] On the authority of very many manuscripts, we have expunged the *it is clear* [patet], which the Vatican edition less aptly prefixes to the word *that* [quod]; edition 1 in place of *it is clear* [patet] has *hence it is* [hinc est]. — (St.) Augustine agrees, in ON THE TRINITY, Bk. V, ch. 14, n. 15: If, therefore, even that which is given a beginning [principium] has that from which it is given ... it must be admitted, that the Father and the Son are the principle [principium] of the Holy Spirit, not two principles; but just as the Father and the Son (are) the One God, and, relatively to the creature, the One Creator and the One Lord, so relatively to the Holy Spirit one principle etc..

He proceeds from the Father; it must be said, that "principally" can be said in a twofold manner: either in respect of a secondary, and thus it conveys the order of prior and posterior, and thus it posits a diversity, and in this manner it is not accepted here; in another manner insofar as "principality" means a certain authority, just as the Father is said to work through the Son. Whence each single [unaquaeque][1] creature is produced by the Father through the Son [a Patre per Filium], inasmuch as They are one; and thus is it to be understood in the proposed.

2. To that which is objected, that a nexus proceeds from several [a pluribus] etc.; it must be said, that the reckoning of a nexus begins from a distinction and tends or leads thoroughly [perducit][2] unto a unity: whence the ultimate and completing reckoning is the unity. Therefore, though a nexus be of two and from two, if it is a perfect nexus, it is from them inasmuch as they are one, not inasmuch as they are several.[3]

3. To that which is objected, that from a unity of subject there is a unity of acting and from a plurality a plurality; it must be said, that that does not have an instance* according to the manner of speaking, because if two terms have been conjoined, their act ought to reckoned [reddi] as numbered;[4] but according to the thing [secundum rem] it must be distinguished, because "subject" is said in a twofold manner: either *through itself* [per se] and *in a first (manner)* [primo], or *not in a first (manner)* [non primo]; and that is true concerning (what is) a subject *through itself* and *in a first (manner)*, not *from another* [de alio]; and by accepting (it) in this manner, the Father and the Son are not the one Principle, or[5] the first Subject of the Spiration, because They do not spirate according to which (They are) Father and Son, but according to which there is in Them one fecundity of Will, and thus inasmuch as (They are) one. — And/or in another way it must be said, that there is a speaking of "act" [actu], as it is an act and/or[6] origin, and of "act", as it is an accident. If we speak of an "act", as it is an *accident*, of necessity one counts according to the number of the subject, because there is not one accident in two subjects. But if we speak of "act", as it is an *act*,[7] in this manner it is compared to a subject as to a principle, and thus it is not counted according to the number of the subject according to which (it is) a subject, but according to which (it is) a principle. Therefore, since, among the divine, Spiration is not an accident,

but a production and/or relation; for that reason it follows the unity of the subject, since (that) is (its) principle, because[8] the Father and the Son, although They are two Persons, yet They are one Principle, because They spirate through the same Virtue: for that reason the Act is not enumerated in Them, for that reason They spirate by one Spiration, although They are two (Persons).

4. To that which is asked last, either inasmuch as (They are) one in substance etc.; it must be said, that inasmuch as (They are) one in the fecundity of the Will, insofar as that Will is treated as being known [ad notionem] through (its) fecundity, which fecundity is by the reckoning of *primacy*, which primacy is signified through that which is *improcessible*. And this is what (St.) Anselm says, that the Father and the Son spirate, according to which Each is the *same* God, not according to which (They are) *God simply*, but according to which God (is) in Each; that is (according to which there is) a considering of the Will in the Persons.

If, therefore, *you ask*, whether (He proceeds) inasmuch as (They are) one in *substance*, or *notion*, or *person*; it must be said, that one can respond in a twofold manner, according to the two opinions previously posited concerning the power of generating, in the Seventh Distinction,[9] because certain ones say, that the power of generating does not differ from generation or paternity except according to the manner of speaking, and thus it means a notion, that is a personal property, such as 'generation', though in another manner. Similarly, these say, that a "fecundity of will" or "spirative force" means the same notion, that "spiration" (does), though in another manner, because one means the spirative force in the reckoning of an aptitude, but "spiration" (means the spirative force)[10] in the reckoning of the act; and thus, according to these, inasmuch as they are (such), (They are) one in notion. Others say, that just as the power of generating means the nature in the person, so (it means) the essence reckoned personally [personaliter], so "spirative force" means 'the Will', inasmuch as [ut] the Will is in the Persons, in Whom It is fecund;[11] and, thus, the Father and the Son spirate inasmuch [in quantum] as (They are) one in Essence or Nature or Will — to speak more properly[12] — in the Will considered in the Persons. Each of these positions seems to me sufficiently probable.

SCHOLIUM

I. For an understanding of this question it must be noted, that the Father and the Son convene in something notional [in aliqua re notionali], that is, in active spiration, in which the Holy Spirit does not convene with Them; whence that ought to pertain to the relation in some manner, since it is established, that the

Three Persons entirely convene in the Essence. For a more accurate explanation of the same question, refer to what the Seraphic Doctor says below in d. 29, a. 2, qq. 1 and 2.

II. In the solution to n. 4, the Seraphic Doctor, (St. Bonaventure of Bagnoregio), returns to that which he said above

---

[1] We prefer the reading of very many manuscripts, such as F G H P Q, *each single* [unaquaeque] in place of *one* [una].

[2] Thus very many codices, such as A D E G H I P Q R T etc. The Vatican edition has *proceeds* [procedit], but less well; the others with edition 1 falsely read *produced* [produxit]. Then codex Z by adding *its* [eius] reads *its ultimate and complete* etc..

[3] See d. 10, a. 2, q. 2, ad 3. — Richard of Middleton, here in q. 3 solves the same objection thus: I say, that that argument concludes no more, except that He proceeds from several, and this is true. From Them, however, He proceeds inasmuch as They are one in spirative potency.

[4] The Vatican edition's *to it* [ei] in place of *to them* [eis], is corrected with the assistance of very many manuscripts and editions 1, 2 and 3, in which place codex X has *in this manner* [sic]. An example of this, of which the Seraphic Doctor speaks, is this: Peter and Paul run; where the act of running is reckoned [in the plural by the subject of each.

[5] The codices do not agree among themselves; many, with edition 1, omit *or* [seu]; codex T omits *principle, or* [principium, seu]; codices G and Z substitute *one* [unum] for *or* [seu].

[6] Edition 1 reads *or* [sive].

[7] The Vatican edition, not trusting in the manuscripts and edition 1, adds *and/or origin* [vel origo].

[8] The Vatican edition, striving against nearly all the more ancient mss. and edition 1, has *why* [quare]; codex I has *and because* [et quia].

[9] Question 1. — Trusting the manuscripts and editions 1, 2, 3 and 6 we have supplied the words *in the Seventh Distinction; because some say, that* [distinctione septima; quod quidam dicunt, quod], in place those of the Vatican edition *because it* [quia ipsa], which edition a little below, after *except* [nisi], disagreeing with many manuscripts, such as A F G I P Q S T V W X etc., has *in a manner of speaking* [in modo loquendi] in place of *by a manner of speaking* [modo loquendi].

[10] Codex V repeats here a *such as* [ut].

[11] Some codices, such as H I and Z, have *in whom there is fecundity* [in quibus est fecunditas].

[12] A few codices, such as F M and X, faultily read *before* [prius] for *more properly* [proprius]. Then from the ancient manuscripts and edition 1, we have substituted *of these* [harum] for *of those* [illarum].

in d. 7, q. 1, concerning the twofold opinion about the power of generating, cf. there the Scholium, and below in d. 27, p. I, q. 2, and d. 28 throughout. For his part the Seraphic Doctor declares, there, that each opinion is probable, even though in this passage He responds according to the second position.

III. The conclusion is, that the Father and the Son produce the Holy Spirit, to the extent that They are one in the fecundity of the Will. For it is evident, that They could not spirate, to the extent that They are one in Essence, because They are also one in Essence with the Holy Spirit, however, as regards Person, they are two, not one; therefore, They produce the Holy Spirit, to the extent that They are one in notion, i. e., in active spiration.

IV. Cf. below d. 29, a. 2, q. 1 and 2. — Alexander of Hales, SUMMA., p. I., q. 70, m. 3, a. 3 ff. — (Bl. John Duns) Scotus, SENT., Bk. I, d. 12, q. 1: and REPORTATIO., d. 12, q. 1 and 2. — St. Thomas, here in q. 1, a. 2 ff; SUMMA., I, q. 36, a. 4; SUMMA CONTRA GENTILES., IV, c. 25. — Bl. (now St.) Albertus Magnus, here in aa. 3, 4, 5; SUMMA., p. I, tr. 7, q. 31, m. 3, q. 1. in passing. — (Bl.) Peter of Tarentaise, here in q. 1. a. 2 ff. — Richard of Middleton, here in q. 3 ff. — Giles the Roman, here in 2. princ., q. 1 and 2. — Henry of Ghent, SUMMA., a. 54, q. 6, n. 50 ff. — Durandus (of Saint-Pourçain), here in q. 3. — (Bl.) Dionysius the Carthusian, here q. 3 and 4. — (Gabriel) Biel, SENT., Bk. I, d. 12, q. 1 and 2.

DOUBTS ON THE TEXT OF THE MASTER

DOUBT I

In this part there are doubts about the text (of Master Peter) and first concerning this which he says. *In the principle councils, which were celebrated amongst them.* Therefore, it is asked, which are those four principle councils?

I RESPOND: And it must be said, that there were four principal[1] Councils of the Apostles in the primitive Church, as a certain Gloss on Acts says.[2] The First was at the election of (St.) Matthias, Acts (chapter) one;[3] the second at the election of the seven deacons, Acts (chapter) six;[4] the third was for not imposing the observances of the Law [legalia] upon the Gentiles, Acts (chapter) fifteen;[5] the fourth to tolerate the observances of the Law for a time, Acts (chapter) twenty-one.[6]

However, the principle Councils of the Fathers, among the Greeks, were similarly four, that is, Nicea, Ephesus, Chalcedon and Constantinople.

DOUBT II

Likewise is asked concerning that exposition, which Master (Peter) puts on that (passage): *He who has taught (something) else and/or preached in another manner* etc.; and he expounds (it thus): *that is, has taught the contrary and/or preached in a contrary manner* etc.; because that exposition of his does not seem probable, for the reason that he who contradicts the articles, has been excommunicated by the law itself [ipso iure]: therefore, it was not necessary [opportebat] to put forth [dare] a sentence on behalf of *the contrary*: therefore, it seems, that (the Fathers of the Council) excluded [tulerunt] a sentence on behalf of a *diverse* (opinion). *Moreover*, whence comes that exposition of his? For God's sake![7] why did they not say "whosoever has contradicted"?

I RESPOND: It must be said, that just as (St.)

Anselm says:[8] Every truth can be said of Sacred Scripture, which does not contradict Sacred Scripture, on account of its generality and dignity; and for that reason the aforesaid exposition has (its) place here. Nor was it unfitting to express the excommunication of heretics, because the holy Fathers used to ordain in the Councils what belonged *to the law*, and on this account[9] it has been said to frighten [ad terrorem]; and they preferred to say *(something) else* [aliud], though they understood *the contrary*, to shut-up [compescerent] more the mouths of the presumptuous, lest they invent novelties in the faith. But, in its truest sense [secundum veritatem] the sentence of excommunication does not extend itself except to those contradicting (the dogma); because it was not their intention, to preclude the way to make a greater explanation of the faith, if God would illumine others more; and if they had said this, it is established that they would not have been well moved, and rightly [merito] their sentence would have to be abolished.[10]

DOUBT III

Likewise is asked concerning this which he says, *that 'that the Holy Spirit is of the Son' is not other than 'that He is from the Son'*. But on the contrary: it is (something) else to say "the hat of Socrates" than "the hat made by Socrates": therefore, similarly it seems in the proposed; or if not, the reason is asked.[11]

And it must be said, that the genitive (case), although it is denominated from a habitude *of principle*, nevertheless it conveys *another* habitude, nay *other (habitudes)*,[12] such as (that) *of possession*; but since among the divine there falls neither a diversity nor a habitude except of origin, since the reckoning of matter among the divine is determined according to the habitude *of principle*; and for that reason in God it is the same to say *the Spirit of the Son*, (and) that *the Spirit proceeds from the Son*.

---

[1] From the older manuscripts and edition 1, we have supplied *principal* [principalia].

[2] Acts 21:21 See (the Gloss) in (Nicolas) de Lyra.

[3] Verse 15 ff.

[4] Verse 2 ff.

[5] Verse 6 ff.

[6] Verse 18 ff. — A little before this edition 1 has *for tolerating* [ad toleranda] in place of *to tolerate* [ad tolerandum].

[7] The Vatican edition, not trusting in the manuscripts and edition 1, in place of this interjection puts *and there is asked* [et quaeritur].

[8] In the book, ON THE CONCORD OF GOD'S FOREKNOWLEDGE WITH FREE WILL, q. 3, ch. 6: Since (Sacred Scripture), as it is the adversary of no truth, so favors no falsity, by the very (fact) that it does not deny, that what is said by reason it acknowledges by its own authority. — And a little after this: And so in this manner Scripture contains the authority of every truth, which reason gathers, since it either affirms it openly or denies it to no extent.

[9] The Vatican edition, contrary to many codices, such as A F G H I T X Z etc. and edition 1, has *moreover* [praeterea] instead of *on this account* [propterea], but less well, because the words *what belonged to the law* [quae iuris erant] here signify the decree regarding discipline, not strictly (that) regarding the Faith. The Vatican edition also a little below this has the indicative instead of the subjunctive for *though the understood* [quamvis intellexerunt]. Then some codices, such as V W X, have *presumptuous mouths* [ora praesumptuosa] for *mouths of the presumptuous* [ora praesumptuosorum].

[10] The Seraphic Doctor speaks only hypothetically and precisely concerning the prohibition of explanation, to the extent that it is a *disciplinary* matter; he does not in the least manner suppose — as the marginal note in the Vatican edition suggests — that the decrees of a general Council are reformable in matters of the Faith.

[11] One or the other codices, such as V and bb, have *why not* [quare non] in place of *the reason is asked* [quaeritur ratio].

[12] In the Vatican edition the words *nay other (habitudes)* are lacking, which however, are had in the manuscripts and edition 1.

Moreover, the other reason is, that *"Spirit"*, according to which it is an *absolute* noun, just as this noun *"God"* (is), does not properly have to be constructed with the genitive, because then it would be the same to say *the Spirit of the Son* as [quod] *the God of the Son*: therefore, it is opportune, that "Spirit" be accepted, according to which it is meant from *spiration*, and in this manner it is a noun conveying origin: therefore, just as it follows: '*The Son of the Father*, therefore, the Son, who is from the Father,' so also it is that to say 'Spirit of the Son', that is, 'the Spirit, who is from the Son.'

DOUBT IV

Likewise, is asked of this which he says: *not without Me and without My judgement* [arbitrio] *and (that) of the Father* etc.. It seems that he speaks badly, because he who has judgement [arbitrium] over anyone has dominion over him:[1] therefore, it seems according to this, that the Holy Spirit is inferior to the Son. *If you say*, that "judgement" (here) means "will"; this is noth-

ing, because,[2] similarly, since the one Will belongs to the Three, the Son, similarly, does not speak without the judgement of the Holy Spirit, and the Father similarly; on which account, it is not said properly (of any one Person).

I RESPOND: It must be said, that the Holy Spirit is consubstantial to the Father and Son, such that He proceeds from the Father and the Son; therefore, the *operation* of the Holy Spirit is common to the Father and the Son, and similarly He equally has "*being*" [esse][3] from the Father and the Son; such that it is not that He speaks, because He has His own speech, nor because He has speech from Himself; and these two the Lord wanted to exclude when He said: *He does not speak on His own,*[4] so that there is excluded the reckoning *of what is proper* [ratio proprii] and the reckoning *of a first principle*. And (St.) Didymus (the Blind), explaining this against (understanding this as what is) proper, says: *Not without Me,* against (understanding this as) a reckoning of a *first principle*: *Without My judgement and (that) of the Father,* and "judgement" does not convey dominion and/or[5] causality, but only authority in the Father and the Son in respect to the Holy Spirit and/or to His operation.

DISTINCTION XII

CHAPTER I

Whether the Holy Spirit proceeds before and/or more fully from the Father than from the Son.

Likewise, there is asked, "Since the Holy Spirit proceeds from the Father and[1] the Son, whether He proceeded before and/or more from the Father than from the Son?"; which the heretic strives to show thus, saying: "if the Holy Spirit proceeds from the Father, He proceeds at least either with the Son already born, (or) before the Son (was) not yet born. However, if He proceeded with the Son already born, the Son was born before [ante ... quam] the Holy Spirit proceeded: therefore, the Nativity of the Son preceded the Procession of the Holy Spirit. But if He proceeds from the Father with the Son not begotten, He proceeds before the Son had been begotten."

To these and questions of this kind, more laborious than fruitful, (St.) Augustine responds in the fifteenth book, ON THE TRINITY,[2] saying: « In that Most High Trinity, which is God, there are no intervals of seasons, through which it can be shown or at least enquired after, whether the Son be born from [de] the Father beforehand, and afterwards the Holy Spirit proceeded from Them both ». « Therefore, we cannot ask, whether the Holy Spirit had already proceeded from [de] the Father, when the Son was born, or whether He had not yet proceeded and, with the latter born, He proceeded from [de] Both? In a word [prorsus], these cannot be asked There, where nothing is begun on account of time, to be perfected in a consequent[3] time. For that reason, let him who can understand the generation of the Son from the Father without time, understand without time the Procession of the Holy Spirit

from Both ». Behold, with these words there is solved that question, by which there was asked, whether the Holy Spirit proceeded from [a] the Father before from the Son.

CHAPTER II

That the Holy Spirit is said principally and properly to proceed from the Father.

Now, must be treated that which was asked second, that is whether the Holy Spirit proceeds more fully and/or[4] more from the Father than from the Son. To which we say, that just as He does not proceed from the Father before (He does) from the Son, so not more nor [vel] more fully does He proceed from the Father than from the Son. However, (St.) Augustine in the fifteenth book, ON THE TRINITY[5] says, that the Holy Spirit does proceed principally from [de] the Father. « Not as a trick », he says, « is it said in this Trinity that the "Word of God" (is) naught but the Son, or the "Gift of God" naught but the Holy Spirit, or "Him from whom the Word has been begotten", and "Him from whom the Holy Spirit principally proceeds", naught but God the Father ». Behold you have heard, that the Holy Spirit proceeds "principally from [a] the Father." But, lest this trouble you, he immediately reveals in which [ex quo ... aperit] sense he spoke, subjoining:[6] « For this reason did I added "principally", because the Holy Spirit is also found to proceed from [de] the Son, but this the Father also gives Him, not as to one existing but not yet having. But, whatever He gave to the Only-Begotten Word, He gave by begetting. Thus, therefore, did He beget Him, that the common Gift would proceed even from Him, and the Holy Spirit would belong to Both ». Behold, he himself has expounded,

---

[1] The Vatican edition, together with codex cc, has *it* [illud], and a little before this *anything* [aliquid] in place of *anyone* [aliquem], but contrary to the authority of the more ancient codices and edition 1.

[2] Codex Z, together with edition 1, adds *then* [tunc].

[3] In codex bb there is added *and speaking* [et loqui].

[4] John 16:13.

[5] From the ancient manuscripts and edition 1, we have substituted *and/or* [vel] in place of *or* [sive].

NOTES ON THE BOOK OF SENTENCES

[1] Only all the editions repeat *from* [a] here. Below after *the Holy Spirit* codices B C D and E read *from* [de] in place of *from* [a].

[2] Chapter 26, n. 45; the quote follow is from *ibid.*, n. 47. — Contrary to our codices and the text of (St.) Augustine, all the editions have

in the first quote *could been shown* [posset ostendi] for *can be shown* [possit ostendi].

[3] The editions, excepting edition 1, have *out of a consequent in time* [ex consequenti ... in tempore]; but the *out of* [ex] must be deleted on the authority of all the codices and the text of (St.) Augustine (to arrive at our reading). A little above this, not a few codices twice have *proceeded* [processerit] for *had proceeded* [processerat].

[4] The Vatican edition, together with a few editions, has *or* [aut]. At the beginning of this proposition after *must be treated* [tractandum est] codex D inserts *concerning this* [de eo].

[5] Chapter 17, n. 29.

[6] The Vatican edition, with not a few editions, has *saying* [dicens], and a little before this, after *sense he spoke* [sensu] adds *this* [hoc].

in what manner the Spirit "principally" proceeds from [a] the Father, not because He proceeds before and/or more from the Father than from the Son, but because, since He does proceed from the Son, this very (thing) does the Son have from the Father.

In the same sense He is also said to "properly" proceed from [de] the Father. Whence (St.) Jerome in (his) exposition of the Catholic Faith and the Nicene Creed[1] says: « We believe in the Holy Spirit, who properly proceeds from the Father ». Likewise: « We find in Scripture that the Holy Spirit (is) the True God, and properly is from the Father ». And likewise: « From the Father, the Son, and the Holy Spirit[2] properly and truly proceeds from the Father ». Behold he openly says, that the Holy Spirit "properly" is from the Father" and "properly proceeds from [a] the Father". Which thus must not be understood, as if He proceeds before and/or more fully from the Father than from the Son, but that the Father has this from Himself, not from an other, that from Him the Holy Spirit is and does proceed; but the Son has this not from Himself, but from the Father, that from Himself[3] the Holy Spirit is and does proceed.

Perhaps according to this understanding, the Holy Spirit is also said "to be sent[4] through the Son" and "to be from the Father through the Son". Whence (St.) Hilary (of Poitiers), speaking to God the Father of the Holy Spirit and the Son, says in the twelfth book, ON THE TRINITY:[5] « In Thy Holy Spirit, (having) come forth from Thee [ex te profecto] and (having been) sent through Him ». Likewise: « Before the ages [tempora] Thy Only-Begotten, born from [ex] Thee, remained, such that Thy Holy Spirit is from [ex] Thee and through Him; whom even if I do not perceive by sense, I yet hold in conscience. For I am stupid in the spiritual affairs which regard Thee [rebus tuis hebes] ». Likewise, in the same (book, he says): « Guard, I pray, this religion of my Faith, that I may always obtain, that which I have professed in the Creed of my New Life [regenerationis]: "May I adore the Father, that is, Thee[6] and Thy Son, as One with Thee; may I merit Thy Holy Spirit, who is from [ex] Thee through Thy Only-Begotten" ». Behold he openly says, that the Holy Spirit "from [a] the Father through the Son" both is sent and is; which is not to be understood, as if from the Father through a minor Son He is sent and/or is, but that from [ex] the Father and the Son He is and is sent by Each [ab utroque]. But this very (thing) the Son has from the Father,

that from Himself the Holy Spirit both is[7] and is sent. Therefore, (St.) Hilary wanted to signify this, making a distinction in speech, to show that the Authorship [auctoritatem] is in the Father. Hence it is also, that the Truth showing, that the Father is the Author of the Procession, by which the Holy Spirit proceeds from the Son, said in the Gospel:[8] *Who proceeds from* [de] *the Father*, when the Holy Spirit proceeds from the Father and the Son. Whence (St.) Augustine in the fifteenth book, ON THE TRINITY (says):[9] « If the Holy Spirit proceeds from the Father and the Son, why did the Son say: *Who proceeds from the Father?* Why do you think, except that He is accustomed [solet] to refer even that which belongs to Himself to Him, from whom He also is, just as He says:[10] *My doctrine is not Mine, but His, who sent Me?* If, here, therefore, the "doctrine" is to be understood (to be) His, which He did not call His own, but the Father's, how much more in that (passage) is the Holy Spirit to be understood to proceed from Him, where he thus says: *Who proceeds from the Father*, since He did not say: "Who does not proceed from Me." From whom, moreover, the Son has, that He is God — for He is God from [de] God — at least from [a] Him He has, that the Holy Spirit also proceeds from Himself. And for that reason the Holy Spirit has from the Father Himself, that He proceeds from [de] the Son even as [etiam sicut] He proceeds from the Father ». « On which account, let him who can understand in this (passage), what the Son says:[11] *Just as the Father has Life in Himself, in this manner has He given even to the Son to have Life in Himself,* not that the Father gave life to a Son, existing without life, but that He thus begot Him without time, so that the Life, which the Father gave to the Son by begetting (Him), is the co-eternal Life of the Father, who gave (It); understand also, just as the Father has Life in Himself, that the Holy Spirit proceeds from Him, so He has given to the Son, that the same Holy Spirit proceeds also from Him, and each without time. Therefore, thus has is been said, "that the Holy Spirit proceeds from [de] the Father," so that there is understood, 'that it has (been) granted) from the Father to the Son that He proceeds also from the Son.'[12] For if whatever He has, the Son has (it) from the Father, He at any rate has it from the Father, such that the Holy Spirit also proceeds from Him. But let no ages [tempora] be thought of There [ibi], which have a "before" and "after", because in that place [ibi] there are entirely none ».

COMMENTARY ON DISTINCTION XII

On the eternal procession of the Holy Spirit, in what kind of manner He proceeds from the Father and the Son.

Likewise, there is asked, "Since the Holy Spirit proceeds from the Father and1 the Son" etc..

THE DIVISION OF THE TEXT

This is the second part, in which Master (Peter) determines, in what manner the Holy Spirit proceeds[1] from the Father and the son; and this part has four short chapters [quatuor capitula] according to the four (questions), which he determines in the four short chapters.[2] For *first* he asks and determines, whether the Holy Spirit proceeds more first from the Father, and He determines that

---

[1] EXPLANATION TO CYRIL, ch. 1 and 3.

[2] All the codices omit *Holy* [sanctus].

[3] Codices D & E, with only the Vatican ed., have *from His very self* [de se ipso], which codex C likewise has before this, where it first occurs.

[4] All the codices add *from the Father* [a Patre], but since this is lacking in all our editions, we have changed nothing in the text.

[5] N. 55; the following passage is n. 56, the third n. 57.

[6] All the editions, against the original and the codices, transpose the words in this manner: *Thee, the Father, that is* [te Patrem scilicet].

[7] The Vatican edition, with a few of the editions, omits *both* [et].

[8] Jn. 15:26; the Vulgate reads *from the Father* [a Patre]. — Then many editions, contrary to editions 1 and 7 and the manuscripts, add *both* [et] after *proceeds* [Trans. Note: in the Latin text after *cum*]; moreover, very many of the editions omit *Holy* [sanctus] in the same phrase.

[9] Chapter 27, n. 48.

[10] Jn 7:16. — Immediately before this the Vatican edition, together with a few of the editions, contrary to the original and the manuscripts, by adding *just as* [sicut] and transposing *and* [et], reads thus: *to*

Him even That which belongs to Himself, as (That) from which He (is) and (That which) He Himself is. [ipsius est, sicut et de quo et ipse est].

[11] Jn 5, 26.

[12] The Vatican edition, together with the other editions, excepting edition 1, faultily and by contradicting the manuscripts and the text of (St.) Augustine, inserts an *and* [et] before *the Son* [Filio: which thus reads *from the Father and the Son*]. The Sense of our text is: so that there is understood, that it has been given by the Father to the Son, that the Holy Spirit proceeds even from Him. — A little after this the Vatican edition, with not a few edd., omits *also* [et] before *proceeds from Him* [de illo procedat]. then edd. 2 & 3 have *But no ages ... are thought of* [Sed ... cogitantur] in place of *But let no ages ... be thought of* [Sed cogitantur].

NOTES ON THE COMMENTARY

[1] Some codices, such as A I S T V Y, have the subjunctive *proceeds* [procedat].

[2] The Vatican ed., without the authority of the mss. and ed. 1, by putting *parts* [partes] in place of *short chapters* [capitula], and having omitted the words *in the four short chapters* [in quatuor capitulis] pro-

(it is) *not*. *Second*, whether more principally and more fully, there (where he says: *Now must be treated that which was asked second*. *Third*, however he determines, whether properly He proceeds from the Father, and he says that (it is) *so*, there (where he says): *In the same sense He is also said to properly proceed from* [de] *the Father*.

Fourth, he determines, whether the Holy Spirit properly proceeds from [a] the Father through the Son, there (where he says): *Perhaps according to this understanding*, where he confirms by the authority of (St.) Hilary (of Poitiers), that the Holy Spirit is sent and proceeds from the Father through the Son.

TREATMENT OF THE QUESTIONS

Having supposed from the preceding, that the Holy Spirit proceeds from the Father and the Son, for an understanding of this part four (things) are asked concerning the procession of the Holy Spirit in comparison to Each.

First there is asked, whether the Holy Spirit proceeds from the Father before [prius quam] (He does) from the Son.

Second, whether (He does) more fully from the Father than from the Son.

Third, whether He proceeds from the Father by means of the Son.

Fourth and last, whether the procession of the Son is prior, according to the order of understanding, to the procession of the Holy Spirit, or the other way around.

ARTICLE SOLE

On the procession of the Holy Spirit in comparison to the Father and the Son.

QUESTION I

Whether the Holy Spirit proceeds from the Father before from the Son?

About the first, that He is from the Father before (He is) from the Son, is shown in this manner:

1. (That) cause is the first, in which there is a standing-still [status], therefore, also (that) principle is first, in which there is a standing-still; but there is a standing-still in the Father: therefore, the Father is the first principle; but the 'first' supposes the 'prior' [prius]:[1] therefore, He proceeds from the Father before (He does) from the Son [prius … quam a Filio].

2. Likewise, (that) cause is first which acts, with another not supposed:[2] if, therefore, the Father produces not through a supposition of another Principle, the Son through a supposition (of One), the Father produces before the Son.

3. Likewise, that which anyone has out of himself, he has through (a consideration of what) is prior to that which he has out of another; but 'that He produces the Holy Spirit' the Father has from Himself, and the Son from the Father: therefore, the Father has (this) through (a consideration of what is) prior to the Son (having it).

ON THE CONTRARY: 1. Where there is no positing of the "posterior", neither of the "prior", because "prior" is said in respect of "posterior", but in the Trinity there is no positing of the "posterior": therefore, neither of the "prior". If therefore the procession of the Holy Spirit from the Father and the Son is eternal, it is clear etc.

2. Likewise, where there is a positing of a "prior and posterior", there is[3] a positing of a diversity of principles; but the Father and the Son produce the Holy Spirit inasmuch as (They are) one, as has been shown above:[4] therefore, there is no reckoning of the "prior" There.

3. Likewise, if He proceeds from the Father through (a consideration of what is) prior to (His procession) from the Son, either[5] He does not proceed from the Son, or He proceeds twice; but He does proceed from the Son and He does not proceed twice: ergo etc..

4. Likewise, it happens that one understands the prior, not having understood the posterior: therefore, if He proceeds from the Father through (a consideration of what is) prior, therefore, it happens that one understands, that He proceeds,[6] with the Son not understood as accompanying [non cointellecto Filio]. *But on the contrary*: the Holy Spirit is a uniting love and a joining love; but there is no accepting of a mutual love according (to what is) lesser than (that which exists) between two, therefore, neither 'that the Holy Spirit is'[7] except 'from Two': therefore, neither does He proceed from One through (a consideration of what is) prior to (His procession) from the Other.

CONCLUSION

The Holy Spirit according to Authorship indeed proceeds from the Father before (He does) from the Son, not however, according to duration, and/or causality, and/or even origin.

I RESPOND: It must be said, that "*prior*" is said in a manifold manner. For "prior" is said according to *duration*, "prior" is said according to *causality*, "prior" is said according to *origin*, "prior" is said according to *authorship* [auctoritate].[8] And in the first two manners the "prior" in no manner occurs [cadit] in God; because (what is) prior according to *duration* is contrary to eternity, (what is) prior according to *causality* is contrary to the unity[9] of the Essence. But (what is) prior according to the *origin*, by which the one (is) out of the other,

---

ceeds thus: *In the first he asks, whether* [In prima quaerit, utrum], and a little below this has *In the second he asks, whether* [In secunda quaerit, utrum]. then after *Third*, it omits *however, he determines* [vero determinat], and then omits the words *and he says that (it is) so* [et dicit quod sic].

[1] Codex K adds: *because the superlative supposes the comparative* [quia superlativum supponit comparativum].

[2] Aristotle, PHYSICS, Bk. IV, text 7 (ch. 1) says: For that, without which nothing else belongs to others, but it itself is without the others, is necessary that it be first. — A little below this after *the Son* in codex O there is added *however* [vero].

[3] Codex I reads *there there is* [ibi est].

[4] Distinction 11, q. 2.

[5] Codex T with edition 1 does well to add here a *therefore* [ergo].

[6] In codex T and edition 1 there is well added here *from the Father* [a Patre].

[7] The Vatican edition, without the authority of the manuscripts and edition 1, reads *neither is the Holy Spirit* [nec Spiritus sanctus est].

[8] Cf. Aristotle, ON THE PREDICAMENTS, ch. "On the Prior", and METAPHYSICS, Bk. V, text 16 (Bk. IV, ch. 11). — In this proposition, from many manuscripts, such as A F G H I K T V W Z aa etc. and edition 1, we have thrice supplied *is said* [dicitur].

[9] Codex X has *to the immutability* [immutabilitati].

and (what is) prior according to the *authorship*, by which the One accepts from the Other,[1] does occur There. But (what is) prior according to *origin* occurs in respect of the *One producing* and the *One produced*, since the One arises out of the Other; however, since *One* arises *from Two*, there does not occur There a "prior" according to *origin*, because Both, then, are the one original Principle; nevertheless there does fall There a "prior" according to *authorship*, because although the Father and the Son are one in producing, nevertheless the Son accepts this from the Father.

If, therefore, there is asked, whether the Holy Spirit proceeds from the Father through (a consideration of what is) prior to (that) from the Son; if "prior"[2] be understood according to duration, it is false; similarly, if the "prior" (be understood) according to causality; similarly, if the "prior" (be understood) according to origin, just as the reasons first brought forward for this prove. But, if the "prior" (be understood) according to *authorship*, so that (what is) *prior* is the same as what (is) *more principal*, it has truth.

1. To that which, therefore,[3] is first objected, that the Father is the first principle and cause (of the procession of the Holy Spirit); it must be said, those reasons have truth, where there is a plurality of causes and/or principles; but in respect of the Holy Spirit there is neither a plurality of causes nor of principles.

2. 3. To that which is objected, that through[4] (the consideration of what is) prior, one has (that) which he has out of himself [ex se]; it must be said, that, if (that) is understood to be (something) *prior*, that is *more principal*, (then) it is true; but, if (it be understood) in another manner, (it is) false, because one and the same (thing) can be had by very many persons, such that (it is had) from one through an other; nor is there such priority (among the Father and the Son) in any of the three aforesaid manners.

SCHOLIUM

I. Having posited a fourfold distinction of *priority*, there is first denied, that the Holy Spirit proceeds from the Father according to *duration, causality*, (or) *origin* before (He does) from the Son. For a priority of *duration* and *causality* cannot be in any manner [esse omnino]; but a priority of *origin* can indeed be said among the divine, but only, to the extent that one Person proceeds from One, and the Other from the Two. Therefore, it is not to be posited between the Father and the Son, to the extent that They produce the Holy Spirit. Next, there is conceded, that the Holy Spirit proceeds from the Father according to *authorship* prior to, and/or even *more principally* than from the Son. For this no other reason is asserted, except that the Father has from Himself [a se ipso] the power of spirating, but the Son from the Father; whence a certain principality befits the Father, which, nevertheless, conveys neither a subjection upon the Son, nor a distinction at the beginning of the spiration [in principio spirativo]. In this matter, what (Bl. John Duns) Scotus says (here at q. 2), is the same: « There is not, therefore, an order of origin between the spiration of the Father and the Son, as if the Father spirates, under [in] some sign of origin, in which the Son does not spirate, rather They spirate together under the same sign of origin. Nevertheless, there is There an order of Ones spirating in spirating, because the Father (with the Term of the first fecundity produced) under that third sign of origin does spirate from Himself [a se], but the Son not by Himself [a se] ».

II. For a greater explanation of the solution to n. 3, it will be useful to hear what Bl. (now St.) Albertus (Magnus) says, there in

a. 3, n. 2: « It must be said, that this (that one property does not belong to two subjects) is true in those supposits, which are divided from each other through (their) essence and substance; for among them, that which is in one the same according to number is not in the other. But for two supposits, which are diverse in nothing, except (that) among them there is an opposition of relation, there can be in them the same, inasmuch are they are not relatively opposed. Moreover, the Father and the Son are such Supposits of the divine Nature; and according to which They are compared to spirative virtue [virtutem spiralem] and to the Holy Spirit, They do not have a relative opposition among them, therefore, according to this They remain the same, and in this manner one in number will be that which in this comparison is in Them. But this is the property of spirating, and thus They are the one principle of spirating of the Holy Spirit ».

III. Cf. below d. 20, a. 2, q. 1 and 2. — (Bl John Duns) Scotus, on this and the following two questions, here in q. 2. — St. Thomas, on this and the following question, here in q. 1, a. 2. — Bl. (now St.) Albertus Magnus,* here in a. 2; on this and the following question, SUMMA, p. I, tr. 7, m. 3, q. 2 incident. — (Bl.) Peter of Tarentaise, here in 1st princ., q. 2. — Henry of Ghent, on this and the two following questions, SUMMA, a. 54, q. 5 and 7; a. 60, q. 9. — (Bl.) Dionysius the Carthusian, on this and the following two questions, here in q. 1. — (Gabriel) Biel, on this and the following two questions, here in q. 3.

QUESTION II

Whether the Holy Spirit proceeds from the Father more fully than and more principally than from the Son?

Second, there is asked, whether He proceeds more fully from the Father than from the Son. And that it is so, seems:

1. Because that on account of which each one (is or acts) also (is or has it) to a greater degree [magis]:[5] therefore, since the Son spirates through the Father, because He has this from the Father, therefore, the Father spirates more.

2. Likewise, « every first cause influences more than the second »;[6] but the Father is the first principle of spirating: therefore, He influences more than the Son.

3. Likewise, more fully does anything proceed, from that which it proceeds properly and principally, than from that which (it) neither principally nor properly (does): but the Holy Spirit proceeds from the Father properly and principally, just as is said in the text (of Master Peter)[7] and (as St.) Augustine also says: ergo etc..

4. Likewise, anyone proceeds more fully from that, from which he has whatever he has, namely, substance and property, than (from that) from which he does not have; but the Holy Spirit

---

[1] Codex R adds *well* [bene].

[2] Trusting in the more ancient manuscripts and edition 1, we have inserted *the "prior"* [prius]. A little below this we follow codex M Y and edition 1, by adding: *similarly if the "prior" according to origin* [similiter si prius origine]. — St. Anselm (of Canterbury) agrees in his ON THE PROCESSION OF THE HOLY SPIRIT, chs. 23-25.

[3] The Vatican edition, contrary to the older codices and edition 1, omits *therefore,* [ergo].

[4] Trusting in the other mss., such as Y & Z, and edition 1, we have supplied *through* [per], which is also had above in this objection. A little before this one or the other codex has *the other* [aliud] for *that* [illud].

[5] Aristotle, POSTERIOR ANALYTICS, Bk. I, ch. 2. Cf. also METAPHYSICS, Bk. II, text 4 (or in the shorter version, Bk. I, ch. 1). — In which text very many codices at *each one* [unumquodque] reads *each such* [unumquodque tale]. Then near the end of the argument, with the help of the manuscripts and the first editions, we have restored *He has* [habet].

[6] BOOK ON CAUSES, proposition 1, in which text very many codices, such as B D E F G M X etc. together with editions 2 and 3, falsely have *prior* [plus] in place of *more* [plus].

[7] Chapter 2; where the words of (St.) Augustine are also had. — One or the other of the codices, such as Y and Z, have *Master (Peter) says* [Magister dicit] in place of *is said* [dicitur].

has from the Father what He is, and that He proceeds from the Father and the Son:[1] but from the Son He does not have, that He proceeds from the Father, because then the Son would give something to the Father: ergo etc..

ON THE CONTRARY: 1. If *more fully* from the Father, therefore, more perfectly: therefore, He does not proceed from the Son most perfectly, therefore, in the Trinity there is something of imperfection.

2. Likewise, if (He proceeds) more fully from the Father than from the Son, He accepts more from the Father than from the Son; but where there is a positing of "more and less", There there is a diversity: therefore, in the Person of the Holy Spirit there is a diversity.

3. Likewise, it seems that (He proceeds) neither *more principally* from the Father, because he who perfectly gives anything to anyone, gives him use[2] and jurisdiction or authority [auctoritatem]; if, therefore, the Father gives to the Son that He is able to spirate, therefore, He gives Him an authorship [auctoritatem] of spirating: therefore, He proceeds equally principally from the Son as from the Father.[3]

CONCLUSION

In a sane sense it can be said, that the Holy Spirit proceeds from the Father principally and or more principally and per se; He does not, however, proceed more fully, nor more perfectly.

I RESPOND: It must be said, that the Holy Spirit is said to proceed[4] from the Father *principally* and *per se*: principally, because (His) authorship [auctoritas] is in the Father; per se, because not only by means of the Son, but also immediately (from Himself). However, He does not proceed *more fully* from the Father nor *more perfectly*, because "*more fully*" posits a grade a perfection,

(and) it also posits a composition of the substance in the one produced, neither of which are among the divine. Whence if this is proposed: 'that that which proceeds from something more principally, proceeds more fully', it simply is to be denied.[5]

1. 2. To that which is, therefore, objected concerning a first cause and a *that on account of which* etc.; it must be said, that just as has been said before,[6] that only has a place, where there is a plurality of causes; but here there is not a plurality, neither of causes, nor of principles: for that reason it does not have a place here.

4. To that which is objected, that the Holy Spirit does not have from the Son, that He proceeds from the Father; it must be said regarding this, that "to have from one's self and/or from an other" does not posit a grade of plenitude. Whence, although the Son has (His) Divinity from the Father, thus[7] nevertheless He is the perfect God as the Father; and for that reason it does not follow, that (the Holy Spirit) proceeds *more fully* from the Father, because (He proceeds) *more principally*. — (To that) which[8] is objected: one has more fully because he has essence and property; it can be responded by denying *the minor*, for the Holy Spirit has from the Son a property, though He does not have (it) according to every respect; for He has (His) Procession from the Son, but not as (He does) from the Father.

To that which is objected, that the Father gives authority [auctoritatem] to the Son; it must be said that while giving authority over the Holy Spirit, nevertheless He has the authority from Himself,[9] because from this ought the Son refer it to the Father, because He has (it) from the Father; and hence it is, that in the Son there is an authorship and a sub-authorship [subauctoritas]. Whence He also principally produces the Holy Spirit,[10] but the Father more principally, because in Him there is only authorship, not sub-authorship. Moreover, among the divine, the *quality of being principal* [principalitas] is said (to be) *the quality of being an author* [auctoritas].

SCHOLIUM

I. In what sense here are to be understood the words, plenius, principaliter, auctoritas, subauctoritas, is sufficiently apparent from the words themselves of the Seraphic Doctor, posited here and below in Doubt 3. It is denied, that the Holy Spirit proceeds *more fully* [plenius] from the Father than from the Son, because this term signifies a grade of perfection; and/or at least connotes a composition in something; on the other hand it is affirmed, that the Father does *more principally* [principalius] produce the Holy Spirit, in the sense and for the reason expressed in q. 1. Moreover, the Son is asserted to *principally* [principaliter] produce the

Holy Spirit, because He gives Him whatever He has, wherefore He is said to have an *authorship* [auctoratem] in respect of the Same, a *sub-authorship* [subauctoritatem], however, in respect of the Father, from whom He has everything. Therefore, to have *authorship* and *the quality of being principal* [principalitas] is the same thing for our Doctor. Whence, at the end of the solution to n. 4, he responds by « interemption », i. e., by denying the false minor. — This manner of speaking, that the Father produces the Son more principally, the Seraphic Doctor, following Master (Peter) and the other ancient theologians, does not reprove. Undeservedly do not a few modern theologians together with

---

[1] Many codices, with edd. 2 & 3, perhaps from this, that the same words immediately occurs after this, unduly omit *and the Son* [et Filio], and, contrariwise, cod. R omits *the Father and* [Patre et], with which codd. aa & bb agree, by reading *and He proceeds also from the Son* [et procedat etiam a Filio]; a reading not to be spurned. Then, after *He does not have, that* [non habet, quod], cod, Y does well to add *He is from the Father and* [a Patre sit et].

[2] We have emended the reading of the Vatican edition and codex cc, from the other manuscripts and edition 1, by putting *use* [usum] for *force* [vim].

[3] The Vatican edition, not trusting in the manuscripts and edition 1, inverts the order of the arguments, by placing this argument last in the fifth place among the arguments for the opposite, though in the margin it has also this reference: Fundament. The reason for this inversion seems to have been, that this argument denies part of the conclusion, namely that the Holy Spirit proceeds *more principally* from the Father. But it is better that, together with the codices, this argument, though it pertains in another respect to the arguments for the opposite, be placed in the last place, because it is a special argument, or a sui generis one, namely, one denying, that the Holy Spirit proceeds *more principally* from the Father, while all the other arguments either prove or deny, that the Holy Spirit proceeds *more fully* from the Father.

[4] One or the other of the codices, such as W and Y, have *proceed* in place of *is said to proceed* [dicitur procedere].

[5] Many codices, with the order reversed, have *that which proceeds from something more fully, proceeds more principally* [quod procedit ab aliquo plenius, procedit principalius]. Though each reading, having attended to the definition of terms, is true in itself, however, one term is verified among the divine, the other is not, and having attend to the order of terms among themselves, it seems that the reading received in the text is to be preferred, which is already found in very many of the ancient mss., such as H L & O, and ed. 1. Cf. response to n. 4. — The Vatican ed., contrary to the mss. and ed. 1, has *is posited* [ponatur] for *is proposed* [proponatur], and after *more fully* [plenius] adds *or if not more fully, neither more principally* [aut si non plenius, neque principalius]. Codices H and Y after *this* [haec] add *question* [quaestio], but it is better that there be understood: this *proposition, that He proceeds more principally*.

[6] In the preceding question, in reply to n. 1.

[7] From the more ancient manuscripts and edition 1, we have supplied the not well omitted *thus* [ita]. (St.) Anselm agrees in his PROCESSION OF THE HOLY SPIRIT, ch. 24.

[8] A few codd., such as H S & ee, read *To that which* [Ad illud quod].

[9] Codd. L & O insert *over the Holy Spirit* [super Spiritum sanctum].

[10] The Vatican edition, without the authority of the mss. and edd. 1, 2, 3 & 6, has *the Son* [Filium] for *the Holy Spirit* [Spiritum Sanctum].

Suarez reject this saying of the Seraphic (Doctor) as erroneous. For they ought to attended (to the fact), that the Seraphic Doctor has explained it in a certainly orthodox sense, nor has he commended it, but only tolerated what is sanely explained, as is apparent from the last proposition in the body (of the response).

To the third counter-objection there is no explicit response, because it has already been solved in the body (of the response).

In which sense it can be said, that the Holy Spirit *properly* proceeds from the Father, cf. below Doubt 3.

II. In regard to the conclusion, cf. St. Thomas, here in q. 1, a. 2; SUMMA , I, q. 36, a. 3, ad 2. — Bl. (now) St. Albertus (Magnus), here in a. 3 and 4. — (Bl.) Peter of Tarentaise, here in q. 1, a. 2. — Richard of Middleton, here in q. 2. — Giles the Roman, 2nd. princ., q. 1. — Durandus (of Saint-Pourçain), here in q. 2.

QUESTION III

Whether the Holy Spirit proceeds from the Father by means of the Son?

Third, there is asked, whether the Holy Spirit proceeds from the Father by means of the Son.

1. That that (it is) so, seems through (St.) Hilary (of Poitiers) in the twelfth (book) ON THE TRINITY,[1] who speaking to the Father says: « May I deserve the Holy Spirit, who is from [ex] Thee through Him »: therefore, the Holy Spirit is from the Father through the Son, therefore, by means of the Son.

2. Likewise, Richard (of St. Victor)[2] says, that among the divine there is a procession only immediate, and one mediate and immediate — one only mediate there cannot be — and he says, that the one mediate and immediate is the procession of the Holy Spirit out of the Father: therefore, since a medium cannot occur (There) except the Son, the Holy Spirit proceeds from the Father by means of the Son.

3. Likewise, similar is the processing in that Trinity to the processing in the created image;[3] but love proceeds from the mind by means of understanding [intelligentia]: therefore, the Holy Spirit proceeds from the Father by means of the Son. *If you say*, that there is not a similitude as much as regards this: therefore, the reckoning of the image is destroyed, because an *image* ought to represent the order and origin of the Persons, not only the number among the Persons, because this[4] is also in the *vestige*.

4. Likewise, if the Son alone spirates,[5] so that the Father (does) not, then the Father would be said to spirate, but by means of the Son, so that there would be only a mediated procession: therefore, since spiration befits the Father per se and befits Him through this, that He is the principle of the Son spirating, therefore, it befits Him both mediately and immediately; and if this,[6] the Holy Spirit proceeds from the Father by means of the Son.

ON THE CONTRARY: 1. More noble is an immediate principle, than a mediate one; but everything more noble is to be attributed to God:[7] therefore, if the Father is a most noble principle of the Holy Spirit, therefore, He produces Him only immediately, not mediately. *If you say*, that He produces at once mediately and immediately; *on the contrary*, the mediate and immediate are opposites; but opposites are not at the same time true of the same and in respect of the same:[8] therefore, it is impossible, that He produces at once mediately and immediately.

2. Likewise, just as *per se* holds itself to *per accidens*, so *the mediate* to *the immediate*; but God is a cause *per accidens* of nothing, of which He is the cause per se: therefore, of nothing, of which He is an immediate principle, is He a mediate principle.

3. Likewise, (a thing) is more immediate, which in no manner receives a medium, than that which receives a medium; but the Son receives no medium in spirating: therefore, more immediately does He produce, than does the Father produce: therefore not entirely uniformly does the Father and the Son produce the Holy Spirit.

CONCLUSION

The Holy Spirit proceeds from the Father both immediately, and by means of the Son.

I RESPOND: It must be said, that, just as Richard (of St. Victor) wants, the production[9] of the Holy Spirit is at once *mediate* and *immediate*: mediate, inasmuch as He is from the Son, and the Son from the Father; but immediate, inasmuch as the Holy Spirit is Himself spirated from the Father Himself.

And an example of this is posited in the going-forth [exitu] of Abel from [de] Adam. For[10] Abel went forth immediately from Adam, because the latter begot him from [ex] his own loins; nevertheless, he went forth mediately, because he went forth from [a] Eve, who was from Adam or drawn from Adam [de Adam deducta]. And it was necessary [oportet] that this manner (of procession) be in God on account of a most high kinship [germanitatem]. For, if there were only a mediated procession of the Holy Spirit, as would be only from the Son, there would not be a most high kinship of the Holy Spirit with the Father. Similarly, if (it were) entirely immediate, as would be only from the Father, there would not be a most high kinship with the Son. And in this manner it must be conceded,[11] that (He proceeds) by means of the Son.

1. To that, therefore,[12] which is objected unto the contrary, that more noble is an immediate principle; it must be said, that there is mediation in three manners. For *a certain* (kind) is the mediation, which excludes only immediation, as when the last effect is not united in an unbroken manner [non continuatur] to the influence

---

[1] At the end. See (here) the text of Master (Peter), ch. 2.

[2] ON THE TRINITY, Bk. V, chs. 7-9.

[3] On the created image, see above d. 3, p. II, especially a. 2, q. 2 and 3.

[4] Trusting in the manuscripts and edition 1, we have substituted *this* [hoc] for *this (similitude)* [haec], which the Vatican edition faultily put there. Under the term "*this*" understand: the representation of number [repraesentare numerum].

[5] From very many manuscripts, such as I aa bb and edition 1, we have changed *spirates* from the indicative to the subjunctive, because this is more congruous with what is subjoined. Then after *the Father would* [tunc Pater] edition 1 adds *not* [non].

[6] In edition 1 there is added *therefore* [ergo].

[7] One or the other codex, such as Y and cc, has *attributed* [attribuendum].

[8] See Aristotle, METAPHYSICS, Bk. XI, ch. 4 (Bk. X, ch. 5), and ON THE PREDICAMENTS, ch. "On Opposites".

[9] Codex E has *procession* [processio].

[10] The Vatican edition, disagreeing with very many manuscripts and edition 1, omits *For* [enim]. — On this example, see Richard of St. Victor, ON THE TRINITY, Bk. V, ch. 6.

[11] Codex V adds the presumed *it must* [est].

[12] With the help of very many manuscripts, such as A F W etc., and edition 1, we have supplied *therefore* [ergo].

of the prior cause, but is produced entirely through a medium, with the prior not cooperating;[1] and this (signification of "mediation") means the *order* and *diversity* and *separation* of the agents. *In another manner* "mediation" is said, insofar as it means the *order* of the causes to each other, not (their) *separation* in acting, but only the *diversity* and order of the agents.[2] *In the third manner,* insofar as it means *order,* not however, the *separation* of the virtues of the agents nor (their) *diversity.*

The *first* mediation does not occur in God, because God is the simply first cause, the influence of whom is so great, that no creature does anything, removed from His influence; and for that reason nothing goes forth from[3] God only mediately. The *second* mediation occurs in God in respect of an effect produced by a created cause, because there is an *order* of causes and a *diversity* of virtues there; and yet there is not a *separation,* because God acts most interiorly, because it (exists) through Himself; nevertheless He acts[4] through the created virtue, which is from it. The *third* mediation occurs in the divine operation, in which the Persons are agents, in which there is attained an *order,* because One has from the Other that He acts, but yet neither is there a *diversity* of virtues There nor a *separation* and/or any distance, nay They act by one virtue and equally most interiorly. And in this manner the Father produces by means of the Son the Holy Spirit, not because there is a medium of distance and/or of a difference, but

because, 'that the Son produces', He has this from the Father, so that, There, there is a certain order. And thus is clear the response to the following, when he says, that the mediate and immediate are opposites; for it is true in the first manner, but not in the second nor in the third.[5]

2. To that which is objected, that of nothing is God a cause <u>per accidens</u>, therefore, neither mediately; it must be said that *to cause anything <u>per accidens</u>* derogates from the truth[6] of the supreme Cause. For something is said to be the cause <u>per accidens</u> of that, of which it is the cause through something else, which is not from it, but from another; if therefore, God would be the cause of anything <u>per accidens</u>, He would not be the most universal and first cause, and thus neither the most noble. But[7] mediation is not repugnant to the nobility of the supreme Cause. For to cause anything[8] <u>per se</u> and through that which *is from itself* does not mean an indignity, nay dignity, because dignity is not only to be able (to do) something <u>per se</u>, but to be able to communicate to another, however, so that the latter can do nothing without it.

3. To that which is objected last, that the Son is a more immediate cause; it must be said, that (that argument) is not valid, because that mediation, which the aforesaid is, is not repugnant to immediation, and for that reason does not diminish it.

SCHOLIUM

I. What (Bl.) Peter of Tarentaise says (here in q. 1, a. 3) can be useful for the elucidation of this question « In looking back to the principle *by which* They spirate, the Holy Spirit proceeds equally immediately from the Father, as from the Son; in looking back to Those *spirating,* similarly He proceeds equally immediately from the Father, as from the Son, but nevertheless He proceeds *mediately* from the Father, because He spires not only through Himself, but also by means of the Son ».

II. The saying: "*to proceed by means of the Son*" is explained in the same sense by St. Thomas (SUMMA, I, q. 36, a. 3, in reply to nn. 1 & 2). — The three manners of mediation, which occur in the solution to n. 1, can be illustrated with more examples. An example of the first manner is the grandfather, who is only a mediated cause of the sons of his own son; and in this manner "*mediately*" and "*immediately*" are contradictorily opposed, nor can such a mediation be attributed to God. An example of the second manner is adduced in the text itself, namely, the cooperation of God with the acts of creatures. For God so works by means of second causes, yet so that that mediation does

not exclude the immediate Divine Operation, by which He touches [attingit] most interiorly both the second cause and its effect; taken in this manner the "*mediate*" and "*immediate*" are not opposed. The third manner of mediation respects only the *order* of the Divine Persons to each Other, or is attained in the Divine Works *ad extra,* which are undivided, and (the former) is given in the spiration of the Holy Spirit, in which there is a order of the Ones spirating.

III. About that which he said at n. 2, that God is not a cause <u>per accidens</u>, cf. SENT., Bk. II, d. 37, q. 2, a. 2, (in reply to n. 4), where he says: A cause <u>per accidens</u> is said in respect of an intention, not to the extent that an accident is a difference of a being.

IV. In regard to the conclusion: Cf. Alexander of Hales, SUMMA, p. I, q. 45, m 6. — St. Thomas, here in q. 1, a. 3; SUMMA, I, q. 36, a. 3. — Bl. (now St.) Albertus (Magnus), here in a. 1. — (Bl.) Peter of Tarentaise, here in q. sole, a. 3. — Richard of Middleton, here in q. 3. — Giles the Roman, here in 2nd. princ., q. 2. — Durandus (of Saint-Pourçain), here in q. 3.

---

[1] Codex A has *operating* [operante]. Edition 1 a little below this, after *In another manner* [Alio modo], has *is* [est] for *is said* [dicitur].

[2] On the authority of the manuscripts and edition 1, we have expunged the *of the virtues* [virtutum], which the Vatican edition prefixed to the words *of the agents* [agentium]. Then after *In the third manner* codex X repeats *mediation is said* [dicitur mediatio].

[3] Trusting in the manuscripts and edition 1, we have substituted *from* [a] for *out of* [ex].

[4] The Vatican edition, with changed punctuation, refers the verb *acts* to the previous phrase, rendering it as *it acts through Himself* [per se ipsum agit], and then inserting an and [et], but against the mss.; ed. 1 in place of *and* [et] repeats well enough *acts* [agit]; cod. F less well after *nevertheless* [nihilominus] adds *there is an action* [est actio], and moreover, puts *according to* [secundum] for the *through* [per] which follows.

[5] Varius codices read variously; codex F in place of *for* [enim] has *but* [sed]; codex H after *for* [enim] adds *in some manner, that is* [aliquot modo scilicet]; many codices, together with editions 1, 2 and 3, erroneously read *for it is true, but not in the first manner but in the second and/or third* [verum est enim, sed non primo modo sed secundo vel tertio]; codex T reads incompletely *for it is true, but mediation does not occur in God in the first manner, but in the second and/or third* [verum est enim, sed non cadit mediatio in Deo primo modo, sed secundo vel tertio], which reading has been changed by a later hand into that which the Vatican edition has. We conjecture that the genuine reading is: *for it is true in the first manner; but mediation does*

not occur in God in the first manner, but in the second and/or third [verum est enim primo modo; sed non cadit mediatio in Deo primo modo, sed secundo vel tertio], by which reading the codices are also reconciled.

[6] In Codex H there is adds *and the nobility* [et nobilitati]; in codex T by a second hand the noun *truth* [veritati] has been changed into *universality* [universalitati]. — On a *cause per se* and *per accidens,* cf. Aristotle, PHYSICS, Bk. II, text 50 (ch. 5), where he says: For as even a being [ens], is indeed one (thing) <u>per se</u>, but another according to accident; so it also happens to be, that his house <u>per se</u> is indeed a cause of the building process [causa aedificativum], but according to accident white or decorated. And thus as a <u>per se</u> cause, it is definite, which, however, according to accident, is indefinite; for infinite (accidents) accede to one (being). Therefore, just as has been said, when among those, which come into being for the sake of any (end), there comes to be this, then it is said (by the common man to be) by cause and by chance.

[7] A few codd., such as V X & Z, add *this* [haec]; codex Y, better, adds after *mediation* adds *which is posited in God* [quae in Deo ponitur].

[8] From the more ancient mss. and edd. 1 & 6, we have substituted *anything* [aliquid] for *another* [aliud]. Then some codd., such as B T & Z, have *that* [illud] for *that* [id], and a little below this cod. Y, together with edition 1, has *of dignity* [dignitatis] for *dignity* [dignitas].

QUESTION IV

Whether the generation of the Son is prior to the spiration of the Holy Spirit, according to the reckoning of understanding?

Fourth and last, there is asked, which of those two emanations, that is, generation and procession, is prior according to the reckoning of understanding. And that the generation of the Son (is), is shown in this manner:

1. In the created image thus it is, that according to the order of understanding the emanation of knowledge [notitiae] from the mind is before (that) of love [amoris], just as (St.) Augustine wants it;[1] « because we cannot love [diligere] things that are uncognized [incognita] », just as (St.) Augustine says in the tenth (book) ON THE TRINITY:[2] therefore, if an order is attained in the image according to (its) conformity to the uncreated Trinity, therefore, according to the reckoning of understanding the processing of the Word is before (that) of love among the divine, most of all [maxime] since through the created image we understand the uncreated Trinity.

2. Likewise, just as the Philosopher wants it,[3] « it is the will, whose beginning belongs in the very one cognizing singulars », therefore, the will as will presupposes cognition: therefore, the emanation of Love (presupposes) the emanation of the Word.

3. Likewise, every beginning, according to the reckoning of understanding, is before the begun; but the Son is the beginning of the Holy Spirit: therefore, according to the reckoning of understanding it is necessary [oportet] that one understand the Son before the Holy Spirit:[4] therefore, also the generation, which is the emanation of the Son, before the procession, which is of the Holy Spirit.

4. Likewise, in every nature[5] acting through a manner of nature and will, the production through the manner of nature is understood before the production of the will: therefore since the Father is an intellectual Nature, producing a connatural Son and through a manner of nature, and the Holy Sprit through a manner of will, as has been touched upon above:[6] therefore, the emanation of the Son is prior according to the reckoning of understanding to the emanation of the Holy Spirit.

ON THE CONTRARY: 1. (St.) Augustine (says) in the ninth (book) ON THE TRINITY:[7] « The appetite precedes the minds' giving-birth [partum mentis], by which (appetite), in seeking that which we want to know, knowledge [notitia] itself is born as an offspring »: therefore, there is an appetite in the created image before knowledge is the offspring, therefore, love (is) before word: therefore, procession (is) also before generation.

2. Likewise, no one seeing a thing cognizes it,[8] unless the intention of (his) will applies the cognizing force to the cognizable itself, as is clear of the man

going along the way, who having gone and thought (himself to be) elsewhere, is thoroughly ignorant of [perfect nescit], (the way) by which he has passed, just as (St.) Augustine says in the eleventh (book) ON THE TRINITY.[9] Therefore, the will precedes cognition itself, therefore, "love" (precedes) "word" among creatures: therefore, for an equal reason, in God, at least according to (their) understanding [secundum intellectum].

3. Likewise, just as the Philosopher wants, the first and the immediate are the same. Whence he himself in the book, THE POSTERIOR ANALYTICS,[10] defining an immediate proposition, says, that « an immediate proposition is that to which the other is not prior »; but equally immediately does the Holy Spirit proceed from the Father, as (does) the Son, therefore, in an equally first manner: therefore, neither according to thing, nor according to the reckoning of understanding does the generation of the Son precede the procession of the Holy Spirit.

4. Likewise, as much as anything (is) more common, so much is it more primary [prior] according to the reckoning of understanding;[11] but the common spiration is more common than the generation, because it convenes with the Father and the Son, but the generation (convenes) with the Father alone: therefore, the spiration is more primary, according to the reckoning of understanding, than the generation.

CONCLUSION

According to the reckoning of understanding, the generation of the Son is prior to the spiration of the Holy Spirit, which is proven with a threefold reason.

I RESPOND: It must be said, that whatsoever concerns the real order, concerning which (more) will be said below,[12] yet, according to the reckoning of understanding the emanation of the Word is prior, both because the Word is a principle of the Holy Spirit, and also because the Word proceeds through the manner of the nature, but the Holy Spirit through the manner of a liberal will, and also because we understand the emanations among the Persons through the emanation found in the image. But, in the image, it is established, that cognition and understanding [intelligentia] precede love and will; yet, I do not want to say, that among the divine the emanation is such that[13] the Nature (is) posterior to the emanation, as we find (it to be) in the created image.

1. To that, therefore, which is objected unto the contrary, that the appetite precedes the mind's giving-birth; it must be said that that appetite has, according to (its) twofold

---

[1] ON THE TRINITY, Bk. IX, ch. 12, n. 18.

[2] Chapter 1, n. 1 ff.

[3] ETHICS, Bk. II, ch. 1, where a (spontaneous) will is defined to belong to him, whose beginning (is) in the one cognizing singulars, among which the action is. — On the will, as will or deliberative (power), to which is opposed the will as nature, see SENT., Bk II, d. 24, p. I, a. 2, q. 3, and Bk. IV, d. 49, p. I, q. 2, ad 1.

[4] Very many codices, together with the Vatican edition, have *than the Holy Spirit* [quam Spiritum Sanctum], but less congruously and contrary to the other codices, such as G T Y etc. together with edition 1; codex X has *to understand the Son before the Holy Spirit* [intelligere Filium prius, quam Spiritum sanctum].

[5] On the authority of the manuscripts and edition 1, we have supplied the *nature* [natura], omitted less well by the Vatican edition on account of what follows.

[6] Distinction 6, q. 2, and d. 10, a. 1, q. 1; and below in d. 13, q. 1 and 2.

[7] Chapter 12, n. 18, in which quote the Vatican edition together with the OPERA S. AUGUSTINI, but contrary to our codices and the first six editions, to *appetite* [appetitus] adds *a certain* [quidam] and after *in seeking* [quaerendo] they add *an finding* [et inveniendo]

[8] The Vatican edition, disagreeing with very many manuscripts and edition 1, has *it* [ipsam].

[9] Chapter 8, n. 15.

[10] Book I, ch. 2.

[11] See Aristotle, PHYSICS, Bk. III, text 2; and METAPHYSICS, Bk. V. text 16 (Bk. IV, ch. 11). — Then in the Vatican edition there is faultily omitted *common* [communis], which however, is had in the manuscripts and in editions 1, 2 and 3.

[12] Here in Doubt 1, and below in d. 20, a. 2, q. 1 and 2. — Immediately after this from the more ancient manuscripts and edition 1, we have inserted *yet* [tamen].

[13] The Vatican edition, together with codex cc, badly and contrary to the other codices and edition 1, omits *such that* [ita].

status, a twofold consideration [dupliciter considerari]:[1] in *one* manner according to the reckoning of one coveting [inhiantis], before the cognition (has) been had; in *another* manner according to the reckoning of one embracing, and this is after the cognition (has) been had, and according to the first state it belongs to imperfection, but as much as regards the second it belongs to perfection. And, for that reason, because we posit in God what belongs to perfection, not what belongs to imperfection, for that reason the appetite according to the second manner is likened to the Holy Spirit, and this has the reckoning of the third. And because the first belongs to imperfection, it is clear, that it belongs to the ignorant and to the one desiring to acquire knowledge [scientia], because it does not befit God.

2. To that which is objected, that intention is required beforehand for cognition; it must be said, that it is true regarding the cognition to be acquired; but knowledge [notitia], insofar as it is in acquiring, does not have a similitude with that Word, as (St.) Augustine wants it in the fifteenth (book) ON THE TRINITY.[2]

3. To that which is objected, that the Holy Spirit proceeds equally immediately; it must be said, that it is true, but yet such does the Holy Spirit proceed immediately, that (He does) also by means of the Son; and thus from that reckoning it is necessary that the emanation of the Son be understood beforehand.

4. To that which is objected, that by as much as anything is common, by so much (is it) more primary [prior]; it must be said, that (this) is true among absolutes, but it does not hold among respectives, as is clear[4] in generation and creation. — However, it can be said, that this is understood of that because it is common[4] by a community of predication, but the common spiration is common by a community, not only of predication, because it is said of the Father and the Son, but also (by a community)[5] of a certain concord and connection; and such a 'common' according to the reckoning of concord and friendship presupposes those in concord [concordantes] and those connected, it does not precede (them); and, thus, that (argument) is clear.

SCHOLIUM

In the conclusion all the ancient Scholastics agree: Alexander of Hales, SUMMA, p. I, q. 46, m. 7. — (Bl. John Duns) Scotus, SENT, Bk. I, d. 11, q. 1. — St. Thomas, here in a. 1. — Bl. (now St.) Albertus Magnus, SENT, Bk. I, d. 28, a. 2 near the end. — Richard of Middleton, here in a. 4. — Giles the Roman, here in 1st princ., q. 1. — Henry of Ghent, SUMMA, a. 54, q. 5, n. 12, and q. 6, nn. 26 and 34. — Durandus (of Saint-Pourçain), here in q. 1. — (Bl.) Dionysius the Carthusian, here in q. 2.

DOUBTS ON THE TEXT OF THE MASTER

DOUBT I

In this part are the doubts about the text (of Master Peter), and first concerning the argument of the heretic, which he makes there: *Either with the Son already born, or with Him not born.* For it seems that that argument of his (is) necessary, because of any contradiction it is necessary that the other part be true;[6] but *"born"* and *"not born"* are opposed contradictorily: therefore, it is necessary to give the other part,[7] that the Holy Spirit proceeds either with the Son already born, or with Him not born: since, therefore, Master (Peter)[8] and (St.) Augustine respond by refuting [interimendo] each part, they seem to respond badly.

I RESPOND: It must be said, that the heretic in his question asked concerning the order of the generation of the Son to the procession of the Holy Spirit, and asked concerning the order according to duration and time, not according to the reckoning of understanding, and he asked, whether the Son was born before the Holy Spirit proceeded,[9] or (if it was) the other way

around. And each was false; for that reason Master (Peter) and (St.) Augustine, considering the intention of the heretic or the interrogation (he made) according to the sense, in which he proposes it, respond simply and well by refuting it.

To that, therefore, which is objected, that the heretic's division is through contradictories; it must be said, that it is false; because a contradictory proposition is accepted by denying the principal composition;[10] but he brings the negation not against the principal composition, but (against it as) understood in this that He *has been born*;[11] and for this reason the cause of its falsity always remains. For this is false: "the Holy Spirit proceeds, with the Son born"; because it is noted, that the nativity of the Son precedes the procession of the Holy Spirit. Again, this is false: "He has proceeded, with the Son not born"; because there is noted, that the nativity of the Son was not together [simul] with the procession of the Holy Spirit. But this is true: "The Holy Spirit has not proceeded, with the Son born beforehand", because the nativity of the Son and the procession of the Holy Spirit were together.

---

[1] Very many codices, together with edition 1, omit the first *twofold* [duplicem], but the Vatican edition omits the second *twofold* [dupliciter], on account of the repetition of the aforesaid terms; our reading, which is congruous with what follows, is exhibited in codex T and by a second hand in codex ff. — Then under the word *of the one coveting* [inhiantis] understand "of the one strongly desiring", just as under the word *of the one embracing* [complectentis] understand "of the one enjoying".

[2] Chapter 13, n. 22. The codices, changing the chapter into the book, falsely read *in the thirteenth and fifteenth* [in decimo tertio et decimo quinto]. — A little before this in the Vatican edition and in codex cc, *plenitude* [plenitudinem] is put in place of *similitude* [similitudinem], but incongruously and against the older codices together with edition 1.

[3] From the manuscripts and edition 1, we have restored the verb *is clear* [patet].

[4] Very many manuscripts, such as I T Y and Z together with edition 1, have *more common* [communius].

[5] The Vatican edition, without the authority of the codices and editions 1, 2 and 3, repeats here *by a community* [communitate].

[6] Aristotle, ON INTERPRETATION., Bk. I, ch. 6 (ch. 8).

[7] In codex Y there is added *namely* [videlicet].

[8] Here, in ch. 1, where the words of (St.) Augustine are also had.

[9] One or the other codex, such as I and bb, together with edition 1, has *the Son would have been born before He had proceeded* [natus esset Filius quam processisset].

[10] That is, the copula (of the sentences), which here becomes the verb *proceeds* [procedit].

[11] Bl. (now St.) Albertus (Magnus), here in a. 2, in reply to the last, says: It must be said, that though "born" and "not born" have the manner of opposition of contradictories, yet the propositions, in which they are posited, are not contradictory, these, that is: "either He proceeded with Him already born, or He proceeded with Him not already born", because the negation is not born to the composition (copula), and for that reason they are both affirmative. — (Bl.) Peter of Tarentaise says similar things, here in a. 1, q. 1, ad 1.

[12] Cf. here, q. 1; and Richard (of Middleton), here in q. 1, at the last reply.

DOUBT II

Is likewise asked concerning this which is said: *Whatever He gave to the Only-Begotten, He gave by begetting.* It seems that he spoke badly, because if this (were true); but[1] He gave Him the spiration, therefore, He gave it by begetting, therefore, the spiration has been begotten. But whatever is said among the divine concretely, is said also abstractly, but it is not converted: therefore, if the spiration has been begotten, the spiration is the generation, which is contrary to (what) all now (say).[2]

I RESPOND: It must be said, that there is a defect in each argument. For this is not valid: 'He gave spiration by generating, therefore, He generated the spiration'; just as there does not follow: 'by generating He gave the Son (His) Essence, therefore, the Essence has been begotten'. For some (things) are said through generation to be given, which are not said to be generated.

And again the other reckoning is not valid: 'the spiration has been begotten, therefore, the spiration is the generation'. For just as shall be clear below concerning the two notions of one Person,[3] it is true, that one is predicated of the other denominatively, not in abstraction, and for that reason that reckoning is not valid, nay rather there is (a fallacy of) the accident. Therefore, regarding what is said [Quod dicitur]: whatever is predicated denominatively and abstractly, is true concerning the Essence, but is not true concerning the property of the Person, and these (points) shall be clearer below.[4]

DOUBT III

Likewise, there is a doubt concerning this which (St.) Jerome says: *We believe in the Holy Spirit, who proceeds properly from* [de] *the Father.* For it seems that he spoke a falsehood, because « the *proper* is that which convenes with one alone »:[5] therefore, if He proceeds from the Father *properly*, therefore, (He does) not (proceed properly) from the Son. *If you say*, that he does not mean "*properly*" as contrary to "commonality" [communitatem], but as contrary to "impropriety": therefore, it seems that He proceeds improperly from [a] the Son.

I RESPOND: It must be said, that "*properly*" does not mean propriety or solitude, but refers to[6] (His) authorship, just as "*principally*" (does). For, just as the Father is said to

"*principally*" spirate, because this He does not have from an other; so also "*properly*", because this condition, the '*not having from an other*', He communicates to no one; thus does Master (Peter) seem to speak.

However, it can be said, that in one manner "*proper*" is meant contrary to "community"; in another manner contrary to "impropriety"; in a third manner it is accepted as an appropriation;[7] and in this manner is it accepted here. For, although the spiration equally truly and properly convenes with the Father and the Son, yet, (St.) Jerome appropriates it to the Father on account of (His) authorship.

DOUBT IV

Likewise, is asked of this which (St.) Hilary says, speaking to the Father: *Out of Thee through Him is Thy Holy Spirit.* For he seems to speak badly, when saying "*through Him*" [per eum], because, as (Peter) Praepositivus says,[9] "*through*" [per], with transitive verbs, signifies sub-authorship, but with absolute (verbs), authorship; as is clear, when there is said: "I am wise through God", in God is noted the authorship (of wisdom). Therefore, when there is said, that the Holy Spirit is from the Father "through the Son", authorship is noted in the Son.

I RESPOND: It must be said, that some want to say, that this is improper: "The Holy Spirit is or proceeds from the Father through the Son"; and (that) it ought to be resolved into this: "The Holy Spirit is spirated by the Father through the Son"; and they agree with the aforesaid reckoning. — But since this is true: "a creature proceeds from the Father through the Son", and this similarly: "it goes forth and/or proceeds": I do not see the reason, why similarly those words of (St.) Hilary cannot be said properly.

And[10] on this account it must be said, that although "to proceed" is not a transitive verb as much as regards (its) manner of signifying, because it is not constructed with the accusative; nevertheless because it is equivalent[11] to a transitive, as when there is said: "He proceeds from the Father through the Son", it must be judged just as a transitive verb; and, for that reason, (the preposition, "through", here) means a sub-authorship.[12]

---

[1] The Vatican edition, without the authority of the manuscripts and editions 1, 2, 3 and 6, has *were true* [esset verum] in place of *but* [sed]; a similar elliptical phrase is often used by St. Bonaventure.

[2] Thus nearly all the codices, together with edition 1; codex cc omits *now* [modo], in place of which the Vatican edition has *modern (authors)* [modernos].

[3] Distinction 33, q. 3 and 4. — Then, after *it is true* [est verum], the Vatican edition, together with codex cc, yet, disagreeing with the other codices and edition 1, adds *to say* [dicere]. A little below this, after *denominatively* [denominative] in codex T there is inserted *but* [sed].

[4] In the passage cited a little above this. — The more ancient codices, together with edition 1, agree in this, that in the last proposition they add the *–er* [melius] to *it will be clear* [patebit], omitted by the Vatican edition and codex cc, but they disagree in this, that some, such as A G H I T etc. together with edition 1, exhibit our reading, others in a singular manner have *and this shall be clearer below* [et hoc infra melius patebit]; codex Z has *and this similarly will be clearer below* [et hoc similiter melius patebit]. — On the solution of this Doubt, see also Bl. (now St.) Albertus (Magnus), here in a. 7.

[5] Aristotle, TOPICS, Bk. I, ch. 4, and Porphyry, ON THE PREDICABLES, ch. "On the Proper". — A little below this, trusting in the more an-

cient manuscripts and edition 1, we have substituted *he does ... mean* [dicit], that is St. Jerome means, in place of *there is meant* [dicitur].

[6] On the authority of nearly all the manuscripts and the three first editions, we have restored the preposition *to* [in]; because this Latin metaphor *to sound for* [sonare in] (for *to refers to*) is a saying familiar to the Seraphic Doctor.

[7] Very many codd. with the three first edd., have *through an appropriation* [per appropriationem]. It would be better to read it *as an appropriated (term)* [pro appropriato]. A little below this, the mss. with the first six edd., faultily read *the Son* [Filius] for *(St.) Jerome* [Hieronymus].

[8] To the solution St. Thomas agrees, SUMMA, I, q. 36, a. 3, ad 2, and (Bl. John Duns) Scotus, here in q. 2.

[9] The Vatican edition, not trusting in the manuscripts and edition 1, has *Priscian* [Priscianus].

[10] In the Vatican edition there is omitted *And* [Et], in disagreement with the manuscripts and edition 1.

[11] Edition 1 has *is equipollent* [aequipollet]. A little below this after *the Son* [Filium], codices H and Y add *it is only valid if it were also said, is produced* [tantum valet ac si diceretur, producitur].

[12] See the explanation of this text of (St.) Hilary and the signification of the preposition, *through* [per], also in St. Thomas, SUMMA, I, q. 36, a. 3 in the body (of the Article), and in reply to n. 4; Bl. (now St.) Albertus (Magnus), here in a. 6; (Bl. John Duns) Scotus, here in q. 2.

DISTINCTION XIII

CHAPTER I

For what reason is the Holy Spirit, since He is from the
Substance of the Father, not said (to be) "begotten",
but only "proceeding"?

After these (things),[1] there must be considered, as much
as it can be understood by such as we are, (that) since the Holy
Spirit proceeds from [de] the Father and is from the Substance
of the Father, why is He not said "to have been born", but
rather "to proceed"; and why is He not said (to be) a "son".
Moreover, the reason why [quare] the Holy Spirit is not said (to
be a "son") and/or (why) He has not been born, and for that
reason is not a son, (St.) Augustine shows in the fifteenth book,
ON THE TRINITY,[2] speaking thus: « If the Holy Spirit would be
said (to be) "a son", "son" would at least be said of Both,
which is most absurd. Indeed no son belongs to two except to
a father and a mother. Moreover, far be it, that between God
the Father and God the Son we suspect anything of the kind
[tale aliquid] ». Therefore, most absurdly would "son" be said
of Both, if Both had begotten Him, which (argument) the
sense of all sane (men) abhors. Therefore, the Spirit has not
been begotten by Each, but proceeds from Each of the Two [a
utroque amborum] ».[3] With these words there is shown, why
the Spirit, since He is from [de] the Father, is not, however,
said (to be) begotten and/or "a son".

CHAPTER II

Why is the Son said "to proceed",
when the Holy Spirit is not said "to be begotten"?

Moreover, since the Holy Spirit is not said (to be) "begotten", but only "proceeding", it is customarily asked
[quare solet], why the Son is not said only (to be) "born",
but also "proceeding", just as He Himself says in the
Gospel of (St.) John:[4] *I have proceeded out of* and/or *have*
come forth from God, and I have come into the world. Therefore,
not only does the Holy Spirit proceed from [a] the Father,
but the Son (does) too. To which we say, that though Each
proceeds from the Father, however, (They do so) dissimilarly. For « the Holy Spirit », as (St.) Augustine says in the
fifteenth book, ON THE TRINITY,[5] « proceeds from the Father not in the manner which (one is) born, but in the manner which (one is) given » and/or (as) the Gift. Moreover,
the Son has proceeded by being born, He has come forth as
the Begotten. And through this, there glitters that, as (much
as) it can, that is, 'why the Holy Spirit is not also a son,
since he also comes forth from the Father', « for this reason, namely[6] 'He is not said (to be) "a son", because neither has He been born, as the Only-Begotten (has), nor
made, as one (who) through the grace of God has been born
unto adoption, as we (are)' ».

CHAPTER III

That a mortal cannot distinguish between the generation of
the Son and the procession of the Holy Sprit.

On the other hand, while we live here, we are not sufficient to distinguish between the generation of the Son and the
procession of the Holy Spirit. Whence, (St.) Augustine responding thus to Maximinus, raising again [refricanti] the aforementioned question, that is, asking, why the Holy Spirit was
not said (to be) "a son", since He was from [de] the Substance
of the Father, says:[7] « You ask from me, if the Holy Spirit is
from the Substance of the Father and the Son is also from the
Substance of the Father, why is One a "son", and the Other is
not a "son". Behold, I respond, whether you grasp it or do not
grasp it: the Son is from the Father, the Holy Spirit is from the
Father, but the Former has been begotten, that (Spirit) of Theirs
(is) proceeding; for that reason that Son is of the Father, from
whom He has been begotten; but that Spirit of Theirs is of
Each, since He proceeds from Each. But for that reason, when
(the Former) speaks of the Latter, He says:[8] *proceeds from the*
Father, since the Father is the Author of His procession, which
(Father) begot such a Son and by begetting gave to Him, that
the Holy Spirit would also proceed from Him. For if He did
not proceed from Him also, He would not have said to the Disciples:[9] *Accept the Holy Spirit*, and would (not) by breathing upon
(them) given Him, as One signifying that He also proceeds from
Himself, (nor) would He have openly shown by exhaling
[flando], that by spirating He was giving (Him) in a secret manner. Therefore, because, if He were born, not only from the Father nor only from the Son, but from Both He would at least be
born; would without doubt be said (to be) the "son" of Both.
And through this, because in no manner is he the son of Both,
it was not necessary [oportuit] that He be born from Both.
Therefore the Spirit[10] is of Both, by proceeding from Both ».

« Moreover, what intervenes [intersit] between "being
born" and "proceeding", speaking of that most excellent Nature, who can explain? Not[11] everything which proceeds, is
born, although everything proceeds, because it is born; just as
not everything which is a biped, is a man, although everyone,
who is a man, is a biped. This I know; but how to distinguish
between that generation and this procession I know not, nor
am I able, nor do I suffice. And through this, that both this
and that are ineffable, just as the Prophet, speaking of the Son,
says:[12] *His generation, who will tell it forth?* such that of the Holy
Spirit there is most truly said: His procession, who will tell it
forth? Therefore, it is sufficient for us that the Son is not
from [a] Himself, but from Him from [de] whom He has
been born, the Holy Spirit is not from [a] Himself, but
from Him from [de] whom He proceeds, and that He proceeds from Each, just as we have already shown ».[13] Concerning the Holy Spirit, in what manner He Himself be

---

[1] Edition 1 alone has *this* [hoc].

[2] Chapter 27, n. 48, and ON THE GOSPEL OF JOHN, Tract 99, n. 9.
— Even the preceding words, according to their sense, have been excerpted from the same passage. — After *Trinity* [Trinitate], the Vatican
edition and editions 4 and 8, omit *thus* [ita]; at the end of the passage,
codices A C and D have *there be suspected* [suspicetur] for *we suspect*
[suspicemur].

[3] (St.) Augustine, ibid., ch. 26, n. 47, in which passage on the Vatican edition after *if both* [si ... ambo] faultily adds *also* [et]. Then codex
B together with (St.) Augustine's text has *by the senses of all sane men*
[ab omnium sanorum sensibus]. Then contrary to (St.) Augustine and all
the mss., the editions read *Therefore,* [ergo] for *Therefore* [igitur].

[4] Jn 16:27, 28. The Vulgate has *I have come forth from God. I*
have come forth from the Father and I have come into the world. [Ego a
Deo exivi. Exivi a Patre et veni in mundum.] But John 8:42 reads: *out*
of God have I proceeded [ex Deo processi]; whence Master (Peter) says:
I have proceeded and/or have come forth [processi vel exivi].

[5] Chapter 14, n. 15, whence have also been taken those which follow the interposed words of Master (Peter).

[6] The Vatican edition and editions 4, 5, 6 and 8, have '*the Spirit*
[Spiritus] in place of *namely 'He*. Then codex C has *has He Himself been*
born [ipse natus est].

[7] Book II, ch. 14, n. 1; in which passage editions 1 and 8 unduly
omit after the first why [cur] the first *is* [est]. Next at *Holy Spirit* [Spir-
itus sanctus] only codices A and C add *also* [etiam].

[8] Jn. 15:26; the Vulgate reads *proceeds from the Father* [a Patre
procedit]. —A little before this only edition 1 together with the original
omits *is* [est] before *of Each* [utriusque].

[9] Jn. 20:22.

[10] Contradicting the manuscripts, edition 1 and the text of (St.)
Augustine, the Vatican edition, together with the other editions, adds *Holy*
[sanctus].

[11] Edition 1 inserts *For* [enim], and a little below this in *that gen-*
eration [illam generationem], inserts *of the Word* [Verbi].

[12] Isaias 53:8.

[13] Loc. cit.. — In the text at the end of the page, passing over into
the next, edition 5 has *God Himself be from God* [ipse Deus sit de Deo]
for *He Himself be from God* [ipse de Deo sit].

from [de] God, and, yet, He is not a son, since is it read that He is from God by proceeding, not by being born, we have disputed above already, as much as has been seen.

CHAPTER IV

Whether the Holy Spirit ought to be said (to be) "unbegotten", since He is not begotten.

Now, there must be considered, since the Holy Spirit has not been begotten, whether He ought to be said (to be) "unbegotten". To which we say, that the Holy Spirit ought to be said (to be) neither "begotten" nor "unbegotten". Whence (St.) Augustine says to (St. Paulus) Orosius: « That the Holy Spirit (is) neither begotten nor unbegotten the certain Faith declares; because if we said (that He is) unbegotten, we will seem to affirm (that there are) two fathers; but if "begotten", we are faulted for [culpamur] believing (that there are) two sons ». For just as a son alone is said (to be) "begotten", so also a Father alone is said (to be) "unbegotten", for the reason that He is not from [a] another. Whence (St.) Augustine in the fifteenth book, ON THE TRINITY (says):[2] « The Father », he says, « alone is not from [de] another, for that reason He alone is named "the Unbegotten", not indeed in the Scriptures, but in the custom of those disputing and of those proffering speech [sermonem] on the matter as much as they are able. But the Son has been born from the Father, and the Holy Spirit proceeds principally from the Father and commonly from Each. And for that reason since we do not say that the Holy Spirit (has been) "begotten", yet we do not dare say (that He is) "unbegotten", lest in this word anyone at all [quispiam] suspect (that there are) two fathers in that Trinity, and/or (that there are) two, who are not from another ». Behold with these words he has openly shown, that the Holy Spirit ought not be said (to be) "begotten" nor "unbegotten".

(St.) Jerome, however, in THE RULES OF DEFINITIONS AGAINST HERETICS[3] says that the Holy Spirit is unbegotten, with these words: « The Holy Spirit is not the Father, but unbegotten and untainted. He is not the Father, because He is of the Father and is in the Father; He has (His) procession out of the Father, and not a nativity;

but He is not the Son, because He has not been begotten ». Behold with these words the Holy Spirit is said to be unbegotten, which seems to be adverse [adversari] to the words of (St.) Augustine.

But so that we may be rid of what seems to be the inconsistency between them [repugnantium de medio abigamus], we say, that (St.) Jerome accepts[4] the name of "unbegotten" [ingeniti] in one manner, and (St.) Augustine in the other. For (St.) Augustine accepts "unbegotten", as 'one who' [qui] and/or 'as something which' [quod] is not from [ab][5] another; and according to this it is said of the Father alone; (St.) Jerome on the other hand means "unbegotten" as 'not begotten'; and according to this it can be said of the Holy Spirit, since the Holy Spirit has not been begotten.

Moreover, that (St.) Jerome accepts it thus, is shown from his own words, which he uses in the same tract,[6] making such a division: « Everything which is, either is unbegotten, or begotten, or made. Therefore, there is that which is neither born nor made; and there is that which is born and has not been made, and there is that which has neither been born nor has been made; and there is that which has been made and has not been born; and there is that which has been made and has been born and has been reborn; and there is that which has been made and has been born and has not been reborn. Now we shall appoint [destinemus] subsistence to each thing of the aforementioned (categories). Therefore, that which has neither been born nor made, is the Father; for He is not from anyone.[7] But that which has been born and has not been made, is the Son, who has been begotten by the Father, and not made. Again, that which has neither been born nor made, is the Holy Spirit, who proceeds from the Father. Moreover, that which has been made and has not been born, (is)[8] the sky and the earth and all the other (things), which are insensible. On the other hand, that which has been made and has been born and has not been reborn, are the animals ». Behold with these words (St.) Jerome shows, that he accepts "unbegotten" as "not begotten". For in other manner the aforementioned division would not be true, that is, that everything which is, is either unbegotten, or begotten, or made. And in the prosecution of this division, put "not born" everywhere "unbegotten" is assigned [in assignatione ingeniti].

---

[1] In the dialogue, namely, of questions under the title "To Orosius", question 2. But this work is spurious. At the end of this passage, edition 8 together with the original has *we will blame* [culpabimus] for *we are at fault* [culpamur].

[2] Chapter 26, n. 47. — In this text after *speech* [sermonem] codex D has *as everso* [qualemcumque] in place of *as* [qualem]. (St.) Augustine himself after *principally from the Father* [de Patre principaliter] inserts *without any interval of time itself being given* [ipso sine ullo temporis intervallo dante] etc. — At the end edition 2 has *are not* [non sint] in the subjunctive, and editions 5 and 9 have *from anyone* [de aliquo] for *from another* [de alio].

[3] Editions 1 and 8, add to the title of this work: *and/or distinctions* [vel distinctionum]. This book does not belong to St. Jerome, nor is it found among the appendices of the editions of his writings. In the appendix to the OPERA S. AMBROSII, (PATROLOGIA., Migne, Lat. tom. 17, col. 510) is printed an anonymous work under the title: DE TRINITATE; ALIAS IN SYMBOLUM APOSTOLORUM TRACTATUS, from which (ch. 3, col. 512) the following text, cited a little below this, has been excerpted in its entirety, with only a few words lacking and/or changed. But the passage cited here is only exhibited according to its *sense*. Moreover, since this work, as the editors think, has been mutilated and interpolated already from ancient times, perhaps (Peter) Lombard accepted even the first text word-for-word from this one. In the previous admonition the Benedictine editors judge of this book,

that it is almost equal to the one published against the Priscillianists and to vindicate the rule of faith of the Council of Toledo, by the Council itself, or if not that of Toledo, at least that of the Second Council of Braga, which is commonly said to have taken place in A.D. 563. — The passage exhibited by Master (Peter) below, Alcuin (DE FIDE SS. TRINITATIS, Bk. II, ch. 9: PATROLOGIA LATINA, Migne, tom. 101, col. 28) reports in its entirety, but with not a few things added and/or changed.

[4] Codices A C D E have *accepted* [acceperit].

[5] The Vatican edition and editions 1, 2, 3, 4, 7, and 9, have *from* [de]. Immediately before this, edition 1 omits *and/or as something which* [vel quod]. Then codices A B C D at *of the Holy Spirit* [de Spiritu sancto] omit *Holy* [sancto]. Then edition 1 omits the last words *since the Holy Spirit etc.* [cum Spiritus etc.].

[6] Chapter 3. — See note 3 above. — Immediately before this the Vatican edition and editions 4, 6 and 8, have *from his words* [verbis eius] for *from his own words* [verbis suis], which though they are less correct, yet all the codices and all the other editions do exhibit. Then where for the first time there is put *neither born* [nec natum] the codices omit *is* [est] contrary to the editions.

[7] The Vatican edition and editions 4, 5, 6, and 9, have *from any other* [ab alio aliquo].

[8] Supply with edition 6 *is* [est]. Immediately after this editions 2, 3, 5, 7, and 9 omit *are* [sunt]. Not much below this at *(St.) Jerome shows* [ostendit Hieronymus] codex C adds *openly* [aperte].

COMMENTARY ON DISTINCTION XIII

On the eternal procession of the Holy Spirit, to the extent that it is distinguished from generation.

After these, there must be considered etc..

THE DIVISION OF THE TEXT

Above, Master (Peter) dealt with the procession through a comparison to that, to which and from which it is. Here, in the third place, he deals with it according to[1] a comparison to the generation, from which it differs. And this part has two parts. In the first, Master (Peter) ask and determines, whether the Holy Spirit ought to be said (to be) *begotten*; in the second, whether He ought to be said (to be) *unbegotten*, there (where he says): *Now there must be considered, since the Holy Spirit has not been begotten.*

Likewise, the *first* part has four (parts). In the *first,* he shows, that the Holy Spirit ought not be said (to have been) born.[2] In the *second,* he shows, that although there is said of the Holy Spirit that He proceeds, nevertheless (this is also) said of the Son, there (where he says): *Moreover, since the Holy Spirit is not said (to be) begotten;* and the reason is, that the Son is said to proceed in another manner than the Holy Spirit. In the *third,* however, he tries to assign a difference between the generation and the procession, there (where he says): *On the other hand, ... between the generation of the Son and the procession of the Holy Spirit* etc..

In the *fourth,* however, and last, he shows the insufficiency of man[3] to track down that difference, there (where he says): *Moreover, what intervenes between "being born" and "proceeding".*

Now, there must be considered, since the Holy Spirit. This is[4] the *second* part, in which Master (Peter) asks and determines, whether the Holy Spirit ought to be said (to be) *unbegotten*, and this part has four parts. In the *first,* Master (Peter) shows and proves with the authority of (St.) Augustine, that the Holy Spirit ought not be said (to be) unbegotten. On the other hand, in the *second* he shows the contrary with the authority of (St.) Jerome, that He ought to be said (to be) unbegotten, and (the argument) is placed there (,where he says): *However, (St.) Jerome among the "Rules for definitions"* etc.. But in the *third,* he determines the aforesaid controversy through a distinction, there (where he says): *But so that we may be rid of what seems to be the inconsistency.* In the *fourth,* he confirms with the authority of (St.) Jerome his own solution, there (where he says): *Moreover, that (St.) Jerome accepts it thus* etc..

TREATMENT OF THE QUESTIONS

For an understanding of those (things) which are said in the text (of Master Peter), four (things) are asked.

First, there is asked, whether, among the divine, there is a positing of 'procession'.

Second, whether the procession of the Holy Spirit is a generation.

Third, whether the procession of the Holy Spirit really differs [differat] from generation.

Fourth, whether the Holy Spirit ought to be said (to be) "unbegotten" [ingenitus] or, whether[5] not.

ARTICLE SOLE

On the procession of the Holy Spirit and on the difference of procession and generation.

QUESTION I

Whether 'procession' is to be posited among the divine?

About the first, that procession is to be posited among the divine, is shown:

1. First, by the authority of the Lord, in the fifteenth chapter of (the Gospel of St.) John,[6] where the

Savior Himself says: *I shall send you the Spirit of truth, who proceeds from the Father* [Mittam vobis Spiritum veritatis, qui a Patre procedit]. If, therefore, the Truth says not but the true, and the Word of God does not say

---

[1] Codex M and edition 1 read *through* [per].

[2] The Vatican edition without the authority of the manuscripts and edition 1 adds *and/or begotten and/or the Son* [vel genitus vel Filius], just as it also next proceeds: *In the second he shows, that since the Holy Spirit is not said (to be) begotten, why the Son, who is said (to be) begotten, is also said to proceed; there (where he says):* [In secunda ostendit, quod cum Spiritus sanctus non dicatur genitus, cur Filius, qui dicitur genitus, etiam dicatur procedere; ibi].

[3] Codices L and O have *that the intelligence of man is insufficient* [humanam intelligentiam insufficientem esse].

[4] The Vatican edition, not trusting in the manuscripts and edition 1, having omitted the words of Master (Peter) *Now there must be*

considered [Nunc considerandum] etc., in place of *This is* [Haec est] puts *Similarly* [Similiter], and, consequently, on account of the varied construction, omits, a little below this, *and this part* [et haec pars].

[5] Trusting in several manuscripts, such as A F G H I T etc. and edition 1, in place of *or,* [aut] we have substituted *or, whether* [an].

[6] Verse 26, where the Vulgate reads: *But when the Paraclete comes, whom I shall send you from the Father, the Spirit of Truth, who proceeds from the Father* [Cum autem venerit Paraclitus, quem ego mittam vobis a Patre, spiritum veritatis, qui a Patre procedit]. — The Vatican edition, striving against the manuscripts and edition 1, has *of (St.) John, through which the Savior says* [Ioannis, per quam dicit Salvator].

(what is) improper [improprium], therefore, truly and properly[1] is there procession among the divine.

2. Likewise, among the divine, there is most truly is an Origin, therefore, also a production; but to every active production there responds a passive production; but procession is a passive production: therefore, from the first,[2] there is among the divine, truly and properly, a procession.

3. Likewise, our love [amor] is both love and[3] from another, and its going-forth from another truly and properly is expressed in the verb for *proceeding*: since, therefore, the Divine Love, Who is the Holy Spirit, truly and properly is a "love" and is from another, just as the noun of "*love*" suits (Him) [competit] most properly, so also does "*procession*" seem to befit Him [ei convenire].

4. Likewise, for a complete reckoning of a "procession" there are required these two, that it be from another and (that) it tend unto another; but the Love, Who is the Holy Spirit, does not proceed from the Father, inasmuch as He loves Himself, nor[4] from the Son, inasmuch as He loves Himself, but inasmuch as the One loves the Other, because He is (Their) nexus: therefore, the Holy Spirit is the Love, by which One loving tends unto the Other: therefore, He is a Love both from Another and unto Another,[5] and those two comprise [complectuntur] the reckoning of perfect "procession": therefore, there is a procession among the divine.

ON THE CONTRARY: 1. "Procession" from the reckoning of its name means an "elongation" and "recession"; whence a "*procession*" (is) a quasi '*marching far away*' [procul cessio], just as a "precession" means a "marching beforehand" [antecessionem]; but, just as among the divine there is not a "marching beforehand" on account of the most high Togetherness [simultatem], so there is not an "elongation" on account of the most high Unity: therefore, just as among the divine there is not posited the name for "*a marching before*" [praecessionis], so neither[6] ought there be posited the noun of "*procession*" [processionis].

2. Likewise, among creatures "procession", from the reckoning of its genus, means "a moving", and thus an "indigence" and "imperfection"; but no such name ought to be transferred to God: therefore, neither "procession".

3. Likewise, "creation" means a special difference of procession and a difference adding a nobility, because it means the "egress" of a thing from the Creator, Who is the Most Noble Cause; but a passive creation is in no manner found among the divine; for no Person is said "to be created": therefore, for an equal reason, neither (is) "procession" (found There).

4. Likewise, "procession" among creatures is not meant except in a two fold manner, namely, the *local* and the *causal*: the local, which is in progressive movement, the causal, which is an effect from a cause. But the local cannot be transferred to divine (things), because no change according to place, neither in general, nor in particular [in speciali], occurs in God. And, *moreover*,[7] since such is from one unto another, one is bound to posit, that the Holy Spirit would not proceed eternally from the Father and the Son; therefore, local procession is not found (in God). But this (procession) is more noble than causal (procession), because it is of a complete being and by an intrinsic principle: therefore, through a topic <u>a maiori</u>,* neither is causal (procession) found in God; and thus no manner of procession is found (There).[8]

CONCLUSION

The reckoning of a procession is truly, properly, and perfectly found among the Divine (Persons).

I RESPOND: It must be said, that "procession" among creatures means a looking-back to *the principle from which* [principium a quo], just a ray is said "to proceed from" the Sun, or a flower "from" a tree; and because it means a change [mutationem],[9] this accedes to it. And, similarly, according to the reckoning of (its) name, it means a looking-back to *the terminus to which* [terminum ad quem]; and because it means an elongation, this accedes to it.

Therefore, since each looking-back [respectus] is found among the divine; for, a Person proceeding has a looking-back to the principle from Whom, (and) Love proceeding[10] has a looking-back to the One loved, that is, that Love, who is (Their) Nexus and Charity: for that reason, there is truly and properly and perfectly found the reckoning of a procession among the Divine (Persons). Whence, there are to be conceded the reasons adduced[11] for this.

1. To that, therefore, which is objected unto the contrary, that "procession" means an "elongation"; it must be said, that this is true among creatures, in which, through an approach [approximationem] to *the terminus to which* there comes to be an elongation from *the terminus from which*, on account of its own finiteness and circumscription and distance; and[12] in this manner it is not in God.

2. To that which is objected, that[13] among creatures ("procession") means a movement; it must be said, that it is not transferred (to God) according to the reckoning of the movement, which it means, but according to the reckoning of (its) twofold looking-back, which, though it cannot be among creatures without movement, on account of (their) imperfection, yet, nevertheless, is in the Creator.

---

[1] The corrupted reading in the Vatican edition: *and the words of God He does not speak except properly truly: therefore, properly* [et verba Dei non loquitur nisi proprie vere: ergo proprie] we have emended with the help of the more ancient manuscripts and edition 1.

[2] The older codices together with edition 1, omit here the *to the last* [ad ultimam] added in the Vatican editino and codex cc.

[3] Codex K again adds *is* [est].

[4] Some codd., such as I S & T with ed. 1, read *but neither* [sed nec].

[5] Thus the more ancient codices, together with edition 1, though very many false read *among others* [in aliis] for *unto Another* [in alium]; but the Vatican edition, together with codex cc, omits the words *therefore, there is* [ergo est] up till *into Another* [in alium].

[6] The Vatican edition, together with very many manuscripts, has less well *not* [non] for *niether* [nec].

[7] Edition 1 *on this account* [propterea]. Then the Vatican edition has *one would be bound* [oporteret] for *one is bound* [oportet].

[8] Codices Y and ee add *among the divine* [in divinis]; codex F adds *in God* [in Deo]. — Concerning this, that procession or local move-

ment is more noble than all other movements, cf. Aristotle, PHYSICS, Bk. VIII, text 54-60 (ch. 7).

[9] The Vatican edition with codex cc reads *it means movement* [dicit motum]; however, several, more ancient codd., such as F H I M X T aa bb & ee, with ed. 1, exhibit our reading, which is confirmed by that false reading of many mss. *it means unity* [dicat unitatem]. Near the end of the response, the Vatican ed. with cod. cc, however, striving against all the other codd. with ed. 1, has *it means* [dicat] (in the subjunctive). Then, many codd. with ed. 1 omit *to it* [ei].

[10] The Vatican edition, contrary to all the codices and to editions 1, 2, and 3, has *as the Love proceeding from the One loving* [ut amor procedens ab amante]. Then codex K after *has a looking-back* [respectum habet] adds *to the One loving and* [ad amantem et], but faultily, because in this member of the division only a second looking-back is attained, namely, the terminus to which.

[11] Very many codices, such as G H I K P Q etc., have *brought forward* [inductae].

[12] Edition 1 *but* [sed] in place of *and* [et].

[13] The Vatican edition inserts, as the subject, *procession* [processio].

---

* *Trans. note*: A "topic <u>a maiori</u>" is syllogism of the form, "If that which is the greater is not in a thing, neither is that which is the lesser". Cf. Aristotle, TOPICS, Bk. I, ch. 1 f., and Pietro Ispano, SUMMULE LOGICALES, tr. V, "On Syllogisms", trans. A. Ponzio, Bompiani, 2006, pp. 172-175.

3. To that which is objected concerning creation, it must be said, that "creation" from its principal imposition [de principali impositioni] means a going-forth from nothing; and for that reason in no manner can its signified be attributed to God [in Deo salvari], neither properly nor transumptively; not so, however, is it concerning generation and procession.

4. To that which is objected, that neither causal nor the local (movement is meant), it must be said, that, nay, (it is meant) *after the manner of causal (movement)*. And causal (movement), in one manner, has agreement [convenientiam] with the local. For causal procession is terminated *in one manner* in the one proceeding, and thus (it is terminated),[1] because it looks back to nothing beyond (that), as when there is said: "a son proceeds from a father"; in *another* manner, insofar as an effect looks back to someone as (its) terminus; and in this manner love proceeds from the one loving unto the one loved, and[2] in one manner *it convenes* with local procession,

because it looks back to the terminus *to which*, in another manner *it differs*, because it does not look back, as if it were being received in it, but as (its) *object*. And, since a looking-back and an emanation are truly found among the divine, hence there is (that), whereby that emanation is said after a similitude of *causal* emanation. But the similitude of *local* procession does not occur There, except in a removed sense [longinque]; and for that reason the Greeks have been deceived.

And to that, that local procession is more perfect; it must be said, that *local* procession always has an imperfection conjoined from[3] the reckoning of (its) name, not so *original* (procession). And it is true, that is more perfect among movements; but "procession" among the divine does not mean "movement", but an 'origin without movement and change', just as has been said above concerning generation.[4]

SCHOLIUM

I. The reckoning of "procession" among creatures contains essentially a twofold looking-back, namely to the terminus *from which* [terminum a quo] and to the terminus *to which* [terminum ad quem]. These looking-backs convey per se no imperfection, whence they can also be posited among the divine. On the other hand, the secondary and per accidens procession does convey imperfections among creatures, (which the Seraphic doctor says "accede to it"), namely both change and movement from the principle *from which*, as well as elongation from the terminus *to which*. These imperfections ought to be excluded from procession among the divine. About this distinction and the other posited in the solution to n. 4, cf. Alexander of Hales, SUMMA, p. I, q. 43, m. 4, in the body.

II. The conclusion touches the Faith: Cf. Alexander of Hales, loc. cit.. — (Bl. John Duns) Scotus, for this and the two following questions in the OXFORD LECTURES and the REPORTATIO, here in q. 1. — St. Thomas, here in q. 1, a. 1; SUMMA, I, q. 27, a. 1. — Bl. (now St.) Albertus (Magnus), SENT, Bk. I, d. 11, a. 1: SUMMA , p. I, tr. 7, q. 31, m. 4. — (Bl.) Peter of Tarentaise, here in q. 1, a. 1. — Henry of Ghent, on this and the following question, SUMMA, a. 61, q. 2, n. 6 ff. — Durandus (of Saint-Pourçain), here in q. 1. — (Bl.) Dionysius the Carthusian, here in q. 2. — (Gabriel) Biel, SENT, Bk. I, d. 14, q. 1.

QUESTION II

Whether the procession of the Holy Spirit is a generation?

Second, there is asked, whether the procession of the Holy Spirit is a generation. And it seems that (it is) not.

1. (St.) Augustine (says) in the fifteenth book, ON THE TRINITY:[5] « Just as the generation presents [praestat] the Essence to the Son without any beginning in time [initio temporis] and without any change, so the procession (does) to the Holy Spirit »: therefore, what presents the Essence to the two Persons is not the same, etc..

2. Likewise, this very (thing) seems *from reason*: because generation is an emanation according to the manner of the nature's fecundity, but, just as has been proven above,[6] the Holy Spirit proceeds through a manner of liberality and love. therefore, He is not generated: therefore, the procession is not a generation.

3. Likewise, nothing one goes forth from two similars through the way of generation,[7] except the one be as a father, the other as a mother, the one as an active principle, the other as a passive

principle; but the Holy Spirit proceeds from Two similars: therefore, if through the way of generation, the One is to Him as a father, the Other as a mother, which is entirely absurd.

4. Likewise, the Son is His own generation and the Holy Spirit is His own procession: therefore, if "to proceed" is "to be generated", the Holy Spirit would be the Son;[8] but the Holy Spirit proceeds from the Son and is said (to be) the Spirit of the Son, just as the Son is said (to be) of the Father: therefore, if the Son is not the Father, neither is the Holy Spirit the Son: therefore neither is the procession the generation.

ON THE CONTRARY: 1. Among these inferiors, generation is a movement according to substance, whence generation is the production of a substance;[9] but the procession of the Holy Spirit is of the Substance, or a production of a Hypostasis: therefore, it is a generation.

2. Likewise, '*to generate*' [generare] is defined by (St. John) Damascene in this manner:[10]

---

[1] Supply: is terminated; the Vatican edition together with codex cc, to remove this addition, omits *and* [et] before *thus* [ita], and reads in English *so that it looks back* etc., but contrary to the more ancient codices and edition 1.

[2] Some codices, such as B T and Y, with edition 1, add *thus* [sic].

[3] We have restored, from the manuscripts and edition 1, *from* [de].

[4] Distinction 9, q. 1.

[5] Chapter 26, n. 47, in which text, trusting in the more ancient manuscripts and edition 1, with the agreement of the edition of St. Augustine's Works, we have put *so* [ita] in place of *in this manner* [sic].

[6] Distinction 10, a. 1, q. 1 and 2.

[7] Many codices, such as A C G H I L R S T U Y Z etc., together with edition 1, faultily omits *through the way of generation* [per viam generationis].

[8] Codex O superfluously adds: *but the Son is not the Holy Spirit nor the other way around; therefore, the generation is not the procession nor the other way around* [sed Filius non est Spiritus sanctus nec e converso; ergo generatio non est procesio nec e converso].

[9] Cf. Aristotle, PHYSICS, Bk. V, text 7 ff. (ch. 1), and ON GENERATION AND CORRUPTION, Bk. I, text 11 ff. (ch. 3). — Then the Vatican edition together with codex cc, contrary to the other codices and to edition 1, has *according to hypostasis* [secundum hypostasim] in place of *of a Hypostasis* [hyupostasis].

[10] ON THE ORTHODOX FAITH, Bk. I, ch. 8: Indeed, generation consists in this, that out of the substance of the one begetting there is produced an offspring of the same substance with the one begetting. — A little below this, on the next page, edition 1 adds *Holy* [sanctus] to *Spirit* [Spiritus].

"to generate" is to produce a similar to one's self in substance; but by the spiration and/or procession the Spirit is produced similar in nature: therefore, the procession is also a generation.

3. Likewise, actions and mutations are denominated by (their) terminus:[1] therefore, whatsoever (things) convene in that which is had through emanation, convene in the manner of emanating; but the Son and the Holy Spirit convene in the Substance, which They have through emanation: therefore, They convene in emanation: therefore, if the manner of the emanating of the Son is a generation, similarly (that) of the Holy Spirit (is) also.

4. Likewise, production is superior to generation;[2] but whatsoever (things) be produced, proceed: therefore, procession is superior to generation: therefore, generation is a procession: therefore, for an equal reason procession is a generation.

If you say, that procession is appropriated to the Holy Spirit: *I ask the reason*: and it seems, that it ought more to be appropriated to the Son, because, if the reckoning of proceeding according to the reckoning of understanding, through (a consideration of what is) prior, is in the Son, therefore procession ought more to be appropriated to that.

5. Likewise, if the One generating is the One spirating, therefore, the One begotten is the One spirated, and the other way around; but passive spiration is a procession: ergo etc..

CONCLUSION

The Holy Spirit's procession is not a generation.

I RESPOND: It must be said, that just as the Holy Spirit is not the Son, so neither is the procession of the Holy Spirit a generation.

1. 2. To that, therefore, which is objected unto the contrary, that generation is the production of a substance; it must be said, that there is a 'producing of a *dissimilar* substance', and there is a 'producing of a substance *similar* according to *the will*',[3] and there is a 'producing of substance *similar* through the manner of *the nature*'. These three manners are distinguished and are diverse and separable, as much as ("producing") concerns itself. Wherefore, it is clear, that in the production of Adam[4] there was a production of a substance, and yet it was not a generation; for God did not generate Adam, but created (him); in the production of Eve from Adam there was a production of a similar substance, not however, a generation, because Adam did not beget

Eve, but in the production of Abel there was a production of a substance according to the way of nature, and for that reason there was a generation there. According to the thing, therefore, these three manners are distinguished,[5] yet in the action of a creature they are not distinguished, because a creature cannot produce a substance, except one similar, and this through natural virtue. And the reason for this is the imperfection of the power and (its) limitation[6] in the creature; but in God there is a most high Power, and for that reason in His operation those three manners have a distinction.

For that reason though there is a *complete reckoning* of generation among inferiors thanks to the matter:[7] there is not, however, a production of a similar substance, and/or a production of a substance, among the divine, nay it must be added: 'through the manner of the fecundity of nature'. And because that condition is lacking[8] in the production of the Holy Spirit, it is clear, that it does not follow.

3. To that which is objected, that each has a similar emanation; it must be said, that emanation differs among those inferiors and in God; because among those inferiors it is terminated at the *essence* and/or substance, which is multiplied; but among the divine it is terminated at *the Hypostases*. Since, therefore, the Hypostasis, at which the procession is terminated, is *Love*, the Hypostasis, at which generation is terminated, is *Image* — and it belongs to both love and nexus to be spirated, not generated, and conversely to an image to be generated, not spirated — since there is not an completely similar proper reckoning of the Hypostases according to Themselves, neither will there be a completely similar emanation. However, He Himself proceeds, even if (His production) is properly terminated at the Substance.

4. To that which is objected, that procession is common to generation, it must be said, that[9] it is common to generation and procession, properly said; and we here speak of procession, insofar as it convenes only with the Holy Spirit; but thus it is not common nor is it in this manner predicated nor[10] subjected; nor is there to be understood there a community of the thing, but only one of proportion, or of a manner of speaking.

On which account, therefore, *there is asked*, "For what reason is (the common name of "procession") appropriated more to the Holy Spirit?": *certain ones* wanted to say, that just as the name of the "*proper*"[11] is common to the definition and to a proper passion,* yet because the *definition* adds upon the name of the *proper*, a proper passion (does) not:[12] for that reason, the definition has the name, the proper passion does not; but the common

---

[1] Aristotle, PHYSICS, Bk. V, text 4: But change is denominated more from "that into which" it is moved than "(that) out of which".

[2] That is: "production" is the genus, a species of which is "generation".

[3] The corrupt reading of the Vatican ed., in which these two prior members of the distinction are exhibited thus: *there is a "producing a substance according to the will" and there is a "producing a substance similar besides nature"* [est producere substantiam secundum voluntatem et est producere substantiam similem praeter naturam], is repaired with the help of the mss. and ed. 1; cod. W after has *a substance dissimilar to the nature* [substantiam dissimilem naturae] for the first member, but cod. Z has *a substance dissimilar through the manner of the will* [substantiam dissimilem per modum voluntatis] instead; next, ed. 1 after *a similar substance"* [substantiam similem] inserts *and this in a twofold manner, for there is a "producing a similar substance* [et hoc dupliciter, nam est producere substantiam similem].

[4] Codex Z has *of Adam* [Adae] for *of Adam* [Adam].

[5] The punctuation of this passage and its reading in the Vatican edition and in codex cc is very much disturbed: *and for that reason there was a generation there according to the thing: therefore, those three manners are distinguished in God. Yet*; [et ideo fuit ibi generatio secundum rem: ergo isti tres modi distinguuntur in Deo. Tamen]; besides, the authority of the more ancient manuscripts and of edition 1 oppose this, not to mention the context.

[6] Edition 1 here repeats *of the power* [potentiae].

[7] That is, a complete and/or sufficient definition of generation.

[8] The Vatican edition, against the more ancient codices, has *defines* [defninit] for *is lacking* [deficit]; edition 1 instead has *was lacking* [defuit].

[9] In codex Y and edition 1 there is added *procession*.

[10] Codex V adds *in this manner* [hoc modo].

[11] Thus very many codices together with edition 1, while the Vatican edition reads *just as this proper name* [sicut hoc nomen proprium].

[12] Peter of Spain, SUMMULA, tract (II), "On the Predicables: on the Proper" says: The "proper" is that which is in one alone and always and conversely is predicated of the thing and does not indicate, what is (the essence) of thing, such as "risible" does. Whence "(that) it *does not indicate what is the 'being' of a thing*" is posited in the definition of *the proper* according to the difference of the *definition*; for a definition is conversely predicated of the thing and indicates, what is the 'being' of a thing. An example: just as "animate, sensible substance" is convertible with "animal" and indicates, what is its 'being'; because every definition is given through substantials; for every superior concerns the essence of its inferior.

---

* *Trans. note*: a *proper passion* is any logical subset of a genus or category: e.g. 'automobile' is a proper passion of 'vehicle'.

name it does retain; thus (it is) in the proposed. — But it is absurd to say this, that the Spirit does not have[1] a proper and singular manner of emanating, just as the Son (does).

For that reason *others* wanted,[2] that it adds another manner; but because that manner is not in creatures, because either rarely or never does any hypostasis proceed in a manner other than through generation, for that reason the sacred doctors did not want to devise [fingere] a proper and/or new name, but rather to appropriate the common one. — But that still does not seem true, because, just as the emanation of the Son is rightly expressed by the word, "generating", so the emanation of the Spirit by the word, "spirating".[3]

And, on account of this, it must be said in one manner, that[4] just as the Father is said (to be) "unbegotten", because generation is entirely removed from Him, because He is neither generated nor is from One generated; similarly the other way around "procession" is said *properly*[5] of Him, in whom there entirely is the reckoning of proceeding; and such is the Holy Spirit, because He proceeds and is from One proceeding, but not so the Son: for that reason it is attributed to the Holy Spirit.

In another manner, it can be said, that the complete reckoning of procession consists in the comparison of the principle *from which* and of the terminus *to which*; and because the Spirit in His own emanation, because He is the Nexus, looks back to Each, the Son to the Other one; for that reason the most complete reckoning of this name is found in the Holy Spirit, although it is found in another manner in the Son;[6] and for that reason it is appropriated to the Son.

5. To that which is objected last, that the One generating is the One spirating; it must be said, that that predication is not formal, but only by reason of the supposit;[7] and because one Person or one Supposit can generate and spirate, for that reason this is true: 'the One generating is the One spirating'; but no single [unica] Person can emanate in more manners all at once [simul]; for that reason it does not follow, that the One begotten is the One spirated.

SCHOLIUM

I. That in God there are two emanations, namely generation and procession, has already been proven above in d. 9, q. 1, and d. 10, q. 1. Here there is asked, whether these two emanations differ, and in the following question, of which nature is this difference. And it deals with generation and procession, to the extent that they are notional acts, or in an active sense. For generation and procession, in the passive sense, are the Second and Third Person of the Trinity. — The conclusion is <u>de fide</u>, since the Athanasian Creed says of the Holy Spirit: « Not made, nor created, *nor begotten, but proceeding* ».

II. To understand the solution to n. 4 more easily, it must be noted, that among the divine the word, *"procession"*, is accepted in a twofold manner, either as a common name, the species of which are generation and spiration, and/or as the special name of the second emanation. For « frequently we find, that something proper is denominated by the common name » (St. Thomas, here in q. 1, a. 3, ad 3). Hence there arises this proposed question, "For what reason is the name, *"procession"*, appropriated to the Holy Spirit rather than to the Son?" The Seraphic Doctor reproves the first solution, with St. Thomas consenting. Ulric defended this, according to the witness of (Bl.) Dionysius the Carthusian, that the *procession* of the Holy Spirit is a procession simply, and that *generation* adds to this common reckoning a specific difference. Those defending this assertion of his illustrate it with the example of the word, *"proper"*, itself. For this name is common both to the definition, which through genus and difference essentially expresses the species, and « to the proper passion », i. e. to that *accidental* condition of any being, which inseparably inheres to a subject, as *risibility* (does) to man. For according to Aristotle the *"proper"* is defined as: « That which does not indicate, what belongs to a thing, but (which) is in it alone and is predicated (of it) conversely » (v. g. 'every man is risible, and every risible is a man'). Therefore, this species of the *"proper"* retains the common name and according to Porphyry (ch. 5) is the fourth predicable, while « genus, species, (and) difference are the first three predicables ». This Bl. (now St.) Albertus (Magnus) confirms (SENT., Bk. I, d. 11, a. 2): « The *"proper"* is said (to be) the convertible predicate; however, since the convertible predicate is twofold, namely the essential, as (is) the definition, and the accidental convertible, the accidental retains the name of *"proper"*, and in this manner it occurs in many ». St. Thomas teaches similarly (here in q. 1, a. 3). On the manifold sense of *"proper"*, cf. St. Bonaventure, SENT., Bk. II, d. 16, a. 1, q. 3. — The second opinion teaching, that on account of the defect of a name expressing this special procession, the common name has been appropriated to the second emanation, again does not please the Seraphic (Doctor), on account of this reason, that in truth such a name is had, namely *"to spirate"* and *"spiration"*. Nevertheless, St. Thomas in his SUMMA (I, q. 27, a. 4, ad 3) retains the aforesaid opinion, saying: « Whence the *procession*, which is not generation, has remained without a special name, but can be named *"spiration"*, because it is a procession of a spirit ». But in his COMMENTARIA (<u>loc. cit.</u>) besides this reason, of which he says, « and I believe it is the better one », he also brings forward the two others, here approved by St. Bonaventure.

III. On the conclusion: cf. Alexander of Hales, SUMMA, p. I, a. 42, m. 2, § 1, and q. 43, m. 2. — St. Thomas, <u>loc. cit.</u>. — Bl. (now St.) Albertus (Magnus), here in a. 1. — (Bl.) Peter of Tarentaise, here in q. 2, a. 2, and q. 1, a. 2. — Richard of Middleton, here in q. 2 and 3. — Giles the Roman, here in 2nd. princ., q. 1. — Durandus (of Saint-Pourçain), on this and the following question, here in q. 2. — (Bl.) Dionysius the Carthusian, on this and the following question, here in q. 1. — (Gabriel) Biel, on this and the following question, here in q. sole.

For "definition" is described thus by Aristotle: a definition is an expression signifying what is the 'being' of the thing; but a proper (name) does not indicate what is the 'being' of the thing. — Then, cod. 1 reads *proper noun* [nomen proprium] for *the name, the proper* [nomen, propria]. Next, the Vatican ed. after *thus* [sic] has, instead, *also do they speak* [etiam dicunt], which, however, is absent from the mss. and ed. 1; some codd. falsely have *just as* [sicut] for *thus* [sic].

[1] The Vatican edition, not trusting in very many manuscripts and edition 1, reads *have* [habet] in the indicative.

[2] The Vatican ed., against the codd. and ed. 1, has *want* [volunt] for *wanted* [voluerunt], then *do not want* [nolunt] for *did not want* [noluerunt].

[3] Edition 1 by adding *and/or "proceeding"* [vel procedendi], elides the force of the argument, that is, that a proper name is given in respect of the emanation of the Holy Spirit.

[4] From very many codices and edition 1 we have substituted *that* [quod] in place of *that* [quia] and a little below this *generation ... entirely* [omnino generatio] or *every generation* [omnis generatio].

[5] In many manuscripts there is lacking *properly* [proprie].

[6] Edition 1 reads more briefly: *the reckoning of this name is not found in the Son* [ratio huius nominis non reperitur in Filio].

[7] In codex X there is inserted: *just as you would say, "the grammarian is an artist"* [diceres, grammaticus est musicus].

QUESTION III

*Whether the procession of the Holy Spirit really differs from the generation of the Son,
and/or only according to the reckoning of understanding?*

Third, there is asked, whether the procession of the Holy Spirit really differs from the generation of the Son, or whether only according to the reckoning of understanding. And it seems, that (it) really (does):

1. Because the Persons differ according to Their emanations; therefore,[1] since the Persons really differ, not only intellectually, because, in every circumscribed intellect, a trinity still remains: therefore, the emanations, which are procession and generation, do really differ.

2. Likewise, what are from diverse principles, really do differ; but generation is from One among the divine, the procession of the Holy Spirit from Two, because from the Father and the Son: therefore, they really do differ.

3. Likewise, according to thing[2] and truth the Divine Substance is principle of some (things) as a *will*, of which It is not the principle as a *nature*, just as is clear, that they have been created by God acting through a manner of *will*, not through a manner of *nature*: if, therefore, procession is of the Will through the manner of will, generation as of the Nature through the manner of nature, procession and generation really do differ.

4. Likewise, in the created image the egress of the word and the egress of love are distinguished, because they *really* do differ; this[3] belongs to perfection, because out of this they make the image's trinity, but because they do differ *essentially*, this belongs to imperfection; but everything which belongs to perfection, is to be posited among the divine: therefore, procession and generation *really* do differ, although not *essentially*.

ON THE CONTRARY: 1. The Father spirates and generates, therefore, either inasmuch as (He is) one (Person), or inasmuch as (He is) many (Persons) and/or many (beings). If inasmuch as *many* (Persons) and/or many (beings), the Father[4] is a composite; if inasmuch as *one* (Person); but because the Father and the Son spirate inasmuch as (They are) one (Being), there are not two spirations, but one: therefore, similarly, if the Father spirates and generates inasmuch as (He is) one (Being), spiration and generation is one production.

2. Likewise, according to all (authors), it is true, that the Father generates by reason of the fecundity of the[5] Nature, He spirates by reason of the fecundity of the Will; but in God the same (Thing) is Will and Nature: ergo etc..

3. Likewise, the emanations[6] are distinguished from within the termini; but the Father gives entirely the same and the whole, which He gives to the Son through generation, to the Holy Spirit through procession: therefore, the spiration and the generation are entirely one emanation.

4. Likewise, this very (thing) is shown per impossibile. If they differ, (they do so) either by their very selves, or by others: *not by their very selves*, because the emanations are neither *from themselves* nor *to themselves*. therefore, if any one whatsoever is distinguished through that which it is, and/or from which (it is),[7] emanations of this kind are not distinguished by their very selves; if *by others*: either *by essence*, or *by notion*, or *by Person*. *Not by the Essence*; it is established, because That does not distinguish nor is It distinguished; *not by a Person*, because it belongs to It to be distinguished, not to distinguish: therefore, if they do differ, this will be *by other notions*; and similarly there will be a seeking from those others, and in this manner unto infinity: ergo etc..

5. Likewise, if they differ, (they do) either by a *substantial* difference, or by an *accidental* one: not *by a substantial* one, because such a difference is not among the divine; not *by an accidental* one, because in God there is not an accident: ergo etc..

6. Likewise, the Son differs more from a creature, than from the Holy Spirit: therefore, the generation differs more from a creature, than from the procession; but generation is not distinguished from creation: therefore, neither from procession. Proof of *the middle*: creation is by the Divine Essence;[8] but person and essence are not distinguished from each other: therefore, neither generation and creation.

CONCLUSION

Generation and spiration do not only differ according to a manner of speaking, but also according to a difference both of origin, and of habitude, and also by their very selves.

I RESPOND: It must be said, that generation and spiration or procession differ not only according to the reason for (their) being said [rationem dicendi], but also according to a difference[9] of origin and habitude, because the manner of their holding themselves is diverse and the manner of (their) origin (is) different; but such a difference is not repugnant to the unity of the Essence.

If, moreover, there is asked the reason for the difference of these emanations, it must be said, that the *first* reason for differing cannot be assigned *on the part of the termini*. For the termini are the Persons, who do not actively convey a reckoning of differing, but passively (do).[10] If, therefore, the Persons

---

[1] From the more ancient manuscripts and edition 1, we have supplied here the *therefore* [ergo] and a little before this the *Because* [Quia].

[2] Edition 1 has *reckoning* [rationem] for *thing* [rem].

[3] Trusting in the manuscripts and edition 1, we have expunged here the *for* [enim] added by the Vatican edition, just as next after *but* [sed] the inserted *according to* [secundum: which had changed the reading to *but according to which* instead of *but because*].

[4] The Vatican edition prefixes *thus* [sic] to *the Father* [Pater], codex cc *because thus* [quia sic], codex Y *therefore* [ergo]; but very many codices together with edition 1 have nothing before it.

[5] On the authority of nearly all the manuscripts and edition 1, we have removed the *intellectual* [intellectualis], here added by the Vatican edition.

[6] The Vatican edition, not trusting in the older manuscripts and in edition 1, adds *of the Father* [Patris], and a little below this after *the same* [idem], it omits *and* [et], contrary to the manuscripts and editions 1, 2, 3, and 6.

[7] A few codices, such as M and Z, add *it is* [est].

[8] In codices O and Z there is added, sufficiently well, *but generation is by a Divine Person* [generation vero est divina persona].

[9] Codices P and Q add *and reckoning* [et rationem] .

[10] The sense is: They do not convey the reckoning itself, which causes the difference, but are the subjects, among which the difference is had. — A little before this codex X after *for* [enim] inserts *properly* [proprie].

do differ, there is asked: by what? and it is necessary to go back to the emanation and relations, which are generation and procession;[1] and thus in this assigning (of a difference) there will be a circle.

Similarly, *on the part of the principles*. For if it be said, that these two emanations differ according to a twofold fecundity of the Nature and the Will, there is asked,[2] in what manner does fecundity differ from fecundity. If you say, that the fecundity *of the Nature* is in the Father alone, *of the Will* in the Father and the Son; this has a further question, whence does this difference come, and one is bound to come to this, that the fecundity *of the Nature* is in *One*, because the Image proceeding through that has been born to be solely from One, the fecundity *of the Will* in *Two*, because a nexus or procession through a manner of a nexus is in two; and thus the difference goes back into the first, and in this there is a circular reckoning. Therefore, it is clear according to this, that the first difference of these emanations is neither to be taken on the part of the termini, nor on the part of the principles.

And for that reason it must be noted, that there is a speaking[3] of emanations of this kind as much as *regards 'being'* and as much as *regards 'being distinguished'*.

And, as much as *regards "being"*, thus they have a reckoning of being [rationem essendi] from their own perfect and fecund Principles. For because in God there is a most perfect *Nature* and a true *Nature*, for that reason a perfect and true fecundity[4] in the Hypostasis, which has a reckoning of a principle. And, because true and perfect and proper is the fecundity of the Nature, for that reason It has a true and proper emanation; and this is the generation. Similarly, it must be understood concerning the spiration as much as regards *the Will*. Whence, *the reason*, why there are[5] truly (emanations) of this kind in God, is the true fecundity of the Nature and Will.

But, if we speak as much as *regards 'differing'*, it must be said, that they differ by their very selves, just as has been shown,[6] because every distinction among the divine comes from the manners *of origin* and *of relation*. Whence, just as two differences differ by their very selves, as "rational" and "irrational", similarly[7] among the divine (do) these two emanations (differ). And just as the differences of the differences become known [innotescunt] to us through the other differences, which arise from them, so also (is it) among the divine. For, because generation and spiration are distinguished by their very selves, according to these there follows [consequitur] a twofold difference according to the reckoning of understanding: *one*, because the generation is from One, but the spiration from Two. For, because the generation is an emanation through a manner of perfect assimilation, for that reason it looks back to one Principle, however, because the spiration is an emanation through a manner of connection, for that reason it is from Two. The *other* difference is in comparison to us. For, because the Holy Spirit is spirated as One joining and thus as One tending unto the Other, for that reason the Holy Spirit

proceeds as One able to be given [ut donabilis]; but the Son is generated, and generation does not look back to a Third.

Through these differences the concomitance of these emanations is necessarily elicited. Because the spiration causes [dat] one to understand beforehand the generation — for They are not joined except as Ones distinct and similar, and thus as those, one of whom is from the other through generation — similarly the generation causes one to understand consequently the spiration; for it is necessary that Those distinct and entirely similar be conjoined through delightful Love [deliciosum amorem].

Therefore, there must be conceded the reasons proving, that they differ, jus as it has been manifested in the reasons (given); but those reasons have not been taken a priori.

Some, however, wanted to assign other differences: and *certain ones* say that they differ through the spirative and generative force, but this difference clarifies [declarat] the unknown through the more unknown; *others* also said, that the Son proceeds through the manner of 'being' [per modum esse], the Holy Spirit through a manner of 'well-being' [per modum bene esse]; but these words are not sane, nor fitting to such a discussion [materiae].

1. To that, therefore, which is first objected, whether the Father spirates inasmuch as (He is) one (God); it must be said, that neither inasmuch as (He is) one (God), nor inasmuch as (He is) many, but inasmuch as One holding Himself in one and another manner [alio et alio modo se habens]; because He holds Himself to the Son in one manner, to the Holy Spirit in another manner. Moreover, this one and another manner of His Holding Himself is not repugnant to the unity of the Substance and/or of (His) Person; but the Father and the Son spirate in this, that One (is) holding Himself in one manner. Hence it is, that twofold is the procession[8] of the Son and of the Holy Spirit from the Father, but one is the spiration or procession of the Holy Spirit from the Father and the Son.

2. To that which is objected, that Nature and Will in God are the same; it must be said, that even if Nature and Will in God are considered absolutely the same, yet the *Will* looks back to something as Will in the reckoning of (its) principle, which *Nature* does not look back to as Nature. And hence it is, that just as it does not follow: 'a creature is from God through a manner of will', because for that reason it would also be through a manner of nature; similarly, because the Nature and Will are compared to those emanations under the reckoning of a *principle*, for that reason nothing prohibits, that those emanations differ, though the Nature and the Will be the same in *substance*.

3. To that which is objected, that the emanations differ from within (their) termini; it must be said, that among these inferiors it is true, where "emanation" means a being in potency [ens in potentia] and thus an 'imperfect one'; but it is not true in God, because There they do not mean a being in potency nor an 'imperfect one';[9] whence among the divine they are the *reason* for distinguishing (the Persons). However, if we want to say, that they differ from within (their) terminus,

---

[1] Thus the manuscripts together with edition 1, while the Vatican edition exhibits the beginning of this proposition, with various words inserted, thus: *If, therefore, the Persons do differ, for what reason and in what do they differ, if we will want to show (that) it is necessary* [Si ergo personae differunt, quare et in quibus differant, si ostendere voluerimus necesse est] etc. Then edition 1 has *would* [esset] in place of *will* [erit].

[2] We follow the older codices together with edition 1, by putting *there is asked* [quaeritur] in place of *I ask* [quaero].

[3] In codex Y there is added *in a twofold manner* [dupliciter].

[4] Cf. above d. 9, q. 1; on the will in d. 10, a. 1, q. 1.

[5] The Vatican edition, striving against very many manuscripts and edition 1, has the subjunctive *are* [sint].

[6] In this question itself; cf. also the preceding question, especially in reply to nn. 1 and 2.

[7] Codex V for *similarly* [similiter] has *in this manner* [sic], codex X has *in this manner also* [sic etiam]. Then, some codd. with editions 1, 2, and 3, have the distorted reading *then* [tunc] in place of *just as* [sicut].

[8] In codex bb there is added *namely* [scilicet].

[9] The Vatican edition, not consistent with itself, and against very many codices, not to mention edition 1, reads *imperfection* [imperfectionem], while codex I both here and a little before this reads *imperfection* [imperfectionem]. Then to *among the divine they are* [in divinis] the Vatican edition adds *not* [not], which the codices together with the first six editions omit, and well so, because the subject of this

we will not accept "terminus" for the Substance and/or Essence, but for Hypostasis, as has been had before.[1]

4. To that which is asked, whether (they differ) by their very selves and/or by others; it is clear, that (they do so) *by their very selves*. And to that[2] which is objected, that they do not have '*being*' *from themselves*, therefore, neither a '*being distinguished*'; it must be said, that that does not hold in regard to the 'being' of an origin. For though the differences have (their) rise from the genus, nevertheless they are not distinguished by the genus, but by their very selves.[3]

5. To that which is objected, in what manner do they differ, either by a substantial or an accidental difference; it must be said, that (this) divides (it) insufficiently, because among the divine there is a difference *of relations*, as (St.) Augustine says in the fifth (book) ON THE TRINITY,[4] which is neither *accidental* nor *substantial*, but rather is said (to be) *original*.

6. To that which is objected concerning creation, it must be said, that by reason of what is connoted [ratione connotati] creation differs more; but by reason of the principal (thing) signified they do not differ so much, because the *Essence* does not differ as much from a Person, as a *Person* (does) from a Person. Whence, the Essence[5] is predicated of [de] the Person and does not cause any number in any manner; a Person, on the other hand, is distinguished from another Person; and for that reason the argument is not valid.

SCHOLIUM

I. In the solution of this subtle question the ancient Scholastics set out in diverse ways. That the state of the question be accurately discerned, it must be attended to, that here it deals with active generation and spiration, not with the passive. Whence, this question differs from both the question concerning the difference between the Second and Third Divine Person (concerning which, see above d. 9, q. 2), and from that, "What is the *power* of generating?" (d. 7, q. 1), with which, however, it is grouped [cohaeret].

Therefore, there is first asked, of what nature is the distinction between active generation and spiration. First, it is resolved with the common sentence, that it is not a distinction merely *of reckoning* or according to a manner of speaking; moreover, in the fundament there is asserted, that these emanations *really differ*. The sense of this *real* distinction is explained by Brülifer and Fr. Bartolomeo de' Barbieri da Castelvetro, 1615-1697 A.D., (CURSUS THEOLOGICUS, disp. 12, q. 7, conclusion 3), that it means the same as Scotus' *formal* distinction. Others understand it in the sense of a *virtual* distinction. For more on this see below d. 26, q. 1, where in the Scholium the mind of the Seraphic (Doctor), by means of a collation of various passages of the same, shall be explained. It is sufficient here to note, that there is not understood under this name a strictly real, *absolute* distinction, but (rather one) « according to the difference of origin and habitude », i. e. « one is distinct from the other, not by an essential reality [re], but by a notional one », as Richard (of Middleton) says (here in q. 3). Moreover, it is established, that the Seraphic Doctor sometimes calls every distinction greater that that which is of the reckoning of one reasoning, a real one.

Then, with this difference of the two emanations supposed, there is again asked, what is *the reason* for this difference, and since very many reasons can be assigned, what is the *first* reason for the same. In this second question chiefly stands the difficulty, which is so great, that (Peter) Aureolus, together with the Nominalists, accuses those of temerity, who presume to explore this matter. Even (St.) Augustine, together with Master (Peter Lombard), here in the text, confesses his own ignorance about it. What the other Scholastics teach about this difference, we shall explain briefly.

II. The chief doctors, both ancient and modern, agree in not a few assertions, and disagree in others.

1. *They agree* (excepting Durandus of Saint-Pourçain) in this, that the *radical* reason for this diversity is to be posited in the different reckoning of each production, since the Son is produced through a manner *of understanding* and *of nature*, the Holy Spirit through a manner *of will* and *of liberality*. St. Bonaventure teaches this above in d. 6, a. 1, q. 2, in d. 19, a. 1, q. 1, here and in the fundament and in the body (of the response). — Commonly theologians, especially after the Council of Florence, teach, that the principium quod of these emanations is the Persons producing, but the proximate principium quo of the first emanation is the Divine Essence with the *Intellect*, or *the fecund Memory* (thus speak many theologians together with the Seraphic Doctor); but the *principium quo* of the second (emanation) is the same Essence with the *Will* or *the fecund Will*.

2. The Divine Nature is equally and through Itself communicated to the Holy Spirit and to the son. Though not a few contradict this position, it seems to be the doctrina certa, which St. Bonaventure teaches especially in d. 10, a. 1, q. 1, in reply to n. 3. Whence it follows, that the root of that difference be sought in the property of this twofold fecundity (cf. here q. 2, in reply to nn. 1 and 2).

3. Several differences for these emanations can and ought to be assigned, namely a difference *of termini*, or of the Persons emanated, which certainly are really distinguished; a difference *of principles*, both because generation is from One, and spiration from Two (here in the 2nd fundament and the body); then there is the difference in *comparison to us* (in the body), because in the second emanation there is some special looking-back to the creature according to (His) *aptitude of donability*, concerning which cf. below d. 18, q. 2 and 5. Nor is the controversy, whether these differences *subsist*, but what is their *first* and quasi a priori reason.

III. On the other hand, theologians disagree about some special determinations.

1. Durandus (of Saint-Pourçain) with not a few others seems to admit no other difference but this, that the generation proceeds from One, the spiration from Two, which sentence the Seraphic Doctor, with the common opinion, meritedly impugns.

2. There is a dispute, whether besides the differences sought *extrinsically* (of *originally* from their own principles, i. e. from the Persons producing, or *consequently* from their termini) these emanations also intrinsically and *formally* (a priori) differ by their very selves, i. e. by the proper reckonings of the (emanations) themselves, in an analogous manner, just as the last difference (v. g. the "rational" and the "irrational") differ. If this be affirmed, this difference ought to be said (to be) the first and quasi formal. The Seraphic Doctor affirms this in the body (of the response) and in reply to n. 4. Besides the others, (Bl.) Peter of Tarentaise, Richard of Middleton and chiefly (Bl. John Duns) Scotus agree, the last of whom even adds: « they differ *by their entire selves* [se totis] ». This last word is explained by the Scotists in this sense, that common to the two emanations there is not some reality through the differences of the contractible, though they do convene in the common concept of being [entis] and relation (Rada, CONTROV., 14, a. 2; Macedo, COLL., 7, diff. 2, who bitterly defends Scotus against the interpretation of him, which Cajetan made). — St. Thomas in the SUMMA, (I, q. 27, a. 4, ad 1) agrees with St. Bonaventure in teaching, that *they differ by the proper reckonings of (the emanations) themselves*, which is the same as *to differ by their very selves*, as Cajetan concedes (on this passage). But the same (Saint) in DE POTENTIA, q. 10, a. 2, does not admit this sentence; on the other hand concerning the other (difference), that they are distinguished from within (their) *principles*, he judges in this manner: « It does suffice, unless something be added »; then he posits a third (difference), that « *the order alone* of the processions, which is attained according

---

proposition is not the *termini*, but the *emanations*, which, as has been said above, in God differ by their very selves and are the reason for distinguishing (the Persons). One or the other codex, such as B and O, together with edition 1, in a singular manner have *among the divine it is the reason* [in divinis est ratio], but not so well on account of the change of subject; one may say the same concerning the reading of codex bb *among the divine they are the reasons* [in divinis sunt rationes].

[1] The preceding question, in reply to n. 3.

[2] Very many codices, such as F H K T etc., have *that* [illud].

[3] The Vatican edition, together with edition 1, has *but from their very selves* [a se ipsis], but the manuscripts oppose this.

[4] Chapter 5, n. 6. — Then cod. Z has *an original difference* [differentia originalis] for *is said (to be) original* [dicitur originalis].

[5] The Vatican ed. and cod. cc have *essentially it is* [essentialiter] for *the Essence* [essentia], which is emended from all the other mss. and ed. 1.

to origin, multiplies the processions among the divine ». In his COM-MENT., (here in q. 1, a. 2, ad. ult.), the same (Saint) speaks wrongly [vitioso] against the reason of St. Bonaventure concerning the circular (argument): « What, therefore, is objected, that the relations are consequent to the processions, whence it rather seems, that diverse processions cause the diversity of relations, than the other way around, and/or what is less that there will be There a circulation; it must be said, that "relation" among the divine has not only, that it be a "relation", but also that it be a *personal* one, that is one constituting a Person, and from this it has a quasi act of the constitutive difference and form of the Person Himself, the operation of which (act) belongs to the generation and spiration; and for that reason it is not unbefitting, that according to the reckoning of "relation" the relations be consequent to those processions and receive a difference from them; but according to which they are proper forms of the Persons Themselves, they cause the difference of the processions ». In what manner the various sayings of the Angelic (Doctor) are to be reconciled, is disputed, and one can confer with Cajetan (at q. 27, a. 4; q. 36, a. 2). Next are the other reasons of St. Thomas, impugned by (Bl. John Duns) Scotus, concerning which, cf. Rada and Macedo, locc. citt.. Otherwise the same difficulty and certain difference of opinion between the Seraphic and Angelic (Doctors) returns below in d. 27, p. I, q. 2, where more will be said in the Scholium on this most subtle matter.

3. There is a diverse manner of speaking about a *proper reckoning* [rationem propriam], why a procession through a manner *of nature* differs from the other through the manner *of will*. In the first, according to (St.) Bonaventure (here in the body of the response), is « an emanation through a manner of perfect assimilation », and before this he says, that through it proceeds the *image*. Which words, if they are brought together with the explanation of the image, which (the Saint) gives in d. 31, p. II, a. 1, q. 2, and with what is said in d. 10, a. 1, q. 2, in reply to nn. 2 and 3, clearly prove, that the Seraphic (Doctor) consented to the sentence of St. Thomas, who (SUMMA, I, q. 27, a. 4) teaches, that in the first emanation there is a reckoning of *similitude* by force *of the procession itself*, (but) not in the second. Hence it follows, that there is falsely attributed to the Seraphic (Doctor) the sentence, which Richard of Middleton (here in q. 3), seems to favor, that that reckoning of his is to be sought in this, that the Son accepts only a fecund *will*, not a fecund *nature*.

4. There is a dispute, whether there is able to be said, that indeed the Holy Spirit proceeds necessarily, but yet *freely* [libere], which (Bl.) Scotus says together with others, and even St. Thomas, DE POTENTIA, q. 10, a. 2, in reply to n. 5 says, although through a manner of will. Certainly this word *freely* is taken here not in the strict and now commonly accepted sense, but for *voluntarily*, to the extent that it does not exclude the necessary, as is (taught) among very many ancient Fathers and Doctors, and even by St. Bonaventure, SENT., Bk. II, d. 25, p. II, q. 2. Whence, Rada (CONTROV., 13) and Macedo (COLL., 7) rightly prove, that this is rather an argument over the name.

5. There is a disputed, whether the Word proceeds through an act *of speaking*, as (Bl.) Scotus wants, which (St.) Bonaventure favors, or whether through an act *of understanding*, as St. Thomas with his own (disciples) teaches. On this controversy cf. below d. 27, p. II, q. 1 and 3 and its Scholium.

IV. The sense of the solution to n. 4 is this. Though these notional acts do not have 'being' from themselves nor an extrinsic distinction from their own original principles, yet intrinsically they are distinguished by their very selves. For that illation, « that that does hold », is to be denied, because in that which has arisen from another, there cannot be intrinsically a distinction. Thus "whiteness" and "blackness", though they are from other causes, differ *by their very selves*. The Seraphic Doctor himself gives an example of the last differences, which are distinguished by their very selves, « though they have their rise from the genus ». For a genus, which according to the Aristotelians contains in itself *in potency* the species and their differences, is in another manner the principle of the differences. Therefore, in the objection there is committed the fallacy of the figure of speech, because the genus of one cause, namely, *the efficient*, has been changed into another genus, namely, *the formal*.

V. Besides the authors already praised, cf. (Bl. John Duns) Scotus, in each version of his Commentary, here in the q. sole. — Bl. (now St.) Albertus (Magnus), here in a. 1, and in d. 11, a. 5. — (Bl.) Peter of Tarentaise, here in q. 2, a. 1. — Richard of Middleton, here in q. 3. — Giles the Roman, here in 1st. princ., q. 2. — Henry of Ghent, SUMMA, a. 60, q. 1, n. 36 ff..

QUESTION IV

Whether the Holy Spirit is unbegotten?

With the difference of generation and procession supposed, there is here asked, fourth, whether the Holy Spirit is unbegotten [ingenitus]. And it seems that (it is) so:

1. *From the authority* of (St.) Jerome, which Master (Peter) puts in the text.[1]

2. Likewise, this very (thing) is shown by *reckoning* of (St.) Jerome:[2] « Because everything which is, either is unbegotten, or begotten, or made »; but the Holy Spirit is not begotten, nor made: therefore, He is unbegotten.

3. Likewise, a privative negation with a constancy of subject is equipollent to a privative term [termino]. Whence 'not equal' [non par] in number is the same as 'unequal' [impar];[3] and, in this manner, since the Holy Spirit is not begotten, therefore, He is unbegotten.

4. Likewise, the Holy Spirit is more distant from the reckoning of generation, than the Father (is), because the Father generates, though He is not generated, but the Holy Spirit neither generates nor is generated: therefore, equally, truly is "being generated" [generatio] lacking from [privatur a] the Holy

Spirit as from the Father: therefore, just as the Father is said (to be) unbegotten, so also the Holy Spirit.

ON THE CONTRARY: 1. (St.) Augustine says (in his letter) to (St. Paulus) Orosius,[4] that « the Father alone is unbegotten »: therefore, according to this (this term) does not befit the Holy Spirit.

2. Likewise, "unbegotten" [ingenitus] is either said according to *substance*, or according to *relation*. If according to *relation*, therefore, it is a notion: therefore, the Holy Spirit has two notions, and thus there would be six (notions in the Trinity), which is contrary to the common opinion. If, according to *substance*: therefore, for an equal reason it would be said of the Son, since that which is said according to substance, convenes with the Three.

3. Likewise, since the Divine Essence is not begotten [ingenita], and the Holy Spirit is not begotten, and the Father is not begotten, and any of These is not made: therefore, the reckoning of '(being) unbegotten' [ratio ingeniti], according to (St.) Jerome, convenes with all; therefore, there is asked, in what manner (does it convene with each) *differently*.[5]

---

[1] Here in ch. 4.

[2] See the text of Master (Peter), ch. 4. — Then some codices, such as A W X Y, have *Because* [Quod] in place of *Because* [Quia].

[3] Cf. Aristotle, ON INTERPRETATION., Bk. II, ch. 1 (ch. 19) and the Commentary of (St. Severinus) Boethius on this passage, where he says: For it is the same to understand what is said (to be) "unjust", as if it were

said (to be) "not just". — A little below with the help of the manuscripts and edition 1 we have inserted *Holy* [sanctus].

[4] See the text of Master (Peter), ch. 4.

[5] We follow many of the codices, by placing *differently* [differenter] in place of *they differ* [differunt]; supply: *does it convene with each* [singulis conveniat].

CONCLUSION

The Holy Spirit can be said (to be) "unbegotten" in the privative sense, but not, to the extent that "unbegotten" is the notion (belonging) to the Father.

I RESPOND: It must be said, that some wanted[1] to distinguish concerning this name, ingenitum ("unbegotten"), which can be written with one (initial) *n*, and thus means only as much as "*unbegotten*" (does); and/or with two (initial n's), and thus is opposed to that which has been properly said (to be) "*begotten*" [genitum]. But this distinction, even if it is valid among the Greeks, it not valid, however, among the Latins, because ingenitum with two (initial) *n's* is not a meaningful word in our language [vox non significativa apud nos]. (St. John) Damascene,[2] however, assigns this difference in his own language, because he was a Greek. *Moreover*, it is not a valid (argument) for the proposed; because nothing here is asked concerning "unbegotten", insofar as it means only as much as "*uncreated*" (does), but insofar as it means only as much as "*not begotten*" or "innascible" (do).

And, on this account, it must be said in another manner, and briefly, that "*unbegotten*", in one manner is accepted *purely privatively*, that is, as 'that which is not generated';[3] and in this manner it is said

of the Holy Spirit and of the Essence; in another manner, insofar as "unbegotten" means only as much as a "*not being from Another*" and[4] a "*from whom the Others (come forth)*"; and in this manner it means the notion of the Father alone, because it means a property and dignity in the Father. And according to the first sense (St.) Jerome speaks, according to the other (St.) Augustine speaks. Whence, moreover, these senses have (their) rise, and for what reason "*innascible*" is a notion and "*improcessible*" (is) not, will be spoken of below.[5]

From these is clear the solution to the *contrariness* (of usages); the objections are also clear.

What, therefore, is objected, that a negation with a constancy of subject is equipollent to a privative term, it is true, if it is *merely*[6] a privative one; but that reckoning concludes only concerning this name according to which *it is privative*, not according to which it *posits* anything.

To that which is objected, "it either predicates[7] the Essence, or a relation"; it must be said, that according to which it is said of the Essence, it is held only privatively or negatively. And for that reason it does not predicate anything, just as where there is said: "the Essence does not generate", (nothing else is meant). All the others[8] have been made manifest.

SCHOLIUM

I. This question seems to have arisen from the diverse manner of speaking, which the most holy Doctors (Sts.) Augustine and Jerome used. St. Bonaventure aptly reconciles their two sentences. Much more concerning the reckoning of innascibility is had below in d. 28, throughout.

II. In regard to the order of the solution for the objections, it must be noted, that the words at the end of the body (of the response): « the objections are also clear » refer to nn. 1, 2, and 4, (and support) the affirmative side. Then he explicitly solves argument n. 3 for the affirmative;

and lastly, he responds to the distinction in the 2nd for the negative.

III. Cf. Alexander of Hales, SUMMA, p. I, q. 69, m. 3. — (Bl. John Duns) Scotus, here in the q. sole, and in d. 28, q. 2. — St. Thomas, here in q. 1, a. 4; SUMMA, I, q. 33, a. 4. — Bl. (now St.) Albertus (Magnus), here in a. 8 ff. — (Bl.) Peter of Tarentaise, here in q. 3, a. 1. — Richard of Middleton, here in q. 4. — Giles the Roman, here in 2nd. princ., q. 2. — Durandus (of Saint-Pourçain), here in q. 3. — (Bl.) Dionysius the Carthusian, here in q. 3.

DOUBTS ON THE TEXT OF THE MASTER

DOUBT I

In the present Distinction there are doubts about the text, and first there is a doubt about the reckoning of (St.) Augustine, which he posits there: *If the Holy Spirit would be said (to be) a "Son", "Son" would at least be said of Both,* and his reckoning seems more for the opposed (argument) than for the proposed: for from this similarly, there would be among creatures a generation, which is out of two.

I RESPOND: It must be said, that although it is more similar as much as regards the duality of (those) producing, there could not, however, as much as regards the manner of producing, be a similitude, because in this manner it would be necessary [oporteret], that One of the two Persons

be a passive principle; but as much as regard this, there can be no[9] similitude.

DOUBT II

Likewise, is asked of this which he says. *Likewise, the Holy Spirit proceeds ... in the manner which (one is) born and/or as the Gift*; because it seems that he speaks badly, because since He has not been given, except in time, it seems that He does not proceed except in time.

I RESPOND: Just as will be clear below,[10] if one understands it of the temporal procession, *given* means the act; but if of the eternal (procession), *given* means the aptitude.

---

[1] In codex V there is added *to say or* [dicere sive].

[2] ON THE ORTHODOX FAITH, Bk. I, ch. 8: For it must be known that the Greek word ἀγένϛον, when it is written with one ν, signifies "uncreated" or "that which is least of all made", but ἀγέννϛον, when it is written with two νν, indicates "that which is not begotten".

[3] The Vatican edition less distinctly, and in disagreement with the manuscripts together with edition 1, reads *that "unbegotten" is said in one manner, insofar as it is accepted privatively, that is, for "that which is not generated"* [quod ingenitum dicitur uno modo, prout accipitur privative, scilicet pro eo quod non generatur].

[4] Codex K reads *as much as a being not from another, but* [quantum ens non ab alio, sed].

[5] Distinction 28, throughout.

[6] Many codices, such as A G H I S T U V W X etc., together with editions 2, 3, 4, 5 and 6, have less well *truly* [vere] in place of *merely* [mere], but edition 1 has *purely* [pure].

[7] Very many codices together with editions 2, 3, 4, 5, and 6, incongruously have *deprives* [privat] in place of *predicates* [praedicat].

[8] From the manuscripts and edition 1, we have supplied *the others* [alia].

[9] Trusting in very many manuscripts and edition 1, we have substituted *no* [nulla] in place of *not* [non].

[10] Distinction 14, a. 1, q. 1.

DOUBT III

Whence, (St.) Augustine responding, thus, to Maximinus, warming up the aforementioned question again.[1] Maximinus warmed up the said question in this manner: 'The Holy Spirit is God, and is not God by being born: therefore, not God naturally: therefore adoptively'. And that this argument is good, seems, because what is in anything naturally, is in it from (its) nativity: therefore, what is not in it from (its) nativity, is not in it naturally: therefore, since the Holy Spirit does not proceed as one born, there is not in Him from a nativity 'that He is God': therefore, He is not God naturally.

And the response of (St.) Augustine to this[2] is, that that argument of his is not valid, except among those which are generated, among others (it is) not. And this is clear, because Adam was by nature a man, just as each of us (are), and, yet, he had through (his) 'being created' [creationem], that which we have through 'being generated' [generationem]; thus God the Father communicates His own Nature to the Holy Spirit through spiration, just as to the Son through generation.

DOUBT IV

Likewise, is asked of this which he says: *The Father is the author of His generation.* For it seems that he speaks badly, because either that which is an "*author*" means *the Essence*, or *a notion*: not *the Essence*, because then it would be said of the Holy spirit; if *a notion*, I ask, *which?* not innascibility, because that one does not mean a looking-back to the procession; likewise, not generation nor spiration, because nothing (then) would be said, as it seems (to be). — Likewise, there is asked, whether the Father could be said (to be) the *author* of the generation? And that (He could) *not*, seems, because the Father is said (to be) the Author of the Son, therefore, just as (St.) Hilary said above and is had in the Ninth Distinction,[3] the sense (of this) is, that He is the *Genitor of the Son*, therefore it would then be the same to say, "*He is the author of the generation*", as "*(He is) the Genitor (of it)*".

I RESPOND: It must be said, that "*author*" means in the Father "fontal plenitude", because He Himself is not from another, but the Others (are) from Him; and hence it means, as I believe, the same notion as "in-

nascible" means, but in a different manner: because "*innascible*" means (the notion)[4] through a privation of (what is) prior, but "*author*" means a fecundity and plenitude in respect of (those) proceeding from Him, which He has from nowhere else; and for that reason there is said "*author*" from "*authorship*". Moreover authorship is in the Father, because what He has, He does not have from another, and this is, what '*innascible*' is,[5] and thus it is clear, that He can be said (to be) "the Author of all the Persons, which are from Him". From these (considerations) the response is clear. For I say, that it means the same notion as innascibility, but in another manner. From this it is clear, that the Son is never said (to be) "the Author of the spiration", though He does spirate, because He does not have (this) from Himself, but from Another; whence an "*author*" properly is said (to be) 'a principle of the other, not from another'.[6]

DOUBT V

Likewise, is asked of this which he says: *How to distinguish between that generation and this procession I know not.* For it seems that such ignorance is a sin, because the distinction of the Persons of necessity belongs to the Faith and to salvation, but he who is ignorant of those things which of necessity belong to the Faith, is damnably ignorant: ergo etc..

I RESPOND: It must be said, that *to know* [scire] is twofold,[7] that is, '*if it is*' and '*just as it is*'. '*To know if it is*'; in this manner is to believe certitudinally that the distinction of necessity belongs to salvation, having taken *to know* in the broad sense. But '*to know just as it is*' does not pertain to the state of merit, but (rather to the state) of reward; and of this knowledge [scientia] Master (Peter) speaks here, and (St.) Augustine (too). And note, that he says three (things): "*I know not*" as much as regards the habit of science; "*I am not able*", as much as regards (his own) genius; "*I do not suffice*", as much as regards each.[8]

DOUBT VI

Likewise is objected concerning this which he says: *He is named "unbegotten", not indeed in the Scriptures, but in the custom of (those) disputing. On the contrary:* Dionysius (the Areopagite says):[9] « One must not

---

[1] That is, a second time and/or urgently *to the one asking, why the Holy Spirit should not be said (to be) the Son, since He is from the substance of the Father.* The words are from the text of Master (Peter), ch. 3. Cf. (St.) Augustine, AGAINST MAXIMINUS, Bk. II, ch. 14 and 15. — The mss. and ed. 1 faultily have *refuting* [refutanti] for *warming up again* [refricanti], just as they also, next, have *refuted* [refutabat] for *warmed up* [refricabat]; the Vatican ed. omits the words *Maximinus ... in this manner:* [Maximinus ... sic].

[2] The Vatican edition, without the authority of the manuscripts and edition 1, has *I respond: It must be said to this, according to (St.) Augustine* [Resp. Dicendum ad hoc secundum Augustinum]. Very many codices ineptly have *the reckoning* [ratio] in place of *the response* [responsio].

[3] In the text of Master (Peter), ch. 4 near the end. — The Vatican edition, disagreeing with the manuscripts and edition 1, has *and* [et] in place of *therefore* [ergo], then it omits *and is had in the Ninth Distinction* [et habetur distinctione nona].

[4] Supply: the notion; the Vatican ed., by not attending to this understanding, contrary to nearly all the codd. and edd., omits *through* [per].

[5] Some codices, such as A T X Z aa and bb, omit *is* [est], which also with edition 1 substitute *because* [quia] in place of *what* [quod].

[6] In these very last words the summation of the solution is contained. For because "*author*" [auctor] does not mean 'any principle of an emanation', but 'such a principle, that whatever it does have, it has not from another', and because this befits the Father alone, for that reason the Father can be said (to be) the Author of the generation (of the Son) and of the procession (of the Holy Spirit). The same is expounded more at length in d. 27, p. I, q. 2, in reply to n. 3, where among other things the Seraphic Doctor says this: Therefore,

since the reckoning of primacy in any genus is the reckoning of the one begun in it, for that reason because the Father is first in respect to the emanation, generation and procession, He generates and spirates. Cf. also d. 2, q. 2, d. 9, Doubt 11, and d. 15, p. II, Doubt 6. — In which manner the Father can be said (to be) *author* is explained also by St. Fulgentius (of Ruspe), FRAGMENT. 35 (Migne's, PATROLOGIA LATINA, tome 65, col. 822), where he says: Indeed, God the Father is not the Author of the Trinity, but He is the Author of the Son and of the Holy Spirit, in this that from Him the Son is born and from Him the Holy Spirit does proceed. For whoever rightly understands the word, "author", will find a name belonging to relation, not to nature. For no one is said to be an "author" of himself, but of the other: whence one is truly named "author" not as regards himself, but as regards the other. Moreover, no one can by any relative name in this manner refer to his own person just as to the other's ... And so we say that God the Father (is) the Author, not of the whole Trinity, but of the Son and of the Holy Spirit: from whom one has the origin both of the eternal nativity of the Only-Begotten Son, and of the eternal procession of the Holy Spirit.

[7] Edition 1 has *in a twofold manner* [dupliciter].

[8] On this last division see above d. 1, a. 1, q. 1, 3rd argument of the fundament.

[9] ON THE DIVINE NAMES, ch. 1, in which text the Vatican edition, contrary to many codices and edition 1, and contrary to the works of Dionysius (the Areopagite), has *Trinity* [Trinitate] in place of *divinity* [divinitate].

dare to say anything of that supersubstantial and holy Divinity except those which have been divinely made clear [claruerunt] to us from the sacred discourses »: therefore, they have done badly, who have invented this name.

I RESPOND: Though that word of theirs is not said in the Scriptures, yet (that which has been) understood by this word is said. And because the word is not profane nor conjoined with error, since the understanding of (its) true (sense) is had from Scripture and by the Faith, it was not against the divine law [contra fas] to attribute it to God, so that by conferring (this name upon Him)[1] we could more openly understand the Trinity Itself.

DOUBT VII

Likewise, is asked of this which Master (Peter) says: *And in another manner (St.) Augustine accepts "unbegotten", as 'one who' and/or 'as something which' ' is not from another';* which means that it befits the Father alone. But this does not seem to be true, because in this manner *unbegotten* befits the Essence: therefore, it is not proper to the Father.

I RESPOND: It must be said, that though Master (Peter) says (what is) understood by (St.) Augustine, yet (he does) not (say it) entirely.[2] For '*unbegotten*', according to which there is meant a property of the Father, is lacking '*being*' *from another*, not is it sufficient for this, that it be a notion, unless it also consequently means, that the other is from Him; because, just as has been objected, '*not being from another*' or '*not being generated*' befits the Essence.[3]

DOUBT VIII

Likewise, against that which (St.) Jerome says: *There is that which is born, and is not made,* Arius objects, that there are twelve manners of generation, of which, with any one granted, it follows, that the Son not only is born, but also made; and he posits these manners, disputing against (Caius Marius) Victorinus (Afer).[4] *The first* manner is through the flowing-down [defluxum] of a line from a point. *The second* is in and through [penes] the immission [immisionem]* of a ray from the Sun and/or from another luminous body. *The third* is in and through the sealing of a character, just as a figure is made in wax by a seal [sigillo]. *The fourth* is in and through immission, as when good will is given by God. *The fifth* is in and through the going-forth [exitum] of a property and/or an accident from the principles of a subject, which are matter and form. *The sixth* is in and through the abstraction of intention or species, just as the species of things is generated in the soul. *The seventh*

is in and through excitation, just as free will [liberum arbitrium] excited by grace proceeds into good works. *The eighth* is in and through transfiguration, just as an statue [statua] is made out of bronze [ex aere], and/or just as in the figure of incision. *The ninth* is in and through production, just as from a prime, immobile, mover movement is produced. *The tenth* is in and through the going-forth of species from[5] a genus through the differences dividing the genus and constituting the species. *The eleventh* is in and through being born [nascentiam], as a man is generated from a man. But in whatsoever of the aforesaid manners the Son is generated, He is[6] not only born, but also made.

To this the response is, that either Arius accepts "generation" *commonly* as regards created and divine, or *specially* in the creature. If *commonly*, I say, that he divides it insufficiently, because beyond those manners (of which he speaks) there is the generation of the Son from the Father according to a singular manner, which[7] is "from the whole substance of the one generating" — just as had been said above in the Ninth Distinction[8] — where, because there cannot be a change, there can be in no manner a making. Moreover, if he divides generation, as it is among creatures, it must be said, that that division is still insufficient, because it omits equivocal generation, which is according to[9] putrefaction. But granted [esto] that he does comprehend that under generation, which is according to being born, however, it still is not valid for the proposed, because, if He is not generated, as a creature is said to be generated, He is in no manner generated. For though a creature be similar to God, yet it is more dissimilar than similar, just as (St.) Augustine says in the fifteenth (book) ON THE TRINITY,[10] and (St.) Jerome[11] similarly: « Every comparison of inferiors is held (to be) more useful to men, than apt to God »; and for that reason the heretics erred, because[12] they used to believe, that it is entirely in God, just as they saw it in the creature. And this is well touched upon in the Gloss on the first (chapter of the Letter) to the Hebrews,[13] where there is said: « Temporals cannot be compared to eternals by a integral collation, but by some tenuous similitude »; and for that reason, just as has been shown above,[14] according to diverse conditions the diverse generations represent that one. For by a reckoning *of conformity* it is similar to the generation of a word from a mind; and by a reckoning *of coevity* (it is) similar to the generation of the splendor from the Sun or from a light; by the reckoning of *equality* (it is similar) to the generation of a living (thing) from a living (thing).[15]

---

[1] Codex Y has instead *by confessing (this name)* [confitendo].

[2] Some codices, such as H M and ff together with edition 1, sufficiently well add the *He does ... say it* [dicit]. Then codices aa and bb have *it is* [est] in place of *there is meant* [dicitur]; edition 1 has *it means a property* [dicit proprietatem].

[3] On the signification of *unbegotten*, see below d. 28, q. 1, and here in q. 4.

[4] The Vatican edition, contrary to very many codices and edition 1, falsely has *Victorianus*. Marius Victorinus, the Rhetor (cf. above d. 1, a. 1, q. 1, in the body of the response), wrote four books against Arius, and disputed with Candid, a defender of Arius, who in his own book, ON THE DIVINE GENERATION, n. 4, proposed these twelve manners of generation.

[5] Trusting in the manuscripts and in three first editions, we have substituted *from* [de] in place of *in* [in].

[6] In the Vatican ed. (in the first clause) there is had an *is* [est: transferred to the first clause, from the second, according to English usage], which, however, is not had in either the mss., nor in edd. 1, 2, 3, and 6.

[7] Many mss., such as A F G H K T V W etc., for *which (manner)* [qui] have

which (generation) [quae]. Edition 1 has *signified* [significatum] for *singular* [singularem].

[8] Question 1. — Then, ed. 1 transposes, reading *because, where* [quia ubi].

[9] Edition 1 has *through* [per] instead of *according to* [secundum].

[10] Chapter 20, n. 39.

[11] ON THE TRINITY, Bk. I, n. 10. — The Vatican ed., not trusting in the mss. and ed. 1, with a changed punctuation, confounds everything by reading *and (St.) Hilary. Similarly, when every* etc. [et Hilarius. Similiter cum omnis etc.].

[12] We prefer the reading of the more ancient manuscripts and of edition 1, by placing *because they* [quia] in place of *who* [qui]. Then codex E after *entirely* [omnino] adds *similar* [simile].

[13] Verse 3. See the Gloss in (Nicolas) of Lyra, on the passage cited, in which after *tenuous* [tenui] there is added *and tiny* [parva].

[14] Distinction 9, q. 1, and Doubt 10.

[15] Cf. HEXAËMERON, Sermon 11. You can find nearly the same words in Alexander of Hales, SUMMA, p I, q. 42, m. 5, a. 3; in Bl. (now St.) Albertus (Magnus' Commentary), here in a. 5, and in Richard (of Middleton), here on the text (of Master Peter).

---

* *Trans. note*: Immission differs from *emission* in that the latter speaks only of diffusion *from* a diffusive source, whereas the former speaks of the projection of that diffusion *upon* an object; though archaic, the English cognates *immit, immission* etc. retain thus the same sense of the Latin verb immittere in all its forms.

DISTINCTION XIV

CHAPTER I

*On the twin procession of the Holy Spirit:
the temporal and eternal.*

Moreover, it must be diligently noted down,[1] that there is a twin procession of the Holy Spirit, namely, the eternal, which is ineffable, by which He proceeds from the Father and the Son eternally and without time, and the temporal, by which He proceeds from the Father and the Son to sanctify a creature. And just as He proceeds from eternity, commonly and at once, from the Father and the Son, so also in time, commonly and at once, from Each He proceeds to a creature Whence (St.) Augustine in the fifteenth book, ON THE TRINITY[2] says: « The Holy Spirit does not proceed from [de] the Father unto the Son and from the Son to sanctify a creature, but proceeds at once from Each; though this the Father has given to the Son, that just as from Himself, so also from Him does (the Holy Spirit) proceed ».

Moreover, of the temporal procession (St.) Bede (the Venerable) speaks thus in (his) HOMILY FOR THE FIRST SUNDAY AFTER THE ASCENSION:[3] « When the grace of the Holy Spirit is given to men, the Spirit is indeed sent from [a] the Father, He is also sent from the Son; He proceeds from the Father, He proceeds also from the Son, because His being sent [missio] is the procession itself ». With these words he openly shows, that the donation of the grace of the Holy Spirit is said (to be) the procession and/or mission of the Same. But since the donation and/or[4] giving is not but temporal, it is established, that this procession or mission is also temporal. (St.) Augustine also hints at this temporal procession of the Holy Spirit in the fifteenth book, ON THE TRINITY,[5] saying in these words, that the Holy spirit proceeded from Christ, when after the Resurrection He breathed upon the Disciples: « When Christ had risen from the dead and appeared to the Disciples, He breathed upon (them) and said:[6] *Accept the Holy Spirit*, to show that He proceeds also from Himself. And He Himself is *the Virtue*, which *used to go forth from Him*, as is read in the Gospel, *and He used to cure all* ». And to show, that this procession of the Holy Spirit is not other than the donation and/or giving of the Holy Spirit Himself, he added:[7] « After the Resurrection the Lord Jesus twice gave the Holy Spirit: once on Earth for the sake of the love [dilectionem] of neighbor, and again from Heaven for the sake of the love

of God; because through the Gift Himself (that) *charity is poured out in our hearts*, by which we love God and neighbor ».

CHAPTER II

That not only the gifts of the Holy Spirit, but also the Holy Spirit Himself is given and sent to men.

Moreover, there are some,[8] who say, that the Holy Spirit, God Himself, is not given, but His gifts, which are not the Spirit Himself. And as they say, the Holy Spirit is said to be given, when His grace, which, however, is not Himself,[9] is given to men. And this they say Bede thought in the words above, with which he says, that the Holy Spirit proceeds, when His grace is given to men, not as if His very Self is given, but His grace. But that the Holy Spirit Himself, who is God and the Third Person in the Trinity, is given, (St.) Augustine openly shows in the fifteenth book, ON THE TRINITY,[10] saying thus: « That the same Holy Spirit (has been) given, when Jesus breathed upon (them), concerning whom He then said: *Go, baptize all the nations in the Name of the Father and of the Son and of the Holy Spirit*, we ought not doubt. He Himself is, therefore, the One who has been given from Heaven on Pentecost Day.[11] In what manner, therefore, is God not the one who gives the Holy Spirit? nay how much is God the one who gives God »? Behold with these words he openly says, that the Holy Spirit, that is God Himself, is given to men by the Father and[12] the Son. And that the Holy Spirit Himself, who is God and the Third Person in the Trinity, is given to us and poured fourth and glides into our minds, (St.) Ambrose openly shows in the first book, ON THE HOLY SPIRIT,[13] saying: « Though many are said (to be) spirits, because there is written: *Who makes spirits His Angels*, one, however, is the Spirit of God. Therefore, the One Spirit Himself have both the Apostles and Prophets sought out; just as also the Vessel of Election says,[14] that *we have drunk of one Spirit*, as the One, who is not able to be torn, but is poured forth into souls and glides into the senses, to restrain the ardor of thirst for this age [saecularis sitis]; which Holy Spirit is not from [de] the substance of corporals[15] nor of the substance of invisible creatures ». With these words he openly says, that the Holy Spirit Himself, who is not a creature, is poured forth in our minds. Likewise, in the same (work he says):[16] « Every creature is mutable, but the Holy Spirit (is) not mutable ». « Why,

---

[1] Edition 2 has *noted* [notandum] for *noted down* [adnotandum].

[2] Chapter 27, n. 48. — A little before this codex D has *to sanctify a creature* [ad creaturam sanctificandam] for *to a creature* [ad creaturam].

[3] Book II, Homily 10.

[4] Editions 1 and 8 have *or* [sive] and then after *it is established* [constat], edition 2 has *that* [quod] in place of *that* [quia].

[5] Chapter 26, n. 48. — The Vatican edition and editions 4 and 6, after *saying in these words* [his verbis dicens], have *the Holy Spirit proceeded* [Spiritus sanctus processit] for *that the Holy Spirit proceeded* [Spiritum sanctum processisse].

[6] John 20:22. — The following text from Sacred Scripture is the Gospel of St. Luke 6:19.

[7] Loc. cit., n. 46; but with not a few (words) transposed and/or omitted.

[8] Codices A C D and E have *others* [alii]; codex B omits both *some* and *others*. Then codices A and D omit *Holy ... God Himself* [sanctum ipsum Deum].

[9] Only the Vatican ed. and ed. 4 adds *who* [qui] and thus changes the construction. Then, codd. A & D and ed. 8 have *to a man* [homini] for *to men*

[hominibus]. — In the following proposition the Vatican edition and editions 4, 6 and 9, have *Himself* [ipse] for *His very Self* [ipsemet].

[10] Chapter 26, n. 26. — Immediately before this, contrary to the codices and to editions 1 and 8, the Vatican edition, together with the other editions, has *says* [dicit] for *shows* [ostendit]. — The text of Scripture is Mt. 28:19. The Vulgate reads: *Going, therefore, teach all the nations, baptizing* etc. [Euntes ergo docete omnes gentes, baptizantes etc.].

[11] Acts, chapter 2.

[12] The Vatican edition, with not a few edd. and codd. C & D, repeats *by* [a].

[13] Chapter 4, nn. 60-62. — The next passage from Scripture is Psalm 103:4.

[14] 1 Cor. 12:13: *And all of us have drunk in the one Spirit* [Et omnes in uno Spiritu potati sumus]. — A little after this in place of *restrain* [restringat] there is read in the original *slake* [restinguat] contrary to our manuscripts and the editions.

[15] The Vatican edition and the other editions, contrary to the codices and the original, add *things* [rerum]; editions 1 and 8 have *nature* [natura] in place of *substance* [substantia].

[16] Ibid., n. 64; the second passage from (St.) Ambrose is ibid., n. 66; the third, n. 72, the fourth, ch. 7, nn. 82 and 81.

moreover, do I doubt to say, that the Holy Spirit is also given, since there is written:[1] *The charity of God has been poured forth in our hearts through the Holy Spirit, who has been given to us*? « Who, though He be inaccessible by nature, is, yet, receivable by us on account of His own Goodness, completing every virtue, but who is shared by the just alone, simple in Substance, opulent in virtues, present to each one, *distributing* [dividens] from His own *to each*[2] and Whole everywhere ». « Therefore, uncircumscribed and infinite (is)[3] the Holy Spirit, who infuses the senses of the separate Disciples, Whom nothing can deceive. Angels used to be sent to a few, but the Holy Spirit used to infuse peoples. Who, therefore, doubts, that it is a divine (work), that He is infused in many at once and (yet) is not seen (by any)? One is the Holy Spirit, who has been given to all the Apostles, though separate ». And here (St.) Ambrose openly says, that the Holy Spirit, who is simple in Substance, since He is one, is given to many. By another authority this same is built up, namely, that the Holy Spirit, who is equal to the son, is given to men. For (St.) Augustine[4] says of the words of the Apostle: « If *the charity of God has been poured forth in our hearts through the Holy Spirit, who has been given to us*: by whom is He given? By Him, who *gives gifts to men*. What gifts? The Holy Spirit, who gives such a gift, as He Himself is. Great is His Mercy: He gives a gift equal to Himself, because the Holy Spirit is His own gift ». With the[5] aforementioned authorities and very many others there is openly shown, that the Holy Spirit, equal to the Father and the Son, is given to us; and for that reason He is not less than the Father or the Son. Whence (St.) Augustine in the fourth book, ON THE TRINITY (says): « Not for that reason »,[6] he says, « is one to judge that the Holy Spirit (is) lesser, because both the Father and the Son have sent Him ».

CHAPTER III

Whether or not holy men could give the Holy Spirit.

Here, there is asked, whether holy men also give and/or could give to others the Holy Spirit. Whom if they do give to others, since His 'being given' [donatio] has been said above (to be His) procession, it seems that the Holy Spirit proceeds and/or is sent from them; but the Creator does not proceed from the creature nor is He sent. Therefore, it remains, that these do not give the Holy spirit nor could they give (Him). Whence (St.) Augustine in the fifteenth book, ON THE TRINITY (says):[7] « None of the disciples of Christ gave the Holy Spirit.

They used to pray, indeed, *that He might come upon them*, on whom they used to impose a hand, they themselves did not use to give Him. Which custom the Church now also observes among Her own overseers [praepositis]. Next, even Simon Magus, offering money to the Apostles, did not say: *Give to me also this power, that I may give the Holy Spirit*; but, (so that) *to whomsoever*, he say, *I shall impose hands, he may receive the Holy Spirit*; because neither did Scripture say above: "but Simon seeing, that the Apostles gave the Holy Spirit", but (rather) it said: *but Simon seeing, that through the imposition of the hands of the Apostles the Holy Spirit was given* ». Behold with these words (St.) Augustine shows, that neither the Apostles nor the other prelates of the Church gave and/or give the Holy Spirit.

And what is more, he says, that one cannot even give (Him), subjoining in the same book:[8] « Of Christ it is written, that *He accepted from the Father the promises of the Holy Spirit and poured (Him) forth*; in which each nature has been demonstrated, that is, the human and the divine. *He accepted*, indeed, as a man, *He poured forth* as God. Moreover, we can indeed *accept* this Gift in our own little measure [pro modulo nostro], but *to pour (Him) forth* upon others we certainly [utique] cannot do, but we invoke God upon us, so that this may come to pass, by Him whom it is effected ». With these words he[9] expressly says, that we cannot pour forth the Holy Spirit upon others, that is, give (Him) to others.

But, to this, there seems contrary what the Apostle, speaking of himself, says to the Galatians:[10] *who granted you the Spirit, and who works virtues among you.* Behold evidently he says, that he granted the Spirit. But it must be understood, that the Apostle spoke this, not because he had the power and authority to give the Holy Spirit, but because he had the ministry, in which the Holy Spirit is given by God. For, as (St.) Augustine says on the same passage, expounding that word of the Apostle:[11] « From the Apostle the Faith has been preached to them, in which preaching they had sensed the advent and presence of the Holy Spirit, just as at that time in the newness of the invitation to the Faith the presence of the Holy Spirit appeared even by sensible miracles, as is read in the Acts of the Apostles ». Here he openly shows, in what manner the Apostle granted the Holy Spirit to them, certainly [utique] not by sending Him upon them, but by preaching the Faith of Christ to them, which (faith), by some visible signs, showed those receiving (it), that the Holy Spirit was in them. Therefore, men, cannot give the Holy Spirit, howsoever holy (they may be).

---

[1] Rom. 5:5. — A little before this the Vatican edition, and editions 8 and 9, omit *also* [et] at *Holy Spirit* [Spiritus sanctus].

[2] A reference to 1 Cor. 12:11. — At the beginning of this passage from (St.) Ambrose, the codd. and ed. 6 have receptabilis for receptibilis (i. e. receivable). A little after this the Vatican ed. alone has *embracing* [complectens] for *completing* [complens]. Then ed. 8 has *opulent* [opulentus] for *opulent* [opulens].

[3] The Vatican edition and editions 1, 4, 5, 6, and 9 add *is* [est]. — Near the end of this passage, codex D has *and is not divided* [nec dividitur] for *and (yet) is not seen (by any)* [nec videtur]; which reading, though it is good in itself, is however, contrary to the text and the context of (St.) Ambrose and contrary to the editions and to the other codices. — Immediately after this, codex D, the Vatican edition and editions 3, 4, 5, 6, and 9, add to the words *One is* [unus est], *therefore* [ergo].

[4] Sermon 128, n. 4 (previously 43); but Master (Peter) transposes and omits various words. — The Vatican edition and editions 1, 5, 6, 8, and 9, badly and contrary to the codices, puts in the text in place of the words *the words of the Apostle* [verbis Apostoli] the words *the words of the Lord* [verbis Domini], though Master (Peter) does not here cite the book of (St.) Augustine, but indicates the words of the Apostle; moreover, contrary to edd. 1 & 8, the Vatican ed. and the other edd. have *Thus*

[sic] for *If* [si]. The words of Scripture are Rm 5:5 and Eph. 4:8 : *He gave gifts to men* [dedit dona hominibus].

[5] The Vatican edition and editions 4, 5, 6, 8, and 9, add *these* [his].

[6] Chapter 21, n. 32. — Then the Vatican edition and editions 2, 3, 4, 6, 7, and 9 superfluously insert *said* [ait] after *Trinity* [Trinitate]. Next, at *lesser* [minorem] only editions 1 and 8 add *is* [esse].

[7] Chapter 26, n. 46. — The reference by (St.) Augustine is to Acts 8:15-19.

[8] Ibid., a little below the former. The citation by (St.) Augustine is Acts 2:33.

[9] Codex D adds *(St.) Augustine* [Augustinus].

[10] Gal. 3:3.

[11] EXPOSITION ON THE EPISTLE TO THE GALATIANS, n. 20. The Vatican edition alone adds, here, the remaining words of the Apostle, from the same verse 5: *Out of the works of the Law have you accepted the Spirit, or out of the hearing of the Faith ?* [Ex operibus legis Spiritum accepistis, an ex auditu fidei ?], to which words of (St.) Augustine the things, which follow immediately, refer. — On the visible mission of the Holy Spirit, see Acts, chapter 2.

COMMENTARY ON DISTINCTION XIV

On the temporal procession of the Holy Spirit, as much as regards (its) principle from which.

Moreover, it must be diligently noted down, that there is a twin procession of the Holy Spirit.

THE DIVISION OF THE TEXT

Having finished the part, which concerns the eternal procession, here begins the second part, which concerns the temporal procession. And, since in this procession it is that one considers three (things), namely, the *principle from which* the Holy Spirit proceeds, and the *manner according to which*, and the *property through*[1] *which* as One apt He is bound [natus est] to proceed: for that reason this part has three parts, in *the first* of which Master (Peter) deals with the temporal procession through a comparison *to the principle from which*; in *the second* he deals with it in comparison to *the manner according to which*, below, in the fifteenth distinction, near the middle, there (where he says): *Here there is asked, whether the Son has only been sent once;*[2] in *the third* through a comparison to *the property through which* He is bound [natus est] to proceed temporally, and this is "gift" or donability, below, in the eighteenth distinction, at the beginning: *Here there is asked, why the Holy Spirit, through whom gifts are divided.*

The first part again has two (parts): in *the first* part he shows,[3] that the Holy Spirit is sent or proceeds temporally from the Father and the son; *second* there is asked, whether He is sent or proceeds from Himself, below, in the fifteenth distinction, at the beginning: *Here there must be considered, since the Holy Spirit is given to men by the Father and the Son.*

The first part belongs to the present distinction and has two parts: in the first he shows, that He proceeds temporally from the Father and the Son; in the second he asks,[4] whether the Holy Spirit is given by holy men, there: *Here there is asked, whether holy men also give and/or could give* etc..

In *the first* part, he again makes three (divisions) according to the three chapters.[5] In the first he shows, that there is a twin procession of the Holy Spirit; in the second, that each procession is from the Father and the Son, there (where he says): *Moreover, of the temporal procession (St.) Bede (the Venerable) speaks thus in (his) Homily* etc.; in the third, because the temporal procession of the Holy Spirit is a being-bestowed [donatio], he shows, that the Holy Spirit Himself is bestowed in His own Person, not only in effect, there (where he says): *Moreover, there are some, who say, that the Holy Spirit.*

Here, there is asked, whether holy men also given and/or could give. This is the *second* part of the present distinction,[6] in which, having shown that the Holy Spirit proceeds temporally or is bestowed by the Father and the Son, Master (Peter) asks, whether He is given by any holy man. And this part has three parts according to the three (divisions) which he shows. For first he declares and proves, that he Holy Spirit *is* not *given* by any holy man. But second he shows by the authority of (St.) Augustine, that *He can* not *be given*, there (where he says): *And what is more, he says that one cannot even give (Him)* etc.. In the third he opposes to the Contrary, that He seems (to have been) given by (St.) Paul, there (where he says): *But to this seems contrary what the Apostle* etc., where he resolves, that He has not been given by him, but by his ministry.[7]

TREATMENT OF THE QUESTIONS

For an understanding of those (things), which are said in the present distinction, two (things) are principally asked.

First, one asks concerning the temporal procession of the Holy Spirit.

Second, concerning His 'being given' [donatione].

As much as regards the first two (things) are asked.

First, there is asked,[8] whether it is, that one posits a temporal procession of the Holy Spirit.

Second, whether the temporal procession adds [ponat] in number with the eternal (procession).

---

[1] Some codices, such as W X and Z, have *according to* [secundum] instead of *through* [per].

[2] The Vatican edition, with the manuscripts and edition 1 striving against it, falsely exhibits the beginning of distinction 16 thus: *Now of the Holy Spirit it must be seen* etc. [Nunc de Spiritu sancto videndum est].

[3] Edition 1 has *is shown* [ostenditur].

[4] The Vatican edition has *there is asked* [quaeritur], but contrary to the manuscripts and edition 1.

[5] From the manuscripts and edition 1, we have substituted *three chapters* [tria capitula] in place of *three parts* [tres partes].

[6] The Vatican edition, not trusting in the manuscripts and edition 1, thus exhibits the preceding proposition: *Similarly the second part, which begins there: Here there is asked, whether holy men also give* etc. [Similiter secunda pars, quae incipit ibi: Hic quaeritur utrum et sancti viri dent].

[7] Codex K has *through his ministry* [per eius ministerium]; codex Y has *in* [in] in place of *by* [ab].

[8] From the more ancient manuscripts and edition 1, we have supplied *First, there is asked* [Primo quaeritur]; some codices however, omit the *there is asked* [quaeritur].

ARTICLE I

On the temporal procession of the Holy Spirit.

QUESTION I

Whether there is to be posited a temporal procession of the Holy Spirit?

That there is to be posited a temporal procession, seems (from the following):

1. Through (St.) Bede (the Venerable), who says in (his) Homily, and (as) there is had in the text:[1] « The 'being sent' [missio] of the Holy Spirit is His procession »; but His mission is temporal: therefore, it is, that one posits a temporal procession of the Holy Spirit.

2. Likewise, this very (thing) is shown *by reason* in this manner: "to proceed" is a 'from one into another'; therefore, since the Holy Spirit is from God and is in a creature, and in the creature He is from God,[2] He proceeds from God into the creature; but this is not, before the creature is, but this is in time [ex tempore]: ergo etc..

3. Likewise, a gift or (something) given by one giving (it) proceeds into the one accepting (it), when it is given; but the Holy Spirit is given in time: therefore, in time He proceeds from the One giving into the one receiving:[3] therefore, it is, that one posits a temporal procession.

ON THE CONTRARY: 1. The procession of the Holy Spirit is the same (thing) which His spiration (is); but His spiration is not said (to be) anything temporal: therefore neither the procession.

2. Likewise, just as the procession holds itself to the Holy Spirit, in the same manner the generation to the Son, and according to the manner in which the Holy Spirit is sent into the mind, so[4] the Son, and Each in time; but the generation of the Son by reason of such a mission is in no manner said (to be) temporal: therefore, neither the procession of the Holy Spirit.

3. Likewise, the procession of the Holy Spirit is not said (to be) temporal, except according to which it is a procession from something into something, as for example [utpote] into a creature; but a procession from something into something is not but in a twofold manner: either according to a processing from something acting into something taking-it-up [ab agente in suscipiens], or according to a processing from place into place. But in the first manner the procession *is not* temporal, because the Holy Spirit is a Person in Himself, fixed and standing still [stans]: therefore, He is not produced in the one taking-Him-up.[5] In the second manner (it is) not (also), because whatever proceeds in such a manner, recedes from (its) principle and accedes to the terminus; but this is not befitting to the Holy Spirit.

4. Likewise, everything which proceeds temporally from another, has a start of being in time [initium essendi ex tempore]; if, therefore, the Holy Spirit proceed temporally, therefore, His[6] '*being*' began.

5. Likewise, the temporal procession is either said (to be) temporal by reason *of the Holy Spirit* or[7] *of a grace*: not by reason *of the Holy Spirit*, because the Person is eternal; similarly it seems, that neither by reason *of a grace*, because (St.) Augustine says in the fourth (book) ON THE TRINITY:[8] « According to which we grasp anything eternal with (our) mind, we are not in this world »: therefore, if grace elevates one to grasp His eternal '*being*', and the procession is not temporal, therefore, neither (is) the procession of the Holy Spirit (temporal) by reason *of a grace*.

6. Likewise, in the procession of the Holy Spirit into a creature there is a procession of the uncreated Gift, which the Holy Spirit is, and of the created gift, which is a grace; but the uncreated Gift is more noble; therefore, since a *denomination* ought to come to be *from the more noble*,[9] the procession of the Holy Spirit into a creature ought to be said (to be) an uncreated procession, but every such is eternal, not temporal: ergo etc..

CONCLUSION

There is to be posited a temporal procession of the Holy Spirit not by reason of That, from whom He proceeds, but by reason of that, into which He proceeds as into (something) susceptive, in which He is received.

I RESPOND: It must be said, that "procession" [processio], according to which it is *commonly* accepted of the Son and of the Holy Sprit, is said (to be) an emanation from Him, that is from the Father, (and) according to which it is said of *the Holy Spirit*, it is said (to be) a procession from One unto the Other. But "proceeding from one unto another" is in a two fold manner: either just as unto *the object*, unto which it is extended forward [protenditur], or just as into *(something) susceptive*, in which *it is received*. And *the first* manner is, indeed, in the eternal procession; for because the Holy Spirit proceeds as mutual Love, for that reason He proceeds from the Two, so that (He proceeds) from One unto Another. « For the Holy Sprit », as (St.) Jerome[10] says and (St.) Augustine (too), « is the Love, by which the Father loves the Son and the Son loves the Father ». *The second* man-

---

[1] Here, in ch. 1, in which text, trusting in the manuscripts and edition 1, we have inserted *His* [eius].

[2] Thus the codices together with edition 1, while the Vatican edition faultily omits *and in the creature He is from God* [et in creatura sit a Deo]. A little before this codex K for phrase *a "from one into another"* [ab uno in alium] has *"to tend from one into another and/or be from one in another"* [ab uno in alium tendere vel a b uno in alio esse].

[3] Very many codices, such as F G and H together with edition 1, have *into the one accepting* [in accipientem].

[4] In not a few manuscripts, such as K bb ff and edition 1, there is added *also* [et].

[5] On the authority of the manuscripts and editions 1, 2, 3, we have expunged here in the Vatican edition the added *but in Himself* [sed in se]. A little before this codex W adds to the first clause, just before the comma, *in respect to the Holy Spirit; for He is a Person* [respectu Spiritus sancti; est enim persona]; but codex Y, in reference to the first manner, inserts *in such a manner* [tali modo] before *a Person* [persona].

[6] In the Vatican edition and codex dd the *His* [eius] is wanting, which however, is had in the other manuscripts and in edition 1.

[7] Codex M here repeats *by reason* [ratione].

[8] Chapter 20, n. 28.

[9] Cf. the Seraphic Doctor's discussion of the Foreword to Book I, q. 4, arg. 2 ad opp.

[10] COMMENTARY ON PSALM 17. — (St.) Augustine, ON THE TRINITY, Bk. VI, ch. 5, n. 7. See above the text of Master (Peter), d. 10, ch. 2. — The preceding words: He proceeds "from One into Another" are to be understood according to what is said in d. 13, a. 1, q. 1, in reply to n. 4.

ner cannot be in that (eternal emanation),[1] though thus did the Greeks understand, that the Holy Spirit is received by the Son and produced from the Father. But in and through [penes] that second manner — since the reception of the Holy Spirit is through the influence of a gratuitous gift,[2] which is in time — a *temporal* procession is attained, according to which the Holy Spirit is said to proceed from Someone into someone, not only as into an object, but as into a tiny dwelling. And in this manner it is to be conceded, that there is a temporal procession of the Holy Spirit, not by reason of That *from which*, but by reason of that *into which* He proceeds.

1. 2. To that, therefore, which is objected concerning spiration and generation, the response is already clear, that neither of those names means a looking-back to[3] the terminus, into which the procession is made.

3. To that which is objected, that the procession of the Holy Spirit cannot be from something into something,[4] as into (something) susceptive; it must be said, that it is true by reason of the Person Himself; but, however, by reason of the (thing) connoted, which is the grace, in which the Holy Spirit is given, He is taken up, because the grace is in someone as in (something) susceptive.

4. To that which is objected: 'what proceeds temporally begins to be'; it must be said, that this is in a twofold manner,[5] because this determination, *temporally*, can be posited about an act of proceeding through a comparison to the *principle from which*, and/or in comparison to the *terminus unto which*. In *the first* manner, the proposition is true; but the Holy[6] Spirit is not said "to proceed temporally" in this manner, for this (reason) that He is produced in time. In *another* manner, through a comparison to the *terminus into which*; thus[7] (the proposition) does not have truth, if 'He proceeds in this (manner) in time, because He has a starting-point [initium]', but only, 'because He begins to be in this (manner)'.

5. To that which is objected, that grace does not proceed temporally, because it elevates to eternity; it must be said, that the *"temporal"* is said in a threefold manner. In *one* manner, the "temporal" is said (to be) that which has a start [initium] and variation and an act in time [in tempore]; and in this manner the "temporal" is said (to be) that which is subjected to time and is corruptible and variable. In the *second* manner, the "temporal" is said (to be) that which has a start of being in time [initium essendi in tempore],[8] but not a variation, such as the soul. In the *third* manner, the "temporal" is said (to be) that which has a start in time, but an act outside of time and elevated above time; and in this third manner there is said (to be) a temporal procession and/or donation of grace.

It can, however, be said, that grace has a temporal "being" by reason of that in which it is, namely, (by reason) of free will [liberii arbitrii],[9] which is changed and is varied; and the word of (St.) Augustine, which says, that we are not in this world, is to be understood as much as regards conformity.

6. To that which is objected, that a denomination ought to be from the more worthy (part); it must be said, that a whole copulate, because it is destroyed by the destruction of any part, has its denomination from the more imperfect part. Whence, if one part of the copulate [copulationis] is *false*, the whole copulate is said to be false: if one *contingent*, the whole is indicated as contingent; if one temporal, the whole (is) temporal.[10] Therefore, because the temporal procession includes the eternal emanation of the Person and the emanation of a grace, which is temporal, for that reason it is said (to be) temporal and not eternal.

And because[11] it is said, that a denomination ought to come to be from the more worthy (part): it must be said, that it is not true, except in that, in which that which is less worthy, is conformed to the more worthy.

SCHOLIUM

I. Having posited this principle, 'that in a procession of love, besides the principle *from which* there is also the terminus *to which*' — because love tends into the other, whence it is in the one loving as in a subject, but in the one loved as in an object or terminus — the very terminus of the procession is distinguished. For either it is simply the object or terminus, or it is something susceptive, i. e. such a subject, that it receives something. This

second manner on account of its imperfection does not befit the Divine Persons considered [spectatis] in Themselves, yet it is found in the temporal mission, to the extent that the rational creature through a grace becomes a little dwelling of the Holy Spirit. For then the Holy Spirit begins to be anew in this creature and/or to be in manner other, than that which He was beforehand; through which, as Richard of Middleton (here in q. 1) says, « there is conveyed

---

[1] In edition 1 there is added as an explanation *eternal emanation* [aeterna emanatione], in which a little below this, together with some mss., such as aa & bb, it also has the subjunctive forms for *is received*, and *is produced*. At the end of this proposition, the Vatican ed., having omitted the punctuation, continues the sentence with the following one.

[2] We follow the very many codices, such as H I aa bb and ee together with edition 1, by placing *gift* [doni] for *good* [boni], which corresponds to the third argument in the beginning of this question. A little below this from the more ancient manuscripts and edition 1, we have substituted *according to that which* [secundum quod] in place of *according to which (procession)* [secundum quam].

[3] From codex Z and edition 1, we have substituted *to* [ad] for the less apt preposition *into* [in], which also recurring immediately after, perhaps offered the occasion of exchanging one for the other.

[4] We have supplied the *into something* [in aliquid], which is required also by the context and confirmed by its being placed in the very objection above, and not without the authority of codex Z. Then trusting in the more ancient manuscripts and edition 1, we have placed *susceptive* [susceptivum] for *receptive* [receptivum].

[5] The reading of the Vatican ed., *that this (procession) is twofold* [quod haec est duplex] is emended with the help of the mss. and ed. 1.

[6] The older codices together with edition 1 exhibit the *Holy* [sanctus], omitted by the Vatican edition and by codex cc.

[7] Edition 1 reads *and thus* [et sic], which also a little after this together with some manuscripts, such as A aa and cc, has the subjunctive form for *He proceeds*.

[8] The Vatican edition, contrary to the more ancient codices and to edition 1, has less well, with transposed words, *a start of being in time* [initium in tempore essendi].

[9] We have substituted, trusting in the manuscripts, on account of abbreviation there are many dubious readings, and in edition 1, and not without the requirements of the grammatical construction, *(by reason) of free will* for *free will* [liberum arbitrium]. — For an explanation of the words of (St) Augustine see below in d. 15, p. II, Doubt 5.

[10] The same is expressed for the syllogism according to the following rule: the conclusion always follows the worse part, i. e. if one of the premises was particular or negative, the conclusion will be particular or negative. — A little before this after *is said* [dicitur] we exhibit the reading of very many manuscripts by adding the *to be* [esse], which the Vatican edition omits, together with edition 1 and one or the other of the codices. Edition 1 together with codex aa has *is judged* [iudicatur] in place of the *is said* [dicitur], in place of which codex V has *will be* [erit] and codex Y *is* [est].

[11] Codex Y has *if* [si] for *because* [quod].

a new real habitude of the terminus to the Holy Spirit, to which there corresponds a new habitude according to our manner of speaking [secundum dici] in the Holy Spirit to the terminus itself. Thus since such a habitude is on account of time [ex tempore], I say, that according to this habitude and/or by reason of this habitude the Holy Spirit proceeds in time [ex tempore] ».

II. So that the solution to n. 2 be understood better, one must suppose, what the same Richard (loc. cit. ad 1) says: « It is not similar concerning generation and procession, because generation conveys only a habitude to the principle *from which*, but the procession of the Holy Spirit not only conveys a habitude to the principle *from which*, but also to the terminus *to which*. Moreover, a Divine Person cannot convey a habitude to anything temporal, as to a principle *from which*; therefore, there cannot be any (temporal) generation of a Divine Person except by reason of a human nature, which is not eternal etc. ».

III. For a more ample elucidation of this Question, see what follows in this article and the following two questions. Cf. also BREVILOQUIUM p. I, c. 5; COMMENTARY ON THE GOSPEL OF ST. JOHN, chs. 1 and 34. (in Bonelli's Supplement, tom. I.). Alexander of Hales, SUMMA. p. I, q. 71, m. 2; and in q. 73 , m. 1. — (Bl. John Duns) Scotus, on this and the following question in either writing, here in the q. sole. — St. Thomas, here in q. 1, a. 1 and 2.; SUMMA., I, q. 43, aa. 1, 2, 6 and 7. — Bl. (now St.) Albertus (Magnus), here in aa. 1 and 10; SUMMA. I, tr. 7, q. 32, m. 1. — (Bl.) Peter of Tarentaise, here in q. 1, aa. 1 and 2. — Richard of Middleton, here in a. 1, q. 1. — Giles the Roman, here in 1st. princ., q. 1. — Henry of Ghent., on this and the following question, SUMMA., a. 61, q. 2, n. 6; and q. 10, n. 6 ff. — Durandus (of Saint-Pourçain), here in q. 1. — (Bl.) Dionysius the Carthusian, here in q. 1. — (Gabriel) Biel, on this and the following question, here in q. 1.

QUESTION II

Whether the eternal procession of the Holy Spirit and the temporal one are numbered as two processions?

Second, there is asked, whether the temporal procession counts [ponat] in number with the eternal. And that it is, seems:

1. Through this, which Master (Peter) says,[1] « that there is a *twin* procession of the Holy Spirit, the eternal and the temporal ».

2. Likewise, *by reason* it seems similarly, because the temporal is more distant[2] from the eternal than the eternal from the eternal; that is established; but an eternal procession with (another) eternal (procession) increases [facit] the number, because the procession of the Son and the procession of the Holy Spirit are two (processions): ergo etc..

3. Likewise, whatsoever (things) have an order, have a number and a distinction; but the eternal and temporal procession have an order, because the eternal (is)[3] before the temporal: therefore, they have a distinction; therefore they increase the number: therefore, the temporal and eternal procession are two (processions).

ON THE CONTRARY: 1. With the processions numbered, the one proceeding is numbered, because one and the same does not proceed twice; therefore, if there are two processions, there are two proceeding: therefore, there are two Holy Spirits;[4] but this is false, because the Holy Spirit proceeding is One: therefore also the first (proposition is false).

2. Likewise, the temporal procession and the eternal, if they differ, either this is from this, that they are diverse emanations, or because (there is) a diverse manner of emanating. Not because (they are) diverse emanations, because then there would be diverse (ones) emanating; nor because a diverse manner, because the Father and the Son spirate always in one manner: therefore, the Holy Spirit always[5] proceeds in one manner: ergo etc..

3. Likewise, a man depicted and a true man are not two men; for they are not numbered except univocally, and because ("man") is said of the two according to (their) one nature;[6] but the temporal and eternal communicate less than a man depicted and a true man: therefore, the temporal procession and the eternal are not to be said (to be) *twin* (processions).

4. Likewise, the temporal procession does not add (anything) above the eternal except a looking-back and/or effect in the creature;[7] but a looking-back and/or effect, added to a cause, does not number it: whence the Sun shining [lucens] and the Sun enlightening [illustrans] or illumining are not two (Suns), similarly God being and God creating: therefore, neither shall the eternal procession and the temporal be twofold.[8]

CONCLUSION

According to an analogous manner of speaking the eternal and temporal procession of the Holy Spirit is not unfittingly said (to be) a twofold procession.

I RESPOND: It must be said, that for an understanding of the aforesaid there must be noted, that a procession is said "to be doubled" [geminari] either by reason of *the ones proceeding*, as for example, when two sons proceed; or by reason of *the manner of proceeding*,[9] as love and word proceed in a twofold manner; and/or by reason of *a manner of speaking*, as a procession is said (to be) a "twin" (generation), that is said in twofold manner.

But one must attend, that there is a threefold manner of speaking, namely the *equivocal*, the *univocal* and the *analogous*.[10] When there is an *equivocal* manner of speaking, there is a doubling about the '*being said*' and not about '*being*'. Whence a man depicted and a true man are said (to be) a "man" *in a twofold manner*, but there is not a twofold man and/or two men. When there is an *univocal* manner of speaking, there is a doubling about '*being*' and not

---

[1] Here in ch. 1.

[2] Codex M has *differs more* [plus differt] instead of *is more distant* [plus distat].

[3] In codex Y there is added an *is* [est]

[4] Edition 1 reads *therefore, two Spirits* [ergo duo Spiritus].

[5] From the manuscripts and edition 1, we have restored the badly omitted *always* [semper].

[6] See Aristotle, PHYSICS, Bk. IV, text 133 (in the other edition, in the last chapter), and in his METAPHYSICS, Bk. V, texts 11 and 20 (Bk. IV, chs. 6 and 15).

[7] Very many codices, together with edition 1, read *unto the creature* [in creaturam], which refers to *a looking-back* [respectum].

[8] With the more ancient manuscripts and edition 1 consenting, we have substituted *twofold* [duplex] for *in a twofold manner* [dupliciter].

[9] In the Vatican ed. and cod. cc there is faultily absent the *of proceeding* [procedendi], which, however, is had in the other codd. and in ed. 1.

[10] Cf. Aristotle, ON THE PREDICAMENTS, at the beginning. — Then, after *manner* [modus], trusting in the older mss. and in ed. 1, we have inserted the incongruously omitted *of speaking* [dicendi]. Then, ed. 1 has *Such as* [Ut] for *Whence* [Unde].

about 'being said'.[1] Whence a true man is numbered in Socrates and in Plato, because there are two men, but it is not said in a multiplied manner. Where there is an *analogous* manner of speaking, because it has part from the nature of the univocal, part from the nature of the equivocal, there is a numbering both[2] in being [in essendo] and in being said [in dicendo].

According to this manner, therefore, it must be said, that *procession*, according to which it is said of the temporal and eternal procession, is not said[3] univocally nor equivocally, but *analogically*, because one manner is closed in the other. For *to proceed* from this into that as into *an object* is the eternal one, but *to proceed* from this into that as into *a little dwelling* is the temporal. Therefore, since the analogous is said (to proceed) in this manner and in that manner,[4] for that reason there is a twofold being-said there, and "one procession" is said in a twofold manner, and thus as a consequence a twofold 'being', so that not unfittingly is the procession of the Holy Spirit said to be twofold.

1. To that, therefore, which is objected unto the contrary, that, with the procession multiplied, the one proceeding is multiplied; it must be said, that it is true, if it is accepted of multiplication according to one manner of speaking. Whence if there were a twin procession, according to which procession is said (to be) a going-forth from something, there would be at least two proceeding, but[5] (it is) not now (being considered) in this manner; on the other hand, there is a *twin* (procession), because in one manner it is from Someone into Someone as into *an Object*, in another manner from Someone into someone as into *a little dwelling*.

2. 3. To that which is objected second: *either* the procession is twofold, because (there is) a twofold emanation *and/or* a twofold manner (of proceeding);[6] it must be said, that he does not divide it sufficiently; for he ought to add a third member, namely, *either* because (it is) a twofold manner of speaking, not an equivocal one. And through this the following one concerning the man depicted and the true one, because there is not an analogy there, but a pure equivocation.

4. To that which is objected last, that an added looking-back does not number etc.; it must be said, that a looking-back added to a *subject* does number the subject; whence the Holy Spirit is not said (to be) twofold,[7] because He is spirated and breathed into. But when a looking-back is added *to the signification of a term*, then it is necessary, that it be said (both) in one and the other manner; and if the looking-back is not distracting — such that it does not cause an entirely diverse signification — but (is) ordered to it, it causes an analogy in the term[8] and a number according to 'being said' [secundum dici] and even a number according to 'being'. Whence if this noun "*illumination*" would signify the *absolute* act of shining and the *compared* act of shining, the Sun would be said "to illumine" in a twofold manner, and there would be a twin illumination by the Sun [solis]; but, nevertheless, more properly would there be a doubling in *being said* [in dicendo] than in '*being*'. Whence Master (Peter)[9] would speak more properly, if he would say: "the procession of the Holy Spirit is said in a twofold manner", than when he says, that there is a twin (procession), because a doubling does not properly occur there.

SCHOLIUM

I. 'To count in number with something' [ponere in numerum cum alio] is the same as 'to be distinguished as a thing from a thing'. Moreover, it must be noted, that this distinction of each procession must be understood in a sane manner. For the temporal procession includes the eternal one and adds upon it a new habitude in the Holy Spirit (according to the reckoning of understanding) to the creature, by connoting some real effect in it, through which there is a new, real relation in the creature to the Holy Spirit. Hence it follows, that *the terms* of these two processions of His differ essentially, because the eternal procession does not look back except to an eternal terminus, but the temporal conveys a looking-back to a temporal terminus. But in the *essence* of these processions there is not other difference except according to the reckoning of the understanding, as Richard of Middleton explains well, here in a. 1, q. 2. — On the threefold manner of speaking: the univocal, equivocal and the analogous, cf. above d. 1, a. 3, q. 1 and its Scholium. — For an understanding of the conclusion the solution to n. 4 helps a great deal; cf. also d. 15, p. II, and d. 16.

II. All the ancient Scholastics agree in the conclusion, except Giles the Roman, who denies, that there can be said to be a twin and/or twofold procession. St. Thomas, here in q. 1, a. 2; SUMMA., I, q. 43, a. 2, ad 3. — Bl. (now St.) Albertus (Magnus), here in aa. 7 and 9; SUMMA., p. I, tr. 7, q. 32, m. 2, a. 2. — (Bl.) Peter of Tarentaise, here in qq. 1 and 4. — Richard of Middleton, here in a. 1, q. 2. — Giles the Roman, here in 1st. princ. q. 2. — Durandus (of Saint-Pourçain), here in q. 2. — (Bl.) Dionysius the Carthusian, here in q. 1, in the second half.

---

[1] The reading of the Vatican edition, *saying* [dicere] for '*being said*' [dici], is corrected with the help of the manuscripts and edition 1. A little before this, codex W has *but not* [sed non] in place of *not* [non].

[2] The Vatican edition, contrary to the manuscripts and edition 1, omits *both* [et]. Codices L and O have *doubling* [geminatio] in place of *numbering* [numeratio].

[3] The Vatican edition, together with codex cc, not trusting in the more ancient manuscripts and edition 1, badly omits *said* [dicta].

[4] Thus with edition 1 all the codices, though some, such as K O V and X, falsely the first time read *just as* [sic] for *in this manner* [sic], but the reading of the Vatican edition is entirely distorted, *just as has been said* [sicut dictum est] for *in this manner said and in that manner* [sic dictum est], i.e. is said to proceed in this manner and in the other manner. Then the codices and editions do not agree amongst themselves, by putting *twofold* [duplex] in place of *in a twofold manner* [dupliciter] and vice versa.

[5] In the Vatican edition and codex cc, there is less aptly omitted the *but* [autem], which in the other codices and edition 1 is had. Then in very many codices and the first six editions, after *but* [sed] there is wanting the verb *it is* [est].

[6] The preceding proposition is more clearly exhibited in this manner: *there is objected second: there is a twofold procession, because either the emanation (is) twofold or the manner twofold*; yet with the editions and codices agreeing with the Vatican edition (except codex H, which after *and/or* [vel] repeats *that* [quia]), we have changed nothing.

[7] The Vatican edition, contrary to very many codices, such as F T X and Y, has *in a twofold manner* [dupliciter]. A little below this in the margin, codex T in a later hand after *of a term* [termini], glossing, puts *such as, namely, because the term in one of its significations is absolute, in another respective* [ut videlicet quia terminus in una sui significatione est absolutus, in alia respectivus].

[8] Many codices, such as A B C D E F G I P Q R S T U etc. together with editions 1, 2, 3 , in place of *in the term* [in termino] have *in the third* [in tertio], concerning which cf. above d. 1, a. 3, q. 1, in reply to n. 1, and below in d. 35, q. 1, in the body (of the response). A little before this edition 1 has *it* [illum], i.e. the *term,* for *it* [illam], i.e. the *signification*.

[9] Cf. text of Master (Peter), here in ch. 1, at the beginning.

ARTICLE II

On the giving of the Holy Spirit.

Consequently, in second place is the principal question concerning the giving of the Holy Spirit. And about this four (questions) are asked.

First, there is asked, whether the Holy Spirit is given in His own Person to men, or whether His is only said to be given for this reason, that His effect is given.

Second, whether the Holy Spirit is given by any holy man.

QUESTION I

Whether the Holy Spirit is given in His own person, or only in an effect?

That He is given in His own Person, is shown in this manner:

1. From the fifth (chapter of the Letter of St. Paul) to the Romans:[1] *The charity of God has been poured out in our hearts through the Holy Spirit, who has been given to us*; but nothing pours out charity except the uncreated Spirit: ergo etc..

2. Likewise, (St.) Augustine in the fifth (book) ON THE TRINITY[2] says, that the Holy Spirit is a gift, and is said to be a gift for this reason, that He is given: therefore, if He personally is a gift, He personally is given.

3. Likewise, this very (thing) is shown *by reason*: The Holy Spirit is love and the first Love, but love is the first gift, in which all[3] other (gifts) are bestowed: therefore, if there is not a positing of the posterior without the prior, there is not a positing that the gifts of the Holy Spirit are given, unless the Holy Spirit Himself be given.

4. Likewise, the Holy Spirit is given to unite[4] and bind together [colligandum] the members of the Mystical Body; but the members of the Mystical Body are members united to one another, just as the Lord sought, in the seventeenth (chapter of the Gospel) of (St.) John:[5] *That they might all be taken up together into the one (Body)*; but a perfect union is not but in one simple (thing): therefore, the members are united through something, which is one and the same in all; but this cannot be a created gift, but (rather) an uncreated one: therefore, it is necessary that with the created gift the Uncreated be given.

ON THE CONTRARY: 1. Virtue[6] is the art of living uprightly, and grace is the gift sufficiently directing the soul unto (its) End: therefore, it seems, a gift other than the gift of created grace is not opportune for the soul: therefore, if one must not posit among the works of God (anything) superfluous,[7] it is clear that it is not necessary that the Holy Spirit be given.

2. Likewise, since one is sanctified through grace, there is nothing in him besides the grace,[8] which was not there before: therefore, since "to give" is 'to cause, that something be among their own, which was not before', naught is given but grace. *If you say*, that the Holy Spirit (is) in him as the Holy One, (but) before (was there) as the Spirit: therefore, (His 'being given') is nothing other than that Holy Spirit causes[9] the grace of sanctification in him.

3. Likewise, what is given after the act of giving [post donationem] is in the power of the one accepting (the gift); but the Holy Spirit cannot be made subject to [redigi sub] the power of anyone:[10] therefore, He cannot be given.

4. Likewise, what is given to anyone differing through essence either is created anew, or multiplied, or is transferred to his possession, as is clear, when I give a cape to anyone, but the Person of the Holy Spirit is neither created nor multiplied nor transferred to his possession, because God always has the Holy Spirit: therefore, the Holy Spirit is not given.

CONCLUSION

The Holy Spirit is given both in His own Person, and in the created gift, which is grace.

I RESPOND: It must be said, that '*to give*' is for the having and/or possessing of something; but '*to have and/or possess something*' is, when something is in the faculty of the one having and/or possessing. Moreover, '*to be in the faculty of the one having* and/or possessing' is 'to be at hand [esse praesto] for enjoying and/or using'. But perfect possession is, when a man has that, which he can use and which he can enjoy.[11] But there is no upright enjoying except of God, and no upright using except through the grace that makes one pleasing [per gratiam gratum facientem]:

---

[1] Verse 5.

[2] Chapter 15, n. 16: The Holy Spirit for the reason that He is given, has not only that He is a gift, but entirely that He is. Cf. also below in Master (Peter's) BOOK OF SENTENCES, Bk. I, d. 18. — Then after *therefore* [ergo] codex bb has *this person* [persona haec] in place of *He personally* [personaliter].

[3] Trusting in the more ancient manuscripts and in edition 1, we have supplied here *all* [omnia] and a little after this *a positing of* [ponere]. Near the end fo the argument, from the more ancient manuscripts and edition 1, we have substituted *Himself* [ipse] in place of *properly* [proprie]. See more on this argument below in d. 18, q. 1.

[4] Codices L and O have *vivify* [vivificandum] for *unite* [uniendum].

[5] Verse 23.

[6] Thus rightly all the codices, together with edition 1, while the Vatican edition has *Grace* [Gratia].

[7] Aristotle, ON HEAVEN AND EARTH, Bk. I, text 32 (ch. 4): But God and nature do nothing in vain.

[8] We follow codex T by putting *besides the grace* [praeter gratiam] in place of *except grace* [nisi gratia], which many codices together with editions 1, 2, and 3, badly omit.

[9] We follow the very many codices, though some, such as A S T V etc. have the less well *causing* [facientem]; the Vatican edition has the secondary clause in direct speech, rather than indirect.

[10] From the more ancient manuscripts and edition 1 we have restored *the power of any one* [potestate nullius] for *any power* [nulla potestate]. Then codex bb has *neither* [nec] for the *not* [non].

[11] Not trusting in the older manuscripts and edition 1, the Vatican edition has less well, twice, *could* [posset] for *can* [possit]. Then codex K has *of an other than* [alio quam], and codex T has *in another than* [in alio a], for the first *except* [nisi].

therefore, perfect is the possession, in which God and His grace are had. But the perfect gift is for the perfect possession: therefore, there not a *best given and a perfect gift*,[1] except there be given the uncreated Gift, which is the Holy Spirit, and the created gift, which is grace. Therefore, one must conceded,[2] that each is given.

1. To that, therefore, which is objected concerning grace, which is the art of living well;[3] the response is clear: for though it is the art, which we use, yet it is not the possession, which we enjoy as object; and for that reason there is not a perfect gift without Him.

2. To that which is objected: nothing more is in such a one than (was) before; it must be said, that 'being given' is not ordered to 'being', but to 'having'. For even though the Holy Spirit was in the sinner before, yet He was not had by him, because the sinner did not have the faculty of enjoying Him.

3. To that which is objected, that the given is in the power of the one accepting, it must be said, that something is given to someone as *one finishing*, just as the reward to the one meriting; something as *one perfecting*, as grace to the one consenting; something as *one subserving*, as the horse to the soldier. But that which is said, that the given is in the power of the one accepting, is true of giving[4] said in the third manner, not in the first and second, because those are two manners of having, in which the one having is had. Whence man is had by grace and is had by the Gift, which he enjoys.

4. From this last is clear: because[5] that is true of that, which is given as a *limited* possession; but of that which is given as *one finishing*, (it is) not, because such can at once be given to many and had by many, because they tend to the same; and for that reason, when it is given, it is not transferred.[6]

SCHOLIUM

I. With wonderful brevity and clarity this question is solved and proven in six propositions. — In the fourth proposition there is said: « Upright using does not happen except through grace »; here the word *upright* [recte] signifies *in a meritorious manner*. For the Seraphic Doctor does not deny, that the sinner can even use something in an upright manner, i. e. in an *honest* manner, nay rather he asserts the contrary in SENT., Bk. II, d. 28, a. 2, q. 3.

II. In solution to n. 2 there is rightly said, that « even though the Holy Spirit was in the sinner before, yet He was not had by him ». For only through charity is the intellectual creature both had in a special manner by the Holy Spirit and has Him to enjoy. This Richard of Middleton (here in a. 2, q. 1) explains with this similitude: « If a poor man had the money of some rich man in his own home, we would not say on this account, that he had that money as his own. Whence notwithstanding, that that money was present in the home of the poor man, it could be given him a new by the rich man; which having been done, he would not only have it now through the presence alone of the money in his home, but he would have it as his own. In a somewhat similar manner I say, that although the Holy Spirit is through (His) Essence present to every thing, yet because the sinner does not have the faculty to enjoy Him, for that reason, notwithstanding that presence, the Person of the Holy Spirit can truly be given by God etc.. ». — Worthy of attention is the doctrine in the solution to n. 3, by which there is declared, that neither is the uncreated Gift to any extent transferred into the power of the one accepting as something subjected to him, nor that having been given as the soul itself to the body is He properly subjected through this to the power of the same.

III. Cf. Alexander of Hales, SUMMA. p. I, q. 73, m. 4, a. 1. — St. Thomas, here in q. 2, a. 1; Summa. I, q. 42, a. 3. — Bl. (now St.) Albertus (Magnus), here in a. 13; and in d. 15, a. 2, in reply to n. 1; on this and the following question, see his Summa., p. I, tr. 7, q. 32, m. 1, qq. 1 and 2, in passing. — (Bl.) Peter of Tarentaise, here in q. 1, a. 5. — Richard of Middleton, here in a. 2, q. 1. — Giles the Roman, here in 2nd. princ., q. 1. — Durandus (of Saint-Pourçain), here in q. 3. — (Bl.) Dionysius the Carthusian, here in quaestiunc. 2. — (Gabriel) Biel, here in q. 2.

QUESTION II

Whether the Holy Spirit is given by any holy man?

Second, there is asked, whether the Holy Spirit is given by any holy man [viro sancto]. And that (this is) so, is proven in this manner:

To give the Holy Spirit is nothing other [non aliud] than to give the grace that makes one pleasing (to God); but there is shown, that to give or infuse the grace which makes one pleasing is *possible* and *fitting* and *true*:

1. And that it is *possible*, seems a minori:* because it belongs to a greater virtue to produce a substantial form than an accidental one; but[7] grace is an accidental form: therefore, since a creature has the virtue of producing a substantial form, much more strongly does it seem concerning grace, which is an accidental form.

2. Likewise, this very (thing) seems to be shown a simili:[8] because grace is a spiritual light; but we see in a corporal light thus, because something is *donative* [dativum], something *receptive*, something *donative* and *receptive*: therefore, if a spiritual light is equally potent, for an equal reason it seems concerning this. But the donative, since He is God, cannot be receptive, because He receives nothing from anyone: therefore, this is to be found in the creature, because he *receives* the spiritual light, which is grace, and *gives* it; and thus etc..[9]

3. Likewise, there are two (things), which cause a creature to have the ability to produce a similar to itself [posse producendi sibi simile], namely (its) *corrupt-*

---

[1] James 1:17.

[2] The Vatican edition, disagreeing with the manuscripts and edition 1, omits *must be* [est]

[3] For this is taken from the first proposition of the objection.

[4] The Vatican edition, contrary to the manuscripts and edition 1, has *donation* [donatione] in place of *giving* [datione], and a little below this, contrary to the more ancient codices and edition 1, omits *two* [duo], then after *the one having* [habens] without the authority of the manuscripts and editions 1, 2, and 3, it adds *both has and* [et habet et]. Codices T and W have *the one having is said to be had* [habens dicitur haberi], very many codices, such as A C G L R S U Y, with a corrupted reading have *the one having is meant* [habens dicitur], however, the other codices, together with editions 1, 2, and 3, exhibit our reading.

[5] From very many manuscripts and edition 1, we have substituted *because* [quia] for the ambiguous *that/because* [quod].

[6] Many codices, such as A B C D F G I L O R S T U W etc., omit the last words beginning at *because they tend to the same* [quia ad idem tendunt].

[7] The Vatican edition together with codex cc less distinctly, and contrary to all the other codices together with edition 1, has *and* [et] for *but* [sed].

[8] A few texts, such as T and aa, have *by a similar reckoning* [ratione a simili].

[9] The Vatican edition and codex cc, yet disagreeing with the other codices together with edition 1, have faultily *concerning the others* [de aliis] for *etc.* [etc.].

---

* *Trans. notes*: Concerning the Latin expressions, a minori and a simili (which is had in the following argument), cf. the first and second trans. footnotes, above, on p. 180.

° Concerning the meaning of the Latin expression, ab oppositis, cf. trans. footnote above, on p. 54.

ibility, on account of which it needs to be conserved in another, and *perfection* in nature, on account of which it can be in perfect act, which is to produce a similar to itself.[1] « For the "perfect" is said (to be) each thing, when it can generate such as it itself is ».[2] If, therefore, grace is a form, which is most swiftly corrupted, and a form of great perfection: therefore, it ought to have the virtue to produce a similar to itself; but not in the subject in which it is: therefore, in another.

4. Likewise, what can perfectly expel a contrary can perfectly engender [aggenerare][3] the contrary habit, because a contrary is not perfectly expelled except through a contrary; but grace can perfectly expel fault: therefore, grace in man can of itself generate grace; but not in the one having, therefore, in another.

5. It is also[4] shown, that it is *congruous*, that grace proceeds from one man into another. And it is shown in this manner: a reason for being proud was the reason for loosing grace, therefore, ab oppositis,° a humiliation is the reason for recuperating (it);[5] but if grace is given by a man, man is humiliated more, than if (it is given) only by God; because if it is given by a man, a man is humiliated under God and under a man, but not, if it is given by God alone, is he humiliated under each: therefore, it seems, that this manner is more congruent.[6]

6. Likewise, if in[7] an act of *justice*, which is a punishment, a sinful soul [anima peccatrix] is subjected to a corporal creature, so that it be ordered in each and every way [in universo]: therefore, in an act of *mercy* it ought to be subjected to some creature, so that it be reordered: therefore, just as it receives a punishment from some creature, so it seems congruous, that it also receive grace.

7. Likewise, a perfect agent not only gives form to the recipient [suscipienti], but also gives a completely similar power;[8] and this is unto the manifestation of its own power: therefore, if God is the most noble agent and the One who most of all ought to be praised in His action, it is congruent, that not only He give form to grace, but also the power of giving (it).

8. Likewise, just as from God there is '*being*' [esse], so also '*well-being*' [bene esse]; but in nothing is there a derogation [derogatur] from God, when He gives the power to a creature of giving '*being*': therefore, in nothing is there a derogation, when He gives the power of giving '*well-being*', therefore, also 'gratuitous being' [esse gratuitum].

9. Moreover, it is shown that it is *true*, because

in the twentieth (chapter of the Gospel of St.) John,[9] the Lord said: *Accept the Holy Spirit; whose sins you shall forgive, are forgiven them* etc..

10. Likewise, in Acts[10] it is said, that through the imposition of the hands of the Apostles the Holy Spirit was given, not through the imposition of the hands of others, as the Gloss says concerning the disciple Philip, in the eighth (chapter) of Acts: therefore, there was some virtue in the Apostles, which was not in the others; but through that the Holy Spirit was given: therefore, the Holy Spirit was given by a man [ab homine].

And, conversely, it is shown that 'that the gift of the Holy Spirit is given by a man' is *false*, is *incongruous*, (and) is even *impossible*.

1. That it is *false*, seems through (St.) Augustine, in the fifteenth (book) ON THE TRINITY:[11] « None of the disciples gave the Holy Spirit, but (rather) they prayed, that He might come upon a man ».

2. Likewise, whosoever gives and/or donates anything, has an active power [posse][12] over it; but no man has power [posse] over the gift of the Holy Spirit: ergo etc..

3. Likewise, that it is *unfitting* [inconveniens], seems, because if a soul is gratified by something other than God [ab alio quam Deo], the 'something other than God' falls as a medium between the soul and God. But, whensoever anything falls as a medium[13] between the soul and God, the soul of the man has been perverted: therefore, according to this, while grace would be given to the soul, it would be perverted.

4. Likewise, grace is able over free will, therefore, if a man could give grace, a man would have an ability [posse] over the judgement [arbitrium] of another; but a judgement, which is subject to another, is not free: therefore, such a donation would take away[14] liberty.

5. Likewise, the greatest glory for God[15] concerns the justification of the impious, but the greatest glory of God ought not to be communicated to another: therefore, if it is communicated, there is a derogation of the divine glory, but if 'something other than God' gives grace, 'something other than God' justifies: therefore, such a donation lessens the glory of God.

6. Likewise, it is just to hope in the one, who can give the merit of salvation; but if man could give grace, he could give the merit of salvation: therefore, it would be just

---

[1] Trusting in the manuscripts and edition 1, here and near the end of the argument, we have substituted the feminine singular [similem] for the neuter singular for *similar* [simile], which even very many of the codd. with ed. 1 exhibit near the beginning of the argument. — On the twofold reason, on account of which the power of producing a similar to itself befits creatures, see above d. 7, q. 2, in the body (of the response).

[2] Aristotle, ON THE SOUL, Bk. II, text 34 (ch. 4), and METEOROL-OGY, Bk. IV, text 19 (ch. 3). Cf. above d. 9, q. 1. — In which text, having examined the more ancient manuscripts and edition 1, we have put *when* [cum] place of *which* [quod]. Then the Vatican edition with the codex cc, yet with the other codices and edition striving against it, has less well *on the other hand* [autem] for *therefore* [ergo]. A little below this codex X has *mostly of* [maxime] in place of *of great* [magnae].

[3] We follow codd. A C H I R S T U etc. with edition 1 by putting *engender* [aggenerare] for *generate* [generare], which the Vatican ed. has.

[4] The Vatican edition, without the authority of the manuscripts and edition 1, has *moreover* [autem].

[5] One or the other cod., such as I & V, repeats here *grace* [gratiam].

[6] Trusting very many mss. and edition 1, we have substituted *this* [iste] for *that* [ille], and *is congruent* [congruat] for *is fitting* [conveniat].

[7] The Vatican edition, contrary to the manuscripts and editions 1, 2, and 3, has *with* [cum], but less well. At the end of the argument, with the help of the manuscripts and edition 1, we have put *so* [ita] and *that* [quod] in place of *in this manner* [sic] and *that* [ut].

[8] Averroës, COMMENTARY ON ARISTOTLE'S PHYSICS, Bk VIII, text 32: For the one generating is that which gives to a simple generated body its own form and all its contingent accidents. — At the end of the argument, codex B adds *grace* [gratiam].

[9] John 20:22-23

[10] Acts 8:17. — The words of the ordinary Gloss, next cited, are: Philip, who evangelized Samaria, was one of the seven (deacons). For if he were an Apostle, he could impose hands, so that they might receive the Spirit, which is licit to Bishops alone.

[11] Chapter 26, n. 46. See the text of Master (Peter), here in ch. 3.

[12] On the authority of very many manuscripts and edition 1, we have expunged, here, the less aptly added *something* [aliquod]; then, we have twice substituted *over* [super] for *above* [supra].

[13] In the Vatican edition and codex cc there is faultily lacking *medium* [medium], which is had in the other manuscripts and edition 1. A little below this, one or the other codex, such as T and ee, have *when* [cum] for *while* [dum].

[14] The Vatican edition, contrary to the older codices and edition 1, has *takes away* [tollit], and, then, contrary to all the codices and edition 1, it adds *of judgement* [arbitrii] (in English at the end of the sentence).

[15] Thus the more ancient codices, together with edition 1, while the Vatican edition has an *of God*, which editions 2 and 3 omit.

to hope in a man; but man is vanity:[1] therefore, such a donation would give trust to vanity [fiduciam vanitatis].

From these four manners* it is clear, that the donation of the Holy Spirit by a man takes away the *order* of the soul itself,[2] takes away *liberty*, lessens the *glory* of God and leads one into *vain confidence*, all of which are (things) unfitting.

7. It is also shown, that it is *impossible*, that such a power be given to a creature: because, just as (St.) Augustine says,[3] « it is greater to make one pious from impious than to create Heaven and Earth ». But the power of creating cannot be received by a creature: therefore, neither the power of giving grace.

8. Likewise, the production of grace is taken up [suscipitur] by the soul through the presence of the agent; but God alone can glide into [illabi] the soul: therefore, God alone can infuse grace into the soul.

9. Likewise, grace is a simple form, both deiform and spiritual, not having (its) rise from the principles of the subject: therefore, since a rational soul by reason of (its) deiformity and spirituality cannot[4] be except from God, it is clear that neither (can) grace, which is equally spiritual, nay more spiritual than the soul itself.

10. Likewise, grace unites (one) immediately to God: therefore, it cannot be but from God immediately, therefore, with no one cooperating: therefore, a creature cannot produce grace.

CONCLUSION

The Holy Spirit cannot be given by a man as by an effective principle, yet He can be given by him as by one preparing and/or obtaining by request.

I RESPOND: It must be said, that, just as those last reasons show, that grace or the Holy Spirit is given by a man as by an *effective* or productive principle, is entirely *false* and *impossible*.

However, for the sake of an understanding of the objections to the contrary it must be noted, that it is in a threefold manner that grace is given by anyone: either as by *one preparing*, or by one administering[5] the Sacraments or by one announcing the admonitions of salvation [salutaria documenta]; and/or as by *one obtaining by request*, either through praying or through good works; and/or as by *one producing*. In the first manner, grace is given by the good and by the bad; in the second manner only by the good; in the third manner only by God.

And, through this, there is manifest the response to the last two,[6] which prove, that the Holy Spirit is given, because, there, the giving is nothing other than a preparation.

1. To that, therefore, which is objected *first*, that a created agent is potent upon a substantial form; I say, that it is not potent upon every substantial, as for example upon that, which is deiform, as is the rational soul. And because grace is deiform,[7] for that reason it cannot be produced by such an agent. But if one argues of other natural forms, the argument is not <u>a minori</u>.°

2. To that which is objected concerning corporal light, it must be said, that it is not similar. For corporal light is diffused through a down-bearing [deferens] medium, and through the same medium there can, again, be engendered[8] what is borne down; but grace is not through a 'being born down' [delationem], but through the gliding-in of the agent and an omnimodal indistance.

3. To that which is objected, that a corruptible creature ought to have a power of generating; it must be said, that it is true of that which is corruptible *from itself*, but grace from itself is never corrupted nor grows old.

And/or say, that that is not the whole cause, mostly in those which are not said (to be) a complete substance, but rather a disposition.

4. To that which is objected, that grace can expel fault: it must be said, that it is in a twofold manner that one expels fault: *effectively*, and/or *formally*. What can expel *effectively*, can effect grace: but it is not necessary [oportet], that (it be) that which *formally* (does such), because it expels by its very self. Therefore, since grace expels formally and by its very self, for that reason it does not follow, that it could generate another grace.

5. To that which is objected, that in justification the sinner ought to be humiliated; it must be said, that it is true, because he ought to be humiliated both beneath man and also beneath visible signs; however, otherwise than under God, because another honor is owed to God than to man; and for that reason, because he is humiliated beneath God as beneath the Principle of salvation and (Him) by whom he is saved, he ought not[9] be humiliated beneath a creature, as (beneath one) by which salvation is given him, but (rather) as (beneath one) by which salvation is administered.

6. And thus is clear even the following (objection) concerning humiliation in punishment. For it is not similar concerning that humiliation, because there the perverse soul, *remaining* in its perversity, by reason of that is subjected to an inferior through nature, *and/or* because it has the relics of perversity; but in the donation of grace the perverse soul is changed from perversity and ordered immediately to God.

---

[1] Psalm 38:6: *Nevertheless, each and every vanity, every man living.* — Then cod. aa with ed. 1 has *giving* [datio] for *donation* [donatio].

[2] The Vatican edition, having omitted *itself* [ipsius], here adds *to God* [ad Deum], and after *takes away* [tollit] adds *judgement's* [arbitrii], but with the codd. and ed. 1 opposed. — At the beginning of this proposition, after *these* [his] cod. M and ed. 1 add, sufficiently well, *therefore* [igitur].

[3] EXPOSITION ON THE GOSPEL OF ST. JOHN, tract 72, n. 3.

[4] Many codices together with three first editions have *after* [post].

[5] From very many manuscripts and edition 1, we have substituted *one administering* [administrante] for *one ministering* [ministrante], and after *the Sacraments* [Sacramenta] the particle *or* [sive] for the ambiguous *or as by* [seu sicut ab]; then after *by one obtaining by request* [impetrante] we have inserted the not well omitted *either* [sive]. Then codices aa and bb after *one producing* [producente] add *and one infusing* [et infundente].

[6] The Vatican edition, not trusting in the older manuscripts and in editions 1, 2, and 3, adds *objections* [obiecta].

[7] The Vatican edition, together with a few codices, superfluously repeats, here, *as is a rational soul* [sicut est anima rationalis].

[8] From very many codices we have substituted *there can, again, be engendered* [aggenerari] for *there can, again, be generated* [generari], in place of which codices L and O have *another can be generated* [aliud generari], and edition 1 *there can, again, be aggregated* [aggregari]. All the codices, with edition 1, after *engendered* [aggenerari] omit the *through* [per], which is falsely adjoined by the Vatican edition.

[9] Trusting the manuscripts and edition 1, we have expunged the *in 'this manner* [sic], which the Vatican edition has prefixed to *not* [non].

---

* *Trans. note*: Here, there appears to be typographical error in the critical text, which reads *means* [mediis] instead of *manners* [modis]; which latter I follow in the English translation, without having checked the editions or any codex.

° Here, <u>a minori</u> is shorthand, for *an argument a minori*. Such is the topical syllogism, which arrives at an affirmative conclusion, by means of arguing from what the lesser could do or has, and concluding that the greater can or has likewise. Cf. Pietro Ispano, TRATTATO DI LOGICA, tract, "De locis", trans. A. Ponzio, (Bompiani, Milano, 2004), p. 172-175, n. 32.

7. To that which is objected, that a perfect agent gives a similar power of acting; it must be said, that it is true, if the patient could take it up in a congruent manner;[1] but, just as has been shown, on the part of a man it is not possible, that such a power be received by him, on account of the nobility of such a form, which cannot be except by a most noble agent.

8. To that which is objected, that to give the power regarding[2] 'being' does not derogate from God; it must be said, that there is an *order* among essences; because some creatures are so noble, that it is not decent that they be produced except by a most noble agent, as are those which are according to the Image (of God).[3] Therefore, since grace concerns (things) most noble, it is clear, that it cannot be produced by a man, just as neither (can) the 'being' of a soul.

9. 10. Those which last are objected have been solved above through the distinction of 'giving', according to the tri-member difference.[4]

SCHOLIUM

I. This Question brings not a little light to bear for the solving of the difficulties, which are proffered against the Catholic doctrine concerning the visible priesthood by the adversaries of the Church. — The word, "*deiform*" [deiformis], (in the solution to n. 1) is taken in a twofold sense, namely, improperly of that similitude, which is naturally in *the image* of God, and properly of the supernatural similitude, which is through the grace of anything which immediately conjoins us to God. Cf. above d. 3, p. I, q. 2, in reply to the last objection, and Book II, d. 16, a. 2, q. 3.

II. Alexander of Hales, SUMMA., p. I, q. 72, m. 4. — St. Thomas, here in q. 3. — Bl. (now St.) Albertus (Magnus), here in a. 16. — (Bl.) Peter of Tarentaise, here in q. 1, a. 7. — Richard of Middleton, here in a. 2, q. 3. — Giles the Roman., here in 3rd. princ., q. sole. — Durandus (of Saint-Pourçain), here in q. 4. — (Bl.) Dionysius the Carthusian, here in q. 2., quaestiunc. 1.

DOUBTS ON THE TEXT OF THE MASTER

DOUBT I

In this part are the doubts about the text (of Master Peter), and first concerning the *positioning* [situ] of this part, because it does not seem, that one ought to here deal with the temporal procession (of the Holy Spirit), because in this part he deals with those which befit God eternally. *Besides*, since the eternal and temporal generation of the Son is determined in one and the other book, because the eternal in the First, but the temporal in the Third, for what reason does he not similarly do (this) concerning the procession of the Holy Spirit?

I RESPOND: It must be said, that because[5] the temporal and the eternal procession are from the same principle, just as Master (Peter) says,[6] and again (because) there is There in a certain manner a conform manner of proceeding, for that reason one works for the declaration of the other; and for that reason here there is posited in passing a treatment on the temporal procession for the manifestation[7] of the eternal procession. But not so does it concern the temporal generation of the Son, because it is not from the same principle, nay (it is) only from (His) Mother, and it looks back to two natures, namely the Divine and the human. For that reason there ought to have been a determination of it after the Divine (Nature), of which it deals in the First (Book), and after human nature, of which (it deals) in the Second.

DOUBT II

Likewise, is asked of the temporal procession, of which Master (Peter) says, that *the Holy Spirit proceeds from the Father and the Son, when He proceeds to sanctify a creature*. For it seems false to say, that the temporal procession is His being-sent [missio]; but the Holy Spirit has been sent in (the form of) a dove and in tongues of fire, which He did not sanctify. *If you say*, that He was not sent *for tongues*, but (was) sent *in tongues to the Apostles*, whom He did sanctify; *on the contrary*: He was sent in (the form of) a dove upon Christ, and He neither sanctified the dove nor Christ.

I RESPOND: It can be said to this, that Master (Peter) does not define here the temporal procession *in a general manner*, but (rather) *in a special one*; insofar as it is the same (thing) which the invisible mission (is), in which the Holy Spirit is given and the creature sanctified. And/or it can be said, that he accepts *sanctification in a general manner*. For "to sanctify" is accepted in a threefold manner: in *one* manner, according to which it is that one makes holy from what is not holy; in a *second* manner, (according to which it is) that one confirms (something) holy in holiness; in a *third* manner, (according to which it is) that one manifests (something) already holy and confirmed. And according to any of these three[8] manners sanctification is found in every sending [missione] of the Holy Spirit by reason of *the terminus to which*, and in this manner does Master (Peter) accept it.[9]

DOUBT III

Likewise, is asked of this which Master (Peter) says of

---

[1] The Vatican edition, together with codex cc, has *in a fitting manner* [convenienter], but the other codices together with edition 1, have *in a congruent manner* [congruenter].

[2] The Vatican edition, not trusting in the manuscripts and edition 1, adds *well* [bene]. Then very many codices together with edition 1 omit *from God* [Deo].

[3] Supply with codex V: *of God*.

[4] The reading of the Vatican edition and codex cc, *nature* [naturam] in place of *difference* [differentiam], we have emended with the help of all the other manuscripts and edition 1.

[5] In the Vatican edition and codex cc there is badly lacking *because* [quia], which, however, is extant in the other codices and edition 1.

[6] Here in ch. 1. — Then from the more ancient manuscripts and edition 1, we have substituted *of proceeding* [procedendi] for the less apt *of producing* [producendi], then after *conform manner of proceeding* [modus procedendi conformis] we have deleted the particle *and* [et], and a little below this in place of *incidentally* [incidentaliter] we have put *in passing* [incidenter].

[7] Codex dd has *declaration* [declarationem].

[8] Trusting in the manuscripts and edition 1 we have supplied *three* [trium].

[9] Codex dd exhibits the solution of this Doubt thus: *I Respond, it must be said, that "to sanctify" is "to understand" in a threefold manner: in the first manner it is "to make (something) holy from a not holy", such as comes to be in the justification of the impius; in the second manner "to sanctify this" is "to confirm (something) holy in holiness", and this was done in the Apostles; in the third manner "to manifest (something) already holy and confirmed", and in this manner it must be understood of Christ, and thus does Master (Peter) accept it. And according to any of these three etc.* [Respondeo, dicendum, quod sanctificare est tripliciter intelligere: primo modo est de non sancto sanctum facere, taliter fit in iustificatione impii; secundo modo sanctificare hoc est sanctum in sanctitate confirmare, et hoc factum fuit in Apostolis; tertio modo iam sanctum et confirmatum manifestare, et sic est intelligendum de Christo, et sic accipit Magister. Et secundum aliquem trium] up to *terminus to which* [ad quem].

the Holy Spirit: *And He is the virtue, which used to go forth from Him.* For he seems to speak badly, because either *virtue* is accepted properly, or in an appropriated manner. *Not* In the first manner, it is established; *not* in the second manner, it seems, because according to the first (chapter)[1] of the First (Letter) to the Corinthians, we say *Christ the Virtue of God and the Wisdom of God* etc..

To this it can be said, that to the Holy Spirit *virtue* is not appropriated simply (speaking), but *sanative virtue* (is), and this, because the grace of health [gratia sanitatum] is a gift of the Holy Spirit,[2] and His grace is the medicine of the soul itself; but to the Son *the virtue of working* is appropriated, because *all (things) have been made through Him.*[3]

In another manner it can be said, that *virtue* has a comparison to that *for*[4] which it is, and in this manner it has the reckoning of a principle; and/or to that *of which* it is, and in this manner it has the reckoning of a complement; and/or to *both*, and in this manner has the reckoning of a mean [medii]. Therefore, just as *from Him* is appropriated to the Father, *through Him* to the Son, *in Him* to the Holy Spirit: so *virtue*, inasmuch as it has the reckoning of *a principle*, is appropriated to the Father, inasmuch as[5] the reckoning of *a mean*, to the Son, inasmuch as a reckoning of *completion*, to the Holy Spirit; because there is a completion in the goodness and delectation of the Holy Spirit, but this will be better said below.[6]

Doubt IV

Likewise, is asked of this which he says, that after *the Resurrection the Lord Jesus twice gave the Holy Spirit.* For it seems, that He gave (Him) *thrice*: because *first* He gave (the Holy Spirit) to them before the Passion, when He gave them the power of casting forth demons and to cure illnesses, according to the tenth (chapter) of (St.) Matthew.[7] *Likewise* after the Resurrection, according to the twentieth (chapter) of (St.) John:[8] *Accept the Holy Spirit. Likewise* after the Ascension, according to the second (chapter) of Acts.[9] Therefore (St.) Augustine insufficiently enumerates (them).

I Respond: To the present it must be said, that the giving [datione] of the Holy Spirit can be numbered as much as regards *act and effect*, and in this manner (Bl.) Rabanus (Maurus)* enumerates (them),[10] and there were three, because He gave thrice and because He gave for three: *first* for the working of miracles; *second* for the absolution of sins; *third* for the conversion of unbelievers. They can also in another manner be numbered as much as regards *place and signification*; and in this manner He gave twice, namely on Earth and in Heaven; likewise[11] on *Earth* to command the precept of the love for neighbor, in *Heaven* to command the affection of love for God, and thus the controversy is clear.[12]

Doubt V

Likewise, is asked of that word of the Apostle: *We have drunk of the one Spirit*; in what trope has this been said? And it seems, that it befits the Son more, because in the fifteenth (chapter) of Ecclesiasticus there is said:[13] *The water of saving wisdom*, and in the ninth (chapter) of Proverbs:[14] *Come, drink the wine*; and this Wisdom Itself says, that is, the Son of God: therefore, etc..

I Respond: It must be said, that the Holy Spirit is said (to be) *drink*, inasmuch as He restrains[15] the ardor of thirst for the age. But this (term) is appropriated to the Holy Spirit, because, just as (Pope St.) Gregory (the Great) says,[16] « having tasted the Spirit, all flesh looses its taste ». But inasmuch as through drinking there is a transfer for the nutriment [delegation nutrimenti] of each member, so it is appropriated to the Son, the appropriated of which is prudence and wisdom, which in a certain manner have a regulative and ordinative force for feeding every power of the soul.[17]

Doubt VI

Likewise, is objected concerning the other word (of the Apostle):[18] *The charity of God has been poured forth* [diffusa] *in our hearts.* For it seems that it has been improperly

---

[1] Verse 24.

[2] 1 Corinthians 12:9.

[3] John 1:3.

[4] From very many manuscripts and edition 1, we have restored the *for* [ad], which the Vatican edition badly omits, which edition a little before this after *virtue* [virtus] adds *either* [vel].

[5] The codices together with edition 1 omit the *has* [tenet], which the Vatican edition here repeats, and a little below this one or the other codex, such as O and V, together with edition 1 have *love* [dilectione] for *delectation* [delectatione].

[6] Distinction 34, q. 3, where it concerns the appropriation of names in common, and d. 32, a. 2, last question, where it concerns the appropriation of this name *virtue* in special. — For more on the appropriation of the Apostle's word *from Him*, etc. see below in d. 36, Doubt 4, and Alexander of Hales, Summa, p. I, q. 67, m. 4.

[7] Verse 1.

[8] Verse 22.

[9] Verses 2-4. — See the words of (St.) Augustine here in the text of Master (Peter), ch. 1.

[10] In the ordinary Gloss on Acts 2 :2 these words are read : « Before the Passion the Holy Spirit was given to the Apostles for the grace of doctrine and healing [sanitatum]; after the Resurrection Jesus breathed the Spirit upon (them) and said: Accept the Holy Spirit, whose sins you shall forgive, are forgiven them etc. ... On Pentecost the Spirit was send from Heaven, so that those who were to be divided on the morrow would accept the knowledge of tongues, lest they be in need of interpreters as they went forth throughout the world. And because God is simple in nature, the Spirit was given once from Heaven; but for the sake of men, who are composed of a twofold substance, namely of body and soul, He is to be loved in a twofold manner. In the third (giving), He is given twice, first in the efficacy of signs for the healing of bodies, afterwards unto the indulgence of sins for the remedy of souls ». These words in the edition of the Opera of (Nicholas) of Lyra (Venice 1588), loc. cit., are attributed to (Bl.) Rabanus (Maurus). — The same text of (Bl.) Rabanus occurs below in d. 15, p. II, q. 1, and in the Commentary on St. John, 20:25 (Bonelli's Supplement.).

[11] Some codices, such as H aa bb and ff, together with edition 1 omit *likewise* [Item], in place of which codex K puts *the reckoning of signification* [ratio significationis]. Then edition 1 in place of *in Heaven* [in caelo] puts *from Heaven* [de caelo], which corresponds more to the words of (St) Augustine, related by Master (Peter) here in ch. 1; and to those of the ordinary Gloss on Acts 2:2 : « *From Heaven* the Spirit is given, so that they might love God; *on Earth*, that they might love neighbor. For twice after the Resurrection was he given to command the two precepts of charity », (cf. a little above this, the other text of the Gloss cited.

[12] This Doubt is solved by Bl. (now St.) Albertus (Magnus), here in a. 12.

[13] Verse 3.   [14] Verse 5.

[15] The Vatican ed., against nearly all the codd. and ed. 1, has *re-extinguishes* [restinguit], then falsely *here it* [Hic] for *this (term)* [Hoc].

[16] These words are not (St.) Gregory's, but (St.) Bernard 's, who in his Epistle 111 to his own parents says: Having tasted the spirit it is necessary to loose the taste for the flesh.

[17] On this doubt, see Bl. (now St.) Albertus (Magnus), here in a. 14.

[18] Supply with codex dd. *of the Apostle* [Apostoli].

---

* *Trans. note*: Bl. Rabanus Maurus, O. S. B., (c. 776 to 856 A.D.), Abbot of Fulda (822-847), Archbishop of Mainz (847-856) was a student of Bl. Alcuin of York, O. S. B., and was famous for leading a revival of Patristic and Biblical Studies in the Carolingian era. He is the likely author of the famous hymn for Pentecost, Veni Creator Spiritus.

said, because what has been *diffused*, has been dispersed, and a virtue dispersed is lesser: therefore, if charity is potent, it ought, therefore, not be said (to be) *diffused*.

I Respond: It must be said, that *to infuse* and *to diffuse* are properly said of a humor. Moreover charity itself is compared to a humor, because just as a tree has branches [fomentum] and life and greenness [viriditatem] from a humor, so the whole spiritual machine (does) from love. Moreover, this love *is infused*, inasmuch as it is received within;[1] but *is diffused*, inasmuch as one proceeding from what is most interior it dilates the affection for a love of the many [ad dilectionem multorum] and moves all the powers of the soul to good operations. « For it works great things, if it is, but if it refuses to work, it is not love », just as (St.) Gregory says.[2] And for that reason the Lord says in the seventh (chapter) of (St.) John:[3] *Rivers of living water flow from His bosom.* — Because, therefore, there is said that it is lessened; it must be said, that it is true among those which have rise from a failing origin;[4] just as in cisterns, in which water is not living. But charity has an unfailing origin, just as a river (does).[5]

DISTINCTION XV

Part I

Chapter I

That the Holy Spirit is given by Himself, and the Son is sent by Himself.

Here, there must be considered, since the Holy Spirit is given to men by the Father and the Son, because it is that He temporally proceeds from Each and/or is sent, whether He also is given by Himself. If He is given by Himself, He also proceeds and/or is sent by Himself. To which we say, that the Holy Spirit both is God and a gift or a given: and for that reason He[1] gives and is given. Indeed, He gives inasmuch as God, as is given inasmuch as gift. Moreover, since the donation or giving of the Holy Spirit is an operation of God and is a common and undivided operation of the Three Persons, thus also the Holy Spirit is not only granted [donatur][2] by the Father and the Son, but also by Himself. Whence (St.) Augustine in the fifteenth book, On the Trinity says,[3] that He gives Himself. « Just as », he says, « the body of flesh is nothing other than flesh, so the gift of the Holy Spirit is nothing other than the Holy Spirit. Inasmuch, therefore, as He is the gift of God, so much is he given to those to whom He is given. On the other hand, on His own [apud se] He is God, even if He is given to no one, because He was God, coeternal to the Father and the son, before He was given to anyone. And not because They given and He is given, for that reason is He less than They. For thus is He given, as the gift of God, so that He also gives Himself, as God. For it cannot be said, that it does not belong to His power, concerning which it has been said:[4] *The Spirit breathes where He wills* ». Behold he openly says, that the Holy Spirit gives Himself. For if the Holy Spirit cannot give Himself, and the Father can give Him and the Son (likewise), thus also[5] the Father can give something and the Son (likewise), which the Holy Spirit cannot. Likewise, if the Father and the Son give the Holy Spirit, and He does not give (Himself): therefore, the Father works something and the Son (likewise), which the Holy Spirit does not work. Therefore, the Holy Spirit does give Himself. But if He gives Himself, then also[6] He proceeds from Himself and is given (by Himself), which is certainly [utique] true. For the temporal procession and/or mission of the Holy Spirit is the donation of the Same, and is itself an operation of God. Therefore, the Holy Spirit proceeds temporally from Himself and is sent by Himself, because He is given by Himself.

But do not wonder, that the Holy Spirit is said to be sent and/or to proceed from Himself. For of the Son of God even (St.) Augustine says in the second book, On the Trinity,[7] that He has been sent not only by the Father, but also by Himself and by the Holy Spirit, asking, in what manner the Son and/or the Holy Spirit has been sent, since Each is everywhere as God. For Each, says (St.) Augustine, is read (to have been) sent. For of the Holy Spirit there is read:[8] *Whom the Father will send in My Name.* And again: *If I go away, I shall send Him to you.* And the Son says of Himself: *I have gone forth from the Father and have come into the world.* And the Apostle says:[9] *God sent His own Son.* Moreover, in the Prophet there has been written in the person of God: *Heaven and Earth do I fill.* And so God is everywhere, therefore, the Son is everywhere, (and) the Holy Spirit is also everywhere. Therefore, the Son has been sent and the Holy Spirit (likewise) to that (place), where They (already) were.

Chapter II

In what manner is the mission of Each to be understood.

« About which there must be asked, in what manner is the mission of the Son and/or of the Holy Spirit understood. For the Father alone », says (St.) Augustine in the same (book),[10] « is never read (to have been) sent »,

---

[1] Not a few codices, such as T V W and X, have *inwardly* [intus].
[2] Homily 20, "On the Gospel", n. 2.   [3] Verse 38.
[4] We prefer the reading of codd. L & O, *from a failing origin* [ab origine deficiente] for *from an origin of failing* [ab origine deficiendi], because it is also more true in itself and is more conformable with the subjoined.
[5] The Seraphic Doctor speaks of this more extensively in his Commentary on the Gospel of St. John, 8:39 (Bonelli's, Supplement, tome I, col. 735).

NOTES ON THE BOOK OF SENTENCES
[1] Codices A B C & E add *both* [et]. A little after this, the Vatican ed. and edd. 4, 5, 6 & 9, add *or given* [sive datum] after *gift* [donum].
[2] The Vatican edition and edition 8 have *is given* [datur]. Immediately after this [in the English text, a little before this] codex D has *certainly* [utique] for *thus also* [itaque].
[3] Chapter 19, n. 36.   [4] John 3:8.
[5] The Vatican edition and editions 3, 4, 6 and 8, together with codices D, have *certainly* [utique] for *thus also* [itaque]. Immediately after this editions 1, 2, 7, and 8 omit *give* [dare] after *the Father* [Pater].

[6] The Vatican ed. and edd. 2, 5 & 9, with cod. D, omits *also* [et]. In the following proposition, at *itself* [ipsa], the Vatican ed. with the other edd., except ed. 6, omits *is* [est], contrary to all the other codices.
[7] Chapter 5, n. 7; but Master (Peter) contracts the popularly known teaching of St. Augustine, transposes words and adds from his own. — A little before this after *the Son* [Filio] the Vatican edition, together with very many editions, omits *of God* [Dei].
[8] John 14:26; the one after this is John 16:7. The Vulgate reads *But if I go away* [Si autem abiero]; edition 1 has: *And thus: if I go away* [Et ita: si abiero]; edition 8: *And if I go away* [Et si abiero], omitting *again* [iterum]. — The next quote is John 16:28.
[9] Gal. 4:4. — Then Jer. 23:24. The Vulgate reads: *"Do I not fill Heaven and Earth?"*, says the Lord [Nunquid non caelum et terram ego impleo, dicit Dominus?]. — Editions 1 and 8 have *there has been said* [dictum est] for *written* [scriptum]. Then the Vatican edition and editions 5, 6, and 9, add *if* [si] after *And so* [Itaque].
[10] Loc. cit., n. 8, and those which follow. — A little before this editions 5 and 9, prefix *as* [ut] to *says* [inquit].

but the Son and the Holy Spirit (are). And of the Son let us see first of all, in what manner (has He been) sent? « The Apostle says:[1] *God sent His own Son wrought out of a woman*, where he sufficiently shows, the Son (was) sent for the very reason, that (He was) wrought out of a woman. Next, He could not be sent by the Father without the Holy Spirit, because the Father is understood to have sent Him, when He wrought (Him) out of a female; which He certainly [utique] did not do without the Holy Spirit ». Behold, here, he says, that the Son (was) sent by the Father and the Holy Spirit.

CHAPTER III

That the Son has also been sent by the Holy Spirit.

And that the Son has been sent by the Holy Spirit, as (St.) Augustine says in the same (book),[2] is confirmed by authorities. Christ Himself says through Isaias: *Now He has sent Me, the Lord and His Spirit.* Of this (St.) Ambrose in the third book, ON THE HOLY SPIRIT[3] says thus: « Who is the one who says: *He has sent Me, the Lord and His Spirit*, except the One who comes from the Father, to save sinners », that is Christ? « therefore, both the Father and the Holy Spirit sent the Son ». The same (is said) in the same (book): « He has been given by the Father, as Isaias says:[4] *A boy has been born for us, and the Son has been given to us.* He is given, I dare say, also by the Spirit, because He has also been sent by the Spirit ». « For the Son of God says:[5] *The Spirit of the Lord (is) upon me, on account of which He has anointed Me: to evangelize the poor He sent me, to preach remission to captives* etc.. Which, when He read from the book of Isaias, He said in the Gospel: *Today this Scripture has been fulfilled in your ears*, to signify that it has been said of Himself. Moreover, He said well, *upon Me*; because as the Son of Man He has been both anointed and sent to preach. For according to the Divinity the Spirit is not above Christ, but in Christ ». Behold with these words (St.) Ambrose shows, that the Son has been sent and given to us not only by the Father, but also by the Holy Spirit.

CHAPTER IV

That the Son has also been given by Himself.

Then he shows, that He has also been given by Himself, saying thus in the same book:[6] « Since it was not defined through the Prophet, from whom the Son is given, it is shown, (that when He is) given by the grace of the Trinity, that the Son Himself also gave Himself ». Behold here he says, that the Son gave Himself, because the Trinity[7] gave Him. But if the Son has been given by Himself, therefore, He has been sent by Himself and proceeded from Himself. And this certainly [utique] is true and must [oportet] be conceded, since His mission is a divine operation.

Moreover, that He is sent by Himself (St.) Augustine adds [astruit] in the second book, ON THE TRINITY, saying:[8] « Perchance someone thinks, that we are saying, that the Son has also been sent by Himself; because (His) conceiving and being-born from Mary is an operation of the Trinity? But, does anyone say, in what manner the Father sent Him, if He sent Himself? To which I respond asking, granted that he says (this), in what manner did the Father sanctify Him, if He sanctified Himself? For each did the Lord say:[9] *Whom the Father*, He says, *sanctified and sent into this world.* And elsewhere: *I sanctify Myself on their behalf.* Likewise I ask, in what manner did the Father hand Him over, if He handed Himself over? For each is read.[10] I believe, he shall respond, if one knows rightly, that there is one Will of the Father and of the Son, and an inseparable operation. Therefore, let him understand in this manner, that that Incarnation and Nativity from the Virgin, in which the Son is understood (to have been) sent, has been wrought by one and the same operation of the Father and the Son, not with the Holy Spirit separated from it. Therefore, the Same Son has been sent by the Father and the Son, because it has been wrought by the Father and[11] His Word, that He was sent, that is, that He appeared Incarnate to men. For He was not sent by changing place, because He was in the world. Wherefore the invisible Father, one with the Son invisible with Himself, by making the same Son visible, is said to have sent Him: who if He became visible thus, that He would cease to be invisible with the Father, that is, if the invisible Substance[12] of the Word, having been changed and passing over, was turned into a visible creature, such that the Son would be understood (to have been) sent by the Father, as only One sent, He would not also be found (to be) sending (Himself) with the Father. On the other hand, since in this manner (the Substance) was accepted *in the form of a servant*, though It remained the incommutable *form of God*,[13] it is manifest, that it has been wrought by the Father and the Son, not by appearances, that It appeared in the Son (Incarnate), that is, (that) the same Son, Himself (now) visible, was sent by the invisible Father with the invisible Son ».

From the aforesaid it is openly demonstrated, that the Son has been sent by the Father and by[14] the Holy Spirit and by Himself, and what is the mission itself, namely, the Incarnation, that is, that He has been made Man, through which He appeared visible, which is a common work of the Father and of the Son and of the Holy Spirit.

---

[1] Gal. 4:4. — A little before this, the Vatican edition, against codd. A B C & D and edd. 1 & 8, has *first* [primo] for *first of all* [primum], and, next, with all the edd., except ed. 3, with changed punctuation, reads badly: *Let the Apostle say that He (was) sent* [missum eum Apostolus dicat].

[2] Loc. cit., n. 8, according to its sense. — The passage from Isaias is 18:16. The Vulgate reads: *Now the Lord God has sent me* etc.[Nunc Dominus Deus misit me etc.].

[3] Chapter 1, nn. 7 and 8. — The following passage is ibid, ch. 2, n. 9; the third from the words *For the Son of God says* etc. [Dicit enim etc.] is ibid., ch. 1, nn. 1, 2 and 6 passim.

[4] Isaias 9:6. The Vulgate reads: *For a little child is born* etc. [Parvulus enim natus etc.].

[5] Lk. 4:18, where Christ, in the synagogue, reads the words of Isaias 61:1-2, and after v. 21 says: *Because today this Scripture is fulfilled* etc. [Quia hodie impleta est etc.]. — Then in place of *signify* [significaret] the Vatican edition together with very many editions has *mark* [signaret], but contradicting codices A C D and editions 1 and 8.

[6] Chapter 2, n. 9. — At the beginning of this passage, the Vatican edition and editions 4, 6, 8 and 9, add *For* [enim]. Then, after *from whom* [a quo datus] we have changed the verb to the subjunctive on the authority of all the codices and editions 1, 5, 6 and 8 (as required by the grammatical construction).

[7] Codex D prefixes to this *whole* [total]; edition 1 adds *equally* [aeque].

[8] Chapter 5, n. 9. — In this text in place of *thinks* [cogat] edition 6 has *asks* [rogat]; and editions 8 and 9 have *thinks* [cogitat]. — Next, the Vatican edition and very many editions by adding *and* [et] before *Mary* [Mariae], contrary to the codices and to editions 1 and 6, [read: ... *and being-born and Mary's*]; (St.) Augustine wrote *that conceiving* etc. [ille conceptus etc.]. A little below this before *He sanctified Himself* [ipse se sanctificavit] we have likewise removed *also* [et] on the authority of the codices and editions 1, 6 and 8.

[9] John 10:36, where the Vulgate omits the *this* [hunc] before *world* [mundum]. — The second passage is John 17:19.

[10] Rom. 8:32, and Gal. 2:20. — Then very many editions after *I believe* [Credo] add *that* [quod].

[11] Codices A and B and editions 1 and 8 repeat *by* [a].

[12] Only the Vatican edition and editions 4, 8 and 9 badly prefix an *in*, by reading: *in the invisible Substance* [in substantia etc.].

[13] A reference to Phil. 2:6,7.

[14] The Vatican edition and edition 6 omit *by* [a]; a little before this, editions 1 and 8 have *above said* [supra dictis] in place of *aforesaid* [praedictis].

CHAPTER V

In what manner this must be understood:
I have not come on My own.

But to this there is opposed: if the Son has been sent by Himself, why, therefore, does He say:[1] *I have not come on My own*? To this (St.) Augustine responds in the second book, ON THE TRINITY,[2] saying: « That this has been said according to the form of a servant, according to which He did not cause Himself to be sent », that is, He did not work the Incarnation (as Man), but according to the form of God.

PART II

CHAPTER VI

Whether the Son has been sent only once, or often.

Here, there is asked, whether the Son has been sent only once, or whether He is sent often. For if the mission of the Son Himself is only the Incarnation, since He has been incarnate only once, He seems also (to have been) sent only once. Or if He is sent often, there is also a mission of His other than the Incarnation. But what is that? Must the eternal begetting [genitura] be said (to be) His mission, or is another mission[3] also to be sought?

CHAPTER VII

On the two manners of the Son's mission.

To which we say, that the Son is said to be sent[4] in two manners, besides that eternal begetting, which is ineffable, according to which He could also be said (to have been) sent, as seems to certain ones, but better and more truly is said (to have been) begotten according to that one. Besides that one, therefore, He is said to be sent in two manners, namely when He appeared visibly to the world as one clothed in flesh, and/or when *He transfers Himself thus into pious souls,*[5] so that He be perceived and cognized by them. These two manners of mission (St.) Augustine openly distinguishes in the fourth book, ON THE TRINITY,[6] saying: « Not for the very reason that He has been born from the Father, is the Son said (to be) sent, but either for the reason that He appeared to this world as the Word made flesh; whence He says:[7] *I have gone forth from the Father and have come into the world,* and/or for the reason that He is perceived in time by the mind of everyone [cuiusquam], just as has been said of Wisdom:[8] *Send Her forth from Thy holy heavens and from the throne of Thy Majesty, so that She might be with me and work with me,* that is, teach me to work. And then He is sent to each one, when He is cognized and perceived by anyone, as much as He can be cognized and perceived by the comprehension [pro captu] of one making his way [proficientis] unto God, and/or of the rational soul perfected in God ».

CHAPTER VIII

That according to one manner He has been sent once, according to the other often; and according to one manner He is said (to have been) sent into the world, according to the other (He is) not.

Behold, there have been distinguished the two manners of the mission of the Son[9], and according to one the Son of God has been sent only once, according to the other He has been sent often and is sent daily. For according to one He has been sent, to be a Man, which only happened once; but, according to the other He is sent, to be with man, in the manner[10] in which He is daily sent to the Saints and Has been sent even before the Incarnation and to all Saints, who were before, and even to the Angels. Whence (St.) Augustine speaking of the Son, that is of the Wisdom of the Father, in the fourth book ON THE TRINITY[11] says: « In one manner Wisdom is sent, to be with man; in another He is sent, to be a man. *For into holy souls does He transfer Himself, and establishes them friends of God and Prophets*; just as He also fills the Holy Angels. But, when the fullness of time came, He was sent, not to fill the Angels nor to be an Angel nor to be with men and/or in men,[12] as He was before in the Patriarch and in the Prophets, but so that the Word Himself might become flesh, that is a Man ».

Besides it must be noted, that since the Son is sent in these two manners, according to one He is said (to have been) "sent" in to the world, according to the other (His is) not. For, He is said (to have been) "sent" into the world in that manner, whereby He appeared visible to the world. Whence (St.) Augustine in the same book[13] says: « When in time He is perceived by any mind, He is, indeed, said to be "sent", but not into this world. For He does not appear sensibly, that is, is not present [praesto est] to the corporal senses. For we too, according to which we grasp anything eternal with our mind, are not in this world, and even the spirits of all of the just living in the flesh, inasmuch as they tasted divine (things),

---

[1] John 7:28 and 8:12. — A little before this editions 1, 2 and 8, have *But still* [Sed adhuc] for *But to this* [Sed ad hoc].

[2] Chapter 5, n. 9.

[3] Codex D repeats *of Him* [eius] after *mission* [missio]; in this proposition edition 3 omits *is* [est].

[4] Codex C has *(to have been) sent* [missus].

[5] An allusion to Wis. 7:27, where the Vulgate reads: *And throughout the nations into holy souls does She transfer Herself, and establish them as friends of God and Prophets* [Et per nationes in animas sanctas se transfert, amicos Dei et Prophetas constituit: in which text *She* refers to Wisdom, since in Latin, *wisdom* [sapientia] is feminine in gender].

[6] Chapter 20, n. 28 and the other words from n. 27. — In this passage, (St.) Augustine and codices A and D read *for the very reason by which* [eo ipso quo] in place of *for the very reason that* [eo ipso quod]; then the Vatican edition and edition 4 omit *either* [vel] after *but* [sed].

[7] John 16:28.

[8] Wisdom 9:10. The Vulgate reads: *Send Her* [mitte illam].

[9] Edition 6 adds here *of God* [Dei] and then reads *He has been sent only once* [semel tantum missus est], omitting *the Son of God* [Dei Filius]; after these words editions 2, 3, 5 and 9 insert *and* [et].

[10] Codex C adds *through grace* [per gratiam]. Below this, editions 1 and 8 omit *and* [et] after *Incarnation* [incarnationem].

[11] Chapter 20, n. 27. — Again Wisdom 7:27 is cited. In the Vulgate, the *for* [enim] is lacking, which however, we put on account of the text of (St.) Augustine, and all the codices and editions, except the Vatican and nn. 3 and 5.

[12] Editions 1 and 8 add *only* [tantum], and immediately before this edition 1 reads *nor* [nec] for *and/or* [vel].

[13] Chapter 20, n. 28. — In this text, codices A C and D add *even* [etiam] after *For we too* [Nam et nos].

tasted divine (things), are not in this world ». From the aforesaid one may clarify [liquet], that besides the ineffable begetting the Son is sent in two manners, namely when He appeared visibly, and/or is perceived invisibly by the mind.

CHAPTER IX

For what reason is the Father not said (to be) sent.

Here, there is asked, why is the Father not said (to be) sent, when in time He is cognized by someone, just as the Son (is). To which we say, that in Him is the authority of a principle, who[1] does not have, from whom He is, by whom the Son is and the Holy Spirit (too). « For the Father is », as (St.) Augustine says in the same book,[2] « the Principle of the whole Divinity, and/or if it is better said, of the Deity », because He is the Principle of the Son and of the Holy Spirit. For, as (St.) Augustine says in the same (book),[3] « if God the Father had also wanted to appear visibly through a subjected creature, most absurdly would He be said (to have been) sent either by the Son, whom He begot, or by the Holy Spirit, who proceeds from Him ». Congruently on the one hand, is He said (to have been) *sent*, who appeared in the flesh; (and congruently) on the other, *to have sent* He, who did not appear in it.

CHAPTER X

That the Son and the Holy Spirit are not as ones lesser than the Father, because (They have been) sent.

And, for that reason, certain heretics thought, since the Father has not been sent, but the Son and the Spirit (have), that the Father is greater or[4] the Son lesser and the Holy Spirit (likewise); and also that the Father as one greater has sent Each as lesser. Which (St.) Augustine disproves in the fourth book, ON THE TRINITY,[5] contradicting them: « Not for that reason », he says, « must it be judged, that the Son is lesser, because He has been sent by the Father, nor for that reason the Holy Spirit lesser, because the Father sent Him and the Son (likewise); for either on account of the visible creature, or rather on account of the commendation of (Him as) Principle, not on account of inequality and/or imparity and/or dissimilitude of substance are these things posited in the Scriptures understood ». Therefore, the Father is not said to have sent the Son and/or the Holy Spirit for the reason, that He was greater and They lesser, but most of all for the sake of commending the authority of the Principle, and because in a visible creature He did not, like Them,[6] appear. Behold, it has been shown, what is the mission of the Son, and in what manners is He sent.

COMMENTARY ON DISTINCTION XV

On mission, as much as regards (its) principle and manner.

PART I

On mission or temporal procession, as much as regards (its) principle.

Here, there must be considered, since the Holy Spirit is given to men by the Father and the Son.

THE DIVISION OF THE TEXT

Above, Master (Peter) deals with the temporal procession of the Holy Spirit Himself, according to which it is from the Father and the Son; here, he shows *second*, that He proceeds temporally from Himself; and he tries to prove [intendit] this in that entire part up to there (where he says): *Here, there is asked, whether the Son has been sent only once*, where he begins to deal (with it) as much as regards *the manner* of the procession.[1]

Moreover, this part has four parts. In *the first*, he shows, that the Holy Spirit is sent by, given by, and proceeds from the Holy Spirit temporally, that this *by a deduction to the impossible* [deducendo ad impossibile], that otherwise the works of the Trinity would not be undivided. In *the second*, he shows, a minori, through authorship, that the Father sent the Son one with the Holy Spirit, such that the Holy Spirit sent the Son, in

---

[1] Contrary to nearly all the codices and edition 6, the Vatican edition, together with the other editions, faultily reads *which* [quae], since the context of the relative must be referred to *in Him* [in eo]. A little before this, codices C and E have *that* [quod] in place of *that* [quia]. Then, after *the Son* [Filius] the Vatican alone omits *is* [est].

[2] Book IV, ch. 20, n. 29.

[3] Chapter 21, n. 32. — The Vatican edition alone reads: *Because even if God the Father had wanted* [Quia etiam si voluisset etc.]. Then all the editions, excepting the Vatican edition and edition 8, read badly *He would appear* [appareret] for *to appear* [apparere]. In favor of our reading are those of the codices and the original. And next, at *who proceeds* [qui ... procedit], codices A C D read well *Him* [ipso] for *Him* [illo].

[4] The Vatican and the other editions, except n. 1, contrary to the codices, except E, add *that ... is* [esse].

[5] Chapter 21, n. 32. — In this passage on the authority of the codices, editions 1 and 8, and the original, after *the Holy Spirit is lesser* [minorem Spiritum sanctum], we have put *because* [quia] in place of *because* [quod], and before *commendation* [commendationem] we have expunged *authority and/or* [auctoritatem vel].

[6] The Vatican edition together with all the editions, except n. 1, faultily reads *like the Former (i.e. the Father)* [sicut ille], contradicting all the codices; *They* [illi] refers to the Son and the Holy Spirit.

NOTES ON THE COMMENTARY

[1] The Vatican edition, not trusting in the manuscripts and edition 1, has *with the manner* [de modo] in place of *(with it) as much as regards the manner* [quantum ad modum], then after *procession* [processioni] it adds *or of the mission of the Son, who is visible and invisible. And this in a certain manner accidentally, since that mission of His befits the Son and the Holy Spirit* [seu missionis Filii, qui est visibilis et invisibilis. Et hoc quodam modo accidentaliter, cum ista missio et Filio conveniat et Spiritui sancto.].

---

* *Trans. note*: Here, a minori is shorthand, for *an argument a minori*. Such is the topical syllogism, which arrives at an affirmative conclusion, by means of arguing from what the lesser could do or has, and concluding that the greater can or has likewise. Cf. Pietro Ispano, TRATTATO DI LOGICA, tract V, "De locis", trans. A. Ponzio, (Bompiani, Milano, 2004), p. 172-175, n. 32.

whom he has in no manner[1] an authorship, therefore, much more strongly does He send Himself; and this he does there (where he says): *But do not wonder, that the Holy Spirit is said to be sent and/or to proceed from Himself.* In *the third part*, on the other hand, he shows this a simili:* for if the Son sent Himself, for an equal reason the Holy Spirit

(sent) Himself; and this he does there (where he says): *Then he shows that He has also been sent from Himself.* However, in *the fourth* and last he opposes (arguments) against the aforesaid, and this there (where he says): *But to this is opposed: 'If the Son by Himself'* etc., where he also solves and briefly concludes the predetermined (arguments).

TREATMENT OF THE QUESTIONS

For an understanding of this part (of Master Peter's text), four (questions) are asked:

First, there is asked, whether there is 'mission' is among the divine.

Second, granted that there is,[2] whether the mission

is on account of time and/or eternal.

Third there is asked, to whom does the mission belong as to one sent.

Fourth, to whom does the mission belong as to the one sending.

ARTICLE SOLE

On mission, among the divine.

QUESTION I

Whether there is 'mission' among the divine?

About the first, that there is 'mission' among the divine, is shown:

1. First through the writing of the Old Testament, in the ninth (chapter) of Wisdom:[3] *Send Her from Thy holy heavens,* and (that) Wisdom is spoken of, which is the Son of God.

2. Likewise, through the writing of the New Testament, in the fourth (chapter) of (the Letter) to the Galatians:[4] *But when the fullness of time came, God sent His own Son.* And afterwards:[5] *Since you are the sons of God, God sent the Spirit of His Son into your hearts.*

3. Likewise, this is shown through the testimony of the Truth, in the sixteenth (chapter of the Gospel) of (St.) John:[6] *but when I go away, I shall sent you the Spirit of Truth.*

4. Likewise, that same is seen[7] *by reason:* because "to send" is nothing other than to lead something forth [producere] into another, just as the Sun sends a ray into the lower heavens [in aëra]; but the Holy Spirit proceeds from the Father and the Son into the creature: therefore, He is sent by Them.

5. Likewise, whensoever anything is given to anyone as to one absent, it is fittingly said that (it) is sent; but the whole Trinity is absent to sinners as much as regards indwelling grace: therefore, whensoever the Holy Spirit is given as much as regards indwelling grace, He is not incongruously said to be sent; if, therefore, *to be given* is among the divine in this manner, as was said,[8] therefore, also *mission.*

ON THE CONTRARY: 1. Wheresoever there is mission, there is *separation,* whence (St.) Jerome (says) on Ezechiel:[9] «What

has been conjoined and united [copulatum] in one body cannot be sent, but what is outside (can be) »; whence a hand is not sent, but a dart [iaculum] (can). But among the divine there is an omnimodal indivision and no separation: ergo etc..

2. Likewise, wheresoever mission is, there[10] is a *subjection* of the one sent to the one sending; which is clear: for a lord sends the servant, and not the servant the lord. But among the divine there is an omnimodal equality and no subjection: therefore, there is not mission There.

3. Likewise, wheresoever mission is, there is *change* [mutatio], because something is not said to be sent, where it is; but among the divine entirely no change occurs: ergo etc..

4. Likewise, mission, passively said, inasmuch as (it is) such, is a work of ministry, but in the Most Noble Nature, inasmuch as (it is) such, ministry does not occur: ergo etc..

CONCLUSION

There is 'mission' among the divine; yet, from the threefold looking-back of mission to (its) principle, to (its) terminus, to the one sent, every imperfection, such as is in a mission among creatures, is to be removed.

I RESPOND: It must be said, that there is "mission" among the divine, just as the aforesaid authorities and reasons show: and it is transferred from creatures to God.

---

[1] Edition 1 has *no* [nullam] for *in no manner an* [nullo modo]. Then codex V reads *did He send* [misit] for *does He send* [mittit].

[2] Codex T repeats here *there is asked* [quaeritur], but ed. 1 omits *granted that it is* [dato quod sic].   [3] Verse 10.

[4] Verse 4, in which text, trusting in the manuscripts and the Vulgate, we have substituted *But when* [At ubi] for *When* [Cum].

[5] Ibid., verse 6.

[6] Verse 7, where the Vulgate reads: *But if I shall go away, I shall send Him (the Paraclete) to you* [Si autem abiero, mittam eum], John 15:26: *Whom I shall send you from the Father, the Spirit of Truth* [Quem

ego mittam vobis a Patre, spiritum veritatis]. — A little before this, one or the other cod., such as S, after *this* [hoc] adds *very same (thing)* [ipsum].

[7] Codex S has *is shown* [ostenditur]. Then edition 1 has *that* [illud] for *that* [istud]. A little below this, having followed the codd. and edd. 1, 2, 3 & 6, we have put *the lower heavens* [aëra] for *air* [aërem].

[8] Distinction 14, a. 1, q. 1, and a. 2, q. 1.

[9] Ezechiel 15:54, among which words in the original there is exhibited *the body* [corpus] after *outside* [extra].

[10] From the more ancient manuscripts and edition 1, we have supplied *there* [ibi].

---

* *Trans. note:* The Latin expression, a simili, is a shorthand, for *an argument a simili.* Such is a topical syllogism, which arrives at an affirmative conclusion, by means of arguing that, if something can do or has such in something, its similar can do or has such in the similar of that something. Cf. Pietro Ispano, TRATTATO DI LOGICA, tract V, "De locis", trans. A. Ponzio, (Bompiani, Milano, 2004), pp. 174-175, n. 33.

Moreover, according to which mission is considered among these inferiors, it has a regard for three (things), namely to (its) *principle*, and to (its) *terminus* and to *the one sent*.

It happens that it is compared to *(its) principle* or to the one sending under a threefold habitude: as to one giving '*being*' and in this manner a ray is sent from the Son; as to the one giving *virtue*, and in this manner a dart is sent by the thrower [proiectore]; as to the one giving *jurisdiction* or authority, and in this manner a messenger is sent by an officer [praetore].[1] According to all these comparisons [omnem hanc comparationem] there is mission among the divine; because the Holy Spirit is sent by the Father and the Son as One having '*being*' and *virtue* and *authority* in operating by Them; and for that reason 'mission' according to this respect is most completely[2] among the divine. For it is not that one posits, that one person receives authority (from anyone), except (from the one) from whom he receives virtue, nor virtue, except (from the one) from whom he receives 'being'.

Similarly, it is compared to *(its) terminus* under a threefold habitude. For something is sent somewhere,[3] namely, where *it comes to rest*, such as [ut] a stone is sent downward; it is also sent to someone, such as by whom *it is had*, just as someone sends someone a gift; it is also sent, as for example [ut], *for something*, which, that is, it works. According to this threefold comparison there is 'mission' among the divine. For the Son and/or the Holy Spirit is sent, as for example, to *indwell* somewhere, as for example, to someone *to be possessed* as a gift, (and) as for example, for *something*, that is, to confer[4] an effect. And for that reason mission through a comparison to (its) terminus is found most completely among the divine, much more than among creatures.

Moreover, if we speak of mission in comparison to *the one sent*, in this manner it posits among these inferiors a threefold condition *of imperfection*, that is, a *separation*, a *subjection*, and a *change* [mutationem]; which, indeed, are not among the divine. However, there is something of perfection corresponding to these There; and the reason for this is clear in this manner:

Among these inferiors, the one sent is separated from the one sending on account of the distance of the terminus from the one sending;[5] as is clear, when I send someone to Rome; because Rome is distant from me, if (the one sent) ought to be at Rome, it is necessary [oportet] that he be separated from me. On the other hand, among the divine, because the God sending is everywhere, there is no distance, and for that reason there is no separation; yet, in place of this there is the egress, or emanation, of the one sent from the one sending.[6]

1. And thus is clear the response to that which is objected concerning the condition of *separation*.

Similarly, among these inferiors there is in the one sent a *subjection* on account of the difference of the one sending to the one sent. For because the one sent receives from the one sending either "being", and/or virtue, and/or operation, it is also separated from it in substance — because a substance entirely the same is not shared by many — it is necessary, that it receive some virtue from it and some jurisdiction inferior to it. But among the divine there is not a substantial difference, and for that reason all (these) are of equal nobility in the One sending and the One sent. But, yet, in place of this there is an emanation[7] of *subauthorship*.

2. And thus is clear the second objection.

Similarly, among these inferiors there is in the one sent a *change* on account of the distance of the one sent from the terminus. For, because[8] it is not at the terminus [in termino], to which it is sent, for that reason it is necessary [oportet] that it change place, and thus that there be in it a change. On the other hand, because among the divine the One sent is absent to no place, it is not required [non oportet], that He approach personally; and for that reason there is *not a change* There. But, yet, in place of this there is the production of some effect anew.

3. And, thus, is clear the third objection. For although among the divine there is not separation, subjection and change, yet in place of these there is emanation, origin of sub-authorship and the production of a new effect.

4. To that which is objected last, that it pertains to ministry; it must be said, that this is true, where the "being sent" [missio] means a "being subjected" [subiectio]; but this is not in the Divine Nature, but (rather) in creatures.

SCHOLIUM

I. In what manner the *temporal procession, mission,* (and) *giving* of the Holy Spirit differ is not determined in the same manner by the ancient Scholastics. Let us hear Richard of Middleton (Sent., Bk. I, d. 14, a. 1, q. 3): « Certain ones want, that they do not really differ, but only according to a reckoning. For the temporal procession principally conveys a looking-back to the *terminus to which*, the mission to the *principle from which*, but the donation *to the effect*. Moreover, some strive to assign a greater difference among these three. For they say, that the *temporal procession* in its principal signified [de principali significato] does not signify except the eternal procession with a certain looking-back according to a reckoning and/or according to a being-said regarding the creature, and in act connotes a new effect in the creature and a new, real relation in the creature to the Holy Spirit. On the other hand, *donation* in its principal signified does not mean some emanation, because the whole Trinity gives Itself — speaking of emanation according to the thing, by which the very Person Himself emanates — but (rather) means the emanation of the gift appropriated

---

[1] Many codices together with edition 1, 2 and 3, faultily read *instructor* [praeceptore].

[2] Codex M adds *also* [etiam].

[3] The Vatican edition among the members of this and the following proposition always exhibits *to someone* [alicui]; the codices are divided among themselves, for some put three times *somewhere* [alicubi], others, such as F H T etc. together with edition 1, exhibit our reading, which also corresponds more with the context.

[4] With the consent of the ancient mss. and ed. 1, we have substituted *confer* [conferendum] for *work* [operandum]. Then some codices, such as A and N, have *according to* [secundum] for *through* [per].

[5] The Vatican edition together with codex cc has *to the one sending* [ad mittentem], but less well and contrary to the other codices together with edition 1. — A little below this after *that* [quod] codex I adds *he be distant and* [distet et].

[6] Codex K, with changed punctuation, has *there is no separation of place; yet a mission of this kind is from one sending* etc. [nulla est separatio loci; tamen huiusmodi missio est a mittente].

[7] The Vatican edition without the authority of the manuscripts and editions 1, 2 or 3, has *origin* [origo]. On subauthorship see below q. 4 in the body of the response, and above d. 12, q. 2, then d. 20, a. 1, q. 2 in reply to n. 4. — A little before this codex W puts *entirely* [omnino] in place of *all (these)* [omnia], which refers to *virtue* and *jurisdiction*.

[8] From the manuscripts and editions 1, 2, and 3, we have substituted *because* [quia] for *when* [cum], and a little below this from the more ancient codices together with edition 1, we have supplied the faultily omitted *thus* [ita].

[9] Codex I reads *yet in place of these there is emanation of a Person* [tamen loco harum est personae emanatio].

appropriated to the Person, in which gift the true (and) very Person Himself is also given to the one receiving that gift. On the other hand, *mission* means a looking-back to the Person emanating through the emanation of some thing visible and/or invisible appropriated to that Person. And thus concerning mission's principal signified there is not an emanation of Person, but there is concerning co-understanding [cointellectu] of mission's signified, just as a nose does not concern the principal signification of simity, although the simity of the nose includes the nose from its co-understanding ». Richard of Middleton himself prefers the second opinion, below in d. 15, p. I, a. 3, q. 1.

With these words there is already manifest, that some thought, that mission *principally* signified the procession of one Person from another (Person), but *connoted* the manifestation of the Same. Thus Alexander of Hales, SUMMA, p. I, q. 71, m. 2 and 4, and not a few moderns, such as Suarez. But St. Bonaventure below (q. 4 in the body of the response and more clearly in reply to n. 3) says: « Mission of itself conveys two (significations), that is emanation and manifestation, and *principally* from the reckoning of its own signification *it conveys manifesta-*

tion ». The same sentence is proffered by St. Thomas (here in q. 1, a. 2; d. 16, q. 1, a. 1; SUMMA., I, q. 43, a. 2 especially in reply to n. 3), Bl John Duns Scotus (SENT. Bk. I, d. 16, q. sole), St. Albertus Magnus, Bl. Peter of Tarentaise, and Richard of Middleton, in the passages cited below.

II. In the response St. Bonaventure teaches, that there is a threefold looking-back included in mission, and he compares these three members again in a threefold manner. According to these multiple looking-backs he resolves, that there are to be removed from the divine missions, whatever (imperfections were) to be posited in them.

III. Alexander of Hales, SUMMA., p. I, q. 71, m. 1. — (Bl. John Duns) Scotus, on this and the following questions here and in the REPORTATIO, q. sole. — St. Thomas, here in q. 1, a. 1; SUMMA., I, q. 43, a. 1. — Bl. (now St.) Albertus (Magnus), SENT., Bk. I, d. 14, aa. 3 and 4. — (Bl.) Peter of Tarentaise, here in q. 1, aa. 1, 2 and 3. — Richard of Middleton, here in a. 1 q. 1. — Giles the Roman, here in 1st princ., q. 1. — Durandus (of Saint-Pourçain), on this and the following question, here in q. 1. — (Bl.) Dionysius the Carthusian, here in q. 1. — (Gabriel) Biel, on this and the following question, here in the q. sole.

QUESTION II

Whether 'mission' among the divine is only on account of time, or whether, also, from eternity?

Second, there is asked, whether mission among the divine is only on account of time [ex tempore], or also from eternity. And that (it is) from eternity, is shown *by authority* and *by reason*.

1. *By authority* in this manner: (Pope St.) Gregory (the Great):[1] « The Son is sent according to that very manner, whereby He is generated »; but He is generated from eternity: therefore, He is sent from eternity: therefore, mission among the divine is from eternity.

2. Likewise, (St.) Bede (the Venerable) in the homily:[2] « The Holy Spirit's being-sent [missio] is His procession »; but He proceeds from eternity: therefore, He is sent from eternity.

3. Likewise, *by reason* in this manner: "mission" (in God), either actively or passively said, is God; but every action, which is actively and passively is God, is from eternity: ergo etc..

4. Likewise, every action, which has God as (its) terminus and as (its) principle, is from eternity, as is clear, when there is said: "God understands God",[3] "God generates God"; but mission is of this kind, because God sends God: therefore, the mission is eternal. *If you say*, that mission requires a twofold terminus, that is 'him who is sent', and 'him to whom he is sent', and the one to whom the mission comes to be, is temporal: *on the contrary*: God can be the One who sends, God, the one who is sent: therefore, for an equal reason God, to whom He is sent; and it seems, that those comparisons of principle and terminus befit God most of all. For God is *the Alpha an the Omega, the Principle and the End*:[4] therefore, more properly is God said (to be the One), to whom it is sent, than God, who is sent.

5. Likewise, whatever is God, is eternal; mission (in God) is God: therefore, it is eternal; but the premises are true: therefore, also the conclusion.

ON THE CONTRARY: 1. In the sixteenth (chapter of the Gospel of St.) John[5] (there is written): *If I will not go away the Paraclete will not come to you; but when I shall go away, I shall send Him to you*. Therefore, the Holy Spirit can be sent and promised; what is eternal cannot be promised: ergo etc..

2. Likewise, (St.) Augustine in the fourth (book) ON THE TRINITY[6] (says): « The Son and/or the Holy Spirit is sent, when in time He is perceived by the mind of anyone ».

3. Likewise, every mission is to[7] something posterior to the one sending; but where there occurs a posterior there necessarily intervenes the reckoning of a principle and of time: ergo etc.. The first proposition is true per se, because the one sending, through (a consideration of what is) prior, has that which[8] he sends, rather than the one, to whom he sends (it), has (it).

4. Likewise, every mission either is by reason of a change, and/or by reason of an operation; but among the divine there is not change: therefore, for this, that there be a mission, it is necessary that an operation intervene; and if an operation, also an effect; and if an effect, also[9] a time: therefore, every mission is on account of time.

CONCLUSION

'Mission' on account of its comparison to the created terminus must be said to be "temporal".

I RESPOND: It must be said, regarding the aforesaid, that "mission" among the divine is in no manner to be said except on account of time [ex tempore]. And the reason for this is, because it means a comparison not only to the principle nor only to the one sent, but

---

[1] HOMILIES ON THE GOSPELS, 26, n. 2: For the Son is said to be sent by the Father for the very reason, that He is generated by the Father. In which text very many codices and edition 1 omit *very* [ipso]. [Trans. Note: in this ambiguous phrase of St. Gregory, the Latin construction *eo ... quo* has both this sense and that understood in n. 1].

[2] See the text of Master (Peter), Distinction XIV, ch. 1.

[3] We leave the second *God* [Deum] in place, though nearly all the codd. and first six edd. have let it fall away, perhaps on account of the immediately following repetition of the noun *God* [God]; likewise it recurs just after *generates* [generat].   [4] Apocalypse 1:8.

[5] Verse 7; the last part of this text is exhibited thus in the Vulgate: *But if I will go away, I shall send Him to you* [Si autem abiero, mittam eum ad vos]. — Then, at the beginning of the next sentence, trusting in very many

mss., such as F H I T X aa bb & ff and ed. 1, we have expunged *When* [Cum], which on account of the form of the argument is better omitted.

[6] Chapter 20, n. 28. See here the text of Master (Peter), chs. 7 and 8. — At the beginning of the words of (St.) Augustine not a few codices, such as I bb and ff together with edition 1, add *Then* [Tunc].

[7] From the manuscripts and edition 1, we have supplied *to* [ad], which the Vatican edition, as is clear from what follows, badly omits. Codex Z prefixes to this *to* [ad] *from someone* [ab aliquo], in place of which codex O has *in some manner* [aliquot modo].

[8] One or the other codex, such as T & cc, have *the one whom* [ipsum quem] for *that which* [quem].

[9] Very many codices, such as F G I K T V Y aa bb ee and ff, together with edition 1, omit *also* [et].

also to the terminus. That terminus[1] of necessity is created, because mission in God, since it does not mean a change, means some operation about the terminus, and thus some effect, and because everything which receives an effect, is created and temporal: for that reason mission of necessity is temporal.

1. To that, therefore, which (St.) Gregory says: « The Son is sent in that manner, whereby is He generated »; it must be said, that he speaks, having presupposed (His) manifestation in a creature.[2] For the Father is manifested in a creature, but is not sent, but the Son is sent. And (St.) Gregory reckons [reddit rationem], that there is no other cause, except that That of His[3] is generated, (and) He, that is, the Father, (is) not.

2. To that which is objected concerning (St.) Bede, it must be said, that (St.) Bede speaks of the procession of the Holy Spirit, insofar as it is in a creature, and thus it is always temporal, as a mission.

3. To that which is objected, that everything which is posited actively and passively, in God, is eternal; it must be said, that it is true, unless it has some further regard to a creature; but mission besides the respect, which is of the One sending to the One sent, conveys some effect in the creature.[4]

To that which is objected, that mission (in God), actively and passively (said), is God; it must be said, that there is a certain action, which looks back to the one alone enduring it, such as « striking you »; a certain one, which (looks back) to the one enduring it and to another terminus, such as « I am teaching you grammar », similarly also « I am sending you to that place ». And that which it objects[5] is true in the action and passion, which look back to nothing else but to the principle and object; but not in the others, which require another terminus, and for that reason it withstands the proposed.

4. Similarly, must it be solved regarding the one following, that it is true, if that action were entirely terminated[6] in God.

But what it objects, that mission looks back to God as its terminus to which; it must be said, that if a terminus, to which there is a mission, would be only in the reckoning *of one finishing*, it would be[7] true; but now it is not so, but rather in the reckoning *of one taking it up*.

5. To the last objection it must be said, that there is a circumlocution [paralogismus] *of accident* there,* just as in this: 'every piece of copper is natural, the statue is copper: ergo, etc.'; because what belonged to the matter is attributed to the statue by reason of craftsmanship. Similarly, here, because what belonged to the Divine Essence is attributed to mission by reason of the connotation.

SCHOLIUM

I. In the conclusion all agree, even those, who with Alexander of Hales stated, that "mission" in its principal signified means something eternal, namely, the eternal procession. Alexander of Hales himself (loc. cit.) solves this objection posited here in the last place: « Of mission there is a speaking as much as regards (its) principal signified and as much as regards (its) connotation: by reason of (its) principal signified it is something eternal; by reason of (its) connotation it is on account of time. But when the eternal is conjoined to the temporal in the same terminus, properly speaking, it ought to be judged temporal, just as, when the necessary is conjoined with the contingent, the whole is judged contingent. For that reason in that argument

there is a fallacy of accident: 'mission is God; and God is eternal: therefore, mission is eternal'; because eternity, which is in the (thing) principally signified by mission, is inferred from what is connoted. For this noun *"eternity"*, when it is an adjective, determines the terminus itself and posits its own meaning by reason of its whole signified ».

II. As regards the question itself: Alexander of Hales, SUMMA, p. I, q. 71, m. 4. — St. Thom as, here in q. 4, a. 3; SUMMA., i, q. 43, a. 2. — Bl. (now St.) Albertus (Magnus), here in a. 1. — (Bl.) Peter of Tarentaise, here in q. 4, a. 3. — Richard of Middleton, here in a. 1, q. 2. — Giles the Roman, here in d. 15, p. II, first princ., q. 3. — (Bl.) Dionysius the Carthusian, here in q. 2.

QUESTION III

Whether "mission", passively accepted, belongs to the whole Trinity, in view of the Father?

Second, there is asked, to Whom mission belongs *as to the One sent*. And it seems, that it belongs to the whole Trinity.

1. (St.) Augustine (of Hippo says) in the fourth (book) ON THE TRINITY:[8] « The Son is sent, when in time He is perceived by the mind of

anyone ». But the whole Trinity is perceived by the mind in time: therefore, the whole Trinity is sent: therefore, even the Father.

2. Likewise, 'that a person be sent' is 'that he come to dwell[9] anew'; but the whole Trinity comes anew

---

[1] We follow the reading of the majority of the codices, such as A F G K S T V X Y cc ee ff and edition 1, while the Vatican omitting the final period of the previous sentences, adds at the beginning of this one *but* [sed], however, the other codices, such as I Z bb add *and* [et], and not a few, such as H and W, add *but* [autem: after terminus in the Latin text]. Then after *does not mean* [non dicat] codex B adds *that there is sent* [mitti], but this seems exceedingly strict of a reading.

[2] As required by the more ancient manuscripts and edition 1, we have substituted *as a creature* [in creatura] in place of *among creatures* [creaturis].

[3] Namely: the Son. — The Vatican edition together with codex cc less congruously and contrary to the other codices and edition 1, has *the One* [ille] for *That of His* [iste]. A little before this after *reckons* [reddit rationem] very many codices, such as A I T bb together with edition 1, have *that* [quod] for *that* [quia], some of which, such as bb and edition 1, then after *except* [nisi] have *that* [quia] for *that* [quod]. — See the

other exposition of the words of (St.) Gregory in the second part of this distinction, Doubt 2.

[4] This solution respects the minor of the third and even the major of the fourth objection, but what follows solves the major of the third objection.

[5] The Vatican edition has *is objected* [obiicitur].

[6] Very many codices, such as A I S & T, with edition 1, have *is terminated* [terminetur]. A little before this, codex W omits *that* [illa].

[7] Trusting the manuscripts and edition 1, we have deleted the *in this manner* [sic], which the Vatican has inserted at this point. — Note, that this solution respects that objection, which is contained in the *Contrary* of the first n. 4.

[8] Chapter 20, n. 28. — At the end of the argument after *therefore* [ergo], we have inserted, from some manuscripts, such as H Q and X, the particle *also* [et].

[9] Codices aa and bb have better *indwell* [inhabitandum].

---

* *Trans. note*: That is, a fallacy of the accident, cf. Aristotle, ELENCHAE, Bk. I, ch. 4 (ch. 5), and Peter of Spain, SUMMULA, tr. *"On Fallacies"*, cited in SENT., Bk. III, d. 7, a. 2, q. 2, p. 179, footnote 1. In the example of copper, supply the conclusion, *ergo, the statue is natural.*

comes anew to dwell in the sinner, when grace is given to him: ergo etc.. *The minor* is clear, according to the fourteenth (chapter of the Gospel of St.) John:[1] *We shall come to him* etc..

3. Likewise, "mission" connotes an effect in the creature; but the rule[2] is, that every word [nomen] connoting an effect is said essentially: therefore "mission", passively said, is said essentially; but what is said essentially befits the whole Trinity: ergo etc..

4. Likewise, when anything is sent, there is sent with it everything which is inseparably conjoined to it;[3] but the Father is inseparably conjoined to the Son: therefore, when the Son is sent, the Father is also sent.

5. Likewise, 'to send' and 'to be sent' either are of equal nobility, or (are) not. If *of equal*, therefore, for the reason for which "*to send*" is said of the Father, for the same reason also "*to be sent*": if[4] *of unequal*: therefore, the One sending is greater than the One sent: therefore, the Son is unequal to the Father.

ON THE CONTRARY: 1. (St.) Augustine in the second (book) ON THE TRINITY[5] (says): « Never is the Father read (to have been) "sent" »; but we ought not assert anything of God, which we do not have from Scripture: therefore, "to be sent" does not befit the whole Trinity.

2. Likewise, (St.) Augustine[6] says, that the Father is most absurdly said (to have been) "sent", but true sayings [sermones] are not most absurd; but rather false: therefore, "to be sent" is not truly said of the Father.

3. Likewise, (St.) Augustine[7] says, that "to be sent" is "to be cognized to be from another"; but the Father is not cognized to be from another: therefore, the Father is not sent.

4. Likewise, every mobile is lead back to the immobile,[8] therefore, the sendable to the unsendable: therefore, among the divine there is some unsendable Person, but (This is) not but the Father: ergo etc..

CONCLUSION

"Mission", passively accepted,
can to no extent be said of the Father.

I RESPOND: It must be said, that "mission", as is clear from the reckoning of (St.) Augustine and (as) shall be clearer below,[9] always has two (things) from its own understanding, that is (its) emanation and manifestation through effect. Therefore, because "mission" passively said (i.e. as 'being sent') always conveys emanation passively, hence it is, that since the Father entirely lacks a beginning, that of Him in no manner can a passive mission be said; whence (such a saying) is not found, and if it were found, it would be as a false (saying) and (would have) to be expounded, as if improper.[11]

1. 2. To that, therefore, which is objected first and second,[12] that mission is a perception by the intellect, and/or a dwelling anew; it must be said, that (each) does not recount [non dicit] the whole reckoning of mission, but only on the part of *the terminus unto*[13] *which*; whence there ought to be added with these *the emanation from another*, and then (each argument) is not valid.

3. To that which is objected third, that it connotes[14] an effect, therefore, it is essential; it must be said, that a word [nomen] connoting an effect either means only a looking-back to the effect, and then is purely essential, such as "*to create*", or means also, with this, a looking-back to a person, and thus can be notional, just as "*to create through the Son*" belongs to the Father alone. In this manner it concerns that it is "*to be sent*", because it does not only mean a comparison of the one sent to the one taking-up[15] the effect, but also to the principle. For it signifies, that it is from another and in another; and in this manner that (objection) is clear.

4. To that which is objected, that inseparables are sent together: it must be said, that that is true of that mission, which is through separation; but of that mission, which is through distinction, it is not that one says, that those which are distinguished are sent together,[16] just as neither are those which are separated in the other mission. And since the Father is distinguished from the Son, 'mission' in the divine means distinction; for that reason it is not required [non oportet], that when the Son is sent,[17] the Father be sent.

5. To that which is objected, that of an equal nobility is 'to be sent' as (is)[18] 'to send'; it must be said, that 'to be sent' is not removed from the Father, because it means ignobility, but because it means the emanation and subauthorship, which though it does not belong to ignobility, yet it does not befit the Father.[19]

---

[1] Verse 23.

[2] The Vatican edition together with codex cc has *thus it* [ita] in place of *the rule* [regula], but contrary to the authority of the other codices and edition 1. Then after *every* [omne], we have inserted, from very many codices, such as H M Y aa bb and ff, together with edition 1, *word* [nomen], which is also had below in the response in all the manuscripts. Then edition 1 has *noting* [notans] in place of *connoting* [connotans].

[3] From the manuscripts and edition 1, we have supplied the unduly omitted *to it* [ei], and a little below this after *conjoined* [coniunctus], we have expunged the *with* [cum], in place of which codex W had *Himself* [ipsi]

[4] The Vatican edition, disagreeing with very many manuscripts and edition 1, adds *it is* [est].

[5] Chapter 5, n. 8. See the text of Master (Peter) here in ch. 2.

[6] ON THE TRINITY, Bk. IV, ch. 21, n. 32; see the text of Master (Peter) here in ch. 9.

[7] ON THE TRINITY, Bk. IV, ch. 20, n. 28; see the text of Master (Peter) here in chs. 7-9.

[8] Cf. Aristotle, PHYSICS, Bk. VIII, text 34 ff. (ch. 5). — Then after the first *therefore* [ergo] codex M together with edition 1 inserts *also* [et]. A little below this, trusting in very many manuscripts and editions 1, 4 and 5, we have substituted *some* [aliqua] for the less apt *another* [alia].

[9] The following Question, in the body of the response, and in reply to n. 3. — Then not a few codices, such as aa bb and ff, together with edition 1, have *concerning* [de] in place of *from* [de], and then codex Y after *emanation* [emanationem] adds for explication *passively* [passive].

[10] From the more ancient manuscripts, such as A H I M T V aa bb and ff, we have supplied *passively* [passive], by which reading all ambiguity is removed. Edition 1 omits the first *passively* [passive].

[11] The reading of codex T seems to be preferred, *it would be false and (would have) to be expounded as if improper* [esset falsa et velut impropria exponenda], since *to be expounded* [exponenda] does not fit so well, in place of which one or the other codex has *it would be false and as if improper, I say* [esset falsa et velut impropria inquam].

[12] Though the manuscripts together with edition 1 omit *and second* [et secundo], we nevertheless retain it, because the response here is for the two first objections.

[13] Codex T has *to* [ad]. At the end of the solution codices L and O in place of *is not valid* [non valet] read *is true* [est vera].

[14] Very many codices together with edition 1 have *notes* [notat].

[15] Codex R has *taking-up of or* [susceptionem seu]. At the end of the response, trusting in very many manuscripts and edition 1, we have inserted *that (objection)* [illud].

[16] On the authority of the more ancient codices and edition 1, we have substituted *together* [simul] for *in this manner* [sic]. A little before this codices N and R have *true* [verum] for *that one says* [dicere]. Codex X exhibits the preceding proposition thus: ... *mission it is not true, which is through distinction, for it is not that one says* [missione non est verum, quae est per distinctionem, non enim est dicere]. A little below this by *the other mission* [alia missione] understand that one, *which is through separation*, in which *the inseparables* are sent *together*, but *not separated*.

[17] The Vatican edition together with some manuscripts has *be sent* [mittatur], but less aptly. Codex T has *if* [si] in place of *when* [cum]. Then after *be sent* [mittatur] codex Z adds *also* [et].

[18] Edition 1 has *and* [et] for *as (is)* [ut].

[19] In codex K there is added *nay it is repugnant to His property, because the Father is not from another* [imo repugnat proprietati eius, quia Pater est non ab alio].

SCHOLIUM

The conclusion is the common sentence [sententia communis]; it is also commonly conceded, that a *manifestation* wrought in some effect, appropriated to Him, does befit Him, v. gr. in an apparition. But, because '*mission*' besides this, connotes in the Person sent, an emanation, and the Father does not emanate, for that reason this manifestation of His is not a mission.

Thus Richard (of Middleton), here in a. 2. q. 1. — Alexander of Hales., Summa., p. I, q. 73, m. 2, a. 1. — St. Thomas, here in q. 2; Summa., I, q. 43, a. 4. — Bl. (now St.) Albertus, here in a. 7. — (Bl.) Peter of Tarentaise, here in q. 3, a. 3. — Richard of Middleton, here in a. 2, q. 2. — Giles the Roman, here in the 2nd princ. q. 1. — Durandus, on this and the following question, here in q. 3. — (Bl.) Dionysius the Carthusian, here in q. 1.

QUESTION IV

Whether "mission", actively accepted, belongs to the whole Trinity?

Fourth and last, there is asked, to whom does mission belong as to the One sending. And that it belongs to the whole Trinity, is shown in this manner:

1. Mission is the same (thing) as temporal donation; but 'to give temporally' befits the whole Trinity, because the whole Trinity gives the Holy Spirit, as (St.) Augustine says:[1] ergo etc..

2. Likewise, (St.) Augustine in the second (book) On the Trinity[2] (says): « The Son cannot be sent by the Father without the Holy Spirit », therefore, the sending [missio] of the Son befits the Holy Spirit: therefore, for the same reason His own [sending]. *If you say*, just as certain ones say, that the former is understood of the mission according to human nature, by which He was sent to preach, according to that (verse) in the sixty-first (chapter) of Isaias:[3] *To announce to the meek has He sent Me*; but not of the mission according to the Divine Nature; *on the contrary*: the mission according to the Divine Nature is a mission into mind, and/or into flesh; but (St.) Augustine understands (his own saying) of the mission into flesh, whence he immediately subjoins: « Because the Father is understood to have sent Him, when He wrought (Him) out of a woman »; therefore, it is established, that he is speaking of the mission according to the Divine Nature.

3. Likewise, Master (Peter)[4] makes such an argument: if the Father can give and/or send the Holy Spirit, and the Holy Spirit cannot, therefore, the Father can do something, which the Holy Spirit cannot. Likewise, if the Father gives and sends the Holy Spirit, and this the Holy Spirit does not do, the Father does something, that the Holy Spirit does not do: therefore, the work of the Trinity is divided.

On the Contrary: 1. The "one given" is said relatively to the "one giving", just as (St.) Augustine says in the fifth (book) On the Trinity:[5] therefore, the Holy Spirit is not given except by those, to whom He is relatively said (to be given); but He is not said relatively (to be given) to Himself: therefore, He does not give Himself, therefore, neither does He send Himself.

2. Likewise, just as the Father is the First Person in the Trinity, before Which there is no Other, so the Holy Spirit, after Which[6] there is no Other; but the Father, because He does not have a Person, from whom He is, is in no manner said (to be) sent: therefore, since the Holy Spirit does not have a Person emanating from Himself, He is in no manner said to send.

3. Likewise, wheresoever there is a passive mission, there is a subauthorship in respect of some principle in the one sent, just as is said by (St.) Augustine and Master (Peter):[7] therefore, where there is an active mission, there is noted an authorship in respect to a Person; but the Holy Spirit does not have an authorship in respect of Himself nor (in respect) of the Other Person: ergo etc..

4. Likewise, wheresoever there is mission, there is truly noted a distinction, just like [sicut] the separation among creatures; but the Person of the Holy Spirit is not distinguished from Himself. therefore, He is not sent by Himself nor does He send the Son, since He does not have an authorship regarding [in] Him: therefore, He does not send.

5. Likewise, every act, according to which a Person is turned back [reflectitur] upon Himself, is essential and said essentially; if, therefore, the Son sends Himself, and/or the Holy Spirit (sends) Himself:[8] therefore, "to send" and/or "to be sent" is essentially said, but every such act is said of the Three: therefore, the Father sends Himself.

CONCLUSION

Improper is the saying, that either the Father or the Trinity sends Itself; entirely proper, that the Person producing sends the One produced; next, less proper, but, yet, to be sustained, that the Persons proceeding send Themselves.

I Respond: It must be said, that in this question the wise opine contrariwise to the wise. For Master (Peter) says expressly and strives to prove by authority and reason, that the Holy Spirit sends Himself and gives Himself;[9] and it is necessary (that this) not (be) according to the same (sense), because between the One sending an the One sent there falls a personal distinction, but only as much as regards a reckoning of understanding, so that the very Same[10] be the One sending inasmuch as God, and the very Same be sent inasmuch as gift.

---

[1] On the Trinity, Bk. XV, ch. 19, n. 36; see here in the text of Master (Peter), ch. 1.

[2] Chapter 5, n. 8.

[3] Verse 1.

[4] Here, in ch. 1. — This argument the Vatican edition together with codex cc, but contrary to all the other codices and edition 1, not to mention the text of Master (Peter), exhibits in a corrupt manner, by omitting the words *and the Holy Spirit* all the way to *and this ... does not do* [et Spiritus sanctus ... et hoc non facit.]

[5] Chapter 14, n. 15: Moreover, because He has been given, and to him who gives is referred etc.. See below, Master (Peter)'s text, d. XVIII, ch. 4.

[6] Understand: *Which Person* [quam personam]. From the manuscripts and edition 1 we have substituted *Which* [quam] this in place of *Whom* [quem], which the Vatican has less well.

[7] Here, in ch. 9, where you will also find the words of (St.) Augustine. — A little below this after *to a Person* [personae] codex O adds as an explanation *sent* [missae].

[8] Codex I here repeats *sends* [mittit].

[9] The Vatican edition, together with codex cc, have (the subjunctive on account of the subordinate clause) *that the Holy Spirit sends Himself and gives Himself* [mittat se et det se].

[10] The Vatican edition together with codex cc, less well and contrary to the other codices and edition 1, reads *so that He be* [ut ipse sit], omitting *Same* [idem].

To other masters and ancients belonged the position, that "to send" and "to be sent" from the reckoning of their name convey a subauthorship and authorship[1] and a distinction; and for that reason it can in no manner be said, that one Person sends Himself and/or is sent by Himself. Therefore, those sayings are improper and are to be expounded (as such), which seem to say this. And they confirm their own position through (St.) Augustine,[2] who says, that the Father in no manner is sent nor is read (to have been) "sent"; this is not because of (anything) else, except because that which has been "*sent*" conveys a subauthorship: therefore, per oppositum,* "*to send*" conveys an authorship, and one Person does not have an authorship over Himself. And they respond to the reasons of Master (Peter), that it is not similar concerning that which is "*to give*" and concerning that which is "*to send*". Because "*to give*" in *one* manner is "to communicate out of liberality or love", and thus is entirely *essential* and connotes no distinction, and in this manner it is conceded, that the whole Trinity gives Itself, and the Father similarly. In *another* manner "*to give*" is "to communicate a gift to someone", not only out of liberality, but also out of authorship, and thus "*to give*" means the notion or is held *notionally*, and in this manner those reasons are not valid: 'if the Father gives the Holy Spirit, and the Holy Spirit does not give Himself: therefore, the Father does something, which the Holy Spirit (does)[3] not'; because it means the notion, and in this sense it is equipollent to that which is "*to send*", and, similarly, passive donation to that which is "*to proceed*". — Similarly, regarding the *similar* (argument), which Master (Peter) brings forward concerning the Son, they say, that it is not similar, because in the Son there is a twofold nature, that is the Divine and the human; and, as much as regards the *human*, He can be sent and is sent by the whole Trinity, because it is less than God and inferior, and not only has a subauthorship, but also a servitude, because (Christ) is the servant of God, although through (the hypostatic) union He is God. But, as much as regards the *Divine* (Nature) He is sent by the Father alone, because He is produced by the Father alone. Therefore, because the Holy Spirit is produced by the Father and by the son, and not by Himself, hence it is, that He is not sent but by the Father and by the Son. And on account of this the reasons of Master (Peter) are not valid, because all the authorities which say, that the Son is sent by the Holy Spirit and/or by Himself, are understood of the human nature.

But, though this position seems more reasonable and easier to sustain, yet — because we ought not draw the authorities of the Saints to our reckoning, but, rather, contrariwise, subject our reckoning to the authorities of the Saints, where they do not contain an express discordance [absurditatem]; and (because) the Saints say, and Master (Peter) says, and most of all (St.) Augustine, who has spoken more on this matter, that the Son is sent by the Holy Spirit and even[4] by Himself, which they cannot expound according to the human nature — *for that reason* the other position both on account of reverence for the Saints, and on account of reverence for Master (Peter) seems rather to be held. For[5] that word of (St.) Augustine, which says, that the Son has been sent into flesh by the Holy Spirit, can in no manner be understood according to the human nature, as is seen, because this mission was for the assumption of a humanity or of the flesh: therefore according to the reckoning of understanding it precedes 'the human nature as already united': therefore, if the Son is in this manner said (to be) sent, it is bound to be attributed to the Divine Nature, and thus by reason of the Divine Nature He has been sent by the Holy spirit; much more strongly, therefore, also *by Himself*, and through this (line of reasoning) even[6] the Holy Spirit *by Himself*.

And, on this account, for an understanding of the objections unto the contrary it must be noted, that "*mission*" of itself conveys two (things), that is *emanation* and *manifestation*, and principally[7] from the reckoning of its own signification conveys a manifestation. And this is clear through (St.) Augustine in the fourth (book) ON THE TRINITY, who says, that "*to be sent*" is "*to be cognized to be from another*", and (as) is had in the present distinction,[8] that « the Son is then sent, when He is perceived in time by the mind of anyone ». Therefore, because it principally conveys a manifestation and connotes an emanation in the one sent, for that reason *manifestation* is signified through that which it is "*to send*" through a manner of action, and through that which it is "*to be sent*" through the manner of passion; but *emanation* (is signified) uniformly in each manner. Whence the sense is: 'the Father sends the son, that is, declares or manifests the emanation of the Son, or that the Son emanates'. On the other hand in the passive, the sense is: 'the Son or the Holy Spirit is sent, that is, is manifested by another to emanate'.

And, since the ablative in respect to a passive (verb), and the nominative in respect to an active verb[9] convey the reckoning of a principle, and the signification of this verb, "*to send*" and "*to be sent*", is a *manifestation* and an *emanation*, for that reason it is *most proper*, when the ablative and/or the nominative convey a habitude of principle in respect to each, as when there is said: "the Father sends the Son", and "the Son is sent by the Father", because the Son emanates from the Father and is manifested by the Father.

On the other hand, because the principal signified by these words is a manifestation, not an emanation, when[10] the nominative and/or ablative is the principle *of the manifestation*, although not *of the emanation*, it is *proper*, but *less* than the aforesaid, and in this sense are conceded

---

[1] Edition 1, having transposed the words, has *authorship and subauthorship* [auctoritatem et subauctoritatem].

[2] ON THE TRINITY, Bk. II, ch. 5, n. 8. See there the text of Master (Peter), ch. 2.

[3] In codex T there is here repeated *does* [facit]. Then after *to send* [mittere] we have inserted from the more ancient manuscripts and edition 1 the particle *and* [et].

[4] In the Vatican edition and codex cc there is faultily absent *even* [etiam], which however, is had in the other codices and edition 1. A little before this edition one has *upon this matter* [super hanc materiam] for *on this matter* [super hac materia].

[5] In codex T for the particle *For* [enim] there is placed by a second hand *However* [tamen].

[6] From many manuscripts, such as A G I K P Q T V X Y aa ee and ff and edition 1, we have inserted the not well omitted *even* [et].

[7] Codex Y *more principally* [principalius].

[8] Chapters 7-9. — Then trusting in the older manuscripts and edition 1, we have substituted *that* [quod] for *that* [quia].

[9] The Vatican edition, striving against the more ancient manuscripts and edition 1, omits *verb* [verbi], which even edition 1 prefixes a little before this to the word *passive* [passivi].

[10] The Vatican edition together with some codices faultily has *since* [quoniam] in place of *when* [quando]. A little below this after *less* [minus], from only some of the codices, such as G H Z and edition 1, we have inserted *than* [quam], for the sake of removing the ambiguity.

---

* *Trans. note*: Here, the Latin phrase, per oppositum, is a shorthand for *through an argument a relative oppositis*. Such is the topical syllogism of the form: 'if this is that, then the relative opposite of this is the relative opposite of that'. Cf. Pietro Ispano, TRATTATO DI LOGICA, tract V, "De locis", trans. A. Ponzio, (Bompiani, Milano, 2004), p. 168-169, n. 28.

those of his : "The Son sends Himself", and "The Spirit sends Himself".

On the other hand, because both *"to send"* and *"to be sent"* convey an emanation about the one sent, and the Person of the Father does not emanate from anyone, similarly neither the Trinity. for the reason the Person of the Father is never read (to have been) "sent" nor (is) the Trinity Itself.

From this it is clear, that this (statement) is simply and *entirely proper.* "The Father sends the Son"; this one is *less proper,* yet does not recede from propriety: "the Son sends Himself"; but this one (is) *entirely improper.* "the Father sends Himself" or "the Trinity Itself (sends Itself)".[1]

1. To that which is objected in the Contrary concerning one given, that it is said relatively; it must be said, that it is true, according to which *"to give"* means 'to communicate through a certain authorship'; in this manner Master (Peter) does not accept it, but (he does) inasmuch as *"to give"* is the same as "to communicate liberally and voluntarily".

2. To that which is objected, that the Father is not sent, because He is[2] not from another; it must be said, that it is not similar, because both *to send* and *to be sent* convey an emanation in the one sent, as is clear to the one expounding (it). For the sense is: 'this person sends that one', that is, 'he manifests the emanation of him'; and: 'this one is sent by that one', that is, 'his emanation is manifested by that one'. But this emanation does not always convey a looking-back[3] to every Person sending, because from Anyone there can be a manifestation of an emanation, from Whom, however, there is not the emanation itself; and for that reason *production* is not in this manner posited in *the One sending,* just as *emanation* (is) in the *One sent;* and for that reason it does not follow, that if the Father is not sent, that the Holy Spirit does not send.[4]

3. To that which is objected: where there is a passive mission, there is a subauthorship; it must be said, that it is true, not by the reckoning, by which (it has a) passive (sense), but by that reckoning, by which both the passive and the active (sense) note an emanation in the One sent, just as was clear in the exposition.[5] And because an emanation is not always in respect to the One sending, for that reason it is not necessary [non oportet], that there always be conveyed an authorship in the One sending, but that reckoning would well be valid, if it were thus, that the principle (thing) signified of that which *mission* is were an emanation or a production.

4. To that which is objected, that *"to send"* conveys a distinction; it must be said, that *"to send"* in *one* manner conveys *a substantial difference,* as when it conveys dominion, as where there is said: "God sends the Angel"; in *another* manner *a personal distinction,* as when it conveys an authorship in the one sending and a subauthorship in the one sent in respect to the one sending, as when there is said: "the Father sends the Son". In a *third* manner it conveys only a distinction as much as regards a *manner of understanding;* just as when there is said: "the will is an instrument moving itself" — because the same is moving and moved — so,[6] when there is said: "the Holy Spirit sends Himself", the Same is the One sending and the One sent, differing (only) in reckoning: *"the One sending",* I say, according to which (He is) God, but *"the One sent"* according to which (He is) gift, just as has be said before.[7]

5. To that which is objected last concerning the reflection of acting, it must be said, that it is true in regard to the principal (thing) signified, but is not necessary [oportet] as much as regards the (thing) connoted, and by reason of the principal (thing) signified there is a reflection of the Person sending upon Himself, such as where there is said [ut dicatur]: "the One sending is sent".

SCHOLIUM

I. The second opinion in the body (of the response) is considered to be that of William of Auxerre. The solution of this question, as the Seraphic Doctor (here in reply to n. 3) rightly observes, depends upon the solution of the other question (q. 1 above, in the Scholium), namely, "What is the principal (thing) signified by a divine mission, *a procession,* or *the manifestation of a procession?*" For this manifestation is an action common to the Three Persons, and if (it is) this, then consequently *"to send"* according to (its) principal signification is something essential, not notional, just as contrariwise *to be sent* is. From these principles the other corollaries follow.

II. Noteworthy is the principle expressed by the Seraphic (Doctor) in the body (of the Response), which is to be observed always as an inviolable rule, namely: « We ought not draw the authorities of the Saints to our reckoning, but rather, conversely, subject our reckoning to the authorities of the Saints, where they do not contain an express discordance ».

III. St. Thomas both in his COMMENTARY and in his SUMMA agrees; likewise (Bl.) Peter of Tarentaise, « even in the same words », as (Bl.) Dionysius the Carthusian reports. All the other masters agree at least in the principal conclusion; however, Giles the Roman impugns the *reasons* given by St. Thomas. — Alexander of Hales, SUMMA., p. I, q. 72, m. 1, a. 1, 2, and . 3. — St. Thomas, here in q . 3, aa. 1 and 2; SUMMA., I, q. 43, a. 8. — Bl. (now St.) Albertus (Magnus), here in aa. 5, 9, and 11. — (Bl.) Peter of Tarentaise, here in q. 2, a. 1; q. 3, a. 1. — Richard of Middleton, here in a. 3, qq. 1 and 2. — Giles the Roman, here in the 2nd. princ, q. 2. — (Bl.) Dionysius the Carthusian, here in qq 1 and 2.

---

[1] The Vatican edition exhibits the propositions in a corrupt manner and contrary to the witness of the manuscripts, thus: *it is clear that this is simply and entirely improper: "the Father sends Himself" or "the Trinity Itself (sends Itself)": because it receded from the property of the Persons and of the Trinity. On the other hand this is simply and entirely proper: "the Father sends the Son", since it recedes from the property of None* [patet, quod haec est simpliciter et omnino impropria: Pater mittit se sive ipsa Trinitas: quia receditur a proprietate personarum et Trinitatis. Illa vero est simpliciter et omnino propria: Pater mittit Filium, cum a nullius proprietate recedatur]. Edition 1 discords with the codices in this, that after *the Son* [Filium] it proceeds thus: *and similarly this one: "the Father and the Son send the Holy Spirit"; and this is less proper: "the Son and/or the Holy Spirit sends Himself", and/or "the Holy Spirit sends the Son"; but this is entirely improper* etc. [et ista similiter: Pater et Filius mittunt Spiritum sanctum; et haec est minus propria: Filius vel Spiritus sanctus mittit se, vel Spiritus sanctus mittit Filium; haec autem omnino impropria etc].

[2] As many manuscripts, such as A G H I K N T V X Y Z aa ee and ff and edition 1 require, we have inserted *He is* [est].

[3] The Vatican edition, contrary to nearly all the codices and edition 1, has not so distinctly *conveys a looking-back* [importat respectum]. A little below this, after *manifestation* [manifestatio] in place of *of an emanation* [emanationis] very many codices together with editions 1, 2 and 3, put *of a mission* [missionis], which however, corresponds less with the context.

[4] The Vatican edition, together with edition 1 and one or the other codex, has *similarly* [similiter], but badly, since it does not correspond with the objection.

[5] Here near the end of the response.

[6] We prefer the reading of not a few of the manuscripts, such as R T X Y and edition 1, of placing *so* [sic] for *similarly* [similiter], in place of which many codices, such as A C F G H I K L O S U W Z etc. have less aptly *just as* [sicut].

[7] Here, in the body (of the Response).

DOUBTS ON THE TEXT OF THE MASTER

DOUBT I

In this part are the doubts about the text (of Master Peter), and first there is the doubt concerning this which he says, that *the Holy Spirit is granted not only by the Father and the Son, but is also given by Himself.* It seems that he says the false, because above[1] the argument was made, that He cannot be given by holy men, because He cannot proceed from them; but He cannot proceed from Him very self: therefore for an equal reason He cannot be given by Himself.

I RESPOND: It must be said, that Master (Peter)[2] argued concerning the temporal procession, and concerning this he well concedes, that He proceeds from Himself, for the reason that it belongs to His own authority, to *spirate* into the one, into whom He wills; but holy men do not have power over Him [posse in eum].[3]

DOUBT II

Likewise, is asked of this which he says, that *the gift of the Holy Spirit is nothing other than the Holy Spirit Himself, just as a body of flesh is nothing other than flesh.* For it seems, if the similitude is a good one, that everything which is a gift of the Holy Spirit, be the Holy Spirit. *But on the contrary*: the fear (of the Lord)[4] is a gift of the Holy Spirit, and is not the Holy Spirit.

I RESPOND: It must be said, that "gift", when it means[5] a relation and through this a distinction in a certain manner, can convey that in a threefold manner: either according to a manner of *understanding*, or according to a manner of *being* [essendi], or according to *the essence*. In *the first* manner *the same* is giving and given, just as « the same understanding and understood »,[6] and *different* by reason of a manner of saying, because the same is given by itself; and in this manner does (St.) Augustine understand it. In *another* manner according to a manner of *being* or of regarding itself, because it is One and Another among the Persons; and in this manner it means a relation of Person to Person. In *a third* manner it conveys a distinction according to *essence*, insofar as it means an effect,[7] and the creature's looking-back to the Uncreated Essence; and in this manner the fear (of the Lord) is said (to be) a gift of the Holy Spirit; but this will be more clear below.[8]

DOUBT III

Likewise, is asked concerning the reckoning of Master (Peter), by which he says: *If the Father and the son give the Holy Spirit, and the Holy Spirit does not give Himself, the Father and the Son can do something, which the Holy Spirit cannot*, because this reckoning of his, as has been said above,[9] is not valid: 'the Father can generate the Son, and the Son cannot: therefore, the Father can do something which the Son cannot': therefore, for an equal reason, since "Holy Spirit" means[10] a Person (just as much) as "Son" (does), its not valid. *If you say*, that it is not similar on account of the act of granting,[11] which is an operation in the creature: *on the contrary*: just as Master (Peter) says in the text,[12] the Holy Spirit's being-given is His procession, but that argument is valid for nothing: 'the Holy Spirit proceeds, and the Father (does) not: therefore, the Holy Spirit does something, which the Father (does) not': therefore similarly neither in the proposed. *If you say* to me, that it is not similar concerning an active and passive (action): *on the contrary*: the inflection of a noun through the cases does not vary (its) signification: therefore, similarly it seems, that neither is there a variation through an active and passive (verb). *And if you say*, that it is not similar; *it is shown*, that (it is) *so*; because every active (action) infers the passive: therefore, it seems, that if it is held[13] essentially in the active voice, that (it is held) similarly in the passive one.

I RESPOND: It must be said, that just as has been predetermined,[14] the reasons of Master (Peter) are good, because he accepts *to give*, according to which it means an effect in the creature; and according to this it is common to the Three Persons necessarily, and this in an active signification. For "to give the Holy Spirit to someone" is "to cause Him to indwell in him"; and for that reason it is not similar concerning the power of generating.

To that, therefore,[15] which is objected, because Master (Peter) says, that (His) 'being given' [donatio] is the same (thing) as (His) procession; it must be said, that he is peaking of passive donation, according to which it is constrained to the Holy Spirit; and his argument is good, because from the same principle the action is, (so) also the passion: therefore, if the active donation is by the Father, similarly the passive donation; similarly if the active donation is by the Holy Spirit, (so) also the passive.

To that which is objected, that what is held in an active

---

[1] Distinction XIV, ch. 3.

[2] One or the other codex, such as ff, together with edition 1, inserts *above* [supra].

[3] Cf. here the text of Master (Peter), ch. 1, and q. 1.

[4] Codex A reads *love (of God)* [amor].

[5] From the more ancient manuscripts and editions 1, 4 and 5, we have substituted the subjunctive form for *it means* [dicat].

[6] Aristotle, ON THE SOUL, Bk. III, text 15 (ch. 4). — Then codex dd reads *by its very self* [a se ipso] for *by itself* [a se].

[7] The reading of the Vatican edition, in which there is omitted *insofar as it means an effect* [prout dicit effectum], is repaired with the help of the manuscripts and edition 1. A little below this, though it is had in not a few manuscripts, such as F T X and dd, we have substituted *the fear (of the Lord)* [timor] for *love (of the Lord)* [amor], as it corresponds more to the objection.

[8] Distinction 18, qq. 2 and 5.

[9] Distinction 7, q. 2, and Doubt 1.

[10] The Vatican edition, contrary to the more ancient codices and edition 1, has *when "Holy Spirit" means* [cum ... dicit].

[11] Trusting in the older manuscripts and edition 1, we have put *of granting* [donandi] in place of *of giving* [dandi].

[12] Here in ch. 1. — Then from very many manuscripts and edition 1, we have substituted *is valid for nothing* [nihil valet] for *not valid* [non valet].

[13] Some codices, such as S X Z, have *it be held* [teneatur].

[14] Here in q. 4, which better explains the entire solution to this Doubt.

[15] From the manuscripts and edition 1, we have restored the particle *therefore* [ergo].

(action) essentially, (is) therefore also (held essentially) in the passive, therefore, similarly it can be said, that the Father proceeds; it must be said, that that argument is not valid, because "to spirate" in the active voice befits Two, in the passive voice it befits One alone; thus "to send" can befit Three, but "to proceed" or "to be sent" only Two.

DOUBT IV

Likewise, is asked of this which he says, that *the Holy Spirit proceeds from Himself.* For it seems false, that *to proceed* is *to be produced*: therefore, if the Holy Spirit proceeds from Himself, He is produced from Himself. *If you say*, that it is not said without a determination, namely *temporally*; on the contrary: *temporally* is a non-diminishing determination: therefore, it follows of necessity, if He proceeds *temporally* from Himself, that He *proceeds* from Himself.

I RESPOND: It must be said, that as has been said above,[1] a procession by reason of (its) comparison to the terminus, in which it is taken-up, that is, the creature which is sanctified, from the reckoning of its name connotes (something) temporal, and for that reason is said (to be) temporal. And since that temporal effect is from the Holy Spirit, for that reason also (that) procession, though not so properly as (the one) from the Father. Nor[2] is it valid *of production*, because a *production* only means a comparison to the *principle from which* and it does not connote an effect. Whence just as: 'He proceeds temporally, therefore, He is produced temporally' is not valid, so also (is it) in the proposed.

DOUBT V

Likewise, is asked concerning the proof of Master (Peter), by which he proves the mission of the Holy Spirit through the mission of the Son, there (where he says): *But do not wonder, than the Holy Spirit is said to be sent and/or proceed from Himself. For even of the Son* etc.. For it seems, that he proves badly, because "mission" means "a subauthorship in the one sent"; but there is more concerning subauthorship in the Holy Spirit than in the Son: therefore, more concerning the reckoning of mission: therefore, it seems, that he ought rather to proceed contrariwise.

Likewise, "mission" means "a manifestation"; but the mission of the Son has been manifested through the mission of the Holy Spirit: therefore, more manifest is the mission of the Holy Spirit: therefore, it seems, that he proves the unknown through the more unknown.[3]

In accord with this, there is asked, concerning which is "to be sent" more properly said, whether,[4] namely, concerning the Son, or whether concerning the Holy Spirit.

I RESPOND: It must be said, that Master (Peter) proves the mission of the Holy Spirit through the mission of the Son, because he has more express authorities for this.[5] Yet, nevertheless, it can be said, that he even proceeds by reasoning well. For, in the mission of a Person there are the considering of two (things): that is, the *emanation*, by reason of which there is subauthorship in the One sent; and, as much as regards this, it is more suitable [magis competit] to the Holy Spirit that He be sent;[6] and, as much as regards this, Master (Peter) argues a minori:* because, if the Son is sent by the Holy Spirit and by Himself, much more strongly also the Holy Spirit. And there is also the considering of the *manifestation*; and, by reason of this, it befits the Son more, because He has more evidently appeared to the world, and as much as regards this Master (Peter) argues *from the more manifest*:[7] and, thus, proceeds in the very best manner [peroptime].

To that which is objected, that the Holy Spirit manifests the Son and His mission; it must be said, that this is not on account of a defect of evidence on the part of the mission of the Son, but on account of the blindness on the part of the ones seeing, which (blindness) the grace of the Holy Spirit removes.

And, thus, it is clear, concerning which (is) more proper.[8] For, in one manner, it is more suitable to the Son, in another manner more to the Holy Spirit according to the two aforesaid conditions.

DOUBT VI

Likewise, is asked of this which he says: *He shows that the Son (has been) sent for the reason that (He has been) made from a woman*: because according to this, since the Holy Spirit has not been made from a woman, it seems that He has not been sent. *Moreover*, if the Son[9] has been *made from a woman*, therefore, He has been made. *On the contrary*: (it is said) in the Creed:[10] *Not made.*

I RESPOND: That is not a common reckoning of 'mission', but only of the visible mission of the Son Himself, and for that reason it is not valid for the Holy Spirit.[11]

---

[1] Distinction 14, a. 1, q. 1, and here in q. 2. — Then edition 1 has *(to) the creature* [creaturam] for *the creature* [creatura].

[2] The Vatican edition together with codex cc has *And not* [Et non] for *Nor* [Nec]. Then after *from which* [a quo] some codices, such as A G T W Z bb and cc, together with edition 1, omit *and* [et], but others, such as F H I and dd, put *nor* for *and ... not* [et non].

[3] The Vatican edition without the authority of the manuscripts and the first six editions, and less well, has *through the unknown* [per ignotum].

[4] In the Vatican edition and codex cc, there is omitted *whether* [utrum], which however, is had in the other codices and edition 1. Not a few texts, such as U Y together with edition 1, a little before hav e *through (a consideration of what is) prior* [per prius] in place of *more properly* [proprius], but falsely, as is clear from the response.

[5] We exhibit the reading of the greater part of the codices, such as A G H I M O T V W X aa bb etc., and edition 1, while the Vatican edition together with the other codices, with changed punctuation, has badly: *authorities. Still after.* [auctoritates. Adhuc post.] Then after *nevertheless* the codices vary in reading; some codices, such as H O T Y Z ff, together with edition 1, exhibit our reading, others add together with the Vatican edition *in some manner* [alio modo], some, such as A S Q faultily have *in no manner* [nullo modo], codex I has *in some manner* [nonnullo modo].

[6] The Vatican edition, contrary to many codices and to edition 1, has *it is more fitting* [magis convenit], which also after, with changed punctuation, puts *that the Holy Spirit be sent* [Spiritum sanctum mitti],

but our reading is exhibited explicitly by many codices, together with edition 1; some on account of abbreviation are of a dubious reading. A little after *much more strongly also* [multo fortius et] codex I adds *by Himself* [a se], while codex dd has *much more strongly is the Holy Spirit sent by Himself* [multo fortius Spiritus sanctus mittitur a se].

[7] In the manuscripts and editions 1, 2, and 3, there is had a minori for *from the more manifest* [a manifestiori], but falsely. Codex dd exhibits the final propositions thus: *There is also the consideration of the manifestation of the one appearing, and by reason of this it befits the Son more, that the kindness of the Son has appeared evidently to the world in the union of the flesh, and as much as regard this Master (Peter) argued from the more manifest and in such a wise proceeds in the very best manner. And through this is it clear regarding the first objection. To that which is objected second etc..* [Est etiam considerare manifestationem apparentis, et ratione huius magis convenit Filio, quia apparuit benignitas Filii evidenter mundo in unione carnis, et quantum ad hoc arguit Magister a manifestiori et taliter peroptime procedit. Et per hoc patet ad primum obiectum. Ad illud quod secundo obiicitur etc.]

[8] The Vatican edition, non consistent with itself and contrary to very many codices and also to edition 1, has *prior* [prius]; a few codices read *through (a consideration of what is) prior* [per prius], which however, is less fitting with the subjoined. Codex dd has *Thus it is also clear, concerning which is more properly said "mission"* [Sic etiam patet, de quo proprius dicatur missio].

[9] In codex W there is added *of God* [Dei].

[10] The Vatican edition, with the manuscripts and the first six editions fighting against it, has *through the Creed* [per Symbolum].

[11] The Vatican edition, not trusting in the manuscripts and edition 1, has *Himself* [se] for *the Holy Spirit* [Spiritu sancto].

---

* *Trans. note*: Here, a minori is shorthand, for *an argument a minori*. Such is the topical syllogism, which arrives at an affirmative conclusion, by means of arguing from what the lesser could do or has, and concluding that the greater can or has likewise. Cf. Pietro Ispano, TRATTATO DI LOGICA, tract, "De locis", trans. A. Ponzio, (Bompiani, Milano, 2004), p. 172-175, n. 32.

To that which is objected, that He has been *made*,[1] it must be said, that that must be understood according to the Human Nature, and for that reason one is bound to add a determination, as (when) there is said "made *out of a woman*" and/or "*according to the Human Nature*", because, on account of avoiding the error of Arius, ecclesiastical speech does not receive that (expression),[2] simply (speaking).

COMMENTARY ON DISTINCTION XV

PART II

On mission of the Son and of the Holy Spirit, as much as regards the manner, which is twofold, namely, visible and invisible.

Here, there is asked, whether the Son has been sent only once.

SEE THE TEXT OF THIS PART, ABOVE ON P. 257.

THE DIVISION OF THE TEXT

Above, Master (Peter) deals with mission as much as regards (its) *principle*, here he deals with it as much as regards (its) *manner*, which is twofold, namely, visible and invisible. And since these two manners befit the mission of the Son and of the Holy Spirit, for that reason Master (Peter) *first* assigns them to [circa] the mission of the Son; *second* to the mission of the Holy Spirit, below at the beginning of the sixteenth Distinction: *Now concerning the Holy Spirit there must be seen* etc..

The *first* part has four parts. In the first[3] he shows by the authority of (St.) Augustine, that the Son has been sent in two manners, that is visibly and in visibly. In the second he assigns a twofold difference for these two manners,[4] there (where he says): *Behold, the two manners of the mission of the Son have been distinguished.* In the third, however, he moves a certain doubt, which has its rise from the predetermined, there (where he says): *Here there is asked, why is the Father not said (to be) sent.* In the fourth, however, he removes or teaches one to beware of the error, proceeding from the solution of that doubt, there (where he says): *And for that reason certain heretics thought.* For from this, that he had said, that the Father is not sent, someone might believe, that He is not an equal among the Divine (Persons). To this Master (Peter), responding, says, that this is not on account of inequality, but on account of the authorship, or connotation, of a principle.

TREATMENT OF THE QUESTIONS

For an understanding of those (things) which are said in this part (of his), three (things) are asked concerning the visible mission of the Son, because the visible is dealt with in (the) third (chapter of Part II). And because the invisible mission of the Son is similar to the invisible mission of the Holy Spirit, for that reason it is at once asked of each.

First, there is asked, whether this mission is according to gifts of the grace which makes one pleasing [dona gratiae gratum facientis], and/or of the grace freely given [gratiae gratis datae].

Second there is asked, whether the Son and the Holy Spirit are said "to be sent" according to the same gifts of grace.

Third, whether each mission is augmented according to the same gifts of grace

---

[1] The error, which has crept into the manuscripts and editions, namely, by adding *not* [non] after *that He has* [quod], which seems to have arisen from the permutation of the last objection with the proposition which comes after *On the contrary* [Contra], we have emended by eliminating the particle *not* [non], which has also conspicuously been expunged in codex H. Likewise, this doubt recurs in SENT., Bk. III, d. 1, Doubt 2, wherein our emendation here is confirmed. Codex I by reading *not made* [non factus] a little below this, puts *divine* [divinam] in place of *human* [humanam], but in a manner incoherent with what is subjoined. The Vatican edition reads *that it is not to be understood except* [non est intelligendum nisi] in place of *must be understood* [est intelligendum], but without the testimony of the manuscripts and edition 1, — Codex cc together with edition 2 retains the *not* [non], but omits the *except* [nisi], but contrary to what follows.

[2] Namely, the proposition: *The Son was made* [Filius est factus].

[3] Trusting in the mss. and ed. 1, we have removed the words *aforementioned question* [praemissa quaestione], which the Vatican ed. added.

[4] In the Vatican edition there is here added *one (difference)* [unam], and then at the end of the quote there is added *The other there (where he says): Moreover, it must be noted* [Aliam ibi: Praeterea notandum]; but manuscripts together with edition 1 withstand this.

ARTICLE SOLE

On the invisible mission both of the Son and of the Holy Spirit.

QUESTION I

Whether the invisible mission is according to the gifts of grace freely given, and/or (of the grace) making one pleasing?

About the first, that this mission is according to gifts of the grace freely given, is shown in this manner:

1. (Bl.) Rabanus (Maurus)[1] says of the Holy Spirit, that the Holy Spirit was given three times. And first he says, that He was given for the working of miracles; but it is established, that the working of miracles is a grace freely given: ergo etc..

2. Likewise, the Holy Spirit is given, when the gift of prophecy is given. Whence in the First (Book) of Kings, tenth (chapter):[2] *The Spirit of the Lord came upon Saul, and he prophesied*; but the gift of prophecy is frequently given to those who do not have the grace which makes one pleasing, just as is clear concerning Saul through the text: ergo etc..

3. Likewise, it seems, that the Son is sent according to gifts of the grace freely given. For then the Son is said to be sent, when there comes to be a revelation of (things) hidden, but a revelation of (things) hidden can come to be without a gift of the grace which makes one pleasing: ergo etc..

4. Likewise, (St.) Augustine says and as is had in the present distinction,[3] that « then Wisdom is sent, when He is perceived by the mind of anyone », or when He becomes known to anyone; if, therefore, He is perceived and becomes known through gifts of the grace freely given, as through unformed faith: therefore it seems that He is given in these: ergo etc..

ON THE CONTRARY: 1. (St.) Augustine[4] says, that the Holy Spirit is then given to someone, when He is given thus, that He makes him (belong) to God and a lover of his neighbor, that is to say, when charity is given to a man, but charity belongs not but to the grace which makes one pleasing: ergo etc..

2. Likewise, this very (thing) seems concerning the Son, because there is said in the seventh (chapter) of Wisdom:[5] *Into holy souls does He transfer Himself, and has established them friends of God*; but they are not said (to be) "friends of God" without the grace which makes one pleasing: ergo etc..

3. Likewise, it is shown *by reason* in this manner:[6] the Holy Spirit is then given and/or sent, when He dwells in a man; but He is not said to dwell in a man without the grace which makes one pleasing: ergo etc..

4. Likewise, when the Son and/or Holy Spirit is sent to someone, He is not sent, to be[7] where He was not before, but to be in him in a manner other than before; but a new manner of being, adding upon 'being' through nature, is not but through the grace which makes one pleasing: ergo etc..

CONCLUSION

In an invisible mission each Person is not given simply, except by a gift of grace which makes one pleasing, according to which, however, He is also given through a grace given freely.

I RESPOND: Some distinguish regarding this, "the Holy Spirit is given and/or sent invisibly", that this[8] can be either inasmuch as (He is) *the Spirit*, and/or inasmuch as (He is) *Holy*. Inasmuch as (He is) *the Spirit*, He is given through a gift of the grace freely given; inasmuch as (He is) *Holy* and/or[9] the Sanctifier, He is given through the gifts of grace which make one pleasing [gratiae gratum facientes]. Similarly, Wisdom and/or the Son can be sent either insofar as (He is) *the One making one know*, and thus through gifts of the grace freely given [gratiae gratis datae], and/or insofar as "*wisdom*" [sapientia] has been said from "*taste*" [sapore], and thus through the gifts of the grace which makes one pleasing. But that does not seem to solve (the question), because it is still possible that the one granting the opposite of this solution solve (it)[10] and ask concerning the Spirit and the Word, in what manner is He said to be given and not indwell.

On this account, it must be said in another manner, both concerning the Son and concerning the Holy Spirit, that[11] "*to be given*" and/or "*to be sent*" is (said) in a twofold manner: either *simply*, and/or *for this*. He is then given *simply*, when He is had simply, namely not only for using, but for enjoying; but this is only through gifts of the grace which make one pleasing; and for that reason only among those is either the Son and/or the Holy Spirit given simply. In another manner, He is said "to be given *for this*", when some gifts are given not for enjoyment, but to help or for some use; and this indeed,[12] when some gifts of the grace freely given are given, in which there

---

[1] See above d. 14, Doubt 4.

[2] Verse 10, where the Vulgate has: *The Spirit of the Lord leapt upon him and he prophesied in their midst* [Et insiluit super eum spiritus Domini et prophetavit in medio eorum].

[3] Chapter 7. — A little below this, after *if therefore, He is perceived* [si ergo percipitur] one or another codex, such as I and T, have *or* [sive] in place of the *and* [et].

[4] ON THE TRINITY, Bk. XI, ch. 17, n. 31: the Holy Spirit ... when he has been given to a man, enkindles him in the love of God and of neighbor, and is this love. — The Vatican edition, with the mss. and the first six edd. striving against it, has *through (St.) Augustine there is said* [per Augustinum dicitur], and then, breaking with the more ancient manuscripts and edition 1, reads *to men* [hominibus] for *to a man* [homini].

[5] Verse 27, where the Vulgate after *does He transfer Himself* [se transfert] omits the *and* [et] and proceeds thus: *friends of God and Prophets does He establish* [amicos Dei et Prophetas constituit].

[6] We have supplied from the older codices and from edition 1: *in this manner* [sic].

[7] Trusting in the manuscripts and editions 1, 2, and 3, we have removed the *there* [ibi] added in the Vatican edition. Then edition 1 has *but to be in* [sed ut insit] for *but to be* [sed ut sit].

[8] From the more ancient mss. and ed. 1, we have inserted *this* [hoc]. Then after *be* [esse] cod. A adds *in a twofold manner*, [dupliciter].

[9] Trusting in many codices, such as F G H I M P Q X Z aa ee and ff, and in edition 1, we have inserted *Holy and/or* [sanctus vel]; some codices, such as F P and Q have *that is* [id est] in place of *and/or* [vel]. A little before this very many codices, such as H M P Q T X aa and ee, together with edition 1, have added *but* [sed] after *the grace freely given* [gratiae gratis datae].

[10] Aristotle, ELENCHAE, Bk. II, ch. 3 (ch. 22), the words of which are above in d. 4, Doubt 3.

[11] Codex A reads sufficiently well *namely that* [scilicet quod].

[12] Thus very many of the more ancient manuscripts together with edition 1, but the Vatican edition together with codex cc has *come to be* [fit] in place of *indeed* [quidem]; codex X has *when* [quando] for *indeed when* [quidem cum].

is manifested the Son and/or the Holy Spirit, and in this manner proceed the reasons for the first part.

1. For,[1] thus, must be understood the word of (Bl.) Rabanus (Maurus); for he also speaks *commonly* of mission; whence he says, that the Holy Spirit (has been) given three times. But (St.) Augustine only speaks of the granting and/or mission, which is to dwell and/or to be had simply.

2. To that which is objected concerning prophecy, it must be said, that in *one* manner the Holy Spirit is given simply in it, insofar as it means a cognition according to the idoneity of the one taking-it-up and according to the piety[2] of the one executing it. In *another* manner, insofar as it is a revelation,[3] the Spirit is not given in it *simply* or is not sent except *for this*. Whence there is not said in the Book of Kings, that the Holy Spirit was sent "*to*" Saul, and/or wrought "*in*" Saul, but "*over Saul*".

3. To that which is objected, that the Son is sent, when there is[4] a revelation of (things) hidden; it must be said, that this is not in any revelation whatsoever; for in some a revelation comes to be, not through the mission of the Son, but through the mission of an Angel; — for many (things) are revealed by the Angels;[5] but it is understood of that revelation, in which there is an enlightening [illustratio] of the soul through a grace; and if through (a grace) given freely, He is not sent simply, but if through (a grace) making one pleasing, then He is sent and had simply.

4. To that which is objected last, that He is then sent, when He is perceived; it must be said, that it is not sufficient to cognize the Son, that He be from Another, nay, it is necessary [oportet], that one cognizes, that He is in him as in His own, little dwelling. But this I say (is) not by a cognition of necessity, but (by one) of conjecture,[6] nor from an actual cognition, but from a habitual one.

SCHOLIUM

I. The more ancient Scholastics used to accept "grace *freely given*" in a sense broader, than modern theologians, thus that every *actual* grace, to the extend that it is distinguished from *sanctifying* grace, would be comprised under this name (cf. SENT, Bk. II, d. 28, a. 2, q. 1, in the *body* of the response, and elsewhere in passing). — The distinction posited in the body (of the response) between *to be given simply* and *(to be given) for this* is the same as *simply* and secundum quid.

II. The first solution, which is also attributed to Bl. (now St.) Albertus (Magnus), SENT., Bk. I, d. 17, a. 9, the Seraphic Doctor does not approve. Bl. (now St.) Albertus says thus: « It must be said, that, as I think, He would not be said to be sent, not in charity simply, but secundum quid in others, as namely He is sent in others as being *the Spirit*, and not as *being Holy* ». But this sentence of (St.) Albertus does not seem to be other than the common one in the matter. St. Bonaventure proposes his own opinion according to the distinction made there in the twofold conclusion, namely that properly and simply the Holy Spirit is not sent nor given except through the gift of sanctifying grace. The reason is, that without this gift and charity we do not have the faculty of enjoying the Holy Spirit. Which, St.

Thomas (SUMMA., I, q. 43, a. 3) explains in these words: « Above the common manner (whereby God is in things) there is a special one, which befits a rational nature, in which God is said to be as One cognized in the one cognizing and One loved in the one loving. And because by cognizing and by loving a rational creature by its own operation attains to God Himself, according to this special manner God is not only said to be in a rational creature, but also to dwell in it as in His own temple ». However, *improperly*, or « having extended the name, "mission" », as Alexander of Hales says, the Holy Spirit is sometimes said to be sent for some act of actual grace and/or of (the grace) freely given. In this doctrine Alexander of Hales, St. Thomas, (Bl. John Duns) Scotus, Richard (of Middleton) and innumerable others, agree.

III. Cf. Alexander of Hales, SUMMA., p. I, q. 73, m. 4, a. 2. — St. Thomas, here in q. 4,. a. 1; SUMMA., I, q. 43, a. 3. — Bl. (now St.) Albertus (Ma gnus), on this and the following question, here in a. 16. — (Bl.) Peter of Tarentaise, here in q. 3, a. 2. — Richard of Middleton, SENT., Bk. I, d. 14, a. 2, q. 2. — Giles the Roman, d. 14, 2nd. princ., q. 2. — (Bl.) Dionysius the Carthusian, here in q. 3. — (Gabriel) Biel, on this and the following question, here in SENT., Bk. I, d. 14, qq. 1 and 2.

QUESTION II

Whether the Son and the Holy Spirit are said "to be sent" according to the same gifts of grace?

Second, there is asked, whether the Son and the Holy Spirit are said "to be sent" according to the same gifts. And that (They are) not, seems in this manner:

1. The 'being sent' [missio] of the Holy Spirit is His donation, and similarly the Son's;[7] but there is another mission of the Son and of the Holy Spirit: therefore, another donation: therefore, another gift.

2. Likewise, this same seems through a simile, be-

cause just as the visible mission of the Son holds itself to the visible mission of the Holy Spirit, so also even the invisible: but the visible mission of the Son and of the Holy Spirit is according to one and another effect and sign in the creature: therefore, the invisible (is) according to one and another gift.

3. Likewise, a mission is for an emanation being cognized and discerned;[8] if, therefore, the Son is discerned by the effect, in which He is sent, (then) the Holy Spirit also; and of this

---

[1] In the Vatican edition *For* [Nam] is wanting, which however, is had in the mss. and in first three edd.. A little below this, having followed a greater part of the codd., such as C G H I R S T U V W aa bb cc and ee, with edition 1, we have substituted *that the Holy Spirit (has been given) three times* [Spiritum sanctum ter datum] for *the Holy Spirit is given three times* [Spiritus sanctus ter datur]. Then, after *But (St.) Augustine* [Augustinus autem], we have supplied *only* [solum], in place of which some codd., such as A V & X, have *only* [solummodo]. Then, very many codd., such as A G I K T etc., have *indwell* [inhabitandum] for *dwell* [habitandum].

[2] In codex K there is added *of the one expounding and/or* [exponentis vel].

[3] Trusting the manuscripts and edition 1, we have deleted the *and in this manner* [et sic] not so well added in the Vatican edition. — Cf. (St.) Augustine, ON DIVERSE QUESTIONS: TO SIMPLICIUS, Bk. II, q. 1.

[4] The manuscripts together with edition 1 read *there is* [est] in place of *there comes to be* [fit]. A little below this codex X has *sometimes* [aliquando] for *in some* [aliqua].

[5] Because the reading of the more ancient manuscripts and edition 1 *for reveal many (things)* [multa enim revelant] is incomplete, if indeed the word *the Angels* [Angeli] has probably fallen away, we have left the reading of the Vatican edition; codex cc and edition 1 have *many (things) are revealed to the Angels* [multa revelantur Angelis], but faultily. A little below this a few codices, such as A I S and cc, together with edition 1, read badly *and thus* [et sic] in place of *and if* [et si].

[6] Codex X has *(by one) of fittingness* [convenientiae], codex Z has *(by one) of congruence* [congruentiae]. [Trans note: here the Seraphic Doctor excludes the transient cognition or vision as a certain confirmation of the presence of the Eternal Word in the believer, a doctrine that reappears in St. John of the Cross, ASCENT OF MT. CARMEL.

[7] Cf. above q. 1.

[8] See above p. I, qq. 1, 3 and 4 of this distinction. — Then codex H has *through the effect* [per effectum], codex T *in the effect* [in effectu] for *by the effect* [effectu]. Near the end of the argument, after *the Son is sent* [mittitur Filius] in codex bb there is added *and* [et].

kind are the gifts of grace: therefore, as much as regards one gift the Son is sent, as much as regards the other the Holy Spirit.

4. Likewise, the same is not appropriated to the Son and to the Holy Spirit, but another (is) among creatures:[1] therefore since the Son is said to be sent in an effect appropriated to Himself, the Son is sent in an effect and/or gift other than the Holy Spirit (is).

ON THE CONTRARY: 1. Every distribution of gifts, both of the grace given freely as well as of the grace which makes one pleasing, is attributed to the Holy Spirit, most of all the gifts of the grace which makes one pleasing, just as is clear in the twelfth (chapter) of the First (Letter) to the Corinthians:[2] therefore, since the Holy Spirit is sent in the gifts appropriated to Him, He is sent in all the gifts: therefore, in the same, in which the Son (is).

2. Likewise, the Son is sent, when wisdom is given, and similarly the Holy Spirit, because the chief [praecipuum] gift of the Holy Spirit is wisdom: ergo etc..

3. Likewise, whensoever cognition is given, the Son is said "to be sent": but in this same gift there is given and/or sent the Holy Spirit, according to the sixteenth (chapter of the Gospel of St.) John:[3] *When He shall have come, He shall teach you all truth*: ergo etc..

4. Likewise, whensoever charity is given, the Holy Spirit is sent, but in this gift the Son is given, according to the seventh (chapter of the Book) of Wisdom:[4] *Into holy souls does He transfer Himself and establish them friends of God*; and (St.) Augustine in the fourth (book) ON THE TRINITY[5] expounds that (verse) concerning the mission of the Son: ergo etc..

CONCLUSION

The Missions of the Son and of the Holy Spirit in themselves and in regard to the root of their gifts are undivided; they are distinguished only in regard to habits and consequent acts.

I RESPOND: It must be said, that in the invisible mission there is a conferral of gifts, among which there is *manifestation* and *indwelling*. And according to this it must be understood, that concerning the gifts of God there is a speaking as much as regards (their) *root*, and/or as much as regards (their) *habit* and/or as much as regards (their) *consequent act*.

Moreover, speaking as much as regards (their) *root*, thus because there is one grace which makes one pleasing, through which the Son indwells and the Holy Spirit (too), which is the root of gratuitous gifts, so They are given and/or sent in (this) same gift.

Moreover, speaking as much as regards *habit*, thus one must distinguish, that[6] certain habits are *purely affective*, certain ones *purely cognitive*, certain ones *intermediary* [medii]. In habits *purely affective*, the Holy Spirit is given or sent, because they are appropriated to Him. In habits *purely cognitive*, neither the Son nor the Holy Spirit are properly "sent", as has been said.[7] But in habits *partly* cognitive, *partly* affective, according to which they contain diverse (objects) in themselves, both the Son is sent and the Holy Spirit. For cognitive (habits) lead unto the manifestation of the Word, affective ones unto the manifestation of Love.

Moreover, if we speak as much as regards (their) *consequent acts*, which are the illumination of the intellect and the inflaming of the affection, in saying "gift" in this manner, They are sent in one and another "gifts".

But, since these[8] are conjoined, for that reason the invisible mission of the Son and (that) of the Holy Spirit are undivided, and, according to this, proceed the reasons for the opposing sides. However, that (argument) which adduces in virtue of the simile [pro simile] in the sensible mission, is by no means a simile, because there is no union and connection among exterior signs so great, as is (that) among interior habits.

SCHOLIUM

I. In regard to "mission" *simply* said, which is according to sanctifying grace, all harmoniously assert, that the missions of each Person are undivided, but in regard to "mission" improperly said or <u>secundum quid</u> some together with Alexander of Hales, (SUMMA., p. I, q. 73, m. 2, a. 3), say, that each Person sometimes is sent and/or given at the same time, however, not always. Alexander of Hales explains this (<u>loc. cit.</u>) in this manner: « Since "mission" passively said is the procession manifested in an effect appropriated to the Person and/or a manifestation of the procession; (and) since the procession of the Son is not the procession of the Holy Spirit, neither (is) the effect the same, in which each procession is manifested, by reason of which the Son and/or the Holy Spirit is said to be sent, nay one effect can be without the other, and the manifestation of one procession without the manifestation of the other: for that reason there can be one mission without the other.

But not so is it concerning "mission" actively said » etc.. To which sentence Richard of Middleton adheres. But (Bl.) Peter of Tarentaise, Giles the Roman, and very many others do not admit this, nor do Sts. Bonaventure and Thomas speak in this manner. For they say, that in regard to the consequent act, these two missions do differ, but yet the one cannot be without the other.

II. Alexander of Hales, <u>loc. cit.</u> and m. 4, a. 2. — St. Thomas, here in q. 4, a. 2; SUMMA., I, q.43, a. 5, especially reply to n. 3., where he uses nearly the same words as St. Bonaventure. — Bl. (now St.) Albertus (Magnus), d. 17, a. 2. — (Bl.) Peter of Tarentaise, here in q. 2, a. 2; q. 3, a. 2. — Richard of Middleton, here in a. 4, qq. 1 and 2. — Giles the Roman, here in 1st. princ., q. 2. — Durandus (of Saint-Pourçain), here in q. 4. — (Bl.) Dionysius the Carthusian, here in q. 3.

---

[1] From the more ancient manuscripts and edition 1, we have substituted *among creatures* [in creaturis] for *in a creature* [in creatura].

[2] Verse 4 ff.

[3] Verse 13, where the Vulgate reads: *But when He will have come, the Spirit of Truth, He shall teach* etc. [cum autem venerit ille Spiritus veritatis, docebit]. — A little before this the Vatican edition together with cc, yet with the more ancient manuscripts and edition 1 struggling against this, omit *same* [eodem].

[4] Verse 27. For the reading of the Vulgate, see the preceding question, fundament n. 2.

[5] Chapter 20, n. 27: For into holy souls does (Wisdom) transfer Himself and He has established them as friends of God and Prophets, just as He also fills the Holy Angels and works all (things) congruous through them by such ministers. But when the fullness of time came, He was sent, not to fill the Angels nor to be an Angel, except inasmuch as He was announcing the counsel of the Father, which was also His; nor to be with men or in men; this (He was) even beforehand both in the Patriarchs and Prophets; but so that the Word Himself might become flesh, that is, might become Man etc..

[6] Edition 1 has *that* [quod] in place of *than* [quia].

[7] Here, in the preceding Question, especially in reply to nn. 2 and 3.

[8] That is, the root, habit and consequent acts of the gifts. — A little below this, trusting in the very many manuscripts, such as C F S Y, we have substituted the singular for the plural of *invisible*.

QUESTION III

Whether the Son and the Holy Spirit are sent, when the gifts of grace are augmented?

Third, there is asked, whether the mission of the Son and the Holy Spirit is according to the same augmented gifts of grace. And that it is, seems *from example*, *authority* and *reason*.

1. By an example in this manner: it is established, that on the day of Pentecost the Holy Spirit was sent to the Apostles, not only visibly, but also invisible, because the visible mission without the invisible does not confer, but they had grace before (this): ergo etc..

2. Likewise, it seems according to the authority of (Bl.) Rabanus (Maurus):[1] « In Baptism the Holy Spirit is given to consecrate a dwelling for God, but in Confirmation He comes into a man with all the fullness of holiness »: therefore, He is given in Confirmation after Baptism: ergo etc..

3. Likewise, the augment of grace is through the addition of grace; but where there is an addition of grace, there is[2] a donation of grace; but « the Holy Spirit is sent and/or given, when His grace is given », as (St.) Bede (the Venerable) says.[4] therefore, in the augment of grace the Holy Spirit is given and/or sent.

4. Likewise, it is no less a gift to consummate charity than to undertake (it) [inchoare]: therefore, if the Son and/or the Holy Spirit is sent, when grace is undertaken, much more strongly (is it) when it is consummated; but it is consummated through an augment: therefore, (Each) is sent in an augment.

ON THE CONTRARY: 1. The Holy Spirit is not sent into a man, to be anew in him, but (rather) to be in another manner in him; but in him, in whom grace is enlarged [augetur], He is not in a manner other than before: therefore, He is not sent to him.[5]

2. Likewise, if He is sent in an augment of grace, either, therefore, because He is sent anew, or because He is sent more abundantly; *not* because (He is sent) anew: therefore, because more abundantly. *But on the contrary*: to be sent is to proceed, therefore, to be sent more abundantly is to more abundantly proceed; but (Each) proceeds always, equally: ergo etc..

3. Likewise, if (Each) is sent in the augment of grace, since, therefore, grace is enlarged in us daily, even without a man knowing it, it seems that the Holy Spirit and/or the Son is sent, without a man knowing it, and[6] that daily (Each) is sent to a man; which is not to be said.

4. Likewise, it happens that the grace of charity is lessened [remitti] in some through negligence: therefore, if the Holy Spirit is sent in an augment, and withdraws in (its) being lessened [in remissione]: therefore, when someone sins venially, He loses [perdit] the Holy Spirit; which is false.

CONCLUSION

The Holy Spirit is not said "to be sent", only when an advance comes to be in a grace already had, but He is (also) said "to be sent" in the conferral of a new use and/or of a new gratuitous gift.

I RESPOND: To this some say, that "that grace be enlarged" is in a twofold manner, namely *perceptibly* and *imperceptibly*. If *perceptibly*, then they say, that in such an augment the Son and the Holy Spirit are given and/or sent; but if *imperceptibly*, then they say, that (Each) is not sent. And the reason for this is, that then He is said "to be given" and/or "to be sent", when He is perceived with the mind.

But it can be said in another manner, that an augment of grace is in a twofold manner: either according to *an advance* [profectum] in a grace had beforehand and[7] its use, or through *the conferral of a new use* and/or even of a gratuitous *gift*. If only through a *progress*, just as the last reasons show, the Holy Spirit is not sent. But if through the *conferral of a new gift*, just as there was among[8] the Apostles on the day of Pentecost, and/or *of a new use*, just as is in Confirmation; then the Holy Spirit can be said "to be sent" and/or "to be given", because in He is there anew in another manner as much as regards that given and/or use of the gift, and because He is more abundantly (there).

1. To that which is objected, that He is not there in another manner of being [alio modo essendi]; it must be said, that even if according to this[9] He is not (there) in another manner of being, He is, however, by a more perfect manner of indwelling and by another manner of using, and for that reason in a new manner.

2. To that which is objected,[10] 'if He is sent more abundantly, He proceeds more abundantly'; it must be said, that "to be sent and/or proceed more abundantly" is in a twofold manner: either *for this*, and/or *in this*; in the first manner there is a "being sent" in a uniform manner, in the second (there is) not.

---

[1] ON THE INSTITUTION OF CLERICS., Bk. I, ch. 30: For the baptized is signed with chrism by means of the priest on the summit of his head, but by means of a pontiff on the forehead, to signify by the first anointing the descending of the Holy Spirit upon him to consecrate a dwelling to God, in the second too, so that by the sevenfold grace of the same Holy Spirit (His) coming into the man might be declared with every fullness of holiness and knowledge.

[2] From the Vatican edition and codex cc there is absent the word *is* [est], which, however, is found in all the other manuscripts and edition 1.

[3] Book II, Homily 10: For when the grace of the same Spirit is given to men, the Spirit is truly sent from the Father. Cf. above p. 242, note 3.

[4] Preferring the reading of edition 1, as that which is confirmed from the true context, we have put in this argument three times *to add together* [consummare] in place of *to conserve* [conservare], which the Vatican edition, together with the manuscripts, exhibits.

[5] From the ancient manuscripts and edition 1, we have substituted *him* [illum] for the less apt *it* [illud], and a little before this *than* [quam] in place of *and* [et].

[6] Very many codices, together with edition 1, in place of *and* [et] put *for the reason* [eo], which reading, however, seems both to shatter the force of the objection and to be less congruous with the response posited below it. — A little above this, after *also* [etiam] codices L and O reads *in a man without knowing it* [in homine nesciente].

[7] The Vatican edition together with codex cc, but with the other codices and edition 1 striving against them, puts *either* [aut] in place of *and* [et], which confounds the members of the distinction.

[8] We have supplied, from the manuscripts and edition 1, the *among* [in].

[9] In the codices there are a variety of readings; for some codices, such as gg, read *there* [ibi] for *according to this* [hoc], but others, such as ff, have *in this* [in hoc], moreover, edition 1 omits *according to this* [hoc]; just before this many read *that if* [quod si] in place of *that even if* [quod etsi], though less well.

[10] Not a few codices and manuscripts, such as I K P Q V and X, (by) adding *that* [quod], (do not require the quotation marks which follow).

3. To that which is objected, that (grace) is daily enlarged; it must be said, that it is enlarged daily as much as regards (its) fervor, but not as much as regard the conferral of new gifts and/or uses.

4. To that which is objected, that with grace lessened, He ought to withdraw, it must be said, that, just as will be clear below,[1] grace is enlarged as much as regards (its) substance, but is not lessened, except only as much as regards (its) fervor; moreover, the Holy Spirit[2] is not said "*to be sent*" in the augment of (its) fervor, but only (in the augment) of the substance of charity.

SCHOLIUM

I. The sense of the question is, whether the Son and the Holy Spirit are always sent, howsoever often the gifts and/or graces are enlarged. — The first opinion, which the Seraphic Doctor neither approves nor reproves, is that of Bl. (now St.) Albertus (Magnus), Richard (of Middleton) and others. On the other hand, (the Seraphic Doctor) does respond under another distinction and with a twofold conclusion, as is clear from his text. — The words in the solution to n. 1 and to n. 4, which seem to insinuate, that in every augment of sanctifying grace there is a mission, ought to be understood according to the doctrine put forth in the body (of the response). St. Thomas follows the sentence of the Seraphic (Doctor), and adds in his commentary: « Certain ones says, that in every augment of the grace which makes one pleasing there is a mission of a Divine Person, which also can be easily sustained ».

II. Alexander of Hales, SUMMA., p. I, q. 73, m. 4, a. 3. — St. Thomas, here in q. 5, quaestiuncula 2; SUMMA., I, q. 43, a. 6, in reply to n. 2. — Bl. (now St.) Albertus (Magnus), here in a. 19; d. 17, a. 9. — (Bl.) Peter of Tarentaise, here in q. 4, a. 1, quaestiuncula 3. — Richard of Middleton, here in a. 4, q. 2. — Giles the Roman, here in 2nd. princ. q. 1, coll. 1. — (Bl.) Dionysius the Carthusian, here in q. 3, at the end.

DOUBTS ON THE TEXT OF THE MASTER

DOUBT I

In this part are the doubts about the text (of Master Peter), and first there is the doubt concerning the *situation* of the first chapter of this part. For it seems, that Master (Peter) ought not place a tract on the mission of the Son here, because the mission of the Son is the Incarnation, but His Incarnation will be dealt with[3] in the Third (Book): therefore, he would have to deal with the mission there, not here.

I RESPOND: It must be said,[4] that Master (Peter) introduces incidentally here a tract on the mission of the Son for the sake of explaining the mission of the Holy Spirit. However, it could be said, that Master (Peter) deals with the mission of the Son here principally in regard to the mind, but of the mission of the Son in regard to the flesh per accidens, to distinguish (it) from the mission of the Son in regard to the mind. But he deals with that mission, which is in regard to the flesh, especially and principally in the Third (Book), and for that reason[5] otherwise than here.

DOUBT II

Likewise, is asked of this which he says: *Not for the very reason, that He has been born of the Father, is the Son said (to have been) sent.* For he seems to say the false and (speak) contrary to (St.) Gregory,[6] who says: « The Son is sent in that manner, whereby He is generated ».

I RESPOND: It must be said, that (St.) Augustine speaks with precision, so that there be understood: *not only for the very reason*; but (St.) Gregory with the presupposition of a manifestation. *And/or in another manner*: (St.) Augustine speaks of the eternal generation, (St. Gregory) of the temporal; whence there is entirely no contradiction there.[7]

DOUBT III

Likewise, is asked of this which he says, that *before the Incarnation He was sent to all the Saints, who were before.* Therefore, it is asked, whether after the Incarnation the Son and the Holy Spirit have been given more fully. And that it is so, it seems, because the state of the Law was a state of imperfection, the state of the Gospel a state of perfection. For the Law lead no one to perfection,[8] but the Gospel says. *Be ye perfect*, in the fifth (chapter of St.) Matthew:[9] ergo etc..

Likewise, this seems specially (true) of the Holy Spirit, because there is written in the seventh (chapter of the Gospel of St.) John:[10] *The Spirit had not yet been given, because Jesus had not yet been glorified*; this is not said, because He had in no manner been given before, but because (He had not been given) so abundantly: ergo etc..

Likewise, there is a greater cognition and dilection in the season of the Law of grace, than in the season of the written Law: ergo etc..

I RESPOND: It must be said, that "*to be given more fully*" can be understood in a twofold manner. either *intensively*, or *extensively*. If *extensively*, thus the Holy Spirit has been given to more in the season of the Law of grace, because *unto every land has their voice gone forth*[11] etc., not only to one nation. If *intensively*, this is as much as regards the *general state*, or as much as regards *special persons*; as much as regards the state in the New Testament,

---

[1] Distinction 17, p. II, qq. 1 and 3.

[2] The Vatican edition, contrary to the codices and edition 1, reads here otherwise than above in the body (of the response): *moreover, the Holy Spirit* [Spiritus autem sanctus]. Then, after *of fervor* [fervoris] codex Y adds *nor in any other augment* [nec in aliquo alio augmento].

[3] Supported by the older manuscripts and edition 1, we have put *will be dealt with* [agetur] for *is dealt with* [agitur]. A little below this, at the end of the argument codex V reads sufficiently well *but not here* [non autem hic].

[4] We have supplied from the ancient codices and edition 1 *It must be said* [Dicendum], and then we have substituted *here a* [hic] for *this* [hunc].

[5] Edition 1 has *thus* [ita] for *for that reason* [ideo].

[6] HOMILIES ON THE GOSPELS., Hom. 26. Cf. p. I of this distinction, q. 2, 1st argument for the opposite.

[7] According to the testimony of the more ancient manuscripts and edition 1, we have inserted *there* [ibi].

[8] Hebrews 7:19 : *For the Law brought nothing to perfection* [Nihil enim ad perfectum adduxit lex].

[9] Verse 48.

[10] Verse 39. — Then, one and the other codex, such as A, together with edition 1, has *because* [quia] in place of *because* [quod], but less well.

[11] Psalm 18:15. — Then, after *this is* [hoc est] the Vatican edition adds *in a twofold manner or* [dupliciter aut], which is lacking in the manuscripts, though some of them, such as V X and Y, together with edition 1, have *or this is as much as* [aut hoc est quantum].

as much as regards special persons in the Old Testament, and thus they hold themselves as things exceeding and things exceeded, because in the Old Testament there were some Evangelical men; and in this manner the reasons for each part proceed. For[1] in the Old Testament there were some abounding in wisdom, as Solomon, some in patience, as Job, some in meekness, as Moses, some in faith, such as Abraham, some in devotion, as David, some in the working of miracles,[2] such as Elias.

Doubt IV

Likewise is asked of this which he says, *that He has been to the Angels.* For it seems false, because an Angel is said (to be) a "messenger" or "one sent": but to one "sent" there is not a sending [missio]: ergo etc.. *If you say*, that He is sent in another manner: *on the contrary*: He who is always present does not need a 'being sent' [missione]; but an Angel always contemplates God as One present: therefore, etc..

I Respond: It must be said, that the mission of Wisdom or of the Son is to enlighten [illustrandam] the creature, just as the mission of the Holy Spirit (is) to sanctify (it). And since the Angels of themselves were not wise nor were of themselves holy, for that reason it was necessary [oportuit], that from the beginning there would be sent to them the Wisdom, which is the Son, and also[3] the Holy Spirit. Whence (St.) Augustine[4] speaks of the state of glorification, but properly He is not said to be sent then, except (when) He is said broadly to be sent for the manifestation of something hidden.[5]

Doubt V

Likewise is asked of this which he says: *According to which we grasp anything eternal with the mind, we are not in this world.* For he seems to say the false, because he either says this[6] according to *the soul*, or according to *the flesh.* Not according to *the flesh*, this is established:

therefore, according to *the soul*: therefore, it seems, that the soul, when it cognizes God, is in Heaven or outside of the world. Likewise, this seems by reason, because "to grasp (something) eternal" is rather "to be grasped": therefore, if what is grasped is located by what is grasping, therefore, the soul is located in eternity, therefore, outside of time. *Besides*, what is cognized and loved, either is drawn to the one cognizing and loving, or the other way around;[7] but while we love God and cognize Him, we do not draw God to us, but ourselves to God, just as is said in the fourth (book) On the Divine Names:[8] therefore, etc..

I Respond: It must be said, that a location [locus] has the nature of one containing and of one quieting.[9] Therefore, "to be in this world" is in a twofold manner: either as much as regards *the truth* and 'being contained' [continentiam], or as much as regards *quiet*. But (St.) Augustine does not say in the first[10] manner, that the soul and body *truly* step forth from this world, when the mind grasps God, but understands (this) as much as regards *quiet*, because the affection of the soul does not rest in the temporal (things), upon which it bears itself, but in the eternal ones,[11] and Dionysius (the Areopagite) understands (it) as much as regard this. — And the second reason is understood (to be), that the one loved draws, not by changing locally, but by conforming to itself, because the one loving is transformed into the one loved, the one cognizing is conformed to the one cognized.[12]

Doubt VI

Likewise is asked of this which (St.) Augustine says: *the Principle of the whole Divinity, and/or if it is better said, of the Deity.* For he seems to speak badly, because either this is through the generation, or through the spiration. But if in this manner: therefore, the Father generates and/or spirates the Deity, which is contrary to Master (Peter), above in the Fifth Distinction,[13] where he says, that the Essence neither generates nor is generated. — *Moreover* there is asked, for what reason does he say: « And/or if it is better said, "of the Deity" »?

I Respond: It must be said, that (St.) Augustine does

[1] The Vatican edition less well, together with codex cc, omits *For* [enim], which however, is extant in the other codices and edition 1.

[2] The Vatican edition reads *work* [opere] for *working* [operatione], but is corrected with the help of the manuscripts and edition 1. — This proposed question will be found more fully treated in Alexander of Hales, Summa., p. I, q. 73, m. 2, a. 4. — St. Thomas, here in q. 5, a. 2. — Bl. (now St.) Albertus (Magnus), here in a. 18. — (Bl.) Peter of Tarentaise, here in q. 4, q. 2. — Richard of Middleton, here in a. 5, q. 1. — Giles the Roman, here in 2nd princ., q. 2. — (Bl.) Dionysius the Carthusian, here in q. 5.

[3] In the Vatican edition and codex cc there is incongruously lacking *also* [etiam], which is found in all the other codices and in edition 1.

[4] On the Trinity., Bk. IV, ch. 20, n. 27, from which the text of this doubt has been taken, see the text of Master (Peter), here in ch. 8.

[5] This is especially treated in Alexander of Hales, Summa., p. I, q. 73, m. 3, a. 2. — St. Thomas, here in q. 5, a. 1, quaestiuncula 3. Bl. (now St.) Albertus (Magnus), here in a. 19. — (Bl.) Peter of Tarentaise, here in q. 4, a. 1, quaestiuncula 2. — Giles the Roman, here in 2nd princ., q. 1, collation 2. — (Bl.) Dionysius the Carthusian, here in a. 5, q. 1.

[6] We have supplied, trusting in the older manuscripts and edition 1, *this* [hoc].

[7] In regard to the first part of this proposition, we follow the reading of many manuscripts, such as F G H I K N T X Y Z dd ee and ff, while the Vatican falsely has *what cognizes and loves* [quod cognoscit et amat], and edition 1 has *what is cognized and loves* [quod cognoscitur et amat]. In regard to the second part, however, we exhibit the reading of codex Y, which is both in itself more distinct and concordant with what follows, from which the reading of codex M does not dissent too much, *is drawn to the one cognizing and into the one loving* [trahitur ad cognoscentem et in amatum], in place of which a greater part of the man-

uscripts together with edition 1 have *is drawn by the one cognizing into the one loving* [trahitur a cognoscente in amantem], but the Vatican edition together with other codices has *is drawn from the one cognizing and loving* [trahitur a cognoscente et amante]. — Then edition 1 has *when* [cum] in place of *while* [dum], and a little below this after *but* [sed] codex dd reads *we are drawn* [nos trahimur].

[8] (Dionysius the Areopagite, *ibid.*,) Chapter 3, § 1: Not that we are drawing the One present everywhere, and never the virtue, but that by memories and invocations we are attaching and uniting ourselves with Him.

[9] Cf. Aristotle, Physics, Bk. IV, texts 41 and 48 (chs. 4 and 5).

[10] The Vatican edition, not trusting in the manuscripts and editions 1, 2, 3 and 6, has *a proper* [proprio] for *the first* [primo], just as also next, contrary to very many older codices, such as A G T Z and dd, it has *steps forth from* [egrediatur] for *step forth from* [egrediantur].

[11] The manuscripts together with five first editions transpose the words *but in (the) eternal ones* [sed in aeternis] after *in the temporal (things)* [in temporalibus], but less well, for the reason that the words immediately following *upon which it bears itself* [quibus superfertur] then would have to be accepted in a sense rarely used, that is in this manner: *through which the affection is brought above temporal things*, which is not concordant with the manner of speaking used by the Seraphic Doctor in respect to this verb superferri [to bear, bring, or carry, up or over or above], cf. below d. 17, p. I, Doubt 5, where there is had *bear one's self above one's passions* [superferri passionibus]. — Then the Vatican edition, without the authority of the codices and edition 1, has *is understood* [intelligitur] for *understands (it)* [intelligit].

[12] St. Thomas expounds the same words of (St.) Augustine, here in q. 5, a. 3. — Bl. (now St.) Albertus (Magnus), here in a. 20. — (Bl.) Peter of Tarentaise and Richard (of Middleton), here on the text (of Master Peter). — (Bl.) Dionysius the Carthusian, here in q. 5, at the end.

[13] Chapter 1. — A little before this edition 1 has *and* [et] for *and/or* [vel].

not say simply, that He is the Principle of the Divinity, but with this determination, "*of the whole (Divinity)*". And since in the most simple there does occur any totality, except when the name of "totality" is extended to a plurality of persons, for that reason "Deity" or "Divinity" stands as "among the Persons"; however, because ("totality") cannot be drawn to the Persons, since it is an abstract noun, the aforesaid saying must be expounded, just as Master (Peter) expounds completely similar sayings above.[1]

Because there is asked: "For what reason is there said better "*of the Deity*"?"; it must be said, that "*divine*" [divinum] can be said of creatures, according to which a man is said (to be) "*divine*"; but "God" is proper to God alone; for that reason "*Deity*" more properly means the form of God than "*Divinity*"; for that reason there is better said "*Deity*" than "*Divinity*".

DISTINCTION XVI

CHAPTER I

On the mission of the Holy Spirit, which comes to be in two manners, visibly and invisibly.

Now, concerning the Holy Spirit, there must be seen, besides that ineffable and eternal procession, by which He proceeds from the Father and the Son, and not from Himself, what is His temporal procession, which is said (to be) a "mission" or "donation".[1] To which we say, that just as the Son is said to be sent in two manners: in one, whereby He has visibly appeared, in the other, whereby He is invisibly[2] perceived by chaste minds; so also the Holy Spirit is said either to be sent or to be given by the Father and the Son and by Himself in two manners: in one visibly, in the other invisibly. For He has been given by the demonstration of a visible creature, just as (He was) on the day of Pentecost and at other times, and He is given daily by invisibly gliding into the minds of the faithful.

And first let us deal with that manner of mission, which comes to be by visible species. Of this (St.) Augustine in the second book, ON THE TRINITY[3] thus says: « It is easy [in promptu] to understand of the Holy Spirit, why He is also said (to have been) sent. For a certain visible species of a creature was wrought in time, in which the Holy Spirit was visibly shown, either when, in the corporal species of a dove, He descended upon the Lord Himself, or when on the day of Pentecost there suddenly came to be a sound from Heaven, like a vehement blowing was put in motion [ferretur], and by them were seen divided tongues, as of a fire, which settled [insedit] upon each of them. This working visibly expressed and offered to the eyes of mortals is said (to be) he mission of the Holy Spirit, not that there appeared to them[4] the Substance Itself, in which He Himself is also invisible and incommutable, just as the Father and the Son (are), but so that men's hearts moved completely by exterior sights [visis] might be converted by a temporal manifestation of the One coming, to the hidden eternity of the One always present ». Behold, with these words (St.) Augustine reveals [aperit] that manner of mission, which is exhibited visibly, even though [cum tamen] the Holy Spirit is not seen in His own Nature, Who was not even in those creatures more than in others, but (rather was there) for another (purpose). For He was in those, so that coming[5] through them to men He might show that He is in those, to

whom those creatures came. For the Holy Spirit did not then come and/or descend into men by a temporal movement, but through the temporal movement of a creature there was signified the spiritual and invisible infusion of the Holy Spirit. And to speak more openly, through that manner of the Holy Spirit's mission, exhibited corporally, there was demonstrated the Holy Spirit's spiritual and interior mission or donation, which is (yet) to be dealt with.

But, before (this), there must be asked, since the Son is said (to be) less than the Father according to the mission, whereby He appeared in a created form, why the Holy Spirit is not also said similarly (to be) less than the Father, since He appeared in a created form.[6] For of the Son, that He be less than the Father according to the form, whereby He appeared as One sent, (St.) Augustine openly shows in the fourth book, ON THE TRINITY[7] saying: « *God sent His own Son, made out of a woman, made under the Law*, even to the extent that (He was) tiny, as one made; and thus sent for the reason that (He was) made. Let us admit, therefore, that (He has been) made less, and inasmuch as (He is) less, insomuch (Has he been) made, and inasmuch as (He has been) made, insomuch (Has he been) sent ». Behold you have, that the Son, inasmuch as He has been sent, that is made, is less than the Father. Why, therefore, is the Holy Spirit not said (to be) less than the Father, when He Himself has assumed the creature in which He appeared? Because, the Spirit assumed the creature, in which He appeared, in one manner, the Son in another manner. For the Son accepted it through a union,[8] but the Spirit (did) not. For the Son accepted the man thus, that He became Man: but the Holy Spirit did not accept the dove thus, that He became a dove. Of this (St.) Augustine in the second book, ON THE TRINITY[9] thus says: « For that reason it has never been written, that God the Father is greater than the Holy Spirit, and/or that the Holy Spirit is less than the Father, because the creature, in which the Holy Spirit appeared, was not assumed in the same manner, as was assumed the Son of Man, in which form the Person of the Word of God Himself was presented, not so that (that Man) would have the Word of God, just as the other wise Saints (did), but because He was Word Itself. For one thing is *the Word in the flesh*, another *the Word (made) flesh*, that is, one thing is the Word in a man, another the Word (made) Man. For *flesh* is posited for *man* in that (verse) which says:[10] *The Word was made flesh*. Not, therefore, in the same manner was

---

[1] Distinction V, chs. 1 and 2.
NOTES ON THE BOOK OF THE SENTENCES
[1] The Vatican edition together with the other editions, except 1 and 8, contrary to the codices, reads *giving* [datio]. A little before this codices A B and E repeat *from* [a] before *the Son* [Filio]. Then after *To which we say* [Ad quod dicimus] editions 1, 6 and 8, have *that* [quod] in place of *that* [quia].
[2] The Vatican edition and editions 2, 4, 5 and 9, contrary to the codices and the other editions, after *invisibly* [invisibiliter] add (the implicitly understood) *by* [a], and contrariwise a little afterwards, before *Himself* [se ipso], codices B C and E, and editions 1 and 8, omit *by* [a]. Then editions 1 and 7 omit *or to be given* [sive dari]. Next editions 2, 3 and 7 read *of a creature visibly* [visibiliter creaturae] in place of *of an visible creature* [visibilis creaturae].
[3] Chapter 5, n. 10. — The Vatican edition and editions 4 and 6 omits *thus* [ita] before *says* [ait].

[4] Codices D and E, together with the original, read *His very Substance* [eius ipsa substantia] for *to them the Substance Itself* [eis ipsa substantia]; codex A reads *to them His very Substance* [eius eis ipsa substantia].
[5] Codices B C D and E and editions 1 and 6 reads *so that through those (creatures) coming to men He might show* etc. [ut per eas ad homines venientes ostenderetur etc.].
[6] The Vatican edition together with the other editions, contrary to the codices and editions 1 and 8, has not so well *when He appeared* [cum apparuit]. A little before this codices C and E and editions 1 and 8 omit *also* [et].
[7] Chapter 19, n. 26. — The passage from Scripture is Gal. 4:4.
[8] Only the Vatican ed. and edd. 5 and 6 add *of Person* [personae].
[9] Chapter 6, n. 11. — The Vatican edition and edition 6 again omit *thus* [ita] before *says* [ait].
[10] John 1:14.

the creature, in which the Holy Spirit appeared, assumed, as was assumed that flesh and human form from the Virgin Mary. For He did not beatify the dove and/or that blowing (of the wind) and/or that fire and join it for ever together with Himself in the unity of (His) Person ». From the aforesaid it has been openly shown, according to what the Son is said (to be) less than the Father, and for what reason the Son is said (to be) less than the Father, and the Holy Spirit not.

CHAPTER II

That the Son according to which (He is) man,
is not merely (less) than the Father,
but (is) also less than the Holy Spirit.

Moreover, it must be noted, that the Son, according to which He has been made Man, is not only said (to be) less than the Father but (less) than the Holy Spirit and even (less) than Himself. And that He, according to the form of a servant, is also said (to be) less than Himself, (St.) Augustine shows in the first book, ON THE TRINITY[1] saying: « Men have erred, transferring those things which have been said of Christ according to the Man, to His Substance, which is sempiternal, as that which the Lord Himself says:[2] *The Father is greater than I*, which the Truth says on account of (His) form of a servant, according to which manner the Son is even less than Himself. For in what manner has He not also been made less than Himself, Who *emptied Himself, accepting the form of a servant* ?[3] For He did not so accept the form of a servant, as to lose [amitteret] the form of God, in which He was equal to the Father. In the form of a servant He is also less than Himself. Therefore, not unmeritedly does Scripture say each, that is, both that the Son (is) equal to the Father, and that the Father (is) greater than the Son; for the former is understood on account of the form of God, but the latter on account of the form of a servant ». On this same (verse St.) Augustine says in the second book, ON THE TRINITY:[4] « The Son of God is

equal to the Father according to the form of God, in which He is, and less than the Father according to the form of a servant, which He accepted, in which He has been found not merely less than the Father, but also (less) than the Holy Spirit, and not this only, but also (less) than Himself ». « On account of which, as he says in (his) Letter to Maximus,[5] He has not only been made less than the Father, but also (less) than Himself and the Holy Spirit and even *lessened for a little while less than the Angels* ». « Therefore, the Son of God is », as he says in the first book, ON THE TRINITY,[6] « equal to God the Father according to Nature, less according to condition [habitu minor], that is in the form of a servant, which He accepted ». With these authorities the Son is openly shown (to be), according to the form of a servant, less than the Father and Himself and the Holy Spirit.

Moreover, (St.) Hilary seems to say, that the Father is greater than the Son, and yet (that) the Son is[7] not less than the Father. For the Father is said (to be) greater on account of authorship, because in Him there is the authorship of generation, according to which (the Son Himself) says:[8] *The Father is greater than I*; and the Apostle: *He has granted to Him a Name, which is above every name*. Therefore, when He says: the Father is greater than I, this is as if He said, 'He has granted Me a Name'. « If, therefore, », says (St.) Hilary in (his) ninth book, ON THE TRINITY,[9] « the Father, in the authorship of one granting, is greater, is not the Son less through the confession of the gift? And thus the One granting is greater, but He is not now less, to whom the One "Being" is granted; for He says: *I and the Father are One*. If it were not granted to Jesus, that He shall be confessed (to be) in the glory of God the Father, He is less than the Father. But if it is granted to Him to be in that glory, where the Father is, you have also in the authorship of the One giving, that He is greater, and in the confession of the given ("Being"),[10] that They are One. And so the Father is greater than the Son and plainly greater (than He), to Whom He grants to be as much as He Himself is, to Whom He imparts the Image of (His own) innascible "Being" by the sacrament of a Nativity, Whom He generates out of Himself in His own form ». You have hear, O reader, what (St.) Hilary says on this (matter), of whose words, wheresoever they occur, diligently take note and piously understand!

COMMENTARY ON DISTINCTION XV

On the mission of the Holy Spirit, in particular, and, indeed, of (His) visible (mission).

Now, concerning the Holy Spirit, there must be seen, besides that ineffable and eternal procession.

THE DIVISION OF THE TEXT

This is the second part of that part, in which (Master Peter) deals with mission as much as regards (its) manner. In this part, he deals with the mission of the Holy Spirit *in particular* [specialiter].[1] And

since the mission of the Holy Spirit is in two manners, that is, the visible and the invisible, just as the mission of the Son (is): for that reason this part has two parts. In *the first (subpart)*, Master (Peter) deals with

---

[1] Chapter 7, n. 14, but with many words omitted by Master (Peter). — A little before this, codex D has *But that* [Quod autem] for *And that* [Et quod]; codex C has *That* [Quod].

[2] John 14:28. — The editions read *says* [ait] for *says* [dicit] contrary to the codices and the original.

[3] Philippians 2:7.   [4] Chapter 1, n. 2.

[5] Epistle 170 (previously 66), n. 9. — All the codices and editions badly cite: *in the book Against Maximinus* (or *Maximianus*) [in libro contra Maximinum (vel Maximianus)]; the Vatican edition has *in the book "The Epistle to Maximus"* [in libr. Epist. ad Maximum]. Maximus was a doctor converted from the Arian heresy. — At the end of this passage, the text of Sacred Scripture is Hebrews 2:9: *who for a little while became lesser than the Angels* [qui modico quam Angeli minoratus est].

[6] Ch. 7, n. 14. — Here the Vatican ed. with all the other edd. reads *in Nature* [in natura], contrary to the original, to our codd. and even to the context,

since *nature* and *condition* are in a parallel construction. Then only the Vatican edition and codex C omit *that is* [id est].

[7] The Vatican edition together with very many editions, but contrary to the codices and editions 1 and 8, omits *is* [sit].

[8] John 14:28; and then Phil. 2:7. — Edition 8, to the verb *says* [dicit], prefaces *the Son Himself* [ipse Filius], which all the others understand.

[9] Number 54. — The text of Scripture is John 10:30.

[10] Against the original, all the codices and editions 6, 8, and 9, the Vatican edition together with the other editions, reads badly *of the One giving* [donantis]. A little after this, the Vatican edition and edition 1 faultily add *even* [et] before *the Son* [Filio].

NOTES ON THE COMMENTARY

[1] The Vatican ed., contrary to the authority of all the codd. and ed. 1, exhibits the first proposition thus: *Above, Master (Peter) dealt with the temporal*

the visible mission of the Holy Spirit. In *the second*, he deals with the invisible mission,[1] and this below in the Seventeenth Distinction: *Now let us proceed immediately to assign the mission of the Holy Spirit*

The first part, again, has two parts. In the first ,Master (Peter) explains the visible mission of the Holy Spirit. In the second, for a greater explanation he moves and determines a certain doubt, there (where he says): *But first there must be asked, since the Son is said (to be) less than the Father* etc.

The first part, again,[2] has two parts. In *the first*, Master (Peter) assigns a twofold manner of the mission of the Holy Spirit according to the twofold manner of the mission of the Son. But, *second*, he proceeds [prosequitur] concerning the other, that is the visible mission, there (where he says): *And first let us deal with that manner of mission, which comes to be visibly* etc., where he says, that the visible mission is an apparition wrought in an exterior sign, through which the interior mission is made manifest [monstratur].

But first there must be asked, since the Son is said to be less than the Father etc.. This is the second part of the Distinction,[3] in which Master (Peter) moves (certain) doubts, and this doubt has its rise from a comparison of the mission of the Son and (of that) of the Holy Spirit. For, since the Holy Spirit is visibly sent, just as even the Son, the question is, 'For what reason is He not said (to be) less than the Father, as the Son (is)?' Moreover, this part, in which he pursues this question,[4] has three parts. In *the first*, he opposes and determines, that the Holy Spirit ought not be said from (His) mission (to be) less, just as the Son (is), because the Holy Spirit has not been united (to a creature). *Second*,[5] having concluded this [occasione huius] he adds a certain truth adjoined to this, that is, that the Son by reason of (His) mission is said (to be) less than Himself, there (where he says): *Moreover, it must be noted, that the Son, according to which He has been made Man*. *Third*, he teaches one to understand sanely a certain doubtful word, which has been conjoined to the present consideration, which (St.) Hilary says, that is, 'that the Father according to the Divinity is greater than the Son, and[6] the Son according to the Divinity is not less', there (where he says): *Moreover, (St.) Hilary seems to say, that the Father is* etc..

TREATMENT OF THE QUESTIONS

For the evidence of this part there are asked three (questions) concerning the visible mission:

First, there is asked,[7] what is it.

Second, for what is it useful.

Third, there is asked, in which manners does it come to be.

ARTICLE SOLE

On the visible mission of the Holy Spirit.

QUESTION I

What is the visible mission?

About the first, (the argument) is advanced in this manner:

First, it is show, that a visible mission is nothing other than an exterior apparition.

1. (St.) Augustine says,[8] that « then the Holy Spirit (and/or) the Son is sent, when in time He is perceived by the mind of anyone »: therefore, then He is visibly sent, when He is perceived visibly; but He is perceived visibly, when He appears in a visible creature: therefore, the mission is nothing other than an apparition.

2. Likewise, this same is seen through a simile, because '*to be invisibly sent*' is nothing other than 'to be manifested invisibly through an invisible effect': therefore, '*to be sent visibly*' is nothing other than 'to be manifested through a visible[9] creature': but this is not other than to appear visibly: ergo etc..

3. Likewise, this again is seen *by an example*, because the Holy Spirit is said (to be) sent to the Son in the appearance [specie] of a dove, just as (St.) Augustine says, and as is had in the text;[10] but then no donation was made to the Son, because He was always full of the Holy Spirit: but (therefore, it was) only an exterior apparition: ergo etc..

BUT ON THE CONTRARY: 1. It seems that a visible apparition itself is not the entire reckoning [tota ratio] of a visible mission, because[11] the Father appeared in a subjected creature, and yet He is not said

---

procession of the Holy Spirit, by which He proceeds and/or is sent by Himself, here he deals with the same as much as regards (its) manner. And since etc.; but falsely, as is clear from the division of the text, d. 15, p. I and II.

¹ In the Vatican edition, contrary to the manuscripts, *mission* [missione] is lacking.

² From the mss. and edition 1 we have supplied *again* [iterum].

³ The Vatican edition, having omitted the words of Master (Peter), begins the proposition thus: *Similarly, the second part, in which* [Similiter secunda pars, in qua], and a little below this puts *which has* [quae habet] in place of *and this doubt has* [et habet haec dubitatio], with the other manuscripts and edition 1 striving against this.

⁴ In the Vatican edition the words *Moreover this part, in which he pursues this question* [Haec autem pars, in qua hanc quaestionem prosequitur], are lacking, yet they are extant in the manuscripts and edition 1.

⁵ The codices together with edition 1 have *And* [Et] for *Second* [Secundo], but less distinctly.

⁶ Trusting in the more ancient manuscripts and edition 1 we have inserted *and* [et].

⁷ From the older manuscripts and edition 1 we have restored *there is asked* [quaeritur]. A little after this at the beginning of the question, we have restored, from the codices and edition 1, the words: *About the first, one proceeds thus* [Circa primum, proceditur sic], which are lacking in the Vatican edition.

⁸ ON THE TRINITY, Bk. IV, ch. 20, n. 28. See these in the text of Master (Peter), d. XV, chs. 7-9.

⁹ The Vatican edition together with codex cc, yet with the other codices and edition 1 striving against this, has *through a creature visibly* [per creaturam visibiliter] in place of *through a visible creature* [per creaturam visibilem], it would be better to read *through a visible creature visibly* [per creaturam visibilem visibiliter]. Codex T has *effect* [effectum] in place of *creature* [creaturam].

¹⁰ Here in ch. 1.

¹¹ We follow the manuscripts and the five first editions, by putting *because* [quia] in place of *thus* [sic]. A little below this after *therefore* [ergo] many codices together with editions 1, 2, and 3, false read *it is a mission before (it is)* [prius est mission quam] for *it is more a mission than* [plus est mission quam].

"(to have been) sent visibly": therefore, it is more a mission than an apparition. The *major* is clear, because (St.) Augustine says in the second (book) ON THE TRINITY:[1] « It is rash to say, that God the Father appeared to the Prophets and Patriarchs through some visible forms ».

2. Likewise, the Son and the Holy Spirit in the Old Testament appeared visibly many times, and yet at that time Neither is said (to have been) visibly sent, just as (St.) Augustine says in the third (book) ON THE TRINITY,[2] where he moves this question: ergo etc..

3. Likewise, everything which appears visibly, is corporeal, since it its perceived by the sense; but God, since He is simple, is entirely incorporeal: if, therefore, if it does not pertain [spectat] to God to appear visibly, therefore, if He is visibly sent, the visible mission is not an apparition. *If you say*, that He does not in Himself appear, but in an effect; *on the contrary*: He appears in the same manner [sic] in every creature both always and everywhere: therefore, according to this He is visibly sent in every creature always and everywhere, which is stupid to say.

4. Likewise, where there is a mission, there is a manifestation of a person, as (St.) Augustine says;[3] but through an apparition alone there is never a manifestation, except a revelation be present [adsit]: therefore, of the reckoning of a visible mission is not only an apparition, but also a revelation: therefore, an apparition is not its entire reckoning.

CONCLUSION

A visible mission is an apparition, in which there is manifested the emanation and indwelling of a Divine Person.

I RESPOND: It must be said, that a 'visible mission' presupposes 'mission' as in the above (sense), and adds upon this a difference, which is the 'visible'. Moreover 'mission' *commonly* said, as was said above in the preceding distinction,[4] presupposes about the one sent *an emanation* and adds above this, *a manifestation*. And since the manifestation of the emanation, according to which the mission is attained, does not come to be except upon him, whom the Holy Spirit indwells through the effect of indwelling grace, hence it is, that 'mission' from a general reckoning means 'a manifestation of an emanation and of an indwelling'.

Moreover, this difference '*visible*', imposed upon [superadveniens] 'mission', contracts it as much as regards (its) principal signification, which is a 'manifestation'; for that reason it means a 'man-

ifestation with an apparition', or an 'apparition manifesting the indwelling of a Person emanating[5] and/or (manifesting) the emanation of a Person indwelling'.

Wherefore, I concede, that the visible mission is an *apparition*; but this is not the entire reckoning (of it), but (rather) an 'apparition, in which there is manifested a Divine Person not only as One *working*, but also as One *indwelling*, and not only as One indwelling, but also as One *emanating*, as if[6] coming from Another'. Through the first it excludes an apparition of God in any creature, through the second an apparition in the Old Testament, through the third the apparition of the Father, because the Father did not appear as One emanating or coming from Another. On the other hand the Son and/or the Holy Spirit in the Old Testament did not appear as One indwelling, but as One showing beforehand that He is going to indwell [se inhabitaturum praemonstrans], wherefore an Angel used to appear in those creatures in the person of God. And this (St.) Augustine proves in the third book, ON THE TRINITY[7] saying: « It is established by the firmness of authority and the probability of reason, that when God is said to have appeared to the ancient Patriarchs, those voices were made by Angels ». And he adduces the authorities of the Apostle in the third (chapter of his Letter) to the Galatians:[8] *The Law ordained through Angels*; and in the second (chapter) to the Hebrews:[9] *For if the speech which has been said through Angels* etc.. And yet I do not say, that this is the reason, for which He has been sent, because the apparition came to be by angelic ministry; because just as (St.) Augustine says in the fourth (book) ON THE TRINITY[10] it is probable, that that dove, in which the Holy Spirit appeared, was moved by the ministry of an Angel. Whence the same in the fourth book, ON THE TRINITY says at the end:[11] « On this it is difficult to find, and not expedient to dare to affirm, anything. However, I do not see, in what manner those (apparitions) of His could be wrought, without a rational and/or intellectual creature ».

1. 2. And thus is clear, that not every apparition is a mission; the response is also clear to the first two reasons.

3. To that which is objected third, that there is no apparition, because God is invisible; it must be said, that "to appear" is in a twofold manner: either *in itself*, and thus it befits (something) corporeal: and/or *in another*, and this in a twofold manner: either just as *a cause* in an effect, and/or just as the *signed* in a *sign* [signatum in signo]; and in this third manner there is an apparition (of God); and according to this manner it does not befit every creature.

4. To that which is objected last, that an apparition is not a manifestation; it must be said, that where there is said: "a mission is[12] a manifestation", ("mission") is not understood

---

[1] Chapter 17, n. 32, among which words the Vatican edition, contrary to the more ancient codices and edition 1 and even the works of (St.) Augustine, omits *God* [Deum].

[2] Throughout, and in Bk. IV, chs. 19 and 20, nn. 25-30.

[3] ON THE TRINITY., Bk. IV, ch. 20, n. 28: When the Son of God was manifested in the flesh, He was sent into this world.

[4] Part I, q. 4. — A little before this after *commonly* [communiter], trusting in the manuscripts, such as H I M Z aa bb and ff and in edition 1, we have supplied *said* [dicta], which perhaps on account of the immediately following words *as has been said* [ut dictum], fell out of the text of the other codices, though less well. Then after *a manifestation* [manifestationem], in codex K there is added *as its principal signified* [tanquam principale significatum suum], which agrees with what follows.

[5] Codex K reads *manifesting an emanation and an indwelling* [manifestatem emanationem et inhabitationem]; the other codices, such as A S T V etc., after *manifesting* [manifestantem] incongruously omit *of a Person* [personae].

[6] Edition 1 reads *that is, as if* [id est, quasi].

[7] Chapter 11, n. 27: And it has also been established by the probability of reason, as much as a man and/or, rather, as much as I could, and by the firmness of authority, as much as the divine sayings of Sacred Scripture made clear, that to our ancient Patriarchs, before the Incarnation of the Savior, when God was said to appear, those voices or corporeal apparitions [species] were wrought through the Angels.

[8] Verse 19.

[9] Verse 2.

[10] Chapter 21, n. 31.

[11] Chapter 21, n. 31, in which text the Vatican edition reads *either with an rational or an intellectual* [sive rationali sive intellectuali], but falsely and contrary to very many codices and even the works of (St.) Augustine.

[12] The Vatican edition together with very many manuscripts here adds *not* [non], which however, we have expunged, trusting in the other manuscripts, such as B I K M Q T Z etc. and edition 1, and as not required by the context. Codex F has *'there is a mission, where there is a manifestation'* [missio ibi est, ubi est manifestatio].

as an act, but *as a habit*, because something comes to be and/or is shown, in which the emanation of a Person can be manifested, and this indeed "apparition" of itself conveys.

1. To that which is, on the other hand,[1] objected unto the contrary, that precisely (speaking "a mission") is not an apparition; it must be said, that (St. Augustine) does not accept (there) the whole reckoning of mission, because "*to be sent*" is not so much "to be perceived by a mind", but "to be perceived by a mind as One emanating from Another and indwelling in someone".

2. Similarly, to this: that "to be invisibly sent" is "to be manifested through an invisible effect"; it must be said, that "to be manifested" does not signify [dicit] (its) whole reckoning.

3. To that which is objected, that in the mission of the Holy Spirit in the appearance of a dove there was naught but an apparition; it must be said, that although there was not a donation of the Holy Spirit there, there was, however, a manifestation of a prior given and of One indwelling in Christ at that time and of One resting and of One proceeding from Another, and thus the entire and perfect reckoning of a "mission"; but from this it does not follow, that an apparition of any kind whatsoever is a visible mission; yet every visible mission is an apparition.

SCHOLIUM

I. A visible mission is declared in a twofold manner, first with the proximate genus '*mission*' and its contracting difference '*visible*', second with the genus '*apparition*' and its contracting difference: 'that which is an emanation and an indwelling of a Person'. Wherefore in a visible mission three (things) are required: the emanation of a Person, the indwelling of the Same and the manifestation of each through some *visible apparition*. — That the same three are required for a visible mission, is taught by St. Thomas, (Bl.) Peter of Tarentaise and others. Through these differences a visible mission is distinguished from the other apparitions enumerated in the text. When [si] he says: « Through the first it excludes the apparition of God in any creature etc. », the words *through the first* refer to the words: « in which a Divine *Person* are manifested », for the operation of God in any creature is common to the Three Divine Persons, whence it is manifestive of no Person (in particular). *Through the second* refers to « is manifested ... as One *indwelling* », *through the third* to « is manifested as One *emanating* ».

II. It must be noted in regard to the order of the solution for the opposite, which first responds to the arguments in the fundament (here the Contrary); then at those which are places in the first position, since each needs

a more accurate determination. — Here it helps to say generally, that the arguments in the *fundaments* of St. Bonaventure and others are not always approved by the author as true in their every part. The genuine doctrine of the author is to be sought out both in the Response to the question, and in the Solution of the objections.

III. All agree on the substance of the response. (St.) Bonaventure, BREVILOQUIUM, p. 1, ch. 5, and COMMENTARY ON THE GOSPEL OF ST. JOHN, ch. 1, v. 34 (Bonelli's SUPPLEMENT, tome I); in regard to the ministry of the Angels concerning apparitions, SENT., Bk. II, d. 10, a. 3, q. 2, in reply to n. 5. — Alexander of Hales, SUMMA., p. I, q. 74, m. 1, and in regard to the ministry of the Angels, m. 4. — (Bl. John Duns) Scotus, on this and the following question, here and in his REPORTATIO, q. sole. — St. Thomas, here in q. 1, a. 1, and in regard to the ministry of the Angels, a. 4; SUMMA., I, q. 43, a. 7, in reply to n. 5. — Bl. (now St.) Albertus (Magnus), here in a. 1 ff.; on this and the following question, SUMMA., p. I, tr. 7, q. 32, m. 2, a. 2. — (Bl.) Peter of Tarentaise, here in q. 1, a. 1 and 2. — Durandus (of Saint-Pourçain), on this and the following question, here in q. 1. — (Bl.) Dionysius the Carthusian, here in q. 1, and in regard to the Angels in q. 3. — (Gabriel) Biel, on this and the following questions, here in a. sole.

QUESTION II

For what is the visible mission of the Holy Spirit useful?

Second, there is asked, for what is the visible mission useful, and it is established that it contributes [confert] to effect nothing, because an exterior apparition works nothing interiorly. That it is also not useful for *making anything known* [ad innotescendum], is shown thus:

1. Either it is for manifesting *the emanation* of some Person, or *the indwelling* (of One). Not *the indwelling*, because *no one knows, whether he is worthy of hatred or love*,[2] and thus no one cognizes, whether God dwells in him. And *again*, what use is it? Let it be that one knows, that God has come, yet, since he knows not that He is going to remain [permansurum], it seems none.[3] If, for manifesting *the emanation* of some Person: therefore, since that knowledge [notitia] is necessary in every season, that is, in the season of the written Law and now, it seems, that both then and now there ought to have

been[4] a visible mission. Therefore, it is asked, for what reason (was it) only in the time of the primitive Church?

2. Likewise, however so much He appear in a creature, He does not become known, unless a revelation be present [adsit]: but when a revelation is present,[5] (the revealed) is for a more true and more certain cognition, than that which is by sensing: if, therefore, the one having a certain cognition does not need to be occupied about an imperfect cognition, therefore, it seems, that an exterior apparition is entirely superfluous.

3. Likewise, it is also proved, that it impedes, in this manner: the affection, occupied about visible goods, rises less to invisible goods, therefore, similarly the intellect: therefore, if it ought to be elevated to the perception of invisibles, there ought not be made for it a show of visibles; because if there is, it seems rather to impede than help.

---

[1] From many codices, such as A F G K T V W X Y etc., and edition 1, we have supplied *on the other hand* [autem], which is omitted less well here, the beginning of the response to the other half of the arguments.

[2] Ecclesiastes 9:1, where the Vulgate reads: And yet man does not know whether he be worthy of love, or hatred [Et tamen nescit homo utrum amore, an odio dignus sit]. — The Vatican edition, together with only some manuscripts, here and below in the response has *and/or* [vel] in place of *or* [an].

[3] Supply with codex X *no utility* [nulla utilitas] for *none* [nulla], and/or with edition 1 *to be no utility* [esse utilitas],* but

codex H adds *therefore, (it is) as a trick* [ergo frustra]. Immediately after this, the Vatican edition has *Not* [Non] for *If* [Si], then *because* [quia] for *therefore* [ergo], but which is emended with the help of the manuscripts some of which read falsely *But* [Sed] in place of *If*, which often happens also elsewhere) and editions 1, 2 and 3.

[4] Not a few codd., such as aa & bb, have *there ought to be* [debeat].

[5] The Vatican edition, not trusting in the manuscripts and edition 1, has less well *be present* [adsit], and adds *interior* [interior] to *revelation* [revelatio]. Then codex K has *a superior* [superiorem], codex W *an interior* [interior] in place of *a more true* [verior].

---

* *Trans. note*: this final phrase *there seems none* [nulla videtur] responds to the question which introduces the hypothetical *of what use it is* [quae utilis est] and, hence, presupposes as it subject *nothing useful* [nulla res utilis)]; for this reason, the supposition suggested by the Quaracchi editors, here, on the basis of codex X or edition 1, is not so good, nor so fitting to the context.

4. Likewise, if the mission is for making (something) known, since there is a threefold cognitive force in us, that is the exterior sense,[1] the imagination and the intellect, and according to this threefold force a threefold prophetic vision is assigned, it seems for an equal reason, that there ought to be distinguished a threefold mission.

Besides, since the mission is for the manifestation of an indwelling, and the Son indwells just as the Holy Spirit (does), for what reason is there not a visible mission to manifest the former?

BUT ON THE CONTRARY: 1. That it be useful for making (something) known, seems, because our cognition begins from sensing [a sensu]:[2] therefore, if we ought to be elevated to the perception of intelligibles, it is congruous and very useful, that in some manner there be a previous excitation in the sense [in sensu] through a sign. And this is, what (St.) Gregory says:[3] « While we visibly cognize God, we are through this snatched up into the love of invisibles ».

2. Likewise, just as miracles show the Divine Power, so signs the Divine Presence; but it was useful and thoroughly necessary, that our faith be led by hand through miracles to the cognition of the Divine Power: therefore, for an equal reason through some visible signs to the cognition of the Divine Presence.

3. Likewise, a mission is to redeem the lost man; but man was lost according to (his) visible and invisible nature: therefore, a mission according to each is useful for him.[4]

4. Likewise, more familiarly does one offer his presence, who offers himself according to sense and intellect, than who (does so) according to one of the two only; but this was most expedient for man who had turned away [homini averso], that he be converted to God: ergo etc..

CONCLUSION

The visible mission of the Holy Spirit was useful to manifest, for persons who would be led by the hand through the senses, (His) indwelling according to the overflow of (His) fullness.

I RESPOND: It must be said, that the visible mission of the Son had the proper and greatest utility, just as will be clear in the Third (Book).[5] But now concerning the Holy Spirit it must be said, that His visible mission is useful for manifesting both emanation and indwelling, but not whatsoever kind of indwelling nor in[6] every genus of person.

On this account,[7] it must be understood, that there is a twofold indwelling, that is (that) according to *sufficiency* of sanctification, and (that) according to *the overflow of fullness*. That which is according to a *sufficiency* of sanctification, lay hidden within invisibly; but that which is[8] according to *an overflow*, appeared exteriorly; and for that reason such an indwelling ought to be manifested in a visible and exterior sign, just as was done among the Apostles.

Similarly, it must be understood, that there is a twofold genus of believers. For certain ones want signs, as ones sensible, certain ones seek understanding, as ones already advanced.[9] Those seeking signs through these are led by hand[10] to intelligibles; and for the sake of such a visible mission is useful. Therefore, a visible mission is useful[11] for manifesting an indwelling of an overflowing fullness, and this for persons being lead by hand through sense.

1. From this is clear the first, that is, for what reason was there no visible mission in the season of the written Law, because there was no mission in fullness, up until *the fullness of time had come*.[12] It is also clear, for what reason He is not now given or sent visibly; because we have already been led by hand to the Faith, whence just as miracles have ceased, so exterior signs.

That which is said, that no one knows, whether he be worthy of hatred, or of love; is true,[13] unless God deigns to show (him); and at that time He used to show (this), and this was very useful for strengthening the Faith and exciting devotion.

2. To that which is objected, that some revelation is necessary; it must be said, that it is true, and yet apparition is not superfluous, because it excites the intellect to an inquisition and by exciting it in this manner prepares it for Revelation, and after Revelation it excites[14] to love [dilectionem]. For a revelation, even if it is an interior cognition, still, however, belongs to the wayfarer, and for that reason it does not prevent [evacuat] cognition of an apparition.

3. To that which is objected, that visibles impede the affection; it must be said, that visibles can

---

[1] The Vatican edition adds *and* [et], which is lacking in the mss. and edition 1. — On the threefold vision of the prophets, see (St.) Augustine, ON A LITERAL EXPOSITION OF GENESIS, Bk. XII, ch. 6, n. 15 ff.

[2] See Aristotle, ON THE SOUL, Bk. III, ext 39 (ch. 8), and ON SENSE AND SENSIBLES, ch. 6. — Then after *to be elevated* [elevari] codex K has *through sense to the cognition of intelligibles* [per sensum ad cognitionem intelligibilium]; and a little below this edition 1 has *there come to be* [fit] for *there be* [sit].

[3] LIBER SACRAMENTORUM, where the last part of these words is exhibited thus: *through this we are snatched up by the love of invisibles* [per hunc invisibilium].

[4] From the more ancient manuscripts and edition 1, we have supplied *for him* [ei].

[5] SENT., Bk. III, d. 1, a. 2.

[6] Very many codices, such as A T etc., together with edition 1, read *according to every genus* etc. [omni genere] for *in every genus* [in omni genere]. Then codex K after *of person* [personae] adds *or of men* [hominum].

[7] As required by the manuscripts and edition 1, we have substituted *On this account* [Propter hoc] in place of *On that account* [Propterea].

[8] The older codices, together with edition 1, exhibit the verb *is* [est], which in the Vatican edition and codex cc is lacking.

[9] An allusion to Mt. 12:39: *An evil and adulterous generation seeks a sign* [Generatio ... signum quaerit]; and to that of Dan. 8:15: *And I sought understanding* [Et quaererem intelligentiam]. — A little before this the Vatican ed., not trusting in the mss. and ed. 1, has *ones sensual*

[sensuales] for *ones sensible* [sensibiles], and, then, against the more ancient codices and edition 1 reads *seeking* [quaerentes] for *seek* [quaerunt].

[10] The Vatican edition faultily and without the authority of the manuscripts and edition 1 (after the first two words of this sentence) reads *so that through these they be lead by hand* [ut per haec manuducantur], and a little after this omits the particle *and* [et]. Very many codices together with edition one have *through this* [per hoc] in place of *through these* [per haec]; but less well; then some codices, such as I P Q Z have *understanding* [intelligentiam] for *intelligibles* [intelligibilia].

[11] The Vatican edition with the codices, by omitting the words *Therefore, a visible mission is useful* [Utilis ergo est mission visibilis] and by conjoining those which follow with the preceding sentence, distorts the teaching of the (Seraphic) Doctor. The reading received in the text is exhibited by many mss., such as A F G H I K N T V W Y ee & ff, however, many of these, perhaps deceived on account of the immediately preceding words *a visible mission is useful* [utilis est mission visibilis], omit with ed. 1 the (first) word (of the Latin sentence) *useful* [Utilis], less congruously.

[12] Gal. 4:4. — On the following proposition, cf. (St.) Gregory (the Great), HOMILIES ON THE GOSPELS, Bk. II, Homily 29, n. 4.

[13] In codex O there is added: *concerning the knowledge of certitude and/or rather is understood concerning the knowledge of (one's) final state* [de scientia certitudinis vel potius intelligitur de scientia status finalis].

[14] Codex T together with edition 1 reads *it exercises* [exercitat]. Then not a few codices, such a W X Y and Z, faultily read *delight* [delectationem] for *love* [dilectionem]; but codex cc reads *to*

be considered in a twofold manner: either as absolute things, and/or as signs or hints [nutus] leading into (something) else.[1] In the first manner if they be loved and considered, they do retard the intellect and affection; in the second manner they help, and so it is in the visible apparition, because there a creature is considered as a sign causing (something) else to come into the intellect.[2]

4. To that which is objected: 'for what reason is there not a threefold genus of mission', (it must be said) that even if 'cognition' concerns the reckoning of 'mission', however[3] not any (cognition) whatsoever nor (a cognition) of anything, but *of One indwelling*. And because there is a twofold manner of indwelling, as has been had before,[4] for that reason there is only a twofold manner of sending, though there are more manners of cognizing. — *And/or in another manner* it must be said, that God is not cognized on the way except in *an effect*, or in *a sign*. If in *an effect*, since that effect is a grace making one pleasing, which occurs in a mind alone, thus it is a visible mission: if in *a sign*, since a sign is that which offers itself to being sensed [sensui],[5] thus it is visible. But, because the power of imagination [imaginaria] belongs to those things, the images of

which are expressed in the exterior sense, but God is not such, for that reason there is no positing of this manner of cognition concerning Him.

To that which is objected last, 'for what reason was there no visible mission for manifesting the indwelling of the Son'; it must be said, that '*that the Son indwell*' is in a twofold manner: either through the grace of union, or through the grace of sanctification. In the *first* manner a manifestation or visible mission was not necessary, because He was most fully in the Man united to Himself, in whom He used to work visible works, in which He was manifested: and for that reason it was not necessary [oportebat], that other visible signs be employed. In the *second* manner, on the other hand, He did not have a mission manifesting such an indwelling, because sanctification is appropriated to the Holy Spirit, whence it used to suffice, that there was a visible mission to manifest the indwelling of Him, to whom sanctification is appropriated,[6] since the indwelling of the Son and of the Holy Spirit are undivided. With it manifested, that the Holy Spirit indwells in man, it is sufficiently shown that the Son (does) too.

SCHOLIUM

I. The Question is resolved along a twofold distinction, namely about the manner of the indwelling and about the genera of believers. Those (things) which are said by St. Bonaventure here of the indwelling according to the overflow of fullness are explained more extensively by his master Alexander of Hales, who (loc. cit) says thus: « (A visible mission) is not for a demonstration of any indwelling whatsoever, but of that indwelling, which is through *a fullness of grace overflowing upon others*, which was in *Christ* and in some manner in *the Apostles* ». Then (master Alexander) teaches, in what manner the influence of the fullness (of grace) was in *Christ* in a twofold manner, namely, through the manner of a cause, and through the manner of doctrine: through the manner of an efficient cause in regard to the Divine Nature, through the manner of a meritorious cause as much as regards (His) human (nature); and in what manner there is an influence *of grace* overflowing in *the Sacraments* in these two manners, just as there is a fullness *of truth* overflowing in the Christ's *preaching*. Then he proceeds: « Therefore, with the coming of the fullness of time, the fullness of indwelling was to be revealed, since that fullness began to overflow, and this for the sensible and for those not yet advanced in faith. But this was, when Christ was baptized and began to preach: that is, a fullness of His *grace* through the manner of influence, because then was the regenerative force given to the water of Baptism; and a fullness of His *truth* through the manner of doctrine, because He then began to preach and to inflow the truth of the Faith. And for that reason, because His fullness began to flow into others, it ought to have been manifested through sensible

signs, so that His doctrine might be believed more swiftly ». — « In *the Apostles*, moreover, there was a fullness of *grace* descending from Christ's fullness, and also in a certain manner a fullness of *influence*, that is, through the manner of doctrine and through the manner of ministry. For we have accepted from the fullness of Christ's *truth* out of the doctrine of the Apostles, from the fullness of (His) *grace* through their ministry in the dispensation of the Sacraments ». Then he concludes, that for showing the indwelling as much as regards the effect of grace overflowing through the manner of ministry the Holy Spirit was visibly given to the Apostles in (Christ's) *breath*, when there was said to them: Accept the Holy Spirit, whose sins you forgive etc. (Jn. 20:22); however, then in *fiery tongues* for showing the indwelling of the Holy Spirit according to the effect of the fullness of *truth* overflowing into others through the manner of (their) doctrine.

II. From the principal conclusion are deduced the two corollaries posited in the text. — The words in the second corollary *just as miracles have ceased* are not understood in the absolute sense, but to the extent that miracles were at the beginning of the Church a quasi-ordinary way of leading souls by the hand to the Faith. — In regard to the threefold vision (in reply to n. 4), cf. SENT., Bk. II, d. 10, a. 3, q. 2; Bk. III, d. 23, Doubt 4; HEXAËMERON, Sermon 9.

III. The conclusion is in fact [in re] the common sentence. — Alexander of Hales, SUMMA., p. I, q. 74, m. 2. — St. Thomas, SUMMA., I, q. 43, a. 7. — Bl. (now St.) Albertus (Magnus), here in a. 10. — (Bl.) Peter of Tarentaise, here in q. 1, a. 2. — Richard of Middleton, here in q. 2. — (Bl.) Dionysius the Carthusian, here in q. 1, near the end.

---

devotion and love [ad devotionem et dilectionem]. Then, from the more ancient manuscripts and edition 1 we have substituted *For* [enim] in place of the *But* [autem], which the Vatican edition and codex cc have, and by which the force of the response is weakened.

[1] An allusion to the words of (St.) Augustine: Woe to those, who love Thy hints for Thy sake etc., quoted above in d. 3, p. I, q. 2, in reply to n. 1; see also the same place, at q. 3 in the last reply, where the same distinction occurs between *thing* and *sign*. — Then after *they be loved* [amentur] the Vatican edition, with the manuscripts and edition one striving against this, reads *and/or if they be* [vel si] in place of *and* [et].

[2] (St.) Augustine, ON CHRISTIAN DOCTRINE, Bk. II, ch. 1, n. 1: For a sign is something besides the appearance, which is born into the senses, causing something else to come into thought out of itself.

[3] The codices, together with edition 1 omit *however* [tamen]. Then, codex V has *of whatsoever* [cuiuscumque] for *of anything* [cuiuslibet].

[4] Here in the body of the Question.

[5] Cf. (St.) Augustine, ON CHRISTIAN DOCTRINE, Bk. II, ch. 1, n. 1. See above in reply to n. 3. — A little below this, one or the other codex, such as aa and bb, reads *exterior* [exteriori] for *interior* [interiori].

[6] Codex O, by adding here *besides* [praeterea], exhibits the words which follow as a new argument, but, as is seen, less well. At the end of the Response, very many codices, together with edition 1, omit *too* [et].

---

* *Trans. note*: Because the Saints of all ages have, do, and shall work them.

QUESTION III

In which manners has the visible mission been accomplished?

Third, there is asked, in which manners the visible mission is accomplished.[1] And diverse manners are accepted from the Scriptures. For the Son visibly appeared in a rational creature, as in a man; however, the Holy Spirit in an irrational one, as for example in the dove, the fire and the blowing-wind [flatu]. Therefore, one asks concerning the diversity of the manners of appearing, and it seems, that the manners[2] were not fitting, in this manner:

1. The Holy Spirit is equally a noble Person, as the Son: therefore, in an equally noble creature He ought to be manifested, as (was) the Son.

2. Likewise, if the Son on account of (His) assumption of humanity or apparition *in the form of a servant* is less than the Father, nay *(has been) made less than the Angels*:[3] therefore, much more strongly (is) the Holy Spirit from (His) apparition in fire not only less than God, but also (less) than man; but this is in no manner fitting: therefore, it is not fitting for the Holy Spirit to appear in an irrational creature. — *If you say*, that the Son appeared in a man assumed and united (to Himself), but the Holy Spirit was not united to the dove and/or to the fire; *on the contrary*: a union takes nothing away from the Divinity: therefore, on account of the union He ought not to be said (to be) lesser. Therefore, if He is said (to be) less, this is on account of the apparition: ergo etc..

3. Likewise, it seems that the Holy Spirit was united,[4] because the Holy Spirit appeared in that dove, and not in another; and *again* He Himself appeared there,[5] not another Person: therefore, He was in it in a manner other than the Father and the Son (were), and otherwise in it than in others; but He could not be in it *otherwise* than another Person (could) as much as regards substance, nor as much as regards operation, because the Same is Substance and operation in the Trinity, therefore, as much as regards union: ergo etc.. *If you say*, that He appeared as in a sign, then I ask: either that was a sign by *nature*, or by *institution*.[6] If by *nature*, then for an equal reason also every other dove; if by *institution*, one asks: "Who instituted it?"

4. Likewise, the Son appeared visibly *in one manner* only and in one creature; one asks, "For what reason (did) not the Holy Spirit (appear) similarly?", and it seems, that it ought to have been thus, because just as in the Son there occurs no variety, nay rather an omnimodal uniformity, so also in the Holy spirit: therefore, He ought to have appeared only in one appearance [species], as the Son (did).[7]

5. Likewise, the Son only appeared *once* visibly, because He was incarnate only one, not more. Therefore, it is asked, "Whence is this, that the Holy Spirit appeared *many times*, as for example not only *once* in the fire?", but also "How long was the Holy Spirit given?"[8] — *If you say*, that those, in which the Holy Spirit appeared, immediately ceased to be after the apparition, and for that reason it was necessary [oportuit] that others be wrought; *then*, therefore, it seems, that neither was that dove a true one, nor the first, since both dove and fire have[9] the virtue to remain; and if this was not in that apparition, then, therefore, they were not true, but false, and they were not apparitions, but deceptions [praestigia] and illusions, just as are the phantasms of the demons and of other mages.

6. Last there is asked, "For what reason did the Holy Spirit appear in so many manners?", and "For what reason in the Head in a form other than in the members, as (He did) in Christ and the Apostles?"

CONCLUSION

The apparition of the Son fittingly came to be once, in the one and rational substance united (to Him); however, the Holy Spirit fittingly appeared many times in many and irrational creatures as signs.

I RESPOND: It must be said, that an end imposes a necessity upon those which are to the end; for that reason the manner of appearing is to be taken up according to the end of the apparition. On the one hand, the Son appeared in the flesh, so that He might be *Mediator*, the Holy Spirit, on the other hand, that (He might be) *Doctor*, according to the sixteenth (chapter of the Gospel of St.) John:[10] *When He comes, He will teach you all truth.* Moreover, for *mediation* there is necessary concourse of separated extremes and a union in one (thing), just as is clear; and for that reason the Son appeared in a creatures as One united (to it). But for the *erudition* of the ignorant a sign[11] intervenes; for that reason the Holy Spirit appeared in a creature as One signed in the sign [signatum in signo].

Therefore, since nothing is perfectly able to be united [perfecte unibile] to God unless (it be) beatifiable, and this only a rational substance; for that reason the Son appeared in a rational substance alone.

However, because an irrational creature is more fit for the use of pure[13] *signification* than the rational, lest perhaps it be believed (to be) united, not only signifying; for that reason the Holy

---

[1] The Vatican edition reads *is the visible ... accomplished* [fiat]; very many codices, such as A T V X, read instead *there be a visible mission* [sit missio visibilis].

[2] From the more ancient manuscripts and edition 1, we have supplied *manner* [modi].

[3] Cf. Philip. 2:7 and Hebr. 2:7,9. — A little before this, in codex T after *in the form of a servant* [servi] there is had *was made* [factus est] for *is* [est], but in edition 1 *is not only* [non solum est], which also a little below this puts *than an Angel* [Angelo] for *than God* [Deo].

[4] Edition 1 reads *was united to that dove* [fuerit unitus illi columbae].

[5] Some codices, such as H and I, add *and* [et].

[6] This division of "sign" is hinted at by Aristotle, ON INTERPRETATION, Bk. I, ch. 2, and by (St.) Augustine, ON CHRISTIAN DOCTRINE, Bk. II, chs. 1 and 2, nn. 2 and 3.

[7] The Vatican edition, breaking with the ancient mss. and ed. 1, omits *as the Son (did)* [ut Filius]. A little before this, cod. W has *if there is in the Son no variety* [si est in Filio nulla varietas] in place of *just as in the Son there occurs no variety* [sicut in Filio cadit nulla varietas].

[8] That is, 'by visible signs', because this happened frequently in the first years of the Church; see Acts 8:17 and 10:14. — The Vatican edition, without the authority of the manuscripts and edition 1, has *once, but also in the appearance of a dove'* [in specie columbae] in place of *once', but also 'how long was the Holy Spirit given'* [quousque dabatur Spiritus sanctus].

[9] The Vatican edition together with very many codices has the verb in the subjunctive.

[10] Verse 13, where the Vulgate has: *But when He comes, the Spirit of Truth, He shall teach* etc. [Cum autem venerit ille Spiritus veritatis, docebit].

[11] For more on this, and on the manner, whereby instruction comes to be through a sign, see (St.) Augustine's book, ON THE TEACHER. — Very many codices, such as A I T W Y Z bb and cc have *a signing* (signification) [signatio (signification)].

[12] Codex T reads *an irrational creature is more fit for the use of signification than* [usui significationis potius fit convenit creatura irrationalis quam].

Spirit appeared in an *irrational* creature, which had in some manner a reckoning to signify and express, just as the blowing signifies (His) spiration, but fire (His) love [dilectionem].

Again, since for a perfect mediation it is required, that the mediator be one, and that the union be inseparable; for that reason[1] the apparition of the Son was *singular* and *indivisible*. But on the contrary, because the Holy Spirit cannot be perfectly signified in one sign, for that reason it was necessary [oportuit] that He be signified[2] through many: and for that reason the son appeared in one manner, but the Holy Spirit in more (manners). With these (reasons) seen, it is easy to respond to the objections.

1. For to that which is objected first, that equally noble is the Person of the Holy Spirit; it must be said, that the nobility of the One appearing causes nothing there, but the end of the apparition (does); because the former as *Mediator*, the latter as *Instructor* [eruditor] or Doctor, for that reason the Son as in a man assumed, the Holy Spirit as in a creature and sign.[3]

2. To that which is objected, that the Holy Spirit ought to be said (to be) less, just as even the Son; it must be said, that that minority is not said of the Son by reason of the Divinity, but by reason of the union and of the communication of idioms; because the Son has become Man who can suffer [homo passibilis], but the Holy Spirit did not become a dove.

3. To that which is objected, that He was united to the dove; it must be said, that there is a union according to *truth*, and there is a union according to *intention*.[5] In the *first* manner those are united which are united in nature and/or person; in the second manner are united the signified and the sign; and in this manner the Person of the Holy Spirit was united to those forms, in which He appeared.

But if one ask, whence has come such a union; it must be said, that (it has come) *according to disposition* [dispositive] from the properties of the creature, in which (the creature) was bound to declare the Person of the Holy Spirit,[6] just as *a blowing* (declares) spirit, *fire* love, *a dove* gifts on account of fecundity. But this[7] came *according to completion* [completive] from the Divine Ordination, which ordained (these) creatures for this, not by instituting, but by forming and instituting (them) simultaneously, because He formed (them) for this alone;

and for this reason both the dove and the fire, simultaneous with the apparition, also began and ceased (to be).[8]

5. From this is clear, for what reason[9] the Holy Spirit not only appeared *once*, but *many times*, however, the Son not (so), because the dove and fire ceased to be immediately after the apparition, but the man (did) not. — From this it is also clear, that even if[10] that dove and fire were a true body, yet neither was the dove a true dove, because it ceased (to be) immediately, but (rather it was) the likeness [similitudo] of a dove; similarly neither the fire a true fire, because it did not burn (anything) up. Yet neither was there any illusion, because there was no falsehood in signifying. For what was offered to sense for signifying, was truly there; and because the reckoning of signifying was attained more than (that) of existing, for that reason it endured as long as it could signify and/or fulfill the office of a sign. And because the dove was formed, moved and conserved by the same force, immediately as that force ceased to move, the dove and fire ceased to be.

6. To that which is asked last, for what reason did the Holy Spirit appear in so many manners; it must be said, that the apparition of the Holy Spirit was for manifesting the fullness of overflowing, as has been had before;[11] and since there can be an overflowing in a threefold manner, for that reason He appeared in three manners. For there can be this fullness through *redemption*, and thus He was in Christ, and this is a grace perfected through every manner. For that reason on Christ He appeared in the dove, because it[12] was the price for the redemption of the first born and was a integral and perfect animal. There can also be (an overflowing) through *the influence of life* as much as regards sense and movement, and this by means of the Sacraments; and this fullness is in priests, and for that reason the Holy Spirit was given to them in the appearance of a blowing-breath [in specie flatus], according to the twentieth (chapter of St.) John:[13] *He breathed upon them saying: Accept the Holy Spirit: whose sins you forgive* etc.. There can also be (an overflowing) in a third manner through *the administration of cognition* or (through) doctrine; and this fullness is in the Apostles and Doctors, and for that reason the Holy Spirit appeared to them in fiery tongues.[14] From these is clear the response and the sufficiency of the manners of appearing and the objections.

---

[1] In codex cc and the Vatican edition there is lacking *for that reason* [ideo], which, however, is had in the other codices and in edition 1.

[2] We have supplied from the older manuscripts and edition 1 *that He be signified* [significari].

[3] Codices aa and bb, having omitted *and* [et], read *as a sign* [ut signo].

[4] Trusting in very many codices and edition 1, we have substituted the more used term *communication* [communicationis] for *communion* [communionis].

[5] That is, according to an act of reason and will, which comes to be either with or without a foundation in reality.

[6] Thus many manuscripts, such as A D F G I K P Q T V W etc. and edition 1, while the Vatican edition together with some codices, has in the passive mood and less aptly *the Person of the Holy Spirit to be declared* [persona Spiritus sancti declarari]. In the reading received in the text *bound* [nata] refers to the previous *creature* [creatura] (and *in which* to *properties*).

[7] We follow the very many codices with ed. 1, while the Vatican ed. with codex cc puts *these came* [veniebant haec]. Codices P and Q *this union came* [viniebat unio haec], but codex S omits the original *this* [hoc]. A little below this, the Vatican ed. with cod. cc, breaking with all the other codd. and ed. 1, has *and* [et] in place of *because* [quia], (and) then puts

because [quia] in place of *and for that reason* [et ideo], whereby the order and connection of the reasons are confounded. Then, some manuscripts, such as H Y and Z, together with edition 1, have *both* [et] for *also* [etiam].

[8] To the special, fourth question, no reply is given by the Seraphic Doctor, for the reason that it is already contained in the body of the question. See also in this regard, below in the reply to n. 6.

[9] We prefer the reading of very many codices, such as I T aa bb and ff, and of edition 1, *for what reason* [quare] in place of *that* [quod]. Codices aa and bb a little before this, after *From this* [Ex hoc] add *it also* [etiam].

[10] The Vatican edition, together with very many codices, has *if* [si] in place of *even if* [etsi].

[11] In the preceding question and here near the end of the body of the question. — Then as required by the more ancient manuscripts and edition 1, we have substituted *in a threefold manner* [tripliciter] for *threefold* [triplex].

[12] Supply: 'a dove', and/or with codices Y and Z put *which* [quia] for *because it* [quia]. — Cf. Leviticus 12:6 ff.

[13] Verses 22-23, where the Vulgate reads: *He breathed upon (them) and said to them. Accept* etc. [Insufflavit et dixit eis etc.].

[14] Acts 2:3.

SCHOLIUM

I. In this one question four problems are solved: 1. how many mission are there both of the Son and the Holy Spirit; 2. for what reason is one attributed to the Son and many to the Holy Spirit; 3. for what reason and in what manner did the Son appear as *One united*, that is by the Hypostatic Union, but the Holy Spirit only as « One signed in a sign »; 4. why is the Son, made man, less than Himself, but the Holy Spirit not so in respect to His own sign (in solution to n. 2).

II. Only three visible missions of the Holy Spirit are enumerated, because Master (Peter) in this distinction mentions only three. By St. Thomas (SUMMA., I, q. 43, a. 7, ad 6) and others there is added a fourth « *in the lucid cloud* » (Mt. 17:5), which is hinted at by the Church in the Office of the Transfiguration (1st Nocturne, 2nd. responsorial) with these words: « In the shining cloud the Holy Spirit was seen ». According to St. Bonaventure, however, (COMMENTARY ON THE GOSPEL OF ST.LUKE, 9:34) that cloud signified the human nature of Christ.

III. In the solution to n. 5 there also occurs a fifth question, whether that dove was merely something fantastic, or at least something corporal, and/or even specifically a real dove. The Seraphic (Doctor) holds a middle position, just as Bl. (now St.) Albertus (Magnus), (Bl.) Peter of Tarentaise, Richard of Middleton and many others do. In the same sense seems to speak even St. Thomas both in his COMMENTARY, here in a. 3, in reply to n. 3, and in his SUMMA., I, q. 43, a. 7. However, the same in his SUMMA, III, q. 39, a. 7 affirms that it was a true dove , which assertion seems to be said only in the sense of one of greater probability, as Cajetan observes on this passage. This opinion even Ulric, « the disciple and imitator of (St.) Albertus (Magnus) » follows, according to (Bl.) Dionysius the Carthusian, who himself also holds this same sentence.

IV. Besides those already mentioned, cf. Alexander of Hales, SUMMA., p. I, q. 74, m. 3 and 5. — Bl . (now St.) Albertus (Magnus), here in a. 4 ff.. — Peter of Tarentaise, here in q. 1, a. 6. — Richard of Middleton, here in q. 5. — Giles the Roman, here in 2nd. princ., q. 1, and 3rd. princ., q. sole. — (Bl.) Dionysius the Carthusian, here in q. 3.

DOUBTS ON THE TEXT OF THE MASTER

DOUBT I

In this part are the doubts about the text (of Master Peter), and first there is the doubt concerning this which he says, that *the Son inasmuch as (He has been) sent, that is made, is less than the Father.* Against which it is objected in this manner: every act, according to which it happens that someone becomes less, belongs to indignity. If, therefore, the Son by reason of (His) mission has been lessened, therefore, (His) mission pertains to indignity.[1] *Likewise,* whensoever anyone from (being) equal becomes lesser, he is changed; but the Son before (His) mission was an Equal, and now He is lesser: ergo etc..

I RESPOND: It must be said, that certain (words) are said of the Son of God through *the Essence*, certain ones through[2] *the (Hypostatic) Union,* which was so great, that it made God man and man God. *Essentially* speaking, in no manner is the Son of God "less"; but this has been said through *the Union,* because all (things) which are said of man, can be said of the Son of God, and thus it is clear, that from this there is no indignity, no mutability in His person; and thus is solved each objection, because each reckoning proceeds, having understood[3] that He became less according to the same Nature, according to which He was an Equal, and thus ceased to be equal. But now He is at once less and equal.[4]

DOUBT II

Likewise, is asked of this which he says, that *the Son is also less than Himself.* For he seems to speak badly, because a greater diversity is conveyed through that which is *greater* and *lesser,* than through that which is *one (person)* and *another (person),* because the first does not occur in the Divine Nature, the second does. If, therefore, this is true: 'the Son is less than Himself', therefore, also this: 'the Son is one and another, and thus two persons', which is not conceded.

I RESPOND: It must be said, that it is true, that *"greater"* and *"lesser"* mean a greater diversity, because (in Him there is) a greater diversity of virtue and of natures; but to this[5] diversity, though it is greater, there does not follow a diversity in person, because many natures can be in one person. Therefore, since in Christ there does occur a diversity of natures and thus of virtues, but not of persons: therefore, *"greater"* and *"lesser"* is said (of Him) by reason of the diversity of virtues, but *"one"* and *"another"* (is) not, since He does not have diverse persons.[6]

DOUBT III

Likewise, is asked of this which he says, that *He was lessened for a little while less than the Angels.* For it seems false, because on that (verse) in the second (chapter of St. Paul's Letter) to the Hebrews:[7]

---

[1] On the authority of the more ancient manuscripts and edition 1, we have removed *of God* [Dei], which the Vatican edition together with codex cc faultily adds.

[2] Edition 1 has *on account of* [propter].

[3] Codex I reads *by understanding* [intelligendo], codex dd has *each objection, because each objection proceeds by understanding* [utraque obiectio, quia utraque obiectio procedit intelligendo].

[4] Cf. here q. 3, in reply to nn. 1 and 2.

[5] Codex reads *such a diversity* [talem diversitatem], the Vatican edition has *the diversity of nature* [naturae diversitatem], but edition 1 *such a diversity of nature* [talem natuae diversitatem]; the other codices exhibit the reading received in the text.

[6] Bl. (now St.) Albertus (Magnus) solves the same doubt, here in a. 1. — Richard (of Middleton) and (Bl.) Peter (of Tarentaise), here in the exposition of the text (of Master Peter).

[7] Verse 9, in which text the Vatican edition, contrary to the Vulgate, to the more ancient codices and to edition 1, has *than the Angels* [ab Angelis] in place of *less than the Angels* [quam Angeli]. The Gloss cited, next, is exhibited by (Nicolas) of Lyra, thus on Hebr. 2:9: « Than the nature of the human mind, which according to the image of God (is) without sin, which Christ assumed, which could be depraved by no sin, God alone is greater ». The Vatican edition, without the authority of any manuscript and edition 1, has *above all* [super omnes] for *God alone* [solus Deus]. A little before this, very many codices after *false* [falsum] omits *because* [quia].

Him who for a little while became less than the Angels, the Gloss says: « Than the nature of the human mind, which Christ assumed, which could be depraved by no sin, God alone is greater ». *Likewise*, the Blessed Virgin, who is purely a creature, has been exalted above all the Angels: ergo etc..

I RESPOND: It must be said, that there is a speaking of Christ in comparison to the Angels as much as regards four (things), that is as much as regards *grace* and as much as regards *the nature of a mind* and as much as regards *the nature of a body* and as much as regards the *state of being able to suffer* [passibilitatis]. As much as regards *grace* He is simply greater; as much as regards *the nature of a mind* He was at least not lesser, because, as the Gloss says:[1] « Less than the Angels was He in body, not in mind »; as much as regards *the nature of a body* He was less; but as much as regards the *state*[2] *of possibility* [passibilitatis] He was less and for a little while lessened, because (His) state of possibility was going to be converted a little while afterwards into a state of glory and honor.[3]

DOUBT IV

Likewise, is asked of this which (St.) Hilary says, that *the Father is greater than the Son*, because if what he says is true, since the Same in God is (His) Wisdom, Power, Goodness and Greatness: therefore, if (the Father)[4] is greater, He is also more powerful and more wise and better. *Besides*, in God there is no magnitude of mass [molis], but (rather one) of virtue: therefore, if the Father is greater, He is more powerful, which cannot stand. *Likewise*, "*greater*" either means *the Essence* or *a notion*. Not *the Essence*, because They are equal in Essence; if *a notion*, (then) I ask: "Which one?" *If you say*, that which (is) the Paternity; *on the contrary*: a comparison according to greater and[5] lesser is not attained except in co-participants, whence there is not said: "the swan is whiter than the raven"; but the Son is not a co-participant in the Paternity [non est comparticipans paternitatem]: therefore, etc.. *Likewise* there is asked: "For what reason is He[6] not said (to be greater) than the Holy Spirit?"

I RESPOND: It must be said, that in the Father there is an authorship in respect to the Son and the Holy Spirit, in the Son in respect to the Holy Spirit, and for that reason (there is) in the Father a greater authorship and a

greater fecundity; and because no noun is competent to express authorship so much, as this noun "*great*": for that reason (St.) Hilary says that the Father is greater than the Son. From this the objections are clear, because "*greater*" does not mean *the Essence*, as (the Divine) "Power" and "Wisdom" (do), but it means *a notion*. If you ask: "Which (notion)?" I say, that it means a notion commonly, but yet in the reckoning of a principle, just as "subauthority" (does) in the reckoning of an emanation;[7] and hence it is, that the Father is said (to be) "greater than the Son", because even if Each has the notion in the reckoning of a principle, yet the Father (has it) in the reckoning of only a principle,[8] and for that reason has more of the reckoning of authorship; but the Holy Spirit is the principle of no Person, and for that reason He is not compared to Them according to greater-ness [maioritatem].[9]

DOUBT V

Likewise is asked of this which he says: *And thus the One granting is greater, but He is not now less* etc.. For it seems false, because in whatsoever manner "*greater*" is accepted, it is said in a manner relative to "the lesser": therefore if there is a positing of the Father as "greater", there is a positing of the Son as "lesser". *Likewise*, the Father is said (to be) "greater", because He has the authorship over the Son: therefore, since the Son has a subauthorship in respect to the Father, He ought to be said (to be) "lesser".

I RESPOND: It must be said, that there is no impediment, for which reason Son may not said (to be) "less than the Father" by reason of (His) subauthority, just as the Father (is said to be) "greater",[10] except that in God names of indignity ought not to be put to use; and/or because holy Doctors, as much as they can, distance themselves from the fallacies of heretics. For that reason when (St.) Hilary said that the Father (is) greater, he was unwilling, that the Son be said (to be) "lesser", lest it seem that greater-ness (be) not only (one) of authorship, but also (one) of inequality. And though (St.) Hilary meant the authorship in the Father, it is not, however, read that he meant (that there was) a subauthorship in the Son; but that true (saying) by masters (of theology) was added into the custom of disputants.[11]

---

[1] In (Nicolas) of Lyra, loc. cit. (the Gloss is cited thus): Therefore, less than the Angels in body, not in mind. However, Angels and men can be said (to be) "greater", because they are greater than the body of a man. They are also greater than the soul, but in this only, that the body having merited original sin weighs down the soul itself; but this was not in Christ etc..

[2] Though very many codices, together with the Vatican edition and edition 1, have *nature* [naturam], we prefer, however, the reading of codices L M and O, as that which responds to the members of the division posited by the Seraphic Doctor above hits.

[3] Cf. Bl. (now St.) Albertus (Magnus), here in a. 12. — St. Thomas, here in the exposition of the text. — (Bl.) Peter of Tarentaise, here in q. 1, a. 7, and in the exposition of the text. — Richard of Middleton, here in q. 6. — Giles the Roman, here on the text. — (Bl.) Dionysius the Carthusian, here in q. 3 at the end.

[4] Supply with some manuscripts, such as F H W Y aa and bb, *the Father* [Pater].

[5] Trusting in the more ancient mss. and ed. 1, we have substituted *and* [et] for *or* [aut]. A little below this, ed. 1 reads *a co-participant with the Father in the Paternity* [comparticipans Patri in paternitate] for *a co-*

participant in the Paternity [comparticipans paternitatem]. — On this reckoning, see above d. 8, p. I, Doubt 4.

[6] In codex bb there is added (as the subject) *each* [uterque].

[7] See above d. 13, Doubt 4, and d. 15, p. I, q. 1, in reply to nn. 2 and 3, and below in d. 20, a. 1, q. 2, in reply to n. 4, and d. 27, p. I, q. 2, in reply to n. 3.

[8] Edition 1 adds *that is, (and) not (in the reckoning) of one begun* [scilicet, non principati].

[9] Thus, the older codices, together with edition 1, while the Vatican edition, with the more recent codex cc, puts *authorship* [auctoritatem], but faultily, because *authorship* [auctoritatem] is the middle term of the conclusion to be elicited. Codex dd has *lesser-ness* [minoritatem], well, and in the same sense with the other codices.

[10] In codex K there is added *than the Son* [Filio].

[11] The Vatican edition, contrary to very many codices and to edition 1, has *in the custom* [in consuetudine]. — This and the preceding doubt are dealt with by Bl. (now St.) Albertus, here in a. 13; by St. Thomas, (Bl.) Peter of Tarentaise and Richard (of Middleton), here in their expositions of the text.

DISTINCTION XVII

PART I

CHAPTER I

That the Holy Spirit is the charity, by which we love God and neighbor.

Moreover, let us now proceed [Iam nunc accedamus] to assign the mission of the Holy Spirit, by which He is invisibly sent into the hearts of the faithful. For the Holy Spirit Himself, who is God and the Third Person in the Trinity, as has been shown above,[1] proceeds from the Father and the Son and Himself temporally, that is, is sent and granted to the faithful. But what is that mission or donation of His, and/or in what manner it comes to be, must be considered.

Moreover, [autem] so that this may be able to be more intelligibly taught and more fully examined [perspici], there must be aforementioned a certain something [quiddam] very necessary for this. It has indeed been said above and shown by sacred authorities,[2] that the Holy Spirit is the Love [amor] of the Father and the Son, by which They love [amant] one another and us. Moreover, it must be added to these, that the very same Holy Spirit is the Love or Charity, by which we love [diligimus] God and neighbor. When this Charity is so great in us, that it makes us love God and neighbor, the Holy Spirit is then said to be sent and/or to be given[3] to us; and he who loves the very love [dilectionem], by which he loves (his) neighbor, in this very (thing) loves God, because *Love* itself *is God*,[4] that is, the Holy Spirit.

Moreover, lest in so great a matter we seem to pour in[5] something of ourselves, let us corroborate what has been said. Of this (St.) Augustine in the eighth book, ON THE TRINITY[6] says: « It follows that [consequens est], he who loves (his) neighbor, loves chiefly that love. But God is love. Therefore, it follows, that he chiefly loves God ». Likewise in the same:[7] « *God is Love*, as (St.) John the Apostle says. How, therefore, are we, as the lowest (of creatures), to run both unto the heights [sublimia] of the heavens and to the lowest (parts) of the earth, seeking Him who is among us, if we would want to be with Him »? « No one says: "I know not, what I love." Let him love (his) brother and let him love the same love. For he knows [novit] more the love, by which he loves, than the brother, whom he loves. Behold you can already have God more known [notiorem] than (your) brother, plainly more known, because more present, because more within, because more certain.

Embrace the God Love[8] and embrace God with love. It is Love Itself, which unites together [consociat] all the good Angels and all the servants of God with the chain [vinculo] of holiness. Therefore, as much as we are healed more [saniores][9] from the tumor of pride, so much are we more full with Love: of which, if not of God, he also is full who is full of love ». With these words (St.) Augustine sufficiently shows, that the very Love, by which we love God and/or neighbor, is God. But still more openly in the same book[10] he adds below this, saying: « Let us attend to fraternal love, as much as the Apostle (St.) John commends it. *He who loves, he says,*[11] *(his) brother remains in the light, and in him there is no scandal.* It is manifest, that in the love of (one's) brother there is posited the perfection of justice. For he in him whom there is no scandal is certainly [utique] perfect. And yet it seems, that he is silent about the love of God, which he would never do, unless because he wants God to be understood in that fraternal love. For most openly does he say in that Epistle,[12] a little after this, thus: *Most beloved, let us love one another, because love is from God* [ex Deo] *: and everyone who loves, has been born of God and cognizes God. He who does not love does not cognize God, because God is Love.* This passage [contextio] declares in a sufficiently open manner, that the very same fraternal love — for fraternal love is that whereby we love one another — (is) not only from God, but even is preached to be God by such a great authority, namely (St.) John. When, therefore, we love (our) brother from Love,[13] we love (our) brother from [de] God, nor can it come about, that we do not love chiefly the same Love, by which we love (our) brother, since God is Love ». Likewise:[14] « He who does not love (his) brother is not in love; and he who is not in love is not in God, because God is Love ». Behold he most openly[15] says, that God is fraternal Love.

CHAPTER II

That fraternal love is God, and not the Father and/or the Son, but only the Holy Spirit.

Moreover, since fraternal Love is God, He is neither the Father nor the Son, but only the Holy Spirit, who in the Trinity is properly said (to be) Love and/or Charity. Whence (St.) Augustine

---

[1] Distinction XV, ch. 1. — Immediately after this codex E and the Vatican edition have *His very self* [semetipso] for *Himself* [se ipso].

[2] Distinction X. — A little before this edition 1 and 2 have *a certain something* [quoddam] for *a certain something* [quiddam].

[3] Codices A and C read *to be granted* [donari].

[4] 1 John 4:8,6. The Vulgate reads: *God is charity* [Deus caritas est]. Master (Peter) follows the reading of (St.) Augustine. — Here Master (Peter) begins to expound his own sentence, commonly reproved as false, which denies that charity is a created habit; concerning which see St. Bonaventure, here in p. I, a. 1.

[5] Only the Vatican edition has *add* [astruere] for *pour it* [influere].

[6] Chapter 7, n. 10. — Immediately before *of this (St.) Augustine* [Augustinus] editions 1 and 8 add *Moreover* [autem].

[7] Ibid., n. 11. The text of Scripture is 1 Jn. 4:16. — The next passage from (St.) Augustine is loc. cit. and ch. 8, n. 12.

[8] Edition 5 reads *the love of God* [dilectionem Dei]. — Then ed. 1 after *embrace* [amplectere] reads *(your) neighbor* [proximum] for *God* [Deum].

[9] Editions 1, 2, 4, 5, 8 and 9, falsely read *more holier* [sanctiores], and codex C *more stronger* [fortiores]; to correct the this error, editions 1 and 8, together with codices B C D and E proceed thus: *we are more holy when more empty of* (codex C reads *more healed from* [saniores]) *the tumor of pride* [sanctiores sumus, quando a

tumore superbiae inaniores]; but our reading is according to the text of (St.) Augustine, cod. A and the Vatican ed., with edd. 3, 6 & 7.

[10] Loc. cit., a little further below. — The Vatican edition alone omits *saying* [dicens].

[11] 1 Jn. 2:10. — A little before this, at *fraternal love* [Dilectionem fraternam] editions 3, 7 and 8, having omitted *fraternal* [fraternam] put *which* [quam] in place of *as much as* [quantum], and together with codices A C D and ed. 6 read *commends* [commendat] in the indicative.

[12] 1 Jn. 4:7,9. The Vulgate reads: *Dearest ones, let us love one another, because charity is of* [ex] *God. And everyone, who loves, has been born of God and cognizes God. He who does not love, knows not God: since God is charity* [Carissimi, diligamus nos invicem: quia caritas ex Deo est. Et omnis, qui diligit, ex Deo natus est et cognoscit Deum. Qui non diligit, non novit Deum: quoniam Deus caritas est]. — Then the Vatican ed. with very many edd. reads *says* [ait] for *says* [dicit]; moreover, after *says* [dicit], editions 3, 5, 6, 7 and 9, with a varied punctuation, badly set aside the particle *thus* [ita] with the quotation. Then, edition 1 has *Sweetest ones* [dulcissimi] for *Most beloved* [dilectissimi].

[13] Only edd. 1 and 3 have *with the love of God* [Dei dilectionem].

[14] Loc. cit., but a little further below.

[15] The Vatican edition, with the other edd., against the codd. and edd. 1 & 8, reads *openly* [aperte] for *most openly* [apertissime]; immediately after this editions 3 and 7 have *said* [dixit] for *says* [dicit].

in the fifteenth book, ON THE TRINITY:[1] « If among the gifts of God nothing is greater than charity, and nothing is a greater gift of God than the Holy Spirit, what follows more [quid consequentius est], than that He Himself is the Charity, which is said (to be) both God and from [ex] God »? « For thus says (St.) John:[2] *Love is from God* [ex Deo]: and a little afterwards: *God is Love*. Where he manifests, that that "love", which is out of God, means "God". Therefore, the God from [ex] God is Love ». Likewise, in the same:[3] « (St.) John, wanting to speak more openly of this matter says: *In this we cognize, that we remain in Him and He in us, because He has given us of His Spirit* [de Spiritu suo]. And so the Holy Spirit, of Whom He has given us, makes us remain in God and Him in us; but love does this. Therefore, He Himself is the God Love. Therefore, He[4] Himself is signified, where there is read: *God is Love* ». From these it appears, that the Holy Spirit is charity.

CHAPTER III

That this (verse): 'God is charity', has not been said in the manner of [per] a cause, as this (verse): Thou art my patience and my hope.

But, lest perhaps someone say, that there has been said through the expression of a cause, this: *God is charity*, for the reason, that is, that charity is from [ex] God and[5] is not God Himself, just as there is said: 'God is our patience and hope', not because He Himself is those (virtues) of ours, but because those of ours are from [ex] God; (St.) Augustine opposes this [occurit] showing, that this has not been said in the manner of [per] a cause, just as that (has been), in the fifteenth book, ON THE TRINITY,[6] saying thus: « We are not going to say, that charity is not on this account said (to be) God, because charity itself is one substance, which is worthy of the name of God, but because it is a gift of God, just as there has been said to God:[7] *Thou art my patience*. Certainly not, for that reason, has it been said, that the Substance of God is our patience, but because ours is from Him. Whence (he says) elsewhere:[8] *From Him is our patience*. For this sense does the very discourse [locution] of the Scriptures easily refute. For such is: *Thou art my patience*, as is: *Lord, my patience*,[9] and: *My God, my mercy*, and many similar (verses). But there is not said: 'God my charity', or: 'Thou art my charity', or: God, my charity'; but it has been said thus:[10] *God is charity*, just as there has been said: *God is spirit*. Let the one, who separates [discernit] his understanding from the Lord, not seek an exposition from us; for we cannot say anything more openly. Therefore, God is charity ». From the aforesaid it grows clear, that the Holy Spirit is the Charity, whereby we love God and neighbor; whence it is more easy for us to show, in what manner the Holy Spirit is sent or given to us.

CHAPTER IV

In what manner the Holy Spirit is sent and / or given to us.

For He is, then, said to be sent and/or given,[11] when He is in us such, that He makes us love God and neighbor, through which we remain in God and God in us. Whence (St.) Augustine, hinting at this manner of mission, in the fifteenth book, ON THE TRINITY,[12] says: « God the Holy Spirit, who proceeds out of God, when He has been given to men, enkindles [accendit] him to love God and neighbor, and He Himself is love. For a man [homo] hast not, whence to love God, except from [ex] God ». Behold in what manner there is given and/or sent to us the Holy Spirit, according to which He is said (to be) a 'given' or a 'gift'. Which gift (St.) Augustine commends, explaining more openly, in what manner He is given, in the same book:[13] « *The love of God* », he says « *has been poured fourth in our hearts*, as the Apostle says, *through the Holy Spirit, who has been given to us*. Nothing is more excellent that that gift of God. It alone is,[14] that which divides between the sons of the Kingdom and the sons of perdition. Other gifts [munera] are also given through the Spirit, but without charity they profit [prosunt] nothing. Therefore, unless the Holy Spirit be imparted to anyone, to make him a lover of God and neighbor, he[15] is not transferred from the left hand (of Christ) to the right hand. Nor is the Holy Spirit properly said (to be) a gift [donum] except on account of the love, which the one who has not, even if *he speaks every tongue, and has prophecy and every knowledge* [scientiam] *and every faith, and would distribute all his substance, and hand his body over, such that it burn, it profits him nothing.*[16] How great, therefore, a good it is, without which such great goods lead no one thoroughly to eternal life? But that very love and/or charity — for of the one thing is each name — leads thoroughly to the Kingdom. Therefore the love, which is out of God and (is)[17] God, is properly the Holy Spirit, through whom *there is poured forth in our hearts the God Charity*, through which the whole Trinity indwells in us. Wherefore most rightly is the Holy Spirit, since He is God, called even "the gift of God". What must be properly understood (to be) that "gift", except the charity, which leads thoroughly to God, and without which whatever other gift of God does not lead thoroughly to God »? Behold here there is revealed [aperitur], what had been said above,[18] that is, that

---

[1] Chapter 19, n. 37. — The next passage from (St.) Augustine is loc. cit., ch. 17, n. 31; but its beginning has been contracted by Master (Peter), who has, besides, changed many words.

[2] 1 John 4:7-8. — Only the Vatican edition reads: *And in the same* [Et in eodem] for *a little after this* [paulo post], and, conversely, has below *a little after this* [paulo post] for *in the same* [in eodem].

[3] Chapter 17, n. 31. — In this phrase, codd. A B & C after *the same* [eodem] add *(St.) Augustine (says)* [Augustinus]. — The passage from Scripture is loc. cit., verse 13. The Vulgate reads: *In this we cognize, that we remain in Him and He in us: since He has given us of His Spirit* [In hoc cognoscimus, quoniam in eo manemus et ipse in nobis: quoniam de Spiritu suo dedit nobis]. Codd. A B C & E and ed. 5 read *we have cognized* [cognovimus].

[4] Supply with ed. 1: *the Spirit* [Spiritus]. — In the previous sentence the Vatican ed., with not a few edd., has *Therefore* [igitur] for *Therefore* [ergo]. Then, after *From these* [Ex his] the Vatican ed. and edd. 3, 5, 8 & 9 insert *therefore* [ergo].

[5] Only the Vatican edition omits *and* [et]. A little after this editions 5 and 8 have *from Him* [ex eo] in place of *from God* [ex Deo].

[6] Chapter 17, n. 27. Next, only the Vatican ed. and ed. 6, with codex C, omit *thus* [ita]. — Then, in the very text of (St.) Augustine after *We are not going to say* [dictari sumus] edd. 1 & 8 add *as certain ones say* [ut quidam dicunt].

[7] Ps. 70:5. — Here the Vatican edition and editions 5, 8 and 9, together with codex E, read *of God* [de Deo] for *to God* [Deo]. — A little

below this, after *has it been said* [dictum est], the Vatican edition, together with the other editions, repeats *Thou art my patience* [Tu es patientia mea], breaking with the codices, with edition 1 and with the original.

[8] Psalm 61:6. — Next only editions 1 and 8 read: *immediately refute* [statim refellit] for *easily refute* [facile refellit].

[9] Psalm 90:9; and the following text is Ps. 58:18.

[10] 1 John 4:16, and then, John 4:24.

[11] Codices A C D and E add *to us* [nobis].

[12] Chapter 17, n. 31.

[13] Loc. cit. and chapter 18, n. 32. — The passage from Scripture is Romans 5:5.

[14] Editions 1 and 8 read *This alone is* [Hoc solum est], edition 2 reads *For it alone is* [Solum enim est].

[15] Codices A B C and E give (the subject of the Latin verb) as *he* [ille], but contrary to the original and the editions.

[16] 1 Corinthians 13:1, at the end of which text the Vatican edition and the other editions, contrary to the codices and the Vulgate, read *not* [non] for *nothing* [nihil].

[17] The Vatican edition and the other editions, contrary to the codices and to editions 1, 2, 3 and 7, add *is* [est].

[18] Here in chapters 1 and 2.

charity is the Holy Spirit and a more excellent gift, and in what manner this gift, that is, the Holy Spirit, is given to us, that is, when He is thus imparted to anyone, that is, He, thus, has (an ability)

to be in someone, to make him a lover of God and neighbor. Which, when He does (this), He is then said to be "given" or "sent" to someone [alicui], and, then, he is said to properly have the Holy Spirit.

PART II

CHAPTER V

Whether the Holy Spirit is increased in a man, and/or is less and more had and/or given, and whether He is given to one having and to one not having.

Here, there is asked, 'if charity is the Holy Spirit, since it is increased [augeatur] and decreased [minuatur] in a man and is had more and less through diverse seasons, whether it must be conceded, that the Holy Spirit is increased and/or decreased in a man and had more and/or[1] less?' For if He is increased in a man, and given and had more and/or less, He seems to be mutable; but God is entirely immutable. Therefore, it seems, that either the Holy Spirit is not charity, and/or charity is not increased and/or decreased in a man. *Likewise,* (that) charity is not given to one not having, so that he have it, and to one having, that he have it more fully.[2] Therefore, if the Holy Spirit is charity, He is both given to one not having, that he have, and to one having, that he have more fully. But in what manner is He given to one not having, since He Himself as God is everywhere and whole in all creatures? and in what manner is He given and/or had more fully without being changed on His own [sine sui mutatione]?

To these we respond thus,[3] saying, that the Holy Spirit or Charity is thoroughly [penitus] immutable and is not increased and/or decreased in Himself, nor receives more and/or less in Himself, but in a man and/or rather for a man is increased and decreased and given and/or had more and/or less; just as God is said to be magnified and exalted in us, Who nevertheless is neither magnified nor exalted in Himself. Whence the Prophet (says):[4] *A man will approach according to a high heart* [ad cor altum], *and God shall be exalted.* On which passage the authority (of Cassiodorus) says:[5] « God not in Himself, but in the heart of a man becomes great [grandescit] ». In this manner, therefore, the Holy Spirit is given to a man and as One given is given more fully, that is, is increased, and is had more and less, and yet exists as One immutable.

And, since He is everywhere and in every creature whole, yet there are many, who do not have Him. For not all, in whom He is, have the Holy Spirit; otherwise even irrational creatures would have the Holy Spirit, which (proposition) the piety of the faith does not admit.

Moreover, so that what we have said, be made more certain, we confirm it with authority.[6] That the Holy Spirit is perceived more and less and is increased in a man and given to one not having (Him), and to one having (Him), so that He be had more, (St.) Augustine shows ON (THE GOSPEL OF ST.) JOHN[7] saying: « Without the Holy Spirit it is established that we do not love Christ and cannot observe His commandments [mandata], and that we can and do act so much the less, as we perceive Him less, but so much more fully, when we perceive Him more fully. And for that reason not only to the one not having (Him), but also to the one having (Him) is He not in vain [incassum] promised: to the one not having indeed, that He might be had, but to the one having, that He be had more fully. For if He were not had less by one and more fully by another, Saint Eliseus would not have said to Saint Elias:[8] *May the Spirit, which is in thee, be double in me.* Moreover, to Christ, who is the Son of God, *the Spirit has not been given according to a measure.*[9] For neither without the grace of the Holy Spirit, is *the Mediator of God and men the Man Christ,*[10] for because the Only-Begotten Son is equal to the Father, He is not (a son) of grace, but (a Son) of Nature; but because the Man has been assumed into the unity of the Person of the Only-Begotten, He is (a son) of grace, not (a Son) of Nature. But to all others (the Holy Spirit) is given according measure and as One given is added, while to each one in virtue of the manner of his own perfection He is completed by the proper measure ». Behold you have an express (argument),[11] that the Holy Spirit is given and/or accepted more and less, and as One given to a man is increased, and is given to the one having and not having (Him), because the Holy Spirit is the Charity, which is given to the one not having and is increased and progresses [proficit] in the one having. Nay, to speak more truly and more properly, a man progresses and fails in it sometimes; and then it is said to progress and/or fail, which yet does not progress nor fail in itself, because it is God. Whence (St.) Augustine in his ninth homily ON THE LETTER OF (ST.) JOHN[12] says: « Let everyman prove himself, how much charity has progressed in him, and/or rather how much he has progressed in charity. For if charity is God, it neither progresses nor fails. Therefore, charity is thus said to progress in you, because you progress in it ». Behold in what manner it must be understood, when the Holy Spirit is said to be increased in us, that we, namely, progress in Him; so also the other things of this kind.

---

[1] The Vatican edition and edition 4 read *and/or more and less* [vel magis et minus]; editions 2, 3, 5, 7 and 9, together with codex D have *and more and less* [et magis et minus]; edition 8 *that is more and/or* [id est magis vel]. We have followed codices A B C and E, and editions 1 and 6.

[2] A reference to Lk. 19:26.

[3] The Vatican edition and the other editions, contrary to all the codices, have *And thus to these we etc.* [His itaque].

[4] Ps. 63:7,8. — The Vatican edition and not a few editions read *A man approaches* [Accedit homo], contradicting even the Vulgate.

[5] That is, (the senator Flavius Magnus Aurelius) Cassiodorus [c. A.D. 490- c. 583], on Psalm 63:6. — A little after this the Vatican edition together with the other editions has *more and less* [magis et minus], but the codices have *more and less* [magis ac minus].

[6] The Vatican edition and editions 4 and 6 read *let us confirm it* [confirmemus]; edd. 1 & 8 have *let us make it firm* [firmemus]. Next only the Vatican edd. and edition 4 after *is given to one not having (Him)* [non habenti detur] add *that He may be had* [ut habeatur]. Then editions 1 and 8 after *be had more* [plus] insert *and/or more fully* [vel plenius].

[7] ON THE GOSPEL OF (ST.) JOHN, Tract 74, nn. 2 and 3.

[8] 4 Kings 2:9. The Vulgate reads: *I beseech, that thy spirit might become double in me* [Obsecro, ut fiat in me duplex spiritus tuus]. Master (Peter) reports these words, as they are had in (St.) Augustine's text. After this quote, all the codices and editions 1 and 6 add, either in the margin, or in the following text, a note, which is

even cited by St. Thomas in his own COMMENTARY (here in the exposition of the text): *In the Book of Kings there is thus read: Elias said to Eliseus: Ask what you will, and I shall do it for you, before I am taken from you: and Eliseus said: I beseech, that thy spirit be made double in me. Which same is thus expounded: Elias was powerful in the spirit of prophecy and in the working of miracles in an excellent manner. Therefore, Eliseus asked to be granted him, the twin grace, which he recognized to be strong in his Master. Whence it is clear, that the disciple did not ask to be above (his) Master* [In libro Regum legitur sic: Elias dixit ad Eliseum: Postula quod vis, et faciam tibi, antequam tollar a te: dixitque Eliseus: Obsecro, ut spiritus tuus fiat duplex in me. Quod ibidem sic exponitur: Elias spiritu prophetali et operatione miraculorum excellenter pollebat. Geminam ergo gratiam, quam Eliseus in Magistro vigere cognoscebat, sibi tribui rogavit. Unde patet, quod non esse discipulus super Magistrum postulavit].

[9] Jn 3:41. The Vulgate reads: *for not according to a measure does God give the spirit* [non enim ad mensuram dat Deus spiritum].

[10] 1 Tim. 2:5. — Next the Vatican edition and very many editions after *Only-Begotten Son* [unigenitus] add *of God* [Dei], with all the codices contradicting and editions 1 and 8 and (St.) Augustine contradicting this, which latter even omits the word *Son* [Filius].

[11] The Vatican ed. and very many edd. read *expressly* [expresse] for *an express (argument)* [expressum], against the codd. and edd. 1 & 8.

[12] Or ON THE GOSPEL OF ST. JOHN, Tract 9, n. 2.

CHAPTER VI

That some say, that the charity of God and neighbor is not the Holy Spirit.

Above, it has been said, that the Holy Spirit is the Father's and Son's charity, by which They love one Another and us, and the very Same is the Charity, which is poured forth in our hearts to love God and neighbor. The former of the two of these [Horum alterum] all Catholics concede, that is, that the Holy Spirit is the Father's and the Son's Charity, but that the very Same is the Charity, by which we love God and neighbor, is denied by very many. For they say: if the Holy Spirit is the Father's and the Son's Charity and our own, therefore, the same Charity is, That by which God loves us, and That by which we love Him. But this the authorities of the Saints seem to deny. For (St.) Augustine says in the book, ON THE SPIRIT AND THE LETTER:[1] « Whence is love, except whence faith itself is, that is from the Holy Spirit? For it would not be in us, unless it *were poured forth in our hearts through the Holy Spirit*. But the charity said to be poured fourth in our hearts is not, that by which He loves us, but that by which He makes us lovers of Him [dilectores suos]. Just as *God's justice* is said (to be), that by which we are made just by His gift [munere], and *the Lord's salvation*, that by which He saves us, and *the faith of Christ*, that by which He makes us faithful ». With these words there seems to be shown a distinction between the charity, by which God loves us, and by which we love. And just our are justice is said (to be) of God [Dei], not because He Himself is just by that, but because by that He makes us just, similarly also faith and salvation; so the charity seems said (to be) God's, which is in us, not because He loves by that, but because He makes us love by that. Of this even (St.) Augustine in the fifteenth book, ON THE TRINITY[2] says the same: « Though (St.) John commemorated the Love of God, (it was) not that by which we (love) Him, but (rather) that by which *He Himself loved us, and sent His own Son as Liberator for our sins* ». Behold here too it seems that he manifestly divides the love, by which we love God, from that, by which He Himself loves us. If, therefore, they say, love is the Holy Spirit, by which God loves, and that by which we love, there is a twofold love, nay the two are diverse [duo diversa est], which is absurd and far from the truth. He is not, therefore, the love, by which we love, but That by which God only loves us.

To these we respond, determining the words of the aforesaid authorities in this manner: 'the charity of God said to be poured forth in our hearts is not that by which He loves us, but that by which He makes us love etc.'. By these words there is not divided nor is there shown (to be) diverse[3] the Charity, by which God loves us, from That, by which we love, but rather, since there is one and the same Charity and It is said (to be) the very Charity of God, It is shown in Scripture to be named the "Charity of God" from diverse

causes and reckonings. For it is said (to be) the "Charity of God", either because God loves us by It, and/or because He makes us lovers of Him by It.

When, therefore, there is said by the Apostle *the charity of God is poured forth in our hearts*, there is not said the "charity of God", by which He loves us, but by which He makes us love, that is, it is named there "the charity of God" not for the reason, that God loves us by it, but for the reason that He makes us lovers of Him by it. And that for this reason it can be said (to be) the "charity of God", because He makes us love by it, he shows[4] from a similar kind [genus] of saying; just as there is said *the justice of God*, by which He justifies us, and *the Lord's salvation*, by which He saves us, and *the faith of Christ*, by which He makes us faithful.

We, also, similarly expound the other authority, where he says, that 'the love of God is commemorated, not that by which we (love) Him, but that by which He loved us', as if he said, he commemorates the "Love of God", not according to which we love God by It, but according to which He loves us by It.

But there is (something) else, they say, which urges more. For above[5] (St.) Augusti ne said, that love is from the Holy Spirit, from whom (is) also faith. Therefore just as faith is not the Holy Spirit, from whom it is, so neither charity. For in what manner is charity[6] the Holy Spirit, if it is from Him? For if it is from Him and is Him, therefore, the Holy Spirit is from Himself. To which we say: the Holy Spirit is indeed not from Himself, but yet is given to us from Himself, as has been said.[7] For the Holy Spirit gives His very Self to us. And from this sense there has been said, that the Charity from Him is in us, and yet It Itself is the Holy Spirit. Moreover, faith is from the Holy Spirit, and is not the Holy Spirit, because He is only the gift and/or given, not the God giving.

They also bring in other reasons to show the same, that is, that charity is not the Holy Spirit, because charity is an affection of mind and a movement of the spirit [animi]; but the Holy Spirit is not an affection of the spirit and/or a movement of the mind, because the Holy Spirit is immutable and[8] uncreated: therefore, He is not charity.

Moreover, that charity is an affection of the spirit and a movement of the mind, they confirm by authorities. For (St.) Augustine in the third book, ON CHRISTIAN DOCTRINE[9] (says): « I call "charity" a movement of the spirit to enjoy God for His own sake and (to enjoy) oneself and neighbor for God's sake ». Likewise, in the book, ON THE CUSTOMS OF THE CATHOLIC CHURCH,[10] treating of that verse of the Apostle: *Neither death nor life will be able to separate us from the charity of God*, says: « The charity of God is here said (to be) the virtue, which is the most upright affection of our spirit, which conjoins us to God, by which we love Him ». Behold with these words there is expressed, that charity is an affection and movement of the spirit, and through this it does not seem to be the Holy Spirit.

To which we say, that this has been said thus, just as there is said: *God is our hope, and our patience*, because

---

[1] Chapter 32, n. 56; at the beginning of the text Master (Peter) has changed the words. For it reads in this manner in (St.) Augustine: *Whence, therefore, that love of His, that is, the charity, through which faith works, except whence faith itself obtains it by asking? For it would neither* etc. [Unde ergo ista dilectio, id est caritas, per quam fides operatur, nisi unde illam fides ipsa impetravit? Neque enim etc.]. — The text of Scripture to which it alludes is Romans 5:5.

[2] Chapter 17, n. 31. The allusion is to 1 Jn. 4:10, in which Master (Peter) has badly *Liberator* [liberatorem]. The Vulgate reads: *the propitiation* [propitiationem]; editions 1 and 8, together with the text of (St.) Augustine have *the One brining an acceptable offering* [litatorem] (in Greek ἱλασμόν).

[3] Editions 2, 3, 5 and 7, have *divided* [divisa]. A little after this the Vatican edition, together with the other editions, except 1 and 8, contrary to the codices, prefaces to the word *diverse* [diversis] the particle *both* [et], but less well. Then the Vatican edition and editions 4 and 8, read *His lovers* [suos dilectores] in place of *lovers of Him* [sui dilectores].

[4] The Vatican edition and editions 1, 4, 6 and 8, together with codex D, have *is shown* [ostenditur] .

[5] At the beginning of this Chapter.

[6] The Vatican edition and the other editions, except 1 and 8, by omitting *charity* [caritas] read *it*, contrary to the codices; immediately before this, the Vatican edition, together with codex D and very many editions, reads *Therefore* [ergo] for *For* [enim].

[7] Distinction XV.

[8] Only the Vatican edition omits *and* [et].

[9] Chapter 10, n. 16.

[10] Book I, ch. 11, n. 19. — The passage, taken from the Apostle, is Romans 8:38-39. — At the beginning, the text of (St.) Augustine, after *The Charity of God* [Caritas Dei inquit], adds *in its sense* [in sensu]; and editions 2, 3, 5, 7 and 9 also omit the following word *here* [hic].

He makes us hope and be patient [pati]; thus, Charity is said to be a "movement" or "affection" of the spirit, because, through it, the spirit is moved and affected to love God. Moreover, do not wonder, if Charity, since it is the Holy Spirit, is said to be a movement of the mind, since even in the Book of Wisdom[1] there is said of the Spirit of Wisdom, *which attains from end even to end*, because He is an Act *mobile, certain, undefiled*. Which is not, for that reason, said, because Wisdom is something mobile and/or some act, but because He attains by His immobility all (things), not by local movement, but as One (who) is always everywhere and[2] is never held enclosed. Therefore, in this manner Charity is said to be a movement of the spirit, not because It Itself is a movement and/or affection and/or virtue of the spirit, but because through It, as if It were a virtue, the mind is affected and moved. But if Charity is the Holy Spirit, *who works in each, as He wills*,[3] since through Him the mind of a man is affected and moved to believe and/or hope and (to other acts) of this kind, just as to love; for what reason is Charity in this manner not said (to be) a movement and/or affection of the mind to believe and/or hope, just as (it is) to love? To which there can sanely be said, that Charity works the other acts and movements of the virtues, that is, the Holy Spirit (works), by means of the virtues, the acts of which they are, as for example the act of faith, that is, to believe by means of the faith, and the act of hope, that is, to hope by means of hope. For through faith and hope He works the aforesaid acts. However, the act of loving, that is "to love", He works through Himself without the medium [medio] of any virtue. Therefore, He works this act in a manner other than the other acts of the virtues. And for that reason Scripture, which grants this especially to Charity, speaks differently of this and of the others. Therefore, Charity is truly the Holy Spirit. Whence (St.) Augustine, treating of the aforesaid verse, says in the same book[4] that Charity is a good, than which nothing is better, and through this he signifies that It is God, saying: « If no thing separates us from His Charity, what can be not only better, but even more certain that this Good »? Behold he says, that nothing is better than Charity. Therefore, Charity is the Holy Spirit, who is God and the gift or given of God, who is divides gifts to each of the faithful and is not Himself divided, but is given to each undivided. Whence (St.) Augustine,[5] where (St.) John says, *not according to measure is the Spirit given to Christ*, says: « However, to all the others there is divided, not indeed the Holy Spirit, but His gifts ».[6]

COMMENTARY ON DISTINCTION XVII

On the invisible mission of the Holy Spirit.

PART I

The invisible mission of the Holy Spirit is determined.

Moreover, let us now proceed to assign the mission of the Holy Spirit, by which He is invisibly sent.

THE DIVISION OF THE TEXT

Having finished the part, in which Master (Peter) dealt with the visible procession of the Holy Spirit, in this part he deals with the invisible one. And this part is divided into two (parts). In the *first* Master (Peter) determines the invisible[1] mission of the Holy Spirit according to his own opinion. In the *second*, however, because his own opinion had many adversaries [impugnatures], he puts the defense of his opinion, there (where he says): *Here there is asked, if charity is the Holy Spirit* etc..

The *first* part, again, has two (parts): in the *first he makes known* the invisible mission of the Holy Spirit; in the *second he confirms it*, there (where he says): *But lest in such a great matter we pout in anything of our own* etc..

Likewise, the first part, in which *he makes known*, has two parts, in the first of which he foretells his intention, there (where he says): *Moreover, let us now proceed to assign*; in the second, having supposed, that the Holy Spirit is the love [amor], by which we love [diligimus] God and neighbor, he shows, that He is invisibly sent, when He works this effect in us; and he does this there (where he says): *Moreover, so that this may be able to be more intelligibly taught* etc..

Moreover, lest in so great a matter. This is[2] the *second* part,

---

[1] Wis. 8:1; and the words which follow are Wis. 7:22, where the Vulgate, having inversed the order of words, reads: *mobile, undefiled, certain* [mobilis, inconinquinatus, certus]. The Vatican ed. with the other edD., except 1 & 8, and cod. D, before *attains* [attingit] reads *who (i.e. the Spirit)* [qui] in place of *which (Wisdom)* [quae], and then codd. A C & D and edd. 1 & 8 again read badly *who* [qui] for *because* [quod].

[2] Only the Vatican edition omits *and* [et].

[3] 1 Cor. 12:11.

[4] ON THE CUSTOMS OF THE CATHOLIC CHURCH, Bk. I, ch. 11, n. 18. — Next codices A B C and E and editions 1 and 5 omit *is* [est] after *than which nothing* [quo nihil melius].

[5] ON THE GOSPEL OF (ST.) JOHN, Tract 74, n. 3. On John 3:34 the words of (St.) Augustine are: *For neither is the Spirit Himself divided, but the gifts through Him: for there are divisions of (their) donations, but the same Spirit* [Neque enim ipse dividitur Spiritus, sed dona per Spiritum: nam divisiones donationum sunt, idem autem Spiritus].

[6] To this Distinction the Vatican ed. and edd. 3, 4, 5, 6, 7, 8 and 9, together with codex E, conjoin the words of the first chapter of the following distinction: *Here, there is asked ... gifts are granted* [Hic quaeritur ... ad donum dona donari], inclusively. But codices A B C & D and editions 1 & 2 rightly begin, here, Distinction XVIII, just as the ancient Commentators also do, especially St. Bonaventure, St. Thomas, Bl. (now St.) Albertus (Magnus), Richard of Middleton, which is apparent from the division of the text, which they make.

NOTES ON THE COMMENTARY

[1] From the manuscripts and the first six editions, we have supplied the badly omitted *invisible* [invisibilem].

[2] The Vatican edition, not trusting in the codices and edition 1, having omitted the words of Master Peter *Moreover, lest in so great a matter* [Ne autem in tanta re], begins the proposition thus: *Similarly, the second part* [Similiter secunda pars]; next, on account of the varied construction, it puts *has* [habet] in place of *and this part is divided into* [et dividitur haec pars in].

in which *he confirms* his own opinion; and this part is divided into four parts. In the first he shows, that the love [amor], by which we love [diligimus] God, is God, and similarly the love, by which we love neighbor. However, in the second he shows, that that love properly is the Holy Spirit, there (where he says): *Moreover, since fraternal Love is God* etc.. In the third he shows, that the Holy Spirit is Charity, not causally, but essentially

and formally speaking, there (where he says): *But lest perhaps anyone say, that there has been said* etc.. Fourth and last, he concludes, as (something) already manifested, that the Holy Spirit is then sent invisibly, when He makes us lovers [dilectores] of God and neighbor, there (where he says): *From the aforesaid it grows clear, that the Holy Spirit is Charity* etc.

TREATMENT OF THE QUESTIONS

For an understanding of this part four (things) are asked.

First, and principally on account of the position of Master (Peter), there is asked, whether besides the gift of uncreated Charity there is a positing of a gift of created charity; and this is to ask, whether the charity, by which we love God, is the Holy Spirit.

Second, granted that there is a created charity, there is asked, whether than charity is to be loved out of charity [ex caritate].

Third, whether charity can be cognized with certitude [certitudinaliter] by the one having charity.

Fourth, if it can be cognized by[3] the one not having (charity).

ARTICLE SOLE

On the gift of the created habit of charity, whether it exist, and in what manner it can be loved and cognized.

QUESTION I

Whether, besides uncreated Charity, there ought to be posited a habit of created charity?

About the first, that there is no positing of a charity other than uncreated Charity,[4] — having supposed the proof through the many authorities, which Master (Peter) adduces in the text[5] — is proven *by reasons*, and *first* by reasons taken from the *essence* of charity, which is (its) goodness, in this manner:

1. No accident is better than a rational substance; but charity is better than a rational soul, because it makes it better: therefore, it is not an accident, therefore, it is a substance. But it is established, that (it is) not irrational, therefore, rational, therefore, a soul and/or an Angel and/or God; but not a soul nor an Angel. therefore, God.[6]

2. Likewise, no created goodness is equivalent to beatitude;[7] but charity is equivalent to beatitude, because through charity a man merits, to be made worthy of eternal life or of beatitude: therefore, charity is not a created good: ergo etc..

3. Likewise, every created good is good through participation; but every good, good by another good, can be understood (to be) not good,[8] and in this manner evil would occur in it through the diminution of (its) beauty [speciei], of (its) standard of measure [modi] and of (its) order:

therefore, if charity is good by a created goodness, charity can be evil and/or at least be understood (to be) evil and/or even become formless [informis]; which is false.

Likewise, this very (thing) is shown by reasons taken from *virtue* in this manner:

4. As much as anything (is) more virtuous, so much does it need fewer means [mediis], therefore, if anything is most powerful, it needs no virtue other than itself: therefore, if the Holy Spirit is of infinite power and is Himself Charity, therefore, by Himself, not by another, He inflames the affection to love [ad amorem]: therefore, there is necessarily no positing of the created charity, which is a habit.

5. Likewise, natural virtue is more distant from God than the will; but God directs natural virtue by no other than Himself [non alio quam sit ipse]:[9] therefore, if no medium falls there, neither does it fall in the will: ergo etc..

6. Likewise, where the always-present-and-not-able-to-err virtue of the Prime Mover moves, it is superfluous to add another virtue, as for example, if hand were always conjoined to rudder [temoni], it would not be necessary [oporteret] that there be another

---

1 We prefer the reading of not a few codices, such as M T and Z (codex H omits the particle *and* [et]), in which there is added *God, and* [Deus et], which corresponds with Master (Peter's) intention to be laconic [ad amussim].

2 The Vatican edition, together with codex cc, but contrary to the more ancient codices with edition 1, has *he shows* [ostendit].

3 The Vatican edition, against very many codices and edition 1, has *by someone* [ab aliquo].

4 Trusting in the more ancient manuscripts and edition 1, we have restored *Charity* [caritas].

5 Here in chapters 1-4 and 6.

6 In this regard (St.) Augustine, 83 Questions, q. 54 says: Nor is anything better than the rational soul, except God. — A little before this codex V prefixes *it is* [est] to *not irrational* [irrationalis].

7 For beatitude, according to (St. Severinus) Boethius, On the Consolation of Philosophy, Bk. III, Prose 2, is the

state perfected with the congregation of all goods. — Next, we follow the many codices, such as B H K O T Z and ff, by substituting *to be made* [ut efficiatur] in place of *and is made* [et efficitur], which the Vatican edition, together with edition 1 and the other codices, has.

8 (St. Severinus) Boethius, On the Seven Rules, says: If they are goods by participation, they are <u>per se</u> in no manner goods; for what is white by participation, <u>per se</u> in that which it is, is not white, and of all the other qualities in the same manner. — Next, after *created* [creata], in the Vatican edition and in codex cc *charity* [caritas] is lacking, which, however, is found in all the other manuscripts and in edition 1.

9 The Vatican edition, together with edition 1, but contrary to nearly all the codices and to editions 2, 3, 4, 5 and 6, has *by Himself* [se ipso] for *Himself* [sit ipso]. A little before this, many codices, together with edition, 1 faultily have *loves* [diligit] in place of *directs* [dirigit].

virtue; but the Holy Spirit is the One directing and helping the will itself and is always conjoined and cannot err: therefore, it is superfluous to posit another charity; but every superfluous (thing) must be cut off [est resecandum]: ergo etc..

Likewise, this same (thing) is shown by reasons taken from *act*.

7. Because it belongs to the act of charity to *recreate* the soul; but it belongs not to a lesser virtue *to recreate*, than *to create*;[1] therefore, if 'to create' is only from the Uncreated, which is of infinite power, therefore, also 'to recreate'; but this is proper to charity [cartitatis]: therefore, it is uncreated.

8. Likewise, to belongs to any act of charity to unite; but no creatures is united through vanity to the truth; but[2] every creature (is) vanity: therefore, no creature is a means for being united to God [medium uniendi Deo]: if, therefore, charity is a means for being united, therefore, it is neither vanity nor a creature.

9. Likewise, it belongs to the act of charity to love [diligere] each single thing in an ordinate manner: therefore, if 'to love in an ordinate manner' is 'to love each single thing, according to what befits it', since the uncreated Good is better than one created unto an infinite degree [in infinitum], therefore, It (is) more lovable unto an infinite degree: therefore, if charity causes one to love God, as He is to be loved, charity causes one to love God unto an infinite degree; but that which goes forth as an infinite act is uncreated:[3] ergo etc..

BUT ON THE CONTRARY: 1. Charity is the principle of reforming the soul as much as regards the power of the will, but the soul as much as regards the other powers, that is the irascible and rational, is reformed through created virtues: therefore, for an equal reason the concupiscible; but its reformation[4] is charity: ergo etc..

2. Likewise, where there is a reformation, there is a conformation and an information, and where there is an information, there is something informing, which holds itself through the manner of a form, but every form of a created thing has been created; for God is the perfecting form of no thing: ergo etc..

3. Likewise, charity is the principle of living; whence Hugo of St. Victor (says):[5] « I know, oh my soul, that love is thy life »; but every life, existing through a participation in something, is by something informing (it), out which and (something else) vivifiable there comes to be one (thing); but out of God and the soul there can not come to be one (thing): therefore, it is necessary to posit

in the soul some created charity, which vivifies (it).

4. Likewise, everything which is in something capable of death [possibili ad mortem], is in[6] it through something separable; but the life of grace is in a soul able to die [possibili ad moriendum] by the death of fault: therefore, through something separable; but this is not God, because it is impossible that the God's presence be separated from anything: therefore, it is something created.

5. Likewise, charity is the principle of being gratified, but gratification is that,[7] in which (someone) good is distinguished from (someone) evil, the just from the impious, not only in act, but also in rest, as a little child and/or adult sleeping: therefore, since the distinction of good from evil is not through uncreated Goodness, because that (gratification) is common to all (rational beings), "charity" means something created.[8] And again, since the distinction of those resting is not through an act and/or use, but habit, it is clear that "charity" means a created habit.

6. Likewise, charity is the principle of meriting; but not because we do good (works), are we for that reason good, but rather the other way around: therefore[9] charity first makes one good before it elicits an act; but since someone from not (being) good is made good, it is necessary that something be posited in him anew, and this cannot be an act: therefore, a habit.

7. Likewise, God cooperates in a meritorious operation in a manner other than natural, because if not in another manner, then returns the error of Pelagius, that a man could merit out of natural (things); therefore, if in another manner, since He cooperates through uncreated virtue with every nature, it is necessary, that in a meritorious, created operation He cooperate by means of some virtue: but this cannot be but a created one: ergo etc..

8. Likewise, it seems, that Master (Peter) has erred, because he who divides the works of the Trinity is a heretic; but Master (Peter) posited, that the charity, by which we love God, is properly the Holy Spirit: therefore, he posits, that our own loving [diligere], which is an effect in a creature, belongs to the Holy Spirit alone; and thus he divides the works of the Trinity.

9. Likewise, he who says, that something created is uncreated, errs; but the charity, by which we love God and neighbor, as is commonly held, is something created: but Master (Peter) said, that this is the Holy Spirit: therefore, he erred.

---

[1] Cf. above d. 14, a. 2, q. 2, fundament 7. — A little before this codices W and Y repeat *recreate the soul* [animam recreare] before *than* [quam].

[2] From the manuscripts and editions 1, 2, 3 and 6, we have substituted *but* [sed] in place of *and* [et]. Next after *every creature* [omnis creatura] codex X adds *is* [est].

[3] Trusting in the very many manuscripts and edition 1, we have expunged the *infinite and* [infinitum et], which the Vatican edition puts before the word *uncreated* [increatum].

[4] Edition 1 reads *reformative* [reformativum].

[5] ON THE EARNEST MONEY OF THE SOUL, at the beginning: I know, that thy life is love. In which text the Vatican edition, breaking with many codices and with editions 1 and 6, reads *I shall know* [Scito].

[6] From nearly all the codices and the first six editions, we have supplied the badly omitted *in* [in].

[7] The Vatican edition, contrary to the more ancient codices and edition 1, has *that* [id] for *that* [illud], and a little below this *and an adult*

[et adultus] for *and/or an adult sleeping* [vel adultus dormiens].

[8] The codices dissent among themselves; very many, together with the Vatican edition and edition 1, not falsely have *charity does not mean something common* [caritas non dicit quid commune]; others falsely *charity means something common* [caritas dicit quid commune], from which the reading of codices O U X, which we have received in the text and which is more distinct, seems to be confirmed. Codex T has by a second hand in the margin *for uncreated Charity means something common* [caritas enim increata dici quid commune], but superfluously, as it is a repetition of the preceding proposition; but the primitive reading of the same, in which the words, which are under consideration, are utterly omitted, is not to be spurned, nay rather would be more pleasing than all the others, if it were supported by a firmer authority; for if this be preferred, the punctuation would have to be changed such that the next following proposition be conjoined with the preceding one.*

[9] In the Vatican edition there is incongruously omitted *therefore* [ergo], which is found in the manuscripts and editions 1, 2 and 3.

---

* *Trans. note*: In the preceding phrase *that* has uncertain reference; if taken as referring to what follows, it would be understood as referring to *charity*, and hence the reading of the second group of codices; if taken as referring to something more distant beforehand, it could only logically refer to *gratification*, because *Goodness* would take *this* [hac] and *distinction* would take *it itself* [ipsa] and, hence, understood as *gratification*, as I have done, which is common to all rational beings, it refutes the misunderstanding among the codices, and supports the received text: the argument being: *Charity is the principle of gratification, gratification the principle of distinguishing the good from the bad; which distinction is on account of created goods, not the uncreated Good; hence, since gratification is common to all created, rational beings, charity itself must be something created.*

CONCLUSION

Besides uncreated Charity there ought to be posited the char-
ity, which is a created habit, informing the soul.

I RESPOND: For the understanding of the aforesaid
it must be noted, that about this there is and was from
ancient (times) a twofold opinion. For of certain ones,
as Master (Peter) and his followers, there is the opinion,
that the Holy Spirit is essentially the Charity, by which
the Father and the Son love [diligunt] us, and even That
by which we love God.

And certain ones wanted to say, that this is the understanding of this position.¹ For they say, that, just as
light can be considered in a threefold manner, that is,
in itself and in (something) transparent and on the extremity of some bright surface [perspicui terminati] —
in the first manner, it is light [lux], in the second manner the light (of the luminous body) [lumen],* in the
third manner a hypostasis of color² — so the Holy Spirit
can be considered *in Himself*, and in this manner is the
Love [amor] of the Father and the Son; He can, again,
be considered *as One indwelling in a human soul*, and in
this manner the Holy Spirit is said (to be) grace; He can
also be considered *as One united to the will*, and in this
manner is the Charity, by which we love God. Whence
they say, that the Holy Spirit is our Charity, not through
an appropriation, but through a union. For according
to the measure the Son alone is Man and/or has been²
incarnate; and yet the whole Trinity has worked the Incarnation, but the Son alone, however, (is) united: in
the same manner, though the whole Trinity works the
union of the Holy Spirit with the will, yet the Holy
Spirit alone is united to the will, and for that reason He
alone is (its) charity.

Moreover, the reason moving one to posit this is
the authority of the Apostle, in the sixth (chapter) of the
First (Letter) to the Corinthians:⁴ *He who adheres to God*
is the one Spirit, and also *a similitude*. For they say, that,
just as the Son proceeds through a manner of nature
and thus is united⁵ to a nature, so the Holy Spirit
through the manner of will, and for that reason unite-
able [unibile] and united to the will. And because the
will is vertible, not so nature, for that reason the Holy
Spirit is united in a separable manner [separabiliter], but
the Son in an inseparable manner [inseparabiliter], and
for that reason in a far inferior manner than the Son,
and to whom He is united in this manner, He by Himself makes (them) love.

But this position cannot stand, because the Holy

Spirit is not unite-able; and *besides*, if He were unite-
able, either (He is such) through Nature, or through
grace. Not through Nature, therefore, through grace:
therefore, it would still be necessary [oporteret]⁶ that
there be a habit of grace disposing the soul to the undertaking of such a union; and thus it contradicts itself
[redit contrarium]. For that reason I do not believe, that
Master (Peter) belongs to this opinion in this manner.

And, on this account, it must be said in another
manner, that that (phrase): *by which we love God*, one is
to accept in a threefold manner: either as 'that by which
we *effectively* love', and in this manner charity or love
[amor] appropriately belongs to the whole⁷ Trinity and
to the Holy Spirit, or as 'that by which we *exemplarily*
love', and in this manner the Holy Spirit, who is the
Union of the Father and the Son and the Nexus of Both,
is⁸ the Unity, to the imitation of Which charity ties us,
according to which the Lord says, in the seventh (chapter of the Gospel of St.) John:⁹ *That they may be one, just*
as We are even One; or as 'that by which we *formally* love',
and in this manner according to the opinion of Master
(Peter) it is an affection of the spirit [animi affectio].

And in all these he said the truth and did not err, but
he was deficient, because beside Him there is a positing of
the charity according to the common opinion, which is¹⁰
a created habit informing the soul. And the reason for
this is taken on part of its *essence*, *virtue* and *operation*.

On part of (its) *essence*, because charity is the goodness of a rational creature, perfecting and distinguishing
and ordering and disposing it to eternal life: therefore
it is necessary, that it be its¹¹ formal perfection.

1. To that, therefore, which is objected first, that
charity is better than the rational soul; it must be said,
that there is no comparison there, because where one
(is said) on account of the other, there (is) only one
(being);¹² whence the one having charity is good on account of charity. *And/or* a comparison does not occur
there, because "good" is not said uniformly. For a rational substance is said (to be) "good", because it can be
ordered [ordinabilis] unto an end, charity "good", because (it is) the one ordering.

2. To that which is objected, that it is equivalent to
beatitude, it must be said, that it is equivalent according to a divine assessment [divinam aestimationem],
which¹³ assesses the work of charity (to be) worthy of
eternal life or of such a great remuneration.

3. To that which is objected, that if it is a good
through participation, then its goodness is thoroughly
changeable into a state of formlessness [permutabilis in
informitatem]; it must be said, that something¹⁴

---

¹ The Vatican edition, not trusting in the manuscripts and in edition 1, reads *can be demonstrated through a similitude* [potest demon-
strari per similitudinem] at the end of this sentence, in place of *this is*
[hic est]. A little before this codex O by omitting *certain ones* [quidam]
reads instead *they*, codex V, however, adds there *also* [etiam].

² This is explained by the words of St. Thomas, here in q. 1, a. 1: because a hypostasis of color is light, and color is nothing other than incorporated
light. — St. Bonaventure has more on this in SENT., Bk. II, d. 13, a. 2, q. 2, and
SENT., Bk. III, d. 23, Doubt 4. Cf. also SENT., Bk. I, d. 3, p. I, Doubt 7.*

³ From the more ancient mss., we have supplied *has been* [est].

⁴ Verse 17, where the Vulgate reads: *But who adheres to the Lord,*
is one etc.. — Next after *also a similitude* [etiam] the Vatican ed., without any authority of the mss. and ed. 1, inserts *moves them* [movet eos].

⁵ Some codd., such as A I T & aa, with ed. 1, read *united* [unitus]
for *is united* [unitus]; cod. aa, furthermore, adds *has been* [est] to this.

⁶ The Vatican edition, together with codex cc, yet breaking with
the more ancient codices with edition 1, reads *it is necessary* [oportet].

⁷ Trusting in the older mss., we have restored the not well omitted *whole* [totius].

⁸ The corrupt reading of the Vatican edition and codex cc, in
which, a little before this having omitted *who* [qui], puts *and* [et] here in
place of *is* [est], and then after *Unity* [unitas] begins a new sentence, is
repaired with the help of the more ancient codices and edition 1. —
Codex Z has *since He* [quoniam] in place of *who* [qui], and very many
codices falsely put *of the Others* [aliorum] for *of Both* [amborum].

⁹ Verse 21.

¹⁰ As required by the more ancient manuscripts and edition 1, we
have substituted the subjunctive form for *is* [sit].

¹¹ In the Vatican edition and codex cc *its* [eius] is wanting, which
the other codices together with edition 1 do well to exhibit.

¹² Aristotle, TOPICS, Bk. III, ch. 2 : If (there is) anywhere one for
the sake of the other; regardless of whether the two are more eligible than
the one: as to become healthy and health, than heath etc..

¹³ Not a few codices, such as A S T W and cc have less congruously *Who* [qui], edition 1 together with one and the other codex, such as
I, has *because He* [quia] instead. Next codex bb has *reputes* [reputat] for
assesses [aestimat].

¹⁴ Codex T adds *is and* [est et].

---

* *Trans. note*: Cf. the Scholium to SENT., Bk. II, d. 13, a. 2, q. 1, for more on the distinction of lux and lumen, and the *Trans. Note* to a. 1, q. 2,
of that same Distinction, for the English translations of these terms.

is said (to be) "a good through participation" in a twofold manner. either because (it is) participating and ordinate, or because (it is) a participation and an ordination. In the first manner it is a good having charity, in the second manner (it is)[1] charity; and for that reason it can *not be*, because it is not the essence itself of a goodness, but (rather) a participation (in it); however, being (a participation),[2] it cannot *not be good* and/or ordinate, because it is the very order of love [est ipse ordo amoris]. Whence it must be solved according to[3] that, through a distinction; and in this are clear the reasons taken from essence.

For on the part of *virtue* it is necessary to posit a created habit of charity. For the charity, by which we love God, is a virtue, not only because[4] God cooperates with us, but also because our will cooperates with God: *For we are God's helpers*;[5] and because, when we cooperate with God, it is necessary that we be conformed to Him, it is necessary, that from that Most High Charity there be left in us some copy [aliquod exemplatum] in our affection, through which it is moved[6] in a manner conformed to It [illi conformiter]. For the will is free and is born to be moved according to what is placed in its way [ad opposita]: and for that reason there is posited the virtue of created charity in us, not on account of a defect on the part of God working with us, but (on the part) of our will cooperating with Him.

4. To that which is objected, that a most powerful virtue does not need an intermediary virtue [virtute media], it is true; but charity is not on account of the need of His virtue, but rather (on account of the need) of the will suscepting (it), which needs some disposing habit.

5. To that which is objected, that God cooperates with a nature without a created virtue; it must be said, that God rules a nature, just as He has instituted (it), and a nature runs uniformly; and for that reason it does not need anything[7] regulating (it). Not so is it concerning the will, which is moved difformly, and for that reason it needs some habit regulating and disposing it. *And/or* it must be said, that one thing concerns a nature and another a will, because a nature does not have to be moved, except according to itself, and/or from below, but the will from above: and for that reason it needs something elevating it.

6. To that which is objected, that the virtue of the Prime Mover is present; it must be said, that (His) presence is not sufficient, but it is necessary, that the one receiving the influence have an ability and a conformity (for Him); and this is through the created virtue.

Also on the part of *operation* a necessity is posited, because a reformation or[8] recreation, a union and a loving [dilectio] are not only by something as by *one effecting*, but also as by *one informing*. Moreover, *informing* charity is created, and from this are clear the objections from the part of act or operation.

7. For what is objected, that a recreation[9] is from the Uncreated; it is true through the manner of (its) efficient (Cause), just as also a creation; but a reformation leaves[10] a further form; and for that reason it is necessary to posit an *informing* habit.

8. To that which is objected, that vanity does not unite[11] to truth; it must be said, that grace can be considered according to which (it is) *from nothing*, and thus is vanity, and in this manner it does not unite, and/or according to which it is *an influence* according to the Divine Presence, and in this manner hit has an expressed similitude of truth, and in such a manner it does unite.

9. To that which is objected,[12] that charity makes one love God, as much as He is to be loved etc.; it must be said, that this can be understood in a twofold manner: either as much as God ought to be loved *in Himself*, and in this manner it is false, because since He is the Infinite Good, He ought to be loved unto an infinite (degree), and in such a manner God alone loves Himself; and/or inasmuch as He is to be loved *by this*,[13] and in this manner it is true, and then one loves to an infinite (degree), not simply, but according to the assessment of the one having charity. For only charity loves God more than a created good, because, if a created good would be multiplied unto an infinite (degree), it would still love God more.

Moreover, what is objected to the contrary, must be conceded, except for the last two, which show that Master (Peter) has erred.

8. Because, therefore,[14] it is objected, that he divides the works of the Trinity; it must be said, that it is false, because that the Holy Spirit is the Charity, by which we love God, has been said either through *appropriation*, or through *union*, or certainly through *exemplarity*, and thus are all the authorities understood, which Master (Peter) adduces on his own behalf;

---

[1] In some mss., such as B and bb, there is inserted *it is* [est].

[2] Trusting in many codices, such as A C G K L O S T U V X Z ee and ff, and in edition 1, we have supplied *being (a participation)* [ens], the sense of which is explained by the reading of codex R *when it is* [cum est] in place of *however, being (a participation)* [tamen ens]; very many codices less aptly *when being* [cum ens]. A little before this, codd. aa & bb have *itself essentially goodness* [ipsa essentialiter bonitas] for *the essence itself of a goodness* [ipsa essential bonitatis], cod. I reads *and in the first manner it can be good* [et primo modo potest esse bonum] in place of *and for that reason it can not be* [et ideo potest non esse], and, next, *in the second manner* [secundo modo] for *however, being (a participation)* [tamen ens].

[3] The Vatican ed., against the mss. and the first five edd., has *that must be solved* [solvendum est illud] for *it ... solved according to that* [solvendum ad illud].

[4] The Vatican ed., with a few manuscripts, twice has *by which* [qua] in place of *because* [quia].

[5] 1 Cor. 3:9. — Next we prefer the reading of a few manuscripts, Q T and ee (by a later hand), which put *to Him* [sibi] in place of *similarly* [similiter], as that which more fully manifests the conclusion; the error of the other manuscripts is explained from this, that the word *similarly* [similiter], when abbreviated, has nearly the same form as *to Him* [sibi].

[6] The codd. do not agree amongst themselves; some, with the Vatican ed., read *it moves* [moveat]; other codices, such as E H I O T Y Z and ee exhibit the reading we have received, which responds to the context.

[7] Very many codd. with ed. 1 have *another* [alio] for *anything* [aliquo]. A little before this, cod. X reads *is moved* [movetur] for *runs* [currit]. In the following proposition, the Vatican edition, not trusting in the mss. and six of the first edd. has *moves* [movet] for *is moved* [movetur].

[8] From the more ancient manuscripts and edition 1, we have restored *or* [sive] in place of *and/or* [vel], and a little below this, after *also* [etiam], we have inserted *as* [ut].

[9] The Vatican edition, together with codex cc, here reads *creation* [creatio] in place of *recreation* [recreatio] and a little below this *recreation* [recreatio] for *creation* [creatio], but the authority of the other manuscripts and edition 1 withstand this; yet a few codices, such as M aa and bb, together with edition 1, by speaking formally, have better *reformation* [reformatio] in place of *recreation* [recreatio].

[10] Thus very many and better codices; the Vatican edition has *requires* [requirit]. The reading received by us is explained above after the solution to n. 3, where there is the argument on the part of *virtue* and it is said: It is necessary, that by that Most High Charity there be left in us some copy in our affection, through which it is moved in a manner conformed to It.

[11] Trusting in the very many manuscripts and in six of the first editions, we have substituted *does unite* [unit] for *is united* [unitur], which responds more to the objection. Next after *according to which* [secundum quod], supply together with codex bb *it is* [est].

[12] As required by very many manuscripts and edition 1, we have substituted *is objected* [obiicitur] for *objects* [obiicit]. Then in many codices and in edition 1 there is less aptly lacking *charity* [caritas].

[13] Very many codices, such as C S V W and X, falsely read *for this* [ad hoc].

[14] The Vatican edition, together with not a few manuscripts, has *moreover* [autem]; edition 1 *for* [enim]. Next, very many codices, such as G H I K T etc., after *it is objected* [obiicitur] put *that* [quod] in place of *that* [quia].

but *formally* speaking they are not understood (to be) true, nor do I believe, that Master (Peter) thus understood (them).

9. And through this is clear the other (objection),[1]

that Master (Peter) says, that (something) created is uncreated, but that the uncreated Gift is sufficient without the created one; and in this there was no error, but only a lack (of consideration).

SCHOLIUM

I. Obsolete and commonly reproved is the opinion of Master (Peter), that there created charity is not in the soul according to habit, but only according to act. For according to this, as is commonly explained, the Holy Spirit perfects the created will through Himself, not only as an inhering form, but as End, Exemplar and Mover, such that the act of charity elicited by the soul has no created habit. (Bl. John Duns) Scotus strives to explain the words of Master (Peter) a little more meekly, that is, that the Holy Spirit is not formally, but only exemplarily and causally our charity, which is very true. (Cf. below Doubt 5).

II. The nine objections of Master (Peter) have been so ordered, that three are accepted on the part of *essence*, three on the part of *virtue*, and three on the part of *act*. Whence St. Bonaventure, under the same threefold regard, apposes contrary reasons, which, having departed from his customary order, he immediately applies to solve the difficulties. In the first place he shows that the explanation of Master (Peter belonging) to certain (authors) is false, (which says) that the Holy Spirit alone unites the created *will* to Himself, just as the Son alone united a human *nature* to Himself. This sense he meritedly reproves as most false, since a unity of operation cannot be except by a unity of supposits, nay of nature; moreover, such a hypostatic and/or natural union of the created will with the Holy Spirit is fictive, nay heretical.

III. In the solution to n. 1, the argumentation is made from the axiom of Aristotle: « Where (there is) one on account of the other, there (is) only one »; from which it follows, that, if a man is accepted by God on account of charity, there is only one goodness there; for that reason a comparison of each separate goodness cannot be made.

IV. In the solution to n. 2 the words: « according to the divine assessment » [secundum divinam aestimationem] mean the same thing as: « according to their being accepted by God » [secundum acceptationem Dei], which according to the common sentence is numbered among the conditions required for condign merit [meritum de condigno]. For more on this see SENT., Bk. II, d. 27, a. 2, q. 3, and BREVILOQUIUM, p. V, ch. 2.

V. On created charity: BREVILOQUIUM, p. V, c. 1. — Alexander of Hales, SUMMA., p. III, q. 61, m. 2, a. 1, 2 and 3. — (Bl. John Duns) Scotus, each version (of his Commentary), here in q. 1. — St. Thomas, here in q. 1,. a. 1; SUMMA., II. II., q. 23, a. 2. — Bl. (now St.) Albertus (Magnus), here in a. 1; SUMMA., p. I, tr. 8, q. 36, m. 3, and p. II, tr. 16, q. 98, m. 1. — (Bl.) Peter of Tarentaise, here in q. 1, a. 1. — Richard of Middleton, here in a. 1, q. 1. — Giles the Roman, here in 1st princ., qq. 1 and 2. — Durandus (of Saint-Pourçain), here in qq. 1 and 2. — (Bl.) Dionysius the Carthusian, here in q. 1. — (Gabriel) Biel, here in q. 1.

QUESTION II

Whether charity is to be loved out of charity?

Second, there is asked, whether charity is able to be loved [amabilis] out of charity; and that it is [et quod sic], is shown in this manner.

1. (St.) Augustine in the eight (book) ON THE TRINITY (says):[2] « No one says: I do not know, what I love [diligam]: he loves (his) brother and he loves love [dilectionem] itself »: therefore, love is to be loved; ergo etc..

2. Likewise, this same (thing) seems *by reason*, because there is no perfect cognition except that, by which one knows [novit] that he knows or knows knowledge [notitam] itself, therefore, neither (is there) a perfect love [amor] except that, by which one loves [amat] that he loves or (loves) love; but charity is perfect love: ergo etc..

3. Likewise, anyone loves (his) neighbor and rightly, because he sees, that he has charity, but « that, on account of which each one (is), (is) even more »:[3] therefore, he ought to love charity, or love [dilectionem], more.

ON THE CONTRARY: 1. (St.) Augustine in the first book, ON CHRISTIAN DOCTRINE[4] says, that only four are to be loved out of charity, namely, God, one's self, (one's) neighbor and (one's) body, but charity or love

is not any of these: therefore, it is not to be loved out of charity.

2. Likewise, love is twofold, namely *of concupiscence* and *of friendship*; if, therefore, charity or love is loved, therefore, either by the love of concupiscence, or of friendship. Not *of friendship*, it is established, because friendship is between similars and (is) the love [amor], by which anyone wishes [optat] good to another; but with charity no one wishes good. Likewise, neither (the love) *of concupiscence*, because concupiscence is not of something had [rei non habitae]: therefore, since no one loves out of charity except[5] the one having charity, therefore, no one can out of charity completely desire [concupiscere] charity. — *If you say*, that one completely desires the augment of charity, this does not solve (the matter), because I am not asking, except whether charity had, according to which it is had, can be loved [amari].

3. Likewise, just as faith is had for believing, and hope for the act of hoping, so love [dilectio] or charity for the act of loving [diligendi]; but no one having faith believes faith and/or in faith, because as (St.) Augustine says: « The one believing knows [scit],

---

[1] The Vatican edition, with very many manuscripts and edition 1 striving against this, has *that (objection)* [illud] for *the other (objection)* [aliud].

[2] Chapter 8, n. 12. See the text of Master (Peter) here in ch. 1.

[3] Aristotle, POSTERIOR ANALYTICS., Bk. I, ch. 2; in which text the Vatican edition, together with some codices, after *each one (is)* [unumquodque] adds *such* [tale]. Cf. above d. 12, q. 2, opposing argument n. 1.

[4] Chapter 23, n. 22: Therefore, since there are four to be loved: one which is above us, the other which we are, the third which is besides us, the fourth which is below us. In which text, as related by St. Bonaventure, the Vatican edition after *neighbor* [proximum] adds *and the body of (one's) neighbor* [et corpus proximi], which many codices also have, yet

with the words *and (one's) own body* [et corpus proprium] omitted; yet other codices, such as F H Y Z and ee, together with edition 1, exhibit the reading received in the text, which is confirmed also by d. 1, a. 1, q. 2, opposing argument n. 1, where the same sentence is quoted. Next codex V has *anything* [aliquid] for *any* [aliquod].

[5] Edition 1 has *not* [non] for *unless* [nisi], in the same sense.

[6] ON THE TRINITY, Bk. XIII, ch. 1, n. 3, where he deals with the manner, by which we cognize the faith, which is in us, and concludes: The most certain science holds it (i.e. faith) and conscience shouts it. And ibid., ch. 5, n. 5: Therefore, anyone sees his own faith itself in himself [apud se]. — Next, codex K, after *concerns* [est de] adds *the things* [rebus], and a little below this, after *hope itself* [spem] the Vatican edition, not trusting in the mss. and edition 1, subjoins *but has (it)* [sed habet].

that he believes, and sees, that he believes »; moreover, credulity concerns (the things) not seen; moreover, similarly, no one hopes hope itself: therefore, a simili,* neither does one love charity, and/or if it is not similar, there is asked: for what reason (is it) not (similar)?

4. Likewise, if the one loving loves love, either *by the same* (love), or *by another*. If *by another*, then for an equal reason he loves another love by another, and thus there will be an infinite regression [abire in infinitum]. If, therefore, it is to stand still and it does not happen to depart unto infinity, if he loves, he loves[1] by the same (love). But if this; *on the contrary*: no special form is reflected upon its very self unless (it) concerns the first intentions (i.e. the transcendentals of being), just as unity, truth, goodness (do); whence in no manner is whiteness said (to be) white: therefore, neither love loved, and thus etc..

CONCLUSION

Created charity is not to be loved with the love of friendship, but with the love both of concupiscence and of complacence.

I RESPOND: It must be said, that accepting "love" [dilectio], according to which God is love, it is at least established, that It is to be loved out of charity. But accepting "love", according to which it is a gratuitous habit, thus at least[2] is it to be loved, but not above all (things).

Moreover, for an understanding of the objections it must be noted, that love [amor] is threefold, namely *of friendship*, by which anyone wishes good to another;[3] *of concupiscence*, by which anyone desires something for himself, and *of complacence*, by which anyone rests and is delighted in the thing desired, when it is present.[4]

I say, therefore, that charity is in no manner able to be loved [amabilis] by the love *of friendship*, because it is not able to be beatified [beatificabilis]; by the love *of concupiscence* it is able to be loved out of charity, according to which the one loving [diligens] desires to love more fully; however[5] by the love *of complacence*, that is, because the one loving accepts the love itself, by which he loves God, by this[6] charity is to be loved, according to which it is already had, for the reason that it is itself a very acceptable good.

1. With these seen, the response to the first two is clear. For that reckoning runs from the authority of (St.) Augustine ON CHRISTIAN DOCTRINE only as much as regards the love of friendship, because (St.) Augustine speaks of the one who is able to be loved, to whom anyone wishes good.

2. That which is objected[7] second is similarly clear: For although (that) of charity had, according to which it is had, is not concupiscence, yet nevertheless it is complacence. — However, it might be said, that spiritual love[8] and possession excites one to desire, while it refects, and refects, while it excites: for that reason concupiscence and complacence remain together.

3. To that which is objected third, concerning faith and hope, it must be said, that it is not similar, because the act[9] of faith of itself means imperfection, similarly also (the one) of hope; for the one is of a thing not seen, the other of a thing not had; and for that reason if such an act is reflected (upon it self), it would diminish in [de] the reckoning of a habit; whence he who believes credulity, does not have it,[10] and (he who hopes for) hope similarly; and for that reason these virtues are emptied out [evacuantur] in the Fatherland. But love is an act of completion and of perfection, just as (is) knowledge [scientia]; whence, just as he perfectly knows [scit], who knows, that he knows, so he perfectly loves who loves love [diligit qui amat dilectionem].

4. To that which is objected, "either by the same, or by another" etc.: it must be said, that by the same as much as regards the habit, but by another as much as regards the act.

And because it is objected, that special (forms)[11] are not reflected; it must be said, that reflection in a form sometimes comes *out of nature*;[12] and so it is in general (forms); sometimes it comes by a reckoning of that, *in which it is*, and thus is in the forms, which are in powers born to be converted upon themselves, and inasmuch as they are converted over themselves. And since the cognitive power cognizes its very self, « and the will is the instrument moving its very self »,[13] for that reason through science someone does know himself and science, and through charity loves himself and it.

And if the reason be asked,[14] why the intellective power has been born to go back upon itself and the will (likewise), it will be said elsewhere;[15] but now it suffices only (to say), that they are simple powers and have been founded in a simple substance and have not been bound to an organ, and for that reason it is clear, that that which is was accustomed to be objected is not similar: 'in the senses there is one power, which sees, and another, which[16] sees, that it sees; wherefore (such a difference) similarly ought to be in the intellect'.

---

[1] Not a few codices, such as G H K T and bb, read *he will love* [diliget]. A little below this, codex O reads *it concerns the transcendentals* [de primis est intentionibus]. On this reflection of the *first intentions* see above d. 3, p. I, Doubt 3 (and the Scholium, here in II.).

[2] Very many codices, with edition 1, omit *at least* [utique].

[3] Some codices, such as A T etc., and edition 1, add *and* [et].

[4] On this threefold love, cf. SENT., Bk. III, d. 29, Doubt 4.

[5] The more ancient manuscripts, together with edition 1, exhibit the particle *however* [vero], omitted in the Vatican edition.

[6] Namely, by the love of complacence. — Many codd., with edition 1, have *this* [haec] in place of *by this* [hoc], but faultily, because he deals with *the same* charity in respect of a threefold love; codex Y has *so* [sic] for *by this* [hoc]; the Vatican edition has *in this manner* [hoc modo].

[7] The Vatican edition, together with the more recent codex cc, reads *is asked* [quaeritur].

[8] Not a few codices, such as B G T Y and ff, together with edition 1, have less congruously *delight* [delectatio] for *love* [dilectio].

[9] The Vatican ed., without the authority of the mss. and ed. 1, beginning a new sentence, has *For the Act* [Actus enim] for *because the act* [quia actus].

[10] Codex O proceeds thus: *as faith, similarly he who hopes for hope, does not have it as hope, similarly, as it seems, these virtues are emptied out* etc. [ut fidem, similiter qui sperat spem, non habet eam ut spem, similiter ut videtur hae virtutes evacuantur etc.].

[11] Codex Y reads *special forms* [formae speciales].

[12] In codex O there is added *of a form in itself* [formae in se].

[13] (St.) Anselm (of Canterbury), ON THE CONCORD OF FORE-KNOWLEDGE AND PREDESTINATION AND GOD'S GRACE WITH THE FREE WILL, q. 3, ch. 11, at the end; among which words the Vatican edition, together with the one or the other codex, has less aptly *its very self (i. e. the will)* [se ipsam] in place of *its very self (i.e. as instrument)* [se ipsum]. Next, we follow cod. T by placing after *anyone* [aliquis] *himself* [se] in place of *knows* [scit], which reading, from what immediately precedes and follows it, is proven as the only one that can be admitted; in the reading of the other codices "reflexive cognition", which it deals with here, is not attained. Then, with the Vatican edition, a few codd. read *and his own science* [et scientiam suam].

[14] Trusting in the more ancient manuscripts and edition 1, we have substituted *be asked* [quaeratur] for *is asked* [quaeritur].

[15] SENT., Bk. II, d. 25, p. I, qq. 1-3; see also Bk. II, d. 19, a. 1, q. 1, fundament 4, and Bk. III, d. 27, a. 1, q. 1 in the body of the response. Next after *but* [sed] in the Vatican edition and codex cc the subject of the verb *it* [hoc] is explicitly had.

[16] The Vatican edition and codex cc have not so well *by which it* [qua], contrary to the codices, such as A B D F G H I P Q T Z ee and ff, together with edition 1. A little before edition 1 after *senses* [sensibus] adds *because out of which* [quia ex quo].

---

* *Trans. note*: For the meaning of the expression a simili, cf. Translator's note, above on p. 257.

SCHOLIUM

I. First the question is resolved in general affirmatively and through a twofold conclusion, that is, in respect of uncreated and created charity. Then in regard to the created habit there is more accurately determined, by which species of the threefold love [amore] is (love) to be loved.

II. The solution to n. 1 presupposes, that the *object* of charity in general has been taken as twofold. For either *the object* is capable of beatitude, and/or is only a *medium*, through which one can be helped, to be beatified. To the first genus pertains those three enumerated by St. Augustine, whence these can be loved [diligi] by the love of friendship [amore amicitiae]; to the second genus pertains every creature, and thus every creature can be loved as a *means* to the Most High Good. Cf. above d. 1, a. 1, q. 2. in reply to n. 1.

The first intentions, which are mentioned in the solution to n. 4,* are the transcendental notions: *being, the one, the true, the good*; which « are reflected upon themselves », i. e. are predicated of themselves, as for example, 'truth is one, true and good'. However, special forms are those, which are established out of genus and difference. These from their own nature cannot be aptly predicated of themselves; yet sometimes this comes to be by reason of *the subject*, in which they are, if it has acts reflected upon itself, just as there is in the two powers of the will and intellect, cf. above d. 3, p. I, Doubt 3.

III. In regard to the question itself, cf. SUMMA DE VIR-TUTIBUS, published under the name of Alexander of Hales, at Paris, in 1507 A. D., by Jean Petit, coll. 63, a. 7. Concerning this Summa a controversy arose on account of those (things), which were written by Fr. Luke Wadding, in his AN-NALES, on A.D. 1245, and by other authors of the Order of Friars Minor, namely that St. Thomas copied much of this work into his SUMMA THEOLOGIAE, especially the *secunda pars secundae*. On the other hand Natalis Alexander, Echardus, and de Rubeis went so far, as to deny that this SUMMA exists in either its manuscript or written form, concerning which claim, one can see de Rubeis' DISSERTATIONES CRITICAE, dissertation 15, which is also published in the modern editions of St. Thomas' SUMMA. But in this these very learned men err, since very many, printed copies of this SUMMA still survive, such as that in the Royal Library of Münich (Germany) and that in our convent of St. Trond, in Belgium. Moreover, it appears from the beginning of this work, that it is not a separate book, but rather part of another work, namely of the great SUMMA of Alexander of Hales, as it seems. But of this SUMMA Alexander of Hales could not himself be the author, because many questions are taken word for word from the COM-MENTARIA of St. Bonaventure. It seems rather that it belongs to William of Meliton, who in 1256, by the order of the Supreme Pontiff, Alexander IV, began to finish the incomplete SUMMA of Alexander of Hales, but who after four years, taken suddenly by his own demise, left the work incomplete. — St. Thomas, here in q. 1, a. 5; SUMMA. , II. II, q. 25, a. 2. — Bl. (now St.) Albertus (Magnus), here in a. 3; on this and the following question, SUMMA., p. I, tr. 8, q. 36, m. 3, incidental question. — (Bl.) Peter of Tarentaise, here in q. 1, a. 4. — Richard of Middleton, here in a. 1, q. 2. — Giles the Roman, here in 3rd. princ., q. 1. — (Bl.) Dionysius the Carthusian, here in q. 2.

QUESTION III

Whether one can know with certitude, that he is in charity?

Third, there is asked, whether charity is cognizable with certitude [certitudinaliter] by the one having (it). And that it is, seems:

1. By the authority of (St.) Augustine in the eighth (book) ON THE TRINITY, and as is had in the text (of Master Peter):[1] « He who loves (his) brother, knows [novit] more the love, by which he loves, than the brother, whom he loves »; but he knows (his) brother with certitude: therefore also charity (with certitude).

2. Likewise, by the second (chapter) of the First (Letter of St.) John:[2] *He who loves his own brother, remains in the light*: therefore, if charity is a light, since nothing is seen more certainly than a light, ergo etc..

3. Likewise, by the second (chapter) of the First (Letter of St.) John:[3] *(His) anointing shall teach you concerning all things*, not, I say, concerning all cognizables, but concerning all (things) necessary for salvation; but charity is most necessary for salvation: therefore, the anointing of the Holy Spirit teaches us it.

4. Likewise, as much as anything is[4] more present to the soul, so much is it more certainly see and cognized; but charity is most present to the soul, because it is in the soul. ergo etc..

5. Likewise, the one having faith is certain, that he has faith, for nothing is more certain to a man than his own faith, as (St.) Augustine says:[5] therefore, for an equal reason the one having charity knows [scit], that he has charity.

ON THE CONTRARY: 1. By the ninth (chapter) of Ecclesiastes:[6] *No one knows, whether he is worthy of hatred, or of love*: therefore, since the one having charity is worthy of love, he knows not [nescit] that he is worthy, ergo etc..

2. Likewise, by the fourth (chapter) of the First (Letter of St. Paul) to the Corinthians:[7] *I am conscious of nothing for myself, but I am not in this justified*: therefore, it seems, that a man not having remorse can not be justified, therefore, not have charity, but no sign is more evident of charity, that the lack of all remorse: therefore, if that is fallible, all the others are fallible.

3. Likewise, to charity[8] it belongs to love God for His own sake and above all (things), such that (one loves) nothing equally and/or above and/or contrary to (Him), but no one knows, whether he loves God before all (else): therefore, no one knows, whether he has charity with certitude.

4. Likewise, the one having charity has been accepted by God, and this[9] is established by us and by all, that these (virtues) of ours are con-

---

[1] Here, in ch. 1.   [2] Verse 10.

[3] Verse 27, where the Vulgate reads: *His anointing will teach you concerning all (things)* [Unctio eius docet vos de omnibus].

[4] In codex Z, there is added *more near and/or* [propinquius vel].

[5] ON THE TRINITY, Bk. XIII, ch. 1 n. 3: It (i.e. faith) does most certain knowledge hold and conscience shout out. And ibid., ch. 2, n. 5: Therefore, anyone sees his own faith in [apud] his very self.

[6] Verse 1; the Vulgate reads: *A man does not know, whether he be worthy of love or hatred* [Nescit homo, utrum amore an odio dignus est].

[7] Verse 4. — A little below this, after *remorse* [remorsum] codex K adds *of conscience* [conscientiae].

[8] The Vatican edition, together with codex cc has *charity is loving* [caritas est diligere] for *to charity it belongs to love* [caritatis est diligere], and next *beneath which* [infra quod] in place of *such that* [ita quod], but faultily (since God in Latin is masculine in gender) and contrary to the more ancient codices, together with edition 1.

[9] According to the more ancient manuscripts and edition 1, we have inserted *this* [hoc].

---

* *Trans. note*: Not explicitly in the solution to n. 4, but rather in the 4th argument of the Contrary.

vertible; but no one knows, whether he has been accepted by God except through a revelation: therefore, no one knows, that he has charity except through a revelation.

5. Likewise, the Apostle says, that he did not know, whether he had a fault, when he said: *but I am not in this justified*; therefore, ab oppositis,* he did not know, that he had grace: therefore, since charity is not without grace, ergo etc..

CONCLUSION

A man in the state of wayfarer, apart from a revelation, can neither of himself nor of another know with certitude, that he is in charity, yet one can probably cognize this through some signs.

I RESPOND: It must be said, *that charity is cognized with certitude*[2] is in a twofold manner: either in the *universal*, what it is and of what kind it ought to be, and thus it can at least be cognized; in another manner that charity is cognized is in *a particular* [in speciali] or in this, and in this manner one can neither of *himself* nor *of another*, so long as a man lives, know (it) with certitude: not of *another*, because one does not *know* [novit], *what are in a man*,[3] except through signs, which are fallible; not of *himself*, and for this there can be a fourfold reason.

One and *chief* (reason) is the implication of the Divine Acceptance; because charity has been joined to the grace which makes one pleasing; which for this reason is said (to be) "making one pleasing", because it renders a man accepted by God, and for that reason charity is so called, not only because it has the dear beloved, but also because it makes a man dear to God. And because we do not know the Divine Acceptance with certitude except through revelation, for that reason we do not know, that we have charity, unless we be taught through revelation.

The *second* reason is the similitude of it to acquired love [dilectionem]. For it can happen, that someone is inflamed to love [ad amandum] God through becoming accustomed [assuefactionem], who will be thrown down [corruet] through some spiritual sin, and yet will always have the affection [afficietur]; just as is expressly clear through blessed Bernard in the book, ON THE LOVE OF GOD,[4] where he reprehends those are proud of (their own) devotion.

The *third* reason is the half-blindness of our eye, because our eye is just like the owl to the most manifest (things) of nature, just as the Philosopher says.[5] Whence just as a half-blind eye would not know how to distinguish between the light of the day and the light of a flame and/or of the Moon, so our spiritual eye (does not know how to distinguish) between the light of grace freely given and (the grace) which makes us pleasing.

The *fourth* reason is the dispensation of the Divine Judgements. For God closes the eyes of His servants as much as regards those (things) which pertain to their dignity, and can be borne off from them. Whence grace is contrary to pride. For pride opens (one's) eyes to see prerogatives and closes (them) to see needs [indigentias] and defects, according to that (verse) in the third (chapter) of the Apocalypse:[6] *You say, that I am rich and have been enriched and am in need for nothing, and you do not know, that your are poor and blind* etc.. But contrariwise the holy man says, that he is nothing, because God closes[7] his eyes to goods and opens (them) to see evils. And this is the reason, why a man does not recognize [cognoscit] the charity, which though it is not sufficient through itself, yet with the others is good. I believe, however, that, which has been said first, is the chief (reason).

Moreover, though charity cannot, with certainty, be recognized [cognosci] to be in someone, even by the one having (it)[8] in respect

---

[1] 1 Cor. 4:4.

[2] Very many codd., with editions 2, 3, 4, 5 and 6, read *essentially* [essentialiter] for *with certitude* [certitudinaliter], but less to the point.

[3] 1 Cor. 2:11: For who of men knows, what (thoughts) belong to a man, except the spirit of the man, which is in him? [Quis enim hominum scit, quae sunt hominis, nisi spiritus hominis, qui in ipso est?]. — A little before this the Vatican edition, contrary to very many codices and editions 1, 2, and 3, *because no one* [quia nemo] for *because one does not* [quia non]. Next trusting in the manuscripts, we have substituted *fallible* [fallibilia] for *fallacious* [fallacia] and *for this* [huius] for *of this very kind* [huiuscemodi].

[4] There are two opuscula among the works of St. Bernard, which regard the love of God. One is entitled, ON LOVING GOD, and it is genuine; the other however, ON THE NATURE AN DIGNITY OF LOVE, at one time used to be ascribed to St. Bernard, but it belongs to William, the Abbot of St. Theodoric. The sentence, which St. Bonaventure here quotes, is not found among the aforesaid works, but seems to have been taken from Guigo's letter or tract TO THE FRIARS OF MONTE DEI (which at one time was attributed to St. Bernard), where at the end of Book I, chapter 14, there is exhibited this definition of prayer [oratio]: « However, prayer is the affection of the man adhering to God, and a certain familiar and pious address, and an illumined state [statio] of mind to enjoy (Him), as long as it is allowed »; and then there is read: « Sometimes even the affection of pure prayer and that good savor of prayer is not found, but (it is) as if one finds (it), when grace precedes the one not seeking (it), not asking for (it) and as if non knowing (it), and like the race of servants is received at the table of sons, and a yet rude and incipient spirit of prayer in one is assumed to be the affection, which is accustomed to be rendered as a reward for holiness according to the merits of the perfect. Which when it comes to be, one considers, that either it is not licit for the negligent to know in his own judgement, what he neglects ... and/or that the provocation of the charity of the one offering (the prayer) enkindles (him) according to the love in him beyond itself. In which, ah the sorrow! very many

fail, because when they feed on the bread of sons, they judge themselves already to be sons, and owing to the fact that they fail to profit from it, *they are emptied in their conscience of the visiting grace, judging themselves to be something*, when they are nothing, and are not emended by the gifts [bonis] of God, but are hardened, and become (like those) of whom the Psalmist says: *The enemies of the Lord have lied and, there will be a time for them unto the ages. And He fed them from the fat of the wheat and from the rock He filled them with honey* (Psalm 80:16 ff.). For servants sometimes are fed by God the Father on the more precious substance of grace, so that they feel to be sons; however, as abusers of God's grace they are made into (His) enemies. For to abuse even the Holy Scriptures in sins and/or in their concupiscences, returning to these (Scriptures) through prayers, they say to themselves that (verse) of the wife of Manue: *If the Lord had wanted to slay us, He would not have taken up the sacrifice of our hands* (Judges 13:23) ».

[5] Aristotle, METAPHYSICS, Bk. II, text 1, which is cited above on p. 72, note 9. — Then the Vatican edition, contrary to the manuscripts and to edition 1, reads *knows not how* [nescit] for *would not know how* [nesciret].

[6] Verse 17, where the Vulgate reads: You say, that I am rich and have been enriched: and you know not, that you are wretched and miserable and poor and blind [Dicis, quod dives sum et locupletatus: et nescis, quia tu es miser et miserabilis et pauper et caecus].

[7] Edition 1 reads *closed* [clausit] and a little after this, together with some manuscripts, has *opened* [aperuit] for *opens* [aperit]. A few codices omit *God* [Deus].

[8] The codices do not agree amongst themselves; many unduly omit the preposition *by* [ab] (perhaps omitted on account of the alliteration of the following word *habente* in the Latin text), codex X omits *even by* [etiam ab]; the Vatican edition however, puts *it* [eam] in place of *even by* [etiam ab]; only a few codices, such as V and hh (codex V having transposed the words *by even* [ab etiam]) together with edition 1, exhibit the reading accepted by us, which both in itself is more distinct and corresponds more to the context.

---

* *Trans. note*: A topic ab oppositis is a proposition which is true in virtue of the truth of a proposition which has the opposite logical form. Here, the first proposition, "he did not know that he had a fault", is converted (cf. above, p. 112, trans. fn.), and the thing affirmed ("fault") is replaced by the affirmation of its opposite ("grace"). Cf. Peter of Spain, SUMMULE, tracts I, "On categoric propositions" and V, "On loci ab oppositis".

to it, yet it can be cognized through probable signs, most of all through the mortification of the concupiscence and of vain or worldly love and through the many other signs, which the Saints speak of and manifest [ponunt].[1]

1. To that, therefore, which is objected unto the contrary, that love [dilectio] is more certain that a brother; it must be said, that "charity" not only means "love", but adds beyond this, namely,[2] that it is gratuitous. And as much as regard the habit of *love* it is cognizable with certitude, but as much as regards that which means *gratuitous*, (it is) not.

2. To that which is objected, that charity is a light; it must be said, that although of itself charity is cognizable, yet it is not cognized by us, because our eye is half-blind.

3. To that which is objected, that (His) anointing shall teach us concerning all (things) necessary for salvation; it must be said, that it is true in the manner, according to which they are necessary; but *knowing* [scire], that one has charity, is not necessary for salvation, but only *having* [it is].

4. To that which is objected concerning the presence of charity, it must be said, that although the substance of the habit be present, yet the condition, which is concomitant with the habit [concomitatur habitum], that is the Divine Acceptance, is not present, nay lies hidden [latens] in God's cognition and judgement.

5. To that which is objected concerning faith, it must be said, that it is not similar, because "faith" means the pure habit, not by the superaddition of acceptance, just as charity (does), and for that reason it is clear, that it is not similar.

SCHOLIUM

I. The threefold conclusion is entirely conformable to the doctrine decided in the Council of Trent (Session VI, ch. 9, and canons 13 and 14). Cf. here Doubt 7; the Prologue, Doubt 4; SENT., Bk. II, d. 38, Doubt 1, and also Bk. III, d. 23, Doubt 4; and St. Bonaventure's COMMENTARY ON THE GOSPEL OF ST. JOHN, Jn. 14:24 (in Bonelli's Supplement).

II. It must be observed, that the Seraphic Doctor in the first reason on behalf of the second conclusion with these words, « Charity has been joined to the grace which makes one pleasing », distinguished charity from habitual grace; cf. also SENT.,

Bk. III, d. 27, a. 1, q. 3. The contrary sentence, but less common and probable, is held by (Bl. John Duns) Scotus.

III. Alexander of Hales, SUMMA, p. III, q. 61, m. 7, a. 3. — St. Thomas, here in q. 1, a. 4; ON TRUTH, q. 10, a. 10. — Bl. (now St.) Albertus (Magnus), here (in his Commentary) in a. 4 and 5. — (Bl.) Peter of Tarentaise, here in q. 1, a. 5. quaestiuncula 1. — Richard of Middleton, here in a. 1, q. 5. — Giles the Roman, here in 3rd. princ., q. 2. — (Bl.) Dionysius the Carthusian, here in q. 5.

QUESTION IV

Whether charity in the universal is cognizable even by one not having it?

Fourth, there is asked, whether charity is cognizable by one not having (it); and that (it is) not, seems:

1. Because everything which is cognized, either is cognized through (its) *essence*, or through a *similitude*. But (charity is cognized)[3] not through *essence*, because it is not essentially in the soul of a sinner [anima peccatrice]; if, therefore, it is cognized, this is through a *similitude*. But on the contrary: the Gloss on the twelfth (chapter) of the Second (Letter of St. Paul) to the Corinthians[4] says: « The third kind of vision, by which love [dilectio] is caught sight of by the intellective (power), contains those things, which do not have images, which are not themselves, similar to themselves », therefore, the similitude of charity is not other than charity: therefore, if anyone lacks charity, he lacks its similitude, and thus never cognizes charity.

2. Likewise, if one not having charity cognizes it, either, therefore, through an *innate species*, or through an *acquired* one, or through an *effect*, or through *the first light*.[5] Not through an *innate* one, because the created soul is as a <u>tabula rasa</u>;[6] not through an *acquired species*, because every acquired species is acquired by means of sense and imagination,[7] but the species of charity does not occur in the sense nor in the imagination. Likewise, not through an *effect*, because no one cognizes anything through an effect, unless he knows, that it is its effect.[8] Wherefore no one recognizes [cognoscit] through an eclipse (of the Moon) the interposition of the Earth, unless he knows, that (the Earth's) interposition its cause. If, therefore, one cognizes (it) through an effect, it is necessary [oportet] that he first know, how then [quoniam][9] charity is its cause,

---

[1] Cf. (St.) Bernard, First Sermon in Septuagesima, Second Sermon in the Octave of Easter and the Second Sermon on Pentecost. — A little before this, the Vatican edition, with one or the other codex reads *through many other probable signs* [per multa alia signa probabilia].

[2] From the manuscripts and editions 1, 2, and 3, we have supplied *namely* [scilicet]. A little below this very many codices, such as A G K I K T etc., together with edition 1, read *that* [id] for *that* [illud].

[3] Supply: *charity is cognized.* — The Vatican ed. with cod. cc omits *But* [Sed], which, however, is extant in all the other codd. and in ed. 1.

[4] Verse 4. — The Gloss has been taken from (St.) Augustine's, ON A LITERAL EXPOSITION OF GENESIS, ch. 6, n. 15, where together with edition 1 there is had *intellected love* [dilectio intellecta] for *love ... by the intellective (power)* [intellectiva], and such an explanation is added: For a man and/or tree and/or the Sun and whatsoever other bodies, whether celestial or terrestrial, are also seen present in their forms, and absent are thought of by images impressed upon the spirit [animo], and cause two genera of (things) seen, one through the senses of the body, the other through the spirit [spiritum], by which those images are contained. But is love never otherwise seen present in the species by which it is, and otherwise absent in some image similar to itself? Certainly

not, but as much as can be discerned by the mind, (love) itself is discerned by one more, by another less; but if something belonging to a corporal image be thought of, it is not discerned.

[5] The Vatican edition, a little after *innate* [innatam] having added *or his own light* [seu lucem propriam], here omits *or through the first light* [per primam lucem], but breaking with all the manuscripts, however, edition 1 has *or in the first light* [aut in prima luce].

[6] Aristotle, ON THE SOUL, Bk. III, text 14 (ch. 4): But it is necessary [oportet] that (it be) thus, as on a tablet on which nothing has been written by the act, which indeed accedes in the intellect.

[7] Cf. Aristotle, ON THE SOUL, Bk. III, text 30 and 39 (chs. 7 and 8) and ON SENSE AND sensibles, ch. 6.

[8] The many codices, such as A G H I N S T V Y Z ee and ff more briefly and very well, in which reading *its* [illius] refers to the preceding *anything* [aliquid], while the others together with the Vatican edition indeed in the same sense, but with a varied construction of sentence, *that the cause is its effect* [quod causa sit illius effectus].

[9] Codex X has *that* [quod] in place of *how then* [quoniam].

and, thus, pre-cognize charity; not, therefore, through the effect. *If you say*, that he cognizes (it) in that *eternal truth*, either this will be *effectively*, or *formally*. If *effectively*, thus all are cognized in that, which causes all to know, whatsoever are known; but if *formally* or exemplarily, therefore, it seems, that either it impresses[1] some species on the intellect, and/or it is necessary, that the truth itself and/or an exemplar is caught sight of; the former (argument) of which is disproved,[2] but the latter (is) manifestly false.

BUT ON THE CONTRARY: 1. Sinners desire charity; but no one desires what he does not cognize, because the unknown [incognita] cannot be loved, just as (St.) Augustine says:[3] therefore, they do cognize charity.

2. Likewise, someone having charity can have cognition of it; but everything which occurs in the apprehending intellect, can be conserved in the memory; therefore, let one suppose [ponatur], that this cognition is impressed upon the memory, and that at length [demum][4] he falls from charity, it is established, that the one lapsed from charity retains his memory: therefore, he still cognizes it, therefore, charity can be cognized by one not having (it).

3. Likewise, if charity is cognized by the one having (it), either this is through (its) *essence*, or through a *similitude*.[5] But I prove, that (it is) through a similitude, because the intellect cognizes nothing, unless it be informed by it; but charity is a habit of the affection, therefore according to essence (charity) does not step forth from it:[6] therefore, if it is united to the intellect and informs it, this is through a *similitude*; but a similitude can be had by one not having charity: ergo etc..

4. Likewise, (St.) Augustine says in the eleventh (book) ON THE TRINITY, that for this, that the intellect understand what is in the memory, it is necessary, that the insight [aciem] of the intellect be informed: therefore, much more strongly for this, that it understand what is in the will: therefore, if it understands charity, the intellect is informed by something;[8] *not* by the substance of charity: therefore, by a similitude, therefore, the same as before.

CONCLUSION

Charity can also be cognized by one not having it, not by the cognition of experience, but by speculative (cognition), and indeed not through a similitude abstracted by the senses, but through a certain innate truth of the soul.

I RESPOND: It must be said, that by the cognition of experience charity is not cognized except by the one having (it); however, by the cognition of speculation it is certain that charity is cognized even by the one not having (it). Moreover, *the manner* of this cognition cannot be through the essence of charity, nor through a similitude acquired by the senses. therefore, it is necessary, that it be through an *infused similitude*, and/or *an innate one*. But both, which are thus cognized by a man, are said by (St.) Augustine[9] to be cognized in the Eternal Truth, or because the Truth infuses cognition (of them), as (He did) in the Prophets, or because He impresses (it) from its foundation [a conditione], according to that (verse):[10] *Sealed upon us is the light of Thy Face, o Lord* etc.. But charity is not cognized by sinners through an infused species: therefore, it is necessary [oportet], that it be cognized through an innate one.

Moreover, there can be an innate species in a twofold manner: either *a similitude only*, just as the species of a stone, or a such a *similitude*, that (there is)[11] a certain *truth* in it. The first species is as a picture; and of this the soul has been created bereft [nuda]. The second species some impression of most high truth in the soul, just as by a grace of the Word there has been given to the soul from its foundation a certain, directive *light* and a certain, natural *direction*; there has also been given to it an *affection*[12] of will. Therefore, the soul cognizes, what is *rectitude*, and what *affection*, and thus, what (is) a *rectitude of affection*, and since charity is this, it cognizes charity through a certain *truth*, which truth, however, is a *similitude* of charity; and then (the soul) rightly has

---

[1] Some codices, such as aa and bb, together with edition 1, have *it may impress* [imprimat]. Next edition 1 after *truth itself* [ipsa veritas] has *or* [sive] for *and/or* [vel].

[2] At the beginning of this argument, where it is argued, that charity cannot be cognized through *an innate species*.

[3] ON THE TRINITY, Bk. X, ch. 1, n. 1: That which anyone in a word does not know, he cannot by any (nuptial) agreement love [amare nullo pacto potest].

[4] Codex X has *then* [deinde].

[5] In the Vatican edition, not trusting in the manuscripts and edition 1, there is added: *Not through its essence, it is established* [Per essentiam non, constat], and next in place of *I prove* [probo] there is had *it is proven* [probatur].

[6] Understand: the affection. The Vatican edition together with codex cc faultily, and breaking with all the other codices together with edition 1, has *it*(*i. e. the similitude, or essence*) [illam]; which also a little below this in place of *but* [sed] puts *and this* [et haec].

[7] Chs. 7 & 8, nn. 11-14, where <u>inter alia</u> he says: But, when it is thought, out of that (species) which the memory holds, it is expressed in the insight [acie] of the one thinking, and by reminiscing there is formed that species, which is a quasi offspring of that which the memory holds.

[8] With the help of the manuscripts and editions 1, 2, and 3, we have expunged here the particle *and* [et], added by the Vatican edition.

[9] See below in the Scholium, where the sentence of (St.) Augustine concerning the manner of human cognition has been propounded more at length. On the cognition of the Prophets, cf. ON A LITERAL EXPOSITION OF GENESIS, Bk. XII, ch. 31, n. 59: Moreover, (something) else is that light, by which the soul is enlightened, to catch sight of all (things) truthfully intellected either in itself and/or in it; for that (light) now is God Himself etc..

[10] Psalm 4:7. — A little before this the Vatican edition, contrary to very many codices and edition 1, faultily reads *among the Prophets* [in Prophetis], and next, contrary to all the codices and editions 1, 2 and 3, has *it may be impressed* [imprimatur] in place of *He impresses (it)* [imprimit].

[11] Codex X adds *there is* [est].

[12] In codex O there is had *a natural affection* [affectio naturalis].

a reckoning *of (its) similitude*, while it is accepted by the intellect; yet, it has a reckoning *of (its) truth*, insofar as it is in the soul.

Wherefore, because (St.) Augustine says,[1] that habits of this kind are cognized in truth itself and through simili-

tudes, which are the same as they (are),[2] he does not say this, because some species comes to be in the intellect of the one cognizing, but because in the soul there is no pure species, but a certain truth impressed by the truth itself, and thus is clear the response to the objections.

SCHOLIUM

I. Having distinguished a twofold cognition, namely, that of *experience* (intuitive) and that of *speculation* (abstractive), he resolves the question itself, which surely is of the greatest importance for the theory of human cognition, with a twofold conclusion. Then he explains the *manner* of this *speculative* cognition with seven propositions. For the confirmation of the response we here subjoin, what (Bl.) Peter of Tarentaise and Alexander of Hales say on this manner. (Bl.) Peter, here in q. 1, a. 5, quaestiuncula 2, (says): « By the cognition *of experience* charity cannot be cognized except by the one having (it), but by *speculative* cognition it can, not through its essence or through a species, which is the same as [quod] it — in this manner it is seen only by the one having (it) — but through the species or through the similitude, which is not the same as it; and this in a twofold manner: either *through an acquired species*, which is its similitude and/or rather its act, left in the memory to make it present [ad eius praesentiam], and in this manner it is seen by the one, who once had it; unless one erases that species by forgetfulness, and in this manner a Saint in the Fatherland (of Heaven) shall see, that he had faith and hope, that is, through a certain vestige of faith, as (St.) Augustine says On the Trinity, Bk. XIV, ch. 3; and/or *through an innate species*, and in this manner it can be seen by anyone whomsoever, not that which is *a species only*, as the species of a stone (is) in the soul, because the soul does not have such a species of charity created with (it), but through an innate species, *which is the thing in itself*, and yet *has a similitude* with charity. For the soul has in itself [apud se] certain seeds of all the virtues and through them has a desire and a certain universal cognition of virtues, just as one comes to cognize a conclusion through principles ». He responds the same to the objection: 'the soul is created as a tabula rasa': « This is understood in regard the to the species, which are only intentions, not (in regard to) things; however, innate habits of this kind are indeed in themselves *things*, however, inasmuch as through them others are cognized as similar, they are quasi *species* ». All these (words) agree nearly word for word [ad verbum] with the doctrine of the Seraphic (Doctor). Alexander of Hales, Summa, p. III, a. 61, m. 7, a. 1 has these (words): « Anyone, whether good or evil, has from (his) creation an enriched [inditam] reckoning of good and evil, according to which (St.) Augustine and (St. Severinus) Boethius speak. Therefore, just as in the notion of the principles *of the true* there is the notion of conclusions in the universal, so in the notion *of the good* there has been impressed in us in the universal the notion of grace in the universal; and from that notion of the good we can know, what grace is in the universal, that is that it is a certain quality in the soul. For since grace is a good, and we have a notion of the good in the universal impressed upon us, from that we can put in clear light [arguere], that grace is; but this will be a notion in the universal, not in a proper reckoning. Cf. ibid., q. 28, m. 1, a. 2. Besides these (authors), cf. Richard of Middleton, here in a. 1, q. 4. From these it is clear, that the intellect can from *an innate light of truth* form an intelligible species, which informs the intellect's insight, to simultaneously have « a reckoning of (its) similitude, while it is accepted by the intellect, and yet a reckoning of (its) truth, in so as it is in the soul », as is had here in the body (of the response).

II. What is said by the Seraphic (Doctor) in this question is of no small importance, for the right understanding of his sentence concerning the manner of human cognition. What it is *to cognize in the eternal truth*, has already been explained above in d. 3, p. I, q. 1 in the Scholium. — What, according to St. Bonaventure, is an *innate species*, and in what sense it can be said (to be) itself innate to the soul, will be here manifestly explained, namely, that this must be understood according to *habit* or the light co-created with the soul,

which is called the natural judgement [naturale iudicatorium], not according to *actual* species or innate ideas. Which is more amply confirmed and explained the same Seraphic Doctor, Sent., Bk. II, d. 39, a. 1, q. 2, where there is asked, whether the conscience is an innate habit, or an acquired one. Having rejected the opinion of Plato, that the cognitive habits of the soul are simply innate, but given to forgetfulness for a time, he asserts, that there are three opinions in this matter, consenting in this, that the cognitive habits are neither entirely innate, nor entirely acquired, but in a certain manner innate, in a certain manner acquired; however, that they disagree in assigning *the manner*, according to which these habits have been acquired and/or are innate. Having rejected two opinions as insufficient, he concludes, that « the cognitive habits are in a certain manner innate in us by reason of the enriched light of the soul, they have also in a certain manner been acquired by reason of the species. And in this indeed the words of the Philosopher and of (St.) Augustine agree. For all agree in this, that to the cognitive power belongs an enriched light, which is called the natural judgement; but the species and similitudes of things are acquired by us by means of the sense, just as the Philosopher expressly says in many places; and this also experience teaches ». Next he says that one must attend to the distinction between the very evident, first principles, of which « the cognition by reason of the light itself is said to be innate in us, *because that light suffices for knowing them* after the reception of the species without any superadded persuasion on account of their evidence », and among the cognition of particular conclusions, the cognition of which has been acquired in virtue of this, that the light innate to us *does not fully suffice* for knowing them, but is lacking some persuasion and new habilitation [habilitatione nova] etc.. — Then by responding to that question, whether every cognition is from sense, he concludes in this manner: « It must be said, that (it does) not. For necessarily one is bound to posit, that the soul knows [novit] God and itself and those (things) which are in it without the support [adminiculo] of the exterior senses. Whence if the Philosopher sometimes says, that nothing is in the intellect, which was not first in sense, and that every cognition has it rise from the sense, it must be understood of those which indeed have being in the soul through *an abstracted* similitude; and they are said to be in the soul after the manner of writing. And on this account the Philosopher very notably says, that nothing *has been written* in the soul, not because there is in it no *knowledge* [notitia], but because there is in it no *picture* and/or *abstracted* similitude. And this is, what (St.) Augustine says in the book, On the City of God: God has inserted in us a noble judgement, where what belongs to light, what to darkness, is cognized in a book of light, which is truth, because truth has been naturally impressed in the heart of men ». — This sentence verbatim, whether in this or in the other book of St. Augustine, we have not found. But it briefly comprises, what St. Augustine proves many times by a longer discourse, especially in The City of God, Bk. XI, ch. 27, n. 2, where among other things he says: « But they (the animals) are not able to touch that incorporeal light, by which our mind is in a certain manner irradiated, so that we are able to rightly judge of all these (things). For inasmuch as we grasp it, insomuch are we able to do that. Nevertheless, there is in the senses of irrational animals, even if it is in no manner a science, but certainly a certain similitude of science ... But we thus grasp them (corporal things) with the sense of the body, that *we judge* of them not by the sense of the body. For we have another *sense belonging to the interior man* [alium interioris hominis sensum]

---

[1] The Vatican edition, not trusting in the manuscripts and in five of the first editions, has *since (St.) Augustine says* [cum Augustinus dicat].

[2] Supply: *things, which in this case are habits* [res, quae hoc in casu sunt habitus]. See above, in the first arg. of the Question. The Vatican ed.

incongruously has *it (is)* [ipse]. As has been noted, in the codd. *it* [ipse] and *these* [ipsae] are written the same. — Next, trusting in the mss. and in ed. 1, we have substituted *comes to be* [fiat] in place of *is* [sit]. At the end of the Resp., ed. 1 has *solution* [solutio] for *response* [responsio].

far more present than this one, by which we sense just and unjust (things): the just through an intelligible species, the unjust through its privation. To the office of this sense not the sight of the pupil, not the aperture of the ear, not the nostrils of the nose, not the taste of the pallet, not any corporeal touch approaches. In this (interior sense) I am certain that I both am and know it, and I love these (acts) and that I love (them) I am similarly certain ».

III. St. Bonaventure completely proves himself (to be) a most faithful disciple of St. Augustine, just as in other questions, so in his whole work concerning the doctrine of human cognition. Wherefore, those things, which he disputes about this matter in this question, exhibit not but a summary of those, which St. Augustine treats, according to his own custom and at length in very many (of his) books, v. g., On Free Will, Bk. II; On the True Religion, ch. 29 ff.; On a Literal Exposition of Genesis, Bk. XII. We consider it worth the while to prove this by example, by proposing from books VIII and IX of St. Augustine's On the Trinity those fundaments of human cognition, which St. Bonaventure here either presupposes, and/or explicitly asserts.

1. There St. Augustine most openly distinguishes between the cognition of the senses (of the fantasy) and (that) of the intellect: « And indeed, when I wish to speak of Carthage, I seek it in myself [apud me], to speak, and in myself I find the phantasm of Carthage, but I accepted that through (my) body, i.e. through the sense of the body ... But not thus do I seek, what is just, nor thus do I find, none thus do I intuit, when I speak of it » etc. (On the Trinity, Bk. VIII, ch. 6, n. 9).

2. He distinguishes in intellectual cognition the concepts formed through abstraction from the sensible things and those not formed through abstraction: « For neither by seeing many minds with corporeal eyes do we gather through similitude a general and/or special knowledge [notitiam] of the human mind, but we intuit the inviolable truth (of it) » (On the Trinity, Bk. IX, ch. 6, n. 9).

3. He asserts, that some intellectual concepts, which we have, suppose experience, whether external or internal: « But what it is to die, and what it is to life, we at least know, because we also live, and we see and have experienced sometimes the dead and the dying » (On the Trinity, Bk. VIII, ch. 5, n. 8).

4. He says, that the knowledge [notitiam] of certain things has been impressed on the human soul: « For neither among all these goods, either which I completely remember and/or which are discerned [cernuntur] or cognized, would we say that one is better than another, when we judge in a true manner, *unless there has been impressed upon us a notion of the good itself,* according to which we would also prove something and prefer [praeponeremus] another to it » (On the Trinity, Bk. VIII, ch. 3, n. 4). For we regularly have a knowledge quasi *infixed* in human nature ... According to the species and genera of things either *implanted by nature* and/or collected by experience, we think of facts of this very kind (miracles and the Resurrection of Christ), so that our faith is not a fiction » (ibid., ch. 4 and 5, n. 7. « What, therefore, do we know [novimus], whether specially or generally, of that Excellence of the Trinity, as there are many such trinities, some of which we have experienced, so that through the *impressed* rule of a similitude, and/or a special and/or general knowledge, we also believe It to be such » etc. (ibid., ch. 5, n. 8).

5. He asserts, that certain (things) can be cognized by man in *the truth*, and even in *the eternal truth*. But he says least of all [minime], that this comes to be through *an immediate* complete sight [conspectum] of eternal reasons, as the Ontologists want; but he ought to be understood according to that interpretation, which the better Scholastics exhibit; cf. above d. 3, p. I, a. 1, Scholium. In On the Trinity, Bk. VIII, ch. 6, n. 9, (St. Augustine) proposes the question, which together with that which is here treated thoroughly by St. Bonaventure, greatly convenes, namely 'in what manner does an unjust man cognize the just spirit [animum iustum], which he loves, and he solves that (question) thus: « What a *spirit* is, as has been said, we know [novimus] out of ourselves; for there is a spirit in us. But what *a just one* is, whence to we know it, if we are not just? ... Or do certain signs show themselves [emicant] through the movement of a body, by which this or that man appears to be just? But whence does he know, that those signs are of a just spirit, not knowing, what entirely a just one is? Therefore, he does know. But where do we know, what a just one is, even when we are not yet just? If we know (this) outside of ourselves, we know in

some body. But this matter does not belong to a body. Therefore, we know in ourselves, what a just one is. I do not even find this elsewhere, when I seek, to speak of this, except in my very self ... And when I want to speak of *Carthage*, I seek it in myself, to speak, and in myself I find the phantasm of Carthage, but I accepted it through the body, i. e. through the sensing of the body ... But I do not thus seek, what a *just one* is, nor do I find (it) thus nor thus do I intuit (it), when I speak of it ... It is (something) wonderful, that a spirit sees in itself, what elsewhere it never sees, and that it sees (something) true, that it sees the true, just spirit itself, and that it is a spirit itself, and that it is not the just spirit, which it sees in its very self. There is not another just spirit in the not-yet-just spirit, is there? ... Or is that which it sees, *an interior truth, present to the spirit,* which prevails to intuit it? Nor do all prevail (to do so); and those who prevail to intuit, even that, which they intuit, they all are not, that is, they are not even just spirits themselves, as they can see and say, what a just spirit is. Wherefore can these be, except by inhering to the very same form, which they intuit, so that from this they be formed and be just spirts, not only discerning [cernentes] ... And whence do these inhere to the form, except by loving (it)? ... Therefore, a man, who is believed (to be) just, is loved *out of that form and truth*, which the one, who loves, discerns and understands in himself; *but that form and truth* he is not, in whatever other manner it be loved. For neither do we find anything such beside that, so that, when it is unknown [incognita], by believing (in it) we love it, for the reason [ex eo] that we already know something such. For whatever such you would look at, it is; and it is not anything such, since it alone is such, as it itself is ». Ibid., ch. 9, n. 13: « However, that one must live in this manner, we believe (has been) heard from the ministers of God, and not from others, but we catch sight (of it) from within in ourselves, and/or rather from above ourselves *in the truth itself.* Therefore, (St. Paul), whom we believe to have lived in this manner, out of this that we see, we love. And unless we would chiefly love this form, which we discern as always stable and incommutable, we would not, for that reason, love him, because his life, when he lived in the flesh, we hold by faith was co-adapted to and congruent with this form ». Book IX, ch. 6, n. 9: « *We intuit the inviolable truth*, from which we perfectly define, as much as we can, not of what kind the mind of any many whatsoever is, but of what kind it ought to be according to sempiternal reasons ». Ibid., n. 11: « That very *form of unshaken and stable truth*, both in which I would enjoy a man, as one believing him (to be) good, and in which I take counsel, whether he be good; that same light of incorruptible and most sincere reason, by (its) imperturbable eternity, pours over the gaze of my mind and that cloud of (my) fantasy, which I discern above, when I think of the same man, whom I had seen ». Ibid., ch. 7, n. 12: « Therefore, in that *eternal truth*, out of which all temporal things have been made, the form, according to which we are and according to which either in us and/or in bodies we work anything by true and right reason, we look upon with the sight of the mind, and from it we have a truthful, conceived, knowledge [notitiam], as a word in us, and by speaking we beget it within, nor does it depart from us by being born ».

6. These last words indicate another part of the Augustinian teaching [sententiae], which St. Bonaventure touches upon at the end of this question, namely, that the habits of the soul, which are cognized in the truth itself and through similitudes, which are the same as themselves (i. e. habits), are not cognized without some species formed in the intellect of the one cognizing (them). In On the Trinity, Bk. IX, ch. 3, n. 3, (St. Augustine) says: « Therefore, the mind itself, just as it gathers knowledge [notitias] of corporeal things through the senses of the body, so (it gathers that) of incorporeals through itself. Therefore, it also *knows* its very self *through its very self*, since it is incorporeal ». In ibid., ch. 11, n. 16:, speaking of the cognition of God, he shows, that in it « there comes to be some similitude of God by that knowledge, however, inferior it is, because it is in an inferior nature; the creature, indeed, the spirit, but the Creator, God. From which is gathered, that when the mind itself knows and approves itself, so there is by the same knowledge a word of it, such as is entirely on par with it and equal and identical [identidem], because neither is it knowledge of an inferior essence, as of the body, nor of a superior, as of God. And since it has by knowledge a similitude to that thing, which it knows, that is, to which the knowledge belongs, this (mind) has perfect (knowledge) » etc..

DOUBTS ON THE TEXT OF THE MASTER

DOUBT I

In this part, there are the doubts about the text (of Master Peter), and first there is the doubt concerning this consequence of (St. Augustine's reasoning): *It follows that, he who loves (his) neighbor, loves chiefly that love.* For this consequence of his does not seem to be valid. For although it is possible, that love be loved, it, however, is not necessary, that anyone love it; for we frequently love many (things), which we do not want to love.

Likewise, there is a doubt concerning this consequence of (the Saint's reasoning): *It follows that he who loves love, loves God*; because, either he understands (this) of *uncreated* (Love), or (of)[1] created (love). If of *created*, it is not at all valid [nihil valet] (to say): 'he loves something created, therefore, (loves something) Uncreated'; if of *uncreated*, then in no manner does this agree [concordat] with the prior sentence, that love, by which we love[2] (our) neighbor, is created love.

I RESPOND: It must be said, that each consequence is good in the proposed (argument). For there is a certain love [amor], in which there is not resting [quietatio] nor delectation nor complacence, as for example that which is from the proneness of corruption, against which reason sits [obsistit]. However, there is a certain love, which is with delectation, complacence and resting; and in such love there is not only acceptance of the thing loved, nay[3] also of love itself; and such love is charity, and for that reason it follows: 'that he who loves [amat] (his) neighbor, loves love [dilectionem], that is, he accepts it [acceptat].

But, since it follows well: 'that he who accepts something out of himself, accepts much more that, in which there is found the reckoning of acceptance';[4] if love [dilectio], for the very (reason) by which (it is) love, is accepted, a greater love is more accepted. Therefore, since our love is an exemplified love [dilection exemplata], and the Divine Love is[5] the Exemplar of every upright love, and in That there is a first and most high reckoning of every acceptance: hence it is, that it follows, that he who loves [diligit] love, loves God. Whence (St.) Augustine[6] argued from this supposition, that the very charity or love of neighbor is love with acceptance, and from this held the first consequence;[7] and from the other supposition, that the first reckoning of

acceptance is in the exemplifying love [dilectione exemplante], not the exemplified one; and from this is clear the second (consequence).[8]

DOUBT II

Likewise, is asked of this which he says: *Behold you already can have God more known than (your) brother.* For it seems false, because in the last (chapter)[9] of the First (Letter of St. Paul) to Timothy there is said of God, that *He dwells in light inaccessible.* Besides, one knows of (one's) brother, *what* he is, but of God one does not know, *what* He is, but *whether* He is; moreover,[10] he does not speak as much as regards the cognition of, *whether* he is.

I RESPOND: It must be said, that 'that something *be cognized with greater certitude*' is in a twofold manner, because the certitude of cognition is according to presence; moreover something is more present in a twofold manner: either as much as regards the *reckoning of a cognizable*, or as much as regards (its) *substance*.[11] As much as regards *substance* God is more present to every thing than any other thing (is); but as much as regards *reason for cognizing*, this is in a twofold manner: either on the part of *the cognizable*, just as the Sun is present to the blind man, and yet the blind man is absent to the light, so God is more present than a brother; but if on the part of *the one cognizing*, thus the brother is more present, because he is present to the eyes of the flesh,[12] on which (things) cognition thrives [viget] according to the present state.

In another manner, it can be said, that something is more present in a twofold manner in the reckoning of a cognizable: either according to *effect*, and/or according to *itself*. According to *itself* a brother is more known, according to *effect* God is more known. Because the divine effect, which is love [dilectio], enters the soul itself and is present to it and more cognized than the brother.[13]

DOUBT III

Likewise, is asked of that (verse) in the fourth (chapter) of the Canonical (Letter of St.) John, which is in the text: *He who loves, remains in the light.* For it seems improperly said, that light

---

[1] Some codd., such as H K aa ee & ff, with edition 1 repeat here *of* [de].

[2] From the mss. and ed. 1 we have put *we love* [diligimus] in place of *one loves* [diligit]. A little before this, cod. O, having put *consequence* [consequentia] in place of *sentence* [sententia], reads *nay love is equivocated, because the* [immo aequivocatur dilection quia] for *that* [quia].

[3] Codex dd has *but* [sed] for *nay* [immo].

[4] We follow not a few of the codices, such as F G H K and T, by putting *acceptance* [acceptationis] in place of *love* [dilectionis], the reading of which is confirmed by the entire progress of the context. Next some manuscripts, such as Y and Z, prefix to the comparative *a greater* [maior] the particle *and* [et], and then after *more* [magis] many codices with edition 1 omit the certainly to be supplied *is accepted* [acceptatur].

[5] The reading of the Vatican edition, in which there is had *and a divine love as* [dilectio divina ut] in place of *and the Divine Love is* [dilection divina sit], is corrected with the help of the manuscripts and editions 1, 2, 3, and 6, from which we also a little below this after *hence* [hinc] supply the *it is that* [est quod]. Some codices, such as A G H I K T etc. with edition 1 prefix to the word *hence* [hinc] the particle *and* [et].

[6] ON THE TRINITY, Bk. VIII, ch. 8, n. 12, from which the text of this doubt has been taken.

[7] That is, that he who loves (his) neighbor, loves love itself. — (A little before this) with the agreement of very many codices, we have substituted *and from this* [et ex hoc] for *and from this* [et ex hac].

[8] Namely: that he who loves love, loves God. — Edition 1 has *from this* [ex hac] in place of *from this* [ex hoc]. — See more on this matter above in q. 2, and in Bl. (now St.) Albertus (Magnus), here in a. 3. — St. Thomas and (Bl.) Peter of Tarentaise, here in the exposition of the text.

[9] Verse 16, where the Vulgate reads *inhabits* [inhabitat] in place of *dwells* [habitat].

[10] Not a few codices, such as A I V and X, with edition 1, omit less well *moreover* [autem]; codex Y adds *Master (Peter)* [Magister].

[11] The Vatican edition and codex cc in this proposition, contrary to many manuscripts and edition 1, have *present* [praesens] in place of *more present* [praesentius], and next contrary to very many codices and to edition 1, having omitted the first *either* [aut] they read *the reckoning for a cognizable* [rationem cognoscibli] in place of *a reckoning of the cognizable* [cognosciblis], which they transfer to after *substance* [substantia]. In place of *a reckoning of the cognizable* [rationem cognoscibilis] it would be more pleasing to have *the reckoning of it being cognized* [rationem cognoscendi], if the codices had favored it.

[12] From the manuscripts and edition 1, we have substituted *to the eyes of the flesh* [oculis carnis] for *to fleshy eyes* [oculis carneis].

[13] On the twofold manner, by which God is present to our intellect, see above d. 3, p. I, a. 1, q. 1. — In the solution of this doubt agree Bl. (now St.) Albertus (Magnus), here in a. 4. — (Bl.) Peter of Tarentaise, here in q. 1, a. 6. — Richard of Middleton in a. 1, q. 3.

respects cognition, just as warmth (respects) affection: therefore, it ought rather to have been said: he remains in warmth, than he remains in the light.

I Respond: It must be said, that it belongs to light to manifest. But 'to manifest something to someone' is in a twofold manner: either just as the way *of things to be cognized*, or just as the way *of things to be done*. The first is through *knowledge* [scientia], and against that light is opposed the shadow [tenebra] of simple ignorance: the second is through *grace*, whence (there is written): *(His) anointing will teach you concerning all (things)*;[1] and against that is the shadow of malice or of sin; and of this light and of those shadows blessed John speaks, as is clear in the text, and in the eleventh (chapter) of Ecclesiasticus:[2] *Error and shadows have been created together for sinners*. And since charity is always with grace, the other virtues not, for that reasons he says: *He who loves, remains in the light*, through appropriation.[3]

Doubt IV

Likewise, is asked of this which (Master Peter) says, that *among divine gifts nothing is greater than charity*. For it seems that he says (something) false, because the gift of *wisdom* is posited as the most excellent among all the gifts, and/or if charity and wisdom are the same, charity will not retain (its) prerogative among the gifts. *Likewise* there is asked of the consequence: if charity is chief among the gifts of God, and there is no one greater than the Holy Spirit: therefore, the Holy Spirit is charity. Therefore[4] either he speaks of *created* charity, or (of) *uncreated* (Charity); if of *Uncreated*, then, therefore, he proves the same through the same; if of *created*, then there seems to be no consequence, because it is not valid, that 'if created charity is greater among the created gifts, that it is the Holy Spirit'.

I Respond: It must be said, that the aforesaid authority of (St.) Augustine can be understood of *created* and *Uncreated* charity; and it is true [habet veritatem] for each. If of *Uncreated*, it is certain; if of *created*, it is greatest among the gifts, because it has more in itself of the reckoning of goodness or of goodness itself, than any gift,[5] speaking precisely. For there are certain gifts, which are without charity; and this indeed is certain, that they are lesser. Certain ones presuppose charity, just as[6] the gift of wisdom (does). For charity is, that which gives sense to taste, so that they taste eternal goods according to it (i.e. to charity). Whence, wisdom adds above (this)

a certain further ability,[7] which compared to charity is a lesser good, but insofar as it encloses [claudit] charity, is a greater good by reason of that which it presupposes. And thus it is clear, that charity, precisely speaking, is the most excellent gift, but wisdom, by presupposing or implying the gift of charity, is said (to be) the most excellent one.

To that which is objected concerning the consequence, it must be said, that in each manner it is good. For if it is understood of *uncreated Charity*, if[8] It is the first and chief gift, and the Holy Spirit is of this kind: it is necessary [oportet] that it be the Holy Spirit, because what is said through a superabundance, convenes with one alone.[9] But if of *created* charity, then the consequence (of St. Augustine) is to be understood on the part of the noun, in this manner: 'if created charity is the greatest (gift)[10] among created gifts, and the Holy spirit is the greatest of gifts: therefore, it is better named with the name of the most excellent Gift than with another'. Therefore it follows, that the Holy Spirit is charity, but not the created one, nay that One which is God.[11]

Doubt V

Likewise, is asked of this which he says: *Certainly not in the same manner has it been said, that the Substance of God is our patience*. For it seems that he speaks badly, because the charity, by which we love God, is not God Himself, unless we understand *by which we love* exemplarily and/or causally: therefore, since it is similar concerning patience, it seems that (St.) Augustine badly destroys[12] that simile: *Likewise*, when God makes us loving, just as patient, for what reason is God said (to be) our charity, as (He is) our patience?

I Respond: It must be said, that God is charity both *essentially* and *causally*: essentially, because in Himself He is Love [amor]; causally, because in us He effects love. But God is not essentially *patience*, but only causally; and for that reason Scripture, hinting at[13] this diverse manner, says, that God is *our* patience, and that God is charity, without adding (anything more than that). Moreover, the reason for this is, that[14] certain habits mean *incompletion*, just as patience, hope and (habits) of this kind (are), which do not occur in God through (His) Essence, but through (Him as their) Cause, because (those) of this kind are from God. Moreover, there are certain habits which

---

[1] 1 Jn. 2:27, where the Vulgate reads: *His anointing shall teach you concerning all (things)*. — The Vatican edition, contrary to the manuscripts, after *whence (there is written)* [unde] adds *through (St.) John* [per Ioannem].

[2] Verse 16.

[3] Cf. Bl. (now St.) Albertus (Magnus), here in a. 6; St. Thomas and (Bl.) Peter of Tarentaise, here in the exposition of the text.

[4] Edition 1 has *for* [enim] in place of *therefore* [ergo], which also next after [in the English text, the second] *either* [aut] repeats *of ... Charity* [de caritate].

[5] Edition 1 reads *any of the gifts* [aliquod donorum], but codex dd has *any other gift* [aliquod donum aliud]. Next a few codices, such as V and Z, omit *which are* [quae sunt].

[6] The Vatican edition, not trusting in the manuscripts and in edition 1, reads *as* [velut]. Edition 1 after *just as* [sicut] adds *is* [est].

[7] We exhibit the reading of nearly all the manuscripts, by putting *ability* [habilitatem] for *virtue, which dwells* [virtutem quae habitat]; edition 1 *enabling* [habilitationem]. A little below this, from many codices, such as A G H I K T W etc. and edition 1, we have substituted *a lesser*

good [minus bonum] for *less good* [minus bona], because the former is more distinct and corresponds more with what is subjoined.

[8] The Vatican edition has *thus* [sic] in place of *if* [sic], and next after *of this kind* [huiusmodi] it adds *therefore* [ergo], but the authority of the manuscripts and of edition 1 withstand this, and do so well, because it deals only with *the consequence to be shown*.

[9] Aristotle, Topics, Bk. V, ch. 3 (ch. 5).

[10] Some codices, such as I and T, add *gift* [donum].

[11] Cf. Bl. (now St.) Albertus (Magnus), here in a. 7. — (Bl.) Peter of Tarentaise and Richard of Middleton, here on the text.

[12] Codex T has the subjunctive form of *destroys* [destruat].; edition 1 reads *builds up* [astruit].

[13] The fault of the Vatican edition, of having *finding* [inveniens] in place of *hinting at* [innuens], we have corrected with the help of the manuscripts. — The text of Sacred Scripture on this diverse manner can be found here in the text of Master (Peter), ch. 3.

[14] From the more ancient manuscripts and edition 1, we have substituted *that* [quia] for *that* [quod] and a little below this *which (habits)* [qui] for *which (virtues)* [quae].

mean a *complement*, and (habits)[1] of this kind are in God essentially, just as charity and wisdom and (those of) this kind are. But it must be noted, that (St.) Augustine wants to say, that God is charity essentially, but he does not want to say, that He is *our* charity essentially, but (rather) *causally* and *exemplarily*.[2] For although all virtues have an cognoscitive [cognoscitivum] exemplar in God and all have an exemplar according to a *distant* similitude, yet certain virtues do not have in God one corresponding to themselves *through all (things)*, just as "patient", which means two (things), namely 'suffering' and 'bearing up under sufferings'. As much as regards the first, it does not have one corresponding in God, but only as much as regards the second. Moreover, charity has in God a corresponding Love [amorem] through all (things), and[3] not only an *essential* Love, but also *a personal One*: and for that reason the authorities say,[4] that "the Holy Spirit is the Charity, by which we love God"; and the ablative, "*by which*", means the habitude not only of an efficient cause, but also of a formal one, not of a perfecting one, but of an exemplifying one.[5]

DOUBT VI

Likewise, is asked of this which he says, that *the gift of charity alone divides between the sons of the Kingdom and the sons of perdition.* For it seems that he speaks falsely, because either he speaks of a division as much as regards *cognition*, or as much as regards *truth*. If as much as regards *truth*, this is false, because not only in charity, but also in gratuitous faith and hope they differ; if as much as regards *cognition*, then least of all does it divide, because it is not known [nescitur], who has this gift.

I RESPOND: It must be said, that all the gifts of the virtues can be formless [informia], except charity. And since they can be formless, they can be in the just and (in) sinners, and for that reason in these they are never separated from one another. But charity never can be formless nor be with sin, because its act is to love God[6] for His own sake and above all (things), which is removed through every sin. For that reason (St.) Augustine says,[7] that charity alone distinguishes (them), speaking of distinction in the universal.

What is objected concerning gratuitous or formed faith, I concede, that it does distinguish, but yet it does not have this, because (it is) *faith*, but because (it is) *gratuitous*; and thus from this, that (it has been)[8] conjoined to charity; and in this manner that (objection) is clear.

DOUBT VII

Likewise, is asked of this which (St. Paul) says: *If I will hand my body over, thus that I burn* etc.. For it seems that he speaks badly, because the Lord says, in the fifteenth (chapter of the Gospel of St.) John:[9] *A greater love than this no one has, to lay down his own life* etc.: therefore, if this is the greatest work of charity, it is impossible, that it be done without charity.

I RESPOND: Some say, that the Apostle speaks by way of [per] the impossible; for with it posited still,[10] that someone would suffer this punishment without charity for Christ's sake, still it would not profit him. Yet I believe, that some[11] out of the industry of (their) natural (powers) and by some grace freely given could sustain death for the sake of faith in Christ [fide Christi] even without charity, just as[12] the heretic sustains (it) through error. And that the Lord says, that that belongs to most high charity, this He says as much as regards sign and exterior show [exteriorem ostensionem]; however, signs are fallible, and for that reason it is not necessarily bound (to be), that if someone sustains death for Christ's sake or for the sake of his faith,[13] he has charity. However, I do believe, that if anyone would suffer death for Christ's sake, who has no great obstacle [obicem], that he would dispose himself to take up the grace, such that charity would be given him.

---

[1] In codex I there is added *habits* [habitus].

[2] In the Vatican edition, this proposition: *Nor it He thus our patience exemplarily* [Nec ita est patientia nostra exemplariter] is faultily lacking, though, it is, however, had in the manuscripts and edition 1.

[3] Codex V has *through* [per] in place of *and* [et].

[4] Which may be seen in the text of Master (Peter), here, in chapters. 1 through 4.

[5] Since a twofold formal cause was then distinguished, namely the intrinsic or informing (perfecting), and the extrinsic or exemplary one. — On this doubt, see also Bl. (now St.) Albertus (Magnus), here in a. 8 and (Bl.) Peter of Tarentaise, here about the text.

[6] Trusting in the older manuscripts and edition 1 we have inserted the badly omitted *God* [Deum]. Next, the relative *which* [qui] refers to *act* [actum]. — For more on this, that charity cannot be unformed, see SENT., Bk. III, d. 27, a. 1. q. 4.

[7] ON THE TRINITY, Bk. XV, ch. 18, n. 32, from which the text of this doubt has been taken.

[8] In edition 1 there is added *it has been* [est]. — You will find the same doubt solved in Bl. (now St.) Albertus (Magnus), here in a. 9.

[9] Verse 13.

[10] The Vatican edition faultily, and breaking with the more ancient manuscripts together with editions 1 and 6, has *in this case* [ad hoc] for *still* [adhuc]. Then editions 2 and 3 read *someone having punishment would suffer* etc. [aliquis habens poenam pateretur etc.].

[11] From very many codices, such as T and X and edition 1, we have inserted *some* [aliqui]. Codex Z has *someone* [aliquis], and a little after this has the singular form for *could* [posset]; codex Y without *someone* [aliquis] has in the singular *one ... (his) powers* [posset].

[12] Codex bb adds the particle *even* [etiam]. Next, codex M has *for the sake of error* [pro errore], and codex ee, together with edition 1, has *for the sake of error* [propter errorem] in place of *through error* [per errorem].

[13] The Vatican edition, together with some manuscripts here repeats *that* [quod], which however, in the greater part of the codices and in edition 1 is lacking.

COMMENTARY ON DISTINCTION XVII

PART II

Master (Peter) puts forth the defense of his own position.

Here, there is asked, 'if charity is the Holy Spirit, since it is increased' etc..

SEE THE TEXT OF THIS PART, ABOVE ON P. 289.

THE DIVISION OF THE TEXT

Above, Master (Peter) dealt with the invisible mission of the Holy Spirit according to his own opinion. Here, *second*, he puts forth the defense of his own opinion, and does this by responding to the objections, which could[1] disprove his own opinion.. And since his own position can be disproved both *by reason* and *by authority* and *last in both ways* [utroque modo], for that reason this part has three parts.

In the *first* part he impugns and disproves this which he had said, that the Holy Spirit is the Charity, by which we love God and neighbor.

However, *second*, through authority, there (where he says): *Above, it has been said, that the Holy Spirit* etc.

Third, through authorities and reasons, there (where he says): *The also bring forward other* etc.. — The first reason against Master (Peter) has been taken out of this, that charity is increased [augetur];[2] the second reason against him has been taken out of this, that charity is from the Holy Spirit, just as (St.) Augustine says; the third reason has been taken from this, that charity is an affection [affectio] of the soul, and this, indeed, is consonant with reason and authority. But, in each of these parts, Master (Peter) first opposes and, second, determines; and the parts (of each of these) are manifest.

TREATMENT OF THE QUESTIONS

For an understanding of this part, there is, here,[3] the question of the augment [augmento] of charity, and about this four (things) are asked.

First, there is asked, whether charity can be increased [augeri] according to substance.

Second, there is asked concerning the augment itself of charity.

Third, there is asked concerning the opposite of its augment, that is, concerning (its) diminution [diminutione], whether charity can be lessened [diminui].

Fourth, of the augment of charity as much as regards (its) terminus or[4] state.

ARTICLE SOLE

On the augment of charity.

QUESTION I

Whether charity can be increased according to (its) substance?

As much as regards the first, it is shown, that charity can be increased according to substance.

1. Through (St.) Augustine, (in his letter) to Boniface:[5] « Charity merits to be increased, as the enacted [aucta] merits to be accomplished [perfici] ».

2. Likewise, this same [hoc ipsum] seems from *reason*: the charity of the way [caritas viae], according to (its) substance, is less than the charity of the Fatherland; but

one happens to pass [devenire] from the charity of the way to the charity of the Fatherland, with (charity) herself saved in (her) 'being', since the *charity* of the way *never passes away* [excidit];[6] but a movement from the lesser to the greater, within the same thing [re salva], is an augment:[7] therefore, it happens that charity is increased.

3. Likewise, it is established, that to diverse (persons) there shall be given greater and

---

[1] With very many codices together with edition 1 striving against it, the Vatican edition has *can* [possunt].

[2] The Vatican edition, contrary to the manuscripts and edition 1, has *may be increased* [augeatur].

[3] With the agreement of very many manuscripts and edition 1, we have supplied the *here* [hic].

[4] The Vatican edition with codex cc repeats *as regards* [ad].

[5] Epistle 189, n. 2, according to its sense, but word for word from Epistle 186, "To Paulinus", ch 3, n. 10. In this text edition 1 together with one or the other codex, such as I, after *merits* [mereatur] adds *also* [et].

[6] 1 Cor. 13:8.

[7] Aristotle, ON GENERATION AND CORRUPTION, Bk. I., text 33 (chapter 5).

lesser rewards; whence the Apostle, in the fifteenth (chapter) of the First (Letter) to the Corinthians (says):[1] *One the clarity of the Sun, another the clarity of the Moon* etc.; and it is established, that for one and the same according to diverse states there ought (to be) a diverse reward, that is greater and lesser; but the magnitude of the substantial reward responds to the quantity of charity, non according to fervor, but according to substance: therefore, if it happens, that a greater reward is owed to someone, therefore, also that charity be increased substantially.

4. Likewise, it happens that charity is becomes better [meliorari], since it is not the most high Good; but charity is a good substantially: therefore, it happens, that charity according to its own substance is made better [fieri meliorem]. But as (St.) Augustine says in the sixth (book) ON THE TRINITY, in the eight chapter:[2] « In spiritual (things) greater and better are the same »: therefore, since charity is something spiritual, it is possible, that according to substance it become greater.

5. Likewise, it is established that in one and same (thing) charity can be unto a greater effect and act: therefore, since greater-ness of an effect comes from the magnitude of the virtue, it is possible, that charity become greater according to virtue. Then I ask. either charity is its own virtue, or not: if *it is*: therefore, with the virtue augmented, it is necessary, that the essence of charity be increased; if *not*, then I ask of that virtue: either it has an essence, or not; if *it does*, similarly I ask of it: therefore, either there will be an infinite regression [abire in infinitum], and/or it is necessary to posit, that something is increased according to substance; but by that reckoning whereby another virtue (is increased), (so) also charity.

But on the Contrary: 1. Charity is a form; but every form consists in an invariable essence:[3] therefore, also charity; but nothing invariable according to essence is increased according to essence: therefore, neither charity.

2. Likewise, where (there is) augment, there a greater and a lesser;[4] but where there is simplicity, there is no greater or lesser: if, therefore, charity is a simple form and not extended, there will be no augment in charity.

3. Likewise, an augment in corporal (things) is according to accident, and not according to substance:[5] therefore, for an equal reason also in spiritual ones: therefore, if charity is increased, this is only according to accident, not according to substance.

4. Likewise, that which is increased is changed,[6] and what is increased according to substance is changed according to substance; but what is substantially changed is now other than before: therefore, what is increased according to substance does not remain: if, therefore, *charity never passes away* [excidit][7] except through sin, and always remains, therefore, it is not increased.

CONCLUSION

Charity can be increased according to substance or according to quantity of virtue.

I Respond: It must be said, that according to the common opinion it is true, that charity can be substantially increased.

For an understanding, moreover, of the objections certain (authors) distinguish augment according to a twofold difference. For an augment is, when a greater succeeds a lesser; but this can be in a twofold manner: either *such*, that that same, which was before lesser, afterwards is made *greater*, just as a man is said to increase and/or any *other* quantum, and in this manner[8] charity is not increased, as they say; and/or *for this reason*, that the greater succeeds the lesser, not the same according to number, but completely similar in form, just as they say the day is increasing, not because the same day is at first[9] lesser; thus they say that charity is increased, ac through this (it is) that one is able to avoid the oppositions.

But this position of theirs, as has been proved above,[10] cannot stand. For it has been shown, that with charity remaining the same there comes to be an increment [crementum] and a perfection.

And for that reason it must be said in another manner, that augment follows quantity. Moreover, "quantity" is said in a twofold manner, namely *properly* and *metaphorically*: properly "quantity" is said of a mass [molis], and this is in corporals; metaphorically "quantity" (is said) of virtue, and this is[11] in spirituals. In the same manner also "augment" is said in a twofold manner: *properly*, namely according to the magnitude of *a mass*, and *metaphorically* according to the quantity of a virtue. Therefore, since in charity there is a quantity of virtue, and not in the greatest degree [in summo], it is established, that charity can be increased. *Again*, since the virtue is the same (thing) which the substance of charity (is), and (since) a quantity belongs[12] to the virtue, hence it is, that of necessity it follows, that charity is increased according to substance; for since it is a virtue, its substance is not other than a virtue.

---

[1] Verse 41.

[2] Number 9: For among these, which are not great in mass, being greater is that, which being better is. — Next codex I has *wherefore* [unde] for *therefore* [ergo].

[3] In the Book, ON THE SIX PRINCIPLES, which belongs to Gilbert of Porretain: A reason or form is that which comes upon the composite, (and is) constant by a simply and invariable essence. Cf. Aristotle, METAPHYSICS, Bk. VII, text. 28, and Bk. VIII, text 10 (Bk. VI, ch. 8 at the end, and Bk. VII, ch. 3). In the first passage cited, he says: « For it is an invisible form »; in the second he compares a substance (essence) to the numbers, in which any addition and/or diminution induces a specific change. — Next after *invariable* [invariabile] codices K and V omit *according to essence* [secundum essentiam], then to the noun *essence* [essentiam] they preface *substance and/or* [substantiam vel].

[4] Aristotle, ON GENERATION AND CORRUPTION, Bk. I, text 31 ff. (ch. 5).

[5] Cf. Aristotle, ON GENERATION AND CORRUPTION, Bk. I, text 30 ff. (ch. 5), and PHYSICS, Bk. V, texts 7-20 (chs. 2 and 3). — Next in the

Vatican edition and in codex cc less aptly, and with the other codices together with edition 1 striving against this, there is omitted *only* [solum].

[6] See Aristotle, PHYSICS, Bk. IV, text 32 (ch. 4) & Bk. VIII, text 55 (ch. 7).

[7] 1 Cor. 13, 8.

[8] Codex X, having varied the punctuation and position (of the words), reads *and/or anything else, and as much as regards this, charity* [vel aliquid aliud, et quantum ad hoc caritas], with which codex R agrees, which however, omits the particle *and* [et] and puts *regards this manner* [ad hunc modum] for *regards this* [ad hoc]. A little below this, codices P and Q have *thus* [ita] in place of *for that reason* [ideo]; and then, trusting in the more ancient manuscripts and edition 1, we have expunged the particle *in* [in] prefixed to the word *number* [numero].

[9] Codex T has *the same, prior day is lesser* [idem dies prius sit minor], and codex K has *can be* [possit esse] for *is* [sit].

[10] Here, in the fundamenta, especially in n. 5.

[11] From the older mss. and edition 1, we have supplied *is* [est].

[12] Very many codd., such as A G I S T W X Y dd and ff read *which*

1. To that, therefore, which is objected unto the contrary, that the essence of a form is invariable; it must be said, that it is true of a universal form, but if it be said of a singular form, it is true considered in itself, but not insofar as in the other.[1]

2. To that which is objected, that simplicity does not admit magnitude; it must be said, that it is true, because it does not admit a magnitude of mass, however, it does admit a magnitude of virtue.

3. To that which is objected, that an augment[2] in corporal (things) is a movement according to accident, the response is clear. For a quantity of *mass* is an accident, essentially differing by a quantum; but not so is it among quanta according to the quantity of *virtue*, nay a quantity of virtue is essential, as has been proven by the opposing argument [in opponendo].[3]

However, it can be said, that when there is said, that[4] the movement of increase [motus augmenti] in corporals is a movement according to accident, that which it is "*according to*" can be accepted in a twofold manner: either (according to) which it means a habitude of a terminus per se or of a formal terminus, and thus at any rate the terminus of an increase is a perfect quantity, or thus, (according to) which it means a terminus

per accidens, and in this manner an augment per accidens[4] looks back to the substance. Which is clear. For when there is added a greater quantity to a lesser, unless it comes to be through a rarefaction and/or through a being-stretched-out [protensionem],[6] it is bound that it be added according to the substance, in which that quantity is, and thus consequently it is terminated at the substance even in corporal (things).

4. And through this what is objected is clear: 'what is changed according to substance is different [aliud et aliud]';[7] it is true, if it means a formal terminus, but (the Apostle) does not mean (it) in this manner.

To that which is objected: 'by that by which it is augmented according to substance, it is also changed according to substance'; it must be said, that[8] to a thing not only does it belongs to be substantial, but also to be perfect [perfectum esse]. Therefore, 'to be changed according to this' can be in a twofold manner: either in respect to '*being*' simply, and thus the changed is now one thing now another; and/or in respect to '*being perfected*' [esse perfecti], and thus it is the same,[9] because when the perfect comes to be from the imperfect, it is not another (thing), but the same one. Hence it is, that charity, although it is substantially increased, is not other, but the same according to substance; whence the objection is not valid.

SCHOLIUM

I. The question is resolved in the affirmative with the common sentence. Then about the *manner* of this argument the Seraphic Doctor mentions [affert] the insufficient opinion of some (authors); then proposes his own and proves it, having employed this axiom, that augment follows quantity. Moreover, quantity is commonly distinguished into proper or (one) of mass, and metaphoric or (one) of virtue; whence it follows, that there ought to be admitted also a twofold augmentation; and hence, that charity can be increased, and that augmentation comes to be according to essence. — So that the reasons and difficulties pertaining to Philosophy, which in this and the following question are touched upon, may be more easily understood, some citation of the various opinions, existing among the ancient schools, concerning the augment and diminution of forms, will be of assistance. According to the testimony of (St. Severinus) Boethius, ON THE CATEGORIES OR PREDICAMENTS OF ARISTOTLE, Bk. III, chapter "On quality", three opinions were already extant among the ancient

philosophers concerning the extension of forms [intensio formarum] or concerning greater and lesser. « For some used to say, that in all (things) there can be discovered a 'more and less' [magis et minus] according to the habitude of matter. For "that it is proper to matter and bodies to grow by being extended [intensione] and to be diminished [minui] by being relaxed [relaxatione]", was the sentence of certain Platonists ». Which words of (St.) Boethius are thus expounded by Bl. (now St.) Albertus (Magnus), in tract. 8, ch. 1: « Indeed one (opinion) of those, who used to say, that in everything, in which a greater and lesser is found, matter is in some manner found, the quantity of which, as they say, consists out of indivisibles: where more similars convene in one, they say it is being extended [id intendi], and where there are fewer, they say it is being abated [illud remiti], and for that reason those are most white, in which concur more indivisibles of whiteness; but that (they) are being abated, where fewer convene. And indeed this opinion, as (St.) Boethius says, was Plato's.

---

the substance of charity *and the quantity of the virtue (are)* [quod substantia caritatis, et quantitas virtutis]; the others, such as H and cc, with edition 1 read similarly, but have *is* [sit] for the *(are)*. Codices L O and Z, a little before this, after *virtue* [virtus] add *"charity"* [caritas], which either must be supplied, and/or the noun *virtue* [virtus] must refer to the following *of charity* [caritatis]; then codd. L and O substitute *and the quantity of virtue, (the same) which the quantity of substance (is)* [et quantitas virtutis, quod quantitas substantiae] for *and (since) quantity belongs to the virtue* [et sit quantitas virtutis]. The manner in which this argument is to be understood, is taken from fundament n. 5, posited above, and below from the response to n. 3. Then some codices, such as D V X and bb, less aptly omits *for* [enim], in place of which codex G has (an explicit subject) *it itself* [ipsa]; codex T then after *virtue* [virtus] inserts *it necessarily follows, that* [necessario sequitur, quod].

[1] On this solution, cf. above d. 8, p. I, a. 2, q. 2, in reply to n. 1. Richard of Middleton says the same, SENT., Bk. I, d. 8, a. 2, q. 2, in reply to n. 2: « Although a form is not variable according to its own absolute 'being', speaking properly of variability, however, because it has a natural aptitude, to be in the matter, in which it can receive variability, it ought not to be said (to be) simply invariable ».

[2] From some manuscripts, such as I and T, we have supplied *an augment* [augmentum], in place of which the Vatican edition, together with codex cc, yet with the other codices and edition 1 striving against this, then puts *of increase* [augmenti] after *movement* [motus].

[3] In the arguments of the fundament, chiefly in the last one, n. 5, and in the body of the question, near the end. — A little above this, after *essential* [essentialis], codex M has *to charity* [caritati].

[4] The Vatican edition, contrary to nearly all the codices and edition 1 omits *that* [quod]. Next in very many manuscripts and edition 1 *of increase* [augmenti] is lacking, yet certainly to be supplied.

[5] We follow the more ancient codd. and ed. 1, by adding *per accidens*.

[6] Cf. Aristotle, ON THE PREDICAMENTS, the chapter "On Quality", and PHYSICS, Bk. IV, text 79 ff. (ch. 9), and ON HEAVEN, Bk. III, text 10, where the definition of "rarefaction" is indicated, namely, that which is a movement, by which a body, remaining the same entity and quantity, acquires a greater local extension. Wherefore, supposing that rarefaction and pretension ("being stretched out") refer to one another, it can be said according to the mind of the Seraphic Doctor, d. 18, Doubt 4, that rarefaction is the natural process, but pretension the artificial process; to the former there would be opposed condensation, to the latter compression.

[7] The Vatican edition badly omits here *now one thing now another* [aliud et aliud]; a little above this, it puts less distinctly *is not increased* [non augetur] in place of *is changed* [mutatur], then at the end of the response *if it means a terminus per accidens* [si dicit terminum per accidens] for *(the Apostle does mean (it) in this manner* [sic dicit], but the authority of the manuscripts and of the first six editions withstands this. — Note above, that the Vatican edition, together with many codices, conjoins with the aforementioned proposition *And through this what is objected* etc. with the response to the third objection; but non well, because it truly pertains with the following response to the fourth objection. A few codices, to establish the connection of these responses (to n. 4), at the end of this first half, add *yet it can be said in another manner* [tamen potest alite dici].

[8] One or the other codex, such as I and Q, has *that* [quod] for *that* [quia].

[9] As required by the context, we have supplied *and thus it is the same* [et sic est idem], though these words are found in a few manuscripts, such as H and I and indeed in the margin (in nearly the same hand). Next, trusting in very many manuscripts and edition 1, we have substituted *Hence it is, that* [Hinc est, quod] in place of *And hence it is, that* [Et hinc est, quia].

Moreover, it seems derived from the ancient Anaxagoras, who said, that like generates like, and all is in all, but is lying hidden; and for that reason everything whatsoever appears to be extended and abated according to a 'more and less' [secundum plus et minus] of this like ». — « But *the other one*, which said that there is not a "more or less" [magis et minus] according to the most certain and most true arts and virtues, but that there can be said to be (one) according to median (arts and virtues), as this very grammar and justice are not said (to be) more grammar and more justice. But that there are certain other mediocre arts, in which the very same could come about (just as a median habit comes to be from a disposition, as St. Albertus adds). *The third* one is, that of which Aristotle speaks, because he indeed thought that those habitudes do not increase [crescere] by any extension [intensione] nor decrease by diminution, but that those participating in (or subject to) them can come under an examination of (their) composition, such that of these a "more or less" is said. For no one says that health itself or justice are each now more or less than the other health or justice, nor that there is more health than another health. But we can say this alone, that someone has more health, i. e. is healthier, and that (something is) more healthful and less healthful. Therefore, we say, that *qualities themselves* do not undertake a "more and a less"; *but those which are said (to be) such according to them*, fall under a comparison, such as "more just" and "more healthy" and "more grammatical" ». — Gilbert of Porretain (ON THE SIX PRINCIPLES, last chapter), mentions three sentences on this matter, which used to be defended by diverse (authors) in his own time and it seems that these correspond to the threefold opinion of the ancient (philosophers). « For certain (authors) say (that quantity is) according to the increment and/or diminution of their *subjects*, which take them up. But indeed in another manner others also announce that that those which are taken up in the one taking them up do diminish and increase. Moreover, others (say that there is) a diminution and augmentation of both according *to each* ». Having adduced very many reasons against this threefold sentence, he concludes: « And so it is clear that nothing is predicated according to a 'more and less' [secundum magis et minus], neither according to the augment and/or diminution of the subject alone, nor according to (that) of the accident; nor by that by which (it is) according to each. Therefore, one is bound to discover by some other means, what (things) are said with "a more and less". But of this kind are those (things), which are in the expression of the affixed [quae sunt in voce eorum quae adveniunt], and not (because they are) according to an increase and/or diminution of the subject and/or of a movable, but since they are nearer to the imposition of those, which are in the expression [in voce], or more remote from the same. For indeed those which are nearer to that imposition which is in the expression itself are said *with (the word) "more"*, but *with (with the word) "less"* those which consist of those more remote, such as (something) white is said to be that, in which there is pure whiteness, therefore, as much as an accident according to the imposition of the expression [vocis] is imbued with a purer whiteness, so much also shall "whiter" be assigned ... But will anyone doubt, why these indeed are said with a "more and less", but substances not at all? But this happens, since the imposition of substances indeed is in a terminus, beyond which it is impossible to transgress. But there is also an addition of certain accidents, which are said without a "more and less", as quadrangular and triangular and the like, for one is not said (to be) more a triangle than the other ».

II. The solution to n. 1 touches upon both sides of the question, disputed among the Scholastics, whether the very substantial forms of the same species, especially the intellectual ones of the soul, receive a 'more or less', or can be of an unequal perfection. Which is to be understood not of the *specific* perfection, which certainly is the same in individuals of the same species, but of *individual* perfection, not of *accidental* perfection, which certainly is diverse in diverse (individuals), but of *substantial* (perfection), according to the grade of perfection consequent to the nature of the individual. Each sentence, i.e. the affirmative and negative, is probable. The supporters of the sentence, that they are unequal, cite for their part that decree of the doctors of Paris, reported by Henry of Ghent (QUODLIBETALS, 3, q. 5) and by Durandus (of Saint-Pourçain) (SENT., Bk. II, d. 32, q. 3): « If anyone says, that all souls are by (their) origin [ab origine] equal, he errs, since otherwise the soul of Christ would not be more perfect than the soul of Judas (Iscariot) ». Durandus (of Saint-Pourçain) strives to restrict this decree to the perfection of the sensitive and vegetative powers, though equally probably, some say that it does not have an irrefragable authority. On the sentence of St. Thomas there is a dispute, though Cajetan (on SUMMA., I, q. 85, a. 7) says, that they are blind, who doubt, that he stands for (their) inequality. But (Bl. John Duns) Scotus, together with very many others, professes that he is one of those blind men. Many testimonies of St. Thomas favor the interpretation of Cajetan, such as SUMMA., I, q. 50, a. 4, q. 85, a. 7; SENT., Bk. II, d. 32, a. 3; Bk. I, d. 8, q. 5, a. 2 in reply to n. 6. — Even St. Bonaventure adheres to the sentence denying (their) parity of perfection, in SENT., Bk. II, d. 3, p. I, Doubt 2, and d. 32, Doubt 6. — But the sentence of (Bl. John Duns) Scotus is doubtful, though it seems to more favor this last sentence, as is clear from the testimonies collected from his writings by Fr. Girolamo da Montefortino, O.F.M., 1662-1738 A.D., in his SUMMA SCOTI, Bk. II, p. I, q. 85, a. 7.

In the solution to n. 3. a twofold response is given. The *first* is: even if it one concedes, that in corporal things there is an augment only according to accident and not according to substance, yet this is not valid in the augment for *virtues*. The *second* response, however, denies, that a movement of increase is in corporals only according to the accident, which is quantity, but that it is added to the substance itself. To prove this there is distinguished a twofold terminus of the increase: *the formal* or per se, and this is the quantity itself, and *the accidental*, and this is the substance itself.

III. Alexander of Hales, SUMMA., p. IV, q. 9, m. 3, a. 2, § 1. — (Bl. John Duns) Scotus, on this and the following question, here in q. 4. and the ff.; REPORTATIO, here in q. 3. et ff.. — St. Thomas, here in q. 2, a. 1; SUMMA., II, II, q. 24, a. 4. — Bl. (now St.) Albertus (Magnus), on this and the following two questions, here in a. 10, and SENT., Bk. III, d.29, a. 10; and Bk. IV, d. 7, a. 5, quaestiuncula 3; SUMMA., I, p. II, tr. 16, q. 101, m. 2, and q. 102, m. 1. — William of Paris , ON VIRTUES, a. 2, q.1. — Giles the Roman, here in q. 2, a. 1. — Henry of Ghent, QUODLIBETALS. 5, q. 19. — Durandus (of Saint-Pourçain), here in q. 5. — (Bl.) Dionysius the Carthusian, here in q. 6. — Biel, here in q. 4.

QUESTION II

In what manner is charity increased?

Second, there is asked, concerning the manner of the augment itself of charity. And that its augment is from elsewhere, is shown:

1. Through (St.) Augustine,[1] who says, that « charity merits to be increased »; but what anyone merits, he has from an other than himself: therefore, if charity merits an augment, it has it from elsewhere.

2. Likewise, that it is augmented through apposition, seems through *the reckoning* of an augment:[2] « for an augment is the addition of a pre-existing quantity »: therefore,

---

[1] EPISTLE TO BONIFACE. Cf. the preced. Quest., 1st arg. of the fundament.
[2] Trusting in very many manuscripts, such as F G H I O and ff, we have inserted *of an augment* [augmenti], in place of which, in many manuscripts and in the fist six editions, there is falsely had *of (St.) Augustine*.

The cited reason or definition is found in Aristotle, ON GENERATION AND CORRUPTION, Bk. I, text 31 (ch. 5): For an augmentation is the addition of an existing magnitude [Augmentatio enim est existentis magnitudinis additamentum].

where there is an augment, there is an apposition of something of the same genus, and where an apposition, there an addition [additio]

3. Likewise, this seems able to be shown through *a simile*, because[1] charity is in the soul, as light (is) in the air; but light in the air is increased through the addition of a new light, as is clear, if one illumining candle overcomes another: therefore, also in charity will there be (an augment) in a similar manner in respect to the soul.

4. Likewise, this seems through the *principle* of the augment; because every single thing [unumquodque] is both nourished and increased out of the same (things):[2] therefore, through a completely similar manner charity has a "to be generated", a "to be conserved" and a "to be increased"; but it is generated in us through a divine influence: therefore, also through a greater same is it increased; but where (there is) a greater influence, something inflows[3] more than before; and where this (is the case), there is an addition: ergo etc..

ON THE CONTRARY: 1. The warmth of spiritual love [amoris] is of greater virtue than (the warmth) of material fire; but fire is increased by itself:[4] therefore, also charity, which is a spiritual fire.

2. Likewise, it seems, that (charity is) not (increased) through apposition, because if the simple is added to the simple, it becomes nothing greater, neither in mass nor in virtue, such as if a point (be added) to a point:[5] therefore, neither if charity is added to charity, will it be greater.

3. Likewise, if something is added, when a composition follows the addition, (there is) also (added) to the greater composition a diminution of virtue:[6] therefore, as much as a greater addition is made, so much does charity become more impotent, and as much as more impotent, so much the lesser: therefore since the augment of charity is as much as regards virtue, charity is not increased through addition.

4. Likewise, if anything is added to a prior charity, either charity is added, or not, if not: therefore, charity is not increased; but if it is, charity (is); but charity is not material in respect to charity: therefore, since from two somethings there does not come to be one, unless one is material in respect to the other,[7] out of a pre-existent and superadded charity there does not come to be one (thing); but for an augment it is necessary that one (thing) come to be out of the one increasing and the one increased: therefore, in no manner is it increased[8] through addition.

CONCLUSION

Charity is increased by divine virtue through the apposition and/or increase of a greater influence.

I RESPOND: For an understanding of the aforesaid it must[9] be noted, that there was about this a twofold opinion. One is, that an augment of charity is through a purification from [depurationem] or through a thorough unmingling with (their) contrary [impermixtionem cum contrario]. But the contrary of chaste love [amoris casti][10] is the love of concupiscence; whence as much as concupiscence is more extinguished in us, so much more is charity purified [depuratur]; and as much as it is more purified, so much more is it assimilated to God and does it approach (its) terminus; and as much as it more approaches, so much more is it increased. And they (who held this) posited, that charity can through itself be increased through a becoming accustomed to [assuefactionem in] the good and (through) a debilitation of concupiscence. Moreover, the reason, which moved them, was the authority of the Philosopher,[11] who says, that forms are extended [intendi] through an approach to (their) terminus and (through) a thorough unmingling with (their) contrary. Together with him was the authority of (St.) Augustine, who says in the book OF EIGHTY-THREE QUESTIONS,[12] that just as concupiscence is lessened, so charity increased; and such an augment through a greater purification [depurationem] is not repugnant to (something) simple.

But that position of theirs is not fitting, since[13] it is an established (opinion), that charity is greater and lesser, with every concupiscence borne away, just as in the First Man and even in the Angels; therefore, since it is thoroughly unmingled there, in any Angel and even in the state of innocence it would be in the highest degree [in summo], which is a foolish thing to say. Whence it must not be said, that as much as regards the remission of concupiscence (charity)[14] is increased according to (its) *substance*, yet it must be conceded, that as much as regards the remission of concupiscence *it is extended through fervor*. And in this manner (St.) Augustine understands (it); and in this manner even the Philosopher speaks of forms as much as regards (their) extension [intensionem], not as much as regards (their) augment.

The other position is, that charity is increased through

---

[1] The Vatican edition less distinctly, and contrary to very many manuscripts, reads *that/because* [quod] for *because* [quia], and next faultily and contrary to the codices and edition 1, it has *is not increased* [non augetur] for *is increased* [augetur], and *illumined* [illuminatae] for *illumining* [illuminanti].

[2] Aristotle, ON GENERATION AND CORRUPTION, Bk. II, text 50 (ch. 8): For all (things) are nourished out of the same, by which they also are. In that proposition the Vatican edition faultily, and contrary to the manuscripts and to edition 1, omits *is* [est].

[3] Codex O in the more usual manner has *is influenced* [influitur].

[4] Cf. Aristotle, ON GENERATION AND CORRUPTION, Bk. I, text 39 (ch. 5): For one happens to cause fire according to this manner, that is, with logs thrown into that which already is (on fire). Truly, thus, indeed, is there an accretion (augmentation); but when the logs themselves are lighted, a generation (edition of Firmin-Didot).

[5] This is the teaching of Aristotle, ON GENERATION AND CORRUPTION, Bk. I, text 8 (ch. 2), where he shows, that points added to points do not make a magnitude or neither "a more" nor "a less". — Next codex T has *is it* [est] place of *will it be* [erit].

[6] The author of THE BOOK OF CAUSES, proposition 17: Every united force is more infinite, than a multiplied virtue. Cf. also Dionysius (the Areopagite), ON THE DIVINE NAMES, ch. 5.

[7] See Aristotle, METAPHYSICS, Bk. VII, text 49 (Bk. VI, ch. 13): For it is impossible, that a substance be out of substances, which are also in act in the same manner; for two which are in act in the same manner, are never one in act;

but if there are two potencies, there will be one (thing), as a double out of the potency of two halves; for an act separates.

[8] The Vatican edition, contrary to the more ancient codices and edition 1, has *can it be increased* [potest augeri]. A little before this very many codices, such as A G H R T U Y Z ee and ff, together with edition 1, have *the one augmented* [augmentato], but others faultily *the augment* [augmento], for *the one increased* [aucto].

[9] Some codices, such as T and X, add explicitly *it must* [est].

[10] The Vatican edition, with codex cc, has *of Christ's love* [amor Christi], but the authority of the more ancient codd. with ed. 1, and the context and the manner of speech of the Seraphic Doctor withstand this, concerning which see above d. 1, a. 2, q. 1, at the end of the body of the Question.

[11] PHYSICS, Bk. V, text 19, (ch. 2): But a "more and less" is out of this, that more or less of the contrary is in it, and not. And TOPICS, Bk. III, ch. 4, near the middle (ch. 5): And those which are thoroughly unmingled with contraries, (are) more such; as indeed (something) more white (is) more thoroughly unmingled with black.

[12] Question 36: Its (i.e. charity's) nourishment is the lessening of cupidity: (its) perfection, no cupidity. — And a little before this: Therefore, anyone wanting to nourish it (i.e. charity), let him insist on diminishing cupidities. Cf. also ENCHIRIDION., ch. 121, n. 32, where (St.) Augustine says: But cupidity diminishes, with charity increasing.

[13] As required by very many manuscripts, together with edition 1, we have put *since* [quoniam] in place of *because* [quia].

[14] Supply together with codex Y *charity* [caritatem].

apposition; and (something) similar to this is had in a light, which is expressly likened to [assimilatur] charity.[1] Whence just as a greater light, added to a lesser one, increases it, so a superadded charity increases a lesser one. And this position posits, that charity is not increased by its own virtue, but by a divine one. For the same is the principle of being increased and of being generated.[2] Whence just as it has it rise from God alone, so as (its) augment.

1. From this is clear that which is objected through (what is) similar in fire. For fire has the power to cause itself (to be) in another and to be increased, not so charity.

2. To that which is objected second, that charity is simple;[3] it must be said, that although charity is simple, because it does not have parts quantitative according to a quantity of *mass*, yet it does have (them) according to a quantity of *virtue*, and as much as regards that[4] it can be increased. If it is objected concerning the point, that it has a quantity of virtue, and yet it is not increased; it must be said, that for this, that something be bound to be increased through an apposition of a completely similar quantity, two (things) are necessary, namely a quantity and a unibility (i. e. an ability to be united). But unibility comes out of an imperfection, for to the perfect, inasmuch as (it is) of this kind, an addition is not possible:[5] and for that reason an addition cannot be made to a point. Therefore, though a point does have a quantity of virtue, it does not have unibility, because it is a certain perfect something [quoddam perfectum] in its genus.

In another manner it can be said, that a point is the most simple (thing) in the genus of *the quantum of mass* [quanti molis],[6] and for that reason it is infinite in virtue; but no charity is most simple in the genus of the *quantum of virtue* [quanti virtualis], unless (it be) divine (Charity), and for that reason That is infinite; and since That cannot be increased through addition, thus neither the virtue of a point. *And if you object to me*, that the virtue of a point is created, therefore, it is not infinite; it must be said, that, because a point is the most simple (thing)[7] *in (its) genus*, not *simply* (speaking), for that reason it does not have infinite virtue *simply*, but *in (its) genus in respect to* lines. *Besides*, a point is not entirely an act, but a terminus in respect to lines, for that reason it does not have an active, infinite power, but a passive one, because a point is not properly said to be able to produce lines, but can be the terminus for the standing still [statui] of a line; and it is not unfitting to posit this in the creature: for that reason the virtue of a point is not augmentable, as the virtue of charity (is).

3. To that which is objected, that as much as something is more composite, so much is it more impotent;[8] it must be said, that generally understood it is false. On this account one must distinguish, that there are material parts, and there are formal parts, which give act and virtue to the whole. Therefore, "*simple*" can be said *more* through *the privation of material* parts; and then the proposition has truth, because such parts give a "to suffer" rather than a "to act", whence as much as something is made more distant [magis elongatur] from matter, so much (is it) more potent. But if it is, *rather*, said (to be) *simple*, because it has fewer *formal* or active parts, it is false, because then a lesser fire would be more potent than a greater one. Then even[9] syrup [sirupus], composed from a few (things), would be more virtuous than that which consists of many; each of which is false; and, for that reason, also the proposed proposition,[10] since as much as charity (is) pre-existent as (it is) added [adveniens], each (charity) has the reckoning of (something) active.

However, in another manner (the objection) can be responded to according to the truth, that augmented charity is not more composite, nay more simple, and this is clear in this manner: because in a contrary manner it is in a quantum *of mass* and[11] a quantum *of virtue*. In a quantum of *mass* the most simple is the least one, such as the point, and for that reason in this genus of quantum an approach [accessus] to simplicity is through diminution, a recess[12] contrariwise through addition. But in the quantum *of virtue* the most simple is the greatest; and for that reason an approach to simplicity is through an addition, and hence it is, that augmented charity is more pure and more simple and more similar to God. And this may not seem[13] unfitting, because to add purity and simplicity and spirituality to anything does not cause a recess from simplicity, but rather an approach.

4. To that which is objected, whether out of them[14] there comes to be one (thing); some say, that — just as diverse lights are in the air distinct and unconfused, but, however, render one greater light on account of (their) concourse in one susceptible (medium), so in the spiritual light, which is grace and/or charity — because they[15] are essentially distinct, yet

---

[1] (St.) Augustine, Epistle 140, or the book, ON THE GRACE OF THE NEW TESTAMENT, ch. 22, n. 54: For what kind of light charity itself is, who can anyone explain with words? ... Or perhaps charity is not light? Hear the Apostle John, indeed he himself said that which I now remember: *Since God is light ... God is charity*. And through this, if God is light, and God is charity, in a word charity is the light itself, which is poured forth in our hearts through the Holy Spirit etc..

[2] See above in fundament 4. Cf. also Aristotle, ON THE SOUL, Bk. II, texts 34-50 (ch. 4).

[3] The Vatican edition, not trusting in the manuscripts and edition 1, omits unduly the words *charity is simple; it must be said, that although* [caritas est simplex; dicendum, quod quamvis].

[4] That is, "the quantity of virtue", in place of which very many codices, such as A C L O P Q R S T Y bb, together with edition 1, here aptly read *that part* [illam partem], just as even the other codices, such as A C R and S, next less well omit *can* [potest]; codices L and O read *is increased* [augetur] for *can be increased* [potest augeri], codex Y has *is said to be increased* [augeri dicitur].

[5] Cf. Aristotle, METAPHYSICS, Bk. V, text 21, and Bk. X, text 13 (Bk. IV, ch. 16, and Bk. IX, ch. 4), and ON HEAVEN, Bk. II, text 23 (ch. 4), where the perfect is defined as that, outside of which it is possible to accept nothing of those, which belong to it. — A little before this edition 1, together with one or the other codex, such as I, has *to perfection* [imperfectioni] for *to the perfect* [perfecto].

[6] Not a few codices, such as B V X Z aa and bb have *of the quantity o mass* [quantitatis molis]. Next after *in virtue* [virtute] in codex O

there is explicitly added *of the quantum* [quantum] and in codex A *in the genus of the quantum* [in genere quanti]. A little below this some codices, such as B and X have *of the quantity of virtue* [quantitatis virtutis] in place of *of the quantum of virtue* [quanti virtualis].

[7] The Vatican edition, against the mss. and the first six edd., reads *something most simple* [quid simplicissimum] for *the most simple (thing)* [simplicissimum]. Next, in very many codd., such as A H I S T X Y Z bb ee & ff and edd. 1, 2 & 3, there is lacking, less well, the adjective *infinite* [infinitam]. A little below this, after *but in (its) genus* [sed in genere], in codex B there is well added *that is* [scilicet].

[8] In very many codices, such as S and cc, there is lacking *as much as is* [qanto est] and then *so much is* [tanto est]; and in edition 1, the first *is* [est] and the *so much* [tanto] are omitted.

[9] From the more ancient manuscripts and edition 1, we have supplied *Then even* [Tunc etiam].

[10] Thus the codd. with ed. 1; the Vatican ed. reads *and, ..., the aforesaid proposition is similarly false* [et ideo praedicta proposition est similiter falsa].

[11] In codex T, there is repeated here *in* [in].

[12] Trusting in very many manuscripts and edition 1, we have expunged the there added *is* [est].

[13] Some codd., such as V & Y, with ed. 1 have *does this seem* [videtur hoc].

[14] Codex T reads *these* [his].

[15] Supply: *spiritual lights*, that is grace added to grace. — The Vatican ed. reads *it must be said that* [dicendum quod] for *because* [quod], against very many codd. and ed. 1. Next, a few codd., such as V & X have [on the following page] *it is made* [efficitur] for *they become* [efficiunt].

they become one (thing) greater in moving the virtue of the free will [liberi arbitrii].

But yet that (example) is not similar, because the distinction of lights in the air comes on the part of (their) diverse origins, as for example when there are many sources of light [lucentia]; not so is it in grace. And for this reason it must be said, that out of them[1] there does come to be one (thing).

Because it is asked,[2] on which account [quod] does it hold itself in the reckoning of the material; it must be said, that an augment happens to come to be in a twofold manner: either through the virtue of the *augmentable itself*, as is clear in a living thing [in animali]; and, then, the augmentable holds itself in the reckoning of the formal and active, the augmenting in the reckoning of the material and passive. It also happens[3] that an augment comes to be through *extrinsic virtue*, solely by the possibility [sola possi-

bilitate] and unibility existing in the augmentable; and, then, the augmentable, because imperfect, holds itself in the reckoning of the passive,[4] the augmenting, because perfect, in the reckoning of the formal and completive, because it gives a perfect quantity.

Because, therefore, it is objected, that the one is not in potency to the other; it must be said, that it is not in potency for conversion, but it is in potency for union; and that potency is in charity by reason of its imperfection; for because it is imperfect, for that reason (it is) possible that it be perfected and for that reason it is unitable to the perfecting thing. Wherefore it does not have a possibility regarding that which is added inasmuch as (it is) charity, but inasmuch as (it is) imperfect; and thus that (objection) is clear.

SCHOLIUM

I. About the question of the *special* manner, by which charity is increased, we observe, that besides the two opinions posited in the text of St. Thomas, (SUMMA., II II, q. 24, a. 5; SENT., Bk. I, d. 17, a. 2, a. 2) he defends a third sentence, namely that charity is increased not through addition ,but through being more rooted [per radicationem maiorem] in the subject, to which Durandus (of Saint-Pourçain) (here in qq. 6 and 7) and (Bl.) Dionysius the Carthusian (here in q. 6) consent. — St. Bonaventure explains his own sentence more in SENT., Bk. II, d. 27, a. 2, q. 2, where besides the three improbable manners he brings forward three other probable ones and wisely concludes: « In whatsoever of these manners of the three following (opinions) it be said, one is not to make much of it [non est magna vis facienda], but (rather) having it as certain, that the grace of God can be increased in us, we ought to work in such a wise, that it increase in us through good works ». The sentence, which the Seraphic (Doctor) more favors, is also defended by Alexander of Hales, Bl. (now St.) Albertus (Magnus), (Bl.) Peter of Tarentaise, Richard of Middleton, Henry of Ghent and most of all by (Bl. John Duns) Scotus and very many later doctors. See more on this controversy in Rada, CONTROVERSIES, n. 18, and Francesco Macedo,

COLLATIONS, coll. 7, difference 3. Here let it suffice to say, that St. Bonaventure least of all understood the *addition of the new grades (of charity)* in that sense, that the new quality differs in number from that which is added to it, and that it retains a numeric distinction, but thus, that all the grades contain the same charity according to number.

II. The distinction of material and formal parts in the solution to n. 3 has been taken from Aristotle's book, ON GENERATION AND CORRUPTION, Bk. I, text 35, (in the Parisian edition, ch. 5). Moreover, here they are called *material* parts, not because they are without form, but because they are passive rather than active; but the others are called *formal*, because they are most of all active.

III. Alexander of Hales, SUMMA, p. III, q. 61, n. 4, a. 2, § 1 and 2; and p. IV, q. 9, m. 3, a. 2, § 1. — St. Thomas, loc. citt.. — (Bl.) Peter of Tarentaise, here in q. 2, a. 2. — Richard of Middleton, here in a. 2, q. 2. — Giles the Roman, here in 1st. princ., q. 2. — Henry of Ghent, QUODLIBETALS, 5, q. 19, 4, q. 15. — (Gabriel) Biel, here in q. 5 and ff..

QUESTION III
Whether charity can be diminished?

Third, there is asked, whether charity can be diminished. And it seems, that (it can) in this manner:

1. Through the nature if *its own opposite* thus: just as (St.) Augustine says:[5] « Charity's poison is cupidity »; whence he also says,[6] that « where great cupidity, there small charity », and in the book of THE CONFESSIONS:[7] « He loves Thee less, who along with Thee loves anything, which he does not love for the sake of Thee ». If, therefore, it happens, that cupidity is not remitted, but only increased, <u>per contrarium</u>,* it happens that charity is diminished.

2. Likewise, a venial (sin) is an evil; but evil is not,

but what takes away [adimit] something of good:[8] therefore, a venial (sin) takes something away. But a natural ability is of much greater inherence than charity: therefore, since a venial (sin) takes away from natural goodness, therefore, also from charity; ergo etc..

3. Likewise, this very (thing) is shown through the nature of *its own subject*; because just as it happens that a man makes progress, so also[9] that he recedes; but through the progress of free will [profectum liberi arbitrii] it happens that charity is increased in us, while one ascends towards perfection: therefore, since it happens that one returns [redire] towards imperfection by the same steps, it happens that charity is diminished.

---

[1] Codex T reads *these* [his].

[2] The Vatican edition has *To that which is objected* [Ad illud quod obiicitur], and next reads *does it not hold* [non habet] for *does it hold* [habet], but the authority of the manuscripts and edition 1 withstand these. Note above, that the Vatican edition, by prefixing the number 5 to this paragraph, exhibits those words which follow as a response to the fifth objection, when in fact they are the response to the other proposition of the fourth objection. — A little below this, form the more ancient manuscripts and edition 1, we have substituted *augment* [augmentum] for *augmentation* [augmentationem].

[3] Not a few codices, such as K V X and ee, have not badly *or it happens* [aut contingit].

[4] In codex M there is added *and* [et]. Then, after *of the formal* [formalis], in codd. M & Y (H and ff in the margin) there is added *active, however, properly speaking, that which augments finally as much as regards the*

terminus of the augmentation itself holds itself in the reckoning of the formal [activi, proprie tamen loquendo, illud quod augmentat finaliter quantum ad terminum ipsius augmentationis se habet in ratione formalis].

[5] In the book OF 83 QUESTIONS, q. 36, n. 1: « But charity's poison is the hope of obtaining and retaining temporal (goods) ». Which hope is by the same a little after this named *cupidity*.

[6] Ibid., and ENCHIRIDION, ch. 121, n. 32; see above q. 2 in the body of the question. — The Vatican edition after *whence* [unde], contrary to very many manuscripts and five first editions, omits *also* [et].

[7] Bk. X, ch. 29, n. 40.

[8] (St.) Augustine, ENCHIRIDION., ch. 12, n. 4: But it (i. e. evil) injures, therefore, it takes away (something) good. — A little before this codex Z incongruously has *because* [quia] in place of *what* [quod].

[9] The Vatican edition, breaking with very many manuscripts and edition 1, omits *also* [et].

---

* *Trans. note*: <u>Per contrarium</u> refers to the conversion of a proposition in the contrary sense: "It is impossible that it be"; *per oppositum*, "It is impossible that it not be". Cf. Pietro Ispano, TRATTATO DI LOGICA, tr. I, n. 25, a cura di Augusto Ponzio, Bompiani Editori, Milano, 2004, p. 35.

4. Likewise, every thing [illud] which by disabling itself[1] in regard to (its) terminus (of movement) is the cause of (its own) corruption, through disabling itself before (its) terminus is the cause of (its own) diminution; but free will disabled through aversion (from God) is the cause of the corruption of charity: therefore, a disabling less than God [sub Deo] (is) the cause of (charity's)[2] diminution.

5. Likewise, this very (thing) is shown through the nature of *charity itself* in this manner: « opposites are bound to come to be about the same (thing) »;[3] but an augment and a diminution are opposites: therefore, if it happens that charity is increased, it happens that it is also diminished.

6. Likewise, that which can be conserved [salvari] in 'being'[4] without the conjunction of it to something, can be separated from it before the conjunction; but charity before addition has a 'being' without an addition [additamento]: therefore, it can be separated:[5] and if this, therefore, (it) also (can) be diminished: ergo etc..

ON THE CONTRARY: 1. Charity is a form, simple and uniform throughout [per totum]; therefore, that which takes away from charity, for the reason that it takes away one part, it takes away[6] also the whole: and if this, therefore, it is never diminished.

2. Likewise, the magnitude of charity is according to the magnitude of the Divine Influence, therefore, its diminution is through a diminution of the influence; but God does not subtract His influence unless offended, and He is not offended except through aversion from Himself and contempt: therefore, charity is not diminished except through mortal sin; but this is not other than (through) charity being taking away [tolli]: ergo etc..

3. Likewise, everything [omne][7] which diminishes the other, is opposed to the other; but venial (sin) and/or cupidity or concupiscence in (something) on the way to [citra Deum] is not opposed to charity, nay it is entirely contingent with it: therefore, it is not diminished.

4. Likewise, what diminishes the other has an ability [posse] over[8] it; but venial (sin) does not have an ability over charity, because charity loves God more, than cupidity (does) a hundred marks of gold and silver:[9] ergo etc..

5. Likewise, this very (thing) is shown through the impossible in this manner: if a venial (sin) diminishes charity, therefore, something diminishes from it: if, therefore, charity is not of an infinite magnitude, therefore, a venial (sin) repeated several times takes away the whole charity, which is false.

6. Likewise, if it diminishes charity according to substance, therefore, it lessens the substantial reward due it; but the substantial reward is the Eternal Good:

therefore, a venial (sin) bears off something from the Eternal Good; but the ablation of the Eternal Good either simply and/or according to a part is the eternal punishment: therefore, a venial (sin) merits eternal punishment, which is contrary to the common opinion. If, therefore, a venial (sin) does not lessen the one, neither the other.

CONCLUSION

Charity, though it is taken away through a mortal sin, however, through a venial sin is not diminished according to substance, but only according to fervor.

I RESPOND: It must be said, that about this there is a twofold opinion, founded on the preceding, twofold opinion concerning the manner of augmenting charity.[10] For certain (authors) say, that charity is increased through a thorough unmingling [impermixtio]; and since a more *thorough unmingling* is according to a greater enabling [habilitionem] of free will and according to the diminution of concupiscence, and contrariwise a *thorough mingling* through a disabling of free will and[11] the augmentation of concupiscence: they say, <u>per consequens</u>, that it is diminished, according to which cupidity and/or concupiscence is increased and free will is disabled; and this is through venial sin. But since venial sin, remaining venial sin, is never repeated so many times, that it increases concupiscence,[12] so that one loves something above God [supra Deum]. for that reason charity can be lessened through venial (sins), but not taken away; but it is taken away through mortal (sin), which increases concupiscence above God.

But this opinion, as has been proven above,[13] does not have a stable foundation, since a substantial augment of charity does not come from free will nor from concupiscence,[14] and for that reason neither a diminution.

And on this account there is posited the other, more probable opinion, that charity is not lessened substantially; and this opinion is founded on this, that the augment of charity has its coming to be through the addition[15] and/or an increase [incrementum] of a greater influence. Which having been supposed it must be said, that charity is not lessened according to substance, but it is increased.

And the reason for this is taken from the part of (its) *opposite* or *agent*. For charity does not have an opposite, except mortal sin, through which, however, it is not lessened, but (rather)

---

[1] Some codices, such as X and Z, read *through disabling itself* [per sui dehabilitationem].

[2] Supply together with codex F *charity's* [caritatis].

[3] Aristotle, ON PREDICAMENTS, ch. "on Opposites", and TOPICS, Bk. II, ch. 3 (ch. 7). — A little before this very many codices, such as A S T W and Z, omit *charity* [caritatis].

[4] Trusting in the manuscripts and six of the first editions, we have inserted *in 'being'* [in esse]. Next codex Y has *another* [aliud] in place of *something* [aliquid].

[5] One or the other codex, such as V and ff, together with edition 1, adds *from that (addition)* [ab illo].

[6] In very many manuscripts and edition 1 there is lacking *it takes away* [adimit].

[7] The Vatican edition, contrary to very many codices and to edition 1, reads *every 'that'* [omne illud]. A little after this very many codices, together with edition 1, have *are opposed* [opponuntur] in place of *is opposed* [opponitur], but not coherently with what is subjoined.

[8] Many codices here and a little below this read *above* [supra].

[9] Nearly all the codices, together with edition 1, exhibit this abbreviation: *c. m. a. ar.*; codex O proffers the full text received (above),

while codex Y (H and ee by the other hand) puts *gold and silver* [aurum et argentum]; but the Vatican edition reads *a creature* [creaturam] for *a hundred marks of silver and gold* [centum marcas auri et argenti].

[10] See the preceding question.

[11] Codex Z adds *through* [per].

[12] Codex V reads *that concupiscence is increased* [quod concupiscentia augeatur]. A little after this very many codices, together with edition 1, have *diminished* [diminui] in place of *lessened* [minui],* and then codex X has *because* [quia] for *which* [quod].

[13] In the body of the preceding question.

[14] Understand this according to the aforesaid proposition: *does not come from the enabling of free will in good nor from the diminution of concupiscence.* The fault of the Vatican edition, which after *will* [arbitrio] puts *for that reason* [ideo] and then omits *for that reason neither* [ideo nec], we have corrected from the manuscripts and from editions 1, 4, 5 and 6.

[15] Some codices, such a I L and O, together with edition 1, read *super-addition* [superadditionem], which reading is corroborated by the mutilated reading of very many codices, which put *over* [super] in place of *through* [per]. Next edition 1 has *or* [sive] for *and/or* [vel].

---

* *Trans. note*: Here, the original footnote transposed <u>diminui</u> and <u>minui</u>, contrary to the received text and the context of the passage.

taken away; but concupiscence or cupidity and venial sin are opposed to charity according to fervor alone, because they stand together and are substantially incontingent[1] to themselves.

1. 2. And for that reason it must be solved according to the first two, because that (saying of St.) Augustine concerning cupidity and a lesser love [amore], (and) similarly[2] that concerning a venial diminution has a place only as much as regards the fervor of charity, and thus the first two are clear.

There is also accepted [sumitur] the reason, why charity is not lessened on the part of *its subject*, because there is free will according to (it's) conversion to God. Moreover,[3] free will disposes itself for the augment of charity through an ability, similarly for a diminution (of charity) through a disability (which is) less than a mortal (sin). But this disposition is from (something) fitting [de congruo], not from (something) completely worthy [de condigno]; and since God is more prone to be merciful than to condemn, and to grant than to subtract.[4] hence it is, that He bestows charity, when free will disposes itself from a fitting (work) [de congruo], but does not subtract (it), except when it necessarily disposes itself to a subtraction of grace. But this alone is through aversion, and then He taken the whole (of its substance) away. And hence it is, that charity is never lessened, but it is increased, because a subject can only prepare itself de congruo for a diminution.

3. To that which is objected, that just as a man makes progress, so does he frequently descend;[5] it must be said, that substantially charity is not in the same manner diminished through a descent, just as it is increased through an ascent.

4. Because it also[6] objects, that it can deprive free will entirely [totum] through a disabling etc.; it must be said, that that is false, because a substantial form is entirely deprived through a disposition to the opposite in the terminus (of movement), it is not, however, lessened through a disposition before[7] the terminus. *Besides*, that has a place, when the disposition in the terminus and before the terminus are of the same genus; but it is not so in the proposed (objection), because one (disposition) is a mortal sin, the other a venial one.

A reason is also taken [sumitur], why (charity)[8] cannot be lessened, on the part of *its own nature*. For (charity) itself is an influence according to the Divine Acceptance; but what God accepts,[9] this is from [ab] Himself and thus, what (has) more He also accepts more, and thus it can be increased from its own nature; but what He accepts less, this is not out of Himself: therefore, it is necessary [oportet] that it come from us: therefore, charity has a 'being increased' of itself, but a 'being lessened' it does not have except from us, as has been shown above.[10] But through us it can be lessened, and for that reason only an augment is due to charity according to its nature [naturaliter].

5. To that, therefore, which is objected, what opposites are bound to be etc.; it must be said, that it is true, unless the other one is in (it) through nature.

6. To that which is objected: it can be without addition, therefore, (it can) be separated; it must be said, that that is true, if it there were something separating (them), but there is nothing which separates (them).

SCHOLIUM

Of the ancient (scholastics Peter) of Auxerre and even, what is remarkable, (Bl.) Dionysius the Carthusian affirm, that charity according to habit can be lessened, which now is most commonly denied. — Alexander of Hales, SUMMA., p. II, q. 108, n. 8, § 3. — (Bl. John Duns) Scotus, REPORTATIO., here in q. 7. — St. Thomas, here in q. 2, a. 5; SUMMA. II II, q. 24, a. 10. — William of Paris, ON THE VIRTUES, c. 11, before the middle. — Bl. (now St.) Albertus (Magnus), here in a. 10. — (Bl.) Peter of Tarentaise, here in q. 2, a. 5. — Richard of Middleton, here in a. 2, q. 5. — Giles the Roman, here in 2nd. princ., q. sole. — Henry of Ghent, QUODLIBETALS, 5, q. 23. — Durandus (of Saint-Pourçain), here in q. 10. — (Bl.) Dionysius the Carthusian, here in q. 9. — (Gabriel) Biel, here in q. 4.

---

[1] Though the reading of the Vatican edition and of the other manuscripts, in which there is put *contingent* [contingentia] in place of *incontingent* [incontingentia], can be explained under some respect, we, however, prefer the reading of the very many manuscripts and edition 1, because they are more consonant with the truth itself and the aforesaid (propositions). A little before this codex Z reads *only* [tantum] in place of *alone* [solum].

[2] Trusting in the more ancient codices and edition 1, we have expunged the here badly added *to* [ad]. Next codices Y and bb read well *concerning the diminution of a venial (sin)* [de venialis diminutione]

[3] Very many codices, such as A T V and Y, omit *Moreover* [autem]; codex X reads *Because free will* [quia liberum arbitrium]; codex Z, however, with a changed punctuation, reads *For according to (its) conversion to God free will* [Secundum enim conversionem ad Deum liberum arbitrium], which does not respond to the subjoined. Next, codex W has *enabling* [habilitationem] for *ability* [habiliatem], just as also a little below this it reads *disabling* [dehabilitationem] in place of *disability* [dehabilitatem].

[4] The Vatican edition together with codex cc has *withdraw* [abstrahendum] and next *withdraw* [abstrahit] for *subtract* [substrahit], then to the noun *a subtraction* [subtractionem] it prefixes *a withdrawal and/or* [abstractionem vel], but the manner of speech (of the Seraphic Doctor) withstands this, just as also the authority of the more ancient manuscripts, together with edition 1. Next codex W has *not according to grace* [non ad gratiam] for *of grace* [gratiae].

[5] From the manuscripts and five first editions, we have substituted *descend* [descendit] for *recedes* [retrocedit], which is more conformable with the subjoined.

[6] The Vatican edition, together with not a few codices, reads *Moreover, because it is objected* [Quod autem obiicitur].

[7] Many codices, such as A B C D F G I P Q S U W and Z, read *within* [intra], but not well nor coherently with the subjoined. What a disposition *in a terminus* and *before a terminus* is, will sufficiently appear from these words of St. Thomas (SENT., Bk. IV, d. 17, q. 1, a. 5, solution to quaestiuncula 3): « The expulsion of a form means the terminus of movement of that, which has been ordered to corruption; and the introduction of a form means similarly the terminus of movement of that, which precedes generation; because both generation and corruption are the termini of a movement. But everything which is moved, when it is in the terminus of (its) movement, is disposed according to that, to which the movement is ordered, and for that reason since the movement of corruption tends unto 'not being' [in non esse], but (that) of corruption to 'being' [ad esse], when a form is introduced, there is a form; but when it is expelled, it is not ».

[8] Supply: charity.

[9] Very many codices, such as A F G H I T Y and bb, together with edition 1, exhibit this proposition thus, *according to which God accepts (it)* [secundum quod Deus acceptat], to which codices V and X prefix *that is* [id est]; codex T, however, next reads *but this* [hoc autem]. A little below this, trusting in the more ancient manuscripts and editions 1 and 3, we have substituted *its own* [sui] for *its own* [sua].

[10] Here, in the body of the question. — Next with the help of the more ancient manuscripts and edition 1, we have supplied *only* [solum], but codex Z reads *to charity alone* [soli ... caritati]; but the Vatican edition together with codex cc badly omit it altogether.

QUESTION IV

Whether charity has a terminus in (its) augment?

Fourth and last, there is asked concerning the augment of charity as much as regards (its) terminus, and there is asked, whether it has a standing-still [status] and/or terminus, beyond which it cannot be increased. And that (it is) so, is shown in this manner:

1. Everything which is in something, does not exceed the capacity of that in which it is; but charity is in the soul: therefore, it does not exceed the capacity of the soul. But the capacity of the soul is finite, because every finite power [potentia] has a finite capacity: therefore, also charity.

2. Likewise, an augment of charity is attained according to a quantity of *virtue*; but a quantity of virtue is similar to a quantity of *mass* and more perfect (than it); but in a quantity of *mass* there is a standing-still in it being augmented, whence the Philosopher (says):[1] « The nature of all constants is a terminus and a reckoning of magnitude and of augment »; therefore, similarly also in a quantity of *virtue*.

3. Likewise, an augment of charity is attained through an ascent to a perfect quantity,[2] therefore, what is always being increased [augetur] never comes to a perfect (state), « but the perfect is, that to which an addition is not possible »;[4] but it happens that charity, since it is a work of God, is perfected, *for the works of God have been perfected*:[4] ergo etc..

4. Likewise, an augment of charity is attained according to (its) drawing near [approximationem] to (its) end, for as much as charity (is) greater, so much (is it) nearer to (its) end;[5] therefore, either it never arrives at (its) end, or if so, it is necessary that it stand still, because otherwise (the end) would be as a trick: ergo etc..

On the Contrary: 1. That there is no standing still, is shown on the part of the *augmenting virtue*. For as much as the augment is extended, so much the augmentative virtue; but the virtue augmenting charity is a divine virtue, which does not have a terminus nor[6] a standing-still: ergo etc..

2. Likewise, this very (thing) is shown[7] on the part of the *one taking it up* [a parte suscipi-

entis]. For just as (something) transparent holds itself to a corporal light, so the capacity of the soul to the light of grace or of charity; but the air never receives so much from a light, that it still cannot receive more: ergo etc..

3. Likewise, this seems to be able to be shown on the part of the *augmentable*, which is charity, because it itself is equally and/or more fully in act than[8] material fire: but material fire by reason of its own actuality is increased in an unlimited manner [in infinitum], if (something) combustible is present, just as the Philosopher says:[9] therefore, in a similar manner charity from itself.

4. Likewise, this very (thing) is shown on the part of the *object of charity*, which is the most high Good, not having a measure: therefore, if a measure of charity ought to be attained through[10] the magnitude of (its) object, and that lacks a standard of measure [modo] and a measure, therefore, also charity: and if this, therefore, it does not have a standing still nor a terminus (in its augment).

CONCLUSION

Charity has a terminus in its augment, which is gathered as much as on the part of the acting virtue, as of the power taking it up, as of the perfecting form.

I Respond: It must be said, that there is a standing still in the augment of charity according to every standard of measure, according to which it happens that there is a standing still and perfection in a movement of increase.

For an augment, just as is clear in corporal (things), has a standing still from three (things): namely from the *acting virtue*, and *the power taking it up* and *the perfecting form*. So[11] it is in man, whose augment stands still, when the *virtue* of warmth and of the flesh according to (his) species cannot circulate [convertere] more fully, than be lost; when the *power* of the radical humor [humidi radicalis] cannot be more extended:[12] when

---

[1] On the Soul, Bk. II, text 41 (ch. 4). — A little before this cod. S, with edition 1, has *in the augment* [augmento] for *in it being augmented* [augmentando]. Next, after *similarly* [similiter], we have substituted, out of many mss., such as A G H I T W X etc., and from ed. 1, *also* [et] in place of *is it* [est].

[2] The Vatican edition, contrary to the manuscripts and edition, has *through an approach to perfect charity* [per accessionem ad caritatem perfectam]; many codices, such as A C F G I L P Q R S T U W etc., together with edition 3 and 6, have *quality* [qualitatem] in place of *quantity* [quantitatem], but in itself less well and contrary to those things which are had in the body of the question near the end. Codices aa and bb read *to quantity and to perfection* [ad quantitatem et perfectionem]; some codices, such as K and X, together with editions 2 and 3, read *an ascension* [ascensionem] for *an ascent* [ascensum].

[3] Aristotle; see above q. 2, in reply to n. 3. — Next edition 1, with some mss., expressly and well, has *happens that charity ... is perfected* [caritatem ... contingit] in place of *it befits charity ... to be perfected* [caritatem ... convenit].

[4] Deut. 32:4.

[5] In this respect Aristotle says, Metaphysics, Bk. V, text 21, (Bk. VI, ch. 16): For according to which they have (their) end, they are said (to be perfected). — Next, out of some manuscripts, such as M T Y and Z, we have inserted the next *either* [aut].

[6] We have substituted, with the help of the more ancient manuscripts and edition 1, *nor* [nec] in place of *and* [et].

[7] The Vatican edition, together with codex cc, has *is seen* [videtur], but breaking with all the other manuscripts and with edition 1.

[8] Trusting in very many manuscripts and edition 1, we have put *than* [quam] in place of *just as* [sicut].

[9] On the Soul, Bk. II, text 41 (ch. 4): For the augment of fire is in an unlimited manner, so long as there will be (something) combustible.

[10] Edition 1 reads *according to* [secundum].

[11] Some codices, such as K Y and cc, together with editions 2, 3, 4, 5 and 6, read *just as* [sicut]; codex Z *and so* [et sic]. Next, codex K after *stands still* [stat] adds *from three (things), namely* [a tribus scilicet].

[12] What a radical humor is according to the opinion of that age, (Bl. John Duns) Scotus explains, Physics, Bk. I, q. 10, n. 23: « Wherefore, note second, that there is a twofold humor, namely the radical and (that) of food. The radical is not fixed within the limits of [determinate in] any part of the body, but is scattered throughout the whole body and is in the whole corporeal matter, in which the soul is introduced at the beginning of generation, in which the soul is fostered and rooted, by the virtue of which afterwards the remaining humors [reliqua] are wrought in the body. And as long as this humor endures, life endures and with it consumed, (life) is consumed, and the soul departs. The humor of food or nourishment is that which comes to be out of food through is conversion into the substance of the one nourished [substantiam aliti], to repair what has been lost from the radical humor through the action of natural warmth. For though the natural warmth resides chiefly in the heart, which is the warmest of all the members, yet from there it is channeled into all the other parts of the body and is scattered throughout the whole body and immersed in the radical humor, in which (parts) it is consumed by its own action, and to the extent, that it is not consumed, it is necessary, that it be continually repaired through the internal taking up of extrinsic alimentation ». — A little before this codex K together with edition 1 has *more fully* [amplius] for *more* [plus]. A little after this codex M has *operation* [operationi] for *perfection* [perfectioni].

the body has been *perfected*, according to what is congruent with the perfection of the soul.

So it must be said, that charity stands still on the part of the *acting virtue*, but a standing still of this kind can be in a twofold manner.[1] For that virtue is either operating *naturally*, or from *design* [proposito]; if *naturally*, then it stands still, when it can not be more full; if *from design*, then it stands still, when it does not more fully dispose; and in this manner the augment of charity stands still, when it has arrived [deventum est] at (its) measure, which God has measured [mensus est] for a man according to the distribution of His Wisdom. And for that reason, although[2] the augmenting virtue is infinite, yet it works according to the disposition of Wisdom, limiting (its) various effects, according to which it is pleased. For He does not work according to (His) omnimodal possibility.

For (charity) stands still on the part of *the one taking it up*, because just as there is said in the twenty-fifth (chapter of the Gospel of St.) Matthew:[3] *He has given to each one according to their own virtue.* And a standing still of this kind can be understood in a threefold manner: either according to *act*, when (charity) does not proceed more fully, and in this manner it stands still in perfect men [viris], who do not rise up to greater (things); or according to *aptitude*, and in this manner it stands still in the blessed, because they cannot dispose themselves more fully and as much as they have, so much have they disposed themselves, whence there is a standing still in them; or according to the *possibility* of the one taking it up, and in this manner (charity) had a standing still in Christ,[4] and I believe also, that (thus it was) in the Blessed Virgin, and some say, that (it was thus also) in the Angels; whether in some others, I do not know. However, I do know concerning Christ, that[5] He has as much of glory, as a united creature can receive, and I believe this very (thing) of (His) Most Sweet Mother.

For (charity) stands still on the part of *the augmentable*, when it arrives [pervenit][6] at the perfect quantity. But it must be noted, that the perfect quantity of a virtue is in a twofold manner: either *simply*, and/or *in genere*. *Simply* the perfect (quantity of charity) is in the most high and most simple (act), as (it is) in God; however, *in genere* (it is) in all (the acts), which[7] stretch out to the complete act, for which they are, and this is *to love God with one's whole heart and with one's whole soul and with all one's virtue.*[8] In the first manner there is not a standing still, but only in the second.

1. To that which is first objected concerning the in-

finity of *the acting virtue*, it must be said, that that reason would hold, if the virtue augmenting charity acts naturally and according to the impetus or according to its own, whole ability [posse]; but now (this divine virtue) acts wisely and thus puts a limit upon each one, (though) it itself in itself not limited.

2. To that which is objected *through (what is) similar* in the air, that the potency of the one taking it up is according to an infinite degree [ad infinitum], it must be said, that '*that a light in the air be increased*', this is in a twofold manner: either through its *being made bright* [clarificationem], and/or through *the aggregation of lights*. In the first manner I believe that it has a standing still;[9] for air could be illumined to such an extent, that even if another light would come upon it, it would not grow more bright. In the other manner light in the air can be increased through *the aggregation of lights*; and thus, because the lights of diverse luminaries are in the same point of the air, they do not constrict [coangustant][10] themselves nor expel themselves, just as many species (do) in one medium; and thus there are never so many species, that there cannot be more; similarly of lights. But then it is not similar concerning charity, since, just as has been touched upon before,[11] in one soul there is only one charity; not so is it concerning the light, which steps forth form diverse luminaries.

3. To that which is objected on the part of the *augmentable*, that fire is augmentable in an unlimited manner; it must be said, that warmth can be increased in a twofold manner: either *intensively*, and thus it has standing still and a most high (degree): and/or *extensively*,[12] so that it is in very many (things), and thus it does not have a standing still on its own part, but on the part of the combustible, which is finite. Similarly, I say, that charity can be increased *intensively*, so that one loves more, and in this manner it has a standing still, just as fire (does); in the other manner *extensively*, as on the part of (things) loved, and in this manner it does not have a standing still on its own part, because (charity) never loves so many, that it is bound [nata est] not to love still more.

4. To that which is objected on the part of the *object*,[13] it must be said, that the object causes nothing regarding this, because the Object is also the same unchanged [non mutatum] and is infinite; and for this reason charity is never commensurate with It nor does it receive an augment according to Its measure,[14] nor a decrease [decrementum].

---

[1] Some codices, such as X and Y, have *twofold* [duplex] for *in a twofold manner* [dupliciter]. A little before this edition 1 has *its standing still* [huius status] for *a standing still of this kind* [huiusmodi status]. On the following division of operative virtue, cf. Aristotle, MAGNA MORALIA, Bk. I, ch. 16 (ch. 17), where it concerns προαιρεξι, which in the more ancient translations was exhibited with the noun *design* [propositum] and/or *choice* [delectus].

[2] The Vatican edition, together with codex cc, reads *though* [licet]. A little before this codex C reads *is going to give to man* [daturus est Deus homini].

[3] Verse 15.

[4] See more on this below in d. 44, Doubt 3, where (the Seraphic Doctor also speaks) of the Blessed Virgin Mary, and in Bk. III, d. 13, a. 1, q. 3.

[5] Out of the more ancient manuscripts and edition 1, we have substituted *that* [quod] for *because* [quia]. A little below this after *Most Sweet Mother* [Mater dulcissima], in codex H there is added *fully of grace, who begot (Him) God and man* [plena gratiae, quae Deum genuit et hominem].

[6] Codex Y reads *it will have arrived* [pervenerit], which also next puts *twofold* [duplex] in place of *in a twofold manner* [dupliciter].

[7] The ancient codices, together with edition 1, have *which (things)* [quae] in place of *which (acts)* [qui]. A little before this some codices, such as H M P Q and T, together with edition 1, add *it is* [est] after *however* [vero], but a few, such as V and X, add *such as* [ut] for the implicit *(it is)*.

[8] Matthew 22:37, and Mk. 12:30.

[9] Codices aa and bb read *it has a 'being illumined' that has stood still* [statum illuminari habeat].

[10] The Vatican edition together with edition cc read *constrain* [angustant].

[11] Above, in q. 2, in reply to n. 4. — Next codex 1 reads *neither* [nec] for *not* [non], and codex Y *as* [ut] in place of *which* [quod].

[12] The Vatican edition adds *that is* [id est], codex cc *and* [et], but the more ancient codices, together with edition 1 omit either conjunction. A little before this in codex S after *has* [habet] there is adds *on (its) part* [a parte], in which addition there has certainly fallen away *its* [sua].

[13] Trusting in the manuscripts and edition 1, we have expunged the *of charity* here added by the Vatican edition.

[14] Codex T reads *nor is it measured according to It nor* [nec ad illud mensuratur nec]; some codices, such as A S V and X, together with edition 1, faultily add *neither* [nec] after *measure* [mensuram].

SCHOLIUM

I. St. Thomas seems to solve this question in one manner in his COMMENTARY, here in q. 2, a. 4, and in another manner in his SUMMA., II II, q. 24, a. 7. Nevertheless, Cajetan on this cited passage rightly asserts, that « the text (of St. Thomas) exhibits one (understanding) on it surface, and in truth teaches another », and he explains his words in this sense, that he only speaks of the charity of the wayfarer [caritate viae], of which there can be no doubt. For the heresy of the Beghards, who asserted that one can acquire such a grade of perfection in this life, that he can make no more progress in grace or charity, has been condemned by Pope Clement V, in the Council of Vienne (PP. Clement, ON HERETICS, chapter "To Our"). But, elsewhere, St. Thomas (SUMMA., III q. 7, articles 7, 9, and 11) seems to teach the common sentence. For because he there (in a. 9) affirms of Christ, that His soul had the highest grade of grace according to intensive quantity etc., he sufficiently shows, that he does not dissent from St. Bonaventure, who (here in Doubt 1) professes the same of Christ together with the sentence of the better Scholastics, which Durandus (of Saint-Pourçain) and a few others contradict.

II. Alexander of Hales, SUMMA., p. I, q. 21, m. 3, a. 5 and 6. — (Bl. John Duns) Scotus, in each version, SENT., Bk. III, d. 13, qq. 1, 2, and 3. — Bl. (now St.) Albertus (Magnus), SENT., Bk. I, d. 44, a. 5. — (Bl.) Peter of Tarentaise, here in q. 2, a. 4. (who expressly says that the sentence of St. Bonaventure is « the more plain and more common »). — Richard of Middleton., here in a. 2, q. 4. — Giles the Roman, here in 1st. princ., q. 4. — Henry of Ghent, QUODLIBETALS., 5, q. 22. — Durandus (of Saint-Pourçain), here in q. 9. — (Bl.) Dionysius the Carthusian, here in q. 8. — (Gabriel) Biel, here in q. 8.

DOUBTS ON THE TEXT OF THE MASTER

DOUBT I

In this part fall [incidunt] the doubts on the text (of Master Peter's second part), and the first concerns this which he says, that *to Christ the Spirit has not been given according to a measure.* For its seems false, because every finite (thing) has a measure: therefore, if the Holy Spirit has not been given to Christ according to a measure, the Infinite Spirit has been given to Christ. But against this is, that all created (things) are of a finite capacity.

I Respond: This will be more clear below,[1] now it just suffices, that this has either been said on account of the grace of *union*, which caused, that all those which belong to God, to belong to that Man; and/or on account of the grace of *the Head*, because in Christ the grace for all acts has not been constrained, just as in (one's) head live [vigent] all the senses. Whence that determination does not deprive (the Man) of finiteness, but deprives the determination according to some act or special gift.[2]

DOUBT II

Likewise is asked of this which (St.) Augustine says, that *charity is the most upright affection of our spirit.* For it seems that he speaks badly, because no habit is an affection; charity is a virtue and thus a habit: therefore, it is not an affection.

I Respond: It must be said, that affection is said in a fourfold manner: in one manner as the affective *force* itself, in another manner affection is said (to be) the *passion* of the affective force, as (is) joy and sorrow and (passions) of this kind; in a third manner it is said (to be) the *act* of the affective power;[3] in a fourth manner it is said (to be) the affective *habit*, just as 'understanding' [intellectus] is in one manner said (to be) the habit of principles, which[4] is the rule of the intellect [regula intellectus]: and in this manner it is accepted, when there is said, that charity is an affection, and in a similar manner does (St.) Bernard[5] accept (it), when he says, that virtue is an ordinate affection.

DOUBT III

Likewise is asked of this which Master (Peter) says, that *charity works the other acts and movements within, by means of the other virtues.* For he seems to speak against that which is said in the fifth (chapter of the Letter of St. Paul) to the Galatians:[6] *Faith works through charity.*

I Respond: It must be said, that although it can be sustained, that charity works by means of the other virtues as (its) ministers, nevertheless the others (are) also through helping and directing charity; yet the solution of Master (Peter), which he makes here, is not valid, because Master (Peter) begs the principle (of his argument) in solving (it). For he supposes, in the solution, the opposite of that which he proves. For since the Holy Spirit does not effect in us the works of the other virtues without intermediary habits, in what manner does He effect in us the work of love [opus dilectionis]? *If you say*, that He Himself is Love, similarly I can say, that the Son is Wisdom and the Word, therefore, for an equal reason without an intermediary habit He ought to illumined the intellect. And on this account the opinion of Master (Peter) is, thus,[7] not probable neither as much as regards (its) reasons, nor as much as regards (its) authorities. Which is clear, if the aforesaid solutions are attended to. For in all the solutions Master (Peter) begs what is in the principle (of his argument).[8]

---

[1] SENT., Bk. III, d. 13, a. 1. — Next, from the manuscripts, we have inserted *now* [nunc], to which codex Y adds (the explicit) *this* [hoc] (for the implicit *it*).

[2] The Vatican edition together with codex cc reads *or special good* [sive speciale bonum], but contrary to the other codices and to editions 1 and 3.

[3] Codex M has *the affective act* [actus affectivus].

[4] Very many codices, together with the Vatican edition, put *and* [et] in place of *which* [qui], others omit *which* [qui], others, such as H T V and Y, together with edition 1, exhibit the reading received in the text.

[5] ON GRACE AND THE FREE WILL, ch. 6, n. 17: So that the virtues are nothing else but ordinate affections.

[6] Verse 6, where the Vulgate reads: *Faith, which works through charity* [Fides, quae per caritatem operatur]. — A little before this, in the text of Master (Peter), very many codices, such as A G I K T etc., omits *means of* [mediantibus].

[7] Codex X omits *thus* [ita], which also a little before this with one or the other codex, such as V, has *for that reason* [ideo] in place of *on this account* [propter hoc]. Next, some codices, such as S and T, after *nor* [the second *nec* in the Latin text], omit less well *as much as regards* [quantum ad].

[8] The last proposition, *For in all* etc., we have supplied out of the more ancient manuscripts and edition 1. — See the solutions presented by Master (Peter) here in his text, ch. 6, and in (St. Bonaventure's COMMENTARIES), p. I, q. 1.

DOUBT IV

Likewise is asked of this which (Master Peter) says, that *the Holy Spirit is not divided*. For it seems that he says the false, because in the eleventh (chapter) of Numbers[1] there is said, that the Lord said to Moses: *I shall take from thy spirit* etc. *Likewise*, in the fourth (chapter) of the First (Letter of St.) John:[2] *Of His Spirit He has given us*; if He have of the Spirit, it seems, that either He gave the whole, and/or He divided (Him) in parts.

I Respond: It must be said, that the Holy Spirit is in His very Self simple and for that reason in Himself undivided; but in (His) effects He is manifold, and for that reason as much as regards effect He is divided, because He is not given to each one [singulis] according to all (His gifts). And hence it is — because[3] He was given more fully to Moses than to others — that for that reason He says: *I shall take from thy spirit*; and because He is not given to us according to all (His gifts), for that reason blessed John (says): *Of His Spirit he has given us*.

DISTINCTION XVIII

CHAPTER I

Whether it must be conceded, that gifts are given through a gift.

Here, there is asked, since the Holy Spirit, through whom gifts are divided (among the faithful), is Himself a gift, whether it must be conceded, that through a gift gifts are divided and given.[1] To which we say, that through a gift, which is the Holy Spirit, (gifts) proper to each are divided, and all the good commonly have that (gift). Whence (St.) Augustine in the fifteenth book, ON THE TRINITY[2] says: « Through the gift, which is the Holy Spirit, the many gifts, which are proper to them, are divided in common to all the members of Christ. For no single one has them all, but these those, and those others, although the gift itself, by which (the gifts) proper to each are divided, all have, that is, the Holy Spirit ». Behold he openly says, that through a gift gifts are granted.

CHAPTER II

Whether the Holy Spirit is said (to be) a "gift" for the same reason, that (He is said to be) "given" or "granted".

Besides, it must be diligently considered, since the Holy Spirit is said (to be) a "gift" and a "given", whether[3] for the same reason each noun befits Him, as it can at least seem (to be). For since it is that the Holy Spirit is given and that the Holy Spirit is granted, the Holy Spirit seems from the same reason to be said (to be) "given" and a "gift". This (St.) Augustine also seems to signify in the fifteenth book, ON THE TRINITY,[4] when he says: « The Holy Spirit inasmuch as He is the Gift of God, insomuch is He given to those to whom He is given, but in Himself [apud se] He is God, even if He is given to no one ». Behold he openly says, that the Holy Spirit is named "gift", because He is given. Moreover, if He is named "gift" only on account of this,

that He is given, He was not from eternity a "gift", because He is not given, except in time.

To which we say, that the Holy Spirit is both said (to be) "a gift" and "a given" or "a granted", but is said (to be) "a given" or "a granted" for this only, that He is given and/or granted, which He has only in time.

On the other hand, He is said (to be) "a gift" not from this only, that He is granted, but from the property, which He had from eternity; wherefore He was also from eternity a gift. For sempiternally He was a gift, not because He was given, but because He proceeded from the Father and the Son. Wherefore, (St.) Augustine in the fourth book, ON THE TRINITY[5] says: « Just as for the Son 'to have been born' is 'to be from the Father', so for the Holy Spirit 'to be the Gift of God' is 'to proceed from the Father and from the Son' ». Here there is openly shown, that the Holy Spirit is a gift for this, that He proceeds from the Father and from[6] the Son, just as the Son is from the Father for this, that He has been born from Him. For it is not the same for the Son and the Holy Spirit to be from the Father, that is, the Son is not said to be from the Father by that property, by which the Holy Spirit (is). For the Son is said to be "from the Father", because He has been begotten from Him; but the Holy Spirit is said to be "from the Father and from the Son", because the Holy Spirit is the Gift of the Father and of the Son, that this, because He proceeds from Each. For[7] He is said (to be) "the Holy Spirit" for this, that (He is) the Gift; and "the Gift" for this, that (He is) proceeding. Wherefore, (St.) Augustine in the fifth book, ON THE TRINITY[8] says: « The Holy Spirit, who (is) not the Trinity, but (rather) is understood (to be) in the Trinity, in this that He is properly said (to be) "the Holy Spirit", is said (to be such) in a relative manner, when He is referred both to the Father and to the Son, because the Holy Spirit is the Spirit of both the Father and the Son. But that relation does not appear in this name, but it does appear, when He is said (to be) "the Gift of God": for He is the Gift of the Father and of the Son, because He proceeds from the Father and from the Son ». Behold with these words there is openly shown, that the Holy Spirit is for the same reason also said (to be) "a gift"; but "a gift", because He proceeds from the Father and the Son. Therefore, the property, whereby He is

---

[1] Verse 17.

[2] Verse 13.

[3] Very many codices, together with the Vatican edition, have *that* [quod] for *because* [quia], but less clearly and distinctly, and for that reason we follow edition 1; codex X, however, has *that because* [quod quia], which can be explained as missing from all the other codices. Next after *to others* [aliis], the codices dissent among themselves; some with the Vatican edition put *and because for that reason* [et quod ideo], others *and for that reason* [et ideo], codex H *for the reason that* [ideo quod], codex F *for that reason He says* [ideo dicit], but a greater part of the codices, such as G I K T V W X etc., together with edition 1, exhibit our text. The reason for this disagreement seems to have been in this, that a little before this very many codices, as we have said, put *that* [quod] in place of *because* [quia]. Cf. d. 18, Doubt 6.

NOTES ON THE BOOK OF SENTENCES

[1] Edition 8 has these two verbs in the indicative: edition 1 also has the particle *or* [aut] for *and* [ac].

[2] Ch. 19, n. 34. — At the end of this text, before *that is* [id est] only

the Vatican ed. has *have* [habent] for *have* [habeant], and ed. 4 even worse *are had* [habeantur]. Then editions 1, 2, 3 & 7 omit *Behold* [Ecce], and for very last word *are granted* [donari] edd. 1 and 8 have *are given* [dari].

[3] Editions 4, 5, 6 and 9 insert *also* [et].

[4] Chapter 19, n. 36. — At the end of the quote, the Vatican edition and the other editions, contrary to the original, to the codices and to editions 1 and 8, have the indicative *is given* [datur].

[5] Chapter 20, n. 29.

[6] The codices, except A, and editions 1 and 8, omit *from* [a].

[7] The codices omit *For* [enim].

[8] Chapter 11, n. 12. — In this text, contrary to the codices, edition 1 and the original, and the Vatican edition, together with the other editions, add *is* [est] before the first *Trinity* [Trinitas]. The same Vatican edition, together with very many editions, before *the Son* [Filium] omits *to* [ad]. The last words of the text: *and from the Son* [et a Filio], are expressed by (St.) Augustine in this manner: *And that which the Apostle says: he who does not have the Spirit of Christ, does not belong to Him* (Rom. 8:9), *at any rate speaks of the Holy Spirit Himself.*

said (to be) "the Holy Spirit" and/or "a gift", is the procession itself, with which we will deal more fully afterwards together with the other (properties).[1] Therefore since He proceeded from eternity from Each, He was also from eternity a gift. Therefore, the Holy Spirit is not said (to be) "a gift" for this only, that He is granted; for He was also a gift before He was granted. Whence (St.) Augustine in the fifth book, ON THE TRINITY (says):[2] « The Holy Spirit always proceeds, and He proceeds not in time, but from eternity; but because He was thus proceeding, to be grantable, He already was a gift, before there was that to which He would be given. For it is understood in one manner, when there is said "a gift", in another when there is said "a granted": for "a given" can also be, before it is given; but "a granted", unless it will have been given, in no manner can be said ». « Therefore, the Holy Spirit is sempiternally a gift, but temporally a granted ». With these words there is openly shown, that just as the Holy Spirit proceeds from eternity, so is He a gift from eternity, not because He was given by the Father to the Son, and/or by the Son to the Father, but because from eternity He has proceeded as "a grantable".

But there is asked, "a grantable" to whom: whether to the Father and to the Son, or whether only to us, who were not yet? But if He was not grantable to the Father and to the Son, but only to us, and was a gift from this, that He was proceeding in this manner as a grantable, it seems that the Son for the same reason always was a gift; because from eternity He proceeded from the Father as grantable to us in time. For it is also read of the Son,[3] that He *is given to us*. To which we say, that the Holy Spirit proceeded as a grantable only to us, not to the Father and/or to the Son, just as also He has only been given to us. And the Son has been truly given to us and has from eternity proceeded from the Father, not only as a grantable; but as One begotten, who also could be granted. Therefore, He proceeded as One begotten and grantable; but the Holy Spirit does not proceed as One begotten, but only as the Gift. Moreover, He always was a gift, not only because (His is) grantable, but because He proceeded from Each, and because[4] He was grantable. Wherefore, (St.) Augustine in the fifth book, ON THE TRINITY[5] says: « By the very fact, that God was going to give Him, He was already a gift, even before He was given », and for that reason (He was)[6] grantable; but grantable in a manner other than the Son; for He (has been) both given and has proceeded in a manner other than the Son. For the procession of the Son is a begetting [genitura] and/or nativity, but the procession of the Holy Spirit is not a nativity; however, each is ineffable.

CHAPTER III

That just as the Son by being born accepted not only, 'to be the Son', but also '(to be) the Essence', so the Holy Spirit by proceeding accepted not only, 'to be a gift', but 'to be the Essence'.

And it must be noted, that just as the Son, by being born, accepted not only, 'to be the Son', but 'entirely to be' and 'to

be the Substance Itself', so also the Holy Spirit by proceeding from the Father and the Son accepted not only, 'to be the Holy Spirit and/or a gift', but also, 'to entirely be' and 'to be the Substance'; which at any rate He did not accept for the reason that[7] He is given. For since He is not given but in time, if He would have this for the reason that He is given, He would have accepted, therefore, in time, to be. Wherefore, (St.) Augustine in the fifth book, ON THE TRINITY[8] says: « The Son by being born not only has this, that He is the Son, but entirely that He is. Therefore, there is asked, whether the Holy Spirit for this, that He is given, has not only, that He is a gift, but entirely that He is. Which if He is not, unless because He is given, that is, if He does not have "being" [esse], unless for this, that He is given, just as the Son by being born has not only, that He is the Son, which is said in a relative manner, but entirely to be the Substance Itself, in what manner was the Holy Spirit the Substance Itself, since He was not given before there was that to which He was given »? Therefore, not for this, that He is given, but by proceeding does He have, that He is a gift, and that He is the Essence; just as the Son not for this, that He has been given, but by being born accepts not only, 'to be the Son', but 'to be the Essence'. Wherefore, (St.) Augustine in the fifteenth book, ON THE TRINITY[9] says: « Just as the generation presents [praestat] the Essence to the Son without the beginning [initio] of time, without any changeability in the Nature of the Father [mutabilitate naturae de Patre], so the procession presents the Essence to the Holy Spirit without any beginning of time, without any changeability of the Nature of Each ».

Here, there arises the question: "If the Son by being born has not only, that He is the Son, but that He is the Essence, and the Holy Spirit by proceeding not only, that He is a gift, but that He is the Essence; is, therefore, both the Son by the nativity the Essence, and is the Holy Spirit by the procession, the Essence?"; since elsewhere there is said, that neither the Father for this, that (He is) God, is the Father, nor the Son for this, that (He is) God, is the Son, nor the Holy Spirit for this, that (He is) God, a gift; because, as (St.) Augustine says in the seventh book, ON THE TRINITY,[10] « with these names those (things) relative to Them are shown, not (Their) Essence ». With which we will more fully deal afterwards.[11]

To which responding briefly, we say, that neither is the Son by the nativity the Essence, but only the Son; nor is the Holy Spirit by the procession the Essence, but only the Gift; and yet Each, both the Former by being born and the Latter by proceeding, accepts, 'to be the Essence'. « For not », as (St.) Hilary says in the fifth book, ON THE TRINITY,[12] « through a defection, or an extension [protensionem], or a derivation from God is He God, but (rather) the Son subsists by the nativity, out of the virtue of the Nature upon [in] the same Nature », and out of the virtue of the Nature upon the same Nature, does the Holy Spirit (also) subsist.

Which can thus be understood: out of the Father, who is the Unbegotten Virtue, the Nature, which He has, the Same the Son by the nativity, that is by being born, and the Holy Spirit by the procession, that is by proceeding, has. Whence, expressing [eloquens] the same more openly,

---

[1] Supply with edition 1 *properties*, with which this and Distinctions XXVI, XXVIII, and XXIX deal.

[2] Chapter 15, n. 16. — And the following passage is ibid., ch. 16, n. 17. — In the first passage, at the beginning of the sentence *For it is understood* etc.[Aliter etc.] there is in the Vatican ed. very many edd., contrary to the original, the codd. and edd. 1 and 8, *He would be given* [donaretur].

[3] Isaias 9:6

[4] The Vatican edition and editions 4 and 6, omit *because* [quia].

[5] Chapter 45, n. 16.

[6] Contrary to the codd. and to ed. 1, the Vatican edd., with the other edd. adds *He is* [est], but *grantable* [donabilis] must rather be referred to the preceding *was* [erat]. A little after this the Vatican edition and edd. 4, 6 & 9, have *is given* [datur] for *(has been) given* [datus], ed. 8 reads *has been given* [datus est]. — The last sentence has been taken according to its sense from AGAINST MAXIMINUS, Bk. II, ch. 14, n. 1.

[7] The Vatican ed. and very many edd., here and a little after this, have *from this that* [ex eo quod] for *for the reason that* [eo quod]. The particle *from*

[ex] is omitted by all the codd. and ed. 1, here and in the following text of (St.) Augustine; *that* [quo] is read here in the text of (St.) Augustine and in codd. B & C. The other codd. in the text of (St.) Augustine indeed have *that* [quo]; except for this, that now one has *that* [quo], now another *that* [quod]. With the original of (St.) Augustine we have always put *that* [quo].

[8] Chapter 15, n. 16, but more diffusely. From codices A C and D we have inserted *says* [ait], which is lacking in the editions.

[9] Chapter 26, n. 47. — A little before this the Vatican ed., by omitting *be* [sit], faultily reads *as the Essence* [ut essentia]. The same Vatican ed., with very many edd., omits in the text of (St.) Augustine *any* [ulla] before *changeability* [mutabilitate].

[10] Chapter 2, n. 3, but with a changed order of words.

[11] Distinctions XXVI, XXVII, and XXIX.

[12] N. 37. — In the original of (St.) Hilary there is better read: *through a dissection* [per desectionem] for *through a defection* [per defectionem], which all the edd., the codd. and even the edd. of the Commentators, such as (St.) Bonaventure, here in Doubt 4, and St. Thomas, in the exposition of the text.

he himself reveals [aperit], what he had said, subjoining:[1] « The nativity of God », he says « cannot not hold that Nature, by which it has come forth [profecta est]. For no Other than God subsists, because from nowhere else than from God does He subsist ». Behold with these words he reveals, in what manner this must be accepted:[2] « From the Father the generation presents the Essence to the Son, and from Each the procession presents the Essence to the Holy Spirit »; not because the Former by the Essence is the Son, and the Latter by the Essence is the Holy Spirit, nay by the personal property (of Each), but because both the Former by being born, and the Latter by proceeding, have the same and the whole Essence, which is in the Father.

CHAPTER IV

That the Holy Spirit is said (to be) a "gift" and a "granted" according to the two aforesaid manners of procession, who, according to which He is a gift, is referred to the Father and the Son, according to which a given, to Him who gives and to those to whom He is given.

From the aforesaid it is clear, that the Holy Spirit is a gift sempiternally, and temporally (is) a given and/or a granted. From which appears that distinction of the twin procession, with which we have dealt above.[3] For according to the latter procession He is said (to be) "a granted" and/or "a given", but according to the former He is said (to be) "the Gift".

And according to this, that He is sempiternally a gift, He is referred to the Father and the Son, but according to this, that He is said (to be) "a given" and/or "a granted", He is referred both to him who gives, and to those to whom He is given, and He is said (to be) of him, who gives, and to those to whom He is given. Whence (St.) Augustine in the fifth book, ON THE TRINITY[4] says: « Because He is "a given", He is referred both to him who has given, and to those to whom he gave. And so the Holy Spirit is said (to be) not only "of the Father" and "of the Son", who gave (Him), but also "*ours*", who accepted (Him). Therefore, the Spirit is both God's, who gave, and ours, who have accepted; not that spirit of ours, by which we are, because (that) is the *spirit of a man, which is in him*:[5] even though that spirit, which is said (to be) "*of man*", we have certainly [utique] accepted; but the Former in one manner, the latter in another, is said (to be) "*ours*". For one is that which we accepted, to be, the Other that which we accepted, to be holy. Moreover, that the Holy Spirit is said (to be) ours, Scripture shows. For it is written of (St.) John (the Baptist), that he came *in the Spirit of Elijah*.[6] Behold the Spirit was said (to be) "of Elijah", that is the Holy Spirit, whom Elijah accepted. And to Moses the Lord says:[7] *I shall take of thy spirit and I shall give (it) to them*, that is, I shall give them of the Holy Spirit, whom I have already given to thee ». Behold here also He is said (to be) the spirit "of Moses". Therefore, it is clear, that the Holy Spirit is said (to be) "our spirit", that is,[8] because (He has been) given to us, and given certainly [utique] for this, that we be holy. However, the created spirit has been given for this, that we be.

CHAPTER V

Whether the Son, since He has been given to us, can be said (to be) "ours", as the Holy Spirit (is).

Here, there is asked, whether the Son also, since He has been given to us, is said and/or can be said (to be) "*ours*". To which we way, that[9] the Son is said (to be) "our Bread", "Our Redeemer" and (things) of this kind; but is not said (to be) "our Son", because "the Son" is said in a manner relative only to Him who begets. And for that reason He cannot be said (to be) "our Son", but the Father's only. Moreover, in this that He is said (to have been) *given*, He is both referred to Him who gave, and to those to whom He has been given, as the Holy Spirit (is);[10] who also, since in the Scripture, as has been said before, is said (to be) "our spirit", and/or "thy spirit" and/or "his", as has been said of Moses and Elijah, yet never in Scripture does it thus occur that there be said: "our Holy Spirit" and/or "thy" and/or "his", but "our spirit" and/or "thy" and/or "his", because He is said (to be) "the Holy Spirit" for this, that (He is) "a gift", and each (name) is said in a manner relative to the Father and to[11] the Son, and this by a sempiternal relation. Yet, if at any time He is said (to be) "our gift", "gift" is accepted as "granted" and/or "given". However, when "gift" is accepted in the manner, whereby (He is) the Holy Spirit, He is said only[12] (to be) the Gift "of the Father and the Son", not "of a man"; thus also the Son cannot be said (to be) "*ours*" under this appellation, that He be said (to be) "our Son", just as neither is the Holy Spirit said (to be) "ours", and yet of the Son there is said "our Bread", and of the Spirit "our spirit". The Former (is) "our Bread", because as One given to us He refects us; the Latter "our spirit", because He breathes into us from the Father and the Son, and breathes in us, as He will. Whence (St.) Augustine in the fifth book, ON THE TRINITY[13] says: « What has been born of the Father is referred to the Father alone, when there is said "the Son"; and for that reason He is the Son of the Father, and not ours. Yet, we do also say "*give us ... our daily Bread*", just as we say, "our spirit" ».

CHAPTER VI

Whether the Holy Spirit is referred to Himself.

After these there is asked, whether the Holy Spirit is referred to Himself: for this seems to be able to be proven from the aforesaid. For if because He is given He is referred to him who gives, and to him to whom He is given, and the Holy Spirit is given by Himself, as has been said before, therefore, He is referred to Himself. The determination of this question we defer to later, when we shall treat of those (things) which are said in a relative manner, on account of time,[14] of God, among which are contained the "given" and the "granted".

---

[1] Loc. cit., with a few words interposed. — The Vatican edition and very many editions read *saying* [dicens] for *subjoining* [subdens], and only the Vatican edition adds *as* [ut] before *he says* [inquit].

[2] Namely, (St.) Augustine, ON THE TRINITY., Bk. XV, ch. 26, n. 47: cf. above p. 320, footnote 9. — Immediately before this, in place of *accepted* [accipiendum] the Vatican edition, together with very many editions, has *understood* [intelligendum].

[3] Distinction XIV.

[4] Chapter 14, n. 15.

[5] (St.) Augustine alludes to 1 Cor. 2:11: *For who of men knows, what are a man's, except the spirit of the man, which is in him?* [Quis enim hominum scit, quae sunt hominis, nisi spiritus hominis, qui in ipso est?]

[6] Lk. 1:17. — Immediately after this the Vatican edition alone, together with the original, omits *Behold* [Ecce].

[7] Num. 11:17. The Vulgate reads: *I shall take of thy Spirit and I shall give to them* [Auferam de Spiritu tuo tradamque eis]. — Only the Vatican edition exhibits a truncated passage, by omitting an entire line, namely: *thy Spirit and I shall give (Him) to them, that is, I shall given them of the Spirit* [tuo et dabo eis, id est, dabo illis de Spiritu].

[8] The Vatican edition and very many editions read *but* [sed], contrary to codices A an D and to edition 1. Codex C by glossing reads: *the Spirit, that which we are, but because He is given to us* [Spiritus, non quod sumus, sed quia nobis datur].

[9] Codices B and E and editions 1 and 8 *that* [quod]. But it is common for Master (Peter) to employ *because* [quia] for *that* [quod]. — Then we follow codices B C D and E according to the position of the words, while the editions read *only in a relative manner* [tantum relative]; the same codices have *to the One* [ad illud] for *to Him* [ad eum].

[10] Only the Vatican edition and edition 4 superfluously adds *is* [et] after *as* [ut]. — Then the same Vatican edition, together with very many editions, reads *has been said above* [supra dictum est] for *has been said before* [praedictum est].

[11] The Vatican edition and editions 1 and 8 omits *to* [ad].

[12] The Vatican edition together with the other editions, but with editions 1, 6 and 8, and the codices contradicting this, omits *only* [tantum]. Next after *also the Son* [et Filius] edition one inserts *of God* [Dei].

[13] Chapter 14, n. 15, but in truncated form in Master (Peter)'s text. This refers to the Lord's Prayer, Mt. 6:11, Lk. 11:3.

[14] Distinction XXX.

COMMENTARY ON DISTINCTION XVIII

On the property of the Holy Spirit, according to which it befits Him to proceed temporally.

Here, there is asked, since the Holy Spirit, through whom gifts are divided, is Himself a gift, etc..

THE DIVISION OF THE TEXT

This is the third part of this part, in which Master (Peter) deals with the temporal procession of the Holy Spirit. For having determined the *principle*, from which the Holy Spirit proceeds, having determined also the *manner*, according to which He proceeds, Master (Peter) determines here the *property*, according to which it befits [convenit] Him to proceed temporally; and this property is "gift", and he intends to deal with this in the entire present distinction. Moreover, this part is divided into four parts, according to the four questions, which he moves.

In the *first*, he asks and determines, whether the Holy Spirit is the Gift, in which[1] the other gifts are granted.

In the *second*, he asks,[2] whether the Holy Spirit is a "given" and a "gift" for the same reason, there (where he says): *Besides it must be diligently considered, since the Holy Spirit is said (to be) a gift and a given.*

In the *third*, he asks, since not only the Holy Spirit, but also the Son has been given, for what reason is (the Latter) not said (to be) *our Son*, just as (the Former) *our Spirit*, there (where he says): *Here there is asked, whether the Son also, since He has been given to us* etc..

In the *fourth*, and last he asks, since the Holy Spirit

is "a gift" in a relative manner, in what manner can He be given by Himself; for if He is granted[3] by Himself, "the Holy Spirit" seems to be said in a manner relative to Himself, and this he does there: *After these there is asked, whether the Holy Spirit is referred to Himself.*

With all the other parts remaining undivided, because he prosecutes in a special manner the aforesaid questions, the middle or *second* part, which concerns the difference of "gift" and/or[4] "given", has four parts. In the first he asks and determines, that the Holy Spirit is not for the same reason said (to be) a "gift" and a "given", because He is a "gift" from eternity, but a "given" in time. However, in the second, contrary to this, that is that the Holy Spirit is eternally a gift, he objects, there (where he says): *But there is asked, to whom (is He) grantable, whether to the Father, and/or to the Son?* But, in the third, because he had spoken in the solution of a certain doubt, he for that reason moves and determines it incidentally, there (where he says): *Here there arises a question, if the Son by being born* etc.. However, in the fourth and last he returns to the first solution, showing, that the Holy Spirit is eternally a gift, because He is a gift for this, that He proceeds from the Father and the Son,[5] and this he does there (where he says): *From the aforesaid it is clear, that the Holy Spirit is a gift sempiternally.*

TREATMENT OF THE QUESTIONS

Having supposed from the aforesaid, that the Holy Spirit is a gift and that He is granted, there are asked, for an understanding of this part, six (questions):

First, there is asked, whether the Holy Spirit is the Gift, whereby all other gives are granted.

Second, whether the Holy Spirit is[6] a gift either from eternity, and/or in time.

Third,[7] what is said more fittingly of the Holy Spirit, that is, "gift" or "given".

Fourth, whether "gift" properly befits [proprie convenit] the Holy Spirit.

Fifth, whether "gift" is a distinctive property [proprietas ... distinctiva] of the Holy Spirit.

Sixth, whether the Holy[8] Spirit is said to be "ours" by reason of (His) donability [ratione donabilitatis].

---

[1] In codex B there is added *all* [omnia].

[2] The Vatican edition, together with the other manuscripts, reads *there is asked* [quaertur].

[3] Codex X reads *is given* [datur].

[4] Edition 1 with one or the other codex has *and* [et] in place of *and/or* [vel].

[5] In the Vatican edition alone there is added *and that He is temporally a "given" and/or a "granted"* [et quod temporaliter est datum vel

donatum], which corresponds to the text of Master (Peter).

[6] From the manuscripts and edition 1, we have supplied *is* [sit].

[7] Trusting in the very many manuscripts and in edition 1, we have expunged the added *there is asked* [quaeritur].

[8] Codices S and V omits *Holy* [sanctus], which reading harmonizes with the manner, in which this question is proposed by all the manuscripts below.

ARTICLE SOLE

On the property of the Holy Spirit, whereby He is a gift.

QUESTION I

Whether the Holy Spirit is the Gift, in Which all other gifts are given?

About the first, that the Holy Spirit is the Gift, whereby all the other gifts[1] are granted, is shown *by authority* and *by reason*.

1. *By authority* in this manner: The Apostle (says) in the twelfth (chapter) of the First (Letter) to the Corinthians:[2] *Divisions of graces there are, but the same Spirit, who divides to each one, as He wills*: and he speaks of gifts not only of the grace which makes one pleasing, but also (of those) which have been freely given: and if through the Holy Spirit each are given, since there is no other difference of gifts, He Himself is the Gift, in which all other gifts are granted.

2. Likewise, (St.) Augustine in the fifteenth (book) ON THE TRINITY (says):[3] « Through the Gift, which is the Holy Spirit, common to all the members of Christ, gifts proper to each are divided ».

3. Likewise, it shown *by reason* in this manner: the Holy Spirit is the first Gift, but every posterior is lead back [reducitur] to the prior: therefore, every gift is lead back to the Gift, which is the Holy Spirit: therefore, in all gifts the reckoning of being granted [donationis] is through the Holy Spirit: ergo etc..

4. Likewise, every gift, inasmuch as (it is) a gift, is given out of love [amore], otherwise it does not have the reckoning of a gift; but « the Holy Spirit is the Love of the Father and of the Son », as (St.) Augustine says, and as is had above:[4] ergo etc..

ON THE CONTRARY: 1. (St.) Isidore (of Seville says):[5] « To many unworthy of the Holy Spirit are the gifts of the Holy Spirit given »: therefore, it happens that other gifts are given without Him. therefore, He is not the Gift, in which all other gifts are given.

2. Likewise, there are some gifts, which are appropriated to the Son, as for example, are those which are given for the act of enlightening the intellect [ad illustrationem intellectus]: therefore, if we are to speak appropriately, such gifts are granted[6] in the Son or through the Son, not by the Gift, which is the Holy Spirit.

3. Likewise, the Son has been given to us, according to the ninth (chapter) of Isaias:[7] *A little boy has been born for us, the Son has been given to us*:

therefore, if He is given through the Holy Spirit, it seems that the Holy Spirit has some authorship and/or influence upon the Son; but this is false: therefore, not all the other gifts are granted through the Holy Spirit.

4. Likewise, this very (thing)[8] is shown through the *impossible*: let it be that there is understood by way of the impossible, that the Holy Spirit is not, yet the Father and the Son are understood as liberal, (then) liberality is in Them in a manner other than from the Holy Spirit, which is false: therefore, if They are understood (to be) liberal, therefore, also as Grantors.

5. Likewise, if the Holy Spirit is a gift, in which the other gifts are granted, therefore, a gift belongs to a gift and a being granted [donatio][9] to a being granted, and if this, a movement belongs to a movement and a relation to a relation, and this the Philosopher[10] holds as unfitting. For since the one dependent cannot terminate the other one, there will be a procession unto infinity [processus in infinitum].

CONCLUSION

This saying, if "in which" is taken in the sense of concomitance, is true only in regard to gratuitous gifts; but if in the sense of causality, and indeed of an exemplar cause, it is true in regard to all gifts.

I Respond: It must be said, that when it is said, that the Holy Spirit is the Gift, "in which" [in quo] all other gifts are granted, that ablative can be accepted in a twofold manner: either such, that it means a *concomitance*, and/or such,[11] that it means a *causality*. If it means *a concomitance*, thus understood *universally*, it is false; because the sense is, that He is given with all gifts. For there are certain gifts, which are *always* with the Holy Spirit, such as charity and wisdom; certain ones, which[12] are *never* with the Holy Spirit, as servile fear; certain ones,

---

[1] In some codices and in the Vatican edition there is lacking here and very often hereafter in this question *gifts* [dona].

[2] Verses 4 and 11, where the Vulgate has *dividing* [dividens] in place of *who divides* [qui dividit]. A little before this the Vatican edition, contrary to the manuscripts and to edition 1, has *and first through the Apostle saying* [et primo per Apostolum dicentem] for *By authority in this manner: Apostle* [Auctoritate sic: Apostolus].

[3] Chapter 19, n. 34: Through the Gift, which is the Holy Spirit, many gifts, which are proper to each, are divided to all the members of Christ in common. — In which text the Vatican, together with codex cc, yet breaking with the more ancient manuscripts and edition 1, has *the many gifts of God, which are proper to each, are divided* etc. [quae sunt quibusque propria Dei dividuntur]

[4] Distinction X, in the text of Master (Peter), chs. 1 and 2.

[5] SENTENCES, Bk. I, or ON THE HIGHEST GOOD, ch. 15, n. 8: Sometimes the gifts of the Holy Spirit are conferred upon the non-worthy and the reprobate. — Codex Z, together with the edition of the works of St. Isidore, has *unworthy of* and *reprobate by* [indignis et reprobis].

[6] Edition 1 with one or the other codex reads *are given* [dantur].

[7] Verse 6.

[8] From the more ancient manuscripts and edition 1, we have inserted *very (thing)* [ipsum].

[9] Trusting in the manuscripts and in edition 1, we have expunged the added *belongs* [est].

[10] PHYSICS, Bk. V, texts 10-18 (ch. 2), and METAPHYSICS, Bk .XI, ch. 11 (Bk. X, ch. 12), where among all the other arguments there is also had this one, that, if a movement belongs to a movement, one that is to stand still belongs to a progression unto infinity, which he reproves. Cf. also PRIOR ANALYTICS, Bk. I, ch. 37 (ch. 35). — Next the Vatican edition, contrary to nearly all the codices and to edition 1, incongruously has *determine* [determinare] for *terminate* [terminare].

[11] From the older manuscripts and editions 1, 2, 3 and 6, we have substituted *such* [ita] in place of *thus* [sic].

[12] Edition 1 here and a little below this omits *which* [quae]. Next codex Z has *not even* [non et] and codex V *however they are not* [autem non sunt] in place of *without* [sine].

which *sometimes* are with the Holy Spirit, *sometimes* without, such as faith, prophecy and (gifts) of this kind.

But, if it be understood *particularly* of the gifts of grace which make one pleasing,[1] in this manner (the concomitance) is true and does not have opposition [instantiam].

Again, this[2] ablative can convey *causality*, and this in a threefold manner: either such, that is means *simply* causality, and in this He is not distinguished neither from the Father nor from the Son, because all gifts are from the Father and from the Son, as[3] (they are) from the Holy Spirit; and/or such, that it means *causality and subauthorship*, and in this He is distinguished from the Father, but not from the Son, because the Father grants (gifts) both through the Son and through the Holy Spirit; and/or such, that[4] it means *causality and subauthority and exemplarity*, and thus it does properly befit the Holy Spirit. For He Himself proceeds through the manner of a first gift, such that every right and gratuitous donation is after that one and accepts a reckoning of donation from that one. It must be conceded, therefore, that the Holy Spirit is the Gift, whereby all gifts, that is, gratuitous ones, are granted through concomitance, and whereby *all* the gifts of God are granted through the Cause of *exemplarity*.

1. To that, therefore,[5] which is objected first from (St.) Isidore, the response is already clear, because he speaks of the gifts of the grace freely given, not (of the grace) which makes one pleasing.

2. To that which is objected second, that certain gifts are appropriated to the Son; it must be said, that there is a speaking of "gifts" in a twofold manner: either by the reckoning *of that which*

is under [subest], or under[6] the reckoning *of a donation*. By the reckoning *of that which is under* some gifts are appropriated to the Son, as wisdom and understanding (are), some to the Holy Spirit, as charity (is). However by the reckoning *of donation*, all are appropriated to the Holy Spirit for the reason already said,[7] because through Him as through the First Gift, the others are granted.

3. To that which is objected, that the Son has been given, and not by the Holy Sprit, it can be responded, that the Son has been given according to (His) human nature, and this was through love, according to the third (chapter of the Gospel of St.) John:[8] *Thus has God loved the world, that He gave His own, Only-Begotten Son.*

4. To that which is objected, that, with the Holy Spirit excluded [circumscripto], there still remains the reckoning of a gift; it must be said, that, with the Holy Spirit excluded, there is an understanding of a causality and subauthority of gifts in God, but not an exemplarity of donation under the reckoning of donation, because the process of love is not understood; and in this last manner it is properly said to befit the Holy Spirit.

5. To that which is objected, that then there is a gift of a gift, it must be said, that a movement does not belong to a movement, as *to a terminus*, similarly neither a relation to a relation; yet as *to a principle* and[9] to a movement a movement does belong, because a movement is a principle of a movement, and a relation of a relation; and in this manner there is said a gift (belongs to) a Gift. And because in causing, one stands still in the first, since He is the First Gift, there is no infinite regression [abire in infinitum]. *Besides*, a "gift" among the divine means a true Hypostasis.

SCHOLIUM

I. Of this name, "gift", which is proper to the Holy Spirit, the Seraphic (Doctor) speaks more abundantly than all the ancient masters on this entire distinction. — The proposition, that the Holy Spirit is the Gift, in which all other gifts are granted, if the words "all gifts" are taken universally, can be understood in a false sense, since there are certain gifts, which indeed are granted *through* the Holy Spirit, but not *with* the Holy Spirit. For the Council of Trent says (Session 14, ch. 4, "On Contrition"): « That fear is indeed a gift of God, yet not of the Holy Spirit indwelling, but of Him impelling ». If the Seraphic Doctor affirms, that servile fear is never with the Holy Spirit, he understands "servile fear" in a servile manner [serviliter], which cannot stand with sanctifying grace, but (rather) the properly, simply servile fear, just as also the hope, which is established from Trent (Session 6, chapter 9). On the fear and its species, see SENT., Bk. III, d. 15, Doubt 5, and d. 34, p. II, articles 1 and 2.

II. For an explanation of the solution to n. 5 there can serve the words of Richard (of Middleton), here in q. 5, in reply to n. 2: « Although a movement does not begin another movement as its *proper* and immediate terminus, yet it is certain, that through one movement another is caused. And far from ad infinitum, through an eternal Gift, which is a subsisting thing, a created gift can be immediately caused ». In nearly the same manner St. Thomas solves this objection, here in q. 1, a. 3; Bl. (now St.) Albertus (Magnus), here in a. 1, in reply to n. 1; (Bl.) Peter of Tarentaise, here in q. 3, a. 1, in reply to n. 6.

III. Besides the authors already mentioned, cf. Alexander of Hales, SUMMA., p. I, q. 64, m. 1. — St. Thomas, loc. cit. and SUMMA CONTRA GENTILES, Bk. IV, ch. 21. — Giles the Roman, here in 1st. princ., q. 3. — Henry of Ghent, SUMMA., a. 61, q. 2. — (Bl.) Dionysius the Carthusian, here in q. 1.

---

[1] The Vatican edition, with codex cc, not trusting in the more ancient mss. and ed. 1, reads *of the gifts making one pleasing* [de donis gratum facientibus]. Next, codex X has *it is true* [verum est] for *(the concomitance) is true* [vera est]: *it* referring to the proposition: *the Holy Spirit is the Gift, in which* etc..

[2] In the Vatican edition there is lacking *this* [iste], which however, is had in the manuscripts (in very many as *that* [ille]) and in edition 1. [Trans. note: here *this* refers to the "*in which*" of the proposition *that the Holy Spirit is the Gift in which all the other gifts are granted*.]

[3] On the authority of very many mss., we have put *as (they are)* [ut] for the less distinct *and* [et], for which edition 1 has *just as* [sicut].

[4] Some codices, such as V and X, together with edition 1, read *that* [quod] for *that* [ut].

[5] From many manuscripts and edition 1, we have supplied *therefore* [ergo].

[6] In codex X there is lacking *under* [sub]. Next after *By the reckoning* [Ratione], we have, together with codex Z and edition 1, omitted the *however* [vero], which many codices together with the Vatican edition have. A little below this in codex X after *some* [aliqua] there is repeated *are appropriated* [appropriantur].

[7] In the body of the question, near the end. Next codex O omits *the others* [alia].

[8] Verse 16.

[9] In codex O there is lacking *and* [et].

QUESTION II

Whether the Holy Spirit is a "gift" from eternity, or in time?

Second, there is asked, whether the Holy Spirit is a gift from eternity, and/or in time [ex tempore]. And it seems that (He is such) in time:

1. (St.) Augustine in the fifteenth (chapter) ON THE TRINITY (says):[1] « He is a gift for this, that He is given to those to whom He is given »; but He is given in time: ergo etc..

2. Likewise, (he says) in the fifth (chapter) ON THE TRINITY:[2] « He is said (to be) a "gift" for this, that God was going to give Him »; but it is established, that He was going to give Him in time: therefore, if He is an eternal "gift", the temporal is the cause of the eternal.

3. Likewise, this[3] seems through *reason*. For "gift" not only means a comparison to the one giving, but also to him to whom it is given: therefore, having posited a "gift", there is posited *one giving* and *one receiving*, because a relation posits (its) extremes;[4] but the one receiving is a creature: ergo etc..

4. Likewise, "gift" adds upon "given", because « a gift is a un-returnable giving »:[5] therefore, if the Holy Spirit has not been given except in time, neither is He a gift except in time.

5. Likewise, just as to the Son it belongs to be generated, so to a gift to be granted; but there is no Son, before He is generated: therefore, neither a gift, before it is granted; but He is granted in time: ergo etc..

ON THE CONTRARY: 1. (St.) Augustine (says) in the fifth (chapter) ON THE TRINITY:[6] « Because the Spirit was proceeding, to be grantable, He already was a gift »; but "that He proceeds as a grantable", this is eternal: therefore (He is) also a "gift" from eternity.

2. Likewise, in the same place (he says) more expressly:[7] « The Holy Spirit is sempiternally the Gift, however, temporally He is given ».

3. Likewise, this very (thing) seems *by reason*, because where there is gratuitous love, there is a reckoning[8] of a gift; but from eternity there is in God a positing of gratuitous love: therefore, also of a gift.

4. Likewise, where there is a perfect reckoning of liberality, there is a gift; but among the divine there is from eternity a perfect reckoning of liberality: ergo etc..

5. Likewise, just as the reckoning of a "word" holds itself to the production of things, so the reckoning of a "gift" to the distribution[9] of graces; but before the production of things at the

beginning there was the Word; therefore, before the conferral of graces at the beginning was the Gift.

CONCLUSION

"Gift" as a "given" is said temporally; however, "gift" as a "sometimes to be given" and/or as a "grantable" is said eternally.

I RESPOND: It must be said, that since "gift" means a looking-back to him to whom it is given, this can be in a threefold manner: either according to *act*, and/or according to *habit*,[10] and/or according to *aptitude*. If according to *act*, in this manner "gift" is meant, because it is given; if according to *habit*, in this manner "gift" is meant, because sometimes (it is) to be given; if according to *aptitude*, in this manner "gift" is meant, because (it is) grantable.

According to the first acceptation it is said temporally; but according to the second and third it is said eternally. And in these three senses does (St.) Augustine accept it. It must be conceded, therefore, that according to any acceptation He is said (to be) a "gift"[11] eternally, just as the reasons brought forward for the second part prove.

1. To that, however, which is objected unto the contrary, it must be said, that it proceeds from "gift", such as it means the *act* of the donation, and thus is meant in time; wherefore the objection is not valid.

2. To that which is objected second, that He is said (to be) a "gift" for this, that He was going to be given etc.; it must be said, that according to that acceptation He is said (to be a "gift") eternally, because (that acceptation) does not mean a looking-back to the creature according to *act*, but according to *habit*, just as even predestination (does).

What, therefore, is objected, that then the temporal is the cause of the eternal ; it must be said, that that participle *"going to give"* [daturus] conveys two (things), namely "an ordination to the one going to give" and "the act[12] of ordination"; and the ordination is eternal, though the act is temporal; and then the ablative does not mean a causality by a reckoning of act, but by a reckoning of the ordination.

---

[1] Chapter 19, n. 36. See the text of Master (Peter here) in ch. 2, at the beginning.

[2] Chapter 15, n. 16. Cf. the text of Master (Peter), ch. 2, near the end.

[3] Trusting in the older manuscripts and edition 1, we have inserted *this* [hoc].

[4] Codex I *each extreme* [utrumque extremum], as is also had below in the response to this objection.

[5] Aristotle, TOPICS, Bk. IV, ch. 4. — The sense is: a "gift" is a "liberal giving", which comes to be without the intention of a retribution.

[6] Chapter 15, n. 16; see here the text of Master (Peter), ch. 2, near the middle.

[7] Chapter 16, n. 17. Cf. the text of Master (Peter), ch. 2, near the middle. — We follow the very many codices, together with edition 1, by substituting *in the same place* [ibidem] for *the same* [idem].

[8] The Vatican edition, together with codex cc, incongruously has *a grace* [gratia] for *a reckoning* [ratio].

[9] Codex X here, as in the immediately following propositions, reads *conferral* [collationem].

[10] Though the manuscripts, together with first six editions, put here, and a little below this, *habitude* [habitudinem] in place of *habit* [habitum]: we, however, prefer the reading of the Vatican edition, both because the noun, *habitude* [habitudo] is commonly accepted by the Seraphic Doctor in another sense (cf. below a. 6), and, because in the following propositions (except response to n. 3, in which many codices exhibit *habitudinal* [habitudinalis] in place of *habitual* [habitualis]), especially in q. 5, all the codices have *habit* [habitum]. Which touches upon the subject, as you may notice, because in this member of the distinction, in respect to the gift, there is hinted at a special determination, which, below, in reply to n. 2, is called the *ordination* [ordinatio], through which it is constituted in the reckoning of the future and is distinguished from the other members.

[11] The Vatican edition, together with codex cc, contrary to the more ancient codices and edition 1, adds *of God* [Dei].

[12] Understand: *the execution* [exsecutionem].

Yet it can be said, that it[1] means a cause of consequence, not of the consequent.

3. To that which is objected, that it means a relation to extremes; it must be said, that an actual relation posits each extreme in act, but a habitual relation[2] (does) not, just as it is clear, that God is said (to be) eternally the Exemplar of the temporal creature.

4. To that which is objected, that "gift" adds above "given"; it must be said, that "gift" in certain (things) is consequent to the reckoning of a "given", as for example are those which of themselves do not mean liberality, except insofar as there is added to them a reckoning of communication, such as book, a small knife [cultellus] and (things) of this kind. In something a "given" is consequent to the reckoning

of a "gift", as for example in that which of itself conveys liberality, even if "gift"[3] is never given, such as love is: and in this manner it befits the Holy Spirit.

5. To that which is objected, that just as to the Son it belongs to be generated etc.; it must be said, that it is false, because to be generated means the emanation of the Son, which according to the reckoning of understanding precedes the Son; whence it is impossible, that He be, unless He is generated; but to be granted does not only mean the emanation of a gift, but means more fully its communication, and this is consequence to the "being" of a gift, and for that reason He is not said (to be) a "gift" in time, though He is granted in time.

SCHOLIUM

I. In regard to the sense of the question it must be noted, that these sayings differ: "to be in time" [ex tempore], "to be with time" [cum tempore], "to be in a time" [in tempore]. The first signifies, that the "being" has a start, and is said of all created things; however, the second, that some being is coexistent to time, which can even be said of God, but the third, that something is measured by time, which properly is said of corruptibles.

II. The threefold conclusion is build upon this fundament, that a "gift" means a looking-back [respectum] to him to whom it is given, and that this looking-back can be threefold. The second and third of which, which is only

according to a reckoning [secundum rationem], is not a relation in act, which always posits even its own extremes in act, but a relation in habit and/or aptitude, as is better explained in solution to nn. 2 and 3. In the principal matter all the Masters agree. Alexander of Hales, SUMMA., p. I, q. 64, m. 2. — Bl. (now St.) Albertus (Magnus), here in a. 6; SUMMA., p. I, tr. 8, q. 36, m. 2, partic. 2. — (Bl.) Peter of Tarentaise, here in q. 2, a. 2, quaestiuncula 1. — Richard of Middleton, here in q. 4. — Henry of Ghent, SUMMA., a. 59, q. 5, n. 32. ff. — (Bl.) Dionysius Carthusian, on this and the following 3 questions, here in q. 2., near the end. — (Gabriel) Biel, on this and the following 3 questions here in article sole.

QUESTION III

Whether "gift" is more fittingly said of the Holy Spirit, than "given"?

Third, there is asked, whether "gift" [donum] is more fittingly said of the Holy Spirit than "given" [datum]. And it seems that "given" is said as fittingly as[4] "gift":

1. Because in the first (chapter of the Letter of St.) James (there is written):[5] *Every best given and every perfect gift is from above*; therefore, by the Holy Spirit there are thus "givens", just as "gifts": therefore just as to Him there is transferred the reckoning of a gift, so also of a given.

2. Likewise, of the movable and the moved there is the same reckoning,[6] therefore, similarly of the given and the grantable: therefore, if "gift" is said in the reckoning of the grantable, but "given" in the reckoning of the actually "given", therefore, the same is the reckoning of "gift" and of "given", ergo etc..

3. Likewise, in every genus act is more perfect than potency:[7] therefore, since "given" means "in act", "gift" "in potency", something is more perfectly expressed when there is said "given" than "gift"; but what is of a greater perfection more properly befits God: ergo etc..

4. Likewise, when any two are said of something, the one of which is the reason for saying the other of the same, that is more fittingly said, which is the reason for saying;[8] but "given" and "gift" are said of the Holy Spirit, and as (St.) Augustine wants,[9] « He is said (to be) a "gift" for this, that He is given »: therefore, He is more properly said (to be) a "given".

ON THE CONTRARY: 1. "*Given*" convenes with [convenit] the Holy Spirit solely [solum]

---

[1] Understand: that ablative *for this that* [eo quod]. On the distinction of *consequence* and *of the consequent* cf. below d. 38, a. 2, q. 1 in the body, and elsewhere in passing. — The explanation of this solution is given by Bl. (now St.) Albertus (Magnus), here in a. 6, in reply to n. 4: It must be said, that it is a causality of consequence and not of the consequent, and in this manner an effect does, indeed, infer the cause; and there is the causality of the consequent, and in this manner an effect does not infer the cause, but rather the other way around, and in this manner is this; wherefore when from a temporal there is inferred the eternal, there is not but a reckoning, of consequence and not of the consequent.

[2] Very many codices, together with edition 1, have *habitudinal* [habitudinalis], some, such as F H P Q X, have *habitual* [habitualis], the Vatican edition, together with editions 2, 3, 4, 5 and 6, has *a relation according to habit* [habitu relatio]. See above in the body of the question.

[3] The Vatican edition, contrary to the manuscripts and first six editions, reads *even if it is never given as a gift* [etiamsi nunquam detur dono] . Next, after *in this manner* [sic] codex M adds "*gift*" [donum] for the subject of the verb.

[4] Codex X has *as* [quam] in place of *as* [ut].

[5] Verse 17. — A little below this, after *Holy Spirit there are* [Spiritu sancto], we have supplied from the more ancient man-

uscripts and edition 1, *thus* [ita], which the Vatican edition, together with codex cc, has less well omitted.

[6] Bl. (now St.) Albertus (Magnus), here in a. 2 exhibits the same proposition, thus: Of the movable and the moved there is one reckoning of substance, not differing except through act and potency. — A little after this not a few codices, such as T and V, have *means* [dicit] for *is said* [dicitur]. Then, the Vatican edition, together with codex cc, less aptly, and not trusting in the other codices together with edition 1, has *of the actuality of the "given"* [actualitatis dati].

[7] Cf. Aristotle, METAPHYSICS, Bk. IX, text 15 (Bk. VIII, ch. 8), where there is proven, that act is according to substance (i. e. according to perfection) before potency.

[8] Similar is the saying of Aristotle, POSTERIOR ANALYTICS., Bk. II, ch. 2: That on account of which each one is, (is itself) also more. And METAPHYSICS, Bk. II, text 4 (Bk. I in the shorter version, ch. 1): But each one itself most of all belongs to the others, according to which there is a univocity in the others. Next, trusting in edition 4, we have also substituted *are said* [dicuntur] for *is said* [dicitur].

[9] ON THE TRINITY, Bk. XV, ch. 19, n. 36; see the text of Master (Peter) here in ch. 2.

in time, but "gift" eternally: therefore, He is more properly said (to be) a "gift".

2. Likewise, even if He were never given by an act, He would be "gift" and "spirit": therefore, it seems, that "gift" more properly befits Him.

3. Likewise, the Gloss on that (verse) in the first (chapter of the Letter of St.) James:[2] *Every best given* etc., says that « "given" is said in regard to natural (gifts), "gift" in regard to gratuitous ones ». If, therefore, the gratuitous are more aptly appropriated to the Holy Spirit, who sanctifies, than the natural ones: therefore, among the divine "gift" is better said of the Holy Spirit than "given".

4. Likewise, « a gift is an un-returnable giving »;[3] but whatever God gives, He gives in an un-returnable manner, because though He gives, He can receive nothing: therefore, among the divine a "*given*" has the reckoning of a "*gift*" and puts on its reckoning: therefore, more fittingly is He said (to be) a "gift" There than a "given".

CONCLUSION

The Holy Spirit is more fittingly said (to be) a "gift" than a "given", which is proved by a twofold reckoning.

I RESPOND: It must be said, that although among the divine each is said, both "*given*" and "*gift*", yet "*gift*" is more fittingly said. And the reason for this is twofold. One indeed is, because "given", since it is either[4] a participle and/or a verbal noun, concerns time; but a "gift" subtracts from time; and for that reason, because all divine (things)[5] are above time, more fittingly is there said among the divine "*gift*", than "*given*". The other reason is, because "gift" adds upon the reckoning of "given" the condition of liberality or un-returnability, which is a condition of great nobility; and for that reason it is most suitable [maxime competit][6]

to the divine. And this is the reason, why "gift" is appropriated to gratuitous gifts, not only to the Holy Spirit Himself, who is the Principle of gratuitous gifts.

1. And from this the response is clear to that (objection) concerning the authority of blessed James.

2. To that which is objected, that[7] of the mobile and the moved there is the same reckoning; it must be said, that it is not similar concerning the mobile and the moved, and concerning "gift" and "given": because that "it has been moved" adds above "the mobile" an *act*[8] and means the whole, which "mobile" means. But "given" does not mean the whole, which "gift" means, as much as it concerns the general understanding[9] of the noun, unless it is appropriated, « for a "gift" is an un-returnable giving », and this will be more clear in the fourth problem.

3. To that which is objected, that an act is the perfection of potency; it must be said, that something is in potency as regards act in a twofold manner: either on account of the imperfection of the *agent*, or on account of the defect of the *one taking it up*. If there is a potency in the first manner, then the act is the perfection of the potency, but if in the second manner, it is not (its) perfection.[10] Whence if there is said, that the shining Sun by act *can* illumine the house, which has is not open, and *does illumine* the house opened, there is noted entirely no greater perfection[11] than before. In this manner it must be understood concerning donability and actual donation.

4. To that which is objected, that[12] "given" is the reason for saying "gift", because (it is) for that reason a "gift", because it is given; it must be said, that it is not the entire reason, just as is said in the text (of Master Peter),[13] but only in comparison to him to whom it is given. — And/or it can be said on the part of our intellect: for this reason is He said (to be) a "gift", because He is given; but yet on the part of the truth[14] of the thing it is the other way around, because for this reason is He given, because He is a "gift".

SCHOLIUM

I. The solution to the last objection can serve to illustrate better the solution to n. 3. We, indeed, name created things *from the grant* or act of donation a "*gift*", but this is not valid concerning the infinite and eternal Gift, which is the Holy Spirit, Who is, least of all, ever in potency, as a gift is, and when He is granted, is not reduced to the act of *a gift*, but only (to that) of *a granted*. But *having been granted*, since the donation comes to be in a time, there is only the extrinsic reckoning of an eternal gift.

II. In the conclusion all agree: Alexander of Hales, SUMMA., p. I, q. 64, n. 2, in reply to n. 3. — St. Thomas, here in q. 1, a. 2; SUMMA., I, q. 38, a. 2. — Bl. (now St.) Albertus (Magnus), here in a. 2. — (Bl.) Peter of Tarentaise, here in q. 2, a. 2, quaestiuncula 2. — Richard of Middleton, here in q. 1, in reply to n. 2. — Henry of Ghent, on this and the following 2 questions, SUMMA., a. 61, q. 3, nn. 19 and 20, and q. 8, n. 5 ff.

---

[1] In codex I there added this other argument: *The same* ("gift") *means a comparison of Person to Person, but "given" of the Person to a creature; but more properly is the Person compared to a Person than the Person to a creature: therefore, more fittingly is there said "gift" of the Holy Spirit, than "gift"* (given) [Idem (donum) dicit comparationem personae ad personam, datam vero personae ad creaturam; sed magis proprie comparatur persona ad personam quam persona ad creaturam: ergo convenientius dicitur donum de Spiritu sancto quam donum (datum)].

[2] Verse 17, in (Nicolas) of Lyra: "Given" is referred to nature, "gift" to grace.

[3] Aristotle, TOPICS, Bk. IV, ch. 4. See above q. 2, 4th opposing argument . — Next codex S has *when He gives* [dum dat] for *though He gives* [cum det].

[4] From many mss., such as A F G I S T X etc. and ed. 1, we have inserted *either* [vel]. This reason is explained by the words of Bl. (now St.) Albertus (Magnus), here in a. 2: "Given" [Datum], which is a particle and consignifies a time, similarly "giving" [datio] and "granting" [donatio] are verbal nouns and thus temporal, consignifying acts, though they do not consignify a time.

[5] Many codices, together with editions 2, 3, 4, 5, and 6, have *gifts* [dona] for *divine (things)* [divina], and edition 1 reads *divine gifts* [dona divina] in place of *all gifts* [omnia divina], but less aptly, as is it is clear; the error of the codices perhaps has arisen from the abbreviation of the word *divine* [divina]. St.

Thomas offers the same reckoning here in a. 2: Hence it is, that "gift" is very suitable to divine (things), which are without time, than (is) "given". — A little before this codices L and O, together with edition 1, have *abstracts* [abstrahit] in place of *subtracts* [subtrahit], which reading is more congruous with the common manner of speaking.

[6] Not a few codices, such as I and W, read *it is most fitting* [maxime convenit].

[7] In very many mss., such as A T & V, and ed. 4, there is lacking *that* [quod]. A little below this, very many mss. with the first six editions, have *"granted"* [donato] for *"given"* [dato], which is less congruous with what follows.

[8] Many codices with edition 1, omit *an act* [actum], and very many, such as A C S V W aa and bb, then, together with editions 3 and 6, put *"moved"* [motum] in place of *"mobile"* [mobile]; but codex cc, together with edition 2, has *"the mobile" a movement* [mobile motum].

[9] Codex V has *intention* [intentione]. A little below this codex Z has *but* [sed] for *and* [et].

[10] In codex V there is added *of potency* [potentiae].

[11] Some codices, such as L O and Z, add well *in the Sun* [in sole].

[12] From very many mss. and ed. 1, we have supplied *that* [quod].

[13] Chapter 2.

[14] The Vatican edition, not trusting in nearly all the manuscripts and edition 1, omits *of the truth* [veritatis].

QUESTION IV

Whether "gift" is an essential name, or a personal one and one proper to the Holy Spirit?

Fourth, there is asked, whether "gift" [donum] *properly* befits the Holy Spirit. And it seems that it does.

1. (St.) Augustine in the fifteenth (chapter) ON THE TRINITY (says):[1] « Just as in the Trinity none is a "truth", but the Son, so also none a "gift", but the Holy Spirit ».

2. Likewise, "gift" means an emanation through the manner of liberality; but this is proper to the Holy Spirit alone: ergo etc..

3. Likewise, "gift"[2] is said in a manner relative to the one granting; but the One granting is not only the Father, nay also the Son, because Each is the One sending; therefore "gift" is said in a manner relative to the Father and the Son: and if this, therefore[3] it is distinguished from Each: therefore neither the Father nor the Son, but only the Holy Spirit is properly said (to be) a "gift".

ON THE CONTRARY: 1. "Gift" is said in regard to a habit [in habitu], but "given" is said in regard to an act, therefore, "given" adds above "gift": therefore, to the one it is fitting to be a "given", the reckoning of "gift" is also fitting.[4] But "given" befits the whole Trinity, because the whole Trinity gives Itself, therefore, also "gift": therefore, it is not properly (said) of the Holy Spirit.

2. Likewise, "gift" means a looking-back to the one giving and to the one to whom it is given: if, therefore, it is proper to the Holy Spirit, (it is) either on account of the looking-back to the *one giving*, or[5] the *one receiving*. Not on account of the looking-back to the *one receiving*, because similarly the *Son has been given to us*,[6] and (He has) been given more than the Holy Spirit. If, on the other hand, to the one giving; *on the contrary*: the Son is said to proceed from the One giving, that is from the Father: therefore ("gift") seems to befit the Son according to the common[7] reckoning. *If you say*, that the Son does not proceed through the manner of a grantable, and not « in the manner He has been given, but in the manner (He has been) born »;[8] *on the contrary*: the Son proceeded from eternity in this manner, that He would be sendable temporally, because « the Son is sent for the reason that He is generated »;[9] but being sent [missio] is not other than being granted [donatio]: therefore, the Son proceeds as a grantable.

3. Likewise, if the Son has been given in time, either He was able for this from eternity, or not. If *so*: therefore, He has proceeded as a grantable; if *not*: therefore, something in time

befits the Son, which is repugnant to the eternal emanation; which is unfitting.

4. Likewise, the rule is, that every noun meaning a looking-back and/or effect towards creatures is common to the Three;[10] but "gift" is of this kind: ergo etc..

CONCLUSION

"Gift" is a personal and proper name of the Holy Spirit; but "given" can be said both essentially of the Three Persons, and personally of the Son and the Holy Spirit, and properly of the Holy Spirit.

I RESPOND: It must be said, that just as is clear from the words of (St.) Augustine, "gift" among the divine is said properly or personally, not essentially, jus as "word" [verbum] is properly said of the Son; but "given" [datum] can be accepted both essentially and personally, or properly and commonly. For the whole Trinity gives Itself, and yet the Father and the Son properly given the Holy Spirit.[11]

On this account it must be noted, that "given" from its own reckoning is the same as "communicated" [communicatum]. Therefore, that which has been given can be said "(to have been) communicated out of *liberality*",[12] and, thus, is common to the whole Trinity; and/or out of *liberality and authorship*, and, thus, it befits the Holy Spirit and the Son, Who have a subauthorship [subauctoritatem] in respect to the Father; and/or the "given" can be said (to have been) not only communicated out of *liberality and authorship* [liberalitate et auctoritate], but also *produced*, and in this manner it is proper to the Holy Spirit, to Whom it is proper to proceed according to the reckoning of liberality, and thus according to the reckoning of a gift and/or a grantable. And in this manner "gift" and[13] "given" are equivalent; however, they do differ, because "given" means a communication in act; but "gift" (a communication) in habit. And, thus,[14] it must be conceded, that, among the divine, "gift" is properly said of the Holy Spirit.

1. To that which is objected, that "given" adds

---

[1] Chapter 17, n. 29: And yet not as a trick is (any) said in this Trinity (to be) "the Word of God" except the Son, nor "the Gift of God" except the Holy Spirit.

[2] Trusting in the more ancient manuscripts and edition 1, we have expunged the here added *of God* [Dei].

[3] In the Vatican edition there is lacking *therefore,* [ergo], which however, is had in very many manuscripts.

[4] From the more ancient manuscripts and edition 1, we have supplied *is fitting* [convenit] and then *whole* [toti].

[5] In not a few manuscripts, such as H K M and U and in edition 1, there is found *to* [ad].

[6] Isaias 9:6. — At the end of the next clause, from some manuscripts, such as H K V and X, we have inserted *Holy* [sanctus].

[7] Edition 1, together with codex Z, has *every* [omnem] in place of *the common* [communem]. Next codex Z has the subjunctive form of *proceed* [procedat], where in codices L and O there is added *from eternity* [ab aeterno].

[8] (St.) Augustine, ON THE TRINITY, Bk. V, d. 14, n. 15. — The Vatican edition, together with codex cc, has *proceeds* [procedit] in place of *proceeded* [processit], but contrary to the other codices and to edition 1.

[9] This is from (St.) Gregory (the Great); see above p. 261, footnote 1.

[10] Codices O and Z adjoin: *because whatever one Person does, All also (do); for the works of the Trinity are undivided. Similarly, in whatsoever habitude one Person holds Himself, All also (do); such (that) if one Person (is) Lord, All also (are); if one the Refuge, All also (are)* [quia quidquid facit una persona, et omnes; indivisa enim sunt opera Trinitatis. Similiter in quacumque habitudine se habet una persona, et omnes; ut si una persona Dominus, et omnes; si una refugium, et omnes].

[11] See above d. 15, p. I, q. 4.

[12] In codex O there is added *alone* [sola], which codex also next has in place of *befits* [convenit] *is only common to* [est commune tantum]. Some codices, such as F H X and Z in the second member of the disjunction and even codex T in the third have *subauthorship* [subauctoritate] for *authorship* [auctoritate], but incongruously; for each Person, though He gives himself out of liberality, is given by the Father out of *authorship*, non *subauthorship*; whence *as One given* (in the passive sense) it befits Each, because the *authorship of the Father* gives the Son and the Holy Spirit.

[13] Very many codices, together with the Vatican edition, have less aptly *and/or* [vel].

[14] From the older mss. and ed. 1, we have supplied *thus* [ita].

above "gift"; it must be said, that according to the common acceptation of *given* and *of gift*, "gift" means something further than "given", and "given" further than "gift". "Gift"[1] further than "given" conveys an emanation through the manner of liberality; but "given" further than "gift" conveys the act of communication, because "gift" means a habit. And for that reason, that which "gift" adds above "given", is personal, for that reason "gift" properly[2] belongs to the Person of the Holy Spirit.

2. To that which is asked, by the reckoning of which respect is "gift" properly said; the response[3] is already clear, because by the reckoning of the respect to the one giving, not, I say, by the reckoning of the respect simply, but by the reckoning of such a respect, that emanates through the manner of a grantable, which is proper to the Holy Spirit.

3. Because, therefore, it is objected, that the Son emanates through the manner of a grantable; it must be said, that it is false. For although grantability or liberality is communicated to the generation of the Son,[4] yet it is not the reckoning of the emanating; and because it is communicated eternally, for that reason it is given temporally; but because it is not the reckoning of the emanating, for that reason the Son does not emanate as a "gift", but only the Holy Spirit (does).

4. To that which is objected last concerning the looking-back to the creature,[5] it must be said, that this is understood of that noun, which conveys only a looking-back to the creature, not of the Person to a Person; but "gift" conveys each, for that reason that[6] rule does not have a place here.

SCHOLIUM

I. The question is not, whether this name in general befits the Holy Spirit, but *under what reckoning* it befits Him, that is, whether it is a *personal* name or a property of the Person, or *an essential one*. — To understand the solution better, it must be understood, that in a divine gift two reckonings are comprised, the one with a real relation to the One giving, the other with a relation of reckoning to the one to whom it is given. The looking-back to the One giving, that is to the Father and the Son, conveys, that the Holy Spirit emanates through the manner of a grantable; and by the reckoning of this looking-back the name, "gift", is *proper* or personal. For Richard of Middleton rightly observes (loc. cit., below): « "Gift" insofar as it is accepted among the divine, is a proceeding thing, to which from its own *manner of proceeding* the *first reckoning* of "gift" befits. But the first reckoning of "gift" is love [amor] ... Moreover, it is proper to the Holy Spirit, because He proceeds as Love ». The other reckoning conveys a looking-back of the reckoning *to creatures*:

« Nor, however, » as St. Thomas rightly observes (SUMMA, I, q. 38, a. 1, in reply to n. 4), « through this, that in a gift there is conveyed a looking-back to the creature, is it necessary [opportet], that it be essential, but (rather) that something essential be included in its own understanding, just as essence is included in the understanding of a Person ».

II. The ancient masters agree here with the Seraphic (Doctor), excepting Durandus (of Saint-Pourçain), who holding to a singular manner teaches, that this name is only appropriated to the Holy Spirit, which is rightly reproved by (Bl.) Dionysius the Carthusian (here in q. 2). — Alexander of Hales, SUMMA., p. I, q. 64, n. 1. — (Bl. John Duns) Scotus, on this and the following questions, in each edition, here in q. sole. — St. Thomas, here in q. 1, a. 1 and 2.; SUMMA., loc. cit. — Bl. (now St.) Albertus (Magnus), here in a. 3; SUMMA., p. I, tr. 8, q. 36, m. 2, partic. 1. — (Bl.) Peter of Tarentaise, here in q. 2, a. 1, quaestiuncula 1. — Richard of Middleton, here in q. 1. — Giles the Roman, here in 1st. princ., q. 1. — On this and the following q., Durandus (of Saint-Pourçain), here in q. 1.

QUESTION V

Whether 'gift' or donability is a distinctive property of the Holy Spirit?

Fifth, there is asked whether 'grantability' [donabilitas] or "gift" is a distinctive property of the Person[7] of the Holy Spirit. And it seems that it is.

1. For (St.) Augustine says in the fifth (book) ON THE TRINITY:[8] « He is a "gift" for this, that (His is) a spirit »; but "spirit" is a distinctive property (of the Holy Spirit): therefore, also "gift".

2. Likewise, (St.) Augustine in the fifth (book) ON THE TRINITY,[9] assigning the difference of the procession of the Son and of the Holy Spirit, posits this, that the Former proceeds through the manner of one born, but

the Latter through the manner of a gift, therefore, if this difference is attained from within the distinctive properties (of Each), as is clear, because 'nativity' is a property of the Son: therefore, also 'donability' [donabilitas] or "gift" is a property of the Holy Spirit.

3. Likewise, this very (thing) seems[10] by *reason*, because every property, according to which a Person differs from the all Others, is a distinctive property of the Person; but "gift" is in the Person alone of the Holy Spirit and always: therefore, it is His personal property.[11]

---

[1] Codex I add *For* [enim]. Then codex W has *means* [dicit] in place of *conveys* [importat].

[2] Edition 1 has *"gift" is proper to* etc. [donum proprium est].

[3] In very many mss. and ed. 1 there is lacking *the response* [responsio].

[4] Some codices, such as T aa etc., and ed. 1, have *accompanies the generation of the Son* [concomitetur Filii generationem], which also a little below this put *accompanies* [concomitatur] in place of *is communicated* [communicetur]. The Vatican ed. has *is communicated to the generation of the Son* [communicetur Filii generationi]. At the end of the Response, trusting in the more ancient mss. and ed. 1, we have substituted *does emanate* [emanat] for *did emanate* [emenavit]. Then some codices, such as I S and aa, with ed. 1, have the *Holy Spirit alone (does)* [solus Spiritus sanctus].

[5] Some codices, such as S and Z, have *creatures* [creaturas] here, which even very many codices, together with edition 1, a little below this, exhibit in place of *creature* [creaturam].

[6] The codices are divided amongst themselves, some, such as F G K M Y and Z, omit *that* [illa], others, with the Vatican edition and edition 1, put *this* [haec] for *that ... here* [hic illa], others, such as

H O and T indeed also present better the reading received in the text.

[7] The Vatican edition, contrary to the manuscripts and edition 1, omits *of the Person* [personae].

[8] Chapter 11, n. 12, and Bk. IV, ch. 20, n. 29. See here the text of Master (Peter), ch. 2, out of which these words have been taken.

[9] Chapters 14, 15 and 16; cf. here the text of Master (Peter), ch. 2, at the end, and ch. 3, at the beginning. — Many codices, together with edition 1, have *in the fifteenth* [decimo quinto] for *in the fifth* [quinto], in which book, ch. 17, n. 29 ff, this difference is also hinted at. — A little below this in many manuscripts and in editions 1, 2, 3 and 6 there is put *of one given* [dati] in place of *of one born* [nati], but faultily, as is gathered from what follows; codex I has *of one being born* [nascientis] in place of *of one born* [nati].

[10] Codex V has *is shown* [ostenditur]. A little below this codex A has *is distinguished* [distinguitur] in place of *differs* [differt].

[11] In this argument according to that statement of the proposition [effatum]: 'that which is constitutive / of a thing is distinctive of it, and

4. Likewise, properties among the divine are relations; but (St.) Augustine says in the fifth (book) On THE TRINITY,[1] that « a relation, according to which the Holy Spirit is referred to the Father and the Son, appears more in this name, "gift", than in this name, "spirit" »;[2] therefore, each is personal.

ON THE CONTRARY: 1. Nothing meaning a looking-back to creatures is a distinctive property of a Person, because, a personal distinction holds, having excluded every looking-back to a creature; but "gift" means a looking-back to him to whom it is given: ergo etc.. *If you say*, that it is not a property according to the comparison, which it has to creatures, but to the One giving, for an equal reason the being-sent [missio] of the Holy Spirit[3] will be a distinctive property, since it means a looking-back to the One sending.

2. Likewise, every distinctive property is said from an act, not from a habit. Wherefore, (One) is said (to be) "the Father", because He generates, (Another) "the Son", because He is generated, but (the Third) "the Holy Spirit", because, He is spirated; but "gift" is not said from the act of granting, but from the habit, otherwise it would not be said from eternity:[4] ergo etc..

3. Likewise, no other Person's distinctive property is accepted in relation to creatures[5] and/or means a looking-back (to creatures); but "gift" means this: therefore, it is not a distinctive property.

4. Likewise, if "gift" is a distinctive property of the Holy Spirit and His notion, then "holy spirit" and "love" is not a property: wherefore if[6] "holy spirit" and "love" is a property, therefore, there are seven notions, which is contrary to the common opinion of all. *If you say*, that the same notion[7] is conveyed through these three names, therefore the names seem (to be) synonymous, as "Marcus", "Tullius", which is equally very unfitting: ergo etc..

CONCLUSION

"Gift" is a distinctive property of the Holy Spirit according to the looking-back to the One giving, yet there is not excluded a reckoning of donability or a looking-back, according to aptitude, to the one to whom He is given.

I RESPOND: It must be said, that as regards this some have said, that there is a twofold considering of "gift" among the divine: in one manner, insofar as it means a looking-back alone to the *granter* [donatorem]; and in this manner (St.) Augustine says,[8] that « He is said (to be) "gift" for this, that He proceeds »; and in this manner they say, that "gift" is a distinctive property of the Holy Spirit. In another manner "gift" is accepted,[9] insofar as it means a looking-back to him to whom it is given, and in this manner it does not mean a distinctive property, but (is) consequent to a distinctive property.

But that does not seem able to stand. For "gift" always means some comparison to him to whom it is given; for having understood, that it is not grantable to anyone, it is impossible to understand, that it is a "gift".

And on this account it must be otherwise said, just as has been touched upon before,[10] that "gift" besides the looking-back, which it conveys to the one giving, conveys a looking-back to him to whom it is given. But this can be in a threefold manner: either according to *act*, as because (He has been) given;[11] and/or according to *habit*, such as because (He is to) be given; and/or according to *aptitude*, as because (He is) grantable. And this looking-back[12] has been so conjoined to the first, that the first without this one cannot be nor be understood, nay it of necessity follows, if He proceeds through the manner of a gift, that He is grantable: and for that reason the following looking-back does not take away from the first, which is not a distinctive property.[13] Therefore, it must be said, that it is a distinctive property by the reckoning of the first looking-back, with the second looking-back not repugnant, but consonant (with this).

---

vice versa', there are commonly employed the terms '*property, according to which a Person differs from all Others*' and '*is in the Person alone and always*' (cf. Porphyry, ON PREDICABLES, ch. "on the Proper"), and '*a distinctive property of the Person*' and '*personal property*', and for that reason on the part of the thing the argument itself is exhibited in an abbreviated manner by many. And/or say, that in the place of the minor, according to the syllogistic form, there must be put: *but "gift" is the property, according to which the Person of the Holy Spirit differs from all Others*, is posited as the *reason* for it.

  [1] Chapter 11, n. 12.

  [2] Codex X adds *holy* [sanctus]; codex O, however, has *therefore, this name, "gift", means a distinctive property more than this name, "holy spirit"* [ergo hoc nomen donum magis dicit proprietatem distinctivam quam hoc nomen spiritus sanctus].

  [3] In the Vatican edition there is lacking *of the Holy Spirit* [Spiritus sancti], which however is found in the manuscripts and in edition 1.

  [4] Edition 1 reads *eternally* [aeternaliter] for *from eternity* [ab aeterno].

  [5] The Vatican edition, not trusting in the more ancient manuscripts and edition 1, has *creature* [creaturam]. Next after *a looking-back* [respectum] supply with codex B (in the margin) *to creatures* [ad creaturas]. At the end of the argument codices L and O add *of the Holy Spirit* [Spiritus sancti], which is certainly to be understood.

  [6] Thus very many codices, together with edition 1; the Vatican edition has *because* [quia] for *wherefore if* [quodsi].

  [7] From very many mss., such as F H M Q T and Z, we have supplied *notion* [notio], for which cod. O has *property* [proprietas], but the

other codd. with ed. 1, having incongruously transposed the words, read *that the same names are conveyed through these three* [quod eadem importantur nomina per haec tria]. A little below this, after *Marcus* [Marcus], with the help of the mss. and first six edd., we have expunged the *and* [et].

  [8] ON THE TRINITY, Bk. IV, ch. 20, n. 29, and Bk. V, ch. 11, n. 12. See here the text of Master (Peter) ch. 2.

  [9] The Vatican edition, with some mss., reads *is said* [dicitur].

  [10] Here in q. 2.

  [11] Understand here and in the following members of the distinction: the Holy Spirit. — The Vatican edition, by referring the participles to *gift*, not trusting in the manuscripts and in edition 1, puts *given, to be given, grantable* [datum, dandum, donabile].

  [12] That is, the third manner of the second looking-back. — Next after *to the first* [primo], edition 1 adds as an explanation *that is, the one which regards the one giving* [scilicet qui est ad dantem], and codex T in the margin has *which is through the looking-back to the one giving* [qui est per respectum ad dantem]. Next, very many codd., such as A F I K R U & V, after *that the first* [ut primus] faultily insert *such that* [ita quod]. Then very many mss., such as C F G H K S V and Z, have *neither* [nec] for *-not* [non], and a little below this cod. Y has *who* [qui] for *if He* [si].

  [13] In codex R there is added *by the reckoning of the first looking-back* [ratione primi respectus]. Next some codices, such as H P Q and Y, read *Wherefore, there must be said* [Unde dicendum] for *Therefore, it must be said* [Dicendum ergo]. A little below this the error of the Vatican edition of putting *according to a looking-back* [respectu] for *looking-back* [respectus], we have corrected with the testimony of the manuscripts and editions 1, 2, 3, and 6.

1. From this the response to the first (objection) is clear, because that looking-back is such, that it cannot be excluded according to aptitude because of the emanation through the manner of liberality. And it is clear that it is not *similar concerning being sent*, because it means a looking-back according to act, not according to aptitude.

2. To that which is objected, that a distinctive property ought to mean an act; it must be said, that "gift" means a twofold looking-back,[1] and by a reckoning of this it means a comparison to a twofold act. By a reckoning of the first looking-back it means the act of *procession*, by the reckoning of the second it means the act of *communication*. It conveys the first act in an act, the second in a habit; and by the reckoning of the first it is a distinctive property, not by the reckoning of the second.

3. To that which is objected, that this is not in another Person, certain ones respond,[2] that the Holy Spirit is the Third Person; for that reason according to the reckoning of understanding (He is) more immediate to us, and for that reason His property is taken in comparison to us, not so among the Others.

Otherwise, it can be solved through interemption, be-cause, just as "gift" means a looking-back to creatures, so also this property, which is *"word"*, as will be clear below.[3]

4. To that which is objected concerning the plurality of notions; it must be said, that "spirit", "love" and "gift" mean the same property, differing by a reckoning. I say, the mean the same notion, because they mean a comparison to the same One and they mean the same emanation, but, however, they name it differently. For "spirit" means it principally through a comparison to the producing force, which is the spirative force; "love" principally as much as regards the manner of emanating, because as a Nexus; but "gift" as much as regards the consequent[4] looking-back. And it happens that the emanation of the Word similarly signifies in a threefold manner, namely, through this name, "son", "image" and "word". For[5] because (He emanates) by the force of nature, (His is called) "the Son"; because through an expressed standard of measure [per modum expressum], "the Image"; because as One expressive of others, for that reason "the Word". Similarly, because (the Third Person emanates) by the spirative force, (He is called) "the Spirit"; because through the manner of a nexus; "Love"; because as One born to connect us, "the Gift". And thus it is clear, that there is one notion named now in one manner, now in another, according to consequent[6] reckonings, for that reason there is no synonymy there.

SCHOLIUM

I. After the Seraphic Doctor has proven in the preceding question, that "gift" is a personal name of the Holy Spirit, not an essential one, he resolves it in this twofold question. The *first* is, whether "gift" not only signifies a property in the Holy Spirit, but a *distinctive* property. For properties among the divine belong to a twofold genus: some are indeed are of the Persons, but not *personal ones* in the strict sense, i. e. *distinctive* and/or even *constitutive* of the Persons; thus there is "active spiration" in the Father and the Son, which has not constituted nor distinguished either Person, since it is common to the Two Persons. Others simultaneously *distinguish* and *constitute* a Person, such as "Paternity", "Filiation" and "Passive Spiration". Whence (St.) Bonaventure says (below in d. 28, q. 3): « For this, that some relation be *personal*, it is necessary that it mean the first and proper habitude of that Person and through the manner of position and completion »; cf. also d. 26, q. 2 and 3. — This *first* question is resolved with the common sentence in the affirmative manner and is proven by the arguments in the fundament. Among the authors there is, however, a difference of opinion about the incidental question, whether this property is not only *distinctive*, but also *constitutive*. Master (Peter) seems to affirm this by teaching, that "gift" formally is the very procession of the Holy Spirit. On the other hand, (Bl. John Duns) Scotus, here in the q. sole, denies this, though according to him "gift" itself signifies first and principally a *looking-back to creatures* and only is something *notional* ex consequenti. But what pertains only ex consequenti to some thing, cannot be *constitutive* of the same, but at most distinctive (of it). But St. Bonaventure and Richard of Middleton, here in q. 2, teach, that "gift" signifies per se a relation to the one giving, but with the superadded respect of grantability, and by a reckoning of the first is a distinctive property per se, and not only

ex consequenti, as Scotus would have it: therefore, (it is) also constitutive.

The *other* question is dealt with in the response itself, which is this: if "gift" is a property of the Holy Spirit, and if in a gift there are two looking-backs, both to the one giving and to him to whom it is given: again there is asked, whether it is a distinctive property only according to the first looking-back, which conveys the origin, or also in some manner according to the looking-back *to creatures*. This looking-back to creatures can be understood in a threefold manner, namely either according to *act* (as a "*given*"), or according to a *habit* (as a "*to be given*"), and/or according to an *aptitude* (as a "*grantable*"). If the looking-back to creatures is understood in the first and second manner, it manifestly cannot be a distinctive property of the Persons. If in the third manner, then there is a controversy, and those sentences, which are expounded in the body, are to be posited. The first opinion entirely excludes this aptitude of the Holy Spirit, that He be granted to creatures, from (being) a distinctive property of His, (and is) chiefly supported by this reckoning, that this grantability is something consequent to the distinctive property. The second opinion, which St. Bonaventure approves together with Richard (of Middleton), asserts, that grantability cannot be entirely excluded from (being) a distinctive property on account of the looking-back to the one giving. In regard to the reason adduced, the Saint concedes (in reply to n. 4), that grantability means a *consequent* looking-back, yet he thinks, that this looking-back is so conjoined to the other regarding the one giving, that "gift" cannot be understood without grantability, or in other words, that it indeed is a consequent, but as something intrinsically *proper*, in a similar manner as the reckoning of *being able to laugh* is proper to man. — The same

[1] In codex T there is added *that is, to the one giving and to the one receiving* [scilicet ad dantem et ad recipientem].

[2] The Vatican ed., with the mss. and edd. 1, 2, 3 & 6 striving against this, has *responds* [respondet]. A little below this, after *the reckoning of understanding* [rationem intelligendi immediatior] cod. I adds *He is* [est].

[3] Distinction 27, p. II, q. 2.

[4] Edition 1 adds *common* [communem]. Next from very many codices we put *signifies* [significare] for *is signified* [significari].

[5] The Vatican edition with codex cc, omits *For* [enim], which is extant in the more ancient mss. and ed. 1. Then, the Vatican ed. falsely, and not trusting in the mss. and the first six edd., reads *through an expressive manner* [per modum expressivum]. Cf. the words of the Seraphic Doctor, in d. 27, p. II, q. 3: For "wisdom" and/or "knowledge"

[notitia] mean (that He is) the First in being understood [primum in intelligendo]; then "the son", which means the Emanation or Conception Itself; then "image", which means the *expressed* Standard of measure [modum expressum] of the emanating; and in the third place "word" [verbum], which means all these and adds above them a reckoning of expressing and of manifesting [rationem exprimendi et manifestandi]. — A little below this, after *Similarly*, [Simliter], we have inserted, from some manuscripts, such as X & Z and edition 1, *because* [quia], which is lacking, less rightly, in many manuscripts and in the Vatican edition.

[6] Codex Y has *differing* [differentes], but less distinctly, as is clear from the words in d. 27, p. II, q. 3, cited here in footnote 5.

sentence does St. Bonaventure also defend in regard to the name, "*Word*", and he explains this more clearly below in d. 27, p. II, a. 1, q. 2. All the other ancient masters either uphold the first opinion, and/or not so accurately distinguish it, as the Seraphic Doctor does. The sentence of St. Thomas Cajetan (commenting on Summa, I, q. 38, a. 2) expounds according to the first opinion; however, the words of St. Thomas in the Summa, loc. cit., a. 1, in reply to n. 4, and Sent., Bk. I, d. 18, q. 1, a. 2 differ only a little from the sentence of St. Bonaventure, nay Forest (de Trinitate, p. 486, col. 2.) would have it that, each teaches

the same. Otherwise, this most subtile question is not of great moment. — In regard to the solution to n. 4 and the explanation of a *notion*, cf. below d. 26, q. 4.

II. Cf. Alexander of Hales, Summa., p. I, q. 64, n. 3. — Bl. (now St.) Albertus (Magnus), here in a. 4; Summa., p. I, tr. 8, q. 36, n. 2, subpart 6. — (Bl.) Peter of Tarentaise, here in q. 2, a. 1, quaestiuncula 2. — Richard of Middleton, here in q. 2. — Giles the Roman, here in 1st, princ. q. 2.

QUESTION VI

Whether the Holy Spirit by reason of (His) donability can be called "our Spirit"?

Sixth and last, there is asked, whether by reason of (His) grantability [donabilitatis] He is called "*our Spirit*". And it seems that He is:

1. Because "*our*" means possession; but we do not have[1] anything divine except through largess [largitionem] and donation: therefore, since "the Holy Spirit" means something divine, that He is said (to be) "*our*", this is by reason of (His) grantability.

2. Likewise, this seems also, because He is[2] said (to be) "our Spirit", but the Son and/or the Father is not said (to be) "ours":[3] therefore, on account of some property, which is in the Holy Spirit and not in the Father and the Son; but this is naught but (His) "grantability": ergo etc..

3. Likewise, before the Holy Spirit dwells in us, He is not said (to be) "*our*"; but He indwells in us through (His) being granted [donationem]: therefore, He is said (to be) "*our*" by reason of (His) grantability.

On the Contrary: 1. If by reason of the grantability: therefore, since grantability is a personal property, not an essential one, it seems that ("our")[4] is said only of the Person of the Holy Spirit; but this (is) false, because there is said, "*our God*".

2. Likewise, if by reason of the grantability: therefore, it is established, that (this is) not through a comparison to the One giving, but to him to whom He is given; but the *Son has been given to us*[5] even more than the Holy Spirit: ergo etc..

3. Likewise, if by reason of the grantability: therefore, fittingly He ought[6] to be said (to be) "our Gift".

4. Likewise, if by reason of the grantability: therefore, since He is grantable to us more inasmuch as (He is) *Holy* than inasmuch as (He is) *Spirit*, He ought[7] rather to be said (to be) "our Holy Spirit", which, however, is not said.

Therefore, there is generally asked, "Of what (things) can "our" be said?"

CONCLUSION

The possessive pronoun "my" and/or "our", with the copula "is", is most properly said of the Holy Spirit by reason of (His) donability and through (the consideration of His) appropriation; the same pronoun, without the copula, is only adjoined to those divine names, which express a looking-back to us according to the reckoning of cause and/or correlation.

I Respond: It must be said, that "*my*" and "*our*" can[8] be attributed to something in a twofold manner: either *by means of a composition*, and/or *immediately*. If *by means of a composition*, thus of themselves they posit a proper habitude about the term, that is a habitude *of possession*,[9] as where there is said: "this is mine"; and in this manner, because everyone who has the spirit of God, has God and all which belongs to God, in this manner "*my*" and/or "*our*" and "*your*"[10] can be said of everything, which is commonly in God, on the one hand more properly of the Son, who[11] has been given to us through the Incarnation, and on the other hand, most of all of the Holy Spirit, *who is the Pledge of an eternal inheritance*.[12] Whence, it must be conceded, that, by reason of (His) grantability between other persons, the reckoning of possessing can be appropriated to the Holy Spirit.

That which is "*ours*" can also be attributed to something *immediately*, and in this manner it does not mean a (proper)[13] habitude, but the reckoning of a habitude conveyed through the term, to which it is united. For in this manner, it is united to none, but what conveys a looking-back *in an explicit manner*, as "our" and/or "my" "father", and/or *in an implicit manner*, as "my[14] book", that is "my possession".

According to this it must be noted, that "*my*" and "*our*"

---

[1] Thus the more ancient mss. with ed. 1, while the Vatican ed. with cod. cc reads *we did not have* [nos non habuimus]. A little below this, the Vatican ed. has *which is said* [quod dicatur] for *that He is said* [quod dicitur].

[2] In very many mss. and the Vatican ed., there is here added *also* [etiam], which however, is lacking cod. X and ed. 1, and seems to be superfluous. Next, some codd., such as S V & X read *Holy Spirit* [Spiritus sanctus] for *Spirit* [Spiritus], but incongruously, as is clear from the body of the Question.

[3] It seems that there is to be supplied *personally*, cf. Alexander of Hales, loc. cit., in reply to n. 4.

[4] Supply: "our", and/or read with codex Y "*our*" *alone is said* [noster soum dicitur]. A little below this after *but this* [hoc autem falsum] one or the other codex, such as bb, adds *is* [est].

[5] Isaias 9:6.

[6] Very many codices, such as A H I T V W X ee and ff, together with edition 1, read *congruently it ought* [deberet congruenter].

[7] The Vatican edition, contrary to very many manuscripts and edition 1, has the indicative *He ought* [debet].

[8] Edition 1, with one or the other codex, such as X, reads *it can be that "my" and "our" are attributed to something in a twofold manner* [meum et nostrum dupliciter potest attribui alicui], and a little below this, with very many codd., such as A I S T Y & Z, it reads *thus of itself it posits* [sic de se ponit].

[9] In other words: *a relation of a thing held to one holding* [relationem rei habitae ad habentem]. See Aristotle, On the Predicaments, at the end, where *Having* is dealt with, and Metaphysics, Bk V, text 29 (Bk. IV, ch. 23).

[10] Thus the greater part of the manuscripts, together with edition1, while some, together with the Vatican edition, transpose the particles *and/or* [vel] and *and* [et], but some, such as I ee and ff, put *and/or* [vel] in place of *and* [et]; codex A, next, has *and/or "his"* [vel suum] in place of *and "your"* [et tuum]. Next, codex G adds after *everything* [omni] *for this reason* [eo].

[11] The Vatican edition, together with some manuscripts has *because He* [quia], and codex I has *in this that He* [in eo quod].

[12] Eph. 1:4, where the Vulgate has *our* [nostrae] for *an eternal* [aeternae]. — A little before this codex M after *on the other hand* [autem] reads *properly* [proprie].

[13] Supply: proper, and/or together with the Vatican edition read *a habitude of possession* [habitudinem possessionis], which edition also after *but* [sed], together with some manuscripts and first six editions, adds *only* [tantum].

[14] One or the other codex, such as G, together with edition 1, has *our* [noster]. Next in many manuscripts and edition 1, there is read "*a possession*" [possessio].

that "*my*" and "*our*" / are not said of something except according to that name, according to which there is said "*this belongs to that*"; *but* "*that this belongs to that*" can be said according to a threefold habitude; either of *being informed*, as white (is) to Peter; and names convey this habitude, which signify in abstraction; and because nothing divine is compared to us according to a habitude of being informed, for that reason there cannot be said of abstractive[1] names "*our*": for that reason there is not said "our Deity" nor "our Eternity".

Second "*that this belongs to that*" can be said according to a habitude *of causality*; and names convey this habitude, which mean an act, as "creator", and because divine (things) have entirely this habitude toward us, as the tail [pene][2] of all such names there is said "*our*".

"*That this belongs to that*" can also be said[3] in a *third* manner according to the habitude *of correlation*; and relative names convey this habitude. But these are in a

twofold manner: because certain ones mean the looking-back of a Person to a *Person*, but certain ones the looking-back to a *creature*. Of those which mean a looking-back to a Person, there is not said "*my*" and/or "*our*". But of those which regard us, as "lord", "master", there is rightly said "*our*".

It must be said, therefore, that *grantability* as much as regards *that*[4] manner of saying "*our*" causes nothing, just as the reasons brought forward second prove; but it does cause a *looking-back*, because "*spirit*" means a looking-back to that into which it is breathed, and we are that; for that reason He is said (to be) "*our spirit*". Similarly, "*God*", because it is imposed by the act, which it has about us, as (St. John) Damascene says;[5] for that reason He is said (to be) "*Our God*".

There is, therefore, a rule, that "*our*" is said of these, which mean a respect to us according to the habitude *of causality* and/or *of correlation*; and thus are clear all the objections.

SCHOLIUM

I. According to the title placed at the beginning there would only be a special question concerning this saying, whether the Holy Spirit by reason of (His) grantability can be said (to be) "our Spirit", but at the end of the arguments unto the contrary, there is posited a *general* question, namely this, 'with what divine names can the possessive "*our*" and/or "*my*" be conjoined', and nearly the whole response pertains to this general question. A twofold manner is sharply distinguished, by which possessive pronouns can be attributed to anything, namely either by means of composition or a copula (such as through the verb *is*, which is not determined by any adjunct, e.g. 'the book is mine'), and/or without a copula, e. g. "my friend". In the first case by a reckoning *of possession* divine (things) can be said (to be) ours, and indeed both the common ones as well as the proper ones, which have been given to us in a special manner; which is most of all verified in the Third Person. In this manner by reason of the grantability there can be most properly said. 'The Holy Spirit is ours'. In the second case the reckoning of grantability does not regard the proposed, or as the text says:

« It causes nothing, just as the reasons induced second prove »; but it rather ought to be attended, which kind of habitude *the term itself* has for us, to which the possessive is conjoined. This habitude to *us* according to the Seraphic Doctor can be threefold. If this is a habitude *of causality* and/or *of correlation* (under this last understand also the reckoning of an *end*), then that possessive can rightly be united to these divine names. But since "*spirit*" means a looking-back to a spiritual effect, namely to inspiration, for that reason there can, not ineptly, be said "*our Spirit*". But there is not rightly said: '*our* Holy Spirit', concerning which, cf. Alexander of Hales and Richard (of Middleton) in the passages cited below.

II. The following teach the same: Alexander of Hales, SUMMA., p. I, a. 63, n. 3. — St. Thomas, here in q. 1, a. 5; SUMMA., I, q. 36, a. 1, in reply to n. 3. — Bl. (now St.) Albertus (Magnus), here in a. 10; SUMMA., p. I, tr. 8, q. 36, m. 2, partic. 3, 4 , and 5. — (Bl.) Peter of Tarentaise, here in q. 4, a. 1. — Richard of Middleton, here in q. 6. — Giles the Roman, here in 3rd. princ., q. sole — Henry of Ghent, SUMMA., a. 59, q. 5, nn. 5 and 17. — Durandus (of Saint-Pourçain), here in q. 3. — (Bl.) Dionysius the Carthusian, here in q. 3.

DOUBTS ON THE TEXT OF THE MASTER

DOUBT I

In this part there are doubts about the text (of Master Peter), and first there is doubted concerning this which he says, that *a relation does not appear in this name*, "*spirit*". For it seems that he says the false, because "spirit" is said, because it is breathed [spiratur]: therefore, it is referred to the one breathing: therefore, a relation does appear in this. *Likewise*, it seems that (in this name, "spirit", a relation) appears more than in

this name, "*gift*", because « those are said (to be) "relative" which, what they are, are this very (thing) of others »;[6] but "spirit" for this, that (it is) a spirit, has "being" from one breathing; on the other hand, it is not necessary that a "gift" have "being" from one giving: therefore, a relation does not seem only to appear in this.

I RESPOND: It must be said, that "gift" as much as "spirit" is said in a relative manner; but yet a relation appears more in this name, "*gift*", than in this

---

[1] Edition 1 has *abstracted* [abstractis]. The Vatican edition, contrary to the mss., has *names of abstraction* [nominibus abstractionis]. Next at the end of the sentence the second *our* [nostra] is omitted by very many codices, with edition 1; however, it is extant in codices F and H.

[2] The Vatican edition, not trusting in the manuscripts and editions 1, 2, and 3, has *for that reason there is rightly of all such names* "*our*" [ideo bene etc.]. Then codex R has *causal* [causalibus] for *such* [talibus].

[3] From some manuscripts, such as G M and Y, we have supplied *be said* [dici]. A little below this edition 1 has *names of looking-back* [nomina respectiva] for *relative names* [nomina relativa]. Next codex Y has *twofold* [duplicia] for *in a twofold manner* [dupliciter].

[4] That is, according to the principal one, when namely "*our*" is attributed to the name, "spirit" *immediately*. — The Vatican ed., against the mss. and ed. 1,

reads *the second* [secundum] in place of *that* [istud]; very many codices, together with editions 2 and 3, have *that* [illum]. Next, codex I has *adduced* [adductae] for *brought forward* [inductae].

[5] ON THE ORTHODOX FAITH, Bk. II, ch. 9. See above, d. 2, Doubt 3.

[6] Aristotle, ON PREDICAMENTS, ch. "on Relatives": But regarding something such are said, whatsoever 'what' they are, are said to be this very (thing) of others. — Some codices, such as V and Y, have *are said (to be)* [dicuntur] in place of the second *are* [sunt]. A little before this, in the Vatican edition, there is badly lacking *than* [quam], but it is extant in the manuscripts and first editions. Then, codex dd at *appears* [appareat] inserts the certainly to be supplied subject *a relation in this name*, "*spirit*" [relation in hoc nominee spiritus].

name, *"spirit"*, because a gift always means a looking-back to the one giving, but a[1] spirit (does) not, nay it can be accepted in an absolute manner.

And/or it must be said in another manner, that (St.) Augustine does not say, that a relation does not appear in this name, *"spirit"*, but that it does not appear in this name, *"holy spirit"*. For although a "spirit" is said to belong to a "breather" [spiratoris], yet a "holy spirit" is not said to belong to a "breather".

To that which is objected, that "spirit" means a habitude looking-back to '*being*' [esse] more than "gift" (does); it must be said, that it is true among those to which 'being[2] a gift' accedes, but in the Holy Spirit, who is for this reason, because (He is) the Gift (of the Father and the Son), that objection does not have a place.

DOUBT II

Likewise, is asked of this which he says, that *the Son by being born accepted, 'to be the Substance Itself'*. For he seems to speak badly, because in all that [in omni eo] which is in the Son through the (eternal) nativity, the Son is distinguished from the Father, because the nativity is a distinctive property: therefore, if[3] the Son by being born accepted, 'to be the Essence and/or Substance': therefore, the Father in substance is distinguished from the Son. *Likewise*, it is bound to be [est natum] that 'the Son by being born accepted (it)' or that 'the Son is by being born': therefore, the Substance has been born, if the Son by being born is the Substance. For everything, which by being born is accepted,[4] has (its) rise from the nativity.

I RESPOND: It must be said, that some *distinguished* that saying of his: 'the Son by being born is the Divine Substance or God', because a gerund[5] can mean *concomitance*, and thus it is simply true; and/or *a cause*, and thus it is[6] manifold (in meaning), because when I say: 'the Son is God or the Divine Substance', I mean three (things), that is, *the subject, the composition* and *the predicate*. Therefore, this gerund *"by being born"* can mean causality in respect to the subject, and/or in respect to the composition, and/or in respect to the predicate. If in respect to *the subject*, then the sense is: 'the Son by being born etc.,' that is,[7] 'He who is the Son by being born, and/or who by being born has, that He is the Son, is God'; and in this manner it is true. If in respect to *the composition*, thus the sense is: 'the Son is God by being born', that is, this predicate befits the subject through the nativity; and in this manner the saying is still true. If in respect to *the predicate*, in this manner the sense is: 'the Son is God or the Divine Substance by being born', such that 'being born' or the

nativity is the principle or origin of the Deity; and in this sense it is false.

However, Master (Peter) *did not distinguish* that saying of his, but simply concedes it, and in a sufficiently probably manner, since the aforesaid distinction does not seem to have a basis [radicem].[8] For since a gerund is bound to determine the composition — because it is entirely nothing to say: *a man by being born* and (sayings) of this kind — and when composition of the predicate, whether of the Essence or of all those which are attributed to the Son, befit the Subject through the nativity, the saying[9] has truth. Nor are the objections adduced unto the contrary valid, because a nativity does not distinguish *that* which through the nativity is had or what is in the one being born, but *him alone*, who is born; and for that reason it does not follow, that the Substance has been distinguished, nor that It Itself is born, even though It is had through the generation.[10]

DOUBT III

Likewise, is asked of this which he says, that *the Son by the nativity is not the Essence*. It seems that he says the false, because since by being born He is the Essence, for an equal reason it seems, that (He is such) by the nativity; and this seems through the authority of (St.) Hilary in the text.

I RESPOND: It must be said, that without a doubt this (saying) of his is to be distinguished: 'the Son by the nativity is the Divine Essence'; because the ablative ('by the nativity') can be construed in the reckoning of a *form*, and/or in the reckoning of a *principle*. If in the reckoning of *a form*, thus it is false, because the nativity is not the formal cause in respect to the essential predicate. If in the reckoning of a *principle*, thus it has truth, because all which befit the Son, befit Him through the origin of the nativity. But Master (Peter), because he accepts the *gerund*[11] in the reckoning of a *principle*, for that reason simply concedes (it) with the gerund; and because he accepts the *ablative* in the reckoning of a *form*, for that reason he simply denies (it) with the ablative; for he judges (it) more according to the[12] usage of speaking than according to the virtue of the saying.

DOUBT IV

Likewise, is asked of this which (St. Hilary) says: *Neither through a defection, or extension, or derivation*; in what manner[13] do those three differ?

I RESPOND: Certain ones say in the following manner [sic], that through a *defection* something is produced from matter through the corruption

---

[1] Many codices, such as A F H K S T V X Y etc., together with edition 1, add *holy* [sanctus].

[2] The Vatican edition, together with codex cc, omits *being* [esse], which also next falsely reads *but the Holy Spirit, because* [sed Spiritus sanctus, quia] for *but in the Holy Spirit, who* [sed in Spiritu sancto qui]; the reading received in the text is exhibited by the more ancient codices (one or the other of which read *because* [quia] in place of *who* [qui]) together with edition 1.

[3] In some manuscripts, such as S and X, and in edition 1, there is aptly omitted the *if* [si].

[4] The Vatican edition, contrary to nearly all the codices and to edition 1, has *accepted* [accepit] for *is accepted* [accipitur], but the reading of the manuscripts is better, because it is more general.

[5] Some codices here, but very many codices together with edition 1 below this, have twice *gerundive* [gerundivum] in place of *gerund* [gerundium].

[6] Trusting in very many manuscripts and edition 1, we have supplied *it is* [est].

[7] The Vatican edition reads *that is* [id est] for *that is* [scilicet].

[8] Codex K has *a reason* [rationem].

[9] The Vatican edition, with codex cc, breaking with the other codd. and ed. 1, has *for that reason it* [ideo] in place of *the saying* [locutio].

[10] The same difficulty is solved in nearly the same manner by Bl. (now St.) Albertus (Magnus), here in a. 7. — St. Thomas, here in q. 1, a. 5. — (Bl.) Peter of Tarentaise, here in q. 1 a. 2. — Richard of Middleton, here in q. 3. — Durandus (of Saint-Pourçain), here in q. 2. — (Bl.) Dionysius the Carthusian, here in q. 4. — And briefly, Alexander of Hales, SUMMA., p. I, q. 42, m. 3, a. 1, in reply to n. 8.

[11] Very many codices, together with edition 1, here and a little below this, read *gerundive* [gerundivum], (cf. Doubt II, above).

[12] In codex N there is added *common* [communem]. Cod. O reads however, *Master (Peter) judges (it)* [Magister tamen], and codex X *for Master (Peter) judges (it) more* [Magister enim plus] in place of *for he judges (it) more* [magis enim]. Next, a few codices, such as X and dd, have *truth* [veritatem] for *virtue* [virtutem]. — In the solution of this doubt, there consent Bl. (now St.) Albertus (Magnus), here in a. 8. — (Bl.) Peter of Tarentaise and Richard of Middleton, here in the exposition of the text.

[13] Many codices, such as A S T V W X etc., have *by what* [quo] for *in what manner* [quomodo].

of a pre-existent form, just as a blade (is) from a grain of wheat [ex grano frumenti herba];* through *extension* [protensionem] something[1] is produced through the permanence of a pre-existing form and the induction of an artificial form, just as a vase is made from silver; through *derivation* (something is produced),[2] which is produced through the permanence of a pre-existing form, solely by a local change, as a river (is) out of a spring and a lake out of a river.

In another manner it can be said, that the material principle, out of which a thing is, is either material and formally transient, and thus there is a defection; or is material and permanent, and thus there is an extension; or is material and permanent and acting, and thus there is a derivation; and their examples have been given [sunt manifesta].[3]

Doubt V

Likewise, is asked of this which is said: *One is that which we have accepted, to be, the Other ... to be holy.* For it seems that he speaks badly, because just as without the Spirit of God we cannot be holy, so neither (can we) be: therefore, it seems, that by the Holy Spirit[4] we not only have accepted, 'to be holy', but also 'to be'.

I Respond: Regarding this, there can be said, that this has been said through appropriation. For although from the Holy Spirit we have "*being*" and a "*being holy*", yet in an appropriated manner we have a "holy being": for that reason it is not said to be accepted in the same manner in the production of our "being", as in the sanctification (of it).

However, it can be said in another manner, that, just as "*to give*" is ordered to having, so "*to accept*"; and because no one has[5] the Holy Spirit, however so much the Holy Spirit works in him, except him who can enjoy Him, and every such (person) is holy: for that reason the Holy Spirit is not said, properly speaking, to be given nor to be accepted, except by the Saints.[6]

Doubt VI

Likewise, is asked of this which He says: *I shall take of thy spirit*, because this cannot be said as much as regards *substance*, therefore, as much as regards *effect* or grace: therefore, it seems that grace is transferred from one to another. *If you say*, that this has been said through conformity; it is objected, that[7] for an equal reason there can be said, that He would take from their spirit and give (it) to Moses.

I Respond: It must be said, that that (verse) is understood of (his) spirit as much as regards (its) *effect*; and this preposition *of* [de] conveys at once[8] a conformity and a partiality, but not as much as regards a *constituent* part according to truth, but according to proportion; since the effect of the Holy Spirit abounded much more in Moses than in the others, so that[9] the others almost seemed to have part of his grace. And there is said "*I shall take*" as much as regards solicitude, because while the gifts of the Holy Spirit have been communicated to the others, the solicitude of Moses was diminished, and part of his solicitude was[10] committed to the others.

DISTINCTION XIX

Part I

Chapter I

On the equality of the Three Persons.

Now, after we have introduced [insinuavimus] the coeternity of the Three Persons according to the little measure[1] of our ability, there now remains to say something of the equality of the Same. For the Catholic

Faith asserts that just as (They are) coeternal, so also (are) the Three Persons coequal. For the Son is equal in all (things) to the Father, and the Holy Spirit to the Father and to the Son; because as (St.) Augustine in the book, ON THE FAITH TO PETER,[2] briefly revealing, in what manner (Their) equality is understood, teaches: « None of Them either precedes the Other in eternity or exceeds (Him) in magnitude or surpasses (Him) in power; because neither than the Son or the Holy Spirit,

---

[1] In many mss. and ed. 1 there is omitted *something* [aliquid]. A little below this, cod. X reads *just as a statue is born from silver* [sicut nascitur de argento statua] for *just as a vase is made from silver* [vas fit de argento].

[2] Supply: *something is produced* [producitur aliquid].

[3] These words of (St.) Hilary are explained in a similar manner by Bl. (now St.) Albertus (Magnus), here in a. 9, and by St. Thomas, (Bl.) Peter of Tarentaise, and by Richard (of Middleton), here in the exposition of the text. St. Thomas, however, understands the words *through extension* [per protensionem] in this manner: when it is produced out of a thing remaining conjoined to itself, as a branch (grows) out of a tree.

[4] Thus the codices and edition 1; codex Y rightly has *by the Holy Spirit* [a Spiritu sancto]; the Vatican edition reads *that we not only have accepted the Holy Spirit* [quod Spiritum sanctum non tantum accepimus].

[5] Codex Y reads *accepts* [accipit], which also a little above this omits *However* [tamen]. Next codex Z reads *has* [habet] for *can* [potest].

[6] The Vatican ed. reads *except to the Saints and by the Saints* [nisi Sanctis et a Sanctis]. See more on this, above in d. 14, a. 2, qq. 1 and 2.

[7] Some codd., such as F G H Z etc., with edition 1, read *because* [quia].

[8] Trusting the mss. and edd. 1, 2 & 3, we have substituted *at once* [simul] for *similarly* [similiter]. A little before this, cod. X, with ed. 1, after *conveys* [importat] adds sufficiently well *there* [ibi]. Next, after *as regards a* [ad partem] we, by placing *constituent* [constitutentem], follow the reading of very many mss., such as G H L O ee & ff, and ed. 1, which in itself

is clearer and seems to be confirmed by the less apt reading of many codices *construing* [construentem], codex R *containing* [continentem]; the Vatican edition has *conferring and containing* [conferentem et continentem]. An explanation for this can be taken from Richard (of Middleton), here in the exposition of the text, where he says: This preposition *of* [de] does not mean there a partition of the substance of the Holy Spirit *and/or of the grace, which was in Moses*, but that the grace of the Holy Spirit would be given them in a lesser abundance, such that they would have a quasi reckoning of a part in respect to the abundance of grace, which was in Moses. And/or he speaks of a removal, in regard to the use of solicitude, not in regard to the habit. — See also St. Thomas and (Bl.) Peter (of Tarentaise), here in the exposition of the text.

[9] The Vatican edition has *such that others almost* [ut quod alii] for *so that others almost* [ut quasi alii], but nearly all the more ancient codices, together with edition 1, withstand this.

[10] Edition 1 omits *was* [est].

NOTES ON THE BOOK OF SENTENCES

[1] Edition 1 reads *the modicum* [modo] in place of *the little measure* [modulo].

[2] Chapter I, n. 4; cf. (St.) Augustine, ON THE TRINITY, Bk. VI, ch. 5, n. 7. — A little above this before *(St.) Augustine* only the Vatican edition and editions 4, 6 and 8, badly add *says* [ait].

---

* *Trans. note*: Concerning *defection*, cf. Master Peter above, in Distinction XVIII, p. 320, footnote 11; here, the Seraphic Doctor's example of *defection* is taken from the evangelical parable of the grain of wheat. But St. Hilary's term *dissection* more accurately speaks to the nature of divine generation, in that it denies that division according to substance, which is common to material organisms.

as much as pertains to the unity of the Divine Nature, is the Father anterior nor greater, nor the Son than the Holy Spirit. Indeed, it is eternal and without a beginning, that the Son exists from the Nature of the Father, and it is eternal and without a beginning, that the Holy Spirit proceeds from the Nature of the Father and the Son. Because of this, therefore, we believes rightly that the Three (are) One and say that (They are) God, because in a word there is, according to nature [naturaliter], one Eternity, one Immensity, one Divinity of the Three Persons». Behold, (St.) Augustine briefly assigned, in what the equality of the Three Persons consists, namely, because One does exceed the Other either in eternity, or in magnitude, or in power.

CHAPTER II

That eternity and magnitude and power in God is one, even if they seem to be diverse.

And, since these are enumerated as diverse, yet in God they are one and the Same, that is, the Divine Essence, simple and incommutable. Whence (St.) Augustine in the seventh book, ON THE TRINITY (says):[1] « He is not by one great, by another God, but (is) great by this, whereby (He is) God; because is it not one (thing) 'to be great', another 'to be God'. Indeed His magnitude is the same, which (His) virtue (is), and (His) Essence is the same, which (His) magnitude is ». Therefore, the Father and the Son are together [simul] the one Essence and the one magnitude. Thus also the power of God is the Divine Essence. Wherefore, (St.) Augustine in the seventh book of THE CONFESSIONS (says):[2] « The will and power of God is God Himself ». The eternity of God is also the Divine Essence. Which (St.) Augustine shows on that passage of the Psalm:[3] *Unto generation and generation Thy years* saying: « There is a generation of generations, which does not pass away, gathered from all the generations, that is from the Saints [sanctis]. In those shall be the years of God, which do not pass away, that is the eternity of God. For the years of God are not one thing, He Himself another, but the eternity of God is the years of God. But the very eternity of God is (His) Substance, having nothing changeable ». Therefore, let us hold unshakably [inconcusse], that It is one and the Same, that is, the Divine Essence, God's Eternity, Power, Magnitude; and yet Scripture is accustomed to posit these and (those) similar to these as if distinct.[4] In these words, therefore, (St.) Augustine briefly comprises [complexus est] the equality of the Three Persons. Because neither in eternity nor magnitude nor power does One surpass the Other. But that Anyone of the Three Persons does not exceed Another, has been shown above,[5] where the coeternity of the Three Persons was introduced.

CHAPTER III

That none of the Persons exceeds the Other in magnitude, because one Person is not greater than the Other, nor (are) Two something more than One, nor Three than Two and/or One.

Now, therefore, it remains to show, that in magnitude and/or in power One doest not exceed the Other; and first let us see concerning magnitude. It must be known, therefore, that the Father is not greater than the Son, nor the Father and/or the Son greater than the Holy Spirit, nor Two Persons together something greater than One, nor Three together something greater than Two, nor a greater Essence in Three than in Two, nor in Two than in One, because the Whole is in Each. Wherefore, (St.) John Damascene[6] says: « We confess all the Nature of the Deity to perfectly be in each one of Their Hypostases, that is, Persons: all in the Father, all in the Son, all in the Holy Spirit. And for that reason the perfect God the Father, the perfect God the Son, the perfect God the Holy Spirit ».

CHAPTER IV

In what manner is the Father said to be "in the Son" and the Son "in the Father" and the Holy Spirit "in" Each.

And, hence it is, that the Father is said to be "in the Son" and the Son "in the Father" and the Holy Spirit "in" Each and Each One "in" Each. Whence (St.) Augustine in the book, ON THE FAITH TO PETER (says):[7] « On account of the natural unity the whole Father is in the Son and Holy Spirit, the whole Holy Spirit, too, is in the Father and the Son. None of These is outside of Any of Them on account of the unity of the Divine Nature ». Behold here he reveals [aperit] to some extent — for something so arcane [tantum arcanum] cannot be fully unbolted by man — out of what understanding Each of the Persons is said to be "whole" "in" the Others. Whence even (St.) Hilary, seeking eagerly after this, interiorly, says in the third book, ON THE TRINITY:[8] « The sermon of the Lord bears off obscurity from very many (of His sayings), when He says: *I (am) in the Father, and the Father is in Me*; nor undeservedly. For the nature of human intelligence does not grasp the reckoning of this saying, nor will a human comparison offer any example for divine things; but what is unintelligible[9] to man, is possible for God's 'To Be' [Deo esse]. And so there must be cognized and understood, what this is: *I (am) in the Father, and the Father is in Me*; if, however, we will prevail to comprehend this such as it is, that what

---

[1] Chapter 1, n. 1.

[2] Chapter 4, n. 6. — Next only the Vatican edition and edition 4 badly omit *Himself* [ipse] after *God* [Deus].

[3] Psalm 101:25; (St.) Augustine's, ENARRATIONS, sermon 2, n. 10. (St.) Augustine reads from the Septuagint: *From generation unto generation* [In generatione generationem], but Master (Peter) according to the Vulgate; the Vatican edition together with the other editions, except edition 8, reads *In generation* [in generatione]. — Next the Vatican edition and very many editions omit *saying* [dicens], with all the codices and editions 1 and 8 contradicting this. — Master (Peter) does not cite (St.) Augustine verbatim, whose words were: « There is a certain generation of generations; in those shall Thy years be. What is that (generation) of Thine? It is a certain one, and if we well acknowledge it, we shall be in it, and the years of God shall be in us. In what manner shall they be in us? In the manner in which God shall be in us; whence there has been said (1 Cor. 15:28), that God is all in all. For the years of God (are) not one thing, and He Himself another, but the eternity of God is the years of God: the eternity itself of God

is the Substance, which has nothing changeable ». — In the text of Master (Peter) edition 1 for *from the Saints* [sanctis] reads *of the Holy Spirit* [Spiritus sancti], and editions 2, 3, 5, ,7 and 9 read *of the Holy One* [sancti]. A little after this, codices A and C have *are* [sunt] for *shall be* [erunt].

[4] The Vatican edition and the other editions, contrary to editions 1 and 8 and codex D, faultily read *distinctly* [distincte].

[5] Distinction IX.

[6] ON THE ORTHODOX FAITH, Bk. III, ch. 6. — The preceding proposition in regard to it sense and the other words have been taken from (St.) Augustine, ON THE TRINITY, Bk. VI, ch. 10, n. 12, and/or even ch. 8, n. 9.

[7] Chapter 1, n. 4.

[8] Number 1. — The text of Scripture is John 14:11.

[9] The Vatican edition, together with all the other editions, reads *not intelligible* [non intelligibile], with all the codices and the original contradicting this. Next, the Vatican edition, together with the editions, except edition 1 and 8, and contrary to the original and the codices, reads *is possible for God* [Deo possibile est].

by the nature of the things be appraised not able to suffer, that, the reckoning of Divine Truth attain [consequatur] ». « (Because) the Father, therefore, is in the Son and the Son in the Father, the fullness of the Divinity in Each is perfect »;[1] « because the fullness of the Deity is in the Son. What is in the Father, this also is in the Son; what is in the Unbegotten, this is in the Begotten; the One by the Other and Each the One »: « He, that is, who is, having nothing which is not also in the One, from whom He is »;[2] « not Two One, but the One in the Other, because non else in Each »; « as the One (Being) in our Faith are Each, not One (Person): we confess neither that Each is the Same (Person), nor Another; because the nativity permits that the God born out of God is neither the Same (Person as the Father), nor an Other (than Himself) ».[3] « Therefore, we confess in Each the same similitude of virtue and fullness of Deity, because the Truth says: *I (am) in the Father and the Father is in Me.* For the Son accepted all from the Father ».[4] « For if He accepted part of the Same, who begot (Him), therefore, Neither is perfect: for it is lacking to Him whence He has departed [decesit], nor will there be a fullness in Him, who will have been established out of a portion. Therefore, Neither is perfect, if both He who begot loses His own fullness, and He who has been born does not attain it ».[5] « Let us say [fateamur], therefore, that the Father is in the Son and the Son in the Father, God in God », as the same (St.) Hilary says in the seventh book, ON THE TRINITY,[6] « not through a twofold conjunction of convening genera, nor through the engrafted [insitivam] nature of a more capable substance, but through the united similitude of nature, through the nativity of a living

Nature out of a living Nature; while the thing does not differ, while the nativity does not degenerate the Nature of God, while not something out of God other than God is born, while None among Them is new, nothing from elsewhere, nothing separable ». Behold by these words, insofar as human infirmity permits, there can be understood,[7] out of which sense Christ said, that He is in the Father and the Father in Him. Out of the same sense too is the Holy Spirit understood to be in Each and Each of the Persons in Each, because, namely, in Each there is the same fullness of the Divinity and the united similitude of nature; because there is not a greater Divine Nature in any of these Persons, but of the one and un-differing Nature are these Three Persons. And for that reason the One is said to be "in" the Other, as has been said beforehand. Whence Ambrose,[8] opening for us the sense [sententia] of the aforesaid words, says on the Second Epistle to the Corinthians, in the fifth (chapter): « Through this the Father is understood to be in the Son and the Son in the Father, because one is Their Substance. For there is a unity, where there is[9] no diversity ». Behold by three testimonies of illustrious men, that is, of (Sts.) Augustine, Hilary and Ambrose, concurring in the same by the revelation of the Holy Spirit speaking in them, there is shown to those willing to believe in a pious manner — yet as *through a mirror and in an enigma*[10] — in what manner it must be accepted, when the Father is said to be "in the Son" and/or the Son "in the Father" and/or the Holy Spirit "in" Each.

PART II

But, now, presently, let us return to the proposed, and, having begun, let us set out, showing, that in magnitude None of the Three Persons surpasses the Other, because None (is) greater than the Others, nor are Two something greater than One, nor Three than Two, nor a God greater than Each of Them; because Each One of Them is perfect, nor is there (anything) whereby that perfection grows.[11]

in the second book, AGAINST MAXIMINUS THE HERETIC,[12] speaks thus: « Do you think, that God the Father cannot be the One God with the Son and the Holy Spirit; for you fear, that the Father may be a part of the One God, who is constituted out of Three. Do not fear this, for no division of parts comes to be in the unity of the Deity. One God is the Father and the Son and the Holy Spirit, that is the Trinity Itself is the One God. Therefore, you ask, "Is God the Father a part of God?"; far be it ».

CHAPTER V

That None of the Persons is a part in the Trinity.

Nor is Any of the Three Persons a part of God and/or of the Divine Essence, because Each of Them is the true and full God and is both the whole and full Divine Essence; and for that reason None of Them is a part in the Trinity. Whence (St.) Augustine

CHAPTER VI

Why are the Three Persons said to be most highly one?

« For there are Three Persons, the Father and the Son and the Holy Spirit, and these Three, because They are of the one Substance,

---

[1] Ibid., n. 23; and what follows is n. 4; in which text the Vatican edition and the other editions, contrary to the codices and to the original, read *of the Divinity* [divinitatis] for *of the Deity* [deitatis].

[2] Ibid., n. 23, and then n. 4; in which text codex C after *not Two* [non duo] inserts *are* [sunt].

[3] Book I, n. 47.

[4] Book III, n. 23. — The text of Scripture is Jn. 14:11.

[5] Book III, n. 8, in which near the beginning the Vatican ed., with a few edd., reads *it would be lacking* [deesset] for *it is lacking* [deest], and, a little below this, after *Therefore, Neither* [neuter ergo] add *of Them* [eorum].

[6] Number 39; but the words: *through the united similitude of the Nature* [per naturae unitam similtudinem], have been taken from n. 37. — In the text, the Vatican ed., with the other edd., contray to edd. 1 & 8 and the codd., after *in the Father* [in Patre] add *and* [et]. Then, the Vatican edition and edd. 4, 6 and 9, badly read *implanted* [insitam] for *engrafted* [insitivam]. Then, after *the nativity of a living* [nativitatem viventis], on the authority of codd. A B & E and edd. 1 & 8, we have inserted *Nature* [naturae]. (St.) Hilary writes: *the nativity of a living Nature out of a Living One* [nativitatem viventis ex vivente naturae].

[7] The Vatican ed. and the other edd., except edd. 1 & 8, has *there is revealed* [aperitur] for *there can be understood* [intelligi potest], contrary to all the codd..

[8] And/or rather *Ambrosiaster*, as he is commonly cited, who, according to the testimony of (St.) Augustine, is a certain *Hilary*, not of Poitiers, but a certain Roman Deacon, as it seems, the author of the COMMENTARY ON THE 12 EPISTLES OF BLESSED PAUL (in the appendix of the Works of St. Ambrose). It is said that St. Jerome wrote against the same in his DIALOGUE OR ALTERCATION AGAINST THE LUCIFERIANS, n. 25. — The passage from the Apostle explained by him is 2 Cor. 5:19. — Before the word *Ambrose* [Ambrosius] editions 1 and 8 rightly add *even* [etiam].

[9] The Vatican edition and the other editions, except edition 5, omit *there is* [est], contrary to all the codices and the original.

[10] 1 Cor. 13:12. — A little above this, only the Vatican edition badly reads *in the same* [in eodem] for *in the same (word)* [idem].

[11] The preceding, in regard to its sense, and the other words, have been taken from (St.) Augustine, ON THE TRINITY, Bk. VI, ch. 8, n. 9, and ch. 19, n. 12. — The Vatican edition, together with very many editions, after *Each* [singuli] and *Each One* [singulus], twice has *of These* [horum] in place of *of Them* [eorum *and* illorum, *respectively*].

[12] Chapter 10, n. 1, and the two following passages, ibid., n. 2.

are the One and are most highly One, where there is no diversity of natures, none of wills. For if They were one *by Nature*, and were not[1] *in agreement*, They would not be *most highly* One; but if They were disparate *by Nature*, They would not be One. These Three, therefore, because[2] They are One on account of the ineffable conjunction of the Deity, by which They are ineffably joined, the One God is ». « Therefore, part of the Trinity cannot be any One[3] whosoever among the Three. Therefore, in the Trinity, which God is, both the Father is God, and the Son is God, and the Holy Spirit is God, and these three together the One God; neither is a third part of this Trinity One (Person), nor is Two something more than One there, nor are All something more than Each, because (Their) magnitude is spiritual, not corporal. *Who can grasp it, let him grasp it*;[4] but who cannot, let him believe and pray, to understand what he believes. For what is said through the Prophet is true:[5] *Unless you will have believed, you will not understand* ». With these words he openly shows the un-differing magnitude of the Three Persons. Likewise, in the same (chapter he says):[6] « You, namely, have said, that the One God has not been composed out of parts, and you want that this be understood of the Father only. He, you say, is the unbegotten, simple, Virtue. And yet in this simple Virtue, you will see many things called to mind [multa commemorare], when you say: "God begot God", "the Good One begot the Good", "the Wise (begot) the Wise", "the Clement (begot) the Clement", "the Powerful One (begot) the Powerful". Therefore, are Goodness and Wisdom and Clemency and Power part of the one Virtue, which you have said is simple? If you will say, they are parts: therefore the simple virtue is established out of parts. And that simple Virtue of yours, by your definition, is the One God: therefore, you say that God has been composed out of parts. I do not say it, you say it, there are, therefore,[7] no parts. If, therefore, in the one Person of the Father you both find those which seem many, and you do not find parts, because the one Virtue is simple: how much more the Father and the Son and the Holy Spirit both on account of the undivided Deity is the One God and on account of the property of each One are Three Persons and on account of the perfection of Each are not parts of the One God! "The Virtue is the Father, the Virtue is the Son, the Virtue is the Holy Spirit." In this you speak the truth; but because you do not want that the virtue begotten from the Virtue, and the virtue proceeding form the Virtue to have the same Nature, in this you say the false, in this you speak against the right and Catholic Faith ». With these words there is openly taught, that those Three Persons are not parts of God and/or of the Divine Essence, and that None of Those[8] is to be said (to be) "a part of the Trinity" nor (is) One (said to be) "greater than" the Others.

CHAPTER VII

When we say, that the Three Persons are the one Essence, neither do we predicate It as a genus of species nor as a species of individuals, because it is not (that) the Essence is a genus and a Person a species, and/or the Essence a species and the Persons individuals.

Here, it must be inserted, that so great is the equality of the Three Persons and indifferent the magnitude, that when we say, that the Three Persons are[9] the one Essence and/or Substance, neither do we predicate (Them) as a genus of species, nor as a species of individuals. For the Divine Essence is not a genus and the Three Persons species, and/or the Divine Essence a species and the Three Persons individuals. Which (St.) Augustine openly demonstrates with probable and irrefragable reasons in the seventh book, ON THE TRINITY,[10] saying thus: « If the Essence is the genus, but a Person the species, as not a few think [sentiunt], one is bound to name the Three substances, as They are named "Three Persons"; just as since "animal" is a genus and "horse" a species, they are named three "horses", and the same three "animals". For There are not said to be species in the plural and a genus in the singular, as if there would be said, "three horses are one animal"; but just as they are said (to be) three "horses" by the name of a species, so three "animals" by the name of a genus ». Therefore, since we say that the Three Persons are the one Essence, not Three essences, since three horses are said (to be)[11] "three animals", not one: it is clear, that by the name, "essence", a genus is not signified, nor by the name, "person", a species.

« On the other hand, if they say, that by the name, "person", a species is not signified, but something singular and individual (is), and by the name, "essence", there is understood a species, as a "person" is not said just as "*man*" is said, but the manner "*this man*" is said, just as Abraham, Isaac and Jacob and/or anyone else, who could also be demonstrated to be present by a finger, so also shall the same reckoning confute them. For just as Abraham, Isaac and Jacob are said (to be) "three individuals", so "three men" and "three animals". Why, therefore, are the Father and the Son and the Holy Spirit, if we discuss Them according to genus and species and individual, not thus said (to be) "three essences", as (They are said to be) "Three Persons" »?[12]

In another manner, (St.) Augustine also proves the same, that is, that the Divine Essence is not a genus, nor the Persons species, and/or (that) the Essence is not a species nor the Persons

---

[1] The Vatican edition and editions 4, 5, 6, 8, and 9 add *one* [unum], with the other editions, codices and the original contradicting this. Similarly, together with the original, the codices and edition 1, we have expunged *most highly* [summe] from this clause, which otherwise would read *and were not most highly in agreement* [et consensione summe non essent].

[2] Editions 1, 6 & 8 and the original read *who* [qui] for *because They* [quia].

[3] The Vatican ed. and the other edd., except edd. 1 & 6, read *whosoever is among the Three* [quicumque unus est in tribus] for *whosoever among the Three* [quicumque unus in tribus], against the codd. and the original.

[4] Mt. 19:12.

[5] Isaias 7:9, according to the Septuagint and (St.) Augustine. The Vulgate reads: *If you will not have believed, you shall not remain* [Si non credideritis, non permanebitis].   [6] *Ibid.*, n .3.

[7] The Vatican ed. and very many edd. omit *therefore* [ergo], against the original, the codd. and edd. 1 & 6. Next, the Vatican ed. and edd. 2, 3, 4, 5, 7 & 9, read *you will not have found* [non inveneris] for *you do not find* [non invenis].

[8] Codices B C D and E have *of Them* [earum], codex A has *of These* [harum]. then at the end before *One* [aliis] only the Vatican edition and editions 4 and 9, add not so well *is* [est].

[9] The Vatican edition and edition 4 omit *are* [esse].

[10] Chapter 6, n. 11. — The Vatican edition, contrary to editions 1 and 8 and the codices, omits *thus* [ita]. But the words of (St.) Augustine are read in the original in this manner: « For if the genus is the Essence, but the species the Substance or Person, as not a few think, I omit that which I have already said, that one is bound to name the Three essences, as the Three are named substances and/or Persons, just as there are said (to be) three horses and the same three animals, since the species is "horse", "animal" the genus. For neither has species been said there in the plural and genus in the singular, as if three horses were said (to be) one animal; but just as (there is said to be) three "horses" by the name of a species, so three "animas" by the name of a genus ».

[11] The Vatican edition and editions 4, 8 and 9, here badly add *to be* [esse, which however, is required in English when *dicere* is rendered as *to say*].

[12] Loc. cit., immediately after this; in which text the Vatican edition and very many editions twice omit *and* [et] after *Isaac* [Isaac].

individuals. « The one Essence », he says,[1] « has no species, just as one animal does not have a species of one essence. Therefore, the Father and the Son and the Holy Spirit are not three species of the one Essence: therefore, the Divine Essence is not a genus. But neither is the Divine Essence a species and the Persons individuals, just as "man" is a species, but Abraham, Isaac, and Jacobs individuals. For if the Essence is a species, as (is) "man", just as one man is not said to be Abraham, Isaac, and Jacob, thus the one Essence will not be said[2] to be the Three Persons. And so not according to genus and species do we say These ».

Chapter VIII

That neither according to a material cause are the Three Persons said to be the one Essence.

It must also be noted, that the Divine Essence is not the matter of the Three Persons, as (St.) Augustine teaches in the same book,[3] « just as if according to a common and same matter the Three Persons were said to be the one Essence, as if there statues were made out of the same gold, we would say that the three statues (are) the one piece of gold [unum aurum]. But not in this manner do we say that the Trinity, that is the Three Persons, (are) the one Essence and the One God, as if a certain Three subsist out of one matter. For in equal statutes three is more gold than each, and one is less gold than two. But in that Essence of the Trinity it is in no manner thus ». Not, therefore, according to a material cause do we say that the Three Persons are[4] the one Essence, just as three statues are said (to be) the one piece of gold.

Chapter IX

Nor are the Three Persons thus said to be the one Essence, as three men (are) one in nature and/or of one nature.

To these, too, must be added, that we do not thus say that the Three Persons are the one Essence, as (St.) Augustine says in the same (book),[5] and/or (are) of the one Essence, « just as we say, that any three men of the same sex and of the same self-control [temperationis] of the body and of the same spirit [animi] are one nature and/or of one nature. For among these things one man

is not as much, as three men (are) together, and two men are something more than one man, just as we have said is also among statues; but in God it is not so. For not greater in Essence is the Father and the Son than the Father alone and/or the Son alone, but those Three Persons together are equal to Each ». From the aforementioned it is clear, that the Three Persons are said (to be) the Divine Essence neither according to a material cause, as three statues (are said to be) the one piece of gold, nor according to a similitude of complexion, as three men (are said to be) of one nature, nor as a genus is predicated of species, and/or a species of individuals, that is as one containing of the contained, more of the less.

On the one hand, to these seem to be opposed (those), which certain Catholic commentators [tractatores] on Sacred Scripture, in their own writings, handed down, among which seem to signify, that the Divine Essence is a certain[6] common and universal, just as a species; on the other hand, (they seem to signify that) the Three Persons are three particulars, three individuals differing in number. Whence (St.) John Damascene, great among the Doctors of the Greeks, in the book, which he wrote on the Trinity,[7] which Pope Eugenius also caused to be translated, says: « Common and universal (names) are predicated of subjects particular to themselves. Therefore, common is the Substance, but particular a Hypostasis, that is a Person. Moreover, there is said "particular", not because it has part of the nature, but (because it is) particular in number, as an atom, that is an individual. For in number and[8] not by Nature are the Hypostases said to differ ». Likewise, in the same:[9] « "Substance" signifies the common and encompassing [circumplectivam] species of <u>homoides</u>, that is of hypostases similar in species, that is persons, as for example "God", "man"; but a "hypostasis" demonstrates an individual, that is the Father and the Son and the Holy Spirit, Peter, Paul and (individuals) of this kind ». Behold he openly says, that a "substance" is universal, but a "hypostasis" particular, and that "God" is a species, as "man", and that the Father and the Son and the Holy Spirit are individuals, just as Peter and Paul, for this that They differ in number; which seems to entirely contradict the aforementioned sentence of (St.) Augustine. What, therefore, shall we say to this? This at least we can and ought to say, that those which (St.) Augustine handed down above, without any [omni] hesitation are to be held.

But, these (words), which are here said, though they seem on the surface [superficie] of discourse to resonate something alien from the Faith, yet they can be sanely understood and do earnestly demand a most pious reader and

---

[1] Loc. cit., a little below; but Master (Peter) contracted the final sentences from the more lengthy doctrine of (St.) Augustine. — Next, on the authority of all the codd. and ed. 1, we have inserted *of one essence* after *animal does not have a species* [animal non habet species]. Then, only the Vatican ed. and ed. 8 after *Therefore, the Father* [Pater ergo] omit *and* [et].

[2] The Vatican edition, with very many editions, contrary to edd. 1, 3, 7 & 8, and codices B C & E, has *is not said* [non dicitur], codd. A & D have well *would not be said* [non diceretur]. At the end, codd. C & D have *are These said* [ista dicuntur] for *do we say These* [ista dicimus].

[3] Loc. cit., immediately after this.

[4] The Vatican edition and the other editions, except edition 1, contrary to all the codices, inserts *the Substance and/or* [substantiam vel].

[5] Chapter 6, n. 11. — The first proposition has already been related a little before this. In the quote, the Vatican edition together with very many editions, contrary to editions 1, 6 and 8, the codices, and to the original, omits *also* [et] before *among statues* [in statuis].

[6] Codex D, together with the Vatican edition, and editions 3, 4, 6, and 8, reads *a certain something* [quiddam] for *a certain* [quoddam]. A little before this after *to be opposed* [adversari] codices A and C do not badly add *those* [ea].

[7] ON THE ORTHODOX FAITH, Bk. III, ch. 6, according to the version

by the Burgundian Pisamus, executed by order of Pope Eugene III, and greatly impugned by John Conon, which, however, after Lombard, was used by the ancient Scholastics of the 13th Century. According to the testimony of Fabricius (BIBLIOTH. GRAEC., tome 9), it was never published in typeface. We offer the words of (St. John) Damascene according to the version of Friar Michael Lequien, O. P., (Migne's, PATROLOGIA GRAECA., tome 94): « Those which are common and universal are predicated of particulars subject to themselves. Furthermore, a common, certain something is an essence, as a species; a particular, a person. I say a particular, not because it claims for itself a certain part of a nature, but because it is particular in number, as an individual. Persons, if indeed not by nature, but in number are said to be distinguished among themselves ». — The Vatican edition, contrary to edition 1 and the codices, reads *the greatest* [maximus] in place of *great* [magnus].

[8] The Vatican edition and editions 4 and 6, omit *and* [et], and immediately after this, contrary to the original, to the codices and to editions 1, 6, and 8, the Vatican edition, together with some editions, has *do ... seem to differ* [differre videntur] in place of *are ... said to differ* [differre dicuntur].

[9] Chapter 4. — Migne's ed.: « Furthermore, that one is a sub-

understander [intellectorem]. In the explanation of which I prefer, as one silent, to hear others, than by speaking offer occasion to the malevolent for detracting (them). However, it seems[1] to me that (they) can be accepted thus. When there is said: "a substance is common, and a hypostasis is particular", he did not accept these (words), when they are said of God, as they are accepted in the philosophical discipline, but they have been spoken through a similitude to those things which are said by philosophers; as just as there, that which is predicated of many is said (to be) "*common*" and/or "*universal*", but what is (said) of one alone (is said to be) "*particular*" and/ "individual"; thus here[2] the Divine Essence has been said (to be) "*universal*", because of all the Persons together and of Each separately It is said, because neither is It predicated of the Others commonly nor of Anyone of the Others singularly. On account of a similitude, therefore, of predication he said that the Substance of God[3] (is) "*universal*", and the Persons "*particular*" and/or "individual". On this account the same also said that the same Divine Essence is « a species common and encompassing of Persons similar in species », because just as this species "*man*" is predicated of its own individuals, as of Peter, Paul and others, neither do they differ in species, but (rather) agree [conveniunt];[4] thus "*God*" is predicated of the Three Persons, who do not differ in Divinity, but agree in all things [per omnia]. Weighing carefully, therefore, this similitude among things sempiternal and things temporal, (St.) John transferred it, in the name of universality and particularity, which properly convenes with temporal things, to eternal things; but (St.) Augustine, seeing a greater dissimilarity, than similarity among the aforementioned things, removed the aforesaid names from the excellence of the Trinity.

CHAPTER X

Whether the Three Persons differ in number, Which have been distinguished by properties.

On the one hand, what (St.) John (Damascene) says, that the Hypostases differ in number, not in nature, in this that he says that They do not differ in nature, he speaks very truly and without scruple; on the other hand, what he says, that They differ in number, one must beware, in what manner it be understood; for in diverse ways are somethings said to differ in number.

For some are said to differ in number, when they so differ, that this is not that nor something, which that is and/or is in that: in this manner Socrates and Plato differ, and (things) of this kind, which among philosophers are said (to be) individuals and/or particulars; according to which manner there cannot be said that the Three Persons differ in number. Also, those are said to differ in number, which are not added [adiunguntur] to themselves in enumeration or computation, but are discerned by themselves, as

when speaking of some things we say "*one, two, three,*" and according to this manner perhaps did (St.) John say, that *the Hypostasis*, that is the Persons, differ in number. For we can say: "the Father is one, the Father and the Son are two, and the Father and the Son and the Holy Spirit are three"; and likewise: "this person is one, this and that are two, this and that and the other are three". However, more fittingly are those Three Persons said to be distinguished by properties only, concerning the distinction of which according to properties there will be treatment in a following (distinction).[5] But now let us return to the undertaking, so that those (things) which have been recently said, might more familiarly become known [innotescant] by being more often turned over (in the mind).

CHAPTER XI

For what reason are the Three Persons together not something greater than One (Person).

It must be known, therefore, « that there is so great an equality in the Trinity », as (St.) Augustine says in the eighth book, ON THE TRINITY,[6] « that not only is the Father not greater than the son, but neither are the Father and the Son together something more than the Holy Spirit, or any Person less something than the Trinity Itself ». Moreover, what thus may be, in another manner, must be demonstrated, if it can come to be. « As much, therefore, as the Creator Himself assists, let us attend », says (St.) Augustine in the same (book),[7] « in what manner in this Trinity Two and/or Three Persons are not something more than One of Them ».

« There what is said (to be) "great", is not great from elsewhere than by this, whereby It truly is; because There the magnitude is Truth Itself and the Truth the Essence; therefore, none is There more greatly [non ibi maius est], because none is there more truly. Moreover, not more truly is the Father and the Son together than the Father alone and/or the Son. Therefore Each together (is)[8] not something greater than Each One of Them. And because equally truly is also the Holy Spirit, for that reason the Father and the Son together are not something more than He, because neither are They more truly. Likewise, in the Essence of Truth "*to be true*" is that, which it is "*to be*", and "*to be*" is that, which it is "*to be great*": therefore, "*to be great*" is that, which "*to be true*" (is). Therefore, what There (is) equally true, is also equally great. Therefore, what There does not have more of Truth, has not more of magnitude. Moreover, what is not more truly, has not more of Truth. Moreover, not more truly is one Person, than Another, and/or Two than One, and/or Three together than Each One. Therefore, One does not have more of truth than Another, nor Two than one, nor Three together than Each One. Therefore, in this manner too the Trinity Itself is not something greater than anyone Person There, but (is) as great as Each One. For there is not a greater There, which is not more true, as Truth Itself is the magnitude ». Behold, it has not been shown by fitting and catholic reason,

---

stance and another a hypostasis, has be said by us many times, and that the "substance" or "essence" signifies the common species comprising also the persons of the same species (ὁμοειδῶν ὑποστασέων), as "God", (or) "man"; but "person" and "hypostasis" denotes an individual, as for example the Father, the Son and the Holy Spirit, Peter, (or) Paul ».

[1] Only the Vatican edition has *they seem* [videntur], and a little below this *does ... accept* [accipit] for *did ... accept* [accepit] and *they are said* [dicuntur] in the indicative.

[2] The Vatican edition and editions 4 and 8, contrary to the other editions and codices, have *this* [haec] for *here the* [hic].

[3] The codices and editions 1 and 8, omit *of God* [Dei], but less well. Next only the Vatican edition after *On this account the same* [Propter hoc idem] omits *also* [etiam].

[4] The Vatican ed. and edd. 4, 5, 6 & 9, against the edd. and codd. add *in all things* [per omnia].   [5] Distinction 26.

[6] Foreword, n. 1. — Next, the Vatican ed. and very many edd., with cod. D, against all the other codd. and the original, has (the indicative) *are* [sunt] rather than (the subjunctive) *are* [sint].

[7] Ibid., and at the beginning of ch. 1, n. 2.

[8] The Vatican Edition, with very many editions, contrary to editions 1 and 3 and the original, add *is* [est], which editions 3 and 7 transpose by reading: *There is not, therefore* [Non est ergo]. Codices B C and E, and editions 2, ,3 and 7, with the original have the neuter form of *Each (thing)* [utrumque] for the masculine *Each (Person)* [uterque].

[9] Those things which precede this, are taken from ibid., ch. 1, n. 2, but with not a few things omitted, transposed and changed by Master (Peter).

in what manner the magnitude of the Three Persons is un-differing, because neither is there One greater than Another, nor Two more something than One,[1] nor Three together something more than Each One.

CHAPTER XII

That God is not to be said (to be) "threefold", but "triune".

Besides, though God is said (to be) "Triune", He, however, ought not be said (to be) "threefold". For there is not a threefold-ness [triplicitas] There, since [uti] the Unity is most high and the Equality un-differing. Whence (St.) Augustine in the sixth book, ON THE TRINITY[2] says: « Not, since God is the Trinity, must He for that reason be thought (to be) threefold: otherwise the Father alone, and/or the Son alone would be less, that the Father and the Son together ». « And when the Father alone and/or the Son alone, and/or the Holy Spirit alone is as great, as is the Father and the Son and the Holy Spirit together, in no manner is God to be said

(to be) "threefold". For the Father with the Son and the Holy Spirit is not a greater God than Each of Them, because there is not (anything) whereby that perfection grows. Moreover, Perfect is the Father and the Son and the Holy Spirit, and Each One of Them is said (to be) the perfect God. And for that reason there ought rather be said "the Trinity", than "threefold".

« In corporeal things one is not as much as three together, and two are more than one thing; but in the Most High Trinity one Person is as much as Three together, and Two are as much as One, and in Themselves They are infinite »,[3] because *there is not end to Their magnitude*. And, through this, there is revealed [aperitur] what we have said above,[4] namely, in what manner both Each are in Each, and All in Each, and Each in All, and One in All, and One All. Behold we have already sufficiently shown, in what manner in the Trinity any Person does not surpass the Other in magnitude.

COMMENTARY ON DISTINCTION XIX

On the equality of the Three Persons in God, in particular in regard to (Their) greatness.

PART I

On the equality, proven through the unity of the Essence.

Now, after we have introduced the coeternity of the Three Persons etc..

THE DIVISION OF THE TEXT

Having terminated the two parts, in which Master (Peter) dealt with those (things) which pertain to the Unity of the Essence and the plurality of the Persons, one by one, here he starts the third part, in which he determines the equality of the Persons, which simultaneously respects[1] the plurality and the Unity. And this part has three parts. In the *first* he proposes, in what (things) does the equality consist. In the *second* he proves (them) in particular [specialiter], there (where he says): *Now it remains to shown, in what manner* etc.. In the *third*, because in proving the propositions he had said (some things) doubtful, for that reason he determines, what kind of *exclusive* sayings [dictiones] are accepted among the divine, below in the Twenty-First Distinction: *Here there arises the question, which treats of the origin of the aforesaid.*

The *first*[2] part, in which he proposes those, in which the equality consists, has two parts. In the first part he proposes, that it consists in three (perfections): eternity, magnitude and power. In the second, lest these three be believed (to be) diverse, he shows that these are the same (thing) in God, in the second chapter:[3] *And since these are enumerated as diverse* etc..

Now, therefore, it remains to show, that in magnitude. This is[4] the *second* part, in which he proves the equality, and this part is divided into two. For having supposed that among the divine there is an equality as much as regards eternity, he shows *first* that (there is) an equality as much as regards magnitude; *second* as much as regards power, below in the Twentieth Distinction: *Now it remains to show, in what manner Any*

---

[1] Codices A C and D, and editions 1, ,2 3, and 7, read *nor Two One* [nec duae una], codices B and E read *nor Two than One* [nec duae quam una].

[2] Chapter 7, n. 9. — The following passage is ibid., ch. 8.

[3] Ibid., chapter 10, n. 12. — The verse of Scripture is Ps. 144:3.

[4] Chapters 3 and 4, at the end, and 11. — The Vatican edition, together with very many editions, contrary to the codices, has *has been said more above* [superius dictum est] in place of *we have said above* [supra diximus]; likewise, the Vatican edition, together with codex C and the other editions, except edition 1, omits *namely* [scilicet], then, after *in what manner* [quomodo] it omits *both* [et], contrary to codices A B C and E, and to editions 1 and 8.

NOTES ON THE COMMENTARY

[1] The Vatican edition, together with codex cc, with the other codices and edition 1 striving against this, has *receives* [recepit]. Next the Vatican edition has *principal parts* [partes principales] for *parts* [partes].

[2] In the Vatican edition there is added *principal* [principalis].

[3] From the manuscripts and edition 1, we have supplied *in the second chapter* [secundo capitulo]. A little before this some codices, such as aa and bb, together with edition 1, after *these are* [haec sunt] insert *one and* [unum et].

[4] The Vatican edition, having omitted the words of Master (Peter), *Now, therefore, it remains etc.* [Nunc superset etc.], in place of *This is* [Haec est] put *Similarly,* [Similiter], then on account of the changed construction it omits the particle *and* [et] and *this part* [haec pars].

etc.. Again, the *first* part has two (subparts). In the first (subpart),[1] he proves the equality of (Their) magnitude through the Unity of the Essence. Second, he proves the equality, by excluding every[2] inequality, there (where he says): *But now presently let us return to the proposed.* The first part, in which he proves the

equality of the Persons as much as regards (Their) magnitude has two (parts). In the first, he proves it through the indivision[3] of the Essence; in the second, through that same he shows, that among the Persons there is an circumincession, there (where he says): *And hence it is, that the Father is said to be in the Son.*

TREATMENT OF THE QUESTIONS

For an understanding of this part, four (things) are asked:

First, there is asked, whether, among the divine, there is a positing of an equality.

Second, granted that (it is) so, whether there is There a most high equality.

Third, whether, among the divine, there is an equality with a conversion.

Fourth, whether there is There an equality with a circumincession.

ARTICLE SOLE

On the equality of the Divine Persons and its properties.

QUESTION I

Whether 'equality' is to be posited among the divine?

About the first, that there is an equality There, it is shown:

1. First through that which is said in the (Athanasian) Creed:[4] « The Three Persons are all coeternal and coequal to Themselves ».

2. Likewise, this very (thing) is shown *by reason* in this manner: every multitude is reduced to a unity,[5] therefore, every inequality to an equality; but the unity, by which there is every multitude, is the uncreated Unity: therefore, even the equality, to which every inequality is reduced, is an uncreated equality: ergo etc..

3. Likewise, everything which belongs to perfection, must be transferred to the divine; but equality in a creature belongs to (its) perfection: ergo etc..

4. Likewise, that (a being is) 'one' in substance [unum in substantia] causes (its) identity; that (a being is) one in quantity [unum in quantitate] (causes its) equality; that (a being is) one in quality [unum in qualitate] causes (its) similitude;[6] but, among the divine, there is not only a unity in substance, but also in quantity, otherwise there would not be a perfect Unity There: therefore, not only is there an identity of substance There, but also[7] an equality.

ON THE CONTRARY: 1. Where (there is) an equality, there (is) a divisibility, because the

simple is not equated to the simple; but, among the divine, there is no positing of divisibility: therefore, neither of equality.

2. Likewise, where (there is) equality, there (is) a quantity, because « it is proper to quantity, that according to it there be said "equal" and/or "unequal" »;[8] but among the divine there is no positing of quantity, because according to (St.) Augustine,[9] « God is great without a quantity »: ergo etc..

3. Likewise, where (there is) equality, there (is) a finity, because there is a commensuration,[10] therefore, the measure and finity; but among the divine there is an infinity: ergo etc..

4. Likewise, where (there is) an equality, there (is) a diversity (of beings), since nothing is the (being) equal to itself; but, among the divine, there is an omnimodal Unity: therefore, there is not an equality There.

CONCLUSION

Among the divine there is to be posited an equality, which is consequent to the quantity of virtue.

I RESPOND: It must be said, that equality is posited among the divine, according to what is said in the (Athanasian) Creed, and (what St.) Augustine says.[11]

---

[1] Not a few codd., such as aa & bb, add sufficiently well *part* [pars].

[2] Trusting in the more ancient manuscripts and edition 1, we have inserted *every* [omnem].

[3] The Vatican edition, without the authority of the manuscripts and edition 1, adds *or Unity* [sive unitatis].

[4] The Athanasian Creed (where there is read, in v. 24: *And in this Trinity nothing prior or posterior, nothing greater or lesser; but the Three Persons are all coeternal and coequal to Themselves* [Et in hac Trinitate nihil prius aut posterius, nihil majus aut minus; sed totae tres personae coaeternae sibi sunt et coaequales.]).

[5] See Dionysius (the Areopagite), ON THE DIVINE NAMES, chs. 5 and 13; (St. Severinus) Boethius, ON ARITHMETIC, where this proposition occurs in a diverse manner. (St.) Boethius, loc. cit., chiefly in Bk. II, ch. 1, also shows, that every inequality of numbers is reduced to an equality.

[6] Aristotle, ON THE PREDICAMENTS, ch. "On Quantity and Quality", and METAPHYSICS, Bk. V, texts 15 (16) and text 20 (Bk. IV, chs. 9 and 15): For the same are those of which (there is) one substance; however, similar, those of which (there is) one quality; moreover, equal, those of which (there is) one quantity.

[7] Many codices, such as A F G H K V W X etc., together with edition 1, omit less well *also* [et].

[8] Aristotle, ON THE PREDICAMENTS, ch. "On Quantity". — A little before this in many ancient manuscripts, such as A C R S T V Y, and edition 1, there is had *but* [sed] in place of *because* [quia].

[9] ON THE TRINITY, Bk. V, ch. 1, n. 2, in which text, trusting in the more ancient manuscripts and edition 1, we have supplied *is* [est].

[10] Bl. (now St.) Albertus (Magnus) and Richard of Middleton, here in a. 1, prove this through the definition taken from (Euclid's) Geometry, and cited below in d. 31, p. I, q. 2, 2nd. opposing argument : The 'equal' is, that which, having supposed the other, does not exceed nor is exceeded'. — Next the Vatican, with nearly all the manuscripts and editions 1, 2, and 3 fighting against this, reads *therefore, where there is a measure, there (is) a finity* [ergo ubi est mensura, ibi finitas], which when posited destroys the progression of the argument.

[11] See here the text of Master (Peter), in which the sayings of (St.) Augustine are quoted.

And to understand this it must be noted,[1] that "equal and unequal" is a proper passion consequent to quantity. Moreover, "quantity" is said in a twofold manner: *properly*, that is, as a "quantity of mass", and *in a transferred manner* [translative], as a "quantity of virtue". And because that[2] is a proper passion of quantity, it is consequent to each quantity; where, therefore, there is a positing of a quantity of virtue, there is a positing of equality and/or inequality. But this quantity of virtue is posited among spiritual (things) and is found in a most high manner [summe] among the divine, because this quantity is not repugnant to simplicity, but is consonant (with it); similarly neither (is) equality consequent to this quantity. And because the other, more complete part of the contradiction is to be attributed to God, and equality goes before inequality: for that reason equality is to be posited among the divine; and the reasons for this are to be conceded.

1. To that, therefore, which is objected unto the contrary, that, where (there is) equality, there (is) divisibility; it must be said, that it is true of the equality, which is consequent to a quantity of mass.

2. To that, therefore, which is objected second: where (there is) equality, there (is) a quantity; it must be said, that it is true either[3] according to genus, and/or according to species; and although the name, "*quantity*", is not transferred, yet the name, "*species*" is transferred, as magnitude.[4]

3. To that which is objected: where (there is) equality, there (is) finity; it must be said, that equality among creatures conveys two (notions), that is *co-termination*[5] and *privation of excess*: the first belongs to incompletion by reason of limitation, the second to perfection; for that reason it is transferred by reason of the second, not the first.

However, it could be said, that the infinite, because it is incomprehensible, according to the truth is comprehensible by the infinite, and for that reason is commensurable to the infinite and is finite *to itself*.[6] And from this there does not follow: 'it is commensurable to the infinite, therefore, (it is) finite'; nay rather '(therefore, it is) infinite': and[7] there is (a fallacy *secundum*) *quid* and *simply (speaking)* there.

4. To that which is objected: where (there is) equality, there (is) a diversity: it must be said, that (there) is a diversity of *supposits* and a diversity of *form*.[8] For an equality and similitude there is required a diversity of *supposits*, but not a diversity of *form*, but a unity (thereof). Moreover, because among inferiors to a diversity of supposits there follows a numbering of form and/or of quantity, this belongs to imperfection; and for that reason the whole, which belongs to perfection, is transferred into God. However, among supposits properly speaking is there not a *diversity*, but (rather) a *distinction*.[9]

SCHOLIUM

I. According to the common sentence, these three common relations of *identity*, *equality* and *similitude* correspond to these three genera: *substance*, *quantity* and *quality*. Alexander of Hales (loc. cit., below) explains this doctrine: « Among these inferior (beings), out of a unity in substance there is caused an identity, out of a unity in quantity an equality, out of a unity in quality a similitude, whence "identity", "equality", "similitude" mean the relations founded through the three predicaments. According to this similitude, since there is a signifying of the Divine Substance as "*essence*", and as "*so great*" [quantam] and as "*of such a kind*" [qualem], there is a positing among the divine of identity, equality and similitude. But quantity among the divine passes over into the genus of substance, and quality similarly, because among the divine there is not positing except of two genera, namely, of *substance* and *for something*. "Equality" and "similitude" mean the relations founded in the substance ». Moreover, just as there is a twofold quantity, namely, the proper or "quantity of *mass*", and the improper or "quantity of *virtue* and/or of perfection" (cf. St. Thomas, SUMMA., I,

q. 42, a. 1, in reply to n. 1), so also is there distinguished a twofold equality, « to the extent that it is consequent to each quantity ». And just as the quantity of virtue (which St. Augustine preferred to name with the name of "magnitude", rather than with the name of "quantity", lest fools take it as an occasion of erring, by estimating that the quantity of mass filling the globe is in God) is more noble than the quantity of mass, so is the equality founded upon the quantity of virtue more noble, than that which is founded upon the quantity of mass. It can also be said, that the one equality is *properly* said, but the other *improperly*. "Equality *properly* taken" is a certain relation of predicament, founded upon the unity, which the thing has in the genus of quantity. But "equality *broadly* taken" is the relation outside of the genus of quantity and cant be founded in any being, finite as much as infinite, to the extent that it has a certain grade among beings. But of God, who is outside of every genus, the relations of identity, equality and similitude are predicated only in the transcendental sense.

---

[1] One or the other codex, such as G, together with edition 1, have the verb in its complete form *it must be noted* [notandum est].

[2] That is, the *equal and unequal* posited a little above this, and/or rather understand: equality and/or inequality; with which agrees the reading of codex X, which next after *of quantity* [quantitatis] adds *that is, of equality and/or of inequality, for that reason* [scilicet aequalitas vel inaequalitas, ideo]; but the reading of the Vatican edition and of codex cc, in which *equality* [aequalitatis] is placed as the subjects of *is consequent* [consequitur], is incomplete and contrary to the more ancient codices and to edition 1.

[3] We have supplied, from the manuscripts and edition 1, the particle *either* [vel].

[4] Cf. above d. 8, p. II, Doubt 4.

[5] Codices aa and bb add *and/or commensuration* [vel commensurationem].

[6] We exhibit the reading of the greater part of the codices, such as A G H I L O P Q S T V Y etc., and edition 1, while all the other codices, together with editions 2 and 3, in place of *to itself* [sibi] put *There* [ibi], and/or falsely *infinite* [infinitum] for *finite* [finitum]; but the Vatican edition omits *and is finite to itself* [et est sibi finitum].

[7] The Vatican edition badly, and not trusting in the mss. and first six editions, omits *and* [et]. Next, codex X for *quid* has the more distinct *secundum quid*: the complete phrase should read: *and there is a fallacy secundum*

quid and simply speaking there [et est ibi fallacia secundum quid er simpliciter] (cf. Aristotle, ELENCHAE, Bk. I, chs. 4 and 5.); if indeed a passing over under any respect from the finite to the finite comes to be simply (speaking). For though an infinite object is comprehended by an infinite intellect, and is commensurable with it, yet on this account there cannot be said, that it is 'finite' simply (speaking), but only *secundum quid*; because only an object infinite in the reckoning of the intelligible responds to a power infinite in the reckoning of the intelligible.

[8] Besides the received text there are found in the manuscripts various readings; codex K after the words *it must be said that* [dicendum quod] adds *it is true where* [verum est ubi]; then very many codices, such as A C R S U W falsely read: *there is an equality of supposits* [est ibi aequalitas suppositorum] for *(there) is a diversity of supposits* [deversitas suppositorum], but codex T originally read *it must be said, that there is an equality of supposits and a unity of form*, [dicendum, quod est ibi aequalitas suppositorum et unitas formae], and afterwards was changed to read *it must be said, that there is an inequality of supposits and a diversity of forms* [dicendum, quod est inaequalitas suppositorum et diversitas formae]. The primitive reading of codex T is not to be spurned. Next codex K reads *Moreover, for an equality* [Ad aequalitatem autem], and after *similitude* [similitudinem] it adds *among the divine* [divinis].

[9] See above d. 4, q. 2, and the doubts on the text; likewise see Alexander of Hales, SUMMA., p. I, q. 65, m. 1.

II. In regard to the solution to n. 2 and the assertion posited there, that « although the name of "quantity" is not transferred, yet the name of "species" is transferred », cf. above d. 8, p. II, Doubt 4. — in regard to the words in the solution to n. 4, that « among (the divine) supposits properly speaking is there not a diversity, but (rather) a distinction », cf. below d. 24, Doubt 1. This solution is explained more by Alexander of Hales (loc. cit., in reply to n. 2) with these words: « Equality among these inferiors is essentially among diverse (things); for among those inferiors the diversity of essence in the supposits follows the diversity of the supposits; not so is it among the divine, where the identity of the Essence is concomitant with the diversity of the Supposits; on which account among the divine there is not a positing of diversity, but of a distinction, just as (St.) Ambrose says. Whence equality among the Divine Persons does not require diversity, but distinction; for distinction does not take away the Unity, or the identity; whence though among the divine there is a most high identity, because distinction is concomitant with that, an identity of this kind does not take away equality ».

III. For more on equality, see below in d. 31, a. 1, qq. 1, 2 and 3. — Alexander of Hales, SUMMA., p. I, q. 47, m. 1. — (Bl. John Duns) Scotus, on this and the following 2 questions, here in q. 1. — St. Thomas, here in q. 1, a. 1, and in d. 24, q. 2, a. 1; SUMMA., I, q. 42, a. 1. — Bl. (now St.) Albertus (Magnus), here in a. 1; SUMMA., p. I, tr. 11, q. 47, n. 1. — Peter of Tarentaise, here in q. 1, a. 1. — Richard of Middleton, here in a. 1, q. 1. — Giles the Roman., here in 1st. princ., q. 1. — Henry of Ghent, SUMMA., a. 70, q. 1. — Durandus (of Saint-Pourçain), on this and the following 2 questions, here in q. 1. — (Bl.) Dionysius the Carthusian, on this and the following 2 questions, here in q. 1. — (Gabriel) Biel, here in q. 1, a. 1.

QUESTION II

Whether, among the divine, there is a most high equality?

Second, there is asked, whether among the divine there is a most high equality. And that (it is) so, seems in this manner:

1. Just as there is said by (St.) Augustine in the book, ON THE FAITH TO PETER,[1] « someone is not said to be greater than another, except either because it precedes (it) in age, or because it exceeds (it) in magnitude, or because it surpasses (it) in power », but nothing of these is among the divine, as (St.) Augustine and Master (Peter) proves:[2] therefore, there is nothing of inequality There: therefore, there is a most high equality There.

2. Likewise, a greater equality cannot be thought,[3] than where one is equated to one and one to many and one to all; but among the divine the Son is as great, as the Father is, and the Son (is) as great, as the Father and the Holy Spirit, and as great also,[4] as all Three (are): ergo etc..

3. Likewise, unity in quantity, just as has been said,[5] causes [facit] equality: therefore, where (there is) most high unity, there (is) most high equality; but this is among the divine; ergo etc..

4. Likewise, there is no standing-still [status] except in the highest [in summo]; but there is a standing-still in that equality through the reduction of all (things) to it: ergo etc..

ON THE CONTRARY: 1. (St.) Augustine in the book, OF EIGHTY-THREE QUESTIONS[6] (says): « If all were equal, all would not be »: therefore, an omnimodal equality takes away perfection.[7] If, therefore, nothing must be posited in God, which is repugnant to perfection, among the Divine Persons there is not an omnimodal equality.

2. Likewise, greater is the equality, which is attained according to a continuous and discrete quantity, than[8] according to a continuous one only;[9] but among the divine there is not a equality according to a discrete quantity, because there is a trinity and thus an inequality [imparilitas]: therefore, among the divine there is not an omnimodal equality.

3. Likewise, greater is the equality, which is attained according to power and wisdom and goodness, than which[10] (is attained) according to wisdom and power only; but among the divine there is not an equality according to goodness: therefore, there is not a most high equality There. Proof of the *minor*: the good is diffusive of itself;[11] but the Son diffuses Himself more than the Holy Spirit, because He produces an Equal to Himself, and also the Father than the Son: ergo etc..

There is asked, therefore, for what reason did (St.) Augustine not show equality in[12] wisdom and goodness? and again, for what reason not on the part of place, just as of magnitude and even of the quantity of the other differences? Which since he did not do this, it seems that he did not assign an omnimodal equality, but only in part;[13] or if he did show an omnimodal one, he proceeds in an insufficient manner.

CONCLUSION

Most high is the equality of the Divine Persons, in eternity in regard to (Their) origin, in magnitude in regard to all which They have in Themselves, in power in regard to (Their) effect.

I RESPOND: It must be said, that among the divine there is a most high equality, and a most high one is also assigned by (St.) Augus-

---

[1] Chapter I, n. 4, where this proposition, applied to the Trinity, is found not as a general one, as it is here exhibited. See the text of Master (Peter), ch. 1.

[2] Here in ch. 1 ff., where the proofs of (St.) Augustine are also found.

[3] The Vatican edition, together with codex cc, has *thought of* [excogitari]. Next codex W has *if* [si] in place of *where* [ubi].

[4] The codices do not agree among themselves; the greater part of them together with edition 1 exhibits the reading received in the text, others, such as V Z aa bb and ff, insert *One* [unus] as the subject of this clause, others together with the Vatican repeat *the Son* [Filius] for the same. See here the text of Master Peter, ch. 11.

[5] In the fourth fundament of the preceding question. — A little below this codex Y has *the former (i. e. most high unity)* [haec] for *this (i.e. this relation of unity to quality)* [hoc].

[6] Question 41: Because all would not be, if all were equal.

[7] Trusting in very many manuscripts and edition 1, we have expunged here the badly added *among the divine* [in divinis], just as a little before this after *nothing* [nihil] we have the explicit *must be* [est] of

the main verb; then we have substituted the indicative form of *is repugnant* [repugnat] for the subjunctive one, and we have inserted *Persons* [divinis] and consequently deleted as superfluous the *There* [ibi] after *there is not* [non est].

[8] In codex bb there is added well *which* [quae].

[9] A *continuous* quantity is that of which the parts have been united; but a *discrete one* that of which the parts have been disjoined from one another, e.g. as is among numbers. Cf. Aristotle, ON THE PREDICAMENTS, ch. "On Quantity".

[10] In many manuscripts, such as A F H I T W X Y Z ee and ff, and edition 1, there is lacking *which* [quae].

[11] This proposition is gathered from Dionysius (the Areopagite), ON THE CELESTIAL HIERARCHIES, ch. 4, § 1 ff., and ON THE DIVINE NAMES, ch. 4, § 1 ff. where he says, that it is proper to the Divine Goodness to communicate Itself to others.

[12] Codices H and M add *power* [potentia].

[13] On the authority of very many mss., such as G H I L O Y Z and ff, we have substituted the ablative form for *part* [parte] for the accusative.

tine, since[1] there is sufficiently shown the removal of every inequality through those three, which are *eternity*, *magnitude* and *power*.

The distinction and sufficiency of these three is accepted[2] by some in this manner. For because among the divine there is no extension of mass nor aggregation of a multitude, for that reason there is no intrinsic,[3] continuous or discrete quantity There, but in its place there is a quantity of virtue, which is touched through that member (of the division), which is *power*. However, because God embraces in His ambit every duration, for that reason there is a quantity of *eternity* There corresponding to time. But because in the ambit of His own immensity there is embraced every place and (everything) placed, for that reason there is a quantity of *magnitude* There corresponding to place. And thus it is clear,[4] though there is no other quantity to accept there, that the equality is sufficiently shown and does consists in those (three).

But this distinction is not fitting, both because there is in God no (quantity) but[5] a quantity of virtue; and thus there ought not have been but one member (of the division) there, nor ought the former be distinguished against the latter; and also, because magnitude among the divine is not only attained as much as regards the ambit of locality, but also as much as regards the intensity [intensionem] of goodness. Whence there is said in the sixth book, ON THE TRINITY,[6] that in « spiritual (things) more and better are the same ». And on this account a quantity of virtue is not only attained in operation, but also, in the matter[7] considered [in re considerata], in an omnimodal absolution.

For that reason we can assign the distinction and sufficiency of these three in another manner. In everything which is, it happens that it has this threefold manner of being considered [triplicem considerationem]. For something can be considered in comparison to its own *origin* or on the part of 'what is before' [a parte ante], and in this manner one is greater than the other, when its origin is prior; and (divided) against this is the equality of *eternity*. Again it can be considered *in itself*; and in this manner one is said (to be) greater than the other, because (it is) of a greater extension, and/or of a greater value: against this[8] there is in God the equality of *magnitude*, so that this equality is not said through a comparison to locality, but also to wisdom and goodness and to everything which causes the one to be said (to be) greater than the other, because[9] (it is) better. Whence (St.) Augustine and Master (Peter) in this distinction prove the equality of magnitude through the equality of virtue or in virtue. Third, it can also be considered through a comparison to *effect*: and in this manner it is said (to be) greater, because (it is) more powerful; and against this is the equality of *power*. Therefore, since it does not happen that the matter [rem][10] be considered in more manners (than these), if there is equality in these (three members), it is most high; and when it is shown (to be) in these, it is shown (to be) most high; and (in this division the argument) is advanced by a perfect induction.

And thus is clear that[11] which was objected last.

1. To that, therefore, which is objected first, that equality is repugnant to perfection; it must be said, that it is true: to the perfection of *each and every one* [universi], which (perfection) has been aggregated out of a diversity; not so is it in *God*.

2. To that which is objected, that there is a greater equality according to each quantity etc.; it must be said, that a most high equality is not in a continuous nor a discrete quantity, because there one is not equated to many; but here[12] there is the most perfect equality: for this reason it is only attained according to the quantity of virtue.

3. To that which is objected concerning goodness, that (it is) diffusive etc.; it must be said, that the emanation of a Person is not attained according to the reckoning of the *goodness* of the Essence, but rather of the *fecundity* of the Person and/or in the Person; and for that reason it does not follow, that if the Holy Spirit does not produce, that on this account He has less of goodness. Whence it must be noted, that there is a twofold diffusion, that is, *within* [intra] and/or[13] *outside of* [extra]. Diffusion *within* is when a person proceeds from a person in[14] the unity of a nature; and this is not properly diffusion, and this is not consequent to the good, because (it is) *good*, but to the good in a *hypostasis*, which is bound to produce another; and for this reason according to this diffusion one Person is not said (to be) better than the Other. The other is[15] the diffusion *outside of*, which is attained in the production of an effect; and according to this reckoning there is attained a diffusion properly (speaking) and the reckoning of the good. And because in this one Person does not exceed the Other, because the works of the Trinity are undivided; for that reason by this One is not better than Another.[16]

---

[1] Codices L and O read *which (most high equality)* [quam], and next they put *he shows by the removal* [ostendit remotione] for *there is shown the removal* [ostenditur remotio].

[2] Codex W reads *is shown* [ostenditur].

[3] The Vatican edition has *extensive* [extensiva] for *intrinsic* [intrinseca], but the authority of the manuscripts and edition 1 withstand this. The reason for this is offered by Alexander of Hales, SUMMA., p. I, q. 47, m. 5, and is cited here in the Scholium. Bl. (now St.) Albertus (Magnus) says entirely the same thing (SUMMA., p. I, tr. 11, q. 47, m. 2): It must be said, that in truth quantity among created things, from within which an equality is attained, is two fold, namely, (that) of magnitude and (that) of virtue. And those which belong to magnitude are twofold, namely, measuring *from within* [intus] and *outside of*; from within: length, width, depth; outside of: place. Similarly the "being" of a thing, as Gilbert (of Porretain) says, is measured by a delay [mora], and this delay is time. But a quantity of virtue is not properly measured except by the object about which the virtue is. And we say that those (are) equal in virtue, which can also be applied to equals [et in aequalia possunt obiecta], whether that virtue is intellectual or operative. Cf. also Bl. (now St.) Albertus (Magnus), here in a. 3.

[4] Trusting in the manuscripts and edition 1, we have expunged the added *that* [quod].

[5] The error of Vatican edition, in which there is omitted *but* [nisi], we have corrected from the manuscripts and edition 1. A little below this, codex I has *ought ... have been* [deberet] for *ought ... be* [debet].

[6] Chapter 8, n. 9.

[7] The Vatican edition less congruously, and contrary to the more ancient codd. and ed. 1, has *as the matter* [ut res] for *in the matter* [res].

[8] Codex X has *on the contrary this* [contra hic] for *against this there* [contra hoc].

[9] Codex Y· has *and* [et] in place of *because* [quia].

[10] The Vatican edition together with codex cc, repeating the fundament of the argument, has less well and contrary to the more ancient codices together with edition 1, reads *Therefore, since the reckoning of equality does not happen* [Quoniam ergo ratio aequalitatis] for *Therefore, since it does not happen that the matter* [Quoniam igitur rem].

[11] From very many mss. and edition 1, we have supplied *that* [illud] and at the beginning of the following proposition *therefore* [ergo].

[12] Trusting in the very many manuscripts and edition 1, we have supplied *here there* [hic] for *this* [haec].

[13] Codex Y has *and* [et] in place of *and/or* [vel].

[14] The Vatican edition with codex cc, with the other manuscripts together with edition 1 striving against this, omits badly *in* [in]. Next after *diffusion* [diffusio], with the consent of many codices, such as A C D E K R S T U X etc., together with editions 2 and 4, we have put *and this (diffusion)* [et haec] for *and this* [et hoc]. Then not a few codices, such as A and Y, have *does not follow* [non sequitur] in place of *is not consequent to* [non consequitur].

[15] In codex M there is added *also* [et].

[16] The Vatican edition together with one or the other codex reads *the Other* [altera]. A little before this codex O after *for that reason* [ideo] reads *in this (Trinity)* [in hac] for *by this (reckoning)* [hac].

SCHOLIUM

I. In the conclusion all agree. But about St. Augustine's proof and about the sufficiency of the members of the division, which he posits, a twofold exposition is given. The first, which belongs to Alexander (of Hales) and (St.) Albertus (Magnus), is not proven (in the response) of the Seraphic Doctor; the second and better even St. Thomas approves with him in SUMMA., I, q. 42, a. 1, in reply to n. 1. So that the foundations of the first opinion be better considered, we cite this passage from Alexander of Hales (loc. cit., below): « Equality looks back to quantity, or to that which is marked though the standard of measure of a quantity. But every quantity either is one measuring-within [mensurans intra], or outside-of [extra]: if within, it is either (one) of virtue, or (one) of mass; but a quantity of mass does not occur among the divine, but a quantity of *virtue* (does); and this is said through "*power*". Likewise, a quantity measuring-outside-of is twofold, namely, time and place; and to the quantity, which is *time* in inferior things, there corresponds *eternity* among the divine; but to that quantity, which is *place*, there corresponds *magnitude* among the divine, not that whereby God is circumscribed in a place, but that whereby He is among all as One not-enclosed; and whereby He contains and locates all things. Therefore, in this manner, quantity among the divine belongs to the *virtue*, which is the (Divine) *Power*, and to the *duration*, which is (His) Eternity; and to the *location* or active continence, whereby He contains and locates all things, and this is said (to be His) "Magnitude". Therefore, because in God there is no positing of quantity in more manners (than this), for this reason equality among the divine is assigned only as much as regards these three ».

II. Alexander of Hales, SUMMA., p. I, q. 47, m. 5. — Bl. (now St.) Albertus (Magnus), here in a. 3; SUMMA., p. I, tr. 11, q. 47, m. 2. — Peter of Tarentaise, here in q. 1, a. 2. — Richard of Middleton, here in a. 1, qq. 1 and 3. — Giles the Roman, here in 1st. princ., q. 3. — Henry of Ghent, SUMMA., a. 70, q. 2.

QUESTION III

Whether the equality of the Divine Persons is reciprocal?

Third, there is asked, whether, among the divine, there is an equality with the conversion (of the Persons). And that (there is) not, seems in this manner:

1. (St. John) Chrysostom[1] on that (verse) in the first (chapter of the Letter) to the Hebrews: *Who, since He is the splendor* etc.: (says), « The Son is equal to the Father, not the Father to the Son ».

2. Likewise, (St.) Hilary (of Poitiers says):[2] « An image, if it perfectly fills that of which it itself is, is co-equated to it, not it to its own image ».

3. Likewise, (St.) Augustine in the first book, ON CHRISTIAN DOCTRINE (says):[3] « In the Father unity, in the Son equality »: therefore, it seems, that the Father is not equal to the Son, as the Son (is) to the Father.

4. Likewise, Dionysius (the Areopagite says):[4] « Among those things which belong to a cause [causalibus] and the caused [causatis] we do not receive a reciprocation »; but the Father is the principle of the Son: ergo etc..

ON THE CONTRARY: 1. Everything relative of an equiparancy [relativum aequiparantiae] denominates extremes according to a completely similar standard of measure [modum];[5] but equality is a relation of equiparancy: therefore, (it is) a similar reciprocation.

2. Likewise, '(being) one in quantity' [unum in quantitate] causes equality; but, just as the Son is one [unum] with the Father, so the Father one with the Son, as much as regards substance and quantity: therefore, there is a reciprocation There.

3. Likewise, a mutual and reciprocated[6] equality is greater than a non-reciprocated one: therefore, if there is a most high equality among the Divine (Persons); it is clear that etc..

4. Likewise, every quantum compared to a quantum either is greater, or lesser, or equal; but the Father is so much in virtue [quantus virtute], and the Son similarly: therefore, either the Father is greater in virtue than the Son, or lesser, or equal; but not greater or lesser: therefore, (He is) equal.[7]

---

[1] In the SECOND HOMILY ON THE LETTER TO THE HEBREWS, n. 2 he says: « However, through *splendor* (St. Paul) shows (His) equality to the Essence and His proximity with the Father ... Then he subjoins: *And the Character or Figure.* For a figure or character is other than the exemplary prototype; but not entirely other, but in this, that it attains to the hypostasis. For this Character also shows, that there is not diversity, but plainly in all things that (He is) the perfect Similitude of Him of whom He is the Character and Figure ». In the Commentary on Book IV of the Sentences, according to the Roman, Hannibaldus of Hannibaldus, which is had among the works of St. Thomas, here in q. 1, a. 2, the same text occurs and is ascribed to *Chrysostom's Gloss.* But it is not found word-for-word in the ordinary Gloss. Ad the end of the Gloss there is said: « But "splendor" and "figure", just as even "*image*", are properly referred to the Person of the Son and are relatively said ». — In the 75th Homily, n. 4, ON THE GOSPEL OF ST. JOHN, there is said by (St. John Chrysostom): « If anyone, however, will have said, that the Father is greater, *as the principle of the Son*, we will not contradict him. According to this, he does not make the son belong to another substance ». Which words, just as also those which have been quoted from the Gloss, are worthy of attention here to this extent, that St. Bonaventure in the body of the question uses the concepts of *imitation* and *subauthorship* to establish the second part of the conclusion, namely, that under some respect there is not a mutual equality among the Father and the son.

[2] (St.) Augustine, ON THE TRINITY, ch. 10, n. 11, referring to the sentence of (St.) Hilary concerning these three names, which are appropriated in the Trinity: "eternity", "image" and "gift" [munus], proposes these words concerning "image". See below in Distinction XXXI, p. 2, at the beginning of Master (Peter)'s text.

[3] Chapter 5, n. 5.

[4] ON THE DIVINE NAMES, ch. 9, § 6, where the beginning of this text is exhibited in the Greek, in this manner: ἐπὶ δὲ τοῦ αἰτίου καὶ τῶν αἰτιατῶν, which is translated diversely by diverse authors: the codices with edition 1 offer the reading received in the text; the Vatican edition has *causes* [causis] in place of *those things which belong to a cause* [causalibus].

[5] A relation of equiparancy is commonly defined: that relation of which the extremes are of the same reckoning and are named with the same name, v. g. "friend" (for a friend is a friend of a friend), "similar", "equal"; to this is opposed the relation of disequiparancy, i. e. the relation of which the extremes are of another reckoning, as the relation of father to son.

[6] As required by the more ancient manuscripts and edition 1, we have substituted *reciprocated* [reciprocata] doe *reciprocal* [reciproca].

[7] The mutilated reading of the Vatican edition and of codex cc, in which the words *but not greater or lesser: therefore, equal* [non maior aut minor: ergo aequalis], is repaired with the help of the older manuscripts and edition 1.

CONCLUSION

The relation of equality among the divine is reciprocal; but the act of co-equation is not said of the Father in respect to the Son.

I RESPOND: It must be said, that there is equality with conversion[1] There, not only because (the quality is) *divine*, but also because equality *from its own reckoning* means a reciprocation inasmuch as (there is) an *equality*. And[2] according to this it must be believed, that the Father is equal to the Son and the Son to the Father.

And for an understanding of the objections it must be noted,[3] that to speak of "equality" is in a two fold manner: either insofar as it means *the respect of equiparancy*, or insofar as beyond (this) respect it concerns the *act of co-equation*.[4] Inasmuch as it means the *respect of equiparancy*, just as the reasons show, it is necessary, that there be a reciprocation There; but inasmuch as it concerns further the *act of co-equation*, thus it means the reckoning of imitation; and in this manner it does not befit

the Father in respect to the Son, because it would convey a subauthority in the Father.[5] Whence the Father is not said "to be co-equated" to the Son, because He does not imitate the Son, neither perfectly nor imperfectly. And (this) is similar, as if there were said: "*this one with that one*". For (this) can be understood in a twofold manner: either[6] insofar as it means a *conjunction* of the two: and in this manner of necessity (equality) is attended according to conversion; for if this one goes with that one, it is also necessary, that it be true the other way around. In another manner "*this one with that one*" means an *association*, and thus a certain subauthority in the one accompanying [associante], and in this manner it is said, that a soldier goes with a king, and not the other way around, because a soldier accompanies a king,[7] and not the other way around. Similarly, must it be understood in "equality".

1. 2. 3. 4. And from these the authorities of the Saints are clear, because[8] they speak of "equality" in the second manner, except that of Dionysius, to which it must be responded, that it has no place in the proposed, because Dionysius speaks properly of "cause", according to which a cause is said (to be) "that of which there follows another 'being'",[9] and thus it differs through (its) essence from (its) effect, and in this manner it does not occur in God in respect to a Person.

SCHOLIUM

I. "Equality *conversely said*" is the same as mutual or reciprocal (equality). — The Saint also employs the distinction between a *simple* relation of equality and equality with the act of *co-equation* below in d. 31, p. I, q. 3. St. Thomas and Alexander of Hales have the same (distinction), loc. citt., below, and even Richard (of Middleton), who to the mind of St. Thomas in regard to the equality with the act of co-equation adds: « But because from the virtue of the expression this name, "*equal*", would not be said to convey but a relation of *equiparancy*, because what conveys a *co-equation* seems (to be) more from the manner of speaking, according to which we are

not accustomed to speak the truth properly: 'a king is with a soldier, but a soldier is with a king'; for that reason from the virtue of the expression, if there were not authorities, which seem to argue for the contrary, it would seem possible that there be conceded simply, that the Father is equal to the Son ».

II. Alexander of Hales, SUMMA., p. I, q. 54, m.1, a. 2 and 3. — St. Thomas, here in q. 1, a. 2; SUMMA. , I, q. 42, a. 1, in reply to n. 3. — Bl. (now St.) Albertus (Magnus)., here in a. 4; SUMMA., p. I, tr. 11, q. 47, m. 3. — Peter of Tarentaise, here in q. 1, a. 3. — Richard of Middleton, here in a. 1, q. 2. — Giles the Roman, here in 1st. princ., q. 2. — Henry of Ghent, SUMMA., a. 68, q. 2.

QUESTION IV

Whether, among the divine, there is an equality with a circumincession?

Third, there is asked, whether among the divine there is an equality with a circumincession. And that (it is) so, is shown:

1. First *by the authority* of the Lord, in the fourteenth (chapter of the Gospel of St.) John:[10] *I (am) in the Father, and the Father is in Me.*

2. Likewise, (St.) Augustine (of Hippo says), ON THE FAITH TO PETER:[11] « On account of the unity of (Their) Nature, the whole Father [totus Pater] is in the Son and (in) the Holy Spirit ».

3. Likewise, this very same (argument) is shown *by reason* [hoc ipsum ostenditur ratione], because in

---

[1] We follow codices I and Z by adding *with conversion* [cum conversione], because the Seraphic Doctor established this question principally concerning this, which however, is lacking faultily in the other manuscripts and in the Vatican edition, and also in edition 1. Codex H (primitive) and K have *reciprocal equality* [aequalitas reciproca] for *equality with conversion* [aequalitas cum conversione]: codex Y (in the margin by a later hand) has *reciprocal equality or (one) one with conversion* [reciproca sive cum conversione]. Next after *because equality* [quia aequalitas], we have, trusting in the manuscripts and editions 1, 2, and 3, expunged *and when equality* [et cum aequalitas], which when added it is necessary that the subjoined (argument) be perturbed.

[2] Se have supplied from the more ancient manuscripts and edition 1 *And* [Et], and a little below this after *the Father* [Pater], trusting in the manuscripts and the first six editions, we have inserted *is* [est].

[3] In codex V there is added explicitly *it must be* [est].

[4] Taken in the passive mood (i. e. as *being made co-eequivalent*).

[5] The reading of the manuscripts and the first six editions *because it conveys authorship in the Father* [quia importat auctoritatem in Patre] is repugnant to the context. Next very many codices, such as A B C D L O R S U Y Z, have *properly* [proprie] in place of *perfectly* [perfecte]. A little below this the Vatican edition, together with codex cc, with the other codices together with edition 1 striving against this, incongruously adds

so [sic] after *And* [Et]. Then, in codex T, by an almost equal hand there is added, in the margin, *goes* [vadit] to the phrase *this one with that one* [hoc cum illo], perhaps on account of the subjoined; in which reading it would have been better to have (the masculine form) *this one* [hic] rather than (the neuter form) *this one* [hoc].

[6] Very many codices, such as A C F L O R S T W etc., omit *either* [aut], in place of which codex U has *that is* [scilicet].

[7] That is, joins himself as a companion to the king. Cf. Robert's, THESAURUS LINGUAE LATINAE, under the verb associare. — In the Vatican edition and codex cc there are badly lacking the words *because a soldier* etc. [quia miles etc.] right up to the end of the sentence, which words are however, extant in the more ancient manuscripts and edition 1. Next, with the agreement of the manuscripts and editions 1, 2, and 3, we have substituted *in* [in] in place of *with* [cum], here at the end of the last sentence.

[8] The Codices disagree among themselves; some, such as F G H and ee, together with edition 1, exhibit the reading received in the text; others, such as A I K S T W Y and ff, put *who* [qui] and the Vatican *which* [quae] in place of *because they* [quia].

[9] Cf. above p. 120, footnote 7.

[10] Verses 10-11.

[11] Chapter 1, n. 4. See, here, in the text of Master (Peter), ch. 4.

whomsoever is the Substance and/or Essence of the Father, there is the Father; but the Substance of the Father is in the Son: therefore, the Father is in the Son,[1] for the same reason the Son is in the Father.

4. Likewise, every cognized is in the one cognized either through truth, and/or through a similitude: but the Father cognizes the Son as much as regards Hypostasis and property: therefore, the Son is in the Father: therefore, either[2] as much as regards *truth*, or as much as regards a similitude *of the truth*. Not as much as regards a *similitude*, because then the Son would be in the Father just as a creature (is): therefore, as much as regards *truth*; for the same reason the Father (is) also[3] in the Son: therefore, there is a circumincession There.

5. Likewise, everything which has been compared to the other, either is *in* it, or *outside of* it. If, therefore, the Son is compared to the Father, either He is *in* Him, or *outside*. If *in* Him, for the same reason the Father (is) also in Him; if *outside of* Him; but those, of which one is outside the other, differ through substance: therefore, the Father and the Son substantially differ.

6. Likewise, there is a greater fittingness [convenientia] among the divine, than is of a genus to (its) species and/or of a whole to (its) parts; but on account of the fittingness of a genus to (its) species a genus is in the species and vice versa [e converso]; and similarly the whole in the parts and vice versa:[4] therefore, much more strongly among the divine is the Father in the Son and vice versa.

ON THE CONTRARY: 1. If the Father is in the Son and vice versa, therefore, the Father is in the Father. For just as it follows in predicating, that whatever is predicated in more and/or equally of anything, is predicated of every 'that' which is under it:[5] therefore, similarly, if anything is in anything, it is necessary, that in the same there be everything which is in that: therefore, if the Son is in the Father, everything which is in the Son, is in the Father: but the Father is in the Son: therefore, the Father is in the Father.

2. Likewise, whensoever two simples of the same genus are together, such that one is in the other, they are not distinguished from one another, just as a point is in a point. If, therefore, the Father and the Son are entirely simple; if the Father is in the Son and the Son in the Father, it does not seem that They are distinguished.

3. Likewise, if there were two Divine Essences, it would be impossible, that One would be in the Other, because One could not glide into [illabi] the Other, since Each would be equally spiritual and most highly spiritual: therefore, if Two Persons are equally and most highly spiritual, it is impossible, that One be in the Other; and that[6] seems, because God cannot be in a creature, unless He glides into it. If, therefore, a Person is in a Person, it seems that He has entirely glided into Him.

4. Likewise, I ask, what does that which it is "*to be in the Father*" signify, whether it be said according to *substance*, or according to *relation*. If according to *relation*, this is against to (St.) Augustine, who says in the text,[7] that « on account of the unity of nature the whole Father is in the Son and in the Holy Spirit ». If according to *substance*; but[8] what are said according to the Substance, befit the Three: therefore, that which it is "*to be in the Father*" befits the Son and the Holy Spirit and the Father: therefore, the Father is in the Father, which is not conceded.

5. Likewise, when there is said. 'the Father is in the Son, and the Son in the Father', either there is conveyed the *same* habitude, or *another*. If the same, since the Son is in the Father as in a principle, then similarly the Father would be[9] in the Son as in a principle; which is simply absurd. If there is not conveyed the same habitude: therefore, just as[10] there is not a circumincession, when there is said: 'a genus is in (its) species, and a species in (its) genus', there would in the proposed similarly be neither a circumincession.

6. Likewise, 'the Son is from [de] the Father and with [apud] the Father', and (this) is not convertible [convertitur]: therefore, for an equal reason it seems, that (this) is not convertible, 'that if the Father is in the Son, that the Son is in the Father'.

7. Likewise, there are nine manners of being "*in*" [novem modi essendi in][11] among crea-

---

[1] One or the other codex, such as G and V, adds *therefore* [ergo].

[2] In the Vatican edition, we have supplied the omitted *therefore* [ergo], from the manuscripts and editions 1, 2 and 3.

[3] With the help of the more ancient manuscripts and edition 1, we have restored the particle *also* [et].

[4] Cf. Aristotle, PHYSICS, Bk. VI, text 23 (ch. 3). See below in the 7th argument of the Contrary. — The words *and similarly* etc. [et similiter etc.] up to the end of the clause are wanting in the Vatican edition and in codex cc, but are found in all the other manuscripts and in edition 1.

[5] Aristotle, ON THE PREDICAMENTS, ch. "On Denominatives", at the end (says): When one is predicated of another, as of a subject, whatsoever of that which is predicated, are predicated, all are said also of the subject. This proposition hints at the principle of the affirmative syllogism, which is called *dici de omni* ["being said of all"]. See Aristotle, PRIOR ANALYTICS, Bk. I, ch. 1 ff. — Aristotle, POSTERIOR ANALYTICS, Bk. II, ch. 14 (ch. 12) says: « But I say that whatsoever "*are in more*" are indeed in each one universally, but, however, (are) also other ». These belong, as is hinted at there, to a twofold reckoning; certain ones are so *in more*, as *to be also outside of the genus*, as are the concepts of first analogy, v. g. "*to be something* in respect of a third"; but certain ones are so *in more*, as yet *not to be outside of the genus*, of which kind are the concepts of a generic univocal, v. g. "*to be an odd number* in respect to a third". Porphyry in his book, ON THE PREDICABLES has *super-abounds* [superabundat] in place of *is in more* [est in plus]. Hence understand by the words *whatever is predicated in more and/or equally* [quidquid praedicatur in plus vel aeque] a predicated, which either is of a greater extension, v. g. a genus, and/or of the same extension as the subject, v. g. a genus with a specific difference and proper (genus). Cf. (St. Severinus) Boethius, FIRST DIALOGUE ON PORPHYRY, ch. "on Genus".

[6] The Vatican edition has *thus it* [ita] on place of *that* [illud], but contrary to the mss., yet very many of them put *that* [istud], and ed. 1 with one or the other cod., such as I, puts *through that* [per illud]. Next, by substituting *because God cannot* [quia Deus non potest] for the ambiguous *that God cannot* [quod Deus non possit], we exhibit the reading of cod. T, with which codd. H & Z and ed. 1 also agree in this, that they have patent for potest, cod. K, having retained (the subjunctive) *can* [possit], substituted *since* [cum] for *that* [quod]; cod. H reads *through this that* [per hoc quod] for *because* [quia]. — A little before this, cod. A has *the Divine* [divinae] for *Two* [duae], and the Vatican ed., contrary to cod. T and the others with ed. 1, reads *be* [sint] for the *are* [sunt], which follows this.

[7] Here in ch. 4.

[8] Trusting in many mss., as A H K M S T W X Y Z etc., and edd. 1, 2 & 3, we have supplied *but* [sed], which is less well absent from the Vatican ed.. — Next, after *Substance* [substantiam] in cod. X there is added *of God* [de Deo].

[9] Ed. 1 reads *will be* [erit]. A little after this, in very many of the more ancient mss. and ed. 1, there is faultily had *similarly* [similiter] for *simply* [simpliciter].

[10] The Vatican edition, not trusting in the manuscripts and the first six editions, reads *if* [si] for *just as* [sicut], and a little before this, contrary to very many codices, has *there is conveyed the other* [importatur altera] for *there is not conveyed the same* [non importatur eadem].

[11] In many mss., just as also in ed. 1 and the Vatican, there is lacking *in* [in], but badly and against codd. H M Y & ff. — Eight of these manners are posited by Aristotle, PHYSICS, Bk. IV, text 23 (ch. 3), and the ninth, as the Seraphic Doctor says a little below this, (St. Severinus) Boethius adds, ON THE CATEGORIES OR PREDICAMENTS OF ARISTOTLE, Bk. I, ch. "on Denominatives".

tures. In the first manner, just as a part in the whole; in the second manner just as a whole in (its) parts; in the third manner just as a species in a genus; in the fourth manner just as a genus in (its) species; in the fifth manner just as a form in matter; in the sixth manner just as one ruled or moved in one ruling; in the seventh manner just as a thing in its end; in the eighth manner just as one contained in one containing; and the ninth (St. Severinus) Boethius adds, namely,[1] just as an accident in a subject. There is asked, therefore, by which of these manners is the Father in the Son and vice versa; and since it is that one grants none of these, it seems that He is in no manner (in the Son).

CONCLUSION

Among the Divine Persons there is a most high and perfect circumincession by reason of a unity of essence with a distinction of persons.

I RESPOND: It must be said, that,[2] just as the authorities and reason prove, there is among the divine a most high and perfect *circumincession*. And this is called[3] a *circumincession*, by which there is meant, that One is in the Other and vice versa: and this properly and perfectly is in God alone, because circumincession in being [in essendo] posits simultaneously a distinction and a unity. And since in God alone there is a most high[4] unity with a distinction, such that the distinction is unconfused and the unity indistinct: hence it is, that in God alone is there a perfect circumincession. And the reason for this is clear, because the reason for circumincession is the perfect Unity of the Essence with a distinction of the Persons. And since this is proper to God alone, for that reason too (is) the circumincession such, according to which (St.) Hilary says and Master (Peter) brings forward in the text.[5]

1. To that, therefore, which is objected, that the Father (is) in the Son and the Son in the Father, therefore, the Father[6] (is) in Himself, certain ones say, that the argument is not valid, because the habitude of that what is "*in*" is changed, because in One it means the habi-

tude of the begun to the beginning, but in the other the habitude of the beginning to the begun. However, one is not bound to say that, because just as will soon be clear,[7] "*in*" does not mean a diverse habitude. Nor yet does it follow, nay it is an accident There, for this because "*in*" notes a distinction, just as the accident is here: 'Peter is similar to Paul, and Paul to Peter: therefore, Peter is similar to Peter'; thus also must it be understood in the proposed.

2. To that which is objected, that[8] simples, existing together, are fused together into a 'one' [confunduntur in unum]; it must be said, that that is true, when the simples have to be distinguished from within *that*, in which they are, just as a point and a unity from that, in which it is. But when they are distinguished *by their very selves* and in[9] their very selves are substantified [substantificantur], then, although they be together, they are not confounded [confunduntur]; and such are the Divine Hypostases. And although it cannot be perfectly found in a creature, Dionysius[10] posits a similar example of this in lights, which are many (and yet) unconfused in the same air; and it is a sign of this (Unity in Trinity), because, when one luminous source [luminare] is taken away, it draws with itself[11] its own light, pulling nothing away [nihil convellens] from the others. And the reason for this is, that lights in the air are not distinguished from within that *in which* (they are).[12]

3. To that which is objected, that an essence is not in an essence except through gliding into it etc.; it must be said, that it is not similar, because where there is a diversity of essences, if one is in the other, it is necessary [oportet] that one in some manner be material to the other; but when[13] persons differ, conserving [salva] a unity of essence, one is in the other, because the essence of one is the essence of the other, and thus, just as the same (thing) does not glide into itself, so there can be no gliding-in There.

4. To that which is objected, what does that which it is "*to be in the Father*" signify; it must be said, that, just as the Saint hint at, just as "*equal*" means a looking-back according to the unity of quantity; and "*similar*" according to a unity of[14] quality, similarly that which it is "*to be in the Father*", (means a looking-back) according to a unity of substance. Whence, just as "*equal*"

---

[1] Very many codd., such as A F G I S T V X Y etc., read *because* [quia] for *namely* [scilicet] and a few, such as H & Z, with ed. 1, have *which (is)* [quod] in place of the same. Next, trusting in the more ancient mss. and ed. 1, we have supplied *manners* [modorum], and then we have substituted *none of these* [nullum horum] for *in none of those* [nullo illorum].

[2] The Vatican edition, contrary to very many codices and edition 1, reads *because* [quia], but less aptly.

[3] In regard to this proposition a great diversity is found among the codices; thus in place of *this* [haec], which is exhibited by very many mss., such as I S T aa & cc, and by ed. 1, others, such as K X Z & bb, with the Vatican ed., put *here* [hic], cod. O *this (concept)* [hoc]; then, only some codd. and the Vatican ed. read *is noted* [notatur] for *is called* [vocatur]; codd. A R & T omit the words *And this is called circumincession* [Et haec vocatur circumincessio]. Next, a few codd., such as K & O, read *because* [quia] for *by which* [qua], and, then, a little below this, cod. T has *this (circumincession)* [haec] for *this (concept, that 'One is in the other etc.')* [hoc].

[4] We offer the reading of the more ancient mss. and of edition 1, by adding *most high* [summa], which the truth of the matter also requires.

[5] Here in ch. 4. — Very many codd., such as A F G H & Z, with edition 1, read *adduces* [adducit] in place of *brings forward* [inducit].

[6] The Vatican edition, contrary to very many mss. and edition 1, adds here and a little before this, after *the Father* [Pater] the verb *is* [est].

[7] Below in reply to n. 5; cf. also Doubt 6.

[8] From the more ancient codd. and ed. 1, we have supplied *that* [quod].

[9] Codices V and X read *thus by their* [ita se ipsis] for *in their* [in se ipsis].

[10] ON THE DIVINE NAMES, ch. 2, § 4: For we also see in a house, with many united lamps, that the lights of all (have been) united to any one light and (that there is) one indiscrete glowing brightness, and that even no one, as I judge, will be able to discern the light of any lamp from the others out of the air containing all the lights, and see without one part the other part, with all mixed properly together [contemperatis] in all, in an unconfused manner. But if anyone will have taken one of the burning (lamps) from the house, with it goes also the whole of its own light [proprium totum lumen], comprising nothing of the other lights, and leaving nothing of itself to the others. For there was of them, what indeed I said, a most perfect unity of all to all, universally un-commingled, and confused in no part: and this, existing in the body "air", and from a light depending on material fire.

[11] In the Vatican edition, not trusting in the manuscripts and editions 1, 2 and 3, there is lacking *with itself* [secum].

[12] Codex Y adds *they are* [sunt]; but codices B D and H add *but from within their own origins* [sed penes suas origines], from which codex I differs only in this, that in place of *from within* [penes] it has *through* [per].

[13] The Vatican edition faultily, and contrary to the manuscripts and also to the first six editions, reads *since* [quoniam].

[14] In codex O there is added *essential and/or substantial* [essentialis vel substantialis], and, a little before this, to the name *of quantity* [quantitatis] there is conjoined *of virtue* [virtualis]. Next, after *in the Father* [in Patre], codex G adds *is* [est], but it would be better to supply *means a looking-back* [dicit respectum].

simultaneously conveys substance with relation, just as will be clear below,[1] so also that which it is *"to be in"*. And just as, when there is said *"equal to the Father"*, it is constrained to stand for the other Persons, so also must it be understood in the proposed.

5. To that which is asked, whether the same habitude would be conveyed; it must be said without prejudice, that *it would be*, as much as concerns the reckoning of the name. For just as, when there is said: 'the Father is similar to the Son and vice versa', there is not conveyed one and another habitude; so neither in that which it is *"to be in"*,[2] because it conveys a relation of identity or of consubstantiality. Whence if there be said: 'the Father is similar to the Son and vice versa', another habitude is not meant; so in the proposed, because that which it is *"to be in the Father"* signifies the same (as) that which it is *"to be consubstantial to the Father"*. And *"consubstantial"* is accepted in a uniform manner, when it is said of the Father and the Son. And this is clear, because if it did not mean a completely similar habitude, there would be no circumincession, just as neither is there, when a creature is said "to be in God", and God "to be in the creature"; because different [alia] habitudes are conveyed in each (proposition).[3]

6. To that which is asked concerning that which it is *"to be with or from"* etc.; it must be said, that certain prepositions convey a habitude of *repugnance*, such as *"against"* [contra]; certain ones (a habitude) of distance, such as that which is *"towards"* [ad] and *"near"* [prope]; certain ones (a habitude) of *cause*, such as *"from"* [de] and *"out of"*, certain ones (a habitude) *of fittingness*, such as *"in"* [in] and *"with"* [cum]. The first and second are in no manner received (among the divine),[4] but the third and fourth are, and the third (are) not conversely (said), but the fourth (are said) conversely, because fittingness is a relation of equiparancy.*

7. To the last it must be explained [solvendum], that that (of the Divine Persons) is a singular manner of being *"in"*, which is not contained among the others, nor can be found properly among creatures.

SCHOLIUM

I. *Circumincession* (in Greek: περιχώρησις) through (its) twofold prefix (circum- + in-) in some manner expresses the twofold sense of the Greek word, namely *"to go in"* [invadere] and *"to grasp"* [capere]. In our times it is often called *circuminsession* [circuminsessio], which word, however, seems to be less apt, to express the profound sense of the Greek word. For an understanding of this question it must be noted, that at least three (things) are required for circumincession: namely an actual non-existence of one in the other; a real distinction of those who are circumincessing; their most interior presence and consubstantiality. Hence it follows, that no creature can be in this manner in another, nor is God Himself properly in any *creature* in a circumincessive manner, but rather that in God alone there is a prefect circumincession, as the holy Doctor teaches in the body (of the Question). Otherwise, as Richard of Middleton (loc. cit. below) teaches, circumincession follows « from this most firmly believed fundament, that among the Three Persons there is one Essence. For from this 'every Person is in the Essence just as a supposit (is) in a nature, and the Essence in is every person just as a nature in a supposit', there follows, that every Person is through His own Essence in the Other, yet in a manner other, than a nature in a supposit and a supposit in a nature » etc., namely because there is required some difference and/or distinction for this, that one be in the other.

II. In regard to the solution to n. 1, the Seraphic Doctor deservedly rejects the first response. For here there is a fallacy of the accident. For *"to be in another"* [esse in alio] conveys the distinction of one from the other; but *"to be in one-self"* [esse in se] bears off every distinction. Therefore, it fallaciously concludes: 'the Father is in the Son, that is, as One distinct from Him, and vice versa: therefore, He is in Himself, since He is entirely indistinct'. For, in this manner, it passes from distinction to identity. The example posited in the text explains the matter more. Thus it is clear, that the Aristotelian Rule: 'whatever is predicated of something, is predicated of all, which are under it', can fail in being applied. Richard of Middleton, however, solves the same objection in another manner.

The fifth objection is solved in the same manner by St. Thomas (here in q. 3, a. 2, in reply to n. 3; SUMMA., I, q. 42, a. 1, in reply to n. 4).

III. In the conclusion all agree; and St, Thomas in his SUMMA uses the same three arguments to prove the conclusion, which St. Bonaventure has as the 3rd., 4th. and 5th. fundaments. — Durandus (of Saint-Pourçain) and (Peter) Aureolus ineptly strive to impugn the 5th. argument (which St. Thomas has in the 2nd. position). — Cf. (Bl. John Duns) Scotus, here in. q. 2; REPORTATIO., here in q. 4. — St. Thomas, here in q. 3, a. 2; SUMMA., I, q. 42, a. 5; SUMMA CONTRA GENTILES., Bk. IV, c. 9, at the end. — Bl. (now St.) Albertus (Magnus), here in a. 8. — Peter of Tarentaise, here in q. 1, a. 4. — Richard of Middleton, here in a. 2, q. 3. — Giles the Roman, here in 2nd. princ., q. 2. — Henry of Ghent, SUMMA., a. 53, q. 10. — Durandus (of Saint-Pourçain), here in a. 3. — (Bl.) Dionysius the Carthusian, here in q. 2. — (Gabriel) Biel, here in q. 2.

DOUBTS ON THE TEXT OF THE MASTER

DOUBT I

In this part there are doubts about the text (of Master Peter); and, first, there is the doubt concerning *the position* of this part. For, since unity in *substance* causes identity, unity in *quantity* equality, unity in *quality* similitude, for an equal reason it seems, that he ought to have determined concerning the identity and similitude; because, if he does not determine concerning these, it seems that neither ought he have done a special tract on equality.

---

[1] Distinction 31, p. I, q. 2. — A little below this after *which it is* [quod est] very many codices, such as A C G I K L O P Q R S T U W Y etc, together with editions 1, 2, and 3, omit *to be* [esse], but badly. Then trusting in the manuscripts, we have substituted in place of *that which it is* [hoc quod est] *when there is said* [cum dicitur], after which codices O and Z add, sufficiently well, *"some person is* [aliqua persona est].

[2] Many codices, such as those a little above, together with editions 1, 2 and 3, faultily omit *to be* [esse]. Next after *Whence* [Unde], on the authority of the manuscripts and edition 1, we have expunged the added *just as* [sicut], which, however, many codices put a little below this in place of *signifies* [significat], and in regard to which codex O (with which codex I nearly agrees) after *consubstantial to the Father* [Patri consubstantialem] adds *so "to be in the Son the same One which is consubstantial to the Son"* [sic esse in Filio idem est quod esse Filio consubstantialem], but less congruously to the matter. Some manuscripts, such as V and X, to the words *in the proposed* [in proposito] add *also*

[et]; then in many codices and editions 1, 2 and 3, after *the same(as) that which* [idem quod] there is omitted *it is* [est], and in very many manuscripts together with editions 1, 2 and 3, there is substituted *there is a consubstantial Father* [esse Patrem consubstantialem] for *to be consubstantial to the Father* [esse Patri consubstantialem].

[3] Supply: proposition; the Vatican edition, contrary to the manuscripts and edition 1, reads *in each (being)* [utroque] for *in each (proposition)* [utraque].

[4] Understand: among the divine. — Next the Vatican edition, breaking with the manuscripts and edition 1, reads *the third in this manner which (is)* [tertiae sic quod] in place of *and the third* [et tertiae], in place of which codex W exhibits *thought the third* [licet tertiae]. In codex O the fourth member of the division is subdivided, inasmuch as certain prepositions convey the habitude of fittingness *simply*, certain ones *with subauthority* and the last *are in no manner reciprocated*.

[5] See above, p. 342, footnote 6.

---

* *Trans. note*: For the definition of *equiparancy*, see below, d. 19, p. I, a. sole, q. 3, p. 347, footnote 5.

I **Respond**: It must be said, that with a perfect equality shown, there is shown, that there is an omnimodal identity and similitude in the Nature; and for that reason with the equality determined, it is not opportune to determine (anything) concerning the others; but he determines more concerning equality on account of extirpating heresies, most of all that of the Arians, who posited inequality [inaequalitatem] among the Divine (Persons); and for that reason a more difficult[1] and useful disputation turns about this.

Doubt II

Likewise, is asked of this which he says, that (Their) *equality consists in eternity*. For he seems to proceed badly, because he divides coeternity[2] against equality: therefore, if it is distinguished from that, (then) as much as regards eternity (Their) equality is not attained.

I **Respond**: It must be said, that perfect equality consists in these Three, and Master (Peter) co-divides equality against coeternity, as much as regards the other two members (of the division), namely magnitude and power.

Doubt III

Likewise, is asked of this which he says: *Not for one (reason) God, for another great* etc., because it seems for an equal reason, since for one (reason) He is God, for another the Father, that by one He is God, by another great. *If you say*, that quantity passes over into the Substance, relation (does) not; it is objected, that does not solve (the matter). For (St.) Augustine[3] speaks of formal predication, and it is established, that formally speaking thus this is false: 'God is great by the Deity, and/or (is) God by (His) magnitude', just as also: '(He is) the Father by (His) magnitude'.[4]

I **Respond**: It must be said, that although according to the reckoning of speaking and/or of understanding on our part "*magnitude*" among the divine is said through a manner of quantity, and "*deity*" through the manner of substance, yet on the part of the thing there is entirely no difference. For nothing is said of the magnitude, which is not said of the Substance. Moreover, in the relation[5] of paternity it is not thus. For something is predicated of the paternity, which cannot be said of the Essence, as "to distinguish" and "to be distinguished".

Doubt IV

Likewise, is asked of this which (St. Augustine) says: *In the generation of generations Thy years.*[6] For he seems to speak badly, because in eternity there falls no variation: therefore, since a year has a variation, it ought not be transferred There.[7] *Likewise*, in that eternity there is an omnimodal simplicity and impartibility: therefore, *years* ought not to have been said in the plural.

I **Respond**: It must be said, that according to the measure of our infirmity we both understand and name the divine eternity.[8] For since "*year*" means a complete revolution of time according to the discourse of the Sun in the Zodiac and (its) regression to the same point, and the divine eternity is perfect and encompasses all other durations. for that reason Scripture has transferred to it the name of "*year*".

Again, because (it[9] has) not been terminated, both on the part of a *before* and on the part of an *after*, for that reason he does not say *of years*, as if it had a terminus, nor a *generation* in the singular, but in the plural *years* and *generations* similarly. Therefore, by reason of (its) perfection and non-termination it is transferred, but not by reason of variation.

Doubt V

Likewise, is asked of this which (St. Augustine) says, that *in the generation of the Saints are the years of God, eternity*. For it seems false, because the duration of the Saints is finite on the part of the "before" and the "after": therefore, the Saints are not in that one.[10] *Likewise*, in what manner of being "*in*"[11] is the generation of the Saints in that one? As a *measure*? no, because God's eternity is the measure of God alone; if as a *cause* in an effect; but in this manner it is in all other creatures: ergo etc..

I **Respond**: It must be said, that[12] that word has not been said through commensuration nor through equality, but through concomitance and conformity. For because the generation of the Saints on the part of the "*after*" lasts unto infinity,[13] it also lasts without variation: for that reason it accompanies [comitatur] that most high eternity forever and is

---

[1] Codex O has *more sufficient* [sufficientior].

[2] Not a few codd., such as I V Y & Z, have *eternity* [aeternitatem].

[3] See there the text of Master (Peter), ch. 2.

[4] The Vatican edition faultily and contrary to the testimony of the manuscripts and edition 1, inverts the order by putting *that just as* [quod sicut] in place of *thus* [ita] and *so is this:* '*the Father is great*' [sic est ista: Pater est mangus] for *just as also:* '*(He is) the Father by (His) magnitude*' [sicut et Pater magnitudine], which also after *and/or* [vel] repeats *God is* [Deus est].

[5] The error of the Vatican edition, which reads *resolution* [resolutione] for *relation* [relatione], we have corrected from the manuscripts and editions 1 and 2.

[6] Thus the codices, together with edition 1, while the Vatican edition, together with all the other editions reads *In generation and unto generation thy years* [In generatione et generationem anni tui]; otherwise see above the text of Master (Peter), ch 1.

[7] Codex dd has *to divine (things)* [ad divina] for *There* [ibi]. A little below this the Vatican edition falsely reads *impartiality* [impartialitas] for *impartibility* [impartibilitas]; very many manuscripts and edition 1 also withstand this.

[8] Many codd., contrary to the context, read *Trinity* [Trinitatem] for *eternity* [aeternitatem]; the Vatican ed. with one or the other cod., has *Trinity*

and/or eternity [Trinitatem vel aeternitatem]; the reading received in the text is exhibited by many manuscripts, such as H ee and ff, and edition 1. Next from the more ancient manuscripts we have supplied *For* [enim].

[9] Understand: *(the divine) eternity* [aeternitas]. — A few codices, such as H and I, add *has* [est], codex X adds *the duration has* [est duratio].

[10] Namely: in that eternity of God. — The Vatican edition, without the authority of the codices and the first six editions, keeping the same sense, reads *therefore that one does not belong to the Saints* [ergo illa non est Sanctis].

[11] Cf. above q. 4, argument 7 unto the contrary, where the nine manners of being *in* are mentioned. Next the Vatican edition has *is it in that generation of the Saints* [est in illa generatione Sanctorum], but contrary to the testimony of the manuscripts and the first six editions, though it conserves the sense.

[12] Trusting in the more ancient manuscripts and edition 1, we have supplied *that* [quod] and consequently have replaced *has been* [esse] with *has been* [est].

[13] Codex I, together with edition 1, adds *and* [et]. Next some codices, such as T and X, together with edition 1 have *is concomitant to* [concomitatur] for *accompanies* [comitatur].

is expressly conformed to it; and for that reason blessed Augustine[1] expounded that (verse) of the Psalm: *In the generation of generations Thy years*: whether (because these years are) in the un-terminated generation, which generation of *the Holy One*, or (because) the Saints are that generation, and because it lasts in perpetuity, and because they have been collected out of many generations.

DOUBT VI

Likewise, is asked of this which (St. Hilary) says, that *the Father is in the Son and the Son in the Father*, because, if whatever is in God is God on account of (His) most high simplicity, therefore, whatever is in the Son is the Son: therefore, if the Father is in the Son, the Father is the Son.

I RESPOND: It must be said, that it is not similar, because, when there is said that something is in God, this preposition "*in*" either means an *essential* distinction, and thus not whatever is in God, is God, because we *in God live, move and are*;[2] or it means *no* distinction except according to a manner of understanding, and this posits an omnimodal identity; and for that reason it follows, that that which is in God is God. But when it is said of a *person*, this preposition "*in*" means a personal distinction, and one person is not predicated of another one; and for that reason it is clear, that it is not similar.[3]

DOUBT VII

Likewise, is asked of this which (St.) Hilary says: *Nor will a human comparison offer any example for divine things*. For it seems false, because an *image* is an expressed similitude, and a *vestige* is every creature: therefore, it seems, that there is an *example* in all (things).

I RESPOND: It must be said, that there is an example which *perfectly* and[4] in an entirely, completely similar manner *expresses* [exemplum exprimens perfecte et consimiliter omnino], and no such (example) is (found) among creatures, because an *image* and all the other creatures have more of a dissimilitude than of a similitude; and there is an example which *leads us by the hand* [exemplum manducens] in some manner, and in this manner there are many, and one is gathered from many, and yet (it is) not entirely perfect.

DOUBT VIII

Likewise is asked of this which (St. Hilary) says: *What is unintelligible to man, for God is able to be*. It seems false, « because our soul is in a certain manner all (things) »,[5] and our intellect does not understand all, though [quin] it could understand more.

I RESPOND: It must be said, that there is a speaking of the *comprehending* intellect, and thus it is not true, that it can understand all, because neither God nor something of God, is comprehensible to us, because (He is) entirely infinite; and one can speak of the *apprehending* intellect, and this in a twofold manner: either in the reckoning of the *possible*[6] and uptaking (intellect), and thus at any rate everything which can come to be, it can understand, because the possible (intellect) is for understanding; or in the reckoning of an *agent* (intellect), and because it does not have a light of such a great power, that it can (act) upon all, namely, (things) present and future, because many are contrary to[7] its judgement, in this manner it does not belong to all.

DOUBT IX

Likewise is asked of this which (St.) Hilary says: *For if He accepted part of the Same, who begot (Him), therefore, Neither is perfect*. For it seems that this does not follow, because a perfect man generates a perfect son, and yet he does not give him but a part.

I RESPOND: It must be said, that there is perfection *simply*, and perfection[8] *in (its) genus*. Perfection *in (its) genus* endures [compatitur secum] well a giving and reception of parts, because in the one giving (perfection) is supplied through a restoration, in the one accepting through augment and addition; but perfection *simply* does not endure a restoration nor an addition. And since in God there is perfection simply, for that reason if He would give part (of Himself), in the One giving there would remain a defect, similarly in the one accepting; for that reason it is not similar concerning a man.[9]

DOUBT X

Likewise is asked of this which (St. Hilary) says: *Not through a twofold conjunction of convening genera* etc.;

---

[1] ENARRATIONS ON THE PSALMS, Psalm 101, Sermon 2, n. 11: From all the generations Though shall gather all the holy offspring of all the generations, and Thou shalt make of them one generation. *In that generation of generations Thy years*, that is, that eternity shall be in that generation, which is gathered from all generations and is brought back into one; that shall be the share of Thy eternity. All other generations are generated with seasons being fulfilled, out of which that one is regenerated in eternity; what has changed shall be vivified; it shall be fit to bear Thee, accepting strengths from Thee. *In the generation of generations Thy years*. — The Vatican edition, just as also above here in Doubt 4, contrary to the codices and to edition 1, reads *In generation and unto generation Thy years* [In generatione et generationem anni tui], which also a little above this adds *thus* [sic] after *for that reason* [ideo], and then it puts *of the Saints or* [Sanctorum sive] for *of the Holy One or* [Sancti sive], contrary to the manuscripts and edition 1. Next codex I has *they last* [durant] and codex dd *the blessed last* [Durant beati] in place of *it lasts* [durat], which also and the end of the response adds *and this is the understanding of this proposition* [et hic est intellectus huius propositionis]. — Bl. (now St.) Albertus (Magnus) solves the same doubt, here in a. 6.

[2] Acts 17:28. — A little below this codex T has *that in this manner God is in God* [quod sic Deus est in Deo] in place of *that that which is in God is God* [quod sit Deus quod est in Deo].

[3] Cf. above q. 4, in reply to n. 1 and in the Scholium.

[4] From the mss. & edd. 1, 2, 3 & 6, we have supplied *and* [et]. Very

many codices, such as C L O R S U V, have *similar* [similiter] for *completely similar* [consimiliter]. — Cf. concerning this division, (d. 3, p. II), Doubt 4, p. 94.

[5] Aristotle, ON THE SOUL, Bk. III, text 37. (ch. 8).

[6] The Vatican edition, with cod. cc, reads *possibility* [possibilitas] for *of the possible* [possibilis], but contrary to the other codd. and to ed. 1. A little after this, trusting in very many mss., such as I S T Y Z & bb, and in ed. 1, we have restored the particle *at any rate* [utique].

[7] The Vatican edition, with the mss. and edd. 1, 2, 3 & 6 striving against this, reads *above* [supra] for *contrary to* [contra]. In the reading of the codd., understand the saying *contrary to the judgement of reason* as concerning *the inferior reason* and that turned toward sensibles, as the Seraphic Doctor himself explains very clearly in SENT., Bk. III, d. 23, a. 1, q. 1, in reply to n. 4. — See more on the comprehending and apprehending intellect, above in d. 3, p. I, q. 1, in reply to n. 1; on the possible and agent intellect, om SENT, Bk. II, d. 24, p. I, a. 2, q. 4, and Aristotle, ON THE SOUL, bk. III, texts 1-20 (chs. 4 & 5). — In cod. O, at the end of the response, there is added *because it has not so great an intellectual light, which can cause all (to be) intellected in potency intellected in act* [quia non habet tantum lumen intellectuale, quod possit omnia intellecta in potentia facere intellecta in actu].

[8] In very many manuscripts, such as A F G I S T W Y etc., and in edition 1, there is lacking *perfection* [perfectio].

[9] From many manuscripts, such as A F G I M N P Q T U Z ee and ff, and edition 1, we have inserted the words *for that reason it is not similar concerning a man* [ideo non est simile de homine].

either he touches upon manners of *being* [modos essendi], or of *being generated*. Not of *being*, because there are much more than those; not of *being generated*; and thus it is insufficient in[1] each manner.

I RESPOND: Some say, that (St.) Hilary assigns those[2] manners of generation, which are in creatures, to exclude those from the Son. But he does not assign but two manners, because he does not speak but of the generation of a living (thing); but a "living thing which can be generated" [vivens generabile] is divided into the vegetable and sensible; and according to that twofold genus, is the twofold manner of being generated, which (St.) Hilary touches upon. For animals are generated through[3] a conjunction of male and female, and plants through being inserted [per insertum]. He touches upon the first, when there is said: « Not through a twofold (conjunction) of *convening genera* », because "masculine" and "feminine" belong to a twofold *genus*, as much as regards sex, and yet are *convening* as much as regards form and nature.[4] He touches upon the second manner when he says: « Nor through the engrafted [insitivam] nature of a more capable substance », just as a young shoot [surculus] is inserted into a tree, « but through the united similitude of nature », that is (through) a similitude entirely un-differing in nature.[5]

In another manner it can be said, that (St.) Hilary does not speak of the manner[6] of being generated, but speaks, according to the manner in which [quomodo] the Father is in the Son; and he excludes the manner of being *in*, whereby a creature is said to be in a creature according to the usual manner; to which manner there concurs a twofold condition of creatures:* the first is the diversity of creatures[7] in regard to nature; the second is the capacity of the one containing. And he excludes the former from that manner of existing, which is among the divine, through those two, which he says: « That the Son is in the Father not through a conjunction of two genera, not through the engrafted [insitivam] nature of a more capable substance ». This is clear through the text of (St.) Hilary,[8] which he immediately subjoins in the original, and (which) Master

(Peter) omits: « Because », says (St.) Hilary, « through corporal necessity exterior (things can) come to be from those, which are contained, interior ones cannot »; and[9] he would have it [vult], that it is impossible in corporal creatures, that they be mutually in themselves, as the Father is in the Son; because on account of corporal necessity and imperfection interiors cannot become exteriors to those which are contained, as if water is inside [intus][10] in a vase, while it is inside, it cannot come to be outside, and thus a vase is not contained, as a vase is in water.

DOUBT XI

Likewise, is asked of this which (St. Hilary) says: *While the nativity does not degenerate the Nature of God*, because not only in God, but in many creatures it does not degenerate (the nature).

I RESPOND: It must be said, that "*to degenerate*" is "to go forth outside of the genus of the one generating". Moreover, "to go forth outside of the genus of the one generating" is this: either as much as regards the *common*[11] *form* and nature; and thus there is a degeneration in equivocal (terms), just as a male horse [equus] generates a hinny [burdonem] from a female donkey [asina], and a male donkey, a mule from a female horse [equa], whence the mule degenerates. In another manner "*to degenerate*" is "to relinquish the properties of the one generating, *with the nature retained*", just a son, who is generated from a noble and handsome father, is homely and ugly [rusticanus et turpis].[12] In a third manner "*to degenerate*" is "to relinquish the nature of the one generating", not through dissimilitude, but through *diversity*: and in this manner every created nativity degenerates, because in every creature the one generating is other than the one generated,[13] and the divine generation alone is, that which does not degenerate, because nothing new is born, nothing added from another, and for that reason the One generating is not separated in substance from the One generated, and for that reason that generation alone is most noble.[14]

---

[1] Trusting in the more ancient manuscripts and edition 1, we have expunged the added *in* [in, *which however, is required in English*].

[2] One or the other codex, such as G, together with edition 1, has *here the* [hic] for *those* [hos].

[3] A few manuscripts, such as G and H, and edition 1, have *out of* [per]. next the Vatican edition, contrary to the more ancient codices and edition 1, adds *And* [Et] at the beginning of the next sentence. Then some codices, such as F G and H, together with edition 1, have *he says* [dicit] for *there is said* [dicitur].

[4] From very many manuscripts and edition 1, we have supplied *nature* [naturam] in place of *matter* [materiam]. A little after this some codices, such as aa and bb, read *there is said* [dicitur] for *he says* [dicit].

[5] The Vatican edition reads *(through) a similitude not differing in nature* [similitudinem non in natura differentem]; but the authority of the older manuscripts and edition 1 withstand this. — The aforesaid exposition of this passage is offered by Bl. (now St.) Albertus (Magnus), here in a. 10; St. Thomas and Richard (of Middleton), here on the text.

[6] Not a few codices, such as F and G, together with edition 1, have *manners* [modis].

[7] In the Vatican edition there is lacking *of creatures* [creaturarum], which, however, is extant in the manuscripts and edition 1.

[8] ON THE TRINITY, Bk. VII, n. 39. — Edition 1, together with one or the other codices, reads *And this* [Et hoc] for *This* [Hoc]. Next from very many manuscripts, such as A H K T Y Z etc. and edition 1, we have substituted *which* [quam] in place of *since* [quoniam].

[9] Very many manuscripts, together with edition 1, exhibit the particle *and* [et], which is lacking in the Vatican edition.

[10] We follow the more ancient codices together with edition 1 by adding *inside* [intus], some of which, however, such as F G I S V W and aa, omit *in* [in].

[11] In codex T there is lacking *the common* [communem].

[12] The Vatican edition, with codex cc, however, breaking with the other mss. and ed. 1, has *homely* [rusticus]. A little before this, cod. T has *from a noble father and mother* [ex patre nobile et matre] for *from a noble and handsome father* [ex patre nobile et pulcro]. Next, after *In a third* [Tertio], we have supplied from not a few mss., such as P Q & dd, *manner* [modo]. Then, after "*to degenerate*" *is* [est degenerare] cod. dd adds *that which (is)* [id quod], in place of which very many codd., such as A F G H P Q T Z ee & ff, with ed. 1, have less well *In a third manner there is* "*to degenerate*" *that is* [Tertio modo est degenerare id est], but some, such as S & V, have *In the third manner* "*to degenerate*" *is also* [Tertio modo est degenerare et].

[13] The error of the Vatican edition and codex cc, *the one generating* [generante] for *the one generated* [generato], here and a little below this, we have corrected from the other mss. and edition 1. A little before this codex T, together with edition 1, has *every nativity degenerates by (something) created* [omnis nativitas creato degenerat] and codex Y has the masculine form for *other* [aliud] rather than the neuter form. Next in place of the reading of the Vatican edition, *and in the divine generation alone there is no degeneration* [et in sola divina generatione degeneratio non est], trusting in nearly all the more ancient manuscripts and in edition 1, we have substituted *and the divine generation alone is, that which does not degenerate* [et sola divina generatio est, quae non degenerat]; in which proposition codices O and Y put *but* [sed] in place of *and* [et], and codex I has *which has not degenerated* [quae non degenerate est] for *which does not degenerate* [quae non degenerat].

[14] Cf. Bl. (now St.) Albertus (Magnus), here in a. 1.

---

* *Trans. note*: The critical edition has *of bowls* [craturarum] for *of creatures* [creaturarum], faultily.

COMMENTARY ON DISTINCTION XIX

PART II

On the equality, proven through the exclusion of inequality.

But, now, presently, let us return to the proposed.

See this Part of the Text, above on p. 337.

THE DIVISION OF THE TEXT

Above, Master (Peter) shows, that the Divine Persons are equal as much as regards magnitude in a positive manner[1] through this, that the one Essence is Whole in Each. Here he shows, that there is in Them a most high equality, and this he does by excluding from Them every[2] reckoning of inequality. And this part is divided into three parts. In the *first* he shows, that there does occur There a reckoning of an integral[3] whole. In the *second* he shows, that there does not occur There a reckoning of genus and species,[4] there (where he says): *Here there must be inserted, that so great is the equality* etc.. In the *third* he shows, that there does not fall There a reckoning of number, there (where he says): *On the one hand, what (St.) John says* etc..[5]

Again the *first* part has[6] two (parts). In the first, because he had made a digression, he continues (the things) said according to (the things) to be said [dicta dicendis]. But in the second he shows, that there does not occur There a reckoning of whole and part, there (where he says): *Nor is Any of the Three Persons* etc..

Likewise, the *second* part, in which he shows, that among the divine there does not occur a reckoning of a universal, or of genus and species, has two parts. In the first he shows, that among the divine there is not accepting of genus nor of species nor of an individual. But in the second he opposes against this, the authority of (St. John) Damascene, there (where he says): *But to these seem opposed certain things.* The first has two (parts): first he shows, that there is no reckoning[7] There of genus and/or species and/or of an individual; second, that there is no reckoning There of a material principle, there (where he says): *It also must be noted, that the Divine Essence is not the matter.* Similarly, the part, in which he objects against this, has two (parts): in the first he shows, that there does occur There a reckoning of universal and individual, according to the reasoning[8] of (St. John) Damascene;

in the second he solves it. The first he makes, there (where he says): *But to these seem opposed* etc.; the second, there (where he says): *But, these (words), which are here said, though in each discourse.*

On the one hand, what (St.) John (Damascene) says etc.. This is the *third* subpart [particula] in which (Master Peter) shows, that among the divine there does not occur the reckoning of number, and this part has four pats. In the first, having aforementioned that in the equality of the Persons there occurs no reckoning of number, he shows, in what manners it does not befit the Persons to differ in number, and in what manner it does befit (Them). In the second he shows, that among the Divine Persons there is as great a magnitude in one Person, as (there is) in the Three, there (where he says): *It must be known, therefore* etc.. In the third he shows, that God cannot be said (to be) threefold or manifold, there (where he says): *Besides, since God is said (to be) Triune.* In the fourth he shows the difference between the plurality, which is in the Trinity, and the plurality,[9] which is in corporal creatures, in the last chapter (where he says): *In corporeal things one is not as much* etc..

And it must be noted, that the whole (distinction) and the fundament of the whole distinction consists, however, in this, that the Divine Essence is one magnitude, not multiplied, and the Whole has not been divided in Any of the Persons; for that reason it is necessary, that the Persons be entirely equal in[10] magnitude. Nor can there occur There a reckoning of a *universal* whole, because that is multiplied in parts, nor of an *integral* whole, because that is divided into parts and is not whole in each part; and, thus, neither the reckoning of a *material principle*, nor the reckoning of *number*.

---

[1] We follow the greater part of the codices by adding *in a positive manner* [positive], but some, such as B U aa &d cc, with ed. 1, read *the magnitude of power* [magnitudinem potentiae], cod. D *magnitude and power* [magnitudinem et potentiam]. In the Vatican edition, breaking with nearly all the mss. and ed. 1, after *regards* [ad] there is inserted *eternity and* [aeternitatem et]. A little before this, very many codd., such as A F G H T & Z, with ed. 1, read *(are) equal* [aequales] for *are equal* [aequari].

[2] The Vatican edition, together with only some codices, has less aptly *the common* [communem] for *every* [omnem].

[3] Trusting in very many mss. & ed. 1, we have removed the added *and* [et].

[4] The Vatican edition adds *and/or of individual* [vel individui], which is lacking in the manuscripts.

[5] The manuscripts have *It must be known, therefore, « that there is so great an equality* [Sciendum igitur est tantam aequalitatem] in place of *On the one hand, what (St.) John says* etc. [Quod autem Ioannes dicit etc.]; but the reading of the manuscripts is false, because it omits that chapter, in which Master (Peter) shows that among the divine there does

not fall a reckoning of number. The same error of the manuscripts recurs a little below, where the subdivision of this part is given, and in which, consequently, the manuscripts exhibit only three parts, having omitted the first part, which is in the Vatican edition.

[6] From the more ancient manuscripts and edition 1, we have substituted *has* [habet] for *(is) in* [in].

[7] Only some manuscripts together with the Vatican read *nature* [natura].

[8] Very many codices, such as H P Q Z and ee, and edition 1, have *authority* [auctoritate].

[9] The mutilated reading of the Vatican edition, in which there is omitted the words *which is in the Trinity, and the plurality* [quae est in Trinitate et pluralitatem], are repaired form the manuscripts and edition 1, just as also a little after this we have substituted *in the last chapter* [ultimo capitulo] in place of *there (where he says)* [ibi].

[10] In the Vatican edition and codex cc there is lacking *in* [in, *which however, would be required in English if it were not in the text*].

TREATMENT OF THE QUESTIONS

For an understanding of this part, four (things) are asked:

First,[1] whether, among the divine, there is a positing of an integral whole.

Second, whether there is a positing of a universal whole.

Third, whether, among the Divine Persons, there is a material principle.

Fourth, whether, among the divine, there is difference according to number.

ARTICLE SOLE

That from God there ought to be excluded all reckonings of inequality.

QUESTION I

Whether, among the divine, there is to be posted a whole integral?

About the first, that there is[2] a positing of a wholeness of integrity [totalitatem integritatis], seems:

1. First, through (St.) Augustine, and (through what) is had in the text:[3] 'The whole Trinity is in Each Person': therefore, either there is an implication of the false there, or there is (an implication) of a totality; but there is not an implication of the false there; therefore, there is (an implication) of a totality.

2. Likewise, this very (thing) is shown *by reason*, because where (there is) a quantity, there (is) a totality and an integrity. But among the divine there is a quantity of virtue: therefore, at least according to that, also an integrity.

3. Likewise, where (there is) plurality, there (is) integrity, because every plurality is established out of unities; but in God there is a plurality, because (there is) a trinity: therefore, in God there is an integrity. *If you say*, that that plurality is not integrated, because there is nothing more in Three than in One — therefore[4] if there is as much in Three, as there is in One, therefore, he believes as much and believes equally fully, that there is one Supposit alone, as he who believes that there are Three Persons; but this is false: ergo etc..

4. Likewise, if anything is equal to something, with the same added (to each), it shall still be equal: therefore, if anything is whole to some-

thing, when added to the same, it shall still be whole; but *three* is whole to one: therefore, three persons to one person.[5]

5. Likewise, everything which is predicated of some (things) together and of nothing by itself [per se], is an integral whole to them;[6] this is established and has no proof [non habet instantiam]; but "trinity" is predicated of the Three Persons together and of None by itself: ergo etc..

6. Likewise, everything which is removed from something, differs from it in genus, and/or species, and/or number, and/or is whole to it; but "*trinity*" is removed from the Father, because the Father is not a "trinity", nor does it differ (form Him) in genus, and/or in species, and/or in number: ergo etc..

ON THE CONTRARY: 1. (St.) Ambrose in (his) book on the Trinity (says):[7] « Among the divine we posit no wholeness, because there is There no quantity nor number ».

2. Likewise, *by reason* it seems, that everything[8] integral has been composed out of parts; but God is most highly simple: therefore, in God there is no wholeness nor integrity.

3. Likewise, every part under the reckoning of a part has to be imperfect in respect to the whole, because out of any

---

[1] Codex X together with edition 1 adds *there is asked* [quaeritur].

[2] In edition 1 there is added *There* [ibi].

[3] Here in ch. 4, where these words of (St.) Augustine are found: « On account of the natural unity, the whole Father is in the Son and Holy Spirit, the whole Holy Spirit, too, is in the Father and the Son. None of These is outside of Any of Them on account of the unity of the Divine Nature ». And in ch. 5, where among all the others (St.) Augustine says: « Therefore, part of the Trinity cannot be any One whomsoever among the Three ». From which words that proposition of the objection seems to have been formed.* — The Vatican edition here and below at the beginning of the response to this objection, not trusting nearly all the manuscripts and the first six editions, has *Essence* [essentia] in place of *Trinity* [Trinitas]; in place of which codices P and Q have *Divinity* [divinitas].

[4] The Vatican edition without the authority of the manuscripts and first six editions, reads *on the contrary* [contra] for *therefore*, [ergo]. — With *therefore* [ergo] the reply to the internal objection begins.

[5] The sense of the argument is: If this axiom is true: 'two things equal remain equal, if to each is added the same thing', this axiom will also be true: 'if anything is a whole to something, it remains the whole', if to the subject and predicate there is added the same thing'; wherefore if in the proposition: '*three* is a whole to *one*', I add the word *person* to "three" and to "one", the truth of it will not be altered.

[6] Aristotle, METAPHYSICS, Bk. V, text 31 (Bk. IV, ch. 26) says: « "Whole" is said of that which no part of them is absent, out of which there is said "the whole by nature" (i. e. according to its own nature); and "that which contains the things contained", as the one which those are; but this in a twofold manner: for either as "anyone thing (is) one", or "out of these that (is) one". For a universal itself and what is entirely said as any whole being, in this manner is a universal, as one containing many, for this, that it is predicated of each ... Otherwise (whole is) continuous and finite, since from very many things existing within [inexistentia] there is one 'what', indeed most of all in potency, not in act ». Which words (Bl. John Duns) Scotus, in his COMMENTARY on this passage, thus explains: And through this he gives one to understand a twofold "whole", to the extent that such a "whole" is predicated of its own parts, by the predication which says: 'this is this'; the other an integral "whole", which is constituted out of its own parts, yet the whole itself is no part of it, because no such whole is predicated of its own parts.

[7] ON THE FAITH, Bk. I, ch. 2, n. 19; ON THE HOLY SPIRIT, Bk. II, ch. 13, n. 93 says: For in what manner does the unity of the Divinity receive plurality, since plurality if of a number, but the Divine Nature receives no number?

[8] In codex M, there is had *every integral whole* [omne totum integrum] for *everything integral* [omne integrum].

---

* *Trans. note:* In this phrase '*The whole Trinity is in the three*', "the whole Trinity" is said according to the Divine Substance or Essence, inasmuch as that which is God is that which is the Trinity; for strictly speaking None is in Himself; but in a transferred sense, in which in each One the same One is reckoned with the Other by circumincession, it can be said. And as regards (St.) Augustine's phrase *'part of the Trinity'*: what is denied is the reckoning of a Person in the Trinity as a "part" therefore, since "part" implies imperfection; not that each Person with the Other Two are that Trinity of Persons.

entirely perfect (things) there does not result a third:[1] therefore, since among the divine nothing must be posited (belonging) to imperfection, there is not a part There: therefore, from relatives,[2] neither a whole.

4. Likewise, every whole is greater than its own part; but where (there is) infinity, there is not "greater and lesser": therefore, neither "wholeness"; but among the divine there is infinity: ergo.

5. Likewise, every whole is can be dissolved again [est resolubile] either according to the thing, and/or according to its understanding [secundum intellectum][3] and everything which can be dissolved again is corruptible: therefore, since in God there is nothing corruptible, there will be nothing which can be dissolved again [non erit resolubile], and thus neither a whole.

CONCLUSION

The reckoning of totality, insofar as it expresses something perfect, befits God; but insofar as it has a regard for parts, neither totality nor partiality can be posited in God.

I RESPOND: "*Whole*" or "wholeness" is said in one manner absolutely; and thus "whole" is the same as "perfect".[4] In another manner "*whole*" is said through a comparison to "part"; and thus what has a part and a part or parts is said (to be) the "whole".[5]

In the first manner there is rightly [bene] a positing of *wholeness* in God, in the second[6] not, nor even of a *partiality*; of a wholeness not, because it bears off simplicity; of a partiality not, because it takes away the perfect; nor of both [neutrum], because it takes away the most high equality.

1. To that, therefore, which is objected concerning (St.) Augustine, who says, that the whole Trinity etc.; it must be said, that he accepts "whole" for "the perfect", and/or "whole" is accepted there privatively, because it deprives [privat] that which it is to be a part outside of a part. Whence "*the whole Essence*" has as much meaning [tantum valet], as "*not having a part* outside and/or inside" does.

2. To that which is objected second, that there is a quantity of virtue There; it must be said, that the quantity of virtue stands still with a most high simplicity; for that reason it abstracts from "totality" and "integrity".

3. To that which is objected, that where a plurality,

there an integrity[7] etc.; it must be said, that "plurality" [pluralitas] in regard to creatures means two (things). For it means *a distinction* of some (things), and *a constitution* of one multitude[8] out of them. The first indeed is found among the divine, because there is truly a distinction There; the second (is) not, because where there is a constitution, there the constituents have less than the whole, which they constitute, and thus differ essentially from one another. But among the divine (it is) not so, because since the Father[9] has the whole Essence, not a part, He cannot have less nor differ essentially. And for that reason it must be said, that among the divine "*plurality*" is received[10] according to the reckoning of distinction. But because "*plurality*" is the "whole" by a reckoning of (its) constitution, and this is not among the divine; for that reason it does not follow, that there is a "*totality*" There; and yet there is truly a unity and plurality There[11], and it is *as much* in the Unity, as in the plurality, but not *in all the manners*. And because faith not only is in respect to (God's) Essence and/or magnitude, but even of (His) manner of being, that which is objected is clear, that he who believes (that there is) one Person does not believe as much, as he who believes (that there are) more.

4. From this the follow (arguments) are clear, because "one" is a part of "three", according to which (one)[12] means a "unity", and "three" a "trinity". But when this name, "*person*", is added, it pulls it apart [distrahitur] and that reckoning of unity does not remain, for that reason neither the reckoning of partiality.

5. 6. To that which is objected, that it is simultaneously *predicated* and *removed*[13] etc.; it must be said, that this not only befits a totality in respect to a part, but even a plurality in respect to a unity; which though it does not have the reckoning of a part[14] on account of (its) diminution and imperfection, yet it does have a reckoning of unity on account of (having a) principle and distinction.

Wherefore, that a whole be removed from parts and not[15] differ, this is not principally by reason of a constitution, but by reason of a distinction. And since among the divine plurality, although there be no constitution of one greater, yet because there is a distinction There, for that reason it is removed in this manner, and is predicated in this manner, just as a "whole" (is) among creatures.

---

[1] Aristotle, METAPHYSICS, Bk. VII, text 49 (Bk. VI, c. 13). See above, d. 17, p. II, a. sole, q. 2, p. 311, footnote 7.

[2] That is, by concluding from the habitude of one relative to the other, namely of a part to a whole.

[3] See (St.) Anselm (of Canterbury), PROSLOGION, ch. 18, and ON FAITH IN THE TRINITY, ch. 3. Cf. above, d. 8, p. I, a. 2, q. 2, p. 161, footnote 1.

[4] Aristotle, PHYSICS, Bk. III, text 64 (ch. 6): However, the "whole" and the "perfect" either are entirely the same, or by nature border on one another [natura inter se affinia].

[5] Aristotle, METAPHYSICS, Bk. V, text 31 (Bk. IV, ch. 6): See above the 5th initial argument.

[6] In codices V and X, there is sufficiently added *manner, however,* [vero modo]. A little below this, codex X has *perfection* [perfectionem] for *the perfect* [perfectum]. Then, edition 1 after *nor of both, because* [neutrum, quia] adds *each* [utrumque].

[7] From codex Y we have supplied *integrity* [integritas].

[8] Thus very many manuscripts, such as F G H P Q and Y, together with edition 1; others, together with the Vatican edition, have *multiplication* [multiplicationis].

[9] Codex O has *any Person* [quaelibet persona] in place of *the Father* [Pater].

[10] Trusting the mss. and ed. 1, we have substituted *is received* [recipitur] for *is found* [reperitur], and, a little below this, from very many

mss., such as A C S T V & ee, and ed. 1, *this (constitution)* [haec] for *this (genus of plurality)* [hoc]. Many codd., such as A F G H I S T V Z etc., with ed. 1, read *was the "whole"* [erat totum] for *is the "whole"* [est totum].

[11] The Vatican edition with cod. cc reads *there is, however, a unity of nature and a plurality of Persons* [est tamen naturae unitas et personarum pluralitas], but the authority of the other mss. and ed. 1 withstand this. A little below this, many codd. with the Vatican ed. have *But because* [Sed quia] in place of *And because* [Et quia], contrary to codd. G and H and to edition 1.

[12] Supply, together with edition 1 *one* [unum], which also next puts *would be added* [adderetur] for *is added* [additur].

[13] Thus, read very briefly the mss. and ed. 1, while the Vatican ed. has *that everything, which is predicated together and of nothing etc.. And to the following: everything which is removed etc.* [obiicitur quod omne, quod praedicatur simul et de nullo etc. Et ad sequens: omne quod removetur etc.].

[14] Codex Z incongruously adds here *namely, among the divine* [scilicet in divinis], and next after *imperfection* [imperfectionem] inserts *which, namely, means a "part"* [quam scilicet dicit pars].

[15] The Vatican edition, faultily, because it corresponds less with the argumentation, and without the authority of the mss. and the first six edd., omits *not* [non]. A summary of this argument is: the reason, for which the "*whole*", i.e. the Trinity, is removed from the Father, and, yet, does not differ from Him, as a whole does from its parts, is not, that the Trinity is something more than the Father (as if there were one Essence among Three), but becaise there is a real distinction There of the Persons.

SCHOLIUM

I. For an understanding of this Question it must be noted, that the Seraphic Doctor here in the body (of the Question) and in reply to n. 1, takes the word, "*whole*" [totum], in three senses. For it can be understood either *positively* and/or *privatively*; if positively, then again either *properly*, i. e. comparatively to the parts, and thus a "*whole*" is the same as the "*one having parts*"; and/or *absolutely*, and thus it signifies the "perfect". But if it is accepted *privatively*, then it signifies a being, which does not have parts, just as are all indivisibles, v. g. the soul. In the first sense "*whole*" can least of all be transferred to God, but rightly so [bene] in the second and third sense. With these things supposed, the question is resolved in regard to "*wholeness*" [totalitatem] with a twofold conclusion; then the negative solution is extended even to "*partiality*".

II. For an understanding of nn. 3, 4 and 5, unto the contrary and the Solution, it must be noted, that the nature of an *integral whole* [totius integralis] conveys, that the whole is predicated of all the parts together, but of not part by itself [per se]. The reason for this is not only, that the parts *are distinguished*, but also that the whole is *unequal* in comparison to its own parts. Indeed, it is true, that even the *Trinity* is not predicated of any Person by Himself, yet from this there does not follow, that the Trinity is an integral whole in a manner related [relate] to Each Person, because not on account of any *inequality* of the Trinity to Each Person, but only on account of the *distinction* of the Persons is that predication (of an "integral whole" to the Trinity) unable to be made. Whence there is rightly replied [replicatur] in the 3rd opposed argument: « That plurality (of

Persons) is not integrated (i. e. does not make an integral whole), because there is nothing more in Three, that in One ». So also the words in the solution: « Where there is a constitution, there the constituents have less than the whole », are easily understood, because it is manifest, that when parts constitute one whole, the parts are less than the whole. Among the divine it is not so, because the plurality of the Persons does not constitute the *Whole*, as is well explained there by the Seraphic Doctor.

For the solution to the reply to n. 4, it must be noted, that "number" among the divine does not have the full reckoning of a "number", because even is the Persons are distinct through Their personal properties, yet They convene in one Essence according to number; but "number" according to its full reckoning conveys a distinction in essence of those numbered. Wherefore three personal unities are indeed more than one, yet they are not more and/or a more *in essence*; thus nearly Richard of Middleton, loc. cit. below, and according to the mind of the Seraphic Doctor, cf. below d. 24, chiefly a. 3, q. 1.

III. (Bl. John Duns) Scotus, on this q. and the following two qq., REPORTATIO, here in q. 5. — St. Thomas, here in q. 4, a. 1. — Bl. (now St.) Albertus (Magnus), here in a. 12; SUMMA., p. I, tr. 11, q. 47, m. 1, incidental question. — (Bl.) Peter of Tarentaise, here in q. 3 and 1. — Richard of Middleton, here in a. 3, q. 1. — Giles the Roman, here in 1st, princ. q. 2. — Henry of Ghent, SUMMA., a. 43, q. 1, a. 4. — Durandus (of Saint-Pourçain), on this 1st and 4th q., here in a. 4. — (Bl.) Dionysius the Carthusian, on this and the following questions, here in q. 3.

QUESTION II

Whether, among the divine, there can be posited a whole universal?

Second, there is asked, whether, among the divine, there is a positing of a universal whole. And that (it is) so, seems:

1. Through (St. John) Damascene,[1] who says, « that, among the divine, the common is, as substance, the particular, as an atom »: therefore, if there is a common and a particular There, therefore, a universal, because to the particular there does not respond a common other than the universal.

2. Likewise, this very (thing) seems through the definition[2] of "universal" and "particular": « For the "universal" is that which is predicated of many; the "particular" of one alone »; but it is that one find these reckonings among the divine: ergo etc..

3. Likewise, everything which is in more and is univocal, is universal to those, in respect of which it is in more;[3] but the Essence or Substance is in more than a Person, and (is) univocal in more, because[4] It means the one Nature found in Them according to identity: ergo etc..

4. Likewise, among the divine, there is the communicable [communicabile] and the incommunicable

[incommunicabile]; therefore, either (these are) *by the same reckoning* [eodem], or by *one* and *another (reckoning)*. Not *by the same* (reckoning); because it is not intelligible, that from the same (reckoning) there comes community and property, convenience and difference formally;[5] therefore, by *one* and *another* (reckonings): therefore, if by one (reckoning) it is communicable, by another incommunicable, therefore, since the communicable is by a reckoning of that *whereby it is* [quo est], the incommunicable by a reckoning of that *which it is* [quod est], therefore, *that whereby it is* and *that which it is*, among the divine, are through a difference; but where these are through difference, there is a universal and a particular: ergo etc..

5. Likewise, as much as anything (is) the more simple, so much (is it) the more universal;[6] but the Divine Essence is most simple: therefore, There, there is a reckoning of the universal in the greatest manner.

ON THE CONTRARY: 1. (St. Severinus) Boethius[7] says, that It is neither universal nor particular.

2. Likewise, this very (thing) seems *by reason*, because wheresoever there is a universal, there is one form, multipliable and/or multiplied;[8] in the sign of which thing, (the word) "*every*",

---

[1] ON THE ORTHODOX FAITH, Bk. III, ch. 6. See here, in the text of Master (Peter), ch. 9. In which text, the Vatican edition, contrary to the manuscripts and edition 3, has *Anthony* [Antonius] for *an atom* [atomus].

[2] The Vatican edition, together with codex cc, has *distinction* [distinctionem], yet, with the other codices and edition 1 exhibiting the *definition* [definitionem], which has been taken from Aristotle, ON INTERPRETATION, Bk. I, ch. 5 (ch. 7).

[3] This definition of a universal is gathered from Aristotle, POSTERIOR ANALYTICS, Bk. II, ch. 14 (ch. 12). See above, p. I, of this Distinction, q. 4, 1st argument unto the contrary.

[4] Trusting in codices K T and Z, we have substituted *because* [quia] for the ambiguous *because/which/that* [quod].

[5] We have restored the certainly better of the more ancient manuscripts and edition 1, of putting *difference formally* [differentia formaliter] for *personal difference* [differentia personalis].

[6] Cf. BOOK ON CAUSES, proposition 4. — At the end of the argument the Vatican edition, together with one or the other codex, has less well *the greatest* [maxima] for *in the greatest manner* [maxime]; very many codices, such as A F H ee and ff, omit *is* [est].

[7] ON THE TRINITY, chs. 1 and 2, where this proposition is contained notionally [sententialiter] or as a conclusion; since (St. Severinus) Boethius shows there, that on account of the most high un-differing-ness [indifferentiam] of God's Substance or unity or simplicity, « there is no diversity in Him, no plurality out of a diversity, no multitude of accidents, and on that account neither number », out of which the aforesaid proposition is the consequent. See Alexander of Hales, SUMMA., p. I, q. 48, m. 4, a. 1. — Next codices F and G after *that* [quod] add sufficiently well *among the divine* [in divinis], but codices H and M add *God* [Deus] for it.

[8] Aristotle, METAPHYSICS, Bk. VII, text 45 (Bk. VI, ch. 13), defines "universal": that which is bound to be in many according to nature. —

which signifies, *"since in a universal manner"*, can be added to every universal; but in God there is not one multipliable Form and/or Nature, nor One multiplied, nor does It receive a universal sign, so that there be said *"every God"*: ergo etc..

3. Likewise, where there is a particular, there is a form and/or nature as a *"here and now"*; but the Divine Nature, whether in Itself, or in the Hypostases, is not a *"here and now"*; but an *"always and everywhere"*: therefore, neither in Itself nor in the Hypostases is a particular There.

. 4. Likewise, where there is a particular and a universal, the universal is more simple than the particular:[2] therefore, since in God the Essence is not more simple than a Person, because in a Person there is no accident, no constitutive principle [principium constitutivum]: ergo etc..

5. Likewise, every nature, in which there is a universal and a particular, is in a determinate genus, and every such (nature) is limited:[3] therefore, since the Divine Nature is infinite, it is clear etc..

CONCLUSION

Though among the divine there is a reckoning of a "common" and a "proper", of a "communicable" and of an "incommunicable", yet, least of all is there a reckoning of a "universal" and a "particular".

I RESPOND: For an understanding of the aforesaid it must be noted, that, since our[4] Faith posits a trinity

and a unity among the divine, it necessarily posits a convening [convenientiam] and a distinction. And because a convening is not but in (something) communicable by many[5] and common, but the distinction is not but in (something) proper and incommunicable, there is necessarily posited among the divine a reckoning of the *common* and *proper*, the *communicable* and *incommunicable*.

But, since in God and[6] creatures there is a distinction of supposits, it is otherwise in God than in creatures. For the distinction of supposits is greater than an accidental distinction; whence although it come to be known through accidents,[7] yet it does not come to be through accidents. For with accidents set aside [circumscriptis], there is still an understanding that supposits differ; and since (this) does not come to be through consequent accidents,[8] it is bound that it come to be from (their) *origin* and/or from (their) *original principle*. It is from (their) *origin*, when one differs from the other, because it emanates from it; for the same cannot emanate from itself. Such a distinction of supposits is in God, but this[9] cannot be in a creature, that is, a distinction solely through an origin; for no creature can give its own essence whole to another. If, therefore, it gives a part, it is necessary, that there be another difference there than (that) of the origin; and for this reason there is a difference from an *original principle*. But this is not the *form* in itself, because (the form) means something communicable,[10] nor (is it) the *matter* in itself, because (that) means something indistinct:[11] therefore, this (original principle) causes *the form, to (be as) one coming upon the matter*. For, because as one coming upon matter it accepts a part, not the whole[12] matter, hence it is, that it distinguishes that, and by distinguishing it is

---

Next by adding the conjunction *since* [quoniam] we offer the reading of the manuscripts and edition 1, which we judge to be the genuine one, because it corresponds to the words of Aristotle, ON INTERPRETATION, Bk. I, ch. 5 (ch. 7), and Bk. II, ch. 1 (ch. 10) in the Greek: τὸ γὰρ πᾶς οὐ τὸ καθόλου σημαίνει, αλλ' ὅτι καθόλου and to the Latin translation authored by (St. Severinus) Boethius (which both the Scholastics and especially the Seraphic Doctor were accustomed to use): For *"every"* does not signify "universal", but *"since in a universal manner"* [Omnis enim non universale significat, sed *quoniam universaliter*], cf. Migne's, PATROLOGIA LATINA, tome 64, col. 322 and 348). See Nicholaus de Orbeliis, O. Min., (fl. c. 1450 A. D.), in EXPOSITIONE LOGICAE SUPRA TEXTUM MAGISTRI PETRI HISPANI, ch. "On the Proposition".

[1] Porphyry, ON THE PREDICABLES, defines "individual" or "particular": « The collection of which properties shall never be the same in any other ». Among these properties *time* and *place* hold the first place. Cf. (St. Severinus) Boethius, ON THE TRINITY, ch. 1, who gives to *place* the first place, and Aristotle, POSTERIOR ANALYTICS, Bk. I, ch. 24 (ch. 31), who makes mentions both of *place* and *time* and concerning the universal through opposition to the particular, according to the translation of (St.) Boethius, adjoins these words: Moreover, the universal, which is in all, is impossible to sense; for it is neither "this something" nor the *"here* and *now"* (οὐ γὰρ τόδε οὐδὲ νῦν); for at any rate, neither would be a universal; for what is "always and everywhere", we say is universal.* — Understand these last words of a *negative* perpetuity and ubiquity, i. e. that which abstracts from every determined time and place; and not of *positive* (perpetuity and ubiquity), i. e. that which extends itself to all times and places, and which befits the Divine Nature alone by Itself as a singular (by no means as a "universal"), which is dealt with in this argument. — Codices L and O read *there is matter and form* [ibi est materia et forma] in place if *there is a form and/or nature* [ibi est forma vel natura].

[2] See Porphyry, ON THE PREDICABLES, ch. "On Species and Difference", and Aristotle, POSTERIOR ANALYTICS, ch. 29 (ch. 24), where from this he deduces, that a universal demonstration is more excellent [praestantiorem] than a particular one.

[3] Cf. above d. 8, p. II, q. 4.

[4] Edition 1 reads *the True* [vera] for *our* [nostra].

[5] Understand these word in the passive sense, such that their sense be: "except in something, which is apt to be communicated or to be had by many". — The Vatican edition, not trusting in the mss. and the first six editions, reads *to/for Many* [pluribus] for *by Many* [a pluribus].

[6] The Vatican edition repeats here an *in* [in], which however, is lacking in the manuscripts and edition 1.

[7] An allusion to the definition of "individual" [individui] cited by us above in the 3rd. argument of the fundament. The collection of accidental properties, by which an individual makes itself known to us, is contained in this saying: "Form, figure, place, time, origin, fatherland, name" [Forma, figura, locus, tempus, stirps, patria, nomen].

[8] Edition 1 has *accidents, consequently* [accidentia consequenter] for *consequent accidents* [accidentia consequentia]. A little below this after *from the other* [ab altero] in edition 1 there is added *only* [solum].

[9] From very many manuscripts, such as A T Y etc., we have substituted *this (distinction)* [haec] for *this* [hoc]. On the reason which the Seraphic Doctor offers here, see more above in Distinction. 9, Question. 1.

[10] Accept the sense of these words of his from the Seraphic Doctor, SENT, Bk. II, d. 3, p. I, a. 2, q. 3 in the body (of the question), where he deals more at length with the principle of individuation: « Again, in what manner a form is whole and the chief cause of the distinction of number, is very difficult to grasp; since every created form, as much as it concerns its own nature, *is bound to have another similar to itself* [nata sit habere aliam sibi similem], just as the Philosopher (METAPHYSICS, Bk. VII, text 55 — Parisian edition, Bk. VI, ch. 15) also says, that there is (a multipliable form) in the Sun and the Moon ».

[11] Under this respect Aristotle, in METAPHYSICS, Bk. VII, text 8 (Bk. VI, ch. 3) describes "matter" [materia]: Moreover, I say "matter" is that "which is said through its very self (to be) neither a 'what' nor a quantum nor some other something, by which s being [ens] is determined". See also METAPHYSICS, Bk. I, text 17 (ch. 8), where he says: For indeed, when nothing had been discerned (the Arabic-Latin translation reads: Moreover, since in the fundament of a nature *there is not anything distinct* [non est aliquid distinctum]), openly, because there was nothing true to say of that substance ... for neither (is it) something of the kind that (is) possible [quale aliquid id possibile] nor (is it) a quantum nor a 'what' [nec quantum nec quid].

[12] In the Vatican edition there is badly omitted *whole* [totam], which however, is extant in the manuscripts and edition 1, from which also, with the exception of only one or the other codex, we have emended the reading of the Vatican edition, which put *it draws* [trahit] in place of *is drawn* [trahitur].

---

* *Trans. note:* For clarity, here, the English translation follows the Greek for *here and now* (as cited here) rather than Boethius' Latin, *now and where* [nunc neque ubi].

drawn into part (of the matter) and is limited and be-comes a "*here and now*" [hic et nunc] and a "one in num-ber" [unum numero] and a "particular".

Therefore, since among the divine there is no ad-dition to matter nor a being-drawn [tractio] into[1] a part, for that reason among the divine there does not occur a universal nor a particular, just as the reasons for this, brought forward in opposition, show.

1. To that, therefore, which is first objected con-cerning (St. John) Damascene, it must be said, that "*par-ticular*" is said improperly for the "*incommunicable*".

2. To that which is objected, that the universal is that which is predicated of many; it must be said, that that (definition) is the reckoning of *the communicable*, but is not (that) of *the universal*, except according to which it is really understood to be multiplied[2] in them. Similarly, must it be solved concerning the particular.

3. To that which is objected, that it is in more and is univocal etc.; it must be said, that the universal is in more, such that (it is) more simple, and it comes to be in[3] less through being added [additionem] to it; but not so (is it) in God.

4. To that which is asked, whether the communi-cable and the incommunicable (in God) is[4] by the same (reckoning); it must be said, that (these are) by one and another (reckoning); because, just as (St.) Au-gustine[5] says, « by one He is God, and by another the Father »; but not by one and by another, according to

thing, but according to a *reckoning*: because by the Deity He is God, by the paternity the Father, and the paternity is *according to thing* not other than the Essence, since the paternity is the Essence; and yet (it is) other *according to reckoning*. And because the ablative (case) means ac-cording to a reckoning, for that reason He is not God by the same, according to which (He is) the Father.[6] — *And if you object*: that either something in the thing [in re] responds to that reckoning, or nothing; it must be said, that that reckoning through a comparison to the Essence, is naught, but a manner (of being regarded), but through a comparison to the other *Person* it is a thing. And this is clear, since "*to have an essence from an-other*" and "*to not have it (from another)*" do not mean an-other thing, but only (another) manner (of having); but "*to have it from another*" and "*to have it not from another*" mean a real difference, because no thing is from itself and from another.[7]

5. To that which is objected last concerning the simple, it must be said, that there is a simple *capable of being added* [possibile ad additionem], and in such a man-ner a universal is simple; in another manner (there is) a simple, because *it deprives composition* and addition, and this repugnance is not consonant with universality; and in such a manner the Divine Essence is simple, which in no manner is able to be drawn [trahibilis] into a part through being added [per additionem], just as a univer-sal is drawn in; and for that reason It is not a universal.

SCHOLIUM

I. The common sentence affirms, that among the divine there is indeed a reckoning of *common* and *proper*, however, least of all a reckoning of *universal* and *particular*, nor of *species* and *individual*. On which account, it must be noted that there is a difference between *universal* and *common*, *particular* and *proper* or *incommunicable*. For, though every universal is common, however, not every common is universal. For a *universal* predicable, with which this discourse concerns itself, is opposed to the particular (predicable), « because », as Alexander of Hales says, « it is said for this, that it grasps part of the common nature », and is something superior, which can be con-tracted through differences to its inferiors, so that in them it is really multiplied. However, (what is) *common* in genus is "one among many"; which can be said in a twofold manner, that is, either as "one multiplied among many", and then it is the same as the universal; and/or as "one not multiplied (among many)", such as (is) the Divine Essence, which is One (Essence) among the Three Persons (cf. above d. 5, Doubt 2). In this special sense "*common*" retains the generic name and is distinguished from "*universal*".

II. For a fuller explanation we cite these words from Alexander of Hales (loc. cit., below): « In God there is no posit-ing of a "universal 'being'" [esse universale], nor of a "singular" and/or "particular 'being'": however, the Divine 'Being' has from each what belongs to perfection. For the "*universal*" is among many and is said of many [de multis], because it is not the whole, which the singulars are, just as "man" is not said to be the whole, which Socrates is, such as (his) quantity and quality and operation, which are yet in the 'being' of Socrates ... But when there is said "God the Father, God the Son, God the Holy

Spirit", the Divine 'Being' is said (to be) *in* Many, but not *of* Many [de multis]. For when I say "*God*", I say the whole 'Being' of the Father, the whole 'Being' of the Son. Therefore, 'to be *of* many' belongs to imperfection in universal 'being', whence it does not befit the Divine 'Being'; but 'to be *in* many' does befit It, because this belongs to virtue and nobility ».

« Similarly, the "*particular*" is said (to be) that which is "in one alone"; however, it is "not of many". What is "not of many" belongs to perfection, because it means the whole 'being'; but "in one alone" be-longs to imperfection, because it is more noble to be in many than in one. For that reason the Divine 'Being' is in Many, not in One alone, I say, that It is in many, *not as One multiplied, but as One*. — Likewise, there is a speaking of the "particular" and "individual" in three manners: in one manner according to which it is said to be "*from matter*" [a ma-teria]; in another manner according to which (it is said to be) "*from ac-cidents*" [ab accidentibus]; in a third manner according to which (it is said to be) from a "*signed and singular form*" [a forma signata et sin-gulari]». Then he proves, that in none of these manners can a singular be in God, and concludes: « Therefore, since the Deity in no manner is plurified in the Father and the Son and the Holy Spirit, the Deity does not hold itself to the Father and the Son and the Holy Spirit as a universal to a singular ». Moreover, (Bl.) Dionysius the Carthusian rightly warns (loc. cit.), that those words "*to be of many*" [esse de multis] have the sense, "to be *part* or *something* of those, which are many and/or in many". This is clear from the whole argumentation of Alexander (of Hales). He himself does not deny that the Divine Essence is predicated of the Three Persons in an analogous manner, just as every universal, which is in many, is predicated of many [de multis].

---

[1] The Vatican edition, not trusting in nearly all the manuscripts and edition 1, puts here *to* [ad] for *into* [in] and next *and/or* [vel] in place of *nor* [nec].

[2] The Vatican edition, without the authority of the codd. and ed. 1, reads *(to be) multiplied* [multiplicatum] for *to be multiplied* [multiplicari].

[3] Very many manuscripts, together with edition 1, exhibit the verb *it comes to be* [fit] in place of *thus* [sic] and of *in* [in], which the Vatican edition omits. Next the Vatican edition, contrary to nearly all the codices and edition 1, badly substitutes *just as* [sicut] for *so* [sic], after which very many codices, such as G H K T etc., add *is it* [est].

[4] Trusting in the more ancient mss. and ed. 1, we have supplied *is* [est].

[5] ON THE TRINITY, Bk. VII, ch. 6, n. 11: On which account, as the Substance of the Father is the Father Himself, not by which He is the Fa-ther, but by which He is. Cf. also above d. 6, Doubt 2, and below in the text of Master (Peter) Dist. XXXIII, near the end, where there is quoted (St.) Augustine's, First Sermon, ON PSALM 68, n. 5.

[6] For more on this see below d. 33, q. 2, and Doubt 4. — Next after *either* [aut], in the Vatican edition and codex cc, there is added *then* [tunc], which is lacking in the other manuscripts and edition 1. [Trans. note: Here the supplying of *being regarded* is according to the reading of the Quaracchi Editors in the d. 26, a. sole, q. 2, Scholium II, 2.]

[7] For a fuller understanding of the aforesaid, see also that which the Seraphic Doctor says above in d. 5, a. 1, q. 1, in reply to n. 1. Cf. Also below d. 26, q. 1, in reply to n. 2, and d. 34, a. 2, in reply to n. 7. — The Vatican edition, without the authority of the manuscripts and the first six editions, incongruously has *that ... be had* [haberi] in place of *to have* [habere] in the preceding first pair of clauses, and then *no one* [nullus] for *no thing* [nulla res]. Codex T has *to be* [esse] in place of *to have* [habere] in the previous second pair of clauses, in which many codices together with edition 1, have less well *and to not have from another* [et non habere ab alio]. Then some codices read *but from another* [sed ab alio] for *and from another* [et ab alio] at the end of the argument.

III. The fundament of the solution to n. 4 is the distinction between *essence* [essentiam] and *property* [proprietatem], concerning which, cf. above d. 13, q. 3 and its Scholium; d. 8, p. II, q. 2; d. 33, q. 2, and chiefly d. 26, q. 1 and its Scholium: — The question on the principle of individuation is touched upon at the end of the argument, concerning which more will be said in SENT., Bk. II, d. 3.

IV. On the question itself: Alexander of Hales, SUMMA., p. I, q. 48, m. 4, a. 1. — St. Thomas, here in q. 4, a. 2; SUMMA., I, q. 3, a. 5. — Bl. (now St.) Albertus (Magnus), here in a. 14 and 15; SUMMA., p. I, a. 47, m. 3, subpart 4. — (Bl.) Peter of Tarentaise, here in q. 3, a. 2. — Richard of Middleton, here in a. 3, q. 2. — Giles the Roman, here in 1st. princ., q. 1. — Henry of Ghent, SUMMA., a. 43, q. 2. — (Bl.) Dionysius the Carthusian, here in q. 2.

QUESTION III

Whether, among the Divine (Persons), there can be posited a material principle?

Third, there is asked, whether among the Divine Persons there can be posited a material principle. And that (it is) so, is shown in this manner:

1. Whensoever anyone and/or anything is from [de] something, such that it itself is distinct, and that, from which it is, (is) indistinct, it is from the latter as from a material principle;[1] but the Person of the Son is from the Substance of the Father, and is distinguished as a person, (and) the Substance means something indistinct: therefore, It is just as a material principle.

2. Likewise, just as the efficient (cause) and the end are correlative causes, so form and matter[2] — for form is said in respect to matter — but in God there is a positing of a formal cause, « for He Himself is a form », as (St. Severinus) Boethius says:[3] therefore, in God there is a positing of matter.

3. Likewise, it seems that a material cause suits [competat] God more than any genus of cause [causarum], because matter among these inferiors gives existence and permanence on account of its own incorruption, whence is the foundation of created existence:[4] if, therefore, God or the Divine 'Being' has existence or permanent through an incorruptible foundation, it seems that the reckoning of a material principle suits God most of all; ergo etc..

4. Likewise, among created things finity come from form, but infinity from matter;[5] but everything which is in God, is infinite: therefore, since the passion consequent to the material principle befits God most of all, the latter (of these two) also suits (Him) most of all.

5. Likewise, although in God there is a most high and omnimodal simplicity, yet we do not truly posit in God (a distinction between) "*what He is*" and "*by which He is*", but (rather), however,[6] (a distinction) through indifference: therefore, for an equal reason it seems, that in God there can be posited matter and form, yet through indifference.

6. Likewise, every distinction is by a form, therefore, having excluded every created form, matter is not distinguished, therefore, is not other than God, therefore, is God, because everything which is and is not distinguished from [a] God, is God: it seems, therefore, that the material principle is God Himself, and thus that it suits the Divine Persons.[8]

On the Contrary: 1. (St. Severinus) Boethius in the book, ON THE TRINITY (says):[9] « Form without matter cannot be a subject », and he is speaking of God: therefore, in God there will not be the reckoning of a material principle.

2. Likewise, matter among all beings is the most imperfect, whence even (St.) Augustine says in the book of CONFESSIONS,[10] that it is nearly nothing; but God is entirely most perfect: therefore, there is found in Him entirely nothing of imperfection: therefore, neither what belongs to matter.

3. Likewise, matter is a principle of suffering,[11] whence suffering is from matter. Everything, therefore, in which there is matter, is born to suffer and to receive; but nothing such is omnipotent; for in this, that it can suffer, it fails from 'being potent' [a posse]: therefore, in the Omnipotent there is in no manner a material principle.

4. Likewise, if is matter in God, (it is) either in respect to

---

[1] This proposition is founded on the sentence of Aristotle concerning matter and form, which hold themselves to one another as potency (indistinct) and act (distinct), and according to which the substantial form of things begotten (except the rational soul) is drawn forth out of the potency of matter.

[2] Cf. Aristotle, PHYSICS, Bk. II, texts 23-31 (ch. 3) and METAPHYSICS, Bk. V, texts 2 and 3 (Bk. IV, ch. 2), where this can be gathered both from the definition of causes, and from this, that the efficient (cause) and the end etc. are posited to be the cause of one another. See the Commentaries of St. Thomas and (Bl. John Duns) Scotus, on these passages. — From very many manuscripts we have substituted *correlative* [correlativae] for *corollary* [corollariae], in place of which edition 1 has *in a corollary manner* [corrolate].

[3] ON THE TRINITY, ch. 2.

[4] See Aristotle, PHYSICS, Bk. I, text 82, (ch. 9), where the incorruptibility of matter is demonstrated, and METAPHYSICS, Bk. VII, text 8 (Bk. VI, ch. 3), where matter is shown (to be) as the extreme [ultimum] or foundation of substance. — With the help of very many manuscripts and edition 1, we have substituted *created* [creatae] in place of *a creature's* [creaturae]. Next the Vatican edition together with only one or the other codex, puts *since* [cum] in place of *if* [si], and *God* [Deum] for *Divine* [divinum], and the subjunctive form of *has* [habeat].

[5] Cf. Aristotle, PHYSICS, Bk. III, texts. 59-72 (chs. 6-7), and Averroës, in his commentary on the aforesaid texts. — A little below this after *passion* [passio], trusting in nearly all the manuscripts and edition 1, we have expunged the repeated *most of*

all [maxime], which codices C and O put in this place, having omitted it after *God* [Deo]. Then codex Z after *suits* [competit] adds *Him* [ei].

[6] The Vatican edition, breaking with the codices and editions 1, 2, and 3, reads *only* [tantum]. Next very many codices together with the Vatican edition have *could* [posset] for *can* [possit].

[7] Aristotle, METAPHYSICS, Bk. VII, text 49 (Bk. VI., ch. 13): For an act separates (in Greek: ἡ γὰρ ἐντελέχεια χωρίζει). — On the indistinction of matter, see the preceding Question, in the body (of the Response).

[8] In the Vatican edition there is wanting the words *thus that it suits the Divine Persons* [et ita competere divinis personis], which however, are extant in all the manuscripts and the first six editions.

[9] Chapter 2: But the form, which is without matter, will not be able to be a subject.

[10] Bk. XII, ch. 7. n. 7: Thou was and nothing else, from which Thou hast made Heaven and Earth, a certain two; one near Thee, the other near nothing. — From many manuscripts, such as A F G K T Y Z etc. and the first six editions, we have supplied *even* [et] after *whence* [unde], and a little below this, trusting in very many codices and edition 1, we have substituted *most perfect* [perfectissimus] in place of *the most perfect (being)* [perfectissimum]. At the end of the argument codex A has *is matter* [est materia] for *belongs to matter* [est materiae].

[11] Aristotle, ON GENERATION AND CORRUPTION, Bk. I, text 53, (ch. 9): For matter is suffering [pati]. — Next the Vatican edition together with codex cc, yet with the other codices and edition 1 striving against this, has *Wherefore, everything* [Unde omne] in place of *Everything, therefore* [Omne igitur].

Himself, or[1] *to others*. If in respect to *others*: therefore, since matter is a being in potency to others, and it is not distinguished by other things, but is perfected through them, then God would receive a complement from [a] creature, and would not be distinguished from it; which is absurd. But, if there is[2] matter in God in respect to Himself, He is either *purely* matter, or something *else*. If *purely* matter: therefore, He not a being [ens].[3] And, *besides*, nothing is the matter of its very self: therefore, it is necessary [oportet], that something be There with the matter: and if this (is so), therefore, the Divine 'Being' [divinum esse] is composite and mixed: therefore, God has neither a *simple 'being'* [esse simplex] and through this neither the *prime 'Being'* [esse primum], and thus is not God.

CONCLUSION

In God in no manner, neither properly nor transumptively, can there be posited a material principle.

I Respond: It must be said, that in God in no manner, neither properly, nor transumptively is a material principle received. And the reason for this is, since "matter" means a passive principle and thus an incomplete one; and since from the Divine 'Being'[4] every incompletion and every passion is to be thoroughly removed, for that reason in no manner is the genus of a material principle to be posited in God.

1. To that, therefore, which is objected, that a Person is *from the Substance*, and It itself is *distinct*, and the Substance not; it must be said, that here there is a defect as much as regards each condition. For *first* this is not received, "that a *Person* is *from the Substance*", just as (St.) Augustine[5] would have it, because « we do not say that Three Persons (are) out of the same Essence »: though this is commonly received, "that *the Son* is from the Substance of the Father", where not matter, but a consubstantiality of origin is designated, just as has

been shown above in the Fifth Distinction.[6] The *other* is the condition, which is deficient: for matter is distinct[7] and able to be distinguished [possibilis ad distinctionem] through form; but the Substance and/or Essence in no manner is distinguished, neither through Itself nor through an accident; and thus it is clear, that the reckoning of matter does not befit Him.

2. To that which is objected, that the efficient (cause) is referred to the end and form to matter; it must be said, that the habitude of no cause occurs in God[8] in respect to Himself, but (rather) in respect to creatures; and the habitudes of the other causes are received in God, with dependence excluded, on account of this, that they pertain to [sonant in] perfection;[9] but matter pertains entirely to imperfection. And what is objected, that form is meant for matter [dicitur ad materiam]; it must be said, that "form" is *constitutive* and *exemplary*. And *constitutive* form is meant for matter; and this does not occur in God, but an *exemplary* form does [sic].[10] And if there be said, that God is a form in Himself, this has been said, because He is the Pure Act, not dependent on the possible. Nor yet is it similar concerning the correspondence of *form* and *matter, the efficient (cause)* and *the end*.[11] For the *efficient (cause)* and the *end* can fall [incidit] upon the same in number; but *form* and *matter* never. However[12] a *constitutive* form does fall with the *efficient (cause)* and the *end* upon the same species, not in number; but an *exemplary* form (does) upon the same in number.

3. To that which is objected, that matter is the foundation of existence; it must be said, that the manner of that foundation does not suit God, because (matter)[13] is the foundation of the 'being' [esse] which it receives from elsewhere, that is from form; but God receives from no one: for that reason matter does not occur in Him.

4. To that which is objected concerning infinity, it must be said, that there is an infinite out of a *defect of perfection*, and this suits matter, but not God; and there is an in-

---

[1] Some codices, such as Y and Z, together with edition 1 repeat here *in respect* [respectu].

[2] From the more ancient manuscripts and edition 1, we have substituted *there is* [est] for *there be* [sit]. A little before this very many codices, such as A G H I S W Z, together with edition 1, read *most absurd* [absurdissimum] in place of *absurd* [absurdum].

[3] See the defintion of "matter" cited by us from Aristotle, in the preceding questions, p. 358, footnote 11. — Next, the Vatican edition, with codex cc, has *it is* [est] for *the Divine 'Being' is* [divinum esse], which is exhibited by the other mss., though very many of them together with edition 1 incongruously read *God* [Deum] for *the divine* [divinum].

[4] Few codices, such as S and W, have *from the divine* [a divinis] in place of *from the Divine 'Being'* [a divino esse]. Next, edition 1 has *has been* [remota] for *is to be* [removenda].

[5] On the Trinity, Bk. VII, ch. 6, n. 11: Therefore, neither do we in this manner say that the Trinity (is) Three Persons and/or Substances, the one Essence and the One God, as if out of one matter a certain Three subsist ..., however, we do say that the Three Persons (are) of the same Essence and/or that the Three Persons (are) the One Essence; but we do not say that the Three Persons (are) out of the same Essence, as if There one thing is what the Essence is, another what a Person (is). — A little below this, after *though* [licet], very many codd., such as A T X & Y, with ed. 1, omit *this (proposition)* [haec].

[6] Article 1, q. 2.

[7] We exhibit the reading of very many mss., which agrees more with the subjoined, while the Vatican ed. with ed. 1 and some codd., has *indistinct* [indistincta], to which codex I adds *from itself* [de se].

[8] The Vatican edition, contrary to the manuscripts and to edition 1, reads *falls upon God* [cadit in Deum] for *occurs in God* [cadit in Deo].

[9] The error of the Vatican edition and ed. 1, and also of some mss., of reading *resound imperfection* [sonant imperfectionem] for *pertain to perfection* [sonant in perfectionem], we have corrected from the other mss. and edd. 2, 3, 4, 5 & 6; codex Y has *it resounds imperfection* [sonant imperfectionem], that is *the dependence* [dependentia], not falsely, but less to the point. Next, many codices together with the Vatican edition

and edition 1, read *resound entirely imperfection* [sonat omnino imperfectionem], which is corrected from the other manuscripts and editions 2, 3 and 6.

[10] Thus many codices, such as A N O R T V W X Y etc., together with edition 1; the Vatican edition, together with some manuscripts, with a varied punctuation, incongruously reads *just as if* [sicut si] for *does. And if* [sic. Et si], codices A and Z omits *does* [sic]. Immediately after this very many codices, such as F G H K L O Y ee and ff, have *that* [quod] for *because* [quia].

[11] Some codices, such as S W and X, here and a little after this read *the final (cause)* [finalis].

[12] Trusting in very many manuscripts and edition 1, we have deleted here the added *only* [tantum]. — Aristotle, Physics, Bk. II, text 70, (ch. 7) says: But for the most part the three (causes) come upon one; for 'that which it is' (the formal cause) and 'that for the sake of which it is' (the final cause) are one; however, 'that whence the first movement is' (the efficient cause) is according to the same species as these; for a man generates a man.

[13] Supply: *matter* [materia]. In the words that follow, next, we offer the reading of nearly all the manuscripts and edition 1, which is also congruous with the sentence of the Seraphic Doctor concerning the essential dependence of matter from form (cf. Sent., Bk. II, d. 12, a. 1, q. 1). Codex F, with transposed words, reads *because it is the foundation, which receives 'being' from elsewhere* etc. [quia est fundamentum, quod recipit esse aliunde etc]; but the Vatican edition, together with editions 4, 5, and 6 has *because "to be a foundation" is "to be what receives the other", and is perfected from elsewhere, that is by form* [quia esse fundamentum est esse quod recipit aliud, et aliunde perficitur, scilicet a forma]; next, codex cc, together with editions 2 and 3, together with the Vatican edition which reads *to be that which it receives from elsewhere* etc. [esse quod recipit aliunde], agrees with the other manuscripts. — A little before this, codex Y has *is not found in God* [in Deo non reperitur] for *does not suit God* [Deo non competit].

finity out of a *privation of limitation*, and this suits God and the most free form [formae liberrimae], not matter; and, thus, that is clear.

5. To that which is objected, for what reason is matter and form not posited through indifference; it must be said, that those two, "*that whereby it is*" and "*that which it is*", from their own reckoning convey no imperfection, but (they do) by reason of this, that they differ. Whence, with their difference withdrawn [sublata], there remains completion, and then[1] they are received among the divine. But matter, not only because it differs from form, means incompletion, but also because it is matter; and for that reason in no manner is it posited in God.

6. To that which is objected last, that with every form excluded, matter is not distinguished; it must be said, that that proposition: 'every distinction is by a form [a forma]', does not have truth, unless it be understood of a perfect distinction — for what has a distinct 'being' has a complete 'being' — but of[2] any kind of distinction whatsoever it is false. For matter differs from form [a forma], and it is established that it differs[3] by its very self from it. In this manner it can be said, even in the proposed, that matter differs from God by its very self; however, on its own part, because it is not perfect, a perfect distinction does not occur; but on the part of God, because He is most perfect, there does occur a perfect distinction. For cause[4] is distinguished by cause, a being-in-act from a being-in-potency; and these are the first and highest differences.

SCHOLIUM

I. This question militates against pantheism or rather materialism, condemned by the Vatican Council (First Constitution "*On God the Creator*", canon 2) with these words: If anyone is not ashamed to affirm that there is nothing besides matter, anathema sit. In view of which it refutes the insanity of David of Dinant (1160 — 1216 A. D.), whose principal argument was that which is read in the last place among the (arguments) opposed [i.e. the first arg. n. 6], that is this: 'if God was not the same as prime matter, it would be necessary [oportet] that they differ by some differences, and in this manner they would not be simple. For in this, that it differs from Him through a difference, that difference causes a composition. Thus (St.) Thomas (SUMMA CONTRA GENTILES, Bk. I, ch. 17) reports the argument of David (of Dinan), and then solves it thus according to the mind of St. Bonaventure: « But this proceeded out of ignorance, by which he did not know, what lies [intersit] between a difference and diversity. For "different", as is determined in the tenth (book) of the METAPHYSICS (text of the commentary n. 12), is said according to something; it is said in an absolute manner from this, that it is not the same. Therefore, a difference is to be sought in these, which convene in something; for it is necessary [oportet] that something be assigned among them, according to which they differ, just as two species convene in a genus, whence it is necessary [oportet], that they be distinguished by differences. But among those, which convene in nothing, one is not to seek, whereby they differ; but (rather) they are diverse by their very selves. For in the same manner even opposed differences are distinguished from one another; for they do not share a genus as a part of their essence; and for that reason one is not to seek, whereby they differ; for they are diverse by their very selves. In this manner even God and prime matter are distinguished, One of which is a pure act, the other pure potency, (both) having a convening [convenientiam] in nothing ». The same argument of David Bl. (now St.) Albertus (Magnus) solves in a similar manner (SUMMA., p. I, tr. 4. q. 20. m. 2, incidental question). — In the same solution to n. 6 by St. Bonaventure, there is posited a twofold species of distinction, namely, the one perfect and specific through form, the other imperfect through the entity belonging to matter.

II. Besides the authors cited, cf. above d. 8, p. II, q. 4. — St. Thomas, SUMMA., I, q. 3, a. 1 and 2. — Bl. (now St.) Albertus (Magnus), SENT., Bk. I, d. 20, a. 1, where he cites and solves many the arguments « of Alexander, a certain Greek, and of David of Dinan, the Latin »; and SUMMA., p. I, tr. 11, q. 47, m. 3, subpart 5. — (Bl.) Peter of Tarentaise, here in q. 3, a. 3 and 4. — Henry of Ghent, SUMMA., a. 28, q. 2, and a. 29, q. 2. — All the other doctors touch upon this question when treading of the simplicity of God, especially concerning that problem, whether God is in any determinate genus, with which Master (Peter) deals in d. 8, p. II.

QUESTION IV

Whether, among the divine, there can be posited a difference according to number?

Fourth and last, there is asked, whether among the divine there is a positing of difference according to number. And it seems that (it is) so.

1. (St. John) Damascene (says) in (his) third book (ON THE ORTHODOX FAITH): « By number, not by nature do the hypostases differ »; and he is speaking of the Divine Hypostases.

2. Likewise, it is necessary that all, which happened to be truly numbered, differ in number; but the Hypostases happen to be truly numbered, as They are said (to be) Two and Three: therefore, there truly occurs among Them a difference according to number.

3. Likewise, all which differ in thing [re], either differ in genus, or in species, or in number, or differ in no manner.[6] But it is impious to say, that the Hypostases differ in no manner: therefore, They at least differ in number.

4. Likewise, unity according to[7] number does not look back to unity of form, but (to that) of the supposit — which is clear: for this white one and this one seated, having been demonstrated (to be) Peter, is one in number — therefore, <u>ab oppositis</u>,* diversity according to number does not look back to diversity of nature, but (to that) of supposits; but in God there is a plurality of Supposits, though there is not a diversity of Nature: ergo etc..

---

[1] From the manuscripts and editions 1, 2 and 3, we have substituted *then* [tunc] in place of *for that reason* [ideo].

[2] In the Vatican edition and codex cc, there is wanting *of* [de], which is found in the other manuscripts and in edition 1. A little above this, codices L and O, read *a perfect, positive distinction* [distinctione positiva perfecta].

[3] The Vatican edition, with the codices and edition 1 striving against this, reads *is distant* [distat].

[4] With the consent of the manuscripts and editions 1, 2 and 3, we have put *cause* [causa] for *the uncaused* [incausatum].

[5] ON THE ORTHODOX FAITH, ch. 6: If indeed the Persons not in nature, but in number are said to be distinguished among Themselves.

[6] Cf. Aristotle, TOPICS, Bk. I, ch. 6 (ch. 5): METAPHYSICS, Bk. V, text 16 (Bk. IV, ch. 9); and (St. Severinus) Boethius, ON THE TRINITY, ch. 1.

[7] In the Vatican edition and codex cc, not trusting in all the other manuscripts and edition 1, there is added *matter or* [material sive], and a little below this, contrary to very many codices, there is put *and this is clear* [et hoc patet] in place of *which is clear* [quod patet], in place of which codex Z has *for this is clear* [hoc enim patet].

---

* *Trans. note*: Concerning the meaning of the Latin expression, <u>ab oppositis</u>, cf. translator's footnote above, on p. 54.

5. Likewise, "same" and "diverse" sufficiently divide being [ens]:[1] therefore everything which is compared to the other, either is the same in species, or diverse; or the same in number, or diverse. Therefore, the Father, compared to the Son,[2] either is *the same* in number, or *diverse*. If *the same*, but whensoever any two are the same in number, one is truly predicated of the other: therefore, I can say: 'the Father is the Son', which is[3] contrary to the Faith. If *diverse* in number: therefore, among the divine there does occur diversity according to number.

BUT ON THE CONTRARY: 1. (St.) Ambrose on the Second Letter to the Corinthians (says), and (as) Master (Peter) recites in the text:[4] « There truly (is) unity, where (there is) *no* diversity »: therefore, there is no diversity according to nature,* though there is *some* diversity, namely, a diversity according to number.

2. Likewise, (St. Severinus) Boethius in the book, ON THE TRINITY, second chapter (says): « There is in God no diversity, no plurality out of a diversity, no multitude out of accidents »: therefore, neither a difference[5] according to number.

3. Likewise, diversity according to number alone comes on the part of matter; whence the Philosopher says, that « matter is entirely in a numerable manner [numerabiliter] »; but not matter occurs among the divine: therefore, neither a diversity according to number.

4. Likewise, whatsoever differ in number, number[7] (by that number) all which are in them, at least all which are there on the part of the formal principle. This is clear, for because Peter and Paul are two, for that reason (they are) two men, two animals, two whites, and thus concerning each: therefore, if the Father and the Son are[8] different in number, therefore, they have two natures, and two essences: therefore they are two gods; which is contrary to the Catholic Faith.

5. Likewise, whatsoever differ in number, are separable in the imagination and/or intellect; but the Father and the Son are in no manner separable, neither in thing[9] nor in intellect, among the divine, because one Person is in the Other and vice versa [e converso]: therefore, neither do They differ in number.

6. Likewise, what is not multipliable nor multiplied is one in number; but the Divine Nature is not multipliable nor multiplied: therefore, It is one in number;[10] but whatsoever are one in number, cannot differ

in number: therefore, if the Divine Essence and/or Nature comprises all the other Persons, it is impossible, that the Persons differ in number.

CONCLUSION

Among the divine there is not to be posited a difference according to number, though the Persons are numbered.

I RESPOND: It must be said, that among the divine there is no positing of a difference according to number. And the reason for this can be taken both *a posteriori* and *a priori*.

A posteriori: since to all which differ in number, there is consequent this passion, which is "number", but "number" is the aggregation of a multitude, in which there is more in the whole than in each of the parts.[11] But this aggregation is only out of those, which have a limited unity, which is more with the other than through itself. But limitation comes through addition. But addition leads thoroughly to composition with matter, which causes it to be '*here and now*' and '*so much* and not more'; and, thus, there is not a diversity according to number except among those, in which there is a distinction through addition and composition and matter. And[12] this distinction does not occur in God, for that reason neither (does) a diversity according to number.

The other reason is *a priori*: because in anything [quolibet], which we understand as complete, we understand under this twofold condition, namely, through the standard of measure "*by which it is*" [quo est] and "*which it is*" [quid est]; and indeed unity or identity according to *species* and/or *genus* comes[13] on the part of that which "*by which* it is", according to diverse states or a greater and lesser completion. However, unity and/or diversity according to *number* comes on the part of that "*which it is*" according to (its) 'to be' [esse], or insofar as it is in an individual[14] supposit. But, in this manner, those two have been conjoined in all which differ in number, because having numbered that "*which it is*", it is necessary, that there be numbered that "*by which it is*". Therefore, since in all which differ in number, there is numbered that "*which it is*", it is necessary, that there be multiplied in them that "*by which it is*".

And, because to a diversity according to number there concurs a diversity of that "*by which it is*" [quo est] and (of that) "*which it is*" [quod est] and (of the one) "*who*

---

[1] See above d. 4, Doubt 2, p. 104, footnote 5.

[2] We prefer the reading of the greater part of the codd., such as A F G H I S T U W Y Z etc. and ed. 1, to the reading of the other codd. and the Vatican ed., *If, therefore, the Father is compared to the Son* [Si ergo Pater comparatur Filio]. Next, after *If the same* [Si idem], we have supplied from many mss. and edd. 1, 2, 3 & 6, the badly omitted *but* [sed].

[3] Codex H adds *false and* [falsum et].

[4] Here in ch. 4, near the end. — A little below this, we have restored the reading of nearly all the manuscripts and edition 1, by adding *though there is some diversity, namely, a diversity according to number* [cum sit aliqua diversitas, scil. diversitas secundum numerum].*

[5] Codex V reads *a diversity* [diversitas].

[6] PHYSICS, Bk. I, text 66 (ch. 7).

[7] Very many manuscripts and edition 1 read *are numbered* [numerantur], but on account of the grammatical difficulty we have not received this reading.°

[8] In codex Y there is added *Two* [duo].

[9] In some manuscripts, and in the Vatican edition, there is here added *nor in manner* [nec modo], but less to the point and with a greater part of the manuscripts and edition 1 contradicting this. At the end of the argument very many codices, together with edition 1, read *therefore, They do not* [ergo non] for *therefore, neither do They* [ergo nec].

[10] The Vatican edition, together with one or the other codex, faultily omits *in number* [numero], which, however, is exhibited in all the other codices and edition 1.

[11] The common definition of "number", taken from Aristotle, PHYSICS, Bk. IV, text 133 (last chapter); METAPHYSICS, Bk. V, texts 11 and 20 (Bk. IV, chs. 6 and 15), and METAPHYSICS, Bk. X, text 21 (Bk. IX, ch. 6), is this: A "number" is a multitude measured through "one". And/or form (St. Severinus) Boethius, ON ARITHMETIC, Bk. I, ch. 3: A "number" is a collection of unity, and/or a heap of quantity discharged out of unities [Numerus est unitatum collectio, vel quantitatis acervus ex unitatibus profusus] (cf. also his ON THE TRINITY, ch. 3).+ — Very many codices, such as A I P Q T V and cc, have *in each one* [in singula] for *in each* [in singulis]. A little before this, codex I has *reckoning* [ratio] in place of *passion* [passio]. Next, codices P and Q read *in those* [in his] for *out of those* [ex his].

[12] From very many, more ancient mss. and ed. 1, we have substituted *And* [Et] for *But* [Sed], though some codd., such as S & Y omit the former.

[13] The Vatican ed. with a few codices has *is coming* [est veniens].

[14] In codex T there is added *and/or a* [vel]. Next some codices, such as A T X Z, together with edition 1, have *joined* [iuncta] for *conjoined* [coniuncta], which some codices, such as S and W, omit.

[15] The Vatican edition with cod. cc, having omitted the particle *And* [Et], conjoin the following proposition with the preceding one, and begin

---

* *Trans. notes:* The critical text reads *according to number* [secundum numerum] for *according to nature* [secundum naturam]: an apparent typographical error, since the argumentation requires a contradistinction between the *according to nature* in the first clause and the *according to number* in the second; this change also corresponds more to the logic of St. Ambrose's saying, and to what the

Quaracchi editors say, here, in footnote 4.

° This error of the manuscripts seems to have arisen by neglecting that the noun "*in number*" [numero] is used in a poetic construction, which requires it to be understood as part of each clause.

+ Here, the "number" defined is not the symbol or the ideal concept, but that which is signified by the former, according to the latter.

it is", that is of the *nature*, of the *thing of the nature*, and of the *supposit* or hypostasis, but principally of that "*which it is*": since among the divine that "*which it is*" or the Essence is in no manner multipliable on account of (Its) most high simplicity, for that reason, it is necessary, that that "*which it is*" similarly remain indistinct: and for that reason it is impossible, that there occur There a diversity according to number. However, neither is It one in number;[1] because in creatures that 'that "*which it is*" (is) one in number' is not sayable of a many; but among the divine that "*which it is*", though it is one, yet is sayable of Many. And the reason for this is, because There the "*whereby it is*" and the "*which it is*" is the Same, as much as (is)[2] on the part of the Thing. And for that reason, just as the "*by which it is*" is communicable to many, though not multipliable, thus (also) that "*which it is*". Wherefore we can say, that a plurality of persons holds a middle position [medium] between "*same* in number" and "*diverse* (in number)". For though that "*which it is*" is not numbered, yet that "*by which it is*" (is); whence there are many *Who's* There.

1. And (St. John) Damascene was to say this, when he says: « In number, not in nature do the Hypostases differ ». For through this addition: "*not in nature*", he contracted the difference according to number or withdrew it [distraxit] from its proper reckoning.[3] Whence he says in the first book, chapter eight: « It is necessary to know [oportet scire], that it is one (thing) to differ in thing, another in reckoning. In all creatures the *division* of hypostases is considered *according to thing* [re], but (their) *community, according to a reckoning*: but in the most high and supersubstantial Trinity it is the other way around [est e converso] ». Whence since diversity according to number causes or notes a diversity *in the thing* and nature, properly speaking, unless the name of "diversity" according to number is withdrawn to the distinction of supposits, it must not be conceded, that there is a diversity There according to number, but (rather) according to the number[4] of *Persons* or Hypostases. And (St. John) Damascene

wants to says this, when he says, that the Hypostases differ in number, not, I say, in the number, which means[5] a diversity *in thing* and nature, but the one which means a difference in *properties* and *relations*, with the Nature always remaining unique and undivided. And from this that (word of St. John) Damascene is clear.

2. To that which is objected second, that those which are numbered differ in number; it must be said, that it is true, that[6] they differ according to that standard of measure, whereby they are numbered; but They are not numbered except as much as regards Persons; and thus They do not differ except in the number of Hypostases and in property.

3. To that which is objected, that what differs in thing etc.; it must be distinguished in this noun "*thing*" [re],[7] because it can mean the "*nature*" or "essence", and it can mean a "*person*". If it means "*essence*" and "nature", it is true; if a "*person*", it is false, and that division does not have a place (among the divine).

4. To that which is objected, that a unity in number looks back to the identity of the supposit; it must be said, that if a supposit be said (to be) that "*which it is*", then it has truth. But if it be said (to be) him "*who is*" or a person, it does not have truth, except in those, in which "*by which it is*" and "*which it is*" differ. Whence properly speaking, a diversity of number follows that "*which it is*"; and for that reason[8] (that argument) does not have a place among the divine.

5. To that which is objected,[9] that "*same*" and "*diverse*" sufficiently divide being [ens], therefore, (They are) the same in number, and/or diverse: it must be said, that that is true in a being [in ente], which is bound to be numbered, such as[10] a created being [ens creatum]; but in an uncreated being this is lacking. Whence (St.) Hilary ON THE TRINITY (says):[11] « The nativity permits that God born out of God is neither the same nor another »: and thus, as has been said before, ("person") holds a middle position between "same" and "diverse".

SCHOLIUM

I. Since the Faith applies the numbers 1 and 3 to the divine, and "number" does not seem to agree with "equality", the Seraphic Doctor aptly deal here with number, precisely under this respect, or in the manner in which "number" can be admitted among the divine, without derogating from the most high, divine equality. More will be said on the reckoning of number among the divine, below in d. 24, a. 2. Since Master (Peter) upholds in this matter an opinion commonly reproved, there was much dispute in that age concerning

the reckoning of 'number' among the divine. Whence Alexander of Hales wrote a whole question on this subject, comprising seven members, in which he expounded that which St. Bonaventure exhibits here in a brief compendium.

II. The Question is resolved with a twofold conclusion. First, it responds with Master (Peter), that among the divine there is no difference according to number. This solution is understood of "number" properly and

---

a new one a little below this, having added *therefore* [ergo], at the words *since among the divine* [cum in divinis], which reading is in itself incongruous and contrary to the more ancient codices and to edition 1.

[1] Trusting in the manuscripts and the first six editions, we have inserted *one in number* [unum numero]. Immediately after this in very many codices, such as A D I L O R S T U etc., there is wanting *in creatures* [in creaturis].

[2] In a few manuscripts, such as Y and Z, there is added *is* [est].

[3] The Vatican edition, which puts *to a difference in* [ad differentiam] in place of *from a proper* [a propria], is corrected from the manuscripts and first six editions. — Very many codices, together with the first editions (except edition 1), read *distinguished* [distinxit] for *withdrew* [distraxit]. Next the Vatican edition, with very many manuscripts and edition 1 striving against this, has *as* [ut] in place of *Whence* [Unde].

[4] The mutilated reading of the Vatican edition, in which there is badly omitted *but (rather) according to number* [sed secundum numerum], is repaired with the help of nearly all the manuscripts and edition 1.

[5] Trusting in very many codices and edition 1, we have substituted here and a little below this (the subjunctive) *means* [dicat] for (the

indicative), and, next, with the help of very many manuscripts, such as F H I T and bb, we have changed *relation* [relatione] to *relations* [relationibus]. Then, a few codices, such as R, S and U, have *undivided in unity* [unitate indivisa] for *unique and undivided* [unica et indivisa].

[6] The Vatican edition, together with codex cc, reads *because* [quia], but with the other codices and edition 1 contradicting this. A little before this, some codices, such as I K T V and cc, have (the subjunctive) *differ* [differant] for (the indicative) *differ* [differunt].

[7] A few codices, such as A D and T, have *of a thing* [rei], and a little below this have (the indicative) form of *it means* [dicit] instead of (the subjunctive) *it means* [dicat]

[8] From the mss. & edd. 1, 2 & 6, we have supplied *for that reason* [ideo].

[9] In the Vatican edition and codex cc there is lacking *which is objected* [quod obiicitur].

[10] Edition 1 adds *is* [est].

[11] Book I, n. 17: Because to the God born out of God the nativity permits neither that He is the same, nor (that He is) another. — In which text, breaking with nearly all the manuscripts and edition 1, the Vatican edition reads *nor other in nature* [nec alium esse natura]. Next, from the codd. with ed. 1, we have put *said before* [praedictum] in place of *said* [dictum].

strictly taken. The Seraphic (Doctor) proves this assertion, common to all the doctors, with a twofold reckoning. The *first* is taken *a posteriori*, i. e. from a consideration of those things, which properly have a numeral difference. This proceeds in this manner: number supposes the aggregation of a multitude, but this a limited unity, limitation (supposes) addition, because a genus (is limited) by the addition of a specific difference, a species by the addition of individuating principles, (and) matter by the addition of forms; but addition implies composition, which is in God least of all and consequently neither (is) a numeral difference. The *second* reckoning is taken *a priori*, or out of the intrinsic conditions of beings and chiefly of an infinite being. This proceeds from the distinction, that must be made in all, completed beings, between "*whereby it is*" and "*which it is*". "*Whereby it is*" signifies the specific and/or generic nature, "*which it is*" however, the individual or the supposit: from this there arises a specific and/or generic unity, however, from this (in turn there arises) an identity (and/or) diversity according to number. But in God "*whereby it is*" and "*what it is*" are multiplied and distinguished lest of all, however, "*who is*" (the Hypostasis) has a distinction and personal number. — With these things supposed the second conclusion, which begins with these words, is easily understood:

« However, neither is It one in number » etc.. For though in God "*whereby it is*" and "*what it is*" are one, yet the plurality of Persons is numbered. Whence among the divine there is not "number" simply, but (there is) with a determining addition, namely, plurality « according to the number of the Persons » (here in reply to n. 1, and Doubt 2). For that reason the Seraphic Doctor does not consent with Master (Peter), who removed number entirely from the divine, but says below (d. 24, a. 2, q. 1, in the body of the question): « "Number" conveys distinction and above this, the composition of aggregation; and though among the divine there is no aggregation, nevertheless there is distinction, for that reason "number" must not be simply removed from the divine, but (only) such a number. And Master (Peter) removes it entirely, for that reason he was lacking in his position. And in that article (his sentence) is not commonly held by the Masters of (the University of) Paris ».

III. Alexander of Hales, SUMMA., p. I, a. 45, m. 1, 2, 3 and 4. — (Bl. John Duns) Scotus, in each edition, SENT., Bk. I, d. 24., a. sole. — St. Thomas, d. 24, q. 1, a. 2; SUMMA., I, q. 30, a. 3. — Bl. (now St.) Albertus (Ma gnus), here in a. 17; SUMMA., p. I, tr. 9, q. 42, m. 1. — (Bl.) Peter of Tarentaise, here in q. 4. — Richard of Middleton, here in a. 3, q. 3. — Giles the Roman, SENT., Bk. I, d. 24, 1st. princ., q. 3. — Henry of Ghent, SUMMA., a. 43, q. 3. — (Bl.) Dionysius the Carthusian, SENT., Bk. I, d. 24. q. 2.

DOUBTS ON THE TEXT OF THE MASTER

DOUBT I

In this part there are doubts about the text (of Master Peter) and first concerning this, which (St. Augustine) says: *Let him pray, to understand what he believes.* For it seems that he speaks improperly, because no one prays for what he does not desire, no one desires what he does not consider, no one considers what he does not cognize and/or understand: therefore, from the first, if he prays, to understand, he (already) understands.[1] *Likewise*, no one assents to a thing, which he does not intuit or conceive in mind: therefore, no one assents to a thing, which he does not understand, because "to understand" is "to intuit with the mind".

I RESPOND: It must be said, that "to understand" is said in a twofold manner: in one manner it is the same as "to cognize, what it is[2] which is said through a name"; in another manner it is the same as "to comprehend by a reckoning". In the first manner it goes before the faith, which *is out of hearing*;[3] in the second manner it is consequent to it, because no human reckoning suffices to manifest the 'things which can be believed' [credibilia]; unless the intellect be enlightened and captivated by faith.[4]

DOUBT II

Likewise, is asked concerning this solution of Master (Peter), by which he says: *Some differ in number, which are not added to themselves in computation.* For he seems to speak badly,

because, either something in *the thing* corresponds [respondet] to that computation, or *nothing* (does). If *something* corresponds: therefore, it does not differ from the preceding difference; if *nothing* corresponds: therefore, our distinction or computation has been founded upon[5] a void [vanum].

I RESPOND: It must be said, that to our computation, when we say, "*one, two, three*", something does correspond. But it is not a numeral diversity, but a personal distinction; whence among the divine there is not said to be a "number" nor a "difference according to number", except one add "according to the number of the Persons", which means a distinction among the Hypostases, not (a distinction) in nature; for that reason, though "Three Persons" be said, yet there is not there a *group of three* [ternarius], but a *trinity*.[6]

DOUBT III

Likewise, is asked of he says, that *though God is said (to be) Triune, He ought not be said (to be) threefold*. For it seems contrary to that which is said in the seventh (chapter) of Wisdom,[7] that *the Spirit of wisdom is manifold*, therefore, twofold and/or fourfold: therefore, etc. *Likewise*, (St.) Isidore[8] says, that « a "trinity" is (something) manifold and numerable ». *Likewise*, it seems *by reason*, that one cloth [pannus], doubled in substance, is said (to be) "twofold", tripled, "threefold":

---

[1] The last part of this argument, the Vatican edition together with codex cc, yet with the other codices and edition 1 striving against this, exhibit in a mutilated form: *no one desires what he does not cognize and/or understand. Likewise.* [nullus desiderat quod non cognoscit vel intelligit. Item.].

[2] The Vatican edition and codex cc read *anything* [aliquid] in place of *what it is* [quid est], but contrary to the common manner of speaking of the Scholastics, and contrary to the manuscripts (some of which, however, such as K W and ee, read less aptly *the something it is* [aliquid est]) and edition 1. Next on the authority of very many codices and edition 1, we have substituted *comprehend* [comprehendere] for *apprehend* [apprehendere]. — Accept the explanation for this distinction from the Seraphic Doctor, who in SENT., Bk. III, d. 24, Doubt 3, resolving the same objection, says: In one manner "to understand" is meant in a broad manner as "to know, what it is which is said through a name"; and that "*understanding*" [intelligere] always precedes the assent of faith, nor is anything believed, which is not first understood in that manner. In the other manner "to understand" is this, "to think according to a previous reckoning", according to which (St.) Augustine

says: « What we understand, we ought for a reason; what we believe, for an authority [Quod intelligimus, debemus rationi; quod credimus, auctoritati] ». And of this (St.) Augustine understands, ... that there are certain (things) which are first believed and are afterwards understood, such as are the articles of the Faith, which are above reason etc.. — A little before this a few codices, such as P and Q, have *is in a twofold manner* [est dupliciter] for *is said in a twofold manner* [dupliciter dicitur].

[3] Rom. 10:17.

[4] Very many codices, such as G H P Q and ff, together with edition 1, have *by the light of faith* [luce fide] for *by faith* [fide]. — See more on this doubt in Alexander of Hales, SUMMA., p. III, q. 68, m. 6, a. 6.

[5] The Vatican edition adds *nothing and* [nihil et], which is lacking in nearly all the manuscripts and editions 1, 2 and 3.

[6] Cf. here q. 1.

[7] Verse 22, where the Vulgate in place of *wisdom* [sapientiae] has *understanding* [intelligentiae].

[8] Cf. below the text of Master (Peter), Distinction XXIV, at the end, where the entire proposition of (St.) Isidore is had.

therefore, if there is one Substance in Three Hypostases, it seems that It is tripled in Them and thus[1] is said (to be) "threefold".

I RESPOND: It must be said, that the distinction of the Persons cannot be signified through the addition of a numeral[2] term to this name, "*God*", except (through the addition) of this name, "*triune*", which has been invented [inventum est] specially for this, to signify the plurality among the Supposits with a unity of form. Therefore, because this name, "*threefold*", means a distinction simply in the term to which it is added, either as much as regards form, and/or as much as regards the multiplication of parts, and because[3] in God there occurs no multiplication, neither as much as regards form, nor as much as regards parts: for that reason in no manner can (God) be said (to be) "*threefold*".

Therefore, because is objected, that[4] (the Spirit of wisdom) is said (to be) *manifold*; it must be said, that that is said in the manner of a cause, because He is the effective principle[5] of many and various gifts, among which there is a true diversity; not so (is it) among the Persons. — What (St.) Isidore says, has been said in an improper manner and is to be expounded (as such). — To that, that the same cloth is said (to be) "threefold";[6] it must be said, that it is true, but yet according to now some parts now others [secundum alias et alias partes]; and because in God there is not an anotherness of parts nor of forms, for that reason He cannot be said (to be) "*threefold*".[7]

Likewise, is asked of this which (St. Augustine) says, that *in corporeal things, two are more than one* [plus sunt duae quam una]. For there seems to be (evidence) withstanding [instantia], because fire together with iron is not[8] greater than fire by itself, or (similarly) light with air. *If you say*, that they are not bodies; it is objected, that the glorified body is simultaneous with the non-glorified one, and the non-glorified one occupies as much space [locum] by itself, as with the glorious one: therefore, they are not greater, because a greater body occupies more space.

I RESPOND: It must be said, that (St.) Augustine[9] speaks of corporeal things, any of which is a body; but fire in iron and light in air is not a body, but a property of a body. *Moreover*, it must be noted, that, here,[10] (St.) Augustine does not accept "*greater*" [maius] extensively, but accepts "*more*" [plus] as much as regards the truth of existence and/or of essence. For, since the Most High Truth is not in every thing [in qualibet re], there is more of the truth of existence in two things, than in one, even though there is not more of the breadth of distance or of the extension[11] of magnitude and/or contentive capacity [capacitatis contentivae].

DISTINCTION XX

CHAPTER I

That None of the Persons exceeds Another in power.

Now, it remains to show, in what manner None of these Persons excels Another in power, so that there be shown, just as one and un-differing is the magnitude of the Three, so one and un-differing the power of the Three. It must be known, therefore, that[1] the Father is not more potent than the Son, nor the Son and/or Father than the Holy Spirit, nor do Two and/or Three have more power than Each of Them; because neither is the Father and the Son together more able [plus possunt] than the Holy Spirit alone, nor are these Three more able than Each of Them, because the omnipotence, which the Father has, both the Son accepts by being born, and the Holy Spirit by proceeding. Which (argument St.) Augustine con-

structs in a manner provable by reasons and authorities in the book, AGAINST MAXIMINUS,[2] who said that the Father (is) more potent and better than the Son.

CHAPTER II

That the Son is no less able than the Father

« Nothing », he says,[3] « less than the Father has He, who says: *All which the Father has, are Mine* ». « For if in power He has anything less than the Father, they are not all His, which the Father Has, but all which the Father has are His; therefore, the Son has as much power, as the Father »: « therefore, He is equal to the Father. For He, who accepts (all), cannot be unequal to Him, who has given (all) ».

---

[1] From the more ancient mss. and ed. 1, we have supplied *thus*. Next, very many codd. with ed. 1 have *in a threefold manner* [tripliciter] in place of "*threefold*" [triplex]. A little above this, (on the preceding page) cod. Z reads *is twofold* [est duplex] for *is said (to be) "twofold"* [dicitur duplex].

[2] The Vatican ed., which has *numerable* [numerabilis] for *numerai* [numeralis], is emended from the mss. and ed. 1. A little below this, cod. T, with ed. 1, has (the imperfect) for *signify* [significaret] instead of (the present) *signify* [significet].

[3] In very many mss., such as A S T W Y etc., and ed. 1, there is omitted *because* [quia], and then there is put *neither a* [nec] for *no* [non].

[4] Here and a little below this, after *because* [quia] supply: the Spirit of wisdom.

[5] The Vatican edition, breaking with the mss. and ed. 1, in this proposition reads *He is the cause of many and because He is the effective principle of various gifts* by adding *He is the cause* [causa est] after the word *because* [quia], and then *because* [quia] after the *and* [et], contrary to very many codd. and ed. 1. Then, some codd., such as A L S Z have *the principle of ... divine effects* [divinorum effectuum etc.] for *the effective principle of ... gifts* [donorum effectivum], yet, some, such as G H K O ee & ff, read like the first group, but omit *divine* [divinorum]. Next, after *not so* [non sic] codex V adds *is it* [est].

[6] The Vatican edition and codex cc read "*manifold*" [multiplex], but contrary to the other codices and edition 1.

[7] See more on this, below in d. 24, a. 3, q. 1. — Alexander of Hales, SUMMA., p. I, q. 66, m. 1, a. 4. — Bl. (now St.) Albertus (Magnus), here in a. 18.

[8] Trusting in the mss. and first six edd., we have expunged the added

something [quid], and then from very many manuscripts and edition 1, we have supplied *you* [tu] after *If* [Si].

[9] ON THE TRINITY, Bk. VI, ch. 10. n. 12, from which the text of this Doubt has been taken. — A little below this, on the authority of the older manuscripts and edition 1, we have inserted after *iron* [ferro] *and* [et].

[10] The Vatican edition reads *there* [ibi], with very many manuscripts and edition 1 striving against this.

[11] Thus nearly all the codices, while the Vatican edition, in place of *the extension of* [de extensione], reads *extensive* [extensivae], with which edition 1 agrees, which, after *magnitude* [magnitudinis] adds, together with codex M, *dimensional* [dimensivae].

NOTES ON THE BOOK OF SENTENCES

[1] Editions 5 and 8 read *that* [quod].

[2] The Vatican edition and the other editions have *in the third book, AGAINST MAXIMINUS* [in librio tertio contra Maximinum]; the codices and edition 1 have: *in the book, AGAINST MAXIM.* [in libro contra Maxim.]. In the printed editions of (St.) Augustine's works there are only two books AGAINST MAXIMINUS. But in the ancient copies of the manuscripts of this work, « COLLATIO AUGUSTINI CUM MAXIMINO », the *first* book was entitled PRIMUS LIBER. C. M., and the other two *the second* and *third* books. The text cited by Master Peter is from the second book, according to the modern reckoning.

[3] Book II, ch. 14. n. 7. — The passage of Scripture is (the Gospel of St.) John 16:15. The two following passages of (St.) Augustine are ibid., nn. 9 and 7.

CHAPTER III

*On the objections of heretics against this,
and the response of Catholics.*

« You, moreover, think this [hoc sapis] concerning power, that the Son is potent, but the Father more potent, since according to your doctrine a potent could beget a potent, and not an omnipotent an omnipotent. Therefore, the Father has an omnipotence, which the Son does not have; but if this is (so), what the Son says is false: *All which the Father has, are Mine* ».[1]

« But, you ask, the Father accepts power from no one; however, the Son (does) from the Father. We say also, that the Son has accepted power from Him, from whom He has been born potent; but no one gave power to the Father, because no one begot Him. For by begetting the Father gave power to the Son, just as all which He has in His own Substance, by begetting He gave to Him whom He begot of His own Substance ».[2]

« But it is asked, whether the Father gave as much power to the Son as was His, or whether less. If as much, the Omnipotent is understood to have begotten not only a potent, but also an Omnipotent; but if less, in what manner are all, which the Father has, the Son's? If the omnipotence of the Father is not the Son's, (it is) not far from doubt that all, which the Father has, are the Son's ».[3] But all are the Son's; therefore, the omnipotence of the Father is also the Son's: therefore, the Father is not more potent than the Son.

Likewise, in another manner he proves against Maximinus[4] that the Son (is) equal to the Father, thus saying: « You say, that the Father begot the Son less than Himself, in which you also derogate the Father, who, if He begot only a lesser [unicum minorem] Son, either could not, or would not, beget an Equal. If you say, that He would not, you have said that He is envious [invidum]; but if He could not, where is the omnipotence of God the Father? Further, according to this article (of your faith) one gathers [res colligitur], that God the Father either could not, or was unwilling to, beget a Son equal to Himself. If He could not, (His was) infirm; if He was unwilling, He is found (to be) envious. But each consequent [utrumque hoc] is false: therefore, the Son is the true equal to the Father.

Therefore, the Father begot a Son equal to Himself and from Each there proceeds an Equal to Each, the Holy Spirit ». « For if the Father could beget », as (St.) Augustine says against the same,[5] « His own full Form in an only Son, and yet did not beget It full, but lesser, we are driven to say that the Father (is) envious ». Therefore, He begot a God full and equal to Himself, the Son.

Moreover, he demonstrates through a similitude to man that this is so, inquiring:[6] « A man, as a father, if he were able, would have begotten an equal Son. Therefore, who dares to say, that the Omnipotent could not (do) this? I add also, because if a man were able, he would beget a Son greater and better than himself. But no one at all can be greater and/or better than God ». « Therefore, why did not God beget an equal, as you say, Son, for whom neither were years, through which an equality would be fulfilled, necessary, nor the omnipotence lacking. Or perhaps He was unwilling? therefore, far be it, He envied (Him); but He did not envy (Him): therefore, He begot an equal Son ».[7] « We believe, therefore, that the Son is equal to Him ».

« But perhaps you will say: the Father is greater than the Son for this very reason, that He has begotten a Begotten from nothing, yet an Equal. To which I swiftly respond: nay, for that reason the Father is not greater than the Son, because He begot an Equal. For this question of yours is (one) of the origin, 'who is from who?'; but (one) of equality is 'of what kind or how much is it?' »,[8] which is to say: to the origin pertains the question, by which there is asked, 'who is from who?'; however to equality that by which there is asked, 'of what kind or how much is Any?'. « Nor when the Son is said (to be) begotten from the Father, is there shown an inequality of Substance, but (rather) an order of nature, not by which the One would be prior to the Other, but by which the One is out of the Other ».[9] Therefore, not according to this, that the Father begot, and the Son has been begotten, and/or the Holy Spirit has proceeded from Each, does equality and/or inequality exist There, because not according to this is one Person said (to be) equal and/or unequal to the Other. Behold the equality of the Trinity and the one and same Substance, as much as we briefly were able, has been demonstrated in the above (sentences),[10] namely, in what manner Any of the Three Persons in neither eternity nor magnitude nor power excels any Other.

---

[1] Ibid., ch. 12, n. 1. — In this text of (St.) Augustine, the Vatican edition, with very many editions, preface the word *beget* [gignere] with *generate and/or* [generare vel], contrary to the codices and the original.

[2] Loc. cit., with a few things interposed. — Here codices A B and C and edition 1 read *Let us say* [Fateamur] for *We say* [Fatemur].

[3] Ibid., immediately after. — At the beginning of the text, after *whether* [utrum] the Vatican edition, with a few edd., badly adds *to Him* [et]. After the citation's end, the Vatican ed., with the other edd., contrary to edd. 1, 2, 3 & 7, and to all the codd., after *all* [omnia] add *which the Father has* [quae habet Pater], which easily can be supplied from the preceding (arguments).

[4] Book. II, ch. 7 and 5. (St.) Augustine teaches the same in the book, 83 QUESTIONS, q. 50.

[5] Ibid., chapter 15, n. 1.

[6] Ibid., chapter 18, n. 3, where the Vatican edition and very many editions, after *I add also* [Addo etiam] omits *because* [quia], breaking with codices B C D and E, edition 1 and the original.

[7] Ibid., chapter. 15, n. 5. — Those which follow, are read in ibid., ch. 18, n. 3.

[8] Ibid., immediately after, where the Vatican edition and editions 4, 8, and 9, read *because He begot an Equal to Himself* [quia aequalem sibi genuit], contrary to the other editions, codices and the original.

[9] Ibid., chapter 14, n. 8. — On the Vatican edition reads badly *is prior* [prior est] for *would be prior* [prior esset].

[10] That is, in this and the preceding distinction.

COMMENTARY ON DISTINCTION XX

On the equality of the Three Persons, as much as regards (Their) Power and Virtue.

Now, it remains to show, in what manner None of these Persons etc..

THE DIVISION OF THE TEXT

Above, Master (Peter) shows the equality of the Persons as much as regards (Their) *magnitude*, here he shows (Their) equality[1] as much as regards (Their) *Power* and *Virtue*. And this part has three parts. In the *first*, he proposes what he intends.[2] In the *second*, he proves (it), there (where he says): *Nothing less than the Father has He* etc.. In the *third*, he dissolves the doubt or objection in the contrary, there (where he says): *But perhaps you will say: the Father is greater* etc..

With the first and last part remaining undivided, the *middle one* is divided into three, according to three proofs or reasons, the first of which has been taken from the authority of the Lord, in the sixteenth (chapter of the Gospel of St.) John:[3] *All, which the Father has, are Mine.* The second has been taken through a deduction ad impossibile, because if He has not begotten an Equal, either He could and was unwilling, and thus was envious; or He wanted to and could not, and thus was impotent; and this is posited[4] there (where he says): *Likewise, in another manner he proves against Maximinus that the Son (is) equal to the Father.* The third reason is demonstrative [ostensiva], taken through the *simile* in created generation and is posited there (where he says): *Moreover, he demonstrates through a similitude to man that this is so.*

TREATMENT OF THE QUESTIONS

For an understanding of those (things), which are said in the present Distinction, two (things) are principally asked:

First there is asked, whether, among the divine, there is a positing of an adequation of power.

Second, whether, among the divine, there is a positing of order.

As much as regards the first two (things) are asked:

First, there is asked, whether, among the divine, there is a positing of an adequation of power[5] as much as regards (its) extension to the possible [extensionem possibilium].

Second, whether there is There an equation[6] as much as regards the intensity [intensionem] of power.

ARTICLE SOLE

On the adequation of Power among the divine.

QUESTION I

Whether, among the Divine Persons, there is equal Power as much as regards (its) extension to the possibile?

That there is a positing of the adequation of power There, as much as regards the number of possibles, is shown in this manner:

1. Whatsoever have the same nature, have the same natural power;[7] but, whatsoever have entirely the same power, whatever one can (do), the other (can) also (do); but the Father and the Son and the Holy Spirit have the same power: ergo etc..

2. Likewise, whatsoever have entirely the same operation, one can work nothing without the other; but the Father and the Son have the same operation: therefore, the Father can (do) nothing without the Son, according to the fifth (chapter of the Gospel of St.) John:[8] *Whatsoever the Father does, all these the Son does similarly.*

3. Likewise, no one can (do) more (things) that an Omnipotent; but the Word of God is omnipotent, just as is said in the eighteenth (chapter) of Wisdom:[9] *Omnipotent Thy Word, Lord* etc. The major is clear, because he who says "all" (i. e. "omni-") excepts nothing.

---

[1] In the Vatican edition and a few codices, there is lacking *equality* [aequalitatem].

[2] The Vatican edition, not trusting in the manuscripts and edition 1, reads *what is intended, that is, that no Person exceeds Another in power* [intenditur, scilicet quod alia persona non excedit aliam potentia].

[3] Verse 15, in which text, the Vulgate has *whichsoever* [quaecumque] for *which* [quae].

[4] Codex T has *this he puts* [hoc ponit].

[5] We have supplied from very many manuscripts and editions 1, 4 and 5, *of power* [potentiae].

[6] Codex V has *adequation* [adequatio].

[7] On this proposition, cf. above Distinction 2, a. sole, q. 1, page 51, footnote 11. — A little below this, codex M prefixes to the terms *the other also* [et alterum] *can* [potest], which certainly is to be supplied.

[8] Verse 19, where the Vulgate (placing the subordinate proposition in the subjunctive) reads: *For, whatsoever He does, these, too, the Son does similarly* [Quaecumque enim ille fecerit, haec et Filius similiter facit].

[9] Verse 15, in which text, the Vulgate omits *Lord* [Domine].

4. Likewise, there is no positing that there are any more[1] than the infinite; but the Son can (do) infinite (things), because He cannot do all, if (He can do) more: therefore, the Father cannot (do) more than the Son, nor for an equal reason (more) than the Holy Spirit.

ON THE CONTRARY: 1. As much as products are more distant, so much in power is the one producing wider or fuller, but the power of the Father extends itself to the created and the uncreated, the power of the Son to the created only, and more distant is the created and uncreated than only created (things):[2] ergo etc..

2. Likewise, the Son of God is one (thing) and a creature another, because a creature is something created, but the Son of God is the uncreated Essence: therefore, if[3] the Son is one (thing) and a creature another, therefore, (together they are) more: therefore, the power, which can (act) upon the Son and a creature, is more potent, than that which can (act) upon a creature only, or is potent upon many (things): but the power of the Father is such (a power): ergo etc..

3. Likewise, it is as much as and/or equally great and/or greater to produce an equal personal, such as a creature; but the Father can without the Son produce a Person and produce a creature: therefore, it seems, that the power in the Father extends itself to more.

4. Likewise, although the Holy Spirit[4] and the Son are not Something more, yet they are More than the Son alone: therefore, since in the Father the power is potent [possit] in the production of Each, in the Son (it is potent) in One of the Two only, the power in the Father is potent upon More[5] than in the Son: therefore, in extension to possibles it is greater.

CONCLUSION

The power of the Essence among the Divine Persons is equal as much as regards (its) extension to possibles.

I RESPOND: It must be said, that in speaking of the power of the Essence [potentia essentiali], which is in respect to the act of the Essence or (that) of production, it, in the Father, extends itself to nothing, to which it does not, on a par [pariter], extend itself, in the Son. And for that reason, because an equality [aequalitas] (of power)[6] consists as much as regards the power of the Essence, it must be conceded without calumny, that the Father and the Son are[7] equally [aequaliter] potent as much as regards (its) extension to possibles.

1. To that, therefore, which is objected unto the contrary, that, wider is the power, which can (act) at a greater distance; it must be said, that that is true of power said in the same manner and as much as regards a completely similar manner of producing; but 'that the Father can produced something created' belongs to the power of the Essence and to the work of creation; however, 'that the Father can produce the Son' belongs to power as (it is) in a Person and to generation; for that reason that reckoning is not valid.

2. To that which is objected, that a creature and the Son are more; it must be said that it is true, that they are *more*, and,[8] yet, they are not *more products*. For, although the Son is other than a creature, yet He is not another product. For the Son is an essence and a nature, but, yet, is not a produced essence and/or nature, because 'to produce a son' is not 'to produce a *something*, but a *someone*'. And for that reason it does not follow, that 'to produce the Son and a creature' is 'to be able to produce more than producing[9] one of the two'.

3. To that which is objected, that He produces a Person without the Son; it must be said, that it is not similar, because since 'to produce a creature' is 'to produce an essence', the production as much as the power belongs to an essence; and because the Essence in the Father and the Son is undivided,[10] for that reason also the power and the action, hence in virtue of this [proinde] also that production. However, because 'to produce the Son' is 'to produce a person', for that reason that production and power means something personal; and since the Father and the Son do not convene in a person, but in the Essence, for that reason[11] it is clear etc..

4. To that which is objected, that the Son and the Holy Spirit are More etc.; it must be said, that it is true, that (the Father) can also (act) upon More, but as much as regards this, equality and/or inequality is not attained, as has been seen.[12]

SCHOLIUM

I. Here one does not deal with *power* [potentia], to the extend that it is (as *potency*) distinguished against *act*, which (potency) is to be entirely removed from God, but with power, to the extent that it is an active principle and the effect of others, or of omnipotence. — The equality of this power can be understood either *extensively* [extensive] or in regard to the number of causable objects, or *intensively* [intensive] or, as Richard of Middleton (loc. cit. below), as much

---

[1] This proposition is commonly exhibited thus: to the infinite an addition cannot be made. — Some codices, such as C I U and cc, read *in the infinite* [in infinitis], and codex U *if ... in the infinite* [si in infinitis] for *than the infinite* [infinitis]. Then a few codices, such as S and Y, omit *any* [aliqua].

[2] Thus, the greater part of the codices, together with editions 2 and 3; others, such as I K X Z aa and ee, read either *the created* [creatum] and/or, together with edition 1 and the Vatican edition, *a creature* [creatura], but less distinctly. A little before this, codex Z reads *of the Holy Spirit* [Spiritus sancti] for *of the Son* [Filii], which reading per se could seem to be preferred, but from the response, posited below, it is clear, that the noun *power* [potentia] is understood, besides the power of *creating*, as the power of *generating*, which suits the Father alone.

[3] By adding the particle *if* [si], we offer the better reading, which also is found in many manuscripts, such as A F G H S T Y etc., and edition 1.

[4] Very many codices, such as A I T W aa and bb, have *the Father* [Pater] in place of *the Holy Spirit* [Spiritus sanctus], but contrary to what follows.

[5] We prefer the reading of some of the manuscripts, such as E X and Z, *More (Persons)* [plures] for *more (beings or things)* [plura], as it is more coherent with the preceding.

[6] Supply: *of power*; but the Vatican edition, contrary to the end intended in this question by the Seraphic Doctor, adds *of the Persons* [Personarum], which is lacking in the manuscripts and edition 1. A little above this, after *in the Son* [in Filio], codices aa and bb add *and the Holy Spirit* [et Spiritu sancto].

[7] The Vatican edition, not trusting in very many codices and edition 1, has the subjunctive form of *are* [sint].

[8] Trusting in many manuscripts, such as A S T V W X Y aa bb and cc, and editions 2, 3 and 6, we have supplied the particle *and* [et], in place of which very many codices, such as G H I K Z, together with edition 1, put *but* [sed], and which the Vatican edition, together with one or the other codex omits. Immediately after this, in the Vatican edition, with the older mss. and ed. 1 contradicting this, there is lacking *they are* [sunt].

[9] Less well, and with the more ancient manuscripts striving against this, the Vatican edition reads *to be able to produce* [posse producere] in place of *producing* [producere], which if the reading of the Vatican edition here is retained, one must add, together with codex K, *to be able* [posse] after *it does not follow that* [non sequitur quod].

[10] Thus the manuscripts together with edition 1, except codex cc, which with the Vatican edition puts *individual* [individua].

[11] From very many codices and edition 1, we have supplied *for that reason* [ideo].

[12] In the body of this Question.

as regards the intensity [intensionem] of the *vigor* of the power. In particular it is asked of the equality of the Three Person in *power*, because the special difficulty about power is to be solved too, since in the Father there is the active power of generating, which is not in the Son nor in the Holy Spirit; similarly one must judge of the power of spirating, which is not in the Holy Spirit. From this difficulty have been taken all the arguments to the opposite, which, however, have already, nearly been solved above in d. 7, qq. 3 and 4. The fundament of this solution is the distinction of power posited in the body (of the question), namely into *essential* and *notional* power (which in the solution to n. 1 is called *the power in a Person*). The former respects the production *ad extra*, which is common to the Three Persons, but the later the production *ad intra*, or the power of generating in the Father and of spirating in the Father and the Son. Indeed *"power"* and *"omnipotence"* can be taken in the broad sense for any productive power, whether it produces *ad intra* or *ad extra*; however, *properly* under *"omnipotence"* there is understood naught but the power of the Essence. To solve the objection, that "to generate" in God is *simply* a power, which does not convene with the Son and the Holy Spirit, Alexander of Hales (<u>loc</u>. <u>cit</u>. in reply to n. 1) rightly observes: « "To generate" in man and in God, is in a dissimilar manner, because among the divine that "to generate" concerns the whole Substance, not a part, and on this account among the divine it is the same as the Substance. But in man it is not so; for there generation does not come to be from the whole substance, but through the falling-off [decisionem] of a part. Whence there the substance of a father is not entirely the same as (that) of the son, though it is the same in specific form: and on this account in the generation, by which a man generates a man, *substance and relation are multiplied*. And for that reason in man there is a *power* [posse] to generate *something* and *according to something* [posse quid et ad aliquid]; *the power (to generate) something* means (to generate) through the multiplication of substance, *the power (to generate) according to something* (means to generate) through the multiplication of relation. However, in generation among the divine the Substance is not multiplied, but only a relation; and on account of this the power to generate among the divine is not a *power (to generate) something*, but a *power (to generate) according to something* ». With these posited, the solution of the same Alexander to the objection is understood: some power is in the Father, which, however, is not in the Son; to which he replies: « It is a change according to predicament, for *(to generate) something* is changed into *(to generate) according to something* ». This power is itself is dealt with below in distinctions 42, 43, and 44.

II. Cf. Alexander of Hales, SUMMA., p. I, q. 21, m. 1, a. 3. — (Bl. John Duns) Scotus, on this and the following q., here in q. sole; REPORTATIO., here in qq. 1 and 2. — St. Thomas, here in q. 1, a. 1. 2; SUMMA., I, q. 42, a. 6. — Bl. (now St.) Albertus, on this and the following q., here in a. 5; on this and the following q., SUMMA., p. I, tr. 11, q. 47, m. 3, partic. 1-3. — (Bl.) Peter of Tarentaise, here in q. 1, a. 1. — Richard of Middleton, on this and the following q., here in q. 1. — Giles the Roman, here in 1, princ., q. 3. — Henry of Ghent, on this and the following q., SUMMA., a. 70, q. 2, nn. 41-63. — Durandus (of Saint-Pourçain), here in q. 1. — (Bl.) Dionysius Carthusian, here in q. 1. — (Gabriel) Biel, here in q. sole.

QUESTION II

Whether, among the Divine Persons, there is an equality as much as regards the intensity of power?

Second, there is asked, whether among the divine there is equality as much as regards the intensity [intensionem] of power. And that (it is) so, seems in this manner:

1. Nothing is more potent than its own virtue; but Christ is the *Virtue of God*:[1] therefore, the Father is not more potent than the Son; similarly, for an equal reason, neither the Son than the Holy Spirit.

2. Likewise, of an equally noble substance[2] there is an equally noble and excellent power: but there is in the Son a Substance equally noble as (the One) in the Father, therefore, also a power equally noble: therefore, the Father can (do) nothing more powerfully than the Son.

3. Likewise, than that power, by which one can (act) over an infinite and most high distance, nothing (is) more potent; but the power of the Word can (act) over the infinite and most high distance, which is between (something) being [ens] and not being [non ens], because *through Him all (things) were made*:[3] ergo etc..

4. Likewise, than that power, which nothing can resist nor anything can retard, nothing is more potent: but nothing can retard the power of the Son, nor can anything resist it, because it works suddenly and freely, (as) the Psalm (says):[4] *He spoke and they were made*: ergo etc..

ON THE CONTRARY: 1. More potent is the power in that which can only act, than in that which (can)[5] act and suffer; but in the Father there is only acting, in the Son acting and suffering: ergo etc..

2. Likewise, anything which is a first principle is more potent, that that which is not a first (principle), because « every primary cause influences [influit] more than a second (cause) »;[6] but the Father is a first principle: therefore the one and same Father (is) more potent than the Son.

3. Likewise, one can act in a more potent manner who has power from himself [a se], than one who (has it) from another [ab alio]; for he who has anything from himself has it in a much better manner, than he who accepts it from another:[7] therefore, since the Son has (His) 'being able' [posse] from the Father, but the Father (has it) through Himself [per se] and from Himself [a se], ergo etc..

4. Likewise, anyone can (do) more, who can (act) both through himself and through another, than the one who (can act) only through himself; but the Father can work through the Son, the Holy Spirit cannot (work) through the Son, nor (can) even the Son Himself, properly speaking: ergo etc..

---

[1] 1 Cor. 1:24. — A little before this, after *than its own virtue* [sua virtute], codices aa and bb add *neither extensively nor intensively* [extensive nec intensive].

[2] The reading, which among the mss. with edd. 1, 2 & 3 is more common, *of an equally noble ...* [nobilis] for *of a ... in an equally noble (manner)*, which the Vatican ed. has. A little below this, codex bb reads *therefore there is also a power* [ergo et potentia est] for *therefore, also a power* [ergo et potentia].

[3] John 1:3.

[4] Psalm 148:5. — The Vatican edition, together with codex cc, but with the other codices together with edition 1 striving against this, has *it is clear because* [patet quia] for *(as) the Psalm (says)* [Psalmus].

[5] Supply with codex V *can* [potest]. Here, in the codd. diverse readings are had: thus in some, such as A and T and in edition 1, there is omitted the second *in that* [in eo], nay there are found manuscripts, such as Z, in which the words *in that which* [in eo qui] are omitted. A little

below this, after *in the Son* [in Filio], codex X adds *there is* [est], and contrariwise very many codd., such as S T & Y with ed. 1, omit *acting and* [agere et].

[6] BOOK ON CAUSES, proposition 1: Every primary cause is more an influence [influens] over its own caused, that a second universal cause. — A little before this, after *that that which* [quam quod non], there is omittedin editions 1, 2, 3 and 6, and in very many manuscripts, such as T V and Y, *is* [est].

[7] We present the ancient reading of edition 1 and the manuscripts, some of which, however, such as A G P and Q, have *receives* [recipit] for *accepts* [accipit], while the Vatican edition reads *than if he receive it from another* [quam si ab alio recipiat]. A little above this, codex Y reads *than one who accepts it from another* [quam qui ab alio accipit], which also with some manuscripts, such as V and X, in place of the second *from himself* [a se], has *through himself* [per se], but codex T reads *from himself and through himself* [a se et per se], which reading is more conformable to the subjoined.

CONCLUSION

The power in the Divine Persons is equally intense.

I Respond: It must be said, that the Power in the Father and the Son is equally intense [intensa], because in Each it is Most High and equally Noble, because (it is) One in Each, not degenerating through nature[1] — (it is) in a similar manner [similiter], also, in the Holy Spirit — and this, speaking of the Son according to the Divine Nature [secundum divinam naturam], according to which He is equal to the Father.

1. To that, therefore, which is objected, that the Son can suffer; it must be said, that that (ability)[2] of His is not according to the Divine Power, but according to (His) human infirmity; and according to that He is inferior to the Father and less potent; but according to the Divine (Nature) He cannot suffer, just as neither (can) the Father.

2. To that which is objected second, that a first principle can (do) more; it must be said, that *"first"* and[3] *"beginning"* [principium]* either means only an *"order"* [orinem], or a *"substantial difference"* [substantialem differentiam]. If only an *"order"*, since it is one and the same on both sides, it not more potent here than there. But if (it means) a *"substantial difference"* with an order, in this manner it is true, that a first (principle) is more potent than a second (principle), because the second adds something to the first, which while it makes it more[4] composite, renders it more limited, and, thus, less potent.

3. To that which is objected third, it has already been solved: because *"to have from another"*, this is either by (something) differing *substantially*, or *personally*. If *substantially*, it is thus[5] true, because, since he has it from another through (its) essence, he does not have it essentially, but by participation; but as much as he has it from *another personally*, yet, by the same essentially, then he has it in an equally noble manner, because totally and essentially. Whence, in the fifth (chapter of the Gospel of St.) John (there is said):[6] *Just as the Father has life in Himself, so has He given to the Son* etc..

4. To that which is objected fourth, that the Father can (act) through Himself[7] and through Another; it must be said that *"to be able (to act) through another"* is in a twofold manner: either through another *inferior cause* acting together (with it), or through another *person*. In the first manner it is more potent to be able (to act) through oneself and through another, than through oneself only; because *"to be able (to act) through another"* means a dominion, and thus power; but *"to be able (to act) through another"* as[8] through a consubstantial *person* does not mean a dominion, but only an authorship [auctoritas]. But *"authorship"* does not mean *"to be greater"* [maioritatem], but only means an origin, just as *"to be able (to act) by another* and *not by another"* does not mean *"to be lesser"* [minoritatem] in power,[9] but only a subauthorship and origin; and in this manner must it be understood in the proposed concerning *"to be able (to act) through another"* and *"to not be able to act through another"*.

SCHOLIUM

I. Of this question we do not find any special treatment except in (Bl.) Peter of Tarentaise, here in q. sole, a. 2. Alexander of Hales, however, solves the same and other objections in Summa., p. I, q. 47, m. 2 and 3. In regard to the 2nd opposed argument, he says among other things: « The descending of created causes is according to (their) greater and lesser distance from the First Cause, on which account, according to which they descend more, they communicate less of the virtue of the First Cause; not so (is it) among the divine, though, There, there is an order according to Nature; for They are entirely the Same according to substance; whence among Them there cannot be a difference of virtue and/or of power ».

ARTICLE II

On order, among the divine.

Consequently, in the second place, there is the question concerning the Second Article, that is,[10] whether, among the divine, there is an order. And about this, two (things) are asked:

First, there is asked, whether an order is to be posited There.[11]

Second, whether (it is) an order of nature.

---

[1] An allusion to the words of (St.) Hilary (of Poitiers), cited above in Distinction XIX, p. I, ch. 4, and explained (by St. Bonaventure in his Commentary) on Doubt 11, of that distinction. — A little below this, the Vatican edition together with codex cc reads *similarly also is it in the Holy Spirit* [similiter et in Spiritu sancto est].

[2] Some codices, such as Y and Z, together with edition 1, read *that (ability)* [illud] for *that (ability) of His* [istud]. Next after *divine power* [potentiam divinam] in codex bb there is added *and/or Nature* [vel naturam].

[3] From very many manuscripts and editions 1, 2, and 3, we have supplied the particle *and* [et], which is put less well by codex V also a little above this, where the same proposition occurs, because above there is only a repetition of the objection, but here its resolution.

[4] Codex T adds reads *while it works more and makes (it) composite and* etc. [dum facit magis compositum et]; a reading not to be spurned. — Cf. above d. 8, p. II, a. sole, q. 2, page 169, footnote 4.

[5] Some codices, such as X and Z, together with edition 1, have *then* [tunc]. Next after *since he has it from another* [cum habeat ab alio] in codex X there is inserted *differing from another* [differente ab alio], and a little below this, there is placed *differing* [differing] before *personally* [personaliter]. Codex Y reads *through participation* [per participationem] for *by participation* [participatione].

[6] Verse 26, in which text the Vulgate, together with the Vatican edition, after *He has given* [dedit] there is added *also* [et], but contrary to the manuscripts and editions 1, 2, 3 and 6.

[7] In all the codices, such as A I T Y Z, and edition 1, there is lacking *through Himself and* [per se et]. Next the Vatican edition, contrary to nearly all the codices and edition 1, after *either through* [aut per] reads *some* [aliqua] for *another* [aliam].

[8] Trusting in very many manuscripts, such as F G H M Y and ee, we have supplied *as* [ut], in place of which codices aa and bb read *that this through a consubstantial person* [per personam scilicet consubstantialem]. A little before this codex Y, after *because to be able* [quia posse], adds *in this manner* [sic], and then edition 1 omits *thus* [et].

[9] Supply: in the one which can (act) by another. A few codices, such as M and N, with edition 1, after *"to be lesser"* [minoritatem] add *and/or "to be greater"* [maioritatem], but one or the other codex, such as S, puts *"to be greater"* [maioritatem] in place of *"to be lesser"* [minoritatem].

[10] In the Vatican edition 1 and the more recent codex cc there is wanting *that is* [scilicet].

[11] From the manuscripts and edition 1, we have substituted *There* [ibi] in place of *among the divine* [in divinis], which the Vatican edition, not trusting in the manuscripts and edition 1, adds a little below this after *Second, whether* [Secundo, utrum].

---

* *Trans. Note*: here principium is rendered *beginning* rather than *principle*, to concord with the citation from Aristotle, made in the following Question, fundament 3 and its footnote 2, on p. 372.

QUESTION I

Whether, among the divine, there is a reckoning of order?

That, among the divine, there is an order, is shown:

1. First through (St.) Augustine (in his work) AGAINST MAXIMINUS:[1] « When the Son is said (to be) from the Father [a Patre], there is not signified an inequality of substance, but an order of nature ».

2. Likewise, this seems by the authority of the Church, because the Church expresses the naming of the Trinity in an ordered manner [ordinate]. For there is said "In the Name of the Father and of the Son and of the Holy Spirit", and this order is never changed: ergo etc..

3. Likewise, "beginning" [principium] means a reckoning of order. « For "first" and "beginning" », says the Philosopher,[2] « I say (are) the same »; but among the divine the Father is the beginning of the Son, therefore, the First (Person). But where this (is), there is an order: ergo etc..

4. Likewise, "order" means a complete reckoning of 'being' and *the good* — « for 'being' », as (St. Severinus) Boethius[3] says, « is that which retains order and preserves [servare] the nature »; similarly also *the good* — but among the divine there is in a most perfect manner a reckoning of 'being' and of *the good*: therefore, there is a reckoning of order There.

5. Likewise, wheresoever there are many, among which there is not an order, they are inordinate; but among the Divine Persons there is a plurality: therefore, if there is not an order There, there is inordinance [inordinatio] and confusion; but inordinance and confusion is[4] repugnant to the divine; therefore, there in an order There.

ON THE CONTRARY: 1. (St.) Eusebius (of Vercelli says):[5] « Among the divine there is number, but not order ».

2. Likewise, this very (thing) seems from the *reckoning of order*. (St.) Augustine (says in his work) ON THE CITY OF GOD:[6] « An "order" is a disposition of equals and disparates [parium disparimque], granting to each one their own places »; but among the divine three is no distinction of places: ergo etc..

3. Likewise, "order" is the contrary of *togetherness* [contrariatur simultati],[7] therefore, where there is an order, there is not an omnimodal togetherness; but where is not an omnimodal togetherness, there is not a perfect equality: therefore, since among the divine there is an omnimodal and perfect equality, there is no order There.

4. Likewise, if there is order among the divine, either it is something *essential*, or *notional*. Not *essential*, because where (there is) order, there (is) distinc-

tion; but among the divine there is no distinction according to the Essence: ergo etc.. Nor (is it) something *notional*, since the same is notion and property, but "order" is the property of no Person:[8] ergo etc..

5. Likewise, where there is order, there is dependence and inclination; for nothing is ordered to anything, unless it has an inclination to it; but among the divine there is no dependence: therefore, (there is) entirely no order There.[9]

6. Likewise, order presupposes number; but among the divine there occurs no difference according to number, as has been shown above:[10] therefore, neither order.

CONCLUSION

'Order' is to be posited among the divine, but an order only according to origin.

I RESPOND: It must be said, that 'order' is threefold, namely, according to *position* [secundum positionem], according to *antecedence* [secundum antecessionem] and according to *origin* [secundum originem].

"Order" according to *position* is said of any, one of which is the superior, another the inferior. And this can be in a twofold manner: either in a place, and/or in dignity. And this "order" does not occur among the divine, just as the first reason taken from (St.) Eusebius shows, and the second taken from (St.) Augustine, just as it clear.

However, "order" according to antecedence is said to be of those, one of which is prior, but the other of the two posterior; and this is said in a twofold manner: either because it goes before [antecedit] in duration or time, or (is) prior in the understanding of its nature [naturali intelligentia] or in cognition. And this "order" is not among the divine, just as the third reason proves, because this "order" takes away equality and togetherness [simultatem], each of which is perfectly among the Divine (Persons).

But "order" according to *origin* or according to an emanation is of one producing to one produced.[11] And that order is among the divine, because there is an order of beginning and

---

[1] Book II, ch. 14, n. 8. See here the text of Master (Peter), ch. 3, near the end. — From cod. T, we put *(in his work) Against* [contra] in place of *(in his letter) To* [ad]. The Vatican ed., with the mss. and ed. 1 striving against this, after *Maximinus* [Maximinum] adds *where he says* [ubi dicit].

[2] POSTERIOR ANALYTICS, Bk. II, ch. 2. — The whole of this third argument is absent from the Vatican edition and codex cc, yet it is extant in the other manuscripts and edition 1.

[3] ON THE CONSOLATION OF PHILOSOPHY, Bk. IV, Discourse 2.

[4] Codex V has *are repugnant* [repugnant].

[5] This is gathered from St. Eusebius of Vercelli, ON THE CONFESSION OF THE TRINITY, where in n. 8 he says: « Therefore, this Holy Trinity, which is the One, True god, does not withdraw [recedit] from number nor is grasped by number. For in the relation of the Persons a number is discerned [cernitur]. But in the substance of the Divinity what is enumerated, is not comprehended ». And ibid., n. 10: « Nor yet are the Three Persons to be estimated separables, since None before Another, None after Another, None without Another is believed either to have existed and/or indeed to have at any time worked ».

[6] Book XIX, ch. 13, n. 1, where the Vatican ed. falsely reads *of parts of disparates* [partium disparium] for *of equals and of disparates* [parium et dispariumque]. Next, codex V reads *disposition* [dispositio] for *distinction* [distinctio].

[7] Cf. Aristotle, ON THE PREDICAMENTS, ch. "On Before and Together".

[8] Codex X, having added at the beginning of this argument a third member of the distinction, namely *or personal* [aut personale], here adds *Likewise, non personal, because order is common, person not* [Item non personale, quia ordo est communis, persona non.] Alexander of Hales, SUMMA., p. I, q. 46, m. 1, in a similar objection posits three members, namely *either it is the essence, or a Person, or a notion* [aut est essentia aut persona aut notio], and in respect of the second member says: « Likewise, neither can it be said, that that order is a Person, nay it its of the Persons, because it means a habitude of the Persons to the Persons ». And Bl. (now St.) Albertus (Magnus), SUMMA., p. I, tract 9, q. 41, m. 2, a. 1, offering three members of the objection, says of the second: « Neither (does order mean) a Person: for the order is of the Persons, but a Person is not of the Persons; just as (things) ordered are not an order, but an order is of (things) ordered ». Nevertheless, it has already been manifested through itself, that *order* does not mean *person*; whence this division could be omitted; and or say, that the *personal* is meant under the *notional*.

[9] Not a few codices, such as V and Z, read *there is entirely no order There* [ibi nullus omnino est ordo].

[10] Distinction 19, p. II, q. 4.

[11] In codd. aa & bb there is added *and this in a twofold manner: either according to which one is from another essentially, and in this manner it is not among*

begun There, or of One producing and One produced, and the first reasons prove that this "order" is among the Divine (Persons).

4. Because it is objected fourth, that the order (There) is not something notional nor essential;[1] it must be said, that it is notional; but it happens that "notion" signifies in a twofold manner: either under a *proper* reckoning, as when "generation" is said (to be a notion); or under a *common* reckoning, by a community, I say, of reckoning, as when there is said *order*,[2] *notion*, *property* — just as "individual" is a common intention — and under this community it does not distinguish, yet among its inferiors it does suppose distinction.

5. To that which is objected: where there is order, there is dependence; it must be said, that "order" conveys habitude, and because "habitude" in creatures according to the reckoning of imperfection means "dependence", for that reason in creatures it conveys dependence; but among the divine "habitude"[3] only posits

a comparison and connection, an no dependence and inclination: for that reason etc..

6. To that which is last objected, that order presupposes number; it must be said, that just as, among the divine, number withdraws [distrahit][4] from the reckoning of number, because, There, there is only a distinction of Hypostases, thus order (withdraws) from the reckoning of order simply (speaking), because, although there is an order There, yet, there is no antecedence There, but only the emanation of origin.

And/or it must be said in another way, that (order) does not always presuppose distinction according to number, unless it is understood of local order or (of an order) according to position. For an 'order according to nature' and 'according to the understanding of nature' [secundum naturalem intelligentiam] is attained between a superior and an inferior, between which there occurs no number. And thus that is clear.

SCHOLIUM

I. Richard of Middleton (here in q. 3) says: « Order simply (speaking) conveys a distinction of (those) ordered and the mutual habitude of a prior and posterior grade of (those) distinguished. But, although the Persons have been distinguished among Themselves and have a mutual habitude among Themselves, yet, They do not have a grade of prior and posterior, because None is prior to Another in duration nor in dignity nor even according to the Nature ». Whence he rightly concludes, that, just as, among the divine, "number" ought not be said except with a determination, namely, the number of the Persons, so it ought not be said, that there is order among the divine, simply (speaking), but with a determination, that is, the order of origin, not by which One is prior to Another, but because One is from Another. The

Seraphic (Doctor), having distinguished the various species of order, defends the same sentence with many conclusions and explains it more clearly in the solution to n. 4. What he says here of numbers, has already been proven above in d. 19, p. II, q. 4.

II. Alexander of Hales, SUMMA., p. I, a. 46, m. 1. — (Bl. John Duns) Scotus, on this and the following questions, QUODLIBETALS., qq. 1 and 4. — St. Thomas, here in q. 1, a. 3: SUMMA., I, q. 42, a. 3 and q. 33, a. 1, ad. 3. — Bl. (now St.) Albertus (Magnus), on this and the following question, here in a. 7; SUMMA., p. I, tr. 9, q. 41, m. 2. — (Bl.) Peter of Tarentaise, here in q. sole, a. 4. — Richard of Middleton, here in q. 3. — Giles the Roman, here in 2nd. princ., q. sole. — Henry of Ghent, SUMMA., a. 52, q. 1. — Durandus (of Saint-Pourçain), on this and the following question, here in a. 2. — (Bl.) Dionysius the Carthusian, on this and the following question, here in q. 2.

QUESTION II

Whether, among the divine, there is an order of nature?

Second, there is asked, whether among the divine there is an order of nature. And that (it is) so, seems:

1. Through (St.) Augustine, who says in the text (of Master Peter),[5] that « when the Son is said (to be) from the Father, there is not meant an inequality of substance, but an order of nature ».

2. Likewise, where (there) is a natural origin, there is a natural order: but among the divine there is a natural origin, therefore, also a natural order: therefore, there is an order of nature.

3. Likewise, where (there) is cause and effect, there is a prior and a posterior; but wheresoever this, there is[6] an order of nature: therefore, since among the divine it happens that one finds cause and

effect, just as (St. John) Chrysostom says on the first (chapter of the Letter of St. Paul) to the Hebrews,[7] and (St. John) Damascene (ON THE ORTHODOX FAITH), in the first book, chapter 8: « The Father is the Cause of the Son », it is clear etc..

ON THE CONTRARY: 1. Of whatsoever the order is, that is ordered: therefore, if among the divine there is an order of nature, the Nature is ordered; but what is ordered is distinguished and numbered:[8] therefore, among the divine the Nature is distinguished and numbered; but this (is) false: ergo etc..

2. Likewise, among the divine[9] the Same is Nature and Essence, because "*the Nature*" is the name of the Essence; but among the divine there is in no manner posited an order of essence: therefore, neither (one) of nature.

---

the divine, but only among these inferiors; and/or according to which one is from another only personally [et hoc dupliciter: vel secundum quod unum est ab alio essentialiter, et sic non est in divinis, sed solum in his inferioribus; vel secundum quod unum est ab alio personaliter tantum.].

[1] Very many codices, together with editions 1, 2, and 3, in place of *essential* [essentiale] put *personal* [personale], which is either a lapse of the copyists, and/or a sign, that here and in the objection itself the third member of the division has been omitted, as not necessary to be enumerated, just as has been observed by us above, from the testimony of codex X. — A little before this, trusting in the more ancient manuscripts and edition 1, we have changed *To that which is objected fourth* [Ad illud quod obiicitur quarto] of the Vatican edition, to *Because it is objected fourth* [Quod obiicitur quarto]. Next codex A has *notional* [notionale] for *"notion"* [notionem].

[2] In codices aa and bb there is added *principle* [principium], mention of which St. Thomas makes, here in q. 1, a. 3, in reply to n. 4.

[3] The Vatican edition, together with codex cc, breaking, however, with the other codices together with edition 1, omits here *"habitude"* [habitudo] and a little below this *for that reason* [ideo].

[4] Codex X reads *is withdrawn* [distrahitur], that is (the word) "number" (when rightly said of God), among the divine, is drawn away from its proper sense to an improper one. Cf. above Distinction 19, part II, article 4, and Doubt 2.

[5] Here in ch. 3, near the end.

[6] In very many manuscripts, such as A T V Z and edition 1, there is omitted *is* [est].

[7] Homily 2, n. 2: for if the Father is His Cause and Author, much more (is He) of those which have been made through Him. — The words of (St.) John Damascene, ON THE ORTHODOX FAITH, cited in the passage cited are: The Father is naturally the Cause of the Son [Pater naturaliter Filii causa est].

[8] The Vatican edition, together with a few codices, adds *if this* [si hoc]. A little below this, after *but this* [sed hoc], in some manuscripts, such as V X and Z, there is added *is* [est].

[9] In very many codices and edition 1, there is lacking *among the divine* [in divinis], but it certainly must be supplied on account of the added reasoning: *the Same is Nature and Essence* [idem est natura et essentia].

3. Likewise, where (there) is an order, there is a prior and a posterior,[1] therefore, if among the divine there is an order of nature, there is a prior and a posterior according to the Nature; but this in no manner is received: therefore neither an order of nature. Moreover, that among the divine there is no prior and posterior according to the Nature, is shown in this manner: « Relatives are by nature together [natura simul] »,[2] therefore, the Father and the Son, according to which (They are) the Father and the Son, are together by the Nature; but the Father is at once by Nature [simul natura] according to That which He is and according to which He is the Father,[3] because among the divine the relations are not adventive [advenientes], nor are they only a reckoning of being referred, but (they are) also (a reckoning) of existing:[4] therefore the Father and the Son according to Their Hypostases are together by Nature, therefore, there is no order of nature There.

4. Likewise, among created causes we see grades, to the extent that[5] according to as much as a created substance can (act) more swiftly [citius], more quickly [velocius] does it work; whence certain (things) work in a time [in tempore], certain ones unexpectedly [repente], certain ones suddenly [subito]; and that cause, which works suddenly, sometimes does not precede in time [tempore], but in nature. Therefore, if God produces the Son according to every nobility and virtue of His power, and the virtue of His power is more infinite than finite: therefore, not only does He produce (the Son) simultaneous in duration, but also simultaneous by nature: therefore, there is no order of nature There.

5. Likewise, we see among cognizables, that certain ones have a cognition of themselves and thought [cogitationem][6] by investigating and posterior in time — and I speak of actual, not of habitual (cognition) — such as the human soul (does); and certain ones simultaneous in duration, as an Angel (does): therefore, if God's cognition and speaking or locution is not an accident, but much more noble and more virtuous[7] than every creature, He has a Word of understanding, not only simultaneous in duration, but also in nature: ergo etc..

CONCLUSION

Among the divine there is rightly said to be an order of nature, that is, an order of natural origin.

I RESPOND: It must be said, that an "order" is said to be[8] of anything in a twofold manner: either as *of that which has been ordered* [sicut ordinati], or as *of the reason for ordering.* "Order" among the divine, as *of that which has been ordered*, is said of the Person of the Father and/or[9] of the Son and/or of the Holy Spirit; as *of the reason for ordering* it is said of the Nature. For "nature" means the productive force, according to which the Philosopher[10] says, that « it is the force implanted in things producing similars out of similars ». But among the divine the order is according to production, for that reason[11] there is said (to be) There an order of nature, that is, of natural origin. Wherefore, that genitive is not construed *subjectively* (i. e. "of the Nature"), as when there is said "the whiteness of Peter", but *from the force of a declaration of essence*, as when there is said "the whiteness of brightness" and/or "a man of authority". And for that reason (the genitive)[12] is resolved into two, so that the sense is: *an order of nature*, that is (an order) of natural origin.

1. From this is clear the first which objects,[13] because it objects, as if the order were said of the Nature as of a thing ordered. The second is also clear, because[14] "essence" is said in an omnimodal abstraction [in abstractione omnimoda], not "as the principle of another"; but "nature" means "as the principle of another", whence it means a comparison to the production or emanation.

Whence[15] it must be further attend to, that "order according to a natural origin" among these inferiors means two (things), namely *emanation* and *antecedence.* And the reason for this is, that emanation among these inferiors posits a diversity of substance [diversitatem substantialem]. Wherefore, what emanates among these inferiors, is an effect, and what produces is a cause; and for that reason *a cause* is said (to belong) to that which the other "being" follows;[16] and

---

[1] We present the ancient reading of the mss. and of ed. 1, while the Vatican edition with the more recent codex cc, in this proposition after *an order* [ordo] adds *of nature* [naturae], and to the word *posterior* [posterius] adds *according to nature* [secundum naturam], and next twice omits *according to nature* [secundum naturam], in which reading the force of the argumentation is weakened. — On the principles of this objections, cf. Aristotle, ON THE PREDICAMENTS, ch. "On the Prior".

[2] Aristotle, ON THE PREDICAMENTS, ch. "On Relatives".

[3] The mutilated reading of the Vatican ed., in which this proposition *but the Father is at once ... He is the Father* [sed Pater ... simul est natura] is omitted, is repaired with the help of the mss. and ed. 1. Next, cod. X has *therefore they are not only* [ergo non sunt] for *nor are they only* [nec tantum sunt].

[4] Cf. above d. 7, Doubt 4.

[5] The Vatican edition, contrary to very many codices and edition 1, has *because* [quia] for *to the extent that* [quod]. A little below this very many codices, such as C E G H K R S and U, read in the singular *a certain (cause) works ... a certain one ...* etc. [quaedam operator etc.].

[6] The codices disagree among themselves, for some, such as B D F I K S V W X & Y, have *cognition*[cognitionem], cod. O *a cognition of others* [aliorum cognitionem], but all the others with ed. 1, read *thought* [cogitationem], which reading both in itself is better and is supported by a greater number of mss.; the Vatican ed. omits *and thought* [et cogitationem]. In cod. Z, there is read *among cognizers* [in cognoscentibus] for *among cognizables* [in cognoscibilibus]. A little below this, after *habitual* [habituali] supply with cod. bb *cognition* [cognitione]. Then, codd. L & O after *duration* [duratione] add *but posterior in nature* [posterius natura].

[7] The Vatican edition, not trusting in the mss. and ed. 1, has *(is) in a much more noble and virtuous manner* [multo nobilius et virtuosius].

[8] In some mss., such as A S T Y etc., there is lacking *to be* [esse].

[9] The Vatican ed., with the more ancient mss. and ed. 1 striving against this, here and a little after this, has *and* [et] in place of *and/or* [vel].

[10] See above d. 7, a. sole, q. 1, page 134, footnote 10.

[11] Some codd., such as L & O, read *and for that reason* [et ideo], oth-

ers, such as K S V and ee, have *and* [et] in place of *for that reason* [ideo]; very many, such as A F H I T bb and cc, with the first six edd., have *that is* [id est] in place of *for that reason* [ideo]. A little below this, as required by the mss. and ed. 1, we have substituted *of Peter* [Petri] in place of *of the wall* [parietis], where there is then added by codd. aa and bb *because order is not ordered and/or order is not that which is ordered* [quia ordo non ordinatur vel ordo non est illud quod ordinatur]. Next, after *of essence* [essentiae] very many mss., such as B E K & V, incongruously add *that is of a natural origin* [id est naturalis originis], and then, trusting in the mss. and ed. 1 we have supplied the words *and/or a man of authority* [vel homo auctoritatis].

[12] Supply: *the genitive.* On the signification of the genitive, cf. above d. 3, p. II, Doubt 3, and below in d. 34, Doubt 5, and in d. 41, Doubt 2: in this last he says: And if it be objected, that one genitive is not constructed from that force (of a declaration of essence); it must be said, that it is true, unless (the word in the genitive) has the virtue of both (manners of signification). Whence there is rightly said: "*a man of the blood*" and "*a man of authority*"; similarly "*the election of grace*", that is "of gratuitous goodness".

[13] The Vatican edition reads *is objected* [obiicitur], but contrary to the manuscripts, many of which, such as I S V and bb, together with edition 1, then faultily omits *because it objects* [quia obiicit].

[14] Trusting in very many mss. and ed. 1, we have substituted here *because* [quia] for the ambiguous *that/because/which* [quod], and a little below, as required by the older codices and edition 1, we have put *whence it means* [unde dicit] in place of *for that reason it means* [ideo dicit].

[15] Some codices, such as F G and Y, together with edition 1, omit *Whence* [Unde], and next in not a few codices, such as S and W, read *an order of substance* [ordo substantia] for *order* [ordo].

[16] See above d. 5, Doubt 3, page 120, footnote 7, where if you except edition 1, which with the Vatican edition reads: *is said according to the being which the other follows* [dicitur causa ad esse etc.]. — A little below this (on the next page), after *posterior* [posterius], in codex Z and edition 1 the *in* [in] is lacking. Next, very many codd. such as A S W & Y, read *there does not follow* [non sequitur] for *there is not consequent* [non consequitur].

because (there is) another in nature, for that reason (there is) a posterior in nature. But among the divine there is an emanation, to which there is not consequent a diversity of essence and/or of nature, for that reason neither "a prior nor posterior" in nature, but a "together" in nature. And for that reason there is not received[1] among the divine a reckoning of *cause* and/or of effect, according to the Latins, but the noun "principle" (is), although the Greeks, as an extended name, use the noun "cause" for the noun "principle". And for that reason among the divine there is a order of nature, not by which the One is posterior to the Other, but by which the One (is) out of the Other. And this is what (St.) Augustine says in the text (of Master Peter).[2]

3. And from this is clear, what is objected third: for although among creatures an order posits a posteriority of nature,[3] yet, (it does) not in God. And for that reason, though there is not a

posteriority There, it does not follow, that there is no goodly order There.

From these are clear the objections to each part. Therefore, it must be conceded, that in some manner there is found among the divine an order of nature, just as the first reasons show; the third,[4] however, is deficient, because the name, "cause", is not found among the divine in a proper (sense) [proprie], according to the Latins.

What is objected in the proposed is clear, because the order is not of the Nature as of a thing ordered.

2. There is also clear, what is objected concerning the Divine[5] "Essence", because it is an absolute name and does not convey a reckoning of origin.

5. The last[6] is clear, because there is no order of nature There, by which the One (is) prior to the Other, but (there is an order) by which the One (is) out of the Other.

SCHOLIUM

I. This question seems to have arisen from the phrase of St. Augustine, cited in Master (Peter's text) here in ch. 3 and in the first argument of the fundament (of this question), that among the divine there is said (to be) *an order of nature* [ordo naturae]. Which if this is understood in that sense, which *the Nature itself* be ordered, would be without a doubt false, since in the Nature there is neither relation nor an order; however, if it is understood, to the extend that the Nature is the *reason for ordering*, it can be understood in a sane sense. For the order of origin, which is among the Father and the Son, is through the Nature. And from Alexander (of Hales) it must be noted, that "*nature*" is said in one manner, "*essence*" in another manner, because "nature" adds above "essence" the reckoning of *productive virtue* or *of a principle of acting*, and by reason of this connotation there can be said (to be) an order of nature. Others understand "order of nature" in the sense of a natural origin, not a voluntary (one). On the twofold signification of the genitive, which is the foundation of the response, see p. 374, footnote 12.

II. In the principal matter all agree; however, (Bl. John Duns) Scotus (loc. cit. below) with not a few others, both ancient and modern, departs in his manner of speaking from all the others by asserting, that the *order* of origin conveys also a habitude according to a *prior and posterior*, which however, is not (one) of *duration*. On the reasons, for which he speaks in this manner, see Rada, controversy 5; Macedo, collation 8, difference 4, section 1. But the Seraphic (Doctor) together with St. Thomas, Richard (of Middleton) and very many others, does not admit the terms "*prior*" and "*posterior*" among the divine. — Alexander of Hales, SUMMA., p. I, a. 46, n. 2. — (Bl.) Peter of Tarentaise, here in q. sole, a. 5. — Richard of Middleton, here in q. 4. — Giles the Roman, the same as in the preceding question. — Henry of Ghent, SUMMA., a. 52, q. 2; a. 54, q. 5, n. 12, and q. 6, nn. 26 and 34. — (Gabriel) Biel, SENT., Bk. I, d. 9, a. 3.

DOUBTS ON THE TEXT OF THE MASTER

DOUBT I

In this part, there are doubts about the text (of Master Peter), and first one doubts concerning the first reason, which Master (Peter) posits: *All which the Father has, the Son has*: therefore, *as much power as the Father has, the Son has*. That argument of his does not seem to be valid, because *what* is changed into *how much*; for "*all*" distributes (logically) for "the Substance", but "*how much*" means "a quantity".

I RESPOND: It must be said, that although such a manner of arguing would not be valid, if quantity and the substance differed, yet, where these are the same, (the truth of the argument) has an omnimodal

necessity; and because this (identity) is[7] among the divine, for that reason the argument is a good one.

Yet it can be said, that the aforesaid argument is in any subject [materiam] good. For someone is not said to have only that which pertains to his substance [habere solum substantialia], but also properties: therefore, it follows, since "*all*" distributes (logically) for "all things had" [omnibus habitis],[8] that He has also properties: therefore, since One has no power, which the Other does not have, therefore, one can (do) nothing, which the Other cannot (do): therefore, if One is omnipotent, the Other (is) also; and thus it is clear, that this (verse) is not a figure of speech, because "*all*" does distribute (logically) for "things of all kinds".[9]

---

[1] The Vatican edition, together with very many mss., has *there is not accepted* [accipitur], but the other codd., such as G H Z aa bb etc., with ed. 1 and the common usage of language, withstand this.

[2] Here in ch. 3, near the end: Nor when the Son is said (to be) begotten from the Father, is there shown an inequality of Substance, but (rather) an order of nature, not by which the One would be prior to the Other, but by which the One is out of the Other.

[3] From many mss., such as A C F G H I L O R S T W etc., and ed. 1, we have supplied *of nature* [naturae], and, a little below this, from nearly all the codd. and ed. 1, we have supplied *for that reason* [ideo]. Next, cod. V has *there can be no goodly order There* [quin bene posit ibi esse ordo].

[4] From the older manuscripts and edition 1 there is absent *reason* [ratio], which the Vatican edition adds here.

[5] Many codices, just as in the objection itself, also omit here *the Divine* [divina], in place of which edition 1 has "*nature*" *and* [natura et].

[6] In codex Y there is added also [etiam]. Next, after *prior* [prior] edition 1 adds *and/or posterior* [vel posterior].

[7] We supply here and in the next clause *is* [est], from nearly all the

manuscripts and edition 1. A little before this in place of *of arguing* [arguendi], not a few codices, such as S W and Y, have *of making an argument* [argumentandi].

[8] The Vatican edition, with only one or the other codex, faultily reads "*all habits*" [omnibus habitibus].

[9] Aristotle, ELENCHAE, Bk. I, ch. 3 (ch. 4), defines the fallacy of a figure of speech thus: « But those which are on account of a figure of speech, when occur (on account of the similitude of one saying with another) the not-same is interpreted as the same, such as the masculine as the feminine, and/or the feminine as the masculine, and/or that which is between these (that is the neuter) as one or the other of these, and/or again "what kind" as "how much", and/or "how much" as "what kind", and/or doing as suffering » etc.. — A (logical) distribution of the term "*all*" [omnis] can be done in a twofold manner, namely for "*each of the genera*" [pro singulis generum], i. e. for "each individual", which is contained under the same genus and under the same species, and for "*genera of each*" [pro generibus singulorum], i. e. for "only the genera and/or species", but not for the individuals contained under the genera and/or species.

DOUBT II

Likewise, is asked concerning this which (St. Augustine) says: *He, who accepts, cannot be unequal to Him, who has given.* For it seems that he says the false, because if this, since every creature is accepting, none would be unequal to God; but this (is)[1] false: therefore, also the first.

I Respond: It must be said, that (St.) Augustine does not speak generally[2] of anyone accepting or of any manner, but of that which accepts all; and such a one accepting cannot be unequal.

DOUBT III

Likewise, is asked of the other reason: *If he could not, therefore, He was impotent.* For it seems that he argues badly, because similarly could it be argued of the Son and the Holy Spirit: if He could not produce an equal Son: therefore, etc..

I Respond: It must be said to this, that generation is the competence [competit] of naught but the Hypostasis of the Father, just as has been touched upon elsewhere;[3] for that reason (the argument) is not valid, nor is it similar.

DOUBT IV

Likewise, is doubted concerning the other part of the authority,[4] because that argument does not seem to be valid: *He could produce an equal, and He did not produce or beget: therefore, He was envious,* because it can similarly[5] be argued: 'He could make that creature better, and He did not: therefore, He envies (it)'. *If you say*, that envy always considers a peer and/or superior, just as (St.) Gregory says on that (verse) in the fifth (chapter) of Job:[6] *The small does envy slay*; it is then objected, that if He would have begotten a lesser Son, envy would have had no place there: therefore, it seems that that solution does not solve (the objection). *Likewise*, it is not valid among creatures: 'this craftsman could make that thing better and did not: therefore, he was envious'; for what reason, therefore, does it hold[7] in God?

I Respond: It must be said, that the envy of a craftsman producing is not attained in the production of an unequal and/or less good thing, unless[8] where the thing from its own nature requires [egixit]

that it be such; for then there is necessarily concluded, that either the one producing could not, or envied, if he could and did not produce, because he did not do, as he ought have. And since a son for this by which he is a son, is bound [natus] to perfectly imitate, if one does not beget a son in perfect imitation, one concludes, that either the one producing was impotent, or he is envious. And for that reason it is clear, that it is not similar concerning the Creator and the creature, a chest [arca] and a craftsman.[9]

DOUBT V

Likewise, is doubted concerning the third reckoning, which (St. Augustine) makes: '*If a man, as father, could beget a son equal to himself,* therefore, *God also* (could)', because this argument is not valid: 'a man has another man equal to himself and/or could have one: therefore, also God similarly'; since God of His own nobility has this, that no one can be equal [aequari] to Him; and thus the reckoning of (St.) Augustine does not seem to be valid.

I Respond: It must be said, that if equality would posit of necessity among equals a diversity in nature, that then (the reckoning of St. Augustine) would not be valid. But with it supposed, that God would generate a Son connatural to Himself, it of necessity follows, that if a man begot an equal, that much more strongly (could) God. For although it belongs to imperfection to be equal to (another), diverse in nature, yet to be equal to (another), connatural (to one's self), belongs to perfection, otherwise the Divine Nature would be in Someone imperfectly;[10] which, if this is impossible, it is clear that etc..

DOUBT VI

Likewise, is asked of this which he says, that the *question of equality is a "of which kind?" or a "how much?"*. For it seems that he says the false, because "*of what kind*" means a quality, according to this a similitude is attained, not an equality, because « it is proper to a quality that (something) be said to be similar and/or dissimilar to it ».[11]

I Respond: It must be said that there is a speaking of "quality" in a twofold manner: in one manner, insofar as the *one denominating* is meant:[12]

---

[1] In codex V there is added *is* [est].

[2] Trusting in the more ancient manuscripts and edition 1, we have expunged here the added conjunctive particle *and* [et]. A little below this after *all* [omnia], codex O adds, not badly, *naturally* [naturaliter].

[3] Distinction 7, q. 2. — A little before this, we have supplied from the manuscripts and edition 1 *It must be said* [Dicendum].

[4] The Vatican edition, contrary to the manuscripts and edition 1, reads *of the reason* [rationis].

[5] Codex dd has *in the same manner* [eodem modo] for *similarly* [similiter], which also next, having omitted *that* [istam], after *better* [meliorem] adds *than such* [tali]; codex V has *could* [posset] for *can* [potest] and a little after this, for *He envies (it)* [invidit] has *He was envious* [invidus fuit].

[6] Verse 2; Morals, Bk. V, ch. 46, n. 84: For we cannot envy, except those whom we think are better than us in something.

[7] Thus, nearly all the codices, together with edition 1, while the Vatican edition reads *does it not also* [etiam non] for *therefore, does it* [ergo].

[8] We prefer the reading of very many manuscripts, such as F G T Z aa and bb to the reading of the Vatican edition, wherein the former puts *unless* [nisi] for *but* [sed], which reading is already commended by the grammatical construction; some codices, such as S and T, together with edition 1, having omitted the particles *not* [non] and *unless* [nisi], exhibit

the proposition in the affirmative, in which a few codices, such as S and Y in place of *a craftsman producing* [artificis producentis] read *an able craftsman* [artificis potentis]. Next very many codices, such as F G H I X Y cc and dd, together with editions 1, 2 and 3, have *of such (a kind)* [talis] for *such* [tale].

[9] Bl. (now St.) Albertus (Magnus) agrees, here in a. 6. — St. Thomas, here on the text. — Richard of Middleton, here in a. 2.

[10] Codex X reads *imperfect in Someone* [in aliquo imperfecta], which then together with codex V has *and* [et] in place of *which* [quod].

[11] Aristotle, On the Predicaments., ch. "On Quality". Cf. also above d. 19, p. I, a. sole, q. 1, page 342, footnote 6.

[12] Namely some accidental form, according to which, as Aristotle says, On the Predicaments, ch. "On Which Kind", they are indeed said to be of such a kind [quales]. — And a little below this he says the same: They are said (to be) of such a kind, which are denominatively said by the said qualities (v. g. "bright" from "brightness", "grammatical" from "grammar"). — Codex T reads *insofar as it is said as one denominating* [prout dicitur ut denominans]. A little after this (on the next page), from many manuscripts, such as F G H S T W Y Z aa and bb, together with edition 1, we have, before *a disposition* [dispositio], put *it is* [est] in place of *it is said (to be)* [dicitur], and then trusting in very many codices and edition 1, we have substituted *better* [melior] for *more noble* [nobilior].

in another manner, insofar as it is a *disposition of nobility*; and according to this there is attained a greater and lesser nobility, and thus a thing is said (to be) better. And because « in spiritual (things), the same is the greater and the lesser »,[1] for that reason the question of equality looks to "quality", not from the proper reckoning of the name, but from the consequent [ex consequenti], as has been seen.[2]

DISTINCTION XXI

CHAPTER I

In what manner can there be said: "the Father alone", and/or "the Son alone" and/or "the Holy Spirit alone", since They are inseparable. *

Here, there arises a question, drawing its origin from the aforesaid. For it has been said above,[1] that as much as is the Father alone [solus] and/or the Son alone and/or the Holy Spirit alone, so much (are) those Three together, and that Two and/or Three Persons together are not something more than One alone. For that reason (St.) Augustine ask in the sixth book, ON THE TRINITY:[2] « In what manner can these be sanely said, since neither is the Father alone, nor the Son, nor the Holy Spirit, but always and inseparably (is) both the Son with the Father and the Father with the Son and the Holy Spirit with Each; for these Three Persons are inseparable ». To which (St.) Augustine responds thus, in the same book:[3] « We say that the Father alone (is) the Father, not because He is separated from the Son and/or from the Holy Spirit, but saying this we signify, that Those together with Him are not the Father ». For the Father alone is the Father. Which is not said, because He Himself is alone, that is without the Son and/or the Holy Spirit, but through this the Son and the Holy Spirit are excluded from a share in the paternity [a paternitatis consortio]. Thus too when there is said: "the Son alone is the Son", and/or "the Holy Spirit alone is the Holy Spirit", the Son is not divided from the Father and/or the Holy Spirit from Each, but the Father and the Holy Spirit are excluded from a share in the property of the Son [filialis], and the Father and the Son from a share in the property of the procession [processibilis]. Since, therefore, there is said: "as much as is the Father alone, so much those Three together", through that which He is said (to be) *"alone"*, the Father is not separated from the Others, but this is the sense: "the Father alone, that is, the Father, because thus is He the Father, because neither is the Son nor the Holy Spirit as much (as those Three).[4] Similarly, understand, when there is said: "He alone is the Son" and/or "He alone is the Holy Spirit". « Therefore, He alone is said (to be) "the Father" », as (St.) Augustine says in the same,[5] « because naught but He is the Father There », and He alone the Son, because naught but He is the Son There, and He alone the Holy Spirit, because naught but He is the Holy Spirit there.

CHAPTER II

Whether there ought to be said: "the Father alone is God", and/or "the Son alone is God", and/or "the Holy Spirit alone is God"; or whether, "the Father is the only God", "the Son is the only God", "the Holy Spirit is the only God".

After this, there is asked, whether, just as there is said: "the Father alone is the Father", and/or "the Son alone is the Son", it can thus be said: "the Father alone is God", and/or "the Son alone is God", thus also of the Holy Spirit; or, "the Father is the only God" [solus Deus], "the Son is the only God". To which we say, that the Father and the Son and the Holy Spirit is said (to be) and is the One God, and this Trinity together is properly said to be the only God, just as "the only Wise One", "the only Powerful One". But it does not seem that by us, using our own words, there ought to be said: "the Father alone is God", and/or "the Father is alone God", except where the discourse of an authority[6] occurs; and thus do we speak of the Son and the Holy Spirit. Wherefore, (St.) Augustine in the sixth book, ON THE TRINITY[7] says: « Since we have shown, in what manner there can be said "the Father alone" and/or "the Son alone", there must be considered that sentence, by which there is said, that the True God is not only the Father, but the Father and the Son and the Holy Spirit ». Behold, you have, that not only the Father is to be said to be the only True God. Likewise, in the same:[8] « If anyone questions, whether the Father alone is God; in what manner shall we respond, that He is not, except perhaps we speak thus, that indeed the Father is God, but that He is not the only God [solus Deus]? But we do say that the only God [solus Deus] is the Father and the Son and the Holy Spirit ». Behold you also have here, that the Father ought not be said to be "the only God" [solus Deus]; and certain ones want to accept, here (in the text of St. Augustine),[9] solus in the part of the subject (i.e. as "the Father is not alone God"), however, if it is in the part of the predicate, they do concede, that the Father is the only God. But from the words of (St.) Augustine it seems to be shown, that properly the only God ought to be said to be the whole Trinity. And this Trinity, as (St.) Augustine says AGAINST MAXIMINUS,[10] is understood, when the Apostle says: *the blessed and only Powerful One*, and there (where he says): *To the only wise God*; and there (where he says): *To the invisible, the only*

---

[1] (St.) Augustine, ON THE TRINITY, Bk. VI, chs. 8 and 9. — In the immediately following proposition we present the true reading and the one more conformable to the context, which codices X and Z exhibit in its entirety; the Vatican edition together with some manuscripts reads *for that reason the questions of quality looks to equality* [ideo quaestio de qualitate spectat ad aequalitatem], other codices, among which is also codex T, faultily reads *for that reason the question of equality looks to equality* [ideo quaestio de aequalitate spectat ad aequalitatem], which also together with editions 4 and 5, at the beginning of the response incongruously puts *"equality"* [aequalitate] for *"quality"*.

[2] See d. 19, p. I, qq. 1 and 2. — Cf. also Bl. (now St.) Albertus (Magnus), here in a. 6, at the end, and St. Thomas, here in the exposition of the text.

NOTES ON THE BOOK OF SENTENCES
[1] Distinction XIX. — Next, only the Vatican edition and edition 4 read *those Three* [illae tres]; supply *Persons* [personae]. Then the Vatican ed., with a few edd., reads *than one Person alone* [una persona sola].

[2] Chapter 7, n. 9, according to its sense; Master (Peter) extends the question even to the Holy Spirit, just as in the following text.

[3] Ibid., with a few (words) interposed. — At the beginning of the editions, besides the Vatican edition and edition 1, badly and contrary to the codices and original, read: *We say that the only God (is) the Father, not because* [Solum Deum Patrem dicimus, non quia].

[4] Supply with codd. A & C: *as much as those Three* [quantum illis tres].

[5] Chapter 9, n. 10.

[6] The Vatican edition and edd. 2, 3 & 7, reads not well *on authorities* [auctoritatibus] for *of an authority* [auctoritatis].

[7] Chapter 9, n. 10; in which text the Vatican ed. and the other edd., contrary to edd. 1 & 8, the codd. and the original, read badly *there could* [posset] for *there can* [possit]. With the text finished, before *True God* [verus Deus], the Vatican ed. and very many edd., contrary to the codd., badly omit *the only* [solus].

[8] Loc. cit.. — The Vatican ed., and edd. 4 & 6, have (the indicative) *questions* [interrogat] for (the subjunctive) *questions* [interroget], with the other edd., the codd., and (St.) Augustine, contradicting this. Then, after *but that* [sed] the Vatican ed. alone reads *there is not a sole God* [non esse solum Deum].

[9] Editions 2, 3, 7 and 9 read *this (word)* [hoc] for *here (in the text of St. Augustine)* [hic]; and edition 6 reads *"solus"* [solus] for solus [solum]. In each, whatever reading, the words of Master (Peter) are somewhat obscure. We can interpret the reading of *"here"* [hic] in this manner: *"here"*, that is in this negative resolution (of the argument), some distinguish, admitting it, if the word, *"solus"*, is accepted on the part of the subject (i. e. "the Father is alone God"). Similarly, also can be understood the reading of *"this (word)"* [hoc]. On this sentence of Master (Peter), cf. St. Bonaventure, here in Doubt 1. — Next, the Vatican ed. and ed. 4 read *thus* [sic] for *if it is* [si sit], and edd. 3 & 7 read worse *if thus* [si sic].

[10] Bk. II, ch. 12, n. 2. Master (Peter) from this and the next three following

---

* *Trans. note*: In this Distinction, and hereafter, the Latin word solus is rendered in English with 2 distinct adverbial expressions: *alone* and *the only*; the disparate senses of *alone* and *only* used in this English translation follow that reckoning confirmed by St. Bonaventure in his COMMENTARIA on this Distinction, q. v., except wherein Master Peter Lombard reads St. Augustine in the contrary sense.

God. For not of the Father alone are these to be accepted, as Maximinus use to contend and the other heretics (too), but of the Trinity. Just as also that (verse): *He alone has immortality,* because according to the right Faith, the Trinity Itself is the one, only God, the Blessed One, the Powerful One, the Wise One, the Invisible One. Whence (St.) Augustine in the same (book says): « Since the one God is the Trinity, this is for us the solution to the question, that we understand that the only wise, the only powerful God (is) the Father and the Son and the Holy Spirit, who is the one and only God ».

CHAPTER III

In what manner is the Trinity said (to be) God alone, since He is with the spirits and the souls.

But, again, there is asked, in what manner we say that the Trinity itself is God alone, since He is with the spirits and the holy souls. To which (St.) Augustine responds in the sixth book, ON THE TRINITY,[2] thus saying: « We say that the Trinity is God alone, although He is always with the spirits and the holy souls, but we say *"alone"* [solum], because no other than

the Holy Trinity is God. For God is not those (spirits and souls) with that (Trinity) », and/or some other (things), but the Trinity itself only [tantum], not they and/or others, is God.

« Nevertheless, », as (St.) Augustine[3] says, « even if the aforesaid were said of the Father alone, yet the Son and/or the Holy Spirit would not be excluded, because *those Three are One*, just as in the Apocalypse there is read of the Son, that *He has a written name, which no one knows, but He Himself.* For not from this [inde] is the Father and/or the Holy Spirit separated. And when there is said: *No one knows the Father but the Son*, not from this is the Father, and the Holy Spirit, separated, because They are inseparable ». Sometimes also the Father and the Son are named, and the nothing is said of [tacetur] the Holy Spirit; just as the Truth speaking to the Father says:[4] *That they may cognize Thee and Him whom Thou has sent, Jesus Christ, to be the one, True God.* « Why, therefore, », says (St.) Augustine,[5] « did he keep silent [tacuit] concerning the Holy Spirit? Because the consequent is, that wheresoever One is named, such as the Father and the Son, there is understood (to be) adhering to Him, with such a great peace, Peace Himself, although He is not commemorated ». Therefore, with One of Them named, the Rest are also understood; which occurs in very many passages [locis] of Scripture.

COMMENTARY ON DISTINCTION XXI

In what kind of manner are exclusive sayings accepted among the divine?

Here, there arises a question, drawing its origin from the aforesaid.

THE DIVISION OF THE TEXT

Above, Master (Peter) proved the equality of the Persons; here, because in the proof he has said (that) certain[1] reasons (were) doubtful on account of (their) exclusive sayings, he moves those doubts and solves (them). And this part has three parts according to the three doubts, which he proposes.

For, *first*, he asks concerning this expression [locutione]:[2] "as much as is the Father alone, so much the Father and the Son", and this in the first chapter (of his Distinction).

Second, he proposes this (doubt) or asks concerning this: "the Father alone is God", and this he does in the second chapter, there (where he says): *After this, there is asked, whether, just as there is said: 'the Father alone* etc..

Third, he asks concerning this: "the Trinity is the only God"; and this he does in the third chapter, there (where he says): *But again there is asked, in what manner do we say that the Trinity itself.* And in any of those parts of his, he first moves the doubt, second he solves it.[3]

---

passages, excerpted the doctrine (St.) Augustine, that one is always to understand the whole Trinity in the cited passages of Sacred Scripture. The words of (St.) Augustine are these: And through this, which the Apostle (1 Tim. 6:15) says: *The blessed and only Powerful One*, I am not driven to accept it in the manner only of the Father, but of the God, which is the Trinity Itself. Chapter 13, n. 2: *To the only wise God* (Rom. 16:27): And so the God, which is the Trinity Itself, is on this account said (to be) the *only* wise One, because He alone according to His own Substance is wise. Chapter 9, n. 1: *To the invisible, the only God* (1 Tim. 1:17): If he had said *to the only Father*, perhaps the question would be solved with more difficulty [difficilius]; however, he who said *to the only God*, is certainly not against us; and indeed the Only-Begotten in the Form of God and the Holy Spirit in His own Nature is invisible. For the one and only God is predicated by us (to be) the Trinity Itself. Chapter 12, n. 2: *the blessed and only powerful One, the King of kings* etc. (1 Tim. 6:16) [Douay-Rheims Challoner edition, v. 15, not v. 16]: I see nothing here said, that does not befit the Trinity. — (St.) Augustine also teaches elsewhere the same (doctrine), cf. ON THE TRINITY, Bk. I, ch. 6, nn. 10 and 11, from which Master (Peter) changed his last words.

¹ Chapter 13, n. 1. To the final words, codices B C and D add these: Therefore, not the Father alone, nor the Son alone, nor the Holy Spirit alone is God, but the Trinity Itself is the one, sole God.

² Chapter 7, n. 9. — The Vatican edition and edition 4 before *saying* [dicens] omit *thus* [ita].

³ AGAINST MAXIMINUS, Bk. II, ch. 13, n. 1; but Master (Peter) has omitted and/or added not a few (words). The three passages of Sacred Scripture occurring in this text are 1 Jn. 5:7; Apoc. 19:12; and Mt. 11:27, where the Vulgate reads: *And no one knows the Son except the Father, nor does anyone know the Father except the Son* [Et nemo novit Filium nisi Pater; neque Patrem quis novit nisi Filius]. St. Bonaventure (here in Doubt 3), reads in Master Peter, what is found in the codd.: *No one knows the Son except the Father* [Nemo novit Filium nisi Pater].

⁴ John 17:3.

⁵ ON THE TRINITY, Bk. VI, ch. 9, n. 10. The preceding proposition has also been excerpted from this, according to its sense. — At the end the Vatican edition alone adds: *as Augustine explains the same* [ut ibidem amplificat Augustinus].

NOTES ON THE COMMENTARY

¹ From the mss. and ed. 1 we have supplied *certain* [quasdam].

² The Vatican ed. with codex cc, but less well and contrary to all the other codd. and ed. 1, reads *reasons* [ratione]. Next, in the Vatican ed. there is lacking *and this in the first chapter (of his Distinction)* [et hoc primo capitulo], which however is extant in the mss. and ed. 1. A similar omission recurs a little below this, namely, *in the second chapter* [secundo capitulo] and *in the third chapter* [tertio capitulo].

³ The Vatican ed. and cod. cc, yet breaking with the other mss. and ed. 1, read *the doubt is moved, second it is solved* [movetur dubitation, secundo solvitur].

TREATMENT OF THE QUESTIONS

For an understanding of this part, there is, here, this question concerning exclusive sayings [diction-ibus exclusivis]. And, about this, there are asked[1] principally two (things):

First there is asked, whether among the divine an exclusive saying is truly added to a substantial term.

Second, whether it is truly added to a relative term.

And as much as regards the first, two (things) are asked:

First:[2] whether an exclusive saying is truly added to a substantial term on the part of a *subject*.

Second, if it is truly added[3] on the part of a *predicate*.

ARTICLE I

On exclusive sayings, added to a substantial term.

QUESTION I

Whether there is said in a true manner: "God alone is the Father"?

That it[4] is, moreover, truly added to this term "*God*" on the part of a *subject*, is shown in this manner: God has something proper; but (something) "proper" is what is in (something) alone:[5] ergo etc.. And because it is established, that an exclusion is truly added to a substantial term in respect to an *essential* predicate, whence there is rightly said: "God alone creates" [solus Deus creat]; there is asked, whether it is truly added to it in respect to a *proper* predicate or[6] a *relative* term, whether, that is, there is truly said: "God alone is the Father" [solus Deus est Pater]. And that (it is) so, seems:

1. Through its exposition, which is: "*God alone is the Father*", that is 'not other than God is the Father':[7] therefore, 'God alone is the Father'. And that this is its exposition, this is had both from common usage and from the Philosopher,[8] who says, that « "*alone*" is that which is *not with another* ».

2. Likewise, this[9] seems from the convertible, since those two are converted: "nothing besides Peter runs", therefore, "Peter alone runs": therefore, also those two: "nothing besides God is the Father", and: "God alone is the Father". But the first is true, because this is false: "nothing is the Father", and (this false proposition) has no instance except in God:[10] ergo etc..

3. Likewise, from whatsoever there is removed what is in

more, there is removed what is in *less*;[11] but "*to be God*" [esse Deum] is in More than "*to be the Father*"; therefore, from whomsoever there is removed "God", (there is) also (removed) "the Father". But whatsoever thus hold themselves in this manner, from whichsoever there is removed one, also the other, one is precisely predicted of the other, nor does it have an instance: therefore, the Father is precisely predicated of God; but if precisely, therefore, with exclusion: ergo etc..

ON THE CONTRARY: 1. An accidental term implicates its own matter [rem] about its own subject — as is clear, when there is said: "a white man runs", about this term "*man*" there is implicated whiteness — therefore, similarly with there is said: "God alone is the Father", about "*God*" there is implicated *solitude*. But (St.) Hilary[12] says, that « God is not to be confessed (to be) solitary »: ergo etc.. And that reckoning of his concludes, that it cannot be truly added, neither with a *proper* nor a *common* predicate.

2. Likewise, it is shown, that (an exclusive term) cannot be truly added in respect to a *common* predicate, as when there is said: "God alone creates". For this name, "*God*", of itself has a quasi indefinite supposition in respect to the Persons,[13] therefore, it renders the saying true for Any: but for Any it is false — for this is false: "the Father

---

[1] The Vatican edition, together with only a few codices, reads *are to be asked* [quaerenda sunt].

[2] Many codices, with edition 1, read *The first is* [Primum est].

[3] Codex I adds *to this term* [huic termino].

[4] Supply: the exclusive saying "*alone*"; the Vatican edition omits the particle *moreover* [autem] and adds *the word, "alone"* [ly solus], but contrary to the testimony of the manuscripts and edition 1.

[5] Porphyry, ON THE PREDICABLES, ch. "On the Proper".

[6] From the more ancient manuscripts and edition 1, we have substituted *or* [sive] for *just as* [sicut].

[7] Very many codices, such as A C G O R U and ee, omit in this proposition the words *that is* [id est], in place of which codices S and Y put *for* [enim]. Codex W omits at the beginning of the proposition the particle *alone* [solus], and in place of *that is* [id est] has *and* [et], a reading not to be spurned, which codex T, corrected by a later hand, conjoins with the reading of the other manuscripts thus: *God alone is the Father, that is, God is the Father and no other than God is the Father* [solus Deus est Pater, id est, Deus est Pater et non alius quam Deus est Pater]. See below, the response to the 3rd. objection, where the same exposition is given.

[8] THE ELENCHAE, Bk. II, ch. 3 (c. 22). — A little above, from many codices, such as A G H I K R X Y aa ee and ff, and edition 1, we have inserted *both* [et] after *is has* [habetur].

[9] In codices V and X there is added *same* [idem], and next in codices S and Y there is put *from* [ex] for *from* [a].

[10] Aristotle, PRIOR ANALYTICS, Bk. II, ch. 26 (ch. 28) says: Moreover, an "instance" is a proposition contrary to the proposition. — Therefore, the sense of the words *and it does not have an instance, except in God* is: the true and contrary proposition to this one: *nothing is the Father* [nihil est Pater] is: *none but (God) or God alone is the Father* [nonnisi seu solus Deus est Pater], which is thus clear, if this: *nothing is the Father* is false, therefore this will also be true: *something is the Father*; therefore, either a creature or God; not a creature or nothing outside of God, as is established; therefore, God alone. — A little before this the Vatican edition, not trusting in many manuscripts, such as A F G H S T X Y etc., and edition 1, has *therefore, God alone (is) the Father* [ergo solus Deus Pater] in place of *and: God alone is the Father* [et: solus Deus est Pater]. [Trans. note: an *instance* here is used in the sense of a *contrary example or evidence*.]

[11] Cf. above d. 19, p. I, q. 4, first opp. arg.. — In this proposition, on the authority of the more ancient mss. and ed. 1, we have expunged the *this* [hoc] after *there is removed* [removetur], which is added in the Vatican ed..

[12] ON THE TRINITY, Bk. IV, n. 18: By us, too, neither is He to be confessed as only "solitary" nor "diverse".

[13] Cf. above d. 4, q. 4. — A little below (on the next page) this the Vatican edition with codex cc, but contrary to all the other codices and edition 1, has *only to One* [solum uni] for *to One alone* [uni soli].

alone creates" — therefore, since every essential predicate convenes with the Three, and not to One alone, in no manner can an exclusive saying be added to a subject in respect to such a common predicate.

3. Likewise, it seems that (it can) not (be truly added) in respect to *a proper* (predicate), because if this is true: "God alone is the Father": therefore, by a simple converse this also: "the Father alone is God"; but that is false: ergo etc.. *If you say*, that it is not converted simply; *on the contrary*: it has an understanding of a universal negative and a particular affirmative (proposition), and each is converted simply: ergo etc..

CONCLUSION

The term " alone" is not said among the divine categorically, so that it be the same sense as "solitary"; but it is said rightly, co-categorically, in respect to both a substantial as well as a personal predicate.

I RESPOND: It must be said, that this saying "*alone*" [solus] can be a *category* [cathegorema]* and/or a *co-category* [syncathegorema].[1] According to which it is a *category*, thus it is an adjectival name [nomen adiectivum], absolutely positing its own matter [rem] about its own substantive, and its own matter is "*solitude*" Whence in this manner,[2] "*alone*" is worth as much as "*solitary*" [solitarius]. And because solitude is in no manner received among the divine as much as regards the Substance, because It is in many Persons, this name, "*alone*", is not received among the divine with substantial terms,[3] as the first reason shows.

However, if it is accepted[4] inasmuch as it is a *co-category*, it thus deprives association and conveys some negation. And in this manner, since some predicate, both substantial and personal, is said[5] precisely of the substantial noun, it is in this manner truly said among the divine and in respect to a *substantial* predicate, as when there is said:

"God alone creates", and in respect to a *personal* (predicate),[6] as when there is said: "God alone is the Father".

1. To that, therefore, which is objected concerning "white", that it posits its own matter about the substantive; it must be said, that it is not similar, according to which this name, "*alone*", is held co-categorically [syncathegorematice], because "*white*" is an absolute disposition of a subject, whence it posits absolutely its own matter about the term, but "*alone*" by reason of its negation does not absolutely; and for that reason it does not posit solitude, but a precision.

2. To that which is objected second, that a substantial term ought to *render the expression true*[7] for any Person; it must be said, that a term, to which there is added an exclusion, has a looking-back to the *predicate*, and has a looking-back to the *exclusion*; and though in respect to the predicate it can have a *personal* supposition, as when there is said: "the man alone runs"; yet the rule among the Sophists[8] is, that through a comparison to the exclusive saying such a term has a *simple* supposition, whence in no manner is it allowed to descend (to a supposit). And this is what is said in the book, ON THE RULES OF THE FAITH,[9] that an exclusive saying causes exclusion as much as regards the *genus of the thing* [genus rei], not as much as regards *matter of the genus* [rem generis], because by reason of the common form, which is the *genus of the thing*, not by reason of the supposit, which is the *matter of the genus*.

3. To that which is objected last, that the converse is false; it must be said, that that is not its converse; because this: "God alone is the Father", has the understanding of an affirmative (proposition), namely "God is the Father", and this is converted simply; and (the original proposition) has the reckoning[10] of this negative (proposition): "none other than God is the Father", and this similarly is converted simply; but this is not its converse: "none other than the Father is God", but (rather) this (is): "nothing which is the Father, is other than God". For the same which was subjected in the first (part), ought to be predicated in the second; and in this manner that (objection) is clear.

SCHOLIUM

I. The questions of this Distinction are sufficiently intricate, but were treated, by the theologians of that age after the Master of the Sentences, in the schools commonly with great dialectical subtlety. These serve

to observe the greater propriety of words in regard to the adoration of the Mystery of the Trinity. The Seraphic (Doctor) supposes in this and the following questions, very many things, which in the ancient logic, concerning exclusive sayings,

---

[1] Very many codd., such as B D Q & S, with ed. 1, here and in the following sentences read *categorical and/or co-categorical* [cathegorematica vel syncathegorematica], insofar as, that is, "*alone*" [solus] signifies, by itself without the addition of the other term and/or only joined to the other, something in a determinate manner. A little below this, the Vatican ed., contrary to nearly all the codd. and ed. 1, has *as an absolute* [absolutum] for *absolutely* [absolute].

[2] The Vatican ed. with cod. cc, faultily reads *here* [hic] for *in this manner* [sic]. Next, at the end of this same sentence, cod. I repeats *is worth* [valet].

[3] From the more ancient mss.s and ed. 1, we have supplied *with* and *terms* [cum terminis], which words are absent, less well, from the Vatican ed. and cod. cc. A little before this, cod. bb at *because It is* [quia est] reads *the Substance* [substantia] for *It*, and cod. Y after *Persons* [personis] adds *for that reason* [ideo].

[4] Codex X has (the indicative) *is accepted* [accipitur] for (the subjunctive) *is accepted* [accipiatur].

[5] Codex T has *is predicated* [praedicatur].

[6] In codex V there is repeated *predicate* [predicati]. Next, at the end of the Response, there is added by codex X *that is, He, who is the only God, is the Father* [id est ille qui est solus Deus est Pater].

[7] On this saying see above d. 4, q. 1 in the Scholium, where you will also find more on *personal* and *simple* supposition and on the *(logical) descent*, of which the Seraphic Doctor speaks a little below this.

[8] Understand (this) in the non-pejorative sense, that is, those men, who were learned in and doctors of logic; it occurs in the same sense in St. Thomas, SUMMA, p. I, q. 31, a. 3, in reply to n. 3. — The rule, which the Seraphic Doctor adduces, is found in the SUMMULA of Peter of Spain, in the "Tract on Suppositions", in the subdivision on simple supposition, where he adduces this example: « "Every animal besides man is irrational"; there that term "*man*" has a simple supposition, because it is not licit that a (logical) descent be made under it; whence it does not follow: 'every animal besides man is irrational, therefore, every animal besides this man is irrational » etc.. — A little below this edition 1 reads *a confused, immobile* [confusam immobilem] for *simple* [simplicem]; se Peter of Spain loc. cit., and not that *a confused, immobile supposition* is also said to be *a (supposition) only confused* [confusam tantum], to which is opposed the *confused mobile or distributive (supposition)* [confuse mobilis su distributiva].

[9] Alan of Lille, in his book, THEOLOGICAL RULES, rule 29.

[10] The Vatican edition, not trusting in the manuscripts and edition 1, reads *(the original proposition) also has the understanding* [habet etiam intellectum] for *and (the original proposition) has the reckoning* [et habet rationem].

---

* *Trans. note*: Here in the critical text there was faultily written categorema(tice) and syncategorema(tice) instead of cathegorema(tice) and syncathegorema(tice), which is corrected in Sent., Bk. IV, d. 1, p. II, Doubt 3, footnote 1, and from Peter of Spain, SUMME LOGICALES.

concerning their species and concerning the five rules to be observed in their exposition, used to be handed down with greater subtlety than utility. Let it suffice to note these few.

1. *An exclusive saying* is that, in which either the *subject* and/or the *predicate* is affixed with exclusive particles, such as *only* [tantum], *alone* [solum], *no more than / no less than* [dumtaxat] etc.. If the exclusive sign affixes the *subject*, then the proposition signifies, that the predicate convenes only with that subject, but not with other subjects, v. g. "only man is risible". However, if the exclusive particle affixes the *predicate*, then (the proposition) signifies, that only that predicate, having excluded all others, convenes with this subject, v. g. "a proud man loves no one but himself".

2. Every exclusive, affirmative proposition is expounded through two propositions, one of which affirms the predicate of the subject, but the other excludes either every other supposit from a share in the predicate, and/or (excludes) another predicate from the subject. Thus the proposition: "God alone is the Father", is thus expounded: 'God is the Father, and nothing, which is not God, is the Father'. Cf. here the solution to n. 3.

3. About the other exclusive terms, such as *only* [tantum] and *at no more than / no less than* [dumtaxat], there is no difficulty, because they do not have no other sense, but the exclusive. However, the term "*alone*" [solus] has an equivocal sense. For it can be understood either *categorically* [cathegorematice], i. e. as signifying through itself something, and then "*alone*" is the same as "*solitary*"; and/or co-categorically [syncathegorematice], when as an adjective it has been adjoined to some substantive. In the first sense it does not make the proposition exclusive nor is it in any manner admitted among the divine. In the second sense it makes the proposition exclusive and it can be added to an essential term (such as "God"), which it posits as a subject in respect to either an essential or personal predicate, which befits God alone.

4. The *conversion* of a proposition is the inversion of the extremes of the proposition, such that, with the truth of the proposition itself retained, from the predicate there is made a subject and from the subject a predicate. Of this conversion there is distinguished a threefold species, namely, *simple*, *per accidens*, and *through contraposition*. Various rules are given in logic, to make this conversion in the proper manner.

II. To explain the solution to n. 2, the words of St. Thomas (SUMMA., I, q. 31, a. 3, in reply to n. 3) can serve: « As the Sophists say: an exclusive saying immobilizes the term, to which it is adjoined, so that there cannot come to be under it a descent on behalf of any of the supposits. For it does not follow: 'man alone is a rational, mortal, animal', therefore '(man) alone (is) Socrates' ». — In the same solution there remains the difficulty, which Brülifer moves here, that in the one and same proposition the same term according to a twofold respect, that is, to the exclusion and to the predicate, cannot have a *simple* supposition (or an excluding descent to the supposits) and a *personal* supposition. To this it must be said, that an exclusive proposition virtually contains two propositions, as has been said above, and which St. Bonaventure does not say, the same (proposition) actually [actu] has a simple and a personal supposition, namely by reason of the matter. In regard to the terms "*simple*" and "*personal*" supposition, cf. d. 4, q. 1, in the Scholium.

III. In the conclusion all agree. — Alexander of Hales, SUMMA., p. I, q. 66, n. 3, a. 2, and the end. — (Bl. John Duns) Scotus, on this and the following 3 questions, here in each version, in q. sole. — St. Thomas, here in q. 1, a. 1, quaestiuncula 2; SUMMA., I, q. 31, a. 3. — Bl. (now St.) Albertus (Magnus), here in a. 3; on this and the following articles, SUMMA., p. I, tr. 9, q. 40, m. 2. — (Bl.) Peter of Tarentaise, here in q. sole. aa. 1 and 2. — Richard of Middleton, here in q. 4. — Giles the Roman, here in 1st. princ., q. 3, collateral 1. — Henry of Ghent., on this and the following questions, SUMMA., a. 75, q. 5. throughout. — Durandus (of Saint-Pourçain), on this and the following 3 questions, here in aa. 1 and 2. — (Bl.) Dionysius the Carthusian, on this and the following 3 questions, here in q. sole. — (Gabriel) Biel, on this and the following 3 articles, here in q. sole.

QUESTION II

Whether an exclusive saying can be truly added to a substantial term on the part of the predicate?

Second, there is asked, whether an exclusive saying can truly be added to a substantial term on the part of a predicate. And that (it is so), is shown in this manner:

1. (St.) Augustine (says) in the sixth (book) ON THE TRINITY:[1] « We say that the Father is God, but not that He is the only God [solum Deum], however we do say that the only God is the Father and the Son and the Holy Spirit ». *If you say*, that the word solum [ly solum] is understood (above) on the part of the subject (i.e. as "He is not alone God"); it is expressly objected through this which (St.) Augustine says AGAINST MAXIMINUS:[2] « The Trinity Itself is the one, only, True God [unus solus verum Deus] »; it is established that in this "*only ... God*" cannot be a disposition on the part of the subject, because in that manner the discourse would be incongruous: ergo etc..

2. Likewise, this very (thing)[3] seems through an *exposition*: the Trinity is 'God and not other than God', therefore, the Trinity is God alone [solus Deus]; the premises are true: therefore, also the conclusion.

3. Likewise, it seems from reason through a *simile*: when the predicate is not in an other than the subject, truly this saying solus is accepted on the part of the subject; therefore, when a subject is not (logically) beneath [non subest] an other than the predicate, truly it is accepted on the part of the predicate; but this subject "*Trinity*" is not (logically) beneath[4] an other than "God": ergo etc..

ON THE CONTRARY: 1. This saying solus is a disposition of a subject, just as this (logical) sign "*all*"; but when "*all*" is added to a predicate, the expression [locutio] is false and improper: therefore, also[5] similarly, when this saying solus is added.

2. Likewise, this saying solus, added to any term, excludes another (person); whence the sense is: '*the man alone*', that is,[6] 'the man and not another (man)'; but "*another*" looks back to the supposit, and the term is subjected by reason of the supposit, and is predicated by reason of a form: therefore, this saying solus of its own reckoning looks back to the subject: therefore, as a false (term), and improperly, is it added to a predicate.

---

[1] Chapter 9, n. 10; see here the text of Master (Peter), ch. 2.

[2] Book II, ch. 9, n. 1: For the one and only God is by preached by us (to be) the Trinity Itself. See also the text of Master (Peter), ch. 2 near the end.' — Next the Vatican edition, not trusting in the manuscripts and the first six editions, reads *the word* solus [ly solus] for *in this (saying) "the only God"* [in hac solus Deus]. Through the words which follows, namely *the discourse would be incongruous* [esset sermo incongruus], understand: that the discourse would be contrary to the rules of grammar.

[3] From very many mss. and ed. 1, we have supplied *very (thing)* [ipsum].

[4] As required by the codices together with edition 1, and also the context, we have put *is (logically) beneath* [subest] for *is in* [in est]. [Trans. note: here *logically beneath*, means *a supposit of the genus of.*]

[5] In the Vatican edition there is lacking the particle *also* [et], which, however, is exhibited by many manuscripts, such as A F G T Y etc., and edition 1.

[6] The Vatican edition, with codex cc, omits less well *that is* [id est]. A little before this some codices, such as S Y and Z, after *excludes* [excludit] reads *another term* [terminum alium].*

---

* *Trans. note*: Which alternate reading is faulty because, as is seen in this argument and in St. Bonaventure's reply, the sense of *alium* here is *another person*, as is gathered from the masculine form of the adjective used here and in the reply.

3. Likewise, according to which it is added to a predicate, it is either held categorically [cathegorematice], or[1] co-categorically [syncathegorematice]. If categorically, then it is an adjectival name (i.e. as in "a lone God" [solus Deus]) and is not received into the divine; if co-categorically, in this manner it conveys an implicit negation; but a negation antecedes what it negates: therefore, it is necessary, that it antecede the composition, which it negates; but when there is said: Pater est solus Deus"; solus[2] follows the composition: therefore, it seems, that (there) it cannot negate it: ergo etc..

4. Likewise, I ask, what does it exclude,[3] when it is added to the predicate. If (it excludes) another from the predicate, so that the sense is: 'He is God alone', that is 'God and not another'; then there is a superfluity there, because the form of the predicate excludes another disparate form, as much as concerns itself — whence there follows: 'that one is a man, therefore, he is not other than a man' — therefore, it seems, that an exclusive saying causes a superfluity and worthlessness [nugationem]: therefore it is not held exclusively, and thus it seems, that it is held only *adjectively* and that it conveys a solitude about that[4] term "God"; and these (conclusions) are false.

CONCLUSION

An exclusive saying can among the divine be added to a predicate of a substantial term truly, but not properly, except with a determination and adjunction of a partitive term.

I RESPOND: To this some want[5] to say, that this saying solus properly ought not be added to a predicate, but only to a subject; and when it is added to a predicate, the expressions are improper, and then it is the same to say solus and "*only*" [tantum]. But yet, if anyone looks into it, not only with this saying solus, but also[6] with this saying "*only*" will he see impropriety and superfluity. For what is it to say: "the Trinity is only God [tantum Deus]", except "It is God, and not another than God"? But[7] this has been said sufficiently improperly, because by this very (reason), that It is God, there is excluded, that It is not other than God. For if It is God, therefore, It is not other than God, and no heretic ever said, that the Trinity is God, who said, that It[8] was other than

God. Whence, it does not seem that (St.) Augustine said anything great, if he wanted to say this.

And[9] on this account it must be said in another manner, that this saying solus can be added in a twofold manner to a substantial term on [a] the part of a predicate: either per se, or with a numeral or partitive term. Per se it is added improperly; and, if it be added according to language [secundum vocem], yet, according to understanding it stands on the part of the subject. For it is the same to say: "He is a man, a white [est homo albus]",[10] and "He is a white man [est albus homo]". Whence the sense is: 'we do not say, that the Father is alone God [Patrem esse solum Deum]', that is, 'we do not say, that the Father alone is God [solum Patrem esse Deum]'. But if it be posited in another manner, the discourse seems to have a superfluity and impropriety, because this (term) excludes, what was excluded from the nature of the predicate itself.

Sometimes[11] this saying solus is added to a substantial term *with a numeral term*, just as with this term "*one*"; and then it excludes plurality, and in this manner it is added well to a predicate; and thus (St.) Augustine accepts it AGAINST MAXIMINUS, when he says: « The Trinity is the one, only, True God », so that (there are) not more (gods); and then the discourse is true and proper and against the heretics, who used to say, that the Trinity is many gods. And there is conveyed through that term solus a privation of multitude, and thus a discretion,[12] and it is more properly said of the Trinity, that the Trinity is the one, only God, than of the Father, since, however, it could be said of Each, because the Father is the One God, and no one every said, that the Father was many; but of the Trinity or of the Three (Persons) some did say (it); and for that reason there is more congruently said: 'the Trinity is the one, only God'. It must be conceded, therefore, that solus can be truly added to the predicate of a substantial term among the divine, but not properly, unless with a determination and an adjunction of a partitive term.

1. To that, therefore, which is objected, that solus is a disposition of a subject, just as this (logical) sign "*all*"; it must be said, that it is not such a proper disposition of a subject, as this (logical) sign "*all*"; because "*all*" distributes on behalf of supposits [pro suppositis], in virtue of which [pro quibus] the term *is subjected*, not in virtue of which[13] it *is predicated*, at least when (the supposits are) taken together; solus, however, not only is said by reason of the supposit, but [verum] also by reason of form, because it excludes *another* and also[14] (because) it can exclude *another*.

---

[1] Codex V adds *is held* [tenetur]. A little below this after *if co-categorically* [si syncathegorematice] very many manuscripts together with editions 1, 2, 3 and 6, add *but* [sed]. Then codex T has *implies* [imiplicat] for *conveys* [importat].

[2] We follow the greater number of mss., such as H I M N P Q Z etc., and edition 1, by putting *solus*, which some codd., such as O R & U omit (in favor of *it* as the subject), but others, such as C L S Y substitute for it *in this manner it* [sic], codex T *here it* [hic], the Vatican edition with cod. cc reads falsely *it does not follow* [non sequitur]. Next, cod. Z with edition 1, with transposed words, reads *therefore, it does not seem, that it can negate it* etc. [ergo non videtur, quod possit ipsam negare etc.].

[3] Edition 1 has the indicative *does it exclude* [excludit].

[4] As required by the more ancient manuscripts and edition 1, we have substituted *that* [istum] for *this* [hunc], and next after *and* [et], we have expunged the added *so* [sic].

[5] The Vatican edition, together with the more recent codex cc, has *wanted* [voluerunt].

[6] From very many mss., such as G H I P Q Z ee ff and edition 1, we have added *also* [etiam]. A little below this after *For what* [Quid enim], the Vatican edition, together with codex cc, adds *another* [alium], which however, is lacking in the other codices and edition 1. Then after *except* [nisi] codex V and edition 1 read *the Trinity* [Trinitas] for *It*.

[7] With the help of the older writings, we have supplied *But* [Sed].

[8] According to the norm of the manuscripts and editions 1, 2, and 3, we have expunged the here added *It* [ipsam: which does not

change the English translation]. A little before this, codex cc and editions 2 and 3 falsely read *because* [quia] for *who* [qui]. Next, the Vatican edition, contrary to nearly all the codices and edition 1, reads *and for that reason* [et ideo] for *Whence* [Unde].

[9] With the more ancient manuscripts and edition 1 favoring it, we have restored the particle *And* [et]. A little after this, in the manuscripts there is wanting the words *on the part of the predicate* [a parte predicati], which certainly are to be supplied.

[10] Aristotle, ON INTERPRETATION, Bk. II, ch. 1: But transposed nouns and verbs, such as "he is a white man" [est albus homo] and "he is a man, a white" [est homo albus], signify the same.

[11] We follow the more ancient codices and edition 1, by putting *Sometimes* [Aliquando] for *In another manner* [Aliter], and next after *just as with* [sicut cum] by adding *this* [hoc], and then by substituting *thus* [ita] for *in this manner* [sic].

[12] The Vatican edition, together with only one or the other codex, reads *distinction* [distinctio], which also a little after this, not trusting the manuscripts and the first six editions, omits these words *because the Father is the One God* [quia Pate rest unus Deus].

[13] In very many manuscripts and edition 1 there is lacking *in virtue of which* [pro quibus], and, contrariwise, in codices aa and bb there is had *but not on behalf of those, in virtue of which* [sed non pro illis, pro quibus].

[14] Not a few codices, together with edition 1, omit *also* [etiam], for which some falsely exhibit *not* [non].

2. And though this the following is clear, because it does not always exclude *another* in the masculine sense [masculine], but it can also exclude *another* in the neuter sense [neutraliter], and/or even a *plurality*, when it is added to a numeral term, as has been seen.

3. To that which is asked, whether it is held co-categorically, and/or categorically,[1] insofar as it is a name conveying a denominating form, so that <u>solus</u> is the same as "*solitary*"; it must be said, that (it is held) co-categorically. What is objected, that it follows the composition; it must be said, that <u>solus</u> conveys two (ideas) in itself, namely, the understanding of this name, "*another*", and the understanding of a negation. As much as regard the understanding of this name, "*another*", it looks back to the term, about which it is posited, and it follows the verb [actum]; as much as (it looks back) to the understanding of the negation, it precedes (the verb according to understanding); and this is not unfitting as much as regards the *diverse* preceding and following. And[2] this is clear to the one expounding it. For if I will say: "I see Peter alone" [video solum Petrum], the sense is: 'I see Peter and I do not see another than Peter'. Similarly, it must be understood in the proposed (objection).

4. To that which is asked, what does it exclude, when it is added to a predicate; it must be said, that when it is added without a determination, it excludes another form; and then in truth there is a superfluity and impropriety there, yet[3] nevertheless (also) a truth. But when it is added with a partitive term, then it excludes plurality; and then the expression can have truth. For the Father and the Son are the One God and not many (gods), and thus (are) the one, only God.

SCHOLIUM

I. The first opinion posited in the body (of question) asserts, that all the propositions, in which the word <u>solus</u> is posited in the predicate, to be improper, and that then this word <u>solus</u> is equivalent to the term "*only*" [tantum]. Against this sentence the Seraphic Doctor argues, that then the words of St. Augustine (cited) in the fundament would be very improper, and that moreover, there would be a superfluity there. How by distinguishing the twofold manner, by which <u>solus</u> can be added to a predicate, he propounds and corroborates his own opinion, he explains more below in Doubt 1. Yet, some, again, distinguish the first member of his distinction, when <u>solus per se</u> is added to a predicate, and they admit in some sense that (it has) been properly said. Thus St. Thomas (here in q. 2, a. 1), Bl. (now St.) Albertus (Magnus) and (Bl.) Peter (of Tarentaise). However, in the SUMMA., I, q. 31, a. 3, in reply to n. 2, the Angelic (Doctor) says that all these propositions are improper, « unless perhaps on the part of the predicate there be understood some implication, so that there be said: "the Trinity is the God, who is the sole God" ». (Bl.) Dionysius the Carthusian (here in q. sole) judges, that St. Thomas in his own COMMENTARY from St. Bonaventure « dissents but a little. Moreover, it seems in this matter that (division) of Bonaventure is more plain and more apt ». This he strives to prove by an argument that is not to be spurned.

II. Besides the authors cited, cf. Alexander of Hales, SUMMA., p. I, q. 66, m. 3, a. 2. — Bl. (now St.) Albertus (Magnus), here in a. 3 and 4. — (Bl.) Peter of Tarentaise, here in q. sole, a. 5. — Richard of Middleton, here in a. 5. — Giles the Roman, here in 2nd. princ., q. sole, collateral 1 and 2.

ARTICLE II

On exclusive sayings, added to a relative term.

Consequently, in the second place is the question concerning the Second Article of the question, namely, whether an exclusive saying can be added to a relative term. And, about this, two (things) are asked:

First, there is asked, whether an exclusive saying is added to a personal term in respect to a proper predicate.

Second, whether it is truly added to a personal term in respect to a common predicate, so that there be truly said: "the Father alone is God".

QUESTION I

Whether the exclusive saying, <u>solus</u>, is truly added to a personal term in respect of a proper predicate?

That it is truly added in respect to a proper predicate, so that, namely, this is true: "the Father alone is the Father" [solus Pater est Pater], seems:

1. Through (what St.) Augustine (says) in the sixth (book) ON THE TRINITY:[4] « In that Trinity the Father alone is said (to be) "the Father", because None but He is the Father There ».

2. Likewise, this seems through the exposition, because the Father is a Person, and no Other is the Father: therefore, this is true: "the Father alone is "the Father".

3. Likewise, nothing is more proper to anything, than what is the same as it in thing and reckoning [idem sibi re et ratione]; but the Father is the same to Himself in thing and reckoning: therefore, ("the Father") is most properly said of Him; but what properly convenes with anything, convenes with (it) alone: therefore, "the Father" is said of the Father alone.

---

[1] We prefer the reading of not a few mss., such as H X aa & bb, in which there is more congruently added the word *categorically* [cathegorematice].*

[2] From the mss. & ed. 1, we have supplied *And* [et], and trusting in the more ancient codd. & ed. 1 we have substituted *Peter* [Petrum] for *Conrad* [Conradum].

[3] The Vatican edition, with the manuscripts and editions 1, 2, 3 and 6 striving against this, reads *there is* [est] in place of *yet* [tamen].

[4] Chapter 9, n. 10. See there the text of Master (Peter), ch. 1, where in this text there is had, in agreement with the original and codex Z, *naught but* [non nisi] for *None but* [nullus nisi],

[5] Cf. Porphyry, ON THE PREDICABLES, ch. "On the Proper".

---

* *Trans. note*: Here in the critical text there was faultily written <u>syncategorematice</u> and <u>categorematice</u> instead of <u>syncathegorematice</u> and <u>cathegorematice</u>, which is corrected in Sent., Bk. IV, d. 1, p. II, Doubt 3, footnote 1, and from Peter of Spain, SUMME LOGICALES.

ON THE CONTRARY: 1. « *"Alone"* [solus] », as the Philosopher[1] would have it, « is the same as *"not with another"* [non cum alio] »; but it is impossible, that the Father not be with Another: therefore, when it is added to this term *"the Father"* and/or to the personal term of another (Person), it is always a false expression.

2. Likewise, solus excludes "another" [alium]: but by one He is "God", by another He is "the Father":[2] therefore, (the exclusive saying solus) added to this term *"the Father"* excludes "God": therefore, if this is true: "the Father alone is the Father", also this similarly: "God is not the Father"; which if this is false: therefore, also the first.

3. Likewise, solus excludes[3] this relative (adjective/pronoun) alius [alius], but thus alius is a relative (adjective) of diversity, which nevertheless implies some identity; whence it follows: 'this one [iste] goes with another [alio] man, therefore, this one is a man.' If, therefore, (solus as a relative pronoun) excludes alius from that which is *"the Father"*,[4] either the one [alium] (is) *"the Father"*, or the other [alium] (is) *"God"*; but in whatsoever manner it be said, the expression is false and an implication of the false: ergo etc..

CONCLUSION

The term solus among the divine is rightly said in respect to a proper predicate, to the extent it excludes association both in respect to the form of the subject term, and in respect to the predicate, whether in participating, or in co-participating.

I RESPOND: It must be said, that according to which this saying solus is held co-categorically [syncathegorematice], it conveys a privation of association; and the expression is simply true, having excluded that sense, whereby it conveys solitude, because in this manner it is not accepted among the divine, just as has been said above.[5]

For, according to which it conveys a privation of association, it is true, because, since it can convey this in a threefold manner, in any sense the expression is true. For this saying solus can convey a privation of association in respect to the *form of a subject term*,[6] so that there is said *"the Father alone"* [solus Pater], that is, "He who is the Father alone"; and in this manner it has without doubt truth: "the Father

alone is the Father". And/or it can convey a privation of association in respect to a *predicate*, and this in a twofold manner: either in *participating*, such as because it does not convene with another; and it is still true, because this predicate which is *"the Father"* convene with only the Person of the Father; for that property convenes with the Father, such[7] that (it does) with no other; and/or it can convey a privation of association in *co-participating*, as when there is said: "Peter eats alone" and/or "goes to Rome alone" [Petrus comedit solus vel vadit Roman solus], not because another does not go[8] to Rome, and/or does not eat, but because no one is a co-participant with him, though he does participate; and in this manner the expression is still true, because the Person of the Father does not participate and/or co-participate with another (Person) in the property of the paternity. And for that reason, according to which solus is held exclusively, the expression is judged true.

1. To that, therefore, which is objected, that solus is the same as *"not with another"*; it must be said, that that negation does not simply exclude another in co-existing, but (rather) excludes another in respect to the form of the subject and/or predicate;[9] as has been seen. And although the Father does exist with Another and cannot be without Another, yet because He does not communicate the property of the paternity with Another, for that reason the expression has truth simply (speaking).

2. To that which is objected, that by one He is "God", by another He is "the Father"; it must be said, that just as it has been said often,[10] alius means a diversity according to the reckoning of speaking and/or understanding in the proposed word; but in the exposition of this saying solus it means a diversity or distinction in the supposit. And because "God"[11] in (its) supposit does not differ from "the Father", nay supposes on behalf of "the Father"; for that reason it does not follow, that an exclusive saying added to "the Father" excludes "God".

3. To that which is objected last, that alius implies some form, according to which it convenes (with the term it modifies);[12] it must be said, that this is not necessary [istud non oportet], that it be a form conveyed through the term (it modifies) — for there truly said: 'a man is (something) other than an donkey [aliud ab asino]' — unless when it comes to that term immediately (proximate), as when there is said "*another donkey*" [alius asinus], it includes a convening in a common nature. But when there is said: "the Father alone" (this) is not to say, that "*the Father*

---

[1] THE ELENCHAE, Bk. II, ch. 3 (ch. 22). — A little below this not a few codices, such as T V and Y, read *when* [cum] for *when* [quando].

[2] (St.) Augustine, ON THE TRINITY, Bk. VII, ch. 6, n. 11, and Sermon 1, on Psalm 68, n. 5. See above d. 19, p. II, q. 2, in reply to n. 4. — Next to *added* [addita] supply *the exclusive saying* solus [dictio eclusiva], and/or add together with codex aa *this saying* [haec dictio] at the beginning of the argument after *Likewise* [Item]; we judge to be less congruous the correction made in codex T by a later hand, by which, namely, there is read *with an exclusive saying added ... it excludes God* [addita dictione exclusive etc.].

[3] We judge the most common reading of the manuscripts and of the editions (except edition 1), by which there is had *includes* [includit], though considered in itself, can be explained (cf. response to n. 3, in the preceding question), yet having considered the end of this argument, it is less apt and incomplete. A little below this, after the first *therefore* [ergo], codex W adds the particle *also* [et].

[4] Codex V has *term "the Father"* [termino Pater] for *which is "the Father"* [quod est Pater], which also next after *it be* [dicatur] adds *always* [semper]. Then, from the more ancient manuscripts and edition 1, we have substituted *an implication of the false* [implication falsi] for *the implication false* [implication falsa].

[5] Here in a. 1, q. 1.

[6] In very many codices, there is lacking less well *subject* [subiecti], better in codex X, where having omitted *term* [termini], *subject* [subiecti] is retained.

[7] On the authority of the mss. and ed. 1, we have deleted the particle *and* [et], which in the Vatican term had been prefixed to *such* [ita].

[8] The Vatican edition, breaking with the manuscripts and the first six editions, reads *go* [eat]; yet very many manuscripts read here *go* [vadit] and a little below his *eat* [comedit] (in the indicative).

[9] Edition 1, together with the Vatican edition, adds *in co-participating* [in comparticipando], which however, is absent from the manuscripts and from the other five first editions. Next after *with* [cum] the Vatican edition, not trusting in very many codices and editions 1, 2 and 3, on account of what follows puts *Others* [aliis] for *Another* [alio], in place of which a few codices, such as S Y and Z, exhibit *the Son* [Filio].

[10] Distinction 6, Doubt 2, and chiefly d. 19, p. II, a. 2, in reply to n. 4. — The Vatican edition, together with one or the other codex, has *above* [supra] for *often* [supra], and contrary to all the codices and edition 1, has alium in place of alius.

[11] In codex T there is added *with "the Father" means no distinction* [cum Patre nullam dicit distinctionem].

[12] A few codices, such as Y and cc, read *it communicates* [communicat]. Next, codex Y has *it* [illud] for *it* [istud].

and not another Father", but *"the Father and not another than the Father"*; and for that reason there is not conveyed a convening in the form of the property of the paternity with anotherness, but it is sufficient, that there be another Person — for the Father is a[1] Person — and/or even another essence: and that (saying alius) excludes this which is *"alone"* [solus]; and thus that is clear.

SCHOLIUM

I. For an understanding of the 3rd argument of the Contrary and its solution, it must be noted first, that the term alius can convey a distinction either about a form (as in "another *God*"), and/or about a supposit (as in "another *Father*"). Second, alius can be added to any term either immediately and/or by means of some proposition, as illustrated by the example in the text. In the first case it posits a specific identity between the extremes; but in the second case it does not convey this identity.

II. The authors (cited here) do not dissent in the substance of the solution. St. Thomas, here in q. 1, a. 1, quaestiuncula 2. — Bl. (now St.) Albertus (Magnus), here in a. 1. — (Bl.) Peter of Tarentaise, here in q. 1, a. 1. — Richard of Middleton, here in q. 2.

QUESTION II

Whether the exclusive saying, solus, is truly added to a personal term in respect of a common predicate?

Second, there is asked, whether an exclusive saying is truly added to a personal term in respect to a common predicate,[2] so that there is truly said: "the Father alone is God" [solus Pater est Deus]. And that (it is) so, is seen *by authority* and *by reason*.

1. *By authority*, in this manner: the Church sings: « Thou alone the Most High, Jesus Christ » [Tu solus altissimus, Iesus Christe]:[3] and that: « to God the Father be the glory and to His only Son » [Deo Patri sit gloria, eiusque soli Filio], and many completely similar (verses) are found.

2. Likewise, in the eleventh (chapter of the Gospel of St.) Matthew:[4] *No one knows the Son but the Father,* but "*no one but the Father*" and "*the Father alone*" are convertible [solus Pater convertuntur]: therefore "the Father alone knows", and this predicate (i.e. "knows") is essential: ergo etc..

3. Likewise, *by reason* it seems, because an exclusive saying added to anything does not exclude but another; but the Three Persons do not have an anotherness in respect to a substantial predicate: therefore, with it added to One, it does not exclude Another in respect to such a predicate; but if it does not exclude, the expression is true: ergo etc..

4. Likewise, an exclusive saying added to anything does not exclude what is in it as a *part*, such as added[5] to "Peter", it does not exclude "Peter's foot": therefore, since the Son is in the Father by a greater identity than a foot (is) in Peter, with it added to "the Father", it does not exclude "the Son".

ON THE CONTRARY: 1. Neither "the Father alone" nor "the Son alone" nor "the Holy Spirit alone" is "God": therefore, it is not truly added in respect to a common term.

2. Likewise, every proposition, in which the predicate is common to the subject, with an exclusion added to the subject, is false, because no such convenes precisely with the subject: but such is this (saying) and (those) completely similar: "the Father alone is God": ergo etc..

3. Likewise, an exclusive saying added to anything excludes everything which posits an association with the term; and this is clear, because it deprives association; but the Son posits an association with the Father: whence "*the Father with the Son*" is "*the Father with Another*".

4. Likewise, an exclusive saying excludes every other, and most of all the opposite; but relatives are one by difference of (their) opposition;[6] therefore, added to one relative (term) it excludes the other: therefore, added to "the Father" it excludes "the Son"; and, if this, all such (expressions) are false.

CONCLUSION

An exclusive saying added to a personal term in respect to a common predicate can then be admitted, if it removes the form of the subject from others; but not, if it removes the form of the predicate.

I RESPOND: It must be said, that[7] here there is a twofold position. For certain ones concede simply and without distinction these (expressions) and (those) completely similar: "the Father alone is God" [solus Pater est Deus]; and their position is, that an exclusive saying added to one of the relatives does not exclude the rest. And the reason for this position is, that (an exclusive saying)[8] does not exclude what is consequent to the term and (what) is understood in the term, such as added to "man" it does not exclude "animal". But one of the relatives is understood in the other and is consequent to the other: therefore, added to one, it does not exclude the other. And, if one opposes, that "*alone*" [solus] excludes the opposite, they say, that there are relatives belong both[9] to a difference of *opposition* and *of being* [entis]: *of opposition*, according to which (they are compared) to *the same*; and

---

[1] The Vatican edition, with codex cc alone, here repeats *another* [alia]. Next from very many manuscripts and edition 1, we have substituted *that (saying alius)* [illa] for *this (other essence) of His* [ista].

[2] In very many manuscripts there is lacking *predicate* [praedicati], in place of which codex X, together with edition 1, has *term* [termini], but contrary to what has been predetermined in the exordium of this article.

[3] In the hymn of the Angels: *Gloria in excelsis Deo* etc.. — The next following strophe is found in the BREVIARIUM ROMANUM, at the end of the hymn for Prime (i. e. *Iam lucis orto sidere*).

[4] Verse 27.

[5] The Vatican edition, contrary to the codices and edition 1, has *such as that if an exclusive saying is added* [ut si diction exclusive addi-

tur], and a little below this, before the (perfect) participle *added* it adds *an exclusive saying* [diction exclusiva].

[6] Cf. Aristotle, ON THE PREDICAMENTS, ch. "On Opposites". — Next, the majority of the codd. have *another (Person)* [alium] for *the other (term)* [aliud], in which reading understand *relative (term)* [terminum relativum].

[7] From the manuscripts and edition 1, we have supplied *It must be said, that* [Dicendum, quod].

[8] Understand: an exclusive saying. A little below this, as required by very many mss. and ed. 1, we have inserted after *and is consequent* [et consequitur] the preposition* *to* [ad].

[9] In the Vatican ed. there is lacking *both* [et], which however, is exhibited by the mss. and edd. 1, 2, 3 & 6. A little below this after *the*

---

* *Trans. note*: here the original footnote, of the Critical Edition, reads faultily *proposition*.

in this manner (the exclusive saying, <u>solus</u>) added to one, it excludes the other; whence it follows: "this One is only the Father, therefore, He is not the Son". According to which[1] they are compared to *diverse* (things), (relatives) belong to a difference *of being*; and in this manner with One posited, there is posited also the Rest; and for that reason One is not excluded by the Other, because an exclusive saying excludes only that[2] other, which is not necessarily concomitant.

But this position does not seem fitting. For an exclusive saying deprives association: therefore it excludes every 'that' which posits (anything) about that association; and for that reason, added to "the Father", it excludes "the Son".

And, on this account, there is another opinion, that an exclusive saying added to "the Father" excludes "the Son"; and this position is more probable. Proceeding according to this position, expressions of this kind are to be distinguished, according to which (St.) Augustine distinguishes (them), and Master (Peter) touches upon;[3] because <u>solus</u> can cause an exclusion in respect to the composition understood about a *subject*, and/or in respect to the *principal* composition. If in the first manner, then the sense is: "*the Father alone is God*", that is, "He who is alone the Father, is God"; and then it removes the form of the *subject* term from the Others, not the form of the *predicate*; and under this sense they are true. And under this sense (St.) Augustine accepts (<u>solus</u>):[4] « The Holy Spirit alone is as much, as is the Father and the Son ».

On the other hand, if it causes an exclusion in respect to the *principal* composition, the expression is false, and all[5] are false, properly speaking, if there is not added a determination, to constrain the exclusion, as is clear, when there is said: « Thou alone the Most High, Jesus Christ, with the Holy Spirit ». Similarly: « To God the Father be the glory and to His only Son » etc..[6]

1. And in this manner the first (objection) is clear.

2. To that which is objected second, that "the Father alone" [solus Pater] is equipollent to this: "*no one but the Father*" [nemo nisi Pater]; it must be said, that it is false, because "*no one*" distributes on behalf of the Nature, not on behalf of a Person;[7] but "*alone*" [solus] is added to the personal term, for that reason it excludes a Person; for that reason properly speaking, this is false: "the Father alone knows the Son", although this is true: "*no one knows the Son but the Father*", because the sense is: "*no one*", that is "no nature,[8] except Him who is of the same Nature, as the Father".

3. 4. To that which is objected, that an exclusive saying excludes another; it must be said, that it excludes every *other (thing)* [aliud] and/or *other (person)* [alius], which is not predicated or subjected, but is associated, whether it be another in form, or in supposit. And since the Father is associated[9] with the Son in respect to a substantial predicate, for that reason in respect to that They exclude one another [excluduuntur invicem]; and because *a part* is not associated, for that reason it is not excluded. Whence a greater and/or lesser identity causes nothing regarding exclusion, but the reckoning of being associated and/or of not being associated (does). And if one objects,[10] that (an exclusive saying) added to a defined (term) does not exclude the definition, and to an antecedent (term), it does not exclude a consequent; it briefly must be said, that if the consequent thus follows, that it does not posit an association, and the definition does not enclose [claudat] in itself (something) diverse, then it does not exclude. However, if it its otherwise, then it does exclude, and opposites are contradictorily implied in the antecedent: whence here a contradiction is implied: "only the Father is". But with this position (St.) Augustine[11] agrees, who denies this (proposition): "the Father alone is God" and (those) completely similar.

SCHOLIUM

I. In the solution to n. 3 and 4, there is again objected: « That an exclusive saying added to a defined (term) does not exclude the definition, and to an antecedent, does not exclude the consequent ». To this St. Bonaventure responds with a distinction. When the consequent is from the reckoning of the antecedent, just as "risible" follows as (something) *proper* to *man*, and the definition is from the reckoning of the defined, such that it adds nothing real, just as "animal" is from the reckoning of "man", then the objection is conceded. For the exclusive addition "*alone*" [solus] added to "man" does not exclude, neither "*animal*" nor "*risible*", when there does not follow: 'a man alone runs, therefore, a risible (animal) does not run'. However, when among each in each case there is a real distinction, just as is among a created father as an antecedent, and his son as a consequent, then the exclusive saying added to the antecedent ex-

cludes the consequent. In God also « even if the Father and the Son are of the same Essence, yet "the Son" is not from the reckoning of "the Father" under the reckoning, whereby He is "the Father" », thus Richard of Middleton, here in q. 3, in reply to n. 3.

II. In the principal sentence all the doctors agree. But St. Thomas in his COMMENTARY (here in q. 1, a. 2) and (Bl.) Peter of Tarentaise (here in q. 1, a. 3) again employ some other distinction, just as in the preceding question. For they want, that if "*another*" [alius] (cf. arguments 3 and 4 throughout this question) is understood in the neuter (i.e. as referring to a discrete being), then « neither the Son nor the Holy Spirit is excluded », and for that reason this expression is true: « the Father by Himself is God » [solus Pater est Deus]. But let this suffice concerning the subtleties here. — Alexander of Hales, SUMMA., p. I, q. 66, m. 3, a. 1. — St. Thomas, <u>loc. cit.</u>, and SUMMA., I, q. 31, a. 4. — Bl. (now St.) Albertus (Magnus), here in a. 2 and 5. — Richard of Middleton, here in q. 3. — Giles (the Roman), here in 1st. princ, q. 2.

---

same [idem], codices O and Z read *they are referred to the same* [ad idem referuntur], codices I aa and bb, together with edition 1 *they are compared to the same* [ad idem comparantur]. Then by *added* [addita] understand: 'the exclusive saying <u>solus</u> added'. Hence the Vatican edition errs a little after this, contrary to the manuscripts and edition 1, by putting *they exclude* [excludant] in place of *it excludes* [exludit].

[1] In a few codd., such as P and Q, there is added *however* [autem].

[2] From the mss. and the first six edd., we have substituted *an exclusive saying excludes only that other* [diction exclusive illud solum aliud excludit] for *that exclusive saying "alone" excludes "the other"* [dictio exclusiva illa solum aliud excludit], in which the reading of the Vatican ed., consequently, the particle *alone* [solum] is considered as the exclusive saying, concerning which the question is, and for that reason exhibits it with italicized letters, but less well. A little before this, the Vatican ed., with the more ancient mss. and ed. 1 striving against this, faultily omits *for that reason* [ideo].

[3] Here, in the text, ch. 1, where the words of (St.) Augustine are also had.

[4] ON THE TRINITY, Bk. VI, ch. 8, n. 9; see above in the text of Master (Peter), d. XIX, ch. 12. — A little before this, after *And* [Et], very many codices together with edition 1 add *in this manner* [sic].

[5] In codex M there is added *such* [tales].

[6] In the Vatican edition and codex cc there is wanting this proposition: *Similarly: « To God the Father be the glory and to His only Son » etc.*, [Similiter: Deo Patri sit gloria eiusque soli Filio etc], which, however, is extant in all the other manuscripts and edition 1.

[7] See the explanation of these words, below, in Doubt 3.

[8] The Vatican edition, together with only one or the other codex, reads *creature* [creatura]; but see below Doubt 1. Next, after *Nature* [naturae], codices H and bb, add *with Him* [cum eo], and then after *as* [ut], codex H adds *is* [est].

[9] Thus some codices, such as I T and Z; the others, together with the Vatican edition, have *are associated* [associantur]. A little below this, after *a greater* [maior], a few codices have *and* [et] in place of *and/or* [vel].

[10] Thus the greater part of the manuscripts, together with edition 1; but all the others read *you object* [obicias]; the Vatican edition has *it is objected* [obiiciatur], which also, next, after *that* [quod], not trusting in the manuscripts and the first six editions, adds *an exclusive saying* [dictio exclusiva], certainly to be supplied.

[11] ON THE TRINITY, Bk. VI, ch. 9, n. 10, here in the text of Master (Peter), ch. 2.

DOUBTS ON THE TEXT OF THE MASTER

DOUBT I

In this part of his (text), there are doubts about the text (of Master Peter), and first there is the doubt [dubitatur] concerning this which Master (Peter) says, that *properly the whole Trinity is the only God*, because it seems that he wants to negate this: « the Father is the only God »; but this seems to be true through the exposition, because the Father is God and not a (person) other than God and/or an other (thing): ergo etc.. *Likewise*, the predicate, which is said of the whole Trinity, cannot be but an essential predicate; therefore, since *the only God* [solus Deus] is an essential predicate[1] — because otherwise it would not be said of the whole Trinity —an essential predicate is also said of each Person singly [singillatim].

I RESPOND: It must be said, that when solus by itself [per se] is added to a predicate, such that it is not understood on the part of the subject, the discourse is improper, whether it be said of the whole Trinity, or of the Father. Nor does (St.) Augustine want to say, that *"the only God"* [solus Deus] is predicated of the whole Trinity, such that (it is) not (predicated) of the Father. But in these expressions: *to God alone the honor and glory*,[2] and (those) completely similar, *"God alone"* [solus Deus] is not accepted on behalf of a unique Person, excluding the other Persons, but on behalf of the whole Trinity, excluding other natures; and Master (Peter) accepts (it) thus, and if (St.) Augustine had[3] wanted to say (this), that this, namely *the only God* [solus Deus], *it would have been predicated* of the Trinity, and not of the Father. But he does want, it to *suppose* for "the Trinity" itself; however, if it supposes for "the Father", it does not precisely suppose for "the Father alone"; and for that reason (St.) Augustine concedes, that the Trinity alone is the only, True[4] God, yet not "the Father alone". Whence also Master (Peter) does not say, that the Father is not "the only God", but that He is not properly said (to be "the only God"). And this has been made manifest, if one looks into (the matter), in what way solus ought to be added to a predicate.[5]

DOUBT II

Likewise, is asked concerning this which (St. Augustine) says: *We say that the Trinity is God alone, although He is always with the Saints*, though He is inseparable from other things and most interior to all: on which account does he say[6] that He is with the Saints more than with others?

I RESPOND: It must be said, that although God is in all and with all, yet He is said specially, to be with the Saints on account of the effect of the indwelling grace, through which they are conformed and become dear and similar to Him. Whence in the eighth (chapter) of Proverbs:[7] *My delights (are) to be with the sons of men*, says the Wisdom of God. Whence *Dominus vobiscum* ("The Lord is with you!") is said to men, not to beasts.

DOUBT III

Likewise, is asked of this expression: *No one* [nemo] *knows the Son but* [nisi] *the Father*, because, since <u>nemo</u> is composed of *not* [non] and *man* [homo], therefore, <u>nemo</u> is the same as *"no man"* [nullus homo]; but an exceptive saying does not except but (what is) contained under the term.[8] Whence nothing is said (in this): 'no man runs except a donkey'. Therefore, since "the Father" is not contained in the supposition of this name, *"man"*, it is clear etc.. *If you say*, that there is amplified from use the distribution conveyed through that term <u>nemo</u> beyond that which regards men; then I ask: on behalf of what does it stand? either on behalf of (something) *created*, or on behalf of (something) *uncreated*? If on behalf of (something) *created*, there is no exception, because (it is) simply true; and *besides*, "the Father" is not contained therein [ibi]. If on behalf of (something) *uncreated*, it is[9] simply and totally false: therefore, through exception it cannot be verified. *If you say*, that (it stands) on behalf of each; in what manner can this be, since they have nothing common? And if they have (something) common, either that which[10] is <u>nemo</u> distributes on behalf of *essences*, or on behalf of *persons*; if on behalf of *essences*: therefore, "the Father" ought not be excepted; if on behalf of persons: therefore, the Holy Spirit ought to be excepted, just as the Father too; otherwise the expression is[11] false.

I RESPOND: It must be said, that <u>nemo</u> distributes commonly for every[12] (being) cognizing or having a cognitive force, and <u>nemo</u> distributes not only on behalf of a supposit or person, but on behalf of a nature. Whence "the Father" is not excepted, because (it is) a Person, but because (He is) of the same Nature with the Son; and for that reason "the Son" and "the Holy Spirit" are implied in that exception, and for that reason the expression has truth.

And/or say, that <u>nemo</u> distributes on behalf of men,[13] and *"but"* [nisi] is not held exceptively, but adversatively, just as there is said in the second (chapter) of the Second (Letter of St. Paul) to Timothy:[14] *It prevails for nothing, but for the subversion of those hearing (it).*

---

[1] In the Vatican edition and cod. cc there is badly omitted *therefore, since the only God is an essential predicate* [ergo cum solus Deus sit praedicatum essentiale], which words, however, are had in the other mss. and ed. 1.

[2] 1 Tim. 1:17. — A little before this in codex G, after *(it is) not (predicated) of the Father* [non de Patre], there is added *only* [tantum], and then codex V for *these* [illis: in the sense of what follows], has *these* [his: in the sense of what is present].

[3] Trusting in the mss. and ed. 1, we have expunged *not* [non], which the Vatican ed. adds, contrary to the mind of Master (Peter), here in ch. 2. Next, a few codd., such as K & dd, after *it would be predicated of the* [praedicaretur de], add *whole* [tota], which cod. X then substitutes for *Itself* [ipsa].

[4] The Vatican edition, with one or the other codex, reads *One* [unus] for *True* [verus]. A little before this, codex X has *the whole Trinity* [tota Trinitas] for *the Trinity alone* [sola Trinitas].

[5] See more on this above in a. 1, q. 2, and in (Bl.) Peter of Tarentaise, here in q. 1, a. 6.

[6] The Vatican edition, contrary to the mss. and ed. 1, has *is it said* [dicitur] for *does he say* [dicit].   [7] Verse 31.

[8] Cf. Peter of Spain, SUMMULA, Tract "On Exponibles".

[9] In very many mss. and edition 1, there is omitted *it is* [est].

[10] The Vatican edition, breaking with the manuscripts and the first six editions, here superfluously adds *this* [hoc].

[11] Codex V reads *would be* [esset].

[12] The Vatican edition, contrary to the more ancient manuscripts and edition 1, faultily has *a common* [communi] for *every* [omni], which also next, not trusting in the codices and the first six editions, has *it* (i.e. the implied subject of the verb) for *nemo*.

[13] The Vatican edition, without the authority of the manuscripts and the fist six editions, reads erroneously *all* [omnibus] for *men* [hominibus]. St. Thomas, here on the text, adducing this manner of solution, says: that the sense is: 'None purely a man knows the Father by the knowledge of comprehension, but only the Son' [Nullus purus homo novit Patrem notitia comprehensionis, sed tantum Filius].

[14] Verse 14, where the Vatican edition together with the Vulgate reads *It is useful* [utile est] for *It prevails* [valet], which the codices and edition 1 exhibit. — On this doubt, cf. above a. 2, q. 2, in reply to n. 2. — Alexander of Hales, SUMMA, p. I, q. 65, m. 3, a. 3. — Bl. (now St.) Albertus (Magnus), here in a. 6.

DISTINCTION XXII

Chapter I

*On the difference of the names, which we use
when speaking of God.*

After the aforesaid, it seems to us that there must be an orderly discussion [disserendum] of the diversity of names, which we use speaking of the Unity and ineffable Trinity. Then it must be shown,[1] in what manners any is said of It. « Therefore, that do we chiefly hold, that there are certain names pertaining distinctly to each Person [singulas personas], as (St.) Augustine says in the eighth book, On the Trinity,[2] which are only said of each Person; but there are certain ones signifying the Unity of the Essence, which are said both of Each singly [singulis singillatim] and of All commonly; however, there are others, which are said of God in a transferred manner [translative] and through a similitude ». Whence (St.) Ambrose in (his) second book, On the Trinity[3] says: « It seems a tripartite distinction (is) to be derived, whereby the Faith may more purely shine. For there are certain names, which evidently show the property of the Deity; and there are certain ones, which express the perspicuous Unity of the Divine Majesty; but there are others, which are said of God in a transferred manner and through a similitude. And so the identifying marks [indicia] of property are "generation", "the Son", "the Word" and (terms) of this kind; but of the Unity of the Eternal Wisdom, "virtue", "truth" and (terms) of this kind; however, (the terms pertaining to) a similitude (are) "character", "mirror", and (those) of this kind ».

Chapter II

*On those which convene with God temporally
and are said relatively.*

To these must be added, that there are also certain names, as (St.) Augustine say in the fifth book, On the Trinity,[4] which convene with God on account of time and are said relatively regarding a creature, certain ones of which are said of all the Persons, such as "Lord", "Creator", "Refuge"; but certain ones not of All, such as "granted", "given", "sent".

Chapter III

On this name which is "Trinity".

Moreover, there is one name, which is said of no Person singly, but of All together, that is *"Trinity"*, which is not said according to substance, but designates as a quasi collective the plurality of the Persons.

There are also certain names, which convene with God in time and are not said relatively, such as "incarnate", "made man" [humanatus] and (those) of this kind. Behold, we have assigned the six differences of the names, which we use speaking of God, concerning each of which one must now deal.

Chapter IV

*On those which properly pertain to the each Person, and on
those which signify the Unity of the Essence.*

It must be known, therefore, that those which properly pertain to each Person, are said relatively to one another [ad invicem], just as "the Father" and "the Son", and the Gift of Each, "the Holy Spirit". However, those, which signify the Unity of the Essence, are said regarding It [ad se]. And those, which are said regarding It, are certainly [utique] said substantially and of All commonly and are said of each Person singly and are accepted singularly, not plurally, in the Most High (Essence), such as "God", "good", "powerful", "great" and (those) of this kind. But those which are said relatively are not said substantially. Whence (St.) Augustine in the fifth book, On the Trinity[5] thus says: « Whatever is said regarding It, is said (to be) substantially that most outstanding and Divine Sublimity; but what is said regarding something, not substantially, is said relatively. And so great is the force of the same Substance in the Father and the Son and the Holy Spirit, that whatever is said of Each regarding Themselves, is not accepted in the Most High (Unity) plurally, but singularly. For we say: 'the Father is God', 'the Son is God', and 'the Holy Spirit is God', which no one doubts is said according to the Substance; yet we do not say, that the Trinity is three gods, but the One God. Thus the Father is said (to be) Great, the Son Great, the Holy Spirit Great: yet (it is not said that there are) three Great Ones, but One Great One. Thus also[6] "the Omnipotent Father", "the Omnipotent Son", "the Omnipotent Holy Spirit"; yet not three Omnipotents, but One Omnipotent. Whatever, therefore, is said regarding It Itself, is said (to be) God and of each Person similarly. And since it is not one (thing) for God *to be* and another *to be great* [magnum esse], but for Him *to be* is the same as is *to be great*, on this account, just as we do not say (that there are) three Essences, so we do not say (that there are) three Greatnesses [magnitudines], but One Essence and One Greatness ».

« For God is not great by that magnitude, which is not that which He Himself (is), to be a quasi participant of it; otherwise that magnitude would be greater than God; but there is nothing greater than God: therefore, He is great by that magnitude, by which He is. And for that reason we do not say (that there are) three Greatnesses, but one Greatness, nor three Great Ones, but

---

[1] The Vatican edition and very many editions, contrary to the codices, read *demonstrated* [demonstrandum].

[2] In the Foreword. — On these three manners of words' signification, (St. Augustine) speaks in ibid., Bk. V, ch. 8, n. 9. — Here and in the following (propositions), both the codices as well as the editions, indiscriminately write sometimes *affixed with seals* [sigillatim], sometimes *singly* [singillatim], sometimes *singledly* [singulatim].

[3] Or, On Faith to Gratian, Prologue n. 2; but for the words: *certain names, which evidently* [nomina quaedam, quae evidenter] there is read *evident identifying marks, which* [evidentia indicia, quae]; yet as the Maurini note, a certain codex reads with Master (Peter): *For there are certain names* [Sunt enim nomina quaedam], and Master (Peter) Himself after *And so* [Proprietates itaque] employs the word *identifying marks* [indicia]. The proposition: *but there are others, which are said of God in a transferred manner* etc. [alia vero sunt, quae translative etc.], Master (Peter) adds, while (St.) Ambrose

rather said: *There are those which, that is, show the similitude of the Father and the Son* [Sunt quae similitudinem Patris et Filii scil. ostendunt]. The Vatican edition and very many editions read *the property and the Person of the Deity* [proprietatem personamque deitatis] for *the property of the Deity* [proprietatem deitatis], contrary to the original and the codices. Then editions 1, 3, 4, 5, 7, 8 and 9, contrary to the context read *express the perspicuous truth* [exprimunt veritatem] in place of *express the perspicuous Unity* [exprimunt unitatem].

[4] Chapter 16, n. 17. — The Vatican edition and editions 4, 5, 8, and 9, a little before this at *certain* [quaedam] omit *also* [etiam].

[5] Chapter 8, n. 9. — Nearly all the editions, contrary to the codices, write *thus* [ita].

[6] Only the Vatican ed. also reads badly *For thus* [Ita enim], ed. 1 and codd. A B C & E have *Thus also* [Ita et], (St.) Augustine has *And so thus* [Ita itaque], cod. D has *Thus* [Ita]. Below, the Vatican ed. and ed. 6, before *same* [idem] omit *the* [hoc], which even (St.) Augustine has.

One Great One, because not by a participation in magnitude is God great, but by His Great Self [se ipso magno] He is great, because He is His own Greatness. Thus must it be said both of the goodness and eternity and omnipotence of God and of all (names) entirely, which can be substantially pronounced of God, by which one speaks [dicitur] regarding Him, not in a transferred manner and through a similitude, but properly, if, however, anything can be said of Him properly by the mouth of man ».[1] Behold, he has openly taught, that names signifying the Unity of the Divine Majesty are both said of God regarding Himself, that is without

a relation, and of all the Persons commonly and are said of Each separately [singulis divisim], and are not plurally, but singularly accepted in the Most High. However, those names, which properly pertain to each Person, relatively, are not said substantially. « For what is properly said according to each Person in the Trinity », as (St.) Augustine says in the same (book),[2] « is in no manner said relatively regarding (the Person) Himself, but (rather) regarding the other (Person) in the relation [ad aliam invicem] and/or regarding a creature: and for that reason it is manifest that they are said relatively, not substantially ».

COMMENTARY ON DISTINCTION XXII

On Faith in the Trinity, to the extent that, having been believed and understood, It is expressed through Catholic expressions, and, indeed, on the Divine Names in general.

After the aforesaid, it seems to us that there must be an orderly discussion of the diversity of names.

THE DIVISION OF THE TEXT

Above, Master (Peter) dealt with the Sacred Trinity, according to which It is believed and understood in a Catholic manner. In this part he deals with It, according to which having been believed and understood It is expressed through Catholic expressions [per catholicos sermones]. Whence, just as Master (Peter) himself says in the text, he intends here to deal with the diversity of the Divine Names. And this part has two parts. In the *first* part (Master Peter)[1] makes a determination [determinat] concerning the Divine Names in general; in the *second* in particular [speciali], and this in the Twenty-Third Distinction: *However, to the aforesaid it must be added, that since all names* etc..

The *first* part is divided into two. In the first part Master (Peter) posits the manifold differences of the Divine Names; in the second he reduces all to two, according that (saying) of (St. Severinus) Boethius, in the book, OF DIVISIONS,[2] that every division is bipartite [bimembris] and/or reducible to a

bipartite, and this there (where he says): *It must be known, therefore, that those which properly pertain* etc..

Likewise, the first part is divided into two (parts). In the first, Master (Peter) posits the differences of the Divine Names according to (St.) Augustine and according to (St.) Ambrose. In the second, for a greater explanation, he adds upon (this) three other differences, there in the second chapter (where he says):[3] *To these must be added, that there are also certain names* etc..

Similarly, the second part, in which he reduces these members to two, has two parts.[4] In the first, he shows, that certain names among the divine are said relatively, and these pertain to the Persons; certain ones regarding (the Deity) Itself [ad se], and these are said of All together. In the second, he shows, that this is true, there (where he says): *For God is not great by that magnitude* etc..

TREATMENT OF THE QUESTIONS

For an understanding of those (things) which are said in this part concerning the Divine Names, four (things) are asked:

First, there is asked, whether God is nameable.

Second, whether He ought to be named by only one[5] name, and/or with many.

Third, having supposed that there are many Divine Names, there is asked, whether all are said in a transferred manner, or (whether)[6] certain ones are also said properly.

Fourth, whether names are said of God according to substance, or whether also in some[7] other manner.

---

[1] From the same loc. cit., ch. 10, n. 11.

[2] Chapter 11, n. 12. — The Vatican edition and editions 3, 4 and 9, read badly *Each Himself* [se ipsum] for *(the Person) Himself* [se ipsam].

NOTES ON THE COMMENTARY

[1] Supply, together with codex Z and edition 1, *Master (Peter)* [Magister].

[2] About the middle (of the Book): « A division too, with the names posited, since it is always separated [sectatur] into two terms » etc.. And a little after that: « therefore, thus every division would be separated into

twins, if for the species and differences the words were not lacking ».

[3] In the Vatican edition, not trusting in the manuscripts and edition 1, there is lacking *in the second chapter* [secundo capitulo].

[4] Edition 1 has *sub-parts* [particulas].

[5] From nearly all the manuscripts and edition 1, we have supplied the badly omitted *one* [uno].

[6] Edition 1 reads *or whether* [an] for *or (whether)* [aut].

[7] Very many codices, such as A F G H K T etc., have *some in another manner* [aliqua alio modo], which reading edition 1 also has, which moreover, after *whether* [utrum] adds well *all* [omnia].

ARTICLE SOLE

On the Divine Names.

QUESTION I

Whether God is nameable?

About the first, that God is un-nameable, is shown *by authorities* and *by reasons* thus:

1. Dionysius (the Areopagite says) ON THE DIVINE NAMES:[1] « It is possible neither to speak of nor to understand God ». And again: « Of God there is neither a noun [nomen], nor a verb [verbum], nor a reason, nor an opinion nor a phantasm [phantasia] »: therefore, God is entirely un-nameable.

2. Likewise, the Philosopher (says) in the BOOK ON CAUSES:[2] « The First Cause is superior to every narration »; but what is superior to every narration can not be told forth [est inenarrabile], and every such is un-nameable: ergo etc..

3. Likewise, it is shown *by reason* thus: a *name* [nomen] has some proportion and similitude to the one named, as the spoke word [vox] to the (thing) signified; but God is entirely infinite, but every spoken word finite: therefore, since there is no proportion,[3] there will be no expression [nulla expressio] through a spoken word: therefore, neither a naming.

4. Likewise, every *name* is imposed by some form;[4] but in God there is no positing of certain form; whence (St.) Augustine (says):[5] « God, who escapes [subterfugit] every form, cannot be pervious to the understanding »: ergo etc..

5. Likewise, every *noun* [nomen] signifies a substance with a quality;[6] but in God there is merely the Substance without quantity and quality: therefore does not happen that one signifies God through a noun.

6. Likewise, that neither[7] (does it happen that one signifies Him) through a *pronoun* [pronomen]. For a pronoun does not have a determinate signification, except through a demonstration and/or relation.[8] But a demonstration comes to be by means of accidents, which can be caught sight of [conspici] with the eyes, but these are not in God: therefore, it seems, that for God there is neither a noun, nor a pronoun.

ON THE CONTRARY: 1. In the Psalm (there is sung):[9] *"The Lord" (is) His Name.* And again:[10] *How admirable is Thy Name in all the Earth*: therefore, God has a Name.

2. Likewise, Dionysius wrote [fecit] a book on the Divine Names: therefore, either God is nameable, or the knowledge handed down there is worthless [cassa][11] and useless.

3. Likewise, it seems *by reason*: because everything which expresses itself by a word [verbo], can be expressed by the sign of a word, but the sign of a word is the voice [vox]:[12] therefore, since God expresses Himself with His own Word, He can be expressed with the voice, but what can be expressed with voice, can be named: ergo etc..

---

[1] Chapter 1, near the middle. Cf. above d. 3, p. I, a. sole, q. 1, p. 67, footnote 6. — You will find the words, which are cited immediately after this, from Dionysius, in loc. cit., and, according to the translation of Scotus Erigena, they are exhibited thus: And neither is there a sense of Him, nor a phantasm, nor an opinion, nor a noun, nor a verb, nor a touch, nor knowledge [Et neque sensus eius est, neque phantasia, neque opinio, nequo nomen, nequem verbum, neque tactus, neque scientia].

[2] Proposition 6.

[3] Namely, between the written word and God. The Vatican edition incongruously and contrary to the more ancient codices and edition 1 adds *of the finite to the infinite* [finite ad infinitum]. — On the major of this argument, see (St. Severinus) Boethius in the first and second edition of his commentary on Aristotle's, ON INTERPRETATION, Bk. I, ch. 1, where among other things he says: Every spoken words [vox] signifies the (things) sensed by the spirit, wherefore out of the (things) understood by the spirit whatever will have come forth, is indicated by spoken words. Therefore, now (Aristotle) says this: There is a certain similitude," he says, "between the thing understood and the spoke word; for according to which measure there are certain simples, which are conceived by the reckoning of the spirit and are constituted by the intelligence of the mind, in which neither any truth nor falsity is found, thus also is in spoken words."

[4] Alan of Lille, RULES OF THEOLOGY, rule 17 says: Since everything has been given a name according to the first institution from a property or from a form, wherefore (St. Severinus) Boethius says: "From the things constituted out of matter and form the human spirit alone stood forth, which insofar as it has willed, has impressed names upon things etc.".

[5] Cf. Sermon 117, on the words of the Gospel of (St.) John, chapter 1: *In the beginning was the Word* etc., ch. 2, n. 3: He can be ineffably understood, (but) not by the words of man does it come to be, that He is understood. We treat of the Word of God and we say, why He is not understood. For He is a certain Form, a Form not formed, but a Form of all (things) formed; an incommutable Form, without fall, without defect, without time, without place, surpassing all, standing forth from all [existens omnibus] and the a certain foun-

dation in which (all) are, and the gable under which (all) are ... We say, "How incomprehensible is what has been read !"; yet it has been read, not so that it might be comprehended by man, but so that many might grieve, because he has not comprehended ... Therefore, He is the Form of all things, the un-fabricated Form, without time, as we have said, and without the dimensions of place [sine spatiis locorum]. For whatever is grasped by place, is circumscribed. A form is circumscribed by its ends, has goal posts [metas], whence and how far it is. Then, what is grasped by place and by a certain mass and space is distended, is less in the part, than in the whole. May God grant that you understand it.

[6] Priscian, GRAMMATICAL INSTITUTIONS, Bk. II, ch. 5, says of the noun: *A noun (is) a quasi signature* [Nomen quasi notamen], because by this noun we note down the quality of each substance. See more on this in (Bl. John Duns) Scotus, SPECULATIVE GRAMMAR., ch. 8. — Next, in codex Z there is omitted *quantity and* [quantitate et]. At the end of the argument, form the manuscripts and edition 1, we have substituted *that one signifies* [significare] for *that ... is signified* [significari].

[7] Supply: *does it happen that one signify God* [contingit Deum significare], and/or with the Vatican edition *God is namable* [Deus sit nominabilis], which however, is lacking in the manuscripts and edition 1.

[8] A reference to the division of pronouns, namely, into *demonstratives* and *relatives*; which according to Priscian, GRAMMATICAL INSTITUTIONS, Bk. II, ch. 1, differ in this, that a demonstration rendered to an interrogation shows the first cognition: Who made it? I did. But a relation signifies the second cognition, as "He, of whom I have already spoken". Cf. (Bl. John Duns) Scotus, SPECULATIVE GRAMMAR, ch. 22.

[9] Psalm 67:5.

[10] Psalm 8:2.

[11] Codices K and V read *superfluous* [superflua].

[12] Aristotle, ON INTERPRETATION, Bk. I, ch. 1: Therefore, those, which are in a voice, are the notes of those which belong to the passions in the soul. — Next, after *God* [Deus] the Vatican edition, contrary to the more ancient manuscripts and edition 1, omits *Himself* [se], and puts *is expressed* [exprimatur] in place of *expresses* [exprimat].

4. Likewise, what happens to understand, happens to signify or enunciate; but it happens that God is cognized by us; this is certain and (has been) proven above:[1] ergo etc..

5. Likewise, what happens to praise, happens to name; but it happens that one praises God, nay, He Himself is[2] most highly praise-able: therefore, also nameable.

CONCLUSION

God is nameable, just as He is intelligible, not indeed perfectly, but imperfectly.

I RESPOND: It must be said, that just as "to understand" is said in a twofold manner, so[3] "effable" and "nameable". For in one manner *"to understand"* is said through a *perfect* comprehension; in another manner through a *semi-full* cognition. So[4] *"effable"* is said in a twofold manner: in one manner through a *perfect expression*, in another manner through a *semi-full narration*. So also "nameable".

If "effable" or "nameable" is said according to the *perfection* of expression, in this manner it must be said, that just as God is intelligible to Himself alone, so is He effable and nameable to Himself also, not[5] by a name other, than He Himself is, nor by word other, than He Himself is; and just as He is incomprehensible *to us*, so also (is He) ineffable, so also (is He) even un-nameable; and through this manner (of speech) does Dionysius and the Philosopher speak.

However, if "effable" and "nameable" are said according to *any kind of* narration[6] *whatsoever*, in this manner, according to the manner which God is cognizable to us, thus (is He) both effable and nameable: and the one who cognizes better, speaks forth [effatur] better and names better and more expressly. Whence the faithful (believer) names more expressly than the infidel,[7] and the writings [scriptura], which support the Faith, such as Sacred Scripture, (more) than reason and/or philosophy. And in this manner proceed the *reasons* and *authorities* for the second part.

1. 2. To that, therefore, which is objected[8] concerning Dionysius and the Philosopher, the response is already clear through that which they say concerning a naming, in which there is a *perfect* expression.

3. To that which is objected, that the voice in a name[9] is proportional to the interior word or the (thing) signified; it must be said, that this is understood of the naming, which includes the whole signification of the thing, otherwise it does not have truth, unless a proportion be understood to be according to the thing under a reckoning of the cognizable; and in this manner it can be nameable. For although God is infinite, yet He is cognized finitely by us.

4. To that which is objected, that God does not have a form; it must be said, that He does not have a form pervious to our intellect, of which kind [cuiusmodi] is the form, the[10] image of which is in the sense; yet, He has a form, because He Himself is the Form, which is the reason for cognizing, which[11] even if we do not cognize (Him) in Himself, He Himself cognizes Himself in Himself, and we Him in created form. Whence from the created form, which we understand and see, we impose names.

5. To that which is objected, that a noun signifies a substance and a quality; it must be said, that there[12] a substance and a quality are not accepted *properly*, but *commonly*; a "substance" is said (to be) *what* is cognized, a "quality" is said (to be) *whereby* it is cognized,[13] and this through a manner of rest; and I say this for the sake of verb and participle and adverb, which is a disposition of a verb. And, since in creatures, as *what* and *whereby* (a thing) is cognized differ very much, for that reason a noun among creatures conveys this (difference)[14] very much through a diversity. However, in God the Same is the One cognized and the Reason for cognizing, as much as (the cognition) concerns Him: for that reason a Divine Name signifies those two through an indifference according to the thing [secundum rem]; and thus the reckoning of substance and quality, as befits a name, is conserved [salvatur] There.[15]

---

[1] Distinction 3, p. I, a. 1, q. 1. — As requested by very many manuscripts and edition 1, we have substituted a little above this, the active verbs *understand, signify, enunciate* for their passive forms. Then codex Y has *as ... above* [ut supra] in place of *and ... above* [et supra].

[2] From very many mss. and edition 1, we have supplied *is* [est].

[3] Edition 1 adds *also* [et].

[4] A few codices, such as P Q and X, have *Similarly* [Similiter] in place of *So* [Sic].

[5] In codex V there is prefixed to *not* [non] the particle *and* [et].

[6] We have restored the reading of the more ancient manuscripts and edition 1, by putting *narration* [narrationem] for *naming* [nominationem], which reading also responds to the division mentioned a little above this. Next after codex Z and edition 1 read *thus (is He) also effable, thus (is He) also nameable* [ita et effabilis ita et nominabilis].

[7] We follow codices T and bb, while all the other codices together with the editions omits *than the infidel* [quam infidelis], and the Vatican edition with only one or the other codex substitutes in addition *the Faith* [fides] for *the faithful (believer)* [fidelis]. We prefer the reading of codex T and bb, both because it is more conformable to the rules of grammar, and because it is indirectly corroborated by the authority of nearly all the manuscripts and first six editions, which read *the faithful (believer)* [fidelis]. Then, in a few manuscripts, such as S and Y, there are omitted the words *which support the Faith, such as Sacred Scripture* [quae fidei suffragatur, ut sacra Scriptura].

[8] In very many codices, except Y, and in the Vatican edition, together with editions 2, 3, 4, 5 and 6, there is unduly added here *second* [secundo], and a little below this the Vatican edition, contrary to nearly all the codices and the first six editions, incongruously puts *he says* [loquitur] for *they say* [loquuntur].

[9] The reading of the Vatican edition and codex cc, *man* [homine] for *a name* [nomine], is contrary to those words which are mentioned in the objection itself, and contrary to the more ancient codd. and edition 1.

[10] Very many codices, such as G H I M Z etc., together with edition 1, have *some* [aliqua] for *the*.

[11] From nearly all the older mss. and edition 1, we have substituted *which* [quam] for the less congruous *since* [quoniam]. Next codex V has the subjunctive form of *we do cognize* [cognoscamus], and a little below this after *Whence* [Unde] in codex Y there is added *also* [et].

[12] The Vatican edition and codex cc omit *there* [ibi], which however, is had in the other manuscripts and edition 1. A little above this, codex W has *with a quality* [cum qualitate] in place of *and a quality* [et qualitatem].

[13] Alexander of Hales, SUMMA., p. I, q. 48, m. 1, in the last reply, expresses the same in these words: « For a substance and a quality, when there is said: "a noun signifies a substance etc.", do not distinguish as in the predicaments, inasmuch as (a noun) is graspable by the intellect ». In other words: a substance and a quality are not accepted here, inasmuch as they are predicaments or other things, but according to the manner of signifying; inasmuch as, that is, substance signified that, upon which the noun is imposed, but quality, that, by which it is imposed, or the respect, under which it is imposed. — A little before this, trusting in the manuscripts and edition 1, we have expunged *insofar as* [prout], which the Vatican edition adds after *commonly* [communiter]. Next, after *verb* [verbum], there is lacking in very many mss. and ed. 1 the particle *and* [et].

[14] The Vatican edition, together with very many manuscripts, has less well *this* [hoc] for *this (difference)* [haec].

[15] To the last objection, which concerns the *pronoun*, no solution is explicitly given; because it is sufficiently contained in the aforesaid (i. e. inasmuch as a *pronoun* stands in the place of a *noun*). — A little before this, we present the plainer reading, which is also the reading of the greater number of codices and edition 1, by putting *according to matter* [secundum rem] for *of matter* [rei], which the Vatican edition with a few mss. has; the others omit either *according to* [secundum] and/or *according to the thing* [rem].

SCHOLIUM

I. The distinction and the two conclusions posited in the body (of the question) have been thoroughly manifested. — In the solution to n. 4 there is conceded, that there is some proportion between the voice and the thing named, but only to the extend that *it is cognizable*. Moreover, the infinite God is only finitely cognizable by us. Proportional to this finite cognition there can also be *finite* name, « speaking of the proportion, which is between any two under the reckoning, whereby one is a sign and the other the (thing) signed ». Thus Richard of Middleton, here in q. 1, in reply to n. 3. — The sentence in the solution to n. 3 must be noted, that we cognized God « in the created form; whence from the created form, which we understand and see, we impose names »; concerning which, cf. above d. 3, p. I, q. 2. Alexander of Hales (loc. cit., below) adds, that from creatures, according to (St.) John Damascene, we impose names in three manners, that is « *as images* and *as forms* and *as marks*. By marks God is named by privations, when God is said (to be) "the Immense One", "the Infinite One", "the Incircumscribable One"; *by images*, when He is named according to the dispositions of spiritual creatures, such as when He is said (to be) "a Spirit", "the Wise One", "the Intelligent One"; *by forms*, when He is named by the similitudes of corporal creatures, as when He is said (to be) "the Lion (of Judah)", "an (unquenchable) fire", and (things) of this kind ».

II. The solution to nn. 6 and 7 is explained more fully in the same sense by St. Thomas (SUMMA., I, q. 13, a. 1, in reply to n. 3), and by Alexander of Hales (loc. cit., below, in reply to the last objection), who explains those words (of St. Bonaventure) which are somewhat obscure on account of their brevity: « and I say this

for the sake of verb and participle and adverb, which is a disposition of a verb », in this manner: « Though a verb and participle signify with a tense, yet, nevertheless God can be noted in a certain sense (by them), not because He Himself falls under time, but because according to the possibility of our intellect, which understands *with motion and time*, we understand and signify (in this manner). Whence also this verb, "*is*" [est], said of God, does not signify with movement and time. Wherefore (St.) Augustine on that (verse) of (the Gospel of St.) John, chapter I: *In the beginning was the Word*, says: "A substantive verb (namely "*is*") has a twofold signification: for sometimes it declares temporal movements according to the analogy of other verbs; sometimes the substance of the one thing, of which it is predicated, it designates by a motion without anything of time; for that reason it is also called a substantive. Such is what is said: *In the beginning was the Word*" » etc.. — Cf. also here below, Doubt 3.

III. Cf. Alexander of Hales, SUMMA., p. I, q. 48, m. 1. — (Bl. John Duns) Scotus, on this and the following questions, here in qq. 1 and 2; REPORTATIO., here in q. sole. — St. Thomas, here in q. 1, a. 1; SUMMA., I, q. 13, a. 1. — Bl. (now St.) Albertus (Magnus), SENT., Bk. I, d. 2, a. 16; SUMMA., p. I, tr. 3, q. 16. — Giles the Roman, here in 1st. princ., q. 1. — Henry of Ghent, SUMMA., a. 73, q. 1. — Durandus (of Saint-Pourçain), on this and the following questions, here in q. 1. — (Bl.) Dionysius the Carthusian, here in q. 1. — (Gabriel) Biel, on this and the following questions, here in q. sole.

QUESTION II

Whether God has only one Name, or several?

Second, there is asked, whether God has only, one Name, or (whether He has) more. And that (He has) more, seems:

1. *By the authority* of Scripture, which names [appellat] Him with diverse names. In the sixth (chapter) of Exodus:[1] *My great Name, "Adonai", I did not make publicly know to them* [non indicavi eis]. In the fifteenth (chapter) of Exodus:[2] *"The Omnipotent" (is) His Name.* And in the Psalm:[3] *"The Lord" (is) His Name.* If, therefore, these are diverse names, it is clear from the authority of Scripture, that God has many Names.

2. Likewise, Dionysius (the Areopagite) in the book, ON THE DIVINE NAMES[4] assigns many Names for God; (St.) Ambrose similarly in the book, ON THE TRINITY,[5] and Master (Peter) similarly in the text.

3. Likewise, this very (thing) seems *by reason*, because no name sufficiently expresses the Divine 'Being' [esse divinum], neither in itself, nor in comparison to our[6] intellect. Which is clear, because every perfection both is and is understood to be in God; and no name expresses the perfection of every

condition: therefore, since it cannot be done through one, we need more.

4. Likewise, that in which things convene and in which they differ, either is necessary to say with many names,[7] or it is necessary that one be equivocated; but equivocation generates ambiguity and is to be taken away: therefore, it is congruous that one express (this) with diverse names. Since, therefore, among the divine there is (something) common and proper and this in many, it is necessary, that there be many Names.

5. Likewise, although one is the First[8] Truth, yet the articles of the Faith are many: if, therefore, faith believes many articles concerning God, and *what is believed in the heart for justice* is bound [oportet] *to be confessed by the mouth for salvation*,[9] one can and ought to confess many articles with the mouth; but with one Name many articles are not expressly and explicitly expressed: therefore, He is bound to have many Names.

ON THE CONTRARY: 1. (St.) Hilary (of Poitiers, in the book, ON THE TRINITY, says):[10] « Not thing to speech, but

---

[1] Verse 3.   [2] Verse 3.   [3] Psalm 67:5
[4] Chapter 1, § 8, where according to their genera he recounts the Names, which are attributed to God by Sacred Scripture, v. gr. "*I am who am*", "*the Life*", "*the Light*", and by wise men, v. g., "*the Good*", "*the Beautiful*" etc..
[5] That is, ON THE FAITH TO GRATIAN, Bk. II, in the Prologue; see here the text of Master (Peter), ch. 1. — Codex W puts *(St.) Augustine* [Augustinus] and edition 1 *(St.) Anselm* [Anselmus] in place of *(St.) Ambrose* [Ambrosus]. Next after *Master (Peter)* [Magister] one or the other codex, such as S and Y, omits *similarly* [similiter].
[6] In the Vatican edition and codex cc there is wanting *our* [nostrum], which is found in all the other manuscripts and edition 1. A little below this, codex X has *the condition of every perfection* [omnis perfectionis conditionem] for *the perfection of every condition* [omnis conditionis perfectionem].

[7] We prefer the reading of codices G and M and edition 1, which put *names* [nominibus] for *manners and/or names* [modis vel nominibus]. Next, after *ambiguity* [ambiguitatem], codex X has *which* [quae] for *and* [et], then after *it is congruous* [congruum est] in codex H there is added *many and* [pluribus et] before *diverse* [diversis], and in codex I there is read *that one say and express (this) with diverse manners and names* [diversis modis dicere et exprimere nominibus].
[8] The more ancient codices, together with edition 1, contrary to the Vatican edition, in this proposition exhibit the word *First* [prima], though some of them either read with transposed words *there is one First Truth* [una prima est veritas] and/or badly omit *one* [una].
[9] Rom. 10:10. — A little below this after *expressly* [expresse] codex bb has *nor* [nec] for *and* [et], which then together with codex aa puts *ought* [debet] for *is bound* [oportet].
[10] ON THE TRINITY, Bk. IV, n. 14.

speech to thing has been subjected »: therefore, since in God there is an omnimodal, real Unity, therefore, also (a unity) of voice and Name.

2. Likewise, everything which is in God, is God, therefore, what signifies anything which is in God, is God; but God is One: therefore, all[1] Divine Names have one Signified; but all such are synonyms; moreover, with synonymous names there is not said more with many than with one: therefore, it seems, that all other than one are more than necessary.

3. Likewise, the multiplication of Divine Names either comes on the part of the *Thing*, or on part of the (human) *intellect*, or on the part of (His) *effects*. If on the art of the *Thing*, then "goodness" and "truth" are not diverse Names, because the Thing (is) entirely One; if on the part of (His) *effects*, then, therefore, "unity" and "eternity" are not diverse, since they do not connote an effect; if on part of the *intellect* alone: therefore it seems, that Names of this kind are worthless [cassa] and vain, since they do not have anything corresponding [respondens][2] in the Thing.

4. Likewise, in Scripture the Name of God is proposed in the singular [singulariter], whether it be added to one, as when there is said: *"The Lord" (is) His Name*,[3] or to many, as when there is said: *In the Name of the Father and of the Son and of the Holy Spirit*: therefore, since there is the same reckoning of Thing and of one Thing, and of Name and of one Name,[4] therefore, God only has one Name.

CONCLUSION

We name God now with one name, now with many, according to the diverse manners, by which "name" is accepted.

I RESPOND: It must be said, that in a name there are three (things), namely *a sound* [vox] and *a signification* and *the reckoning under which one is made known* [ratio innotescendi]. On which account, "name" is accepted in a manifold manner: sometimes on behalf of a signifying *sound*, as when there is said: '"Peter" is the name of an Apostle'; and in this manner it is established, that in God there are many Names. Sometimes "name" is accepted on behalf of the *thing signified* [res significata], as when there is said: "the good and the honest are the same in name"; and in this manner, among the divine, there is in a certain manner a saying of one name, in a certain manner of many. For, if the thing signified is said essentially, in this manner all (Divine Names) are one;

if personally, in this manner (there are) many (Persons) and many corresponding Names. Sometimes "name" is accepted on behalf of *the mark itself* [ipso notamine] or the reckoning under which one is made known; and in this manner it must be said, that[5] in a certain manner (God has) one Name, in a certain manner many.

For, if the reckoning under which one is made known is accepted on the part of *God*, in this manner He is made known through the Virtue, which is one and great; and thus the Name of God is "the Great One" or "the Greatest One". Whence, in the tenth (chapter) of Jeremias (there is written):[6] *Great art Thou, and "the Great One" (is) Thy Name*, as much as regards the reckoning under which one is made known or the Virtue, through which He is made known, according to which there is said in the Psalm:[7] *God is known in Judah, in Israel "the Great One" (is) His Name*.

But, if the reckoning under which one is made known is accepted by reason[8] of (His) *effects* or creatures, in this manner there are diverse Names. For God is made known to us in a threefold manner, namely through *causality*, through *ablation* and through *excellence*;[9] and according to this there is a multitude of Names. For, if He be named through *causality*, there are many Names, because He has many effects; if through *ablation*, there are many Names, because many (names) are removed (from Him), that is all created ones; if through *excellence*, (there are) many, because in many, in all, that is, the conditions of nobility, He exceeds creatures.[10]

4. From the aforesaid, the objections are clear. For, because it objects, that Scripture expresses the Name of God in the singular; it must be said, that Scripture, as it very much preaches the Name of God (as) *the Great, the Admirable*,[11] *the Holy* and *the Praise Worthy*; and in this manner does not speak of "name" [nomine], according to which (it is) *a spoke word* [vox], but according to which it is a *reckoning under which one is made known* on the part of God; and in this manner (expresses) one (Name of God). However, it does not follow: 'it speaks in the singular, therefore, (God has) only one (Name)', because frequently what is said in the singular is also said universally, as is clear in the many examples in the Law, when there used to be said: *a man of the House of Israel*,[12] and/or *the man who made* this and/or that, it was understood of any man.

3. To that which is objected, that the *unity*[13] is on the part of the Thing; it must be said, that there is a Plurality on the part of the Thing,

---

[1] From the manuscripts and first six editions, we have supplied *all* [omnia]. A little above this, after the first *therefore* [ergo], in codex T there is read *everything which* [omne quod] for *what* [quod]. At the end of this argument the Vatican edition, not trusting in the manuscripts and edition 1, has *are not necessary* [non sunt necessaria] for *are more than necessary* [sint praeter necessaria].

[2] The Vatican edition, contrary to very many codices and edition 1, has *corresponding* [correspondens].

[3] Psalm 67:5; Mt. 28:19. — A little before this, from very many more ancient manuscripts and edition 1, we have substituted *it be added* [addatur] in place of *is it added* [dicitur], and (a little before this) codices G H and M, together with edition 1, after *is* [singulariter] add well *always* [semper].

[4] Aristotle, METAPHYSICS, Bk. IV, text 3 (Bk. III, ch. 2): For the same is one man, and a man and the one being a man [ens homo]; and it shows nothing diverse according to the repeated saying 'a man and a being, a man and one man'.

[5] The Vatican edition together with codex cc, but breaking with the other codices and edition 1, omits *that* [quod].

[6] Verse 6, after which text in the Vatican edition and in codex cc there is added *that is* [id est] in place of *(there is written)*.

[7] Psalm 75:2.

[8] Codex M together with edition 1 has *on the part* [a parte] for *by reason* [ratione].

[9] Dionysius (the Areopagite), ON THE DIVINE NAMES, ch. 7, § 3, which is cited above, in d. 3, Doubt 1, page 77, footnote 10.

[10] Codex aa adds: *A fourth manner can be added, as (when) there is said, that God is made known to us through a similitude; and in this manner there are similarly many names, such as "Lion", "Lamb", "Rock" and (those) of this kind* [Quartus modus potest addi, ut dicatur quod innotescit nobis Deus per similitudinem; et sic similiter sunt multa nomina, ut leo, agnus, lapis et huiusmodi] The same words are found in cod. bb along the margin. The aforesaid two codd. add examples for each of the three manners of cognizing God; thus, for the way of causality after *names* they insert, *such as "Creator", "Founder" and (those) of this kind* [ut creator, conditor et huiusmodi]; for the way of ablation, after *Names* [nomina], they put *such as "Incorporeal", "Immense", and (those) of this kind* [ut incorporeus, immensus et husiusmodi]; for the way of excellence, after *many* [multa], they add *as "Supersubstantial", "Super-good", and (those) of this kind* [ut supersubstantialis, superbonus et huiusmodi]. Codex X adds here (i.e. before *many* [multa]?) the verb *there are* [sunt]. Codex Y at the beginning of this proposition has *if He is named* [nominatur] for *if He be named* [nominetur].

[11] Very many mss., such as A S T V etc., with ed. 1, read *Wonderful* [mirabile]. A little below, this cod. W reads *there is* [est] for *(expresses)*.

[12] Leviticus 17:8. — Trusting in the more ancient manuscripts and edition 1, we have restored *the House* [domo].

[13] The Vatican edition with codex cc reads *plurality* [pluralitas] for *the unity* [unitas], but contrary to the scope of the obj. and the other codd., with edition 1. Next, cod I, with transposed words, reads:

such that the *Thing* is accepted on behalf of a *Person*. But if on behalf of *the Nature*, even if there is no plurality in Itself, yet[1] (there is) inasmuch as It becomes known. And for that reason (there are) many Names.

2. To that which is objected, that such names are synonyms: it must be said, that names[2] are then synonyms, when they differ solely on the part of the *spoke word* [vocis]. But here there is a difference according to the reckoning under which one is made known, and for that reason they are not synonyms. The other reason has been given above, in the Eighth Distinction, in the first problem.[3]

3. To that which is objected, that if (the multiplication of Divine Names) comes *solely* on the part of the *understanding*, therefore, such names are vain; it must be said, that it does not come form this solely, since to that reckoning under which He is made known there corresponds [respondet] the plurality in creatures, and in God there corresponds a true Unity,[4] comprising that whole plurality. Wherefore, because we understand the Power and Wisdom of God through diverse (things), we name in a diverse manner; and because in God there is truly a Wisdom and Power, for that reason there is no vanity There.[5]

SCHOLIUM

I. The Seraphic Doctor distinguishes in the term ("name") three (things), namely a signifying sound [vocem], a signifying thing [rem], the reckoning under which a thing is made known [rationem innotesscendi]. To illustrate this last member there used to be offered this popular example regarding that which "man" [homo] notes, (namely) that he has been made out of *humus* [ex humo]. But the Divine Essence, in Itself one, most simple and infinite, is the reckoning under which He is made known in respect to many (things), since our intellect cannot express that one most high Perfection with a unique concept, but forms another concept from that Infinite One under the reckoning of *wisdom*, another under the reckoning of *goodness*, and thus of the other attributes. — According to the said distinction the question is solved with five principal propositions and with not a few (others) adjoined. For an explanation there can serve (what has been said) above in d. 8, p II, q. 2, and in regard to the solutions to nn. 2 and 3, ibid., p. I, a. 1, q. 1, near the end; St. Thomas, SUMMA., I, q. 13, a. 4; SUMMA CONTRA GENTILES, I, ch. 35.

II. It must be noted, that the order in the solution of the opposed arguments has been changed. The 1st opposed (argument) is not explicitly solved, since the principles of the solution have already been exhibited in the body (of the response). The first solution respects the 4th opposed (argument); but the second respects the 3rd opposed (argument), in regard to its first member. Then, there follows the solution to the 2nd; and in the last place, (the solution) to the third member of 3rd opposed (argument).

III. In the conclusion (to the question), all agree: Alexander of Hales, SUMMA TEOLOGICA ., p. I, q. 48, m. 2, a. 1, and m. 3. — St. Thomas (Aquinas), here in q. 1, a. 3. — Bl. (now St.) Albertus (Magnus), d. 8, a. 3; (and in his own) SUMMA., p. I, tr. 14, q. 59, m. 4. — (Bl.) Peter of Tarentaise, here in q. sole, a. 2. — Richard of Middleton, here in a. 2. — Giles the Roman, here in 1st. princ., q. 2. — Henry of Ghent, (in his own) SUMMA., a. 73, q. 9. — (Bl.) Dionysius the Carthusian, here in q. 3.

QUESTION III

Whether all the Divine Names are said in a transferred manner?

Third, there is asked, whether all Divine Names are said in a transferred manner [translative], or whether certain ones are also said properly. And it seems, that all are said in a transferred manner.

1. In THE RULES OF THE FAITH[6] there is said: « Every simple is properly, and is said improperly »; but what is improperly said, is improperly named: since, therefore, God is simple, He is improperly named; but impropriety is lead back [reducitur] to a property: therefore, the Divine Names are said of God improperly, (and) of others properly; but what is said of anything improperly, is said in a transferred manner, if (it is said)[7] of another properly: ergo etc..

2. Likewise, just as one happens to understand[8]

any one thing [unumquodque], one happens also to signify (it); but one does not happen to understand God except through the properties and conditions of creatures, therefore, neither to name (Him); but what is named according to the properties of others is always named in a transferred manner: ergo etc..

3. Likewise, there is naught but a twofold theology, that is, the mystical and the symbolic, according to which Dionysius (the Areopagite) would have it;[9] but each names God in a transferred manner — for the mystical (names Him) through spiritual and invisible creatures, but the symbolic through corporal ones — therefore, every naming of God is a transferred one [translativa est].

4. Likewise, every Divine Name has been imposed for the sake of our instruction;[10] but all our

---

it must be said, that if the Thing is accepted on behalf of a person, the plurality is on the part of the thing [dicendum, quod si accipiatur res pro persona, pluralitas a parte rei est].

[1] Supply: *is* [est], which codices Z aa and bb prefix to the word *yet* [tamen].

[2] From very many manuscripts and edition 1 we insert *names* [nomina], and next trusting in the more ancient manuscripts and edition 1, we have substituted *differ* [differunt] for the inept *are said* [dicuntur], and a little below this, we have supplied *they are* [sunt].

[3] Namely, in p. I, q. 1, in reply to the last objection.

[4] Codex T reads *one Truth* [una veritas], with which codex S agrees, which having omitted *one* [una], reads *the Truth* [veritas]; codex Y, having omitted *true* [vera], has *a Unity* [unitas], and codices aa and bb after *Unity* [unitas], add *or Truth* [sive veritas].

[5] Edition 1 adds *but (rather) truth and unity* [sed veritas et unitas], which, also, a little before this, reads *in God One (Being) is truly Wisdom and Power* [in Deo est unum vere sapientia et potentia].

[6] Alan of Lille, THEOLOGICAL RULES, rule 20. — Codices aa and bb after *of the Faith* [fidei] add *and/or Theology* [vel theologiae]. ·

[7] In codex aa there is added *it is said* [dicatur]; but codices P and Q read instead *but of anything properly* [sed de aliquot proprie] and transposes these after *improperly* [improprie].

[8] The Vatican ed. with cod. cc, but with the other codd. and ed. 1 striving against this, reads *as any one thing happens to be understood* [unumquodque, sicut contingit intelligi]. A little before this, a few codd., such as P Q & V, prefix *so* [sic] aptly before *one happens also to signify* [contingit et significare]; cod. T, however, for these same words puts *thus (one happens) also to name* [ita et nominare], a reading which, if one looks at the form of the argument, is to be preferred.

[9] Epistle 9. Cf. also ON THE DIVINE NAMES, ch. 1, near the end, and ON MYSTICAL THEOLOGY, ch. 1. — A little below this, after *spiritual* [spirituales], ed. 1 omits *and* [et] and then in some codd., such as V W & X, the particle *but* [sed] is lacking; at the end of the argument very many mss. with edd. 2, 3 & 6, exhibit less congruously *in a transferred manner* [translative] for *a transferred one* [translativa]; next cod. O puts *is said (to be)* [dicitur] and codd. P & Q *is said to be* [dicitur esse] in place of the final *is* [est].

[10] A reference to Rom. 15:4: *Whatsoever has been written, has been written for our instruction* [Quaecumque scripta sunt, ad nostram doctrinam scripta sunt].

learning [doctrina] begins from sense;[1] therefore, every Name of God is accepted according to some sensible; but in God there is no sensible property according to truth, but solely in a transferred manner: ergo etc..

ON THE CONTRARY: 1. The Apostle says in the third (chapter of his Letter) to the Ephesians,[2] speaking of God: *From whom every paternity in Heaven and Earth is named*; but if paternity on earth [in terris] is named from the paternity of God: therefore, God is more properly and more principally said (to be) "Father" than others, therefore, not in a transferred manner. This very (thing) does Dionysius[3] and (St. John) Damascene say, supporting (themselves) upon this authority of the Apostle. For (St. John) Damascene says:[4] « It must be known, that there is not transferred from us to the Blessed Deity the name for 'paternity' and 'filiation' and 'procession', just as the divine Apostle says: *From whom every paternity* »: ergo etc..

2. Likewise, Blessed Ambrose says, as it is had in the text,[5] that there is a threefold difference of Divine Names, and one of those are transferred [translativa] names: therefore, not all are said in a transferred manner.

3. Likewise, certain (names) are said of God, which have an opposite in every creature, such as "eternity" and "immensity"; but a transferred name is attained according to some similitude:[6] therefore, such names are not transferred ones.

4. Likewise, certain (names) are said of God, the signified of which is properly in God alone, as this name, "*the Good*" and "*He who is*", according to the eighteenth (chapter of the Gospel of St.) Luke:[7] *No one (is) good, except God alone*. And (St.) Augustine[8] says, that « God alone truly is, in comparison to Whom all others are not ».

CONCLUSION

Not all names are said of God in a transferred manner: for when they signify a thing, the truth of which is in God and the opposite in a creature, they are in no manner transferred; when they signify a thing, the truth of which is in God and the similitude in a creature, they are transferred according to imposition, not according to thing; finally when they signify a thing, the truth of which is in a creature and a completely similar property in God, they are properly transferred.

I RESPOND: To this certain (authors) wanted to say, that there are certain names, which God imposed upon Himself, certain ones, which we imposed upon Him. If we speak of the names, which God imposed upon Himself, since He Himself understands Himself properly, names of this kind are proper; and such are said to be "*the Good*" and "*He who is*". Whence Dionysius[9] seems to want, that that name, "*the Good*", is alone the proper and principal (name); however, (St. John) Damascene,[10] that that name, "*He who is*", is alone the proper and principal one; and one stretches out in name to the perfection (of God), the other to (His) absolution (from all things), each, however, to (Divine) property.[11] But, if we speak of the names, which we have imposed upon Him, thus since we do not cognize God except through creatures, we do not name Him except through the names of creatures; and[12] for that reason (such names are said of God) solely in a transferred manner, whether because they more properly and first convene with a creature, or because the have been first imposed upon a creature, though they do not more properly convene with a creature. And this is

---

[1] Cf. Aristotle, POSTERIOR ANALYTICS, Bk. I, ch. 14 (ch. 18), ON THE SOUL, Bk. III, text 39 (ch. 8), and ch. 6, "On Sense and the Sensible", and also METAPHYSICS, Bk. I, ch. 1. — Next very many codices, such as A S T W Z etc., have *something* [aliquid] for *some* [aliquod].

[2] Verse 15, in which text the Vatican edition, together with the Vulgate, reads *From whom* [Ex quo] for *From whom* [A quo], and then the Vulgate exhibits *in the Heavens* [in caelis] for *in Heaven* [in caelo], contrary to the codices and edition 1.* — A little below this, codex V has *another (father is)* [alius] for *others* [alia: in the sense of *other beings are*].

[3] ON THE DIVINE NAMES, ch. 1 § 4: Whence in nearly every theological action we see the Thearchy divinely praised, such that the Monad is indeed also named "the One" on account of (His) simplicity and unity ... so that, however, the Trinity on account of the subsistent expression of the thrice super-essential fecundity, out of which every paternity in Heaven and on Earth is, is also named.

[4] ON THE ORTHODOX FAITH, Bk. I, ch. 8: It is also interesting to know that, the vocabulary [vocabula] of paternity, filiation and procession has not been transferred by us to the Blessed Deity, but on the contrary has been communicated to us from There, according to the extent that the Apostle says: *On this account I bend my knees to the Father, from whom every paternity* etc. [Propterea flecto genua mea ad Patrem, ex quo omnis paternitas].

[5] Here in ch. 1. — Next cod. V has *of those* [illarum] for *of those* [ex illis].

[6] Cf. above Foreword, p. 1, footnote 8.

[7] Verse 19. Because those words are thus read in St. Luke, in the very passage cited by us, though in the mss. and edd. there is had *Matthew 19:14*, where there is read: *One is good, God* [Unus est bonus Deus].

[8] ON THE CITY OF GOD, Bk. VIII, ch. 11: « *I am Who am; and you shall say to the children of Israel: He Who is has sent me to you*; as if in the comparison to Him who truly is, because He is incommutable, those which have been made mutable, are not ». For the rest of this, cf. above

Master (Peter's) text, Distinction VIII, ch. 1, where the same passage recurs, and he attributes it to (St.) Jerome.

[9] ON THE DIVINE NAMES, ch. 3, § 1: And, if He is seen, we weigh the name, "the Good", as the first, perfect (name) and as that which manifests all the emanations of God. (in Corderius' version). Cf. also ch. 4.

[10] ON THE ORTHODOX FAITH, Bk. I, ch. 9, where he also adds a reason: For He Himself contains within His own embrace 'being' in its entirety [totum esse] as a certain immense open sea of essence and defined with no limits. — From nearly all the more ancient manuscripts and edition 1 we have supplied the particle *however* [vero].

[11] In other words, Dionysius in the name, "*the Good*" [bonum], intends the Divine 'Being' [divinum esse], to the extent that, as One existing most completely in Itself, It is the cause comprehending all or the principle and end of all. For good out of its own nature is diffusive of itself and has the reckoning of an end; but the perfect is that which, being had before all, can make a similar to itself (cf. loc. cit. chs. 4 and 13). But (St. John) Damascene in the name, "*He who is*", considers the Divine 'Being' according to Itself and absolutely, to the extent that it is an infinite, open sea of essentiality. Yet each designates such in these names, that it convenes truly and properly to God. Cf. Alexander of Hales, SUMMA, p. I, q. 49, m. 4, a. 2.

[12] In the Vatican edition and codex cc, there is lacking *and* [et], which is exhibited by the other codices and edition 1. In the previous two clauses we have expunged the explicit subjects of the verb *we* [nos], which followed the words *since* [cum] and *creatures* [creaturas], on the testimony of the manuscripts and edition 1. Next, codex T has *not because they* [non quia] for *though they do not* [quamvis non]. One or the other codex, such as Y, in this and the following proposition, has *through (a consideration of what is) prior* [per prius] for *more properly* [proprius].

---

* *Trans. note*: According to the classical conception, which distinguished Heaven from the sky, the former was <u>caeli</u> and the latter <u>caelum</u>; which distinction of terms frequently is absent in post-classical Latin.

a certain transferal [translatio quaedam], though, properly speaking, there is a transferal, when (the names) properly convene with those, from which they are transferred, such as "to laugh" (convenes) more properly with men, than with meadows.

But this position does not seem to stand.[1] For since[2] we cognize God in a threefold manner, that is through an *effect*, through *excellence* and through *ablation*, it is established, that in all these manners one happens to name God. If through an *effect*, there is no transferal;[3] similarly, if through *ablation*, since a transferal is attained according to some similitude: « for all transferring according to some similitude transfer ».[4]

And, on this account, it must be otherwise said, that there are *certain* names, which signify a thing, the truth of which is in God and the opposite in a creature, such as "the Immense One" and "the Eternal One"; and such are in no manner transferred, neither according to thing nor according to imposition. *Certain ones*[5] signify a thing, the truth of which is in God and its similitude in a creature, such as "Power", "Wisdom", and "Will"; and such names are transferred from creatures to God, not according to thing, but according to imposition; because they have been imposed upon creatures before (they have) upon God, thought they are first in God. There are *certain* names, which signify a thing, the truth[6] of which is in a creature and a completely similar property in God, such as "Rock" and "Lion" — for the thing signified is in a creature, but the similitude of the property, such as "stability" and "fortitude" is in God — and these

are properly transferred [translativa]. It must be conceded, therefore, that among the divine some are transferred names, not all.

1. To that, therefore, which is objected, that a simple is said improperly, it must be said, that there "*to say*" is not "*to name*", but (rather)[7] "*to enunciate*", because for the simple there is no composition in being [in essendo], but there is a composition in enunciating, and for that reason (it is said) improperly; not so in naming. — And/or say, that not everything said improperly has been said in a transferred manner.

2. To that which is objected, that He is understood solely through creatures; it must be said, that although He is understood solely through creatures, yet not solely through a similitude,[8] nay (rather) He is (also) cognizable through negation and dissimilitude

3. To that which is objected, that symbolic and mystical theology name God in a transferred manner; it must be said, that although mystical (theology) does name[9] God in a transferred manner, as much as regards the properties of (His) excellence, yet it does not solely name (Him) in this manner, but also through abnegation; and for that reason not solely in a transferred sense.

4. To that which is objected, that all our learning begins from sense; it must be said, that it is true; and[10] every name has something sensible, namely, a spoken word [vocem], so that it is heard; but it is not bound [oportet], that it have a sensible signification, because a word [verbum] of understanding, which is insensible, puts on the sensible, spoken word.

SCHOLIUM

I. Here "*proper*" is not accepted, to the extent that among the divine it is distinguished against "*common*", but to the extent that it is distinguished against "*metaphorical*" or "*transferred*". — The Seraphic Doctor together with the Angelic (Doctor) rejects the sentence noted in the first opinion, that all names, imposed upon God *by us*, are naught but metaphorical; this he proves through induction, by enumerating the three ways or manners, by which we form Divine Names, that is, (by way) of causality, negation and eminence. In the way of eminence a transferal indeed comes to be according to a certain similitude, which, however, differs from a metaphorical similitude. — In regard to the manner of conceiving the divine perfections, Richard of Middleton (loc. cit. below) makes these observations: « There are certain names, which signify, and/or rather through which we intend to signify and hint at distinctly (although we do not attain to signify it in this manner) a thing, which are in God through (a consideration of what is) prior and in a creature through (a consideration of what is) posterior; and such names more properly are said of God than of a creature, not by a reckoning of this, that through the name *we understand* that He has

been distinctly hinted at, but by the reckoning of this, that through the name *we intend* to hint at it; and in this manner they are not said of God in a transferred manner ». Then, the same says in the solution to n. 4: « Though we understand God through His effects, which are certain similitudes of God, yet, our cognition does not stand still in these effects, but ascends to cognize the Virtue and Divinity of God, though in general and in an obscure manner ». — However, (Bl.) Dionysius the Carthusian, (here in q. 2), does not entirely consent to the solution of Sts. Thomas, Bonaventure, Albertus (Magnus) and others, chiefly in regard to this, that all names have been imposed upon God from creatures and, as much as regards the spoken word [vocem], transferred from creatures to the Creator; in particular, he makes certain exceptions against the reproof of the first opinion, which St. Bonaventure has in the Response, and he asserts, that frequently there is a *transferal*, while we name God, both through (His) *effect*, as well as through an *ablation*, and through *eminence*. But one can respond, that St. Bonaventure least of all denies, that certain names have been imposed upon Him, by not but God the Revealer, but

---

[1] A few manuscripts, such as I and X, together with edition 1 prefix to the word *to stand* [stare] the word *able* [posse].

[2] In cod. O there is added *according to Dionysius* [secundum Dionysium], for the words of which, see above d. 3, Doubt 1, p. 77, footnote 10.

[3] The Vatican edition adds *Equi-formally, if through excellence* [Pariformiter si per excellentiam], which words, however, are omitted in the mss. and ed. 1; see the reason for this omission a little below this, in the solution to n. 3.

[4] Aristotle, TOPICS, Bk. VI, ch. 2, concerning which see above, Foreword, p. 1, footnote 8.

[5] Edition 1 reads instead *There are certain names, which* [Quaedam sunt nomina, quae] for *Certain ones* [Quaedam].

[6] Codices K and V read *the property* [proprietas]; a little below this after "*fortitude*" is [fortitudo] in codex A there is added *properly* [proprie], and then many codices, such as A C F G H K L S etc., put *thus* [ita] for *these* [ista], among which codex T, which, having omitted many words, briefly reads *and thus some are transferred names, not all* [et ita sunt aliqua nomina translativa, non omnia].

[7] Codex T has *except* [nisi] to *but (rather)* [sed]. — It must be noted, that "*to name*" [nominare] respects a *term*, but "*to enunciate*" [enuntiare] a *proposition*, which is always something complex or composed.

[8] In codex O there is added *of a creature* [creaturae].

[9] Codex V, after *mystical* [mystica], having added *and symbolic* [et symbolica], consequently has the verbs of *naming* which follow in the plural. Next, in some manuscripts, such as A T etc., and edition 1, there is lacking *God* [Deum]. Then, codex X has *negation* [negationem] in place of *abnegation* [abnegationem].

[10] The Vatican edition, together with codex cc, having changed the punctuation, reads *that* [quod] in place of *and* [et] and, next, reads *according to* [secundum] in place of *namely* [scilicet], but less distinctly and contrary to the other codices, together with edition 1. A little below this, codex W has *an intelligible word* [verbum intelligibile] in place of *a word of understanding* [verbum intelligentiae].

he denies, that for this reason there can be aptly distinguished *proper* names from *metaphorical ones*. Likewise, St. Bonaventure does not deny, nay expressly affirms, that certain *effects* of God and the names signifying these effects cannot be said but *metaphorically* of God. Finally, according to the mind of the Seraphic Doctor it can be said, that even the names which *properly* convene God in regard to the *thing signified* (such as "wisdom"), are yet not properly to be attributed to God in regard to the *manner of signifying*, to the extent that not in that manner, by which we conceive them in this life, but through the manner they convene with God in the more eminent and more perfect, infinite degree. But this does not cause, those names to be transferred (metaphorical), except in an improper sense. For, as Richard rightly says (loc. cit., in reply to n. 4), « a name is not said (to be) *transferred* [translatum], except where there is a transferal by reason of the *thing signified* ».

II. For more on the necessity and rules for a transferal, see below d. 34, q. 4. — On the Name of God; "He who is", the Seraphic Doctor speaks magnificently in the ITINERARIUM MENTIS IN DEUM, ch. 5. Cf. Alexander of Hales, SUMMA., p. I, q. 49, m. 4, a. 1 and 2. — St. Thomas, SENT., Bk. I, d. 8, q. 1, a. 1 and 3; SUMMA., I, q. 13, a. 11. — Bl. (now St.) Albertus (Magnus), SENT., Bk. I, d. 3, a. 13 and 14. — Richard of Middleton, here in q. 6.

III. In regard to the conclusion: Alexander of Hales, SUMMA., p. I, q. 48, m. 2, a. 2. — St . Thomas, here in q. 1, a. 2; SUMMA., I, q. 13, a. 3. and 6. — B l. (now St.) Albertus, on this and the following question, here in a. 1; SUMMA., p. I, tr. 14, q. 56 and 59, m. 1 and 2. — (Bl.) Peter of Tarentaise, here in q. 1, a. 3. — Richard of Middleton, here in q. 4. — Giles the Roman, here in 1st. princ., q. 3. — Henry of Ghent, SUMMA., a. 32, q. 2, and a. 73, q. 2. ff. — (Bl.) Dionysius the Carthusian, here in q. 2.

QUESTION IV

Whether all the names said of God are said according to the Substance?

Fourth and last, there is asked, whether all the names said of God are said according to substance. And that (they are) not, nay (it is) the otherwise, is shown:

1. *By the authority* of (St.) Augustine in the fifth (book) ON THE TRINITY:[1] « This chiefly let us hold, that whatever *regarding Itself* that most outstanding and Divine Sublimity is said (to be), is said substantially; but what (is said) *regarding something*, (is) not substantially, but relatively (said) »; but "the Father" and "the Son" are said regarding something: ergo etc..

2. Likewise, (St. Severinus) Boethius (says) in the book, ON THE TRINITY:[2] « God is great without quantity, good without quality, but is not related without a relation »: therefore, relation truly and properly remains [manet] in God, therefore, also the manner of speaking relatively.

3. Likewise, this very (thing) seems *by reason*, because in the Divinity some names are incommunicable, as is clear in all[3] personal (names); but the Substance is communicable, since It is One in the Three: therefore such names do not indicate the Substance: therefore, among the divine there is a manner of speaking other than according to substance.

4. Likewise, among the divine, there is one and another manner to hold oneself [se habere], because the Son holds Himself to the Father in a manner other than the Holy Spirit, but there is not one and another 'being' [esse] or 'subsisting' [subsistere]: therefore, since one happens to understand this and to speak of it understood, it is necessary, that there be There another manner of speaking and of understanding than according to substance: ergo etc..

ON THE CONTRARY: 1. Everything which is said, is either said according to *substance*, or according to *accident*, because substance and accident sufficiently divide being [ens];[4] but among the divine nothing is said according to *accident*: therefore, according to *substance*.

2. Likewise, everything which is said, either is said per se, or *not* per se. If per se, then according to substance; if *not* per se, then, therefore, through another and in another; but all (names) which are said of God, are said per se: therefore, all are said according to substance.

3. Likewise, to be said according to substance and[5] according to relation either means diversity on the part of the *thing*, or on part of the *manner of understanding* or of the manner of speaking. If on the part of the *thing*: therefore, in God there is diversity and composition; if on part of the *manner of speaking*. then since there is a diverse manner of speaking in that which is *good* and in that which is *great* and in that which is *God* — because one is asked: "How big is God [quantus est Deus]?", one responds,[6] "*Great*", one does not respond "*Good*"; similarly if one is asked: "What is God like [qualis est Deus]?", one responds, "*Good*", not "*Great*" — therefore, not only are there two manners, but even many more than two.

4. Likewise, what[7] responds [respondetur] to the question made *through something* [per quid], is said according to substance, both as much as regards the thing and as much as regards the manner; but relative names respond [respondentur] to the question made *through something* concerning God: therefore, they are said according to substance. A proof of the *minor*. (St.) Augustine in the book, ON CHRISTIAN DOCTRINE (says):[8] If one is asked, "What is God?", one fittingly responds: "The Father and the Son and the Holy Spirit".

5. Likewise, since there are certain (names employed) in regard to the divine, which

---

[1] Chapter 8, n. 9. Cf. the text of Master (Peter) here in ch. 3, in which words the Vatican edition, contrary to the original and the manuscripts, and also to edition 1, having put the indicative *is said* [dicitur] for the infinitive [dici] with *substantially* [substantialiter], and *regarding another* [ad aliud] for *regarding something* [ad aliquid], it adds *is said* [dicitur] both after *but what* [autem] and after *relatively* [relative]. At the end of the argument, from the more ancient manuscripts and edition 1, we have substituted *regarding something* [ad aliquid] for the incongruous *another* [aliud].

[2] Chapter 4, where according to the *sense* this proposition is contained, inasmuch as, namely, (St. Severinus) Boethius shows there, that when anyone changes the other predicaments besides relation into divine predication, all the rest are translated into (the category of) substance. Which, if you attend to the words of the proposition, they seem taken from (St.) Augustine, ON THE TRINITY, Bk. V, chs. 1 and 5.

[3] Edition 1 reads *names* [nominibus] for *all* [omnibus].

[4] Cf. above d. 5, a. 2, q. 1, page 116, footnote 6.

[5] The Vatican edition, together with codex cc, incongruously and contrary to the other codices, together with edition 1, reads *either* [aut] in place of *and* [et].

[6] In codex V there is here and next after *one does not respond* [non respondetur] adds *That which is* [quod est], and a little below this after *manners* [modi] adds *of speaking* [dicendi].

[7] Codices P and Q read *whatever* [quidquid]. Edition 1, together with codex cc exhibit the minor in this manner: *but through relative names one responds to the question* etc. [sed per nomina relative respondetur ad quaestionem etc], and then edition 1 adds to the noun *God* [Deo] *Himself* [ipso].

[8] Book I, ch. 5, n. 5; according to the sense. The words of (St.) Augustine are: For not easily can there be found a name, which befits so great an Excellence, unless that which is thus better said: This Trinity, the One God out of Whom all (have their being), through Whom all (made), in Whom all (remain in being); thus the Father and the Son and the Holy Spirit etc..

are not said according to substance nor[1] according to relation, such as this name, *"incarnate"*, (and) this name, *"unbegotten"*, it seems that that division does not comprise all the Divine Names.

CONCLUSION

Not all names are said of God according to the Substance, but certain ones even through the manner of quantity and/or quality and, in addition, certain ones according to relation.

I RESPOND: For an understanding of the aforesaid it must be noted, that a *diverse manner of being spoken of* [dici diversimode] is according to a threefold difference.

In one manner, a *diverse manner of being spoken of* is attained according to the diverse manner of *being* [diversum modum essendi], which is per se and per accidens: and indeed in this manner there is no *diverse manner of being spoken of* among the divine, because that diversity of manner posits an essential[2] diversity in the thing said; and, as much as regards this, there is only one manner of speaking in God. For all (the Names) which are said of God, are God Himself and His Substance.

In another manner, a *diverse manner of being spoken of* is according to a diverse manner of *being understood*, which indeed is attained according to one and another reckoning or medium[3] of cognizing; and in this manner not only is there a *diverse manner* of being spoken of among the Divine Names, nay *an omnimodal* one, because God is not only cognized through diverse (Names), nay through all genera of things, and in this manner the Names said of God, certain ones are said through the manner of *substance*, such as "God"; certain ones through the manner of *quantity*, such as "Great";[4] certain ones through the manner of *quality*, such as "Good"; and in the same manner concerning all the others.

In a third manner, a *diverse manner of being spoken of* is according to a diverse manner of *being regarded* [se habendi]; which[5] indeed is attained as much as regards *absolute* (being) and as regards *compared* or related (being); and indeed this manner of diversity is *less* than the first (manner), and *greater* than the second. *Less* than the first, because according to the first there is attained

an essential diversity and composition; *greater* than the second, because according to that there is attained entirely no[6] distinction in the thing. But according to this (third) manner there is attained in this (manner) a unity and plurality: a unity according to (what is) absolute, a plurality according to (what is) looked-back-to. And as much as regards this manner there are only two manners of speaking, namely, according to *substance*, such as those which are said regarding (the thing) itself,[7] and according to *relation*, such as those which are said regarding something. However, because these (Names) do not mean another manner of *being*, for that reason these are predicated of the former and are one; and because they mean another manner of *being regarded*, for that reason according to the former (one speaks of) a unity, according to the latter a plurality.[8] From these (arguments) the objections are clear.

1. For because there is objected, that everything which is said, is said according to substance and/or according to accident; it must be said, that among the divine (the objection) has an instance, where a relation is not an accident, nor yet is said according to substance.

2. To that which is objected second, that everything which is said among the divine, is a per se being [ens per se]; it must be said, that it is true, but yet there does not follow: 'it is said as a per se being, therefore, (it is said) according to substance', because there is not said: "that a name is said according to *substance*", such that *the substance* is said *through itself* [per se], but such that it is said *regarding itself* [ad se].[9]

3. To that which is objected, of what kind is this diversity, either according to thing, or according to the manner of being understood; it must be said, that (it is) according to a manner of *being regarded* [se habendi],[10] which is not only in our intellect, but also in the thing.

4. To that which is objected fourth, that relative names respond [respondetur] to the interrogation made concerning substance; it must be said, that "substance" is said in a twofold manner: either (as) "a per se being", or (as) " a (being) *regarding itself* [ad se].[11] If as a per se (being), thus all (names) both relative and absolute, mean in God the Substance; and because in this manner "*substance*" responds to the question made through "*What?*" [per quid], for that reason all (names) can respond. But if "substance" be said as an *absolute* being [ens absolutum], not as one compared, in this manner what is said *regarding itself*, is said according to substance. And in this manner (St.) Augustine does not[12]

---

[1] Very many codd., such as A I K M S etc., contradicting the context, have *but* [sed] in place of *nor* [nec]; the Vatican ed. with a few mss., reads *but neither* [sed nec]; all the other mss. with ed. 1 exhibit the reading received in the text. Next, after *"incarnate"* [incarnatus] codd. O and X add *and* [et], and, then, very many mss., such as A F H T V etc., with edd. 1, 2, 3 & 6, have (the indicative) *comprise* [complicitur], rather than (the subjunctive) *comprise* [complectatur].

[2] Codex R reads *a diversity of being* [diversitatem esendi] for *an essential diversity* [diversitatem essentialem]. Next a few codices, such as F O and X, have *concerning God* [de Deo] for *in God* [in Deo]. — Cf. Aristotle, METAPHYSICS, Bk. V, text 13 (Bk. IV, ch. 7).

[3] Thus very many and indeed the better known codd., such as A G H K R T V W ee & ff, with ed. 1, while the Vatican ed. has *manner* [modum].

[4] The Vatican edition, not trusting in nearly all the manuscripts and edition 1, faultily omits *certain ones through the manner of quantity, such as "Great"* [quaedam per modum quantitatis, ut magnus].

[5] Codices I O and Z, with edition 1, read *which (manner)* [qui] instead of *which (diverse manner of speaking)* [quod]. Next, codex R reads *relative* [relativum] for *related* [relatum].

[6] In the Vatican edition there is substituted *no* [non] for *no* [non], but less aptly and contrary to nearly all the codd. and edd. 1, 2 and 3.

[7] The undue omission of the words *such as those which are said* [ut illa quae dicuntur], which omission is had in the Vatican ed., is repaired with the help of the mss. and ed. 1. Next, some codices with ed. 1 have *Which because* [Quae quia], another has *Because which* [Quia quod], a few have *Because* [Quia] for *However, because these (names)* [Quia vero haec], which all the others, with the Vatican edition, exhibit.

[8] The most common reading of the manuscripts and the first six

editions, in which, with the words *the former* [illa] and *the latter* [haec] (some codices, such as A H I and K, together with editions 2, 3, 4, 5, and 6, have *this* [hoc]) transposed, there is had *according to latter unity, according to the former plurality*, is proved from the context to be rejected.

[9] The sense is: in this proposition '*that a name be said according to substance*', the words *according to substance* are not taken in that sense, whereby through "substance" there is understood "*a* per se *being*" [ens per se], but rather "*a being regarding itself*" [ens ad se], and for that reason the Divine Relations, though they are per se, but not *regarding themselves* [ad se], are not said according to substance. See a little below this, in reply to n. 4.

[10] From the manuscripts and editions 1, 2 and 3, we have restored the faultily omitted se [se]. A little before this codex V has *is asked* [quaeritur] for *is objected* [obiicitur].

[11] Very many codices, such as F M X Y Z, together with edition 1, this twofold member thus: *either a* per se *being or a* per se *and ad se being* [aut ens per se au tens per se et ad se]. A little before this codex I has *that through relative names one responds* [quod per nomina relativa respondetur] in place of *that relative names respond* [quod nomina relativa respondentur], and codex K has *question* [quaestionem] for *interrogation* [interrogationem]. Next, trusting in the more ancient manuscripts and edition 1, we have placed *thus* [sic] for *then* [tunc]. Then codex S has *are said in God according to substance* [dicuntur in Deo secundum substantiam] in place of *mean in God the Substance* [dicunt in Deo substantiam].

[12] Nearly all the codices, with edd. 1, 2 & 3, omit *not* [non], but badly, as is clear from the context. Next (on the following page), from the older mss. and ed. 1, we have supplied *names* [nomina], which the Vatican edition with cod. cc omits, and instead of which codex X reads *all relatives* [omnia relativa] for *relative names* [nomina relativa].

accept it; and in this manner "the Father" and "the Son", and relative names are not said according to substance.

5. To that which is objected last, that many (names) are said of God, which are not said according to substance nor according to relation; it must be said, that *being spoken of in a relative manner* among the divine can be in a twofold manner. For certain names are said relatively out of *the principal understanding* of the name, certain ones out of the *consequent (understanding of it)*.

And[1] the first difference is divided into three: because certain (names) signify a relation and *are said relatively*, such as "the Father"; certain ones signify a relation,[2] such as "paternity", which *are not said regarding the Other*, but (which) is that itself by which the Other is referred; certain ones are said relatively, because *they deprive relation*, such as "unbegotten", "improcessible"; yet that is not a pure privation, as shall be seen below.[3]

But those which convey a relation out of a *consequent* understanding, are similarly according to a threefold difference. For *certain* (names) are said to be said relatively, because they are posited on behalf of relatives, as when there is said: "God generates God" [Deus generat Deum], that is, "The Father (generates) the Son". *Certain ones* are said relatively, because they enclose [claudunt] the relation interiorly in their own signified, as when there is said "*incarnate*" [incarnatus] — for the sense is, that "He is united to the flesh"; for the Union means a relation, which respects a singular Person — or "to assume the flesh" [assumere carnem] and (expressions) of this kind. *Certain ones* are said relatively, because they enclose the relation in the Supposits [suppositis], such as "similar" and "equal"; for They are not similar, unless as Those Which are referred and distinguished.

SCHOLIUM

I. For an easier understanding of the state of the question we note, that "*substance*" [substantia] is taken in a twofold sense, as is clear from the solution to n. 2. For it is understood either as a thing standing *through itself* [res per se stans]; and in this it is distinguished against the "accident", whereby it is in another, and in this sense the substance is whatever is in God; and the relations themselves do not remain in the predicament of accident, but pass over into the predicament of substance. And/or "substance" is taken as the absolute thing [res absoluta] or *regarding itself* [ad se], and in this manner it is distinguished against relation; in this second sense the principal question is understood, as is clear from the arguments in the fundament. Besides this doubt, other questions are also solves. For St. Bonaventure asked above (in the division of the questions), whether names said of God are said according to substance, or whether also in any *other manner*. For which reason he here explains in the first place the three diverse manners of speaking of God and responds to the question according to this threefold distinction.

II. To better understand that is here said of the manner of speaking according to substance and according to relation, we note these (words) from Alexander of Hales (loc. cit. below, § 3): « It must be said, that (in God) all the predicaments are changed; but yet dissimilarly. For predicaments other than *substance* and *relation* are changed in a twofold manner: according to the reckoning of their own *genus*, and according

to the reckoning whereby they are *in a creature* ... However, (the predicaments) *substance* and *regarding something* [i.e. relation] are changed in one manner; for they are changed by the reckoning, whereby they are in a creature, but remain according to the first intention of their genus. For "substance", such as is in a creature subsisting under accidents, it not among the divine; yet there is among the divine a "substance", such as (is) a per se being [ens per se]. Again in a creature *regarding something* there is an accident, according to which manner it is not among the divine; but yet there is among the divine a *regarding something*, that is a 'holding itself regarding another', and/or rather 'One holding Himself regarding *Another*' ».

III. What is taught here in the body and in reply to n. 5 concerning the various species of difference or of distinction and concerning the names signifying relation is worthy of attention. Cf. above d. 13, a. 3; d. 19, p. II, q. 2, in reply to n. 2, and especially d. 26, q. 1. Alexander of Hales teaches the same, in SUMMA., p. I, q. 48, m. 4, a. 3, § 4 and 5.

IV. In regard to the conclusion all agree. Alexander of Hales, SUMMA., p. I, q. 48, m. 4, a. 3. — St . Thomas, DE POTENTIA., q. 7, a. 4 and 5; SUMMA., I, q. 13, a. 2. — Bl. (now St.) Albertus (Magnus), SUMMA., p. I, tr. 14, q. 57, — (Bl.) Peter of Tarentaise, here in q. 1, a. 4. — Richard of Middleton, here in q. 5. — Giles the Roman., here in 1, princ., q. 4 near the middle. — Henry of Ghent, SUMMA., a. 32, q. 5. — Durand., here in q. 2. — Dionysius the Carthusian, here in q. 4.

DOUBTS ON THE TEXT OF THE MASTER

DOUBT I

In this part, there are doubts about the text (of Master Peter), and first there is doubted concerning this which he says: *To these must be added, that there are also certain names* etc., because either the divisions of (Sts.) Augustine and Ambrose are sufficient, or (they are) not. If they are: therefore, Master (Peter) superfluously adds; if insufficient (divisions) are said, it must be regarded as unfitting [pro inconvenienti est habendum].

I RESPOND: It must be said, that neither the division of (St.) Augustine nor of (St.) Ambrose has been diminished; nor (is) the addition of Master (Peter) superfluous, since[4] the members of the division of Master

(Peter) are included in the members of the division of (St.) Ambrose. For the former is through (things) immediate; for since it has three members [sit trimebris], it is reduced to those divisions; because every Name of God is either *proper*, or *transferred*, if *proper*, either it looks to the *Substance*, or to the *Persons*. But Master (Peter) specifies those members more, because any name can look to the unity of the *Substance*[5] from eternity, and/or in time; similarly to the *Persons* from eternity, and/or in time; and to the *Persons* in a twofold manner: either dividedly [divisim], as this name, "*the Father*", and/or together and conjoined, as this name, "*Trinity*"; and thus[6] there are six members.

---

[1] In the Vatican edition there is lacking the particle *And* [Et], which the more ancient codices and edition 1 exhibit.

[2] In codex X there is added *and are not said relatively* [et non dicuntur relative]. A little below this after *they deprive relation* [privant] codex X adds *itself* [ipsam].

[3] Distinction 28, q. 1.

[4] As requested by very many mss. and ed. 1, we have substituted *since* [quoniam] in place of *for* [nam]. A little before this, in very many

mss., such as A S T V etc., and ed. 1, there is lacking the words *(St.) Augustine nor* [Augustini nec].

[5] In very many mss. and ed. 1, here and a little below this, after *Persons* [personas] there is omitted *and/or* [vel], which the Vatican ed. adds.

[6] The Vatican ed., with one or the other cod., has *those* [ista] for *thus there* [ita]. — On the reconciliation of the diverse divisions, see also Bl. (now St.) Albertus (Magnus), here in a. 1. — St. Thomas, here in q. 1, a. 4. — (Bl.) Peter of Tarentaise, here in a. 5. — (Bl.) Dionysius the Carthusian, here in a. 3.

Doubt II

Likewise, is asked concerning this which (Master Peter) says, that *the Trinity is a quasi collective (name)*. For he seems to speak badly, because « a collective unity », as (St.) Bernard (of Clairvaux) says,[1] « is the least unity; but the Unity of the Trinity holds the citadel [arcem] among all unities »: ergo etc.

I Respond: It must be said, that this name, "*Trinity*", falls short [deficit][2] in two (aspects) from a properly collective name. *First*, because those which a collective name gathers together, have a diversity simply; and *second*, because they have a unity <u>secundum quid</u>: but[3] it is the other way around in the name for the *Trinity*. Yet, in this there is a similitude, because just as a collective name at once says many and is predicated of none per se, so neither is this name, "*Trinity*", predicated of Any of the Persons, and yet conveys All together; and[4] for that reason Master (Peter) does not say, that it is a collective (name) *simply*, but *quasi*.[5]

Five Rules on the Divine Names

It must be known, therefore, that those which properly etc.. About this it must be noted, that from the words of (St.) Augustine, which are posited here and in the book, On the Trinity,[6] there are elicited five rules concerning Divine Names. The *first* is this: every name, which is said of God, is said according to substance and/or according to relation, except this name, "*man*" [homo]. The *second* is this: every name, which is said of the Three Persons, such that (it can be said) of Any singularly, is said according to substance,[7] except partitive names. The *third* is this: every name said according to substance is predicated of the Three Persons together, taken singularly, except this name, "*Person*" [persona]. The *fourth* is this: every name said of God in respect to a creature indicates the Essence, except those which pertain to (something) lesser. The *fifth* is this: every name, which is said of God in time and is not said of each Person, predicates a *notion* and/or an "*as if*" [quasi]: this[8] is said on account of this name, "*sent*" [missus], which means "to be from another" [esse ab alio].

Doubt III

Likewise is asked of this which (St. Augustine) says: *Not three Omnipotents, but One Omnipotent*; because since we say[9] that *the Three* (are) *potent*, it seems that for an equal reason we can say that (there are) *Three Omnipotents*.

I Respond: It must be said, that a verb [verbum] always signifies adjectively and upon adjacents, and for that reason always draws its number from the subject [supposito], similarly (does) the participle [participium], remaining a participle, because it has the nature of a verb. But a name [nomen], because is signifies in rest, sometimes becomes a substantive [substantivatur], and when it is numbered, then it is numbered just as a substantive noun [substantive nomen] on the part of its form. And for that reason, because <u>potens</u> can be a participle (i.e. "being able"), (and)[10] "*omnipotent*" is only noun: for that reason there is not received in the same manner, "three omnipotents", just as "*the three (are) able*", unless "*omnipotent*" is an adjective [adiectivum] and/or[11] retained adjectively. Moreover, the reason, for which "*omnipotent*" cannot be a participle, is on account of (its) composition, which does not admit the verb. For a participle, as the Grammarian says,[12] passes over into a name in four manners: namely, *by composition*, as in "untrained" [indoctus], *by comparison*, as "more learned" [doctior]; *by construction*, as in "the one loving that" [amans illius]; *by loss of time*, as in "the one to be loved" [amandus], according to which the same signifies and/or[13] the same sounds, as "*the one worthy to be loved*" [amari dignus].

Doubt IV

Likewise, is asked of this reckoning of (St.) Augustine: If He is great by participation, therefore, greatness is greater than He, and he posits (this) there (where he says): *God is not great by that magnitude* etc. And that reckoning of his seems not to be valid. For (this) is not valid: 'that is white by whiteness through participation: therefore, whiteness is whiter and/or greater[14] that it'.

I Respond: It must be said, that the reckoning of (St.) Augustine is good and is founded upon the very exposition of the name, because "*to participate*" is "*to grasp*" [capere] a "*part*" [partem], and if one grasps a part, therefore, it is less than the whole. Because, therefore, it is objected concerning *whiteness*, it must be said, that there is a "*being greater*" [esse maius][15] in a twofold manner; either as much as regards "*being*" [esse], and/or as much as regards

---

[1] On Considerations, Bk. V, ch. 8.

[2] The Vatican edition, without the authority of the manuscripts and editions 1, 2, and 3, reads *differs* [differt] for *falls short* [deficit], which also a little before this, with the more ancient codices and edition 1 contradicting it, omits *It must be said* [Dicendum].

[3] The Vatican edition, with codex cc alone, has *and* [et] for *but* [sed]. Next after *similitude* [similitudo], a few codices, such as A W and Y, have *which* [quod: which refers to *this*] in place of *because* [quia].

[4] With the approval of very many codices, together with edition 1, we have supplied *and* [et].

[5] See more on this in Alexander of Hales, Summa., p. I, q. 66, m. 1. — Bl. (now St.) Albertus (Magnus), here in a. 3.

[6] Book V, ch. 8 ff, n. 9 ff. — Next, on the authority of the older mss. and ed. 1, we have substituted *five* [quinque] for *certain* [quaedam].

[7] In codex H, there is added *such as "God", "Powerful", "Good", "Great", and (names) of this kind* [Deus, potens, bonus, magnus et huiusmodi]; in codex O, however, after *partitive names* [nominibus partitivis], there is added *such as "one", "any", and distinctive ones, such as "distinct", "distinction", "discretion"* [ut unus, aliquis; et distinctivis ut distinctus, distinctio, discretio].

[8] The Vatican edition prefixes the word *and* [et], and a little before this edition 1 reads *the Three single Persons* [tribus personis singulis] for *each Person* [personis singulis]. — You will find the same rules ex-

pounded in B. (now St.) Albertus (Magnus), here in a. 6. — Richard of Middleton, here in q. 7. — (Bl.) Peter of Tarentaise, here in a. 6.

[9] Not a few codd., as G T & ee, read *when we* [cum dicimus] for *since we* [cum dicamus], and next cod. Y *would be able* [possemus] for *can* [possumus].

[10] By codices V and X, there is here added *and* [et].*

[11] The Vatican edition, contrary to the more ancient codd. and ed. 1, reads *and* [et], and next has *held* [tentum] for *retained* [retentum].

[12] Cf. Priscian, Grammatical Institutions, Bk. V, ch. 11, where he deals with the first manner, that is *composition*, and Bk. XI, ch. 1, where he deals with the other manners, and Bk. VIII, ch. 10, where he also speaks of the last manner. — A little after this, we have supplied from the more ancient manuscripts and edition 1 *namely* [scilicet].

[13] Some codices, such as A S X etc., read *as* [quod] in place of *and/or* [vel], edition 1 has *according to which the same also* [secundum quod diem et] for *and/or the same* [vel idem], and contrariwise codex W omits *signifies and/or the same* [significant vel idem].

[14] The Vatican edition, breaking with the manuscripts and editions 1, 2, 3, and 6, omits *and/or greater* [vel maius].

[15] In the Vatican ed., and one or the other cod., there is badly lacking *being* [esse]. Cod. T reads *that "being greater" is said in a twofold manner* [quod esse maius dicitur dupliciter]. A little before this, codex X has *but if* [sed si] for *and if* [et si].

---

* *Trans. note*: In this response, the argument concerns the structure of Latin Grammar and the formation of participles; which is not identical in English. The English translation here, therefore, should be regarded only as an aide in understanding this argument, and an argument not entirely coherent in regard to the English language. For in Latin the word for "noun" [nomen] is the same as that for "name", and, yet Latin names as "nouns" all the words that can be declined in cases, which includes adjectives. And thus a participle, which can also be declined in Latin, can be a termed a "noun", when it is used as a substantive, or an "adjective", when modifying the noun it is adjacent to.

"*being able*" [posse]. It must be said, therefore, that the participation of a subject is attained in respect to a universal form; and, although that is whole in the subject as much as regards (its) "*being*", yet, (it is) not as much as regards (its) "*being able*", because it can be in others. But[1] nothing can be greater than God, neither as much as regards (its) "*being*", nor as much as regards (its) "*being able*". And, for that reason, the argument of (St.) Augustine holds rightly, that God can participate in nothing.

In another manner, it can be said, that the argument of (St.) Augustine holds rightly in those forms, which have been born to denominate some-thing through (their own) essence; and, in such, what is through participation, is reduced to that which is through essence; and, whensoever it is thus, that which is a 'being through (its own) essence' [ens per essentiam], excels that which a 'being through participation' [ens per participationem] has.[2] If, therefore, greatness is great through essence, and God (is God) through participation, it necessarily follows, that greatness is greater than God. Not so is it concerning whiteness, because it is not bound to denominate itself nor to be predicated of anything through[3] (its own) essence, by denominating it.

DISTINCTION XXIII

CHAPTER I

On this name which is "Person", since it is said according to substance, it is accepted not singularly, but plurally in the Most High.

To the aforesaid[1] there must be added, that since all the names, which are said of God according to substance, are said singularly and not plurally of all the Persons in the Most High (Trinity), as has been shown above,[2] there is, however, one name, that is "person", which is said according to substance of Each Person and is plurally, not singularly, accepted in the Most High (Trinity). For we say: "the Father is a person, the Son is a person, the Holy Spirit is a person", and this is said according to the substance. And yet there is not said: "the Father and the Son and the Holy Spirit are one person", but (rather) "are three persons". Therefore, this name is excepted from the aforesaid[3] rule for the names, which are said of God according to substance, because since this is said regarding Itself and according to substance, yet it is accepted plurally, not singularly, in the Most High (Trinity).

Moreover, that "person" is said according to substance, (St.) Augustine shows in the seventh book, ON THE TRINITY[4] saying: « It is not one thing for God *to be*, another *to be a person*, but (it is) entirely the same (thing) ». Likewise:[5] « In this Trinity, when we say "the Person of the Father", we do not say (something) other than the Substance of the Father. On which account, as the Substance of the Father is the Father Himself, not whereby He is the Father, but that He is; thus also the Person of the Father is not other than the Father Himself; indeed "person" is said regarding Himself, not regarding the Son and/or the Holy Spirit, just as "God" and "great" and "good" and "just" and (names) of this kind are said regarding Himself. And according to the measure which for Him *to be* is that, which (is) *to be God*, which (is) *to be great*, which (is) *to be good*; so for Him *to be* is that, which (is) *to be a person* ». Behold you expressly have, that "person" is said according to substance, such as when there is said: "the Father is a Person", here the sense is: 'the Father is the Divine Essence'; similarly, when there is said, "the Son is a person", "the Holy Spirit is a person", that is "is the Divine Essence".

For this reason, there arises here an indeed difficult, but not unuseful, question, by which there is asked, why these Three are not said (to be) one person, just as (They are said to be) one Essence and one God. Which question (St.) Augustine diligently treats and congruously explains in the seventh book, ON THE TRINITY,[6] thus saying: « Why do we not say (that) these Three together (are) one person, just as (we say that They are) one Essence and one God, but we say (rather that They are) Three Persons, though we do not say (that They are) three gods, or three essences? Because we want also [vel] that some, one word [vocabulum] serve this signification, by which "Trinity" is understood, lest we would be entirely silent to one interrogating us, "What are the Three?", when we say that there are Three ». « When, therefore, there is asked, "What (are) the Three?" », as (St.) Augustine says in the fifth book, ON THE TRINITY,[7] « human speech labors head-on in great need [magna prorsus inopia]. Yet there has been said "Three Persons", not so that that would be said, but lest one would be entirely silent ». For the eminence of the ineffable subject [rei] does not prevail to be explained by this word. Behold, he shows, by what necessity there is said in the plural "persons", namely, so that we may respond[8] with this one name to those asking (us) concerning the Three.

---

[1] From nearly all the codices and edition 1, we have substituted *But* [autem] for *However* [tamen].

[2] The Vatican edition reads *is a being through participation* [est ens per participationem], but contrary to the manuscripts and the first six editions.

[3] Codex G has *as much as regards* [quantum ad]. — The same doubt is resolved by Bl. (now St.) Albertus (Magnus), here in a. 8, where he holds the first solution. Alexander of Hales, SUMMA., p. I, q. 48, m. 4, a. 3, § 6 says: Wherefore, (St.) Augustine ON THE TRINITY, (Bk. V, ch. 10) says: "That when "*great*" is said of a creature, such as of a house and/or of a mountain, "great" is said by participation, and the creature is not its own greatness; but when "*great*" is said of God, (His) greatness is said through (His) Essence, and He Himself is His own greatness. But here (St.) Augustine accepts "*great*", according to which it is common to "great in dimension" and "great in virtue"; for in God there no "great in dimension", but (only) a "great in virtue"; thus must it also be understood, when "*good*" and (names) of this kind are said. Therefore, in this manner (St.) Augustine want to says, that names of this kind are properly said of God by abstracting from the manner, by which they are in creatures" etc.. — The last proposition, which St. Bonaventure, posits concerning *whiteness*, St. Thomas, here on the text, demonstrates in this manner: We say a white thing (is) white, but we say "whiteness" is "whiteness" (i. e. it is not denominated "white"). For it is not necessary that, what is in (something) caused, be in the cause in the same manner, but (rather) in a more eminent manner. — See also (Bl.) Peter of Tarentaise, here on the text.

NOTES ON THE BOOK OF SENTENCES

[1] Codices B and E add *however* [tamen].

[2] Distinction XXII, ch. 3.

[3] Codices A B and E read *the afore-written* [praescripta].

[4] Chapter 6, n. 11, where the Vatican edition alone faultily reads *that it is not one thing to be God* [non aliud Deum esse], and edition 8 and codex C *there is a being-God* [est Deum esse] for *It is not one thing for God to be* [Non enim est aliud Deo esse].

[5] Ibid.

[6] Ibid., immediately after. — Here the Vatican edition and the other editions, contrary to the codices, to edition 1 and to the original, after *though* [cum] add *yet* [tamen]. A little after this the same Vatican edition and a few editions have *we be entirely silent, having been interrogated* [taceamus interrogati] for *we would be entirely silent to the one interrogating* [taceremus interroganti].

[7] Chapter 9, n. 10.

[8] The codices and edition 1 read *we would respond* [responderemus], and a little before this only edition 8 reads *by what necessity "persons" are said in the plural* [qua necessitate dicantur pluraliter personae].

CHAPTER II

By what necessity has there been said by the Latins
"Three Persons", and by the Greeks "Three Hypostases and/or
Substances".

By which necessity not only the Latin language [Latinus sermo], but also the Greek, laboring upon this matter, is constrained by nearly [pene] the same penury of names. Whence (St.) Augustine revealing [aperiens], what has been said of necessity by the Greeks and/or by the Latins of the ineffable Trinity, says in the seventh book, ON THE TRINITY:[1] « For the sake of speaking of ineffable (things), so that we might be able to speak in some manner, there has been said by the Greeks "*one essence*, three *substances*, that is, one *ousia*, three *hypostases*". For the Greeks accept substance in another manner than the Latins. But by the Latins there has been said "*one essence* and/or *substance*, *three persons*", because "essence" is not accustomed to be understood in another manner in our language, that is Latin, than "substance" (is). And to understand at least in an enigma, it has pleased (them) that it be said thus, so that something would be said, when there is asked, "What are the Three, which the True Faith pronounces to be[2] "three", when both one says that the Father is not the Son, and one says that the Holy Spirit, that is the Gift of God, is neither the Father nor the Son?" When, therefore, it is asked, "What (are) the *three* (things)?" and/or "What (are) the *three (persons)*?", we confer to find some name, by which we comprise those Three. Nor does (a word) occur to (one's) spirit, because the supereminence of the Divinity exceeds the faculty of accustomed speech. For God is thought more truly than is said, and is more truly than is thought ».

« Therefore, the Father and the Son and the Holy Spirit, since They are Three, let us ask, "What "three" are they?", and "What common (name) do They have?". For They cannot be said (to be) "three fathers", because only the Father is the Father There, nor "three sons", since neither the Father nor the Holy Spirit is the Son There, nor "three holy spirits", because the Holy Spirit by His own signification, by which He is also[3] said to be "The Gift of God", is not the Father nor the Son. Therefore, what (are) the Three? If They are said to be three persons, that which a "person" is, is common to Them ». « For certainly, because the Father is a person, and the Son a person, and the Holy Spirit a person, for that reason They are said (to be) "three Persons" ». « On this account, therefore, we say (that there are) Three Persons, because that which a "person" is, is common to Them ».[4] From the aforesaid it can be openly understood, by what necessity there has been said by the Latins "*three persons*", since "person" is said according to substance. Whence also that which a "person" is,[5] is common to the Three.

CHAPTER III

For what reason do we not say that the Father and the Son and the Holy Spirit are "Three Gods", since (we do say that they are) "Three Persons".

But, here, there is asked, since we say, that the Father and the Son and the Holy Spirit are Three Persons, because what a "person" is, is common to Them, that is, because the Father is a person, and the Son is a person, and the Holy Spirit is a person: why do we not similarly say (that there are) "three gods", since the Father is also God, and the Son is God, and the Holy Spirit is God? Because, namely, Scripture contradicts the latter; but the former, even if it does not say (it), yet it does not contradict (it). Whence (St.) Augustine moving and defining this question in the seventh book, ON THE TRINITY[6] thus says: « If, for that reason, we say, that the Father and the Son and the Holy Spirit are Three Persons, because that which a "person" is, is common to Them; why do we not also say (that They are) "three gods"? Certainly, as has been said before, because the Father is a person, and the Son is a person, and the Holy Spirit is a person, for that reason They are said (to be) "three persons". Therefore, because the Father (is) God, the Son God, and the Holy Spirit God, whey are They not said (to be) "three gods" »? Behold, he has proposed the question; pay attention to what he responds, as he continues [subdens]:[7] « Or whether, for this reason, They are not said (to be) "three gods", because Scripture does not say (that They are) "three gods"? But neither does the text of Scripture anywhere commemorate "three persons". Or whether for this reason it was licit from the necessity of speaking and disputing to say (that They are) "three persons", not because Scripture says (it), but because Scripture does not contradict (it)? But if we were to say (that They are) "three gods", Scripture would contradict (us), saying:[8] *Hear o Israel, thy God, is one God* ». Behold the resolution [absolutio] of the question, for what reason do we say (that They are) "three persons" rather than "three gods", because, namely, Scripture does not contradict it.

CHAPTER IV

Why we do not say "Three Essences", as (we do) "Three Persons".

However, there also emerges here the other question, which (St.) Augustine consequently connected (with the former), saying:[9] « Why », he says, « is it not licit to say (that They are) "three essences", because similarly Scripture, just as it does not say (it), thus does not contradict (it)? But if you say, that on account of the Unity of the Trinity They are not said (to be) "tree essences", but "the one Essence"; I ask, why on account of the same Unity of the Trinity are They not said (to be) "one person", and not "three persons"? For as the name for the Essence is common to Them, such that any single One is said (to be) the Essence, in the same manner, the word for a Person is common to Them ». « What remains, therefore, unless that we say, that these words (were) born by the Greeks and Latins from the necessity of speaking against the traps [insidia] and/or errors of heretics? And since the human need for speaking strives to proffer to human sense, what it holds in the sacristy [secretario] of the mind concerning God, whether through pious faith or through any understanding whatsoever, it feared to say (that They are) "three essences", lest there would be understood in that most high Equality any diversity. Again it could not say, that there were not a certain Three; which because Sabellius has said (there were not), he had fallen into heresy. Therefore, it asked, what it would say (that) the Three (are), and it said (that They are) "three persons" or "three substances", according to the Greeks ».

---

[1] Chapter 4, n. 7. — A little before this, the Vatican ed. with not a few edd., omits *by* [a] before *the Latins* [Latinis]. The words in the text *that is ... than the Latins* [id est ... quam Latini] has been interpolated by Master (Peter).

[2] Only the Vatican ed. and edd. 4 & 6, read badly *which ... the Three to be "three"* [quae tria esse tria etc.]; edd. 5 & 9 read *because* [quia] for *which* [quae].

[3] The Vatican edition and editions 4 and 8 omit *also* [etiam].

[4] The three passages from (St.) Augustine are read in loc. cit., nn. 7 and 8.

[5] Here the Vatican ed. and the other edd., contrary to ed. 1 and all the codd., add (faultily) *that is, this name, "person"* [id est hoc nomen persona].

[6] Chapter 4, n. 8. — From the codd. and very many edd., we insert *thus* [ita] before *says* [ait]. At the end of the text, the Vatican ed. and edd. 2, 3, 4 & 5 twice add *is* [est], namely after *the Father* [Pater] and after *the Son* [Filius].

[7] Ibid., with a few (words) interposed. — A little before this, the Vatican ed., contrary to the codices and very many editions, adds *this* [hanc] before *question* [quaestionem] in place of *the*.

[8] Deut. 6:4. The Vulgate reads: *Hear o Israel, the Lord, our God, the Lord is One* [Audi Israel, Dominus Deus noster, Dominus unus est]. (St.) Ambrose in ON THE FAITH TO GRATIAN, Bk. I, ch. 1, n. 6 and ch. 3, n. 23, reads (the verse in the same way) with Master (Peter) and (St.) Augustine; and (St.) Hilarly (likewise), ON THE TRINITY, Bk. IV, n. 8. — Immediately after this codex D has *solution* [solutio] in place of *resolution* [absolutio]. Then ed. 6 has *it* [illi] for *it* [illud].

[9] Ibid. immediately afterwards, and what follow is from n. 9. — At the end of the first quote, ed. 1 adds *and predicates the essence* [et essentiam praedicat].

« For what one is bound to understand of "persons" according to our (language), this (one understands) of "substances" according to (that) of the Greeks. For in the same manner they say "the Three Substances" (are) "the one Essence", that is, "the Three Hypostases", "the one Ousia"; according to which manner we say "the three Persons" (are) "the one Essence and/or Substance" »;[1] « though they also, if they want, just as they say "three substances" (are) "three hypostases", they can say "three persons" (are) "three prosopa". But they preferred to say the former, because perhaps, according to the custom of their own tongue, it is more aptly said ».

CHAPTER V

That in the Trinity there is not a diversity and/or singularity and/or solitude, but a Unity and a Trinity and distinction and identity.

It has already been sufficiently shown, I think, by what necessity we say (that They are) "three persons", and for what reason we (do) not (say that They are) "three gods and/or essences", because, namely, in the one Scripture goes against it, in the other the understanding of a diversity (does); because there is thoroughly no diversity There, just as (there is) neither singularity and/or solitude, but (rather) a unity and trinity. Wherefore, (St.) Augustine in the seventh book, ON THE TRINITY[2] says: « Human need seeking, what it would say that the Three (are), said (that They are) "three persons and/or substances", by which names it wanted that a diversity not be understood, but (similarly) it did not want a singularity, so that not only a unity be understood There from that, which is said (to be) "the one Essence", but a trinity from that, which the Three Persons are said (to be) ». (St.) Hilary also in the seventh book, ON THE TRINITY[3] says: « The Lord says:[4] *He who sees me, sees also the Father.* When He says this, there is excluded the understanding of a singular and also a unique, that is, a solitary. For neither does (His) discourse signify a solitary (Person), yet (His) profession does teach an un-differing Nature. For the Father has been seen in the Son through a united similitude of nature. For one (Being) [unum] are the One born and the One Generating, They are one (Being) and not one (Person) [unus]. And so the Son is not solitary, nor singular nor disparate ». Likewise, in the same (book):[5] « Just as in the Father and the Son it is impious to believe (that there are) two gods, so it is a sacrilege to preach that the Father and the Son (are) a singular God. Nothing among Them is new, nothing diverse, nothing alien, nothing separable ». Of this also (St.) Augustine in the book, THE QUESTION ON THE OLD AND NEW LAW[6] says: « God is one, but not singular ». Likewise, (St.) Ambrose in the book, ON THE FAITH[7] says: « What is of one substance cannot be separated, even if it belongs not to a singularity, but to a unity ». « When there is said "the One God", there is not at all excluded the Trinity of the Deity and for that reason there is preached not what (belongs) to a singularity, but what (belongs) to a unity ». Behold, from the aforesaid it is shown, that God is neither to be confessed (to be) "singular", nor "diverse" nor "unique" and/or "solitary", because singularity and/or solitude excludes the plurality of Persons, and diversity bear off the Unity of the Essence. A diversity induces a separation of the Divinity, a singularity takes away the distinction of the Trinity. For that reason (St.) Ambrose in the second book, ON THE FAITH[8] says: « The equality is neither diverse nor singular »; « nor (is it an equality) according to the Sabellians, confounding the Father and the Son, nor according to the Arians, separating [secernens] the Father and the Son. For the Father and the Son have a distinction, but They do not have a separation ». Likewise in the same (work):[9] « The Father and the Son according to the Divinity are one (Being), nor is there a difference of substance nor any diversity There; otherwise in what manner do we say (that there is) one God? For diversity causes many (things to be) ». It is established, therefore, from the aforesaid, that in the Trinity there is no diversity; yet if, at some time, there is found said in Scripture (that there are) *three diverse Persons* and (sayings) of this kind, it means (that) the diverse (Persons are) distinct (Persons).

CHAPTER VI

That God ought not be said (to be) "manifold".

And just as in the Trinity there is no diversity, so neither a multiplicity, and for that reason God is not to be said (to be) multiple [multiplex], but (rather) Triune and Simple. Whence (St.) Ambrose in the first book, ON THE FAITH[10] says: « There is in the Father and the Son a Divinity, not discrepant but one, nor can What is one be confused, nor (can) What is un-differing [indifferens], (be) manifold ». And, thus, God is not multiple.

---

[1] Ibid. n. 8; but the words *that is, "the Three Hypostases", "the one Ousia"* [id est tres hypostases, unam usiam] have been inserted by Master (Peter). The following passage is ibid., ch. 6, n. 11.

[2] Chapter 4, n. 9. — A little below this the Vatican edition alone reads *says* [dicit] for *said* [dixit].

[3] Numbers 38 and 39. — But Master (Peter) has woven this text together from seven passages of (St.) Hilary; which, to illustrate his method by an example, we here submit to the eyes of the reader: The first sentence and the second are from n. 38; the third is also from n. 38, a little before it; the fourth likewise, but a little after it; the first half of the fifth from n. 39; the second half from n. 38; the first half of the sixth from n. 39, the second half from n. 38.

[4] John 14:9. — A little below this, the Vatican ed. and the other edd., contrary to ed. 1, to all the codd. and to the original, read *there is excluded a singularity and also the understanding of a unique, that is, a solitary* [exluditur singularitas atque unici, id est solitarii intelligentia].

[5] Ibid., n. 39, but with the order of the propositions changed. For *a sacrilege* [sacrilegum], some codices and editions 1 and 2, have *sacrilegious* [sacrilegium].

[6] MIXED QUESTIONS FROM THE OLD AND NEW TESTAMENT, question 122. These do not belong to (St.) Augustine, but rather to a heretical author, perhaps Hilary the Deacon, of whom, we have spoken in Distinction XIX, p. I, ch. 4, p. 337, footnote 8. In the text, the Vatican edition together with the original, but contrary to all the codices and the other editions, has *solitary* [solitarius] for *singular* [singularis].

[7] Book V, ch. 3, n. 46. — The following passage is loc. cit., Bk. II, ch. 1. n. 18. After the end of the texts, all the codices and edition 1 have *that* [quod] for the *that* [quia], which the Vatican edition and the other editions have.

[8] Chapter 8, n. 69. — The following quote is ibid., ch. 3, n. 33.

[9] In the same work, but Bk. II, ch. 2, nn. 18 and 19.

[10] Chapter 2, n. 17.

COMMENTARY ON DISTINCTION XXIII

On substantial Divine Names, in particular.

To the aforesaid there must be added, that since all the names, which are said of God according to substance, etc..

THE DIVISION OF THE TEXT

Above, Master (Peter) dealt with the diversity of Divine Names in general. Here he begins the second part, in which he deals with the same[1] in particular [in speciali]. And since certain names are substantial, certain ones relative, and it happens that one considers them absolutely, and regarding one another:[2] for that reason this part has three parts. In the first he deals with substantial names. In the second with relative ones, below in the Twenty-sixth Distinction (where he says): *Now of the properties of the Persons, which we have frequently* etc. In the third with those[3] relative to one another, below in the Thirty-third Distinction (where he says): *After the above said, it is necessary that there be considered more interiorly* etc..

And, since among substantial names, this name, *"person"*, is excepted from the general rule, which is, that a substantial (name) is said of the Three singularly: for that reason he first excepts that name of Theirs[4] from the general rule, showing, that we ought to say (that there are) Three Persons; and this (he does) in the present distinction. But second, he determines what is signified through this name, "Three", and through this name, "Persons", when we say (that there are) "Three Persons", below, in the next Distinction (where he says): *Here there must be a diligent inquiry* etc..

The first part has four (parts). In the first, Master (Peter) excepts that name from the general rule. In the second, he investigates the reason for this exception, there (where he says): *For this reason, there arises here an indeed difficult, but not unuseful, question*, showing, that it was the need of human speech. In the third, Master (Peter), opposes and determines (questions) contrary to the assigning (of this name), there (where he says): *But here there is asked, since we say, that the Father and the Son and the Holy Spirit are Three Persons* etc.. In the fourth, he summarizes what has been determined [epilogat determinata], to add, there (where he says): *It has already been shown sufficiently, I think* etc.. The subdivisions of these parts are clear through themselves. For every part is subdivided into the two chapters, which it contains.[5]

TREATMENT OF THE QUESTIONS

For an understanding of those (things) which are said in the present distinction of the names: *"person"*, *"substance"* and *"essence"*, two (things) are principally asked.

First, there is asked concerning the transferal of those names to the divine.

Second, concerning the numbering of the same among the divine.

About the first three (things) are asked.

First, whether the name for 'person' ought to have been transferred there.[6]

But second, whether the name for 'substance' (ought to have been transferred there).

Third, whether the name for 'essence' (ought to have been transferred there).

ARTICLE I

On the transferal of the names, "person", "substance", (and) "essence" to the divine.

QUESTION I

Whether the name of 'person' has been fittingly transferred to the divine?

First, therefore, there is asked, whether the name for *'person'* ought to have been transferred there,[7] to the divine. But, that the name for 'person' ought not be said among the divine, is shown in this manner:

1. (St.) Augustine (says) in the fifth (book) ON THE TRINITY, and (as) it is had in the text:[8] « There has been said: "Three Persons", not so that that would be said, but lest one would be silent »: therefore, it seems,

---

[1] In very many manuscripts and edition 1, there is lacking less congruently *with the same* [de eadem].

[2] The reading of very many codices and edition 1, in which there is read *regarding themselves* [ad se] for *regarding one another* [ad se invicem], generates ambiguity and is contrary to what is subjoined; codices aa and bb, having made this change, reads *through a comparison to themselves* [per comparationem ad se].

[3] The Vatican edition, not trusting in the manuscripts and the first six editions, reads *with substantial (names) and (names) relative* [de substantialibus et relativis].

[4] Codices V and Y reads *that name* [illud nomen] for *that name of Theirs* [istud nomen].

[5] In the Vatican edition there is wanting this last proposition, *For every part is subdivided* etc. [Nam quaelibet etc.], which, however, is extant in the manuscripts and edition 1.

[6] The Vatican edition reads *whether there is a transferring of the name for 'person' to the divine* [utrum ad divina transferri nomen personae], but contrary to the codices, many of which, however, together with edition one have the indicative form, instead of the perfect subjunctive, for *ought to have* [debuit].

[7] Though the particle *there* [ibi] seem to be superfluous, yet as required by very many mss. and ed. 1 we have inserted it. [Trans. note: It seems that *there* here and just before footnote 6 in the text, signifies *in Master Peter's text* rather than *in God*, and thus is not superfluous. Indeed ignorant of this reason, perhaps, the Vatican edition in footnote 6 changed the reading to remove this apparent superfluity.] Next, in very many mss. and ed. 1, there is omitted less congruously *the name for 'person'* [nomen personae]. Then, the Vatican edition, contrary to the mss. and ed. 1, reads *And that* [Et quod] in place of *But, that* [Quod autem].

[8] Here in ch. 1, at the end.

---

that *"person"* is said among the divine solely to flee heretics and not according to the truth or propriety.

2. Likewise, this very (thing) seems *by reason,* because *"person"* names a particuliar and not anything whatsoever, but (that) of a rational nature; but from whatsoever a superior is removed, (there is) also (removed) the inferior: therefore since among the divine there is not speaking of a *particular,*[1] similarly neither will there be a speaking of a *person.*

3. Likewise, a particular of a rational creature is the most composed among all created (beings). For it has been composed from a corporal and spiritual substance, and again, among all, the corporal is seen to have more composition: therefore since *"person"* is the name of a particular, and this of one most highly composed, and among the divine there is a most high Simplicity, it is clear that among the divine the name for 'person' ought[2] not be said.

4. Likewise, our vocabulary [vocabula nostra] ought to respond to the Greeks, so that the unity of the Faith be shown; but the Greeks do not use the word *"prosopon"* among the divine, which is the same as "person": therefore, since they have a more proper vocabulary than we (do),[3] neither ought we use (it).

ON THE CONTRARY: 1. A *"person"* is said like one "making a sound through himself" [per se sonans], or "one through itself" [per se unum];[4] but a "one through itself" is most properly received in God: therefore, also 'person' according to its own name.

2. Likewise, a *"person"* is said (to be) one "having his own intellectual nature distinct from others"; but in God there is a positing of "one having an intellectual nature and (that) distinct from others", just as has been shown above concerning the plurality of the Persons:[5] ergo etc..

3. Likewise, *"person"* names for me the last the genus of rational nature; but a rational or intellectual nature is more noble among[6] created (beings), and again, the last among them is the most complete, because to it no

addition can be made: therefore, if whatever belongs to completion, must be posited in God most properly, it is clear etc..

4. Likewise, *"person"* means dignity. Whence among ecclesiastics "persons" are said (to be those) having some notable dignity:[7] therefore, since dignity is most properly in God, the name for 'person' most properly is to be posited in God.

CONCLUSION

The name for 'person' is fittingly and properly said among the divine to signify the distinction and most noble property of the Supposits.

I RESPOND: It must be said, that *"person"* from its own reckoning means "a supposit[8] distinct by a property pertaining to dignity". And this is clear in its *etymology* and in its *equipollent* (term).

In *etymology,* because a "person" is said like "one through itself" [per se unum].[9] But a "one through itself" is properly said to be "one, which is entirely distinct from others and indistinct in itself".[10] *Again,* "person" is said from "sounding throughout" [personando], as if from "resounding itself" [se resonando]; but "to resound" is said (to be) that which in sound is preeminent to others; and for that reason a *"person"* is said (to be) "a distinct supposit having a dignity", and by reason of this dignity, since (this) ought to be said through the nature of the word, <u>persona</u>, with the penultimate syllable said slowly [penultima correpta], a person is meant when the penultimate syllable (has been) drawn out.[11]

Similarly, the reckoning for this signification is accepted from the *equipollent* (term) in the Greek tongue, which is *"prosopon"*. Among the Greeks *"prosopon"* used to mean, just as (St. Severinus) Boethius relates, a "masked man" [homo larvatus], which indeed used to be done in tragedies; and it was done for the sake of two (reasons): one reason was to represent distinctly the one, from whom the discourse

---

[1] Cf. above d. 19, p. II, q. 2. — Next we judge the reading, by which *simply* [simpliciter] is put in place of *similarly* [similiter], which is most common in the manuscripts and editions 1, 2 and 3, less fitting, unless the words *simply neither* [simpliciter nec] are taken for *entirely neither* [omnino nec] or *in no manner* [nullo modo].

[2] Trusting in the more ancient manuscripts and edition 1, we have substituted *ought* [debet] for *it is necessary* [oportet].

[3] The Vatican edition, together with only one or the other codex, repeats here the words *and they do not use (it)* [et non utuntur]. A little before this codex V reads *this* [hoc] for *the* before *word* [vocabulo], and codex O puts *through (a consideration of what is) prior a* [per prius] for *a more proper* [proprius].

[4] The Vatican edition and the more recent codex cc have the feminine form for *one* [una]. Then edition 1 after *but* [sed] adds *a "being' through itself"* or [esse per se sive], while contrariwise codex T has briefly *this* [hoc] for *a "one through itself"* [per se unum].

[5] Distinction 2, q. 2. — A little before this, trusting in many manuscripts, such as F G H I P Q S T V W X etc., and edition 1, we have inserted after *intellectual* [intellectualem] the particle *and (that)* [et], which codex S also exhibits in the same manner in the major proposition. Then not a few codices, such as T and W, in the minor reads *a distinct (being)* [distinctum] for *(that) distinct* [distinctam].

[6] Codex aa adds *all* [omnia]. A little below this the more common reading of the manuscripts and editions, 1, 2, and 3, puts *what* [quod] for *whatever* [quidquid].

[7] In his COMMENTARY ON THE GOSPEL OF ST. JOHN, 1:23, n. 50 (Bonelli, SUPPLEMENT, tome I) St. Bonaventure says: *Worthy and eminent, ecclesiastical persons are called "persons".* — The Vatican edition and some editions in this argument, just as below in the body of the question, read *in the Churches* [in ecclesiis] for *among ecclesiastics* [in ecclesiasticis]; very many codices, on account of the abbreviation have an ambiguous reading; codices H and ee, together with edition 1, in the body of the question clearly exhibit the written form *ecclesiastics* [ecclesiasticis], which reading, both from the context and

the definition given in the COMMENTARY ON ST. JOHN just cited and from the custom of canon law, is confirmed.

[8] In many manuscripts there is read *(something) distinct* [distinctum] for *a supposit distinct* [suppositum distinctum], but less congruently; edition 1 has *something* [quid] for *supposit* [suppositum]. Next the Vatican edition, contrary to the manuscripts and edition 1, faultily reads *(and) pertaining* [pertinens] for *pertaining* [pertinente]. — Below in d. 25, a. 1, q. 2, in reply to n. 4, having cited the three definitions of "person", the Seraphic Doctor adds a fourth with these words: By the masters (of sacred theology) it is defined in this manner: a "person" is a "hypostasis distinct by a property pertaining to nobility".

[9] Thus St. Isidore, if you accept what Bl. (now St.) Albertus (Magnus says), SUMMA., p. I, tr. 10, q. 44, m. 1, but the same is ascribed here in d. 23, a. 2 to Simon of Tournay. — The Vatican ed., contrary to nearly all the codd. and ed. 1, reads in the feminine *one* [una], but less well.

[10] Aristotle, METAPHYSICS, Bk. V, text 11 (Bk. IV, ch. 6): For universally however, many do not have a division, to the extent that they do not have (it), to that extent are said (to be) one. From Bk. X, text 9 (Bk. IX, ch. 3): However, what (is) indivisible or not divided, (is) one. In PHYSICS, Bk. III, text 68 (ch. 7): Since "one" is indivisible, any "one" whatsoever is. — A little below this after *as if* [quasi], we exhibit the more common reading of the manuscripts and edition 1, by substituting *from "resounding itself"* [a se resonando] in place of *"resounding through itself"* [per se resonando]; perhaps it would be better to read *from "resounding through itself"* [a per se resonando]. Then some codices, together with edition 1, have *is eminent* [eminet] in place of *is preeminent* [praeeminet].

[11] This etymology of the name, "person", is found in (St. Severinus) Boethius, ON THE ONE PERSON AND TWO NATURES OF CHRIST, ch. 3, in these words: However, "person" has been said from "sounding throughout" [personando], with the penultimate syllable circumflexed [circumflexa penultima]. Which if the antepenultimate is accented, it will openly seem (to have been) said from "sound".

[12] Loc. cit..

was being made; the other reason was to better resound and/or sound throughout. And those two befit the two said[1] properties: and for that reason from this name, *"prosopon"*, among the Greeks, there has been drawn this name, <u>persona</u>, among the Latins.

And because among ecclesiastics a distinction of dignity is attained most of all, it was drawn *first* to signify honor among ecclesiastics. *Then*, because a individual of rational nature is distinct from others, and by this property of dignity among creatures, hence it is, that it has been extended to signify a supposit of rational nature. *Finally*,[2] because in God there is a finding of a supposit distinguished by a most noble property, at the dictation of the Holy Spirit [dicante], it has been transferred to the divine, because There is found more properly the Thing for the name [res nominis], though the name itself had been imposed upon others before. It must be conceded, therefore, that among the divine the name for *'person'* is properly and fittingly accepted.

1. To that, therefore, which is objected, that it has been *said*, not to be said; it must be said, that (St.) Augustine speaks on behalf of[3] that time, in which the name for *'person'* was equivalent, according to use, to "substance"; and for that reason it was said, not so that what "person" was accustomed to signify would be said, but it has been said like a transferred (name); *lest one remain silent*, that is, lest the confession of the faith be proved to have been diminished.

2. To that which is objected, that *"person"* names a particular; it must be said, that 'particular' from the reckoning of its name conveys 'a part' and 'an imperfection'; but 'person' from the reckoning of its name conveys 'a completion'; for that reason it is posited among the divine, though "particular" (is) not; and rightly, because among the divine the name of a species is properly said, and the name of a genus improperly.[4]

3. To that which is objected, that "person" names (something) most composed; it must be said, that this happens [accidit], because an individual of a created, rational nature is in a genus and for that reason is distant (from it) by many differences, since it is distinguished by a quality; but among the divine there is solely distinction by origin, and besides, He[5] is not in a genus; and for that reason it is not necessary, that there be There an aggregation of differences.

4. To that which is objected, that among the Greeks[6] they do not use the equipollent (term), namely *"prosopon"*; it must be said, that the reason for using (it) among the Latins was not so much propriety as penury, because they did not have something to respond with. And the reason for this was, because "substance" according to common use sounds the same as "essence"; but the Greeks had a proper word, namely "hypostasis", which they use: and for that reason they were not constrained to transfer ("prosopon" to the divine), as we (were).

SCHOLIUM

I. The affirmative conclusion is proved through the definition of *"person"*. This definition is built both from the etymology of the Latin word, and from the equipollent Greek term *prosopon* (πρόσωπον).*

On the words in the solution to n. 2: « among the divine the name of a species is properly said, and the name of a genus improperly », cf. above d. 8, p. II, Doubt 4; and Alexander of Hales, SUMMA., p. I, q. 48, m. 4, a. 3, § 4; and in regard to *particular and universal*, d. 19, p. II, q. 2.

On the concept of "person", cf. below d. 25, throughout, and d. 34, a. 1, q. 1.

II. On the conclusion: Alexander of Hales, SUMMA., p. I, q. 56, m. 1, and q. 57, m . 1 — (Bl. John Duns) Scotus, on this and the following questions, REPORTATIO, d. 25, q. 1. — St. Thomas, here in q. 1, a. 2; SUMMA., I, q. 29, a. 3. — Bl. (now St.) Albertus (Magnus), here in a. 1; SUMMA., p. I, tr. 10, q. 44, m. 1 and 2. — (Bl.) Peter of Tarentaise, here in q. 1, a. 1. — Richard of Middleton, here in a. 1, q. 1. — Giles the Roman, here in q. 2. — Henry of Ghent, SUMMA., a. 53, q. 1 and 2. — Durandus (of Saint-Pourçain), on this and the following question, here in q. 2. — (Bl.) Dionysius the Carthusian, here in q. 2. — (Gabriel) Biel., here in q. 1.

QUESTION II

Whether one shall use fittingly, among the divine, the name for 'substance' and 'subsistence'?

Second, there is asked, whether the name for *'substance'* ought to be said among the divine and/or even (that) for *'subsistence'*. And it seems, that (it is) so.

1. (St.) Augustine, in the fifth (book) ON THE TRINITY[7]

(says), « God, without any doubt, is said (to be) a "substance", and/or, if He be better named, an "essence" ».

2. Likewise, both (Sts.) Boethius[8] and Augustine say of the Trinity, that the genera of the other names, such as

---

[1] The Vatican edition, together with codex cc, reads *aforesaid* [praedictis].

[2] From many manuscripts, such as F G T etc., and edition 1, we have substituted *Finally* [Demum] for *Then* [Deinde].

[3] The Vatican edition, together with codex cc, but with the other codices and edition 1 striving against this, reads *of* [de] in place of *on behalf of* [pro].

[4] In codices aa and bb there is added: *On account of which (St.) Augustine says, that God is great without quantity, good without quality* [Propter quod dicit Augustinus, quod Deus sine quantitate est magnus, sine qualitate bonus]; in codex H, however, there is added *a name of a species, such as "good" and "great", a name of a genus, such as "what kind" and "how much"*, which exhibit the addition, which we note from codices aa and bb, in the margin.

[5] Supply: "God", and/or "a Divine Person". — A few codices,

such as Z bb and ee, have *on this account* [propterea] for *besides* [praeterea], a reading not to be spurned; a few codices, such as K and V, have *a person* [persona] for *besides, He* [praeterea]. — On this response see Richard of St. Victor, ON THE TRINITY, Bk. IV, chs. 13-16.

[6] Thus nearly all the codices with the first six editions, contrary to the Vatican edition, which reads *Greeks* [Graeci] in nominative. A little below this, trusting in the mss. and edition 1, we have substituted after *they did not have* [non habebant] *something* [quid] for *what* [quod].

[7] Chapter 2, n. 3.

[8] In his book, ON THE TRINITY, ch. 4; and Augustine, ON THE TRINITY, Bk. V, ch. 10, n. 11 ff. — Next, some codd., such as V & X, read (the subjunctive) *pass over* [transeant]. Then, trusting in the more ancient mss. and ed. 1, we have twice placed (the indicative) *pass over* [transit] (for the subjunctive). Codices Y and aa read sufficiently well *there the name* [nomen ibi].

---

* *Trans. note*: Here the original text of the Scholium had faultily πρόςωπον.

"greatness", "goodness" etc., pass over into the Substance: if, therefore, "substance" *does* not *passover* into another, it is established that the name for 'substance' is properly said; for if (it is) not properly (said), equally well would there be said, that "substance" passes over into other (names), just as (they do) the other way around.

3. Likewise, the reckoning of a substance according to the Philosopher[1] is "that which is a *being through itself* [ens per se]"; but God alone is most properly a *being through Himself*; therefore, the name for 'substance' is most properly in God.

4. Likewise, the reckoning of a substance according to (St.) Augustine[2] is "a being said *regarding itself* and absolutely"; but there is properly a "being said regarding itself", where there is no dependence; therefore, if this is in God, ergo etc..

ON THE CONTRARY: 1. (St.) Augustine in the seventh (book) ON THE TRINITY (says):[3] « It is unfitting to say of God, that He stands beneath [substet] His own goodness »; but if (this be said) of (His) goodness, by the same reckoning also of any property: therefore, simply speaking, it is unfitting to say, that He is a substance.

2. Likewise, (St. Severinus) Boethius in the book, ON THE TRINITY (says):[4] « God is not a substance, but above every substance »; therefore, the name, "*substance*", is properly in creatures and not in God.

3. Likewise, this very (thing) seems *by reason*: because[5] everything which stands beneath [substat], has something inhering (to it); but in God there is no inherent nor inherence; therefore, neither substance.

4. Likewise, everything which stands beneath another,[6] is composed with it: therefore, where there is no composition, nor a name for 'composition', there (is) neither the name for 'substance': therefore, since among the divine there is no composition, it is clear etc..

CONCLUSION

"Substance", to the extent that it means "to stand through itself, not through another", is properly said among the divine; to the extent that it means "to stand beneath an inherent accident", it is not admitted; to the extend that it means "to stand beneath either another distinguishing or another perfecting" it is received, but more on account of the imperfection of our intellect than according to a property of the Divine 'Being'.

I RESPOND: It must be said, that the name for 'substance' can be said from twofold property, namely, from "*standing through itself*" [per se stando], not through another; and[7] in this manner it is among the divine, and even more properly than among creatures; and/or from "*standing beneath another*" [substando alii] and/or others, and this is[8] in a threefold manner: either "(standing beneath) another *inhering* (in it)", and in this manner it is falsely and improperly said among the divine, because properties among the divine are not accidents nor inherent; and/or "(standing beneath) another *distinguishing*", and in this manner it is said not entirely improperly nor entirely properly among the divine, because that property does not inhere, but it does distinguish,[9] and for that reason it does not cause it to subsist or stand beneath, as if *standing under another*, but to exist, as if *to be from another* — and hence it is, that Richard (of St. Victor) days in the book, ON THE TRINITY,[10] that « it is better said (to be) an "existence" than a "substance" » — and/or because it stands beneath another as *one perfecting*, and in this manner *a thing of the nature* [res naturae] is said to stand beneath in respect of (its) essence. And that manner is more about our understanding than about the Divine 'Being' [divinum esse], because,[11] just as will be clear in the following problem, such a manner of speaking comes forth form our intellect, not from the property of the Divine 'Being'.

---

[1] Aristotle commonly defines "substance" *negatively*, as in his book, ON PREDICAMENTS, ch. "On Substance": « Nor is it said of any subject, nor is it in any subject »; and METAPHYSICS, Bk. V, text 15 (Bk. IV, ch. 8): « The last subject, which is not said of another »; but *positively* in PHYSICS, Bk. I, text 27 ff (ch. 3), where he calls it: « that which truly is » [illud quod vere est]; and in METAPHYSICS, Bk. VII, text 4 (Bk. VI, ch. 1): « a being simply » [simpliciter ens]. From these words and/or even those (said) in opposition to "accident", which according to Aristotle, METAPHYSICS, text 35 (Bk. IV, ch. 30) "is in another" [aliteri inest], or "the being of which is to be in another", this popular definition of "substance" seems to have been formed, which occurs in (St.) John Damascene, DIALECTICS, ch. 4, and in Averroës, COMMENTARY METAPHYSICS, Bk. VII, text 48: Substances, because they are existing through themselves [Substantiae, quia sunt existents per se]. — At the end of the argument, from the older manuscripts and edition 1, we have supplied the proposition *therefore the name for ' substance' is most properly in God* [ergo nomen substantiae propriissime est in Deo], which in the Vatican edition and the more recent codex cc is faultily lacking. A little before this, on the authority of very many manuscripts, such as H L M N O Y and Z, we have inserted after *is a* [est] *being* [ens].

[2] ON THE TRINITY, Bk. VII, ch. 4, n. 9: « But it is absurd, that "substance" is said relatively: for every thing subsists according to itself: how much more (then does) God »? And ibid., ch. 5, n. 10: « Each (i.e. "essence" and "substance") is said regarding itself, not relatively to something ». — Next codices W and Y read *but* [sed] in place of *therefore if* [ergo si], and codices V and X have *difference* [differentia] for *dependence* [dependentia].

[3] Chapter 5, n. 10: It is forbidden, however, to say, that God subsists and stands under His own goodness.

[4] Chapter 4: For the 'substance' in Him is not truly a substance, but beyond substance.

[5] The Vatican edition together with codex cc omits *because* [quia]. A little below this in not a few manuscripts, such as B X W Y and aa there is read *there is nothing inherent* [non est aliquid inhaerens].

[6] The Vatican edition, contrary to the authority of the manuscripts and edition 1, has less distinctly *something* [aliquid] for *another* [alii].

[7] The codices do not agree among themselves; the greater part of them, together with edition 1, exhibit *and* [et], in place of which some, such as A T V and X have *but* [sed], some with the Vatican edition have *if* [si]. Next after the following *and* [et] in many manuscripts, such as A F G I T V X Y Z etc., and edition 1, where is added *even* [etaim], which the Vatican edition omits.

[8] Some codices, such as A T and W, with edition 1, omit *is* [et]. Then after *inhering (in it)* [inhaerens] codex O adds *and this is the proper acceptance of "substance"* [et haec est propria acceptation substantiae].

[9] See more on this below in d. 33, q. 2. — In the Vatican edition and codex cc, there is wanting *but it does distinguish* [sed distinguit], which words, however, are extant in the other codices and edition 1. Next codex O prefaces to the words *to be from another* [ab alio esse] the words *to stand still beneath another, that is* [sub alio sistere id est], where also many codices, such as A C F I K R S T U X Y, together with editions 2, 3, 4, 5, and 6, read *because* [quia] for *as if* [quasi].

[10] Book IV, ch. 20: « Persons are more rightly said (to be) "existences", than "substances" and/or "subsistences" ». — From which last words the Vatican edition selects "subsistence" for the text, while the codices together with the first six editions exhibit "*substance*". Next from codices W and bb (ee by a second hand) for the sake of clarity we have added *another* [alii] after *it stands beneath* [substat].

[11] The Vatican edition with codex cc, with all the other codices and edition 1 striving against this, reads *and* [et] for *because* [quia]. At the end of the response codd. X and Z have *of the Divine Essence* [divinae essentiae] in place of *of the Divine 'Being'* [divini esse].

SCHOLIUM

I. According to the twofold property, which can be attended to in a substance, namely *to stand through itself* and *to stand beneath* (cf. above d. 8, p. II, Doubts 5 and 6), there is also given to the question a twofold response. According to the first property "substance" is rightly transferred to the divine; "substance" in the second sense or as one *standing beneath another* can, again, be understood in a threefold manner, to which distinction there corresponds a threefold response.

II. In regard to the sentence of Richard of St. Victor, that among the divine there is better said *"existence"* than *"subsistence"*, it must be observed, that he understands a *"subsistent"* in the strict sense for "that which has been distinguished through itself by that property, which is in it as *in a subject"*, *"existent"*, however, for "that which has been distinguished through itself out of the manner of an *origin"*. « But other doctors of Sacred Scripture accepts "subsistences" broadly for "hypostases existing through themselves in any manner whatsoever", and for that reason they call the Divine Persons "subsistences" and/or "substances" ». Thus Bl. (now St.) Albertus (Magnus), here in a. 1, in reply to n. 2; cf. also St. Thomas , SUMMA., I, q. 29, a. 3, in reply to n. 4.

III. The term *"a thing of the nature"* [res naturae], occurring here in the body of the question, and elsewhere frequently, has been taken from St. Hilary (ON HE TRINITY, Bk. IX, n. 3) and signifies a *supposit*. Cf. below d. 34, q. 1. — St. Thomas, SUMMA., I, q. 29, a. 2, in the body of the question, says: « A substance is said (to be) *a thing of the nature*, according to which it supposes for some common nature, just as this man is a thing of the human nature ».

IV. In the conclusion all agree: Alexander of Hales, SUMMA., p. I, q. 48, m. 4, a. 3, § 1, and q. 57, m. 1. — St. Thomas, here in q. 1, a. 1 and 3. — Bl. (now St.) Albert us (Magnus), on this and the following question, here in a. 4; SUMMA., p. I, tr. 10, q. 43, m. 1. — (Bl.) Peter of Tarentaise, on this and the following question, here in q. 2, a. 1. — Richard of Middleton, here in a. 1, q. 2. — Giles the Roman, q. 2, collaterals 1 and 2. — Henry of Ghent, SUMMA., a. 32, q. 5, n. 51 ff.; a. 68, q. 5, n. 4. — (Bl.) Dionysius the Carthusian, here in q. 1 and 2.

QUESTION III

Whether the name for 'essence' is fittingly employed among the divine?
Moreover, there is asked concerning the difference of the names: essence, subsistence, substance *and* person.

Third, there is asked, whether the name for *'essence'* ought to be said among the divine. And it seems that (it is) so.

1. (St.) Augustine (says) in the seventh (book) ON THE TRINITY:[1] « "Essence"[Essentia] is truly and properly said among the divine, such that, perhaps, it is opportune [oporteat] that God alone be said (to be) an "essence" ».

2. Likewise, this name, *"He who is"* [qui est], is the name, which God Himself imposed upon Himself;[2] therefore, if He names Himself properly, God is properly said (to be) *"He who is"*, but of whomsoever there is properly said *"He who is"*, there properly can be said (that) in him[3] (there is) an *essence*: therefore, "essence" is said among the divine.

3. Likewise, among all names, the name for *'essence'* is the most absolute, whence an "essence" according to Avicenna[4] is said (to be) "the quiddity of the thing according to an absolute name" [rei quidditas nomine absoluto]; since, therefore, among the divine there is an omnimodal absolution: therefore, (there is) also the name for *'essence'*.

ON THE CONTRARY: 1. We do not understand [intelligimus] 'God' except in creatures and through creatures; but the naming of God is through[5] our understanding: therefore, no entirely absolute name ought to be posited in God.

2. Likewise, I ask, in what do the name for 'substance' and[6] for 'essence' differ? For "substance" either means (something) *common*, or a *supposit*. If a *supposit*: therefore, the name for 'person' is superfluous; if (something) *common*: therefore, the name for *'essence'*

---

[1] Chapter 5, n. 10; in which text, trusting in very many manuscripts, such as G H U and ee, and edition 1, not without the original, we have expunged before an *"essence"* [essentiam] *through* [per].

[2] Ex. 3:14.

[3] The Vatican edition has *of him (that he is)* [de ipso] for *(that) in him (there is)* [in ipso]. A little before this, after *"He who is"* [qui est] thre is omitted by not a few manuscripts, such as A S T V X and Y, and edition 1, *properly* [proprie].

[4] We have made a review of only the more principle works of Avicenna (Venetian Edition, undated), namely, LOGIC, BOOK ON SUFFICIENCY, ON HEAVEN AND THE WORLD, ON THE SOUL, ON ANIMALS, ON INTELLIGENCES and THE FIRST PHILOSOPHY (Metaphysics). Though the sentence, which St. Bonaventure cites here, is not literally found in all the other works of Avicenna, just as it does not occur in the aforesaid works word-for-word, yet it seems that it can be gathered from the doctrine of Avicenna concerning universals. For, according to him, the essences of things can be considered under a threefold respect. « One respect of an essence is, according to which it is *not related* to any third "being" nor to that which follows it, according to which it is thus. The other respect is, according to which it is among these singulars; and the other, according to which it is in the intellect » (LOGIC, p. I, ch. 1). « Avicenna defends that an essence considered in itself, or to the extent that it is an essence, is most absolute, i. e. such that it excludes any respect. Thus, in THE FIRST PHILOSOPHY, tract 5, ch. 1, when dealing with the "being" of universals, he says: « We, therefore, posit two considerations (concerning the essence of "humanity") in this (one man), one consideration concerning it, according to which it is, and the other consideration concerning

its consequents. But according to the first consideration, it is naught but only a humanity; whence, if anyone will ask, whether the humanity, which is in Plato, out of this that it is a humanity, be other than that (humanity), which is in Socrates, and we necessarily will say: "No, one is not bound to consent to that, so as to say: 'therefore, this one and that one are one in number'"; since that negation was absolute, and we understood in that, that that humanity, out of this that it is a humanity, is only a humanity ... We will say, therefore, that this (one man) is a certain sensible, which is an animal and/or a man with matter and accidents, and this is a natural man; and this is a certain (man), which is an animal and/or a man considered in itself according to that which it itself is, not accepted with that "this" which is mixed with itself, without the condition of "common" or "proper" or "one" or "many", not in an effect nor in a respect even to (its) potency, according to which it is something in potency; for an animal from this that it is an animal, and a man out of this that he is a man, namely, as much as regards his own definition and his own understanding without the consideration of all others, which accompany him, is naught but an animal and/or a man » etc. Cf. St. Thomas, ON BEING AND ESSENCE. — In the conclusion of this argument, trusting in the older manuscripts and edition 1, we have inserted *also* [et].

[5] Thus the better reading of the manuscripts together with editions 2, 3, 4, 5 and 6, while the Vatican edition, together with edition 1 has *on account of* [propter]. A little before this in some manuscripts, such as A S T etc., there is lacking *and through creatures* [et per creaturas], but less well and contrary to the response to this objection, posited below.

[6] The Vatican edition, here, repeats *the name* [nomen].

is superfluous: therefore, since we ought to circumscribe our lips in speaking of God, by no means ought this name be posited in God.[1]

3. Likewise, there is asked on this account concerning the necessity and sufficiency and difference of those four names: "essence", "subsistence", "substance" and "person".

CONCLUSION

The name for an essence is fittingly employed among the divine; the reason and sufficiency of the four names is explained.

I RESPOND: For an understanding of the aforesaid it must be noted, that those four names or words [vocabula][2] respond to the four words in Greek, which are: "ousia", "ousiosis", "hypostasis", and "prosopon", such that "ousia" corresponds to "essence", "ousiosis" to "substance", "hypostasis" to "subsistence", and "prosopon" to "person".

But the reason and sufficiency for these[3] four names is accepted from other important reasons [ab aliquibus] in this manner. Among the divine there is an accepting of the *communicable* and the *incommunicable*, and this out of the truth and necessity of the Faith, which says that God (is) Triune and One.

And since we[4] ought to understand in God, what truly is, through that which we see among these inferiors, most of all according to (their) noble and first and chief conditions, since there is found in *common* among inferiors *what it is* and *whereby it is*,[5] by the reckoning of which it is signified in concretion and in abstraction, so that there be said "*man*" and "*humanity*": in the same manner among the divine *do we understand*, since we do not understand the two in that difference. For that reason also in abstraction *we signify* (Him)[6] through this name, "*Deity*", and in concretion through this name, "*God*". And for that reason we have imposed upon Him the name, by which there is signified that *whereby He is*, and this is "essence"; and that *which He is*, and this "substance"; and thus those two names are accepted on the part of (what is) *common*.

And, among the divine, there is also an accepting of what is *incommunicable*, and this is what (is) distinct, or Who (is) distinct. And this, indeed, happens to be understood or signified in a twofold

manner: either inasmuch as (it is) *distinguishable*, and this through the name for 'subsistence' or 'hypostasis'; and/or inasmuch as (it has been) distinguished, and this through the name for 'person'. And though in God the distinguishable and the distinct differ in nothing, because in Him potency is always conjoined to act, yet it does happen that they are signified[7] with a twofold name.

Wherefore, those four names differ according to (their) manner of being understood, just as *whereby it is, what it is, which it is, who it is* (do).[8] And since in God the same is *whereby He is* and *what He is* on one part, and the *distinguishable* and the *distinguished* on the other according to the thing, the Saints accept both "*substance*" and "*essence*" for the same (thing); similarly the Greeks also use the name, "*hypostasis*", for a "*supposit distinguished by an act*". Whence the distinction through *where by (it is)* and *what it is*, and through *the distinguishable* and *the distinguished* does not cause among Divine Names[9] a diversity, except according to the reckoning of understanding.

There were also[10] others wanting to say, that "*substance*" and "*essence*" are accepted on the part of (what is) *common*, but differently, because that *common* happens to be understood under a twofold reckoning: one is, "what all lack[11] for this, that they be"; the other is, "that which does not need others". In the first manner there is said "*essence*", from that and through that which all are; in the second manner "*substance*", since it stands through itself, with all[12] others excluded. However, "*subsistence*" or "*hypostasis*" and "*person*" are accepted on the part of the *incommunicable* and they do differ. For though each name means something distinct, yet "*hypostasis*" means a "*distinct supposit of a substance*", but "*person*" means a "(supposit) distinct by a noble property".

There were[13] others, who wanted to say, that those four names are distinguished through the *communicable* and the *incommunicable*, according to which each one can be signified in a twofold manner: either in *abstraction*, and/or in *concretion*. For the *communicable* can be signified[14] in *abstraction*, and in this manner it is said (to be) an "essence"; and/or in *concretion* to a supposit, and in this manner it is said (to be) a "substance". Similarly, the *incommunicable* can be signified in *abstraction*, and in this manner it is said (to be) a "subsistence" or "hypostasis"; and/or in *concretion*, and in this manner it is said (to be) a "person".

---

[1] Codex X has these last words in the active mood: *by no means ought we posit this name in God* [nequaquam debemus hoc nomen ponere in Deo].

[2] In many manuscripts, such as A F G H I K T V W X and Y, and edition 1, there is omitted *names or* [nomina sive], but in codex S there is omitted *or words* [sive vocabula].

[3] Some codices together with the Vatican edition have *these four names of ours* [istorum quatuor nominum], but next the Vatican edition, contrary to the more ancient mss. and edition one, has less distinctly *sometimes* [aliquando] for *from other important reasons* [ab aliquibus].

[4] The Vatican edition, together with codex cc, breaking with the other codices and edition 1, omits the explicit subject *we* [nos]. Next, as required by very many codices and edition 1, we have substituted *that* [id] for *that* [illud], and then from nearly all the manuscripts, we have changed *notable* [notabiles] into *noble* [nobiles].

[5] Trusting in very many manuscripts, such as H I K W X and ee, and edition 1, we have inserted *it is* [est], as these two are commonly exhibited. A little below this codex H has *with that difference* [cum differentia illa] for *in that difference* [in differentia illa].

[6] The Vatican edition, together with only a few codices, reads *He is signified* [significaretur], and a little below this, contrary to nearly all the codices and edition 1, it has *we signify* [significaremus] for *there is signified* [significaretur], where codices L and O read *what signifies* [quod significaret] in place of *by which there is signified* [quo significaretur]. In very many manuscripts and edition 1, after *we have imposed* [imposuimus] there is lacking *upon Him* [ei].

[7] Very many codd. with ed. 1 have *one signifies (them)* [significare]

for *they are signified* [significari], but less coherently with the preceding. Edition 1, moreover, has *reckoning* [ratione] for *name* [nomine].

[8] Trusting in the greater part of the codices and edition 1, we have omitted three times the particle *and* [et], with which the Vatican edition conjoins the sayings *where by it is, what it is* etc.; a few codices exhibit the particle *and* [et] only twice, namely between the first two sayings and between the last two.

[9] The Vatican edition, with some mss., reads less distinctly *all Divine (Names)* [omnibus divinis] for *Divine Names* [nominibus divinis].

[10] Not a few codices, such as A and Z, together with edition 1, have *also* [et] for *also* [etiam].

[11] Edition 1 has *need* [egent].

[12] The Vatican edition, less well and contrary to the more ancient manuscripts, together with edition 1, omits *all* [omnibus]. Very many codices, such as F H I P Q T Z and aa, and edition 1 have *it is through itself* [per se est] in place of *it stands through itself* [per se stat], and some codices, such as V W X after *in the second manner* [secundo modo] repeat *there is said* [dicitur]. A little below this codex L has *they are distinguished* [distinguuntur] for *they do differ* [differunt].

[13] Codex Z together with edition 1 here adds *also* [et], and next codices A S T and Y, together with edition 1, have *according to* [secundum] for *through* [per].

[14] We have corrected the reading of the Vatican edition from the manuscripts and edition 1, by putting *be signified* [significari] for *signify* [significare]. Then, after *concretion* [concretione], very many codices, such as A C O R S T W and Y, do not badly omit *to a supposit* [ad suppositum].

However, all these manners have been calumniated [habent calumnia]. The *first* indeed, which is taken through the distinguishable and the distinguished, because the Greeks use the word "hypostasis", where we use "person", and thus for a distinct supposit. And (St. John) Damascene[1] says, that « a "hypostasis" is a "substance with properties" »; and thus he signifies "one distinguished by an act". The *second* manner similarly has been calumniated, because "essence" does not seem to be signified in a manner other (than) as in the reckoning of "a cause in respect to others", since it is a most absolute name. The *third* manner has been calumniated similarly[2], because "substance" signifies in abstraction, just as "essence" (does), and *moreover* there is a doubt, whether there is an understanding of hypostases, abstracted from properties; and for that reason if there is not an understanding, in what manner does it happen that they signify?

And, on this account, there is a *fourth* manner of speaking, that says with the Faith, that God is Triune and One, inasmuch as it says "*One*", we cannot understand "one", if we do not understand *what it is*[3] and *whereby it is* one; and *whereby it is* one is that *which it is*, and *what is* one is that *which it is*. The first is the Essence, the second the Substance.

If we understand "*Triune*", it is necessary, that[4] we understand Him *who* is distinguished, and *what* is distinguished. *Whereby* He is distinguished is a property; but that One *who* is distinguished is always signified as One distinct. And this can be in a twofold manner: either as One distinct by *whatsoever* property, and/or as One distinct by a *noble* or notable property.[5] The first is signified by the name for '*subsistence*', which is said (to be) the first substance,[6] and it convenes not only with the individual man, but even with the donkey. The second is signified through this name, "*person*", which conveys a noble property and convenes with naught but a supposit of a rational creature.[7] Because the Greeks use the name for '*hypostasis*', just as we (do) the name for '*person*', for that reason (St. Severinus) Boethius[8] says, that the Greeks use the name, "hypostasis", for a supposit of a rational nature. With these things seen, the objections are clear.

1. Moreover,[9] because it is objected, that we ought not name God *absolutely*; it must be said, that although we do name God through creatures, yet we also cognize through creatures, that He has an absolute "being". The other (objections) are (thus) clear.

SCHOLIUM

I. For an easier understanding of some of the terms, occurring in this and the following distinctions, we note these things from the common doctrine of the ancients.

1. *Essence, substance, nature*, though in God they are the same (Thing) and are also often confounded in respect to creatures by (many) authors, yet in strict signification they do differ. "*Essence*" « is taken from <u>esse</u> ["to be", "being"], which is the most common » (St. Thomas, SUMMA., I, q. 29, a. 1, in reply to n. 4), and simultaneously most of all abstract and « most absolute » (St. Bonaventure, here in the 3rd fundament.), i. e., that which excludes every dependence and respect ad extra, and is « most of all most interior to each » (St. Thomas, SUMMA., I, q. 8. a. 1). An essence is properly that « which is signified through the definition » (St. Thomas, SUMMA., I, q. 29, a. 2, in reply to n. 3). Whence it can be said of the definitions [res] of every predicament. — "*Substance*" belongs to a more contracted signification, since it is said only of that, which is in the first predicament, and is distinguished against "*accident*", because it is that which is through itself and sustains the other. — "*Nature*" has a signification still more contracted. St. Bonaventure says (SENT., Bk. III, d. 5, a. 2, q. 1, in reply to n. 4): « In this does "essence" differ from "nature", that "essence" names the form of a thing in a certain abstraction, "nature" names that being in motion and matter, as the principle of natural operations ».

2. The *communicable* and *incommunicable* is twofold. One is the *communicable* through *identity*, by which something superior is thus communicable to its inferiors, such that it is predicated of them in a right manner. Thus "*man*" is communicable to every human individual. The other is the communicable through *being informed* or « through being constituted as one », by which something is thus communicated, such that it belongs to another thing by either a substantial and/or accidental form, just as a soul is communicated to a body, and any accident to its subject; cf. SENT., Bk. III, d. 5, a. 1, q. 2, in reply to n. 1. — In each manner the Divine Essence is conceived by us (as) communicable and communicated to the Persons, that is, as *that whereby It is* and as *that which It is*. For "the Divine Essence" is predicated in a right manner of the Persons (e.g. 'the Father is the Divine Essence'), and is conceived by us also as the reckoning, by which the Persons Themselves are God (e. g. 'the Father according to the Divine Essence is God').

3. The *particular* and *singular*, the *individual*, a *supposit* and a *person* differ. The "*particular*" can also be said in respect to a genus; but the "*singular*" or "individual" is always opposed to the "species". However, the "singular" is twofold: either in the genus of *accident*, and this is communicable to the subject as an accidental form; and/or in the genus of *substance*, and in this manner the singular and/or individual is *naturally* incommunicable in each of the above said manners. It is from the reckoning of the individual, that it has been divided from the others, which are and/or can be in the same species, (and that it is as) one existing undivided in itself. whence <u>de facto</u> an individual in the genus of substance (if we prescind from the Human Nature of Christ) coincides with a *supposit*, from the reckoning of which there is incommunicability; according to *concept*, however, both are distinguished. However, in what manner a supposit and the subsistence are distinguished in a singular nature, or what they add to the same both among created things and among the divine, is a difficult and controverted question, concerning which see below, d. 25, Scholium on q. 1, and in regard to a supposit in the divine, d. 34, q. 1. — Next *person* again contracts further the signification of "*supposit*"; for a *supposit* is also found among material things; but a *person* adds (to it) the nobility of an intellectual nature and for that very reason a higher grade of subsisting in itself. For

---

[1] ON THE ORTHODOX FAITH, Bk. III, ch. 6: For a "hypostasis" is defined (as) "an essence with its accidents".

[2] On the authority of very many manuscripts and edition 1, we have here supplied *similarly* [similiter], and next we have substituted *signifies* [significat] for *is signified* [significatur]. A little below this after *there is not an understanding* [non est intelligere] codex aa repeats *of hypostases, abstracted from properties* [hypostases abstractis proprietatibus].

[3] In codex T there is added here *one* [unum].

[4] Edition 1 reads *that* [ut].

[5] The Vatican edition, not trusting the manuscripts and edition 1, omits *or notable* [sive notabili].

[6] See more on *the first substance* or the individual substance in Aristotle, ON THE PREDICAMENTS, ch. "On Substance".

[7] Edition 1 has *nature* [naturae]. A little before this, very many codices, such as A T and Z, together with edition 1, have *notable* [notabilem] for *noble* [nobilem].

[8] ON THE ONE PERSON AND TWO NATURES OF CHRIST, ch. 3. — The Vatican edition at the beginning of this proposition, contrary to the manuscripts and first six editions, has *On behalf of which* [Pro qua] for *Because* [Quia], and then, not trusting in very many manuscripts and edition 1, it reads *as (St. Severinus) Boethius says, who says* [ut dicit Boethius, quis ait] for *for that reason (St. Severinus) Boethius says* [ideo dicit Boethius], and also a little after this, has *creature* [creaturae] for *nature* [naturae].

[9] Codices V and X read *for* [enim]. Codex V at the end after *The other* [Alia] repeats *objections* [obiecta].

material things subsist less in themselves than spiritual ones do, speaking _per se_. Whence intellective natures are said (to be) and are in a more eminent manner _subsistent forms_. On the person, cf. below d. 25, throughout.

II. About the difference and sufficiency of the four names, with which he deals in the body of the question, three opinions are cited, which all proceed from the same fundament, namely, from that distinction between the _communicable_ (the common) and _the incommunicable_ (the proper); ut they are explained further in slightly diverse ways, as is expounded in the text. The Seraphic Doctor considers all three opinions deficient in some manner (« they have been calumniated »). Against the first opinion he himself urges this reason, that theologians together with St. John Damascene accept "hypostasis" and "person" in the same sense; against the second, that the name, "essence", is being abused and that it causes it _to refer_ to creatures, though it is « most absolute »; which reckoning is confirmed by St. Thomas (SUMMA., I, q. 59, a. 2 in the body of the question); against the third he brings forward two reasons, the first of which has some difficulty. For the Seraphic Doctor seems to deny, that "substance" can be accepted in the concrete, though elsewhere (in a. 2, q. 2) he clearly teaches with St. Thomas, saying, that "person" can name a substance. Perhaps, he brought forward only a usage of speech on behalf of the argument; whence he also immediately added another reason. — Next, he explains his own opinion in an outstanding manner, with Alexander (of Hales) and St. Thomas agreeing.

III. Alexander of Hales, SUMMA., p. I, q. 49, m. 1; q. 57, m. 1 and 2. — St . Thomas, here in a. 1; SUMMA., I, q. 29, a. 2. — Richard of Middleton, here in a. 1, q. 3. — Giles the Roman, here in. q. 2, collateral 3. — Henry of Ghent, SUMMA., a. 68, q. 5; n. 4. a. 53, q. 4. — (Bl.) Dionysius the Carthusian, here in q. 2.

ARTICLE II

On the numbering of the four Names.

Consequently, in the second place,[1] there is the question concerning the numbering of the aforesaid Names; and, having supposed that this name, "_person_", is numbered, there is asked about this:

First, whether, among the divine, this name, "_substance_" [substantia], is numbered.

Second, there is asked, if "_essence_" is numbered.

Third, if this name, "_God_" [Deus], (is numbered), whether, that is, we can say in a Catholic manner [catholice] that there are "several Gods" [plures deos].

QUESTION I

Whether, among the divine, there can be said (to be) several Substances?

Moreover, that this name, "_substance_" [substantia] is numbered, is shown in this manner:

1. (St.) Hilary (of Poitiers says), ON SYNODS:[2] « They are, indeed, Three through substance, but One through consonance ».

2. Likewise, (St.) Anselm (of Canterbury says) at the end of the MONOLOGION:[3] « The Three are more aptly said (to be) "substances" ».

3. Likewise, (St. Severinus) Boethius (says) in the book, ON THE TWO NATURES AND ONE PERSON OF CHRIST:[4] « We say that (there is) one Essence and three Substances ».

4. Likewise, this very (thing) seems _by reason_, because the substance is the mean [medium] between the essence and the person; but a mean tastes [sapit] the nature of the extremes:[5] therefore, for the equal reason, by which there is said (to be) "one Substance" from the unity of the Essence, there will be able to be said (to be) "_several_" [plures] from the plurality of the Persons.

5. Likewise, every number is reduced to a substance after the manner of an origin [originaliter] — for accidents and/or properties are never numbered except through substance[6] — but acts are numbered and are said in the plural [pluraliter] among the divine: therefore, it is necessary to posit a number according to substance. But, that they sare said in the plural, is clear; for there is said: "the Father and the Son and the Holy Spirit create" [Pater et Filius et Spiritus Sanctus creant].

6. Likewise, "_the same_" [idem] is relative to substance, just as "_such_" [talis] and "_what kind of_" [qualis] (is) to quality; but this is false: 'the Father is the same with the Son', because (St.) Hilary[7] says, that we cannot say that God (the Father is) "the same": therefore, it is necessary, that a distinction occur [cadat] in substance; therefore, if, on account of the distinction of the Persons, we say (that there are) "several" Persons [plures personas], therefore, also "several" Substances.

ON THE CONTRARY: 1. Nothing is said more according to substance than this name, "_substance_": therefore, if substantial names are said singularly of All (the Persons), just as is clear from the rule of (St.) Augustine posited above,[8] it is clear that etc..

---

[1] From the manuscripts and edition 1, we have supplied: _in the second place_ [loco secundo], and a little below this, from the more ancient codices and edition 1, _About this: First_ [circa hoc: Primo].

[2] Number 31: They are, indeed, through substance Three, but, through consonance One.

[3] Chapter 78: « For these two Names (i.e. "person" and "substance") are more aptly chosen to signify the plurality in the most high Essence ». And a little after this: « Therefore, by this reason of necessity, that Most High and One Trinity or Triune Unity can be said (to be) one Essence and Three Persons or Three Substances ».

[4] Chapter 3: Whence we also say (in Greek), that there is one οὐσίαν and/or ουσίωσιν, that is Essence and/or Subsistence of the Deity, but Three ὑποστάσεις, that is Three Substances.

[5] Aristotle, POLITICS, Bk. IV, ch. 9, (ch. 7): For in this (medium) each of the extremes appears.

[6] Cf. Aristotle, TOPICS, Bk. I, ch. 6 (ch. 5), where he deals with the diverse manners, by which "_the same_" is said, among which is that, according to which an accident is [facit] one in number with its subject, in respect of which in the book, ON THE AUTHORITIES OF ARISTOTLE., there is added: whence accidents are numbered by the numbering of the subjects. — Edition 1 after _properties are never numbered_ [proprietates numerantur] adds _in themselves_ [in se].

[7] ON THE TRINITY, Bk. I, n. 17: But we, having been divinely instructed, to preach neither "two gods" nor "a lone (God)", will cite this reason of the Evangelical and Prophetic pronouncement in the confession of God the Father and God the Son, that in our Faith They each are the One (Divine Being), not the One (Person); nor Each the Same (Person), nor confessing Another between the True and the false. Cf. above d. 19, p. II, a. sole, q. 4, p. 364, footnote 11.

[8] Distinction 22, Doubt 2, near the end.

2. Likewise, among whatsoever there occurs a distinction according to substance,[1] there occurs a true diversity; but between the Father and the Son a "diversity" is not to be confessed, therefore, neither a "number" according to substance: therefore, there is no saying of several substances.

3. Likewise, (St.) Augustine[2] says: « that it is the same for God *to subsist* and *to be* »; therefore, since one is the "*to be*" [esse], one is the "*to subsist*": therefore, just as from the one "*to be*" there is said "one *Essence*" and/or the other way around, so also from the one "*to subsist*" there ought to be said "one *substance or subsistence*".

4. Likewise, (St.) Jerome (says) to Pope Damasus: « Who ever, except with a sacrilegious mouth, preached that (there were) Three Substances »?

CONCLUSION

"Substance" and "subsistence", as they mean "essence" are not plurified; if they are accepted in the sense of "hypostases", they are said in the plural.

I Respond: It must be said, that the name for '*substance*' as much as for a '*subsistence*' is accepted in a twofold manner among the divine, because each of these has in itself an understanding of the *act* and of the *preposition*. Therefore, a "*substance*" can be said (to be) a "quasi *standing through itself*" [per se stans], and/or[4] a "*(standing) under another*" [sub alio] or under a property. In the *first* manner there is only one (Substance) or it is not numbered, because There the "*what It is*" is one. In *another* manner, insofar as it means a looking-back to a property,[5] it is numbered or plurified. In the first manner it is worth [valet] only as much as "*ousiosis*", in the second manner it is worth only as much as "*hypostasis*". In entirely the same manner this name, "*subsistence*",[6] is distinguished, and according to the first [alterum] understanding it is equipollent to "*ousiosis*", according to the second "*hypostasis*"; and according to the first it is plurified, but according to the second least of all [minime].

And, because "substance" and "subsistence" can be said in a twofold manner, for that reason there comes (about) a diversity of manner of speaking among the Doctors. For (Marcus) Tullius (Cicero) and (St. Severinus) Boethius[7] say, that "*subsistence*" is equipollent to "*ousiosis*", and for that reason (St. Severinus) Boethius says, that it is not plurified; but they say that "*substance*" is equipollent to "*hypostasis*", and for that reason (St. Severinus) Boethius says, that it is plurified, and according to this manner do (Sts.) Hilary, Anselm and Boethius speak. But (Sts.) Jerome and Augustine want, that "*substance*" be equipollent to "*ousiosis*", and for that reason they say that it is not plurified, but[8] "*subsistence*" to "*hypostasis*", and for that reason they say that it is plurified. From these (considerations) the response to each part is clear.

It is also clear, why the Greeks did not transfer the name, "*prosopon*", (to the divine), just as the Latins (did); because it was necessary for us to transfer the name for *person* on account of the ambiguity (of our two terms "substance" and "subsistence"); and for that reason the Church[9] preferred to respond that (there are) "*Three Persons*" rather than "*Three Substances* or *Subsistences*".

However, to the argument which it makes, that substance holds a medium: it must be said, that "substance", insofar as it is equipollent to[10] "hypostasis", holds itself more with "person", and for that reason is numbered or plurified, just as "person" (is): but insofar as it is equipollent to "ousiosis", it holds itself more with "essence", and for that reason is neither numbered nor plurified, just as neither (is) "essence". Moreover, all those reasons, both[11] preceding and following (that one) speak of "substance", insofar as it is equipollent to "hypostasis" or "supposit", and in this manner it is plurified.

Moreover, the reasons for the opposite side run according to the other acceptation of this name, "*substance*". Similarly, must it be judged[12] concerning this name, "*subsistence*". But since the authority of (St.) Augustine, and the custom of those using (it), accepts that name, that is, "substance", more in that acceptation, in which it means that *which it is* or according to the ousia [usiosim] or that (which is) common: for that reason it is not commonly received, that there be said (to be) "*Three Substances*" among the divine.

SCHOLIUM

I. Since the terms "*substance*" [substantia] and "*subsistence*" [subsistentia] have been composed from the preposition *sub-* and the verb *stare* ("to stand") or *sistere* ("to cause to stand"), they can have a twofold sense from (their) etymology, or as St. Bonaventure says

(here in the body of the Question), they have « in themselves an understanding of an act and of a preposition » [in se intellectum actus et praepositionis]. Whence it happened, that the Holy Fathers, before these had accepted a determinate sense from the ecclesiastical custom, used them in a two-

---

[1] In some manuscripts, such as A P Q and Y there is wanting *according to substance* [secundum substantiam]. At the end of the argument, codex T reads *according to substance* [substantia] for *substances* [substantias].

[2] ON THE TRINITY, Bk. VII, ch. 4, n. 9: It is for God (the same) "to be" as "to subsist". — A little below this, after *so* [ita] in not a few codices, such as A I and T, and edition 1, there is lacking *also* [et] and in codex V there is then lacking *there ought to be said* [debet dici].

[3] Epistle 15, n. 4: « Will any, I ask, with a sacrilegious mouth, preach Three Substances »? In which text very many codices, together with edition 1, read *Has ... preached* [praedicavit].

[4] The Vatican edition, having put *and* [et] for *and/or* [vel], then repeats *a quasi standing* [quasi stans], but contrary to the first six editions and the manuscripts, of which, however, codices C O and T, repeat only *as if* [quasi]; codex cc and editions 2, 3, 4, 5, and 6, have less well *or* [sive] in place of *and/or* [vel].

[5] Trusting in the more ancient manuscripts and edition 1, we have expunged the here added *then* [tunc].

[6] In the Vatican edition and codex cc there are wanting the words *this name* [hoc nomen], which, however, are exhibited in the other manuscripts and edition 1; and contrariwise a little below this, after *ousiosis*, the Vatican edition, contrary to very many codices and edition 1, adds *and* [et].

[7] ON THE ONE PERSON AND TWO NATURES OF CHRIST, ch. 3, where (Marcus) Tullius (Cicero) is also cited. — Next, the mutilated reading of the Vatican edition, by which for the words *is equipollent to* [aequipollet] to *is equipollent to* [aequipollere] there is substituted *and "substance" are equipollent to* [et substantia aequipollent], is repaired on the testimony of the mss. and ed. 1.

[8] The Vatican ed., not trusting in the mss. and ed. 1, has *and* [et] for *but* [sed].

[9] The Vatican edition, with only codex cc, adds *also* [etiam].

[10] Codex S and W have *it is equivalent to* [aequivalet]. A little below this, after the second *for that reason* [ideo], we have substituted from very many manuscripts and edition 1, *neither* [nec] for *not* [not].

[11] In the Vatican edition and codex cc there is lacking *both* [et]; in codices aa and bb, however, after *those* [illae] there is added *authorities and/or* [auctoritates vel]. Next, very many manuscripts, such as A F G H I T Y etc., with edition 1, have *equivalent* [aequivalet] for *equipollent* [aequipollet].

[12] The Vatican edition with codex cc has the complete verbal form for *must it be judged* [iudicandum est], and a little below this has reads *of those using that name, namely "substance", it is accepted* [utentium nomine illo .. accipitur etc.] for *has of those using (it), accepts that name, namely substance* [utentium nomen illud ... accipit etc.]; but the authority of edition 1 and of the other manuscripts withstand this, very many of which have *accepted* [accipit] for *accepts* [accipit].

sense in their vocabularies, and consequently were able to respond to this question either in the affirmative or negative.

II. Alexander of Hales, SUMMA., p. I, q. 57, m. 3. — St. Thomas, here in q. 1, a. 1, in reply to nn. 4 and 5; SUMMA., I, q. 29, a. 2, in reply to n. 2. — Bl. (now St.) Albertus, here in a. 3;

on this and the following question, SUMMA., p. I, tr. 10, a. 43, m. 1. — (Bl.) Peter of Tarentaise, here in q. 2, a. 2. — Richard of Middleton, here in a. 2, q. 2. — Giles the Roman, here in q. 4. — Henry of Ghent, on this and the following question, SUMMA., a. 53, a. 5, n. 37, and a. 75, q. 2, n. 8. — (Bl.) Dionysius the Carthusian, here in q. 2.

QUESTION II

Whether, among the divine, there can be numbered several Essences?

Second, there is asked, concerning the numbering of that name, "*essence*". And that it is not numbered, is shown in this manner:[1]

1. Because among the divine there is a most absolute Unity, which is not multiplied: therefore since no name is absolute to such an extent, as the name for '*essence*', therefore, through that there is signified a non-multiplied unity: therefore, the name for '*essence*' is not numbered; and this is what (St.) Augustine says, what reason resists [repugnat].

2. Likewise, this very (thing) seems a minori.* For this name, "*God*", is a name for the Essence in comparison to a Person, but according to Scripture, in the Law, that is, in the sixth (chapter) of Deuteronomy,[3] God is said (to be) One and not several: and according to the Creed:[4] « Not three gods, but one is God »: therefore, also this name, "*essence*", is much less plurified, since is it said more absolutely.

3. Likewise, the Divine Nature is not multiplied in the Three; but this name, "*essence*", is a name for the Divine Nature, as (is) this name, "*substance*": therefore neither the Essence nor the Substance are multiplied[5] under their own names, as it seems.

ON THE CONTRARY: 1. (St.) Augustine in the seventh (book) ON THE TRINITY (says):[6] « Why are these Three [tria] not said (to be) one Person ? », and he is speaking of the Three Persons; but the neuter gender (of the word "Three") respects the Essence: therefore, since They are said (to be) "Three", therefore, (They are) "Three essences".

2. Likewise, it seems *by reason*: (St.) Augustine in the same book, (ON THE TRINITY),[7] says, that « the Father and the Son and the Holy Spirit

are said (to be) "three persons", because that which is a *person* is common to Them »; but this name, "*essence*", is a common one: therefore, "*three persons*" can be said.

3. Likewise, in the same place he says, and (as) is had in the text,[8] that « for that reason They are said (to be) "three persons", because the Father is a person, and the Son is a person, and the Holy Spirit a person ». Therefore, similarly, They are "three essences", because the Father is an essence etc..

4. Likewise, the Father and the Son are several beings [entes], therefore, several having entity — for it follows: 'there are several gods, therefore, several deities'[9] — similarly: 'the Father and the Son are: therefore, (They are) several 'beings' [plura esse]', therefore, several essences.

CONCLUSION

"Essence" is not numbered among the divine, because in the Three Persons the One and Same Nature has not been numbered.

I RESPOND: It must be said, that in every substance, of which there is a 'being' [esse] and an operating [operari], we necessarily understand a *nature* and *one having* a the nature. Therefore, since this[10] is in God, we understand in God a Nature and One having the Nature. And we say that "the Nature" (is) "the Substance" and/or "the Essence"; we say that "the One having the Nature" (is) "a Person". Therefore, since[11] in a rational creature it happens, that one person has several natures, that is, the corporal and the spiritual: so in a contrary sense, in God, on account of (His) most

---

[1] Not a few codices, such as A T X and Y, have *this is shown* [hoc ostenditur] and edition 1 has *here it is shown* [hic ostenditur] for *is shown in this manner* [ostenditur sic].

[2] See here in the text of Master (Peter), chs. 4 and 5. Cf. also below in dubium 3, on the text.

[3] Verse 4: *Hear o Israel, the Lord our God, the Lord is One* [Audi Israel Dominus Deus noster, Dominus unus est].

[4] Namely, the Athanasian Creed; in the words cited from it, very many codices together with edition 1 omit *is* [est]. Next after *therefore* [ergo], trusting in very many manuscripts and edition 1, we have inserted *also* [et] and then, from many codices, such as A F H M N T Z etc., and edition 1, we have inserted *much* [multo], but very many codices, such as K V X aa and bb, conserving the same sense, put *much more strongly not* [multo fortius non] for *much less* [multo minus]. Finally, at the end of the argument, the codices are divided amongst themselves: for some, and indeed good ones, such as A F G S T Z, together with edition 1, put *it speaks* [dicat], but others *is it said* [dicatur].

[5] From very many codices, such as A S T V W etc., with editions 1, 2, 3, and 6, we have substituted *are multiplied* [multiplicantur] for *is multiplied* [multiplicatur]. A little before this very many codices, together with edition 1, have *and ... (is likewise)* [et] for *as (is)* [ut].

[6] Chapter 4, n. 8: Or since on account of the ineffable conjunction these Three (namely, the Father, the Son, and the Holy Spirit) together (are) the one God, why (are They) not also one person etc.. — See also here in the text of Master (Peter), ch. 4, where another text of St. Augustine taken from the same chapter is cited, in which the verb *are ... said (to be)* [dicantur] is repeated, in place of which both the original and very many codices, together with edition 1, have the indicative form *are ... said (to be)* [dicuntur]. In respect of these words of (St.) Augustine

there is found a great variation in the manuscripts; thus very many, such as B D F G H I Q T and V, together with edition 1, read *Though/Since* [Cum] for *Why* [Cur], which is omitted in a few, such as P and Z; then some codices, such as A P S and T, omit the particle *not* [non], and not a few, such as V X and bb, after *said* [dicantur] read *of* [de] for *(to be)*. Next after *Persons* [personis], we exhibit the reading of codices T aa and bb; nearly all the other codices, in place of *but the neuter gender (of)* [sed neutrum genus], have *therefore, properly* [ergo proprie], which reading is either reflects corruption of the text, and/or an omission of several words.

[7] Chapter 4, nn. 7 and 8. See here, the text of Master (Peter), ch. 3.

[8] Here in c. 3; to which only in the text of the Vatican edition, together with codex X, there is prefixed to each of the three recurrences of *person* [persona] the word *one* [una], though many codices, together with edition 1, omit it only once, that is, the first time, but very many codices, such as G H M and Y omits these entirely, which reading we follow, as it convenes with both that of the original and the text of Master (Peter). Next, trusting in very many mss., such as H M P Q X and Z, and as required by the form of the argument, we have inserted *Therefore* [Ergo].

[9] Thus the mss. and the first six editions, contrary to the Vatican edition, which omits *several* [plures] from *several beings* [entes plures] and then in place of *several having entity* [plura habentes entitatem] reads *the Several have entities* [plura habent entitates]. A little below this after *similarly* [similiter] codex O repeats *there follows* [sequitur].

[10] Namely: a 'being' and operating founded in a substance. — Next after *we ... understand* [intelligimus], in codices aa and bb there is added another *necessarily* [necessario].

[11] We follow the very many codices and edition 1, by substituting *since* [Quoniam] for *in that manner in which* [Quomodo], and a little below this after *so* [sic], by expunging the *also* [et].

---

* *Trans. note*: Here, a minori is shorthand, for *an argument a minori*. Such is the topical syllogism, which arrives at an affirmative conclusion, by means of arguing from what the lesser could do or has, and concluding that the greater can or has likewise. Cf. Pietro Ispano, TRATTATO DI LOGICA, tract, "De locis", trans. A. Ponzio, (Bompiani, Milano, 2004), p. 172-175, n. 32.

high simplicity it happens, that the one Nature is had by several (Persons), since[1] it happens that It is had in one and another manner; and this cannot be by the Same. Therefore, because there is only one Nature had and (It is) not numbered, for that reason there is only said (to be) "one Substance and Essence"; however, because (there are) Several having (It), for that reason (there are) several Persons, with entirely no existing repugnance.

1. To that, therefore, which is objected concerning "essence" through this which (St.) Augustine says: "*these Three*"; it must be said, that he speaks less expressly and improperly; and for that reason his word must be explained.

2. 3. To that which is objected, that therefore, *Three*

Persons,[2] because "person" is common, and Any is a *person* etc.; it must be said, that ("person") does not mean the whole reckoning, but the part as much as regards the exterior word; for that reason one is bound to understand, that there is added there:[3] 'because what is distinguished is common'. Whence the Father is a person, and the Son is a person, not for the same (reason), but for another.

4. To the last which is objected, it must be said, that sometimes *being* [ens] is said as a substantive [substantive], and thus does not draw a number from elsewhere; sometimes[4] it is held as an adjective [adiective], and thus draws (its) number from (its) subject [supposito], and thus is not numbered in form; and in this manner it does not follow, that there are *several entities*, nor from this word, "They are" [sunt], that (there are) *several 'beings'* [plura esse].

SCHOLIUM

I. For an understanding of the solution to n. 3 it must be noted, that a community of *essence* is accepted in a sense other than a community of *person* or of persons. The former is a community of one same thing, but the latter a communion only of reckoning; cf. St. Thomas, SUMMA, I, q. 30, a. 4; Bl. (now St.) Albertus (Magnus), here in a. 5. Whence the latter means something common, which is *distinct* in the Three Persons. Thus there is understood, what is had in the solution to n. 3, namely, that the reckoning, which here is cited from St. Augustine, touches only part of the cause, whereby They are said (to be) "Three Persons". For in the reckoning of "person" there is included "property", and for this reason the Persons are plurified.

II. In the solution to n. 4, the words: « it does not draw a number from elsewhere » [non trahit numerum aliunde]

are to be understood in this manner: since <u>ens</u> *in the masculine gender* here (i.e. when there was said in n. 4, "several 'beings' " [sunt entes plura]) signifies a "supposit", it draws its number, from itself, not from another supposit. But <u>ens</u> in the neuter gender does not signify a supposit, but an essence or form; whence if numeral or partitive terms, such as <u>aliud</u> ("other"), <u>alterum</u> ("the other of two"), are adjoined to it, there is signified a multiplication of the essence or form, which among the divine is entirely false.

III. Alexander of Hales, Summa., p. I, q. 49, m. 3. — St. Thomas, Sent., Bk. I, d. 25, q. 1, a. 4; Summa., I, q. 39, qq. 1 and 2. — Bl. (now St.) Albertus (Magnus), on this and the following q., here in aa. 6 and 7. — (Bl.) Peter of Tarentaise, here in q. 2, a. 3. — Richard of Middleton, here in a. 2, q. 3. — (Bl.) Dionysius the Carthusian, here in q. 2, at the end.

QUESTION III

Whether we can say in a Catholic manner that there are "several Gods"?

Third, there is asked, whether in a Catholic manner we can say that there are "several Gods" [plures deos]. And that it is so, seems in this manner:

1. This name, "*God*" [Deus], receives a distinctive term by reason of (its) supposition, as when there is said, "God generates God": therefore, since the same distinction is conveyed through that which "*generates*" is and through that which "the Three" is, because (it is) a personal (distinction), therefore, for an equal reason this[5] is Catholic: "the Three are Gods".

2. Likewise, "*God*" is the same as "*One having deity*" [habens deitatem]; but there are Several "Ones having deity" — this is said in the Catholic manner — therefore, similarly the Several are "Gods".

3. Likewise, this name, "*God*", though it is substantial, yet it has been imposed from (His) Operation. But it happens, that (the Divine) Operation is said in the plural [pluraliter] of the Persons, as is clear in the first (chapter) of Genesis: *Let us make man* etc. [Faciamus hominem]:[6] therefore, also this name, "*Gods*".

4. Likewise, for the true numbering of anything, more [plura] are not required than a true multiplication of supposits and forms; but this is in God, because the Three are Divine Persons [tres sunt personae divinae]; "*Person*" [personae] means a supposit, "Divine" [divinae] (means)[7] a form: ergo etc..

5. Likewise, since every general (name) happens to be

---

[1] A greater number of the manuscripts, together with edition 1, read *since* [quoniam] in place of *because* [quia]. A little below this after *Therefore, because* [Quia ergo], on the authority of the more ancient codices and edition 1, we have put *one* [una] for *the same* [eadem], to make the sense more coherent with the preceding. Next after *Essence* [essentia] codices aa and bb repeat *and (it is) not numbered* [et non numerata], and after *and for that reason* [ideo] codex K reads *the Several are said (to be) "Persons"* [plures dicantur personae].

[2] From codices K P Q and aa, and edition 1, we have inserted *Persons* [personae], and next from codex H and edition 1, we have substituted the masculine form for *Any* [quilbet] for the feminine *Any* [quaelibet], to indicate the Father and the Son and the Holy Spirit, just as is exhibited in the third objection; as if the Seraphic Doctor proposes the *second* and *third* objection briefly. By which, both the reading received in the text is confirmed as true (from the very words of the objections), and the reason for the diverse readings in the manuscripts is suggested. For beside the reading of the Vatican text now cited, by some codices, such as A and T, there is put *for that reason* [ideo] for *Any* [quilibet], by others in place of the same there is had *He is a person*, *He* [est persona], but in codices P and Q the words *and Any is a person* [et quilibet est persona] is simply omitted.

[3] (St.) Augustine, ON THE TRINITY, Bk. VII, chs. 4-6, where this proposition is contained according to its sense among those, which he says against Sabellius, which passage is had by Master (Peter) in chapter 4. It is explained more clearly by (St.) Augustine in chapters 5 and 6, that "person" means 'something common which is distinguished', but "essence" 'something common undistinguished'. — At the end of the response in place of *but for another (reason)* [sed alia], the Vatican edition together with codex cc, less aptly, and contrary to the more ancient codices together with edition 1, reads *but for one (reason) and another* [sed alia et alia].

[4] Very many codices, together with edition 1, have less congruently *in another manner* [alio modo] for *sometimes* [aliquando]. At the end of the response, on the authority of codices H P Q Z and aa, we have supplied "*They are*" [sunt], which the context entirely requires.

[5] In very many manuscripts, such as I and I, there is had *it is* [est] for *this is* [haec est].

[6] Verse 26. — Next, after *therefore* [ergo], from many mss., such as A F G I M S T etc., and ed. 1, we have supplied the particle *also* [et].

[7] In the more ancient manuscripts and edition 1, here there is not repeated *means* [dicit], though in the Vatican edition and codex cc it is present.

specified, and "person" is a general name, it seems that it can be specified, when there is said: "Three Persons", to say in a still more special manner *which Three*, but this cannot be, unless a common name is added to the Three, nor is there a giving (of a name) other than this name, "*God*": ergo etc..[1]

ON THE CONTRARY: 1. That it is not said in a Catholic manner, is clear from the Commandments, according to the sixth (chapter) of Deuteronomy:[2] *Hear o Israel, thy God is one God* [Audi Israel, Deus tuus Deus unus est]. Likewise, in the Creed (there is said):[3] « Not three gods, but one is God » [Non tres dii, sed unus est Deus].

2. Likewise, this very (thing) seems by *reason*, because this name, "*God*", means the Divine Nature; but the Divine Nature is not numbered or plurified:[4] therefore, neither (is) this name, "*God*".

CONCLUSION

Though there are Three Persons, yet, according to the Catholic Faith, we cannot say, that there are "Three Gods".

I RESPOND: It must be said, that there is no saying of "several gods" [plures deos] in a Catholic manner, because a plural number signifies the plurification of the term according to supposit and form in a substantive name, since the plural doubles [geminet] its singular. And for that reason, since the form conveyed through this name, "*God*", is not multiplied, it ought not be said that (there are) "*several gods*".

1. To that, therefore,[5] which is objected, that in a Catholic manner there is said: "God generates" [Deus generat]; it must be said, that it is not similar, because "*generates*" conveys a distinction together with a convening; but "*that the Several (are) Gods*" [plures deos] conveys simply a distinction as much as regards supposit and form.

2. To that which is objected, that "*God*" is the same as "*One having deity*"; I respond in a two fold manner: that[6]

"*One having deity*" can be said in one manner *in the neuter (gender)* [neutraliter], and in this manner there is only the One, and it is equipollent to that, which is "*God*", which indeed means *what He is*; in another manner *in the masculine (gender)* [masculine], and in this manner it has not equipollent (expression), and thus is multiplied.

However, it can be said in another manner, that "*God*" does not signify "*One having*", but signifies (rather) "*the Deity*" in comparison to the One having; and for that reason it is not multiplied.

3. To that which is objected[7] concerning (the divine) operation, it must be said, that a name can signify an operation through the manner of an *adjacent* [per modum adiacentis], and in this manner it draws (its) number from elsewhere; and/or through the manner of a *substantive*, and in this manner it is not multiplied, and this name, "*God*", signifies in such a manner.

4. To the last which is objected, that there is a multiplication of supposits and forms There; it must be said, that this name, "*Divine*", is a quasi possessive; wherefore it is imposed by a twofold form, that is, (by the form) of *possession* and (by the form) of *the possessor*. And the form of deity is in the reckoning of a *possessor*, and the individual, existing form of a possessor, is numbered according to the form of *possession*, such as "*the sheep of Socrates*" [oves Socraticae]; thus (is it) also in the proposed (in its own manner);[8] whence the form had is not numbered.

5. To that which is objected, that a general (name) happens to be specified; it must be said, that a person, since it names[9] an individual of an intellectual nature, can be specified in a twofold manner, namely, through (the names) *proper to the Persons*, as when there is said: "the Three Persons, that is, the Father and the Son and the Holy Spirit"; it can also be specified through a *determination of nature*, as if there be said: "divine and/or angelic and/or human persons".

And *if you ask*,[10] for what reason it is not specified through one name, just as it is among creatures; because three angelic persons are said (to be) three angels; it can be responded, that this is on account of the need of human speech, under which both the Greek tongue and the Latin labor, but

---

[1] The sense is: in this saying "*Three Persons*" the name for '*person*', since it is a generic name, ought to be specified, so that there is cognized, what kind of or *which* are the Three; but this cannot be done except by the addition of this name, "*God*", which is common to the Three, by saying, "*Three Gods*".

[2] Verse 4, where the Vulgate reads: *Hear o Israel, the Lord our God, the Lord is One* [Israel, Dominus Deus noster Dominus unus est]. — The reading received in the text is exhibited by the codices and the text of Master (Peter), here in ch. 3. Cf. also the text of Master (Peter), d. II, ch. 4.

[3] The Athanasian (Creed). — In which versicle, very many codices together with edition 1, omit *is* [est]. A little before this the Vatican edition together with codex cc, reads *Wherefore* [Unde] for *Likewise* [Item].

[4] The Vatican edition has *specified* [specificatur], but contrary to the testimony of the manuscripts and edition 1, codex V reads *nor multiplied* [sive non multiplicatur] for *or plurified* [sive plurificatur], with which codex X agrees, by reading *or multiplied* [sive multiplicatur].

[5] Trusting in many manuscripts and edition 1, we have inserted *therefore* [ergo]. Next after *generates* [generat] in codex X there is added *God* [Deum]. Then in codex O after *because "generates"* [quia generat] there is added *conveys a distinction among the supposits, not in the form, because it* [importat distinctionem in suppositis, non in forma, quia]. Finally, codex bb put *and/or the Three* [vel tres], codices A S and T, *the Three* [tres] for *Gods* [deos].

[6] The Vatican edition, with not a few codices, has *as* [ut] in place of *that* [quod]; the reading received in the text is confirmed moreover, by the words posited above in the objection itself. Next the Vatican edition has *I respond, that that expressing is twofold, because* [respondeo, quod ista locutio est duplex, quia] for *I respond in a twofold manner: that* [responde dupliciter: quod], but contrary to edition 1 and to the codices, which, however, in congruously transpose the words *in one manner* [uno modo] after *in a twofold manner* [dupliciter] on account of the confusion of what is subjoined.

[7] The Vatican edition together with codex cc reads *is said* [dicitur]. Next after *a name* [nomen] in the manuscripts and edition 1 there is lacking the particle *either* [vel], added by the Vatican edition. At the end of the response codices aa and bb read *plurified* [plurificatur] for *multiplied* [multiplicatur]. — Alexander of Hales, SUMMA., p. I, q. 50, m. 2, resolving the same objection, says: It must be said, that though this name, "God", is a name of an operation, besides this it has the understanding of a perfect substance and (of) one standing through itself. But the divine operation is signified in a twofold manner: *as an adjective* [adiective] or as a verb [verbaliter], because verbs signify upon adjacent (subjects), and for that reason on account of the plurality of the Persons, it is signified in the plural [pluraliter], when there is said: *Let us make man to Our image* [Faciamus hominem ad imaginem]. But sometimes *as a substantive* [substantive] and as a name [nominaliter], not through the manner of an adjacent [adiacentis], which operation indeed is the same as the Divine Substance, and for that reason it will not receive the plural [pluralitatem].

[8] Understand: in its own manner. For in the cited example the form of the possessor (Socrates) is unique, the form of the possession (the sheep) is plural. Whence (according to the rule of Latin syntax) the plural adjective (Socraticae) is referred not to the possessor, but to the possession. It is otherwise in the expression "the Divine Persons", where the one form "divine" is in the Three Persons. Whence the plural adjective (divinae) is referred to the Three Possessors, who are numbered, not to the form or the Divine Nature. — Edition 1 after *reckoning of a possessor* [ratione possessoris], in place of *and* [et] puts *but it happens that* [contingit autem quod].

[9] The Vatican edition, together with codex cc, has *when it names* [cum nominat], and a little below this it reads *that is* [scilicet] for *namely* [videlicet]. Very many codices in the following propositions twice exhibit *be signified* [specificari] for *be specified* [specificari], but faultily.

[10] The Vatican edition, together with codex cc, has the indicative form *ask* [quaeris], which edition also a little below this, after *creatures* [creaturis], contrary to the manuscripts and edition 1, has *where* [ubi] for *because* [quod].

more the Latin. — And/or it can be said, that the nature of those names does not permit this, since a special name is imposed by a special form. Therefore, either it has been imposed by *the common Nature*, or by *a property of a Person*. If it has been imposed by *the common Nature*, since That is not multiplied, it cannot[1] be specified through one name. But if it has been imposed by *a property of a Person*,

since that does not convene with the Three, it cannot be specified through that. And for that reason the Church, compelled by necessity, responds (with)[2] a general name, or (with) what conveys the community of name, which is common and multipliable; and for that reason one is not to seek a specification through another name, except either through an adjective [nomen adiectivum], and/or through the Names of the Persons.

SCHOLIUM

I. The unity of God has already been dealt with above in d. 2, q. 1, and the plural form of this name, "*God*", in d. 4, q. 3, Scholium.

In the 3rd opposed argument it is said, that the name, "*God*" (Θεός), has been imposed from (the Divine) *operation*. This (argument) has been taken from (St. John) Damascene, ON THE ORTHODOX FAITH, Bk. I, ch. 9 (see above d. 2, Doubt 3, p. 60, footnote 2). The distinction employed by St. Bonaventure in the solution to n. 3 is explained in other words by Alexander of Hales (SUMMA., p. I, a. 50, m. 1, a. 2) in this manner: « A name for an operation is said in two manner: in one manner the name (has been) *imposed by the operation*, in another manner (the name is) *signifying an operation*. In the first manner (St. John) Damascene says, that this name, "*God*", is a name of an operation, because it has been imposed and is taken from the operation of fostering, seeing and/or consummating, through which opera-

tions *from the created things of the world there is cognized His sempiternal virtue and divinity* [a creatura mundi cognoscitur sempiterna virtus eius et divinitas] (Rom. 1:20). In the second manner, ("God") is not a name for an operation, nay it signifies the Divine Nature Itself, inasmuch as (It is) of this kind, and it has been imposed to signify this. Therefore, as much as regard that *by which* it is imposed, it is said by (St. John) Damascene (to be) a name of an operation; as much as that upon which it is imposed, (St.) Ambrose says, that it is a name of the Nature ».

II. Few of the ancient authors treat of this question explicitly: Alexander of Hales, SUMMA., I, q. 14, m. 2; q. 50, m. 2. — Bl. (now St.) Albertus (Magnus), SUMMA., p. I, tr. 13, q. 51, incidental q. 4. — Giles the Roman, SENT., Bk. I, d. 2, 1st. princ., q. 1.

DOUBTS ON THE TEXT OF THE MASTER

DOUBT I

In this part, there are doubts about the text (of Master Peter) and first concerning this which (St. Augustine) says: *One ousia, three hypostases*. For this seems contrary to that which (St.) Jerome says:[3] « Let us pass over in silence [taceamus] the "three hypostases"; it is not a name of good esteem [bonae suspicionis] »: therefore, it ought not be said. — *Besides* it seems, that the name, "*hypostases*", ought in no manner be received, and/or the name, "*ousia*", because (St. Severinus) Boethius says on the BOOK OF PREDICAMENTS,[4] that 'hypostasis' is 'matter', 'ousiosis' 'form', 'ousia' a 'composite'; but in the divine neither matter nor a composite is received: ergo etc..

I RESPOND: It must be said, that (St.) Jerome does not say, that it must not be said,[5] that there are "three hypostases", because it would be false and/or erroneous, but because the name used to be uncustomary, and used to seem to sound the same as "substance"; and "substance" according to the common acceptation is not said plurally of the Persons: and for that reason he wanted at that time to pass over it in silence, lest heretics take occasion to malign (it). But now that name has been specified and expressed; for that reason it is now conceded.

To that which is objected second, it must be said, that names of this kind are accepted in one manner in Philosophy, in another in Theology; and this is clear through (St. Severinus) Boethius himself,[6] who accepts it in one manner, speaking as a philosopher, and in another, speaking as a theologian in the book, ON THE TWO NATURES AND ONE PERSON OF CHRIST.[7]

DOUBT II

Likewise, is asked concerning this which (St. Augustine) says, that *God is more truly, than is thought*. For he seems to say the false, because every faithful (Catholic) thinks, that God is Triune and One, and nothing is more true than that: therefore, He is not more truly, than He is thought. Likewise, it seems false, what he says, that *He is more truly thought, than is said*; for we say many (things), which we do not understand: therefore, the truth of speech [veritas sermonis] extends itself more than (the truth) of interior thought. Likewise, I say, that God is most highly True; but nothing can be more truly thought than this nor be *greater*[8] than most highly true: ergo etc..

I RESPOND: It must be said, that the discourse [sermo] of (St.) Augustine is twofold (in sense). For there can be a comparison of a being to the

---

[1] From the more ancient manuscripts and edition 1, we have substituted *can* [potest] for the less apt *could* [potuit]. Next, after *But if it* [Si autem] very many codices with edition 1 have the verb in the subjunctive.

[2] The Vatican edition reads *imposes* [imponit], but contrary to the testimony of the mss. and edd. 1, 2 & 3; ed. 1, with some codd., reads *responded (with)* [respondit]. Near the end of the response, the Vatican ed., with not a few codd., having omitted *either* [vel], puts *and* [et] for the following *and/or* [vel].

[3] Epistle 15, "To Pope Damasus", n. 4, where in the original has *Let the "three hypostases" be passed over in silence* [Taceantur tres hypostases] for *Let us pass over in silence the "three hypostases"* [Taceamus tres hypostases], and then omits *a name* [nomen].

[4] In the chapter, "On Substance", where there, indeed, occurs the division of 'substance', into 'matter', 'species' (i.e. 'form') and that which is confected out of each ('the composite'), but not the appropriation of the Greeks names, "hypostasis", etc.. — A little before this codex bb and edition 1 has *nor* [nec] for *and/or* [vel].

[5] The Vatican edition, with one or the other codex, omits *it must be said* [dicendum]. Next, a few manuscripts, such as W and bb, have *which* [quod] for *because it* [quia], and then some codices, such as A S Y and aa, together with edition 1, have *and* [et] and codex T *or* [aut] for *and/or* [vel].

[6] Trusting in the more ancient manuscripts and edition 1, we have supplied here *himself* [ipsum], and, next, after *philosopher* [philosophus], we have inserted *and* [et], which codex O prefaces with *in (his) commentary* [in commentario].

[7] Chapter 3. — See more on this, above (St. Bonaventure's COMMENTARY), in a. 1, q. 3, and a. 2, q. 1.

[8] We offer the more common reading of the manuscripts and edition 1, by substituting *greater* [maius] in place of *more true* [magis verum]; codex cc, together with editions 2, 3, 4, 5 and 6, reads *nor be more highly true* [nec esse magis summe].

thought [cogitatum] itself, and of the thought to the *saying* [dictum]; and in this manner it does not have truth, because one and the same and equally true is the God, who *is* and *is thought* and *is said*.[1] Again there can be made a comparison to the *act* of being and of thinking and of speaking; and in this manner the discourse of (St.) Augustine has truth: since God in His own 'to be' [esse] has most high Truth; but our thinking since it is created and exemplified by the most high Truth, cannot be most highly true; similarly neither (our) speaking, and for that reason it has less of truth. — And *again*, since there is more assimilated to the most highly[2] True [summe vero] the interior act of thinking than the exterior act of speaking, thought has more of truth than speaking, because God is more similar (to it). But the reasons for the opposite proceed according to the first way.[3]

Doubt III

Likewise, is asked of this which (St.) Augustine says, that *the necessity of speaking and disputing allowed one to say "three persons", because Scripture did not contradict (this)*; but similarly, if there are not said to be "three persons", Scripture does not contradict (this): therefore, it is licit to say, that the Father, the Son and the Holy Spirit are not "three persons"; but it is not licit to say but the true [verum]: therefore the opposite of this is[4] false.

I Respond: It must be said, that that was not the whole reason that it was said, but (St.) Augustine left out [subticet] part of the cause. For the reason was, just as he himself reveals [aperit] in the following (passages), that

reason was consonant (with it), and Scripture did not contradict (it). For if Scripture contradicted (it), howsoever much reason dictated (it), it would not be said. And on this account it was not licit to say "three essences", because reason was not consonant (with it). But it is clear, why [quare] reason is more consonant in this name, "*person*", than in this name, "*essence*", if one attends to the signified of each. From the words of (St.) Augustine, therefore,[5] which Master (Peter) posits, it is clear, for what reason "*three persons*" was said by the Church, that it was a threefold reason. The first was, because the necessity was imminent; the second, that reason was consonant; the third, that Scripture contradicted (it) in nothing, nay even was consonant (with it). Wherefore, (St. Augustine) says less and understands more, when he says, that Scripture does not contradict (the saying that "there are not three persons".).

Doubt IV

Likewise, is objected against that which (Master Peter says): *there is thoroughly no diversity There, just as (there is) neither singularity*; because if this is true, therefore, there is every[6] identity There: therefore, (an identity) of Nature and of Person.

I Respond: It must be said, that the force (of the expression) is to be wrought in the word.[7] For "*diversity*" is attained as much as regards essential or substantial principles. Because, therefore, among the divine as much as regards substantial (principles) there occurs no difference; for that reason he says, that (there is) no diversity; for that reason it does not follow, that there is thoroughly an omnimodal[8] identity, unless there be added a determination, namely, in regard to the essential (principles); and in this manner that (objection) is clear.

---

[1] The Vatican edition, together with codex cc, reads *and who is thought and who is said* [et qui cogitator et qui dicitur].

[2] The Vatican ed., against the codd. & ed. 1, has *most high* [summo].

[3] (Bl. John Duns) Scotus, Sent., Bk. I, d. 22, q. 1, together with Ockham, Thomas of Strasbourg and not a few moderns, asserts, that it can come to be, that something is *more distinctly* named, than cognized, which seems able to be conceded under some respect, to the extent that *de facto* someone cognizing in a confused manner, while using a name signifying in a precise manner, can do this. But in this sense it is not opposed by the sentence and solution given by St. Bonaventure.

[4] The verb *is* [est] is wanting in very many manuscripts. Next, after *I respond* [Respondeo], we have supplied, from the more ancient codices and edition 1, *It must be said* [Dicendum].

[5] The codd. disagree amongst themselves; very many, among which are G H O Y Z and aa, with ed. 1, exhibit the reading received in the text; very many, such as L T bb ee & ff, have *moreover* [autem] for *therefore* [igitur]; then some, with the Vatican ed., omit any word. Moreover, trusting in the mss. and ed. 1, we have changed *the punctuation* in this passage; indeed the Vatican ed. conjoins this same sentence with the preceding and forms a new proposition beginning with the word *for what reason* [quare]. But then the sense does not con-

vene with the words of (St.) Augustine, related by Master (Peter) here in ch. 3, which do not explain the diverse signified of the words "*person*" and "*essence*", but the reasons, why the "Three Persons" are confessed by the Church. — A little above this, codex T has *was more consonant* [magis consonabat] for *is more consonant* [magis consonet].

[6] Codex X has *entirely* [omnimo]; perhaps better and more conform, since the response itself reads *omnimodal* [omnimoda].

[7] That is, the word "*diversity*" is to be accepted in the strict sense. In this manner Aristotle accepts it saying, in Metaphysics, Bk. X, text 12 (Bk. IX, ch. 3): But a difference is one thing and a diversity another. For it is not necessary that the diverse and that, from which (it is) diverse, be diverse in something; for indeed everything, whatever is a being, is either the same or diverse. But the one differing from the other, is different in something; for which reason it is necessary that something be the same by which they differ; but in this it is either the same genus or species, etc..

[8] From the older manuscripts and edition 1, we have substituted *omnimodal* [omnimoda] for *entirely* [omnino]. Then, very many codices omit the verb *there is* [est: *in the English translation, this refers to the prior verb*]. — On this solution, cf. below d. 24, in the Doubt sole.

A NOTE TO THE READER

FROM THE QUARACCHI EDITORS

With the first published distribution of this edition, it has been observed by very many erudite men, that it would be expedient, that from here on we restrict to some extent the number of the *critical* notes: it has already been sufficiently proven, that the Vatican edition dissents often and very often in minutia from the ancient codices; moreover, the readers of the works of St. Bonaventure nearly all care but a little, that in the notes an account be given of the small changes of words made in the text, when they touch upon the sense in a minimal way. Encouraged by the authority of these men, we shall from now on more frequently correct the errors [menda] and defects of the Vatican edition, without making mention of the matter in the notes. We shall, however, change nothing in the text, unless supported by the authority of the more ancient codices, at least of those which are more worthy of trust.

DISTINCTION XXIV

Chapter Sole

What is signified by these names: "one", "two", "three", "triune" and/or "trinity", "several" and/or "plurality", "distinction" and/or "distinct", when we use them, speaking of God. *

Here, it is opportune that a diligent inquiry be made [inquiri], since in the Trinity there is no diversity and/or singularity, nor multiplicity and/or solitude, into what is signified by these names, that is, by "*one*", "*two*", "*three*", "*triune*" and/or "*trinity*", "*several*" and/or "*plurality*", "*distinct*" and/or "*distinction*", when there is said: "one God", "Two Persons" and/or "Three Persons", "several Persons" [plures personae], "the Persons are distinct" [distinctae sunt personae]; and/or when there is said: "the distinction of the Persons", "the plurality of the Persons", "the Trinity of the Persons" and (sayings) of this kind. For, by this, we seem to be saying [videmur dicentes] that one posits in God quantities of numbers and a multitude of things and/or a multiplicity. Therefore, by revealing [aperiente] that of which we speak, let us take care to review [insinuare], what these signify There.[1]

If we diligently look into [intendimus] the aforesaid words of the authorities, to grasp the understanding of the (things) said, the use of these words seems (to have been) introduced by reason of removing and excluding from the simplicity of the Deity (those things) which are not There, rather than of positing any.

For, when there is said: "*one God*", a multitude of gods is excluded, nor is there posited in the Divinity a quantity to be numbered, as if there were said: "God is, nor are there many [multi] or more [plures] gods". Whence (St.) Ambrose in the first book, On the Faith,[3] says: « When we say "one God", the unity excludes a number of gods and does not posit a quantity in God, because neither number nor quantity is There ».

Similarly, when there is said: "*one is the Father*", and/or "one is the Son", and (sayings) of this kind, this is the reckoning of the saying, that there are not many fathers and/or many sons, thus also concerning similar (expressions).

Likewise, when we say: "that there are *several* [plures] Persons", we exclude singularity and solitude, (and) we do not posit a diversity and/or multiplicity[4] There, as if there were said: "we confess the Persons without solitude and singularity". Whence (St.) Hilary in the fourth book, On the Trinity[5] thus says: « God said: *Let Us make man to Our image and similitude*. I ask now, whether you estimate that a lone God spoke to Himself, or do you understand this sermon of His to have been given [extitisse] for another? If you say that He was alone, you are convicted [argueris] by the Voice Itself, saying: *Let Us make* and *Our*. For the profession of company [consortii] takes away the understanding of singularity

and solitude, because there cannot be any company with a solitary itself, nor does the solitude of a solitary receive a "*Let Us make*" nor to an alien to one's self would one say "*Ours*" ». Attend to these words, reader, and see, that (God) has signified a plurality by the name of '*company*'. The profession, therefore, of company is a profession of plurality, which (God) has professed saying "*Let Us make*" and "*Our*". For each is said in the plural; but by the profession of this plurality (God) has not posited a diversity and/or a multiplicity, but has denied a solitude and a singularity. Thus, therefore, when we say: that there are "several" Persons and/or a "plurality" of Persons, we exclude the understanding of a singularity and solitude.

Thus, too, when we say: "*Three* Persons" [tres personae], by the name of *a group of three* [ternarii] we do not posit a quantity of number in God and/or any diversity, but we signify that the understanding (is to be) directed to no other (being) except to the Father and the Son and the Holy Spirit, so that the understanding of the saying [dicti] is this:[6] 'there are Three Persons', and/or 'the Three are the Father and the Son and the Holy Spirit', that is, 'not only the Father, nor only the Son, nor only the Father and the Son, are in the Deity, but also the Holy Spirit, and no other (person) than These'. Similarly, 'not only is this Person and/or That, and/or This and that (Person) is There, but this (Person) and That and That,[7] and no other (person)'. And (St.) Augustine sufficiently shows that thus this will be understood, where he says,[8] that by that name (human need) wanted no diversity to be understood, but was (similarly) unwilling that a singularity (be understood).

Similarly, when we say:[9] "the Father and the Son are two [duo]", we do not posit the quantity of duality There, but signify this, that there is not only the Father nor only the Son, but the Father and the Son, and this One is not that One; and thus of the other (sayings) of this kind. Thus also, when we say: "the Father and the Son are two [duae] Persons", we signify this, that not only the Father is a Person, nor only the Son is a Person, but the Father is a Person, and the Son is a Person, and this (Person) is not that (Person).

Moreover, when we say: "the Persons are[10] *distinct*" [distinctae], and/or "there is a distinction among the Persons", we exclude (Their) confusion and thorough mingling [permixtionem], and we signify that this (Person) is not that (Person). And when we add: "the Persons are distinguished by properties or (are) different by properties", we signify that One is this Person and the Other (is) that (Person) by Their own properties. And when we say: "*the One and the Other*" [aliam et aliam], we do not posit a diversity and/or alienation (of Persons) There, but we do exclude the Sabellius' confusion (of the Persons).

Thus, too, when the Persons are said (to be) "*discrete*" [discretae], and/or when a discretion [discretio] is said to be among the Persons, we cause the same signification. For "*distinction*" is accepted There in that[11] manner,

---

[1] Only the Vatican edition and edition 6, together with codex D, has not so well *to themselves* [sibi] for *There* [ibi].

[2] Namely, in d. XXIII. The sentence of Master (Peter) which says, that unity and numbers are only to be accepted in the divine *privatively*, not *positively*, is not held more commonly by the other Scholastics; cf. St. Bonaventure's Commentaria, here in a. 1, q. 1, and in a. 2, q. 2.

[3] Chapter 2, n. 19; according to its sense. For thus there is read in (St.) Ambrose: « A diversity makes several [plures], a unity of power excludes a quantity of number, because a unity is not a number ». (St.) Ambrose repeats the same opinion in On the Holy Spirit, Bk. III, ch. 13, n. 93. — All the codices and edd. 1, 2, 3, 7 and 9, cite the *book of St. Ambrose* under the title *On the Trinity* [de Trinitate]. A little before this only the Vatican edition and edition 1 insert *if* [si] after *as if* [tanquam].

[4] The Vatican edition and the editions, except nns. 1 and 6, contrary to the codices, read *we posit neither a diversity nor a multiplicity* [nec diversitatem nec multiplicitatem ... ponimus].

[5] Number 17. However, the final words differ not a little from

the original, with (St.) Hilary saying: He took away the understanding of *a singular* by the profession of *company*. But there cannot be any company with a solitary to itself. Nor, again, does the solitude of a solitary receive a "*Let Us make*"; nor does anyone say "*Our*" to an alien to oneself. — The passage of Scripture is Gen. 1:26.

[6] The Vatican edition and very many editions have *of this saying is* [est huius dicti], contrary to all the codices and edition 1.

[7] The Vatican edition and edition 1 omits *and That* [et illa], which here signifies the Third Person of the Trinity.

[8] On the Trinity, Bk VII, ch. 4, n. 9. [Trans. note. *human need* is supplied, from the context of the passage in St. Augustine.]

[9] The Vatican edition, together with very many editions, reads *there is said* [dicitur] for *we say* [dicimus].

[10] Only the Vatican edition and edition 4 omit *are* [sunt].

[11] The Vatican edition and very many editions have *the same* [eodem] for *that* [eo], and a little before this *Thus also* [Ita et] in place of *Thus also* [Ita etiam].

---

* *Trans. note*: Here Master Peter Lombard discusses, among other things, the differing significations of the Latin words for *one* [unus, una], *two* [duo, duae] and *three* [tres, tria], which on account of having gender in Latin, implicate more than a merely numerical signification.

in which "*discretion*" (is). And congruously there is said to be a "discretion" and/or a "distinction" There, not a "diversity" and/or a "division" or a "separation". Whence (St.) Ambrose in the first book, ON THE FAITH (says):[1] « It is not the Father Himself, who is the Son, but between the Father and the Son there is an expressed distinction ».

However, when there is said:[2] "*the Trinity*", it seems that there is signified that, which is signified, when there is said: "*the Three Persons*", as, just as there cannot be said: "the Father is the Three Persons", and/or "the Son is the Three Persons", so there ought not be said: "the Father is the Trinity", and/or "the Son is the Trinity".

Here, it must not be overlooked, that, since as has been said above,[3] God is not to be confessed to be singular nor manifold, and that has been confirmed by the authorities of the Saints, (St.) Isidore seems to think in the contrary, saying:[4] « One must distinguish between a trinity and a unity. For a unity (is) simple and singular, but a trinity (is) manifold and numerable; because a trinity is a unity of three ». Behold, he says that a unity is singular, and a trinity manifold and numerable. But to this we say, that he accepts "*singular*" [singularem], just as the others accept "*one*" [unum]; but "*manifold*" [multiplex] and "*numerable*" [numerabilem],[5] just as the others say "*triune*" [triunum].

COMMENTARY ON DISTINCTION XXIV

What does a numeral name signify among the Divine?

Here, it is opportune that a diligent inquiry be made, since in the Trinity there is no diversity.

THE DIVISION OF THE TEXT

Above, Master (Peter) excepted[1] this name, "*person*", from the general rule for substantial names, showing, that there must be said "*Three Persons*", not "*Three Essences*" and/or "*Three Substances*". Here he begins the *second* part, in which he determines, what is signified, when there is said "*Three Persons*"; and this part has two parts. In the *first*, he shows, what is signified[2] through a numeral saying; in the *second*, what is signified through this name, "*person*", below in the Twenty-fifth Distinction (where he says): *Moreover, one must consider, since this name, "person", as has been said before* etc..

The *first* part, again, has two (parts): in the first, he asks and solves in a general manner; in the second, he adapts his own solution to the distinctive[3] names in particular [in speciali], there (where he says): *For when there is said, "one God"*. And this second part has four parts. In the first, he determines, what "*one*" and "*several*" signify; in the second, what "*two*" and "*three*" signify, there (where he says): *Thus also, when we say "Three Persons" by the name of a group of three*; in the third, what "*discrete*" and "*distinct*" signify, there (where he says): *Moreover, when we say: "the Persons are distinct"*; in the fourth, what "*trinity*" and "*triune*" signify, there (where he says): *Therefore, when there is said "the Trinity"* etc..

TREATMENT OF THE QUESTIONS

For an understanding of those (things), which are said in the present distinction , there is the question concerning numeral terms [terminis numeralibus], in what manner they are accepted among the divine. And about this three (things) are principally asked.

First there is asked concerning the numeral and partitive term, just as is this name, "*one*" [unus].

Second, concerning a simply numeral term, just as is this name, "*three*" [tres].

Third, concerning the name[4] comprising each, such this name, "*triune*" [trinus].

And as much as regards the first, two (questions) are asked:

First there is asked, whether this name, "*one*", is said positively, and/or privatively, among the divine.

Second, whether it is said according to substance [secundum substantiam], and/or according to relation [secundum relationem].

---

[1] That is, ON THE FAITH TO GRATIAN, ch. 2, n. 16.

[2] Editions 2 and 5 add "*the Triune God*" and/or when there is said [Deus trinus vel cum dicitur].

[3] Distinction XXIII, ch. 6.

[4] We have not found this passage in the editions of (St.) Isidore, cited even by the other Scholastics: A unity is simple and singular, but a trinity manifold and numerable.

[5] Only the Vatican edition has *numeral* [numeralem], and afterwards reads *they* for *the others* [alii]. Edition 8, just as after *accept "one"* [accipiunt unum] by glossing it adds *in regard to the Essence* [in essentia], so at the end adds *in regard to the Persons* [in personis].

NOTES ON THE COMMENTARY

[1] The Vatican edition alone reads *Master (Peter) excepts* [excipit]. Next, very many codices, together with edition 1, have *general* [generalium] for *substantial* [substantialium], but this responds less to the words of Master (Peter), in the preceding distinction, ch. 1. A little below this the Vatican edition, together with one or the other codex, after *and/or* [vel] adds "*Three Gods*" and/or [tres dii vel].

[2] In the Vatican edition, with nearly all the mss. and ed. 1 dissenting, there is added *through a numeral name or* [per nomen numerale sive].

[3] The Vatican edition faultily reads with some mss. *distinct* [distinctis]. Next, after *this* [haec], trusting in very many mss. and ed. 1, we have inserted *second* [secunda], by which word the reading is rendered more distinct. In the subjoined propositions, the Vatican ed. with a few codd. twice reads *what is signified through* [quid significetur per] for *what ... signify* [quid significent], and the third time *signifies* [significet].

[4] Codex bb has *term* [termino]. A little further, after *just as* [sicut], edition 1 adds *is* [est].

---

* *Trans. note*: At the end of this paragraph, the final citation from the text of Master Peter is rendered according to St. Bonaventure's reading; whereas in the critical edition of Lombard, accompanying this edition, there is had *However* [vero] for *Therefore* [vero]. These kind of variations, from the critical text of Lombard's SENTENCES, occur frequently throughout the Divisions of the Text, presented by the Seraphic Doctor; on account of the fact that the text of Lombard which he used, was not one known to the Quaracchi editors; let the reader remember this, when cross referencing to Lombard.

ARTICLE I

On numeral and partitive term, "one" [unus].

QUESTION I

Whether this name, "one", is said positively, and/or privatively, among the divine?

Moreover, that ("one")[1] is said privatively in all (things), seems by this:

1. Through its reckoning. For the Philosopher[2] says, that '*one*' [unum] is that which is not divided; but that reckoning has been given through a privation: therefore, 'one' is said privatively.

2. Likewise, the Commentator says on (Aristotle's) METAPHYSICS,[3] that 'one'* and 'many' [multa] are opposed just as 'privation' and 'having' [habitus] (are), because 'one' means a privation, a 'multitude' means a having; which if (this) is true, 'one' is not only said privatively in God, but even in all (things).

3. Likewise, this very (thing) seems by *reason*, because 'one' is opposed to that which is 'many': therefore, either *contradictorily*, or *contrarily*, or *privatively*, or *relatively*. Not *contradictorily*; this is clear. Again[4] neither *relatively*, because relatives are together, and one (relative) depends from the other mutually; but 'one' does not depend upon 'many'. Not *contrarily*, because one of (two) contraries is not the principle of the other; but 'one' is the principle of 'many':[5] therefore, through a topic a divisione° it is opposed *privatively*. But it is established, that "*many*" means a positing [positionem] (of number): therefore, "one" means naught but a privation (of number).[6]

4. Likewise, it seems, that it is especially said privatively *in God*, because 'one', according to which it is said positively, is the principle of multitude and of quantity:[7] but in God there is no quantity: therefore, neither is 'one' said positively.

5. Likewise, this very (thing) seems, because, if God is positively one and a stone one, therefore, God and the stone are two: therefore, God and a creature constitute a number; and if this, God is part of a number, which has been disproved [improbatum] above.[8] *If you say*, that it does not follow, because 'one' is not said univocally; for[9] that (argument) is nothing, as it seems, because, if ('one') adds [ponit] anything, when that can convene with a creature, to (what is) lesser analogically, the numeration is also attained according to an analogy, as when there is said: "humanity and whiteness are two essences": therefore, this does not solve it.

ON THE CONTRARY: 1. Anything has '*being*' [esse] and '*being one*' [esse unum] by the same,[10] since the form, which gives 'being', gives a distinct 'being'; if, therefore, (the adjective) "*being*" [ens] is not said privatively, but positively, for an equal reason neither is (the adjective) "*one*" said privatively of anything.

2. Likewise, what resounds [sonat] unto a complement, resounds unto a having [habitum], not unto a privation; but 'one' resounds unto a complement, because how much anything (is) more perfect, so much more does it approach [accedit] to a unity:[11] therefore, 'one' is not said privatively.

---

[1] Supply together with edition 1 *"one"* [unus]. Next, from the manuscripts and edition 1, we have inserted *this* [hoc] and *its* [eius].

[2] You will find the words of Aristotle quoted above in d. 23, a. 1, q. 1, p. 405, footnote 10. — At the end of the argument codex Y has *through a privation* [per privationem] for *privatively* [privative].

[3] Book X, text 9: Therefore, "many" and "one" are contraries by that contrariety, according to which "privation" and "holding" [habitus] are contraries ... because indivisibility is a privation of divisibility, and divisibility is a quasi holding. — At the end of the argument, with nearly all the manuscripts and edition 1 striving against this, the Vatican edition, having omitted *even* [etiam], reads *means not only a privation* [non tantum ... dicit privationem] for *is not only said privatively* [non tantum ... dicitur privative].

[4] The Vatican edition, together with very many codices, reads *Likewise* [Item] codex Y omits both. Next after *together* [simul] codex X adds *by nature* [natura], which is also added by Aristotle, ON THE PREDICAMENTS, ch. "*Regarding something*" or "*On Relation*".

[5] Cf. Dionysius (the Areopagite), ON THE DIVINE NAMES, chs. 5 and 13. See also the immediately subsequent argument. — A topic a divisione, concerning which is this argument, is defined by Peter the Spaniard in his SUMMULA ON THE BOOK OF TOPICS, near the end, in this manner: It is the habitude of one of those being co-divided to the remainder, such as: 'if Socrates is an animal, he is either a rational animal or an irrational (animal); but he is not irrational: therefore, (his is) a rational (animal).' Most of all: 'having posited one of the members of those being divided in any subject, the remainder are removed (and with one removed, the remainder are posited)'.

[6] You will find more on this fourfold opposition and its principles in Aristotle, ON THE PREDICAMENTS, ch. "*On Opposites*".

[7] Cf. Aristotle, METAPHYSICS, Bk. V, text 12 (Bk. IV, ch. 6), and Bk. X, text 21 (Bk. IX, ch. 6). (St. Severinus) Boethius, ARITHMETICS, Bk. I, ch. 7, says: For which reason it is established, that the first is the unity of all the rest, which are in the natural disposition of numbers, and is even rightly [rite] acknowledged as the begetter of the whole plurality, though as (of the whole) lured forth. — A little before this, the Vatican edition, without the authority of any manuscripts nor of edition 1, omits *according to* [secundum]. Next, at *there is no* [nulla est], the Vatican edition together with some manuscripts reads *there is entirely no* [nulla est omnino].

[8] Distinction 19, p. II, q. 4. — At the beginning of this argument, in very many codices and edition 1, there is lacking *very (thing)* [ipsum]. Then the Vatican edition, contrary to more ancient manuscripts and edition 1, has *therefore, it seems, that the stone and God* [videtur quod lapis et Deus] for *therefore, God and the stone* [ergo Deus et lapis].

[9] From very many mss. and editions 1, 2, 3 and 6, we have restored *for* [enim], in place of which the Vatican ed. has *certainly* [certe].

[10] Cf. Dionysius (the Areopagite), ON THE DIVINE NAMES, chs. 5 and 15; (St. Severinus) Boethius, ON UNITY AND THE ONE. On the added reason, see above d. 3, p. II, a. 1, q. 3, p. 84, footnote 7. — The Vatican edition, together with codex cc, breaking with the other codices and edition 4, omits the second *being* [esse].

[11] In the book, ON CAUSES, proposition 47: « Every united virtue is more infinite than a multiplied virtue ». See also Dionysius (the Areopagite), in the passage cited just above.

---

* *Trans. note*: The Quaracchi editors are accustomed to denote a term understood as a word by italicizing the term — though italicization is used also by them for emphasis — yet, here they do not italicize *one* [unum], because in the neuter it refers to the number or the concept of the number, rather than the word or adjective. To make this clear in the English translation, '*one*' [unum] will refer to the number 1 and or the concept of the number 1, and "*one*" [unus] as the word or adjective, which represents the number, when this adjective is reckoned as a word, rather than used as an adjective. (Likewise, the single quote ' ' is used in the English translation to signify concepts rather than things or words.) However, since this question concerns the use of the adjective, *one*, its title uses the masculine form; whereas, since the Seraphic Doctor speaks of the number, he expressly calls its *name* [hoc nomine] in the first paragraph of the Response, with the neuter form. Cf. unum in the Rationale for the Translation of Peculiar Latin Terms, in the Introduction to this English translation.

° See footnote 5, here above, for an explanation of this term: cf. also Aristotle, TOPICS, Bk. I, ch. 1 f., where the forms of argumentation or *loci*, by which probable arguments are constructed, are expounded.

3. Likewise, if 'one' is privative, it is established that (it is) not but (privative)[1] of a multitude. *But on the contrary*: no privation antecedes having naturally,[2] but 'one' naturally antecedes 'many': therefore, 'one' is not a privation.

4. Likewise, no privation constitutes its own having nor is saved in it: but 'one' is saved in 'the many' and constitutes them:[3] therefore, ('one') is not opposed as a privation: therefore, ('one') is not accepted privatively.

CONCLUSION

In God "one" is only said positively, and not privatively; but in creatures, (it is said) sometimes positively, sometimes privatively, even according to the thing (understood).

I RESPOND: It must be said, that the opinion of certain (authors), and of Master (Peter) principally, was, that, whatever concerns this name, *"one"* [unum], in creatures, is in God not said positively, but privatively, as he says in the text and assumes the authority of (St.) Hilary (teaches); though (St.) Hilary does not say expressly, but that the use of these names in God was invented more for the sake of depriving than for positing anything. And the *reason* was, that 'one', said positively, is the principle of quantity and number; but God does not have in Himself a quantity, nor is He in Himself numerable nor co-numerable with another.

But, though this position seems[4] probable, yet commonly it is not held. And the reason for this is, because, since 'one' is much more completely in God than in creatures, much more strongly is it said positively There. And *again*, since every unity is reduced to the first unity, and there is no reduction of a having to a privation, it is necessary, that *"one"* [unus][5] posit something in God.

And, on this account, it must be said, that there is a speaking of this name, *"one"* in creatures as much as regards *the thing understood*, and/or as much as regards *the reckoning of understanding*. If we speak as much as regards the *reckoning of understanding*, thus I say,

that it is said *privatively*; whence also its reckoning is assigned through the privation of division or of multitude. And this is, because 'one' is the first [primum], and firsts do not have (their) being-understood from us nor (have they their) being-made-known [notificari] except through posteriors; and hence it is, that it is said privatively.[6] Whence a unity in substance, and/or in quantity, and/or in quality, because it has something prior, through which it can be understood, is said positively, as (is) "identity", "equality", "similitude", and their opposites (are said) privatively.[7]

If, on the other hand, we speak as much as regards *the thing understood*, thus 'one' has a looking-back to *matter* and has a looking-back to *form*. By reason of the looking-back to *matter* it is in itself undivided, yet in potency it is divisible; and because the potency of matter holds itself through a manner of privation, similarly also 'one'. By reason of the looking-back to the *form*, which gives a distinct and limited "being", thus it means a positing (of number).[8] Therefore, since in God 'one' is entirely according to form, in creatures it is attained both according to form and according to matter, hence it is, that in God it is only accepted *positively*, in creatures sometimes *positively*, sometimes *privatively*, even[8] according to the *thing* (understood).

1. To that, therefore, which is objected first, that ('one') is defined or made known [notificatur] privatively; the response is clear, because according to the reckoning of its name, by reason that (it is) the first, it ought to be made known in this manner.

2. To that which is objected second, that it is opposed as a privation; it must be said, that 'one' through (its) looking-back to *matter* is accepted privatively, and thus the Commentator accepts (it); through (its) looking-back to *form*, it is accepted contrarily, according to which a multitude is formally accepted; through (its) respect to *the consequent act*, which is "to measure", it is accepted relatively and according to the genus of relatives, in which 'one' does not depend upon the other, just as is clear in knowledge [scientia] and a knowable [scibili];[10] and, thus, the diverse opinions on this are true.

3. To that which is objected, that in God there is no

---

[1] Supply: *privative* [privativum], and/or with the Vatican edition and some codices *in respect to* [respectu] for *of*.

[2] Aristotle, in ON HEAVEN AND THE WORLD, Bk. II, text 18, says (in the Greek): καὶ τῆς στερήσεως πρότερον ἡ κατάφασις (i.e an affirmation), (which) according to the Arabic-Latin translation (is): "A having is before a privation, as (what is) hot (is) also (before what is) cold" [Habitus est ante privationem, ut calidum et frigidum]. And in text 22 (ch. 4), the following proposition is found: But since 'one' is prior in nature in any one genus to 'many' and the 'simple' to the 'composite' etc..

[3] In this respect Dionysius (the Areopagite), ON THE DIVINE NAMES, ch. 13, § 1, says: « For there is no multitude not participating in 'one'. See also above, d. 19, p. II, q. 4, for the definition of 'number' in Aristotle and (St. Severinus) Boethius. — You will find many more similar arguments in Avicenna, METAPHYSICS, Bk. III, c. 6.

[4] The Vatican edition with only the more recent codex cc has *is held (to be)* [habeatur], and further on *much more formally* [multo formalius] for *much more strongly* [multo fortius].

[5] The Vatican edition, together with codex cc, reads *'one'* [unum: but faultily, because here the Seraphic Doctor discusses the use of the *adjective* for the number, rather than the word in all its general uses or the number itself, which discussion continues in the next paragraph].

[6] Aristotle, METAPHYSICS, Bk. X, text 9 (Bk. IX, ch. 3): Moreover, 'one' itself is said from (its) contrary, and the 'indivisible' is signified from the 'divisible', for this, since that a multitude is and (is) divisible is more sensible than that it is indivisible. — A little before this, breaking with the more ancient manuscripts and edition 1, the Vatican edition has *and* [et] for *nor* [neque]; but here, contrary to nearly all

the codices and edition 1, having changed the punctuation, it reads *that 'one' is said privatively. But a unity in substance* etc.. [privitive dicitur unum. Unitas autem in substantia etc.]. Codex O reads *that 'one', simply (speaking) is said privatively; but 'one' and a unity in substance* etc.. [privative dicitur unum simpliciter; sed unum et unitas in etc.].

[7] Aristotle, *loc. cit.* text 10: Likewise, to 'one' indeed belongs ... 'the same', 'the similar' and 'the equal': but to 'multitude' belongs 'the diverse', 'the dissimilar' and 'the unequal'. Cf. also METAPHYSICS, Bk. V, text 27 (Bk. IV, ch. 22).

[8] (St.) Augustine, ON A LITERAL INTERPRETATION OF GENESIS, unfinished book, ch. 10, n. 32: « The force itself of a form is commended by the name of "unity". For 'to be truly formed' is this, 'that something be brought back into one'; since the most highly One is the principle of every form ». Cf. also the book, ON THE TRUE RELIGION, ch. 36, n. 66. — Bl. (now St.) Albertus, here in a. 1, says: For there are three acts of form or of that, by which a thing is that which it is: the first is 'to give "being"', but the second 'to give a reckoning of the nature', and the third is 'to terminate'; and from that last act of form is its definition, and this the Philosopher intends, when he said, that that which is not divided, is said (to be) "one", according to which it is not divided; in this manner we rightly say, that this thing (is) "one", this and that thing are "two", and in this manner we rightly say, that "God is one".

[9] In the Vatican edition there is wanting *even* [etaim], which is exhibited in the manuscripts and edition 1.

[10] On this cf. Aristotle, METAPHYSICS, Bk. X, texts 2-22, (Bk. IX, chs. 1-6).

principle of numbering etc.; it must be said, that 'one' means a privation of multitude according to the general reckoning of the name; but that privation, even if, nominally [nomine tenus] it is a "privation", yet really is a positing (of number), because as much as there is more a privation of division in anything, so much is that more complete and more perfect. Therefore, since in God there is a most perfect Unity, it is accepted There according to an omnimodal privation of multitude. But in this manner there is said the '*one*', which does not have in itself[1] a multitude *according to act* [actu], nor is *in potency* to a multitude, neither through division nor through aggregation. But this 'one' is the most perfect and most high and infinite,[2] and it is not in potency to number, and it is not co-numerable with another; and in this manner it is in God alone. And so it is clear, that "*the one God*" is said positively, and in what manner His Unity differs from a creature.

4. Because, therefore, it is objected, that 'one' is the principle of 'multitude'; it must be said, that it is true in a created unity, but it is not true in a perfect and uncreated Unity — I mean a principle *within*, just as a part (is).[3]

5. Whence if there be said: "God and a creature are two", either this has been said improperly, and "*two*" occurs by a reckoning of number according to the thing; or, if it means a number, this is solely on the part of the one understanding; because, when one understands diverse and distinct (things), one accepts (them) under the reckoning of a *number*, just as, when our intellect understands (these), it distinguishes (them) with *time* [concernit tempus].[4]

SCHOLIUM

I. For an understanding of this Question we first note the following:

1. "*One*" is accepted in a twofold manner: either to the extent that it is converted with *being* [ente], and/or to the extent that it is formally *the principle of number*. The first transcends every genus, just as *being*, *the true*, *the good*, and this *essential* unity is found in all things; the second is in the predicament of quantity and is called "*accidental* unity". That *accidental* unity is not in God, is the one sentence of all (authors). Whence the whole question concerns *essential* unity.

2. There is a controversy among philosophers and theologians regarding what this '*one*' according to (its) reckoning adds upon being [ens]. The difference of the sentences of the principle doctors has been determined by many authors in the following manner: St. Thomas (Summa., I, q. 11, a. 1), Henry of Ghent (Quodlibetals, I, q. 1) and others, following Aristotle and his commentator Averroës, are resolved: « that 'one' does not add any thing [rem aliquam] upon being [ens], but only a negation of division ». And St. Thomas (Summa., I, q. 11, a. 1, in reply to n. 3) says: « 'One' does add something [aliquid] *according to reckoning* upon a being [ens] ». — Avicenna taught the entirely opposite, according to St. Thomas (loc. cit.), by asserting, that 'one' adds some thing [rem aliquam] positive upon the substance of a being, as 'white' (does) upon 'man'. For he himself held the false opinion, that it is not to be granted [dari] but an accidental unity, which is the principle of number. — St. Bonaventure, Alexander of Hales (Summa., p. I, q. 13, m. 1 and 2, and q. 65, m. 2, a. 1), Bl. (now St.) Albertus (Magnus), here in a. 3, (Bl.) Peter of Tarentaise (who here in q. 1, a. 2 brilliantly contracts the teaching of the Seraphic Doctor), and Richard of Middleton (here in a. 1, a. 1, especially in his reply to n. 1) hold a middle position between the opinion of Avicenna and Averroës. They teach, that '*one*' does convey something [aliquid] positive, but only *virtually* distinct from being [ab ente]. (Bl. John Duns) Scotus (On Aristotle's Metaphysics, Bk. IV, ch. 2, and Sent., Bk. II, d. 3, q. 2), with his own, thinks that 'one' is something [quid] positive and by the nature of (its) thing *formally* distinct from being.

II. St. Bonaventure, besides a twofold species of unity, distinguishes a twofold manner of speaking of unity, that is, in regard to the *thing understood* [rem intellectam], that is, according to the reckoning of being [essendi], and in regard to the *reckoning of understanding*, that is, according to the manner, by which the reckoning of unity makes itself known to our intellect. For the human intellect always understands and makes known the most simple (things), which are less obvious to sense, *a posteriori*, wherefore it also explains '*one*' and/or a *point* through the negation of division. And so the holy Doctor concedes, that a unity according to the reckoning of *being made known* means a *privation of division*. — On the other hand, according to the reckoning of *being* [essendi] he again distinguishes '*one*' itself in a twofold manner: first, to the extent that it has a looking-back to *matter*, which is both *divisible* by potency, and holds itself to form *through the manner of privation*; and in this manner again he concedes, that '*one*' does not mean something [quid] positive. Second, to the extent that '*one*' looks back to *form*, under this respect '*one*', according to his sentence, does convey something [aliquid] positive, yet identified with its subject, as some act of the form; and in this manner '*one*' adds upon being a reckoning of positive perfection. On this controversy, cf. Cajetan (commenting on Summa., I, q. 11, a. 1) and Forest (de Trinitatis Mysterio, q. 5, p. 255 ff.), who strives to thus interpret the sentence of St. Thomas, especially that in On Truth, q. 1, a. 1, thus, that departs but a little and/or nothing in meaning [in re] from the Seraphic (Doctor).

III. The solutions to n. 2, 3, and 4 are founded in this, that '*one*' and '*many*' under a diverse reckoning are opposed either *privatively*, and/or *contrarily*, and/or *relatively*. In respect to matter '*one*' *deprives* the division and actual multitude, according to which by reason of the matter it is in potency; in respect to the form, which confers both '*being*' [esse] and '*being one*' [unum esse], 'one' is taken positively and *contrarily* regarding 'many'; in respect « to the consequent act, which is "to measure" », since 'one' is the measure of 'many', it is accepted *relatively*; for in this manner it is a part of the multitude and not a privation. This relative opposition to a multitude pertains to the genus of relatively imperfectly, which (relatives) are neither always together, nor (where) one depends upon another; and example of which is in knowledge and a knowable. — On this species of relation, cf. below d. 30, q. 3 and the Scholium.

This doctrine of the Seraphic Doctor is more fully explained by Bl. (now St.) Albertus Magnus (here in a. 3), with these words: « It must be said, that there is a 'one' indivisible, reduced to the matter and/or to a disposition of matter, and a 'one' reduced to the nature of the form, just as we say "one by continuity" [continuitate unum]; and when we says "one by continuity", we say "one by matter" [materia unum] and "one by form" [forma unum], because continuity is a disposition of matter. But whatever is by continuity one, is in potency many [multa]; but every potency is in the genus of privation, chiefly the potency of matter, which is a potency of a continuum; which is clear, because a continuum is a 'many' [multum] by passive potency, and not by active potency. Therefore, 'one' reduced to the unity of matter has an opposition to 'many', just as 'privation' (does) to 'having' [habitum]; because such a unity is susceptible of a multitude; and this is the intention of the Philosopher and of the commentary (of the Commentator) saying this. But the 'one', which has been reduced to form, has three considerations, namely, according to the formal reckoning of 'one', and according to that which it is, and according to that which is proximate and

---

[1] The more ancient codices, together with edition 1, exhibit *in Itself* [in se], which the Vatican together with codex cc, less aptly omits.

[2] Codices G and Z and edition 1 add '*One*' [unum]. Next codices V and X have *for that reason It* [ideo] for *That* [illud].

[3] That is: 'one' is then the principle of 'multitude', when it enters a multitude as a part. — The Vatican edition, contrary to nearly all the manuscripts and edition 1, after *within* [intra], faultily adds *itself* [se], and next after *Whence* [Unde] it adds *it is not true* [non est verum].

[4] Aristotle, On Memory and Remembering, ch. 1: It does not happen that one understands anything without a continuum [sine continuo], nor without time [sine tempore], those (things), which are not in time [in tempore] etc..

consequent to it. Considered in the first manner, it has an opposition of contrariety to 'the many', because each is posited in the species, and they mutually expel themselves from the same susceptible ... But if 'one' is accepted according to that which it is, it has no opposition to 'many', but rather is the principle of 'many' and is salved substantially in that 'many'. And Avicenna argues for this [hoc attendit], saying, that it does not have opposition, because privation neither causes a having nor is saved in it ... If 'one' is accepted according to the reckoning consequent to the nearest to itself, which is the reckoning of measure; then the 'one', which a certain, is the one measuring the 'many', which is uncertain; and in this manner ('one' and 'many') are opposed as 'measure' and 'measured'. And this Aristotle, in (Book) X, of his First Philosophy and the Commentator on the same and Avicenna in his own METAPHYSICS say, that 'one' and 'many' are opposed relatively. But he distinguishes in the same place among relatives, because there are certain ones, each of which depends on the other, and each of those posits the rest, as a father and a son, and a lord and a servant; but there are certain ones, one of which depends upon the other, and not the other way around, and for that reason there one posits the other and not the other way around, as knowledge and a knowable; and in this manner 'one' and 'many' are opposed relatively, because 'many' posits 'one' and is not convertible with it [et non convertitur] ».

IV. In regard to the conclusion, besides those cited, cf. Bl. (now St.) Albertus (Magnus), here in a. 1, 2, and 3. — Giles the Roman, here in 1st, princ. q. 2. — Henry of Ghent, SUMMA., a. 25, q. 1. — Durandus (of Saint-Pourçain), here in q. 1 and 2. — (Bl.) Dionysius the Carthusian, here in q. 1 and 2. — (Gabriel) Biel, here in q. 1.

QUESTION II

Whether "one" [unus] *is said, among the divine, according to substance or according to relation?*

Second, there is asked, whether "*one*" [unus] is said according to substance, or whether according to relation. And it seems, that (it is said) according to substance:

1. Because « being [ens] and the 'one' [unum] are convertible », just as the Philosopher[1] wants and (St. Severinus) Boethius (teaches); but "*being*" [ens] is said according to substance: therefore, also "one" [unum].

2. Likewise, this is conceded: « The Father and the Son and the Holy Spirit are one God [unus Deus] »; but if They are the one God, since God does not diminish from the reckoning of 'one' [unius], therefore, They are One [unus]. But nothing is said in the Most High of the Three singularly, which is not said substantially:[2] ergo etc.. *If you say*, that, when it is held as an adjective, then it is not said substantially: *on the contrary*: the signification of the term is the same, when it is held as an adjective, and when it is held as a substantive. *Likewise*, when it becomes a substantive in the *neuter*,[3] it is said substantially; since, therefore, the signification of the term is the same in the masculine and in the neuter, since the imposition is one, therefore, it is said substantially, in the masculine. *Moreover*, other names in the masculine are said substantially, as this name, "*eternal*" [aeternus]; whence (there is said) in the Creed:[4] « Not Three Eternals, but One Eternal »: therefore, similarly (They are) one.

3. Likewise, when there is said: « the Father is one», either it is held *substantially*, or *notionally*. If *substantially*, I have the proposed; if *notionally* — but the Father has two notions: therefore, He ought not to be said (to be) "one" [unus], but "two" [duo].

4. Likewise, a notion and a property are the same: therefore, since a property is said (to be), « that which convenes to One alone »,[5] no notion can be said of the Three. But this name, "*one*" [unus], is predicated of any Person: therefore, it does not mean a notion.

ON THE CONTRARY: 1. The rule had above in the Twenty-second Distinction is:[6] « Everything which predicates substance and/or essence, is said in the Most High of the Three singularly »; but this does not convene with this name, which is[7] "one" [unus]: ergo etc..

2. Likewise, nothing pertaining to essence or substance is multiplied or plurified; but that which is "*one*" is plurified, because the Father is one, and the Son is one, and They are two, because (They are) one and one: ergo etc..

3. Likewise, "that He is one" and "that He is distinct" is the same; but when I say, "the Father is distinct", that which is *distinct* is not said substantially: therefore, neither that which is *one*.

4. Likewise, in respect to whatsoever term there is a saying of "*another*" [alium], that term means a relation — whence "*another God*" [alius Deus] is not said — but in respect to that which is "*one*" there is a saying of "*another*", for the Father is one and the Son is Another: ergo etc..

---

[1] METAPHYSICS, Bk. IV, text 3 (Bk. III, ch. 2): « And so, if being and 'one' are the same and one in nature, on account of this, that they follow one another etc. ». Cf. also Bk. X, text 8, (Bk. IX, ch. 2). — (St. Severinus) Boethius, ON THE ONE PERSON AND TWO NATURES OF CHRIST, ch. 4: « For what is not one, neither can entirely be; for "to be" and 'one' are convertible ». See also his book, ON UNITY AND ONE.

[2] See above in the text of Master (Peter), d. XXII, ch. 3, and (St. Bonaventure's), dubium 2 on the same text. — Below, after *then* [tunc] very many manuscripts, together with edition 1, omit *not* [non], but falsely, because contrary to the scope of the objection. The Seraphic Doctor perhaps alludes to the last part of the words of Alan of Lille's, THEOLOGIC RULES, rule 23: But for that reason we apposite *in a substantive manner*, because names signifying substance and/or the circumstance of a substance, if held as an adjective, such as this name, "*powerful*" [potens], this name, "*just*" [iustus], *are said* of the Three Persons *in the Most High in a plural number*, as: the Father and the Son and the Holy Spirit are *just* [iusti], are *powerful* [potentes].

[3] The Vatican ed., with one or the other cod., adds *gender* [genere], & a little below this, with codex cc, in place of *one* [una] exhibits *the same* [eadem].

[4] The Athanasian (Creed).

[5] Porphyry, ON THE PREDICABLES, ch. "On the *Proper*". — Very many codices, such as A V X and Y, together with edition 1, have *because* [quia] for *that which* [quod].

[6] In the text of Master (Peter), ch. 4, and in Doubt 2 on the text.

[7] We follow the more common reading of the manuscripts and edition 1, by adding *which is* [quod est].

CONCLUSION

Since in God there is both an essential and a personal unity, by which one Person is distinguished from Another, the term <u>unus</u>, if used as an adjective, can signify each unity, but if as a substantive, then <u>unus</u> is attributed to a personal unity, but <u>unum</u> to an essential (unity).

I RESPOND: It must be said, that, since the reckoning of unity is a reckoning of distinction with indivision, but among the divine we posit also[1] an Essence distinct from other essences through Itself, and (so) that a Person be distinguished from the Others through a property, it is necessary that among the divine one posit both an *essential* and a *personal* unity. Therefore, since a person is not other than an essence, the unity of essence and person are not two unities according to thing, but one, differing by a reckoning: for that reason the unity of the latter and the former is not said equivocally, since neither this one nor that is imposed in the manner of a species [specialiter].

Therefore, because the concrete accepts a special signification from the abstract, this name, "*one*" [unus], conveys among the divine an essential and personal unity. And when it is held *as an adjective*, it conveys each indifferently; but it determines through the adjoined (word). Therefore,[2] when it is added to an essential term, it conveys an essential (unity); when it is added to a notional (term), it conveys a personal (unity).

However, when *it becomes a substantive*, then[3] it is necessary, that it be determined by itself. And for that reason, since the neuter gender conveys, what it means, under an indistinction, in the *neuter* gender it has fittingly been attributed or appropriated to essential unity. But in the *masculine*, because it conveys a distinction and a certain supposit and means the reckoning of one producing, it has been appropriated to personal unity.

1. And for that reason it[4] is clear, that in this manner it is not accepted as a being nor as convertible with it, but solely in the neuter (gender is it such).

2. The second is also clear, because there is a fallacy of a figure of speech [figurae dictionis] there out of an exchange [commutatione][5] of that term "*one*" [unus]. For although the *signification* is not varied through substantiation nor through a diversity of gender, nevertheless the *manner of* supposition can be varied, most of all if the use (of the term) causes this, and the reckoning is fitting with the use.

To that, therefore, which is objected, that "*eternal*" [aeternus] is said essentially; the response is clear, because eternity is said only essentially, but unity (is also[6] said) personally. — However, some say, that it is (for this reason) in this name, "*one*" [unus], because it is a partitive name and (a name) having the article in itself.

3. To that which is objected:[7] either it predicates a notion, etc.; it must be said, that it does predicate a notion; but one must pay attention, that (it does(not (predicate) any (notion) whatsoever, but (rather) a *personal* (notion), which causes Him to be one, and that (notion) is one in any Person.

4. To that which is objected, that a notion is said of one (Person); it must be said, that there is a signifying of notion under a *proper* reckoning, as through this name, "*paternity*", and *commonly*, as through this name, "*relation*", "*notion*", "*unity*" and "*property*", which mean the same under diverse reckonings. For the sense is: « a Person is[8] one », that is, "a unique (Person), by a personal property (both) indistinct in Himself and distinct from the Others".

SCHOLIUM

In regard to the solution to n. 1, cf. Alexander of Hales, SUMMA., p. I, q. 65, m. 2, a. 1, and Richard of Middleton, here in a. 1, q. 3, in reply to n. 3. — Besides these, in regard to the conclusion, cf. St. Thomas, here in q. 1, a. 4; SUMMA. , I, q. 30, a. 3, in reply to n. 1. — Bl. (now St.) Albertus (Magnus), here in a. 4. — (Bl.) Peter of Tarentaise, here in q. 1, a. 3. — Giles the Roman, here in 1st. princ., q. 4. — (Bl.) Dionysius the Carthusian, here in q. 3.

ARTICLE II

On purely numeral names.

Second there is principally asked concerning the second article,[9] that is, concerning names purely numeral, such as are "*two*" and "*three*" etc.. And about this similarly there are asked two (questions):

First, there is asked, whether they are said positively, or privatively.

Second, whether they are said according to substance, or according to relation.

---

[1] The Vatican edition, together with very many codices, omits *also* [et], and a little below this after *it is necessary* [necesse est] adds *also* [etiam].

[2] Thus the greater part of the manuscripts, while all the others, together with edition 1 and the Vatican edition, put *For* [enim].

[3] From the more ancient manuscripts and edition 1, we have supplied here *then* [tunc], and little below this after *in the neuter* [in neutro] we have added *gender* [genere]. For *by itself* [se ipso], edition 1 has *in itself* [in se ipso], codices K aa and bb have *it determines itself* [ipsum determinet] pro *it is determined by itself* [se ipso determinetur]. Then, several manuscripts, such as G I M V Y & Z, together with edition 1, have *without distinction* [sine distinctione] in place of *under an indistinction* [sub indistinctione].

[4] In edition 1 there is added *the first (objection)* [primum].

[5] The Vatican edition, with not a few mss. and ed. 1, has *change* [mutatione] for *exchange* [commutatione]. Then after *can* [potest] the same with cod. cc alone adds *however* [tamen], and then it puts *be diversified* [diversificari] for *be varied* [variari], and has (the indicative) *causes* [facit] for (the subjunctive) *causes* [faciat].

[6] Supply: *also* [etiam]; and next after *it is* [hoc est], understand: for that reason, for which the Vatican ed., without the mss. & ed. 1, adds *special* [speciale].

[7] In codex Y there is read *that "one" either* [quod unus aut] for *either it* [aut]. — On the *personal* notion, which is referred to here, see below d. 26, q. 1 and 4.

[8] From very many manuscripts and edition 1, we have inserted (the copula) *is* [est] (which in Latin is very often omitted).

[9] In the Vatican edition and codex cc there is wanting here *concerning the second article, that is,* [de secundo articulo, scilicet].

QUESTION I

Whether purely numeral names are said, among the divine, in a positive or privative manner?

And that they are said only privatively, seems:

1. Through the authority of Master (Peter) in the text,[1] which says, that « the use of these has been introduced [inductus] more for the sake of depriving than of positing »; and the authority of Master (Peter) seems to be strengthened [firmari] through the authorities of others. For (St. Severinus) Boethius says in (his) book, ON THE TRINITY:[2] « That truly is one, in which there is no number »; but among the divine there is most truly a One: therefore, among the divine there is no number: therefore those terms among the divine either are said falsely, or they do not predicate a number, if they do posit something: ergo etc..

2. Likewise, (St.) Isidore[3] says, that number is the virtue of the member [memeris], that is, of a division, according to (its) etymology; but in God there occurs no division, therefore, neither a number; therefore, the same as before.

3. Likewise, the Philosopher[4] says, that « number is a multitude measured through 'one' »; but in God there occurs no measuring, since He Himself is immense: ergo etc..

4. Likewise, this seems through *reason*: because from whatsoever there is removed a genus, (there is) also (removed every) species; but the genus of quantity is removed from God: ergo etc..

5. Likewise, in whatsoever there is a genus, it is necessary to posit someone of the species:[5] therefore, if number is in God, either it is There a group of two [binarius], and/or a group of three [ternarius], and/or some of the other (groups of number). But the Saints deny every species (of number in God), therefore, also the genus (of number): therefore, the same as before.

On the Contrary: 1. If the *Three* are only said privatively, because They are not One and/or Two, then for an equal reason it could be said: "There are three chimera", because there are not one and/or two (chimera); but that is not said: ergo etc..

2. Likewise, it seems that it does mean *a number*. (St.) Eusebius[6] says: « Among the divine there is a number, but not an order »; but if there is a number There: therefore, it happens that there is a signifying. And if this: therefore, the saying, which signify that, are held positively.

3. Likewise, (St.) Bernard (of Clairvaux says):[7] « If there is one Essence, Three Persons, who denies (there is) number »? as if to say, "No one (does)": ergo etc..

4. Likewise, this very (thing) seems *by reason*, because a discrete quantity is of a greater abstraction than a continuous (one): therefore, also a discretion more than a duration. But the name meaning a duration is said positively in God, as (is) "*eternal*": therefore, also the name meaning a discretion.

5. Likewise, in whatsoever there is a positing of species positively, there is a positing of genus; but in God there is a positing of a Trinity: therefore also of a plurality.

CONCLUSION

Among the divine, number is indeed said positively, but it is not There simply, but (rather as) the number of the Persons.

I RESPOND: For an understanding of the aforesaid, it must be said,[8] that the *position* of Master (Peter) was, that, among the divine, numeral names of this kind do not posit anything [aliquid], but (rather) deprive, just as is clear in the text. And the *reason* for this position was, because names of this kind, if they do posit something [aliquid], posit at least a number; but both reason says and the authority of the Saints confirm, that number is not to be posited among the divine. For since among the divine there is no *division* and separation, (and) there is also no *aggregation*, (and) there is also no *measuring*; and (since) a number does convey a *separation antecedently*, and an aggregation and measuring *consequently*: number among the divine does not seem to be[9] posited. And for that reason, among the divine, numeral sayings do not mean anything [aliquid], but rather deprive, that is, a greater and lesser number.

But neither the *position* nor the *reason* for the position is[10] fitting, if it is attended to interiorly. For the *position* destroys

---

[1] Near the beginning. — In the Vatican edition and codex cc, having omitted the words *in the text* [in littera], there is read *By the authority* [auctoritate] for *Through the Authority* [per auctoritatem]. A little below this not a few codices, such as A T U and X, together with edition 1, read *authority* [auctoritatem] for *authorities* [auctoritates].

[2] Chapter 2.

[3] The passage cited as from (St.) Isidore can be neither found nor emended; the greatest part of the codices have virtus memeris or nutus memeris, a few read mutus memoriae. The same passage occurs in Bl. (now St.) Albertus (Magnus), here in a. 1: nutus memeris: and in his Commentary on the Posterior Analytics, Bk. I, tract 2, ch. 1 he says: « For a number comes to be out of an iteration of a unity accepted according to the mind, on account of which a "number" is also said (to be) a "*nod of the mind*" [nutus mentis] and/or "(a nod) *of a member*" [memeris], that is "of a division" »; and among the ancient editions of the Commentary of St. Thomas, here in a. 2 there is read: *a merely unique, that is, of a division* [unicus merus scilicet divisionis], which reading through the felicitous conjecture of Fr. Nicholas, was changed into "*a part of one and/or a partition of one, that is a division*" [unius meros vel unius merismos, scilicet divisio], adjoining: "what is subjoined from (St.) Isidore, occurs nowhere among him". — (St.) Isidore in his ETYMOLOGIES, Bk. III, ch. 3 says: « Number is a multitude constituted out of unities; for (they want) that 'one' be the seed of number, not (that it be) a number. The (coin), the "*nummus*", gave (its) name to number [numerus] and conferred it by its frequency ». — At the end of the argument before *a number* [numerus] the Vatican edition, faultily and not trusting in the manuscripts and editions 1, 2, and 3, omits *neither* [nec].

[4] METAPHYSICS, Bk. X, text 21 (Bk. IX, ch. 6).

[5] Aristotle, TOPICS, Bk. II, ch. 2 (ch. 4): (It is) necessary, that of those which a genus is predicated, someone of the species also be predicated.

[6] Cf. St. Eusebius of Vercelli, ON THE CONFESSION OF THE TRINITY, n. 8. — A little after this, from very many manuscripts and edition 1, we have inserted *there is* [esse].

[7] ON CONSIDERATIONS, Bk. V, ch. 7, n. 17: Since to those Three Persons belongs that Substance, and that One Substance to those Three Persons, who denies a number? [Trans. note: Regarding *discretion*, a little below this, cf. the "Rationale for the Translation of Peculiar Latin terms" in the Introduction to this English translation.]

[8] The Vatican edition has *it must be noted* [notandum].

[9] The Vatican edition, with a few codices, reads *is* [est] for *to be* [esse], and then *Therefore also* [ideo etiam] for *And for that reason* [Et ideo]; after *sayings* [dictiones] it adds *and/or reckonings* [vel rationes].

[10] The Vatican ed., with cod. cc, reads *seems to be* [videtur esse]. Cod. W reads *one containing the truth* [continens veritatem] for *fitting* [conveniens].

* *Trans. note*: Here memeris has been translated *member*, inasmuch as, according to Dr. Calvert Watkins, reconstruction of proto Indo-European, AMERICAN HERITAGE DICTIONARY OF THE ENGLISH LANGUAGE, "Indo-European and the Indo-Europeans", pp. 1497 ff., *mems-*, means "a piece of meat", and is the root of the Latin membrum, a member or part; and evidently, also, of the Greek *meros* and *merismos*, "a part" and "a partition".

itself. For it posits, that names designating plurality are said privatively, similarly too the names designating[1] unity. And, if this, if in this manner they are mutually opposed [invicem opponuntur], so that each is the privation of the other, there will be a circular dependence in being made known [circulatio in notificando]; and, if each is the privation of the other — since a privation is not of a privation, but of a having — each posit something: and thus, if they are said privatively, they are said positively; and on account of this[2] the position is not fitting.

The *reckoning* of the position is similarly not fittingly taken up. For number conveys a *distinction* and above this a *composition of aggregation*; and though among the divine there is no *aggregation*, nevertheless there is *distinction*; and for that reason number is not to be simply removed from the divine, but (only) *such* a number (is). And Master (Peter) removes (it) entirely; for that reason he failed in his position. And in this article (his sentence) is not commonly supported[3] by the Masters of Paris.

Therefore, it must be conceded, that names of this kind are said positively, just as the reasons induced for this prove. And it must be conceded, that among the divine in some manner there is number, in some manner not. For according to which it means a *distinction of the Persons*[4] according to origin, in this manner, (number) must be said to be among the divine; but according to which it means an *aggregation* and a substantial *division*, number is not to be posited among the divine.

From these the objections are clear. For the reason for the first side proceed from number according to that acceptation, by which it is taken in these inferiors as much as regards the aforesaid conditions. Whence, in their own sense they conclude truly, that there is not a number There.

Similarly, the reasons for the opposed side procede, according to which number conveys a certain [certam] distinction, and this indeed is a positing (of number) among the divine; and for that rasion they conclude truly in their own sense. Whence, among the divine, one must deny that there is number simply, but one must concede that there is a number of the Persons.

4. 5. To that, however, which is objected concerning continuous quantity, and concerning the species of number, it must be said, that neither is there continuous quantity in God, because eternity is not a quantity, nor is the Trinity a species of number.

SCHOLIUM

I. About the question, what do numbers among the divine formally signify, the same difference of opinions returns, which we have observed above (a. 1, q. 1) about the reckoning of *'one'*. The sentence of Peter Lombard, which St. Bonaventure judges to be less sufficient, St. Thomas, both in his COMMENTARY (here in q. 1, a. 1), and in his SUMMA. (I. q. 30, a. 3), approves and explains in this sense, that number among the divine is a transcendental, which adds to the numbered Persons a twofold negation, namely, the negation of division in oneself and indivision from another, and that beside this negation it signifies nothing else. What, however, is objected against this sentence, namely, that it falls into « a circular dependence », that is, circular reasoning [circulum vitiosum], the Angelic (Doctor), SUMMA., loc. cit., in reply to n. 3, strives to solve by this asserting, that it is not *'one'* and *'many'* [multum] that are opposed formally, but *'one'* and *'divided'* that are. To which the assertors of the contrary sentence respond, that *'divided'* and *'many'* are the same (according to their reckoning). — Otherwise, the two sentences convene in this assertion, that number adds to entities that twofold negation; but they differ about this, that *'one'* and *'the many'* [plura] signify formally in God. Here, again, St. Bonaventure asserts, that *'one'*, just as other terms of simple things, is cognized and defined through a negation as something more known [quid notius], but that that negation is rather something [aliquid] consequent to the constitution of *'one'* and *'the many'*; just as incommutability is also consequent to a person already constituted, as is taught in the following Distinction. St. Thomas agrees with Master (Peter) in the conclusion, but differs from him to some extent, by proceeding from another fundament, concerning which one can refer to Cajetan (commenting on SUMMA., I, q. 30, a. 3).

II. Cf. besides the (authors) already praised, Alexander of Hales, SUMMA., I, p. I, q. 65, m. 2, a. 1. — (Bl.) Peter of Tarentaise, here in q. 2, a. 1 and 2. — Richard of Middleton, here in a. 2, q. 2. — Giles the Roman, here in 1st. princ., q. 2. — Henry of Ghent, SUMMA., a. 73, q. 11, n. 8 and the following; a. 74, q. 5, n. 11; a. 75, q. 4, n. 9. — (Bl.) Dionysius the Carthusian, here in q. 2 and 3.

QUESTION II

Whether purely numeral names are said, among the divine, according to substance, or according to relation?

Second, there is asked, whether the aforesaid names are said[5] according to substance [secundum substantiam], or according to relation [secundum relationem]. And it seems, that (they are said) according to substance:

1. Just as (Sts. Severinus) Boethius[6] and Augustine (say): « Quantity passes over into the substance »; but a number means a quantity, therefore, it passes over into the substance: therefore, numeral sayings are said according to substance.

2. Likewise, every name, which is said *regarding (the thing) itself* [ad se], is said according to the substance;[7] but *"two"* [duo] and *"three"* [tres]

---

[1] On the authority of the older codices and edition 1, we have put *designating* [designantia] for *signifying* [significantia].

[2] Codex Z, together with edition 1, reads *on account of this* [propter hoc] for *on account of this* [propterea], codex F has *thus* [ita], the Vatican edition, together with some codices, has *in this manner* [sic].

[3] The Vatican edition has *is held* [tenetur], but contrary to nearly all the codices and edition 1.

[4] The Vatican edition, contrary to very many codices, together with edition 1, has *a personal distinction* [distinctionem personalem]. Next after *it must be said* [dicendum est] supply with the Vatican edition *number* [numerum].

[5] The Vatican edition, not trusting in the mss. and edition 1, adds *among the divine* [in divinis], for which codex Y has *of God* [de Deo].

[6] In his book, ON THE TRINITY, ch. 4. — (St.) Augustine, ON THE TRINITY, Bk. V, ch. 1, n. 2, and ch. 8, n. 9.

[7] See above in Master (Peter)'s text, d. XXII, ch. 4.

is a name, which is said *regarding (the thing) itself*, not regarding another: therefore, they are said according to the substance.

3. Likewise, when there is said: "the Father and the Son and the Holy Spirit are Three",[1] that which is "*Three*" is either said *notionally* [notionaliter], or *essentially* [essentialiter]; not *notionally*, because there is no notion, which is commonly said of the Three: therefore, it is said *essentially*.

4. Likewise, there are five notions: but if[2] numeral terms convey the plurality of the notions, therefore, there will be a group of five [quinarius] among the divine: therefore, there are not Three, but Five. But this (is) false: therefore, they are not said notionally, therefore, they are said essentially or substantially.

ON THE CONTRARY: 1. Every name pertaining to the Substance is not said plurally, but singularly; but[3] "*Three*" is only said plurally: therefore, in no manner is it said according to substance, therefore, it is said according to relation.

2. Likewise, every substantial name is predicated of any Person; but "*Three*" is predicated of no Person: ergo etc..

3. Likewise, if this name, "*Three*", is said according to substance, therefore, it is licit to add to it[4] a substantial term: therefore, we can say that (there are) "Three Gods" and/or "Three Substances", each of which is contrary to the Faith.

CONCLUSION

Among the divine, numeral names are said according to relation and convey the notions.

I Respond: It must be said, that some wanted to say, that numeral terms of this kind in God mean nothing other than this name, "*Persons*", in the plural. Whence if there be said: "the Persons are Three", the same is subjected and predicated. And here the *reckoning* and manner of understanding is: because if the forms were posited to be from eternity, just as is imposed upon Plato, who posited (this);[5] then They would be many [plures] and in some, certain number. But that number would not be a property nor a consequent passion, but *numeral*[6] *forms* themselves. And through this manner to say "*Three*" among the divine is not but to say "the Persons Themselves".

But that is not opportune [non oportet] to say, since if it were entirely the same, then it would seem to be a trifle, if the Three Persons were said to be one Person; and it would seem that nothing[7] more is said, when there is said: "the Three are Persons", than: "the Persons are Persons".

And, on this account, there is another manner of speaking, wherefore numeral terms of this kind are said according to relation and convey the notions themselves:[8] And this is clear, because among the divine they convey a distinction; but the distinction is from the properties; whence "*Three*" conveys the property of the Three Persons in concretion. But a notion, inasmuch as it convenes to a sole (Person), is said (to be) *a property*: but inasmuch as it distinguishes (one Person) from another, it is said (to be) the *unity* (of the Person):[9] whence the Three Persons are said (to be) distinct by Their own properties. *And if you ask*, what is said, when there is said: "three notions"; it must be said, that the properties are distinguished by themselves, for that reason it means naught but the notions themselves.

1. To that, therefore, which is objected, that quantity passes over into substance; it must be said, that a number among *creatures* is a quantity, but in *God* it means a relation; and this is clear in this manner. A distinction among *creatures* is through an *apposition* of some property and/or quality, and thus through an addition; but where (there is) an addition, there (is) a limitation; where (there is) a limitation, there is a division of one from another, and where these are, there (is) an aggregation of diverse (things) and a measuring. And because it belongs to quantity *to measure*, according to a distinction among inferiors there follows a number and it is a *standard of measure of being* [modus essendi], consequent to matter with form. But among the *divine* there is only[10] distinction through an *origin*, not through the addition of something, and for that reason (there is) no addition, no limitation; and where this is not, neither (is there) a measuring, and therefore, neither a quantity. But where (there is) an origin, there (is) a habitude and a relation; and for that reason among the divine, number does not mean a quantity, but rather a relation. And since relation does not pass over into substance, for that reason neither (do) numeral terms.

---

[1] The Vatican edition, together with codex cc, breaking with the other codices and edition 1, badly omits *Three* [tres]. Next, very many codices, such as F G H I M W and X, have *but* [sed] for *that* [hoc], but incongruously.

[2] The Vatican edition alone omits *if* [si], and, a little below this, after *therefore*, [ergo] it reads *the number will be* [erit numerus] for *there will be* [erit], and *is* [est] before *false* [falsum].

[3] Very many codices, such as A C R S Y and Z, together with edition 1, having omitted the particle *not* [non], put *and* [et] in place of *but* [sed], which reading perhaps could be explained by the words of Alan of Lille, cited above in a. 1, q. 2, p. 423, in footnote 2; but the reading received in the text agrees with the aforesaid of d. XXII of Master (Peter)'s text, ch. 4, and with (St. Bonaventure, below in) Doubt 2 on the text, and exhibits the general rule.

[4] The Vatican edition, together with very many manuscripts, omits *it* [ei], which however, is exhibited by the other codices and edition 1. Next, codex X has *unfitting* [inconveniens], and codex Y *false* [falsum] for *contrary to the Faith* [contra fidem].

[5] Cf. (Plato's Dialogue), TIMAEUS, near the beginning (Basil edition of 1578 A. D., tome III, p. 28 f.), and PARMENIDES (ibid., p. 132), and ON THE SOUL OF THE WORLD, at the beginning (ibid., p. 93). — (Cf. also) Aristotle, passim, especially METAPHYSICS, Bk. VII, text 56 ff., and Bk. XIII, ch. 4 and 5 (Bk. VI, ch. 16, and Bk. XII, ch. 4 and 5).

[6] The Vatican edition, contrary to the mss. and the first six ed., faultily reads *numbered* [numeratae]. Next, the Vatican ed., with codex cc, reads "*the Three Persons*" [tres personas] for "*the Persons Themselves*" [ipsas personas], but contrary to the testimony of very many mss. and ed. 1; all the other codices read "*the Three Themselves*" [ipsas tres].

[7] Trusting in nearly all the mss. and ed. 1, we have substituted here *nothing more is said* [nihil plus dici] for *more is not said* [non plus dici], and a little before this, from the mss. and edd. 2, 3, 4, 5 & 6, the plural of the verb *were said* [dicerentur] for the singular [diceretur]. Very many codices, such as T and X, prefix to the word *it would seem* [videretur] the word *again* [iterum], and next after *than* [quam] codices H K V X Z aa and bb add *if there were said* [si diceretur]. Some mss., such as A S & V, with ed. 1, read *and* [et] for *than* [quam].

[8] In the Vatican edition and codex cc there is wanting *themselves* [ipsas], which is extant in the other manuscripts and edition 1.

[9] See the explanation for this below in the response to n. 4. — The Vatican ed., with cod. cc, prefixes *to be* [esse] before *a property* [proprietas] and *the unity* [unitas]. Next, the Vatican ed., breaking with the more ancient mss. and ed. 1, has *three* [tirbus] for *Their own* [suis], and (the indicative) *you ask* [quaeris] for (the subjunctive) *you ask* [quaeras].

[10] In the Vatican ed., and cod. cc alone, there is less well omitted *only* [solum]. A little below this very many codd., such as A G H S T V Y & bb, after *and where* [et ubi] read *this (limitation)* [haec] for *this (consequential series)* [hoc]. — See more on this, above in d. 19, p. II, a. sole, q. 4, on p. 362.

2. To that which is objected, that they are said regarding (the thing) itself; it must be said, that *"that a name be said regarding another"*, this[1] can be in a twofold manner: either *within* and/or *outside*, either *implicitly* and/or *explicitly*. And that name is said substantially, which is not said regarding another, neither within nor outside, nor implicitly nor explicitly. But a numeral term means a relation to another *within*, because it conveys a distinction of (Those) numbered and implies 'relation'.

3. To that which is objected, that no notion is said of the Three; it must be said, that it is true: no *determinate* notion; but (something) *common* to the notions according to (their) reckoning is said of the Three, as this name, *"related"*, and this name, *"distinct"*, and completely similar names.

4. To that which is objected, that there are five notions; it must be said, that *"Three"* conveys not any notions whatsoever, but only *personal* ones.[2] For that notion which makes,* a Person to be a Person and (makes Him) distinct from all (the Others), that is said to be the *unity of the Person* [unitas personae], inasmuch as it gives (Him) a distinct "being"; and that notion is one for One, just as there is one unity for One; and those (notions) are only three. And, for that reason, since there are only[3] three unities in the Three Persons, hence it is that the Persons are only said (to be) "Three".

SCHOLIUM

I. That numeral names in God are only said according to relation, is the most certain and most common doctrine; but there is a controversy concerning what those names convey among the divine; this matter is treated with in the Response. The first opinion posited there, which the Seraphic Doctor reproves, indeed concedes, that these names are said according to relation, but thus, that that expression, *"there are Three Persons"*, signifies nothing other than this: *"there are Persons"*. The defenders of this opinion seemed to have feared, that, if it were said, that numeral names convey something distinct from the Divine Persons Themselves, they would fall into the error imposed by Plato, that the forms of numbers are eternally subsistent. — Here it must be noted, that St. Bonaventure favors the milder explanation of the Platonic Ideas, which even St. Augustine has in his book, ON EIGHTY-THREE QUESTIONS, q. 46, n. 2. For St. Augustine thinks,

that Plato taught, that the ideas are separate from things, but not subsistent in themselves, but in the mind of the Creator. However, Aristotle wants, that Plato taught, that the ideas are subsistent through themselves. Concerning the true sentence of Plato, the controversy has not yet in our own days been settled.

That the notions or personal properties are distinguished from themselves, is the established teaching of the Seraphic Doctor (here in the body of the question; above in d. 13, a. 2 and 3, in the Scholium; and below in d. 26, q. 1 and 3).

II. The common sentence of the other doctors agrees with the Seraphic Doctor in the conclusion: Alexander of Hales, SUMMA., p. I, q. 65, m. 2, a. 2. — St. Thomas, here in q. 2, a. 2; SUMMA., I, q. 31, a. 1. — Bl. (now St.) Albertus, here in a. 4. — (Bl.) Peter of Tarentaise, here in q. 2, a. 3. — Richard of Middleton, here in a. 2, q. 3. — Giles the Roman, here in 1st. princ., q. 4. — (Bl.) Dionysius the Carthusian, here in q. 3.

ARTICLE III

On the name, "triune" *and* "trinity".

In the third place, is the principal question concerning the difference[4] of the numeral names, such as is this name, *"triune"* [trinus] and *"trinity"* [trinitas]. And about this two (things) are asked.

First, there is asked, whether names of this kind convey 'unity'.

Second, grated that they do, there is asked, of which kind is that unity, which they convey.

QUESTION I

Whether the names, which signify, at once, 'one' and a number, convey a unity?

Moreover, that they do convey a unity, seems:

1. First through (their) etymology: for a "trinity" is said (to be) a "quasi unity of three" [trium unitas],[5] similarly also "triune".

2. Likewise, this seems, because among the divine this name, *"trinity"*, is received, but not this name, *"a group of three"* [ternarius]; but these two convey the same plurality: therefore,

---

[1] From the more ancient manuscripts and edition 1, we have here supplied *this* [hoc], and next after *in a twofold manner* [dupliciter] we have substituted *either* [vel] for *in one manner* [uno modo], and, near the end of the Response, after *a relation* [relationem] *to another* [ad aliud] for *to something* [ad aliquid].

[2] Codex aa reads *does not convey any notion whatsoever, but only a personal one* [non quamcumque notionem importat, sed solum personalem]; codex T has *does not convey any relation and/or notion whatsoever* [non quamcumque relationem vel notionem importat]. Next, after *causes* [facit], trusting in the older manuscripts and edition 1, we have expunged *that* [illam].

[3] In the Vatican edition and codex cc alone there is unduly omitted *only* [tantum]. A little before this, codex Y after *unity for One* [unitas unius] adds *among the Three Persons* [in tribus personis].

[4] The Vatican edition, not trusting in the manuscripts and edition 1, reads *Third, there is principally asked concerning the difference* [Tertio principaliter quaeritur de differentia], and, next, together with codex cc after *"triune"* [trinus] it has *and/or* [vel] for *and* [et].

[5] (St.) Isidore, ETYMOLOGIES, Bk. VII, ch. 4 : A "trinity" is named, because one whole comes to be out of certain three, as if a *tri-unity* [tri-unitas].

---

* *Trans. note*: Here St. Bonaventure speaks of the causality of the notions in the essential order and according to our reckoning; because in God there is no causality in the proper sense of the term.

this[1] is not by reason of a plurality: therefore, this name, "*trinity*", conveys something beyond plurality; and (this is) naught but a unity: ergo etc..

3. Likewise, among the divine the name, "*triune*", is received, but the name, "*threefold*" [triplex], is not received — for God is not said (to be) "threefold", just as Master (Peter) says in the text,[2] but the Faith commonly says that God (is) Triune — therefore, ("triune") means something beyond that, which is "*threefold*"; but (this is) not a plurality: therefore, (it is) a unity.

4. Likewise, Master (Peter) said above, in the Twenty-second Distinction,[3] that this name, "*trinity*", is a collective name; but a collective name not only conveys a plurality, but also a unity: ergo etc..

ON THE CONTRARY: 1. Out of three persons nothing comes to be one; but from three created unities there does result one[4] something; therefore, number, when said among creatures, ought rather convey a unity than (when said) among the divine. But when "*a group of two*" and/or "*a group of three*" [binarius vel ternarius] is said among creatures, it conveys number thus, that (it does not convey) a unity: therefore, neither ought this name, "*trinity*", convey (a unity) among the divine.

2. Likewise, if "*triune*" and "*trinity*" convey plurality and unity; since no name so distinct and indistinct has[5] a plurality of distinction and a unity of indistinction, it will be able to be said of no name among the divine.

3. Likewise, if it[6] conveys a unity: therefore, since the same ought not be joined to itself, there is badly and frivolously said in the Hymn for Confessors, at the end:

Who, remaining seated above the peak of the sky,
Governs the machine of the whole world,
The Triune and One.[7]

CONCLUSION

The name, "triune" and/or "trinity", conveys with the plurality of the Persons also the Unity of the Essence, but not (Their) collective (unity).

I RESPOND: It must be said, that because there is number among the divine in a singular manner, namely, out of the distinction of the Supposits with a unity of form, it ought to have been expressed in a special manner[8] with a name, which means simultaneously a plurality and a unity. — Therefore, because names of this kind convey a plurality and a unity;[9] for that reason they are similar to collective names. But because the unity of collectives is a unity of aggregation, which is consequent to the plurality; but here there is a unity of form, which is not consequent to the plurality (of the Persons): for that reason such a name is not a collective one. And for that reason Master (Peter) says, that it is a *quasi* collective (name).

1. And on this account the first (objection) unto the contrary is clear. It must be conceded, therefore, that it does convey a plurality and a unity.

2. To that, therefore, which is objected, that no name simultaneously conveys[10] plurality and unity; it must be said, that this is true according to the reckoning of the form; but since (a name) is one in form, it can have a plurality of supposits; and this is not unfitting and/or impossible.

3. To that which is objected concerning frivolity, it must be said, that, just as this word, "*cede*", has the understanding of this word, "*giving*", and "*of place*", but when there is said; "*cede a place*", it falls under the understanding of the second of the two; similarly (is it) in the proposed, and similarly must it be understood among[11] relatives, when there is said: "*the son's father*".

SCHOLIUM

All the other ancient masters treat of this and the following question together and agree in the same solution. Alexander of Hales, SUMMA., p. I, q. 66, m. 1 and 2. — (Bl. Duns) Scotus, REPORTATIO., here in q. sole, near the end. — St. Thomas, here in q. 2, a. 2: SUMMA. , I, q. 31, a. 1. — Bl. (now St.) Albertus, here in a. 8; SUMMA., p. I, tr. 10, q. 45, m. 1 and 2. — (Bl.) Pete r of Tarentaise, here in q. 3, a. 1. — Richard of Middleton, here in a. 3, q. 1. — Giles the Roman, here in 2nd. princ., q. 2. — Henry of Ghent, SUMMA., a. 75, q. 4, n. 16, and ff.. — (Bl.) Dionysius the Carthusian, here in q. 5.

---

[1] Namely, that among the divine the name, "*trinity*", is received. — The Vatican ed. with cod. cc, with the other mss. and ed. 1 striving against this, here reads in an exceedingly restricted manner: *therefore, this name, "Trinity", if it is received among the divine, this* etc. [ergo hoc nomen Trinitatis, si recipiatur in divinis, hoc etc], and, a little before this, it has *is found* [reperitur] for *is received* [recipitur], and *a trinitarian group* [trinitarius] for *a group of three* [ternarius].

[2] Distinction XIX, ch. 12. — The Vatican edition, contrary to very many codices and edition 1, has *is said in a manifold manner* [dicitur multipliciter] for *Master (Peter) says* [dicit Magister].

[3] Chapter 3. — The Vatican edition, not trusting in the manuscripts and edition 1, omits *in the 22nd Distinction, that this name* [distinctione 22, quod hoc nomen]; but one must note, that this is omitted, because its sense is explained in the body (of the Question).

[4] The reading of the Vatican ed. and cod. cc, *there does comes to be or result* [fit sive resultat] for *there does result one* [unum resultat], is exceedingly arbitrary and contradicts all the other codd. and ed. 1. A little below this, the Vatican ed. has *a trinarian group* [trinarius] for *a group of three* [ternarius].

[5] The Vatican edition, contrary to the more ancient codices, reads *neither does it have* [nec habeat], in place of which, in edition 1, there is read *has no* [nullam habeat]. A little before this, the Vatican edition reads *is* [sit] for *so* [sic].

[6] Supply: "trine" and/or "trinity"; codex X reads *they convey* [important], just as is had in the preceding argument.

[7] As found in the Gothic Breviary, according to St. Isidore, in the OFFICIO UNIUS CONFESSORIS PRAECIPUI, NON PONTIFICIS.

[8] In the Vatican edition, less well and contrary to the manuscripts and edition 1, there is lacking *manner* [modo]. A little before this codex R has *in* [in] for *out of* [ex].

[9] Codex Y adds *simultaneously* [simul].

[10] Codex T together with edition 1 reads *has* [habet], which also next after *that* [quod], together with very many, other codices, such as A I and Y, reads *it* for *this* [hoc].

[11] The Vatican edition, together with codex cc alone, reads *concerning* [de].

QUESTION II

Whether the unity, which the names, "Trinty" and "Triune" convey, is the unity of the Essence, or of a Supposit?

Second, there is asked, of which kind is that unity, which this name, "*Trinity*" [trinitas] and/or "*Triune*" [trinus] conveys, whether, namely, (a unity) of Supposit, or of Essence. And it seems that (it is that) of the Essence:

1. Because That which is a *Trinity* is said of All together and[1] in the singular; but this alone befits a term conveying a substantial unity: ergo etc..

2. Likewise, no unity is of three except an essence and/or an essential (unity);[2] but a trinity is a unity of three: therefore, this name, "*Trinity*", means an essential unity; for an equal reason also this name, "*Triune*".

3. Likewise, neither this name, "*Trinity*", nor this name, "*Triune*", is said of a Person: therefore, it does not convey a personal unity. For (this)[3] is not conceded: 'a Person is Triune', and/or 'a Person is a Trinity'.

ON THE CONTRARY: 1. Names of this kind convey simultaneously a plurality and a unity; but the unity alone of a Person is plurifiable, not (that) of an essence: therefore, they convey[4] the unity of a Person.

2. Likewise, the Unity of the Essence is predicated of the Father; but neither this name, "*Triune*", nor this name, "*Trinity*", is predicated of the Father: ergo etc..

3. Likewise, the Unity of the Essence is predicated of the Essence; but this is never said: "the Divine Essence is Triune", nor:[5] "the Trinity is Triune": therefore, it does not mean an essential unity.

Therefore, there is asked, which unity do they convey, and whether those names are said according to substance, or according to relation. And since they are said of All together in the singular, it seems that they are said according to substance; again, since they are said of Any singly, they do not seem to be said according to substance.

CONCLUSION

The unity, which the terms "Trinity" and "Triune" convey, is not a personal unity, but an essential one.

I RESPOND: It must be said,[6] that regarding this it is customarily said, that this name, "*Trinity*", has a twofold et-ymology. In one manner "*Trinity*" is said (to be) "*a unity thrice*" [unitas ter]; and, thus, a numeral name does occur in it as a complement, and thus it is said according to relation, just as numeral terms (are); and the unity, which it conveys, is a *personal* unity, not an essential one, because the former is plurified. The other etymology is: "*Trinity*" is "*the unity of Three*" [unitas trium];[7] and then the unity is not numbered, but is signified as communicable by the Three; and since this unity is essential, for that reason it conveys an essential unity.

And, indeed, this last[8] etymology without a doubt has truth; but the first does not seem to have the truth. For since "*Triune*" and "*Trinity*" have the same signification, if the former: "*a unity thrice*" is the etymology,[9] then "*triune*" would be said (to be) "*one thrice*". But this, namely "*thrice one*", cannot be said of God, when, nevertheless, He is said (to be) "*Triune*".

On this account, it must be said, that names of this kind convey a formal unity or (a unity) of essence with a plurality of supposits; and for that reason they have in a certain manner the nature of a substantial term in this, that they are said of the Three singularly, and (have in a certain manner the nature) of a numeral term in this, that they are said of None through Himself.

1. To that which is objected, that the unity alone of a Person is plurifiable; it must be said, that "*Trinity*" does not convey a plurality about the unity directly [in recto], but solely obliquely [in obliquo], because it is of Three and/or by Three; and this (the unity) of the Essence.

2. To that which is objected, that the Unity of the Essence is predicated of the Father; it must be said, that it is true, but not for this reason, that several [plures] convene in Him — just as "animal" is predicated of "man", yet not for the reason, by which diverse species convene in him[10] — and because "*Trinity*" convey that unity as in Several, for that reason etc..

3. To that which is objected, that the Essence is not said (to be) "Triune", nor the Trinity "Triune";[11] it must be said, that this name, "*Triune*", conveys a unity in concretion, and such as inhering in Several. And for that reason it is said of Him (i.e. God) alone, because it conveys a unity as in concretion,

---

[1] In the Vatican edition and cod. cc alone there is lacking *and* [et].

[2] The Vatican edition alone here repeats *unity* [unitas].

[3] The Vatican edition and one or the other codex add here *this (proposition)* [haec].

[4] The Vatican edition faultily reads *it conveys* [importat].

[5] The words *nor: "the Trinity is Triune"* [nec trinitas est trina], we have inserted from codices P and Q, especially for this, that they occur below in the solution to this objection. Next codices W and Y have *the Unity of the Essence* [unitatem essentiae] for *an essential unity* [unitatem essentialem].

[6] The Vatican ed. with codex cc alone prefaces this with: *For an understanding of the aforesaid* [Ad praedictorum intelligentiam]. Next, the Vatican ed., without the authority of the mss. and ed. 1, has *it is fitting that it be said* [convenit dici] for *it was customarily said* [consuevit dici].

[7] Thus St. Isidore, ETYMOLOGIES, Bk. VII, ch. 4. See the previous question, p. 428, footnote 5. — A little below this after *communicable* [communicabilis], as requested by many manuscripts and editions 1, 2 and 3, we have supplied the preposition *by* [a], which is often conjoined to the word *communicable* [communicabilis] by the Seraphic Doctor.

[8] In the Vatican ed. and cod. cc alone there is omitted *last* [ultima].

[9] In the Vatican edition, and in some codices, there is prefixed to the words *a trinity (is)* [trinitas] the words *a unity thrice* [unitas ter].

[10] The equivalent example is this: just as of man "animal" is not predicated, to the extend that it comprehends under itself other diverse species of animals, namely, rational and rational, as if in man diverse species of animals convened, but because 'man' is a species of 'animal': so of the Father there is not predicated the Unity of the Essence, to the extent that It is in the Other Persons, as if more Persons convened in the Father, but because He is one of the Persons, to Whom the unique Divine Essence convenes. — The Vatican edition, a little before this, contrary to nearly all the codices and the first six editions, has *by which* [qua] for *that* [quia], and then after *several convene in* [plures in] has *It* [ea] for *Him (the Father)* [eo]. Next, below this, the Vatican edition, with nearly all the manuscripts and edition 1 dissenting, omits *yet* [tamen], and faultily exhibits *by which diverse species, they* etc. [qua diversa specie conveniunt] for *by which diverse species* etc. [qua diversae species conveniunt].

[11] Codices V and Z omit the words *nor the Trinity "Triune"* [nec trinitas trina].

as this name, *"God"*, which indeed supposes the Persons. And because such[1] is this name, *"God"*, for that reason there is conceded: *"God belongs to Three"* [Deus est tribus], not: *"the Deity is Triune"*; because (the word), *"Deity"* [deitas], does not suppose a Person; similarly, neither, this name, *"Trinity"* [trinitas]; and, in this manner, all (the objections) are clear.

SCHOLIUM

In the solution to n. 3 the Seraphic Doctor rejects the saying *"the Deity is Triune"*. Yet in the hymn SACRA SOLEMNIS IUNCTA SINT GAUDIA (in the Office for Corpus Christi), whose author is reported to be St. Thomas, there is read: « Te trina Deitas unaque poscimus » [Thee, the Triune and One Deity, we earnestly beseech]. Here it can be said, because the abstract term ("Deity") is taken as the concrete (term, "God"). For other authors on this, see the Scholium of the preceding Question.

NOTES ON THE TEXT OF THE MASTER

In this part, there must be noted about the text (of Master Peter), on this which he says: *When we say: "that there are many Persons", we exclude singularity and solitude*; that[2] among the divine we do receive a *unity*, not a *singularity* nor a *solitude*; because *singularity* excludes communicability, *solitude* excludes plurality; and we posit one Essence in Many (Persons): for that reason we (as Catholics) do not receive these.[3]

Similarly it must be noted on the part of plurality, that we do receive (amon the divine) these four, namely[4] *anotherness, plurality, discretion* and *distinction*; but these four on the contrary we do not receive, namely, *diversity, multiplicity, division* and *separation*.

Moreover, the *reason* for this is, that *separation* supposes a division, division a *multiplicity*, multiplicity a *diversity*, but diversity posits a *distinction of form* and/or of nature. And, because among the divine there is an omnimodal unity of *Nature*, for that reason, since a diversity (of Nature) is not received, neither (are) any of those four. Contrariwise, *discretion* presupposes[5] a *distinction*, distinction a *plurality*, plurality an *anotherness*. But anotherness is not only attained as much as regards form, but also as much as regards supposit;[6] and because the Hypostases are many, for that reason the aforesaid four are received among the divine.

But, the *distinction* of the aforesaid names is this. For of the first four *"anotherness"* and *"plurality"* convey a distinction on the part of the thing; but *"distinction"* and *"discretion"* (convey the same) through a comparison to our cognition; but *"anotherness"* (does so) through a manner of *substance*, *"plurality"* through a manner of *quantity*, although there is truly no quantity There. But *"distinction"* and *"discretion"* differ, because *"discretion"* is said in comparison to *sight*, but *"distinction"* in comparison to *touch*.

Moreover, the other four differ in this manner: for[7] a *"diversity"* is attained according to *substance*; a *"multiplicity"* (is attained) as much as regard a true *quantity*; a *"division"* (is attained) as much as regards a *position* or as regards a *discontinuation*; but a *"separation"* (is attained) as much as regards a *'where'*. — And or *in another manner*: *"diversity"* (is attained) as much as regards *an intrinsic principle*; *"multiplicity"* as much as regards a *number*; a *"division"* as much[8] as regards a *terminus*; but a *"separation"* is attained as much as regards an *interjected medium*.

DISTINCTION XXV

CHAPTER I

What is signified by this name, "Person", in the plural number, that is, when there is said "Persons".

Moreover, one must consider, when this name, "person" [persona], as has been said, is said according to substance, what is the understanding of the saying, when it is proffered *in the plural* [pluraliter profertur]: "Three Persons", and/or: "Two Persons", and when there is said: "one [alia] is the Person of the Father, another is the Person of the Son, another [alia] is the Person of the Holy Spirit". For, if among these expressions the word for '*person*' causes an understanding of the Essence, we seem to confess that (there are) several Essences, and thus several Gods. However, if it does not have the signification of 'essence' There, one is the reckoning of this name, when there is said: "the Father is a Person", and/or "the Son is a Person"; and another (is the reckoning of it), when there is said: "the Father and the Son and the Holy Spirit are three Persons"; and when there is said: "one is the Person of the Father, another (that) of the Son", and (expressions) of this kind.

« For "person" », as (St.) Augustine says above, « is said regarding Itself, and it is the same for God *to be a person* as *to be*,

---

[1] In codex T there is added *a name* [nomen]. At the end of the response, we have substituted from very many manuscripts *all (the objections)* [omnia] for *the objections* [obiecta].

[2] The Vatican edition, not trusting in the manuscripts and edition 1, reads *It must be noted that* [Notandum quod] for *that* [quia].

[3] The Vatican edition, together with very many codices, has less aptly *this (consequence)* [hoc] for *these (i.e. singularity and solitude)* [haec].

[4] In the Vatican ed. and cod. cc alone, there is wanting *namely* [scilicet].

[5] Trusting in the manuscripts and editions 1, 2, 3, and 6, we have substituted *presupposes* [praesupponit] for *supposes* [supponit]. A little before this very many codices, such as A I T etc., after *for that reason* [ideo] insert less congruously *also* [et], and codex Z puts *of the aforesaid* [praedictorum] for *of those* [istorum].

[6] See above d. 4, a. 1, q. 2 and Doubt 9. — Next, the particle *and* [et] is less well absent from very many codices and the first six editions.

[7] The Vatican edition, together with codex cc alone, reads *because* [quia] in place of *for* [nam]. Next, edition 1 has *as much as regards* [quantum ad] for *according to* [secundum]. A little below this, codex X has *number* [numerum] for a *'where'* [ubi] (that is, a separation is according to a diversity of location).

[8] Out of many manuscripts and editions 1, 4, 5, and 6, we have supplied *as much* [quantum].

NOTES ON THE BOOK OF SENTENCES

[1] Distinction XXIII, ch. 1.

[2] Distinction XXIII, ch. 1. Cf. in the same, p. 401, footnote 4. — Then after *that is* [id est], on the subsequent page, the codices and edition 1 omit *Divine* [divina].

just as it is the same for Him *to be* as *to be God*». From which there is manifestly gathered, that we do predicate the Divine Essence, when we say: "the Father is a Person, the Son is a Person, the Holy Spirit is a Person, that is, the Divine Essence; and entirely one and the same (thing) is signified by the name for '*person*', that is the Divine Essence, when there is said: "the Father is a Person, and the Son is a Person", as there is signified by the name for '*God*', when there is said: "the Father is God, the Son is God". Thus also the same is signified, when there is said: "God is God", and "God is a person"; for by each name the Divine Essence is understood, because each is said according to substance.

On the other hand, when there is said: "the Father and the Son and the Holy Spirit are three Persons", what do we signify by the name, "*Persons*"? Or (do we signify) the Essence? For this seems (the case), if we diligently scrutinize the words of (St.) Augustine posited above.[1]

For above he said, that « for this reason do we say that (there are) "Three Persons", because that which a person is, is common to the Three ». And again, « because the Father is a Person, and the Son is a Person, and the Holy Spirit is a Person, for that reason the Three are said (to be) "Persons" ». Therefore, it seems, that this name, "*person*", has the same signification, when there is said: "Three Persons", as it has, when there is said: "the Father is a Person, the Son is a Person, the Holy Spirit is a Person"; because, as (St.) Augustine shows, the former is said — that is, "Three Persons" — on account of the latter,[2] because that which a person is, is common to Them. Therefore, that which is common to Them, that is, to the Father and to the Son and to the Holy Spirit, seems to be signified by the name for '*person*', when there is said "*Three Persons*".

In another manner it can also be shown, that There the Essence is signified by the name for '*person*', when there is said "*Three Persons*". For, as (St.) Augustine said above,[3] for this necessity did we say that (there are) "*Three Persons*", to respond to those asking, "*What (are) the Three (Persons)?*" [quid tres], and/or "*What (are) the Three?*" [quid tria]. Therefore, when there is asked, "*What (are) the Three (Persons)?*", and/or "*What (are) the Three?*", there is a fitting response [convenienter respondetur], when there is said, "three Persons". But when there is asked, "*What (are) the Three (Persons)?*", and/or "*What (are) the Three?*", through "*What*" one asks concerning the Essence. For what those Three are, naught is found but the Essence. If, therefore, we respond rightly to the question, it is necessary [oportet] that in responding we signify the Essence; otherwise we do not show, what the Three are. If, on the other hand, responding, we signify the Essence, we understand the Essence Itself by the name for '*person*', when there is said: "*Three Persons*".

To certain ones it seems, that by the name for '*person*' there is signified the Essence, when there is said "*Three Persons*", on account of this, that (St.) Augustine says,[4] that the Three are said (to be) "Persons", because that which is a "person" is common to Them, so that such is the understanding: 'the Father and the Son and the Holy Spirit are three Persons', that is, 'are Three having that, which a person is, common (to Them)', that is, 'there are Three, Anyone of which is a Person, that is the Essence'. But in what manner according to this understanding will there be said: "one [alia] is the Person of the Father, another (that) of the Son?" And

this, too, do they thus want to understand, namely, 'One [alius] is the Father, and Another is the Son, yet (They) having that which a person is, common (to Them both)'. And they confirm this by the authority of (St.) Augustine, who in the seventh book, ON THE TRINITY[5] says: « We say that the Three Persons (are) of the same Essence, and/or that the Three Persons (are) the One Essence. But we do not say that the Three Persons (are) out of the same Essence, as if there something is that which is the Essence, another that which (is) a Person ». — With this authority and the aforesaid they strive to assert in the aforesaid expressions, that the name for '*person*' signifies the Essence.

But what shall they respond to that which (St.) Augustine says in the book, ON THE FAITH TO PETER,[6] « namely, that the Father is one in person, or according to person [personaliter], the Son another according to person, the Holy Spirit another according to person »? For in what manner (is) the Father one according to person, the Son another according to person, the Holy Spirit another according to person, if They entirely convene in *being a person* [in esse personam], that is if "person" causes only the understanding of the Essence? For that reason it seems to us that it can be said in another manner more congruently according to the authorities of the Catholic Doctors.

CHAPTER II

On the threefold acceptance of this name, "Person",
in the Trinity.

It must be known, therefore, that this name, "*person*", causes a multiple understanding, not only one. And as (St.) Hilary (of Poitiers) says in the fourth book, ON THE TRINITY:[7] « The understanding of sayings is to be assumed from the causes for speaking [ex causis dicendi], because thing has not subjected to speech [sermon], but speech to thing ». Therefore, discerning the causes for saying this name, that is, "*person*", we distinguish the signification, saying, that this name, that is, "*person*", is said properly according to substance and signifies an *essence*, just as (St.) Augustine shows above,[8] when there is said: "God is a person, the Father is a person". However, for a certain necessity, as (St.) Augustine said above, this name has been transferred, so that in a plural manner there is said "*Three Persons*", when there is asked, "*What (are) the Three (Persons)?*", and/or "*What (are) the Three?*"; where it does not signify an *essence*, that is, the Divine Nature, which is common to the Three Persons, but the *Subsistences*, and/or the Hypostases according to the Greeks. Indeed, the Greeks, as (St.) Augustine said above,[9] accept "substance", that is, "hypostasis", in one manner, we in another. For we says that a "substance" (is) an "essence" or a "nature". But we say "persons", just as they say, "substances", that is, "hypostases". If,[10] therefore, we accept "persons" thus, as they accept "substances" and/or "hypostases"; but they accept "hypostases" in another manner, than we (do) "substance"; therefore, we accept "persons" in another manner than "substance". Therefore, when we say: "Three Persons", we do not signify there by the name for '*person*' the Essence. What, therefore, do we signify? We say, that

---

[1] Distinction XXIII, ch. 2. The passages indicated are found on p. 402, in footnotes 1 and 4.

[2] Codices A and D and edition 1 add not so well *that is* [id est].

[3] Distinction XXIII, chs. 1 and 2, where the passages of (St.) Augustine are cited. — A little before this, the Vatican ed. and the other edd., except ed. 1, contrary to the codd., read *it seems that it can* [videtur posse] for *it can* [potest]. — In the following sentences, very many edd. have *we say* [dicimus] for *we said* [diximus], and *we shall show* [ostendemus] for *we show* [ostendimus].

[4] ON THE TRINITY, Bk. VII, ch. 4, n. 7.

[5] Ch. 6, n. 11. — At the end, at *a Person* [persona], the Vatican ed., with the other edd., except ed. 1, add *is* [est], contrary to the codd. and the original.

[6] Chapter 1, n. 5.

[7] Number 14.

[8] Here in ch. 1, and in Distinction XXIII, chs. 1 and 3; the following passage is also ibid., ch. 2.

[9] See Distinction XXIII, ch. 2. — A little before this codices C D and E have *Substances* [substantias] for *Subsistences* [subsistentias], which reading is not false, so long as *Substances* is understood as the *First Substances*, or as the *Hypostases* among the Greeks, as is said in the following clause.

[10] The Vatican edition and edition 8 faultily read *Thus* [Sic]. Next, the Vatican edition and edition 2 have *and they* [et illi] in place of *but they* [at illi].

there are three Persons, that is three Substances,[1] namely three Beings, for which the Greeks say: "three Hypostases".

And, here, the sense is assisted from the aforesaid words of (St.) Augustine, if they are understood more interiorly. For because the Father is a Person, that is the Essence, and the Son a Person, and the Holy Spirit a Person; for that reason They are said (to be) "three Persons", that is "three Subsistences",[2] "three Beings" [tres entes]. For They cannot be said (to be) "three Subsistences and/or Beings", unless each One of Them [singulus eorum] were a Person, that is, the Essence. Therefore, because that, which a person is, is common to Them; for that reason They are rightly said (to be) "three Persons", that is, "Subsistences" and/or "Subsistents", as, just as the Essence, which is common to Them, truly and properly is, so those Three are truly and properly understood (to be) Subsistences and/or Beings [entes]. And for that reason (St.) Augustine,[3] discerning the causes of the sayings, says, that the Three Persons are the One Essence and/or of the same Essence, not out of the same Essence, lest There a Person be understood to be one (thing), the Essence another. For the Three Persons, that is, Subsistences, are one in essence and of the One Essence, but They are not one in person and/or of one Person, though "person" is sometimes said according to substance. For if this would be said, there would be a confusion among the Persons.

But to this, which they say: when there is asked, "What (are) the Three (Persons)?", and/or "What (are)[4] the Three?", one asks concerning the Essence, because what those Three are, naught is found but the Essence — wanting through this to induce us, to understand the Essence by the name for 'person', when we respond: "Three Persons" — thus we say: indubitably it is true, that there is not found one Something [unum aliquod], which those Three are, except the Essence. For those Three are the One [unum], that is the Divine Essence. Whence the Truth says:[5] I and the Father are One [unum]. Nevertheless, when there is asked, "What (are) the Three (Persons)?", and/or "What (are) the Three?"; one does not ask concerning the Essence, nor does "What" refer there to the Essence; but when the Catholic Faith professed that there are Three, as (the Apostle) John says in the canonical Epistle:[6] There are Three, who give [perhibent] testimony in Heaven, it used to ask, what those Three are, that is, whether They were three things [tres res], and what three things, and by what name are those three things signified. And for that reason by the necessity of speaking this name, "person", was found to respond, and there was said: "three Persons".

But let it not move you, that we have said "three things". For saying this, we do not posit a number of diverse things in the Trinity, but we thus says "three things", to confess that the same are one, certain, most high Thing. Whence (St.) Augustine in the first book, On Christian Doctrine,[7] thus says: « The Things, therefore, which must be enjoyed, are the Father and the Son and the Holy Spirit. And the same Trinity is one, certain most high Thing and (is) common to those enjoying It, if, however, (It is) a Thing, and not the Cause of all things, if, however, (It is) even a cause.[8] For there can not easily be found a name, which befits so

great an Excellence, except that which is better said: "This Trinity (is) the One God" ». Just as, therefore, They are said (to be) "three things", and These are the one Thing, so They are said (to be) "three Subsistences",[9] and These are one Substance. — Behold, it has been shown, what is the understanding of this name, "person", when we say: "Three Persons".

CHAPTER III

Out of which sense is there said: One, the Person of the Father, Another, (the Person) of the Son, Another, (that) of the Holy Spirit; or the Father (is) one in person, the Son another, the Holy Spirit another.

Now, let us look into, whether according to the same reckoning and cause there is said: "One is the person of the Father, another (that) of the Son, another (that) of the Holy Spirit. Which at least can be sanely understood, so that the sense is such: "One is the Subsistence and/or Hypostasis of the Father, another (that) of the Son, another the Subsistence of the Holy Spirit; and one Subsistence (is) the Father, another (is) the Son, another (is) the Holy Spirit.

Then there is asked, whether according to the same reckoning there is accepted, when there is said: "the Father is one in person, the Son another in person, the Holy Spirit another"; or "the Father is one according to person [personaliter], the Son another according to person, the Holy Spirit another according to person".

To which we say, that even if it can be accepted in the same manner, yet more congruently is another understanding said differently from the reckoning of the saying, so that here by the name for '*person*' the property of a Person is understood, so that the sense is such: 'the Father is one in person and/or according to person' [personaliter], that is, the Father by His own property (is) Other than the Son, and the Son by His property is Other than the Father, for by the property of the paternity [paternali proprietate] the Hypostasis of the Father is distinguished from the Hypostasis of the Son, and the Hypostasis of the Son by the property of the filiation [filiali proprietate] is discerned from the Father, and the Holy Spirit is distinguished from Each by the property of the procession [processibili proprietate].

In the same manner, too, "person" can be sanely accepted in the aforementioned expressions, when there is said: "one is the Person of the Father, another (that) of the Son",[10] that is, "one is the property, by which the Father is the Father, another that by which the Son is the Son, another that by which the Holy Spirit is the Holy Spirit". Thus also by the name for '*person*' certain ones want to understand the properties, when the Three are said (to be) "Persons"; but it is better, that we understand the Subsistences and/or Hypostases, when we say "Three Persons".

From the aforesaid there is gathered, that the name for '*person*' in the Trinity has a threefold reckoning. For there is where it causes the understanding of the Essence, and there is where it causes the understanding of a Hypostasis, and there is where it causes the understanding of a property.

On the one hand, that it is said according to substance and sometimes signifies the Essence, we have shown openly from the sayings of (St.) Augustine above. On the other hand, that it is accepted on behalf of a hypostasis and a property, must be shown from the authorities of the Saints,

---

[1] The Vatican ed. and edd. 1, 4, 5, 8 & 9, read *Substances* [substantiae]; codd. A B D & E *Subsistences* [subsistentiae], and C *Subsistents* [subsistentes].

[2] Codex C and edition 8, here and below more frequently, have *Substances* [substantiae] for *Subsistences* [subsistentiae]; codices C and E and edition 8 add *and/or* [vel] before *three Beings* [tres entes].

[3] On the Trinity, Bk. VII, ch. 6, n. 11; see the preceeding chapter.

[4] The Vatican ed. and edd. 4, 6 and 9, omit *What (are)* [quid].

[5] Jn. 10:30.

[6] 1 John 5:7. The Vulgate reads: *Since there are Three, who give testimony in Heaven* [Quoniam tres sunt, qui testimonium dant in caelo]. Also codex X, with the Vulgate reads *give* [dant] for *give* [perhibent]. Cf. above Dist. II, ch. 5, p. 49, footnote 3. — Below this, the Vatican with the other edd., except ed. 1, transpose the Latin *to respond* [ad respondendum] after *"person"* [persona].

[7] Chapter 3, n. 3. The following passage is ibid., ch. 5, n. 5. — Above, before *three things* [tres res], the Vatican edition together with editions 4 and 5, has *we say* [dicimus] for *we have said* [diximus].

[8] The Vatican edition, together with the other editions, except editions 1 and 6, omits *if, however, (It is) even a cause* [sit amen et causa], contrary to the original and to the codices.

[9] The Vatican edition, together with editions 2, 3, 7 and 8, and codex C, read *Substances* [substantiae], and next only the Vatican edition together with the other editions, except edition 1, has *Essence* [essentia] for *Substance* [substantia].

[10] Only cod. A & edd. 1 & 6 add *another (that) of the Holy Spirit* [alia Spiritus sancti]; but these words can be easily supplied from the preceding.

[11] Here in ch. 1, and in Distinction XXIII, ch. 1.

lest according to our own conjectures we seem to say something daring [aliquid ausi]. On this (St.) Jerome in (his) exposition of the Catholic Faith, To Damasus,[1] thus says: « There is not, in a word, any grade in the Trinity, and nothing which (is) inferior or superior can be said (to be There), but the whole Deity is equal in Its own perfection, so that excepting the words, which indicate the property of the Persons, whatever is said of one Person, can be most worthily understood of the Three. And also as confuters of Arius, we say that there belongs to the Trinity one and the same Substance, and we say that the One God (is) in the Three Persons; thus deflecting [declinantes] the impiety of Sabellius, we distinguish the Three Persons expressed under a property: not saying that He is a Father to Himself, that He (is) a Son to Himself, that He (is) a Holy Spirit to Himself, but that one is the Person of the Father, another (that) of the Son, another (that) of the Holy Spirit. For we confess not only the names, but even the properties of the names, that is, the Persons, and/or as the Greeks express (it), the Hypostases, that is, the Subsistences. Nor does the Father sometimes exclude the person of the Son and/or of the Holy Spirit; nor the Son and/or the Holy Spirit received the name and Person of the Father, but the Father (is) always the Father, and the Son (is) always the Son, and the Holy Spirit (is) always the Holy Spirit. And so They are one in substance, but They are distinguished according to Persons and names ». Behold, here (St.) Jerome openly says, that the properties are the Persons, and the Persons are Subsistences. Whence what we have said has been made manifest, namely, that by the name for 'person' there is signified both *Hypostasis* and *property*. — (St.) John Damascene[2] also says that the Persons are "*Hypostases*", and he says that These (are) "*Beings*" [entes], thus saying: « In the Deity we confess (that there is) One Nature and that Three Hypostases (are), according to the truth, Beings, that is, Persons ».

COMMENTARY ON DISTINCTION XXV

What does the name, *"person"*, signify?

Moreover, one must consider, when this name, "person".

THE DIVISION OF THE TEXT

Above, Master (Peter) shows,[1] what is signified through a numeral term, when we say *"Three Persons"*, here, second, he subjoins, what is signified through this term *"person"*. And this part is divided into two (parts). In the first (part), he asks and opposes (objections); in the second he solves (the objections), there (where he says): *To certain ones it seems, that by the name for 'person' etc..*

The *first* part has three parts. In the first, he moves a doubt; in the second he opposes (an objection) through the authority of (St.) Augustine, showing, that it is said according to substance, there (where he says): *For "person", as (St.) Augustine says above*; third he opposes (this) through a reckoning, in the third chapter,[2] there (where he says): *In another manner it can also be shown*: where he shows that it (is) the same.

To certain ones it seems, that by the name for 'person'. This is the *second* part, in which he solves (the doubt); and this part is divided into two (subparts). In the first, he solves (the doubt) according to the opinion of others, who say, that "person" is accepted according to the Essence, yet related to a Supposit. In the second, he solves (the doubt) according to his own opinion through a distinction, there (where he says): *It must be known, therefore, that this name, "person", causes a multiple understanding.* And this part is divided into two (subparts). In the first part, he says, in what manner this name, "person", is accepted in the plural; in the second, in what manner it is accepted in the singular, when there is said: "One is the Father, Another the Son in person",[3] there (where he says): *Now let us look into, whether according to the same reckoning.* — The first part has three parts. In the first, he posits a distinction, through which he solves (the doubt); in the second, he confirms (the solution) through the authority of (St.) Augustine, there (where he says): *And here the sense is assisted from the aforesaid words etc.*; in the third, he responds to the objection, there (where he says): *But to this, which they say.* — Similarly, the following part has three parts. In

---

[1] All the codices and edd. 1, 2, 3, 5, 7 and 9, read: *to Alipius and Augustine, Bishops* [ad Alipium et Augustinum, Episcopos]. But among the words of St. Jerome the book is entitled: *To Damasus* [ad Damasum]. — In this text, contrary to the ed. of (St.) Jerome's works, codd. A B and C and ed. 1, the Vatican ed., with the other edd., have *Divinity* [divinitas] for *Deity* [deitas]. Then, contrary to the original, codd. A B C and E, and ed. 1, the Vatican ed., with the other edd., add *Essence and/or* [essentiam vel] before *Substance* [substantiam], and, after this, before *impiety* [impietatem] add *too* [etiam].

[2] On the Orthodox Faith, Bk. III, ch. 5, where he speaks in this manner: *We confess One Nature in the Divinity, but we say (that there are) truly existing Three Persons* [Unam in divinitate naturam confitemur, tres autem personas vere existentes dicimus.]

NOTE WELL: The codices add a fourth chapter to this Distinction, beginning: Nunc de proprietatibus, which is found at the beginning of Distinction XXVI. But it has been put there, because St. Bonaventure, in the Division of the Text cites this chapter as part of Distinction XXVI.

NOTES ON THE COMMENTARY

[1] The Vatican edition, with the codices and edition 1 fighting against this, reads *responds* [respondet], and a little below this it has *is said* [dicitur] for *we say* [dicimus]. Then after *here* [hic], which indeed is wanting in not a few codices and edition 1, it omits *second* [secundo], which is extant in nearly all the codices and edition 1.

[2] The Vatican edition omits *in the third chapter* [tertio capitulo], which words in many codices, such as I P T Y etc., are had, in place of which words there is exhibited in other codices, such as A Q S V X Z, *in the fourth chapter* [quarto capitulo]; in our edition of Master (Peter's Book of Sentences), it is the *first chapter*.

[3] The words *in person* [in persona], suppressed by the Vatican edition, we have restored on the authority of very many manuscripts, such as A B D F G H K P Q T Y Z etc., and ed. 1.

the first he determines, in what manner "person" is accepted, when there is said: "one is the Person of the Father"; second, in what manner it is accepted, when there is said: "the Father is one in person"; third, he confirms this by authorities. The first he does, there

(where he says): *Now let us look into* etc.; the second, there (where he says): *Then, there is asked, whether according to the same reckoning*; the third, there (where he says): *But that it is said according to substance*.

TREATMENT OF THE QUESTIONS

For an understanding of this part two (things) are principally asked:

First, there is asked concerning the quiddity of this name, "person".

Second, there is asked concerning the commonality [communitate] of the same.

As much as regards the first, two (things) are asked:

First, there is asked concerning 'person', what is it according to the thing.

Second, what is it according to (its) definition.

ARTICLE I

On the quiddity of the name, "person".

QUESTION I

Whether this name, "person", among the divine, is said according to substance, or according to relation?

And that *"person"* is said according to substance, seems:

1. From the words of (St.) Augustine in the seventh (book) On the Trinity:[1] « It is the same for God to be and to be a person ». And again: « When we say "the person of the Father", we say nothing other than "the Substance of the Father" ». therefore, "person" means nothing other than "substance", therefore, "person" is said according to substance.

2. Likewise, (St.) Anselm (of Canterbury) at the end of the Monologion (says):[2] « As many as there are persons, so many are there substances »: therefore, the name for *'person'* is said according to substance.

3. Likewise, Hugh of Saint Victor in the book, On the Sacraments, in the first part of the second book (says):[3] There is only one substantial name, which is said of each singularly, yet in the Most High (Trinity) is not said singularly, but is pronounced plurally, such as (is) "person": therefore, this name, *"person"*, is a substantial name.

4. Likewise, (St. Anicius Manlius Severinus) Boethius in the book, On the Two Natures and One Person of Christ,[4] defining "person", says,

that « it is an individual substance of a rational nature »; but if "substance" is in its right sense [in recto] predicated, and not per accidens, but according to (the thing) itself: then, therefore, "person" means "substance" according to all the Doctors.

5. Likewise, this very (thing) seems *by reason*, and this through a *division*. For (St. Severinus) Boethius,[5] hunting for a definition of *"person"*, says, that either it is a substance, or an accident; and he says, that it is not an accident: therefore, (it is) a substance. If, therefore, "person" among these inferiors means "substance" and "something existing through itself" [quid per se existens]: therefore, (it means these) also in God.

6. This (also) seems *through its abstraction* [per eius absolutionem], since every name, which is said *according to (the thing) itself*, means the Substance among the divine, because such is not said according to relation; but this name, *"person"*, is of this kind. This is clear; and (St.) Augustine says in the seventh (book), On the Trinity:[6] « Indeed, *"person"* is said regarding (the thing) itself, as (is) "good" and "great" »: ergo etc..

7. Likewise, this seems through *the response of the Church*: because every name, which is fittingly responded

---

[1] Chapter 6, n. 11. — The following text is also found in the same place. Cf. here the text of Master (Peter) chs. 1 and 2. — The Vatican edition omits the first conclusion: *therefore, "person" means nothing other* etc. [ergo persona etc.].

[2] Chapter 78.

[3] Chapter 4: Indeed, "person" is said regarding (the thing) itself, not regarding the Son and/or the Holy Spirit, just as "God" and similar (names are said). For this name alone is, which when it is said of Each regarding Himself, is accepted plurally, not singularly, in the Most High (Trinity). For we say, that the Father is a Person, and the Son a Person, and the Holy Spirit a Person. However the Father and the Son and the Holy Spirit are not one Person, but Three.

[4] Chapter 3. — A little below this, after *in its right (sense) predicated* [praedicatur in recto], codices H and bb add *of a Person* [de persona].

[5] Loc. cit., ch. 2: Therefore, these are to be investigated by those inquirers in this manner: since apart from a nature there cannot be a person, since what are said (to be) natures, are other substances, other accidents; and we see, that a person cannot be constituted in accidents. For who says, that any (nature) of whiteness and/or blackness and/or magnitude is a person? Therefore, it remains, that a "person" is said to come together in substances. — Immediately before this, the Vatican edition badly and contrary to the testimony of the codices, except codex cc alone, has *definition* [definitionem] for *division* [divisionem].

[6] Chapter 6, n. 11. — On the major of this argument, see (St.) Augustine, On the Trinity, ch. 8, n. 9. — Understand *through its abstraction* [per eius absolutionem] as "because it has an absolute 'being', not a relative one. — A little above this footnote, codex W adds *a name* [nomen] after *such* [tale].

to a question made through (the interrogative), "*What?*", indicates a substance,[1] because "*What?*" seeks a substance; but this name, "*person*", is the response of the Church to heretics asking, "What (are) the *Three?*", just as (St.) Augustine says and Master (Peter too):[2] therefore, it indicates a substance.

8. Likewise, this seems *by the abstraction of relation*. Let us understand, that there is no relation among the divine, and that the Divine Nature is in one, sole Hypostasis, just as the Gentiles understand (It); then it is established,[3] that there is still an understanding of an intellectual Nature and of One having That, therefore, both of a Person and a Nature: therefore, if, excluding every relation, there is conserved [salvus est] the understanding of a *Person*, "*person*" is not said according to relation. And it is said according to relation and/or according to substance: therefore, it is said according to substance.

ON THE CONTRARY: 1. (St. Severinus) Boethius (says) in the book, ON THE TRINITY,[4] at the end: « If the Persons are divided, it is necessary, that a word, which draws (its) origin from the Persons, not pertain to the Substance ». If, therefore, (those words) which draw (their) origin from the Persons not pertain to the Substance, much more strongly (does) neither the name for '*person*'.

2. Likewise, Richard of Saint Victor[5] says, that « '*person*' is the same as a 'one existing through itself, according to a certain manner of singular existence of a rational nature' »; but a singular manner of existence is a relation among the divine: ergo etc..

3. Likewise, it seems *by reason*, that every name, which receives a multitude and/or a plurification, pertains to relation, because, according to all, the Substance always remains undivided. And (St. Severinus) Boethius[6] says, that « the Substance contains a unity, a relation multiplies (that as) a Trinity »: if, therefore, the name for '*person*' is multipliable, it is clear that it is said according to relation.

4. Likewise, every name of itself, conveying a distinction, is said according to relation; but the name for '*person*' of itself conveys a distinction, because a person is a hypostasis distinguished by a property; and (St. Severinus) Boethius[7] says, that « it is an individual », and individuation is not other than distinction: ergo etc..

CONCLUSION

Among the divine, "person" is said both according to substance, and according to relation; from a general understanding it is said more principally according to substance than according to relation; but from a special understanding it is said in God according to relation.

I RESPOND: It must be said, that some wanted to solve (this question) by distinguishing the signification of "*person*" according to the *diversity of number*, such that in the singular it would be said according to substance, in the plural according to relation.[8] — But this solution is neither valid *in itself*, nor *as regards the proposed*. Indeed *in itself* it is not valid, because every plural doubles its own singular,[9] therefore, it does not change the signification. *As regards the proposed* it is not valid, because there is said in the singular: "one is the Person of the Father, another (that) of the Son", which could not be said, if it were a substantial term, since there is not one substance of the Father, another of the Son.

Some wanted to solve (it) through a distinction of the signification *according to diverse times*, namely, that before the response of the Church it would be said substantially and according to substance, after the response it would be said according to relation. — But this solution is not valid *in itself* nor *as regards the proposed*. *In itself* it is not valid, because the Church with some reason responded[10] more (with) that name than (with) another substantial (term); and then She did not impose the signification: therefore, the response of the Church caused nothing regarding the change of signification. It is not valid *as regards the proposed*, because according to the signification, which it has after the response of the Church, the Doctors speak, and reasons run, for each side.

And, besides, it must be understood, that a *person* is said (to be) "a supposit of a rational nature distinguished by a property", according to all, who understand its special signification; but a *supposit* of a rational nature is established to be a substance, the *property* (whereby it is) to be distinguished is established to be a relation. Since, therefore, "*per-*

---

[1] Cf. Aristotle, POSTERIOR ANALYTICS, Bk. II, ch. 1 ff.

[2] Here in the text, ch. 2, where the words of (St.) Augustine are also indicated.

[3] The Vatican ed. with cod. cc alone, reads *it happens* [contingit].

[4] Rather, in the book entitled, WHETHER "THE FATHER" AND "THE SON" AND "THE HOLY SPIRIT" ARE SUBSTANTIALLY PREDICATED OF THE DIVINITY, otherwise known under the title ON THE PREDICATION OF THE THREE PERSONS, which he wrote to John, a Deacon of the Roman Church. — In the text itself, after *are divided* [divisae sunt] the edition adds *but the substance (is) undivided* [substantia vero indivisa]; very many codices, such as I S ee and ff, together with edition 1, have *draws* [trahat] in the subjunctive.

[5] ON THE TRINITY, Bk. IV, ch. 24: Perhaps it will be plainer and expedite the understanding, if se say, that a person is "one existing through itself solely according to a certain singular manner of rational existence". — The Vatican edition, together with codex cc, has *Whence* [Unde] for *Likewise* [Item].

[6] ON THE TRINITY, ch. 6; in which text after (before in English) *relation*

[relatio], codex bb, together with the more ancient editions of Boethius, adds *but* [vero]. — A little before this, the Vatican edition together with codex cc, omits *always* [semper].

[7] In the book, ON THE TWO NATURES AND ONE PERSON OF CHRIST, ch. 3. See above the 4th opposed argument. — On the definition of 'person' mentioned immediately before this, cf. the text of Master (Peter), ch. 3, and below in a. 1, q. 2, in reply to n. 4. — A little above this, after *but* [sed] some codices, such as G K P O aa and bb, has *this* [hoc] for *the*, and codices aa and bb after *name* [nomen] add *that is* [scilicet]; then the Vatican edition together with codex cc alone, after *for 'person'* [personae] omits *of itself* [de se].

[8] Neither this nor the second sentence, following below, seems to have been that of Master (Peter), here in ch. 2. Cf. St. Thomas, ON POTENCY, q. 9, a. 4.

[9] See Priscian, GRAMMATICAL INSTITUTIONS, Bk. V, ch. 9.

[10] The Vatican edition, together with some codices, has *responds* [respondet]; next codex R reads *any substantial name* [aliquod nomen substantiale] for *another substantial (name)* [aliud substantiale].

son" conveys each, that is, 'supposit' and 'property', it is necessary that it be said according to substance and according to relation. And, since it is said according to substance and according to relation, it is said more principally according to substance, as much as *concerns the general* and first understanding of the name. For *"person"* means a "certain substantial supposit", whether in God or in creatures. And, to this, is consonant the very[1] manner of speaking on the part of the name. But, as much as *concerns the special* and ultimate understanding of the name, because it means "a supposit distinguished by the property, which is relation", it is said in God according to relation. And, hence, it is, that the Saints and Doctors say, that the name for *'person'* is said according to substance, though it is also said according to relation.

But, someone will object: since those manners, namely, that is, 'being said according to substance', and 'being said according to relation', divide Divine Names[2] out of an opposite (reckoning), as it seems (they do); either they will not be able to be found in the same (thing), or that name implies opposites in itself. — And, besides, it must be understood, that, just as Richard of Saint Victor[3] says, *'being said according to substance'* is twofold: either by indicating substance according to *a common nature*, and in this manner *"man"* is said according to substance; or by indicating substance as *a certain supposit* [suppositum certum], such as *a certain man* [quidam homo]. In the first manner, to say "substance" is to say *"what (it is)"*, in the second manner it is to say *"someone"*. I say, therefore, that the name for *'essence'* and/or for *'substance'* is said according to substance, because it indicates the common nature; but *"person"* is said according to substance, because it indicates a certain and distinct supposit. But a common nature is not multiplied nor referred; and for that reason what means a substance according to a common nature is thus said regarding (the thing) itself, which in no manner can be said according to relation; and indeed in this manner it is divided out of an opposite (reckoning). But a *supposit* or a hypostasis it bound to be plurified and compared to another, and thus to be referred. And, because it is said according to substance in this manner, nothing impedes by reason of the superadded relation that it be said according to relation; and this (is what) Richard of Saint Victor wants to say.

The response, therefore, it clear to all the objections, according to each side. For it must be conceded, that the name for *'person'* is said according to *substance*, as has been explained, just as the Saints say and reasons prove;

for thus they understand *that it is said according to substance*. It must be conceded, nevertheless, that it is said *according to relation*, though not thus principally, just as the following reasons proves, since a multitude of relations plurify 'person' itself.

7. To that, however, which is objected, that ("person") responds to the question made *through "What (it is)?"*, because from this there could be concluded,[4] that it not only means 'substance', as a supposit, but also as a common nature; it must be said, that *"What?"* sometimes asks the *essence*, having supposed that "What?" is that which is said through the name, as: "What is man ?" And what responds to this question indicates *purely the substance* and the essence, when it is a question concerning substance. Sometimes, with (the interrogative) supposed in an indeterminate voice, it asks, what *is said through the name*, just as if there is said: "Brunello runs", and there is asked: "What (is) "Brunello" ?", that is, whether (he be) man, and/or donkey. Sometimes, having supposed the quiddity and signification, it asks concerning that, *in respect of which* a dependent name is said, as if there is said: "The white ones run", and[5] there is asked, "What white ones?", one can respond: "men", and/or "donkeys". And in this manner the heretics asked, "What (are) the Three?" Because Blessed John (the Apostle) had said in (his) first Canonical (Letter), in the fifth chapter:[6] *There are Three who give testimony* etc., they asked: *"What (are) the Three?"* — since ("Three") is an adjective without a substantive; and then one asks for a *supposit* more than for an *essence* — and for that reason a *supposit* is the response, and this through the name, *"person"*. Whence, at the suggestion of the Holy Spirit, the Church responded in the very best and noble and catholic manner, just as Richard says;[7] and this name responded very well and more to the impulse of the Holy Spirit, as Richard says, than another.

But then it could be asked: for what reason did the heretic not ask through this interrogative, *"Who?"*, and it seems, that he should have. For if he used to ask concerning a *supposit*, and *"Who?"* asks concerning a supposit; he ought to have asked: *"Who (are) the Three?"*.

And to this is the response, that *"Who?"* asks concerning a *certain* or real supposit [supposito certo, sive reali], and concerning that they did not use to ask, because in the same authority there is subjoined:[8] *the Father, the Word, and the Holy Spirit*; but they did use to ask of a supposit, in respect of which that which is *Three* is signified in the adjacents: and for that reason they asked: *"What (are) the Three?"*, rather than *"Who (are) the Three?"*. For in this manner one was bound to respond (to them) with a unique name, and this is was they were seeking.

---

[1] The Vatican edition with codex cc alone omits *very* [ipse].

[2] Many codices, such as A C G K L O T Y etc., together with the ancient editions (except edition 1), read *a Divine Name* [nomen divinum]. Then not a few codices, together with edition 1, exhibit *could not* [non potuerunt] for *will not be able to* [non poterunt], and omit besides *either* [aut].

[3] ON THE TRINITY, Bk. Iv, ch. 19, where he says: And so fearing, where there is not fear, they rightly feared to say, that "persons" is said according to substance, if "person" simply signified a substantial 'being', and did not consignify anything. But it does signify 'one having a substantial 'being' out of some singular property'. Therefore, for that reason, we confidently say, that "persons" is said in the Divinity according to substance and signifies the Substance, and that there are several Persons There, not several Substances; because There there are Several having the one and undiffering 'Being' out of a different property. And so There the Unity is according to a manner of being [modum essendi], the plurality according to a manner of existing; a Unity of

Essence, because (there is) one and an undiffering 'Being'; several Persons, because several existences.

[4] The Vatican edition, breaking with the codices and edition 1, reads *and from this it can be concluded* [et ex hoc potest concludi].

[5] The Vatican edition, together with codex cc, does not incongruously repeat here *if* [si].

[6] Verse 7.

[7] ON THE TRINITY., Bk. Iv, ch. 5 (according to its sense), where even the following citation is found. — In this first citation, codex O has *in a notable manner* [notabiliter] for *(in a) noble (manner)* [nobiliter], and some codices together with the Vatican edition, here in the second citation, have *responds* [respondet] for *responded* [respondit]. — A little before this the Vatican edition, together with codex cc, has *and in this manner through this name* [et sic per hoc nomen] for *and this through the name* [et hoc per nomen].

[8] 1 Jn 5:7. — Next the Vatican edition, not trusting in the codices and edition 1, has *signifies* [significat] for *is signified* [significatur].

8. To the last argument, because it does not proceed rightly, the response will be more clear below.[1] However, it can be said, that, even if the understanding of "*person*" can be abstracted from *this determinate* property, yet from its own general understanding, it encloses [claudit] the understanding of a property; and because among the divine a property is a relation, for that reason from a general[2] understanding it encloses a relation. Whence just as among the divine *this Person*, which is the Father, cannot be abstracted from the paternity, which is a personal relation, with the personality itself preserved [salva]; so neither (can) "*persons*" (be abstracted) from a understanding of relation in general.[3] And thus it is clear, that it does not follow, that it is said only according to substance.

SCHOLIUM

I. Above, in d. 23, a. 1, q. 1, not a few things have already been said concerning the etymology and signification of the term, "*person*". Here special questions regarding the same matter are solved, and not a few things are posited concerning its own reckoning. We do not think it unuseful, to add to those things, which have been said above in the Scholium of Distinction 23, a. 1, q. 3, concerning the conception of this term.

1. In the response there is read, « that "*person*" is said (to be) a supposit of a rational nature distinguished by a property [rationalis naturae suppositum proprietate distinctum] ». This definition, repeated often by the Seraphic (Doctor), has been taken from Alexander of Hales, Summa., p. I, q. 56, m. 3. Concerning the Angels, St. Bonaventure says in Sent., Bk. II, d. 3, p. I, a. 2, q. 2: According to the measure that there is an *individual* discretion by the existence of a natural form in the matter, so there is a *personal* discretion by the existence of a noble and supereminent nature in supposit »; and ibid., q. 3: « Therefore, *individuation* in a creature rises up out of a twofold principle; but a "*personal* discretion" means 'singularity' and 'dignity'. Inasmuch as it means 'singularity', it means this out of the conjunction itself of the principles, from which there results that which it is; according to *dignity* it means principally the reckoning of a form ». It also must be attended to, that according to the Seraphic (Doctor) spiritual substances obtain a higher grade in the genus of substance and subsistence than corporal ones. For in Sent., Bk. II, d. 3, p. I, a. 1, q. 2, in the body (of the question), he says: « And since what is purely in the genus of substance shares more of the nature of one standing through itself and independent, but what accedes more to the nature of accidents is more drawn away: hence it is, that spiritual substances are substances through (a consideration of what is) more prior and true, next (come) superior bodies, last inferior bodies ». Cf. Sent., Bk. III, d. 1, a. 1, and ibid., d. 5, passim, but chiefly a. 2, q. 2, in reply to n. 1, where the Seraphic Doctor, gathering together the whole of his own doctrine on this matter into an epitome, says, that « the *individual* in making known a person conveys a threefold distinction, namely, (that) of *singularity*, (that) of *incommutability* and (that) of a *super-eminent dignity* »; which members of the division are then more accurately explained.

2. The orthodox Faith concerning the Trinity and Incarnation teaches, that some distinction must be made both in God, and in intellectual creatures among 'person' and 'nature'. Speaking of created persons, this distinction ought to be such, that in Christ there can be a *complete*, singular, human nature, which does not have a *human* personhood [personam humanam]; out of which it is clear, that personality or subsistence does not pertain to the constitutive predicate of the *nature*. In this all the doctors also agree, that it conveys some ultimate act, perfecting and/or terminating the substance, by which it is rendered entirely incommunicable. But what precisely that is, which *person* adds upon nature, whether (it be) something *real*, or *a being of reason* [ens rationis]; whether (it be) a *thing*, or a *manner (of being)*; whether (it be) something *positive*, or *negative*, this question greatly divided the doctors and Schools. The two extreme opinions are commonly reproved, namely, both the opinion, which is attributed to Durandus (of Saint-Pourçain), that nothing is added but *a being of reason* [ens rationis], and the opposite of Cajetan, that it adds to nature an absolute entity, really distinct from the nature. (Bl. John Duns) Scotus thinks that it is *probable*, that the formal reckoning [rationem formalem] of a person consists *in the privation* of a twofold communicability, namely, as *what is* (communicated) [ut quod est] and as *whereby it is* (communicated) [ut quo]: cf. here in the following question, in reply to n. 3, which (privation), however, connotes a positive reality, upon which those negations are founded. But it is clear from his own words and those of very several Scotists, such as Lychetus, Rada (controversy 22, a. 2), Mastrius and others, that (Bl.) Scotus also judges the other sentence (to be) probable (Sent., Bk. III, d. 1. q. 1). The more common sentence, which St. Bonaventure and St. Thomas favors, asserts, that a person adds upon a *nature* something positive, which is distinguished from the nature, not as a thing (is) from a thing, but as a substantial *standard of measure* [modus substantialis] (St. Bonaventure, Sent., Bk. I, d. 34, q. 1, in the body of the question, near the end). St. Bonaventure (here in a. 2, q. 1, in the body of the question) in respect of the opinion approved by (Bl.) Scotus, explicitly says: « Because that privation in a person is more a positing than a privation » (cf. ibid., q. 2, in reply to n. 3; a. 1, q. 2; and Bk. III, d. 10, a. 1, q. 2; and on 'person' in God, Bk. I, d. 34, a. 1. q. 1). Hauzeur (collation, tome II, cols. 267-277) strives by a longer discourse to bring each sentence back together in harmony.

II. The first question of this distinction has two parts. In the *first* part the problem, indicated in the title of the question, after the two false solutions have been rejected, is resolved in this sense, that "person" conveys each, i. e., '*supposit*' (or the 'first substance') and '*relation*'. But which more principally? St. Bonaventure responds with the same distinction, which St. Thomas uses (Summa., I, q. 29, a. 4), namely, that "person" accepted in the *general* and first understanding of this name (St. Thomas says: « in the common (understanding) » means more principally "the substance", but in the *special* (understanding of it), as *this* Divine Person, it signifies a relation.

In the *second* part the objection, that the manners of predicating are so opposed according to substance and relation, that they cannot be composed in the same subject, is solved. The response is built up from the Aristotelian distinction between *first* (« a certain supposit ») and *second* substance (i.e. the essence). — From the words of the Seraphic Doctor it least of all follows (though not a few have wanted to assert this), that the Divine Persons are constituted through absolute realities. For the Seraphic (Doctor) constantly teaches, that in the understanding of a Divine Supposit there is enclosed the understanding of the property, which among the divine is a *relation*. Therefore, even if a "person" in its right sense [in recto] means a "first *substance*", yet it connotes a *relation* (cf. solution to n. 1 and to the last objection). — But it must be noted, that just as "*substance*" is accepted in a twofold sense, so also "*relation*"; for either (it is accepted) to the extent that it is a relation *referring by an act*, and/or (it is) as a *subsisting* relation, or through the manner of a Hypostasis (St. Thomas, Summa., I, q. 29, a. 4). If it is accepted in the first manner, a relation in the reckoning of a 'person' is manifestly conveyed only *in its oblique sense* [in obliquo]; but if it is accepted in the second manner, there is rightly said with St. Thomas (ibid.), that "person" in God signifies 'relation' in its right sense and 'essence' *in an oblique sense*. With this distinction supposed, the diverse manner of speaking about this manner is explained by St. Bonaventure and the same St. Thomas (De potentia, q. 9, q. 4).

The seventh objection is solved in the same manner, by St. Thomas (Summa., loc. cit., in reply to n. 2).

---

[1] Distinction 27, p. I, q. 3. — A little before this the Vatican ed., with a few codd., has *which does not* [quod non] for *because it does not* [quia non].

[2] The Vatican ed. reads *special* [speciali], breaking with the codd. and also the first six edd., and besides this in a manner also repugnant to the context.

[3] The codices and editions read *special* [speciali]. But, from the context and doctrine explained in the Response, it seems to be consistent, that there be placed *in general* [in generali] instead.

III. Alexander of Hales, SUMMA., p. I. q. 56. m. 2. — (Bl. Duns) Scotus, here in q. sole; REPORTATIO., here in q. 1. — St. Thomas, SENT., Bk. I, d. 23, q. 1, a. 3; SUMMA., I, q. 29, a. 4. — Bl. (now St.) Albertus, SENT., Bk. I, d. 23, a. 2; SUMMA ., p. I, tr. 10, q. 44, m. 1. — (Bl.) Peter of Tarentaise, SENT., Bk. I, d. 23, q. 1, a. 2. — Richard of Middleton, here in a. 1, q. 1. — Giles the Roman, SENT., Bk. I, d. 23, q. 3. — Henry of Ghent, SUMMA., a. 53, a. 4 and 5. — Durandus (of Saint-Pourçain), SENT., Bk. I, d. 23, q. 1. — (Bl.) Dionysius the Carthusian, SENT., Bk. I, d. 23, q. 3. — (Gabriel) Biel, here in q. sole.

QUESTION II

Whether "person" has been rightly defined by Boethius, as that which is an individual substance of a rational nature, and whether this reckoning befits the Divine Persons?

Second, there is asked, concerning this name, "*person*", what is it according to (its) definition; and (St. Severinus) Boethius[1] defines it in this manner: « A person is an individual substance of a rational nature ». And that this definition of his is fitting for a Divine Person is shown:

1. Through the intention of the author, because (St. Severinus) Boethius intends to deal with the Person of Christ; but it is established, that the Person of Christ is uncreated: therefore, he intends to assign a reckoning to a Divine or Uncreated Person.

2. Likewise, it seems that this is the reckoning of a Person[2] among the divine: for in God it is established, that there must be posited that a *Supposit* is *incommunicable*, and this Supposit is the Divine Substance, and it is also of a *rational Nature*; and (this) does not befit but that of which a "*person*" is said: therefore, it is its reckoning, as it seems.

ON THE CONTRARY: 1. Every definition means an *aggregation*, since it is established out of many (parts),[3] otherwise in this it would be worthless; but in a simple (thing) there is no aggregation: therefore, no simple (thing) is definable. But a Person among the divine is entirely simple: ergo etc.. *If you say*, as [secundum quod] some say, that although It is simple according to reckoning; *on the contrary*: either there responds to that reckoning something in the thing, or nothing; if something: therefore some composition is in the thing; if nothing: therefore, the reckoning is entirely vain. But on account of a vain reckoning there is nothing to be defined: ergo etc..

2. Likewise, by reason of *its own parts* it does not seem to befit a Divine Person. For 'rational' is the difference of 'animal': therefore, to that, to which 'animal' does not convene, a rational nature does not convene. But 'animal' does not convene with God, since it is a species of body: therefore, neither that which is *rational*.

3. Likewise, it seems that "*substance*" is not said in its right sense of a person, because, with the defined multiplied, it is necessary that there be multiplied[4] the definition and the parts of the definition: therefore, if a person is a substance, since there are many Persons, therefore, many Substances. — *If you say*, that "substance" stands there for [pro] a hypostasis; *on the contrary*: a hypostasis is said (to be) "an individual substance", just as (St. Severinus) Boethius says: therefore, just as it is worthless, if there would be said: "a rational man", so also in the aforesaid notification. — Therefore, there is asked, whether this name, "*substance*", stands for (something) common, and/or for a hypostasis.[6]

4. Likewise, it seems that it is not *convertible*. For the soul of a man is an individual substance of a rational nature: ergo etc.. — Last there is asked, since diverse definitions of "person" are assigned,[7] in what manner do they differ.

CONCLUSION

That definition of Boethius is good and fitting for the Divine Persons.

I RESPOND: It must be said, that just as is clear from the intention of the author, this definition of "person" befits and is assigned to a Divine Person.

1. To that, however, which is objected, that a simple (thing) is not definable; some say that to define anything is in a twofold manner. In one manner in its right sense and through a difference meaning a *positing*, as when there is said: "man is a rational, mortal animal"; and in this manner it is true, that a definition means an aggregation and composition, and in this manner the aggregated alone is definable.[8] In another manner it happens that one defines something in its oblique sense and through a difference meaning a *privation*, as when there is said: "simity is the curvature of a nose"; and then there is not signified, that the substance of the thing is aggregated out of diverse (things), since what is posited in an oblique sense does not, of necessity, enter into the essence (of the thing). *Furthermore*, a *depriving* [privans] difference does not posit some composition or apposition; and such is the said

---

[1] In the book, ON THE TWO NATURES AND ONE PERSON OF CHRIST, ch. 3.

[2] We have inserted, from cod. W, *of a Person* [personae]. — A little below this, cod. M, with ed. 1, has *an individual* [individua] for *the Divine* [divina]; cod. T in the margin exhibits this reading: *this Supposit is the same as the Divine Substance* [hoc suppositum est idem quod substantia divina].

[3] According to Aristotle, METAPHYSICS, Bk. VII, text 33 and 43 (Bk. VI, chs. 10 and 12), a definition is a reckoning (discourse) having parts, which (parts) are a genus and a difference.

[4] The Vatican edition, with one and/or another codex, reads *that one multiply* [multiplicare] for *that there be multiplied* [multiplicari].

[5] In the book, ON THE TWO NATURES AND ONE PERSON OF CHRIST, ch. 3.

[6] The codices together with edition 1 omits this question, to which, however, a response is given below in the solution to n. 3; for which reason we have, together with the Vatican edition, received it into the text.

[7] The Vatican edition, supported by codex cc alone, reads *since the definitions are diverse or are assigned concerning a "person"* [cum diversae sint definitiones sive assignentur de persona].

[8] Codices P and Q, together with edition 1, reads *only what is aggregated is definable* [solum quod est aggregatum est definibile] for *the aggregated alone is definable* [solum aggregatum est definibile].

reckoning. For that which (belongs) to *a rational nature*[1] falls (to it) in its oblique sense, and this difference, '*individual*', does not posit (something), but deprives it. — But this response cannot stand. First, indeed, because what is defined through an oblique sense, either is defined just as an *accident* (is) through a *substance*, or just as (an accident is) through a *thing of the same genus*; but either ("person" is defined) in this manner, or in this manner there is an addition there. For definitions of *accidents*, just as the Philosopher says,[2] are out of something added [additamento]. Similarly, if (it is defined) through a *thing of the same genus*; then, therefore, it does enter into the essence and does not mean the whole, since it is a part of the definition: therefore, it is necessary, that that which is apposed, add something according to the thing, and thus either in its right sense, or in its oblique sense it is necessary that it mean an aggregation.

And on this account it must be said in another manner, that this reckoning, understood of a *created* person, is a notification meaning an aggregation. But in *God* it does not mean an aggregation according to thing, but according to the reckoning of understanding; which, however, is not vain for this, that all (the parts of the definition), which are said in the reckoning of 'person', are found in God, though not through a diversity. — And this indeed can be understood thus. In creatures *specification* is through a completing addition,[3] *individuation* through an addition or contracting apposition. And for that reason, when there is said "*an individual substance*", '*individual*' really does add upon 'substance', whence[4] even '*individual substance*' (adds) upon 'nature'; and for that reason it is necessary, that in the *creature* a person be composite. But in *God* there is individuation and/or distinction through *origin* alone. And because a Person arises by His very self, for that reason there is There entirely no addition,[5] but (rather) a plurification, and through the plurification (of Persons) a distinction and individuation; and for that reason (in God) neither does "individual" adds upon the Substance, nor "*substance*" upon the Nature. For that reason (that definition of St. Boethius)[6] is truly said and the reckoning of (its) understanding is true; and that notification of his befits a Divine Person, and in it there is not signified any composition; whence it has the reckoning of a certain *notification** and occurs by reason of the *defi-*

nition, because neither God nor a Divine Person is definable, and yet (They are) cognizable, and can be made known [notificabilis].

2. To that which is objected concerning the differences posited, or concerning the members (of the definition), it must be said, that the "*rational*" is said *in one manner* (to be), that which it has the power of discerning good from evil, true from false — and in this manner it convenes with God and creature;[7] *in another manner* (to be), that which has the power of discerning through an inquisition and a gathering and discourse — and this belongs to a soul conjoined to the flesh. And in this manner such a difference is posited in the definition in the first manner, but objected to in the second manner.

3. To that which is objected, that "individual substance" is said in its right sense; it must be said, that it is numbered, just as (is) 'person'. For, just as (St.) Anselm says,[8] as many as there are individual substances, so (are there) many persons.

To that which is asked, whether this name, "*substance*", stands for (something) common, or for a hypostasis; it is customary to respond in a threefold manner.[9]

In the first manner yes, that "*substance*" does stand for (something) common. *And if you object*, that it is not individuated; they say, that an adventive difference looks back to substance by reason of the *supposit*, not by reason of the *form*, as is clear, when there is said: "an individual animal". — But this response does not seem fitting, because[10] this name, "*substance*", according to which it stands for (something) common, does not suppose a *person*. Whence this is false: "the Essence generates"; and this (too): "the Substance generates".

In the second manner it is said, that "*substance*" there is worth only as much as "hypostasis"; nor is it worthless. For *individuation* is attained in a person as much as regards a threefold incommutability,[11] namely, *through predication*, and this befits a hypostasis; and *through composition*, because it is not composeable with the other; and *through union*, insofar as something is united to (anything) more worthy. And thus *the difference 'individual'* means those two incommutabilities. Whence it is clear, that there is nothing worthless there: it is also

---

[1] In very many codices there is wanting *nature* [naturae], and next after the word *difference* [differentia], edition 1 adds *which is* [quae est].
[2] METAPHYSICS, Bk. VII, text 12 (Bk. VI, ch. 4). — A little above this, some codices, such as S T and Z, have *through a subject* [per subiectum] for *through a substance* [per substantiam]. Below this, after *the whole* [totam], codex R adds *reckoning* [rationem].
[3] Codex Y reads: *In creatures, specification comes to be through a difference and/or through a completing addition* [In creaturis specificatio fit per differentiam vel per additionem complentem].
[4] From codex O there is absent *whence* [unde].
[5] The Vatican edition, together with codex cc, having prefaced he word *and* [et] to the word *for that reason* [ideo], omits *entirely* [omnino]. Immediately before this, codex O has *has (His) origin from His very self* [originem habet a se ipsa] for *arises from His very self* [oritur se ipsa].
[6] Supply: *that definition of (St.) Boethius* [definitio illa Boethii]. — Next, the word *that ... of his* [ista] is wanting in very many manuscripts, and also in edition 1.
[7] Cf. (St.) Augustine, ON ORDER, Bk. II, ch. 11, n. 30 ff.
[8] MONOLOGION, ch. 78: As many persons, so many are the individual substances.
[9] The Vatican edition, with codex cc, has *in a twofold manner* [dupliciter], and a little before this many codices have "*person*" [persona] for "*substance*" [substantia], but faultily. See the preceding page, footnote 6. — A little below this, codex O reads *what stands for the essence* [quod stet pro essentia] for *that "substance"* [quod substantia].
[10] Very many codices, such as G H T and Z, have *since* [cum], and consequently, then, have the verb *suppose* [supponat] (in the subjunctive).
[11] *Incommutability* is opposed to that *communicability*, which is

twofold, namely *as what* (is communicated) and *as whereby* (it is communicated) [ut quod et ut quo]. Through the first a superior is communicated to an inferior through an identity and essentially, as '*animal*' is communicated to 'man' and is predicated of 'man'. Communicability *as whereby* (something is communicated) comes to be through *being informed*, and/or at least according to the manner of the form. This (communicability) is threefold, and to it is opposed a threefold incommutability. The first comes to be through an *identity*, such as (when) a nature is communicated to its own supposits and a universal to (its) inferiors; and then what is communicated *as whereby* is also the one communicated *as what*; whence there is also a predication in the first manner of speaking, such as "Peter is a man". The second comes to be through a *composition* in the reckoning of form and matter, and/or of accident and subject. Buy this communication that to which it is communicated, does not come to be the very thing communicated, but something such, v. g. a body, a living thing etc.. The third comes to be through a *union*, such as (when) the Human Nature of Christ is communicated to the Word, to be sustained by Him, which union is not properly through a being informed except according to a certain analogy. To these three manners of communicability there corresponds a threefold *incommunicability*; and in these three manners a *person* is incommunicable. Cf. St. Thomas, here in q. 1, a. 1, in reply to n. 7, and (Bl. John Duns Scotus), SENT., Bk. III, d. 1, a. 1, n. 9, and ff. — A little below this codex S has *another* [alii] for *the other* [alteri].
[12] That is, the second and the third. — The Vatican edition, together with very many codices, here and a little below this, has *incommunities* [incommunitates] for *incommunicabilities* [incommunicabilitates].

---

* *Trans. note*: A notification is a verbal expression which makes the thing refered to, understood, though not necessarily in a sufficient manner as definition would.

clear, that the definition is convertible (among creatures and God). Through that twofold incommutability there is excluded the soul of man, which is composeable with another, and the Human Nature in Christ, which is united to (Something) more worthy. — But yet, though that has been reasonably said, still there remains the question of the *hypostasis*, because a hypostasis is an *individual substance*. Similarly, there is asked, in what manner is "*substance*" accepted there, and (yet) it cannot be accepted for (something) common, nor for a hypostasis.[1]

And on this account there is said third, that this name, "*substance*", stands there, according to which 'substance' is divided into first and second 'substance',[2] and thus in a certain commonness [communitate] to universal and particular 'substance'; and they gather this from the words of (St. Severinus) Boethius, when he hunts for the definition of "person" through the aforesaid division of 'substance', as is clear there.[3] Whence this name, "*individual*", constrains that definition of this name, so that it stands for 'first substance'; and thus there is nothing worthless there nor (is) the individuation of a common substance.

4. To that which *is asked* last concerning the assignation of the definition, it must be said, that a "person" is defined by (St. Severinus) Boethius in this manner: "a person is an individual substance of a rational nature"; by Richard (of St. Victor)[4] in this manner: "a person is an incommunicable existence of an intellectual nature". It is also defined in another manner, thus: "a person is one existing through himself alone according to a certain, singular manner of rational existence". By the masters (of theology) it is defined thus: "a person is a hypostasis distinguished by a property pertaining to nobility". — And the difference of these definitions is to be noted: because (St. Severinus) Boethius considers more the reckoning of the *thing*, but the masters still[5] (consider) the reckoning of the *translation*. However, the definitions of Richard belong to a person, insofar as it is chiefly among the divine; but one is the proper assignation, but the other the exposition or correction of the definition of (St. Severinus) Boethius.[6] — However, it can be said, that all mean the same (thing), yet they differ according to the manner of speaking; because the definition of (St. Severinus) Boethius was given and seemed to sound improper [improprietatem sonare]; for that reason Richard (of St. Victor) posited another through more proper words; and (it was defined) in this manner even as regards the fourth (definition).

SCHOLIUM

I. (Bl. John Duns) Scotus, in SENT., Bk. I, d. 23, q. sole, reproves the definition of (St. Severinus) Boethius posited here, and substituted the other (definition) of Richard, that « a "person" is an incommunicable existence of an intellectual nature ». Yet this one, as St. Bonaventure says (in reply to n. 4), is « an exposition or correction of the definition of (St.) Boethius ». The definition of (St.) Boethius is commonly received with some exposition, as it is explained in the same manner by the Angelic and Seraphic Doctors. In particular the words "*substance*" and "*individual*" need explanation, concerning which see the solution to n. 3. Concerning the first word the Seraphic Doctor, together with St. Thomas (SUMMA., I, q. 29, a. 1, in reply to n. 2), asserts, that it is accepted neither precisely for a '*first* substance' (a hypostasis), nor for a '*second* substance' (« for (something) common », that is, an essence), but « is accepted commonly, insofar as it is divided through first and second (substance) » (St. Thomas, loc. cit.). — Here the word "*individual*" cannot signify "*singular*"; for then it would follow, that the Human Nature of Christ was a human person, which is heresy; and moreover, that a soul separated (from a body) was a person, which is commonly not approved. Therefore, it must be said, that "*individual*" stands for "*incommunicable*".

The final words of the solution to n. 1 are to be noted. — The last objection has not been solved for this reason, because from what has been said it is already manifest, that "*individual*" there is said on behalf of "*incommunicable*".

II. Alexander of Hales, SUMMA., p. I, q. 56, m. 3. — (Bl. John Duns) Scotus, in each version, SENT., Bk. I, d. 23, q. 1. — St. Thomas, here in q. 1, a. 1; SUMMA. , I, q. 29, a. 1. — Bl. (now St.) Albertus (Magnus), here in a. 1; SUMMA., p. I, tr. 10, a. 44, m. 2. — (Bl.) Peter of Tarentaise, here in q. 1, a. 1. — Richard of Middleton, here in a. 1, q. 2 and 3. — Giles the Roman, here in 1st. princ., q. 3. — Henry of Ghent, SUMMA., a. 53, q. 1. — Durandus (of Saint-Pourçain), SENT., Bk. I, d. 23, q. 1. — (Bl.) Dionysius the Carthusian, SENT., Bk. I, d. 23. — (Gabriel) Biel, SENT., Bk. I, d. 23. q. 1.

ARTICLE II

On the commonality of the name, "person".

Second there is asked concerning the second article, that is, concerning the commonality [communitate]* of this name, "*person*". And about this two (things) are asked:

First, there is asked, whether this name, "*person*", is truly common to the uncreated Persons.

Second, whether it is a common, univocal (term) for created and uncreated persons.

---

[1] Codex O adds: *because then the same (term) would be defined* [quia tunc idem definiretur].

[2] Aristotle, ON PREDICAMENTS, ch. "On *Substance*", posits this division, understanding under '*first* substance' the individual itself, as a certain man, under '*second* (substance)', the species, such as man. — A little before this the Vatican edition, together with codex cc, after *according to which* [secundum quod] inserts *this name* [hoc nomen], and then after *is divided* [dividitur] it omits *substance* [substantiam].

[3] Loc. cit. (page 439), ch. 2. — This sentence even St. Thomas, here in q. 1, a. 1, prefers. — Next, after *of this name* [illius nominis] the Vatican alone, supported by no codex, adds "*substance*" [substantia].

[4] ON THE TRINITY, Bk. IV, chs. 22 & 23. — The following definition is found also in Richard (of St. Victor), loc. cit., ch. 24; but the last one is gathered from the text of Master (Peter), here in ch. 3.

[5] Supply: *consider* [considerant]. — For *still* [adhuc], which we have recalled from the more outstanding codices, the Vatican edition, together with codex cc, has *add* [addunt]. And in truth, because in a Person there is a property pertaining to nobility, for that reason this name, "*persons*", can be transferred to the divine.

[6] Cf. Richard (of St. Victor), ON THE TRINITY, Bk. IV, ch. 21 ff., where he thoroughly treats of the definition given by (St. Severinus) Boethius. — Very many codices, such as A T W X together with edition 1 *shortening* [correptio] for *correction* [correctio]. — Next, after *was* [fuit], codex I inserts *first* [prius].

---

* *Trans. note*: Here St. Bonaventure speaks of the *common-ness* [communitas] of the name, "*person*", that is, of that characteristic of the name which makes it applicable to all the Divine Persons; in English there is still retained this Scholastic notion of common-ness as *community*; but in philosophical terms, it is more common today to use the term *commonality*, when speaking of shared characteristics, than of *community*. Nevertheless, during the discussion, St. Bonaventure shifts between the senses of *community*, as of one in which there is a sharing of some characteristic, and of one in which there is a sharing of nature or of being, which is properly a *community*. For this reason the English translation will employ each term, *community* and *commonality*, to render the one Latin term, communitas.

QUESTION I

Whether the name, "person", is common to the uncreated Persons?

Moreover, that it is truly common to the uncreated Persons, is shown:

1. *Through (St.) Augustine* in the seventh (book) ON THE TRINITY:[1] « For that reason », he says, « They are said (to be) "*Three Persons*", because what a "*person*" is, is common to Them »; but it is established, that for a plurification (of Persons) a commonality of name only is not sufficient: therefore, it is truly common according to the thing.

2. Likewise, this very (thing) seems *by reason*, because every name, which receives upon itself a distributive sign, is truly common to those, in which it is distributed;[2] but such is the name, "*person*": therefore, it is common to the Three. For (with) it is fittingly said: any Person is referred to.

3. Likewise, everything which is said according to the same name and according to the same reckoning of many, is truly common to them; but '*person*' is of this kind, because according to the same name[3] and the same reckoning, namely the afore-assigned one, it is said of the Three: ergo etc..

4. Likewise, when I say: "the Father is a Person", this name, "*person*", is predicated; therefore, either as a *being from the reckoning* of "Father", or as (something) *accidental*.[4] It is established that (it is not predicated) as (something) *accidental*: therefore, (it is) as *a being from the reckoning* of "Father". Therefore, either it means the whole which the Father is, or (it does) not; if the whole, therefore just as "father" is predicated of the Father alone, so also "person"; which is false. Therefore, it does not mean the whole, therefore, that which a *Person* is, is in More than (that which) "*father*" (is); both in more,[5] because it *concerns the reckoning of "Father"*, and similarly (because) it *concerns the reckoning of "Son"*: therefore, it is truly common (to Them all).

ON THE CONTRARY: 1. Every (name) common to any (group), which is numbered in them, is truly universal to them, most of all if it is not said accidentally of them. This is clear, because (St.) Augustine used to say, above, in the Nineteenth Distinction,[6] that an essence is not universal, on account of naught, but that it is not numbered in the singulars. If, therefore, "*person*" is common *to the Three*, and furthermore is numbered or plurified in Them: therefore, it is universal, therefore, among the divine there is the positing of a universal; which is contrary to the what has been predetermined and contrary to (St.) Augustine,[7] who wants, that among the divine there is neither [non] universal nor particular.

2. Likewise, nothing is common, which from its own reckoning and name deprives a community; but "*person*" means an individual or incommunicable from the reckoning of its name: ergo etc..

3. Likewise, every (name) which is said according to substance and is common, is said according to a common substance; but nothing which is said according to a common substance, is plurified: therefore, "*person*" is not plurified. But it is established that it is plurified, and, yet, it is said according to substance: therefore, it does not mean something common.

4. Likewise, if it means something common, either (a commonality) *of name* only, or *of name and of reckoning* only, or *of name and of reckoning and of thing*. If only *of name*: therefore, it is equivocal,[8] therefore, it is not common (to Them all). If only *of name and of reckoning*, such that nothing is common *in the thing*: therefore, it is only a vanity (of expression). But if *of name and of reckoning and of thing*; but a real community, as (St. John) Damascene wants it,[9] is not but a community of substance and of nature, and this is in no manner plurified: therefore, this name, "*person*", in no manner can be common (to Them all).

CONCLUSION

The name for 'person' is common to the uncreated Persons, but by another commonality than that, by which "essence" is common to Them.

I RESPOND: For an understanding of the aforesaid it must be noted, that "*person*" without doubt is common to the Three, and (there is) a common *Essence*; but, yet, there is different [alius] manner of commonality in *essence* and *person*. And the sign of this is, that "*Person*" is plurified, "*Essence*" is not.

But the difference of these[10] commonalities is accepted differently from diverse (reckonings). For certain ones say, that in a twofold manner something happens to be common, that is, according to a *being posited*, and according to a *privation*; according to a *being posited*, as "animal" is[11] common to man and donkey; but according to

---

[1] Chapter 4, n. 8. — On the principles of these arguments, see above d. 19, p. II, q. 2.

[2] Cf. Peter of Spain, SUMMULA., tract "On *Distribution*", where distributive signs are divided into distributives of *substance*, v. g., "every" [omnis], "none" [nullus], and those of *accidents*, v. g., "whatsoever kind" [qualiscumque], "any you please" [quilibet]. — A little above this, the Vatican edition, favored by codex cc, exhibits *name* [nomen] for *sign* [signum], and then a little below this after *the Three* [tres], it omits the last proposition of this argument.

[3] In the Vatican edition and codex cc alone there is lacking this proposition: *because according to the same* etc. [quia secundum idem etc.].

[4] Codex bb adds *or extraneous* [sive extraneum].

[5] Understand: both indeed in more. On the sense of the words *is in more* [in plus est], see above, d. 19, p. I, a. sole, q. 4, p. 348, footnote 5.

[6] The text of Master (Peter), ch. 7 ff.

[7] ON THE TRINITY, Bk. VII, ch. 6, n. 11, concerning which, see the text of Master (Peter) above, in Distinction XIX, ch. 7 ff, and ibid., in the COMMENTARIA, p. II, q. 2.

[8] Thus very many codices; the Vatican edition with codex cc reads *an equivocation* [equivocatio]. A little further below this, the Vatican edition alone has *an analogy* [analogiam] for *only a vanity (of expression)*.

[9] ON THE ORTHODOX FAITH, Bk. I, ch. 8. Cf. also above the text of Master (Peter), d. XIX, ch. 9. — A little above this, after *But if of name* [Si vero nominis] the codd. and ed. 1 badly omit *and of reckoning*.

[10] From the Vatican edition there is absent *these* [harum], which on the authority of very many codices, such as G H M O aa and bb, and of edition 1, we have restored.

[11] The Vatican edition, together with codex cc, has *as "animal" is said to be* [dicitur animal esse].

a privation, as *"non-animal"* is common to *stone* and *wood*. And they say, that a community according to a *being posited* is in nature and essence and in a name signifying this; but a community according to a *privation* is in a person, because a person is said (to be) a quasi-incommunicable, that is, (it is said) according to a privation of community.

Others say, that there is a twofold community: a certain one according to the *unity of an absolute nature*, a certain one according to the *similitude of a compared habitude*. A community according to the *unity of an absolute nature* is *humanity*[1] in respect of Peter and Paul; because the one universal nature is found in each. But a community according to a *similitude of related habitude* is that which is attained in a completely similar comparison,[2] just as the manner of ruling is common to a mariner for ruling a ship, and a doctor for ruling schools, because each out to be an expert not by chance [sorte], but by art. And indeed the *first* manner is attained in an *essence*, but the *second* is attained in a *person*. For a *"person"* is said (to be) distinguished by a property; and thus it means a habitude to a property, which is completely similarly in any of the Persons. It[3] does not mean, as much as it is of itself, the one natural Form except in its oblique sense; but *"essence"* or *"substance"* means the absolute Form and Nature, in which They communicate.

Some say, in a third manner, that there is a twofold community, namely *of thing* and *of reckoning*: *of thing*, just as a universal regards singulars, but *of reckoning*, just as some intention (is) accepted by the soul according to a completely similar manner of accepting; and in this manner this name, *"individual"*, is common, according to reckoning, to Peter and Paul. In the *first* manner they say that the *Essence* is common; in the *second* manner they say that *"person"* is common, because that which is an individual among creatures means a *"person"* among the divine.

But all these manners of speaking, if we attend (to them) more diligently, are fitting, and have been taken from the signification of this name which is *"person"*, or from (its) distinction.[4] For *"person"* means 'an incommunicable' according to (its) reckoning; and this means a privation of community. *"Person"* furthermore, because it has an incommunicability by reason of this, that it is subordinate [subest] to a distinguishing property, means a habitude to a property, just as (it does)

through the name, *"hypostasis"*. Again, from these it is had that *"person"* posits about the supposit, of which it is said, an intention of *being subjected*, and not of *being predicated* of many. And thus it is clear, that from the reckoning of its name it conveys a *privation of community*, a *similitude of habitude*[5] and an *intention of reckoning*. And because its *commonality* is accepted according to the reckoning of the name, for that reason it conveys a community according to *privation*, and to *proportion* or analogy, and to *reckoning*. — However, among all these manners, the middle one approaches the nature of the thing more, because in truth that privation in a person is more a *positing* than a *privation*. And *again*, the *intention* of the name has (its) foundation and root in the thing.

Therefore, the reasons,[6] that *"person"* means (something) common among the divine, are to be conceded.

1. To that, therefore, which is objected, that it is plurified; the response is already clear: because a *universal* means a community according to a *positing* and according to the *unity of the nature* and according to the *thing*, not only according to a reckoning; and since *"person"* in his manner does not convey a commonality, for that reason it is not a universal. — Nevertheless, however, the reckoning is not valid, because a *universal* is plurified, such that it is truly numbered on account of a true addition, through which it is contracted to an individual; but '*this person*' does not add upon '*person*', since, as has been said before,[7] there is among the divine no distinction through addition, but (only) through origin: for that reason *"person"* is neither truly numbered, nor is it drawn aside [trahitur in partem] in that manner, according to which a *universal* (is),

2. To that which is objected, that it deprives a community; it must be said, that that which deprives a community, is not common according to that community, which it deprives; but *"person"* deprives a community of *thing*, but not a community of *reckoning*, and according to that it is not common, but according to a community of reckoning (it is).

3. To that which is objected: what is common and said according to substance, is said according to a *common* substance;[8] it must be said, that this is the *(fallacy of) the accident*, just as this: 'this one is white, and he is a monk, therefore, he is a white monk'; because this term *"white"* conveys one reckoning of denominating in the premises and another in the conclusion. In this manner one must rightly say of this term

---

[1] Some codices, such as F G I R S and V, together with edition 1, have *(one) of humanity* [humanitatis].

[2] The Vatican edition, not trusting in the manuscripts and edition 1, has *operation* [operatione] for *comparison* [comparatione].

[3] The Vatican edition adds *For* [enim].

[4] Codex Y has *definition* [definitione]; codex T has *distinction and/or definition* [distinctione vel definitione].

[5] On the authority of codex T we have inserted the words *similitude of habitude*, which are wanting in the Vatican edition. Our reading is corroborated both from the context (because the Seraphic Doctor exhibits the preceding words in summation) and from the mutilated reading of the other codices, *conveys a privation of habitude* [importat privationem habitudinis].

[6] Codex V subjoins *which prove* [quae probant].

[7] Distinction 19, p. II, q. 2. — A little above this, the Vatican edition together with codex cc has *as* [ut] for *such that* [ita quod], and then it exhibits *on account of which* [propter quam] for *through which* [per quam]. Next, for the words *but 'this person' does not add upon 'person'* [sed haec persona non addit supra personam] the Vatican edition substitutes *and here 'person' does not add upon the Essence* [et hic persona

non addit supra essentiam], with which either reading the reading of edition 1 convenes: *but 'this person' does not add upon the nature* [sed haec persona non addit supra naturam]; but each reading, even if in itself it is not false, yet it does not regard the proposed, because, as follows from the objection, one deals not with the looking-back [respectu], which person has for the essence, but with the looking-back, which this person in particular has for 'person' taken in common or in general. The codices rightly have *person* [personam] for *Essence* [essentiam], but very many of them read rightly *is added* [additur] for *adds* [addit].

[8] The mutilated reading of the Vatican edition, which omits the words *is said according to a common substance* [dicitur secundum communem substantiam], we have repaired with the help of the manuscripts, and most justly, because those words are had in the objection. — The word, *accident* [accidens], which occurs just hereafter, is accepted for *the fallacy of the accident* [fallacia accidentis]. — A little further below this, the Vatican edition together with codex cc has *therefore* [ergo] for *because* [quia].

"*common*", that (in this argument) it is first accepted according to habitude, second according to the unity of the nature.

4. What is asked: either there is a commonality of thing, or of reckoning, or of name; it must be said, that (there is a commonality) according to all

these manners; but a real community is twofold, just as has been seen, namely, according to the *unity of the nature*, and according to a *similar habitude*: and in the first manner (St. John) Damascene speaks, and for that reason all the others are clear.

SCHOLIUM

I. This question arose from a sufficiently subtle difficulty, *by which reckoning* can the name for '*person*' be common to the three Divine Persons. For it is clear, that it is not common by a community of *thing*, just as the *Essence* is common to those Three Persons; it cannot also be common to Them *through the manner of a universal*, since in God there is no reckoning of a universal. — St. Bonaventure cites three probable solutions, but prefers the second. His sentence is explained more in the following question with these words: « (A "person") is said according to the comparison of things of the same nature, for that reason (it is said) *analogically* and *equally* and for that reason *in a certain manner univocally* ». — St. Thomas (loc. cit., infra) chooses and explains well the third solution, against which (Bl. John Duns) Scotus argues, by saying, that nothing posited in the definition is a being of reckoning [ens rationis].

The *fallacy of accident* in the solution to n. 3 consists in this, that in the *major* the term, "*common*", is accepted according to a *similitude of habitude* (according to the second solution): but in the *minor* (it is accepted) absolutely according to the unity of the nature.

II. Alexander of Hales, SUMMA., p. I, q. 56, m. 4, a. 2. — (Bl. John Duns) Scotus, on this and the following q., REPORTATIO., here in q. 2. — St. Thomas, here in q. 1, a. 3; SUMMA. , I, q. 30, a. 4. — Bl. (now St.) Albertus (Magnus), here in a. 3; SUMMA., p. I, tr. 10, q. 44, m. 1. — (Bl.) Peter of Tarentaise, here in q. 1, a. 3. — Giles the Roman, here in 1st. princ., q. 1 and 2. — Henry of Ghent, SUMMA., a. 53, q. 7. — Durandus (of Saint-Pourçain), here in q. 2. — (Bl.) Dionysius the Carthusian, SENT., Bk. I, d. 23, q. 2. — (Gabriel) Biel, on this and the following q., here in q. sole.

QUESTION II

Whether the name for 'person', said of created and uncreated persons, is a common univocal (term)?

Second, there is asked, whether this name, "*person*", is a common univocal (term) for created and uncreated persons. And it seems, that (it is) so:

1. Because there is the same reckoning and the same name for '*person*', according to which it is said of the former and the latter.

2. Likewise, this seems, because a community of *person* is a community of a *completely similar habitude*; but he completely similar habitude, which is found in God, is found also[1] in a creature, because just as the Father is a Supposit of the Divine Nature, so Peter (is) of the human (nature): ergo etc..

3. Likewise, the complement of the reckoning of a *person* consists in incommunicability; but incommunicability is common to the Divine Persons and to created ones: ergo etc..

ON THE CONTRARY: 1. God and creatures are most highly distant: therefore, they have nothing common, therefore, nothing univocal.

2. Likewise, a *person* is a substance: therefore, those which are univocated [univocantur] in person, are univocated in substance. But the Creator and the creature are not univocated in substance, because then God would be in a genus:[2] therefore, neither in person.

3. Likewise, those which are univocated in something, are equally in that; but a creature shares nothing equally with God: therefore, that which a *person* is, is not said univocally of God and creature.

4. There is asked, therefore, of what is "*person*" said, (of creatures, or of God,) through (the consideration of what is) prior;[3] and it seems, that through (the consideration of what is) prior it is said of creatures, because from them it was translated to the divine. *On the contrary*: intellectual nature and substance and distinction are, through

(a consideration of what is) prior, in God rather than in creatures; and they are not More from the reckoning of *person*: ergo etc..

CONCLUSION

The name for 'person' is said of created and uncreated persons analogically, and indeed of the Divine Persons, compared to Themselves, by an analogy according to equality, but of the Divine and created persons together by a distant analogy.

I RESPOND: It must be said, that this name, "*person*", as has been seen before,[4] does not mean but a *commonality of habitude* [communitatem habitudinis], upon which there is founded a *commonality of reckoning* [communitas rationis]. Therefore, since a completely similar habitude is found in created persons and in uncreated Ones, hence it is, that this name, "*person*", is not said equivocally, but analogically.

But one must attend (to this), that a commonality of habitude can be through a looking-back to a thing *of the same genus*; and then it is a univocation and an analogy according to equality — as Peter is an individual (being) and Paul (likewise) — and the reckoning of an individual befits these equally. It can also be through a comparison to things[5] *of diverse genera*, as Peter and the whiteness of Peter are united in that, which is an individual "being"; and the reckoning of an individual befits Peter through (a consideration of what is) prior to his whiteness. In this manner, it must be said, that this name, "*person*", said of *Divine Persons*,

---

[1] From many codices and edition 1 there is absent *also* [et].

[2] Cf. above d. 8, p. II, q. 4.

[3] Supply, together with codex G and edition 1, *of creatures, or of God* [de creaturis, an de Deo].

[4] In the preceding Question.

[5] In many codices there are lacking the words *to things* [ad res]; in edition 1 there is read *of things* [rerum]. — Next after *which* [quod] codex T omits "*being*" [esse].

because it is said according to a comparison of things of the same Nature, for that reason (it is said) *analogically*[1] and *equally*; and for that reason, (it is said) in a certain manner univocally; similarly, when it is said of *created* persons. But when it is said of *created and uncreated* persons, it is said through a comparison of things of diverse natures, and for that reason through (a consideration of what is) *prior* and *posterior*. And thus "person" is first said of created persons according to the *name*, but according to the *thing* (belonging to) *the name* it is said, through (a consideration of what is) prior, of uncreated Persons.

And because it is asked, whether "person" is common to created and uncreated persons; it must be said, that if it said (as) a common univocal (term), (it is) not. And the reason for this are to be conceded.

1. Because, therefore, there is objected, that there is the same reckoning etc.; it must be said, that there is not the same reckoning except according to analogy; because intellectual nature and hypostasis and distinction and property is in a by far more noble and another manner in God than in creatures.

2. To that which is objected, that there is a completely similar habitude; it must be said, that it is not a similitude of *equality*: and on this account such a similitude does not cause a univocation, but solely an analogy.

3. To that which is objected concerning incommutability, it must be said, that it is not a pure privation, nay it conveys a distinction; and since[2] the other reckoning of distinguishing, very distant from that, is in God, and this not only according to thing, nay also according to a right reckoning, the intellect does not attribute to God a manner of being distinguished which befits [competit] composites. For that reason neither is it univocal by reckoning, but solely analogous.[3]

SCHOLIUM

I. From the solution to the preceding question anyone could argue, that the name for 'person' is a common *univocal* (term) for Divine (Persons) and created persons, since the commonality of a similar habitude, which is asserted to be between the Divine Persons, seems to also be established among created (persons) and Divine Persons. The question itself is specified, while the Seraphic Doctor distinctly responds both by comparing the Divine Persons among themselves, and (by comparing) created (persons) with created (persons), and created (persons) with Divine (persons). — And it must be noted, that by comparing created persons with created ones, that *common univocal* cannot be understood of the *generic* and/or *specific* unity, which many human individuals have, but (can be) of the commonality in the *reckoning of singularity*. But the singular in the concrete does *differ* from a singular, yet, as is said in the body of the Question, the reckoning of an individual equally convenes with them. — On the two fold analogy, cf. above, d. 1, a. 3, q. 1, and d. 7, q. 4. — To the question posited in the fourth argument of the fundament, responds the 3rd conclusion.

II. Alexander of Hales, SUMMA., p. I, q. 56, m. 4, a. 1. — St. Thomas, here in q. 1, a. 2; on the principles of the solution, cf. SUMMA., I, q. 13, a. 6 and 10. — B l. (now St.) Albertus (Magnus), here in a. 2. — (Bl.) Peter of Tarentaise, here in q. 1, a. 2. — Richard of Middleton, here in a. 2, q. 1. — Giles the Roman, here in 2nd. princ., q. 1. — Henry of Ghent, SUMMA., a. 53, q. 3. — Durandus (of Saint-Pourçain), here in q. 1.

DOUBTS ON THE TEXT OF THE MASTER

DOUBT I

In this part there are doubts about the text (of Master Peter) and, first, there is asked of this which Master (Peter) says: *We say, that there are "three Persons", that is, "three Subsistences"*;* because (St. Severinus) Boethius says the contrary in the book, ON THE TWO NATURES AND ONE PERSON OF CHRIST,[4] assigning the difference between *"to subsist"* [subsistere] and *"to stand under"* [substare], because « that, which does not need another to be, subsists; but that, which (having been) subjected to others, so that they prevail to be, serves beneath (these), stands under ». It seems, therefore, that *to subsist* is the same as *to be*, and *subsistence* the same as *essence*: therefore, in no manner can it be said, that there are several *Subsistences*.

I RESPOND: It must be said, that (St. Severinus) Boethius accepts this name, *"subsistence"*, there according to Marcus Tullius (Cicero),[5] insofar as he accepts the signification from the act of *standing still* [sistendi] or of *standing through itself* [per se standi]; and, in this manner, there is only One Substance. But now the doctors of Sacred Scripture accept (it), insofar as it rather conveys a looking-back to the property, under which it stands, and in this manner it is plurified. But the reason for this is common usage [communis usus]. Because they accept *"substance"* [substantia] for 'the nature of the thing' [natura rei]; for that reason they wanted rather to accept "subsistence" [subsistentia] on behalf of the *supposit* [supposito].

DOUBT II

Likewise, is asked concerning this which (St. Augustine) says, that *the Three Persons are the One Essence and/or of the same Essence, not out of the same Essence*. For it seems false, because the Father generates the Son from His own Substance and spirates the Holy Spirit: therefore, it seems, that all the Persons are of the same Substance.

Likewise, there is asked: for what reason is there not conceded this, that the Persons are *out of the same Essence*, just as there is conceded this, that They are *of the Same Essence*? And it seems, that it ought to be conceded, because *"out of"* [ex] means among the divine a habitude of origin, and, similarly, the genitive (case) conveys an origin. *If you say*, that (it is) on account of transitions, because

---

[1] Codices aa bb and cc, with ed. 1, read *antonomastically* [antonomastice], not entirely faultily, because antonomasia is that figure of speech, which comes to be, as often as an epithet is substituted for a proper name (i. e. as when the Pope is spoken of as "His Holiness"; or a king, as "His Majesty").

[2] Edition 1 adds *also* [etiam].

[3] Codex G reads *(is) an analogy alone* [sola analogia].

[4] Chapter 3: For that which does not need accidents, so that it can be, subsists; but that which as a certain subject to other accidents, so that

they prevail to be, ministers under (them), stands under. — A little before this, after the words *to subsist is the same as* [subsistere sit idem quod], we have restored from the mss. the words omitted by the Vatican ed.: *to be, and subsistence the same as* [esse et subsistentia idem quod].

[5] See above, d. 23, a. 2, q. 1, p. 412, footnote 7. — Immediately after this the Vatican edition, supported by codex cc, has *according to the act of subsisting* [secundum actum subsistendi] for *from the act of standing still* [ab actu sistendi].

---

* *Trans. note*: The quote from Master Peter is taken from the beginning of the second paragraph to ch. 2 of his text (p. 433 above), according to its sense. The second quote, that of St. Augustine, at the beginning of Doubt 2, is found toward the end of this same paragraph.

prepositions are transitive[1] — thus even oblique cases are transitive. *Moreover*, this is received: "the Persons are in the same Essence", and yet this which I am saying, "*in*", is a preposition.

I RESPOND: It must be said, that that when[2] anything is compared to another, as one *informing* or *denominating* (the other), there is not posited on account of this a diversity or distinction of one to the other; for in this manner 'deity' is compared to God. In another manner the other is compared[3] just as a *beginning* to a begun; and then of necessity a distinction is conveyed. Since, therefore, this preposition "*out of*" [ex] conveys a habitude of cause and/or at least of beginning, for that reason of necessity it means a distinction between extremes: and for that reason this cannot be true, that the Persons are *out of the same Essence*. But because the genitive (case) is not only construed in the reckoning of a *beginning*, nay (also) out of the *force of the declaration of the essence*, when there is said: "a woman of egregious form", as Priscian says;[4] for that reason with the genitive this is true: "the Three Persons are of the same Essence".

DOUBT III

Likewise, is asked of this which (Master Peter) says: *Three things*, and he accepts this from (St.) Augustine in the first book, ON CHRISTIAN DOCTRINE.[5] For it seems that he speaks badly by saying "*three things*", because "thing" is an absolute and general name: therefore, it seems, that if it means anything among the divine, that it means the Essence or Substance: therefore, just as in no manner is "*three Essences*" received, so in no manner ought "*three things*" be received. *And if you say*, that "*three Beings*" [tres entes] is received;[6] this is not similar, because ens is a participle, and thus it draws its number from another and is not numbered according to its own form of entity; but "thing" [res] is a substantive name. *If you say*, that "*thing*" names for me the form on the part of the soul; this is nothing, because those names are names for *intentions*, and a "*thing*" is divided against an "*intention*".

I RESPOND: It must be said, that any one [unaquaeque] thing[7] can be considered in a threefold manner: either according to the properties, which it has in its own nature; or according to the manner, through which it comes to be in [apud] the soul; or according to the consequent property, which is in it from the acts of the soul, which are *to subject* and *to predicate*, *to compose* and *to divide*.[8] Therefore, according to this threefold acceptation [acceptionem] it happens that a thing is named in a threefold manner: *In one manner* through the name, which indicates an existence on the part of its own nature, just as white and black and (accidents) of this kind. *In another manner*, according to which the soul accepts (it); and thus, because the soul accepts all (things)[9] through the manner of a being, it names a thing in this manner. Whence, every that is said (to be) "*a thing*", which the soul thinks of as an existent in a nature. *In another manner*, it happens that (the soul) names (it) through second intentions, just as *genus, species, subject* (and) *predicate* are said.

Since, therefore, this name, "*thing*", means a quasi medium between the name, which means the form of the *intention*, for that reason it not only befits an essence, but also persons; and for that reason we say that the Three Persons are "*three things*", not so, "*three Essences*"; and this name alludes to this signification. For a "*thing*" [res] is said from "*I reason, you reason*" [reor, reris], which means an act on the part of the soul; and in another manner "*thing*" comes from that which has been *ratified* [ratus], which means a stability on the part of the nature; and in this manner "*thing*" means a stability or ratification [ratitudinem] on the part of the entity. And thus the objections are clear, because in one manner it is a name for *a nature*, in another manner it is a name for *a reckoning*.[10]

DOUBT IV

Likewise, is asked of this verse of (St.) Jerome: *There is not, in a word, any grade in the Trinity*. For he seems to speak against that which (St.) Augustine says in the ninth (book) of the CONFESSIONS:[11] « The Father an the Son do not differ in substance, but in cause and in grade ». — Likewise, among the divine there is subsistence,[12] therefore, there is a "*under*" [sub] There; and "*under*" is said in manner relative

---

[1] Cf. above d. 5, a. 1, q. 2, 1st. opposed argument, and the solution to this argument.

[2] The Vatican edition alone reads *sometimes* [aliquando], and next after *denominating (the other)* [denominans] it adds *and yet* [et tamen]. — A little below this codex O has *but in this manner* [sic vero] in place of *for in this manner* [sic enim].

[3] Thus the older codices together with edition 1; the Vatican edition, together with codex cc, reads *something is compared to another* [comparator aliquid ad aliud].

[4] GRAMMATICAL INSTITUTIONS, Bk. XVIII, ch. 1. Cf. also above d. 3, p. II, dubium 3; and Alexander of Hales, SUMMA., p. I, q. 56, m. 7, a. 3, in reply to n. 1; and also Bl. (now St.) Albertus (Magnus), here in a. 5; and St. Thomas, here about the text.

[5] Chapter 5, n. 5.

[6] The Vatican edition, together with codex cc, omits the words *that ... is received* [quod recipitur], substitutes for the word *this* [hoc], which follows immediately, *here* [hic], and a little below this changes *its own form of entity* [formam propriam entitatis] into *the form of its own entity* [formam propriae entitatis].

[7] In the Vatican edition and codex cc there is read *a thing* [res] for *any one thing* [unaquaeque res].

[8] We note, that to a thing considered in the first and third manner there responds the concept, which will be called by the Scholastics the *first intention* and the *second intention*, but by the moderns the *real and logical* idea. Therefore, the *first* intention is the concept, by which the thing is represented to the intellect, insofar as it is in itself, or according to its properties, which convene with it, without any reckoning of the operation of the intellect being had, v. gr.

man, insofar as it is a rational animal. But the *second* intention is the concept, by which the thing is represented to the intellect, not insofar as it is, but under the properties attributed to it by the intellect, v. g. *man*, to the extent that it is a *species*, and/or to the extend that it is a *subject* in a proposition. The middle manner, by which a thing can be considered, namely, according to St. Bonaventure, through which a thing comes to be in the soul, comprises the general conditions, which are concomitant with the act of the intellect, v. g. that the intellect cognizes the thing through a manner of abstraction, of universality, of being etc. — A little above this, the Vatican edition together with codex cc has *common* [communem] for *consequent* [consequentem], breaking with the older codices and also in a manner repugnant to the Scholastics manner of speaking.

[9] The words received in the text: *and thus, because the soul accepts all (things)* [et sic, quia anima omnia accipit], which have been suppressed by the Vatican edition; we have restored on the authority of very many codices, such as G H M O T Z bb and edition 1.

[10] Cf. above d. 1, Doubt 7; Bl. (now St.) Albertus (Magnus), here in a. 6; St. Thomas, here in a. 4.

[11] Even if the codices and edition together cite Book 9 (and/or 11) of the CONFESSIONS, nevertheless, the words cited are not extant there, but are had in the book, which once was faultily considered to be among the works of St. Augustine, and which is entitled: QUAESTIONES EX UTROQUE TESTAMENTO MIXTIM, q. 122: « Does the Son differ in nothing from the Father? He differs plainly in the Substance, which the true Son is; but He does differ in the grade of causality (others read: in cause and/or in grade) ». Tertullian, AGAINST PRAXEAS, ch. 2 says: « But (there are) Three not according to status, but grade, nor according to substance, but form; not according to power, but species ».

[12] The Vatican edition, together with only a few manuscripts, has *substance* [substantia].

to a superior : therefore, there is an *"under"* and a *"over"* [super] There, therefore, an inferior and a superior, therefore, also a grade. — Therefore, wheresoever there is an authority and a subauthority, there is a grade; but this is in the Father and the Son: ergo etc..

I RESPOND: It must be said, just as the Gloss says, on the twentieth (chapter) of Exodus:[1] « *Thou shalt not ascend by way of the steps to the altar* etc. Through *steps* [gradus] he ascends to an altar, who says that the Father is greater than the Son, and the Son than the Holy Spirit, just as Arius says ». Whence since a *step* from the reckoning of its name takes away the equality of the Persons, for that reason (St.) Jerome rightly says, that there is not in a word, in the divinity, a grade [gradus]; nevertheless an *order* is posited. For a *grade* and an *order* differ, just as a point and a unity. For a point is a positioned [posita] substance; for that reason it is only in corporals. But a unity is a substance not having a position;[2] for that reason it is among

spirituals. In this manner a *"grade"* means a super-positioning [superpositionem] either of place, and/or of dignity. But *"order"* means a habitude to a principle without a super-positioning.[3]

To that, therefore, which *(St.) Augustine* says, it must be said, that he speaks in an improper sense [improprie] in each verse, and *"cause"* is taken there for *"principle"*, but *"grade"* is taken for *"order"*.

To that which is objected concerning *"under"* [sub], it must be said, that *"under"* [sub] among the divine does not mean inferiority, but only a habitude according to the reckoning of understanding. — To that which is objected concerning <u>auctoritas</u>, it must be said, that it is true, according to which <u>auctoritas</u> is said [sonat] in the reckoning of a dominion (i.e. as *"authority"*, which posits a grade; but thus it is not among the divine, but only insofar as it is said [sonat] in the reckoning of a principle (i.e. "authorship"); and this posits and order in being cognized.[4]

DISTINCTION XXVI

CHAPTER I

On this name, "hypostasis".

Now, concerning the properties of the Persons, which we have frequently called to mind in this treatise, it is necessary for us to say something. But, first, let us hear, what (St.) Jerome says concerning this name, *"hypostasis"*. For he says, that under this name there lies hidden a poison. But he says this, according to which the heretics used to use it, to seduce the simple, that is, for a *Person* and for the Essence, so that, whether there was only said (to be) one Hypostasis or Three, they would lead the less experienced to an unfitting (conclusion), then this name was not so common [vulgatam] among Catholics, nor (was) its signification so determined, as (it is) now. And for that reason (St.) Jerome says, that this name is not to be used without a distinction and/or an exposition, at that time, that is, when he use to contend with heretics, writing thus of the Catholic faith to Pope Damasus:[1] « From the Dancer of the Arians there was exacted by me, a Roman man, a novel noun, *"hypostasis"*. We sought by questioning [interrogamus], "What do they judge three "hypostases" to be understood (to be)?", "Three subsistent Persons", they said. We responded, that thus do we believe (Them to be). The *sense* was not sufficient for them, they urgently asked for the *name* itself; because I was ignorant of what (kind) of poison lay hidden in its syllables. We shouted: "If any of the three Hypostases, that is, subsistent things, is not confessed (to be) Persons, anathema sit! But if anyone, understanding a hypostasis (to be) an <u>ousia</u>, does not indicate [indicit] the Three Persons to be one Hypostasis, he is alien to Christ,

who, that is, saying (that there are) "three hypostases", strives to assert under a name of piety three natures. Let it suffice for us (Catholics) to say that (there is) one Substance and Three Persons, perfectly equal; let us be silent regarding "three hypostases", if you please. This name is not one of good esteem [bonae suspicionis], when in the same word the (various) senses (of it) disagree. Either, if you think that it is right, that we ought to say that (there are) three "hypostases" with their interpretations, we do not deny it. But believe me, a poison lies hidden beneath the honey: *for an angel of Satan transfigures himself into an Angel of light* ».[2] With these words he does not deny, that the name, *"hypostasis"*, is to be used, but he shows that the heretics used it in a depraved manner, against which there was a need for caution in distinguishing the signification (of it); otherwise the one who confessed that (there are) "three hypostases", would have contradicted himself.

CHAPTER II

On the properties of the Persons and on the names relative to these.

Let us now see, concerning the properties of the Persons, which are also said in Scripture, for the most part, (to be) the notions or relations in that Holy Trinity; which, for that reason, is recalled [repetitur] by us, so that It may be more tenaciously infixed in our heart.[3] (St.) Augustine says in the book, ON THE FAITH TO PETER:[4] « 'To have begotten' is other than 'to have been born' and 'to proceed' is other than 'to have begotten' and/or 'to have been born'. Whence it is manifest, that One is the Father, Another the Son, Another the Holy Spirit ». « And it is proper to the Father alone, not that He has not Himself been born, but that

---

[1] Verse 26. — The Gloss in (Nicholas of) Lyra on this passage (reads): Thou shalt not make a grade in the Trinity as Arius (did), who taught that the Father (is) the greater, the Son the lesser, the Holy Spirit the least.

[2] Aristotle, POSTERIOR ANALYTICS, Bk. I, ch. 23 (ch. 27): « A unity according to substance is without a position, but a point (is) a positioned substance ». A similar (statement) is had in METAPHYSICS, Bk. V, text 12 (Bk. IV, ch. 6). St. Bonaventure, SENT., II, d. 2, p. II, q. 3, fundament 2, says: « A point is a positioned substance, as the Philosopher says, i. e., one having a position according to its essence, in which it differs from a unity ».

[3] Cf. above d. 20, q. 2, q. 1 and 2. — The Vatican edition, together with codex cc, has *positioning* [positionem] for *super-positioning* [superpositionem].

[4] Cf. above d. 16, Doubts 4 and 5. — This doubt is also solved by St. Thomas, here commenting on the text.

NOTES ON THE BOOK OF SENTENCES

[1] Epistle 15, n. 3; in which text edition 2 has *induce* [inducit] for *indicate* [indicit]; the original has *say* [dicit], but it inserts the particle *in* [in] before *the three persons* [tribus personis]. Then, codd. A C D E and ed. 1, with the original, read *let us be silent regarding "three hypostases", if you please; it is not (a name) of good esteem* [taceamus; tres hypostases, si placet non bonae suspicionis est], which reading, though less clear, perhaps is genuine. Immediately after this in the original there is read *the words disagree in the same sense* [in eodem sensu verba dissentiunt] for *in the same word the (various) senses (of it) disagree* [in eodem verbo sensus dissentiunt]; however, this latter reading of Master (Peter) is entirely to be preferred.

[2] A reference to 2 Cor. 11:14.

[3] Only edition 2 reads *are recalled by us, so that they may be more tenaciously infixed in our heart* [a nobis repetuntur, ut cordi nostro tenacious infigantur], that is, "the properties of the persons"; in our text this proposition is referred to the *Holy Trinity* [Trinitate sancta].

[4] Chapter 1, n. 6. The following passage is <u>ibid.</u>, ch. 2, n. 7.

He begot one Son; and (it is) proper to the Son alone, not that He did not beget, but that He has been born from the Essence of the Father; but it is proper to the Holy Spirit, not that He has neither Himself been born nor has He begotten, but that He alone proceeds from the Father and the Son ». Behold he briefly assigned the three properties of the Three Persons, of which one is not the other. For he signified this, when he said: " 'To have begotten' is other than to have been born, and 'to proceed' (is) another", that is, one property or notion is generation, and another (is) nativity, another procession, which by other names are said (to be) the paternity, the filiation, (and) the spiration.[1] These properties those names of the Persons designate, namely, "Father", "Son" and "Holy Spirit", which are relative (names) and are said regarding one another; because they note the relations, which are not accidental to God, but belong immutably to the Persons Themselves from eternity, so that the *appellations* are not merely [modo] relative, are also the relations or notions *in the Things Themselves*, namely, in the Persons.

CHAPTER III

That not all (names) are said of God according to substance; for certain ones (are said) according to relation, however, nothing (is said) according to accident.

About which it must be known, that not every (name) which is said of God, is said according to *substance*; because certain ones are said according to a *relation*, which is not an accident, because it is not mutable. For as (St.) Augustine says in the fifth book, ON THE TRINITY:[2] « Nothing in God is said according to accident, because nothing accedes to Him; nor, however, is every (name) which is said, said of God according to substance. It remains that, in created and mutable things what is not said according to substance, is said according to accident. But in God nothing, indeed, is said according to accident, because nothing in Him is mutable or able to be lost [amissibile]; nor, however, is everything which is said of God, said according to *substance*. For 'as regards something', which is not an accident, is said, just as "the Father" (is said regarding) "the Son", and "the Son" regarding "the Father"; because both the Former (is) always the Father, and the Latter (is) always the Son; and thus always, because the Son has always been born, not has the Son every begun to be. Wherefore, if He at any time had begun to be, or (if) at any time the Son had ceased to be, it would be said according to accident. And because the Father is not said (to be) the Father, except out of this, that the Son is His, and the Son is not said (to be) the Son, except out of this, that He has a Father; these (names) are not said according to substance, but these (names) of Theirs are said regarding one another, and yet not accord-

ing to accident, because both that He is said (to be) the Father, and that He is said (to be) the Son is eternal and incommutable to Them ».

Behold, with these words there is openly shown, that certain (names) are said of God according to *substance*, certain ones according to *relation*, yet nothing according to *accident*. The property of the Father is also shown to be, that He has a Son, and the property of the Son, that He has a Father. And for that reason, when he said,[3] that it is eternal and immutable, that one is said (to be) the Father, and that (the other) is said (to be) the Son; he wanted that it be understood thus, that is: the property, by which the Father is the Father, and the property, by which the Son is the Son, is eternal and incommutable, because both the Father is always the Father, and the Son always the Son. Whence even (St.) Hilary, assigning the properties of the Person in the twelfth book, ON THE TRINITY[4] says: « If it is always proper to the Father, that He is the Father, it is necessary that it always be proper to the Son, that He is always the Son. For where there is always a Father, there is always a Son: therefore, he who is not always the Father, has not always begotten ». Likewise, in the same (he says): « It is manifest that it is proper to the God (who has been) born, that He is the Son ».

CHAPTER IV

For what reason is it said that it is proper to the Only-Begotten, to be the Son of God, since even men are the sons God.

Here, there is asked, in what manner is it said that it is proper to the God (who is) born, that He is the Son of God and/or begotten out of God, since men are said (to be) and are sons of God, according to that (verse): *(you are) all sons of the Most High*.[5] And to Moses the Lord said of the people of Israel:[6] *My first born son, Israel*. But there is a great distance: for men are sons of God by a making [factura], not (they are not such) by a property of (their) nativity; but God the Son by the property of (His) origin is the Son and by the truth of (His) nativity, not by a making and/or by an adoption; and indeed they are before they are sons of God; for they become the sons of God,[7] they are not born sons of God. Whence (St.) Hilary, showing that the God (who has been) born (is) alone a son of God by the property of (His) origin, distinguished between Him and the men (who are) sons of God in the twelfth book, ON THE TRINITY,[8] thus saying: « However, He alone who is born out of Him is truly the Son of the Father. And we, indeed, are God's sons, but through a making. For we were *at one time sons of wrath*, but *we have been made* sons for God through adoption rather than *being born such* [quam nascimur]. And because everything which comes to be, before it comes to be, was not, we, when we were not sons, were made (such). For before we were not sons, but through grace we have been made, not born, nor generated, but acquired (as such). For God acquired us for Himself, and

---

[1] Excepting edition 8, the other editions and codices omit less well *(and) the spiration* [spiratio]. Codex A (in the margin by another hand) repeats *procession* [processio] for *spriation* [spiratio]. Immediately afterwards before *names* [nomina] we have inserted *those* [illa], on the testimony of all the codices and edition 1.

[2] Chapter 5, n. 6. — A little above this the Vatican edition, together with very many editions and codices D and E, has *from this (St.) Augustine* [Unde Augustinus] for *as (St.) Augustine* [Ut Augustinus]. In the second half of the text the Vatican edition, together with the other editions, except ed. 1, by adding the verbs reads *the Former is always the Father, and the Latter is always the Son* [et est ille semper Pater, et est ille semper Filius], breaking with the codices and the original.

[3] Only the Vatican edition, together with editions 4 and 6, reads *since he said* [cum dixerit].

[4] Number 23; however, Master (Peter) changes the order of the propositions. — The following passage is *ibid.*, n. 15.

[5] Psalm 81:6. — A little above this after *it is said* [dicatur], trusting in all the codices and editions 1, 2 and 5, we have inserted *it is* [esse], and before *according to that (verse)* [secundum illud] we have, contrary to the Vatican edition alone, put *are* [sint] for *become* [fiant].

[6] Exodus 4:22.

[7] From the Vatican edition alone there is omitted *the sons of God* [filii Dei], and not ineptly read instead *for they become, they are not born, sons of God* [fiunt enim, non nascuntur filii Dei]. All the codices and the other editions add at least *sons* [filii], codices D and E and edition 1 add *the sons of God* [filii Dei], which reading more accurately expresses the sense; a little above this at *before they are sons of God* [quam filii Dei sint], codex C and very many editions have (the indicative) for *they are* [sunt] rather than (the subjunctive) [sint].

[8] Numbers 12 and 13; in which text only editions 2, 3, 7 and 8, after *However* [Vero] add the dative for *God* [Deo]; and the same and not a few other editions read *out of God* [ex Deo] for *out of Him* [ex eo]. The text of (St.) Hilary omits *truly* [vere]. Trusting in the same original and codices A B and C, we have posited the better reading *God's sons* [filii Deo sumus], though all the editions and codices D and E have *the sons of God* [filii Dei sumus]. We have corrected the same a little below this, placing *sons for God* [filii Deo per] for *sons of God* [filii Dei per]. The words *at one time sons of wrath* [aliquando filii iracundiae] respect Eph. 2:3: *And we were by birth sons of wrath* [Et eramus natura filii irae].

through this He is said to have begotten us. For we know [cognoscimus] that it has never been said that God begot sons, with the signification of the property. For out of an adoption[1] man has been made a son of God, not out of a generation; nor is it his property, but (rather) a naming, and through that he is not truly a son, because neither is he said properly (to be) "born", nor was he always a son. But the Only-Begotten God neither was at one time not a son, nor was something before (being) a son, nor (was) He Himself anything but a son. And so thus, He who always is a son, by the property of (His) nascibility and by truth is the son of Him alone, who begot (Him); and only He who begot, is His father; because just as the Former (is) a son by origin, so the Latter a father by generation ».

CHAPTER V

That a man is said (to be) a "son" of the Trinity, and the Trinity, the "father" of men.

On the other hand, the man, who is a son of God, is by a making not only a son of the Father, but also (a son) of the Son and of the Holy Spirit, that is, of the whole Trinity; and the Trinity Itself can be said to be his Father. Whence (St.) Augustine in the fifth book, ON THE TRINITY[2] says: « The Trinity cannot be said to be a father, except perhaps in a transferred manner regarding the creation on account of the adoption of sons. For that which has been written:[3] *Hear o Israel, the Lord Thy God, is one God*, must at any rate not be understood, with the Son or the Holy Spirit excepted; which One Lord, Our God, we rightly say (is) also Our Father, regenerating us through His grace ». On this even (St.) Hilary in the sixth book, ON THE TRINITY[4] says: « Through faith God is father to all, to whom He is the father through that Faith, by which we confess Jesus Christ (to be) the Son of God ». Behold it has been shown, for what reason it is said that it is proper to the God (who has been) born, that He is a son, because, that is, He alone is properly said (to be) "*born*". Whence (St.) Hilary in the third book, ON THE TRINITY[5] says: « The Lord saying: *Glorify Thy Son*, has not witnessed by name alone, that He is a son, but also by (His) *property*. We are the sons of God, but He (is) not such a son. For He is a true and proper son by origin, not by adoption; by truth, not by being named [nuncupatione]; by a nativity, not by being created ».

CHAPTER VI

That the Holy Spirit is said (to be) "the Gift" by the same property, by which (He is said to be) "the Holy Spirit", and in each manner relatively to the Father and the Son.

Thus, too, it must be said of the Holy Spirit, that He is properly said (to be) "*the Gift*" of God, yet though there are also many gifts of God. But the Holy Spirit is thus by (His) immutable and eternal property a gift,[6] just as the Son by (His) property is a son. For, He is said (to be) "*a gift*" for this, whereby (He is said to be) a "*holy spirit*", and He is at least said (to be such) by each name in a relative manner, and He is said by the same relation (to be) a "*holy spirit*" and a "*gift*"; though

the relation itself does not appear so much in this name, "*holy spirit*", just as (it does) in this name, "*gift*". Whence (St.) Augustine in the fifth book, ON THE TRINITY[7] thus says: « The Holy Spirit, who is not the Trinity, but is understood in the Trinity, in this that He is properly said (to be) a holy spirit, is said (to be such) relatively, when He is referred both to the Father and to the Son, because the Holy Spirit is a spirit of both the Father and of the Son. But the relation itself does not appear in this name, but it does appear, when He is said (to be) a *gift* of God; for He is a gift of the Father and the Son, because He proceeds both from the Father and from the Son. And perhaps for this reason He is thus named, as we have already said, nor is it annoying to repeat, that the same appellation can befit the Father and the Son. For by this He is properly said (to be) what They (are) commonly: because both the Father (is) a spirit and the Son a spirit, and both the Father (is) holy and the Son holy. Therefore, so that out of the name, which befits Each, the communion of Each be signified, the gift of Both is called a holy spirit ».

Behold you have, for what reason the Holy Spirit is properly said (to be) a gift, and that He is relatively said (to be) either a gift, or a holy spirit, and that He has a proper name for Himself, which commonly befits the Father and the Son, but separately [divisim]. And it must be known, that[8] when the Father and/or the Son is said (to be) a "spirit", or "holy", neither is said in a relative manner, but (rather both are said) according to substance.

CHAPTER VII

Whether the Father and/or the Son and/or the Trinity Itself can be said (to be) a "holy spirit".[9]

Here there can be asked, whether the Father and/or the Son and/or even the Trinity Itself can be said (to be) a "holy spirit", just as separately [disiunctim] it is said (that They are) both a "*spirit*" and "*holy*". On this (St.) Augustine in the fifth book, ON THE TRINITY[10] speaks in this manner: « The Trinity in no manner can be said (to be) a "son", but It can, indeed universally, be said (to be) a "holy spirit", according to that which is written: *Since God is a spirit*. And so the Father and the Son and the Holy Spirit, since God is one, and certainly [utique] God is holy, and God is a spirit, can be named a "*trinity*", and a "*holy spirit*". But yet this "*holy spirit*" will not be said in a relative manner, but according to essence, because properly (speaking) the Holy Spirit, who is not the Trinity, but in the Trinity, is said (to be such) in a relative manner ».

CHAPTER VIII

That not all (the names), which are said relatively, respond, according to their terms, to one another in reverse.

However, certain (authors) think, that "*holy spirit*" and/or "*gift*" are not said relatively to the Father and/or to the Son. For if, they say, these are said relatively to one another, they respond to one another [invicem sibi] according to (their own) terms [vocabulis]: so that, just as there is said:

---

[1] These are read ibid., n. 15, but with many (words) omitted and/or changed by Master (Peter).

[2] Chapter 11, n. 12. — Above, the Vatican edition and editions 1, 4, and 6 omit *also* [et] after *of the Father, but* [Patris, sed].

[3] Deuteronomy 6:4. — The Vulgate reads: *Hear o Israel, the Lord our God, the Lord is One* [Audi Israel, Dominus Deus noster, Dominus unus est].   [4] Number 30.

[5] Number 11. The passage cited from Sacred Scripture is Jn. 17:1.

[6] Only codices A and D add *of God* [Dei]; then the codices and edition 1 omit *is* [est] before *a son* [filius].

[7] Chapter 11, n. 12.

[8] Codices A B D and E and editions 1, 2, 3 & 7, read *that* [quia]. Even elsewhere, Master (Peter) uses the Latin quia [because] for quod [that].

[9] Codices D and E, begin, here, Distinction XXVII.

[10] Chapter 11, n. 12, with not a few things changed and omitted by Master (Peter). — The passage of Sacred Scripture is John 4:12. — Near the end of the text of (St.) Augustine, only the Vatican edition and editions 4 and 5 have *is not said* [non dicitur] for *will not be said* [non dicetur].

"the Father of the Son (is) a father", and "the Son of the Father (is) a son", so there is said "*a father of the Holy Spirit*" and/or "*the father of the Gift*", and "the Holy Spirit and/or the Gift of the Father (is) a spirit and/or a gift". But not so is it among all relative (names). For not all (names), which are said relatively, respond to one another according to their own terms. Whence (St.) Augustine, shattering their opinion, (says) in the fifth book, ON THE TRINITY:[1] « Let it not move (you) », he says, « since we have said, that the Holy Spirit is said in a relative manner not (to be) the Trinity Itself, but Him who is in the Trinity, though the term for Him, to whom He is referred, does not respond to Him in reverse [vicissim]. For we say that (He is) the Holy Spirit of the Father, but we do not say in reverse that (the Latter is) the Father of the Holy Spirit. Likewise, we say that (He is) the Holy Spirit of the Son, but we do not say that (the Latter is) the Son of the Holy Spirit, lest the Holy Spirit be understood (to be) His father. For in many relative (names) it happens, that a term is not found, by which they respond to themselves in reverse. When, therefore, we say "*the gift of the Father and of the Son*", we indeed cannot say that "(One is) *the father of the gift*" or "(the Other is) *the son of the gift*", but so that these respond in reverse, we say that (the Holy Spirit is) "the gift of the granter", and that (Either is) "the grantor of the gift", because in the latter case [hic] a customary [usitatum] term could be found, in the former case [illic] it could not ». « When, therefore, we say "*the gift of the grantor*" and "*the grantor of the gift*", we say each relative to one another ». « However, God was not only [non nisi] a "*grantor*" in time, since the Holy Spirit is "*a gift*" also from eternity ».

COMMENTARY ON DISTINCTION XXVI

On the properties of the Persons, according to which they are sealed upon the Persons Themselves.

Let us now see, concerning the properties of the Persons etc..

THE DIVISION OF THE TEXT

Above, Master (Peter) dealt[1] with those (names) which are said of God according to *substance*; here, second, he deals with those which are said of God according to *relation*. Moreover, this part is divided into two. In the first he deals with those which are said of God *properly* and *eternally*. In the second, he deals with those which are said of God *temporally* and *commonly*,[2] below in the Thirtieth Distinction: *For there are certain (names), which are said of God in time.* The first part, again, is divided into two; because certain ones are *personal* properties or relations, and of these he deals first; certain ones (are) *not personal*, and of these he deals second, below in the Twenty-Eight Distinction: *Moreover, it is necessary that one consider, that there are not only three etc..* The first part, again, is divided into two. In the first, he assigns the properties of the Persons, according to which they are assigned in the Persons Themselves. However, in the second, he deals with these, according to which it happens that they are expressed with diverse names, below in the Twenty-Seventh Distinction: *Here there can be asked, whether the properties etc..*

The *first* part has two (parts). In the *first*, Master (Peter) assigns the properties of the Persons. However, in the *second*, he moves a doubt about the assignment, there (where he says): *Here there is asked, in what manner is it said that it is proper to the God (who is) born etc..*

The *first* part has three parts according to (its) three chapters.[3] In the first, he determines, to what the prop-

erties are assigned, because (they are assigned to) hypostases. In the second, he assigns, what those properties are, there (where he says): *Let us now see, concerning the properties of the Persons.* Third, he shows, what those properties are, since they are relations or (are) said according to relation, not only according to accident, and this he does in the third chapter, there (where he says): *About which it must be known, that not every (name) etc..*

Here there is asked, in what manner is it said that it is proper to the God (who was) born. This is the *second* part, in which he moves doubts according to the aforesaid assignments [assignationes], and this part has two (parts). In the first, he moves a doubt against the assignment of the property of the Son. In the second, against the assignment of the property of the Holy Spirit, there (where he says): *Here there can be asked, whether the Father.* The first part has two (parts). In the first, he proposes a question and solves (it) by the authority[4] of (St.) Hilary (of Poitiers). In the second, also he applies that solution about the property of the Holy Spirit, which is "*gift*", there (where he says): *Thus, too, it must be said of the Holy Spirit.*

Similarly, the second part has two parts. In the first, he asks and solves; in the second he reproves the position of certain (authors). The first he does there (where he says): *Here there can be asked, whether the Father* etc.; the second he does there (where he says): *However, certain (authors) think, that the Holy Spirit etc..*

---

[1] Chapter 12, n. 13; the following passages are ibid., chs. 15 and 16, nn. 16 and 17. — The Vatican edition, together with a few editions, reads (at the end) *also from eternity* [et ab aeterno] for *also from eternity* [etiam ab aeterno].

NOTES ON THE COMMENTARY

[1] The Vatican edition, not trusting in the codices and edition 1, prefixes *in a manifold manner* [multipliciter] to the verb *dealt* [egit].

[2] Thus the codices, not without edition 1 and the Vatican edition, omit the words *and commonly* [et communiter], and a little above this before *temporally* [temporaliter] adds *properly both* [proprie et].

[3] In the Vatican ed. alone there are wanting the words *according to (its) three chapters* [secundum tria capitula], and which those which follow below this: *and this he does in the third chapter* [et hoc tertio capitulo facit].

[4] In place of *(it) by the authority* [auctoritate] very many codd., with ed. 1, faultily read *the authority* [auctoritatem]. — The Vatican ed. alone reads: *(it) by the authority of (Sts.) Augustine and Hilary* [auctoritate Augustini et Hilarii].

ARTICLE SOLE

On the properties, in general.

For an understanding of those (things), which are said in this Distinction concerning the properties, four (things) are asked:

First, there is asked, whether among the divine there is a positing of properties.

Second, granted that there is, there is asked, what are those properties.

Third, there is asked, what is their act.

Fourth and last there is asked concerning their number.

QUESTION I

Whether, among the divine, there are to be posited properties for the Persons?

Moreover, that among the divine there is a positing of properties not only verbally [vocaliter], but also really, is shown in this manner:

1. (St.) Jerome says, and (as) there is had at the end of the preceding Distinction:[1] « We confess not only the Names, but even the properties of the Names »: ergo etc..

2. Likewise, (St.) Augustine says in the book, ON THE FAITH TO PETER:[2] « It is proper to the Father, that He begot one Son »: therefore, a coniugatis, generation is a property of the Father; but it is established, that generation is really in God, (and) it is also established, that it befits the Father alone: therefore, according to thing it is a property of the Father.

3. Likewise, it belongs to a property to distinguish, therefore, where there is a true distinction, there is a true property; but among the divine there is a true distinction: whence (St. John) Damascene (says):[3] « We recognize the difference of the Hypostases, that is, of the Persons, in three properties, the paternal, the filial and the processible ».

4. Likewise, this very (thing) seems *by reason*, because just as there is one manner of asking concerning essence and person, so there is another manner of asking concerning essence and property. For one asks concerning an essence through (the interrogative) "*What?*", concerning a property through (the question) "*In what manner does it hold itself?*": therefore, just as among the divine there is posited both 'essence' and 'person' according to truth, so ought there be posited 'property'.

5. Likewise, above it has been proved, that generation [generatio] and procession [processio] really differ — otherwise, the Persons will not differ — therefore, generation and spiration [spiratio] really

differ. But generation as much as spiration is in one Person, not multiplied, such as in the Person of the Father: therefore, since a Person is really one, and the properties really many, therefore, there is a positing of properties really different among the divine; but not by an *essential* nor a *personal* difference, since they are in the same Person: therefore, by a *notional one*. Wherefore, if generation [generatio] and spiration [spiratio] do not differ, then, just as this is true: 'the Father spirates the Holy Spirit', so also this (would be true): 'the Father generates the Holy Spirit'; and it would follow, that the Holy Spirit would be the Son.

6. Likewise, the Father and the Son are the one principle of the Holy Spirit, this has been proven above,[5] and the reason (for this) is in the One coming forth [in promptu], because He who is spirated is entirely One. That which is one (here) means a unity not of essence nor of person: therefore, it is necessary [oportet], that (it be one) of property; and if this, it is necessary [necesse est] to posit that among the divine (there) really (are) properties, not nominally or only in word [in voce].

7. Likewise, in the Father there is paternity and innascibility: therefore, either (they are) the same property, or (they are) different [alia]. If (they are) the same property, therefore, (they are) also the same relation; but according to paternity [paternitatem] He is referred to the Son: therefore, also according to innascibility [innascibilitatem]. But this is false; therefore, (innascibility) is another (property);[6] and the Person (who has these two properties) is one [una]: therefore, it is necessary to posit also that (there) really (are) different properties in the Divine Persons.

ON THE CONTRARY: 1. (St.) Hilary (says), ON THE TRINITY:[7] the Father and the Son and the Holy Spirit differ in (Their) Names alone: therefore, if They differ in (Their) Names alone, the properties There are not real, but verbal [vocales].

---

[1] Chapter 3.

[2] Chapter 2, n. 7. See the text of Master (Peter), ch. 2. — Next, understand the words, a coniugatis, thus: An (Aristotelian) topic [locus] or manner of arguing from the concrete to the abstract, and/or vice versa. The concrete and abstract (terms of which) are said to be conjugated (lit. "yoked together"), i. e. posited under the same yoke of signification, because they convene in the principal signified and do not differ except according to the manner of signification.*

[3] ON THE ORTHODOX FAITH, Bk. III, ch. 5. Cf. also Bk. I, ch. 8. — On the major of the argument, cf. below q. 3.

[4] Distinction 13, q. 3.

[5] Distinction 11, q. 2. — At the end of the argument, the Vatican edi-

tion, without the authority of the codd. and ed. 1, has *that there be posited* [poni] for *to posit* [ponere], and then, contrary to codd. B D H K P Q V aa & bb, it reads *nor* [nec] for *or* [sive]; cod. F reads *and/or* [vel]. — Many codd. read *in speech* [voce] for *in speech* [in voce]; in codd. aa & bb there is read *nominally only or according to speech* [nominaliter tantum sive secundum vocem].

[6] Thus codd. F H P Q T ee & others; cod. O reads *therefore, (paternity is) one (property) and (innascibility) another* [ergo alia et alia]; the Vatican ed. with cod. cc, reads *therefore (innascibility is) another (property)* [igitur alia].

[7] (St.) Hilary constantly teaches the contrary (of this). Therefore, this sentence seems to have been formed from those passages, which occur in the individual books of the work cited above, in which the holy Doctor urges the substantial unity of the Divine Persons, and/or from the opposition of the heretics (to this Catholic dogma), v. g. in his ON THE TRINITY, Bk. II, n. 5 (cf. reply to n. 1).

---

* *Trans. note*: Cf. Peter of Spain, SUMMULE LOGICALES, tract 5, "On Topical Arguments". Note, however, that in Pietro Ispano, TRATTATO DI LOGICA, a cura di A. Ponzio, Bompiani, 2004, p. 181, the Italian for the example is faulty: it should read, *La giustizia è buona; dunque, un giusto è buono.* The translation, as Ponzio gave it, fails to notice the transition from the abstract to the concrete terms, though admittedly Peter's explanation is deficient.

2. Likewise, (St. John) Damascene says in the first book: « It is necessary [oportet] to know, that it is one thing to differ in thing, another in reckoning », and he means, that among creatures there is a difference *according to thing* [re] and a fittingness [convenientia] according to reckoning, but among the divine (it is) the other way around. Since, therefore, there is a distinction according to properties, it seems, therefore, that they are There only according to a manner of speaking and/or of understanding: not, therefore, on the part of the thing.

3. Likewise, this very (thing) seems by *reason*, because in a most highly simple (thing) there does not occur any difference; but a Divine Person is most highly simple: therefore, either in Him there is no property, or it is only by a manner of speaking [solo modo loquendi]: ergo etc..

4. Likewise, a Person is simple, just as the Essence (is); but the properties of the Essence do not differ except only in a manner of speaking, not according to thing: therefore, similarly the properties of a Person.

5. Likewise, the Divine Essence, on account of (its) most high Simplicity, is referred by Itself [se ipsa] to a creature, and for that reason an essential relation differs from the Essence only in a manner of speaking, as when there is said *"Lord"*, for (this name) passes over entirely into the Substance:[2] therefore, for an equal reason a Person is referred by Itself to a Person.

6. Likewise, a creature on account of (its) essential comparison to its own principle is referred by itself to its Creator — otherwise between the Creator and creature there would fall a medium, which would be neither the Creator nor the creature — therefore, if more essential is the comparison of a Person to a Person, therefore, (a Person) is referred by Himself (the other Person). And if this: therefore, it seems, that a property itself and/or a relation does not differ except only in a manner of speaking from a Person.

CONCLUSION

Properties of the Persons are to be posited among the divine, which differ not only according to speech, but also really from one another, and in some manner even from the Persons.

I RESPOND: It must be said, that all Catholics writers [catholici tractatores] posited that (there are) properties of the Persons among the divine. For, since there are many Persons and (These) distinct, it is necessary, that there be There (something) *distinguishing* (Them), but this we name a "property" [proprietatem]. But (these) have been diversified in the manner that they are posited [in modo positionis].

Since, therefore, some[3] see the most high Simplicity in a Person, just as in the Essence, they posited, that just as in the Essence *whereby It is* [quo est] and *what It is* [quod est] is entirely the Same, so in a Person *who* is distinguished and *whereby* (He is distinguished is)[4] entirely the same, and thus a Supposit and a property (is entirely the same thing), but (the latter) differing only by a manner of speaking; just as if there is said: "I beg you, kind, Sir" and/or "I beg your kindness".

But that position cannot stand, since, just as has been proved in the opposing (argument),[5] in the same Person there are properties differing not only by a manner of speaking, but also really. For we see, that *one* Person in one manner is compared to One, as the Father (is) to the Son; and we see, that one Person in one manner or according to one habitude is compared to Many, as the Holy Spirit (is) to the Father and the Son; and again, that one Person in many manners is compared to Many, as the Son (is) to the Father and the Holy Spirit. Similarly, we see, that *many* Persons in the same manner are compared to One, as the Father and the Son (are) to the Holy Spirit: therefore, the unity of habitude cannot be accepted on the part of the Essence — (that) is certain — nor on the part of the Person, who is referred; not on the part of the Person, to whom He is referred. It remains, therefore, that there is another manner of speaking, taken on the part of the thing.

And, for that reason, the common opinion now holds, that among the divine there are properties of the Persons *really* differing from one another, and through this also differing from the Persons *in some manner*. For just as, because in the one Essence, not plurified, we posit many Persons, the manners[6] of speaking *essentially* and *personally* differ not only by a difference taken on our part, but even on the part of the thing; in this manner must it also be said concerning the manner of speaking *personally* and *notionally*. And for that reason the masters (of theology) distinguish three manners of speaking among the divine, which are taken[7] on the part of the thing, namely, an *essential*, a *personal*, and a *notional* (manner). And it is said commonly, that there are three manners of predicating (among the divine), namely in *"What?"*, in *"Who?"* and in *"What or in what manner it holds itself"*. And the sin according to a figure of speech occurs (in an argument) from switching between [ex commutatione][8] these manners (of speech), just as among creatures (it occurs) from switching between the predicaments. Therefore, just as among the divine there is a true Essence, and there are true Persons, so there are true properties of the Persons.

1. To that which is first objected unto the contrary, from (St.) Hilary (of Poitiers), it must be said, that (St.) Hilary accepts "Names"

---

[1] ON THE ORTHODOX FAITH, ch. 8: Moreover, knowing, that it is one (thing) to be considered in regard to thing and another by a reckoning or by thought, makes a difference. Certainly in all creatures a certain discretion of persons in regard to thing is considered ... but a community and conjunction and unity by a reckoning and by thought is perceived [perspicitur] ... However, in the Sacrosanct Trinity thing holds itself in a contrary manner.

[2] That is, it is entirely the same as the Substance Itself and/or Divine Essence. — Next after this codex T has *through Itself* [per se ipsum] for *by Itself* [se ipsa].

[3] Among who is (Peter) Praepositivus; cf. below d. 33, q. 1; and Alexander of Hales, SUMMA., p. I, q. 68, m. 1, a. 1.

[4] Supply with the Vatican edition *is* [est], and next after *property* [proprietas] with the same edition supply *is entirely the same (thing)* [omnino est idem].

[5] In the seventh argument of the fundament. — A little below this after *really* [realiter], codex I interposes *because one is the manner, whereby the Father holds Himself to the Son, another whereby He holds Himself to the Holy Spirit* [quia alius est modus, quo se habet Pater ad Filium, alius quo se habet ad Spiritum sanctum].

[6] Very many codd., such as A S T V X & Y, have *the manner* [modus].

[7] The Vatican edition, favored only by a few codices, has *are* [sunt] for *are taken* [sumuntur]. — Next after *of predicating* [praedicandi], supply with the Vatican edition alone *among the divine* [in divinis]. — On the three manners of predicating, which follow, see Alan of Lille's book, RULES OF THEOLOGY, rule 50.

[8] Thus the more outstanding codices, together with edition 1. The text of the Vatican edition sounds badly: *And it falls into a sin, namely, the figure of speech out of a switching between* [Et incidit in peccatum, scilicet figuram dictionis ex commixtione].

not for the words themselves, but for the (things) understood or signified, conveyed through those three Names. For there they convey the properties. For "*alone*" does not exclude the truth of a property there, but excludes a diversity of form and/or of substance and/or of nature.

2. To that which is objected from (St. John Damascene), that They differ only by a reckoning; it must be said, that *to differ by a reckoning* is *in a threefold manner*. In one manner on the part of *our apprehension*, just as in God (His) Goodness and Greatness (differ). In another manner to differ by a reckoning is according to a *difference of attribution*, because some manner is posited about one (thing) and/or is attributed to one (thing), which is not attributed to the other; and in this manner *the Essence* and *a Person* and *a notion* differ by (their) reckoning. In a third manner to differ by a reckoning is to differ according to a *plurality of distinction*, which does not induce a diversity in essence and/or nature, yet does induce such a difference, that one is not said of the other; and in this manner *Person* from *Person* and *property* from *property* differ by a reckoning. And indeed the first difference according to reckoning is the least, because nothing responds to it on the part of the thing; but (something) does respond to the last one. Therefore, (St. John) Damascene does not want to divide '*thing*' against '*reckoning*', except according to which "*thing*" is accepted for "*nature*"; nor does he divide (them) entirely in this manner, but denominates (them) as if from (their) principle. For among creatures there is not only a community of *reckoning* [rationalis],[1] nay also of *nature* [naturalis]. For Peter and Paul not only convene in a *reckoning*, but also in a *common nature*.

3. To that which is objected, that this[2] excludes [tollit] a most high simplicity; it must be said, that a certain difference of reckoning is founded upon something *absolute*, whether substantial or accidental, a certain one upon a *respect* or manner of being regarded [modum se habendi]. And the first difference is entirely repugnant to simplicity, and cannot be in God; but the second is not repugnant. For we see, that concerning (something) new, there is some respect about something, with it in no manner being changed.[3] We also see, that something has many respects, without it existing in composition (with many things). It must be said, therefore, that the personal properties are *respective*, not *absolute*; and for that reason they can

differ by a reckoning of respects; because a "Person" means a Supposit or a Hypostasis, but "properties" mean a habitude to the Other.

4. From this the following (objection) is clear. For because *essential* properties are absolute, they cannot mean a real difference, unless they have an essential (signification); and for that reason they differ only in a manner of speaking. Not so *personal* properties. Wherefore, essential properties pass over entirely into the Essence, but personal ones (do) not.

5. To that which is objected, that the Essence is referred by itself; it must be said, that the Divine *Essence* cannot be referred except to another essence; but to that it is not referred, since "relation" means an order and a habitude. But just as the Philosopher would have it:[4] « God is not ordered to things, but things to Him »; and for that reason there is no relation there, except in the manner alone of speaking. But when a *Person* is referred to a Person, there is truth an order of origin, and for that reason a habitude, and for that reason a true relation. And thus that (objection) is clear.

6. To that which is objected, that a creature is referred by itself (to God);[5] it must be said, that '*to be referred by oneself*' can be understood *in a threefold manner*; either because between the looking back to the thing and the essence there falls no medium, because *it depends essentially on the essence itself*, and in this manner it is indeed found in creatures. For, thus, matter is referred to form and form to matter; whence the Philosopher says,[6] that « matter is that which is for the other »; yet, neither is matter its looking-back, nor (is) form, because they do not have an omnimodal simplicity. In another manner, there is a '*to be referred by oneself*', because between that which is referred and its correlative there falls no medium, which *is not their other* [non sit alterum eorum]; and in this manner the Father is referred by Himself to the Son, and conversely. For the Father is His own paternity, and this on account of (His) most high simplicity. In a third manner, there is a '*to be referred by oneself*', because that which is referred *is naught but a relation* and a pure looking-back; and to be this is not possible [impossibile], neither in God nor in a creature, because, just as (St.) Augustine says,[7] « everything which is referred is something, except that which is relatively said »; otherwise a relation would belong to a relation.[8] And thus it is clear, that every

---

[1] The Vatican edition, contrary to the editions and three first editions, reads *of reckoning* [rationis] for *of reckoning* [rationalis].

[2] Supply: difference.

[3] Understand: by a change, which they call *regarding itself* [ad se] or according to some absolute entity. On this matter (St. Severinus) Boethius, ON THE TRINITY, says: For let anyone move, (and then) stand still; therefore, if I approach him on the right, he will be on the left compared to me; not that he himself is on the left, but that I have approached on the right. Again, I approach on the left, likewise, he comes to be on (my) right, not that such that he is per se on the right, and (not) so that which is, is least of all (measured) from me or out of me, but least of all out of itself. Wherefore those which according to the property of any thing, in that which it is, do not cause a predication, can alternate and/or change nothing, and can entirely vary no essence.

[4] (Aristotle), METAPHYSICS, Bk. XII, text 52 (Bk. XI, ch. 10): For He (the Ruler of the universe) is not for the sake of order, but order for the sake of Him.

[5] Supply with codices V and X *to God* [ad Deum].

[6] (Aristotle), PHYSICS, Bk. II, text 26 (ch. 2): « Matter belongs to those which (are) for something; for another matter (is) for another form ». But in the

book, ON PREDICAMENTS, ch. "*On Relation*", Aristotle defines relatives, or those which are for something, as: Whatsoever that which they are, are said to be of others and/or, in any manner your please, in another manner for the other. — See more on that which neither by matter nor by form is its own respect, above in d. 3, p. II, q. 3, 4th opposed argument, and also the solution on p. 87. — A little below this after (in the English before) the word *form* [forma], the Vatican edition, together with codex cc, breaking with the other codices and edition 1, reads *nor is form it own looking-back* [nec forma est suus respectus], and below this for *they do not have* [non habent] it substitutes *it does not have* [non habet].

[7] ON THE TRINITY, Bk. VII, ch. 1, n. 2: Every essence, which is said relatively, is also something, except the relative. Cf. also ON THE CITY OF GOD, Bk. XI, ch. 10. — A little above this, codex T read *is a pure looking-back* [respectus est purus].

[8] Which is impossible. Cf. Aristotle, PHYSICS, text 10 ff. (ch. 2), where he proves six reasons similar to this, namely, that movement is not of a movement, nor is generation of a generation, nor is change of a change. One reason is, that if change is of a change, one must establish an infinite regression [processus in infinitum], which is repugnant.

relative property, whether it be in God or in a creature, necessarily differs in some manner from that of which it is the property, and more so in the creature than in the Creator. And all these (Names) are understood, just as has been assigned before, since every respective (name) is founded upon something absolute.

SCHOLIUM

I. In this question *personal properties* are accepted in the broader sense, to the extent that they are opposed to *essential properties*; whence even *innascible* and *active spiration* are numbered among the personal properties. However, below in d. 28, q. 3 *personal properties* are called those, which both *distinguish* and *constitute* a Person. For there it is said: « For this, that any relation be *personal*, it is necessary that it mean the *first* and *proper* habitude of that Person and (these) through a manner of *positing* and completion ». In this sense *innascibility* and *active spiration* are not *personal* properties.

A twofold question is treated here. The first is, whether among the Divine Person *there are* properties; on the other hand, the second, by which reckoning *are they distinguished* among themselves and from a Person. In affirming the first question catholic theologians agree. On the second question there were diverse sentences, which here and more accurately below in d. 33, q. 1, are reviewed. The sentence posited first in the Response of d. 33 is attributed to (Peter) Praepositivus (cf. above d. 4, dubium 3, p. 105, footnote 3), but by (Bl.) Dionysius the Carthusian to (William) of Auxerre, which (sentence) the Nominalists also professed. These did not admit among a property and a Person and the Essence but a distinction of *reckoning alone* or according to a manner of speaking; whence, retaining the name for a property, they removed the thing (which it is). This opinion is reproved by St. Bonaventure, by Alexander of Hales, by St. Thomas, by (Bl. John Duns) Scotus and by others. — Gilbert of Porretain went in the opposite direction, by teaching that there is to be posited a properly, *real* distinction There, asserting as he did, that the properties are not of a Person nor in the Persons, but *assisting* the Persons (cf. d. 33, q. 1). — On this distinction not a few things are said above in d. 13, q. 3, in the Scholium; but here there will a more accurate investigation of the sentence of the Seraphic Doctor, *by which reckoning* the properties are distinguished from a Person, from the Essence, and among themselves, when there are many properties in the same Person.

II. The *manner of speaking* concerning the nature of this distinction, which St. Bonaventure uses, differs to a little extent from that, which is not common in the Schools.

1. It is often said by the Seraphic Doctor, that the properties in the same Person differ among themselves *really* (cf. here in the 5th argument of the fundament; d. 13, q. 3, d. 33, q. 1). The word *really* [realiter] least of all ought to be understood in the sense of a *real* distinction and *absolutely*. This is manifest in many passages, such as here in reply to n. 3; d. 33, q. 1; d. 25, a. 1, q. 2; d. 7, q. 3; d. 19, p. II, q. 2, in reply to n. 4. Moreover, this distinction is called *real*, because it is greater than that which belongs to a *purely virtual reckoning*; yet it does not convey an *absolute* reality, but (only) a *relative* one, that is, a looking-back to diverse termini. Which to understand better, one must attend to the *threefold* manner of speaking (about the Divine Persons), here at the end of the Response, namely the *essential*, the *personal* and the *notional* (manners). The *notional* manner is, when the predicate does not convene, either with One nor with Three, but only with Two Persons, v. g. *the Father and the Son spirate*; but when there is said, *"the Father generates"*, then the manner of speaking is *personal*. On the diverse manners of speaking among the divine more is said in d. 22, q. 4, in reply to n. 5. — Also one must note, that this is not a difference, neither *substantial* nor *accidental*, because, as is well observed in d. 13, q. 3, in reply to n. 5, « among the divine there is a difference of the relations, which is neither accidental, nor substantial, but rather is said (to be one) of origin ».

2. Therefore, the distinction between a property and a Person is described by the Seraphic Doctor (d. 33, q. 1, at the end of the body of the question), thus: « A property is a Person and in a Person, because it is the same through its essence or *manner of being* [modum essendi], yet it differs as much as regards the *manner of being regarded* ». Ibid., q. 2, in reply to n. 2: « A property distinguishes in this, that (it is) different not according to *essence*, but according to *manner*; which *manner* does not mean a composition, because it passes over into the Substance, not means only an understanding, because it is

a *thing* and remains *in respect of (its) object* » (or to its terminus). And of the distinction between a property and the Essence there is said (d. 19, p. II, q. 2, in reply to n. 4): « That paternity is according to *thing* not other than the Essence, yet it is other according to *reckoning* ... and that reckoning through a comparison to the Essence is naught but a *manner* (that is, of being regarded), but through a comparison to another Person it is a *thing* ». This formula he often repeats, as in d. 22, q. 4, in the body of the question; cf. d. 13, q. 3. Alexander of Hales speaks in the same manner, in his SUMMA., p. I, q. 68, m. 1; and so does Richard of Middleton, here in q. 1, and (Bl. John Duns) Scotus and others.

3. What this difference according to *thing* and a *manner of being regarded* is, is determined more (precisely) here in the solution to n. 2, which must be consulted together with the other passage above in d. 22, q. 4. For there is distinguished a threefold grade, by which something can *differ by a reckoning*. The *first* grade turns about absolute attributes and is « on the part of our apprehension », and « nothing responds to it on the part of the thing ». These words are to be understood precisely of the *actual difference*, but not of the *foundation* of the difference apprehended by us, as is manifestly established from those (things), which are read above in d. 22, q. 2, at the end (cf. above d. 8, p. II, q. 2, Scholium). The *second* grade is « according to the difference of attribution », which obtains between the Essence, a Person and a notion. The *third* grade is a *real* distinction, but only according to a *relation*, and this is between Persons and personal properties regarding themselves.

From the text itself it is manifest, that St. Bonaventure teaches, that there is a *greater* distinction between the Essence and the properties or Persons, than that which is commonly said to be a *virtual* one, which is between absolute attributes regarding themselves and regarding the Essence, but that the same is *less*, than that which is between the Persons Themselves. The reason, why a difference of *attribution* is greater than the difference of the first grade, posited in that (grade), is because a *property* has a relation to an other, which *the Essence* does not have; and this *manner of being regarded* is not only in our intellect, but also in the part of the thing. With eloquent words the Seraphic Doctor asserts this, below in d. 27, p. I, q. 3, in reply to nn. 1, 2 and 3, saying: the paternity « as much as regards the comparison to the subject is entirely the same, for that reason in no manner is it abstractable on the part of the thing. Nevertheless, it can still differ in some manner through a comparison to (its) object, *which difference, indeed, is taken on the part of the thing* » (cf. d. 33, q. 2 in reply to n. 2). But this difference of reckoning conveys least of all a composition in God, because « the paternity is according to *the thing* not other than the Essence, yet it is other according to a *reckoning*. And if you object: that either something in the thing [in re] responds to that reckoning, or nothing; it must be said, that that reckoning through a comparison to the Essence, is naught, but a manner (of being regarded), but through a comparison to the other *Person* it is a thing. And this is clear, since *"to have an essence from another"* (such as it is in the Son) and *"to have it not from another"* (such as it is in the Father) mean a real difference, because no thing is from itself and from another ». Thus does St. Bonaventure speak above in d. 19, p. II, q. 2, in reply to n. 4, which is explained more in d. 5, a. 1, q. 1, in reply to n. 1, and below in d. 34, q. 1, and q. 2, in reply to n. 7. Moreover, that the difference of *attribution* is less than the difference of the third grade, is already clear through itself and is reviewed in the same cited passage.

4. St. Thomas, as we know, does not distinguish the difference of *attribution* with express words as a middle grade of difference among the first and second kind; but he expresses the same doctrine with these words (SUMMA., I, q. 28, a. 2, in corp.): « A relation really existing in God is the same as the Essence according to thing, and does not differ except according to a reckoning of understanding, insofar as in a relation there is conveyed a looking-back to its opposite, which is not conveyed in the Name for the Essence ». The words in this passage: "according to a reckoning of understanding" [secundum intelligentiae rationem], are not understood of the distinction of the reckoning of reasoning, which is very clear from the words themselves (SENT., Bk. I, d. 2, a. 1, a. 2):

« It remains, that they are diverse by a reckoning, not only on the part of reasoning itself, but from the property of the thing itself ».

(Bl. John Duns) Scotus, (SENT., Bk. I, d. 2, q. 7, n. 41, and QUODLIBETALS., 5 § *Circa tamen*) here uses his own *formal* distinction, which he, as Brülifer (on this passage) would have it, formed from the distinction of *attribution*, which St. Bonaventure here and above in d. 8, p. II, in reply to n. 4, and in d. 13, q. 3, taught. Bartholomew de Barbieri (CURSUS THEOLOGICUS, tome I, disputation 13, p. 210) rightly says, that he faultily and contrary to very many interpreters of the clear words of the Seraphic (Doctor), reduced that distinction of *attribution* to a *pure virtual* distinction. Likewise, Bartholomew observes concerning the dividing line between (Bl.) Scotus' *formal* distinction from the nature of the thing and St. Bonaventure's distinction of *attribution* the following: « Scotus would have it, that there is an absolute formality, or distinction between formalities; but St. Bonaventure, that it is only according to a *comparison*, or according to a diverse manner of being regarded, for this that a relation among the divine according to a reckoning of "*in*" (that is, to the extent that it is in the Nature) is identified formally with It, but retains a *looking-back to its object* [respectum ad obiectum], and thus differs through that comparison to it ».

III. In the solution to n. 6 there is distinguished a threefold manner of immediate relation, namely, a relation *through the essential*, relation of *correlatives*, a relation of a relation, concerning which one can confer SENT., Bk. II, d. 1, p. I, a. 3, q. 2. One must also note the difference between a *relation*, which is a *reckoning* of being referred, a *relative*, which is formally referred, such as a father is to his son, and a *related*, which is the fundament of a relation itself, such as the *man* in the father and the son.

IV. Alexander of Hales, SUMMA., p. I, q. 68, m. 1. — (Bl. John Duns) Scotus, in each edition, here in q. 1. — St. Thomas, SENT., Bk. I, d. 33, q. 1, a. 2, and here in q. 2, a. 1 and 3; SUMMA., I, q. 28, a. 1, and q. 40, a. 1. — (Bl.) Peter of Tarentaise, here in. q. 2, a. 1. — Richard of Middleton, here in a. 3, q. 1. — Giles the Roman, here in 2nd. princ., q. 1 and 2. — Henry of Ghent, SUMMA., a. 55, q. 1. — (Bl.) Dionysius the Carthusian, on this and the follow question, here in q. 1, and in d. 27, q. 1.

QUESTION II

What, among the divine, are the properties of the Persons?

Second, there is asked, concerning the properties, *what* they are. And that they are relations, seems:

1. Because (St.) Hilary (of Poitiers) says in the twelfth (chapter) ON THE TRINITY:[1] « It is proper to the God (who has been) born that He be a son »; but filiation is a relation: ergo etc..

2. Likewise, (St. John) Damascene (says):[2] « We say, that the Divine Hypostasis of the Word, in a manner (belongs) to the nativity and in habitude differs from the Hypostasis of the Father »; but a manner of habitude is a relation: ergo etc..

3. Likewise, Richard of Saint Victor in (his) book, ON THE TRINITY[3] says, that the Persons are distinguished by the property of origin; but origin among the divine is not a movement, but a habitude, therefore, a relation: ergo etc..

4. Likewise, this very (thing) seems *by reason*, because the proper is what befits one alone [convenit soli];[4] but nothing absolute is incommunicable among the divine and befitting to one alone: therefore, every personal property is relative, ergo etc..

ON THE CONTRARY: 1. Just as paternity is a *relation*, so magnitude a *quantity*, and thus goodness a *quality*, but the Greatness of God is not a quantity, nor the Goodness a quality:[5] therefore, neither is the paternity (of the Father) a relation. But paternity is a property: ergo etc.. *If you say*, that it is not similar, because the others pass over into the Substance, a relation (does) not; the contrary is shown first in this manner:

2. Likewise, just as quantity is one genus of *accident*[6] distinct from substance, so also relation; but because in God there occurs no diversity, for that reason necessarily the genus of quantity passes over into the Substance, since There there is no accident nor a diversity of genera: therefore, for an equal reason relation (passes over similarly).

3. Likewise, just as God is His own greatness, so (is He His own)[7] paternity; but because God is His own Greatness, for that reason quantity (in God) does not differ from the Substance, but passes over into It: therefore, also the paternity similarly.

4. Likewise, it seems that relation passes over more, because between all general of accidents relation conveys a greater *dependence*, because (it exists) regarding subject and object; but God is entirely independent: therefore, a relation too remains least of all in God.

5. Likewise, among all the genera of beings relation has less of *entity*,[8] just as is clear, because it comes and goes [advenit et recedit] without a change of that which is referred; but in the Most High Being [summo ente] there ought be posited naught, but what has much of entity [multum de entitate]: ergo etc..

CONCLUSION

The properties of the Persons are relations.

I RESPOND: It must be said, that it is necessary that the personal properties (be) relations. And this for a twofold reason, both because they are incommunicable and befit one alone, and also because they really differ, as

---

[1] Number 15. See here the text of Master (Peter), ch. 3.

[2] ON THE ORTHODOX FAITH, Bk. III, ch. 7.

[3] Book IV, ch. 15: To no extent can They differ alternatively according to any property of quality; it remains, that They be believed to have some difference according to the manner of (Their) origin.

[4] Cf. above d. 8, p. I, a. 1, q. 1, p. 152, footnote 1.

[5] See above d. 8, p. II, dubium 4, and (St. Severinus) Boethius, ON THE TRINITY, ch. 4.

[6] The Vatican edition and codex cc omit *of accident* [accidentis].

[7] Supply with the Vatican edition: *is He His own* [Deus est sua].

[8] Cf. Aristotle, METAPHYSICS, Bk. XIV, ch. 3 (Bk. XIII, ch. 1), where this is proven at greater length; and Averroës in METAPHYSICS, Bk. XII, text 19, says: Because (a relation) belongs to a weaker "being" than the other predicaments, in which certain (authors) reputed, that it is from things understood second [ex secundis intellectis]. — On the reckoning cited next, cf. the preceding question, solution to n. 3. — Codices K V and cc and editions 2, 3, 4, 5 and 6 falsely read *to which it is referred* [ad quod refertur] for *which is referred* [quod refertur].

has been shown before.[1] But (of all the categories of predicament) relation alone remains among the divine.

For an understanding of which, it must be noted, that relation in some (things) *convenes* with other genera,[2] in some (things) *it differs*. For *it convenes* in that, which is a predicament and a genus of being, and in that which is an accident; and *it does not convene* [disconvenit] in that, which unlike [praeter] the other genera has a looking-back not only to the subject, but also to the object, according to a habitude and a dependence.

As much as regards the first conditions, it is impossible that relation remain among the divine, just as the other genera (do),[3] and this on account of the most high Simplicity. For in God relation is not a predicament nor an accident, but is the Substance. On the other hand, as much as regards the conditions, which it has in respect to (its) *Object*, it is necessary that it *remain* in a certain manner, that is, as much as regards a *habitude*,[4] and this on account of the true distinction (of Persons), which is among the divine, and the true origin and habitude (of the Persons); and it is necessary that it *not remain* in a certain manner, that is, as much as regards dependence, and this on account of the omnimodal absolution, which is among the divine. Therefore, the other genera pass over simply (into the Substance), but relation remains in a certain manner There, in a certain manner passes over. But beyond (this),[5] relation means a looking-back to (its) *object*, and ac-

cording to that looking-back it means the plurality (of Persons), which is truly among the divine; and thus relation remains. It is also clear, that it passes over in a certain manner (into the Substance), namely, as much as regard everything which means a composition. Whence, it is neither a genus, nor in a genus, not is it an accident, nor is it (something) else.

1. 2. 3. And thus are clear the first[6] three objections about this, because one is taken from the nature of a *genus*, the other from the nature of an *accident*, the third from the *predication of identity*. It is also clear, in what manner it remains, that is, as much as regards that which means a distinction, not as much as regards that which means a dependence and inclination, because in this manner the perfection of absolution deprives (these).

4. And through this is clear the fourth argument, which objects concerning the *dependence* of relation.

5. To that which is objected, that it has less of being [ente]; it must be said, that this is true, since it differs essentially from substance; but in God it is not so. — Yet, besides the aforesaid reason this reason could be given [reddi], that it does not pass over: for, because it has the least amount of being [minimum de ente], for that reason it causes the least and/or no composition, even when[7] it remains according to its own property. On the other hand, the others, which have something of absolute being [ente absoluto], cause a composition; and hence it is, that relation signifies more [melius valet] in the Most High Simple than any of the others.

SCHOLIUM

I. Besides the solution to the principal question, the nature of relation in common is also explained, not without the difference, which there is between relations in God and relations in creatures. — From this passage it manifestly appears that it is false, what some impose upon S. Bonaventure, namely, that he taught, that the Divine Persons are constituted through something absolute, concerning which, see the following Question, and d. 33, q. 1.

II. Alexander of Hales, Summa., p. I, q. 68, m. 2. — (Bl. John Duns) Scotus, Reportatio., Sent., Bk. I, d. 33, q. 3. — St. Thomas, Summa., I, q. 40, a. 1. — Bl. (now St.) Albertus (Magnus), here in a. 9. — (Bl.) Peter of Tarentaise, here in q. 2, a. 2. — Richard of Middleton, here in a. 4, q. 1. — Giles the Roman, here in 1st. princ., q. 2, and in d. 27, 1st. princ., q. 1.

QUESTION III

Whether the act of the personal properties is 'to distinguish the Hypostases',
or whether (it is) 'to show (that They are) distinct?

Third, there is asked, concerning the properties, as much as regards (their) act. And there is asked, whether the act[8] of properties of this kind is *to distinguish* the Hypostases, or *to shown that (They are) distinct*. And that it is *to distinguish*, seems:

1. Through (St. Severinus) Boethius, On the Trinity, (saying):[9] « Substance contains the Unity, relation multiplies the Trinity »: but, if it multiplies, therefore, it distinguishes.

2. Likewise, Richard of St. Victor, On the Trin-

---

[1] In the preceding Question.

[2] For *genera* [generibus] the Vatican edition, without the authority of the codices and edition 1, has *predicaments* [praedicamentis], i. e. with the supreme genera of things, which can be predicated of an individual, which (genera) are 10 (in number) according to Aristotle. — In place of *For* [enim], at the beginning of the next sentence, edition 1 has *Indeed* [quidem].

[3] The sense is: just as the other predicaments (in God) are identified with the Divine Essence, so also relation, both as much as regards (its) conditions, as will be said a little below, (and) as much as regards any condition special to it, namely, dependence. — Edition 1 immediately before this, after the word *just as* [sicut], aptly inserts *neither* [nec: because, inasmuch as the predicaments are the same according to thing with the Divine Essence, they do not remain].

[4] On the authority of the more outstanding manuscripts and edition 1, we have restores here *that is, as much as regards a habitude* [scil-

icet quantum ad habitudinem], which words are lacking in the Vatican ed..

[5] Codex V adds *this* [hoc]. Not much after this, for *it means the plurality (of the Persons), which is truly* [dicit pluralitatem, quae vere est], very many codd., such as F G M T Z aa bb & ff, read *it remains, what it truly is* [manet, qui vere est]; some codd., such as A H & R, omit *it means the plurality (of the Persons)* [dicit pluralitatem], thus exhibiting *which (looking-back)* [qui] for *which (plurality)* [quae]. A little below this, for *thus* [ita] cod. cc, with edd. 2, 3, 4, 5 and 6, reads *that* [illa].

[6] In very many codices and edition 1 there is lacking *first* [prima]. Next codex M has *against* [contra] for *about* [circa], and then codex Y reads *the second* [secundum] for *the other* [aliud].

[7] The Vatican edition, with only a few codd., reads badly *and yet* [et tamen] for *even when* [etiam cum]. Near the end of the solution, not a few codd., such as G H O & aa, and ed. 1, read *remains* [manet] for *signifies* [valet].

[8] In many codices and edition 1 there is read *whether it belongs to properties of this kind* etc. [utrum huiusmodi proprietatum sit].

[9] Chapter 6.

says,[1] that a Person is distinguished by the property of (His) origin; but a property means an origin and a relation: ergo etc..

3. Likewise, this very (thing) seems by *reason*,[2] because, since the Persons are distinguished, either They are distinguished through something *absolute*, or (something) *respective*.* Not through (something) *absolute*, because, just as (St.) Augustine would have it,[3] « what is said regarding It [ad se] is said as regards Each [singulis] »: therefore, it is necessary, that They do differ through something *respective*.

4. Likewise, the property of the Father either *accedes* to the Hypostasis Itself, or is *consubstantial* to It; wherefore if[4] it accedes, therefore there are some accidents There; therefore, there is some composition There. But, if it is *consubstantial* and connatural: therefore, since it is not consequent to the 'being' of the Hypostasis, it is not only the reason for (its) being made known [ratio innotescendi], but also for (its) being distinguished [distinguendi].

5. Likewise, in the Most High Simple the reason for being [ratio essendi] and for being cognized [cognoscendi] is the same; but the Person of the Father is most highly Simple: therefore, He is distinguished by the same, by which (His) being distinguished is cognized. But this is through (His) property: ergo etc..

ON THE CONTRARY: 1. Everything respective is led back [reducitur] to an absolute;[5] but what is reduced to something according to a reckoning of understanding is consequent to that (something): therefore, since the properties are respective,* the Hypostases absolute, the properties are lead back to the Hypostases: therefore, the Hypostases are prior.[6] But what is prior is not distinguished by that which is posterior, because by the same is (its) 'being' and (its) 'being distinct' [esse distinctum].

2. Likewise, everything[7] which distinguishes something, gives to it such a 'being', as it is and/or has; but the properties have of themselves only a respective 'being': therefore, if the Hypostases are distinguished through the properties, They have only a respective 'being'. But this is false, because since the Supposits are essential, They have an absolute 'being' for (Their) substance.

3. Likewise, among the Divine Persons the plurification is *through origin*, but the distinction (is) too. But "*origin*" means an emanation and/or going-forth; but a "*relation*" per se does not emanate without (something) else emanating first, because in an "*regarding something*" [ad aliquid] there is no movement:[8] therefore, a Hypostasis arises from a Hypostasis according to the reckoning of understanding before there is an understanding

that there is a relation. And if this, a relation is consequent to the 'being distinct' in the Hypostases: ergo etc..

4. Likewise, « everything which is said relatively, is something, except that which is relatively said », just as reason dictates, and (St.) Augustine says in the seventh book, ON THE TRINITY.[9] But the Father and the Son are said relatively: therefore, Each of Them is Something, except that which is relatively said; therefore, abstracting from relation, one happens to understand (that Each is) Something. I ask, therefore, what that is: either the Essence, or a Hypostasis. If the Essence, therefore, there is a relation in the Essence: therefore, it multiplies It. If a Hypostasis: therefore, either One, or Two. Not One, because it is impossible to understand, that the Father and the Son are one Hypostasis: therefore, (it is) two (Hypostases). And if this, it is clear that etc..

5. Likewise, abstracting from all the properties of two individuals, such as Peter and Paul, with only the hypostases remaining, one still happens to understand, that (their) distinction remains: therefore, for an equal reason in the Divine Hypostases. Which if (this) is true, then, therefore, (the properties) are[10] only a reason for (Their) being distinguished in regard to us.

CONCLUSION

The properties of the Persons are the reckonings not only by which the distinction (of the Persons) is manifested, but also by which (the Persons) are distinguished.

I RESPOND: It must be said, that about this was a twofold opinion. For certain (authors) said, that abstracting from the properties, it is impossible to understand the Hypostases as distinct, because properties of this kind among the divine not only give the Persons (Their) 'being made known' [innotescere], nay they also give (Them Their) '*being*';[11] whence with these borne away [abstractis], (Their) '*being*' and '*being distinct*' is borne away.

The opinion of the others was, that abstracting from the properties, there is still an understanding of distinction among the Hypostases, since the properties, according to them, are not the reckoning by which They are distinguished [ratio distinguendi] according to thing, but (rather are the reckoning whereby Their) distinction is manifested [distinctionem manifestandi].[12] Whence they say, that abstracting from the paternity and filiation, one still happens to understand *one from another*, and *from one, the other*. — *And if your ask*, in way manner They are distinguished, they say,[13] that (They are) by Their very Selves, just as princi-

---

[1] Book. IV, ch. 15. See the previous Question, p. 455, footnote 3. — The minor of this argument is exhibited by nearly all the more ancient codices, with edition 1, thus: *but a habitude mans a relative origin* [sed habitude dicit originem relativum] (very many codices have *respective* [respectivum] for *relative* [relativum]; the reading of codex O is better: *but an origin means a relative habitude* [sed origo dicit habitudinem relativum]; but each reading here does not seem to be fitting; they seem to be taken from the 3rd. fundament of the preceding Question.

[2] The words *very (thing)* [ipsum] and *by reason* [ratione] are lacking in the more ancient codd. and ed. 1. With the Vatican edition we retain them, because they are customarily put there by the Seraphic Doctor.

[3] ON THE TRINITY, Bk V, ch. 8, n. 9: Whatever, therefore, God is said (to be) regarding Himself, is said of each Person singularly.

[4] Very many codd. with the Vatican ed., read *because if* [quia si].

[5] Aristotle, ETHICS, Bk. I, ch. 6: Moreover, that, which per se is also the substances, according to this, that it regards something, is prior to the nature; for it seems that this is a certain appendix and accident of that which is.

[6] Edition 1 adds *to the properties* [proprietatibus]. Next, in place of *is distinguished by that* [distinguitur eo], nearly all the codices, together with the first six editions, read *is distinguished from that* [distinguitur ab eo], which sounds bad in Latin; better the reading of codex O: *is distinguished through that* [distinguitur per illud].

[7] In many codd. there is *what* [quod] for *everything which* [omne quod], and, a little below this, after *But this* [Sed hoc], *is* [est] is lacking.

[8] Aristotle, PHYSICS, Bk. V, text 19 (ch. 2).   [9] Ch. 1, n. 2.

[10] Codices F P and Q substitute *are naught but* [non sunt nisi] for *are* [sunt], which reading very many codices favor, with the first six editions, by exhibiting *are not* [non sunt], but omitting faultily the *but* [nisi].

[11] Understand: *personal 'being'* [esse personale].

[12] The words *(rather are the reckoning whereby Their) distinction is manifested* [distinctionem manifestandi] are wanting in the Vatican edition: we have restored them from the older mss. and edition 1.

[13] Among whom is (Peter) Praepositivus. — Following on the next page we have restored *genera* [genera] from codex T.

---

* *Trans. note*: What is *respective* has the quality of *looking-back to* or of *respecting* or *regarding* another; and so, what is related to another, is related in a respective manner or under a certain respect.

-ples and the most general genera are distinguished and differ by their very selves. Whence this is the immediate (conclusion of their reasoning): the Substance is not a quantity.

And if we consider (the matter) interiorly, each opinion contains something of probability; and this is clear in this manner. For in the Divine Hypostases we understand an *origin* or emanation, we also understand a *habitude*. According to the reckoning of understanding an *origin* precedes that which originates [oritur]; and according to the reckoning of understanding a *habitude*[1] is consequent to that which is referred. Therefore, a relative property can convey solely a *habitude*; and in this manner it is consequent to a reckoning of distinction and is a reckoning whereby the distinction *is made known*, not of *distinguishing*, just as the second opinion says, and the reasons induced for the second part, concerning relation itself, prove. For a distinction can then be understood, because *one is understood from another*, and *from one, another*. — A property can also convey *each*, namely, a *habitude* and an *origin*; and then not only is it a reckoning whereby They are made known, but also (a reckoning whereby They) are distinguished. For with the *origin* or emanation excluded, it is impossible to understand a plurality among the divine: nay, just as there is one Essence, so also there is understood one Hypostasis. And in this manner the first opinion and the reasons for the first part proceed.

But it must be noted, that since it is the same for the Divine[2] Persons *to originate* and *be* and *to hold Themselves to the Other*, yet according to the reckoning of understanding (these) are ordered, so that first is the *originating*, then the '*being*' is understood in those which have 'being' from another, and then *holding oneself to the other*. But because they are the same in God, for that reason they are designated by the same name. Whence the generation means an *origin* and a *habitude*, yet properly speaking the generation means the *origin*, and the paternity the *habitude*.[3] Since, therefore, a divine property according to the common usage of speaking conveys *habitude* and *origin*, for that reason it must be held, that the properties not only are the reckoning by which Their distinction is made known, but also by which They are distinguished.

1. And, to that which is objected, that (everything) respective is led back to an absolute; it must be said, that to be led back to something is in a twofold manner: either as to a *principle*, or as to a *terminus*. A property of origin in these two manners is lead back to an absolute: innascibility[4] is lead back to the Hypostasis of *the Father* as to a *principle*, but (it is led back) to the Hypostasis of *the Begotten* and of *the Spirit* as to a *terminus*. Since, therefore, what is led back to something as to a *principle* is consequent to it, for that reason, abstracting

from the origin, solely God is understood as *innascible*, not being from another, and thus in a unity of hypostasis. On the other hand, because what is led back to something[5] as to a *terminus*, is understood to precede; hence it is, that abstracting from the origin, there is not yet an understanding of the preceding Hypostasis. — *And/or* that must be understood, where "respective" means a dependence by reason of which[6] it fails from a most high simplicity, that it is not in God.

2. To that which is objected, that (something) respective only gives a respective 'being'; it must be said, that this is true of the "respective", which means only a habitude; but it is not true of the "respective", which means an origin.

3. To that which is objected, that a relation does not arise through itself; it must be said, that *relation* is a property, according to which it is itself, but *origin* (is a property), insofar as it is that which originates; and because an origin properly does not originate,[7] but is that by which the one originating originates, such that it is not consequent, by time and/or by nature, but according to the reckoning of understanding, it is either necessarily *together* and/or *precedes* it. For this reason that (objection) is clear.

4. To that which is objected, that everything which is said relatively is *something*, except that which is said relatively;[8] it must be said, that it does not have truth in (what is) most highly simple, that 'to be' and 'to be referred' so differ, that one can be separated from the other according to *thing* — because there is one (thing) There — but[9] only according to *our intellect*; nor still, does our intellect abstract in this manner, that it understands distinct hypostases, abstracting from properties and relations. For if from the Hypostases of the Father paternity is abstracted, and/or the other way around, it already does not have[10] something *special*, which is the principle for understanding it: and thus it is considered under a *general* and incomplete *reckoning*. Whence also they seem to me to speak well, who says, that the understanding of this name, "*thing*", remains, according to which it is a *general* term [vocabulum]. And in this manner *it is clear*, that, abstracting from the properties, there remains no distinction, neither in thing nor in understanding; and for that reason in each manner they are a reckoning of distinguishing.

5. To that which is objected, that Peter and Paul are understood to be distinguished, abstracting from (their) properties; it must be understood, that it is not similar. For there, there is a distinction on the part of their own matter and their own form, which is made known through accidental properties; but among the divine there is only a distinction through origin. For that reason that (objection) is clear.

---

[1] The Vatican edition alone reads *relation* [habitudo].

[2] Very many codices, such as F H X Z bb ee, read *in the Divine* [in divinis] in place of *for the Divine* [divinis]; codex cc together with editions 2, 3, 4, 5 and 6 read *among the divine* [in divinis] in place of *for the Divine Persons* [divinis personis].

[3] Cf. below d. 27, p. I, q. 1 at the end of the body of the question.

[4] Thus the Vatican edition, which we follow contrary to the reading of the manuscripts and edition 1,which have *innascible* [innascibilis].

[5] The Vatican edition together with codex cc has *another* [aliud].

[6] In place of *by reason of which* [ratione cuius] codex T has *for then* [tunc enim].

[7] Very many of the more ancient codices omit *and because an origin properly does not originate* [et quia origo proprie non oritur], faultily substituting *origin (is) not (a property)* [origo non] for the previous *but*

origin (is a property) [origo vero]. Next, some codices, such as F I T, have *it follows* [sequitur] for *is consequent* [consequitur].

[8] The more ancient codices, with edition 1, read more briefly in this manner: *it objected, that (everything) is something, except what is relatively said* [obiicitur, quod est aliquid excepto quod relative dicitur].

[9] Nearly all the codices, together with edition 1, read *except* [nisi] for *but* [sed]; less congruently. A little above this, after the verb *be separated* [separari], the Vatican edition, together with not a few codices, adds *or be abstracted* [sive abstrahi].

[10] The Vatican edition, not trusting in the codices and edition 1, reads *there is already not had* [iam non habetur] for *it already does not have* [iam non habet], and a little before this, supported by only a few codices, it reads *were abstracted* [abstraheretur] for *is abstracted* [abstrahatur].

SCHOLIUM

I. To 'difference' three acts are attributed, namely, to divide a genus, to constitute a species, to distinguish. Hence there is the occasion of asking, which acts among the divine does a personal property have, which is a quasi locus of difference. That first act of dividing a genus is manifestly impossible in God. But of the other two acts one can inquire, whether, that is, the properties both distinguish and constitute the Hypostases, or as adventive denominations [quasi adventitiae] only manifest the Hypostases as already distinct, such as the name, "Socrates", notes a person already distinct. This question coincides nearly with the most difficult, and more subtle than useful, question, through what precisely are the Divine Persons constituted. But since a right understanding and solution of many questions in Distinctions 27, 29 and 33, depends on this question, not a few things seem to have to be said, first of the status of the question, then of the principal sentences of the masters.

II. For clarifying the state of the question, we note the following:

1. In God four (things) are distinguished: the absolute Divine Nature; the immediate Principles of the two emanations, which are the (Divine) Intellect and Will; the emanations themselves or the origins; and next the relations, both subsistent and formal, which are the quasi termini of those emanations or origins.

2. The (Divine) Nature is absolute and without relation to anything; the (Divine) Intellect and Will are also absolute, yet regard in some manner the Emanations Themselves, of which They are the Principles. The emanations or origins are in Themselves, indeed, not something relative, but are themselves « a certain way to a Person » (St. Thomas, SUMMA., I, q. 40, a. 2 and 4.

3. In the divine the reckoning of a Hypostasis is relative. Moreover, since in every relation there must be distinguished a fundament of the relation (the 'being in' [esse in]) and the relation itself (the 'being to' [esse ad]), even the divine relations are considered, both to the extend that they consist in the Divine Nature, and to the extent that they are referred to one another. But under this last respect they are naught but something relative; however, under the first, (they are) in a certain manner something absolute.

4. It is entirely established, that the Divine Persons are not constituted, neither through the Nature, nor through the Intellect or Will; therefore, three remains only the two reckonings, of which one can ask, whether they, that is, the origins and relations, are distinctive and constitutive of the Persons, and indeed these according to a 'being in' and a 'being to'.

III. There are diverse sentences defended concerning the question thus proposed.

1. (Peter) Praepositivus, whom Peter Lombard favors, and others, thought, that the Persons are distinguished through (Their) origins alone; moreover, that the properties do not distinguish the Persons, but show (that They are) distinct. This opinion, according to the passage in the posited response, is reproved by St. Thomas and (Bl. John Duns) Scotus, and it is not approved by St. Bonaventure, regardless of what not a few have said, contradicting the explicit words of the Seraphic Doctor.

St. Thomas, (Bl.) Scotus and others commonly hold the opinion posited in the first place, that the Persons are both constituted and distinguished through the relative properties. The same sentence does St. Bonaventure support, as is proven especially from the last proposition of the Response. Yet he himself so explains it, that he demonstrates that there is something of truth also in the second sentence.

2. In the latter explanation of this sentence in the manner of speaking of the principle doctors, which we judge to agree entirely in the manner, there is not a little discrepancy, and what is surprising, that the latter expositors of St. Bonaventure, St. Thomas and (Bl.) Scotus understand their words in a different sense. — Not a few gravely judged that (Bl.) Scotus, taught with John of Ripa, that the Persons are constituted through something absolute. But from the words of (Bl.) Scotus himself (SENT., Bk. I, d. 2, q. 2 and 4; d. 28, q. 3; REPORTATIO., d. 26, q. 1) and from his better commentators it is established, that he holds the common opinion, that the Persons are constituted through the relations. Moreover, John of Ripa, in a sense different from that, which the censors of this opinion suppose, admits it as probable (cf. REPORTATIO, here in q. 3; Rada, controversy 23, Macedo, collation 7, difference 4, sections 4-5). How-

ever, in not a few more special matters Scotus dissents from both St. Thomas and St. Bonaventure, concerning which his Commentators can be consulted.

3. St. Thomas (SUMMA., I, q. 40, a. 2) reproves the opinion of (Peter) Praepositivus and adds: « Whence it is better said, that the Persons or Hypostases are distinguished by the relations through (Their) origin. For though They are distinguished in each manner, yet prior and more principally (are they such) through the relations according to the manner of understanding » (cf. ibid., a. 2, and SENT., Bk. I, d. 26, q. 2, a. 2). — However, in what manner do the relations constitute the Persons? To explain this St. Thomas (ibid., a. 4) uses the distinction between a property, to the extent that it is a relation, which presupposes a notional act, and a property, to the extent that it is constitutive of a Person and is understood before the notional act. This distinction is impugned by (Bl.) Scotus (SENT., I, d. 28, q. 3); but the sentence of St. Thomas is not expounded in the same manner by his commentators, who can be consulted concerning this matter.

4. To St. Bonaventure there is faulty imputed by many authors the opinion of John of Ripa, that the Persons are distinguished through (Their) origin alone and through something absolute; nay it is asserted by the same, that Scotus himself (here in q. 1, nn. 23 and 24) thus understood St. Bonaventure. Among these, Lychetus says on this passage: « It belongs to the Divine Bonaventure and John of Ripa »; even Cajetan (commenting on St. Thomas' SUMMA, I, q. 40, a. 2) reprehends (Bl.) Scotus, for having falsely attributed this sentence to St. Bonaventure. But in truth neither did St. Bonaventure teach this, nor did (Bl.) Scotus reprove him for it: cf. the author of the Scholia and of the marginal notes in the edition of (Bl. John Duns) Scotus' works, Lyon: 1639, and Macedo, collation 7, difference 4, Prologue. Whence it must be said, that Scotus neither asserted that of St. Bonaventure, nor disproved his genuine sentence. For (loc. cit.) after he pronounced the sentence, « that the properties, according to which they are habitudes, do not distinguish the Persons, but according to which they are origins (do) », adds: « Which word, though perhaps he himself did not understand it in this manner, can be expounded (to say), that the origins do not distinguish the persons formally, but in a quasi beginning manner [principiative] ». And in d. 28, q. 3, n. 3 he says, that an origin is a quasi way to a Person; then he subjoins: « Yet, if that way is understood concerning the distinguishing in a quasi beginning manner of any corresponding effective cause in creatures, just as has been expounded in d. 26, neither would this argument be against that one ».

The genuine sentence of St. Bonaventure does not differ from the common sentence, except in this, that (to in some manner sanely expound the opinion of the ancient doctors, especially Master Peter) he holds a middle way in the manner of speaking, namely, that the Persons are constituted both through (Their) origins, and through (Their) properties: through (Their) origins, indeed, inchoatively, through (Their) relations formally. Moreover, he understands relations, not to the extent that they are bare relations, but with (their) origins, and again (he understands) the origins not without the relations. This assertion of our is already sufficiently clear from the collection of those thing which are proffered in the body of the question and in reply to nn. 1, 2, and 4; in d. 27, p. I, q. 2; and in d. 28, q. 2, and peremptorily is proven authentic by the interpretation of his own sentence, which the Seraphic Doctor gives below in his own Preface to the Prologue of Book II of his COMMENTARIA, where he speaks of the question treated below in d. 27, p. I, q. 2 (see the Scholium). With St. Bonaventure there is in agreement, besides (Bl.) Dionysius the Carthusian, Richard of Middleton, who reconciles the two opinions touched upon, in his response, saying, that the emanations are the quasi effective principle of the distinction of the Persons, but the relations (are) the formal principles of it. St. Thomas, as is clear from the passage cited above from him, namely SUMMA., I, q. 40, a. 2, teaches the same thing.

IV. Alexander of Hales, SUMMA., p. I, q. 58, m. 7. — (Bl. John Duns) Scotus, here in q. sole, and in d. 28, q. 3; REPORTATIO., here in q. 2. — St. Thomas, here in q. 2, a. 2; q. 1. a. 2; SUMMA., loc. cit. — Bl. (now St.) Albertus (Magnus), here in a. 5. — (Bl.) Peter of Tarentaise, here in q. 2, a. 3. — Richard of Middleton, here in a. 3, q. 2. — Giles the Roman, here in 1st. princ., q. 2 and 3. — Henry of Ghent, SUMMA., a. 36, q. 3. — Durandus (of Saint-Pourçain), here in q. 1. — (Bl.) Dionysius the Carthusian, here in q. 2 and 3. — (Gabriel) Biel, here in q. 1. and ff..

QUESTION IV

How many properties of Persons are there among the divine?

Fourth and last, there is the question [quaeritur] concerning the properties, as much as regards (their) *number*. And it seems:

1. That *they are infinite*, because the properties are the respects, through which God is made known to us; but those are infinite, just as is clear concerning[1] ideal respects: ergo etc..

2. Likewise, the Father and the Son are likened to one Another according to all essential conditions [conditiones essentiales]; therefore, according to all (essential conditions) They are compared and, according to all, They are made known to us; but those are indefinite in number: ergo etc..

3. Likewise, by as much something is more simple, by so much does it have more respects [respectus],[2] such as a point (has more respects) than a line, and a line than a surface; but the Divine "Being" is most simple: therefore, in It there are infinite respects. But all are a reckoning of being made known [ratio innotescendi]: therefore, the notions are infinite.

4. But that *there are only three*, seems through (St. John) Damascene,[3] who says, that among the divine all are one besides the generation, the non-generation [ingenerationem] and the procession; but those are naught but three properties: ergo etc..

5. Likewise, it seems *by reason*, because a property is convertible [convertitur] with that of which it is a property;[4] but a property is of a Person: therefore as many as there are Persons, there are properties and not more. But the Persons are three: ergo etc..

6. Likewise, let this reckoning be made: every Person is any of the three properties[5] — this is true — every notion is a Person, therefore, every property or notion is any of the Three: ergo etc..

But that *there are three more*, is shown in this manner:

1. The notions or properties are relations. But in every habitude there are two relations according to the two extremes; but among the divine there are two origins: therefore, (there are) at least four relations.

2. Likewise, a property is what befits one alone;[6] but innascibility befits the Father alone: therefore, it is

a property. And it is none of those four relations: therefore, there are five.

There is sought [quaeritur], therefore, the *sufficiency* and *number* of the notions among the divine, and *from within what* are they accepted, and whether there is the *same* number of properties and relations.

CONCLUSION

Properly speaking, among the divine, there are four relations and properties, and five notions; in a less strict sense the Names are confounded and they have an equal number, five.

I RESPOND: It must be understood regarding that *last* (objection), that[7] a difference of meaning [vim] is accustomed to be made among these three nouns: "*property*", "*relation*" and "*notion*". For (something) is said (to be) a "*property*", inasmuch as (something) convenes to (one) alone: a "*relation*", inasmuch as it means a habitude to another, a "*notion*", inasmuch as it is a principle of being cognized. And because every property is a reckoning of being cognized,[8] similarly also every relation; for that reason the name for a notion is in more than those two. Because a certain *property* is a relation, such as paternity; a certain one (is) not, such as innascibility, which does not mean a looking-back, but deprives (this); similarly, a certain *relation* is a property, such as filiation, a certain one (is) not, such as active spiration — for this reason, that it befits More, not One alone — and[9] hence it is, that the name for a *property* and a *relation* hold themselves as ones exceeding and ones exceeded. But the name for a *notion* is in more. Whence there are more notions than properties, even more than relations. But the *properties* and *relations* mutually and equally go forth from themselves [se excedunt]; for that reason they are equal in number.

Yet, one is not bound to make (this) difference of meaning. For every *relation* distinguish in some manner from another, and, thus, is in some manner *a property*. Similarly, everything which distinguishes, in some manner conveys *a relation*, therefore, every *relation* (is) a property, and every *property* a relation. But every *notion* is a property and/or a relation: therefore, every

---

[1] Cf. below d. 35, q. 5. — The Vatican edition, together with one or the other codex, reads *from* [ex] for *concerning* [de].

[2] Thus Avicenna, if you accept what Bl. (now St.) Albertus (Magnus) says in his SUMMA., p. I, tr. 9, q. 39, m. 1.

[3] ON THE ORTHODOX FAITH, Bk. I, ch. 8: And again, on account of the Father, the Son has whatever the Spirit also has, that is, on account of this, that the Father has these, yet, provided that [modo] you except the properties of 'unbegotten', of 'begotten', and of 'procession'. For in these personal properties the Three Persons of the Holy Trinity are distinguished amongst Themselves, not according to the Essence, but by (that which is) peculiar to any discrete Person, known in a manner undivided (from the Others). — Cf. also ibid., Bk. III, ch. 5, which is cited below in the text of Master (Peter), d. XXVII, ch. 3.

[4] Aristotle, TOPICS, Bk. I, ch. 4, and Porphyry, ON THE PREDICABLES, ch. "*On the Proper*". — Next, the Vatican edition, together with codex cc, omits the conclusion: *therefore, as many*

as there are Persons, there are properties and not more [ergo quot sunt personae, tot sunt proprietates et non plures], which conclusion is extant in the more ancient manuscripts.

[5] In the Vatican edition alone there is wanting *properties* [proprietatum]. A little further below this, the codices and edition 1 have *but* [sed] for *therefore* [igitur]. But since the argumentation is confounded by this reading, we have retained the text of the Vatican edition, especially because this argument is proposed in nearly the same form in Alexander of Hales, SUMMA., p. I, q. 68. m. 3.

[6] Cf. above, d. 8, p. I, a. 1, q. 1, p. 152, footnote 1.

[7] The Vatican edition, contrary to the older codices and edition 1, reads more briefly: *It must be noted that* [Notandum quod].

[8] Cf. above, d. 8, p. I, a. 1, q. 1, p. 152, footnote 1.

[9] It would be better to omit *and* [et] or by putting it after *hence it is* [hinc] read it as *also* [et]. Perhaps this arose a weakness in the codices, on account of the prior *for this reason* [ideo].

notion is a property and similarly a relation. And thus by an *extended* name they are equal; for that reason both the *number* and the *reckoning* of assigning the number is the same in all these names.

It must be understood, therefore,[1] that about the *number* of the properties there were three opinions. Certain (authors) said, that they are *infinite*; certain ones, that (there are) *three*; certain ones, that (there are) *five*. — But the reason for this[2] diverse opinion was, that they considered the notions *in a diverse manner* [diversimode]. Those who considered them in comparison to those by which they are made known, said, that they are infinite, because through infinite comparisons and similitudes and respects God is made known to us. — Those, however, who considered (them) in comparison to the Hypostases, which are distinguished and/or made known, said, that there are only three, because there are only Three Persons; for that reason They have[3] only three things proper [tres propria], through which They are sufficiently made known. — Those, however, who considered (them) through a comparison to the reckonings, by which they are made known, said, that there are five.

For the reckoning of *being made known* and of *distinguishing* is the same. But the reckoning of being distinguished is accepted on the part of the origin: therefore, either *positively*, or *privatively*. If *privatively*; either it deprives the origin through a manner of *one producing*, and this does not mean a nobility, that is, 'to not produce' (does not mean some quality of nobility), for that reason it is not a notion; or it deprives the origin through a manner of *one produced*, and this either *specially*, and/or *generally*. If *specially*, it does not mean a nobility; if *generally*, thus it does mean a nobility; and thus there is only one *notion*.[4] But if it is accepted on the part of an origin *positively*, since there is a twofold origin, and to any (of the two) there responds of necessity a twofold habitude; of necessity there will be four, namely, active and passive generation, and active and passive spiration; and all together [universo] five.[5]

The first opinion took up the reckoning in a more distant manner [magis a longinquo], and for that reason it receded more from the truth; the second, in a more proximate one [magis de proponquo], and for that reason it approached the truth more; the third, (did) just as it ought to, and for that reason it posited and found the truth. And this is the position, which the common opinion of the masters holds, that there are five notions; and the reason for this has already [prior] been seen.

1. 2. 3. To that, therefore, which is objected concerning *infinite* respects and comparisons, it must be said, that neither properties nor relations are notions, except those which convey a respect distinguishing a Person from a Person, and this is the respect of origin, because one can only compare (Them) in five manners, pertaining [spectantibus] to dignity; for that reason that (objection) is clear.

4. To that which is objected, that (there are) only *three*, through the word of (St. John) Damascene; it must be said, that under "generation" he comprehends the two generations,[6] similarly under "procession".

5. To that which is objected, that a property ought to be convertible [converti] with a Person; it must be said, that it is true of that which is the personal property, causing the Person to be a Person;[7] however, it does not follow, that if it is convertible, that there are so many, and not more, since one and the same can have many convertible (names).

6. To that which is objected concerning that syllogism, it must be said, that in that (logical) process there is a *fallacy of the accident*, just as here: 'the Father is the innascibility, and the Father is the paternity; therefore, the paternity is the innascibility'; because what is attributed to the subject or Hypostasis (of the Father) is attributed to the habitude (of the Same). — However, a *figure of speech* can be posited from the change in the manner of speaking, because among the divine the Essence is predicated as a *what*, a Person as a *who*, and a notion as a *of which*; and it proceeds from a Person to a notion.

SCHOLIUM

I. Under a twofold respect the Seraphic Doctor inquires concerning the *number* of the properties. For *first* the words "*property*", "*relation*", and "*notion*" are distinguished amongst themselves, and each one is accepted in its proper and strict sense (« a difference of meaning is accustomed to be made among these three nouns »); *second* those three words are accepted in an extended sense as synonyms (« Yet one is not bound to make this difference of meaning »). From these words the second part of the Response begins to the *last* question. But in the Vatican edition a new proposition indeed begins there. — According to the first way there are numbered four properties and five relations, but (also) five notions; according to the other, second way the number "five" befits those three words. — (Bl. John Duns) Scotus (SENT., Bk. I, d. 28, q. 1, a. 3) doubts, whether *inspirability* ought to be added as a sixth notion; but in his REPORTATIO (SENT., I, d. 28, q. 5), as if retracting this doubt, he affirms that it is not a notion. — The three other question treated here are sufficiently clear. — There is more on notions above in d. 24, a. 1, q. 2, in reply to n. 4, and below in d. 27, p. I, q. 1, at the end of the body of the Question.

II. Alexander of Hales, SUMMA., p. I, q. 68, m. 3. — (Bl. John Duns) Scotus, REPORTATIO, d. 28, q. 4. — St. Thomas, here in q. 2, a. 3; SUMMA., I, q. 32, a. 3. — Bl. (now St.) Albertus (Magnus), here in a. 10 and 13. — (Bl.) Peter of Tarentaise, here in q. 2, a. 4. — Richard of Middleton, here in a. 4, q. 2. — Giles the Roman, here in 2nd. princ., q. 2. — Henry of Ghent, SUMMA., a. 55, q. 3. — Durandus (of Saint-Pourçain), here in a. 2. — (Bl.) Dionysius the Carthusian, here in q. 4.

---

[1] Codex bb reads *But it must be understood* [Sed intelligendum est]. — In favor of the first opinion, which is touched upon next, Bl. (now St.) Albertus (Magnus), here in a. 10, cites Gilbert of Porretain and Simon of Tournai, who asserted too, that the infinite relations of this kind, existing from eternity, were assistants in God, and not God; concerning which see below d. 33, q. 1.

[2] From the Vatican ed. and cod. cc there is absent *this* [huius]. In place of the following word *opinion* [opinionis], some codd., such as P Q & aa, and ed. 1, have *position* [positionis], some, such as A T & Y, have *reckoning* [rationis].

[3] Very few codices, together with codex cc and the Vatican edition, substitute *there are* [sunt] for *They have* [habent], and a little above this, after *they said* [dixerunt], they omit *there are* [esse], and also below in place of the words *through a comparison to* [per comparationem ad] exhibit *as much as regards* [quamtum ad].

[4] Thus the codices almost unanimously against the Vatican edition, in which there is read: *and for that reason there is only one privative notion, namely, innascibility* [et ideo notio privativa est una sola, scilicet innascibilitas]. Not a few codices, such as P and Q, prefix to the word *notion* [notio] the word *this* [haec].

[5] Codex P and Q read more clearly: *and thus all together there are five* [et ita in universo sunt quinque].

[6] Namely, active and passive generation. — The Vatican edition, together with some codices, reads *relations* [relationes] for *generations* [generationes]. Then, after *"procession"* [processione] codex Q in the margin exhibits the added words *two processions* [duas processiones].

[7] In very many manuscripts, such as A C I L O R S T etc., there are wanting the words *to be a Person* [esse personam].

DOUBTS ON THE TEXT OF THE MASTER

DOUBT I

In this part, there are doubts about the text (of Master Peter) and first of this which (St.) Jerome says: *From the Dancer of the Arians there was exacted by me, a Roman man, a novel word, "hypostasis".* For, if it is novel, since the Apostle says in the last (chapter) of the First (Letter) to Timothy,[1] *to avoid the novelties of words*, in no manner ought he have conceded it. *Moreover*, (St. John) Damascene says, that « a hypostasis is s substance with accidents »; but among the divine there occurs no accident, therefore, neither the name for 'hypostasis': ergo etc..

I RESPOND: It must be said, that a "novelty" [novitas] in one manner means [sonat in] a vice, in another manner (it does) not. When there is such an discovery [adinventio], that also causes a sentence, which does not have its rise from ancient truth, then it is truly novel; and thus the Apostle says that it must be fled from, whence he adds (to that verse, the word), *"profane"*. But that word, as much as regards a sane understanding, was not new, but (only) as much as regards the understanding, which the heretics supposed. — *What is objected* concerning the authority of (St. John) Damascene, it must be said, that the name for 'hypostasis' of itself does not convey a looking-back to an accident, but only to a distinguishing property, which, because among creatures (this) is an accident, for that reason he says (that a "hypostasis" is) "a substance[2] with accidents"; but it is not so in God.

DOUBT II

Likewise, is asked concerning this which (St. Jerome) says, that *poison lies hidden beneath the honey*; because, since he does not say this except on account of the conjoined error, it seems, that such names[3] are to be fled from entirely.

I RESPOND: It must be said, that poison did not lay hidden beneath the name, but beneath the intention, or occasion,[4] of those who from it wanted to induce (others) into heresy, when the occasion presented itself [occasionaliter]. — *And/or* it can be said, that poison did lie hidden, not as much as regards (its) signification, but on account of the doubting (it caused); and for that reason, now, since its signification has been determined, it is without doubt to be used.[5]

DOUBT III

Likewise is asked of this which (St.) Augustine says, that *'to have begotten' is other than 'to have been born'*. For he seems to speak badly, because since *"other"* means a diversity in essence, according to this it seems,[6] that active generation and nativity differ through (their) essence; which is against the Faith.

I RESPOND: It must be said, that *"other"* does not mean there a diversity on the part of the absolute thing, but through a comparison to the one speaking and understanding, as if to say:[7] *"to say*, that the Father generates, is other than to understand (that He does)", and (sayings) of this kind; but beneath this anotherness there is not a diversity of essence, but an anotherness of property.

DOUBT IV

Likewise, is asked of this which (St. Augustine) says, that *it is proper to the Father, not that He has not been born.* For he seems to speak contrary to that which is said below in the Twenty-eighth Distinction,[8] where it is said, that that which is *unbegotten* is proper to the Father, but to say *"unbegotten"* is not other than (to say) *"not begotten"*.

I RESPOND: It must be said, that (St.) Augustine speaks of that which is *not born*, according to which it means a pure negation; and in this manner it does not mean a property. For *"unbegotten"*, insofar as it is a property, is not a pure negation.

DOUBT V

Likewise, is asked concerning this reckoning of (St.) Augustine, by which he says, that *in God nothing is said according to accident, because nothing in Him is mutable or able to be lost.* For the reckoning, by which some accidents are inseparable,[9] does not seem to be valid; and such are not able to be lost [amissibilia].

I RESPOND: It must be said, that just as the same (St.) Augustine[10] himself says, every accident is either through its own nature able to be lost, or can be increased and/or decreased [indendi vel remitti] about its own subject. And he does not say, that it is an accident only, because it can be lost, but because it could come upon a thing a pre-existing thing [rei prius existenti] and/or recede from a thing already existing, and/or at least be increased and/or decreased or varied. — *And if you object*, according to (St. Severinus) Boethius,[11] that accidents cannot be altered; it is true concerning (their) being altered from subject into subject, yet it is certain, that they are increased and decreased in the same (subject). — In another manner,

---

[1] Verse 20. — See the words of (St. John) Damascene above in d. 23, a. 1, q. 3, p. 410, footnote 1.

[2] The greater part of the codices, together with the Vatican edition, have *subject* [subiectum] for *substance* [substantiam], but codex T rightly, with what precedes this, has more fittingly *substance* [substantiam].

[3] He is speaking of *"hypostasis"* and *"ousia"*. — Very many codd. and ed. 1 have *all such names* etc. [talia nomina omnia], instead of *such names* ... *entirely* [talia nomina omnino etc.]. A little above this, the Vatican ed., with some mss., has not so well *through the conjoined error* [per errorem coniunctum] for *on account of the conjoined error* [propter errorem coniunctum].

[4] Codices aa and bb omit *or occasion* [sive occasione].

[5] The Vatican edition, breaking with the more ancient codices and edition 1, and the words of Master (Peter), has *to be held* [est tenendum].

[6] The verb *it seems* [videtur], exhibited in the manuscripts and edition 1, is absent from the Vatican edition.

[7] Codices G and Y, together with edition 1, read *one would say* [diceret] for *to say* [dicat]. Then after *of this kind* [huiusmodi], the Vatican edition has *and* [et] for *but* [sed].

[8] In the text of Master (Peter), ch. 1 ff. Cf. ibid., in (St. Bonaventure's) COMMENTARY, q. 1 and 2.

[9] Cf. Aristotle, PHYSICS, Bk. I, text 28, (ch. 3), and Porphyry, ON THE PREDICABLES, ch. "On the *Accident*".

[10] ON THE TRINITY, Bk. V, ch. 4, n. 5 ff., where he also makes mention of the division of separable and inseparable accidents.

[11] COMMENTARY ON THE CATEGORIES OR PREDICAMENTS OF ARISTOTLE, Bk. I: « But if anyone also objects, that accidents can change

it can be said, that an accident can be compared to a *prime* subject and to a *proximate* subject.[1] And when it is had regarding a *prime* subject, every *accidens* means (something) coming-upon (the subject), which is also possible to be absent, though not in respect to the subject, which is (its) subject and cause.[2] — The third manner of speaking (about this) is this, that that alone is immutable through nature, which is entirely simple If, therefore, God is entirely immutable, therefore, He is entirely simple;and in nothing simply is there an accident:[3] therefore, in no immutable is there a positing of accident. If, therefore, the Father is immutable, and the paternity is in Him: therefore, it is not an accident.

DOUBT VI

Likewise is asked concerning this which (Master Peter) says, that *we are the sons of God through a making* [per facturam]; because according to this manner of speaking, of his, since a donkey has been made, it seems that it can be said (to be) a "son of God"; and likewise, that a chest, which has been made by a craftsman, can be said (to be) a "daughter of the craftsman", neither of which is conceded. *If you say*, that it is necessary that it be made to the image of God: *on the contrary*: the devil has been made to the image of God: therefore, the devil is a "son of God".

I RESPOND: It must be said, that this *"son"* which I mean, means two (things), namely *a rising* and *an imitation*. It must be said, therefore, that there is an imitation *through an omnimodal assimilation*; and in this manner the natural Son imitates the Father, and because He has no companion in imitating (Him) in this manner, for that reason He Himself is alone the natural Son. And again,[4] there is an *expressed* imitation; and this consists in the image, and this still has the reckoning of a son and of a making. And again, (there is) the *distant* imitation; and this has only the reckoning of a making, not of a son. But one must attend, that an *expressed* imitation either[5] consists in its own condition, or is marked out [insignita] furthermore by its own perfection and ornament, or it is

deprived of honor and deformed by its own condition. In the first manner a son is said (to be) by a making; in the second manner, a son (is said to be) by a making and an adoption; in the third manner, in no manner is a son said (to be), except very improperly and with a distracting addition; because the Lord in the eighth (chapter of the Gospel of St.) John says,[6] *that sinners have as (their) father, the Devil*, on account of this, that they withdraw from God, and imitate him.

DOUBT VII

Likewise is asked concerning the distinction of those three (distinctive characteristics), which (St.) Hilary posits, namely, *"origin"*, *"truth"* and *"nativity"*; and it must be said, that he says these three to exclude three heresies. Against *Photinus* he says *"by origin"*, not *"by adoption"*; because Photinus used to say, that Christ is the adopted son of God. Against *Sabellius* he says *"by truth"*, not *"by being named"*; because he used to say, that the very Same was named[7] "father", (and was) afterwards (named) "son". Against *Arius* he says *"by a nativity"*, not *"by being created"*; because Arius used to say, that the Son of God is a creature.

DOUBT VIII

Likewise is asked of this which (St. Augustine) says, that *though the term for Him, to whom He is referred, does not respond to Him in reverse*. For (this) seems (to be) false, because « it is proper for relatives to be said conversely [ad convertentiam] »:[8] therefore, if they are not said conversely, they are not said relatively.

I RESPOND: It must be said, that that is true, if a name has been imposed upon each extreme; otherwise if it fails on one side, it is not said: just as if there be said, *"an oar of a ship"* (and not *"a ship of an oar"*).[9] Similarly, (St.) Augustine wants to say, that *under those names of Theirs*, "the Father" and "the Son", They are not referred to the Holy Spirit. But yet, where names fail, the Philosopher teaches that one is to devise (one);[0] but *among the divine*

---

place, and indeed if he holds an apple in his hand, his hand will be completely filled with the scent of the apple, to this extent that the scent which is an accident, can pass over into another subject. But Aristotle does not say this, since an accident cannot change place, nor did he say thus that it is impossible to be "without that in which it was", but (rather) "without that in which it is"; for this signifies that it can indeed change place, but that it cannot subsist without any subject ». In his COMMENTARY ON PORPHYRY., Bk. V, reviewing the commonalities and differences of a genus and accident, (St. Boethius) says: « However, the sharing in an accident is both increased and decreased. For you will find that someone walks a little longer, is a little darker (in complexion), and if you consider (those) among the Ethiopians themselves, you will find that not all are equally cover over in the color black ». He repeats the same in the book, ON THE PROPER AND THE ACCIDENT..

[1] A prime subject is prime matter; a proximate subject is composed out of matter and form.

[2] In (his Commentary on) SENT., Bk. II, d. 26, a. 1, q. 3, the Seraphic Doctor says: It must be noted, that there is some accident, which is compared to something as to a subject and cause; some, which is only compared to something as to a subject and another as to a cause; v. g., the blackness in a raven is compared to the raven itself as to a subject and cause; a light in the air and/or a refection in a mirror is compared only as to a subject, not as to a cause, because even if it is received in that (medium), yet, it has its rise from elsewhere.

[3] Cf. (St. Severinus) Boethius, ON THE TRINITY, ch. 2. — This doubt is also solved by St. Thomas, commenting here on the text (of Master Peter).

[4] Codex F has *also* [etiam], codex O *yet* [tamen], very many codices faultily read *therefore* [igitur].

[5] The Vatican edition, with some mss., has *also* [et], ed. 1 has *as* [ut] for *either* [aut]; perhaps the genuine reading is *either is or* [aut est ut].

[6] Verse 41. — A little above this after *in the second manner* [secundo modo], codex V repeats *is said* [dicitur]. — This doubt is also solved by Bl. (now St.) Albertus (Magnus), here in a. 15; and St. Thomas, commenting here on the text.

[7] Some codd., such as F G T & W, read *is named* [nuncupatur]. Next, the error of the Vatican ed., of placing *by being named* [nuncupatione] for *by a nativity* [nativitate], we have corrected on the authority of the codd.. — St. Thomas exhibits the solution to this doubt, commenting here on the text.

[8] Aristotle, ON THE PREDICAMENTS, ch. "On *Relation*".

[9] Aristotle, loc. cit., says: For neither by this, that a vessel [navigium] is, is it, by this, said (to be) its oar [temo]; for there are vessels, of which there are no oars; wherefore, it is not convertible; for a vessel is not said to be "a vessel of an oar".

[10] Thus codices P and Q; the Vatican ed. reads *it is fitting that one devise names* [nomina decet fingere]. Very many other codd., with edition 1, favor the reading received by us, by putting *teaches* [docet] for *it is fitting* [decet], though omitting *the Philosopher* [Philosophus]. In truth the Philosopher, loc. cit., says: But sometimes, perhaps, it will even be necessary to devise a name, if one has not been imposed, to fittingly be assigned. — A little after this (on the next page), many codd., with ed. 1, have *to lack (one)* [carere] for *to remain silent* [tacere].

it is better to remain silent, than to devise (a new name), for the sake of avoiding error.

DOUBT IX

Likewise is asked concerning this which *in the former case a customary term could not be found.* For (this) seems (to be) false, because <u>spirator</u> (i. e., "breather") is as rightly said according to <u>spiritus</u> (i. e. "spirit"), as <u>donator</u> (i.e. "grantor") according to <u>donum</u> (i.e. "gift").

I Respond: There is one manner of speaking, because (St.) Augustine does not speak simply of this name, "*Spirit*" [Spiritus], but of the whole (name), "*the Holy Spirit*". — *And/or in another manner,* he says this,

because <u>spirator</u> was not at that time a customary name, as <u>donator</u> (was).

DOUBT X

Likewise is asked of this which (St. Augustine) says, that *He is not only said (to be) a grantor in time;* because according to this He is not only said (to be) a gift in time, since relatives are together by nature.[1]

And to this it must be said, that He can be spoken of from the act of granting and/or from being held. In the first manner He is said (to be "a grantor") only in time, thus also[2] a "*gift*"; in the second manner He is said (to be such) from eternity.

DISTINCTION XXVII

PART I

CHAPTER I

What are those properties, by which the Persons are distinguished.

Here, it can be asked, whether the properties, which (St.) Hilary assigned above,[1] namely, that the Father is always the Father, and the Son is always the Son, are those same properties, which (St.) Augustine distinguished above, saying, that it is proper to the Father, that He begot the Son; and proper to the Son, that He has been begotten by the Father; and to the Holy Spirit, that He proceeds from Each. And then, whether also these (of St. Augustine) are those (of St. Hilary), which are said (to be) *the paternity, the filiation,* (and) *the procession.* It seems that the same are not the properties, which (St.) Hilary posits, and those, which (St.) Augustine posits. For if they are the same, it is the same, therefore, for the Father to be the Father and to have begotten the Son; which at least certain (authors) do concede. But if this is; therefore, to the one to whom it befits to be the Father, to that one it befits to have begotten the Son. Therefore, if the Divine Nature is the Father, It begot the Son; if, however, It did not beget (Him), It is not the Father. But who dares to say, either that It begot the Son, or that It is not the Father. But if It is the Father, and has not begotten the Son, therefore, it is not the same to say, that something is the Father and begets the Son. And thus there does not seem[2] to be one and the same property.

To which, without prejudice to others, we say, that each noted the same properties, though with diverse words. For what (St.) Hilary says, thus ought to be understood: it is proper to the Father, that He always is the Father, that is, the property of the Father is, that by which He is always the Father; however, He is always the Father, because He always begot the Son. Thus also it is proper to the Son, that He is always the Son, that is, the property of the Son is, that by which He is always the Son; however, the Son is al-

ways, because He is always begotten. Therefore, the property, by which the Father is a father, is because He always has begotten; and this same is said (to be) the paternity and/or generation. And the property, by which the Son is always a son, is because He has always been begotten by the Father, and this same is said (to be) the filiation and/or begetting [genitura] and/or the nativity and/or the origin and/or the nascibility. Thus too, the property, by which the Holy Spirit is a holy spirit and/or a gift, is because He proceeds from Each; and this same is said (to be) the procession. In the aforesaid expressions, therefore, the same properties have been signified.

CHAPTER II.

That it is not entirely the same to say, that He is the Father and that He has begotten and/or has a Son.

Nor, yet, does it seem to us, that it is entirely the same to say that Something is the Father and that It has begotten the Son; and/or that Something is the Son and that It has a Father, and/or that (Something) is the Holy Spirit and that It proceeds from Each. Otherwise the Father would not be the name of a Hypostasis, that is, of a Person, but only a property; similarly the Son and the Holy Spirit: and thus through[3] three Names there would not be signified three Persons. And for that reason we say, that the Name of the Father does not only note a relation, but also a Hypostasis, that is, it signifies a subsistence, thus also the Son and the Holy Spirit. However, the words for the relations, that is, "the paternity", "the filiation", "the procession", and/or "to beget", "to be begotten", "to proceed", signify only the *relations* themselves, not the *Hypostases*, or (that is, that they signify, for example) 'to have a son' and 'to have a father'. For the sake of an example [ut verbi gratia], when we say: "God is a father", by the name for father we both note the *relation* and signify the Divine Hypostasis, so that the understanding is such: 'God and/or the Divine Essence is the Father', that is, 'He who begot', namely[4]

---

[1] Aristotle, <u>loc. cit.</u>.

[2] Thus the greater part of the codices, together with edition 1; some, such as L P Q W and Z, have *just as also* [sicut et]; the Vatican edition together with codex cc reads *and thus* [et sic].

NOTES ON THE BOOK OF SENTENCES

[1] In the preceding Distinction, ch. 3, which quotes from his own ON THE TRINITY, Bk. XII, n. 23. — Codices B and E have *had assigned*

[assignaverat] for *assigned* [assignavit]. — The passage of (St.) Augustine is had <u>ibid.</u>, and is found in his ON THE TRINITY, Bk. V, ch. 5, n. 6.

[2] The Vatican edition, together with editions 4, 6 and 8, reads *there will not seem* [videbitur].

[3] The Vatican edition adds *these* [haec].

[4] The Vatican edition and all the other editions have *that is* [id est], contrary to the codices.

the Hypostasis, which has a son. Similarly, God is a son, that is, a Hypostasis begotten and/or having a father. Thus too, God is a Holy Spirit, that is, a Hypostasis proceeding from Each, or He who proceeds. When, however, we posit the names of the relations in the predicates (of sentences), we signify only the notions themselves, not the Hypostases, such as when there is said:[1] "God begot, that is, has a son"; and "God has been begotten, that is, has a father". And then it is necessary that there be understood in the subjects (of the sentences) only the Hypostases, not the Essence, which is determined by those properties.

CHAPTER III

That the properties determine the Hypostases, not the Substance, that is, the Nature.

For those properties each properly convene with each Person, and through them those Persons are determined and differ from One another, but do not secede from Themselves. Whence (St.) John Damascene (says):[2] « The Hypostases do not differ from One another according to substance, but according to Their own characteristics [characteristica idiomata], that is, the determinative properties. However, the characteristics, that is, the determinatives, are of the Hypostases, and not of the Nature; for indeed they determine the Hypostases ». Likewise, (he says):[3] « Indeed, we say that there is atemporally [intemporaliter] and eternally a Hypostasis of the Word, simple, having all, which the Father has, as (One who is) homoousion to Him, that is, consubstantial (to Him), differing by the manner of the nativity and by habitude from the Hypostasis of the Father [a paternali hypostasi], but never seceding from the Hypostasis of the Father ». The same, expressing more openly the personal properties, says in the same (book):[4] « We recognize the difference of the Hypostases, that is, of the Persons, in three properties, that is, (that) of the Father, (that) of the Son and (that) of the One processing, moreover, (we recognize) the Hypostases Themselves, unable to secede [insecessibiles] and unable to be made distant from One another [indistabiles invicem] and united, indeed, in a manner in which They cannot be confused [inconfusibliter] — for They are three, even if united — but divided in a manner without distance [indistanter]. For indeed Each is a perfect Hypostasis and possesses His own property, that is, His own mode of existence; but They have been united according to substance and are not distant nor do they secede from the Hypostasis of the Father ». Behold here you have those three, distinct properties, which have been signified in diverse manners above.[5]

PART II

Here, it must not be overlooked, that just as "the Father" and "the Son" and "the Holy Spirit" are the Names of the Persons and designate the personal properties, so also there are other names for the Persons, that is, which signify the Persons Themselves and denote Their properties, the same (properties), which (are) also the aforesaid names, whence they are also said relatively, namely, *Begetter, Begotten, Word, Image*. Whence (St.) Augustine in the fifth book, ON THE TRINITY (says):[6] « It must be seen », he says, « that when "*begotten*" is said, there is signified that, which is signified, when "*son*" is said. For, a son (is) for that reason, that (he has been) begotten, and because (he is) a son, (he) certainly [utique] (has been) begotten ». « Moreover, just as a son is referred to a father, so a begotten to a begetter, and just as a father (is referred) to a son, so a begetter to a begotten ». The same (says) in the sixth book, ON THE TRINITY:[7] « The *Word*, indeed, is taken (to be) the Son alone, not the Father and the Son together, as if Both are the one Word. For "*the Word*" is said in thus, as *Image*, but the Father and the son (are) not Both and *image*, but the Son alone is *the Image* of the Father, according to the measure that (He is) also a *son* ». The same (says) in the seventh book, ON THE TRINITY:[8] « The Word, according to which He is *Wisdom* and *the Essence*, is that which the Father (is); according to which (He is) *the Word*, He is not that which the Father (is), because a word is not a father, and a "*word*" is said relatively, just as "*son*" (is) ». Likewise, in the same (book he says): « Just as a *son* is referred to a father, so also a *word* is referred to him to whom the word belongs, when the word is said. And on that account He is not said (to be) a "*word*" according to that, according to which (it is said to be) "*wisdom*"; because "*word*" is not said regarding itself, but only relatively regarding him to whom the word belongs, just as a son (is said) regarding a father ». « Indeed He is a son by that, according to which (He is) a word, and He is a word by that, according to which (He is) a son; but (He is) Wisdom (by that), according to which (He is) the Essence, and for this reason, because the Father and the Son are the One Essence and the one Wisdom ». Likewise, in the same (book he says):[9] « The Father Himself is not a word, just as (He is) neither a son nor an image ». « Moreover, what (is) more absurd than that an image be said regarding itself »? The same (says) in the fifth (book):[10] « "Son" is said relatively, "word" and "image" are also said relatively, and in all these words He is referred to the Father, but none of these is a father said (to be) ».

There has been openly shown, that just as "*son*" and/or "*begotten*" is said relatively to "father", so "*word*" and "*image*"; and that He is said (to be) a "word" or "image" by that, according to which (He is) a son, that is, He is said (to be) a "*word*" and "*image*" by the same property or notion, by which (He is) a "*son*"; but not by that, according to which (He is) a "*word*", is He said (to be) "*wisdom*" and/or "*the Essence*", because not by the notion, according to which He is said (to be) a "*word*", is He said (to be) "*wisdom*". For He is said (to be) "*wisdom*" according to *essence*, not according to *relation*.

---

[1] The Vatican edition and the other editions, except ed. 1, have *we say* [diximus] for *there is said* [dicitur], contrary to the codices.

[2] ON THE ORTHODOX FAITH, Bk. III, ch. 6. In the new version there is read: By which it comes to be, that persons do not differ among themselves by a reckoning of essence, but (by one) of accidents, which, indeed, are proper and certain notes, by which a hypostasis is marked out [sigillatur], not a nature; for a hypostasis is defined as an essence with accidents [ἄτινά εἰσι τὰ χαρακτηριστικὰ ἰδώματα· χαρακτηριστικὰ δὲ ὑποστάσεως, καὶ οὐ φύσεως. Καὶ γὰρ τὴν ὑπόστασιν ὁρίζονται, οὐσίαν μετὰ συμβεβηκότων].

[3] Ibid., ch. 7, with a few things omitted here; the version of all the others responds nearly word for word with the original.

[4] Ibid., ch. 5. The ancient version is faithful; yet some (words) are omitted: for *We recognize ... (that) of the Father, (that) of the Son and (that) of the One processing* [paternali et filiali et processibli recognoscimus] there is read in the original τῇ ἀναιτίῳ καὶ πατρικῇ καὶ τῇ αἰτιατῇ καὶ υἱϊκῇ, καὶ τῇ αἰτιατῇ καὶ ἐκπορευτῇ ἐπιγιγνώσκομεν (or in Migne's LATIN PATROLOGY: we acknowledge that there has been posited that there is both One without cause, the Father, and Another from a Cause, the Son, and Another Same from a Cause and proceeding [quod unus sine causa sit et Pater, alter a causa et Filius, alter idem a causa et procedens esse positum agnoscimus]).

[5] Distinction XXVI, ch. 2, and here in ch. 1.

[6] Chapter 7, n. 8. The following passage is ibid., ch. 6, n. 7.

[7] Chapter 2, n. 3.

[8] Chapter 3, n. 4, and the passage which follows is ibid., ch. 2, n. 3, from which ch., the passage following it has also been taken. In the second quote, after *only relatively* [tantum relative], the Vatican ed. and very many edd. add *is said* [dicitur]; in the third, after *for this reason* [ideo], the Vatican edition alone omits *because* [quia].

[9] Ibid., ch. 1, n. 1. The final proposition is ibid., n. 2.

[10] Chapter 13, n. 14; in which text the Vatican ed. with cod. C & edd. 4 & 5, omits *also* [etaim]; in the original there is read both "*word*" and "*image*" are relatively said [relative dicitur et verbum et imago].

CHAPTER IV

*On the general rule for those which regard themselves,
and for those which are said relatively.*

And, here, one must adverted to a certain general rule for those which regard themselves, and for those (names) which are said relatively of the Father and the Son. « For whatever are said regarding themselves », as (St.) Augustine says in the sixth book, ON THE TRINITY,[1] « the one is not said (to be) without the other, that is, whatever are said (to be that) which shows their substance, both are said (to be) together. Therefore, neither is the Father God without the Son, not the Son (God) without the Father, but Both together (are) God », but not Both together (are) a *father* nor Both together a *son* and/or *word* and/or *image*.

CHAPTER V

*Or whether according to substance there is said,
"God from God ", and (sayings) of this kind.*

Here, there is asked, when there is said: "God from God, Light from Light", and (expressions) of this kind, whether they are said according to *substance*. For according to relation it is established that these are not said. If, however, they are said according to substance, Both, namely, the Father and the Son, can be said together (to be) "God from God, Light from Light", according to the aforesaid rule. — To which we say, that though *"God"* is said according to substance, and *"Light"* and *"Wisdom"* and (Names) of this kind, and (though these) are never accepted relatively; yet sometimes they are accepted on behalf of relatives, that is, on behalf of Persons, but not relatively, as when there is said: "God begot God", we posit the former on behalf of the Father, the latter on behalf of the Son; similarly, when there

is said: "God from God, Light from Light". Also, in the other expressions there are often found Names for the Essence deduced for the signification of the Persons, as when there is said: "the *God* (who has been) *born*" [Deus natus], "the *God* (who has) *died*" [Deus mortuus], "the *God* (who has) *suffered*" [Deus passus], where only the Son is signified. Thus also, when there is said: "God of God", and (expressions) of this kind, it is understood of the Son alone. Whence (St.) Augustine seeking, in what manner (expressions) of this kind are said, says in the sixth book, ON THE TRINITY:[2] « in what manner is there said, "God from God, Light from Light"? For not Both together (are) "God from God", but the Son alone (is) from God, namely, (from) the Father; nor (are) Both together "Light from Light", but the Son alone (is) from the Light of the Father ».

And it must be known, that only according to the Names for the Substance is there said a *"that from that"*, though there those Names do not signify the Substance. However, according to the same Names for the Persons there is never said *"that of that"*, just as (there is never said) "the Word from the Word", and/or "the Son from the Son", because the Names of this kind cannot convene with diverse Persons. Which (St.) Augustine, though obscurely, in the same book[3] thus says: « This alone of Them cannot be said, *"that from that*, which Both together are not" »: that is, we cannot use that name alone to show that *One* (is) from *One*, which does not befit Both, « just as "the Word from the Word" cannot be said, because together Both (are) not the Word, nor "the Image from the Image", nor "the Son from the Son", because together Both (are) not the Son, and/or the Image ». — And just as the Names for the Substance sometimes cause the understanding of distinct Persons, so also (they cause) now and then (an understanding) of the whole Trinity together. Whence (St.) Augustine in the fifth book[4] says: « In the Name of "the Father", the Father Himself per se is pronounced, but in the Name of "God", both the Father Himself and the Son and the Holy Spirit, such as when there is said: *No one (is) good, except God alone*, because the Trinity is the One God ».

COMMENTARY ON DISTINCTION XXVII

PART I

On the properties of the Persons, to the extent that they are expressed through more usual words.

Here, it can be asked, whether the properties etc..

THE DIVISION OF THE TEXT

Above, Master (Peter) assigned the personal properties, here, second,[1] he deals with the properties themselves, according to which they are expressed through diverse words [vocabula]. And since it happens that they are expressed through words more and less usual, for that reason this part has two parts. In the *first* he deals with the expression of the properties through

more[2] usual words, in the *second* through less usual words, below in the same Distinction (where he says): *Here there must not be overlooked* etc..

The *first* part has four (parts). For, since (Sts.) Hilary and Augustine assign the properties to some words and to others, yet, each to ones customary,[3] because the one, name-

---

[1] Chapter 2, n. 3. In the original there is read: Therefore, neither is God the Father without the Son, nor the Son God without the Father, but Both together (are) God.

[2] Chapter 2, n. 3.

[3] Ibid., just as also (is) the following passage.

[4] Chapter 8, n. 9. — The passage of Sacred Scripture is Lk. 18:19. — At the end of the text, the Vatican edition, together with very many editions, reads *the one, only God* [unus solus Deus].

NOTES ON THE COMMENTARY

[1] In the Vatican edition and codex cc, there is wanting *second* [secundo].

[2] The codices, not without edition 1, omit *more* [magis].

[3] Many codices, among which are A T V X and cc, and edition 1, read *customary (properties)* [consuetas] for *to ones customary (i. e. customary words)* [consuetis].

-ly, (St.) Augustine (assigns them) through *"to generate"* and *"to be generated"*, the other, namely (St.) Hilary, through *"to be the Father"* and *"to be the Son"*, for that reason Master (Peter) first asks, whether the properties assigned by each are the same. Second he solves (the question), showing, that they are the same, there (where he says): *To which, without the prejudice of others etc..* Third, lest anyone believe, that they are entirely the same, he shows, that they are the same[1] according to thing,

but differ as much as regards the manner of signifying, namely, in concretion and in abstraction, there (where he says): *Nor yet does it seem to us, that it is entirely the same etc..* However, fourth, because he has said, that the properties are signified in composition, because[2] there could be asked: "in respect of whom?", he shows, that (they are signified) in respect of the Hypostases, there (where he says): *For those properties each properly convene with each Person etc..*

TREATMENT OF THE QUESTIONS

For an understanding of this part, four (things) are asked:

First, there is asked, whether *'to be the Father'* [esse Patrem] and *'to generate'* [generare] is one[3] notion.

Second, there is asked, which of these is the reckoning of the other.

Third, whether the properties happen to be abstracted.

Fourth, whether it is licit to opine in a contrary manner about these.

ARTICLE SOLE

On the property of the paternity, on the abstraction of the properties, (and) on the certitude of this doctrine.

QUESTION I

Whether 'to be the Father' and 'to generate' are one and the same notion?

As much as regards the first, that it is the same notion, is shown in this manner:

1. To a hypostasis there belongs one sole property, which gives it a distinct 'being' [esse distinctum]. For it is not there in the reckoning of an accident, but of a form, but that (form) is only one for One [una sola unius]. But *'to generate' is a property*, through which the Hypostasis of the Father is distinguished, similarly also *'to be a father'*: therefore, it is the same notion.

2. Likewise, of the Father to the Son there is only one relation, because (there is) only one origin and one manner of emanating; but *"to generate"* means the relation of the Father to the Son, similarly also *"to be a father"*: therefore, it is the same relation and/or notion.

3. Likewise,[4] if there are diverse properties, then, therefore, there are more notions than five, nay (they are) infinite. For just as *'to be a father'* follows after *'to generate'*, so *'to be distinguished from a father'* follows after *'to be referred to a father'* etc.; which if they are other notions, then, therefore, the number of the notions is infinite. But this is unfitting, and it follows, (from) 'if those properties are diverse': ergo etc..

ON THE CONTRARY: 1. If *'to be a father'* and *'to generate'* [generare] is the same property: therefore, entirely the same is conveyed by the name for *'father'* and the name for *'begetter'* [genitoris]. Therefore, just as one has been baptized, if one is baptized in the Name of the Father, so if in the Name of the Begetter; but this is commonly denied.

2. Likewise, the properties and notions are diverse and are cognized to be diverse, because they are predicated of diverse (Persons) — because one is predicated of One, of which another is not predicated — but this is conceded: "the Essence is the Father"; this denied: "the Essence generates":[5] ergo etc.. *If you say*, that this is on account of a diverse manner of signifying; *on the contrary*: this is nothing, because *'to be a father'* as much as *'to generate'*, each is said in concretion.

3. Likewise, the properties are proved to be diverse, when one is not predicated of the other, such as the paternity and the innascibility; but *"to generate"*, as will be clear below,[6] is not said of the paternity — for this is not admitted: "the paternity generates" — therefore, they are diverse.

---

[1] The Vatican edition alone reads *the same* [eaedem] in the plural.

[2] With no codex supporting it, the Vatican edition omits *because* [quia], and then after *of whom?* [cuius], it subjoins *and* [et].

[3] Codices Z and aa, together with edition 1, read *the same* [eadem], a reading a little more elegant, because below at the beginning of the question there is also read *the same notion* [eadem notion].

[4] Thus very many codd. with ed. 1; cod. V reads *But* [Sed]; the Vatican ed. with cod. cc reads *And/or* [Vel]; codd. R S & U omit *Likewise* [Item].

In the following proposition, to avoid ambiguity, we have retained with the Vatican edition the particle *after* [ad], before the verbs *'to generate'* [generare] and *'to be referred'* [referri], even if they are lacking in the more ancient manuscripts.

[5] Cf. above d. 5, a. 1, q. 1.

[6] Distinction 33, q. 4. — A little above this, in place of *when* [quando], which we have put on the authority of codices G H P Q and X and of edition 1, the Vatican edition reads *because* [quia].

CONCLUSION

The paternity and the generation are one property according to thing; but according to the manner of signifying there is a threefold difference among them.

I Respond: It must be said, that they are entirely the same property[1] according to thing; and the reason for this is manifestly apparent. For one is said of the other not only in concretion, such as "the Father generates", but also in abstraction, such as "the paternity is the generation"; which would not be, if they were different.

Moreover, though it is the same property, yet it is signified in a different manner, and this as much as regards three (things). First, indeed, because *generation* expresses more generally the property of the Person than that which is a *father*. For, just as (St.) Augustine says and (as) is had in Book Three, Distinction Four,[2] *'to generate'* follows after *'to be a father'*, but is not convertible (with it). For a man is said to generate lice, yet he is not said (to be) their father. Another reason is, because that which is a *father* conveys within itself a hypostasis, about which it notes a property; but this verb, "*generates*", does not convey a hypostasis, nay it needs (something) be placed beside it from outside; and Master (Peter) posits this in the text.[3] The third is, because — since a property con-veys two (things), namely, an emanation and a habitude, which although they are the same according to thing, yet they differ by a reckoning of understanding — because that which it is *'to generate'* conveys a *production*, and 'the generation' an *emanation*; but that which it is *'to be a father'* properly conveys a *habitude*.

1. From these the objections are clear. For, because there is no baptism in the Name of the *Begetter*, this is not on account of a diversity of thing, but of a manner of expressing; and each is considered there, just as will be clear in the Fourth (Book).[4]

2. To that which is objected, that it is not predicated etc.; it must be said, that this is on account of a diverse manner of signifying. For that which it is *'to generate'*, because it does not have a supposit within (it), posits its subject [rem] about the Essence, and for that reason it signifies that It is distinguished; not so, however, that which is a *father*, since it has a supposit within (itself). For the sense is: 'the Essence is a father, that is, is the One who generates'.[5]

3. To that which is objected last, that one is not predicated of the other; it must be said, that there is predication through a manner of *denomination*, and this is through concretion [per concretionem];* and there is predication[6] through a manner of *identity*, and this is through abstraction [per abstractionem]. Since, therefore, *'to generate'* and *'to be a father'* is one and the same property, for that reason it is predicated not only through a manner of denominating, but (also) through abstraction, such as "the paternity is the generation".

SCHOLIUM

I. One must attend to the difference between this question and that, which is treated in d. 33, q. 3, "Whether two notions of themselves can be predicated of one Person?" This difference is touched upon in the solution to n. 3. — On the twofold predication, through the manner of denomination and of identity [per modum denominationis et identitatis], cf. below d. 33, q. 3 (Scholium), and d. 34. q. 2.

II. Alexander of Hales, Summa., p. I, q. 68, m. 5, a. 6, § 1. — (Bl. John Duns) Scotus, on this and the following question, Reportatio., here in q. 1. — St. Thomas touches upon this question, here in q. 1, a. 1; Summa., q. 33, a. 2, ad 2. — Bl . (now St.) Albertus (Magnus), here in a. 1. — Peter of Tarentaise, here in q. 1, a. 2. — Richard of Middleton, here in a. 1, q. 2. — Henry of Ghent, on this and the following question, Summa., a. 58, q. 3, — (Gabriel) Biel, here in q. 1.

QUESTION II

Whether the generation is the reason for the paternity, or whether (it is) the other way around?

Second, there is asked, which of these is the reason for understanding [ratio intelligendi] the other, that is, whether the Hypostasis of the Father or the Father generates for this reason, because He is a father, and/or is a father for this reason, because He generates. And it seems that He is a father for this reason, because He generates:

1. By the authority of Master (Peter) in the text:[7] « He is always a son, because He has always been begotten »: therefore, the passive generation is the reason for being a son: therefore, for an equal reason too, the active generation is the reason for being a father, ergo etc..

2. Likewise, according to a reckoning of understanding [secundum rationem intelligengi] *'to generate'*

---

[1] The Vatican edition, together with a few codices, reads non congruously, *the same properties* [eaedem proprietates].

[2] Where these words of (St.) Augustine from the book, Enchiridion., ch. 39, n. 12, are cited by Peter Lombard, thus: Therefore, it must not be conceded, that whatever is born from some thing, is, as a consequence [continue], to be named of the same thing. For, as will omit, that in one manner a son is born from a man, in another a hair, a louse, (and) an earthworm [lumbricum], none of which is a son. — A little above this, codex S after *First, indeed* [Primum quidem] subjoins *is* [est].

[3] Chapter 2.

[4] Sent., d. 3, p. I, a. 2, q. 3. — A little before this, from the more outstanding manuscripts, we have read *there is no baptism* [non sit baptisum], in place of which the Vatican edition has *one is not baptized* [non sit baptizatus].

[5] See more on this above in d. 5, a. 1, q. 1, in reply to n. 3, p. 113.

[6] Very many codices, together with edition 1, have *a predicating* [praedicare], but since in the subsequent proposition all the codices and the editions unanimously exhibit the word *predication* [praedicatio], we have preferred with the Vatican edition here to read *predication* rather than the gerund *a predicating* [praedicare]. — On this twofold predication, cf. above d. 5, a. 1, q. 1, in reply to n. 2.

[7] Chapter 1.

is before 'to be', and 'to be' is before 'to be referred': therefore, 'to be generated' is before 'to be a son': therefore, for an equal reason 'to generate'[1] is before 'to be a father', according to the order of understanding. If, therefore, the latter reckoning is prior, not the other way around: ergo etc..

3. Likewise, the Hypostasis of the Father is a father: therefore, either because (He is) God, or because (He is) God generating. Not because (He is) God, because for an equal reason (He would be) also the Son: therefore, because (He is) God generating, ergo etc..

ON THE CONTRARY: 1. None but a distinct person generates, since 'to generate' does not befit an essence, but a person; but the Person of the Father is not distinct except through the paternity: therefore, 'to generate' does not befit that Hypostasis except through the paternity: therefore, He generates for this reason,[2] because (He is) a father.

2. Likewise, among those which are not acquired through an act, the habit is before the act according to the reckoning of understanding — for because we are not good through works, but rather, the other way around, we are good, before we do good works [operemur bona][3] — but paternity in God is not acquired through an act: therefore, in the order of understanding He is understood to be a father before He generates.

3. Likewise, "*the Father generates*", this is a certain divine act, which per se is in the Father alone; I ask, "Through what?" For, either because (He is) *God*, or because (He is) *God, a father*, or because (He is) *innascible*. Not because (He is) *God*,[4] because then (the divine act) would also be in the Son; not because (He is) *innascible*, because innascibility means a privation of nativity, not a positing (of it):[5] therefore, a divisione, because (He is) *God* (and) *a father*.

CONCLUSION

The generation is rather the reason for the paternity,
than the other way around.

I RESPOND: For an understanding of this it must be noted, that, in this [hic], there is a twofold opinion. Certain ones say, that,

since properties are relative in God, in a contrary manner [e contrario] than in creatures — because among creatures (they are)[6] as ones arriving [advenientes], in God as ones standing within [insistentes] — that among creatures an *act* is the reason for a relation, whence among inferiors one is a father for this reason, because one generates; but among the divine, contrariwise [e contra], a *relation* is the reason for an act. Whence they simply concede, that the Father generates, because (He is) a father; and they deny (it) conversely [conversim].

But, although that could be in some manner grasped by the intellect on the part of the Father, yet if we would consider that in the Son, it does not seem entirely intelligible, that for this reason, because (He is) a son, He is generated.[7] For it is commonly said, and reason agrees [concordat], that the Son has this, both 'that He is' and 'that He is a son', through generation: therefore, the generation according to the reckoning of understanding precedes the filiation; and relatives are together by nature in understanding, not only in being [in essendo]:[8] therefore, the generation is the reason for saying (that) the paternity (is) in God the Father. For just as the passive generation holds itself to the filiation, so the active (generation) to the paternity.

And on this account there is another opinion, that (He is) a father for this reason, because He generates. And that this is well said, is clear through the difference assigned between *generation* and '*being a father*' [esse patrem].[9] For according to its proper reckoning "*generation*" means an emanation or origin, "*paternity*" means a habitude. Moreover, it is established, that an *origin* is the reason for a habitude, a *habitude* is not the reason for an origin. And for that reason the generation is the reason for the paternity, not the other way around. For that reason the reasons for this are conceded.

1. To that, therefore, which is objected unto the contrary, that none generates but a distinct person; it must be said, that it is true, that according to the reckoning of understanding it is necessary that a *hypostasis* be understood before a generation — I am speaking according to the order of understanding[10] — but it is not necessary [non oportet] to understand beforehand that it (has been) *distinguished by an act*, because (a person) is distinguished through a property of generation by a complete distinction, just as will be clear better

---

[1] The Vatican edition reads '*to be generated*' [generari], which error we have corrected from the more ancient manuscripts and edition 1.

[2] The Vatican edition, together with not a few codices, reads in the negative *therefore, He does not generate except* [ergo non generat nisi].

[3] Aristotle, ETHICS, Bk. II, ch. 4: Therefore, things are sanely said (to be) just and temperate, when they were such, as the just and/or temperate man would act; but the just and temperate man is not the one who doest these (things) alone, but the one who also so act, as the just and temperate are accustomed to do. — In very many codices, such as A F G S T Y and Z, and edition 1, there is read *we work* [operemur] for *we do good works* [operemur bona]. The Vatican edition, before *are good* [sumus boni], inserts *also* [etiam], not so well; and a little before this codex X omits *because* [quia].

[4] For this sentence, Bl. (now St.) Albertus (Magnus), SUMMA., I, tr. 8, q. 34, m. 1, and St. Thomas, here in q. 1, a. 2, cite St. Anselm, ON THE PROCESSION OF THE HOLY SPIRIT, ch. 7, who teaches, that the Holy Spirit does not proceed from the Father, because He is the Father, but because He is God. — For *would also be in* [etiam inesset] codices F H P Q T aa and bb have *would convene with* [conveniret]; the other codices together with edition 1 entirely omits these words.

[5] Besides the reason, which Bl. (now St.) Albertus gives in his SUMMA., I, tr. 8, q. 34, m. 1, the same author proposes another in his Commentary, here in a. 2, saying: Yet there are certain (authors) who says, that He generates, because (He is) innascible, that in this manner he seeks a companion [socius], to whom he communicates his delights. But those, in all charity, do not understand the question, because, when there is asked, whether (it is) because (He is) the Father and/or the other

way around, one asks of the *reckoning* of the One generating, as One generating, and not *for what reason* He generates. — The words *by elimination* [a divisione], which immediately follow, signify the place or manner of arguing, concerning which, see above d. 24, a. 1, q. 1, p. 420, footnote 5.

[6] Supply w. cod. bb: *they are* [sunt]. — Next, the Vatican ed., not trusting in the codd. and ed. 1, w. a varied punctuation, reads: *ones standing within. For among creatures an act is* [insistentes. In creaturis enim actus est]. Then, cod. T has *the cause of* [causa relationis] for *the reason for* [relationis ratio], and a little below this after *the Father generates* [quod Pater] it inserts *for this reason* [ideo]. Then for *(it) conversely* [conversim], ed. 1 has well *the converse* [conversam].

[7] In the Vatican edition there is read: *that for this reason He is the Father, because the Son is generated* [quod ideo sit Pater, quia Filius generetur]. The words *He is the Father* [sit Pater] smack of the work of an interpolator, and corrupt the text. For the discourse concerns passive generation, in which, as all agree, the notional act precedes that property according to (its) understanding. Cf. Scholium of this Question. — A little below this after *has this* [hoc habet], codex K inserts the words *from the Father* [a Patre].

[8] Concerning which, cf. Aristotle, ON THE PREDICAMENTS, ch. "On Relation". — Not much after this, cod. T after *so* [ita] repeats *the generation* [generatio].   [9] In the preceding q..

[10] The text, which we have restored from the better mss., the Vatican ed. exhibits in a very mutilated form. For omitting *that* [quod] after *that it is true* [quod verum est] & changing the punctuation, it begins a new sentence at *it is necessary* [necesse est], proceeding thus: *For it is necessary, that before the generation there be a Hypostasis (I am speaking according to the reckoning of understanding)* [Necesse est enim, ante generationem esse hypostasim (secundum rationem intelligendi loquor)]. Then, after *one is bound* [oportet] codd. L & O read *to understand before in time* [tempore praeintelligere].

below;[1] yet according to the reckoning of understanding the reason for distinguishing (the Person of the Father) *is begun* [inchoatur] in the innascibility, and for that reason He generates, not as One distinguished *by the paternity* beforehand, but as One distinguished in a certain manner *by the innascibility*.

2. To that which is objected, that (the paternity) is not acquired through an act; it must be said, that among the divine no property is acquired, because each [quaelibet] is the Essence. Yet according to the reckoning of understanding an *origin* or emanation of an origin is the *reason* for a *relation*, just as among these inferiors *a reckoning is according to 'being'*. Whence just as the act of generation is eternal, so also the property of the paternity (is)[2] eternal. Whence, although it is not *acquired* through an act, yet *it is in* (the Father) through an act; whence that proposition is false and ought to be proposed generally in this manner: "among those which are not in (another) through an act" etc., and then the *minor* is false. — Yet it can be said, that that is true of an act, which is elicited out of that habit, just as a meritorious work (is elicited) out of a grace; but the act of generation is not elicited nor is it understood to be elicited from the paternity: for that reason it is not necessary [non oportet] to understand *the paternity* prior to this, that (the Father) is understood *'to generate'*.

3. To that: either He generates, because (He is) *God*, or because (He is) *a father* etc.; it must be said, that He generates, because (He is) *the innascible* God, and He spirates, because (He is) *improcessible*.[3] — *Because it is objected*, that the innascibility is said according to a privation, some say, that a *pure* privation is not the reason for a habit, but *some* privation with a substrate habit is a reason. Whence just as any generous [liberalis][4] man invites (others) to dine (with him), because (he is) alone, so the Father generates on account of liberality, and so that He may not be alone; and for that reason when He has generated and spirated once, He generates no more, because He is not longer alone, although He is (still) generous.

Yet in another manner it must be said, just as had been said before,[5] that the innascibility is a *privation*, which according to the thing is a *perfect position*. For the Innascible is said (to be) the Father, because He is not from another; and *'to not be from another'* is *'to be first'*, and primacy is a noble *position*. For 'the first' by a reckoning of first means a noble position and condition to such an extent, that, as will be seen, the positing of a

second follows after the positing of a first. Wherefore, because (He is) first, for that reason He is a beginning [principium];[6] because (He is) a beginning, for that reason, either by an act and/or by a habit, He has begun. Since, therefore, *the reckoning of primacy* in some genus is the reckoning of a beginning[7] in it, for that reason, because the Father is first in respect to emanation, generation and procession, He generates and spirates. And since (He is) the first in the genus of generation, because (He is) innascible, (He is) first[8] in the genus of spiration, because (He is) the improcessible God; for that reason He generates, because (He is) the innascible God; and beyond this there is no positing (of the question): "For what reason is He innascible?" For since the innascibility means a primacy, and there is a standing still in the first, for that reason etc.. And this is what is said below, in the Twenty-Ninth Distinction,[9] near the beginning: « The Father is the beginning of the whole Divinity, because (He is) from no One »; and this is what has been presupposed in many passages above.[10]

But what moves one to say this, is first the ancient position of the great *Doctors*,[11] who said, that the innascibility in the Father means a *fontal plenitude*. But the fontal plenitude consists in producing. But it is established, that a fontal plenitude is said to be in Him not for this reason, because He produces a creature, because this convenes with the Three (Persons);[12] nor for this reason, because He produces the Holy Spirit, because this convenes with the Son: therefore, the fontal plenitude in the Father posits the generation in the Same. If, therefore, the innascibility is a fontal plenitude, it is clear etc..

(What) moves (one to say this is) also the *common opinion*, which says, that innascibility is proper to the Father; but what means a notion, according to which it conveys a *pure privation*, cannot be proper[13] and most of all proper; for thus it convenes with the Essence and the Holy Spirit: therefore, *it posits something*: not absolute — it is established, that by reason of that it cannot[14] be a property — but it cannot posit a positive respect in respect to the *One producing*: therefore, from its own reckoning it posits (it) in respect of the *One produced*. But according to the reckoning of understanding the first reason for looking-back to Anyone as to One produced is the generation: therefore to the positing of innascibility there follows the positing of generation: ergo etc..

(What) moves (one to say this) is also the word of *(St.) Hilary*, in the twelfth (book) ON THE TRINITY,

---

[1] Distinction 28, q. 1, 2 and 3. — At the end of the solution of this argument, the Vatican edition, with the codd. and edition 1 striving against this, reads *not as One distinguished beforehand in a certain manner by the innascibility* [non ut prius distincta quodam modo *innascibilitate*].

[2] Supply with codex G *is* [est].

[3] With the principal question solved, the Seraphic Doctor, from the occasion of this objection, solves in the sentences which follow, the connected question, namely, what is the ultimate reason, *for which* God generates and spirates. Cf. above d. 7, q. 2, the conclusion and here in the Scholium.

[4] In very many codices, such as A I O Q S T and Y, there is read *a generous being* [liberalis ens] for *a generous man* [homo liberalis].

[5] Above, in d. 2, q. 2, in the body of the question, and d. 11, q. 2 in the body of the question, and d. 13, dubium 4; cf. also below, d. 28, q. 1 and 2. — Next after *privation* [privatio], codex Q adjoins *according to the spoken word* [secundum vocem].

[6] Cf. above d, 11, a. sole, q. 2, p. 215, footnote 9.

[7] Thus many codices, such as G K M N P Q Y ee and ff; the others with the Vatican edition have *a begun* [principiati].

[8] The Vatican edition, with no codex nor edition 1 supporting it, reads *And since the first 'being' in the genus of generation, because (it is) innascible, is also the first 'being' in the genus of spiration* [Et quoniam esse primum in genere generationis, quia innascibilis, et esse primum in

genere spirationis]. Not much after this for *posting (of the question)* [ponere], not a few codices, such as P Q bb and ff, have *asking* [quaerere].

[9] In the text of Master (Peter), ch. 1.

[10] Above, in d. 2, q. 2, and d. 11, q. 2.

[11] For *of the great Doctors* [magnorum doctorum], some codices, such as A R S (T by the first hand) T and cc, read *of the teachers of doctors* [magistrorum doctorum]; codex G has *of our doctors* [nostrorum doctorum], codices I P Q and V, omit both and reads only *of the masters (of theology)* [magistrorum].

[12] Supply with codices aa and bb *Persons* [personis]. — A little before this, very many codices, among who is also codex T, together with edition 1, have the subjunctive form *produces* [producat], and a little below this *that He produces* [quod producat] for *because He produces* [quia producit].

[13] Codex T adds here *to the Father* [Patris]. Not much after this (in the English before this), some codices such as W and Y, have the subjunctive form for *means* [dicat]; in place of which the Vatican edition, breaking with the more ancient codices and also edition 1, substitutes the verb *conveys* [importat].

[14] Not a few codices, such as A F G H I T V X and Y, together with edition 1, have *could* [posset]. A little below this, after *from its own reckoning it posits* [de ratione sua ponit], codices Q and Z repeat *a respect* [respectum].

TRINITY,[1] where he says, that the Father is the *author* of the Son. But it is established, that through *"author"* he does not understand "maker" [factorem], but *"begetter"*. Therefore, it befits the Father to be a begetter by this, whereby it befits Him to be an author; but 'to be an author' befits Him through that which means that there is authorship in the Father; but a most high Authorship is in the Father by reason of (His) *innascibility*: therefore, it befits the Hypostasis of the Father by reason if (His) *innascibility* to generate. And it seems that the words of (St.) Hilary, in the twelfth (book), ON THE TRINITY, mean this, if one attends (to them), and similarly (those) in the fourth (book).[2]

(What) moves (one to say this is) also the word of the Philosopher,[3] who says, that principles as much as they are more first, so much (are they) more potent — and that a first cause inflows more — and (that the cause) which (is) simply first, has a most high inflowing through every manner. If, therefore, we see in the order of causes, among which is the *essential* order, that a primacy causes, there to be a most high influence in a cause, and (causes its) influence (to be) greater according to essence: for an equal reason, where there is an order of *persons*, the primacy in the first person is a reason for producing the others; and because 'innascible'[4] means a primacy, hence it is, that it means a *fontal plenitude* in respect to the production of a person. And we see that the sign of this (is), that the first ones in the genera are the principles of the others,[5] and what are simple, so as (to be) in many, such that there is a standing still in them, have an infinite power, just as the point (does) in respect to lines, and unity in respect to numbers; so also the Divine Essence, because (It is)[6] first in respect to creatures. Whence, perhaps, because the Divine Essence is first, for that reason It is most Omnipotent. And because every essence follows the Essence of the Three Persons, it is impossible, that one Person produce anything without the Other. Moreover, although the power of producing ought not be in respect to infinite Persons, just as has been demonstrated above,[7] nevertheless, if it were posited hypothetically [per impossibile], that a thousand Persons were produced, it would be necessary, that All proceed immediately from the Person of the Father. Because, just as a first cause works immediately in every, following production, so in His own manner (the Father does) in the Persons.

Reason also[8] moves (one) to this. For just as it is impossible that the Hypostasis of the Father and of the Son be understood, with the Hypostasis of the Holy Spirit not understood; so also it is possible that the Hypostasis of the Father be understood, with no other Person understood. And then, indeed, He would be understood, with the paternity not understood. And it is certain, that it is possible that this is understood. For we can, with the plurality of the Persons not understood, understand the Divine Nature and the One having It, and that He does not have it from another; and thus do the Gentiles understand (God).[9] By understanding (God) in this manner, therefore, it happens that one says and understands of Him, that He can generate. Through what, therefore, can He (do this)? I find nothing in that Hypostasis except (what is) common, besides the innascibility: therefore, if the generation cannot be in Him through that which is common, it is in Him through that which is proper; but this is the innascibility: ergo etc..

Again, just as we see many Persons in the one Nature, so many properties in one Person: therefore, just as for the most complete perfection it is necessary, that all the Persons be lead back [reduci] to One, who is the beginning of the Others, so (it is necessary that) all the properties of one Person (be led back)[10] to one, by which is the reason for the others. But in the Father there is the *paternity*, the *innascibility* and the *spiration*, but the *innascibility* is not reducible to the others: therefore, it is necessary, that the others be reduced to the *innascibility*, which is, as (the great Doctors) have said, a fontal plenitude.

Furthermore, the property of the paternity and the generation, as much as it concerns its general signification, is *communicable*; which[11] is clear among creatures, because a begotten generates, and a son of one becomes the father of another. But among the divine the paternity is *incommunicable*: therefore, since

---

[1] Number 21: For in the enunciation of discourse [sermonum] when we say " born" [natum], we do not, however, speak beforehand of "one not born" [non natum]. For "not born" and "to be born" are not the very same (thing); because the latter is from the other, but the former from no one. And the One is an eternal 'Being' without an author always, the Other what is coeternal to the Father, that is to the Author. For where the Father is an author, that is also a nativity; but, on the other hand, where there is an eternal Author, there is also an eternal nativity, because just as a nativity is from an author, so also from an eternal author there is an eternal nativity. He says nearly the same thing ibid., n. 51.

[2] Number 6: In the One, *from Whom* (the Church) understands the authorship of innascibility; in the One, *through whom* She venerates the power no different from the Author. Cf. also Bk. IX, n. 31.

[3] Not Aristotle, but the author of the book, ON CAUSES (cf. above, d. 8, p II, q. 2, 3rd opposed argument), who posits the three reasons adduced by the Seraphic Doctor here, and indeed the second of these, explicitly, in proposition 1: « Every primary cause is more inflowing upon its own caused, than a universal second cause ». But the first reason he insinuates in the same place, in his manner: « Therefore, it is already manifest and plain, that a distant cause is first, and the first is more comprehending and more vehemently the cause of the thing than a proximate cause » (cf. also propositions 16 and 17). Finally, the same author speaks of the third reason in proposition 20: « The First Cause rules all created things, except that which is commingled with them », which he ex-

plains thus: « The First Cause is fixed, standing with Its own pure Unity always, and It rules all created things and inflows upon them the virtue of life and goodnesses according to the manner of the virtue of those able to receive them and (the manner) of their ability. For the First Goodness inflows goodnesses upon all things by one inflowing, yet each thing receives from that inflowing according to the manner of its virtue and of its 'being' ».

[4] Codex H has *innascibility* [innascibilitas].

[5] Cf. Aristotle, METAPHYSICS, Bk. II, text 4 (in the shorter version, Bk. I, ch. 1), and Bk. X, text 2 ff. (Bk. IX, ch. 1). — On the potent infinity of a point, by which it can terminate infinite lines, see above d. 17, p. II, q. 2, in reply to n. 2. — The Vatican edition, without the authority of the codices and editions, proceeds thus: *and what are simply first, so that in them there is a standing-still as in many* [et quae sunt simpliciter prima, ita quod in eis sit status ut in pluribus].

[6] Supply together with codices G M and bb *It is* [est].

[7] Above, in d. 2, q. 3, and d. 7, q. 2.

[8] For *also* [etiam], which we have replace from codices I P and Q and editin 1, the Vatican reads *moreover* [autem]; codices Y and cc read here *Moreover, still, reason moves (one)* [Adhuc autem].

[9] Cf. above d. 26, q. 3. — A little below this after *Hypostasis* [hypostasi] the Vatican edition, not trusting in the codices and edition 1, reads *not* [non] for *except (what is)* [nisi].

[10] Supply: *it is necessary that ... be lead back* [reduci necesse est]. — The Vatican ed. alone, having suppressed *one* [unius], inserts *be lead back* [reduci], and it substitutes *for them* [illarum] in place of *for the others* [aliarum].

[11] The Vatican ed. with codex cc reads *as* [ut] for *which* [quod].

this (incommunicability) does not concern the reckoning of the paternity inasmuch as (it is) a paternity, it will be by reason[1] of something, which is incommunicable; but this is the *innascibility* or *primacy*, because the *first* cannot give a primacy to another, and the *innascibility* cannot generate an Innascible: therefore, it seems, that among the divine the Hypostasis of the Father generates for this reason, because (He is) innascible.

Last, since '*first*' and '*beginning*' [principium] is the same, just as is clear and (as) the *Philosopher* says,[2] either He is first for this reason, because (He is) the beginning, or the other way around. It is established, that the reckoning of a beginning befits Him for this reason, because He is first; for that reason He has this through Himself. And it is established, that there is a standing still in a first principle [in primo principio], not because (it is) *a principle*, but because (it is) *first*. And it is established, that that is a condition of

nobility: therefore since the Father is « the beginning of the whole Deity », as (St.) Augustine says,[3] this is, because He is the First Person, and (He is such) through this, because (He is) innascible.

This has been said without prejudice to the others. For each of these positions is great, and none is to be contemned; but *this one*[4] seems to fall more in the intellect than the *first one*, most of all if the proper acceptance of the *paternity* itself is considered [respiciatur], which is truly a relation and simultaneous in nature with the filiation, nor can it be abstracted from the nature and property of a relation; whence it thus conveys a habitude to the Son, just as '*to generate*' (does). For that reason, this position also seems more intelligible, and this will be more clear below,[5] when the innascibility is dealt with.

SCHOLIUM

I. St. Thomas treats of the same question (SUMMA., I, q. 40, a. 4) under the title. « Whether the notional acts are understood before the properties ». In the solution of this problem, St. Bonaventure disagrees at least in words with Alexander of Hales (SUMMA., p. I, q. 59, m. 3), with whom St. Thomas agrees. Alexander of Hales and St. Thomas make a distinction between the paternity as a *relation* (and thus according to understanding it presupposes generation) and as a *property* (and thus it is understood before generation). Alexander of Hales would also have it, that "*God*" be added in this formula, such that there is said: "the Father, inasmuch as (He is) God (and) father, generates. But (Bl. John Duns) Scotus (SENT., Bk. I, d. 28, q. 3, nn. 2 and 3) opposes arguments against the application of this distinction and against the sentence of St. Bonaventure. — The principal argument of St. Thomas is the 1st opposed argument in St. Bonaventure's question. The sentence of St. Thomas, which is not explained by all in the same manner, seems to have been expressed rightly by (Bl.) Peter of Tarentaise (here in q. 1, a. 3): « According to understanding the paternity is understood first, as the constitutive form of the Father, by which He personally subsists in Himself; then as the generative power, by which He acts; then as the act of generation; and last as a relation ».

II. The sentence of St. Bonaventure, to which Richard of Middleton consents, by taking the middle road, judges each sentence as probable, nay strives to put them into concord with a successful outcome. For it distinguishes in the paternity both the *fecundity*, which it conveys, and the *relation* to the Son; and again in the innascibility it distinguishes both the *privation* and the *fontal plenitude* or fecundity. To the extent that the innascibility means a *fontal plenitude*, it is the root of the generation; and thus it is true, that the Father, because He generates, is a father, that is, has a relation to the Son. But it is also true, that He generates, because (He is) a father, to the extent that the paternity includes fecundity. On innascibility, that it conveys more than a mere privation (as Bl. Scotus would have it), cf. d. 28 throughout; on origin and relation, above in d. 26, q. 3.

That we have rightly interpreted the doctrine of the Seraphic Doctor, is thoroughly proven both from the unpublished Prologue of St. Bonaventure to the Second Book of Sentences, and by the other unpublished addition to this question. We have subjoined each here in the Scholium.

III. Alexander of Hales, SUMMA., p. I, q. 59, m. 3. — (Bl. John Duns) Scotus, REPORTATIO., here in q. 1. — St. Thomas, here in q. 1, a. 1; SUMMA., I, q. 40, a. 4. — Bl. (now St.) Alber-

tus, here in a. 2. — (Bl.) Peter of Tarentaise, here in q. 1, a. 3. — Richard of Middleton, here in a. 1, q. 3. — Giles the Roman, here in 1st. princ., q. 2. — Henry of Ghent, SUMMA., a. 58, q. 3. — Durandus, here in q. 1. — (Bl.) Dionysius the Carthusian, here in q. 2.

(PREVIOUSLY) UNPUBLISHED (CONFIRMATIONS OF THIS DOCTRINE)

I. St. Bonaventure explains his own sentence concerning this question most clearly in a certain Prologue to Book Two of the Sentences, mention of which we have made in the Prolegomena, p. LVIII, and on pp. 90 and 137. Moreover, he says these words: « But perhaps it will seem to some, that I have deviated from his (i.e. Alexander of Hales) sentence, when there was a discussion of the eternal generation in the First Book, d. 27. For when there was written in his SUMMA (loc. cit. in the Scholium), that He generates for this reason, because He is *the Father*, I seemed rather to adhere to that opinion, which says, that the Father generates for this reason, because (He is) *the innascible God*; when, again, there was written by the same, that there is a saying of something among the divine, to which a word does not respond, I adhered more to that opinion, which says, that there is no *saying* without a word, and through this that I have receded from his path. But if anyone understands rightly, I did not disagree with him, neither in the first, nor in the second, because truth is not contrary to truth.

« But I judge it to be true, both that the Father generates, because (He is) *innascible*, and that He generates, because (He is) *God* (and) *father*, and this is clear in this manner. For it is plain and according to the common opinion true, that the Power of the Father generates for this reason, because It is *fecund*. Therefore, rightly is that said to be the reason for generating, which conveys the fecundity of the Power of the Father. But the fecundity is conveyed both by the name for the *innascibility* and by the name for the *paternity*, but in different manners [aliter et aliter]. For the *paternity* conveys the fecundity as if by *presupposing* and by understanding (it) beforehand, though principally it is imposed *by a habitude*. For the paternity is said to be the habitude of the Father to the Son. But the *innascibility* conveys the fecundity *out of (its) consequent understanding*: for from (its) first understanding it conveys a *privation of habitude* to the prior; but out of this privation alone it could not be a property, since (that privation) is consequent to the Essence. And for that reason the Innascible one is not only said (to be) the Father, because *He does not accept (His) 'being' from Another*, but because He does not accept (His) 'being' from Another and because *He has whence He gives 'being' to Another*.

« Who, therefore, superficially understands by attending and/or looking into (the reason), by which the name is first imposed, will deny each, saying that the

---

[1] The Vatican edition faultily reads *it will concern the reckoning of something* [erit de ratione alicuius], contradicting codices A F G P Q T W Y and Z, and also edition 1.

[2] See above d. 11, a. sole, q. 2, p. 216, footnote 9. — Next after *It is established, that* [constat quod], the Vatican edition and codex cc omit *for this reason* [ideo].

[3] ON THE TRINITY, Bk. IV, ch. 20, n. 9. See below d. 29, ch. 1, in the text of Master (Peter). — Immediately following this, the Vatican ed. with codex cc has *the first* [primum] for *the first Person* [prima persona]

[4] Codex Y has *the second* [secunda] for *this one* [haec].

[5] Distinction 28, q. 1 ff. — A little above this, after *whence* [unde], codices aa and bb have *it (i.e. the paternity)* [ista] for *it*. Then in place of *For that reason this position also* [Ideo et ista positio] very many codices together with edition 1 read *And for that reason the other position* [Et ideo alia positio], by which reading the sense is confounded, wherefore we have retained the reading of the Vatican edition. — Note, that here codices G aa and bb enrich the text with a very long addition, which you will find in the Scholium, II.

Father does not generate for this reason, because He is a *"father"*, nor that He generates for this reason, because He is *"innascible"*, because neither a habitude nor a privation is a reason for producing a Person. And as much (he speaks) according to this, he will speak the truth, but not *fully*. But, he who grasps the full [plenarium] understanding of each, by attending (to the fact) that the fecundity is conveyed through each name, will say each: both that He generates, because (He is) the innascible God, and that He generates, because (He is) God (and) a father. For it is true, that the Father generates, because He has nothing from Another, but He (also) has whence He gives to Another. It is also true, that the Father generates, because He has a fecundity in producing One similar to Himself in all things [per omnia] through the manner of nature.

« When, therefore, I said, that the Father is a father for this reason, because He generates, and not that He generates for this reason, that (He is) a father, I did not say this according to the reckoning of *fecundity*, which this name, *"paternity"*, conveys among the divine, but according to the reckoning of the *habitude*, by which the name for a father is imposed; and for that reason I did not contradict Master (Alexander), *but there I did omit to say this and I now add it*, that the paternity means not only a *habitude*, but also a *fecundity*. Whence though the reasons induced there show, that He does not generate for this reason, because (He is) a father, and (though) it is conceded, that they conclude *truly*, according to which *"father"* is imposed from a *habitude*; it had to be added, that they *do not* conclude, according to which the name for a father conveys a *fecundity*. Moreover, when I said, that the Father generates, because (He is) the innascible God, I did not say this, inasmuch as that which is *innascible* conveys a privation of habitude; for thus Master (Alexander) denies it, but I said this, inasmuch as in a man the power of *innascibility* encloses one of *fecundity*. And that is necessary to posit for this, that the innascibility is a property, just as has been shown there in a manifold manner. Moreover, I adhered rather to this position, that the Father generates, because (He is) the *innascible* God, not because the innascibility is more the *reason for generating* than the paternity, but because there is a greater *standing still* in it, beyond which it is not fitting to seek. For, if there is asked, "Why (*for what reason?*) does the Father generate?", and there is answered: "Because He is a father, that is, (He is) fecund by a fecundity of nature", still there will be a doubt and one will ask, "For what reason is *that* power more fecund than *another*? And there will be the response: "This is (so), because it has 'being' from no other". For, for this reason « the Father is the beginning of the whole Deity, because (He is) from none », as Master (Peter) says. With this reckoning rendered, the argument stands [ibi status est] nor is there further proceeding. And for that reason I said, that the Father generates, because (He is) the innascible God, not to assign a *proper reckoning* of the generation, but rather for the sake of *ending the inquiry*. For in the name for a father there is conveyed the reckoning of generation, as a *proper* (reckoning), but in the name for the *innascibility*, as a *prime* (reckoning); in the one *antecedently*, in the other *consequently*; in the one *commonly*, in the other *specially* ».

II. As has already been said above on p. 472, in footnote 5, and in the Prolegomena, p. LXIII, footnote 2, that codices G aa and bb add to this question a sufficiently lengthy disquisition to explain and defend the sentence of the Seraphic Doctor. Therefore, one asks, whether this addition was written by St. Bonaventure himself. It is manifest from the preceding fragment of the unpublished Prologue, that it was not written as part of the Commentaria, such as this was initially edited by the author. Then from the words of the addition « Above, in the Ninth Distinction », and « just as will be seen below », (that is in d. 28) it can be argued, that it is to be considered as part of some Commentary on the Book of the Sentences. Next it is clear, that this disquisition is also naught but a longer, yet faithful, exposition, agreeing frequently with his own words, of his doctrine, which is contained in the said Prologue, and that it is not unworthy of so great a Doctor. Nevertheless, the authority of the three codices, though they are ancient, does not seem to us to be sufficient, for us to affirm that St. Bonaventure is the author of this writing. For it could be, that from the very words of the Seraphic (Doctor), spoken in class, as that Prologue testifies, one of his students composed this addition and added it to one of the copies of his Commentaria, and/or that it has been inserted from some writing of his students on the Sentences after the time of the Commentaria. We have, indeed, examined very many works of the disciples of the Seraphic Doctor treating of this matter, but in vain. Moreover, it remains doubtful, whether it will be able to be found among other works. — Nevertheless, it is not improbable, that St. Bonaventure after having edited this Commentary added to it what he had taught verbally in class, since in the Prologue he says: « I omitted to say this there and now I supply it ». Therefore, it seems to him, that some words, which had omitted before, were necessary to explain his own

sentence. In whatever manner the matter is understood, this addition of the three codices is a worthy one, and for that reason we insert it here. We cite some variant readings contained in the uncials of codex G.

« Moreover, it must not be overlooked, that when there is said, whether a father generates, because (he is) a father, or whether the other way around, a distinction is customarily made, from this, that the paternity, by which the name for a *father* is conveyed, can be considered as a *property*, and/or as a *relation*. If it is considered as a *property*, thus it is the perfection of the Person of the Father, inasmuch as (He is) such a person, and this, because it is a personal property, and because every act, which convenes with a supposit, is understood to convene by reason of some property and quality and form. Accepting (the paternity) in this manner, '*to generate*' convenes with the Person of the Father and is understood to convene (with Him), because (He is) a father. But if the paternity is considered as a *relation*, since a relation means a looking-back to the other, namely to a son, thus it necessarily supposes the understanding of *a son*, and the understanding of *a son* (supposes) the understanding of *a generation*, and through this, as much as regards the reckoning of understanding, the understanding of *paternity* presupposes the understanding of *generation*. And as much as regards this understanding it is true, that He is a father for this reason, that He generates. And according to those two ways, the reasons, which are given for the opposed sides, seem to be able to be set forth [declinari] ».

« But to this distinction many things seem to run contrary. For such a distinction neither seems *in itself* to be valid, nor *as regards the proposed*.

« 1. *In itself*, indeed, it seems to deviate from rectitude, first, because among the divine a relation is superior to a property or *in More*, because (it is) more common; although among the divine there is properly no inferior and superior; for every personal property is a relation, but not vice versa [e converso]. But between an inferior and superior there falls no distinction. For it is nothing to say, that "whiteness" can be a name for a color, and/or a name for a quality. Therefore, in a completely similar manner there is no distinction, when one distinguishes, that "the paternity" can be the name of a *property*, and/or of a *relation*.

« 2. Again, no name among the divine can be proper to a Person, if it does not mean a looking-back to Another. Also, every (name), which among the divine is said absolutely, is necessarily said of the Three, just as (St.) Augustine would have it. If, therefore, the paternity names the property of a Person, this is not, except because it means the looking-back of a Person to a Person: therefore, with the relation excluded from its understanding [per intellectum], it will now not be a property. Therefore, the understanding of relation among the divine cannot be excluded from the understanding [ab intellectu] of a property neither according to the *thing* nor according to a *reckoning*. If, therefore, there falls no distinction between those, one of which is the reason for understanding the rest, neither (will there be) a distinction among those, one of which cannot be understood in any matter, with the other excluded: therefore, the result is [redit], that there is no aforesaid distinction, namely, that the paternity can be a property and/or a relation.

« 3. Furthermore, the paternity, insofar as it is a property among the divine, is in some manner predicated: therefore, either unto a *what* [in quid], or unto a *which* [in quale], or *in the manner in which One holds Himself* [in quomodo se habet]. If unto a *what*: therefore, that name is the name of the Substance more than of a property. If unto a *which*, but every (name) which is predicated among the divine as unto a *which*, passes over into the Substance, just as (Sts.) Boethius and Augustine would have it. And no such (name) is proper to a Person: therefore, the paternity is not proper to a Person. Therefore, it remains, that it is predicated as *in a manner in which One holds Himself*, because there is no other manner to assign, according to which, what is said by the paternity, is predicated. And that appears more clearly, because it does not respond to the question made through "*Which?*" [quale], but through "*In what manner does One hold Himself?*" Therefore, as it is a property, it conveys a habitude to Another, and thus a relation: therefore, it seems impossible to sustain the aforesaid distinction.

« 4. Last, when one distinguishes, that the paternity can be a relation and/or property, either this is according to a diversity on the part of *the thing*, or according to a diversity on the part of *the one understanding*: non according to a diversity on the part of *the thing*; this is established, because there is entirely a most high Simplicity There, and for that reason '*to generate*' and '*to be a father*' are the same, and *the paternity* and *the generation* (are the same). Therefore, it will be according to a diversity on the part of *the one understanding*. On the contrary: just as our intellect imposed a word upon the *general* production and emanation itself, so it imposed the word for *paternity* upon the habitude

and relation itself. Therefore, just as one does not distinguish, that '*to generate*' can name the property of a Person and/or (name) a production, similarly neither does it seem that a distinction can rationally be made in that which (He is) a father.

« Nevertheless, the aforesaid distinction does not seem to be valid *as regards the proposed*.

« 5. For it is said, that the understanding of the paternity, as a relation [ut est relatio], presupposes the understanding of the generation, and this according to the reckoning of understanding, although, inasmuch as it is a property, it is the other way around. *But on the contrary*: whatever is prior to something according to thing and/or understanding, which is prior to a third according to thing and/or understanding, the first one is necessarily prior to the third, conserving the same manner of priority. But that, from which there turns out no consequence (cf. Aristotle, ON THE PREDICAMENTS, ch. "On the Prior") and that which has the reckoning of a superior, is prior. Therefore, since relation so holds itself to a property, that the understanding of the paternity, as a *relation*, is a preamble to the understanding of the paternity, as a *property*, and the understanding of the generation is a preamble to the understanding of the paternity, as a *relation*, according to the aforesaid distinction: therefore, it is a preamble to the understanding of the same, as a property, through that maxim: "whatever is prior to a prior, is also prior to a posterior". Let this be accepted sanely as much as regards our understanding, because among the divine one does not happened to find properly a prior and a posterior.

« 6. Again, a *positive* understanding in the same and in respect to the same antecedes a *privative* understanding, just as a convening antecedes a difference, and just as an affirmation antecedes a negation; but the paternity, as a *relation*, means a looking-back and a habitude to a son, as a *property*, it means the distinction of the Father from the Son, because the proper is what convenes with (one) alone: therefore, the understanding of the paternity, as a *relation*, is a preamble to the understanding of the same, as a *property*: therefore, if the paternity is consequent to the understanding of the generation according to our understanding inasmuch as (it is) a *relation*, it remains that it is (also) consequent inasmuch as (it is) a *property*.

« 7. Furthermore, in whatsoever manner paternity is accepted, it is a true saying, concerning him who begets, that he is a father, even if he does not generate by an act nor generates in the future [de futuro]: therefore, paternity can be understood to be in anyone without this, that he generates in an act. If, therefore, the proper reason for anything both according to thing and according to understanding posits that, of which it is the reckoning, it seems that in no manner is the paternity the reason for generating. *If you say*, that this is true of paternity in a creature, not in the Creator; *against this* is, that "paternity" is not taken equivocally here and There: therefore, the understanding and the reckoning of understanding is completely similar, just as also the reason for naming and for imposing (a name upon), whatever is on the part of a thing.

« 8. Last, thus is the filiation the *property* and *relation* of the Son, just as the paternity (is) also of the Father. But in whatever manner the filiation be accepted, whether as a *property* or as a *relation*, it is always a true saying, that the Son is a son, because (He has been) begotten; and this (St.) Augustine often saying both in his Sermon on the Purification of the Blessed Virgin and in his book, ON THE TRINITY, and this same does (St.) Gregory say, and it is has above in the Ninth Distinction. Therefore, in whatever manner the paternity be accepted, it is always a true saying, that He is a father, because He generates.

« It seems, therefore, that the aforesaid distinction neither *in itself* nor *as regards the proposed* has an efficacy. On each side [haec et illa] more objections can be made against the aforesaid distinction.

« *Response*: If anyone, therefore, understands the aforesaid distinction in a superficial manner, I judge, that he will find very many obstacles [plurima obviantia] for himself; but if we attend to the force of the word, it will become sufficiently clear [lucidum], that it seems ambiguous. For it is plain, that the word for the paternity insinuates two (things) about the Person, of which it is said: both a *fecundity*, through which He is the principle of the Son, and a *habitude*, according to which He is referred to Him. If, therefore, in the aforesaid distinction, by which there is said, that the paternity can be considered under a reckoning of a property and of a relation, a distinction can be understood to be made between the understanding of *fecundity* and (that) of the *consequent habitude*, the calumny of words and the importunity of objections ceases. For no one of sane mind doubts, that a *fecundity* of nature according to

the reckoning of understanding precedes the very production of the generation, and that the *habitude* itself is consequent according to the reckoning of understanding to the generation itself: for a father is never understood to generate a son, unless because a fecundity is understood to be in him; never is he understood to be referred, unless he is understood to have a son. And thus the understanding of the paternity by reason of *the fecundity* is a preamble to the understanding of the generation or to the act of generating according to the reckoning of understanding; however, the understanding of the *habitude* and of the relation is the other way around. Thus, therefore, it is manifest, that if we speak of this name, "*father*", as much as regards its *ultimate* understanding, by which the name is imposed, whatsoever kind of distinction is made, that He does not generate for this reason, because (He is) a father, but rather the other way around; though we can concede, that He does generate for this reason, because (He is) a father, as much as regards the understanding of *the fecundity*, which is a quasi preamble; and through this we can avoid all the preceding objections.

« A completely similar manner of distinguishing is also valid for many other questions, such as, whether a father generates, because (he is) *innascible*, because as much as regards (its) first understanding, which is a privative one, innascibility is not a reckoning of generating, but (it is one) as much as regards (its) consequent (understanding), which (understanding) is a fontal plenitude. — It is also valid for the question, whether the *power of generating* is said according to substance, or according to relation. — Nevertheless, it is valid for the question, when there is asked, whether by abstract properties there is an understanding of a distinction among the Hypostases. And through this many opinions can be reduced to a harmony, which (otherwise) seem repugnant (to one another). For in questions of this kind concerning the properties, not a small measure of force is constituted in the understanding, which the name chiefly cause, and for that reason one must not adhere exceedingly on one side of this kind (of question), for the reason that controversies *concerning names* are to be left to the pertinacious, according to the teaching of the Philosopher [iuxta philosophicum documentum] (cf. TOPICS, Bk. VIII. ch. 4, at the end).

« From these, therefore, it is clear, that one of the aforesaid positions or opinions does not impugn the other; since it rather helps to elucidate [dilucidandam] the truth. For while each posits, that the act of generation befits [competit] the Person of the Father by reason of (His) *fecundity* through a manner of nature, they entirely agree; but while they say, that that fecundity is conveyed through these two names "*paternity*" and "*innascibility*", they do not contradict (one another), because "*paternity*" conveys the fecundity as much as regards the first understanding or as a preamble; but (it conveys) the "*innascibility*" only as much as regards the consequent (understanding). For "*paternity*" conveys fecundity in respect to an act of generating *determinately*, and thus signifies (it) as the *proper* reckoning of generating; but "*innascibility*" (signifies it) as the *first* (reckoning), since just as Master (Peter) says below: « The Father is the principle of the whole Divinity, because (He is) from no one ». — And if there be asked, why the Person of the Father is more fecund to generate than another Person; the reason is this, because that One is first and thus from no One; and this name, "*innascible*", conveys this, just as will be seen below, nor does any further question remain, why, that is, an innascible Person is innascible, nay there is a *standing-still* there. But, if anyone shall not find a standing-still or rest in the *first*, when he investigates the reckoning of the first and most primordial emanation, that is, (that) of the generation of the Son of God, I do not know if one is to ever find it in another place ».

The last proposition is extant in codex G alone, in which here there is terminated what is adjoined. But in codices aa and bb there are very many other things added, which do seem to be written by St. Bonaventure. For contrary to the custom of the Seraphic Doctor, who strives in all things for brevity, not a few things, from what has already been said and nearly in the same words, are repeated. There is also added the other question, namely, whether the fecundity in the Father is said according to substance, or according to relation, and the distinction posited above is applied to the two questions: whether the power of generating is said according to substance, or according to relation (above in d. 7, q. 1), and whether abstracting from the properties, one happens to understand the Persons (in the following question). But among these scarcely worthy of being noted is contained, except that sentence, which we have transcribed in the Prolegomena, p. LXIII, ch. 1.

QUESTION III

Whether the properties can be abstracted from the Divine Persons?

Third, there is asked, whether it happens that the properties are abstracted. And that it does not, seems:

1. Because every abstraction supposes a concretion; but there is properly a concretion only among those, in which there is a denominative predication:[1] therefore, if this is in accidents only, it seems, that wheresoever there is a positing of an abstractable property, there is a positing of an accidental property. But such is in no manner posited among the divine: ergo etc..

2. Likewise, wheresoever there is abstraction, the abstracted is more simple than the concrete[2] — this has no instance* — but among the divine there is no greater and lesser simplicity, since everything which is There, is most simple and in fine belongs to the whole Simplicity: therefore, among the divine there occurs no abstraction.

3. Likewise, every abstraction is of a universal from a particular, or is of a form from matter;[3] but among the divine there is neither a universal nor a particular, nor form nor matter: therefore, among the divine there is no abstraction.

4. Likewise, whensoever anything is abstracted from anything, what remains is less, than there was before the abstraction, because each is something — for nothing is not abstracted from something, nor nothing from nothing, but something from something — therefore, if the paternity is abstractable from a Person and/or Hypostasis, therefore, It would have less of entity than with the paternity. *But on the contrary*: with the paternity abstracted, a Hypostasis is understood to be God: therefore, if It would have less of entity than with the paternity, God would not be understood to have a most high "being".

ON THE CONTRARY: 1. Master (Peter Lombard) says in the text:[4] « "The paternity", "the filiation", (and) "the procession" signify only the relations themselves »: therefore, either something responds to this in the thing, or nothing. If nothing: therefore, they signify falsely and in an empty manner [inaniter]; if something: therefore, it seems, that they are abstractable on the part of the thing.

2. Likewise, with the Son not understood [non intellecto],° the Hypostasis of the Father can, nevertheless, be understood to be; but with the Son not understood, the paternity cannot be understood: therefore, with a[5] property abstracted, that Hypostasis, of which the property was, can still be understood to be. But, whensoever any two so hold themselves, that one can be understood without the other, one can be abstracted from the other: therefore, truly a property can be understood to be abstracted from a Hypostasis.

3. Likewise, when I say *"person"*, I understand 'one having a nature with[6] a incommunicable property'; but it is established, that that this whole is not understood together, therefore, first one, afterwards the other: therefore, first I understand a nature, then the one having it, and third the incommunicable property: therefore, each one is intelligible through itself, therefore, also the property without (its) subject: therefore from this it is abstractable. *If you say to me*, that on the part of the *understanding* [intellectus] it can be abstracted, but not on the part of the *thing; on the contrary*: then according to this, if there is an abstraction on the part of the manner of understanding, therefore, the notion and the person do not differ except in the manner alone of speaking; and this has been disproved above.[7]

4. Likewise, relation among the divine is a true relation, because, as (St. Severinus) Boethius says:[8] « God is not related without a relation »; but where there is a true quantity and quantum, there is a true abstraction, not only on the part of the *understanding*, but even (on the part) of the *thing*: therefore, for an equal reason, where there is a true relation or one truly related, there is a true abstraction.

5. Likewise, whensoever any property has a being distinguished from another according to *thing*, from which it is not distinguished according to *supposit*, there the abstraction is not only on the part of the *understanding*, but also on the part of the *thing*; but the paternity differs from the innascibility, however, the Father does not differ from the Innascible One:[9] therefore, truly and properly a property or notion is abstractable from a Person, not only on our part, but also on the part of the thing.

---

[1] Aristotle, ON THE PREDICAMENTS, ch. 1 says: « However, they are said (to be) denominatives which differing in case from something according to name have an appellation, such as "grammarian" from "grammar", and "strong" from "strength" ». Therefore, two (things) are required for this, that something be a denominative or be denominatively predicated of something, namely, that it be concrete adjectively (non substantively, as "man"), and that it be derived from some abstract accident. Hence it is also easily understood, that the Seraphic Doctor immediately adds: « therefore, if this is in accidents only ». Cf. also above, d. 5, a. 1, in reply to nn. 2 and 3, and below in d. 33, q. 3.

[2] For the abstract means the form alone, but the concrete a form and a subject.

[3] Cf. St. Thomas, SUMMA., I, q. 40, a. 3: It must be said, that a *twofold* abstraction comes to be through the intellect. *One*, indeed, according to which the universal is abstracted from the particular, as 'animal' from 'man'. But *the other*, according to which a form is abstracted from matter, just as the form of a circle is abstracted through the intellect from every sensible matter. —

Cf. also Aristotle, PHYSICS, Bk. II, text 18, (ch. 2); ON THE SOUL, Bk. III, texts 10 ff, 35, and 39 (chs. 4, 6, and 8), and METAPHYSICS, Bks. XIII and XIV throughout (Bk.s XII and XIII); and St. Thomas and Averroës in their commentaries on these passages.

[4] Here in ch. 2. — A little below this, for *to this* [huic], which is extant in very many codices and also in edition 1, the Vatican edition with a few codices has *still* [adhuc], codd. A H N X & Y have *here* [hic].

[5] Codex W reads *this* [hac] for *a*.

[6] In place of *with* [cum], which even the Vatican edition exhibits, together with codex cc, many codices with edition 1 have *out of* [ex].

[7] Distinction 26, q. 1.

[8] See above, d. 22, a. sole, q. 4, p. 397, footnote 2. — The minor of the argument is hinted at by Aristotle, ON THE SOUL, Bk. II, in those texts, which we have just cited. — At the end of the argument, before *abstraction* [abstractio], the Vatican ed. with cod. cc alone omits *true* [vera].

[9] The Vatican edition, breaking with the more outstanding codices and edition 1, reads *however, it does not differ from the innascible Father* [non autem differt ab innascibili Patre].

---

* *Trans. notes*: Here *instance* [instantia] is the technical scholastic term for a contrary proof or example, or an instance in which the contrary occurs or is obtained.

° Throughout this Question, St. Bonaventure speaks of intellectus, which word, since it is a supine, is a verbal noun, having the sense of both a power (i.e. the intellect or the understanding) and the consequence of that power (an understanding), and, thus, in English can be rendered as either *intellect* or *understanding*. This ambiguity allows the Seraphic Doctor to speak of the intellectual power of the soul (the intellect) and that which it obtains (an understanding of something), while using the same Latin term. It is in the latter sense that intellectus noster is composed and/or resolvable, since the understanding which our intellect obtains is by a composition of *what something is* [quid est], i.e. the nature or species, with *that by which it is* [quo est], i.e. the genus or difference, and is resolvable according to the reckoning of these two, in which it abstracts the latter from the former. It should be noted, that the failure to make this distinction, is the cause of innumerable misunderstandings of Scholastic Theology, regarding intellectus. For the same power and that which it obtains by its act, is really the same according to thing [re], because it is the very nature of the intellect to obtain an understanding of an

CONCLUSION

The abstraction of the properties among the Divine Persons is not on part of the thing, but on the part of our understanding.

I Respond: It must be said, that '*something be abstracted from something*' is in a twofold manner. In one manner there is the abstraction,[1] which has its rise *from the nature of the thing*; and in this manner the universal is abstracted from the particular, and form from matter, since in each manner there is composition and diversity. In another manner there is the abstraction, which has its rise from *our intellect* [ab intellectu nostro]. For our intellect when it understands anything complete, of necessity understands in a twofold manner or by a twofold reckoning, namely, through the manner of that *which is* and of that *by which (it is)*.[2] For always, when it understands anything, it considers it intelligible through some reckoning, through which it also grasps it; and thus our understanding [intellectus noster] is resolvable into the understanding of that *which is* and of that *by which (it is)*,[3] because there was a composition about it.

Since, therefore, a real abstraction presupposes a composition, which in no manner is in God, neither as much as regards the Essence, nor as much as regards a Person; for that reason in no manner is there an abstraction There on the part of the *thing*. *Again*, since we understand God according to the ability [possibilitatem][4] of our intellect, for that reason our intellect understands God through the manner of that *which (He is)* and of that *by which (He is)*; and our understanding is resolvable, and because (it is) resolvable, (it is) also composed, though the thing is not composed. As much as regards this there can be an abstraction and separation, to understand that *by which He is, what He is*, with (Him) not being understood [non intelligendo].[5] And since the manner of *signifying* is consequent to the manner of *understanding*, for that reason it happens that *one signifies* that *which (He is)* in abstraction, and this on the part of the communicable, as when there is said "*the Deity*",[6] and on the part of the incommunicable, as when there is said "*the paternity*".

I concede, therefore, just as the first reasons manifest, that there is There no *real* abstraction.

1. 2. 3. To that which is objected unto the contrary, concerning signification, it must be said, that something does respond on the part of our understanding; nor is it necessary [oportet], that an abstraction respond.[7] For just as our understanding, though it is composed, truly understands the simple through the manner of a composed, because it posits that composition about *itself*, not about *the thing understood*; thus entirely must it be understood concerning abstraction. And through this, the two following (objections) are clear, which have been taken from the reckoning of understanding.

To that which is objected, that they then differ solely in the manner of speaking; it must be said, that, just as has been touched upon in the preceding Distinction,[8] a relation according to comparison passes over to the *subject*, (a relation) according to *object* or terminus remains; and this is, because abstraction is of a form from a *subject*, not from a *terminus*, because the paternity is abstracted[9] from the Father, not from the Son; and as much as regards the comparison to the *subject* it is entirely the same, for that reason in no manner is it abstractable on the part of the thing. Nevertheless, it can still differ in some manner through a comparison to the *object*, which difference is indeed taken on the part of the *thing*; but just as that difference causes nothing regarding a *composition*, so it causes nothing regarding *an abstraction*.

4. 5. And in this manner are clear the two following (objections), because the relation remains and it is distinguished by the other (Person); but this is through a comparison to the *object*, not to the *subiect*.[10]

SCHOLIUM

I. Since the properties of the divine persons, such as *the paternity*, are expressed with an *abstract word*, the question arises, in what sense does the abstraction come into being. *Abstraction*, just as *distinction*, can be both *real* (i.e. on the of the thing), by which it conveys the composition (that is) in the thing, from which it abstracts, and according to the *manner of understanding*, which does not suppose such composition. A twofold *example* of the first species of abstraction is made, both according to the 3rd argument of the fundament and St. Thomas, Summa., I, q. 40, a. 3, this species is again divided into *two inferior species*, namely, to the extend that there is abstracted a *universal* from a particular, and/or a *form* from matter. This distinction belongs to Aristotle, and is explained by St. Thomas in his Commentary on Aristotle's Physics, Bk. II, text 18, lecture 3, in these words: « One must consider, that there are many (things) conjoined according to thing, one of which does not concern the understanding of the other ... and for that reason one can be understood separately without the other. And according to this it is that one understanding is abstracted from the other. Moreover, it is manifest, that posteriors do not concern the understanding of priors, but vice versa. Whence priors can be understood without posteriors, and not vice vera: just as is clear, that '*animal*' is prior to '*man*', and

---

[1] For *there is the abstraction* [abstractio est] the Vatican edition has *(it is) by the abstraction* [abstractione], a corrupt reading. Immediately after this, just as a little below, we have replaced, from codices I P Q and aa, *its rise* [ortum] for *whole* [totum], which the Vatican edition with the other manuscripts puts instead.

[2] Codex K reads *and by which it is* [et quo est] for *and of that by which (it is)* [et ipsius quo].

[3] Codices K P Q and X have explicitly *it is* [est].

[4] That it, its potentiality or imperfection. — Not much after this, on the authority of codices T and Z and edition 1, we have restored *for that reason* [ideo], which is absent from the Vatican edition. Somewhat further below this, for *(it is) also composed* [etiam compositus], codex I has *it is composed* [est compositus], and many codices together with edition 1 have less distinctly *and (it is) composed* [et compositus].

[5] The Vatican edition together with codex cc has *with (Him) not understood* [non intellecto].

[6] The codices, excepting one or the other, just as also the first six editions, prefix to *the Deity*" [deitas] the phrase "*God is*, which reading, however, does not convene with that which has been said in d. 5, a. 1, q. 1.

[7] Codex O adds *on the part of the thing* [a parte rei].

[8] Question 2. — A little above this, codex V has *in the manner alone of speaking* [solo modo loquendi] for *solely in the manner of speaking* [solum modo loquendi]. A little below this, we have restored the words *and this is* [et hoc est], from codd. C F L O R S U & W, which had been suppressed in the Vatican ed., in place of which codd. X & Y read *and the reason is* [et ratio est], cod. X reads *and the reason for this is* [et ratio huius est], and codd. A G H K T V Z bb ee & ff, with ed. 1, have *and (this) is* [et est].

[9] Thus codices I O and T, together with edition 1; the Vatican edition has *abstracts* [abstrahit] for *is abstracted* [abstrahitur]. A little after this codex R has *differs* [differt] for *can differ* [differre potest].

[10] For *the subject* [subiectum], codd. E K V & X have *the thing* [rem]; edd. 2, 4 & 6 have *to the thing and this is the subject* [ad rem et hoc est subiectum].

---

object; and being a power in the soul which as a form is an act [quae ut forma actus sit], the intellect is to this extent not only a power but also an act and, hence, can be considered both as a thing and as that which it actually obtains. But, here, it must be carefully noted, that "that which the intellect obtains" can be considered in a twofold manner, either properly and/or terminally as that intelligible species or reckoning which it abstracts from the thing it understands, or consequentially and/or relationally, as that understanding that it obtains in itself through that intelligible species, which species as an accident in the intellect, enters into composition with the intellect; and which consequent understanding is, under one aspect, the relation of the intellect, considered as a power, to that intelligible species, since as St. Thomas observes, "truth is the adequation of intellect and thing". These dis-

'man' is prior to 'this man'. For 'man' holds itself from an addition to 'animal' and 'this man' form an addition to 'man'. And on this account 'man' does not concern the understanding of 'animal', nor 'Socrates' the understanding of 'man': whence 'animal' can be understood without 'man' and 'man' without 'Socrates' and other individuals; and *this is what abstracting a universal from a particular is* ». Then he explains the abstraction, which mathematicians make from sensible and natural matter: « Moreover, similarly too among all accidents, which come upon a substance, first there comes upon it quantity, and then the sensible qualities, and the actions and passion and movements, consequent to the sensible qualities. Therefore, if *quantity* does not include in its own understanding the sensible qualities and/or passions and/or movements, yet it includes in its own understanding the substance ... And for that reason quantities of this kind, and what accede to them, are according to understanding abstracted from movement and from sensible matter, as is said in METAPHYSICS, Bk. VII. Therefore, because they have been so abstracted from movement according to understanding, that they do not include in their understanding the sensible matter subjected to movement; for that reason the mathematician can abstract (them) from sensible matter, and it differs nothing as much as regards the truth of the consideration, whether they are considered in this manner or in that ». In the same place, the Angelic (Doctor) speaks also of the error of Plato, who taught, that all which are abstracted according to understanding, are abstracted according to thing.

Brülifer (on this passage) understands the abstraction of form from matter of the separation of the soul from the body, with the intervention of death. It is more aptly understood of mathematical abstraction, « just as the form of a circle is abstracted through the intellect from every sensible matter » (St. Thomas, SUMMA., loc. cit.) — For more on abstraction see in St. Bonaventure, SENT., Bk. IV, d. 50, p. II, a. 1. q. 12, where in the 1st argument of the fundament and in the body of the question he distinguishes a threefold grade of abstraction according to the act of *sensing*, *imagining* and *understanding*.

II. Though real abstraction and/or (abstraction) on the part of the thing, is not admitted (in God), yet it follows least of all, that the properties are distinguished from the Essence and among themselves only in a manner of speaking, as (Peter) Praepositivus wants it. This opinion is explicit reprobated in the solution to n. 3, and below in d. 33, q. 1 (cf. also above d. 26, q. 1, Scholium). — St. Thomas, SUMMA., q. 32, a. 2, and q. 40, a . 2 teaches the entirely same doctrine from the same principles.

III. Alexander of Hales, SUMMA., p. I, q. 68, m. 5, a. 6, § 2. — (Bl. John Duns) Scotus, REPORTATIO., Bk. I, d. 26, q. 3; QUODLIBETALS., q. 4. — St. Thomas, SENT., Bk. I, d. 26, q. 1, a. 2; SUMMA., I, q. 40, a. 3. — Bl. (now St.) Albertus (Magnus), SENT., Bk. I, d. 26, a. 5. — (Bl.) Peter of Tarentaise, SENT., Bk. I, d. 26, q. 1, a. 4. — Richard of Middleton, SENT., Bk. I, d. 26, a. 2, q. 1 and 2. — Giles the Roman, SENT., Bk. I, d. 26, 1st. princ., q. 3. — Henry of Ghent, SUMMA., a. 56, a. 3, n. 7 ff. — (Bl.) Dionysius the Carthusian, SENT., Bk. I, d. 26, q. 3.

QUESTION IV

Whether it is licit to opine in a contrary manner concerning the notions or properties?

Fourth and last, there is asked, whether it is a sin to opine in a contrary manner concerning the notions and properties. And it seems, that it is not:

1. Since the Saints had contrary opinions concerning the Scriptures, and yet did not sin, but for them (having contrary opinions) was only a punishment. Whence (St.) Augustine (says):[1] « To approve the false for the true is not the nature of man as established [hominis instituti], but a punishment for the damned ».

2. Likewise, (St.) Jerome (says):[2] « That what does not have truth from the Scriptures, is contemned with the same facility, by which it is approved »; but the notions do not have (their) truth from the Scriptures, but have been invented by the masters (of theology): therefore, it is licit to contemn many things in this regard [ibi] by the same reckoning, by which (it is licit) to prove (them).

3. Likewise, this seems *by reason*, because the number of the notions and (things) of this kind does not concern those (things) which are necessary for salvation; but it is licit to opine in a contrary manner among those (things) which do not pertain to the way of salvation, and this without sin: therefore, also among the notions.[3]

4. Likewise, if there is a sin in this [ibi], therefore, (it belongs) either *to faith*, or *to morals*. Not *to faith*, because it is not contrary to the articles (of the Faith); not *to morals*, because 'to be believe the false' does not respect morals: therefore, (there is) no sin.

ON THE CONTRARY: 1. Of two opining in a contrary manner about the notions it is necessary that one of the two say the false about divine (things); but a lie about divine (things) is a lie in the Christian Religion, and this is a most grave sin:[4] ergo etc..

2. Likewise, with two opining in a contrary manner about the notions, it is necessary that one of the two be deceived and err; but error about divine (things) is the most dangerous. Whence (St.) Augustine in the first book, ON THE TRINITY (says):[5] « Neither does one err anywhere more dangerously, nor is anything found more fruitfully ». If, therefore, an error about the Humanity of Christ is a sin: therefore, also much more strongly about the notions.

3. Likewise, since the properties are God Himself, he who says and/or believes, that the properties are not, and/or that they are not what they are, says of God what He is not; but he who says, that God is not what He is, and/or the other way around, errs by the error of sin: therefore, since one of the two opining in this manner[6] is of such a kind, ergo etc..

4. Likewise, just as (St.) Augustine says:[7] « Not only does the one who says the false, lie, but also who asserts a doubt »; but each of those opining says what (is) a doubt, because neither opinion of the two is certain: therefore, each lies. But who lies about God

---

[1] RETRACTATIONS, Bk. I, ch. 9, n. 5.

[2] ON THE GOSPEL OF ST. MATTHEW, Mt. 23: 35, in which text and also a little below this in the minor of the argument, codices G H Z aa and bb exhibit *authority* [auctoritatem], which word is extant even in the original, for *truth* [veritatem].

[3] In the Vatican edition and codex cc there is wanting the conclusion: *therefore, also among the notions* [ergo et in notionibus], which in all the other codices is had.

[4] Cf. (St.) Augustine, ON THE LIE, ch. 3, n. 4 and passim.

[5] Chapter 3, n. 5. — The Vatican edition, in the text cited, reads *elsewhere* [alibi] for *anywhere* [alicubi]; codex G a little further above

this, for *but error about* [sed error circa] substitutes *but to err about* [sed errare circa] and then consequently changes *the most dangerous* [periculosissimus] to *most dangerous* [periculosissimum].

[6] With some codices, such as H and Z, and edition 1, we have inserted *in this manner* [sic], which was wanting in the Vatican edition.

[7] ON THE LIE, ch. 3, n. 3, according to its sense. — Near the end of the argument, the Vatican ed. with cod. cc falsely substitutes *True* [Veram] for *God* [Deum], and then the Vatican ed. after *when very much* [ut plus] inserts *who* [qui]; the reading *when very much* [ut plus], which signifies the same as *when very much* [ut plurimum], we have taken from cod. T; the other codd. with the Vatican ed. omit *when* [ut], but ed. 1 omits *but when ... mortally* [sed ut plus mortaliter].

---

tinctions are evident in the text of the Seraphic Doctor when he says in the reply to nn. 1-3, « because (the intellect) posits that composition about *itself* »: in which the power is that which "posits", and the intelligible species is that which is "that composition", and the relation of the two is signified by "about itself". The English translation of this term, intellectus, therefore, follows the context. This understanding of intellectus, as a power and the consequence of that power, is confirmed by St. Bonaventure's usage of this term intellectus in 3rd opposed argument above, where there is objected within the argument that there can be an abstraction a parte intellectus, using the supine for the thing or power, as a noun, and the argument proceeds, through the admission of an abstraction a parte modi intellgendi, using the gerund for the same, but at the end of the first paragraph of the response

sins mortally and/or venially but when very much, (he sins) mortally: therefore, each sins.

CONCLUSION

In those things which have not been determined about the notions by the Church, it is licit to opine contrary (things), but not to presumptuously assert (them).

I RESPOND: It must be said, that *to opine in a contrary manner* can be either about those (things) which pertain to the doctrine of *the Christian Religion*, and/or about those which pertain to the doctrine of *human investigation* [humanae inquisitionis]. About those which pertain to the doctrine of *human investigation* it is licit *to opine* and *to assert* in a contrary manner; *to opine* indeed,[1] because these are not made [illa faciunt] for salvation, *to assert*, for the reason that they are subject to our inquisition. — Among those which pertain to the doctrine of (our) *Religion* one must make a distinction. For certain (doctrines) are from the *necessity of the Faith*, certain ones from *the certitude[2] of Scripture*, certain ones are *adjoined* to these latter, as are those which are made for the explanation of the Faith and (for) the exposition of Scripture.

About those (doctrines) which are from *the necessity of the Faith*, to opine contrary (things) simply (speaking) is a sin in one of the two, namely, the one who opines *the false*. And if it is a simple opinion, there is the sin of an error; but if (there is) the assertion and defense (of it), (it is) not only an error, but is to be said (to be) "a heresy".

Among those (doctrines), however, which are from[3] *the certitude of Scripture*, it is licit that *those ignorant* of the Scriptures opine in a contrary manner; nor is it a fault, that the one simple man believes, that Jacob was the father of Isaac, the other of the two (does) not, but (believes) the other way around. And the first one, though indeed he suspects this and/or opines (it), he does not sin,[4] because he is ignorant of Scripture. But for *those knowing* Scripture it is not licit, nay one of the two sins if he *simply* opines (contrarily). But if *he defends* (his contrary opinion), he is to be judged a heretic, since he contradicts Sacred Scripture.

Among those (doctrines), however, which are *adjoined* to the Faith and/or to Scripture, either one opinion *follows after the Faith* and Scripture, and the other follows the opposite; and then it must be said, that *before* a thorough treatment [pertractationem][5] it is licit to opine in a contrary manner, but *after* a thorough treatment it is not licit, nay it is a sin, just as among those (doctrines), which have been determined through the Faith and Scripture, just as was (the one) concerning the opinion of (Gilbert) of Porretain about the (divine) properties. For he said, that they were not God, and the consequence of this was [ad hoc consequitur] contrary to the Faith. For when the Church adores a (divine) property, She then would not adore God, but then, God would not have been adored (since God and His divine properties are the same according to thing). Whence if, after it was shown to him that (this was) unfitting, he had not retracted (his) error, he would have been judged a heretic by the Church; but he did retract (it) in the Council of Rheims, as (St.) Bernard (of Clairvaux) says.[6] — Among those (doctrines), however, which are *adjoined* to the faith and *do not follow (after)* nor are repugnant (to it),[7] because there are doubts, it is licit *to opine*, but it is not licit *to assert*, because *to opine* belongs to the reason of one conferring, but *to assert* a doubt about God belongs to the reason of the proud.

It must be conceded, therefore, that each one opining, if *he asserts*, he sins, not on account of error, but on account of presumption; and thus it must be conceded, that it is licit in this manner [ibi] to opine contrary (things).

1. To that which is objected, that (it is) a lie in the Christian Religion etc.; it must be said, that it is not *a lie*, because neither (of the two) speaks against credulity; (it is) not (a lie)[8] in the Christian Religion, because it does not concern the necessity of the Faith and/or of morals.

2. To that which is objected, that that error is dangerous; it must be said, that it is true, inasmuch as it is contrary to the Faith; but if it concerns those which do not pertain to the Faith, it is not true.

3. To that which is objected, that he sins, because he says, that God is not what He is etc.; it must be said, that that is true, if it has been determined through the Faith and/or Scripture; otherwise he does not sin, unless he asserts and/or defends (the contrary opinion as true).

---

[1] The text, which the Vatican edition, exhibits thus distorted and mutilated is: *to assert, because these do not make for salvation. To assert, however, contraries in those which* etc. [asserere, quia illa non faciunt ad salutem. Asserere autem contraria in his quae etc], we have restored from the manuscripts and edition 1. Next, codex V reads *of the Christian Religion* [christianae] for *of (our) Religion* [religionis].

[2] Edition 1 has *the rectitude* [rectitudine]; the Vatican edition together with the editions and codices reads *the necessity* [necessitate], but below, where the same formula is repeated, they read *the certitude* [certitudine], which word certainly expresses the sense more correctly.

[3] Codices G K and aa after *from* [de] insert *the necessity and/or* [necessitate vel]; then codex O substitutes *necessity* [necessitate] for *certitude* [certitudine], and a little after this edition 1 reads *for the ignorant ... to opine* etc. [ignorantibus].

[4] The words *he does not sin* [non peccat] is wanting in not a few codices; in codices aa and bb, in their place, there is read *he is not a heretic* [non est haereticus]. A little before the Vatican edition, without the support of the codices, after *though indeed* [licet quidem] omits *this* [hoc], and after *opines* [opinetur] it has *a falsehood, yet* [falsum] for *(it)*,.

[5] The Vatican edition without the authority of the codices and edition 1 here and a little below this has *thorough confrontation* [percontationem] for *thorough treatment* [pertractationem].

[6] ON THE CANTICLE OF CANTICLES, Sermon 80, nn. 8 and 9. See also below d. 33, a. 1, q. 1, where more is said of the opinion of Gilbert of Porretain.

[7] This is the second member of the distinction, which the Seraphic Doctor makes regarding those which are adjoined to the Faith; wherefore, cod. T, which we follow, after the words *Among those (doctrines)* [in his], inserts *however* [autem]. For *and do not follow (after)* [et non sequuntur] very many codd., such as A C F G K & O, exhibit *and it does not follow* [non sequitur], and codd. H I P Q T & W have *and error does not follow* [nec sequitur error]. Then after *are repugnant* [repugnant], the Vatican edd., with no codex supporting it, inserts explicitly *it* [ei], and a little below this after *to assert* [asserere] with a few codd., it reads *a doubt about God* [dubium circa Deum]. — The words immediately following: *to opine belongs to the reason of one conferring* [opinari est rationis conferentis], are to be accepted in the sense of what the Seraphic Doctor says in SENT., Bk. III, d. 24, a. 1. q. 2: « In one manner an opinion is said (to be) the assent to one side with fear for the other; in another manner an opinion is said (to be) an assent of the soul generates from more probable reasons », thus, it is understood to be the act of the reason, by which, having made a comparison among the probable arguments of the diverse sentences, one adheres to one sentence, not excluding the possibility, that the other sentence is true.

[8] Supply: *it is ... a lie* [est mendacium]. The Vatican ed. has the corrupt reading: *credulity; in the Christian Religion* [credulitatem in Christiana religione].

---

saying, in intellectum ipsius *quod est* et ipsius *quo*, using the supine for the consequent understanding obtained by the action of the power. However, it should be noted that the Seraphic Doctor in second proposition of the reply to nn. 1, 2 and 3, uses the term in both senses simultaneously, not making this distinction, since he speaks according to the unity of the thing, since the power and the consequent act of the power are the same thing according to thing [secundum rem]. Cf. Aristotle's distinction, regarding the possible (passive) intellect and the agent (active) intellect.

4. What is objected last, must be conceded. For he, who, on his own authority [propria auctoritate], asserts and/or affirms of God, what neither Scripture nor the Faith says nor (what) follows after these,[1] is to be judged *presumptuous*, even if he speaks the true; and if he doubts in his heart and affirms with his mouth, he is *mendacious*; if he asserts in each manner, he is *proud*.

SCHOLIUM

Gilbert of Porretain, thinking that the relations and properties are *assistant* in God, argued from this, that they are not God (cf. below d. 33, q. 1). Whence the question arose, whether the doctrine concerning the notions pertained to the Faith. What here touches upon *the Faith*, is explained diffusely in SENT., III, d. 25, chiefly, a. 1, q. 1 and 3. — The other masters are in agreement:

Alexander of Hales, SUMMA., p. I, q. 68, m. 1, a. 2. — St. Thomas, SENT., Bk. I, d. 33, q. 1, a. 5; SUMMA., I, q. 32, a. 4. — Bl. (now St.) Albertus (Magnus), SENT., Bk. I, d. 26, a. 14. — (Bl.) Peter of Tarentaise, SENT., Bk. I, d. 33, q. 1, a. 1. — Giles the Roman, here in the 2nd. princ., q. 2. — (Bl.) Dionysius the Carthusian, SENT., Bk. I, d. 26, q. 5.

DOUBTS ON THE TEXT OF THE MASTER

DOUBT I

In this part, there are doubts about the text (of Master Peter) and, first, concerning this which (St.) Hilary says: *It is proper to the Father, that He always is a father.* For he seems to say the false, because every property differs from Him of whom it is a property, either *according to thing* and/or *according to reckoning*;[2] but a *father* and a *father* convene in *thing*, *reckoning* and *name*: therefore, one is not the property of the other.

I RESPOND: It must be said, that in the Father we understand both Him *who* is a father, and (that) *by which* He is a father. Therefore, when a father is predicated of a father [de se], by the reckoning of one it is subjected and by the reckoning of the other it is predicated. Similarly, when '*to be a father*' is assigned (as) proper to the Father, because it is assigned as in the reckoning of (something) attributed, for that reason by reason of the property itself it is attributed to the Hypostasis Itself. Whence[3] he says, that '*to be a father*' is proper to the Father, not because the Father is a father.

DOUBT II

Likewise, is asked concerning this (which Master Peter says): *The same is said (to be) the nativity and/or the origin.* For he seems to speak contrary to that, which has been said above, in the Third Distinction, in the chapter on the vestige,[4] and (against what) has been treated of by (St.) Augustine ON THE TRUE RELIGION, namely, that 'origin' is appropriated to the Father.

I RESPOND: It must be said, that "*origin*" is always said in a relative manner.[5] Therefore, "origin" can be accepted either in respect to a *creature*, and/or in respect to a *person*. If, in respect to a *creature*, thus, it belongs to the whole Trinity and is appropriated to the Father, but if in respect to a *Person*, thus, it can be accepted

actively, and/or *passively*: if *actively*, thus it is (proper) to the Father and the Son, but is appropriated to the Father; if *passively*, thus (it is proper) to the Son and the Holy Spirit, and is appropriated to the Son, not according to which it is said simply, but according to which "*origin*" means an emanation through the manner of nature. For thus, since that (manner) is proper to the Son, similarly too (is) "origin", according to which it is accepted thus; and in this manner it is accepted here, and for that reason (this latter saying of Master Peter) is not contrary to the former one.

DOUBT III

Likewise, is asked of this which (Master Peter) says, that '*to beget*' and '*to be begotten*', *signify only the relations, not the Hypostases.* For it seems false, because since the relations are signified in concretion, they do not only[6] convey the relations, but also a Supposit; but when they only convey the relations, they are signified *abstractly*. If, therefore, that which is '*to beget*' and '*to be begotten*'[7] do not convey a relation *abstractly*, but *concretely*: it seems, that they do not convey only the relations.

I RESPOND: It must be said, that *concretion* is conveyed differently. For in one manner it is conveyed through *a verb*, in another through *an adjective* [nomen adiectivum]. For because a verb conveys an *act as stepping forth*, for that reason (it signifies) at a certain *distance* [in quadam distantia]; and for that reason it also[8] conveys under a certain inclination. And on account to this, because it conveys at a distance, it does not include within itself a supposit, nay it is necessary [oportet], that (something) extra be added, unless the place of the exterior addition is supplied by a demonstration, which in act properly belongs to the first or second person (of the verb), since (these persons) are always present and demonstrative (in the form of the verb). And for that reason, although (verbs) convey in concretion, yet they do convey naught but a *relation*,

---

[1] The Vatican edition, together with one or the other codex, has *these (testimonies of Scripture and Faith)* [illa] for *these (i. e. Scripture and Faith)* [illas].

[2] Cf. above d. 8, p. I, a. 1, q. 1, p. 152, footnote 1.

[3] Codices P Q and Q add *in the manner of signifying* [signanter].

[4] Chapter 1, where the words of (St.) Augustine are also had.

[5] The Vatican edition, together with codex cc, reads *(to be) a relation* [relatio] for *in a relative manner* [relative]. — Next, after this codices L and O have *Moreover* [autem] for *therefore* [ergo]. A little further below this, the Vatican edition, contrary to nearly all the codices and edition 1, reads *it is in respect* [respectu] for *it belongs*.

[6] Thus, rightly, in codices P and Q; the remaining codices, together with edition 1 and the Vatican edition, have less well: *because the relations signify in concretion and for that reason do not only convey* [quia relationes significant in concretione et ideo non solum important].

[7] The Vatican edition omits *and 'to be begotten'* [et gigni], contrary to codices L O P Q W X etc., and then together with codices L and O, and as required by the contest, we have substituted the plural for *convey* [important].

[8] Many codices together with the Vatican edition omit *also* [etiam], contrary to codices M P Q T and edition 1.

as much as it concerns itself, *(they do) not (convey) a supposit.*[1] — But an adjective, signifying the same, signifies as *an informing property*, and for that reason in a certain *union* and *without distance* [indistantia]; and for that reason (adjectives) convey *a form* and *a supposit* together, as when there is said "white" (i.e. as in "White was the winner of the race"), unless (this form) is signified[2] in abstraction, as when there is said "*whiteness*" [albedo]. Attending to this, Master Peter says, that "*the paternity*" and "*the filiation*", "*to beget*" and "*to be begotten*" mean only the relations.

Doubt IV

Likewise is asked of this which (Master Peter) says: *When, however, we posit the names of the relations in the predicates (of sentences), we signify only the notions themselves, not the Hypostases*; because if this is true, when there is said: "the Essence is the Father", since "the Father" is posited in the predicate, it stands then[3] for the notion: therefore, it is the same to say: "the Essence is the Father", as if there were said: "the Essence generates"; but this is false: ergo etc..

I Respond: It must be said, that certain (words) are placed in the predicate through *their own nature* and signification; and such are those which of themselves convey a composition, just as are *verbs*;[4] and of such Master (Peter) speaks. Certain (words) are thus placed in the predicate, which are bound *to be subjected*, such as this noun "*father*" and this noun "*son*"; and such, because they not only are bound *to be predicated*, but also *to be subjected*, can convey an

understanding of *a hypostasis*. Whence the word of Master (Peter) must be understood with precision, namely, of those[5] which are thus bound *to be predicated*, that (they are not bound) *to be subjected*, and, thus, (his argument) has nothing to withstand it [non habet instantiam].

Doubt V

Likewise, is asked concerning this which (St. John Damascene) says: *However, the characteristics, that is, the determinatives, are of the Hypostases, and not of the Nature* etc.. For he seems to speak badly, because the properties, which do not determine the *Nature*, are not natural; because every natural property, by the very reason that it is natural, determines *the nature*: therefore, if the properties in the divine do not determine *the Nature*, they are not natural, therefore (they are) besides the nature: therefore, (they are) *accidental*.

I Respond: It must be said, that just as there is said (to be) an "*order of nature*" in a twofold manner: either (as that order) in which nature *is set in order* [ordinatur], or (as that order) whereby nature is a *reckoning for setting in order* [ratio ordinandi];[6] and in this manner it must be understood concerning *the properties*: and when we say a "*natural property*", it is not necessary [non oportet], that the property have the nature as *a subject*, but that it be *consonant to the nature* of the subject itself, just as "a natural son" is not said, because he is from the nature and/or essence, but (because he is) from a father producing[7] naturally; in this manner, too, is it to be understood in the proposed.

COMMENTARY ON DISTINCTION XXVII

Part II

On the properties of the Persons, to the extent that they are expressed through less usual words.

Here, it must not be overlooked, that just as "the Father" and "the Son" etc..

THE DIVISION OF THE TEXT

Above, Master (Peter) dealt with the personal properties, according to which they are expressed through more usual names; here he deals, second, with the same, insofar as they are expressed through less usual words [vocabula]. And this part has four parts. In the first, Master (Peter) assigns differences for the names, through which it is fitting that the properties be expressed, confirming by authorities, that those names are proper ones. In the second, however, he assigns a certain

---

[1] This question concerning the signification of grammatical forms is of no small moment for the exact explanation of abstruse expressions. Much more on the most subtle matters of this argument is had in (Bl. John Duns) Scotus, « Speculative Grammar ». In the forms of *a verb* the subject is signified only indeterminately (in Latin), apart from the first and second persons (e. g. amo, amas); for the third person (e.g. amat, amant) signifies no distinct subject, unless one is added. — Next codices L and O, with transposed words, has *a property as one informing* [proprietatem ut informantem] for *as an informing property* [ut proprietatem informantem].

[2] The Vatican edition, with nearly all the codices and editions striving against this, has *(the adjective) signifies a form* [significet formam] for *(this form) is signified* [significetur].

[3] The Vatican edition with codex cc has *only* [tantum] for *then* [tunc].

[4] Cf. the preceding Doubt. — A little above this, the Vatican edition and not a few codices and edd. omit the words *of themselves* [de se].

[5] For *those which are thus* [illis quae illa], codd. P & Q have *for those of which it is established that they are thus* [illis de quibus constat quod ita].

[6] Cf. above d. 20, a. 1, q. 2, in the body of the question. — A little after this for *when* [quando], the Vatican edition has *since* [quoniam], breaking with codices F L O P Q T and Y, and also with edition 1.

[7] For *producing* [producente] very many codices, such as A G K T W T and aa, faultily read *proceeding* [procedente], codices L and O more rightly read *(because he is) as one proceeding from a father naturally* [a patre naturaliter procedens].

rule, in which proper (names) are discerned from common ones, there (where he says): *And here one must advert to a certain general rule.* In the third, he opposes (an objection) against the aforesaid rule and determines (it), there (where he says): *Here there is asked, when there is said, "God from God"* [Deus de Deo]. In the fourth, he elicits from that solution another rule, there (where he says): *And it must be known, that only according to the Names for the Substance* etc..

TREATMENT OF THE QUESTIONS

For an understanding of those (things) which are said concerning (the name), "word" [verbo], in this part four (questions) are asked:

First, concerning the signification of "word".

Second, concerning (its) connotation.
Third, concerning its comparison.
Fourth, concerning its transferal.

ARTICLE SOLE

On the name for a word.

QUESTION I

Whether, "word" be said essentially, or notionally, among the divine?

Therefore, as much as regards the first, there is first asked, whether "*word*" [verbum] is said essentially, and/or notionally. And that it is said *notionally*, is shown:

1. First by the authority of the Canon (of Scripture). Blessed John (the Apostle),[1] expressing the Incarnation in a most elegant manner, says: *The Word was made flesh*; but the Union was not made but in the Person of the Son: therefore, "the Word" does not express but the Person of the Son, and *in a manner proper* (to Him): ergo etc..

2. Likewise, (St.) Augustine (says) in the fifteenth (chapter), ON THE TRINITY:[2] « In the Trinity none is said (to be) a word, except the Son, nor a gift, except the Holy Spirit ».

3. Likewise, (St.) Anselm (says) in the MONOLOGION:[3] « It is most manifest [apertissimum], that neither he to whom the word belongs, can be his own word, nor (that) a word can be he of whom it is the word ».

4. Likewise, it seems *by reason*, because a word is what emanates from a mind through the manner of a conception; therefore, a word of itself means one concieved;[4] but '*to be conceived*' and '*(to be) begotten*' are the same, but (the adjective) '*begotten*' is a notional one: ergo etc..

5. Likewise, what emanates through the manner of a perfect expression is said (to be) a "word";[5] but '*to be an image*' is proper to the Son: therefore, also '(to be) a word'.

6. Likewise, every word means a looking-back to the one speaking;[6] but "that (something) is respective" among the divine has been said notionally, if one speaks of a respect to a Person; but the One speaking cannot be but a Person: ergo etc..

ON THE CONTRARY: 1. That it is said *essentially*, is shown in this manner. Just as (St.) Augustine says in the ninth (book), ON THE TRINITY, in the tenth chapter:[7] « A word is, with love, a knowledge »: but "knowledge" is essentially said: ergo etc..

2. Likewise, a word is (that), by which a thing is manifested and expressed;[8] but 'to be manifested' belongs to each [cuiuslibet] Person, and a manifestation is essential: therefore, a word (is) too. *If you say*, that "manifestation" is not meant simply, but (rather) a "manifestation of the Other"; then *there is objected*, that the Holy Spirit is manifestive of the Son, according to the sixteenth (chapter of the Gospel of St.) John:[9] *He shall glorify me* etc..

3. Likewise, this very (thing) is shown through a comparison to the *one speaking* [ad dicentem]; but the Ones speaking are Three, just as (St.) Anselm says in the MONOLOGION:[10] « Each One in the Trinity speaks

---

[1] John 1:14. — Next for *but* [sed] codices A and T have *if* [si].

[2] Chapter 17, n. 29. In the original this passage begins thus: And yet not in vain in this Trinity is non said (to be) a word etc..

[3] Chapter 38.

[4] Cf. (St.) Augustine, ON THE TRINITY, Bk. IX, ch. 7, n. 12 ff.; and (St.) Anselm (of Canterbury), MONOLOGION, ch. 11. — Then codices aa and bb, to the word *conceived* [conceptum], which occurs twice, twice adjoin the word *of the mind* [mentis].

[5] Cf. (St.) Augustine, ON THE TRINITY, Bk. IX, ch. 11, n. 16; and (St.) Anselm, MONOLOGION, ch. 10. — Codices P Q and Q add *which (manner) is 'to be an image'* [quod est esse imaginem], and codex O adjoins *therefore, a word is said (to be) what emanates through the manner of an image* [ergo verbum dicitur quod emanat per modum imaginis].

[6] Cf. (St.) Augustine, ON THE TRINITY, Bk. IX, ch. 2, n. 3; and (St.) Anselm, MONOLOGION, ch. 38.

[7] Number 15.

[8] Cf. (St.) Augustine, ON THE TRINITY, Bk. IX, ch. 7, n. 12; and (St.) John Damascene, ON THE ORTHODOX FAITH, Bk. II, ch. 21, where a "word" is called a "*messanger of the spirit*" [animi nuntius]. — Next for *essential* [essentialis], which the Vatican edition and edition 1, together with codices A F L and T have, the other codices and editions have *equal* [aequalis], codices aa and bb have *equally* [aequaliter].

[9] Verse 14.

[10] Chapter 62: The Father and the Son and Their Spirit, each says Himself and both Others.

speaks Himself »: therefore, a word belongs to the Three. But nothing belongs to the Three but (what is) essential: ergo etc..

4. Likewise, just as (St.) Anselm (says) in the MONOLOGION:[1] « 'To say' [dicere] is nothing other than 'to look upon attentively by thinking [cogitando intueri]' »; but this is essential: therefore, a word (is) also. *If you say*, that 'to say', according to which it is essentially said, does not have a corresponding word; *on the contrary*: just as (St.) Anselm says,[2] « The Father, by speaking Himself [se dicendo], generates the Word »; but every act, according to which a Person is reflected upon Himself, is an essential one: therefore '*to say*', insofar as it is an essential (act), also responds to a word: ergo etc..

5. Likewise, this is shown through a comparison to *that which is said through a word*. No medium [nihil medium] between a creature and the Creator is a notion and/or notional, since a medium is equally distant from the extremes; but the Word is the medium (between creature and Creator), since *all (things) have been made through* the Word:[3] ergo etc..

CONCLUSION

*The "Eternal Word" is said only notionally,
not essentially, among the divine.*

I RESPOND: To this some said, that "*to say*" is accepted in a threefold manner among the divine. In one manner "*to say*" [dicere] is the same as "*to understand*" [intelligere]; in another manner, (it is) the same as "*to generate*" [generare]; whence (St.) Augustine[4] expounds that (verse) in the first (chapter) of Genesis: « *He spoke*, that is He begot the Son, in Whom He set all things in order [omnia disposuit] »; in a third manner, "*to say*" is the same as "to create" [creare]; and (in this manner) a word does not respond to that which is *(the act of) saying* [dicere], inasmuch as (it is) uncreated, except according to which *(the act of) saying* is the same as (the act of) generating; and thus it convenes with the Father alone. — But it does not seem intelligible, that there is a *speaking* [loqui] without *a word*, and that there is some *(act of) saying*, to which there does not respond *a word*, just as neither that (there is) an *(act of) generating* without *a begotten*, nor *(an act of) knowing* [nosse][5] without *a knowledge*. And by this, too, the very manner of speak-

ing and understanding abhors, that anyone say and speak without any word [sine omni verbo].

For that reason some wanted to say, that just a "*to say*" is accepted *essentially* and *personally*, because there are Three who speak [dicunt], just as (St.) Anselm says,[6] so "word" is also meant essentially and personally. And according to this way, they strive to solve the objections to each side. — But this is contrary to (St.) Augustine and contrary to (St.) Anselm expressly. For (St.) Augustine[7] says, that « a word, by this that (it is) a word, is said regarding the other ». And this is also clear through the authorities of (St.) Augustine, which Master (Peter) adduces in the text,[8] and (because St.) Anselm in the MONOLOGION expressly denies this.

On account of this, it must be understood, that "to say" [dicere] is the same as "to speak" [loquere]; but "to speak" is in a twofold manner, either *to oneself*, that is *with oneself* [apud se], and/or *to the other* [ad alterum]. "To speak *to oneself*" is nothing other than "to conceive something in one's mind". But the mind conceives by understanding, and by understanding another it conceives without another, by understanding itself it conceives a similar to itself, because understanding [intelligentia] is likened to the understood [intellecto]. The mind, therefore, by speaking itself with itself conceives one similar to itself in all things [per omnia]; and this is the conceived word.[9] — In another manner "to speak *to the other*" [dicere ad alterum] is "to express the (word) conceived by the mind [mentis]"; and to this "*speaking*" [dicere] responds the pronounced word [verbum prolatum].

It must be said, therefore, that just as "*to say*" [dicere] is accepted in a twofold manner in us, so also in God. For God's "*speaking with Himself*", this is (His) "conceiving by understanding"; and this is (His) "generating an offspring similar to Himself", and to this "*speaking*" responds the word born, that is the Eternal Word. In another manner "*to say*" is "*to express oneself exteriorly*", and in this manner "*to say*" is the same as "*to declare* oneself through a creature", and to this "*speaking*" responds the created word and the temporal word.

It must be conceded, therefore, that "*word*" is accepted just as "*to say*" (is), that is, eternally and tem-

---

[1] Chapter 63: But to a most high spirit a 'to say' of this kind is nothing other than a quasi 'to look upon attentively by thinking' [quasi cogitando intueri], just as the speech [locutio] of our mind is nothing other than the inspection of the one thinking.

[2] MONOLOGION, ch. 33, where having shown generally, that the rational mind, by thinking, forms an image and word, he says: And so in this manner who denies, that the Most High Wisdom, when by speaking He understands Himself, begets One consubstantial to Himself, His own Similitude, that is His own Word?

[3] Jn. 1:3.

[4] ON THE LITERAL EXPOSITION OF GENESIS, Bk. II, ch. 6, n. 13: Therefore, God has not said: "Let there be this and/or that creature", as many times as there is repeated in this Book: *And God said*. Indeed, one Word has He begotten, in which He has said all, before each (thing) was made. Cf. also *ibid.*, Bk. I, ch. 3, n. 8, and ch. 6, n. 12; and also ENARRATIONS on Psalm 61, v. 12, n. 18, which is cited in the following question.

[5] The Vatican edition, together with codex cc, faultily reads *(an act of) being known* [nosci].

[6] See the words of (St.) Anselm cited here, above in the 3rd. opposed argument. — The Vatican edition, referring to the text of (St.) Anselm in ch. 63, where this Doctor says, *that there are not Three saying ... nor more, which are said*, after the words immediately preceding *who speak* [qui dicunt] adds *and who are spoken* [et qui dicuntur], with the codices and also the editions withstanding this. A little above this, the

same Vatican edition, by itself, has *since "to say" is accepted* [cum dicere accipiatur] for *just as "to say" is accepted* [sicut dicere accipitur], and consequently after this has *for that reason* [ideo] in place of *so ... also* [ita et], which is our reading, which is supported by codd. O T W & even codex F, in which, having transposed the words, there is read instead *and thus* [et ita]. The other codices, with the first xis editions, for *so ... also* [ita et] substitute *that a* [quod].

[7] ON THE TRINITY, Bk. VII, ch. 2, n. 3. — The entire text of (St.) Anselm is had above in the 3rd. argument of the fundament.

[8] Chapter 3. — The passage cited from the MONOLOGION is ch. 63, where (St.) Anselm says: Though, therefore, each one speaks [dicere] Himself, and All together (speak) Themselves; yet it is impossible, that in that Most High Essence there be a Word other than the One, concerning which it has already been established, that He is born in this manner out of Him, of Whom He is the Word, so that He can be said to be His True Image, and is truly His Son. In which I see a certain, wonderful and inexplicable something. For, behold, since it is manifest, that each One, namely the Father and the Son and the Spirit of the Father and of the Son, equally speaks Himself and both the Others, and that there is only one Word of all Three There; yet to no extent does it seem that the Word Himself can be said (to be) the Word of all the Three, but only of One of Them. For it is established, that He is His Image and Son, of Whom He is the Word. — Not a few codd. after *Monologion* [Monologio] omit *this* [hoc], in place of which the other codd., such as A G K V & X, read *(it) too* [et].

[9] Cf. (St.) Anselm, MONOLOGION, ch. 10 and 32. — For the following words *In another manner* [Alio modo], the Vatican edition alone substitutes *But "to speak" or* [Loqui autem sive].

porally. And a word, created temporally,[1] is neither God nor is in God, but (is) a creature in respect to God. The Eternal Word is God and is of Him alone, of whom there is a "being conceived" [concipi], just as "to say" is of Him alone, of whom there is a "to conceive". For that reason, the reasons proving that a word is said notionally, are simply to be conceded.

1. 2. To that which is objected, that a word is *a knowledge*, and a word is *manifestive*; it must be said, that this is not the whole reckoning of a word, just as neither is "to know" [nosse] the whole reckoning of "*to say*" and/or[2] "*to manifest*", but it is necessary, that a concept [conceptum] occur there; for that reason since *a conceived knowledge* and *a manifestation* through a concept is through the Son alone, not (through) the Holy Spirit, for that reason that which is objected is clear.

3. To that which is objected concerning a word in comparison to the one speaking, it must be said, that "*to say*" is not said essentially, except according to which it is said in respect to a created word, and according to which it notes a temporal effect; however, according to which it means an eternal respect, thus there is only one speaking.

4. Therefore, because it is objected, that "*to say*" is not other than "to intuit by thinking"; it must be said, that it is true, where the intuited is not without a concept,[3] as (is) in us and in the Father; but (this) is not in the Son, similarly neither (is it) in the Holy Spirit. For although They understand Themselves, yet They do not conceive an offspring, because in Them there is not fecundity for generating. — If *you ask* the reason for this,

(St.) Augustine teaches (it) in the fifteenth book[4] ON THE TRINITY; because we do not understand except through understanding, and that is always begotten. But in that blessed Trinity it is otherwise than in the image, because each Person understands. And for that reason "to understand" does not mean There a reckoning of *conceiving*, and through this it does not comprise *the whole reckoning of saying* and/or *of a word*, in God, as in us.

5. To that which is objected, that an act reflected upon itself (is essential) etc.; it must be said, that, whether it is said *with oneself*, or *exteriorly* to the other, in each manner ("speaking") implies an *absolute* and *respective* act with itself. For "to speak with one's self" [dicere apud se] is "to beget a concept [conceptum] by thinking about or understanding oneself"; and by a reckoning of the first there is a *reflection*, but by a reckoning of the second there is a *relation*. Similarly, "to speak *exteriorly*" [dicere exterius] is "to form something outside by declaring oneself and/or a concept". Whence the "*speaking*" [dicere] in each manner is reflected upon the one speaking and the one spoken: upon the one speaking, according to the reckoning of an absolute act;[5] upon the one spoken, according to the reckoning of a compared (act). And in this manner there is made manifest that objection, since "*to speak*" is not only absolute; and for that reason it is not always an essential (act).

6. To that which is objected, that the Word is a medium; it must be said, that there is twofold medium [medium], namely, *of essence* and *of understanding*; and the Word is not a medium in being [in essendo] — but an extreme, since the Word Himself made all (things) — but only in understanding, because the Father made all things through the Word. And this will be spoken of more clearly below.[6]

SCHOLIUM

I. The name and reckoning of a word (which in man be either the pronounced, exterior word, and/or the one produced in the mind) has been transferred to God, concerning which, see q. 4 below. By the Seraphic (Doctor) himself, below in q. 3, in the body of the question, the mental word [verbum menti] is accurately defined, as that which is « an expressed and expressive similitude, conceived by the force of the spirit of the one understanding, according to which it understands itself and/or another »; in which definition four (things) are touched upon, as are expounded there. With the Seraphic (Doctor) and many others, convenes St. Thomas (Summa, I, q. 27, a.1) saying: « Whosoever understands, out of this, that he understands, there proceeds something within him, which is the conception of the thing understood, out of the knowledge of which it proceeds » (cf. ibid. q. 34, a. 1). — But St. Thomas and (Bl. John Duns) Scotus disagree in a secondary matter. The former teaches, that the word of the created, understood (thing), formally speaking, is not the intellection itself, but is a formal and expressed similitude of the thing cognized through the act of understanding. But (Bl.) Scotus (Sent., Bk. I, d.27,q. 1) affirms, that it is the actual intellection itself. On this difference of opinion, one can confer with Cajetan, commenting on Summa, I, q. 27, a. 1, and Rada, tome I, controversy 7.

II. In transferring the name for a *word* to the divine, one must attend to the difference between a word in God and in creatures, and also exclude all (those things), which belong to *imperfection* (below in q. 4). Among the others, which mark a dividing line [discrimen important] between the created word and the uncreated (Word), we

note these two: *first*, that the created word is an *effect*, the uncreated is only a *terminus* of production. *Second*, the *created* word does not presuppose intellection, but is produced, so that there may be intellection; however, the *uncreated* (Word) presupposes *essential* and unbegotten intellection, and It Itself is the terminus of the conception and production, by which the Father expresses for Himself such a Concept entirely similar to Himself.

III. "*To speak*" [dicere] in God is distinguished (here in the body of the question) in a twofold manner, namely, eternally and temporally, which is explained more at length in SENT, Bk. II, d. 13, dubium 3. — Speaking of the eternal act of speaking [dictione aeterna], all concede, that it is the act of the (Divine) Intellect, and that a twofold act of intellect is to be posited in God, the one *essential* and common to the Three Persons, by which each Person understands Himself and the other Persons and all (things); the other *notional*, by which the Father produces or speaks the Word through a fecund memory. However, (Bl.) Scotus dissents from St. Thomas in a secondary matter; for the former wants, that the *essential diction and intellection* to be two distinct and/or disparate acts, while the Angelic (Doctor) posits, that the (Divine) diction is contained in the essential intellection and that it only adds an expression and relation. On this controversy, which seems to concern more the name than any matter of moment, see Cajetan, commenting on SUMMA, I, q. 34, a. 1, and Rada, controversy 8. — Bartholomew de Barberii (tome I, disputation 12, a. 6, n. 376) observes,

---

[1] The Vatican ed. reads *has been created temporally, nor is* etc.[temporaliter creatum est nec etc.], which we have corrected on from codd. T & Z.

[2] The Vatican edition with cod. cc, has *and* [et], edition 1 together with codex ff has *and not of* [nec]. Then the Vatican edition, contrary to the codices and to edition 1, puts *because* [quia] in place of *for that reason* [ideo], has *comes to be* [fit] for *is* [sit], and after *is objected* [obiicitur] adds *second* [secundo]. Then in place of *for that reason ... is clear* [ideo patet] very many codices incongruously read *and thus* [et sic].

[3] Codex O has *a conception* [conceptione], codex bb together with

edition 1 *concepts* [concepta] for *a concept* [conceptum].

[4] Chapter 17, n. 12.

[5] In the Vatican edition there is lacking the word *act* [actus], which we have restored from the older codices and edition 1.

[6] In the following question. Cf. also d. 32, a. 2, q. 2. — A little above this, after *the Word Himself* [ipsum Verbum], very many codices, together with edition 1, omit *all (things)* [omnia], which at any rate must be supplied with the Vatican edition. — Cf. (St.) Anselm, MONOLOGION., ch. 37.

that St. Bonaventure convenes more with (Bl.) Scotus, contrary to (the opinion of) Forrest and others; which is sufficiently hinted at in this question in the body and chiefly in reply to nn. 3 and 4, and in q. 3, in the body (cf. also d. 32, a. 1, q. 1, in rep ly to n. 4, and a. 2, q. 1, in reply to n 5).

IV. *The first opinion*, which is commemorated in the Response, is proposed also by Bl. (now St.) Albertus (Magus), here in a. 6. Alexander of Hales (SUMMA., p. I, q. 62, m. 2) proffers six manners, in which "*word*" and "*to say*" can be accepted in God, namely, essentially, not connoting anything in the creature (e.g. "the Father speaks Himself"); essentially, co-understanding in some manner a word (because the Understanding, which is appropriated to the Son, is co-understood); notionally (e.g. "the Father speaks the Word"); notionally and connoting an effect in the creature (e.g. "the Father speaks to us in the Son"); essentially and connoting an effect indistinctly of the Three Persons (e. g. "the Lord has spoken to Satan"). Likewise, in the solution to n. 2 he distinguishes in God the speaking of *the word* [dicere verbum] and the speaking of a *thing* [dicere rem].

Nevertheless, among the Seraphic Doctor and Alexander (of Hales) there is no contradiction, except in (their) manner of speaking, as St. Bonaventure in his often cited Prologue (cf. p. 472, col. II) evidently demonstrates with these words: « Moreover, in the second no one judges that I have disagreed, who knows how to distinguish between *propers* and *transumptives*. For just as one saying, that there is no true smile without a mouth, nor that one is truly flying without wings, does not contradict him, who says, that the field smiles without a mouth, and that arrows fly without wings; so he who says, that the name for *speaking* and/or saying, *properly* taken, is not without a word, just as neither (is) a *generating* without a son, does not contradict him, who says, that speaking and saying can be taken transumptively and, according to some signification, be said transumptively of anything without a generated word. In these, therefore, and in all others, if one diligently and piously takes a look, he will find, that I have not dared to withdraw from the footsteps of my fathers and elders ». (Cf. also, what is said of a word, improperly said, in the following question, in the body).

The second opinion is favored by St. Thomas in his Commentary (here in q. 2, a. 2). But in the SUMMA (I, q. 34, a. 1) he consents entirely with the Seraphic (Doctor) saying: « A "word" among the divine, if properly taken, is only a personal name ». — Indeed, singular and false is the opinion of Durandus (of Saint-Pourçain) (here in q. 3), who asserts, that *properly* "word" in God is said essentially, and not except *through an appropriation* (is it said) of the Son; which doctrine follows out of his other singular opinion, that neither the Son proceeds through the intellect, nor the Holy Spirit through the will.

V. Alexander of Hales and St. Thomas, locis citt. — (Bl. John Duns) Scotus, in each writing, here in q. 2, and REPORTATIO., q. 4. — Bl. (now St.) Albertus (Magnus), here in q. 6; SUMMA., p. I, tr. 8, q. 35, m. 3, a. 3. — (Bl.) Peter of Tarentaise, here in q. 2, a. 2. — Richard of Middleton, here in a. 2, q. 2. — Giles the Roman, here in 2nd. princ., q. 2. — Henry of Ghent, SUMMA., a. 58, q. 2. — Durandus (of Saint-Pourçain), here in q. 3. — (Bl.) Dionysius the Carthusian, on this and the following questions, here in q. 3. — (Gabriel) Biel, on this and the following question, here in q. 3.

QUESTION II

Whether "the Eternal Word" connotes anything on the part of a creature?

Second, there is asked, concerning the connotation of "the Eternal Word", and there is the question, whether "the Eternal Word" connotes something on the part of a creature. And that it does, seems:

1. First by the authority of the Psalm:[1] *He spoke* [dixit] *and they were made*; and by the first (chapter) of Genesis: *God said* [dixit], *"Let it be!", and it was made*: therefore, since "*to say*" is not other than "to proffer a word", and to *saying* there follows a *making*, and to a *making* the *made* itself, therefore, to a word there follows (something) made: therefore, it seems, that "the Word" connotes something created. *If you say*, that this is not said of "*to say*", insofar as it is accepted eternally and (insofar as) the Eternal Word responds to it,[2] but insofar as it is accepted temporally and a created word responds to it; *on the contrary*: (St.) Augustine (says) in the eleventh (book) of the CONFESSIONS:[3] « By Thy Eternal Word Thou sayest whatever Thou sayest, and there comes to be whatever Thou sayest, nor does Thou do otherwise than by saying »: therefore, it seems, that that must be understood of the Eternal Word.

2. Likewise, (St.) Augustine in the book of EIGHTY-THREE QUESTIONS,[4] treating of that (verse) of the Gospel: *In the beginning was the Word*, says: « In a better manner, we interpret "the Word" in this passage, to signify not only a looking-back [respectus] to the Father, but also to those which have been made by (His) operative Power »: therefore, "the Word" signifies a looking-back to (things) made. But it is established, that he is speaking of the Eternal Word, that is, which *was in the beginning*.

3. Likewise, on that (verse) of the Psalm: *Once has God spoken*, (St.) Augustine says:[5] that is, He begot the Son, in Whom He has disposed all (things). If, therefore, "the Word" conveys not only a generation, nay also even the disposition of all (things), therefore, ("the Word") means a looking-back to all (things).

4. Likewise, (St.) Anselm (says) in the MONOLOGION:[6] « When the Most High Spirit speaks Himself, He speaks all (things), which have been made »: therefore, by the same Word He speaks Himself and creatures. But "the Word" means a looking-back to that which is said through the Word: therefore, ("the Word") means a looking-back not only to the Father, but also to those which have been made: ergo etc..

ON THE CONTRARY: 1. Every (word) which con notes (something) temporal, is said temporally; but "the Word" is not said temporally among the divine, because *in the beginning was the Word*:[7] therefore, "the Word" does not connote (something) temporal, because every creature and/or created (thing) starts *temporally*, accepting *time* in the broad sense [large]: therefore, "the Word" connotes nothing in comparison to creatures. *If you say*, that ("the Word") connotes in

---

[1] Ps. 32:9 and 148:5. — In the Vatican ed. there are wanting the words exhibited by the codd.: *and by the first (chapter) of Genesis: God said, "Let it be!", and it was made* [et primo Genesis: Dixit Deus: fiat, et factum est].

[2] Thus the codd.; the Vatican ed. omits the *not* [non] in the phrase *that this is not said* [hoc non esse dictum], and, then, it also omits the words: *insofar as it is accepted eternally and (insofar as) the Eternal Word responds to it, but* [prout accipitur aeternaliter, et respondet ei Verbum aeternum, sed].

[3] Chapter 7, n. 9, where the original reads: By Thy Coeternal Word Thou sayest at once and sempiternally all which Thou sayest, and there comes to be whatever Thou sayest is to be, nor doest Thou do otherwise than by saying, nor yet does all which Thou doest by saying come to be both at once and sempiternally.

[4] Question 63. In the original (text of St. Augustine), the final words of the cited passage are: *but to those too, which have been made through the Word, by (His) operative power* [sed ad illa etiam, quae per Verbum facta sunt, operativa potentia] instead *of but also to those which have been made by (His) operative Power* [sed etiam ad ea quae facta sunt operativa potentia].

[5] ENARRATIONS, Ps. 61:12, n. 18; not literally, but according the sense.

[6] Chapter 34.   [7] John 1:1.

habit, not in act, just the eternal *disposition* and *predestination* (differ); *on the contrary*: if there would never come to be and/or never had been made anything, the Father still would speak Himself, therefore, He would also in mind[1] conceive the Word: therefore, the Word would be, if there never were any future and/or present creature: ergo etc..

2. Likewise, *that He speak the Word* is necessary, since, just as has been proven in the preceding, in the Sixth Distinction,[2] the production of a Person is necessary; but the production of a creature is voluntary, whence when He produces it, He was able not to produce (it). If, therefore, the simply necessary does not include in itself the contingent, "the Word" does not mean a any looking-back to a creature.

3. Likewise, the Creator and the creature are most highly distant, therefore, they communicated in nothing; if, therefore, the Word of the Father is one, and most highly one, therefore, when God the Father is said in that Word, it is impossible that the creature be said. Therefore, if the creature is not said in that Word, ("the Word") does not, therefore, mean a looking-back to the creature.

4. Likewise, if "the Word" means a looking-back to the creature, therefore, He will be able to be said (to be) "the Word of a creature"; which (St.) Anselm expressly denies in the MONOLOGION:[3] « The Word, by which He speaks the creature, is in no manner the Word of a creature ». *If you say* to me, that ("the Word") means principally a looking-back to the One speaking, whence ("the Word") cannot be said (to be) but the Word of the Father; for the same reason, since "the Spirit" means principally a looking-back to the One spirating, (the Spirit) will not be able to be said (to be) "the spirit of Moses", and/or "the spirit of Elijah"; which is contrary to Scripture.[4]

5. Likewise, if ("the Word") means a looking-back to the creature, since every name, meaning a looking-back to a creature, is essential, not personal; (therefore,) "the Word" is in no manner said personally; which is contrary to (what has been) predetermined.[5]

CONCLUSION

"The Eternal Word" conveys also a looking-back to the creature, through the manner of dispositive exemplarity and of operative virtue.

I RESPOND: It must be said, just as (St.) Anselm says,[6] that a word is then said and/or generated, when in the mind

the similitude and/or image of anything cognizable is conceived; and the word looks back [respicit] to that, to which the conceived similitude looks back. Since, therefore, our mind does not see itself and others together, nor (under) one and the same (aspect),[7] for that reason it speaks itself by one word, and others by another, nay by (many) others: for as many as are the words in it, so many (the things) understood. The Most High Spirit, however, in the Father cognizes Himself and all (under) one and the same aspect; and when He understands Himself and others, He cognizes Himself[8] as the Principle of the others. And because in Him the conceptive force conceives a Similitude, encompassing all under one attentive gaze [sub intuitu uno] or aspect, He conceives or generates one Word, which is the imitative Similitude of the Father and the exemplative Similitude of things and (their) operative Similitude; and thus (the Word) holds a quasi middle (ground), and *the Father* is said *to work through the Word*; and furthermore, there is attributed to the Word Himself, that He is *the Virtue* of God and *the Wisdom* of God.[9]

And thus it is clear, that "the Divine Word" means a looking-back to the very *Father* (who) speaks, from whom there is generated, One (who is) completely similar through all (things). ("The Eternal Word") means also a looking-back to *the creature* through a manner of dispositive exemplarity and operative virtue. And because these do not mean a looking-back in *act*, but only in *habit*, I say, that just as an *exemplar* means a looking-back in habit, and *power* similarly — because God knows and is able (to do) many (things), which He does not do — so also the Eternal Word. Whence just as has been said above[10] of the Gift (of God), so also it must be now understood of the Word.

Therefore, the reasons proving, that ("the Word") *means a looking-back* (to creatures) are to be conceded; but not that ("the Word") *actually connotes an effect*. Whence the first reason,[11] which proves concerning an actual effect, is to be solved, just as in the opposing (argument) it has been touched upon, because there he speaks of *"to say"*, according to which a *created* word responds to it, which is a quasi brought-forth word [prolatum]; but yet that *"to say"* is through the *uncreated* Word, just as the Father is said to work through the Son; and this is what (St.) Augustine says, « that by Thy Eternal Word Thou sayest whatever Thou sayest, and there comes to be whatever Thou sayest ». — However, it can be said, that that *"to say"* is eternal, and is only worth as much as a *"to dispose"*; and it has been conceded, that "the Word" means this. And that this is the understanding [intellectus] of (St.) Augustine, is clear through the following text: « And at once and sempiternally Thou does speak. Nor, yet, at once and

---

[1] Codex T omits *in mind* [mente], and then it substitutes *any* [aliqua] for *any* [ulla].

[2] Question 1. — A little after this the Vatican edition alone has *contingent* [contingens] for *voluntary* [voluntaria], which change in the text the same Vatican edition makes below also, in the solution to this objection.

[3] Chapter 33.

[4] Num. 11:17, 25, concerning which, see above d. 17, p. II, dubium 4, and d. 18, dubium 6. On the spirit of Elijah, cf. Kings 2:9,15. Cf. also the text of Master (Peter), d. XVIII, ch. 4 and 5.

[5] In the preceding question.

[6] MONOLOGION, ch. 31 and 33. The propositions which follows contain a summary of those which (St.) Anselm teaches in chs. 32-36 of the same. — The Vatican edition faultily reads *Augustine* [Augustinus] for *Anselm* [Anselmus].

[7] Codices L and O insert *aspect* [aspectu] after *one* [uno], and codex V likewise *word* [verbo] after *the same* [verbo]. Next codices C F G I L O R S U Y Z and aa and others ineptly read *in one manner* [alio modo] for *by one word* [alio verbo].

[8] From many codd., such as F G I L O P Q T V X Z aa & cc, and the first six edd., we have restored the word *Himself* [se], which is absent from the Vatican ed.. Next, cod. W has *comprising* [complectentem] for *encompassing* [cicumplectentem]. A little below this, not a few codd., with edd. 2, 3, 4, 5 & 6, adds to the verb *He conceives* [concipit]* the word *also* [et].

[9] Cf. 1 Cor. 1:24; and below d. 32, a. 2, q. 2.

[10] Distinction 18, especially q. 2 and 5.

[11] See the first argument of the fundament, where the entire text of (St.) Augustine is cited. — A little above this, codex cc has *connotes an actual effect* [connotat effectum actualem] for *actually connotes an effect* [connotat effectum actualiter].*

---

* *Trans. note*: Here in original text of footnote 8, there was faultily written *He conceived* [concepit] for *He conceives* [concipit]. — And in footnote 11, in the second half, there was faultily had *A little below this* [Paulo inferius] for *A little above this* [Paulo superius]. Both corrections are made from the critical text here above, by understating the discrepancies of the footnotes as typographical errors.

sempiternal are[1] whatever Thou does make ». And from this authority the truth of the response is clear, that the Word means a *habitual* looking-back.

1. To that which is objected unto the contrary, that nothing eternal connotes (something) temporal; it must be said, that it is true (of something) in act; whence "the Word" properly speaking does not *connote an effect*, but *does mean a looking-back* not to a creature already being [iam entem][2] and/or even to one only going-to-be [futuram], but even to one able to come to be [possibilem fieri]. And in this manner the response is clear to the instance, which it adduces unto the contrary.

2. To that which is objected, that the production of the Word is necessary and eternal, but (that) of the creature voluntary; it must be said, that although the *actual* production of a creature is voluntary, yet the *power* of producing (it) and the *knowledge* [scientia] (to do so) is necessary. For it is impossible, that God not *be able*, and it is impossible, that God *not know how* to produce creatures.

3. To that which is objected, that they do not communicate in anything; it must be said, that it is true of an essential commonality [communitate] and of (common) predication; and in this manner they do not communicate in the Word, because the Word is God, not a creature; nevertheless, according to some reckoning they can still have a looking-back to the same. For nothing impedes, that God be the principle of one and the same (Word), and the creature be (Its) effect; and thus it is concerning "the Eternal Word", which means a looking-back to the Father as to a principle, but to the creature as to an effect.

4. To that which is objected, that (the Eternal Word) will then be able to be said (to be) the Word of a creature; it must be said, that, just as is clear from the reckoning of the name, a word means a looking-back as[3] to the one producing, because it is said (to be) *the word of the one speaking*; similarly the gift; and because the principal respect, conveyed through the name, is said only in respect to a Person, for that reason neither is the Son said (to be) the word of a creature, nor the Holy Spirit the gift of a creature. *And if you object* concerning this name,

"*spirit*", it must be said, that insofar as it is said of the spirit of Elijah, it is not accepted from a *personal act* — because[4] the Holy Spirit is said (to be) "the spirit" of the Father and the Son only — but it is accepted from *the act of inspiring* [actus spirandi], concerning which (there is said) in the third (chapter of the Gospel of St.) John:[5] *The Spirit, where He wills, breathes*; and this is an *essential act*. Whence just as He is said (to be) "*the God of Elijah*", because He favors Elijah, and/or from some other act, so "the *spirit* of Elijah", because He breathes upon Elijah; thus, too, He could be said (to be) "*the holy spirit* of Elijah", just as there is said in the thirteenth (chapter of the Book) of Daniel:[6] *The Lord stirred up the holy spirit of the younger boy.* Nor is this contrary to Master (Peter), because he himself speaks of the "Holy Spirit", insofar as it is a name imposed from a personal property. And more determinate is that whole name, which stand on behalf of a Person, that this name, "*spirit*", (is) per se; for that reason we more frequently find that "*spirit*" is said of some man, that "*holy spirit*" (is said) of some man. But yet somewhere it is found, because, just as He is said (to be) "*the spirit* of Elijah", because He breathes into him and inspires (him),[7] so also "*the holy spirit* of Elijah", because He inspires holy (deeds) in him. And for that reason, perhaps, it was said there,[8] that *He stirred up a holy spirit*, because it was not to preach future (things), but to withdrawn (him) from an iniquitous judgement.

5. To that which is objected, that a name meaning a looking-back to a creature is not a notional one; it must be said, that it is true, if it *purely* means (this); but "the Word" does not *only* mean this nor does it *principally* meant (this), but principally it means a looking-back to the Father, just as has been said concerning the Gift.[9] Moreover, the Son and the Holy Spirit are named by names meaning more a looking-back to creature than to the Father, since according to the reckoning of understanding and appropriating, They are a quasi medium between us and God, and according to the reckoning of appropriating They are the Ones leading (us) back to God. Whence according to (St.) Augustine:[10] « The Father is the beginning, to which we are lead back; the Son the form, which we follow; and the Holy Spirit the grace, by which we are reconciled ». Whence They are also more properly said to be given to us than (is) the Father.

SCHOLIUM

I. In the Response there is distinguished a threefold similitude in the Word, namely, an *imitative* or expressive (similitude) of the Father, an *exemplative* (similitude) of created things, and an *operative* (similitude) of the same. These have been accepted from (St.) Augustine, EIGHTY-THREE QUESTIONS, q. 63, and have been approved by Alexander (of Hales), SUMMA, p. I, q. 62, m. 1. a. 3, and by the Angelic (Doctor), SUMMA., I, q. 34, a. 3; cf. also the following question, in reply to n. 2. — The first argument

of the fundament, which requires explanation, is explained in the Response in a twofold manner, beginning at the words: *Therefore, the reasons proving, that ("the Word")* [Concendendae igitur sunt]. — For the whole question, cf. above d. 18, q. 5, and for the solution to n. 4, ibid., q. 6.

II. Along with this question there is a certain controversy, principally conducted between the Thomistic and Scotistic schools, namely

---

[1] For *are* [sunt], which we have placed on the authority of all the codices and editions, the Vatican edition together with the original has *does there come to be* [fiunt]. Next for *habitual* [habitualem] many codices, such as C H K M R S T U V Y Z and bb, have *habitudinal* [habitudinalem], and codices A G L O have *habitude* [habitudinem], but not rightly; see above d. 18, a. sole, q. 2, p. 325, footnote 10.

[2] The Vatican edition together with codex cc has *existing* [existentem] for *being* [entem].

[3] Codex O omits *as* [ut].

[4] Very many codices, such as G H P Q and ff, rightly adjoin *in this manner* [sic].

[5] Verse 8. — *The act of inspiring* [actus spirandi], of which the Seraphic Doctor speaks a little above this, is to be accepted as the same as the *act of inspiring* [actus inspirandi]. — After the words *concerning which* [de quo], which follow next, edition 1 subjoins *there is said* [dicitur]; the Vatican edition, apart from the authority of the codices, then re-

peats the same after the word *so* [ita]. Then for *He breathes upon Elijah* [spirat Eliae], codex O has *He is breathed upon Elijah* [inspiratur Eliae], and edition 1 has *He inspires Elijah* [inspirit Eliae]. — On the etymology of the word, "*God*", see above d. 2, Doubt 3, p. 60, footnote 2.

[6] Verse 45. — On the sentence of Master (Peter), which the Seraphic Doctor cites next, see above d. XVIII, ch. 5, and the latter's COMMENTARY, ibid., q. 6.

[7] Cod. T reads *he is inspired* [inspiratur] for *inspires (him)* [inspirat].

[8] Dan. 13:45 reads: The Lord stirred up the holy spirit of the younger boy, whose name (was) Daniel [Suscitavit Dominus spiritum sanctum pueri iunioris, cuius nomen Daniel].

[9] Above, in d. 18, q. 4 and 5.

[10] ON THE TRUE RELIGION, ch. 55, n. 113, where the original reads *we run back* [recurrimus] for *we are lead back* [reducimur]. — A little before this, codices P and Q, both after *and God* [et Deum], and after *to God* [ad Deum], add *the Father* [Patrem].

(regarding the question) out of which cognition is the Word produced, whether from some *actual* cognition of the Persons and of creatures, or whether out of a *presupposed* cognition of the Divine Essence and of the Persons, but not of creatures; and whether this cognition is presupposed as the *principle by which* of the Word, or whether it is presupposed only by the order of nature, which (order) is the principle of the production. This difference arises out of that diverse manner of speaking, concerning which we have spoken in the Scholium of the preceding question. St. Bonaventure is read by his interpreters in favor of each side, since when he writes (in the body of the question): *The Most High Spirit, however*, etc., they think that he favors each side. However, more probably, as it seems to us, Bartolomeo de' Barbieri (disputation 14, q. 9)

asserts, that he speaks according to the manner of Scotus. But the matter requires more explanation than can be given here.

III. In the solution of the question itself it seems that all agree. Alexander of Hales., SUMMA., p. I, q. 62, m. 1, a. 4. — (Bl. John Duns) Scotus, on this and the following questions, here in q. 3; REPORTATIO., here in q. 6. — St. Thomas, here in q. 2, a. 3; SUMMA., I, q. 34, a. 3, and q. 37, a. 2, in reply to n. 3. — Bl. (now St.) Albertus (Magnus), on this and the following question,. SENT., Bk. I, d. 28, q. 10; SUMMA., p. I, tr. 8, q. 35, m. 3, a. 5. — (Bl.) Peter of Tarentaise, here in q. 2, a. 3. — Richard of Middleton, here in a. 2, q. 3. — Giles the Roman, here in 2nd. princ., q. 4. — Henry of Ghent, SUMMA., a. 59, q. 5. — (Bl.) Dionysius the Carthusian, here in q. 3, near the end.

QUESTION III

Whether there is a comparison of the Word to wisdom or knowledge?

Third, there is asked, concerning the comparison of *the Word* to *wisdom*. And since the Son is a *word* and a *wisdom*, there is asked, which of these is *prior* according to the reckoning of understanding. And it seems that *wisdom* is prior.

1. (St.) Augustine, in the ninth (book) ON THE TRINITY, in the tenth chapter (says):[1] « A word is, with love, a knowledge [notitiam] », therefore, "*word*" according the reckoning of understanding adds (something) above knowledge; but what is had [se habet] through an addition to something, presupposes it: ergo etc..

2. Likewise, "*knowledge*" means (something) *essential*, but "*word*" (means something) *personal*: therefore, since the essential is more common, and everything more common according to the reckoning of understanding is prior:[2] ergo etc..

3. Likewise, "*word*" means a *looking-back* to creatures, but "*wisdom*" means something *absolute* from the reckoning of its name: therefore, since the "*absolute*" according to the reckoning of understanding is prior to *the respective*, therefore, wisdom (is) also (prior) to word.

ON THE CONTRARY: 1. (There is written) in the first (chapter) of Ecclesiasticus:[4] *A fount of wisdom, the word of God on high*; "*fount*" means the reckoning of a principle: therefore, a word is the principle of wisdom. But what is a principle is prior according to the reckoning of understanding: therefore, necessarily, a word is prior to wisdom.

2. Likewise, just as (St.) Augustine says in the book, OF EIGHTY-THREE QUESTIONS,[5] « the Word means

an operative power »: but power, just as Richard (of St. Victor) says, is prior to wisdom according to the reckoning of understanding: ergo etc..

3. Likewise, a "*word*" means a similitude, conceived interiorly, "*wisdom*" means a habit and/or ability to cognize;[6] but the conception of a similitude and of a species precedes the ability itself: therefore, a word precedes wisdom in being understood.

In accord with this, there is asked, since the Son is said (to be) a "*word*" and a "*wisdom*", on account of what is "*wisdom*" only an appropriated (name), not a proper one, but "*word*" is a proper (name). — And again, since the Son is properly a "*son*" and an "*image*" and a "*word*", there is asked, what is the difference of those names of His. For if there is no difference but in their sound [in voce], then they seem to be synonymous names.

CONCLUSION

According to the reckoning of understanding, the understanding of "wisdom" and "knowledge" is prior to the understanding of a word.

I RESPOND: It must be said, that in the understanding of a word there occur these conditions, namely, *the cognition* of the one understanding, a similitude *in concept* and *an expression* of something. And this is clear, if we would consider the generation of a word according to (St.) Anselm in his MONOLOGION,[9] who speaks thus: « When I think of an absent, known man, the insight [acies] of my

---

[1] Number 15. — Some codices, together with the Vatican edition, a little above this, after *wisdom* [sapientia], have (the neuter) for *prior* [prius] instead of (the masculine) *prior* [prior].

[2] Under this respect Aristotle, TOPICS, Bk. VI, ch. 3 (ch. 4) says: These (i.e. genus and difference), moreover, are simply more known and prior than the species; for the genus and difference take away the species, for which reason these (are) prior to the species. But they are more known; for with the species (is) indeed know, it is necessary that the genus and differences be cognized; for one cognizes a man, and one cognizes an animal that can walk [anima gressibile]; but with the genus and difference known, it is not necessary that the species also be cognized; for which reason the species (is) not more known. — A little before this, for *everything more common* [omne communius], which we have replaced from manuscripts B O P and Q, the Vatican edition has *more common "being"* [esse communius].

[3] See above d. 26, a. sole, q. 3, p. 457, footnote 5.

[4] Verse 5.

[5] Question 63. — The words of Richard (of St. Victor), ON THE TRINITY, Bk. VI, ch. 15., who is cited next, are these: Therefore, it is established, what has already been said above, that power can be

manifold, where there can be no wisdom, v. gr. as in inanimate things and brutes; and on the contrary, moreover, where there is no power, there can be no wisdom in (the thing). For to be able to know, without a doubt, is to be able to do something. And so wisdom does not give "being" (and/or) "being able" to power, but power to wisdom.

[6] Cf. Aristotle, ETHICS, Bk. VI, ch. 3, where the five intellectual habits, namely art, science, prudence, wisdom, (and) understanding are mentioned; and ch. 7, where there is a more lengthy explanation of wisdom. — Next for *of a species* [speciei], in the Vatican edition and codex cc there is had *of species* [specierum].

[7] Chapter 33. — Next, the Vatican edition, citing the text of (St.) Anselm, being supported by only a few codices, has *the insight of thinking in oneself forms such* [format acies cognitionis in se talem] for *the insight of my thinking is formed upon such* [formatur acies cogitationis meae in talem]. — In place of our reading of *my* [meae], the words *in oneself* [in se], which are extant in not a few manuscripts and in edition 1, have been falsely placed; our reading is supported by codex O, together with the original.

thinking is formed upon such an image of him, as that which I have drawn into my memory through the sight of my eyes, which image in thinking is the word for the same man, which I say in thinking. Therefore, the rational mind has, when by thinking it understands itself, its own image with itself, born out of itself, that is the thought of itself, according to its own similitude, formed as if by the impression of itself [sua impressione]; which image of it is the word. And so in this manner who denies that the Most High Wisdom, when He understands Himself by speaking, begets a Similitude consubstantial to Himself, that is His own Word »? But a word is not other than an *expressed* and *expressive* similitude, conceived by the force of the spirit of the one understanding, according to which it intuits [intuetur] itself and/or another. Whence it is clear, that the understanding of *a word* presupposes the understanding of *knowledge* and of *generation* and of *an image*: the understanding of *generation* in the interior conception; the understanding of *an image* in a similitude conform in all things [per omnia], and it adds upon these all the understanding of an *expression*.

Since, therefore, the intuiting of the one understanding does not mean a looking-back, for that reason the "*wisdom*" itself and the "*knowledge*" do not mean (something) proper. But since the conception and the similitude mean a looking-back,[1] for that reason it is necessary, that the name for a *son* as much as for an *image*, and as much as for a *word* be *properly* said.

And, *again*, the *order* in speaking is clear, and even the *reason* for the different manner of speaking is clear. For "*wisdom*" and/or "*knowledge*" mean (something) first in understanding; then "*son*",

which means the emanation itself or the conception; then "*image*", which means an expressed manner of emanating, and in the third place[2] "*word*", which means all these, and adds above (them) a reckoning of expressing and manifesting.

With these seen, it is easy to respond to the objections. For I concede, that, according to the reckoning of understanding, the understanding of 'knowledge' and 'wisdom' is prior.

1. To that which is objected, that the Word is a fount of wisdom; it must be said, that this is understood of created wisdom.

2. To that which is objected, that (the Word) means an operative power; it must be said, that the Word, even if He has omnipotence, just as the Father (does), yet the Word Itself does not mean an operative power from the reckoning of His own Name, except inasmuch as that power is operative by a previous[3] *disposition*; and since disposition is an act of wisdom, for that reason "*wisdom*" is prior in understanding.

3. To that which is objected, that a similitude is prior to an ability in understanding; it must be said, that that is true,[4] (in those) in whom wisdom is through an acquisition, just as (it is) among us; but not so in God, nay the other way around, because out of the intuiting of the Mind of the One most highly wise there arises the Word, which is said to be Most High Wisdom, such that the conceived Similitude does not give wisdom to the One conceiving, nay rather It accepts (it). What is objected last, has already been determined.

SCHOLIUM

Besides the solution to the proposed question, there is, in the Response, both an accurate investigation into the reckoning for *a word*, and an assertion, that "the Word" is *properly* said (of the Son), and a description of the *difference* between the four Names for the Second Person. On the name, "*wisdom*", cf. below d. 32, Doubts 1-5. On the name, "*image*", cf. below d. 31, p. II, a. 1, qq. 1 and 2, and Doubts 2, 3 and 4.

On the question itself: Alexander of Hales, SUMMA., p. I, q. 62, m. 1, a. 2. — St. Thomas touches upon the question in (his) SUMMA., p. I, a. 34, a. 1, in reply to n. 2. — (Bl.) Peter of Tarentaise, here in q. 2, a. 1, quaestiuncula 3. — Richard of Middleton, here in a. 2, q. 4. — Henry of Ghent, SUMMA., a. 58, q. 2, n. 14 ff.. — (Bl.) Dionysius the Carthusian, here in q. 3.

QUESTION IV

Whether the name for a word has been rightly transferred to the divine?

Fourth, there is asked, concerning the transfer [translatio] of this name, "*word*" [verbum], to the divine. And, that it ought in no manner be transferred, is shown:

1. Every transfer (of a name to the divine) is according to a similitude;[5] but nothing in a creature is more vain than a word, because immediately when it comes to be, it passes over and is not, *but the word of the Lord remains in eternity*:[6] ergo etc..

2. Likewise, since there is an *intelligible* and *sensible* word according to the twofold (act of) *speaking* [secundum duplicem dicere], there is asked, "Which of these is transferred?" And (St.) Augustine in the fifteen (book), ON THE TRINITY, wants,[7] that the *exterior* one (is) not: « An exterior word is not a word, but a sign for a word »: therefore, if the Divine Word is a true word, ergo etc..

---

[1] Nearly all the codices, together with edition 1, contrary to the context, have *(something) proper* [proprium] for *a looking-back* [respectum]. Just before this codex T after *similitude* [similitudo] inserts *and the expression* [et expressio].

[2] Very many codices, together with the first six editions, have ineptly *manner* [modo] for *place* [loco], as can be seen.

[3] Very many codices, together with editions 2 and 3, have *paternal* [paterna], for *previous* [praevia]; an evidently corrupt reading.

[4] Edition 1 subjoins *in those* [in his].

[5] Cf. above, p. 1, footnote 8, and p. 72, footnote 3. — Then, edition 1 has *among created (beings)* [inter creata] for *in a creature* [in creatura].

[6] 1 Peter 1:25.

[7] Chapter 11, n. 20: The word which sounds outside, is a sign of the word which shines within, to which the name for a word is more fitting. — A little before this very many codices, together with edition 1 and 6, omit *of these* [istorum].

3. Likewise, an *exterior* word goes forth from the one speaking, but the Divine Word is always in the One speaking, because *I am in the Father*, says the Truth, in the fourteenth (chapter of the Gospel of St.) John:[1] ergo etc..

4. Likewise, it seems that neither (is the Divine Word said) according to the similitude of an *interior* thought [interioris cogitationis], because (St.) Augustine says in the fifteenth (book) ON THE TRINITY:[2] Thought is something inconstant [volubile]; but in God nothing is inconstant: ergo etc..

5. Likewise, *the thoughts* [cogitationes] *of mortals are timid*, Wisdom (chapter) nine,[3] *and uncertain (are) our foresights* [providentiae]; but in the Divine Word there is no falsity, no doubtfulness [dubietas]: ergo etc..

6. Likewise, we think of many (things), which *are displeasing* to us; but the Divine Word is pleasing to the Father in all things [per omnia]:[4] ergo etc..

7. Likewise, we think of many (things), which we *cannot* (do); but the Divine Word is omnipotent:[5] ergo etc..

ON THE CONTRARY: 1. Among all created (things) *the image* is more expressed [expressior],[6] therefore, among all emanations that is more expressed, which is in the image; but in the image, the emanation of (something) similar to the uncreated Word, is the emanation of a word from a mind: therefore, (it is) most expressed, therefore, it is fittingly transferred.

2. Likewise, what is said through a comparison of a word of *the intellect*, this seems (to be) through a comparison to a thing outside (it), since Ecclesiasticus,[7] according to the other translation of the Septuagint, (says): *The principle of every work, the word*; but through the Son of God all (things) have been made: ergo etc..

3. Likewise, that the word of *the voice* is similar, seems, because He is said (to be) "the Word", because (He is) expressive and manifestive — whence *neither does anyone know the Father but the Son, and (him) to whom the Son wishes to reveal (Him)*, Matthew (chapter) eleven[8] — but this most of all is in the word of *the voice*, for the *interior* word does not lie open except through the word of *the voice*: therefore, He is said (to be) "the uncreated Word" according to the similitude of an exterior word.

4. Likewise, (St.) Basil (the Great says):[9] To the Son of God there is attributed (the names) "*sense*",

"*wisdom*", "*virtue*", "*word*" and "*light*": the Sense, by which all things are thought; the Wisdom, by which (all) are disposed; the Virtue, by which (all) come to be; the Word, by which (all) are announced; the Light, by which (all) are grow bright. If, therefore, He is said (to be) "the Word" by reason of (His) being announced [annuntiationis], and this pertains to a word *of the voice*, it is clear that He is said (to be) that "Word" according to the similitude of a uttered word [verbi prolati].

CONCLUSION

The name for a word, understood with certain conditions, is fittingly transferred to the divine.

I RESPOND: It must be said, that just as the reckoning of *paternity*, through (a consideration of what is) prior, is found in God (rather) than in creatures, yet, the name itself has been transferred by us to God;[10] thus, the reckoning of *light*, thus, (the reckoning) of *wisdom*, and (the reckoning) of those similar (names), thus, too, the reckoning of a *word*. And (its) signified is in God, through (something) prior and more noble than in us; yet, the name has been transferred by us to God.

Moreover, a *translation* is done for the sake of two (things): one reason is for the sake of an expressed similitude, the other reason is for the sake of our instruction; and these two are (present) here.

First, indeed, is a *similitude* of the created word to the uncreated One, according to which (similitude) the blessed Augustine distinguishes the *word*, in the fifteenth (book) ON THE TRINITY,[11] according to a threefold difference. For one is the *sensible* word, the other is the *intelligible* word, the third is the *middle* word [verbum medium]. A *sensible* word is attained in an utterance of the voice [in prolatione vocis], the *intelligible* word in the thought of the thing [in cogitatione rei], the *middle* word in the thought of the voice [in cogitatione vocis]. — And there is an order (among these), because a man first thinks *what* something *is*, second, *in what manner* he ought to *pronounce* the (thing) thought, third, *he pronounces* (it).

Therefore, just as the reckoning of *a trinity* is found in the sense, (and) is found in reason turned toward sense [in ratione conversa ad sensum], (and) is found even in reason according to itself, so also the reckoning of a *word*. And according to this standard of measure [quemadmodum], the *trinity*, in which consists the expressed

---

[1] Verse 11.

[2] Chapter 15, n. 25: What is it, I ask, this formable and not yet formed, except a certain something of our mind, which we thrown by this and a certain revolving motion [volubili motioni], when now this, now that, is thought by us, just has will have been found and/or occur? — And ch. 16: On which account, thus, it is said (to be) the Word of God, so as to not be said (to be) the thought of God, and to not be believed to be something quasi inconstant [volubile] in God.

[3] Verse 14. — Edition 1 places *just as is said in* [sicut dicitur] before the scriptural citation.

[4] Cf. Mt. 3:17 and 17:5. — The word *to the Father* [Patri], which is wanting in the Vatican edition, we have replaced on the authority of the more outstanding manuscripts and edition 1.

[5] Wis. 18:15.

[6] Cf. above d. 3, p. I, q. 2, in the last reply, and p. II, a. 1, q. 2. — At the end of the argument, the Vatican edition, together with some codices, has *expressive* [expressiva] for *most expressed* [expressissima].

[7] Ecclesiasticus 37:20, where the Vulgate reads: *Before all (thy) works let a truthful word precedes thee* [Ante omnia opera verbum verax praecedat te].

[8] Verse 27.

[9] This text is cited even by other Scholastics, such as Bl. (now St.) Albertus (Magnus) and St. Thomas, but they do not indicate, in which writing of (St.) Basil it is had. The editors of the works of those Scholas-

tics would have it that the text has been taken from (St.) Basil's work AGAINST EUNOMIUS, in Bk. II, n. 17 of which work, indeed some of those names, which are here attributed to the Son of God, do occur, but not all, nor are these names explained there, just as is done in our text. More of the aforesaid names are found expounded in (St.) Gregory of Nazianzen, ORATIONS, n. 36 and 49. — However, Tertullian in his APOLOGIA, ch. 21 says: « And we also ascribe [inscribimus] to *the Word* [Sermoni] and also to the *reason* and likewise to the *virtue*, through which we declared that God (has) constructed all (things), His own Substance (as) a spirit, in which there is also the One pronouncing *the Word*, and (for Whom) disposing *reason* is at hand [adsit], and (to Whom) perfecting *virtue* is present ». — In the text cited (by St. Bonaventure) after *the virtue, by which* [virtus qua] the codices, together with editions 1, 2 and 3, do not have *all others* [cuncta] for *(all)*.

[10] See above d. 22, q. 3, chiefly in the 1st. argument of the fundament. — A little below this after *than* [quam], the Vatican edition alone interposes *in men and/or* [in hominibus vel].

[11] Chapter 10, n. 19, and ch. 11, n. 20. — A little above this, the Vatican edition, together with a few codices, reads *an expressed similitude* [expressa similitudo] for *a similitude* [similitudo].

[12] ON THE TRINITY, Bk. XV, ch. 3, n. 5, where the holy Doctor exhibits a summary of those things which he has taught in other books on this threefold trinity, the first and second of which in Bk. XI, ch. 2 and 3, and the third in Bk. IX, ch. 4, and Bk. X, ch. 11.

similitude, is not in sense, nor in the inferior part of reason, but in reason according to itself; thus, when *"word"* is said in (this) threefold manner, the expressed similitude consists in none, but in the *intelligible* word; and this is the word, which pertains to no language [linguam]. Whence (St. Augustine) says,[1] that « he who can see this, in some manner sees the similitude of that word ».

Moreover, the similitude *of this* word (of which St. Augustine speaks) he assigns to Him as much as regards three (considerations), namely, as much as regards an *emanation* or *origin*, as much as regards a *disposition*, as much as regards a *union*. For there is a considering of these three in the Son of God: that of *an origin*, according to which He is said (to be) a "son"; that of an eternal *disposition*, according to which He is said to be the elegant archetype [mundus archetypus] and the art full of the reasons of all living (things);[2] and that of *a union*, according to which He is said (to have been) "made man".

It is a similitude in *origin*. For just as the Son proceeds through the manner of nature (as) One similar to the Father in all things [per omnia], so the word of the intellect proceeds from the mind through the manner of nature (as) similar and equal to it in all things; whence it is said (to be) the concept of the mind [mentis conceptus].

As much as regards a *disposition*, it is a similitude.[3] For just as a man works nothing reasonably, which he does not think about beforehand [praecogitet] and conceive in his mind, so God the Father disposed all things in the Word. And just as our disposition and/or preconception can be, even if a work does not follow, so also the eternal disposition and precognition does not depend on a work.

However, as much as regards a *union*, it is a similitude. For just as the word of the mind is united to the voice, so that it be made known, and yet does not pass over into the voice, but remains whole in the mind; so in every way [per omnia] in the Eternal Word it must be understood, that He has been united to the flesh and does not pass over into the flesh, but remains whole with the Father. This, therefore, is a similitude.

But, yet, this similitude is not attained in a word of the mind *generally*. For, just as the same (St.) Augustine says,[4] we frequently think of (those things) which *we know not*, and in this manner a fallacy is conjoined to our word; frequently, of (those) which *we do not want*, and then displeasure is joined (to it); frequently, of (those) which *we cannot*, and then impotence is joined (to it). But a divine word is *most true, most pleasing, most omnipotent*; for that reason the expressed similitude of

it does not consist in our word, except it be a word of *certain knowledge* and of *complete pleasure* and of *power*, and this is the word, which consists in thinking, with an affective and operative (power) joined to it. Whence (St.) Augustine in the ninth (book) ON THE TRINITY (says):[5] « A word is, with *love*, a knowledge »; and if *virtue* be added (to this definition), then it is a perfect reckoning (of what a word is), and in this manner a word is with love and virtue a knowledge. — Therefore, "word" has been transferred (to the divine) from the interior word according to the aforesaid similitudes and predetermined conditions; and this is the reckoning (of a word) *on the part of the thing*.

On the other hand, the reason *on out part* is, because we understand divine (things) through created ones.[6] Since, therefore, when we hear of the Father and the Son, we think of a carnal father and son, so that we are raised up to think of spiritual generation; for that reason the most divine John,[7] who was entirely elevated in the contemplation of the Divinity, used the name for a *word*, saying: *In the beginning was the Word*; which Word, who understands (It), profits much in cognizing the Son of God.

With these seen, the objections are clear. For I do concede, that an *exterior* word does not have an *expressed* similitude, both because (it is) vain, and because it proceeds exteriorly, and also because it is not a word, but the sign for a word; but an *interior* word has the opposite of these. I also concede, that an interior word (which is) *doubtful*, and/or *false*, and/or *impotent*, and/or *displeasing*, does not have an expressed similitude, but (only) the word, which has the opposite conditions (does).

To that which is objected on the opposite (side), that an intelligible word has a similitude (to the Divine Word): it must be conceded. However, what is objected concerning the *sensible* word, it must be said, that it has some kind of similitude [aliqualem similitudinem], but not an expressed one; for that reason there is no transferal according to that one, but according to the *interior* (word),[8] which is more similar, as is clear. Moreover, no word can be likened to that One in all things. For that One alone has a substantial *identity* and natural *togetherness* [simultatem] with the One speaking, because It is together in nature and duration (with Him): which conditions, as the blessed Augustine[9] says, are not in our word. And, for that reason, although there is a similitude, yet, there is not a little [nonnulla] dissimilitude; and for that reason it can be rightly said (to be) a *transferal*, because (the word) is not similar in all things. And in this manner all (the objections) are clear.

SCHOLIUM

On the transference (of terms to God) and its species, see above d. 22, q. 3, and St. Thomas, SUMMA THEOLOGIA, I, q. 13, a. 6. — Since the arguments alleged, (above), on each side convey too much, since the first series strives to prove, that *no* species of created word ought to be transferred, but the other (series), that *all* species (ought to be); hence, it is, that the Seraphic Doctor, (St. Bonaventure), imposes on each series of arguments some restrictions. — The Response

---

[1] ON THE TRINITY, Bk. XV, c. 10, n. 19. That which followed this citation is taken from ch. 11, n. 20 of the same.

[2] Cf. above d. 6, a. sole, q. 3, p. 130, footnotes 1 and 5.

[3] For *it is a similitude* [est similitudo], many codices have *(it is) similar* [similis], edition 1 has *it is similar* [est similis].

[4] Loc. cit., ch. 14, n. 23, and ch. 15, n. 24.

[5] Chapter 10, n. 15.

[6] Cf. above d. 3, p. II, q. 2.

[7] John 1 :1.

[8] Supply together with cod. X *word* [verbum], and little below this after *that One* [illud], supply together with codices A aa and bb *namely, the eternal One* [scilicet aeternum].

[9] ON THE TRINITY, Bk. XV, chs. 13-16, nn. 22-26. — Immediately after this the Vatican edition together with codex cc has *they are not in* [non insunt] for *are not in* [non sunt in], and at the end has *(the transferal) is not similar* [similis] for *(the word) is not similar* [simile].

of the author is quite clear, especially concerning the similitude and dissimilitude between the Word of God and our (word); not a few things are explained through those thing which have been said concern the difference between *the vestige* and *the image* etc., above in d. 3, p. I, q. 2, and p. II, a. 1, q. 1 and 2.

Alexander of Hales, SUMMA., p. I, q. 63, m. 1, a. 1 and 3. — St.

Thomas touches upon the question here in q. 2, a. 1; SUMMA., I, q. 34, a. 1; DE VERITATE., q. 4, a. 1. — Bl. (now St.) Albertus (Magnus), here in a. 3, 4 and 7. — (Bl.) Peter of Tarentaise, here in q. 2, a. 1. quaestiunculae 1 and 2. — Richard of Middleton, here in a. 1, q. 1. — Giles the Roman, here in 2nd. princ., q. 1. — Henry of Ghent, SUMMA., a. 59, q. 2 passim, especially in n. 41.

DOUBTS ON THE TEXT OF THE MASTER

DOUBT I

In this part, there are doubts about the text (of Master Peter) and first of this which (St. Augustine) says: (*The Word), according to which He is Wisdom and the Essence, is that which the Father (is); according to which (He is) the Word, He is not that which the Father (is)*, because either "*that*" (here) is held *essentially*, or *personally*. If *essentially*, not only according to which (He is) *wisdom*, is He one with the Father through the Essence, but also inasmuch as (He is) *the Word*. If *personally*, then it is false, that *according to which (He is) wisdom*, He is *that* which the Father personally (is). — Likewise, since "*that*" (in the citation above) is of the neuter[1] gender, it seems that it stands for *the Essence*, and thus the Word always is that which the Father (is), namely, the one (with Him) through the Essence and/or Substance.

I RESPOND: It must be said, that there "*this*" stands for (what is) signified by the term, so that the sense is: 'the Word, according to which (He is) *wisdom*, is that which the Father (is)'; because according to which (He is) wisdom, there is attributed to Him something, which (is) also (attributed) to the Father, namely, (that which is) signified by this name, "*wisdom*". In a similar manner, the other (proposition) is true: 'the Son, according to which (He is) *the Word*, it not that which the Father (is)', because something is attributed to the Son, according to which (He is) the Word, which does not convene with the Father. Whence "according to" [secundum] means there a habitude under a forma reckoning, and the pronoun "*this*" conveys and demonstrates the proper (thing) signified by the term; and for that reason, because "*wisdom*" signifies (something) *essential*, it is held in the first (proposition) essentially; because (what is) signified by "*the Word*" is *personal*, it is held in the second (proposition) personally.

And/or in another manner it can be said, that it is held essentially, and "*according to which*" [secundum quod] means a habitude through a manner of form [modum formalis]; whence just as in one (manner) He is God, in another He is the father — because by the Deity He is God, by the paternity the Father,[2] such that (He is) neither by the paternity God, nor by the Deity the Father — thus (St.) Augustine accepts (it), when he says: "according to which (He is) *the Word*, He is not that which *the Father* (is)",[3] not so that (their) unity in nature is denied, but so that the habitude of that which is a "*according to*" is denied; because the Word, inasmuch as (He is) a word, does not mean the Unity of the Essence, but a distinction of Person, on the other hand (He does as) wisdom.

DOUBT II

Likewise, is asked concerning this which (Master Peter) says: *By the same property or notion He is said (to be) "word"* [verbum], *"image"* [imago] *and "son"* [filius], because if this is true, therefore, there is a *synonymy* there and/or an flourish of words [inculcatio verborum], or (there is) some *difference* (among them).

I RESPOND: It must be said, that there is a *difference*, and the one difference can be accepted in this manner, so that He is said (to be) *the word*, which[4] proceeds from the interior (things), *the image*, which is imitated in exterior (things), and "*son*" comprises each; and for that reason He is more and more commonly said (to be) *a son*, than any of the others.

And/or in another manner: all these three (names) convey a similitude of the other (Person); but "*son*" conveys that similitude (as) naturally emanating, "*image*" as expressly imitating, "*word*" as expressing others, as much as it is of itself [de se] or born to express to (them); for that reason, that Person is more frequently named a "*son*" on this account, that it conveys the emanation itself and that habitude by a proper name.

And/or in another manner: "*image*" conveys that similitude as *conform*, "*word*" conveys it as *mental* or *spiritual*, but "*son*" (as) *connatural*. And in this manner the diverse reckoning of signifying the same habitude is made clear, and thus it is the same property, nor, however, (is there) a synonymy. — And in the first acceptation the intention of a *word* takes precedence [praeit], in the second the intention of a *son*, in the third the intention of an *image*, yet among all (these) the middle manner (of speaking) is more fitting.[5]

DOUBT III

Likewise, is asked of this which (St.) Augustine says, that *the Son alone is "God from God"* [Deus de Deo]. For he seems to say the false, because « the Holy Spirit is God from God »:[6] therefore, the Son (is) not the sole ("God from God").

I RESPOND: It must be said, that this exclusion is required on account of the manner of speaking [acrtatur ex modo loquendi]. Which is clear, because he does not simply mean this, but speaking of the Father and the Son he says:[7] « not Both (are) "God from God", but the Son alone », such

---

[1] (Here St. Bonaventure uses) the more ancient form for *of neither* [neutri] rather than the classical *of neither* [neutrius], which occurs more often thant not among the ancient grammarians.

[2] Cf. above d.19, p. II, a. sole, q. 1, p. 359, footnote 5.

[3] Codex O ends the proposition at this word. Then it adds: In another manner it seems that the can be said, that the word "*this*" always stands personally and is only worth a "*this is the Father*", as if there were said: *is the Father*. For Wisdom, according to which (It is) the Essence, is the father; according to which It is the Word, It is not the Father, not so that etc.. [Aliter videtur posse dici, quod stat semper ly *hoc* personaliter et tantum valet *hoc est Pater*, ac si diceretur: *est Pater*. Sapientia enim, secundum quod essentia, est Pater; secundum quod est Verbum, non est Pater, ut non etc.]

[4] Edition 1 here, and again a little below this after *image* [imago], substitutes *because* [quia] for *which* [quod], in which second occurrence very many codices, together with edition 1, also concur. Codex Y then reads *and a son, because He comprises each* [et filius quia complectitur utrumque].

[5] Cf. above q. 3 of this distinction.

[6] See the words of (St.) Augustine above in the text of Master (Peter), d. X, ch. 2.

[7] This passage of (St.) Augustine is had here in the text of Master (Peter), ch. 5. — This doubt is also solved by Bl. (now St.) Albertus (Magnus), here in a. 9, and Richard (of Middleton), here (commenting) on the text (of Master Peter).

that on account of the manner of saying *"alone"* [solus] one is constrained to make an exclusion vis-à-vis the Father [pro Patre].

DOUBT IV

Likewise, is asked of this which (Master Peter) says: *According to the Names for the Substance is there said a "that from that".* For it seems false, because there is rightly said *"the Son from the Father"* through names, which are not Names for the Substance. *If you say,* that (that proposition) is understood according to the same name; *there is objected,* that there is rightly said *"One proceeding from one Proceeding"*, and *"The Principle from the Principle"*, or *"One spirating from One spirating"*, yet these names are not said according to the Substance.

Likewise, there is asked of this, which he immediately adds there: *Though there those Names do not signify the Substance*; because if this (is true), therefore, they signify a relation, therefore, this name,

"God", signifies a relation. *And again,* if they do not signify the Substance, but a relation, therefore, relative names can be posited on behalf of them: therefore (one can say) *"the Father from the Father"*.

I RESPOND: It must be said, that *that there be said a "this from this"* is in a twofold manner, namely according to *the same* name, and/or according to *another* (name). According to *the same* it cannot be, unless it convenes with two; and because the Names convening with two Persons are nearly all essential ones, though some are notional; for that reason the rule of Master (Peter), that (there are) very many (names for the Substance for which this is true), has truth. However, only [maxime][1] certain books have (this rule); (in those) in which it is not (found), it can be posited as a gloss; and in this manner the objection ceases, because Master (Peter) does not intend to exclude but proper names, which are said of One alone. — Because *it is objected*, that the Names do not signify the Substance; it must be said, that he accepts *signification* (there) on behalf of *supposition,* and *"they do not signify"* is only worth as much as *"they do not suppose"*.[2]

DISTINCTION XXVIII

CHAPTER I

That there are not only three properties of the Persons.

Moreover, it is necessary [oportet] to consider, that there are not only the three aforesaid properties or notions in the Persons, but even others, which are noted with other names. For even this name, *"unbegotten"* [ingenitus], is said relatively of the Father only, and it designates another notion than 'Father' and/or 'Begetter' (does). For *'to be a father'* and *'to be unbegotten'* is not the same, that is, not by the same notion is *"father"* said, as (is) *"unbegotten"* (said). For *"father"*, as has been said before,[1] is said according to the property of generation, but *"unbegotten"* according to the property of innascibility. Therefore, the Father differs from the Son by the authorship of the generation, He differs too by the property of innascibility, that is, because (He is) unbegotten. Whence (St.) Augustine, distinguishing between the property, by which He is said (to be) a *"father"*, and that, by which He is said (to be) *"unbegotten"*, thus says in the fifth book, ON THE TRINITY:[2] « To say that one (is) *"unbegotten"* is not that which it is to say that one (is) a *"father"*; because even if He had not begotten the Son, nothing would prohibit saying that He (is) *"unbegotten"*. And if anyone begets a son, not from this is he *"unbegotten"*, because men (who are) begotten beget other (men) ». Therefore, not for this reason is He said (to be) a *"father"*, because (He is said to be) *"begotten"*; and for that reason,[3] since « of God the Father each is said, one is the notion, by which He is understood (to be) a *"begetter"*, another that by which (He is said to be) *"unbegotten"*. For *"begetter"* is said as regards a begotten, that is a son. However, when He is said (to be) *"unbegotten"*, He is said (to be), not that which He is, but (rather) that which He is not ». « This must be made clear by examples. That He is said (to be) *"unbegotten"*, by this it is shown, that He is not a son; but *"begotten"* [genitus] and *"unbegotten"* are fittingly [commode]

said, moreover, <u>filius</u> (i.e. son) is said in Latin, but to say <u>infilius</u> (i.e. un-son), the custom of speaking does not admit; yet it does not diminish the understanding (of the term), if there be said *"not a son"* [non-filius]; according to the same standard of measure, too, if *"not-begotten"* is said on behalf of tat which is said (to be) *"unbegotten"* [ingenitus], nothing other is said. For that reason one must not consider in (such) things, what either may [sinat] and/or may not be said by the use of our speech, but (rather) let every [quis] understanding of these things shine forth. For at present we not only say *"unbegotten"*, but also *"not-begotten"* [non-genitum], which is worth the same. For what else do we say, than *"not a son"*? Furthermore, the negative particle *"not"* causes, that there be said substantially, that which is said relatively without it, placed before the same; but that only is denied, which was said without it, just as in the other predications [praedicamentis], when we say: *"there is a man"*, we designate a substance. He who, therefore, says, *"there is no man"*, expresses in words [enuntiat] no other genus for the predication, but only denies it. Therefore, just as I speak according to substance (when I say): *"there is a man"*, so I deny according to substance, when I say: *"there is not a man"*. But, if that which is said (to be) *"begotten"* is only worth, as much as what is said (to be) a *"son"*, therefore, just so is that which is said (to be) *"non-begotten"* worth as much, as what is said (to be) *"not a son"*. Moreover, (since) we deny relatively, by saying *"not a son"*, therefore, we deny relatively, by saying[4] *"not-begotten"*. Furthermore, what is an *"unbegotten"* except an *"not-begotten"*? Therefore, one does not withdraw from the predicament of relation [a relative praedicamento], when one says *"unbegotten"*. For just as *"begotten"* is not said regarding itself, but (rather is said to be) 'that which is out of a begetter', when *"unbegotten"* is said, it is not said regarding itself, but (rather) it is shown (to be)' that which is not out of a begetter'. Moreover, what is relatively pronounced, does not indicate a substance. Therefore, though *"begotten"* and *"unbegotten"*

[1] For (this use of) <u>maxime</u>, one now reads *only* [tantum]; see the text of Master (Peter), here in ch. 5.

[2] Cf. above d. 4, a. sole, q. 2, p. 98, in the Scholium.

NOTES ON THE BOOK OF SENTENCES

[1] Distinction XXVI, ch. 2, and d. XXVII, ch. 1 and ff..

[2] Chapter 6, n. 7. In the same chapter occur those which follow, but with many (words) omitted and transposed.

[3] The Vatican edition alone has *The same* [Idem] for *an for that*

reason [ideoque], and next with ed. 8 it has *when ... is said* [cum ... dicitur] for *since ... is said* [cum ... dicatur], and then with the other edd., excluding ed. 1, after *For* [enim], it reads *is shown* [ostenditur] for *is said* [dicitur], contrary to the codd. and the original.

[4] These words: *"not a son", therefore we deny relatively, by saying* [*non-filius, relative igitur negamus dicendo*], are omitted faultily in the Vatican edition and in the other editions, except edition 1. They are extant in the original and in all the codices.

are diverse, yet it does not indicate a diverse substance, because just as a "*son*" is referred to a "*father*", and "*not-a-son*" to "*not-a-father*", so is it necessary that "*begotten*" be referred to "*begetter*", and "*not-begotten*" to "*not-begetter*" ».[1] Behold he evidently shows, that "*unbegotten*" is said relatively and is accepted of the Father alone, and that one is the notion, by which He is said (to be) "*unbegotten*", another, by which (He is said to be) a "*father*".

CHAPTER II

Whether the Father alone ought to be said (to be) "not-begotten" and/or "not a son", just as He is said (to be) "unbegotten".

For this reason one is accustomed to ask: "Whether, just as the Father alone is said (to be) "*unbegotten*", ought He alone to be said, thus, (to be) "*not-begotten*" and/or "*not a son*", that the Holy Spirit cannot be said (to be) "*not a son*" and/or "*not-begotten*"?" To certain (authors) it seems, that the Father alone ought to be said (to be) "*not-begotten*" and/or "*not a son*"; however, the Holy Spirit, just as He is not said (to be) "*unbegotten*", thus, they say, is not to be said (to be) "*not-begotten*" and/or "*not a son*". Indeed, the Holy Spirit ought to be said and to be believed to not be begotten, and/or to not be a son, but He ought not be said to be "*not-begotten*" and/or "*not a son*". — But to others it seems, that though the Holy Spirit cannot be said (to be) "*unbegotten*", yet He can be said (to be) "*not-begotten*" and/or "*not a son*". On the other hand, what (St.) Augustine says above, that when there is said "*unbegotten*", it is only worth, as much as, when there is said "*not-begotten*" and/or "*not a son*", they say that he said this by showing the etymology of the name, not (that he said this) according to the reckoning of predication [ratione praedicationis].

CHAPTER III

On the property, which "unbegotten" notes.

If, however, you wish to know, what the property, according to which the Father is said (to be) "*unbegotten*", is, hear (St.) Hilary calling the same "*the innascibility*", in the fourth book, ON THE TRINITY,[2] thus saying: « There is One from One, that is, a Begotten from an Unbegotten, by a property in each one, both (that) of innascibility and (that) of origin. With the understanding, therefore, of the Persons, signified in the Scriptures, and having distinguished the sense of innascibility and nativity, a solitary God must not be thought of [non est opinandus]. A discretion, therefore, and/or a distinction of Persons has been posited in the Scriptures, but in no manner [in nullo] a distinction of Nature ».

CHAPTER IV

The response of (St.) Ambrose against the Arians concerning the Unbegotten.

One also must not be silent about this, that the Arians strove to prove from this (name), that the Father was of one substance, the Son of another, because the Former is said (to be) "*Unbegotten*", and the Latter "*Begotten*", since 'to be unbegotten' and 'to be begotten' is (something) diverse.

Whence (St.) Ambrose, responding to their question, says, he has not read in the divine Scriptures of this name, namely, "*unbegotten*", thus saying in the book, ON THE SACRAMENT OF THE LORD'S INCARNATION:[3] « Since some time ago, certain (persons) heard, that we said, that the Son of God, who has been generated, cannot be unequal to the Father, though the Former has been generated, the Latter generated, because generation (is) not of a power, but of a nature; they indeed judged for themselves that that question (had) a concealed meaning [vocem occlusam], but by a damnable backsliding [tergiversatione] they changed course [vertunt vestigium] on the same spot, so that they think, that a change of question comes to be by a change of speech, saying: "In what manner can an *unbegotten* and a *begotten* be of one nature and substance?" Therefore, to respond to my own proposed question, first of all I never find, I have not read, (and) I have not heard (the word) "*unbegotten*" in the divine Scriptures. Therefore, of what mutability are men of this kind, that they say that we have put into use those (words), which have not been written, though we do say those which are written, and they object that it has not been written? Do they not turn against themselves and derogate the authority of their own calumny »? Attend, o reader, since (St.) Ambrose does not want to use this name, "*unbegotten*", on account of heretics. Thus too is it opportune [oportet] that, on account of the snares of calumniators, we remain silent concerning certain (things) [subticere quaedam], which can be believed securely by catholic and pious readers. For indeed, there are certain (things), which are not of such great religion and authority, that it is opportune for us to be a slave to them by confessing and receiving (them) always, but (which) can sometimes be passed over in silence; nor, yet, are they of that perversity, which, when it is opportune, that we not have free use of them.[4]

CHAPTER V

Whether 'to be a father' and 'to be a son' is diverse.

Moreover, one is accustomed to ask, since it has been said above,[5] that it is one (thing) to say that He (is) "*unbegotten*", another that He (is) a "*father*", and that "*begotten*" and "*unbegotten*" are diverse, whether similarly 'to be a father' and 'to be a son' are diverse, or the same. — To which we say, that out of the same sense, by which "*begotten*" and "*unbegotten*" is said (to be) diverse, and by which there is said, that it is not the same to say "*begotten*" and "*unbegotten*", it can be said, that it is not the same, but diverse 'to be a father' and 'to be a son', and/or 'to be a holy spirit', because not by the same notion is the Father a father, by which the Son is a son, and/or by which the Holy Spirit is a holy spirit. And for that reason out of this sense we do concede, that it is one (thing) 'to be a father', and it is another 'to be a son', because one is the notion, by which the Father is a father, another, by which the Son is a son. But if transposing, so that[6] you say, it is one (thing) that a father *is*, another that a son *is*, the understanding is varied; and for that reason it is not conceded. For the sense is such, as if there be said, 'that by which the Father *is*', is one (thing), not indeed (whereby He is) *a father*, but (whereby He) *is*, another, 'that by which the Son *is*', not indeed *a son*, but (that He) *is*; which is thoroughly false. For the Father *is* by this, by which

---

[1] All the preceding from the words: *This must be made clear by examples* [Hoc exemplis], (on the preceding page), have been taken from ON THE TRINITY, Bk. V, ch. 7, n. 8, with a few things changed. — A little after this the Vatican edition faultily reads *that one* [alia] for *and that one* [aliaque], edition 1 has *that one also* [alia quoque].

[2] Number 33. The final proposition is from n. 35, and reads thus: A discretion *only* of a Person, regarding "*Thee*" and "*Thy*", as been posited, however, in no manner a *distinct confession* of nature.

[3] The codices and editions 1, 2, 3, 5, 6 and 8, read: ON THE HOLY SPIRIT, *Bk. IV* [IV. de Spiritu sancto], but it is rather the book on the Incarnation of the Lord, ch. 8, n. 79. In which text after (before in the English) *Scriptures* [Scripturis], the Vatican edition, together with all the other editions, reads *I have not heard of an unbegotten* [ingenitum], breaking with the codices and original. Near the end, only the Vatican edition omits *themselves* [sibi].

[4] Codices B and C read *that we have not free judgement to use them* [eis uti liberum habeamus arbitrium].

[5] Chapter I.

[6] Codices A and D have *and* [et] for *so that* [ut].

the Father is God, that is, through the Essence and/or the Nature; but the Son is God by this, by which the Father is God: therefore, the Son *is* by this, by which the Father *is*, and thus that the Father *is* and[1] that the Son *is*, is the same, but 'to be a father' and 'to be a son' is not the same. Whence (St.) Augustine in the fifth book ON THE TRINITY[2] says: « Although 'to be a father' and 'to be a son' is diverse, yet (Their) substance is not diverse, because this is not said according to substance, but according to a relative (name); which relative, however, is not an accident, because it is not mutable ». Behold he says that 'to be a father' and 'to be a son' is diverse; which must [oportet] be accepted in accord with the aforesaid reckoning, namely, because one is the notion, by which (the Father) is *a father*, another, by which (the Son) is *a son*. For the Father is not said (to be) a "father" according to essence, nor (is) the Son (said to be) a "son", according to relation.

CHAPTER VI

Whether wisdom is said (to be) begotten according to relation, and/or according to substance.

It also must be known, that just as the Son alone is said (to be) a "*word* " and/or "*image*", so also He alone is said (to be) "*wisdom born*" and/or "*(wisdom) begotten*" [sapientia nata vel genita]. And for that reason there is asked, whether this is said relatively, and if it is said relatively, whether according to the same relation, by which He is said (to be) a "*word*" and "*image*". Of this, (St.) Augustine in the seventh book, ON THE TRINITY[3] thus says: « Let us accept that, when He is said (to be) a "*word*", that this is said, as if He is said (to be) "*born wisdom*" [nata sapientia], so that He is both *the Son* and *the Image* (of God); and these two, when they are said, that is "*born*" "*wisdom*", in one of them, by that (name) which is "*born*", both the Word and the Image and the Son is understood — and (so that) in all these names there is shown the Essence, because they are said relatively — but in the other (name), which is "*wisdom*", the Essence would also be demonstrated, since it is also said regarding Itself. For by Its very self It is wise, and this (name) belongs to that "*being*" which (is) *being-wise* [eius esse quod sapere]; whence the Father and the Son together (are) one Wisdom, because (They are) the One Essence ». — Be on guard, reader, in what manner you understand that, which (St.) Augustine says here. For he seems to say, that when "*born wisdom*" is said, there "*wisdom*" signifies the Essence, and "*born*" notes a relation. Which, if

it is thus, we are driven to say, that the Divine Essence has been born; which is repugnant to what has been said above [superioribus repugnat]. — But to this we say, that in the one, that is in that (name) which is "*born*", the same notion is understood,[4] which is noted when there is said "*word*" and "*image*". However, in the other, namely "*wisdom*", the Essence is demonstrated, that is, there is demonstrated, that the Son is the Essence, because "*wisdom*" is said according to essence. And, for that reason, when He is said (to be) "*born wisdom*", one understands, that He Himself, because He has been born, is the Essence. However, there "*wisdom*" does not cause an understanding on behalf of the Essence, but on behalf of a Hypostasis, so that, just as when He is said (to be) a word and/or a son, a Hypostasis is understood with its property, thus, when He is said (to be) "*born wisdom*", the same be understood,[5] that is a begotten hypostasis (is understood). For that reason, he say vigilantly, that the same must be understood, when He is said (to be) a "*word*", and when He is said (to be) "*born wisdom*", that is the same relation and the same Hypostasis, in which that property is. And from this that which we have said above[6] is aided, namely, that when there is said "*the Father*" and/or "*the Son*" and/or "*the Holy Spirit*", not only are those properties signified, as when there is said "*the paternity*", "*the filiation*", but also the Hypostases with their properties.

CHAPTER VII

On "image".

This, too, must be known [sciri oportet], because though it was said above,[7] that he says "*image*" [imaginem] relatively of the Son, just as "*word*" and "*son*" (are), yet now it is found that it is said according to substance. Whence (St.) Augustine in the book, ON THE FAITH TO PETER[8] says, that there is essentially one Divinity and image of the Holy Trinity, according to which [ad quam] man has been made. (St.) Hilary too in the fifth book, ON THE TRINITY[9] says in the same manner: « Man is made according to a common image. The name (for 'image') does not differ in sound [discrepat], the nature (of 'image') does not differ. For there is one species according to which man has been created ». From these words it is shown, that "*image*" sometimes causes the understanding of an essence, and then it is said regarding (the Essence) itself and not relatively.

---

[1] The Vatican edition and edition 4, 6, 7, 8 and 9, read thus *that the Father is, is the same as that the Son is, etc.* [ita idem est Pater esse quod Filius esse etc.]., contrary to the codices and the other editions.

[2] Chapter 5, n. 6. [3] Chapter 2, n. 3.

[4] The Vatican ed. with the other edd., contrary to the codd.s and edd. 1 & 8, reads faultily, *let the same notion be understood* [eadem notio intelligatur] for *the same notion is understood* [eadem notion intelligitur].

[5] The Vatican ed. with the other edd., reads *the same is understood* [idem intelligatur] for *the same be understood* [idem intelligitur], breaking with the codices and edition 8.

[6] Distinction XXVII, part II, at the beginning. — The Vatican edition, together with very many editions, has *above* [superius] for *above* [supra], and after *namely* [scilicet] it omits *that* [quod].

[7] Ibid., part II, ch. 3, near the end.

[8] Chapter 1, n. 6. That this book is not by St. Augustine, but by (St.) Fulgentius of Ruspe, has been said, above, in the Prolegomena, p. LXXXIV.

[9] Number 8.

COMMENTARY ON DISTINCTION XXVIII

On the non-personal property, which is innascibility.

Moreover, it is necessary to consider, that there are not only etc..

THE DIVISION OF THE TEXT

Above, Master (Peter) dealt with the properties, which belong to the Persons and (are) personal; here he begins the second part, in which he deals with the non-personal properties or relations. And this part is divided into two, because there is a twofold non-personal property, namely, the innascibility and the common spiration, which is signified through this name, *"beginning"* [principium]. For that reason, first he deals with the innascibility, second with the common spiration, below in the Twenty-Ninth Distinction (where he says): *There is, moreover, another name* etc. The first part has two (parts). In the *first*, he determines (what) concerns the property of the innascibility; in the *second*, because opposites shine forth[1] more clearly about opposites, he touches incidentally upon (what) concerns the property of *nascibility* and of the *nascible*, below (where he says) in the same Distinction: *It also must be known, that just as the Son.*

Likewise, the *first* part has four parts. In the first, he shows, what is (that which is) signified by this name, *"unbegotten"*, in itself, showing, that it is proper to the Person of the Father and (is) different from the paternity and (is) said according to relation. Second, he determines its signification in an equipollent (term), as in this name, *"not-begotten"*

[non genitus], and in this name, *"innascible"* [innascibilis], there (where he says): *For that reason it is accustomed to be asked, whether, just as the Father alone* etc..[2] Third, he determines the use of this name, showing, that although it does not have (its) rise out of Scripture, that yet it is licit to use it, even though (St.) Ambrose seems to say the contrary — for he does this to reprehend the heretics — and he does this there (where he says): *One also must not be silent about this* . In the fourth, however, he determines[3] a certain doubt, which has (its) rise out of (what has been) predetermined, there (where he says): *Moreover, one is accustomed to ask* etc..

It also must be known, that just as the Son alone etc.. This is the *second* part of this part,[4] in which he incidentally determines (what) concerns the property of the Son or the Born (God); and this has two parts according to the two (names), which he touches upon there. For, because there had been said above, that *"wisdom"* meant (something) common, and *"image"* (something) proper; for that reason, because this could generate doubt, because we sometimes find (them used) contrariwise [e contrario], for that reason he first shows, that *"wisdom born"* is properly said of the Son. But, second, he shows, that *"image"* is sometimes accepted essentially, there (where he says): *This too must be known.*

TREATMENT OF THE QUESTIONS

For an understanding of those (things) which are said in the present Distinction, four (questions) are asked:

First, there is asked, whether this name, *"unbegotten"* [ingenitus] or *"innascible"* [innascibilis], is said according to substance, and/or according to relation.

Second, having supposed that it is said according

to relation, there is asked, whether it means the same relation as this name, *"father"* [pater].

Third, there is asked, whether the innascibility is a personal property or relation of the Father.

Fourth and last there is asked, whether the improcessibility [improcessibilitas] means some notion in the Father.

---

[1] Or, as Aristotle says in ELENCHAE, Bk. I, ch. 14 (ch. 15): Having been set out according to their contraries, they appear lesser and greater and worse and better to men. And in ON HEAVEN AND THE WORLD, Bk. II, text 40 (ch.6) he says: For more understandable are the (things) placed along side themselves. — Next, the Vatican edition with a few codices has *innascibility* [innascibilitatis] for *nascibility* [nascibilitatis].

[2] The Vatican edition alone adds here: *Adioining, what is the prop-*

erty according to which the Father is said (to be) "unbegotten", there (where he says): Moreover, if you want to know [Adiungens, quae sit proprietas secundum quam Pater dicitur ingenitus, ibi: Si autem vis scire].

[3] Codices P Q and W read *he solves* [solvit].

[4] The words *It also must be known* up to *of this part* [Sciendum quoque ... huius partis] inclusively have been suppressed in the Vatican edition with the words: *Similarly, the second part* [Similiter secunda pars].

ARTICLE SOLE

On innascibility and improcessibility.

QUESTION I

Whether the name, "unbegotten" *or* "innascible" *is said according to substance, and/or relation?*

Therefore, as much as regards the first, that this name, "*unbegotten*" [ingenitus], is said according to relation, is shown:

1. Through (St.) Augustine, who says in the fifth book, ON THE TRINITY[1] and (as) is had in the text (of Master Peter): « One does not withdraw from the predicament of relation, when one says "*unbegotten*" »: therefore it is said according to relation.

2. Likewise, in the same book:[2] « Just as a "begotten" (is said) regarding a "begetter", so an "unbegotten" regarding a "not-begetter" »; but what is said regarding another is said relatively or according to relation: ergo etc..

3. Likewise, this very (thing) seems *by reason*, because every "that", in which a Person differs from a Person, is said according to relation — this is clear — but according to that (name) which is "*unbegotten*" the Father differs from the Son: ergo etc..

4. Likewise, no negation deprives the manner of signifying or of saying;[3] but "*begotten*" is said according to relation, therefore, with a negation added, (a relation) is still said: ergo etc..

ON THE CONTRARY: 1. Every relation among the divine posits something — that is certain — but "*unbegotten*" posits nothing: ergo etc.. *Proof of the middle*: if this name posits anything, therefore, either according to which it is held *negatively*, or according to which (it is held) *privatively*. Not according to which (it is held) *negatively*; this is established. If, therefore, according which it is held *privatively*; but a privation takes away act and posits an aptitude:[4] therefore, according to this, "*unbegotten*" will be the same as "*apt to be generated, and not begotten*"; but this befits None: ergo etc..

2. Likewise, every relation among the divine signifies in concretion conveys a distinction, and for that reason none is said of the Essence according to the manner of denomination — but "unbegotten" is said of the Essence, for the Divine Essence is not begotten,[5] since [cum] its opposite, namely "begotten", is not predicated of the Essence: ergo etc..

3. Likewise, negations hold themselves contrariwise from affirmations; but "*begotten*" is in less than "*related*" (is), and "*generation*" (is in less) than "*relation*": therefore, "*unbegotten*" is in more than "*not-related*", and "*not-being-generated*" [ingeneratio] (is in more) than "*not-being-related*" [non-relatio]. But "*not-related*" and/or "*not-being-related*" is not said according to relation, because then it would imply (its) opposites: therefore, since that (name) which is "*unbegotten*" is in more, it is not in the genus of relation: ergo etc..

4. Likewise, every relation among the divine is either in respect of a *beginning*, or in respect of a *begun*: therefore, if that (name) which is "*unbegotten*" means a relation, either[6] (it does so) in respect of a *beginning*, or in respect of a *begun*. But not in respect of a *beginning*, because then the Father would have a beginning, which is unfitting. If in respect of a *begun*, then, therefore, there is no negation of that, of which there was an affirmation — for "*begotten*" is said in respect of a *beginning*, because (it is) from something — therefore, if "unbegotten" is not said in respect of a *beginning*, then, therefore, the negation is not said in respect of that, in respect of which there was an affirmation. Therefore, it neither means a relation to *the begun*, because the name does not permit (that), nor to *a beginning*, because the thing does not permit (that).

CONCLUSION

The name, "unbegotten", in (its) principal understanding means a relation privatively, but out of (its) consequent understanding (it means something) positively, that is, a fontal plenitude.

I RESPOND: It must be said, that about this there are diverse positions. For all posited, that that (name) which is "*unbegotten*" is said according to relation, but differently.

For *certain* (authors) said, that "*unbegotten*" only means the *privation* of relation; and for this there suffices this alone, that it be said notionally, since a privation can be a principle of distinguishing and making known,

---

[1] Chapter 7, n. 8, and here in the text of Master (Peter), ch. 1.

[2] Loc. cit.. — The Vatican edition alone after *Just as* [Sicut] adds *is said* [dicitur], in place of which in the original (text of St. Augustine) there is read *is referred* [refertur].

[3] (St.) Augustine proves this proposition in ON THE TRINITY, Bk. V, ch. 7, n. 8, by expounding examples from all ten genera of predicaments, some of which Master (Peter) adduces here in the text, in ch. 1. St. Bonaventure, moving a doubt below concerning the words of (St.) Augustine (dubium 2), approves them and fortifies them with this reason: Since a term denied draws (its) signification from the (term) affirmed, there is the same manner of speaking, as much as regard signification, in the denied term and the affirmed one. —

Cf. also Aristotle, ELENCHAE, Bk. II, ch. 6 (ch. 31), where he says, that making is included in not-making and an affirmation too entirely in the negation.

[4] Cf. Aristotle, On the Predicaments, ch. "On Opposites", and Metaphysics, Bk. V, text 27 (Bk. IV, ch. 22), not without Metaphysics, Bk. IV, text 4 (Bk. III, ch. 2), where the difference between negation and privation is shown. — Next, the Vatican edition, without the authority of the codices, and not supported by edition 1, has *but not yet begotten* [sed nondum genitus] for *and not begotten* [et non genitus].

[5] Codex Y *unbegotten* [ingenita].

[6] Codex V adds *this will be* [hoc erit]. A little below this, after *would have* [haberet] codices F and T read *some* [aliquod] for *a*.

just as a unbranded sheep from a branded one [non signata a signata]. *And again*, a negation means a nobility, just as the "*not being ruled*" in a king, the "*not being caused*" in a cause, (and) the "*not being produced*" in a principle. — But that position cannot stand, because a pure negation neither *distinguishes* nor *means a nobility*:[1] it does not distinguish, for a negation of relation is said of the Essence; it *does* not *mean a relation*, for every nobility posits something through a manner of a position.

Others posited, that that (name) which is "*unbegotten*" is said according to relation and *in a positive manner* [positive], because by depriving the one it posits the other: just as "*unequal*" deprives equality and posits the relation opposed to that, similarly that (name) which is "*dissimilar*", whence it also conveys a relation positively; thus that (name) which is "*unbegotten*" by depriving the relation regarding a begetter posits the opposite relation regarding a non-begetter. And this they say (St.) Augustine thought, who says, that « just as a "*begotten*" is said regarding a "*begetter*", so a "*not-begotten*" regarding a "*not-begetter*" ».[2] — But that position of their cannot stand, because "not-begotten" is said either regarding a *beginning*, or regarding a *begun*. If regarding a *begun*, therefore, in respect of that this name, "*unbegotten*", cannot be said, since "*begotten*" is said in respect to a beginning, and there is the same signified in this name, "*begotten*" and "*unbegotten*", and "*unbegotten*" differs by a negation alone: therefore, it is necessary, that this name, "*unbegotten*", be said in respect of a *beginning*. If, however, this is true: therefore, according to this the Father would be posited[3] to have a beginning, in respect of which it is said. *And again*, that "beginning" does not mean a beginning, but a privation of that.

The third manner of speaking is, that which this name, "*unbegotten*", according to which the notion of the Father is assigned, is said according to relation *partly* privatively, *partly* positively. On this account it must be noted, that, just as (St.) Augustine says,[4] « "*unbegotten*" and "*non-begotten*" is the same ». "*Not-begotten*", moreover, can be accepted in a threefold manner, just as "*not-white*" (can), because the negation can be *in the genus*,

and/or *outside the genus*, and/or partly *in the genus* and partly *outside the genus*.[5] According to which the negation is *outside the genus*, thus generally it deprives and does not posit any quality, just as the "*not-white*" can be said (to be), that which is not in the genus of color nor of quality. According to which the negation is *in the genus*, thus it deprives whiteness and posits the contrary quality, as the "*not-white*", because it lacks whiteness, but yet is black. According to which (the negation is) partly *in the genus*, partly *outside the genus*, namely in a remote[6] genus and outside a proximate genus; thus the not-white is said (to be) that which lack both whiteness and color, yet has a *quality* nevertheless.

Through this standard of measure it must be understood in the proposed. For that which is *unbegotten*[7] conveys an order in the reckoning of a *remote* genus, and an order to a principle in the reckoning of a *proximate* (genus), and such an order through the manner of nature in the reckoning of a *completive* (genus). If, therefore, "*unbegotten*" is a negation *outside the genus*, thus the "*unbegotten*" is said (to be) that which is not generated nor even has an order and/or[8] a relation; and in this manner it means a privation *purely*, and is said of the Essence and it not said according to substance nor according to relation, for this, that it is only a privation. — In another manner the negation can be *in the genus*; and then the "*unbegotten*" is said (to be) that which is not generated, yet has an order to a principle, and in this manner it means a *substrate relation*; but yet out of this it does not mean a *nobility*, and thus it does befit the Holy Spirit, and yet it is not a notion. — In a third manner, the negation can be in a certain manner *in the genus*, in a certain manner *outside the genus*; and thus the "*unbegotten*" is said (to be) that which is not generated, yet has an order, but not to a principle; and in this manner it means a privation of relation in respect of a *principle*. For if it has an order, and not to a principle, therefore, it itself is *first* and *a principle*; and in this manner it means a nobility, just as also a *beginning*. And it was proper [decuit] that that be signified through a negation, because first things [prima] are cognized through a negation,[9] and in this manner it is a *notion*.

---

[1] The Vatican edition corrupts the text of the codices, and even that of edition 1, by substituting *is distinguished* [distinguitur] for *distinguishes* [distinguit], then after *nobility* [nobilitatem], by adding *nor distinguishes* [nec distinguit], and then a little below this after *a position* [positionis] by inserting the proposition: *It doest not distinguish, because it is not a relation* [Non distinguit, quia non est relatio].

[2] See above, in the 2nd argument of the fundament. — The explanation of this saying of (St.) Augustine is found below, in dubium 3. — Next, for *not-begotten* [non genitus] codex R has *unbegotten* [ingenitus].

[3] Very many codices, such as A T V and Y, together with edition 1, read *will be posited* [ponetur].

[4] ON THE TRINITY, Bk. V, ch. 7, n. 8: Furthermore, what is an "*unbegotten*", but a "*not begotten*"? — A little before this *is assigned* [assignatur] the Vatican edition alone faultily reads *is likened to* [assimilatur].

[5] This division of 'negation' is insinuated by Aristotle, POSTERIOR ANALYTICS, Bk. I, ch. 4: For it is a contrary or a privation or a contradiction in the same genus, as 'equal' and 'unequal' (are) among numbers, according to which it is obtained. And in METAPHYSICS, Bk. IV, text 4 (Bk. III, ch. 2) he says: However a negation and privation of one is a glimpsing [speculari], on account of which in each manner there is glimpsed one that of which the negation or privation is; for either we simply say, that it is not in that (genus), or we establish (it in) some genus. If indeed in that (genus) there is a difference for one according to which (it is) in a negation, for a negation is the absence of that; however, a privation comes to be by a certain subjected nature, of which the privation is said (ed. Firmin-Didot). And ibid., text 27, (ch. 6): Moreover, a pri-

vation is a negation by a certain determinate genus. — (Bl. John Duns) Scotus, commenting on (Aristotle's) METAPHYSICS, Bk. IV, text 4, says: For it must be noted, that there is a twofold negation: a certain one is in a simple manner and *outside the genus*, through which (negation) there is said absolutely, that this is not that; the other is a negation *in the genus*, or non-limiting [infinitans], through which (negation) something is not absolutely denied, but (is said) within the goal-posts of some genus, just as the blind is said (to be), what does not have sight; yet not everything not having sight is blind, but (only that which) is in the genus of animals, which has been born to have sight. Whence a negation *outside the genus* can be verified both of a non-being [non ente], which has been born to have and does not have. Whence both the chimera, and the stone, as even a man can be said (to be) "*not seeing*"; but not so concerning a privation, which is a negation *within a genus*, because not everything not-seeing can be said (to be) blind, but only that which is apt, having been born to have sight. Cf. also the Commentary of (Bl.) Scotus, SENT, Bk. I, d. 28, q. 2, n. 4. — Next after codex K reads *any, contrary quality* [aliquam qualitatem contrariam] for *some quality* [aliquam qualitatem].

[6] The Vatican edition, supported by editions 4 and 5 alone, omits *remote* [remoto] and a little below this *nevertheless* [nihilominus].

[7] Codices M and Z have *begotten* [genitum], codex O reads *begotten* [genitus].

[8] Edition 1 has *nor* [nec].

[9] Cf. above d. 24, a. 1, q. 1, p. 421, footnote 6.

But, since *"unbegotten"* from the reckoning of its name does not seem to mean but a privation and/or a negation of generation, on this account it must be said *in a fourth manner*, that this name, *"unbegotten"*, according to which it befits the Father properly, means a relation *privatively*, but out of (the name) itself it means *positively* a relation *out of a consequent*. Which is clear in this manner. For the one who is *simply* not generated is said *"not to be generated"*; and thus it befits not only the Father, but the Essence and the Holy Spirit. But beyond this understanding, insofar as it properly befits *the Father*, it adds (something), because the Father *is not generated*, nor *is accepted through generation*; and in this manner there is excluded the Essence, which is accepted through generation, but still befits the Holy Spirit. However, insofar as it befits the Father alone, thus He is said (to be) *"unbegotten"*, because He *is* not *generated*, nor *is accepted through generation*, nor *is consequent to a generation*. Through the first member (of this division) the Son is excluded, through the second the Essence, through the third the Holy Spirit, the procession of Whom presupposes generation according to the order of (its) origin, because He proceeds as a nexus from the Father and the Son.[1] For though among the divine there is no *prior* and *posterior*, yet according to origin and the reckoning of understanding the generation of the Son is before the procession of the Holy Spirit, as has been shown above,[2] and yet they are simultaneous according to nature [simul sunt natura].

In this manner, therefore, with the verb 'to be consequent' [verbo consequendi] accepted in the broad sense [large], since properly there is no *preceding* and *following* There, Any (Person) is said to be *"unbegotten"* in a threefold manner: either because *He is* not *produced* through generation, or because *He is* not *produced* through generation nor *is had* or accepted through generation, or because *He is* neither *produced* nor *accepted* nor *is consequent* through a generation. Therefore, in this manner *"unbegotten"* conveys *in no manner* a 'being from another' [esse ab alio], and thus (it conveys) a primacy and through this a fontal plenitude, just as has been shown in the beginning of the preceding Distinction,[4] and just as is clear from the beginning of the following Distinction, where there is said, that « the Father is the beginning of the whole Deity, because He

is from None »; and thus in (its) *principal* understanding it means a relation *privatively*, out of (its) *consequent* (understanding it means a relation) *positively*; and thus it does not mean a negation, which posits nothing.

Wherefore, the reasons for this are to be conceded.

1. To that, therefore, which is objected, that it posits nothing according to which (it is held) negatively; it must be said, that (that) is false, because there is no negation *outside the genus*, as if there be said: "a chimera is unbegotten", nay there is a negation with a constancy of subject; and such a negation leaves in the subject a most high nobility.

2. To that which is objected, that it is said of the Essence; it must be said, that it is true, but according to which is said *only privatively*, and in this manner it is not a property of the Father; but according to which it is a property of the Father, it is not said of the Essence.

3. To that which is objected, that negations hold themselves contrariwise to affirmations; it must be said, that that is not always true of a negation *in a genus*, but (it is of one) *outside a genus*. For *"not-white"*, insofar as it is a negation in a genus, is not said (to be) superior to that which is *"not-of-the-kind-that"* [non-quale]; similarly *"unbegotten"* is not superior to that which is *"not-related"*.

4. To that which is objected last, that[5] it means a relation; it must be said, that according to which it conveys a relation privatively, it is said in respect of a *beginning*; and out of this it does not follow, that the Father has a beginning, nay that He does not have (one), because it is not said according to the positing (of a beginning), but according to the removal (of one). Whence (St.) Augustine says well, « that it is said regarding a not-begetter », because *"unbegotten"* signifies the removal of 'begetter'. However, according to which it conveys a relation *positively* and out of a consequent (understanding), thus (it is said)[6] in respect of *a begun*; and in this manner it is not unfitting, that some privative name convey something out of a consequent (understanding), which an affirmative one does not convey to its opposite. And in this manner all the rest (of the objections) are clear.

SCHOLIUM

I. It seems that some things must be noted concerning the *multiple sense* of the word *"unbegotten"* [ingenitus] — concerning the signification of this *notion* in the Father — and whether it is the *constitutive property* of the Father.

1. The multiple *sense* of this *word*, as (Bl. John Duns) Scotus rightly observes (here in q. 2, n. 3), flows from a twofold sources, since *"begotten"* [genitus] can be accepted in a diverse sense, and the particle *"un-"* [in-] (can) signify a threefold manner of privation (cf. St. Thomas, SUMMA., I, q. 34, a. 4, in reply to n. 2; Aristotle, METAPHYSICS, Bk. V., texts 17 and 22; in the Parisian edition, Bk. IV, chs. 12 and 22). Four senses of the word *"unbegotten"* must especially be attended to: *a)* with *a proper*

privation, which posits an aptitude to some form and denies the form itself — this sense is entirely excluded from God; *b)* with a *simple negation* of form, and in this manner it is said of the Person of the Father and the Holy Spirit and even of the Divine Essence, to the extent that It is not generated, though It is communicated through generation; *c)* with the name, *"to be generated"*, extended to *"to be communicated"*, (and in this sense) the Divine Essence is not unbegotten; *d)* by denying entirely, that a Person is from Another in any manner, and/or, as the Seraphic (Doctor) says, by positing « that He is not generated, nor is accepted through generation, nor is consequent to

---

[1] See above d. 10, a. 2, q. 2.

[2] Above, in d. 12, q. 4.

[3] Thus the cleared codices. In the Vatican edition and not a few of the manuscripts the second member (of the division) is wanting: *or because he is not produced through generation* [aut quia non producitur per generationem]. — In codex F the hand of an interpolator has lengthened the text thus: *"unbegotten", either because it is not produced through generation, but is communicated through generation, as the Essence (is); or because He is not produced through generation nor is had or accepted through generation, but is consequent to a generation, as the Holy Spirit (is); or because He is not produced nor accepted nor*

is consequent, as the Father (is) [ingenitus, aut quia non producitur per generationem, sed per generationem communicatur, ut essentia; aut quia non producitur per generationem nec per generationem habetur sive accipitur, sed generationem consequitur, ut Spiritus sanctus; aut quia non producitur nec accipitur nec consequitur, ut Pater].

[4] Part I, q. 2, a. 3. — The saying of (St.) Augustine, which is cited next from the following Distinction, namely, that the Father is the beginning of the whole Deity, is found there in the text of Master (Peter), ch. 1, and is explained there in dubium 1.

[5] Codex T has *in respect of which* [respectu cuius] for *that* [quod].

[6] Supply: *it is said* [dicitur].

a generation »; and in this manner it befits a principle without a principle and is proper to the Father alone. — Hence the apparent contradiction between the words of the Holy Fathers and doctors (cf. d. 13, q. 4) can be easily reconciled.

2. On the signification of the notion "*unbegotten*" in the Father the doctors do not thoroughly agree. Not a few said, that something positive is signified by the innascibility, namely the positing of a relation, which is the opposite to the relation of a begetter. St. Thomas and (Bl.) Scotus want, that formally it means a pure negation. However, since very negation and/or privation is founded upon something positive, those two doctors disagree in voice in assigning a *fundament* of this negative concept. (Bl.) Scotus teaches, that the formal fundament of this negation is the paternity under the reckoning of paternity. St. Thomas is not expounded in the same sense by his interpreters. Moreover, it seems that he teaches, that by this name there is conveyed a negation of a principle *from another*, (which negation is) founded in the reckoning of a principle *to another*. Vasquez thinks, that he agrees with St. Bonaventure, who according to his custom takes a middle path and teaches, that the innascibility *primarily* and *formally* means a negation, but *secondarily*, *consequently* and even *fundamentally* (means) a positing, as is manifestly clear from the following question, in the body (of the question), and above in d. 27, p. I, q. 2, in reply to n. 3. This positive (signified), connoted in the reckoning of an unbegotten, according to him is the *fontal plenitude* in the Father (cf. loc. citt., and d. 7, q. 2, and d. 13, q. 3, and passim).

3. That *the constitute property* of the Father is formally the paternity, is the common sentence, and is manifestly taught by the Seraphic Doctor (here in q. 3). Yet, the Seraphic (Doctor), consistent with his own (doctrine), adds, that even the innascibility in some manner, that is out of (its) consequent understanding, means a relation *positively*, and in this manner it constitutes the Father, but only *in the manner of a root* [radicaliter] or *of a beginning* [inchoative]. For according to him (d. 27, p. I, q. 2) the paternity presupposes the generation as (its) root, but the generation (presupposes) a fecundity, which is conveyed in the innascibility, to the extent that it means a fontal plenitude in the Father. This is conceived as the *common* root of two emanations and as fecund, not in the second act, but in the first, or, as Richard of Middleton says, in *habit*. This doctrine has (its) firm foundation in that common doctrine, which was consecrated at the Council of Florence (Decree of Union for the Jacobites), that « the Father, whatever He is or has, does not have from another, but out of Himself is also the *principle without a principle*. The son, whatever He is or has, has from the Father and is the *principle from the principle* etc. » (cf. d. 29, a. 1 and 2, and Doubts 1 and 2).

II. With these things supposed, both the three solutions, which St. Bonaventure does not approve, and the fourth one received by him and posited at the end of the Response, are easily understood. This sentence, that the innascibility *fundamentally* means a fontal plenitude in the Father, and out of (its) consequent (understanding means) a quasi common relation to the two emanating Persons, was the ancient position of the great Doctors (above in d. 27, p. I, q. 2 and 3), which Alexander of Hales (SUMMA, p. I, q. 69, m. 2 and 4), and (Bl.) Peter of Tarentaise (here in q. 2, a. 3) favor, and which Richard of Middleton defends (here in a. 2, a. 1 and 2). Nevertheless, this ancient solution was abandoned by the later Scholastics, nay by (Bl.) Scotus (here in q. 2, n. 6 ff.) it was impugned by three arguments, the principal one of which concludes nothing, since it supposes (an understanding) contrary to the mind of the Seraphic (Doctor), that in that fontal plenitude there is conveyed some *real* relation, *distinct* from the generation and active spiration. Even St. Thomas (here in q. 1, a. 1, in reply to n. 2; and in the SUMMA, I, q. 33, a. 4, in reply to n. 1) objects: « It does not seem true, because thus *the innascibility* would not be another property from the paternity and spiration, but would include them, just as a proper is included in a common ». To which it will be able to be responded according to the mind of the Seraphic (Doctor), with a distinction: by speaking of a *principal* and formal signification of innascibility, which means the *negation* of a beginning, this notion is not the same with the paternity and spiration; by speaking of a *secondary* signification, which conveys that fontal plenitude, « it really is the same with the paternity and active spiration ... yet it differs according to reckoning » (Richard of Middleton, here in a. 2, q. 2). Thus according to sense, even St. Bonaventure, here in q. 2, and in Doubt 1, and q. 3, in reply to n. 2; cf. also d. 29, Doubt 1, near the end.

III. Besides the authors already cited, cf. Bl. (now St.) Albertus (Magnus), here in a. 1 and 2; and in d. 13, a. 9 and 10; SUMMA., p. I, tr. 9, q. 39, m. 1, subpart 1. — (Bl.) Peter of Tarentaise, here in q. 1, a. 1 and 2. — (Bl.) Richard of Middleton, here in a. 2, q. 1. — Giles the Roman, here in 1st. princ., q. 2. — Henry of Ghent, SUMMA., a. 57, q. 1. — Durandus (of Saint-Pourçain), here in q. 1. — (Bl.) Dionysius the Carthusian, here in q. 2. — (Gabriel) Biel, on this and the following questions, here in the q. sole.

QUESTION II

Whether innascibility and paternity convey the same relation?

Second, having supposed that this name, "*unbegotten*", is said according to relation; there is asked, whether it conveys the same relation, as this name, "*the Father*", whether, that is, *the innascibility* and *the paternity* is the same relation. And that (it is) not, is shown in this manner:

1. (St.) Augustine in the fifth (book) ON THE TRINITY (says):[1] « It is one (thing) to say *that He is a father*, and another (that He is) *unbegotten* »; but (this is not said) according to essence: therefore, according to relation.

2. Likewise, this seems *through a reckoning*, because it is possible, that someone be understood *to be unbegotten*, and not *to be a father*, as in Adam,[2] and conversely, as in Cain. If, therefore, one relation can be understood, with the other not understood, and conversely; (one can) be posited too, with the other not posited: therefore, they are diverse relations.

3. Likewise, relations are diversified from within terms, because a relation, according to which (it is) of this kind, regards the other (terminus);[3] but "*unbegotten*" is said through a privation of (something) prior, namely, of a father, and "*father*" (is said) according to the positing of an offspring [germinis] or son: therefore, they mean a looking-back according to different sides [aliam et aliam partem]: ergo etc..

4. Likewise, generation and non-generation [ingeneratio] differ more than generation and spiration — for in the former [hic] there is a proper opposition, but in the latter [ibi] there is only a disparity [disparatio] — but the generation is (one) relation and the spiration another: therefore, also the generation and the non-generation. But the generation and the paternity is the same (relation), as has been shown above:[4] therefore, the innascibility and the paternity are not the same relations.

ON THE CONTRARY: 1. Every relation among the divine [relatio in divinis] is of a Per-

---

[1] Chapter 6, n. 7. Cf. here the text of Master (Peter), ch. 1.

[2] Codex Y reads *as Adam in paradise* [quod Adam in paradise]. Next the Vatican edition has faultily *Abel* [Abel] for *Cain* [Cain].

[3] Cf. Aristotle, ON THE PREDICAMENTS, ch. "On *Relation*", and METAPHYSICS, Bk. V, text 20 (Bk. IV, ch. 15).

[4] Distinction 27, p. I, q. 1. — At the beginning of the argument edition 1 has the plural form of the verb *differ* [differunt]; at the end the words *are not the same relations* [non sunt eaedem relationes] are omitted by many codices; codex T substitutes for them *are diverse relations* [sunt siversae relationes].

son to a Person; if, therefore, "*unbegotten*" means a relation, therefore, either (a relation) to the Son, or (to)
the Holy Spirit, or to Each. Not to Each, because the
Father is not compared by a unique relation, but by
diverse ones to the Son and (to) the Holy Spirit; not to
the Person of the Holy Spirit — this is established —
therefore, to the Son. If, therefore, the paternity is a
relation to the Son: therefore, the innascibility is the
same relation.

2. Likewise, relations among the divine do not accede to the Persons, but *bestow the 'to be' of a Person*:[1]
therefore, if one Person there is a unique 'to be', there
will be a unique relation of Him. But the Father is one
Person, and the innascibility and the paternity convene
with Him: ergo etc..

3. Likewise, just as the nascibility in the Son holds
itself to the filiation, so the innascibility in the Father to
the paternity; but in the Son the nascibility and the filiation are the same relation: ergo etc..

4. Likewise, the Philosopher (says):[2] « I say that a
first and a beginning (are) the same »; but "the innascibility" means that which it means in the reckoning of a
first, "father" (means what it means) in the reckoning
of a *beginning*: therefore, they mean the same habitude
and relation: therefore, they are not two relations, but
one only.

CONCLUSION

*The innascibility is a notion other than the paternity, since
each conveys a different relation both according to (its)
principal understanding, and according to (its)
consequent understanding.*

I RESPOND: It must be said, that this (name)
which is "*innascible*"[3] conveys another relation, than this
(name) which is "*father*", both as much as regards (its)
principal understanding, and as much as regards (its) *consequent* (understanding). As much as regards (its) *principal* (understanding), it is manifest, that ("innascible")[4]
conveys a looking-back to a beginning through a manner of a *privation*, but "father" conveys a looking-back
to a begun through a manner of a *position* and a *generation*; and thus they mean diverse habitudes, one of
which is a true habitude, the other the privation of a
habitude. — As much as regards (their) *consequent* understanding they similarly differ, though not as much.
For "*father*" means a relation[5] of a beginning only in re-

spect of the Son and through a manner of *generation*,
but "*innascible*" means a universal principality or fontal
plenitude in producing, not only as much as regards
generation, but also as much as regards spiration, not
only in respect of the Son, but also in respect of the
Holy Spirit. And this is clear, because He is said (to be)
"*innascible*", for this, that He is not generated nor is He
consequent to generation: therefore, in the name, "*innascible*", the reckoning of being born and of being produced is borne away; and if this, (then) there is posited
the reckoning of an omnimodal principality, and for
that reason (a reckoning) of a fontal plenitude.

1. To that, therefore, which is objected, that it
means the looking-back of a Person to a Person; it must
be said, that *privatively* or negatively[6] it does not mean a
looking-back to a Person. And that which says, that
every relation means a looking-back to a Person, is understood of that which means a *position*. But according
to which it is accepted as much as regards (its) *consequent understanding*, it means a looking-back to each Person. — That which is objected, that there is not
common relation; it must be said, that it is true as much
as regards (their) *principal* understanding, yet there can
rightly be (a common relation) as much as regards
(their) *consequent* (understanding), so that any name
means a plenitude in respect of each.

2. To that which is objected, that a relation grants
a Person to exist; it must be said, that not *any (relation)
whatsoever* (does this), but (only) that which is a *personal*
relation. But what that is, will be seen below.[7]

3. To that which is objected, that in the Son the
same is the nascibility and the filiation: ergo etc.; it
must be said, that it does not follow, because they are
not opposed in the same genus of opposition; because
the paternity and *the filiation* are opposed relatively, not so
the nascibility and the *innascibility*, nay (they are opposed)
more contradictorily and/or contrarily.

4. To that which is objected, that a first and a beginning is the same; it must be said, that "*first*" is said in
a twofold manner: either through a *privation of (something) prior*, and thus a first and a beginning are the same
according to thing, and not according to reckoning. In
another manner a "first" is said (to be) *in respect of a second*; and thus a first and a beginning are the same according to thing and reckoning, and thus a first is not
signified through this name, "*innascible*". For it conveys
a primacy through the privation of (something) prior,
as it clear from the very imposition of the name.[8]

SCHOLIUM

This Question is explained by the preceding (one).
The authors, who do not admit the *consequent* understanding, connoted in this notion and declared in the preceding Question, also approve, here, only the first part of
the Response.

Alexander of Hales, SUMMA., p. I, q. 59, m. 4. — St. Thomas,
SUMMA., I, q. 33, a. 4. — Bl. (now St.) Albertus (Magnus), here in.
q. 3. — (Bl.) Peter of Tarentaise, here in q. 1, a. 3. — Richard of
Middleton, here in a. 2, q. 2. — Henry of Ghent, SUMMA., a. 57, q.
2. — (Bl.) Dionysius the Carthusian, here in q. 3.

---

[1] See more on this above in d. 26, q. 3.
[2] (Aristotle), POSTERIOR ANALYTICS, Bk. I, ch. 2. — Near the end
of the argument, many codices prefix to the word *relation* [relationem]
the word *not a* [non], in place of which particle codices L and O put
naught but a [non nisi].
[3] Very many codices, together with the first six editions, read *innascibility* [innascibilitas].
[4] Codex F adds "*innascible*" [innascibilis].

[5] Thus very many codices, such as A C L N O P Q R S T U V Y;
the Vatican edition has *reckoning* [rationem].
[6] Codex W adds *not positively according to (its) principal understanding* [non positive secundum principalem intellectum].
[7] In the following question.
[8] Codices K and Y have *of the spoken word* [vocis]; codices S and
V read *by the very exposition of the spoken word* [ex ipsa vocis exposi-
tione].

QUESTION III

Whether the innascibility, or the paternity, is the personal property of the Father?

Third, there is asked, whether the innascibility is the personal property or relation of the Person[1] of the Father, or whether the paternity (is). And that the paternity is, seems:

1. Because that is a personal property, through which a Person is separated from all (the Others), but such is this relation *the paternity*: ergo etc..

2. Likewise, that is a persona property, through which a Person is more properly named and expressed; but the Person of the Father is most properly expressed through the paternity: ergo etc..

3. Likewise, just as the filiation holds itself to the Son, so the paternity to the Father; but the filiation is the personal relation of the Person of the Son: therefore the paternity too (is the personal relation of the Person) of the Father.

4. Likewise, that is a personal property, which speaks[2] through a manner of position and proper habitude; but among all the relations, which are said of the Father, the paternity alone is such: ergo etc..

ON THE CONTRARY: 1. A personal property or relation gives the 'to be' to the Person; but the paternity does not give a 'to be' to the Person of the Father, because he has no 'to be' out of this, that He gives the 'to be' to the Other; but the Person of the Father is said (to be) "a father", because He gives the 'to be' to the Other: ergo etc..

2. Likewise, with the personal property not understood, it is impossible to understand the Person; but with the paternity not understood, there is an understanding of the One having deity and innascibility: therefore, since the innascibility is a property of the Person of the Father, ergo etc..

3. Likewise, a personal property ought to mean the whole "*being*" of a Person; but the paternity does not name the Person of the Father according to every plenitude of fecundity, but the innascibility (does): ergo etc..

4. Likewise, (St. John) Damascene (says):[3] « Among the divine, all are 'one' [unum] except the generation, the non-generation and the procession »; it is established, that he does not name all the properties, therefore, only the personal ones: therefore, the non-generation is a personal property, and (it belongs) not but to the Father: ergo etc..

CONCLUSION

The personal property of the Father is the paternity, not the innascibility nor the active spiration.

I RESPOND: It must be said, that, just as the common opinion says and (as) is had from the words of Master (Peter)[4] and of the Saints, that is, of Hilary and Augustine, the paternity is the personal notion of the Father. For, for this, that any relation be a personal one, it is necessary [oportet] that it mean the *first* and *proper* habitude of that Person, and (that it speak) through a manner of *position* and *completion*; but it is established, that *the innascibility* as much as regards (its) *first* understanding does not mean a position, as much as regards (its) *consequent* understanding it does not mean a *special* relation, but the fontal plenitude. Similarly, *the spiration* does not mean the *proper* relation of the Father;[5] and for that reason it is necessary [necesse est], that the paternity mean (this). On which account, the reasons induced for this are also to be conceded.

1. To that, therefore, which is objected, that a property gives the 'to be' to a Person; it must be said, that that must not be understood if a 'to be' *simply*, but of the personal 'to be' or of being distinct [esse distincto];[6] and the very authorship of the paternity among the divine does not accede to that Hypostasis, nay it means the complement of that Person, by reason of whom He is. Therefore, although the Father does not have a 'to be' out of this, that He gives a 'to be' to the Other, yet nothing impedes, that out of this He is a distinct Person.

2. To that which is objected, that there is an understanding of the Person of the Father etc.; it must be said, that having understood by apprehending *fully* and proceeding rationally, there is no understanding of the Person of the Father and/or (His) Hypostasis, without the paternity;[7] because if "*innascible*" is understood, such that the paternity is not present, "*innascible*" means a privation and does not say anything about the Father, which it does not also say about the Essence; and for that reason it is not understood as a personal property nor is it another one,[8] and for that reason

---

[1] Codices P and Q omit the word *of the Person* [personae], the other codices, together with the editions omit the word *personal* [personalis]. — The principles, which are employed in the following arguments, are to be deduced from d. 26, qq. 1-4.

[2] The Vatican edition, together with some manuscripts, reads *is said* [dicitur].

[3] ON THE ORTHODOX FAITH, Bk. I, ch. 8. See above d. 26, q. 4, the 4th. opposed argument.

[4] Distinction 26, ch. 2 ff., and here in chs. 1-3, where the words of (Sts.) Hilary and Augustine are also had.

[5] In the Vatican edition and codex cc alone there is read *a proper relation* [propriam relationem] for *the proper relation of the Father* [propriam relationem Patris].

[6] Cf. above d. 26, q. 3, in the Response. — On the subsequent proposition see above, d. 27, p. I, q. 2, reply to nn. 1 & 3, and here, in Doubt 1. — A little below this after *does not have* [non habeat] very many codices, less fittingly, omit *a 'to be'* [esse].

[7] Very many codices omit *and/or (His) Hypostasis, without the paternity* [vel hypostasim sine paternitate], editions 2, 3, 4, 5, and 6 omit only the words *and/or (His) Hypostasis* [vel hypostasim]; edition 1 in place of *without the paternity* [sine paternitate] exhibits *unless the paternity (has been) understood* [nisi intellecta paternitate]. — On understanding by apprehending [intellectu apprehendente], consult Doubt 1 below.

[8] The Vatican edition and edition 1 here add *nay they are natural properties* [immo sunt proprietas naturales], which words, because they do not respond to the context and are lacking in all the codices and editions, except edition 1, we have not received into the text.

the Person of the Father is not understood as distinct or (as) "that" Hypostasis. For the property of innascibility, as a property, includes the properties and relations in respect of a begun; otherwise, as has been shown above,[1] it is not a property.

3. To that which is objected, that a personal property means the whole "being" of a Person; it must be said, that if it meant *the whole "being"*, that is *the perfect*, *the complement* and *the proper* ("being"), in this manner it has truth. But if it is understood, that it means *the whole "being"*, that is *every habitude*; in this manner it is false, because it ought not mean

every (habitude), but it is necessary, that it mean *one determinate* (habitude), or it would mean[2] *none determinately*, and thus will not be a *personal* notion.

4. To that which is objected concerning (St. John) Damascene, it must be said, that he does not enumerate all the personal properties, according to which (they are) personal, but intends to comprehend the relations under them: and under *"generation"* he comprehends the two personal (relations), under *"procession"* two (more relations), one personal, the other not personal; but[3] under *"non-generation"* he mans only the innascibility, which is a property, though not a personal one.

SCHOLIUM

I. In the Response it is explained, that four (things) are required, so that a property be a *personal* one, namely, that it be a *first* property, because it distinguishes first, *a proper* one, not a common one (such as the active spiration), through a manner of *position*, and *of completion*, by which the Person is perfectly constituted in (His) personal 'to be'. The last two differences do not convene with the innascibility; whence it is indeed a property, but not a personal one (cf. above d. 26, q. 4). — The solution to n. 1 supposes, that the personal 'to be' in God is a *relative* 'to be', because

in God relation alone distinguishes the Persons. Whence the relation of paternity results out of the begotten Son (cf. here Doubt 1).

II. Alexander of Hales, SUMMA., p. I, q. 69, m. 2 and 5. — (Bl. John Duns) Scotus., here in q. 2; REPORTATIO., here in q. 2. — St. Thomas, here in q. 1, a. 2; SUMMA., I, q. 33, a. 2. — Bl. (now St.) Albertus (Magnus), on this and the following q. here in a. 4. — (Bl.) Peter of Tarentaise, here in q. 1, a. 4. — Giles the Roman, here in 1st. princ., q. 1 and 3. — Henry of Ghent, SUMMA., a. 57, q. 4. — Durandus (of Saint-Pourçain), here in q. 2. — (Bl.) Dionysius the Carthusian., here in q. 1,. at the end.

QUESTION IV

Whether improcessibility means the notion in the Father just as innascibility?

Fourth, there is asked, whether improcessibility is a notion of the Father, just as the innascibility. And that it is, seems:

1. Because, just as the Father differs from the Son through innascibility, so from the Holy Spirit through improcessibility: therefore, just as the innascibility is a notion of the Father, similarly it seems, that improcessibility (is also).

2. Likewise, just as it belongs to the nobility of the Father not to be generated, so also not to be spirated:[4] therefore, if on account of a reckoning of nobility the innascibility is posited (as) His notion, similarly the improcessibility ought to be posited (such).

3. Likewise, just as 'to generate' befits the Father through this, that (He is) innascible, so also 'to spirate' through this, that (He is) improcessible, or inspirable [inspirabilis]: therefore, just as innascibility is a notion, because it means not only a privation, but also a position (of nobility), thus it seems, that improcessibility (is a notion). *If you say*, that improcessibility is included under innascibility; *there is objected*: because[5] improcessibility convenes with the Son, and yet innascibility

never (does): therefore, it is another notion at least in the Son, therefore, at least in Former it ought to be a notion (too). *If you say*, that it does not mean a nobility; *on the contrary*: every (name) which is said among the divine, pertains to nobility, otherwise it would not be said There: therefore, if the improcessibility is said of the Son, it seems that it resounds unto a nobility.

In accord with this there is asked: since the Father communicates to Someone[6] (His) improcessibility or inspirability, for what reason does He not similarly communicate (His) innascibility?

ON THE CONTRARY: 1. If improcessibility is a notion: therefore, the notions are more than five, which is contrary to the common opinion.[7]

2. Likewise, if improcessibility is a notion, either this is because it simply deprives *"being" from another* [esse ab aliquo], or because it deprives[8] *being spirated* [spiratio]. If in the first manner, it does not differ from the innascibility; if in the second manner, then it does not differ from active spiration, for because He is not spirated, He who does spirate, spirates.

---

[1] Question 1. — A little before this, in place of *For the property of innascibility* [Nam proprietas innascibilitatis] edition 1 has *For innascibility* [Nam innascibilitas].

[2] Codices I S W Y and bb (T by a second hand) have *will mean* [dicet]; edition 1 has *or if it would mean* [si ... diceret]. Just after this, in place of *will be* [erit] some codices, together with edition 1, read *is* [est].

[3] In several codd., such as A I T Z & cc, there is lacking *but* [sed].

[4] Superfluous and useless is the addition, which the Vatican ed. here exhibits, supported by no codex (except cod. cc): *therefore, if on account of a reckoning of nobility it belongs to the Father 'to not be generated', thus 'to not be spirated'* [ergo si propter rationem nobilitatis est Patris non generari, ita est non spirari]. A little before this, the same Vatican ed. reads *the nobility of* [nobilitas est Patris] for *it belongs to the nobility of* [nobilitatis est Patris].

[5] Codices S V W and Z have *that* [quod]. A little below this, in place of *it ought to be* [debet esse] some codices, such as I T and Z, have *it should be* [deberet esse].

[6] Codex Y reads *to Another* [alteri] for *to Someone* [alicui].

[7] Cf. above d. 26, q. 4.

[8] Thus, even the Vatican edition; in the codices and editions there is incongruously extant *posits a* [ponit] for *deprives* [privat], which does not respond to the context. A little below this, the genuine text, which the codices and first six editions have, is changed by the Vatican edition in this manner: *because He who spirates is not spirated* [quia non sipratur qui spirat] for *because He is not spirated, He who does spirate, spirates* [quia non spiratur, spirat qui spirat].

3. Likewise, if '*to not proceed*' were a notion, (it would be) for the same reason (as) '*to not produce*'; but this is false: ergo etc.. *If you say*, that it is not similar, because '*to not produce*' does not mean a nobility; *on the contrary*: 'to not produce a person' means a standing-still in being emanated [status emanationis]; and just as the reckoning of a *beginning*, before which there is not something, does mean a nobility, similarly the reckoning of a *standing-still*, beyond which[1] there is no proceeding: therefore, it does mean a nobility: if, therefore, there is no other (argument), for which reason it is not said notionally, it seems, that '*to not produce*' is a notion, just as '*to not be spirated*'.

CONCLUSION

Improcessibility is not a notion of the Father.

I RESPOND: For an understanding of the aforesaid it must be noted, that nothing can be a notion among the divine, unless it means a positive respect, either out of (its) *first* understanding, and/or out of (its) *consequent* (understanding). For if it only deprives a relation, thus it is said of the Essence just as of a Person. Whence, just as it is said, that the Father is not produced, nor (that) the Holy Spirit produces a Person; so also one does not say that the Essence is produced, nor that It produces a Person. And just as that which is *unbegotten* cannot be a notion, unless it posits a positive respect out of (its) *consequent* (understanding) — and this it does posit, just as has been seen[2] — similarly neither can that which is *inspirable* be a notion, unless it posits a positive respect. Moreover, it does not posit this, except according to which it posits a primacy in respect of spiration, just as the innascibility (does) in respect of generation, so that, just as He who is neither generated nor is consequent to a generation is said (to be) "*innascible*", so He who neither proceeds nor is consequent to a procession (is said to be) "*improcessible*".

And, since every emanation is either a generation, and/or consequent to a generation, because a generation means a prime emanation; for that reason the 'innascible' deprives *every* emanation, and for that reason it means a *fontal plenitude*, not only in respect of a generation, but also of a spiration; and for that reason the innascibility is neither the generation nor the spiration. But He is said (to be) "*improcessible*",[3] because He is neither spirated nor consequent to a spiration, and in this manner the Son or a generated (Person) is not excluded. For the Son is generated, and yet is not spirated nor is consequent to a spiration. Therefore, the "*improcessible*" does not deprive except only one emanation, and for that reason it means only *part* of that fontal plenitude of His; and for that reason improcessibility cannot be a distinct notion in the Father from the innascibility, nor in the Son from the spiration, nor does it convey a *fontal* plenitude, but only (a plenitude) *in spirating*. Therefore, although improcessibility can mean a nobility, yet because it is not distinguished[4] from the other assigned (notions), for that reason it is not counted [ponit in numerum] with them.

1. 2. 3. And thus are clear the first three objections, that improcessibility *distinguishes*, and *means a nobility*, and *means a fecundity*; because (their) reasons are not valid, for this, that this whole (meaning) is enclosed in the other assigned reasons, for that reason (improcessibility) is not distinguished against the others.

To that which *is asked*, why [quare] the innascibility is not communicated, just as the improcessibility (is); it must be said, that, just as is clear, (it is) because improcessibility does not enclose in its understanding a 'not being from another' [non esse ab alio], just as the innascibility does, but means only a '*not being spirated*'. Moreover, the Father can communicate to None, that He is not from another;[5] however, He can communicate to Another, that He is not spirated.

To that which *is asked*, "Why [quare] '*to not produce*' is not a notion?"; it must be said that it does not belong to *nobility*, and if it would be [esto, quod esset] — because that does not seem to be principally considered in the reckoning of a notion[6] — it must be said, that the reason is this: because it does not mean a positive respect, as much as concerns the reckoning of its name; and for that reason it simply convenes with the Essence, and for that reason it is not a notion. Not so, however, is it concerning the innascibility, as has been seen in the preceding.[7]

SCHOLIUM

I. From the principles established by St. Bonaventure it is easily understood, that *improcessibility* is not a notion of the Father. Moreover, when the other sentence is held, namely, that it consists in a pure negation, concerning which it can be doubted, and indeed (Bl. John Duns) Scotus in his Oxford Commentary (here in q. 2, in reply to n. 3) doubted, whether perhaps it is to be admitted as a sixth notion. But in his later writing or REPORTATIO (here in q. 4) he himself adhered to the common doctrine (cf. Macedo, collation 8, difference 3, section 8). — After the solution to the objections the solution of the incidental question follows at the end of the opposed arguments, and then there is the response to the question posited implicitly in the final (argument) of the fundament.

II. Alexander of Hales, SUMMA., p. I, q. 69, m. 3, reply to the last. — (Bl. John Duns) Scotus, here in q. 2, ad 3. — St. Thomas, SUMMA., I, q. 33, a. 4, in reply to n. 5, and q. 32, a. 3. — Giles the Roman, here in 1st. princ., q. 1, collat. 1. — Henry of Ghent, SUMMA., a. 60, q. 10. — Durandus (of Saint-Pourçain), here in q. 2. — (Bl.) Dionysius the Carthusian, here in q. 1, near the middle.

---

[1] Very many codices, such as I S and V, with edd. 1, 2 & 3, have (the adjective) *which* [quod] instead of (the pronoun) *which* [quem].

[2] Question 1.

[3] The codices and editions read *But "improcessibility" is said* [Sed improcessibilitas dicitur], but lest aptly.

[4] The Vatican ed. with cod. cc, faultily reads *it distinguishes* [distinguit].

[5] See above d. 27, p. I, q. 2, in reply to n. 3, near the end.

[6] For *of a notion* [notionis], the Vatican edition, not trusting in the more outstanding codices, has *of its name* [sui nominis].

[7] Question 1.

DOUBTS ON THE TEXT OF THE MASTER

Doubt I

In this part, there are doubts about the text (of Master Peter) and first of this which (St.) Augustine says, that, *if He had not begotten the Son, nothing would prohibit saying that He (is) unbegotten.* For it seems, according to this, that there accedes to the Person of the Unbegotten[1] a *generating* and thus a '*being a father*' [esse patrem]. — Likewise, from this there seems to follow, that with the paternity removed, there still remains the Person of the Father; and thus (that) the paternity is not (His) personal property.

I Respond: It must be said, that there is a speaking of the intention of this name "*unbegotten*" and "*father*" either *simply*, and/or insofar as they are posited in a *Divine Person*. If we speak *simply*, thus they are diverse intentions, and one is intelligible apart from [praeter] the other and separable according to thing,[2] just as is clear in the generation of men. *In another manner* there is a speaking of these, insofar as they are posited about a Divine Person, and in this manner they mean a different [aliam et aliam] reckoning of being understood; and those two *according to thing* are entirely inseparable, yet *according to understanding* one can be accepted apart from the other. And in this manner (St.) Augustine says, not that they can be separated *according to thing* [re], but as much as *regards our (act of) understanding (them)* [ad intelligere nostrum].[3]

But that something can be understood apart from the other, this can be in a manifold manner: either as much as regards an *apprehending* understanding, or as much as regards a *resolving* understanding. If in the *first* manner, thus something cannot be understood without anything, which is its *reckoning of understanding*, just as God (cannot be understood) apart from deity, and man apart from humanity; yet, an *effect* can be understood, with (its) *cause* not understood, and an *inferior*, with (its) superior not understood, because one can apprehend '*man*', with none of (his) superiors understood. And thus the Philosopher says,[4] that he who says "*one*" in a certain manner says "*many*", not *simply (speaking)*, but *in a certain manner*, because (he does so) implicitly.

In another manner one happens to understand something apart from the other, by a *resolving* understanding; and this understanding considers those which are the essentials of a thing, just as a subject can be understood without its proper passion. And this can be in a twofold manner: either by an understanding resolving *fully* and perfectly, or by an understanding failing and resolving *semi-fully*.[5] With an understanding resolving *semi-fully*, something can be understood to be, with the first being [ente] not understood. But with an understanding resolving *perfectly*, something cannot be understood, with the first being not understood.

According to this threefold understanding of the comparison of the Father and the Unbegotten one happens to speak *in a threefold manner*. For if we speak of an *apprehending* understanding, it is possible that these two[6] be understood, with one of the two not apprehended, for this (reason), that one is the signified of the other, the other (the signified) of the former [alterius]. If we speak of a *resolving* understanding, if it still resolves *semi-fully*,[7] by accepting the understanding of this name "*unbegotten*" only privatively, just as the gentiles accept (it); in this manner one can be understood without the other. If we speak of an understanding *fully* resolving, since "*unbegotten*", according to which it is a property of the Father, is not said only privatively, nay it posits a *positive* respect; of necessity it posits *the paternity*. And in this manner it is true, that in saying that something[8] is "*unbegotten*", there is necessarily posited that it is a "*father*", since a fontal plenitude is posited through that (name) only.

When, therefore, (St.) Augustine says, that he is not said (to be) a "*father*" for this reason, because (He is) unbegotten, he speaks of an *apprehending* understanding, because the one is not the proper and first reckoning of understanding of the other, nay each, namely "*unbegotten*" and "*father*", mean a different [aliam] reckoning of being made known; yet according to a *full*[9] resolution one does posit the other necessarily. Whence the distinction of the Person of the Father is quasi *undertaken* [quasi inchoatur] in the innascibility and *is consummated* in the paternity; and for that reason, with the paternity not understood, that Person cannot be understood as completely distinct. And for that reason the paternity is a personal notion, though in the reckoning of understanding the innascibility occurs first.[10]

---

[1] The Vatican edition reads *to the Unbegotten Person* [personae ingenitae].

[2] Nearly all the codices, together with the six first editions, have *reckoning* [rationem] for *thing* [rem]; but faultily, as is clear form the subjoined. — Cf. above q. 2, 2nd. argument of the fundament.

[3] Thus codices A C F G H R S T U Y ee and ff, together with edition 1; the Vatican edition, together with a few codices, has *as regards our understanding* [ad intellectum nostrum].

[4] (Aristotle), Physics, Bk. I, text 21 (ch. 2). — Just above this in place of *And thus* [Et sic] very many codices and editions read *and just as* [et sicut], the Vatican edition has *just as* [sicut], and codices P Q S V and W (just before this) read *with no superior understood* [non intellecto superiori].

[5] Thus codex O (codex L in the margin); all the other codices, with edd. 1, 2 and 3, omit *and perfectly* [et perfecte], and then *and resolving semi-fully* [et resolvente semiplene]. The Vatican edition does the same, yet it reads *by an understanding semi-full and* etc. [intellectu semipleno etc.]. A little above this, after *the essentials* [essentialia] the Vatican edition, together with codex cc, reads *thus* [sic] for *just as* [sicut]. A little below this before *resolving* [resolvente] the more ancient codices with edition 1 insert *however* [autem]. Then, after *with the first being not understood* [non intellecto primo ente] codices S and T add *to be* [esse], which verb, namely

to be [esse], edition 1 a little after this adjoins after *something cannot be understood* [non potest intelligi aliquid]. — We note, that this division of understanding is had also in the Seraphic Doctor's Itinerarium Mentis in Deum, ch. 3, and 5.

[6] The Vatican edition alone has *one of these* [unum istorum] for *these two* [haec duo].

[7] The Vatican edition, breaking with the mss. and ed. 1, having omitted the word *if* [si], has (the indicative) *it resolves* [resolvit].

[8] For *in saying that something is* [dicendo aliquid esse], which we have placed on the authority of the mss., the Vatican ed. alone reads *for being* [ad esse]; the greater part of the codices, with ed. 1, incongruously read *it means that something is* [dicit aliquid esse]; cod. R has more truly *when it means that something* etc. [quando dicit aliquid], and cod. T *when it means that something* etc. [cum dicit aliquid]; codd. V and Y have omits *in saying* [dicendo]; finally codd. L and O read *it means according to which (it) regards being* etc. [dicit secundum quod ad]. Next, in place of *a fontal plenitude* [plenitudo fontalis] many codd., such as F G I K P Q T Y Z etc., with ed. 1, read *a plenitude of fontality* [plenitudo fontalitatis], and then for *that (name) only* [ipsum tantum], codd. P and Q read *that term* [ipsum terminum].

[9] The word *full* [plenam] is omitted in the more ancient codices and in edition 1.

[10] You will find more on this in the first three questions of this Distinction, and in d. 27, p. I, q. 2, in reply to nn. 1 and 3.

DOUBT II

Likewise, is asked concerning this which (St. Augustine) says: *Furthermore, the negative particle "not" causes, that there be said substantially* etc.. For it seems false, because "*man*" is said according to substance, yet "*whiteness*" can be said to be a not-man: therefore, because "*man*" and "*not-man*" are contradictorily opposed, and of anything (there is) an affirmation, and/or an negation:[1] therefore, "*whiteness*" is a "*not-man*" and whiteness is a quality: ergo etc.. *If you say,* that (St.) Augustine speaks, according to which it causes a negation *in the genus*; then *there is objected* concerning this, that it is a *not-substance*; it is established, that it cannot cause a negation *in the genus*: therefore, since "*not-substance*" is not said except of the other genera, it is clear etc..

I RESPOND: It must be said, that the manner of speaking according to *substance* about a denied[3] or infinite term is an accepting (of that term) in a twofold manner: either as much as regards *the signified*, or as much as regards *(something) supposed*. If as much as regards *the signified*, because a denied term draws (its) signification from an affirmed one,[4] there is the same manner of speaking as much as regards the signification in the term denied and affirmed. Whence just as "*man*" is said according to substance as much as regards (its) signification, so also "*not-man*". For when I say: "Here is a man", I preach a substance: when I say: "Here is a *not-man*"; I remove a substance. If, however, we speak as much as regards *(what is) supposed*, then a denied and an affirmed term supposes on behalf of (something) else. In this manner (St.) Augustine opposes (it), and in this manner does not understand (it).[5]

DOUBT III

Likewise, is asked of this which (St. Augustine) says, that *a "not-begotten" is referred to a "not-begetter"*. For he seems to say (something) false, because every relation posits two extremes: therefore, if a "*not-begotten*" is referred to a "*not-begetter*", there is necessary for this, that something be the "*unbegotten*", which the two are, the one of which is a "*not-begotten*", the other of the two a "*not-begetter*". *On the contrary*: let it be through the impossible, that there is naught but one alone, he at least would be the not-begetter.

I RESPOND: It must be said, that 'that one be referred to someone' this can be in a twofold manner: either according to a reckoning of *existing*, or according to a reckoning of *understanding*; according to a reckoning of *existing*, when a real habitude is conveyed; according to a reckoning of *understanding*, when a

real habitude is deprived. For, for this, that there be understood a *privation* of habitude, it is necessary that there is an understanding of a habitude; and for this, that a *habitude* be understood, it is necessary that the two extremes be understood as affirmed; and thus for this, so that[6] a *privation of habitude* or of relation be understood, it is necessary that the two extremes be understood (to have been) denied. And as much as regards this (St.) Augustine says, that a not-begotten is referred to a not-begetter, because the understanding of the former cannot be grasped except through the understanding of the latter; and thus as much as regards the reckoning of *speaking* it is said according to relation, just as "not-a-man" is said according to substance.

DOUBT IV

Likewise, is asked of this which (Master Peter) says, that *when "born wisdom" is said, "wisdom" signifies the Essence*. Therefore, according to this it will be licit to posit "*the Essence*" in place of "*wisdom*", since it causes the understanding of that; which is false.

I RESPOND: It must be said, that there is a speaking of the name for *wisdom* as much as regards (its) *signified*, and/or as much as regards (something) *supposed*. As much as regards the *signified* it means the Essence, but yet *it supposes* a Person; and thus the adjective respects the same by the reckoning of a *Supposit*, when there is said "*wisdom born*", not by a reckoning of the *signified*. Nor does it follow on this account, that in place of "*wisdom*" there can be posited "*the Essence*", because since "*wisdom*" is of (the category) of middle names, it can suppose on behalf of a Person and be drawn to a Supposit; but "*the Essence*", since it is a most abstract name, not (so).[7]

DOUBT V

Likewise, is asked of this which (Master Peter) says, that *"image" sometime causes the understanding of the Essence, and then it is said regarding (the Essence) itself.* For it seems false, because "*image*" always connotes an *imaged*; but the same cannot be "*image*" and "*imaged*": therefore, it is always said relatively.

I RESPOND: It must be said, that "*image*" always means a looking-back either to (something) created, and/or to (something) uncreated; and when it means a looking-back to (something) uncreated, it is said personally and relatively according to thing; but when (it means) the looking-back of a creature (to the Uncreated), it is said essentially and regarding (the Essence) itself, not as much as regards a manner of speaking, but because it convenes with the whole Trinity.[8]

---

[1] Aristotle, METAPHYSICS, Bk. IV, text 15 (Bk. III, ch. 4).

[2] Cf. here q. 1, in the body (of the Question).

[3] Some codices, among which is codex T, together with edition 1, have *negative* [negativum] for *denied* [negatum].

[4] Cf. above d. 28, a. sole, q. 1, p. 496, footnote 3.

[5] You will also find the solution to this doubt in Bl. (now St.) Albertus (Magnus, COMMENTARY), here in a. 5.

[6] Edition 1 has *that* [quod] for *so that* [ut].

[7] Cf. above d. 5, a. 1, q. 1, in the body (of the Question), where there is propounded the threefold genus of names signifying the Essence, namely, those which signify It in *concretion*, in an *omnimodal abstraction* and in *a middle manner*.

[8] This is expounded at greater length below in d. 31, a. 1, q. 1, in the body (of the question). — A little before this, in place of *(it means) the looking-back* [respectum creaturae], many codd., such as F G H I K S T Y etc., with ed. 1, have *(it is said) in respect* [respectu creaturae]; an incongruous reading.*

---

* *Trans. note*: That which is "the looking-back to something uncreated", which is said personally, is the Image of the Father, which Image is the Son; that which is "the looking-back of the creature to the Uncreated", is the image of God, which image is in man. Note, that whereas St. Bonaventure begins his Response with a twofold distinction, he omits the first member in his discussion, because that image which is said in respect to a creature is a work of artifice, such as a painting. But, here, the Seraphic Doctor speaks only of those images which have a divine origin. Furthermore, an "image" is not said in respect of something, but rather in respect to something, because it is made according to a proto-type which is other than, not the same as, the image itself according to thing and being: thus no image, as a single thing, is an image of itself.

DISTINCTION XXIX

CHAPTER I

On principium.

There is, moreover, another name, noting à manifold relation, namely, principium (i.e. "beginning" or "principle"). For a principium is always said regarding something. And the Father is said (to be) a principium, and the Son a principium, and the Holy Spirit a principium; but differently. For the Father is said (to be) a principium regarding the Son and regarding the Holy Spirit. Whence (St.) Augustine in the fourth book, ON THE TRINITY,[1] says: « The Father is the beginning [principium] of the whole Divinity, and/or if it is better said, of the Deity, because He Himself is from None. For He does not have a from Whom He is and/or a from Whom He proceeds »; but from Him the Son has been begotten, and the Holy Spirit proceeds. He is not, therefore, said (to be) the beginning of the whole Deity, because He is the principle [principium] of Himself and/or of the Divine Essence, but because He is the principle of the Son and the Holy Spirit, in Each of which is the whole Divinity. The Son is said (to be) a principium regarding the Holy Spirit. But the Holy Spirit is not said (to be) a principium, except as regards creatures, regarding which even the Father is said (to be) a principle and the Son and the Trinity Itself together, and each Person[2] is said (to be) the Principle of creatures. « Therefore, the Father is the beginning without a beginning, the Son the beginning from a beginning, the Holy Spirit the beginning from each (beginning), that is from the Father and the Son ».[3]

CHAPTER II

That from eternity the Father is a principle and the Son, but not the Holy Spirit.

And the Father from eternity is the principle of the Son, and the Father and the Son the principle of the Holy Spirit, because the Son is from the Father, and the Holy Spirit from Each. But the Holy Spirit is not from eternity a principle, but began [coepit] to be (one), because He is not said (to be) a principle except as regards creatures. When, therefore, creatures began to be, the Holy Spirit also began to be their Principle. Thus too the Father and the Son began to be, with the Holy Spirit, the one Principle of creatures, because creatures began to be from the Father and the Son and the Holy Spirit; and these Three are not said (to be) three (principles), but the one Principle of all creatures, because in one and the same manner They are the Principle of things. For things are not in one manner from the Father and in another from the Son, but (are) in thoroughly the same manner (form Both). For that reason the Apostle understanding, that this Trinity is the one Principle of things, says:[4] *From Him and through Him and in Him are all (things)*. « When, however, we hear, that all things are from God », as (St.) Augustine says ON THE NATURE OF THE GOOD,[5] « we ought at any rate understand all natures,

and all which are naturally.[6] For not from Him are the sins, which do not serve nature, but vitiate (it), which (sins) are born out of the will of (those) sinning ». Of all (things), therefore, which naturally are, the one Principle is the Father with the Son and the Holy Spirit, and this He began to be. Moreover, from eternity the Father is the principle of the Son according to generation, and the Father and the Son the one principle of the Holy Spirit. Whence (St.) Augustine in the fifth book, ON THE TRINITY,[7] thus says: « He is said relatively (to be) *"the Father"*, and the Same is said relatively (to be) a *"principle"*. But He is said (to be) "the Father" as regards the Son, but a "principle" as regards all those which are from Him. And the Son is said (to be) a "beginning". Since there was also said to Him:[8] *What are you?* He responds: *The Beginning, I who also speak to you.* But is the Father not the Beginning? Nay He wanted to show that He (is) the Creator, when he said that He is the Beginning, just as the Father is the Beginning of creatures, because all are from Him. However, when we say that both the Father (is) a beginning and the Son a beginning, we do not say (that there are) two principles of creatures, because the Father and the Son together are the one Principle regarding a creature, just as (They are) the one Creator. If, however, anything remains in itself and begets and/or works something, He is the principle of the that thing which begets, and/or of that which works, we cannot deny, that the Holy Spirit[9] also is rightly said (to be) a *"beginning"*, because we do not separate Him from the appellation of "Creator": because it has been written[10] of Him, that *He works*, and He works certainly [utique] remaining in Himself. For not into something of those which He works, is He Himself changed and turned. Therefore, the one Principle regarding a creature, with the Father and the Son, is the Holy Spirit, not two and/or three principles ». Behold (St.) Augustine openly shows, that the Father and the Son and the Holy Spirit are the one Principle of created things, that is, that in one and the same manner They are the Principle; and that manner he sufficiently revealed, because, namely, all (things) are worked, and because similarly[11] those Three work, for that reason They are said to be the one Principle.

CHAPTER III

In what manner the Father (is) the principle of the Son, and He with the Son (the principle) of the Holy Spirit.

Then, in the same book he immediately [continue] shows, in what manner the Father is said (to be) a principle regarding the Son, and (in what manner) regarding the Holy Spirit He and the Son (are said to be the same), saying, that the Father is the principle of the Son for this reason, because He begot Him, and that the Father and the Son are the principle of the Holy Spirit, because the Holy Spirit proceeds and/or is given by Each. For he thus says:[12] « If the one betting regarding that which is begotten is a principle, the Father regarding

---

[1] Chapter 20, n. 29. The words: *He Himself is from None* etc. [ipse est a nullo etc.], are from n. 28.

[2] The Vatican edition, together with the other editions, has *of the Persons* [personarum], contrary to codices A B D and E, and to ed. 1.

[3] (St.) Augustine, AGAINST MAXIMINUS, Bk. II, ch. 17, n. 4.

[4] Rom. 11:36.

[5] Chapter 28. Even those which precede, according to (their) sense, have been taken from (St.) Augustine's, ON THE TRINITY, ch. 13, n. 14.

[6] The Vatican edition and the other editions, except edition 1, have *natural* [naturalia], but contrary to the codices and original.

[7] Chapter 13, n. 14. See also ENARRATIONS on Psalm 109, n. 13.

[8] John 8:25.

[9] Codex C adjoins *is a beginning and* [esse principium et]. A little below this edition 9, together with the original, after *of "Creator"* [creatoris] it has *and* [et] for *because* [quia].

[10] 1 Cor. 12:11: But all these does one and the same Spirit work [Haec autem omnia operatur unus atque idem Spiritus].

[11] Codd. A & D, edd. 1 & 5 (in the margin), have *together* [simul].

[12] ON THE TRINITY, Bk. V, ch. 14, n. 15. At the beginning of the text editions 1, 2 and 3, together with the original have *regarding that which he begets* [ad id quod gignit] for *regarding that which is begotten* [ad id quod gignitur]. The passage of Sacred Scripture is Jn. 15:26.

the Son is a principle, because He begot Him. Moreover, whether also regarding the Holy Spirit the Father is a principle, because it was said: *From the Father He proceeds*, is no small question. Which if He is thus, He is not now the principle to only that[1] Thing, which He begets and or makes, but also to the That, which He gives and which proceeds from Him. If, therefore, what is given and/or what proceeds has a principle, from which it is given and/or proceeds, it must be professed [fatendum est], that the Father and the Son are the principle of the Holy Spirit, not two principles. But just as the Father and the Son regarding a creature are said relatively (to be) the one Creator and one Lord, so relatively regarding the Holy Spirit They are one principle. However, as regards a creature the Father and the Son and the Holy Spirit are the one Principle, just as (They are) the one Creator and the one Lord ». Behold, you have, that the Father is said (to be) the principle of the Son, because He begot Him. Therefore, He is the Father by that notion, by which He is said (to be) the principle of the Son, that is, by the generation, according to which He is also said (to be) the "*author*" of the Son. Whence (St.) Hilary in the fourth book, ON THE TRINITY[2] says: « By that very (name) by which He is said (to be) "the Father", of Him whom He begot, He is shown (to be) an author, having that Name, which is indeed neither understood from another, and out of which the One who has been begotten, is taught to have subsisted ». « The Church knows the One Innascible God, She knows the Only-Begotten Son of God. She confesses the Father free from origin, She confesses too the origin of the Son from a beginning [ab initio], not that He Himself (is) from a beginning, but from an Uninitiable One [ab ininitiabili], not through Himself, but from Him who is from no one, born from eternity, that is, taking up a nativity from the paternal eternity. Here is published the profession of the Faith, but the reason for the profession has not yet been expounded »; and for that reason it must be asked, namely, in what manner, that which he says, that the origin of the Son is from a beginning, and that He Himself is not from a beginning, but from an Uninitiable One, is to be understood. At any rate subjoining this he determined, in what manner he accepted a "*beginning*" [initium], saying, that the origin of the Son is from an beginning, as if

he said: do not understand (it) thus, that the origin of the Son is from a beginning, as if the Son Himself has a beginning, but because He Himself is from an Uninitiable One, that is from the Father, from whom are all (things). Nor though the Son is the beginning [principium] from a beginning, yet it must not be conceded, that the Son has a beginning. And since the Son is the Beginning from a Beginning, and the Father the Beginning not from a beginning, the Beginning from a Beginning is not the Beginning without a beginning, just as the Son is not the Father, nor yet (are They) two beginnings, but one, just as the Father and the Son (are) not two Creators, but the one Creator.

CHAPTER IV

Whether the Father and the Son are the principle of the Holy Spirit according to the same notion.

Moreover, the Father and the Son are the one principle not only of creatures, as has been said above, but also of the Holy Spirit; for that reason it is customarily asked, whether the Father and the Son is the principle of the Holy Spirit by the same notion, or is it one notion, by which the Father is said (to be) the principle of the Son, and another, by which the Son (is said to be the same). — To which we say, since the Father is said (to be) the principle of the Holy Spirit and the Son (is too) — because the Holy Spirit proceeds and/or is given by Each, nor does He proceed and/or is given otherwise by the Father than by the Son — sanely can it be understood, that the Father and the Son are said (to be) the principle of the Holy Spirit by the same relation and/or notion. — However, if one asks, what that notion is, which "*principle*" notes there, we do not have a name for it,[3] but it is not the paternity itself and/or the filiation, nay (it is) a certain notion, which[4] belongs to the Father and to the Son, by which from eternity the Father and the Son are the one principle of the Holy Spirit. But, as has been said before,[5] the Father and/or the Son is said (to be) "the Giver" (of the Holy Spirit) in time, just as the Holy Spirit (has been) given and/or granted (in time).

COMMENTARY ON DISTINCTION XXIX

On the non-personal property, which is the common spiration, signified through the name, <u>principium</u>.

There is, moreover, another name, noting a manifold relation etc..

THE DIVISION OF THE TEXT

Above, Master (Peter) dealt with the non-personal[1] property, which is the *innascibility*. Here, second, he deals with the non-personal property or notion, which is the common spiration, signified through this name <u>principium</u>.* And, since that name is accepted not only *no-*

tionally, nay even *essentially*, for that reason he *first* distinguishes the multiplicity of this name, *second* he manifests the unity of this name, according to which it is said of the Father and the Son in respect of the Holy Spirit, showing, that They are the one principle [principium]

---

[1] Thus here and a little below all the codices, together with the original; but all the editions have, twice, *of that* [eius] for *to that* [ei]. then after *that the Father and the Son are the* [Patrem et Filium], all the editions, except edition 1, add *one* [unum], but contrary to the original and codices. Then very many codices and editions 2, 3 and 4, together with the original, omit *are* [sunt] before *just as (They are) the one Creator* [sicut unus creator].

[2] Number 9. The other passage is <u>ibid.</u>, n. 6.

[3] The name received now is *spiration* [spiratio], consecrated by

the Second Council of Lyons (A. D. 1274): « The Holy Spirit ... not by two spirations, but by a unique spiration, proceeds ».

[4] The Vatican edition alone omits *which* [quae]; a little further below this, the same edition together with codex C and the other editions, except edition 1, has *is* [est] for *are* [sunt].

[5] In Distinctions XIV, XV, and XVII.

NOTES ON THE COMMENTARY

[1] In not a few manuscripts and edition 1 there is wanting (the suffix) *non-* [non].

---

* *Trans. note*: Since the Latin term, <u>principium</u>, means both *principle* and *beginning*, and this question regards the multiple meanings of the Latin word <u>principium</u>, in the English translation it shall be left in its Latin form, when spoken of as a word, but translated as *principle* or *beginning*, whenever the argument turns on that meaning of the term. Likewise, further below, the Latin word <u>initium</u>, means both a *beginning* and a *start*, however, here in the English translation, when spoken of as a word it will be left untranslated. Cf. more on <u>principium</u> in the Rationale for the Translation of Peculiar Latin Terms.

of the Holy Spirit; and this there (where he says): *Then in the same book he immediately shows.*

The *first* part has two (parts). In the first he distinguishes the multiplicity of this name; in the second, however, he explains through authorities the members of his distinction, that principium has all those acceptations, and this there (where he says): *And the Father from eternity is the principle of the Son.*

Then in the same book etc.. This is the *second* part, in which he deals with this name principium specially, insofar as it is said notionally and essentially. And first he shows, that the Father and the Son are the one principle of the Holy Spirit; second, by what unity They are one, namely, by the unity of the notion, in the last chapter: *Moreover, the Father and the Son* etc., where he shows, that by the same notion They are a principle,[1] and that that notion is the spiration.

TREATMENT OF THE QUESTIONS

For the evidence of those (things) which are said in the present Distinction concerning this name, principium, two (questions) are asked:

First, there is the question concerning it, as much as regards (its) multiplicity (of meaning).

Second, as much as regards (its) unity (of meaning).

And as much as regards the first, two (questions) are asked

First, having supposed that this name, principium, is accepted essentially, there is asked, whether it can be accepted personally [personaliter] or notionally [notionaliter].

Second, granted that (it is accepted) essentially and notionally, there is asked, concerning those two manners, whether it is accepted univocally [univoce], and/or equivocally [aequivoce].

ARTICLE I

On principium, *as much as regards the multiplicity (of its meaning).*

QUESTION I

Whether the name, principium, *among the divine, can be accepted personally or notionally?*

Moreover, that it is accepted notionally, is shown in this manner.

1. (St.) Augustine (says) in the fifth (book) ON THE TRINITY:[3] « The Father regarding the Son is a principle, because He begot Him »; therefore, the same is conveyed by the name for a *principle*, which (is conveyed) by the name for *generation*: therefore, it is held personally or notionally.

2. Likewise, this seems by *reason*, because wheresoever there is a true[4] reckoning of emanation and origin, there is a true reckoning of a *principle*; but among the divine there is truly and properly the reckoning of emanation: therefore, there is truly and properly the reckoning of a *principle* There.

ON THE CONTRARY: 1. A *beginning* [principium] and a *first* [primum] are the same:[5] therefore, where the reckoning of a beginning occurs there is a saying of a "*first*"; and where there is a saying of a "*first*" there is a saying of a "*prior*" [prius] — because the superlative (i. e., "*first*") presupposes the comparative (i. e., "prior")

— and where (there is) a first, there (is) a posterior: therefore, from the first (proposition), where there is a reckoning of a beginning, there is a reckoning of a posterior. But among the divine it is in no manner received, that one Person is posterior to the Other:[6] therefore, in no manner is a Person the beginning of a Person.

2. Likewise, among creatures the same is a *beginning* and a *start* [initium], just as is clear through the Philosopher,[7] therefore, where a start is not received, neither (is) a beginning; but all the Persons among the divine are without a start, therefore, also without a beginning: therefore, principium does not mean the looking-back of a Person to a Person: therefore, it is not accepted personally or notionally.

3. Likewise, the same is the *cause* and the *principle* according to thing, differing by a reckoning, because "*principle*" [principium] is said as much as regards 'being done' [fieri], "*cause*" [causa] as much as regards 'being' [esse]:[8] therefore, if 'being' is of a greater nobility than 'being done', there ought to be more properly

---

[1] Very many codices, such as K S V and W, together with edition 6, read *one principle* [unum principium] for *a principle* [principium].

[2] Codex T has *an understanding* [intelligentiam] for *the manifestation* [evidentiam].

[3] Chapter 14, n. 15.

[4] In the Vatican edition and codex cc there is lacking *true* [vera].

[5] Codices aa and bb add *according to the Philosopher* [secundum Philosophum]. — The complete quote from Aristotle is found in d. 11,

a. sole, q. 22, p. 215, footnote 9. Cf. also TOPICS, Bk. IV, ch. 1, where he says: A beginning is first, and a first is a beginning.

[6] Codex Y reads thus: *because no Person is posterior to the Other* [quia nulla persona est posterior altera].

[7] Cf. METAPHYSICS, Bk. V, text 1 ff. (IV. ch. 1).

[8] Cf. Aristotle, METAPHYSICS, Bk. V, text 1 ff. (Bk. IV, ch. 1). — A little below this many codices have *the prior one* [prius] for *more properly* [proprius]; a reading not to be preferred.

There the reckoning of a cause than of a principle, but it is not received, that one Person is a cause, and Another is the effect: therefore, the intention of a principle ought not be received There.

4. Likewise, God is *the Alpha and Omega, the Beginning and the End*,[1] and each (extreme) is of equal nobility; but the intention of an end is said of God essentially thus, that in no manner (is it said) personally — for God is thus the End of the creature, that He is not the end of a Person — therefore, similarly it seems, that He is thus the beginning of a creature, that in no manner is He the beginning of a Person.

CONCLUSION

The reckoning of a <u>principium</u> *is received among the divine, chiefly in regard to the Person of the Father, but not the reckoning of a cause nor of an effect, nor of a prior and a posterior, nor of a start and a started, nor of an end and of that which regards an end.*

I RESPOND: It must be said, that among the divine there is a true origin or emanation, and not only a true one, but also a most complete one. But for this, that it be most perfect,[2] it is necessary, that the One emanating have with the One producing an omnimodal equality and unity in substance, because nothing can be equal to God except God. If, therefore, the emanation and origin ought[3] to be expressed fittingly and in a catholic manner [catholice], there ought to be received names meaning the truth of an origin, and not be received names conveying an imperfection and/or a diversity and/or an inequality.

Since, therefore, *"beginning"* [principium] and *"begun"* [principiatum] mean the truth of an origin, for that reason each is received among the divine, but most of all the intention of a *beginning*. But since *"posterior"* means an imperfection, and *"start"* [initium] similarly, because it means an imperfect duration, namely, an inception; and (since) the intention of a *cause* conveys a diversity, because it is a cause of that 'being' which follows another;[4] and the intention of an *"end"* (conveys) an inequality, because an end is better than those which are to the end: for that reason neither the intention of a *"prior"* and a *"posterior"*, nor of a *"start"* and a *"started"* [initiati], nor of a *"cause"* and an *"effect"*, nor of an *"end"* and of that *which is "to an end"*, is received in a Person in respect of a Person. But the intention of *"one producing"* and *"one produced"*, because it is possible, that One produced be most highly perfect and[5] equal to the One producing, is for that reason received among the divine, similarly also the intention of a *"beginning"*.

1. To that which is objected, that to a *"beginning"* there follows a *"prior"*, and according to this a *"posterior"*; it must be said, that just as is said according to (St.) Hilary,[6] « the Father is greater than the Son, yet the Son (is) not lesser » — because that which is *"lesser"* resounds unto imperfection — for that reason, although it is received, that the Father is prior to the Son, because the Latter is from the Former, not the other way around, yet it is not received, that the Latter is posterior. But yet neither is a reckoning of the *prior* entirely received properly; because since among the divine there is an *order* and an *origin*, there is an *origin* properly, and less properly an *order*, nor is it except only by a reckoning of origin.[7] Therefore, since <u>principium</u> conveys principally an origin, and *"prior"* an order; for that reason there is simply received the intention of a *principle*, but the intention of a *prior* (is received) less properly and with a determination; but the intention of a *beginning*, insofar as it deprives an anterior, is most properly received in God, most of all as much as regards the Person of the Father. And for that reason it does not follow, that *"prior"* is said so property, that it means only looking-back to a *"posterior"*.

2. To that which is objected concerning <u>initium</u>, it must be said, that <u>initium</u> is accepted in one manner broadly for a principle of being and enduring [essendi et durandi]; in another manner properly for a principle of enduring, as that is said to have a start, which began to be. In the first manner (i.e. as a "beginning") it can be accepted among the divine, and thus (St.) Hilary accepts in the text (quoted by Master Peter);[8] but in the second manner (i. e. as a "start") it cannot (be accepted), and thus it is not equivalent to <u>principium</u>.

3. To that which is objected concerning *"cause"*, that it is the as a principle; it must be said, that among creatures the same is *"principle"* and *"cause"*; and this is, because the one produced differs form the one producing, and for that reason it can be said to be its effect, and that (principle) of it can be said (to be) a *"cause"*; and to the same concur the intention of a cause and of a principle, and similarly the name; but not so (is it) among the divine, because There the One producing can be of one substance with the One produced. For that reason that (objection) is not valid.

4. To that which is objected concerning *"end"*, the response is already clear, because *"end"*, as much as it concerns itself, means an excess of goodness in respect of that which is to the end, not so a beginning in respect of that which is from it; and for that reason God cannot be the *end* except of an unequal creature,[9] yet He can be and is the *beginning* of an entirely equal Person. And for that reason a Person is not the *end* of Another; yet He is a *beginning*.

---

[1] Apoc. 22:13: *I am the Alpha and the Omega, the First and the Last, the Beginning and the End* [Ego sum Alpha et Omega, primus et novissimus, principium et finis]. — Next, after *thus the End of a creature, that* [ita finis creaturae, quod] codex Q in place of *not* [non] repeats *in no manner* [nullo modo].

[2] Codices P and Q read thus: *most complete. But that it be most complete, it is necessary* [completissima. Ut autem sit completissima, necesse est].

[3] Codex bb has *ought* [debent] in the plural.

[4] Cf. above d. 5, Doubt 3, p. 120, footnote 7. — On the subsequent proposition Aristotle, TOPICS, Bk. III, ch. 1, says: An end seems to be more eligible than those which are to the end, and of two (the more eligible is) that which is nearer to the end.

[5] Codices S W and T read *since it is equal* [cum aequetur] for *and equal* [et aequetur].

[6] ON THE TRINITY, Bk. IX, nn. 54 and 56. On the words of (St.) Hilary, cf. the text of Master (Peter), d. XVI, ch. 2, and ibid., in (St. Bonaventure's) Commentary, doubts 4 and 5.

[7] Cf. above d. 20, a. 2, q. 1 and 2. — Somewhat above this, after *posterior* [posterior] codex K supplies *to the Former* [illo], and many codices together with the editions omit the verb *is* [sit] before *posterior* [posterior] at that point. Next, the Vatican ed. with some codd. has *there is an origin more properly* [proprius est origo] for *there is an origin properly* [proprie est origo], and, then, after *nor is it* [nec] codd. B P & Q repeat *an origin* [origo], to which word cod. B, moreover, adjoins *There* [ibi].

[8] Chapter 3. — A little before this many codices, together with edition 1, omit *among the divine* [in divinis], in place of which words codex T substitutes *here* [hic].

[9] For *of an unequal creature* [creaturae inaequalis] codex M has *in respect of an unequal creature* [respectu creaturae inaequalis].

SCHOLIUM

I. Here (the Seraphic Doctor) deals with a *producing* principium, which according to the common sentence can be accepted among the divine in a threefold manner (cf. the following question), namely, *essentially*, as the Three Persons are the Principle of a creature, *personally*, because the Father alone is the principle of the Son, *notionally*, because the Father and the Son spirate the Holy Spirit. Here there is the question only of the second and third acceptation of this term. — Having purified the concept of a principium from all *imperfection, diversity*, and/or *inequality* (concerning which, see above d. 20, a. 1, q. 2, in reply to n. 2), we can use the word principium even in regard to the emanations ad intra, nay the Seraphic Doctor does not refuse to admit, with the Greek Fathers, even the « intention of a *begun* [principiati] ». On this the Angelic (Doctor) says, SUMMA, I, q. 33, a. 1, in reply to n. 2: « But this is not in use among our Doctors ». — That the reckoning of a *prior* and a *posterior* is not received (d. 12, q. 2), nor of a *start* and a *started*, nor of an *end* and a *middle*, nor of a *cause* and a *caused*, is reviewed here in the body (of the question) and more accurately in the solution to the objections. In regard to the solution to n. 1, cf. S. Thomas, loc. cit., in reply to n. 3. — In the solution to n. 3 a certain, ancient difference between the Latins and Greeks is touched upon. The Latins, to shut off the way to the error of Arius in words, rejected the name for a *cause* in respect to the Termini of the emanations ad intra. The Greeks, on the other hand, in according with the axiom of Aristotle, which is cited in the 3rd opposing argument (in Greek: αἱ ἀρχαὶ καὶ αἴτια), say that principium and *cause* signify the same. The manner of speaking of the Greeks has also been approved by Florence (Decree of Union for the Greeks).

II. Alexander of Hales, SUMMA., p. I, q. 70, m. 1 and 3. — (Bl. John Duns) Scotus, on this and the following question, in each writing, here in q. sole. — St. Thomas, here in q. 1, a. 1; SUMMA., I, q . 33, a. 1. — Bl. (now St.) Albertus (Magnus), on this and the following question, here in a. 1; SUMMA., p. I, tr. 9, q. 41, m. 1, a. 1 and 2. — (Bl.) Peter of Tarentaise, here in q. sole, a. 1. — Giles the Roman, here in 1st. princ., q. 1. — Henry of Ghent, SUMMA., a. 52, q. 2, n. 10 and 11, and q. 3, n. 5; a. 54, q. 6, n. 55. — Durand, on this and the following question, here in q. 1. — (Bl.) Dionysius the Carthusian, here in q. 1.

QUESTION II

Whether this name, principium, *if taken essentially and notionally, is said univocally, or equivocally?*

Second, there is asked, whether the name principium, when it is accepted essentially and notionally, is said univocally, and/or equivocally. And it seems that (it is said) *univocally*.

1. (St.) Basil (the Great) says,[1] that the Son of God's *accepting* is *common* with creatures, but (His) *having* through (its) essence (is) *proper* (to Him). If, therefore, there is a common accepting: therefore also a giving; and if this, since from within this is accepted the reckoning of a principium in respect of the Son and in respect of a creature, it seems, that it is said *univocally*.

2. Likewise, principium said essentially and notionally differs in the same manner, just as "wisdom" and "begotten wisdom"; but "wisdom" is not said equivocally in this and in that [sic et sic]: ergo etc..

3. Likewise, nothing is said in a multiple manner[2] from this, that it is said of a genus and of a species, or from this, that it has one supposit or more — because multiplicity respects diverse significations, not supposits — but principium said essentially is in more and convenes with more than (when said) notionally and convenes with the very same: therefore, it is not said in a multiple manner, but *univocally*.

4. Likewise, that it is not said *analogically*, seems, because where there is an *analogy*, there is a *prior* and a *posterior*, but among the divine there is not a *prior* and a *posterior*: therefore, neither an *analogy*. — And again it seems, that neither (is it said) *equivocally*, because where there is equivocation, there is a diversity of signification; but a Person and the Essence are not diverse: therefore, it cannot be accepted *equivocally*.

BUT ON THE CONTRARY: 1. That it is said *in a multiple manner*, seems first through Master (Peter) in the text,[3] who says, that this name principium causes a multiple understanding: therefore, it is said *in a multiple manner*.

2. Likewise, this very (thing) seems *by reason*, because those acts of Theirs, *to generate, to spirate*, (and) *to create*, are of the same principium, according to which it is accepted differently; but there is not one common reckoning to be found for those acts of Theirs: therefore, neither for a principium, which means thus a different looking-back.

3. Likewise, there is a rule of the Philosopher,[4] that if any (name), in one acceptation of it, has one opposite (name), and in another, another, it is said in a multiple manner; but principium essentially is said in respect of a created, and notionally in respect of an Uncreated: therefore, (it is said) in a multiple manner in the former and latter acceptations [sic et sic].

---

[1] AGAINST EUNOMIUS, Bk. II, n. 23 ff., but not literally.

[2] Cf. Aristotle, TOPICS, Bk. I, ch. 13. — Next for *because* [quia], the Vatican edition has *and this because* [et hoc quia].

[3] Chapter 1. — After this argument in codex O alone two others are inserted, namely: *Likewise, the* principium *of a creature is essential, the* principium *of the Son personal: therefore, since there is not the same univocal for the Essence and for a Person, the name for a* principium *will be equivocal.* — *Likewise, nothing (is) univocal to the Creator and to the creature: therefore, "begun", since it is common vocally to the Son and to the Holy Spirit and to creatures, therefore, (it is) univocal. But if one of the opposites is said in a multiple manner, the rest (are) too: therefore,* principium *in respect of those will be said equivocally* [Item, principium creaturae est essentiale, principium Filii personale: ergo cum non sit idem univocum essentiae et personae, erit nomen principii aequivocum. — Item, nihil univocum Creatori et creaturae: ergo principiatum cum sit commune vocaliter Filio et Spiritui sancto et creaturis, ergo aequivocum. Sed si unum oppositorum dicitur multipliciter, et reliquum: ergo principium respectu horum dicetur aequivoce]. Then at the beginning of the following argument, codex O omits *by reason* [ratione], and justly, because the two interposed arguments in this codex have already been argued thus.

[4] This is elicited from the general rule, which Aristotle posits in TOPICS, Bk. I, ch. 13, with these words: Indeed, the first in a contrary must be examined carefully, if it is said in a multiple manner, or if it is dissonant in species or name. — At the end of the argument after *therefore* [ergo] codex M repeats *it is said* [dicitur].

4. Likewise, <u>principium</u> essentially said is said *temporally*, notionally said (it is said) *eternally*, sub nothing is a common *univocal* to an eternal and to a temporal: ergo etc..

CONCLUSION

The name, principium, said essentially and notionally, is accepted neither univocally nor equivocally, but analogically.

I RESPOND: It must be said, that *that a name be accepted differently* among the divine can be in a threefold manner: either as much as regards (something) *supposed*, or as much as regards the *signified*, or as much as regards the *connoted*. In the first manner this name *"God"* is accepted differently, when there is said: "God is the Trinity", and "God generates", because in the first it stands for *the Nature*, in the second for *a Person*; and that (manner) does not induce any *multiplicity*.[1] — In another manner it happens that a term *is accepted differently* as much as regards *the signified*, according to which the term itself in one acceptation of it signifies the Essence, in another a Person, just as this name *"father"*, insofar as God is said (to be) *"the Father of the Son"*, and insofar as He is said (to be) *"Our Father"*; and this induces an *equivocation*, because there is a diversity of signification not in the thing itself, but in signifying. — In a third manner it happens that *it is accepted differently* by a reckoning of (what is) *connoted*, as for example this name <u>principium</u>, said essentially, connotes a created effect,[2] said personally, it connotes nothing created; and that (manner) induces a multiplicity according to *analogy*, not according to *equivocation*: according to *analogy* indeed, because it is accepted for diverse (Persons) or diverse (things), which do not have but a unity[3] of proportion, and for that reason it necessarily required [necessario oportet], that there fall an *analogy* there; but not an *equivocation*, because equivocation has many constructions [institutiones] and is accepted determinately on behalf of anything, just as is clear in this name <u>canis</u> (i.e. "a dog", "the dog fish", "the Dog star, Sirius").

But not so does this name, <u>principium</u>, hold itself.

For <u>principium</u> from its imposition has been imposed from the act of *producing*, not of creating nor of generating. Whence just as *"to produce"* is not said *equivocally* of the production of the Son and of a creature, but analogically,[4] so also this name <u>principium</u> is accepted differently according to these three comparisons.

I concede, therefore, that there is a *certain multiplicity* in this, though there is not a multiplicity *simply* (speaking), just as (there is) of an equivocation properly said; and the reasons for this (side) are to be conceded, because they do not conclude, that there is a true equivocation. However, that word of the Philosopher is understood (to apply), when a name has diverse opposites, which are not united in any (name), neither *univocally* nor *analogically*, which is opposed to that term, but are opposed in (their) *first* (sense) and <u>per se</u>. But not so is it in the proposed, because <u>principium</u> is not said *first* regarding the Son and/or regarding a creature, but regarding that[5] which has been produced or begun [principiatum]; which indeed is said of the Son and of a creature, though not univocally, but analogically.

1. To that which is objected concerning (St.) Basil, it must be said, that (St.) Basil accepts the *"common"* for the *"analogous"*, which is a medium between the purely equivocal and univocal.

2. 3. To that which is objected concerning "wisdom" and "wisdom born", it must be said, that it is not similar, because there is no diversification *there* except solely as much as regards the One supposed, but *here* there is as much as regards the connoted. — And through this (the objection) following (it) is clear.

4. To that which is objected last, that a prior does not occur There etc.; it must be said, that although a prior and posterior do not occur There *in themselves*, yet it does occur in respect of *an effect*, because in comparison to an effect an analogy is accepted. — But what is said,[6] that there is no diversity There; it must be said, that it is true *in the thing*; yet in *signifying* and *understanding* it is one (thing) to understand *the Essence*, another to understand *a Person*; thus also *to say*, and through this also *to signify*. And for that reason, although there is no diversity on the part of the *absolute thing*, nevertheless there can be on the part of the *signification*.

SCHOLIUM

I. When <u>principium</u> is said *essentially*, the act of *creating* responds to it; when it is said *personally*, the act of *generating* (does); but when *notionally*, the act of *spirating*. Hence there arises the question, whether this name in those relations is taken *univocally*, and/or *equivocally*. The first assertion, namely that it is said *univocally*, is argued through the three first, opposed arguments, but is overturned by the four arguments of the fundament, by which there is proven, that <u>principium</u> in God is said *in a multiple manner*. However, since, as is clear from the end of the Response, there is a twofold *multiplicity* of signification, namely a multiplicity *simply*, i.e. an *equivocation*, and a multiplicity *according to analogy*,

again there is asked, what *species* of multiple signification obtains here, and concerning this the whole Response deals. The solution of this question depends both on the threefold distinction posited at the beginning of the Response (which St. Thomas also has, here in a. 2), and on the difference between *equivocal* and an *analogous* (names). These names convene in this, that they signify diverse reckonings in many, but they differ in this, that *the equivocal* have been instituted to signify many and entirely diverse reckonings, such as a <u>canis</u> is said to be a domestic animal, a certain (kind of) fish, (and) a star (i. e., the Dog star, Sirius); but *the analogous* signify indeed diverse reckonings, but thus that they convene in a *similitude* and/or

---

[1] That is, neither a multiplicity *simply*, or (that is) an equivocation, nor a multiplicity according to *analogy*.

[2] The word *created* [creatum], exhibited even by the Vatican edition and edition 1, is wanting in very many codices.

[3] Very many codices, such as K V W and Y, have *identity* [identi-

tatem], incongruously.

[4] See above d. 7, q. 4.

[5] In the Vatican edition and edd. 4 & 5, there is lacking *that* [hoc].

[6] Codices F I K S V and Y, and others with edition 1 have *is objected* [obiicitur].

a proportion (cf. above d. 1, a. 3, q. 1, Scholium). However, there can be a certain *equivocation* in *the same thing*, yet under a distinct and diverse, signified reckoning, an example of which id adduced, in the body (of the question), in regard to the name "*father*", in the expressions: "God, the Father of the Son", "God, Our Father".

II. The 3rd. argument of the fundament, taken from Aristotle, is expounded through a certain restriction at the end of the body (of the question). — The solution to n. 3 is not given explicitly, because the principles posited in the solution to n. 2 suffice. For the *major* in the 3rd objection is true; but the *minor* false. For not from *this* reason, that a principium, essentially taken, is in Three Persons, notionally taken, in Two, but personally, in One, can it be argued, that the word principium is not taken univocally; but this follows from *another* reason, namely, because in the first saying a creature is connoted, but in the others, not. By this difference of connotation there is conveyed a *multiplicity* of signification, however, not of *equivocation*, but of analogy.

III. Among the ancient authors there is no dissension in regard to the Response itself. But very many Scotists do not concede, according to the doctrine of (Bl. John Duns) Scotus, SENT, Bk. I, d. 8, q. 3, n. 12, the proposition of the Seraphic (Doctor), here in reply to n. 1, that the *analogous* is a mean between the *purely univocal* and the *equivocal*; which difference of opinion Brülifer reduces to a harmony, by saying that St. Bonaventure speaks of the univocal, in which the same reckoning is equally shared in by those in which there is a common name, but (Bl.) Scotus of that, in which the same reckoning is unequally shared. Mastrius (PHILOSOPHIA AD MENTEM SCOTI, tome I, disputation 2, q. 5, a. 3) teaches, that « the analogous, *formally* taken, mediates thus between the univocal and equivocal, that it never coincides with the other; but *materially* taken, always coincides with the other one.

IV. Alexander of Hales, SUMMA., p. I, q. 70, m. 1. — St. Thomas, here in q. 1, a. 2. — (Bl.) Peter of Tarentaise, here in q. sole, a. 2. — Richard of Middleton, here in q. 2. — Giles the Roman, here in 2nd. princ., q. 1. — (Bl.) Dionysius the Carthusian, here in q. 2. — (Gabriel) Biel, here in q. sole.

ARTICLE II

On principium, *as much as regards the unity (of its meaning).*

Consequently, there is the question of the second article, that is, of the unity of this name, principium, and about this two (questions) are asked.

First, there is asked, whether the Father and the Son can be said (to be) "*the one principle*" of the Holy Spirit.

Second, whether They can be said (to be) "*the one spirator*" and/or "*the same principle*" of the Holy Spirit.

QUESTION I

Whether the Father and the Son can be said (to be) "the one principle" of the Holy Spirit?

Moreover, that They can be said (to be) the "*one principle*" of the Holy Spirit:

1. In the text (of Master Peter)[1] there is said: « It must be professed, that the Father and the Son are the one principle of the Holy Spirit ».

2. Likewise, *by reason* it seems, that of one begun there is one beginning in one genus; but there is one Holy Spirit: therefore, He has one beginning. Therefore, if He is immediately and perfectly from the Father and the Son,[2] therefore, the Father and the Son are one beginning.

3. Likewise, the Father and the Son spirate: therefore, either by one power, or by two. It is established that (it is) by one (power), because when there is one *Essence* in Them, there is also one *Power*: therefore, since the Three[3] are said to be a principle by a reckoning of power, and there is one power in the Father and the Son, it is clear that, etc..

4. Likewise, just as the Three Persons create by a unique act of creation [unica creatione], so Two spirate by a unique act of spiration [unica spiratione]; but the Three, because They create by a unique act of creation, are the one Principle of the creature: therefore, the Two the one principle of the Holy Spirit.

ON THE CONTRARY: 1. When there is said: "They are the *one principle* of the Holy Spirit", either "*one*" means the Unity of *the Essence*, or the unity of *a Person*, or of *a notion*. Not of *the Essence*, because then the Holy Spirit would be the principle of the Holy Spirit; not of *a Person*, because then the Father and the Son would be one Person: therefore, of *a notion*. But *on the contrary*: if the Father and the Son on account of the unity of a notion are said (to be) *the one principle*, therefore, ab oppositis,* the Father on account of a plurality of notion can be said (to be) many principles.

2. Likewise, if the Father is a principle of the Holy Spirit, and the Son a principle (of the Holy Spirit),[4] and this principle is not that one: therefore, there are two principles.

3. Likewise, the Father and the Son are the one principle, therefore, the one principle is the Father and the Son: and if this, therefore, the Father is the Son.

4. Likewise, if They are the one principle: either the one, which is the Father, or the one, which is not the Father. If the one, which is the Father: therefore, the Father and the Son are

---

[1] Chapter 3. — A little above this before (after, in the Latin) "*the one principle*" [unum principium] the Vatican edition adjoins *to be* [esse].

[2] Cf. d. 12, q. 2.

[3] Codex T has *the Three Persons* [tres personae]; codex O and edition 1 read *a thing is said* etc. [res dicatur etc.]; the Vatican edition and the other editions, together with codex cc, have sufficiently well *They* [ipsi]. All the other codices read as in the text; which reading is not false, since the reckoning of *principle* in respect of *creatures* also befits the Holy Spirit (cf. here Doubt 2 and 3).

[4] Supply together with codices aa and bb *of the Holy Spirit* [Spiritus sancti].

---

* *Trans. note*: Concerning the meaning of the Latin expression, ab oppositis, cf. translator's footnote above, on p. 54.

the Father. If the one, which is not the Father: there-fore, the[1] principle of the Holy Spirit is not the Father: therefore, the Father is not the principle of the Holy Spirit.

CONCLUSION

The Father and the Son are rightly said (to be) "the one principle" of the Holy Spirit, by which there is signified the unity of the notion, yet in comparison to the Unity of the Essence and of the spirative power.

I RESPOND: It must be said, that all concede this: "The Father and the Son are the one principle of the Holy Spirit", since (St.) Augustine[2] proposes and says that; but they are diversified in *the manner of understanding.*

For *certain (authors)* say, that this name, "*principle*", does not mean the Essence nor a notion nor a Person there, but means the *convening* of the Two Persons in a unique notion. And they say, that this name, "*triune*", has been imposed specially to insinuate a trinity of sup-posits, such as convene in the unity of a nature; and thus in the proposed they say ("*principle*") is held. — But since it is not easy to accept this kind of positing or transference from the virtue of the word, this position is diagnosed to have no firmness.

And for that reason there were *others*, who said, that this name, principium, conveys a notion unto *adjacent (terms)*, and (that) it is a name, retained as an ad-jective [adiective]; and for that reason this numeral adjective, which is "*one*", (belonging) to the name, oc-curs by reason of the name and is held adverbially, so that the sense is: "the Father and the Son are one prin-ciple, that is, produce or spirant in one manner the Holy Spirit. — But since this name, principium, from its im-position is a substantive name, as is clear, that position of their still does not seem reasonable.

And, for that reason, there were *third*, those who said, that this name, "*principle*", as much as concerns itself, stands for *the Essence* and (that) it happens through addition to be drawn to a Person. And when there is said: "the Father is the principle of the Son", it is drawn to the Person of the Father; but when there is said: "the Father and the Son are the one principle of the Holy Spirit", it stands for the Essence and/or Nature, inasmuch as it is in the Two Persons, however. And that seems to be con-sonant with (St.) Anselm[3] saying, that « the Father and the Son spirate, inasmuch as Each (is) the same God ». And they say, that "one" means the unity about this term, "*principle*", not (the unity) of a Per-son, but of the Essence and/or of the Nature, as is

in the Two Persons. — But since (St.) Augustine[4] seems to say, that principium, said of the Father and the Son, means a *common notion*; similarly Master (Peter) says in the last chapter, that it means the unity of a *notion*; and (since) "*principle*" conveys a *notion*,[5] and the *Essence* is not referred (to): for that reason neither is this manner of theirs yet entirely fitting, though it is more probable than the others.

And for that reason there is a *fourth* manner of speaking, that this name, "*principle*", stands on behalf of a *notion*, yet not[6] in comparison to a *Supposit*, but to the *Nature* and the *spirative force*; and "*one*" conveys a unity about that, according to which it befits the ac-ceptance of that.

And this is clear in this manner: for since the Fa-ther and the Son spirate the Holy Spirit, inasmuch as (They are) *the one improcessible God*; and inasmuch as (They are) *the one God*, there is in Them a *unity* of will; inasmuch as (They are) *improcessible*, there is a *fecundity* of will (in Them), and inasmuch as (They are) *the one improcessible God*, there is in Them *one fecundity*[7] of will, and the one fecundity means a unity of principle: it must be said, that without a distinction it must be con-ceded, that the Father and the Son are the one principle of the Holy Spirit.

1. And regarding that which *is asked*, which unity does that which is "*one*" about the "*principle*" mean; it must be said, that since this name, "*principle*", is said of Many together, it cannot stand for a *Person*; and again, since it means a looking-back to a Person, it cannot stand for the *Essence*: therefore, it is necessary, that it stand for a *notion*. Therefore, when there is said: "the Father and the Son are the one principle", "*one*" means the unity of *notion*, yet in comparison to the unity of the Nature and of the spirative force, just as will be clear in the other problem[8] and is clear, too, from the aforesaid.

2. To that which is objected presently, having demonstrated the Father and the Son, that this principle is not that one; one can respond in a twofold manner. First, indeed, that *this and that* cannot be said, because through the rule a distinction does not occur, except where there is a union out of diverse causes.[9] There-fore, since an omnimodal union is in the name for a principium, such that it is not multiplied, for that reason there is no saying of a *this and that* there. — *In another manner* it can be said, that when there is said a "*this and that*", either it demonstrates a *form*, or a *Supposit*, or *both*: if a *form*, it is false; if a *Supposit* and/or both, it is true according to the reckoning of a Supposit;[10] and for that reason it does not follow, that (there are) two (prin-ciples), because the form is not multiplied. Similarly, can it be argued in this name "*God*".

---

[1] Codex O inserts *one* [unum].

[2] See here the text of Master (Peter), ch. 3.

[3] ON THE PROCESSION OF THE HOLY SPIRIT, ch. 21: But no sense grasps, that the Holy Spirit is the Spirit of the Father or of the Son, ac-cording to which the Father is One, the Son Another, but according to which Each is one and the same God. Cf. ibid., ch. 7, and MONOLOGION, ch. 54.

[4] See here in the text of Master (Peter), ch. 3.

[5] The Vatican edition together with codex cc has *relation* [rela-tionem].

[6] Not a few ancient codices, such as A S T Z etc., together with edition 1, have *not only* [non tantum] for *yet not* [non tamen], which read-ing, though it is more difficult, is not false.

[7] Here the codices disagree among themselves, some by omitting the first *one* [unus], others *in Them* [in eis]; the Vatican ed. omits both; the entire text is exhibited well by codices L M O Z, with edition 1.

[8] The following q.. — Next, the Vatican ed. omits *too* [etiam].

[9] See the explanation of this rule above, in d. 4, q. 2, in the body (of the Question). Hence it is clear, that just as the Three Divine Persons are united in the name "*God*" [Deus], so the Father and the Son in the name "*principle*" [principium]. — A little below this after *there* [ibi] in the Vatican edition and codex cc there is read *not a this and a that there* [non est ibi hoc et illud] for *not a saying of a this and that there* [non est ibi dicere hoc et illud].

[10] Codex T adjoins well *false according to the reckoning of a form* [falsa ratione formae].

3. To the two following (objections) *certain (authors)* respond, that this name, <u>principium</u>, cannot be a subject, nor can it become a relation to Him, that it is held *as an adjective.* — But that is nothing, because the name is a *substantive* one: therefore, it can be a subject and be predicated and become a relation to Him.[1] — *And if they say,* that for this it has been invented; it is nothing, because it cannot be proven. And again, an invention ought to have a reason, and we do not see, that it can *become* a relation, as if there be said: *"In the beginning was the Word,*[2] in which beginning was the Spirit", because He as not in Another, but in the Same. *It can also be a subject.* because if the Father is the principle of the Holy Spirit, by the simple converse, the principle of the Holy Spirit is the Father.

On this account one must respond *in another manner,* because, when there is said *"one principle"*, *"one"* means the unity of *notion,* which is common to the Two; and because it means a common unity, for that reason here there is (a fallacy of) the consequent:[3] "the one principle of the Holy Spirit is the Son and the Father: therefore the Son is the Father", just as here: "the one God is the Father and the Son: therefore, the Father is the Son".

4. To that which is objected last: either the one, which is the Father etc.; it must be said, that because the *"one"* means the common spiration, as it is in More, for that reason it does not happened to divide: 'either the one which is the Father, or the one which is not the Father' — as if there be said: "ever many is an animal; either an animal which is white, or an animal which is not white", there is a granting[4] of *neither,* because "animal" commonly stands for a white animal and a not-white one, such that for each together it renders the expression true. Similarly, in the proposed, <u>principium</u> stands for the *principle,* which is the Father, and which is the Son; and for that reason it is not licit there *to divide* and *to descend,* nay there is a figure of speech there out of a change of supposition.[5]

SCHOLIUM

I. On this question the Church afterwards proposed (two) definitions pertaining to the Faith. For the Second Council of Lyon says, that « the Holy Spirit proceeds eternally out of the Father and the Son, not as out of two spirations, but by a unique spiration »; and Florence (Decree of Union for the Greeks) decreed, that the Holy Spirit « proceeds out of Each as from one principle and a unique spiration ». — The Seraphic Doctor already treated the same question above in d. 11, q. 2; but here he resumes it, chiefly to solve a certain difficulty (1st. opposed argument), nor does he explain more accurately, in what sense here *"one principle"* [unum principium] is to be understood. On this sense the theologians of that age used to disagree; wherefore here four sentences are posited.

II. The fourth opinion , received by the Seraphic Doctor, consists in two propositions. The first is: *"principle"* here stands for a *notion,* but yet in comparison to the *Nature* and *spirative force,* or to the principle *from which* of the spiration, both the *remote* (principle), which is the Nature, and the *proximate* (principle), which is the power of spirating. The second is: *"one"* here conveys the unity of the notion in comparison to the spirative force. Whence according to St. Bonaventure *"principle"* conveys here two (things), namely, both the notion (active spiration), and the power of spirating. To this consents (Bl. John Duns) Scotus, who, however, thinks, that it *principally* conveys the power of spirating and that there is connoted a notion or the active spiration; but the Seraphic (Doctor) affirms rather that principally there is signified the notion itself. Nor does St. Thomas dissent (SUMMA., I, q. 36, a. 4, in reply to n. 1) saying, that the Holy Spirit proceeds from the Father and the Son, inasmuch as They are one in the spirative virtue, which in a certain manner signifies the Nature with a property. Otherwise the difficulty about the same *power of spirating* and the variety of opinions, which we have observed above (d. 7, q. 1) about the *power of generating,* returns, namely, whether it conveys something *absolute,* and/or *relative.* That the same, middle sentence, which we have vindicated in d. 7 according to the Seraphic (Doctor), is also to be held in regard to the power of spirating from the same, is sufficiently clear from the final proposition in the solution to n. 1, and from the response to the following question, especially from the words: « For that reason we say: the Father and the Son are » etc..

III. In the 1st. opposed argument after the words: *But on the contrary* [Sed contra], an argument is proffered, which militates against the sentence of the Seraphic Doctor; yet which is not solved here, but in the following Question (in the body of the Question) at the words: « Hence it is, that the Father is not said to be *several principles* » etc. (cf. also St. Thomas, <u>loc. cit.</u>, in reply to n. 2). — To the 2nd. opposed (argument) a twofold solution is given: the first is constructed from that certain general rule handed down there; the second from this principle, that among the divine the plurality of form does not follow out of the plurality of Supposits. An example is, that the *Deity* (a form) is not multiplied, though it is in Three Persons. Similarly, there can be one *fecundity of producing* or one notion in the Person of the Father and the Son. And in a similar manner this opposed argument is solved from this principle, that in God a *unity of Persons* does not follow out of a *unity of form.* — The solution to n. 4 is worked out in the same manner by St. Thomas, <u>loc. cit.</u>, in reply to n. 4.

IV. Alexander of Hales, SUMMA., p. I, q. 70, m. 3, a. 3 and 6. — (Bl. John Duns) Scotus, on this and the following q., SENT., Bk. I, d. 12, q. 2: REPORTATIO, ibid. q. 1 and 2. — St. Thomas, SENT., Bk. I, d. 11, q. 1, a. 3 and 4; SUMMA., I, q. 36, a. 4. — Bl. (now St.) Albertus (Magnus), here in a. 4; SUMMA., p. I, tr. 7, q. 31, m. 3, q. 1, incidental. — (Bl.) Peter of Tarentaise, here in the q. sole, a. 5. — Richard of Middleton, SENT., Bk. I, d. 11, q. 3, and here in q. 1. — Giles the Roman, here in 1st. princ., q. 3. — Henry of Ghent, SUMMA., a. 60, q. 7. — Durandus (of Saint-Pourçain), here in q. 2. — (Bl.) Dionysius Carthusian, d. 11, q. 3, and here in q. 4.

---

[1] Thus also Alan of Lille, RULES OF THEOLOGY, rule 51: But this seems (to be) no reason. For although it is an adjective according to (its) signification, yet it its is a substantive word, just as this name *"lord"* [dominus], (and) this name *"author"* [auctor]. — In place of *and ... to Him* [et ad ipsum], all the codices and editions here put *and to Him* [et ad eum]; even a little above this, the codices and edition 1 have *nor ... to Him* [nec ad eum] for *nor ... to Him* [nec ad ipsum] (i.e. to the Holy Spirit), which the Vatican edition and the other editions have.

[2] John 1:1. — Next for *It can also* [Potest etiam] codex T has *It can be predicated and* [Potest praedicari et].

[3] Understand: a fallacy of the consequent. — For *here* [hic] codex Q *there* [ibi].

[4] The Vatican ed. with codex cc has *being granted* [dari], faultily.

[5] On the terms pertaining to Logic, which occur in this solution, cf. the Scholium above d. 4, a. sole, q. 2, p. 98 ff.

QUESTION II

Whether the Father and the Son can be said (to be) "the one spirator", and or even "the same principle" (of the Holy Spirit)?

Second, there is asked, whether these are to be conceded: "the Father and the Son are the one spirator", and/or: "are the same principle of the Holy Spirit". And that that this is to be conceded: "They are *the one spirator*", seems:

1. Because the Father and the Son are not the one principle, except because They spirate by a unique act of spiration [unica spiratione]: therefore, since this name "*spirator*" [spirator] conveys the spiration itself, the Father and the Son are the one spirator.

2. Likewise, because the Father and the Son create by a unique act of creation [unica creatione], They are not only said (to be) "*the one principle*" of a creature, but also "*the One Creator*": therefore, since They similarly spirate by one act of spiration, They are "*the one spirator*".

3. Likewise, that They are "*the same principle*", seems, because a non-multiplied unity causes an omnimodal identity; but the Father and the Son are the one principle of the Holy Spirit, such that the unity of the principle in no manner is multiplied in Them:[1] therefore, They are "*the same principle*".

4. Likewise, this is true: "the Father and the Son spirate by the same act of spiration", but the same is conveyed by this name "*principle*", which (is conveyed) by this name "*act of spiration*" [spiratio]: therefore by an equipollent (substitution), the Father and the Son are *the same principle*.

ON THE CONTRARY: 1. A "*spirator*" and "*he who spirates*" are equipollent: therefore, if there is one spirator, therefore, there is[2] also one who spirates. But this is false: "One spirates", because not One, but Two are They who spirate: ergo etc..

2. Likewise, "*spirator*" conveys the spiration itself in concretion regarding a supposit: therefore, either it is the *Essence*, or a *Person*. Not the *Essence*, therefore, a *Person*: therefore, if the Father and the Son are the one spirator, They are one Person and/or Hypostasis.

3. Likewise, it seems, that it is not to be conceded, that They are "*the same principle*". For if They are the same principle, they are the *same*; but it is false, that the Father and the Son are the *same*: therefore, the first (proposition) is false. Moreover, it is manifest, what follows; for it follows rightly: 'they are the same animal, therefore, (they are)[3] the same'. It is clear, again, that this is false: "they are the same", because they are *distinct*, therefore, they are not the same.

4. Likewise, that which "*the same*" [idem] is, is a *relative* pronoun: therefore, since a pronoun designates a certain person, and a *relative* is a (name) noting the identity in that, on be-

half of which it refers, (relative pronoun) signifies the identity in the supposed (noun);[4] but that is not an essence, but a person: therefore, (here) it signifies, that They are the same Person, which since (this) is false, it remains, that that expression is false.

CONCLUSION

The expressions are not to be approved, nor that the Father and the Son are "the one spirator", nor that They are "the same" principle of the Holy Spirit, though they are the "one" principle of Him.

I RESPOND: It must be said, that this expression: "the Father and the Son are *the one principle* of the Holy Spirit" [Pater et Filius sunt unum principium], is received simply; but this one: "the Father and the Son are *the one spirator*" [Pater et Filius sunt unus spirator], is not received; and this one similarly is not admitted: "the Father and the Son are *the same principle*" [Pater et Filius sunt idem principium]. For, though they seem to be equipollent to the former, yet, they are not equipollent. For the notion of spiration is signified in a different manner in these expressions.

On which account, it must be noted, that the notion can be signified in a twofold manner, that is, in *abstraction* and in *concretion*, as if to say a "*principle*" and/or a "*spirator*". Moreover, in concretion it can be signified either in comparison to a subject in the reckoning of a *supposit*, and/or in comparison to a subject in the reckoning of *one who is active* [in ratione activi], and/or *in both manners* [utroque modo].

Therefore, the notion of the spiration is signified in concretion in comparison[5] to a subject in the reckoning of a *supposit* [in ratione suppositi] through this name "*spirator*", which is a verbal name. And because a supposit of this notion is a Person and not one Person, but Two, for that reason we say that (there are) *two*[6] spirators, not *one*. Nor is it similar concerning that which is a "*creator*" [creator]: because, since it is an essential name, it signifies in concretion regarding a subject, which is a substance — and that is the One (Being) in the Three [unum in tribus] — but the notion (signifies in concretion) regarding a person, which of itself is multiplied,[7] is not the One (Nature) in the Two [una in duabus].

The notion is also signified in comparison to a subject in the reckoning of *one who is active* [in ratione activi], as through this name "*prin-*

---

[1] The Vatican edition and codex cc omit *in Them* [in illis].

[2] From codices F G H I P Q T X and Z we have restored *there is* [est], which is lacking in the Vatican edition. Next for *One spirates* [unus spirat], codices P and Q have *(there is) One who spirates* [unus qui spirat].

[3] Supply together with codex X *they are* [sunt].

[4] Priscian, GRAMMATICAL INSTITUTIONS, Bk. II, ch. 4: It is proper to a pronoun to be posited on behalf of some proper name and to signify certain persons. — And ibid., Bk. XVII, ch. 12 (he says): Moreover, the aforesaid is a cause, on account of which one pronoun is accepted for all the names, that is, which have a demonstration of and/or relation to some certain substance, which in all the proper names is to be signified in one

and the same word [voce].

[5] In the Vatican edition there are wanting the words *in comparison*, which the context presumes and which are also exhibited by codex T. Several codices, such as W X aa and bb, together with edition 1, substitute *in comparison* [in comparatione] for *in concretion* [in concretione].

[6] Thus the manuscripts and editions 1, 2, and 3; the Vatican edition omits *two* [duos].

[7] For *is multiplied* [est multiplicata] the Vatican edition, together with some codices, has *is multiplied* [est multiplicatur]; moreover, it alone and faultily adds *for that reason* [ideo]; not a few codices have *which of itself it, is multiplied* [quae de se est multiplicatur].

ciple", which means an origin. And since a subject acts through *virtue*, and *virtue* respects *nature*, since in the Father and the Son there is *one* Nature and *one* Virtue, not multiplied; through this name *"principle"* there is signified the notion of the spiration, as in no manner multiplied. For that reason we say: "the Father and the Son are the *one* principle of the Holy Spirit", so that *"one"* means the unity of the notion and of the spirative force and of the Nature in the Ones spirating. Hence it is, that the Father is not said (to be)[1] *several principles*, though He has several notions, because He does not have (them) according to diverse forces [vires] and natures.

The notion is also signified in comparison to a subject in the reckoning of a *Supposit and One who is active*, when there is said *"the same principle"*, since the pronoun *"the same"*, which wants to signify a certain Person, respects a *Supposit*; and *"principle"*, just as has been said, respects Him as *One who is active*. And since the Supposit *is not the same* nor one, for that reason this is false: "the Father and the Son are *the same principle"*.

This therefore, is true: "the Father and the Son are *the one* principle"; but this is false: "They are *the one spirator"*; again, this (is) false: "They are *the same* principle of the Holy Spirit". And the reason for all of these is clear from the aforesaid.

1. And regarding that which is first objected, that They are the one principle, because They spirate by a unique act of spiration; it must be said, that this is not the *whole* reason; rather [sed] the whole reason is this, because by an unique act of spiration and by a unique virtue and in the Unity of the Nature They spirate the same One; and *"principle"* in this manner conveys that notion: and for that reason They are the one principle. But not so is that notion signified through the name *"spirator"*, which is a verbal name and descends from a verb, which concerns a personal supposit. For a *"spirator"* is said (to be) the one who spirates, and that is a Person.

2. To that which is objected concerning the act of creation, the response is already clear, because the act of creation does not only have (its) coming-to-be [fieri] *by one virtue*, but also has *one supposit*,[2] and that is the Substance — for the Father does not create as a proper subject, but the Divine Substance Itself, which is one, (does) — but the supposit of the act of spiration cannot be the Substance, but a Person: for that reason it is not said, that the Father and the Son are the one spirator.

3. To that which is objected, that an *identity* is not-multiplied unity; it must be said, that that is not sufficient, unless there be *such* a unity, that it is neither multiplied nor is there compatible [compatiatur] with it a plurality of supposits, which an identity excludes. And because the unity of a principle is compatible with a plurality of Persons, for that reason that (objection) is clear.

4. To that which is objected, that They spirate by the same act of spiration; it must be said, that it does not follow from this, that They are *"the one spirator"*, for although it is the same notion, yet it is not the same Supposit. And when there is said *"the same principle"*, there is noted an identity in Each; when there is said *"by the same act of spiration"*, there is noted an identity in the Other: for that reason the latter does not follow out of the former, nor does the one infer the other.

SCHOLIUM

I. Alexander of Hales, Bl. (now St.) Albertus (Magnus), (Bl.) Peter of Tarentaise, Ulric — according to Bl. Dionysius the Carthusian — and even St. Thomas, in his Commentary (here in q. 1, a. 4, in reply to n. 2), think with the Seraphic Doctor, that the expression *"two spirators"* is to be received. But St. Thomas in the SUMMA (I, q. 36, a. 4, in reply to n. 7) thinks « that it is better to say », that « there are two spirators on account of the plurality of Supposits, but not two spirators on account of the one act of spiration. For adjectival names have a number according to supposits, but substantives from themselves according to the form signified ». In the principal assertion (Bl. John Duns) Scotus agrees with the Angelic (Doctor), yet not in the *reason* added (concerning which, see Macedo, collation 6, difference 3). The author of the 65th opusculum among the opuscula of St. Thomas (Parma edition) strives to reconciles each sentence. But this opusculum, according to the testimony of De Rubeis (Dissertation 29, ch. 1), does not belong to St. Thomas.

The decision regarding this difference pertains rather to the tribunal of grammarians; but their judgement does not concord with this rule (of St. Thomas) .

II. The other form of expression, by which there is said *"the same principle"*, is asserted by St. Thomas (loc. cit.) « to be fittingly said, according to which the word, *"principle"* [ly principium], supposes in a confused and indistinct manner on behalf of the Two Persons together ». St. Bonaventure, however, with the others cited above, does not admit this formula. — The others, such as Richard of Middleton, repute each sentence probable.

III. Alexander of Hales, SUMMA., p. I, q. 70, n. 3, a. 1, 4, and. 5. — St. Thomas, loc. cit.. — Bl. (now St.) Albertus (Magnus), here in a. 5 and 6. — (Bl.) Peter of Tarentaise, here in a. 4 and 5. — Richard of Middleton, SENT., Bk. I, d. 11, a. 5,* here in q. 1. — Giles the Roman., here in 1st. princ., q. 2, and d. 11, princ. 2, q. 1. — Henry of Ghent, SUMMA., a. 60, q. 6. — Durandus (of Saint-Pourçain), here in q. 3. — (Bl.) Dionysius the Carthusian, SENT., Bk. I, d. 11, q. 4.

DOUBTS ON THE TEXT OF THE MASTER

DOUBT I

In this part, there are doubts about the text and, first, concerning this which is said, that *"the Father is the*

beginning of the whole Deity" [principium totius deitatis]. Therefore, one asks, what this name, principium, stands for there. For it cannot stand for *the Essence* nor for a *Person*, because each means, as much as it is of itself, an absolute. Therefore, either it stands

---

[1] The Vatican edition together with codex cc reads *the Father means many* etc. [Pater dicit plura etc.]. Next, after *because He does not have* [quia non habet] codd. I K V W aa & bb repeat *several* [plures], in place of which codex Y has *diverse* [diversas], and then codices P Q and X with edd. 2, 3, 4, 5 & 6 incongruously omit *according to* [secundum].

[2] Here *"supposit"* [supposit] signifies a *subject*, as is apparent from the following and preceding propositions, though it may perhaps be an error in the codices.° — Below the Vatican edition, together with cod. cc, has well *which is unique* [quae unica est] for *which is one* [quae una est].

* *Trans. notes*: Here the original Scholium faultily read *q. 5* for *a. 5*.

° The Quaracchi editors are not entirely correct. Here *supposit* signifies that which is the locus of an action, and is not said in the terminology of grammarians, as a *subject* [subiectum], and hence *"supposit"*, as St. Bonaventure has it, is correct, since that which is a supposit is the individual of a species, the species being in this case, the Creator, and the locus of this power of creation is the Divine Substance, which is one.

for *the paternity*, and this is false, because He is not the father[1] of the Holy Spirit; nor for *the spiration*, because the spiration is not in respect of the Son; nor *commonly* regarding Each, because They have nothing common except the Essence; neither for *the innascibility*, because the innascibility does not mean a looking-back to a Person, but a privation of a looking-back: therefore, in every manner[2] it is false.

I RESPOND: It must be said, that the sense of this expression is this: "the Father is the beginning of the whole Deity, that is of all the Persons in the Deity"; and there is an *apt distribution* [distributio accommoda],[3] just as when there is said: "Heaven contains all (things), that is, except itself". — But if one asks, what does this name "*beginning*" stand for; it must be said, that it stands for the paternity and the spiration together, because through the paternity He is the beginning of the Son, through the spiration the beginning of the Holy Spirit, and through each the beginning of Each. — What, therefore, *is objected*, that They do not have (anything) common; it must be said, that[4] They do not convene in a unique notion by a convenience of *form*; yet They do convene by a convenience of *origin* in the same Person and by the property of the same Person. For because the Person of the Father is from None, as is said in the text,[5] for that reason He produces by every manner of production, and for that reason He is the beginning of the whole Deity. Whence the same is conveyed by the name for a *beginning*, when He is said (to be) "the beginning of the Deity", *in (its) principal* understanding, that is conveyed by the name for the *innascibility*[6] as much as regards (its) *consequent* understanding. And from this word and from this reckoning of the word that position receives (its) confirmation, which says, that *the innascibility* in the Father means a plenitude of fontality or a fontal plenitude, though out of (its) *consequent* understanding.[7]

DOUBT II

Likewise, is asked concerning circumlocutions of this kind, in what manner this name principium is accepted there, when there is said: "*beginning without a beginning*", "*beginning from a beginning*". For either it is accepted *essentially*, or *personally*: not *personally*, as it seems, because the Holy Spirit is said to be "*the beginning from a beginning*", and "*beginning*" does not befit Him except temporally. — *Moreover*, just as Master (Peter) says in the Twenty-Seventh Distinction,[8] *a this* cannot be said *of that*, except as much as regards names for the Substance: therefore "*beginning*" cannot be accepted notionally. — *And again*, on behalf of what notion would it be accepted,[9] when the Son is said (to be)

"the beginning from a beginning"? because (it would not be accepted) for *the filiation*, because it (name) befits the Holy Spirit, that is, to be "the beginning from a beginning"; not for *the common spiration*, because the common spiration befits the Father, whom being a "beginning from a beginning" does befit. — *If you say*, that it is accepted essentially; *on the contrary*: the Essence is not the beginning of a Person nor does it mean a looking-back to a Person: therefore, since "beginning" means a looking-back to a person, it cannot be accepted essentially, and thus in no manner (can it be).

I RESPOND: It could be said, that this name principium is accepted in comparison to a creature, and is drawn to the Person through the added prepositions, just as if to say: "God from God", and "God not from God", and completely similar (expressions): and in this manner the objections cease. — *In another manner* it can be said, that this name principium has not been imposed to signify an essential and/or personal respect, as much as it is of itself, but holds itself indifferently to each, and its acceptation is determined through the adjunct. Therefore, when it is said of the Father, it stands for the notion of *the paternity* and of the spiration commonly, and is constrained through the property of *the innascibility* through this, that He is said (to be) "*not from a beginning*". Similarly in the Son it stands for the common spiration with the filiation, which is conveyed through this, that He is said (to be) "*from a beginning*". But of the Holy Spirit it must be said, that stands only essentially and is constrained to the Person through this, that He is said (to be) "*from each*".[10]

DOUBT III

Likewise, is asked of this which (Master Peter) says, that *the Holy Spirit began to be the Principle of creatures*. For he seems to speak against that which has been said above in the Third Distinction:[11] « From the perpetuity of creatures there is understood (their) eternal Founder [Conditor aeternus] ». If, therefore, the Holy Spirit is an eternal Founder, therefore, (He is) eternally a principle. — Likewise, in the hymn: *Aeterne rerum Conditor*.[12] — Likewise, *by reason* it seems, that things from eternity were in God; but not but as in a principle: therefore, from eternity He was a principle.

I RESPOND: It must be said, that the name, which mean an effect in a creature, can mean that *in act* and/or *habit*: if *in act*, they are said in time; if *in habit*, they can be said eternally. And since principium can resound unto an act, and/or as a habit, for that reason it can

---

[1] For *father* [pater]* codex T has *in respect* [respectu]. The Vatican edition reads, *because the Holy Spirit is not a father* [quia non est pater Spiritus sanctus].

[2] Codices A I K S V W Y aa and cc, together with edition 1, have *entirely* [omnino] for *in every manner* [omni modo].

[3] That is, a distribution, in which a term is not distributed for all its inferiors simply, because from the custom of speaking one is excepted, namely, the very subject of the proposition. Cf. above d. 7, q. 4, in the body (of the question), and below in d. 45, a. 1, q. 4, in the body (of the question). — Next for *contains* [continet] codex V has *covers* [tegit].

[4] Codex O here subjoins: *just as those two personal acts, 'to generate' and 'to spirate', convene in that common one, which is 'to produce', so those relations in that which is a "principium"* [sicut isti duo actus personales generare et spirare conveniunt in hoc communi, quod est producere, sic istae relationes in eo quod est principium].

[5] Chapter 1.

[6] Very many codices, such as A T W X T Z and cc, together with edition 1, *the Innascible one* [innascibilis] .

[7] Cf. above d. 15, p. II, Doubt 6. — This doubt is solved also by St. Thomas, here about the text, and in the SUMMA., p. I, q. 33, a. 1, and by Richard (of Middleton), here about the text.

[8] Chapter 5.

[9] Codices A and Z have *is it accepted* [accipitur] for *would it be accepted* [acciperetur].

[10] Cf. Alexander of Hales, SUMMA., p. I, q. 70, m. 3, a. 1. — Bl. (now St.) Albertus (Magnus), here in a. 3 and 8. — (Bl.) Peter of Tarentaise, here in a. 7. — Richard (of Middleton), here in q. 4.

[11] Chapter 1. — The proposition, which then follows: *If, therefore, the Holy Spirit is an eternal founder* [Si ergo Spiritus sanctus est aeternus Conditor] is wanting in many manuscripts.

[12] Which is attributed to St. Ambrose, and is had in the (traditional) BREVIARIUM ROMANUM, in the Office for Sunday, at Lauds.

---

* *Trans. note*: Here the footnote original read *the Father* [Pater], faultily if the received text above is without error; but the received text is more fitting to the context, than if *the Father* was read, since "*the Father*" is the proper Name of the Person, but such is denied properly by St. Bonaventure.

be said not only *temporally*, nay even *eternally*. But since (the customary) use accepts this name, principium, more, insofar as it is said in an act, than in a habit, for that reason Master (Peter) says, that it is said *temporally*.

What is objected, that He is said (to be) the "*eternal Founder*": it must be said, that this[1] expression is twofold: both on the part of that which is a "*Founder*", because it can mean an act, and/or a habit; and on the part of that which is "*eternal*", because it can be held *as an adjective*, and/or *as a substantive*. And if "*eternal*" be held *as a substantive*, in this manner it does not posit an eternity about the founding, but about the supposit, and (then) the expression is true. If ("eternal" is held) *as an adjective* and "*Founder*" is held in the manner of a habit [habitualiter],[2] the expression is still true; if in the manner of an act [actualiter], then (it is) false. The senses are manifest. For in one manner the sense is: "*the eternal Founder*, that is, the *Eternal One*, who is the Founder". In another manner, "*the eternal Founder*, that is the One able from eternity to found in time". In a third manner, "*the eternal Founder*, because He has founded eternally." In the first two senses the expression is true, but in the third sense it is false.

Doubt IV

Likewise, is asked of this which (Master Peter) says, that *the Father from eternity is the principle of the Son*; but the Father and the Son and the Holy Spirit are not a principle, except in time: therefore, according to this, since the eternal is before the temporal, through (a consideration of what is) prior "principle" is said *notionally* among the divine rather than *essentially*. *But on the contrary*: everything essentially said is more common; and as much as anything (is) more common, so much (is it) prior:[3] therefore, through (a consideration of what is) prior "principle" ought to be said *essentially* rather than *notionally*.

I Respond: It must be said, that there is a twofold speaking of this name, "*principle*": either in respect of a *subject*, or in respect of a *terminus*. If in respect of a *subject*,[4] thus since the understanding of the Essence is before the understanding of a Person, thus "*principle*" essentially said according to the reckoning of understanding goes before [praeit] "principle" notionally said, just as (the objection) opposes. But if in respect of a *terminus*, in this manner "principle" *essentially* said respects something diverse through (its) essence, and thus[5] (something) created; however, "principle" *notionally* said respects a consubstantial

and uncreated and eternal Person; and for that reason "principle", *notionally* said, is said eternally, and as much as regards this way it is said (to be) prior in God not only as much as regards (its) *understanding*, but even as much as regards (its) thing. And thus it is clear, concerning which acceptation this name, "principle", is said through (a consideration of what is) prior according to diverse comparisons.[6]

Doubt V

Likewise, is asked of this which (St. Augustine) says, that *when the Son said that He (is) the Beginning, He wanted to show that He (is) the Creator*. For it seems false; because He Himself responds to the question of the Pharisees asking. *Who are you?*[7] But "*Who?*" asks concerning a *person*; but "*the Beginning*", according to which it is accepted on behalf of the Creator, is held *essentially*: therefore, either the Lord does not respond fittingly, or "*the Beginning*" does not stand for the Creator there. — *If you say*, that (the word) is appropriated to the Son; *on the contrary*: both the reckoning of creation and the reckoning of a beginning is appropriated to the Father:[8] not, therefore, to the Son.

I Respond: It must be said, that "*beginning*" is held essentially there, just as is said in the text (of Master Peter);[9] but it has been drawn to the Person of the Son. — But what *you object*, that it is appropriated to the Father; it must be said, that "*beginning*" from the reckoning of its name is not appropriated to the Son except through an addition; and thus (it is) in the proposed, because it is appropriated through the act of a verb. For He did not say simply: "*I (am) the Beginning*", but "*I, the Beginning, who also speak to you.*[10]

Doubt VI

Likewise is asked of this which (Master Peter) says, that *it must not be conceded, that the Son has a beginning, since He also is the Beginning from the Beginning*. For it seems that he ought to concede (this), because every relative ought to have a correlative responding to itself:[11] therefore, if the Son, when He is said (to be) "*the Beginning from the Beginning*", is said relatively (to be such), He ought to have a correlative, which is a "*beginning*".

I Respond: It must be said, that 'having a beginning' is in a twofold manner: either as a *correlative*, just as a son

---

[1] In the Vatican edition and codex cc there is lacking *this* [haec].

[2] Very many codices faultily have *in the manner of a habitude* [habitudinaliter], cf. above d. 18, a. sole, q. 2, p. 325, footnote 10. — A little below this, after *that is* [id est], the Vatican ed. with codex cc distorts the text in this manner: *the Founder, Thou who art eternal* [conditor, qui est aeternus], and cod. I in this manner: *who is eternal, is the Founder* [qui est aeternus, est conditor]. At the end of the solution, codd. P & Q have explicitly *in* [in] before the *first two senses* [Duobus etc.] and codd. I S V W & Y before *the third* [tertio].

[3] Cf. Aristotle, Physics, Bk. III, text 2, and Metaphysics, Bk. V, text 16 (Bk. IV, ch. 11), and above in d. 27, p. II, a. sole, q. 3, p. 487, footnote 2.

[4] In the Vatican edition and codex cc there are wanting the words *or in respect of a terminus. If in respect of a subject* [aut respectu termini. Si respectu subiecti].

[5] The word *thus* [ita] is absent from the Vatican ed., but in very many codd. and in ed. 1 it is had; in not a few codd., however, it has been placed not before *(something) created* [creatum], but after. A little further above this, for *something* [quid] the Vatican ed. with cod. cc has *what is* [quod est]. A little below this, in place of *for that reason* [ideo], codd. S V & W have *thus* [ita].

[6] The distinction, which St. Bonaventure makes in this solution, is also used by (Bl.) Peter of Tarentaise, here in q. 1. But Richard of Middleton (here in q. 2), together with the Angelic (Doctor), absolutely concedes, that through (a consideration of what is) prior He is said (to be) "the principle" of the Persons [principium personarum] in a manner related to the Principle of creatures [principium creaturarum]. Alexander of Hales (Summa., p. I, q. 70, m. 1, § 1), St. Albertus Magnus (here in a. 2), and St. Thomas, (here in a. 2, quaestiuncula 2) respond, making the same distinction in regard to the matter, which St. Bonaventure uses.

[7] Jn. 8:25.

[8] Cf. below Distinction 31, a. 1, q. 3, and d. 34, q. 3. — Somewhat above this some codices, together with edition 1, have *reckoning of a creator* [ratio creatoris] for *reckoning of creation* [ratio creationis].

[9] Chapter 2.

[10] John 8:25.

[11] Cf. Aristotle, On the Predicaments, ch, "On *Relation*".

is said to have a father, and in this manner the Son does have a beginning; or as *its own disposition*, and in this manner (something) is said to have a beginning which began to be, and in this manner the Son does not have a beginning,[1] because He did not begin. — And/or in another manner: both having a beginning *of being* and *of enduring*; in the first manner the Son has a beginning, in the second manner (He does) not.[2]

DISTINCTION XXX

CHAPTER I

On those (names), which are said of God temporally and relatively according to an accident, which accedes not to God, but to creatures.

For there are certain (names), which are said of God on account of time [ex tempore] and befit Him temporally without His being changed [sine sui mutatione] and are said relatively according to an accident, which accedes not to God, but which accedes to creatures, such as *"creator"*, *"lord"*, *"refuge"*, *"given"* and/or *"granted"* and (names) of this kind. Of these (St.) Augustine says in the fifth book, ON THE TRINITY:[1] « *"Creator"* is said relatively to a creature, just as *"lord"* to a servant [servus] ». Likewise, (he says elsewhere):[2] « Let it not move (you), that the Holy Spirit, though He is co-eternal to the Father and the Son, yet is said (to be) something on account of time, even as we said of that (name) which (is) *"granted"*. For the Spirit sempiternally is a *"gift"*, but temporally a *"granted"*. And if one is not said (to be) a *"lord"*, except when one begins to have a servant, that is also a relative appellation for God on account of time. For sempiternal is not the creature, whose Lord He is: therefore, He does not have the sempiternal *"being"* of a *"lord"* [dominum esse], lest we be driven to say that the creature (is) also sempiternal, because He ruled (it) as a lord [dominaretur] sempiternally, or (because) it also served in His household [famularetur] sempiternally. Moreover, just as one cannot be a *"servant"*, who does not have a lord, so neither a *"lord"*, who does not have a servant ».

But here someone will say, that this appellation, by which He is said (to be) a *"lord"*, is not due [competit] God on account of time, because He is not only a lord of things, which began in time [ex tempore], but even of that thing, which did not begin in time, that is, of time itself, which did not begin in time, because there was no time before[3] it began: and for that reason He did not begin to be a lord on account of time.

To which it can be said, that though He did not *begin on account of time* to be a lord of time, yet *He did begin* to be a lord of time, because time was not always; and of

man himself He began to be a lord in time.[4] Of this (St.) Augustine in the same book[5] thus immediately says: « Whoever will stand forth, who says that God alone (is) eternal, but that the seasons [tempora] are not eternal on account of (their) variability and mutability, but yet that the seasons themselves did not begin to be in a time [in tempore], because there was no time, before the seasons began, and for that reason that it did not accede[6] to God in a time, to be a lord, because He was lord of those seasons, which at any rate [utique] did not begin to be in a time — what shall he respond concerning *man*, who has been made in a time, whose Lord at any rate He was not, before he was? Certainly, to have been the lord of man, accedes to God on account of time, and to remove all controversy, certainly to have been *your* lord and/or *mine*, we who began to be a little while ago, He had on account of time. In what manner, therefore, shall we obtain, that nothing is said of God according to accident? Except because *to the Nature of Him* there accedes nothing, by which He is changed; so that those accidents are *relatives*, which accede with some change *of the things*, of which they are said, jut as *"friend"* is said relatively. For one does not begin to be a friend, except when he begins to love: therefore, let there be some change of will, so that one be said (to be) a friend. However, a *coin* [nummus], when it is said to be *the price*, is said (such) relatively; nor yet has it been changed, when it began to be *the price*, nor when it is said (to be) *a pledge* and (things) of this kind. If, therefore, *a coin* can be said relatively without any change of its whole self, so that neither when it begins, nor when it fails to be said (such), there comes to be something of a change in its nature and/or form, by which it is a coin; how much more easily ought we accept concerning that incommutable Substance of God, that thus something is said relatively to the creature, so that, although it begins to be said temporally, yet nothing is understood to have acceded to the Substance of God Itself, but (something is) to the creature itself, regarding which it is said. In what manner, also, is He said (to be) *"our refuge"*:[7] for God is said (to be) "our refuge" relatively: for He is referred to us, and then He comes to be our refuge, when we flee back [refugimus] to Him. Does something, then, come to be in His Nature, which was not

---

[1] For *does not have a beginning* [non habet principium] the Vatican edition, together with codex cc, faultily reads *does not begin to be* [non incipit esse]; not a few codices, after *beginning* [principium], adjoin an *and* [et], and codex T (in the margin), after *begin* [incipit] adds *to be* [esse].

[2] Cf. above d. 9, q. 3, in reply to n. 3.

NOTES ON THE BOOK OF SENTENCES

[1] Chapter 13, n. 14. — A little above this, trusting in codices B C E and edition 1, we have put *which accedes not to God* [non quod accidat Deo] for *which accedes not to God* [non quod accidit Deo].

[2] Ibid., ch. 16, n. 17; in which text the Vatican edition, together with the other editions, except edition 1, reads *Let it not move anyone* [Non aliquem moveat], contrary to the codices and the original, and a little after this the same, together with the other editions, has *the Holy Spirit* [Spiritus sanctus] for *the Spirit* [Spiritus].

[3] Codex A and edition 1 transpose the words well in this manner: *time was not, before it began* [non erat tempus, antequam inciperet].

[4] Our codices here add this short note: *When time began, God began to be a lord, nor was He a lord before time, but with time not on account of time, and/or in a time, because time was not before He (was) a lord, but (they were such) together.* [Quando coepit tempus, Deus coepit esse dominus, nec ante tempus fuit dominus, sed *cum* tempore non *ex* tempore, vel *in* tempore, quia non ante fuit tempus quam ispe dominus, sed simul.] Cf. S. Bonaventure, here Doubt 2.

[5] Loc. cit.. But not a few (words) have been omitted and/or changed by Master (Peter).

[6] All the codd. and edd. 1, 2, 3, 7 & 8, have *accede* [acciderit] in the perfect subjunctive, but incongruously [trans. note: because the clause must be in indirect discourse, which requires an infinitive].

[7] Ps. 17:2, and passim; the other passage from Sacred Scripture is Jn. 1:12.

before we fled back to Him? In us, therefore, there comes to be some change, we who, by fleeing back to Him, are made better; but in Him nothing (does). Thus too He began to be *Our Father*, since we are regenerated through the grace of Him, who *gave us power to be made the sons of God*. Therefore, our substance is changed for the better [in melius], when we become His sons. Similarly, too, He began to be *Our Father*, but without any commutation of His own Substance. What, therefore, God began to be said temporally, which He did not used (to be said to be), is manifest that it is said relatively, yet not according to an accident *in God* [Dei], because something accedes to Him, but plainly according to an accident *in that* [eius], regarding which God is said to be something relatively ». — From these he openly shows, that certain (names) are said of God temporally in a manner relative to creatures without a change *of the Deity*, but not without a change *of the creature*; and thus it is an accident in the creature, not in the Creator, and the appellation, by which the creature is said relatively to the Creator, is a relative one and notes a relation, which is in the creature itself. But that appellation, by which the Creator is said relatively to the creature, is indeed a relative one, but does not note a relation, which is in the Creator.

CHAPTER II

Whether the Holy Spirit is said (to have been) given and/or granted relatively to Himself, since He is given by Himself.

Here there can be solved the question proposed above,[1] where it was asked, since the Holy Spirit is said (to have been) *given* and/or *granted* — moreover, what is given is referred to him who gives, and to the one to whom it is given — and since the Holy Spirit (is also said to be such) from Himself, whether, when He is said to be given and/or granted, He is said (to be such) in a manner relative to *Himself*. To which question, responding, we say, that the Holy Spirit is said (to have been) given and/or granted in a manner relative, both to the One giving, and to the one to whom He is given.[2] Moreover, the One giving, or the Grantor, is the Father with the Son and the Holy Spirit. And yet we do not say, that the Holy Spirit is referred *to Himself*, but the appellation of a given and/or a granted is referred both to the One giving and to the one receiving, because nothing can be said (to have been) *given*, unless it is given from someone and to someone. Moreover, when the Holy Spirit is said *to be given* and/or (to have been) *given by Himself*, He indeed is said (to be such) in a manner relative to the one to whom He is given; and the appellation is a relative one, and in the one to whom He is given there comes to be a change, not in the One giving.

COMMENTARY ON DISTINCTION XXX

On relative names, which are said of God temporally and commonly.

For there are certain (names), which are said of God on account of time etc..

THE DIVISION OF THE TEXT

Above, Master (Peter) dealt with relative (names), which befit God properly and eternally. Here he deals with those (names), which befit God temporally and commonly, and this part has two (parts). In the first, Master (Peter) deals with the relative (names), which are said of God on account of time [ex tempore].* In the second, with those which befit the several Persons, but, yet, can be appropriated, such as "*similar*" [similis] and "*equal*" [aequalis], below in the Thirty-First Distinction (which beings): *Moreover, it is necessary that one consider, that since the Three Persons* etc..

The first part has four parts. In the *first* he shows, that some names are said of God on account of time [ex tempore], giving examples [exemplificans] of many. In the *second*, because the example for this name, "*lord*" [dominus], seemed unfitting, he opposes and solves, there (where he says): *But here someone will say, that this appellation* etc.. However, in the *third*, because the saying seemed false, that something is said of God on account of time, for that reason he moves and solves a doubt, there (where he says): *In what manner, therefore, shall we obtain, that nothing is said of God according to accident?* In the *fourth*, however, from what has been predetermined [ex praedeterminatione] he solves a certain[2] doubt asked in the preceding, there (where he says): *Here can be solved the question proposed above*, etc..

---

[1] Distinction XVIII, ch. 6.

[2] Codices D and E have *is granted* [donatur].

NOTES ON THE COMMENTARY

[1] For *eternally* [aeternaliter] very many codices have *essentially* [essentialiter], and next for *temporally and commonly* [temporaliter et communiter] the Vatican edition alone has faultily *properly and temporally* [proprie et temporaliter].

[2] For *a certain* [quoddam], codices A F G I (T by the primary hand) V and cc have *(it) according to the* [ad], codex Z has *another* [aliud], codex Y *that* [illud].

---

* *Trans. note*: Cf. ex tempore, under the entry for tempus in the *Rationale for the Translation of Peculiar Latin Terms*, in the Introduction to this English Translation, on p. E-25.

TREATMENT OF THE QUESTIONS

For an understanding of those (things) which are said in this Distinction, three (questions) are asked:

First, whether anything is said of God on account of time [ex tempore].

Second, granted that it is, there is asked, whether those (names) which are said of God on account of time, are said *per se* and/or *per accidens*.

Third, whether they are said according to substance [secundum substantiam], or according to relation [secundum relationem].

ARTICLE I

On those (names), which are said of God on account of time.

QUESTION I

Whether anything is said of God on account of time?

Moreover, that some (names) are said of God on account of time [ex tempore], is shown thus:

1. « He is not a lord, unless he has a servant », just as (St.) Augustine says;[1] but God is said (to be) a "*lord*" and He did not have a servant from eternity, therefore, on account of time: ergo etc..

2. Likewise, a passion responds to an action, such that they are together;[2] but God creates, therefore, something is created; but something is not created except in time [ex tempore], therefore, He does not create except in time [ex tempore]: ergo etc..

3. Likewise, '*being a man*' [esse hominem] convenes with no one except on account of time [ex tempore], for this (reason) that '*being a man*'[3] has a beginning; but '*being a man*' does convene with God: therefore, (it does so) on account of time.

4. Likewise, jut as the temporal holds itself to the temporal, so the eternal to the eternal: therefore, with the proportion changed, jut as the eternal holds itself to the temporal, so the temporal to the eternal. But the eternal thus holds itself, that it is said of the temporal, as when there is said. "Peter has been predestined": therefore, the temporal will also be able to be said of the eternal.

ON THE CONTRARY: 1. Everything temporal is created, but God is uncreated, and among these [horum] there is a most high distance; but of these, among which there is a most high distance, the one is not predicated of the other: ergo etc..

2. Likewise, everything temporal is changeable and variable; but every that, of which a changeable is predicated, is itself[4] changeable: therefore, since God is not changeable and variable, it is clear that etc..

3. Likewise, nothing[5] eternal is on account of time; but everything which is predicated of God, is God, and thus eternal: therefore, nothing such can be said on account of time.

4. Likewise, everything which is something in time [ex tempore], began to be something, which it was not before; and every such[6] is changeable: therefore, nothing such is in God, ergo etc..

If you say, that something is not predicated of God on account of time [ex tempore] by a predication through the *Essence* and/or *inherence*, but through a *cause*, which does not posit something in God, but in the effect; *on the contrary*: when there is said: "God is a *creator*", this is said on account of time, and not *through a cause*: therefore, that is no response. *Proof:* Everything which is said of something through a cause, is said of another through an essence, and/or inherence; but "*creator*" is said of no other that of God, neither through an essence, nor through inherence: ergo etc..

Likewise, what is said of another *through a cause*, can be inferred through the manner of the habitude of the cause [habitudinis causalis], such as: "a day is the sun shining upon the earth",[7] therefore, the day is from the sun: therefore, if *through a cause* God is a creator, for an equal reason God (is) from the creature, and/or the other way around.

Likewise, what is predicated solely *through a cause* is not the same as that, of which it is predicated; but when there is said: "God creates", the action of God is God: therefore, it is not predicated through a cause.

Likewise, when God is said (to be) a "*lord*", "*lord*" does not mean any *genus of cause*, and yet it is said of God: therefore, the aforesaid response is not sufficient.

---

[1] ON THE TRINITY, Bk. V, ch. 16, n. 17. See here the text of Master (Peter), ch. 1.

[2] Cf. Aristotle, METAPHYSICS, Bk. V, text 20 (Bk. IV, ch. 15), where action and passion are placed among relatives; and his PHYSICS, Bk. III, text 19 (ch. 3) where it is said, that action and passion are one movement in the one suffering as the subject. And Gilbert of Porretain, ON THE SIX PRINCIPLES, ch. on *Action* (says): Every act of a passion is effective, and everything inferring a passion is an action.

[3] Codex M reads *every human 'being'* [omne esse humanum].

[4] Very many codices, such as C F G H K O R S T U V X and cc, together with editions 1, 2 and 3, read *there is (something) mutable about it* [circa ipsum est mutabile].

[5] Codex I has *no* [nullum].

[6] Codices C F R S T and U read *such 'to be'* [esse tale] for *every such* [omne tale].

[7] A similar definition is had in Aristotle, TOPICS, Bk. VI, ch. 3 (ch. 4): A day is the Sun's lying upon the earth. — Next after *for an equal reason God* [pari ratione Deus] in codex I there is repeated *is* [est].

CONCLUSION

*Some names are said of God on account of time not by reason
of the principal (thing) signified, but by reason of (the
thing) connoted in the creature.*

I RESPOND: It must be said, that '*that something be
said ex tempore*' is in a twofold manner: either because
it is *temporal* (i.e. "in time"), or because it means a *looking-back to a temporal* (i.e. "on account of time").

In the first manner nothing is predicated of God
through (His) *essence* and/or through *inherence*, just as
the four reason induced for this prove, yet (something) is predicated *through a cause*, as if to say: "God
is my patience",[1] and/or *through the union*, as if to
say: "God is a man"; and this does not posit a
change and/or a temporal 'being' about God, but
about the creature.

In the other manner something is said on account of time, for this (reason), that from the reckoning of its name it means a *comparison to something
temporal*, as "*lord*" and "*creator*", but yet from its principal signification it conveys the *Essence*. For "*lord*"
conveys dominion, which is the power of coercing
subjects [subditos]; and this is the Divine Essence.
Similarly, "*creator*" conveys the Divine Action, which
is the Divine Essence. Yet each signifies in respect
to a creature, and thus connotes (something) created
and temporal.

Therefore, since the whole which conveys in itself the contingent and necessary, is denominated a
contingent; similarly, the whole which (implies it itself) the eternal and temporal, is denominated a *temporal* on account of the nature of the whole copulate,
which posits each part and is falsified in virtue of

each part and in virtue of the other (part);[3] hence it is,
that such (names) are said on account of time, not by
reason of the principal (thing) signified, but by reason
of (what is) connoted in the creature. And in this manner the four following arguments are clear.[4] For it must
be conceded, that not everything which is said of God
on account of time, is said through a *cause*, but it is said
either through a *cause*, and/or through *the union*, and/or
through a certain *comparison to the temporal*. And in this
manner all (the objections) are clear.

1. 2. To that, therefore, which is objected, that the
temporal is *created*, and *changeable*; it must be said, that
it is said of the temporal in the first manner; and this is
not said of God, except through a cause and/or through
the union.

3. To that which is objected, that everything which
is predicated of God is eternal, it must be said, that this
is twofold, because "*eternal*" can be held *as an adjective*,
and/or *as a substantive*. If *as an adjective*, in this manner
it is false: 'for anything is predicated of God, the duration of which is not eternal'. If *as a substantive*, it is true,
and the sense is: 'everything which is predicated of
God, is something eternal'. Nor yet does it follows: 'it
is[5] eternal'; nay there is the fallacy of the accident there,
just as here: 'the act of creation [creatio] is God; and
God is eternal; therefore, the act of creation is eternal';
thus also in the aforesaid. For something, which is eternal by reason of the principal (thing) signified, that is,
which is something eternal, by reason of (that which is)
connoted is said (to be) temporal.

4. To that which is objected, that that which is on
account of time, begins to be something; it must be said,
that that is not in God on account of any change made
in Him, but in the creature: and that has been determined above, in the Eighth Distinction.[6]

SCHOLIUM

I. On the difference, which is between beginning <u>ex tem-
pore</u>, <u>in tempore</u>, <u>cum tempore</u>, cf. here Doubt 2. — *Five manners* of predicating something of God are enumerated in the
Response, namely, through *the Essence* (such as, "God is his own
'being' "), through *inherence* (i. e. *quasi* inherence, such as "God
is wise"), through *a cause* ("God is my hope"), through *the union*
("God has become man"), through a certain *relation* to the temporal ("God is the Creator"). Cf. SENT., Bk. III, d. 7, a. 1, q. 1,
in the body (of the question). By others only *four* manners are
enumerated, such as (Bl.) Peter of Tarentaise does (SENT., Bk. I,
d. 30, q. 1, a. 1): « In four manners something is found to be
predicated of anything: in the first, through *essence*, as "man is
an animal"; in the second manner, *through a denomination* and/or
accidental *inherence*, such as "the man is white"; in the third
manner, *through a cause*, such as "the sun is the day"; in the
fourth manner, through a *respect* or habitude, such as "this one is
his right hand" ». Richard of Middleton (here in q. 1), has
eight, namely: « That, which is said of anything either signifies

its essence, or something concerning the essence, or some,
absolute accident, inhering in it, or the cause of that, or the
effect of that, or the reckoning denominating it, or the transient action of that in an exterior thing, or the other's action
signified in a passive manner, or a thing united to that of
which it is said ». These eight manner can be reduced to
those five. See more on this below in d. 33, q. 3, and in d.
34, q. 2.

II. There did not fail to be those who accepted the names
"*lord*" and "*creator*" for the *habit* or *power* of ruling as a lord
and/or of creating; whence they concluded, that those are to be
said of God from eternity (cf. here Doubt 1). But the common
sentence holds, that those are accepted in virtue of the *act* and
are said only on account of time.

With Alexander of Hales (SUMMA., p. I, q. 53, m. 3,
and m. 4, a. 3), St. Bonaventure says, that both the name
"*lord*", and the name "*creator*" « from their principal (thing)
signified convey the Essence ». But St. Thomas,

---

[1] Psalm 70:5: *Since Thou art my patience, Lord* [Quoniam tu es
patientia mea, Domine].

[2] (St. Severinus) Boethius, ON THE TRINITY, ch. 5 defines "lord" in
this manner: A certain power, by which a servant is coerced. Cf. also (St.)
Ambrose, ON THE FAITH, Bk .I, ch. 1, n. 7, whose words can be found above
in (Lombard's BOOK OF SENTENCES, Bk I, d. II, ch. 4, p 46, footnote 3.

[3] Alexander of Hales, SUMMA., p. I, q. 53, m. 1 (says): For it is more
easy to destroy that to construct (something) entirely, as Aristotle says (TOPICS,
Bk. VII, ch. 3). For, for this, that I be a white man, two (things) are necessary,
namely, that I be a man, and that I be white; and for this, that I not be white, it

suffices, that I not be white. Cf. also above d. 14, a. 1, q. 1, in reply
to n. 6, and Aristotle, PRIOR ANALYTICS, Bk. I, ch. 15, where the
same is taught in respect of a syllogism, one proposition of which is
necessary, the other contingent. — A little above this, *similarly,
the whole which* [similiter, quod] supply, together with codex I, *implies in itself* [in se implicat].

[4] Namely the final arguments, which reply to the instance made
in the 4th opposed argument.

[5] Codices M and bb read *therefore, it is* [ergo est].

[6] Part II, q. 1 and 2.

(SUMMA., I, q. 13, a. 7, in reply to n. 1) distinguishes between the name "*lord*" and "*creator*". That "*creator*" « signifies an action of God, which is His Essence », he himself concedes; but "*lord*", as he says, « does not signify the Divine Substance directly, but indirectly ». Nevertheless, there seems to be hardly a dissention among each sentence. For the one is that it signifies something *more principally*, the other that it signifies it *directly*.

III. The *fallacy of the accident*, which is noted in the 3rd. opposed argument consists in this, that there the difference between the twofold signification, which is in the name for a *lord* and/or for a *creature*, is not attended to. For to the extent that these words signify the Divine Essence, they mean something eternal; but not, to the extent that they signify a looking-back to the creature, which convenes with God per accidens.

IV. It must be noted, that in the 4th. opposed argument there is affirmed regarding an instance, that those (names) which are said of God on account of time, are said of Him through a *cause*. To elude this insufficient result, (the opponent) makes objection, by bring to bear four arguments, to prove, that the names "*creator*" and "*lord*" are not predicated of God *through a cause*. St. Bonaventure does not respond explicitly to these arguments, but only *generally* at the end of the Response, by conceding, that not everything said of God on account of time is said *through a cause*, but very many (things are said) either through *the union* (such as, "God is a man"), and/or through a *looking-back* to a creature (such as, "God is the Creator"). For it is manifest, that the name "*creator*" cannot convene with God on account of time on the part of the *Divine Action*, which is the eternal Essence of God. Moreover, so that the two first arguments of the Reply, which are sufficiently subtle, may be understood better, it must be noted, that 'that some (names) are said of God by a predication *of cause*' can be understood in a twofold manner: *first*, because God causes that which is signified by the predicate; in this manner there is said: "God, my patience", which expression responds to the cited example: "a day is the Sun shining upon the earth"; and then there is rightly inferred: "the day is from the Sun", "patience is from God". *Second* it can be understood, not because the predicate itself is caused, but because in that there is implied the *habitude* of a cause. In this manner, in the name "*creator*" there is conveyed a *habitude* to that which is caused, namely, to *the creature*, but there is manifestly not conveyed, that the Creator Himself is caused. The other two arguments have no difficulty.

V. Alexander of Hales., SUMMA., p. I, q. 53, m. 1, 2 and 3. — (Bl. John Duns) Scotus, here in q. 1. — S. Thomas, here in q. 1, a. 1 and 2; SUMMA., I, q. 13, a. 7. — Bl. (now St.) Albertus (Magnus), here in a. 1; SUMMA., p. I, tr. 13, q. 52 and 53. — (Bl.) Peter of Tarentaise, here in q. sole, a. 1. — Richard of Middleton, here in q. 1. — Giles the Roman, here in 1st. princ., q. 1. — Durandus (of Saint-Pourçain), here in q. 1. — (Bl.) Dionysius the Carthusian, on this and the following q., here in q. 1 and 2.

QUESTION II

Whether the names, which are said of God on account of time, are said per se, and/or per accidens?

Second, there is asked, whether (the names) which are said of God on account to time, are said per se, and/or per accidens. And that (they are said) according to *accident*, is shown in this manner:

1. (St.) Augustine (says) in the fifth (book) ON THE TRINITY and (as) is had in the text (of Master Peter):[1] « That He would be a lord of man, accedes to Him on account of time [ex tempore] ».

2. Likewise, this very (thing) seems *by reason*: because everything which is *present* and *absent*, except the corruption of that, of which it is said, is predicated according to accident[2] — this is known per se — but all these which are said of God temporally, are of this kind: ergo etc..

3. Likewise, what is predicated per se of anything, is always in it, therefore, ab oppositis,* what is predicated of anything and is not always in (it), is predicated not per se, therefore, per accidens, but such are the names of this kind: ergo etc..

4. Likewise, everything which is predicated of something, either is convertible with the subject, or from the reckoning of the subject, or is predicated per accidens;[4] but names of this kind are neither from the reckoning of God, nor (are) convertible, as is clear from this name "*lord*": ergo etc..

ON THE CONTRARY: 1. (St.) Augustine (says) in the fifth (book) On the Trinity:[5] « Nothing is said of God according to accident ».

2. Likewise, it is shown *by reason*: because in whatsoever there is a positing of an accident, there is a positing of a composition [compositionem][6] and consequently [per consequens] a variety; but neither is in God: ergo etc..

3. Likewise, everything per accidens is lead back [reducitur] to a per se;[7] but a 'being led back' [reductio] is of a posterior to a prior, not the other way around [non e converso], but God does not have a prior, neither simply nor secundum quid:* therefore, nothing is said of God according to accident.

4. Likewise, everything which is said of two, (is said) of one per se, (and) of the other of the two per accidens, (and) is said in a more perfect manner of that, of which it is said per se;[8] but whatever is said of God is said most perfectly: therefore, nothing is said of God according to accident [secundum accidens], therefore, names of this kind are not said of God per accidens, therefore, per se.

CONCLUSION

The names, which are on account to time said of God, are predicated per accidens only in that sense, in which per accidens is opposed to "necessary".

I RESPOND: It must be said, that '*to be said according to accident*' is in a threefold manner. In one manner "*accident*" [accidens] is said through opposition to "*substance*" [substantiam]; and in this manner an "*accident*" is said (to be) "a property *inhering* in another" [proprietas alii inhaerens], which (property) is not from the essence

---

[1] Chapter 1.

[2] Aristotle, TOPICS, Bk. I, ch. 4.

[3] Aristotle, POSTERIOR ANALYTICS, Bk. I, ch. 4.

[4] Aristotle, TOPICS, Bk. I, ch. 4.

[5] Chapter 16, n. 17. See the text of Master (Peter), here in ch. 1.

[6] Aristotle, METAPHYSICS, Bk. VII, text 21 (Bk. VI, ch. 6): But it is not true to say, that what is said according to accident, such as "(he is) musical" or "(the wall is) white", on account of this, that it signifies

(something) twofold (i. e. the form and subject), is itself even the same "*being*" (i.e. essence) as *what it used to be*. Cf. also his PHYSICS, Bk. I, text 26 ff. (ch. 3).

[7] Aristotle, PHYSICS, Bk. II, text 66 (ch. 6): But nothing according to accident is prior to those which are per se. Cf. METAPHYSICS, Bk XI, ch. 7 (Bk. X, ch. 8).

[8] Cf. Aristotle, TOPICS, Bk. III, ch. 1.

---

* *Trans. note*: Concerning the meaning of the Latin expression, ab oppositis, cf. translator's footnote above, on p. 54.

° The technical term, secundum quid, which literally means "according to something", indicates that manner of speaking in which a term signifies according to some standard of measure, e.g., a wall painted white is white not per se, but secundum quid, that is, it is white according to which it is painted.

of the thing".[1] And in this manner, indeed, « nothing is said of God according to accident », just as (St.) Augustine says, for this (reason), that in this manner an *accident* posits a composition and a variety in that, of which it is said. — In another manner '*to be said according to accident*' is through opposition to per se; and in this manner, there is said according to accident, either what is said through an other in essence, as if to say: "the wall distracts";[2] either through something, to which it is in a certain manner the same, in a certain manner diverse, as for example, when it is said of a superior through an inferior, as: "the figure has three (angles)", and/or of an inferior through a superior: as, "an isosceles (triangle) has three (angles)". In this manner nothing is said of God according to accident. For this '*to be said according to accident*' posits in something a posteriority and an imperfection, just as the reasons induced fro this show; but God has nothing *imperfectly*, has nothing *from another*,[4] which is entirely other, neither from a superior and/or an inferior, because these do not occur in God. — In a third manner '*to be said according to accident*' is through opposition to *the necessary*, so that there is said to accede that, which is not in (it) necessarily.[5] And in this manner (names) of this kind are said of God *according to accident*, because they are not said of Him necessarily; but are said of Him per se, because (they are said) through a comparison (of Him) to a creature. Moreover, the comparison to a creature

is per se, because God is His own action; but yet, because God acts through (His) Will, which is not always nor of necessity conjoined to act,[6] for that reason (His action is) *not necessary*; and as much as regard this there occurs There a reckoning of speaking according to accident. Whence this manner of speaking per accidens is opposed to (the manner of speaking) per se in creatures by reason of this, that to the '*speaking* per se' (in creatures) there follows the necessary in creatures; but in *God* (there does) not, since He does the[7] same by Himself and *voluntarily*; and for that reason in God (this manner of speaking per accidens) does not have an opposition to (the manner of speaking) per se.

Therefore, the reasons showing, that they are not said of God according to accident, proceed according to the first and second acceptation.

1. What, moreover, is objected, that '*to be a lord*' does accede (to Him); must be understood in this manner, that is, it convenes (with Him) neither *necessarily* nor *always*.

2. To that which is objected, that they are[8] absent except corruption; it must be said, that that definition is *of an accident*, according to which '*being present*' is through inherence; but in this manner it does not befit God, as has been seen, but only creatures: whence that (objection) is clear.

3. 4. To that which is objected concerning per se, it must be said, that (a per accidens) is said of a per se in creatures. For to a per se in creatures there follows a necessary, but not so in God.

SCHOLIUM

I. St. Thomas (here in q. 1, in reply to n. 2) posits only two manners, according to which something is said per accidens (i.e. in the category of an accident). But St. Bonaventure distinguishes here a threefold manner, according to which something is said both per accidens, and per se (i.e. through itself). — To the three principal conclusions the Seraphic (Doctor) adds a *corollary* here, by which he teaches, that those (names) which are said of God *contingently* and thus per accidens, are nevertheless predicated of Him per se. For, among creatures, that which is said of anything per accidens and therefore, contingently, cannot be said

of it per se, because that which is said per se, is necessary (cf. text of Aristotle, in the 3rd. opposed argument).

II. Alexander of Hales, on this and the following q., SUMMA., p. I, q. 53, m. 3 and 4. — St. Thomas, loc. cit.. — Bl. (now St.) Albertus (Magnus), here (in his Commentary), in a. 2; SUMMA., p. I, tr. 13, q. 52, q. 3, incident. — (Bl.) Peter of Tarentaise, here in the q. sole, a. 2. — Richard of Middleton, here in q. 2. — Giles the Roman, here in 1st. princ., q. 2. — (Bl.) Dionysius the Carthusian, here in q. 1.

QUESTION III

Whether the names, which are said of God on account of time, convey a real relation in God?

Third, there is asked, whether (the names) which are thus said of God on account to time, are said according to substance, or according to a relation, which is a *true* relation.[9] And that (they are said) according to *relation*, seems in this manner:

1. Just as the Father generates by His very self, so He creates by His very self; yet, although He generates by His very self, the generation and paternity are said truly (to be) in Him according to relation: therefore, for an equal reason, although He creates and rules as a lord by His very self,

---

[1] Cf. Aristotle, METAPHYSICS, Bk. VII, text 2 ff. (Bk. VI, ch. 1). — For *essence* codex K reads *substance* [substantia]. A little before this the Vatican edition and very many codices have *as the opposite* [per oppositum] for *through opposition* [per oppositionem].

[2] Understand: the sight, by reason of (its) whiteness. For as Aristotle says, METAPHYSICS, Bk. X, text 23 (Bk. IV, ch. 7), bright-white is « indeed a disgregative* color, and the former (i.e. black), on the other hand, an congregative color ». If, therefore, there is said: "the wall distracts", this befits a wall not by the reckoning of itself, but by the reckoning of the whiteness (which is) distinct from itself.

[3] Supply: here and a little above this after *three* [tres], the word *angles* [angulos]. For to the figure, which is the *genus*, there befits the having of three angles by reason of the *species*, that is, of triangle; but an isosceles (in Greek: τὸ ἰσοσκελές) or a triangle, which has only two equal sides, is the *species* inferior to the "triangle", simply said, and a having of three angles befits it by reason of the superior (genus), that is, of the triangle. — On this second

manner of speaking per se and per accidens, cf. Aristotle, POSTERIOR ANALYTICS, Bk. I, ch. 4-8, and METAPHYSICS, Bk. V, text 23, (Bk. IV, ch. 18).

[4] Cod. Y reads *from anyone* [ab aliquo].

[5] Cf. Aristotle, METAPHYSICS, Bk. V, text 13 (Bk. IV, ch. 6), and Bk. VI, text 5 (Bk. V, ch. 2). — A little below this after *but* [sed] codex T subjoins *yet* [tamen].

[6] Understand this of an act of the Will, to the text that *it passes over* into the creature or looks back to it, not to the extent that it is in God Himself. — Immediately after this, to the particle *not* [non] some codices, such as V W Y and aa, adjoin *is* [est]. Then, for *according to accident* [secundum accidens] codices P and Q have per accidens.

[7] Codex M adds *very* [ipsum].

[8] Codex K interjects here rightly *present and* [adsunt et]. Then, codex Q (in the margin) after *except* [praeter] adds *the subject's* [subiecti].

[9] That is, a *real* relation [realis relatio].

---

* *Trans. note*: Here the rare English word *disgregative* [disgregat, disgregativus], means "that which is, or is conducive to, separating, disjoining, dissolving" in the sense opposed to "gathering a flock together", from dis- "apart" and a verbalized, grex, gregis, for "flock". A white wall distracts [disgregat] the sight, by giving it the appearance of indefiniteness, and hence, gives no definite point of view, thus distracting the sight from a consideration of its proximity. The example of a white wall was used perhaps, because in the Mediterranean world, interior walls are generally white, on account of the plaster which is used to finish them.

yet, because (these actions)[1] are regarding the other, they are said *really* relatively.

2. Likewise, names of this kind either mean *purely* the Divine Substance, or *add above* (this) some respect. If they mean *purely* the Divine Substance — but the Substance is eternal and from eternity: therefore, they are said of God from eternity, which is false. Therefore, *they add above* (this) some respect, therefore, a relation. *If you say*, that they do not add a looking-back according to *thing*, but according to *a manner*,[2] *on the contrary.* either to that manner responds something in the *thing*, or *nothing*. If something in *the thing*: therefore, they are really said relatively; if *nothing*: therefore, the manner of understanding is false and the manner of speaking unfitting.

3. Likewise, there are certain relative (names said) according to "*being*", certain ones according to 'being said' [dici]. But among relatives according to "*being*" there is the *truth* of a looking-back; but "lord" and "servant" are relative (names) according to "*being*": therefore, each conveys a looking-back, not only according to a *manner*, but even according to *thing*: ergo etc..

4. Likewise, "*dominion*", said of God, thus means rightly [bene] a 'being placed over' [superpositionem],[3] just as (when it is) said of the creature; therefore, that 'being place over' either is posited in *God*, or in a *creature*; not in the *creature* — it is established, because then the same would be placed over itself — therefore, it is posited in *God*. But a 'being placed over' is truly a relation: ergo etc..

5. Likewise, when I say: "God creates", there is noted in this a twofold looking-back, that is, of a cause to an effect, and vice versa [e converso]. Therefore, either each is in the *creature*, or each in *God*, or one (is) in *God*, the other in the *creature*. It is established that it is impossible that each is in *God*, because God is not an effect; and similarly (it is impossible that each is) in the *creature*, because a creature is not the cause of itself, therefore, it is necessary, that the other (be) in God: ergo etc..

6. Likewise, when I say: "God creates", God is most truly a cause: and if a true reckoning of cause posits a true relation, the names of this kind, (when) said of God, posit a true relation.

ON THE CONTRARY: 1. Dionysius (the Areopagite says):[4] « In those caused [In causalibus] and causes we do not receive a reciprocation »: therefore, since God is the most perfect cause of a creature, He is not referred to the creature, although, conversely [e converso], the creature is referred to Him.

2. Likewise, the Philosopher says,[5] that knowledge [scientia] according to (its) "being" is referred to the knowable, but is not convertible with it [non convertitur]: therefore, if the dependence of God regarding the crea-

ture is lesser than of the knowable regarding knowledge, therefore, there is no relation in Him.

3. Likewise, *by reason* it seems, because names of this kind, if they mean a relation about God, either that is *purely the Essence* of God, or something *added above* (It). If (that which they mean is) *purely the Essence* of God, therefore, (it is) something eternal, therefore, the looking-back of the names of this kind is eternal: therefore, of necessity they are said from eternity [ab aeterno]. But, if they mean something *added above*: therefore, in God there is some composition.

4. Likewise, every relation means a dependence and/or at least an order and habitude to that, in respect of which it is said; but God is not ordered nor terminated (by a creature):[6] therefore, nothing is said of God relatively in respect of a creature.

CONCLUSION

The names, which are on account to time said of God, do convey some relation according to thing in God, but only according to a manner of understanding.

I RESPOND: Regarding this, it must be understood,[7] that '*to be said according to relation*' is in a two fold manner: either according to *thing*, or according to a *manner*. Moreover, a *real* relation is threefold. For sometimes it is founded upon an *accidental property*, as the similitude in a twofold whiteness;[8] sometimes upon an *essential dependence*, just as the Philosopher says,[9] « by matter, that itself which it is, is for the other » — sometimes upon a *natural origin*, just as an effect regards (its) cause, and a son regards a father.[10]

The first relation cannot be in God, because in God there is no *accidental property*. The second cannot be in Him, because in God there is no *dependence* [dependentiam]. The third is in God, but not in respect of the creature, but in respect of a Person; for this one does not mean a *composition* nor the inclination of a *dependence*, just as the first and second (do), but posits a *distinction* and an *order*. And since one Person is truly ordered to Another and has a habitude (to Another) and in another manner, according to thing [secundum rem], holds Himself to One rather than to Another; for that reason this relation is in a Person in respect of a *Person*;[11] but not in respect of a *creature*. For God has no order

---

[1] Edition 1 adds *these* [ista].

[2] Namely, of understanding or of speaking. We note, that in this question the Seraphic Doctor promiscuously uses the words, "a relation according to *a manner*" [relation secundum modum], "according to a *reckoning*" [secundum rationem], "according to '*being said*'" [secundum dici], to signify the same thing, namely a relation of *reckoning* [relatio rationis], which is opposed to a *real* relation [relation realis], as is apparent from the body of the question and from the solution of the arguments. The same occurs above in d. 28, Doubt 3, and below in d. 34, q. 2, a. 6. — Many codices omit the *not* [non] at the beginning of this sentence, and then for *but* [sed] substitute *and also* [et etiam], faultily.

[3] That is, an order of superiority.

[4] ON THE DIVINE NAMES, ch. 9, § 6. Cf. above d. 19, p. I, a. sole, q. 4, p. 346, footnote 4.

[5] ON THE PREDICAMENTS, ch. "On *Relation*", and METAPHYSICS, Bk. V, text 20 (Bk. IV, ch. 15.).

[6] Understand both followed by *by a creation* [a creatura]. — See above d. 26, a. sole, q. 1, p. 453, footnote 4.

[7] The Vatican edition, having changed the punctuation, adds *that it must be known* [sciendum], in place of which codices X and Z have *that it must be noted* [notandum].

[8] Hence Aristotle calls similars, those « which are one in *quality* ». Cf. above d. 19, p. I, a. sole, q. 1, p. 342, footnote 6.

[9] Cf. above d. 26, a. sole, q. 1, p. 453, footnote 6.

[10] Aristotle, METAPHYSICS, Bk. V, text 20 (Bk. IV, ch. 15).

[11] Cf. above d. 8, p. II, q. 1, in reply to n. 2; d. 20, a. 2, q. 1; and d. 26, q. 1.

to a creature nor does He have one or another habitude (to it). And for that reason in no manner is there *really* in God a relation in respect of a creature. — But a creatures does have an order and habitude to God, by means of an *accidental property* and an *essential dependence* and a *natural origin*:[1] for that reason according to every manner the creature is referred to God.

Since, therefore, our intellect, when it understands that something is referred to anything, understands also that it is compared to it: for that reason it understands God through a manner of looking-back and of relation, to which looking-back nothing responds in God except the Divine Essence; on the part of the creature it does (something)[2] does respond, and for that reason it is not vain. — It must be conceded, therefore, that names of this kind, when said of God, do not convey a relation in God according to *thing*, but only according to a *manner of understanding*. From these, those (things, which were) sought, are clear.

1. For that which is objected concerning the Father, it must be said, that it is not similar, because there is an order and habitude of the Father to the Son, and a habitude to the Son other than (that) to the Holy Spirit: moreover, God, just as the Philosopher says,[3] does not have an order nor any habitude. For « the First Cause holds itself in the same manner to all (things), though the others hold themselves in one and another manner to It », and in the twelfth (book) of the First Philosophy[4] it says, that the first and most high Good is not ordered to these created (things).

2. To that which is objected, if they do not mean a relation, therefore, (they mean) purely the Substance [pure substantiam]; it must be said, that (names of this kind) about God mean purely the Substance according to *thing*, but the relation (is) according to a *manner of understanding*; however, in a creature (the relation is) according to thing.[5]

And what it objects, that the (manner of) understanding is vain; it must be said, that (this) is false, because the understanding is founded upon something, namely, upon the relation of the creature, to which there responds a relation according to a 'being said' in God.

3. To that which is objected, that certain (names) are relative (said) according to "being" etc.; it must be said, that there are certain relative (names said) according to "being" on the part of each extreme, such as "*lord*" and "*servant*" in a creature; certain ones on the part of one of the two, such as "*the knowable*" and "*knowledge*", and "*the measurable*" and "*the measure*";[6] thus (it is) in the proposed.

4. 5. To that which is objected, that "*lord*" means a 'being placed over', and similarly "*creator*"[7] (means) a causality; it must be said, that 'being placed over' in God is truly a '*being placed over*', and truly a *causality*, because truly God is placed over another, and truly He effects (things). Yet that 'being placed over' is not *truly a relation*, similarly neither a causality, but is truly the Divine *Essence*, because It Itself[8] is placed over and effects (all other beings).

6. To that which is objected, that there is, There, the looking-back of cause and effect; it must be said, that the looking-back of an *effect* is, There, truly a looking-back and truly a relation, but the looking-back of a *cause* is not a looking-back nor a relation in God according to *thing*, but according to a *manner of understanding*, however, according to thing (it is) the Substance and/or the Essence.

SCHOLIUM

I. Those things which are here said of the diverse *species* of relation, are taught by Aristotle and sufficiently explained by St. Thomas, SUMMA., I, q. 13, a. 7. That a relation does not always induces a change in each extreme, is explained here in Doubt 3, and more diffusely by Richard (of Middleton), here in q. 4. — For an understanding of the solutions to the opposed arguments, it must be noted, that though the *relation* itself to the creature in God is only one of a *reckoning*, yet it has its real *fundament* in Him (cf. the solution to nn. 2 and 5.).

II. Only the Nominalists contradict the conclusion, by asserting that in God there is a real relation to creatures, acquired in time, but without a change in Himself. — (Bl. John Duns) Scotus does not deny, that in God there is a relation of reckoning to creatures (as faultily asserted by Cajetan, in his commentary on SUMMA., I, q. 13, a. 7), but rather he agrees in the matter itself with the Angelic and Seraphic Doctors, though he makes some objection against the *form* of the reckoning employed by St. Thomas (cf. Lychetus on Scotus, here in q. 2.).

III. (Bl. John Duns) Scotus, loc. cit.; REPORTATIO, here in the q. sole. — St. Thomas, here in q. 3; SUMMA., I, q. 13, a. 7; SUMMA CONTRA GENTILES, Bk. II, chs. 12-13. — (Bl.) Peter of Tarentaise, here in the q. sole, aa. 3 and 4. — Richard of Middleton, here in qq. 3 and 4. — Giles the Roman, here in the 1st princ., qq. 2, 3 and 4. — Henry of Ghent, SUMMA., a. 29, q. 3, n. 4. — Durandus (of Saint-Pourçain), here in q. 3. — (Bl.) Dionysius the Carthusian, here in q. 3. — (Gabriel) Biel, here in q. 5.

---

[1] Cf. below Doubt 1.

[2] Supply: something [aliquid]. — Only the Vatican edition reads: *yet on the part of the creature something does rightly respond* [ex parte tamen creaturae bene aliquid respondet].

[3] Understand: the author of the BOOK OF CAUSES, who in proposition 24 says: « The First Cause exists in all things according to one disposition, but all things do not exist in the First Cause according to one disposition ». Richard of Middleton, here in q. 4 adjoins these words to his: « But if those (names), which are said of God on account to time, would posit in God real relations to a creature, He would not exist in all according to one disposition: therefore, they do not posit in God any real relation to the creature ». — A little above this after *a habitude* [alia habitudo] the older codices together with edition 1 omit *to the Son* [ad Filium].

[4] Aristotle, METAPHYSICS, Bk. XII, text 52. You will find his words above in d. 26, a. sole, q. 1, p. 453, footnote 4.

[5] For *thing* [rem] the Vatican edition together with codex cc has '*being*' [esse].

[6] Aristotle, METAPHYSICS, Bk. V, text 20 (Bk. IV, ch. 15) says: But the measurable and the knowable and the intelligible, for this, that the one is said regarding the other, are said according to something (i.e. as relatives). For the intelligible signifies, that which belongs to its understanding; but there is no understanding regarding that of which it is the understanding; for the same, in a word, has been said twice. — For *the measurable* [mensuarbile] many codices have *the measuring* [mensuratio], codex K and edition 1 have *the measured* [mensuratum]; but incongruously.

[7] The Vatican edition, together with codex cc, has '*being created*' [creatio].

[8] Codices A S T V X Y and others together with edition 1 read *He is placed over by Himself* [se ipso].

DOUBTS ON THE TEXT OF THE MASTER

DOUBT I

In this part, there are doubts about the text (of Master Peter) and, first, concerning these names, *"creator"*, *"lord"* and (those) of this kind, which Master (Peter) says: *are said of God on account of time.* For (this) seems false, because, as (St. Severinus) Boethius[1] says, « *dominion* is the power of coercing subjects », but this is in God from eternity: ergo etc.. — Likewise, as (St.) Ambrose says: « *"Lord"* is a name for the Nature »: therefore, if the Nature is eternal, therefore, also the dominion. — Likewise, concerning this name *"creator"* there is an objection, because[2] one is not said (to be) a *"lector"*, because he is *actually* [in actu] reading, but because he is *able* [habilis] to read; but God is from eternity able to create: ergo etc..

In accord with this *there is asked* concerning the *signification* and *connotation* of these names, and whence do they have (their) *reckoning* of connoting, since the Divine Essence is (their) principal (thing) signified.

I RESPOND: It must be said, that although the Divine Essence does not *truly*[3] have a looking-back to the creature, yet it does happen that one *understands* and *signifies* It through the manner of a looking-back; and yet the understanding (of it) is not vain, on account of this, that it posits the whole reckoning of a real looking-back in the creature.[4] Since, therefore, names of this kind mean the looking-back, from which they are imposed — though they are imposed upon the Essence — for that reason they are said according to the exigency of that looking-back. For that reason it must be understood, that certain (names) mean *the looking-back alone*, such as "lord"; certain ones[5] *the effect*, such as "creator" and "just", and both are under a twofold difference, because they either convey the looking-back to a thing *present*, or to a thing *future*, or to a thing in act and/or in habit. In the first manner, because they posit a creature in act, they mean the looking-back alone,[6] when the creature begins (to be); in the second manner (they mean it) from eternity.

According to this, therefore, if *"lord"* and *"creator"* convey a looking-back in *act*, they cannot be said from eternity; but if in *habit*, they can. Yet, the common usage accepts names of this kind, as connoting

in *act*; and for that reason (St.) Augustine says,[7] that they are said with time. — Therefore, what (St. Severinus) Boethius says, must be understood, that (dominion)[8] is the power of coercing subjects had, not (those) not had. — What (St.) Ambrose says, it is clear that it is not compelling [non cogit], because although ("lord") is imposed upon the Nature, yet it is imposed from a property[9] of the Nature, such as means a looking-back to creatures, and for that reason it connotes something created. — And in this manner all (the objections) are clear, because a *reckoning* of connoting is a manner of signifying.[10]

DOUBT II

Likewise, is asked concerning this which (Master Peter) says, that *time did not begin in time* [ex tempore].* For (this) seems false, because everything which begins, is temporal, and every temporal is measured by time, and ever such began in a time [in tempore]:[11] ergo etc.. *If you cite* [des] *the instance* (of that which exists) in perpetual time [in perpetuis], *there is the objection*, that nothing is more variable than time; but every such is temporal: ergo etc. — Likewise, if time did not begin in a time, therefore, it began outside of time [extra tempus], therefore, there was a time outside of every time.

I RESPOND: It must be said, that as much as regards the present (objection) — because of the beginning of time one ought to speak in the Second (Book)[12] — to begin *in* time [ex tempore] and *in a* time [in tempore] and *with* time [cum tempore] differ, because the <u>ex</u> means an order, and thus it presupposes an anterior time; and for that reason nothing begins in time except that which follows time. "In a time" means an existence of time;[13] but time was not in its own beginning [initio], since it is successive. For that reason (those) which are of an equal duration *with* time, did not begin, neither in time, nor *in a* time, but *with* time, that is, when time began.

If *you ask*, in what manner did time begin; it must be briefly said, that in none of the aforesaid manners, but it began in its own beginning [principio], and for that reason it did not begin outside of time.

To that which is objected, that the temporal is measured by time; it must be said, that the temporal, which

---

[1] The entire text of (St. Severinus) Boethius can be found above in d. 30, a. sole, q. 1, p. 522, footnote 3, and the entire text of (St.) Ambrose, cited just after this, is found above in Master Peter Lombard's, BOOK OF SENTENCES, Distinction II, chapter 4, p. 47, footnote 3.

[2] Codex S has *that* [quod].

[3] Edition 1 reads *does not have a true looking-back* [non habeat verum respectum].

[4] See more on this here in q. 3. — A little after this in place of *for that reason they are said* [ideo dicuntur] many codices together with edition 1 have *for that reason they mean* [ideo dicunt], in an evidently corrupt manner.

[5] The Vatican edition alone adds *also* [etiam].

[6] Some codices, such as H O cc and ff, read *they are only said* [dicuntur solum] for *they mean the looking-back alone* [dicunt respectum solum], a less congruous reading. A little below this codices F G I T V and Y, together with edition 1, have the subjunctive form for *convey* [importent].

[7] ON THE TRINITY, Bk. V, ch. 16, n. 17. See here the text of Master (Peter), ch. 4.

[8] Supply: *dominion* [dominium]. — The Vatican edition, not trusting in the codices and editions, after *that (dominion) is* [quod] subjoins *not* [non], suppressing the same particle next after

but [sed]. Not a few codices, together with editions 4 and 5, exhibit *not* [non] twice, in both position; which is evidently false.

[9] Codices A T and Y and others, with edition 1, read *is imposed appropriately upon the Nature* [imponitur appropriate naturae] for *is imposed from a property of the Nature* [imponitur a proprietate naturae].

[10] Cf. here q. 1. — Alexander of Hales, SUMMA., p. I, q. 53, m. 1. — Bl. (now St.) Albertus (Magnus), here in a. 6; and SUMMA., I, tr. 13, q. 52. — St. Thomas, here in a. 2. — (Bl.) Peter of Tarentaise, here in a. 5. — Richard (of Middleton), here in q. 3. — A little before this codex T has *the objections* [obiecta] for *all (the objections)* [omnia].

[11] Cf. Aristotle, PHYSICS, Bk. IV, text 114 ff. (ch. 12), where that which follows here is also hinted at.

[12] Namely, SENT., Bk. II, d. 1, p. I, a. 1, q. 2, in reply to n. 3.

[13] For the words *an existence of time* [existentiam temporis] codex O exhibits *one containing time and/or at least the co-existence of time* [temporis continentem vel saltem temporis coexistentiam], and then after *successive* [successivum] it adds: *for that reason it did not begin in a time as (in) a coexisting (time). Likewise, there was no time before its own beginning, for that reason it did not begin in time as in one containing (time), for that reason etc.* [ideo non coepit in tempore tanquam coexistente. Item tempus non fuit ante sui initium, ideo non coepit in tempore tanquam in continente, ideo etiam quae etc.]

is exceeded[1] by a time [a tempore], is measured and begins in a time [in tempore], but that which is not exceeded, begins with time [cum tempore]; and the reason is the aforesaid one.[2]

DOUBT III

Likewise, is asked of this which (St. Augustine) says, that *a coin is not changed, when it begins to be the price* (of something). For (this) seems false, because 'to be the price (of something)' is an accident of the coin, and now it is in it, and before it was not in it, therefore, the coin has been changed.

I RESPOND: It must be said, that a *relation* does not predicate something absolute, but predicates an order to the other; but an *order* looks back to the disposition of the ones ordered. Therefore, certain (things) are able to be put in order [ordinabilia], such that each (extreme) is in *potency*; and then the relation is introduced through a change made in each. Certain (things) are able to be put in order, such that one (of the two extremes), as much as it is of itself, is in *act*, but the other in *potency*; just as is clear concerning the two, one of which, which is actually white, has the property in act, according to which a similitude is attained, and for that reason, with the other (of the two) made white from not-white, a perfect similitude is made. — Therefore, it is not necessary [non opportet], that a relation always induce a change in *each* of the extremes on account of its corruption and/or inception;[3] but it is sufficient, that (it does) in one (of the two). And the reason has been seen, because it looks back to a double extreme; and because one can be of itself in *act*, with the other existing in *potency*: just as in a coin, which is in the power of the one possessing (it), to be the pledge and/or price and/or pledge-money [arrha] according to the change made in it; nor does something absolute come upon the coin, but (rather) an order, which on the part of coin was in *act*, on the part of that (use), which was in *potency*, comes to be in act; and for that reason that (use) is changed, without the coin having been changed.

DOUBT IV

Likewise, is asked of this which (Master Peter) says, that *it is an accident in the creature, when the relation is of the creature to the Creator*. For it seems false, because it does happen that a thing is understood, with (its) accident removed: therefore, if a relation to the Creator accedes to a creature, therefore, with that (accident)[4] removed, it happens that the created thing is understood *to be*, even with the looking-back to the Creator excluded. — Likewise, if the *relation*, by which the creature is referred to the Creator, is an accident, since it is *created*, it is referred, and thus through (another) accident: and in this manner of the other (accident), and thus there is[5] an infinite regression [abire in infinitum].

I RESPOND: It must be said, that a creature, as much as regards (its) *first act of being* [esse primum] is essentially dependent, and such a relation, which expresses that dependence, is not accidental to the creature, but ration *essential*. But, as much as regards *the second act of being* [esse secundum] or (its) well-being [bene esse], it is not dependent essentially, because that *well-being* is accidental; for that reason such a relation is said according to *accident*, as filiation (is), according to which it means an adoption; and (St.) Augustine understands (it) of such.

To that which is objected, that a relation is referred by another relation; some want to say, that a creature is referred by itself. — Yet it seems that this must not be said, because no creature is its own relation, since it is not most highly simple, nay by this very (thing), that it is referred, it bears off (its) simplicity.[6] — For that reason it must be said, that (names), which mean a substrate thing with (its) looking-back, are referred properly as relatives, but the relations themselves or the looking-back are not referred, nay rather those are referred by others, because they are not beings, but of beings:[7] so it must be said in the proposed, that the relations themselves are not referred through themselves, but with (their) subjects, so that the one with the other and through the other (is referred). For that reason there is no seeking of another beyond (that), by which they are referred.

DOUBT V

Likewise is asked of this which (Master Peter) says: *And yet we do not say, that the Holy Spirit is referred to Himself*. For it seems that He can be referred (to Himself),[8] because the Holy Spirit is a *gift*, and a *gift* is referred to the one granting; and He Himself is *the One granting*: therefore, it is necessarily concluded, that He is referred to Himself.

I RESPOND: It must be said, that this name "*spirit*" means a relation according to '*being*'; and for that reason, because by a relation according to '*being*' nothing is referred to itself according to the same (manner), in no manner is the Holy Spirit, inasmuch as (He is) a *spirit*, referred to Himself. But "*gift*" does not only convey a relation according to '*being*', as for example, when it means the authorship in the one giving, but also according to a *manner of being said* [modum dicendi], as when it means the largess and power in the one communicating;[9] and because in such a manner He can be compared according to a manner of understanding to Himself, as a *given*, inasmuch (He is) a *given*, it is said in regard to Himself, (but) inasmuch as (He is) the *One giving*, (it is) not. For that reason (Master Peter)[10] concedes, that the appellation of "*given*" and/or "*granted*" is referred to the Holy Spirit, but not "*holy spirit*".

---

[1] For *is exceeded* [exceditur] many codices read hear *is delayed by time* [extollitur a tempore] and, a little after this, *is not delayed* [non extollitur], codd. L and O, with ed. 1, have *is excelled* [excellitur]. Next, the Vatican edition alone reads corruptly thus: *begins from time; but that is not exceeded which* [incipit a tempore; sed illud non exceditur quod].

[2] Cf. Alexander of Hales, SUMMA., p. I, q. 53, m. 2. — Bl. (now St.) Albertus, here in a. 4 and 7. — St. Thomas, here about the text.

[3] Thus the greater part of the codices with edition 1, the Vatican edition has *defection* [defectionem]; codex L has *ceasing* [desitionem].

[4] Understand: *accident* [accidente]; and/or read: *with that removed, namely, the relation* [illa remota, scil. relatione].

[5] Codex W has *there will be* [erit].

[6] Cf. above d. 8, p. II, a. sole, q. 2, p. 169, footnote 4.

[7] Aristotle, METAPHYSICS, Bk. VII, text 2 (Bk. IV, ch. 1). says of accidents generally, that the are only « said (to be) beings, for this (reason), that they are truly something of a being [quid entis] » (i.e. of a substance), or, as is commonly said, that accidents

[accidentia] are not *beings* [entia], but *something of a being* [quid entis]. Moreover, among accidents, just as has been said above in d. 26, q. 2, a relation « has the least of entity », the unique duty of which is, to refer those, to which it accedes, to each other.

[8] Supply together with the Vatican edition: *to Himself* [ad se]. — At the end of the objection very many codices, together with edition 1 have *is referred* [referatur] in the subjunctive.

[9] For *communicating* [communicante] the Vatican edition together with codex cc has *granting* [donate].

[10] Understand: *Master (Peter)* [Magistri]. — Codex dd together with edition 1 has *it is conceded* [conceditur]. At the end of the solution, after "*holy spirit*" [autem], codices N W X Z aa and bb add *itself* [ipse]. — The principles upon which this solution is founded, are found, explained more at length, above in d. 10, a. 2, q. 3 in the body (of the Question), and in (Master Peter's text), Distinction XV, ch. 1, and also in (St. Bonaventure's Commentary), d. 18, q. 4, in the body (of the Question).

DISTINCTION XXXI

PART I

CHAPTER I

Whether the Son is said (to be) "equal" and/or "similar" to the Father according to substance.

Moreover, one must consider, since the Three Persons are coequal to Themselves, whether this is said relatively, or according to substance; and if relatively, whether the equality is to be considered according to relation, or according to essence; then, what is the equality itself. — To which we say, that, just as nothing is *"similar"* to itself, « for a similitude », as (St.) Hilary says,[1] « is not to itself »; thus also something is not said (to be) *"equal"* to itself, and through this, just as *"similar"*, so is *"equal"* also said relatively. Therefore, the Son is said relatively (to be) "equal" to the Father and the Holy Spirit ("equal") to Each. — The Son, however, is equal to the Father and the Holy Spirit to Each on account of the most high Simplicity of the Essence and (its) Unity. The Son, therefore, is equal to the Father according to substance, not according to relation. Whence (St.) Augustine in the fifth book, ON THE TRINITY says:[2] « We ask, "according to what is the Son equal to the Father?" Not according to this, that the Son is said (to be such) *regarding the Father*, is He equal to the Father; it remains, therefore, that He is equal according to That, which He is said (to be such) *regarding Himself*. Moreover, whatever is said *regarding itself*, is equal according to substance. There is, therefore, the same Substance of Each ».

Likewise, in the sixth book (he says):[3] « It is sufficient to see, that in no manner is the Son equal to the Father, if in anything, that is, which pertains to signifying His Substance, He is found (to be) unequal. In all (things), therefore, the Son is equal to the Father and is of the same Substance ». From these (words) it becomes perspicuous, that the Son according to substance is equal to the Father and the Holy Spirit to Each, and the appellation (of equality) alone is relative. — Therefore, the equality of the Father and the Son is not a relation and/or a notion, but an indisparity on account of a unity of nature.[4]

We also say the same thing [hoc] concerning *"similar"* and *"similitude"*. For when the Son is said (to be) "similar" to the Father, He is indeed said (to be such) relatively, but He is similar to the Father on account of a unity of essence. Therefore, the appellation is only a relative one, but the similitude is (Their) « undiffering Essence ».[5] Whence in a not unlearned manner it seems to certain ones, that by the name of *"equal"* and/or *"similitude"* something is not posited, but is removed, so that according to this reckoning the Son is said (to be) *"equal"* to the Father, because He is neither greater nor lesser than He, and this on account of a unity of essence. Thus, too, He is said (to be) *"similar"*, because (He is) neither diverse nor from another [alienus] nor dissimilar in anything, and this on account of a simplicity of essence. Therefore, not according to which the Son is begotten from the Father, is He equal and/or unequal to the Father, nor similar and/or dissimilar, but (He is) equal and similar according to substance.

PART II

CHAPTER II

On the sentence of Saint Hilary, by which he shows (the names) proper to the Persons in the Trinity.

Here, it must not be overlooked, that the illustrious man, (St.) Hilary, assigning the properties of the Persons, says,[6]

that *eternity* is in the Father, *sightliness* [speciem] in the Image, *use* in the Gift [Munere]. Of such great difficulty are (these) words (of his), that (St.) Augustine labored vehemently in their understanding and explanation, as he himself shows in the sixth book, ON THE TRINITY,[7] thus says: « A certain (author), since he wanted to insinuate in the briefest manner the (names) proper to Each of the Persons in the Trinity, said that eternity is in the Father, sightliness in the Image,

---

[1] ON THE TRINITY, Bk. III, n. 23.

[2] Chapter 6, n. 7. — A little above this the Vatican edition and editions 4 and 6, together with codex D, have *according to essence* [secundum essentiam] for *according to substance* [secundum substantiam].

[3] Chapter 4, n. 6. The following text is ibid., ch. 6. n. 7.

[4] On the authority of all the codices and edition 1 (edition 5 in the margin), we have put *an indisparity on account of a unity of nature* [propter naturae unitatem indisparitas] for *a natural unity and identity* [naturalis unitas et identitas], which St. Bonaventure follows, here in a. 1, q. 2, 1st. opposed argument; cf. the following footnote.

[5] This definition has been taken from (St.) Hilary, ON SYNODS, n. 73: « A natural similitude co-equates things themselves through the similitude of a not-undiffering essence » (cf. ibid. nn. 13-19). On this passage refer to what Alexander of Hales (SUMMA., p. I, q. 55, m. 1, a. 1) says of (Peter) Lombard: « Certain (authors) say, that these names *"equal"* (and) *"similar"* are only accepted in a removed manner, just as when there is said: "the Father and the Son are *equal"*, that is, "They are not unequal"; and "They are *sim-*

ilar", that is, "They are not dissimilar". In which sentence Lombard seems to have been. *For in the first edition of the Sentences he said:* "The similitude is (Their) undiffering Substance"; *and in the second, as if correcting (himself) he said:* "The similitude is (Their) indifference", as if to say: "The Father and the Son are said (to be) similar, because They are not different ». — From this testimony of Alexander (of Hales), it is evinced, that Peter Lombard in the second edition of the Sentences changed some (things). From this it is also explained, where those *Brief Notes* [notula] have arisen, which have been added to the text now and then, as the three *Brief Notes* adjoined to this Distinction; we have noted another already, above, in Distinction VI.

[6] ON THE TRINITY, Bk. II, n. 1, at the end.

[7] Chapter 10, n. 11. I this text there is found no small difference with the original, namely in the words (near the end of the passage on the following page): *but (they are) the same, that is, one thing* [sed idem, hoc est unum] for which in the original there is read: *but that which is the 'to understand', this is the 'to live', this (is) the 'to be', all (are) one: as* [sed id quod est intelligere hoc vivere, hoc esse est, unum omnia: tanquam].

Image, use in the Gift. And because he stood forth (as) a man of no mediocre authority in the treatment of the Scriptures and the assertion of the Faith — for (St.) Hilary posited this in his books — having scrutinized [scrutatus] the concealed understanding of these words, that is, of "*the Father*", and "*Image*" and "*Gift*", "*eternity*", "*sightliness*" and "*one*", as much as I am able, I judge that (I have) not followed him in the word for *eternity*, except that the Father does not have a father, of which He is; but the Son is of [de] the Father, so that He is and is coeternal to Him. For an image, if it perfectly fulfills that of which it is the image, is itself co-equated to it, not it to its own image; in which image he names a "*sightliness*" [speciem], I believe, on account of the beauty, where there is so great a *congruence* and a first equality and a first similitude, dissident in no thing and in no manner unequal and dissimilar on no side [nulla ex parte], but responding to the identity of Him whose image He is; where there is a first and most high *Life*, for which 'to live' is not one (thing) '*to be*' another, but (they are) the same; and a first and most high *Intellect*, for which '*to live*' is not one (thing) '*to understand*' another, but (they are) the same, that is one [unum], just as a perfect word, to which nothing is lacking, and a certain Art of the Omnipotent and Wise God, full of all, living, incommutable reasons, and all (are) one [unum] in that (Art), just as that (Art is) the One from the One, with whom (there is) the One; therefore God knows all (things), which He made through It ».

A Brief Note: (St.) Hilary in (his) book, ON SYNODS (says):[1] « The image of that, according to which it is imaged, is an undiffering appearance [species]. For neither is anyone himself his own image; but it is necessary, that that of which the image is, the image demonstrate. Therefore, an image is an imaged [imaginata] and indiscrete similitude of a thing for co-equating the thing. Therefore, it is the Father, (and) it is also the Son, because the Image of the Father is the Son; and because an image is, to be the image of a thing, it is necessary (that) the Appearance have in itself both the nature and essence of the Author, according to which It is an image ».

« Moreover, there is a certain ineffable embrace [complexus] of the Father and the Image, which is not without a thorough enjoyment [perfruitione], (not) without charity, (not) without joy. Therefore, that love [dilectio], delectation, felicity and/or beatitude — if, yet, by any human voice it is worthily spoken of — has been briefly named "*use*" by him, and is in the Trinity the Holy Spirit, not begotten, but (rather) a sweetness [suavitas] of the Begetter and Begotten, pouring over all creatures to capture them [pro captu earum] by (His) vast largess and fruitfulness [ubertate]. And so those Three both seem to be determined by one Another, and are in Themselves infinite. He who sees this either *in part* and/or *through a mirror and in an enigma*,[2] rejoices as one knowing [cognoscens] God, and gives thanks. But the one who does not see (this), tends through piety to see (it), not through blindness to calumniate (it), since God is one, but yet a Trinity ».[3] — Behold, you have, in what manner the aforesaid words of (St.) Hilary are to be accepted, though they be of such a great profundity, that even with the employed exposition, human sense hardly prevails a little to understand them, since even the explanation itself of them, which (St.) Augustine here gives forth, has in itself a very great (share) of difficulty and ambiguity.

For not according to the aforementioned exposition are there distinguished, here, those three *properties* assigned above,[4] but the *Hypostases* Themselves are shown (to be) distinct from one Another. However, by the name of "*eternity*" there seems to be designated the same *property*, which this name "*unbegotten*" notes. — But let us see, what is that which he says: « For an *image*, if it perfectly fulfills that of which it is the image, is itself co-equated to it, not it to its own image ». For he seems to say, that the Son, who is the Image of the Father, is co-equated to the Father, not the Father to the Son, though the Son is also said (to be) equal to the Father in Scripture, and the Father to the Son; but the Son has this from the Father, to be equal to Him, but the Father does not have (this) from the Son, and yet the Son is fully and perfectly equal to the Father, that is, is an image of Him of whom He is the Image.

Therefore, in the aforesaid words (St.) Hilary is said to have assigned (names) proper to *the Persons*, because he posited the relative names of the Persons, namely, "father",[5] "image" and "gift", which are said relatively of the Persons and note the properties, by which the Persons are distinguished. — For thus the Holy Spirit is said relatively (to be) a "*gift*" [munus], just as a "*gift*" [donum]. Nevertheless, he did not signify those *properties* by three other names, according to the aforesaid exposition of (St.) Augustine, except by the sole name of "*eternity*", by which he wanted not that the paternity itself be understood, but that notion, by which He is said (to be) "*unbegotten*".

It must also be known [sciri oportet] , that (St.) Augustine wanting to show the distinction of the same Three *Persons* without the expression of those three *properties* commemorated above, thus says in the first book, ON CHRISTIAN DOCTRINE:[6] « In the Father there is *unity*, in the Son *equality*, in the Holy Spirit the *concord* of unity and equality: and these three (names are) all *one*, on account of the Father, all *equal* on account of the Son, all *connected* on account of the Holy Spirit. And thus the Father and the Son and the Holy Spirit and any single One of These is God, and together All (are) the one God, and any single One of These is the full Substance, and All together (are) the one Substance. The Father is neither the Son nor the Holy Spirit; the Son is neither the Father nor the Holy Spirit; the Holy Spirit is neither the Father nor the Son, but the Father (is) only a father, the Son only a son, and the Holy Spirit only a holy spirit. Of the Three [tribus] (there is) the same eternity, the same incommutability, the same Majesty, the same Power ». — In this words he openly insinuates the distinction of the Three Persons.

CHAPTER III

For what reason is "unity" attributed to the Father.

But it disturbs [movet] very many, that he attributes to the Father a *unity*, to the Son an *equality*. For since "*unity*" is said according to substance, it is not only in the Father, but also in the Son and in the Holy Spirit; and there is one "*equality*"

---

[1] Proposition 1, n. 13. This and the two following *Brief Notes* [Notula] are lacking in not a few editions, such as. edition 8; in some, such as the Vatican and edition 7, they are exhibited in the margin, in others, such as edition 9, they are inserted into the text itself. Even in our codices they are not put in the same place. The more ancient Commentators on Lombard often make mention of them. They seem to originate with the second edition of Lombard's work, of which we have spoken above on p. 529, in footnote 5.

[2] 1 Cor. 13 :12. The Vulgate and even very many editions, together with the Vatican edition, omit in this text *and* [et], contrary to the codices and original.

[3] (St.) Augustine, ON THE TRINITY, Bk. VI, ch. 10, nn. 11 and 12; in which text the edition of (St.) Augustine's (works) has *according to one Another* [ad se invicem] for *by one Another* [a se invicem], which the ancient editions have. For *through piety* [per pietatem] the Vatican edition and editions 4, 5, 6, 7, 8 and 9 read *through the piety of the faith* [per pietatem fidei], breaking with the codices and the original.

[4] Distinction XXVI.

[5] The Vatican edition omits "*father*" [patris], and a little after this it faultily puts *notes* [notat] for *note* [notant].

[6] Chapter 5, n. 5, with not a few (words) omitted and/or added.

of the Father and of the Son and of the Holy Spirit. Therefore, why is "*unity*" attributed to the Father and "*equality*" to the Son? Perhaps "*unity*" is attributed to the Father according to (St.) Augustine for the same reason, for which "*eternity*" (is attributed), above, to the Same according to (St.) Hilary: because, namely, the Father is such, that He is not from Another, and because He begot the Son, (to be) the one God with Himself , and (because) the Holy Spirit proceeds from Him (to be) the one God with Him. Therefore, a "*unity*" is said to be in the Father, because neither is there anything other, than which He is — for He is not from Another — nor is there anything or anyone from Him from eternity, which is not one (thing) [unum] with Him; for the Son and the Holy Spirit are one (thing) with the Father. Whence the Truth says: *I and the Father are one* [unum].[1]

A Brief Note. (St.) Hilary in the book, ON SYNODS (says):[2] « If anyone says that the Son (is) innascible without a beginning [sine initio], as if saying that two without a beginning [sine principio] and two innascibles and two unborns makes two gods: anathema sit. For the Head, which is the beginning of all (things), (is) the Son; but the Head, which is the beginning of Christ, (is) God. For thus do we refer all (things) through the Son to the one uninitiable Beginning of all [ininitiabile omnium initium]. To confess the Son innascible, is most impious. For now there will not be one God, because that one God be preached, requires [exigit] the Nature of one innascible God. Therefore, since there is one God, there cannot be two Innascibles; since there is one God for this reason [idcirco] — since the Father is God, and the Son of God is God — because innascibility alone is from within the One [penes unum]. Moreover, the Son (is) God for this reason, because He exists (as) One born from the innascible Essence. Therefore, the Holy Faith rejects that there be preached an innascible Son, so that it may preach through the one innascible God the One God, to embrace the only-begotten Nature, begotten out of the innascible Essence, in the one Name of the Innascible God. For the Head of all (things) is the Son, but the Head of the Son is God, and to the One God all (things) are referred by this step and this confession, since from Him each and every (thing) takes (its) beginning [principium], the beginning of which He Himself is ». The same (says) in the same (book): « To all creatures the Will of God brings to bear the Substance, but a perfect nativity gave to the Son the Nature out of the innascible and not born Substance. For such are all created (things), as God has willed (them) to be. But the Son, born out of God, subsists (as) such, as God is, nor has He brought forth a nature dissimilar to Himself according to nature; but out of the substance of God the begetting of the Nature has brought to bear the Essence, according to origin, it (has) not (brought to bear) the Essence according to a creature of the Will ».

CHAPTER IV

For what reason are the Father and the Son said to be unum and/or unus Deus, but not unus.

Here, it must be said [dici oportet], that the Father and the Son and the Holy Spirit are rightly said to be "*one*" [unum] and "*one God*" [unus Deus], but not "*one*" [unus]. For two and/or more things can rightly be said to be "*one*" [unum], if they are of one essence, and theirs is one nature. But "*one*" [unus vel una] cannot be said of diverse things, unless there be added, *what one* (is) [quid unus vel una]; with

which added, it can rightly be said of things both of one and diverse substance. Whence (St.) Augustine in the sixth book, ON THE TRINITY, in the third chapter,[3] says thus: « I know not, whether there be found in the scriptures the saying, *they are one* [unum], of those which are diverse in nature. But if there are both any more *of the same nature*, and *they think diverse (thoughts)*, they are not one [unum], inasmuch as they think diverse (thoughts). When, therefore, if there is said "*one*" [unum], not to add, *what unum* (is), and many are said (to be) one [unum]; there is signified (that they are) the same (thing) by nature and essence, not dissident nor dissenting ». « Whence (St.) Paul and Apollo, who were both men and used to think the same, are said to be "*one*" [unum], when there is said: *He who plants and he who waters are one* [unum].[4] However, when there is added, *what unum* (is), something can be signified (to have been) made one out of many, though diverse in nature: just as the soul and body cannot certainly [utique] be said (to be) 'one' — for what is so diverse (as they)? — unless there be added and/or understood [subintelligatur], *what unum* (is), that is, "one man". Whence the Apostle (says): *He who adheres*, he says, *to the Lord, is one spirit (with Him).* He did not say: "*is one*" [unus est], and/or "*are one*" [unum sunt], but added "*spirit*". For diverse in nature are the spirit *of a man* and the spirit *of God*, but by inhering the spirit of the man becomes one spirit with God », because it comes to be a sharer [particeps] of His truth and beatitude. If, therefore, of those which are of a diverse substance, there is rightly said, that they are "*one spirit*", how much more those, who are of one Substance, rightly said to be the "*one God*"? « Therefore, the Father and the Son are 'one', at any rate, according to the Unity of the Substance, and (are) the one God ». In which there is also damned the *Arian* heresy, which does not want that the Father and the Son and the Holy Spirit, as (St.) Augustine says in (his) book, ON HERESIES,[5] be of one and the same Substance and Nature and/or, to speak more expressly, Essence, which in Greek is said "*ousia*", but that the Son be a creature. And also the *Sabellian*, which, as (St.) Augustine says in the same book, used to say, that the same Christ Himself is both the Father and the Holy Spirit, so that there is a trinity of *names* without the subsistence of *persons*. « Each pest », as (St.) Augustine says ON THE GOSPEL OF ST. JOHN,[6] « the Truth destroys, saying: *I and the Father are one* [unum]. Hear each (word) and turn away (from each error), both "*one*" [unum] and "*we are*" [sumus], and you shall be freed from Charybdis and Scylla. For that He said "*one*" [unum], he frees you from Arian; that He said "*we are*", He frees you from Sabellius. If '*one*': therefore not diverse; if "*we are*": therefore, the Father and the Son. For "*we are*" would not be said of one, nor "*one*" [unum] of (something) diverse. Therefore, let the Sabellian blush, who say, that the very Father is, He who is the Son, confounding the Persons, who have also been called the Patripassians, who[7] say, that the Father has suffered. However, the Arians say, that the Father is one (thing), the Son another, not one substance, but two; that the Father (is) greater, the Son lesser. Do not say this, you (who are) Catholic! Sail in the midst, therefore, avoid each dangerous side and say: "the Father is a father, and the Son a son: *one* [alius] (is) the Father, *another* the Son, but not *another* (thing) [aliud], nay the very (same), because (They are) the one God ». — Behold, it has been shown, for what reason unity is said to be in the Father, when those Three are 'one'.

---

[1] John. 10:30.

[2] Proposition 26, nn. 59 and 60, and the following text is proposition 24, n. 58. In the original there is read *from the impassible Essence* [ex impassibili essentia] for *from the innascible Essence* [ex innascibili essentia].

[3] Number 4, but with very many (words) interpolated and changed by Master (Peter).

[4] 1 Cor. 3:8. The following passage is ibid., 6:17. — Near the

end of this text of (St.) Augustine, the Vatican edition together with very many editions has *the Unity of the Essence* [unitatem essentiae] for *the Unity of the Substance* [unitatem substantiae].

[5] Article 49; the following passage is articles 36 and 41.

[6] Tract 36, n. 9.

[7] Editions 1, 2, 3, 4, 5, 6, 8 and 9 read *because they* [quia] in place of *who* [qui].

A Brief Note. (St.) Hilary in (his) book, On Synods (says):[1] « Perhaps it seems that the Faith has spoken less expressly of the undiffering similitude of the Father and the Son, since of the Father and the Son and the Holy Spirit it thought that Their own [propiam] Substance and order and glory (were) so signified in the names of each One named, that They indeed are Three through substance, but One [unum] through consonance. Therefore, the gathered Synod of the Saints, wanting to thoroughly crush that impiety, which mocked [eluderet] the Unity of the Father and of the Son and of the Holy Spirit with a number of names, so that, not by the subsisting cause of each name, a threefold naming [nuncupatio] would obtain a union under the falsity of names, and the Father Himself would have the one and only same Name of both the Holy Spirit and the Son. For that reason (the Saints) said that there are three *substances*, thoroughly teaching through *"substances" persons of subsistences*, not separating the Substance of the Father and the Son by a diversity of a dissimilar Essence. Moreover, what has been said, that They are indeed *"Three through substance, but One through consonance"*, is not worthy of calumny [non habet calumniam]; because by the surname of the Spirit [connominato Spiritu], that is, "the Advocate" [Paracleto], it is fitting that a unity of *consonance* rather than of *essence* be predicated through a similitude of substance ». Likewise, in the same (book he says): « When we confess God (to be) the Father, we also preach Christ (to be) the Son of God, and between these let the confession of two gods be irreligious; They cannot according to an indifference of nature and an undiffering Name be one in the genus of essence, for Whose Essence is not licit that there be but one Name ». « For the religious unity of the Name, constituted out of the essence of an undiffering Nature, does not take away the Person of the begotten Essence, so that the unique and singular Substance of God is understood through the union of the Name, since the one Name of each Essence, that is, "the one God", is preached on account of the indissimilar substance of the Nature in Each ».

Chapter V

Why there is said to be an equality in the Son.

Now, let us see, for what reason is *"equality"* said to be in the Son, since there is a one and most high equality of the Three. This has, perhaps, been said, for this reason, because the Son has been begotten by the Father (to be) equal to the One Begetting and to the Gift, which proceeds from Each, and for that reason those Three are said to be equal on account of the Son. For the Son has from [a] the Father, that He is equal to Him and to the Holy Spirit; and the Holy Spirit has from Each, that He is equal to Each. But we say this without the arrogance [supercilio] of an assertion and prejudice against a greater understanding, preferring in the explanation [apertione] of such reserved discourses [clausarum sermonum] to hear those more expert that to pass on [influere] anything to others.

Chapter VI

Why in the Holy Spirit there is said to be virtue, concord and/or a connection.

Moreover, that in the Holy Spirit there is said to be the *"concord"* of Each and that through Him *all (things have been) connected*, the understanding is easier for us, who recall [revocantibus] the aforesaid to mind. For above,[2] according to the authorities of the Saints, it has been said, that the Holy Spirit is the *"love"* [amor], by which the Father loves [diligit] the Son, and the Son the Father. Therefore, rightly is the Holy Spirit said (to be) the *"connection"* [connexio] and/or *"concord"* of the Father and the Son, and that through Him *all (things have been) connected*. Whence (St.) Augustine in the sixth book, On the Trinity (says):[3] « The Holy Spirit is a certain consubstantial communion of both the Father and the Son ». Likewise, in the seventh book, On the Trinity (he says): « The Holy Spirit is most high Charity, joining Each together, and joining us from below ».

COMMENTARY ON DISTINCTION XXXI

On the relative (names), which are said of God commonly and eternally.

Part I

On the signification of these names

Moreover, one must consider, since the Three Persons are coequal to Themselves etc..

THE DIVISION OF THE TEXT

In the previous, preceding subpart, Master (Peter) dealt with the relative (names), which are said of God *properly* and *temporally*. In this part, he deals with those, which are said of God *commonly* and *eternally*. And, since these can be appropriated [sunt appropriabilia], for that reason this part has two parts.

In the *first*, he determines their *signification*; in the *second*, their *appropriation*, there (where he says): *Here it must not be overlooked* etc.. The *first* part has two (parts). In the first, he determines the signification of this name, *"equal"* [aequalis]; in the second, of this name, *"similar"* [similis], and this he does in the second chapter:° *We also say the same thing concerning "similar" and "similitude"* etc..

---

[1] This *Brief Note* [Notula] has been composed from three passages from this book, namely, nn. 31 and 32, n. 41, and n. 42. Near the end of the *Brief Note*, the edition of (St.) Hilary's (works) has *the Substance of the unique and singular God* [unici ac singularis Dei substantia] for *the unique and singular Substance of God* [unica ac singularis Dei substantia].*

[2] Distinction X.

[3] Chapter 5, n. 7: Therefore, the Holy Spirit is something common to the Father and to the Son, whatever that is. But the communion itself (is) consubstantial and coeternal. And in Bk. V, ch. 11, n. 12 (St. Augustine says): Therefore, the Holy Spirit is a certain ineffable communion of the Father and the Son. — The following passage is ibid., Bk. VII, ch. 3, n. 6.

---

* *Trans. notes*: Cf. here St. Bonaventure's Commentary, Doubt 8 throughout, on this passage of St. Hilary.

° By *second chapter* [secundo capitulo], St. Bonaventure intends the second paragraph of the first chapter of Master Peter's Distinction.

TREATMENT OF THE QUESTIONS

For an understanding of this part there is the question concerning these names "*similar*" and "*equal*", and about this three (questions) are asked.

First, there is asked, whether these names are said according to a positing, or according to a privation.

Second, there is asked, whether they are said according to substance [secundum substantiam], or according to relation [secundum relationem].

Third, there is asked, whether they mean a mutual relation [mutuam relationem] in the Father and in the Son.

ARTICLE SOLE

On the names, "similar" *and* "equal".

QUESTION I

Whether equality and similitude are said of God positively and/or privatively?

And that they are said according to a privation [secundum privationem], seems:

1. Through the authority of Master (Peter) in the text:[1] « It seems to certain ones, that by the name of "*equality*". [aequalitatis] and "*similitude*" [similitudinis] something is not posited, but is removed, so that the Son is said (to be) "equal" to the Father, because He is neither greater nor lesser than He ».

2. Likewise, it can be proven in this manner: Euclid[2] defines the *equal* thus: « The equal is what does not exceed the substitute for the other [alteri suppositum], nor is exceeded (by it) »: therefore, since this definition has been given according to a privation, it is clear that etc..

3. Likewise, "*equal*" and "*similar*" do not only mean a unity, but also a diversity;[3] but there is not positing of a diversity among the divine: therefore these names are not said according to a positing, but according to a privation.

4. Likewise, "*equal*", according to which it means the positing (of something), means a commensuration;[4] but among the divine there is no commensuration nor excess: therefore they are said through the privation of excess, not through a positing (of it).

On the Contrary: 1. "*Similitude*" and "*equality*" among these inferiors are said positively; but these are more completely in God, because, as (St.) Augustine[5] says, in the Son there is found first a reckoning of similitude and equality: therefore, much more strongly do they mean in God a positing (of the same).

2. Likewise, every negation, which is not a *pure* negation, is founded upon the positing (of something): therefore, since that which I say (is) "*equal*", conveys the removal of an excess and does not convey a *pure negation* — because then the equal of God would be a chimera — it is necessary [oportet], that it convey a positing (of something).

3. Likewise, this is false: 'the Father and the Son are unequal': therefore, that which is "*unequal*" [inaequale] deprives something which is in God; but this is not but (what is) conveyed through equality: therefore, "*equality*" posits something, because if its opposite deprives, it is necessary that it posit (the same).

4. Likewise, the heretics say that this[6] (is) false: 'the Father is equal to the Son', therefore, either because something *is posited*, or because something *is removed*. Not because *it is removed*, because they say that this (is) true: 'the Father is unequal (to the Son)', which *removes* (something): therefore, because something *is posited*, ergo etc.. — And each of those reckonings[7] is founded upon the opposition of "*unequal*" to "*equal*". For if "*equal*" and "*unequal*" were accepted in a manner (that) removes (something), then, for this (reason), that (they) are opposites, they would be accepted positively.

---

[1] Chapter 1. — For *and* "*similitude*" [et similitudinis] codex W, together with the text of Master (Peter), has *and/or* "*similitude*" [vel similitudinis].

[2] THE ELEMENTS, Bk. I, § On the conceptions of the soul: If any thing is substituted for another and applied to it and the one does not exceed the other, they will be equal to one another (Venetian edition of 1509). — In the text itself, in place of *the substitute for* [suppositum] codices A F G K P Q W X Y, together with edition 1, have *the one superimposed upon* [superpositum].

[3] That is, diverse things, among which there is an equality and similitude. Under this respect (St.) Hilary, ON THE TRINITY, Bk. III, n. 23 says: There is not similitude to itself.

[4] For "*equal*" accepted thus means a real relation, founded in the unity of a determined quantity. Cf. Aristotle, METAPHYSICS, Bk. V, text 20 (Bk. IV, ch. 15).*

[5] ON THE TRINITY, Bk. VI, ch. 10, n. 11: Where (i.e. in the Son) there is already such a great congruence and first equality and first similitude, dissident in no thing and in no manner unequal and dissimilar on no side, but responding again and again [ad identidem] to Him of whom He is the Image.

[6] Codex V here and a little below this after *this* [hanc] inserts *is* [esse], and below this after *unequal* [inaequalis] it adds *to the Son* [Filio].

[7] From the older codices and edition 1, we have restored *reckonings* [rationum], in place of which word the Vatican edition, together with codex cc, has *positings* [positionum]; a false reading, because this respects the two last arguments. A little below this in place of the *for this (reason) that (they) are* [eo quod], which reading is proven from very many manuscripts and edition 1, the Vatican edition has *their* [eorum]; even codex W has *their* [eorum], but less badly, since a little before this it exhibits *similar* [simile] for *unequal* [inaequale].

---

* *Trans. note*: A "commensuration" [commensuratio] in Latin and English is the comparison of measure made among two measurables. What is, thus, commensurate to another, has the same or similar measure as it.

CONCLUSION

*"Equality" and "similitude" are not said of God
privately, but positively.*

I RESPOND: It must be said, that according to what is favored [innuitur] in the text (of Master Peter) and (as) the ancient doctors say, the position of Master (Peter) was, that the names, which do not mean a personal property and/or the Unity of the Essence,[1] are accepted *privatively*. On which account, because "*similar*" and "*equal*" mean the looking-back of the Father to the Son, and that looking-back is not a personal property nor the Essence; he wanted to posit, that all such, such as "*two*", "*three*", "*similar*" and "*equal*", are said according to a privation, and (are said) just as has been proven above[2] concerning the unity and plurality of the Divine Names. For, if among the divine there is positively a unity and plurality, and these two cause a similitude and an equality, it is necessary, that these be accepted positively among the divine. And the reasons brought forward for this are to be conceded.

2. To that, therefore, which is objected, that the equal is what does not exceed; it must be said, that underlying[3] that negation is an affirmation and positing, which is make known through the privation of (its) opposite, namely, an excess.

3. To that which is objected, that there is no diversity among the divine; it must be said, that (these names) of themselves indicate a diversity of naught but of a *Supposit*,[4] not *of form*; and because among the divine there is a plurality of Supposits, it is clear that etc..

4. To that which is objected, that according to which they are said positively, they mean a *commensuration*; it must be said, that among the divine there is not, simply (speaking), a commensuration,[5] but yet there is a commensuration in respect of the infinite, and this does not posit a commensuration simply.

In another manner it can be said, that "*equal*" and "*similar*" from their first understanding posit a unity of quantity and of quality; moreover, that which is "*equal*" is what posits the commensuration, because that quantity is a *measured one*. Therefore, since among the divine (quantity)[6] is *immense*, it means There a convening in the quantity of virtue, though it does not posit There a commensuration.

SCHOLIUM

I. St. Bonaventure, who has already treated of *equality* among the divine in d. 19, p. I, q. 1 and 2, here, following Master (Peter), returns to discuss the same matter, under another reckoning, because of what is said below in Doubt 1. — In regard to the reckoning of a *similitude*, it must be noted, that not a few Fathers (of the Church) did not want to admit it in God, out of fear, that the Arians had substituted ὁμοούσιον ("similar in substance") for the Church's term ὁμοιούσιον ("consubstantial"). But with the end of the danger of error, this expression is commonly received (cf. St. Thomas., SUMMA., I, q. 42, a. 1, in reply to nn. 2 and 3).

Not withstanding, that in God, in whom there is the *same* Nature, the reckoning of *equal* and/or *similar* seems to be excluded. For these three relations are distinguished, as Aristotle has already observed (cf. above in d. 19, p. I, a. sole, q. 1, p. 342, footnote 6), and, indeed, in this manner, so that *the same* is founded upon a unity of *substance*,

the *similar* upon a *quality*, but the *equal* upon a *quantity*. Whence, they can aptly be transferred to the divine. And (Bl. John Duns) Scotus rightly observes (here in q. 1, n. 6), with St. Thomas consenting (loc. cit.), that *equality* among the divine also includes in itself a *similitude* and adds something, namely, that it excludes an excess. — In regard to the obsolete opinion of Master (Peter) on this matter and in regard to the reckoning of unity and plurality, cf. above d. 24, a. 1, q. 1, and a. 2, q. 1.

II. Alexander of Hales, on this and the following q., SUMMA., p. I, q. 54, m. 1, a. 1. — (Bl. John Duns) Scotus, here in the q. sole; REPORTATIO., here in q. 2. — St. Thomas, here in q. 1, a. 1; SUMMA., I, q. 42, a. 1. — Bl. (now St.) Albertus Magnus, here in a. 4. — (Bl.) Peter of Tarentaise, here in q. 1, a. 1. — Richard of Middleton, here in a. 1, q. 1. — Giles the Roman, here in 1st. princ., q. 3. — Henry of Ghent, SUMMA., a. 70, q. 1, n. 46. ff. — Durandus (of Saint-Pourçain), here in q. 2.

QUESTION II

Whether "equality" and "similitude" are said among the divine according to substance, or whether according to relation?

Second, there is asked, whether the abovesaid names are said according to substance, or according to relation. And that (they are said) according to substance, seems:

1. By the authority of Master (Peter) in the text:[7] « Equality »,

he says, « is not a relation and/or a notion, but the unity and/or identity of nature »; and (St.) Hilary ON THE TRINITY (says):[8] « The similitude is (Their) undiffering Essence »: therefore, both "*similitude*" and "*equality*" mean the Divine Essence.

---

[1] Codex R has *an essential unity* [essentialem unitatem] for *the Unity of the Essence* [essentiae unitatem]. Then immediately afterward many codices together with edition 1 read *because they* [quod].

[2] Distinction 24, a. 1, q. 1, and ibid., a. 2, q. 1. — A little above this, after "*two*" [duo] codex T inserts *and* [et].

[3] Codex V reads *underlying* [subiacet] for *underlying* [substernitur].

[4] Which "*diversity*" among the divine is called "*distinction*". Cf. above d. 24, Doubt 1.

[5] The greater part of the codices, together with edition 1, have *measuring* [mensuratio].

[6] Supply, together with codices L and O *quantity* [quantitas], that is, the quantity of virtue, concerning which,

see above d. 19, p. I, qq. 1, 2 and 3, where there occur very many other considerations, which concern this question.

[7] Chapter 1; but we have received the other reading; confer ibid., footnote 1.

[8] (St.) Hilary (of Poitiers) in his work, ON THE TRINITY, more often than not, especially in Books VII and VIII, demonstrates the equality and similitude (according to him, in his book, ON SYNODS, these names have the same force) of the Son of God from this, that in the Son of God there is « a Nature or Essence undiffering ». You will find a more exact definition of similitude in his book, ON SYNODS. Cf. also here the text of Master (Peter), ch. 1, page 529, footnote 5.

2. Likewise, "*equal*" is said according to quantity, and "*similitude*" according to quality;[1] but among the divine, quality and quantity pass over into the Substance: ergo etc..

3. Likewise, everything which is said according to relation, conveys a distinction concerning its principal understanding; but "*similar*" and "*equal*" mean a convening: therefore, they are not said according to relation.

4. Likewise, nothing which is said according to relation, is said of two, unless it conveys a relation in *common* — I say this on account of this name "*related*" and "*distinct*" — but the "*similar*" and the "*equal*" do convey a *special* relation, if they convey it,[2] because there is no assigning of more special (names) under them, and they are said of many: ergo etc..

ON THE CONTRARY: 1. (St.) Hilary, ON THE TRINITY, (says):[3] « A similitude is not to itself »; but everything which is said according to substance, is said regarding itself: ergo etc..

2. Likewise, everything which is said according to substance, is said of many singularly; but "*similar*" and "*equal*" is said plurally: ergo etc..

3. Likewise, the Father is referred according to an equality to the Son, and the Son to the Father, but not according to essence: therefore, (Their) equality does not mean the Essence.

4. Likewise, , either the Father is the equality of the Son to the Father, or not. If *so*: therefore, since the Son by that equality is equal to the Father,[4] the Father is equal to Himself; which is not conceded. Wherefore, if the Father is *not* the equality of the Son to the Father, therefore "equality" is not said of All (the Persons): therefore, it does not mean the Essence; for the Essence of the Son is the Father.

CONCLUSION

"Similitude" and "equality" are said in some manner both according to substance and according to relation, but properly and principally according to relation, ex consequenti *and causally according to substance.*

I RESPOND: It must be said, that according to the common opinion of all, since the "*similar*" and the "*equal*" mean a convening of many in one, that[5] they of themselves mean a *distinction* among the Supposits and a *union* or unity in essence. And because a *distinction* of persons pertains [spectat] to a manner of speaking according to relation, a *unity* of being [unitas essendi] to a manner of speaking according to substance, for that reason names of this kind are neither said entirely according to substance, nor entirely according to relation, but in a certain manner according to substance, in a certain manner according to relation. But because they cannot, according to this twofold manner, be said *principally* (of either one), but it is necessary, that (they be said principally) according to one of the two, for that reason one is bound [oportet] to seek further, according to which manner of speaking they are (principally)[6] accepted among the divine. And here there are diverse opinions.

For *certain* (authors) say, that names of this kind, signified according to *concretion*, are said *principally* according to *relation*. For *similars* are said to have the same quality. Therefore,[7] because (a name of this kind) looks back to a Supposit per se, according to which (it is) concrete, for that reason it is said according to *relation*. But in *abstraction*, because a *similitude* is a unity of nature and/or of essence, because it looks back to the unity of form first, not to a distinction of the Supposits except out of its consequent meaning [ex consequenti], it is said principally according to *substance*. — But that manner of solving (the difficulty) is not fitting. For there is the same signification in the concrete and in the abstract in the principal (thing) signified: therefore, if one is said according to substance, the rest too, similarly:[8] therefore this does not solve what has been said.

The *second* opinion is, that names of this kind both in *concretion* and in *abstraction* are said principally according to *substance* and connote a distinction among the Supposits. And the reason for these is, because since a similitude looks back to those two, namely, to the convening and the difference, it looks back more immediately and more completely to the convening.[9] For (those) *different* are said to be *similar*, inasmuch as they convene, but (those) *convening* are not said to be similar, inasmuch as *they differ*. Therefore, a similitude looks back to a distinction through the manner of *matter*,[10] but through the manner of *form* it looks back to unity according to essence; and for that reason there is said completely [completive] according to *substance*, both "*similitude*" and "*similar*". — But that position cannot stand. For it is certain, that a "*similitude*" is said (to be) the looking-back of the some to one another; but among the divine there is naught but a looking-back of a Person to a Person. Moreover, a looking-back of a Person to a Person cannot be said according to *substance*: therefore, it is necessary, that this name "*similar*", which is imposed from a similitude, not be said according to *substance*.

---

[1] Cf. above d. 19, p. I, a. sole, q. 1, p. 342, footnote 6. On *the minor* (of the argument), see above d. 22, a. 4.

[2] Understand: *if they do convey a relation* [si aliquam relationem important]. — The Vatican ed., after *if they do* [si eam], inserts , *I say,* [inquam], codd. K V & X put *equally* [aeque].

[3] Bk. III, n. 23.

[4] Very many codices, such as G I T V W Y Z aa bb and ee, here interpose *the Father is equal to the Father* [Pater est aequalis Patri].

[5] Only the Vatican edition omits *that* [quod]; but it is the custom of the Seraphic (Doctor), in similar constructions, to repeat the *that* [quod].

[6] Supply, with the Vatican edition, *principally* [principaliter]. — A little above this, before *it is necessary* [necesse est], form the manuscripts we have restored the *but* [sed], which is absent from the Vatican edition.

[7] Thus, rightly, the Vatican edition; for *the principal (thing) signified* [principali significato] the codices, together with edition 1, substitute *even the Supposit* [et supposito], or *and in the Supposit* [et in supposito] and/or *and in the assumed (term)* [et in sumto], which readings have been corrupted.

[9] Codices C L W and Y add *than to the difference* [quam differentiam], codices R S U and V have faultily *and to the difference* [et differentiam], codex X adjoins *and secondarily to the difference* [et secundario differentiam].

[10] Or *materially*, i.e., less principally and as if by connoting.

And for that reason there is a *third* opinion, that names of this kind are said according to relation, formally speaking. For they mean the looking-back of distinct Supposits, convening in some one (thing); and thus There the looking-back occurs through the manner of *form*, but the unity of essence and the plurality of the Supposits[1] occurs through the manner of *cause*.* For that reason they are said properly and principally according to relation, but out of their consequent meaning [ex consequenti] according to substance, causally speaking. And this is more clear, if we would consider the signification of these names in creatures, from where the transferal (of these names) is made. For a *similitude* is (a relation)[2] according to *quality*; and a "*similitude*" means a relation *formally*, but a quality *causally*, similarly "*equality*" means a quantity *causally*, but a relation *formally*. For a similitude is not a quality, but a relation, which is attained according to a quality.[3]

1. To that which is objected concerning Master (Peter) and (St.) Hilary, that (the similitude) is the Essence; it must be said, that all such discourses are understood *causally*.

2. To that which is afterwards said,[4] that "*equal*" is said according to quantity; it must be said, that "*according to*" [secundum] means an efficient cause, it does not mean a form; in the same manner concerning "*similar*".

3. To that, however, which is objected, that relative (names) convey a distinction; it must be said, that *certain*

(names) among the divine are said according to relation, which are *distinctive* of the One related, such as "the Father" and "the Son"; and such convey a *distinguishing* looking-back, and such convey a distinction as *exercised*. But *certain ones* are said according to relation, which are *relative* of the One distinguished, such as "similar" and "equal"; and such convey a looking-back, but that looking-back is not a *distinguishing* notion, but a distinguishing consequent. For it conveys a distinction not as *exercised*, but as *conceived*. For a distinguishing looking-back is of one Person to Another, according to which it is from the Former. However, in names of this kind there is conveyed the looking-back of one Person to Another, according to which They communicate the one Nature. And because (this) looking-back is a relation, for that reason it is plurified, however, because (it is) the looking-back of the one Essence, for that reason it is said of Many.

4. And for that reason, what is said last, is clear, that no relative (name) is said of many, unless it means a relation in common. For it must be said, that this is not only among those names, which convey a distinction in common, as "*related*" and "*distinct*", but also among those,[5] which mean the looking-back of many, as they communicate in something. For such a name means a looking-back in common, yet specified by reason of the communication in one; whence *similars* are said (to be) related to one another; participating in one quality.

SCHOLIUM

I. It is established, that the names "*similar*" and "*equal*" in God convey both a distinction among persons and a unity in essence. But the question arises, what manner of speaking do they convey *more principally*, whether that, which is according to relation, or the other, which is according to substance. — The third sentence in the Response, which belongs to the author, seems to not be the common one. St. Thomas even agrees in this, that « the unity of essence and the plurality of the Supposits occurs *through the manner of a cause* ». For in his Commentary (here in q. 1, a. 1) he says: « The unity of quantity is *its cause* » (i.e. Their equality is the cause), and in the SUMMA., I, q. 42, a. 1, in reply to n. 4 (he says): « because the Persons are each equal to Themselves *out of this*, that They are of one magnitude and Essence ».

II. There is a controversy concerning the nature of these relations. (Bl. John Duns) Scouts (here in q. 3, n. 2, and in d. 19, q. sole; QUODLIBETALS, n. 6) teaches, that these are real, and this seems to respond to his own *formal* distinction. St. Thomas (loc. cit., in reply to n. 4) holds entirely, that they are only distinguished according to a reckoning. In the Vatican edition, in the margin (alongside the solution to n. 4) there is read: « From these one may see, that in St. Bonaven-

ture such are real relations. Scotus consents to the divine (St.) Bonaventure in this; but Bassol. says, that it cannot be inferred, that the Doctor posits these relations to be real ». And in truth we do not see, by what right there can be construed from this solution, that Saint Bonaventure taught this sentence of (Bl.) Scotus.

III. In regard to the solution to n. 1, cf. here Doubt 3. — The solution to n., 4 is founded upon this, that *common relations* can be understood in a twofold sense: namely, either to the extent that "*common*" means some *superior genus*, which has under itself inferior species, such as the distinct, the related; and/or to the extent that "*common*" is opposed to "*proper*", and thus many persons are said to be equal and/or similar, according to which they convene in one essence.

IV. Besides those already cited: (Bl. John Duns) Scotus, REPORTATIO., here in q. 1. — Bl. (now St.) Albertus (Magnus), here in a. 3; SUMMA., p. I, tr. 11, q. 47, m. 1, in reply to n. 3. — (Bl.) Peter of Tarentaise, here in q. 1, a. 2. (whose doctrine St. Bonaventure nearly repeats). — Richard of Middleton, here in a. 1, q. 2. — Giles the Roman, here in 1st. princ., q. 1. — Henry of Ghent, SUMMA., a. 68, q. 4, n. 8 ff. — Durandus (of Saint-Pourçain), here in q. 1. — (Gabriel) Biel, on this and the following question, here in the q. sole.

---

[1] In the codices and in editions 1, 2 and 3 there is wanting *of the Supposits* [suppositorum], in codex T there is also wanting *and the plurality* [et pluralitatem], which words are certainly, together with the Vatican edition, to be supplied.*

[2] Supply with the Vatican edition *a relation* [relatio]. A little after this for *and a similitude* [et similitudo] many codices, together with edition 1, have *but a similitude* [sed similiduto], less congruously. Then not a few codices, together with edition 1, omit the proposition beginning at

similarly [similiter] and ending with the word *formally* [formaliter], some codices omits only the first part of this proposition.

[3] Codices P and Q adjoin *nor is equality a quantity, but a relation, which is attained according to a quantity* [nec aequalitas est quantitas, sed relatio, quae attenditur secundum quantitatem].

[4] Codices I P and Q have *objected* [obiicitur].

[5] Codices P and Q repeat here *names* [nominibus].

---

* *Trans. note*: Each pair is said in relation to the Supposits, thus, the sense here and where this phrase occurs below in the Scholium, I, is: *the unity of the Supposits in essence, and Their plurality* etc..

QUESTION III

Whether "equal" and "similar" are said among the divine according to a mutual relation?

Third, there is asked, whether the aforesaid names, namely *"equal"* and *"similar"*, mean a mutual relation, according to which the Father is equal to the Son, and the Son to the Father. And that (they do) not, seems:

1. Because according to Dionysius (the Areopagite):[1] « In what regards causes [In causalibus] we do not receive a reciprocation »; but the Father is the principle of the Son: therefore, no a reciprocation occurs There, for [ut] the Father to be said (to be) equal to the Son.

2. Likewise, this seems *by reason*, for because the Son is similar to the Father, for that reason He is said to be the Similitude of the Father: therefore, if, conversely, the Father is similar to the Son perfectly, therefore, the Father is the Similitude of the Son. But this is not received: ergo etc..

3. Likewise, who is equal to another is adequated according to his own equality: if, therefore, the Father is equal to the Son, therefore, He is adequated to Him;[2] I ask: by whom? either by *Himself*, or by *Another*. Not by Himself, because whosoever equates himself to another, does something in himself; but the Father does nothing in Himself, therefore, He is not adequated, neither by Himself; nor is He equated by Another: therefore He is not equal to the Son.

ON THE CONTRARY: 1. The similar and the equal are relative to an equiparancy;° but those denominate each extreme in a completely similar manner:[3] therefore, if the Son is similar to the Father, for an equal reason the Father is similar to the Son.

2. Likewise, a reckoning of a similitude is a *convening* and/or an *indifference* in quality and/or substance; but a *convening* looks back equally to each extreme, and an *indifference* (similarly):[4] therefore, if the Son is undiffering from the Father and conversely (the Father is undiffering from the Son), the Father is similar to the Son.

3. Likewise, every plural replicates its own singular; but this is conceded: "the Father and the Son are similars

and equals", therefore, the Father is similar; I ask: "To whom?" either *to Himself*, or *to Another*.[5] Not *to Himself*: therefore, *to Another*.

CONCLUSION

"Similar" and "equal" among the divine are said according to a mutual relation, insofar as they simply mean a convening in quantity and quality; however, not, insofar as they add above (this) a reckoning of origin.

I RESPOND: It must be said, that *"similar"* [similis] and *"equal"* [aequalis] are accepted in a twofold manner: either insofar as they mean a *convening* in quantity and/or quality, or insofar as they *add* upon (this) convening an imitation and/or perfect expression. Indeed, in the first manner they are relatives of an equiparancy [relativa aequiparantiae], and are said conversely [ad convertentiam], according to which the reasons brought forward second prove. In another manner *"similar"* and *"equal"* add upon this[6] a reckoning of *origin* — whence the *"equal"* is said as if *"adequated"* [adaequatus], and the *"similar"* as if *"assimilated"* [assimilatus] — in this manner it befits naught but him who is from another [ab altero], and in this manner the first reasons proceed, that the Father is not said (to be) the "Similitude" of the Son through imitation, nor is He equated to the Son through an emanation from Another, but equals the Son by Himself [aequat sibi Filium].

However, what Dionysius says, that we do not receive a reciprocation etc.; he speaks of a cause[7] properly, insofar as it differs from an effect through essence [ab effectu per essentiam]; but in this manner the Father is not the cause of the son, nay there is rightly a habitude of the Son to the Father, just as (there is) the other way around [e converso]; and thus all (the objections) are clear.

SCHOLIUM

The same distinction, which is employed in this Response, is expressed by the Seraphic Doctor above in d. 19, p. I, q. 3 in this manner: « Either insofar as it means *the looking-back of equiparancy*, or insofar as beyond the looking-back it concerns the *act of co-equation* ». The solution is the common sentence.

Alexander of Hales, SUMMA., p. I, q. 54, m. 1, aa. 2 & 3. —

(Bl. John Duns) Scotus, REPORTATIO., here in q. 3; SENT., Bk. I, d. 19, q. 1. — St. Thomas, SUMMA., I, q. 42, a. 1, in reply to 3. — Bl. (now St.) Albertus (Magnus), d. 19, a. 4. — (Bl.) Peter of Tarentaise, d. 19, q. 1, a. 3. — Richard of Middleton., d. 19, a. 1, q. 2. — Gi les the Roman, here in 1st. princ., q. 2. — Henry of Ghent, SUMMA., a. 68, q. 2.

---

[1] See d. 19, p. I, a. sole, q. 3, p. 346, footnote 4.

[2] For *He is adequated to Him* [ei adaequatur], which is the reading of nearly all* the codd., the Vatican ed. with cod. cc has *if He is adequated* [si adaequatur], codd. G & S read *if He is adequated to Him* [si ei adaequatur]. Near the end of the argument, the Vatican edition reads *therefore He does not adequate Himself, nor is He equated to Another* [ergo non adaequat se, nec alii aequatur] for *therefore, He is not adequated neither by Himself; not is He equated by Another* [ergo non adaequatur nec a se; nec ab alio aequatur], which codd. K M T & ff have, and also differently by omitting by [a, ab]; cod. P reads *therefore, He does not adequate Himself to Another, nor is He equated by Another* [ergo non adaequat se alii nec ab alio aequatur], with which reading ed. 1 is in agreement, omitting only *to Another* [alii].

[3] Cf. d. 19, p. I, a. sole, q. 3, p. 346, footnote 5. — Just before this,

the Vatican ed. badly omits *in a completely similar manner* [consimiliter].

[4] Supply: *similarly* [similiter], i.e. the indifference looks back equally to each extreme. — For *and* [et] edition 1 has *also* [etiam].

[5] Codex V reads *whether to Himself, or to Another* [an sibi an alii].

[6] Very many codices, such as A F G H I K (T by the first hand) V etc., omits *this* [hoc], in place of which codices P Q (T by a second hand) Z and ee substitute *the convening* [convenientiam]; in edition 1 for *add upon this* [addunt super hoc] there is read *add above (this)* [superaddit].

[7] Codex O here adds *and of those causes, which do not fully and perfectly receive the similitude of its cause* [et de causatis illis quae non plene et perfecte recipiunt similitudinem suae causae]. Cf. d. 19, p. I, q. 3, in reply to n. 4.

---

* *Trans. note*: Here the original footnote read faultily <u>ferme</u> for *nearly* [fere].

° For the definition of *equiparancy* see d. 19, p. I, a. sole, q. 3, p. 347, footnote 5.

DOUBTS ON THE TEXT OF THE MASTER

Doubt I

In this part, there are doubts about the text (of Master Peter) and first there is the doubt concerning *the location* [de situ] of this part, because when equality was treated of above in the Nineteenth Distinction,[1] it seems that Master (Peter) here superfluously repeats (what was said there).

I Respond: It must be said, that of equality and similitude there is a speaking in a twofold manner, namely, on the part of *the thing*, and/or on the part of *the name*. And in the first manner equality and similitude were dealt with in the preceding (Distinctions), in the second manner here.

Doubt II

Likewise, is asked concerning this which (Master Peter) says, that *nothing is similar to itself*. For it seems false, because someone does differ from himself, just as the old man Socrates from himself as a boy: therefore, for an equal reason something can be similar to itself. — Likewise, Christ the man is similar to Himself,[3] because no one is blessed, unless He be assimilated to God; but Christ is assimilated to God most of all: ergo etc..

I Respond: It must be said, that, just as a *difference* sometimes notes an anotherness of a *supposit* from a supposit, as when there is said: "Peter is other than Paul"; sometimes an anotherness in *nature*, as when there is said: "Christ according to which (He is) *a man* differs from Himself[3] as God"; sometimes an anotherness of a *status* from a status, as the old man Peter differs from himself as a boy: through this manner (of division) must it be understood concerning a *similitude*. Therefore, when "*similar*" means a similitude of a *supposit* to a supposit, the same cannot be similar to itself; but when it means the similitude of a *nature* to a nature; and/or of a *status* to a status, the same can be similar to itself, because they concur in the same person; and thus does Master (Peter) understand (it).

Doubt III

Likewise, is asked of this which (Master Peter) says, that *the equality of the Father and of the Son is not a relation and/or a notion*, because just before this he had said, that "*similar*" and "*relative*" is a relative (name): therefore, a similitude is relation.

I Respond: It must be said, that Master (Peter) understands (this) of the notion, which is a *property* of a Person, non of a relation understood in the common manner. — *And/or in another manner* it must be said, that the word of Master (Peter) is to be understood causally, just as is clear from the preceding, because the *equality* does not consist in personal properties, but rather in the essential ones, which have been shown above.[4]

COMMENTARY ON DISTINCTION XXXI

Part II

On the appropriation of relative names, which are said commonly and eternally.

Here, it must not be overlooked, that the illustrious man, (St.) Hilary etc..

THE DIVISION OF THE TEXT

Having terminated that part, in which he deals with the *signification* of these names "*similar*" and "*equal*", here the *second* part begins, in which he deals with the appropriation of these names, and this part has two parts. In the first, he assigns the appropriations; in the second, he moves and solves a doubt, which has its origin from an appropriation of this kind, below in the Thirty-Second Distinction: *Here there arises a question deduced from the aforesaid.*

The first part is divided into two parts: in the *first*, he assigns (the names) appropriated according to (St.) Hilary; in the second, (those appropriated) according to (St.) Augustine, there (where he says): *It must also be known, that (St.) Augustine wanting to show the distinction of the same Three Persons* etc. The *first* part has three (parts). In the first, he assigns (St.) Hilary's appropriation and his explanation on account of its obscurity. In the second, he shows, that those (names) which (St.) Hilary assigns, are not proper (names), but appropriated ones,

---

[1] Chapter 1 ff. — Codex T together with the other codices and edition 1 reads *since* etc. [cum ... sit] for *when* etc. [cum ... est].

[2] Codex W adds *as God* [Deo].

[3] The Vatican edition alone omits *Himself as* [se].

[4] Distinction XIX, ch. 1 ff, and (St. Bonaventure's) Commentary, d. 19, p. I, q. 1 and 2.

there (where he says): *For not according to the aforementioned exposition* etc.. However, in the third he shows, that those to which he appropriates these, are proper (names). For an appropriation is common in respect of a proper (name), and this he does there (where he says): *Therefore, in the aforesaid words (St.) Hilary is said to have assigned (names) proper to the Persons* etc..

It must also be known , that (St.) Augustine wanting to show the distinction of the same Three Persons etc.. This is the *second* part of this part, in which Master (Peter) assigns the appropriation of (St.) Augustine, and this part has two parts. In the first, he puts the appropriation itself; in the second, he puts its expo-

sition, there (where he says): *But it disturbs very many, that he attributes to the Father* etc. And this part has three (parts) according to those three appropriated (names). In the first he shows, in what manner *"unity"* is appropriated to the Father, showing also, incidentally, in what manner some are said to be *one* [unum]. However, in the second he shows, in what manner *"equality"* is appropriated to the Son, there (where he says): *Now let us see, for what reason is "equality" said to be in the Son* etc.. But in the third he shows, in what manner *"concord"* is appropriated to the Holy Spirit, there (where he says): *Moreover, that in the Holy Spirit there is said to be the "concord" of Each* etc..

TREATMENT OF THE QUESTIONS

For an understanding of those (things) which are said in this part, two (questions) are principally asked:

First, there is the question concerning (St.) Hilary's appropriation.

Second, concerning (St.) Augustine's appropriation.

And as much as regard the first, three (questions) are asked.

First, there is asked, whether "image" is said among the divine according to substance, or according to relation.

Second, granted that (it is said) according to relation, there is asked, whether "image" is a proper (name) of the Son.

Third, there is the question concerning the reckoning of the appropriation of those three (names), namely, of "eternity", "sightliness", and "use".

ARTICLE I

On (St.) Hilary's appropriation.

QUESTION I

Whether "image", among the divine, is said according to substance, or according to relation?

Moreover, that *"image"* is said according to substance, is shown in this manner:

1. (St.) Hilary (says) in the fourth (book) ON THE TRINITY:[1] « God, according to the image and same similitude, common to Himself with God, is found to make man ».

2. Likewise, (St.) Bede (the Venerable says) on that (verse):[2] *Let us make man* etc.: « In this, that he says "the image", is noted the one and equal Substance of the Trinity »: therefore, "image", since it pertains to the community and unity of the Substance, is said according to substance.

3. Likewise, this very (thing) seems *by reason*, because that same, which means[3] an *exemplar* actively, means an *image* passively; but "exemplar" among the divine is said according to substance, not according to relation.

4. Likewise, an *image* consists in representing [consistit in repraesentando] something not only in substance, but also in the distinction

and order of (those) distinguished: if, therefore, among the divine there occurs no distinction in one Person, it is necessary, that among the divine an image be attained, according to which the Unity of the Essence is in the Three Persons: therefore, not notionally, but essentially is there said (to be) an *image* among the divine.

ON THE CONTRARY: 1. (St.) Augustine in the seventh (book) ON THE TRINITY (says):[4] « What (is) more absurd, than that (something) be said (to be) an *"image"* regarding itself »? but everything which is said according to substance, is said regarding (the thing) itself: therefore, since (something) is not said (to be) an *"image"* regarding itself, ("image") is not said according to substance.

2. Likewise, (St.) Hilary (says) in the third (book) ON THE TRINITY:[5] « An image is not alone », therefore, among the divine the image is with (something) else; but the Essence is not with (something) else; ergo etc..

3. Likewise, this very (thing) seems through the *definition* of an image, because (St.) Hilary[6] says, that « an image is

---

[1] Number 18. The sense of the words cited is: God (the Father) is found to work or have made man according to the image common to Himself with God (the Son). Cf. above, d. XXVIII, ch. 7.

[2] In HEXAËMERON, Bk. I (on Genesis 1:26): However, in that which follows *to Our image and similitude*, the one and equal substance of the same Holy Trinity is indicated.

[3] The Vatican edition, having omitted *which* [quod], here and immediately after this twice exhibits *is said* [dicitur] for *means* [dicit].

[4] Chapter 1, n. 2.

[5] Number 23. — Codex W prefixes the first *therefore* [ergo] with an *if* [si].

[6] ON SYNODS, n. 13; in which definition the Vatican edition alone reads *is the co-equation of a thing to a thing* [est rei ad rem conaequatio] for *of a thing ... the thing* [est rei ad rem coaequandam] — You can find the whole definition in the text of Master (Peter), here in the Brief Note in ch. 2. — Next, the Vatican edition, together with codex cc, omits *of One* [unius].

of a thing to *co-equate* the thing » etc.; but the Thing, which is co-equated to the Thing, is a Person: therefore, the Image is of a Person to a Person. But what means the looking-back of One to the Other is said according to relation: therefore, also "*image*".

4. Likewise, this seems through the *etymology*. For an "*image*" is said to be a quasi imitation [quasi imitago],[1] therefore, where there is the reckoning of an image, there is an imitation; but the Divine Essence does not imitate anything, because everything such is from something; therefore "*image*" is not said according to substance and/or essence.

CONCLUSION

Properly speaking, there is said (to be) an image, not according to substance, but notionally.

I RESPOND: It must be said, that just as "*exemplar*", according to the property of the word, means an expression through the manner of (something) *active* — whence an "exemplar" is said (to be that) according to the imitation of which something is made[2] — so, contrariwise, "*image*" (means an expression) through the manner of (something) *passive*; and an image is said (to be that), which expresses and imitates the other. And in this manner "image" is accepted in a twofold manner, according to which the expression is twofold, namely, either in a *unity* of nature, and/or in a *diversity* of nature: in the community or unity of a nature, just as the son of the Emperor is said (to be) an image of (his) father; in a diversity of nature, just as the image of the Emperor is on a coin.[3]

Thus, in respect of God, "*image*" is said through an expression according to *an identity of nature*; and thus it is the uncreated Image and is said notionally or according to relation, because image means an emanation, but there is no emanation in a unity of nature except of a Person. "Image" is also said through an expression in *the diversity of nature*; and thus there is said (to be) a created image in respect of the whole Trinity. And in this manner it is clear, that "*image*", accepted among the divine, is said according to the relation of a Person to a Person; and this according to the property of the word, just as the reason brought forwards for this prove.

But, since it happens that the name for "*exemplar*" (is) abused,[4] so that what is made according to the imitation of the other, is said (to be) an exemplar, so contrariwise it happens that "*image*" (is) abused, so that (that) according to the expression of which something is made, is said (to be) the image; and thus since a creature is made according to the expression of the Unity of the Essence in the trinity of Persons, it can be said (to be) the image of the whole Trinity; and in this manner it is said (to be) an *imaging* image, since from the reckoning of its name it means[5] (something) *imaged* [imaginatum]; just as an exemplar is abusively said (to be) an exemplified [exemplatum], though an exemplar is the one exemplifying. And according to this manner (Sts.) Hilary and Bede seem to have accepted ("*image*"), as Master (Peter) says in the Sixteenth Distinction of Book Two.

Yet, it can be said, that each is said of the *created* image, which since it is less in respect of the Essence, is a common image of the Three Persons and indicates the unity of substance in the Three. Wherefore, neither is "image" said purely *regarding (the thing) itself*, because it always means a *looking-back* either to some Person, or to a creature,[6] or of a creature to the Divine Nature. It is also never said purely according to *substance*, because it always notes a distinction either interiorly, and/or exteriorly. Wherefore, an "image" is not said (to be) according to the Essence simply, but according to the Essence as considered in the Three Persons. — However, conserving the propriety of speech, an the "image" (of God)[7] is said (to be) according to a personal relation, insofar as it is said (to be) the Eternal Image.

1. 2. According to the authorities for the opposite (side) the response is clear.

3. To that, therefore, which is objected, that "*exemplar*" is said essentially, ergo etc.; it must be said, that it is not similar, because the whole Trinity is a beginning [principium]. And for that reason because "*exemplar*" means the reckoning of *one producing* — whence it is said according to substance and befits the whole Trinity, but the whole Trinity is not a begun [principiata] — and because "*image*" means the reckoning of *one produced* properly: for that reason it does not befit the whole Trinity nor is it said according to substance.

4. To that which is objected, that for this, that there be an image, it ought to express the distinction and the order (of things distinguished); it must be said, that that is true in the image, which is an image of a thing having a distinction and an order (among things distinguished), just as a man has among his members [in partibus],[8] and the whole Trinity among the Persons; but when the thing, of which the image is, does not have a distinction, as for example one Person, it is not necessary [oportet] that it be expressed

---

[1] This etymology of the name imitago is attributed to Sextus Pompeius Festus, who redacted the book of Verreus Flaccus, ON THE SIGNIFICATION OF WORDS into a compendium in the 3rd. or 4th. century after Christ (cf. Forcellini's, LEXICON). Aristotle, TOPICS, Bk. VI, ch. 1 (ch. 2) says: For an image is that, the generation of which is through imitation.

[2] And if this exemplar is in the mind of the artisan, it is called an *idea* [idea], which is defined thus, by (Lucius Annaeus) Seneca in his 65th Epistle, to Lucilius: an exemplar (is that), to which the artisan looks back, (as) he makes, that which he destined (to make) [exemplar, ad quod respiciens artifex, id quod destinabat, effecit]. — Codex T, together with very many others, a little before this reads *through an active manner* [per modum activum] and then *through a passive manner* [per modum passivum].

[3] (St.) Augustine, SERMONS, IX (on the Ten Chords), ch. 8, n. 9: For the images in men are also diverse. The son of a man has the image of his own father, and this is that which his father (is), because a man is just as his father; but in a mirror your image is not that which

you are ... For just as on a coin the image of the Emperor is in one manner, in another in (his) son; for the image is also an image, but the image of the Emperor has been impressed in one manner on the coin, in another manner in the son, in another manner on a golden aureus; thus also as the coin of God is etc..

[4] That is: accepted improperly and/or falsely.

[5] The Vatican edition, together with a few codices and edition 1, has *is meant* [dicatur]. A little below this for *the one exemplifying* [exemplans], the codices together with editions 1, 2, and 3 have not rightly *of an exemplar* [exemplaris], and then for *seem* [videntur] the Vatican edition, favored by not a few codices, reads *is said* [dicitur] (erroneously).

[6] The Vatican edition alone thus supplies the text: *and/or of a Person to another Person, and/or of the Essence to a creature* [vel personae ad alium personam, vel essentiae ad creaturam]. Next after *It is* [Numquam] codex R has *therefore* [ergo] for *also* [etiam].

[7] Codex W inserts *of God* [Dei].

[8] Codices aa and bb read *in the parts of (his) soul, that is in (its) powers* [in partibus animae, id est in potentiis], codex T (in the margin) adds *and/or in (his) powers* [vel in potentiis].

in this manner. — And/or it can be said, that that is true, when an image differs substantially. For, then, for this, that it express expressly, it is necessary [necesse est] that it imitate the substance in (its) consequent conditions; and when it imitates in the same form of substance, it is not necessary [oportet].

SCHOLIUM

I. The *created* image of God is dealt with above in d. 3, p. I, q. 2, at the end, and in p. II, a. 1 and 2, and more diffusely in Bk. II, d. 16. However, here there is the treatment of the *uncreated* Image, which is a proper name of the Son. First (in the Response) the name "*image*" is defined and explained in (its) *proper* sense, then the same name in (its) *improper* sense (« it happens that "*image*" is abused », to the extent that it is an *imaging* image or one causing an image (cf. SENT., Bk .II, d. 16, Doubt 3). — At the end of the Response the author concludes, that "*image*", in whatever sense it be understood, always includes a *looking-back*, and indeed in God Himself a looking-back according to a *personal* relation, if it is understood in (its) proper sense. — From this question and Doubts 2 and 3 and other passages, it is construed, that according to the mind of St. Bonaventure three (things) are required for the perfect reckoning of an image, namely, that it be something *similar* to that, which it represents, either in appearance [in specie], and/or at least as a sign of the appearance — so that *it imitates* and *expresses* the other (wherefore, with this condition lacking, the egg is not an image of an egg, as St. Augustine says in OF EIGHTY-THREE QUESTIONS, q. 74) — so that the image *is referred* to the one imaged as to its *prototype* really distinct from itself. St. Thomas teaches the same (thing) in other words, in SENT., Bk. I, d. 28, q. 2, a. 1; SUMMA., I, q. 35, a. 1.

II. That "*image*" [imago] is said both according to relation, and « according to the *property* of the word » and that it is a *proper* name of the Son (cf. following question), is the common sentence among the Latin Doctors, contrary to a few, among whom is Durandus (of Saint-Pourçain) (SENT., Bk. I, d. 28, q. 3), who teaches the same concerning "*word*" [verbum] (cf. above d. 27, p. II, q. 1) as of "*image*", that « it does not *properly* befit the divine, yet insofar as it does befit, it is said personally, not essentially ».

III. Alexander of Hales, SUMMA., p. I, a. 61, m. 1 and 2. — St. Thomas , locis. citt.. — Bl. (now St.) Albertus (Magnus), on this and the following q., SENT., Bk. I, d. 28, a. 9; SUMMA ., p. I, tr. 8, q. 35, m. 2. — (Bl.) Peter of Tarentaise, SENT., Bk. I, d. 28, q. 3, a. 1. — Richard of Middleton, SENT., Bk. I, d. 28, a. 3, q. 1. — Giles the Roman, SENT., Bk. I, d. 28, 2nd. princ., q. 2. — Henry of Ghent, SUMMA., a. 68, q. 2, n. 21 ff.. — Durandus (of Saint-Pourçain), loc. cit.. — (Bl.) Dionysius Carthusian, on this and the following q., SENT., Bk. I, d. 28, q. 4.

QUESTION II

Whether "image" among the divine is said properly of the Son?

Second, there is asked, whether "*image*" is a *proper* (name) of the Son. And that it is, seems:

1. Through (St.) Hilary[1] in the proposed appropriation: « Eternity (is) in *the Father*, sightliness [species] in the *Image*, use in the *Gift* ». "Father" is said properly, similarly "*Gift*": therefore, if they are rightly posited, from an equal reckoning [ex aequo] "*Image*" is said properly of the Son.

2. Likewise, (St.) Augustine (says) in the sixth (book) ON THE TRINITY:[2] « The Son alone is the image of the Father », and more expressly: « (He is) a son by this, by which (He is) image and word »: therefore, according to this, since "son" means a personal relation, it is clear that etc..

3. Likewise, an *image* is an expressed similitude and among the divine a most expressed similitude;[3] but a most expressed similitude cannot be of many distinct (persons): if, therefore, the Son is from One, the Holy Spirit equally from Two, therefore, there will not be able to be an *image*.

4. Likewise, among the divine, an *image* is attained [attenditur] according to the imitation of a Person, not of the Essence, because[4] it is not an image of the Essence, but of a Person: therefore, for this, that one Person be the image of the Other, it is necessary, that He imitated that One in this, that He looks back to a Person as a Person; but the emanation and/or production of a Person looks back to a Person as a Person; for the production of a creature looks back to the Substance. Since, therefore, the Son alone imitates the Father in the production of a Person, the Son alone is an *image*.

ON THE CONTRARY: 1. (St. John) Damascene[5] says, that « the Holy Spirit is an image of the Son »: therefore, it is not *proper* to the Son to be an image.

2. Likewise, this seems through each of (St.) Hilary's definitions.[6] And the *first* is: « An image is, of that thing according to which it is imaged, the undiffering appearance [species] »; but this befits the Holy Spirit: therefore (He is) also an image. The second is: « An image is the imaged and indiscrete similitude of a thing to co-equate the thing »; but his befits the Holy Spirit: ergo etc..

---

[1] ON THE TRINITY, Bk. II, n. 1, where in the original there is thus read: In the Father ... infinity in eternity, sightliness etc. See here the text of Master (Peter), ch. 2, where these appropriated (names) are also expounded.

[2] Chapter 2, n. 3. — The subsequent text is had ibid., Bk VII, ch. 2, n. 3: Indeed, the Son by this, by which the Word, and by this the Word, by which the Son ... And these two, when they are said, that is, "*born wisdom*", in one of them, by that which is "*born*", both word and image and son is understood, and in all these names the Essence is not shown, because they are said relatively etc.. Cf. (the text of Master Peter), above d. XXVII, ch. 4, near the end.

[3] Cf. (St.) Augustine, OF EIGHTY-THREE QUESTIONS, q. 74. In what manner the immediately, following proposition is to be understood, is explained in the body of the question. — Very many codices, such as A H I L M O (Q T in the margin) and Z, together with edition 1, after *cannot be* [potest esse], adds *but* [nisi], erroneously.

[4] The Vatican edition adds *a Person* [persona].

[5] ON THE ORTHODOX FAITH, Bk. I, ch. 13: The image of the Father is the Son and the Spirit of the Son.

[6] ON SYNODS, n. 13. See here the text of Master (Peter), ch. 2. The second definition, unduly omitted by the Vatican edition and by very many codices, and even by edition 1, we have supplied from codices P and Q; codex T exhibits it in the margin.

3. Likewise, this seems through *a reckoning*, because for an image these two suffice, namely, an imitation according to *similitude*, and according to *equality*;[1] but there is a finding of these two in the Person of the Holy Spirit: ergo etc..

4. Likewise, just as the Son proceeds from the Father, as One expressing the Father, so the Holy Spirit from the Son, as One expressing the Son: therefore, according to the manner which the Son is the image of the Father, so the Holy Spirit is the image of the Son.

CONCLUSION

The Son alone, properly speaking, is an image.

I **RESPOND**: It must be said, that an *image* among the divine not only means the expression of a Person, but also an expression in *the highest degree* [in summo]. But an expression in *the highest degree* posits two (things), namely, that it is *of one to one*, and that it is according to *every manner*. That it is *of one to one*, it posits through this, that « that which is said through superabundance, convenes with One alone »;[2] and if (the expression) be essential, of the Essence; if personal, of a Person. For 'one' in *the highest degree* cannot *express* many (things) and/or many (Persons);[3] the 'one', I say, in which there is no diversity. Similarly, 'one' cannot *be expressed* most highly by the Many, as They are many, because then They would be entirely undiffering. — It posits also (something) else, namely, that it is an expression according to *every manner*. For if it does not have an expressing out of some respect, it would not express *most highly*.

On account of the first reckoning the Son alone is an image, because He alone proceeds from *One*, but the Holy Spirit from Two, and for that reason He equally expresses Each, and for that reason Neither (is an expression) in the highest degree. On account of the second reckoning the Son alone is an image, because according to *every respect* He has a reckoning of expressing,[4] both inasmuch as He is

compared to that One *from whom* [a quo] He is, and inasmuch as He is compared to that One *who* is from Him [ex quo]. Inasmuch as He is compared to that One *from whom* He is, because He goes forth through the manner of nature, and thus through the manner of a word and appearance [species] and through a manner of an expressed similitude. Inasmuch as He is compared to that One *who* is from Him, because the Son spirates through all and in the same manner, as the Father. Moreover, the Holy Spirit convenes in none of these; for that reason the reckoning of an image is in the Son alone, because only He proceeds from *One*, and because through the manner of *nature*, because He too *produces*[5] *in a completely similar manner* the Holy Spirit. — Yet the middle reckoning, because (it is made) through the manner *of nature*, is a proper reckoning, however, the others argue [faciunt] according to congruity.

It must be conceded, therefore, that the Son alone, properly speaking, is an *image*, and by that, by which (He is) *a son*, by that is He an *image*, and *by the same* [eo ipso] a *word*. But as "*son*" He means only a looking-back to the Father, as "*image*" principally to the Father, but consequently a looking-back to another Person, as "*word*" principally a looking-back to the Father, and consequently a looking-back to the creature. Whence the same notion belongs to the Son Himself, yet signified in one and another manner. Wherefore there is no superfluity.

1. To that, therefore, which is objected concerning (St. John) Damascene, it must be said, that (St. John) Damascene was a Greek; but the Greeks do not accept thus the reckoning of image properly, as the Latins, because neither do they understand in this manner, sanely, (what) concerns the origin of the Persons. — And/or it can be said, that the discourse of (Sts.) Augustine and (John) Damascene is understood causally, because (the Holy Spirit) reforms us according to the image of Christ.[6]

2. To that which is objected, that each definition of image befits the Holy Spirit; it must be said, just as will be clear below,[7] that species and similitude, as it is accepted there, befit the Son alone.

---

[1] Cf. (St.) Augustine, OF EIGHTY-THREE QUESTIONS, q. 74, where the concepts of image, equality and similitude are expounded and compared amongst themselves.

[2] Aristotle, in TOPICS., Bk. V, chs. 2 and 3 (ch. 5) says in the Greek: τὸ γὰρ καθ' ὑπερβολὴν ἑνὶ μόνῳ ὑπάρχει. The words, καθ' ὑπερβολὴν, which are rendered into Latin by (St. Severinus) Boethius as *through a superabundance* [per superabundantiam], are rendered by others as *in (its) excellence* [in excellentia], have the same force, as that which is termed by grammarians a "superlative".

[3] Thus the Vatican edition with ed. 1. The codd., with all the other edd., after *and/or many (Persons)* [vel plures] adds '*one*' [unum], with which word added, causes the construction to be a disjunctive one, and it posits a member of the divine, which is expressed in the passive construction with the words: Similarly, 'one' etc. [Similter unum etc.]. Moreover, then it would be necessary to supply: '*One*' (can) not (express) many (things in the highest degree) [Non unum plura (in summon exprimere potest)], which words, perhaps, have been omitted by the copyists. — A little further below this, for the *different* [differentes], which the Vatican edition exhibits, we have restored from codd. F I P Q T and Z *undiffering* [indifferentes], as required by the context.

[4] Codex K proceeds thus: *For He expresses, inasmuch as He is compared to the Father, from whom He is, and inasmuch as He is compared to the Holy Spirit, who is from Him, and inasmuch as He is compared to that One from whom (He is), because He goes forth* etc. [Exprimit enim, in quantum comparatur ad Patrem, a quo est, et in quantum comparatur ad Spiritum sanctum, qui ex ipso est, et in quantum comparatur ad illum a quo, quia exit etc.].

[5] Codex K reads *in a manner completely similar as the Father (does)* [consimiliter ut Pater producit].

[6] (St. John) Damascene explains the sentence, which is cited in the first objection, with the words which he subjoins (in his own work): Through which Christ, dwelling in man, grants that the image of God be in the same. — A little above this, the agreed reading of all the codices and editions, which we have also retained, together with the Vatican edition, is *that the discourse of (Sts.) Augustine and (John) Damascene* etc. [quod sermo Augustini et Damasceni etc.]. But since the Seraphic Doctor makes no mention, in the first of the preceding objections, of (St.) Augustine, but

only of (St. John) Damascene, one does not understand, why he here names (St.) Augustine. For which reason it seem rightly to be conjectured, that the *discourse of (St.) Augustine* has been left out through an error of copyists, in place of which words in the original perhaps there used to be read: *which according to (St.) Augustine the word of (St. John) Damascene* etc. [quod secundum verbum Damasceni etc]. This passage of Alexander of Hales favors this conjecture (SUMMA., q. 61, m. 3, a. 2): « To that of (St. John) Damascene, that the Holy Spirit is an image of the Son; it must be said, that the Son is said to be an image of the Father in a multiple manner. In one manner quasi effectively: for just as an artisan, having the image of Hercules in mind, works that in the material through the same; so the Father is said to work the created image through the Son, the Image. Whence *(St.) Augustine* (in his letter) to Januarius (says): The image of the invisible Father is Our Savior: as much as regards the Father He is the Truth, as much as regards us, to whom He reveals (Himself), He is an image. But just as the Father works the created image, through the Son, the Image, so through the Holy Spirit, the image of recreation; and thus the Holy Spirit is an image, just as the Son, that is, quasi effectively. According to this, therefore, it must be said of the Holy Spirit, that He is not said (to be) an image simply, but quasi effectively, that is, in respect of the image of recreation. Whence "image" conveys two (things) concerning *the Holy Spirit*: that He is from the Son, and that He is the gift from Him, according to which there is in us the image of recreation; but absolutely He is not an image, just as the Son, because He is not from the Father as One having a conformity in the production of a Person out of Himself ».

[7] In the following Question. — The Vatican edition, which in this objection omits many (words), here, together with very many codices, omits *each* [utraque] before *definition* [definitio], and also *and similitude* [et similitudo] before *as it is* [ut ibi]. We have supplied, from codices P and Q, the words which were suppressed.

3. 4. To that, therefore, which is objected concerning assimilation and equality, it must be said, that the Son is not said (to be) an *"image"* on account of an assimilation in substance, but on account of

(His) manner of emanating; and in this the Holy Spirit does not have a most expressed similitude, neither with the Son nor with the Father, for that reason He is the image of Neither.

SCHOLIUM

I. That the name *"image"* is rightly said of the Son, is established from Sacred Scripture (Col. 1:15, 2 Cor. 4:4, Heb. 1:3); that it is a *proper* name for Him, is commonly taught, against Durandus (of Saint-Pourçain) and a few others, by the Latin doctors, while the Greeks attribute this name to the Holy Spirit. — Nevertheless, concerning *the reasons for assigning*, why this name is properly said of the Son, our doctors do not agree. St. Thomas (SUMMA., I, q. 35, a. 2) approves only this, that « the Son proceeds as a word, from the reckoning of which He is the similitude of an appearance [species] to that One from whom He proceeds, but not from the reckoning of love » etc.. The same reason, which (Petrus) Aureolus and others impugn undeservedly, St. Bonaventure also cites as a « *proper reckoning* », and the several others, which can be reduced to these two, he adjoins as *congruent* reasons (cf. 3rd. and 4th. argument of the fundament, and in the body of the response). The first is: the Son is from One, and an image most highly expressive cannot be but of one to one, and/or, (as Alexander of Hales, St. Albertus Magnus, and (Bl.) Peter of

Tarentaise say in slightly a different manner), of an image there is no image. St. Thomas asserts that this reckoning (loc. cit.) is worth nothing. The second is, because the Son convenes with the Father in the one spiration, but the Holy Spirit does not, concerning which reckoning St. Thomas says: « But this does not seem *to be sufficient* ». This can be easily conceded according to the mind of St. Bonaventure. Moreover, (Bl.) Dionysius the Carthusian (d. 28, q. 4), warns that these two reasons, commended by the authority of Richard of St. Victor, Alexander (of Hales), (St.) Albertus (Magnus) and of others, are not to be thoroughly neglected.

In what manner *"son"*, *"word"*, (and) *"image"* differ, is touched upon at the end of the Response; cf. d. 27, p. II, Doubt 2, and q. 2.

II. On the question itself: Alexander of Hales, SUMMA., p. I, q. 61, m. 3. — St. Thomas, SENT., Bk. I, d. 28, q. 2, a. 3; SUMMA., loc. cit.. — (Bl.) Peter of Tarentaise, SENT., Bk. I, d. 28, q. 3, a. 2. — Richard of Middleton, SENT., Bk. I, d. 28, a. 3, q. 2. — Giles the Roman, SENT., Bk. I, d. 28. 2nd. princ., q. 3. — Henry of Ghent, SUMMA., a. 69, q. 4.

QUESTION III

Whether eternity is appropriated to the Father, species to the Image, and use to the Gift?

Third, there is asked, for what reason is "eternity" [aeternitas] appropriated to the Father, "sightliness" [species] to the Image and "use" [usus] to the Gift. It seems, that (St.) Hilary's appropriation is not good:[1]

1. Because all the Divine Persons together are eternal and coequal; and *"eternity"* abstracts from the act of a Person: therefore, it is not appropriable.

2. Likewise, there is asked, for what reason is species appropriated to an image? For either it is taken there as "species", as species is said (to be) a *form*, or as (species is said to be) a *"beauty"* [pulcritudo]; if as a *form*; but just as *"nature"* is appropriable to None,[2] so neither (is) "species". But if as *"beauty"*; but the beauty of an image is referred to (its) prototype, therefore, to the Father: therefore, it ought to be appropriated to Him.

3. Likewise, Dionysius (the Areopagite) says,[3] that « the good and the beautiful is the same »: therefore, since *"goodness"* is appropriable to the Holy Spirit, therefore, also *"beauty"*.

4. Likewise, (St.) Hilary (of Poitiers) says,[4] that « it is necessary [oportet] that an image have the essence and nature and species of the original [auctoris] ». Therefore, for what reason does he define an image through a *species* rather than one of the others?

5. Likewise, one is not to use God, but only the creature:[5] therefore, *"use"* is appropriable to no Person, therefore, neither to the Holy Spirit.

CONCLUSION

"Eternity" [aeternitas] *is congruously appropriated to the Father, on account of (His) lack of a beginning;* "use" [usus], *as it means generally the acting of the will, to the Holy Spirit, on account of (His) manner of emanation, that is, according to will; but* species *to the Son, because* species *means a similitude, a reckoning of being cognizing, and a beauty: all of which are congruent to Him, because He emanates through a manner of nature.*

I RESPOND: It must be said, that this appropriation of (St.) Hilary was to explain the *origin* or emanation of the Persons. Since, therefore, the Person of the Father lacks both an emanation and an origin, for that reason there ought to have been appropriated to Him that (name), which conveys a privation of a beginning. But

---

[1] You will find the words of (St.) Hilary (here) above in q. 1, p. 541, footnote 1. — A little above this, codices X and Z read *For it seems* [Videtur enim]. After this argument, in codex O the following is found inserted: *Likewise, an appropriation is to exclude error: therefore, since men can err more about the eternity of the Son than (that) of the Father, it ought rather be appropriated to the Son* [Item, appropriatio est ad excludendum errorem: ergo cum magis possunt homines errare circa aeternitatem Filii quam Patris, magis Filio debet appropriari].

[2] For *to None* [nulli], which we have put on the authority of codices O Q and Y, and of edition 1, the Vatican has *by None (i.e. no Person)* [nulla]. A little before this, after *as a species is said (to be) a form* [ut species dicitur forma], codices aa and bb add *and/or an essence* [vel essentia].

[3] ON THE DIVINE NAMES, ch. 4, § 7 (according to the Greek text): *The beautiful is the same as the good* [ταὐτόν ἐστι τἀγαθῷ τὸ καλόν]. — After *is the same* [idem est], codices aa and bb adjoin *and/or follow after one another* [vel se consequenter]. — This argument, placed in the last position by the Vatican edition, we have put here, in the first position, on the authority of the codices and edition 1.

[4] ON SYNODS, n. 13: To be an image of a thing, it is necessary (that) it have the species and nature and essence of the original [auctoris], according to which it is, in itself, an image.

[5] Cf. above d. 1, a. 1, q. 3. — At the end of the argument, the Vatican edition, together with some manuscripts, reads faultily *the Holy Spirit* [Spiritus sanctus] for *to the Holy Spirit* [Spiritui sancto].

such is this name "*eternity*". For the eternal is that which lacks a beginning.[1] And though from its own name it does not mean but a privation of the duration of a start, yet through appropriation it means a privation of every beginning.

1. And thus is clear the first objection.

However, the Holy Spirit proceeds through a manner of will and love; and thus there ought to have been appropriated to Him the name, which expresses the acting [actus] of the will; but this is this name "*use*". « For '*to use*' is 'to assume something into the faculty of the will' »[2] to either use or enjoy (it). Since, therefore, taking up (something) to enjoy (it) is through love, similarly to use (it), because love is a weight and an order:[3] for that reason "*use*" rightly is appropriated to the Holy Spirit.

5. And in this manner (what was) sought last is clear, namely, that "*use*" is accepted here, not insofar as it is divided against "*fruition*", but insofar as it means the embrace of love and[4] a free act.

However, the Son emanates through a manner of nature;[5] and because He emanates through a manner of nature, for that reason He emanates through the manner of a *perfect* and *expressed similitude*. For nature produces a similar and equal to itself. And because He has in Himself the reckoning of an *expressed similitude*, for that reason, also (one) of *an act of cognition* [cognitionis], because an expressed similitude is a reckoning of being cognized.[6] And because through the manner of a *perfect similitude* and *reckoning* He has in Himself the reckoning and exemplar of all (things), hence it is, that He has the reckoning of perfect *beauty*. For because He is the *perfect* and *expressed similitude*, for that reason He is beautiful in comparison to *Him* whom He expresses. However, because He has the *reckoning of being cognized*, and not only of one (thing), but of the whole universality [totius universitatis]; for that reason as « the most beautiful One bearing in (His) mind a beautiful world »,[7] He has beauty in comparison to *every exemplified beauty*. From these two there is bequeathed [relinquitur] a most perfect beauty. For, just as (St.) Augustine says:[8] « Beauty is not other than a numerous equality ». Since, therefore, in comparison to *the Father* He has a beauty of equality, because He expresses perfectly, as a beautiful image; but comparison to *things* He has all the reasons, according to which (St.) Augustine says,[9] that « He is the Art full of all living reasons »: for that reason it is clear, that in the Son there is rightly found the reckoning of *every beauty*. — Therefore, by that, by which the Son emanates through a manner of nature, He has the reckoning of a perfect and expressed similitude; by this, that He has the reckoning of a perfect similitude, He has the reckoning of an act of cognition [rationem cognitionis]; and by reason of each He has the reckoning of beauty. Since, therefore, the name for a species conveys a *similitude* and conveys a *reckoning of being cognized*, it conveys also a *beauty* — so that « indeed, the sightliness of Priam is worthy of empire »[10] — for that reason it is most elegantly appropriated to the Son.

2. 4. It is clear, therefore, for what reason (St.) Hilary appropriates that name to *the Son* rather than another, (and) also for what reason He defines an *image* through that name than through any other.

To that, therefore, which is objected, that the beauty of an image is referred to (its) prototype; it must be said, that (that) is true, but, yet, the *honor* (of the image) is referred in one manner, the *beauty* (of it) in another: because the honor of an image or a picture is so referred to (its) prototype, that there is no honor in it according to itself, just as is clear, if an icon of blessed Nicholas is honored; but the beauty is thus referred to the prototype, because, there is, nevertheless, a beauty in the image, not only in that of which it is an image. And there can be found there a twofold reckoning of beauty, though in that of which it is (an image), naught but one is found. Which is clear, because an image is said (to be) "beautiful", when it represents well that, according to which it is. And that this is another reckoning of beauty, is clear, because it happens that one is without the other: according to which standard of measure [quemadmodum] there is said[11] (to be) beautiful an image of a devil, when

---

[1] Richard of St. Victor, ON THE TRINITY, Bk .II, ch. 4: For it seems that the sempiternal is, that which lacks a start and an end; the eternal, that which lacks each and every mutability.

[2] (St.) Augustine, ON THE TRINITY, Bk .X, ch. 11, n. 17. Se above (Master Peter), d. I, ch. 2, and the Seraphic Doctor's explanation there in a. 1, q. 1.

[3] (St.) Augustine, CONFESSIONS, Bk. XIII, ch. 9, n. 10: My weight (is) my love, by the one I am moved [feror], wheresoever I am moved. Cf. also ON THE CITY OF GOD, Bk. XI, ch. 28, and Bk. XV, ch. 22, where there is also taught, that in love an order is required.

[4] Codices K V and X insert *thus* [ita].

[5] The words *and because He emanates through a manner of nature* [et quia emanat per modum naturae], which are extant in very many codices and edition 1, are wanting in the Vatican edition and in some codices. — On the next added reckoning, see above d. 7, a. sole, q. 1, p. 134, footnote 10.

[6] Cf. above d. 6, q. 3, in reply to n. 4, and below in d. 35, q. 1, in the body (of the question), and Aristotle, ON THE SOUL, Bk. II, text 38 (ch. 8), and his book, ON MEMORY AND REMINISCENCE, ch. 2 (ch. 1). — A little below this after *a reckoning* [rationem] the Vatican edition repeats *of being cognized* [cognoscendi], supported by neither the codices nor editions 1, 2 and 3.

[7] (St. Severinus) Boethius, ON THE CONSOLATION OF PHILOSOPHY, Bk. III, metr. 9. — The Vatican edition, without the authority of the codices and edition 1, adds *as (St. Severinus) Boethius says* [ut dicit Boethius], and next for *every exemplified beauty* [omne pulcritudinem exemplatam] it reads *every extraneous beauty* [omnem pulcritudinem extraneam], supported by only a few codices. Codex O has *every beauty of the One exemplified* [omnem pulcritudinem exemplati].

[8] ON MUSIC, Bk VI, ch. 13, n. 38: Or do you judge (beauty) to be other than a numerous equality? Cf. also ON THE CITY OF GOD, Bk. XXII, ch. 19, nn. 2 and 3.

[9] ON THE TRINITY, Bk. VI, ch. 10, n. 11.

[10] Porphyry, ON THE PREDICABLES, ch. on *Species*, according to the faulty, ancient translation, which the Scholastics used — even Averroës reads it thus. The words *the sightliness of Priam* [species Priami], Bl. (now St.) Albertus (Magnus), who did not suspect that the *of Priam* had arisen through the error of copyists, attempted to explain in his Commentary ON THE PREDICABLES OF PORPHYRY in this manner: « According to which we say, that the sightliness of Priam, the Trojan King (whose form was most elegant), was worthy of empire; because out of an elegant form there is demonstrated a disposition to virtues » etc. But (St. Severinus) Boethius, according to the edition of Migne, renders the Greek text of Porphyry into Latin rightly, reading *sightliness, indeed, is first worthy of empire* [species quidem primum digna est imperio], which other interpreters rendered as *sightliness, indeed, is the first worthy of empire* [species quidem prima digna est imperio], the first reading of which is had in Euripides, from whom those words cited have been taken. The words of Euripides, (translated into English) are:

Indeed, it happens to me to see the nephews of their nephews,
First, indeed, in form worthy of a kingdom:
For this most high virtue exists in life,
A body to have, to merit something beautiful.

[11] The Vatican ed. alone here adds *beautiful an icon of blessed Nicholas, because it represents his comeliness, and then it is pleasant, and* [iconia beati Nicolai pulcra, quia decorum illius representat, et tunc placida est, et.].

it represents well the foulness [foeditatem] of the devil, and then (the image itself) is foul. And for that reason (St.) Hilary, appropriating *sightliness* [speciem] or beauty to the Son, appropriates more under the name of "*image*" than under the name of "*son*".

3. 4. To that which is objected, that the same is the good and the beautiful; it must be said, that Dionysius does not want to say, that they are 'one' *according to reckoning* [ratione], but that they are 'one' *according to thing* [re]. But, since they differ *according to reckoning*, for that reason one can be appropriated to one, which is not appropriated to the other.

SCHOLIUM

I. On the reckoning itself of *appropriation* and on its twofold root, cf. below d. 34, q. 3, were there is also a discussion concerning the appropriation, by which power is attributed to the Father, wisdom to the Son, goodness to the Holy Spirit; see the third appropriation here in a. 2, q. 3 (cf. BREVILOQUIUM., p. I, ch. 6). In this question there is expounded in an outstanding manner the appropriation taken from Saint Hilary.

It must be noted, that in the Son there is a reckoning of most high *pulchritude* from a twofold source [ex duplici capite]: on the part of the Father, whom He expresses by a most perfect similitude, and on the part of (what are) exemplified. See more on the reckoning of beauty in SENT, Bk. II, d. 9, q. 8; SENT., Bk. IV, d. 49, p. II, a. 2, q. 1, in the fundament; ITINERARIUM, ch. 2; HEXAËMERON., Sermons 6 and 20. — The doctrine in the solution to n. 2 is also worthy of attention.

II. Alexander of Hales, SUMMA., p. I, q. 67, m. 1. — (Bl. John Duns) Scotus, REPORTATIO., Bk. I, d. 34, q. 3. — St. Thomas, here in q. 2, a. 1; SUMMA., I, q. 39, a. 8. — Bl. (not St.) Albertus (Magnus), here in a. 5, 6 and 7.; SUMMA., p. I, tr. 12, q. 48, m. 2. — Giles the Roman, here in 2nd. princ., q. 2. — (Bl.) Peter of Tarentaise, here in q. 2. a. 1,. 2 and 3. — Richard of Middleton, here in a. 2, q. 1. — Henry of Ghent, SUMMA., a. 71, q. 4. — Durandus (of Saint-Pourçain), here in q. 3. — (Bl.) Dionysius the Carthusian, here in q. 1. — (Gabriel) Biel, here in the q. sole.

ARTICLE II

On (St.) Augustine's appropriation.

Consequently, there is the principal question concerning (St.) Augustine's appropriation,[1] which is: « In the Father unity, in the Son equality, in the Holy Spirit the concord of unity and equality ». And about this three (questions) are asked:

First, there is asked, whether God can be said to be "one" [unum] with a creature.

Second, whether a creature can be said to be "one" [unum] with another creature.

Third, concerning the reckoning of appropriation of those three (names).

QUESTION I

Whether God can be said (to be) "one" with a creature?

Moreover, that God can be said to be "one" [unum] with a creature, is shown:

1. Through the Authority of the Apostle, in the sixth (chapter) of the First (Letter) to the Corinthians:[2] *He who clings to the Lord is one spirit (with Him).* If one spirit: therefore, one being and one thing; and if this, therefore, 'one' [unum].

2. Likewise, the man, who *clings to God, is one spirit.* therefore, either a *created (spirit),* or an *uncreated* (one); not a *created* (one), because God is not a creature: therefore, one[3] *uncreated.* But the uncreated Spirit is entirely one: therefore, the man clinging to God is simply one [unum] with God.

3. Likewise, a mean [medium] is united more to an extreme, than an extreme to an extreme; but the Holy Spirit is the medium uniting just men, and just men, united through Him, are 'one' [unum] — according to the seventeenth (chapter of the Gospel of St.) John:[4] *That they may be one* [unum], *just as even We are one* [unum] — therefore, the just man can be said to be "one" [unum] with the Holy Spirit.

4. Likewise, a member is united more to (its) head, than a member with a member: therefore, since the members of Christ are "one" [unum] in Christ, much more strongly is the member the same to the Head. But Christ is the Head, not only according to (His) Humanity, but also according to (His) Divinity: ergo etc..

ON THE CONTRARY: 1. From that word, which is said in the tenth (chapter of the Gospel of St.) John:[5] *I and the Father are 'one'* [unum], the Saints impugn the Arian heresy, and most of all (St.) Augustine, concluding from this, that Arius errs, who says, that the Son

---

[1] ON CHRISTIAN DOCTRINE, Bk I, ch. 5, n. 5.

[2] Verse 17.

[3] For *one* [unus] the Vatican edition together with codex cc has <u>ad minus</u>, and a little lower *by clinging* [adhaerendo] for *clinging* [adhaerens]. Somewhat above this, before *not a created (one)* [non creatus], codices W and X interject *but* [sed].

[4] Verse 22. — For *are 'one'* — *according to the seventeenth*

(chapter of the Gospel of St.) John [sunt unum — Ioannis decimo septimo] the Vatican edition, together with some manuscripts, has *are. Whence (St.) John in the seventeenth (chapter of his Gospel says)* etc. [sunt. Unde Ioannes] .

[5] Verse 30. — You will find (St.) Augustine's reason, which this regards, here in the text of (Master) Peter, ch. 4. Cf. also ON THE TRINITY, Bk. IV, ch. 9, n. 12, and AGAINST MAXIMINUS, Bk. II, ch. 20, n. 1.

has another nature. If, therefore, the reckoning of (St.) Augustine is good, <u>unum</u> means a unity in nature; but in such a manner God is not one [unum] with a creature: ergo etc..

2. Likewise, this seems *by another reckoning*, because (those) which are most of all distant are least of all one [unum]; but the Creator and creature are most of all distant: therefore, they cannot be simply said (to be) one [unum].

3. Likewise, if they are one [unum], therefore, one something; but if they are one something, therefore, God and the creature have something common; and if this, they are univocated in some (name). Therefore, since the univocal is more simple, than those which are univocated in it,[1] something is more simple than God.

4. Likewise, if God and the creature are one [unum], since He is distant from anything in an infinite degree [in infinitum], by that reckoning by which He is said to be "one" [unum] with one (creature), (He is said to be such) with any. But whatsoever are the same to one and the same, are the same amongst themselves:[2] therefore, ˙cording to this all (things) are one [unum].

CONCLUSION

God cannot be said simply (to be) "one" with a creature, but with a certain determination, such as "one spirit", this expression is rightly put to use.

I RESPOND: It must be said, that just as (St.) Augustine says,[3] regarding this, that some be 'one' [unum], a conformity of *will* is not sufficient, but it is necessary that there be presupposed a convening in *nature*. Since, therefore, God and the creature are most highly different in nature, for that reason they ought not be said (to be) "one" [unum], just as the reasons brought forward for this prove.

However, because the just man is[4] conformed through charity to the Divine Will and clings to It more than to anything else, he is rightly said (to be) "one" [unum] *with a determination*, as for example "one spirit". For the will and love are said (to be) spirit,[5] whence *he who clings to God is one spirit (with Him)*, because he is of one (will) and of a conform will (with God).

1. To that, therefore, which is objected: he is one spirit, therefore, one thing; it must be said, that there is a fallacy <u>secundum quid</u> and *simply (speaking)* there. For "*one*" is withdrawn from its reckoning through that which is "*spirit*", and means there a unity, not through the indivision or unity of nature, but through a conformity of will.

2. To that which is objected: either one created spirit, or (one) uncreated etc.; it must be said, that neither a created (spirit), nor an uncreated (one). For "*spirit*" there does not stand for a substance, but for an act of the will; and "*one*" does not convey but a conformity of human affection toward the Divine Will or toward the Divine Love, because love transforms the one loving into the one loved.

3. To that which is objected, that the[6] Spirit is uniting medium; it must be said, that He unites as much as regards the will, but not as much as regards a conformity of nature; and they are not said (to be) "*one*" [unum] by reason of a conformity of will alone. For that reason it is not valid, because the binding of the Spirit is not the whole cause why they are one [unum].

4. To that which is objected, that the members of Christ are "one" [unum]; it can be said, that the members of Christ are not said (to be) "*one*" [unum] *simply*, but "*one body*", and in this manner Christ is one [unum] with (His) members,[7] but this is by reason of (His) assumed Humanity.

SCHOLIUM

I. Before there is a treatment of *unity*, to the extent that it is appropriated to the Father, two questions concerning the unity, which can be between God and creatures, and (the unity) between a creature and a creature, are considered. — On Christ, to the extent that He is the Head of the Church, mention of which is made in the solution to n. 4, cf. SENT, Bk. III, d. 13, a. 2, q, 1, 2 and 3.

II. Alexander of Hales, SUMMA., p. I, q. 23, m. 4, a. 1, § 4. — Bl. (now St.) Albertus (Magnus), SUMMA., p. I, tr. 6, q. 29, m. 1, a. 2, in reply to n. 4. — (Bl.) Peter of Tarentaise, here in q. 3. a. 4. — Giles the Roman, SENT., bk. I, d. 8, p. I, 1st. princ., q. 2. — (Bl.) Dionysius the Carthusian, in this and the following question, here in q. 2, writes only of St. Bonaventure.

QUESTION II

Whether one creature can be said simply (to be) "one" with another?

Second, there is asked, whether one creature can be said (to be) "one" [unum], with another (creature); and that (it is) so, is shown in this manner:

1. The Apostle (Paul) in the third (chapter) of the First (Letter) to the Corinthians (says):[8] *He who*

plants and he who waters are one [unum]; but one is the one planting, another the one watering, such as Apollo: therefore according to this it is clear, that one creature can be said to be "*one*" [unum] with another.

---

[1] Or, to use more general terms: *since a universal is more simple than the particulars, which are contained under it.* Cf.* Aristotle, POSTERIOR ANALYTICS, Bk. I, ch. 20 (ch. 24). — At the beginning of this objection, for *if they are one* [si sunt unum], codex T, together with not a few others, has *if they be one* [si sint unum].

[2] Aristotle, POSTERIOR ANALYTICS, Bk. I, ch. 25 (c. 32): The same to the same are the same. Cf. TOPICS, Bk. VII, ch. 1, and PHYSICS, Bk. I, text 17 (ch. 2).

[3] See here the text of Master (Peter), ch. 4.

[4] Codex M, together with edition 1, adds *most highly* [summe].

[5] See above d. 10, a. 2, q. 3 in the body (of the Question).

[6] Supply, with codd. W & Z, *Holy* [sanctus]. A little further below this, for *and they are not* [et non] codd. K O S & X have *and for that reason they are* etc. [et ideo], cod. W has *and for that reason they are not* etc. [et ideo non], and, at the end of the solution, for *why* [quare] the Vatican ed. has *that* [quod].

[7] For *with (His) members* [cum membris], the Vatican edition, with nearly all the codices striving against this, has *co-member* [com-membrum].

[8] Verse 8. On the following words, cf. *ibid.*, v. 6. — Next for *one creature* [una creatura], the Vatican edition has *every creature* [omnis creatura].

---

* *Trans. note*: Here Cf. has been added, according to the context; as it did not appear in the original text of the footnote.

2. Likewise, (St.) Augustine says and Master (Peter) posits in the text,[1] that they are rightly said (to be) "one" [unum] which convene in nature and will; but this, one creature has with another: ergo etc..

3. Likewise, the Lord (says) in the nineteenth (chapter of the Gospel of St.) Matthew:[2] *And so they are presently not two, but one flesh*; He said this of man and wife; but if they are, and they are not two, therefore, they are one [unum]: therefore, man and wife can be said to be "one" [unum], and thus etc..

4. Likewise, from the unity of a material principle comes a unity simply (speaking), which is a unity in number;[3] but in man the body is a material principle — *but he who clings to a prostitute, becomes one body* (with her), just as is said in the sixth (chapter) of the First (Letter of St. Paul) to the Corinthians — therefore, one [unum] simply, and thus etc..

ON THE CONTRARY: 1. "*The same*" [idem], said simply, stands for the same in number,[4] therefore, "*one*" [unum] said simply, stands for one in number; but two creatures are not one in number, howsoever they convene: therefore, they ought not be said to be 'one' [unum].

2. Likewise, if some (things) are said (to be) one [unum] on account of (their) convening in nature, then, therefore, since a man and a donkey convene in nature, they are one [unum]; which is not conceded. *If you say*, that beyond this there is required a conformity of will; (on the contrary):[5] therefore, since men (,who are) sinners, convene in nature and in will, therefore, they ought to be said (to be) one [unum]: which, since they are not said (to be such), therefore, a conformity of nature and will is not sufficient.

3. Likewise, if a man, from being joined with a whore, is made one [unum] (with her), since every unity is from the first Unity,[6] this unity will be from the first Unity; but such a unity is detestable: therefore, the first Unity makes (their) unity detestable, therefore, it itself is blamable [vituperabilis].

CONCLUSION

Those, which retain a conformity of nature, will and operation, can be congruously said (to be) "one" simply; yet with the lack of any of these conditions, they can only be said (to be) "one" secundum quid.

I RESPOND: It must be said, that two distinct creatures cannot have a unity except through a conformity; but not every [quaelibet non] conformity causes (them) to be said (to be) "*one*" [unum] *simply*, but (only) that which is a conformity simply (speaking), not secundum quid. Moreover, for a *full* conformity there is required a threefold conformity, namely, in *nature*, in *will*, and in *operation*;

and when those three concur for any two (creatures), then those two[7] are said (to be) "*one*" [unum]: just as (St.) Paul and Apollo in nature were conform, because each (was) a man; similarly in will, because each desired the salvation of the faithful; similarly in action, because each use to exert himself to procure that, the former by planting and the latter by watering, and each action (was) conform, because each was through the preaching of the divine word. For the divine word, first scattered, is the seed, then it accepts the irrigation of rain. — But if there is a conformity in *nature* alone, they ought[8] not be said (to be) one except secundum quid, that is, with a diminishing determination, such as "one in genus and/or in species". If only in *will*, then they are "one spirit", which means (one) love. If one in *nature* and *will*, then (they are) "one body and one soul". If one in *nature* and *action*, they can be said to be "one" [unum] with a determination, such as a fornicator with a whore can be said (to be) one body; yet he cannot be said to be "one" [unum] simply, just as a man and a wife (are). Nor are evil men thus one [unum], as good men, because they disagree [disconveniunt] principally in what they intend to will [in volitis intentis]. For any evil (man) seeks *his own* good and not the common (good).

From these the (things) sought are clear. For it must be conceded, that if they have a conformity, just as has been said, that any two (can) be said (to be) "one" [unum] simply, just as the first[9] reasons prove.

Moreover, to that which is objected fourth, it must be said, that it does not conclude, because a fornicator and a whore are not said (to be) one body by reason of the corporal substance, but by reason of the carnal work, in which they are united: and for that reason it does not follow, that they ought to be said (to be) "*one*" [unum] *simply*.

1. To that which is objected concerning one in number, it must be said, that there is a twofold unity, namely, of *indivision* and *of conformity*. The unity of *indivision* is attained in one in number, and this is a unity simply (speaking); but the unity of *conformity* is not in one in number, but in those to whom it happens that they are conformed with others, as has been said.

2. To that which is objected, if they are said to be "one" [unum] on account of a conformity in nature etc.; it must be said, that (they are said to be such) on account of a conformity in *nature* and *will*; and not only in the nature, according to which there is the essence of a thing, but *out of which the one sprouting up, sprouts up*,[10] that is, inasmuch as it is the principle of the operation; in this manner it is clear, that a man and a donkey are not said to be "one" [unum]. It is also clear, that evil men are not said to be "one" [unum], because even if

---

[1] Here in ch. 4. — At the end of the argument, in place of *creature* [creatura], which word we have restored from codices K Q T (ee in a second hand), the Vatican edition has *nature* [natura].

[2] Verse 6.

[3] Aristotle, METAPHYSICS, Bk. V, text 12 (Bk. IV, ch. 6): In number, indeed, (they are one), whose matter (is) one. — The text of Sacred Scripture cited he is found loc. cit., v. 16.

[4] Aristotle, TOPICS, Bk. I, ch. 6 (ch. 5): However, most undoubtedly, what is one in number, seems to be said (to be) "the same" by all.

[5] Supply, together with the Vatican edition: *on the contrary*: [contra].

[6] Dionysius (the Areopagite), ON THE DIVINE NAMES, ch. 13,

§ 1 ff., and (St. Severinus) Boethius, ON UNITY AND ONE.

[7] The Vatican ed. and cod. cc omit *then those two* [tunc illa duo].

[8] Some codices, such as F H K T and Z, have *it ought not have been said (that they are)* [deberet dici].

[9] The Vatican edition, together with codex cc, adds *three* [tres].

[10] Aristotle, METAPHYSICS, Bk. V, text 5 (Bk. IV, ch. 4) says: « However, a nature is said, indeed (to be), in one manner, the generation of things being born ... but in another, (that) out of (something) which at first (is) not existing there is generated what is begotten ». These words in the Arabic-Latin version are rendered thus: « And "nature" is said in one manner of all (things) sprouting up; and "nature" too is said (to be) that, with

---

* *Trans. note*: The technical term, secundum quid, which literally means "according to something", indicates that manner of speaking in which a term signifies according to some standard of measure, e.g., a wall, painted white, is white not per se, but secundum quid, that is, it is white according to which it has been painted.

they do concord in the *proximate* end [fine propinquo] and in work, yet they differ in the *remote* (end), because each *seeks what is his own*.[1] But the just (act) the other way around; for if sometimes their wills disagree in the *proximate* end, they convene in the *remote* (end).

3. To that which is objected, that unity with a whore is in no manner from God; it must be said, that just as in a sin there is a substance of the action — and this is from God — and a deformity — and this is not from God; so in such a unity it must be understood.

SCHOLIUM

I. For a right understanding of this Question there must be noted the *distinction*, posited in the solution or rather more accurately in the determination in the 1st. opposed argument, and in the following question, in the reply to n. 1, namely, that there is a twofold unity: the unity of *indivision* (of a nature), by which something is indistinct in itself, distinct from anything else; the unity of *conformity*, which conformity can again be threefold, as is expounded in the text. In the rigorous sense only the unity of *indivision* is unity *simply (speaking)* [unitas simpliciter]. Nevertheless, in the broader sense

sometimes, even with the lack of a unity of indivision, a unity of *conformity* can be said (to be) a unity *simply (speaking)*, that is, when the conformity is perfect in nature, in will, (and) in action, as is explained in the body (of this question). Thus the various passages of Sacred Scripture are aptly expounded. — In regard to the solution to the last (objection), that the *substance* of an action, which is the quasi substrate of the *deformity*, is from God, cf. SENT., Bk. II, d. 37, a. 2, q. 1.

The question itself is explicitly treated only by Bl. (now St.) Albertus (Magnus), here in a. 13.

QUESTION III

According to which reckoning is "unity" appropriated to the Father, "equality" to the Son, (and) "concord" to the Holy Spirit?

Third, there is asked, concerning the reason for the appropriation of (these) three, aforesaid names.

1. And first concerning "*unity*". And it seems, that it is not appropriable, because 'one' and being [ens] are convertible,[2] therefore, "unity" and "essence" (are convertible); but "essence" is appropriable to None: therefore, neither "unity".

2. Likewise, if ("unity") is appropriated, since the Holy Spirit is the unity of Both, as (St.) Augustine[3] says, it seems, that it ought to be appropriated to the Person of the Holy Spirit.

3. Likewise, there is the objection concerning the "*equality*", which is appropriated to the Son. For nothing is more undiffering among equal things than that equality; but the undiffering is not appropriable: therefore, neither is "equality" appropriable.

4. Likewise, if ("equality") is appropriated, it ought to be appropriated to the Father, because equality is not other than 'one' or a unity in quantity;[4] but "unity" is appropriated to the Father: therefore, also "equality".

5. Likewise, there is the objection concerning the "*concord*", which is appropriated to the Holy Spirit. For if concord reduces the many to unity, it seems rather to make the common from the *proper* than the proper from the common: therefore, if 'to appropriate' is 'to make the proper from the common', "concord" is appropriable to None.

6. Likewise, it seems that ("concord") ought to be

appropriated to the Son, since the Son *is our Peace, who made each (of our nations, Jew and Gentile) one* [unum], according to the second (chapter of St. Paul's Letter) to the Ephesians.[5] Likewise, in the first (chapter of his Letter) to the Colossians (there is written):[6] *Pacifying through the Blood of His Cross, both those which are on earth, and those which are in Heaven.*

7. Likewise, there is the objection against the reckoning of (St.) Augustine:[7] « All (are) equal on account of the Son etc. », therefore, the Father is equal on account of the Son: therefore, He has something from the Son, which is false. — Likewise, I ask, which cause does "*on account of*" [propter] mean, whether the *efficient*, or the *final*? Whichsoever of these it does mean, since the whole Trinity is *the One effecting* and *the End* of every thing, both *unity*, and *equality*, and *concord* is on account to the Father, (and) similarly on account of the Son: therefore, there is no reason for appropriating (the terms).

CONCLUSION

To explain the order of the Persons, "unity" is appropriated to the Father, "equality" to the Son, "concord" to the Holy Spirit.

I RESPOND: It must be understood, that just as (St.) Hilary's appropriation was to explain the *origin* of the Persons, so this one (of St. Augustine) is to explain (Their) *order*.

---

which *the one sprouting up, sprouts up* at first » [Et dicitur natura uno modo de omnibus pullulantibus; et etiam dicitur natura illud, cum quo *pullulat pullulans* primo]. Which words Averroës comments on in this manner: « And he intended through "*the one sprouting up*" [pullulans], the "one growing out of some thing and distinct from it" in the creature, though it is continuous with it ... and (in another manner) everything which grows in another and is continuous with it, either according to touch, or according to consolidation, is said to sprout up ». Bl. (now St.) Albertus, here in a. 13, applies this definition of nature, « the one sprouting up, sprouts up » to the Apostles, in whom (their) « faith was in the reckoning of (their) nature ».

[1] And allusion to Phil. 2:21: *For all seek what are their own, not what belongs to Jesus Christ.*

[2] See d. 24, a. 1, q. 2, p. 423, footnote 1. — In the following conclusion supple: *are convertible* [convertuntur].

[3] ON THE TRINITY, Bk. VI, ch. 5, n. 7. Cf. above d. 10, a. 2, q. 2.

[4] Cf. above d. 19, p. I, a. sole, q. 1, p. 342, footnote 6. — A little above this, codex M has *it seems* [videtur] for *it ought* [debet].

[5] Verse 14. — A little before this codices aa and bb have *because "concord" and "peace" (are) the same* [quia concordia et pax idem] for *since* [quoniam].

[6] Verse 20.

[7] ON CHRISTIAN DOCTRINE, Bk. I, ch. 5, n. 5.

Since, therefore, the Person of the Father is the first, before which there is no Other, and which is not out of Another; for that reason there is appropriated to Him the "*unity*", which is first in number, and before which nothing is in number.[1]

1. 2. From this the response to the first two (objections) is clear, because here "*unity*" is accepted according to that reckoning, by which it means a *primacy*, not an *indivision* of essence — because[2] thus it is convertible with being — or a *conformity* of will — because thus it is appropriated to the Holy Spirit. However, as the first (reckoning) it is appropriated to the Father.

Similarly, because the Person of the Son according to the reckoning of understanding is second and the One perfectly expressing the Father, and this causes an equality; for that reason "*equality*" according to a reckoning of order is first found in the Son. For it is then first understood, when the Son is understood to be born.

3. 4. And from this the objection is clear. For that "*equality*" be appropriated, this is not by a reckoning of unity, but by a reckoning of a first an perfect association. For "*equality*" is then first understood, when association is understood; and this is understood first in the Son, who is the second Person.

Similarly,[3] the Person of the Holy Spirit, according to the reckoning of understanding, is the third (Person); but "*concord*" posits two concordables and also a concordant; for that reason concord first begins, where the third Person is first understood to arise.

5. 6. And in this manner it is clear, that "*concord*" is appropriated to anyone, not because it makes the proper from the common,[4] but because it connects (those) distinct, and this according to the reckoning of its own emanation; which does not convene with the Son by reason of (His) *emanation*, but by reason of (His) *mediation*, because (He is) *the Mediator of God and men*.[5] From this all the objections are clear.

7. To that, however, which is objected last: « All are one [unum] on account of the Father, all (are) equal on account of the Father »;[6] it must be said, that if "*all*" [omnia] distributes for (all) "*created*", then "*on account of*" [propter] means the *formal, exemplary* cause according to *thing* and appropriation, because every equality has an exemplar in the equality of the Son; and thus concerning the others.[7] But if it distributes for (all) "*created and uncreated*", then "*on account of*" means the *formal, exemplary* cause according to the appropriated *reckoning of understanding*; because our intellect does not understand equality in the Father except on account of this, that He has a Son expressing His Nature and Power through all (manners); similarly concerning the others. And then "*on account of*" does not mean a cause of exemplarity according to *thing*, but according to *the reckoning of understanding*. And in this manner there is not noted, that the Father has anything from the Son, but that our intellect cognizes something of the Father through this, that it cognizes the Son.

SCHOLIUM

I. Just as St. Hilary's appropriation (here in a. 1, q. 3) serves to explain the *origin* and production of the Persons, so this one of St. Augustine to understand the *order* of the Three Persons. — Here (in reply to nn. 1 and 2) there is rightly distinguished a threefold unity. Concerning the reckoning of *unity* among the divine , cf. above d. 24, a. 1. — Here "*concord*" [concordia] signifies the same as "*nexus*" [nexus], concerning which see above d. 10, a. 2. a. 2.

II. Alexander of Hales, SUMMA., p. I, q. 67, m. 2. — (Bl. John Duns) Scotus, REPORTATIO., Bk. I, d. 34, q. 3. — St. Thomas, here in q. 3, a. 3; SUMMA., I, q. 39, a. 8. — Bl. (now St.) Albertus (Magnus), here in a. 9, 10, and 11. — (Bl.) Peter of Tarentaise, here in q. 3, a. 1, 2, and 3. — Richard of Middleton, here in a. 2, q. 2. — Giles the Roman, here in 2nd. princ., q. 3. — Henry of Ghent, SUMMA., a. 71, q. 4. — Durandus (of Saint-Pourçain), here in q. 3. — (Bl.) Dionysius the Carthusian, here in q. 2. — (Gabriel) Biel, here in the q. sole.

DOUBTS ON THE TEXT OF THE MASTER

DOUBT I

In this part, there are doubts about the text (of Master Peter) and first concerning the *location* of this part, because since Master (Peter) deals with appropriation in the Thirty-Fourth Distinction, and with appropriated (names) in the Thirty-Fifth Distinction all the

way to the end, it seems, that he badly situates here[8] a tract on appropriated (names).

I RESPOND: It must be said, that from a twofold cause Master (Peter) places here a tract on appropriated (names). *One (reason)* is, that whereby he had dealt with the names, which mean a relation according to a *common* relation, according to

---

[1] Codex D here adds *and from which flows every number; whence in (this) unity there is a primacy and a fecundity in respect of all numbers* [et a qua fluit omnis numerus; unde in unitate est primitas respectu omnium numerorum et fecunditas].

[2] Many codices, together with edition 1, here, others a little below this, substitute not well *and* [et] for *because* [quia]. For *or a conformity of will* [aut voluntatis conformitatem] codices L and O read *not insofar as it means a conformity of will* [non prout dicit voluntatis conformitatem]; codex Y has *or according to which it means a conformity of will* [aut secundum quod dicit voluntatis conformitatem]. A little after this codices T and Y omit *as* [Ut] before *the first (reckoning)* [prima].

[3] The Vatican edition alone here inserts *because* [quia].

[4] Codices L and O, having inverted the sense, read thus: *not because it makes something common from the proper* [non quia de proprio commune aliquid faciat]. — The Vatican edition, together with a few

codices, reads *it makes something proper* [aliquid faciat proprium].

[5] 1 Timothy 2:5.

[6] In the Vatican ed. alone, there are wanting the words *one on account of the Father* [unum propter Patrem], but in nearly all the codd. and edd. 2, 3, 4, 5 & 6, there are wanting the subsequent words *equal on account of the Son* [aequalia propter Filium]; in ed. 1 the words *on account of the Father, all (are) equal* [propter Patrem, omnia aequalia] are wanting. The integral reading, which we have restored, is found in cod. Z. Next, after this for "*all*" [omnia] many codices, with edition 1, have faultily "*one*" [unum].

[7] Understand (the names): "unity" and "concord".

[8] Codex bb reads *this* [hunc] for *here a* [hic].

[9] Codex T omits *a relation according to* [relationem secundum]. Next, for *which (names)* [quae] (on the following page), the Vatican edition, with very many codices and edition 1 striving against this, has *which (relation)* [quam].

which (names) the appropriation is attained, just as are "*similar*" and "*equal*"; and thus here this part is introduced incidentally. *The other* reason is that, because appropriated (names) serve to evidence proper ones [faciunt ad evidentiam propriorum]; for that reason immediately after the tract on proper (names), he dealt with appropriated ones, and this most of all, insofar as they serve to evidence proper (names). For that reason he dealt with these here, which do not man a looking-back to creatures; however, below, he deals with those appropriated (names), which mean a looking-back to creatures: and thus the distinction of this part is clear from that one. Whence (St.) Hilary' s three appropriated (names) manifest to us the *emanation* of the Persons, but (St.) Augustine's three appropriated (names) manifest to us the *order* of the Persons, if one looks into (the matter).[1]

DOUBT II

Likewise, is asked concerning this which (St. Augustine) says, that *He is a certain Art of the omnipotent and wise* etc.. For He seems to speak badly, because each one, with art not understood, is untrained [iners]: therefore, if the Son is the Art of the Father, with the Son not understood to be, the Father is untrained: therefore, it seems, reasonably that the Father has to work by His Son.

I RESPOND: It must be said, that the meaning is according to the context [facienda est vis in verbo], because he does not say, that He is *art simply*, but that He is *a certain art*, because He is not the Art, *by which* the Father knows, but *where* He knows; there is no art of the Father, by which the Father is wise, but (there is an Art) which is from the wise Father, through which the Father works all (things), because He produced all (things) through the Son. And it must be noted, that since "*art*" includes the intention[2] of both "*virtue*" and "*wisdom*", similarly also "*word*"; yet differently, because "*word*" means an emanation and a looking-back, for that reason it is a proper (name), but "*art*" an appropriated one.[3]

DOUBT III

Likewise, is asked of this which (St. Hilary) says, that *the Holy Spirit pours over all other creatures with (His) vast largess*; therefore, according to this it seems, that the Holy Spirit is granted to all.

I RESPOND: It must be said, that the Holy Spirit is not said "*to be given*" by reason of any effect, but properly by reason of that, which causes the Holy Spirit to be had, and thus to indwell in someone as in a temple.[4] And because a rational creature alone is capable of this kind (of having), and (because) the just alone grasp (Him); for that reason it is clear, that to them alone is the Holy Spirit given. Moreover, for this reason the Holy Spirit is said *to pour over all other creatures*, not because there is attributed to Him the act of creating, but because there is attributed to Him the act of conserving.

DOUBT IV

Likewise, is asked concerning the reckoning of (St.) Hilary, which is posited in the Brief Note: *An image is of that thing, according to which it is imaged, an undiffering appearance.* First *that* reckoning *of his* does not seem convertible, because the whole seems to befit the Holy Spirit. — Likewise, "appearance" [species] is accepted either essentially, or personally. If *essentially*: therefore, that which[5] is an "*undiffering appearance*" is understood [sensus est] (to be) the same, as that which is (understood), if there would be said "*an undiffering essence*"; but this befits the Father, not only the Son. And again, the Essence is not said as *of Anyone*. If it stands *on behalf of a Person*: therefore, the "*undiffering appearance*" is understood (to be) the same, as that which is (understood), when there is said "*undiffering Person*", but this (is)[6] false.

Likewise, there is the objection concerning the *second* reckoning, which is such: *An image is the imaged and indiscrete*[7] *similitude of a thing to co-equate the thing.* For (this definition) seems false, because frequently an image does not equate that of which it is an image. — Likewise, if it is to co-equate a thing, then there seems to be an *equality*, not a similitude. — Likewise, it seems that he says the false, when he says "*indistinct similitude*", since every image and similitude is distinguished from that of which it is an image.

Likewise, since of one thing there is one definition,[8] *there is asked*, according to which standard of measure [quomodo] are those reckonings of his differently assigned?

I RESPOND: It must be said, that here there is defined the *uncreated Image*, insofar as it is proper to the Son alone, and in this manner it always means a looking-back to the Father; and for that reason in the *first* reckoning the genitive is posited, as in the reckoning of a *principle*, in the second it is posited in the reckoning of a *terminus*: since the Image has a being-compared to the Father, not only as to Someone, *to whom* or in whom *He leads*,[9] but also *from whom He emanates*. And thus is clear the distinction and order of these reasons.

And the *first* reckoning contains three conditions. Through the first the Son is noted *to be from Another* — when there is said: "*An image (is) of that thing, according to which it is imaged*" — and through the genitive, and the verb, which is passive. Through the second there is noted, that He is according to an *expressed* manner *of emanating*, namely, through this, that He is said (to be) an "*appearance*" [specie], which includes a perfect[10] similitude of cognizing.

---

[1] This doubt is also solved by Bl. (now St.) Albertus (Magnus), here in a. 1.

[2] Codex W has *the reckoning* [rationem].

[3] Cf. BREVILOQUIUM, p. I, ch. 3. — Bl. (now St.) Albertus (Magnus), here in a. 8. — St. Thomas, SUMMA., p. I, q. 39, q. 8.

[4] See above d. 14, a. 2, q. 1, and d. 15, p. II, q. 1. — A little after this, from the older manuscripts and edition 1 we have restored the word *alone* [sola], suppressed by the Vatican edition. Without the authority of the codices, the Vatican edition transposes this doubt, together with the preceding one, after the fifth doubt.

[5] Codices dd and ee omit *that which is* [qui est]. Next for *as that which is (understood)* [qui etiam est] the Vatican edition has *as that which would be (understood)* [qui esset etiam].

[6] Codex T, together with not a few others, adds *is* [est].

[7] Many codices read *indistinct* [indistincta], but below in the explanation of this word they have *indiscrete* [indiscreta].

[8] Aristotle, TOPICS, Bk. VI, ch. 3 (c. 4.), where he also adds this reason: For to each of those which are, one is the 'to be that which it is'. — Immediately before this for *one* [una], codex T has *a unique* [unica]; codex T reads *only one* [una tantum].

[9] Our reading, which is supported by the authority of very many codices and edition 1, differs not a little from the reading of the Vatican edition, which is: *to some thing, or to something or into something He leads* [ad aliquam rem sive ad quid sive in quid ducit]. Codex F O T X, other than consenting with our reading, omits *to Someone* [ad aliquem], while codex S reads *to some Terminus* [ad aliquem terminum]. — A little further below this, for *the distinction and order of these reasons* [harum rationum distinctio et ordo] the Vatican edition has *the reckoning and order of these definitions* [harum definitionum ratio et ordo], with nearly all the codices and edition 1 disagreeing.

[10] Codex M has *an expressed* [expressum] for *a perfect* [perfectam].

But through the third there is noted, that He is *undiffering according to substance*, namely, through this that He is *"undiffering"*. And through the first condition He differs both from the Essence and from the Father, through the second, from the Holy Spirit, through the third, from the created image.

And through this it is clear,[1] that *"appearance"* [species], even if of itself it is (a name) for the Essence, yet it is accepted there as drawn to a *Person*; and *"undiffering"* does not mean an indistinction in this name *"appearance"*, but in substance. And in this manner the objections concerning the *first* reckoning are clear.

With this seen, the *second* reckoning is similarly clear, which is given in comparison to the Father Himself as to a *terminus*. And this is clear, when it is said (to be) *"of a thing to co-equate a thing"* [ad rem coaequandum rei], that is, the Person of the Father; through this that it is said (to be) *"imaged"*, there is excluded the Person of the Holy Spirit; through this that is said (to be) *"indiscrete"*, there is excluded the created image itself, and *"indiscrete"* does not mean (His) personal undiffering quality [indifferentiam], but only (His) essential one.

To that, therefore, which is objected concerning *equality*, it must be said, that that is not necessary concerning a created image. And *again*, since an image from the reckoning of its name means a quality in a quantity, for that reason[2] the first is said (to be) a *"similitude"* to co-equate a thing, that is, a similitude, according to which a thing is co-equated to thing.

DOUBT V

Likewise, is asked concerning the difference of these three (names), which (St. Hilary)[3] attributes (to the Most Holy Trinity), namely "appearance" [species], *"nature"*, *"essence"*.

I RESPOND: It must be said, that the substantial and completive form of each (thing) is said to be (its) *"appearance"*, *"nature"* and *"essence"*, and this according to a threefold consideration. For it can be considered *in itself*, and in thus it is said (to be) an *"essence"*; it can[4] be considered in comparison to *its own operation*, and thus it is said (to be) a *"nature"*; it can, again, be considered in comparison to *our cognition*, and thus it is said to be its *"appearance"*.[5] The Image of the Author has (His) *Appearance*, by this, that (He is) a begotten and or naturally imaged similitude; but (He has His) *Essence*, because (He is) an indiscrete similitude, that is, (undiffering) through substance.

DOUBT VI

Likewise, is asked concerning this which (St. Hilary) says: *If anyone says that the Son (is) innascible and without a beginning* [sine initio]. For it seems, that (St.) Hilary does not say rightly, that *he who says that (there are) two innascibles, says that (there are) two gods*; because innascibility among the divine is not a property of the Essence, but of a Person: therefore, it does not follow, that if there are two innascibles, that (there are) two *essences*, but (rather) that (there are) two *Persons*. — Likewise, "innascibility" means a privation of that which has been *born*, whence *"innascible"* is only worth as much, as *"not a son"*; but it does not follow: 'there are two sons among the divine, therefore, two gods': therefore, for an equal reason it does not follow, 'there are two innascibles, therefore, two gods'.

I RESPOND: It must be said, that *"innascible"*, just as has been said above,[6] deprives or negates *'being from another'*, and from this it posits a *fontal plenitude* in the one who is said (to be) *"innascible"*; and from *each* part there is concluded, that if there are two innascibles, that there are two gods. For it follows: 'there are two, any of which is not *from another*, therefore, they are not distinguished through origin: therefore, it is necessary, that they be distinguished through substance'. Likewise, if there are two, among which any is a *fontal plenitude*: therefore, any can be the beginning of the Trinity and is « the beginning of the whole Deity »,[7] just as has been said of the Father. But if there are distinct beginnings, and beguns: therefore, if any is the beginning of the whole Deity, and there are two: therefore (there are) two deities. Therefore, although *"unbegotten"* is not a property of the Substance, but of a Person, yet because it is (a property) of the *first* Person, and in a unique Person there cannot be but one innascibility: for that reason it posits of necessity a diversity of gods.[8]

DOUBT VII

Likewise, is asked of this which (St. Hilary) says: *For the Head of all (things) is the Son.* For he seems to speak badly, because either *"the Head"* is said by a reckoning of *deity*, or by a reckoning of *conformity in nature*. If by a reckoning of *deity*, for the same reason the Holy Spirit can be said (to be) *"the Head"*. Likewise, if by a reckoning of *deity*, then *"the Head"* of the Son cannot be said (to be) God, because *"the Head"* rises above [superexcellit] and holds a greater nobility, which the Father does not have in respect of the Son. *If*

---

[1] In the Vatican edition and codex cc there is wanting *it is clear* [patet].

[2] Codex T (in the margin) reads *in the first it is said* [in prima dicitur] for *the first is said* [prima dicitur]. — On these definitions of an image, cf. also Alexander of Hales, SUMMA., p. I. q. 61, m. 2. — Bl. (now St.) Albertus (Magnus), here in a. 6. — St. Thomas and (Bl.) Peter of Tarentaise, here on the text. — (Bl. John Duns) Scotus, SENT., Bk. I, d. 28, q. 2, a. 1.

[3] Understand: *(St.) Hilary* [Hilarius], from whom the doubts, which follow, have also been taken. — For *"essence"* [essentiam] the codices, together with edition 1, faultily read *"image"* [imaginem].

[4] To the verb *it can* [potest] not a few codices, together with edition 1, 2, and 3, add *again* [iterum].

[5] Cf. Aristotle, PHYSICS, Bk. II, text 11 ff., and text 28 ff.

(ch. 1 and 3); METAPHYSICS, Bk. V, text 3 and 5 (Bk. IV, ch. 2 and 4), where the substantial form [forma substantialis] is called, in Greek, ὁ λόγος τοῦ τί ἦν εἶναι (the reckoning of the essence), ἡ φύσις (the nature) and τὸ εἶδος καὶ τὸ παράδειγμα (the species and exemplar).

[6] Distinction 27, p. I, a. 1, q. 2, in reply to n. 3; and d. 28, q. 1.

[7] The text is from (St.) Augustine, ON THE TRINITY, Bk. IV, ch. 20, n. 29; in which text after the word *the beginning* [principium], very many codices and edition 1, together with the original, subjoin *is* [est], which is omitted by the Vatican edition.

[8] Cf. Alexander of Hales, SUMMA., p. I. q. 69, m. 5. — Bl. (now St.) Albertus (Magnus), here in a. 14, where it also concerns the following doubt. — St. Thomas and (Bl.) Peter of Tarentaise, here on the text.

you say, that "*the Head*" does not mean a nobility and superexcellence; *there is the objection* from the following text, where[1] there is said: « *all (things) are referred by this step* »; but it is established, that between the Father and the Son by reason of *the Deity* there is no step: therefore, it cannot be accepted according to a reckoning of *deity.* — If by a reckoning of *conformity,* since the Son does not have a conformity in nature with all (things), but only with men, He will not be "*the Head*" of all (things).

I RESPOND: It must be said, that "*the Head*", according to which it is accepted property, conveys a reckoning of *influence,* and of *conformity of nature*: and in this manner Christ is said to be "the Head of the whole Church"; but (St.) Hilary in an more extended manner accepts (it), insofar as "*the Head*" means the original beginning. And since God the Father is the beginning of the Son, and the Son the beginning of all (things), such that the Son is produced and produces, for that reason *He is* the Head, and *He has* a Head. But the Father, since He does not have a Head, since He is innascible, is the Head of all; and for that reason He is said (to be) *the Fontal Principle,* from Whom all and in Whom all are lead back through the Son. And in this leading-back there is a *step,* by comparing *creatures* to the Son; but further by comparing *the Son* to the Father *there is no step*; but (there is) an order and an origin. And for that reason (St.) Hilary does not say "*by these steps*", but "*by this step*". — What is objected concerning the Holy Spirit, it must be said, that the Holy Spirit Himself, since He proceeds from the Son, is with (all) other (things) lead back through the Son to the Father, and on this account the *leading-back* is appropriated to the Son.

DOUBT VIII

Likewise, is asked of this which (St. Hilary) says: *That They are Three through substance, but One* [unum] *through consonance*; because this confession of faith does not seem to be fitting, because it can be said of three men, when agreeing [concordantibus],[2] that they are "three" through substance, but "one" [unum] through (their) consonance [per consonantiam].

Likewise, there is asked of the reckoning of (St.) Hilary, by which he says, that *it ought to be said through consonance on account of the Holy Spirit, because, that is, by the surname of the Spirit, it is fitting that a unity of consonance rather than of essence be predicated.* For that seems false, because the Holy Spirit is of the same Essence with the Father, as the Son.

I RESPOND: It must be said, that[3] (St.) Hilary intends to show that the confession of the Fathers (is) catholic, when they said, that « there are Three [tria] according to substance, One through consonance ». For the holy Fathers, wanting to crush the heresy of Sabellius — which *crushed,* that is emptied the truth of the Father and Son through a *sole nomination,* which he said was there, *not (a sole) thing* — to this extent confessed expressly a *plurality,* as they confess less expressly a *unity of essence*; yet they did not recede from the truth, because tria is understood (to be) "three *things*", that is three Hypostases; but "through *substance*"[4] there is not understood "*ousia*", but "*Person*": and for that reason from this (first) part (of the expression) they spoke the truth. — On the part of *consonance* they spoke the truth in a similar and irreprehensible manner. For, just as through the Name of the Father and of the Son there is hinted unity *of nature,* because the Son is connatural to the Father, thus through the Holy Spirit, who is Love, one is given to understand a unity *of consonance.* And for that reason it was truly not worthy of calumny, and on this account they said it: and this (St.) Hilary wants to say, when he says, that (a unity) of consonance rather than of essence (be predicated); not because each is not true, but because the former is more expressed and is less worthy of calumny. Yet it still follows, that,[5] if the Father and the Son produce out of Themselves one Spirit,* by reason of this that there is a unity of consonance, it is necessary, that They have a unity in essence.

DISTINCTION XXXII

CHAPTER I

Whether the Father and/or the Son love by that love, which proceeds from Each, that is, by the Holy Spirit.

Here, there arises a question, deduced from the aforesaid. For it has been said, above,[1] and shown by the authorities of the Saints, that the Holy Spirit is the *communion* of the Father and of the Son and (is) *the Love* [amor], by which the Father and the Son love [diligunt] one Another. For that reason there is asked, whether the Father and/or the Son love through the Holy Spirit and/or by the Holy Spirit.[2] Indeed, it seems that it must be said [oportere dici], according to the authorities posited above, by which it is shown, that the Holy Spirit is He by Whom the Begotten is loved by the One begetting and loves His own Begetter. *But on the contrary*: if the Father and/or the Son is said *to love* through the Holy Spirit, it seems *to be* through the Holy Spirit, because

---

[1] See here the text of Master (Peter), ch. 3, *Brief Note.* For *where* [ubi] the codices, together with edition 1, have *because* [quia], and then in the text for *are referred* [referuntur], which is read in the original and in Master (Peter's text), the others, together with edition 1, have *are brought down* [deferuntur], others *are differed* [differuntur], others, which the Vatican edition also follows, *differ* [differunt].

[2] Many codices, such as A F G H I S T etc., together with edition 1, have *agreeing* [concordibus].

[3] The Vatican edition, and not a few codices, here very incongruously subjoins *just as* [sicut], by conjoining the following proposition with this one and by omitting *For* [enim] before *the Holy Fathers* [Sancti Patres]. Our reading is supported chiefly by the authority of codex Y. A little after this for *crushed* [elidebat], the Vatican edition, together with codices A L O T X Y Z and edition 1, reads *mocked* [eludebat].

[4] For *substance* [substantiam] nearly all the codices, together with editions 1, 2, and 3, have *consonance* [consonantiam]; faultily, as is clear from the subjoined.

[5] Very many codices, among which are G H and S, together with edition 1, have *because* [quia]. — The solution of this doubt is also had in St. Thomas, here on the text.

NOTES ON THE COMMENTARY

[1] Distinction XXXI, ch. 6.

[2] The Vatican edition and the other editions, breaking with the codices and edition 1, omit *and/or by the Holy Spirit* [vel Spiritu sancto]; codices C and D and edition 8, have the plural form for *love* [diligant]; and codex C, moreover, adds *Themselves* [se].

---

* *Trans. note*: Here the original text of the Quaracchi edition faultily read *spirit* [spiritum] for *Spirit* [spiritum], contrary to the context, which requires that the *unity in essence* be had by the Father and the Son and the Holy Spirit.

it is not one (thing) for God *to be*, and another *to love*, but (they are) the same; because, as (St.) Augustine says in the fifteenth book, ON THE TRINITY:[1] « Whatever seems to be said according to *qualities* in that simple Nature, must be understood according to *essence* », such as "good", "great", "immortal", "wise", "loving", and (names) of this kind. And for that reason, if the Father and/or the Son love through the Holy Spirit, it seems to be through the Holy Spirit. Nor does (the Father or the Son) love only by Their Essence, but also by (Their) Gift.

To this question, since it contains a depth of exceeding profundity, we respond this alone, that (St.) Augustine seems to signify, that is, that the Father and the Son love Themselves and guard (Their) unity not only by Their own Essence, but by Their own, proper Gift; which, though it has been posited above,[2] yet it is no annoyance [non piget] to repeat (it), because it is thus expedient. Therefore, (St.) Augustine speaks in the sixth book, ON THE TRINITY,[3] thus: « It has been made manifest, that Any of the Two is not, the One by whom Each is conjoined, by whom the Begotten is loved by the One begetting and loves His own Begetter, and that They are not by participation, but by Their own Essence, nor by the gift of Anyone superior, but by Their own (Gift) *the Ones preserving* [servantes] *the unity of peace* ».[4] Behold, here he says, that by Their own Essence and by Their own Gift They preserve [servant] unity. Likewise, in the tenth book, ON THE TRINITY[5] he says: « In that Trinity, who dares to say, that the Father loves neither Himself nor the Son nor the Holy Spirit except through the Holy Spirit »? — Here he openly shows, that the Father loves not only through the Holy Spirit; however, he does simply say, that the Father does not love through the Holy Spirit.

CHAPTER II

Whether the Father is wise by the Wisdom, which He begot.

Moreover, one must diligently investigate, whether the Father is wise by the Wisdom, which He begot, which is only the Son. Which it seems can be proven *by a simile*. For if the Father loves by the Love [amore], who proceeds from Him, why is He not wise [sapit] and/or does not understand also by the Wisdom and/or Intelligence, which He Himself begot? « There seems to urge this question », as (St.) Augustine says in the seventh book, ON THE TRINITY,[6] « that which the Apostle wrote, saying, *Christ, the Virtue of God and the Wisdom of God*, where there is asked, whether thus there is a Father of His own wisdom and virtue, that He is wise by this Wisdom, which He begot, and powerful by this Virtue, which He begot. — But far be it, that it be thus; because, if There 'to be' is that which (it is) 'to be wise', the Father is wise not through that Wisdom, which He begot, otherwise That is not from Him, but He from That. For if the Wisdom, which He begot, is the cause for Him, to *be wise*, (then) it is the very cause for Him, to *be*; which cannot come to be, except by begetting or by making Him; but neither has anyone said in any manner that Wisdom (is) the begetter or founder of the Father. For what is more insane? Therefore, the Father is also the very Wisdom, by which He is wise; but the Son is said to be "*the Wisdom*" of the Father and "*the Virtue*" of the Father, not because the Father through Him is wise and/or powerful, but because the Son, (who is) Wisdom and Virtue, is from the Father, (who is) Wisdom and Virtue ». — From these, therefore, it is clear,

the Father is not wise by begotten Wisdom, but by Himself, the unbegotten Wisdom.

A Brief Note. (St.) Augustine in the book, OF EIGHTY-THREE QUESTIONS (says):[7] « When God is said (to be) wise, and said (to be) wise by the Wisdom, without which, is forbidden to believe, that at some time He either was and/or can be, He cannot be wise by participation in wisdom, just as a soul (is), which can both be and not be wise; but because He Himself begot That, by which He is said (to be) wise by Wisdom ». Observer, o reader, that the Father is said (to be) *wise by begotten Wisdom*, which is obvious [obviat] by other testimonies. But (St.) Augustine corrects this in the first book of RETRACTATIONS, saying: « I said in the book, OF EIGHTY-THREE QUESTIONS, in the twenty-third question, which concerns the Father, that He begot That by which the Wise one is said (to be) Wisdom; but I treated that question afterwards, better, in the book, ON THE TRINITY ».

After these, there is customarily asked by certain (authors), whether *the Son* is wise by begotten or unbegotten Wisdom. For if He is not wise by *begotten* Wisdom, neither is He wise by Himself; however, if *begotten* Wisdom is wise, He does not seem to be wise by *unbegotten* Wisdom; and thus He does not seem to be wise by the Father, since He has all from the Father. — To which we say, that there is one Wisdom of the Father and of the Son and of the Holy Spirit, just as (there is) one Essence, because the Wisdom in the simplicity of that Nature is the Essence; and only an *unbegotten* Wisdom; and the *begotten* Wisdom is *from* [de] the *unbegotten* Wisdom and/or *by* [a] the unbegotten Wisdom. And since it is the same There 'to be' as 'to be wise', it remains, that the begotten Wisdom is wise from the unbegotten Wisdom. Therefore, the Son is sot said (to be) the Wisdom of God, as if He alone is the One understanding [intelligens] and/or discerning [sapiens] Himself and the Father and the Holy Spirit; because, as (St.) Augustine says in the fifteenth book, ON THE TRINITY:[8] « If the Son alone understands There both Himself and the Father and the Holy Spirit, there is this absurd result [ad illam reditur absurditatem], that the Father is *not* wise from Himself, but from the Son, and Wisdom has not begot Wisdom, but the Father is said to be wise by that Wisdom, which He begot. For where there is not intelligence, neither can there be wisdom. And for that reason, if the Father Himself does not understand Himself, but the Son understands the Father, the Son indeed makes the Father wise. And if for God 'to be' is that which (it is) 'to be wise', and that Essence of His is what Wisdom (is); it is true that the Son does not have the Essence from the Father, but rather the Father from the Son; which is most absurd and also most false. Therefore, God the Father is wise by That which He Himself is as His own Wisdom; and the Son, the Wisdom of the Father, is wise from the Wisdom, which is the Father, from whom the Son has been begotten. Thus the Father is also intelligent by That which He is as His own Intelligence. For one would not be wise, who was not intelligent. Moreover, the Son, the Intelligence of the Father, has been begotten from the Intelligence, which is the Father, from whom He is intelligent ».

Therefore, [proinde], the Father is Wisdom, and the Son Wisdom, and Each the One (is) Wisdom, and yet the Father alone is the unbegotten Wisdom, and the Son alone the begotten Wisdom, and yet the Father is not one Wisdom, the Son Another, but there is one and the same Wisdom:

---

[1] Chapter 5, n. 8.   [2] Distinction X, ch. 2.

[3] Chapter 5, n. 7. — A little above this, after *but* [sed] codex D adds well *also* [etiam], then codices B and E have *it will be no annoyance* [non pigebit] for *it is no annoyance* [non piget].

[4] Ephesians 4:3. Codices A B D and E read *unity in the bond of peace* [unitatem in vinculo pacis] for *the unity of peace* [unitatem pacis]. The Vulgate reads: *Solicitous to preserve the unity of the spirit in the bond of peace* [Sollicti servare unitatem spiritus in vinculo pacis].

[5] Chapter 7, n. 12.

[6] Chapter 1, n. 1. The last proposition is ibid, n. 2. — The passage of Sacred Scripture is 1 Cor. 1:24.

[7] Question 23. — The passage from (St. Augustine's) book on RETRACTATIONS, is ch. 26. In his work ON THE TRINITY, this question is dealt with in Bk. VI, ch. 1, n. 1 ff; Bk .VII, chs. 1-4; and in Bk .XV, ch. 7, n. 12.

[8] Chapter 7, n. 12.

just as the Father is the unbegotten God, and the Son is the begotten God, and the begotten God is not the unbegotten God; yet nor for that reason is the Father one God, the Son another, but the one God (is) Each, but (They are) not one [unus]. For One is the Begotten, the Other the Unbegotten, but (there is) not other God, nay Each (is) the One [unum] or the One God. Thus the begotten Wisdom is not the unbegotten Wisdom, but One is the begotten Wisdom, the Other the Unbegotten; yet there is no other Wisdom, but one and the same Wisdom.

CHAPTER III

Whether the Son is wise by Himself* and/or through Himself.

From the aforesaid it is established, that the Son is not wise *by Himself* nor *from Himself*, but by the Father and from the Father. Moreover, there is customarily asked, whether the Son is wise *by Himself* and/or *through Himself.* — Certain (authors) says, that here a multiple understanding is caused, and for that reason one will have to distinguish, so that, when you say, that the Son is wise *by Himself* and/or *through Himself*, if you understand that (He is) wise by the Nature and Essence, (your) understanding is true; but if you understand that He is wise *by Himself* and/or *from Himself*, you have an understanding subjected to falsehood. — However, others simply and without a determination concede expressions of this kind: "the Son is wise *through Himself*, but not *by Himself* and/or *from Himself*"; and "the Son is *God through Himself* and *is through Himself*, but not *by Himself* and/or *from Himself*"; confirming this by the words of (St.) Hilary, who says in the ninth book, ON THE TRINITY,[1] that the Son acts not *by Himself*, but *through Himself.* « Of the Nature », he says, « which you contradict heretically, is this Unity, so that the Son acts *through Himself*, lest He act *by Himself*, and thus He does not act *by Himself*, to act *through Himself.* Understand the Son acting, and *through Him* the Father acting. He does not act *by Himself*, when the Father is shown to remain in Him; He does act *through Himself*, when according to the nativity of the Son He Himself does (those things) which are pleasing. He would be infirm, by not acting by Himself, unless He acts by God; but He would not be in the Unity of the Nature, if He did what He did and in which He pleases (to do what He did), not through Himself ». Therefore, just as, they say, the Son acts *through Himself*, but not *by Himself*; so the Son ought to be said (to be) wise *through Himself*, but not *by Himself*; in the same manner also is He[2] and/or is He to be said to be, as they say, *through Himself God*, but not *by Himself* and/or *from Himself.*

CHAPTER IV

Whether there is only one Wisdom of the Father.

After these, there is customarily asked by certain (authors), whether there is only one Wisdom of the Father; which they strive to prove that there is *not*, in this manner: the Son, they say, is the begotten Wisdom of the Father, by which the Father is not wise: therefore, there is some wisdom of the Father, by which He is not wise; moreover, there is also a unbegotten wisdom of the Father, and by this the Father is wise. therefore, there is a certain wisdom of the Father, by which He is wise, and it is not that Wisdom of the Father, by which He is not wise: there is not, therefore, only one wisdom of

the Father. — Likewise, the unbegotten Wisdom is the Wisdom of the Father, and the begotten Wisdom is the Wisdom of the Father; moreover, the unbegotten Wisdom is not the begotten Wisdom: therefore there is not only one Wisdom of the Father. — This and (those) similar to these we reject as sophistries [sophistica] and as far from the truth and as clear to all other experts in theology, adverting to (what are) unworthy of a response [responso indigna],[3] yet applying [adiicientes] one, because there is one Wisdom of the Father, but It is not said in one manner. For the Wisdom of the Father is said to be That which He begot, and the Wisdom of the Father is said to be That by which He is wise: therefore, the reckoning of the saying is diverse. For *the Former* is said (to be) of the Father, because He begot It; and *the Latter* is said (to be) of the Father, because He is wise by It. Yet, there is one Wisdom of the Father, because the begotten Wisdom is the same Wisdom and That by which He is wise, or That by which the Person of the Father, or the Essence of the Father, is understood (to be) wise; because the Person of the Father, which is understood, when there is said "*the unbegotten Wisdom*", and the Person of the Won, which is signified, when there is said "*the begotten Wisdom*", is the one and same Wisdom, which is understood (to be) the Divine Essence, common to the Three Persons.

CHAPTER V

Just as in the Trinity there is the Love, which is the Trinity, and yet the Holy Spirit is the Love, which is not the Trinity, and for that reason there are not two Loves; so also concerning Wisdom.

And just as in the Trinity there is a Love [dilectio], which is the Father, the Son and the Holy Spirit, which is the very Essence of the Deity; and yet the Holy Spirit is the Love, which is not the Father and/or the son, and there are not, for this reason, two Loves in the Trinity — because the Love, which properly is the Holy Spirit, is the Love, which is the Trinity, yet He Himself[4] is not the Trinity — thus in the Trinity there is a Wisdom, which is the Father and the Son and the Holy Spirit, which is the Divine Essence; and yet the Son is the Wisdom, which is not the Father and/or the Holy Spirit. And, not for this reason are there two Wisdoms There, because the Wisdom, which properly is the Son, is the Wisdom, which is the Trinity, yet It Itself is not the Trinity; just as the Son is the Essence, which is the Trinity, yet He Himself is not the Trinity.

CHAPTER VI

For what reason is the Father not said (to be) wise by the Begotten Wisdom, just as He is said (to be) loving by the Love, which proceeds from Him.

Moreover, it must be diligently noted, that for this reason, by which the Father is not said to be wise by the Wisdom,[5] which He begot, it seems that it will have to be said, that the Father does not love the Son, and/or the Son the Father by that Love, which proceeds from Each, namely, which is properly the Holy Spirit. For just as it is the same for God 'to be wise' as (it is) 'to be', so it is same for Him 'to love' as (it is) 'to be'. And for that reason, just as the Father is denied to be wise by the Wisdom, which He begot — because if He would be said (to be) wise by That, That would not be understood to be from Him, but He from That — thus it seems that it ought not be conceded, that the Father and/or the Son loves by the Love, which only

---

[1] Number 48. The edition of (St. Augustine's works) has at the beginning: Of the Nature, oh you who contradict, is this Unity [Naturae, qui contradicis, haec unitas est]. Below, it also reads: ... which are pleasing, He would belong to the infirm by not acting by Himself, unless *to this extent* He Himself acts, *so that (those things) which He does be pleasing* [infirmis sit non a se agendo nisi adeo ipse agit, ut quae agit placeant]. — The reading of Master (Peter) is more agreeable.*

[2] The Vatican edition, together with very many editions, adds *Himself* [ipse], and a little before this after *so* [ita] it adds *also* [et].

[3] The Vatican edition faultily reads *response* [responsio] in the nominative, codex D (has correctly) *response* [responsione] in the ablative.

[4] The Vatican edition and editions 4, 5 and 8, have *It itself* [ipsa].

[5] Thus the codices; the Vatican edition, together with very many editions, has *(to be) wise by that Wisdom* [ea sapientia] for *to be wise by the Wisdom* [esse sapientia].

---

* *Trans. note*: In the English translation, "*by Himself*", in this paragraph and throughout this Distinction and St. Bonaventure's COMMENTARY on it, is not said in the sense of *apart from all others*, but in the sense of *by means of Himself, by his own power or nature or being*.

the Holy Spirit is; because if the Father and/or the Son loves by That, the Holy Spirit does not seem to be from [a] the Father and the Son, but the Father and the Son from the Holy Spirit, because it is the same There '*to love*' as (it is) '*to be*'. — But above[1] it has been said and sanctioned by the authority of (St.) Augustine, « that in the Trinity there are Three: One loving Him who is from [de] Him, and One loving Him from whom He is, and Love Itself »; « and Any of the Two is not, He by whom the Begotten is loved by the One Begetting and loves His own Begetter ». With which words there is openly signified, that the Father loves the Son, and the Son the Father, even[2] by that Love, which is not Any of Them, but only the Holy Spirit. Therefore, since it is the same There '*to love*' as (it is) '*to be*', in what manner is the Father and/or the Son said not to be by that Love, by which the One loves the Other, since for that reason the Father is denied to be wise by the Wisdom, which He begot, lest He be understood to be by It?

I admit [fateor] that this question is difficult for me,[3] chiefly since it arises from the aforesaid, which seem to have the same reckoning, which as the infirmity of my intelligence attends to, is troubled, desiring more *to report* [referre] from the sayings of the Saints than *to contribute* [afferre] (to them). « For the best reader » as (St.) Hilary says in the book, ON THE TRINITY,[4] « is he who *looks forward to* the understanding of sayings from sayings, rather

than (who) *imposes* (it), and (who) *reported* more, than *he contributed*, and (who) does not think that there seems to be contained in the sayings, what he presumed to understand before (his) reading (of them). Therefore, when there is a discourse [sermo] concerning of the things of God, let us concede to God the understanding [cognitionem] of Himself and serve His sayings with pious veneration ». — Therefore, let the pious reader diligently investigate the reason for the sayings, if perchance it is worth while [valeat] to find for the sayings some cause, by which when known,[5] the aforementioned question might be able to be explained to some extent. But I, not resolving [absolvens] the question, but excluding error, profess, that thus it has not been said, that the Father loves the Son, and/or the Son the Father by that Love, which proceeds from Each, which is not Any of Them, but only[6] the Holy Spirit, as if the Father and/or the Son is by that Love. But thus does the Father loves the Son by This, and the Son the Father, that the Father also loves through Himself by that Love, which He Himself is — so also the Son — but not in this manner, that the Father does not love through Himself and the Son (likewise), but only through That. « Who presumes to opine and/or affirm, » says (St.) Augustine,[7] « these (things) in that Trinity »? — Yet this question, we, being less sufficient for this, leave to the diligence of the readers, to more fully adjudicate and resolve [diiudicandam atque absolvendam].

COMMENTARY ON DISTINCTION XXXII

The doubts about the two expressions, pertaining to appropriation, are solved.

Here, there arises a question deduced from the aforesaid etc..

THE DIVISION OF THE TEXT

Above, Master (Peter) posited the appropriated (names), in explanation of which he said, that the Holy Spirit is concord, because the Father and the Son love Themselves by the Holy Spirit; for that reason he here moves a question regarding that expression. And this he does in this Distinction. But this Distinction has three[1] parts.

In the *first*, Master (Peter) moves the principal question posited above, namely, whether the Father and the Son love Themselves by the Holy Spirit. But in the *second*, he moves another question, completely similar to this one, which he makes to explain it, and this he does there (where he says): *Moreover, one must diligently investigate* etc., and that question is:

"Whether the Father is wise by begotten Wisdom?" In the *third*, he returns to determine the principal question, and this he does there (where he says): *Moreover, it must be diligently noted* etc..

The *first* part has two parts. In the first, Master (Peter) moves the question and opposes (it). But in the second, he responds to the question, but he does not respond to the objection, there (where he says): *To this question, since it contains a depth* etc..

Moreover, one must diligently investigate etc.. This is the *second* subpart, in which Master (Peter) determines the adjoined question, namely, "Whether the Father is wise[2] by begotten Wisdom?" And, because for the determination

---

[1] Here in ch. 1. The passage from (St.) Augustine is ON THE TRINITY, Bk. VI, ch. 5, n. 7.

[2] The Vatican edition, together with very many editions, has *that is* [scilicet].

[3] The Vatican edition reads *(is) a most difficult one for me* [difficillimam mihi]; codices B and E, together with edition 1, read *It is difficult for me, I admit, to solve this question* [Difficile est mihi fateor hanc quaestionem solvere]; codex C has *I admit, that it is difficult for me, this question* [Difficile esse mihi fateor hanc quaestionem]; codex D, together with editions 3, 4, 5, 6, 7, 8 and 9, has *I admit, that this question (is) difficult for me* [Difficilem mihi hanc fateor quaestionem].

[4] Number 18.

[5] Codices B and E has *by which when cognized* [qua cognita]. The Vatican edition, with very many edd., has *the aforesaid question itself* [ipsa praemissa quaestio], and then *this question* [hanc quaestionem].

[6] The Vatican & ed. 1 have *yet* [tamen]; a little before this, the same Vatican ed. with a few edd. omits *thus* [ita] before *it has not been said* [dictum esse].

[7] ON THE TRINITY, Bk. XV, ch. 7, n. 12.

NOTES ON THE COMMENTARY

[1] The manuscripts with edition 1 have *four* [quatuor], faultily.

[2] The Vatican ed. alone amplifies the text here by adding after *wise* [sapiens] the words *that is, whether the Son is wise* [utrum Filius sit sapiens], and then after *begotten Wisdom* [sapientia genita] the words *and/or the Wisdom, which He begot* [vel sapientia, quam genuit]. These last words it also adds a little

of this question three other doubts concur, for that reason this part has four parts according to the four doubts, which he moves and determines. And first he determines that question of his: "Whether the Father is wise by begotten Wisdom?", which he determines on the negative side. But, second, he determines another question: "Whether the Son is wise by unbegotten Wisdom?", which he determines on the affirmative side,[1] there (where he says): *After these there is customarily asked* etc.. Third, he moves this question: "Whether the Son is wise through Himself and/or by Himself?", which he determines through a distinction, that "*by Himself*" can be held originally, and/or formally, and this there (where he says): *Moreover, there is customarily asked, whether the Son* etc.. Fourth, he moves this question: "Whether the Father has a twofold Wisdom?", which he determines on the negative side, showing, that this question and its reckoning is not worthy of a response, and this he does there (where he says): *After these, there is customarily asked by certain (authors), whether there is only one Wisdom* etc..[2]

Moreover, it must be diligently noted etc.. This is the *third* part, in which Master (Peter) returns to the question first posited, and this part has two parts. In the first he objects, accepting a reckoning from the determination of the other question. But in the second, in place of a solution he shows his own insufficiency and leaves this question to the reader[3] to be determined, and this there (where he says): *I admit this question is difficult for me* etc..

TREATMENT OF THE QUESTIONS

For an understanding of the present Distinction two (things) are principally asked according to the two questions, which Master (Peter) determines.[4]

First, there is the question concerning this expression: "the Father and the Son love Themselves by the Holy Spirit".

Second, there is the question concerning this other one: "the Father is wise by begotten Wisdom".

As much as regards the first, two (questions) are asked.

First, there is asked, whether that expression is to be admitted.

Second, there is asked, in which habitude [habitudine] is that ablative construed.

ARTICLE I

On the expression: "The Father and the Son love Themselves by the Holy Spirit".

QUESTION I

Whether the Father and the Son love Themselves by the Holy Spirit?

Moreover, that (this expression)[5] is to be admitted, is shown *by authority* and *by reason*.

1. First *by authority*, in this manner: (St.) Augustine in the sixth (book) ON THE TRINITY (says):[6] « Not Any of the Two is (He), by whom the Begotten is loved by the One Begetting and loves His own Begetter »: if, therefore, there is Someone, and He is not the Father and/or the Son, therefore, He is the Holy Spirit.

2. Likewise, (St.) Jerome on the Seventeenth Psalm (says):[7] « The Holy Spirit is the Love [amor] of the Father for the Son, and of the Son for the Father »; but by the Love, which is of the Father for the Son, the Father loves the Son, and vice versa: ergo etc..

3. Likewise, (St.) Bernard (of Clairvaux says), ON THE LOVE OF GOD:[8] « Thou doest love Thyself », he says, « oh Amiable Lord, when from the Father and the Son

---

above this to the words *begotten Wisdom* [sapientia genita], and again a little below this (on the next page) after at words *wise by begotten Wisdom* [sapiens sapientia genita] it reads *wise by the Wisdom, which He begot, and/or by begotten Wisdom* [sapiens sapientia quam genuit, vel sapientia genita].

[1] The proposition which begins with *But, second* [Secundo vero] and ends with *customarily asked etc.* [solet etc.], the Vatican edition transforms in this manner: *Second, he moves this question, "Whether the Son (is) wise by begotten, and/or unbegotten, Wisdom. And he determines it in the affirmative as much as regards the first part, that is, what He is wise by begotten Wisdom* [Secundo movet hanc quaestionem, utrum Filius sapiens sapientia genita, vel ingenita. Et determinat eam affirmative quantum ad primam partem, scilicet quod sit sapiens sapientia genita]. St. Thomas, here in the division of the text, says: « In the second part he inquires, whether the son is wise by begotten and/or unbegotten Wisdom, and he determines it first, showing, that He is not wise by begotten Wisdom, but by unbegotten Wisdom; second, showing, that He is wise through begotten Wisdom ».

[2] The Vatican edition adds: *And he determines (it) with this, that in the Trinity there is the Love, which is the Trinity, and in the Holy Spirit there is the Love, which is not the Trinity. And this, there (where he says): And just as in the Trinity* [Et determinat cum hoc, quod in Trinitate est dilectio, quae est Trinitas, et in Spiritu sancto est dilectio, quae on est Trinitas. Et hoc ibi: Et sicut in Trinitate].

[3] Codices P Q aa and bb, together with edition 1, prefix to the word *reader* [lectori] the word *prudent* [prudenti].

[4] Codices P and Q add *here* [hic].

[5] Supply, together with the Vatican edition, *this expression: "the Father and the Son love Themselves by the Holy Spirit"* [ista locutio: Pater et Filius diligunt se Spiritu sancto].

[6] Chapter 5, n. 7, concerning which, see Master (Peter) here, ch. 1.

[7] Verse 1. See above Distinction X, ch. 2.

[8] Understand the work ON CONTEMPLATING GOD, ch. 7, n. 14, which book is falsely attributed to St. Bernard. In the text itself, after the word *Lord* [Domine], the original adds *in Thyself* [in te ipso].

there proceeds the Holy Spirit, the Love of the Father for the Son, and of the Son for the Father, and so great a Love, that there is a unity ».

4. Likewise, it is shown *by reason*, in this manner: Master Hugh of St. Victor reckons thus [facit talem rationem] in a certain Epistle to Bernard:[1] « If you rightly say that you love [amare] by love, because it proceeds from you, why are the Father and the Son not rightly said to love by the Love, who proceeds from Them »? And again in the same place: « If the Holy Spirit were the love of your heart, just as (He is) of the Father's and Son's, who, I ask [quaeso], could deny, that you love [diligere] yourself by the Holy Spirit, that is, by your own loved »?

5. Likewise, it seems by another reason, in this manner: just as a word holds itself to *speaking*, so love to *loving* [amor ad diligere]; but the Father by His own Word, which proceeds from Him, speaks Himself and all (things),[2] because the Father by His own Word, which proceeds from Him, declares His very Self: therefore, the Father and the Son, by the Love, which proceeds from Them, love Their very Selves.

6. Likewise, just as a son cannot be produced except by being generated [generando], so neither love except by loving [diligendo]: therefore, the Father and the Son by loving Themselves produce the Holy Spirit,[3] who is personal Love: therefore, either by loving by the Love, which is the Holy Spirit, or (by the love), which is not the Holy Spirit. If by the love, which is not the Holy Spirit, either that love is *essential*, or *personal*: not *personal*, because then there would be two Person among the divine, to whom (the name) "Love" properly befits, which is impossible; similarly neither *essential*, because the Holy Spirit is that. And again, if *essential*, then, therefore, since (this) befits the Holy Spirit, the Holy Spirit would similarly produce (a Person). Therefore, it remains, that They produce the Holy Spirit by loving them [se] by the Love, which is the Holy Spirit: either, therefore, by loving *Themselves*, or by loving *an other than Themselves*. Not an other, because then an other would be required for the production of the Holy Spirit: therefore, by loving Themselves *by the Holy Spirit*, They produce the Holy Spirit: therefore, the Father and the Son love Themselves by the Holy Spirit.

ON THE CONTRARY: 1. 'To love' is the same as 'to will good',[4] and 'to will' (in God is) the same as 'to be': therefore, since this is false: 'the Father and the Son are by the Holy Spirit', (also) this similarly: 'They love Themselves by the Holy Spirit'.

2. Likewise, just as 'to be wise' holds itself to the Father in respect of the Son, so 'to love' to the Father and the Son in re-

spect of the Holy Spirit; but this is false: 'the Father is wise by begotten Wisdom': therefore, the former similarly.

3. Likewise, every plural infers the singular; but this is false: 'the Father loves Himself by the Holy Spirit': therefore, also the first. *If you say*, that 'to love' is held *notionally*; *on the contrary*: according to no notion does it happen that one Person be mutually *reflected* upon Another;[5] but according to love [dilectionem] there is a mutual reflection in the aforesaid expression: therefore, 'to love' is not held notionally: therefore, (the conclusion is) the same as before.

4. Likewise, no notion befits the Three: but 'to love by the Holy Spirit' befits the Three. For the Father loves by the Holy Spirit, and the Son loves by the Holy Spirit, and the Holy Spirit loves by the Holy Spirit, because (He loves) by Himself: therefore, it is not held notionally: therefore, (the conclusion is) the same as before.

5. Likewise, the Father and the Son by the same Love [amore] love Themselves and us; but God' love [dilectio] for us is essential, since it connotes an effect in the creature: therefore, similarly, (it is essential) when there is said: "They love Themselves".

6. Likewise, if it is held notionally, I ask, on behalf of *which notion*? There is no positing (of a notion there), except of the spiration: therefore, either *actively*, or *passively*. If actively: therefore, "*They love Themselves*" is the same as "*They spirate*"; but this is false: "They spirate by the Holy Spirit", therefore, also the first.[6] If passively; *on the contrary*: that is not predicated of the Father and the Son, but of the Holy Spirit alone. *If you say*, that it is predicated denominatively; *on the contrary*: every property, which is predicated of a Person among the divine in concretion, is predicated also in abstraction:[7] therefore, since the procession does not convene with the Father and the Son in abstraction: therefore, nether denominatively.

CONCLUSION

*This expression is false, if it is held essentially,
but true, if it is held notionally.*

I RESPOND: For the understanding of the aforesaid it must be noted, that *certain* (authors) denied the aforesaid expression simply and said, that all completely similar (expressions) had been retracted by blessed Augustine in (his retraction of) his own similar (expression), namely in this: « the Father is wise by begotten Wisdom ».[8] — But this solution cannot stand, because not on-

---

[1] Which is had in Richard of St. Victor's work, entitled, "In what manner the Spirit is the Love of the Father and the Son", where the following text is also found, transcribed word for word, with the sole exception of the verb *were* [esset], in place of which the original has *were said (to be)* [diceretur].

[2] Codices L and O insert *according to (St.) Anselm in the MONOLOGION* [secundum Anselmum in Monologio], concerning which, cf. above d. 27, p. II, q. 2, 4th argument of the fundament. You will find this explained there and in the questions which follow, in this Distinction. — The Vatican edition, supported by codex cc alone, omits the words from *all (things)* up to the conclusion *therefore, the Father* etc. [ergo etc.]. The same Vatican edition, at the beginning of this argument, substitutes *another reason is formed* [alia ratio formatur] for *it seems by another reason* [alia ratione videtur].

[3] For *the Holy Spirit* [Spiritum sanctum] codices L O and aa have *the Love* [amorem].

[4] Aristotle, in ON RHETORIC, Bk. II, ch. "On Love" (ch. 4) says: 'To love', therefore, is 'to will good (things) to another'. — After the words which follow, *and to will* [et velle] supply: *in God* [in Deo]. — Immediately after the verb *'to be'* [esse], codices aa and bb adjoin *there-*

fore by this, that the Father and the Son love Themselves, They are; but They are not the Holy Spirit, etc. [ergo eo quod Pater et Filius se diligunt, sunt; sed non sunt Spiritus sanctus, etc.].

[5] (Bl. John Duns) Scotus, here in q. 1, a. 1, propounds this thus: No notional act is conversive upon the same agent, from which it is and/or proceeds, on account of the distinction, which such an act requires between the agent and (its) end.

[6] For *by the Holy Spirit* [Spiritu sancto] the Vatican edition, together with one or the other codex, has *Themselves* [se]. — Next after *that* [illa] supply: *passive spiration* [spiratione passiva], and/or with the Vatican edition read *notion* [notio].

[7] Cf. above d. 27, p. I. a. 1. q. 1, and on *denominative* predication see above d. 5, a. 1, q. 1, in reply to n. 2, and also d. 27, p. I, a. sole, q. 3, p. 475, footnote 1. — For the words *in abstraction* [in abstractione] and *in concretion* [in concretione], which occur in this proposition, many codices substitute, respectively, *abstractly* [abstracte], others *abstractively* [abstractive], and *concretely* [concrete], not a few, *concretively* [concretive].

[8] Concerning which, cf. the text of Master (Peter) here, ch. 2 in the *Brief Note*. The sayings of the other Saints, mention of which is next made, you will find here in the arguments of the fundament.

-ly did (St.) Augustine say it, but even other Saints, the saying of whom (St.) Augustine did not retract.

For that reason there were *others*, who conceded it simply, saying that this expression ought to be understood through *appropriation*, not through *property*, so that the sense be: "the Father and the Son love Themselves [se] by the "love", which is appropriated to the Holy Spirit".[1] — But that solution of theirs cannot stand, because then similarly this would have to be conceded: "the Father and the Son are good by the Holy Spirit"; since "goodness" is appropriated to the Holy Spirit,[2] which, however, is in no manner conceded. Therefore, the first opinion cannot stand, which denies such expressions simply, since multiple authority says them; similarly the next, which concedes them simply, cannot stand, since a multiple reckoning contradicts (it).

It remains, therefore, that one chooses the *middle* position, namely, that in one manner it is true, in another false. For this (name) which it is *'to love'* [diligere] can be held *essentially*, and/or *notionally*. According to which it is held essentially, thus it means the complacency of Will, which is common to the Three. According to which it is held *notionally*, thus it means the fecundity of the Will to produce a Person out of Itself, which fecundity, indeed, is only in Two, although the Will is in Three. If, therefore, it is held *essentially*, the expression is false, because then it follows, that the Father and the Son are by the Holy Spirit.[3] And in this sense the pronoun ("Themselves" [se]) is construed with the verb *reciprocally* (i.e. as "Each loves Himself"). But if *notionally*, it is true, just as the reasons for the opposed (side) prove. And in this sense the pronoun is construed with the verb *retransitively* (i.e. as "They love one Another"). Whence the sense is: "the Father and the Son love Themselves, that is, the Father loves the Son and the Son the Father"; and then the expression is true, because the Love, which is the Holy Spirit, is the Love joining the Father with the Son and conversely (the Son with the Father); and then it is not licit to infer: 'therefore, the Father loves Himself by the Holy Spirit'.

1. 2. 3. From this the first three (objections) are clear. For the first proceeds according to which 'to love' is held *essentially*, the second similarly, for 'to be wise' is not said *notionally*, as 'to love' (is), but it is either *common*, and/or *appropriated*; the third similarly, because it proceeds according to which the oblique (case)[4] is construed reciprocally, and then 'to love' is held *essentially*.

To that which is objected, that it cannot be held *notionally*, it must be understood, that just as generation can be signified in a twofold manner, on one manner, as it means the *emanation*, in another manner, as it means the *manner* of emanating with a superadded expression; and in the first manner through this verb "*to generate*", in the second manner through this verb "*to say*", (this) is signified, thus also spiration can be signified in a twofold manner. In the first manner through this verb which is "*to spirate*"; in the second manner through this verb which is "*to love*". For according to the manner which "*to say*" conveys the generation and further a certain expression about a Person, so also "*to love*". Whence just as "*to love*" conveys the act of generating and of declaring[5] or of expressing, and by reason of the act of declaring there is said: "the Father speaks Himself by the Word", that is, by declaring or expressing Himself He generates the Word, and/or by generating the Word He expresses Himself by the Word; so also in the proposed "*to love*" conveys the act of connecting or of agreeing [concordandi] and of spirating; and by reason of the act of connecting there is said: "the Father and the Son love Themselves by the Holy Spirit", that is, by agreeing with one Another They spirate the Holy Spirit, and/or by spirating the Holy Spirit They are connected with one Another. And from these the objections are clear.

For what is objected concerning mutual *reflection*, the response is clear, because this is by reason of the co-intellected, essential act.[6]

4. 5. To that which is objected, that 'to love by the Holy Spirit' convenes with Three and is said in respect of a creature; it must be said, that it does not convene with Three by reason of the spiration, which it conveys; and for that reason, although it is said in respect of a creature, yet it is not said entirely, essentially, but connotes something essential; yet it does mean the notion by reason of the looking-back, which it conveys to a Person, just as has been said above concerning the Word and concerning the Gift.[7]

6. To that which is objected last, on behalf of which notion it stands; it is clear, that it stands on behalf of the common spiration; yet it is not licit to posit for it the verb for *spirating*, because it conveys that notion in another manner. Whence just as this is conceded: "the Father speaks by the Word", yet not this: "the Father generates by the Son", and yet "to speak" conveys that generation; so[8] in the proposed must it be understood.

---

[1] Perhaps the genuine reading is that which is had in Codex T: *the Father and the Son loves Themselves by the Holy Spirit, to whom "love" is appropriated* [Pater et Filius diligunt se Spiritu sancto, cui appropriatur amor], which reading many codices seem to favor, since in them is found the words *to whom is appropriated* [cui appropriatur] for *which is appropriated* [qui appropriatur].

[2] A greater part of the codices and edition 1 read thus: *to which Holy Spirit "goodness" is appropriated* [cui Spiritui sancto appropriatur bonitas], less congruously.

[3] Very many codices, together with the first editions, have *the Holy Spirit* [Spritus sanctus] for *by the Holy Spirit* [Spiritu sancto]. — On the twofold construction, namely *reciprocal* [reciproca] and *retransive* [retransitiva], we noted, that a *reciprocal* construction is that, in which the action of the verb returns immediately to the substance, from which it had come forth, e. g., "Socrates loves himself"; and with this construction formed, the sense of the expression, which is dealt with here, would be: "the Father loves Himself, and the Son loves Himself; Both by the Holy Spirit"; which is false. On the other hand, a *retransitive* construction is that, in which the action of the verb goes forth from one subject into the other, and again it returns to the first subject, e. g., "I love you, so that you may love me". Cf. Priscian, GRAMMATICAL INSTITUTIONS, Bk. VII, chs. 10 and 17.

[4] Understand: *case*, that is, the accusative (case) of the word, *Themselves* [se].

[5] For *of declaring* [declarandi], the Vatican edition, together with some codices, here and a little afterwards, after *of saying* [dicendi], has *by saying* [dicendo] for *by declaring ... Himself* [declarando se].

[6] For the verb 'to love' [diligere], taken notionally, not only signifies the production of Holy Spirit in the precise manner, which is properly signified by the verb 'to spirate', but signifies something more: for it connotes together with the emanation of the Holy Spirit an act of love or *an act of concordance*, which is something essential; and by reason of this the reflection is had. — For *this is by reason of the ... act* [haec est ratio actus] many codices faultily have *here there is an ... act* [hic est actus], and then for *co-intellected, essential* [essentialis cointellecti] the Vatican edition has *notional* [notionalis] (codex cc and editions 2, 3, 4, 5, and 6, have *essential* [essentialis]) *commonly intellected* [communiter intellecti]. The reading of edition 1 and codices L and O is: *because by this there is a common essential act of understanding* [quia hoc est actus essentialis communis intelligendi]; the reading of codex I is this: *because this is common by reason of a common, co-intellected essential act* [quia haec est communis ratione actus essentialis communis cointellecti].

[7] Distinction 27, p. II, q. 2; and d. 18, q. 2 ff.. — A little above this, the Vatican edition and codex cc, reads *yet the looking-back, which it conveys to a Person, does mean the notion* [dicit tamen notionem respectus, quem importat ad personam] for *yet it does mean the notion by reason of the looking-back, which it conveys to a Person* [dicit tamen notionem ratione respectus, quem importat ad personam].

[8] Codex Z adds *also* [et].

SCHOLIUM

I. This Question supposes, that the Holy Spirit proceeds through the manner of mutual charity and as the Nexus of the Father and the Son, concerning which see above d. 10, a. 1, qq. 2-3,, and a. 2, q. 2. — On the sense of this expression Peter Lombard (here in ch. 1) has not dared to define anything, and many opinions have arisen, of which (St.) Albertus (Magnus) cites five, St. Thomas (in his Commentary, here in q. 1, a. 1) cites nine, (and) St. Bonaventure cites, here, three. The *first* opinion posited here, that St. Augustine retracted this very expression, is ascribed to a certain Gottfried; the *second* Durandus (of Saint-Pourçain) follows, who (here in q. 1) says, that « all the aforesaid propositions are simply false, if the *loving* is taken *notionally*; but if it is taken *essentially*, thus they are true, though they are improper and for that reason are to be expounded » (that is, to be accepted through appropriation, because "love" is appropriated to the Holy Spirit). This sentence is overturned by the two arguments posited in the body of the Question (but in different places). The *third* opinion is that of Hugo of St. Victor, who is supported by St. Bonaventure, St. Thomas, Bl. (now St.) Albertus, Alexander of Hales (to whom the sentence of Durandus is falsely attributed), (Bl.) Peter of Tarentaise, Richard of Middleton and others. This is *optimally* explained in the solution to n. 3 (cf. above d. 27, p. II, q. 1, and d. 10, Doubt 3). — (Bl. John Duns) Scotus uses the foundations established by St. Bonaventure in the reply to n. 3, by distinguishing between essential and notional love (as between 'to *understand*' and 'to *say*'), and resolves, that the expression is false, both if the loving is taken *purely essentially*, or if it is taken *purely notionally*, but that nevertheless it is true, if taken *in a middle manner*, so that the sense be: "They produce the Holy Spirit, as One having a certain habitude to the One producing, whose *Love* He is". The same also argues against the reckonings of St. Thomas, in a sufficiently subtle manner. For those who are pleased by those disquisitions which are more subtle than useful, cf. Cajetan (commenting on SUMMA, I, q. 37, a. 2); the Commentator on Scotus, Lychetus (here in q. 1), Rada, controversy 17; Macedo, collation 9, difference 1, and many other authors of each School.

II. In the solution to n. 5 the *minor* is denied, that is, that God's love for us is *entirely* essential, though *it does connote* something essential. The same is more expressly taught by St. Thomas (loc. cit., in reply to n. 3), where he says: « It must be said, that the Father does not only *love* the Son, but also *Himself and us* by the Holy Spirit ». However (Bl.) Scotus (loc. cit. n. 14) in his own way does not approve this, and even Suarez thinks, that this expression is not proper nor easily put to use. On the foundation of the sentence of the Angelic and Seraphic (Doctors), cf. above d. 27, p. II, q. 2, and d. 18, qq. 2 and 5. — However, this proposition: *the Father loves Himself by the Holy Spirit*, the Seraphic Doctor (at the end of the body of the question) does not seem to concede, yet St. Thomas (SUMMA., I, q. 37, a. 2, in reply to n. 3) and (Bl.) Scotus do not doubt to admit it. However, St. Bonaventure speaks there of purely essential love and of the Holy Spirit personally, but not of *loving* to the extent that « it conveys also a produced Person through the manner of a love, which has a habitude to the thing loved » (thus St. Thomas loc. cit.). St. Bonaventure treats with the *loving* which is not *entirely* essential in the solution to nn. 4 and 6, where in an orderly manner he speaks of the *loving* accepted *notionally*, and as connoting something essential, and as distinct from *spirating*, just as *speaking* (is distinct) from *generating*. For the terms 'to *spirate*' and 'to *love*' signify indeed the same thing, but by a diverse reckoning. For they differ just as the *act*, by which a Person is produced, differs from the *manner* of His production. But passing from the *thing* to the *manner* is contrary to the rules of logic. In regard to the solution to n. 6, cf. St. Thomas, loc. cit., in reply to n. 2.

III. Other authors treat this question together with the one which follows. Alexander of Hales, on this and the following question, SUMMA., p. I, q. 67, m. 3, a. 3. — (Bl. John Duns) Scot., on this and the following q., here and in REPORTATIO., q. 1. — St. Thomas, here in q. 1, a. 1; SUMMA., I, q. 37, a. 2. — Bl. (now St.) Albertus (Magnus), on this and the following q., here in a. 1 and 2.; SUMMA., p. I, tr. 12, q. 50, m. 1, q. 3, in passing. — (Bl.) Peter of Tarentaise, on this and the following q., here in q. 1. — Richard of Middleton, on this and the following q., here in a. 1 and 2. — Giles the Roman, on this and the following q., here in 1st. princ., q. 1. — Henry of Ghent, on this and the following q., SUMMA., a. 61, q. 7. — (Bl.) Dionysius the Carthusian, here in q. 1. — (Gabriel) Biel, on this and the following q., here in q. 1 and 2.

QUESTION II

In what habitude is that ablative construed, if there is said: "The Father and the Son love Themselves by the Holy Spirit"?

Second, there is asked, in what habitude is that ablative (i.e. "by the Holy Spirit" [Spiritu sancto]) construed, when there is thus said: "The Father and the Son love Themselves by the Holy Spirit". And that (it is said) in the habitude of a form, seems:

1. Through a *simile*, because Peter[1] loves by the love [amore] formally proceeding from himself: therefore, for an equal reason the Father and the Son love Themselves formally by the Holy Spirit.

2. Likewise, nothing denominates something, to which it is compared as to (its) *sole principle*, unless it is compared (to it) as *one informing* — for though running is from God, yet God is not said "to run" — but Love is from the Father and the Son, and They are said to love by Him:[2] therefore, Love is (there) in the reckoning of a form.

3. Likewise, by every nexus some are connected formally; but the Holy Spirit is the Nexus: therefore, some are connected by Him, and naught but the Father and the Son: ergo etc..

4. Likewise, by every whiteness someone is white formally, therefore, by every love someone is loving formally; but none has been loved formally by love, except him for whom the love is: since, therefore, the Holy Spirit is (the mutual Love) of the Father and the Son, it is clear that etc..

ON THE CONTRARY: 1. Everything which loves formally by another than itself, has a loving solely through participation: therefore, if the Father and the Son love formally by another than Themselves, therefore, They love through participation. But this is unfitting: ergo etc..

2. Likewise, if anyone loves by someone formally, with the latter excluded, it is impossible to understand that he loves the same or the love in him [amorem in eo sive ipsum amare]: therefore, if the Father and the Son[3] love

---

[1] The Vatican edition alone has *the Father* [Pater].
[2] Very many codices have *for that reason* [ideo], faultily.

[3] Codex O subjoins *formally* [formaliter] well, and then very many codices, together with edition 1, omit *Themselves* [se].

Themselves by the Holy Spirit, it is impossible to understand that the Father love, with the Holy Spirit not understood; but this is false: therefore, also the first.

3. Likewise, no hypostasis is a form;[1] but the Love, which is the Holy Spirit, is a Hypostasis: therefore, It is not a form, therefore, no one loves formally by that Love.

4. Likewise, no relative can but the form of its correlative — because from the form and the formed there comes to be one (being), but a relative is distinguished from (its) correlative — but the Love, which is the Holy Spirit, holds it self in the manner of a correlative to the Father and the Son: ergo etc..

5. Likewise, every form is before that of which it is the form; therefore, if the Father and the Son love Themselves[2] by the Holy Spirit formally, that Love precedes the loving of the Father and of the Son. But this is false, because love [dilectio] is produced: ergo etc..

CONCLUSION

When we say, that the Father and the Son loves Themselves by the Holy Spirit, that ablative is construed in the reckoning of a quasi, formal effect, and for that reason in some manner in the reckoning of a form.

I RESPOND: It must be said, that the position of some was, that that ablative is construed in the reckoning of a *sign*, not in the reckoning of a *form*. For the Holy Spirit holds Himself through the manner of One produced in respect of the love [dilectionis] of the Father and the Son, and for that reason He is a sign of that. Whence they say, that this is the sense of the expression: "the Father and the Son love Themselves"; and the sign of this is, that They spirate concordantly [concorditer] the Holy Spirit, who is (Their) unique and undivided Love. — But this position is not sufficient. For if the ablative could be construed truly in the reckoning of a *sign* with a verb, then this would be true: "the Father and the Son love Themselves by created love" [amore creato], because created love is a sign of that; which no one concedes. — *If you say*, that that (ablative) is not such a proximate [ita propinquum][3] sign; *it is objected*, that then this would simply be true: 'the Father is wise by begotten Wisdom', since begotten Wisdom is in the greatest manner the sign of the Wisdom in the generating Father.

The position of others was, that that ablative is construed in the reckoning of a form. For they say, that '*to*

love themselves', said of the Father and the Son, is other than '*to be connected One to the Other*' [invicem connecti]. And since They are connected formally by a nexus, and the Holy Spirit is that nexus; for that reason, formally speaking, this is true: "the Father and the Son loves Themselves by the Holy Spirit", just as this is formally true: "the Father and the Son are connected by a nexus". — But this position cannot entirely stand, because, when there is said: "the Father and the Son are connected", either "*are connected*" means something, which is in the Father and the Son *from* [a] *the Holy Spirit*, or (something) which is in Them as the *principle* of the Holy Spirit. If (something) which is in Them *from the Holy Spirit*: therefore, the Father and the Son receive something from the Holy Spirit; if *something*, since They cannot receive a part, therefore, *the whole*: therefore, They are from the Holy Spirit, which is unfitting. It remains, therefore, that that which "*are connected*" is, means something, which is in the Father and the Son as the *principle* of the Holy Spirit — for though it is passive according to the manner (of speaking),[4] it is active according to thing — and if this, (then) the Holy spirit is compared to the being connected [connexionem] as to a *principle*, not, therefore, as in the reckoning of *a form* entirely.

It is clear, therefore, that the first position speaks less sufficiently; the second speaks less abundantly, because it expresses too much. And the first belonged to Master Simon of Tornai;[5] the second belonged to Master William of Auxerre. And though neither (opinion) is entirely sufficient, yet each has in itself something of the truth. For the first says, that the Holy Spirit holds himself to the Father and the Son through the manner of *One produced*; and this, indeed, is true. The second says, that *love* is compared to the ones loving as in the reckoning of *a form*; and this, indeed, is true.

And for that reason from these two positions, one of which is insufficient and the other excessive [excedens], there is gathered a *middle* position, (both) sober and sufficient; namely, that that ablative is construed in the reckoning of a *formal effect*, if it is licit[6] to name as an "effect", that which is out of a principle. And this was the position of Master Hugh of Saint Victor,[7] who clearly saw the truth here. Whence he argued against those, who reputed this question unsolvable. Whence he says, that, just as when there is said: "I love you by the love proceeding from me", the construction there is in the reckoning of a *formal effect*; so in the proposed. Yet, in this there is a difference, because the love proceeding from you is resting

---

[1] Supply together with codex O: *of another* [alterius].* Likewise, codex O, a little below this, reads *therefore, it is the form of None* [ergo nullius etc.] for *therefore It is not a form* [ergo non etc.].

[2] Very many codd. with ed. 1, omit *Themselves* [se], as above.

[3] The Vatican edition, with codex cc, omits *such* [ita], not well.

[4] Supply together with codices aa and bb *of speaking* [dicendi]. — Next the Vatican edition inserts *yet* [tamen] before *it is* [est].

[5] Concerning whom, see the Prolegomena, p. LXXXVI.

[6] For *if it is licit* [si licet], codd. G I K S T bb and ff have *it be licit* [liceat], having omitted *if* [si]. Cod. Y exhibits this passage in an amplified form: *of a formal effect, not according to which a form has a matter to be perfected, but to be connected, so that it be licit* [effectus formalis, non secundum quod forma habeat materiam perficiendi, sed connectendi, ut liceat].

[7] Which is not found in Hugh (of St. Victor), but in an opusculum published among the works of Richard of St. Victor, the title of which is: "In what manner is the Holy Spirit the Love of the Father and the Son" [Quomodo Spiritus sanctus est amor Patris et Filii], where there is read: « Sim-

ilarly, that the Father is said to love by the Holy Spirit, is not understood thus, as if the Holy Spirit exists as the Author and Origin of love [dilectionis], which the Father is, and in virtue of (His own) judgement loves [pro arbitrio amat] what He loves, but that the Father spirates that Love [dilectionem], by which the Son is loved and the Holy Spirit is, and is the Author and Origin of That ... The human spirit is not love, but love does proceed from it, and for that reason it does not love by itself, but by the love, which proceeds from it. But the Father is Love, and the Holy Spirit is His Love, and for that reason the Father loves by Himself, He loves by the Holy Spirit; He loves Himself by His own Love, He loves by His own love ... If you rightly say that you love by the love, which proceeds from you [de te], why are the Father and the Son not rightly said to love by the Love, which proceeds out of Them? Is this, brother, the question, which they think (is) unsolvable, (which) they both say and write (is) unsolvable?

---

* *Trans. note*: Such a supplement weakens the argument, since a hypostasis as a hypostasis is never a form, not just never a 'form of another'.

in you as (something) *uniting* and *inhering*, because it is an accident; but among the divine the Love proceeding from the Father and the Son is resting in Them as (*Someone) unique*, yet not as (something) *inhering*, because It is not an accident, the Substance and a Hypostasis; and for that reason it has, still less, the reckoning of a form.

Therefore, the reasons brought forward for this are to be conceded, because the ablative has in some manner the reckoning of a form. — Yet, what is objected last, is not valid, because every whiteness is a form; but some love is a Hypostasis.[1]

1. 2. To that, therefore, which is objected unto the contrary: if They love formally by another, therefore, (The love) through participation; it must be said, that *'to love by another through essence'* causes a participation, but *personal anotherness* (does) not. Whence Hugh (says):[2] « The human spirit is not love, but love does proceed from it, for that reason it does not love by itself; but the Father is Love and the Holy Spirit is His Love, for that reason He loves by Himself; He also loves by the Holy Spirit »; and for that reason it is clear, that (They) do not (love) through participation. — And for

that reason the following (objection) is clear; for, because the Father loves Himself by an essential Love, for that reason the Father can be understood to love, with the Holy Spirit not understood; but not so is it concerning a notional love.

3. 4. The reasons which follow proceed from form, according to which it has the *perfect act* of a form. For it belongs to form to inhere, and for that reason it is not a Hypostasis; for that reason too it is not distinguished.[3] However, *there* (i.e. in that above quoted expression), the ablative occurs from the act of a form, which is '*to inhere*', and it has the act of the form, which is '*to unite*'.

5. To that which is objected last, that a form precedes that of which it is the form; it must be said, that it speaks of form, according to which it has a reckoning of a cause, because thus it does precede; but the ablative occurs from the reckoning of *causality*, because it is construed through a manner of a *formal effect*. Therefore, it is clear, that in a certain manner there is a reckoning[4] of a *form* there, in a certain manner the reckoning of a *sign*; and in this the response to all (the things) sought is clear.

SCHOLIUM

I. The sentence of the Seraphic Doctor on this question is explained thus by (Bl.) Peter of Tarentaise (here in q. 1, a. 1): « The ablative means the habitude of an *effect* according to thing, but a habitude of *form* only according to the manner of signifying, that is, according to denomination, just as when there is said: "these speak by word", and/or "run by running", and/or "act by an action". The same, indeed, is signified through a verb and an ablative, but through an ablative as a denominating quality, through a verb as an act coming forth from a subject, just as when there is said: "the Father speaks the Word" and/or "loves the Holy Spirit". For each means both a notional act and the Person, which is signified as a quasi denominating form, when the name of a Person is added ».

II. The solution is built up from a twofold distinction. The first is about the expression "*other than oneself*" [alio a se], to the extent that it is understood either as "*other in essence*" [aliud in essentia], and/or "*other in person*" [alius in persona]. The second, taken from Hugh (of St. Victor), is about the twofold *manner*, by which someone loves anyone, namely, either by the love, which the one loving produces as an accident and (something) other than himself, and/or by the essential love, which is the same as the one loving. — The solutions, which follow, suppose, that in the Father and the Son there is a twofold Love, the *essential* and the *notional*; of the manners of which the one can be understood without the other, though in these Persons they are not really distinct.

See (the citations to) other authors in the preceding Scholium.

ARTICLE II

On the expression: "The Father is wise by begotten Wisdom", *
and concerning the other: "The Father is powerful by the Virtue, which He begot".

Consequently, the principal question concerns this expression: "the Father is wise by begotten Wisdom" [Pater est sapiens sapientia genita]. And about this two (questions) are asked.

First, there is asked, whether that expression is to be admitted.

Second, for an understanding of this,[5] whether this is to be admitted: "the Father is powerful by the Virtue, which He begot".

QUESTION I

Whether there can be rightly said: "The Father is wise by begotten Wisdom"?

Moreover, that the first expression is to be admitted, is shown in this manner:

1. In the first (chapter) of the First (Letter of St. Paul) to the Corinthians (there is written):[6] *We say that*

Christ (is) the Virtue of God and the Wisdom of God; but each one is wise by his own wisdom: therefore, if Christ is the Wisdom of the Father and is begotten Wisdom, the Father is wise by begotten Wisdom.

---

[1] The Vatican edition more fully and more perfectly reads thus: *but some love is not a form, but is a Hypostasis* [sed aliquis amor non est forma, sed est hypostasis].

[2] See the text cited a little above this, from *Richard* (of St. Victor). — At the beginning of the solution, the Vatican edition changes the text for the worse, thus: *To that, therefore, which is objected, that They love formally* [Ad illud ergo quod obiicitur, quod formaltier diligunt].

[3] The Vatican edition, together with one or the other codex, has *it*

does not distinguish [non distinguit] for *it is not distinguished* [non distinguitur]; falsely, as is clear from the 4th objection.

[4] For *there is a reckoning of form there* [est ibi ratio formae], codices O and X have *it is there in the reckoning of a form* [est ibi in ratione formae], and, a little after this, have *in the reckoning* [in ratione] for *the reckoning* [ratio].

[5] Edition 1 has *for an understanding of this* [ad intelligentiam huius] in place of *for an understanding of this* [ad intellectus huius].

[6] Verse 24.

---

* *Trans. note*: Here the title of the article in the Quaracchi Edition faultily omitted *wise* [sapiens], as is evident both from the text which follows, and from the title of the Question, which has the complete expression, and from the text of Master Peter here, in ch. 2.

2. Likewise, (St.) Augustine (says) in the sixth (book) ON THE TRINITY:[1] « The Son is a certain Art of the omnipotent and wise God, where He knows all (things) »; but each artisan is wise by his own art: therefore, the Father is wise by the Son: ergo etc..

3. Likewise, this seems *by reason* through a simile: because every one loving, from whom love proceeds, is one loving by a love proceeding from himself: therefore every wise one, from whom wisdom proceeds, is wise by the wisdom emanating from himself; but the Father is of this kind: ergo etc..

4. Likewise, (St.) Augustine in fifteenth (book) ON THE TRINITY (says):[2] « God the Father knows all in Himself, He knows too in the Son »; but 'to know all' and 'to be the most wise' is the same: if, therefore, He knows all in the Son, not only by Himself, but also by the Son, is He wise.

5. Likewise, God the Father says all by the Word, just as (St.) Augustine says in the eleventh (book) of THE CONFESSIONS:[3] « By Thy coeternal Word Thou doest say whatsoever Thou doest say »; but as (St.) Anselm says, « 'to say' is 'to understand' »: therefore, the Father understands all by means of the Word: therefore, since 'to be wise' and 'to understand' is the same, it is clear that etc..

ON THE CONTRARY: 1. Among the divine 'to know' is 'to be':[4] therefore, if the Father is wise by begotten Wisdom, therefore, He is begotten Wisdom; but this is false: therefore, the first (is) also (false).

2. Likewise, with the generation not understood, there is still an understanding of God as wise: therefore, the begotten Wisdom is not the reason for the Wisdom of God.

CONCLUSION

The expression: "The Father is wise by begotten Wisdom", is simply false.

I RESPOND: It must be said, that without a distinction, since 'to be wise' [esse sapientem] is said *essentially*, that the expression is simply false; and if it is read (to have been written) anywhere by any Saint, it is to be expounded. Whence (St.) Augustine in the book of RETRACTIONS[5] retracts it, saying, that he treated that question better in the book, ON THE TRINITY, where, that is, he says the contrary, showing, that this reckoning is not valid: "if the Father was without the Son, since the Son is His Wisdom, the Father was a fool [inspiens]"; because wisdom does not only convene with the Son, but with the Father and the Son

and the Holy Spirit. And this he says (in his work) ON THE TRINITY in very many places, but most of all in the sixth and fifteenth (book).[6]

1. 2. 3. To that, therefore, which is objected, that the Son is the Wisdom and Art[7] of the Father; it must be said, that this is conceded: "the Father is the Wisdom of the wise Father"; and yet not this: "the Father is wise by begotten Wisdom". Whence it must be noted, that when *wisdom* is said (to be) *of anyone*, this is said in a twofold manner: either just as of (its) *subject*, as "the whiteness of Peter", or just as of (its) *principal*; for the genitive (case) conveys origin.[8] Therefore, since the Son is the Wisdom having (Its) origin from the Father, for that reason this is true: "the Son is the Wisdom of the Father". But where there is said: "the Father is wise by begotten Wisdom", the ablative ("by begotten Wisdom") is construed in the reckoning of the causality of something, and/or in the habitude of a form and/or of a principal, and most of all of a form; and for that reason it is false, because the Sin is neither the form nor the principle of the Father. — *If you ask*, for what reason is it not construe in the reckoning of a *formal effect*, just as love is with the one loving, from whom it proceeds:[9] it must be said, that it is not similar. And there is a twofold reason for this, one *common*, the other *special*: the *common*, which is taken from creatures; since there are certain acts, which mean a movement from things to the soul, as *wisdom*, certain ones from the soul to thing, as 'to love'.[10] For that reason a comparison of *love* to the one loving is in the reckoning of (something) *coming forth*, not in the reckoning of (something) *imparting*, and for that reason love of itself conveys a *form* and an *effect*; but because (St. Augustine) says "*wisdom*", as *regarding* One who is intelligent [ut ad intelligentem], not as *from* One who is intelligent [ut ab intelligente], for that reason the ablative ("by begotten Wisdom") conveys only a *form*, *not an effect*; and for that reason the expression is false. — The other reason is a *special* one among the divine, because proceeding *Love* is Love *properly*, not through an *appropriation*, and "*to love*" similarly has been said *notionally*, whence it conveys origin, as has been demonstrated above;[11] but "*wisdom*" (is) always (said) *essentially*, and that which it is "*to be wise*" is in no manner said *notionally*, because in no manner does it convey an origin. And for that reason the expression is false.

4. To that which is objected, that the Father knows all in the Son; it must be said, to say: "*He knows by the Son*" and "*in the Son*" differ. For, when there is said: "*He knows by the Son*", the ablative conveys the reckoning of a form and/or of a principle of cognizing; and for that reason it is simply false. Yet this: "*He knows in the Son*", is to be distinguished, because the pre-

---

[1] Chapter 10, n. 11. See the entire passage above, in the text of Master (Peter), Distinction XXXI, ch. 2.

[2] Chapter 14, n. 23.

[3] Chapter 7, n. 9. — The text of (St.) Anselm is found in his MONOLOGION, ch. 32: If (the Most High Spirit) said nothing among Himself — since for him it is thus the same *to say* something as it is *to understand* (it) — He would not understand anything. Cf. above d. 27, p. II, q. 1 ff..

[4] (St.) Augustine, ON THE TRINITY, Bk. VII, ch. 1, nn. 1 and 2. See here the text of Master (Peter), ch. 2.

[5] Book I, ch. 26, where this sentence, proven in the book, ON 83 QUESTIONS, q. 23, is retracted. — Then very many codices, together with edition 1, have *reads* [recitat] for *retracts* [retractat].

[6] Book VI, ch. 1, n. 1 ff., and Bk. XV, ch. 7, n. 12. Cf. also Bk. VII, chs. 1-4.

[7] For *Art* [ars] the Vatican edition and not a few codices have *Virtue* [virtus]; not well, because this solution respects the second objection also, which deals with *art*.

[8] Cf. above d. 3, p. II, Doubt 3, and d. 11, Doubt 3. See also (Bl. John Duns) Scotus, SPECULATIVE GRAMMAR, ch. 19.

[9] Concern which, see the preceding article, q. 2.

[10] Cf. Aristotle, ON THE SOUL, Bk. II, texts 38, 46, and 54 (chs. 8-10). He says the same in METAPHYSICS, Bk. VI, text 8 (Bk. V, ch. 4) in respect of the object of these acts, that good and evil are in things, but true and false in the mind. — A little further below this, the Vatican edition, together with codex cc, has *there is said* [dicitur] for *(St. Augustine) says* [dicit].

[11] Distinction 10, a. 2, q. 1, and here in a. 1, q. 1. — A little above this, after *has been said* [dictum] codex O adds *not essentially only, but* [non essentialiter tantum, sed].

position "*in*" [in], with what accompanies it in its phrase [cum suo casuali], can determine this verb "*knows*" in comparison to the *subject*; and then it is false: for the sense is, that the Son is Father's reason for cognizing. And/or it can determine the verb in comparison to the *object*; and, then, it is true, and the sense is, that the Son is for things cognized the Reason and Exemplar and Cause of (their) being exemplified. And that this could be the sense of the expression, is clear. For he who perfectly cognizes anyone, cognizes everything which is in him: if, therefore, the Father perfectly cognizes the Son, and all are in the Son, therefore, He cognizes all in the Son. And, yet, there does not follow from this, that He[1]

is wise by the Son, because then there is signified, that the Son is the very Father's reason for cognizing.

5. To that which is objected last, that the Father says all by the Word; it must be said, that that which it is "*to say*" [dicere] conveys an *origin*, it also conveys an *effect* in the creature, which He effects through the Word;[2] but "*to understand*" [intelligere] conveys, of itself, naught but only an Act of the Essence [actum essentialem], such that it conveys of itself a looking-back neither to the Person, nor to the creature. For that reason it is not entirely the same to say, "*He says all by the Word*", and "*He understands all by the Word*": for "*to say*" is the same as "*to understand*", but it conveys more amply.

SCHOLIUM

I. Since "*wisdom*", which is an attribute of the (Divine) Essence and common to the Three Divine Persons, is appropriated to the Son, who is called "*the begotten Wisdom*", in this question there is a treatment of "wisdom" as appropriated to the Son. — About the retraction, which St. Augustine made, there is asked, in what sense ought it be understood, since it must be supposed, that it never dawned on this Doctor, that the Father is wise through His own *essential* Wisdom. Perhaps he used to believe, that the Father can in some manner *be denominated* by the begotten Wisdom, which, as (this is) very improper, he retracted (cf. here Doubt 3).

II. On the solution to n. 1 and the signification of the genitive, see Doubt 7. — In the solution to n. 4 the Seraphic Doctor distinguishes a twofold sense of the expression "*to know in some-one*". St. Thomas explains the same distinction (here in q. 2, a.

1, in reply to n. 3) in this manner: « "*To see in something*" [Videre in aliquo] is said in a twofold manner: either of him whose cognition he accepts in him, just as ... a disciple (sees) in the word of the teacher, spoken and/or written; or to intuit a thing cognized, represented in another, just as a builder sees his own art in the house, which he makes ».

III. The (same) conclusion is established among all (authors). Alexander of Hales, SUMMA., p. I, q. 67, m. 3, a. 2, § 3. — (Bl. John Duns) Scotus, in each version, here in q. 2. — St. Thomas, here in q. 2, a. 1; SUMMA., I, q. 39, a. 7, ad 2. — Bl. (now St.) Albertus (Magnus), here in a. 3 and 4; SUMMA., p. I, tr. 12, q. 50, m. 2. — Giles the Roman, here in 2nd. princ., q. 1. — Henry of Ghent, SUMMA., a. 38, q. 2, and a. 40, q. 6, n. 8. — Durandus (of Saint-Pourçain), here in q. 2. — (Bl.) Dionysius the Carthusian, here in q. 2. — (Gabriel) Biel, here in q. 1.

QUESTION II

Whether there can be rightly said: "The Father is powerful by the Power or Virtue, which He begot"?

Second, there is asked, whether this expression is to be admitted: "the Father is wise by the Power or the Virtue, which He begot". And it seems that (it is) in this manner:

1. Because whosoever works [operatur] through anyone can cannot work without him, has power from him; but the Father works through the Son and cannot work without the Son:[3] ergo etc..

2. Likewise, among the divine *virtue* and *working* [operatio] is the same,[4] therefore, since the Father works through the Son, He is able through the Son; but whosoever is able through the other, is also able by his power: therefore, the Father is powerful by begotten Power.

3. Likewise, just as *knowing* [nosse] holds itself to wisdom, so *working* to power; but there rightly follows: "this one knows through that one, therefore, he is wise through him":[5] therefore, there rightly follows: "this one works through that one, therefore, he has power from him or through him": ergo etc..

4. Likewise, when there is said: "the Father works through the Son", this preposition "*through*" [per] either conveys a *cause*, or an *instrument*. Not an *instrument*, because then the Son would not truly cooperate with the Father; and again, (the Father) would be[6] in want [indigens], if He acted through an instrument:: therefore, in the reckoning of a *cause*. And if this, therefore, the Son gives (the act of) *working* [operari] to the Father: therefore, also the *power* of working.[7] *If you say*, that it does not mean the reckoning of a causality, but of sub-authority; therefore, since the Holy Spirit similarly has a subauthority in working, just as the Son (does), by the reason whereby the Father is said "*to work through the Son*", by the same reason (is He) also (said "to work) *through the Holy Spirit*". *If you say*, that this has been said through an appropriation; I ask the reason for appropriating. For since the work is through a power, and the power is appropriated to the Father, not to the Son, therefore, there will not be able to be appropriated to the Son that (the Father)[8] *works through the Son*.

---

[1] Codex M adds explicitly *He Himself* [ipse].

[2] The Vatican edition, together with codex cc, has *which He says or effects through the Word* [dicit per Verbum sive efficit].

[3] Cf. the text of (St.) Hilary here in the text of Master (Peter), ch. 3, and that of (St.) Augustine, in ON THE TRINITY, Bks. VI and VII, at the beginning, and Richard of St. Victor in the opusculum: "In what manner is the Holy Spirit the Love of the Father and the Son".

[4] See above d. 7, a. sole, q. 1, p. 135, footnote 5. — Next for *He is able through the Son* [potest per Filium] edition 1 has *He is powerful through the Son* [est potens per Filium].

[5] Very many codices, such as I W X Y and bb, add *and/or by him* [sive ab illo].

[6] Supply: the Father [Pater].

[7] The Vatican edition, not trusting in the manuscripts and edition 1, *power* [potentiam] for *the power of working* [potentia operandi], and next for *of subauthority* [subauctoriatis] it substitutes *subauthority* [subauctoritatem], supported by a few codices.

[8] Understand: the Father [Patrem]. — Immediately before this for *to the Son* [Filio] the Vatican edition, together with one or the other codex, has *to the Father* [Patri], falsely.

5. Likewise, since the immediate cause of an operation [operationis] is the will, and that is appropriated to the Holy Spirit, it seems that there ought rather be said that "*(The Father)¹ works through the Holy Spirit*", than "*through the Son*".

ON THE CONTRARY: 1. '*To be powerful*' and '*to be*' is the same:² therefore, if the Father is powerful by begotten Power, therefore, He has His '*to be*' from It.

2. Likewise, "power" is appropriated to the Father, therefore, it befits the Son neither through *property* nor through *appropriation*: therefore, such an expression is more improper that this one: "the Father is wise by begotten Wisdom".

3. Likewise, the power, by which anyone is powerful, according to the order of understanding antecedes '*being able*' [posse]; but generation according to the order of understanding follows '*being able*': therefore, this is entirely false: "the Father is powerful by begotten Power".

CONCLUSION

The expression: "the Father is powerful by begotten Power", is simply false; but the other is true: "the Father works through the Son".

I RESPOND: It must be said, that this is simply false: "the Father is powerful by begotten Power", and more improper than any of the aforesaid. — But for an understanding of the objections it must be noted, that this rule is accustomed to be given concerning this preposition "*through*" [per], which with an *absolute* verb conveys authorship, as when there is said: "this one is good *through that one*", and/or wise and/or powerful ("through that one"). However, with a *transitive* verb it conveys a subauthorship, such as "the king punishes through the bailiff [ballivum] ".³ It must be said, therefore, that this is false: "the Father is powerful through the Son"; yet this is true: "the Father works through the Son". And the argument: 'he works through him, therefore, he is able through him', is not valid, because "*through*" first conveys a causality in respect of an effect, and after this [postmodum] in respect of the Father.

1. To that, therefore, which is first objected, that he who works through someone, is able through him; it must be said, that it is false, because it is not, that he has

power from him, but that he has power undivided with him and gives to him a 'being able'; for that reason, he works through him and he cannot without him.

2. To that which is objected, that working [operatio] and power does not differ in God; it must be said, that through a comparison to God it is true; however, (each) does differ as much as regards the connoted effect.

3. To that which is objected, that it follows: "He knows through the Son, therefore, He is wise through the Son":⁴ ergo etc.; it must be said, that it is not similar concerning "*to know*" and "*to work*". For although "*to know*" is a transitive verb, yet it does not connote an effect, just as "*to work*" (does); and for that reason "*through*" cannot convey with it a subauthorship: for where there is a subauthorship, there is noted, that something is from two and from one through another. And thus that is clear.

4. 5. To that which is objected, whether it means the reckoning of a cause and/or of an instrument; it must be said, that it means neither properly, but a subauthorship, which conveys the reckoning of each as much as regards that which belongs to completion There.

What is objected, that "(the Father)⁵ works through him" is not appropriated to the Son: the response is, that working [operari] is through *virtue*, and "*virtue*" is appropriated to the Son, just there is said in the first (chapter of St. Paul's) First (Letter) to the Corinthians:⁶ *We say that Christ (is) the Virtue of God and the Wisdom of God.* Moreover, the reason, why "*virtue*" is appropriated to the Son, is, that virtue is the ultimate (point) of power [ultimum potentiae]* or is finished power [potentia ultimata].⁷ Therefore, since the Son is produced by the Father according to an omnimodal perfection of power, because 'to generate' is an act of perfect power — « each one is perfect, when it can generate a such as it itself is »⁸ — because, the Son, therefore, accepts the power of producing an equally Perfect, just as He Himself and the Father is, such as the Holy Spirit: for that reason "*virtue*" is appropriated to Him; for that reason He is said (to be) "*the Virtue of the Father*" and "*the Right Hand* (of God)",⁹ and *the Father* (is said) "*to work through the Son*".

In another manner it can be said, that "*virtue*" means a more immediate ordination to act than "*power*" (does), because "*power*" is ordained to work through a disposition, and "disposition" is appropriated to the Son, for that reason "*disposed power*" also.¹⁰ And in this manner all the (reasons) sought are clear.

---

¹ Supply together with edition 1: *the Father* [Pater].
² Cf. (St.) Augustine, ON THE TRINITY, Bks. VI and VII, ch. 1 ff..
³ This rule is ascribed to (Peter) Praepositivus, above in d. 12, Doubt 4, with whom Alexander of Hales is in agreement, SUMMA., p. I, q. 67, m. 3, a. 3. — A little above this, after *authorship* [auctoritas], codex Y adds *about what accompanies it in its phrase* [circa suum casuale].
⁴ This conclusion, *therefore, He is wise through the Son* [ergo est sapiens per Filium], is wanting in the Vatican edition, and also in very many codices.
⁵ Understand: *the Father* [Patrem]. On this sentence see the 4th. objection at the end, from which it also appear, that the reading of the Vatican edition, from which *not* [non] is (here) absent, is false. Equally false is the reading of codices P and Q, which, having omitted the particle *not* [non], after the end of the clause add *not to the Father* [Patri non]. Our reading is supported by the authority of codex T. — For *is objected, that* [obiicitur, quod] codices P and Q (T by a more recent hand) have *is objected, for what reason* [obiicitur, quare].
⁶ Verse 24.
⁷ Aristotle, ON HEAVEN AND EARTH, Bk. I, text 116 (ch. 14) says (in Greek): Ἡ δὲ δύναμις τῆς ὑπεροχῆς ἐστίν, i. e. « But virtue (power) belongs to its own excession [excellence] ». Which words St. Thomas expounds (lecture 25), saying: The virtue of a thing is not attributed ex-

cept to (its) excellence, i.e. (that) according to which the virtue of the thing is attained, which is the most excellent of all things unto which it can (be). And this is what is said in the other translation: « Virtue is the ultimate point of power [ultimum potentiae] », as if, that is, the virtue of a thing is determined according to the furthest (point), unto which it can (be).*
⁸ See above d. 9, a. sole, q. 1, p. 180, footnote 5. — Next for *such as* [ut], codex K has *namely* [scilicet].
⁹ (St.) Hilary in (his) exposition of Psalm 137:7, n. 15, on the words, *and He saved me by Thy Right Hand* [et salvum me fecit dextera tua], says: Virtue is signified in the right hand; and for that reason the Lord, who is the Virtue of God and the Wisdom of God, is sometimes named with the epithet [cognominatur] "the Right Hand of God", through Which we are protected against all (our) enemies in the war of all (our) tribulations. — In the Vatican edition and not a few codices, there is prefaced to the words *and the Right Hand* [et dextera] the words *both the Arm* [et brachium], concerning which (St.) Augustine, ENARRATIONS on Psalm 43, n. 4, (says): *Thy Right Hand*, Thy Power, *Thy Right Arm*, Thy very Son.
¹⁰ Codices F I aa and bb add: *Through this is also clear that (objection) concerning the will* (i.e. objection n. 5), *because just as Hugh says, « the will does not go forth unto a work, except by means of a virtue, and for that reason the virtue is more immediate »* [Per hoc etiam patet illud de voluntate, quia sicut dicit Hugo, « voluntas non exit in opus nisi mediante virtute, et ideo virtus est etiam immediatior ».]

---

* *Trans. note*: Here <u>ultimum potentiae</u> is translated as "*ultimate (point) of power*", according to the sense in which this Latin term is understood by St. Bonaventure in SENT., Bk. III, d. 34, p. I, a. 1, q. 3, in reply to n. 3, p. 743.

SCHOLIUM

I. In the solution to n. 4, there is a response to the question, "For what reason is there not said, that the Father works through the Holy Spirit, just as there is said, that He works through the Son?" It is certain, that the Father communicates to the Holy Spirit the same virtue of acting, which He communicates to the Son. Therefore, the reason, why the one is said, the other is not, can be gathered from this only, that to the Son alone is "*virtue*" appropriated, for which St. Bonaventure gives a twofold reason.

II. Treating of this question are: Bl. (now St.) Albertus (Magnus), here in a. 7. — (Bl.) Peter of Tarentaise, here in q. 2, a. 2. — Richard of Middleton, here in a. 2, q. 1, in reply to n. 5. — Henry of Ghent, Summa., a. 39, q. 7. — (Bl.) Dionysius the Carthusian, here in q. 4.

DOUBTS ON THE TEXT OF THE MASTER

DOUBT I

In this part, there are doubts about the text (of Master Peter) and first concerning the reckoning of (St.) Augustine, which is posited in the text (of Master Peter): *If the Father is wise by the begotten Wisdom, which He begot, and for Him 'to be' is that which (it is) 'to be wise', therefore, He is by begotten Wisdom.* For it seems that that argument of his is not valid, because this is not valid: "for the Father 'to be' is that which (it is) 'to work'; but *He works* through the Son: therefore, *He is* through the Son". Therefore, neither, similarly, is that argument valid. *If you say*, that it is not similar, because "to work" connotes an effect; *there is objected*, that it is the same for the Father *to be* as (it is) *to be the Father*; but this argument, however, is not valid: "the Father by the Deity is God, therefore, by the Deity He is the Father": therefore, similarly, this argument is not valid: "He is wise by begotten Wisdom, therefore, He is by begotten Wisdom".[1]

I RESPOND: It must be said, that the argument of (St.) Augustine is necessary: since 'to be wise' and 'to be' among the divine do not differ according to the manner of speaking on the part of the thing, but solely on our part. But not so is 'to be' and 'to work', since, even if 'to work', as much as regards its principal signified, is the same as 'to be', yet as much as regards what it connotes [ad connotatum] it does differ, and can be extraneous, and thus it can be a (fallacy of) *accident* there.[2] Yet that which it is 'to be God' and 'to be the Father', although they do not differ as much as regards essence and/or the manner of *being*, yet, they do differ as much as regards the manner *of being regarded* [se habendi], which truly is among the divine, namely[3] an *absolute* (manner of being regarded) and a *compared* one; and for that reason the paternity does not pass over into the Substance, as "Wisdom" (does); for that reason it has another manner of being said, which can be extraneous in respect of some attribute. For that reason it is (a fallacy of) *accident* there, but not on the argument of (St.) Augustine.

DOUBT II

Likewise, is asked concerning this which (Master Peter) says, that *the Father is not wise by begotten, but by unbegotten Wisdom*. For he seems to speak badly, because just as "*eternity*" is appropriated to the Father, so "*wisdom*" to the Son; but Eternity ought not be said (to be) "*unbegotten*", just as (St.) Anselm says in the book, ON THE INCARNATION OF THE WORD:[4] therefore, neither can nor ought wisdom be said (to be) "*unbegotten*". *Likewise*, if wisdom can be said (to be) "*unbegotten*",[5] for an equal reason wisdom can be said (to be) "*proceeding*", and thus it seems, that "wisdom" is appropriable to the Holy Spirit, just as to the Son.

In accord with this *there is asked*, for what reason is *Power* not said (to be) "*from Power*", just as *Wisdom* (is said to be) "*from Wisdom*"?

I RESPOND: It must be said, that "*wisdom*" is (one) of the middle names,[6] which is bound *to suppose* on behalf of a Person. And for that reason, just as there is said "*God from God*", and "*the begotten God*" and "*the Unbegotten*", so there is also said "*Wisdom*"; yet not so properly, because it is an abstract name

---

[1] The Vatican edition, together with editions 4 and 5 alone, omits *therefore, He is by begotten Wisdom* [ergo est sapientia genita].

[2] Understand here, as well as below near the end of the solution: *a fallacy of accident* [fallacia accidentis].

[3] On the authority of very many codices, we have restored *namely* [scilicet], which is wanting in the Vatican edition. For *namely* [scilicet] codex Z has *that is* [id est], edition 1 has *according to* [secundum], and not a few manuscripts have *but* [sed]. Immediately before this for *which (being regarding)* [qui], the Vatican edition, together with codex cc, has faultily *which (manner of being regarded)* [quod].

[4] The entire title is: ON FAITH IN THE TRINITY AND ON THE INCARNATION AGAINST THE BLASPHEMIES OF RUZELIN OR ROSCELIN [de Fide Trinitatis et de incarnatione Verbi contra blasphemias Ruzelini sive Roscelini], in which book, in ch. 9, (St.) Anselm, speaking in an orderly manner of the Eternity of the Three Divine Persons, says: « And since that nativity and that procession are without a beginning; otherwise Eternity born and Eternity proceeding have a beginning, which is false: we ought or we can think that God has never begun to be the Father and the Son and the Holy Spirit ». Thus the original text, which Alexander of Hales, SUMMA, p. I, q. 67, m. 1, reports in a little different manner, thus: « (St.) Anselm (says): There is One God, the Father and the Son and the Holy Spirit. And a little while after speak-

ing of the nativity and procession he says, that the nativity and the procession are without a beginning, otherwise there would be an Eternity born and proceeding: — which is false — we ought to think that God never has a beginning or began (to be) the Father or the Son or the Holy Spirit. From this, therefore, there seems to remain, that since Eternity ought not be said to be born and/or proceeding, because it befits the Father alone ». It seems that this passage of (St.) Anselm, as exhibited in Alexander of Hales, St. Bonaventure had before his eyes and took from it in the sentence, that Eternity ought not be said "*to be born*" nor (be) "*unbegotten*", which sentence he proves in the body of the solution. [Trans. note: In the English translation "Eternity" is a name of the Divine Nature, appropriated to the Father, not the concept.] — The Vatican edition, with the manuscripts and edition 1 striving against it, substitutes *begotten* [genita] for *unbegotten* [ingenita], and destroys the argument by this reading. A little above this for *because just as* [quia sicut] many codices, together with edition 1, have *because if* [quia si], which also then omit *so* [ita], incongruously.

[5] In codex Y there is added here *as much as regards the Son* [quantum ad Filium], and a little below this after "*proceeding*" in the same codex Y and in codices B and D there is inserted *as much as regards the Holy Spirit* [quantum ad Spiritum sanctum].

[6] Cf. above d. 5, a. 1, q. 1, in the body (of the question). — A little below this after "*Wisdom*" [sapientia] codex dd adds well *from Wisdom*" [de sapientia].

in a certain manner. Yet "*Wisdom from Wisdom*" is said rather than "*Eternity from Eternity*", because "*eternity*" signifies in greater abstraction than "*wisdom*" (does), and for that reason it abstracts more from the reckoning of origin. According to this, it must also be conceded, that "*Wisdom*" can be said (to be) "*proceeding*", though still less properly. Nor is that argument valid; for although "*wisdom*" is not appropriable to the Holy Spirit,[1] yet it can be drawn (to Him) through an adjoined determination.

Regarding that (which is asked):[2] for what reason is "*Power*" not said (to be) "*from Power*"? it must be said, that it is not said as properly as "*Wisdom from Wisdom*". Since "*wisdom*" is appropriated to the Son, who is from Another and has from Another all that He Has, therefore, He also has Wisdom from Him:[3] for that reason "*begotten Wisdom*" from its appropriation presupposes "*unbegotten Wisdom*". But "*power*" is appropriated to the Father, who is not from Another; for that reason, thus, there is not said "*Power from Power*", and/or "*begotten Power*".

DOUBT III

Likewise, is asked of this which (St.) Augustine says in (his) book of RETRACTATIONS and (which) is posited in the text (of Master Peter): *I treated that question, better, in the book, On the Trinity.* For he seems not to speak rightly, because, since a comparative (adjective) in each of the extremes presupposes the matter of its positive (form),[4] if (it is) there *in a better manner*, therefore, in each (it is) *in a good manner*: therefore, if he says there, that the Father is wise by the Wisdom, which He begot, it seems that he says (something) true.

I RESPOND: It must be said, that the comparison is abusive,[5] since in the book, ON THE TRINITY he says the contrary of this, and for that reason if (he speaks) *well* (there), it is established that (he speaks) *badly* here. However, as much as regards this, that he said some true (things) in the book of 83 QUESTIONS on this question, for that reason (he did not speak) *entirely badly*, but in a certain manner well, in a certain manner badly: and for that reason he says, that *there* (he treated of the question) *better*, hinting that something had been said there badly. For he who builds up one of the opposites, consequently [per consequens] destroys the other of the two.

DOUBT IV

Likewise is asked concerning this response of Master (Peter), that *begotten Wisdom is wise from unbegot-*

ten Wisdom. For it seems not to be good, because it does not seem to respond to the question. For there is not asked, that begotten Wisdom or the Son is *from* the Father, but this is asked, whether the Son is wise[6] by unbegotten Wisdom.

I RESPOND: It must be said, that Master (Peter) responds well, though with few words, in which he hints at this distinction, that '*that one is wise by someone*', this is in a twofold manner: either thus, that the ablative is held *formally*, and in this manner the Son is wise by begotten Wisdom, and the Father by unbegotten Wisdom; or thus, that it is held *originally*, and in this manner, since begotten Wisdom is *from* unbegotten Wisdom, the Son is wise by unbegotten Wisdom. But because the ablative for the most part [ut plurimum] is construed in the reckoning of a *form*, for that reason Master (Peter), having spoken cautiously, said,[7] that the Son, who is begotten Wisdom, is wise *from* unbegotten Wisdom, so that the verse would not be calumniated; and for that reason he responds well.

DOUBT V

Likewise, is asked concerning this which (Master Peter) says, that *each is the one Wisdom, and yet the Father alone is the unbegotten Wisdom.* For he seems to say two opposite (things), because those two properties[8] contract "wisdom", and since the properties are distinct, they distinguish — and this is clear, because the Father alone is the unbegotten Wisdom — wherefore if "wisdom" is distinguished, therefore, there is one and another Wisdom, therefore, not one. *Likewise*, it seems false to say, when he says, that the Father alone is the unbegotten Wisdom. For either "wisdom" is said *essentially*, or *personally*: if *personally*; therefore, the one Wisdom is not begotten and unbegotten, since the Father and the Son are not one Person; however, if *essentially*, therefore, the Father alone is not the unbegotten Wisdom.

I RESPOND: It must be said, that in this name "*wisdom*" there is a considering of two (things), namely, *the signified* and *the supposed*. And as much as regards *the signified* it means the essence; but (as much as regards)[9] *the supposed* it is a Person. And those determinations, "*begotten*" and "*unbegotten*", do not respect *the signified*, but *the supposed*, and thus they do distinguish *the supposed*, while remaining one in *the signified* or form; and the begotten Wisdom is one and the unbegotten Another, namely, Person, but there is not one and another Wisdom, just as there is no other Essence. And for that reason Master (Peter) gives [ponit]

---

[1] The Vatican edition, having inserted a comma after *appropriable* [appropriabilis], reads *yet the Holy Spirit can be drawn (to it)* etc. [Spiritus sanctus tamen etc.].

[2] In codices K P Q W and Y there is is read *Regarding that which is asked* [Ad illud quod quaeritur], in codex T *Regarding that which is objected* [Ad illud quod obiicitur].

[3] For *therefore, He also has Wisdom from Him* [ergo et sapientiam ab illo habet] the Vatican edition reads *therefore also Wisdom from Another* [ergo et sapientiam ab alio].

[4] That is, an adjective *in the comparative (degree)* presupposes, what can be said of each extreme *in the positive (degree)*, or as Aristotle says in TOPICS, Bk .II,c h. 4 (ch. 11): If something is more or less said, (then) it is also (there) simply. — Immediately after this not a few codices have *but* [sed] for *if* [si].

[5] For the comparative "*better*" in the saying of (St.) Augustine is to be accepted improperly. — On the retraction of (St.) Augustine, see above a. 2, q. 1, in the body (of the Question).

[6] From codd. F K L & O we have replaced *wise* [sapiens], which the Vatican ed. omits. A little further above this, for *that* [quod] cod. S has *for what reason* [quare], cod. Y *whether* [an], and not a few other codd., with the Vatican ed. read *of begotten Wisdom or whether* etc. [de sapientia genita sive an etc.] for *that begotten Wisdom or* [quod sapientia genita sive], and then after *Master (Peter)* [Magister], with codex cc, it omits *well* [bene].

[7] Some codices, such as B I and M, together with edition 1, read *spoke cautiously and* (ed. 1 has *when* [cum]) *said* [caute est locutus et dixit]. — In the same sense this doubt is solved by Alexander of Hales, SUMMA, p. I, q. 67, m. 3. a. 2, § 4: Bl. (now St.) Albertus (Magnus), here in a. 4; St. Thomas, here in q. 2, a. 2; (Bl.) Peter of Tarentaise, here in q. 2. a. 3; Richard (of Middleton), here in a. 2, q. 2.

[8] Namely, *begotten* and *unbegotten* Wisdom. — Next for *distinct* [distinctae] edition 1 has *distinctive* [distinctivae] and below, rightly, *wherefore if* [quod si] for *because if* [quia si], which the codices and editions have.

[9] Codex M here repeats *as much as regards* [quantum ad].

a good example in this term "*God*", which signifies the Essence and supposes a Person. — Therefore, when there is asked, whether it is said *essentially* or *personally*, it must be said, that as much as regards the signified it is said *essentially*, but as much as regards the supposed it is said *personally*, and for that reason there is no controversy.[1]

DOUBT VI

Likewise, is asked concerning this which (St. Hilary) says, that *the Son does not act by Himself, when He is shown to remain in Him*, but similarly the Son remains in the Father: therefore, for an equal reason the Father does not act by Himself. *Likewise*, he seems to say the false, when he says: *He would be infirm, by not acting by Himself, unless He acts by God*, because according to this, since every creature acts by God, then the one acting seems to be *infirm*, and in this the Son does not seem to differ from others.

I RESPOND: It must be said, that (St.) Hilary intends to shown two (things) from the words of the Lord in (the Gospel of St.) John, and those two he shows by deducing (them) to the impossible. For the Lord Himself says in the fourteenth (chapter of St.) John:[2] *The words, which I speak to you, I do not speak by Myself; the Father, remaining in Me, Himself does (these) works.* Therefore, from this he argues, that the Son *does not act by Himself*, but by the Father remaining in Him, not only as (One who is) *consubstantial* (to Himself), but as (His) *principle*; but *in this manner* the Son does not remain in the Father, but (is) only as (One who is) *consubstantial* (to Him). — The other is the authority of the Lord, in the eighth (chapter of the Gospel of St.) John,[3] where He says: *He who sent Me has not left Me alone, because those (things) which are pleasing to Him, I do always.* If He Himself acts always as one [una] with the Father, then, therefore, *He acts through Himself.* — He proves these two through a deduction *to the impossible*: because every power is from

the First Power, which first resides in the Father: therefore, if the Son is not able *by God*, He is simply impotent and/or infirm, because (one who is) infirm has the power to fail from himself, not from God. Likewise, if the Son does not act *through Himself*, He does not act through His own virtue, connatural to Himself: therefore the virtue of the Father and the Son is different [alia]. For "*by himself*" [a se] and "*not by himself*" [non a se], does not cause a distinction in nature, but only in person, because it means the reckoning of a principle and/or of an origin. But "*through himself*" [per se] and "*not through himself*" [non per se] — because <u>per se</u> is said against <u>per accidens</u>, or against <u>per alius</u> (i.e. "through another") — posits a diversity in nature;[4] and for that reason the Son acts *through Himself*, although not *by* Himself.

DOUBT VII

Likewise, is asked of this which (Master Peter) says, that *there is one Wisdom of the Father, but it is not said in one manner.* For he seems to speak badly, because "wisdom" is always (said)[5] essentially: therefore, he says the false, when he says: "(it is) not said in one manner".

I RESPOND: Master (Peter) does not want,[6] that "*wisdom*" be said in a multiple (sense), but that "*the Wisdom of the Father*" (be): because the genitive can be construed in the reckoning of an *origin*, and in this manner *the Son* is said (to be) "the Wisdom of the Father", and/or *the begotten Wisdom Itself* "the Wisdom of the Father", because it is from the Father, and/or ("the genitive") can be understood in the reckoning of a *subject*, so that "the Wisdom of the Father" be said, just as "the whiteness of Peter" (is), and in this manner "*the begotten Wisdom*" is not said to be of the Father, but of the Son.[7] Therefore, because the passive reckoning, conveyed through this adjective "*begotten*", is not one in the Person of the Father and the Son, the expression is false by reason of *the determination*, not by reason of that which is "*the Wisdom*": because the one and the same Wisdom is the Father and the Son and the Holy Spirit, and that Wisdom is of the Father and of the Son and of the Holy Spirit.

DISTINCTION XXXIII

CHAPTER I

Whether the properties of the Persons are the Persons Themselves, and/or the Divine Ousia?

After the abovesaid, one is bound to more interiorly consider and subtly inquire, whether the properties of the Persons, by which the Per-

sons Themselves are determined, are *the Persons Themselves* and are God, that is, the Divine Essence, or whether they are *in the Persons*, such that they are not *the Persons*, and through this neither the Divine Essence. — For that the properties are in the Persons, no one dares to cast any doubt [inficiari], since authority openly shouts, that « in the Persons is the property, and in the Essence the Unity ». We have also constructed above with many testimonies of the Saints, that the

---

[1] This doubt is also solved by Bl. (now St.) Albertus (Magnus), here in the last article.

[2] Verse 10. — In the Vulgate there is read *but the Father* [Pater autem], in ed. 1 *but the Father* [Pater vero], in the Vatican *for the Father* [Pater enim]. Then, after *remaining in Me* [in me manens], we have inserted *Himself* [ipse] from very many mss., with the Vulgate consenting.

[3] Verse 29, in which the Vulgate, after the words *sent Me* [misit me], has *is with Me and* [mecum est et], and then after *because* [quia] has explicitly *I* [ego]. — A little below this, after *with the Father* [cum Patre], the Vatican edition, together with codex cc alone, adds *therefore*,

there is one Virtue of Him and of the Father, and thus They act by one Virtue [ergo est una virtus eius et Patris, et sic agunt una virtute].

[4] See more on this above in d. 30, q. 2, in the body (of the Question). — On this doubt, cf. St. Thomas and Richard (of Middleton), here on the text.

[5] In codices P Q X aa and bb, together with edition 1, there is had *is said* [dicitur] for *is (said)* [est].

[6] In codices N P W and add there is added *to say* [dicere].

[7] On the twofold sense of the genitive, cf. above a. 1, q. 1, in reply to n. 1. — For *but of the Son* [sed Filii], many codices, together with edition 1, have *and of the Son* [et Filii]. — This doubt is solved in the same sense by St. Thomas and Richard (of Middleton), here on the text.

persons are distinguished and determined by properties, and we express the properties themselves, namely, three (of them), with their own terms [propriis vocabulis].[1] Therefore, since the very properties, by which the Persons Themselves are determined and differ, are from eternity; in what manner are they, if they are not in Them; and in what manner are they in Them, and are not the Persons Themselves, so that there is no multiplicity There? About which, we confess that just as the properties are in the Persons, so also are they the Persons, just as we have protested above by the authority of (St.) Jerome,[2] thus saying — so that recalling it to mind may not be noisome [pigeat] — in the exposition of the Faith: « Turning away from the heresy of Sabellius, we distinguish the Three Persons expressed under a property. For we confess not only the Names, but also the properties of the Names, that is, the Persons and/or, as the Greeks express (it), the Hypostases, that is, the Subsistences ». — Behold he openly says, that the Persons are distinguished by the properties, and that the properties themselves are the Persons; the words of whom we here touch upon, because above we have cited them without comment [latius posuimus].

And, since we spoke above[3] in an orderly manner of the Simplicity of the Deity, by the authority of the Saints, namely, of Augustine, of Hilary, of Isidore and also even of (St. Severinus) Boethius, we evidently demonstrated, that God is entirely that which He has in Himself, except that the Father has a Son, nor is He the Son, and the Son has a Father, nor is He the Father; and that in this manner (God) is in Nature of the Three, so that He who has This is what He has, and that the Whole *is One, is the One Life*; which we do not repeat now, lest we engender disgust [fastidium ingeramus] in the reader. If, therefore, there are properties There, each one of them is That in whom it is, and they are one [unum] and the same Life of each One. We say, therefore, both that the properties are in the Three Persons, and that they are the Persons and the Divine Essence.

For that a property is also the Divine Nature, (St.) Hilary shows, saying, that the nativity of the Son is the Nature. Whence in the seventh book, ON THE TRINITY[4] he says: « The Nature of Each does not differ: the Father and the Son are One [unum]. Therefore, by this sacrament the nativity has, that it embraces in itself both the Name and the Nature and the Power (of the Person), because the nativity cannot not be this Nature, whence the Son is born ». Likewise, in the sixth (book he says):[5] « The nativity, is a property, is the Truth ». Likewise, in the seventh (book) he says, « that the nativity of the Nature is to be understood to be in the Nature of God ». Above,[6] he also says, « that it is proper to the Father, that He is always the Father, and proper to the Son, that He always is the Son », signifying that the property of the Father is the Father, and the property of the Son is the Son. — There seem to be openly signified, by this and very many other authorities, that the property of the Son is a son, and thus (is) God; thus (it is) also the property of the Father and the property of the Holy Spirit.

But some deny this, saying, that indeed the properties are in the Persons, but they are not the Persons Themselves, because thus they say that they are[7] in the Persons and/or in the Divine Essence, so that they are not within, just as those (names) which are said (to be) of God according to substance, such as goodness, justice, but have been affixed extrinsically. And that they are thus, they strive to prove by

reasons. For if, they say, the properties are the Persons, the Persons are not determined by them. — Against which we say, that the Persons also differ by Themselves, just as (St.) Jerome says above,[8] speaking of the Father and the Son and the Holy Spirit: « They are one [unum] according to substance, but they are distinguished according to Persons and Names ». — But again they add: If the properties themselves are the Divine Essence, since the Three Persons do not differ according to essence, neither do They differ according to properties. For in what manner does the Father differ from the Son, by this, since They are in essence the One, which is the Divine Essence?

To their new and human doctrines I respond with the word of (St.) Hilary:[9] « Immense is that which is required and incomprehensible: it is outside the signification [significantiam] of speech, outside the intention of sense; it is not enunciated, not attained, not held; the nature of the thing itself consumes the significance of words; there blinds the contemplation of sense a Light which cannot be looked through [imperspicabile lumen]; (a Light) which is contained by no limit [fine nullo], exceeds the capacity of the intelligence. For me, therefore, it is in sense a stain, it is in understanding a stupor, but in speech I confess not now an infirmity, but a silence; exceedingly perilous is it to proffer anything concerning things so great and so recondite beyond the celestial Prescript, so that there be a discourse concerning God beyond God's foredetermination [praefinitionem]. The form of the Faith is certain. Therefore, nothing is to be added, but a measure (is) to be established against audacity [constituendus audaciae]; whatever further is asked, is not understood ».

The depravity of all the other heretics, excited by the instinct of diabolic fraudulence, has not yet quieted, but in so great a questioning of things it adds: if the paternity and the filiation are in God, or in the Divine Essence, therefore, the same Thing is its own Father and Son. For (He) in whom the paternity is, is the Father, and (He) in whom the filiation (is), is the Son. If, therefore, one and the same Thing has in Itself the paternity and the filiation, It also generates and is generated; which saying, they were drawn into [per trahuntur] the Sabellian heresy, extending the Father into the Son, since they propose the Same (to be) Its own Son and Father. However, if they denied, that the paternity and the filiation are in the one Essence of God, in what manner, therefore, do they say that they are God? — These and other cutting remarks [aculeis] of arguments do they use in the assertion of their opinion, to dissect the form of the Truth.

Resisting the audacity and foreseeing the ignorance of whom, we dare to say something about this. The paternity and filiation are not said to be thus in the Divine Substance, as in the Hypostases Themselves, in which they are thus, that they determine Them, as (St.) John Damascene says:[10] « They are proper [idiomata] characteristics, that is determinative properties of the Hypostases, and not of the Nature; for they do indeed determine the Hypostases and not the Nature ». And for that reason, though the paternity and filiation are in the Divine Essence, since they do not determine It; it cannot for that reason be said, that the Divine Essence both generates and is generated, and/or that the same Thing is There[11] the Father and the Son. For thus the properties deter-

---

[1] Cf. Distinction XXVI, ch. 2, and d. XXVII, ch. 1.

[2] Distinction XXV, ch. 3, at the end. — Below this, codices A B and E have *he openly shows* [aperte ostendit] for *he openly says* [aperte dicit].

[3] Distinction VIII, part II.   [4] Number 21.

[5] Number 40. The passage following this is Bk. VII, n. 22.

[6] Distinction XXVI, ch. 3. The passage from (St.) Hilary, is taken from ON THE TRINITY, Bk. XII, n. 23. — The Vatican edition has *For above he said* [Supra enim dixit] for *Above, he also says* [Supra etiam dicit].

[7] Codices C and D read *they are said to be* [dicuntur esse] for *they*

say that they are [dicunt esse]. A little below this, codices A B D and E, and editions 1, 2, 3, 5, 7 and 9 have *(which names) have been affixed* [affixa sunt] for *(which properties) have been affixed* [affixae sunt].

[8] Distinction XXV, last chapter.

[9] ON THE TRINITY, Bk. II, n. 5, but with not a few (words) omitted, transposed and changed by Master (Peter).

[10] ON THE ORTHODOX FAITH, Bk. III, ch. 6. See above, d. XXVII, p. I, ch. 3.

[11] Thus codd. C & D, and ed. 1, in all the others there is read *is Its own Father and Son* [sit sibi Pater et Filius] for *is There the Father and the Son* [sit ibi Pater et Filius].

-mine a Person, that by this property a Hypostasis is generating, and by that another Hypostasis is begotten, and thus not the Same generates and is generated, but a different One of the Two [alter alterum].

CHAPTER II

In what manner can the properties be in the Nature of God, and not determine It?

But perhaps you ask, since these properties cannot be in the Persons, and not determine Them, in what manner can they be in the Divine Essence, so that they do not determine It. — I respond to you here too with (St.) Hilary:[1] « I do not know (it), I do not inquire after (it), and yet I shall console myself: the Archangels do not know (it), the Angels have not heard (it), the ages do not hold (it), the Prophet has not sensed (it), the Apostle has not questioned (it), the Son Himself has not spoken of [edidit] (it). Therefore, let the pain of quarrels cease; let man not think by his own intelligence that he is able to follow after the sacrament of the generation. Yet, in an absolute manner, is the Father, and the Son », and the Holy Spirit « to be understood ». « The understanding of the words stands on this boundary [in hoc fine]: from the Father is the Son, who is the Only-Begotten from the Unbegotten, the Progeny from the Parent, the Living One from the Living One, not according to the Nature of the Deity One and Another, because Both (are) the One ». « By believing this, begin, run the course, persist; even if I do not know that I am going to arrive, yet shall I congratulate (myself) for setting out. For who seeks after the infinite in a pious manner, even if he does not attain it, nevertheless sometimes makes progress by going forward. But do not insert yourself into that hidden and enclosed (sacrament) of the unsearchable [inopinabilis] nativity, lest you submerge [immergas] yourself, presuming to comprehend the Height of intelligence; but understand that they are incomprehensible ». With these and many others there is evidently shown, that it is to no extent licit for us to *thoroughly scrutinize the Majesty,*[2] to posit a right to Power, to circumscribe a measure for the Infinite.

Nevertheless, agitated by the spirit of impatience they still do not desist, but strive even to fortify their own opinion with the authorities of the Saints, by which they wish to show, that the property, by which the Father is the Father, and the property, by which the Son is the Son, are not God, bringing forward for this the words of (St.) Augustine on that passage of the Psalm: *And there is no substance,* thus says:[3] « God is a certain substance. Whence we are also thus edified in the Catholic Faith, to say, that the Father and the Son and the Holy Spirit are of the One Substance. What is of the One Substance? Whatever is the Father, what *God* is, this is the Son, this is the Holy Spirit. But when He is *the Father,* He is not that which[4] *He is.* For he is said (to be) "*the Father*" not regarding Himself, but regarding the Son; but regarding Himself He is said (to be) "*God*". Therefore, by this, that He is *God,* and/or whereby (He is God), He is the Substance. And because the Son is of the same Substance, without doubt [procul dubio] the Son is also God. But, on the other hand, because that which is "*the Father*", is not a Name for the Substance, but is referred to the Son, we do not say thus, that the Son is *the Father,* as we say, that the Son is *God* ». — From this words they say it is signified, that the property of the Father and/or the property of the Son is not God and/or the Divine Essence. For when he says: "By this, that He is *God,* He is the Substance, but that which *the Father* is, is not the substance";[5] he openly shows, they say, that that by which He is God, is the Substance; but that by which He is the Father, is not the Substance. Likewise, when he says: "*the Father* is not that which *He is*", he shows, that when by that whereby He is the Substance, He is not the Father. For He did not simply say: "the Father is not that which He is", but said: "*when He is the Father*, He is not that which He is", signifying, that (that) by which He is *the Father* is not That by which *He is,* that is, the Essence. These thus expounding this, make their comments seem true to the simple and incautious. — However, we say that these are to be understood in another manner. For saying: "by this, that He is *God,* He is the Substance; but that which *the Father* is, is not the Substance", he wanted that this be understood, that by the Essence He is God and by the Deity He is the Substance. For He is *the Substance* by that, by which He is *God,* and vice versa, whose Deity is that, which is the Substance, and the Substance, that which (is) the Deity; but that which is *the Father,* it not *the Substance,*[6] that is, that by which He is *the Father,* is not that by which He is *the Substance,* because the property of the generation, by which He is not the Substance, He is the Father. However, he did not deny that the property is the Substance. That which he says must also be understood thus: "When He is *the Father,* He is not that which *He is*", that is, He is not *the Father* by that, which and/or by which He Himself *is,* that is the Essence, but by the notion.

Likewise, by these words of (St.) Augustine, posited above,[7] they vehemently insist, namely, that the Word, according to which He is *Wisdom,* (is) also *the Essence,* that is what the Father (is); according to which (He is) *a word,* is not that, which the Father (is). If, they say, the Word is not that which the Father (is), according to which He is a *word,* that, therefore, which[8] a *word* is, is not that which *the Father* is: therefore, the property by which He is a *word,* is not that which *the Father* is, is not, therefore, the Divine Essence. — To which we say, that, though according to which (He is) *a word,* He is not that which *the Father* is, yet that property, by which *He is* a word, is that which the Father *is,* that is the Divine Essence, but is not the Hypostasis of the Father.

---

[1] ON THE TRINITY, Bk. II, nn. 9, 10, and 11, but with very many (words) omitted and transposed by Master (Peter).

[2] A reference to Proverbs 25:27: *He who is a scrutinizer of the Majesty, will be oppressed by the Glory* [Qui scrutator est maiestatis, opprimetur a gloria].

[3] (St.) Augustine, ENARRATIONS ON THE PSALMS, Ps. 68:3, sermon I, n. 5.

[4] The Vatican edition and the other editions, except ed. 1, add *and/or whereby* [vel quo], breaking with the codices and the original. A little below this, for *that He is God and/or whereby (He is God)* [quod vel quo Deus est] the original has: *that He is God, by this* [quod Deus est, hoc ipso]. After this, for *is not a Name for the Substance* [non substan-

tiae nomen est] the codices, contrary to the Vatican edition and to editions 6 and 8, and the original, have *does not belong to the Substance* [non substantiae est].

[5] Codd. A B C & E and ed. 1 read *does not belong to the Substance* [substantiae non est] for *is not the Substance* [substantia non est]. A little after this cod. D has twice *that which* [quod] for *that by which He* [quo].

[6] The codd. & edd. 3 and 7 have *does not belong to the Substance* [non est substantiae] for *is not the Substance* [non est substantia], and below they have *He is not that which belongs to the Substance* [non illud est quod est substantiae] for *He is not that which He is* [non illud est quod est].

[7] Distinction XXVII, p. II, ch. 3.

[8] Thus codd. A C D & E and ed. 1; cod. B & other edd. have *by which* [quo].

COMMENTARY ON DISTINCTION XXXIII

On the properties in comparison to the Essence and to the Persons.

After the abovesaid, one is bound to more interiorly consider and subtly inquire etc..

THE DIVISION OF THE TEXT

Above, Master (Peter) dealt with the Names for the Substance, and with the properties (considered) *through themselves* and singly. Here in the third place he deals with these[1] *in comparison*, and this according to (their) convening and difference; and this part of his has two parts. In the first, Master (Peter) asks concerning the properties in comparison to the Essence and the Persons. However, in the second, he deals with the comparison of a Person or of the Thing of the Nature to the Nature, below in the Thirty-Fourth Distinction (where he says): *To the aforesaid there must be adjoined* etc..

The first part has two (parts) according to the two works of the wise man, the first of which is « not to lie, about [de] those (things) which he knows »; and the second is « to be able to manifest the one lying ».[2] Whence, in the *first* part, he first shows and proves the truth; in the *second* he defends it against falsehood, there (where he says): *But some deny this* etc..

The *first* part has four parts.[3] In the first, he shows, that the properties are the Persons and in the Person, through the nature of a property itself, because it is eternal and distinct. In the second, he shows that same by the impetuosity [violentiam] of authority,[4] there (where he says): *Turning away from the heresy of Sabellius*, where he puts the quotes [auctoritates] from (St.) Jerome. In the third, he shows this very (thing) through the nature of the Divine Simplicity, there (where he says): *And since we spoke above in an orderly manner of the Simplicity of the Deity*. In the fourth, he shows, that the properties are not only the Persons, but (are) also the Divine Essence. And this he proves by the efficacy of authority, there (where he says): *For that a property is also the Divine Nature*, where he puts the quote from (St.) Hilary.

But some deny this, saying etc.. This is the *second* part, in which Master (Peter) puts the defense of the proven truth, by positing the reasons of others and his own responses. And since twofold is the manner of impugning the truth, namely, through reasons and authorities, for this reason this part has two parts. In the first he posits the reasons and responses; in the second the authorities, there (where he says): *Nevertheless, agitated by the spirit of impatience they still do not desist* etc..

The first part has four parts.[5] In the first, he posits the objection, that the properties are not the Persons; and because (the objection) was a *rational* one, he responds to the truth. But, second, he subjoins another reason, and because it seems *curious*, he responds ad hominem, not ad orationem,[6] there (where he says): *But again they add* etc.. Third, he takes up their reckoning yet again and responds according to the truth, there (where he says): *The depravity of all the other heretics*, etc.. Fourth and last, he subjoins their interrogation, and because it was *curious*, he fixes beforehand the limit [terminum] for human inquisition, there (where he says): *But perhaps you ask, since these properties* etc.. And each of these parts can be subdivided, that is, according to this, that first he posits the opposition and second the response, and that has been made manifest in the text.

Nevertheless, agitated by the spirit of impatience they still do not desist, etc.. This is the last part, in which Master (Peter) responds to the authorities, which they bring forward; and this part has two parts, according to the two quotes of (St.) Augustine, which they bring forward: and the first has been taken from (his) Exposition of the Psalms, but the second has been taken from (St.) Augustine, in the seventh (book) ON THE TRINITY. The first part is posited there (where he says): *Nevertheless, agitated by the spirit of impatience* etc.; the second part is posited there (where he says): *Likewise, by these words of (St.) Augustine*, etc.. And each of these parts can be subdivided, because first he posits the authority or reason, but second he dissolves (it).

---

[1] Codices aa and bb add *(which) are said* [dicuntur].

[2] These 2 texts are found in Aristotle, ELENCHAE, Bk. I, ch. 2 (ch. 1).

[3] Codices I X aa and bb, together with edition 1, have *subparts* [particulas]. Somewhat further below this, for *distinct* [distincta] codices aa and bb read *distinctive* [distinctiva].

[4] The Vatican edition has *through the violence of (its) author, Sabellius* [per violentiam auctoris Sabelii]. Next it reads *he posits the authority of (St.) Jerome* [point auctoritatem Hieronymi] for *he puts the quotes from (St.) Jerome* [ponit auctoritates Hieronymi].

[5] Codices X aa and bb, together with edition 1, have *subparts* [particulas]. A little further below this, for *a rational one* [rationalis], codices G Y and Z, together with edition 1, have *reasonable* [rationabilis].

[6] For *ad orationem* The Vatican edition has *ad rationem* (i.e. "to the reckoning"); each reading has the same sense. Our reading is had by all the codices; the term ad orationem (i.e. "to the discourse, argument, request") has been taken from (St. Severinus) Boethius, cf. above d. 6, Doubt 3, p. 131, footnote 6.

TREATMENT OF THE QUESTIONS

For an understanding of the present Distinction four (questions) are asked.

First, there is asked concerning the comparison of a property to a Person.

Second, of the comparison of a property to the Essence.

Third, of the comparison of one property to another.

Fourth, of the comparison of the same property to itself.

ARTICLE SOLE

On the diverse comparisons of a property.

QUESTION I

Whether a property is a Person?

Therefore, as much as regards the first, there is asked concerning the comparison of a property to a *Person*. And there is asked, whether a property is a Person. And that (it is not), is shown in this manner:

1. Wheresoever there is truly a determining and a determined according to thing, there the one determining differs from the one determined — for if it does not differ, it is not truly a determining, but the whole is a determined — but a *Person* among the divine is truly a determined, and a *property* truly a determining, because a property truly, and not according to a manner of speaking alone, distinguishes a Person: therefore, a property differs from a Person. But a difference is not predicated of itself in abstraction:[1] therefore, neither a property of a Person, and/or vice versa.

2. Likewise, wheresoever there is truly an abstract and a concrete, there what is abstracted differs from that, from which it is abstracted;[2] but a property is signified in concretion regarding a Person, when there is said "*the Father*", and in abstraction, when there is said "*the paternity*", and not only is there a difference in the manner of speaking, because something is said of the Father, which (is) not (said) of the paternity: therefore, the paternity truly differs from the Person. But what truly differs from another is not predicated of it in abstraction: ergo etc..

3. Likewise, wheresoever there is an absolute and a respective, the absolute is not the looking-back itself, howsoever much it is referred by itself — whence although matter is referred to form by itself, yet it is not the very looking-back to the form[3] — therefore, though among the divine a Person is truly an absolute substance, (and) the relation is a true looking-back, howsoever much a Person is referred by Himself, He is not the true looking-back or the looking-back itself, nor vice versa: therefore, a property is not the Person Himself.

From these three suppositions (Gilbert) of Porretain use to argue, that a Person is not a property, nor vice versa. And because everything which is in a Person, is the Person on account of the Most High Simplicity, he used to argue *furthermore*, that the properties are not in the Persons, but stand alongside (Them) [assistunt].

4. And that this position of his is fitting, seems *by the authority* of (St. Severinus) Boethius ON THE TRINITY.[4] For he says, that « a relation does not consist in that which is the '*being*' (of that which is related), but in (its) *comparison* ».

5. Likewise, this very (thing) is shown *by reason*, because everything which comes to something and recedes without its own mutation, does not predicate anything, which is in that, but (is)[5] only standing alongside; but a relation is of this kind, as is clear in the right and left hands: ergo etc.. Since, therefore, the properties are relations, they are not the Persons nor in the Persons, but they stand alongside.

---

[1] Thus there is not said: rational is rationality. This argument of Gilbert of Porretain is hinted at here in the text of Master (Peter), ch. 1, near the middle.

[2] Concerning which, see above d. 27, p. I, q. 3.

[3] See above d. 3, p. II, a. 1, q. 3, in reply to n. 4. — Next after *absolute substance* [substantia absoluta] codices I X and b, together with edition 1, insert *and* [et]. A little below this codex T omits the words *a true looking-back or* [verus respectus sive].

[4] Chapter 5: « The whole of which does not consist in that which is the 'being' (of the thing related), but in that which is (its) 'holding of itself' [se habere] in comparison in some manner ». In the same place there is also hinted the next following argument, concerning which, see d. 26, a. sole, q. 1, p. 453, footnote 3. Cf. also the Commentary of Gilbert of Porretain, on this passage. — The Vatican edition alone faultily omits in this citation the *not* [non].

[5] The Vatican edition, together with codex cc, adds *is* [est].

ON THE CONTRARY: 1. « Everything most simply is that which it has, except that, according to which it is said relatively ». This is (the sentence) of (St.) Augustine in the eleventh (book) ON THE CITY GOD[1] and it is self-evident [per se nota]; but a Divine Person is most simple, otherwise He would not be God, and He is not said in a manner relative to a property: therefore, He is a property.

2. Likewise, everything most perfect is every that by which it is perfected and denominated — this is self evident, because otherwise the one denominating and the one perfecting would be more perfect that it; and (St.) Augustine propounds this in the fifth (book) ON THE TRINITY,[2] saying, that because God Himself is the greatest, for that reason He is His own greatness — but a Divine Person is something most perfect and is denominated by His own property: therefore, a Person is His own property, and the Father is the paternity.

3. Likewise, everything simply first is whatever it has, except that which is out of it[3] — for if it has anything which is not from it, and/or which it itself is not, that is as equally first as itself: therefore, it will not be simply first — but the Father has paternity, and the paternity is not from Him, and He Himself is simply the First: therefore, the Father is the paternity, for the same reason the Son is the filiation, and the Holy Spirit the procession.

From these it is concluded, that the properties are not only *the Persons*, but (are) also *in the Persons*.

4. That that this is true, seems *by the authority* of (St.) Jerome in the book, ON THE EXPOSITION OF THE CATHOLIC FAITH TO POPE DAMASUS:[4] « We distinguish », he says, « Three Persons, expressed under the properties ».

5. Likewise, this seems *by reason*. Because everything which is, either is a being *through itself* and *in itself*, or *in another*.[5] The properties, therefore, are either beings *through themselves*, and thus substances; or *in another*. If *in another*, naught but in the Persons, because a property is naught but in Him of whom it is the property. If *through itself*, therefore, a property is a substance: therefore, either a *created* (substance), or an *uncreated* one, or a *middle* one. But not a *created* one, nor a *middle* one — that is established — it remains, therefore, that (it is) *an uncreated* (substance): therefore, (the properties) are Persons.

CONCLUSION

A property is a Person and in a Person, yet a property and a Person differ according to (their) manner of holding themselves.

I RESPOND: It must be said, that concerning the comparison of a property to a Person there was a three-fold opinion.

The *first* position was, that the properties are not *the Persons* nor *in the Persons*, but *stand alongside* the Persons, just as the relations (do). And the reason, which moved those of this (position), was the plurality of the Persons and the Divine Simplicity. For because the Persons[6] are many, They have many properties, which are truly different. And because they are different, if they were in a Person, they would bear off His simplicity. Which, since it cannot be born off from the divine, the posited, that the properties are *standing along side* the Persons, that they are not *the Persons*. And to this seems consonant the nature of a relation, which does not seem to be in a substance[7] nor to predicate anything in the subject, but to mean a looking-back to another. — And this position, even if it was in some manner reasonable, yet it cannot stand, because it posited, that the relations among the divine are neither God nor a creature. Whence even if at its beginning it contained a modicum of error, yet it lead to a great (error);[8] and for that reason it was retracted at the Council of Rheims, and Master Gilbert of Porretain retracted (it) with his own mouth.

For that reason there was a *second* opinion,[9] differing much from this (first) one, namely, that the properties are entirely the Persons and do not differ except only in a manner of speaking, and (that) there are only three properties, just as there are Three Persons. And this position was founded similarly upon the Divine Simplicity. For, because the Persons are most simple, They are distinguished by Themselves, and They Themselves are Their own properties, nor do They have others different (from these) according to thing, but only in a manner of speaking. And this position was (that) of Master (Peter) Praepositivus, and it is more probable than the preceding one. — But yet it has been disproved above, in the Twenty-Sixth Distinction,[10] because one Person has many rela-

---

[1] Chapter 10, n. 1: For (the nature of the Good) is said (to be) "simple", since what It has, that It is, except that any Person is said relatively to the Other. — In codex O after *This is* [Haec est] there is added *the rule* [regula].

[2] Chapter 10, n. 11: But God, because is not great by that greatness, which is not that which He Himself is, as if God is a participant in that, when He is great — otherwise that will be a great greatness than God, but there is nothing greater than God — therefore, He is great by that greatness, by which He Himself is the same greatness. Cf. also Bk. VI, ch. 7, n. 8 ff.. — Next, after *that* [quod], we have restored, from codd. I M W X Z & bb, the conjunction *because* [quia], which is wanting in the Vatican ed.. Codd. I X & bb omit *Himself* [ipse]. A little before this, for *otherwise the one denominating* [aliter denominans] many codices, with ed. 1, incongruous read *then the one denominating* [tunc denominans]. Then, after *that it* [eo] codex O (L in the margin) adds *according to what is less secundum quid; and if secundum quid: therefore, simply, most of all in a most simple, where there is not a this and that* [ad minus secundum quid; et si secundum quid: ergo simpliciter, maxime in simplicissimo, ubi non est quid et quid]. At the end of the argument cod. I reads *His own paternity* [sua paternitas] for *the paternity* [paternitas].

[3] Codices I M and bb, together with edition 1 *from it* [ab illo].

[4] See above, d. XXV, ch. 3. — For *to Pope Damasus* [ad Damasum] the codices and editions, except editions 4 and 5. have *to Philip* [ad Philippum].

[5] Cf. above d. 5, a. 2, q. 1, p. 116, footnote 6. — Next for *substances* [substantiae] the Vatican edition, together with a few codices, has *a substance* [substantia].

[6] In codex bb and edition 1 there is added here *truly* [vere].

[7] Codices E F I M X aa and bb read *subject* [subiecto].

[8] Aristotle, ON HEAVEN AND THE WORLD, Bk. I, text 33 (ch. 5.): « On which account what at the beginning is a little, at the end becomes very great », which sentence Averroës in his Commentary on this passage expresses thus: « the least error in the principles and/or at the beginning of a thing is a great one in the end ». These words of Averroës were afterwards very frequently quoted among the Scholastics. — A little before this, in place of *it contained* [contineret] the Vatican edition, together with some codices and edition 1, has *it contains* [continet].

[9] Codices I and Y and edition 1 have *position* [positionis].

[10] In Questions 1, 2 and 3. — After *But yet it* [Attamen], at the beginning of the proposition, codex I and edition 1 subjoin *too* [et].

tions, which are true relations; and many Persons have one Property; and one Person holds Himself to the Son in one manner and to the Holy Spirit in another, even according to thing. From which there necessarily follows, that a property really differs in some manner from a Person, and not only in a manner of speaking, as Master (Peter) Praepositivus used to say.

And on this account it must be understood, that each of the aforesaid positions said something of the truth and in something is deficient. For the *first*, which said, that the properties differ in some manner from the Persons, spoke the truth; but (spoke) badly in this, that it said that they differ *simply*. The *following one*, which said, that the properties are the Persons, spoke the truth; but went to far [excessit] in this, that it said, that they differ *in no manner* from the Persons.

For that reason, from these two positions there is conflated[1] one true and *common* position, which the masters (of theology) not commonly hold, that the properties are *the Persons* and *in the Persons*, yet differ in some manner from the Persons. — And that this position is fitting, it clear, if one inspects the nature of the properties. For it has been said above,[2] when there was asked, what a property is among the divine, that it was a *relation*. It has also been said, that a relation by reason of the comparison, which it has to (its) *subject*, passes over into the Substance among the divine; and for that reason it is entirely predicated of its own subject, such as "the Father is the paternity". However, by reason of the comparison, which it has to (its) *object*, it remains most truly among the divine and has in a certain manner a difference from a Person; nor does it, according to this, cause a composition, but a distinction in respect of Whom it is. For a composition is attained through a comparison of a property to a *subject*, a distinction (is attained) in respect of an *object*. And from this it is clear, that a property is a *Person* and in a *Person*, because it is the same through essence or the manner[3] of *being* [modum essendi], yet it differs as much as regards the manner *of holding itself*. — Therefore, the reason, that the properties are the *Persons* and *in Persons*, are to be conceded.

1. And from what has been said the response to the first argument is clear. For because a property and a Person have a small difference in [penes] the manner of being regarding, for that reason a property truly determines and distinguishes; yet this does not take away (its) being predicated (of a Person),[4] because that manner (of holding itself) does not add another essence.

2. To that which is objected second, concerning abstraction, it must be said, that there is no abstraction according to *thing*, but only according to a *manner of understanding* and *of speaking*: because abstraction respects the *subject* in which (it is), and according to that looking-back it passes over (into the substance);[5] yet because it remains in the comparison to the *terminus*, hence it is, that a relation not only differs in a manner of speaking, and yet it is not necessary, that there be There a true abstraction.

3. To that which is objected third, that an absolute is not said of a respective; it must be said, that (this) is true in a *creature*, because a true looking-back is itself either other through essence, or in comparison to another through essence, as matter and form (are), neither of which is among the divine: whence a looking-back in creatures posits a dependence, and for that reason it deprives a most high Simplicity, and for that reason it is not predicated (of its subject) among creatures. For everything most simple is entirely independent.[6] But among the *divine* relations do mean a looking-back without a dependence; and for that reason they do not deprive a most high Simplicity, and for that reason they are said of the Hypostases.

4. To that which is objected afterwards, that all relations are standing alongside; it must be said, that (relations)[7] are said *to be in comparison* by (St. Severinus) Boethius, not because they are not in the thing, but because, though they are in the thing, they are not in it *absolutely*, but in *comparison to the other*, indeed, with which (other) changed and corrupted, it happens that the relation is equally corrupted and ceases on account of this, that it is not in the subject *absolutely*, but as regarding the other; yet nevertheless it is in the subject.

5. From this is clear the response to that which is objected. For that does not have truth but in an absolute being, not a respective one. And that[8] is drawn from *reason* and *the words* of (St. Severinus) Boethius; from *reason*, because when I say, that this has been ordered to something, I say nothing of that, of which it is said, and when of something, which has no order, there comes to be (something) having an order, because it was not that to which it was ordered — and for that reason there was an order in potency in this not[9] by reason of itself, but by reason of that to which it is (ordered) — as much as it is on its own part, it was in act; and for that reason, with no change being made in *it*, but in the *object*, it is brought into being [in esse] and ceases (to be). And this is clear from *the words* of (St.) Boethius, because (St.) Boethius does not simply deny, that a relation does not consist in that which is the *'being'* (of the thing related), but that it does not totally consist (in that). Whence he says:[10] « A relative predication, which does not consist whole in that which is the *'being'*, cannot through itself add, and/or diminish, and/or change the whatever of the thing, of which it is said ». From this he hints, that in some manner it does consist; and for that reason neither among creatures nor in God is it true to say, that a relation is not in something; but it is true to say, that it is not absolutely the *whole* (thing) in something.

---

[1] Codex bb has *confected* [conficitur]. [Trans. note: "to conflate" in English, in this context, means to compose a verbal proposition by means of adding two other propositions together.]

[2] Distinction 26, q. 2.

[3] Codices T and X to the word *the manner* [modum] prefix the word *according to* [secundum]. A little after this to the word *reasons* [rationes] codex K adds well *showing* [ostendentes].

[4] That is, (the predication) by which a property is predicated of a person, and <u>vice versa</u>.

[5] Supply together with the Vatican edition *into the substance* [substantiam]. At the end of the solution, before *true* [vera] the Vatican edition, together with a few codices, omits *There* [ibi].

[6] Cf. above d. 8, p. II, a. sole, q. 2, p. 169, footnote 4.

[7] Understand *relations* [rationes]. — Immediately after this, for *in comparison* [in comparatione] very many codd., with edd. 2, 3, 4, and 5, faultily have *in relation* [in relatione]; cod. Y reads thus: *that relations are not said to be, not because* etc. [quod non esse relationes dicantur, non quia etc.].

[8] Codex T has *this* [hoc], codex L has *the same* [idem], the other codices have falsely *for that reason* [ideo]. A little above this, after *an absolute being* [ente absoluto] cod. T and not a few others insert *and* [et].

[9] For *in this not* [in hoc non] codices M P Q and X have *and this not* [et hoc non], codices C and O have *not this* [non hoc], codex T reads briefly thus: *in this, yet by reason of itself it was in act, and for that reason* etc. [in hoc, tamen ratione sui erat in actu, et ideo etc.].

[10] ON THE TRINITY, ch. 5. — In the passage cited, the Vatican edition, with both the codices and edition 1 and even the text of the original striving against this, by changing *which* [quae] into *because* [quia] reads: *A relative predication cannot through itself add, and/or diminish, and/or change the whatever of the thing, of which it is said, because it does not consist whole in that which is the 'being' (of the thing).*

SCHOLIUM

I. That there are *properties* among the divine, has already been proven above (d. 26, q. 1), and along with that something has been said of their *nature* and of the two extreme and false opinions of Gilbert of Porretain and (Peter) Praepositivus. In this Question the nature of the properties is more accurately determined. — *Gilbert*, the Bishop of Poitiers († A.D. 1154), addicted in philosophy to immoderate realism, wanted to infer, from the sentence of (St. Severinus) Boethius, cited in the 4th opposed argument, that a relation has 'being' only *in comparison*, that is in an order *to a terminus*, that the relations are not *the Persons*, nor are reduced through identity to the Essence; likewise, that they are not, neither *in the Persons* nor *in the Essence* (that is denominatively, and according to our manner of understanding, as if through information), but that they are only standing alongside [assistentes], as is, for example, a looking-back to another. So that his sentence be better understood, we transcribe this (passage) from Bl. (now St.) Albertus (Magnus), SUMMA, p. I, tr. 13, q. 52: « (Gilbert of Porretain's disciples) distinguish between *subsistent*, *existent*, *insistent* and *assistant*. They say that a *subsistent* is that which is sufficient for itself to be and is not in want of another, just as is the Divine Essence. Moreover, they say that an *existent* is that which is in want of a certain other, as a cause, out of which (other) it is, just as (something) caused and created. Moreover, they say that an *insistent* is that which flows to another as to a subject, in which it is. But they say an *assistant* (is) that which is not in, but (which), through the habitude of something extrinsic, means a looking-back to the other, just as relatives, the '*being*' of which regards another. And such looking-backs mean the 'being' in those names "*Lord*" and "*Creator*". — The principal arguments on behalf of this sentence are found here in the first 3 opposed arguments. This error was condemned by the Council of Rheims, celebrated in the year (of Our Lord) 1148 by (Pope) Eugene III, with these words: « We believe and confess, that God, the Father and the Son and the Holy Spirit, is alone eternal, and there are not said to be present in God any three, whether relations, or properties, or singularities and/or unities, and/or anything of this kind, which are from eternity and are not God ». — (Master) *Praepositivus* conversely inferred from the same principle of the Divine Simplicity another extreme opinion, namely, that the properties are indeed *the Persons*, but are not *in the Persons*, since they do not differ from the Persons except

in a *manner of speaking*. This error is refuted in the 3rd and 5th arguments of the fundament and in the body (of the question). — Therefore, the *middle* and true sentence established, both that the properties *are the Persons* through identity, and that they are *in the Persons* on account of a certain distinction, *necessarily* made by our intellect and at least with a *foundation from the part of the thing*. On the nature of this distinction the doctors differ in (their) manner of speaking, concerning which, see above d. 26, q. 1, Scholium, and here in the solution to n. 1.

II. In regard to the solution to n. 2, cf. above d. 27, p. I, q. 3, where it is denied, that in the properties there is a *true* abstraction. The best reason for this assertion here and there, in the reply to n. 3, namely, that an abstraction looks back to the *subject*, in which the relation is; and under this looking-back the relation (as an *in which*) passes over into the Substance and is identified with it. But the relation as a *toward* (or in regard to the looking-back to a terminus) indeed remains, and the relative distinction among the Persons is real, but this is not by reason of an *abstraction*. For nothing among the divine is abstracted, which really differs, and nothing really differs, which is abstracted. — The 3rd objection, that a relation can to no extent be predicated of the Divine Essence, contains no small difficulty, is solved by the Seraphic (Doctor) from this principle, that the concept of a relation, transferred from creatures to God, ought to be purified from all which it has among created imperfections, and from all which are repugnant to the Divine Simplicity. In a manner, a little different, but in the same sense, St. Thomas (SUMMA., I, q. 28, a. 2, ad 3) solves the same difficulty. — The solution to n. 4 explains well the definition of relation given by (St. Severinus) Boethius; cf. St. Thomas, *loc cit*. a. 3.

III. Alexander of Hales, SUMMA., p. I, q. 68, m. 1, a. 1, and m. 5, a. 1 and 6, § 4. — (Bl. John Duns) Scotus, here in the q. sole; REPORTATIO., here in q. 3. — St. Thomas, here in q. 1, a. 2; SUMMA., I, q. 40, a. 1. — Bl. (now St.) Albertus (Magnus), here in a. 2; SUMMA., p. I, tr. 9, q. 39, m. 2, a. 3. — (Bl.) Peter of Tarentaise, here in q. 2, a. 1 and 2. — Richard of Middleton , here in a. 1, qq. 1 and 2. — Giles the Roman, here in 1st. princ., qq. 1 and 4. — Henry of Ghent, SUMMA., a. 56, q. 1. — Durandus (of Saint-Pourçain), on this and the following q. here in q. 3. — (Bl.) Dionysius the Carthusian., on this and the following q. here in q. 1. — (Gabriel) Biel, on this and the following q. here in the q. sole.

QUESTION II

Whether a property is the Essence?

Second, there is asked concerning the comparison of a property to *the Essence*, and there is asked, whether a property is the Essence. And that it is, seems:

1. Because the Church chants:[1] « there is adored property in the Persons »;* but nothing is to be adored with latria but the Divine Essence: ergo etc.. Whence (St.) Bernard (of Clairvaux says):[2] « That property, which is not God, I do not believe is adorable by me ».

2. Likewise, the Essence is in a Person, similarly[3] also a property: therefore, either they are There through a *difference*, or through an *indifference*. If through *difference*: therefore, a Person is composed, which is unfitting. If through an omnimodal *indifference*: therefore a property is the Essence, and the Essence is a property.

3. Likewise, a property either is *something*, or *nothing*. If *nothing*: therefore, either a Person is not distinguished, or the distinction of a Person is nothing. If it is *something*; but everything which is something is an essence, either created, and/or uncreated; but a property is not a created essence, this is manifest: therefore, the uncreated (Essence).

4. Likewise, everything which is, either is *God*, or (is) *better*, or *more* or *less* good, than God: therefore, a property either is God, or (is) better or less or greater. But it cannot be *greater*, because God is that than which a greater cannot be thought.[4] It cannot be *less*, because then the Father would be less, that He Himself is (as God): therefore, it is *God*.

ON THE CONTRARY: 1. (St.) Augustine says and it is had above, in the Eighteenth Distinction: « He is not God by that,

---

[1] (In the MISSALE ROMANUM), in the Preface of the Most Holy Trinity, the author of which preface is reported to be either Pope Pelagius, or St. Ambrose.
[2] ON CONSIDERATIONS., Bk. V, ch. 7, n. 15: If it pleases one to posit a fourth divine being [quartam divinitatem]; I am persuaded, in the meantime, that that, which is not God, is least of all to be adored by myself.

[3] In very many codices and editions 2, 3, 4, 5 and 6, there is wanting *similarly* [similiter].
[4] (St. Severinus) Boethius, ON THE CONSOLATION OF PHILOSOPHY, Bk. II, prose 10.
[5] In the text of Master Peter, ch. 3. Cf. above d. 6, Doubt 2, and d. 19, p. II, q. 2, in reply to n. 4.

---

* *Trans. note*: The passage in the Missal reads fully: *So that in the confession of the true and sempiternal Deity, there is adored both property in the Persons, and unity in Essence, and equality in Majesty* [Ut in confessione verae sempiternaeque Deitatis, et in personis proprietas, et in essentia unitas, et in maiestate adoretur aequalitas].

by which (He is) the Father, but He is God by the Deity, He is the Father by the paternity »: therefore the Deity is not the paternity, nay (they are) one (thing) and another.

2. Likewise, this seems *by reason*. There is this per se true[1] concept of the spirit [conception animi], that the principle of distinguishing and of uniting is not the same, formally speaking; but the Essence is the Reason for uniting, a property, however, a reason for distinguishing: therefore the Essence and the property are not the same.

3. Likewise, no property is predicated properly of any essence or substance, unless it be in it: therefore, if the properties are said of the Divine Essence, therefore, they are in It. But a property posits its own thing about the subject, in which it is: therefore, since a property of a thing is a looking-back, and to a looking-back there follows a distinction, the properties, of necessity, posit a distinction about the Divine Essence, if they are in It. But this is unfitting: ergo etc..

4. Likewise, if the Essence is a property, therefore, (it is such) either *per se*, or *per accidens*:* if *per se*, therefore, in whatsoever the Essence is, the paternity (is) also, but this is false: therefore, if it is true (that the Essence is a property), it is true per accidens. Therefore, since among the divine there is no positing of an *accident* nor of a *per accidens*, it is clear that etc..

5. Likewise, if a property is the Divine Essence, since the Divine Essence and/or Substance is the Creator and creates,[2] therefore, the property creates; which is not conceded. Therefore, *there is asked*, "For what reason is it conceded, that the paternity is the Essence, and that it is also to be adored, and yet not, that it is the Creator and/or wise?"

CONCLUSION

Though the Essence and a property have a diverse manner of holding themselves, because the Essence means an absolute, but a property a looking-back to a terminus; nevertheless the Essence is the property, and vice versa.

I RESPOND: Just as Master (Peter) touches upon in (his) text,[3] of some there was the position, and it is first posited [imponitur] by (that man) of Poitiers, that a property is neither the Essence nor in the Essence, but (is) only standing alongside [solum assistens]. — But that position is manifestly blameworthy [improbata],

because it is necessary, that it be the Divine Essence, if it is anything.

On this account, for an understanding of the objections, it must be understood, just as has been noted before,[4] that a relation by reason of (its) comparison to (its) *subject* passes over into the substance, and for that reason a property is the Divine Substance; however, by reason of (its) comparison to (its) *terminus* or object it remains; and as much as regards this it is distinctive[5] and differs from the Essence, not because it means another *essence*, but another *manner of holding themselves*, which through a comparison to the Essence and/or to a Person means a *standard of measure*, adding nothing; however, in comparison to (its) correlative it truly means *a thing*[6] and *a distinction*; and for that reason there is no vanity in the reckoning of (its) understanding nor a composition in the thing, but a true distinction. And since that looking-back does not mean other than *the Essence*, (when it is) compared to It, similarly neither other than *the Person*: for that reason it is truly *the Essence* and *the Person*. — But because that looking-back further is not *of the Essence* to another, but *of a Person* to a Person; for that reason the looking-backs and the relations, properly speaking, are *in the Persons*, not *in the Essence*: because *the Persons* are referred and distinguished according to them, but not in *the Essence*, because[7] It is neither referred nor distinguished. However, they are in the Divine Essence, speaking commonly and improperly, as there is said to be in the Divine Essence everything which is the Divine Essence, and/or everything which is in the Essence and/or in a Person.

1. To that, therefore, which is objected, that by one He is God, by another He is the Father; it must be said, that the ablative means a reckoning of being said and/or of being denominated; whence also the anotherness, signified through the ablative, is attained only as much as regards the manner, not as much as regards the Essence, as is clear.

2. To that which is similarly objected, that the principle of distinguishing and of uniting is not the same; the response is clear, because a property distinguishes in that, which (is) differing not *according to essence*,[8] but *according to a manner*, which manner does not mean a composition, because it passes over into the Substance; nor does it mean only an understanding, because it is a thing and remains in respect of (its) *object*.

3. To that which is objected, that naught is predicated of a substance, except[9] what is in the substance; is must be

---

[1] For *per se true* [per se vera] codices L and O read *quasi self-evident* [quasi per se nota]. A little below this, for *, however,* [autem] the Vatican edition, together with a few manuscripts and edition 1, has *is* [est].

[2] Cf. (St.) Anselm (of Canterbury), MONOLOGION, ch. 13.

[3] Chapter 1. — (The man) *of Poitiers* [Pictaviensis], who is subsequently mentioned, is not that Peter of Poitiers († A.D. 1205), who was Chancellor of the University of Paris and who wrote the « QUINQUE LIBROS SENTENTIARUM », in the first of which, ch. 25, he impugned the opinion, which follows here, but Gilbert of Porretain, the one time Bishop of Poitiers. — A little below this to the words *the Divine Essence* [divina essentia] codex Y prefixes *in* [in].

[4] In the preceding question and in d. 26, q. 2. — A little after this for *the Divine Substance* [divina substantia] codex bb has *the Divine Essence* [divina essentia].

[5] Thus codices G H K R T V X Y ff and others, the Vatican edition has *distinct* [distincta]. A little below this for *which* [qui], codices I and bb have *because* [quia],and then after *a Person* [personam] the Vatican edition interjects *only* [solum].

[6] Understand: anything, or a relative entity, which, while is opposed to nothing, is called "*a thing*" [res].

[7] The Vatican edition, having omitted the words *not in* and *because* [in ... non, quia] reads thus: *but the Essence is neither referred* etc. [essentia autem nec refertur etc.]. Our reading is the common one of the codd. and edd. 1, 2, 3, 4 & 5. A little above this, after *according to them* [secundum eos], codex Y adjoins *only* [tantum]. For *However, they are in the Divine Essence* [Sunt tamen in essentia divina] codd. G H K P Q S T V and others have *but yet in the Divine Essence* [sed tamen in divina essentia]. At the end of the body (of the Question), before *the Essence* [essentia] codex T omits *in* [in].

[8] Codd. aa & bb read more clearly: *because a property does not distinguish in that which they differ in essence* [quia proprietas non distinguit in eo quod differunt in essenita]. Cod. M reads *is differing* [differens est].

[9] As required by the context, we have restored from cod. Z, the *except* [nisi]. Very many codd., such as X Y aa bb & cc, for *except what is* [nisi quod est] exhibit the less well *which is not* [quod non est]. Next, after *it must be said, that* [dicendum, quod] supply: *property* [proprietas]. Then, for *as of a subject* [ut de subiecto] not a few codd. faultily have *and/or of a subject* [vel de subiecto], cod. L *as a substance* [ut substantia].

said, that (a property) is not predicated of the Substance as of a subject, nor through inherence, but it is only predicated of a Person in this manner. Whence it is predicated of the Essence, because the Essence and the property are one [unum] in the Person, not because one is in the other.

4. To that which is objected, whether it is predicated per se, or per accidens; it must be said, that (a property is not predicated) per se, because (it is predicated) through a Person: not per accidens, because a Person is not other than the Essence. Since, therefore, divine things superexceed inferior things, so also (this) predication the predication (that prevails here below).

5. To that which is objected last, that if the Essence creates, a property also (creates); it must be said regarding this, that although a property is the Essence, yet the Essence does not suppose[1] the property, nor vice versa. Whence it does not follow, that that which convenes with the Essence, convenes with a Person, and/or vice versa: yet some do convene with the Essence and a property, some (do) not.

Wherefore it must be noted that *certain* (names) are said of the Divine Essence in Itself, as for example those which are said in opposition to a creature, such as "Immense", "Uncreated", and (Names) of this kind; and these are said of the properties. *Some* are said of the Divine Essence as (It is) in the Persons, such as that It is communicable, and that It is the One in the Three; such befit the Essence, as (that which) has the reckoning of a form,[2] and in this the reckoning of the Essence and of a property differ; and such (expressions) are not said of the properties. Again *some* are said of the Essence, such as that It is the principle of action,[3] such as that It is powerful, wise, willing, such as that It creates; and such are not said of the properties. Whence it must be noted, that essential adjectives, which respect the Essence in Itself as diverse from a creature, are said of the properties; but those which (are said) of It formally, whether (inasmuch) as It is a form, and/or (inasmuch) as It is a principle, are not said. And in this manner all the things sought are clear.

SCHOLIUM

I. In this question there is taught, in what manner the properties hold themselves to the *Essence*. The principle difficulties in the preceding question and above in d. 26, q. 1, are explained. The conclusions themselves are determined further by two corollaries, namely, in what manner the properties are *in* the Persons and *in* the Essence.

II. The sense of the solution to n. 1 is: though the ablative conveys a habitude in the reckoning of a formal cause, which is not according to thing in God, yet it is to be posited according to a reckoning of understanding; and this is sufficient, so that one may say: "He is *God* not by this (that is not by that reckoning or formality), by which He is *the Father*". But Gilbert (of Porretain), distinguishing the paternity really from the Deity, falsely understood those words in this sense: "as much as regards that which is *the Father*, it is not *God*" (cf. here Doubt 4). — On predication through *inherence*, in the solution to n. 3, cf. the following question, and below in d. 34, q. 2. — The solution to n. 4 is constructed from this principle, that, since divine things infinitely exceed the created intellect, the rules of logic also sometimes are deficient, such as this rule, that every predication is either *per se*, and/or *per accidens*. For each is denied in regard to (this) proposition: "the Essence is the property". In regard to predication

per se, it seems that this must be understood of such a predication in the strict sense, since St. Thomas (SUMMA., I, q. 39, a. 6, in reply to n. 2) admits this predication in a similar case. — Worthy of special attention is that which is had in the solution to n. 5. — There are two questions pertaining to this, which are not explicitly treated by St. Bonaventure, which among the Scholastics, especially the Thomists and the Scotists, used to be disputed, namely, whether a relation is included in the reckoning of the Essence, and vice versa, which (Bl. John Duns) Scotus denies together with many other (authors). The other is whether the relations, taken precisely, mean a perfection, which again (Bl.) Scotus denies. The interpreters of St. Bonaventure want to draw him to both sides. It seems more probable to us, that at least in the second question he favors rather (Bl.) Scotus, as Bartolomeo de' Barbieri, tome I, disputation 13, q. 3, would have it.

III. Alexander of Hales, SUMMA., p. I, q. 68, m. 5, a. 2. — (Bl. John duns) Scotus, here in the q. sole; REPORTATIO., here in q. 1. — St. Thomas, here in q. 1, a. 1; SUMMA., I, q. 39, a. 1 and 2. — Bl. (now St.) Albertus (Magnus), here in a. 3, 5, and 6; SUMMA., p. I, tr. 9, q. 39, m. 2, a. 2. — (Bl.) Peter of Tarentaise, here in q. 3, a. 1 and 2. — Richard of Middleton, here in a. 2, qq. 1 and 2. — Giles the Roman, here in 1st. princ., qq. 2 and 3. — Henry of Ghent, SUMMA., a. 55, q. 5.

QUESTION III

Whether a notion is predicated of a notion?

Third, there is asked concerning the comparison of one notion to another. And there is asked, whether one notion or property of one Person is predicated of another (notion of the same Person).[4] And that it is, seems:

1. By an expository syllogism. For of necessity it follows, as is said in the PRIOR (ANALYTICS),[5] 'this A is B; this A is C with the same demonstrated: therefore, C is B'; and this syllogism of his is founded upon that *principle* (which is)

---

[1] Or "include in its own formal signification". For as Alexander of Hales says a the end of SUMMA, I, q. 56, m. 5: « The former is said to be supposed, with the other supposed, because it is in its intention directly [in rectitudinem], such as with a man supposed, there is supposed an animal, and with Peter supposed there is supposed a man: but the Essence is not directly [secundum rectitudinem] in the reckoning of a Person, but obliquely. Similarly, with a notion supposed a Person is not supposed. And/or if the intention of a "supposed" is constrained, the former is said to be supposed with the other supposed, when what is attributed to the one is attributed to the other; for that reason the ancients said, that though a Person was the Essence, because, nevertheless, a Person generates, the Essence (does) not, with a Person supposed, the Essence is not supposed; therefore, there does not follow: "a Person begets; the Essence (does) not; therefore, the Person is not the Essence"; but because (there is) another reckoning of understanding in this name ("Person") and in this name "the Essence".

[2] Which is the Deity Itself. — From codices X and T (by a second hand) we have restored *has* [habet] for the *have* [habent], which is reading the Vatican edition, since the context demands the singular form.

[3] For *of action* [actionis] the Vatican edition, with cod. cc, has *of operations* [operationum]. Next, at the end, for *of the properties* [de proprietatibus] cod. Y has *of the personal properties, nor properly of the Essence, but of the Persons: because actions belong to supposits, properly speaking* [personalibus, nec proprie de essentia, sed de personis: quia actiones sunt suppositorum propropie loquendo]; but cod. G, in the margin, has *of the properties, because a property does not act, but it does suppose* [quia proprietas non agit, sed supponit].

[4] Understand: *notion of the same Person* [notione eiusdem personae], v. g. the paternity of the innascibility.

[5] Aristotle, PRIOR ANALYTICS, Bk. I, ch. 6, proves the useful means of the third form of the syllogism, in a twofold manner: through deduction to the impossible, and through an *exposition* (ἔκθεσις). A proof through *exposition* is that, in which, as Bl. (now St.) Albertus (Magnus) says in (his) COMMENTARY on this passage (tract 2, ch. 11),

self-evident [per se notum]: "whatsoever to one and the same are the same, are the same among themselves". Therefore, let there be such a syllogism: 'the Father is paternity; the Father is innascibility: therefore, paternity is innascibility'. *If you say*, that (a fallacy of) *accident*[1] sins against that consequence and against that principle, as is clear here: 'Peter is an individual; Peter is a man: therefore, man is an individual'; *against this there is objected*, that where there is (a fallacy of) *accident*, there is an accidental predication; but when there is said: "the Father is paternity", "the Father is innascibility", there is no accidental predication, because (each) is (said) in abstraction: therefore, there is no (fallacy of) the accident there. — Likewise, there rightly follows in a concretive manner: "the Father generates; the Father is innascible: therefore, the innascible One generates"; and yet the predication is thus[2] more conveyed through the manner of an accident: therefore, it follows much more strongly in the abstract: therefore, this is true: "paternity is innascibility".

2. Likewise, this is shown *a minori*° in this manner: there is a greater union[3] of properties in one Person or in an incommunicable Supposit than of the properties in the common Nature; but so great is the union of properties in the one common Nature, that one is the other, just as Goodness is Wisdom: therefore, much more strongly in a Person is one property predicated of the other.

3. Likewise, there is a greater union of properties in one Person than of a property and of the Essence in a Person — because there is an equal union as much as regards the thing, and as much as regards manner a property convenes more with a property, than a property with the Nature or the Essence — but so great is the union of the Essence and of a property in a Person, that the one is predicated of the other, just as "the paternity is[4] the Deity": ergo etc..

4. Likewise, there is a greater union of properties[5] in one Person than of the two natures in the same Person; but on account of the convening of natures in the one Person of Christ there is a communication of idioms, because God is a man, and a man God: therefore, for an equal reason, on account of the convening of properties in one Hypostasis, one is predicated of the other.

ON THE CONTRARY: 1. Just as a Person holds Himself to a Person, so a notion to a notion; but one Person is not predicated of another Person: therefore, neither one notion of another notion.

2. Likewise, what is predicated of anything in abstraction does not add to it according to number [non facit numerum cum illo];[6] therefore, if a notion is predicated of a notion, there are not more notions, but one.

3. Likewise, if a notion is predicated of a notion, therefore, spiration is generation, and to spirate is to generate: therefore, since this is true: "the Father spirates the Holy Spirit", this, similarly, will be true: "the Father generates the Holy Spirit".

CONCLUSION

The two notions of one Person can be predicated of one another in the concrete, but not in the abstract.

I RESPOND: It must be said, that there is predication through *identity* and predication through *inherence*. Predication through *inherence* is in concretion [in concretione], and this is[7] by reason of a supposit, such as "the white one is the musical one". However, predication through *identity* is in abstraction [in abstractione] and by reason of a form, not of the supposit, such as "justice is goodness".ª

I say, therefore, that a notion can be compared to a notion in a twofold manner: either in *concretion*, and/or *in abstraction*. If in *concretion*, thus one is predicated of the other, such as "the One generating is the One spirating", and "the Father is innascible", and this, because they convene in a Supposit. However, if in *abstraction*, because then a notion conveys purely a looking-back itself, and in one and the same Person there are diverse looking-backs without composition in Himself [sui], and this according to diverse comparisons; thus one is not predicated of another.

1. To that, therefore, which is objected concerning the syllogism, it must be said, that against that syllogism (a fallacy of) *accident* does sin, just as is clear in the example posited before; whence the form of the syllogism has no value. Similarly, that *principle*[8] must be understood *according to (what is) the same*. For it does not follow, that if any two are similar to one, that they are similar amongst themselves, unless they are similar according to the same. Similarly, it is necessary [oportet] also among relations for this, that there be an identity of the one to the other, that they not only be in the same[9] and according to the same, but also regarding the same.

---

something sensible is taken up, of which each extremity is predicated universally and/or particularly; or, as (Bl. John Duns) Scotus says, (in his Commentary on the) PRIOR ANALYTICS, Bk. I, q. 11: « An *expository* syllogism is that, the middle of which is a discrete (singular) term ». It is called *"expository"*, because the matter, which it concludes, it expounds or manifests to the senses themselves. On the principle, upon which this syllogism is supported, see above d. 32, p. II, a. 2, q. 1, p. 546, footnote 2.

[1] That is, a fallacy of accident.*

[2] Codices L and T have *here* [hic], many codices faultily have instead *just as* [sicut]. Next for *it follows* [sequitur] codices I aa and bb have *it would follow* [sequeretur].

[3] Codex W has *unity* [unitas].

[4] Some codices, such as H V and Y, together with edition 1, have *and* [et] for *is* [est].

[5] The Vatican edition, with very many codices and edition 1, has *of property* [proprietas], less rightly. To the word *union* [unio] codices B E I X aa and bb prefix the words *unity and/or* [unitas vel]. Next, after *the convening of* [convenientiam] in codex bb there is repeated *two* [duarum].

[6] Because through abstraction the reason for the composition (v. g. the subject, in which the many, diverse among themselves, can be united) is removed.

[7] Many codices here read *in the reckoning* [in ratione] for *by reason* [ratione], but less congruously.

[8] Understand: the principle of identity, cited in the objection.

[9] The Vatican edition, with cod. cc, reads *that they are not only the same and are the same according to* [non tantum eadem sint et sint secundum etc.], though the older codices, with edition 1, exhibit our reading, yet with this difference, that not a few of them, such as A C F H K L R S T U and V, for *the same (subject)* [in eodem] substitute *in the same (Person)* [in eadem]. — Cf. (Bl. John Duns) Scotus, PRIOR ANALYTICS, Bk. I, q. 11, where the question: "Whether an expository syllogism holds in sake of a form", is resolved in this manner: that an expository syllogism holds in sake of a form in all terms, yet while the premises are duly regulated, through *being said of all* and/or *of none*, so that the discrete term is distributed by means of those sayings (i. e. so that the discrete or singular term is accepted *according to the same* in the premises).

---

* *Trans. note*: On a fallacy of the accident, cf. Aristotle, ELENCHAE, Bk. I, ch. 4 (ch. 5), and Peter of Spain, SUMMULA, tr. *"On Fallacies"*, cited in SENT., Bk. III, d. 7, a. 2, q. 2, p. 179, footnote 1.

° Cf. the translator's footnote, above on p. 413.

ª For an explanation of the terms *in concretion* and *in abstraction*, see the Rationale for the Translation of Peculiar Latin Terms, in the Introduction to this English Translation, pp. E-15 and E-13, respectively.

Since, therefore, the diverse relations in the same Person are not regarding the same (thing) or the same (One), for that reason it does not follow, that if they convene in a Supposit, that on this account they convene among themselves. And in this manner it is clear, that neither the *syllogism* nor the *principle* are fitting.

To that which is objected, that there is no (fallacy of) accident there; it must be said, that *a fallacy of accident* is not only attained as much as regards an accidental predication, but is also attained as much as regards the variation of the principle,[1] so that it convenes in only one acceptation, in the other it is extraneous; thus it is in the proposed. For the Father according to one comparison is innascible, according to another is the paternity;[2] so that the paternity is no manner means a comparison to the prior, neither positively, nor privatively, as much as concerns its own reckoning: and for that reason it is clear that etc..

2. 3. To that which is objected through the similitude of the union of two (thing) in a third, it must be said that predication through identity can be in a threefold manner: either so that *the Essence* is compared to *the Essence*, or *the Essence* to a *property*, or a *property* to a *property*. When, therefore, there is a predication through identity through the comparison of *the Essence* to *the Essence*, there is noted an essential identity, as when there is said, "greatness is goodness". When, again, through a comparison of *the Essence* to a *property*, there is noted, similarly, an essential identity. However, when there is a comparison of a *property* to a *property*, because a property does not convey but a reckoning and a relation or looking-back; there is then noted an identity of reckoning. And hence it is, that one essential property is predicated of the other, and a property of the Essence, because there is a uniform manner of predication among these regarding one another and regarding that in which they convene, because (they convene) through an identity of essence. But it is not thus, when a property is predicated of a property. Nor when a property is predicated of a property, there is noted a convening in substance and essence and supposit.[3] But when it is predicated of another property, there is noted a convening in reckoning and in a looking-back. And for that reason it is not similar, nay there is (this fallacy of) *accident* there: 'they convene in substance, therefore, (they convene) in a looking-back'.

4. To the last (objection) concerning the convening of natures in one Person, the response is clear, because there is no communication of idioms in abstraction, but (there is) in concrete, because *deity* is not humanity, but *God* is a man; similarly is it in the proposed. For that reason all (the objections)[4] are clear.

SCHOLIUM

I. The question concerns notions in the same Person, v. g. the paternity and active spiration in the Father. For when divine attributes, virtually distinct among themselves, are predicated of one another, and a property of the Essence, it seems, that the properties of the same Person can be predicated of themselves (which reckoning is solved in the reply to nn. 2 and 3). But the negative response (to this question) is common (in theology). But the School of St. Thomas does not admit here but a virtual distinction; (Bl. John Duns) Scotus employs his own formal distinction, St. Bonaventure the distinction of attribution, concerning which we have spoken above in d. 26, q. 1.

II. On the diverse species of predication, see above d. 30, q. 1, in the Scholium. — On the difference between predication through *identity* and the other (predication) through *inherence* or denomination, which is called by (Bl.) Scotus *formal (predication)*, see more (above) in d. 5, a. 1, q. 1, in reply to n. 2, and in d. 34, q. 2, and in SENT., Bk. III, d. 8, a. 1, q. 3, in the body (of the question). A predication through identity is made between abstract terms, or at least with one abstracted, not by reason of (its) *supposit*, but (by reason of its) *form*, as "wisdom is goodness", "the Essence is the Father". This does not exist [valet] properly among created things (d. 5, a.1, q. 1, in reply to n. 2), but is truly employed among the divine (d. 34, q. 2), whether (the two signified) are the same according to substance, but diverse according to the reckoning of understanding (such as "Goodness is Wisdom"), or are the same according to substance, diverse according to a manner of holding themselves and/or of not holding themselves, such as a Person and the Substance (ibid. in reply to n. 5). Yet a predication through identity observes less the propriety of predication than the other one (SENT., Bk. III, d. 5, Doubt 1).

A denominative predication is made in the concrete [in forma concreta] and by reason of the supposit. As is said (by St. Bonaventure) in SENT., Bk. III, d. 6, a. 1, q. 3, in reply to n. 4, this « can be in four manners: through a manner of *inherence* or through a manner of accident, as when there is said: "this one is white"; through a manner of *transmutation*, as when there is said: "Peter has become pale"; through a manner of *possession*, as when there is said: "the donkey of Socrates"; through a manner of *union*, as when there is said, "the fiery iron", that is, "(iron that) has been united to fire", and "an animated body", that is "(a body) united to a soul" ». — The word "*denominative*" [denominativum] has been taken from Aristotle, ON THE PREDICAMENTS, ch. 1, who distinguishes: homonyms (ὁμώνυμα), synonyms (συνώνυμα), and denominatives (παρώνυμα).

III. The (other) authors agree in the conclusion: Alexander of Hales, on this and the following q., SUMMA., p. I, q. 68, m. 5, a. 4, 5 and 6, § 6. — (Bl. John Duns) Scotus, REPORTATIO., here in q. 3, in reply to n. 3. — St. Thomas, SENT., Bk. I, d. 27, q. 1, a. 1, in reply to n. 3;: SUMMA., I, q. 32, a. 3, in reply to n. 3. — Bl. (now St.) Albertus (Magnus), here in a. 4 and 7. — (Bl.) Peter of Tarentaise, on this and the following question, here in q. 4, a. 1 and 2. — Richard of Middleton, on this and the following q., here in a. 3, qq. 1 and 2. — Henry of Ghent, SUMMA., a. 75, q. 2. — (Bl.) Dionysius the Carthusian, d. 26, q. 1. (the q. is briefly touched upon).

---

[1] The Vatican edition faultily reads *of the predicate* [praedicati], contrary to the codices and the other six editions. — The subject *the Father*, accepted according to a comparison of *the paternity* and/or *innascibility* does not mean formally the same. This is hinted at by codex W, which to the word *principle* [principii] adjoins *and/or of a comparison or of the looking-back* [vel sive comparationis sive respectus]; the same codex a little below this, after *acceptation* [acceptione], which word is omitted by very many manuscripts, adds *and/or comparison* [vel comparatione], at the same time changing, together with codex P and W, the word *only* [sola] into *its own* [sua].

[2] Codex L and O proceed thus: *the innascibility deprives the comparison to the prior, but the paternity in no manner* etc. [innascibilitas privat comparationem ad prius, paternitas vero nullo modo].

[3] Many codices, together with editions 2 and 3, have *in supposit* [in supposito] for *and supposit* [et supposito], others, such as C L O R U and bb, have *and in supposit* [et in supposito]. A little above this, after *there is noted* [notatur], codex V inserts *an identity and/or* [identitas vel].

[4] For *all (the objections)* [omnia] some codices have *the objections* [obiecta]; codices B and X have *all the objections* [omnia obiecta].

QUESTION IV

Whether the same property can be predicated denominatively of its very self?

Fourth, there is asked concerning the comparison of the same property to itself. There is asked, therefore, whether the same property or notion is predicated of itself denominatively.[1] And that it is, seems:

1. Through a *simile*, because *essential* adjectives denominate abstract (Names), as "Greatness is great", and "Goodness (is) good": therefore, for an equal reason, "the generation generates", and "the spiration spirates".

2. Likewise, because there is a standing still in *first* (forms),[2] for that reason they are denominated by themselves — whence "the Unity by Itself is one" — therefore, since the personal properties do not have prior (properties), nay they themselves are first, then they denominate themselves.

3. Likewise, an indefinite affirmative (predication) is equipollent to a particular one,[3] therefore, they are simply convertible; but this is conceded: "the One generating is the paternity or the generation": therefore, "the generation is the One generating".

4. Likewise, if this is not conceded: "the paternity is[4] the One generating", either this is on account of a repugnance on the part of the *thing*, or on part of *the manner*: not on part of the *thing*, because it is the same thing; not on the part of *the manner*, because the same property and relation is conveyed: therefore, in no manner is there a repugnance there: therefore, the expression is simply true.

ON THE CONTRARY: 1. Just as it is proper for a property to distinguish, so it is proper for a Person to produce Another; but this is false: "a Person distinguishes", because He does not distinguish, but is distinguished: therefore, this also is false: "a property generates".

2. Likewise, « everything which is referred, is something, except that, which is said relatively »;[5] but a property is naught but a relation: therefore, a property is not referred. But 'to generate' is 'to be referred': therefore, a property does not generate.

3. Likewise, a property conveys an origin and a relation: therefore, if it is reflected upon itself and denominates itself, then, therefore, there will be an origin of an origin and a relation of a relation; which the Philosopher[6] and all reason holds as (something) unfitting.

4. Likewise, when there is said: "the generation generates", either the verb is constructed by reason of *the supposit*, or by reason of *the form*: not (by reason) of *the form*, because a looking-back does not act;[7] nor by reason of *the supposit*, because with the notion supposed the Person is not supposed — for something convenes with the Person, which (does) not (convene) with the notion, as has been shown above[8] — therefore, the expression is simply false.

CONCLUSION

No property can denominate itself.

I RESPOND: It must be said, that the aforesaid expression are false; for no notion denominates itself.

And the reason for this is, because the denomination of a notion conveys an *emanation* as an act, it also conveys a *relation*.[9] And since *production* is properly of a supposit, not of a form, similarly the *relation* is of something as of a supposit; for that reason every such denomination concerns a supposit. Not so is it concerning the essential properties — and/or (inasmuch) as it concerns the first (intentions),[10] such as 'one' and 'true' — nay they look back to form; for that reason they denominate themselves. Wherefore, because it is not present among adjective notions of this kind, they cannot be true expressions by reason of a *form*. However, by reason of a *supposit* they cannot be true, because a notion does not suppose a Person, because there are many notions in the same Person. However, the Essence does suppose the Substance, because the one Essence is also the one Substance; and for that reason this is true: "the Deity creates", because the Deity supposes God; but this is false: "the paternity generates", because it does not suppose the Father.

1. 2. What is objected concerning *essential conditions*, and concerning *first (forms)*, it is clear, that it is not similar for the reason[11] already said. — However, another reason can, nevertheless, be assigned, because the looking-back of a reflection upon an absolute rests in that, such that the absolute gives a fundament to the looking-back, and the looking-back gives a complement. But, when a looking-back is reflected upon itself, because each

---

[1] Or in other words: « Whether personal acts are predicated of the properties through a denominative manner, so that there can be said: "the generation generates", "the spiration spirates" ».

[2] Understand: *forms*, and/or *intentions or conditions* [formis, vel intentionibus sive conditionibus]. Cf. above d. 3, p. I, Doubt 3, p. 78, footnote 13.

[3] Thus, this indefinite affirmative proposition: "a man is just", is equivalent to this other: "some man is just". For the first proposition: "a man is just", is equivalent to its own converse proposition: "something just is a man", which proposition as particular is simply convertible [simpliciter convertitur] into this one: "some man is just". From which it follows, that this proposition: "a man is just", can also simply be converted into this one: "a just one is a man".

[4] Not a few codices, together with editions 1, 2, and 3, read *is not* [non est], but faultily, as follows from the preceding argument.

[5] (St.) Augustine, ON THE TRINITY, Bk. VIII, ch. 1, n. 2. — Next many codices, together with editions 2, 3, 4, 5, and 6, read *is not a relation* [non est relatio] for *is naught but a relation* [non est nisi relatio]; but

codices T Z and ee, together with edition 1 read *but a property is a relation* [sed proprietas est relatio].

[6] Concerning which, see above d. 26, a. sole, q. 1, p. 453, footnote 8. — A little above this, the words *if it is reflected upon itself* [si supra se relectitur] signify the same as *if it is predicated of itself* [si de se predicatur].

[7] For actions are of supposits. — A little before this, for *not (by reason) of the form* [non formae], codices V and X read *not by reason of the form* [non ratione formae]. — On the following proposition, see here q. 2, p. 576, footnote 1.

[8] Here in qq. 1 and 2. — A little before this, to the words *which ... not* [quod non] codex bb adjoins *does ... convene* [convenit].

[9] Codex Y adds *as a manner* [ut modum].

[10] Understand: *intentions* [intentionibus].

[11] Many codices incongruously read *that is it not similar concerning the already said reason* [quod non est simile de ratione iam dicta], codex bb has more truly *that it is not similar from the already said reason* [quod non est simile ex ratione iam dicta].

means a comparison to the other, one cannot give a fundament, nor the other a compliment; and for that reason it cannot be reflected. But in *simple first* (forms), of the kind of which is truth, because they either do not convey a relation, or if they do convey (one), they convey a relation, which looks back commonly[1] to the Substance and to Its properties, as for example 'to be from God' [ut puta esse a Deo], for that reason they are reflected upon themselves; not so (is it) in the proposed, because production looks back to a Person.

3. To that which is objected, that this is true: "the One generating is the paternity"; it must be said, that "the One generating" is held be the subject [subiicitur][2] by reason of the *Hypostasis*, and thus there is noted a predication through identity; but when it is the predicate [praedicatur], it is accepted by reason of a *form*, for that reason the manner of accepting is changed: for that reason it does not follow (that the One generating is the paternity). If, however, it would be understood to be the predicate by reason of *a supposit*, it would be true; for then the sense would be:[3] "the paternity is the One who generates"; but then "the generation generates" does not follow, nay there is (a fallacy of) *accident* there.

4. To that which is objected, that there is no repugnance there;[4] it must be said, that there is repugnance there on the part of the manner of understanding. For a notion does not denominate but a supposit, whence such a manner does not befit a notion. Whence just as this is false: "whiteness is white", so must it be understood in the proposed.

SCHOLIUM

I. It is established, that the same notion can be predicated *of itself* through *identity*, that is in the abstract, whence there can be said: "paternity is active generation". There is only asked (here), whether this can be done *in the concrete* or *denominatively*, v. g. by saying: "the generation is the one Generating or generates". The same question is propounded by Richard of Middleton and others in these words: « Whether personal adjectives are predicated of properties ». The principle reasons for the false opinion are the 1st and 2nd opposed arguments, which conclude from a parity, that namely essential adjectives denominate abstract ones; and also that first intentions, that is, the transcendentals (of being), such as one, true, good, are denominatively predicated of themselves. It is proven in the body (of the question) and in reply to nn. 1 and 2, that this parity does not subsist. Richard of Middleton (here in a. 3, q. 2) approves and further explains the sentence of the Seraphic (Doctor) in these words: « Although "*to generate*" and "*generation*" signify the same thing, yet, (they do so) in a diverse manner: because "*to generate*" signifies an act and through the manner of an act, but "*generation*" not so, but through the manner of a certain form. And, because acts are of supposits, though through forms, but not properly of the forms themselves as of agents, but as of principles, through which the supposits act: for that reason, though this is to be conceded: "the Father generates", yet, this is not to be conceded: "the paternity generates" ». — That the *first* intentions (the transcendentals of being) are reflected upon themselves, that is, are predicated of themselves, has already been said above in d. 3, p. I, Doubt 3, and in d. 17, p. I, q. 2, in reply to n. 4.

II. St. Thomas, here in q. 1, a. 4; Summa., I, q. 40, a. 1, in reply to n. 3. — Bl. (now St.) Albertus (Magnus), here in a. 8. — Giles the Roman, here in 2nd. princip., q. 1. — (Bl.) Dionysius the Carthusian, here in q. 2.

DOUBTS ON THE TEXT OF THE MASTER

Doubt I

In this part, there are doubts about the text (of Master Peter) and first concerning the response of Master (Peter), which he posts there (where he says): *To their new and human doctrines* etc.. For he seems to respond insufficiently, because he does not solve (their) argument, but says, that it is incomprehensible; and it seems, that this evasion of his is no (response). For either the argument concludes *necessarily*, or *as a sophism* [sophistice]: if *necessarily*, then, therefore, since it proceeds from true (propositions), the conclusion is true; if *not necessarily*, then, therefore, it is a sophism; but one sophism is not incomprehensible: and thus[5] it seems, that he applies badly the quote from (St.) Hilary.

I Respond: It must be said, that it is easy to respond to the argument, because there is a sophism there according to (a fallacy of) *accident*: 'a property is the Essence; and the Essence is not distinguished:[6] therefore, neither a property (is distinguished)'. But Master (Peter) does not say that *this* (argument) is incomprehensible, but dismisses it as a sophism and unworthy of discussion by scholars [maiorum]. But that *seeking after truth*, which follows, is incomprehensible according to the state of a wayfarer [viae]: since, if the Essence is predicated of a property through an omnimodal identity, and <u>vice versa</u>, the latter is distinguished and the Former (is) not; and this is incomprehensible to us. For because *we see through a mirror*,[7] we understand through a similitude taken from creatures; and this (about which we speak) has no similar under Heaven, nay it is proper to God alone on account of (His) most high Simplicity: for that reason Master (Peter) says that it is incomprehensible. — Nor is it similar concerning a *genus* and (its) *difference*: because the genus is predicated of the difference, and the latter distinguishes, and the former

---

[1] For *commonly* [communiter], codex R has *similarly* [similiter].

[2] Or: "is the subject in this proposition". Similarly, <u>praedicatur</u>, which follows next, has the meaning of: *is the predicate*, i.e. as in this proposition: "the paternity is the One generating". — Very many codices and also editions 2, 3, 4 and 6 faultily read "*the Father*" [Pater] for *it* in this proposition, edition one has "*the paternity*" [paternitas] instead.

[3] Very many codices, such as G S T W ee ff, together with edition 1, having changed the punctuation, read thus: *it would then be true, and the sense would be* [vera esset tunc, et esset sensus].

[4] Codices A P Q and T, together with edition 1, have *what repugnance is there* [quae repugnantia sit ibi]; not a few other codices, together with editions 2 and 3, have *that there is repugnance there* [quod repug-

nantia sit ibi]. — On the last proposition of the solution, see above d. 17, p. I, q. 2, objection 4.

[5] In many codices there is lacking *thus* [ita], in place of which codex X and edition 1 have *for that reason* [ideo].

[6] The Vatican edition here and below this has *distinguishes* [distinguit] for *is distinguished* [distinguitur].

[7] 1 Corinthians 13:12. — A little above this, codices L and O read after *vice versa* [e converso] thus *why is the latter distinguished and the Former not* [cur haec distinguitur, et illa non]. A little further below this, the Vatican edition omits *it is* [est], in the phrase *it is proper to God alone* [solius Dei est proprium], which verb is congruous added in very many codices, such as I T aa etc., and in edition 1.

does not, because it is not predicated through identity. For that reason (Master Peter)[1] with (St.) Hilary says, that it is incomprehensible, and he describes incomprehensibility as much as regards a threefold power [vim]: as much as regards *the receptive (power)*, when he says "*incomprehensible*: etc."; as much as regards *the expressive (power)*, when he says, "*outside the signification of speech*"; as much as regards *the (power) of judgement* [iudicativum],[2] when he says "*outside the intention of sense*". And the other (words), which follow, befit [aptantur] these three, as is clear to the one looking into (the matter).

DOUBT II

Likewise, is asked concerning the response of Master (Peter), which he makes there (where he says): *Whose audacity resisting* etc.. For he says, that the properties are in the Hypostases and determine Them; (that) they are in the Essence, but do not determine It. For there seems to be an opposition (here), because every property is determinative of that in which it is, otherwise it is not in it: therefore, if the properties do not determine the Essence, they are not in the Essence.

I RESPOND: It must be said, that Master (Peter) responds well, because this preposition "*in*" notes diverse habitudes. For in one manner the Father is said (to be) in the Son, in another manner the paternity in the Father. For the Father is said to be in the Son not as distinctive properties (are), but as a consubstantial Person; the paternity (is said to be) in the Father, as distinctive properties (are). In this manner Master (Peter) wants to say, that the properties are or are said to be in *the Essence* in a manner other than in *a Person*. For they are said to be in *the Essence* on account of identity, so that "*in*" means entirely an identity; they are said to be in *the Persons*, just as true properties in hypostases and (as) determinations in (those) determined. However, among *creatures* there is not one manner without the other, because a property is not entirely the same with that of which it is a property: and for that reason among creatures a property is not said to be in something, except in that in which it inheres; not so (is it) among the divine.[3]

DOUBT III

Likewise is asked concerning the other response of Master (Peter), which he makes there (where he says): *I respond to you here too with (St.) Hilary* etc. For what he says, that the Archangels do not know the solution to this question, seems false. For since they are comprehensors (of the Divine Vision), it is established that they cognize all, which concern the substance of the Glory: therefore, they cognize the distinction of Persons and the Unity and Measure of the Essence: therefore, they see, for what reason the properties determine the Hypostases, not the Essence. And *again*, if there will be[4] a comprehension concerning which there is now faith;

and (which) we no hold by faith: therefore, we shall cognize (this) in the Fatherland.

I RESPOND: It must be said, that, just as (St.) Augustine says ON THE TRINITY:[5] « Just as a pit is said to be "blind", not because it cannot see, but because what it has it does not show to others »; so the Angels and Saints are said not to know on account of this, that they do not reveal such (things), but rather (those which are) intelligible; and because such (things) do not have (anything) similar in a creature, nay rather a dissimilar: for that reason they are said to be incomprehensible to us. And (St.) Hilary removes the threefold cognition, which we have of divine things: one is through the revelation *of the Angels*, the other through the enlightenment *of the Prophets*, the third through the preaching *of the Apostles*. And he says, that the Angels *do not hear*, because they themselves receive revelation from greater (Angels) and do not express it to us.[6] — Therefore, Master (Peter) responds well, by showing (his) insufficiency. For if there is asked, for what reason a property is in *a Person* as (something) distinguishing (Him), not in *the Essence*; there is the response, that *a Person* holds Himself and is referred to Another and is distinguished (regarding Another). And if this is the response, there still remains the question, *for what reason* is a Person referred: and the response is, that the Essence is one, the Persons Three. If you ask (something) entirely *similar* to this kind (of question), you will not find (the answer); and for that reason it is necessary [oportet] to stand still upon the foundation of faith.

DOUBT IV

It must be noted on this solution of Master (Peter), which he posits here: *However, we say that these are to be understood in another manner*, that those expressions, which (St.) Augustine propounds,[7] namely, « the Father is not *the Substance* by that, by which He is *the Father* » and (those) completely similar, are twofold, because the ablative conveys a habitude in the reckoning of a *form* or of a formal cause, though among the divine there occurs no habitude of a cause truly, as much as regards the thing, however, (there does) as much as regards the reckoning of understanding. Therefore, a causality can occur under a negation, so that there is a *negation of causality*; and then the expression is true, and in this sense (St.) Augustine accepts (it), and Master (Peter) propounds (it). For the sense is: "not *by this* is He God, by which (He is) the Father"; because by the paternity He is the Father as by a reckoning of saying and/or of understanding; but the paternity is not in this manner a reckoning of saying and/or of understanding, that He is God; and thus the expression is true and it in no manner supports [nihil facit pro] (Gilbert) of Porretain. It can also be *a causality of negation*; and then it is false, and the sense is: "not by this *is He* God by which (He is) the Father", that is, as much as regards this, that *He is the Father, He is* not *God*; and in this sense (Gilbert) of Porretain accepts (it), and thus (his) understanding is false and in this manner (St.) Augustine does not accept (it).[8]

---

[1] Supply together with codex O: *Master (Peter)* [Magister].

[2] The Vatican edition, with very many codices and editions, reads *the indicative (power)* [indicativum], but faultily, as appears also from Richard (of Middleton), here on the text. On this doubt cf. above q. 2.

[3] You will find more on this above in qq. 1 and 2. Cf. also St. Thomas and Richard (of Middleton), here on the text.

[4] Codex T has *there is* [est].

[5] Book I, ch. 12, n. 23: For indeed expressions of this kind one is said not to know, because (the meaning) is hidden, according to which (kind) a ditch, which is hidden, is said to be blind. — Next to the word *Saints* [Sancti] very many codices, such as I X aa and bb, prefix *other* [alii].

[6] Codex B reads more clearly in this manner: *because though they themselves receive revelation from greater (angels), yet they do not express it to us* [quia licet ipsi recipiant revelationem a maioribus, tamen nobis non exprimunt]. For *because they themselves* [quia ipsi] ed. 1 has *as much as they themselves* [quantum ipsi]. Before *express* [exprimunt] not a few coddices, together with editions, 2, 3, 4, 5 & 6, falsely omit *not* [non].

[7] See there the text of Master (Peter), ch. 2, and (St. Bonaventure's) COMMENTARY, q. 2, 1st. opposed argument.

[8] This doubt is also solved by Bl. (now St.) Albertus (Magnus), here in a. 9; St. Thomas and Richard (of Middleton), here on the text.

DISTINCTION XXXIV

CHAPTER I

On the words of (St.) Hilary, by which he seems, according to the intelligence of the depraved, to say, that the Divine Nature and the Thing of the Nature is not the Same, and that God and what God is, is not the Same.

To the aforesaid it must be added, that certain men of a perverse sense leapt forth into so great an insanity, as to say, that the Nature of God and a Person or Hypostasis is not the Same, saying, that the same Essence cannot be the Father, and the Son without a confusion of Persons. For if, they say, that Essence, which the Father is, is the Son, the Same is Its own Father and Son. If you say that this Thing is the Father, ask what (is) the other, which you say is the Son. If, however, you do not ask (what) the other (is), but say that (it is) the same; (then) the same begot and was begotten. On account of these (those) of this kind divide between the Nature and a Person, so that they do not receive that the one and simple Nature of the Divinity is the Three Persons. And this they strive to defend by the testimony of (St.) Hilary, who in eighth book, ON THE TRINITY, seeking whether the Apostle, naming *"the spirit of God"* and *"the spirit of Christ"*, signified the same with each word, said thus: « The Preacher of the Gentiles, wanting to teach the Unity of the Nature in the Father and the Son, says: *The spirit of God is in you. If, however, anyone does not have the spirit of Christ, he does not belong to Him. But if the spirit of Him, who raised up Jesus* etc.. We are all spiritual, if there is in us the spirit of God, but this is both the spirit of God and the spirit of Christ. And when the spirit of Christ is in us, the spirit of Him, who raised up [suscitavit] Christ, is in us. And when the spirit of Him who raised up Christ is in us, the spirit of Christ is also in us; nor, however, is it not the spirit of God, who is in us. Discern, therefore, o heretic, the spirit of Christ from the spirit of God, and the spirit of Christ roused [excitari] from the dead from the spirit of God rousing Christ from the dead; which spirit of Christ, when it dwells in us, is the spirit of God, and the spirit of Christ roused from the dead is only the spirit of God rousing Christ from the dead. And I ask now, whether *in the spirit of God* you estimate (to be) signified a *nature*, or *a thing of nature*. For a *nature* [natura] is not the same as *a thing of nature* [res naturae], just as a man also is not the same as what is of a man; nor a fire also the same as that which is of the fire itself: and according to this *God is also not the same as what is of God* ». — By the occasion of such a saying the aforesaid heretics taught the dogma [dogmatizaverunt], that a Person and the Nature of God is not the Same, asserting, that the Nature of God is not the Three Persons, understanding in these aforementioned words of (St.) Hilary

through *"the thing of the nature"* a Person, and by the name of *"nature"* the Divine Nature. And for that reason they say, that (St.) Hilary asked the heretic, whether through *"the spirit of God"* he thought there was signified *the Nature*, or *the Thing of the Nature*, so as to show, that one must distinguish between *the Nature* and *a Thing of the Nature*, that is a Person.

This, indeed, they say, not understanding by pious diligence the circumstance of the Scripture, with which considered, one can thoroughly see, *in what manner* (St.) Hilary said the aforementioned (words). For subsequently, in the same series,[2] he shows, that in *"the spirit of God"* there is sometimes signified the Father, as when there is said:[3] *The spirit of the Lord is upon me"*; there is sometimes signified the Son, as when there is said: *In the spirit of God I cast out demons*, demonstrating that He casts out demons by the power of His own Nature; sometimes the Holy Spirit, as there (where it is written): *I shall pour forth of My spirit upon all flesh*. Which He says had been consummated, when the Apostles, with the Holy Spirit sent, spoke in all tongues. Then he shows openly, *for what reason* he made this distinction, and that in the words above of the Apostle the same Spirit was signified, and that He Himself is a Thing of the one Nature of the Father and the Son, saying thus:[4] « These have been demonstrated for this purpose [idcirco], that by whatsoever heretical part of falsehood one is born off, one might be enclosed by the borders of truth. For in us dwells Christ, with whom dwelling there dwells God, and when there dwells in us the spirit of Christ, there yet dwells no other[5] than the spirit of God. Wherefore if through the Holy Spirit Christ is understood to be in us, yet this spirit of God is to be known as *"the spirit of Christ"*. And since through the Nature of God the Nature itself dwells in us, the nature of the Son is believed to be undiffering from the Father, since the Holy Spirit, who is the spirit of Christ, and the Spirit of God is demonstrated (to be) a Thing of the One Nature. I now, therefore, ask, in what manner They are not out of nature one [unum]. From the Father proceeds the Spirit of Truth, from the Son He is sent and from the Son He accepts. But all which the Father has, are the Son's; and for that reason He who accepts from Him, is the spirit of God, and the same is the spirit of Christ. He is a Thing of the Nature of the Son, but also the same Thing and of the Nature of the Father, and He is the spirit of God rousing Christ from the dead, and He is the same spirit of Christ roused from the dead. In something the nature of Christ and of God differ, so as not to be the same, if it can be presented, that the spirit, which is of God, is not of Christ ». « There is, therefore, in us the spirit of God, and there is in us the spirit of Christ; and when the spirit of Christ is in (us), the spirit of God is in (us). Thus, when that which is of God, is also of Christ, and that which is of Christ is of God; Christ cannot be another diverse something, than God is. Therefore, the God Christ is one spirit with God », « according

---

[1] Numbers 21 and 22. — The passage from Sacred Scripture is Rom. 8:9-11.*

[2] Ibid., n. 25. — A little before this codex C has rightly *not understanding* [non intendentes] for *not understanding* [non intelligentes].

[3] Isaiah 61:1; the second passage is Mt. 12:28; the third Joel 2:28; then there is an allusion to Acts 2:17. — Next for *in the words above* [in superioribus verbis] the Vatican edition and other editions, breaking with the codices and edition 1, have *in the above through the words* [in superioribus per verba].

[4] Ibid., n. 26. In this text there is a reference to Eph. 3:17: *that Christ dwell through faith in your hearts* [Christum habitare per fidem in cordibus vestris]; and 1 Cor. 3:16: *And the Spirit of God dwells in you* [Et Spiritus Dei habitat in vobus].

[5] The Vatican edition, together with very many editions, has *nothing other* [non aliud] for *no other (Person)* [non alius], with the original, the codices, and editions 1 and 4 contradicting it. (St.) Hilary has *through the nature of the Thing* [per naturam rei] for *through the Nature of God* [per naturam Dei].

---

* *Trans. note*: In this and the subsequent paragraph, capitalization in *"the spirit of God"* [spiritum Dei] and *"the spirit of Christ"* [spiritum Christi] follows the habit of capitalization of the Latin, rather than that employed in this English translation, so as to not forejudge the discussion of Master Peter, who through this ambiguity leads the reader to understand that both are said properly of the Holy Spirit.

to that (verse): *I and the Father are one* [unum]. In which the Truth teaches, that there is a unity of nature, not a solitude of union ».[1] — Behold, if you diligently attend to these words, you find, that the Holy Spirit is said (to be) *a Thing of the Nature* of the Father and the Son, and that the same is said to be *the Nature* of God, where there is said: « through the Nature of God the Nature itself dwells in us, if through the Holy Spirit Christ is in us ».* And so in the Trinity one must thus not distinguish between *the Nature* and a *Thing of the Nature*, as among created things, because, as (St.) Hilary says:[2] « there is no comparison of earthly (things) to God, and if sometimes they are brought forward as examples of comparisons, no one esteems them to contain absolutely in themselves the perfection of (such) a reckoning ». « For not according to human sense is one to speak of God ».

Therefore, looking back to the nature of created things, he says:[3] « A nature is not the same as a thing of the nature », subjoining examples from creatures themselves. Showing from this, that it is an error, to measure the Creator under the measure of creatures, he adds: And according to this « God, and what God is, is not the same », as if to say: "you sense the likeness [instar] of creatures from the Creator, you are driven to say, that God and what is God is not the same; which is an impious (thing) to say, since the Spirit of God is God, and the Son of God is God."

Therefore, not according to corporal standards of measure, as he subjoins in the same series, are those which are said of God to be accepted. Where, emptying the opinion of those, who thus think that '*to be God*' is one (thing),[4] and '*what is of God*' another, and another *the Nature* of God and a *Thing of the Nature*, as is it among creatures, he openly teaches, that 'to be God' and what are His (are) not an other, thus that they are in Him, saying thus:[5] « A man or something similar to him, when it will be somewhere, it will not be elsewhere, because that which it is, is contained therein, where it was in form, so that that which stands still in some place, is not everywhere. But the God of immense virtue, the living Power, which is never not present nor is ever lacking, teaches *that He (is) All* through *His own*, and He signifies that *His own* is not other than *Himself*, so that where *His own* are, *He Himself* is understood to be *through His own*. However, not in a corporal manner, when He is somewhere, is He believed not also to be everywhere, since He does not cease to be in all through His own. Moreover, those which are His own, would not be other, than what He Himself is. And these (words) have been said on account of the understanding of the Nature ». With these words he openly signifies — if you, yet, understand, o heretic — that the Divine Nature is not other than those which are Its own, thus that they are in (It), and through them It is in all Its own, which are not in (It). For they are also Its own, which are not in (It), that is all creatures; and They are Its own which are in (It), as the Three Persons, which are of the same Nature and (are) the same Nature, just as confirmed [firmavimus] above by the testimony of (St.) Augustine,[6] saying: « that the Three Persons are of the same Essence and/or (are) the same Essence, but (are) not out of the same Essence, lest the Essence be understood (to be) one (thing), a Person another ».* — Yet we do not disavow [diffitemur],

that some distinction will have to be made according to the reckoning of the intelligence, when there is said "*Hypostasis*", and when there is said "*Essence*"; because in the Latter there is signified what is common to the Three, in the Former not (so). Yet a Hypostasis is the Essence, and vice versa. Therefore, we say, that the Three Persons are one and the same according to essence, but differing by properties. Whence (St.) Augustine on the passage from the Psalm touched upon beforehand [praetaxatam][7] says: « Ask, "What is the Father?" The response is: "*God*." Ask, "What is the Son?" The response is: "*God*." Ask, "What is the Father and the Son?" The response is: "*God*." Interrogated concerning each one, respond "*God*." Interrogated concerning both, respond, not "gods", but "God". Not so (is it) among men. For so great is there a unity of Substance There, that it admits an equality, it does not admit a plurality. If, therefore, there were said to you, when you say, that the Son is what the Father is: "in a word the Son is the Father", respond: "I have said to you, according to substance, that the Son is what the Father is, not according to that which is said *regarding another*." For *regarding Himself* He is said (to be) "God", *regarding the Father* He is said (to be) "the Son". And again the Father *regarding Himself* is said (to be) "God", *regarding the Son* He is said (to be) "the Father". What is said regarding the Son (to be) "the Father", is not the Son; what is said (to be) "the Son" regarding the Father, is not the Father; what is said (to be) "the Father" regarding Himself and "the Son" regarding Himself, this is the Father and the Son, that is, God ».

CHAPTER II

Whether there can be said, "one God of three Persons", as there is said, "one essence of three Persons", and (whether there can be said) "three Persons of one God", as (there is said) "three Persons of one essence"?

Here, there must be considered, since God is the Divine Essence, and thus the One God is said to be three Persons, just as the One Essence is said (to be) three Persons, whether thus one prevails to say sanely, "one God of three Persons", and/or "three Persons of one God", just as there is said "one essence of three Persons", and "three Persons of one essence." — In these expressions it seems that the usage [usus] of Scripture is to be emulated by us, where there is frequently found (to be) said thus: "one is the Essence of the Three Persons", and "the Three Persons are of one essence"; but it never happens that one has read, that (there is) "one God of three Persons",[8] and/or "three Persons of one God". Which I think the holy Doctors avoided for this reason, lest thus perhaps there be accepted among the Divine Persons, as it is accepted, when something similar is said of creatures. For there is said, "*the God of Abraham, Isaac and Jacob*",[9] and "*the God of every creature*". Which indeed is said on account of the Principle of creation and/or the privilege of grace,[10] and the subjection and/or servitude of the creature. Since, therefore, in the Trinity there is nothing created and/or serving and/or subjected, the Faith has not admitted such

---

[1] Those which precede this are found ibid., nn. 27 and 28. — The passage from Sacred Scripture is Jn. 10:30.

[2] ON THE TRINITY, Bk. I, n. 19. The last proposition is Bk. VIII, n. 14.

[3] On this and the following passage, see p. 582, footnote 3.

[4] The Vatican edition and editions 4 & 6 add the gloss: *and what is of God another, and the Nature of God another* [et aliud, quod Dei est, aliudque naturam Dei], breaking with all the codices and the other editions.

[5] Ibid., n. 24. In which text for *it was in form, so that* [fuerit in forma, ut] the edition of (St.) Hilary's (works) has *it was; its nature infirm for this, that* [fuerit; infirma ad id natura eius, ut]. Then, the Vatican

edition, with very many edd. adds *which* [quae] after *is every lacking* [desit usquam], but contrary to the original, the codd., and ed. 1. At the end, contrary to the codd., the Vatican with the other editions, except ed.n 8, has *are not other* [autem aliud sunt] for *would not be other* [aliud autem sint].

[6] ON THE TRINITY, Bk. VII, ch. 6, n. 11. Cf. Distinction V, ch. 2, p. 110, footnote 7, and d. XXV, ch. 1, p. 432, footnote 5.

[7] ENARRATIONS ON THE PSALMS, Ps. 68, sermon 1, n. 5. Cf. Distinction XXXIII, ch. 2.

[8] The codices and edd. 3, 5, 7, 8 & 9, omit *Persons* [personarum].

[9] Ex. 3:6; the other passage is Judith 9:17.

[10] The Vatican edition alone has *of glory* [gloriae].

---

* *Trans. note*: Here the critical edition faultily omits the quotations marks, « », about these passages from St. Hilary and St. Augustine, contrary to its own custom. I have restored them, having consulted the Grottaferrata Edition of Lombard's First and Second Books, 1971, p. 250.

a manner of expression. Thus, too, there is not said, the other way around, of *the Essence* of God, that It Itself is of the essence of Abraham, Isaac and Jacob and/or of any creature, lest we seem to confound the nature of the Creator and of the creature.

CHAPTER III

That power, wisdom, (and) goodness are sometimes referred in Scripture to the Persons distinctly.

From the aforesaid[1] it is established, that just as "essence", so "power", "wisdom", and "goodness" are said of God according to substance. Moreover, what are said of God according to substance, befits the Three Persons equally. Therefore, there is one Power, Wisdom, (and) Goodness of the Father and the Son and the Holy Spirit, and these Three (are) the same Power, the same Wisdom, (and) the same Goodness. Whence there appears to be a most high perfection in the Trinity. For if, there were lacking There power and/or wisdom and/or goodness, He would not be the Most High Good [summum bonum]. But because there is There a perfect Power, an infinite Wisdom, (and) an incomprehensible Goodness, He is rightly said and believed (to be) the Most High Good. And though the Power, Wisdom, (and) Goodness in God is thoroughly one [unum] and the same; yet in Sacred Scripture these names are accustomed to be frequently referred in a distinct manner to the Person, so that "power" is attributed to the Father, "wisdom" to the Son, (and) "goodness" to the Holy Spirit. Wherefore, it is not boring [otiosum] to inquire for what reason this is done.

CHAPTER IV

For what reason is power attributed to the Father, wisdom to the Son, goodness to the Holy Spirit, since there is one Power, Wisdom, (and) Goodness of the Three.

« Therefore, the prudence of the Sacred Speech took care to do this, lest we measure the immensity of God by the similitude of a creature. For Sacred Scripture had said, that God is the Father, and that God is the Son; and man, who saw man as a father, did not see God as a father, and he began to think, that thus it is in the Creator, as he saw (it) among creatures, from whom these names have been transferred to the Creator, among which a father is prior to a son, a son is posterior to a father, and there is accustomed to be noted a defect from the antiquity in the father, and an imperfection of sense from the posteriority [posteritate] in the son. For that reason Scripture runs against this, saying that the Father (is) powerful, lest He seem (to be) prior to the Son, an for that reason less powerful, and that the Son (is) wise, lest He seem posterior to the Father, and for that reason less wise ».[2]

« The Holy Spirit is also said (to be) "God", and God is said to have "a spirit"; and this (term, "spirit") used to seem (to be) a quasi name for being puffed-up [inflationis] and of a growing wrath [tumoris] — wherefore the human conscience feared to approach God on account of (His) rigor and cruelty — for that reason Scripture tempered its own speech, naming (Him) *"the good spirit"*, lest He, who was meek, be thought cruel; not that the Father alone is powerful and/or more powerful, and the Son alone wise and/or more wise, and the Holy Spirit alone good and/or more good. One, therefore, is the Power, Wisdom, (and) Goodness[3] of the Three, just as one (is Their) Essence; and for that reason, just as the Son is said (to be) *homoousios*, that is "consubstantial" to the Father, so also "*co-omnipotent*" ».

CHAPTER V

On this name homoousion, where is it received in authority, and what does it signify.

Here, there must not be overlooked, what (St.) Augustine in the second[4] book, AGAINST MAXIMINUS says concerning this name *homoousion*, which Latin writers [tractatores] frequently use. « The Father », he says, « and the Son are of one and the same Substance. This is that *homoousion*, which was confirmed [firmavit] in the Council of Nicea against the Arian heretics by the Catholic Fathers with the authority of truth; which afterwards in the Council of Rimini, on account of the novelty of the word, understood less than it was able — which, however, the ancient Faith begot — heretical depravity, having deceived many by the fraud of the few, under the heretical emperor, Constantius, tried to cause to totter [labefactare]. But after not a long time with the liberty of the Catholic Faith prevailing, after the force of the word, as was ought, had been understood, this *homoousion* was defended and diffused fare and wide by the sanity of the Catholic Faith. For what is *homoousion* except "of one and the same substance"? What is homoousion, I say, except: *I and the Father are one* [unum]? Therefore, it is not to be shunned among the profane novelties of spoken words ».

Moreover, it must be known, that in the assigning of the distinction of names, among the others, which we have diligently explained [executi], we have said[5] that certain ones, such as *"mirror"*, *"splendor"*, *"character"*, *"figure"* and (names) of this kind, are to be said of God in a transferred manner and through a similitude. Concerning which I hand over to the pious reader what I think [sentio], so that, namely, having considered (them) by the reckoning of (their) similitude, he may take up (not only) an understanding of the said (names) from the reasons to be said, but a catholic (understanding of them).

Of the sacrament of the Most High and Ineffable Unity and Trinity we have already said much. Yet we profess that we have handed down nothing worthy of His ineffability, but rather that *wonderful* knowledge of Him out of ourselves, not even we have been able to reach.

---

[1] Distinction XXII, ch. 4.

[2] All the preceding has been taken from Hugo of St. Victor, ON THE SACRAMENTS, Bk. I, p. II, ch. 8, with a few (words) changed and/or transposed by Master (Peter). What follows is also taken from the same place.

[3] Codices A B C and E, and edition 1, have *Kindness* [benignitas].

[4] Chapter 14, n. 3. In which text the modern edition of (St.) Augustine reads (in reference to "the word") *understood less than was necessary* — which [oportuit intellectum quod] for (our reading in reference to "novelty") *understood less than it was able* — which [potuit intellectam quam]; the Vatican edition alone follows the modern edition, but omits *which* [quod]. Ancient editions of (St.) Augustine concord with our text. Then all the editions faultily have *Constantine* [Constantino] for *Constantius* [Constantio], breaking with the codices. Next the Vatican edition and editions 4 and 8 have *expanded* [distensum] for *defended* [defensum].

[5] Distinction XXII, ch. 1.

[6] Only the Vatican edition and editions 2 and 3 have *wonderful* [mirificam] for *wonderful* [mirificatam]. — This is a reference to Psalm 138:6: *Wonderful has knowledge of Thee become out of me: it is strengthened, and I was not able for it* [Mirabilis facta est scientia tua ex me: confortata est, et non potero ad eam].

---

* *Trans. note*: This "wonderful knowledge" of God which is "out of oneself" is the mystical apprehension of the Trinity, which is granted to the Saints and to other souls, sometimes entirely gratuitously, sometimes partly gratuitously and partly meritoriously, and is worked by grace alone, being above the natural powers of the soul. It is said to be "*out of oneself*" because it is worked in the substance of the soul itself, and is essentially incomprehensible to the powers of sense.

COMMENTARY ON DISTINCTION XXXIV

On the comparison of the Persons to the Nature.

To the aforesaid it must be added, that certain men of a perverse sense etc..

THE DIVISION OF THE TEXT

Above, Master (Peter) dealt with the comparison of the properties to the Persons and (to) the Essence; here, second, he deals with the comparison of the Persons to the Essence. And this he does in this distinction, which is divided into three parts. In the *first* he deals with the comparison according to predication; in the *second* according to appropriation, there (where he says): *From the aforesaid it is established, that just as "essence", so "power"* etc.; in the *third* he adjoins a chapter on the transferal (of names), so that in this manner that tract may lead thoroughly to its consummation, and this there (where he says): *Moreover it must be known, that in the assigning* etc..

The *first* part has three parts.[1] In the first, he puts the error of certain ones saying, that the Persons are not the Nature, and this together with their confirmation, namely, with the authority of (St.) Hilary. In second, he elicits the sane understanding of the very authority[2] from the words of (St.) Hilary which follow [sequentibus], through which he also crushes their error, there (where he says): *This, indeed, they say, not understanding* etc.. In the third, he dissolves a certain incidental objection [oppositionem incidentem],[3] "For what reason are the Three Persons not said (to be) of one God, just as the Three Persons are said (to be) of one essence?", there (where he says): *Here there must be considered, since God is the Divine Essence* etc..

From the aforesaid it is established, that just as "essence" etc.. This is the *second* part, in which Master (Peter) deals with the appropriation (of names), and this part has three parts. In the first, he says and shows, that common (names) are appropriated. In the second, he gives an account of [rationem reddit] the appropriation, there (where he says): *Therefore, the prudence of the Sacred Speech took care to do this* etc.. In the third, because this name, *homoousion*, means a comparison of the Essence or Nature to the Persons, he determines that its use is catholic and is consonant with the truth of the Faith, there (where he says): *Here there must not be overlooked, what (St.) Augustine* etc..

Moreover, it must be known, that in the assigning of the distinction etc.. This is the *third* subpart, in which Master (Peter) deals with the translation of names, which (part) could be divided against the whole preceding tract on the Divine Names. But, because Master (Peter) determines little or nothing, for that reason it[4] is rather posited incidentally with the conclusion [epilogatione]. Whence this subpart has two parts. In the first, he hands down a certain general instruction concerning transferable names [nominibus translativis]. In the second, however, he posits a conclusion for the aforesaid, in which he finishes (his) tract on the Sacrament of the Trinity and Unity, showing that in this tract he was deficient rather than sufficient on account of the height of the material, and this he does there (where he says): *Of the sacrament of the Most High and Ineffable Unity and Trinity* etc..

TREATMENT OF THE QUESTIONS

For an understanding of the present Distinction four (questions) are asked:

First, there is asked, whether among the divine there is a positing of addition.

Second, whether among the divine there is a positing of predication.

Third, whether there is a positing of an appropriation There.

Fourth, whether there is a positing of a transferal There.

---

[1] Codices I bb and the others, together with edition 1, read *subparts* [particulas]. Next for *their confirmation* [sua confirmatione], which we have restored from codices I O T and X and edition 1, the Vatican edition has *a most high confirmation* [summa confirmatione].

[2] For *of the very authority* [ipsius auctoritatis] codex T has *of this authority* [huius auctoritatis]

[3] The Vatican edition has *question* [quaestionem] for *objection* [oppositionem].

[4] The Vat. has *it (this subpart)* [posita] for *it (little or nothing)* [positum].

ARTICLE SOLE

On the comparison of Person to Nature and on the appropriation and transferal (of names to the Divine).

QUESTION I

Whether, among the Divine, a Thing of the Nature adds upon the Nature?

Therefore, as much as regards the first there is asked, whether there is among the divine a positing of addition, that is, whether the Three of the Nature add upon the Nature. And that it is so, seems in this manner:

1. (St.) Hilary ON THE TRINITY (says):[1] « A nature is one (thing), a thing of a nature another »; but the understanding of the Nature is enclosed in a Thing of the Nature: therefore, if It is (something) else, it is necessary, that (It be) in the reckoning of something added.

2. Likewise, (St. Severinus) Boethius (says) ON THE TWO NATURE AND ONE PERSON OF CHRIST:[2] « Nature and person are to be distinguished and separated by Their own reckonings »; but whose definitions are diverse, they themselves are diverse: therefore, since the Nature occurs in the definition of a Person, it is necessary, that the diversity come from the reckoning of (something) added, ergo etc.. If *you say*, that the definitions of the Nature and a Person are not diverse according to thing, but according to the reckoning of understanding; then one concludes, that that understanding is[3] hollow [cassus] and vain, since nothing in the Thing responds to it.

3. Likewise, this very (thing) seems *by reason*, because as much as anything is found in many, so much it is more simple (that they);[4] but the Essence and/or Nature in many, but a Person in One alone: therefore, *the Nature* (is) more simple. But something is not less simple than (something) else, unless through some addition: ergo etc..

4. Likewise, as much as anything is of a greater abstraction, so much is it more simple;[5] but *the Nature* is of a greater abstraction than *a Person*, since with the properties removed [abstractis] there is an understanding of *the Nature*, but not *of a Person*: therefore, a Person adds something upon the Nature, ergo etc..

5. Likewise, this is a self-evident [per se notum] principle: « Of no same is there both a true affirmation and negation according to the same »;[6] but something is truly affirmed of a Per-

son, such as *that He is distinguished*, which is denied of *the Nature*, therefore, not according to the same: therefore, in *a Person* there is something, which is not in *the Nature*, and/or the other way around. And if this, therefore, the one adds upon the other.

6. Likewise, this is a self-evident principle: « Whatsoever are the same to one and the same according to an omnimodal indifference, are also the same among themselves »:[7] therefore, since (Their) Nature is one and the same, if *the Persons* are entirely the Same with *the Nature* and add nothing (to It), therefore, the Persons are the same to one another; and thus the error of Sabellius, that one Person according to thing is the Other, returns; ergo etc..

ON THE CONTRARY: 1. (St.) Augustine in the seventh (book) ON THE TRINITY (says):[8] « It is not one (thing) for God *to be*, and another *to be a Person* »: therefore, *a Person* adds nothing upon the '*to be*', therefore, neither upon *the Nature*.

2. Likewise, in[9] a most highly simple there can be no addition; but a Divine Person or Thing of the Nature is most highly simple: ergo etc..

3. Likewise, whatsoever two so hold themselves, that whatever is in one, is the other through essence, the one adds nothing upon the remainder [reliquum]; but what ever is in a Person is the Deity: ergo etc.. The *major* is manifest; the *minor* is clear in this manner: in a Person there is naught but the Substance and a property, and that Substance is the Deity, because He is God, and God (is) no other than He Himself — because then[10] He would be through participation — therefore, by Himself He is God and by the Deity He is God; and *the Substance*, which concerns the understanding of *a Person*, is through essence the very Nature, and similarly *the property* is the Essence, as has been proven above.[11] Therefore, there remains the first, that It adds nothing.

4. Likewise, if (a Person) does add, either It adds (something) *else*, or *the same*. 'That It adds *the same* to Itself' is not intelligible. If (something) *else*,

---

[1] Book VIII, n. 22. See the text of Master (Peter) here, in ch. 1.

[2] In the Foreword: « However, since there is a doubt in the whole question of heresies contrary to themselves concerning the Persons and Natures, the latter are first to be defended and segregated by their own differences ». In the text, for *reckonings* [rationibus], which we have placed on the authority of codices B D T and X, and edition 1, the Vatican edition has *names* [nominibus]. — On the minor proposition, cf. Aristotle, TOPICS, Bk. VI, ch. 3 (ch. 4): But these are not the same, for this reason, that (their) definitions (are) diverse.

[3] In codex O there is added *according to (St. Severinus) Boethius, ON THE CONSOLATION (OF PHILOSOPHY)* (Bk. III, Prose 10).

[4] Cf. above d. 8, p. II, q. 1, in reply to n. 1.

[5] See Aristotle, METAPHYSICS, Bk. XI, ch. 1 (Bk. X, ch. 1) et above in d. 27, p. I, q. 3, 2nd. arg. of the fundament, and concerning the reason added to the minor proposition, cf. d. 26, q. 3, in the body (of the Question).

[6] Aristotle, ON INTERPRETATION, Bk. I, ch. 6 (ch. 7), and METAPHYSICS, Bk. IV, texts 9-19 (Bk. III, chs. 3-5)., where this principle is proven at greater length.

[7] Cf. above d. 31, p. II, a. 2, q. 1, p. 546, footnote 2.

[8] Chapter 6, n. 11.

[9] Codex T and not a few others read *to a most highly simple* [summe simplici] for *in a most highly simple* [in summe simplici].

[10] Understand: if He would be God by another than Himself.

[11] Distinction 33, q. 2. — A little above this, after *and similarly* [et similiter] codices A G T and X, with edition 1, subjoin *even* [et].

therefore, either (something) else *substantially*, or *accidentally*: not *accidentally*, because there is no accident among the divine; nor *substantially*, because then there would be diverse substances. Therefore, *the Nature* according to essence does not[1] differ from *a Person*, and this is manifest.

5. Likewise, if (a Person) does add something, either it is *material*, or *formal*, because the formal is not but in respect of the material. Therefore, since in God there is nothing material, It will not be able to add something formal: therefore, (It adds) in no manner.

6. Likewise, if (a Person) adds something upon the Divine Nature, either it is *better* than the Divine Nature, or *equal*, or *less*: not *better*, it is established; it is also established, that (It does) not (add something) *worse*, because then It would be a creature; not (something) *equal*, because nothing can be equal to the Divine Nature: therefore, (It adds) entirely nothing.

CONCLUSION

A Person or Thing of the Nature adds nothing according to thing upon the Nature, yet differs from It according to a reckoning, because a Person has a relation to Another, but the Nature (does) not.

I RESPOND: It must be said, that when there is asked, whether *a Person* or Thing of the Nature adds something upon *the Nature*, one must respond, that there is a speaking of addition in a twofold manner: either as much as regards *the Thing*, or as much as regards *the understanding*.

If as much as regards the *understanding*, since the understanding of this name "*person*" or "*hypostasis*" or "*thing of nature*" includes the understanding of *the Nature* and still gives an understanding of something; it thus must be said,[2] that necessarily there is a *composition* about the understanding and an *addition*. And this is clear. For a "*person*" is said (to be) "a supposit of a rational nature distinguished by a property."[3] Behold, the understanding of *a person* is composed out of many understandings; and the understanding of *a nature* occurs in that: therefore, (this) established, that as much as regarding the understanding "*person*" does add upon "*nature*". — For that understanding is not false, because it neither *distinguishes the Nature* through that addition, nor *composes the Person*. It does not *distinguish the Nature*, since, even if it adds upon the understanding of *the Nature* a property, it does not add[4] (it) in a right sense [in recto], so that you understand, that a Person is *the Nature* distinguished by a property; but one must understand in an oblique sense [in obliquo], that a Person is *a distinct Supposit* of the rational

Nature, or that It is a distinct Hypostasis; and for that reason it does not posit a distinction about the Nature, nor does It understand That to be distinguished. — Again, *it does not compose a Person* nor does it impose something upon That, which is not in Itself. And this is clear, because a sane and faithful intellect understands and believes, that a[5] Person is *most simple*; it understands that It is, nevertheless, *most perfect*. Whence just as about *the Essence*, on account of this, that It is most perfect, it understands all the conditions of nobility and (these) in a true manner, because they are there; and yet it understands those conditions to (be) many, that is, power, wisdom, goodness, since it believes and knows, that all these are one [unum] in God; nor is that understanding false nor vain, because it does not posit in God what He is not, nor (does it posit) the understanding of a Person. Whence it says that It (is) simple, because, though it says that there is in It the Nature, and the Nature in a true manner, and a Supposit, which is truly a supposit, and a property, which is truly a property; yet it says, that all these are one [unum], and that the one is the other. Therefore, according to the most simply existing thing, there is truly an addition and composition about *the understanding*, without vanity and falsity.

If, however, we speak on the part of *a thing*, thus it must be said, that since an addition on the part of a thing posits a composition, and a Divine Person is most simple, that it is entirely impossible, that there be any addition There, and thus according to *thing* a Thing of the Nature adds nothing upon the Nature.

But, then, it seems that it is not intelligible, that *a Person* is *distinct* according to thing, and *the Nature*[6] (is) not, and yet there is no *addition* and no *difference* according to *thing* between a Person and the Nature. — And regarding this, in whatsoever manner it is to be understood, since this is above the powers [vires] of the human intellect, it must be noted, just as Richard (of St. Victor)[7] would have it, that there is a distinction through *quality*, and a distinction through *origin*. A distinction through *quality* is in creatures, nor can it be without an addition, because this distinction has its rise out of an addition of matter to form. But there is said (to be) a distinction through quality, when one is distinguished from another through *absolute* properties, as is clear, when one is white, and the other black. A distinction through *origin* is, when one produces, and the other is produced. And according to the manner which the distinction through *quality* is a true distinction and according to *thing*, so a distinction through *a true origin* is a true distinction. For just as one cannot be at once white and black, so one and the same cannot produce itself. Sin-

---

[1] The Vatican edition omits *not* [non], and then for *manifest* [manifestum] has *manifestly false* [manifeste falsum], which reading is evidently false, since, with these changes, the conclusion of the proposition does not respond to the aforementioned (arguments). The particle *not* [non] is found in the most outstanding codices L O and T, and the word *manifest* [manifestum] in many others. In codices I aa and bb, for *Therefore the Nature according to essence* [Ergo natura secundum essentiam] there is read *Therefore, the Nature and/or Essence according to substance* [Ergo natura vel essentia secundum substantiam].

[2] The words *it thus must be said* [sic dicendum], which are wanting in the Vatican edition, we have restored from codices I X (Z has *it must be said* [dicendum]. A little before this, the Vatican edition for the words *and still gives* [et adhuc det], not trusting in the codices, substitutes *yet it still gives* [adhuc tamen dat], by which the sense of the proposition is distorted.

[3] Cf. above d. 25, a. 1, q. 2, in reply to n. 4.

[4] Codices L and O have *occur* [cadit] for *add (it)* [addit]. The Vatican edition adds to the beginning of this clause *yet* [tamen].

[5] Supply, together with codex B and bb and edition 1, *Divine* [divinam].

[6] Very many codices, together with the Vatican edition, read *the Essence* [essentia], codices B and I have *the Essence or Nature* [essentia sive natura], a few others have faultily *a Person* [persona]. Immediately after this for *yet* [tamen] the Vatican edition, not trusting in the codices and edition 1, *with this* [cum hoc], and a little above this has *yet* [tamen] for *then* [tunc].

[7] ON THE TRINITY, Bk. IV, ch. 13, where three members of the division are distinguished: « For (existence) can be varied either according to the quality alone of the thing, or according to the origin alone of the thing, or according to a combination [concursionem] of each ».

-ce, therefore, among the divine there is understood a true origin, for that reason there is understood to be There a true *distinction*. — Again, when I understand, that the Father produces, I understand, that He produces by Himself, just as when I understand, that the Divine Substance acts, I understand, that It acts by Itself,[1] for an equal reason also that the Son is produced by Him: therefore, the production *adds* nothing. — Similarly, it posits no *composition* about the Son. Therefore, since, where there is a true origin, there is a true *distinction*, and the origin is understood to be without *an addition*; the distinction is also understood to be there without *an addition*.

Moreover, though a Person or a Thing of the Nature does not hold Itself to the Nature through an *addition*, yet it nevertheless differs according to *a reckoning*; otherwise it would not be intelligible, that with the Nature existing unique, It is plurified according to person. But the difference is according to a reckoning, because *the Essence* does not arise from an essence, nor does It hold Itself to another essence; but *a Person* rightly arises from a Person and holds Himself to Him. — *If you ask* the reason for this, I respond, that the Unity and Nobility of the Divine "Being" does not admit a plurification about the Essence, just as about a Person; and the reason for this has been said above, in the Ninth Distinction.[2] Since, therefore, the manner of holding Itself to Another and of arising from Another does not posit a composition in a Person according to thing, but a real distinction from the other Person; for that reason that manner, compared to the Essence and/or the Person, of which it is, is only *a manner*; but compared to the One, to whom it is, since it causes a distinction according to thing, it is truly *a thing*, and thus in one manner it causes a differing *according to thing*, in another manner *according to a reckoning*. Hence it is, that, though one Person is not Another, yet *a Thing of the Nature is the Nature*. It is clear, therefore, that, that a Person be simple and add nothing upon the Nature, nor that They differ except according to a reckoning, these are co-possibles; and yet the Latter is communicable, namely, the Nature, the Former incommunicable, namely, the Person; the Latter (namely a Person) distinguished, the Former (namely the Nature) not distinguished.

Therefore, the reasons proving, that a Person or Thing of the Nature adds entirely nothing according to thing upon the Nature, are to be conceded.

1. 2. To that which is objected, that a thing of the nature is one (thing), the nature another, and similarly (that) 'person' and 'nature' have a different [aliam] reckoning; it can be said, that (Sts. Severinus) Boethius and Hilary are speaking (of person and nature) among creatures. But if we understand (them) in God, then we will say, that there is a diversity of reckoning, which is founded not upon (something) absolute, but upon (something) respective, which[3] induces no composition. For the Essence is not referred, but a Person is referred and arises, and yet It is not composed, because It is Its own looking-back.

3. To that which is objected, that the more simple is that which is found in many; it must be said, that 'to be found in many', this is in a twofold manner: either thus, that one of them can be anywhere, where the other is not, as a man and among many men, and in this manner the proposition has truth; or thus among many, that the one is not without the other, and in this manner is it among the Persons — for the One is not without the Other — and in this manner it does not have truth. For just as the Nature is always and everywhere, so also a Person; and thus it is clear, that (the Person), by whom (the Nature) is constrained, adds nothing (to the Nature).[4]

4. To that which is objected, that (the Nature) is of greater abstraction etc.; it must be said, that that has truth where that, from which it is abstracted, causes some composition with that which is abstracted;[5] but (the Nature) is not in God in this manner.

5. To that which is objected, that an affirmation and negation are not both [simul] true of the same; it must be said, that howsoever small the difference of reckoning it suffices for an affirmation and negation.[6] Whence the proposition is to be understood of the same according to thing and reckoning; and a Person differs in another manner from the Nature, though not through a real addition.

6. To that which is objected, that whatsoever are the same to one and the same, are among themselves the same etc.; it must be said, that that fails, where there is a convening of many as in a common, as of differences in a genus. It also fails, where any many are distinguished through their origins, as the rays of diverse stars are united in one point of the air, and yet are distinguished regarding one another. Since, therefore, the Divine Persons convene in the Nature as in one common, and moreover[7] are distinguished regarding One another through origin; for that reason (this) makes it clear, that it is not valid. — Yet, it can be said, that the rule is true everywhere, if it is sanely understood. On account of which it must be noted, that certain (things) are *absolute*, certain (things) *respective*. But a diversity among *respectives* comes not only on the part of the subject, but also (on the part) of the terminus;[8] among these the rule does not hold, unless it is understood according to the same. Since, therefore, the Persons are referred through Their properties, though They are *one* [unum] in nature, yet because They are not *regarding one* [unum], for that reason it does not follow, that They are the Same. And in this manner that (objection) is clear.

---

[1] Not a few of the older codices and even edition 1 omit *by Itself* [ipsam se ipsa]; codex X reads *that It is and* [esse et].

[2] In qq. 1 and 2.

[3] Codices W and X read *upon a looking-back, which* [super respectum, qui], codices A and V have *which (diversity of reckoning)* [quae]; not a few other codices, together with editions 1, 2 and 3, incongruously read *which* [qui] (in the masculine). Next for *and yet It is not* [nec tamen] codex W reads *and yet a Person is not* [nec tamen persona]. [Trans. note: Something *respective*, is something inclined to *look back*.]

[4] Cf. above d. 8, p. II, q. 1, in reply to n. 1.

[5] This difficulty is solved in nearly the same manner above in d. 8,

p. II, q. 1, in reply to n. 1; but the question is treated more diffusely above in d. 27, p. I, q. 3.

[6] Aristotle, Topics, Bk. I, ch. 14 (ch. 16). For in finding any difference among the proposed, we will show, that (they are) not the same.

[7] For *moreover* [praeterea] very many codices, together with the Vatican edition, have *Persons* [personae].

[8] From codex I (T in the margin) and edition 1, we have restored *of the terminus* [termini], in place of which the other codices *of the thing* [rei], but the Vatican edition, together with codex cc, has *of the thing, to which they are referred* [rei, ad quam referuntur].

SCHOLIUM

I. The *Nature* here spoken of is the Divine Essence Itself, to the extent that it is communicable to the Three Persons; a *thing of a nature*, according to St. Hilary, spoken of by the Scholastics is *a hypostasis* or supposit (cf. above d. 23, a. 1, q. 2, Scholium). — On the *addition* to *the Nature*, which the reckoning of a person conveys, cf. above d. 25, a. 1, q. 1, Scholium. — That the question on this passage (of St. Hilary) is solved under a twofold respect, is clear from the text itself. Under the second respect (on the part of the thing), it is manifest, that, there can be posited no difference between the Nature and a Person. But then there arises a doubt, not, at least adequately, (to be) solved by the human intellect, "In what manner with such a supposition a real distinction of Person can stand?" To solve this doubt to a little extent the Seraphic Doctor recurs to this principle, which is evinced by many reasons, that a created person differs very much from an uncreated One. Yet the principal difference is this (in reply to n. 1), that a created hypostasis differs from the nature through something *absolute*, but a Divine Hypostasis differs from the Nature through something *relative*. Richard of Middleton (here in a. 1, q. 1) explains this in this manner: « A Person differs from the Essence according to a reckoning, not as we say, that attributes differ according to a reckoning, but on account of a different *manner of holding Itself*, because in the manner of holding oneself to the other They differ according to affirmation and negation, because a Person holds Himself to Another, but the Essence does not, and the Essence holds Itself absolutely, but a Person (does) not »

II. Alexander of Hales, SUMMA., p. I, q. 56, m. 7, a. 1 and 2. — (Bl. John Duns) Scotus, in each version, here in q. 1. — St. Thomas, here in q. 1, a. 1; SUMMA., I, q. 39, a. 1. — Bl. (now St.) Albertus (Magnus), here in a. 1 and 2; SUMMA., p. I, tr. 10, q. 44, m. 4, and q. 43, m. 2, a. 1. — (Bl.) Peter of Tarentaise, here in q. 1, a. 1 and 2. — Richard of Middleton, here in a. 1, qq. 1 and 2. — Giles the Roman, here in 1st. princ., q. 1. — Durandus (of Saint-Pourçain), here in qq. 1 and 2, and in d. 33, q. 1. — (Bl.) Dionysius the Carthusian, here in q. 1. — (Gabriel) Biel, here in the q. sole.

QUESTION II

Whether, among the divine, a Person is predicated of the Nature, and the Nature of a Person?

Second, there is asked, whether among the divine there is a positing of predication, namely, so that a Thing of the Nature or Person is predicated of the Nature, and/or vice versa. And it seems, that (there is) not.

1. (St. Severinus) Boethius (says) in (his) book, ON THE TRINITY:[1] « God is a form without a subject »; but where there nothing is subjected, nothing is predicated: ergo etc..

2. Likewise, Dionysius (the Areopagite) says,[2] that « negations concerning God are true, but affirmations (are) not in complete agreement [incompactae] »; but where there is truly a predicating of something of anything, there is truly an affirming; but in God one does not happed to affirm (anything) truly: ergo etc..

3. Likewise, this very (thing) seems *by reason*: because wheresoever there is predication, there is a combination [complexio] and a composition;[3] but in God there is no combination, therefore, also no composition: therefore, also no predication.

4. Likewise, in every predication the subject holds itself according to the manner of matter; but among the divine there is neither a finding of matter nor of the manner of matter: therefore, neither of predication.

5. Likewise, if there is predication There, either *the same* is predicated *of the same*, or *something of (something) else* [aliud de alio]. If *the same* (is predicated) *of the same*, there is grasped from this no other understanding, than if there were no predication, as is clear when there is said. "a man is a man". If *something* (is predicated) *of (something) else*: therefore, among the divine there is something and (something) else, therefore, a composition.

6. Likewise, if there is predication There, either *a Thing of the Nature* is predicated of *the Nature*, or the other way around. *A Thing of the Nature* cannot be predicated of *the Nature*, because a *Thing of the Nature* holds Itself through the manner of a supposit: therefore, it belongs to It to be the subject [subiici], not to be the predicate [praedicari]: therefore, if it is predicated, then, therefore, *the Nature* (is predicated) of *the Thing of the Nature*. *But on the contrary*: the Nature is a form; but every form is said relatively regarding the one informed, but no relative is said of (its) other.[4] therefore, *the Nature* is not predicated of a Thing of the Nature: therefore, there is no predication (There).

7. Likewise, (of) those which have opposite properties, the one is not predicated of the other; but the property of the Essence and/or the Nature is communicability; but (the property) of a Person (is) incommunicability: therefore, the one is not predicated of the other, nor (is) one Person (predicated) of the Other: therefore, it is established, that there is no predication There.[5]

---

[1] Chapter 2: The Divine Substance is a form without matter ... for It is a form; however, forms cannot be subjected.

[2] ON THE CELESTIAL HIERARCHIES, ch. 2, § 3, (where the Greek text reads): Αἱ μὲν ἀποφάσεις ἐπὶ τῶν θείων ἀληθεῖς, αἱ δὲ καταφάσεις ἀνάρμοστοι. In the text, Corderius substitutes *incongruous* [incongrue] for the *not in complete agreement* [incompactae], which is in Scotus Erigena's Latin translation.

[3] Cf. Aristotle, ON PREDICAMENTS, near the beginning, where he deals with *complex* and *non-complex* expressions; and ON INTERPRETATION, Bk. I, ch. 3 ff.., where he deals with *word* and *enunciation*. — The Vatican ed. with cod. cc, after *there is a combination* [ibi est complexio] interjects *therefore* [ergo]. In many codd. & ed. 1 there is wanting the final conclusion: *therefore, also no predication* [ergo et nulla praedicatio].

[4] For *(its) other* [alio] the Vatican ed. and cod. cc have more clearly *its correlative* [suo correlativo], concerning which, cf. Aristotle, ON PREDICAMENTS, ch. "on *Opposites*". Next, after *therefore, there no predication* [ergo non est] codd. B C & bb with ed. 1 rightly insert *There* [ibi].

[5] Codices P Q and W, having omitted the verb *it is established* [constat], read more briefly: *therefore, there is no predication There* [ergo nulla est ibi praedicatio].

ON THE CONTRARY: 1. (St. John) Damascene (says): « The Substance is predicated of the Hypostases ».[1]

2. Likewise, it seems *by reason*: because faith has (as its) object the true and has (as its) object God, therefore, there is a positing of the true among the divine; but truth and falsity (are) about a composition,[2] the truth, I say, about which there is credulity and/or opinion: therefore, among the divine there is a positing of composition, therefore, also of predication.

3. Likewise, wheresoever there is truly[3] (something) common and (something) proper, there is truly a positing of predication; but among the divine there is truly a finding of a common and of a proper, because the Nature is common, and a Person proper or incommunicable: ergo etc..

4. Likewise, this verb "*is*" is a note of identity:[4] but every predication is by means of this verb "*is*": therefore, every predication is a sign of identity. But where there is truly a signified, there is truly also a sign; but in God there is most properly and most truly an identity, just as has been proven;[5] because *a Thing of the Nature* does not add upon *the Nature*: therefore, (there is) most properly a predication. And this is what (St. Severinus) Boethius says, that « (there is) no predication more true than that, in which the same is predicated of itself »: if, therefore, there is this among the divine, therefore, all predications among the divine are most true.

CONCLUSION

A Person is predicated of the Nature and vice versa, *by a predication through identity; but by a predication through the manner of inherence only the common is predicated of the proper.*

I RESPOND: It must be said, that there is predication through *inherence*, and there is predication through *identity*, and there is a finding of each in God: through *inherence*, such as when there is said: "the Father generates", and/or "God creates"; through *identity*, such as when there is said: "the Father is the generation", and/or "God is (the act of) creation". Moreover, there is a finding of predication through *identity* most properly in God, on account of the quality[6] of the Thing Itself, since there is a most high identity There: whence all expressions conveying 'unity', are most true there. Moreover, there is a finding There of predication through *inherence* on account of the defectibility[7] of our intellect, since, though an *act* among the divine is God's Substance and also the very *property*, yet, because our intellect understands through inferior things, and enunciates through words for inferior things, it has the manner of enunciating, which it has about inferiors; and for that reason it predicates through the manner of *inherence*, although all which are in God, really have the manner of *substance*.

Yet its understanding is not false; since, according to the manner an intellect abstracting a line from matter is not false,[8] because it does not posit that manner about the thing, but about its own act of understanding [intelligere], similarly our intellect does not posit among the divine a combination [complexionem] about the Thing, but about its own act of understanding and its own act of expressing. For, although there is in God a most high Simplicity, yet, It cannot be expressed except through a combination. And for that reason (St.) Augustine[9] says rightly, « that God is more truly than He is thought (to be), and is thought (to be) more truly than He is said (to be) ». For, even if the intellect in some manner ascends through understanding to the contuiting [contuitum] of simplicity, yet it cannot express this with a simple spoken word, but (must do so) with a composite.

1. To that, therefore, which is objected, what in God there is not subject; it must be said, that it is true as much as regards *the Thing*; yet, there is[10] (a subject) as much as regards the manner of understanding and/or of enunciating.

2. To that which is objected, that affirmations (about God) are not in complete agreement [incompactae]; it must be said, that this is said, because no name expresses the Divine Essence, as It is, entirely. — *And/or*, say, that in an affirmation there is

---

[1] ON THE ORTHODOX FAITH, Bk. II, ch. 6, (the Greek text of which reads): Κατηγορεῖται δὲ ἡ οὐσία τῆς ὑποστάσεως, i.e. and thus the Essence is predicated of the Hypostases.*

[2] Aristotle, METAPHYSICS, Bk. VI, text 8 (Bk. V, c. 4.): « For indeed the true has (its) affirmation in the composed, but (its) negation in the divided; however, the false (causes) contradiction of this partition ». And afterwards he shows, that the truth and false are not in things, just as good and evil (are), but in intellects, not every (intellect), but in the one composing and/or dividing. Cf. also ON INTERPRETATION, Bk. I, ch. 1 ff., where he teaches, that truth and falsity are neither in nouns nor in verbs (because they exist without composition and division), but only in enunciation. — The Vatican edition, together with codex cc, to the word *about a composition* [circa compositionem] adds *are* [sunt]. The first proposition of the argument in codex T (by the first hand) sounds thus: *because faith has as (its) object God, as true* [quia fides habet obiectum Deum ut verum].

[3] Edition 1 adds *a finding of* [reperire], which is also had in the minor.

[4] Aristotle, ON INTERPRETATION, Bk I, ch. 3.

[5] In the preceding Question. — A little before this for *there is truly also* [vere est et] edition 1 had *there is truly* [ibi est vere]. — The proposition of (St. Severinus) Boethius, which is next commemorated, is found in his Commentary on (Aristotle's) ON INTERPRETATION, first edition, Bk. II, near the end, where the author, dealing with this proposition:

"the good, since (it is) good, also (has its) opposites", says: « The good », he says, « is also good, and not evil, the one of which is according to itself and in a proximate manner and naturally, that, namely, which is good; but the other is accidentally, i. e. because evil is not .... Wherefore if this is (so), that proposition is more true, which affirms, that it is according to itself ». This predication is accustomed to be called a "natural" (predication) or a "*formally* identical" (predication) to distinguish it from the other, which is named a "*really* (identical predication)" or "materially identical" (predication), v. g. "animality is rationality". Cf. Mastrius, CURSUS PHILOS., tome I, disputation 5, n. 107, and disputation 10, n. 63.

[6] Codex V has *the equality* [aequalitatem].

[7] Codex R has *the defect* [defectum].

[8] Cf. Aristotle, PHYSICS, Bk II, text 18 (ch. 2), where the Philosopher, dealing with mathematical abstraction, says: « nor does a lie come to belong to those abstracting ». See also ON THE SOUL, text 35 (ch. 7). — A little below this for *combination* [complexionem], which edition 1 reads as *that combination* [complexionem illam], codex T has *combinations* [complexiones], the Vatican ed. has *composition* [compositionem].

[9] ON THE TRINITY, Bk. VII, ch. 4, n. 7. Cf. above (Master Peter's), d. XXIII, ch. 2, and (St. Bonaventure's) Commentary (on the same), Doubt 2. — Immediately after this for *except through a combination* [nisi per complexionem] codices S and T have *there through a non-combination* [ibi per incomplexionem].

[10] Supply: *a subject* [subiectum].

---

* *Trans. note*: Here the original footnote renders the Greek less accurately than St. Bonaventure does, reading: *i. e. and thus the Essence is predicated of a Person (Hypostasis)* [i. e. predicatur itaque essentia de persona (hypostasi)].

noted an *identity*, and this truly is in God on the part of the thing; and there is a *composition*,[1] and in respect of this there is lack of complete agreement [incompactio], because there is no real composition There.

3. To that which is objected concerning combination, it must be said, that that a combination (of words) in speech signifies a composition in understanding, but a unity in the Thing.

4. To that which is objected, that the manner of matter does not occur in God; it must be said, that it is true, because[2] the manner of matter does not occur as an *out of which* [ex qua]; but the manner does rightly occur as an *concerning which* [de quo] and an *in which* [in quo].

5. To that which is objected: "Either the same is predicated of the same" etc.; it must be said, that sometimes the "same" is *according to thing*, yet diverse according to *a reckoning of understanding* and *saying*, such as "Goodness is[3] the Substance"; sometimes (it is) the same according to *substance*, (and) diverse according to *the manner of holding itself*, such as "a Person is the Substance", or "a relation is the Substance", and "God generates": and for that reason some understand is grasped from the combination (of words), which is not grasped from a simple spoken word.

6. To that which is asked, whether a Thing of the Nature is predicated of the Nature; it must be said, that by a predication through *identity* Each is predicated of the Other, nor is there a composition[4] in the reckoning of form nor in the reckoning of matter; but if (They are predicated by a predication) through *inherence*, then the Common (Nature) is predicated of the Proper (i.e. a Person), such as "the Father is God".

What, therefore, is objected, that the Nature is a form; is to be responded to in a twofold manner:[5] that "form" in one manner is said *relatively* regarding the one informed, and in this manner there is no accepting (of form) in God; in another manner (there is said) *absolutely*, that (form) lacks matter, and in this manner there is (form) in God; and thus that (objection) is clear. — *In another manner*

it can be said, that '*to be said relatively*' is in a twofold manner: either according to 'being' [esse], and/or according to '*being said*' [dici]; according to '*being said*', as "seeing" (is said) regarding sight, and "understanding" regarding the intellect, and in this manner one is predicated of the other; (or) according to 'being', as "the Father" (is said) regarding the Son, and in this manner it is not predicated. For "*the Nature*" does not mean a looking-back to a Person according to 'being', but according to '*being said*'; and such a looking-back is conveyed, when it is said, that the Nature is a form in respect to a Thing of the Nature. Hence it is, that there is said by reason of that looking-back: "three Persons of one *essence* and/or nature", and "one Nature of three Persons"; yet there is not said: "three Persons of one God". For this name "*God*" does not convey a looking-back according to a '*being said*' to a Person, but only to a creature. For that reason there is said "*the God of Abraham, Isaac and Jacob*".[6]

7. To the last it must be said, that communicability and incommunicability are not opposed properties, but differ in this manner, as '*to have* a property' and '*to not have (one*' differ).[7] For because *a Person* has a relative property, for that reason He is distinguished and is incommunicable; but because *the Essence* lacks that property, for that reason it is common, and communicable to Many; and for that reason They are not distinguished regarding One another. — *And/or* it can be said, that communicability[8] is not even a distinguishing property among creatures; wherefore, although "*man*" is common, and "*Peter*" proper, yet (this) does not impede, that "*man*" be said (to be) "in *Peter*"; how much more in God (is communicability not a distinguishing property).[9] Moreover, that proposition is understood of properties which separate and distinguish those, in which they are, regarding one another.

SCHOLIUM

I. On the species of predication, cf. d. 30, q. 1, and d. 33, q. 3. — It must be observed, that the first five opposed arguments strive to prove, that in a word that *no* predication is to be admitted among the divine; but the sixth and the seventh exclude only the predication, concerning which the question is. Wherefore, in the *Response* many outstanding things are said concerning predication *in general*, that it is to be admitted among the divine (cf. St. Thomas, SUMMA., I, q. 13, a. 2, 4, and 12); but the solution to the *special* question, indicated in the title (of the question), is only explicitly exhibited in the solution to the 6th objection. The Seraphic Doctor responds in a twofold manner, first denying, that in God "form" is said in a relative manner regarding the informed, second distinguishing (what) it (is) '*to be said relatively*'. If this is understood of a *real* relation, there is certainly not real relation between the Nature and a Hypostasis in God, but only between a

Person and a Person; but if it is understood of a relation *according to a 'being said'*, it can be conceded, that the Nature is a form in respect of a Person, and that by reason of this looking-back this expression can be conceded: "three Persons of one essence", concerning which proposition see Doubt 5 there, and above in d. 3, p II, Doubt 3, and St. Thomas, here in q. 2; SUMMA., I, q. 39, a. 2, and other (authors) commonly. — In regard to the solution to n. 7, cf. above d. 19, p. II, q. 2, in reply to n. 4.

II. Alexander of Hales, SUMMA., p. I, q. 56, m. 7, a. 3. — (Bl. John Duns) Scotus, SENT., Bk. I, d. 4, q. 2; REPORTATIO., here in q. 2, and in d. 4, q. 2. — St. Thomas, SENT., Bk. I, d. 4, q. 2; SUMMA., I, q. 39, a. 6. — Bl. (now St.) Albertus, SENT., Bk. I, d. 4, a. 8. — Peter of Tarentaise, here in q. 2, a. 1 and 2. — Richard of Middleton, here in a. 1, q. 1. — Henry of Ghent, SUMMA., a. 75, q. 2. — Durandus, here in q. 3. — (Bl.) Dionysius the Carthusian, here in q. 1.

---

[1] Edition 1 reads *and there is no composition* [et non est compositio]; codex I has *and this composition is truly not even in God on part of the thing* [et haec vere est in Deo a parte rei non etiam compositio] for *and this truly is in God on part of the thing, and there is a composition* [et haec vere est in Deo a parte rei; et est compositio]. For *and this truly is* [et haec vere est] codices H & T have *and this is true* [et hoc verum est].

[2] Codex T with not a few others & ed. 1 has *that* [quod]. Next, after *the manner* [modus] there is wanting in several codd. & in ed. 1 *of matter* [materiae].

[3] Against the Vatican edition, which here puts *and* [et], we judge, with codd. L O T & X, that there must be read *is* [est], because the verb *is* [est] responds to that other *is* [est] in the following proposition: *such as "a Person is the Substance"*. A little further above this, for *the "same" is according to thing* [idem est re] some codd., such as T & V with ed. 1 read *the "same" according to thing* [idem re]. If one prefers that reading *the "same" according to thing* [idem re], he can supply (after *the "same"*) from the preceding *is predicated* [praedicatur], for the suppressed *is* [est].

[4] For the word *composition* [compositio], which is found in very many codices, the Vatican edition has *predication* [praedicatio]; codices F G P R S U cc ee and ff, with edition 1, have *comparison* [comparatio].

[5] Very many codices have *the response is twofold* [responsio est duplex] for *it must be responded to in a twofold manner* [respondendum est dupliciter]; the Vatican edition has only *I respond* [respondeo]; codex X (codex I in the margin) reads thus: *it must be responded, that "form" is said in a twofold manner: in one manner* etc. [respondendum est, quod forma dicitur dupliciter: uno modo etc.]

[6] Exodus 33:6; Mt. 22:32

[7] Cf. above d. 5, a. 1, q. 1, in reply to n. 1, and d. 19, p. II, q. 2, in reply to n. 4.

[8] Codex bb (T in the margin), together with edition, has *the property of communicability* [proprietas communicabilitatis].

[9] Understand: is communicability not a distinguishing property [communicabilitas non est proprietas distinguens].

QUESTION III

Whether there is a positing of appropriated (names) among the divine?

Third, there is asked, whether among the divine there is a positing of appropriation. And that there is, seems:

1. Because it is through (things) common that one comes unto the understanding of (things) proper, just as it is clear, that through *memory, intelligence,* and *will* one comes unto the cognition of the Trinity; similarly (one comes unto the same) through *unity,* through *truth* and *goodness,* in which consists the reckoning of the vestige;[1] but one does not come from (things) common to (things) proper, unless (those) common are in some manner appropriated: therefore, since it is that one comes in the divine through (things) common to the cognition of (what is) proper, there is appropriation There.

2. Likewise, for this there is the authority of Sacred Scripture, which appropriates common (names) to the Persons, such as "power" to the Father, "wisdom" to the Son, and "goodness" to the Holy Spirit.[2]

But on the Contrary: 1. Just as the proper holds itself to the common, so the common to the proper; but the proper cannot be communicated except to the false: therefore, neither (can) the common be appropriated. Therefore, just as (what is) proper to the Father never comes to be common to others, so neither (does) the common (become) proper.

2. Likewise, if there is appropriation among the divine, either it is according to *thing,* or according to *understanding* [secundum intellectum]: if according to *thing,* but where[3] there is appropriation according to *thing,* something is said through (a consideration of what is) prior of that to which it is appropriated: therefore, among the divine there is a prior and a posterior as much as regard essentials, which is unfitting. If according to *understanding,* but the intellect [intellectus] appropriates to that, with which it judges that (something) more convenes: therefore, since the intellect judges more that wisdom is in the Father, as in One more ancient, (wisdom) ought to be appropriated to Him. But it is appropriated in a contrary manner [in contrarium]: therefore, appropriation is contrary to understanding [contra intellectum]: therefore, it is not attained according to understanding.

3. Likewise, where there is appropriation, a proper (name)[4] is prior according to the reckoning of understanding [secundum rationem intelligendi] to the appropriated (name) — for the reason for the appropriation, is, through (a consideration of what is) prior, in the proper (name) — therefore, since the appropriated (name) is a common (name), according to the reckoning of understanding the proper (name) will be prior to the common one; which is unfitting.

CONCLUSION

Common (names), which to some extent connote the origin of the Persons, have a reckoning of appropriating on the part of the thing; to the extent that they do not connote an origin, they are not appropriable, except perchance for the sake of removing error from our understanding.

I Respond: It must be said, that there is a speaking of appropriated (names) in a twofold manner: either as much as regards *that which they signify,* or as much as regards *the order,* which they connote.

If as much as regards *the signified,* since that is common, and convenes entirely[5] through indifference, it does not happen that (a name) is appropriated according to a reckoning taken up on the part of *the thing* [ex parte rei], yet it is appropriated according to a reckoning on the part of *our understanding* [ex parte intellectus nostri] for the sake of removing error [propter errorem amovendum]. For, since a carnal understanding sees in a carnal father a defect of power, and in a son a defect of wisdom, and in a spirit it understands [intelligit] the fury of wrath; for that reason a spiritual understanding, to raise[6] (the mind) from carnality, attributes "power" to the Father, though it does not befit Him more, but so that it may not be seen to befit (Him) less; and, thus, concerning the others.

But, if we speak as much as regards the *order* and/or origin, which they connote, thus (names) are appropriated on the part of *the Thing* on account of (their) fittingness with the proper (Names) of the Persons. Whence, because the Father is from no One, and the Son from the Father, and the Holy Spirit from Each, an order of this kind is also attained in "power", "wisdom" and "goodness"; for that reason the reason for appropriating (these names) is clear. Whence, those (names), which do not[7] connote in any manner an order and/or origin, are not appropriable.

1. To that, therefore, which is objected, that a proper (name) is not communicated, ergo etc.; it must be said, that it is not similar, because from this, that a common (name) is appropriated, it is not attributed except to That to which it convenes; but, if the proper (name) becomes a common (name), then it is attributed to That with which it does not convene: and for that reason it is not similar.

2. To that which is *asked,* whether there is appropriation according to thing [secundum rem] and/or according to understanding [secundum intellectum];

---

[1] Cf. above d. 3, p. I, q. 2, in reply to n. 4, and q. 4, and Doubt 3, and also p. II, q. 1 ff.

[2] See the text of Master (Peter) here, in ch. 3.

[3] Codex T has *wheresoever* [ubicumque].

[4] Very many codices, together with edition 1, prefix *there* [ibi] before *the proper* [prius].

[5] For *convenes entirely* [omnino conveniat] the Vatican edition alone has *convenes with all the Persons* [omnibus conveniat personis]. Next, for *our understanding* [intellectus nostri] codices R and V have *the understanding only* [intellectus tantum].

[6] Understand: *the mind* [mentem], and/or read with codex Y *so that it may be raised* [ut elevetur] for *to raise (the mind)* [ut elevat]; codex K has *as one elevated* [ut elevatus] in place of the same. A little further above this, for *spirit* [spritu] many codices, together with editions 2 and 3, faultily have *holy spirit* [spiritu sancto]. — The reckoning, which the Seraphic Doctor gives here, is that of Hugo of St. Victor and is found above in the text of Master (Peter), ch. 4.

[7] In not a few codices there is wanting the *do not* [non].

it must be said, that through that (word), which is *"according to"* [secundum], there can be said (to be) an appropriative force or an appropriating principle, and/or that (word), which is *"according to"*, can convey a *reckoning* of appropriating. If in the *first* manner, thus since 'to appropriate' belongs to the virtue of the one cognizing, thus appropriation is according to our understanding. But, if *"according to"* means a *reckoning* of appropriating, thus, in one manner it is according to *thing*, that is, as much as regards the order connoted; in another manner according to *understanding*, as much as regards the signified. Whence, understanding appropriates[1] for the sake of understanding, but not the same understanding for its own sake; but a sane and faithful understanding for the sake of a carnal understanding, not so that it concords with that, but so that it obviates that.

And for that reason since a carnal understanding believes little of the Power in the Father, a spiritual (understanding) appropriates power to Him. Yet (that) understanding is not false, because it does not understand that there is *more* power [plus de potentia] in the Father, but that (it is) *not less* than[2] (it is) in the Son. But if it would appropriate power to the Son, then a carnal understanding would believe that there is more (power) in the Son, and for that reason it would be false; and thus that (objection) is clear.

3. To the last (objection) it must be said, that an appropriated (name), according to that which *it is*, is prior according to a reckoning of understanding to a proper (name); but the appropriated under *this intention*[3] is consequent to the reckoning of the proper; and according to this there is nothing unfitting.

SCHOLIUM

I. *Appropriated* (names, according to the reckoning of what they signify) in God are the « essential » attributes « considered in the Persons » (thus the Seraphic Doctor below in d. 36, a. 1); these always mean a « relation and a thing and signify God as a cause » (ibid.). — A twofold reckoning for making an appropriation is proposed: the one is wholly on the part of our very imperfect understanding, namely, for the sake of removing error; and this proceeds « through the manner of a dissimilitude » (St. Thomas, SUMMA, I, q. 39, a. 7); this reckoning is explained more here in the solution to n. 2. The other is on the part of the thing on account of a certain fittingness to (those which are) proper to the Persons, namely, by reason of the

order, which the attributes connote. — On the various manners of appropriates (names), cf. above d. 31, p. II, a. 1, q. 3, and (its) Scholium.

II. Alexander of Hales, SUMMA,* p. I, q, 67, chiefly m. 3, a. 1. — (Bl. John Duns) Scotus, REPORTATIO., here in. q. 2. — St. Thomas, SENT., Bk. I, d. 31, q. 1, a. 2; SUMMA., I, q. 39, a. 7. — Bl. (now St.) Albertus (Magnus), SENT., Bk. I, d. 31, a. 2, and d. 34, a . 5; SUMMA., p. I, tr. 12, q. 48, m. 1. — (Bl.) Peter of Tarentaise, here in q. 3, a. 1 and 2. — Richard of Middleton, SENT., Bk. I, d. 31, a. 2, qq. 1 and 2. — Giles the Roman, SENT., Bk. I, d. 31, 2nd. princ., q. 1. — Henry of Ghent, SUMMA., a. 72, q. 1 ff... — Durandus (of Saint-Pourçain), SENT., Bk. I, d. 31, q. 3. — (Bl.) Dionysius the Carthusian, SENT., Bk. I, d. 31, qq. 1 and 2.

QUESTION IV

Whether a transferal (of names) is to be posited among the divine?

Fourth, there is asked, whether among the divine there is a positing of a transferal [translatio] (of names). And that there is, seems:

1. Through (St.) Ambrose in the book, ON THE TRINITY:[4] « There are names, which are said of God in a transferred manner [translative] and through a similitude [per similitudinem] ».

2. Likewise, Dionysius (the Areopagite says) in (his) book, ON THE DIVINE NAMES:[5] « Theologians praise God, as One unnamable, out of every name »; but this cannot be except through a transferal (of names): therefore, among the divine, there is a positing of a transferal (of names).

3. Likewise, this seems *by reason*, because Sacred Scripture[6] says, that God grows angry and grieves [dolere]; but this cannot be said properly: therefore it is necessary, that it be said in a transferred manner. But among all (the names), which it happens to name,

grief and wrath are most distant from God: therefore, if it happens to transfer these, (it transfers) all other names too.

4. Likewise, through those through which one happens to understand a thing, one happens also to signify (a thing), and through those through which one happens to signify (a thing), one happens also to name (a thing); but through all created (things) one happens to understand God: therefore, also to name (Him).

BUT ON THE CONTRARY: 1. « All speaking in a transferred manner [transferentes] transfer (names) according to some similitude »;[7] but there is no similitude of God to a creature, since there is a most high distance (between them): ergo etc..

2. Likewise, a similitude is a relation of equiparancy:[8] therefore, if on account of a similitude it happens that the names of creatures are transferred to the Creator, for a equal reason also the other way around. But those are not transferred: therefore, neither these.

---

[1] On the authority of the codices, we have emended the false reading of the Vatican edition and codex cc, which have *an understanding is appropriated* [intellectus appropriatur].

[2] For *but that (it is) not less than* [sed non minus quam] the Vatican edition has *and that (it is) less* [et minus].

[3] Understand: to the extend that it is appropriated or that the appropriated is formally accepted, to which the 'materially accepted' is opposed, that is, that which is appropriated, namely an essential attribute.

[4] Or ON THE FAITH, Bk. II, Prologue, n. 2. See what is noted on this text above, in Master Peter's, d. XXII, chapter I, p. 388, footnote 3.

[5] Chapter 1, § 6.

[6] Gen. 6:6, and Ex. 4:14. — At the beginning of this argument, after *this* [hoc] codices P and Q add *very (thing)* [ipsum], and, near the end, codex T, together with not a few others, substitute *more* [magis] for *most* [maxime].

[7] Aristotle, TOPICS, Bk. VI, ch. 2. Cf. above St. Bonaventure's Foreword to his Commentary, p. 1, footnote 8.

[8] Cf. above d. 17, p. II, a. sole, q. 4, p. 316, footnote 5.° — At the beginning of this argument codex V and edition 1 put *every* [omnia] in place of *a*.

---

* *Trans. note*: Here, in the text of the original Scholium, there was faultily omitted *Summa.*, [S.], and below near the end of the citations, after *Durandus (of Saint-Pourçain)*, [Durand.] there was likewise omitted *Sent.*, *Bk. I*, [I. Sent.].

° For the definition of *equiparancy* see above, d. 19, p. I, a. sole, q. 3, p. 347, footnote 5.

3. Likewise, a similitude is a reason for a transferal (of names):[1] therefore, the names of things more similar to God ought to be transferred to God more; but such are the names of the Angels: therefore, those (more similar) are transferred; (but those less similar are not transferred). — Therefore, one asks, "Which names ought to be transferred, and which (ought) not?"

CONCLUSION

A transferal (of names) is to be posited among the divine for the sake of a twofold reason.

I RESPOND: It must be said, that the reason and/or end for the transferal (of names to the Divine) is twofold: one, I say, is *the praise* of God, the other *the leading* of our intellect *by the hand* [manuductio intellectus nostri]. — For the sake of *the praise* of God a transferal is necessary. For since God is very praiseworthy, lest it would happen that one cease from praise on account of a lack of words, Sacred Scripture teaches, that the names of creatures are to be transferred to God,[2] and this in an indefinite number, so that, just as every creature praises God, so God may be praised out of every name for a creature; and (so that) He who will not be able to be praised with one name, as One superexcelling every name, might be praised out of every name. — The other reason is *the leading* of our intellect *by the hand*. For because we come[3] through creatures to cognize the Creator, and, as (they are) very many, nearly all creatures have noble properties, which are a reason for understanding God, just as the lion (has) fortitude, the lamb meekness, a rock solidity, the serpent prudence, and those completely similar; for that reason it was necessary [oportuit], that many names be transferred to God.

Since, therefore, the end imposes a necessity upon those which regard the end, since there is a transferal as regards the *praise* of God; for that reason names conveying a deformity, such as "devil", "toad", "wolf", ought not be transferred, because they are transferred more for blame [ad vituperium] than for praise. — Again, because the transferal is for the sake of *our instruction*, and a similitude starting from (what is) more known is a way for cognizing; for that reason there is a transferal (of names) from creatures, as from (things) more known, to the Creator, but (this) is not done the other way around [non convertitur]. And because a great similitude is the mother of falsehood,[4] for that reason names (which are) very similar are not transferred, such as are the names for the Angels, lest perhaps an Angel be believed to be God. — From this it is clear, that there is a transferal (of names) among the divine, and as much as regards the multiformity of names, for which reason God is said (to be) *All-Namable* [omninominabilis];[5] and (thus) all (the objections), except the first, are clear.

For because is objected, that there is no similitude, because there is a most high distance; it must be said, that there is no similitude through the participation of one nature (in another), yet there is a similitude according to an analogy and habitude, and this in comparison to (God's) effects. But concerning this, more is had elsewhere.[6]

SCHOLIUM

I. The *transferal* (of a name) is the same as a metaphor (e.g. "at the right hand of God"); it is accepted in general from the properties of all created things, which *by reason of a similitude* are employed to signify divine things. This is explained more above in d. 22, q. 3, where the same, as what is here taught in the body (of the question) is also taught (in reply to n. 2), namely, that names very similar are not aptly transferred to the divine: cf. Dionysius the Areopagite, ON THE CELESTIAL HIERARCHIES, ch. 2; and St. Thomas, SUMMA, q. 1, a. 9, in reply to n. 3.

II. Alexander of Hales, SUMMA., p. I, q. 55, and q. 48, m. 1, 2 and 3, and q. 1, m. 4, a. 5. — St. Thomas, here in q. 3, a. 1 and 2; SUMMA., I, q. 1, a. 2. — Bl. (now St.) Albertus (Magnus), here in a. 6; SUMMA., p. I, tr. 14, qq. 56 and 59. — (Bl.) Peter of Tarentaise, here in q. 4, a. 1 and 2. — Richard of Middleton, here in a. 3, qq. 1 and 2. — Giles the Roman, here in 2nd. princ., q. 1. — Henry of Gent, SUMMA. a. 32, qq. 1 and 2. — Durandus (of Saint-Pourçain), here in q. 4. — (Bl.) Dionysius Carthusian, here in q. 1, at the end, and in d. 22, qq. 2 and 3.

DOUBTS ON THE TEXT OF THE MASTER

DOUBT I

In this part, there are doubts about the text (of Master Peter) and first concerning this which Master (Peter) says: *By the occasion of such a saying the aforesaid heretics* etc.. For it seems, that Master (Peter) judges [reputet] those heretics badly, who use to say, that the Nature is not said of the Persons: Because (St. John) Damascene[7] seems to say the same (thing) which they used to say, when he says: « There is no saying of "the Deity" concerning a Hypostasis »: therefore, since "the Deity" means "the Nature", it is clear that etc..

---

[1] Cf. above d. 3, p. I, a. sole, q. 2, p. 72, footnote 3. — A little below this after *are transferred* [transferuntur] one must supply: « but those (less similar) are not transferred » [sed illa non transferuntur]; which words seem to have fallen out (of the text).

[2] See Dionysius (the Areopagite), ON THE DIVINE NAMES, ch. 1, § 6, where you will find the more principle names which are attributed to God by Sacred Scripture.

[3] Cf. above d. 3, p. I, q. 2.

[4] Aristotle, ELENCHAE, Bk. I, ch. 6 (ch. 7): Deception, indeed, (is) out of a similitude.

[5] See Dionysius, ON THE DIVINE NAMES, ch. 1, § 7. — Then for *all (the objections)* [omnia] edition 1 has *(all) the objections* [obiecta].

[6] Distinction 1, a. 3, q. 1, in reply to n. 1; d. 7, q. 4; d. 25, a. 2, q. 1. Cf. also d. 35, q. 1 and SENT, Bk. II, d. 16, a. 1. q. 1, where

four species of similitude are given, namely, the similitude through a convening in nature: thus in the Trinity one Person is similar to the Other; a similitude through participation in some universal nature: thus a man and a donkey are alike in the animal; a similitude according to proportionality; thus the captain and charioteer are similar to themselves in ruling a vehicle; and a similitude through the convening of order: thus the exemplified is likened to (its) exemplar. — Codex B here adds *that is, above in d. 3, in the second problem* [scilicet supra d. 3. in secundo problemate], that is in d. 3, p. I, q. 2, in reply to n. 3; and a little above this after *it must be said, that* [dicendum quod] the editions, except edition 1, insert *even if* [etsi].

[7] ON THE ORTHODOX FAITH, Bk. III, ch. 11: But the word for divinity we cannot usurp for a Person.

I RESPOND: It must be said, that the word of (St. John) Damascene understood simply, generates a sinister understanding [sinistrum intellectum], and who thus understands (it), as it sounds, would be a heretic. But (St. John) Damascene himself understands (it) with a precision, namely, that "deity" is not only said of a unique Hypostasis, nay of All.

DOUBT II

Likewise, is asked concerning this which (Master Peter) says: *In "the spirit of God" there is sometimes signified the Father, as when there is said: The spirit of the Lord is upon me"* etc.. For he seems to speak badly, because (St.) Jerome says on that passage [ibi] in the Gloss, that it is understood of that spirit, of which there is said in the eleventh (chapter) of Isaias:[1] *the Spirit of the Lord shall rest upon Him* etc.; it is established, that there ("the Spirit of the Lord") is accepted on behalf of the Holy Spirit. Likewise, this seems by another authority, because the other Evangelist, (St.) Luke, says in the eleventh (chapter of his Gospel):[2] *If in the finger of God I cast out demons*, and the Gloss expounds *"finger"* as *"the Holy Spirit"*, which is the Third Person in the Trinity.

I RESPOND: It must be said, that those reasons do not enclose contrarieties,[3] because one Scripture can be expounded in many manners. For in that quote, in which there is said in the sixty-first (chapter) of Isaias: *the Spirit of the Lord is upon me* etc., the mission of the Son is dealt with; and since the Son can be understood (to have) been sent according to (His) *Divine Nature*, and in this manner He is understood, properly speaking, (to have) been sent by the Father only; for that reason *"the Spirit of the Lord"* stands there on behalf of the Father.[4] But if it is understood of the mission according to (His) *human* nature, thus it is understood of the Holy Spirit, insofar as He is the Third Person in the Trinity. — Similarly, it must be understood concerning the following quote (from Isaias), which can be understood in each manner, but yet *"spirit"* is accepted in one manner and in another.

DOUBT III

Likewise, is asked concerning this which (St.) Hilary says, that *in something the nature of Christ and of God differ, so as not to be the same, if it can be presented, that the spirit, which is of God, is not of Christ.* For in this manner he seems to speak badly, because this argument is not valid: 'the Son is the son of the Father and not of the Holy Spirit, therefore, the Nature of the Father and the Holy Spirit differ': therefore since *"spirit"* means a person, that argument, which (St.) Hilary makes, is not valid.[5]

I RESPOND: It can be said, that (St.) Hilary is speaking of *"spirit"*, according to which it names a *nature*; but in this manner his word has nothing to withstand it [non habet instantiam]. — Nevertheless, however, if it is understood of *"a spirit"*, insofar as (this word) is said *in the manner of a Person*, it still has truth. For since the Word cannot be without *"a spirit"*, then the Father and His Word have two "spirits", and thus (as two "spirits") They would not belong to one nature (but to two Persons). — Moreover, if the spirit of the Father were not (that) of the Son, it would not arise from Christ, and if it did not proceed from Him, it would not be distinguished *according to origin* [originaliter],[6] therefore, *according to essence* [essentialiter], but the spirit of God and God are one [unum] essentially: therefore, it would be necessary [oporteret], that *the spirit* and *God* differ essentially or are distinguished from the Son.

DOUBT IV

Likewise, is asked concerning this which Master (Peter) says, that *the word of (St.) Hilary: "A nature is not the same as a thing of the nature", is understood only among creatures.* It seems that that solution is not fitting, because (St.) Hilary speaks of "the spirit of God", insofar as it signifies *the Nature* and *a Thing of the Nature*; which if there is no difference, he ought not have made a distinction [vim facere],[7] as he seems (to have done); which if he urges a distinction in *"spirit"*, insofar as it signifies *"the Nature"* and *"a Thing of the Nature"*, therefore, it seems that a distinction [distinctio] is to be made among (names) of this kind.

I RESPOND: It must be said, that when there is said by (St.) Hilary: "nature is one (thing), a thing of a nature another", either it is understood of an anotherness on the part of *the thing*, just as those heretics used to understand (it); and in this manner (his axiom) has truth only in creatures. In another manner it can mean an anotherness or difference *according to reckoning*; and in this manner it has truth among the divine, and thus (St.) Hilary understands (it), and (thus St.) Augustine says,[8] that « it is one (thing) 'to be the Father', another 'to be God' »: not, I say, one (thing) according to *thing*, but one (thing) according to the reckoning of signifying and understanding and holding itself.

DOUBT V

Likewise, is asked concerning this response of Master (Peter), that there ought not be said, *"a Person of one God"*, because *there is nothing in the Trinity there is created and/or serving and/or subjected.* For he seems to speak badly, because the genitive from its own reckoning does not convey subjection nor a dominion: therefore, (his) reason does not seem sufficient. *If you say*, that this (sufficiency) comes on the part of the *term*; this is nothing, because the term does not of itself convey a looking-back to a lord.

---

[1] Verse 2. — The gloss of (St.) Jerome on this passage is found in (Nicholas) of Lyra's work.

[2] Verse 20. — The gloss is found in (Nicholas) of Lyra's work.

[3] Codex Y and edition 1 have *a contrariety* [contrarietatem]. A little further above this, for *those reasons* [istae] codex V has *those authorities* [illae auctoritates].

[4] Concerning which, see above d. 15, p. I, q. 4.

[5] The argument of (St.) Hilary is this: If it would be true, that the "spirit of God" is not also "the spirit of Christ", then it would follow, that the nature of Christ and God differ.

[6] Cf. above d. 11, q. 1, 4th. arg. of the fundament, & ibid., Scholium, n. V.

— At the end of the solution, on the authority of codex Z, and as required by the context, we have inserted *from the Son* [a Filio], which is lacking in the Vatican edition. — This doubt is also solved by St. Thomas, here on the text.

[7] Understand vim facere in the sense of *have urged that distinction* [urgere istam distinctionem]. — A little before this, after *it signifies* [significat] codex V has *the Nature Itself* [naturam ipsam].

[8] ON THE TRINITY, Bk. VII, ch. 6, n. 11. See also here the text of Master (Peter), ch. 1, at the end, and d. XXXIII, ch. 2. — More is had on this doubt above, in q. 1.

Likewise, there is asked, "For what reason does this name "essence" not convey a superexcellence in the genitive, just as this name "*God*" (does)?"[1] — Likewise, for what reason is there not said: "three Persons of essence", just as (there is said: "three Persons) of one essence"?

I RESPOND: It must be said, that for this, that the genitive be construed truly and properly, it is necessary that some habitude be conveyed either according to *thing*, and/or according to *a manner of understanding*. But the genitive conveys a habitude of a begun to a beginning, and/or vice versa, such as of one possessing to one possessed, and/or of a form to one informed, and/or of one specifying to one specified. But it does not convey the habitude of *a form* except with an abstract term, because[2] (an abstract term) signifies through the manner of a form; and since a form holds itself through the manner of one expressing and of a declaration: for that reason such a construction is not attained except with the genitive of an abstract noun in a determinate manner. Whence there is fittingly said: "*a woman of egregious form*", but there is never said: "*a woman of form*". For that reason there is rightly said: "three Persons of one essence", but not: "three Persons of essence".[3] — But "*God*" is not an abstract noun, for that reason it is not constructed with the genitive, except either in the habitude of a *subject*, as "the form of God", and/or in the habitude of *one specifying*, as "a Person of God", just as (there is said): "a creature of salt"; and/or in the habitude of a *principle*, as "a creature of God". And since, when there is said: "three Persons of one God", none of the habitudes is conveyed properly except the habitude of a *principle* or of *one possessing*; hence it is, that since in that sense the expression is false, it is not to be received. — Another reason is this, because an expression, which is in the force of a declaration of an essence, is convertible, so that, when there is said: "a woman of egregious form", there can be said: "the egregious form of a woman". Therefore, if there would be said: "three Persons of the one God", there would (also) be said: "one God of three Persons"; and that understanding is not sane, as it is seen: for it can be said in this manner, just as there is said: "one God of three men".[4]

DOUBT VI

Likewise, is asked concerning this which (Master Peter) says, that *in those three consists the Most High Good*, namely Power, Wisdom, Goodness. It seems that he speaks badly, because "*the Most High Good*" specifies "*the Good*": therefore, if "goodness" is distinguished against "power" and "wisdom", for an equal

reason "*the Most High Good*" (is similarly distinguished). Likewise, It does not seem to be in these three, because the Most High Good is the aggregative and collective of *all* goods:[5] therefore, not only of those three.

I RESPOND: It must be said, that "*the good*" is distinguished in one manner against "*power*" and "*wisdom*", in another manner (it is) not. For if it is accepted on behalf of the goodness of morals, thus it consists in the will and is distinguished against the other two. But if "*the good*" is accepted commonly, thus it comprises all. For there is the good *of nature*, and this regards power; and the good *of grace*, and this either perfects the intellect, and thus is *science*, or the affection, and thus (is) *goodness*; and *the good* comprises these three in its own universality, and *the Most High (Good)* in its own integrity. Therefore, since every good is reducible to these (three), for that reason the Most High Good consists in these three.

DOUBT VII

Likewise, is asked concerning this which (Hugo of St. Victor) says, that *Scripture appropriates "power" to the Father, lest He seem less powerful*. It seems that this, *that He (be) less powerful*, ought to be said more of the Son, since He has suffered and has died: therefore, "power" ought to have been appropriated to Him more.

I RESPOND: It must be said, that, because on account of the Passion He seemed to have done (something) foolish and not to have had power [habuisse impotentiam] — on account of which the preaching of the Cross was to the Jews a scandal and to the Greeks foolishness[6] — for that reason the very Apostle, the egregious Doctor, not only appropriates "*wisdom*" to Christ, nay also "*virtue*", to exclude infirmity in this manner from the Divinity: and he preferred to appropriate "*virtue*" to Him than "*power*", because "*virtue*" means a final power and the sum of power, just as the Philosopher would have it,[7] that « virtues is the end of power »; for that reason he preferred to appropriate "virtue" to Him. Nor is it unfitting that the same be appropriated out of diverse considerations now to One, now to Another, since it equally convenes with the Three. Whence *to the Father* we attribute power, lest He seem impotent on account of (His) antiquity: *to the Son* virtue, lest He seem not (to be) powerful or (to be) debilitated on account of the assumed infirmity. Nevertheless, however, a distinction is to be made [facienda est vis] between "*power*" and "*virtue*", just as has been said in the Thirty-Second Distinction.[8]

---

[1] The sense of the objection is (this): Since in that expression, according to Master (Peter), there is implied in the genitive "*of God*" a superexcellence in respect of the nominative "*three Persons*", who are considered as *Ones serving* and/or *subject*, it seems that the genitive "*of essence*" also conveys the same.

[2] Accept quod here as *because (an abstract term)* [quia]; we prefer reading *which (term)* [qui] for *because* [quia]. A little further above this, for *as of one possessing* [ut possidentis] codices L and O, together with edition 1, have *and/or of one possessing* [vel possidentis]. A little further below this, for *of a declaration* [declarationis] codex T, together with edition 1, has *of one declaring* [declarantis], codices L and O *of one determining* [determinantis]; very many others have *through the manner and declaration of one expressing* [per modum exprimendi et declarationem] for *through the manner of one expressing and of declaration* [per modum exprimendi et declarationis].

[3] In the Vatican edition there are wanting the words *but not: "three Persons of essence"* [non autem: tres personae essentiae], and a little below this, after *the genitive* [genitivo], the words *except either* [nisi vel].

[4] Cf. above q. 2, in reply to n. 6. — On the meaning of the genitive, see above d. 3, p. II, Doubt 3; d. 11, Doubt 3, and d. 25, Doubt 2.

[5] Wherefore, (St. Severinus) Boethius, in ON THE CONSOLATION OF PHILOSOPHY, Bk. III, prose 2, thus defines the beatitude, which is the supreme good: the state perfected by the congregation of all goods.

[6] 1 Corinthians 1:23: *But we preach Christ crucified, to the Jews indeed a scandal, but to the Gentiles foolishness, but to those called, Jews and Greeks, Christ the Virtue of God and the Wisdom of God* [Nos autem praedicamus Christum crucifixum, Iudaeis quidem scandalum, gentibus autem stultitiam, ipsis autem vocatis Iudaeis atque Graecis Christum Dei virtutem et Dei sapientiam].

[7] ON HEAVEN AND THE WORLD, Bk. I, text 116 (ch. 11), concerning which, see above d. 32, a. 2, q. 2, p. 564, footnote 7.

[8] Article 2, q. 2, reply to the last objection. Cf. also here in q. 3. — A little before this for *infirmity* [infirmitatem] the Vatican edition has *humanity* [humanitatem]. — The words facienda est vis etc. have the sense of: *one must distinguish, by accepting each word in its strict sense.*

DISTINCTION XXXV

CHAPTER I

On God's knowledge, foreknowledge, providence, disposition and predestination.

And, since above[1] we have spoken in an orderly manner and said several (things) concerning those (names) which are said commonly of God according to substance, yet certain of these demand [efflagitant] a special treatment; concerning which there is now [amodo] to be a treatment, that is, concerning (God's) *Knowledge* [scientia], *Foreknowledge* [praescientia], *Providence, Disposition, Predestination, Will* and *Power*. — Therefore, it must be known, that God's Wisdom and/or Knowledge, since it is one and simple, yet, on account of the various states of things and (its) diverse effects, is allotted [sortitur] many and diverse names. For it is not only said (to be) a "knowledge", but also a "foreknowledge" and/or "disposition", a "predestination" and[2] a "providence".

CHAPTER II

What does (His) foreknowledge and/or foresight concern?[3]

And (His) *foreknowledge* or *foresight* [praevidentia] only concerns (things) futures, and indeed [sed] all, namely, the good and the evil.

CHAPTER III

What (does His) disposition concern?

However, (His) *disposition* concerns (the things) to be done.

CHAPTER IV

What (does His) predestination concern?

(His) *predestination* concerns the men[4] (who are) to be saved and the good, which are both freed here and are crowned in the future. For God from eternity has predested men to good (things) by electing (them), and He has predested good (things) for them, by preparing (them). That He has predested men, the Apostle[5] shows, saying: *He has predestined those whom He foreknew to be conformed to the image of His Son.* And in another place: *He has elected us before the foundation* [constitutionem] *of the world, to be holy and immaculate.* Moreover, that He has prepared good (things) for them, the prophet Isaias shows, saying: *Eye has not seen, o God without Thee, what Thou has prepared for (those who) love and/or*

wait for [exspectantibus] *Thee.* Therefore, from eternity He has predestined certain ones to be good and blessed, that is, He has elected, that they be good and blessed, and He has predestined, that is, He has prepared, good (things) for them.

CHAPTER V

What (does His) Providence concern?

Moreover, (His) *Providence* is of (those) to be governed, which (Providence) seems to accepted in the same manner, in which (His) *disposition* (is). However, sometimes (His) Providence is accepted for (His) Foreknowledge.

CHAPTER VI

What (does His) Wisdom and/or Knowledge concern?

However, (His) *Wisdom* and/or Knowledge concerns all, namely, the good and the evil, and (things) present, past and future, and not only (things) temporal, but also eternal. For God does not thus know these temporal (things) of ours, as one (who) knows not Himself, but He Himself alone perfectly knows Himself, in comparison to which knowledge the knowledge of every creature is imperfect.

CHAPTER VII

Whether foreknowledge and/or disposition could belong to God, if there were no future (things)?

Here, it is necessary [oportet] that one consider, whether there could be knowledge, and/or foreknowledge, and/or disposition, and/or predestination in God, if there would have been no future (things). For since foreknowledge is of (things) future, and disposition of (things) to be done, and predestination of (those) to be saved, if there were no future (things), if God was going to make nothing, and/or save none, it does not seem that there could be in God a foreknowledge, and/or disposition, and/or predestination; moreover, God could foreknow no future (things), could not create anything, and/or save anyone: therefore, there could not be in God a foreknowledge, and/or disposition, and/or predestination. — But to this, there is objected by certain (authors): "If," they say, "God's Foreknowledge could not be in God from eternity, it also could not be; but if it could not be, since God's Foreknowledge is His Knowledge,

---

[1] In Distinctions VIII, XIX, XXII, and XXX.

[2] The Vatican edition and edd. 4 and 6, omit *a "foresight", and/or "disposition", a "predestination" and* [praevidentia, dispositio, praedestinatio et], contrary to all the codices and to edition 1 and the other editions, which however, differ to some extent among themselves.

[3] Thus codd. A B & D, the others, with very many edd., read better *providence* [providentia] for *foresight* [praevidentia]. In the chapter itself very many edd. falsely have *not only concerns (things) future, but* [non de futuris tantum, sed] for *only concerns (things) future, and indeed* [de futuris tantum, sed].

[4] Thus codd. A B D & E and edd. 1 & 6; cod. C and the other edd.

have *all* [omnibus] for *the men* [hominibus]. Not that the Angels are to be excluded, but because Master (Peter) speaks explicitly in the following (passages) only of men. Immediately after this, the Vatican edition, with very many editions, repeats *all* [omnibus] before *the good* [bonis].

[5] Romans 8:29. The Vulgate reads: *For those whom He has foreknown, He has also predestined to become conformed to the image of His own Son* [Nam quos praescivit, et praedestinavit conformes fieri imaginis Filii sui]. — The other passage is Eph. 1:4, where the Vulgate has *in Him* [in ipso] after *us* [nos]; the third passage is conflated from Isaias 64:4 and 1 Cor. 2:9.

and (His) Knowledge is His Essence: therefore, that which is the Divine Essence could not be from eternity." Thus also do they object concerning (His) disposition and predestination, which is the Divine Essence. They also add even other (arguments), saying thus: "If God was able to not foreknown some (things), since it is the same for God '*to foreknow*' as '*to know*', and '*to know*' and '*to be*'; therefore, He was able not to be. Likewise, since it is the same for God[1] '*to be foreknowing*' and '*to be God*', if He was able to not be foreknowing, He was able to not be God; moreover, He could not be foreknowing, if He could foreknow nothing [nulla]; but He could foreknow nothing, because He could make nothing."

To this, in accord with the small measure of our intelligence, we thus say: "Foreknowledge", and/or "disposition", and/or "predestination" seem to be said *regarding something*. For just as "*creator*" is said relatively regarding the creature, so "foreknowledge" and/or "foreknowing" seems to be referred to (things) future, and "disposition" to (things) to be done, and "predestination" to (things) to be saved. Nevertheless, "*creator*" is said in a relative manner thus, that it does not signify the Essence. However, "foreknowledge" and/or "foreknowing" is also said in respect of (things) future, and designates the Essence; thus also "disposition" and "predestination". And for that reason when there is said: "if there were no future (things), there would not be foreknowledge in God, and/or God would not be foreknowing", because the cause for saying that varies [vaira est ibi], it is necessary [oportet] that one distinguish the reason for the saying. Therefore, when you say: "if there were no future (things), there would not be foreknowledge in God, and/or He[2] would not be foreknowing", if in saying this you attend to the cause, namely, because there would be no subjects of His Foreknowledge, of which there could be said (to be) a foreknowledge, and/or (that) He Himself (is) foreknowing, because each is said on account of (things) future; the understanding is true. But if, however, [Sin] for this reason you say this, "that there is not in Him a knowledge, by which He foreknows (things) future, and/or which is not God Himself, who is foreknowing of (things) future", the understanding is false. These expressions are also to be similarly determined: "God's Foreknowledge could not be", and/or "He could not be foreknowing", and "God could not foreknow anything"; that is, it could be, that there would be no future subjects of His Knowledge, and thus He could be said (to be) not "*foreknowing*" and/or (not) "*to foreknow*", and/or His Knowledge (could be said not to be) a "*foreknowledge*"; yet, not for this would He and/or His Knowledge been less, but He could be said (to be) not "*foreknowing*" and/or (not) "*to foreknow*" and/or (not to have) a "*foreknowledge*", if there were to be no future subjects of His Knowledge. Similarly, concerning (His) disposition and predestination and/or Providence. For these, as has been said, are referred to (things) temporal and only concern (things) temporal.

Chapter VIII

That God's Knowledge concerns (things) temporal and eternal.

However, (God's) *Knowledge* and/or Wisdom concern not only (things) temporal, but also (things) eternal; and for that reason, even if there were no future (things), yet there would be in God the same knowledge, which there is now, nor would it be less than now, nor is it greater than it would be.[3] Therefore, God from eternity knew eternity and everything which was going to be, and He knew (both) immutably. He also knows (things) past and/or future no less than (things) present, and by His eternal and immutable wisdom He Himself knows all which are known. « For every reckoning of supernal and terrestrial wisdom », as (St.) Ambrose[4] says, « is in Him, because He grasps by His own immense wisdom every wisdom ».

Chapter IX

In what manner are all said to be "in God" and (to be) "life in Him"?

On which account,[5] all are said to be and to have been "in God" from eternity. Whence (St.) Augustine (says) ON GENESIS:[6] « These visibles », he says, « before they came to be, were not. In what manner, therefore, were they, which were not, known to God? And again: In what manner did He make them, which were not known to Him? for He did nothing as one ignorant. Therefore, He made (them) known, He did not cognize (what had) been made. Consequently, [Proinde], before they came to be, they both were and were not: they were in God's Knowledge, they were not in their own nature. Moreover, regarding God Himself I do not dare to say that they were known in another manner, when He made them, than that, in which He had know them, to make (them), *with Whom there is no transmutation, nor overshadowing of alteration* ». — Behold, here you have, that these visibles, before they came to be, were in the knowledge of God. In this sense, therefore, all are said to be "in God", and everything which *had been made* is said[7] to be "*life in Him*": not for this reason, that the creature is the Creator, and/or that those temporal (things) are essentially in God, but because they are always in His knowledge, which is Life.

Hence it is, too, that all are said to be present to Him, not only those which are, but also those which have passed away, and those which are to be, according to that (verse): *Who calls those which are not, as those which are*: « because », as (St.) Ambrose says in (his) book, ON THE TRINITY,[9] « He cognizes thus those which are not, as those which are ». And, for this reason, all are said to be in Him and/or with Him or present to Him. Whence (St.) Augustine (says) on that passage of the Psalm:[10] « *And the beauty of the field is with Me*, He says "it is with Me" for this reason, that with God nothing passes away, nothing is to be. With Him are all future (things), and from Him past (things) do not detract. With Him are all by a certain, ineffable cognition of God's wisdom ». — Behold here (St.) Augustine reveals [aperit], out of what understanding words of this kind are to be accepted. "all are present in God", "in God are all (things)", and/or "with God [cum Deo vel apud Deum] and/or in Him (is) life"; because the ineffable cognition of all (things) is in Him.

---

[1] The Vatican edition, together with very many editions, has *that God is foreknowing and that God is* [Deum praescium esse et Deum esse] in place of *for God 'to be foreknowing' and 'to be God'* [Deo praescium esse et Deum esse], contrary to the codices and edition 1.

[2] Codex D has *God* [Deus] for *He*, and, a little below this, the same, together with codices A and E, and edition 1, has *for this reason* [ex ea ratione] in place of *for this reason* [ea ratione].

[3] Thus rightly codices C and D, with all the editions; codex A has *nor would it be greater than now* [nec maior esset quam modo], codices B and E have *or greater than now* [nec maior quam modo].

[4] ON THE EPISTLE OF ST. PAUL TO THE COLOSSIANS, 2:3; with not a few (words) changed. In which text, trusting in codd. A B D & E, ed. 1 and the original, we have restored *terrestrial* [terrenae] for *aeternal* [aeternae].

[5] Codices A C and E have *Moreover* [Praeterea] for *On which account* [Propterea].

[6] Book V, ch. 18, n. 36. — The passage from Sacred Scripture is James 1:17.

[7] John 1:3-4, according to the ancient reading: *what has been made, in Him was life* [quod factum est, in ipso vita erat].

[8] Romans 4:17.

[9] That is, ON THE FAITH TO GRATIAN, Bk. V, ch. 16, n. 198.

[10] Psalm 49:11; (St.) Augustine on this Psalm, n. 18, with not a few (words) omitted and/or changed by Master (Peter).

COMMENTARY ON DISTINCTION XXXV

On God's Knowledge in general, according to Itself.

And, since above we have spoken in an orderly manner and said several (things) etc..

THE DIVISION OF THE TEXT

Above, Master (Peter) dealt with the sacrament of the Trinity and Unity; in this part, he deals with the conditions, according to which there is in God a reckoning of causality, which are, that is, *power, wisdom* and *will*. Moreover, this part has three parts. In the first of which, he deals with (God's) knowledge; in the second with (His) power, below in the Forty-Second Distinction, (where he says): *Now the omnipotence of God must be dealt with*; in the third with (God's) Will, below in the Forty-Fifth Distinction: *Now something must be said concerning God's Will* etc..

The first part has three (parts).[1] In the first, he deals with (God's) knowledge in general, *according to itself*. In the second, he deals with *the manners* of the divine cognition, whether God cognizes mutably and/or immutably, and in what manner, in the Thirty-Eighth Distinction, (where he says): *Now, therefore, returning to the proposed* etc.. In the third, however, he speaks [agit] as much as regards the special *effects* (of God's knowledge), below in the Fortieth Distinction, (where he says): *However, predestination concerns salutary goods* etc..

The first part is divided into three (parts). In the first, Master (Peter) makes a determination [determinat] concerning the knowledge of God itself. In the second, because things are acknowledge in the one knowing through the manner of the one knowing, he determines, in what manner things are in God, below in the Thirty-Sixth Distinction, (where he says): *Here one is accustomed to ask, since all are said to be in God's cognition* etc.. But, in the third, he incidentally determines, in what manner God is in things, below in the Thirty-Seventh Distinction, (where he says): *And since it has been demonstrated in part* etc..

The first part, which contains the present Distinction, has three (parts).[2] In the *first*, since God's Knowledge is one, he determines, in what manner it obtains many names. In the *second*, since God's Knowledge and/or Foreknowledge is eternal, he determines, in what manner it holds itself to temporal and/or created things, there (where he says): *Here it is necessary that one consider, whether there could be knowledge and/or foreknowledge* etc.. In the *third*, since God's Knowledge is a being, in what manner He cognizes non beings [non entia], there (where he says): *On which account all are said to be and to have been "in God"* etc..

In the *first* part, continuing with what he has been saying [se ipsum continans], he says, that the Divine Essence has many names on account of those which it connotes [propter connotata].[3] In the *second*, he says, that God would have knowledge, if nothing were going to be, and (that) it would be a knowledge, but would not be said (to be) a foreknowledge. In the *third*, he shows, that all things[4] have their reasons in God, through which they are cognized and are in Him, and thus all are present to Him; and in this manner the division and the sentence (of Master Peter) is clear. For[5] the subdivisions of the parts are manifest in the text.

TREATMENT OF THE QUESTIONS

For an understanding of the present Distinction there is the question [quaeritur] concerning the reckoning of the Divine Cognition, which is accustomed to be named an "*idea*".

First, there is asked, whether in God there is to be posited the reckoning of an idea [ratio idealis].

Second, granted that there is, there is asked, whether it has a plurality according to thing.

Third, whether it has a plurality according to reckoning.

Fourth, whether it has a plurality according to the number of universals, or (according to the number) of singulars.

Fifth, whether it has a plurality according to a finite and/or infinite number.

Sixth, whether among ideas there is a plurality according to an ordered and/or 7confused number.

---

[1] Codex I subjoins *parts* [partes].
[2] The Vatican edition adds *parts* [partes].
[3] The Vatican edition has *on account of (its) connoted names* [propter nomina connotata], with out the support of the codices.

[4] For *all things* [omnes res], which reading we have restored from codices P and Q, all the other codices, together with edition 1, substitute only *all (things)* [omnes], the Vatican *all (beings)* [omnia].
[5] Codex V has *But* [autem].

ARTICLE SOLE

On ideas.

QUESTION I

Whether in God there are to be posited ideas?

Therefore, as much as regards the first there is asked, whether there is in God a positing of ideas. And that there is, is shown:

1. First by the authority of (St.) Augustine in the book, OF EIGHTY-THREE QUESTIONS:[1] « Ideas are eternal and incommutable forms, which are contained in the Divine Intelligence ». From these three conditions one concludes, that there is an idea is in God.

2. Likewise, it is shown *by reason* in this manner: everything acting in a rational manner,[2] not by chance, and/or out of necessity, cognizes a thing before it is; but everyone cognizing has the thing cognized, either according to truth, and/or according to a similitude; but things, before they are, cannot be had by God according to truth: therefore, according to a similitude. But the similitude of a thing, through which a thing *is cognized* and *produced*, is an idea: ergo etc..

3. Likewise, everything which leads in a determinate manner unto the cognizing of the other, has within itself a similitude of the (thing) cognized, and/or is itself a similitude of it; but the Eternal Mirror leads the minds seeing It into the cognition of all created (things), just as (St.) Augustine says,[3] that they more rightly cognize There than elsewhere: therefore, it remains, that in Him reside the similitudes (of things). And it is established, that they are in Him as in One cognizing, because He not only represents (them) to others, but to Himself; but this is the whole reckoning of an idea: ergo etc..

4. Likewise, because things are produces by God, for that reason they are in God as in *One working* [in efficiente], and God is most truly efficient; similarly, because *they are finished* by Him, for that reason He is most truly (their)[4] End: therefore, for an equal reason, because *they are cognized* and *expressed* by Him, God is through Himself (their) *Exemplar*. But an exemplar is not, but (that) in which are the exemplified ideas of things: ergo etc..

ON THE CONTRARY: 1. Dionysius (the Areopagite says), ON THE DIVINE NAMES:[5] « The Divine Intellect does cognize, but out of Itself, and through Itself, not directing [immittens] Itself according to an idea unto singulars [singulis], but knowing and containing all according to one cause of excellence »: therefore, God does not know singulars through an idea.

2. Likewise, it seems *by reason*: because "idea" means the reckoning of a similitude, and a "similitude" means the reckoning of a convening; but there[6] is no convening of God to the creature, since there is a most high distance, or if there is (a convening), it is the smallest: therefore, either (there is) no similitude, or the smallest. Therefore, either there is no idea in God, or if there is, it is according to an imperfect reckoning; but nothing imperfect is to be posited in God: ergo etc..

3. Likewise, the most noble manner of cognition is to be attributed to God; but cognition through the essence of a thing is more noble than through the similitude of a thing: therefore, God cognizes through the essence of the thing, not through a similitude. But an idea is a similitude, not the essence of the thing: and thus etc..

4. Likewise, an idea is not necessary except for directing (one) in cognizing and regulating (one) in working;[7] but nothing needs one directing and/or regulating, except that which can err and/or deviate. But God has nothing of these: therefore, in vain [frustra] are ideas posited in God.

---

[1] Question 46, n. 2, in which passage th e text of the original exhibits *principal* [principales] for *eternal* [aeternae].

[2] In codices aa and bb there is here inserted *either out of design or out of will* [vel ex proposito sive ex voluntate], and then after *a thing before* [rem antequam] there is added *it is made, but God is acting in a most rational manner, not by chance and/or by necessity, therefore, He cognizes a thing, before it is made or* [rem antequam additur fiat, sed Deus est agens rationabilissime, non a casu vel ex necessitate, ergo cognoscit rem, antequam fiat vel]. — On this major proposition, cf. Aristotle, METAPHYSICS, Bk. I, ch. 1, where there is taught, that those acting through understanding, who do not know the reason for their work, do not act, but make, just as fire burns; and PHYSICS, Bk. II, text 39 ff. (ch. 5), and METAPHYSICS, Bk VI, ch. 7 (Bk. X, ch. 8), where *fortune*, which is other than choosing and understanding, is distinguished through opposition to a per se cause. On the first *minor*, see above d. 3, p. I, q. 1. You will find a summary of this argument in (St.) Augustine, RETRACTATIONS, Bk. I, ch. 3, n. 2; and ON THE CITY OF GOD, Bk XI, ch. 10, n. 3; and also in (St.) Anselm, MONOLOGION, ch. 9.

[3] ON THE CITY OF GOD, Bk. XI, ch. 29. — Immediately after this codices D P T and Z, together with edition 1, have *they (i.e. things) are more rightly cognized There* [rectius ibi cognoscuntur] for *they (i.e. minds) more rightly cognize There* [rectius ibi cognoscunt].

[4] Codex Q prefixes *their* [earum] to *End* [finis]. — On this argument, cf. Dionysius (the Areopagite), ON THE DIVINE NAMES, ch. 5, and the Scholium of St. Maximus (in Migne's edition) on this passage.

[5] Chapter 7, § 2. In the text itself the Vatican edition here and below in the solution to this objection substitutes *leaning ... upon* [innitens] for *directing Itself ... unto* [se immittens]. Our reading, which is also had in Scotus Erigena, is favored by many codices, which exhibit the *directing unto* [immittens], but which omit the word *Itself* [se].

[6] The Vatican edition and codex cc here add explicitly *there* [ibi].

[7] A reference to (Lucius Annaeus) Seneca's definition of idea, which is had in (his) Epistle n. 65 to Lucilius: An idea is an exemplar, looking back to which a craftsman effects that which he destined (to do). In the same place this Platonic definition of the idea is found: An idea is the eternal exemplar of those which are made naturally. — For a confirmation of this argument there is commonly cited Aristotle, METAPHYSICS, Bk. I, text 31 (ch. 9): However, to say that they are exemplary (forms) is idle talk and to speak poetic metaphors. For what is it, that one does, looking upon ideas? — A little further below this, for *and/or deviate* [vel deviare] the Vatican edition and codex cc have *and deviate* [et deviare].

CONCLUSION

God cognizes through ideas and has in Himself the reasons for and similitudes of the things, which He cognizes.

I RESPOND: It must be said, that about this there was a twofold opinion.[1]

For certain (authors) said, that God does not cognize according to the reckoning of an *idea*, but according to the reckoning of a *cause*. And they posit (this) simile: 'just as if a point cognized its own virtue, it would cognize lines and circumferences; similarly, if a unity had a cognitive power, through which it could turn itself upon itself, it would cognize all numbers'. For since God has the virtue of producing all and cognizes the whole of His own virtue, for that reason He cognizes all. And this they say, Dionysius (the Areopagite) thought, when he says, that « He cognizes all not according to an idea, but according to one cause of excellence ». — But this position cannot stand. First indeed, because God does not cognize through the conference of that which reaches [collationem deveniendi] from a beginning to a begun, but by a simple gaze [simplici aspectu]. And *again*, everything cognizing, inasmuch as (it is) of this kind, is similar to the cognizable: therefore[2] (God too) has His similitude, and/or is Himself a similitude. *Again*, everyone cognizing produces distinctly for this reason, because he cognizes distinctly, and not the other way around: therefore, a reckoning of *producing* is not a reckoning of *cognizing*. And *again*, He cognizes some (things), which are not from Him.[3] On account of these (considerations) and (those) similar, one must speak in another manner.

For that reason there is another position, both according to the Saints, and according to philosophers, that God cognizes through *ideas* and has in Himself the reasons for and similitudes of the things, which He cognizes, in which not only does He Himself cognize (things), but also those looking upon Him: and these reasons (St.) Augustine calls "ideas" and "primordial causes".[4]

For an understanding, however, of the objections, it must be understood, that an idea is said (to be) "the similitude of the thing cognized". But "similitude" is said in a twofold manner: in one manner according to the convening of two in a third, and this is the similitude according to *univocation*; in another there is the similitude, according to which one is said[5] (to be) "*the similitude of the other*"; and this similitude does not concern a convening in something *common*, because the similitude is by itself similar, not in a third; and in this manner the creature is said (to be) "the similitude of God", and/or conversely God (is said to be) "the Similitude of the creature". Taking similitude in this manner, a similitude is the reason for cognizing, and this (similitude) is said (to be) an "idea". — But it is in us in one manner, in God in another. Indeed, in us the reason for cognizing is a *similitude*, the cognized is *a truth*. For in us the similitude has been accepted and impressed by (something) extrinsic, on this account, that our intellect, in respect of the cognized, is possible and not a pure act; for that reason it comes to be in act through something of the cognized, which is its similitude.[6] But in God it is the other way around, because the reason for cognizing is *the Truth Itself*, and the cognized is *a similitude of the Truth*, that is, a creature itself. And because the reason for cognizing consists in the First Truth Itself,[7] for that reason the reason for cognizing in God is *most highly expressive*. And since every that which expresses most highly, assimilates most perfectly the cognized by an assimilation suitable to [competente] (its) cognition, for that reason it is clear, that *the Truth Itself* from this, that It causes the act of cognizing [cognoscere], is *an expressive[8] similitude and an idea*. It is the other way around in us, because by this very (thing), that it is a *similitude*, it causes the act of cognizing. And from these the objections are clear.

1. For what is objected, that (the Divine Intellect cognizes)[9] not directing Itself according to an idea unto singulars; it must be said, that Dionysius from this does not want to remove the reckoning of an idea from God, but wants to say, that (in the Divine Intellect) there is not in this manner a multitude and difference of ideas according to singulars, as (there is) in us.

2. To that which is objected, that there is no convening, and/or (it is) the least; it must be said, that there is a similitude of *univocation* or of participation, and a similitude of *imitation*, and (a similitude) of *expression*. There is entirely no similitude of *participation*, because nothing is common (to God and a creature).[10] There is a limited [modica] similitude of *imitation*, because in a limited manner (something) finite can imitate (something) infinite, wherefore there is always a greater dissimilitude than a similitude. But there is a most high similitude of *expression*, because (this convening) is caused by the intention of a truth, which, as has been seen, is itself an expression (of the First Truth); for that reason God cognizes all most highly.

---

[1] In codex Y there is here added. *since according to (its) etymology an "idea" is said from "eidos"* (εἶδος), *which is a form; but "form" is said in a threefold manner: either that by which a thing is formed, such as the form of a agent, from which the formation of the effect proceeds; or that through which something is informed, as the soul is the natural form of a man; or that according to which something is formed, and this is the exemplary form, according to the imitation of which something is produced. And in this third manner a form is said (to be) an "idea", and concerning this certain (authors) indeed said* etc.. [quoniam secundum etymologiam idea dicitur ab ydos, quod est forma; forma autem dicitur tripliciter: aut a qua res formatur, ut forma agentis, a qua procedit formatio effectus; aut per quam aliquid informatur, ut anima est forma naturalis hominis; aut ad quam aliquid formatur, et haec est forma exemplaris, ad cuius imitationem aliquid producitur. Et hoc tertio modo dicitur forma idea, et de hac quidam dixerunt etc.]

[2] Supply: *God too* [et Deus]. — Next, the Vatican ed., with nearly all the codd. contradicting this, reads *it is* [ipsum est] for *is Himself* [ipse est]. Then, cod. Z reads *His similitude* [similitude eius] for *a similitude* [similitudo].

[3] In cod. O there is added *such as the evils of fault* [ut mala culpae].

[4] Concerning ideas, cf. above 1st. argument of the fundament and ff.; concerning primordial causes, cf. (Augustine's) ON THE LITERAL EXPOSITION OF GENESIS, Bk. V. ch. 4, n. 10, and Bk. VI. ch. 145, n. 25, and Bk. IX, ch. 17, n. 32 ff. — You will find an explanation of (St.) Augustine's doctrine in (St.) Bonaventure, SENT., Bk. II, d. 18, a. 1, q. 2.

[5] For *is said (to be)* [dicitur] the Vatican ed. with codex cc has *is* [est]. A little below this, before *third* [tertio] the Vatican ed. alone has *to a* for *in a* [in]. — On this twofold sense of "similitude", cf. d. 34, a. sole, q. 4, p. 594, footnote 6.

[6] Supply: whence the immediate *reckoning of cognizing* is not the cognized object (i.e. a truth), but a similitude of it. — In the following proposition *the other way around* [e converso] it to be accepted as *contrariwise* [e contrario], which is also extant in edition 1.

[7] The older codices, together with edition 1, have *first in the Truth Itself* [in ipsa veritate primo] for *in the First Truth Itself* [in ipsa veritate prima]. Next for *assimilates ... the cognized* [assimilat cognitum] codex bb has *is assimilated ... to the cognized* [assimilatur cognito], and then for *suitable to (its) cognition* [competente cognitioni] very many codices, together with edition 1, have less clearly *to a suitable cognition* [competenti cognitioni].

[8] Codex Z has *most expressed* [expressissima]. A little below this after *it causes* [facit] it reads *one to cognize the truth, which is outside; but it was contrariwise in God, because in Him the truth, which is below, causes Him to cognize a similitude, which is outside* [veritatem, quae est extra; e contrario autem erat in Deo, quia in ipso veritas, quae est infra, facit cognoscere similitudinem, quae est extra]. Then before *the objections* [obiecta] codex S adds *all* [omnia].

[9] The Vatican edition here subjoins *is* [est], in place of which it would be much better to substitute: *the Divine Intellect cognizes* [cognoscit intellectus divinus]. A little further below this, the same Vatican edition, favored by not a few codices, changes *a multitude* [multitudo] into *a similitude* [similitudo].

[10] Supply together with codex X *namely to God and a creature* [scilicet Deo et creaturae].

3. To that which is objected third, that cognition through an essence is more noble; it must be said, that there is a similitude *caused by the truth* of a thing outside, and concerning this it is true, that it thus never perfectly expresses the thing, just as the thing itself (would be), if it were by being present [praesentialiter][1] in the soul; and by this similitude God does not cognize. There is another similitude, which is the very *expressive truth* of the cognized and (is) a *similitude* by this, by which (it is) *a truth*; and this similitude expresses the thing better, than the thing itself expresses it, because the thing itself accepts a reckoning of expression from it; and according to this it is a more perfect cognition, and in this manner God cognizes.

4. To that which is objected, that an idea is for regulating and directing; it must be said, that there can be a 'to be regulated' and a 'to be directed' in a twofold manner: either through a rule *differing* from the one directed and regulated, and this posts an imperfection and a possibility of error; or through a rule, which is *the same* as the one regulated, and this posits the impossibility of error. For because the rule cannot wander [errare], and (because)[2] God is the very Rule and Idea; for that reason it is impossible, that He err. And thus it is clear, that an idea in God does not posit[3] an imperfection, but (rather) a complement.

SCHOLIUM

I. The doctrine of ideas, which is famous, both on account of the gravity of the matter and the multitude of controversies about it, has been taken from St. Augustine, chiefly from his books OF EIGHTY-THREE QUESTIONS, q. 46, and ON THE CITY OF GOD, Bk. VII, ch. 28. In the first place St. Augustine asserted, that Plato was the first to employ the *name* of "idea", but not the first to understand the thing itself; then (in n. 2) he teaches: « Therefore, in Latin we can say "*ideas*" and/or "*forms*" and/or "*species*", as it seems to us to translate the word from the word. But if we call them *reasons* [rationes], we indeed depart from the propriety of translation — for in Greek rationes are named λόγοι, not ideas — but yet anyone who would want to use this word, would not err in this matter. For ideas are also certain principal forms and/or reasons for things, stable and incommutable (in themselves), which have not themselves been formed, and through this eternal and always holding themselves in the same manner, which are contained in the Divine Intelligence. And though they neither arise themselves nor are lost [intereant], yet everything, which can arise and be lost, and everything, which arises and is lost, is said according to them ». — Moreover, all Catholic doctors convene in this, that ideas are to be posited in God, because otherwise it would follow, that He acts either *by chance* and/or *by the necessity of nature*, not *by the judgement of the Will* [arbitrio voluntatis]. For 'to act through *the will*' presupposes, that the (things) to be done are predefined through the intellect. For « one acting according to *nature* produces through forms, which are truly of the nature, just as a man (produces) a man, and a donkey a donkey; one acting through *understanding* produces through forms, which are not anything of a thing, but ideas in the mind, just as a craftsman produces a chest [arcam] » (St. Bonaventure, SENT., Bk. II, d. 1, p. I, q. 1, in reply to n. 3). « A creature steps forth form the Creator, but not through nature, because it is of another nature, therefore through art, since there is no other, noble manner of emanating than through nature, either through art or from the will; and that Art is not outside of Him: therefore, He is acting and willing through (His) Art: therefore, it is necessary, that He have expressive reasons. For if He gives *form* to this thing, through which it is distinguished from another thing, and/or (gives) *a property*, through which it is distinguish, it is necessary, that He have the ideal form, nay ideal forms » (HEXAËMERON., Sermon 12, at the beginning). Since the doctrine concerning ideas is of the greatest moment, so that the sentence of St. Bonaventure concerning God's foreknowledge and knowledge (below in d. 38 and 39) may be rightly understood, we will mention here not a few things, both concerning the many *terms*, which occur here, and concerning *the differences* of the principal opinions, all of which are nearly founded upon this, that the authors do not all think the same thing *concerning the formal reckoning of an idea*.

II. On the various *terms*, nearly all synonymous, the Seraphic (Doctor) thus says in (his) BREVILOQUIUM. (p. I, ch. 8): The Divine Wisdom « inasmuch as It is the reason for cognizing all (things) cognized, is said (to be) "*the Light*"; inasmuch as It is the reason for cognizing (things) seen and approved, is said (to be) "*the Mirror*"; inasmuch as It is a reason for cognizing (things) foreseen and disposed, is said (to be) "*the Exemplar*"; inasmuch as It is the reason for cognizing (things) predestined and reproved, is said to be "*the Book of Life*". Therefore, It is *the Book of Life* in respect of things, as returning, *the Exemplar* (of things), as going forth, *the Mirror* (of things), as they go, but *the Light* in respect of all. — But to an exemplar looks an *idea*, *a word*, *an art*, and *a reckoning*: an *idea* according to which (it is) an act of foreseeing, a *word* according to which (it is) an act of proposing, an *art* according to which (it is) an act of prosecuting, a *reckoning* according to which (it is) an act of perfecting, because it adds upon an intention of the end. However, because all these are one [unum] in God, for that reason one is frequently accepted on behalf of the other ».

Ulric (quoted by Bl. Dionysius the Carthusian in, SENT., Bk. I, d. 36, q. 1) speaks a little differently of the same: « (The Divine Wisdom) is called an "*idea*", that is a first form, because an idea is a form of all the forms, in which the formality of it is by participation; (It is called) an "*exemplar*", inasmuch as all imitate It; a "*reason*", inasmuch as It is the similitude of the things in the intellect; a "*species*", inasmuch as It is a means of cognizing [medium cognoscendi]; a "*paradigm*" [paradigma], inasmuch as God works according to Its looking-back to the thing — for "paradigm" is said from *para-*, which (means) "*in accord with*" [iuxta] and *–dogma* (sic), as if "one teaching to work" [the Greek παράδειγμα is derived from παραδείχνυμι]. It is also called *the World Archetype* by Plato in the Timaeus, that is "the principal Exemplar" ». — Similar things are read in Alexander of Hales, SUMMA., p. I, q. 23, m. 4, a. 1; and in p. II, q. 3, m. 3; and in Bl. (now St.) Albertus (Magnus), SUMMA., p. I, tr. 13, q. 55, m. 2, a. 4. — However, it must be noted, that properly speaking a ratio cognoscendi* is accepted rather on the part of the power as a disposition, by which it is rendered equipped [expedita] for understanding, or is that *according to which* (the object) is cognized. In the human intellect this is both an *intelligible species*, and *the light* of the agent intellect, and/or also an illumination effected by a superior cause. But in God, His own Essence Itself is alone the ratio cognoscendi *of Itself and all*. Moreover, (the term) "*idea*", as will be clear from what is to follow, is now accepted by very many as that *which* is cognized, or as that which is the object of the intellect as its term, looking back toward which, an agent works and produces a thing; and in this manner it is properly (speaking) an "*exemplar*". Nevertheless, St. Thomas and chiefly St. Bonaventure accept "*idea*" also as a principle, *according to which* (an object) is cognized, and in this manner it is the same as a *reckoning* of cognizing.

III. About the *formal* signification of ideas there is exists a great debate [magna opinionum pugna] among the Schools.

1. According to the sentence of (Bl. John Duns) *Scotus*, here in the q. sole, with which there nearly agree Durandus (of Saint-Pourçain) (SENT., I, d. 36, q. 3) and many Nominalists,

---

[1] A few codd., such as A T & V with ed. 1, have *presently* [praesenter], others, such as X Z & aa, *present* [praesens]. To the word *the soul* [animam], which follows immediately, cod. R adds *itself* [ipsam]. Then, after *another similitude* [alia similitudo], cod. O adds *caused by truth* [causata a veritate], and,

a little below this, at *a similitude by this* [eo similitudo] cod. x inserts *is* [est].

[2] Supply together with codex bb *because* [quia].

[3] The Vatican edition, not trusting in the codices and edition 1, here interposes *a defect and* [defectum et].

---

* *Trans. note*: As that « by which an intellect is rendered equipped for understanding », a ratio cognoscendi is a "reason for cognizing", but as « that according to which (a thing) is cognized » it is a "reckoning of cognizing". See ratio in the Rationale for the English Translation of Peculiar Latin Terms, in the Introduction to this English translation.

and which Richard of Middleton (SENT., Bk. I, d. 36, a. 2, q. 2) judges (to be) not improbable, that ideas are *the creatures themselves, according to (their) possible 'being', cognized in the Divine Mind,* or as Mastrius says (DISPUTATIONES THEOLOG., tome I, disputation 3, q. 2): « they are creatures precognized by God as able to be made, to this extent that objectively they are only contained in the Divine Intelligence as real, objective concepts ». For (Bl.) Scotus teaches (SENT., Bk. IV, d. 50, q. 3, n. 4): « If an idea is posited in respect of the Divine Essence ad extra, the cognition of those, to which that looking-back is, is necessarily presupposed: for the Essence is never compared, unless that to which that comparison is made is first understood; for no comparison is made regarding an unknown ». — In this sentence ideas are not precisely the Divine *Essence,* which however, is presupposed, neither to the extent that "the Divine Essence" accepted *absolutely,* nor to the extent that It includes a *relation* to creatures or a respect of *imitability.* Yet the same says (loc. cit.) that all are cognized « through that Essence, which perfectly represents all, which (Essence), as One representing them in this manner, as cognized objects, has the reckoning of an idea ». — From this it follows, that from (Bl.) Scotus' point of view ideas cannot be posited as a ratio cognoscendi of creatures, except terminatively and secondarily, but only as the reckoning or principle of producing them, and indeed not *effectively,* but only *exemplarily.* — For it follows, that ideas per se do not have a looking-back except to things conceived as *possibles,* not as *produced* and/or *to be produced* in time. — But since (Bl.) Scotus names that cognized 'being', which things have in the Divine Intellect, a « *diminished 'being'* [esse diminutum] » and a « *'being'* secundum quid », these words ought not be understood in the sense of *Wycliffe,* who is reported to have taught, that creatures in God had from eternity a real *'being'* of essence and existence; nor in the sense of *Henry of Ghent,* who attributed to creatures in God a certain 'being' of *essence,* but not of *existence* (which sentence Scotus impugns with many arguments), nor in that sense, which Cajetan (commenting on the SUMMA., I, q. 14) and others impose upon (Bl.) Scotus, that that 'being' holds a middle (position) between real being and a being of reason [ens rationis]. For from the words themselves of (Bl.) Scotus (loc. cit. and in d. 45, q. sole, n. 5, and d. 3, q. 4, n. 18) and of the principal Scotists it sufficiently appears, that that *diminished 'being'* is to be posited among the beings of *reason* (cf. Mastrius, loc. cit.; Rada, loc. cit., a. 3; and among the authors of our own day, cf. Fr. Kleutgen: DIE PHILOSOPHIE DER VORZEIT, tom. II. Abhandl. 6. n. 582. 583).

2. The other doctors agree in this, that they state, that the ideas of creatures are *the Divine Essence,* but concerning *the manner,* according to which It is an idea, or concerning *the formal reckoning* (of an idea), they disagree. *St. Thomas* (DE VERITATE, q. 3, a. 2) first says: « (God's) Essence is the Idea of things, as It is *understood* », and then: « The Divine Essence, *with the diverse proportions of things to It co-intellected,* is the Idea of each one » (cf. SUMMA., I, q. 15, a. 1 and 2; SUMMA CONTRA GENTILES, I, ch. 45). According to St. Thomas, therefore, as Cajetan interprets him, an idea is the Divine Essence, as *It is formative of the thing according to a middle understanding,* or is the Divine Essence, to the extent that It is understood by God as imitable by the creature. Whence the Essence, considered *in Itself* with all Its attributes, is the *prime, proper,* and *motive* Object of the Divine Intellect; but considered in comparison *to others to be produced* outside of God, It is the secondary Object of the (Divine) Intellect. — Furthermore, ideas are referred both to merely *possible* things, and to things *existing* in any difference of time, but yet not in the same manner (DE VERITATE, q. 3, a. 6; SUMMA. , I, q. 15, a. 3, in reply to n. 2). — Likewise, an idea is not only a principle of *producing,* but also of *cognizing* (SUMMA., I, q. 15, a. 3). Moreover, ideas are an *exemplar,* to the extent that they are in an intellect as *a similitude* of others; but they are a *reason,* to the extent that they are in an intellect as *understood in themselves,* namely, by a quasi reflex act (ibid., a. 2, in reply to n. 2). — Finally, the *distinction* of ideas results from the diverse looking-backs, which are in things, to the Divine Essence.

All these, at least in regard to (their) substance, are approved by Alexander of Hales, Bl. (now St.) Albertus (Magnus), (Bl.) Peter of Tarentaise, Richard of Middleton and even St. Bonaventure.

3. Nevertheless, St. *Bonaventure* in not a few (things) employs another manner of speaking and proceeding, which on account of the gravity of the matter we exhibit (here) in a contracted manner from many passages:

a) *The Father by understanding Himself expresses Himself and all (things) in the Word.* « The Father by His own Word, which pro-

ceeds from Him, speaks Himself and all (things), because the Father by His own Word, which proceeds from Him, declares His very Self » (above in d. 32, a. 1, q, 1, 5th argument of the fundament, p. 557). « The Most High Spirit, since He is a pure act and is not only intelligent, but also an intellect, cannot not understand Himself. Since, therefore, an intellect is equated to one understanding, it understands whatever *it is* and whatever *its is able*: therefore, also *the reckoning of one understanding* is equated to an intellect, because it is its similitude. Moreover, this similitude is the Word, because according to (Sts.) Augustine and Anselm, the similitude of a mind turning itself upon itself, which (similitude) is in the insight [acie] of the mind, is a word. If, therefore, this similitude is equal (to the mind itself), it is God. Therefore, the Species originated represents the One originating according to everything which *is,* and according to everything which *can be*: therefore, It represents many (things). Likewise, when It represents the virtue of the Father, It represents a most immense virtue » etc.. « Therefore since the Most High Intellect is an active principle, in His own Similitude *He disposes* all, *He expresses* all, *He sets* all in motion » (HEXAËMERON., Sermon 3).

b) *An idea is the Divine Essence in comparison to creatures.* It signifies « the Divine *Essence* in comparison to the creature » (here in q. 3, in the body of the question); or « in respect to that which is to be, and/or can also be » (ibid., in reply to n. 5).

c) *But an idea is not the Essence, precisely to the extent that It is the Essence, but with an order to understanding, to the extent that It is the truth*: cf. here in the body of the question and passim. Moreover, *the Truth* is conceived as a *property* of the Divine Essence, to the extent that It expresses Itself to an intellect, or as « a property, which is a reason for signifying and understanding the Uncreated Essence » (above in d. 8, p. I, a. 1, q. 1, in reply to the last objection; cf. d. 3, p. I, Doubt 4). For just as a being is said (to be) "*good*" through a comparison to a final cause, so (is it said to be) "*true*" through a comparison to an exemplary cause. « Just as the good is said according to a reckoning of an *order* (unto an end), so the true according to a reckoning of an *expression,* and a reckoning of expressing belongs to the exemplar itself » (ibid., in reply to nn. 4 and 7).

d) *The Divine Truth is a light and (is) most highly expressive.* « The Truth is a *most high Light,* which nothing can hide [occultari], nor are even shadows hidden [obscurantur] from It » (below in d. 39, a. 1, q. 2), It Itself is « expressive of all » (here in the body of the question). « The Divine Truth by one and a most high expression expresses Itself and others; for that reason there is a most high assimilation not only in respect of Itself, but also in respect of others » (below in d. 39, a. 1, q. 1, in reply to n. 4).

e) *An idea is the expressive similitude of the (thing) cognized.* « An idea is said (to be) "the similitude of the thing cognized" » (here in the body of the question). « An idea according to thing is the Divine Truth, according to the reckoning of understanding it is a *similitude of (the thing) cognized* » (here in q. 4, in the body of the question). Moreover, (it is) not « an *impressed* and/or *expressed* similitude » as some later Scholastics thought, « but an *expressing* one. Because (it is) entirely expressing, for that reason it expresses most highly, *according to all conditions* » (here in q. 2, in reply to n. 3); it means « the immensity of the Divine Truth in expressing and cognizing everything which is possible *to God* » (here in q. 5, in reply to n. 3) and *to others* (d. 39, a. 1, q. 2; d. 40, a. 2, q. 1, in reply to nn. 1, 2 and 3).

f) *This similitude differs from the similitude of univocation and imitation.* It is not a similitude of *univocation,* by which each extreme convenes through a participation in another third, nor only a similitude of *imitation,* by which a finite in a limited manner imitates an infinite, but (it is) rather a similitude of *expression,* and indeed « a most high one, because (this convening) is caused by the intention of a truth, which is itself an expression (of the First Truth) » (here in reply to n. 2).

g) *An idea as a similitude is a ratio cognoscendi,* but it differs from the similitude, which is in our intellect. « But it is in us in one manner, in God in another. Indeed, in us the reason for cognizing is a *similitude,* the cognized is *a truth.* For in us the similitude has been accepted and impressed by (something) extrinsic, ... But in God it is the other way around, because the reason for cognizing is *the Truth Itself,* and the cognized is *a similitude of the Truth,* that is, a creature itself » etc. (here in the body of the Question).

h) *This similitude is the expressive reason for cognizing all (things).* « This similitude is the expressive reason for cognizing not only the universal, but also the singular » (here in q. 4, in the body of the question). « It is the very expressive *truth* of the (thing) cognized, and a *similitude* by that, by which (it is) a *truth* ... it expresses the thing better, than the thing itself expresses it » (here in reply to n. 3); it « is a pure act and the truth itself (of the thing cognized) »; it is « outside a genus », « not constrained nor limited, but it extends itself to all, just as the Divine Essence (does) »; it itself is a *common* (universal) similitude

as much as regards (its) indifference and amplitude, but *a proper* one as much as regards (its) most discrete expression » (here in q. 2, in reply to n. 3). Therefore, while a created thing through a similitude (species) caused by itself can express naught but itself (SENT., Bk. II, d. 3, p. II, a. 2, q. 1), and this indeed naught but in part; on the contrary « the Divine Truth by one and a most high expression expresses Itself and others; for that reason there is a most high assimilation, not only in respect of Itself, but even in respect of others » (below in d. 39, a. 1, q. 1, in reply to n. 4).

i) *All truths depend from the First Truth.* Just as all beings depend from the First and Most High Being, so all truths from the First and Most High Truth. « For all are true and are bound to express themselves through an expression of that Most High Light; which if it would cease to shine upon them [influere], all others would cease to be true. For that reason no created truth is true through (its) essence, but through participation » (above in d. 8, p. I, a. 1, q. 1, in reply to 4 and 7.). In the same sense St. Thomas says (SUMMA CONTRA GENTILES, I, ch. 68): « Just as the First Essence is the principle of every essence, so the First Intellection and Volition (is the principle) of every intellection and volition ».

k) *An idea is the similitude of a thing, through which the thing is cognized and produced* (here in the 2nd. argument of the fundament). Therefore, it is not only a *terminus* of cognition (that *which* is cognized), and a exemplary principle *for producing* as « the reckoning, according to which a craftsman produces his own works » (SENT., Bk. II, d. 11, a. 1, q. 2), but also a *principle* of cognition (that *according to which* it is cognized), or the *reckoning*, by which God cognizes all others (cf. d. 39, a. 1, q. 1, in reply to n. 3).

l) *The properties of ideas.* « An idea, though it is (something) *absolute* in God, yet according to the manner of understanding it means a middle respect between the One cognizing and the cognized », which « according to thing holds itself more on the part of *the One cognizing*, who is God, yet according to the reckoning of understanding or of saying a similitude holds itself more on the part of *the one cognized* » (here in q. 3, in the body of the question). *The plurality* of ideas is according to the reckoning of understanding (ibid.).

m) *The definition of an idea.* Therefore, according to the mind of the Seraphic (Doctor) the definition of an idea seems to be, that which is read in the unpublished compendium of his Commentary, written by Fr. Guglielmo de Marra, on SENT, I, d. 35, q. 3 (National Library of Florence, codex n. 727, A. 2): « An idea is the Divine Essence or the Eternal Truth in a determined manner imitable and expressive of this imitability in the Divine Intellect: that (it is) *imitable*, this is (its) *the material* (aspect) in (its) being reckoned as an idea; that (it is) *expressive of imitability*, this (is its) *formal* (aspect). Whence in the reckoning of an idea there is a considering of *that which* it is, namely, the Divine Essence and/or Truth; of *that for which* it is, namely the ideated (thing); and of *that according to which* it is, and this is a reckoning of expressing in the Divine Intellect ».

IV. If one asks, whether the doctrine of St. Bonaventure entirely convenes with the sentence of St. Tomas, Fr. Petrus Trigosus de Catalayud, O.F.M. Cap., (SUMMA, q. 11, a. 2, dubium 2) and other expositors assert, that each Saintly Doctor teaches the same (thing) with different words; but Fr. Bartolomeo de' Barbieri (CURSUS THEOL., tome I, disputation 5, q. 2, and q. 6) strives very much to prove, that there is a notable difference between each position. He explains this difference asserting, that according to « the Thomists » an idea is God's Essence, to the extent that It is a reason eminently containing all creatures *only in being* [in essendo], « or insofar as It contains things eminently and virtually through the manner of an equivocal cause, and insofar as (It is) cognized directly by the Divine Intellect under diverse respects of imitability by creatures ». (He asserts) moreover, that this containing of things in God according to eminence and causative power *is not sufficient*, to be perfectly a reason for cognizing creatures in the individual, to the extent that they are, contracted through finiteness, but that under this reckoning the Divine Essence is only *radically*, and as if under the reckoning of matter, an idea; and that things

are thus in God not *in act*, but *in potency*. Moreover, (he asserts) that St. Bonaventure, besides that containing of an eminence and causality in *being* [in essendo], requires an eminential containing in *cognizing*, which the Divine Essence has out of a twofold source [capite]: first, to the extent that It is the First and Most High *Truth*, most highly and infinitely expressing Itself and all other truths; second, to the extent that It has the reckoning of a universal and particular cause and of a common and proper similitude (species), as is explained here in q. 2, in reply to nn. 2 and 3. He asserts, that this is the reason, why St. Bonaventure so often connects a twofold reason, namely, that (there is) a *virtual* containing of things in God's power, and an *exemplary* containing (of them) in the Most High Truth (as is said in SENT., Bk. I, d. 36, a. 1, q. 1, in reply to n. 2, and a. 2, q. 1; d. 39, a. 1, q. 2), and why (here in the reply to n. 2) he says that not precisely a similitude of imitation, but a similitude *of expression* pertains to the idea. Next he says, that an idea is at once a reason *for cognizing* an ideated thing and *for producing* it, and that according to its first reckoning it is properly said (to be) an "*idea*", according to the other and "*exemplar*". We have excerpted what he says here from the author's longer discourse.

However, whether the doctrine of the Angelic and Seraphic Doctors, besides the difference in their manner of speaking and proceeding, truly differ thus, as de' Barbieri would have them, would require a more subtle and longer disquisition, which we freely relinquish to those wiser (that ourselves). However, it is manifest, that St. Thomas, St. Bonaventure and (Bl. John Duns) Scotus himself in agreement teach the following: ideas are in the Divine Intellect through the manner of forms or of a similitude — they have a threefold comparison, namely, to the Divine Essence, to the (Divine) Intellect, (and) to the things ideated outside of God, which they connote — in God the Essence, Intellect, Truth, (and) an idea are *really* the same. It is also manifest from the aforesaid, that there is chiefly urged by St. Bonaventure, that (an idea is) *a property* of the Uncreated Essence (in which the ultimate root of every truth is to be sought), by which the Divine Essence infinitely expresses and declares Itself to Itself as to One understanding; whence it is, that the Uncreated Essence is the First and Infinite *Truth*. Moreover, just as created things have accepted from the First *Essence*, *to be*, so from the First *Truth*, to be able *to express* themselves, or to be *true* through a participation in the First Truth. Moreover, these cannot express but themselves, and through an imperfect similitude. But the First Truth, which is (truth) through essence, by expressing Itself expresses also all (things) other than Itself, and in this manner is their Idea. — This doctrine is most profound.

V. In regard to the first opinion, disproved in the Response, it must be noted, that 'to cognize through a cause' ought to be understood under the addition "in *the reckoning of a cause*" or "*by inferring an effect from a cause*". Alexander of Hales makes this observation (SUMMA, p. I, q. 23, m. 2, a. 2) thus saying: « God can be considered as *that which is* a cause, and/or in *the reckoning of a cause*. If He is considered, as a cause, He knows all through a cause, because He knows all through Himself, as the Cause of all. But He does not know all in the reckoning of a cause. For where the one understanding and the intellect are the same, no middle cause is necessary, as is clear, since the soul understands itself, it does not understand itself through a cause ». Otherwise "*cognition through a cause*" is not opposed to "*cognition through an idea*", which rather is supported in causality (cf. St. Thomas, DE VERITATE, q. 2, a. 4).

VI. Besides the authors already cited: Alexander of Hales, SUMMA., p. I, q. 23, m. 2, aa. 1 and 4, and m. 4, a. 1. — (Bl. John Duns) Scotus, on this and the following two questions, here in the q. sole; REPORTATIO., on this and the following two questions, here in q. 2. — Bl. (now St.) Albertus (Magnus), here in a. 7; SUMMA., p. I, tr. 13, m. 2, a. 1. — (Bl.) Peter of Tarentaise, SENT., Bk. I, d. 36, q. 2, a. 2. — Richard of Middleton, d. 36, a. 2, qq. 1 and 2. — Giles the Roman, d. 36, 2nd princ., q. 1. — Henry of Ghent, SUMMA., a. 68, q. 5, n. 6 f.. — Durandus (of Saint-Pourçain), SENT., Bk. I, d. 36, q. 3. — (Bl.) Dionysius the Carthusian, here in q. 1. — (Gabriel) Biel, here in q. 5.

QUESTION II

Whether, among ideas, there is to be posited a plurality according to thing?

Second, there is asked, whether there is a positing among ideas of a plurality according to thing [secundum rem]. And that there is, seems:

1. Because (St.) Augustine[1] says, that « ideas are eternal and incommutable forms ». If there are many forms, since "form" means that which is an "*idea*" absolutely, then it seems, that they are many, according to that which they are absolutely.

2. Likewise, an idea is a *similitude* expressing the ideated according to the whole; but whatsoever to one and the same according to the whole are similar, in no manner differ according to one another:[2] therefore, if there is an idea of all, according to that which it is, it would be one, then all would be undiffering.

3. Likewise, an idea is *one something*, either one *common*, or one *proper* similitude: if one *common* (similitude): therefore, through that things are never be distinguished; if one *proper*: therefore through that many are never cognized.

4. Likewise, if an idea is a *reason for cognizing*; but each one cognizing cognizes according to the exigency of the reason for cognizing: therefore, if an idea is one something, since no distinction occurs in one, God does not cognize things distinctly, but indistinctly.

ON THE CONTRARY: 1. (St.) Augustine (says) in the sixth (book) ON THE TRINITY: « The Son is a certain Art of the omnipotent God, full of all the reasons of living (things), and all (things) are one [unum] in Him ».

2. Likewise, what is more perfect is to be attributed to God; but it is more perfect to be able to cognize and work many by one than by many:[4] therefore (this) is to be attributed to God: therefore, God cognizes all by one idea.

3. Likewise, in every genus of cause there is a *standing still* in one simple (thing), as for example, in the genus of an efficient (cause there is) also an end:[5] therefore, since God is the Exemplar, in which there is an standing still in an omnimodal manner, there is, therefore, in God a most high unity. But an exemplar, which contains many, is not entirely one and simple: therefore, in the Divine Exemplar there is naught but one idea according to thing.

CONCLUSION

Ideas in God are the Divine Truth Itself, and for that reason, according to thing, there is one Idea.

I RESPOND: For an understanding of the aforesaid it must be noted, that in this there was a twofold opinion.

For certain (authors) said, that ideas in God, according to thing, have a distinction. For they said, that there is a considering of a university of forms in God, in *the soul* and in *the world* or in matter. And in *matter* or in the universe [in universo] they have distinction, composition and opposition, because they are there materially. However, in the human *soul* they have distinction and composition, but they do not have opposition, and this, because they are (there) in some manner spiritually, yet not entirely, because they are from things outside;[6] for that reason, there is a composition; for they differ from the soul. In *God* they have distinction, but not a composition, nor an opposition on account of (His) Most High Simplicity. And, although in God they are distinct, yet, they are the one Exemplar, just as many particular forms, in one seal, make the one seal. — But this position of theirs, although, at its start, it seems probable, yet, at the end contains an error. For, if, in God, there would be posited ideas really differing or distinct, then, there would be There a real plurality [pluralitas realis] other than (that which) the personal plurality [pluralitas personalis] is; which is abhorrent to pious ears. *If you say*, there is not posited another[7] absolute plurality, but (only) a respective one; then, *I ask* concerning that looking-back [respectu]: either it is *something*, or *nothing*: if *nothing*, there is no real distinction There; if *something*, there is no granting but (something) of the Divine Essence; but all essentials in God are one [unum].

For that reason, there is another position, that ideas are one [unum] according to thing. And this is clear in this manner: an "idea" in God means a *similitude*, which is a reason for cognizing; but that

---

[1] See above here q. 1, p. 602, in the Scholium, I. — After the words cited from (St.) Augustine the Vatican edition, having interjected the particle *but* [sed], proceeds thus: *but if there are many forms: and since* etc. [sed si formae sunt plures: et cum etc.].

[2] Cf. above d. 31, p. II, a. 2, q. 1, p. 546, footnote 2. — This argument can also be formed in this manner: 'what are similar to one-third, are similar among themselves; but all created (things) are supposed (to be) similar to one idea: therefore, all are similar among themselves; but the consequence is false: therefore, also the antecedent'.

[3] Chapter 10, n. 11.

[4] Cf. Aristotle, ON HEAVEN AND THE WORLD, Bk. II, text 63 ff. (ch. 12), where it is shown, that what shares goodness according to fewer acts, is more noble than that which (shares goodness) according to many (acts). — At the end of this objection, the Vatican edition, together with codex cc, omits *all* [omnia], which is extant in all the codices and in edition 1.

[5] In codices L and O there is adjoined *and matter* [et materiae]. — Cf. Aristotle, ON HEAVEN AND THE WORLD, Bk. II, text 22 (ch. 4), and METAPHYSICS, Bk. II, text 5 (in the shorter version Bk. I, ch. 2).

[6] Cf. (St.) Augustine, ON THE TRINITY, Bk. XI, ch. 5, n. 9. — The sense is: Cognized objects in the soul have a spiritual 'being', because whatever is received, is received through the manner of the one receiving; but (they are) not entirely spiritual, because they are species accepted from material things. — A little above this, before the words *in some manner* [aliquo modo] the Vatican edition alone, not badly, prefixes *there* [ibi]. Then, after *for that reason there is* [ideo est] codices L and O proceed thus: *there a distinction; however, because (the cognized is) other than the soul, for that reason there is a composition there. In God they have* etc. [ibi distinctio; quia vero aliud ab anima, ideo est ibi compositio. In Deo habent etc.].

[7] In the Vatican edition and codex cc, there is lacking *other* [aliam]; not rightly, because the defenders of that opinion indeed posit *another* plurality, yet not an *absolute* one.

according to thing is the Divine *Truth* Itself, just as has been demonstrated above;[1] and because That is one, it is clear, that according to thing all ideas are one [unum]. And this (St.) Augustine[2] says expressly, that all (things) are one [unum] in that Art.

1. To that, therefore, which is objected, that they are forms; it must be said, that a form is twofold, that is, the form, which is the perfection of a thing, and the exemplary form. And (St.) Augustine accepts "ideas" in the reckoning of a form for an "*exemplary* form". Yet each is said *relatively*: the former regarding the matter, which it informs, but the latter regarding the exemplified. And for that reason, because a form speaks[3] as to the other of the two [ut ad alterum], just as a similitude (does), when there are said (to be) *many* forms, there is not noted from this, that among idea there is a plurality according to thing or according to that which they are, but according to that regarding which they are.[4]

2. To that which is objected, that an idea is a similitude expressing according to the whole: ergo etc.; regarding this *one* manner of speaking is, that an idea does not mean some similitude, through which the one cognizing is assimilated to others, but (means) that to which many are assimilated; and many can be assimilated to one, just as if from the form of a seal there is made the same expression of a figure in wax, there will be able[5] to be, from the same one form, many and various impressions, according to which the seal is more or less impressed. Thus do they understand (the idea) in God: since the multitude among things comes according to *steps* and *approximation* to the Divine 'Being' Itself. — But it is not sufficient to say that, because God *makes* all diverse according to *form*, not only according to *a step* and a dignity; and *He cognizes* them through one, according to thing, which indeed is a similitude of the cognized. — *If you say*, that this is, because God cognizes by Himself, just as He acts by Himself, for that reason, just as by one He does many, so by one He cognizes many; it still has not been solved, because there still remains the question, in what manner can God Himself be assimilated to many.

On this account, it must be said, that a *certain* similitude is according to *a property of the genus*; and concerning this one there is no doubt, that it cannot be one according to the genus of many different (things); and this is the similitude, which *is expressed* and is caused by a thing of a determinate genus.[6] The *other* is the Similitude simply *outside of genus*, and This, because it is not constrained to this genus, for the reason that It belongs to this one, for that reason It belongs to that one, and by the reason It belongs to this one according to part, by the same reason according to the whole; and such a similitude is the Divine Truth and the idea in God. — *If you ask*, in what manner this can be understood; in a certain manner it can be understood, though the simile cannot be entirely adapted. For since that Similitude is a pure act and the Truth Itself, just as has been said,[7] and all other cognizables, howsoever much (they are) noble according to that which they are, are compared to It through the manner of the *possible*: just as *one* according to *form* can be assimilated *to many, diverse* according to *matter*,[8] so in the proposed there can be one real Similitude of all cognizables. And in some manner *an example* can be posited in light, which (being) one, according to number, expresses many and various species of colors. But in our cognition, since it holds itself through the manner of the possible in respect of the cognized and in a certain manner (is) informable by it, a similitude cannot be found, nay there is found a dissimilitude; and for that reason by looking at (this explanation) according to our cognition it seems to us that in God it is not intelligible.

3. To that which is *asked*, whether that similitude is proper and/or common; it must be said, that God is not said (to be) *a universal cause* nor *a particular one* simply; but has something of the nobility of a *universal* cause, because He is capable of [potest in] very many effects; similarly[9] (He has) something of *a particular* cause, because He is immediately and sufficiently capable of any effect. Thus, in God's *cognition* in must be understood, that there is neither entirely (a similitude) in *the universal*, nor entirely in *the particular*. Similarly concerning *similitude* and idea it must be understood, that (each) is *common* as much as regards indifference and amplitude, but *proper*[10] as much as regards a most discrete expression. — The reason for this is, because (an idea) is an *expressing* similitude, not an impressed nor an expressed one;

---

[1] In the preceding Question. — Next, for *according to thing* [secundum rem], which reading we have received into the text on the authority of codd. P Q aa & bb, the Vatican ed. has less distinctly *through That* [per eam].

[2] Cf. above 1st. argument of the fundament. — Immediately after this the Vatican edition has *because* [quia] for *that* [quod].

[3] The Vatican edition, breaking with nearly all the codd. and edd. 1, 2 & 3, has *"form" is said* [forma dicitur] for *a form speaks* [forma dicit].

[4] The final words *but according to that regarding which they are* [sed secundum id ad quod sunt] are absent from the older codd.. Perhaps they were considered superfluous by copyists and were omitted on account of (their) consonance with the immediately antecedent words. In the Vatican ed. and also in ed. 1 they are extant, and moreover, in the Vatican ed. there is adjoined to them: *that is, regarding those which are outside, namely, by reason of (what they) connote, such as are the (things) ideated themselves* [id est, ad ea quae sunt extra, scilicet ratione connotatorum, ut sunt ipsa ideata]. A little before this, for *or* [sive] codd. aa & bb have *but only* [sed solum], badly.

[5] The Vatican edition reads *there can be* [possunt] for our reading *there will be able to be* [poterunt], which is that of cod. Z, and which is not obscurely persuaded by very many codd., which read *there will be able to be* [poterit] in the singular, and by cod. O, which exhibits *there could be* [potuerunt].

[6] The Vatican ed. alone has *determinately* [determinate], and, a little below this, *the same reason* [eadem ratione] for *that reason* [ea ratione].

[7] In the body of the Question.

[8] For *matter* [materiam] very many codd. and all the first edd., except ed. 1, have faultily *nature* [naturam], codex U *number* [numerum]. After *diverse* [materiam] edition 1 inserts *also* [etiam]. Then, for *one real* [una realis] codex T has *the same real* [eadem realis].

[9] For *similarly* [similiter] codices A T X and edition 1 have *at the same time* [simul], which codex T, without the semicolon, connects with the preceding, putting a comma after it. The same construction, with the order of words changed only a little, is found in codex X: *in very many effects at the same time* [in plurimos simul effectus], which reading is less favorable to our own, because it constrains exceedingly the concept of a universal cause. On this (Bl. John Duns) Scotus, (commenting on Aristotle's) PHYSICS, Bk. II, q. 8 (says): It is said (to be) a "universal cause" in causing [causa universalis in causando], and then the universality of the cause is attained from within the diversity of *the effects*, which that cause can produce; second, (it is said to be a "universal cause") from within the diversity of *places*, in which it can at the same time produce diverse effects; and, third, (it is said to be such) from within a diversity of *times*, in which it can produce diverse effects successively: such that that cause is said (to be) more universal, which can at the same time produce many effects in many places, or can in many times produce many effects.

[10] Codex X has *particular* [particularis], and then *a most distinct* [distinctissimam] for *a most discrete* [discretissimam]. A little below this, after *nor an expressed one* [nec expressa] codex R adds: *because (it is) entirely expressing, not impressed nor expressed* [quia omnino exprimens, non impressa nec expressa].

because (it is) *entirely* expressing, for that reason it expresses most highly and according to all conditions. And *again*, from this that it is not an expressed (similitude), for that reason (it is) not constrained nor limited, but extends itself to all, just as the Divine *Essence*; though the whole (of the idea) is in one (ideated thing), yet not thus is it in one,[1] that it is not in another.

4. To that which is objected last, that one cognizes according to the exigency of the reasons (for cognizing); it must be said, that just as *the Reason for cognizing* [ratio cognoscendi] is one, and, yet, represents

many cognized most distinctly according to their proper conditions [secundum proprias conditiones]; so the Divine *Cognition* as much as regards *the manner* of cognizing, which is in It, is one and simple, not distinct; but in comparison to an *object*, It cognizes distinctly. When, therefore, there is said: "God cognizes all *distinctly*" [Deus cognoscit omnia distincte]; if a *distinction* is posited in cognition through a comparison to *the One cognizing*, it is false; but, if through a comparison to the *one cognized*, thus, it has truth.

SCHOLIUM

I. For an understanding of the doctrine concerning ideas, which the Seraphic (Doctor) proffers, the solutions to nn. 2 and 3 are of the greatest moment. (Bl. John Duns) Scotus completely approves (this) profound doctrine in SENT, Bk. IV, d. 50, q. 2, and in very many other passages. — The five differences, which obtain between God's cognition and ideas and ours, are here hinted at. **1.** The Divine Intellect is a pure act, and (its) cognizable is in the reckoning of potency to It, while our intellect is a power and in potency to (its own) cognizable. **2.** Intellect and intellection in God is the Divine Substance; our intellection, as an act, is an accident. **3.** The Divine Intellect does not accept from things any impressed and/or expressed species, but rather as a similitude *expressive* of things It expresses and grants an assimilation, or, as Alexander of Hales says (SUMMA., p. I, q. 23, m. 1), « It cognizes through a similitude, which is not *from things* but *regards things* »; our intellect from thing borrows an impressed species and forms an expressed species. **4.** An idea is really one in God and (is) a most perfect similitude *of all* cognizables, whether actuals or possibles (cf. here q. 4, in reply to n. 2).

5. Our ideas do not express the thing except in part, but a divine idea expresses the thing with all the manners, pertaining to the object in whatsoever manner. The Seraphic (Doctor) expresses this briefly in the BREVILOQUIUM. (p. I, ch. 8): « Because an exemplar (in God) is most simple and most perfect, for that reason (it is) a pure act; however, because (it is) infinite and immense, for that reason (it is) outside of every genus. And hence it is, that existing one, it can be an expressive similitude of many ».

II. Nearly all the other authors treat this and the following question. Alexander of Hales, SUMMA., p. I. q. 23, m. 4, a. 1, and q. 14, m. 4; p. II, q. 3, m. 2. — St. Thomas, SENT., Bk. I, d. 36, q. 2, a. 2; SUMMA. , I, q. 15, a. 2; SUMMA CONTRA GENTILES., I, ch. 54. — Bl. (now St.) Albertus (Magnus), on this and the following question, here in a. 9; SUMMA., p. I, tr. 13, q. 45, m. 2, a. 2. — (Bl.) Peter of Tarentaise, on this and the following question, d. 36, q. 2, q. 3. — Richard of Middleton, SENT., Bk. I, d. 36, a. 2, q. 3. — Giles the Roman, on this and the following question, SENT., Bk. I, d. 36, 2nd. princ., q. 2. — Henry of Ghent, SUMMA., a. 68, q. 5, n. 9. — Durandus (of Saint-Pourçain), on this and the following question, SENT., Bk. I, d. 36, q. 4. — (Bl.) Dionysius the Carthusian, SENT, Bk. I, d. 36, q. 2.

QUESTION III

Whether, among ideas, there is a plurality according to reckoning?

Third, there is asked, whether there is a positing among ideas of a plurality according to a reckoning. And that there is, is shown in this manner:

1. (St.) Augustine (says) in (his) book, OF EIGHTY-THREE QUESTIONS: « Man was established according to one reason, the horse according to another »:[2] therefore, if an "idea" means the very reason for cognizing, it is necessary, that it be plurified according to reckoning.

2. Likewise, this very (thing) is shown from the manner of saying and defining (the term), because (St.) Augustine[3] says in the plural and defines in the plural those ideas, saying that *they are forms*: therefore, they are plurified *according to thing*, and/or *according to reckoning*, but not *according to thing*: therefore, *according to reckoning*.

3. Likewise, an "idea" means a similitude to the cognized, and a "similitude", though it is something absolute in God, has a manner of being said regarding the other or a looking-back (to the other);

but the plurification of a relative similitude is from the thing, to which it is assimilated:[4] therefore, since there are many ideated things, there are many ideas according to the reckoning of saying.

4. Likewise, God, before He produces things, cognizes (them) distinctly and by an act; but there is no distinction in God cognizing nor in the cognized: therefore, it is necessary [oportet], that there be (one) in the reckoning of cognizing.

ON THE CONTRARY: 1. If there is[5] a plurification (of ideas) according to reckoning, since there is none according to thing, then that plurality is not other than a vanity.

2. Likewise, if there is a plurality in this name "*idea*", either (this is) according to a reckoning of that *which it is*, or according to a reckoning of that *regarding which it is*: not according to a reckoning of that *which it is*, because (an idea) is the Divine Essence; if according to the reckoning of that *regarding which it is*, therefore, since "word" and "exemplar" and "art" mean a looking-back to the

---

[1] After *one* [uno] the Vatican edition, together with codex cc, repeats without reason *thus* [sic].

[2] In Question 46, n. 2.

[3] Loc. cit.. See above q. 1, p. 602, Scholium, I.

[4] For the rule is, that for a plurality of relations there suffices a plurality of one of the terms; whence in one point in respect to diverse

lines there can be many relations. Cf. here q. 4, in reply to nn. 3 and 4. — A little further above this, for *has* [habet] reads *yet it has* [habet tamen].

[5] Codex Z and edition 1 after *is* [est] subjoin *There* [ibi]. Next, for *since there is none according to thing* [cum on sit re], codex T has *since there is none according to thing* [cum secundum rem non sit].

creature, at least according to name it ought to be plurified, which, however, is false.

3. Likewise, if there are many ideas, not on account (what is) signified, but on account of (what is) connoted, then *I ask*: either that connoted is *eternal*, or *temporal*: if (it is) *eternal*, therefore, it seems, that there are many (ideated things) from eternity; if *temporal*, therefore it seems, that an "idea" is not said of God except on account of time, just as neither "*lord*" nor "*creator*" are said (of God) except on account of time.

4. Likewise, ideas, if they are many on account of the ideated, therefore, either according to the "*being*", which the ideated have in *God*, or in *their own genus*. If on account of the "*being*", which they have in *God*; *on the contrary*: in God they are one [unum], therefore, by a reckoning of that "*being*" they cannot be said (to be) many. If, on account of the "*being*", which they have in *their own genus*; but they do not have (this)[1] except in time: therefore, either ideas are not many except in time, and/or the temporal is the cause of the eternal; each of which is unfitting.

5. Likewise, "idea" either means *something*, or *nothing*; if *nothing*, therefore, it has neither a plurality nor a unity; if it means *something*, therefore if there are many ideas, there are many things: therefore, if there are many ideas from eternity, there are many things from eternity; but there are not many things personally, because "idea" does not mean something personal: therefore, many essentially.

CONCLUSION

Ideas in God are one according to thing, but many according to the reckoning of understanding.

I RESPOND: It must be said, that, just as is clear from (what has) been said before in the Thirtieth Distinction,[2] although in God there is no looking-back to the creature on the part of the thing, yet it does happen, that the Essence Itself is signified in respect to the creature through many names. Nor, however, is the name or word ("idea")[3] vain. It must be understood, therefore, that this name "*idea*" signifies the Divine Essence in comparison or in respect to a creature. For an idea is a similitude of a cognized thing, which (idea) though it is (something)[4] absolute in God, yet according to the manner of understanding it means a middle looking-back between the One cognizing and the cognized. And although that looking-back according to thing holds itself more on the part of the One cognizing, because (the One cognizing) is God Himself, yet according to the reckoning[5] of understanding or saying a similitude holds itself more on the part of the cognized. And, since the One cognizing is one [unum], and the cognized are many [multa];

for that reason all ideas in God are one [unum] according to thing, but, yet, many [plures] according to the reckoning of understanding or saying. Whence it must be conceded,[6] that all reasons in God are one something, but (there is) not one idea or reason, but many.

1. To that, therefore, which is objected, that nothing underlies that reckoning (of an idea) on the part of the thing; it must be said, that it is false, because on the part of God the Essence, not a looking-back, underlies the looking-back[7] (of the idea); but on the part of the creature a true looking-back (to God) underlies (the reckoning of the idea), and for that reason that signified looking-back (of the idea) does not induce a falsehood [falsitatem]. In this manner, though on the part of God no plurality underlies the plurality of respects, yet one does on the part of the connoted; whence that looking-back thus plurified has no falsehood nor vanity.

2. To that which is objected, that "word" and "art" mean a looking-back (to the creature); it must be said, that they do mean (that), but in a manner other than "idea" and/or "reason"[8] (do). For "*idea*" or "a reason for cognizing" holds itself more according to the reckoning of understanding on the part of the cognized. For a "*similitude*", according to which (it is) of this kind, does not mean a looking-back to that in which it is, but (to that) of which it is; but "*word*" holds itself more on the part of the one speaking, similarly both "*art*" and "*exemplar*" on the part of the one producing: and because the cognized are many, and the one cognizing one, for that reason there are many *ideas* and only one *Art*. — And/or in another manner (it must be said, that) "*reason*" and "*idea*" mean a looking-back to things inasmuch as they are distinct, not so the other words.

3. To that which is objected, that there are not[9] many connoted from eternity; it must be said, that the plurality among ideas is by reason of the connoted. But there is a speaking of "the connoted" in a twofold manner: either inasmuch as *they are*, or inasmuch as they have been *connoted*. Inasmuch as *they are*, thus they are solely in time; but inasmuch as *they are connoted*, thus they can be connoted both *eternally* and *temporally*: eternally, when[10] the looking-back (of the idea to the connoted) is conveyed as in habit, just as through this name "*predestination*" — for that reason predestination is eternal, because it connotes an effect not in act, but in habit — but *temporally*, when the looking-back is conveyed in act, just as through this verb "*to create*". Since, therefore, (things) temporal are connoted thus, as they are going to be, and they are going to be many; for that reason they are connoted as many. But yet in this manner the (things) connoted, though they are connoted[11] from eternity, are not from eternity, but in time; thus the "multitude" of the connoted, though it is said (to be) from eternity, yet it does not posit a real multitude except in time.

4. To that which *is asked*, whether ideas are many according to the "*being*" of the ideated; it must be said, that

---

[1] Supply, with codices Z aa and bb, and edition 1: *this* [hoc].

[2] In Question 3. — Next the words *looking-back on account of the thing* [respectus a parte rei] signify the same as *real looking-back* [respectus realis].

[3] The Vatican ed. alone reads thus: *Nor, however, is this name or word, "Idea", vain* [Nec tamen hoc nomen sive vocabulum Idea est vanum].

[4] The Vatican edition alone adds here *something* [quid]. At the beginning of this proposition, in place of *is* [est] codex bb, together with edition 1, has *is said (to be)* [dicitur].

[5] For *according to the reckoning* [secundum rationem] the Vatican edition, with codex cc alone, has *according to the reckoning* [ratione].

[6] The Vatican ed. faulty has *they must be conceded* [concedendae sunt].

[7] In codex O there is added to the text *and/or reckoning* [vel rationi].

[8] Codex V and W add *for cognizing* [cognoscendi].

[9] The particle *not* [non] is absent, faultily, from the Vatican edition and from codex cc. The (third) proposition in codex V begins *If inasmuch as they are* etc. [Si in quantum sunt etc.].

[10] For *when* [quando], codices A F G H I W X and Y have less well *because* [quia]. A little below this, codex R reads *for, for this reason* [ideo enim] in place of *for this reason* [ideo].

[11] Codices A C F G H K L R S W and X, together with the first editions, read *they connote* [connotent]. A little before this, codex R has *just as* [tamen sicut] for *in this manner* [tamen sic].

(they are) according to the "*being*", which ideated things are going to have in their own genus.[1] And although they do not have that except in time, yet they were going to have it from eternity; and they are the ideas of things as they are going to be: for that reason they are not only understood (to be) many in time, but also from eternity. Thus the understanding that there was a predestination and reprobation from eternity differs, not by a reckoning of that which was from eternity, but by a reckoning of that, which was going to be in time.

5. To that which is objected: 'if (there are) many ideas, therefore, (there are) many things';[2] it must be said, that an "idea" not only means that which (the ideated) *is*, but a looking-back *to that* which (the ideated) is going to be, and/or even can be; and, by a reckoning of that looking-back, ("idea") receives

a plurification. And because that posits nothing in act, but only in potency, hence it is, that the plurality of ideas does not posit any actual plurality; just as no (plurality) is posited, if one says, that (God)[3] can make many (things). But this name "*thing*", which (the objection) says, conveys (a plurality) absolutely; and for that reason when there is said, that there are many *things*, there is posited a plurality in act; and for that reason that argument is not valid, nay there is there (a fallacy secundum) quid and *simply*,[4] just as if there be said: "many (things) are possible to God, and/or there are many cognized (things): therefore, there are many (things). Thus neither is (the argument:) 'there are many ideas: therefore, there are many things', valid; because *ideas* are not many by a reckoning of that which *they are*, but by a reckoning of that *regarding which they are*.

SCHOLIUM

By the conclusion, the error of Avicenna is crushed, who imagined, that in God there is only one idea in respect of the First Intelligence emanated from God, in which are the ideas of other things. — In the conclusion the catholic doctors agree, but not in its determination and explanation. Durandus (of Saint-Pourçain) (d. 36, q. 4) asserts that there are many ideas

for this reason, because many creatable things, understood by God from eternity, are signified; with whom (Bl. John Duns) Scotus, with others, nearly agrees, according to their own sentence about the proper reckoning of ideas (cf. Scholium, here in q. 1). See (these) authors in the preceding Scholium.

QUESTION IV

Whether ideas are plurified through a comparison to the ideated, to the extent that these are diverse in species and/or in individual?

Fourth, there is asked, whether ideas are plurified through a comparison to ideated (things), according to the multitude of the ideated as much as regards the diversity of universals or of singulars. And that (it is according to a diversity) of singulars, seems:

1. Since the reason for distinguishing is through ideas; but God does not only distinguish a universal from a universal, but also a singular from a singular. But because He distinguishes the universal from a universal, for that reason He has many ideas and reasons of many universals. Whence « by one reason there is established the horse, by another reason there is established man »:[5] ergo etc..

2. Likewise, the cognition of a thing is most true according to the totality of the thing;[6] but a singular adds something upon the universal: therefore, since God cognizes the whole, He not only has the idea of the universal, but also of (what is) superadded,

namely, of the singular; similarly also of the other singular. Therefore, if (these) are added according to the reckoning or multitude of ideas [idealem], it is clear that etc..

3. Likewise, God predestines certain men [quosdam ex hominibus], (and) reproves certain (others); but by one reckoning He predestines, and by another reckoning He reproves: therefore, according to one reckoning and idea they are foreknown and (according to another they are) predestined in God. But this is an individual or numeral diversity: ergo etc..

4. Likewise, among the divine an idea is multiplied by reason of a looking-back and relation to the (thing) ideated, therefore, with one (ideated)[7] multiplied, the rest is multiplied: therefore, since man, who is an ideated, is multiplied among diverse individuals according to thing, the idea (of man) is multiplied in respect of them according to reckoning (of their number).

---

[1] Or: according to the *actual "being"*, which they will have in themselves and which is contradistinguished from the *ideal "being"*, which they have in God. — A little below this, for our reading which is that of the more outstanding codices, codex cc, together with editions 2, 3, 4, and 5, omit *the understanding* [intelligere]; the Vatican edition does likewise and has *is said* [dicitur] for *differs* [differt].

[2] Many codices have faultily *reasons* [rationes] for *things* [res]. Next for *that which (the ideated) is* [quod est] the Vatican edition, together with codex cc, has *what (the ideated) is* [quid est].

[3] Supply together with codices W and Z and edition 1 *God* [Deus]. Next for *when there is said* [cum dicitur] the Vatican edition has *when it says* [cum dicit].

[4] Codex V reads more completely: *there is a fallacy secundum quid and simply there* [est ibi fallacia secundumquod et simpliciter], concerning which see Aristotle, ELENCHAE, ch. 4. (ch. 5).

[5] (St.) Augustine, OF EIGHTY-THREE QUESTIONS, q. 46, n. 2. — A little above this, after *He has* [plurium] many codices insert *both* [et].

[6] The Seraphic Doctor wants to say: a thing is most perfectly and most truly cognized, when it is cognized according to the whole, which (perfect) cognition is said by (St.) Augustine (to be) a comprehension, concerning which see above d. 3, p. I, a. sole, q. 1, p. 69, footnote 4. On the following proposition, cf. Aristotle, POSTERIOR ANALYTICS, Bk I, ch. 20 (ch. 24).

[7] Namely, an ideated. — In codices F Q and W, and edition 1, there is adjoined to the word *one* [uno] the word *of the relatives* [relativorum], which addition seems exceedingly general. Next for *therefore, since* [cum ergo], which reading we have assumed from codices V X and Z; the Vatican edition has *and since* [et cum]; codices A F G H I K T and others with the first editions omit *therefore* [ergo].

ON THE CONTRARY: 1. (St.) Augustine (says) to Nebridius: « I say, as much as it pertains to man, that there is there only the reckoning of man, not of my and/or your (humanity) »; therefore, the multiplication and/or distinction of ideas is attained solely according to the diversity of universals.

2. Likewise, a created craftsman through one idea produces many (things): therefore, since this belongs to nobility, God through one idea produces many diverse² in number according to thing and reckoning.

3. Likewise, the singular as a singular is more composed than the universal: therefore, if there is in God an idea of the singular as a singular, then, therefore, there is another idea more simple; but this is unfitting: ergo etc..

4. Likewise, a singular is more proper than a universal:³ if, therefore, in God there is an idea of the universal as a universal, and of a singular as a singular, therefore, one idea (is) common, the other proper. But the common is prior to and is more simple than the proper: therefore, one idea is prior to and more simple than the other: therefore, in God there is a positing of order and of composition of the Essence, ergo etc..

CONCLUSION

Ideas are plurified not only according to the multitude of universals, but also of singulars.

I RESPOND: It must be said, that in God an idea according to thing is the Divine Truth, according to the reckoning of understanding it is a similitude of the (thing) cognized. But this similitude is an *expressive reason* for cognizing not only the universal, but also the singular, though it itself is not universal nor singular, just as neither (is) God.⁴ And for that reason not only is it a similitude of a universal, as it is a universal, but also of the singular, as (it is) a singular, and for that reason, because it is a similitude of each, not only is it multiplied according to the multitude of universals, but

also (according to the multitude) of singulars. And this is what (St.) Augustine says to Nebridius: « I say, that as much as⁵ regards making man there is not only a reckoning of man, but as much as regards the world [orbem] of time there lives various reckonings of men in that wholeness [sinceritate] (of the Eternal Truth) ».

1. And, from this, the solution to that word of (St.) Augustine is clear, because (St.) Augustine says, that although of the universal, as it is a universal, there is one idea, yet of singulars, as singulars, there are many. Whence in the same place he says,⁶ « that if one wants to make an angle, it suffices to have the reckoning of an angle. But if one want to paint a quadrangle, it is necessary, that he have the reckoning of four angles ».

2. To that which is objected, that a created craftsman produces many (things) through one idea; it must be said, that he does this through the application of that to diverse matters. Wherefore, if he has only one idea, it is impossible to understand, that according to that he cognizes by a simple gaze diverse (things); but God by a simple gaze cognizes singulars as diverse,⁷ such that (He cognizes them) according to (their) whole and according to (their) proper differences and properties; for that reason it is not similar.

3. 4. To that which is objected concerning composition and priority, it must be said, that neither according to *thing*, nor according to *reckoning* it is necessary [oportet] that the idea have the properties of the ideated (thing). For of the corporal⁸ there is a spiritual similitude, and of the composed there is a simple similitude, even in creatures; for that reason it is not necessary, that one idea be more simple than and/or prior to the other. Yet a similitude according to a reckoning of understanding has the property of the ideated according to *distinction*, both on account of correlation, because it is necessary that, with one of the relatives⁹ multiplied, the rest also be multiplied, at least according to reckoning; and also, because that similitude is a reason for expressing and distinguishing; and for that reason, although a property of distinction is received, yet it is not necessary concerning the others.¹⁰

---

¹ Epistle 14, n. 1. — In the cited text, the Vatican edition has *to make man* [ad hominem faciendum] for *to man* [ad hominem], with neither the codices nor edition 1 supporting it; and, then, for *not of my* [non meam] not a few codices faultily substitute, *as of my* [ut meam]. Next, for *of ideas* [idearum] the Vatican ed. with cod. cc has *of ideated (things)* [ideatorum].

² Many codices, such as A C F G I K R S T U etc, with edd. 1, 2 & 3, have *by a diverse number* [diverso numero] for *diverse in number* [diversa numero]; codex V reads *by a distinct number* [distincto numero].

³ This is established from the definition of what is proper, which according to Aristotle, TOPICS, Bk. I, ch. 4, convenes with it *alone*: « For no one says that the proper (is) that which happens to be in another ». And in ON INTERPRETATION, Bk. I, ch. 5 (ch. 7): « But I say that a universal (is) that which is bound to be predicated among *many*; but the singular, that which (is) not ». — Next after *one idea* [idea communis] codices V and W subjoin *is* [est].

⁴ Cf. here q. 2, in the reply to n. 3, and d. 19, p. II, q. 2, where there occur many of those things to which these objections refer.

⁵ The Vatican ed. here adds *it pertains* [pertinet], which in the original

text is *it concerns* [attinet], and reads *regards* [ad] as *to*. A little after this, the Vatican edition, together with edition 1, with the codices and the original text striving against this, has *order* [ordinem] for *world* [orb].

⁶ Epistle 14, n. 4, where the original text reads: And so as often as I wish to demonstrate an angle, naught but one reckoning of an angle occurs to me, but I would never draw a quadrangle [quadratum], unless I intuited the reckoning of four angles at once.

⁷ Codices K L O T and aa adjoin *singulars* [singularia]; a little below this, codices L and O prefix tot he word *properties* [proprietates] the word *diverse* [diversas].

⁸ The Vatican edition has *For of a natural thing* [Nam rei naturalis]. Next the same Vatican edition, together with codex cc, omits *to the other* [altera].

⁹ Codex T, together with not a few other codices and edition 3, has *correlatives* [correlativorum].

¹⁰ That is: it is not necessary, that the other properties of the ideated be received into the understanding (of an idea), besides that property of distinction.

SCHOLIUM

I. The conclusion is contrary to not a few, who following Plato, « deny that there are in God the ideas of all singular goods, saying, that singulars have no other idea than the idea of the species, and that God cognizes through the idea of species all singulars contained under the species » (Richard of Middleton, SENT., Bk. I, d. 36, a. 2, q. 4). Henry of Ghent seems to favor this sentence (QUODLIBETALS, 5, q. 3). But the common sentence with Sts. Bonaventure and Thomas (SUMMA., I, q. 15, a. 3, in reply to n. 4) and the same Richard reproves that opinion. Nevertheless, St. Thomas in another place (DE VERITATE, q. 3, a. 8, in reply to n. 2) reconciles each sentence thus: « If we speak of an "*idea*" *properly*, according to which it is of a thing in that manner according to which it is in (its) "being" producible; thus one idea responds to the singular, to the species, and to the genus, individual in the singular itself, by this that Socrates, a man and an animal, is not distinguished according to "being". But if we accept "idea" *commonly* on behalf of a similitude and/or reason, thus, since the consideration of Socrates, as he is Socrates, and as he is a man, and as he is an animal, is diverse, there will respond to him many ideas and/or similitudes ». This agrees with the principles of St. Bonaventure.

In the solution to nn. 3 and 4 there must be noted the exception, made there, in the general rule, that an idea does not have the properties of the ideated; for there is excepted the property of *distinction*. At the same time one must attend to the proof of this exception, confirmed by a twofold reason. The difficulty about the property of ideated (things) is explained more here in q. 6.

II. Besides the passages cited: Alexander of Hales, SUMMA., p. I, q. 23, m. 3, a. 6. — (Bl. John Duns) Scotus, on this and the following question, REPORTATIO., Bk. I, d. 36, a. 3 and 4. — St. Thomas, SENT., Bk. I, d. 36, q. 2, a. 3; SUMMA CONTRA GENTILES., I, ch. 63. — (Bl.) Peter of Tarentaise, SENT., Bk. I, d. 36, q. 2, a. 4. — Richard of Middleton, SENT., Bk. I, d. 36, a. 2, q. 4. — Giles the Roman, SENT., Bk. I, d. 36, 2nd. princ., q. 4, collat. 3. — (Bl.) Dionysius the Carthusian, SENT., Bk. I, d. 36, q. 2.

QUESTION V

Whether the ideas in God are finite in number, or infinite?

Fifth, there is asked, whether in God there is a positing of a multitude of ideas according to a finite number, and/or an infinite one. And it seems, that (it is) according to an infinite number.

1. (St.) Augustine (says) in the eleventh (book) ON THE CITY OF GOD:[1] « There is one Wisdom, in which are infinite treasures of all intelligible things ».

2. Likewise, (St.) Augustine says in the sixth (book) ON THE TRINITY,[2] that « the Son is the Art full of the all living reasons »; but it is established, that that Art is infinite: therefore, it is not filled, except by (things) infinite, therefore, there are infinite reasons There.

3. Likewise, it seems *by reason*, because it is established, that God cognizes all species of number, therefore, they all have ideas in God; but the species of number are infinite:[3] ergo etc.. *If you say*, that the species are infinite in regard to *us*, not according to *thing*; *on the contrary*: let it be posited,[4] that all species of number exist in reality [sint in re]; with this posited, it follows of necessity, that they are simply infinite in act: therefore if of all the species of number there are in God ideas according to act, it is clear that etc..

4. Likewise, God can produce infinite (things);[5] but He can produce nothing, of which he does not have a cognition and an idea: therefore, He has the ideas of infinite (things). But of many (things) there are many ideas: therefore, of infinite (things) there are infinite (ideas).

5. Likewise, more can be thought of than all finite (things), because something greater than every finite can be thought of; but neither God, nor man has[6] a thinking of more (things) than those which God cognizes, because then God's knowledge would not be most high: and if this, since He cognizes through ideas, it is clear that etc..

ON THE CONTRARY: 1. (St.) Augustine (says) in the twelfth (boo) ON THE CITY OF GOD:[7] « Whatever is known, is bounded [finitur] by the comprehension of the one knowing »; but it is established, that the reasons for cognizing are known: therefore, they are bounded. But whatsoever are bounded, are finite: ergo etc..

2. Likewise, the multitude of ideas is according to the multitude of ideated (things); but it is established, that all other (things) from God are finite in act: therefore, similarly also ideas.

3. Likewise, where there is an infinity, there is a confusion and inordinance [inordinatio]; but in the Eternal Exemplar there occurs no confusion nor inordinance: ergo etc.

---

[1] Chapter 10, n. 3. In the passage cited the original text, after the words *in which* [in qua], adjoins *certain immense and* [immensi quidam atque].

[2] Chapter 10, n. 11.

[3] Aristotle, in PHYSICS, Bk. III, text 36 (ch. 5), and in METAPHYSICS, Bk. XI, ch. 9 (Bk. X, ch. 10) calls the *passion* (i.e. property) *of number* infinite.

[4] Which, however, in itself it not possible. For though God by an act cognizes infinite numbers, it does not follow, that He can produce by an act infinite (numbers) outside (Himself). Cf. below d. 43, q. 3. — Immediately before this, for *not according to thing* [non secundum rem] codex T has *but finite according to thing* [sed finitae secundum rem],

codex V has *finite according to thing* [finitae secundum rem]. At the end of the argument the Vatican edition reads: *therefore, if of all species of number in God there are ideas and they are infinite according to act* [ergo si omnium specierum numeri sunt in Deo ideae et sunt infinitae actu, patet etc.] for , which extension is had also in edition 1, yet with the omission of the word *and* [et] and with the placing of a common after *ideas* [ideae].

[5] Understand: "infinite" in potency, that is, He cannot produce so many, that He could not (produce) more. Cf. below d. 43, q. 3.

[6] Codex T, with edition 1, has *can think more (things)* [potest plura cogitare] for *has a thinking of more (things)* [habet plura cogitare].

[7] Chapter 18. The original text of the cited passage is this: Whatever is comprehended by knowledge, is etc..

4. Likewise, to posit an infinity in act in a creature is to posit an imperfection, wherefore every created is bounded by that, by which (it is) perfected;[1] but every condition of imperfection is to be removed [releganda] from God: ergo etc..

CONCLUSION

Divine ideas do not exist in a finite number,
but in an infinite one.

I RESPOND: It must be said, that, just as there is said in the Psalm,[2] *of the Divine Wisdom there is no number*, and through this, neither (is there a number) of the reasons, through which the Divine Wisdom cognizes; and since they have no number, they are not numerable: for that reason they do not exist [non sunt] in a finite number, but an infinite one. And the reasons and authorities brought forward for this are to be conceded.

1. To that, therefore, which is objected, that every knowable has been bounded, ergo etc.; it must be said, that everything knowable through comprehension has been bounded according to the one comprehending; but eternal reasons are known through comprehension by God alone, for that reason they have been bounded according to God alone. But to the extent that (this) does not follow: 'this is equated to an infinite, therefore, it is bounded', nay there is (a fallacy <u>secundum</u>) <u>quid</u> and *simply* there,[3] and the opposite rather follows: 'therefore, it is not bounded'; so also must it be judged in the proposed. But those reasons are not comprehensible by any finite intellect; for that reason that (objection) is clear.

2. To that which is objected, that the multitude of ideas is from the multitude of ideated (things); it must be said, that just as has been said,[4] it does not come from the multitude of ideated (things) inasmuch as (they are) created, but inasmuch as (they are) connoted. Moreover, an idea does not connote an ideated (thing) according to (its) actual existence, but only according to (its) potency. And because God can make infinite (things), though He never makes but finite (things), for that reason the ideas and/or reasons for cognizing are in God infinite, because they are not only of beings and/or future (things), but of all (things) possible to God. For God can (do) nothing, which He does not cognize by an act.

3. To that which is objected, that an infinity posits a confusion; it must be said, that there is a positing of an infinity according to a real diversity; and thus it deprives both distinction and order, if it is posited according to act. But the multitude of ideas is not of diverse things, but means the immensity of the Divine Truth in expressing[5] and cognizing everything which is possible to God, and indeed, this, according to thing and act, is one [unum]: for that reason there is no confusion.

4. To that which is objected, that an infinity in a creature belongs to imperfection; it must be said, that although it does belong to imperfection in a creature, yet it does[6] not in the Creator, because there is a understanding of infinity through *defect* and through *excess*. An infinity through *defect* can be in a creature as in matter,[7] and this belongs to imperfection; but this is to no extent in the Creator. Moreover, an infinity through *excess* cannot be in a creature simply, since it has a created and composed and limited 'to be'; but God has nothing of these, and for that reason He has an infinity, and this belongs to most high perfection.

SCHOLIUM

I. The solution of this question depends upon the solution of the other question, namely, whether it is also to be established that there are in God the ideas of things merely possible; which all concede, but explain with a certain difference. St. Thomas (SUMMA, I, q. 15, a. 3, in reply to n. 2) distinguishes the "idea" in the strict sense as an exemplar and principle of *working* [principium operandi], and in the broader sense as a principle or reason *for cognizing* [principium seu ratio cognoscendi]. The same says (DE VERITATE, q. 3, a. 6): « That an "idea" *properly* said respects the practical cognition not only in act, but also in *habit*. Wherefore, since God has *virtually* a practical cognition of those which He can do, though they never have been done nor are going to be; it remains, that there can be an idea of that, which neither is, nor was, nor will be » etc..

From the principles posited here, another question can be solved, whether an idea pertains to *speculative* knowledge, or to the practical. For it must be resolved, that it pertains to the practical, to the extent that it is a principle of working; but to the speculative to the extent that it is a principle of cognizing. St. Thomas, DE VERITATE, q. 3, a. 3 agrees; yet he adds also another manner of speaking, according to which, *properly* speaking, the "*idea*" respects practical knowledge either in act and/or *in virtue*, while the word "*similitude*" and "*reason*" respect both speculative and practical knowledge.

II. Alexander of Hales, SUMMA., p. I, q. 23, m. 3, a. 2. — Richard of Middleton, SENT., Bk. I, d. 36, a. 2, q. 5. — Durandus (of Saint-Pourçain), SENT., Bk. I, d. 43, q. 2, n. 12. f... — (Bl.) Dionysius the Carthusian, SENT., Bk. I, d. 36, q. 3.

---

[1] Cf. Aristotle, METAPHYSICS, Bk. V, text 21 (Bk. IV, ch. 16), where among others things, those which have or acquire a boundary [finem], (are) perfect.

[2] Psalm 146:5. — A little below this the words *but an infinite one* [sed infinito] are wanting in the Vatican edition alone.

[3] Codices O and V read *there is (a fallacy)* <u>secundum quid</u> *and simply there* [ibi secundum quod et simpliciter], concerning which see above d. 19, p. I, a. sole, q. 1, p. 343, footnote 7. Next for *so also* [sic etiam] codices A S T X and not a few others, together with edition 1, have only *so* [sic].

[4] In q. 5. —A little below this, for *an ideated (thing)* [ideatum] very many

codices, together with editions 2 and 3, have *ideity* (i.e. the quality of being *ideated*) [ideitatem], and, then, in a corrupted manner, *exigency* [exigentiam] for *existence* [existentiam].

[5] Codex O reads thus: *but it means also the infinity of the manners of imitating the Divine Essence, just as has been said elsewhere, of the Divine Truth in impressing and cognizing* etc. [sed dicit infinitatem vel modorum imitandi divinam essentiam, sicut alias dictum est, divinae veritatis imprimendo et cognoscendo etc.].

[6] In codex T and not a few others there is omitted *it does* [est].

[7] Aristotle, METAPHYSICS, Bk. VII, text 40 (Bk. VI, ch. 11): Since, indeed, matter is not, it indeed is indefinite (ἀόριστον) etc..

QUESTION VI

Whether the ideas have an order?

Sixth and last, there is asked, whether among ideas there is a positing of an ordered number. That that there is,

1. (St.) Augustine[1] seems to say: « Man was established according to a reason other than (that by which) the horse (was) », because a man is one (being), a horse another: therefore, since a man is more noble than a horse, for an equal reason man was established according to a more noble idea and/or reason than the horse (was). But where there is (something) more and (something) less noble, there is an order: ergo etc..

2. Likewise, just as God cognizes and produces distinct things through ideas, so[2] He cognizes and produces ordered things: therefore, just as there is posited a plurality among ideas out of a plurality of (things) cognized and ideated, so there ought to be posited an order out of (their) order.

3. Likewise, where (there is) a plurality or a distinction, there is either an *order*, or an *inordinance* [inordinatio]; but in God there occurs no *inordinance* nor confusion: therefore, in God (ideas)[3] have an *order*.

ON THE CONTRARY: 1. Ideas are many, because through them God cognizes distinctly; but[4] God does not cognize one after the other, but all together: therefore, ideas have in God a togetherness [simultatem].

2. Likewise, if there is an order, therefore, either (it is an order) of priority, or of dignity, or of origin:[5] not of priority, because then one idea would be posterior to another, which is unfitting to say; not of nobility, because any (idea) in God is most highly noble; not of origin, because if one (idea) arises from the other, then there would be There a true distinction according to thing: therefore, in no manner, as it seems, is there an order among them.

3. Likewise, every infinity either entirely deprives order, or bears off perfection from order, because it bears off a standing-still and a complement; but among ideas there is an infinity, as has been seen in the other problem:[6] therefore, either (there is) no order (among them), or an incomplete one; but not an incomplete one, therefore, none.

CONCLUSION

Among ideas there is no order regarding one another, neither according to thing, nor according to a reckoning, but only (an order) regarding ideated (things).

I RESPOND: It must be said, just as has been touched upon in opposing,[7] there is no order among ideas or the reasons for cognizing [rationibus cognoscendi] regarding one another, neither according to *thing*, nor according to a *reckoning*. Indeed, ideas do have an order regarding (things) ideated, but not regarding one another, since neither (is) one prior to the other, nor posterior, nor is one from another, nor it is more noble; and for that reason no order is posited There. — And the reason for this is, because "ideas" mean a looking-back to things cognized, from the reckoning of their name.[8] And because those are many, for that reason ideas from the first respect of the name are many. But "order" means a new respect and a new habitude, when one idea is compared to another. And since, with that[9] respect excluded, which regards ideated (things), ideas in God are simply one [unum] and they do not have an order regarding one another; for that reason it must not be conceded, that ideas have a plurality with an order to one another.

1. To that which is objected, that it is another idea, because man (is) another: therefore, (it is) more noble, because man (is) more noble than the horse; it must be said, that it is not similar. For a similitude, by this, that (one thing) is compared to the other, has a '*being distinguished*' [distingui], but it does not have a '*being ennobled*' [nobilitari] from that, unless it receives something from that to which it is compared. And, since the idea of a man receives nothing from a man, and the idea of a horse (receives) nothing from a horse: for that reason one (idea) is not said (to be) more noble than the other.

2. To that which is objected, that God cognizes ordered things; it must be said, that although He cognizes ordered (things), yet He cognizes (them) together and in an equally noble manner; and for that reason, just as there was posited a distinction among ideas, because He cognizes distinctly through them, so there ought to be posited a togetherness [simultas] and equal nobility (among them), because He cognizes together and in a equal noble manner; and thus no order ought be posited. For just as, though God cognizes white things, there are no white ideas in God, so though He cognizes ordered (things), it is not necessary [non oportet], that there be in God ordered (ideas).

3. To that which is objected, that where there is a plurality without an order, there is confusion and inordinance; it must be said, that it is false, because there can be a togetherness there; and thus it is among ideas. — *And/or* it must be said, that that has (its) place, where there is real plurality; such it is not among ideas, because all are one [unum] (according to thing); and for that reason there cannot be an inordinance.

---

[1] In his book, OF EIGHTY-THREE QUESTIONS, q. 46, n. 2.

[2] Codex T reads *so He also* [ita etiam].

[3] Supply, together with codices F P Q and W: *ideas* [ideae].

[4] Many codices, such as A C G H I L R S T Z etc., for *but* [sed] have faultily *therefore* [ergo], codex O has better *if, therefore,* [si ergo].

[5] Cf. above d. 20, a. 2, q. 1, in the body of the Question.

[6] In the preceding Question.

[7] In the arguments of the fundament (i. e., here in the Contrary),

especially in n. 2. — At the beginning of the Response after *It must be said* [Dicendum] codices A F I and V insert *that* [quod]. Next, after *according to thing* [secundum rem], which reading we have restored from codices. F T and W, the Vatican edition has *according to origin* [secundum originem]; codices A C L O R & S and several others have *according to order* [secundum ordinem]. Then, after *a reckoning* [rationem], the Vatican edition adds *of priority or of dignity* [prioritatis aut dignitatis].

[8] Cf. above q. 3, in the body of the Question.

[9] For *that* [illo] very many codices have *one* [uno], faultily.

SCHOLIUM

I. The Response to this Question and the solution to nn. 1 and 2 is elicited from this principle, that ideas have neither a *nobility*, nor an *order*, nor *any properties* from *ideated (things)*, but only a *distinction** (cf. here q. 4, in reply to nn. 3 and 4). But, that ideas accept a distinction from ideated (things), comes from this, that ideas convey a looking-back to distinct ideated (things). Moreover, *the foundation* of that looking-back is the very perfection of the Divine Essence, which eminently contains and expresses all as the First and Most High Truth.

II. This question is found to be treated by only a few of the ancient Scholastics, namely by (Bl.) Peter of Tarentaise, SENT., Bk. I, d. 36, q. 2, a. 4, in reply to n. 9. — (Bl.) Dionysius the Carthusian, SENT., Bk. I, d. 36, q. 4, after the beginning.

DOUBTS ON THE TEXT OF THE MASTER

DOUBT I

In this part, there are doubts about the text (of Master Peter) and first concerning this which Master (Peter) says: *Yet certain of these demand a special treatment.* For either these (names)[1] demand a special treatment, because they are *difficult*, or because they have been *appropriated*. If, because they are *difficult*; but others are also difficult, such as "simplicity", "truth" and "immutability". If, because they have been *appropriated*; but "unity" and "equality" are similarly.

I RESPOND: It must be said, that these demand a special treatment from a threefold cause: both because they are difficult; and because many of them have been determined in Scripture; and also because they mean a looking-back to a creature, and according to these conditions there is attained a reckoning of cause in the Divine Nature. For that reason, because (Master Peter in his treatment of the material) ought to have passed over [facere transitum][2] to creatures or to creation, and for this there is required beforehand in the Cause a *being able* [posse], a *knowing* and a *willing*, which cause [facere] the Cause to be perfect: for that reason he locates this Tract in the midst, between the Tract on the Trinity and the Tract on the University of Things. But because (actions) of this kind hold themselves more with God, and hold themselves to this extent,[3] that they are God; for that reason this Tract is placed in the First Book.

DOUBT II

Likewise, is asked concerning this which (Master Peter) says: *There is now to be a treatment ... concerning (God's) knowledge ... and will and power.* For he seems to order (the tract) badly, because power precedes knowledge and will:[4] therefore, he badly orders (the tract) in proposing (this order) and badly (orders it) in executing (the order he proposes).

I RESPOND: It must be said, that there is a speaking of these in a twofold manner: either in their *generality*, or as *they concur* for one effect. If in their generality, thus since *knowledge* is in respect of the good and the bad to be done, it is according to the reckoning of understanding prior to [quam] power; and *power*, since it is in respect of (things) to be done and not to be done, is prior *to will*, which is only in respect of the good to be done. But if we speak of these, insofar as *they concur* for one effect; thus *power*, inasmuch as one (is) potent, is first, inasmuch as one (is) executing, is last: for *being able* is first, then *knowing*, and after *willing*, and last is *doing*, which is (the act) of power itself.[5] And as much as regard this act Master Peter puts power here in the last place; but considers the order in execution according to a greater and lesser generality.

DOUBT III

Likewise, is asked concerning this which (Master Peter) says, that *the Divine Knowledge obtains names,* which namely are "*knowledge*",[6] "*foreknowledge*" and/or "*foresight*", "*disposition*", "*predestination*", (and) "*providence*". One asks (therefore),[7] "In what manner are these names distinguished?"; and it seems, that he enumerates (them) insufficiently, because there is not only a positing among the divine of a predestination, but also of a reprobation.

I RESPOND: It can be said, that names of this kind are distinguished in this manner: the Divine Cognition can be considered in *Itself*, or in *comparison* to creatures. If in *Itself*: either insofar as It means purely a cognition through a manner of *speculation*, or insofar as it means a speculation *joined to affection*. In the first manner, It is knowledge, in the second manner it is wisdom. And/or in this manner: either[8] It means a *simple* cognition,

---

[1] Namely, "knowledge", "foreknowledge", "providence", "disposition", etc.. — Next, after the first *If* [Si] in codices P and Q there is added *on this account* [propter hoc].

[2] Codex X subjoins well *from the Creator* [de Creatore]. Then for *to creation* [ad creationem] nearly all the codices have *to the Creator* [ad Creatore]; not well.

[3] For *and hold themselves to this extent, that* [et adeo se tenet] the Vatican edition has *and (are) from God, when* [et a Deo, cum]. After *that* [quod] many codices add *because* [quia], but superfluously.

[4] Concerning which see above d. 27, p. II, a. sole, q. 3, p. 487, footnote 5. — Next, we have corrected the reading of the Vatican edi-

tion, *proposed* [proposito], with *in proposing* [proponendo], from codices D T aa and bb.

[5] For *(the act) of power itself* [ipius potentiae] codex E has *the act of its own power* [actus sua potentiae].

[6] Codex W adds "*wisdom*" [sapientia].

[7] Codex bb adds *therefore* [ergo]. Then codices V and Y have *are distinguished* [distinguantur] in the subjunctive.

[8] Codex V subjoins *insofar as* [prout], and a little below this after *a most noble reckoning* [rationem nobilissimam] the Vatican edition, together with a few codices, adds *or through most noble causes, which are themselves God* [sive per causas nobilissimas, quae ipsae Deus sunt].

---

* *Trans. note*: Supply here: *in regard to the ideated.* Because the distinction among things comes from the Divine Will which creates distinct things according to the ideas of things possible and distinct; and, thus, this distinction is not *according to* the ideated, because this implies that the ideated are primary, the distinction of ideas secondary; nor really *from* the ideated, since nothing outside of God is the cause of anything in God, but only *notionally* from the ideated, since each relative implies its correlative. — Throughout this Distinction, the term "*ideated (things)*" [ideata] does not mean *things* as "real things", but all that depends upon any idea in God, whether things or notions or forms or properties or qualities, whether substantial, actual, potential, virtual etc..

or (a cognition) through a *most noble* reckoning. In the first manner (It is) "knowledge", in the second manner "wisdom".[1] — But if It be considered in *comparison* to things, this can be in a twofold manner: either It connotes an *event*, and thus (is) "foreknowledge"; or an *effect*, and this in a twofold manner: either in *conserving* or *governing*, and thus (It is) "providence"; or in *effecting*, and this in a twofold manner: either as much as regards a good *of nature*, and thus (It is) "disposition"; or as much as regards a *superadded* good, and thus (is) "predestination", or as much as regards its *privation*, and thus (is) "reprobation". And because the privation of grace is not a (divine) *effect*, but a *defect* (of the creature), for that reason "reprobation" is not enumerated here, but is contained under the name for foreknowledge, and that (name) is appropriated to It.

Whence the division can be formed in the manner: God's Cognition either is in Itself, or in a comparison: if in Itself, either (It is said to be a "cognition") through a most noble reckoning, and thus (is) "*Wisdom*"; or through some kind of [qualemcumque] reckoning, and thus is "*Knowledge*". If in comparison: either to events, and thus (is) "*foreknowledge*", or to events and effects, and this either in governing, and thus is "*providence*"; and/or in effecting, and thus, if (the comparison) is in respect of a whatever of nature, It is "*disposition*"; if in respect of a rational (creature), thus (It is) "*predestination*"; or to events and effects and defects, and thus (It is) the "*reprobation*", which is named "foreknowledge".[2]

DOUBT IV

Likewise, is asked concerning this which (Master Peter) says, that "*creator" is said in a relative manner thus, that it does not signify the Essence*. For he seem to say the false: for "*creation*" signifies a manner of action, not (a manner) of relation, therefore, "*creator*" similarly: therefore, it is not said according to a relation on the part of the manner, nor on the part of the thing; that is established: therefore, (it is said relatively) in no manner. — Likewise, he seems to say the false, when he says, that it does not signify the Essence, because "*creation*" [creatio] signifies something: therefore, either (something) created, or uncreated. If created: therefore, it is not said of God; if uncreated: therefore, since it does not signify a Person, it signifies the Essence.

I RESPOND: It must be said, that '*that something be said relatively*' is in a twofold manner: either because it signifies a relation, just as names, which are in the predicament of relation; or because it has a looking-back (to something else) adjoined (to it): thus, since every action means a looking-back to (what) suffers (it) or the (thing) done, and (what)

suffers (it) to the one acting, thus it is said in a manner relative (to the other), and thus Master (Peter) understands (it) concerning this name "*creator*"; and well.[3]

Even the other (thing), which he says, that *it does not signify the Essence*, he says on account of this, that though (the act of creation) is imposed upon the Divine Essence — and for that reason is said of the Essence alone, according to all (authors) — yet concerning that, by which it is imposed, there was a controversy. For certain (authors) wanted to say, that names (belonging) to the six genera[4] do not *predicate* anything in God, but *co-predicate*. Whence "action" does not seem to say anything *in* the one acting, but (something) *by* the one acting. And reason seems consonant with this, because action and passion seem to be the same. And again the word of (St. Severinus) Boethius ON THE TRINITY,[5] that « the other genera of things are predicated neither of the Creator, nor of creatures », seems consonant with this. — This opinion was sufficiently probable, and Master (Peter) was of this (opinion);[6] and for that reason he says, that "*foreknowledge*" according to the reckoning of knowledge conveys the Essence, but "*creator*" (conveys) only a relation.

Nevertheless, today this is not commonly held. For we say, that God is His own action, as for example, (His act of) creation. And since the Divine Essence is an action, and this name "*creator*" is imposed from an action; for that reason not only has it been imposed upon *the Essence*, but also *by the Essence*, but it signifies That in relation. Nor does (St. Severinus) Boethius intend to say, that such (names) are not predicated, but (that) they are not predicated absolutely. — However, if we wish to sustain Master (Peter) according to the common opinion, we say, that Master (Peter) does not want to say, that "*creation*" does not convey the Divine Essence, but that, as much as (it signifies) out of the force of the word, it does not mean the Essence absolutely, but through the manner of relation or under a relative appellation. But "*foreknowledge*" means two (things): both a knowledge and a precedence [praecessionem].[7] According to the reckoning of knowledge it means the absolute Essence, whence it remains a knowledge, with the thing itself not remaining. Not so does it concern "*creation*", for there is no (act of) creation, unless there is also a creature. And according to this (explanation), the word of Master (Peter) is not worthy of calumny [non habet calumniam].[8]

DOUBT V

Likewise, is asked concerning this which (Master Peter) says: *If there were no future (things), yet there would be in God the same knowledge*. For he seems to speak badly, because our knowledge posits

---

[1] Cf. Aristotle, METAPHYSICS., Bk. I, ch. 1 ff., and ETHICS, Bk. VI, chs. 6 and 7.

[2] The Vatican edition alone adds *through appropriation* [per appropriationem]. — The Seraphic Doctor treats of the diverse names attributed to the Divine Knowledge more at length below in d. 38 ff. Alexander of Hales also speaks of them in his SUMMA, p. I, q. 23, m. 1, near the end, and also Bl. (now St.) Albertus (Magnus), here in a. 4.

[3] Cf. above d. 30, q. 3.

[4] Understand: belonging to the higher genera or to the predicaments, which are: action, passion, where, when, layout [situs] and habit. According to those, of whom the Seraphic Doctor speaks here, these names are not said of any thing in the same manner, in which the names (belonging to) the four first predicaments, which are: substance, quantity, quality, (and) relation, are said. For those four are said of a thing, to the extent that what is signified by those names is contained intrinsically in the thing itself, of which it is predicated; but those six (are said), to the extent that what is signified by

them is something, which affect extrinsically the thing, of which it is predicated. Or, as (St. Severinus) Boethius says, ON THE TRINITY, ch. 4: « Some (predications), indeed, quasi demonstrate the think, but others quasi (demonstrate) the circumstances of the thing; and that the former indeed thus are predicated, to show that something is a thing, but the latter (are predicated), not (to show) that it is (a thing), but rather affix something (to it) extrinsically in a certain manner ». This difference is briefly insinuated (by St. Bonaventure) by the verbs *predicate* [praedicare] and *co-predicate* [compraedicare].

[5] Chapter 4: However, the rest are neither predicated of God nor of all others.

[6] In chapter 7 of this Distinction.

[7] For *a precedence* [praecessionem] nearly all the codices, together with the first editions have faultily *predestination* [praedestinationem]; codex O has better *a fore-ordering* [praeordinationem].

[8] This doubt is also solved by Bl. (now St.) Albertus (Magnus), here in a. 6, and by St. Thomas and Richard (of Middleton), here on the text.

things, and when it does not posit (them), it is not knowledge, but an opinion and/or another accepting [acceptio] less noble:[1] therefore, since it is of the nobility of knowledge to posit a thing, it seems much more strongly, that the Divine Knowledge, which is the most noble (knowledge), posit (a thing).

I Respond: Regarding this it must be briefly said, that there is a knowledge, by which I have a cognition of the thing, and there is a knowledge, by which I know, that the thing is.[2] The first knowledge, neither in us, nor in God posits the existence of the thing in its own genus, neither concerning the present, nor concerning the future; which is clear, because a craftsman has the cognition of making a house, which he never will make. However, the second knowledge posits the thing both in God and in us; but in us,[3] because (the knowledge) *depends* (upon the thing), in God, because *it connotes* (it). And as much as regard the first manner Master (Peter) says, that it would be the same knowledge, but not in respect of the same, and as much as regard the second manner (that it would be a knowledge) in respect of as many, as it is in respect of now.

Doubt VI

Likewise, is asked concerning this which (Master Peter) says, that *all are present to Him, not only those which are, but also those which have passed away*. In what manner is that understood?

For either it is understood of presence according to *truth*, or of presence according to *cognition*. In the first manner it is false: (for) it is established, that the Antichrist is not present in God according to the truth. If according to *cognition*, because He has a cognition of (things)[4] past and future; but thus a soul has (it): therefore, similarly all are present to it.

I Respond: It must be said, that all are not said to be present to God according to *the truth of the existence* of things, but (rather) according to *cognition*, because *by an act* He cognizes (things) present, past, and future; and about *the act* of His Cognition there is always a quality of being present [praesentialitas], so that there is no succession in *the now* of God's Cognition, which (now) comprises every succession without mutation: and for that reason all are present to It from a *twofold cause*.[5] Moreover, although a creature has a cognition of (things) past, yet because its cognition passes over into the past, and a new cognition is generated out of the existence of the thing: for that reason one does not say, that all are present to a creature, just as one says, that all are present to God. And for that reason there is posited in God no *memory*, since the memory looks back to the past,[6] not only in *the thing* (remembered), but as even *the act* of that cognition passes over into the past; but "*foreknowledge*" does not mean a reckoning or act of knowledge as a future (act); and for that reason in God it is fittingly posited.

---

[1] Cf. Aristotle, Posterior Analytics, Bk. I, ch. 2: There is no knowing of that which is not, such as that a diameter is a symmeter; and ibid., ch. 26 (ch. 33), where the differences between knowledge and opinion are examined.

[2] The first knowledge is commonly called, in respect of God, the knowledge *of simple understanding* [scientia simplicis intelligentiae], the other the knowledge *of vision* (cf. below d. 39, a. 1, q. 3, and d. 41, a. 2, q. 2).

[3] Codex O adds: *just as an effect posits (its) cause; in God, just as a cause posits the effect* [sicut effectus ponit causam; in Deo, sicut causa ponit effectum]. — More concerning this doubt will be found below in d. 38, a. 1, qq. 1 and 2.

[4] The Vatican edition here inserts the word *present* [praesentium], for no reason, since the question does not concern things present. Next for *but thus a soul has (it)* [sed sic habet una anima] the same Vatican edition, dissuaded by all the codices, has *but if thus, since a soul also has this* [sed si sic, cum hanc habeat etiam anima].

[5] Not a few have interpreted this passage to mean, that St.

Bonaventure taught the sentence of (Bl. John Duns) Scotus, which opposed the doctrine of St. Thomas concerning the presence of things in eternity; concerning which see below d. 39, a. 2, q. 3. But this interpretation seems to be alien to the mind of the Seraphic (Doctor), who offers a twofold reason for this, that all are present to God, that is, one (reason) on the part of *the Divine Cognition*, the other on the part of *the eternity of God*; and in proffering this second reason he entirely convenes with St. Thomas, saying « that (the *now* of eternity) comprises every succession without mutation [omnem successionem sine mutatione] », which words are explained at greater length below in d. 39, a. 1, q. 3, in St. Thomas' sense (cf. the Scholium there). — Next the Vatican edition dilates the text by inserting after *a cognition of (things)* [cognitionem de] the word *present* [praesentibus], after *past* [praeteritis] the words *and future* [et futuris], and after *to the past* [praeteritum] the words *and the future* [et futurum].

[6] Cf. above d. 3, p. II, a. 1, q. 1, in reply to n. 3. — The Vatican edition alone adds *as past* [ut praeteritum].

DISTINCTION XXXVI

CHAPTER I

Whether all ought to be said to be in the God's Essence, as they are said to be in God's Cognition and/or Foreknowledge?

Here, there is customarily asked, since all are said to be in God's Cognition or Foreknowledge[1] and/or in God through cognition, and His Cognition and/or Foreknowledge is the Divine Essence, whether it must be conceded, that all are in the Divine Essence and/or in God through essence. — To which we say, that God's Cognition is indeed His Essence, and His Foreknowledge, in which are all (things), is His Cognition, and yet not all, which are in His Foreknowledge and/or Cognition, ought be said to be in His Essence. For if this would be said, they would be understood to belong to the same Essence with God.[2] For in God there is said to be through essence, that which is the Divine Essence, which is God. Therefore, God has with Himself in His own Foreknowledge those which He does not have in His own Nature. Whence (St.) Augustine thus says of the words of the Apostle:[3] « *He has elected us before the constitution of the world.* Who is sufficient to explain this? They are elected, who are not, nor does He err, who elects, nor does He elect in vain; yet, He elects and has as elected, those whom He is going to create to be elected, which He has with His very self, not in His own Nature [in natura sua], but in His own foreknowledge ». They were not yet, those to whom He promised (the Kingdom),[4] but they too have been promised, they to whom He has promised. — Behold he openly says, that God has the elect with Himself before the world, not in His own Nature, but in His Foreknowledge, yet though His Foreknowledge is not other than His Nature, because His foreknowledge is His Knowledge [notitia]. Yet it can be referred to the elect, when he says: in natura sua, that is, (in) *their* (nature).* Indeed He had them from eternity with Himself, not in their own nature [in natura sua],[5] that is, (in that) of them, who were not yet, but in the foreknowledge of them [in sua praescientia], because He thus knew [novit] them, as if they were.

CHAPTER II

By what reckoning are good (things) said to be in God, and not evil ones?

After the aforesaid, there is asked, since all are said to be in God, not through the essence of the Nature, but through the cognition of knowledge, and God knows (things) good and evil, whether it must be simply conceded, that there are evil (things) in God, or that they are in God through cognition. For God knows [scit] and has known always all (things), both good and evil, even before they are made, and He foreknew them as future from eternity. And for that reason since we said that all goods are in God on account of the foreknowledge of (His) Cognition, for the same reason it seems that there must be said, that all evils are in Him, since He has always known [noverit] them, and they were through cognition present to Him. For God cognized beforehand from eternity that certain ones (were) going to be wicked and, as (St.) Augustine says,[6] He foreknew their malice, but He did not prepare (it). Therefore, since He knows the sins of all, must it not be understood, that these are included in that generality of expression, by which the Apostle said,[7] that all are in God? He says, *from Him and through Him and in Him are all.* — But who, except the insane, has said, that there are evil (things) in God? For those are understood to be in God, which are *from Him* and *through Him*; but these are *through Him* and *from Him*, whose Author He is; but He is the Author of naught but the good. Therefore, naught is *from Him* and *through Him*, but good (things); thus, therefore, naught are *in Him* but good (things): therefore, evil (things) are not in God, because, though He knows [noscat] them, yet He does not thus entirely know (them), as good (things). Evil (things) He cognizes as from afar, as (King David) the Prophet says,[8] *and the heights He cognizes from afar*, that is, pride. And elsewhere speaking to God of the wicked he says: *Of those hidden from Thee has their belly been filled.* Which (St.) Augustine expounds: « The hidden things », he says, « are the sins, which are hidden from the Light of Thy Truth ». But in what manner are sins hidden from the Light of Divine Truth, when they are known [sciantur] by God? For if He did not know (them), in what manner would He judge of them and damn the wicked for them. Elsewhere the Prophet (says):[9] *Because neither from the East, nor from the West* is He absent [deest]. Which expounding (Flavius Magnus Aurelius) Cassiodorus says: « Neither from the good, nor from the wicked is God absent, but He is present to and the cognizer of all ». Therefore, God cognizes both good (things) and evil ones through knowledge, but He also cognizes good (things) through approbation and good pleasure [beneplacitum], but evil ones (He does) not. Whence Cassiodorus says on the Psalm: « Sins have been hidden from God, because He knew [novit] (them) not, that is, He does not approve (them) ». And in this sense (St.) Augustine said that they (have been) hidden from the Light of God. He who in (his) Epistle to Evodius[10] insinuated, that God's "cognition" is to be accepted various manners, saying: « If you refer

---

[1] Here and in this entire chapter and the following, all our codices and editions, except the Vatican edition and editions 2 and 8, for *foreknowledge* [praescientia] put *presence* [praesentia]; which in indeed in itself is not false, as is explained by Master (Peter) in Distinction XXXV, ch. 9, even though it is less congruous.

[2] Codices B C and E, together with very many editions have *Him* [eo] for *God* [Deo].

[3] Ephesians 1:4; (St.) Augustine's 26th Sermon, ch. 4, n. 4. In which text the Vatican edition, together with a few editions and codices A B and E, has *elects, nor did He elect in vain* [eligit, nec vane elegit] for *elects, nor does He elect in vain* [eligit, nec vane eligit].

[4] Codices B C D and E (A in the margin) add *the Kingdom* [regnum]. A little after this only the Vatican edition and editions 4 and 5 have *the constitution of the world* [mundi consitutionem] for *the world* [mundum].

[5] Thus codices A C & D and edd. 2, 3, 5 & 7; the Vatican ed., with others, has *there own* [sui] for *there own* [sua]. Immediately after this editions 1, 2, 3, 5, 7, and 8 have *because they* [quia] for *who* [qui].

[6] ON THE PREDESTINATION OF THE SAINTS, Bk. I, ch. 10, according to sense.

[7] Romans 11:36.

[8] Psalm 137:6; the second citation is Ps. 16:14. The citation from (St.) Augustine is ENARRATIONS ON THE PSALMS., Ps. 16, n. 13.

[9] Psalm 74:7; Cassiodorus, EXPOSITION ON THE PSALTER, on this passage: The following citation of the same (author) is Ps. 16:14.

[10] Our codices and editions have *book to Helvidius* [libro ad Helvidium], but in truth the passage is found in his EPISTLES., 169, n. 2 "to Evodius", with not a few (words) omitted, however, by Master (Peter). A little before this the codices have *are hidden from the Light* [abscondi a lumine] for *(have been) hidden from the Light* [abscondita a lumine].

---

* *Trans. note*: In accord with Master Peter assertion, which distorts the plain sense of the text, that in natura sua can be construed as referring to the elect, rather than to God, in natura sua is rendered here as *in their own nature*, and, then, in sua praescientia as *in the foreknowledge of them*. — Master Peter seemingly does this to reconcile two truths, namely that the elect pre-exist in some manner in God prior to creation, and, yet, the elect are not God; and he uses St. Augustine's denial of their identity with the Divine Nature and his affirmation of their existence in God's Foreknowledge, un-

to (His) knowledge [scientiam], God is not ignorant of some and/or some (things), who, however, says to certain ones in judgement: *I have not known you* [non novis vos],[1] but (rather) by this verse their disapproval is insinuated ». — Behold, God is said not to cognize those which[2] He does not approve, which are not pleasing to Him. And thus it appears, that what we said is true, namely, that in a certain manner God cognizes good (things), in which (manner) He does not cognize evil ones. Indeed He knows [noscit] each equally and in the same manner as much as regards being known [notitiam], but He cognizes good (things) also by approbation and good pleasure.

And hence it is, that good (things) are only said to be in God, not evil ones, and the former *from up close* [prope], the latter *from afar* [longe], because though somethings are said to be in God on account of the presence of cognition, and (since) God cognizes good (things) and evil ones, yet He does not cognize evil ones except through (their) being known [notitiam], but good ones not only through knowledge [scientiam], but also through approbation and good pleasure. And because of such a cognition some are said to be in God, that is, because He thus knows [scit] them, as to also approve them, and they are pleasing, that is, He thus knows [scit] (them), that He is their Author.

CHAPTER III

Whether it is the same that all are "from God" and "through Him" and "in Him".

Consequently, if we diligently look into (it), *"from God"* [ex Deo] and *"through Him"* [per ipsum] and *"in Him"* [in ipso] seems to be the same. Whence (St.) Ambrose in the third book, ON THE HOLY SPIRIT (says):[3] « We have said above, that these three: *"from God"* and *"through Him"* and *"in Him"*, are *all* one [unum]. When (St. Paul) says, that all are *"through Him"*, he did not deny, that all are *"in Him"*. All these have the same force, namely *"with Him"* [cum ipso] and *"in Him"* and *"through Him"*, and one among them is also understood to be completely similar (the others), not contrary (to them) ». — Behold you have it, that from the same understanding Scripture says, that all are *"in Him"* and *"through Him"* and *"from Him"* and/or *"with Him"*. Therefore, since on account of this[4] reckoning all are said to be *"from God"* and/or *"through Him"*, not only because He knows [scit] (them), but also because He is their Author; it entirely follows [consequitur], that they are said *"to be in God"* according to the same reckoning, namely, because He knows[5] (them) and He is their Author: it is said, that *in Him we live and are moved and are*, because by Him as Author we are, we are moved and we live. Therefore, since He is not the Author but of the good, deservedly are good (things) alone said to be *"in Him"*, just as (they are said to be) *"from Him"* and *"through Him"*. Therefore, since in His Cognition and/or foreknowledge are all, namely (things) good and evil, yet in Him are said to be naught but the good (things), of which He is the Author. Whence (St.) Augustine in the book, ON THE NATURE OF THE GOOD (says):[6] « When we hear », he says, « that all are *"from God"* and *"through Him"* and *"in Him"*, we indeed ought to understand "all natures", and "all which are naturally". For neither are there from Him the sins, which do not serve nature, but vi-

tiate it, which are born from the will of sinners ». — Here he openly says, that in that generality of expression only good (things) are contained.

CHAPTER IV

That all are in Any of the Three both through Him and in Him.

Moreover, it must be known, that though the distinction of the Persons is indicated there, when there is said: *"from Him"* and *"through Him"* and *"in Him"*, yet all are from the Father and through the Father and in the Father; similarly it must be accepted concerning the Son and concerning the Holy Spirit. Whence (St.) Augustine in (his) book, ON THE TRINITY (says):[7] « One must not », he says, « accept in a confused manner, what the Apostle says, *"from Him and through Him and in Him"*: saying *"from Him"* on account of the Father, *"through Him"* on account of the Son, *"in Him"* on account of the Holy Spirit ». But vigilantly attend, lest, because he said *"from Him"*, wanting the Father to be understood (thereby), you understand, that all are from the Father, so as to deny, that all are from the Son and/or from the Holy Spirit, since all can sanely be said to be from the Father and through the Father and in the Father; similarly must it be said both of the Son and of the Holy Spirit.

CHAPTER V

That not all which are ex Deo, are also de ipso.

This also must be adjoined[8] here, that not all which are said to be *from* God [ex Deo], ought to be also said to be *of* Him [de ipso]: « because », as (St.) Augustine says in the book, ON THE NATURE OF THE GOOD,[9] « ex ipso does not mean entirely the same (thing) as de ipso. For that which is *of Him*, can be said to be *from Him*, but not everything which is *from Him*, can be said to be *of Him*, because it is not of His Substance. For Heaven and Earth are *from Him*, because He made them, but not *of Him*, because (they are not) of His Substance. Just as any man, if he generates[10] a son and makes a house, the son is *from him*, and the house is *from him*, but the son (is) *of him*, however, the house is *of earth and wood* », not *of him*.

In[11] the aforementioned it has been revealed, that in God's cognition or foreknowledge are all, namely (things) good and evil, but the evil are not there in every manner, in which good (things are); and that in God only good (things) are, as *from Him* and *through Him*, not evil ones; and (that) there has been assigned, in what sense these are to be accepted; and that naught is said properly to be *of Him* which is other than Him: but all, which are by Him as Author, are said to be *from Him*.

---

[1] A reference to Mt. 7:23: *I have never known you* [Nunquam novi vos]; and Lk. 13:17: *I do not know you* [Nescio vos].

[2] Only the Vatican ed. and ed. 2 have, sufficiently well, *He who* [qui] for *those who* [quae]. Our reading is explained by ed. 8 which inserts *and/or* [vel] after *approve* [approbat]. Then, below this, trusting in the codd. and ed. 1, we have restored *and in the same* [eodemque] for *in the same* [eodem].

[3] Chapter 11, n. 84, but with the order of the propositions changed. The passage of Sacred Scripture is Rom. 11:36.

[4] Contrary to the codices and edition 1, the Vatican edition, together with the other editions, has *the same* [eadem] for *this* [ea].

[5] Here the passage seems to be corrupted in all the edd.; the Vatican ed. has *namely because He also is said to be their Author, because* [scilicet quia et eorum auctor esse dicitur, quia]; the other editions have *namely, because He knows (them) and is said to be their Author, because* [scilicet quia scit et eorum auctor esse dicitur, quia]. Our codd. put *is* [est] in place of *to be* [esse]. — The passage from Sacred Scripture is Acts 17:28.

[6] Chapter 28. At the end of this text (after *which* in the English) the Vatican edition and very many editions add *all* [omnia], contrary to the codices, edition 1 and to the original.

[7] Book VI, ch. 10, n. 12, whence are taken the first words; the others are from Bk. I, ch. 6, n. 12. The original reads: "From Him", from the Father; "through Him", through the Son; "in Him", in the Holy Spirit.

[8] Thus the Vatican edition, together with codices B and E and the other editions, except edition 1, which has *must be averted to* [advertendum] for *must be adjoined* [annectendum], codices C and D have *must be attended to* [attendendeum]; in the Division of the Text St. Bonaventure as *one must turn his attention to* [adnimadvertendum].

[9] Chapter 27, with not a few things changed.

[10] The original has *begets* [gignat] for *generates* [generat] and, then, *makes* [faciat] for *makes* [facit]; the edd. have *generates* [generat] and, then, with the exception of edd. 3, 7 & 8, they incongruously read *makes* [faciat].

[11] The Vatican edition, together with codex E, has *From* [ex].

---

derstanding, since the Divine Foreknowledge is the Divine Nature, so that St. Augustine can be understood to use sua not in reference to God, as he plainly is, but in reference to *the elect*. This problematic interpretation proposed by Master Peter is addressed more properly by St. Bonaventure in his own tract on divine ideas in the preceding Distinction, for it involves the foreknowing of something by God in God, which is not God according to His Essence in itself, but in some sense is the Essence in relation to creatures, inasmuch as they are known by God from eternity. And this, it seems, is the reason for the Seraphic Doctor placing his tract on divine ideas, which is unique among the ancient Scholastics, here in the prior Distinction.

COMMENTARY ON DISTINCTION XXXVI

In what manner are things in God?

Here, there is customarily asked, since all are said to be in God's Cognition etc..

THE DIVISION OF THE TEXT

Above, Master (Peter) dealt with God's Cognition, by which He cognized all created (things). And, since the cognized is said to be in the one cognizing, for that reason he determines here, second, the manner, in which things are in God. And, since created tings are not only said to be *in God* [in Deo], but also *from God* [ex Deo] and *through God* [per Deum], for that reason he *first* deals with the existence of things in God; but, *second*, compares (them) to the other habitudes, namely "*from Him*" and "*through Him*", there (where he says): *Consequently if we diligently look into (it)* etc..

The first part has two (parts). In the first, (Master Peter) shows, in what kind of manner things are said to be in God on the part of that in which they are, whether, that is, they are in God's Essence, just as they are in God's foreknowledge. In the second,[1] in what kind of manner they are said to be in God on the part of those things, there (where he says): *After the aforesaid there is asked, since all are said to be in God* etc., where he asks, whether there are evil (things) in God, and he solves (the question), that (there are) not. Any of these parts could be divided: since he asks and opposes, and afterwards he determines, and the parts are manifest in the text. •

Consequently, if we diligently look into (it). This is the *second* part, in which he compares that which it is "*to be in God*" to other habitudes, conveyed through other prepositions, and this part has four parts according to the four chapters. In the first, he shows the agreement of these three; in the second, (their) difference and appropriation, there (where he says): *Moreover, it must be known* etc.. In the third, he shows the difference of that which is said (to be) "*of Him*" [de ipso] regarding that which is said[2] (to be) "*from Him*" [ex ipso], there (where he says): *Here one must also turn his attention[3] to this* etc.. In the fourth, he briefly summarizes [epilogat] the aforesaid, there (where he says): *From the aforementioned it has been revealed* etc.; and these can be divided against the entire preceding (part). The understanding of the parts is clear in the text.

TREATMENT OF THE QUESTIONS

For an understanding of this part, there is the question of the existence of things in God, and about this three (questions) are principally asked.

First, there is asked, whether creatures were in God eternally.

Second, there is the question concerning the manner of the existing of those things in God.

Third, as much as regards the generality[4] of things existing in God, whether, namely, all which God cognizes, were and are in God. — Thus, that first (there is the question) concerning (their) existence, second concerning the manner, and third concerning (their) number.

Therefore, as much as regard the first Article, two (questions) are asked.

First there is asked, whether there were things in God from eternity.

Second, whether they are in God according to a reckoning of essence, and/or of person.

---

[1] For *In the second* [In secunda] very many codd. have *Second* [Secundo].

[2] For *is said* [dicitur] codices P Q and V have *is* [est]; in not a few codices there is neither *is said* [dicitur] nor *is* [est].

[3] Codex T has *attend* [attendedum] for *turn his attention* [animadvertendum].*

[4] Cod. A has *universality* [universalitatem]. A little after this, the Vatican ed. with cod. cc, has *cognizes beforehand* [praecognoscit] for *cognizes* [cognoscit].

---

* *Trans. note*: As frequently occurs, St. Bonaventure quotes a version of Lombard's text, which differs from the critical edition presented by the Quaracchi editors. The original text of Lombard, here, reads *This also must be adjoined here* [Illud etiam hic annectendum est]. Cf. here the text of Master Peter, ch. 5, footnote 8.

ARTICLE I

On the existence of things in God.

QUESTION I

Whether things were in God from eternity?

Moreover, that things were in God from eternity, seems:

1. Because an active cognizer [agens cognoscens] acts through the species of the thing, which he has from within himself [penes se];[1] but a thing is in the soul, because its similitude is in it: therefore, also in God similarly. *If you say*, that that exemplar is nothing of the thing, therefore, according to that there ought not be said, that things are in God; *on the contrary*: what is *cognitive* and *productive* causes an exemplar of a thing more to *be*, than what has *been produced* by the thing:[2] if, therefore, according to the reckoning of an exemplar *produced* by the thing, a thing is in the soul, much more strongly ought it to be said to be in God according the reckoning of a producing exemplar; but this is from eternity: ergo etc..

2. Likewise, a produced similitude is not truly *something*, but *of something*;[3] but the exemplar, through which God cognizes, is truly God Himself: therefore, the exemplar of the thing in God is more true than (the one) in the soul: therefore, much more strongly is a thing in God than it is in the soul, and thus etc..

3. Likewise, because a thing can go forth from matter, a thing is in matter, and, yet, it is not totally in the potency of the matter, nay of the agent:[4] therefore, if things, which are in God's Power, are There totally, must more strongly ought they be said to be in Him, and thus etc..

ON THE CONTRARY: 1. What goes forth through being created [per creationem] is entirely nothing, before it is created; but creatures go forth in this manner: therefore, they are entirely nothing, before they are produced. But what is not, neither is here nor there:[5] therefore, it is not in something, and thus neither in God.

2. Likewise, what is in something, is in it either according to *itself*, and/or according to *something of its own*; but a thing is not in God according to *itself*, because then the essence of the thing would be in God;[6] nor according to *something of itself*, because nothing of itself is eternal, but the whole (of it is) in time [ex tempore]: ergo etc..

3. Likewise, what is in something is in it according to *actual 'being'* [esse actuale], and/or *potential* ('being'): but a creature is not in God according to *actual 'being'*, because then it would be by an act: therefore, if it is in God, it is according to *potential 'being'*. But every *potential 'being'* [esse potentiale], according to which (it is) of this kind, is thoroughly mutable [permutabile]: therefore, if a creature from eternity is in God according to potential 'being', it is in God from eternity according to mutable 'being'. But this (is) false: therefore, the first (is) also (false).

4. Likewise, if a creature is said to be *"in God"*, because it can be (created) *by God* [a Deo]: therefore, since it is impossible that it be (created) *by God* from eternity,[7] a creature will not be in God from eternity according to a reckoning of power.

CONCLUSION

Things are in God from eternity according to the presence of (their) similitude and also according to (God's) causative power, but not according to a real existence.

I RESPOND: It must be said, that something is said *"to be in something"* [esse in aliquo] in a threefold manner: either[8] according to *actual*

---

[1] Cf. above d. 35, q. 1. — Concerning the minor of this argument, see Aristotle, ON THE SOUL, Bk. III, text 38. (ch. 8).

[2] In this proposition the idea created in the (human) mind is said to be something *"produced by the thing"*, to the extent that the intelligible species, produced in the soul by the object, concurs, as a principle *by which*, with the action of the soul for the production of the exemplar or (created) idea. This does not pertain to divine ideas. Cf. Dionysius (the Areopagite), ON THE DIVINE NAMES, ch. 5, § 8.

[3] Aristotle, METAPHYSICS, Bk. VII, text 8 (Bk. VI, ch. 3) says: καὶ γὰρ τὸ χωριστὸν καὶ τό τόδε τι ὑπάρχειν δοκεῖ μάλιστα τῇ οὐσίᾳ, which words in the ancient Venetian version (A.D. 1489) were rendered thus into Latin: « For indeed it seems that there is, most of all, in a substance a separable and *this something* [Etenim separabile et *hoc aliquid* inesse videtur maxime substantiae] ». Cf. also his book, ON PREDICAMENTS, ch. "On Substance", from which much is cited below in d. 37, p. I, a. 2, q. 1, 3rd argument of the fundament. Hence the Scholastics call a *substance* "this something" [hoc aliquid]. Similarly, Aristotle calls it "that which *truly is*" [quod vere est], concerning which see above d. 23, a. 1, q. 2, p. 407, footnote 1. But an *accident* is said to be *of something*. Similarly, Aristotle, METAPHYSICS, Bk. VII, text 2 (Bk. VI, ch. 1) also teaches, that accidents are not so much *beings* [entia], as *something of a being* [quid entis], that is, either the quantity and/or quality of a substance. The sense of the Seraphic Doctors' words is: the similitude (exemplar, or idea) pro-

duced in the soul is not a substance, but an accident. — At the end of the argument, codex V has *and if thus* [et si sic] for *and thus* [et sic].

[4] For an agent by transmuting matter by its own action draws forth out of that, which per se is undiffering to diverse forms, a form similar to itself.

[5] Aristotle, PHYSICS, Bk. IV, text 1 (ch. 1): And indeed those which are, all estimate to be somewhere, however, that which is not, (they estimate) never to be. — Next for *and thus* [et ita] codices T and X have *therefore* [ergo].

[6] And consequently the essence of the creature would be the Essence of God. — For *the essence of the thing* [essential rei], which reading is had in codices C F K T and others, not a few codices falsely have *the essence of God* [essential Dei], the Vatican edition has *essentially it* [essentialiter]. A little further above this, for *in it* [in illo] many codices have *by it* [ab illo], to which reading the context is repugnant. — On the major of this argument, cf. Aristotle, PHYSICS, Bk. IV, text 24. (c. 3.).

[7] Or, since it is repugnant, that things be created by God from eternity.

[8] For *either* [vel] codices T and Z have *namely* [scilicet]. The same codices, together with very many others, then omits the following *and/or* [vel], and for the next *and/or* [vel] substitute *and* [et].

existence, and/or according to *the presence of a similitude*, and/or according to *causative power*. In the first manner things are in the universe, in the second manner in a cognitive substance, in the third manner in their own cause. In these two last manners things are in God, because He is the One cognizing things, before they come to be, and the One able to produce (them). Whence because *He cognized* (them) from eternity, and (because) *the power*, by which He produced (them) in time, was in God from eternity, for that reason things are said to be in God from eternity.

1. To that which is objected: what is[1] nothing is not in anything; it must be said, that it is true in the first manner of existing, but false according to the second and according to the third (manner), because that which is nothing now, God can make.

2. To that which is objected, that that which is in something,[2] is in it according to itself etc.; it must be said, that as much as regards the *second* manner things are in God according to *something of themselves*, because (they are there) according to *an exemplar*. But "*something of a thing*" [aliquid rei] can be said in a threefold manner, namely *essentially, effectively* and *causatively*, that is,

just as a *part*, an *effect* and/or a *cause*. In this third manner that exemplar is *something of the thing*.[3] — As much as regards the *third* manner, namely, causative power, the thing is (in God) according to itself not in an *act*, but *according to potency*, because its own 'being' can be produced by God.

3. Similarly, to the following (objection), it must be said, that according to the reckoning of an *exemplar*[4] things are *actually* in God; according to the reckoning *of being created* [creationis] (they are in God) *potentially*, because they can be produced.

What is objected: what is in God is immutable; it must be said, that this is true of that which is in God *by an act*; but what can be produced by God is mutable. — *And/or* it must be said, that the possible[5] has a comparison to the Divine Power, which is immutable, and thus it is immutable; and/or to the temporal (thing) connoted outside (of God), and thus has a mutable 'being'.

4. To that which is objected concerning creation [de creatione], it must be said, that although the act of creating [actus creandi] could not be from eternity, yet the power of creating [potentia creandi] was in God.[6]

SCHOLIUM

I. In this Distinction the whole doctrine concerning the existence of things in God is most accurately treated by St. Bonaventure. — For an understanding of the first Question it must be noted, that the expression "*to be in God*" can be understood in a threefold manner, as is well explained here in Doubt 1. — Then one must observe, that the word, <u>esse</u>, can be accepted in a threefold sense, that is, for *essential* [essentiale], (or quiddative 'being' [esse quidditativo], as the Scholastics called it), for *the 'to be' of existence* [esse existentiae], and for *that 'to be'* [illo esse], which signifies *the truth of a proposition* or the connection of a subject and predicate, which connection is in things *fundamentally*, but in the intellect *formally*. In propositions, which have a necessary relation of terms — whence they are said (to belong to) *perpetual truth* — the actual existence of the subject is not required for the truth of the proposition. Nor yet does that ideal and eternal necessity suppose, that something is from eternity, except in God. The contrary doctrine, namely « that there are many truths from eternity, which are not God », is the seventh article reprobated by the University of Parisian Masters, to which St. Bonaventure refers in SENT., Bk. II, d. 23, a. 2, q. 3, at the end; cf. St. Thomas, SUMMA., I, q. 16, a. 7, and q. 10, a . 2, in reply to n. 3. — On the sentence of Henry of

Ghent and others, that God communicated to the *essences* of things some intelligible 'being' from eternity, and on *diminished 'being'* according to the doctrine of (Bl. John Duns) Scotus, cf. above d. 35, q. 1, in the Scholium.

II. To the two manner, according to which things are in God, that is, as in an exemplary and efficient cause, there is to be added a third, « as in a conserving *end* » [ut in fine conservante], from a. 2, q. 1, of this Distinction. — The 4th opposed argument falsely applies the principle, established by the Seraphic (Doctor), namely that a creation wrought by an eternal act is impossible. On this sentence cf. SENT., Bk. II, d. 1, p. I, a. 1, q. 3, and Bk. I, d. 43, q. 3.

III. Alexander of Hales, SUMMA., p. I, q. 23, m. 4, a. 1, § 5 and 6. — (Bl. John Duns) Scotus, here in the q. sole. — St. Thomas, here in q. 1, a. 3; SUMMA., I, q. 18, a. 4, in reply to n. 1. — Bl. (now St.) Albertus (Magnus), here in a. 1 and 2; SUMMA., p. I, tr. 15, q. 60, m. 4, a. 1, subpart 1. — (Bl.) Peter of Tarentaise, here in a. 1, q. 1. — Richard of Middleton, here in a. 1, q. 3, and d. 35, q. 5. — Giles the Roman, here in 1st princ., q. sole. — Durandus (of Saint-Pourçain), here in q. 2. — (Bl.) Dionysius the Carthusian, here in q. 5. — (Gabriel) Biel, here in q. sole.

QUESTION II

Whether things are in God according to a reckoning of essence, and/or of person?

Second, there is asked, whether things are in God according to a reckoning of essence, and/or of person. And that (they are) according to a reckoning of essence, seems:

1. Because what is in (a thing) according to a reckoning of person is proper (to it), what is in (a thing) according to a reckoning of essence is common: if therefore, this[7] is common to the Three, it is clear that etc..

---

[1] Codices aa and bb subjoin *entirely* [omnino].

[2] The words *that which is in something* [illud quod est in aliquo] are wanting in many manuscripts. Somewhat below this, codices L O V and cc have *can be* [potest esse] for *can be said* [potest dici].

[3] The Vatican edition here inserts *namely, as (its) cause, that is* [videlicet ut causa, scilicet]. Then, after *the thing is* [est res] codex W adds *in God* [in Deo], and then for *according to itself* [secundum se] codex V exhibits *according to 'being'*, and, after a few words, codex M prefaces *its own 'being'* [suum esse] with *according to* [secundum se: and hence *it* must be added after *'being'* in English].

[4] The Vatican edition has *exemplarity* [exemplaritatis] for *an exemplar* [exemplaris].

[5] For *the possible* [possibile], which we recall from the more outstanding codices, the other codices have *the potential* [potentiale]; but the Vatican edition, for the same, substitutes *according to potency* [potentia], and, then, reads *it holds itself through* [se habet per] for *has* [habet].

[6] Supply together with the Vatican edition *from eternity* [ab aeterno].

[7] Understand: 'that things are in God'.

2. Moreover, things are in God according to a reckoning of exemplarity; but in God the exemplar of a creature is the Divine Essence, because God cognizes and produces by Himself: ergo etc..

3. Likewise, the rule is, that whatever is said of God in relation to a creature [in relatione ad creaturam], is said essentially;[1] but that things are in God is said in such a manner: ergo etc..

ON THE CONTRARY: 1. That (it is) according to a reckoning of *person* seems, because things are in God, inasmuch as they can go forth from Him; but '*to produce*', since it is an act, belongs to its supposit:[2] therefore, to a Person.

2. Likewise, just as (St.) Augustine (says) in (his) book, OF EIGHTY-THREE QUESTIONS:[3] « "Word" means an operative power »: if, therefore, things are in God according to a reckoning of operative power, they are in Him according to the reckoning of the Word [ratione Verbi]: therefore, since the Word is a Person, they are in God according to the reckoning of person.

3. Likewise, (St.) Augustine says in the eleventh (book), twenty-fourth chapter, ON THE CITY OF GOD,[4] that « when there is said: "He spoke" [Dixit], such as "*Let there be*" [fiat], there is understood the Father: in the verb of *speaking* the Son, in the *vision* the Holy Spirit »: therefore, since it belongs to Him, in whom they are, *to produce*, therefore, it is clear, that they are (in Him) according to a reckoning of person.

CONCLUSION

Things are in God not according to a reckoning of essence, nor of person, but they are in God as in a cause.

I RESPOND: It must be said, that among the divine there is a considering of the Essence, which is common as *common* and absolute, there is a considering of *the properties*, and there is a considering of the common as *in relation* to the proper. The first is said in an omnimodal absolution; the second, namely, a property, means a relation to a person; the third means a relation to things; and those appropriated signify God as a *cause*. — Therefore, when there is asked, whether things are in God according to a reckoning of essence, and/or of person; it must be said, that properly speaking (they are) neither in the former nor in the latter manner [nec sic nec sic], but they are in God as *in a cause*, and thus according to a reckoning of the appropriated (names), which are (names) for the Essence (as they are) considered in the Persons.

Therefore, when it is objected, that[5] (things) are in the Essence; it must be said, that those reasons conclude, that they are in the Essence commonly said, according to which It comprehends appropriated (names), not according to which It is considered in an omnimodal absolution.

What is objected in opposition, does not conclude concerning a Person according to a reckoning of proper (names), but according to a reckoning of appropriated ones.[6]

SCHOLIUM

Since creatures are in God according to a threefold reckoning of *causality*, that is, efficient, exemplary, and final (causality), and since actions are *of supposits* (here 1st. opposed argument), a doubt has arisen, whether '*that things are in God*' is to be attributed according to a reckoning of *essence*, or of *person*, or of *each*, that is, according to a reckoning of appropriated (names). This question, posited in this manner, we do not find discussed, except by a few, namely by (Bl. John Duns) Scotus, COLLATIONS, col. 31, and SENT., Bk. II, q. 1; Bl. (now St.) Albertus (Magnus), here in a. 11, and Giles the Roman, here in 2nd princ., q. 2. The whole reckoning of the Response is founded upon these two principles, that things are in God *as a cause*, and that *appropriated* (names or properties) signify God as a cause.

ARTICLE II

On the manner, in which things exist in God.

Consequently, as much as regard the second Article, there is the question of the manner of the existence of things in God, and about this two (questions) are asked.

First, there is asked, whether all which are in God, are in Him life.

Second, there is asked, whether things are more truly [verius] in God than in the universe or in their own genus.

---

[1] See above d. 22, Doubt 2, where among the five rules, derived from the words of (St.) Augustine, this one holds the fourth place. — Next for *in such a manner* [taliter] codex T has *essentially* [essentialiter].

[2] In accord with that axiom: 'actions are of supposits'.

[3] In q. 63. The entire text is had above in d. 27, p. II, q. 2, 2nd argument of the fundament.

[4] The words of (St.) Augustine are these: He, indeed, is understood (to be) the Father of the Word, who said: *Let there be* [qui dixit: Fiat]. But with Him saying *it was done*, without a doubt it was done through the Word. On the other hand, In that (verse) which is said: *God sees, that it is good*, there is sufficiently signified, that God without any necessity ... but with goodness alone made what has been made ... Which goodness, if it is also rightly understood (to be) the Holy Spirit, the whole Trinity is intimated to us in His works. — In codex F (and T in the margin) the text begins thus: *He said, He saw, let there be; through "let there be" there is understood* etc. [Dixit, vidit, fiat; per fiat intelligitur etc.]. Next for *to produce* [producere] codices P Q and V read *to produce things* [res producere]. Then, after *that they are* [quod sunt] codex O not incongruously adds *in God* [in Deo].

[5] For *that* [quod] many codices have less rightly *whether* [utrum], and at the end of the Response for *It is considered* [consideratur] they have faultily *they are considered* [considerantur].

[6] In codex V (W in the margin) there is added: *What it says, that to produce is an act of a person, is true, according to which it is proper, that is, in respect of a Person; but according to which it is common, that is, in respect of a creature, it belongs to the Essence, because the Essence and the One having the Essence is the Same* [Quod dicit, quod producere est actus personae, verum est, secundum quod est proprium, scilicet respectu personae; sed secundum quod est communis, scilicet respectu creaturae, est essentiae, quia idem est essentia et habens essentiam.].

QUESTION I

Whether all in God are life?

Moreover, that all are life in God, seems:

1. According to the first (chapter of the Gospel of St.) John: *What was made in Him was life*: but every creature has been made: therefore, every creature is in Him life.

2. Likewise, (St.) Augustine (says) in the fifth (book) ON A LITERAL EXPOSITION OF GENESIS:[2] « All are said to have been "life" in Him, not in their own nature, because He knew all, before they were made ».

3. Likewise, it seems *by reason*, because the Divine Essence is life, therefore, what is the Divine Essence is also life; but a creature in God is the Divine Essence, because whatever is in God is God: therefore, it is life. And this is what (St.) Anselm says in the MONOLOGION,[3] « that a creature in God is the creative Essence [creatrix essentia] ».

4. Likewise, 'to understand' is one difference of that which it is 'to live', since "to live" is said in a fourfold manner according to the Philosopher:[4] therefore, if 'to understand' is 'to live', therefore, every reason for understanding is a reason for living. But things are living in God; but not through participation: therefore, they are simply life.

ON THE CONTRARY: 1. According to the seventeenth (chapter) of Acts:[5] *In Him we live, move and are.* Therefore, if because we live, we are in God *life*, therefore, also because we move, we are in Him *movement*; but this is not said: therefore, neither ought that be said.

2. Likewise, if things in God are said (to be) "life", therefore, either by a reckoning of *power*, or of *being known* [notitiae], or of *will*. Not by a reckoning of *power*, because a thing from this, that it can be produced through being created [creationem], before it is produced, is entirely nothing, because it is produced according to the whole; if it is nothing, therefore neither (is it) life. Nor by a reckoning of *being known*, because then, since evil (things) are cognized by God, then evils would be in God life; which is absurd. If by a reckoning of *will*, but God's Will is not but of futures: therefore, future (things) alone live in God. But (things) other than futures are in God through an idea: therefore, not everything which is in God, is in Him life.

3. Likewise, this[6] seems, because an eternal exemplar represents things most expressly, according to which they are and go forth from Him: therefore, since certain (things) live, certain ones (do) not, it represents certain (things) through the manner of the living, certain ones through the manner of the non-living: therefore, certain (things) are in God life, certain ones not.

4. For this reason there is asked, for what reason are things said to be in God "*life*" rather, than "*wisdom*", and/or "*essence*", and/or "*intelligence*"?

CONCLUSION

All which are in God (are) as in an exemplar, in which they are life.

I RESPOND: To this some wanted to say, that not all which are said to be in God, are in Him life; but only those, which are thus in God as disposed to be made.[7] And the reason for this is, that "*word*" and "*life*" mean an act and a disposition. And for that reason (St.) Anselm[8] says, that a word is naught but of those which are, and/or are going to be; and for that reason only those are in God life. And for that reason they say, that for a reckoning of *saying "life"* there necessarily concurs, that things are in God as much as regards *power*, *being known* and the *will* to produce (them). — But this cannot stand according to (St.) Augustine. For the Son, as he himself says in the sixth (book), ON THE TRINITY,[9] « is the Art full of all living reasons »; but it is established, that He is not filled except with infinite reasons: therefore, the infinite reasons of things live in God, therefore, not only (the reasons) of beings and/or of futures, but also of all possibles. And again (St.) Augustine in the book, OF EIGHTY-THREE QUESTIONS,[10] says, that « a reason is, even if something is never made through it »; but it is established, that a design [ratio] in the mind of a craftsman lives, not because a thing is produced outside (of his mind): for it lives, even if the thing is corrupted, and (even if) it causes entirely nothing exteriorly regarding life. And for that reason it is clear, that not only (things) present and/or future live in God.

And, on this account [propterea], it must be said in another manner, that things are

---

[1] Verse 4.

[2] Chapter 14, n. 31: Thus, therefore, it must be distinguished, that, when we had said: "what was made", we then infer: "in Him was life", not in itself namely, that is in its own nature, according to which it was made, such as would be the condition and the creature, but in Him it was life, because all which have been made through Him, He knew, before they were made.

[3] Chapter 34: « And indeed in themselves they are a mutable essence, created according to an immutable reason, but in Him they are the very first essence and first truth of existing ». This first essence is called ibid., ch. 36 f., the « essentia creatrix ».

[4] (Aristotle,) ON THE SOUL, Bk. II, text 13 (ch. 2): Moreover, having said that "to live" (is understood) in a manifold manner, we both say that, if any one of these is alone in (some-

thing), that it itself is alive, such as understanding, and sense, and movement and standing-still according to place, (there is), however, still movement according to nourishment [alimentum] and increase and decrease.

[5] Verse 28.

[6] Codex V and X have *this very (thing)* [hoc ipsum].

[7] That is, willed by God, to be.

[8] MONOLOGION, ch. 32: For of that which was not, nor is, nor is going to be, there can be no word.

[9] Chapter 10, n.11.

[10] Question 63: Moreover, a reason, even if nothing is made through it, is rightly said (to be) "a reason".

in a threefold manner, namely, as in a *producing principle*, as thus they are in the reckoning of power; as in an *expressing exemplar*, as thus they are in the reckoning of being known; and as in a *conserving end*, in the reckoning[1] of will. In the first manner — because (they are) in a producing principle — since God produces the whole (of the thing) out of nothing, they are entirely nothing, neither life nor anything. However, because they are in God as *in a conserving end*, since they are conserved according to the "being", which they have, thus certain (things) are life, certain ones not. Whence only certain ones *are*, certain ones *are* and *move*, certain ones, such as men, both *are* and *move* and *live*. However, because they are (in God)[2] as in an *expressing exemplar*, they are thus in Him life. And because not only in that Exemplar are beings [entia] expressed, but also all (things) cognizable by God, for that reason all are in God life, which are in Him. And for that reason blessed John (the Apostle) says: *What has was made in Him was life.* — And thus it is clear, that 'to be in God' is attained according to the threefold genus of cause; and similarly it is clear, in what manner (things are in God) by a reckoning of power, and of being known, and of will; and[3] that question is solved, according to which genus of cause (they are there), and/or according to which of the three conditions things are said to be in God. It is also clear, which (things) are said (to be) "life" in God, namely, all which are in Him as in an exemplar.

1. To that which is objected, that in God we move etc.; it must be understood as much as regards the third manner of being [modum essendi] in God, namely, through conservation. For God conserves in us life and operation and essence; and it is understood that that word (has) been said as much as regards this.

2. To that which is said: by a reckoning of what are things said (to be) in God "life" ; it must be said, that (they are said to be such) both [simul] by a reckoning of power and of being known, because those two concur for the reckoning of an exemplar; for God is not an exemplar but of those which He cognizes and is able (to make).

3. To that which is objected, that in that exemplar things are represented as they are; it must be said, that it is true, yet it is not necessary [non oportet], that the reckoning of representation be entirely such, as is the represented, just as has been shown above:[4] and for that reason just as there is a spiritual idea of corporal (things), so a living (idea) of non living (things).

4. To that which *is asked* last, for what reason are things said to be in God "life" rather than the others;[5] it must be said, that although the aforesaid verse, by which there is said: *What was made in Him was life*, has many expositions; yet there must be especially considered about this verse *the truth of the saying*, and *the reason for saying* (it). *The truth of the saying*, as (St.) Augustine[6] says, is, that all things, made by God and/or even possible to be made, have reasons in God, through which they are understood; which reasons indeed are said *"to live"*, because they are *in a living substance*, according to which (it is) living, and (because) they are also *a reason for understanding*, which (understanding) is an act of life: and for that reason in a created craftsman they are said *"to live"*, but in God they are not only said *"to live"*, but also (be) *"life itself"*, because in God the very reason for cognizing is the very understanding. — Moreover, the *reason for saying* (it) was this. For since things have a "being" in God and also in the universe, and *in a diverse manner*, because they have some properties according to (their) existences in the world, which do not suit them, according to which they are in God: for that reason (the Apostle) not only said. *"What has been made in Him was"*, but (added) *"life"*, so that all those conditions would be excluded. For creatures in the world have a corporal, variable and corruptible "being". For since « life is a *spiritual* and continual act, flowing from a *resting* [quieto] and *sempiternal* being »,[7] it has been said perfectly, that things are in God life, so as to exclude through *spirituality* corporeity, through *resting* variability, through *sempiternity* corruptibility.

SCHOLIUM

I. This Question is coherent to some extent with the words of St. John, (Jn. 1:3-4), which in many ancient copies of Sacred Scripture and by many Fathers, especially the Latins (such as Tertullian, St. Ambrose, and St. Augustine), were thus parsed, so as to read: *what was made in Him was life* (see 1st. argument of the fundament). The Vulgate together with St. Irenaeus, St. Jerome and the other Fathers now reads: ... *which was made. In Him was Life* etc. — To be noted is the difference (posited in the solution to n. 4) between 'to live' and 'to be life'. *The former*

---

[1] For *in the reckoning* [in ratione] the Vatican edition here reads *and thus they are there by a reckoning* [et sic sutn ibi ratione], and a little before this twice has *there by a* [ibi] for *in the* [in]. Next after *In the first manner because* [Primo modo, quia] the Vatican adjoins *they are in God just as* [sunt in Deo sicut]; then after *they are entirely nothing* [nihil omnino sunt] the Vatican edition, contrary to codex T together with very many others and edition 1, adds *in God* [in Deo].

[2] Supply together with the Vatican edition *in God* [in Deo]. Somewhat further below this, for *cognizable by* [cognoscibilia] codices aa and bb have well *possible to* [possibilia]. Understand our reading thus: which are cognizable through *their own idea*. For evil (things), though they are cognizable to God, do not have *their own idea* (in God; that is, as *an evil thing*). By the name "beings" [entia] there is noted those which exist whether actually or in the future.

[3] Thus codex T and very many other codices, not without edition 1; the Vatican edition adds *in this manner* [sic].

[4] In codex O there is rightly added here *in Distinction 35, q. 4* (in reply to nn. 3 and 4) [dist. 35. q. 4.].

[5] Codex W subjoins *namely, "wisdom", "essence", (and) "understanding",*

and a little below this, together with codex T and very many others, and also edition 1, it substitutes *which is said* [quod dicitur] for *by which there is said* [quo dicitur].

[6] In his book, OF EIGHT-THREE QUESTIONS, q. 46, and more at length in his TRACT ON THE GOSPEL OF ST. JOHN, Bk. I, n. 16 f.. — Somewhat further below this, for *which (understanding) is an act* [qui est actus] codex Y has *which (reason) is an act* [quae est actus].

[7] BOOK ON CAUSES, proposition 18: « Because life is a procession proceeding out of a first, resting, sempiternal being, and similarly a first movement ». Which proposition recurs also in the book, ON THE MOVEMENT OF THE HEART (written by Alfredus Angelicus, circa A.D. 1220 and edited by Master Alexander Neckam, which book the Scholastics very often used), in these words (in ch. 1): Therefore, life is first and equal and continuous, for it is the first act of a form. For it is the first movement flowing from a resting and sempiternal (Barach edition; Innsbruck, A. D. 1878). — At the end of the solution for *sempiternity* [sempiternitatem] many codices, together with edition 1, have faultily *simplicity* [simplicitatem].

can even be said of the designs in the mind of a created crafts-man; but *the latter*, naught but of reasons in a divine exemplar. St. Thomas agrees in his Quaestiones Disputatae de Veritate, q. 4, q. 8, in reply to n. 2.

II. St. Thomas too, together with the Seraphic (Doctor), and very many other doctors disprove the first opinion posited in the Response. Conform to the common opinion is also the distinction, that things are in God in *one* manner as in a *producing* principle, by a reckoning of power, in *another* manner as in *one cognizing* or as in an expressing exemplar (and in this manner things are in God life), in a *third* manner, as in a *conserving end*, by a reckoning of will, because *the disposition* of a will looks to a final cause, as is taught below in d. 40, Doubt 7. — Notable is also the solution to n. 4. That the reasons of things in God « are also a reason for understanding », St. Thomas (De Veritate, loc. cit., in reply to n. 4) explains thus: « For the similitudes in the Word, just as they are for things the cause of (their) existing, so they are for things a cause of

their being cognized, inasmuch as, namely, they are impressed upon intellectual minds, so that they may be able to cognize things; and for that reason, just as they are said (to be) "*life*", insofar as they are principles of existing, thus they are said (to be) "*light*", insofar as they are principles of cognizing ». — The definition of the "*life*" posited here is found also found in Alexander of Hales, Summa, q. 87, m. 1, a. 1, and in a. 2 § 3 (cf. the previous page above, footnote 7).

III. Alexander of Hales, Summa., p. I, q. 23, m. 4, a. 1, § 4, and p. II, q. 3, m. 3, a. 2, collateral question. — (Bl. John Duns) Scotus, on this and the following question, here in the q. sole, n. 20. — St. Thomas, here in q. 1, a. 3; Summa., I, q. 18, a. 4; De Veritate., q. 4, a. 8. — Bl. (now St.) Albertus (Magnus), Sent., Bk. I, d. 35, a. 12. — (Bl.) Peter of Tarentaise, here in q. 1, a. 3, in reply to n. 4. — Richard of Middleton, here in a. 1, q. 3. — Giles the Roman, here in 2nd. princ., q. 1. — (Bl.) Dionysius the Carthusian, here in q. 1. — (Gabriel) Biel, here in the q. sole.

QUESTION II

Whether things have 'being' in God more truly than in their own genus?

Second, there is asked, whether things are in God more truly [verius] than in the universe or in their own genus. And that they are more truly in God, seems:

1. Through (St.) Augustine in the fifth (book) On the Literal Exposition of Genesis:[1] « All, before they were made, were in the knowledge [notitiam] of the One making and certainly [utique] (they are) better there, where (they are) eternal, where (they are) more true and incommutable ».

2. Likewise, « each one, just as it holds itself to 'being' [esse], so to cognition »;[2] but creatures are more truly cognized in God than in their own genus: therefore they are also more truly in God.

3. Likewise, « everything which is in something, is in it through the manner of that in which it is »;[3] but God is to an infinite (degree) more noble than the world: therefore to an infinite (degree) things are in God in a more noble and more true manner than in the universe.

4. Likewise, the 'being' of life is more noble and more true [verius] than (that) of the non-living; but all live in God, as has been demonstrated above,[4] but not (all live) in their own genus: ergo etc..

On the Contrary: 1. A thing is more truly, where it is simply, than where it is only secundum quid; but in God it is only said to be secundum quid — because it does not follow: '(that if) the donkey is in God, therefore, the donkey is' — but in its own genus (it is) *simply*: therefore, (it is) there more truly.

2. Likewise, a thing is more truly, where it is according to intrinsic and proximate principles, than where it is[5] in an extrinsic and remote principle; but things are in the world according to intrinsic principles, but in God as in an extrinsic principle: ergo etc..

3. Likewise, a thing is more truly, where it is according to

its own entity, than where (it is) only according to a similitude; but a man and a stone and others are in God according to a similitude: ergo[6] etc..

CONCLUSION

Things, if they are compared to themselves according to a diverse manner of existing, have a more true 'to be' in their own genus than in the one cognizing (them); but, if they are compared with their own similitude, which is in God, then the similitude more truly has 'being' than the thing itself in the world.

I Respond: It must be said, that there is a *threefold* existence of things, that is, in an eternal *exemplar*, and in a created *intellect*, and in *the world* itself.[7] In an eternal *exemplar* and in a created *intellect* things are according to a similitude; in *the world* itself (they are) according to their own entity. — When, therefore, it is asked, "In what are they more truly?", this can be asked in a twofold manner: either thus that a comparison is made *of the same thing to itself* according to a diverse manner of existing, so that the sense is: "Where does the stone have more truly a 'to be' [verius habet esse], either when it is in the *one cognizing* and/or[8] producing, and/or when it is *in itself*?"; and in this manner it must be conceded, that each thing is more truly in its own genus than in God, just as the reasons brought forwards for this prove. In another manner a comparison can be made *of the thing to its own similitude*, so that the sense of question is: "What has a *more true and more noble 'being'* [habet esse verius et nobilius], whether the thing itself, and/or its similitude?" And in this manner it must be simply

---

[1] Chapter 15, n. 33.

[2] Aristotle, Metaphysics, Bk. II, text 4 (Bk. I *in the shorter version*, ch. 1). In the original text for *cognition* [cognitionem] there is extant *the truth* [veritatem].

[3] On which account there is commonly said, together with the author of the Book of Causes, in propositions 10, 12, 20 and 24: Everything which is received in something, is in it through the manner of the one receiving, and not of the one received. Cf. also (St. Severinus) Boethius, On the Consolation of Philosophy, prose 5. The words of this axiom seem to have been altered

here, because in God nothing can be received. — Next, for *than the world* [mundo] codices V and W have *than a creature* [creatura].

[4] In the preceding Question. — A little further above this, for *of life* [vitae] codex O has *of a living (being)* [viventis].

[5] Codices aa and bb after *it is* [est] interject *as* [ut].

[6] This argument is hinted at by (St.) Anselm in (his) Monologion, ch. 36.

[7] According to (St.) Augustine in his Literal Exposition of Genesis, Bk. II, ch. 8, n. 16.

[8] Codices P Q and Z, together with edition 1 have better *and* [et].

conceded, that *the similitude* of the thing has a more true and more noble 'being' in God, that *the thing itself* (does) in the world, according to a reckoning of that which it is; because (a similitude in God) is God Himself. And the reasons brought forward for this are to be conceded.

Yet, the similitudes of things in a created intellect have more truly and more nobly a 'being' than things in the universe, as (St.) Augustine says ON THE TRINITY,[1] not by a reckoning of that *which* they are, but by a reckoning of that *in which* (they are), because in a more noble and more spiritual manner similitudes are in a cognizing intellect, than are things themselves contained in the world. And thus the reasons for each side are clear.

2. However, regarding that argument, which is made concerning the comparison of 'being' to cognizing; it must be said, that that (saying) understood generally, that a thing is there more truly, where it is cognized more truly, does not have truth. For it happens that one cognizes that which is not; and for that reason just as '*being*' [esse] does not follow after '*being cognized*' [cognosci];[2] so neither '*being truly*' after '*being cognized truly*', nor '*being more truly*'' after '*being cognized more truly*'. Therefore, when it is said, that each one, just as it holds itself to 'being', so to cognition, this is understood, because the same principles, which are the principles of being [essendi], are the principles of being cognized [cognoscendi]; but yet the principles of being confer 'being' through themselves, but they do not confer a cognition through themselves, but through their similitudes.[3]

SCHOLIUM

I. In the solving of this question the ancient Scholastics do not use the same distinctions and manners of speaking; yet in the doctrine itself they hardly differ — that which not a few others say, notwithstanding. St. Bonaventure, having supposed the common doctrine, which affirms a threefold existence of the 'being' of things, distinguishes a twofold comparison. In the first, the diverse manner of being *of the same thing* is compared, thus that <u>verius</u> (reckoned as a comparative adverb) is referred to a grade of being [ad gradum essendi] *ideally*, and/or *really*; and then a thing really existing « has *more truly* a 'to be' » [verius habet esse]. In the second, *the truth* and *nobility* of being of a thing [essendi rei] really, is compared (to the truth and nobility of being) of the similitude ideally existing, and then <u>verius</u> (reckoned as a comparative adjective) is referred to the grade of *perfection* in being [in essendo], and the thing ideally existing « has a *more true and more noble* 'being' » [habet esse verius et nobilius]. Here, (his) manner of speaking nearly convenes with the distinction, which St. Thomas employs in (his) QUAESTIONES DISPUTATA DE VERITATE, q. 4, a. 6, saying: « the word, <u>verius</u>, can designate either the truth of a *thing*, and/or the truth of *predication*. If it designates the truth of a *thing*, thus without doubt there is a greater truth of things in the Word, than in themselves. But, if the truth of *predication* is designated, thus it is the other way around ». In a slightly different manner, but in the same sense, St. Thomas teaches in the SUMMA., I, q. 18, a. 4, in reply to n. 3, and here in q. 1, a. 3, in reply to n. 2, that things « have *a more true 'being'* simply in the Divine Mind »; « '*to be this*', as for example a man and/or a horse, they have *more truly* in their own nature than in the Divine Mind ». — In the solution to n. 2, there is masterfully explained (by St. Bonaventure) the saying of Aristotle, badly applied by not a few, namely, that each one, just as it holds itself to 'being', so to cognition.

II. St. Thomas, <u>locis citt</u>. — Bl. (now St.) Albertus (Magnus), SENT., Bk. I, d. 35, a. 11. — (Bl.) Peter of Tarentaise, here in q. 1, a. 4. — Durandus (of Saint-Pourçain), here in q. 2, n. 7. — (Bl.) Dionysius the Carthusian, here in q. 5.

ARTICLE III

On the number or generality of existence, which things have in God.

In the third place is the question of the third Article, namely, concerning the generality of the existence of things in God, and about his two (questions) are asked.

First, there is asked, whether evils (things) are in God.

Second, whether in God there are imperfect (things), according to which (they are) of this kind.

QUESTION I

Whether evil (things) are in God?

Moreover, it seems, that evil (things) are not in God.

1. (St.) Augustine (says in his book), ON FREE WILL:[4] « Inasmuch as things are rightly blamed [vituperantur], insomuch does the blamer of them see the art, in which they have been made, so that he blames in them that, which he does not see in the art ». If, therefore, they are blamed as much as regards (their) wickedness or inasmuch as (they are) evil; and in this manner they are not seen in God: therefore, in this manner they are not in God.

---

[1] Book IX, ch. 4, n. 4: « The being known [notitia] of a body is greater than the body itself, which is known by that being known. For thus there is a certain life in the reason of the one cognizing, but the body is not life. And the certain life in any body is greater, not by mass, but by force ». And *ibid*., ch. 11, n. 16: « Yet the imagination of a body in the soul is better than that species of the body, inasmuch as the former is in a better nature, that is, in a vital substance, just as if it is a spirit ». Cf. also (St.) Anselm, MONOLOGION., ch. 36. — Somewhat below this for *than are* [quam sint] codices I X have *than are* [quam sunt], and then *in the world containing (them)* [in mundo continente] for *contained in the world* [in mundo continentae].

[2] Aristotle, ON INTERPRETATION, Bk. I, ch. 7 (ch. 9): For not on account of denying and/or affirming will (a thing) be and/or not be.

[3] Cf. Aristotle, METAPHYSICS, Bk. I, text 5 ff. and text 25 ff. (chs. 6 and 9), and Bk. VII, texts 23 and 44 ff. (Bk. VI, chs. 7 and 13), where the Platonic system is refuted, which supported a false understanding of that axiom.

[4] Bk. III, ch. 15, n. 42.

2. Likewise, « everything which is in God, is from Him and through Him », as (St.) Augustine says, and Master (Peter) in the text;[1] but evil (things) never are *from* God nor *through* God: therefore, neither (are they) *in* God.

3. Likewise, everything which is in God, either is as in a producing *principle*, or as in an expressing *exemplar*, or as in a conserving *end*;[2] but it is established, that God is not a *principle* producing evils, nor even *conserving* (them). Likewise, He is not an *exemplar* expressing (them), because the reckoning of an exemplar is attained according to an assimilation; but there is no assimilation of God to (something) evil: therefore, evil (things) are in no manner in God.

4. Likewise, as much as anything is better, so much is it more distant from evil; but God is the best, than Whom nothing better can be thought: therefore, He differs[3] by as great a distance, as no greater can be thought. But that which has neither the truth of wickedness nor (its) similitude is more distant from evil, than that which has at least the similitude (of wickedness), and (that) in which evil is in no manner (is more distant from it), than (that) in which it is in any manner: ergo etc..

ON THE CONTRARY: 1. Everything which is cognized by something, which is its own cognition, is in that as in one cognizing; but God cognizes evil (things), because He punishes and reproves them, and God is His own Cognition: therefore, evil (things) are in God. The *minor* is clear, the *major* similarly, because every cognized is in a cognition:[4] if, therefore, the cognition and the one cognizing are the same, therefore, if it is in the cognition, (it is) also in the one cognizing.

2. Likewise, everything which is cognized in something, is in that in which it is cognized; but evil (things) are cognized by God: therefore, they are in God. The proof of the *minor*: evil (things) are cognized by God — it is established — either *within Him*, or *outside*: not *outside*, this is established, because the Divine Gaze [aspectus] does not go forth outside, for then it would need another to cognize.[5] *And again*, the Angels cognize evil (things) in God. Whence (St.) Augustine ON A LITERAL EXPOSITION OF GENESIS (says):[6] The

Angels see in Him our good (deeds), which please them, and our evil ones, which displease them.

3. Likewise, everything which is cognized in something, and not through an accident [per accidens], is in some manner in that as in an exemplar; but evil (things) are cognized by God, and not through an accident, because He cognizes nothing through an accident, but all through Himself: therefore, evil (things) are in God.

4. Likewise, everything which is cognized by something not through a privation, is cognized through a similitude and an idea; but in God there occurs no cognition through a privation, because there can be in that Exemplar no privation, since He is a pure act:[7] therefore, if He cognizes evil (things), He does not cognize through a privation, but through a similitude. But the similitude (of a thing) is an idea in God: therefore, evil (things) have an idea in God.

CONCLUSION

God cognizes evil (things), yet they are not in God nor do they have an idea in Him, but they are cognized through an idea of the good, of which they are privations.

I RESPOND: It must be said, that evil (things) *are cognized* by God, yet they do no *exist* in God according to which (they are) *evil*, because thus do we (Catholics) speak in the proposed. — For that reason, I say, *they are cognized*, because just as « the straight (line) is the judge of itself and of the oblique »,[8] so the Most High *Truth* and *Light* and *Act* is the reason for cognizing not only *the truth*, and *the light* and *an act*, but also *obliquity*, *shadow* and *privation*. Whence light by itself knows darkness.[9]

However, evil (things) *are not* in God, since they are said to be in God, according to which God co-opts them according to some genus of cause, and most of all according to the genus of a formal and exemplary cause; but evil does not have God as (its) cause,[10] nor as

---

[1] In chapter 2, where the words of (St.) Augustine are also had.

[2] In the Vatican edition there is read *in one conserving* [in conservante] for *in a conserving end* [in fine conservante], which we have restored on the authority of codices K V W X aa and bb, and also with the authority of the text had above in a. 2, q. 1, in the body (of the Response).

[3] Codices P and Q read *He is distant* [distat] for *He differs* [differt]

[4] Cf. above d. 3, p. I, a. sole, q. 1, p. 68, footnote 2, and Aristotle, METAPHYSICS, Bk. XII, text 61 (Bk. XI, ch. 9), where he treats especially with God's intellection

[5] Cf. (St.) Augustine, ON A LITERAL EXPOSITION OF GENESIS, Bk. V, ch. 13, n. 29: Furthermore, if He had known (all), where except with Himself, with whom was the Word, through which all were made? For if He had known them outside of Himself, who taught Him? For who as known the thought [sensus] of the Lord, or who was His counselor? (Rom. 11:34). — The Vatican ed. with edd. 2, 3, 4, 5 & 6, adds here: *Therefore, it remains, that (evil things are cognized) within Him* [Restat ergo, quod intra se].

[6] Book II, ch. 8, n. 17: For the Angels also did not set out to perceive wisdom, as we (do), to catch sight of the invisible (things) of God, understood through those which have been made, they who, from (the moment) in which they were created, enjoyed thoroughly the very eternity and pious contemplation of Word, and hence looking upon these, according to that which they seen within, either rightly approving deeds, and/or disproving sins.

[7] In favor of the reckoning, which is here adduced, the Scholastics are accustomed to cite that which Averroës says on that text of Aristotle, ON THE SOUL, Bk. III, text 25: If, however, there is nothing contrary in something, it

cognizes itself. « For he says: that is, if there were any understanding, when the one understanding was not found (to be) in potency and in act, then that understanding would not understand entirely a privation, nay it would understand nothing outside of itself ».

[8] Aristotle, ON THE SOUL, Bk. I, text 85 (ch. 5): For one side of the contrariety is sufficient to judge about itself and (its) opposite; for by a straight (line) we cognize both it and an oblique one; for (it is) the judge and rule of each; but the oblique (line is the judge and rule) neither of itself, nor of the straight (line).

[9] Dionysius (the Areopagite), ON THE DIVINE NAMES, ch. 7, § 2: For the Divine Spirit did not know, learning of existing (things) from existing (things), but from Himself and in Himself ... not contemplating each according to (their) species, knowing and containing all according to one circumstance of cause, just as light too according to the cause in itself comprises beforehand [praeambivit] a cognition of shadows, not seeing shadows otherwise than by (its) light.

[10] For with (St.) Augustine, ON THE CITY OF GOD, Bk. XII, ch. 7, it is customary to say: « Evil does not have an *efficient* cause, but a *deficient* one, which is not God ». — Less clear and reproved by the codices and edition 1 is the reading of the Vatican edition: *as a formal cause and as an exemplar* [pro causa formali et pro exemplari]. A little below this the same Vatican edition, together with codex cc, recklessly suppresses the words: *Since, therefore, a privation , according to which (it is) of this kind, can be assimilated to nothing* [Quoniam igitur privatio secundum quod huiusmodi nulli est assimilabilis].

(its) exemplar, because "evil" [malum] according to the reckoning of wickedness means only a *privation*, but "exemplar", according to which (it is) of this kind, means an *assimilation*. Since, therefore, a privation , according to which (it is) of this kind, can be assimilated [est assimilabile] to nothing, hence it is, that neither evil [malum] nor falsehood has an idea in God; moreover, its opposite can be assimilated. Whence since God cognizes by one and the same (act) *the good* [bonum] and *the evil* opposed to it, He cognizes *the good* according to the reckoning of assimilation; and for that reason the good is in God as in an exemplar and as a one cognized through itself and through the manner of a position. But *evil*, since it is cognized by God, it does not have in Him an idea, for that reason it is not in God, though it is in God's Cognition: because, though it is cognized by God, it is not cognized through its own idea, but (through that of) the good, of which it is the privation. And, for that reason, it is said to be *cognized* per accidens and through a privation.

1. To that, therefore, which is objected, that evil is in God's Cognition, and the Cognition is God: ergo etc.; it must be said, that in this there is a *fallacy according to accident*.[1] For though God's Cognition *is the same* as God, yet *It connotes (something) else*, just as power and wisdom (do). Whence just as (this) does not follow: 'it is in God's knowledge [notitia], therefore, also in (His) power', nay there is (a fallacy of) *accident* and (of) *the consequent* there; so also in the proposed.

2. To that which is objected, that evil is cognized in God, therefore, it is in God; it must be said, that nether does that follow: for "*to be in God*" [esse in Deo]

means more than "*to be cognized by God* and/or *in God*". For, when something is said "to be cognized by God", there is understood through this, that God is *the reason for cognizing* it; but when there is added, that this is "*in God*", there is signified, that God is the reason for cognizing (it) as an *exemplar* and through assimilation; and for that reason there is (a fallacy of) *the consequent* there.

3. To that which is objected, that He does not cognize evil (things) through an accident etc.; it must be said, that '*to be cognized through an accident*' is in a twofold manner: either on the part of the *one cognizing*, or of the *one cognized*. In God there occurs no cognition through an accident on the part of the *One cognizing*, because[2] He cognizes all by Himself; yet it does occur on the part of the *one cognized*, since He cognizes one thing [aliquid] through its own similitude, as a good, another thing [aliquid] through the similitude of its opposite; and thus there is a per accidens There, not in *having recourse (to another)* [in decurrendo], but in *assimilating*. For when God cognizes evil, He is not understood to be assimilated to it, but to its opposite.

4. Similarly, must it be solved concerning 'privation': because '*to cognize through privation*' is in a twofold manner: either thus, that there is a privation in the *cognizing virtue*, just as anyone cognizes the silence and darkness through ear and eye,[3] and thus it posits an imperfection; or thus, that there is a privation in the *cognized*, not in the one cognizing, just as light would know darkness, (and) sound silence, if it had a cognitive power [vim]; and thus God cognizes, since He is *a pure Act* and *Light* and *Truth*.

SCHOLIUM

I. Here (St. Bonaventure) deals with evils « according to which (they are) evil », that is according to the *formal (being belonging to)* evil, which is a privation, not according to the *material* or substrate (being) of it (cf. SENT, Bk. II, d. 34, a. 2 throughout, and d. 35, a. 2, throughout; d. 37, a. 2, q. 1). The entire solution is constructed from this principle, that '*to be cognized by God*' is one thing, '*to be in God*' another, which is explained in the solution to n. 2, and here in Doubts 1 and 2. — That (something) evil does not have an idea in God, and that it is cognized through the idea of its opposite, is commonly taught by the

ancients. On the manner, in which God cognizes evil (things), cf. d. 39, a. 1, q. 2 and (its) Scholium.

II. Alexander of Hales, SUMMA., p. I, q. 23, m. 3, a. 3, and m. 4, a. 2. — (Bl. John Duns) Scotus, on this and the following question, REPORTATIO., here in q. 3. — St. Thomas, here in q. 1, a. 2; SUMMA., I, q. 15, a. 3, in reply to n. 1; ON THE TRUTH., q. 3, a. 4. — Bl. (now St.) Albertus (Magnus), here in a. 6; SUMMA., p. I, tr. 13, q. 55, m. 2, a. 3, q. incid. — (Bl.) Peter of Tarentaise, here in q. 1, a. 1 and 3, in reply to n. 2. — Richard of Middleton, here in a. 1, q. 2. — Durandus (of Saint-Pourçain), here in q. 1. — (Bl.) Dionysius the Carthusian, here in q. 5.

QUESTION II

Whether imperfect (things) are in God?

Second, there is asked, whether imperfect (things), according to which (they are) of this kind, are in God. And it seems that (they are) not:

1. Because evil (things) as evils cannot have a similitude with the Most High Good: therefore, for an equal reason,

since imperfect (things) do not have a similitude with a most perfect (thing), they will not be in God.

2. Likewise, those alone are in God, which can be by God [a Deo] and through God [per Deum]; but imperfect (things) are not

---

[1] Concerning which, see above d. 2, a. sole, q. 4, p. 58, footnote 5. — By the word *the consequent* [consequens], at the end of this and the following solution, there is signified *a fallacy of the consequent* [fallacia consequentis], which according to Aristotle, ELENCHAE, Bk. I, ch. 4 (ch. 5): « is (a fallacy) for this reason, that they think that the consequence is convertible ».

[2] In place of all the words of this reply to n. 3 up to this point, codex O reads instead: *To that which is objected: in God there occurs no cognition through an accident; it must be said, that (this) is true concerning those which are bound to be cognized through themselves and through being posited; but evil has through itself neither a cause nor a will nor a cognition, but (does) through the good, according to Dionysius,*

in the fourth chapter ON THE DIVINE NAMES, because [Ad illud quod obiicitur: in Deo nulla cadit cognitio per accidens; dicendum, quod verum est de his quae nata sunt cognosci per se et per positionem; sed malum per se nec causam nec voluntatem nec cognitionem habet, sed per bonum, secundum Dionysium, capitulo quarto de Divinis Nominibus, quia]. For *there occurs no* [nulla cadit] codices V and W have *there occurs no* [non cadit aliqua]. Somewhat below this, after for *of its opposite* [sui oppositi], codices aa and bb insert *just as an evil is* [ut malum est]; and then for *not in having recourse (to another)* [non in decurrendo] the Vatican edition, together with not a few codices, no less rightly has *not in running about (to another)* [non in discurrendo].

[3] Cf. Aristotle, ON THE SOUL, Bk. II, text 103 (ch. 10).

(created) by God, because there is said in the thirty-second (chapter) of Deuteronomy:[1] *God's works are perfect*.

3. Likewise, one objects especially concerning *matter* and *passion*,[2] *diversity* and *composition*. For since an exemplar under the reckoning of an exemplar is a form, if (it is) a pure act, and thus entirely simple, it seems that the reckonings of matter and passion and diversity and composition are repugnant to the exemplar; and if this, since nothing is said to be in God except according to the reckoning of an exemplar, it is clear that etc..

4. Likewise, just as *truth* and *goodness*[3] is a general condition of beings, so also *unity*; but the opposite of *truth* does not have an idea in God, similarly too (that) of *goodness*: therefore, for an equal reason (neither does) the opposite of *unity*. But the opposite of *unity* is a multitude: ergo etc..

ON THE CONTRARY: 1. (St.) Augustine (says) to Nebridius:[4] « He who established the whole could not, not have the reasons of the parts »: therefore, since the parts under the reckoning of parts are imperfect, it is clear that He has the reasons of imperfect (things).

2. Likewise, every Divine cognition is by (something) prior [a priori]: therefore since in every creature there first [prius] occurs the reckoning of the imperfect, such as (the reckoning) of matter to (that) of form, (the reckoning) of beginnings to (that) of a begun, of parts to (that) of a whole, therefore, God cognizes these through the prior. Therefore, if perfect (things) have an idea in God, it is necessary, that imperfect ones also have (one).

3. Likewise, a divine exemplar expresses a thing according to (its) whole, otherwise (God) would not perfectly cognize (the thing), therefore, whatever concerns a thing, has an exemplar;[5] but matter concerns the constitution of a thing, and (things) imperfect concern the constitution of the perfect: ergo etc..

4. Likewise, every effect is assimilated to its own cause by some assimilation; but the least assimilation suffices for the reckoning of an exemplar: therefore everything which is by God has an idea in God, through which, before it is made, it is in God.[6] But *matter* and *passion* and *composition* and *diversity* is (created) by God, because they all mean being [ens]: therefore, all are in God.

CONCLUSION

Imperfect (things) are in God, not by reason of imperfection, which means a privation, but by reason of that which underlies the imperfection.

I RESPOND: To this some said, that imperfect (things) are not in God, and they are not cognized by God through some proper idea, but through the idea of their opposites, such as *matter* through the idea of form, *passion** through the idea of act, *multitude* through the idea

of unity. — But that cannot stand. For since all those mean some entity and thus truth, of necessity they have some assimilation to the First Truth, and thus a reckoning of exemplarity; and for that reason they are necessarily in God.

On which account it must be understood, that when there is asked, whether imperfect (things) have an idea in God, this can be understood in a twofold manner: either by reason of that which *underlies* (them), or by reason of (their) *imperfection*. If by reason of (their) *imperfection*, since imperfection is a privation, and privation does not mean being [end] nor something by God nor (something) able to be assimilated, thus (imperfection) does not have an idea. But, if by reason of that which *underlies* (them), just as matter is said (to be) something imperfect, and matter means some essence, so it has an idea, but not an imperfect one, but a perfect one;[7] since, just as of the non-living there is a living idea, and of (things) corporal a spiritual (idea), so of (things) temporal an eternal (idea), and of (things) imperfect a perfect (idea).

Nor, however, is there a good idea of evil (things). Whence it must be noted, that an idea, just as had been said above in the question concerning ideas,[8] means an assimilation outside the genus (of a thing). Moreover, the first assimilation is in the reckoning of entity in God. Therefore, everything which of itself means a reckoning of *entity*, or (which) has been composed, whether imperfect, or material, or passible, or in act, or in potency, can be assimilated to God and produced (by God); and for that reason it has 'being' in God. Moreover, that which means *a privation* by this very (thing) looses the reckoning of a true effect and the reckoning of assimilation; and for that reason falsehood and wickedness do not have an idea, nor are they *in* God, nor (created) *by* God. — From this it is clear, that imperfect (things) are in God; clear too are the (things) asked.

1. For that which is objected concerning evil, the response is clear, because "evil" means simply a privation in that which (is) evil, not "imperfect".

2. To that which is objected, that imperfect (things) are not (created) by God: it must be said, that imperfect (things), according to that which they are, are (created) by God, though imperfection does not remain in them, because God perfects (them).[9]

3. To that which is objected, that they do not have an assimilation; it must be said, that although (imperfect things) do not have (such) in (their) special conditions, yet they do have (one) in (their) general (conditions); and this is sufficient. For all (things) have a reckoning of the good and of the beautiful and of being [entis].[10]

4. To that which is objected concerning the opposite of unity, it must be said, that it is not similar. For *unity* is conserved [salvatur] in a multitude, not so *goodness* in wickedness, nor *truth* in falsehood, because the latter are privations; moreover, a multitude is not a privation of unity in the same manner;[11] and for that reason the whole (objection) is clear.

---

[1] Verse 4. — On the major proposition, cf. the text of Master (Peter), here in ch. 2.

[2] That is, concerning the passible or passive potency. — For *passion* [passione] the Vatican edition has *potency* [potentia].

[3] The words *and goodness* [et bonitas], suppressed by the Vatican ed., we have restored from codd. L O P Q V W and Z and ed. 1. Next, after *for an equal reason* [pari ratione], supply with cod. O *neither does* [nec].

[4] Epistle 14, n. 4: Therefore, if Nebridius is a part of this universe, just as he is, and every universe is made up of parts, God, the Founder of the universe, could not not have a reckoning of the parts.

[5] In the Vatican ed. and not a few mss., this conclusion is wanting.

[6] The Vatican edition, together with codex cc, reads *is an exemplar in God* [est exemplar in Deo].

[7] The Vatican ed. and cod. cc omit *but a perfect one* [sed perfectam].

[8] Distinction 36, q. 2, a. 2.

[9] The sentence would be more clearly expressed in this manner: "Though the imperfection would remain not *from this*, that God perfects (the imperfect thing), but *from elsewhere*"; for a creature does not have this, that it is imperfect, properly from God, but from itself, because (it has been made) out of nothing. Wherefore (St.) Augustine, ON FREE WILL, Bk. II, ch. 20, n. 54, says: « On the one hand, everything good (is) from God ... But every defect is from nothing ». Cf. SENT., Bk. II. d. 34, a. 1, q. 2; Alexander of Hales, SUMMA, p. II. q. 94, m. 3. a. 3.

[10] Cf. Dionysius (the Areopagite), ON THE DIVINE NAMES, ch. 4, § 7 ff.. At the end of this chapter you will find a long explanation of the nature and cognition of evil, by which those things which have been said here are confirmed.

[11] See above d. 24, a. 1, q. 1.

---

* *Trans. note*: Here the critical edition faultily had <u>dassio</u> for *passion* [passio].

SCHOLIUM

I.* That imperfect (things), to the extent that they formally mean a *privation*, do not have their own idea (in God), is established among all (authors). But whether imperfect (things) by a reckoning of the *positive* thing, which stands beneath the privation, are not only cognized through some idea, but through *their own* idea, this question is discussed here, and it principally deals with prime matter. The first opinion denies, with Plato (who also thought falsely that matter was not created by God), this entirely. St. Thomas (ON THE TRUTH., q. 3, a. 5) says against Plato: « But we (Catholics) posit, that matter has been caused by God; whence it is necessary to posit, that in some manner there is an idea for it in God, since whatever is caused by Him, retains a similitude of Him in howsoever a manner ». Then the same (St. Thomas) distinguishes "idea" taken *properly*, which « looks back to the thing, according to which it is producible in 'being' », and thus he assigns a proper idea neither only to matter, nor only to form, but to *the whole composite*; and (he also distinguishes) "idea" accepted *broadly* for a similitude and/or reason, « and thus nothing prevents, that there even be an idea of prime matter according to itself ». In the same manner the same (St. Thomas) resolves SENT, Bk. I, d. 36, q. 2, a. 3, in reply to n. 2; which sufficiently convenes with the doctrine of the Seraphic (Doctor). However, in the SUMMA, I, q. 15, a. 3, in reply to n. 2, the Angelic (Doctor) simply says: « Matter does indeed have an idea in God, yet no other than the idea of the composite: for matter according to itself neither has 'being', nor is cognizable ». The interpreters of St. Thomas do not agree, whether he here retracted (as Cajetan thinks) what he said, or whether he was speaking only of the idea in the strict sense. (Bl. John Duns) Scotus and Richard of Middleton follow St. Bonaventure in (his) manner of speaking.

II. Besides the mentioned authors: Bl. (now St.) Albertus, here in a. 7, and d. 35, a. 10. — Giles the Roman, here in 2nd princ., q. 3. — (Bl.) Dionysius the Carthusian, here in q. 5, at the end.

DOUBTS ON THE TEXT OF THE MASTER

DOUBT I

In this part, there are doubts about the text (of Master Peter) and first concerning this solution of Master (Peter), by which he says, that *God's Cognition is His Essence, and yet not all, which are in His Cognition, are in the Essence.* For he seems to speak badly, since this argument seems to be necessary: 'if any two are entirely the same; if anything is in one, (it is) also in the other'. *If you say*, that (God's Cognition, or foreknowledge, and His Essence) differ in virtue of (the things which they) connote [penes connotata]; it seems false, because God's foreknowledge does not connote (anything). — *And/or if you say*, that the foreknowledge does connote; *there is the objection* concerning this name "*God*", that it does not connote, and yet all are said to be "in God": therefore, for an equal reason, also "in the Essence". — *Moreover*, against Master (Peter) seems to be the verse of (St.) Anselm in the MONOLOGION,[1] that « the creature in the Creator is the creative Essence »: therefore, it seems, that they are truly in God's Essence.

I RESPOND: It must be said, that this preposition "*in*" sometimes connotes *inherence*, as if to say, "an accident in a subject"; sometimes it notes *identity*, as if to say, "the ideas of things are in God", since they are *God*, not (created) *by God*; sometimes it notes *causality*, as if to say, "creatures are in God Himself": and this preposition "*in*" can be said according to the four genera of causes, but in God it is not said except according to three.[2] — Since, therefore, "*cause*" means a looking back to a creature according to a reckoning of understanding, for that reason this preposition "*in*", according to which it means *causality*, is not added except to terms meaning a looking-back to the creature. And since the name for the Substance and/or Nature and/or Essence does not mean a looking-back, for that reason if there is said: "creatures are in God's Substance", this preposition "*in*" either notes *identity*, or *inherence*, each of which is false: and for that reason such expressions are not received; and in that argument there is a sophism according to (a fallacy of the) accident. For that reason Master (Peter), that it is not valid; for though they are the same according to thing, yet they differ according to the manner of signifying and understanding.

To that which is objected, that "*God*" does not mean a looking-back (to creatures); it must be said, that it is false, because it is imposed by the act, which He has regarding creatures, just as (St. John) Damascene says;[3] whence there is rightly said: "the God of creatures".

To that which is objected, that a creature in the Creator is a creative essence; it must be said, that "*that a creature is in the Creator*" is "*that (it is) an idea and/or similitude of that which God is*"; and (St.) Anselm wants to say, that that *similitude* is the creative Essence, not that that *creature* is the Essence. Whence it must be conceded, that the ideas of things are in the Divine Essence, because "*in*" notes identity, and truly; but this cannot be said of a creature according to the 'being', which it has in its own genus.

DOUBT II

Likewise, is asked concerning this which (Master Peter) says, *that those are understood to be in God, which are from Him* [ex ipso] *and through*

---

[1] See above in d. 36, a. 2, q. 1, p. 623, footnote 3.

[2] Namely, according to an efficient, exemplary (formal) and final cause [causae efficientis, exemplaris (formalis) et finalis]. Cf. above a. 2, q. 1, in the body (of the Question). That the reckoning of a material cause is to no extent transferred to the divine, has been proved above in d. 19, p. II, q. 3.

[3] See above d. 2, p. 60, Doubt 3, footnote 2.

---

* *Trans. note*: In the original text of this Scholium, there are omitted, perhaps by oversight, the Roman numerals which number each paragraphs.

Him etc.. For it seems that he speaks badly, because such are not but present, therefore, in God they are naught be those which presently exist; which is manifestly false and against (St.) Augustine,[1] who says, that things are in God from eternity. *If you say*, that he accepts *"to be in God"* as in one conserving (them), because thus the Apostle, in the aforesaid quote accepts (it):[2] *From Him and through Him and in Him*; then one does not address the proposed [nihil facit ad propositum], because Master (Peter) accepts *"to be in God"*, according to which things are said to be in God eternally. — *If you say*, that things are *actually* from God and/or through God in time, but (are) *habitually*[3] from eternity; then I *ask*, "For what reason are they *actually in* God from eternity, and not *from God* and/or *through* God?"

I RESPOND: It must be said, that *"to be from*[4] *God"* and/or *"through God"* can be accepted either according to *aptitude*, and/or according to *act*, and/or according to *habit*. If according to *act*; thus the aforesaid quote, that those alone are in God, which are *from* god and/or *through* God, is not going to be understood precisely, because God cognizes many (things),which are *in* God, which are, however, not *from* Him nor *through* Him, nor will be. Again it can be accepted according to *habit*; and thus it still is not going to be understood precisely, because God cognizes and can make many (things), which He will not make; and yet they are *in* Him, and shall not ever be *from* Him nor *through* Him. Again it can be understood according to *aptitude*; and then it precisely has truth, because nothing is *in* God, unless it (be) apt to be *from* God and *through* Him; and in this manner it is valid for the proposed, and thus does Master (Peter) understand (it), and through this are excluded evil (things), because God cannot make evils, nor can they be *from* Him nor *through* Him.

That which is asked, "For what reason are things not said to be eternally *from* God" etc. ; it must be said, that it is not similar, because those prepositions signify through the manner of *becoming* [fieri] and of *movement* and of *act*; but this preposition *"in"* through the manner of *rest* [quietis].[5] And since God did not make (anything) but in time, and was not *actually* a Cause causing but in time, though *habitually* (He was) from eternity; for that reason things are said (to be) eternally *"in* God", rather than *"from* God".[6]

DOUBT III

Likewise, is asked concerning this reckoning of Master (Peter), by which he says, that *evil (things) are not in God, because God does not* *cognize them through approbation.* For he seems to speak badly, because *approbation* looks back to will; but *'being in God'* looks back from eternity to exemplarity: therefore, 'being known through approbation' [notitia approbationis] does not address this. — Likewise, Master (Peter) seems (to be) insufficient in (his) division of Cognition, because just as good (things) are cognized by being known through *approbation*, so evil (ones) by being known through *reprobation*. — Likewise, *approbation* either *adds* something upon being known simply, or (does) *not*; if (it does) *not*: therefore, in God there is[7] no distinguishing of a *being known*, and a *being known through approbation*. Likewise, if it adds nothing, therefore, just as there are in God those which He cognizes *by approving*, so also those[8] which He cognizes *simply*. If it does *add* something: therefore, it seems, that being known in God [divina notitia] is composed. *If you say*, that it adds according to understanding — but our understanding does not cause things to be in God: therefore neither (does evil's) being known through approbation (add anything).

I RESPOND: It can be said, that *approbation* according to understanding adds upon cognition *the good pleasure* of the will; but this good pleasure connotes goodness in that,[9] in respect of which it is; because naught pleases God but the good, and every good, inasmuch as (it is) of this kind, is similar to God. If, therefore, an idea means a reason for cognizing according to an assimilation, all which God cognizes by (their) being known through approbation, are in Him.

But, it must be noted, that *"approbation"* [approbatio] can connote goodness in *act*, and thus it is not precisely true, that everything which is in God, is cognized by (its) being known through approbation. Again it can connote goodness in *potency*, just as an exemplar connotes the entity of a thing, not because it is, but because God can make it; and in this manner nothing is in God, except that which He cognized by (its) being known through approbation, because thus He cognizes every good, which *is* and/or which *He can make*, and of that He has an exemplar; and for that reason that only is in God.

What, therefore, *it objected*, that the (Divine) Will does not make what is in God; it must be said, that this is not, because the Will (is) in *act*, but because God can do nothing, which He does not approve as good, whence *"approbation"* rather means There the judgement of the (Divine) Reason, rather than an affection of the Will.[10]

What *it asks*, if (approbation) *adds* (anything upon cognition): it must be said, that it does add on the part of our *understanding* and on the part of *the connoted*, not on the part of *God* Himself. Moreover, *reprobation* does not add in this manner; and, for that reason, Master (Peter) does not posit as a member (of the division) a 'being known through *reprobation*' [notitiam reprobationis].

---

[1] See above a. 2, 1st argument of the fundament in both q. 1 and q. 2. Cf. also ON A LITERAL EXPOSITION OF GENESIS, Bk. V, ch. 18, n. 36, and ENARRATIONS ON THE PSALMS, Ps. 49: 11, n. 18.

[2] Romans 11:36.

[3] For *habitually* [habitualiter] nearly all the codices, here and near the end of the solution, have *habitudinally* [habitudinaliter], but faultily. Cf. on this above d. 18, a. sole, q. 2, p. 325, footnote 10.

[4] For *from* [ex] nearly all the codices and edition 1 have *in* [in]; faultily, as is clear from the subjoined.

[5] Cf. above d. 19, p. I, q. 4, in reply to n. 6.

[6] From this and the preceding Doubt it follows, that it is one (thing) to be *in God's Essence*, another to be *in God*, another to be in *God's knowledge*. For, of divine ideas, it is said, that (their) being [ens] is in God's Essence, which cannot be said of creatures, which indeed, to the extent that they are, are in *God as (their) Cause* and in *God's Cognition*; but evil (things) are indeed in God's Cognition, but not in God, and much less in God's Essence. Cf. Alexander of Hales, SUMMA., p. I, q. 23,

m. 4, a. 1, § 5, and a. 2, in reply to n. 2; Bl. (now St.) Albertus (Magnus), here in a. 2 and a. 10; St. Thomas, here in q. 1, a. 2; Richard of Middleton, here on the text.

[7] For *there is no distinguishing* [non est distinguere] codices F T W and edition 1 have *there not lacking a distinguishing* [non deest distinguere], codex R reads *he ought not have distinguished* [non debuit distinguere]. If one prefers this reading, let him understand *Master (Peter)* for *he*.

[8] For *those* [illa] codex O has *those evil (things)* [ista mala]. A little further below this, for *does not cause things to be* [non facit res esse] nearly all the codices, together with edition 1, read *does not grasp, that things are* [non capit res esse], which reading the context reproves.

[9] The Vatican edition and codex cc have *God* [Deo] for *that* [eo], which is manifestly false.

[10] Cf. (St.) Augustine, in the last, unfinished book, ON A LITERAL INTERPRETATION OF GENESIS, ch. 5, n. 22, where the signification of the word *"approbation"* is expounded. See also in the same work, Bk. I, ch. 5, n. 11, and Bl. (now St.) Albertus (Magnus), here in a. 9.

Doubt IV

Likewise, is asked concerning this which (St.) Ambrose says: *All these have the same force, namely "with Him" [cum ipso] and "in Him" and "through Him"*. For it is objected, that if they have the same force, therefore, there seems (to be) here a flourish of words [inculcatio verborum]. — Likewise, either *"being in Him"* is accepted just as "in *an exemplar*", or just as "in *a conserving cause*". If as "in *an exemplar*", it is established that '*to be in Him*' is one (thing), and '*(to be) from Him*' (another), just as has been shown before. If as "in *a conserving (cause)*", '*to be produced*' is still one (thing), '*to be conserved*' another.[1] — Likewise, if they have the same force; (then) just as "*from Him*" is appropriated to the Father, so it can be appropriated to the Son, and (then) similarly there will be an appropriating of "*in Him*" to the Father.

I Respond: It must be said, that there is a speaking of these three circumlocutions as much as regards that *which they signify*, or as much as regards *the order*, which *they connote*. If we speak as much as regard that *which they signify*, thus all (things) are said to be "*from God*", as from a first principle, not moved from elsewhere [aliunde]; all (things) are

said to be "*through God*", as through a most sufficient principle, which does [agit] all through itself; (and) all (things) are said to be "*in God*", as in an infinite principle, which cannot do anything outside of itself, but whose [eius] virtue surrounds all. And in these three circumlocutions there is signified, that God is the first and most sufficient and most infinite Principle. And because all these are one [unum] in God and convene with the Three, for that reason as much as regards the *signified* (St.) Ambrose says, that they have the same force; nor yet is there a multiplication (of words),[2] because they convey the same in a diverse manner, according to the reckoning of understanding. — But, if we speak as much as regards *the order*, which the habitudes of the prepositions *connote*, thus they are appropriated to the Three: because "*from Him*" means a reckoning of a first, and "*through Him*" means the reckoning of a middle, and "*in Him*" means the reckoning of a last or of one restive [quietative].[3] And for that reason "*from Him*" is appropriated to the Person of the Father, which is the first (Person) in the Trinity; "*through Him*" is appropriated to the Son, who is the middle Person; and "*in Him*" to the Holy Spirit, who is the third Person. From these (considerations) the objections are clear.

DISTINCTION XXXVII

Part I

Chapter I

In what manners God is said to be in things.

And, since it has been demonstrated, on the one hand [ex parte], in what manner all (things) are said to be in God, it seems that there must be added here, in what manners *God* is said *to be in things*, supposing , nevertheless, that [si tamen] the human mind for its part [ex parte] is even strong enough to think worthily of it, and/or the tongue sufficient to speak (of it). — Therefore, it must be known, that God, existing incommutably always in Himself, is by means of (His) presence, power, (and) Essence in every *nature* or essence without His own limitation [sine sui definitione], and in every *place* without circumscription, and in every *time* without mutability. And, moreover, He is in holy spirits and souls *in a more excellent manner*, namely, through indwelling grace, and in the Man Christ *in a most excellent manner, in Whom the fullness of the Di-*

vinity indwells corporally, as the Apostle says.[1] For in Him God dwelt, not through the grace of adoption, but through the grace of union. Moreover, so that none may presume to accuse these of falsehood, because they exceed the capacity of human intelligence, they seem to me that (they must) be fortified by the authorities of the Saints. Blessed Gregory (the Great), On the Canticle of Canticles (says):[2] « Though God is in all things in a common manner according to presence, power, and substance, yet He is said in a more familiar manner to be through grace in those, who consider more keenly [acutius] and faithfully the wonderfulness [mirificentiam] of God's works ». For of this same (passage) (St.) Augustine says to Dardanus[3] in the book on the presence of God: « Since God is an incorporeal nature and (is) incommutably alive, remaining in Himself by an eternal stability, He is present [adest] whole to all things, and whole to each; but they in whom He dwells, have Him in virtue of their own diversity of capacity, some more fully, some less,

---

[1] Here in Doubts 2 and 3. Cf. also above here in a. 2, q. 1.
[2] Supply, with codex V: *of words* [verborum]. — Then, after *because* [quia] we have inserted *the same* [idem] from the more ancient codd. and ed. 1. The word *in a diverse manner* [diversimode], which follows immediately, is absent from many codd. and from ed. 1; and in codd. F I O T & Y there is not rightly read: *because they do not convey the same* etc. [quia non idem important etc.].
[3] For *restive* [quietativi] codices L and O have *locative* [locativi]. — On this doubt, cf. Alexander of Hales, Summa., p. I, q. 67, m. 4; Bl. (now St.) Albertus (Magnus), here in a. 10, and Summa., p. I, tract 12, q. 50, m. 4; Richard (of Middleton), here on the text.

NOTES ON THE BOOK OF SENTENCES
[1] Colossians 2:9.
[2] Master (Peter) errs in citing (Pope St.) Gregory (the Great), since he badly understood the Ordinary Gloss (on Cant. 5:17), only part of which is from (St.) Gregory (the Great), the other words not so. This error of Master (Peter) was followed by the other Scholastics, even St. Bonaventure, here in p. I, a. 2, q. 2, 1st argument, and St. Thomas, Summa., I, q. 8, a. 3; cf. De Rubeis, Dissertationes, dissertation 31, ch. 1.
[3] Epistle 187, ch. 6, n. 19.

whom He Himself builds up by the grace of His Goodness as a most beloved temple for Himself ». (St.) Hilary (of Poitiers) also teaches most openly in the eighth book, ON THE TRINITY,[1] that God is everywhere: « The God », he says, « of immense virtue, the living Power, which is nowhere not at hand [adsit], nor is ever missing [desit], by Himself instructs thoroughly [edocet] all through His own, so that where His own are, He Himself is understood to be. But though He is *nowhere* in a corporal manner, not even *everywhere* He is believed to be, though He also does not cease to be in all ». (St.) Ambrose, in the first book, ON THE HOLY SPIRIT,[2] proves that the Holy Spirit is not a creature, because He is everywhere, which is proper to Divinity, saying thus: « Since every creature has been circumscribed by certain limits of its own nature, in what manner does anyone dare to name the Holy Spirit a creature, He who does not have a circumscribed and determined virtue, because[3] He is both in all and always everywhere? which is certainly [utique] proper to divinity and lordship [dominationis] ». The same (says) in the same (book):[4] « It belongs to the Lord to fill completely [complere] all, He who says: *I fill Heaven and Earth.* If, therefore, the Lord is He who fills Heaven and Earth; who, therefore, can judge that the Holy Spirit (has) no share in divine lordship and power, He who fills the world again? and what is more, (who) has also filled Jesus, the Redeemer of the whole world ». From these and very many other authorities there is openly demonstrated, that God is everywhere in every creature, by means of (His) Essence, presence, (and) power.

CHAPTER II

That God does not dwell, wheresoever He is,
but the other way around.

On the other hand, He also dwells in the Saints, in whom He is through grace. For not, wheresoever He is, does He dwell there, but where He does dwell, there He is. He dwells in the good alone, who are His temple and His seat [sedes]. Whence through Isaias[5] the Lord says: *Heaven is My seat, but Earth the footstool for My Feet,* because in the Elect, who are a heaven, God dwells and reigns, the devout who submitted to His Will; but the wicked, who are an earth, He treads upon by separating them for judgement [iudicii districtione]. Whence there is also said in the Book of Wisdom:[6] *A throne of Wisdom the soul of the just,* because He is more especially in the just than in other things, in which all, however, He is whole. « According to which manner the soul », says (St.) Augustine in (his) Letter to Jerome[7] on the origin of the soul, « is at once present whole in all the subparts [particulas] of the body, neither less in (those) lesser, nor greater in (those) greater, but yet works more intensely in some, and more remissly in others, though in each sub-

part of the body it is essentially whole », thus God too, since He is in all essentially and whole, yet He is said to be more fully in those, in whom He indwells, that is, in those He is thus, that He makes them His own temple. And these such are *with Him* already in part [ex parte], but (shall be) perfectly in beatitude; but the wicked, even if they are, where He Himself is, Who is nowhere missing, yet they are not *with Him.* Whence (St.) Augustine ON (THE GOSPEL OF ST.) JOHN (says):[8] « It was not enough to say: *Where I am, they too are,* but He added *with Me,* because even the wretched can be, where He too is, who is nowhere missing; but the Blessed are *with Him,* because they are not but the blessed of Him [ex eo] ». *With*[9] Him are they who enjoy Him and see Him, just as He is; but the wicked are not *with Him,* as the blind, in the light, are not with the light. Nor are the good thus now with Him, to see (Him) through a *vision* [speciem], even if they are in some manner with Him through *faith.* Moreover, in what manner God dwells in the good, we shall prevail to understand to some extent from those (things), which have been said above,[10] when the temporal procession of the Holy Spirit was dealt with, where, though in part [ex parte], there is expounded — *for we know in part, and we prophesy in part* — in what manner the Holy Spirit dwells in us, He who indwells not without the Father and the Son.

CHAPTER III

Where God was, before there was a creature.

But, if you ask, where did God dwell, before the Saints were; we say, that He dwelt in Himself. Whence (St.) Augustine in (his) book, AGAINST MAXIMINUS says:[11] « God dwells in His own temple », « namely in the Saints, who are God's temple now, walking (as they do) according to *the Faith*; and (who) also shall at last be the temple of God according to *vision* [speciem], in which manner the Angels are now the temple of God. But someone says: before God made Heaven and Earth, before He made the Saints, where did He dwell? God dwelt in Himself, He dwelt with Himself, and He is with Himself. Therefore, the Saints are not thus the house of God, that, with them subtracted, God falls; nay they are thus the house of God, that, if He should depart, they fall ».

« It must also be known, that », as (St.) Augustine says in (his) book to Dardanus,[12] « there cannot be said, except in a most stupid manner, that the Holy Spirit does not have a place in our body, the whole of which our soul fills. There is also more stupidly said, that the Trinity is impeded somewhere by narrow (places), so that the Father and the Son and the Holy Spirit cannot be together in some place ». « However, much more wonderful is this, that since God is everywhere whole, yet He does not dwell

---

[1] Number 21.

[2] Chapter 7, n. 81.

[3] Editions 1 and 3 have *who* [qui] for *because He* [quia]; the Vatican edition, together with the other editions, has faultily *which (virtue)* [quae].

[4] Ibid., n. 86. — The passage from Sacred Scripture is Jer. 23:24. The Vulgate reads: *Do I not fill Heaven and Earth?* [Nunquid non caelum et terram ego impleo?].

[5] Is. 66:1. The Vulgate reads: *Heaven is My seat* etc. [Caelum sedes mea etc.].

[6] A reference to Wis. 7:27: *Wisdom transfers Herself into holy souls* [Sapientia in animas sanctas se transfert], and Wis. 9:10: *so that She may be with me and work with me* [ut mecum sit et mecum laboret].

[7] Epistle 166, ch. 2, n. 4.

[8] Tract 111, n. 2. — The passage from Sacred Scripture is Jn. 17: 24. — What follows is only taken according to sense from (St. Augustine, ibid.,) nn. 3 and 4.

[9] The Vatican edition, together with the other editions, by adding (before this) *wherefore*[quod], conjoins this proposition with the text of (St.) Augustine. A little after this codex D and edition 1

have *but the wicked (are) not with Him, (are) not in the light, but neither (are they) with the light* [mali non cum illo, non in luce, sed nec cum luce], but edition 1 omits *but* [sed] and has explicitly *are they* [sunt] just after it. Codex A has *but the wicked are not with Him, not in the light, (and) are not with the light* [mali vero non sunt cum illo, non in luce, non sunt cum luce]; codex B reads *but the wicked (though they are) with Him, as in the light, are not with the light* [mali vero cum illo ut in luce non sunt cum luce]; codex E has *but the wicked (are) not with Him and are not in the light* [mali vero non cum illo et in luce non sunt]. We have retained the reading of the Vatican edition and of the other editions.

[10] In Distinction XIV. — The passage from Sacred Scripture is 1 Cor. 13:9.

[11] Book II, ch. 21, n. 1, and then ENARRATIONS ON THE PSALMS, Ps. 122:1, n. 4. In which text very many editions, together with the Vatican edition, omit *also* [etiam] after the semicolon of the first sentence; and then contrary to the original and to editions 3, 5, 7, and 8, the Vatican edition and the other editions have *He dwells with you* [apud te habitat] for *He dwelt with Himself* [apud se habitabit].

[12] Epistle 187, ch. 4, n. 15, and ch. 5, n. 16. — At the end of the passage from Sacred Scripture is Mt. 6:9, and Lk. 11:2.

in all. Furthermore who dares to opine, except (the one who) is thoroughly ignorant of the inseparability of the Trinity, that the Father and the Son can dwell in someone, in whom the Holy Sprit dwells not, or (that) in someone the Holy Spirit (dwells), in whom the Father and the Son do not dwell? It must be said, therefore, that God is everywhere through the presence of Divinity, but not everywhere through the grace of indwelling. For on account of this indwelling of grace we do not say: *Our Father, who art everywhere*, though this too is true; but *who art in the Heavens*», that is in the Saints, in whom He is in a certain more excellent manner.

« Wonderful too is this, that », as (St.) Augustine says in the same (book),[1] « God is an indweller in certain ones who do not yet know [quorundam cognoscentium] God, and (is) not (an indweller) in certain ones who do know God. For the latter do not pertain to the temple of God, who *knowing God, do not glorify (Him) as God*. To the temple of God there does pertain the little ones sanctified by the Sacrament of Christ and regenerated by the Holy Spirit, who are not yet able to know God. Therefore, Him whom the former could *know* and did not *have*, these could *have*, before they (could) *know*. Moreover, most blessed are those, for whom *to have God* is that which (it is) *to know (Him)*». — Here (St.) Augustine reveals [aperit] to some extent, in what manner God dwells in someone, that is, is had (by someone), when, namely, He is thus in someone, as to be cognized and loved by him.

From the aforesaid it is clear, that God is everywhere whole through essence and dwells in the Saints through grace. And since it has been shown above, though briefly [tenuiter], *by which reckoning* He is said to dwell in certain ones, a reckoning of order would demand,[2] that there also be assigned, *in what manner* He is everywhere and whole through essence, if the sublimity and immensity of this consideration did not entirely exceed the sense of the human mind. For as (St. John) Chrysostom says ON THE EPISTLE TO THE HEBREWS:[3] « Just as we understand many (things) of God, which we do not prevail to express thoroughly; so we express many (things), which we are not fit [idonei] to understand, v. g., we know and say, that God is everywhere; but in what manner He is everywhere, we do not grasp by (our) intellect. Likewise, we know that there is a certain incorporeal virtue, which is the cause of all the good, but in what manner, and/or what that is, we are thoroughly ignorant ».

However, certain (authors), presuming to measure by their own immense genius, have handed down that this is thus to be understood, that God is said to be everywhere through essence, not that God's Essence properly is in every place and in every creature, but because every nature and everything which naturally is, in whatsoever place it be, and every place, in which He is, has "being" through Him. The same also say,[4] that God is said to be everywhere through presence and/or through power for this reason, that all [cuncta] places are present to Him, and (because) those which are in them, He does not cease to also work something in them. For, the very places, too, and whatever is in them, if He Himself did

not conserve, they could not remain. In them, therefore, God is said to be through substance, as they say, because through the virtue of His own Substance He causes (these) places and all, which are in them, to be. — But though these (things), which they assert in explaining the understanding of the aforesaid, are true, yet in those words, by which God is said to be everywhere through essence, more must be believed to be contained; which man, while alive [vivens], is not able to grasp.

CHAPTER IV

That God, though He is in all things essentially,
yet, He is not befouled with sordid things.

« There is also customarily asked by the same, in what manner is God substantially in all things, and is not contacted by the befoulments [inquinationibus] of sordid bodies. Which is so frivolous, as to not even be worthy of a response, since even a created spirit cannot be befouled by the sordid (things) of a body,[5] even one leprous and/or however so polluted. But even (the Sun) pours forth its own rays, without being itself polluted [sine sui pollutione], upon places and bodies not only clean, but even unclean and stinking with sordid (things), by contact with which men and certain other things are infected; however, the rays of the Sun, touching [contingentes] them, exist unpolluted and uncontaminated. It is, therefore, not to be wondered, if the Divine Essence, entirely simple and incommutable, (which) fills all places again, and is in all creatures essentially, is yet not even contaminated and/or in contact [contingatur] with the filth of whatever thing ». Whence (St.) Augustine in the book, ON THE NATURE OF THE GOOD (says):[6] « Though in God », he says, « are all which He established, yet those who sin do not befoul Him. Of whose Wisdom too, which *reaches from end unto end mightily*, there is said: *She stretches to all on account of Her own cleanliness, and incurs nothing foul in Her*. « Some indeed fear that which cannot come to pass [fieri], namely, that by human flesh the Truth and Substance of God be befouled; and yet they preach, that this visible Sun scatters its own rays through all dung [faeces] and sordid (things), and keeps [servari] them clear and pure [sinceros]. If, therefore, clean visible (things) can be in contact with unclean visible (things) and not be befouled, how much more (can) the invisible and incommutable Truth » (not be)?

Finally, let them say in response [respondeant], what they estimate rather must be said in response of God: either that He is *nowhere* through essence, and/or that (He is) *everywhere*, and/or *somewhere*, such that (He is) not everywhere? But who dares to say, that the Divine Essence is *nowhere*, and/or that It is *somewhere*, and not everywhere? For if It is thus *somewhere*, that (It is) not everywhere, therefore, It belongs to a place [localis est]. Therefore, *everywhere whole* is that which contains the whole and penetrates the whole, which can neither in virtue of Its own Simplicity be divided, nor in virtue of Its own Purity be stained, nor in virtue of Its own Immensity be in any manner comprehended. Whence, (St.) Augustine (says):[8] God is everywhere, Whom we approach not by places, but by actions.

---

[1] Chapter 6, n. 21. — In the text the reference is to Rom. 1:21: *Who, when they had known god, did not glorify (Him) as God* [Qui cum cognovissent Deum, non sicut Deum glorificaverunt].

[2] The Vatican ed. with several edd., prefaces this with *now* [nunc].

[3] Homily 2, n. 1.

[4] Thus codex D; codices A B and E have *They themselves also say the same* [Ipsi idem etiam dicunt]; all the editions have not well *They also say the same* [Idem eitam dicunt].

[5] The Vatican edition and the other edd., except ed. 1, together with codex C, read *of the body* [corporeis] for *of a body* [corporis]. Below the Vatican ed. alone has in the final sentence of the quote the subjunctive form for the verbs in its first two clauses. Then, very many edd. have the indicative forms of the final two verbs in the same sentence.

[6] Chapter 29. Even those (words), which precede this paragraph

have been taken according to sense from (St.) Augustine, ON CHRISTIAN WARFARE, chs. 18, n. 20.

[7] The first passage is a reference to Wis. 8:1; the second to Wis. 7:25. — Those (words) which follow up to *Truth* [Veritas] have been taken from (St.) Augustine, ON CHRISTIAN WARFARE, chs. 18 and 20. This text is placed in codices A B C and D, and not a few editions, at the end of the chapter; in edition 7 it is read in the margin; in edition 9 it is before *Whence (St.) Augustine* [Unde Augustinus]. Therefore, it seems, that it is rather a brief note added in the second edition of this book. Cf. above D. XXXI, p. 529, footnote 5. Nevertheless, we have not removed it from the place, which it obtains in the Vatican edition and in edition 8.

[8] ENARRATIONS ON THE PSALMS, Ps. 34, sermon 2, n. 6; and ON CHRISTIAN DOCTRINE, Bk. I, ch. 10, n. 10.

PART II

CHAPTER V

Since God is everywhere and always,
yet, He (does) not belong to a place, nor is He moved
according to place nor according to time.

And, since the Divine Nature is truthfully and essentially in every place and in every time, yet is not moved through places and/or through times,[1] nor belongs to a place, nor to a time. It does not belong to a place, because It is not thoroughly circumscribed by a place, because It is also, thus, not in one place, that It is not in another, nor does It have a dimension, just as a body (does), to which according to place there is assigned a beginning, middle, and end, and a before and behind, a right and left, an up and down, which (body) by its own interposition sets itself off from its surrounding [facit distantiam circumstantium].*

CHAPTER VI

In what manners is something said (to belong) to a place,
and/or (be) circumscribable.

For, in these two manners something is said in Scripture (to belong) to a place or (be) circumscribable, and vice versa, namely either because grasping a dimension of length, height and width, it sets itself off in place, as a body; and/or because it is delimited [definitur] and determined according to place, since, when it is somewhere, it is not found everywhere; which befits not only a body, but also every created spirit. Therefore, every body belongs to a place in every manner; but in a certain manner a created spirit belongs to a place, and in a certain manner it does not belong to a place. Indeed it is said (to belong) to a place, because it is terminated by the delimitation [definitione] of a place, since when it is present to somewhere, the whole is not found elsewhere; however, it does not thus belong to a place, that grasping a dimension, it sets itself off in a place. Therefore, the Divine Essence alone belongs entirely to no place [omnino illocalis] and is uncircumscribable, nor is It moved in any manner according to places — that is either by a finite determination, and/or by an undertaken dimension — nor according to times, that is, in affection and cognition. For in these two manners, namely, according to place and time, change comes to be in a creature [creaturae], which is far from the Creator. Whence (St.) Augustine says, ON GENESIS:[2] « The Omnipotent God », he says, « always the Same according to (His) incommutable Eternity, Will, (and) Truth, moves a spiritual creature through time; He also moves a corporal creature through time and place, so that by that movement He might administer the natures, which He established. Therefore, since He does something such, we ought not opine that His Substance, by which He is God, is, according to times and places, mutable, or through times and places mobile, since He Himself is also interior to every thing, because in Him are all; and exterior to every thing, because He is above all; and anterior to all, because He is before all; and newer than all, because He is the same after all », that is after the beginnings of all. — Behold here there is openly shown, that God is changed and/or moved neither according to places nor according to times. Moreover, a spiritual creature is moved through time, but a corporal one also through time and place.

CHAPTER VII

What is it to be changed according to time.

Moreover, 'to change through time' is to vary according to the interior and/or exterior qualities, which are in the thing itself, which is changed, such as when it undertakes an alteration in [vicissitudinem] joy, sorrow, knowledge, forgetfulness, and/or a variation of form or of any exterior quality. For this change, which comes to be according to time, is a variation of qualities, which comes to be in a corporal and/or spiritual creature, and for that reason is called the season (of the thing).

However, concerning *change of place* a great debate exists [versatur] among inquirers [conquirentes]. For there are those who say, that no spirit can in any manner be changed according to place, wanting (as they do) to remove place universally from every spirit, since they assert that a place is established only according to dimension and circumscription, and say that that belongs only to a place and/or is *in a place*, which receives dimension and sets itself off in a place. And they say that (St.) Augustine thought, that a change *of time* is only to be attributed to a spiritual creature, but *of place and of time* to a corporeal one.

But, as we have said above, a thing is said to belong to a place and/or be circumscribable in a twofold manner, namely, either because *it receives a dimension* and sets itself off, and/or because *it is delimited* by a terminus of place, each of which convenes with a corporeal creature, but the latter of the two with a spiritual one only. For, as we have said above, a corporal creature belongs to a place and/or is circumscribable thus, that it is determined by a delimitation of place, and because it receives dimension it sets itself off; but a spiritual one is only enclosed by the delimitation of a place, since it is thus somewhere, that (it is) not elsewhere; but it neither receives a dimension, nor sets itself off in place, because if there were many spirits here, there would not by this crowd [coangustarent] the place, by which it would contain fewer bodies [minus de corporibus]. And for that reason (St.) Augustine attributes a change *of place* to a body, not to a spirit, because though a spirit passes from place to place, yet not thus, that being circumscribed by dimensions, it would by its interposition set itself off from its own surroundings, just as a body (does).

CHAPTER VIII

Whether created spirits belong to a place
and are circumscribable.

Therefore, created spirits are in a place and pass from place to place [transeunt de loco ad locum], and in a certain manner (they belong) to a place and are

---

[1] These (words) have been taken according to sense from (St.) Augustine, ON A LITERAL EXPOSITION OF GENESIS, Bk. VIII, ch. 20, nn. 39 and 40.

[2] In Bk. VIII, ch. 26, n. 48.
[3] Here in ch. 6.

---

* *Trans. note*: See this idiom in the Rationale for the Translation of Peculiar Latin Terms, in the Introduction to this English translation, at the tope of page E-23.

circumscribable, but not in every many, in which corporeal [corporeae] creatures (are). But the uncreated Spirit, who is God, is indeed in a place and in every place, but belongs entirely to no place and (is) uncircumscribable. Whence (St.) Bede (the Venerable), On (THE GOSPEL OF ST.) LUKE,[1] says: « When the Angels come to us, they thus fulfill (their) ministry exteriorly, that they yet assist before God interiorly through contemplation, because, even if an Angel is a circumscribed spirit, yet the Most High Spirit, who is God, is uncircumscribed, within Whom the Angel runs, wheresoever he is sent ». — Behold, here there is said, that an angelic spirit is circumscribed, but the Spirit, who is God, (is) uncircumscribed. In other place even (St.) Ambrose, showing the distance between the uncreated Spirit and a created spirit, says, that the Seraphim pass from place to place, thus saying in (his) book, ON THE TRINITY:[2] « Isaias said: Because there was *sent to me one of the Seraphim*. And indeed the Holy Spirit is said (to be) "*sent*", but the Seraphim (are sent) to *one*, (the Holy) Spirit, however, to *one*. The Seraphim* are sent *in ministry*, (the Holy) Spirit works a *mystery*. The Seraphim pass from place to place — for he does not completely fill all — but he himself is filled again by (the Holy) Spirit ». Here there is openly demonstrated, that the Angels in a certain manner belong to places.

CHAPTER IX

That God is everywhere without local movement.

And so, let us say, that the Divine Nature in virtue of Its own immensity is nowhere missing, and that It alone, belonging entirely to no place and uncircumscribable, is enclosed by no place, but *reaches from end unto end*,[3] yet not by a spacious magnitude nor by a local movement, but by the immensity and immobility of Its own Essence. Whence (St.) Augustine says to Dardanus:[4] « We do not opine that God is diffused through all (places) as if by a spacious magnitude, just as soil or light is according to this diffused, but rather just as in two wise men, the one of which is grander in body than the other, but is not wiser, there is one wisdom, and it is neither greater in the greater, nor lesser in the lesser, nor lesser in one than in the two; so God, without labor ruling and containing the world, is whole in Heaven, whole on Earth, and whole in each, and contained by no place, but in Himself whole everywhere ». The same also says on the Psalm:[5] « To the Word of God there pertains not 'being in part', but 'being everywhere through Himself'. For this is the Wisdom of God, who *reaches from end unto end mightily*, yet, not by local movement, but by His own immobility: just as if (when) any rocky

mass fills up any place, it is said, that it reaches from (one) end of that place unto the (other) end, yet though it does not desert the one by occupying the other. Therefore, that Word has no local movement, and that Wisdom is unmoving [solidus] and everywhere ». — From the aforesaid it is known, that God is thus everywhere through essence, that He is neither diffused by a spacious magnitude, nor, having deserted one place, does He occupy the other, because He has no local movement. And for that reason (St.) Augustine, wanting to prescind[6] every local movement and local circumscription from God's purity, says rather, that all are in Him, rather than that He is somewhere, and yet that He is not a place, Who is in no place, thus saying in the book, OF EIGHTY-THREE QUESTIONS:[7] « God is not somewhere. What is somewhere is contained by a place, what is contained by a place is a body, but God is not a body: therefore, He is not *somewhere*. And yet, because He is and is not in a place, all are in Him rather than He (is) somewhere; and yet (they are) not thus in Him, that He is a place. For a place is in a space, which is occupied by the length and width and height of a body, and God is not such a something. Therefore, all are also in Him, and He is not a place, yet the place of God is said (to be), though [sed] improperly, God's temple, not that by which He is contained. Moreover, this is understood (to be) nothing better than a clean soul ». — Behold here he says, that God is not in a place. But it must be understood, that He is not in a place locally, that is, because He has neither a circumscription nor local movement.

But to this there is customarily opposed thus: Everyday creatures are made, which before were not, and God is in them, though He was not in them before: therefore, He is where He was not before, and for that reason He seems (to be) changeable. — But though everyday He begins to be in the creatures, in which He was not before, because they were not; yet, this comes to be without His own change, in the manner which He began to be in the world which He made, yet without His own mutability; similarly, He ceases to be in those which were before, without His own change, and, yet, He Himself does not desert a place, but the place ceases to be.

It seems already that (there has been) sufficiently demonstrated, in what manner all are said to be in God, and God in all; which debate we have undertaken quasi incidentally, because the matter, about which our discourse turned, seemed to demand it. For we were speaking in an orderly manner of the Knowledge and Wisdom of God, and though we said,[8] that God knows all, it was asked, whether on account of the Cognition, which He has of all, all were said to be in God, or whether Scripture said this for another reason. The occasion of this question, therefore, led us into the aforesaid disputation.

---

[1] In chapter 1. (St.) Bede has taken these words, with a few variations of expression, from St. Gregory (the Great's), HOMILIES ON THE GOSPELS, Homily 34.

[2] Or rather ON THE HOLY SPIRIT, Bk. I, ch. 10, n. 115, and ch. 11, n. 116. — The passage from Sacred Scripture is Isaias 6:6: *and there flew to me* etc. [et volavit ad me etc.]. — In the text of (St.) Ambrose, codices A B and C have thrice *Seraph* [Seraph] for *Seraphim* [Seraphim].* At the end of the chapter, the Vatican edition, together with very many editions has *shown* [ostenditur] for *demonstrated* [monstratur].

[3] A reference to Wis. 8:1.

[4] Epistle 187, ch. 4, n. 11. — In which text, the Vatican edition and the other editions have *smoke* [fumus] for *soil* [humus], breaking with all the codices, with editions 1 and 8, and with the

original, in which there is read: just as soil, as humor, or air, or light is diffused by this.

[5] ENARRATIONS ON THE PSALMS, Ps. 147, n. 22, but many (words) have been omitted here and in the preceding passage by Master Peter.

[6] Codices A B C and E have *foresee* [praevidere].

[7] In Question 20. — The Vatican edition, together with a few editions, has at the beginning of the second sentence of this quote *For what* [Quod enim] instead of *What* [Quod]. Near the end after *He is not a place* [locus non est] all the editions, except the Vatican, add *nor is He in a place* [nec in loco est], but breaking with the codices and the original.

[8] Codices A and D, and editions 2, 3, 7, 8, and 9 have *we taught* [doceremus].

---

* Trans. note*: Here Master Peter employs "*Seraphim*", as a collective name, and thus uses singular forms of the Latin verbs; in the English translation, to avoid misunderstanding, the name "Seraphim" is used as a simple plural, and, therefore, the verbs have been changed, likewise, to the plural.

COMMENTARY ON DISTINCTION XXXVII

PART I

In what manner is God in things and in corporeal places?

And, since it has been demonstrated, on the one hand, in what manner all (things) are said to be in God etc..

THE DIVISION OF THE TEXT

Above, Master (Peter) dealt with the manner in which all (things) are in God. Here, second, he deals with the manner in which God is in things and in corporal places. And, since to *being in a place* and in a changeable thing there follows a change in that which is in that (place or thing), for that reason (Master Peter) deals, second,[1] with God's immutability in place, below in the same Distinction beyond the midpoint, there (where he says): *And since the Divine Nature etc..* The first part has three parts. In the *first*, he tells, in what manner God is places and things, and confirms (this) through authorities. In the *second*, he strives to reveal the understanding of the sayings, there (where he says): *Moreover, in what manner God dwells in the good* etc. In the *third*, he shows the insufficiency of our intellect to grasp this, there (where he says): *From the aforesaid it is clear, that God is everywhere whole etc..*

The *first* part has three (parts) according to (its) three chapters.* In the first, (Master Peter) shows the manners of being of God in things. But, in the second, he confirms by authorities, that God is everywhere through essence, there (where he says): *Moreover, so that none may presume to accuse these of falsehood* etc. In the third, he shows, that God dwells through grace in the Saints alone, there (where he says): *On the other hand, He also dwells in the Saints etc..*

Moreover, in what manner God dwells etc.. This is the *second* subpart, in which he excites (the reader) to an understanding of the sayings, and this part has three parts. In the first, he leads (one) by hand reasonably. In the second, he excludes a foolish reckoning, there (where he says): *It must also be known, that, as (St.) Augustine says* etc. In the third, he arouses (the reader) to admiration, there (where he says): *Wonderful too is this.* For the divine sacraments are more admirable than intelligible.

From the aforesaid it is clear, that God is everywhere whole etc.. This is the *third* part, in which (Master Peter) shows (our) insufficiency to cognized, in what manner God is everywhere through essence; and this part has three parts according to (its) three chapters. For, first, he shows, that our intellect is not sufficient. Second, he excludes those who presumptuously solve (the question), there (where he says): *However, certain (authors), presuming to measure by their own immense genius* etc.. But, third, he sends away [abiicit] those who unreasonably questioned (the matter), there (where he says): *There is also customarily asked by the same, in what manner is God* etc.; where he shows, that their question (is) frivolous and unworthy of a response.

TREATMENT OF THE QUESTIONS

For an understanding of this part there is the question of the existence of God everywhere; and about this three (questions) are principally asked.

First, there is asked, whether it befits God to be everywhere.

Second, there is asked, whether it is proper for God to be everywhere.

Third, there is asked, in what manner it befits God to be everywhere.

And as much as regards the first, because "to be everywhere" can distribute on behalf of all things and on behalf of all places, two (questions) are asked.

First, whether God is in all things.

Second, whether He is in all places.

---

[1] The Vatican edition suppresses *second* [secundo], which word we have recalled from the more ancient manuscripts and from edition 1, and indeed justly, as is evidently apparent from the slightly longer reading of codex R: *for that reason he first deals with the manner in which God is in things, and second* etc. [ideo primo agit, quomodo Deus sit in rebus, et secundo etc.].

---

* *Trans. note*: St. Bonaventure, as almost always happens, presents a Division of the Text which does not correspond to the division of Parts, Chapters, or paragraphs in the critical edition. Thus in saying *chapters* [capitula], this evidently does not signify the chapters found in the critical edition; but either refers to those in the edition which he was using, or he uses capitula in the sense of *headings*, that is, "subjects under consideration".

ARTICLE I

Wherefore does it befit God to be everywhere?

QUESTION I

Whether God is in all things?

Moreover, that He is in all things, is shown in this manner:

1. The Philosopher (says) in (his) First Philosophy: « As much as anything (is) more simple, so much is it needed by many and found in many »;[1] but God is the Most Simple on the confines of simplicity: therefore, He is found in all. But He is not discovered except where He is: therefore, He is in all.

2. Likewise, as much as a cause (is) prior, so much (is it) more universal, therefore, the First Cause is the most universal; but as much as anything (is) more universal, so much does it inflow into many: therefore, since the First Cause is the most universal, It inflows into all.[2] But everything which inflows into something, is present to it according to virtue — for nowhere and never does one acting work except through the presence of virtue — but God on account of His Simplicity is the same as His Virtue: therefore since God's *Virtue* is in all, (His) *Substance* is also in all.

3. Likewise, this seems <u>per impossibile</u>: because everything which is in one limited thing, thus that it is not in another, is limited and constrained [arctatum]; but this is impossible concerning [circa] God: therefore, He is not in one thing, unless He is in all.

4. Likewise, if God is in one thing, thus that (He is) not in another, either *He can* be in that, in which He is not, or (He can) *not*: if He can *not*, therefore, He is not omnipotent; if *He can* be, and He is not, since the thing does not change, therefore, He can be changed. Therefore, if God is not in all things, either He is not omnipotent, or not immutable; each of which is impossible.

ON THE CONTRARY: 1. As much as anything is more disjoined [seiungitur] from a shadowy nature, so much does it cognize in an more unmingled [impermixtius] manner and under a more noble light; but God cognizes in a most clear manner: therefore, He is disjoined most of all from shadowy nature. But every creature (is) a shadow: therefore God either is in none, or is in the fewest created things.

2. Likewise, as much as a mover is more distant from the movable, so much more sufficiently does it move — whence a soul moves more sufficiently than a natural form,[3] and an Intelligence than a soul — but God is the most sufficient Mover and Worker: therefore, He is most highly distant from every movable: therefore, either He is not in things [in nullis rebus], or (He is) in a few.

3. Likewise, « every united virtue is more infinite than a multiplied one »;[4] but Divine Virtue is most infinite: therefore, most united. But, as much as anything is more united, so much (is it) more scattered [diffusum] and discovered in fewer: ergo etc..

4. Likewise, there is asked: what necessity is there, that one posit[5] that God (is) in all things? It seems, that (there is) none on God's part. For there is nobility in the one acting, which can act where it is not, similarly, which cause a standing effect through itself — otherwise the words of God are more weak than the works of created craftsmen, which are conserved in *"being"*, with them absent — therefore, if there is no necessity, it seems, therefore, that it is a superfluity (to posit such in God). But it is impossible, that there be any superfluity in God: ergo etc..

CONCLUSION

God is in all things, the reason for which is both His perfection, and the indigence of things.

I RESPOND: It must be said, that God is in all things, just as (King) David[6] himself testifies, saying: *If I ascend into Heaven, Thou are there* etc..

Moreover, the necessity that God exist in all (things) is taken both on the part *of His perfection*, and on the part *of the indigence of things*. On His part, on account of (His) Most High *Immensity* and Most High *Power;*

---

[1] This proposition seems to have been gathered from that, which Aristotle says in METAPHYSICS, Bk. XI, ch. 1 (Bk. X, ch. 1) concerning first principles, namely, that they are more simple, contain all, and that, with these entirely removed, all others at once perish. — The subsequent words, *on confines of simplicity* [in fine simplicitatis], have been taken from the BOOK OF CAUSES, proposition 20 (in Bardenhewer edition, prop. 21). In several editions of the BOOK OF CAUSES it is read thus: the Infinite Simple of simplicity [infinita simplicitatis simplex].

[2] Cf. the BOOK OF CAUSES, propositions 1 and 20, cited above in d. 27, p. I, a. sole, q. 2, p. 471, footnote 3. — On the immediately subsequent proposition Aristotle says in

PHYSICS, Bk. VII, text 9 (ch. 2): That from which the beginning of the movement is, is at once with that which is moved. Cf. also, ON GENERATION AND CORRUPTION, Bk. I, text 54, (ch. 7). — Somewhat below this in place of *His Simplicity* [suam simplicitatem] codd. S & Z have *(His) most high Simplicity* [suumam simplicitatem], cod. K has *His most high Simplicity* [summam suam simplicitatem].

[3] The Vatican edition prefixes to the word *natural* [naturalis] the words *material and/or* [materialis vel].

[4] BOOK ON CAUSES, proposition 17.

[5] Codices L and O read *that God is* [Deum esse] for *that one posit that God (is)* [Deum ponere].   [6] Psalm 138:8.

and the reason for each is (His) most high *Simplicity*. For because He is most highly simple, constrained to nothing, for that reason He is found in all as *One immense*; because (He is) most highly simple, for that reason (He is) to an infinite degree [in infinitum] *the most virtuous*, and for that reason His Virtue (is) in all; and (His) Virtue is the Same as (His) Substance, and for that reason it is necessary, that He be in all.[1]

On the part of *the creature* there is a necessity, because a creature has in itself *possibility* and *vanity*, and it is the cause of each, because it has been created from nothing. For because a creature is and accepted[2] a '*to be*' from another, which causes it to be, when it was not before; from this it is not its own '*to be*', and for that reason it is not a pure act, but has a *possibility*, and for this reason it has an ability to be in flux and to vary [fluxibilitatem et variabilitatem], for that reason it lacks stability, and for that reason it cannot be except through the presence of that which granted it *to be*. An example of this is revealed [apertum] in the impression of the form of a seal in water, which (form) is not conserved for a moment, unless with the seal present. — And again, because a creature has been produced from nothing, for that reason it has a *vanity*; and because nothing vain is supported in itself, it is necessary,[3] that every creature be held up [sustentetur] through the presence of *the Truth*. And there is a simile: if one would place a ponderous body in the air, which is (itself) vain, it would not be held up. Thus also in the proposed.

1. To that which is objected concerning distance and commingling [permixione], it must be said, that something is united to something in a threefold manner: either according to *presence* only, or according to *presence* and *dependence*, or according to *presence* and *dependence* and *concomitance* in matter. In the first manner a ray (of light) is in the air, in the second a soul in a body, in the third manner a liquid in a liquid. What is in something in the first manner is not thoroughly mixed, similarly what is in the second manner is not thoroughly mixed properly, but only that which (is) in the third. And,

indeed, in the first manner God is in things, not in the second and/or the third.

2. To that which is objected concerning the distance of a mover from a movable, it must be said, that there is a distance through absence, and this impedes, (and) not assist [iuvat ad] movement; and there is a distance through independence, and this helps [iuvat], because as much as the mover is more perfect and more absolute, it depends less and is more sufficient, and in this manner God, even (as) present, is distant.

3. To that which is objected, that a united virtue is more infinite; it must be said, that a united virtue which causes according to its magnitude, is attained per se in respect of *the subject*, per accidens in respect of *the object*. Moreover, in respect of *the subject* it is attained through the simplicity of the subject, but in respect of *the object* through an indistance [indistantiam] from the virtue, because as much as the virtue (is) more powerful, so much (is it) nearer to the object.[4] Since, therefore, Divine Virtue in substance is most simple and is never elongated from the Substance, for that reason It is most infinite in many, because (It is) most united in many, as in one. « For everywhere is the center of that Power », just as Trismegistus says.[5]

4. What is objected last has already been solved, because the necessity is on the part of God and the creature, as has been seen. — Therefore, what is objected, that a created agent [agens creatum] works, where it is not, and produces an effect, which stands without it; it must be said, that in God it is not similar. For if this is attained in a created craftsman, this comes from a defect of perfection: for because the created agent is *limited*, and *differs* from its own virtue, it can work through virtue where it is not; again, since it acts *upon what is subjected to it* [agit ex suppositione] and cannot (act) upon the whole, for that reason the effect does not depend totally from it. But God has the opposite conditions, because (He is) *infinite*, and in Him Virtue and Substance are *the Same*, and He produces *the whole*; for that reason it is not similar.[6]

SCHOLIUM

I. Together with the principal Question, there is solved another connected question, proposed in the 4th opposed argument, namely, concerning *the cause*, why God is in all things.

That God *is in* all things and places, is by faith certain [fide certum est]. This *inexistence* of God [inexistentia Dei] is according to all doctors utterly singular and contains *supereminently* all manners of presence [omnes modos praesentiae],

according to which creatures, both corporal and spiritual, can be present to themselves, but excludes every imperfection, which accompanies those manners (of presence) in creatures. Wherefore God's presence implies 1.) a certain « indistance of (His) manner of being present [praesentialitatis] » (below in a. 2, q. 2) and/or a *coexistence*, but not that, by which *corporal* substances, endowed with quantity, *coexist* to themselves, thus that one (is) *outside* the other,

---

[1] In an admirable manner the Seraphic Doctor speaks of this in his ITINERARIUM MENTIS IN DEUM, chs. 5 and 6.

[2] Not a few codices, such as F I V and cc, have *accepts* [accipit]; the Vatican edition and* edition 1 have *it has been created* [creata est] for *a creature is* [creatura est]. A little further below this, for *but* [sed] the Vatican edition, together with codex cc, faultily has *because it* [quia].

[3] Codex T inserts here *therefore* [ergo], and a little above this before *nothing vain* [nihil vanum] it omits, together with very many other codices and edition 1, *because* [quia]. A little further below this, for *of the Truth* [Veritatis] codd. X bb & cc, with edd. 2, 3, 4, 5 & 6, have *of (Divine) Virtue* [virtutis]. On the reasons alleged here, cf. above d. 8, p. I, a. 2, q. 2, in reply to n. 7, and (St.) Anselm, MONOLOGION, chs. 13, 14, 20 ff..

[4] Very many codd., with the first six edd., read *subject* [subiecto]; a depraved reading, because it does not correspond to the context.

[5] We do not find these words in the works of Hermes Trismegistus, but rather in Alan of Lille's, RULES OF THEOLOGY, rule 7, where there is thus read: « God is an intelligible sphere, whose center (is) everywhere, (and whose) circumference (is) nowhere », which words are also cited by Alexander of Hales, in his SUMMA, p. I, q. 7, m. 1, and attributed to Trismegistus. However, Bl. (now St.) Albertus (Magnus), in his commentary, SENT., Bk. I, d. 3, a. 18, says: I do not know who this Trismegistus was, and I believe, that the book is a forgery. For all which Trismegistus is said to have said, I find in a certain book of Master Alan, which is composed of certain general propositions and which is subjected to a commentary on the same.

[6] Cf. (St.) Augustine, ON A LITERAL EXPOSITION OF GENESIS, Bk. IV, ch. 12, n. 22.

---

* *Trans. note*: Here it appears that the footnote in the critical edition omitted *and* [et], faultily, and after the numeral *1* it erroneously puts a period, for it reads incongruously *Vat. ed. 1 creata pro creatura*, though the reading *Vatican edition and edition 1 has* etc. is only my supposition.

and only a part of the one contacts a part of the other; 2.) It implies « an existence *of intimacy*, as that which is being contained within, as a soul in a body » (ibid.), excluding, however, every dependence, in an analogous manner, just as light is in the air; 3.) It implies a *causality*, by which God works immediately « through the influence of (His) Virtue » (ibid.) « bearing all (things) through the Word of His Virtue » (Hebr. 1:3). It is also established, that the most simple Essence of God is His Power and Operation.

II. Nevertheless concerning the *proper* and *formal* reckoning of God's ubiquity there is a controversy between (Bl. John Duns) Scotus and his School and the School of St. Thomas. For St. Thomas (SUMMA, I, q. 8, a. 1, and elsewhere) from God's presence through *operation* concludes His presence through *essence*. All concede, that this method of argument is true, if it is *a posteriori*, since Essence, Power and Operation in God can least of all be separated and/or distinguished *in thing* from on another; however, if it its understood *a priori*, thus that the very *reason for operating* is the formal reason of the Divine ubiquity, (Bl.) Scotus (here in q. sole, and SENT., Bk. II, d. 2, q. 4) contradicts it, asserting, that, if per impossibile God *would* not *work* in some thing, He would yet be there, and vice versa, if He *would* not *be* in some place, yet He could work there, that is at a distance. On this controversy, cf. Cajetan on the passage cited; Rada, controversy 28; Macedo, collat. 9, diff. 3, and very many others draw St. Bonaventure from diverse (passages) to their own side; but he himself proves God's presence in each manner, namely, indeed *a priori* through God's Im-

mensity and Simplicity, which is constrained to nothing in regard to the presence of intimacy; but *a posteriori* through (His) causality and Operation, from which the very essence and power and operation of creatures most interiorly depends. These fundaments are conceded by all. Action at a distance, which, contrary to (Bl.) Scotus, St. Thomas (loc. cit. in reply to n. 3) admits in no agent, St. Bonaventure (in the solution to n. 4) denies, at least in regard to God. Below in a. 3, q. 2 he also asserts, that « (a manner of existing) ... *by means of a presence* [praesentialiter] does not principally respond to operation; for something is present to something, even if it does not operate (upon it) ». — It must be noted that what is said in the solution to n. 4 of the threefold difference between a created and uncreated agent, namely that a created agent has a limited 'to be', whence it cannot be present except in one place — that its virtue differs from itself — that it acts out of a supposition and not in the whole, that is, by supposing the matter, about which it acts; whence the effect too depends from it in *becoming*, not in *being*.

III. Alexander of Hales, SUMMA., p. I, q. 9, m. 3. — (Bl. John Duns) Scotus, on this and the following question, here in the q. sole; REPORTATIO., here in qq. 1 and 2. — St. Thomas, here in q. 1, a. 1; SUMMA., I, q. 8, a. 1; SUMMA CONTRA GENTILES., Bk. III, c. 68. — Bl. (now St.) Albertus (Magnus), on this and the following question, here in a. 1, 2, 3, and 7. — (Bl.) Peter of Tarentaise, here in q. 1, a. 1. — Durandus (of Saint-Pourçain), here in p. I, q. 1. — (Bl.) Dionysius the Carthusian, on this and the following question, here in q. 1. — (Gabriel) Biel, on this and the following two questions, here in the q. sole.

QUESTION II

Whether God is in all places?

Second, there is ask, whether God is everywhere locally, that is, whether He is in all places. And it seems that (He is) not.

1. (St. Severinus) Boethius (says) in (his) book, ON THE TRINITY: « God seems to be said to be thus everywhere, not because (He is) in every place, but because He cannot be entirely in a place ».

2. Likewise, this very (thing) seems *by reason*, because, just as the Philosopher wants,[2] a place is compared to the one placed [ad locatum] more in the reckoning of form; but God is the most excellent Form; therefore, in respect of Him there is no form, therefore, no place.

3. Likewise, it seems according to another reason, because fourfold is the condition of a place in respect to the one placed, namely, *to contain*, *to guard* [salvare], *to measure* and *to terminate*.[3] A place contains as a vessel, measures as a quantity, guards as a nature, terminates as a boundary [finis]; but God is compared to a place according to none of these conditions; ergo etc..

4. Likewise, the first and proper passion of being in a place is dimension,[4] therefore what recedes more from dimension, is less in a place; and what (recedes) most of all, (is) least of all (in a place); and what recedes entirely, is in no manner in a place; but God is of this kind: ergo etc..

ON THE CONTRARY: 1. Jeremias (chapter) twenty-three:[5] *Heaven and Earth do I fill full*; but everything which is itself in a place by filling (it) full, is in a place according to which (it is) a place.

2. Likewise, this seems *by reason*, because there is an indigence of a place, according to which (it is) a place, regarding the one in the place, that (the former) be fulfilled [repleatur] by the latter;[6] but every creature (is) an emptiness [vanitas], moreover, an emptiness does not fulfill except through the presence of truth: therefore, for this, that a place be fulfilled, it is necessary, that God be at hand. But with this posited, God is posited to be in a place, as it is a place.

3. Likewise, there is a greater indivision[7] of form according to matter than of the one placed to a place; but a form is not united to matter nor remains throughout except through God's presence:

---

[1] Chapter 4: That He is everywhere, seems thus to be said, not because He is in every place (for He cannot be entirely in a place), but because to Him every place is at hand for Him to seize, since He is not taken up in a place; and He is also said to be nowhere in a place for this reason, since He is everywhere, but not in a place.

[2] (Aristotle), PHYSICS, Bk. IV, text 14 (ch. 2): « For what reason shall a species and form of anything seem to be a place, according to which a magnitude and the matter of a thing is terminated; for (a place) is the terminus of each one ». And ON HEAVEN AND THE WORLD, Bk. IV, text 35 (ch. 4) he says: « Moreover, we say that that which contains, belongs to form, but that which is contained, to matter ». — A little below this after *of form* [formae] the Vatican edition, together with codex cc, adds *rather than in the reckoning of another genus of cause* [quam in ratione alterius generis causae].

[3] Aristotle, PHYSICS, Bk. IV, text 30 (ch. 4).

[4] See Aristotle's text here in footnote 2.

[5] Verse 24.

[6] What follows (is taken) from the definition of 'place' in Aristotle, PHYSICS, Bk. IV, text 41 (ch. 4): « A place is the first immobile terminus of (something) containing », which definition according to Aristotle befits a place, *as it is a place*, not a place, *as it is a vessel*: for thus a place is not immobile. — The subsequent proposition alludes to Rom. 8:20:* *For to emptiness has creation been subjected* [Vanitati enim creatura subiecta est]. — A little after this, for *does not fulfill* [replet], codices G K T and ff faultily read *is not fulfilled* [repletur].

[7] Or union. — Somewhat below this the words *as a nature* [ut natura] do not pertain to the word God [Deus], but to *any thing* [qualibet re], thus that the author intends to say: God is in any thing, to the extent that the thing is a nature.

---

* *Trans. note*: Here the original note read faultily *8:10* for *8:20*. In passage from Scripture, the Latin, vanitas, which is traditionally rendered as *vanity*, is rendered in its other sense, as *emptiness*, on account of what St. Bonaventure says in the second paragraph of the Response, regarding *the vacuity of (the place's) distance* [vacuitatem distantiae], as compared to the *emptiness of (the place's) essence* [vanitatem essentiae].

therefore, much less neither the one placed to the place. But because through God's presence a form is united to matter, God is in any thing, as (its is) a nature: therefore, since through God's presence the one placed is united and conserved in place, God is in the place, as it is a place.

4. Likewise, presence and togetherness is according to place and according to time; but God is most perfectly present to any thing: therefore, according to place and time. But what are present according to time, are in the same time: therefore, also those which are present according to place, are in the same place: if, therefore, God is present to every place, God is in a place, not only, as it is *a thing*, but also, it is *a place*.

CONCLUSION

God is in every place, but not circumscriptively, nor in a delimited manner, but according to excellence and through a presence supplying the indigence of the place.

I RESPOND: It must be said, that there is a threefold condition, according to which the one placed is compared to the place. *One*, according to which[1] (the one in the place) is excelled (by the place), and this is (its) property of being guarded [salvationis]; for in this manner the one placed needs a place, and the place completes its indigence and conserves (its) nature, and according to this property corporal (beings) alone are in a place, but not spiritual ones, because (the latter) do not receive an influence from a corporeal place.

The *other* is the property, according to which the one placed is equated and proportioned to the place; and this is (its) property of commensuration, and according to this condition corporal (beings) are properly in a place, because they alone are completely measurable [commensurabilia], whence they are circumscribed. But spiritual (beings are in a place) less properly; for they are not in a commensurative manner* in respect of the parts (of the place), yet they are in delimitive manner in respect to the whole (of the place).[2] The *third* is the condition, according to which the one in the place excels the place, namely, that through its presence it fills again and supplies the indigence of the place. For a place without one in the place is deprived and indigent, just as (is) the concavity of the eye without the organ.

Since, therefore, God is compared to no creature, neither according to a reckoning of *inferiority*, nor (to a reckoning) of *equality*, but (according to one) of *superiority* and of excellence; God is not in a place as much as regards the *first* and *second* property, but only as much as regards the *third*, that is, He supplies the indigence of the place through (His) presence. For the one placed through (its) presence fills again the vacuity of (the place's) distance; but God through (His) presence fills again the emptiness of (the place's) essence, and those (places) indeed without this cannot be.[3]

From these, the response to the objections is clear. For the reasons proving, that God is in a place, as it is a place, proceed according to the third condition, as is clear; but the reasons for the opposite (side proceed) according to the first and second, that is (according to the properties) of being guarded and of being limited [terminationis].

SCHOLIUM

I. This question differs from the preceding one, since St. Bonaventure (4th. opposed argument) distinguishes place, as it is a *thing*, under which respect it pertains to the preceding question, and as it is a *place*, under which (its) special difficulties are to be discussed. On this subject Alexander of Hales (SUMMA., p. I, q. 9, m. 3, in the collateral question) says of the difference between the expression: "God is *in every thing*", and the other: "God is *everywhere*": « When I say: "God is in every thing", I speak of the habitude of one conserving to one conserved. But the one conserved is more in the one conserving than vice versa, because the one conserving contains the one conserved at least virtually. Therefore, from this, that there is said: "God is in every thing", there is posited, that things are in God and are contained by Him, and not the other way around. But when I say: "God is everywhere", I posit nothing in God, but I do posit, that He fills again all *wheres* ». — For an understanding of the question the fourfold condition of a place regarding the one in the place must be noted (3rd argument of the fundament, and below in p. II. a. 1. q. 1, in the body of the question; SENT. Bk .II, d. 2, p. II, q. 2, q. 1).

II. There is commonly distinguished a fourfold manner of being in a place: *circumscriptively*, when the whole of the one in the place responds to the whole of the place, and the parts of the one in the place respond to the parts of the place, just as bodies are in a place; *in a delimited manner* [definitive], when a thing is in one place thus, that (it is) not in another, but yet (is) whole in

the whole place and whole in the parts of the place; thus a soul is in a body and an Angel in a place; *sacramentally*, just as the Most Sacred Body of Christ is whole under the whole species and its parts, but at once also under the other species, but not everywhere (in space); *in a fulfilling manner* [repletive], as St. Bonaventure and Alexander of Hales mean it to signify the utterly singular manner, in which God unconfusedly and in an unmingled manner *is in*, *fills again*, *contains* and superexcels all (places) to an immense degree. This manner of speaking seems to have been borrowed from Jeremias 23:24 and St. Augustine (CONFESSIONS, Bk. I, ch. 3): « All which Though does fill full, by containing Thou does fill full ... all which Thou dost fill full, Thou doest fill full all by Thy whole Self ». — The words at the end of the body (of the Response), « God through (His) presence fills again the vacuity of essence » etc., are explained well by St. Thomas (SUMMA, I, q. 8, a. 2): « God fills again every place, not as a body; for a body is said to fill a place again, inasmuch as it does not suffer with itself another body; but through this that God is in any place, there is not excluded, that others are there, nay He fills all places again through this, that He gives *being* to all in all the places, which He fills again ».

III. Alexander of Hales, SUMMA., p. I, q. 9, m. 2. — St. Thomas, here in q. 2, a. 1. — (Bl.) Peter of Tarentaise, here in q. 2, a. 1. — Giles the Roman, here in the 2nd princ., q. 2. — Durandus (of Saint-Pourçain), here in p. I, q. 2.

---

[1] The Vatican ed. & ed. 1 here repeat *the one in the place* [locatum].

[2] Supply, here and a little above this, after *parts* [partium] the word *of the place* [loci]. — The Vatican ed. has *completely measurable* [commensurabilia] for *in a commensurative manner* [commensurative], and *delimitable* [definibilia] for *in a delimitive manner* [definitive].

[3] The sense is: and that fulfilling, by which the one in the place

fulfills the vacuity of distance (of the place), cannot be without this fulfilling, by which God fulfills the emptiness of the creature's essence. Cf. (St.) Anselm, MONOLOGION, ch. 13 f. and ch. 20 ff. — A little before this, for *emptiness of (the place's) essence* [vanitatem essentiae] the Vatican edition, together with not a few codices, has *vacuity of (the place's) essence* [vacuitatem essentiae].

---

* Trans. note: A *commensurative manner* is a manner of being which causes that which exists in this manner to be capable of being completely measured; similarly a *delimitive manner* is a manner of being which causes that which exists in this manner to be capable to being delimited.

ARTICLE II

It is proper to God to be everywhere.

Consequently, as much as regards the second Article there is asked, whether '*to be everywhere*' is proper to God. And, because the proper is that which befits one alone and always,[1] for that reason, as much as regards this, two (questions) are asked.

First, whether '*to be everywhere*' [esse ubique] befits God alone.

Second, whether it befits Him always [semper] or from eternity [ab aeterno].

QUESTION I

Whether 'to be everywhere' befits God alone?

Moreover, it seems, that it befits [conveniat] God alone.

1. (St.) Augustine (says) in (his) book, ON THE CREED:[2] « 'To be everywhere' is 'to be God' »; but it befits no creature to be God, nay this is most proper to God: therefore, it befits no creature to be everywhere.

2. Likewise, (St.) Ambrose (says) in (his) book, ON THE HOLY SPIRIT:[3] « Since every creature has been circumscribed by the certain limits [limitibus] of its own nature, 'to be everywhere and in all things' is proper to the Divinity and to Lordship [dominationis] ».

3. Likewise, this very (thing) seems *by reason*, because every creature, existing *through itself* and *in itself*, is this something;[4] but everything which is this something, is a singular, and every singular is here and now, and nothing such is bound to be everywhere: therefore, it belongs to God alone to be everywhere.

4. Likewise, that condition, by which God is everywhere, befits God by reason of His immensity; but immensity is a property of God alone, which can convene with no creature: therefore, neither (does) 'to be everywhere'.

AGAINST THIS: 1. one objects concerning a *universal*, since a universal is always and everywhere,[5] and, yet,

is not God. — *If you say*, that it is everywhere in respect of its singulars and not simply; *it is* then *objected*, that there is some universal, the singulars of which are everywhere, and it is impossible that anything come to be, which is not its singular and/or in a singular, such as this universal '*substance*': therefore, it is everywhere.

2. Likewise, there is the objection concerning the *number*, which is in all beings, and nothing can come to be, in which there is no number;[6] and, *moreover*, among all beings there is *one number*: therefore, since God is not a number, 'to be everywhere' is not proper to God alone. — *If you say*, that (number), there, is not whole, but according to part and part; *there is the objection* concerning a voice, which is, in the ears of diverse (men), whole and in the whole air: let it be that the voice would be so loud [magna], that it would be heard throughout the whole world, then it would be everywhere whole and one. *Proof:*[7] because, if (there were) many (voices), since the parts of the air are infinite, and in any part (there is) a voice: then, therefore, there are infinite voices in act; which is impossible.

3. Likewise, there is the objection concerning a *soul* [de anima], which is in any

---

[1] According to Aristotle, TOPICS, Bk. I, ch. 4, and Bk. V, ch. 1, and Porphyry, ON THE PREDICABLES, ch. "On *the Proper*", the "proper" can be taken in four manners: either (as) that which befits one alone, but not all; and/or (as that which befits) all, but not one alone; and/or (as that which befits) one alone and all, but not always; and/or (as that which befits) one alone and all and always. Here, the "proper" is taken in the fourth manner or, as one customarily says, in the strict sense.

[2] TO CATECHUMENS., or Sermon III, ch. 7, n. 7: For 'to be God' is this, 'to be whole everywhere'.

[3] Book I, ch. 7, n. 81. Cf. here, the text of Master (Peter), ch. 1. In the text cited here, in place of *to the Divinity* [divinitatis] the Vatican edition, together with codex cc, has *to God's Virtue*, and then in place of *to Lordship* [dominationis] very many codices, together with edition 1 has *to (His) duration* [durationis].

[4] Or a substance. Cf. above d. 36, a. 1, q. 1, p. 620, footnote 3. — What pertains to the *minor* (of the argument), is noted here from Aristotle, ON THE PREDICAMENTS, ch. "On *Substance*": « But it seems that "*this* something" signifies all substances. In the first (i. e. in singulars) substances, therefore, it is indubitable and true, that they signify *this something*. For that which is signified is individual and one in number. But in second substances (i. e. genera and species) it seems, indeed,

similarly ... yet, it is not true, but rather they signify *something of the kind* [quale aliquid]; for neither is one that which is the subject, according to the manner (it is) first substance, but "man" and "animal" is said of many ». And in POSTERIOR ANALYTICS, Bk. I, ch. 24 (ch. 31) he says: « Nor is there a knowing (of it) through sense; for if there is a sense of this such (i. e. of a singular thing) there is also no (sensing) of this something (i. e. the universal); but it is necessary that one sense *this something*, both here and now. Moreover, the universal, which is in all, it is impossible to sense; for it is not *this something*, neither now nor here [ubi], for neither would it, at any rate, be a universal; for that which is always and everywhere we say is a universal ».

[5] See the preceding footnote.

[6] For any produced being, by this very (thing) that it is a singular, will be one in number. — This sentence is supposed by the subsequent proposition: in all beings *collectively* taken there is a determined number. — In the conclusion, codex T reads *one number* [unus numerus] for *a number* [numerus].

[7] For *Proof* [Probatio] the Vatican edition reads *extension* [prolatio], which it places in the previous sentence immediately after *one* [una], having suppressed the punctuation between them. Next, after *in any part* [in qualibet parte] codex V inserts *of the air* [aëris].

part of the animal whole, as has been demonstrated above:[1] therefore, let it be, that there would come into being an gigantic animal as great as the whole word, then (its) soul would be everywhere: therefore, that (a soul) is not (everywhere), this is on account of a defect of the body, and not its own. — *If you say*, that it is in many as in one place, whence there is never one soul except in one body; *there is the objection* concerning the Body of Christ, which is whole and entire on diverse, distinct altars.

4. Likewise, it is objected *through reason*. For though it is of the nature of a singular to be *here and now*, yet God does grant a 'to be *always*' to something, such as to the Angels: therefore, for an equal reason He will grant a 'to be *everywhere*' to something.

5. Likewise, if any two are inseparably united, wheresoever one is, (there is) also the other; but the Human and Divine Nature in Christ have been inseparably untied: therefore, where the Divine (Nature) is, (there is)[2] also the Human. But the Divine Nature is everywhere: therefore, also the Human; and in this manner etc..

CONCLUSION

'To be everywhere' befits God alone properly and singularly.

I RESPOND: It must be said, that 'to be everywhere', just as the Saints say, befits God alone properly and singularly, thus that it befits no other, nor can it be understood to befit (another), if it is rightly understood. — For God is said "to be everywhere", thus that on God's part there is understood[3] an *identity* and a *totality*, no the part of place a *plurality* and a *universality*. Through the condition of *identity* there is excluded a universal, which though it is in all (its) singulars, yet according to one and another supposit, and thus (it is) numbered. Through the condition of *totality* there is excluded number; for although number is everywhere, yet according to one and another part. Through the condition of *plurality* on the part of place there is excluded the created spirit, which, though it is in many parts of a body, yet,[4] (is) not in all except as (they are) united. Through the condition of *universality* there is excluded the Body of Christ under the Sacrament, which (Body) though it is in many (places in virtue of the Sacrament), yet, is not in all (places simply) nor can it be, because this only befits Him under the Sacrament.

1. 2. 3. And thus a clear the first opposing examples [instantiae]. What, however, is objected concerning a voice, it must be understood, that the generation of sensibles in a medium is through diffusion, whence a voice is not numbered, just as neither light (is), except according to the being numbered [numerationem] of the one taking it up — whence as many as there are ears, so many are there voices, since the voice in the air was multipliable, and not multiplied — and for that reason it is clear, that (a voice) is neither *whole* everywhere before being numbered, just as neither (is) light diffused, nor (is it) *the same* after being numbered. And for that reason the example of the existence of a voice is not very similar to God.

4. To that which is objected, that God grants a sempiternity; it must be said, that both "to be *everywhere*" and "(to be) *always*", conveys a certain infinity; and the infinity of *sempiternity* is an infinity of duration, which is according to power, and this is not repugnant to a creature, because it does not impede the duration of a creature to be *finite* according to act and *infinite according to potency*; and for that reason for every duration of the creature it is necessary that something be adjoined. But "to be *everywhere*" means an *immensity according to act*, because it conveys a togetherness of places; and this is repugnant to a creature, and for that reason it cannot be entirely communicated to it. However, it is communicated according to the possibility of a creature, according to which it participates more or less in the nature of spirituality. For nothing is entirely spiritual except God alone, just as (St.) Augustine says ON THE CUSTOMS OF THE CHURCH:[5] « God alone is incorporeal, because He fills all again ». But certain creatures are spiritual through *abstraction*, such as a universal and a number; and these can be in many on account of (their) commonality to many, and according to their own plurification. Certain (creatures) are spiritual through *separation from corporal matter*, such as the soul; and these are in many, (and) yet (are) not multiplied. Moreover, certain (creatures) are spiritual through *union*, such as the Body of Christ is a food of a spiritual nature,[6] though it is a true body, and for that reason it is a quasi medium between the soul and God, and for that reason inasmuch as food (can), it tastes more the nature of spirituality; and for that reason it is in many (places), as they are many places, yet not in all, because a reason for being fed [cibationis] does not extend itself to all (places). And, thus, it is clear, for what reason it is in many (places) under the Sacrament.

5. What is objected concerning the inseparably united, must be solved through interemption,[7] when the one exceeds the other, as is clear in a genus and species. What is objected, through *union*, "a man is God"; it must be said, that this is understood through the communication of idioms; similarly too 'to be everywhere' befits (Christ) through the communication of idioms [per idiomatum communicationem].

---

[1] In d. 8, p. II, q. 3. — A little after this, for *as the whole* [quasi totus] codex T, together with some other codices, has *as the whole* [ut totus], and at the end of the argument, for *its own* [suum] codex K has *of the soul* [animae].

[2] Supply, together with the Vatican edition, *there is* [est].

[3] Codex Z has *so that ... there is understood* [intelligatur] for *thus that ... there is understood* [intelligitur]; codex W then adds *to be* [esse].

[4] Codex T subjoins *is* [est].

[5] The words cited are not had in the bk., ON THE CUSTOMS OF THE CHURCH, but in the book by Gennadius (of Marseille), ON ECCLESIASTICAL DOGMAS,, in ch. 11, which at one time was attributed to (St.) Augustine, in which there is read: One must believe that nothing is incorporeal and invisible in nature, except God alone, the Father and the Son and the Holy Spirit; who is believed (to be) incorporeal from this, that He is everywhere and fills and constrains all.

[6] The Vatican edition, together with codex cc, has *soul* [animae] for *nature* [naturae].

[7] Cf. above d. 3, p. II, a. 1, q. 3, p. 87, footnote 4.

SCHOLIUM

I. The four conditions, which befit the Divine Ubiquity alone, result from the very eminence of Divine Perfection, and are easily understood through the opposed arguments. — The words in the solution to n. 2: « as many as there are ears, so many are there voices », are to be understood of *the received appearances* (of the one voice) in the medium and in the organ, not of *a voice itself.* Nearly the same solution to the question and to the objections is found in Alexander of Hales, St. Thomas, Richard of Middleton and others.

II. Alexander of Hales, Summa., p. I, q. 9, m. 5. — St. Thomas, here in q. 2, a. 2; Summa. , I, q. 8, a. 4; Quodlibetals., 11, q. 1, a. 1. — Bl. (now St.) Albertus (Magnus), here in a. 8; Summa., p. I, tr. 13, q. 55, a. 3, incidental q.. — (Bl.) Peter of Tarentaise, here in q. 2, a. 2. — Richard of Middleton, here in a. 1, q. 3. — Giles the Roman, here in 2nd princ., q. 2. — Durandus (of Saint-Pourçain), on this and the following q., here in p. I, q. 2. — (Bl.) Dionysius the Carthusian, here in q. 2.

QUESTION II

Whether 'to be everywhere' befits God from eternity?

Second, there is asked, whether *'to be everywhere'* befits God always or eternally. And that it does, seems:

1. Because, just as He holds Himself *always* to time, so *everywhere* to place; but before all time God was *always*: therefore, before every place God was *everywhere*.

2. Likewise, what is proper to God [proprium Dei] befits Him more essentially than a proper passion to any subject; but on account of the necessary fittingness of a passion to a subject the distribution of supposits includes the distribution of times[1] — whence « that is said of every [dici de omni est], which is not in a certain one thus, in a certain one not, nor sometimes thus, sometimes not », but in any and always — therefore, similarly that which is *everywhere* includes sempiternity: therefore, 'to be everywhere' befits God always, therefore, from eternity.

3. Likewise, things are in God, and God in things; but things are in God from eternity: therefore, a relativis, since this are said through conversion [conventiam],[2] God is in things from eternity, but not except in all: ergo etc.. *If you say*, that these are not said correlatively; *on the contrary*: when there is said: "God is in things", there is not signified a looking-back nor a dependence of God to things, but of things to God: therefore, it is nothing other to say, that God is in things, than that things are in God.

4. Likewise, if God was not everywhere from eternity, and He was, therefore, He was *elsewhere* than *everywhere*; and now He is *everywhere*: therefore, He changed place, therefore in God there is a change. But this is false: therefore, also the first. *If you say*, that the change is in what it connotes [in connotato]; *on the contrary*: when there is said: "God is in a place", there is not noted[3] an effect, but only the presence of God: therefore, it seems, that according to this there is not signified a change in the what it connotes, but only in God Himself: therefore, it remains per impossibile, that God is everywhere eternally.

Against This: 1. *'Everywhere'* presupposes *'where'*, and *'where'* presupposes *'place'*; and *'place'* is not posited except in time: and, therefore, there is no positing that God is everywhere, except in time.

2. Likewise, there rightly follows: 'God is everywhere, therefore, He is in Heaven', therefore, with the consequent destroyed, there is also destroyed the antecedent; but from eternity He was not in Heaven: ergo etc..

3. Likewise, there rightly follows: 'God is everywhere, therefore, in this house of yours'; but this house of yours was not except in time and after the start of time: therefore, also (His) 'being everywhere'.

CONCLUSION

'To be everywhere' befits God from the beginning of things and places, which are connoted, not eternally, unless 'to be everywhere' is understood to be the Divine Immensity's quality of being present.

I Respond: It must be said, that "to be everywhere" can be accepted of God in a twofold manner, just as "to be always". For, in one manner, "always" conveys the Divine Immensity according to duration, and thus it is the same as "eternity", and it befits God eternally; in another manner, it connotes a *togetherness of time*, and in this manner it befits Him from the beginning of time. Thus, "to be everywhere" in one manner conveys the Divine Immensity's quality of being present [praesentialitatem],* through

---

[1] The sense is: but a proper passion of a created thing does not only befit *every* and one alone, but also *always*. Cf. here above in q. 1, p. 642, footnote 1. On the notion of distribution see above in d. 4, a. sole, q. 2, p. 99, Scholium, I, n. 2. — The words, which are next cited, are from Aristotle, Posterior Analytics, Bk. I, ch. 4. Cf. also Topics, Bk. V, ch. 1.

[2] Cf. Aristotle, On Predicaments, ch. "On *Relation*". — By the

words a relativis there is signified the manner of arguing, which is supported in the habitude of one of the relatives to the other, and generally is expressed with these propositions: with one of the relatives posited, there is posited also the rest, with one of the relatives removed, there is removed also the rest.

[3] Codex Z has *connoted* [connotatur] for *noted* [notatur].

---

* *Trans. note*: Cf. praesentialitas in the Rationale for the Translation of Peculiar Latin Terms, in the Introduction to this English Translation, on p. E-20.

which He is present to every *that* which is, whether to Himself, or to another; and in this manner 'that God *is everywhere*' is the same as 'that God *is immense*'. And thus it befits God *eternally*; and according to this the *first* reason proceeds.

In the other manner, insofar as it connotes a *created place* or *thing*; and then it befits Him *from the start* of things and places on account of what it connotes [propter connotatum], and it befits (Him) *always*; and yet it is proper, because it befits (Him) alone, and always in one manner, though not eternally; just as (it is) in the demonstrative (sciences in their own manner).[1] And in this manner the *second* reason proceeds. And this manner of accepting that "God is everywhere", is more usual [usitatior], and according to this manner it does not befit Him eternally.

3. On the other hand what is objected against this, that it befits (Him) eternally through its converse; it must be said, that it is not its converse.[2] For when it is said, that things are in God, this is understood in the reckoning of exemplarity, and nothing is connoted in act; but when God is said "to be in things", something created is connoted. For, there is nothing in that[3] which is not: therefore, if God is in things and places, there are things and places; yet a non-being [non-ens], according to itself, is rightly [bene] in an exemplar as in a princi-

ple. Wherefore, this: "God is in things", is not the converse of this: "things are in God", but this (is): "God is the exemplar of things", and each is true eternally. And of this: "God is in things", the converse is: "things are contained by God and are conserved by Him".

4. To that which is objected, that if God was not everywhere, and now He is, therefore, He has changed; it must be said, that it does not follow, because this is not on account of a change in God.[4]

What is objected, that "everywhere" [ubique] does not connote an effect, but only a presence; it must be said, that a presence conveys a habitude to two, namely, of that which is present, and that to which it is present, and, for that reason, the inception (of the Divine presence) can be in the reckoning of the thing to which He is present, and not (in the reckoning) of a new effect.

What is objected for the opposed, proceeds according to which *"everywhere"* connotes a created place.

What, however, is objected last, is not valid, nay there is a fallacy of accident there, just as in this: 'that triangle begins to have three (angles): therefore, not every triangle always has three (angles)', because the distribution (of "every" in this argument) is not made on behalf of the parts (of a triangle)[5] as (they exist) now, but simply (speaking).

SCHOLIUM

I. The conclusions are easily understood, having supposed that distinction about the sense of the terms *"to be everywhere"* and *"to be always"*. In the *absolute* sense, which however, is less usual (in reply to n. 2), the first signifies the Divine Immensity, to the extent that It conveys a presence in *habit* and *in a first act*; but when it is taken, insofar as it connotes created tings and a place, it conveys a presence in a *second act* and it presupposes creation. In a similar manner *"to be always"* signifies either in an absolute manner eternity, and/or by connoting time and presupposing the start of time. — The last argument for the negative side is deservedly rejected on account of a *fallacy of accident*, which is committed, when that which is truly predicated of the subject in respect of an accident, which it has, is also predicated of the subject as such. Thus in the proposed example (at the end of the reply to n. 4), when a triangle is drawn on a tablet, it is true, but only <u>per accidens</u>, that that figure *begins* to have three angles, but absolutely *from eternity* it suits a triangle to have three angles.

Wherefore, there is a fallacy of the accident (in that objection), « because the distribution (of "every triangle" in this argument) is not made on behalf of parts as (they exist) now, but simply (speaking) », that is, the expression *"every triangle"* does not suppose on behalf of a triangle, to the extent that it is drawn through the accident of the *now*, but *simply* (speaking) on behalf of a triangle as such (i.e. in abstraction from any given particular actual triangle). In the same manner in that false argument there is a passing from the *absolute* sense of the proposition: "God is everywhere", to a sense (that is) <u>per accidens</u> true, when the house began to be built. — St. Thomas (here in q. 2, a. 3, in reply to n. 2) and others accept *"to be everywhere"* only in the *more usual* sense, to the extent that it connotes a created place; whence they do not distinguish the major of the 1st argument on behalf of the affirmation, but simply deny it. Yet in the doctrine itself there is no difference.

II. Alexander of Hales, Summa., p. I, q. 9, m.

---

[1] Understand: *sciences in their own manner* [scientiis suo modo est.]. For, in these, a proper passion is shown to always be in or convene with the subject, even though it is something created. Regarding this, (St. Severinus) Boethius, in his Commentary on Aristotle's Book on Interpretation, second edition,, Bk. II, at the beginning says: However, there are other (propositions), which (while) non signifying sempiternal (truths), yet are also themselves necessary, so long as there are those subject, of which the proposition affirms or denies anything, such as when I say: "man is mortal", as long as there is a man, so long it is necessary that man be mortal. For, if anyone says: "fire is hot", as long as there is fire, so long is the proposition (: "that fire is hot",) true of necessity. — A little below this, some codices, such as I and Z have *it does befit Him temporally* [convenit ei temporaliter] for *it does not befit Him eternally* [non convenit ei aeternaliter].

[2] Namely the proposition: "things are in God", does not signify

the same as this one: "God is in things". On the difference of these propositions, cf. above d. 36, Doubt 1, and Alexander of Hales, Summa, p. I, q. 9, m. 3, and Giles the Roman, here (in this distinction). — Next for *and nothing* [et nihil] codices X and Z have *yet nothing* [nihil tamen].

[3] Many codices, with edd. 2 & 3, faultily read *in God* [in Deo] for *in that* [in eo]; codices F L and O read *For God is in none* [Nam in nullo est Deus] in place of *For there is nothing in that* [Nam nihil est in eo].

[4] The Vatican ed. with a few mss. adds *but in things* [sed rerum].

[5] Thus nearly all the codices; codex S reads *on behalf of things* [pro rebus], codex T by the first hand has *in things* [in rebus], the Vatican edition, with codex cc, has *of three (angles)* [de tribus]. The sense of our reading is: the distribution through the sign "every" is referred to the subjective parts (or the inferior parts under the whole universal), insofar as they are *simply* according to their nature, not insofar as they come to be *here and now*, v. g. to form a triangle. — A little above this, the Vatican edition alone has *was not* [non fuit] for *is not made* [non fit].

ARTICLE III

In what kind of manner is God in things?

In the third place, one asks principally concerning the third Article, namely, in what kind of manner is God in things. And, about this, two (questions) are asked.

First, there is asked, whether God is in all things equally or uniformly [aequaliter sive uniformiter].

Second, there is asked, in which manners [quibus modis], and in what kind of manner is God in things.

QUESTION I

Whether God is equally in all things?

Moreover, that He is uniformly (in all things), seems:

1. Because, just as the Philosopher says,[1] « the First Cause holds Itself in one manner to all (things), though all do not hold themselves in one manner to It »; but all are in God uniformly, because they are life and the creative Essence: therefore, much more strongly God is in all things equally and uniformly.

2. Likewise, what is everywhere whole, is equally and uniformly;[2] but since God is most simple, He is everywhere whole: therefore, He is equally and uniformly in all things.

3. Likewise, to each thing [unicuique rei] matter and form are the most interior [intima]; but form is not united to matter except by means of an appetite, but an appetite has its rise from essence;[3] but this could not (be) except through God's presence: therefore, God is more "the most interior" to every thing than its own form. But form is most highly "the most interior" to each thing: therefore, God in a terminal degree [in termino] is most interior to anything [cuilibet]. But what has being in a terminal degree is uniformly: ergo etc..

4. Likewise, this is shown per impossibile: because, if God is not equally in things, therefore when[4] He is more intimately in one than in another, therefore, in some He is not intimately in a most high manner: therefore something in the thing is intrinsic (to it), in which God is not: therefore, God is not the most interior (thing), which there is. But this is impossible: therefore, the first (is) too.

BUT ON THE CONTRARY: 1. « Everything which is received in something, is there through the manner of the one receiving, and not of the one received »;[5] but creatures are not equally able to grasp God [capaces Dei]: therefore, God is not in them equally.

2. Likewise, just as *the intellect* holds itself to the First Light, so *a being* to the First Essence, and *a living (thing)* to the First Life;[6] but a greater *intellect* participates more in the Divine Light [divinam lucem]: therefore, a more perfect *being* [ens] and a more perfect *living* (thing participate more) in the Divine Essence and Life: therefore, God is more perfectly in one than in another.

3. Likewise, the existence of God in things is the conservation of things; but not all things are equally conserved:[7] therefore, He is not equally in all.

4. Likewise, though God is everywhere, He is said to dwell only in the just; but this would not be, if He were equally and uniformly in all: ergo etc..

CONCLUSION

God is uniformly in things, to the extent that there is not connoted an effect; but to the extent that God gives to one creature more than to another, He is said to be more in one than in another.

I RESPOND: For an understanding of the aforesaid it must be noted, that *God can be understood to be in things*

---

[1] The Philosopher understood here is the author of the BOOK OF CAUSES, who in prop. 24: The First Cause exists in all things according to one disposition, but all things do not exist in the First cause according to one disposition. — On the minor of the argument see above d. 36, a. 2, q. 1.

[2] Codex T in the margin adds, not incongruously, *in all* [in omnibus].

[3] What this sentences wants to say, is explained by Alexander of Hales, as you can see below in the Scholium adjoined to this Question. — Next, after *could not* [non posset], codices O and V have explicitly *be* [esse]. At the end of the argument, on the authority of very many codices, we have placed *in a terminal degree is most interior* [in termino intimus est], and then *in a terminal degree* [in termino], i. e. most highly or as much as possible, for which the Vatican has first intimior intimo est intimus, and then in intimo for *in a terminal degree* [in termino]. Codex T in the first place has intimior est intimo, and codex W has *most highly and in a terminal degree is most interior* [summe et in termino est intimus].

[4] In very many codd., such as H P Q & V, there is wanting the *when* [cum]. A little further below this, for *the most interior (thing)* [intimum], the Vatican ed., with not a few mss., reads *in everything* [in omni]; cod. T by a second had has *the most interior (thing) to everything* [intimum omni].

[5] BOOK OF CAUSES, propositions 10 and 20 ff.. Cf. also (St. Severinus) Boethius, ON THE CONSOLATION OF PHILOSOPHY, Bk. V., prose 4.

[6] Cf. BOOK OF CAUSES, proposition 18 ff.. — Immediately after this, for *a greater intellect* [maior intellectus], codices M P and Q have *one more intelligent* [magis intelligens], and codex T, with some others, has *the more the understanding the more it participates* [magis intellectus magis participat] for *a greater intellect participates more* [maior intellectus magis participat]. At the beginning of the argument, codd. P & Q have *an intelligent (being)* [intelligens] for *the intellect* [intellectus].

[7] Cf. here in a. 1, q. 1 f.. — To the word *the existence* [existentia] at the beginning of this proposition, codices A D Z aa ff and many others prefix *from* [ex], with which added, the thought of the proposition appears clearly.

in a twofold manner: in *one* manner, so that (His) 'being present' is the same to any thing, *with it not connoting* an effect; and in this manner He is uniformly in all things, by this, that He is most interior to any thing and most highly present and whole in any thing. In *another manner* it can *connote an effect*, just as a craftsman is said to be in (his) artifice through the connotation of an effect and through the impression of his own similitude; and in this manner, since He gives to one creature more than to another, He is more in one than in another. — And this can be in a threefold manner:[1] either *extensively*, as much as regards those which have a *more long lasting* 'to be' [esse diuturnius], such as (is) in an incorruptible body more than in the sensible soul; and/or *intensively*, as much as regards those which have a *more noble* "being" [esse nobilius], such as (is) in a sensible soul (more)[2] than in an incorruptible body, and/or *in each manner*, such as (is) in a rational soul than in a corruptible body.

With these (things) seen, the objections to each side are clear. For they proceed by these two ways, as is clear, except the first two to each side.

For, what is objected, that God holds Himself uniformly to all things; if the *uniformity* is understood on the part of the *Divine "Being"*, it is true; but if it is understood on the part of the *effect*, it is false. Since God, existing in a uniform and stable manner, moves[3] all others and produces both many and various effects, He also by effecting diverse (effects) in things causes, that things do not hold themselves uniformly to Him. Therefore, since when God is said to be "*in things*", in one manner there is connoted an effect, in another manner (there is) not; for that reason in one manner it is conceded, that He is uniformly, in another manner that (He is) not. Similarly, the other way around, when it is said, that all are "*in God*", in one manner an effect can be connoted, just as is clear in predestination and reprobation, and thus He is not uniformly (in all things), in another manner an effect is connoted, and thus (He is) uniformly.

What is again objected for the opposed, that everything which is received, is through the manner of the one receiving; it must be said, that (this) is true, where the received depends upon the one receiving, as a (an intelligible) species[4] (does) upon the cognizing virtue; but in the proposed it is not thus. Whence, the Divine Essence, existing in the thing, does not accept the manner of the thing; and, thus, that (objection) is clear.

SCHOLIUM

I. This question, treated explicitly by few ancient (Scholastics), paves the way to the following connected question. — In the 3rd argument of the fundament the difficult passage: « but form is not united to matter except by means of an appetite, but an appetite *has its rise from the essence* » (of the thing), is explained profoundly by Alexander of Hales, SUMMA, p. II. q. 86, m. 2, a. 2, § 1: « In every movement, whether to form or to a location [ad situm] the first intrinsic principle of the movement is an appetite. This is indeed a force endowed to all creatures by the Creator, through which they are ordered to their complement and in their complement stand still and are rooted. Nor is it only in creatures, but also in *the essential principles* of creatures, which are matter and form, act and potency. For neither is *matter* moved by itself to form, because, it determines nothing, it would not be moved more to this than to that; nor does *form* cause it self in matter; but *through an implanted appetite* [per appetitum insitum] each is ordered to one another and through an appetite of this kind they are inseparably conjoined. Nor does the appetite seek only a *thing completed in "being"*, but is rooted and founded in the very *essential principles* of things. And just as it is in a movement to form, so it is in every non-violent movement: for in every movement an appetite excites the mover to the movement. From which it is clear, that it is *the universal, intrinsic principle of movement* ». He continues, explaining the differences of appetites and of those in which there is an appetite, according to which they have more and/or less of form and/or matter. Moreover, that intrinsic principle of movement and life excludes least of all the influx of the First Cause, nay it demands it, as is proven, ibid., a. 1. §1. — From this passage from (Master) Alexander it is clear, that Trigosus (SUMMA., q. 6, a. 5) errs, who, without the support of any codex and/or edition, changed the text (of St. Bonaventure), by placing *has its rise from the "being"* [ortum habet ab esse] for *has its rise from the essence* [ortum habet ab essentia], supporting himself by this reason, namely, that the ancient reading made no sense.

That a sensible soul has "being" more perfectly than a corruptible body is explained more in SENT., Bk. III, d. 21, a. 2. q. 2, in reply to n. 3 (cf. St. Thomas, SUMMA, I, q. 70, a. 3, in reply to n. 2).

II. In regard the question itself: Alexander of Hales, SUMMA., p. I, q. 10, m. 5. — (Bl. John Duns) Scotus, on this and the following q., REPORTATIO., here in q. 2. — Bl. (now St.) Albertus (Magnus), here in a. 6. — (Bl.) Peter of Tarentaise, here in q. 1, a. 2. — Richard of Middleton, here in a. 1, q. 2. — Durandus (of Saint-Pourçain), on this and the following q., here in p. I, q. 1. — (Bl.) Dionysius the Carthusian, here in q. 2., near the middle.

QUESTION II

In what manners is God said "to be in" things?

Second, there is asked, in what manners [quibus modis], and in what kind of manner [qualiter] is God in things. And Master (Peter) assigns in a twofold manner the manners of the existing of God in things. And he accepts one manner from (St.) Augustine, who says (in his letter) on God's presence TO DARDANUS,[5] that « in one manner God is in all creatures, in another in the Saints, in another in Christ. In crea-

---

[1] The Vatican edition, together with many codices, faultily reads *in a twofold manner* [dupliciter].

[2] Supply, together with codex H: *more* [plus].

[3] A reference to that verse in (St. Severinus) Boethius', ON THE CONSOLATION OF PHILOSOPHY, Bk. III, meter 9.

Of lands and sky the Sower, who time from the aevum
Doest command to go, and stable remaining grant all others to move.

[4] That is the intentional (species), which concur for an act of cognition.

[5] Epistle 187, ch. 12. See here the text of Master (Peter), chs. 1 and 3. — The words of the cited text: *In creatures each through (its own) nature, in the Saints through indwelling grace, in Christ* [In creaturis singulis per naturam, in Sanctis per inhabitantem gratiam, in Christo] are missing in the Vatican edition.

-tures each [singulis] through (its own) nature, in the Saints through indwelling grace, in Christ through union ». He accepts another manner from (St.) Gregory, who says on the fifth (chapter) of Canticles,[1] « that God is in things in a threefold manner, namely, *by means of (His) Power* [potentialiter], *presence* [praesentialiter] and *Essence* [essentialiter] ». There is asked, therefore, concerning the *distinction, sufficiency* and *order* of these manners.

1. And there is objected against *(St.) Augustine's* assignation: for either those manners are accepted as much as regards *the Divine Substance*, or as much as regards *the creature*, or as much as regards *effects*. If as much as regards *effects*, since they are innumerable, (His) manners of being are innumerable. If as much as regards *the suscipient creature* [creaturam suscipientem], since there is only a twofold suscipient, namely a nature and a will, it seems, that there are only two manners, namely, through nature, and through grace. If as much as regards *God's Substance*, since no diversity occurs in It, there will be only one manner.

2. Likewise, just as grace is an effect superadded to nature, so a miraculous operation: therefore just as in those having grace God is in a manner other than in those not having (it), so also in a thing, in which He works miraculously, such as in Balaam's donkey,[2] He will be in a manner of being other (than in the thing, in which He does work miraculously).

3. Likewise, just as the grace which makes one pleasing [gratia gratum faciens] is above nature, so a grace freely given [gratia gratis data], such as prophecy, so also punishment and glory: since these differ according to genus and species, the diverse manners of being ought to be distinguish according to this: therefore Master (Peter) does not distinguish sufficiently.

4. Likewise, there is objected against *(St.) Gregory's assignation*: for either that assignation is according to *effects*, or (according to) *God's conditions* and *properties*. If according to *effects*, then since (God's) Essence connotes not effect, it ought not be posited (as a manner of presence). If according to God's *conditions*; but there is not only God's Power, but also (His) Wisdom and Will: therefore, it seems, that he assigns (them) insufficiently.

5. Likewise, there seems to be a *inversion* [praeposteratio] *in the order*. For, according to thing and to the reckoning of understanding, essence precedes power, and power presence: therefore, he badly orders (them).

6. Likewise, there seems (to be) a *flourish of words* [verborum inculcatio], because in God, Power, Essence and presence are the same: therefore, (their) distinction is sought.[3]

CONCLUSION

Each assignation of the manners of the being of God in things is fitting, both that which belongs to (St.) Augustine, and that which (belongs) to (St. Gregory): for the former looks back to the diversity of (His) manners of being in things, the latter to the conditions of the same manners.

I RESPOND: It must be said, that (St.) Augustine's assignation looks back to *the diversity* of the manners of the being of God in things, but (St.) Gregory's assignation looks back to *the conditions* of the manners of being. For wheresoever God is, whether through nature or through grace, He is *by means of (His) Essence, Power, (and) presence*.

But *the diversity* of the manners of being is accepted from within the diversity of *effects*, and not any kind (of diversity), but only a three-membered one [trimembrem]. For there is a certain effect, according to which a thing[4] is compared to God through the manner of *one going forth*, and all these (effects) are contained under the manner of nature, in an extended sense [extenso nomine]. A certain (effect is) through the manner of *one returning*; and this is the effect of inchoate and/or consummated grace, and/or of glory, and as much as regards this (effect) is the second manner of being. There is (also) a certain effect, according to which the creature is compared to God as *arriving* [perveniens],[5] and this is the effect of *Union*, in which there are united in the unity of a (Divine) Person, a creature and the Creator, as the God-Man [homo-Deus]. Since, therefore, there are three manners of effects, according to which a creature is compared to God in a diverse manner; for that reason He is said to be in things only in three manners. — And the first, which is attained as much as regards a *going-forth* [exitus], is likened to a straight line; the second, as much as regards a *return*, to a reflected line; the third, as much as regards *perfection*,[6] is likened to a circle. And the first manner (of going-forth is) indeed similar to *a line*; the second, because it includes the first, is similar to a *surface* [superficiei]; the third, because (it includes) each, is similar to a *solid* [soliditati]. And for that reason the Apostle in the second (chapter of his letter) to the Colossians[7] says best of all [optime], that *in Christ dwells the whole Divinity corporally*: for (God's manner of being) is most perfectly (in Him), because it is (there) according to the manner of a *circle*, which is a perfect nature, and through the manner of *altitude*,[8] which is a perfect quantity. And from these is clear sufficiency and *distinction* (of God's manners of being), and the solution of the objections.

But blessed *Gregory's* assignation is accepted as much as regards *the conditions* of the manners of being [conditiones modorum essendi]. For in these

---

[1] On this text, which is falsely attributed to (Pope St.) Gregory (the Great), cf. here the text of Master (Peter), ch. 1. This threefold manner of being is hinted at by (St.) Anselm, ON FAITH IN THE TRINITY, ch. 1 and by Richard of St. Victor, ON THE TRINITY, Bk. II, ch. 23.

[2] Num. 22:23 ff.. — Thus, the Vatican edition; all the codices, for *He will be* [erit], have *He was* [erat], which seems to us less congruous. After *other* [miraculose], supply, together with codices K V and X, *than in the thing, in which he does not work miraculously* [quam in re, in qua non operatur miraculose].

[3] Some codices, such as C I aa and bb read *therefore, for what reason (is there) a distinction?* [quare ergo distinctio] for *therefore, (their) distinction is sought* [quaeritur ergo distinctio].

[4] Codices F R (T in the margin) have *a creature* [creatura].

[5] The Vatican edition, without any authority of the codices, adds

and/or perfecting [vel perficiens], then after *the effect* [effectus] codices D and W add *of the grace* [gratiae]. A little below this, we have received the reading of codex T *God-Man* [homo-Deus] for that of the Vatican edition, *man and God* [homo est Deus].

[6] Codex T (in the margin) has *arriving* [perventionem]. Next after *the third, because* [tertius, quia] codex S repeats *it includes* [includit].

[7] Verse 9: *Because in Him dwells every plenitude of Divinity corporally*. — Next, after *most perfectly* [perfectissime], supply together with the Vatican edition and codex cc *in Him* [in eo]. Then for *nature* [natura] the Vatican edition, together with some manuscripts, has *figure* [figura]. — Cf. (St.) Augustine, ON THE QUANTITY OF THE SOUL, ch. 12, n. 19, and ch. 16, n. 27, where he deals with the excellence of the circle.

[8] Codex T in the margin has *of a solid* [soliditatis], which seems to be a more fitting term.

---

* *Trans. note*: In English it is customary and more proper to say *God-Man*, than *Man-God*, because in English the precedent position is for the more noble member, whereas the emphasis in Latin is placed on the final member of syntactical constructions, as it is the more final and hence dramatic part; to this extent, the English translation, by reversing the word order, preserves the entire meaning of the Latin phrase, <u>homo Deus</u>.

three blessed Gregory speaks about the perfection of the manners of the existing of God in all (thing), in which He is in this manner. For something is in something according to *the indistance of the quality of being present* [praesentialitatis indistantiam], as a contained in one containing, such as water (is) in a vessel; something (else) according to *the influence of virtue* [virtutis influentiam], such as a mover in a movable; something (else) according to *the existence of intimacy* [intimitatis existentiam], as that which is containing (is) within, such as the soul (is) in the body.[1] And it is necessary that everything which is *perfectly* in a thing be according to this threefold condition; and in this manner God is (in things). And for that reason He is said to be (in things) *by means of (His) Power, Presence* and *Essence,* because (He is in things) according to the indistance of (His) quality of being present, according to the influence of (His) Virtue, (and) according to an existence of intimacy.

And *the distinction, sufficiency* and *order* (of these) is clear:

since according to the reckoning of understanding those conditions hold themselves through an addition, and for that reason blessed Gregory orders (them) well, first by means of (His) presence [praesentialiter], etc..

However, some want to distinguish conditions of this kind from within *the (Divine) Substance, Virtue* and *Operation.*[2] But though the manner of existing *by means of the Essence* [essentialiter] responds to the Substance, and (that) *by means of power* [potentialiter] to the (Divine) Virtue, yet (that) *by means of (the Divine) presence* [praesentialiter] does not respond to the (Divine) Operation, for something is present to something, even if it does not work.

Some accept (them) from within *the genera of causes.* But neither does this seem fitting, because '*to consist by means of essence*' does not connote a genus of causality.

Some from within *the trinity of the vestige,* namely (according to) *the standard of measure, species,* and *order,** but *essence* precedes all these according to the manner of reckoning.

SCHOLIUM

I. In *St. Augustine's* assignation there are connoted the diverse *effects* of the Divine presence, and according to these there are distinguished three grades; wherefore in this manner God is not *uniformly* in created things (cf. preceding question). — The threefold comparison of a creature (to God), through the manner of *one going forth, one returning* (and) *one arriving,* is familiar to the Seraphic (Doctor) under various forms, and has been taken from Dionysius the Areopagite (ON THE DIVINE NAMES, ch. 4, § 4, 10 and 14; ON THE CELESTIAL HIERARCHIES, ch. 1). — The words posited in the first member of the division: « these (effects) are contained under *the manner of nature, in an extended sense* [extenso nomine] », insinuate, that "*nature*" here is understood in the broader sense, so that it comprehends together even graces freely given [gratias gratis datas], such as the working of miracles. — The example of the threefold line has been taken from Dionysius (ON THE DIVINE NAMES, ch. 4, § 8). — On the circle, which is « the most simple, capable, and beautiful figure » (SENT., Bk. IV, d. 24, p. I, a. 1, q. 1), to the extent that it represents Christ, cf. SENT., Bk. III, d. 1, a. 2, q. 1. — On the other example, taken from the threefold quantity, cf. above d. 2, q. 4.

II. In explaining *the second* assignation, which is founded upon the words attributed erroneously by the Scholastics to St. Gregory (see Master Peter's text here, p. 632, footnote 2), the ancient masters went off in diverse directions, which (directions), because they (all) say something true, have more or less of probability. The position of St. Bonaventure is profound and plain; by it he very clearly explains *the distinction* of these manners, their *order* (because the following manner expresses through *addition* a certain gradation) and *sufficiency.* — The manner of distinguishing, posited in the second place, is that of Alexander of Hales (SUMMA., p. I, q. 10, m. 4), who says: « In God there are three (things): essence, virtue, operation ... through the Essence He is in things by means of (His) Essence [essentialiter], through Virtue He is in things by means of power [potentialiter], through

operation by means of (His) presence ». This manner of distinguishing is pleasing also to Durandus (of Saint-Pourçain) and Giles the Roman, but not to St. Bonaventure. — The third manner is « from within the genera of causes », that is according to an efficient, exemplary, and final cause. Against this the Seraphic (Doctor) argues, that "*by means of essence*" [essentialiter] does not connote any genus of causality. — The fourth manner is according to the distinction of *a standard of measure, of beauty* and *of order* (cf. above d. 3, p. I, q. 2, and Doubt 3), which three according to Alexander of Hales, (SUMMA., p. I, q. 18, m. 2) in this sense are essential (properties), because they refer the thing to its essential causes. « For "*a standard of measure*" [modus] means a relation to God as to One effecting, "*beauty*" [species] as to form (that is, an exemplary form), "*order*" as to an end ». Whence in this sentence "*by means of essence*" [essentialiter] responds to a standard of measure, "*by means of presence*" [praesentialiter] to beauty, "*by means of power*" [potentialiter] to order. But the Seraphic Doctor disproves this with these words, obscure because of their brevity: « But essence precedes all these according to the reckoning of understanding ». The sense (here) is: since the essence of things precedes those three relations, it would follow, that in respect of the *essence* of things there would be no presence of God, which is most false. — St. Thomas (SUMMA, I, q. 8, a. 3), together with many others, distinguishes in this manner: « He is in all through *power,* inasmuch as all are subjected to His Power; He is in all through *presence,* inasmuch as all are bare and open to His eyes; and He is in all through *essence,* inasmuch as He is at hand to all as the Cause of (their) being ».

III. Besides the passages cited above: Alexander of Hales, SUMMA., p. I. q. 10, m. 2, 3 and 4. — St. Thomas, here in q. 1, a. 2. — Bl. (now St.) Albertus (Magnus), here in a. 5 and 10. — (Bl.) Peter of Tarentaise, here in q. 1, a. 3. — Richard of Middleton, here in a. 1, q. 1. — Giles the Roman, here in. 1st princ., q. 2. — (Bl.) Dionysius the Carthusian, here in q. 2.

DOUBTS ON THE TEXT OF THE MASTER

DOUBT I

In this part, there occur [incidunt] doubts about (Master Peter's) text and first concerning this which Master (Peter) says, and it is a verse from (St.) Augustine, namely, that *the wicked are not with Him, as the*

blind, in the light etc.. For he seems to speak badly, because the wicked are *in God,* because in Him they live, move and are:[3] therefore, if a greater convening [convenientia] is not conveyed [importatur] through that which it is '*to be with someone*' than '*in someone*', it seems, that just as the wicked are said to be *in*

---

[1] Aristotle, ON THE SOUL, Bk. I, text 90 (ch. 5): For it seems that the soul, on the contrary, rather contains the body, for with it stepping forth, (the body) expires and begins to rot.

[2] See more on these in the Scholium added to this question. — A little below this, after *by means of the (Divine) presence* [praesentialiter]

the Vatican edition, without cause and without the authority of the codices, adds *principally* [principaliter], and after a few more words it substitutes *somewhere* [alicuibi] for *to something* [alicui].

[3] Acts 17:28: *For in Him we live and move and are* [In ipso enim vivimus et movemur et sumus].

---

* *Trans. note:* Here, the translation of the terms regarding the *trinity of the vestige,* namely *the standard of measure* [modum], *species* [speciem], and *order* [ordinem], is taken from St. Bonaventure, ITINERARIUM, I, n. 11.

God, so they ought to be said to be *with God*. — Likewise, what is more improper, "God is *with the wicked*", and/or "the wicked *with God*"? It seems, that (it is) the latter: "the wicked are with God". Whence (St.) Augustine in (his) book of CONFESSIONS:[1] « Thou was with me, and I was not with Thee »; spoke on behalf of the state of sin. *But on the contrary*: "*with*" [cum] means an authorship in what belongs to a cause [auctoritatem in causali],[2] therefore, it seems, that it is better to say: "a man (is) *with God*", than the other way around.

I RESPOND: It must be said, that this preposition "*with*" means an *association*. But in a society two (things) are considered, namely, a mutual *assistance* [mutuum auxilium] and a *conformity of will*. Since, therefore, *the good* alone have a conform will and are co-helpers [coadiutores] with God,[3] for that reason of them alone it is properly said, that they are *with God*, and <u>vice versa</u>; because then that which is "*with*" does not mean an authority. However, because *the wicked* are not conformed nor assisted by God in their salvation, but contradict (Him), and yet God helps them in many (things); for that reason (St.) Augustine says: "Thou were with me" etc..[4]

DOUBT II

Likewise, is asked concerning this which (St. Augustine) says: *He dwells with Himself* [apud se] etc.. For he seems to speak badly, because prepositions are *distinctive*, because (they are) *transitive*:[5] if, therefore, God is not distinguished from Himself, there is badly said, that He was *with Himself*. *If you say*, that they convey [dicunt] the transition as much as regards a manner; *on the contrary* there is the Gloss on the first (chapter of the Gospel of St.) John,[6] which says, that "*with*" [apud] notes a distinction of the Father regarding the Son.

I RESPOND: It must be said, that God is not only *in* creatures, but also *with Himself* [apud se]. Whence (St.) Augustine in (his) book of CONFESSIONS (says):[7] « God is in Himself as the Alpha and the Omega, in the world as the Creator and Ruler, in the Angels as taste and decoration, in the Elect as Liberator and Helper, in the reprobate as terror and horror ». — *What is objected*, that a preposition means a *transition* and a *distinction*; it must be said, that as much as it concerns the virtue of its signification, it does not mean but a *transition* as much as regards a *manner*; moreover, what it means as much as regards the *thing*, this is by reason of the matter or of the terms, to which it is added.[8]

DOUBT III

Likewise, is asked concerning this which (Master Peter) says, that *God dwells in someone, when He is thus in someone, as to be cognized and loved by him*. It seems that he does not speak well, because He dwells in the little ones, who do not cognize Him: therefore, this reason does not seem (to be) fitting.

I RESPOND: There is a cognizing *in act*, and there is a cognizing *in habit*; and though little ones do not cognize (God) *in act*, yet they do cognize (Him) *in habit*, by this, that they have grace and the virtues, just as is said in the Fourth Book.[9]

DOUBT IV

Likewise, is asked concerning this which (St. John Chrysostom) says: *But in what manner He is everywhere, we do not grasp by (our) intellect*. For it seems that he says (something) false, because « what we understand, ought (to be) for a reason », just as (St.) Augustine says;[10] but we have reasons, through which we know, that God is in things by means of (His) Power, presence and Essence. *If you say*, that (we know but) we do not comprehend;[11] (it is) similarly (objected) that neither do we comprehend the others, which are said of God: therefore, Master (Peter) ought not have said more concerning this than concerning the abovesaid, (namely) that it is ineffable.

I RESPOND: It must be said, that *certain ones* are purely intelligible, and such the imagination does not contradict, but fails; *certain ones* are sensible, and in such it is sufficient; *certain ones* are in a certain manner imaginable, and in a certain manner intelligible, and in such the intellect frequently fails, and the imagination contradicts and fails: such as when we consider [cogitamus], that God is everywhere, we grasp God with our intellect alone, but the place we imagine. And since our imagination does not grasp the example,[12] that some one (thing) is in many places, and (our) intellect does not look upon it in the clarity of light; hence it is, that such are judged by us (to be) not intelligible more than others.

DOUBT V

Likewise, is asked concerning this which (Master Peter, paraphrasing St. Augustine,) says: *created spirit is not befouled by the sordid (things) of a body*.

---

[1] In Bk. X, ch. 27, n. 38.

[2] Cf. above d. 19, p. I, q. 3, in the body (of the Response).

[3] 1 Cor. 3:9: *For we are God's helpers* [Dei enim sumus adiutores].

[4] This doubt is also solved by Bl. (now St.) Albertus (Magnus), here in a. 11, and by Giles the Roman, here on the text.

[5] Prepositions are called *transitive* [transitivae], inasmuch as they say something outside of the subject. Cf. above d. 5, a. 1, q. 2, in reply to n. 1 and its Scholium.

[6] Verse 1. The Gloss is exhibited by (Nicholas) of Lyra thus: "*He was with God*", as One with Another.

[7] The words cited here are not found in the book of Confessions, nor in the Sermons of (St.) Augustine on (the Gospel of St.) Matthew, chapter 6: "*Our Father* etc." as is suggested by others. Bl. (now St.) Albertus (Magnus), SUMMA., I, tr. 18, q. 71, cites a similar (verse) from (St.) Bernard (SERMON, 6, "On the Dedication of Church"), which, however, does not convene with this text in all (its words). In the cited text the

Vatican edition, together with codex cc, prefixes *the liberated and/or* [liberatis vel] to *the Elect* [electis].

[8] Cf. on this doubt, Bl. (now St.) Albertus, here in a. 12 and 13; (Bl.) Peter of Tarentaise, here on the text; and Giles the Roman, here in the 1st princ., q. 3.

[9] Distinction 4, p. II, a. 2. q. 2. Cf. also SENT., Bk. III, d. 23, q. 2, in the body (of the Response) and in the reply to n. 5; Alexander of Hales, SUMMA., p. I, q. 11, m. 5: Bl. (now St.) Albertus (Magnus), here in a. 15, (Bl.) Peter (of Tarentaise) and Richard (of Middleton), here on the text.

[10] In the book, ON THE UTILITY OF BELIEVING, ch. 11, n. 25, where the original text has *we ought to* [debemus] for *ought (to be)* [debetur]. Cf. also his RETRACTATIONS, Bk. I, ch. 14, n. 3.

[11] Supply with the Vatican ed.: *it is objected, that* [obicitur, quod].

[12] In the Vatican ed. there is wanting *the example* [exemplum]. Next, many codd. read *only something is* [aliquod tantum est] for *some one (thing) is* [aliquod unum est]. — The solution of this doubt is of great moment.

For it seems to be contrary to that which is said in the ninth (chapter) of Wisdom:[1] *The body, which is corrupted, weights down the soul.* And again, the soul contracts original (sin) from the flesh and is infected by it.

I RESPOND: Just as the generation, which is of a similar out of a similar, is *univocal*, and (the generation) which is of a dissimilar thing, (is) *equivocal*, so infection is according to a *univocal* reckoning, such as a leper making a leper, and according to an *equivocal* reckoning, such as the infection (of the body) generating the infection (of the soul).[2] Master (Peter) speaks in the first manner, because the soul of a leper is not of a leper; (but) he objects in the second manner.

DOUBT VI

Likewise, is asked concerning this which (St. Augustine) says: *In God are all which He established, yet those who sin do not befoul Him.* For he seems to speak badly, because sordid corporal (things) do befoul corporal things, therefore, (sordid) spiritual (things do befoul) things spiritual. *Likewise*, if they do not befoul God: therefore, it seems, that it can be said, that God is in a devil, which is contrary to every usage [usum].

I RESPOND: It must be said, that, just as Master (Peter) touches upon in the text,[3] sordid corporal (things) do not befoul a body, which neither communicates in matter nor depends, as is clear in a ray (of light), which is not infected by dung [faecibus], because it neither depends nor communicates in the transmutable matter. And since God has neither, for that reason that (argument) is not valid. — *What is objected*, that God is in sinners; it must be said, that it would not be unfitting to say (this); yet because this seemed[4] to sound of contumely, for that reason a determination is to posited, by the reckoning of which a sane understanding of the expression may appear: so that if there be said, "God is in a devil and/or in an adulterer", (it is said) as much as regards the conservation of (their) nature.

COMMENTARY ON DISTINCTION XXXVII

PART II

On the immutability of God, as much as regards place.

And, since the Divine Nature is truthfully and essentially etc..*

SEE THE TEXT OF MASTER (PETER), ABOVE ON P. 635.

THE DIVISION OF THE TEXT

Above, Master (Peter) showed, in what kind of manner God is in places and in all things; and, since 'to existence in a place' [existentiam in loco] there follows a circumscriptibility [circumscriptibilitas] and a 'belonging to a place' [localitas][5] in the placed creature, for that reason he intends here to remove these conditions from God. And this part is divided into two. In the *first*, he shows that God (is) uncircumscribable and immutable. However, in the *second*, he concludes and confirms (this) through authorities, there (where he says): *And so let us say, that the Divine Nature* etc..

The *first* part has three parts. In the first, he shows, that immutability and incircumscriptibility befit God. In the second, he removes this from angelic nature and from every created nature, there (where he says): *But in a certain manner a created spirit belongs to a place* etc.. In the third[6] he infers his own conclusion, that the uncreated Spirit is alone uncircumscribable, there (where he says): *Therefore created spirits are in a place* etc..

And so let us say etc.. This is the *second* part, in which he resumes his own conclusion, to add (to it), and this part has three parts. In the first, he concludes (what have been) predetermined and confirms (these) with authorities. But, in the second, he moves a doubt and solves it, there (where he says): *But to this there is customarily opposed* etc. In the third, he briefly summarizes [epilogat] (what have been) predetermined and shows the reason for the position of the present chapter, there (where he says): *It seems already that (there has been) sufficiently demonstrated* etc..

---

[1] Verse 15.

[2] That is, the infection of the flesh generates the infection of the soul. On equivocal generation, there is said above in d. 13, Doubt 8 (that it is): « that (generation) which is according to putrefaction ». The common opinion of that age used to admit this generation in regard to some, imperfect forms of life [viventia]. — A little before for *univocal* [univocam] many codices have <u>univocatam</u>. The words, which then follow, *and according to an equivocal reckoning* [et secundum rationem aequivocam], are badly omitted in very many codices and edition 1.

[3] In chapter 4. — The words immediately subjoined by the Vatican edition have changed the text into something worse: *sordid corporal (things) do not completely befoul a spiritual body, because then neither communicate matter nor depend (upon it)* [sordes corporales non coinquinant corpus spirituale, quia nec communicant in materia nec de-

pendent]. A little below this, for *because it neither* [quia nec], not a few codices have less congruously *which neither* [qui nec], and then for *the transmutable* [transmutabili] codices L and O have *a completely similar* [consimili].

[4] Edition 1 has *seems* [videtur]. — Cf. on this doubt, Bl. (now St.) Albertus (Magnus), here in a. 17, and St. Thomas, here in q. 1, a. 1, in reply to n. 5.

[5] The Vatican edition reads *a locability* [locabilitas].

[6] The Vatican ed., having put *four parts* [quatuor partes] for *three parts* [tres partes] above, here inserts in its own name: *he posits the opinion of certain (authors) who say, that created spirits do not move according to place, nor belong to a place, there (where he says): However, concerning change of place* etc.. *In the fourth* etc. [ponit opinionem quorundam qui dicunt, spiritus creatos non moveri loco, nec esse locales, ibi: De mutatione vero loci etc. In quarta suam etc.].

---

* *Trans. note*: Here, the titular citation of the first sentence of part II of Master Peter's Distinction read *substantially* [substantialiter] for *essentially*. Since the Latin text accepted by the Quaracchi editors above, in the critical edition of Lombard reads *essentially* [essentialiter], the English translation has followed this, rather than this seemingly faulty subtitle.

TREATMENT OF THE QUESTIONS

For an understanding of this part two (things) are principally asked.

First, there is asked concerning God's incircumscriptibility or quality of not belonging to a place [illocalitate].

Second, concerning an angelic spirit's change of place [per locum]; for (Master Peter)[1] discusses [prosequitur] these two in the text.

And, as much as regards the first Article three (things) are asked.

First, there is asked, whether God belongs to a place within a place.

Second, whether He is able to change [mutabilis] from place to place.

Third, whether He is separable from place or is outside of every place.

ARTICLE I

On the incircumscriptibility of God.

QUESTION I

Whether God belongs to a place?

About the first, (the argument) proceeds in this manner. That God belongs to a place [est localis], is shown in this manner:

1. "To be in a place" [esse in loco] and "to be placed" [esse locatum] are convertible; but God is in a place, as has been proven in the preceding:[2] therefore, God has been placed. But "to be placed" is "(to belong) to a place": therefore, God belongs to a place.

2. Likewise, what is in one place only belongs to a place: therefore, if all places can (be) more than one, and that which has being in the whole tastes more of the nature of a thing, than that which has (it) in part, much more does that which is in every place belong to a place. But God is in every place, because (He is) everywhere: therefore, it seems that He most of all belongs to a place.

3. Likewise, 'God is everywhere: therefore, He is here', a toto (in loco);[3] but what is here, is in a determinate place, and what is in a determinate place belongs to a place: ergo etc..

4. Likewise, God is in some determinate place, therefore, either according to (His) *whole*, or according to *part*. If according to *part*: therefore He has one part and another part [partem et partem], which is unfitting. If according to (His) *whole*; but, what is according to a whole is comprehended in something

by it, and, what is comprehended by some determinate* place, belongs to a place: therefore, God belongs to a place.

ON THE CONTRARY: 1. Master (Peter says) in the text. « He does not belong to a place, because He is not thoroughly circumscribed by a place ».

2. Likewise, it is proven *by reason* thus: nothing is said (to be) temporal, except that which is exceeded by time — for temporals are corruptible in time [in tempore] — therefore, nothing is said (to belong) to a place, except that which is exceeded by a place;[5] but God is not exceeded by a place: ergo etc..

3. Likewise, place is an *accident*, therefore, ("place") denominates naught, but that which is compared as an accident;[6] but, to God, it cannot be compared as an accident (is): therefore, it does not denominate God: therefore, God does not belong to a place.

4. Likewise, a place is a continuous, divisible quantity, but a point is the indivisible principles of quantity,[7] therefore, a point convenes with God more than a place (does), as much as regards (its) properties; but God is not said (to belong) to a point [punctualis], except improperly and falsely: therefore, He ought not be said (to belong) to a place.

---

[1] Supply with ed. 1: *Master (Peter)* [Magister]. A little further above this, for *quality of not belonging to a place* [illocalitate] the Vatican ed. has *inability to belong to a place* [illocabilitate], and *ability to change through place* [mutabilitate per locum] for *change of place* [mutatione per locum].

[2] In Part I, of this Distinction, a. 1, q. 2. — The adjective "of/to a place" [localis] here has the same meaning as "circumscribable by place" [loco circumscriptibilis]. — A little further below this, for *But "to be placed"* [Sed esse locatum], the Vatican ed., with some codd., has *but everything placed* [sed omne locatum], and then after *is* [est] it interject *to belong* [esse].

[3] By the words a toto (in loco) there is signified a topic [locus] or manner of arguing, which according to the diversity of "*whole*" is manifold, that is, a topic (which argues) from a whole universal, from an whole integral, from a whole *in a manner*, from a whole *in time*. « The totum in loco (which is what is spoken of here) is a saying comprehending every place adverbially, such as "*everywhere*", "*nowhere*". A pars in loco is a saying comprehending some place adverbially, such as "*here*", "*there*". A topic (which argues) a toto in loco is the habitude of that (whole) to its own part and it is held [tenet] constructively and destructively. Constructively in this manner: "God is everywhere, therefore, God is here". The maxim (for this usage) is: "Whatsoever suits the whole *on the topic (being asserted)* [totum in loco], (suits) also every part of it. Destructively in this manner: "Caesar is nowhere, therefore, Caesar is *not* here". The maxim (for

this usage) is: "Whatever is removed from a whole on the topic (being asserted) [a toto in loco], (is) also (removed) from any part of it". A topic (which argues) a parte in loco is a habitude of the same to its whole; and it is always destructive, as for example: "Caesar is not here, therefore, he is not everywhere". The maxim (for this usage) is: "Whatever does not suit the part on the topic (being asserted) [pars in loco], (suits) neither its whole » (Peter of Spain, SUMMULA., tract "On the topical syllogism"). — The Vatican edition omits a toto (in loco).°

[4] In chapter 5.

[5] Aristotle, PHYSICS, Bk. IV, text 117 (ch. 12): Moreover, since 'to be in time' [esse in tempore] is, as '(to be) in number'; "any time" [aliquod tempus] will be accepted as greater than every that, which in time. On which account it is necessary that all those which are in time, be contained by time [contineri a tempore], just as even any whatsoevers in something, as those which are in a place, are (contained) by a place.

[6] Cf. above in d. 27, p. I, a. sole, q. 3, p. 475, footnote 1.

[7] See Aristotle, ON THE PREDICAMENTS, ch. "on *Quantity*", and PHYSICS, Bk. VI, text 1 ff..

---

* *Trans. note*: Here the critical edition faultily omits the hyphen after *de* [de], which ends one line, so as to connect it to *terminate* [terminato], which begins the next, and thus reads as two separate words.

° Below in footnote 4, Cf. Aristotle, TOPICS, Bk. I, ch. 1, for the use of the term locus (topic) for a method or form of argumentation.

CONCLUSION

Though God is in some manner in a place, yet,
He is to no extent said (to belong) to a place.

I RESPOND: It must be said, that what (belongs) to a place [est localis] is said (to be) that which follows the laws of place, just as *the temporal* (is) that which follows the laws of time. Moreover, the laws of place are as much as regards an act *of containing, measuring, conserving* [salvandi], *terminating*, according to which the place holds itself to the one placed through the manner of one imparting, and the one placed holds itself to the place through the manner of a suscipient. And since God is thus present to a place, that He receives entirely nothing from it, but only supplies its indigence and gives to the place a virtue of containing and to the one placed the virtue of filling (it) again: hence it is, that God is in no manner to be said to belong to a place, just as Master (Peter) says in the text. And the reasons brought forward for this are to be conceded.

1. To that, therefore, which is objected, that "*to be in a place*", and "*to be placed*" are convertible; it must be said, that they are convertible by reason of the matter about a body itself (which is in a place), yet by reason of the virtue of the word (they are) not. For this determination "*in a place*" [in loco], for this, that the expression has truth, does not require nor posit but a quality of being present and an indistance; but "*to be placed*" posits a being surrounded [ambitum] and a containment [continentiam], "*to belong to a place*" posits a idoneity to the properties of place and some indigence. And for that reason this is conceded: "God is in a place"; yet it has something of impropriety, on account to this, that this preposition "*in*" seems to convey a surrounding containment. But this is more improper: "God has been placed". And this is still more improper: "God belongs to a place"; and for that reason it is not to be received, but explained [exponenda].

2. To that which is objected, "what is in *one* place (only)[3] belongs to a place"; it must be said, that this is, because the place superexcels the very one placed, whence the former determines and defines (the latter); but when it is in *all* (places), all places superexcel it. And for that reason all places cannot (superexcel) so much over *this*, as much as one place can over the *that*, which is only in one place. And for that reason God is not to be said (to belong) to a place.

3. To that which is objected, that God is here etc.; it must be said, that "*here*" can be held in a twofold manner: either *only demonstratively*, or *demonstratively* and *discretively*.[4] If *only demonstratively*, thus it is true, that God is here, because (in this expression) there is no signifying [signare] of a place, to which God is not present. But if *discretively*, it is false that He is here; and it does not follow from the first (proposition, namely: "God is here"), and in this sense its reckoning proceeds.

4. To that which is asked: "God is either (in a place) according to (His) whole" etc.; it must be said, that in God there is *simplicity* and *infinity* together. When, therefore, when a name conveying a totality is applied to [apponitur circa] "God", it can be applied in a twofold manner: either by reason of (His) *simplicity*; and thus it deprives this part and that part, and in this manner it is signified through a name,[5] as if to say: "God (is) whole" [totus Deus]. And since God in every place is simple, and anything [quodlibet] is capable of the Divine Simplicity; for that reason by reason of (His) Simplicity God is in any place whole. Again, a totality can be applied by reason of (His) *infinity* and this comes to be through an adverb, as if to say: "God is totally in this place or (is) according to (His) whole". Therefore, when there is asked: "(Is He there) either according to *part*, or according to *whole*?"; it must be said, that (the question) does not divide through the immediate (members of the division),[6] because God is (in a place) neither according to a part, because (He is) simple, nor according to a whole, because (He is) infinite. And for that reason He is to be said (to be) whole in any place, yet not totally; and for that reason He is in a place, yet not as belonging to a place [localiter].

SCHOLIUM

I. The Questions of this Article are discussed, so as to remove from the Divine Ubiquity those imperfections, which accompany the presence of creatures in a place, as the Seraphic Doctor himself observes above in the Division of the Text of the present Distinction. — The solution to n. 4 is constructed from the commonly received distinction between *whole simply* [totum simpliciter] and *whole and totally* [totum et totaliter], which is employed to solve many theological questions. St. Thomas exhibits the same distinction in other words, in his SUMMA., I, q. 8, a. 2, in reply to n. 3.

II. The authors (who discuss this are): Alexander of Hales, SUMMA., p. I, q. 9, m. 1 and 2. — Bl. (now St.) Albertus (Magnus), here in a. 14 and 18. — (Bl.) Peter of Tarentaise, here in q. 3, a. 1. — Henry of Ghent, SUMMA., a. 32, q. 5, nn. 39-42. — Durandus (of Saint-Pourçain), here in p. I, q. 2. — (Bl.) Dionysius the Carthusian., here in q. 2. — (Gabriel) Biel, here in the q. sole.

---

[1] Cf. Aristotle, PHYSICS, Bk. IV, text 30 (ch. 4).

[2] Chapter 5, ff.. — Cf. also (St.) Anselm, MONOLOGION., ch. 22.

[3] Codex T adds well *only* [tantum], which is had in the objection.

[4] That is, by discerning this place from another, such that *here* it is, and *elsewhere* it is not. At the word *from the first* [ex prima], which occurs in what is subjoined, understand: *proposition, namely: "God is here"* [propositione, nempe: Deus est hic]; and then accept *its reckoning* [sua ratio] in the sense of *the reckoning of the one objecting* [ratio obiicientis].

[5] Which is "*whole*" [totus], in place of which the Vatican has less congruously "*the Whole*" [totum]. — Next after *of the Divine Simplic-*

ity [simplicitatis divinae] very many codices, together with edition 1, adjoin *and/or saying* [vel dictum], omitting at the same time the subsequent *for that reason* [ideo], which however, codex T retains.

[6] He wants to say: the one objecting does not divide through the immediate members (of the logical division: as for example in the argument: 'Socrates is a man: Therefore, either Socrates is a writer or Socrates is a carnivore.'). — At the end of the solution the Vatican edition, together with codex cc, omits the words *and for that reason He is in a place, yet not as belonging to a place* [et ideo est in loco, non tamen localiter]. For *as belonging to a place* [localiter] many codices have *totally* [totaliter], faultily.

QUESTION II

Whether God is able to change according to place?

Second, there is asked, whether God is able to change [mutabilis] according to place. And that (He is) not, seems in this manner:

1. Master (Peter) in (his) text[1] says and accepts from (St.) Augustine ON A LITERAL EXPOSITION OF GENESIS: « God is in every time, and in every place, yet He does not move through places and/or times ».

2. Likewise, it is shown *by reason*, because « movement is an imperfect act »;[2] but in God there is no imperfection: therefore, neither change according to place.

3. Likewise, through every movement something is acquired;[3] but God can acquire no place, because He is everywhere: therefore, it is impossible, that God be changed according to place.

4. Likewise, rest [quies] is a more noble disposition than movement;[4] but what is more noble is to be attributed to God: therefore, it is impossible, that God be changed according to place, because He is always at rest [semper quiescit].

ON THE CONTRARY: 1. (St.) Augustine (says) to (Paulus) Orosius:[5] « God moves Himself without time and place », therefore, it seems that God moves; but the most perfect of movements is movement according to place: ergo etc..

2. Likewise, (St.) Isidore (of Seville says):[6] « Since God does not belong to a place [illocalis], yet as belonging to a place [localiter] He walks in the Saints »: therefore, it seems at least that He is changed per accidens.

3. Likewise, this seems *by reason*, because « with us moved, there are also moved those which are in us ». The Philosopher says this,[7] and he says (it) on account of the forms, which are not in one (place) determinately: therefore, if God is in us, God is moved in us at least *according to an accident*.

4. Likewise, although God as much as regards (His) existence does not through (His) Essence determine (for Himself) a place,[8] yet, as much as regards (His) dwelling He definitely is in some,

such that (He is) not in others: therefore, at least as much as regards this manner He is able to change.

CONCLUSION

God neither through Himself, nor through an accident, is changed through place.

I RESPOND: It must be said, that just as Master (Peter) says in the text,[9] God is in no manner changed through place; and this is true, because neither *through Himself*, nor *through an accident* is He changed, and this is on account of (His) most high Immensity, by which He is at hand to all and absent from none. And if He starts to be in a thing, and/or ceases, this is only according to the change of the thing, not according to a change of Him: as for example, if, with the air illumined, a crystal is understood to be created, a ray (of light) starts to be in it, and with the crystal removed, it ceases to be, with no change made in the ray.

1. 2. To that, therefore, which is objected, that God moves Himself; it must be said, that (St.) Augustine does not say *simply*, that He moves Himself, but:[10] *"without time and place"*. And, since every movement according to (St.) Augustine is comprehended under change according-to-*time* and according-to-*place*; for that reason there is a saying of that, as much as there would be a saying of (this): "He moves Himself without movement", and, thus, He does not move Himself truly, nor is a contradiction implied. But, since in movement there are two (things), namely that which is *the act* and that which is *the variation* or imperfection,[11] (St.) Augustine wants to say, that He moves Himself without movement, because He is always in *act*, but not in an imperfect act, nay (in) a perfect one. — What (St.) Isidore says must be understood

---

[1] In ch. 5. The passage from St. Augustine (is taken) according to sense from ON A LITERAL EXPOSITION OF GENESIS, Bk. VIII. ch. 20, nn. 39 and 40.

[2] Aristotle, PHYSICS, Bk. III. text 15 (ch. 2): A movement indeed seems to be some act, however, imperfect.

[3] Otherwise it would be possible, that someone « at once *moves* and *has moved*, by that which he was moved, when he was moved, as if one goes to Thebes, it is impossible, at once to go to Thebes and to have gone to Thebes », as Aristotle, says in PHYSICS, Bk. VI, text 7 (ch. 1).

[4] Aristotle, TOPICS, Bk. VI. ch. 3 (ch. 4): For prior and more known is that which is remaining and delimited than that, which is undelimited and in movement. — At the end of the argument for *because* [quia], which together with the codices, even editions 1, 2 and 3 have the Vatican edition has *but* [sed].

[5] Or THE DIALOGUE OF 65 QUESTIONS, q. 41. On *the minor*, cf. Aristotle, PHYSICS Bk. VIII, text 57 ff. (ch. 7).

[6] In the book of CONSIDERATIONS, or ON THE MOST HIGH GOOD, Bk. I, ch. 2, n. 5.

[7] TOPICS, Bk. II, ch. 3 (ch. 7), where also the subsequent words: « and he says this on account of the forms, which are not in one (place) determinately », are explained. For Aristotle, treating of Platonic ideas, says: For it will befall the same (ideas) both to be moved and to be at rest and also to be sensible and insensible; for ideas seem to be at rest and immobile

and intelligible to those who posit, that ideas are; but yet since they are in us, it is impossible that they be immobile; for with us moved it is necessary, that all those too which are in us be moved together. Cf. above d. 5, a. 2, q. 1, p. 116, footnote 8.

[8] That is, He is not determinately in some only, but in all. — Next for *dwelling* [habitationem] codex Y has *indwelling* [in habitationem].

[9] Chapter 5 f.. — After a few (words) for *through place* [per locum] codex V has well *according to place* [secundum locum].

[10] Very many codices, such as F N W & X (T in the margin), here repeat the preceding words *that He moves Himself* [quid movet se], but the Vatican edition, together with codex cc, here subjoins *but with these being added* [cum his additionibus]. — On the following proposition consult Master (Peter) here in ch. 6, where the very words of (St.) Augustine are also had.

[11] Aristotle, in PHYSICS, Bk. III, text 6 ff. (ch. 1), defines movement in this manner: movement is an act of a being in potency insofar as (it is) in potency, i. e. the actual tendency of a mobile thing regarding a terminus. — A little before this, for *move Himself truly* [movet se vere] a greater part of the codices, together with edition 1, have *move truly* [movet vere], which reading does not correspond to the context; the Vatican edition has *move* [movetur]. A little below this, after *that He moves* [quod movet], not a few codices, again faultily, omit *Himself* [se].

metaphorically, and/or in the manner of a cause, because He makes the Saints walk, that is, through faith, *from virtue unto virtue.*[1]

3. To that which is objected, that with us moved etc.; it must be said, that that does not have truth, except in those which are in others through a *dependence* and a *delimitation* [definitionem]. Wherefore because a ray is in the air, but does not *depend* upon the air, for that reason it is not moved, with the air moved; and because the soul is in the hand, and is not *delimited* [definitur] by the hand, for that reason it is not moved, with the hand moved. But God does not depend upon things nor is He delimited (by them); for that reason He is not moved by the movement of things.

4. To that which is objected concerning God's dwelling, it must be said, that He is determinately in some not by reason of (His) Immensity, but by reason of the influence of grace; and for that reason God Himself is not determined, but only the effect (is). Hence it is, that He is not *through Himself,* nor *through an accident* moved nor can He be moved, because He depends upon none and cannot depend,[2] He is delimited by none and cannot be delimited; and non only it is not possible, but it is not even intelligible.

But someone *will object* thus: let us understand that a[3] body leaves [egredi a] a place, without (anything else) entering, then there remains a vacuum; therefore, either God *is* there, or (He is) *not:* if *so,* therefore, in Him is that which is nothing, which is a stupid (thing) to say; if He is

not, and before He was there, therefore, it seems that He has been changed, at least per accidens: therefore, it seems, that God goes forth with the thing and with the thing enters [ingrediatur], because if the thing only would go forth, God would not go forth.[4] — To this I respond, that, if per impossibile it be posited, that the place is evacuated, then, the deprived *capacity* of the place is understood to remain; a *capacity* is something, and God is in that; but a *privation* is nothing, and God cannot be in that: therefore, God does not cease to be in[5] that, which *remains* after the withdrawal of the body; but when *the thing is deprived,* the comparison of it to God is borne away. For what is nothing, has no comparison.

But, when *the thing moves, it does* not leave [dimittit] God, nor *does it approach* to God, nor does God *come* with the thing; because He is thus in the thing, as to be the same outside of the thing; for that reason neither does the thing leave Him nor does it find (Him) anew. And this is intelligible, if one can understand, that God is *simple,* and infinite and *immense.* For because He is *immense,* He is thus within, that (He is) outside;[6] because (He is) *simple,* He is according to one and the same (thing) within and outside: for that reason neither does He leave [dimittitur], nor does He acquire [acquiritur] another (place) in the thing; nor does He go [itur] from one to another (place) [ab ipso ad ipsum], when[7] He leaves, so as to be found in one and another place [alibi et alibi].

SCHOLIUM

There is a twofold movement or change according to place, namely *through itself* [per se] and/or *through an accident* [per accidens], as Aristotle teaches, chiefly in ON THE SOUL, Bk. I, text 37 ff.. Neither manner befits God. That some thing be moved per accidens, there is required, that it be in another thing, which is moved through itself, in a *circumscriptive* manner, such as a body on a ship, and/or at least in a *delimitive* (manner), such as a soul is in the body. — The term *is at rest* [quiescit] in the last argument of the fundament is said of God in an *improper* sense, since neither *movement* nor a *privation* of movement *properly* befits God. — In the solution to n. 4 there is a sufficiently subtle reply. The Seraphic (Doctor) solves the

example for the opposite [instantiam] with this distinction: if anything *positive* (i.e. the capacity of the place) would remain, then this positive (thing) has a relation to God; but to the extent that through a privation *nothing* remains, « the comparison (of the thing) to God is borne away », that is the looking-back, which the existing thing *really* has regarding God, and God (has) *according to a reckoning* to the thing, is thoroughly born away, yet God is neither moved *through Himself* nor *through an accident.*

The authors (who also discuss this question are): Bl. (now St.) Albertus (Magnus), here in a. 19. — (Bl.) Peter of Tarentaise, here in q. 3, a. 2. — Henry of Ghent, SUMMA, a. 30, q. 5.

QUESTION III

Whether God is separable from every place and/or (is) outside of every place?

In this third place, there is asked, whether God is separable from every place [ab omni loc separabilis] and/or (is) outside of every place [extra omnem locum]. And that (He is) not, seems:

1. Because outside of every place there is nothing [nihil est]: therefore, if God is outside of every place, therefore He is nothing [nihil est][8] and/or in nothing [in nihilo].

2. Likewise, that which *"outside of"* [extra], is an adverb for place: therefore, if God is outside of every place, He is in a place and beyond [praeter] every place; but this is false and not intelligible: therefore, God cannot, neither *according to thing* [re] nor *according to understanding* [intellectu], be separated from every place.

3. Likewise, when there is said: "God is outside of the world" [Deus est extra mundum],

---

[1] A reference to 2 Cor. 5:7: *For we walk through faith* [Per fidem enim ambulamus]; and to Ps. 83:8: *They shall go from virtue unto virtue* [Ibunt de virtute in virtutem]. — For *through faith* [per fidem] the Vatican edition, together with edition 1, has *make progress* [proficere].

[2] Cf. Aristotle, PHYSICS, Bk. VIII, text 46 ff. (ch. 6), where he teaches, that the prime mover is entirely immobile and is not moved per se nor per accidens.

[3] Codex T has *some body* [corpus aliquod] for *a body* [corpus].

[4] And, thus, God would be in nothing, which is absurd to say.

— Before *go forth* [exiret], we have recalled from codices L and O *not* [non], which is wanting the Vatican edition, but is required by the context.

[5] From cod. R we have restored *in* [in] for *by* [ab], which the Vatican has.

[6] Codex K reads *He is thus within the thing, that He is outside (it)* [ita est intra rem, quod est extra].

[7] Thus the codices, together with editions 1, 2 and 3, in which reading there is to be entirely supplied *the thing* [res], namely, which leaves a place for a place.* The Vatican edition has *nor* [nec] for *when* [cum], which reading smiles upon our own.

[8] The Vatican edition alone omits *He is nothing* [nihil est]

---

* *Trans. note:* This rationale of the Quaracchi editors, of reading *the thing* [res] as the subject of the clause, fails to recognize that from *for that reason* [ideo] onwards, the passive forms of the verbs are employed in the middle voice and, therefore, have *God* as their subject.

"*outside of*" either stands for something, or for nothing: if not nothing, therefore, "*outside of the world*" is a chimera; if for something, therefore, for (something) *created*, and/or *uncreated*: not for (something) *created*; (this) is established:[1] therefore, for (something) *uncreated*: therefore, '*to be outside of the world*' is 'to be in God'. But all are in God: therefore, all are outside of the world.

4. Likewise, God is in no (place), which is not in Him; but nothing is in God, which is outside of the world: therefore, God is not outside of the world.

ON THE CONTRARY: 1. That place *can* be separated from God according to understanding, seems, because it is possible according to understanding, that a place be deprived of every placed (thing) and to remain a vacuum; but a vacuum is a privation, (and) moreover God is in no (being), which is not in Him; but a privation is not in God: therefore, neither (is) God in a privation, therefore, neither (is He) in a vacuum, and thus He is separable from place.

2. Likewise, that God *is separated* from place according to thing, seems, because, just as the eternity of God holds itself to every time, so (God's)[2] Immensity to every place; but the eternity of God was before every time: therefore, God's Immensity was *outside of every place*. But what is outside of something is separate [est separatum] from it: ergo etc..

3. Likewise, if God is only in created places, since those are of a finite dimension, and what completely measures [commensurat] itself by a finite is delimitable and finite: therefore, God would be finite.

4. Likewise, God is good to such an extent, that a better cannot be thought of, therefore, (He is) great and immense to such an extent, that a greater cannot be though of than He; but a line greater than the whole world* can be thought of, if it be understood to extend outside of the circumference of the sky: therefore, if God is there, God is outside (the world), or He is not the greatest.

5. Likewise, an Angel can be outside of the world; but not outside of God: therefore, God is outside of the world.

CONCLUSION

God according to distance cannot be separated, neither according to thing nor understanding, from every place, but according to independence He is separate, both according to thing and understanding, from place.

I RESPOND: It must be said, that '*that something be separated from another*' is in a twofold manner: either according to *distance*, and/or according to *independence*.[3] In the first manner any two, which are in the same place, are separated, when one is elongated from the other. And in this manner it is impossible to be,

nor to be understood, that God is separated from every place. For that separation includes a distance *of space*, and this of necessity includes a *place*; and thus two opposites are implied, namely, that God is in a place, and is distant from every place. But if we speak of a separation through *independence*; thus it must be said, that *God* both according to thing and according to understanding is separate from place, because in Himself He is entirely independent from a place, just as (He is) before the production of a place. But *the place* contrariwise is not separable from God, neither according to thing nor according to understanding, just as the reasons brought forwards for this prove.

2. Similarly, when there is asked, "Whether God is *outside of every place?*"; it must be said, that "*outside of*" in one manner means a site and a position; and in this manner it is impossible,[4] just as it is impossible, if "*before*" [ante] means "*time*", that He be "*before time*". In another manner "*before*" and "*outside of*" mean an the *excess* and a superexcellence of the Divine eternity and Immensity in respect of time and place; and in this manner it must be conceded, that God is *before time* and *outside of every place*. Nor does it follow from this, that *He is separated* from place, but that (His) most high Immensity *superexceeds* every place and is not constrained to it. And by this (St.) Gregory wants to say,[5] that God is *outside of* all, (as) the One not excluded, because He is not distant; and *inside* all, (as) the One not included, because He is not constrained, because being[6] in Himself, He is entirely immense, such that outside of Him nothing can be nor be thought of, or nothing can be thought of so immense, as God is in His very self.

3. From this the following (objection) is clear, because that He is not *outside*, is not on account of His own limitation, but (on account of) the deficiency [defectionem] of the place.

4. To that which is objected concerning the line, it must be said, that immediately, as there is understood (to be) something outside of the world, from this there is given to be understood, that God is there, just as if a new world is understood to be made, without doubt God would be in it. Yet it does not follow, that He is there, because nothing is that.

5. Similarly, if an Angel be made outside of the world;[7] God then is outside, not according to His own movement, but (that) of the Angel. But perhaps it belongs more to fiction than to truth, that an Angel goes forth outside of the universe, just as will be clear.[8] Nevertheless, one must think of that, which is the Divine '*To Be*', just as It cannot be thought to have a terminus in *duration*, so It cannot be thought nor ought it have a terminus in *existence* and (Its) *quality of being present* [praesentialitate]; and just as It cannot be thought to have an interruption [intercisionem] in *duration*, so neither in (Its) *quality of being present*. This understanding is to be held; yet, beware, in what kind of manner one imagines and expresses (it) through a sermon.

---

[1] Codices T and V have *this is established* [hoc constat].

[2] Codex T has *God's Immensity* [Dei immensitas]

[3] Some codices, such as M V and Y have *dependence* [dependentiam]; erroneously.

[4] Understand here: that God is outside of every place.

[5] MORALS ON THE BOOK OF JOB, Bk. II, ch. 12, n. 20.

[6] Or *existing* [exisens]. — The Vatican edition omits *being* [ens]. A little after this for *or* [sive] codex T has *just as* [sicut].

[7] The word *the world* [mundum], which we have restored from codex Y, is lacking in all the other codices, and even in the Vatican edition; in very many codices there is also lacking *outside of* [extra]; in these readings one must supply an *etc.* [etc.]

[8] Below in a. 2, q. 2, in reply to the last objection; and in SENT., Bk. II, d. 2, p. II, a. 2, q. 3. In these passages there is proven, that the Angels cannot be outside of place and consequently not outside of the world. *

---

* *Trans. note*: It is apparent in this Question that the Seraphic Doctor understands the term *the world* [mundum] without distinguishing its differing senses: *the Universe, creation, the Earth*; using the term, as he does, in the general sense of the Greek term, *cosmos*.

SCHOLIUM

I. From the title of this Question it appears, that here two problems are treated; but with these other questions are solves through the manner of corollaries. The first principal question respects places *really existing*, and whether *God* is separable from them. To this it responds by distinguishing the term "*to be separated*" [separari]. Through the manner of a corollary there is solved the question, whether *a place* is separable from God. To this pertain the 1st and 2nd opposed arguments. — The second question in the solution to n. 2 respects *imaginary* places, or those which are supposed to be outside of the world. It responds with a distinction of the preposition "*outside of*" [extra]. In the solution to nn. 4 and 5 two connected questions in regard to a new world and an Angel created *outside of the world* are determined. But that an Angel in truth can be outside of a place in an indivisible point, and thus outside of the world, the Seraphic Doctor does not concede.

II. The response to the second question in the solution to n. 2 is explained more by Richard of Middleton (here in a. 1, q. 4) in these words: « 'That God is *outside of* the word' can be understood in a twofold manner: in one manner thus, that His Immensity exceeds the world and does not depend upon the world; and in this manner it is true, that God outside of the world is infinite, because He exceeds the finite, nor does He depends upon the finite, nor is He enclosed by the finite .... In another manner it can be understood, that God is *outside of* the world thus, that there is a granting of space outside of the world, in which God is; and in this manner it is false ». But if there be said, that outside of the world there is, indeed, no real space, but (only) imaginary (space), according to the mind of the Seraphic (Doctor) one would have to respond, that space is *in act* nothing, and only *in potency* is there a place, in which God is also understood to be *in potency*, « not on account of His own limitation, but (on account of) the deficiency of the place ». This manner of speaking of God's presence in imaginary spaces is approved also by Alexander of Hales (SUMMA, p. I, q. 9, m. 4), by (Bl. John Duns) Scotus (here in the q. sole) and by St. Thomas according to (his) more common exposition (cf. Gotti, THEOLOG. SCHOLASTICO-DOGM., tome I, tr. 2, q. 4, d. 5, § 3). However, certain Thomists, especially on account of (what St. Thomas says in) QUODLIBETALS., 11, 5, want to argue, that the Angelic (Doctor) teaches, that God is in act and truly in imaginary spaces; which seems to us improbable.

III. Alexander of Hales, SUMMA., p. I, q. 10, m. 3. — Bl. (now St.) Albertus (Magnus), here in a. 21. — (Bl.) Peter of Tarentaise, here in q. 3, a. 3. — Richard of Middleton, here in a. 1, q. 4. — Durandus (of Saint-Pourçain), here in p. I, q. 2. — (Bl.) Dionysius the Carthusian, here in q. 2.

ARTICLE II

On the ability of the Angels to move through place.

Consequently, concerning the second Article there is asked, namely, concerning an Angel's change[1] (of place), and, about this, three (questions) are asked.

First, there is asked, whether an Angel can move locally without a body.

Second, there is asked, whether (an Angel) moves through a medium [per medium], and/or (does) not.

Third, whether (an Angel) passes through [pertranseat] a medium by a sudden movement [motu subito], and/or by a successive one [succesivo].

QUESTION I

Whether an Angel can move locally without a body?

As much as regards the first, that an Angel cannot move without a body, is shown in this manner:

1. (St.) Bernard (of Clairvaux says) ON THE CANTICLE OF CANTICLES:[2] « To run about and to pass [transire] from place to place belongs to naught but bodies »: therefore, if it befits an Angel, it befits (him) not but through an assumed body.

2. Likewise, it seems *by reason*, because what moves, either moves per se, or per accidens;[3] but an Angel does not move *through himself* locally, since that is proper to bodies, and a thing per se is in the latter alone, which it is in properly: therefore, if (an Angel) moves, this is per accidens. But what moves per accidens, is moved by some movement, such as a sailor moved by a ship: therefore, it seems, that an Angel cannot be moved, except with a body moved, and thus an assumed body.

3. Likewise, everything which moves, moves on account of indigence;[4] but in the blessed Angels there is no indigence: ergo etc.. *If you say*, that (they move) on account of our indigence: therefore, with our indigence excluded, it does not seem, that an Angel can move: if, therefore, our indigence gives no virtue to the Angel, it is clear that etc..

4. Likewise, « everything which is moved, differs from the mover », just as the Philosopher proposes;[5] but an Angel

---

[1] The Vatican edition, together with codex cc, reads *ability to move* [mutabilitate] for *change (of place)* [mutatione].

[2] Sermon 5, n. 2.

[3] Cf. Aristotle, PHYSICS, Bk. V, text 1; Bk. VIII, text 27 (ch. 4), and ON THE SOUL, Bk. I, text 37 ff. (ch. 3).

[4] Cf. Aristotle, ON THE MOVEMENT OF ANIMALS, ch. 4 ff. (ch. 6 ff.), where he establishes the end of movement in the pursuit of some good.

[5] PHYSICS, Bk. VIII, text 27 ff. (ch. 4); but word for word it is found in Averroës' Commentary (on the same). In that text, Aristotle recollects what he has taught in diverse places, especially in PHYSICS, Bk. VII.

is not distant from itself: therefore, an Angel is not moved by itself nor by another: therefore, it can not move except by moving another, such as by moving a body.

ON THE CONTRARY: 1. In the first (chapter of St. Paul's Letter)[1] to the Hebrews (there is said): *They are all administering* [administratorii] *spirits, sent on account of them* etc.; but they execute some ministry without a body, such as suggesting [suggerere] good (works), and (things) of this kind: therefore, they can move without a body.

2. Likewise, (St. John) Damascene (says):[2] « Immediately they are found where the Divine Nod commanded (them to be), by the swiftness of (their) nature [velocitate naturae] »: if, therefore, velocity is a disposition to movement, from their own nature they are mobile.

3. Likewise, an Angel is in one place only and he is there, where he works: therefore, his virtue either is constrained to one (place) alone, or if it is not constrained, neither is (his) substance constrained to one place. But he cannot be in many (places)[3]: therefore, when he is in one place, he is in potency to another (place). But what is in potency to one does not come to be in act in that, except through a movement according to place: ergo etc..

4. Likewise, that it moves without an assumed body, is shown *through (what is) similar* in the soul. For a soul, having been stripped from the body, is born locally into Heaven and/or descends into Hell; but it is established, that a soul does not assume another body than its own: therefore, it moves without a body, therefore, for an equal reason (so does) an Angel.

5. Likewise, an Angel can be in the Empyrean (Heaven) without a body, for an equal reason (he can also be) on Earth: therefore, if through the same force, through which he is at rest on Earth, he makes himself be on Earth or transfers (himself to Earth),[4] therefore, it seems, that (he does so) without a body.

CONCLUSION

An Angel can move both without a body, and with an assumed body: without a body by crossing a place delimitively, but with an assumed body circumscriptively.

I RESPOND: It must be said, that an Angel, just as Scripture says, has (the ability) to move itself [habet moveri]. Moreover, he moves not only by an assumed body, but also not with an assumed body, since it is of no less liberty or virtue or nobility (to move) without a body, than it is (to move) with a body.

Moreover, for an understanding of the objections it must be noted, that just as there is a *'being in a place'* [esse in loco] or a *'belonging to a place'* [esse locale] in a twofold manner — just as Master (Peter) touches upon in the text[5] — namely, because *one is circumscribed* and because *one is delimited*, and *properly* that which is circumscribed belongs to a place, but the other *in a certain manner* belongs to a place, (and) *in a certain manner* (does) not: thus *'to move through place'* [moveri per locum] in one manner is 'to bear oneself [ferri] from place to place' through the circumscription (of the place), and in this manner it belongs only to bodies; in another manner *'to move'* is less properly *'to go across'* [transire] according to *delimitation*, and in this manner it belongs to spirits. *Properly*, therefore, an Angel does not move through the circumscription (of a place), except by an assumed body, *less properly* an Angel moves through the delimitation (of the place) even without a body.

1. From this is clear the response to the first objection, and[6] (St.) Bernard accepts *"to run about"* and *"to pass"* [transire] according to the property of place, which is *circumscription*.

2. To that, therefore, which is asked, whether (an Angel moves) <u>per se</u> or <u>per accidens</u>; it must be said according to the aforesaid distinction[7] concerning movement, that according to the *first* movement a spiritual (being) does not move except <u>per accidens</u>, by some movement. For just as a sailor, with the ship moved, moves, so a spirit, with the body moved, in which it is. As much as regards the *second* movement, just as an Angel through himself and without a body is delimited by a place, so through himself is he transferred, such that (he moves) without another moving, nor through another movement. Moreover, (St. John Damascene) objects concerning the first movement only, which <u>per se</u> befits a body alone.

3. To that which is objected, that everything which moves, moves on account of indigence; it must be said, that that is true in a natural movement, in which a nature does not move except through an appetite for some thing, which (appetite) posits an imperfection in the nature — because a nature, with its perfection had, is at rest — but it is not true in a voluntary movement, in which someone moves either on account of acquiring (something) else,[8] or to demonstrate (his) virtue, just as a soldier moves in a stadium. — *And/or* it must be said, that that is true in every movement, accepting *"indigence"* generally for *"its own* indigence" and *"another's"* and *"its own"* as much as regards that of which the privation posits an *imperfection*, and/or of that which the privation does not posit an imperfection, but a *limitation*;[9] and in this manner it is in the Angel. For an Angel, wanting to work something on Earth, needs to pass over to the Earth, because he cannot at once be in Heaven and on Earth on this account,

---

[1] Verse 14, in which text the Vulgate reads *sent to minister* [in ministerium missi] for *sent* [missi]. — Next, for *they execute* [exsequuntur], which we have restored from codices P Q bb and edition 1, the Vatican edition had badly *they pursue* [consequuntur]. Then, after *good (works)* [bona], the same Vatican edition, together with codex cc, insert *and reveal (things) hidden away* [et revelare secreta].

[2] ON THE ORTHODOX FAITH, Bk. II, ch. 3. For *they are found* [inveniuntur], which is in the original text, and in codices P and Q and edition 1, the Vatican edition reads (the entire sentence in the singular, with) *it is found* [inveniuntur].

[3] Supply. together with the Vatican edition: *together* [simul].

[4] The sense is: if an Angel can rest on Earth without a body, and consequently (be there) by his spiritual force alone, it follows, that by his spiritual force alone he can also transfer himself to Earth.

[5] In chapter 6.

[6] For *and* [et] the Vatican edition, with ed. 1, has *because* [quia].

[7] For *distinction* [distinctionem] very many codices have *definition* [definitionem], a few, with the Vatican ed., have *division* [divisionem]; our reading is supported by codd. D P Q R Y & cc and ed. 1, and also by the context. Then, after *concerning movement* [de motu], not a few codices omit *that* [quod], and after a few words the Vatican ed. prefixes *that is* [scilicet] to the words *by some movement* [alio moto].

[8] For *(something) else* [aliud], codex T has *something* [aliquid].

[9] Here he wants to say: "indigence" means in the needy subject either a privation properly said, that is, a need for a *due* perfection, and/or a simple negation of a *further* perfection or a limitation; the former is not in an Angel; but only the latter. — Somewhat further above this, for *and "its own"* [et suam] codex V has *for "its own"* [ad suam].

that he has a finite virtue. And in this manner it is clear, that limitation is not repugnant to the highest [summae] perfection of a creature.

4. To that which is objected, that everything which is moved, differs from the mover; it must be said, that in natural movement it is true, where nothing moves itself, because nothing is reflected upon itself on account of being bound up [alligationem] with matter; but it is not true in the will, which is the instrument moving itself [instrumentum se ipsum movens];[1] and the virtue, which is a substantial spirit, can be reflected upon the substance, and thus the one moving (can) be the same with the one mobile, yet not according to the same: because an Angel is able *to move itself* [habilis est ad moveri] on the part of *that which* belongs either to (its) substance and/or to (its) matter, if it has matter, but (it is able) to *move* (another) on the part of the form, whether of that *by which* it is, and/or of (its) active virtue.

SCHOLIUM

I. Following the footsteps of Master (Peter), the Seraphic Doctor here deals incidentally with the movement of Angels in regard to place. For an understanding of this question there must be presupposed the doctrine concerning the manner, in which Angels are in a place, wherefore we refers the reader to SENT., Bk. II, d. 2, p. II, a. 2, qq. 1-4. Here let it suffice to briefly note, that, though all concede, that Angels are not in a place *circumscriptively*, but *delimitively*, yet from the Angels' *formal reckoning* of presence in a place there is an wonderful disagreement among the schools and even among the authors of the same school. Prescinding from the opinion of those who, with Vasquez, think, that the Angels can also be in an indivisible point, the multitude of opinions can be reduced to these principal positions: namely, the fundament of (their) presence is posited, either in the *application* of the Angels' *virtue*, and/or not in (their) operation, but in the proper and finite *substance* of the Angels. The first sentence is that of St. Thomas, which yet is not explained in the same manner by his disciples; the second of that of (Bl. John Duns) Scotus, Richard of Middleton and many others, which is favored by the manner of speaking of St. Bonaventure. — One must also note the thesis reprobated by the University of Paris in the time of Alexander of Hales: "An Angel in one instant can be in diverse places, and even everywhere, if it wants" (cf. SENT, Bk. II, d. 23, a. 2, q. 3, at the end).

II. That the Angels not per accidens, but even per se move, yet in a manner other than bodies (do), the Seraphic (Doctor) here holds and explains well, with the common sentence of theologians, against the Peripatetics. — In the solution to n. 4 the Seraphic Doctor supposes, that a spiritual substance can be reflected upon itself and move itself, but not according to the same (cf. SENT., Bk. II, d. 24, p. I, a. 2, q. 2, in reply to n. 4; d. 25, p. I, q. 1), and that it moves itself actively on the part of (its) *form*, passively on the part of (its) *matter*. In regard the last, however, he speaks problematically, adding: « If it has matter ». This refers to the sentence, that he himself in SENT., Bk. II, d. 3, p. I, a. 1, qq. 2 and 3, defends as probable, namely, that in the Angels there is to be admitted in some manner the definition of matter and form.

III. Alexander of Hales, SUMMA., p. II, q. 33, m. 1 and 3. — (Bl. John Duns) Scotus, SENT., Bk. II, d. 2, q. 9. — St. Thomas, here in q. 4, a. 1; SUMMA., I, q. 53, a. 1. — Bl. (now St.) Albertus (Magnus), here in a. 2. — (Bl.) Peter of Tarentaise, here in q. 5, a. 1. — Richard of Middleton, here in a. 3, q. 1. — Giles the Roman, here in 2nd princ., q. 1. — Durandus (of Saint-Pourçain), on this and the following qq., here in q. 4. — (Gabriel) Biel, on this and the following questions qq., here in q. 3.

QUESTION II

Whether an Angel moves through a medium?

Second, there is asked, whether an Angel moves through a medium, and/or not. And it seems that (he does move) through a medium.

1. (St. John) Damascene says, that « An Angel quickly passes through [pertransit] by the swiftness and power of (his) nature »: but 'to pass through' is 'to pass [transire] through a medium': ergo etc..

2. Likewise, when an Angel moves from the terminus *from which* to the terminus *unto which*, either he moves in the terminus *from which*,[3] or in the terminus *unto which*; but in the terminus *from which* there is no 'being moved' [motum esse]; but in the terminus *unto which* there is a 'being moved': therefore, since moving [moveri] is a medium between each, it is necessary [oportet] that (the moving) be in an intermediary space.

3. Likewise, that he can move through a medium, seems, because it is certain, that an Angel existing at Paris[4] can be at Rome, by the same virtue and in any intermediary place, and first in one nearer and then in each single place had in consequence to it [consequenter se]: but this is to pass through a medium: ergo etc..

4. Likewise, whensoever between any extremes there falls a medium, which has a natural order to the extremes, it is impossible, that an agent of finite virtue can pass through from (one) extreme into the (other) extreme without the medium, as is clear — because (since) between white and black there is a intermediary [medius] color, it is impossible, that any created agent make black from white, if he does not do (so) through an intermediary color[5] — but between Heaven and Earth according to the natural order there are other intermediary bodies: therefore, it is impossible, that he come to be or move from Heaven unto Earth without the transition of a medium.

---

[1] (St.) Anselm (of Canterbury), ON THE CONCORD OF GOD'S FOREKNOWLEDGE WITH FREE WILL, q. 3, ch. 11: On which account, (the will) can be said (to be) the instrument moving itself. Cf. above d. 17, p. I, q. 2, in reply to n. 4. — Next, after *and thus the one moving* [et ita movens] codex T and X repeat *can* [potest]; the Vatican edition reads *and thus the one moving is the same* etc. [et ita movens idem est].

[2] ON THE ORTHODOX FAITH, Bk. I, ch. 13.

[3] The Vatican ed. adds a third member: *or in intermediary space* [in spatio intermedio]. On this arg., cf. Aristotle, PHYSICS, Bk. VI, text 7 (ch. 1).

[4] The codd. with ed. 1 have *an Angel existing as a Parisian* [Angelus existens Parisius] for *an Angel existing at Paris* [Angelus existens Paris].

[5] See Aristotle, PHYSICS, Bk. Vi, text 32 (ch. 4). — A little further below this, for *come to be* [fiat] the Vatican edition has *come* [veniat]. In codex V there is read *that a movement be made* [quod ... motus fiat] for *that he come to be* [quod ... fiat].

ON THE CONTRARY: 1. (St.) Augustine (says) ON THE LITERAL EXPOSITION OF GENESIS, and Master (Peter) posits in the text[1] (that): God moves a spiritual creature through times, not through places: therefore, although it comes to be from one place into another, this is not through an intermediary place.

2. Likewise, the conclusion has been proven in the sixth (book) of the PHYSICS,[2] that it is impossible, that an impartible [impartibile] move over a magnitude (of space); but an Angel, not having assumed a body, is an impartible: ergo etc..

3. Likewise, it seems *by reason*, because, if (an Angel) does pass through (a medium), therefore either through *simple* (places), or through *composed* (places): if through *composed* (places), therefore, he is composed; if through *simple* ones: but those are infinite in any continuous (space), and it is impossible to pass through infinite (places):[3] ergo etc..

4. Likewise, if through *simple* (places); but from simple (places) there does not come to be any continuum:[4] therefore, that movement will not be continuous, therefore, by passing through them it never passes through a space: therefore, if he moves through a medium, he never arrives at terminus.

5. Likewise, « it is impossible, that something pass through a space greater than itself, if does not first pass through a space less than and/or equal (to itself) »:[5] therefore, if an angelic spirit passes through space, he passes first (through a space) equal to himself and/or less than one greater (than himself). But (that which is) equal to a simple does not make a greater:[6] therefore, there is (movement) in the first transit only, and if it passes nothing, similarly (there is) also none in the second transit, therefore, also none in the third: and in this manner (the Angel) never passes through any amount of space [spatium aliquantum].

CONCLUSION

It is reasonably said, that an Angel moves through a medium.

I RESPOND: It must be noted here, that about this diverse (authors) have spoken in diverse manners.

For certain (authors) have said, that since an Angel is simple, he cannot pass through a medium; whence he moves from (one) extreme into (another) extreme without a medium, and every place, to which he moves, holds itself to him through the manner of (something) immediate. Wherefore change according to place in an Angel is not a movement, but only a change without a medium. — But that position does not seem fitting. For it is certain, that an Angel, which is a guardian of a man, can thus guard (him), that he does not desert him, and without a body it can guard (him): therefore, he can inseparably ac-

company him: therefore, when the man goes through a medium, and the Angel does not desert him, the Angel also equally goes through the medium.

And for that reason there were others who said, that an Angel can move through a medium and without a medium, because his movement is at the nod of his own will, according to the virtue divinely conferred upon him; and for that reason,[7] when he wants, he causes himself (to be) in (one) extreme immediately, and when he wants, he passes over (to that place). And they posit (this) simile, that our intellect can think of Paris and of Rome in a twofold manner: either thus that it immediately thinks of one and afterwards of the other, and/or thus, that (it) first (thinks) of one and afterwards of the way (to the other) and third of the third.[8] And because it is as easy for an Angel to bear himself [ferri], as (it is) for us to think, since he is not bound to a body, they say, that he has self-movement in the former and latter manner [sic et sic]. — But whatever concerns the position, *the example* is not fitting: since the one thinking within himself has a species of Rome and a species of Paris, nor do these have a location [situm] in the soul nor an *order* according to location, nay any is equally present to (the soul's) gaze; and for that reason at its pleasure [ad libitum] it can think of one and the other. But in the thing there is a natural *order* and *location* [situm], and necessarily there lies between one city and the other a medium. And on this account that example is not fitting, nor on this account is there opened for us a way to understanding.

And, since that is in a certain manner intelligible,[9] that (the Angel) bears himself [feratur] *through a medium*, and reason and authority concur [concordat]; for this reason it seems reasonably that it is to be said. But that member (of the division), which says, that (the Angel) can (move) *without a medium*, I judge must be rejected, not because I assert it to be false, but because there is no authority at hand, which says this, and reason does not urge (it), nay it does not grasp (it). However, it is possible, that God granted something to those spiritual (beings), which carnal intellects do not understand. — Therefore, the reasons proving, that an Angel does move through a medium, are to be conceded.

1. To that, therefore, which is objected, that God does not move an Angel through place; it must be said, that the meaning given to the word [vis in verbo] according to the understanding of (St.) Augustine is to be had [facienda est], which is clear from the text. For he said that a spirit does not move through places, because he does not obtain *the properties of place*, namely circumscription and dimension, when it transfers (itself) from place to place; but *the property of time*, which is variation and some innovation, a spirit truly and properly admits. For new affections come upon [succedunt] spirits through nature and thoughts [cogitationes], and

---

[1] Here in ch. 6.

[2] Texts 86-90 (ch. 10), where more reasons are given. Accept the word *impartible* [impartibile] as « an indivisible according to quantity », as Aristotle interprets it loc. cit., and the words *over a magnitude* [super magnitudinem] for the notion: *extended space* [spatium extensum].

[3] Aristotle, ON HEAVEN AND THE WORLD, Bk. I, text 35 (ch. 5), and Bk. III, text 19 (ch. 2).

[4] Aristotle, PHYSICS, Bk. VI, text 1, and METAPHYSICS, Bk. XI, ch. 9 (Bk. X, ch. 10).

[5] Aristotle, PHYSICS, Bk. VI, text 89 (ch. 10). — Next, after *it passes first* [prius transit] codd. aa & bb add *through a space* [per spatium].

[6] Aristotle, METAPHYSICS, Bk. III, text 16 (Bk. II, ch. 4): But all the others in a certain manner, when added, do indeed make a greater ... but a point and a unity least of all ... indeed (one) of this very kind, when added, does not make a greater, but to does produce a more. Cf. ON GENERATION AND CORRUPTION, Bk. I, text 8 (ch. 2).

[7] The Vatican edition and codex cc omit *for that reason* [ideo].

[8] For *of the third* [de tertio], codex I (by a second hand), together with editions 1, 4 and 5, have *of the terminus* [de termino]; a fitting reading. Immediately before this, for *the way (to the other)* [via], the codices, such as F L O V X and Z, have *the other* [alio].

[9] Codex X subjoins *namely* [scilicet].

furthermore [ulterius] they intend and remit these, such that there can truly be an ability to participate [partibilitas] on the part of a form or of a property to be acquired.

2. To that, therefore, which is objected from the Philosopher, that an impartible does not move over a magnitude (of space); it must be said, that the Philosopher proves and concludes concerning an impartible, which has a location [situm] in a magnitude (of space), that it is an impartible and is situated in an impartible (place).[1] This cannot move over a magnitude (of space), because if it moves, it moves to acquire a location [situm]; and what is acquired through movement, it acquired, thus that (one) part (is) after (the other) part; and[2] a an impartible location cannot be acquired, such that (one) part (of it) is acquired after (another) part: and for that reason it is true, that such an impartible cannot move over that magnitude. But an Angel is such an impartible, that he does not have a location in an impartible (place), nor is there a saying, that an Angel is in an impartible place, just as will be clear:[3] and for that reason the demonstration of the Philosopher do not have a place here.

3. 4. To that which is asked: either (an Angel) passes over through simple (places), or through composed ones; it must be responded, that he does pass through *composed* (places), because he is not in a simple place, but in a composed (place); this I suppose for the present, but in its own place it shall be proven.[4] Nor is (this) valid: 'he passes through composed (places), therefore, he is composed', just as neither is (this) valid: 'a soul is in a composed (place), therefore, it is composed':

because thus is (the Angel) in that, that he is not a part in a part, but that whole is simple in every part, yet thus that those parts are one place.

However, it can be said, that if anyone wants to imply (something) of this kind, that even if (an Angel) passes thoroughly through simple (places), yet[5] it does not on this account pass through infinite (places). And this is clear, because if one imagines, that a sphere moves over a plane, it does not touch (it) but in on a point: therefore, it does not touch (it) but through simple (places), yet, neither does it pass through (places) infinite according to act, since that sphere bears itself over the plain and does not rest in any location; and thus it does not rest in any location; and, thus, it is not co-measured in any point, but neither does it number the points in that (plane), but, since it is in a continuous conveyance [in continua latione], it looks back to those indivisible (points) as united, and thus as they are in a continuum; and in this manner, since a continuum is finite according to act and infinite in potency, and (since) that potency is not reduced to act, it (the sphere) does not pass through (places) infinite according to act, because it does not look back to these as numbered according to act. — Yet truly, because the example has (its) calumny, and the saying does not seem to be consonant with the saying of the Philosopher, who says entirely, that an impartible does not move; I adhere more to the prior response.

5. And through that (response) the following one is clear. For it objects, as if an Angel were in a point, which I believe (to be) entirely false, because he would not be in a place, since a point is not a place, nor is he actually [actu] in a continuum. But this entire (matter) will be more clear in the Second Book.[6]

SCHOLIUM

I. To solve this Question there is to be distinguished a twofold movement, namely, *the continuous*, by which the mobile successively deserts through parts *the terminus from which* [terminum a quo] and through parts acquires *the terminus to which* [terminum ad quem], and *the non-continuous* (or discrete), by which the mobile at once deserts the whole *terminus from which*, and immediately acquires the whole *terminus to which*. A *continuous* movement* implies a transit through intermediary places; but a *non-continuous* movement excludes this transit, whence it seems to be a simple *change* of place rather than a *movement*.

St. Bonaventure here speaks only of the movement of the Angels according to their natural manner, prescinding from the Divine Power. About this question three opinions are posited here. The first, which is here and commonly reproved, asserts, that the Angels cannot move themselves except by a *non-continuous* movement; the second, on the contrary, asserts, not but by a *continuous* movement; but the third, in each manner. The third sentence is taught by St. Thomas according to the principles, which he has about the manner, by which Angels are in a place. The second is held by Alexander of Hales and nearly all outside the School of St. Thomas. St. Bonaventure prefers this one, with a certain restriction, and indeed for reasons worthy of our attention. Moreover, (Bl. John Duns) Scotus approves the second opinion with a distinction. For he distinguishes extremes into *continuous* extremes, or those which are included in a whole place, adequate to the virtue of an Angel, and extremes *so distant* [ita distantia], that they have a medium distinct from the extremes. With these supposed, he teaches, that in a place with *continuous* extremes Angels can, if they want, moves themselves or change place, not

having passed through the medium; but in the others « it seems probably, that (they do) not », as he says in SENT., Bk. II, d. 2, q. 12, n. 3.

II. For an understanding of the solution to n. 2 there is to be noted the definition of a *point*, which Aristotle (ON THE SOUL, Bk. I, text 68: cf. footnote 1 on his present page): « A point is a unity having a position ». The whole solution of this difficulty is founded upon the distinction between *the indivisible* (an impartible) *in itself* and *in regard to a place*, such as the point, and indeed between the indivisible *in itself*, but in regard *to the virtue of occupying a place* as if virtually divisible, such as the soul, which, indivisible in itself, coexists with the quantity of the whole body. Aristotle's axiom is true in regard to [relate] to the first divisible (cf. SENT., Bk. II, d. 2, p. II, a. 2, q. 3, and St. Thomas, SUMMA., I, q. 53, a. 1, in reply to n. 1): — The second solution to the last (objection) is constructed from this principle, that when a body is moved through a place composed by means of points indivisible and infinite in *potency*, it is not moved by a *non-continuous* movement form one such point to another. For then it would follow, as St. Thomas observes (loc. cit., a. 2), that « either (an Angel) does not pass through all the intermediary points [omnia media], and/or that he numbers by an act infinite intermediary points; which is impossible ». But it is manifest, that it moves by a *continuous* movement and through intermediary [media] places, which are in *potency* infinite, but *according to act* are united to form one finite continuum.

III. Alexander of Hales, SUMMA., p. II, q. 33, m. 2. — (Bl. John Duns) Scotus, SENT., Bk. II, d. 2, q. 12. — St. Thomas, here in q. 4, a. 2; SUMMA., I, q. 53, a. 2. — Bl. (now St.) Albertus (Magnus), here in a. 23. — (Bl.) Peter of Tarentaise, here in q. 5, a. 2. — Richard of Middleton, here in a. 3, q. 2. — Giles the Roman, here in 2nd princ., q. 2.

---

[1] Or in an indivisible point.° — Under this respect a point is defined by Aristotle as a placed substance or (a substance) having a position. Cf. above d. 25, Doubt 4, p. 447, footnote 2. — For *in an impartible (place)* [in impartibili] the Vatican edition substitutes *according to an impartible location* [situ impartibili], and then reads *For this* [Hoc enim] for *This* [Hoc]; codex R a little above this to the words *that it is an impartible* [quod est impartibilis] prefaces *for* [nam].

[2] Codex T (by a second hand), with edition 1, has *but* [sed].

[3] Here in reply to the last (obj.), and more at length in SENT., Bk. II, d. 2, p.

II, a. 2, q. 3. — A little before this, for *a location in an impartible (place)* [situm in impartibili] codex T, not a few others, and even ed. 1 and the Vatican ed., read *a location in a partible (place)* [situm in partibili].

[4] Cf. loc. citt. in the preceding footnote.

[5] Breaking with very many codd., the Vatican ed. omits *yet* [tamen], in place of which some codd. faultily have *only* [tantum]. Next, after *over a plane* [super planum] in cod. O there is added *for a sphere thus moved does not touch the plane* [sphaera enim sic mota, planum] for *it does not touch it* [non tangit].

[6] In Distinction 2, p. II, a. 2, q. 3.

---

* *Trans. notes*: Here the original Scholium has *manner* [Modus] for *movement* [Motus], which change has been made on account of what follows, namely *non continuous movement* [motus non continuus], and which responds better to the sense of the argument.

° Cf. footnote 2 on the previous page.

QUESTION III

Whether an Angel passes through a medium by a sudden movement, and/or by a successive one?

Third, there is asked, whether an angelic spirit passes through a medium by a sudden movement,[1] and/or by a successive one. And it seems, that (he does so) by a successive one.

1. In any instant he is in the terminus *from which*, and in another instant he is in the terminus *to which*; but between any two instants there falls an intermediary time [tempus medium], and in the midst of these instants there is self-movement [moveri]: therefore, the self-movement of the Angel is in time: therefore, he moves by a successive movement.

2. Likewise, this very (thing) is shown on the part of *space* thus: an Angel, if he passes through a medium in any instant, is[2] in the medium and in the parts of the medium; but it is impossible, that any one (being) besides God and the Body of Christ be together and at any time [simul et semel] in many places: therefore, it is impossible, that an Angel in the same instant be in the whole medium and at the end, therefore, he does not move suddenly: therefore, it is bound to be [oportet] necessarily, that (he moves) in a successive manner.

3. Likewise, this is shown on the part *of the virtue* [a parte virtualis]. Just as the Philosopher would have it [vult],[3] if so great a virtue moves in so great a time, and a greater in a lesser, and the greatest in the least, and the infinite in the now, therefore, according to which the virtue is more powerful, according to this is the movement more swift; but an *instant* exceeds a time improportionably: therefore, also the *virtue*, which moves in an instant, superexceeds that, which moves in a time unto an infinite (degree). But no created virtue superexceeds another unto an infinite (degree), and angelic virtue is created: therefore, since every natural, local movement is successive, it is clear that the movement of an Angel is successive.

4. Likewise, if an Angel moves, therefore, either that movement is *truly a movement*, or *a change*.[4] If (it is) *a change*: therefore, generation, and/or corruption, (is a change), which is established to be false. If (it is) *a movement*; but every movement properly said has a before and after [prius et posterius], and a location and time, and every such is successive: ergo etc..

ON THE CONTRARY: 1. (St.) Augustine in the book, OF FIVE RESPONSES, (says):[5] « A ray (of light) does not arrive more swiftly at nearer places than at more remote places », and it is established that it passes through a medium: therefore, if angelic virtue is not less powerful, but more, it is clear that etc..

2. Likewise, the Philosopher proves, « that if there were a vacuum,[6] there would not be movement »; but the same causes the very space for the Angel, which causes the vacuum for a moving body, because it resists him in no manner, just as neither a vacuum (does): therefore, it seems, that the Angel himself passes through it suddenly.

3. Likewise, everything which moves in a successive manner, is partly in the terminus *from which*, partly in the terminus *to which*;[7] but everything such is partible: therefore, it is necessary, that an Angel be partible, or he does not move in a successive manner.

4. Likewise, everything which transfers itself together and whole together, does not move in a successive manner; but an Angel transfers himself together [simul], since he is entirely simple: therefore, in an instant, and (thus) he does not move in a successive manner.

5. Likewise, a successive movement is composed and an accident,[8] and no composed accident is in a simple subject; but an Angel is simple: therefore, he is not the subject of a successive movement, but the movable is the subject of a movement, ergo etc..

CONCLUSION

An Angel moves through a medium by a successive movement, by reason of the distance of the space and by reason of the finite virtue of the one moving.

I RESPOND: It must be said, that about this some thought in diverse manners.

For certain (authors) said, that because and Angel is simple, and space composed, that both an Angel and its virtue is improportionable[9] to space; and, for that reason, its virtue entirely surpasses [vincit supra] space, to such an extent that suddenly and by an improportionable movement it passes through space, and a movement of this kind is above

---

[1] Very many codices, together with edition 1, have *act* [actu], which reading does not convene with the title of this article.

[2] To the word *is* [est], the Vatican edition adds *together* [simul].

[3] As can be gathered from (Aristotle's), PHYSICS, Bk. VI, text 13 ff. (ch. 2), and Bk. VIII, text 79 f. (ch. 10). — Near the end of the argument, after *natural* [naturalis] codex T inserts *and* [et].

[4] According to Aristotle, PHYSICS, Bk. V, texts 7-9 (ch. 1), every transmutation is either from a non-subject into a subject [a non-subiecto ad subiectum], and/or from a subject into a non-subject [a subiecto in non-subiectum], and/or from a subject into a subject [a subiecto in subiectum]; the first is called "generation", the second "corruption", the third "movement". The first two species of transmutation are comprehended, here, by the Seraphic Doctor under the word "*change*" [mutatio]. On the sentence next cited, that in a movement, properly said, there is a before and after, cf. Aristotle, PHYSICS, Bk. IV, text 99 (ch. 11).

— After the words *If (it is) a movement* [Si motus] the Vatican edition omits *but every movement* [sed omnis motus], and reads the first part as *Thus every movement* [Sic omnis motus].

[5] Question 1, n. 5 (this work is also known as Epistle 102 "to Deogratias"): For as the ray of our eye arrives no more swiftly at (things) nearer, (no) more tardily at (things) further, but happens upon each interval with equal swiftness.*

[6] (Aristotle,) PHYSICS, Bk. IV, text 66 ff. (ch. 8).

[7] Cf. Aristotle, PHYSICS, Bk. VI, text 32 (ch. 4). See also ibid., text 87 (ch. 10), where from the cited he proves, that an impartible cannot move.°

[8] See Aristotle, PHYSICS, Bk. III, text 18 ff. (ch. 3).

[9] Codex T has *improportional* [improportionalis]. Next, for *entirely surpasses* [vincit supra] codex R has *is said to be entirely above* [omnino dicitur esse supra], and a little below this (on the following page) for *But* [sed], the Vatican edition and the other codices, except codex Y and edition 1, have *And* [Et].

---

* *Trans. notes*: St. Augustine speaks in the terms of the optics of his day, which held that the human eye contained its own source of light, by which it illumined all that it saw, thus confounding the intelligibility of light as seen by the eye, with an intelligible light.

° An "impartible" is an "indivisible according to quantity"; a "partible" is a "divisible according to quantity".

nature. — But since it seems difficult to understand, that it passes through a medium, if it is not in many parts of the medium; and to posit, that it moves suddenly and is many parts of the medium, is to posit movement in that, which is in many places together; and this is entirely absurd to say of an Angel, just as the Saints say, and philosophers and Catholic doctors agree in this:[1] for that reason it must be said, that an Angel does not move through a medium suddenly, but successively.

On which account, it must be noted, that in a movement, which is successive by a perfect succession, there is a succession from a fourfold cause: the first is *the distance of the medium*, the second *the resistance of the medium*, the third is *the ability of the movable to participate (in space)* [partibilitas mobilis], the fourth is *the limitedness* [finitas] *of the virtue* (of the one moving), by this, that it properly belongs to a finite virtue to move in time, most of all through a medium.[2] Therefore, it must be conceded, that the movement of an Angel through a medium is not successive by a perfect succession, because there is lacking there *the resistance of space* and *the ability of the movable to participate (in space)*; it is, however, successive by reason of *the distance of the space*, in which it cannot be at once through the whole (quantity), and (by reason) *of the limitedness of the virtue* of the one moving, which does not exceed improportionably the medium, and for that reason it does not cause a movement entirely improportionable to the medium. — And the reasons proving, that that movement through space is successive, are to be conceded. Yet the first reason is a sophistry [sophistica]; but (this sophistry) is dissolved elsewhere, when one deals with the transition of bread into the Body of Christ, where (the reason) has its place.[3]

1. To that, therefore, which is objected, that a ray (of light) does not arrive more swiftly; it must be said, that (St.) Augustine speaks according to the perception of sense,[4] because (our) sense does not perceive, that a ray arrives more swiftly at nearer places than at more remote ones, not because there is not, according to thing, truly a before and after there. Whence, if it be said that a ray moves suddenly, "*suddenly*" [subito] is understood on behalf of "*in an unnoticed manner*" [repente], and (what is) "*unnoticed*" [repentinum] is said (to be) that which has a self-movement in an imperceptible (quantity of) time. — But it can be said in another manner, that light moves suddenly, because the movement of light in a medium is not only a local movement, but is the movement of a diffusion, which is a generation, just as a likeness [idolum][5] is generated

from an object; and because light, at once, is and lights, at once when it is, it generates a splendor, and thus in the same instance; similarly it can be understood of the former (splendor),[6] and thus one after another. Whence if a man, at once, would be and would generate, in the first instant the world would have been full of men. In this manner he who knows no better can respond.

2. To that, therefore, which is objected concerning a vacuum, that if there would be a vacuum, there would not be movement; it must be said, that about this many (authors) have said many (things), the saying of which would be long. Now, however, it can be said, by supporting the Philosopher, that if there would be a vacuum, there would not be successive movement, with "vacuum" rightly understood, according to which I believe the Philosopher understands (it), that it means simply "*privation*": if there is[7] a vacuum there — where we understand a vacuum (to be), there we understand nothing to be — therefore, there would not only be missing the resistance of a body, but there would also be *no distance* there; but where there is no distance, there is no near nor far; but where there is local movement, there is necessarily an approach and/or withdrawal [elongatio]: therefore, if there is a vacuum, there is no movement, not on account of a defect of *resistance*, but *of distance*. But since the medium, compared to the *Angel*, has a reckoning of distance, because it truly causes a distance between the extremes (of any movement), for that reason there suffices for the succession whatsoever kind of (medium) for the sake of distance; but where there is a *vacuum*, there is no distance, and this is necessarily required beforehand for a local movement. For the ability of the movable to participate (in space) and the limitedness of (its) virtue do not cause a succession, unless there is a before and after in the magnitude (of the space), over which there is (a movement), or in that which is acquired through the movement.

3. To that which is objected, that that which moves in a successive manner, is partly in the terminus *from which*, and partly in the terminus *to which*; it must be said, that in a successive (movement), where there is a full succession, there is a positing of (this) part and (that) part, both as much as regards *the substrate magnitude*,[8] and as much as regards *the moved magnitude*, and as much as regards *the acquired disposition*. Because a natural movement to a location [ad situm], is a movement according to form in a certain manner; but in the movement of an Angel there is no succession according to a omnimodal completion, and, for that reason, (there is) no

---

[1] Codices A and I, and not a few others, prefix to the word *agree* [concordat] the word *now* [modo].

[2] The first and second cause of a succession in movement is hinted at by Aristotle, PHYSICS, Bk. IV, text. 66 ff. (ch. 8), where from the defect of this twofold condition there is shown, that a successive movement is impossible in a vacuum. The two other causes of succession are briefly touched upon this the arguments of this Question. — In a manner repugnant to the context, the Vatican edition and codex cc here add *Fifth can be the limitedness and limitation of the movable* [Quinta potest esse finitas et limitatio mobilis].

[3] SENT., Bk. IV, d. 11, p. I, q. 5, in reply to n. 4, where he deals more at length concerning this difficulty.

[4] The Vatican edition, together with not a few manuscripts, has less well *the perceptibility of sense* [perceptibilitatem sensus], and then *that* [quod] for *because* [quia]. In favor of our reading stands codices A T and V, in favor of *because* [quia] there is also codex X.

[5] The Greek εἴδωλον (an image, simulacrum, appearance) signifies here in general the species expressing the thing. — A little before this for *but is a movement* [sed est motus] codices A and T have *but also a movement* [sed etiam motus].

[6] Understand: *splendor* [splendore]. — For *the former* [illo] the Vatican edition, together with not a few codices and edition 1, has *another* [alio].

[7] For *if there is* [si est] codices A G I S T Y aa and ff, together with edition 1, have *but there is* [sed est], codex H has *wherefore, if there is* [quod si est], the Vatican edition has *if there were* [si esset], codex X has *because* [quia] and then omits *a vacuum there* [vacuum ibi].

[8] This and those which follow, have been more clearly stated at the end of the solution to the preceding objection. — On movement to a location [motu ad situm] and on movement according to form [motu ad formam], which are next mentioned, cf. here in Doubt 2. Movements according to form in *the broader* sense are said (to be) those, through which a thing is either disposed to the reception and/or corruption of a substantial form, or through which it receives or loses its own substantial form. And they are five: *generation* and *corruption*, *augmentation* and *diminution* (which body respect quantity) and *alteration* (which respects quality and in itself comprehends *intension, remission* and *alteration* as subspecies). In *the stricter* sense, generation and corruption are excluded. Understand a "movement to a location" as a "local movement" or a "change according to place". Cf. Aristotle, ON THE PREDICAMENTS, ch. "on *Movement*", and PHYSICS, Bk. V. texts 9-17 (ch. 1 f.). — Next, after *in a certain manner* [quodam modo] in codex Y there is added: *because completion belongs to a form* (i. e. the form is complete), *when it arrives at its own natural place* [quia completio est formae, cum pervenit ad suum locum naturalem].

(movement)[1] according to all these differences, but only according to a priority and posteriority of the magnitude *over which*. — What, therefore, is said, that it is partly in the terminus *from which*, partly in the terminus *to which*, this is not according to a diversity of the parts of the movable, but is only through (its) access and recess.

4. To that which is objected, that (the Angel) transfers himself together whole; it must be said, that although on his own part he transfers himself together whole, yet he does not transfer himself together upon the whole (medium), on account of the distance of the medium, in which whole (distance) he cannot be at once.

5. To that which is objected, that a composed accident cannot be in a simple thing; it must be said, that it is true concerning the composed, which has parts according to act; but of the composed, which is in a succession, it is not true. For just as a successive duration can be in an Angel, according to which it remains, by this, that concerning that (duration) there is never but a *now*, so a successive movement can be in (an Angel), according to which he bears himself; and this indeed has nothing unfitting with it. With these (things) seen, the objections are clear.

For the summary [summa] of the aforesaid is, that an Angel does "move" without an assumed body, and that he moves in a medium or through a medium, and that he moves by a successive movement, though not one composed by an[2] omnimodal succession, as has been said before.

SCHOLIUM

I. Every *continuous* movement is also *successive*, but not *vice versa*. For a *successive* movement is opposed to an *instantaneous* one; but a *continuous* to a *non-continuous* or discrete one. — The first opinion, mentioned in the text, is rightly reproved, because from it there would follow, that an Angel could be at once in a delimitive manner in many places adequated to himself. Therefore, the Seraphic (Doctor) teaches, that an Angel moves not *in an instant*, but by a successive movement, which, however, differs from the successive movement of bodies, just as is explained in the body (of the Response) and in the reply to n. 3. St. Thomas (here in q. 2, a. 3; and in the SUMMA, I, q. 53, a. 3) also denies, that the local movement of the Angels, whether it be *continuous* or *non-continuous*, can come to be in the same instant; but in regard to a *non-continuous* movement, which he upholds for the Angels, he uses other reasons. (Bl. John Duns) Scotus, according to his distinction, mentioned in the preceding Scholium, thinks, that only a simple *change of place* within the sphere of a place adequated to the Angel, can come to be in an instant. — In the solution to n. 1 it seems worthy of observation, that the Seraphic Doctor had already conjectured, that the movement of light does not come to be in an instant. The other solution (which he gives) to the same objection is approved by St. Thomas, in his SUMMA., I, q. 53, a. 2, in reply to n. 2.

II. (Bl. John Duns) Scotus, SENT., Bk. II, d. 2, q. 11. — St. Thomas, here in q. 1, a. 3; SUMMA. , I, q. 53, a. 3. — Bl. (now St.) Albertus (Magnus), here in a. 24. — (Bl.) Peter of Tarentaise, here in q. 5, a. 3. — Richard of Middleton, here in a. 3, q. 3. — Giles the Roman, here in 2nd. princ., q. 3.

DOUBTS ON THE TEXT OF THE MASTER

DOUBT I

In this part, there occur [incidunt] doubts about (Master Peter's) text and first concerning this which Master (Peter) says: *nor does It have a dimension, just as a body (does)* etc.. For he seems to speak badly, because there is said in the third (chapter of the Letter of St. Paul) to the Ephesians:[3] *So that you may be able to comprehend with all the Saints, what is the length, breadth* etc., and the Gloss expounds that of God.

I RESPOND: Master (Peter) speaks *properly* and according to the letter, but the Apostle speaks *metaphorically*. Whence those words are expounded in a multiple manner. For in God there is a *length* of longanimity, a *breadth* of charity, a *sublimity* of mercy, and a *depth* of justice or of wisdom as much as regards God's judgements.

DOUBT II

Likewise, is asked concerning this which (St.) Augustine says in the text, that *He moves a corporal creature through time and place*. For that division of (St.) Augustine's is bad, first, because no change according to time is posited by the Philosopher. *And again*, his division does not seem sufficient, because the Philosopher posits six species of movement.[4]

I RESPOND: It must be said, that according to the Philosopher every species of movement is reduced to this twofold movement, namely to movement to *a location* [motum ad situm], and to movement according to *form* [motum ad formam]; moreover, (St.) Augustine understands through "movement according to *place*", a movement to *a location*, which belongs to a perfect and complete being, without waste [deperditione] and/or innovation about the quality or property of the substance, to the extent that by this (property the movement) regards a location, unless it equally regards a form.[5] But he comprehends "movement according to *form*", which is subdivided into [per] five species, under a change according to *time*, on this account, that of itself it means a measure, variable and (belonging to) a variable thing.[6] Whence every change, which is according to the absolute and intrinsic properties of a thing, whether according to the corporal

---

[1] Supply, together with codices P Q and W: *there is ... movement* [est motus], or with codex T read: *it does not pass* [non transit].

[2] For *one composed by an* [composito] the Vatican edition, together with codex cc, read *with a posited,* [posita].

[3] Verse 18. — The Gloss, which is next mentioned, is found in (Nicholas) of Lyra, on the cited passage.

[4] ON THE PREDICAMENTS, ch. "on *Movement*": But the species of movement are six: generation, corruption, augmentation [augmentum], diminution, alteration and change according to place. Cf. here q. 3, p. 663, footnote 8, where you will also find explained, those things which are next referred to in the solution of this Doubt, concerning the doctrine of Aristotle.

[5] Cf. Aristotle, PHYSICS, Bk. VIII. texts 55-60 (ch. 7).

[6] Aristotle, PHYSICS, IV, text. 98 ff. (ch. 11).

qualities or according to the spiritual ones, such as are affections in souls, he calls a "change according to *time*". And thus is clear the reason of the division and (its) sufficiency.[1]

DOUBT III

Likewise, is asked concerning this which (Master Peter) says, that *a spiritual creature moves through time*. For it seems that he says (something) false, because a spiritual creature is measured by the aevum, since he is perpetual: therefore, if he moves, he does not move through time, but through the aevum. — Likewise, the angelic intellect is deiform, just as the Philosopher would have it [vult],[2] therefore, it understands in an instant; for an equal reason it is also affected: therefore, not in time. — Besides, time through (a consideration of what is) prior is the measure of the movement of the first mobile (sphere): therefore, that alone is measured by time, which underlies that movement; but such is not an Angel nor its movement: ergo etc..

I RESPOND: For the present it must be noted,[3] that "time" in one manner is said *properly*, and in this manner it means the measure of a changeable thing, inasmuch as (it is) changeable, yet under the reckoning of a continuum; and, since the movement of the first mobile (sphere) is the most evident and continuous movement among all; for that reason "time" in this manner is said properly to be in the first mobile (sphere), just as in a subject, in which it is first and in which it first appears. In another manner, "time" is said (to be) the measure of *any changeable thing*, according to which (it is) changeable, whether it moves instantaneously or continuously; and in this manner it is not only in the movement of the first mobile (sphere), and in those which underlie that, but also in every created (thing), about which a variation accedes; and in this manner it is in the Angels. And through this the objections are clear.

For what is objected concerning the aevum, it must be said, that *the aevum is the measure of the Angels as much as regards (their) substantial "being"*, which is invariable and incorruptible; but *time* (is their measure) as much as regards the *properties*, which vary, and certain ones suddenly, certain ones successively, just as some affection is revealed [patet][4] in the Angels, to be intended through nature little by little [paulative]. And, thus, all the other (objections) are clear.

DOUBT IV

Likewise, is asked concerning this which (St. Augustine) says, that *there is the same wisdom in the two, neither greater nor lesser*. For he seems to say the false, because wisdom is an accidents and a quality of the wise man, and an accident is numbered through substance.[5]

I RESPOND: It must be said, that regarding this some wanted to say, that the same created wisdom was in two wise men, and this they give to understand through two suppositions. One is, that species of a thing in the soul do not differ through essence from the thing outside (the soul). The other supposition is, that two wise men can know the same (thing), namely, one enunciable, which is said (to belong) to each one [dictum est singulare]. And this last is in need of no persuasion; but they show the prior one, that it is the same, because it is cognized through the same things, through which the thing has "being".[6] If, therefore, it has "being" through its own form, therefore, also a 'being cognized'; and the form of the thing is truly in the soul, and since the intellect is knowing through that form, and it happens that some two know and think of entirely the same (thing), that is not only a true form, but also one (form). And that this is true, they persuade through this, that if the form can, according to truth, produce a completely similar form in matter and cause it to be in the matter of another, why [quare] it is not similar in the soul, which is more able to receive (it)? Wherefore, they also say that (St.) Augustine thought this. Whence, they say, that wisdom is not according to the manner of the other properties. — But this position deviates from (St.) Augustine, because (St.) Augustine would have it,[7] and the other Saints (too), that to be in many entirely distinct does not befit one and the same creature except through a miracle. *And again*, that position[8] has been founded upon a falsehood: because if the truth of a donkey would be in a soul, why would the soul not be said to be a donkey? *And again*, if the truth (of a donkey) would be there,[9] still, it would not be the same, because no form, when it generates itself, generates itself entirely the same, but of necessity an essence is plurified in the one generating and the one generated, except that (Essence) which (is) in God: and (therefore) it is not valid for the proposed.

---

[1] This doubt is also solved by Bl. (now St.) Albertus (Magnus), here in a. 20, and by (Bl.) Peter of Tarentaise, here on the text, where he also treats of the following two Doubts.

[2] Cf. BOOK OF CAUSES, prop. 10, where there is taught, that the first intelligences, which are nearer to the One, the True, (and) the Pure, are of greater virtue. — Yet this expression seems to be better attributed to Dionysius (the Areopagite), who in divers passages of ON THE DIVINE NAMES, v. g., ch. 4, § 22, and ch. 5, § 8, calls the Angels, "deiform" (θεοειδεῖς). St. Bonaventure too, in SENT., Bk. II, d. 3, p. II, a. 2, q. 2, in the 1st opposed argument, cites Dionysius as the author of this expression.

[3] For more on the aevum and time, cf. SENT., Bk. II, d. 2, p. I, throughout.

[4] *Is revealed* [patet] for *seems* [videtur]. — The Vatican edition reads *just as it is clear that some affection in the Angels is intended by nature little by little* [patet ... paulatim intendi aliquam affectionem] for *just as some affection is revealed in the Angels, to be intended through nature little by little* [patet ... paulative intendi aliqua affectio]. Without reason and without the authority of the codices the Vatican edition changes *little by little* [paulative] into *little by little* [paulatim], even though it is established, that the word *little by little* [paulative] was familiar to the writers of the Middle Ages, according to Du Cange's, GLOSSAR. AD SCRIPTORES MEDIAE ET INFIMAE LATINITATIS..

[5] See above d. 23, a. 2, q. 1, p. 411, footnote 6. Cf. also (St. Severinus) Boethius, ON UNITY AND THE ONE. — For *substance* [substantiam] the Vatican edition and edition 1 has *subjects* [subiecta].

[6] Bl. (now St.) Albertus (Magnus), here in a. 27, expresses this sentence in these words: Just as Aristotle says, in (his) FIRST PHILOSOPHY, Bk. VII, text 20 (Bk. VI, ch. 6), that if forms are absolute by the things, to which they belong, as Plato used to say, wherefore nothing is then known through them; therefore, if a form, which is in the soul, is other than the form, which is in the thing, the thing with not be known through it. — A little above this, at *but they show the prior one* [sed prius ostendunt], codex T has *the first* [primum] for *the prior one* [prius]. A little further below this, for *it happens* [contingat] nearly all the codices and edition 1 faultily read *it does not happen* [non contingat]; we say faultily, because, with the particle *not* [non] inserted the force of the argumentation is corruption. Codex I before *it happens* [contingat] repeats *since* [cum].

[7] Epistle 187 to Dardanus, n. 10, and ON THE CITY OF GOD, Bk. XXII, ch. 29, n. 3. Cf. also (St. John) Damascene, ON THE ORTHODOX FAITH, Bk. II, ch. 3, and the opusculum, which once was attributed to St. Anselm, ELUCIDARIUM, Bk. I, ch. 3. — After a few (words), for *again* [itergum] the Vatican edition, together with codex cc, has *for that reason* [ideo].

[8] The Vatican edition, together with codex cc, adds *is founded and* [fundatur et].

[9] Codex Y adds *that is, (the truth) of the thing in the cause* [scilicet rei in causa]. Somewhat below this before *it is not valid* [non valet] the Vatican edition, together with some codices, inserts *therefore* [ideo].

And, for that reason, there is a second manner of speaking, which (St.) Augustine understands of uncreated Wisdom, which is in wise men and *reaches everywhere on account of Its own cleanliness*.[1] — But, since (St.) Augustine intends to posit an example among creatures, it still does not seem that this is according to his understanding. *And again*, he himself says, that that wisdom is equal in two (men), who are equally wise, but not in others: therefore, it seems that he is speaking of the habit (of wisdom).

And, for that reason, there is a third manner, which he says concerning the unity (of wisdom) through conformity. — But, that still did not seem to be sufficiently said, because, then, there would be greater (wisdom) in two than in one, just as is clear among two rich men, who are conform and equal in (their) riches.

On this account, it must be said, that a similitude or intention in the soul has (an ability) to be compared [habet compari] to *the soul*, in which it is, and to *that* of which it is. And, since it has (its) rise from that of which it is, and is said regarding that; for that reason, the similitudes of one thing are many in souls, because they lead unto one and the same truth, and one (similitude is) as much, as two, hence it is, that[2] through a comparison to *that* of which they are, they have a unity, nor are two greater than one, similarly neither (is one) wisdom (greater than two wisdoms); but in a comparison to *the souls*, which cognize through them, they have a plurality, and two are more than one. And, for that reason, it is clear, that one cannot posit entirely a simile, because things differ by intention or similitude;[3] but in God, in Whom they do not differ, it is clear, that One can be in Many. And, thus, all the other objections are clear.

DISTINCTION XXXVIII

Chapter I

Whether the Knowledge and/or Foreknowledge of God is the cause of things, and/or the other way around?

Now, therefore, returning to the proposed, let us pursue what has been taken up [coepto insistamus]. Above[1] it has been said, that God's Foreknowledge is only [tantum] of (things) future, but of all, both of the good and of the wicked; however, (His) Knowledge and/or Wisdom (is) not only [modo] of (things) past,[2] but also of (those) present and future, nor only [tantum] of (things) temporal, but also of (those) eternal, because God knew Himself. Here there arises a question not to be ignored [dissimulanda], whether, namely, (His) Knowledge and/or Foreknowledge is *the cause* of things, or whether things are the cause of God's Knowledge and/or Foreknowledge. For God's Foreknowledge seems to be the cause of those which are beneath [subsunt] to Him, and to cause the necessity of their coming forth [eveniendi], because neither were any (things) going to be, unless God foreknew them, nor can they not come forth, after God will have foreknown them. Moreover, if it is impossible, that they not come forth, because they are foreknown, therefore, (His) Foreknowledge Itself, by which they are foreknown, seems to be their cause of coming forth. But it is impossible, that they not come forth, when they have been foreknown, because if they did not come forth, when they are foreknown, God's Foreknowledge would fail. But God's Foreknowledge cannot fail. Therefore, it is impossible,

that they not come forth, since they have been foreknown. Thus, therefore, (His) Foreknowledge seems to be the cause of those, which have been foreknown. This same is also said of (His) Knowledge, namely, that, because God knew some, for that reason they are. To which sentence (St.) Augustine seems to attest in the fifteenth book, ON THE TRINITY,[3] saying thus: « God did not cognize these *in some time* [ex aliquo tempore]; but all (things) temporal (that were) going to be and even in regard to these, for what and when we were going to ask from Him, and whom and concerning which things, either He was to hear [exauditurus] and/or not hear, He foreknew beforehand *without a beginning*. Moreover, each and every creature, both spiritual and corporal, not because they are, for that reason did He know them, but they are for this reason, because He knew (them). For He was not ignorant of those which He was going to create: therefore, because He knew, He created, not because He created, did He know; nor did He know created (things) otherwise than (they were) to be created. For nothing accedes to His Wisdom from them, but with those existing, just as it was opportune [oportebat] and when it was opportune, the Former remained as It was. Whence, in Ecclesiasticus (it is written):[4] *Before they were created, all have been known* [nota] *to Him, thus too after (all) have been consummated* ». — Behold with these words (St.) Augustine seems to hint, that God's Knowledge and Foreknowledge are the cause of those which are made, when he says, that they are for this reason, because God knew (them). The same too, in the sixth book,[5] does he seem to say: « Though », he says, « the seasons withdraw and approach, nothing withdraws and/or approaches God's Knowledge,

---

[1] Wisdom 7:24, where the Vulgate reads: *but She stretches everywhere on account of Her cleanliness* [attingit autem ubique propter suam munditiam].

[2] The phrase *hence it is, that* [hinc est, quod] is a certain repetition of the particle *for that reason* [ideo], located a little above this. — A little before this for *and one (is) as much* [et tantum una] the Vatican edition alone has *one is as much* [est tantum una].

[3] The sense is: the same things have diverse intentions or similitudes in diverse souls, and diverse things have diverse intentions in the same soul. — A little before this, to the word *intention* [intentioni], the Vatican edition prefixes explicitly *by* [ab], and edition 1 has *by their own* [sua], codex T *by their own* [a sua]. — This doubt is also solved by Bl. (now St.) Albertus (Magnus), here in a. 27, and by St. Thomas, (Bl.) Peter of Tarentaise, and Richard (of Middleton), here on the text.

NOTES ON THE BOOK OF SENTENCES

[1] Distinction XXXV, ch. 1.

[2] Thus, in codices A B and E and in editions 1 and 6; in the others, there is read not well *of (things) future* [de futuris]. Then, breaking with the codices and edition 1, the Vatican edition, together with very many editions, has *are the causes of God's Knowledge* [sint causae scientiae etc.] for *are the cause of God's Knowledge* [sint causa scientiae etc.].

[3] Chapter 13, n. 22. — A little before this the Vatican edition, together with a few editions, has *will have known* [noverit] for *knew* [novit].

[4] Ecclesiasticus 23:29. The Vulgate reads: *For to the Lord God, before they were created, all have been known: thus too after (time has been) perfected He looks back upon all* [Domino enim Deo, antequam crearentur, omnia sunt agnita: sic et post perfectum respicit omnia].

in which He knew all which He made through It. For those which have been created, are not for this reason known [sciuntur] by God, because they have been made, but rather they have been made for this reason, because they are immutably known by Him ». — And he also seems to signify, that God's Knowledge is the cause of those which are made, saying, that not for this reason did God know [novisse] them, because they were made, but for this reason (have they been) made, because God knew them. And, for this reason, God's Knowledge and/or Foreknowledge seems to be the cause of those which He knew.

Which, if It is thus, It is, is therefore, the cause of all evils, since all evils are known and foreknown by God; which is far from the truth. For if God's Knowledge and/or Foreknowledge would be the cause of evils, God would at any rate be the Author of evils, which is thoroughly false. Therefore, God's Knowledge and/or Foreknowledge is not the cause of all which are beneath Him.

Nor are future things the cause of God's Foreknowledge: for though they were not going to be, unless they were foreknown by God, yet they are not foreknown for this reason, because they are going to be. For if this were, then of That, which is eternal, something would exist as (Its) cause other than It, diverse from It, and the Creator's Foreknowledge[1] would depend from creatures, and a created would be the cause of the Uncreated. Yet Origin ON THE LETTER (OF ST. PAUL) TO THE ROMANS[2] says: « Nothing shall be on account of this, because God knows it (is) going to be, but because it is going to be, for that reason it is known by God, before it is made ». This seems to obviate the aforementioned words of (St.) Augustine. For here there seems to be signified, that future things are the cause of (God's) Foreknowledge; but in the former, that (His) Foreknowledge is the cause of future things.

Therefore, desiring to remove from the midst that which seems (to be) a repugnance, we say, that future things are to no extent the cause of God's Foreknowledge and/or Knowledge, nor for that reason are they foreknown and/or known, because they are going to be and/or have been made; thus expounding what Origin says, 'because it is going to be, for that reason it is known by God, before it is made', that is, 'what is going to be, is known by God, before it is made, nor would it be known, unless it were going to be', so that no cause is noted there, except *that without which* it would *not* be made.[3] Thus too do we say, that God's Knowledge and/or Foreknowledge is not the cause of those which are made, unless (as) the such, without which they are not made, if, however, we only refer "knowledge" to a "*being known*" [ad notitiam]. However, if by the name for knowledge there is included also good pleasure and disposition, then It can rightly be said (to be) the cause of those which God makes. For in these two manners, as has been touched upon before, above,[4] God's Cognition and/or Knowledge is accepted, namely for a being-known [notitiam] alone, and/or for a being-known and a good pleasure [beneplacito] together. In this manner, perhaps, (St.) Augustine accepted (it), saying: They are for this reason, because He knew (them), that is, because it pleased the Knower (to know them), and because Knowing (them) He set (them) in order [sciens disposuit]. And this sense is assisted from this, because (St.) Augustine deals only with the good there, namely with creatures, and with those which God makes, all of which He knew not only by (His) Knowledge, but also by (His) good pleasure and disposition. Therefore, in this manner is God's Cognition accepted there, to not only signify being-known, but also God's good pleasure.

However, God knows[scit] and foreknows [praescit] evils, before they come to be, but by their being-known alone, not by (His) good pleasure. For God foreknows

and foretells even those which He Himself is not going to cause [non facturus], just as He foreknew and foretold the infidelity of the Jews, but did not cause (it). Nor for that reason, because He foreknew (it), did He drive them to the sin of infidelity, nor would have he foreknown and/or foretold their evils, if they were not going to be had. Whence (St.) Augustine ON (THE GOSPEL OF ST.) JOHN (says):[5] « God », he says, « foreknowing (the things that are) going to be, He foretold through the Prophet the infidelity of the Jews, but He did not cause (it), nor would He have foreknown their evils, unless they had them. For not for this reason does He drive anyone to sin, because He foreknew [praenovit] the future sins of men; for He foreknew [praescivit] their sins, not His own. And for that reason if those which He foreknew (were to going to belong) to them, do not belong to them,[6] He did not truly foreknow (them). But because His Foreknowledge cannot fail, without doubt no other, but they themselves sin, whom God foreknew were going to sin. And for that reason, if they willed to do not evil, but good, (those who were) going to do no evil would have been foreseen by Him who knew, what anyone is going to do ». — With these words there is openly shown, if we diligently attend (to them),[7] that God's Foreknowledge is not the cause of the evils, which He foreknows, because He does not foreknow them as One (who is) going to cause (them) nor as His own, but (as belonging) to those who are going to do and/or have them. Therefore, He foreknew these by (their) being-known alone, not by the good pleasure of an author. Whence one is given to understand, that God, conversely, foreknows good (things) as His own, as those which He is going to do, so that in[8] foreknowing them there was together (their) being-known by Him [ipsius notitia] and the good pleasure of (their) Author.

CHAPTER II

Whether God's Foreknowledge can fail?

But regarding that, which has been said above, namely that God's Foreknowledge cannot fail [falli non posse], it was customarily opposed by certain (authors), in this manner: 'God foreknew this one (was) going to read, and/or something of this kind; but it can be, that he does not read: therefore, it can be otherwise than God foreknew, therefore, God's foreknowledge can fail'. — Which is entirely false. Of course it can (be) that something does not come to be, and, yet, that it has been foreknown to come to be; yet, for this reason God's Foreknowledge cannot fail, because, if that were not to come to be, neither would it have been foreknown by God to come to be.

But they still urge the question saying: either it can come to be [fieri] otherwise, than God has foreknown, or not otherwise; if not otherwise: therefore, necessarily all shall turn out (as God foreknows it) [cuncta eveniunt]; if, however, otherwise: therefore, God's Foreknowledge can fail and/or be changed. But it can come to be otherwise, because it can come to be otherwise, than it comes to be; but thus does it come to be, as it has been foreknown: therefore, it can come to be otherwise, than it has been foreknown. — To which we say, that that expression, namely: "it can come to be otherwise, than God foreknew", and (those) of this kind, can cause a multiple understanding, to (signify): "what God foreknew cannot be", and "it is impossible, that what God has foreknow not be", and "it is impossible, that all the foreknown which come to be, not be", and (expressions) of this kind. For these can be understood *conjointly* [coniunctum], so that

---

[1] Thus, in the codices and edition 1; in the Vatican ed. and others, there is had *Knowledge* [scientia]. Immediately before this, (in the Latin, and after this in the English), the Vatican edition and editions 4, 5, 7, 8, and 9, have *would depend* [depederet] for *would depend* [penderet].

[2] Book VII, n. 8 (on Romans 8:30).

[3] Codices A B and C and edition 1 (ed. 5 in the margin) have *it is made* [fit] for *it would be made* [fieret]; codex E has (the subjunctive) *it is made* [fiat].

[4] Distinction XXVI, ch. 2.

[5] Tract 53, n. 4; but only according to its sense.

[6] Thus codices A C D & E, edd. 1 & 6, and Augustine's original;

in the others there is read *are not* [non sunt] for *do not belong to them* [non sunt ipsorum]. Then codices A B C and E and all the editions, except the Vatican, have *He did not foreknow (them) as true* [non vera ille praescivit] for *He did not truly foreknow (them)* [non vere ille praescivit], but contrary to the original and codex D. Then, contrary to original and edition 1, the Vatican edition, together with the others, has *are sinners* [peccatores esse] for *were going to sin* [peccaturos esse].

[7] Codices B C D and E and edition 1 have *understand (them)* [intendamus], codex A has *look into (them)* [inspiciamus].

[8] The Vatican ed. & the other edd., except ed. 1, breaking with the codd., have *by foreknowing* [praesciendo] for *in foreknowing* [in ... praesciendo].

there is an implicit condition, and *disjointly*. For, if you understand: "it cannot come to be otherwise, than God has foreknown", that is, so that each cannot be together, namely that 'God thus will have foreknown it to come to be, and it comes to be otherwise', you understand (it) truly. However, if you understand (it) through a *disjunction*, as to say, that 'this cannot turn out otherwise, than it did turn out and[1] in that manner God foreknew (that it was) going to be', it is false. For it can turn out otherwise, than it did turn out, and yet God foreknew that (it was) going to be in this manner. Similarly, also the other de-termination, namely, 'it is impossible, that that not turn out, which God foreknew, and/or though He foreknew (it)'; if you understand (it) *conjointly*, you speak the truth; if *disjointly*, a falsehood. Thus, also, even this: 'it is im-possible, that everything which comes to be not have been foreknown', that is, that each cannot be together, namely, 'that it come to be', and '(that) it not have been foreknown', this is the true sense. However, if you say, that 'God could not foreknow everything which comes to be', it is false. For He could cause it not to come to be, and thus it would not have been[2] foreknown.

COMMENTARY ON DISTINCTION XXXVIII

On the causality, infallibility and necessity of the Divine Foreknowledge.

Now, therefore, returning to the proposed, let us pursue what has been taken up etc..

THE DIVISION OF THE TEXT

This is the second part of this whole part, in which the Divine Knowledge is dealt with. For having termi-nated the first part, in which It was dealt with as much as regards (Its) substance and in general, here It is dealt with as much as regards (Its) standard of measure [modus]. And since the standard of measure of a noble cognition is twofold, namely, (its) *certitude* and *perfection*, or (its) infallibility and immutability, for that reason this part has two parts. In the first (Master Peter) deals with the infallibility or certitude of the (Divine) Foreknowl-edge, but in the second of Its immutability or perfec-tion, there (in the Thirty-Ninth Distinction,[1] where he says): *Moreover, it is customarily asked, whether God's Knowledge* etc..

The *first* part pertains to the present Distinction, in which Master (Peter) intends to ask and determine, whether the Divine Foreknowledge infallibly posits the foreknown. And this Distinction has two parts. In the *first* part, re-turning to the proposed on account of the digression made before, he briefly summarizes (what have been) predetermined. In the *second* he prosecutes his own principal proposed (question), there (where he says): *Here there arises a question not to be ignored* etc.. And *this* part has two (parts). In the first Master (Peter) in-quires, whether (God's) Foreknowledge posits the foreknown through the manner of a cause, and/or of an effect; in the second, whether through the manner of necessity, and/or of contingency or infallibility, in the last chapter, there (where he says): *But regarding that, which has been said above* etc.. The first part has two (parts). In the first he oppose for each side, namely, that (His) Foreknowledge is the cause of the foreknown and also (its) effect, for and against. In the second he solves (it), there (where he says): *Therefore, desiring to remove from the midst* etc.. Similarly, the sec-ond also has two (parts): in the first he opposes, in the second he solves (it), there (where he says): *To which we say, that that expression* etc..

TREATMENT OF THE QUESTIONS

For an understanding of the present Distinction two (questions) are principally asked.

First concerning the Divine Foreknowledge as much as regards (Its) causality.

Second as much as regards (Its) necessity.

And concerning the first, two (questions) are asked.

First, there is asked, whether the Divine Fore-knowledge is the cause of things.

Second, whether It is caused by things.

---

[1] The codices and editions 1, 2, 3, 5, 7 and 9, omits *and* [et].
[2] Thus codd. B C & D; in the other codd. and in all the edd., there is read *thus not to have been* [esse] for *thus it would not have been* [esset].

NOTES ON THE COMMENTARY
[1] Supply, together with the Vatican edition: *below in Distinction 39* [infra distinct. 39].

ARTICLE I

On the causality of the Divine Foreknowledge.

QUESTION I

Whether the Divine Foreknowledge is the cause of things?

And, that It is the cause of things, is shown thus.

1. (St.) Augustine (says) in the fifteenth (book), ON THE TRINITY:[1] « Things are going to be for this reason, because God knew them ».

2. Likewise, *by reason* in this manner: every that, which antecedes another, and with it posited, there is posited the other, is the cause of the latter — this is clear through the definition of a cause[2] — but the Divine Foreknowledge precedes every future (thing), and again posits the future (thing), in respect of which (positing) it is: therefore, (God's) Foreknowledge is (its) cause.

3. Likewise, every thing either is from [a] *God*, or from *nature*, or from *free will* [libero arbitrio], and I accept these causes broadly, insofar as they comprehend cause and fortune; but no thing ca be from nature nor from free will, except with God working: therefore, every thing or every future (thing) is from God. But it is not from God acting unless (He is acting) according to art and cognition: ergo etc..

4. Likewise, everything which is known, in some manner is in itself, and/or in its cause,[3] therefore, what is foreknown by God is in God as in a cause; but everything which is in God, is from God: therefore, every future foreknown is from the Divine Precognition as from a cause: ergo etc..

5. Likewise, everything which is known, either is known through (its) *cause* or through (its) *species*, or through (its) *effect*: therefore, if God foreknows, therefore (He does so) in any of these manners. Not through an *effect*, because an effects follows; not through a *species* or similitude, because that is together (with the thing) and/or even after the thing, of which it is the similitude: therefore, through a *cause*, therefore the Divine Foreknowledge is the cause of the foreknown.

ON THE CONTRARY: 1. God is the cause of none except through (His) Will; but He foreknows many, regarding which He has no will: ergo etc.. *Proof of the middle*: He foreknows, that you are lying, and, yet, there is no saying, that He wants you to lie: therefore, He is not the cause of that.

2. Likewise, if (His) Foreknowledge is a cause, either by reason of (Its) *knowledge* [ratione scientiae], or by reason of (Its) *antecession* [ratione antecessionis]. Not by reason of this,[4] that it is *before* [prae], because (that) does not mean but an order. Similarly, not by reason of (Its) *knowledge*, because God cognizes more, which He will never do: therefore, It is in no manner a cause.

3. Likewise, if (His) Foreknowledge is the cause of the foreknown, since He foreknows evils, God will be the cause of evil; but this is false.

4. Likewise, if It is a cause, since He communicates (His) Foreknowledge to some thing to be created, consequently [per consequens] He communicates the causality in respect of that; but this is impossible: ergo etc..

5. (St.) Anselm (of Canterbury), ON THE CONCORD OF (GOD'S) FOREKNOWLEDGE AND FREE WILL[5] says, that « there is as much as the saying of (this): "if God foreknows (it), it will be", as (there is of) this: "if it shall be, of necessity it will be »; but in the latter [hic] there is noted no causality: therefore, neither in the former [ibi].

CONCLUSION

The Divine Foreknowledge and Knowledge always conveys a causality in some manner, but not always in respect of the foreknown.

I RESPOND: It must be said, that "foreknowledge" means a precognition of the future. Therefore, there is a speaking of "foreknowledge" either as much as regards *the thing signified*, or insofar as *it is signified through this name*.[6] If as much as regards the reckoning of *the name*, thus it does not signify in the reckoning of a cause; if as much as regards *the thing conveyed*, thus it means a cause; but yet not always in respect of *the foreknown* or of (something) future.

For the "future" is in a threefold difference. For

---

[1] Chapter 13, n. 22. See here the text of Master (Peter), ch. 1.

[2] Concerning which, see above d. 5, a. 2, q. 2, 2nd argument of the fundament, and ibid., Doubt 3.

[3] The Vatican edition, with edd. 4 & 5 reads: *is in the one knowing as in its cause* [est in sciente ut in sua causa]. Our reading is confirmed from the solution to the last argument. — Next, for *as in a cause* [ut in causa] codices D E and K have *as its cause* [ut sua causa], the other codd., with edd. 1, 2 & 3, have *as a cause* [ut causa]. — On the minor proposition: *but everything which is in God, is from God*, see above Distinction XXXVI, ch. 2 f., and St. Bonaventure's COMMENTARY on the same, a. 1. q. 1, and also a. 3, q. 1 f. — Then, after *every future foreknown is* [omne futurum praescitum est] the Vatican ed. adds *necessarily* [necessario], and immediately after this cod. T substitutes *Cognition* [cognitione] for *Precognition* [praecognitione].

[4] The Vatican edition reads thus: *Not by reason of (Its) antecession, because that which is "before", does not mean* etc. [Ratione antecessionis non, quia hoc quod est ante, non dicit etc.]

[5] Question 1, ch. 2: Wherefore when I say, that if God foreknows something, it is necessary, that it is going to be; which is the same as if I say: "if it will be, of necessity it will be".

[6] Namely "*foreknowledge*" [praescientia], which term signifies naught but the antecession of knowledge. Similarly Alexander of Hales (SUMMA., p. I, q. 24, m. 2) says: (God's) Foreknowledge of approbation can mean a cause by reason of the *approbation* understood, not by reason of the *antecession*, which is understood through (the suffix) "ante-".

in a certain manner (something future) is, that of which *God* is the whole cause, such as are those which are created; in a certain manner, that of which *a creature*, such as a will, is the whole cause, such as are defects and sins; in a certain manner, that of which *God and a creature* are together the cause, as are natural works and moral works, because God cooperates with the creature.

According to this, it must be understood, that in respect of the first future (thing) the Divine Foreknowledge is the cause and the whole cause; but in respect of the second future (thing) It is neither the cause nor the whole one, because (that) does not have an *efficient* cause, but a *deficient* one;[1] it is, however, the cause of its opposite; however, in respect of the third It is a cause, but not the whole one. Therefore, it must be conceded, that the Divine Knowledge and/or Foreknowledge is the cause, in some respect, of future (things). However, if It is accepted in its generality, it must be said, that the Divine Foreknowledge always conveys some causality, but not always in respect of the foreknown, as for example when the foreknown is an evil. And in this reckoning proceed the arguments showing, that It is not a cause.

1. To that, therefore, which is first objected, through the word of (St.) Augustine, that It is a cause of the foreknown; it must be said, that (St.) Augustine speaks of the knowledge of things or the good, which proceed from God.

2. To that which is objected, that a cause is that which precedes and posits another: it must be said, that '*to posit another*' is in a twofold manner, namely[2] according to a *production*, and/or according to a *consequence* [consecutionem]; and what posits (another) according to a *production* is truly a cause in being [in essendo], however, what posits (another) according to a *consequence* is not a cause in being, but only in (its) following after [in consequendo].

3. To that which is objected, that that which is from free will is from God; it must be said, that it is true of that which is from *efficient* free will, vices and sins are from *deficient* (free will).

4. 5. To that which is objected, that of necessity every future (thing) is known by God through (its) cause; it must be said, that, just as has been touched upon above[3] concerning the (Divine) Cognition of evil, in every cognition there is an assimilation; but nothing is assimilated to God but that which is from Him: and for that reason in every act of God's Cognition [in omni cognitione Dei] there is causality. And when,[4] indeed, it is in respect of that which means *entity* simply, It is a cause and an idea in respect of that; but when there is a precognition in respect of a *privation*, then the reckoning of causality and of an idea is in respect of (its) opposite. Therefore, it must be said, that for this, that something be cognized, it is necessary, that it and/or its opposite have 'being' in *a thing* and/or in *a cause*. Moreover, not only the opposite of the evil, even the very *will* (for it), which is the principle of evil, is in God as in a cause; yet the evil is not in God as in a cause, neither <u>per se</u> nor <u>per accidens</u>, because the reckoning of causing is changed, just as will be said afterwards.[5] — And there is a manifest example of this. If a craftsman will work on a piece of knotty wood [materiam nodosam], which was not suitable [idonea] for the reception of an image [speciei], he would foreknow, that there is going to be a defect in the image, but (that it would) not (be) from himself. Similarly, it must be understood in God and free will, which causes a vice in a work, so long as it does not conform itself to and obey God working; but for this reason it is sufficient, that the opposite of the evil, or that from which the evil is, be in God as in a cause, for this, that it be foreknown.

SCHOLIUM

I. In this and the following Distinction a most difficult matter is treated of, concerning the Divine Foreknowledge and Knowledge, concerning which the (First) Vatican Council (Dogmatic Constitution on the Faith, ch. 1) said: « All (things) are bear and revealed to His eyes (Hebr. 4:13), even those which are going to be by the free action of creatures ». On this question there have been agitated among catholic theologians most grave controversies, which, though they have arisen from a difference of opinions concerning the concord to be established between divine grace and free will, yet in this passage they have found a most ample field for disputations. For so great is the difference between the Divine Cognition and our own, so much does the immense *height of the riches of the Wisdom and Knowledge of God* (Rom 11:33) exceed our capacity, that the difficulties and obscurities are more augmented for us, the more one descends to special questions and quasi recedes from the immense and most simple unity of that most pure Act, which is at once the Divine *Knowledge* and *Substance*. But yet, all catholic theologians do suffi-

ciently agree in the chief *principles*, employed for the explanation of the same Faith. While in human cognition there are really distinguished *the one cognizing* and *the one cognized*, *the reckoning* of cognizing *the power* of cognizing and *the act* of cognizing, all concede, that « in God the Intellect understanding, and That which is understood, and the intelligible Species, and the very Act of understanding [ipsum intelligere] are entirely one and the Same » (St. Thomas, SUMMA., I, q. 14, a. 4; cf. St. Bonaventure, d. 39, a. 2, q. 1) — (all also concede) that the same Divine Essence is *the very Light* illumining all, in comparison of which « every cognition, by which we knew any creature in itself, can not unworthily be said to be a "night" » (St. Augustine, ON A LITERAL EXPOSITION OF GENESIS, Bk. IV, ch. 23) — (likewise all concede) that the Divine Knowledge neither is caused nor arises from a thing; for that reason It does not depend from it nor does It run about cognizing an effect *from (its) cause*, but rather It cognizes the effect *in the cause* (St. Thomas, loc. cit., a. 7, in reply to n. 2) — (and likewise all agree) that the Divine Knowledge cognizes things under the measure of eternity, both equally (those which are) past, present and future. But we conceive

---

[1] Cf. (St.) Augustine, ON THE CITY OF GOD, Bk. XII, ch. 7, and ENCHIRIDION ch. 23, n. 8. — Next for *opposite* [oppositi] codex T has *supposit* [suppositi].

[2] Codex T has *either* [vel].

[3] Distinction 36, a. 3, q. 1.

[4] Not a few codices, together with editions 2, 3, 4, and 5, have transformed the word *when* [cum] into *yet* [tamen]. A little further below this, for *but when* [sed cum] not a few codices and the aforesaid editions have *but yet* [sed tamen], the Vatican edition has *however, if* [si autem].

[5] Distinction 46, q. 3, where there is expounded the difference between 'leading unto an end' through the manner of a *cause*, and/or through the manner of *chance* [casus], and/or through the manner of an *occasion*, and in what manner in chance, which is dealt with here, the reckoning of causing is changed, inasmuch as, that is, it passes from the reckoning of a cause properly said to the reckoning of an occasion. — Next, for *will work* [operetur] codices A and H have *would work* [operaretur], and then for *on* [super] the Vatican edition, together with codex cc, has *according to* [secundum].

things under differences of time and space, and *by intuiting* we cognize naught but things *present* imperfectly, but *by remembering* we know *somethings past* still more imperfectly, and *by conjecturing* we divine *a few(thing) future*, rather than know (them).

II. This one, most simple Knowledge (which is) God's, « is in itself in no manner diversified, though It is allotted diverse names. For inasmuch as It is cognoscitive of all possibles, It is said (to be the "Divine) *Knowledge*" or "*Cognition*"; inasmuch as it is cognoscitive of all which will be in the universe, it is said (to be "God's) *Vision*"; in as much as It is cognoscitive of all which will come to be rightly, It is said (to be "His) *approbation*"; inasmuch as it is cognoscitive of those which are going to be, It is said (to be "God's) *Foreknowledge*" or "*Foresight*" [praevisio]; inasmuch as It is cognoscitive of those which are to be done by God Himself, It is said (to be "His) *disposition*" (or "*arrangement*"), inasmuch as It is cognoscitive of those (acts) which are to be rewarded, It is said (to be the "Divine) *predestination*", but inasmuch as It is cognoscitive of those (acts) which are to be damned, it is said (to be "His) *reprobation*" » (St. Bonaventure, BREVILOQUIUM, p. I, ch. 8). — First of all one is to note the threefold species of the Divine Knowledge, commonly received in the Schools and explained by the Seraphic Doctor below in d. 39, a. 1, q. 3 (cf. here in Doubt 3, and d. 39, a. 1, q. 2; and d. 36, Doubt 3), namely the Knowledge *of simple understanding*, which is terminated ad things merely possible and/or even ad « a sole event » (here in Doubt 3), the Knowledge *of approbation*, and the Knowledge *of vision*. The Knowledge *of approbation* « connotes the complacency of the (Divine) Will » (d. 39, a. 1, q. 2), and (its) « effect and goodness » (here in Doubt 3, and in d. 36, Doubt 3), whence It is not in respect of evils; It is also said (to be) *practical* (d. 40, a. 1, q. 2, in reply to n. 2, and in Doubt 3). For that reason the Knowledge *of vision*, which is of all which ever were, are and will be, extends Itself to more than the Knowledge of approbation (does); and not a few theologians (such as Gotti) subdivided the Knowledge *of vision* into the Knowledge *of approbation* and *reproof* [improbationis]. — But one must chiefly observe, that properly speaking, there is to be attributed to God a *knowledge* rather than a *foreknowledge*. For in a *foreknowledge* there is noted not only the order of (what is) prior, but also a certain *distance* between the knowledge of the one cognizing and the coming forth of the thing [rei eventum], since time is conceived as a certain *medium* between each. However, in truth this medium does not exist between God's cognition and the cognized, wherefore « there is (nothing) future in respect of the Divine Knowledge, which, existing in the moment of eternity, holds Itself to all by means of being present [praesentialiter] » (St. Thomas, SUMMA CONTRA GENTILES, Bk. I, ch. 67. Cf. St. Bonaventure, below in d. 39, a. 2, a. 3; St. Thomas, DE VERITATE, q. 3, a. 12).

III. In regard to the Question proposed here all theologians agree on these (points): 1. That God's « Knowledge, according to the reckoning of knowledge, does not mean any *causality*, otherwise every knowledge would be a cause; but inasmuch as It is the knowledge of a Craftsman working things, in this manner It has the reckoning of a cause in respect of the thing worked through (the Divine) Art ... It is clear also,

that the principle of causality consists within the (Divine) Will » (St. Thomas, here on q. 1, a. 1). 2. In regard to God's causality in respect of (things) *future* all admit the distinction posited here in the body (of the Response), that of some (things) God is the whole and sole cause, of some He is a cause together with secondary causes (cf. below d. 45, a. 2, q. 2, in reply to n. 1), of some, namely of evils, He is in no manner to be said to be the cause. 3. Prescinding from (His) Cognition of evils, very many say, that God's Knowledge, to the extent that It has the Will conjoined (to It), « in Its generality always conveys some causality » (here in the body of the Response) and that « in every act of God's Cognition [in omni cognitione Dei] there is a causality » (cf. below d. 46, q. 4, in reply to n. 4). However, there is a controversy concerning *the manner* of this causality, whether it is not only *directive* (concerning which there is no doubt), or whether, moreover, (it is) proximately and immediately *effective*, which is denied by many, lest it prejudice the liberty of the created will. 4. In respect of *an evil*, formally taken as a *privation*, no *efficient* cause is granted, but only a *deficient* one, and to no extent is there in God any cause of an evil, whether an efficient, or exemplary, or final one; yet in *the cognition* of an evil the reckoning of *causality* is implied in a multiple manner. For there is here manifestly valid a causality *improperly* said, which is called "(the causality) of consequence", concerning which the solution to n. 2 deals, and which is explained below in a. 2, q. 1. For this does not posit a thing *by producing*, but simply *by inferring* the consequence, namely, either from the coming forth the knowledge, and/or from the knowledge the coming forth. But the reckoning of causality is implied in other manners in the (Divine) *Cognition*, namely in respect of the good, of which an evil is the corruption, just as is explained here in the reply to nn. 4 and 5. See more on this in d. 39, a. 1, q. 2, in the Scholium.

For the illustration and confirmation of (these) conclusions serve (these) words of St. Thomas (DE VERITATE, q. 2, a. 14): « Knowledge inasmuch as (it is) knowledge does not mean an active cause, just as neither (does) form inasmuch as it is form ». « Between God's Knowledge, which is the cause of a thing, and the thing caused itself there is found a twofold medium; one on the part of God, namely, the Divine Will; the other on the part of the things themselves, as much as regard certain effects, namely, second causes, by means of which things come forth [proveniunt] from God's Knowledge, but even intermediary (causes); and for that reason things known by God proceed from His Knowledge through the manner of will and through the manner of second causes, not is it necessary [oportet], that in all (things) they follow the manner of knowledge ».

IV. Alexander of Hales, SUMMA., p. I, q. 24, m. 2. — St. Thomas, on this and the following question, here in the q. sole, a. 1; SUMMA., I, q. 14, a. 8. — Bl. (now St.) Albertus (Magnus), here in a. 1; SUMMA., p. I, tr. 15, q. 61, m. 2. — (Bl.) Peter of Tarentaise, here in q. 1, a. 1. — Richard of Middleton, here in q. 2. — Giles the Roman, here in 1st princ., q. 1. — Henry of Ghent, SUMMA., a. 36, q. 4. — Durandus (of Saint-Pourçain), here in q. 1. — (Bl.) Dionysius the Carthusian, on this and the following question, here in q. 1. — (Gabriel) Biel, SENT., Bk. I, d. 35, q. 6.

QUESTION II

Whether the Divine Foreknowledge is one caused by things?

Second, there is asked, whether the Divine Foreknowledge is one caused by things. And that (It is) so, is shown thus.

1. Origin, ON THE EPISTLE (OF ST. PAUL) TO THE ROMANS,[1] says: « Because something is going to be, for that reason it is known by God, before it comes to be ». "*Because*" [Quia], therefore, either means a cause *of (it) being* [causa essendi] or *of (it) being consequent* [consequendi]. If *of (it) being consequent*, just as it follows: 'this is going to be, therefore, (it is) foreknown', so the other way around [e converso]: therefore, just as he says: "because it is *going to be*, for that reason it is foreknown", thus

he ought to have said the other way around: "because *it is known*, for that reason it is going to be"; and (yet Origin)[2] denies this in the text: « Not on this account shall something be, because God knows (it) »: therefore ("because") means a cause *of (it) being* [causa essendi].

2. Likewise, it seems *by reason*, because with it understood, that God foreknows nothing, something "future" (in itself)[3] can (still) be understood, but not the other way around: therefore, the latter is the reason and the cause of the former.

---

[1] See, here, the text of Master (Peter), ch. 1, where you will also find the exposition of the text from Origin cited here. — Somewhat below this, after *thus conversely* [ita e converso], there is wanting in very many codices *therefore* [ergo].

[2] Understand: *Origin* [Origenes]. For the words, which follow, are

Origin's, loc. cit.. — Codex Z has *Master (Peter) denies* [negat Magister], even though he does not deny the converse.

[3] Codex M and edition 1 read '*that something is going to be*' [aliquid futurum esse] for *something "future"* [aliquid futurum]. — The sense of this argument is this: in the hypothesis, that God foreknows nothing,

3. Likewise, this argument is a good one: 'this one lies, therefore, God foreknew, that he lies': therefore, there is some habitude of a topic [habitudo localis][1] (being argued) there, and none can be found except (that) of a cause to an effect. But God is not the cause of a lie [mendacii]: therefore, it remains, that the future (thing) is the cause of (His) Foreknowledge.

4. Likewise, whatever two so hold themselves, that they are consequent to one another, either both are caused by a third, or one is the cause of the other; but thus do those two hold themselves, namely, 'that he lies', and 'that God foreknows', and there is no saying, that both are caused by a third: therefore, one is the cause of the other.

ON THE CONTRARY: 1. (St.) Augustine (says):[2] « For God did not for this reason know (the things) which were created, because they were made ».

2. Likewise, it seems by reason, that It is not caused by things, because every cause is more noble than its own effect:[3] if, therefore, the Divine Foreknowledge is caused by any thing, since the Divine Foreknowledge is uncreated, and the thing created, therefore, the created (would be) more noble than the uncreated.

3. Likewise, the Divine Foreknowledge is eternal: therefore, since the thing is temporal, if It is caused by things, the temporal is the cause of the Eternal; and since a cause if prior to the effect,[4] therefore, the temporal (is) prior to the Eternal.

4. Likewise, if things are the cause of (God's) "Foreknowledge", either by reason of (Its) principal signified [principalis significati], or by reason of what It connotes [connotati]; if by reason of (Is) principal signified, since that is the Divine Essence, therefore, things are the cause of God; if by reason of (what It) connotes, since the connoted are the things themselves, then they are their own cause.[5]

CONCLUSION

The Divine Foreknowledge, only according to a reckoning of inferring and speaking, has to some extent a cause among things.

I RESPOND: Some[6] wanted to say, that "cause" is said in a twofold manner: *properly*, and *commonly*;

properly, as that which gives "being" to another; and thus things are in no manner the cause of the Divine Foreknowledge. In another manner, a "cause" is *commonly* said (to be) that, without which a thing is not, and in this manner it is said (to be) a "*sine qua non*" cause; and in this manner, because God's Foreknowledge is not, if things are not going to be, for that reason in this manner they are said (to be) a cause. — But, since this name "*cause*" always conveys a honorableness, in respect of that which it is said (to be) a "cause", and a certain super-imposition [superpositionem]; for that reason that does not still seems to be entirely sane to say, that (a future thing)[7] is a "*sine qua non*" cause. *And moreover*, that does not solve (the matter) regarding the authority of Origin, because he himself denies the converse.[8]

And on this account it must be said in another manner, that there is an accepting of "*cause*" according to a threefold manner, namely according to a reckoning of *being* [essendi], and according to a reckoning of *inferring*, and according to a reckoning of *saying*. Therefore, I say, that according to the reckoning of *being* the (Divine) Foreknowledge can be the cause of some foreknown, though not entirely,[9] but in no manner the other way around. According to the reckoning of *inferring*, they are mutually causes, because they mutually antecede and are consequent; and the antecedent is the cause of the consequent.[10] According to the reckoning of *saying*, the future (thing) is the cause of (God's) Foreknowledge, and not the other way around. For foreknowledge is said (to be) "*knowledge before a thing*". It is established, therefore, that It conveys an order to the posterior; and since, if a known would always be present, there would be *knowledge*, but not *foreknowledge*; for this,[11] that It be said (to be) a "*foreknowledge*", comes from the futurition of the thing. And thus does Origin understand (it), and (thus) the first (objection) is clear.

3. To that which is objected third concerning the habitude of the topic (being argued), it must be said that it is a topic (argued) a convertibili.[12]

4. To that which is objected last, it must be said, that it has a contrary example [instantiam] in the proposed, and because in God[13] alone there is a contrary example, for that reason it is to be borne (in mind). But the reason for this is, because God's Foreknowledge is in respect of the true, and in respect of every true; for this reason *It posits* and *is posited*. And, because It can be in respect of the true, which is not from Him

---

one can still understand something "future"; but in the hypothesis, that there is nothing future, a foreknowledge neither can be understood nor can be hand: therefore (something) future is the cause of the Foreknowledge. Or, as Alexander of Hales says, SUMMA., p. I, q. 24, m. 3: Likewise, that with which it posited, the one is posited, and that with which it is removed, the other is removed, this is in some manner the cause of the latter; but with a future thing posited, It is posited, and with a future thing removed, the Foreknowledge is removed: therefore, the future thing is the cause of God's Foreknowledge.

[1] By the name, "topic" (τοπός),* the Scholastics signify the seat of the argument and/or that, by which the argument is drawn to the proposed question, and a topic consists in the habitude of some terms among themselves. Thus, v. g. a topic (argued) from a cause, which is next mentioned by the Seraphic Doctor, is the habitude of a cause to its effect.

[2] ON THE TRINITY, Bk. XV, ch. 13, n. 22. See there the text of Master (Peter), ch. 1.

[3] Avicenna, METAPHYSICS, Bk. VI, ch. 3: A cause is more worthy than the one caused.

[4] Aristotle, POSTERIOR ANALYTICS, Bk. II, ch. 17 (ch. 14).

[5] Which would be absurd to say. For nothing itself generates itself, as Aristotle says in ON THE SOUL, Bk. II, text 47 (ch. 4).

[6] Among whom is the Master of the Sentences, here in ch. 1.

[7] Understand: "a thing" or "a future (thing)", and/or substitute *they are* [sint], that is "future things", with codex R for *it is* [sit].

[8] Namely, of the proposition: 'because something is going to be, for that reason it is known by God'. The converse is: 'because it is known by God, for that reason is going to be'.°

[9] Codex Z has *though not for every one* [licet non omni]. We prefer *of all* [omnium] for *entirely* [omnino].

[10] Supply with cod. O: *according to the reckoning of inferring* (not of being) [secundum rationem inferendi]; for: 'God foreknows this, therefore, it shall be', concludes equally well as: 'this shall be, therefore, God foreknows (it)'. This is what in the solution to n. 4 he calls the *It posits and is posited* [ponit et ponitur]. Cf. Aristotle, ON THE PREDICAMENTS, ch. "On the Prior", where this priority is called the priority « of those which are convertible according to being a consequence (of one another) », and (where) this example is proposed: « If there is a man, the saying, by which we say, that there is a man, is true; and it is convertible; for if the saying, by which we say that there is a man, is true, there is a man ».

[11] Codex R has *for this reason, for this* [ideo ad hoc]; codex W has *for this, therefore* [ad hoc ergo].

[12] Richard of Middleton, here in q. 3, in reply to n. 1 solves a similar objection in this manner: I say, that it is true (namely, that there is some habitude of a topic being argued there); but that habitude is the habitude of a relative to a relative, just as this (is): 'there is a foreknowledge: therefore, something is foreknown', and conversely, and I speak of a relation according to reckoning. — For *third* [tertio] the codd. with the edd. have falsely, *second* [secundo].

[13] From cod. X we have restored *God* [Deo], which word all the other codd. & ed. 1 omits, reading *in (Him) alone*, and for which the Vatican ed. has *Him* [hoc].

---

* *Trans. notes*: Here the Latin reads locus, which I have translated throughout as *topic*.
° Here the note faultily has *will be going to be* [erit futurum] for *is going to be* [est futurum].

according to this that it is beneath (Him), and not the other way around;[1] for this reason It is neither the *cause*, nor *is It caused*. Therefore, (God's) Foreknowledge is in respect of the *true*, because (It is) Divine; (It is) in respect of *every true*, because nothing lies hidden to God: for this reason It *posits* and *is posited*. *Again*, because It is a knowledge, which means simply a being known [simplicem notitiam], for this reason *It does not cause*; because (It is) Divine, for this reason *It is not caused*. For that reason, It posits and is posited, and does not cause, nor is caused [non causat, nec causatur].

SCHOLIUM

I. The occasion for this Question was given by the words of Origin, cited by Master (Peter) and St. Bonaventure (here in the 1st opposed argument), and also repeated by the other Fathers (of the Church) according to (their) sense, that to future things it seems that a certain causality in respect of the Divine Knowledge be attributed. On the understanding of these sentences there has been much dispute from that time down to our own age.

The first solution, which is (that) of Master (Peter) himself, distinguishes between a cause in the *proper* sense, which manifestly implies a dependence of the Divine Knowledge upon future things and can to no extent be admitted, and a cause in the *improper* sense, namely, a "*sine qua non*" cause, by which there is expressed not so much a cause, as rather an *occasion, disposition* or *some prerequisite*, which not a few think can be admitted in this matter. This solution of Master (Peter)'s does not seem to be sufficiently sane to the Seraphic (Doctor); with whom Alexander of Hales (SUMMA., p. I, q. 24, n. 3) agrees, who even does not admit the word for cause in the sense of *a concomitance*, « because it must not be conceded, that the temporal is in some manner the cause of the eternal, because (it is such) neither per se nor per accidens ». The same do St. Thomas, Bl. (now St.) Albertus (Magnus), (Bl. John Duns) Scotus, Richard (of Middleton) and others hold. The Seraphic (Doctor) says well (below in d. 40, a. 2, q. 1, in reply to n. 1), that God's Knowledge « depends *in no manner* from the precognized; for He does not cognize according to its exigency, but according to the exigency of the Eternal Light and Glory [claritatis], in which there occurs no doubt, but (rather) a most high certainty ».

II. St. Bonaventure's solution with (its) threefold distinction can scarcely be reproved by anyone. Sanely, according to the reckoning of *saying*, the noun "*foreknowledge*" is said for this reason, because it refers to (things) future; and not the other way around is something said (to be) "*future*" for this reason, because it is foreknown. Wherefore if (things) were no *future* (things), but only a *foreknowledge*, it would be ineptly said (to be) a "*foreknowledge*", since it would be naught but a "*knowledge*". Likewise, it is manifest, that according to the reckoning of *inferring* it is licit to conclude from the existence of (something) future, that God has foreknown it, and vice versa [e contrario].

verso]. This explanation is approved by St. Thomas (DE VERITATE, q. 2, a. 14, in reply to n. 1) saying, that the saying of Origin « there is not conveyed a cause of being, but a cause of inferring » (cf. SUMMA., I, q. 14, a. 8, in reply to n. 1). But then a difficult remains, because the words of Origin « deny the converse », i. e. they do not admit this proposition: "because things are known by God, for that reason they are going to be" [quia res a Deo sciuntur, ideo futura sunt]; which, however, if "*because*" [quia] and "*for that reason*" [ideo] are taken in the *illative* sense, and not the causal (sense), he must have conceded it. — In the third manner, according to the reckoning of *being*, it is conceded by all, that to no extent can future (things) be the cause of the Divine Foreknowledge; but it seems scarcely able to be denied, that in all foreknowledge of future (things) there is in some manner implied a causality, since no being can be future, unless the approbation of the Divine Will be supposed, and no evil without Its permission.

Even other explanations of these sayings are cited by the ancient doctors to solve, as it seems, that difficulty just touched upon, that, namely, the converse is denied. Whence Alexander of Hales (loc. cit.) says: « And/or it must be said, that Origin did not posit an active (verb), but a passive one; wherefore (this) must not be conceded: 'because it is going to be, *for that reason* God *knows (it)*', but (rather) *'for that reason it is known by God'*. For in this manner there is noted a cause of *aptitude* to know *on the part of the knowable*. But in the active (voice) there is rather noted a cause in respect of something *in the One knowing* ». The same (solution) is repeated by Bl. (now St.) Albertus Magnus (SUMMA., p. I, tr. 15, q. 61, m. 3). St. Thomas, in addition to the manner of explaining already related above, says (SUMMA., loc. cit.): « Origin spoke, attending to the reckoning of knowledge, with which the reckoning of causality does not convene, except as adjoined to the (Divine) Will »; and (DE VERITATE, loc. cit.): « The intention of Origin is to say, that God's Knowledge is not the cause, which induces a necessity in the one known ».

III. Alexander of Hales, SUMMA., p. I, q. 24, m. 3. — Bl. (now St.) Albertus (Magnus), here in a. 3: SUMMA., p. I, tr. 15, q. 61, m. 3. — (Bl.) Peter of Tarentaise, here in q. 1, a. 2. — Richard of Middleton, here in q. 3.

ARTICLE II

On (the Divine) Foreknowledge, as much as regards the reckoning of (Its) necessity.

Consequently, there is the question concerning the second Article, namely, concerning the Divine Foreknowledge as much as regards the reckoning of (Its) necessity. And, about this, two (questions) are asked.

First, there is asked, whether the Divine Foreknowledge posits a necessity about the foreknown.

Second, whether the Divine Foreknowledge has a necessity in Itself.

---

[1] The sense is: foreknowledge can be in a related manner to something true, which is not from Him as much as regards malice, but which is beneath (Him), nor can there be by malice itself the foreknowledge of such a truth. — A little above this, before *according to this* [secundum it], the Vatican edition inserts *except* [nisi], which reading would be true, if one dealt here immediately with an evil *action*. A little below this, after *nor is caused* [nec causatur], the same Vatican edition, together with codex dd and edition 1, subjoins *because* [quia].

QUESTION I

Whether God's Foreknowledge imposes a necessity upon the things foreknown?

And, that the Divine Foreknowledge posits a necessity is shown in this manner:

1. (St.) Anselm (says) in the book, ON THE CONCORD OF (GOD'S) FOREKNOWLEDGE AND FREE WILL:[1] « It is necessary, that those which God foreknew, are going to be ».

2. Likewise, *by reason* in this manner: « from *a major* concerning a necessary and *a minor* concerning a 'being in' [inesse], one always concludes concerning a necessary », just as the Philosopher says in the first (book) of the PRIOR ANALYTICS.[2] Therefore, let there be such a syllogism: 'it is necessary that every foreknown (is) going to be' — this is clear through (St.) Anselm — but with it demonstrated in any (manner), (that) 'this has been foreknown': therefore, it is necessary that 'it is going to be'.

3. Likewise, everything which God foreknows, is true; but as the Philosophers says in the first (book) ON INTERPRETATION,[3] « everything which is, when it is, it is necessary that it is »: therefore, if the foreknown is now true, it is necessary, that it is now true. And the foreknown is going to be: therefore, now it is necessary that it is going to be: therefore, of necessity it comes forth.

4. Likewise, this very (thing) is shown per impossibile: God foreknows something in the affirmative [in partem affirmativam]; therefore, I ask, whether that can not be; if (it can) not: therefore, it is necessary; if it can [si sic]: therefore, it can turn out [evenire] otherwise, than God foreknows: therefore, the Divine Foreknowledge is fallible and uncertain. And this is the argument of (St.) Augustine[4] and also of (St. Severinus) Boethius in the fifth book, ON THE CONSOLATION (OF PHILOSOPHY): « If things foreseen are able to be turned aside [detorqueri valent] in a manner other [aliorsum] than they have been foreseen, there will already be no firm Foreknowledge of the future »

5. Likewise, God foreknows, that something is going to be: therefore, either it is *possible*, that it is not going to be, or *impossible*. if (it is) *impossible*, that it not be, therefore, it is necessary that it be; but if (it is possible); but every possible (is) able to be posited [ponibile], and having posited a false possible in a 'to be', that it follows, is not impossible.[5] Let it be posited, therefore, that this is not; and God foreknew that this is: therefore, God foreknew a falsehood. But this is impossible: therefore, it is impossible that something (belong) to the preceding.

ON THE CONTRARY: 1. That it does not infer a necessity, is shown by the authority of (St.) Augustine, taken *from a simile*, in the book, ON FREE WILL:[6] « Just as my memory does not compel [cogit], that those which have passed away, are made, so God's Foreknowledge does not compel, that those which are going to be, come to be ».

2. Likewise, the same is shown *by reason*: let us understand, that God foreknows nothing, therefore from this nothing accrues [accrescit] to free will: therefore, the positing of a foreknowledge bears nothing away from it:[7] therefore, since free will of itself, regarding each [ad utrumlibet], is the cause of things and of contingents, the Divine Foreknowledge does not take this away.

3. Likewise, just as has been proved above,[8] the Divine Foreknowledge in many (things) either is not the cause, or is not the whole cause; but that which grants a necessity to something, has the reckoning of a cause, because that from which is (its) '*being*', (is) also (its) '*being necessary*' [esse necessarium]: therefore, since the Divine Foreknowledge of many

---

[1] Question 1, ch. 1. — A little before this to the word *a necessity* [necessitatem] codex V adjoins *about the foreknown* [circa praescitum].

[2] Chapter 9. — Generally the two species of propositions, starting with Aristotle (loc. cit., ch. 2), are distinguished, namely, as absolute and modal. The former is that, in which there is said *simply*, that the predicate convenes with (or is in), and/or does not convene with the subject; but the latter is that, in which there is also expressed *the manner*, in which the predicate convenes with, and/or does not convene with the subject. The former is also called a proposition concerning '*being in*' [de inesse], which is twofold, namely, concerning '*being in*' *simply*, and concerning '*being in*' *as now*, insofar as the predicate convenes with the subject either necessarily (v. g. 'a man is a soul'), or contingently. Similarly, a proposition concerning a *necessary* is twofold, namely, concerning *the necessary simply*, and concerning *the necessary as now*. — Alexander of Hales, SUMMA, p. I, q. 28. m. 4. a. 3, in reply to n. 2, and St. Thomas, DE VERITATE, q. 2, a. 12, objection 4, according to the more ancient expositors of Aristotle, Theophrastus, Eudemus and Themistius, say, that in such a syllogism the conclusion *does not* follow concerning a necessary. But St. Bonaventure and even St. Thomas, here in q. 1, a. 5, objection 5, say the contrary, with Aristotle himself and also with Averroës, who in his Commentary on this text, discussing this controversy, impugns those interpreters with many words. Otherwise, these two contrary opinions can be well reconciled, if one says, that one opinion speaks of 'being in' simply, the other of 'being in' as now. Cf. (Bl. John Duns) Scotus, PRIOR ANALYTICS, Bk. I, q. 28, where he approves both the one and the other opinion with a distinction. — The words of (St.) Anselm, regard which the Seraphic Doctor next refers, have been cited in the preceding argument.

[3] Chapter 7 (ch. 9), where he deals with the truth and falsity of the propositions, which respect future contingents. « Therefore, the Philosopher says there, that it is necessary that which is, when it is, is, and that that which is not, when it is not, is not ».

[4] Cf. here the text of Master (Peter), ch. 1 at the end. The words of (St.) Severinus Boethius are found loc. cit., prose 3. — Somewhat above this, after *whether that can-* [utrum illud] the Vatican inserts –*not*, which is repugnant to the thought of the argument and to codices H P Q T Z etc..

[5] A reference to that definition of a contingent, which Aristotle proposes in POSTERIOR ANALYTICS, Bk. I, ch. 12: « Moreover, I say, that the contingent, by according to which it (is) not necessarily existing, is also contingent, but when (it has) been posited in a 'to be', nothing will be on this account impossible »; and PHYSICS, Bk. VIII, text 36 (ch. 5): « If we posit, therefore, that it is possible, nothing impossible accedes, but perhaps a falsehood », which words the Scholastics were accustomed to render in this manner: With a possible posited in a 'to be', nothing impossible follows (cf. Gilbert of Porretain, ON THE SIX PRINCIPLES, near the end.)

[6] Book III, ch. 4, n. 11. In the original text the cited words sound like this: For just as you by your memory do not compel, that those which have passed aware are made etc..

[7] The sense is: just as if we were to imagine, that God foreknew nothing, nothing would accrue to free will, or that free will is entirely indifferent to each: so, with the (Divine) Foreknowledge posited, nothing is taken away from it, but it remains indifferent.

[8] In the preceding Article, q. 1. — Cf. also (St.) Anselm, ON THE CONCORD OF GOD'S FOREKNOWLEDGE WITH FREE WILL, q. 1, ch. 7.

future (things) is not the cause, such as of evil (things), It imposes no necessity upon things.

4. Likewise, the Divine Foreknowledge foreknows things, just as they are going to turn out, since It foreknows naught but (what is) true: therefore, when It does foreknow, that someone (is) going to sin, since a sin is not but through a will, It foreknows, that this one through (his) will does this, and It foreknows, that he can do (something) else. Therefore, if everything which It foreknows, is true, it is true, that this one, through (his own) will, will do this and will be able to do (something) else; and if this is contingent: therefore, if with[1] the Divine Foreknowledge there is a contingency about things, therefore, no necessity (is imposed with It).

5. Likewise, this very (thing) is shown by reasons leading *to the impossible*. If the Foreknowledge imposes a necessity upon things, therefore, chance [casus] and fortune perish. Second, it is impossible, that free will and counsel perish. Third, (it is impossible) that merit and demerit perish. Fourth, (it is impossible) that praise and blame [vituperium] perish.[2]

CONCLUSION

The Divine Foreknowledge does not impose a necessity upon things, but It does foreknow the very manner of the contingence of contingent things.

I RESPOND: It must be said, that there were three positions about this.

For certain (authors) said, that the (Divine) Foreknowledge necessarily, since It is infallible, imposes a necessity, and for that reason they took away [abstulerunt] free will and sin. — And that position of their was heretical and iniquitous, because it destroyed good morals.

The other position was, that the Divine Foreknowledge, if there was (such), would impose a necessity, and thus every virtue and praise would perish.[3] And because they loved the State [rem publicam], for that reason they removed [abstulerunt] foreknowledge from God, and they removed truth from propositions concerning the future. — And this was heretical and impious, because it derogated from the Divine Nobility.

The third position is the Catholic one, which honor God and conserves good morals [bonos mores conservat], and for that reason (it is) just, pious and

true: that[4] there is a Divine Foreknowledge, and yet It does not impose a necessity upon things. For in this manner He foreknows that they are going to turn out, just as they are going to turn out; and for that reason, since many are going to turn out contingently, such as those which are from free will and chance and fortune, just as He foreknows, that the former are going to be from the latter, so He foreknows the manner of (their) contingency, according to which they are from the latter.

Moreover, for an understanding of the objections it must be noted, that there is a twofold necessity, namely, *the absolute*, and *the respective*. An *absolute* necessity, which is opposed to contingency, is said (to be) the necessity of *the consequent*. A *respective* necessity is said (to be) the necessity of *the consequence*, and this is not opposed to the contingent. For something contingent necessarily follows, so that if one walks, it necessarily follows, that he moves.[5]

It must be said, therefore, that in the foreknown there is no *absolute* necessity, but only (a necessity) of *consequence*, because there necessarily follows: 'God foreknows this, therefore, this will be'. And in this manner the authority of (St.) Anselm is understood, and (those) completely similar authorities, which are proposed with a manner of necessity; and in this manner the first (objection) is clear.

2. To that which is objected second concerning a syllogism (formed) from *a major* concerning a necessary and *a minor* concerning 'being in'; it must be said, that just as is clear, and (as) the Philosopher expounds (it), this is understood of that proposition, which concerns *'being in' simply*, which is equivalent to the necessary; but *the minor* of this syllogism, namely: 'this has been foreknown', does not concern *'being in' simply*; for just as will be clear below,[6] it is not necessary.

3. To that which is objected concerning the foreknown, that it is true, and if it is true, it is now necessarily; it must be said, that the Philosopher makes that reckoning to shown, that among future (things) there is no truth; and it is a sophistic one [sophistica].[7] For when there is said: "everything which is, when it is, is necessarily"; it is understood of that, which posits something in act about a supposed, to the extent that [quod] it is impossible that, that from which it has been posited, not have been posited, but the true concerning a future posits nothing about a subject, because[8] it is not true for the present, but only for the future: and for that reason there is no necessity, neither *simply*, nor *as now*, because it posits nothing *as now* [ut nunc].

---

[1] Very many codices, and also editions 1, 2, and 3, unduly omit *with* [cum]. — Concerning this argument cf. (St. Severinus) Boethius, ON THE CONSOLATION OF PHILOSOPHY, Bk. V, prose 3 f., and (St.) Anselm, ON THE CONCORD OF GOD'S FOREKNOWLEDGE AND FREE WILL, q. 2, ch. 3.

[2] Concerning these, cf. Aristotle, ON INTERPRETATION, Bk. I, ch. 7 (ch. 9), and (St. Severinus) Boethius' Commentary on this passage, and also (St.) Augustine, ON FREE WILL, Bk. III, ch. 2, ff., and ON THE CITY OF GOD, Bk. V, ch. 9 f., where the diverse opinions, which are next adduced in the body of the Question by the Seraphic Doctor, are reviewed.

[3] In codex T there is added *and it was imposed by (Marcus) Tullius (Cicero) and his followers* [et imponitur Tullio et sequacibus eius].

[4] Codex T has *namely, that* [scilicet quod]; the Vatican edition, together with codex cc, has *because* [quia].

[5] According to (St. Severinus) Boethius, ON THE CONSOLATION OF PHILOSOPHY, Bk. V, prose 3 and 6, this twofold necessity is called *absolute* and *conditional*; according to (St.) Anselm, CUR DEUS HOMO, Bk. II, ch. 17, and his ON THE CONCORD OF GOD'S FOREKNOWLEDGE AND FREE WILL, q. 1, ch. 3, there is said (to be) a *antecedent* and *consequent* (necessity). Next, after *It must be said* [Dicendum] in many manuscripts and edition 1 there is wanting *therefore* [ergo].

[6] In the following Question.

[7] That reckoning is sophistic not in the sense, that that principle of Aristotle is false, but to the extent that it is applied to prove, either that in propositions concerning the future there is *no* truth, even when supposed in respect to the First Cause (as the 2nd opinion related in the body of the Response would have it), and/or that even a foreknown, contingent future (thing) *necessarily* comes forth (as the 1st opinion and the objection would have it). Otherwise, that « in a future (thing), as much as it is *on the part of the contingent thing*, there is no certitude » St. Bonaventure, together with St. Thomas, teaches, below in q. 2. One must speak in another manner concerning the future (thing) under *the reckoning of the Divine Foresight*. — Codices R and X read thus: *there is no determined truth; and that reckoning is sophistic* [veritas determinate; et ista ratio est sophistica]. For *a sophistic one* [sophistica] edition 1 has *a sophism* [sophisma]. Next, for *everything which* [omne quod] many codices, and editions 1, 2 and 3, have *the 'being' which* [esse quod].

[8] Codex T moves the particle *because* [quia] after *for the present* [pro praesenti]. At the end of the solution the words *because it posits nothing as now* [quia nihil ponit, ut nunc] are to be explained thus: because it posits no subject existing in act [quia nullum ponit subiectum actu existens].

4. To that which is objected per impossibile, that, if it could be otherwise, It could fail; it must be said, that[1] *falsehood* [falsitas] comes from the discord of an intellect regarding the cognized, similarly *the potency to fail* [potentia fallendi] from the potency to be discordant [potentia discordandi]. Therefore, I say, that since (it is) necessarily foreknown: it follows after the Foreknowledge, for that reason they cannot be discordant: and for that reason It never fails, nor can It fail.

5. What, therefore, is objected, whether it can be otherwise; it must be said, that it can be otherwise, because God is able to have foreknown (it) otherwise; and when it is posited, that *it is*[2] otherwise, it is posited, that *He foreknows* (it) otherwise. Therefore, when it is inferred: 'it can be otherwise, than it is; and God thus foreknew (it): therefore, (this can be)[3] otherwise, than God foreknows (it)', the conclusion must be distinguished: because it can be understood *separately* [divisim], and thus it is true: and the sense is: 'God foreknows that this comes forth', and 'it is possible, that it does not come forth'; but if *conjunctively*, (it is) false; and the sense is: 'it is possible, that God foreknows (it) in one manner, and it turns out in another'. And there is a *fallacy of composition* in that (manner of) proceeding, just as here: 'the one running can not move: therefore, it is possible, that someone runs and does not move'; (which) does not follow. Similarly, when there is asked, "Whether it may be posited (etc.)?"; it must be posited (that 'everything possible (is) able to be posited'); but when it assumes: 'God foreknew (it)', this is opposed to the (thing it) posits:[4] and for that reason it must be denied.

SCHOLIUM

I. Each opinion which either denies the liberty of the creature, to save the Divine Foreknowledge, or takes away the Foreknowledge, to save the liberty, it is established by the Catholic Faith, that it must be rejected as impious. However, since with the Divine Foreknowledge there convenes an omnimodal *infallibility* and *immutability* in knowing, and in those too there is implied a certain *causality* in respect of the known, it does seem that from each source [capite] the liberty of created judgement can be prejudiced. This *second* difficulty the Seraphic Doctor, here in the 3rd and 5th argument of the fundament, briefly destroys; see more on this in a. 1, q. 2, in the body (of the Response), and below in d. 40, Doubt 7, and ibid., a. 2, q. 1, and in d. 45, a. 2. q. 2. It is entirely established, that that causality, by which God influences [influit in] second causes and cooperates with the free acts of intellectual creatures, is congruent with the nature of (free) agents and does not take away (their) liberty, but rather posits (it); yet concerning *the manner*, in which this concursus comes to be and in which liberty is saved, there is a debate among Catholic theologians. — However, the *first* difficulty is evidently solved here together with the common sentence, by employing that distinction between the necessity of *a consequent* and *of a consequence*, which the Catholic Schools received from (St. Severinus) Boethius (ON THE CONSOLATION OF PHILOSOPHY, Bk. V, pros. 6) under various names. The words of (St.) Boethius are these: « There are two necessities: one *simple*, as that it is necessary, that all men are mortal; the other *of a condition*, such as whether you know that someone is walking, when it is necessary that he is walking. For it is not possible, that anyone knew, that it was other than it was known. But this condition draws with it that simple (necessity) least of all. For its own nature does not cause the latter necessity, but the adjunction of a condition (does). For no necessity compels that one walking voluntarily go forward, though it is necessary, however, that when he walks, he goes forward ». Then, the same author employs this distinction to demonstrate, that the Divine Providence does not injure created liberty. — the same distinction is employed by the Seraphic Doctor below in d. 40, a. 2, q. 1 and 2, and in d. 47, q. 1 and elsewhere.

II. The solutions to nn. 2 and 3 are founded on the distinction of a thing exiting in act [rei actu existentis] and of a thing going to be [rei futurae]. In regard to the existing thing the sentence of Aristotle is true, that everything which is, when it is, it is necessary that it is, by a necessity, namely, which is consequent from the supposition, that the subject *now exists* (whence it is called by the Seraphic Doctor « the necessity as now »), because existence excludes non-existence; but it is not true of that, which is not yet, but is going to be, because in virtue of the *now* nothing is posited *in the thing* about the subject. — In the 5th opposed argument there is supposed, that something has been foreknown by God, and yet is not going to be. To elude the sophism of the objections, the Seraphic Doctor uses the celebrated distinction of *the composed* and *the divided*, as is clear from the text. St. Thomas (here in a. 5, in reply to n. 5) solves the same objection, by employing the distinction, « that (the proposition) can concern *the saying*, and/or *the thing*; and if it concerns the *saying*, it is true (that is, that it is necessary, that everything known by God, be), and if it concerns *the thing*, it is false ».

III. Alexander of Hales, SUMMA., p. I, q. 24, m. 4 and 5. — (Bl. John Duns) Scotus, SENT., Bk. I, d. 39, q. sole; DE RERUM PRINCIPIO, q. 4, a. 2, section 5. — St. Thomas, here in the q. sole, a. 5, SUMMA., I, q. 14, a. 13; SUMMA CONTRA GENTILES. I, c. 67; DE VERITATE., q. 2, a. 12. — Bl. (now St.) Albertus (Magnus)., here in a. 4; SUMMA., p. I, tr. 15, q. 61, m. 5. — (Bl.) Peter of Tarentaise, here in q. 2, a. 1. — Richard of Middleton, here in q. 6. — Giles the Roman, here in 2nd princ., q. 3. — Durandus (of Saint-Pourçain), here in q. 3, n. 19. ff.. — (Bl.) Dionysius the Carthusian, here in q. 2. — (Gabriel) Biel, here in the q. sole.

---

[1] The Vatican edition, with edd. 4 & 5, supported by no codex, adds: *just as truth comes from the concord of an intellect regarding the thing cognized, but this concord is not other, than the adequation of thing and intellect:* so [sicut veritas venit ex concordia intellectus ad rem cognitam, haec autem concordia non est aliud, quam adaequatio rei et intellectus: sic]. Next, for *I say, therefore* [Dico igitur] codd. H & T insert *Wherefore* [quod].

[2] Trusting in codd. A F H K T and several others, as required moreover, by the context, we have substituted, with ed. 1, *it is* [sit] for *He knows (it)* [scit], which is the vitiated reading of the Vatican ed.. A little before this, for *is able to have foreknown* [potest praescisse] cod. V has *can foreknow* [potest praescire].

[3] Understand: this can be or come forth [hoc potest esse sive evenire].. — The words, which follow next: *it can be understood separately ... but if conjunctively,* [potest intelligi divisim ... coniunctim],

want to say: the conclusion can be understood in a divided and a composite sense.

[4] The Vatican edition reads *to (the thing) posited* [ponento], and a little before this, it has *what is posited* [quod ponitur] for *whether it may be posited* [quod ponatur]. Each reading is obscure on account of the brevity and ambiguous sense of the verb *to posit* [ponere], which can signify either *to infer* [inferre] or *to suppose* [supponere]. The easier explanation seems to be this: after *it be posited* [ponatur], supply: *etc.*, namely *that this is not* [hoc non esse], as is read in the 5th* opposed argument. The words *it must be posited* [ponendum est] concede the application of the principle cited there: 'everything possible (is) able to be posited' [omne possibile ponibile].°

---

* *Trans. note*: Here the original note faultily reads *4th* for *5th*.

° The supplementation, suggested here by the Quaracchi editors, has been made in the text, within parentheses.

QUESTION II

Whether God necessarily foreknows what He foreknows?

Second, there is asked, whether the Divine Foreknowledge has in Itself a necessity, that is, whether it is necessary, that God foreknows what He foreknows. And that it is, is shown:

1. First through the authority of (St.) Anselm in the book, ON THE CONCORD OF PREDESTINATION AND FREE WILL:[1] « What God foreknows, it is impossible that He does not foreknow »: therefore, ab aequipollenti, it is necessary that He foreknows.

2. Likewise, it seems *by reason*, because every saying concerning (something) past is a true necessary — wherefore if he ran, it is necessary that he ran — but if (God) foreknows, He foreknew: therefore, since this is a saying concerning (something) past, therefore, (it is) necessary.

3. Likewise, though God's Power is indifferent to going forth and/or to not going forth, yet from (the moment) in which It went forth into act, it is necessary that It went forth. Whence, although It could create and not create, before It did create, yet from (the moment) It creates, it is necessary that It did create: therefore, from (the moment) in which He foreknew, it is necessary that He foreknew.

4. Likewise, if a man willed and foreknew something, it is necessary, that the man knew and willed: therefore, if about God's Knowledge there is no lesser certitude, nay greater, than (that which there is) about man's knowledge, much more strongly is it necessary. *If you say*, just as some say,[2] that in this (expression): "*God foreknew*", the whole is on account of the future [ex futuro] according to thing, even though it is understood under the reckoning of the past, whence: "God foreknows" is naught more than to say: "God is, and this will be"; *on the contrary*: then, let it be that God has no cognition, yet while a thing was going to be, (and) this would be true: "God foreknows"; which is manifestly false. *Moreover*, let it be that to (God's) Foreknowledge there is added an act passing over into the past, such as (an act of) promising[3] and/or predicting and/or prophesying [prophetatio], (then) there passes over into the past something, and the same sophism and the same doubt is formed [fit]: therefore, this does not solve (it).

5. Likewise, *to be* and *not to be* are more distant, than *the necessary* and *the contingent*; but something, which simply is, has (its) 'to be' in God's foreknowledge: therefore,

much more strongly can something, which in itself is contingent, be necessary in the God's Foreknowledge: ergo etc..

6. Likewise, everything immutable is necessary; but when there is said: "God foreknows", (this) is immutable: therefore, it is necessary. The first is manifest, the second is clear, because when there is said: "God foreknows", if it is changed, so that He comes to be not foreknowing, either (this will be)[4] according to a change of *the thing* or of *God*. Not of *the thing*, because the thing is yet nothing, therefore, it is not changed nor can it be change. If according to *His own* change, therefore, God is changed.

7. Likewise, everything eternal is necessary, because there is only one Eternal, and It is That in which there occurs no contingency, but (rather) a most high necessity; but God's *foreknowing* is eternal: therefore, it is necessary, that God foreknows what He foreknows.

ON THE CONTRARY: 1. The rule is, if the antecedent of a good conditional is necessary, the consequent (is) also; and if the consequent is not necessary, neither (is) the antecedent.[5] But: 'if God foreknows, that this is going to be, it will be' does follow, whatsoever contingent be demonstrated, because the opposite cannot stand: therefore, since the consequent is not necessary, therefore neither (is) the antecedent.

2. Likewise, the rule is, that a necessary suffers itself with every possible. For everything repugnant to a necessary is impossible;[6] but with it demonstrated in any (manner), that one has been foreknown to be damned, it is possible, that he be saved. therefore, those two can stand together, 'that he is foreknown to be damned', and 'he may be saved'; and this is impossible; ergo etc..

3. Likewise, the rule is, that the opposite of a contingent is contingent, and the opposite of a necessary is impossible. And the rule *again* is, that if to an antecedent there follows a consequent, to the opposite of a consequent there follows the opposite of the antecedent.[7] From these I argue thus: let A be a contingent foreknown by God, if God foreknows (A), A will be: therefore, through the (second) rule,[8] if A will not be; God does not foreknow (A). But, 'that A is not', was contingent, 'that God did not foreknow' was impossible;

---

[1] The sentence of (St.) Anselm in the book cited, is not found expressed in the same words as it is here. But there, especially in q. 1, chs. 1, 2 and 5, there are had other propositions which teach, that God foreknows future (things) and indeed (does so) immutably in eternity; from the likeness of which truth this sentence has been formed.

[2] See here in the body of the Question.

[3] Edition 1 *foreseeing* [praevisio]; in the body of the Question there is posited *credulity* [credulitas].

[4] The Vatican ed. adjoins *this will be* [hoc erit]. A little above this, to the words *is immutable* [est immutabile] cod. V prefixes *the foreknowing* [praescire]. A little further below this, the Vatican ed. has *God's* [Dei] for *His own* [sui].

[5] This rule, as much as (it) regards simply syllogisms, is insinuated by Aristotle, PRIOR ANALYTICS, Bk. I, ch. 8 ff. and is derived from that general principle of Aristotle, PRIOR ANALYTICS, Bk. II, ch. 2: "Of the true there is no false syllogizing", which is hinted at in POSTERIOR ANALYTICS, Bk. I, ch. 6: But when the middle (term) is

from necessity, the conclusion is always from necessity, just as the true from the true. — For *of a good conditional* [bonae conditionalis] the Vatican edition, together with editions 4 and 5, has *of a good consequence* [bonae consequentiae].

[6] On this and the following rule, cf. Aristotle, ON INTERPRETATION, Bk. II, ch. 3 (ch. 12 f.), where he deals with the consequences and opposition of modal propositions [propositionum modalium], and PRIOR ANALYTICS, Bk. I, ch. 12.

[7] This rule is had in PRIOR ANALYTICS, Bk. I, last chapter, where the Philosopher, dealing with propositions, simple and privatory of order and consequences, says: "But simply, when they hold themselves in this manner etc..". — In many codices and edition 1 this is read in reverse order, thus: *to the opposite of an antecedent there follows the opposite of the consequent* [ad oppositum antecedentis sequitur oppositum consequentis].

[8] Namely, the one which is posited here in the last place.

therefore, to the contingent there follows an impossible. But this is contrary the art[1] (of logic): therefore, it is necessary, that the latter be contingent, namely 'that God foreknows this'.

4. Likewise, every Divine action, which respect an object, which can not be, can cease. Wherefore since God conserves the created thing, He can cease to conserve (it): therefore, since (His) foreknowing is in respect of a contingent, it will be contingent.

CONCLUSION

In the saying, "that God foreknows that contingent (is) going to be", though the act of God in itself is eternal and necessary, it is to be judged contingent in the whole saying, by reason of the connoted contingent.

I RESPOND: It must be said, that, just as has been proved necessarily,[2] this is established and there is no doubt, that 'that God foreknows some contingent' — when it is antecedent to a contingent and connotes something, which has a contingent truth — that it must be judged (to be) contingent.

But some wanted to judge it (to be) contingent, because the whole which it says, it says concerning a future. — And that has been disproven,[3] because it is false, and not intelligible. For every in intellect, which understands this, though it does not understand time about God, it does understand, that the act of the Divine Foreknowledge was in God from eternity, and it does differ from the future thing. And moreover, just as has been said,[4] this does not solve (it).

Others wanted to judge it (to be) contingent, because, though it has been said concerning (something) past, yet it depends from (something) future. And they say this in regard to [in] (those propositions) believed, and prophesied, and said by Christ, and (those) completely similar, which they infer from the necessity of propositions concerning (something) future. — And that is improbable,[5] as it seems, since if an act of the Divine Precognition depends from (something) future, then, since in the future, as much as it is on the part of the contingent thing, there is no certitude, neither would there be (any certitude) in the Divine Precognition.

Moreover, in what manner does It depend, since it is not caused by it in any manner? *And again*, in what manner does that which is necessary *to have been*, such as an act of cognizing and believing and predicting, depend from that which *is going to be?* It does not seem either probable or intelligible.

And, for that reason, it must be said in another manner, that there is a certain saying *of the past*, and *on behalf of the past*, just as if it be said, that "Peter has read"; (there is) a certain (saying) *of the past*, but *on behalf of the future*, such as "the Antichrist was going to be born"; (there is) a certain (saying) *of the past* and *on behalf of the past*, yet (which) *depends from the future*, such as this saying: that "Peter said the truth, that there will be a naval battle"; for, for this, that the saying have truth, *the coming forth* of the battle is required; and from that depends the truth of our assertion and cognition, which is caused by the thing;[6] (and finally) there is a certain saying *of the past*, which *does not depend (from the future)*, but connotes (it), just as if there is said: "God foreknew that this (is) going to be".

For, because God's Knowledge is only in respect of the true, for that reason It connotes the truth about that future saying; but since the Divine Cognition[7] does not have certitude from the thing, because It is neither cause or arises from it, for that reason It does not depend upon it; and on this account It cannot fail, even though It does connote (something) future. Whence in "the Foreknowledge" these two are meant, namely *an act* of the Divine Cognition, and this is necessary *to be* or *to have been*, and an *ordination of the future* regarding that act, and this ordination of the future regarding that act is not necessary. And it is to be judged contingent in the whole saying, not by reason of the totality or of the principal signified,[8] but (by reason) of the connoted. And if it is posited, that "God does not foreknow something, which He does foreknow", it can and ought to be understood not through the removal of the principal signified, but (through a removal) of the connoted itself or of that order of the temporal to the eternal, which indeed is contingent by reason of the other, namely of the temporal. Therefore, there is a contingency in the whole saying, because it connotes that something is true concerning the future, which (future) is indeed contingent.

And this is clear in this manner. For, when there is said: "God foreknows that you are going to be saved"; in this a twofold act and composition

---

[1] Namely: logic, and/or especially syllogistic logic (cf. d. 40, a. 2, q. 1, in reply to n. 4), in which is had the contrary rule, to that posited in the first place in this argument. To understand better the aforesaid, we cite here the words of Mastrius, from his work CURSUS PHILOSOPHICUS., tome I, tr. 2, ch. 9, n. 77, on this subject: « Just as *"ever"* and *"none"* are contraries, so *"necessary"* and *"impossible"*; and just as *"certain ones"* and *"not certain ones"* are subcontraries, so *"possible"* and *"not possible"* are subcontraries. And again, just as *"none"* and *"certain ones"*, and *"all"* and *"not certain ones"* are contradictories, so *"impossible"* and *"possible"* or *"contingent"* are contradictories, likewise *"necessary"* and *"not possible"* or *"not contingent"*; and finally, just as *"all"* and *"some"*, *"none"* and *"not some"* are subalternates, so also *"necessary"* and *"possible"* or *"contingent"*, and *"impossible"* and *"non possible"* or *"not contingent"* ».

[2] Here in the fundament. — In the Vatican ed. there is lacking *necessarily* [necessario]. Next, ed. 1 has the subjunctive, reading *since it is antecedent* etc. [cum antecedat ... connotet] for *when* [cum antecedit ... connotat].

[3] Here in the 4th opposed argument. — Next many codices, together with edition 1 read *that (is) not intelligible* [non intelligible illud] for *not intelligible* [non intelligibile].

[4] Here in the 4th opposed argument. — For *moreover* [propterea] the Vatican edition has *on this account* [propterea].

[5] Codex O has *impossible* [impossibile]. For *And that* [Et illud] codex R has *But even that* [Et etiam illud].

[6] Cf. Aristotle, ON INTERPRETATION, Bk. I, ch. 7 (ch. 9). — The Vatican edition, together with codex cc, in the third member of this proposition, omits *of the past and* [praeterito et], and then for *yet (which) depends* [tamen dependet] codex R has *yet as depending* [tamen dependenti]. A little below this after *of our assertion* [nostrae assertionis] the same Vatican edition omits *and our cognition* [et cognitionis], and after a few (words), in the fourth member of the same proposition, after *but connotes* [sec connotat] adds in place of *(it)* the words *the truth about that future (thing)* [veritatem circa illud futurum]; edition 1 adds here *the future (thing)* [futurum] only.

[7] Codices L and O have *Precognition* [praecognitio].

[8] Just as they who follow the opinion, impugned at the beginning of the body of the Question, contend. — A little above this, after *and this ordination* [et haec ordinatio] very many codices, such as AI T V and Z, together with edition 1, omit *of the future* [futuri].

is included, namely this:[1] 'you will be saved', and this: 'God has a cognition of your salvation and had (this) cognition from eternity'. *Indeed to have a cognition* is (in God) an eternal and necessary act, because it does not depend upon the thing; but *'to be saved'* is a future and contingent act. Since, therefore, an act of the Divine Cognition does not depend upon the cognized, for that reason there can be a certitude in it, according to a contingent,[2] existing thing. But since, as it signifies through the manner of foreknowledge, it connotes a future contingent, and every saying, which encloses in itself a contingent, must be judged contingent; for that reason the whole (saying) is judged (to be) contingent. — And this solution is true and general. For an act of credulity, an act of prophesying and an act of Divine Assertion, on this account, that they run according to the enlightenment [illustrationem] of the Divine Foreknowledge, for that reason they connote, and do not depend; for that reason they are certain and infallible concerning things not certain in themselves.

1. To that, therefore, which is objected concerning (St.) Anselm, that it is necessary that He foreknow what He foreknows; it must be said, that he understands this as much as regards an act of (His) Precognition, which is necessary to have been, but not as much as regards the connotation of a futurition [futuritionis].[3]

2. 3. To that which is objected, that the saying concerns (something) past: it must be said, that as much as it concerns the reckoning of being past [praeteritionis], it is necessary; but since (something) future is connoted, for that reason it is contingent. And from this the follow is clear, because as much as regards that future the (Divine) Power is not[4] yet in act, nay it can still go forth, for that reason etc..

4. 5. To that which is objected, that there is a (Divine) cognition without the existence of the thing, therefore, (a cognition) of a necessity without the necessity of the thing; it must be said, that it is true, that in an act of cognition there is a necessity, but not in the whole (saying). Nor is it similar, because the Precognition does not connote the actual existence of the thing, but connotes the futurition of the thing, and for this, that the saying be necessary, it is necessary, that there is a necessity in the (thing) connoted.

6. To that which is objected, that every immutable (is) necessary; it must be said, that for *the 'to be' of a mutable* two (things) concur: that it holds itself in one manner *before*, and in another manner *after*; and through (its) opposite, *the immutable*, it can be said in a twofold manner: either because nothing is in act, or because it is in act and cannot hold itself otherwise. Therefore, that immutable, which is and can-

not hold itself otherwise, is convertible with the necessary; but that which is said (to be) "immutable", which is not something in act, is not convertible.[5] And in this manner a true (saying) concerning a future (thing) is contingent, before the thing is. This saying, "that the Antichrist will be", is now a true immutable (saying), because if one posits, that it is true, one posits, that it was always (true); and similarly if (one posits that it is) false, and for this (reason), because (when false) it posits nothing in act. Since, therefore, *"that God foreknew"* connotes a future contingent, for that reason the saying is immutable; nor does it follow from this, that it is necessary, as has been seen.

Yet, some want to say in another manner, that *"that God foreknows this contingent (is) going to be"* is immutable on the part of the One foreknowing, but on the part of the thing foreknown it is mutable, and for that reason on that part (it is) contingent. But yet that is difficult to say; for what is foreknow once has been foreknown always, and God is able to not[6] foreknow that a contingent (is) going to be, so that nothing comes to be about the future (thing), and thus (there is) no change. And for this reason the other manner of speaking is the more reasonable one [rationablior].

7. To that which is objected last, that nothing which is eternal [nihil ens aeternum] is contingent; it must be said, that "being eternal" [ens aeternum] is in a twofold manner: either *purely eternal*, or that which *connotes (something) temporal* concerning (something) future; and the *purely eternal* is necessary, but (that which) *connotes (something) temporal* concerning (something) future by reason of the connoted can be judged (to be) contingent, just as for that reason it can also cease.

The sum of the sayings is this, that *"that God foreknows that a contingent (is) going to be"* is a certain saying, which encloses in itself an eternal act of the Divine Cognition, and means an ordination to a future contingent. And though the act of the Divine Cognition posits something existing, necessary and eternal; yet that ordination posts a future (thing), which is contingent. And again, though it means an ordination, yet it does not mean a dependence, but only a connotation; and for that reason it does not posit[7] an uncertainty [incertitudinem]. And hence it is, that *"that God foreknows that (something) is going to be"* is *contingent* by reason of the connotation regarding a contingent; it is *immutable* by reason of the ordination to the future (thing), which is able to not be, with no change having been made (in Him);[8] it is *certain* by reason of (its) independence from the same. And this will be more plainly clear below in the Distinction concerning predestination.[9]

---

[1] For *this (saying)* [hic] codices A M S aa and bb, with ed. 1, both here and in the following, exhibit *this* [haec], that is *this composition*.

[2] Codex T has *according to a thing existing contingently* [re contingenter existente]. Then, for *since, as* [quoniam, ut] the Vatican edition has *when* [quando]. A little below this after *for that reason the whole* [ideo totale], supply together with codex R *saying* [dicutm].

[3] For *of a futurition* [futuritionis] codex K has *of the future contingent* [futuri contingentis]. [Trans. note: The "futurition" of a thing is "the future act of existence" of a thing.]

[4] Codices L and O have *has not yet gone forth* [non exivit]. Next to the verb *go forth* [exire] the Vatican edition prefixes *not* [non]. Codices R and X supply to the text here: *It can go forth and not go forth* [potest exire et non exire]. — The sense of this proposition is this: Though the Divine Power, considered *in Itself*, or to the extent that it is God Himself, is a pure act and is to no extent changed, by passing from potency to act,

to produce an effect; yet *in a manner related to the future (thing)*, which has not yet been produced, it can be said to be not in act, that is, not in that transient act.

[5] Codices G and aa have *is not convertible with the necessary* [non convertitur cum necessario]. Next, before *This saying* [Hoc dictum] the Vatican edition inserts *And so* [Et sic], codices R and X *just as* [sicut]. A little after this codex A has *nothing is posited in act* [nihil actu ponitur] for *(when false) it posits nothing in act* [nihil actu ponit].

[6] The Vatican edition, having inverse the order of the words has *cannot* [non potest] for *is able not* [potest non]; codex V has *is cannot not* [non potest non].

[7] Codices Z and bb read *it does not deprive and/or posit a certitude* [non privat certitudinem vel ponit].

[8] Codex O adds here *in Him* [in eo].

[9] Distinction 40, a. 2, qq. 1 and 2.

SCHOLIUM

I. Alexander of Hales treats of the same question under the title: "Whether God's Foreknowledge is immutable"; and Richard of Middleton under the title: "Whether it is possible, that God does not foreknow and/or did not foreknow that which He foreknows". The question does not concern *the principal signified* of the Divine Foreknowledge, or the Divine act in itself, which is manifestly eternal and necessary, but (rather) the ordination of the connoted, which is the contingent, to the Knowledge; and/or more clearly, it concerns complex propositions (or *sayings*), which contain the assertion, that God foreknows and/or foreknew that something contingent was going to be, v. g. "God foreknows and/or foreknew, that the Antichrist is going to be". Since the act of foreknowing in the past and/or present is able at once not to be, when it in truth was and/or is, this seems to convey, that the whole proposition is necessary; and if it (is), it seems to follow, that all future (things), even (those) contingent, are necessary. Moreover, it is clear, that this question pertains rather to logic; nor does it discuss certain subtle difficulties, which (Bl. John Duns) Scotus (Sent., Bk. I, d. 39, q. sole, n. 25) urges against the distinction employed at the end of the body (of the Response), and below in d. 39, a. 2. q. 2, namely that the proposition: "God knows necessarily", is in the composite sense false, in the divided sense true.

II. To the Question there is a twofold response. St. Thomas (Summa., I, q. 14, a. 13, in reply to n. 2; and Sent., Bk. I, here in q. 1, a. 5, in reply to n. 4) teaches, that the proposition: "God knew, that this contingent is going to be", is « necessary absolutely » (which seems to be understood not of a necessary absolute in (its) *rigor*, but of a necessary pertaining to *immutability*). — St. Bonaventure, however, together with (Bl. John Duns) Scotus (Sent., Bk. I, d. 39, q. 4), Richard of Middleton (d. 39, a. 1, q. 2) and very many others, even not a few from the School of St. Thomas, want the proposition to be *simply* contingent, and only necessary secundum quid. But St. Bonaventure (in reply to n. 6)

distinguishes an *immutable* saying from a *necessary* saying, so that some saying can be *immutable*, but not *necessary*. — For a fuller explanation see below d. 41, a. 2, q. 2; and what is hear said of the difference of the four sayings (in the body of the Response), pertains to the last of these according to thing.

III. In the Response itself there is more to be noted, v. g., that « if an act of the Divine Precognition depends from (something) future, then, since in the future, as much as it is on the part of the contingent thing, there is no certitude, neither would there be (any certitude) in the Divine Precognition », which sentence is approved by St. Thomas (loc. cit.). But with these words there is least of all denied, that there is a determined truth in future contingents according to *the habitude*, which they have to the First Cause and Truth. Likewise, it must be noted, what is said at the end of the Response concerning the certitude of the Divine Knowledge in regard to things contingent and not certain in themselves. — In the solution to n. 6 there is added another response, which is (that) of Alexander of Hales (Summa, p. I, q. 24, a. 7, § 1, in reply to n. 3), but less approved by our Doctor.

It must be observed, that the Seraphic (Doctor) distinguish between *connoting* and *having a respect*. For in God something can *have a respect* to things merely possible and existing within God; but what *it connotes* is always an *effect* ad extra, whether existing or future. The Seraphic (Doctor) teaches (this) in the same manner as above in d. 27, p. II, q. 2, in reply to n. 1.

IV. Alexander of Hales, Summa., p. I, q. 24, m. 7. — (Bl. John Duns) Scotus, Sent., Bk. I, d. 39, q. sole; Reportatio., d. 39, qq. 1 and 2. — St. Thomas, Sent., Bk. I, d. 39, q. 1, a. 1; Summa., I, q. 14, a. 15. — Bl. (now St.) Albertus (Magnus), Summa., p. I, tr. 15, q. 61, m. 6. — (Bl.) Peter of Tarentaise. here in q. 2, a. 3. — Richard of Middleton, Sent., Bk. I, d. 39, a. 1, q. 2. — Giles the Roman, Sent., Bk. I, d. 39, 1st princ., q. 1. — Durandus (of Saint-Pourçain), here in q. 3, n. 22. ff., and in d. 39, q. 1.

DOUBTS ON THE TEXT OF THE MASTER

Doubt I

In this part, there occur [incidunt] doubts about (Master Peter's) text and first concerning this which (St.) Augustine says: *Nor did He know created (things) otherwise than (they were) to be created.* For he seems to speak badly, because a thing, if it is truly cognized, is cognized as it is; but they were otherwise, when they were to be created, than when they had been created — for first things were in (their) *Cause* and secundum quid, afterwards in *their own genus* and *simply* — therefore either God does not truly cognize, or He cognized in another manner.

Likewise, an Angel cognizes things in the Word, he also cognizes them in their own genus, and the one and the other manner of cognizing is a this from that [hic ab illo]:[1] therefore, since what an Angel knew cannot be concealed from God, it seems, that God cognizes in each manner, and thus in the one manner and in the other.

I Respond: It must be said, that when I say, that a thing *is cognized otherwise*, it can be understood in a twofold manner. either thus that the adverb means an

anotherness as much as regards *the cognition*, or as much as regards *the "being" of the thing cognized*. If as much as regards *the "being" of the think cognized*, thus it is true;[2] and the sense is: "God cognizes, that this thing is and/or that He holds otherwise, than He held it before"; and in this manner (St.) Augustine does not understand (it). But if it means an anotherness as much as regards *the cognition*, thus it is false; and the sense is: "God cognizes the thing made otherwise, than He cognized before that (it was) to be made!; and thus it is false, because in this manner the Divine Cognition is signified (as) altered, and that It received something from the thing outside. And through this the first objection is clear.

What is objected, that God cognizes things in their own genus, just as an Angel (does); it must be said, that *"to cognize things in their own genus"* is understood in a twofold manner: either so that that 'to be', which it has in its own genus, is cognized, and this belongs to perfection, and it does not lie hidden from God, and thus it does not mean a new manner of cognizing from the cognition (had) in the Word; or so that the gaze of the intelligence or cognitive force is deflected[3] upon

---

[1] Cf. Sent, Bk. II, d. 4, a. 3, q. 1 f..* — A little above this to the word *things* [res] codex X adjoins *created* [creatas].

[2] Codices V and X have *it (the proposition) is true* [est vera] for *it (the saying) is true* [est verum]. Next, codices T and cc have (the sub-

junctive) for *than He held it before* [quam se prius habuerit] rather than (the indicative) *than He held it before* [quam se prius habuit]

[3] The Vatican edition, contrary to the codices and to edition 1, has *is reflected* [reflectatur].

---

* *Trans. note*: By *is a this from that* [hic ab illo], St. Bonaventure means that the latter manner of knowing is from the former manner of knowing.

the thing as it is in its own genus, and this belongs to imperfection, because, that is, then[1] the one cognizing steps forth outside himself; and this can in no manner be posited in God, and thus He works in the Angel another manner of cognizing. And thus that (objection) is clear.

DOUBT II

Likewise, is asked concerning this which (Master Peter) says: *Then of That, which is eternal, something would exist as (Its) cause* etc.. For he wants to say, that *"foreknowledge"* (in God) means something eternal; but this seems (to be) false, because *"foreknowledge"* means a looking-back to a future creature; but nothing is future according to the *"being"*, which it has in God, but (rather) in its own nature: therefore, it connotes something temporal, therefore, it seems, that it is cognized[2] on account of time. — Besides, that looking-back means nothing on the part of God except only out manner of understanding: therefore, that looking-back then began, when our understanding began, it was not, therefore, from eternity.

I RESPOND: Just as Master (Peter) says, *"foreknowledge"* (in God) means something eternal and from eternity. For since it does not convey but two (significations), namely *antecession* and *knowledge*, and (since) the *antecession* of every creature is before every creature, and *the knowledge* (of every creature is) naturally, it is clear that *"foreknowledge"* (in God) means[4] something eternal. — What, therefore, is objected, that it conveys the futurition of the thing; it must be said, that a futurition conveys in one manner *a succession of time*, and thus does not concern the reckoning of foreknowledge; for in this manner the future (thing) began (to be) with time. In another manner the future (thing) conveys *an order of a temporal to an eternal* according to a *consecution* [consecutionem], just as the Foreknowledge (does according to) *an antecession*; and since that order requires only the first extreme (to be) in act, and That was from eternity, for that reason (there is) both a futurition and a foreknowledge.[5]

What is objected, that that looking-back on the part of God means nothing according to *thing*; it must be said, that (that) is false, because that looking-back is the Divine Essence; but it is true, that it means nothing *respective* or dependent, but only according to a manner of understanding; and for that reason it did not begin according to thing, but only the manner of signifying began. And when Master (Peter) says, that *"foreknowledge"* (in God) means (something) eternal, he is not speaking of the reckoning of naming, but (rather) of that which is signified through the name.[6]

DOUBT III

Likewise, is asked concerning this which (Master Peter) says: *that God's Knowledge and/or Foreknowledge is not the cause ... if, however, we only refer "knowledge" to a "being known". However, if by the name for knowledge there is included also goodwill and disposition, then It can rightly be said (to be)* etc.. For he seems to speak badly, because either *"knowledge"*, said in this or that manner, means *the same* manner of knowing, or *another one*; if *the same*, therefore, if in one manner It is a cause, (it is) also in the other; if *another* manner, therefore, in God there is a multiple manner of knowing, therefore, not a uniform one through all (things). — Likewise, the knowledge *of a simple being-known* [scientiae simplicis notitiae] is God; and God is the cause of all; therefore, that knowledge is the cause of all.

I RESPOND: It must be said, that in us a *"simple being-known"*, and the *"being-known of good pleasure"* mean diverse cognitions and diverse manners of cognizing, and consequently connote diverse (concepts): but in God there is only one Cognition, but God does by that one (cognition), what we (do) by many; and for that reason that one can be signified in a twofold manner.[7] And since when it is signified through a manner of *approbation*, it connotes an effect and a goodness; but when through a manner of *a simple being-known*, only a coming forth. And since *"to be a cause"* of something connotes an effect or looking-back — even though it is the same knowledge or wisdom on the part of the principal signified — for that reason there is said, that this[8] is the cause of those which He foreknows, and the that (is) not. And this is said, not because the thing signified is not a cause, but because, thus as [ut sic] it has been signified, it is not signified through the manner of a cause, since it is compared to those which are in no manner from God. And thus that (doubt) is clear.

DOUBT IV

Likewise, is asked concerning this word of (St.) Augustine: *God through the Prophet foretold the infidelity of the Jews*; because, though the Prophet's saying was certainly [certitudinaliter] true, it seems, that God revealed to the Jews their own downfall [casus] or damnation; which is contrary to that (word of his), ON THE LITERAL EXPOSITION OF GENESIS,[10] which says, that (this) ought to be revealed to none, lest he be driven to despair.

I RESPOND: It must be said, that a downfall can be fore-

---

[1] The words *that is, then the one* [scilicet tunc], which we have substituted for the reading of the Vatican edition and codex cc, *the force* [vis], are found in edition 1, and are favored by not a few codices, among which there is instead read, even if incongruously, *though then the one* [licet tunc]. In codex O there is read: *because then the cognizing is through another or is through innate species and/or (those) received from the thing, (and) it steps forth* etc. [quia tunc cognoscere est per aliud sive sit per species innatas vel receptas a re egreditur etc.].

[2] For *it is cognized* [cognoscatur] the Vatican edition, with a few codd., has *it is said* [dicatur]. A little before this for *something temporal* [aliquod temporale] codex Y has *something temporal* [quid temporale].

[3] Here in ch. 1 near the middle, and above in d. XXXV, ch. 8, and also below in d. XXXIX, ch. 2.

[4] Codices V and X have the subjunctive form *means* [dicat].

[5] Here the twofold manner, according to which the futurition of the thing is considered, serves not a little to understand the question concerning the manner, in which God cognizes all by means of being present.

[6] Cf. Alexander of Hales, SUMMA., p. I, q. 24, m. 1; Bl. (now St.) Albertus (Magnus), SUMMA., p. I, tr. 15, q. 61, m. 1.

[7] The Vatican edition adds here: *namely, through a manner of approbation and through a manner of a simple being-known* [scilicet per modum approbationis et per modum notitiae simplicis].

[8] Understand: *the knowledge of approbation* [scientia approbationis]. — A little above this after *signified* [significati], in the Vatican edition there is adjoined *yet diversely signified* [tamen diversimode signatur].

[9] The saying of the Prophet, which (St.) Augustine refers to (ON THE GOSPEL OF ST. JOHN, Tract 53, n. 5, on account of which this doubt occurs), is Isaias 6:10: Blind the heart of this people and weigh down its ears and close its eyes: lest perchance it see by its eyes, and hear by its ears, and understand in its heart, and be converted, and I heal it.

[10] Book XI, ch. 18, n. 24 f., and ch. 26, n. 33. Immediately after this the Vatican edition, together with not a few codices, has *where he* [ubi] for *which* [qui].

told; but not, on account of this, is it revealed, either because one does not believe the one speaking, or because it is understood (to have been) said of[1] a condition, or, the one understanding (it) understands (it) of another, not of himself. And, because the word of Isaias the Prophet was said in a threatening and general manner [comminatorie et generaliter], and with incredulous men, on the one hand, not adverting to (it) at that time, it could have been understood in all these manners, to have been a prediction [praedictio], not a revelation.

DISTINCTION XXXIX

CHAPTER I

Whether God's Knowledge can be increased and/or lessened and/or in any manner be changed?

Moreover, there is customarily asked, whether God's knowledge can be increased and/or lessened. For each seems to be able to be proven. For that the Divine Knowledge can be increased and/or changed,[1] is proven in this manner: because God can know [scire] what He never knows. For there is someone, who is not going to read today, and yet it can be, that he reads today; for he can read today. But nothing can come to be, which cannot be known by God. Therefore, God can know, that this one (is) going to read today, therefore, He can know something, which He does not know: therefore, His Knowledge can be increased and/or changed. And the Same seems able to be lessened. For there is someone going to read today, whom God knows (is) going to read. But it can be, that he does not read, therefore, God is able not to know, that he (is) going to read, therefore, He is able not to know something which He does know: therefore, His Knowledge can be lessened, and/or changed. — To which we say, that God's Knowledge is entirely immutable nor can it be increased and/or changed. For, as (St.) Augustine says in the fifteenth book, ON THE TRINITY:[2] « God's Knowledge is Wisdom Itself, and Wisdom is the very Essence or Substance of God; because in the wonderful Simplicity of that Nature it is not one (thing) 'to be wise' [sapere], another 'to be', but that which it is 'to be wise', that it is 'to be' ». « And for that reason the Word knew [novit] all, which the Father knew; but His *knowing* of the Father is, just as (His) '*being*'; for 'to know' and 'to be' is one (thing) There. And for that reason, just as the Father's '*being*' is not from the Son, so neither (His) *knowing*. Consequently [Proinde], as One speaking His very self, the Father begot the Word coequal to Himself through all (things). For He would not have spoken Himself integrally and perfectly, if there were something less or more ample in His Word than in His very Self. Therefore, this Word is entirely, what the Father (is), yet He is not the Father, because the Former (is) the Son, the Latter (is) the Father. Therefore, the Father and the Son know One another, but the Former by begetting, the Latter by being born. And all which are in Their Knowledge, in Their Wisdom, in Their Essence, each one of these He sees together, not piece by piece [particulatim] or one by one [singillatim], as if alternately by a gaze on this side (and) that side, and from there to here and then back, and/or from there unto one and another, as if He cannot see some, without not seeing others; but He sees all together, none of which is, that which He does not always see » and know [sciat]. « And so His Knowledge is incapable of being lost and varied [inamissibilis et invariabilis]. But our knowledge is capable of being lost and of being received, because for us 'to be' is not that which (it is) 'to know'. On this account, just as our knowledge is dissimilar to that Knowledge (which is) God's, so also our word, which is born from our knowledge, is dissimilar to that Word, which has been born from the Father according to knowledge ». — From this authority there is clearly shown, that God's Knowledge is entirely invariable, just as the very Essence of God is entirely invariable; and that the Father and the Son with the Holy Spirit know and see all at once. Therefore, just as the Divine Essence cannot be increased and/or lessened, so neither the Divine Knowledge. And yet it is conceded, that He can *know* what He does not know, and that He is able *not to know* what He does know; because something could be the subject of His Knowledge, which is not, and something could not be a subject, which is, without a thorough change [permutatione] of the Knowledge Itself.

CHAPTER II

Whether God can newly either know in time and/or foreknow something?

This is opposed by certain ones thus: if God can know and/or foreknow what He never knew and/or foreknew, He can, therefore, know and/or foreknow something on account of time. — To which we say: God can indeed know and/or foreknow everything which He can make, and He can make what never will come to be. Therefore, He can know and/or foreknow, what will never come to be, nor is, nor was. Nor that does He know and/or did He know, nor does He foreknow and/or did He foreknow, because His Knowledge is naught, but of those which are and/or were and/or will be; and (His) Foreknowledge is not but of future (things). And though He can know and/or fore-

---

[1] The Vatican edition, together with editions 3 and 5, have *under a condition* [sub conditione] for *of a condition* [de conditione].

NOTES ON THE BOOK OF SENTENCES

[1] Codex D has *lessened* [minui], codex E has *lessened and/or changed* [minui vel mutari].
[2] Chapter 13, n. 22. The following passage is ch. 14, n. 23, but some propositions have been transposed and others omitted by Master (Peter). The third passage is, again, ibid., ch. 13, n. 22. — In the last text, only the Vatican edition and editions 4, 5, 6, 8 and 9, after *incapable of being lost* [inamissibilis] add *and varied* [et invariabilis], breaking with even the original. Immediately after this, for *that which (it is) 'to know'* [quod scire] the Vatican edition reads *that which (it is) 'to be wise' and/or 'to know'* [quod sapere vel scire]; the original reads *that which (it is) 'to know' and/or 'to be wise'* [quod scire vel sapere].

know what never is nor will be; yet, He cannot know and/or foreknow something on account of time. He can, certainly [utique], know and/or foreknow what never is nor will be, nor has that been known and/or foreknown from eternity; yet He cannot *start* to know and/or foreknow that, but He can thus now know and/or foreknow, just as He is able to have known and/or foreknown from eternity. *For if you say*, that He now can know and/or foreknow what He did not know and/or foreknow from eternity, that is, so that from eternity He did not know and/or foreknow, as if each can be together; it is false. *However, if you say*, that He can now know and/or foreknow what He did not know and/or foreknow from eternity, that is, that He has a power of knowing and/or foreknowing from eternity even something now, and yet it has not been foreknown nor is going to be; it is true. Therefore, He cannot newly either on account of time know and/or foreknow something, just as He cannot newly and/or on account of time will something; and yet He can will what He has never willed.

CHAPTER III

Whether God can know more, than He knows?

Likewise, by certain ones God is said to be able to know more, than He knows, because He can know all which He knows, and He can make some, which never will be, and those He can know. For He can make some (which are) unknown [incognita]. But if all were, which now are, and He would make certain others, which are not nor will be, and would know them all, for certain [pro certo] He would know more, than He now knows. And yet His Knowledge cannot be increased,[1] because all this [hoc totum] can come to be without the changeability of knowledge. Therefore, it is established, that God's Knowledge is entirely immutable nor can it be increased and/or lessened, but Its subjects (can).

CHAPTER IV

That God, both always and together, knows all.

However, that which has been aforesaid, that is, that God sees all always and together, seems to obviated, what

(St.) Jerome says in (his) EXPOSITION OF HABACUC:[2] « It is absurd », he says, « to lead the Majesty of God to this, that He knows through single moments, how many gnats [culices] are born, or how many died, how many is the multitude of flees [pulicum] and flies, or how many fish swim in the waters and similar (things). Let us not be flatterers of God's utterance, as to be injurious unto ourselves, while we push back His Providence to the lowest depths [ad ima], saying that there is the same Providence for irrational and rational (things) ». Here (St.) Jerome seems, to say, that God does not have a Knowledge or Providence for those least (of things). Which if this is (true), then He does not know all together and always. — And so let us know that that has been said in such a sense, as to deny that God knows them alternately and/or piece by piece, nor did He cognize them thus through diverse moments of the seasons, just as through various moments certain of them fail, certain ones begin. Nor does He thus provide for those and other irrational (beings), according to the measure which (He does) for rational ones. *For is not God's care*, as the Apostle says,[3] *ever for the cattle?* And just as God's care does not concern the cattle, so neither (does it) concern the other irrational (things). Yet Scripture says, that that *care if for all*. Therefore, He has a providence and care *universally* for all, which He has founded, so that each one has what is due to and convenes with it. But He has a *special* providence and care for rational (beings), concerning whom[4] He has handed down [tradidit] the precepts and for them He prescribed a Law for living uprightly and promised rewards. This providence and care He does not have for irrational (beings). For this reason the Apostle says, that [quia] *God's care is not for the cattle*. Yet He provides and cares for all, that is, He governs all, *He who causes His sun to rise and grants rain*[5] for all. And so God knows, how many are the multitude of fees, gnats and of flies and fish, and how many are born, and how many die; but He does not know this through single moments, nay all together and always,[6] nor thus does He knows that He has the same providence for irrational and rational (beings), that is, that He provides in thoroughly the same manner for irrational and rational (beings). For to (those) rational He gave both precepts and delegated Angels for (their) guard.

And so God knows together and immutable all which were and are and will be, both good and evil; He also foreknows all future (things), both good and evil.

---

[1] Codex D adds *and/or lessened* [vel minui].

[2] Habacuc 1:14.

[3] 1 Corinthians 9:9; the other passage is Wis. 12:13.

[4] Understand: in respect of those which He gave the seven final precepts of the Decalogue [respectu quorum dedit septem praecepta posteriora decalogi]. This is the reading of the codices and edition 1; the other editions, less well, omit *concerning* [de], because, then, the sense of the words is the same as that,

which the following words express: *and to them He prescribed a Law for living uprightly* [eisque recte vivendi legem praescripsit].

[5] A reference to Mt. 5:45: He who causes His sun to rise upon the good and the wicked and rains upon the just and unjust [Qui solem suum oriri facit super bonos et malos et pluit super iustos et iniustos].

[6] Only the Vatican edition and editions 4, 5, 6, 8 and 9 have *once* [semel].

COMMENTARY ON DISTINCTION XXXIX

On the perfection of the Divine Knowledge.

Moreover, there is customarily asked, whether God's knowledge can be increased and/or lessened etc..

THE DIVISION OF THE TEXT

Above, Master (Peter) dealt with the *certitude* of the Divine Knowledge, here he deals with (Its) *perfection*. And since the truly perfect is that to which there is no possible addition,[1] for that reason Master (Peter) asks, whether the Divine Knowledge can be increased and/or lessened. And this part has three parts. In the *first* Master (Peter) asks and determines, wherefore does the Divine Knowledge not receive an increase or diminution nor an alteration, but cognizes all together and with one gaze. In the *second* he opposes against this, that the Divine Knowledge cannot be increased, through this, that it seems able to know something on account of time [ex tempore], and

he determines (it), and this he does in the second chapter, there (where he says): *This is opposed by certain ones* etc.. In the *third* he objects, by the authority of (St.) Jerome, against that which had been said, that the Divine Knowledge is in respect of all, and this there (where he says): *However, that which has been aforesaid, that is, that God* etc.. And any of these three parts can be subdivided, because in them he first opposes and second solves (the objections); yet in the second he posits a twofold response, and in the third after the response he subjoins an summation [epilogationem], in the last chapter.[2]

TREATMENT OF THE QUESTIONS

For an understanding of the present Distinction there is asked concerning the perfection of the Divine Cognition, and about this two (questions) are principally asked.

First, there is asked concerning the perfection of the Divine Cognition as much as regards the number of cognizables.

Second, there is asked concerning It as much as regards the manner of cognizing.

And, concerning the first, three (questions) are asked.

First, there is asked, whether God cognizes (those) other than Himself.

Second, there is asked, whether God cognizes all others than Himself.

Third, whether God can know and/or foreknow more, than He knows.

ARTICLE I

On the perfection of the Divine Cognition, as much as regards the number of the cognizables.

QUESTION I

Whether God cognizes (things) other than Himself?

Moreover, that God cognizes (those) other than Himself, is shown *by authority* [auctoritate]and *by reason* [ratione].

1. *By authority*, in this manner: the Psalm (says): *Will He who planted the ear not hear: or will He who formed the eye not*

consider? as if to say, it is impossible, that He gives others the power of cognizing, and does not Himself cognize.

2. Likewise, (there is written) in the twenty-third (chapter) of Ecclesiasticus:[4] *All, before they were created, (are) at once acknowledged by the Lord God, thus too*

---

[1] Cf. above d. 17, p. II, a. sole, q. 3, p. 312, footnote 5.
[2] Supply, together with the Vatican edition: *there (where he says): And so God knows together* [ibi: Simul itaque].

[3] Psalm 93:9.
[4] Verse 29.

after (the world has been) perfected, does He look back to all: therefore, if He does not create Himself, but another, He not only cognizes Himself, but also another.

3. Likewise, this is proven *by an ostensive reckoning* thus: everything producing things according to an *order* and *liberty* produces them as one precognizing (them)[1] — for if one produces *in an ordinate manner*, it is necessary, that one produce according to wisdom; again, if *according to liberty*, it is necessary, that (one produce) according to one's own wisdom, not another's — therefore, in this there is a cognition of all.

4. Likewise, among *beings* there is a *standing-still*,[2] therefore, for an equal reason (there is such) among *(those) able to cognize*; but the first *being* [ens], in which there is a standing-still, is the Principle, from which is every entity, and without which nothing is, nor is anything except from That: therefore, for the same reason in the first *One cognizing*, if there is a standing-still, it is necessary, that from Him be every cognition, and that through Him all be cognized, and without Him nothing. If, therefore, « (that) on account of which each one (is), that One (is) even more »:[3] it is clear that etc..

5. Likewise, this very (thing) is shows *through the impossible*, because if He does not cognize an other than Himself, therefore, either (He does so) because *He cannot*, or because *He will not*. Not because *He will not*, because in God the Will does not precede the Cognition: therefore, because *He cannot*. But everything cognizing, which cannot cognize something, which is cognizable, has a deficient and constrained cognition; which "being" is impossible in God: ergo etc..

6. Likewise, God can (do) nothing, except that which He knew, otherwise He could (do) something as One ignorant, which is absurd: therefore, if He did not know something other than Himself[4] and he cannot (do it) in Himself; since He is not above Himself, therefore, He can (do) nothing in the whole world: therefore, God is the most impotent, which is the most absurd (thing) to say.

BUT ON THE CONTRARY: 1. This is opposed according to *the reckoning of the Philosopher* in the twelfth (book) of (His) METAPHYSICS:[5] « The intelligible is the perfection of the intellect »: therefore, if God understands an other than Himself, His Intellect is perfected by the other; and if this, then there follows a threefold unfitting (result):

first, that His Cognition is cheapened [vilescit], since It is perfected by a thing less noble, that God is (Himself); second, that His Cognition and/or God Himself is transmuted, for everything which is perfected by another, has a passive potency, which is the principle of being transmuted; and the third unfitting (result) is, that God is not His own action, since action is from a perfection, and God is perfected by another etc..

2. Likewise, if God cognizes an other than Himself, since everything which is in God,[6] is the same as God, it is necessary, that that which He cognizes, be outside of God: therefore, if He cognizes another, He cognizes something outside of Himself. And from this there similarly arises a threefold unfitting (result), namely, that His cognition is in need of the exterior (thing), (that) it is also transmutable, and that it is other than Himself; all of which are unfitting.

3. Likewise, this same is shown through *the reason for cognizing*, since the reason for cognizing (a thing) is a truth itself; but (this) truth is the same as the entity of the thing, as (St.) Augustine says:[7] therefore, nothing is cognized by God except a being. But God cognizes nothing but from eternity: therefore, nothing is cognized by Him except a being, which is from eternity; but such is one alone, namely, God Himself: ergo etc..

4. Likewise, *the reason for cognizing* is an assimilation — for where there is a cognition, it is necessary, that there be there an assimilation of the one cognizing to the one cognizable[8] — therefore, where (there is) a most high cognition, there (is) a most high assimilation; but God's Cognition is most high and most perfect (assimilation): therefore, it ought to be attained according to a most high assimilation. But nothing is assimilated to God most highly except Himself: therefore, He cognizes Himself alone.

5. Likewise, it seems that there is no necessity to posit, that God cognizes (those) other than Himself, since, just as power holds itself to production, so intelligence to cognition; but God's Power, even if It produces nothing, is not less potent: therefore, if God's Intelligence cognizes nothing other than Himself, It is nevertheless most highly intelligent.

---

[1] On this proposition cf. above d. 35, a. sole, q. 1, p. 600, footnote 2. The words *according to an order* [secundum ordinem] are to be explained thus: in an ordered manner by destining (them) unto a determined end. On the context between order and wisdom, which is next made mention of, refer to that verse of Aristotle, METAPHYSICS, Bk. I, ch. 2: It is necessary that wisdom order (επτάττεσθαι), not be ordered (επιτάττειω).

[2] Cf. above d. 3, p. I, Doubt 1, p. 78, footnote 2. — After a few (words) for *(those) able to cognize* [cognoscibilibus] very many codices, such as K V Y and Z, have well *(those) cognizing* [cognoscentibus].

[3] Aristotle, POSTERIOR ANALYTICS, Bk. I, ch. 2.

[4] The Vatican edition, together with codex cc, here adds *and He cannot (do it) upon another than Himself* [nec potest supra aliud a se]; codex bb adds *He cannot do something other than Himself* [non potest aliquid aliud a se]; in all the other codices and edition1 nothing is added. Next for *since He is not* [cum non sit] many codices have *since He is* [cum sit], faultily.

[5] Text 51 (Bk. XI, ch. 9), where on behalf of an erroneous sentence, that the First Intellect does not understand others than Itself, this reason is brought to bear: « Then (it is) clear, that something else would be more honorable than the Intellect, namely: that which is understood ». Averroës in his Commentary on this text says: « On which account there will be another being more noble that this one; for the one understood is the perfection of the one understanding ». — The threefold unfitting (result), which the Seraphic Doctor next mentions, is insinuated also by Aristotle, loc. cit.. — For *by the other* [ab alio]

codices A I and T have *by that* [ab illo], codex b has *by something* [ab aliquo]. At the end of the argument for *from a perfection* [a perfectione], i. e. from a form (concerning which, cf. above d. 3, p. II, a. 1, q. 3, p. 84, footnote 7), the Vatican edition, together with editions 4 and 5, has *by one perfecting* [a perficiente], and then the same Vatican edition, together with codex cc, omits *by another* [alio].

[6] The Vatican edition , not without the authority of the codices, has changed the words *is in God* [est in Deo] into *God cognizes* [cognoscit Deus], and together with this it inserts *not* [non] after the previous *since* [cum], to render its own reading more reasonable. But that our reading, which we have restores from codices K V and X, is the true one, is evident and is also proved from the context.

[7] SOLILOQUIES, Bk. II, ch. 5, n. 8: For to me the true seems to be that which is. — The major of this argument is customarily expressed in this manner: Whatever is cognized, is cognized under a reckoning of the true. — For an understanding of the last proposition of this argument: *but such is one* etc., it will not be unuseful to refer to that verse of (St.) Augustine in (his book), OF EIGHTY-THREE QUESTIONS, q. 46, n. 2, where the holy Doctor, impugning the falsely accepted Platonic ideas, speaks thus: For He did not use to intuit something placed outside of Himself, so that according to that He constituted, what He was constituting; for to opine this is a sacrilege.

[8] Aristotle, NICOMACHEAN ETHICS, Bk. VI, ch. 1: If indeed from a certain similitude and affinity there is exists a cognition by these (the powers of the soul).

6. Likewise, the goodness of a creature compared to the Goodness of the Creator is as a point to a line, therefore, similarly the truth (of the one) to the truth (of the Other); but if a point is understood to be removed from a line, the line is no less nor more imperfect: therefore, if God cognizes His own Truth without the truth of a creature, His own Cognition is nevertheless perfect.

CONCLUSION

God does cognize an other than Himself, yet not through another, but through Himself.

I RESPOND: It must be said, that it is *pious* and *necessary* to say, that God cognizes an other than Himself: *pious* indeed, because every upright spirit says this, because what our spirit cognizes it is not hidden from God; *necessary*, since a work cannot be hidden from the most wise Worker. And for that reason to say the opposite is impious and impossible.

And, on that account, for an understanding of the objections it must be noted, that '*to cognize an other*' is in a twofold manner: either through *an other than oneself*, the one cognizing, or *through oneself*. When the one cognizing cognizes another and *through another*, then it is true, that it has (its) perfection from another, and then its intellect is in potency and receives from another (its) perfection and for that reason an addition and transmutation, and this is entirely impossible about God. There is, again, a 'to cognize *through oneself*'; and then there is a cognizing act[1] in respect of the cognizable, and then it does not receive a perfection from the cognizable, but rather the other way around. And in this manner we posit that God cognizes an other than Himself *through Himself*.

1. And, in this manner, the first reckoning does not proceed, but (it does) according to the first way, and the Philosopher understood (it) thus, if he spoke the truth.

2. To that which is objected second, that if God cognizes an other than Himself, therefore, something outside of Himself; it must be said, that 'to cognize something *outside of oneself*' is in a threefold manner: either through something conceived[2] from the outside, and thus the cognition *depends* from (something) extrinsic, and in this manner it is not possible to posit (it) in God; or (it is) 'to cognize something outside', because the gaze of the one cognizing *is deflected outside*, just as an Angel cognizes; or because that which is other and diverse, *has (its) rise from within*, and thus what is outside is cognized through (something) entirely intrinsic, and in this manner God cognizes, that is, through an exemplar, which

is the same as Himself, (and) by which things are cognized. And, in this manner, the objection has no value [nihil valet].

3. To that which is objected third, that from eternity there was only one being; it must be said, that there is a twofold *"being"* of a thing, that is, *in itself* and *in its own cause*, that is in its own genus, and in (its) exemplar. And for the cognition of a thing there suffices its existence in a cause or in an exemplar; and because through the exemplar it is represented, just as it is going to be in its own genus, for that reason through (its) existence in the exemplar it is entirely cognized, just as it is going to be, nor is it cognized in another manner, after it has been made. What, therefore, *is objected*, that from eternity there was only one being; it must be said, that it is true, in Its own genus or in (Its) actual 'to be'; yet there were many (things) in (It as) cause, and that "being" was the reason for cognizing (them) according to each manner of being.

4. To that which is objected fourth concerning assimilation, it must be said, just as had been said above in the Question concerning ideas,[3] that for a cognition there is required an assimilation, not through a convening in genus and/or species, but according to a reckoning of *expressing*. And, since the Divine Truth by a one and most high expression expresses Itself and others; for that reason there is a most high assimilation, not only in respect of Itself, but even in respect of others. And thus that (objection) is clear.

5. To that which is objected, that a power is said (to be) perfect, even if it makes nothing, ergo etc.; it must be said, that it is not similar concerning an act of *making* in respect of a *power*, and of *knowing* in respect of an *intelligence*. For '*to make*' is an act as an act and as one stepping forth, which does not cause a perfection, but is consequent (to it) and attests (to it); but '*to know*' is an act as a habit, which is signified as the perfection of a power.[4] Therefore, since the Divine Intelligence is the most perfect, for that reason it not only *cognizes* some (things), but everything which can be cognized, but It does not *make* everything which can be made.

6. To that which is objected last, that the truth of a creature causes nothing regarding the First Truth etc.; it must be said, that it is true, and for that reason the First Truth is equally noble and perfect before the creation of the truth of others, just as before. But yet to posit, that there is some truth, and it is not from the eternal Truth, is to posit that the First Truth is not a most high one; thus[5] to posit, that some truth is, and that it is not cognized, takes away the reckoning of a perfect truth, such as is the reason for cognizing. And for that reason it is clear, that (His) Cognition of a creature is from the perfection of the most high Truth, just as (is) also (His) Power of producing (it).

---

¹ Cod. T reads *the one cognizing is in act* [cognoscens est actu] for *there is a cognizing act* [cognoscens est actus].

² Edition 1 has *accepted* [acceptum].

³ Distinction 35, q. 1, in the body (of the q.) and in reply to n. 2.

⁴ Aristotle, METAPHYSICS, Bk. IX, text 16 (Bk. VIII, ch. 8), proposes the difference between a transient action and immanent one, which is here referred to, in this manner: « And so of whatsoever (acts) there is a certain other (something) which comes to be, besides (their) use, *it belongs to those acts in which it comes to be*, such as building in that which is built, and weaving in that which is woven; similarly both concerning the others, and entirely of a moving in a moved.

However, to these there belongs no other certain work besides the action, (for) *the action is in these very ones*, such as seeing in the one seeing, and speculation in the speculator, and life in the soul ». From these the Response of the Seraphic Doctor is easily understood. For '*to make*' [facere], as a transient action, presupposes the perfection of the power, and, for that reason, *the power* [potentia], whether it causes (it) or not, can be most perfect and a pure act; but '*to know*' [scire], as an immanent action, cannot be most perfect and a pure act, except (when) in it there is comprehended an actual cognition of all things.

⁵ Codices A I and Y have *but* [sed].

SCHOLIUM

I. That God cognizes created things not only according to (their) intelligible "being", which they have from eternity in God Himself, but also according to that, which they have in their own genus, is the common sentence of the Scholastics — except, as it seems, (Peter) Aureolus — and is manifestly asserted by the Seraphic Doctor (here in reply to n. 3). Therefore, things are also cognized *in themselves* [in se ipsis], to the extent that they are a *terminus* of the Divine Cognition. But it must be said in another manner, if the words "*in themselves*" [in se ipsis] are understood of *the medium of* or *reason* for cognizing. Therefore, one distinguishes the medium *by which* [medium quo] and the medium *in which* [medium in quo]. The medium *by which* is that which renders the cognizing power proximately able to cognize, and it is also called the *non-cognized* medium, which in us is the intelligible species and also the light of the agent intellect. The medium *in which* (the *cognized* medium) is that which (when) cognized leads unto the cognition of the other thing, such as things seen in a mirror, and conclusions in principles. — However, that the Divine Essence alone is the medium, *by which* God cognizes, is evident and received by all; that the Same is *alone* also the medium *in which* (God cognizes), such that God cognizes all created (things) in His own Essence as in a cognized medium, is the sentence of the ancient Scholastics. Whence Alexander of Hales (SUMMA., p. I, q. 23, m. 3, a. 4) says: « God's Knowledge, which is *regarding things*, is not *through things*; whence since He Himself is an immutable cause, He cognizes through an immutable and necessary cause even contingent (things) ». St. Thomas (SUMMA CONTRA GENTILES, I, ch. 48), Bl. (now St.) Albertus (Magnus), Richard (of Middleton), and St. Bonaventure (here in the reply to n. 2 and to n. 6, and in a. 2, q. 1, in the arguments of the fundament and in the body of the Response) agree. — But it must be noted well, what (here in the reply to n. 2) is said of the threefold manner, by which something existing outside the one cognizing can be cognized, lest anyone think, that God cognizes created things thus, that His Knowledge is, just as ours, discursive, and/or so that the gaze of the One cognizing is deflected <u>ad extra</u>, « just as an Angel cognizes » (which is explained in SENT, Bk. II, d. 3, p. II, a. 2, q. 1).

Very many authors think otherwise, after the rise of the controversies of the XVI Century concerning the divine assistance, teaching, that God cognizes created things, insofar as they are in themselves, not in Himself as in a cognized medium, but *immediately in themselves*. These same, with Suarez, apply this principle to the cognition of conditionally contingent futures, and they say, that these are cognized in *their objective truth*, before and independently from every decree of the Divine Will. This sentence is contradicted by many, and even by not a few of the defenders of the <u>scientia mediae</u>, among whom is Father P. Kleutgen, S. J., in his outstanding work: INSTITUTIONES THEOLOG., Regensburg, 1881, tome I, n. 548.

II. Here we come upon a most difficult question, and one considered very much by theologians throughout three centuries, concerning *the reason* or *medium*, by which God cognizes absolutely free contingents and/or conditionally future (contingents). It is not for us to judge concerning all the sentences, proffered about this matter in the meantime; but it does suffice, that *first* we refer briefly to the other principle opinions, besides that which has already been named, and *then* to propound the sentence of St. Bonaventure.

1. The *Nominalists* affirm that this question is insolvable by the human intellect, and they recur to the infinite perfection of the Divine Intellect, whose « eternal eye has an intuitive vision of all things, nay, speaking on my own [ut proprius loquar], It is a certain incomprehensible intuition, which is at once born immediately over any thing actually and/or possibly existing » (Gregory of Rimini, here in q. 2, a. 2). — *Not a few* among the ancient *Thomists*, among whom (are) Capreolus and Cajetan, think that the key to reveal this secret was to be found among the words of St. Thomas (SUMMA., I, q. 44, a. 13), that God's « intuiting is born from eternity upon all, insofar as *they are in their quality of being present* », concerning which sentence there will be said not a few things here in the Scholium to a. 2, q. 3. — The *others* devoted to the School of *St. Thomas* now commonly hold, that God cognizes free, *absolutely* future (things) in His own Will's intrinsically efficacious decrees [decretis ab intrinseco efficacibus], but that (He cognizes) free, *conditionally* future (things) in (those) decrees (of His Will which are) absolute on the part of (their) subject, (but) conditioned

on the part of (their) object (Gotti, THEOLOG. SCHOLAST., tome I, tr. 4, q. 5, Doubt 5, and q. 6, Doubt 2). — (Bl. John Duns) *Scotus* (here in the q. sole, n. 23, and in d. 41, a. sole, n. 10; REPORTATIO, d. 40, q. sole) teaches, that the Divine Essence represents things, to the extent that they are going to be in a determinate manner, out of *the determination* of His own Will. This determination Mastrius (DISPUTAT. THEOLOG., tome I, d. 3, q. 3, a. 8) strives to explain in the sense of a concomitant decree, which exposition was afterwards received by many. But both those words of (Bl.) Scotus, and the authority of his better interpreters, such as Lychetus, Rada, Frassenius and very many others, gave another more probable interpretation, which understands that determination in the sense of antecedent decrees, so that this determination is the cause, wherefore things pass from a state of mere possibility to have indeed infallibly an existence in the future, but so that they proceed contingently and freely from their own proximate cause.

2. St. Bonaventure use s another manner of speaking, namely, that God « has *ideas* of all, present and at once, through which He cognizes future things so certainly, just as if they were present » (here in a. 2, q. 3), or in other words: « because through the exemplar (the thing) is represented, just as it is going to be in its own genus, for that reason through (its) existence in the exemplar it is entirely cognized, just as it is going to be, nor is it cognized in another manner, after it has been made » (here in the reply to n. 3). This formula of saying, that God cognizes all future (things) in His own *ideas*, pleased even not a few of the more ancient disciples of St. Thomas (cf. Mastrius, <u>loc</u>. <u>cit</u>., a. 1), but was reproved by (Bl. John Duns) Scotus (here in the q. sole, n. 7), chiefly for this reason, because ideas represent only things merely *possible*; likewise because they represent them only as *simple termini*, not however, to the extent that these terms are contingently joined in complex propositions. These reasons proceed from that doctrine of ideas which (Bl.) Scotus professed, but they are not valid, supposing the acceptation of "*ideas*", which St. Bonaventure professes, as we have mentioned above in the Scholium of d. 35, q. 1. For an *idea* is accepted by him in a broader sense, to the extent that it represents not only things in a state of *possibility*, but even those, to the extent that they exist in their own genus and presuppose the determination of the Divine Will. (St. Bonaventure) took this signification of ideas from Dionysius (ON THE DIVINE NAMES, ch. 5, n. 8 at the end), who according to the edition of Corderius teaches: « We say that exemplars (παραδείγματα) are in God the substantifying and unitedly [substantificas et unite] preexisting reasons of things, which the Divine Speech calls the "predefinitions" and the "divine and good wills" [voluntates], the definers and effecters of things, according to which He, who is above substance, predefined and produces all, which are ». Even St. Thomas accepts ideas in the same broader sense, as in DE VERITATE, q. 3, a. 6, where he distinguishes « ideas (which are) in a certain manner *indeterminate* », which look back to those which never are nor will be nor were, and the idea, which « to produce those which are and/or will be and/or were *is determined* out of a proposal of the Divine Will » (cf. <u>ibid</u>., a. 1, where the same passage from Dionysius is cited, and SUMMA, I, q. 14, a. 13). Also favoring this is Bl. (now St.) Albertus Magnus (here in a. 12), who distinguishes a twofold reckoning in an idea, to the extent that it is *light*, as a reason for cognizing, and *life*, as a principle of movement; and as life and light is « the principle of each and every created "being" ». Moreover, in his SUMMA, p. I, tr. 15, q. 60. m. 4, a. 1, part. 5, he explicitly says, that God « cognizes through exemplary reasons, just as Dionysius says ».

Moreover, that St. Bonaventure, when he says that ideas are for God a reason for cognizing all others than Himself, does not exclude the causality of the Divine Will, but presupposes (it), is manifestly apparent from many passages: v. g. here in a. 2, q. 1, among others, he says, that God's Knowledge is compared « to a creature according to a reckoning of diversity and of *causality*, and for that reason (is compared) to a creature according to the reckoning of (its) being ideated [secundum rationem ideandi] » (cf. above d. 36, a. 1. q. 1, especially in the 1st argument of the fundament and in the reply to n. 2, and in a. 2, q. 1). — This is entirely confirmed by the same's profound doctrine concerning the (Divine) *Will* as the Cause of things, below in d. 45, a. 2, q. 1,

where he says in reply to n. 2: « In the (Divine) Will there is first found the reckoning of actuality. For power and knowledge, even if they have a reckoning of a habitual cause, yet (they do) not (have one) of an actual (cause) except through a will. Whence (God's) Will causes from the Knowledge a disposition or causes, that the Knowledge be a disposing and executing power » (cf. d. 40, Doubt 7). He also teaches in d. 45, a. 2, q. 2, in what sense the Divine Will is the immediate cause of all which are, not excluding secondary causes, and he affirms there (in reply to n. 4), that God's Will, fully cognized, is the sufficient cause for cognizing all other (things). Whence the Seraphic Doctor does not dissent from St. Thomas, who so frequently says, that God cognizes all others outside of Himself, inasmuch as He is their cause (SUMMA CONTRA GENTILES, I, chs. 49, 65, and 67), « and that inasmuch as God's Knowledge extends Itself, insomuch does His causality extend itself » (SUMMA, I, q. 14, a. 11). The same is frequently taught by Bl. (now St.) Albertus (Magnus), such as in his SUMMA, p. I, tr. 15, q. 60, m. 4, a. 1, part. 3, in reply to n. 1, and by Alexander of Hales, SUMMA., p. I, q. 23, m. 3, a. 4.

Moreover, it must be noted, that according to the words of St. Bonaventure it does not seem that this *causality* is to be restricted to an *efficient* cause alone, which supposes the good pleasure of the (Divine) Will (d. 40, Doubt 7), but rather is to be extended to a threefold genus of cause, according to which things are said *to be in God*, « namely as in a *producing principle*, and thus they are there by reason of the (Divine) Power; as in an *expressing exemplar*, as thus they are there by reason of (their) being known; as in a *conserving end*, and thus they are there by reason of the (Divine) Will » (above in d. 36, a. 2, q. 1). He explicitly says, that two (things) concur for the reckoning of an exemplar, namely, a reckoning of *power* and of *being known*, « for God is not an exemplar but of those which He cognizes and can (make) » (ibid., in reply to n. 2, and

d. 36, Doubts 1 & 4, and the many arguments in the fundaments of the Questions in dd. 35 and 36). Hence it is, that he teaches very frequently, that everything true depends from the first exemplary Cause (here in reply to n. 6). just as every being (depends) from the first efficient Cause, (and) every good from the first final Cause; and that in Distinctions 36, 36, 38, 39, and 40, he very frequently names (God), besides "the efficient Cause", "the First Truth expressing every truth". Especially, when he deals with the cognition of future contingents, he appeals to the perfection and clarity of the Eternal Light, as in d. 40, a. 2, q. 1, in reply to n. 1, 2 and 3, and in d. 39, a. 2. q. 2.

The foundation of this doctrine, namely, that the one, most simple Essence of God under diverse reckonings of understanding is the efficient, exemplary, (and) final Cause of the whole order of real and ideal things, has not been questioned. The dissension among theologians began only, when one descends to species and to the determining of the diverse manners of this causality; and nor has there been found up to now a system, which is approved by (their) common estimation.

III. Alexander of Hales, on this and the following q., SUMMA., p. I, q. 23, m. 3, throughout. — (Bl. John Duns) Scotus, on this and the following q., SENT., Bk. I, d. 36. q. 1, and d. 38, qq. 1 and 2. — S. Thomas, on this and the following q., SENT., Bk. I, d. 38, q. sole, a. 2, 3 and 5; SUMMA., I, q. 14, a. 5 and 6. — Bl. (now St.) Albertus (Magnus), on this and the following q., SENT., Bk. I, d. 36, a. 4, and d. 39. a . 9; SUMMA., p. I, tr. 15, q. 60, m. 3. — (Bl.) Peter of Tarentaise, SENT., Bk. I, d. 35, q. 1, a. 4. — Richard of Middleton, SENT., Bk. I, d. 35, q. 3. — Giles the Roman, on this and the following q., SENT., Bk. I, d. 35, 1st princ., qq. 1 and 2; d. 38, p. II, q. 1; and d. 39, 1st princ., q. 3. — Durandus (of Saint-Pourçain), SENT., Bk. I, d. 35, q. 1. — (Bl.) Dionysius the Carthusian, on this and the following q., SENT., Bk. I, d. 35, q. 1. — (Gabriel) Biel, on this and the following q., SENT., Bk. I, d. 36, qq. 2 and 4.

QUESTION II

Whether God cognizes all others than Himself?

Second, granted that God cognizes (those) other than Himself, there is asked, whether He cognizes all others than Himself. And that He does, seems:

1. By the authority of Jeremias, (chapter) seventeen:[1] *Depraved is the heart of man* etc., and afterwards: *I, the Lord, scrutinizing hearts and minds* [corda et renes];* but nothing (is) more uncertain, nothing more hidden from our thoughts: therefore, if He cognizes these, (He) also (cognizes) all others.

2. Likewise, in the fourth (chapter of St. Paul's Letter) to the Hebrews (there is written):[2] *All are bare and open to the eyes of Him, regarding Whom (is) our speech.* And again: *The Word* [sermo] *of God is living and efficacious*, up to this, *and no creature is invisible in His sight.*

3. Likewise, in the last (chapter of the Gospel of St.) John (there is written): *Lord, Thou knowest all.*

4. Likewise, (St.) Augustine in the third (book) ON THE TRINITY (says):[4] « Nothing becomes visible nor intelligible, which from the interior and invisible court [aula] of the Most High Emperor is not commanded, or permitted, according to the ineffable justice of punishments and rewards, and graces and merits ». And if this (is so): therefore, He cognizes all (things).

5. Likewise, it seems *by reason*, because as much as a substance is more spiritual and more simple, so much is it cognitive of more;[5] but God is the most simple and most spiritual substance: therefore, He is cognitive of all.

6. Likewise, God is the Creator and Remunerator; but inasmuch as a creator is a craftsman, insomuch (is) a remunerator a judge; but a perfect craftsman cognizes all products, a perfect judge all to be remunerated: if, therefore,[6] every creature pertains to craftsmanship, and every good and evil to judgement, therefore, God cognizes every creature, and all goodness and wickedness.

7. Likewise, it is impossible, that something be, in which God is not through the presence of (His) Essence, as has been proven above;[7] but to whatsoever He is present through essence, (He is) also (present through) cognition: therefore: it is impossible, that something be uncognized by God.

8. Likewise, if He were in one thing thus, that (He was) not in another, His Essence would be limited: therefore, if He thus cognized, that others were uncognized, His Cognition would be limited and constrained, and thus imperfect.

---

[1] Verses 9-10, where the Vulgate exhibits *of all* [omnium] for *of man* [hominis], and placing *probing* [probans] before *minds* [renes]. — Next, for *more uncertain* [incertius] codd. I & O have *more interior* [interius].

[2] Verse 13. The following text is ibid., vv. 12 and 13, where the Vulgate has *no* [non ... ulla] for *no* [non ... aliqua].

[3] Verse 17.

[4] Chapter 4, n. 9. In the original text for *becomes visible nor intelligible* [fit visibile nec intelligibile] there is read *comes to be visibly and sensibly* [fit visibiliter et sensibiliter], and at the end the same has *retributions* [retibutionem] for *merits* [meritorum].

[5] Cf. the BOOK OF CAUSES, proposition 10, and Aristotle, ON THE SOUL, Bk. III, text 3 ff. (ch. 4.).

[6] Together with codd. D P Q (T by a second hand) and ed. 1, we have put *if, therefore,* [si ergo] for the *but* [sed], which is extant in the Vatican ed..

[7] Distinction 37, p. I, a. 1. q. 1 ff.. — In the minor proposition, which follows, among the words *also cognition* [et cognitionem] supply *He is present through* [praesens est per]. The reason enunciated in this minor proposition for the sentence is, that in God the Essence is the same as the Cognition. For *to whatsoever* [cuicumque] many codices, together with edition 1, have less well arranged.

---

* *Trans. note*: For the Hebrews, the seat of a man's conscience and will was in the kidneys and heart, respectively; but in English, we place these seats, respectively, in the heart and mind. Since the intent of the metaphor is to refer to things spiritual and not to the organs of the body, I have taken the liberty to replace the Hebraic metaphor, conserved in the Vulgate, with the English one.

BUT ON THE CONTRARY: 1. Everything more noble is to be attributed to God; but « not knowing certain (things) is better than knowing (them) », just as (St.) Augustine says in (his) ENCHIRIDION:[1] therefore, it is necessary to posit, that God does not know those.

2. Likewise, our intellect on account of its immateriality does not understand singulars — wherefore, as the Philosopher[2] says, « there is an understanding of universals, and a sensing of singulars » — but the Divine Intellect is much more immaterial than our own: therefore, if our own does not understand singulars, neither (does) the Divine.

3. Likewise, our habit of knowledge [habitus scientialis] on account of its certitude is not but of necessaries, and not of contingents, because (St. Severinus) Boethius[3] says, that « knowledge is of those which are allotted their own immutable existence ». If, therefore, the Divine Cognition is much more certain than our knowledge, it is clear that etc..

4. Likewise, what necessity is there to posit that God cognizes all? And it seems that (there is) none, because our cognition is not said (to be) less perfect, if it does not cognize one fly: if, therefore, the Divine Cognition is much less perfected by a knowable, It will not be imperfect, if It does not cognize those of little worth [ista vilia].

5. Likewise, just as God is[4] omniscient, so is He omnipotent; but the power of evil does not concern omnipotence nor the perfection of power: therefore, similarly also the cognition of evil does not concern the perfection of knowledge, ergo etc..

6. Likewise, this very (thing) is shown by authorities, and first by the authority of Habacuc:[5] *Clean are Thine eyes, Lord, lest they see evil* etc. Likewise, of the wicked there is said in the twenty-fifth (chapter of the Gospel of St.) Matthew:[6] *I do not know you.*

CONCLUSION

God, by a cognition of a simple being known, cognizes all (things), good and evil, but (by that) of approbation only good (things).

I RESPOND: It must be said for an understanding of the objections, that in God there is the being known of *approbation* [notitia approbationis], and (that) of *a simple being known* [simplicis notitiae]. And the being known of *approbation* connotes the complacency of the (Divine) Will. By this God does not cognize all, because (with this God cognizes) neither evils nor the wicked, but only

good (things) and the good; and concerning this are understood the last two authorities.[7] And the other (is) the cognition of *a simple being known*; and this because (the thing) has (its) reason for being cognized from the Truth, which is a most high light, which nothing can cover over [occultari], nor are even *shadows darkened by It,*[8] for that reason He cognizes of necessity all, great and small, good and evil, just as the reasons for the first side shown.

1. To that, therefore, which is first objected, that everything more noble is to be attributed to God; it must be said, that there is a better *simply*, and there is a better *that this* and (a better) according to a standing-still. I say, therefore, that to know all *simply* is better and more noble; but *to a corrupt man*, who accepts an occasion for sinning from a cognition, not knowing certain (things) is better. For that reason it does not follow, that it is to be attributed to God.

2. To that which is objected concerning the immateriality of the intellect, it must be said, that this, that it does not cognize singulars, does not only come from (its) immateriality, nay from the materiality of (its) conjoined (body) and its own immateriality. For, since it is conjoined to a body, for that reason it has powers, according to which it depends from the body as much as regards (its) operation, and through which the intellect, so long as it is in the body, goes forth to exterior (things), because those (powers) are (its) media, namely, the sense of the particular and the imagination. Therefore, since a singular does not come to [pervenit ad] the intellect except through those powers, and the ascending through these is according to an abstraction and a purification from [depurationem] (matter), and the abstraction makes of the singular a universal,[9] for that reason it cannot cognize singulars as an intellect, unless the intellect be separated and/or divine.

3. To that which is objected concerning the certitude of (our) knowledge, it must be said, that this is not on account of certitude *simply*, but on account of the certitude *caused by the thing*. And since certitude is caused in our cognition and/or[10] depends out of the thing [ex re], for that reason our cognition cannot be certain, unless the thing be necessary. But the Divine Cognition, since it is not caused by nor depends from the thing [a re], for that reason it can be certain of a contingent thing [de re contingenti].

5. To that which is objected, that the power of evil does not concern omnipotence: ergo etc.; it must be said, that it is not similar, because rectitude, remaining rectitude, is not a reason for *cognizing* evil; but rectitude is not a *cause of evil*, unless by declining from rectitude and

---

[1] Chapter 17, n. 5. And Aristotle, METAPHYSICS, Bk. XII, text 51 (ch. 9): And indeed certain (things) it is better not to see than to see.

[2] In many passages. Cf. POSTERIOR ANALYTICS, Bk. I, chs. 14, 20, and 24 (chs. 18, 24, and 31); ON THE SOUL, Bk. II, text 60 (ch. 5), METAPHYSICS, Bk. I, ch. 1.

[3] ON ARITHMETIC, Bk. I, ch. 1: « For wisdom is of the things, which are and are allotted their own immutable substance, the comprehension of the truth ». The same is taught by Aristotle, POSTERIOR ANALYTICS, Bk. I, last chapter, and ETHICS, Bk. VI, ch. 3, 6.

[4] The Vatican edition, together with codex cc, has *is said (to be)*. Next after *of power* [potentiae] the Vatican edition adjoins *naturally* [naturaliter].

[5] Habacuc 1:13, where the Vulgate, having omitted *Lord* [Domine], procedes thus: *lest Thou see evil* [ne videas malum]. Our reading, as the ed. of (St.) Jerome's (works) attests, was the other in use.

[6] Verse 12.

[7] Which are cited in the 6th opposed argument.

[8] Psalm 138:12: *Because the shadows shall not be darkened by Thee* [Quia tenebrae non obscurabuntur a te].*

[9] Just as the intellect in eliciting by a cognition of exteriors through intermediaries, i.e. the sensible powers, quasi goes forth and descends to exteriors, so *the singular* or species which the singular generates in the intermediary and organ, enters and ascends from the sense of a particular to the common sense and thence through the fantasy even unto the understanding. So the ascending species is abstracted and purified from singular or individuating conditions. Cf. ITINERARIUM MENTIS IN DEUM, ch. 2, and Aristotle, ON THE SOUL, Bk. III, text 39 (ch. 8). — Next for *it cannot cognize singulars as an intellect* [non potest singularia cognoscere ut intellectus] codex O has *our intellect cannot cognize singulars* [non potest singularia cognoscere noster intellectus], and then many codices, such as C G H K L O R S U V Y, proceed thus: *not so a separated and/or divine intellect* [non sic intellectus separatus vel divinus].

[10] Pro *and/or* [vel] codex O has *it necessarily* [necessario].

---

* *Trans. note*: That is, the Light of God is not like those impotent material lights, which when lit, cast darker shadows because of the paucity of the magnitude of the dimension of their source.

failing. For that reason, '*to know* evil' [scire malum] does concern the perfection of knowledge, but '*to be able (to do)* evil' [posse malum] does not concern the perfection of power.

4. To that which is asked,[1] "What is the necessity for cognizing that God (knows) all?"; It must be said, that (it is) the infinity and immensity of the Truth, which does not suffer, that anything be hidden from God, just as the immensity of the Divine Presence does not suffer, that anything be absent from God.

SCHOLIUM

I. In this general question the Seraphic (Doctor) solves also special problems, which are treated by the other masters (such as Alexander of Hales, SUMMA., p. I, q. 23, m. 3, a. 1-7) in distinct questions. In particular he solves the question (in the reply to n. 2), whether God cognizes *singulars*, where he also touches upon the question, whether *our* intellect in virtue of the state of a wayfarer *directly* cognizes singulars; which the Seraphic Doctor denies, together with Alexander of Hales (loc. cit., a. 6, in reply to n. 1) and St. Thomas (SUMMA., I, q. 86, a. 1). (Bl. John Duns) Scotus thinks otherwise (SENT., Bk. I, d. 3, q. 2 and passim), together with Durandus (of Saint-Pourçain) and others. This difference of opinions is coherent with the controversy concerning the adequate object of the human intellect, whether it is the quiddity of a material thing, as the School of St. Thomas teaches, or whether (it is) being taken *most commonly*, such as is a *real* being in common, not only the quiddity of the sensible thing, as (Bl.) Scotus judges it; concerning which there is a copious disputation in the books of Philosophy of each School.

II. In the Response and in the solution to n. 5 the cognition of *evil* is briefly discussed. Those which are touched upon here are explained more above in d. 36, a. 3, qq. 1 and 2, and below in d. 46, qq. 4 and 5. The ancient scholastics agree in this, that evil is not cognized by God except through another, « because it is of the reckoning of evil, that it is a privation of a good, and thus it can be neither defined nor cognized except through a good » (St. Thomas, SUMMA., I,

q. 14, a. 10, in reply to n. 4). The fundament of this doctrine is, that « an evil is substantified [substantificatur] in a good, and not only in a good, but also in the good opposed to it in a certain manner ». (St. Bonaventure, SENT., Bk. II, d. 34, a. 2. q. 2), and that *pure* evil is not possible, according to the same (loc. cit., q. 1): « To posit that there is something evil, which has nothing of the good, does not only belong to a heretical perversity, but also to a manifest blindness and stupidity ». Hence it is, that « though evil is not the subject of a divine *production*, yet it is the subject of the (Divine) *foresight* » (below in d. 46, q. 5, in reply to n. 3); and though as a *privation* it has naught but a *deficient* cause and (has) to no extent any cause *in God*, yet it can « be in God's Foreknowledge, which is naught but of the true. However, for this, that something be in God's Foreknowledge, it is sufficient, that *it*, and/or its *cause*, and/or its *opposite* be in God as in a cause » (ibid., q. 4, in reply to n. 4). That '*to be able* to do evil' does not concern the reckoning of power, is explained below in d. 42, q. 2.

III. (Bl.) Peter of Tarentaise, SENT., Bk. I, d. 36, q. 1, a. 1 and 2; d. 38, q. 2, a. 2; and d. 39, q. 2, a. 1 and 2. — Richard of Middleton, SENT., Bk. I, d. 35, q. 5; d. 36, a. 1, qq. 1 and 2; and d. 38, q. 5. — Durandus (of Saint-Pourçain), SENT., Bk. I, d. 35, qq. 1 and 2, and d. 38, q. 3.

QUESTION II

Whether God necessarily foreknows what He foreknows?

Third, there is asked whether God can know and/or foreknow more, than He knows. And that He can know more, is shown in this manner:

1. Nothing is known except being and the true [ens et verum];[2] but many can be, which are not, and be verified, which are false: therefore, many can be known by God, which, however, are not known.

2. Likewise, it seems that He can foreknow more, because (His) Foreknowledge [praescientia] is only of (things) future; but many (things) can be future, which never will come to be nor shall be: therefore, many (things) can be foreknown, which are not foreknown: therefore, God can foreknow more, than He knows.[3]

BUT ON THE CONTRARY: 1. It seems that He cannot know more, because God's Knowledge is of (things)

infinite, since It is infinite, just as has been proven above; but there cannot be nor be thought more (things) than (those) infinite: ergo etc..

2. Likewise, if He can foreknow more, either more *non-complex* (beings) or more things, or more *complex (beings)* or enunciable (propositions). Not more *non-complex* (beings), because God knows things, even if they never are, for He knows all which can come to be. Similarly, not more *complex* (beings), because of any contradiction one part is always true, the other false: therefore, concerning complex (propositions) there are as many true ones as there are false ones:[5] therefore, he who knows all (propositions) cannot know more, because there cannot be more true (propositions).

3. Likewise, it seems that He cannot foreknow more, than He foreknows, because whatsoever God foreknows, He foreknows together nor can He foreknow except together: if,

---

[1] The codices, posting this solution in the last place, perhaps to respond to the incidental question.

[2] Aristotle, POSTERIOR ANALYTICS, Bk. I, ch. 2, speaking in an orderly fashion of the conditions required for *knowing*, says: True (principles) indeed, therefore, there must be, since of that which is not, there is no knowing.

[3] The Vatican ed., with a few mss., has *He foreknows* [praesciat].

[4] Distinction 35, q. 5.

[5] Cf. Aristotle, ON THE PREDICAMENTS, ch. "On *Opposites*", and ON INTERPRETATION, Bk. I, ch. 6 (ch. 7), and METAPHYSICS, Bk. IV, text 9 ff. (Bk. III, ch. 3). — At the beginning of this argument after *Likewise* [Item] we have restored, on the authority of codices H M Y and bb, the *if* [si], which the Vatican edition omits, which (edition) also then exhibits *know* [scire] for *foreknow* [praescire].

therefore, He can foreknow more, than He foreknows, therefore, either *together*, or *successively*. *Together* is impossible, *successively* (is) similarly impossible, because in eternity there is no succession: therefore, in no manner.

4. Likewise, if He can foreknow more, therefore, since there is a greater foreknowledge of a more, at least extensively, and that which can be more can be increased, therefore, the Divine Foreknowledge can be increased; but where (there is) an increase, there (is) a change and variation: therefore, the Divine Knowledge[1] can be changed and varied.

CONCLUSION

There can be a knowledge of approbation and of vision of more, but not a knowledge of simple understanding.

I RESPOND: It must be said, that when it is asked, whether God can foreknow and/or know more, one must judge concerning *the (Divine) Foreknowledge* in a manner other than concerning *the (Divine) Knowledge*. For, just as is accustomed to be said, God's Cognition is threefold, not as much as regards the diversity of the cognition, but (as regard the diversity) of the (things) connoted (by It),[2] namely, the cognition of *approbation*, of *vision* and of *understanding* [intelligentiae]. The cognition of *approbation* is only of those to which the good pleasure of the (Divine) Will extends itself, and this is only of those which come to be and are good; and this (cognition) without doubt can be of more. However, the cognition of *understanding* is said (to be) the cognition, by which God cognizes everything possible both to Himself and to others, and by this God cognizes infinite (things); and this can in no manner be of more. The cognition of *vision* is of those of which there was from eternity a (Divine) Foreseeing [praevisio],[3] and this is only of those which are and/or were and/or will be; and this cognition can be of more, than it is. And because this cognition is of the same, of which the Foreknowledge is,

there can be a Foreknowledge of more. — There must be conceded, therefore, that a certain Knowledge can be of more, a certain One not. And through this the response to the objections concerning the (Divine) Knowledge is clear.

1. 2. For what it objects, that God's Knowledge is of (things) infinite, and that It connotes nothing about the non-complex; it must be said, that this is true of the knowledge of *understanding*, but it is not true of the knowledge of *vision*. — Moreover, what is objected concerning the Foreknowledge, it must be conceded, that It can be of more.

3. On the other hand, what is objected regarding the opposite, that if He can know more, either together, or not together; it must be said, that togetherness [simultas] can be attained in a twofold manner: either as much as regards *the substance* of the foreknown[4] or (as regards) the cognition; thus it is true, that (He foreknows them) *together*, because from eternity He foreknew certain ones and from eternity He could foreknow more and is able to have foreknown more. But if the togetherness is attained as much as regards a *reckoning of paucity and plurality*, thus there is a implication of opposites, and in this manner the sense is, that He foreknows more and fewer together. And in the first sense the objection has truth.

4. To that which is objected, if He can foreknow more, that (His) Foreknowledge can be increased; it must be said, that let it be, that *the foreknown* could be increased, yet *the Foreknowledge* would not be increased, because God foreknows by one and the same both many and one, both the more and the few. Yet though the foreknown can *be more*, yet they cannot *be increased*, because 'to be increased' concerns the fewer becoming more; but this: "*to be able to be more*" has two causes of (its) truth: either because of the fewer there can come to be more, or because from the start there could be more; and in this last sense the saying is true. And for that reason, since (the objection) proceeds from many causes of truth to one, it causes a sophism according to the consequent.[5]

SCHOLIUM

I. To solve this Question one must use the distinction between the knowledge of *simple understanding* and the knowledge of *vision*. St. Thomas proposes the same question (SUMMA, I, q. 14, a. 15) under the title: "Whether God's Knowledge is variable?" The difference, which there is between the solutions of the ancient doctors, seems to consist in only a manner of speaking. For it is commonly received: 1. that (God's) Knowledge of *simple understanding* is entirely invariable; 2. likewise, too the Knowledge of *vision* and of *approbation*, to the extent that It is considered on the part of the *One cognizing*, 3. but, to the extent that It is considered on the part of *things cognized*, since God could have proposed to Himself from eternity the creating of more in time, the Knowledge of vision and « of foreknowledge can be of more » (here in the body of the Response; cf. St. Thomas, SUMMA., I, q. 14, a. 15, in reply to n. 2). This is also valid concerning the Knowledge of *approbation*, if It is ac-

cepted in respect of the things which have, are, or will every exist [rerum unquam existentium]. The other say the same thus: the Knowledge of vision is *invariable* in the *composed sense*, that is, having supposed that determination of the (Divine) Will has already been made; but (It is) *variable* in the *divided sense*, or as separated from that determination. — For a better explanation, cf. above d. 38, a. 2, q. 2; below in d. 412, a. 2. q. 2; and in regard to the solution to n. 2, below in d. 42, q. 2. qq. 1 and 2. For what it objects in regard to the Knowledge of *complex (sayings)*, as many (parts) of which are false as are true, and the false are foreseen just as the true, excited the subtility of the ancient Scholastics not a little and moved them, to deny the solution given here. But the general response of the Seraphic Doctor seems to be sufficient. — To the 4th objection there is given a twofold solution. The first is clear, the second proceeds from the distinction between '*being more*' and '*being increased*' or '*becoming more*'; *the former* can be

---

[1] Codex T has *Foreknowledge* [praescientia].

[2] For *of the (things) connoted (by It)* [connotatorum] the Vatican edition, together with codex cc, has *of the cognized* [cognitorum].

[3] Codex T has *a (Divine) Foreseer* [praevisor].

[4] Namely, to the extent that they have been foreknown. — For *of the foreknown* [praescitorum] the Vatican ed. alone has *of the Foreknowledge* [praescientiae]. Next, for *is able to have foreknown* [potest

praescisse] the Vatican ed., with some mss., has *could have foreknown* [potuit praescisse].

[5] Concerning which, see Aristotle, ELENCHAE, Bk. I, ch. 4 (ch. 5), where to show the falsehood of this sophism he offers, among other things, this example: According to which manner (of error is the following), 'if (he who is) not fevered (be) hot, it is also necessary that (he who is) hot be fevered'.

conceded, because the expression admits of a *divided sense*; but *the latter* (does)not, because it conveys the *composite sense*.

II. Alexander of Hales, Summa., p. I, q. 23, m. 4, a. 5. — St. Thomas, here in q. 1. a. 1. 2; Summa., I, q. 14, a. 15. — Bl. (now St.) Albertus (Magnus), here in a. 1 and 8; Summa., p. I, tr. 15, q. 61, m. 7. — (Bl.) Peter of Tarentaise, here in q. 1, a. 2. — Richard of Middleton, here in a. 1, q. 3. — Giles the Roman, here in 1st. princ., q. 2. — Durandus (of Saint-Pourçain), here in q. 1. — (Bl.) Dionysius the Carthusian, here in q. 1. — (Gabriel) Biel, here in the q. sole.

ARTICLE II

On the manner of the Divine Cognition.

Consequently, there is the question concerning the second Article, namely, concerning the manner of the Divine Cognition. And about this three (questions) are asked.

First, there asked, whether God cognizes Himself and others uniformly [uniformiter].

Second, whether He cognizes mutables immutably [immutabiliter].

Third, whether He cognizes all (things) presently [praesenter].

QUESTION I

Whether God cognizes in the same manner Himself and others than Himself?

Moreover, that He cognizes Himself and others in the same manner or uniformly, is shown in this manner:

1. God's Knowledge is His own Essence, and His *knowing* [scire] is His own '*being*' [esse], therefore, too (His) manner of cognizing [modus cognoscendi] is (His) manner of being; but there is one manner of essential being [essendi essentialis] in God: therefore (there is) also one manner of cognizing.

2. Likewise, God by Himself and not by another cognizes Himself, and by Himself and not by another He cognizes others,[1] therefore, by one and the same reckoning He cognizes Himself and others; but a manner of cognizing is attained from within the reckoning of cognizing: therefore, if there is the same reckoning of cognizing Himself and others, (there is) also the same manner, and thus etc..

3. Likewise, this very (thing) seem per impossibile, because if He cognizes Himself in one manner, (and) creatures in another manner: therefore, when He cognizes Himself and others, He varies [variatur] in cognizing; therefore, with God there is a *transmutation and alternation and overshadowing*.[2]

4. Likewise, if in another manner, then I ask: either that manner is *the Creator*, or *a creature*. Not *a creature*, because (God's) Cognition and manner of cognizing is eternal; if *the Creator*, either (that manner) means something *personal*, or something *essential*. Not (something) *personal*, because every cognition is common to the three, therefore, it means something essential: therefore, if (there is) one manner and another, therefore, one Essence and another; but this is impossible: therefore, the first (is) also.

ON THE CONTRARY: 1. God in cognizing (those) other than Himself [cognoscendo alia a se], cognizes through an idea, but Himself He does not cognize through an idea:[3] therefore, if "cognizing through an idea" means a manner of cognition [modum cognitionis], and He does not cognize Himself through an idea, it is clear, that (He does so) by another manner of cognizing; and thus etc..

2. Likewise, in the Cognition, by which God cognizes Himself, the same is the One cognizing and the One cognized and the Reason for cognizing; but in the Cognition, by which He cognizes creatures, the reason for cognizing is not the same with the one cognized: therefore, (it is) not the same manner (of cognizing).[4]

3. Likewise, there is nothing common to God and creature according to the reckoning of being, therefore neither according to the reckoning of being cognized [cognoscendi]: therefore, since the '*being*' of the creature is other than (that) of the Creator, and (there is) another *manner of being*, therefore, (the creature) is cognized by another cognition and in another manner than the Creator (is). If, therefore, (the creature)[5] is cognized in another manner than God, and it is the same '*that the creature is cognized*' and '*that God cognizes*': therefore, God cognizes Himself in one manner and others (in another).

4. Likewise, every cognition, in which the one cognized is more noble, more present and more intelligible, is a more noble cognition, that is, as much as regards *thing* and *manner*. As much as regards *thing*, because (it is) of a more noble thing; as much as regards *manner*, because (it is) of a more present thing. But in the Cognition, by which God cognizes Himself, the One cognized is more noble, more present, and more intelligible than in the cognition of a creature: therefore, (it is) a more noble cognition as much as regards thing and manner.

---

[1] Cf. Aristotle, METAPHYSICS, Bk. XII, texts 39 & 51 (Bk. XI, chs. 7 & 9).

[2] James 1:17: *Among Whom there is no transmutation nor the alteration of overshadowing* [Apud quem non est transmutatio nec vicissitudinis obumbratio].

[3] Cf. above d. 35, q. 1 and ff..

[4] Supply, together with codex Z: *of cognizing* [cognoscendi]. Immediately before this, for *not* [non] codex V has *neither* [nec].

[5] Understand, together with codex O (in the margin): *the creature* [creatura]. A little below this, after *the creature is cognized* [creaturam cognosci], in codices L and O there is found *by God* [a Deo].

CONCLUSION

By one cognition and in the same manner God cognizes Himself and (those) other than Himself.

I RESPOND: It must be said, that there is a certain cognition, which is caused by and has its rise from the cognizable; and this, since it is caused by and depends from the cognizable, varies according to the exigency of the cognizable as much as regards *thing* and *manner*.[1] And there is another cognition, which according to thing is the same as the One cognizing and is not caused by the cognizable nor depends (from it); and this accepts an identity as much as regards *thing* and *manner* on the part of the One cognizing, not on the part of the one cognized.

Therefore, since the Divine Cognition does not depend from things nor is caused (by them), but is the same as God, and God holds Himself (to each) according to the same Essence and in the same manner: for that reason by one cognition and in the same manner God cognizes Himself and (those) other than Himself; because (He cognizes) *through Himself*, (being) in no manner varied nor diversified.

For an understanding, moreover, of the objections, it must be noted, that through a looking-back to *the One cognizing* the Cognition is compared in the same manner and is in the same manner, because according to that comparison it has (its) '*being*';[2] and in this manner the first reasons proceed, showing that God cognizes Himself and others in the same manner. Through the looking-back to the *one cognized*, though (the Divine Cognition) is in the same manner,[3] yet It is compared in another manner: for (It is compared) to God according to a reckoning of *identity*, (but) to the creature according to a reckoning of *diversity* and *causality*, and for that reason (It is compared) to the creature according to the reckoning of (its) being ideated, but to God least of all; and the reasons brought forward for the second side prove this, that It is compared in another manner, and in this manner it must be conceded.[4] If, therefore, one infers, that It is in another manner, the reckoning is not valid, because God's Cognition does not receive a manner of being nor a nobility from the (thing) cognized.

1. 2. And thus the two objections concerning the idea (of the thing) and (its) diversity are clear.

3. To that which is objected third, that there is nothing common to the Creator and the creature; it must be said, that it is true concerning the commonality [communitate][5] (which is) according to the same comparison; but according to the one and the other nothing prohibits, that something be the truth of the creature and a similitude of God, similarly, that something be the truth of God and the similitude of a creature. And since the reckoning of cognizing is accepted from within each manner, for that reason there can be a common cognition.

4. To that which is objected last, it must be said, that it holds, when the cognition is caused, as in the proposed.

SCHOLIUM

I. That on the part of *the One cognizing,* God does, in one and the same manner and according to the same reason for cognizing, cognize all, is evinced from that axiom (at the end of the body of the Response), that « God's Cognition does not receive (its) manner of being and nobility from the (thing) cognized » (cf. above d. 35, q. 4, in reply to n. 4, and q. 6, in reply to n. 2). This is coherent with another principle: Whatever is received, is received through the manner of the one receiving, though *the reception* of anything from outside can in no manner be said of God, whose Intellect is the (Divine) Substance and a most pure Act. — In the solution to n. 3, it is said, that the *truth of a creature* can be a similitude of God, which is explained above in d. 3, p. I, q. 1, in reply to n. 1, and in q. 2, in reply to nn. 3 and 4; and that a *truth of God* can be the similitude of a creature, concerning which, see d. 35, qq. 1 and 2.

II. Alexander of Hales, SUMMA., p. I, q. 23, m. 2, a. 1 and 3, and m. 4, a. 4. — (Bl. John Duns) Scotus, REPORTATIO., Bk. I, d. 36, q. 1; DE PRIMO PRINCIPIO, ch. 4., concl. 9; COLLAT. 21. — St. Thomas, SENT., Bk. I, d. 38, q. 1, a. 2; SUMMA. , I, q. 14, a. 5. and passim in the ff.; SUMMA CONTRA GENTILES., I, c. 46, and passim; DE VERITATE., q. 2, a. 13. — Bl. (now St.) Albertus Magnus), here in a. 2, and in d. 36, a. 3; SUMMA., p. I, tr. 15, q. 60, m. 2. — (Bl.) Peter of Tarentaise, SENT., Bk. I, d. 36, q. 2, a. 1. — Richard of Middleton, SENT., Bk. I, d. 35, q. 7, in the solution to the arguments. — Giles the Roman, on this and the following question, in d. 39, 1st princ., q. 2. — Henry of Ghent, SUMMA., a. 40, q. 45. — Durandus (of Saint-Pourçain), SENT., Bk. I, d. 35, q. 1. — (Gabriel) Biel, SENT., Bk. I, d. 35, qq. 2 and 3.

QUESTION II

Whether God cognizes mutables immutably?

Second, there is asked, whether God cognizes mutables immutably. And that (it is) so, is shown:

1. First, by the authority of Dionysius (the Areopagite), ON THE DIVINE NAMES,[6] (where he says): « God cognizes all material (things) immaterially, (all) divided (things) in an undivided manner [impartite partita], the many uniformly, (and) mutables immutably ».

---

[1] For the cognition of a more noble *thing* is more noble than of a ignoble thing, and the *manner* of cognizing a thing through presence (intuitively) is more noble than the manner of cognizing through a similitude and/or through an abstraction. See above, d. 3, p. I, q. 1, 3rd argument of the fundament.

[2] Understand: as a Divine Cognition. — In other words: God cognizes Himself and others uniformly, because He cognizes Himself and others by one and the same medium [uno eodemque medio], namely, His own Essence.

[3] From codices R (T by a second hand) V aa and edition 1, we have restored the word *manner* [modo]. The Vatican edition, which, supported by a few manuscripts, suppressed this word, reads *the same* [eadem] for *in the same manner* [eodem modo]. A little further below

this, after *least of all* [minime], cod. X repeats *according to a reckoning of being ideated* [secundum rationem ideandi].

[4] Codices U and X have *and this must be conceded* [et hoc concedendum est]; the Vatican edition has *in this manner they must be conceded* [hoc modo sunt concedendae]. The same Vatican edition then has *that It is thus in another manner* [quod alio modo sic] for *that It is in another manner* [quod alio modo sit].

[5] Very many codd., such as R S T W & X, have *(that which is) communicated* [communicato] for *the commonality (which is)* [communitate].

[6] Chapter 7, § 2: Therefore, cognizing according to the Divine Wisdom He knows once for all, all (things), material (things) immaterially, both the divided in a non divided manner, and the many universally (ἐνιαίως), cognizing and adducing all by the one same (act) [ipso uno].

2. Likewise, (St.) Augustine (says) in the fifteenth (book) ON THE TRINITY: « His Knowledge is incapable of being lost and varied [inamissibilis et invariabilis] »; but every such (is) immutable: ergo etc..

3. Likewise, this very (thing) is shown *by reason*, because what is more noble is to be attributed to God; but the cognition, by which a thing is immutable cognized, is more noble than that by which it is cognized mutably: ergo etc..

4. Likewise, what is in something is in it through the manner of that, in which it is,[2] and this is true most of all in God, in Whom everything which is, is itself or God Himself: therefore, since the Knowledge of things and the things cognized themselves are in God, and He is entirely immutable: therefore they are in God immutably.

5. Likewise, for this there is the reckoning of (St.) Augustine,[3] leading *to the impossible*: « For God's knowing is His own 'being', and His own Knowledge is His own Essence »: if, therefore, He would know mutably, He would be mutable, which is in itself entirely impossible.

6. Likewise, where there is mutability, there is no certitude, therefore, if God would know things mutably, He would know them uncertainly; but incertitude is a condition dishonoring [dedecorans] cognition: therefore, God's Cognition would not have a perfect nobility.

ON THE CONTRARY: 1. When a thing is present, God knows, that it is present; and when (it has) past away, He knows that it has past away; and when it is going to be, He knows that it is going to be, not that (it has) passed away: therefore, it seems, that just as we cognize things mutably, so God also cognizes (them).[4]

2. Likewise, for that that knowledge be true, it is necessary, that the knowable and the knowledge be proportioned, otherwise it is not true knowledge: therefore, since of the mutable there is no proportion to the immutable, but (there is) of the mutable to the mutable, therefore, God does not cognizes mutable things immutably, but mutably; otherwise He does not cognize, as it seems, truly.

3. Likewise, « whatever is known, is true »,[5] therefore, what is immutably known, is immutably true; but mutable things do not have immutable truth: therefore, they cannot be known immutably.

4. Likewise, because things are contingent, for that reason 'that God foreknows future contingents' is contingent, just as has been shown in the preceding:[6] therefore, because things are mutable, 'that God knows immutable things' is mutable: therefore, God cognizes mutables mutably. Or, if this is not true, I ask, for what reason (is it) not? And *again*,

in what manner can it be understood, that of a mutable thing there be an immutable knowledge?

CONCLUSION

God cognizes mutables immutably according to (His) act of knowing, though things are mutable according to (their) act of being.

I RESPOND: It must be said, that when there is asked, "Whether God knows things immutably?", this is in a twofold manner: because this disposition[7] "*immutably*" can determine the act of *God's knowing* [actum sciendi Dei], and/or the act of *the things' being* [actum essendi rerum]. If the act of *God's knowing*, thus it is entirely true, that He knows immutably, because about His act and cognition there falls no *transmutation nor alternation of overshadowing*.[8] But if it determines the act of *the things' being*, thus it is false concerning mutable things, because God knows these mutables and He knew [novit] their mutability, and He knows [scit], that they hold themselves now in another manner[9] than before; but nevertheless *He knew (this) immutably*.

And the reason for this is, since in His Cognition there is no *reception*, there is no *succession*, nor is there a *forgetfulness* [oblivio]; and for that reason, howsoever much things are mutable, He Himself[10] is not changed [mutatur] in cognizing their mutability. And though there is nothing similar, yet one can be *thought of*, if one understands and/or thinks of an eye fixed upon a wall [in pariete], which by itself sees (those) passing by, without a reception and by one gaze sees all and all the movements of these, howsoever the things are changed, yet neither is the eye changed nor its cognition; and thus it is in God.[11] But *an example* to understand this can be taken contrariwise [a contrario] in this manner. For because a *caused knowledge* depends from the knowable, and not the other way around, for that reason there can be a change [mutatio] about *the knowledge* through forgetfulness and error and a successive consideration, with no change having been made in *the knowable*. Thus (too) in a contrary manner,[12] because *the Divine Knowledge* does not depend upon the thing known, there can be a change about *the knowable*, with no existing change in the Divine *Knowledge*; and yet according to that Knowledge He knows the whole.

1. And, through this, the response to the first objection, concerning that which He knows to have been and to be, is clear. For it must be said, that this means a mutation on the part of *the knowable*, not (on the part) of *the knowledge*.

2. To that which is objected concerning proportion, it must be said, that in special conditions it is not

---

[1] Chapter 13, n. 22. See here the text of Master (Peter), ch. 1.

[2] Cf. above d. 36, a. 2, q. 2, p. 625, footnote 3. On the argument itself, cf. (St.) Augustine, ON THE CITY OF GOD, Bk. XI, ch. 10, n. 2.

[3] ON THE TRINITY, Bk. XV, ch. 13, n. 22, where the principles of this argument are had. See here the text of Master (Peter), ch. 1.

[4] Codex V reads *cognizes them* [eas cognoscat].

[5] Cf. Aristotle, POSTERIOR ANALYTICS, Bk. I, ch. 2. The words of the Philosopher are had above, d. 39, a. 1, q. 3, p. 690, footnote 2.

[6] Distinction 38, a. 2, q. 2.

[7] For *disposition* [dispositio] edition 1 has *saying* [dictio], the Vatican edition has *determination* [determinatio]. A little before this for *in a twofold manner* [dupliciter], the Vatican edit ion has *twofold* [duplex]; codex cc reads *this (question) is twofold* [haec est duplex] for *this is in a twofold manner* [hoc est dupliciter].

[8] James 1:17.

[9] Very many codd. with ed. 1 read incongruously *that the cognition holds itself now rather than before* [se habere nunc cognitionem quam prius] for *that they hold themselves now in another manner than before* [se habere nunc cognitionem quam prius]; not a few codd., such as I (in the margin) and V, having retained the *in other manner* [aliter] prefix *the cognition* [cognitionem], and by this addition render the reading equivocal.

[10] Codices F S and T, together with edition 1, have *It (i.e. His Cognition)* [ipsa]. Next, ed. 1 reads *no similar example* [nullum exemplum sit simile] for *is nothing similar* [nullus sit simile].

[11] Cf. (St.) Boethius, ON THE CONSOLATION OF PHILOSOPHY, Bk. V, prose 6. See also, St. Bonav., below in d. 40, a. 2, q. 1, in reply to nn. 1, 2 & 3.

[12] Codex O reads *Thus, (it is) the other way around in God* [Sic e contrario in Deo].

necessary [oportet] that even caused knowledge be proportioned, because of a corporal thing there is a spiritual knowledge; but it is sufficient, that there be a proportion in the truth.

3. To that which is objected, that whatever is known, is true: therefore, what is knows immutably, is immutably true; it must be said, that there is a (fallacy of) *accident* here.[1] For though knowledge requires truth in the one known from the reckoning of its own general intention, knowledge (requires truth) most of all in respect of an enuncible; yet knowledge does not always mean a conformity in immutability, most of all the Divine Knowledge, which does not depend from a knowable (mutable).

4. To that which is objected, that God does not foreknow a future contingent necessarily; it must be said, that it is not similar both on the part of *the act of foreknowing*, and on the part of *the disposition*. On the part of *the act*, it is not similar, because "*to foreknow*" always notes[2] the coming forth of a thing; but "*to know*" does not always connote the existence of the thing; for God knows (those) which He can make and will never make. *Moreover*, it is not similar concerning *the disposition*, because the manner of immutability looks back to the act, but the contingent (thing) looks back not only to *the act*, but to *the ordination* to the future; and, indeed, *the act* of the Divine Cognition is immutable and necessary, but the comparison to the future contingent is contingent.

SCHOLIUM

The solution of this and the following Question depends from the commonly received principle, that God, whose Knowledge does not depend from things, as ours (does), does not cognize things according to their manner, but according to His own manner; therefore, mutables immutably, contingents infallibly, temporals eternally. — Among the ancient Scholastics this question is especially treated by Alexander of Hales, SUMMA., p. I, q. 23, m. 4, a. 6, who illustrates the point also with examples taken from other creatures, and Bl. (now St.) Albertus (Magnus), SUMMA., p. I, tr. 15, q. 60, m. 4, a. 1, subpart 5. On certain difficulties objected to by Scotists, we have mentioned these above in d. 38, a. 2, q. 2, in the Scholium. — For an understanding of the solution to n. 4, it must be noted that *the*

Foreknowledge of future (things) differs from the *Knowledge of mutables* from a twofold source, namely, on the part of the act, because the act of foreknowing connotes the coming forth of the thing, the act of *knowing* (does) not (connote) the existence of the thing; and « on the part of the disposition », because in *the Foreknowledge* there is implied an *ordination* of those which are contingent, but *the Knowledge* only respects the act itself through a manner of *immutability*.

Alexander of Hales, SUMMA., p. I, q. 23, m. 4, a. 6. — St. Thomas, SUMMA., I, q. 14, a. 15. — Bl. (not St.) Albertus (Magnus), here in a. 3; SUMMA., p. I, tr. 15, q. 61, m. 6. — (Bl.) Peter of Tarentaise, here in q. 4, a. 1. — (Bl.) Dionysius the Carthusian, SENT., Bk. I, d. 38, q. 2.

QUESTION III

Whether God cognizes each and every (thing) presently?

Third, there is asked, whether God cognizes all (things) presently [praesenter]. And it seems, that (it is) so.

1. On that (verse) from the last (chapter) of the Second (Letter of St.) Peter:[3] *A thousand years* etc., the Gloss (says): « In the acknowledgement of the Divine Truth, (things) past and present and future are equally present ».

2. Likewise, (St.) Augustine (says) ON (THE GOSPEL OF ST.) JOHN:[4] « In the Truth, which remains, I find not the past and the future, but only the present, and this uncorrupted ».

3. Likewise, as much as a thing is *more present*, so much is the cognition more noble, because this works towards the nobility of the cognition;[5] but God cognizes all in a most noble manner: therefore, all which He cognizes, He cognizes in a most present manner.

4. Likewise, if He does not cognize all *presently*,

therefore, He does not cognize all *together*, wherefore if (He does cognize all) *together*, then, therefore, He cognizes all in the same *now*, and thus presently. But if He does not cognize (all) *together*, therefore, (He cognizes all) one after the other; but in every such cognition there is a transmutation: therefore in God's Cognition there would occur a transmutation, which is entirely false and impossible.[6]

ON THE CONTRARY: 1. Foreknowledge is not but of (something) future, and as it is going to be: therefore, if God cognizes all presently, therefore, He foreknows nothing entirely; but He does foreknow, ergo etc.. *If you say*, that He is said improperly "to foreknow"; *on the contrary*: in *foreknowledge* there is naught but two, namely *knowledge* and *antecession* in respect of the cognized; but it is established, that in God there is properly knowledge, it is also established, that in Him there is properly an antecession, because God properly antecedes all others: therefore, if He cognizes

---

[1] On this fallacy, cf. above d. 2, a. sole, q. 4, p. 58, footnote 5. — Codices aa and bb add: *such as here, 'I know that God is in a multiple manner: therefore, it is true, that God is in a multiple manner'* [ut hic, scio Deum esse multipliciter: ergo verum est, Deum esse multipliciter].

[2] Edition 1 has *connotes* [connotat].

[3] Verse 8, where in the Gloss of (Nicholas) of Lyra there is had *Virtue* [virtutis] for *Truth* [veritatis], and *stand together* [constant] for *are* [sunt].

[4] Tract 38, n. 10, where, in the original text, there is had *in an uncorrupted manner* [incorruptibiliter] for *uncorrupted* [incorruptum].

[5] Cf. above d. 3, p. I, q. 1, 3rd argument of the fundament.

[6] On this argument, see (St. Severinus) Boethius, ON THE CONSOLATION OF PHILOSOPHY, Bk. V, prose 6.

(those) other than Himself properly, therefore, God foreknows others,[1] therefore, that is no response.

2. Likewise, everything present according to the status of its own quality of being present [secundum statum praesentialitis] is necessary: therefore, if God cognizes all presently and always presently, therefore, He cognizes all necessarily. Therefore, just as that which is present cannot not be, so, if God foreknows something, it is necessary that He has foreknown (it), and if He has foreknow (it), it will be: therefore, that it is, is necessary.[2]

3. Likewise, this is shown *through the impossible*, because if He cognized all presently, therefore, several together [plura simul]; therefore, He turns Himself completely at once to many [simul ad multa]; but as the Simple (Being), to which He turns himself completely, He turns Himself completely totally: therefore, when He understands the one, He cannot (turn Himself completely) unto the other.

4. Likewise, if He cognizes all presently: therefore, He knows together two (things) opposed contradictorily; but whatever is knows is true:[3] therefore, the two opposed contradictorily are together true.

CONCLUSION

God cognizes all presently, yet the quality of being present is not to be accepted on the part of the cognized, but (on the part) of the One cognizing.

I RESPOND: It must be said, that "*to cognize all presently*" can be understood in a twofold manner: either[4] because [quod] there is noted a quality of being present [praesentialitas] on the part of *the cognized*, and in this manner it is false, because He does not cognize, that all are true *presently* and *together*; or thus, that there is noted a quality of being present on the part of *the One cognizing*, and in this manner it has truth.

And the reason for this is, that God has the ideas of all (things) present (to Himself) and together, through which He cognizes future things so certainly, just as if they were present (to Him). *And again*, He turns Himself completely upon all these together and presently, and thus He cognizes (them) together and presently. *And again*, the One present to His own Cognition is the most simple Present, which embraces [circumplectitur] all times.[5] And from these three reasons joined together God is said "to cognize all presently". — And these reasons have (their) whole from this, that the quality of being present of the Divine Cognition, which (quality) indeed is eternity, is *simple* and *infinite*. Because it is *simple*, for that reason (the Divine Cognition is) always present; because (it is) *infinite*, for that reason all are present to It. An *example* of this is posited in God's quality of being present as much as regards the *existence* of things, according to which (quality) God is whole in one (thing),[6] so that He is, nevertheless, also in other (things); and this is, because (He is) simple and infinite. — For this reason God judges, that something *is future*, but (is) not *future to Him*; and He cognizes all *presently*, and yet He, nevertheless, *foreknows* (them).

1. 2. And through this the first and second (objection) is clear, because they proceed, according to which the quality of being present is a disposition of the thing cognized in *its own nature*, not in *the Divine Cognition*.

3. The third (objection) is also clear, because this (Being)[7] is simple and infinite, and (because) It cognizes many in one; for that reason It turns itself completely together over many.

4. What is objected concerning opposites, is similarly clear, because although He cognizes opposes together on His own part, yet He knows, that the one is uncomposeable with the other, (and) yet that the one can succeed the other.

SCHOLIUM

I. That God cognizes all *presently*, is taught by all Catholic theologians; but there is a great dispute concerning two connected questions, the *first* of which is, "In what manner *is that presence to be understood*?"; but the *second*, "Whether *the reason for cognizing* created things is the same for God?"

In regard to the first question, St. Thomas (SUMMA., I, q. 14, a. 13, q. 57, a. 3; SUMMA CONTRA GENTILES., I, chs. 66 and 67; DE VERITATE., q. 2, a. 13; SENT., Bk. I, d. 38, q. sole, a. 5) teaches: « All (things) which are in time, are present to God from eternity not only by the reckoning, by which He has present to Himself the reasons for things, as certain (authors) say, but because His intuition is born from eternity over all, insofar as *they are in their own quality of being present* [in sua praesentialitate] (SUMMA, I, q. 14, a. 13). This second reason (advanced by St. Thomas) displeased many, among whom Peter John Olivi, O. F. M., went so far, as to censure it as

heretical. But on the other hand, the judges (who condemned) the same Peter John, reproved his own censure as *erroneous* (D'Argentré, COLLECTIO IUDICIORUM tom. I. p. 229, ed. Paris. 1728). Even (Bl. John Duns) Scotus, here in the q. sole, n. 9, does not admit but the first reckoning of presentiality and he teaches, that the infinite duration of eternity, which surpasses every time, has naught but in potency, least of all *in act*, a relation of coexistence to future things; indeed because that which does not *exist*, in no manner can *coexist* and/or be the fundament of a *relation* of coexistence. (Bl.) Scotus is favored also by Alexander of Hales (SUMMA., I, q. 23, m. 4, a. 3), and not only do Durandus (of Saint-Pourçain) and the Nominalists follow him, but also very many later theologians from nearly all schools.

Nevertheless, the sentence of St. Thomas, rightly understood, we repute as most true and most worthy of God, and entirely conform

---

[1] In the Vatican ed. and cod. cc there is wanting the conclusion: *therefore, if He cognizes (those) other than Himself properly, therefore, God foreknows others* [ergo si cognoscit alia a se proprie, ergo Deus praescit alia]. A little before this (on the preceding page), cod. W has *by which* [qua] for *because* [quia].

[2] Cf. (St.) Anselm (of Canterbury); ON THE CONCORD OF GOD'S FOREKNOWLEDGE WITH FREE WILL, q. 1, ch. 4.

[3] Cf. above in this Distinction, a. 1, q. 3, p. 690, footnote 2.

[4] Cod. R after *either* [aut] reads *thus that* [ita quod] for *because* [quod].

[5] Cf. (St.) Augustine, OF EIGHTY-THREE QUESTIONS, qq. 17 and 19, and also ON THE GOSPEL OF ST. JOHN, tract 38, n. 10, and ENARRATIONS

ON THE PSALMS, Ps. 110, n. 10, and Ps. 121, n. 6; (St.) Anselm, PROSLOGION, ch. 20, and ON THE CONCORD OF GOD'S FOREKNOWLEDGE WITH FREE WILL, q. 1, ch. 5. — A little further above this, for *which* [quod] codices A and I have *because it* [quia], and a little further below this, for *(their) whole* [totum] the Vatican edition, together with a few manuscripts, has *(their) rise* [ortum].

[6] For *in one (thing)* [in una] codex M has *in each one thing* [in unaquaque re].

[7] Namely that simple thing, which converts itself totally upon the object of its own cognition, which is here said of God.

with the doctrine of Sts. Augustine, Gregory (the Great), Anselm and Bonaventure. The whole difficulty turns around the right understanding of this profound position. Whence we note, beforehand, these few (points).

1. One is the *now* (or present instant) of time, another the *now* of the aevum, another the *now* of eternity, as Alexander of Hales well explains (SUMMA, p. I, q. 13, m. 9, a. 4, § 3). It suffices here to say, that the *now of time* is an indivisible instant, rapidly fleeing, which joins time before with (time) after; the *now of eternity* is eternity itself, which according to the reckoning of (its) infinite simplicity is *at once whole* and *indivisible*, and according to this reckoning similar to an instant of indivisible time, but according to the reckoning of (its) unlimited immensity it comprises in itself and superexceeds all durations of time and of the aevum in a most eminent manner.

2. The Divine Intellection, since It is the Substance, has the same measure, which the Divine Substance Itself (has), whence too « the quality of being present of the Divine Cognition, which (quality) indeed is eternity, is simple and infinite » (here in the body of the Response). But human intellection, which is an accident, is measured by time, but the substance of the soul is measure by the aevum.

3. One is the presence, by which *corporal* things, and/or things in (their own) genus, which are measured, are coexistent with themselves, another, that by which *God* coexists with things, another, that by which *temporal* things and differences of time coexist with God. So that corporal things be present to themselves, there is required besides an indistance of *place*, that they be together in the same instant of *time*, whose measure is broken up into parts successive to one another or into the differences of (instants) past and future, and (which) does not exist except in the instant. Whence in this coexistence *part* of the duration of the succeeding (instant) is outside of the other of its part, and no *instant* can coexist except *with one sole instant* of the coexistent duration of the thing. If the measure of each duration is equal and in the same flux of time, then the whole duration of one coexists with the whole duration of the other, but thus, that part of the duration of one coexists with only part of that of the other. But if the measure of each is diverse, then not only *according to parts*, but even *on account of a part* [ex parte] they coexist with themselves, and/or coexist to no extent: v. g. the measure of a hour indeed does coexist with the measure of a *year*, whose part it is, but yet not *with the whole year*, nor with a proportioned part of it in an unseparated manner [indivisim], but through a succession of parts.

That God coexists in one manner with all things and measures of times and places, is manifest. The whole of (His) eternity *exists* through the manner of one *indivisible* instant, remaining throughout without succession and comprising and exceeding, by (this) act, all successions and measures of time. *In this manner* it is the measure of the Divine Life and Action ad intra: *in this manner* it also measures ad extra all measures of created things, whence in the same, most simple and immense *now* of eternity *He coexists* with all things, not only with those which in a measure of *time* are present according to the *now* of time and/or according to a certain *part* of eternity, which we *imagine*, but even with those which in a measure of time and place are distant to one another according to the difference of past and future (times). (His) immense and undivided eternity indeed coexists with finite things whole on account of (its) *indivision*, but not *totally* on account of (its) *excess*, because it also coexists with (all) other things ever existing, and with (all) other (things) possible in *potency*.

That *created things* and their measure (i.e. time) coexist in another manner with (God) eternity, must be held. It is manifest, that the same, in virtue of the measure of time, in which they are, and in virtue of that state, in which their duration in every instant flows from a difference of a future to a difference of a past, respond least of all to the whole (of God's) eternity, nor that these can in virtue of *their own duration* coexist with the same eternity. But to the extent that this infinite measure of time is embraced and quasi included in the higher and supereminent measure of eternity, according to which whole time is not but the least instant, it can be said, that temporal things also coexist with *the whole eternity*, but not *totally*. But "*not totally*", said of the coexistence of *temporal things*, has a reckoning other than when said of *God's* coexistence. For the former *coexistence* convenes with God per se (i.e. through itself), and "*not totally*" by reason of the *excess* of His own measure. But creatures, since they are not eternal nor coeternal to God, do not have that coexistence ex se (i.e. out of themselves) and by reason of their own duration, but by reason of the immensity and simplicity of *the Divine eternity*, and "*not to-*

tally" befits them on account of a *defect*, namely, on account of the *finite* measure of their own duration.

II. Though St. Bonaventure is drawn by very many authors to the sentence of (Bl. John Duns) Scotus, especially on account of (his) solution to the 5th Doubt of Distinction 35 (to which side even Bartolomeo de' Barbieri, CURS. THEOL., tom I, disputation 5, q. 7, holds tenaciously); yet the very words of the Seraphic Doctor (here and below in d. 40, a. 2, q. 1, in reply to n. 4, and d. 41, a. 2, q. 1, in reply to n. 4; ITINERARIUM MENTIS IN DEUM, ch. 5 near the end) sufficiently demonstrate, that he fully agrees with the sentence of the Angelic (Doctor), when sanely understood. In the ITINERARIUM he thus says: « Because (the Absolute 'Being') is *eternal* and *most present*, It for that reason comprises [ambit] and enters all durations, as if existing at the same time as their center and circumference. — Because It is *most simple* and *the greatest*, for that reason wholly within all and wholly outside, and through this "it is an intelligible sphere, whose center is everywhere and circumference nowhere" ». Moreover, the explanation of this doctrine, which the Seraphic Doctor makes in a certain unedited Disputed Question, to be published by us in its own time, leaves nothing to doubt, for which purpose we transcribe here only one of its propositions: « Just as the Divine Incircumscriptibility has all places present to Itself, and is not distended through them, though they are truly distended, so the Divine Eternity has all times present to Itself, and yet It does not succeed with them, though they truly succeed ». — The very many objections, which are customarily made against this sentence, are solved best of all, among the ancient masters, by Richard (of Middleton), here in a. 1, q. 1, and in d. 41, a. 4, q. 2; who, however, censures the sentence of (Bl.) Scotus as not entirely improbable. About the fundaments of each position one can confer with Rada, contr. 30, a. 2; Macedo, coll. 9, diff. 4, and the other defenders of each sentence.

III. The words, by which the Seraphic Doctor distinguishes at the beginning of the Response the twofold sense of the expression "*to cognize presently*" [praesenter cognoscere], seem to need some explanation. If "*presently*", as an adverb, determines the Divine *Act of knowing* Itself, all concede, that the same (Act) is outside of every measure of time in the most simple now of eternity, thus that neither *the past* nor *the future* nor *the present of time* can convene with It. But if "*presently*" is drawn to "*all things*", then a twofold sense can again be distinguished: either to note « *the quality of being present of the cognized* [praesentialitas cognitorum] », such as is « the disposition of the thing cognized in its own nature » (here in reply to nn. 1 and 2); as if the future things are not really distant in the measure of time among themselves, but are together and present, which is manifestly false — and/or (that the things) cognized themselves can be compared not to the now *of time*, but to *eternity's quality of being present*, which is together with the Divine Cognition's quality of being present; and if it is taken in this sense, that twofold opinion of the Schools ceases. Thus nearly Richard (of Middleton), d. 41, a. 4, q. 2.

IV. In regard to the *second* question, "Whether this quality of being present is for God the reason for cognizing future contingents?", there were not lacking a few, as we have noted above in the Scholium to q. 1, who thought that the knot of the difficulties, which concern the Divine Foreknowledge, could be solves thus, among whom are numbered even the Salamancans. St. Thomas himself often proffers the reckoning, which (B.) Scotus (here in the q. sole, n. 9) stove to overturn. But the sentence of St. Thomas is more commonly explained in another manner, namely that he did not want to establish this reckoning of his *a priori* as the unique and proper *medium in which*, but that rather (he wanted to establish it) *a posteriori*, having already supposed the Foreknowledge, as that from which he would take the best arguments, to lead one by hand to understand, that God's Foreknowledge is *intuitive, infallible, immutable*, and does not *derogate the contingency of things*. He insinuates this, among other things, with these words (SUMMA CONTRA GENTILES, I, c. 67, in the beginning): « From these, moreover, it can *in some manner* already be clear, that God had an infallible knowledge of contingents from eternity, and yet they do not cease being contingents ». — And in truth, if God's Knowledge is not, as ours, *from things*, but rather *for things*, that quality of being present of things, at least *alone*, cannot be *the proper reckoning* of the Divine Foreknowledge.

V. Besides the authors already cited: Alexander of Hales, SUMMA., p. I, q. 23, m. 4, a. 3. — Bl. (now St.) Albertus (Magnus), SUMMA., p. I, tr. 15, q. 60, m. 4, partic. 3. — (Bl.) Peter of Tarentaise, SENT., Bk. I, d. 41, q. 4, a. 2. — Durandus (of Saint-Pourçain), SENT., Bk. I, d. 38, q. 3, n. 11, ff...

DOUBTS ON THE TEXT OF THE MASTER

DOUBT I

In this part are the doubts about (Master Peter's) text and first concerning this which (St.) Augustine says: *Therefore, the Father and the Son know One another, but the Former by begetting, the Latter by being born.* For it seems that he speaks badly, because *knowing* is an essential (act) among the divine: therefore, if He knows by being born, since *"to be born"* means a personal property, a personal property is the reason for an essential thing,[1] which is not sanely nor truly said.

I RESPOND: Some wanted to say, that Gods *knowing* [scire], related to creatures, and/or such that one Person knows Himself, is said *essentially*; but according to which one Person knows Another, means the looking-back of a Person to a Person and is said *notionally*. — But this has not been said fittingly, because, just as is had in the preceding,[2] only *"wisdom"* and *"being wise"* [sapere] are said essentially.

And, on this account, it must be said, that that ablative not only means a cause or reckoning of saying, but (also) a reckoning of concomitance. For gerunds, just as Priscian says,[3] are expounded [habent exponi] through an *"if"*, and/or through a *"while"* [dum], and/or thorugh a *"because"* [quia]: and in the first manner they mean a convening, in the second a concomitance, and in the third a cause.

DOUBT II

Likewise is asked concerning this which (St. Augustine) says: *And all which are in Their Knowledge, in Their Wisdom, in Their Essence, each one of these He sees together.* But, above in the Thirty-Sixth Distinction,[4] it was said, that creatures are in God's self-knowledge [notitia], but not in God's Essence: therefore, there is a contradiction.

I RESPOND: It must be said, that in the Divine Knowledge [divina scientia] there are knowables, but in the Divine Essence there are attributes, such as power, wisdom and goodness. And (St.) Augustine wants to say, that the Father and the Son together see all cognizables, created and to be created, and all attributes of the Essence. Whence, the text is to be read *in a separated manner* [divisim]: "all which are in Their Knowledge, as for example (things) created, Each knows together; similarly all which are in Their Essence, as for example the attributes,

They know or Each knows together". And, for that reason, he does not want to say, that creatures are in the Divine Essence.[5]

DOUBT III

Likewise, is asked concerning this which (Master Peter) says, that *God's Knowledge is naught but of those which are and/or were and/or will be.* For this seems to be false, because God knows everything which He can make; but He can make what never was nor is nor will be: therefore, God's Knowledge is of something, which never was and/or is and/or will be. *And moreover*, It is of (things) infinite, just as (St.) Augustine would have it in the eleventh (book), ON THE CITY IF GOD,[6] not only those which are and/or were and/or will be.

I RESPOND: It must be said, that Master (Peter) is speaking of the Knowledge of *vision*, which is only of those, of which there was a prevision from eternity; but he himself objects concerning the Knowledge of *understanding*, which connotes the existence of nothing: which is clear. For God understands everything which He can (do), and thus the objection does not argue [currit] rightly.[7]

DOUBT IV

Likewise, is asked concerning this which (Master Peter) says, that *He cannot start to know and/or foreknow* etc. For he seems to speak badly, because nothing is known but (what is) true:[8] therefore, before it is true, it is not known: therefore, if something begins to be true, something begins to be known by God: therefore, God can begin to know something. — Likewise, *the Act of creating* [creatio] is the Divine Essence, and yet by a reckoning of (what is) connoted (by this Act) God can begin to create something: therefore, similarly also (being) to know something.

I RESPOND: *"To know"* is said in a twofold manner. In one manner, *"to know"* is that which (it is) to have the cognition of something; and in this manner it does not connote the actual existence of the cognized, and thus God cannot begin to know anything, that is (He cannot) begin to have the cognition of anything. In another manner *"to know"* is that which (it is) *to know that something is true*, and then this is first known to be true, when it begins to be; and just as[9] God begins to know, so He also ceases to foreknow, not by a reckoning of the principal signified, which is (His) Knowledge, but by reason of the connoted, which indeed is the truth of the thing known.

---

[1] Edition 1 adds *and/or something essential* [vel quid essentiale].

[2] Distinction 32, a. 1, q. 1, in reply to n. 2, and a. 2, q. 1 in the body.

[3] Cf. GRAMMATICAL INSTITUTIONS, Bk. VII, chs. 9 and 13. — For *gerunds* [Gerundia] many codices, together with edition 1, have *gerundives* [Gerundiva], and a little further below this, for *they mean* [dicunt] they have faultily *it means* [dicit]. — On this doubt, cf. also Alexander of Hales, SUMMA., p. I, q. 23, m. 4, a. 4, in reply ton. 2; (Bl.) Peter of Tarentaise and Richard (of Middleton), here on the text.

[4] Chapter 1, and ibid., in his own Commentary, Doubt 1.

[5] See Alexander of Hales, SUMMA., p. I, q. 23, m. 4. a. 3.

[6] Chapter 10, n. 3.

[7] The solution to this doubt is also found in (Bl.) Peter of Tarentaise and Richard (of Middleton), here on the text.

[8] Cf. above here in a. 1, q. 3, p. 690, footnote 2.

[9] The Vatican edition, together with very many codices, reads *so* [sic]. A little before this, for *first* [primo] codex X has *properly* [proprie]. — More on this doubt is found above, in a. 1, q. 2, and in a. 2, q. 2; in Bl. (now St.) Albertus (Magnus), here in a. 6; St. Thomas, here in q. 1, a. 2; and in (Bl.) Dionysius the Carthusian, here in q. 1.

Doubt V

Likewise, is asked concerning this which (Master Peter) says: *Nor can He newly and/or on account of time will something, and yet He can will what He has never willed.* For here he seems to say two contradictorily opposed (things), since the former is new, which before was not and now is: therefore, if He could will what He did not will before, it seems that He begins to will.

I Respond: It must be said, that when I say, that God wills this,[1] I mean two (things): both an act of the Divine Will, and furthermore an ordination of that effect to that Act. And the first, indeed, is necessary and always, nor can it begin nor cease. For the Divine Will is always in its own act, such that It cannot lack that nor have another; but the ordination of any effect to that Act is the ordination of a future thing, which is not yet, and for that reason it can be and not be, and (can) be ordered and not ordered. When, therefore, there is said: "God can will what He has never willed, and yet not on account of time"; the understanding is, that that effect could be ordered to the Divine Willing; and since the ordination of the effect is an ordination of a future thing, both what is once future always was future, and what is[2] once ordered, always was ordered to

that (Will). When, therefore, it is said, that God can will something, it is the same to say, that something could be future or have an order to the Divine Will, which does not, yet, have an order;[3] but if it had, it would have it from eternity, and for that reason it does not begin on account of time. And for that reason Master (Peter)'s example is a good one, if God's Willing conveys an order to the willed in the reckoning of the *future*; but according to which It conveys a concomitance in the reckoning of the *present*, God can on account of time will this to be, or approve this today, not because[4] the Act begins, but because (what it) connotes begins.

Doubt VI

Likewise, is asked concerning this which (Master Peter) says, that *He has a special providence and care for rational (beings)*; because (this) seems contrary to that which is said in the sixth (chapter) of Wisdom:[5] *Equal is His care for all.*

I Respond: It must be said, that there *"equally"* does not deprive the order of Divine distribution, but deprives the acceptance of persons. And *"all"* distributes[6] there only on behalf of men, yet for the great and small, the poor and the rich; and thus His care is equally for all, because He wants the salvation of the poor as much as of the rich.

DISTINCTION XL

On the other hand,[1] predestination concerns the goods of salvation [bonis salutaribus] and the men to be saved. For, as (St.) Augustine says in the book, ON THE PREDESTINATION OF THE SAINTS,[2] « predestination is a preparation for grace, which cannot be without (God's) Foreknowledge. But (God's) Foreknowledge can be without predestination. Indeed by predestination God foreknows those, which He Himself was going to make, but God also foreknew (those) which He was not going to make, that is all evils ». He predestined those whom He elected, but the rest He reproved, that is, He foreknew that they (were) going to sin unto [ad] eternal death.

Chapter I

Whether anyone predestined can be damned, and/or (anyone) reprobate be saved.

None of the predestined seems to be able to be damned, nor do any of the reprobate [reproborum] (seem) to be able to be saved. Whence (St.) Augustine (says) in the book, ON BLAME AND GRACE:[3] « In the Apocalypse »,[4] he says, « there is said: *Hold what you have, lest another accept your crown.* If another is not going to accept (it), unless he loses

---

[1] The Vatican edition, having placed a comma after *wills* [velle], substitutes *here* [hic], indeed on the authority of very many codices, but faultily, as is clearly understood from what is subjoined. The copyists, when transcribing the manuscripts, seem to have read in this passage, as very often occurs, *here* [hic] for *this* [hoc], since they are truly very similar in form.

[2] The Vatican edition has *was* [fuit]. — Understand the preceding *and* [et] as *therefore, also* [ergo etiam].

[3] Codex Z, here and a little before this, has *ordination* [ordinationem]. A little further below this, for *example* [exemplum] edition 1 has *saying* [dictum]. That our reading is the true one, is clear from the entire text of Master (Peter), ch. 2: « Therefore, He cannot newly either on account of time know and/or foreknow something, *just as* He cannot newly and/or on account of time will something; etc. ».

[4] Many codices, together with the Vatican edition, after *not because* [non quia], read *the Act does not begin* [non incipiat actus] for *the Act begins* [incipiat actus], which is repugnant to the context and also to codices D F M and Y and to edition 1. — On this doubt read Alexander of Hales, SUMMA., I, q. 25; Bl. (now St.) Albertus (Magnus), here in a. 7; and (Bl.) Peter of Tarentaise, here on the text.

[5] Verse 8, where the Vulgate has *Equally* [Aequaliter] for *Equal* [Aequalis]. A little after this for *equally* [aequaliter] the Vatican edition has *equality* [aequalitas].

[6] Or is accepted. Cf. above d. 4, q. 1, Scholium. — Next for *yet* [tamen] the Vatican edition has *both* [tam]. — This doubt is also solved by (Bl.) Peter of Tarentaise and Richard of Middleton, here on the text.

NOTES ON THE BOOK OF SENTENCES

[1] In codices C D and E and in edition 1, distinction XL begins with the chapter which follows: *Non of the predestined* etc.. And in truth, according to the distribution of chapters these 5 sentences pertain to the last chapter of the preceding Distinction. But St. Bonaventure, as is clear from (his) Division of the Text, begins Distinction XL here.

[2] Chapter 10, 19; but the final words are from the Gloss on (St. Paul's Letter to the) Romans 8:29.

[3] Chapter 13, n. 39. In the codices and editions, except edition 9, it is entitled the book, ON CORRECTION AND GRACE [de Correction et gratia] for ON BLAME AND GRACE [de Correptione et gratia].

[4] Apocalypse 3:11.

(it), there is a certain number of the Elect », that is, it cannot be increased and/or lessened. — But to this certain (authors) object, striving (as they do) to prove, that the number of the Elect can be increased and lessened, thus: "God could not apportion [apponere] grace to those whom He apportions (it), and He could subtract (grace) from those whom He does not subtract (it); which if it were done,[1] they certainly [utique] would be damned. Therefore, those could be damned, who will yet be saved. And so the number of the Elect could be lessened; thus too it could be increased, because the grace, through which they are saved, could be apportioned to those whom it is not apportioned. Therefore, they could be saved, having the grace, who yet without it shall be damned: and so the number of the Elect could be increased." — To which we respond, that for this reason it has been said and is true, that the number of the Elect cannot be increased and/or lessened, because each cannot be *together*, namely, that someone be saved and not be predestined, and/or that someone be predestined and be damned. For the understanding of the implicit *condition* causes the truth in the *saying*, and (causes) an impossibility in *a true one* [in vero]. However, if it is *simply* understood, the impossibility is not admitted, such as when there is said: "the one predestined can and/or cannot be damned", and "the reprobate can be saved". For in these expressions and (those) of this kind the thought of the saying [sententia dictionis] is to be judged from the reckoning of the saying [ex ratione dicti]. And indeed one understanding comes to be, if these sayings are accepted *through a conjunction*, and another, if *through a distinction*, as was touched upon above,[2] when (God's) Foreknowledge was dealt with. For if, when you say: "the one predestined cannot be damned", you thus understand: "that is, it cannot be, that he be predestined and be damned", you understand the truth, because you understand (it) *conjointly*; but false, if (you understand it) *disjointly*, such as if you understand, that there cannot be damned, (him) whom I say (has been) predestined. For He could be not predestined, and thus be damned.

Nevertheless, they still insist [instant] and by arguing *according to the conjunction* proceed thus. "For it cannot be", they say, "that someone be predestined and be damned. *Each* of these cannot be together; but *one of the two* of these can *not be*, namely, that he is not predestined: for from eternity he has been predestined and he cannot now not be predestined. Therefore, since it is impossible, *that each be together*, and (since) it is impossible, *that one of the two not be*, it seems, that it cannot be *that the other of the two be*, namely that he be damned. Which if it is, therefore, it cannot be, that he not be saved." — In the solution of this question we prefer to hear others, than to teach. Yet we say, that a similar question can be moved concerning (God's) *Foreknowledge*; and for that reason, both in this and in that, we will make [facimus] one response, saying, that that must be determined, upon which this whole question is supported, namely, "*it is impossible, that one of the two*[3] *not be*", namely, that he is now predestined; for from eternity he has been predestined. For it must be distinguished, when he says: "this one cannot now not be predestined" and/or "it cannot now be, that he is not predestined". For this can be un-

derstood both *conjointly* and *disjointly*. For it cannot be, that from eternity he be predestined and now not be predestined, nor can it be *together*, that he be predestined and not be predestined; but yet it could be from eternity, that he was not predestined. And, just as *from eternity* God was able not to predestine him, so it is conceded by certain (authors), that even *now* God is able to not have predestined him. Therefore, from eternity *God is able to not have predestined* him: therefore, he is able *to not have been predestined*. However, if he *had not been predestined*, neither would he *now* be predestined: therefore, he is able *now* to not be predestined. Thus they speak both of *the Foreknowledge* and of *the foreknown*; which in God's and men's *actions* and/or operations they concede to no extent. For from this, that something *has been made* and/or said, they do not concede, that it can *not be* and/or *not have been*, nay it is impossible, that that which has been made and/or said, not be and/or not have been, referring (as they do) the possibility and/or impossibility to *the nature of the existing thing*. However, when dealing with God's *Foreknowledge* and/or *predestination*, possibility and/or impossibility is referred to *God's power*, which always was and is[4] the same, because predestination, Foreknowledge, and Power are one [unum] in God.

CHAPTER II

What is God's reprobation, and in whom is it considered, and what is the effect of predestination?

And, since predestination is a preparation for grace, that is, a divine election, *by which He elects those whom He willed before the constitution of the world*, as the Apostle says;[5] reprobation, conversely, is to be understood as the foreknowledge of the iniquity of certain ones and the preparation for the damnation of the same. For just as *the effect of predestination* is that grace, in which we are justified in the present and are assisted to live uprightly and persevere in the good, and that according to which we are beatified in the future; so God's *reprobation*, by which from eternity, by not electing certain ones, He reproved (them), is considered according to two (aspects), the one of which *He foreknows* and *does not prepare*, that is (their) iniquity, the other *He foreknows* and *prepares*, namely, (their) eternal punishment. Whence (St.) Augustine (says) To PROSPERUS and To HILARY:[6] « This rule », he says, « is to be held in an unshaken manner, that sinners *have been foreknown* in (their) sins, not *prepared*, but (their) punishment has been prepared ». « For God prepared », as (St.) Augustine says in the book, ON THE GOOD OF PERSEVERANCE,[7] « in His Foreknowledge, (those) for whom He willed His own goods; and to whomsoever He grants (it), far from doubt, He foreknew that He is going to give Himself ». « God also prepared », as (St.) Fulgentius (of Ruspe) says,[8] « for the wicked an eternal fire, for those at any rate, whom He justly prepared to pay the penalty [ad luenda supplicia]; yet, He did not

---

[1] Thus in the codices and edition 1 (edition 5 in the margin); in the others *He were to do* [faceret] for *it were done* [fieret].

[2] Distinction XXXVIII, ch. 2. — A little above this, the Vatican edition and editions 4, 6, 8 and 9 omits *another* [alia].

[3] The Vatican edition and the other editions, contrary to the codices and edition 1, add *of these* [istorum].

[4] Codex D adds *and will be* [et erit].

[5] Ephesians 1:4.

[6] (Which) is not found in the cited books, but in HYPOGNOSTICON, Bk. VI, ch. 6. See also the Gloss on Rom. 8:29 in (Nicholas) of Lyra,

from which Master (Peter) has transcribed more of what follows, having changed not a few)words).

[7] And/or ON THE GIFT OF PERSEVERANCE, ch. 17, n. 41.

[8] To MONIMUS, Bk. I, ch. 25; according to its sense, but literally in the Gloss (loc. cit.). In which text codices B and E before *to commit sins* [ad facienda peccata] prefix *them* [eos]. — A little below this, codices A B and D, and editions 2, 3, 7 and 8 (5 in the margin) have *admit injustice* [iniustitiam admittendam] for *lose justice* [iustitiam amittendum].

prepare (them) to commit sins [ad facienda peccata]. For God prepared, that the Divine Equity would render (punishment), not that human iniquity would be admitted. For not, just as He prepared the Saints to lay hold of justice [ad iustitiam percipiendam], did He thus prepare the iniquitous to lose justice, because He never was a preparer of depravity ».

Therefore, just as God's *predestination* is properly a foreknowledge and preparation for God's benefices, by which there are most certainly liberated whosoever are liberated;[1] so God's *reprobation* is a foreknowledge of the malice (which is) not to end in certain ones and the preparation of a punishment (which is) not to be terminated. And, just as *the effect of predestination is an apportioning of grace,* so *the effect of the* eternal *reprobation* seems in a certain manner to be *the obduration* (to grace). « For God does harden (sinners) against (grace) », as (St.) Augustine (says), TO SIXTUS,[2] by imparting [impertiendo] malice, but by not imparting grace, just as neither are they worthy. For (those) to whom He does not impart (grace) are neither worthy (of it) nor merit (it); rather that He does not impart (it), this they are worthy of, this they merit ». Wherefore the Apostle[3] says: *On whom He wills God has mercy, and whom He wills He hardens;* calling *"mercy"* a predestination and chiefly the effect of predestination, that is an apportioning of grace, but "obduration" a privation of grace. « For it must not be understood », as (St.) Augustine says To SIMPLICIANUS,[4] « that God thus hardens, as if to drive anyone to sin; but, yet, He does not bestow [largitur] to certain sinners the mercy of His justification, and because of this He is said to harden them, because He does not have mercy upon them, not because He impels them, to sin. But He does not have mercy upon them, to whom He judges grace not to be proffered according to an equity most secret and most removed from human senses »; « which the Apostle does not reveal [aperit], but wonders at, saying: *O height of the riches of the Wisdom and Knowledge of God* »!

COMMENTARY ON DISTINCTION XL

On predestination and reprobation, as much as regards (their) active cause.

On the other hand, predestination concerns the goods of salvation etc..

THE DIVISION OF THE TEXT

This is the third part, in which Master (Peter) deals with the Divine Knowledge, constricted [contracta] to (its) special effects. And this part is divided into two parts. In the first predestination and reprobation are dealt with as much as regards (their) *active* causality. In the second there is inquired, whether they have a passive causality, whether, namely, they are from our merits, below in the next Distinction: *But if we seek what merits obduration* etc..

The first part has two (parts). In the *first,* he deals with predestination; in the *second* with reprobation, there (where he says): *And, since predestination is a preparation for grace* etc.. Again, the *first* part is divided into two (parts). In the first, he deals with the quiddity of predestination; in the second, he inquires concerning its necessity, there (where he says): *None of the predestined seems to be able* etc.; in which part he first moves a doubt and opposes (it), and, then, solves (it), in the third he opposes against the response, and last he solves (it). The parts (of each) manifestly appear in the text.

And, since predestination is the preparation for grace etc.. This is the *second* part of the Distinction, in which Master (Peter) deals with reprobation, and this part has two (parts). In the first, he shows, what it is and what it connotes, inasmuch as (it is) a precognition. In the second, however, he shows, what is its cause, or what[1] is its effect, and this there (where he says): And, just as *the effect of predestination is an apportioning of grace* etc..

TREATMENT OF THE QUESTIONS

For an understanding of the present Distinction three (questions) are principally asked.

First, there is asked concerning predestination.

Second concerning election.

Third concerning reprobation.

The first Article has two (questions):

---

[1] (St.) Augustine, ON THE GIFT OF PERSEVERANCE, ch 14, n. 35.
[2] Epistle 194, c. 3, n. 14.
[3] Romans 9:18.
[4] Book I, q. 2, n. 16; but with very may (words) omitted by Master (Peter). The final words, *which ... does not reveal* etc. [quam non aperit etc.], have been taken from the just cited epistle, TO SIXTUS, ch. 2, n. 5. — The passage from Scripture is Romans 11:33.

NOTES ON THE COMMENTARY
[1] Cod. W has better *what* [quid].

For, first, there is asked concerning predestination, as much as regards (its) entity.

Second, as much as regards (its) necessity.

Moreover, concerning (its) entity two (questions) are asked.

First, there is asked, whether predestination is something eternal, or temporal [quid aeternum, an temporale].

Second, what is predestination according to thing [secundum rem].

ARTICLE I

On predestination, as much as regards (its) entity.

QUESTION I

Whether predestination is something eternal, or temporal?

Moreover, that predestination is something eternal, seems:

1. Because, what is before the constitution of the world is something eternal [quid aeternum]: (but) predestination is of this kind, because predestination is election, according to the first (chapter of St. Paul's Letter) to the Ephesians:[1] *He elected us before the constitution of the world*: ergo etc..

2. Likewise, « predestination is a foreknowledge of benefices »;[2] but whatever God foreknows, He foreknows eternally: therefore, since every foreknowing [praescientia] is eternal, and every predestination is a foreknowing, every predestination is eternal.

3. Likewise, « predestination is a proposal to have mercy [propositum miserendi] »;[3] but a proposal is something of the one proposing, preceding the things, which are proposed: therefore, since it is God's proposal, and God proposes eternally, it is clear etc..

4. Likewise, from the reckoning of its name predestination means a precession or antecession, but naught but of the one predestining to the one predestined; but the One predestining is eternal: therefore, it means the order and the antecession of an Eternal to a temporal. But that antecession is eternal: ergo etc..

ON THE CONTRARY: 1. Predestination conveys a *relation* to the one predestined; but every relation posts a true[4] looking-back [respectum verum] either in each of the extremes, and/or at least in one of the two; but predestination cannot posit a true looking-back in the One predestining: therefore, it posits a true looking-back in the one predestined. But a true looking-back is not founded except upon something created [quid creatum]: therefore, "predestination" means something created and temporal [quid creatum et temporale].

2. Likewise, predestination conveys an *action*, and to every action there responds a passion:[5] therefore, since the action and passion are not in the same, because *the One predestining* and *the one predestined* is not the same, it is necessary, that (the predestination) be in the other. But the other is naught but something temporal and created: therefore, predestination conveys something temporal and created: therefore, it is not eternal.

3. Likewise, predestination conveys an *order* of the One predestining to the one predestined, therefore, either (an order) according to the 'being' [secundum esse], which it has in *God*, or according to the 'being', which it has in *its own genus* [in proprio genere]. Not according to the 'being', which it has in *God*, because in this manner it is God and it does not follow God: therefore, according to the 'being', which it has in *its own genus*. But the 'being', which it has it its own genus, is something temporal and created: therefore predestination (is) similarly: and thus etc..

4. Likewise, every Divine act, which is not reflected upon the Essence and/or a Person, *passes outside*, and every act passing outside is said of God on account of time: therefore, since predestination does not pass into a Person and/or the Essence, but outside, therefore, it is temporal.

5. Likewise, predestination is a *preparation*;[6] but nothing is said to be prepared, before something begins to come to be according to intrinsic principles — for a craftsman is not said "to prepare a house", by thinking alone, before (he has) the lumber [ligna] and stones — therefore, it is necessary, that it be posited in a thing [in re].

---

[1] Verse 4, where in the Vulgate after *us* [nos] there is added *in Him* (i.e. in Christ) [in ipso]. — You will find more on this, that predestination is an election, below in a. 3, q. 2.

[2] This definition is (St.) Augustine's, ON THE GIFT OF PERSEVERANCE, ch. 14, n. 35. Cf. the following Question, in the body (of the Response).

[3] This definition is also (St.) Augustine's, ON THE PREDESTINATION OF THE SAINTS, ch. 17, n. 34, and is founded upon the words of the Apostle to the Romans, 9:15-18, where he concludes: « *Therefore He has mercy upon whom He wills* » [Ergo cuius vult misereri], and to the Ephesians, 1:5: *Who has predestined us .... according to the proposal of His*

own Will [Qui praedestinavit nos ... secundum propositum voluntatis suae]. Cf. the following question, in the body (of the Response).

[4] That is a real one, concerning which see above d. 30, q. 3. — At the end of the argument, the Vatican edition, together with codex cc, omits the words of the conclusion: *therefore "predestination" means something created* [ergo praedestinatio dicit quid creatum].

[5] Cf. above d. 30, a. sole, q. 1, p. 521, footnote 2.

[6] A reference to the definition of predestination taken from the book of (St.) Fulgentius (of Ruspe), ON FAITH TO PETER, ch. 35, n. 78. Cf. the following Question.

CONCLUSION

Predestination is eternal, by reason of (its) principal signified and (its) antecession to the connoted.

I Respond: It must be said, that in predestination there are naught but two (things), namely *the principal signified* and *the connoted. The principal signified* is the Divine Essence, but *the connoted* is a creature, such as grace and glory and the person to be saved.[1] And these two does predestination convey with an order of antecession of the one to the other by reason of the preposition, ("pre-").

Since, therefore, *the principal signified* is eternal, thus predestination is something eternal.[2] *Again*, since it conveys the antecession of the signified to the connoted, and that antecession is from eternity: for that reason predestination is something eternal and from eternity. And the reasons for this are to be conceded.

1. To that which is objected concerning *relation*, it must be said, that a thing[3] or relation can be signified in God in a twofold manner: either in respect of one existing in *act*, and/or in respect of one existing *in potency*, in act sometime in the future; and when in respect of one existing *in act*, then it is necessary, that a true looking-back respond in act; but when in respect of one existing *in potency*, it suffices that it respond in potency, and such is founded upon a being in potency; and for that reason it posits nothing according to act except God.

2. To that which is objected concerning *action*, it must be said, that there is an action according to *thing*, and there is an action according to a *manner* (of understanding).[4] To the action according to *thing*, which is the principle effecting something, there responds a passion differing according to thing, such as to the act of creating [creationi-actioni] (there responds) the act of being created [creatio-passio].[5] But to the action according to a *manner* (of understanding) there responds naught but a passion according to a differing manner (of understanding), such as to the act of cognition [cognitioni-actioni] of God Himself there responds the very *'being cognized* (of the thing)' [ipsum

cognosci]; and this, indeed, is really not another (action according to thing), but according to a manner (of understanding). Therefore, since *"predestination"* does not convey but a precognition, whether actively or passively, for that reason it is something eternal and it is not other than God.

3. To that which is objected concerning *order*, it must be said, that there is an order according to *nobility*, and according to *duration*;[6] and the order according to *nobility* posits (its) extremes together, but an order according to *duration*, by this very (thing) that it is an order, posits, that (its) extremes are not together; and an order according to a reckoning of *anteceding* is together with the one anteceding or with the one preceding, similarly (the one) according to the reckoning of *following after* [subsequendi] is together with the one subsequent. Since, therefore, predestination conveys an order according to a reckoning of *preceding*, for that reason it is eternal, although it is in respect of a temporal; since it is not together with that, but antecedes (it).

4. To that which is objected, that predestination *passes outside*; it must be said, that 'to pass outside' is in a twofold manner: either into something which is outside, or into something which *is* inside, but *will be* outside. And in the first manner it connotes something in act and means something temporal, such as "to create" and "to conserve"; in the second manner (it does) not, such as "to predestine".[7]

5. To that which is objected concerning the *preparation*, that it is attained[8] according to intrinsic principles, not according to an efficient cause; it must be said, that there is a certain efficient principle, which works according to *the matter lying before (it)* [materiam praeiacentem]; and this indeed, because it is in need of another, is not said "to prepare", when it only wills and disposes from within, but when it readies the matter outside. There is a certain efficient cause, which *is in need of nothing* to work, but immediately, when it wills, it works; and in such *"to prepare"*[9] is nothing other than *"to dispose"* and *"to propose"*; and such is God, because He is in need of no other than Himself to work.

SCHOLIUM

I. « To predestine is to preordain unto an end ... Predestination connotes three (things), namely, the preordained, and this is a man; and the reckoning of preordaining, and this is grace, and the reckoning of the end, and this is glory: and thus there are three, namely *what*, and *through what*, and *for what* » (below in a. 3, q. 2, in reply to n. 3). Predestination according to (St.) Au-

gustine (On the Gift of Perseverance, ch. 14, n. 35) is « a foreknowledge and a preparation of God's benefices, by which there are certainly liberated, whosoever are liberated »; according to St. Thomas (Summa., I, q. 23, a. 1) it is « a reckoning of the sending of a rational creature over unto the end of eternal life »; according to (Bl. John Duns) Scotus, (here in the q. sole, n. 2), it is

---

[1] And, indeed, grace as the medium *through which*, glory as the terminus *to which*, the person to be saved as *the subject*. What follows: *these two* etc. [haec duo etc.] refers to the *principal signified* and *the connoted*.

[2] It could be objected concerning *creation*, which taken actively even in regard to the principal signified is the Divine Essence, and yet is not said to be eternal; but see below the solution to n. 2 and 4, and St. Thomas, here in q. 1, a. 1, in reply to n. 1.

[3] For *a thing* [res] codex X (V in the margin) has *a looking-back*. Somewhat below this after *a true looking-back* [verus respectus], the Vatican edition, together with codex cc, omits not so well *in act* [in actu].

[4] That is, a manner of understanding. This distinction of action is founded in that, by which action is distinguished into a transient or immanent action. To a transient action there responds a passion in the ef-

fect, but not to an immanent (action), even if it respects an external thing, v. g. to the an act of the (Divine) Vision (there is no corresponding passion) of the thing seen. Cf. above d. 39, a. 1, q. 1, p. 686, footnote 4.

[5] Alexander of Hales, Summa, p. II, q. 6, m. 2, a. 5, uses the same manner of speaking.

[6] Cf. above d. 20, a. 2, q. 1, in the body (of the Response).

[7] This is explained more above in the solution to nn. 2 and 3. — A little before this, for *it connotes something* [connotat aliquid], which reading is found in codices A T and Y, the Vatican edition, together with the other codices and edition 1, has *it connotes another* [connotat aliud].

[8] Codex O has *which is attained* [quae attenditur] for *that it is attained* [quod attenditur]; the Vatican edition, together with codex cc, has *that it antecedes* [quod anteceditur].

[9] The Vatican edition, with cod. cc, for *in such "to prepare"* [in tali praeparare] reads *in such a preparation there* [in tali praeparatione].

« the order of the election through the Divine Will of any intellectual and/or rational creature to grace and glory ». With these definitions the threefold description of predestination, which is proposed below in q. 2 by St. Augustine convenes. For a more ample explanation there can serve what is said in a. 3, q. 2, of the difference between *the proposal, the election* and *the predestination*, and also here in Doubt 7 of the threefold causality, which is conveyed in predestination, and in Sent. Bk. III, d. 11, a. 1, qq. 1, 2, and 3 on the predestination of Christ.

The Catholic Doctrine concerning predestination takes a middle path among the innumerable errors, which have sunk to the extreme, while some distort predestination into a most pernicious *fatalism*, which suffocates free will and the merits of good works, but others *eliminate* the same under the appearance of human independence, and/or at least so *infirm* (it), as to exceedingly derogate from God's gratuitous gifts of *grace, final perseverance* and *election*. But in this all catholic doctors agree, that the predestination of the Elect is infallible and immutable, but thus, that it wounds least of all the liberty of creatures; likewise, that God has from eternity prepared good works, « so that we may walk in them » (Eph. 2:10), but thus, that « God's *gifts* are also the good *merits* of the justified himself » (Trent, session 6, canon 32), since « so great is (God's) goodness towards all men, that He wills, that which are His gifts, to be their merits » (ibid., ch. 16); and finally, that God's discretion between the Elect and the reprobate is eternal, but thus, that no adult is reproved except on account of *his own fault*, but no one, except through the Divine Mercy, is saved. — On the other hand, if one descends to the more special questions, especially regarding those which depend from the manner, in which a created will cooperates with divine grace, and in general from the deter-

mination of the Divine concursus to the free actions of creatures, the difficulties and the controversies of the Schools grow to almost an immense degree, such that in not a few things wise men stand against wise men, and as ones wiser still, confiding in their own ignorance, to say with the Apostle (Rom. 11:33): *O the height of the riches of the Wisdom and Knowledge of God! how incomprehensible are His judgements!* See the excellent words of the Seraphic Doctor below in d. 41. a. 1. q. 2, at the end.

II. That predestination is *eternal* not only in regard to the *act* itself of the One predestining, but even by reason of the eternal *connotation* regarding the person predestined, to grace and to glory (cf. here in Doubt 1), is commonly taught (cf. Alexander of Hales, Summa, p. I, q. 28, m. 1. a. 1; St. Thomas, Summa, I, q. 23, a. 2, q. 2). — The solution to n. 2 is founded upon this, that an action according to *thing*, which is the principle *effecting* something, that is, which *passes* into the extraneous matter, and the action according to the *manner* of understanding, not passing outside the subject, such as in God is the act of cognizing the creature, differ. To this there responds in the creature naught but a passion according to a *manner*, because a creature precisely as cognized receices only a *denomination*, not something real from outside (cf. St. Thomas, here in q. 1, a. 1, in reply to n. 1). — Notable also is the solution to n. 5, concernign which one can confer Alexander of Hales, loc. cit., a. 2; St. Thomas, here in q. 2, a. 1, in reply to n. 2; Richard of Middleton, here in a. 1, q. 2, in reply to n. 2.

III. Besides the cited authors: Bl. (now St.) Albertus (Magnus), here in a. 2 and 5; Summa., p. I, tr. 16, q. 63, m. 1, incidental question 1. — (Bl.) Peter of Tarentaise, here in q. 1, a. 1, quaestiunc. 1, and a. 3. — Richard of Middleton, here in a. 1, q. 2. — Giles the Roman, on this and the following question, here in 1st. princ., q. 1, a. 1 and 2. — Durandus (of Saint-Pourçain), on this and the following question, here in q. 1. — (Bl.) Dionysius the Carthusian, here in q. 1. — (Gabriel) Biel, on this and the following questions, here in q. sole.

QUESTION II

Whether predestination is according to God's Knowledge, or Will?

Second, there is asked, what is predestination, whether, namely, (it is) according to God's Knowledge, and/or Will [Dei scientia, vel voluntatis]. And with it supposed, that it means something, which is in each genus — for it is, as (St.) Augustine says,[1] *a foreknowledge* of benefices, and *a proposal* to have mercy — there is asked, which of these does it convey more principally and through the manner of a complement. And that it conveys a knowledge, seems:

1. Because a composite draws (its) signified from (its) components; but *"destination"* [destinatio], since it means both a mission and an ordination, is accepted in the reckoning of "predestination" as an *ordination* — for, just as (St.) Augustine says,[2] *"to predestine"* [predestinare] is the same as *"to preordain"* [praeordinare] — but though a *willing* and *knowing* craftsman preordains, yet he does not order inasmuch as (he is) *willing*, but inasmuch as (he is) *knowing*: ergo etc..

2. Likewise, knowledge is not divided according to the reckoning of (its) being accepted [secundum rationem accipiendi] into the virtues and/or into those which be-

long to the will, but into those which belong to the cognition; but we divide the Divine Knowledge into predestination and reprobation: therefore, predestination, according to which (it is) of this kind, pertains to the (Divine) Knowledge.

On the Contrary: 1. Predestination is the cause of grace and glory;[3] but grace and glory are immediately from the (Divine) Will: therefore, predestination of itself means something in the genus of the will. *If you say*, that from the force of the name it does not convey that causality; *on the contrary*: let it be, that God would foreknow, that someone (is) going to have grace and glory from elsewhere than from Himself, (then) He would not be said to predestine: therefore, of itself it means a *causality*.

2. Likewise, predestination conveys a knowledge and a will; but as often as these two are conveyed in anything, the will holds itself through the manner of one consequent and adding to knowledge;[4] but what is consequent and adds, holds itself through the manner of a difference and a complement, and by such the thing is to be denominated: therefore, it seems,

---

[1] See above the preceding Question, 2nd and 3rd arguments of the fundament, and here in the body of the Question. — A little before this, by the words *in each genus* [utroque genere], there are signified (the genera of) knowledge and will.

[2] (In the work) once attributed to (St.) Augustine, Hypognosticon, Bk. VI, ch. 2: « Predestination is indeed said from *foreseeing* [praevidendo] and *preventing* [praeveneiendo] and/or *preordaining* [praeordinando] something future ». In this respect, in the book, On the Gift of Perseverance, ch. 17, n. 41, he says: And indeed in His own Foreknowledge, which cannot fail nor be changed, *to arrange* [disponere]

His own works, that is entirely, and not anything else, to predestine (them). — A little above this, for *signified* [significatum], codex K, together with edition 1, has well *signification* [significationem].

[3] Thus taken, "predestination" is commonly defined as "a preparation for grace in the present and for glory in the future". Cf. the text of Master (Peter), here in ch. 2.

[4] For the will, because it is the rational appetite, presupposes and follows the reason and knowledge. Hence it is, that in relation to knowledge it holds itself through the manner of one fulfilling and specifying [per modum complenttis et specificantis], adding,

that it conveys more completely a will, and thus that Master (Peter) badly situates (it).

CONCLUSION

Predestination, which is the cause of grace and glory, conveys both a knowledge and power and will, but it is more principally in the genus of the will.

I RESPOND: It must be said, that since *"predestination"*[praedestinatio] signifies the Divine Essence as the cause of grace and glory, and this according to the ordained distribution of grace and glory, as much as it concerns itself, it does not only convey a *knowledge*, but also a *will* and a *power*. But, since the causality of grace and glory is attributed properly to the (Divine) *Will* as effecting, but to the (Divine) *Knowledge* as disposing, and to the (Divine) *Power* as executing; for that reason, even if predestination conveys those three, yet it is more principally in the genus of the *will*. And, for that reason, predestination is defined by (St.) Augustine through those three: first through that which respects *power*, in the book, ON FAITH TO PETER:[1] « Predestination is the preparation for a gratuitous donation »; second through that which respects *knowledge*, in the book, ON THE GOOD OF PERSEVERANCE:[2] « Predestination is the foreknowledge of God's benefices »; third through that

which respects *will* and most properly, in the book, ON THE PREDESTINATION OF THE SAINTS:[3] « Predestination », he says there, « is a proposal to have mercy ».

1. To that, therefore, which is objected, that it means an order; it must be said, that the (Divine) Order is twofold: one, *the disposition of things* in the universe, and this is appropriated to the (Divine) Knowledge; the other, *the directing (of things) unto (their) end*, and this is appropriated to (God's) Goodness or Will, and in this manner it concerns the reckoning of predestination.

2. To that which is objected, that (predestination) is a part of the Foreknowledge; it must be said, that according to the manner that faith and prudence are in the genus of *cognition*, yet they add something upon cognition, which draws it off [distrahit] into the genus of *virtue*, which respects the will; through this manner and in the proposed, it must be understood. And, since *"knowledge"* [scientia] is not only accepted for *"a simple being known"* [simplici notitia], but even, as (it) frequently (is), for *"practical (knowledge)"*, and, in this manner, it comprises knowledge with will, and thus Master (Peter) accepts it generally; for that reason, he enumerates predestination among those which belong to the (Divine) Knowledge. — However, some wanted to say, that it is more principally in the genus of *knowledge*, by this, that in the reckoning of predestination there occurs in a right sense [in recto] a knowledge, but in an oblique sense [in obliquo] a will; for predestination is the knowledge of good pleasure. Each manner of speaking is sufficiently probable, but the first (is) more (so).

SCHOLIUM

I. All Catholic doctors teach, that in predestination there is included both an act of the Divine Intellect, and an act of the Will; but among the same there is a controversy regarding what is more principally signified in it. St. Thomas (SUMMA., I, q. 23, a. 1 and 4) teaches, according to his own principles, that formally it consists in an act of the (Divine) Intellect as *commanding*, which supposes an end willed and the means chosen [media electa]. This sentence St. Bonaventure (here at the end) judges to be sufficiently probable, and Alexander of Hales (SUMMA., p. I, q. 28, m. 1, a. 2), Bl. (now St.) Albertus (Magnus), (Bl.) Peter of Tarentaise, Richard of Middleton, Durandus (of Saint-Pourçain) and others likewise hold. Nevertheless, St. Bonaventure reputes as *more probable* the manner of saying, that the same consists rather in an act of *the (Divine) Will*, by which God approves that order, proposed by (His) Intellect, and proposes that it be executed, so that *the act of directing unto an end* is appropriated to the Will (here in the reply to n. 1). This is also the sentence of (Bl.) Scotus (here in q. sole, n. 2) with his School and not a few others. Father Trigosus (q. 18, a. 2. Doubt 4), supported by Father Marc de Baudun, O.F.M., Cap., (1606-1692 A. D.), PARADISUS THEOLOGICUS., tome I, q. 23, a. 2), would reconcile each sentence in this manner: Predestination *completively* [completive] consists in an act of the Will, just as St. Bonaventure (2nd argument of the fundament) himself says, that « it *more completely* conveys

a will »; but *essentially* (it consists) in an act of the Intellect, since the of the Will, by which God *loves* and *elects*, is also in the manner of St. Bonaventure not formally *predestination*, but is presupposed for it, as is clear from his words (here in a. 2, q. 3, in reply to nn. 2 and 3). However, to us it seems that there here occurs the same, certain kind of difference between the two Saintly Doctors, which we have observed above in d. 1, a. 2, q. 1, in the Scholium, in regard to the concept of Beatitude. — On the Doctrine which grants a causality « properly *to the Will* as effecting, but *to the Knowledge* as disposing, and *to the Power* as executing », cf. below d. 45, a. 2, q. 1 (chiefly in reply to n. 3) and in q. 2. — In the solution to n. 2, to explain, the manner in which an addition upon *cognition draws* predestination from the genus of the intellect into the genus of the will, a twofold example is offered: first concerning *faith* (cf. SENT, Bk. III, d. 23, qq. 1 and 2), second concerning *prudence* (ibid, d. 33, q. 3).

II.* Alexander of Hales, SUMMA., p. I, q. 28, m. 1, a. 2. — (Bl. John Duns) Scotus, here in the q. sole. — St. Thomas, here in q. 1, a. 2; SUMMA., I, q. 23, a. 1. — Bl. (now St.) Albertus (Magnus), here in a. 1. — (Bl.) Peter of Tarentaise, here in q. 1, a. 1, quaestiunc. 2. — Richard of Middleton, a. 1, q. 1. — (Bl.) Dionysius Carthusian, here in q. 1, at the beginning.

---

that is, an efficacy in respect of those, which through knowledge had been simply cognized. — A little before this, for *as often as* [quoties] codices A and V has *however so often as* [quotiescumque]. — By the final words of this argument, *that Master (Peter) badly situates (it)* [quod male situet Magister], there is indicated, that Master (Peter) faultily placed the question concerning predestination in the Tract on God's Knowledge, since according to this argument it should pertain to the Tract on (God's) Will. — For *situates (it)* [situet], codex I has *insinuates (it)* [insinuet].

[1] Chapter 35, n. 78.

[2] Now named, ON THE GIFT OF PERSEVERANCE, ch. 17, n. 41, where this definition is had according to its sense. The very words of (St.) Augustine are exhibited here in the text of Master (Peter), ch. 2.

[3] Chapter 17, n. 34, where the sentence cited, if one regards the words, is not indeed found, but it can be easily constructed from the words which are read there: "And so they have been elected before the constitution of the world ... those, that is, by a vocation according to a proposal". Cf. also HYPOGNOSTICON, Bk. VI, ch. 6 f..

---

* *Trans. note*: Here the original text of the Scholium had *III* for *II*, faultily.

ARTICLE II

On predestination, as much as regards (its) necessity.

Second, as much as regards this first article (to be considered), there is asked concerning the necessity of predestination. And about this two (questions) are asked.

First, there is asked, whether it infers a necessity of salvation for a free will [libero arbitrio].

Second, whether it infers a certitude in the outcome [certitudinem in eventu].

QUESTION I

Whether predestination infers the necessity of salvation?

Moreover, that it does infer a necessity, is shown in this manner.

1. Every cause, which is necessary in itself and posits an effect necessarily, *infers* simply a necessity of the effect; but predestination in respect of salvation is of this kind: ergo etc.. The *minor* is clear. For predestination, since it is in itself God, means something necessary; and again, it necessarily infers the effect, because: 'if he has been predestined", there necessarily follows: 'he shall be saved": ergo etc..

2. Likewise, every cause, which can in no manner *be cancelled* [cassari], posits a necessity about the production of (its) effect — for a cause is said "to be cancelled", when it posits no effect — but predestination can in no manner be cancelled: therefore predestination posits a necessity.

3. Likewise, however so often two causes concur to some effect, which (two), it is impossible, that *they be discordant* [discordare], if one is immutable, it is necessary, that the other be immutable, and consequently [per consequens] the effect (too). This is manifest through itself: for if one of the two is mutable, with the remaining one [reliqua] existing immutably, it is possible, that they are discordant. But it is impossible, that predestination and free will be discordant: therefore, since predestination is an immutable cause, it is necessary, that free will be immutable; and if this, since the whole is immutable, it therefore, remains, that predestination imposes a necessity for salvation and upon free will [libero arbitrio et saluti].

4. Likewise, it seems, that the one predestined can in no manner be damned, and if this, then he is necessarily saved; and (this) is shown by this reckoning: these two are convertible: 'to have been foreknown' and 'to be damned', (and) 'to have been predestined' and 'to be saved'; but the one predestined cannot have been foreknown: therefore, he cannot be damned. *Proof of the middle.* When any two so hold themselves, that it is impossible, that one succeed the other, and they cannot be in (something) together, if one of the two is in (it), it is impossible, that the one remaining be in (it), but 'to have been predestined' and

'to have been foreknown' so hold themselves, that it is impossible, that they be together in the same (man); it is also impossible, that one of the two succeeds the other of the two, namely, that a man first have been predestined and afterwards (have) been foreknown: therefore, when he has been predestined, in no manner has he been foreknown: ergo etc..

5. Likewise, concerning everything which is eternal, when it is not, it is impossible that it be, because it is impossible, that (something) *not being* be eternal; but the foreknow, if he is, has been eternally foreknown: therefore, the one who has not been foreknown, it is impossible that he have been foreknown. But the one predestined has not been foreknown: ergo etc..

6. Likewise, of that which is not, it is the same to say, that it *can be*, and that *it can begin to be*; but a foreknown is something not being [quid non ens] in respect of one predestined: therefore, it is the same to say, that the one predestined *can be* foreknown, as *that he can begin* to be foreknown or to be damned. But he cannot begin to be foreknown, ergo etc..

ON THE CONTRARY: 1. Divine predestination causes no one to be saved unworthily: therefore, since dignity in being saved respects merit, and merit free will, therefore predestination does not take away the liberty of judgement [libertatem arbitrii], according to which (there is) free will: therefore, it neither imposes a necessity.

2. Likewise, predestination bears off nothing from free will, but only posits grace in it; but grace infers no necessity upon free will, therefore, neither (does) predestination: if it imposes no necessity upon it,[2] therefore, since salvation depends out of free will, it is clear that etc..

3. Likewise, if predestination imposes a necessity, therefore, since, with every contingent occurrence [casu], it is necessary, that the one who has been predestined, be saved, therefore, in vain does anyone work to do good [laborat benefacere]; because, whether he does good or evil, it is necessary, that he be saved.

4. Likewise, no one is praised in that which is of necessity, nor is he blamed:[3] therefore, if it is necessary,

---

[1] Many codices faultily omit the second *it can* [posse].

[2] The Vatican edition and codex cc there are lacking the words *if it imposes no necessity upon it* [si nullam ei imponit necessitatem].

[3] Cf. Aristotle, ETHICS, Bk. II, ch. 5: On which account (the virtues) are neither the faculties nor the powers, indeed, since we say that (we are) neither good nor evil because of this, that we can act absolutely; nor are we

that the one predestined be saved and the one fore-known be damned, neither is the one predestined to be praised, if he is saved, nor the one foreknown to be blamed, if he is damned; which (saying) is contrary to the state of glory and punishment.

CONCLUSION

Predestination neither by reason of (its) causality nor by rea-son of (its) foreknowledge infers a necessity, whether in respect of salvation or in respect of free will.

I RESPOND: It must be said, that predestination neither infers a necessity *for salvation*, nor infers a ne-cessity *upon free will*, since predestination is not the cause of salvation except when including merits, and thus in saving free will.

For an understanding of the objections, more-over, it must be noted, that "predestination" [praedestinatio] conveys two (things): both a reck-oning of *foreknowledge* and a reckoning of *a cause*. Inasmuch as it means the reckoning of *a cause*, it does not necessarily posit an effect, because it is not a cause through necessity, but through a will; and again, it is not *the whole* cause, but (is a cause) with another contingent cause, namely with free will. And the rule is, that however so often as an effect de-pends out of a necessary and variable cause — from a necessary one as from a universal one, from a vari-able one as from a particular one — it is denomi-nated from the variable one, because denomination is from a particular cause;[1] and the effect, which de-pends from the contingent cause, is contingent. — Besides the reckoning of *a cause*, (predestination)[2] conveys the reckoning of *foreknowledge*, and *fore-*

knowledge indeed includes *the whole* in the cognition, be-cause (it includes) free will and its cooperation and vert-ibility, and the whole. *And moreover*, it is not but of the true, and concerning the true contingent it is also infalli-ble, just as has been demonstrated above in the Question on the Foreknowledge.[3] For that reason predestination does infer salvation and cannot be cancelled nor be dis-cordant from free will. And because the Foreknowledge imposes no necessity of *a consequent*, but only of *a conse-quence*, similarly neither (does) predestination.

1. 2. 3. From this the first three objections con-cerning the necessity of *inferring*, the impossibility of *being cancelled*, (and) the impossibility of *being discordant*, are clear. For these all mean a necessity of consequence only, because they are in predestination not through the reckoning of *causality*, but (through the reckoning) of a *precognition*, which is *concordant* [concors], *certain* and *in-fallible*. *Concordant*, because (God's) Foreknowledge or Precognition[4] (is) true: for He who cognizes, cognizes truly, that the thing is present, just as it is, and that the one going to be comes forth, just as it will come forth. For truth is the adequation of thing and intellect.[5] It is, again, *certain*, because (it is) independent, because it de-pends in no manner out of the one precognized. For He does not cognize according to its exigency, but accord-ing to the exigency of the Eternal Light and Glory, in which there falls no doubtfulness [dubietas], but the most high certitude; and for that reason it is equally cer-tain concerning all. Again, it is *infallible*, since it is the one comprising the whole possible-being [posse] of the foreknown; and for that reason it can fail in noth-ing nor (can it) be circumvented. — And there is the example of (St. Severinus) Boethius in the fifth (chap-ter) ON THE CONSOLATION (OF PHILOSOPHY),[6] that if anyone would gaze [aspiceret] from an eminent

---

praised nor blamed. Add that we have been endowed with a faculty and are strong by nature, we are made good or evil, just as we have said above, lest of all by nature.

[1] The reason is, because an effect is more assimilated to a partic-ular cause than to a universal one. Thus, to cite an example from the Scholastics, a man begotten is more assimilated to the man generating than to the Sun, because the Sun is a universal generator. Cf. also above in d. 38, a. 2, q. 2, in the body of the Response near the end, and in d. 14, a. 1, q. 1, in reply to n. 6, where a similar (argument) is had concerning the necessary and the contingent.

[2] Supply together with codex R *predestination* [praedestinatio].

[3] Distinction 38, a. 2, q. 2; d. 39, a. 1, q. 2, in reply to n. 3, and ibid., a. 2, q. 2. — On the last proposition of the body of the Response, cf. above d. 38, a. 2, q. 1.

[4] Codex T reads *Cognition* [cognitio].

[5] This definition of truth used to be commonly attributed by the Scholastics to Aristotle, or to a certain Isaac, who wrote a book, ON DEF-INITIONS. If one regards the words alone, the definition of truth proposed here by the Seraphic Doctor occurs in neither the one nor the other, but if one attends to the meaning, that definition is had among each. Aristotle speaking in many places of the truth and falsity of speech teaches, that an expression is true if it enunciates the thing, just as it is; but false, if it enunciates the thing, not as it is. Cf. his books ON PREDICAMENTS, ch. "On *Substance*", ON INTERPRETATION, Bk .I, ch. 7 (ch. 9); ON THE SOUL, Bk. III, text 21 ff. (ch. 6); METAPHYSICS, Bk. IV, text 27 (Bk. III, ch. 7), and also Bk. V, text 34 (Bk. IV, ch. 29). But in METAPHYSICS, Bk. IX, text 21 (Bk. VIII, ch. 10) he says: « On which account the true means, that which reputes [putat] the divided to be divided and the composed to be composed; but the false, that which (is) contrary to that (manner in) which things hold themselves, either when they are or (when) they are not ». That which is attributed to Isaac, we have found at Münich, in the Royal Library, codex n. 8001, lat., which from folio 151 verso up to folio 154 verso contains Isaac's famous book, ON DEFINITIONS. In which

book we find this definition of truth and falsity: « Truth is that which the thing is; according to others, truth is an expression [sermo], which confirms a demonstration either according to sense or according to understanding [vel sensibliter vel intellecutaliter]; but that expression thus is, as a definition, since it is enunciative of the nature and essence of the thing; similarly also the expression of the one speaking: (its) truth indeed is enunciative of the nature and of the essence of truth, as much as by itself (it is) that which the thing is, it truly is, and (its) truth is naught but what is. Falsity is that which the thing is not, and it is said (to be) the speech, by which there is said of something the contrary of it. The true is the affirmation of the thing concerning the thing, by which it is (not) truly removed; but the false is its contrary; the right is that which is impossible to be removed ». — The definition of truth, pro-posed by the Seraphic Doctor, in regard to (its) words, agrees more with that definition, which Averroës proposes in the book « The Destruction of De-structions », disp. metaph. I, near the end (dubium 22): « For indeed the truth, as has been declared in its declaration (i. e. definition), is to equate a thing to the understanding, that is, which (understanding) is found in the soul, just as it is outside the soul » (Venice: 1495) — and with the definition of Avi-cenna, METAPHYSICS, Bk. I, ch. 9, which is: Moreover, truth ... is understood (to be) the disposition of a saying and/or of the intellect, which signifies [sig-nat] the disposition in the exterior thing, when it is equal to it. Cf. also (St.) Anselm's book, ON TRUTH. — A little after this for *it depends* [pendet] very many codices, such as X Z aa and bb, have *depends* [dependet]; then for *its exigency* [eius exigentiam] the Vatican edition, together with codex cc, reads *its* (i.e. the precognized) *existence* [eius existentiam]; finally for *and for that reason ... concerning all* [et ideo de omnibus] many codices, together with edition 1, have faultily *and for that reason ... for all* [et ideo omnibus].

[6] Prose 6, where the author speaking of Providence says: « that which constituted long before infirm things, looks out upon all the rest as if from the exalted peak of things » ... And, ibid., to the one impugning the immutabil-ity of Providence he responds: That your proposal indeed can deflect you, but since that which you can also (do), and whether you do, or whither you turn, the present truth of Providence intuits, (and I say) that the Divine Fore-

place upon the region lying round about [circumiacentem], where there is a multitude of roads [viarum], all of which he saw together and with one gaze [uno aspectu], one walking through that place, though he could go through diverse roads, yet, he could not hide from the sight of the former one [eius], in virtue of this that he could go through no road, which that one did not see. If, therefore, there be understood to be one vision, which can foresee all the ways and the whole *possible-being* of the one going, in no manner could anyone circumvent that prevenient (vision).[1] And such is the gaze of the Divine Foreknowledge, because He cognizes from eternity what *we could think* and/or *will*, and He sees together with this, unto which side our will and operation would be inclined. And because predestination includes the Foreknowledge, hence it is, that *it is concordant* with free will, and cannot *be discordant*, and (that) it cannot *be cancelled*; and (that) it necessarily *infers* salvation, but not necessarily *effects* (it).[2]

4. To that which is asked, "Whether the one predestined can be damned?"; it must be said, that (it is) *so*, without distinction, because although *this (expression)*: "it is possible that the one predestined be damned" can be distinguished concerning *thing*, and/or *saying*,[3] just as this one (can): "it is possible that the white one be black"; yet, *this (expression)*: "the one predestined can be damned" is not to be distinguished according to the art (of logic), just as neither (is) this: "a white man can be black." For it cannot concern a *saying*, since it has not *been said.**

On account of which it must be understood, that this (expression): "the one predestined can be damned", has[4] three causes of truth, just as this (expression): "the one predestined can be foreknown" (does): because either the form of the predicate can be in the subject *with* an implied form, and/or *after* an implied form, and/or *without* an implied form. For in whatsoever manner the predicate can be in (the subject), the expression is to be judged simply true; and I say, that in the *third* sense the expression: "the one predestined can be foreknown", is true.[5] For the one predestined is able not to have been predestined, and it is necessary, that every man have been predestined, and/or foreknown; and for that reason it follows, that he is able to have been foreknown. And that this be posited is indeed necessary. For the Faith and reason say, that: "if he has been predestined", it follows (that), "he will be saved". *Again*, the Faith and

reason say, that '*that this one is saved*' is contingent; and he who would say and assert the contrary, would have to be rejected, according to the certain judgement of all. *And again*, the art (of logic) says, that if a consequent is contingent, it is impossible, that (its) antecedent be necessary, and this has been proven above through the three rules;[6] and he who would say the contrary of this, would destroy the entire syllogistic art, whose virtue belongs to the illation, that the opposite of a consequent cannot stand with (its) antecedent. Moreover, it is certain, that the opposite of a contingent stands with a necessary.[7] Therefore, 'that this one has been predestined' is not necessary. And it is (either) *necessary*, and/or *contingent*, and/or *impossible*; and it is not *impossible* nor *necessary*: therefore, it is *contingent*; and a *contingent* can not be: therefore, this one who has been predestined, is able not to have been predestined.

And, indeed, I believe this, that it is necessary that one posit (this); yet, it is difficult for one to understand this. However, it can be thus grasped, if we presuppose four truths. The *first* is, that the present of the Divine eternity embraces every time, the same and uniformly; and this does (St.) Anselm say in the book, ON THE CONCORD OF (GOD'S) FORE-KNOWLEDGE AND FREE WILL,[8] that « just as *the present time* embraces every place, and everything which is in a place, so *the present of eternity* every time ». And it is necessary that one posit this, though we cannot fully understand it. For we see, that its opposite is false and impossible: because if this were not, then the present of the Divine eternity would be changed. — The *second* is this, that God by one and the same (gaze) cognizes all, thus that God's Cognition is unique, because He cognizes this and that by which He cognizes its opposite. And this has been proved above[9] by authority and reason, not only as much as regards that *through which* it is cognized, but even as much as regards *the act* of the Divine Cognition. — The *third* is, that when we say, that the Divine Cognition and/or Will is ordered to this cognizable and to another, an order and/or looking-back is not posited in God's act, but solely on the part of the created and/or cognized thing; and that (order and/or looking-back) indeed, as has been seen before,[10] is not posited in act, but in habit, nor (does it) concern the present, but the future. — The *fourth* is, that the future (thing) under

---

knowledge cannot also be avoided, just as one cannot flee from the intuition of a present eye, though you turn yourself in various actions by a free will [libera voluntate] ... For the Divine Intuition runs before and It bends back and recalls to the presence of Its own cognition everything future. Cf. also ibid., Meter 2. — A little further below this, for *through that place* [per locum illum] the Vatican edition, together with codex cc, has *through his own place* [per locum suum].

   [1] Understand: vision. — For *prevenient* [prevenientem] the Vatican edition alone has *foreseeing* [praevidentem], and somewhat below this *is inclined* [inclinatur] for *would be inclined* [inclinaretur].

   [2] Or, to use other words, it is necessary in the following after, but not in the effecting. Cf. above d. 38, a. 2, q. 1.

   [3] Cf. here the text of Master (Peter), ch. 1, where *a saying* is distinguished *from a true (thing or event)* [a vero], and a *composed* sense from a *divided* one.**

   [4] And/or rather: can have.

   [5] For an easier understanding of the this passage it will not be unuseful to accept this proposition as the major of the syllogism: *For in whatsoever manner a predicate can be in (the subject), the expression is*

to be judged simply true, and, then, to add, as the minor, these words: *but in this proposition the form of the predicate cannot be in the subject, except in the third sense, i. e. without an implied form*, and, then, to make this the conclusion. *therefore, I say, that in the third sense* etc..

   [6] Distinction 38, a. 2, q. 2, 1st to 3rd arguments of the fundament. — A little before this, in place of the word *above* [supra] there is falsely read in very many codices *by a sophism* [sophisma].

   [7] See *loc. cit.*, according to the second and third rule. — The Vatican edition, together with one or the other codex, faultily has *does not stand* [non stat] for *stands* [stat].

   [8] Question I, ch. 5: According to the manner which present time contains every place and those which are in any place, so in the eternal present there is enclosed every time and those which are in any time.

   [9] Distinction 39, a. 1. q. 1, and q. 3, in reply to n. 4, and also a. 2, q. 1, and q. 3, in the last reply. — A little above this, after *by one and the same* [uno et eodem] codex Z supplies *respect and/or manner* [respectu vel modo].

   [10] Distinction 38, a. 2, q. 2, and here in a. 1, q. 1.

   ** *Trans. note*: In saying, at the end of this argument, *because it has not been said*, the Seraphic Doctor means to say, that the proposition is said simply, and not subordinated to a main verb, as the previous one is.

the reckoning of a future (thing), which is posited to be true once, is posited to have been true always, and that which is posited to be false once, is posited to have been false always; and for that reason when one posits *that it can be*, one does not posit that *it is changed* nor *that it begins*.[1]

With these supposed, it is easy to understand, that the one predestined can be foreknown, and that God could have predestined him whom He foreknew. For it is established, that the salvation of this one who has been foreknown, was able to be foreseen from eternity, since it can be and or come to be in time; and if it could from eternity be ordained to the Divine Cognition and Will, it can also now. For indeed because the present is whole, and nothing passed into the past, and nothing has been made, which is necessary to have been made; hence it is, that just as it can be thought, that He truly can (predestine)[2] and that He has predestined *from eternity*, so also, that He can *now*, in His own, that is, *now* of eternity, not have predestined. And this Master (Peter) says in the text. However, the eternal act of the Divine Cognition cannot be thought to not have been, but (it can be thought)[3] to not have been ordered to this future contingent; and if this is posited, there is posited no change in *the eternal present*, because no succession is posited; nor is a change in the (Divine) *Cognition* posited, because there not posited in God any cognition neither in an order on the part of *the One cognizing*, because no order is posited in God, nor an order on the part of *the one cognized*, because on that part there is posited naught but a future (thing); and that (future thing), when it is not, can be understood to be, and it can be future without a change.[4]

And this entire (argument) appears more clearly, if we come to the signification of these words "*foreknown*" and "*predestined*". For "*predestined*" and "*foreknown*" are two words, and as much as regards (their) *principal signi-*

fied they convey the Divine Essence, as much as regards (their) *connoted* they convey future contingents. Therefore, as much as regards (their) *principal signified* they are the same, but as much as regards (their) *connoted*, because they are contingents, which are not in (something) of necessity, the one can be the other.[5] But because *the connoted* are not only *contingents*, but also *concern the future*, which (contingents) posit nothing in act, they can *not be in* and *be in* (something) without a change (in God's Cognition). For when they are posited *to be in* true (things) concerning the future, they are posited to have been always, and when they are posited *not to be*, they are posited to have never been, just as is clear; and (St.) Anselm[6] says, that is one says, that something is going to be concerning a contingent, it is established that it is possible, that it is not going to be; and if it is going to be, it always was true, that it was going to be. And for that reason this: "the one predestined can be foreknown" is true without a change (in God's Foreknowledge) and without a beginning (of its being true). For there is no repugnance, neither on the part of the signified, nor on the part of the connoted, and this is clear, if they[7] be resolved. For the sense is: "this one has been predestined", that is, "this one has been precognized by God and he will be saved through God's grace". Similarly: "this one has been foreknown", the sense is: "this one has been precognized and will be damned through his own fault". For it is established, that in the Divine Cognition there is no difference in itself, but only in the connoted. Therefore, since the one to be saved can be damned, the one predestined can be foreknown without any change (in God's Foreknowledge).

4. 5. 6. From this the other three objections are clear: for the first and last is understood in regard to forms, which posit something in act about a subject; but the second of that which is so eternal, that it connotes nothing temporal. But such are not "to have been foreknown" and "to have been *predestined*".[8] And thus all (the objections) are clear.

---

[1] Cf. Distinction 38, a. 2, q. 2, in reply to the last two (objections), where there is distinguished a twofold immutable and eternal, one namely, which is convertible with necessary being, the other, which is not convertible with necessary being, since it is not something in act, since it is a future contingent.

[2] Supple: *predestine* [praedestinare]. — For *can* [posse] the Vatican edition has *could* [potuisse]. The particle *and* [et], which follows the verb, is lacking in edition 1 and, in codex T it has been expunged by a second hand. A little further above this, for *passed* [transiit] many codices, together with edition 1, have *passes* [transit]. — See the sentence of Master (Peter) here in ch. 1.

[3] Understand: *it can be thought* [potest cogitari]. Cf. above d. 38, a. 2, q. 2, in the body (of the Response). — A little further above this, for *but* [sed] not a few codices have *that is* [scilicet] and the Vatican edition, together with codex cc, has *and/or* [vel]. The same Vatican edition a little below this after *and if this is* [et si hoc] inserts into the text *not* [non]; faultily. Then Cod V reads *in eternity* [in aeterno] for *in the eternal present* [in aeterno praesenti], which omitted word is also lacking codex T, but has been added after a second consideration.

[4] Namely, because that which is not is not changed, even though it comes to be; for a change supposes existence. The Vatican edition less aptly to the context, a little above this, puts *not to* [non] for *it can* [potest].

[5] That is, because they are contingent in a manner related to, v. g., a man, it is not necessary, that one of them in a manner determined out of itself convene with him, but either one and/or the other can convey with him. — A little before this, for *(their) connoted* [connotatum] edition 1 has *(their) connoteds* [connotata].

[6] In the book, ON THE CONCORD OF GOD'S FOREKNOWLEDGE WITH FREE WILL, q. 1, ch. 2: Just as 'that a thing is white' and 'that a white thing is white' is not the same; for wood is not always by necessity white, because at some time, before it becomes white, it could not become white; and afterwards it is white, it can become not white; however, it is necessary always that white wood be white, because neither before it is, nor after it is white, can it come to be, that as white it be at the same time not white ... In the same manner any thing, such as a certain action, is not going to be by necessity, because before it is, it can come to be, such that it is not going to be; but it is necessary that a future thing be future, since a future (thing) cannot at the same time not be future. Cf. also ibid., ch. 3. — A little before this, for *to be in true (things)* [inesse] edition 1 has *to be true* [esse vera].

[7] Understand: *the two following propositions*; and/or read with the Vatican edition *(that proposition) be resolved* [resolvatur]; edition one reads *(that proposition) is resolved* [resolvitur].

[8] Concerning which, cf. above d. 38, a. 2, q. 2, in reply to the last (objection).

SCHOLIUM

I. Having supposed the distinction between an *absolute* necessity or (a necessity) of *the consequent*, and a *hypothetical one* or (a necessity) of *a consequence* or of *an illation* (above in d. 38, a. 2, q. 1), in this question (the Seraphic Doctor) deals principally with the *absolute* necessity, but at the end of the body of the Question, also with a *hypothetical* necessity. Moreover, in the solution to n. 4 he treats a special question, "In which sense can it be said, that the one predestined can be damned?" — Manifestly heretical and condemned by the Council of Constance, approved by (Pope) Martin V, is the proposition (prop. 27) of Wycliffe: « All come forth from an absolute necessity ».

II. To better understand the Catholic dogma, the Seraphic (Doctor) proves through (its) parts, that neither the reckoning of *causality*, nor the reckoning of *knowledge*, which are implied in predestination, infer a necessity upon free will. It is noted, that besides the ancient heretics, (John) Calvin and very many others so exaggerated the causality and efficacy of predestination, that the true causality and contingency of free will *was taken away*, as if being moved by God, it did not move and determine itself. Which most pernicious error was reproved by the Council of Trent, Session 6, canon 4. Whence catholic doctors unanimously teach, that the action of the First Cause does not exclude the true and free cooperation of a second cause, nor does the motion or efficacy of grace impede, that a created will also truly moves and determines itself. But among the Catholic Schools it has also been a bitter dispute concerning *the manner* and *reckoning* of that cooperation, chiefly among those two celebrated Schools, opposed in this question as adversaries. For the School, which is said to belong to the Thomists, affirms that the true doctrine of Sts. Augustine and Thomas is, that the Divine Will by Its own causality infers by its intrinsic efficacy a free consent upon a created will, not only [nedum] in regard to the substance of the act, but even in regard to the manner of liberty (cf. S. Thomas, SUMMA., I, q. 19, a. 8; q. 83, a. 1, in reply to n. 3; q. 105, a. 4; SUMMA CONTRA GENTILES, Bk. III, ch. 89; DE VERITATE., q. 6, a. 3, in reply to n. 3). In this sentence the certitude of the Divine *Foreknowledge* is also explained from the efficacious decrees of the Divine Will. The other School, to explain the infallibility and efficacy of the divine decree of the One predestining together with the indifference of free will, uses *intermediary knowledge* [scientia media], by which there is foreseen, that which the will is going to do of itself, but with the assistance of *prevenient* grace, antecedently to every absolute Divine decree; and the this way defends (the thesis) that divine concursus (is) congruent to liberty and (is) an indifferent motion, which does not antecede the determination of the will, but is simultaneous with it and/or as some seem to teach, rather consequent to it. — St. Bonaventure, on the *causality* of the Divine Will, says nothing in this passage, which is not generally received. See more below in d. 45, a. 2, qq. 1 and 2; and on the Divine motion, SENT, Bk. II, d. 25, p. II, qq. 4 and 5; d. 37, a. 1, q. 1; d. 26, q. 6; d. 14, p. I, a. 3, q. 1.

But, in regard to the other reckoning, namely, (that) of *foreknowledge*, it is manifest, especially from the solution to nn. 1, 2, and 3, that St. Bonaventure traces back [refundere] *the certitude*, which is in predestination, not to the causality implied in it, but to the nobility of the Divine Knowledge, whence he recurrs rather to *the Foreknowlede*, to show the concord of predestination with the liberty of creatures; nay his words found in this passage, when he says: « not through a reckoning of causality », thoroughly exclude the reckoning of causality. But St. Thomas (DE VERITATE, q. 6, a. 3, in the body of the Question) in regard to the certitude of predestination seems to hold otherwise, since he says: « Wherefore, besides the certitude of the Foreknowl-edge, the very *order of predestination* has an infallible certitude, and yet the proximate cause of salvation, namely free will, is not ordered according to it necessarily, but contingently » (cf. SUMMA., I, q. 23, a. 7). But we think, that St. Bonaventure in this does not precisely dissent from St. Thomas, since elsewhere (in the following Question, in the body), besides the certitude of *infallible knowledge*, he refers also to the certitude of *the immutability*, arisen from the Divine disposition and ordination, which includes a decree of the Will; wherefore there is said below (in d. 45, a. 2, q. 1, in reply to n. 2): « *the Will* causes a disposition of *the Knowledge* ». Moreover, that the very Foreknowledge of God is founded in *causality*, according to St. Bonaventure, has already been said above in d. 39, a. 1. q. 1, in the Scholium. But that this causality is not understood by him in the sense of an efficient cause alone, is sufficiently manifested too here in the solution to nn. 1, 2, and 3.

III. In the solution to n. 4 there is subtly discussed the expression "Whether the one predestined can be damned?", and very many profound and noteworthy (things) are brought to bear to prove the path of the Seraphic Doctor, which (path) differs to some extent from that, which the other masters (of theology) hold. For he distinguishes two propositions: (one) modal, in which the signified of the saying is posited in (its) *right sense* [in recto], and such is the form of (this) proposition: "the one predestined can be damned", and (another) modal, in which the signified is posited in (its) *oblique* sense [in obliquo], through an accusative and an infinitive verb, such as is the proposition: "it is possible, that the one predestined be damned". That the proposition in this *second* form ought *to be distinguished*, the Seraphic (Doctor) affirms with the common sentence. For either that proposition is understood of *the saying* and in a *composed* sense, and then it is false (such as: "that something white is black" is possible in the sense, (that) this proposition (is true): "something white is black"); and/or *of the thing* and in a divided sense (such as: "a thing, now white, can become black"). The disjunction of *thing* and *saying*, which is used even by Master (Peter) in this Distinction, is explained by St. Thomas, in his SUMMA, I, q. 14, a. 13, in reply to n. 3. — However, the *first* form of the proposition St. Bonaventure admits *without a distinction* as true, while Master Peter (here in ch. 1), St. Thomas (SUMMA., I, q. 23, a. 6, in reply to n. 3), (Bl. John Duns) Scotus, Richard of Middleton, Durandus (of Saint-Pourçain) and others also employ in this form the distinction of a composed and divided sense. But the Seraphic (Doctor) proves his own assertion, by supposing a threefold sense of that proposition (« it has three causes of truth »); and this (proposition) can be true, if one of the three senses is simply true. For the subject, "*the one predestined*", can be understood either « under a implied form », i. e. reduplicatively, "the one predestined *as predestined*" and/or « after an implied form », i. e. "he who *before* had been predestined, *afterwards* comes to be reprobate", and in this manner it is again false; and/or « without an implied form », i. e. by considering the subject *absolutely*, and then the predicate, "*can be damned*", is rightly said of the subject, as is proven in the following (Question) and here in Doubts 4 and 5; which is there to some extent explained with four profound and very notable principles. — The solution to nn. 4 and 6 is also made according to the same principles, which St. Thomas employs, DE VERITATE, q. 6, a. 3, in reply to n. 8.

IV. Alexander of Hales, SUMMA., p. I, q. 28, m. 4, throughout. — (Bl. John Duns) Scotus, here in the q. sole; and REPORTATIO., here in the q. sole. — St. Thomas, on this and the following q., here in q. 3; SUMMA., I, q. 22, a. 4; q. 23, a. 6; DE VERITATE., q. 6, a. 3. — Bl. (now St.) Albertus (Magnus), here in a. 14, 15 and 16; SUMMA., on this and the following q., p. I, tr. 16, q. 63, m. 3, a. 2. — (Bl.) Peter of Tarentaise, here in q. 2, a. 1. — Richard of Middleton, here in a. 2, qq. 1 and 2. — Giles the Roman, here in 1st. princ., q. 2. — (Bl.) Dionysius the Carthusian, on this and the following q., here in q. 2.

QUESTION II

Whether predestination posits certitude in the outcome?

Second, with it supposed that predestination does not infer a necessity upon free will, which could not otherwise be, there is asked, whether it posits a certitude in the outcome [certitudinem in eventu], namely, so that it never comes forth otherwise, except just as God has predefined (it). And that it does, is shown:

1. First *by authority* according to the thirteen (chapter of the Gospel of St.) John:[1] *I know, whom I have elected*; and in the second (chapter) of the Second (Letter of St. Paul) to Timothy: *God knew, who belonged to Him*: therefore, if the Divine Cognition is certain and infallible, and it would fail, if those, whom He knew certainly to be His own, would not be saved, therefore, it is true, that it comes forth in the same manner, just as God has predefined (it), and thus that etc..

2. Likewise, according to the second (chapter) of the First (Letter of St.) John:[2] *They went forth from us, but they were not of us.* Therefore, that (verse) is put as a sign: wherefore the sign, that a man has not been elected, is this, when he has not persevered finally in the good. If, therefore, that sign is right, it is certain, that all the predestined and they alone persevere finally in grace; and if this is certain, what they alone are salved and all (of them): therefore, there is a certitude in the outcome

3. Likewise, (St.) Augustine in the book, ON THE GOOD OF PERSEVERANCE (says):[3] « Predestination is the foreknowledge of God's benefices, through which there are most certainly liberated whosoever are liberated ». If, therefore, they are most certainly liberated, it is clear that there is a certitude of salvation in respect of persons, and thus that etc..

4. Likewise, (St.) Augustine in the book, ON CORRECTION AND GRACE (says):[4] « There is a certain number of the elect, which cannot be lessened nor increased »: therefore, it seems, that there is certitude in a determined number [in quoto numero].

5. Likewise, this seem by *reason*, because *in the Father's House there are many mansions*, just as is said in the fifteenth (chapter of the Gospel of St.) John;[5] therefore, either God foresees, who ought to dwell there, or not. It is established that He does foresee, who ought to be there: therefore, if any of them is lacking, some mansion will remain empty. But this is unfitting and indecent in the Supernal City: therefore, it is certain, that each predestined will have his own place.

6. Likewise, the number of the elect has been limited beforehand [praefinitus] by God according to the best and most fitting [decentissima] reckoning and proportion — for if He made all in a most ordinate manner, much more strongly (did He make) the Supernal City — but the best proportion is defiled and lost through augment and diminution: therefore, if it cannot be, that there be a defect of order and of congruent proportion There, (then) certainly there will be saved as many, and not more nor fewer, than[6] God foresees.

BUT ON THE CONTRARY: 1. That there is not a certitude of outcome as much as regards *persons*, seems thus: In the third (chapter) of the Apocalypse (there is written):[7] *Hold what you have, lest another accept thy crown*; (Pope St.) Gregory (the Great says) on this: « While one falls, another is promoted in his place [in locum eius subinducitur] »: therefore, if one claims for himself the place of the other, it does not come forth thus, just as God ordained, nay an exchange [transmutatio] (of places) is made all the time [tota die].

2. Likewise, on that (verse) in the thirty-fourth (chapter) of Job:[8] *He shall crush many*, (St.) Gregory (says) in the same place: « When some fall down, others are allotted (their) place of life ».

3. Likewise, that there is no certitude as much as regards *number*, seems from the fifth (chapter of the Gospel of St.) Luke:[9] *The net was breaking*; (where) the Gloss (says): « Not as many enter of the Jews, as have been predestined »: therefore, fewer are saved, than are predestined.

4. Likewise, in the first (chapter) of Deuteronomy (where there is written):[10] *May God add to this number many thousands*; the Gloss (says): « To this number, predefined in the Foreknowledge of the God, Who *knew, who are His own* »: therefore, if God adds to a predefined number, there is no certitude as much as regards the number of (those) to be saved.

5. Likewise, it seems that, as much as regards *neither* (the number of the saved or of the damned), is there

---

[1] Verse 18. — The following text is loc. cit., verse 19, which text the Vulgate exhibits in this manner: *The Lord has known, who are His own* [Cognovit Dominus, qui sunt eius]. — About the end of the argument for *it comes forth* [evenit] the Vatican edition, together with some manuscripts, has *it will come forth* [eveniet].

[2] Verse 19, where the Vulgate has *they went forth* [prodierunt] for *they went forth* [exierunt]. — The Vatican edition after *as a sign* [pro signo] inserts *namely* [scilicet] and reads *that* [quod] for *wherefore* [quod].

[3] Which is now named, as has been said above, ON THE GIFT OF PERSEVERANCE, ch. 14, n. 35; just as the ON CORRECTION AND GRACE (as is read in the following argument) is now named ON BLAME AND GRACE; cf. (the text of Master Peter) above, d. XL, ch. 1, p. 699,* footnote 3.

[4] Chapter 13, n. 39. See the text of Master (Peter) here, in ch. 1. — At the end of the argument, for *a determined* [quoto] for *a certain* [quodam]. The adjective, quotus, signifies the same as determinatus, just as the name, quota [quota], signifies a certain determined (amount), « which one is held to offer a prince or lord in tribute and/or valuation » (Du Cange, GLOSSAR. MEDIAE ET INFIMAE LATIN.).

[5] Verse 2.

[6] For *than* [quam] the Vatican edition has *as* [quot].

[7] Verse 11, where the Vulgate has *so that no one may* [ut nemo] for *lest another* [ne alius]. — The text next cited and ascribed to (St.) Gregory, is found according to its sense in his MORALS ON THE BOOK OF JOB, Bk. XXV, ch. 8, n. 20, and ch. 13, n. 31; but the words themselves, as cited, are had in the ordinary Gloss on the aforementioned words of the Apocalypse, wherefore the Vatican edition for *(Pope St.) Gregory (the Great)* [Gregorius] substitutes *the Gloss* [Glossa].

[8] Verse 24. — The words of (St.) Gregory are had in MORALS ON THE BOOK OF JOB, Bk. XXV, ch. 8, n. 19, where in the original text there is read *they* [illis] for *some* [aliis].

[9] Verse 6. — The entire text of the ordinary Gloss is: Not as many enter of the Jews, as have been preordained to life with God.

[10] Verse 11. — In its entirety the ordinary Gloss reads thus: *To this number, defined before God. He knew who are His, He who numbers the multitude of the stars.*

---

* *Trans. note*: Here the original footnote omits *p.* [pag.].

certitude. Let us understand that A, B and C are the number of the predestined, (and) D, E and F the number of the foreknown; then I ask: "A can thus rightly be damned, just as D, and, <u>vice versa</u>, D, thus,[1] (can) be saved, just as A": therefore, there is no certitude as much as regards the persons. Again, "A can be damned, and, then, only two remain, and D (can) be saved, and then there will be four": therefore, there is no certitude as much as regards number.

6. Likewise, this very (thing) is shown by deducing *to an unfitting* (conclusion). For if it is certain, who and how many will be saved, so that it comes forth thus, and not otherwise, though it can (be) otherwise:[2] therefore no predestined will be damned in any case and/or outcome, and no foreknown will be saved: therefore, no one ought to care, whether he does well and/or badly, because if he has been foreknown, whatever he does, in the end he will be damned; if predestined, whatever he does, in the end he will be saved; one is stupid, therefore, who does not *eat and be glad*, and (who) does not *have good (things) in his own life*.[3]

CONCLUSION

Predestination on the part of the thing coming forth does not have a certitude in the coming forth, on the part of God precognizing and disposing it has both the certitude of infallibility and immutability.

I RESPOND: It must be said, that there is a saying of certitude on the part of *the thing coming forth*, and on the part of *God foreordaining*.[4] If we speak of the certitude on the part of *the thing*, since this is said against contingency, in this manner I say, that there is no greater certitude in the number of the elect, than there is in the number of other future contingents, because the outcome of our salvation and damnation depends out of our liberty. But if we speak of the certitude on the part of *God precognizing*, in this manner the outcome of[5] salvation is certain with the certitude of *infallibility*, because the Divine Foreknowledge does not fail, and for that reason it always comes forth, as He has foreknown. It is also certain with the certitude of *immutability*, because the Divine disposition and ordination does not vary, so that now He elects one and now another, but he who once has been elected, always was and will be, and not another.

The reasons brought forward for the first side proceed from the certitude *of the outcome*, not as much as regards the

necessity, but as much as regards *the infallibility* of the eternal precognition, and as much as regards *the invariability* of the eternal preordination.[6]

1. 2. To that, therefore, which is objected, that the one accepts the place and crown of the other; it must be said, that the place of an eternal mansion and the crown of retribution is due someone according to (his) *reputation for justice*,[7] to another according to *the predefinition of (God's) Foreknowledge*. And it does happen, that one place is owed to someone according to (his) *present justice*, to this extent [eo] that, with him falling, another enters, to whom it is owed according to an *eternal predefinition*. However, when the place is owed to someone according to an *eternal predefinition, he can* indeed fall down and loose the place, and another, who has not been predestined, *can* acquire (it); but yet this *never* comes about [evenient]. Therefore, because the foreknown just (man) frequently loses the place of (his) eternal mansion, which another of equal merit acquires; and (because) no one knows, whether he has been foreknown, and/or predestined: for that reason, though he may know, that he is just, he ought to fear, that he may lose (his) place. And to this fear blessed John in the aforesaid quote from Apocalypse exhorts (us). And this fear is good for all, both for the foreknown and the predestined, because it humbles and disquiets (the soul). On the other hand, a certitude concerning (one's) election *elevates* (one) unto the swelling (of pride) and *depresses* (one) into torpor; for that reason according to the most ordinate dispensation[8] it has been established [hoc factum est], that it is revealed to none, whether he has been predestined, unless he has been confirmed in the good by God, so that he cannot be elevated through pride and/or according to torpor through negligence. Therefore, it is clear, that that quote does not signify that a change comes to be in the Foreknowledge, and/or that (something) comes forth otherwise, than God has foreknown, but that he who is actually just can lose the place, which is worthy of, by losing justice, and that he who is a sinner can acquire a place not owed [indebitum][9] him, by acquiring justice; and this happens all the time. — An example (of this) is manifest in the Old Testament concerning Saul and David in the kingdom, for which there could rightly be said to Saul: *Hold what you have*, that is (your) humility and justice, *lest another accept thy crown*, that is the one due you according to your present state, yet due another according to an eternal disposition.[10] There is also an example in the crowns of the Forty Martyrs.

3. 4. To that which is objected concerning a diminution

---

[1] Codex X after *thus* [ita] repeats *rightly* [bene].

[2] The Vatican edition, having omitted the words *though it can (be) otherwise* [quamvis posit aliter], after the following word *therefore* [ergo] it interjects *it is certain, that* [certum est, quod], which insertion is not had in either edition 1 or in the codices. In nearly all the codices the words suppress by the Vatican edition, *though it can (be) otherwise* [quamvis posit aliter], are found, but the codices faultily prefix to these *therefore* [ergo], but not codex T (in which the *therefore* has been expunged by a second hand) nor in edition 1, which two codices we have followed. Codex X, which in all other things convenes with the rest of the codices, omits the *therefore* [ergo] before *no predestined* [nullus praedestinatus].

[3] A reference to the words of Wisdom 2:6 ff.; Isaias 22:13, Luke 12:19. — For *have* [habet] edition 1 has *partake of* [sumit].

[4] Codex W reads *predestining* [praedestinantis]. Next, after *the thing* [rei], the Vatican edition adds *coming forth* [evenientis]. Then, for *is said* [dicatur], codices P Q and X (T in the margin) have *is divided* [dividatur].

[5] The Vatican edition and codex cc here add *our* [nostrae], and a little below this, after *and for that reason it* [et ideo] omits *always* [semper].

[6] Edition 1 has *precognition* [praecognitionis], the Vatican edition has *predestination* [praedestinationis].

[7] The Vatican edition, together with edition 1, prefaces the word *present* [praesentis] to *justice* [iustitiae]. Codices A and I, in this proposition, read *in one manner according to a reputation ... in another according to the predefinition* [aliter ... aliter] for *someone according to (his) reputation ... to another according to the predefinition* [alicui ... alicui]. A little further below this, for *to this extent that* [eo quod] the Vatican edition, together with a few codices, has *and which* [et quod].

[8] The Vatican edition and not a few codices have *disposition* [dispositionem]. Next for *by God* [a Deo] very many manuscripts have *to this extent* [adeo].

[9] The Vatican edition, together with one or the other codex, has *owed* [debitum] for *not owed* [indebitum], which reading can be well explained.* A little further above this, for *has foreknown* [praescivit] the Vatican edition has *foreknows* [praescit], edition 1 reads *will have foreknown* [praesciverit].

[10] Cf. 1 Kings 15 ff.. — On the example of the Forty Martyrs, cf. BREVIARIUM ROMANUM, March 10th.

---

* *Trans. note*: By understanding this in terms of *the state obtained by justification*; whereas, otherwise it is to be understood as *the state prior to obtaining justice*, that is, the state of Original Sin.

and augment, it must be said, that that whole (of each verse) must be referred to the state of present justice. For that Gloss: « Not as many of the Jews enter », is understood according to the time of the primitive Church, because many will enter in the time of the end [in tempore finalis] of the Church. Similarly, what is said, that *May God add to this number*, is understood by (His) justifying more and calling (them) to the Faith.

5. To that which is objected, that there can be more and fewer and others, than have been foreknown: therefore, there is no certitude; it must be said, that there is no certitude of *necessity*, however, there is a certitude of *infallibility*. For though there can be others and more, yet there never will be; and if there were, then they were predestined from eternity: for that reason no change can occur there.

6. To that which is objected, that, if it thus came about, then, the one foreknown and the one predestined work in vain [frustra]; it must be said, that that is the argument of fools,[1] which leads them into torpor and the excuse of impiety. And, for that reason, one must, first, show, that they argue in a foolish manner,

by inferring *from a simile*, by speaking thus: "God foreordained, whether you ought to live tomorrow, or not; therefore, for what (purpose) do you eat and drink?" He who would so argue and consent to such a reckoning, would argue from dementia; similarly (is it) in the proposed. — Second on responds *against* (this) *by arguing*: "You say, that God predestines; and I say, that God remunerates justly as a just Judge. « Therefore, no good (will go) unrewarded, no evil unpunished »:[2] therefore, no one works without fruit, not one grows torpid without damage [damno]. — And on this account it must be said, that the aforesaid argumentation *fails*. for it proceeds, as if God would predestine and foreknow unto every outcome; but He does not predestine a man to salvation except through merits, nor does He reprove (him), so that he arrives unto damnation without merits (worthy of this). And for that reason not only is our salvation on the part of God, but also on our own part; and since He Himself wills, that all come to be[3] saved and (wills) to impart grace to all, the defect of our salvation comes only from our malice and/or negligence.

SCHOLIUM

I. This question is added, lest anyone from the previously established principles be able to derogate from *the certitude* of the Divine predestination. With it there is resolved, in the solution to nn. 3 and 4, another question, whether, namely, the number of the predestined can *be increased*; and in the solution to n. 6 by a strong and threefold argumentation there is checked the foolishness of those, who abused this doctrine to excuse (their own) impiety.

II. The distinction of a certitude on the part of *the thing coming forth*, and on the part of *God predestining* is also employed by St. Thomas (SUMMA., I, q. 116, a. 3; DE VERITATE., q. 6, a. 3, at the end of the body of the Response, and elsewhere). This in general

is conceded by all, though there is disagreement concerning *the reckoning* of the certitude on the part of God. — That no one, excluding by revelation, can know *in a certain manner*, that he has been predestined, is taught by the Council of Trent (Session 6, c. 12) and confirmed by the Seraphic Doctor below in d. 41, a. 1, q. 2, and elsewhere.

III. Alexander of Hales, SUMMA., p. I, q. 28, m. 2, a. 3. — Bl. (now St.) Albertus (Magnus), here in a. 11 and 12. — (Bl.) Peter of Tarentaise, here in q. 2, a. 2 and 3. — Richard of Middleton, here in a. 2, q. 3.

ARTICLE III

On Divine election.

Consequently, as much as regards the second[4] article (to be considered), there is the question concerning Divine election. And, about this, two (questions) are asked.

First, there is asked, whether election is in God eternally, and/or on account of time [ex tempore].

Second, there is asked, what is election according to thing [secundum rem].

---

[1] The Vatican edition omits *of fools* [stultorum], and a little below this, together with codex cc, substitutes *predestined* [praedestinavit] for *foreordained* [praeordinavit].

[2] This axiom seems to have been formed from what (St. Severinus) Boethius says ON THE CONSOLATION OF PHILOSOPHY, Bk. IV, prose 1 and 4, and under his name it was widely cited. Cf. the passages from Aristotle, of which we have already made mention above d. 4, a. sole, q. 3, p. 101, footnote 5. Somewhat further above this, for *against (this) by arguing* [contra arguendo] the Vatican ed. has *by making (this) argument* [argumentando].

[3] 1 Timothy 2:4: *Who wishes all men to be saved and come to the acknowledgement of the Truth* [Qui omnes homines vult salvos fieri et ad agnitionem veritatis venire]. — Here it helps to cite that which (St.) Augustine in ON THE GIFT OF PERSEVERANCE, ch. 15, n. 38, tells of a certain

monk: "There was a certain (monk) in our monastery, who having been corrected by the brothers, why he would do certain (things that are) not to be done, and would not do (those which are) to be done, used to respond: Howsoever I am now, such shall I be, so God has foreknown that I am going to be. Who, indeed, also used to speak the truth, and this, however, did not profit him unto the good, but he progressed to such an extent in evil, that, having deserted the society of the monastery, be became as a dog returning to its own vomit, and, yet, still, what he is going to be, is uncertain."

[4] Since the first Article was divided into two (cf. d. 40, Treatment of the Questions, p. 701), we have entitled this one as Article III, as the other editions (have done).

QUESTION I

Whether election is in God from eternity, or on account of time?

Moreover, that election is in God eternally, is shown:

1. First by the authority of the Apostle in the first (chapter of his Letter) to the Ephesians:[1] *He elected us before the constitution of the world, to be holy and immaculate before Him.*

2. Likewise, in the thirteenth (chapter of the Gospel of St.) John (there is written):[2] *I know, whom I have elected*; but He had elected temporally, who were His disciples: therefore, there is another election in God than the temporal one.

3. Likewise, that election is in God, seems through *reason*, because everything acting discretely and ordinately, is acting through an election;[3] but God is of this kind: therefore, in God there is a positing of election.

4. Likewise, it seems that (it is) *from eternity*, because every 'choosing of' [dilectio],° which is specially of some, is not only a 'choosing of', but also a 'picking out of' [electio];[4] but God's predestination is not of all men, but only of (those) to be saved, and predestination is not without a 'choosing of', therefore, neither without an election; but the former is from eternity: therefore, this too.

BUT ON THE CONTRARY: 1. (St. John) Damascene (says):[5] « Election does not occur to God, because the Divine Nature is not possible regarding ignorance ».

2. Likewise, "*to elect*" is "to choose one (thing) before another"; but God *wishes all men to be saved*:[6] therefore, it seems, that election is not in God.

3. Likewise, it seems that it is only in God *temporally* — for election would not be, if man had stood firm, therefore, it seems, the fall of man is a cause regarding [faciat ad] election — but the temporal is not a cause regarding the '*being*' of an eternal:[7] therefore, election is not eternal, but temporal.

4. Likewise, election is of beings in a dissimilar manner [dissimiliter];[8] but all in God are eternally one [unum] and in a similar manner [similiter]: therefore, election is of things existing in their own

genus. But in their own genus they are not but on account of time: therefore, neither (is) election.

5. Likewise, election is a choosing beforehand; but God chooses nothing of another beforehand as much as regards an intension of the affection:[9] therefore, only as much as regards the excellence of the effect. But there is no positing of an effect except on account of time: therefore, etc..

6. Likewise, vocation is in regard to more [in plus] than (is) election. *For many have been called, but few elected*, according to the twenty-second (chapter of the Gospel of St.) Matthew;[10] but the vocation is temporal: therefore, it seems similarly that election (is also).

There is asked, therefore, since *vocation* is temporal, but *predestination* eternal, whence is it, that *election* is both temporal and eternal.

CONCLUSION

Election, but not deliberative (election), is in God from eternity, the manifestation of which is temporal election.

I RESPOND: It must be said, that "*election*" is said in a twofold manner. in one manner, insofar as it means a 'choosing of' with *only a discretion*,[a] in another manner, insofar as it means a 'choosing of' with *a preceding discretion* and *deliberation* and *inquisition*. And in the first manner it is in God, in the second manner[11] in the creature, in which there can occur ignorance; and in this second manner (St. John) Damascene speaks.

2. To that which is objected, that God's Will and 'choosing of' [dilectio] is without discretion; it must be said, that there is an *antecedent* Will and a *consequent* (Will): *the antecedent*, by which He wills as much as is in Himself, *the consequent*, by which He wills with the Foreknowledge of our salvation; and the first indeed is of all, but the second (is) not.[12] According to this manner (of speaking), there is a twofold 'choosing of': one, which looks back to the *antecedent*

---

[1] Verse 4, where the Vulgate reads: *He elected us in Him* etc. [Elegit nos in ipso etc.]; and, below, for *before Him* [coram ipso], which (St.) Ambrose reads as *before Him (i.e. the Father)* [coram eo], the Vulgate reads *in His sight* [in conspectu eius].*

[2] Verse 18. — For *Likewise* [Item] the Vatican edition alone substitutes *On the contrary* [Contra], and then after *therefore* [ergo] reads *there is no other* [non est alia], faultily, because with this reading, the argumentation of the (Seraphic) Doctor is disturbed and rendered void.

[3] Cf. above d. 35, a. sole, q. 1, p. 600, footnote 2. Cf. also Aristotle, ETHICS, III, ch. 2, and MAGNA MORALIA, Bk. I, ch. 16, (ch. 17), where he deals with prohaeresis (περὶ προαιρέσεως) which Greek verb (προαίρεσις) in the ancient Latin versions was sometimes rendered by the word *election* [electio], as e.g. loc. cit, here in the ETHICS, sometimes by the word *proposal* [propositum], as e.g. loc. cit. here in the MAGNA MORALIA; in the more recent Parisian edition (Firmin-Didot) the verb προαιρεσις is consistently rendered as *counsel* [consilium].

[4] Concerning which see above d. 10, Doubt 1.

[5] ON THE ORTHODOX FAITH, Bk. II, ch. 22: In God we indeed say (that there is) an act of willing, but not election properly (χυρίως) taken. God

indeed does not deliberate, because it belongs to the ignorant to make plans.

[6] 1 Timothy 2:4: *Who wishes all men* etc. [Qui homines vult etc.]. In regard to the major of this argument we are reminded of the words of Aristotle, ETHICS, Bk. III, ch. 2: « For an election is with a reckoning and a thinking; which the noun itself (προαίρεσις) seems to signify, as if from certain proposals some one is bound, i. e. grasped ».[+] Cf. also (St. John) Damascene, ON THE ORTHODOX FAITH, Bk II, ch. 22.

[7] The Vatican edition, together with a few manuscripts, reads *eternal 'being'* [esse aeternum] for *the 'being' of an eternal* [esse aeterni].

[8] Which is also hinted at by (St.) Augustine from diverse QUESTIONS TO SIMPLICIANUS, Bk. I, q. 2, n. 4: For in what manner is it just and what kind of election (is it) entirely, where there is no distance? And ibid., n. 6: For no one is chosen unless (he is) distant form him who is rejected.

[9] Or, to use other words: but God as much as regards the intension of the affection equally holds Himself to all men.

[10] Verse 14.

[11] Edition 1 interjects *it is only* [est solum].

[12] You will find more on this distinction below in d. 45, q. 1, in the body (of the Response).

---

* *Trans. note*: Here and in the Vulgate, *Him* refers to Christ, *He* to the Father, inasmuch as election is appropriated to the Father. The Greek text, at the end, reads *down in His sight* (κατενώπιον αὐτοῦ), which markedly distinguishes between a *before Him* which is one of equivalence and a *before Him* which is of subordination. And, hence, supports St. Bonaventure's doctrine that the elect are chosen in Christ, as Exemplar, to be in an eternal relation to Him by means of their ideal being, which being God the Father sees in the Son from all eternity, and on which basis He elects them, before a prevision of their merits. It is in the more diligent consideration of this, that many problems of grace and predestination are adequately addressed.

° The Latin, dilectio, properly means "to chose of or from", but customarily is rendered in English as *love* or *dilection*: here to preserve the rationale of the argument, the English "*choosing of*" is employed, since the sense throughout is clearly in regard to election, not to love.

+ The Latin term, electio, also similarly has this sense, because etymologically what is electus is *bound* [-ligatus] *out of* [e-] a group; a verb that perhaps has arisen from the setting of animal husbandry. In theological terms, both are apt verbs for the elect, whom God takes in Christ to be His own flock, and thus by selecting them from many possibles, binds them up in Christ by an eternal choice.

[a] Cf. *discretion*, cf. the RATIONALE FOR THE TRANSLATION OF PECULIAR LATIN TERMS, above on p. E-16.

Will, and by this He chooses [diligit] all; and there is another, which looks back to *the consequent* (Will), and by this He chooses all (those) to be saved, and this is election.

3. To that which is objected, that there would be no election, if man had not sinned; it must be said, that there is an election, by which there is elected and separated *the good from the bad*, and there is an election, by which there is separated *the better from the less good*. This second (kind) would be, if man had not sinned, but the first would not be, if man had not sinned, not because (his) *fall* causes anything regarding the reckoning of (his) being elected, but *the prevision of (his) fall* (does); and although the fall of man was temporal, yet the prevision of it was eternal.

4. To that which is objected, that election is of beings in a dissimilar manner; it must be said, that just as there is a twofold '*choosing of*': a certain one, which *arises out of a consideration* of goodness, a certain one, which is *the principle* of goodness; so there is a twofold *election*: a certain one, which *is caused by the diversity* and preeminence of the eligibles, and this is consequent to the eligibles, such as (is) human election; a certain one, which is *the reason for the diversity* in electing, such as (is) the divine one, and this is of dissimilars, which are not, but which are going to be. And such precedes and is eternal;[1] for except for the Divine Election, we would all be reprobated and wicked. And thus that is clear.

5. To that which is objected, that election is a *choosing beforehand*; it must be said, that a 'choosing beforehand' by reason of the superiority [maioritatis] of the effect can be in a twofold manner: either through a manner of *approbation*,[2] or through a manner of *disposition* and preordination. Through a manner of *approbation* it does posit an effect *in act*, through a manner of *preordination* and disposition it posits only *in potency*; and just as (God's) disposition (of all things) is eternal, so also (His) 'choosing beforehand'.

6. To that which is objected concerning *vocation*, that it is only temporal; it must be said, that "*vocation*" means an act as *exterior*, "*election*" means an act as *interior*, "*predestination*" means an act as *anterior*. Therefore, since an act as *exterior* connotes an effect as exterior, for that reason the (Divine) vocation (of the many) is only temporal. Again, since an act as *anterior* does not have the reckoning of being initiated, for that reason the predestination (of the elect) is only eternal. But since an *interior* act comes to be exterior through a manifestation, hence it is, that (God's) election and 'choosing of' (the few)[3] is eternal and temporal.

Therefore, what is objected concerning *vocation*, that it is in regard to more, therefore, prior; it must be said, that it is prior according to a reckoning of understanding as more common, but not as much as regards the order of enduring [ordinem durandi]; for it is not an essential superior, but a consequent effect.[4] And thus all (the objections) are clear.

SCHOLIUM

I. What *election* is and in what manner it differs from (God's) *proposal* (to have mercy) and from *predestination*, is explained in the following question, in reply to nn. 2 and 3 and to some extent here in reply to n. 6; but more diffusely by Richard of Middleton, Sent., Bk. I, d. 41, a. 1, q. 1, and by St. Thomas (Sent., Bk. I, d. 41, q. 1, a. 2), where he says: « The Divine Ordination itself, by which certain ones are preferred to others regarding the pursuit of beatitude, is said (to be) "the Divine Election" »; and in the same, in the reply to n. 1: « *Election* is, that by which some are ordered out of the order of His own Wisdom to the end of beatitude; but *predestination* is, (that) according to which there are prepared for them those things which lead thoroughly unto the end »; and in reply to n. 2: « Election *requires beforehand* [praeexigit] a diversity of nature in the Divine Cognition, and *it causes* a diversity of grace, just as the (Divine) disposition causes a diversity of nature ». — The distinction between eternal and temporal election is approved by St. Thomas, Sent., Bk. I, d. 41, q. 1, a. 1, who also in the 2nd opposed argument solves the same distinction of the antecedent and consequent Will (Summa., I, q. 23, a. 4, in reply to n. 3). On the antecedent and consequent will see more below in d. 46, a. 1, q. 1. — The solution to n. 3 has been taken from Alexander of Hales, Summa., p. I, q. 30, m. 1. ad 2; and Bl. (now St.) Albertus (Magnus) is in agreement, Summa., p. I, tr. 16. q. 66, 4th incidental question. This solution favors those, who teach, that in the supposed hypothesis, that Adam has not sinned, none would have been born reprobate; but common sentence with St. Thomas (Summa, I, q. 100, a. 2) holds the contrary. — From the words: « Not because (his) fall causes anything regarding the reckoning of (his) being elected, but *the prevision of (his) fall* (does) », and from the solution to n. 4 it seems to follow, that the Seraphic (Doctor) together with the Angelic Doctor (de Veritate., q. 6, a. 2, in reply to n. 9; Summa., I, q. 23, a. 5, in reply to n. 3) sup-

pose, that according to our manner of understanding the efficacious election of the predestined was wrought by God after the prevision of original sin. But (Bl. John Duns) Scotus, (Sent., III, d. 7, q. 3) seems to think otherwise and according to his sentence, that Christ would have been incarnate, even if Adam had not sinned.

II. In the solution to n. 2 there is taught, that the discretive election pertains to the *consequent* Will, not *to the antecedent* (Will), concerning which distinction, cf. below d. 46, q. 1. Moreover, it must be strongly noted, that in the solution to n. 4 there is said of the difference between *our* 'choosing of' and election, which *supposes* a goodness an preeminence in the chosen and elected and hence *is caused*, and the Divine *'choosing of'* and Election, which contrariwise is *the cause* of the goodness and diversity in the chosen and elected. St. Thomas teaches entirely the same (thing), Summa., I, q. 23, a. 4; and Bl. (now St.) Albertus (Magnus) also, in Summa., p. I, tr. 16, q. 65, 2nd incidental question, saying: « In the eternal Election, which to which no merit is prevenient, God looks back to nothing in us, but only to the communication of His own Goodness in His very Self ». And this is confirmed by canon 12 of the Second Council of Orange: « God loves us as we are going to be by His gift, not as we are by our merit » (cf. below d. 43, Doubt 7).

III. Alexander of Hales, Summa., p. I, q. 28, m. 1, a. 1, and q. 30, a. 1. — St. Thomas, Sent., Bk. I, d. 41, q. 1, a. 1; Summa., loc. cit. — Bl. (now St.) Albertus (Magnus), here in a. 17; on this and the following question, Summa., p. I, tr. 16, q. 65. — (Bl.) Peter of Tarentaise, Sent., Bk. I, d. 41, q. 1, a. 2. — Richard of Middleton, Sent., Bk. I, d. 41, a. 1, q. 1. — Giles the Roman, on this and the following question, Sent., Bk. I, d. 41. 1st. princ., qq. 1 and 2. — Durandus (of Saint-Pourçain), on this and the following question, Sent., Bk. I, d. 41, q. 1. — (Bl.) Dionysius the Carthusian, Sent., Bk. I, d. 41, q. 2.

---

[1] Cf. (St.) Augustine, On the Predestination of the Saints, ch. 17, n. 34 ff..

[2] For the words *through a manner of approbation* [per modum approbationis] the Vatican edition, without any authority of the codices, here and a little below this, exhibits *through a manner of appropriation* [per modum appropriationis] and at the same time in the first place adds to these words *or operation and/or application*, i. e. which posit an effect in act.

[3] In the Vatican edition and codex cc there are wanting the words *and 'choosing of'* [et dilectio].

[4] For *a consequent effect* [effectus consequens], which is clearly read in codd. H I R & aa, and in ed. 1, the Vatican ed. reads *consequent according*

to effect [effectu consequens]. Many codices are of a dubious reading, and one cannot discern, whether they exhibit one or the other reading. — In this regard one can refer to what (St.) Augustine, On the Predestination of the Saints, ch. 17, n. 34, proffers concerning the Elect and their vocation. For having made the distinction, in ch. 16, n. 32, between the called [vocati], who even if they are called, do not want to come, and those, who have been also predestined and elected, says loc. cit.: "And so they have been elected before the constitution of the world by that predestination, in which God foreknew His own future deeds; moreover, they have been elected from the world [de mundo] by that vocation, by which God fulfilled that which He predestined (to do)."

QUESTION II

Whether election is the same as predestination?

Second, there is asked, what is election, and it seems, that it is the same as predestination.

1. Master (Peter) says in the text:[1] « Moreover, sine predestination is (a divine) election, by which God elected whom He willed, before the constitution of the word »: ergo etc..

2. Likewise, it seems *by reason*, because everyone predestined has been elected, and everyone elected (has been) predestined: therefore, predestination is election, since they are predicated through one another regarding one another.[2]

3. Likewise, whose opposites are the same, they themselves are the same;[3] but the opposite of election is reprobation, and the latter is the opposite of predestination: ergo etc..

ON THE CONTRARY: 1. Whichsoever are of diverse, they themselves are diverse; but predestination is only of the good, however, election (is) of all (those) to be saved and of some to be damned: ergo etc.. *The proof of the minor* is had in the sixth (chapter of the Gospel of St. John):[4] *Have I not elected twelve, and one of you is a devil? If you say*, that that is understood of the temporal election; *on the contrary*: the temporal election is a sign of the eternal one: therefore, either it is concordant (with it), or it is a false sign.

2. Likewise, if there never were anyone wicked, there would be a predestination, but there would not be an election; according to this, therefore, election looks back to one objected, predestination to another: therefore, they are not entirely the same.

3. Likewise, one acting according to a proposal is said (to be) acting through an election,[5] and he is not said to act according to a predestination: therefore predestination and election differ.

There is asked, therefore, what is (their) *difference*, and which is *prior* according to the reckoning of understanding [secundum rationem intelligendi].

CONCLUSION

Election according to the affection of love is the same as predestination, but election according to the effect of being given the final grace is the infallible sign of predestination.

I RESPOND: It must be said, that "*election*" is said in a threefold manner. For there is an election according to *the affection of love* [affectum dilectionis], and according to *the effect of being at last made pleasing (to God)* [effectum finalis gratifications], and according to *a state of being preferred* [statum praelationis]. The first is eternal and is the same as predestination; the second is temporal and the infallible sign of the first; the third similarly (is) temporal, and is not an effect nor a sign of the eternal election. For many wicked an reprobate (men) are set over others [praeficiuntur]; and would that the wicked ones were not more than the good!

1. To that, therefore, which is objected concerning the word of the Lord, in the sixth (chapter of the Gospel of St.) John, it must be said, that it is understood of the election *of being preferred*, and this is not only of the good nor of all the good; and for that reason it is clear, that it is not the same as predestination. — And what is objected, that it is a sing; it must be said, that it is not a certain sign, nor does the Lord give (it) as a sign, and foolish is he, who trusts [credit] this sign. But election according to *the effect of being given the final grace*, this is a certain sign simply (speaking), but it is not certain to us. And this differs from the *vocation*, because grace is given to many, who do not persevere; for that reason they are said (to be) "*called*", but not "*elected*"; and of these there is said in the twenty-second (chapter of the Gospel of St.) Matthew:[6] *Many are called, but few are elected*.

2. To that which is objected, that election looks back to evil, and convenes with everyone acting from a proposal, not so predestination; it must be noted, that in God *the proposal, the predestination* and *the election* are the same according to *thing*, yet they differ according to *the reckoning of understanding*. For a "*proposal*"[7] simply means the will to do something. For one is said to propose, who firmly wants to do something. But *the election* and *the predestination* add upon the conception[8] (of the Will),* but differently, because *the predestination* adds an order and direction unto the end, but *the election* a discretion or separation from their opposite. Whence "*the proposal*" means the firm conception of the Will, "*the predestination*" with the conception means a preordination, and "*the election*" a certain discretion. According to this, therefore, it is clear, that *the proposal* is prior according to the reckoning of understanding, and then *the election*, because one must understand that something is separated from evil or from the mass (of the damned),[9] before it is directed unto the end; and thus *the diversity* and *order* (of each) is clear.

3. And, from this, is clear, that which is asked last, "For what reason is the one acting from a proposal [a proposito] not always said "to act"

---

[1] Chapter 2.

[2] Argumentation from concrete to abstract is only valid, when the concrete is accepted formally, that is, according to a form, which indicates the abstract, just as in this argument; for the one predestined as predestined has been elected as one elected.

[3] This proposition, just as also the major of the following argument, has been gathered from the rules, which Aristotle, TOPICS, Bk. I, ch. 13, proffers concerning distinguishing equivocal (terms) from univocal ones.

[4] Verse 71, where the Vulgate reads: *Have I not elected you* etc. [Nonne ego vos etc.]. — A little above this, for *however, election* [electio] very many codices have *and* [et], and, then, *for and of some to be*

damned [et aliquorum damnandorum] not a few codices, such as Y aa bb and cc, read *but election (is) of some to be damned* [election autem aliquorum damnandorum] and codices I V and X read *and election (is) of some to be damned* [et election aliquorum damandorum]. Our reading has been taken from codex T and edition 1, with which the Vatican edition also convenes, except for its omission of *of all* [omnium].

[5] Cf. here above q. 1, page 714, footnote 3.

[6] Verse 14.

[7] In codex O there is added or "*disposition*" [sive dispositio].

[8] Supply, together with the Vatican edition: *of the will* [voluntatis].

[9] A reference to the words of (St.) Augustine, ENCHIRIDION, ch. 99, n. 25: For only grace discerns the redeemed from the lost, which the

---

* *Trans. note*: The *conception* of an will is its making of a decision or choice. It is said to be a "*conception*" because what is *conceived* is, according to the etymology of the word, "completely grasped or taken in hand". Regarding *discretion*, a little below this, cf. the "Rationale for the Translation of Peculiar Latin terms" in the Introduction to this English translation.

according to a predestination, just as according to an election" is clear; because everyone acting from a proposal, deliberating, accepts one of the two sides of a contradiction beforehand, for that reason everyone such is said to elect,[1] but not everyone acting thus orders an effect unto an end, but, as very frequently (occurs), (orders) himself. But 'to predestine' is 'to preordain one of two unto an end', and this, indeed, suits God properly; and for that reason that is clear. For *predestination* connotes three (things), namely, *the one preordained*, and this is a man; and *the reckoning of the preordaining*, and this is grace; and *the reckoning of the end*, and this is glory: and in this manner there are three, namely, *the "what"* [quod], and *the "through what"* [per quod], and *the "toward what"* [ad quod].

SCHOLIUM

I. In the Response there is said, that election according to the affection of love « is the same as predestination »; this must be understood not according to the formal *reckoning of understanding* [secundum formalem rationem intelligendi], but according to *thing* [secundum rem]; which is explicitly stated here in the solution to n. 2. St. Thomas (SUMMA, I, q. 23, a. 4) agrees, where he explains, that « predestination, according (its) reckoning, presupposes election, and election, love [dilectionem] ». — In regard to the intention of the end, which is touched upon in the solution to the last (objection), cf. SENT., Bk. II, d. 28, Doubt 4.

II. The (other) writers (on this subject are): Alexander of Hales, SUMMA., p. I, q. 28, m. 1, a. 1, and q. 30, m. 4. — St. Thomas, SENT., Bk. I, d. 41, q. 1, a. 1; SUMMA., I, q. 23, a. 4. — Bl. (now St.) Albertus (Magnus), here in a. 18 and 19. — Peter of Tarentaise, SENT., Bk. I, d. 41, q. 1, a. 2. — Richard of Middleton, SENT., Bk. I, d. 41, a. 1, q. 1.

ARTICLE IV

On reprobation, and, in particular, on obduration.

Consequently, there is the question concerning the third[2] article, namely, concerning reprobation. And, since those what have been said of eternal predestination, are to be said (of), and/or can be adapted to, reprobation, there is asked in particular [specialiter] concerning obduration [obduratio], which is its connoted, concerning which two (things) are asked.

The first is, whether (obduration) is a punishment, or a fault.

The second, whether obduration is from God.

QUESTION I

Whether obduration is a punishment, or a fault?

Moreover, that obduration is a punishment, is shown in this manner.

1. On that (verse) in the ninth (chapter of St. Paul's Letter) to the Romans:[3] *He will have mercy upon whom He wishes* etc., the Gloss of (St.) Augustine (reads): « Obduration is not wanting to have mercy »; but '*not wanting to have mercy*' is not a fault, but a punishment: ergo etc..

2. Likewise, in the same (there is written):[4] « He will have mercy according to the grace, which is given freely; but He hardens against (the good) [obdurat] according to the judgement, which is rendered to merits »; but it is established, that it is not rendered to good merits, therefore, to evil ones; but that which is rendered to evil merits is punishment: therefore, obduration is a punishment.

3. Likewise, this very (thing) seems *by reason*, because in this fault and punishment differ, because a fault is a voluntary affection, but a punishment is an involuntary affection; but the obduration of a heart is involuntary, because no one wishes to be disabled or hardened against (the good): ergo etc..

4. Likewise, just as *being made entirely blind* [excaecatio] holds itself to understanding, so *obduration* to affection; but *"being made entirely blind"* means a punishment, not a fault: therefore, also *obduration*.

ON THE CONTRARY: 1. On that (verse) in the second (chapter of St. Paul's Letter) to the Romans:[5] *According to the hardness* etc., the Gloss (says): « Hardening [induratio] belongs to a mind hardened [induratae] in a pertinacious malice, through

---

common cause (of our damnation), drawn from the origin (of our race's fall), collects into one mass of perdition. Cf. To SIMPLICIANUS, Bk. I, q. 2, n. 17, ff.; in which question you will find many of those things which are treated of here by the Seraphic Doctor. — The Vatican edition changed, on its own, the word *the mass (of the damned)* [massa] into *wickedness* [malitia]. A little above this, after *then election* [deinde electio] codex Y interjects *and then predestination* [et deinde praedestinatio].

[1] Cf. Aristotle, ETHICS, Bk. III, ch. 2 f., and MAGNA MORALIA, Bk. I, ch. 16 (ch. 17). — Next, for *himself* [se ipsum] codices F P and Q have not so well *unto himself* [in se ipsum].

[2] See above here in a. 3, q. 2, p. 713, footnote 4.

[3] Verse 18. — The quote from (St.) Augustine is had in To SIMPLICIANUS, Bk. I, q. 2, n. 15.

[4] The words of the ordinary Gloss on Rom. 9:16 had here seem to have been excerpted from (St.) Augustine's, To SIMPLICIANUS, Bk. I, q. 2, n. 15, or from his book, ON GRACE AND FREE WILL, ch. 23, n. 45, or from his unfinished work AGAINST JULIAN, Bk. II, sent. 141 (at the end of the book).

[5] Verse 5. — The Vatican edition, having neglected the authority of the codices and of the original text, renders the words of the Gloss thus: *Hardening is the persevering of the mind in pertinacious wickedness, through which* etc. [Induratio est perseveratio mentis in malitia pertinaci, per quam etc.].

which the man becomes impenitent »; but this means a fault: ergo etc..

2. Likewise, (St.) Augustine (says) ON THE PRE-DESTINATION OF THE SAINTS:[1] « Obduration is nothing other than obviating God's commandments »; but "*to obviate commandments*" means disobedience [inobedientiam]: but, as (St.) Ambrose says, « a sin is nothing other than a prevarication of the Divine Law and disobedience against the celestial commandments »: therefore "obduration" means a sin.

3. Likewise, it seems *by reason*, because no temporal punishment, according to which (it is) of this kind, is opposed to sanctifying grace; but obduration is opposed to the grace which makes one pleasing [gratiae gratificanti] and most of all to the final grace: therefore, obduration is not a punishment, but a fault.

4. Likewise, in this is the difference between punishment and fault, because, as (St.) Augustine[2] says, « a punishment is an evil, which we suffer, but a fault is an evil, which we do »; but each one causes his own obduration, just as (St.) Augustine says in the book, ON GRACE AND FREE WILL: « The Lord hardened [induravit] the Pharaoh by a just judgement, but he (hardened) himself by free will ». And that obduration is from us, is clear: because in the Psalm one is dissuaded: *Do not*, it says, *harden* [obdurare] *your hearts*: ergo etc..

CONCLUSION

"Obduration", as it means a heart unfit for the impression of grace, is a punishment for sin; as it signifies a heart established in sin, is a the disposition of a preceding sin; but as it means a rebellious heart, it is a sin against the Holy Spirit.

I RESPOND: It must be said, that "obduration" among spirits has been said in a manner transferred from obduration among bodies. But among bodies a threefold property follows from hardness [duritiam], even though it is in a body through the same nature; not so in a spirit.[3] For (what is) "hard" [durum] is '*unable* to take up' [inhabile ad suscipiendum], (and) is '*stable* to remain throughout' [stabile ad permanendum], again, it is '*strong* to rebel or resist' [forte ad rebellendum sive resistendum].

According to this threefold manner a heart is said to be hardened against (the good) in a threefold manner. In the first manner a heart is said (to be) "hardened against (the good)" from this, that it is *unable* to take up the impression of grace; and in this manner it means [sonat in] a passion and is a punishment consequent to a fault. In the second manner a heart is said (to be) "hardened against (the good)", which has been *established* in sin, which, namely, has been very compacted for the love of sin; and in this manner obduration is a sin with a disposition or a disposition of a preceding. In the third manner a heart is said (to be) "*rebellious*", which wants to impugn God and His commandments and grace; and in this manner it is a special genus of sin, that is, the sin against the Holy Spirit.

1. 2. And according to this threefold manner the diverse authorities, which seem to run contrary [obviare] to themselves, proceed concerning obduration: but they proceed by diverse ways according to the members of the aforesaid distinction. It must be conceded, therefore, that obduration in one manner is a punishment; it but nevertheless be conceded, that in the other manners it is a fault or the disposition of a fault.

3. 4. To that, therefore, which is objected, that a punishment is not repugnant to grace and that it means [sonat in] a passion; it must be said, that punishment is threefold. For there is a certain punishment (for sin which is) *inflicted*, a certain one (which is) *contracted*, a certain one (which is) *done*. For the punishment *inflicted* (for original sin) is simply a passion and not repugnant[4] to grace, such as (is) hunger, thirst, and sickness. The punishment *contracted* (from original sin) is the fomes (of sin) and concupiscence, and this indeed is a passion, and for that reason a punishment, but yet it inclines to an evil action; and for that reason it is repugnant to grace not as much as regards (its) substance, but as much as regards inclination. The punishment *done* (by a personal sin) is just as a hardening against [sicut obduratio] and an expulsion of grace, and this indeed is a punishment, because it is a passion; but because it is from an evil action or from sin, and is concomitant with it inseparably, for that reason it is opposed to grace. And thus it is clear, that nevertheless it is a punishment and a passion; for thought it happens through one's own action, nevertheless it is a punishment, just as is clear in a man with scabs [in scabioso], who delights in scrapping himself, but afterwards feels a burning in (his) flesh.

SCHOLIUM

I. Alexander of Hales (SUMMA., p. I, q. 29, m. 3, 4, and 5) enumerates and explains well the three effects of reprobation, which are *the subtraction of grace*, *a being thoroughly blinded* [excaecatio], (and) *obduration* (i. e. being hardened against the good). In the solution to n. 3 the first member of this division is touched upon by the Seraphic Doctor, and he well distinguishes the *threefold punishment*; but he makes mention of *being blinded thoroughly* [excaecationis] in the 4th argument of the fundament. On *punishment* and its order to fault, cf. SENT., Bk. II, d. 36, throughout. — The

---

[1] It would be better to read ON PREDESTINATION AND GRACE, in which book, which is of an uncertain author, there is said in ch. 4: For what other is hardness than obviating God's commandments? — The following quote, cited from (St.) Ambrose, is found in his book, ON PARADISE, ch. 8, n. 39.

[2] AGAINST ADIMANTUS, a disciple of Mani, ch. 26: Evil in this passage is not to be understood as sin, but a punishment. For evil is named in a twofold manner: the one, which a man does, the other, which he suffers; what he does, is a sin, what he suffers, a punishment. Cf. also ON THE TRUE RELIGION, ch. 20, n. 39, and ON FREE WILL, Bk. I, ch. 1, n. 1, and also Bk. III, ch. 15 and 15, n. 44 ff. — The text next cited

is loc. cit., ch. 23, n. 45 sounds like this: And through this God also hardened through a just judgement, and the Pharaoh himself through free will. — The Psalm, from which the words next cited, is 94:8.

[3] The sense is: Although *the nature* of a body is a remote cause of hardness and of that threefold property, which is attributed to (its) hardness; yet, the hardness is its proximate cause. But, in a spirit, hardness and (its) consequent properties are to no extent in it by a reason of its own *nature*. — On the threefold property of hardness, cf. Aristotle, ON THE PREDICAMENTS, ch. "On *Quality*"; ON HEAVEN AND THE WORLD, Bk. III, text 11 (ch. 1), and METEOROLOGY, Bk. IV, ch. 5 (ch. 4).

[4] Codices R and V read *is not repugnant* [non repugnant].

doctors (of theology) agree in this doctrine, and (Bl.) Peter of Tarentaise follows our Doctor nearly word for word.

II. Alexander of Hales, loc. cit. — St. Thomas, on this and the following question, here in q. 4, a. 2; SUMMA CONTRA GENTILES., Bk. III, ch. 161; and in regard to the principles, SUMMA., I, II, q. 79, a. 1, I, q. 23, a. 3. — Bl. (now St.) Albertus, SUMMA., p. I, tr. 16, q. 66, m. 2. — (Bl.) Peter of Tarentaise, here in q. 3, a. 2. — Richard of Middleton, here in a. 3, qq. 1 and 2. — Durandus (of Saint-Pourçain), on this and the following question, here in. q. 2. — (Bl.) Dionysius the Carthusian, here in q. 2.

QUESTION II

Whether obduration is from God?

Second, there is asked, whether obduration is from God or is an effect of God reproving. And that it is, seems:

1. According to the ninth (chapter of St. Paul's Letter) to the Romans:[1] *He will have mercy upon whom He wills, and He hardens whom He wills*: but that something be done by God as Author and by God willing is the same: therefore, if obduration is by God willing, therefore, (it is) also by God as author.

2. Likewise, on the same in the Gloss (there is said):[2] « Obduration is *not wanting to have mercy* »: therefore, either this is a predication through a *cause*, or through *inherence*, or through *essence*. Not through *inherence* and/or through *essence* — for in God there is a will to have mercy, yet not an obduration — therefore, it has been said through a *cause*; but God does not want to have mercy upon some as foreknown, as (St.) Augustine says: therefore, their obduration is from Him.

3. Likewise, on that (verse) of Exodus:[3] *I shall harden his heart*, (St.) Augustine says: « God hardened the Pharaoh by a just judgement », therefore according to this it was just, that the Pharaoh was hardened; but every just (judgement) proceeds from the Most High Justice, which is God: ergo etc..

4. Likewise, it seems *by reason*, because everything which is *something*, is from God; obduration is something: therefore, according to that which it is, it is from God. That it is *something*, is clear, because "hard" means a natural power;[4] but "soft" means an impotence. Therefore, if softness both in bodies and spirits is something, which has God (as its) cause, it is clear that etc..

5. Likewise, whosoever has the care of another, if he permits him to do evil [malefacere], when he can prohibit (him), and/or (permits him) to perish, when he can help, is not unfittingly said (to be) the cause of his evil-doing and/or of his sin or evil (deed). Wherefore the prelate, who does not correct (his) subjects [subditos], is said (to be) the cause of the evils in (his) subjects; similarly, he who has whence to feed one dying of hunger, and does not feed (him), is the cause of this death. If, therefore, God can prohibit, that our affection hardens,[5] and can feed (it), so that it does not fail, and does not do (this); it seems, that to Him there is to be attributed the reason and cause of (his) being hardened.

6. Likewise, the Philosopher gives the maxim:[6] « If anything is the cause of something, the opposite is also the cause of (its) opposite », such that, if *to have* a lung is a cause of breathing, *not having* (one) is also the cause of not breathing. But (His) 'wanting to have mercy' is the cause of (our) being made pleasing [causa gratificationis]: therefore (His) 'not wanting to have mercy' is the cause of (our) obduration.

7. Likewise, « if anything through its own presence is the cause of something, through its absence it is the cause of the opposite », this is another maxim of the Philosopher;[7] but God through His presence is the cause of the softening of (our) heart: therefore, through His absence He is the cause of (our) obduration.

8. Likewise, if any two are entirely similar, either

---

[1] Verse 18.

[2] You will find the saying from the Gloss in (St.) Augustine's, TO SIMPLICIANUS, Bk. I, q. 2, n. 15. — On the threefold predication, of which mention is next made, see above d. 30, q. 12, in the body (of the Response), and in the Scholium. — The sentence of (St.) Augustine, which is cited at the end of the argument, has been taken from his ON DIVERSE QUESTIONS TO SIMPLICIANUS, Bk. I, q. 2, n. 13, where the saintly Doctor says: Because if (God) would also have mercy upon some, He could thus call (them), in a manner in which it would be apt for them, to both be moved and understand and follow. And ibid., n. 16: And so thus let it be most tenaciously and most firmly believed, that this, that God has mercy upon whom He wills, and hardens whom He wills against (the good), that is, He has mercy upon whom He wills, and He does not have mercy upon whom He wills not, that (this) belongs to some equity hidden and untraceable [investigabilis] by human measure etc. — For *a will to have mercy* [voluntas miserendi], which words occur in the midst of the argument, the Vatican edition alone has faultily *a will to not have mercy* [voluntas non miserendi].

[3] Exodus 4:21 — The words of (St.) Augustine are had, ON GRACE AND FREE WILL, ch. 23, n. 45. Cf. the previous Question, p. 718, footnote 2.

[4] Aristotle, ON THE PREDICAMENTS, ch. "On *Quality*", among the various species of quality posits in the second place a natural power and impotency and supposes for this second species *"the hard" and "the soft"* saying: For "the hard" is said (to be), that which has a power not easily wounded [secari]; but "the soft", that which has an impotency (belonging) to the very same (quality). — Next, for *Therefore if softness* [Ergo si mollities] the Vatican edition has *Therefore, if hardness* [Ergo si durities], which reading does not respond so well to the context, because that argument proceeds from the lesser to the greater.

[5] The Vatican edition omits non here, breaking with the codices. — The Latin particles placed separately here ut ... non are to be accepted as ne. See the references on Latin Grammar. — On this argument, cf. (St.) Anselm, ON THE DOWNFALL OF THE DEVIL, ch. 1.

[6] This maxim is constructed from (Aristotle's) POSTERIOR ANALYTICS, Bk. I, ch. 10 (ch. 13), where there is denied by the Philosopher that the demonstration, in which a remote cause is posited as not convertible nor sufficient to cause the effect through itself, is a demonstration propter quid, with this example as proof: « Such as *on account of what* [propter quid] does a wall not breathe? Because it is not an animal; for if the cause of not breathing is this, it is necessary that being an animal (be) the cause of breathing. So that if the negation (is), "it is the cause of this not being", the affirmation (is), "it is the cause of this being" ». Cf. also Averroës on this passage, where you will also find the same example of the lung, which St. Bonaventure here cites.

[7] (Aristotle), PHYSICS, Bk. II, text 30 (ch. 3): But more fully there is the same cause of contraries; for what (when) present is the cause of this, (when) absent we also make sometimes the cause of the contrary, such as the absence of a pilot (is the cause) of the subversion of a ship, whose presence was the cause of (its) salvation. — For *but* [sed] which immediately follows, the Vatican edition has *therefore, if* [ergo si], breaking with the codices and edition 1. Then before the words *through His absence* [per sui absentiam] not a few codices, together with the Vatican edition, omits *therefore* [ergo], which we have restored from codex Z and edition 1.

some property is not in one, which is not in the other, or if it is in (one), it is in (it) from the other. Therefore, let there be posited here two little ones, such s Jacob and Esau.[1] God hardens one against (the good), such as Esau, the other He does not harden against (the god), such as Jacob: therefore, since they are entirely similar as much as regards nature and as much as regards merits, the obduration come from elsewhere. But there is no giving (of obduration) except by God, ergo etc.. *If you say*, that (it comes) from a devil; *on the contrary*: let it be that a devil in no manner intervenes [se intromittat], nevertheless the former is hardened against (the good).

9. Likewise, every effect, whether positive or defective, has a proximate and immediate cause: therefore, I ask, what is the proximate cause of obduration: for either (it is) *the original fault*, or *an actual one*, or *the use of free will*, or *something else*. Not *the original fault*, because then all would be hardened against (the good); similarly, neither *an actual fault*, because then everyone actually sinning would be hardened against (the good); nor *the use of free will*, because obduration, as it is the connoted of reprobation, is in little ones, in whom there is not use of free will. It remains, therefore, that *God's Will* is the cause, and this seems, because with It posited there is posited the effect. For, if God did not want to have mercy upon this one, it is necessary, that he be hardened against (the good).

On the Contrary: 1. In the sixth (chapter of the Gospel of St.) John (there is written):[3] *All who come to Me, I shall not cast outside*: therefore, the Lord is prepared to embrace all: therefore, the defect of enlightenment [illustrationis] does not come from the part of God, but from our part.

2. Likewise, in the third (chapter)[4] of the Apocalypse (there is written). *Behold, I stand at the door and knock, if anyone opens to me, I shall enter into that* etc.. But, if a foreigner, wishing to be given hospitality [volens hospitari], does not recline (at table) in the house, the cause is not on his part, but only (on the part) of the doorkeeper [ostiarii]: therefore, similarly obduration, too, is not the cause, without the one who does not receive God knocking.

3. Likewise, (St.) Augustine (says) on that (verse of the Gospel of St.) John:[5] *The Light shines in the darkness*, says: « Just as light is present to a blind man (who has been) placed in the sun, and he himself is absent to the light, so to every iniquitous (man), who is blind at heart, Wisdom is present, and he himself is absent ». If, therefore, the good is similar, since blindness or the privation of the act of seeing is not from the Sun, it is clear that neither is obduration from God.

4. Likewise, (St.) Anselm (of Canterbury says):[6] « A man has not grace for this reason, because God does not give (it), but because man does not accept (it) »: therefore, obduration ought not be said to be from God.

5. Likewise, it seems *by reason*, because « it belongs to the best to bring forth the best [optimi est optima adducere] »;[7] but obduration is the worst among all evils: therefore, God, who is the Best, does not effect it.

6. Likewise, the obduration of the soul renders the soul impotent to the good, therefore, it is a defect; but a defect either does not have a cause, or if it has (one), it has a deficient cause,[8] but God is the deficient cause of nothing: therefore, obduration is in no manner from God.

CONCLUSION

Obduration, insofar as it is a defect, is not from God; but insofar as it is ordained by the Divine Justice in retribution as a punishment for sin, it is from God.

I Respond: It must be said, that obduration, inasmuch as (it is) a punishment, means an ineptitude of the soul, and, thus, it means a penal *defect*; and every punishment, inasmuch as (it is) such, is just and *ordinate* [iusta et ordinata]; for that reason it means an *ordinate defect* [defectum ordinatum]. Inasmuch, therefore, as it is a *defect*, it does not have but a deficient cause; but this is not God, because God is not a deficient cause, but (rather the deficient cause is) a destitute free will. However, inasmuch as (it is) *ordinate*, it has a *meriting* cause, that is, the fault itself, and an *ordering* cause, that is, the Divine Justice granting retribution [retribuentem divinam iustitiam].

1. 2. 3. Therefore, those three quotes, that is, from the Apostle, (St.) Augustine and the Gloss, and (those) completely similar, which say, that God has hardened someone against (the good), are understood as much as regards the reckoning of the *order*, not as much as regards the reckoning of the *defect*, because through a comparison to *the defect* He is compared only in the reckoning of *one permitting*, not of *one effecting*. And there is an example: if anyone would be worthy to perish by hunger, and another could feed him, and by a just judgement did not want to feed him; if it were asked, which was the cause of death in the former one, the response would be, that (it was) a defect of food; but the latter would not be said to have killed (the former), but (only) to have permitted (his death). If *again* it were asked, whether the latter did (what he did) justly, it would be said, that he did; yet, though *he did nothing*, because it[9] had been ordained [ordinatum] by his authority for the merits of the former, and consequently that

---

[1] Romans 9:11 ff.. Cf. (St.) Augustine, On Diverse Questions to Simplicianus, Bk. I, q. 2, n. 4, ff..

[2] Just as predestination connotes grace as (its) temporal effect, so reprobation obduration, which, as Alexander of Hales, Summa, p. I, q. 29, m. 5, a, 3 says, is twofold: one is *general* for all, who descend from Adam through seminal concupiscence, and this follows original sin ... the other is *special*, which, I say is in adults, who have a will and proposal to resist God's benefices.

[3] Verse 37, where the Vulgate reads *Him* [Eum] for *All* [Omnis].

[4] Verse 20.

[5] John. 1:5. — (On the Gospel of St. John), tract I, n. 19: In which manner a blind man placed in the sun, to him the Sun is present, but to the Sun he is absent; so every fool, every iniquitous, every impious (man) is blind at heart. Wisdom is present, but when He is present to a blind man, his eyes are absent; not because He is absent to him, but because he is absent to Him. — Next, for *the good* [bonum] edition 1 has *this* [hoc], and at the end of the argument codices P and Q read (in the subjunctive) *is* [sit] for *is* [est].

[6] On the Downfall of the Devil, in which that which, indeed, is here said of man, is taught concerning the Devil and proven throughout the whole book, with these prefatory words of chapter 1: see, if it can be said, not only *for a man*, but also for an Angel, because he does not have that which he has accepted. Cf. also his book, On the Concord of God's Foreknowledge with Free Will, q. 3, ch. 5 ff., where the same sentence is hinted at, but in relation to man.

[7] Dionysius (the Areopagite), On the Divine Names, ch. 4, § 19. Cf. below d. 44, a. 1, q. 2, where this sentence is confirmed from Plato.

[8] Cf. above d. 36, a. 3, q. 1, p. 672, footnote 10.

[9] That is, that he merit death on account of (his) fault.

had been ordained as a punishment due him. Through this manner (of speaking) it must be understood in the proposed.

4. To that, therefore, which is objected, that "obduration" means the positing (of something); it must be said, that among bodies it does means a *positing* (of something), because through their own nature they are bound to resist themselves [sibi];[1] but among spirits it means a *defect*, because it ought to be of the natural aptitude of a spirit to be able for the susception of the Divine influence. Whence such an ability belongs to a power and habit,[2] but on the other hand, obduration, and ineptitude, is through the manner of a privation.

5. To that which is objected, that he who permits, a subject to perish, is the cause etc.; it must be said, that it is true, if he is bound and ought to do (something); but if he is not bound nor ought to do this, nay rather the contrary, there can to no extent be imputed to him the danger (of perishing), but the justice (of his act can be);[3] and thus it is in God.

6. 7. To that which is objected, that if anything is the cause of something, that (its) opposite is the cause of the opposite; it must be said, that that holds in natural and necessary (things), just as in '*having a lung*' and '*not having (one)*' and *breathing* and *not breathing*; but it does not have a place among voluntary (things), just as (St.) Anselm says.[4] Moreover, the cause, why this one has grace, is because God gives (it); the cause, why he does not, is because he does not accept (it). — But this solution does not seem suitable [competens], since if the maxim of the Philosopher is a good one, it is necessary, that it hold in every matter.

And on this account it must be said, that he is speaking of a proximate and immediate cause, which is the *whole* cause, not requiring [exigens] another one,[5] and in every such (his maxim) holds. But though God's Will is the efficient cause of (his) being made pleasing, yet, (his) free will concurs to (his) sal-

vation as one consenting. Therefore, because those two do concur, any of them can cause the defect; and the Divine Will, which is most liberal, does not cause (it), but the free will, which, though it cannot nor is it sufficient *to effect* (it), yet it can be the *deficient cause*, which is sufficient for the defect of the effect. For in regard to the good « it is easier to destroy than to construct ».[6]

8. To that which is objected concerning absence, it must be said, that when the absence of anyone is an evil, either he is the cause of his own absence, or (he is) not. If he is the cause of his own absence, he is said consequently to be the cause of that which is incurred from the absence; but if he is not the cause, nay, as much as it concerns him, he is always prepared to be present; then in truth he is in no manner to be said to be the cause, but that, by reason of which he justly absents himself, (is), for that reason our sin (is the cause), and not God. *For our sins have set up a division* [diviserunt] *between us and Our God*,[7] and they are as most dense clouds, bearing off from us the enlightenment of grace.

9. To that which is asked, "What is the efficient cause, according to the reckoning of which it is in (a soul)?"; it must be said, that the[8] cause is free will, *the meritorious (principle)* is a sin, whether original or actual. But *the deficient cause*, which posits the defect, is the free will, deficient and remaining thoroughly in its own defect, whether because it neglects this, or because, when in the commission of sins [peccatis exigentibus], another does not run to help (it). However, because, with two existing similars, one can have an encouraging [sublevantem][9] hand, the other not; for that reason one *is hardened against (the good) out of itself*, but the other *is encouraged by another*. And through this manner (of speaking) it must be understood in Jacob and Esau; for Esau lay sick [iacuit] with his own infirmity, but Jacob was revealed by another's virtue.

SCHOLIUM

I. As (Fr. Stephanus) Brülifer (O.F.M., † 1497 A.D.) has already observed (on this passage), the solution of this Question is very clear and contains very many (things), most worthy of being noted, especially in the solution to the objections. St. Thomas (SENT., Bk. I, here in q. 4, a. 2) entirely agrees. Moreover, it deals with the first member of the division posited in the Response of the preceding Question, that is with obduration, to the extent that it is *a punishment*. According to the Seraphic Doctor this is, on the part of *man*, a disposition and/or act of a will obstinate in evil, the whole *deficient* cause of which is in him alone; on *God's*

part it is a certain subtraction of *efficacious* grace, but not of *every grace*, which subtraction is on the supposition of preceding sin. Which St. Thomas confirms (SUMMA CONTRA GENTILES, Bk. III, ch. 162): « Therefore, when (God) subtracts these helps from anyone in virtue of the merit of their own action, according to which His Justice requires (it), He is said to harden them against and thoroughly blind them to (the good) » (cf. Richard of Middleton, SENT., Bk. I, d. 41, a. 3, q. 3). — One must chiefly note, 1) that one must speak differently of the causality of a defect, to the extent that it is *a defect*, and to the extent

---

[1] The Vatican edition omits *themselves* [sibi]; codex R exhibits *one another* [sibi invicem].

[2] Which are the first two species of quality, cited by Aristotle in his book, ON PREDICAMENTS, ch. "On *Quality*", concerning which see above d. 3, p. II, a. 1, q. 3, in the body of the Response, and in a. 2, q. 1, in reply to n. 1. — Codex O before the words *and habit* [et habitus] interjects *or to a power* [et potentiae], and then after *obduration* [obduratio] it omits *and* [et]. Next after *through the manner* [per modum] the Vatican edition inserts *of a prevision and* [praevisionis]; finally, codex cc for *privation* [privationis] substitutes *prevision* [praevisionis].

[3] The Vatican edition reads *of justice* [iustitiae] for *the justice (of his act can be)* [iustitia].

[4] These probative propositions, which follow immediately here, occurred already above in the 4th argument of the fundament.

[5] Many codices have faultily *another* [alium], edition 1 *another* [aliud] for *another one (i.e. another cause)* [aliam].

[6] Aristotle, TOPICS, Bk. VII, ch. 3 (ch. 4).

[7] Isaias 59:2: You *iniquities have set up a division between you and your God* [Iniquitates vestrae diviserunt inter vos et Deum vestrum]. — A little above this, after *for that reason* [ideo] the Vatican edition, with some codices, subjects *truly* [vere]; in place of *for that reason out sin (is the cause)* [ideo peccatum nostrum] cod. Z has *but this is our sin* [hoc autem est peccatum nostrum], codd. F & V read *that is* etc. [illud est etc.] instead.

[8] Codex Z adjoins *efficient* [efficiens]. The Vatican edition alone omits *is the free will* [est liberum arbitrium], and then for *meritorious (principle)* [meritorium] it exhibits *meritorious (cause)* [meritoria]. Even in not a few codices, such as I P & Q, which in the rest convene with our reading, and also edition 1, there is read *meritorious (cause)* [meritoria]. The words, which follow next, *which posits the defect, is the free will, deficient* [quae ponit defectum est liberum arbitrium deficiens] are wanting in many codices. Then, after *it neglects* [negligit] cod. Z adds *to detest* [detestari], and after a few (words) for *run to help (it)* [succurrut] many codd., with ed. 1, substitute *relieve (it)* [succedit], cod. Y has *come up to aid (it)* [subvenit].

[9] A reference to Ecclesiastes 4:10: *Woe to the one alone, because when he has fallen down, he does not have one to support him* [Vae soli, quia cum ceciderit, non habet sublevantem se].

that it is *ordained* (here in the body of the Response, and St. Thomas, here loc. cit.). 2. To *posit the effect* there is required a concurrence of *all* causes, (but) to *impede the effect* the defect (the occurrence) of *one* cause suffices, upon which axiom is founded the solution to nn. 6 and 7 (cf. St. Thomas, loc. cit., in reply to n. 3); whence the cause, which suffices to impede the effect, does not yet suffice to posit the same. 3. Hence it follows, that though a will dissents freely from the motion of divine grace, and freely consents to the same, yet in one manner one must speak of the causality, to the extent that the act of the will *is deficient*, the defect of which is it-

self the first and sole deficient cause (of obduration), in another manner the will *is proficient* [proficit] for a good act, the first *efficient* cause of which *proficiency* [profectus] is God, but together with the second cause (here in reply to n. 9). This is explained in SENT., Bk. II, d. 34, a. 1, q. 2; and by St. Thomas, SUMMA CONTRA GENTILES, Bk. III, c. 159.

II. Besides those already cited: Alexander of Hales, SUMMA., p. I, q. 29, m. 3 and 4. — St . Thomas, locc. citt. and SUMMA., I, q. 23, a. 3. — Bl. (now St.) Albertus (Magnus), here in a. 23. — (Bl.) Peter of Tarentaise, here in q. 3, a. 3. — Richard of Middleton, here in a. 3, q. 3.

DOUBTS ON THE TEXT OF THE MASTER

DOUBT I

In this part, there are the doubts about (Master Peter's) text and first concerning this verse, which is posited, namely, "*predestination concerns the goods of salvation*". Therefore, there is asked, "What is understood through "the goods of salvation"[bonis salutaribus] ?" *If you say*, that grace and glory (are); *therefore*, just as a man is said (to be) "predestined", so grace ought to be said (to be) "predestined".

I RESPOND: It must be said, that predestination is a preordination. But in an ordination three (things) occur, *a what* is ordered, both *through a what*, and *to a what*. The first is, man, the second is grace, the third is glory. And, since the former alone is said (to be) "predestined", who is ordered by a predestination, for that reason it is clear, that grace and glory ought[1] not be said (to be) "predestined", but the man only, who is predestined to salvation.

DOUBT II

Likewise, is asked concerning this which (Master Peter) says: *And the men to be saved.* For he seems to speak insufficiently: because since predestination is a preparation for grace and glory,[2] therefore it is not only of men, but also of Angels.

I RESPOND: It must be said, that "predestination" [praedestinatio] in one manner means a preparation of the good [praeparationem boni],[3] and in this manner it convenes with men and Angels and, even, with Christ; *in another manner* it means a preparation of the good and a liberation from evil [liberationem a malo], and in this manner predestination is said (to be) a "proposal to have mercy", and in this manner it is properly of men, and thus Master Peter accepts (it) here.[4]

DOUBT III

Likewise, is asked concerning this which (St. Augustine) says, that *(God's) predestination cannot be without (God's) Foreknowledge.* For he seems to speak badly, because the Foreknowledge is of the wicked, whence the foreknown are said (to be) wicked; but predestination, of the good: therefore, there can be a predestination without the Foreknowledge, just as the other way around.[5] *If you say* to me, that predestination is special, but the Foreknowledge is common and special; *then I ask*, "For what reason is the *Foreknowledge* appropriated more to reprobation than to predestination?"

To this there is one manner of responding, which, because predestination *adds*, for that reason it had its own name: but reprobation *does not* (add), for that reason it retained the common name. — But in what manner does that have truth, since reprobation is the foreknowledge of punishment, the cause of which is God?[6]

And for that reason it must be said, that it not *only* adds, (it must be said) that it also withdraws.[7] For predestination gives one to understand a *good pleasure*, which draws it into the genus of *practical* knowledge *simply* (speaking), by this, that the good pleasure is simply and absolutely in respect of the whole connoted (by the predestination). But not so is it concerning reprobation, because (God's) Will is not in respect of the evil of *fault*, and, in respect of *punishment*, It is *consequent*, not antecedent, and quasi drawn (away).[8] And on this account, because it is more withdrawn from the reckoning of *knowledge*, it retained for itself the name of *the Foreknowledge*.

DOUBT IV

Likewise, is asked concerning this response of Master (Peter): *To which we respond, that for this reason it has been said* etc.

---

[1] Edition 1 has *ought* [debent] in the plural. — More on this doubt is had above in a. 1. q. 1. Cf. also (Bl.) Peter of Tarentaise and Richard (of Middleton), here on the text.

[2] And/or, more accurately: since predestination is a preparation for grace in the present and for glory in the future. Cf. here the text of Master (Peter), ch. 2.

[3] Codex Y here interposes: *according to which predestination is said in the present* [secundum quod dicitur praedestinatio in praesenti].

[4] Cf. Alexander of Hales, SUMMA, p. I. q. 28, m. 2, a. 4; Bl. (now St.) Albertus (Magnus), here in a. 7; St. Thomas, here in q. 2, Richard (of Middleton), here in a. 1; Giles the Roman, here in 1st princ., q. 3.

[5] In other words: the reprobate are called "the foreknown": therefore, if the foreknown have not been predestined, it seems, that foreknowledge is not contained in predestination.

[6] The sense is: not only does predestination add something to the Foreknowledge, but reprobation (does) too, namely, the punishment, which is inflicted upon the reprobate by God.

[7] He wants to say: reprobation indeed adds something upon the Foreknowledge, but not as much, as predestination adds, which withdraws the foreknowledge (in predestination) from the genus of knowledge into another genus, namely, (that) of the Will.

[8] What the Seraphic Doctor wishes to say with these words, see below d. 46, q, 2, especially in the reply to the last objection. — The Vatican edition reads less rightly: *is not in respect of the evil of fault, but in respect of punishment. It is also consequent* etc. [non est respectu mali culpae, sed respectu poenae. Est et consequens etc.]. — On this doubt, cf. Alexander of Hales, SUMMA, p. I, q. 29. m. 1: Bl. (now St.) Albertus (Magnus), here in a. 10; St. Thomas, here in q. 4, a. 1.

For it seems, that (that) does not solve (the matter) on account of his own distinction regarding the question concerning *increase*, since having demonstrated that someone (is) to be damned, it is true to say, that he can be saved, therefore, it can (be) that he was predestined: therefore, there can be more predestined, than there are: therefore, the number of the predestined can be increased.

I RESPOND: It must be said, that Master (Peter) in this first response principally responds to the first question, whether it is possible that one predestined be damned; and *rightly* [bene], that is, through *composition* and *division*.[1] And through that solution (his) response to that concerning an increase is in some manner clear, but not fully; for that reason he annexes a following solution, which is an explication of this one, in which there is said, that someone cannot *start* to be predestined, though it can (be) *that he was* predestined, because this is to say, that he could (be) *from eternity*. And since "*increase*" means a greater number than before with the presupposition of a prior and (with) a new addition, for that reason it is clear, that from its own reckoning it means a distinction and a succession in parts. Whence if any (number), immediately when it is, were as great, as it is going (to be), it would not be said "*to be increased*", but yet it could have *been greater*, thus must it be understood in the proposed. — *And/or* it can be solved in another manner through a composition and a division, just as Master (Peter) solves it; for there can be more, than there are,[2] therefore, the number can be increased.

DOUBT V

Likewise, is asked concerning this which (Master Peter) says, that *the understanding of the implicit condition causes the truth in the saying, and (causes) an impossibility in a true one*, in what manner is that able to be understood. For the same is not the cause of (its) opposites, and (if) an "*implicit condition*" causes truth, in what manner does it cause an impossibility?

I RESPOND: It must be said, that Master (Peter) wants to say, that this, demonstrated in any manner, is false: "it is impossible, that this one is damned and/or saved"; but if there be added and implied *the condition of predestination*; it causes truth *in the saying* and an impossibility *in a true one*, that is, it causes that saying with the manner of impossibility to be true, as for example if there be said: "it is impossible, together that this one is damned and has been predestined". *And/or* it can be said in another manner, the false saying of any condition by implication comes to be true:[3] such as with it demonstrated I disprove, "*that this one is saved*" is false; add *the condition*

of predestination, and it will become true: "*that this one is saved, if he has been predestined*," is true. Likewise, with the same demonstrated, "*that this one is damned*" is true; add *the condition of predestination*, and it becomes impossible: "that this one be damned, if he has been predestined", is impossible, understanding (this) conjunctively.[4]

DOUBT VI

Likewise, is asked concerning this which (Master Peter) says: *For from this that something has been made and/or said, they do not concede, that it can not be* etc. For (this principle) seems false: because Christ said, that Peter (was) going to sin:[5] therefore, after He said (it), it was necessary *that He said (it)*, and there necessarily follows: 'if Christ said (it), it will be', because *grant the opposite*, and then it would follow,[6] that Christ had lied, which is impossible: therefore, it seems, that since the antecedent is necessary, that it was necessary, that Peter deny (the Lord).

I RESPOND: It must be said, that in Christ's saying there are two (things), namely *the proffering of the word* and an *assertion*. And *the proffering of the word* is simply past and necessary, and from that no consequent follows. For it does not follow. 'Christ said this, therefore, it will be'; for He proffered this word: *I shall be a liar similar to you*.[7] Again there is *an assertion*, and that follows the enlightenment [illustrationem] of the Divine Foreknowledge (which He enjoyed as Man). Therefore, just as the Divine Foreknowledge is certain and infallible, to which nothing false can be subjected, and yet It looks to the future and connotes a[8] truth about it, and for that reason it is not *necessary*, that God foreknew what He has foreknown, though it is *certain* and *infallible*: thus it must be understood of Christ's assertion, that it has a *certitude* and *infallibility* from the Divine Foreknowledge; but yet it is not necessary, that Christ asserted this; and for that reason, if it be posited, that this did not happened, it is posited, that Christ also did not assert it. And in this manner that and (those) completely similar is clear. For in Christ's assertion there are two (things), namely the *act* of the mind,[9] and a *relation* or ordination to a future contingent. And though the one is necessary, the rest is contingent.

DOUBT VII

Likewise, is asked concerning this which (Master Peter) says: *Just as the effect of predestination is that grace, in which we are justified in the present* etc.. From this it is shown, that predestination is a *cause of grace*. Therefore, one asks: in what genus of cause (is it)? For, since it is a knowledge, it

---

[1] Or as is now accustomed to be said: through a distinction in the composite sense and in the divided sense.

[2] Codices W and W read *there are* [sunt] in the indicative. — Cf. above a. 2, qq. 1 and 2. — Alexander of Hales, SUMMA., p. I, q. 28, m. 2, a. 3, and m. 4, a. 3; Bl. (now St.) Albertus (Magnus), here in a. 11, ff..

[3] The Vatican edition reads *implicitly is true* [implicite verum sit] for *by implication comes to be true* [implicatione fit verum].

[4] Cf. above a. 2, qq. 1 and 2. — The same solution of this doubt is found in Bl. (now St.) Albertus (Magnus), here in a. 15; St. Thomas, (Bl.) Peter of Tarentaise, and Richard (of Middleton), here on the text.

[5] Matthew 26:34. — Next, after *it was* [fuit], codices A and X interject *still* [verum].

[6] The Vatican edition, together with not a few codices, has *it does follow* [sequitur].

[7] John 8:55.

[8] Codex Y adjoins *contingent* [contingentem]. A little below this, after *assertion* [assertione], codex T has *which* [quae] for *that it* [quod].

[9] Codex T has *of the truth* [veritatis]. — On this doubt, cf. above d. 38, a. 2, qq. 1 and 2, and here, in a. 1, in last two questions.

seems to mean an *exemplary* cause. *And again*, this does not seem to suffice, because an *exemplar* does not necessarily infer the exemplified, but *the Foreknowledge* does posit (it). *And again*, if it is a cause, (it is) either a *universal one*, or a *particular one*:[1] not a *universal one*, because then it would need another particular, helping (cause); not *a particular one*, because then it would have been determined to one effect only. *And again*, either a *necessary* (cause), or a *contingent one*: not a *necessary one*, since it works through the Will; not a *contingent one*, since this is fallible and uncertain.

I RESPOND: It must be said, that predestination is a cause of *grace*, just as (Master Peter)[2] says, and *the whole* cause, but not the (whole) cause of *salvation*, such that there is excluded a cooperating (cause) and a disposing (cause). *For we are Christ's helpers*,[3] and no one is saved unwilling. — What, therefore, *is asked*, "In which genus of cause is it?"; it must be said, that predestination encloses in itself *knowledge* and the *good pleasure* of the Will and *the disposition* of the Will, through which it pleases God to save us, which (disposition) is the Most High Goodness (as It is) to be manifested. By reason of the first it means a cause in the genus of *form*,[4] by reason of the second (a cause) in the genus of *one effecting*, by reason of the third (a cause) in the genus of *an end*.

What is asked, whether (predestination is) a *necessary* (cause), and/or a *contingent one*; a *universal* (cause), and/or a *particular one*; it must be said, that of all these manners of causing it has what belongs to (their) *perfection*, not what belongs to (their) imperfection. For of the property of a *universal* (cause)[5] it has an extension to many; of the property of a *particular one* a sufficiency for singulars; of the property of a *contingent one* it has a liberty of judgement, because (God) can cause and not cause. Moreover, it does not have (their) conditions of *imperfection*, because it has neither an insufficiency, just as a universal cause (does);

nor a limitation, just as a particular one (does); nor an inevitability, just as a necessary (cause does); nor a vertibility, just as a contingent (cause does).[6]

DOUBT VIII

Likewise, is asked concerning this which (Master Peter) says, that *the effect of predestination* is *an apportioning of grace*. For he seems to speak badly, because "*cause*" and "*effect*" are correlative (terms); therefore, since relatives are together by nature, whensoever there is a predestination, there is an apportioning of grace: therefore, no one has been predestined, unless he has grace. *But on the contrary* there is this, that predestination is *not of beings*, just as (St.) Augustine says in the book, ON FAITH TO PETER.[8]

I RESPOND: It must be said, that predestination is not always a cause in *act*, but (it is) in *habit*; and for that reason it is not necessary [non oportet], that an effect respond (to it) in *act*, but in *habit*.

On which account, from this, there is clear what is accustomed to be asked, "Whether predestination posits something in the one predestined?"; for it must be said, that it does not necessarily posit anything *concerning the present* or *an act*;[9] since many have been predestined, who are not (now) wicked, and many (have been predestined), who are (now) wicked; but it does posit something according to *habit* or *concerning the future*, by reason of which a man can *rejoice*, namely *because his name has been written in Heaven*.[10] And, when that will have been posited, it will be a great good; and that will be the reason for persisting in the good and for coming thoroughly to the Great and Most High Good; and, for that reason, this habitual good [bonum habituale] must be posited before the grace, which is according to the justice present.[11]

---

[1] A particular cause is that, which produces only one species of effect, v. g. fire (produces only) fire; on the other hand a universal cause is that, which produces various species of effects, v. g. the Sun, by whose influence, concurrent with other particular causes, diverse effects are produced.

[2] Understand: Master (Peter). — Then after *but not* [sed non] supply, together with codex Y, *whole* [tota].

[3] 1 Corinthians 3:9: *For we are God's helpers* [Dei enim sumus adiutores].

[4] Or (in the genus) of a formal, extrinsic (cause), i.e. an exemplar. Cf. above d. 3, p. I, a. sole, q. 2, p. 73, footnote 7. — A little above this, after *the Most High Goodness* [summa bonitas] the Vatican editions omits *(as It is) to be manifested* [manifestanda].

[5] Codex O subjoins this *cause* [causa].

[6] Cf. Alexander of Hales, SUMMA., p. I, q. 28, m. 4, a. 1; Bl. (now St.) Albertus (Magnus), here in a. 21; (Bl.) Peter of Tarentaise, here about the text.

[7] Aristotle, ON THE PREDICAMENTS, ch. "On *Relation*".

[8] Chapter 34, according to (its) sense; for he teaches, that the men predestined by God have been predestined *before all ages* and *before the constitution of the world*. This clearer sentence is proffered in his 26th Sermon, ch. 4, n. 4. Cf. above the text of Master (Peter), d. XXXVI,* ch. 1.

[9] The Vatican edition alone reads the word *act of evil* [mali actu] for *act* [actu].

[10] Luke 10:20: *Moreover, rejoice, that your names have been written in Heaven* [Gaudete autem, quod nomina vestra scripta sunt in caelis]. — Immediately after this for *a great good* [magnum bonum], which reading is that of codices M T aa and bb (ee by a second hand); the Vatican edition has only *great* [magnum].

[11] On this doubt and also on the question treated in it, whether predestination posits anything in the one predestined, cf. above a. 1. q. 1; Alexander of Hales, SUMMA., p. I. q. 28, m. 2. a. 1, and m. 4, a. 2; Bl. (now St.) Albertus (Magnus), here in a. 4; St. Thomas, here in q. 1, a. 1, and SUMMA., I, q. 23, a. 2; Richard (of Middleton), here in a. 1, q. 1 and on the text.

---

* *Trans. note*: Here the original footnote employed Arabic numerals instead, contrary to the custom of the Quaracchi editors, who in citing the text of Master Peter, always used Roman numerals.

DISTINCTION XLI

CHAPTER I

Whether there is any merit of obduration and/or mercy?

But, if we seek what merits [meritum] *obduration* and *mercy*, we find what merits obduration, but we do not find what merits mercy, because there is nothing meriting mercy—lest grace be emptied out—if it is not granted[1] freely, but is rendered according to merits. And so *He has mercy* according to the grace, which is given freely; but *He hardens against* (the good) according to the judgement, which is rendered according to merits. « Wherefore it is given to be understood, that just as God's reprobation is a '*not wishing to have mercy*', so God's obduration is a '*not having mercy*', so that nothing is imposed by Him, by which a man is worse, but there is only not paid out [erogetur] that which is better ».[2] — From these there is openly shown, what the Apostle[3] understood *mercy* (to be), (and) what (he understood) *obduration* (to be), and that [quia] he advocates nothing meriting *mercy*, however, *obduration* is not without merit, but has (as its cause God's) '*not wanting to have mercy*'. And predestination is accepted here for the word for *mercy*, and chiefly the effect of predestination, but God's eternal reprobation itself (is) not (accepted here for the word for) *obduration*, because there is nothing meriting that, but (obduration is) the privation or subtraction of grace, which in a certain manner is the effect of reprobation. Yet sometimes "*reprobation*" is accepted for "*obduration*", just as even "*predestination*" (is) for its effect, which is apportioned grace.[4] For the grace, which is apportioned, is the effect of predestination. — Therefore, since there are no (works) meriting the grace, which is apportioned to a man for justification; much less even (meriting) the predestination itself, by which God from eternity elected whom He wills, there can thus neither exist some meriting the reprobation, by which from eternity He foreknows certain ones (are) going to be wicked and (are) going to be damned: just as He elected Jacob, and reproved Esau,[5] which was not in virtue of their merits, which they then had, because they had none, since they themselves neither existed; nor on account of the future merits, which He foresaw, did He either elect the former, and/or reprove the latter.

CHAPTER II

On the various opinions of carnal (men) on this (matter).

However, certain (authors) have opined, that God had elected Jacob for this reason, because He foreknew that (he was) going to be such, as would believe in Him and serve Him. Which (St.) Augustine says in the book of RETRACTATIONS,[6] that he at one time thought, where he openly shows, that if he had been elected on account of (his) future merits, (his) election would already not be out of grace. Therefore, (St. Augustine says that) he was not for this reason elected by God, because he was going to be such, but he was made such out of (his) election, thus saying: « Disputing, what God elected in the one not yet born, whom He said, that the elder [maiorem] will serve, and what similarly He reproved in the same elder, not yet born, to this I have lead the reasoning, to say: "Therefore, God in (His) Foreknowledge did not elect anyone's works, which He himself is going to give (them), but He elected in (His) Foreknowledge (his) faith, and whom He foreknows is going to believe Him, him He elects, to give His own Holy Spirit, so that by working good (works) he might arrive at eternal life" ». — Behold here he openly says, that He did not elect him on account of (his) works, but on account of the faith, by which He foreknew[7] that he was going to believe. But because there is also merit in faith, just as in works, he retracted this, saying:[8] « I had not yet more diligently sought nor had I then found, what the election of grace is, concerning which the Apostle says: *The remainder shall be saved through the election of grace*; which certainly [utique] is not a grace, if it proceeds from merits, as that which is already given not according to grace, but is rendered according to a debt to merits, rather than being granted [donatur]. Consequently, that which I said immediately afterwards [continuo]: "For the Apostle[9] says the same: *The same God, who works all in all*." Never, however, was it said: "*God credits* [credit] *all in all*." And then I subjoined: "Therefore, that on which account [quod] we believe, is ours; but the good which we work, is His, who gives the Holy Spirit to (those) believing (in Him)." Indeed I would not say, if I did not already know, that faith itself is found among God's gifts [munera], which are given in the same spirit. Therefore,

---

[1] The Vatican edition and several edd., with cod. C, read *if it were not granted ... but is rendered* [donetur ... reddatur] (in the subjunctive).

[2] (St.) Augustine, To SIMPLICIANUS, Bk. I, q. 2, n. 15.

[3] Romans 9:18: *Therefore, He has mercy upon whom He will, and He hardens whom He wills* [Ergo cuius vult miseretur, et quem vult indurat]. — A little below this, codices B and D and edition 1 read *is not always without merit* [non est semper sine merito]. Immediately after this, the Vatican edition and the other editions also omit the words *but has (as its cause God's) 'not wanting to have mercy'* [sed habet nolle misereri].

[4] Codex A has *the apportioning of grace* [gratiae appositio].

[5] A reference to Malach. 1:2-3: *"Is Esau not the brother of Jacob?", says the Lord, and I have loved Jacob, but Esau I have held in hatred* [Nonne frater erat Esau Iacob, dicit Dominus, et dilexi Iacob, Esau autem odio habui]. Cf. Rom. 9:13.

[6] Bk. I, ch. 23, nn. 2 and 3. The retraction refers to what he said in his EXPOSITION OF THE EPISTLE OF ST. PAUL TO THE ROMANS, ch. 60. Cf. To

SIMPLICIANUS, Bk. I, q. 2, n. 8, and ON THE PREDESTINATION OF THE SAINTS, ch. 3, n. 7. — A little further below this, the Vatican edition, together with editions 2, 4, 5, 6, 8 and 9, has *such out of such an election* [ex tali electione talis] for *such out of (his) election* [ex electione talis].

[7] The Vatican edition and the other editions, except edition 1, *foresaw* [praevidit], breaking with the codices.

[8] Loc. cit.. — The passage from Sacred Scripture is Rom. 11:5. The Edition of (St.) Augustine's (works) has further down: *which certainly is not a grace, if any merits precede it, lest presently* [quae utique non est gratia, si eam merita ulla praecedant, ne iam]. The Vatican edition has: *which indeed (is) not out of grace, if merits precede it* [quae utique non ex gratia, si eam merita praecedant]. Our text is exhibited by editions 1, 6, and 8, to which the other editions and our codices consent, except that some editions have *(is) also not out of grace* [non et ex gratia], others *(is) not out of grace* [non ex gratia] for *is not a grace* [non est gratia].

[9] 1 Corinthians 12:6.

each is *ours* on account of the judgement [arbitrium] of the will, and each has been *given* through the spirit of faith and charity. — And that which I said a little afterwards: "For it is ours to believe and to will, but His to give to (those) believing and willing the faculty to work well through *the Holy Spirit, through whom charity is poured fourth in our hearts*",[1] is indeed true, but by the same rule each is also *His*, because He prepares (our) will, and each (is) *ours*, because (each) does not come to be, unless with us willing »: therefore, the merit of faith also comes from God's mercy. Therefore, not on account of faith and/or any merits did God elect some from eternity nor apportion the grace of justification[2] in time, but He has elected by His own gratuitous Goodness, that they would be good. Whence (St.) Augustine (says) in the book, ON THE PREDESTINATION OF THE SAINTS:[3] « Not because He foreknew that they were going to be such, did He for that reason elect (them), but (He elected them) so that they would be such through the election of His grace, *by which He has made us pleasing in His Beloved Son* ».

However, it seems that to these there can be opposed [adversari], what (St.) Augustine[4] says on the Prophet Malachias, where it is written: *Jacob I have loved, but Esau I have held in hatred*: « On whom He wills », he says, « He has mercy, and whom He wills, He hardens. But this will of God cannot be unjust. For it comes from the most secret merits [ocultissimis meritis], because sinners themselves, after having made (themselves) one mass on account of the general sin, yet there is among them no[5] diversity. Therefore, something takes precedence [praecedit] among sinners, by which, though they are not yet justified, they are made worthy of justification. And again there takes precedence among other sinners, that by which they are worthy of being dulled [obtusione] ». — Behold here (St.) Augustine seems to say, that the very will of God, by which He chooses some, (and) reproves others, comes about [proveniat][6] on account of merits, but *most secret ones*, that is, that in virtue of merits He willed to elect some, reprove others, and that in virtue of merits the grace of justification is apportioned to some, to others not, whence they are dulled. But what he wanted to understand, is not known, unless perhaps this be said, that he understood, that which we said above he retracted. For in the same place he also subjoined immediately certain other (things), which in the book of RETRACTATIONS[7] he openly retracts; which will be clear to one reading each. Whence it is verisimilar, that even in the aforementioned, he retracted it.

However, certain (authors) accept that it is to be said in this sense, not because anyone is predestined in virtue of (his) merits (and/or) merits the grace of justification, but because some are not to such an extent wicked, as to merit that grace is not imparted to them. For no one can merit God's grace, through which he is justified, yet, he can merit, that it not be apportioned, such that he be thoroughly cast off. And, indeed, some came to so great a depth of iniquity, as to merit this, such that they were worthy of it; but others live thus, even if they do not merit the grace of justification, yet, they do not entirely merit to be repelled nor that grace be subtracted from them. And, for that reason, he said, that among certain

sinners there takes precedence that by which they are worthy of justification, and among others that by which they are worthy of being dulled. — But this (understanding) is frivolous.

« On the other hand, many seeking to give a reckoning concerning this depth, and striving according to the conjectures of their own heart to think of the inscrutable height of God's judgements, went off into the fables of vanity, saying that souls sin on high in Heaven and according to their sins are directed to bodies in virtue of their merits, and are enclosed in (them) as quasi prisons worthy of them. Such as these went after their own thoughts, and wanting to dispute concerning God's depth, they were overturned into a depth, saying, that souls lived [conversatas] before in Heaven and there they did something of good and/or evil and in virtue of their merits they were thrust down to earthly bodies. But this the Catholic Faith rejects on account of the evident sentence of the Apostle, by which he says:[8] *When they were not yet born, nor had done anything of good and/or evil* »[9] etc. Therefore, faithful ignorance is better than temerarious knowledge. « Therefore, He elected those whom He willed by a gratuitous mercy, not because they were going to be faithful, but so that they would be faithful, and He have them grace, not because they were faithful, but so that they would come to be (such). For the Apostle says:[10] *I have laid hold of mercy, that I may be faithful*; he did not say, because I was faithful. He indeed is given and as one faithful, but it has also been given before, so that he would be faithful ». Thus, He also reproved those whom He willed, not on account of (their) future merits, which He foresaw, yet by a truth most righteous [rectissima] and removed from our senses.[11]

But one askes, whether, must as there is said that *He has elected* certain ones, so that they would come to be good and faithful, so it ought to be conceded, that *He has reproved* certain ones, to be wicked and unfaithful, and *that He hardens (them) against (the good)*, so that they sin; which is in no manner necessary [oportet] to be conceded. For *reprobation* is not thus the cause of evil, as *predestination* is the cause of good; nor does *obduration* so make a man wicked, according to the manner which *mercy* makes (him) good.

CHAPTER III

Whether those which God once knows and/or foreknows, He always knows and foreknows, and always knew and foreknew?

Moreover, it is necessary [oportet] that one consider, whether all those which God once knows and/or foreknows, He always knows[12] and knew, and foreknows and foreknew; or whether He formerly [olim] knew and/or foreknew what He now does not know and/or foreknow. — Concerning (His) *Foreknowledge* we first respond, saying, that He *foreknew* many (things), which He does not now foreknow. For, since His Foreknowledge is not but of future (things), out of which those which were going to be, come to be present and/or pass away, cease to be under God's *Foreknowledge*, but always are under (His) *Knowledge*

[1] Romans 5:5.
[2] The Vatican edition alone has *of sanctification* [sanctificationis].
[3] Chapter 19, n. 38. — The passage from Sacred Scripture is Eph. 1:6.
[4] In his book, OF EIGHTY-THREE QUESTIONS, q. 68, n. 4. — The passages from Sacred Scripture are Malach. 1:2-3 and Rom. 9:18. The Vulgate and (St.) Augustine read: *On whom He wills* [Cuius vul] for *On whom He wills* [Vui vult]. — The Vatican edition and editions 4, 6 and 8, having omitted very many (words), exhibit: *(St.) Augustine's book OF EIGHTY-THREE QUESTIONS: on whom He wills* [Augustinus lib. 83 Quaestionum: cui vult].
[5] Thus the codices, editions 1 and 6, and the original. The Vatican edition, together with very many editions, has *yet among them there is not a little* [tamen nonnulla inter eos].
[6] The codices and edition 1 have *comes* [veniat].
[7] Bk. I, ch. 26. — A little before this the Vatican edition and editions 4 and 6 omit *also* [etiam].

[8] Romans 9:11-12. The Apostle continues thus: *so that God's proposal according to election might remain, not out of works, but out of the One calling it has been said to him: Because the elder shall serve the younger* [ut secundum electionem propositum Dei maneret, non ex operibus, sed ex vocante dictum est ei: Quia maior serviet minori.].
[9] What precedes this has been taken from (St.) Augustine's, 165th Sermon, ch. 5, n. 6, but with not a few things transposed and/or changed.
[10] 1 Corinthians 7:25. — In regard to (their) sense, these propositions have been taken from (St.) Augustine's, RETRACTATIONS, Bk. I, ch. 23, n. 4, and from his ON THE PREDESTINATION OF THE SAINTS, ch. 3, n. 7.
[11] ON DIVERSE QUESTIONS TO SIMPLICIANUS, Bk. I, q. 2, n. 16, with a few (things) changed.
[12] The Vatican edition and editions 2, 4, 6, 7 and 9 have less congruously *does know* [scit] in the indicative, but breaking with all the codices.

Therefore, God foreknew from eternity all, which (things) were going to be, nor does He cease *to foreknow*, except when the cease to be future. Nor when He ceases to foreknow somethings, which He used to foreknow before, does He know them less, than He cognized (them to be) before. For it is not said from the defect of His Knowledge, that He foreknew somethings at some time, which He does not now foreknow, but (it is said) from the reckoning of the word which is "*foreknowledge*". For "*to foreknow*" is "*to know beforehand*" how [quam] something comes to be. And for that reason God cannot be said to foreknow, except what are going to be.

However, of (God's) *Knowledge* we speak otherwise. For God knows always all which He knows at any time. For every knowledge, which He at any time has, He always had and has and will have. — But to this there is thus opposed: "He formerly knew, that this man, who has been born, (was) going to be born, (and) now He does not know, that he (is) going to be born: therefore, He knew something, which now He does not know"; and other infinite (objections) of this kind could be brought forward.[1] — But to this we say, that of the nativity of this man and the creation of the world He now also knows the same, as He used to know, before they came to be, though at that time and this [tunc et tunc] it is necessary to express with diverse words the understanding [sententiam] of this. For what then was going to be, now has passed away; and for that reason (one's) words are to be commuted to designate this; just as (when) speaking of diverse times we designate the same day now through this adverb "*tomorrow*", while it is still future, now through "*today*", while it is present, now through "*yesterday*", while it is past. And for before the world was created, God used to know that it (was) to be created, before it was created, for He knew (it as) created. Nor is it that He *knows diverse (things)*, but (He knows) entirely *the same (thing)* concerning the creation of the world; jut as the ancient Fathers believed, that Christ (was) going to be born and going to die; but we believe, that He has already (been) born and (has) died; and yet we and they do not believe diverse (things), but the same (thing). « For the times », as (St.) Augustine says,[2] « have varied; and for that reasons the words have changed, not the Faith ». Therefore, let us hold undoubtedly, that God always knows all, which He at any time knows.

COMMENTARY ON DISTINCTION XLI

On the passive causality or the meritorious cause of predestination and reprobation.

But, if we seek what merits obduration and mercy etc..

THE DIVISION OF THE TEXT

Above, Master (Peter) dealt with the active causality of predestination and reprobation. In this part, he inquires concerning (its) *passive* causality, whether, namely, predestination and reprobation have in us a meritorious cause; and this, indeed, he principally intends in this Distinction, which has two parts. In the *first*, Master (Peter) investigates the principal proposal; in the *second*, he moves a certain question, which has (its) rise from the preceding, namely, whether God ceases to know and/or foreknow something. From the manifestation of which he makes clear the interminability of the Divine Knowledge, there (where he says): *Moreover, it is necessary that one consider* etc..

The *first* part has four parts. In the first, Master (Peter) determines the truth, showing that *reprobation* has a meritorious cause as much as regards what it connotes [connotatum], which is obduration; not so *predestination* as much as regards what is connotes, which is 'being made pleasing' [gratificatio]. But, in the second, Master (Peter) removes a certain opinion, which could lead a man into error, there (where he says): *However, certain (authors) have opined* etc. In the third, he removes its defense, there (where he says): *However it seems that to these there can be opposed* etc. In the fourth, he removes a presumptuous inquisition in this question, showing that some, wanting to give a reckoning of this depth of Divine predestination had fallen into a depth of error, there (where he says): *On the other hand, many seeking to give a reckoning concerning this depth* etc..

Moreover, it is necessary that one consider, whether all those which God once knows etc.. This is the *second* part, in which Master (Peter) determines the question, whether God ceases

---

[1] The Vatican and the other edd., except ed. 1, have *can be said* [dici possunt], contradicting the codd., (some) of which, however, (such as) codices A B and D have *can* [possunt] for *could* [possent]. — Concerning the following sentence of Master (Peter) and the Nominalists, that they are entirely the same propositions concerning the same thing, but proffered under diverse differences of tenses, it must be said, that (this explanation) is insufficient and in part false, cf. (St. Bonaventure's) Commentary, here in a. 2, q. 2. — Master (Peter) speaks of the same matter, also, below in d. XLIV, ch. 2.

[2] ON THE GOSPEL OF ST. JOHN, tract 45, n. 9, according to (its) sense. — A little before this, the Vatican edition and editions 2, 3, 4, 7, 8 and 9 omit *already* [iam] before *(been) born and (has) died* [natum et mortuum].

to know and/or foreknow something; and similarly there is the question, whether He ceases to predestine someone; and this part has two parts. In the first he determines concerning (God's) Foreknowledge, that it does happen to cease to foreknow something. But, in the second, he determines concerning (God's) Knowledge, there (where he says): *However, of (God's) Knowledge we speak otherwise*, where he says, that God ceases to know nothing; and in each part he first moves a question, (and) second determines (it).

TREATMENT OF THE QUESTIONS

For an understanding of the present Distinction, two (questions) are principally asked.

First, there is asked concerning the causality of predestination.

Second, concerning the sempiternity or interminability of the Divine Knowledge.

As much as regards the first, two (questions) are asked.

First, there is asked, whether predestination and/or reprobation have, in us, a meritorious cause.

Second, whether they have in God a motive reason [rationem motivam].

ARTICLE I

On the causality of Divine predestination.

QUESTION I

Whether predestination and/or reprobation has, in us, a meritorious cause?

Moreover, that they have in us a *meritorious cause*, is shown in this manner:

1. First concerning *reprobation*. In the ninth (chapter of St. Paul's Letter) to the Romans,[1] on that verse: *Esau I held in hatred*, the Gloss (says): « Esau, with grace subtracted, has been reproves through justice »; but justice respects merits: therefore, reprobation is out of merits.

2. Likewise, through "reprobation" naught is meant but these three, namely, "*an eternal hatred*", "*a temporal obduration*" and "*final damnation*"; but all these have in us a merit, because God hates no one except on account of (his) demerits nor does He harden (anyone) against (the good) nor does He damn (them): ergo etc..

3. Likewise, by (His) antecedent Will *God wishes all men to come to be saved*:[2] if, therefore, He reproves anyone, this is by (His) consequent Will, for no one, of himself, does He create for torment [ad supplicium]; but (His) consequent Will is a concession *on account of us, as a cause* [concessio ex nostra causa]; but there is nothing on account of a cause [non est ex alia causa] other than merits: ergo etc..

4. Likewise, concerning *predestination* it is similarly shown. (Pope St.) Gregory (the Great)[3] says and (St.) Augustine (too), that predestination is helped by the prayers of the Saints; but one's own faith is worth more than the faith of another: therefore, by one's own merit and (that) of another anyone can by asking obtain [impetrare], that he be predestined.

5. Likewise, no one has been predestined unless as one persevering finally in grace, and[4] vice versa: therefore, they are convertibles; but anyone can merit final perseverance: therefore, he can merit, that he is predestined.

6. Likewise, what is able unto greater [potest in maius] is able unto less and/or an equal [potest in minus vel aequale], for an equal reason; but a man can merit to have God, which is the greatest (merit) among all; he can

---

[1] Verse 13. — The words of the Gloss, in (Nicolas) of Lyra, are these: Jacob (was) elected by grace, not by merit, Esau with grace subtracted (interlinear Gloss; and the ordinary Gloss adjoins: He reproved through justice).

[2] 1 Timoth 2:4. — The argument itself has been taken from (St. John) Damascene, ON THE ORTHODOX FAITH, Bk. II, ch. 29, where there is said: It is necessary to know this, that God (by His primary and) antecedent Will wills that all come to be saved and (become) co-shares of His Kingdom. For he did not establish us, to punish (us), but because He is Good, (he made us) for this, to be participants in His own Goodness. Furthermore He wants sinners to be punished, because He is just. And so that first, antecedent Will is also said (to be His) Good Pleasure, of which He Himself is the cause; but the second, consequent Will (is) also (said to be) a permission having its rise *out of us as cause* (τὸ δὲ δεύ-

τερον ἑπόμενον θέλημα καὶ παραχώρησις, ἐξ ἡμετέρας αἰτίας). Cf. below d. 46, q. 1. — Next, after *this is* [hoc est] edition 1 interjects *only* [solum]; after a few (words) the Vatican edition alone has *is a consequent* [est consequens] for *is a concession* [est concessio].

[3] In his DIALOGUES., Bk. I, ch. 8 (where he says): « Those (things), which holy men worked by praying, were thus predestined, to be obtained by prayers ». (St.) Augustine, ON THE GIFT OF PERSEVERANCE, ch. 22, n. 60: For why is it not rather said: and if they are not yet called, let us pray for them so that they may be called? For, perhaps, they have been thus predestined, so as to be conceded to our prayers and (so that) they may accept the same grace, by which they want (to be) and are made elected. Cf. also ENARRATIONS ON THE PSALMS, Ps. 105:23, there under n. 21.

[4] For *and* [et] very many codices, together with edition 1, have *nor* [nec], faultily.

also merit salvation, which is equal to that which it is to be predestined: ergo etc..

BUT ON THE CONTRAY: 1. Every merit antecedes that of which it is the merit, because it disposes to that; but predestination and reprobation precede our 'being': therefore, they do not fall under our merit.[1]

2. Likewise, every merit is in some manner the cause of that which is merited; but predestination and reprobation are eternal, but merits are temporal: therefore, the temporal is the cause of the eternal; which is impossible.

3. Likewise, in particular concerning *predestination* seems (that which is said) in the third (chapter of St. Paul's Letter) to Titus:[2] *Not on account of the works of justice, which we have done, but according to His own mercy has He saved us.*

4. Likewise, grace is an effect of predestination; but the first grace antecedes every merit and is the cause of every merit: therefore, it does not fall under merit, and it is grace by this very (fact), because it is given without merits: therefore neither (does) predestination (fall under merit).

CONCLUSION

Neither predestination nor reprobation in regard to (their) eternal proposal *fall under merit, but in regard to* what they connote *reprobation falls under merit simply, but predestination* secundum quid.

I RESPOND: To understand this it must be noted, that in predestination three (things) are understood: the first is an *eternal proposal*; the second is *a temporal 'being made pleasing'* [temporalis gratificatio]; but the third (is) an *eternal glorification.* Similarly, in reprobation three (things) are understood, namely an *eternal proposal,*[3] and a *temporal obduration*, and an *eternal damnation.* — As much as regards the *first* and *last*, it must be similarly judged: for the last ones, namely *the punishment* and *the glory*, simply fall under merit; but the first, namely the eternal proposal, by the very (fact) that it is eternal, cannot have a meriting [meritum]. However, as much as regards *the middle one*, which is *'being made pleasing'* [gratificatio] and *obduration*, it must be judged differently. For *obduration* simply falls under demerit or under an evil merit [malo merito], but *'being made pleasing'* (falls) simply neither under merit, nor simply outside of (it). — For there is the merit of *the fitting*, of *the worthy* and of *the completely worthy*. The merit of *the fitting* [meritum congrui] is, when a sinner

does what is *in himself* and *on behalf of himself*. The merit of *the worthy* [meritum digni], when a just man does (something) *for another*. The merit of *the completely worthy* [meritum condigni], when the just man works *on behalf of himself*, because grace is ordained for this on account of the one completely worthy [ex condigno]; but to merit grace for another (is) not entirely *on account of the one completely worthy,*[4] because the sinner (for whom he merits) is unworthy of every good, nor (is it) only *on account of the fitting* [ex congruo], because the just man is worthy to be heard out. — Therefore, *'being made pleasing'* can fall under the merit of *the fitting* in regard to him being made pleasing, (and) under the merit of *the worthy* as much as regards another holy man, (and) under the merit of *the completely worthy* as much as regards neither, and this, properly speaking, is merit.

Therefore, one must respond to the question, whether predestination and reprobation fall under merit, that[5] simply speaking, as much as regards (their) principal signified, neither falls under merit: but as much as regards what (they) connote, reprobation falls under merit simply, but *predestination*, secundum quid.

Therefore, the reasons proving, that predestination does not fall under merit, are to be conceded; similarly (those proving), that neither (does) reprobation.

1. To that, therefore, which if first objected concerning the Gloss, that Esau has been reproved through justice; it must be said, that "reprobation" there is accepted on behalf of what it connotes,[6] which is obduration.

2. To that which is objected, that eternal hatred falls under merit; it must be said, that *"eternal hatred"* means two (things): both *what it principally signifies* [principale significatum] and *what it connotes* [connotatum], because God hates no one as much as regards (His) *affection*, but only as much as regards (their) *effect*. And the first is not out of merits, but the second (is); which is clear, if it is resolved, because hatred is a *proposal to punish*; but no one merits a *proposal*, but (one can merit) *a punishment*.

3. To that which is objected, that He reproves no one except[7] by (His) consequent Will; it must be said, that (His) Will is not said (to be) "consequent", because it is consequent to our merits according to a reckoning of *will*, but only according to a reckoning of *the willed* — for God wills something, which we do merit — and for that reason because *the willed* is what is connoted, it is clear that etc..

4. To that which is objected concerning predestination, that it is helped by the prayers of the Saints; it must be said, that that is understood according to the reckoning of *what it connotes*, which is the grace, which holy men can by asking obtain by their own prayers; and yet it does not follow, that a man can by asking obtain (it) for himself, because for this that he obtains (it) by asking,

---

[1] On this and the following arguments, cf. (St.) Augustine, ON DIVERSE QUESTIONS TO SIMPLICIANUS, Bk. I, q. 2, and ON THE GIFT OF PERSEVERANCE. Cf. also the text of Master (Peter) here, in ch. 2. — In the minor proposition, codex O after the words *and reprobation* [et reprobatio] proceeds thus: *antecede every merit, because they precede our 'being'* [antecedunt omne meritum, quia praecedunt nostrum esse]; codex T (in the margin) reads thus: *precede all our merit and even our 'being'* [praecedunt omne meritum nostrum et etiam nostrum esse].

[2] Verse 5.

[3] For *proposal* [propositum] the Vatican edition, together with codex cc, has *hatred* [odium], perhaps because in the 2nd opposed argument this is also read; but since it is exhibited in what is subjoined and even in the response to n. 2, we have judged the reading of the codices to be received into the text. Then, for *temporal obduration* [temporalis obduratio], very many codices have *temporal ordination* [temporalis ordinatio], to which reading the subjoined is repugnant.

[4] This second part of the proposition: *but to merit grace* etc. [ad gratiam autem], the Vatican edition, having changed the punctuation, transformed into a new principal proposition: *A grace to be merited for another is not entirely* etc. [Gratia alteri promerenda non est omnino etc.].

[5] Very many codices, together with edition 1, have less congruously *because* [quia].

[6] Codices L and O read *an effect or what it connotes* [effectu sive connotato].

[7] The Vatican edition and codex cc omit *except* [nisi], faultily. — On (God's) consequent Will, which always connotes the coming forth of an effect, cf. below d. 46, q. 1, in the body (of the Response). — At the end of the response, after *it is clear* [patet] codices L and O continue thus: *that merit is not in respect of will, but in respect of the willed* [quod meritum non est respectu voluntatis, sed respectu voliti].

it is necessary, that he be *worthy* to merit (it), and this is not but through grace.

5. To that which is objected, that it is the same to have been predestined and to persevere finally in grace; it must be said, that it is not *the same*, but (it is) *convertible*. But it does not follow, that if anyone can merit one of the convertibles, that he can also (merit) the rest;[1] just as it does not follow, that if something is the cause of one of the convertibles, that it is the cause of the other; this is manifest.

6. To that which is objected: what is able unto greater, is able unto less; it must be said, that this is true, if *it is* equally *ordered* to each. For if it has an ordination to the greater, and does not have an ordination to the lesser, even though it is able unto the greater, yet it does not follow, that (it is such) unto the lesser; similarly in the proposed. For grace is ordered to merit God as the One glorifying, not as the One predestining, similarly (it is ordered) to glory, not to the first grace.

SCHOLIUM

I. For understanding this and the following Question more easily, it helps to note beforehand the following.

1. One must distinguish between the reason for *willing* and the reason for *the willed*. For God by a unique act wills the end and all those which are for the end; whence « '*to will the end*' is not for God a cause of willing those which are for the end; but yet He does will, that those which are for the end be ordered unto the end. Therefore, He wills, *that this is on account of that*, but *He does not will this on account of that* » (St. Thomas, SUMMA., I, q. 19, a. 5; cf. Cajetan's Commentary; and the SUMMA CONTRA GENTILES, Bk. I, ch. 86). — The same distinction between the reason for *willing* and the reason for *the willed* is employed by St. Bonaventure, below in d. 45, Doubt 3, and he explains the difference between our will and the Divine (Will) thus, « that our will, when it is excited by a willed, has (its) cause and reason from it both as much as *regards itself* and as much as *regards the willed*, most of all when it wills something, which is for the sake of an end; but God's Will, the act of which He Himself is, because It is not excited for any reason *other than Itself*, cannot have a cause as much as *regards Itself*. But (Its) *willed* sometimes has a cause other than the Will, sometimes only the Will, as in the creation of the world. *The (Divine) Will* has a reason, but not a cause, because It is not irrational ». Wherefore etc.. — (Bl. John Duns) Scotus uses the same distinction (REPORTATIO, here in the q. sole, nn. 3-7), to persuade his own sentence, that on *God's* part there is neither in predestining nor in reproving any other reason except the Divine Essence; and that on the part of *the effect* there is a reason for *reprobation*, but not for *predestination*.

2. An *efficient cause*, a *meritorious cause*, (and) a *motive reason* differ. God alone is the *efficient* cause of grace and glory; the *meritorious* cause, which either is reduced to a disposition and/or in some manner to an efficient cause, cannot *be* except in the creature, but it has been *foreseen* by God. A *motive reason* [ratio motiva] differs from a *meritorious cause*. For a *reason* opens more broadly [latius patet] than a *cause*, which is conceived as one influencing [influens] the effect; whence one divine attribute can be conceived by us as *the reason* for the other, but least of all as *(its) cause*. Likewise, the term "*motive*" [motiva] opens more broadly than "*meritorious*" [meritoria], as is manifest. Hence it is, that a *motive reason* can be conceived both on the part of *God*, v. g. as a showing of His mercy, and on the part of *the one predestined*; and on his part (it) again (can be conceived) in a twofold manner: either to the extent that this reason is founded in some *merit* (and then it coincides with the meritorious cause), and/or as it supposes only something motive of a *congruity*.

3. In predestination *what is principally signified* [principale signifcatum] and *what is connoted* [connotatum] is distinguished by the Seraphic Doctor. The former is *the eternal preordination* or *proposal* of the Divine Will either to have mercy and/or to punish (cf. here in reply to n. 2, and in q. 2, in the body of the Response); but *what it connotes* comprehends *the effects* of the Divine predestination, which (effects) as *the willed* are ordered to the Divine Will through a real relation; and consequently

even God's Will is terminated through a relation of *the reason* for these willed, which are the secondary object of the same Will. The principal *effects* of predestination are three: *vocation*, which in adults implies a series of actual graces; *justification*, through the infusion of habitual grace; *glorification*, which implies the grace of final perseverance.

4. That these *effects* or these *willed* are ordered *to one another* according to a reckoning of some causality [secundum rationem alicuius causalitatis], is the common sentence: that is, that the effect « (is) indeed a posterior (cause and reason) for the prior according to the reckoning of a *final* cause; but the prior (is a cause of a reason) for the posterior according to the reckoning of a *meritorious* cause, which is reduced to the disposition of the matter » (St. Thomas, SUMMA, I, q. 23, a. 5). It is also certain, that *the vocation* in regard to the first grace and even in regard to the series of actual graces does not fall under merit; nor does *justification* (fall) under *condign* merit, though adults « *are disposed* by freely assenting and cooperating » to justification (Trent, Session 6, ch. 5). Likewise, it is certain, that the one justified by the assistance of grace « *truly merits the increase* of grace, an *eternal life* and *the attainment* of eternal life itself, *yet, if he passes away in grace* » (ibid., can. 32). Finally it is certain, that *the execution* of this condition: "yet, if he passes away in grace", or « *that great gift of perseverance unto the end* » (ibid., can. 16) « without the special assistance of God » (ibid., can 22) can neither be obtained nor merited de condigno by the justified. But since neither the first nor the last of the temporal effects of predestination, namely, vocation and final perseverance, fall under merit, *the whole series* of the effects of predestination ought to be judged gratuitous, even though in them there is implied in a multiple manner the cooperation and causality of a free will.

5. In meritorious acts « what is from free will and from predestination is not distinct » (St. Thomas, loc. cit.), because « the whole effect is from the created cause, and the whole (is) from the infinite, uncreated Will » (St. Bonaventure, below in d. 45, a. 2, q. 2, in reply to n. 1), yet *not totally* . Whence it follows, that the same meritorious act is *the whole effect of predestination* and *God's gift*, though under another respect *the whole* can even be *from free will*; it also follows, that those same which are *God's gifts* can be *our merits* (Pope Celestine I, Epistle 21, ch. 12).

6. The effects of predestination, both each singly and all collectively, just as they have an order to one another, so, too, on their own part they have a real relation to God, who is the first efficient, exemplary and final cause of each one and of all together; whence God is by theologians rightly said (to be) "the *first* and *principal* cause of salvation"; yet, not *the sole* (cause), since He least of all excludes the actions of second causes, nay rather He implies them and orders (them) to His own effects. Otherwise there would be no merit nor demerit,

---

[1] Codex I here inserts: *for of convertibles there is frequently a cause of one of the two, but not of its very self, such as the truth of the thing is the cause of the truth of the proposition, and man is the cause of (his being) risible* [nam convertibilium est causa alterius frequenter, non tamen sui ipsius, ut veritas rei est causa veritatis propositionis, et homo est causa risibilis]; and similarly in codex T (in the margin) there is read: *for one of the convertibles is often the cause of the other, yet it is not the cause of itself, such as man is the cause of (his being) risible* [nam unum convertibilium saepe est causa alterius, non tamen est causa sui ipsius, ut homo est causa risibilis].

nor would the ancient sentence (The Epistle of the Synod of Bishops in exile in Sardinia) be true: « God saves freely and damns justly ».

II. In the Response there is distinguished a threefold merit, namely, in addition to the merit of *the completely worthy* [meritum condigno], and of *the fitting* [de congruo], (there is) also the merit of *the worthy* [meritum digni] (which now is commonly subsumed under the merit *of the fitting*), by which a just man through his own suffrages obtains graces for others from God. On this threefold division and the other subdivisions, cf. SENT., Bk. II, d. 27, a. 2. qq. 2 and 3, and SENT., Bk. III, d. 4, a. 2. q. 2, d. 18, a. 1, q. 2.

The words in the body (of the Response): « The merit of the fitting [Meritum congrui] is, when a sinner does what is in himself », gave certain (authors), such as Vasquez, occasion to blame the Seraphic Doctor, as if he taught, that through the works of the natural order a disposition to justification can be wrought. That this interpretation is entirely alien to the mind of the Seraphic Doctor, can be gathered even from the words just following: « a sinner is unworthy of every good », and more clearly from Doubt 3 of this Distinction. In other passages the Saint manifestly teaches, that the disposition to justification requires « a grace prevenient and assisting the will »; cf. SENT., Bk. II, d. 28, a. 2, q. 1, d. 27, a. 2, qq. 1 and 2, SENT., Bk. IV, d. 15, p. I, q. 5; and St. Thomas, SUMMA., I, II, q. 109, a. 6, q. 112, a. 2. On the celebrated axiom: "To the one doing what is in himself, God does not deny grace", SENT., Bk. II, d. 28, a. 2. q. 1, in reply to n. 4. — Moreover, because those words posited in the body (of the Response) were not said precisely of the disposition to justification, Father Trigosus thinks that they can be expounded also of *vocation* in general, by accepting *"the merit of the fitting"* [meritum congrui] in the broader sense, to the extent that he who naturally lives well, rather than the impious, who by continuous sins provokes more the wrath of God daily, may seem *less unworthy* of grace.

III. That that which *is principally signified* in predestination, namely, *the eternal proposal* of the Divine Will, is gratuitous, though by a reckoning of *the willed* the glorification and reprobation are consequent to our merits and demerits, is manifestly taught here in the body (of the Response) and in the solution to n. 3 and in the final words of the reply to n. 6; St. Thomas (here in q. 1, a. 3, in reply to n. 5), (Bl. John Duns) Scotus and the other ancient doctors are entirely in agreement. — In the solution to n. 4 there is taught, with the common sentence, that predestination in regard to *the effect* of grace is helped by the prayers of the Saints (cf. St. Thomas, here in q. 1, a. 4; SUMMA, I, q. 23, a. 8; DE VERITATE, q. 6, a. 6.). — In the solution to n. 6 there is supposed, that not all convertibles are formally the same, as is clear in (this) example: "the risible is rational". Hence it follows, that in this manner one infers falsely: 'anyone can merit final perseverance, therefore, also predestination'. But neither can a man *properly merit* final perseverance, yet, when he does not lack grace, he can by asking suppliantly obtain it from God.

IV. Alexander of Hales, SUMMA., p. I, q. 28, m. 3, a. 1. — (Bl. John Duns) Scotus, on this and the following question, in each version, here in the q. sole. — St. Thomas, here in a. 3; SUMMA., I, q. 23, a. 5; DE VERITATE., q. 6, a. 2; SUMMA CONTRA GENTILES., Bk. III, c. 163. — Bl. (now St.) Albertus (Magnus), here in a. 2; SUMMA., p. I, tr. 16, m. 3, a. 2. — (Bl.) Peter of Tarentaise, here in q. 2, a. 1, and q. 3, a. 1. — Richard of Middleton, here in a. 2, q. 1, and a. 3, q. 1. — Giles the Roman, on this and the following question, here in 1st princ., q. 2, a. 1, and d. 40, 2nd princ., qq. 1 and 2. — Durandus (of Saint-Pourçain), on this and the following question, here in qq. 2 and 3. — (Bl.) Dionysius the Carthusian, on this and the following question, here in q. 1. — (Gabriel) Biel, on this and the following question, here in the q. sole.

QUESTION II

Whether predestination and reprobation have, in God, a motive reason?

Second, there is asked, whether predestination and reprobation have, in God, a *motive reason*. And that (it is) so, seems:

1. Through the Canon of Genesis, in the eighteen (chapter):[1] *The Lord said: Will I be able to conceal from Abraham what I am going to do, since he is going to be unto a great nation, and is going to precept his own house, to keep My covenant?* Therefore, the Lord wanted to reveal (it) to Abraham himself on account of the consideration of (his) future good (deeds): therefore, since He foresees these from eternity, for an equal reason He predestines out of a foreknowledge of future good (deeds).

2. Likewise, (St.) Ambrose (says) on the ninth (chapter of St. Paul's) Letter to the Romans:[2] « I shall give grace to him, whom I will have known (is) going to return to me, after (his) error, with (his) whole heart »; speaking in the person of the Lord: therefore, the reason, why [quare] the Lord proposes to give grace, is, because He foresaw something future in the man.

3. Likewise, it is shown *by reason*, that every will, by the very (fact) that (it is) a will, is rational:[3] therefore, if this belongs to perfection in a will, that it is on account of a reason [ex ratione], this is found most of all in the Divine Will: therefore, since "predestination" means a "divine proposal", it will be on account of a reason.

4. Likewise, everyone electing wisely elects those among (his) household servants, in which he sees better past morals, and similarly, whom He knew were more faithful; and if he could cognize (things) future, much more would he elect and reject on account of (his) prevision of future goods and evils than of ones past. Therefore, if God is the One electing most wisely, therefore, He accepts the reason for electing or reproving from (His) Foresight or Foreknowledge.

5. Likewise, no one electing wisely elects beforehand (things) entirely indistant (to one another),[4] most of all, if he can accept all in an equally congruous manner; but God prefers one to another in election: ergo etc..

6. Likewise, if the Divine proposal or predestination only had (as its) reason God's will, and no other, then, therefore, it seems that (there is) a parcity in the Divine

---

[1] Verses 17-19, in which text the older codices, with ed. 1, have *from* [ab] explicitly before *Abraham* [Abraham]. In the conclusion, for *He foresees* [praevideat] the Vatican ed., with cod. cc, has *provides* [provideat].

[2] Verse 15. — The commentary, which is cited here as (St.) Ambrose's, is denied to be his by critics, cf. above the text of Master Peter, d. XIX, p. I, ch. 4, p. 337, footnote 8. — At the end of the argument for *He foresees* [praevidit] not a few codices, among which is even codex T, and also edition 1, read *He foresaw* [praevidet].

[3] Aristotle, ON THE SOUL, Bk. III, texts 42 and 50 (chs. 9 and 19),

and (St. John Damascene), ON THE ORTHODOX FAITH, Bk. II, ch. 22. — St. Anselm, ON THE TRUTH, ch. 12, teaches the same, saying: Every will just as it wills something, so wills on account of something.

[4] Cf. above d. 40, a. 3, q. 1, p. 714, footnote 8. For the interpretation of the word *(things) indistant (to one another)* [indistantia], there is cited (St. Severinus) Boethius, ON THE DIFFERENCES OF THE TOPICS, Bk. III: « Of (things) similar there is the same judgement ». — The Vatican edition after *indistant* [indistantia] adjoins *or indifferent* [seu indifferentia].

Will — for if He wanted to save all, all would be saved, and there is no other reason, except because He does not want (it) — therefore, His Will is not most liberal nor the best.[1]

7. Likewise, if there were no other reason than[2] (His) Will, therefore, when God proposes to damn (someone) by reproving (him), if He would will to damn someone without any reason by (His) Will alone, therefore, He seems (to be) most cruel, and that He has made men for punishment [ad supplicium].

8. Likewise, if by (His) Will alone He predestines and reproves, not by a precognized reason, it seems, therefore, according to this, that He is an acceptor of persons; which is contrary to that which is said in the tenth (chapter) of Acts:[3] *In truth I have found* [comperi], *that God is not an acceptor of persons.*

BUT ON THE CONTRARY: 1. In the thirty-third (chapter) of Exodus (there is written):[4] *I shall have mercy to whom I have mercy, and I shall be clement upon whom it has pleased Me*: therefore, the first and most powerful reason for Divine mercy and predestination is God's good pleasure and Will.

2. Likewise, in the eleventh[5] (chapter of the Gospel of St.) Matthew the Son says: *Thou hast revealed to these little ones, and has hidden these from the wise; thus Father, since in this manner was it pleasing before Thee*: therefore if the Son gives [reddit] the best reason, the Divine pleasure alone is the reason.

3. Likewise, the Apostle, on this question, says in the ninth[6] (chapter of his Letter) to the Romans: *Does a potter not have the power, to make of the same mass (of clay) some vessels, indeed, unto honor, others unto contumely?* For if one would seek from the craftsman, why of one part of the mass he makes a beautiful vessel and from the other a vile one, since the whole mass is equally good, there is no other reason, except because it pleases him: for thus would he work well, if he worked contrariwise: ergo etc..

4. Likewise, (St.) Augustine (says), ON THE PREDESTINATION OF THE SAINTS:[7] « Not because He knew that they (were) going to be such, did he for that reason elect (them), but so that they would be such ».

5. Likewise, it seems *by reason*, because God's will is the Cause of causes,[8] therefore, there is a *standing-still* in It [ibi]; but where there is a standing-still, there is no further [non ultra] seeking of a reason: ergo etc..

That there is a *standing still* [status] There, it clear. That a *standing-still* also does not suffer the seeking of a reason, seems, because as often as we seek a cause and/or reason, we seek (it) as (something) distant; for if the cause and the reason for it were entirely the same, immediately, with that (standing-still) seen, there would be seen (its) cause and no (other) would be sought. But there is no *standing-still* except in the Most Highly Simple [summe simplici], and thus (there is) no distance (There): therefore, neither a reason, nor a seeking (for reasons).

6. Likewise, if God predestines this one on account of a prevision, therefore, either of *good (works)* or of *evil ones*, or of *indifferent ones*; not on account of a prevision of *indifferent* ones and *evil* ones: therefore, on account of a prevision of *good (works)*. But there are going to be no good (works), except those which God is going to do by His own Will:[9] therefore, the prevision is on account of (His) Will, and not the other way around [et non e converso].

7. Likewise, if anyone would ask: "Since God could produce one other world similar to this one, for what reason (has He produced)[10] this one more than that one?", there would be no question, that this one alone was, because He willed (it): therefore, for an equal reason there is no cause, why He predestines and reproves, except because He wills (it).

CONCLUSION

Predestination and reprobation as much as regards the ordination of the willed to the Divine Will, though they do not have a meritorious cause, do, however, have a reason in general and in particular, but in particular naught but the reasons of congruence and (those) unknown to us.

I RESPOND: It must be said, that when there is asked, whether God's eternal proposal or election and/or reprobation has *a reason*, this is not understood as much as regards the Divine *Will* and/or Its *Act*, which is God, but as much as regards *the ordination of the willed* to His Will.[11] And, if there is sought a *causal* and/or *meritorious* reason, there is responded, that (there is) not.

---

[1] On this and the following argument, cf. the words of (St. John) Damascene, here above in q. 1, p. 728, footnote 2.

[2] In codex V, for *(His) Will* [voluntas], there is here read: *God's Will to predestine and/or reprove* [voluntas Dei praedestinandi vel reprobandi]. At the end of the argument, for *and that* [et quod] the Vatican edition has *for this, that* [eo quod], cod. F has instead *because* [quia].

[3] Verse 34, where the Vulgate reads *that* [quia] for *that* [quod].

[4] Verse 19. In the text cited the Vulgate has *I will* [voluero] for *I have mercy* [misereor], and *unto whom* [in quem] for *upon whom* [super quem]. Cf. Rom. 9:15. — Then for *Divine mercy* [divinae misericordiae] not a few codices have *God's mercy* [Dei misericordiae].

[5] Verse 25 f., where the Vulgate reads: *Thou has hidden these from the wise and prudence, and hast revealed them to little ones; thus Father, etc.* [Abscondisti haec a sapientibus et prudentibus, et revelasti ea parvulis; ita Pater, etc.].

[6] Verse 21 f., where the Vulgate after *potter* [figulus] adjoins *of clay* [luti], and, then, for *some vessels indeed etc.* [alia quidem vasa] it substitutes: *one vessel, indeed, unto honor, but another unto contumely* [aliud quidem vas in honorem, aliud vero in contumeliam].

[7] Chapter 19, n. 38.

[8] (St.) Augustine, ON THE TRINITY, Bk. III, ch. 2, n. 7, and ch. 4, n. 9. Cf. below d. 45, a. 2. q. 2. — At the end of the argument, for *and thus (there is)* [et ita] edition 1 has *and there (is)* [et ibi].

[9] Cf. (St.) Augustine, ON DIVERSE QUESTIONS TO SIMPLICIANUS, Bk. I, q. 2, n. 4, ff., and ON THE PREDESTINATION OF THE SAINTS, ch. 17, n. 34, ff.. Cf. also the text of Master (Peter), here in chs. 1 and 2.

[10] Understand: *has He produced* [produxit], as is read in codices aa and bb. — (St.) Augustine's book, OF EIGHTY-THREE QUESTIONS, q. 28: He who asks: "For what reason has God willed to make the world?", seeks the cause of God's Will. But every cause is efficient. Moreover, everything efficient is greater than that which it effects. But nothing is greater than God's Will. Therefore, one is not to seek a cause for It.

[11] The willed [volitum], as it is an effect of the Divine Will, is really ordered to It, and on the other hand the Divine Will according to the reckoning (of understanding) is referred to the willed as to Its secondary object. Though under this respect it could be said equally well, that the willed is ordered to the Divine Will, and the Divine Will is ordered to the willed; yet it is better to use the first manner of speaking, which the Seraphic Doctor employs here, both because the greater is not ordered to the lesser, but on the contrary the lesser to the greater, and because on the part of the willed there is a real relation, on the part of God (there is) not. But (God's) Will is rightly said *to be terminated* at the willed. — A little above this, after *reprobation* [reprobatio] codex R adds *in God* [in Deo], the Vatican edition reads here *in God has a motive reason* [in Deo motivam habet rationem]. Below this at *And if there be sought* [Et si quaeratur] codex Y reads instead *And if there be asked, whether there is for this* [Et si quaeratur utrum si ad hoc], and after a few (words) for *that (there is) not* [quod non] the Vatican edition exhibits *that it cannot be given* [quod dari non possit].

However, if *a reason of congruity* and *fittingness* [decentiae] is sought, certain (authors) respond, that God's Will Itself is its own reason, nor is there another reason, why He elected this one, except because it pleases (Him); and this is sufficient through every manner (of reckoning), because He is the Cause of causes, and the Reason for reasons; and by the very (fact) that it pleases (Him) it is upright on account of the most high rectitude of His Will, because It is not only *upright*, but also *a rule*. — But one must beware, lest, when we wish to magnify God's Will, we rather derogate His Will. For if there were no other reason, why God elected this one and not that one, except because it pleases (Him to do so),[1] certainly the Divine Judgements would not be said (to be) "*hidden*" [occulta], but "*manifest*", since anyone grasps this reason; nor would they be said (to be) "*wonderful*", but rather "*voluntary*".

And, on this account, it must be said, that that eternal *proposal* — just as (St.) Augustine says, and as is had in the text (of Master Peter)[2] — and that *Will* is most reasonable and has a reason; and just as it was from eternity, it had a reason from eternity, not another (reason) on account of essence, but on account of what it connotes.[3] Moreover, what that is in the election and/or reprobation of men, is not entirely known to us, nor entirely unknown.

On account of this, it must be noted, that there are certain works, which go forth from the Divine Will with (something) else ordained to this by an order of *necessity*, whether we take "necessity" in *causing*,[4] or in *meriting* and/or *disposing*, such as *raining* and *remunerating*, or *damming* and *saving*; and in respect of such the Divine Will has a reason in *general* and in *particular*. Wherefore, if it be asked: "For what reason does God will *that it rain*?", the response is: "On account of our utility." Similarly, if it be asked: "For what reason does He will to remunerate some?", the response is: "For the sake of His Glory."[5] — Similarly, It has a reason in *particular*, so that if there be asked: "For what reason does God will that it rain in the winter, not in the summer?", then the response is: "Because watery vapors are more abundant in the winter than in the summer." Similarly, if it be asked: "Why does He will to save Peter more than Judas?", the response is: that "The former had good merits, but the latter evil ones." — Moreover, there are certain works, which are from the Divine Will with (something) else[6] ordained to this by an order of *congruity*, just as is our 'being made pleasing' and/or justification, which is from the Divine Will

with the cooperation and preparation of free will; and this, because « He who created thee without thee, will not justify thee without thee ».[7] And this has been said according to a congruency; *for we are God's helpers*. Nevertheless, God justifies without preparation and cooperation, as is clear concerning those justified in the womb, and as they say of (St.) Paul. And in respect of such works (His) Will[8] has a reason in *general* and it has (one) in *particular*, but in general a certain one, in particular a hidden one.

For, if there is asked: "For what reason does God want to justify?" the response is: "To show His Mercy". And if there is asked: "For what reason does He not want to justify all men by the will of (His) *good pleasure*?", it must be said, that this is for the sake of showing His Justice. Whence (St.) Augustine in the twenty-first (book) ON THE CITY OF GOD (says):[9] « If all would remain in punishment, there would not appear the grace of the Merciful Redeemer [misericordis redimentis]. Again, if all were transferred from darkness to light, in no one would there appear the severity of retribution, in which (severity), on that account, there are more than in that (light), so that there might thus appear, what was owed to all ». — If it be asked in *particular*: "For what reason does He want to justify one rather than another, with the two demonstrated (to be) similar?", because there can be many reasons of congruency, for that reason there is no certitude on *the part of the thing*. And for that reason since our cognition depends from the certitude of the thing, no one can find a certain reason, unless he has certain (signs) through revelation of that for which there are doubts. And because that cognition was not expedient for our salvation, but (its) 'being hidden' was necessary[10] for the sake of (our) humility; for that reason God does not wish to reveal (it), and the Apostle did not dare to inquire, but showed the defect of our understanding, when he exclaimed in the eleventh (chapter of his letter) to the Romans:[11] *O height of the riches of the Wisdom and Knowledge of God, how incomprehensible are His judgements, and unsearchable His ways* etc.!

1. To that, therefore, which is asked, whether predestination has a reason; it must be said, that it does have (one) in *general*, similarly in *particular*, and[12] this reason is known to the Divine Foreknowledge, not to us, for the aforesaid reason.

2. 3. To that which is objected concerning Sacred Scripture, that it assigns (God's) good pleasure as the reason; it must be said, that although it does assign (it) as the reason and does not express

---

[1] For *it pleases (Him to do so)* [placet] codex Z has *the Lord has willed (it)* [Dominus voluit]. The same codex, with several others, and with edition 1, has a little before this *elects* [eligit] for *elected* [elegit].

[2] Chapter 2.

[3] The sense is: from eternity it has a reason and for diverse willed a different [aliam et aliam] reason, not, indeed, on its own part or on the part of the Divine will, but on the part of the willed which is connoted [voliti connotati].

[4] Edition 1 with some mss. reads thus: *whether we take (it as) "necessity" or (as) "necessity in causing"* [sive necessitatem sumamus sive necessitate in causando]. Next, after *raining* [pluere] codd. L & O rightly insert *punishing* [punire].

[5] Trusting in the more outstanding codices and edition 1, we have restored the final proposition, beginning with *Similarly* [Similiter], which (proposition) is absent from the Vatican edition.

[6] Codex T reads *something* [aliquo] for *(something) else* [alio].

[7] (St.) Augustine's 169th Sermon, ch. 11, n. 13: Therefore, He who made thee without thee, does not justify thee without thee. — The passage from Sacred Scripture next cited is 1 Cor. 3:9; and on St. John the Baptist, cf. Lk 1:41, and on the conversion of St. Paul, see Acts, chapter 9.

[8] For *(His) Will* [voluntas], the Vatican edition has *of (His) Will He* [voluntatis], faultily, as is clear from the context. In agreement with our reading is also codex O. Codex T for *(His) Will* [voluntas] exhibits *of congruity He* [congruitatis].

[9] Chapter 12. In the original text the passage here cited sounds thus: If all would remain in the punishments of a just damnation, in no one would the merciful grace of the Redeemer appear ... in which (punishments) there are many more than in that (grace), so that there may be shown in this manner, what was owed to all.

[10] The reading *(its) 'being hidden' was necessary* [occultation fuit necessaria] we have taken from codices A L O and T. Codex L prefaces to these words *furthermore* [ulterius]. In a good many codices there is read: *the former (ignorance) was necessary* [ulterior fuit necessaria]; in the Vatican edition and codex bb, and also in edition 1, there is read: *ignorance* (codex bb and edition 1 have *not-knowing* [nescientia]) *was more useful* [utilior fuit ignorantia].

[11] Verse 33.

[12] Codex R has *but* [sed].

another, it must not be concluded, that *there is no* other, because not all has been written, but (all which has been written is) useful for us.[1] Moreover, it was useful to know, that the Divine good pleasure is a *cause* and a *reason*, so that we may learn to fear Him and to attribute nothing of merit to ourselves.

4. 5. To that which is objected, that He did not elect, because He foresees such; it must be said, that (St.) Augustine denies (this), according to which that which is a "*because*" means a "*cause*", not according to which it means a "*reason*"; because although the Divine Will can have a *reason*, out of which It is congruently said to work, yet It does not have a *cause* or causal reason, since It is the Cause of causes, and most of all in respect of *the willed*, which indeed is on account of the pure [mera] liberality of God, as for example is grace, justifying the impious. And through this the following (objection) concerning a *standing-still* is clear.

6. To that which is asked: "On account of a prevision of what?", it must be said, that *it can be* on account of the prevision of good (works), such as are in some manner from free will; yet, determinately, on account of a prevision of which, I do not *know*[2] nor *do I want to ask*, nor is there a reason except (one) of *congruity*. Whence there can also be others than these.

7. To that which is objected concerning the creation of the world, it must be said, that it is not similar, because the creation of the world by the Divine Will and good pleasure is as from *a whole cause*. *And again*, through creation nothing is presupposed.

On the other hand, the reasons for *the opposite* proves, that the Divine Will works reasonably and that It has a reason of congruity (for acting) by reason of *the willed*. And because this is true, for that reason they are to be conceded. Though some of them can be calumniated, yet the principal conclusion has no calumny. For (St.) Augustine says this in (his) book of RETRACTATIONS[3] after all the reconsiderations [rectractationes], that « He proposes and elects and reproves by a truth most certain and most removed from our senses ». And because it is most removed from our senses, for that reason no one ought to inquire after it, because in this life we cannot arrive (at it).[4] And for that reason in the insufficiency of our understanding (this) discourse on predestination is to be closed, *so that every mouth may be shut, and all the world subjected to God*,[5] whose judgements are not scrutable, but (are) to be venerated by a dreadful silence.

SCHOLIUM

I. This Question differs from the preceding one, in which the order of *the effects* of predestination to one another, and the *meritorious cause*, which could be among the same, were dealt with. Here one deals with *the Divine proposal itself* or with *the preordination* in electing and/or reproving, not indeed of the Will and/or Its Act in Itself, since It is the Divine Essence, but « as much as regards the ordination of the willed to His Will », or in other words, to the extent that the Divine Volition is terminated at the effect, either of predestination and/or of reprobation. That indeed in this sense a *meritorious cause* cannot be conceded for that preordination, is explicitly taught here and in the preceding question, with the now common sentence. But there is asked, whether there is to be assigned at least *some motive reason* « *of congruency and fittingness* ». Moreover, this difficulty is chiefly discussed not about the reason of predestination in *general*, but in *particular* and comparatively. For which reason Richard of Middleton (here in a. 2. q. 2) proposes the question in this manner: « Whether in God there is any reason, whatsoever it be, that He has predestined some and not others ». — It helps to note before hand (therefore), what follows.

1. This matter is obstructed by grave difficulties. On the one part one ought to save God's Justice, Equity and Goodness, and (His) earnest, antecedent Will to save all men; on the other part one must beware, lest one derogate *the gratuitousness* of God's gifts, namely, of grace, final perseverance and predestination, and also of *the independence* of the Divine Will. For just as the Divine Intellect in Its Act does not depend upon any reason for cognizing, what is outside of God, though It is terminated at things existing outside of God, since God's Cognition is not *from things*, but *regards things*; in a similar manner the Volition of the Divine Will, though it is terminated at the objects willed outside

of God, cannot be excited by any *motive reason* nor (can It) depend upon anything, which is other that Itself, as is rightly taught below in d. 45, Doubt 3.

2. Already among the ancient Scholastics there was a great dispute, *whether* and *in what manner* the foreknowledge of merits can be accepted as the reason for predestination. Richard of Middleton lists very many opinions, loc. cit., q. 1. — Alexander of Hales (SUMMA, p. I. q. 28, m. 3. a. 1) rightly says: « On the part of predestination neither what is principally signified is on account of merits, nor even the first (thing) which it connotes, which is the infusion of grace, but *the conferral of glory* is on account of merits ». But ibid., a. 2, in reply to n. 2, he says: « The *conferral* of grace and glory can be a reason for the foreknowledge of merits ». On which words (Bl.) Dionysius the Carthusian makes this note: « This response of such a great doctor engenders in me admiration and fear »; and he strives to prove, that it is contrary to the intention of St. Augustine and the Fathers. But, if we are not mistaken, (Alexander of Hales) had already said in the preceding Article that it is sanely expounded. For he speaks precisely of *justification*, and the words "*foreknowledge of merits*" are to be understood of the mere supernatural *disposition* to the infusion of habitual grace, through which actual graces (are) acquired. Thus understood, the sentence of Alexander means the same as that which Bl. (now St.) Albertus Magnus (mentioned below in part II of this Scholium) teaches concerning *the preparation for grace*.

Henry of Gent (QUODLIBETALS, 4, a. 19) teaches, that predestination, to the extent that it is *from God acting*, has no reason except God's Goodness and Will; but to the extent that it is in *the receiving subject*, has some reason, namely, *the foreseen* good use of free will. For he thus distinguishes this good use, as if (it is) indeed an *effect* of (not reason for) predestination, to the extent that it is

---

[1] John 21:25, and Rom. 15:4.

[2] The Vatican edition reads *a prevision of which I neither know how to determine* [propter quorum tamen praevisionem nec scio determinare] for *yet, determinately, on account of a prevision of which, I do not know* [propter quorum tamen praevisionem determinate nec scio].

[3] In this book of RETRACTATIONS the words cited are not found; yet the sentence is had, expressed in these words, in another work of (St.) Augustine, ON DIVERSE QUESTIONS TO SIMPLICIANUS, Bk. I, q. 2,

n. 16, in which the saintly Doctor also retracts some of the things he said. Cf. here the text of Master (Peter), near the end of chapter 2, and ON THE GIFT OF PERSEVERANCE, ch. 11, n. 25, and ch. 14, n. 35 and 37.

[4] Understand: *at it* (i.e. at that truth). — The Vatican edition has *find* [invenire] for *arrive* [pervenire], contrary to the codices and edition 1.

[5] Romans 3:19. The subjoined refers to Rm 11:33: *How incomprehensible are His judgements!* [Quam incomprehensibilia sunt iudicia eius!].

on account of *grace*, but with it there is a motive reason (but not a meritorious one) for the same (use), to the extent that it is on account of *free will*. Which doctrine displeased (Bl. John Duns) Scotus (here in the q. sole, n. 8) and very many others.

For *(Bl.) Scotus*, together with St. Thomas, teaches that the reason for predestination, as it is God's *act of predestination*, is to be referred unto the Divine Will only as unto an *adequate* cause. Yet (Bl.) Scotus (ibid., n. 13) wisely adds: « Of all these opinions, because the Apostle, disputing of this matter (in his Letter) the Romans, in the end seems to relinquish the whole (saying): *O height of the riches ...*, for this reason, lest by scrutinizing a depth, according to the saying of Master (Peter), one go off into a depth, let one choose which is more pleasing, *so long as, however, the Divine Liberty be saved* without any injustice, and (that there be saved) the others which are to be saved about God, such as His freely electing » etc.. Therefore, the ancient school of (Bl. John Duns) Scotus, O.F.M. (i. e. Nicholas of Lyra, O.F.M. (1270-1349 A. D.), Nicholas of Niesse, O.F.M., Peter of Aquila, O.F.M. († 1361), Alfonso de Castro, O.F.M. (1495-1558), and Franciscus Lychetus de Brixia, O.F.M. (1465-1520)) and even the very many later theologians (v. g. Bartolomeo Mastri de Moldola, O.F.M. Conv. (1602-1673), Juan de Rada, O.F.M. (1545-1609), Francisco Macedo, S. J. (1596-1681), Mathias Hauzeur, O.F.M. (1589-1676), Johann von Schmising (fl. 1517-1560), Henricx, and the most learned Corbinianus Luydl etc.) deny, that foreseen merits are the reason for the efficacious predestination. That nearly the whole school of *St. Thomas*, and the very celebrated theologians (St. Robert) Bellarmine, S. J. (1542-1621), Francisco Toledo, S. J. (1532-1596), Francisco Suarez, S. J. (1548-1617), Diego Ruiz de Montoya, S. J. (1562-1632), and Luis de Molina, S. J. (1535-1600) proffer the same sentence, but do not explain it in the same manner, is very well known. But Philip Faber, O.F.M., Conv. (1564-1628), John Punch, O.F.M. (c. 1599-1672) and Claude Frassen, O.F.M. (1620-1711), among the Scotists, wrote in the favor of the other sentence.

3. It must be observed, that in the celebrated controversy, which has been conducted among Catholic Schools for three centuries, whether, that is, predestination to *glory* is on account of foreseen merits, the *state of the question* is not the same, as that which St. Bonaventure and his contemporaries commonly used to treat, with that, which is disputed in the Schools of our age. They used to ask, whether predestination in general, that is, the preordination according to *all* its effects, taken collectively, has in God any motive reason, whether in *general*, or in *particular*, i. e., comparatively to one man before another; nay they principally used to consider the first effects of predestination, namely, vocation and justification, and predestination in *particular*. But now one deals precisely with the last effect of predestination or with the predestination *to glory*, not indeed in the order of *execution*, but of *intention*. For it is conceded by all, that in the order of *execution* the last effect is de facto rendered to adults on account of (their) preceding merits; whence *the attainment* of glory and also *the divine decree*, of giving in time « the crown of justice », presuppose in God a prevision of good works. But that which is last in execution is first in the order of *intention*; wherefore *the intention* of giving glory is conceived as antecedent to the Will of giving the means [media]. And so about this *intention*, by which some are efficaciously and absolutely elected to glory, there have arisen two sentences, opposed against each other. Moreover, very many other (opinions) follow one and/or the other side with a certain restriction and/or diverse exposition. Therefore, the first sentence distinguishes *the conditioned* intention of giving glory, and *the absolute* one. By the *conditioned* and antecedent Will God predestines *all* men gratuitously to glory under the condition, that they are going to use well the graces given (them). However, by (His) *absolute* and *efficacious* Will He preordains not all, but not a few elect absolutely to glory before the others. This *discretion* according to this sentence presupposes the foreknowledge of merits as *absolutely* future, such that the predestined according to the reckoning (of understanding) are elected *first* to grace and to merits, and *afterwards* are and/or even, as many would have it, are *on account of* (their) foreseen merits, elected by (His) consequent and absolute Will to glory. Whence the *discretion* of (those) to be saved and (those) to be reproved, even in the order of *intention*, is made by God according to a prevision of merits and from the motive of justice. Thus very many later (theologians), with Leonard Lessius, S. J. (1554-1623), Gabriel Vasquez, S. J. (1549-1604), Martin Becanus, S. J. (1563-1624), and (the Jesuit Fathers) of Würzburg. — The contrary sentence also distinguishes between the order of *intention* and *execution*, or between the first *election* to glory and the *attainment* of glory itself; but it speaks in another manner of *the order* of election and of *the motive* of the same. As the defenders of this sentence would have it, *the intention* not only *as conditioned*, but even *as absolute*, by which some are ordered by the consequent Will to *glory*, precedes according to the reckoning (of understanding) the prevision of merits, such that this Divine Volition does not have a motive except the gratuitous Divine Mercy; but the ordination *to grace*

and to *merits* (which are the means to the end, that is, to glory) presupposes the election to glory, whose effects they are. Whence the motive *for intending* glory is gratuitous, but the motive *for giving* it in execution is out of justice; or in other words: "God, not on account of merits, but freely, *wills first to ordain* (one) to glory, yet He does want *to give it on account of merits*. This sentence considers good works under the reckoning of *a divine gift*, because God is their first and principal Cause, and as a consequence, to the extent that they are the effects of predestination. But the first sentence considers the same good works under the respect of *merit*, to the extent that they also proceed from free will as its effects.

It is not ours to judge of the truth of these sentences, which we have only proposed, to more easily establish, that St. Bonaventure does not here treat of the matter under these distinctions, since he does not speak either of the order of *intention* and *execution* (as Bl. Scotus has already done), nor precisely of the election to *glory*, nor of *the order* of priority and posteriority, which according to our manner of understanding is supposed to exist among the divine decrees.

Hence it is not to be wondered, that St. Bonaventure and very many ancient Scholastics are drawn by diverse (authors) to each side, and that the words of St. Bonaventure (in dd. 40 and 41, and below in d. 46, a. 1, q. 1) are understood diversely, that is, either of the order of *intention*, and/or of the order of *execution*. For Petrus Trigosus de Catalayud, O.F.M. Cap., 1533-1593 A. D., (SUMMA THELOG., q.18, a. 6, dubium 1) disputes at length to prove that St. Bonaventure teaches the predestination to glory before the prevision of merits, to which Hauzeur consents (COLLATIONES., I, col. 516) and others too. These propositions, which speak of the prevision of merits, they understand not of the order of *intention*, but of *execution*. But, on the other hand, Bartolomeo de' Barbieri and Frassen (DE DEO, tract 2, disp. 2, a. 2, sect. 2, q. 3), together with very many others, make St. Bonaventure the patron entirely of the other sentence.

However, it is manifest, that the Seraphic Doctor speaks according to the common state of the question in his own age and proposes his own sentence also with an the highest moderation and wisdom.. While he speaks of a motive reason in respect of predestination in *general* (here in the body of the Response), he does not mention the prevision of merits, but (rather) the showing of mercy and justice. Moreover, while he speaks of predestination in *particular* and comparatively (in the body of the Response, and in reply to n. 6) he does not intend to prove but: a) that one must suppose that there is some motive reason as much as regards the ordination of *the willed* to the Divine Will, with which it works congruently; b) that this is not a meritorious cause, but only a reason of congruence; c) that the same is not *certain* nor determined to us, « because there can be *many* reasons of congruence »; d) *that it is possible*, that besides the others the prevision of goods is *also* a motive reason, (what however, these goods are, the Seraphic Doctor confesses to be ignorant); e) that the assertion, that merits in Jacob are *the reason of congruency* for his election, smacks of a certain temerity (here in Doubt 1); f) that beside the principal conclusion (that the Divine Will « has a reason of congruity according to the reckoning of the willed »), others are not to be inquired after, and he concedes, that the arguments cited for it in the fundament can in part be calumniated (in reply to n. 7). See also below in d. 46, q, 1, d, 47, q. 1.

II. Hence it is clear, that the Seraphic Doctor proposes in a most cautious manner the common sentence of his own age, and that he does not depart from St. Thomas even in (his) manner of speaking *except in this*, that in respect of predestination in *particular* he asserts, that *there is*, indeed, a reason of congruity, which, however, on account of our ignorance (of it) cannot be assigned in a determinate manner. Nevertheless, St. Thomas (SUMMA., I, q. 23, a. 5, in reply to n. 3), who (Bl.) Scotus follows in this, explicitly says: « Why He elected these unto glory and reproved those, has no reason except the Divine Will ». If these words are understood in that sense, which he hints at with the other formula (ibid., in the body of the Response): « There is no *assigning* (by us) of a cause for the Divine Will on the part of (Its) Act of willing »; then each Saintly Doctor says the same (thing) with different words. Moreover, perhaps this manner of speaking in the Angelic (Doctor) proceeds from that principle (SUMMA., I, q. 19, a. 5), that 'willing an end' cannot then be a cause of willing those which are for the end, when someone « by one ct wills an end and those which are for the end », as happens in God. — Otherwise St. Thomas does not deny, that « God's Will is

never unreasonable » (St. Anselm, Cur Deus homo, Bk. I, ch. 8), but he himself says (here in q. 1, a. 3): « Predestination does not have a cause, but it does have a reason on the part of (its) effects, according to which (reason) it is said (to be) rational and just ». Therefore, one seeks only concerning *the assignation* of the motive reason, which is not itself the (Divine) Will. Richard of Middleton exhibits the arguments for each side, here in a. 2, q. 2, though he follows rather St. Thomas in (his) manner of speaking. — Alexander of Hales convenes with the Seraphic (Doctor), but that he does not speak so cautiously and moderately, we have already observed. — Bl. (now St.) Albertus (Magnus), in (his) Summa., p. I, tr. 16, q. 65, frequently uses nearly the same manner of speaking, which the St. Bonaventure (does). Indeed he says (there in the 2nd incidental question, in reply to n. 1): « The Divine Election is the *Cause* of merit, and it is a cause in respect to future merits »; but also: « For certain the merits in God's Foreknowledge are most hidden merits, but these cannot be *the cause* of the eternal Election, but they can be *the reason, on account of which the Election is reasonable* »; and ibid, in reply to n. 2: « For the work of the Divine Will is Election, and It has no other cause, though (His) *foreknowledge of merits shows that the Election (is) reasonable* ». Moreover, concerning the *preparation* itself *for grace* (which he names *the principal signified* of predestination) he says: « It cannot have a cause except God's Will; yet because the foreknowledge of merits according to the reckoning of understanding informs the Will preparing the grace ... I do not see, what prohibits, that the foreknowledge of merits be the reason » (ibid., q. 63, 1st incidental question). Which words respond rather to the manner, in which Alexander (of Hales) speaks, than that which St. Bonaventure uses.

(Bl.) Dionysius the Carthusian (here in q. 1 at the end) concludes: « However, although the position of (St.) Thomas is probable, nevertheless (if it can be said, with the authority of Scripture guarded) I think the position of (St.) Bonaventure (is) more reasonable, as much as regards this, that he says, that predestination has a reason in particular or in the singular, just as in common, so that God's Will *as a will* is not alone the reason, why this one is predestined more than that one, but a certain and even legitimate reason, on account of which the Will acts thus, especially since God's Will is essentially the very infinite Wisdom and Justice, on account of which It can consist neither as One irrational nor as One unjust »; which he proves there with many reasons.

III. The words in the solution to n. 6: "Yet, determinately, on account of a prevision of which (good works), I do not *know* nor *do I want to ask*," etc. seems to respect the passage of (St.) Augustine (Of Eighty-Three Questions, q. 68, n. 4, and in Master (Peter)'s text, here in ch. 2), concerning the sense of which both for some time and more so throughout three centuries there has been a very great dispute. Therefore, St. Augustine says, that God's Will, by which He has mercy upon whom He wills, and hardens whom He wills, « comes from most hidden merits ». Master (Peter) thinks, that St. Augustine retracted this in his own similar (manner), which even St. Thomas (de Veritate, q. 6, a. 2, in reply to n. 10) mentioned, but he adds: « Or if it ought to be sustained, it must be referred to the *effect* of reprobation and/or of predestination, which has some meritorious and/or dispositive cause ». Matthew of Aquasparta, who in a certain unpublished, disputed question: "Whether predestination has some cause?", entirely follows St. Bonaventure, and explains the same text « not of the eternal Election, but of those called to penitence ».

IV. Besides the authors cited: Bl. (now St.) Albertus, here in a. 3 and 4. — (Bl.) Peter of Tarentaise, here in q. 2, a. 2, and q. 3, a. 2. — Richard of Middleton, here in a. 2, q. 2, and a. 3, q. 2.

ARTICLE II

On the sempiternity of the Divine Cognition.

Consequently, as much as regards the Second Article there is asked second concerning the interminability of Divine Cognition. And, about this, two (questions) are asked.

First, because he has a doubt through a comparison to *complex (sayings)*, there is asked, whether God cognizes things through the manner of an complexion.*

Second, there is asked, whether the enunciable or complex (sayings),[1] which God once cognizes, He always cognizes.

QUESTION I

Whether God cognizes things through the manner of a complexion?

Moreover, that God cognizes through a manner of complexion, is shown in this manner.

1. The same thing, which sense cognizes, the intellect cognizes,[2] but sense (does so) through the manner of a non-complexion [per modum incomplexionis], the intellect, however, through a manner of complexion; but the intellect is more potent in cognizing than sense (is); therefore, 'to cognize through the manner of complexion' belongs to power. But every such is to be attributed to God: ergo etc..

2. Likewise, a thing is signified differently through a non-complex utterance [vocem in complexam] and through a complex one, because through a non-complex utterance (it is signified) as much as regards (its) *'being' simply*, through

---

[1] Thus codices L O and Y. The Vatican edition, together with the other editions and codices, omits *complex (sayings)* [complexa]; however, since they have *or* [sive], the former word can hardly be omitted.

[2] Thus also Aristotle, On the Soul, Bk. III, texts 9-12 and 12-40 (chs. 4 and 6-9); On Sense and Sensation, and Metaphysics, Bk. VII, texts 53 ff., and also Bk. XIII, ch. 5 f. (Bk. VI, ch. 15, and Bk. XII. ch. 4 f.), where the Philosopher, impugning Platonic ideas, proffers also this argument, that, with these ideas admitted, there would be had a knowledge not of the things which are about us, but of (things) entirely other. Cf. also (St. Severinus) Boethius, Commentary on Porphyry, Bk. I, (his own translation), near the end, where there is said: One is indeed a subject according to singularity and universality, but in one manner it is a universal, when it is thought; in another a singular, when it is sensed in these things, in which it has its own 'to be'. Cf. besides (St.) Boethius', On the Consolation of Philosophy, Bk. V, prose 4. — On the minor proposition, cf. Aristotle, On the Soul, Bk. III, texts 21 ff. (ch. 6).

---

* *Trans. note:* According to Cassell's Latin & English Dictionary, New York, 1987, a *complexion* [complexio] is, in terms of logic, the statement of a proposition in syllogistic form. And, thus, *through the manner of complexion* [per modum compexlionis] is equivalent to saying *through the manner of syllogistic reasoning*. However, from the context of this article, we can see that St. Bonaventure uses it in a more general sense in which *through the manner of complexion* means *through the manner of composition*, wherein "composition" refers to the combination of concepts in an intellectual proposition, such as is signified in a verbal statement. In addition, complexio is from the Latin verb complector, -teri which is generally rendered as *to comprise*, and properly as *to embrace*, which meanings are also employed in this Question for the verb.

a statement [orationem] or complexion as much as regards (its) *being 'such and/or such'* [esse tale vel tale];[1] but God does not only cognizes things as much as regards (their) *'being' simply*, but also as much as regards (there) *being such and/or such*: therefore, He cognizes (them) according to complexion.

3. Likewise, the order of one thing to another, to which it is conjoined in the thing, causes a composition in cognition and/or a complexion in a discourse [in sermone]; but God does not only understand the thing itself in itself, but also in (its) order to the other thing, to which it is united: therefore, (He does) not only (cognize) through a simple manner,[2] but (also through the manner) of composition.

4. Likewise, God understands our *understanding* and our *speaking*; but we say and understand a thing through the manner of a complexion: therefore, God understands in this manner.

BUT ON THE CONTRARY: 1. Dionysius (the Areopagite says), ON THE DIVINE NAMES:[3] « God cognizes all material (things) immaterially, the divided [partita] in a undivided manner, the many uniformly, (and) mutables immutably ». If, therefore, He cognizes the divided in an undivided manner, therefore composites through a simple manner; but the manner of simplicity and (that) of complexion are opposed: therefore, He cognizes through the manner of complexion.

2. Likewise, since the intellect cognizes[4] through the manner of complexion, either that manner is in *the thing*, or in *the understanding*. Not in *the thing*, because since sense apprehends the same thing, it would apprehend it through the manner of a complexion: therefore, it is in the understanding. But every such understanding in which there is a complexion, is really complex and composed; but the Divine Understanding is not of this kind: ergo etc..

3. Likewise, if He cognizes things through a manner of complexion, since the manner of the Divine Cognition is coeternal to It,[5] He cognized from eternity through the manner of complexion: therefore, the complexion was from eternity. But He understood many (things), therefore, there are many complexions from eternity: therefore, *true*, and/or *false* ones; if *true* ones: therefore, there are many truths from eternity; if *false* ones: therefore, there are many falsehoods from eternity.

4. Likewise, if He cognizes through a manner of complexion, since the same thing is now truly cognized under a reckoning of being future [ratione futuritionis], now under a reckoning of being past [ratione praeteritionis], now under a reckoning of being present [ratione praesentialitatis]: therefore, God cognizes in all these manners. *But on the contrary*: He cognizes all as present; whence in the last (chapter)[6] of the Second (Letter of St.) Peter there is said: *One day with God (is) as a thousand years* etc.; therefore, He does not cognizes in these manners.

CONCLUSION

The Divine Cognition of things is not through the manner of complexion, insofar as the complexion is accepted about the Divine Intellect, but insofar as falls about things both looked at in themselves, and expressed through our intellect.

I RESPOND: It must be said, that *"to cognize things through a manner of complexion"*[7] can be understood in a threefold manner. For either the manner of complexion falls about *the thing*; and in this manner the sense is: "God cognizes, that things exist and/or hold themselves through a manner of complexion or composition" and this is true, for He does cognize that things are, just as they are. In another manner, as the manner of complexion falls about the thing, as (the thing) is *expressed through our understanding*; and then the sense is, that God cognizes things not only as they are, but also as (our) understanding expresses (them) — for He cognizes things and utterances [voces] or understandings signifying the former[8] — and this is true. In the third manner it can be understood, that the manner of complexion falls about *the Divine Understanding*; and in this manner it is false. For it pertains to an intellect, which understands many (things) through many (things), that it is bound to embrace [oportet complecti] (them); but God understands many (things) in one and thus a simple manner,[9] nor is His understanding more simple understanding one (thing) rather than many. Whence 'to understand many through a manner of complexion' does not entirely belong to virtue, nor entirely to imperfection; and for that reason it is not posited, neither in *the lowest* cognition, such as the sensitive, nor in the *supreme* cognition, such as in the Divine, and perhaps it is not even in the *supreme* cognition of *the soul itself*, which is said (to be) "intellective", insofar as it is in its own highest (degree): for it cognizes through the manner of a simple gaze.

The reasons proving, that He cognizes through a manner of complexion, proceed according to the first and second way; for that reason they conclude truly, except the first, regarding which it has already been solved.

2. To that which is objected, that complexion comes from the (human) intellect; it must be said, that *complexion* can be compared to an intellect in a twofold manner: either as to a *cause*, or as to a *subject*. If as to the *subject*, in which and which it informs and denominates, thus it is compared to the human intellect, from which is the complexion, which (intellect) also embraces (its comprehension).[10] If as to a *cause*, thus it is compared to the Divine Intellect.

---

[1] Cf. Aristotle, ON THE PREDICAMENTS, at the start, where he speaks of the complex and non-complex, ON INTERPRETATION, Bk. I, ch. 1 ff., and also (St. Severinus) Boethius' Commentary on this. Understand, by *'being' simply* [esse simpliciter], the essence or quiddity of the thing, to which the concept responds, and which is expressed by an utterance. — For *through a statement* [per orationem] ed. 1 has *through a conjunction* [per coniunctionem].

[2] Ed. 1 *of a simple (saying)* [simplicis].

[3] Chapter 7, § 2. Cf. above d. 39, a. 2, q. 2, p. 693, footnote 6. — A little further below this, for *the manner of simplicity* [modus simplicitatis] edition 1 has *the manner of the simple* [modus simplicis].

[4] Edition 1 reads (in the indicative) *when ... cognizes* [cum...cognoscit] for (the subjunctive) *since ... cognizes* [cum .. cognoscat].

[5] Codices P Q & Y, together with edition 1, have *to God* [Deo] for *to It* [ei], which could also be read as *to Him* [ei]. Next, for *He cognized* [cognovit] codices X and Y have *He cognizes* [cognoscit].

[6] Verse 8.

[7] Codex T has *of composition and/or of complexion* [compositionis vel complexionis].

[8] That is intellectual concepts, which are the similitudes and signs of things. Aristotle, ON INTERPRETATION, Bk. I, ch. 1: Therefore, those which are in the voice, of those which are known as passions in the soul and of which the former (are) similitudes, are also the same things.

[9] Cf. above d. 39, a. 1, q. 3, in the reply to the last objection, and a. 2. q. 1.

[10] Or in other words: which also comes to be composed by conjoining and dividing its own concepts. — At the end of the solution (on the next page), for *in understanding* [in intelligendo] codices I and O have *in understanding* [intellectu].

For the Divine Intellect cognizes the complexion not about Itself, but about our understanding; since the complexion is not from our intellect, except when the Divine (Intellect is) cooperating in (its) understanding.

3. To that which is objected, that if He cognizes things through the manner of complexion, that then the complexions are eternal; it must be said, that in the first and/or second sense it does not follow, that the complexions are eternal, because there is no complexion about God; but it does well follow, that the truth signified through any complexion is eternal, just as the truth of this, that the world is going to be; yet a proposition[1] and complexion is from out intellect understanding that eternal truth. Whence just as a temporal utterance signifies an eternal thing, such as this name "*God*", it does not, however, follow, that it is eternal; just as many enunciables signify an eternal truth, and, yet, they are not eternal.

4. To that which is objected, that He then cognizes things under a reckoning of being future and of being past; it must be said, just as has been touched upon, that "the manner" of the Divine Cog-

nition can be accepted according to *Itself*, and/or on the part of *the cognized*. If on the part of *the cognized*; thus it must be said, that He cognizes entirely, that the thing is just as it is, and thus that it is in a mutable manner,[2] and thus that it is in a composed manner, and thus concerning all (things): and in this manner He cognizes, that a thing past has passed away, and that a future one is going to be, and that one not past is present. Again it can be accepted on *Its* part; and thus, since God's Cognition is entirely simple, entirely present, It cognizes all through a manner of simplicity and through a manner of being present. Whence, what it says: "all are present with God", this has been said regarding the Cognition, in which there occurs no succession, for that reason neither a new nor an old, nor a past nor a future. Yet in the act of angelic and human cognition there does occur a succession, and for that reason a past and future. And on this account[3] all are not said (to be) thus present to a cognizing soul, as to God. And this is manifest, because *the now of eternity*, which is always present, comprises all temporals; and for that reason it is clear, in what manner it must be understood.[4]

SCHOLIUM

I. Following the order of the Book of Sentences, the Seraphic Doctor returns to the treatment of the Divine Knowledge. The same question is entitled by Alexander of Hales: "Whether God's Knowledge is of enunciables?", and by St. Thomas and others in a similar manner. The same St. Thomas (SENT., Bk. I, d. 38, q. 1. a. 3) manifests even the occasion for disputing this matter, with these words: « According to the position of Avicenna and from the sayings of Al-Ghazahli it seems to follow, that God does not know enunciables ».

II. The words (here at the end of the Response): « and perhaps it is not even in the supreme cognition of the soul itself » etc. touch upon the common doctrine, that in a human soul there is a certain participation in that simple cognition, which is in the Angels, according to the principle of Dionysius the Areopagite (ON THE DIVINE NAMES, ch. 7), that God conjoins the boundaries of inferiors with the principles of superiors. See more on this in SENT., Bk. II, d. 39, a. 1. q. 2; BREVILOQUIUM, p. II, ch. 12 at the end; ITINERARIUM MENTIS IN

DEUM, ch. 1; Alexander of Hales, SUMMA, p. II, q. 69, m. 4, a. 3; St. Thomas, DE VERITATE , q. 13, a. 3, in reply to n. 7, and q. 15, a. 1; SENT., Bk. I, d. 3, q. 4, a. 1; SUMMA, I, q. 79, a. 8 and 9. — One is to note the sentence at the end of the solution to n. 2, that the Divine *Intellect* cooperates with our intellect in understanding; which is said according to that sentence of the Seraphic Doctor, by which he establishes a *special* Divine cooperation for our intellectual acts (cf. above d. 3, p. I, q. 1, Scholium).

III. Alexander of Hales, SUMMA., p. I, q. 23, m. 3, a. 5. — (Bl. John Duns) Scotus, REPORTATIO., Bk. I, d. 38, q. 1. — Bl. (now St.) Albertus (Magnus), SENT., Bk. I, d. 39, a. 5; SUMMA., p. I, tr. 15, q. 60, m. 3, q. incidental 6. — (Bl.) Peter of Tarentaise, SENT., Bk. I, d. 38, q. 1, a. 3. — Richard of Middleton, SENT., Bk. I, d. 38, q. 4. — Giles the Roman, here in 2nd princ., q. sole. — Henry of Ghent, SUMMA., a. 36, q. 6. — Durandus (of Saint-Pourçain), SENT., Bk. I, d. 38, q. 2. — (Bl.) Dionysius the Carthusian, SENT., Bk. I, d. 38, q. 2. — (Gabriel) Biel, on this and the following question, SENT., Bk. I, d. 39, q. sole.

QUESTION II

Whether the enunciables, which God cognizes once, He cognizes always?

Second, there is asked, whether the enunciable or complex (sayings), which God cognizes once, He cognizes and/or knows *always*. And that (it is) so, seems:

1. Because God does not cognize an enunciable (saying) except according to the reckoning of (its) truth;[5] but an enunciable truth, which once

was, always was and is and will be: therefore, the enunciable, which He cognizes once, He always cognizes. *Proof of the middle*: every truth of a complex (saying) is founded upon an non-complex thing; but the same thing is first future, afterwards present, then past, and one and the same:

---

[1] Codex K has *a composition* [compositio].

[2] Codex T (V in the margin) reads *and thus that it is mutable* [et ita mutabilem esse] for *and thus that it is in a mutable manner* [et ita mutabiliter esse]. Immediately before this the Vatican edition omits *just as it is* [sicut est]. Somewhat further below this, for *a manner of simplicity* [modum simplicitatis] edition 1 has *the manner of a simple (act)* [modum simplicis].

[3] The Vatican edition, together with codex cc, has *besides* [praeterea] for *on this account* [propterea].

[4] Codices A and T read *it is clear, that it must be understood thus* [patet, quod sic intelligendum].

[5] Codices L and O here insert: *as signified and/or according to the reckoning of the enunciable in itself; if according to the reckoning of the enunciable in itself, since this is some thing etc.; if according to the reckoning of (its) truth: but etc.* [signatae vel ratione enuntiabilis in se; si ratione enuntiabilis in se, cum ipsum sit aliqua res etc.; si ratione veritatis: sed etc.]. A little further below this, for the false reading of the Vatican edition, *upon a complex thing* [super rem complexam], we have substituted on the authority of the better codices and edition 1, *upon a non-complex thing* [super rem incomplexam]. At the end of the argument, codex T has *of those* [istorum] for *of these* [horum].

therefore, one and the same truth is in it according to all these manners. But it is necessary, that it always be under any one [aliquo] of these manners: ergo etc..

2. Likewise, this very (thing) seems for another reason: because whatsoever God knows, He knows immutably — otherwise, since God's *knowing* is His *'Being'*, if His *knowing* would be changed, (His) 'Being' (would) also (be changed),[1] which is impossible — but everything which has immutability, has sempiternity, because, if it ceases, it is changed: therefore, what God cognizes once, He cognizes always.

3. Likewise, what has been written in that Book cannot be deleted; but God cognizes, not by gazing outside, but by reading in the Book of His own Foreknowledge: therefore what He cognizes once, He cognizes always. The *first* is clear, because on that (verse) in the thirty-second (chapter) of Exodus: *Either delete me from Thy Book* etc., the Gloss (says):[2] « As one secure he says this, because he will not be deleted ». And it says the same on the Psalm.

4. Likewise, what ceases and/or is lost by something ceasing, of necessity depends out of that; but the Divine Cognition does not depend out of a truth to be created:[3] therefore, though an enunciable (saying) ceases to be truth, yet God does not cease to know it; and if this: therefore, what He knows once, (He) also (knows) always.

BUT ON THE CONTRARY: 1. Just as *foreknowing* holds itself in respect of (something) future, as it is going to be, so *knowing* in respect of (something) true — for if it is known in act, it is true in act — but, just as Master (Peter) says,[4] God ceases to foreknow a thing, when the thing from the future comes to be present: therefore similarly He ceases to know, when from (being) true it comes to be false.

2. Likewise, just as the Divine *Accepting* looks back to goodness, so the (Divine) *Vision* to truth; but God ceases to accept a man, when he looses (his moral) goodness: therefore, He ceases to cognize[5] a thing or enunciable, when it looses (its) truth.

3. Likewise, this very (thing) is shown per impossible, because, if He knows whatsoever enunciable He knew, He also knew, that Christ is going to die, therefore, He also knows (it) now; but whatever is known is true:[6] therefore, that Christ is going it die is true, which is contrary to the Faith.

4. Likewise, if He knows now, whatever He knew; but at some time He knows that you are not, when you were not; therefore, He knows that you are not, and He knows that you are, because it is true: therefore, He knows two contradictorily opposed (truths) together, therefore, two contradictorily opposed (truths) are true together, which is false and impossible.

CONCLUSION

Inasmuch as "knowing" means a bare understanding, whatsoever God knows once, He knows always; but inasmuch as "knowing" connotes the truth in the object, according to the reckoning of what it connotes, which is variable, God does not know once whatsoever He knows.

I RESPOND: It must be said, that *"to know"* [scire] is said in a twofold manner: in one manner, insofar as *it is reflected upon itself;*[7] and thus the sense is: "this one knows this", that is, "he has a cognition of this"; and in this manner it must be said, that *"to know"* connotes nothing actual on the part of the known, neither a truth nor a presence. For God has a perfect cognition of every enunciation, whether the enunciation be perfect and congruous, whether true, and all other similars. In another manner, *"to know"* is said, according to which it is a proheretic [prohaereticum][8] verb and passes into an act outside, and thus it connotes the truth in an object; therefore, "to know an enunciable" is, then, the same as "to know, that this is true". Wherefore *"I know that you are sitting"*, this is to say: "I not only have a cognition of this, but I also cognize, that it is true." — In the first manner *"knowing"* conveys a bare[9] understanding; in the second manner, an understanding with an assent.

If, therefore, "to know" is accepted in the *first* manner, thus I say, that whatever is, both every enunciable, and everything which He knew, He still knows and has a cognition of that, because of every that which is and what can be, He has cognition. Nor does it follow: 'he knows this, therefore, it is true'; nay there is a (fallacy of) *the consequent* there.[10] — But if "to know" is accepted in the *second* manner, insofar as it connotes the truth

---

[1] Understand: *His own 'Being' would also be changed* [etiam suum esse mutaretur].

[2] Verse 32. — The Psalm, which is next mentioned, is Ps. 105, and the verse, which is referred to is v. 23. — The Gloss, in which the words: *As one secure he says this* etc. [Securus hoc dicit etc.] is the interlinear Gloss, and the Gloss, which « say the same on the Psalm », is the ordinary Gloss and is taken from (St.) Augustine, QUESTIONS ON EXODUS, q. 147, and ENARRATIONS ON THE PSALMS, Ps. 105, n. 21. — On the minor proposition of the argument, cf. (St.) Augustine ON THE CITY OF GOD, Bk. XX, ch. 15. — For *The first is clear* [Prima patet] the Vatican ed., with several codd., has faultily *Moreover, it is clear* [Praeterea patet].

[3] Edition 1 has *out of a created truth* [ex veritate creata] for *out of a truth to be created* [ex veritate creanda].

[4] Here in chapter 3. The exposition of this saying of Master (Peter) is given below, in Doubt 4. — Master (Peter), loc. cit., distinguishes between God's *Foreknowledge* and *Knowledge*, and affirms that (His) Foreknowledge can cease; but that (His) Knowledge cannot. But St. Bonaventure affirms the latter later on, namely, that God's Knowledge can cease, deriving this from the principle, by which Master (Peter) taught, that God's Foreknowledge can cease.

[5] Ed. 1 has *to think* [cogitare].

[6] Cf. above d. 39, a. 1, q. 3, p. 690 , footnote 2. — For *is known* [scitur] the Vatican has *He knows* [scit].

[7] That is, insofar as it consists in itself, or, as is said a little below

this, insofar as *it conveys a bare understanding,* that is, a mere apprehension without a judgement concerning the objective truth of the cognition. In this manner, God cognizes all which can be cognized, even all (those) false and impossible. — A little further below this, for *a presence* [praesentiam] not a few codices, together with editions 2, 3, 4, and 5, have *a foreknowledge* [praescientiam].

[8] In Greek, προαιρετικόν (from προαίρεσις, which is mentioned above in d. 40, a. 3, q. 1, p. 714, footnote 3), i. e., an elective and/or adhesive one. Therefore, the verb *"to know"*, accepted as a proheretic verb, signifies a cognition with an election or adhesion (i.e. an assent) in a manner related to a cognized thing, that is, to the extent that there is judged together with this, that the cognized thing is true, and (this) "to know" *passes over into the act outside* by connoting *the existence of the cognized outside of the intellect.* — Codex M to the word *proheretic* adjoins: *that is a voluntary one, whence a prohaeresis is that which the will is* [id est voluntarium unde prohaeresis id est voluntas].

[9] Together with the Vatican edition we retain *bare* [nudum], even though the codices, together with the six first editions, exhibit *divine* [divinum], which seems to constrict the sense exceedingly.

[10] That is a fallacy of the consequent, for inasmuch as *"to know"* is accepted in the antecedent in the first sense, explained here, and in the consequent in the second sense. Cf. Aristotle, ELENCHAE, Bk. I, ch. 4 (ch. 5).

about the enunciable, in this manner were they who said, that He ceases to know some enunciable; because they posited, that the enunciable, which is true, could be false.

Others said the contrary, because they posited, that the enunciable, which is once true is always true, and thus is always known. And so that may be more [melius] clear, their[1] *position* and the *reason* for (their) position must be seen. There were those who said, that albus, alba, (and) album, since they are three spoken words [voces] and have three manners of signifying, yet, because they convey the same signification (i.e. "white"), they are one name. Through this manner they said, that the unity of an enunciable[2] is to be accepted not on the part of *the spoken word* and/or the manner of signifying, but (on the part) of *the thing signified*; but there is one *thing*, which first is future, then present, third past: therefore, *to enunciate*, that this thing is future, then present, third past, will not cause a diversity of enunciables, but of spoken words. — *Again*, since the same *time* is first future, then present, third past, that is, the time which is the measure of the thing, which is *signified* through a statement; though "*that it is*" and/or "*that it has been*" and/or "*that it will be*" consignify three times, by reason of the *consignified (time)*[3] they do not diversify the enunciable, but it is varied only on the part of the time of *the signified*. Wherefore if I say together: "Socrates runs today", and tomorrow I say: "He runs"; since this verb gives (one) to understand *another time*, and thus *another action*; the enunciable is not the same, howsoever much the signification (has been) *changed*.[4] And because, with the same signification *retained*, the enunciable is always true, and it not the same, except with the same signification is retained: for that reason they said, that that which is once true, is always true. And for that reason, since God forgets nothing, they say, that every enunciable, which God knew, He knows. — And they respond to this reckoning: 'every enun-

ciable, which He knew, He knows; but He knew, that you are going to be born and/or that you are:[5] therefore, etc.'; there ought not be inferred in this manner: 'therefore, He knows, that you *are*', but in this manner: 'therefore, He knows, that you *were*'. Otherwise there is a *figure of speech* there, because it proceeds from an identity in the manner of signifying to an identity of thing. — And in this manner Master (Peter) solves (it).[6] And that was the opinion of the Nominalists, who were said to be Nominalists [Nominales], because they used to found their own position upon the unity of the name.

But that position of theirs was against *the Philosopher*, who says in (his) PREDICAMENTS,[7] that the same statement is first true, afterwards false. It was also against *the common position*. It was also against *the truth*. And the reason for this is, because neither does it have a good *foundation*, nor a good *adaptation*.

For, first, if it be asked, whether albus, alba, (and) album are three names, one must respond: "either you are speaking *grammatically* or *logically*". If *grammatically*, since a grammarian considers the imposition of a name, and (its) principal manner of signifying a substance with a quality,[8] thus, he will say, that there is one name. If *logically*, since the logician considers a name, inasmuch as it is an expressive, spoken word [vox], wherefore he defines a *noun* [nomen], a *verb* [verbum], and *statement* [orationem] through *the spoken word* as through (their) genus; and with a superior multiplied, it is necessary, that the inferior be multiplied: if there are many, significative *spoken words*, there are of necessity many *names*. And for that reason it is clear, that they used to badly accept the unity of the name, according to which it is fitting for the proposed.

The *adaptation* was also bad, because the enunciable does not signify *the thing*, but *(its) manner of holding itself*,[9] and since through a verb of the present, past and future (tense) there is signified, that things hold themselves in a different [alio] manner: it is clear of necessity, the enunciable, "that you are *going to be born*" is other (than), "that you *have been born*". — *Again*, they use to be deficient in the last one,[10] because, just as "*man*" [homo] does not signify this man

---

[1] Nearly all the codices, together with edition 1, have less harmoniously *their* [sua] for *their* [eorum].

[2] Codex R has *of an enunciation* [enuntiationis].

[3] Namely, *time* [temporis]. — For *by reason of the consignified (time)* [consignificati] the Vatican edition has *yet by reason of the signified* [ratione tamen significati]. The same Vatican edition a little before this for *which (time) is signified* [quod significatur] substitutes *which (thing or measure) is signified* [significatur], which reading we have corrected from many codices and from the six first editions.

[4] This proposition interprets the preceding words: *but it (i. e. the enunciable) is varied only on the part of the time of the signified*; for, afterwards, v. g., howsoever little the action is diverse in diverse times, it is necessary that the enunciable be diversified. The Vatican edition alone refers this proposition to these words: *by reason of the consignified (time) they do not diversify the enunciable*, wherefore it has also transformed it, in this manner: *Socrates runs today, and tomorrow I say, "He ran", since this verb does not give one to understand another time* and thus neither another action, the enunciable has not been changed, howsoever much the consignification (has been) changed [Socrates currit hodie, et cras dicam cucurrit, cum hoc verbum non det intelligere aliud tempus (?) et ita nec aliam actionem enuntiabile non est mutatum quantumcumque mutata consignificatione]. The codd. convene with our reading, except that not a few of them exhibit *has not changed* [non est mutatum] for *is not the same* [non est idem], in a manner repugnant to the context. For *is not the same* [non est idem] edition 1 reads *however, is the same* [tamen est idem], and a little further above this, for *tomorrow I say: "He runs"* the same edition has *tomorrow I say, "He has run"*. A little below this, in the following proposition for *is always true* [semper est verum] the Vatican ed. has *is always the same* [semper est idem], and at the end of the other proposition for *which God knew, He knows* [quod Deus scivit, scit] cod. Z has a little more perfectly *which God once knew, He knows* [quod Deus semel scivit, scit]. — The expression *the time signified* [tempus significatum] and *the time consignified* [tempus consignificatum] has been taken from Aristotle, ON INTERPRETATION, Bk. I, where in ch. 2,

there is said of a *name*: Therefore, a name is a significative spoken word etc., and in ch. 3, there is said of a *verb*: But a verb is that which consignifies a time.

[5] The Vatican edition alone, here and a little below this, after *that you are* [te esse] and *that you were* [te fuisse] repeats *going to be born* [nasciturum]; codex L, here and a little after this, prefixes *not* [non] to the verb *are* [esse] and then to the verb *were* [fuisse].

[6] Here in ch. 3. — On the fallacy of the figure of speech, cf. Aristotle, ELENCHAE, Bk. I, ch. 3 (ch. 4), which (error) is founded « in a similitude of speech in a part with another saying not signifying the same (thing) » (Peter of Spain), v. g. "that he is going to be born", "that he was going to be born." — For *it proceeds* [procedit] codex V and edition 1 have *one proceeds* [proceditur].

[7] In the chapter, *on Substance*: For the same statement seems to be true and false, just as if the statement, "that someone sits", is true, (but) with him rising up, the very same will be false. — Below many codices read *do they have* [habent] for *does it have* [habet].

[8] On the grammatical definition of a *name* [nominis], cf. above d. 22, a. sole, q. 1, p. 390, footnote 6; on the logical definition of *name*, *verb* and *statement*, cf. Aristotle, ON INTERPRETATION, Bk. I, ch. 1 ff..

[9] Namely, the connection of the predicate with the subject.

[10] That is, in regard to the consignification of time [consignificationem temporis], concerning which the Seraphic Doctor has spoken a little above this, in the proposition which begins: *Again, since the same time is first future* etc. [Rursus, cum idem tempus sit etc.]. The reason, which the Seraphic Doctor here proffers to refute the Nominalists, is founded in this, that our concepts and the propositions formed from them on account of the abstraction [propter abstractionem], which befits them, do not designate singular objects; and (those propositions) which are applied here serve for the same signification, such that

---

* *Trans. note*: Here the Quaracchi editors have placed a question mark (?), since evidently they have understood, less well, the signified of tempus to be that for the *tense* of a verb, rather than the actual *time* in which the original action occurs.

and/or that one, so *a verb of the present tense* does not signify, or join [sive copulat] and/or consignify, this and/or that present, but the present in common. And hence it is, that, just as *"man"* does not have another signification nor is it another name nor an equivocal one, if it is now supposits on behalf of Peter, now on behalf of Paul; thus neither does *a verb of the present tense*, whether pronounced today or tomorrow, have another signification, and for that reason it does not make another enunciable. And on this account[1] it is clear, that in whatever tense it be proffered, that you are going to be born, that it is the same enunciable, what was first true, now false. Therefore, according to which *"to know"* connotes the truth about the enunciable, that known, which He knew, now He does not know, without any change being caused in God's knowledge, but only in what is connoted. — Therefore, it must be con-

ceded, that in the second acceptation not every (enunciable) which He knows, He knows always.

1. To that, therefore, which is objected, that the truth is one in the present, past, and future; it must be said, that although it is reducible to one truth of the thing, just as an accident to a subject,[2] and the manner of being to an entity [modus essendi ad entitatem], yet, since the manner of being has its own truth, and there are three manners of being (there), for that reason there are three truths.

2. 3. 4. To that which is objected concerning indelibility and immutability and independence, it must be said, that it has already been solved, because no transmutation comes to be in God's Cognition, nor does He cease to know an enunciable on account of a change in Himself, but (on account of a change) in what it connotes.

SCHOLIUM

I. Master (Peter) posited this question here in chapter 3, both in regard to (God's) *foreknowing* and in regard to (His) *knowing*, and concerning the same matter he also speaks below in d. XLIV, ch. 2. Lombard's solution in regard to (God's) *Foreknowledge* is right, but in regard to the second members it is in part false. For St. Bonaventure, together with Alexander of Hales (SUMMA., p. I, q. 15, m. 7, in reply to the objections), St. Thomas (here in q. 1, a. 5; SUMMA, I, q. 14, in reply to n. 3), and Richard of Middleton (here in a. 4, q. 1), responds to this with a distinction. He indeed concedes, that if God's Knowledge is referred to *things*, God knows every *thing*, which He knew; but if it is referred to *enunciables*, then he teaches, that the sentence of Master (Peter), which is that of the Nominalists, is lacking and supported by a false foundation. For the Nominalists thought, that the enunciable is the same, when *the same* thing and/or action is enunciated in three propositions of diverse tenses, so that of *the same* running there is said *today*: "Peter *runs*", and *yesterday*: "He will run", and *tomorrow*: "He has run", whence they said « it is the same enunciable, that Christ *is born*, and *is going to be born* and *has been born* » (St. Thomas, SUMMA., loc. cit.). On the contrary, by the same proposition, said at diverse times, there can be rightly signified diverse actions, so that of Peter's three runs, which he made yesterday and today and tomorrow, there is rightly said on each day: "Peter runs." — It is true, that this question pertains to (the art of) dialectic; yet it is not unuseful to avoid (certain) errors. For, if the sentence of the

Nominalists were true, it would follow, that the differences of time would be of no moment in enunciating the truth of any proposition, and that just as there is no succession *on the part of God*, who has all things present to Himself, so also the things themselves and the differences of times do not *really* succeed *one another*. For if the differences of times on the part of *things* have truth, the *enunciation* or signification of this difference also ought to have truth, and this truth God knows. Therefore, it is not the same enunciable, that Christ *is born* and/or that He *has been born* and/or *that He is going to be born*. Wherefore Richard of Middleton (loc. cit.) concludes rightly: « By the knowledge of *simple understanding*, whatever God knew, He now knows both in regard to things as in regard to enunciables. But if *"to know"* signifies "to cognize the truth", thus not every enunciable, which God knew to be true, He now knows to be true ». Cf. also St. Bonaventure, above in d. 38, a. 2. q. 2, and in d. 39, a. 1. q. 3.

II. Besides the authors (already) cited: Alexander of Hales, SUMMA., p. I, q. 23, m. 3, a. 7, and m. 4, a. 6. — St. Thomas, besides the passages already cited, QUODLIBETALS. 4, a. 17. — Bl. (now St.) Albertus (Magnus), here in a. 6 and 7. — (Bl.) Peter of Tarentaise, here in q. 4, a. 1. — Richard of Middleton, here in a. 4, q. 1. — Durandus (of Saint-Pourçain), SENT., Bk. I, d. 39, q. 1.

DOUBTS ON THE TEXT OF THE MASTER

DOUBT I

In this part are the doubts about (Master Peter's) text and, first, concerning this which Master (Peter) says: *However, certain (authors) have opined, that God had elected Jacob for this reason, because He foreknew that (he was) going to be such* etc.. It seems that this position is not an

opinion, but a manifest heresy, because he who posits this, posits, that grace is to be given by God to a man, not freely, but on account of (his) merits; and that is the worst error, namely, the error of Pelagius.

I RESPOND: It must be said, that the *"for this reason"* [ideo] can mean *a meritorious cause* [causam meritoriam] and/or *a reckoning of congruity* [rationem congruitatis]. If

---

any proposition, considered *in itself*, is the same, howsoever it be proffered according to time; thus v. g., this proposition: "Socrates runs", considered *in itself* is the same, whether it is pronounced today or tomorrow. But the matter holds its in another manner, if the proposition is not considered *in itself*, but in a manner related to *the thing*, or inasmuch as it is *true*. For then the same proposition, which first was true, can come to be false, insofar as the thing itself is changed. Therefore, what the adversaries say, *that with the same signification retained, the enunciable is always true* etc., is false. —

A little below this (on the present page), for *or join* [sive copulat], which reading, with that of the Vatican *join* [copulet], and codd. A C L S T U W & Y we retain; not a few codd. with ed. 1 have *or does not join* [sive non copulet].

[1] The Vatican ed. with cod. cc has *moreover* [praeterea] for *on this account* [propterea]. A little further below this, for *that known, which He knew, now He does not know* [scitum illud quod scivit, modo non scit], which reading, with the Vatican ed., even cod. T exhibits; very many codd. with ed. 1 have *that known He indeed knew and not does not know* [scitum illud quidem scivit et modo non scit].

[2] Edition 1 reads *a substance* [substantiam].

it means a meritorious cause, thus, though at first sight [prima fronte] it does not mean an error, yet an error follows after it. But, if it means a *reckoning of congruity*, thus it does not mean an error; but yet it does have a certain temerity, because it strives to render an account of God's hidden depth; and for that reason it was worthy of retraction in each manner.[1]

Doubt II

Likewise, is asked concerning that word of the Apostle, which (St.) Augustine says: *The remainder shall be saved through the election of grace* (Rom. 11:5): "In which habitude is there construed that genitive (i.e. "of grace")?"; because grace seems (to be) neither *electing* nor *elected*; and, again, grace is only in time [ex tempore]: therefore, also the election.

I Respond: It must be said, that if it be understood of the *temporal* election, then "*the election*" is said (to be) "*of grace*", because it comes to be through grace; but if of the *eternal* (election), thus "*the election*" is said (to be) "*of grace*",[2] not as "*grace*" means a habit, but as it is construed as a genitive from *the force of the declaration of the essence*; wherefore "*the election*", which does not consider merits, is said (to be) "*of grace*", that is "*gratuitous*". *And, if there is objected*, that *one* genitive is not construed out of the force of the latter [ex illa vi];[3] it must be said, that (that) is true, unless it has the virtue of two (names). Whence, there is rightly said "*a man of the blood*" [vir sanguinis], and "*a man of authority*" [homo auctoritatis], similarly there is said "*the election of grace*", that is "*of gratuitous goodness*".

Doubt III

Likewise, is asked concerning this which (St. Augustine) says: *Something takes precedence among sinners, by which ... they are made worthy of justification.* For it seems that he says the false, because a sinner before justification remains in sin, and so long as he is in sin, he is unworthy of the bread, by which one is fed, just as the authority says,[4] and even of life itself, so that he is reckoned [ut puta] God's enemy: ergo etc..

I Respond: It must be said, that that word of (St.) Augustine was retracted, and is understood (to have been) retracted in the aforementioned retraction, which is posited in the preceding chapter;[5] or, there *the dignity* (of precedence) is only worth as much as a *fittingness* [congruitas]; and, regarding the grace which makes one pleasing, there can be many 'qualities of fittingness' [congruitates] among sinners through the multiple grace freely given (them).

Doubt IV

Likewise, is asked concerning this which Master (Peter) says, that *God ceases to foreknow future (things), when they cease to be future.* For it seems that he says the false, because (God's) "*Foreknowledge*" means something eternal; but nothing eternal ceases to be: therefore neither does the One foreknowing cease to foreknow. — Likewise, Richard (of St. Victor) says,[6] that since there are four combinations, that there is a *certain* (something) which has a beginning [principium] and an end, *a certain one* which lacks beginning and end, *a certain one* which has a beginning and not an end, such as the soul, (but) *the fourth*, namely, which has an end and not a beginning, is impossible. For that which lacks a beginning does not have (its) 'being' from another; but what is such, is by itself: therefore, it is entirely immutable, therefore, it cannot cease. If, therefore, (God's) Foreknowing lacks a beginning, it is necessary, that it lack an end.

I Respond: It must be said, that without doubt Master (Peter) says well, that God ceases *to foreknow* somethings, when the come to be present. for if *He used to foreknow* (them), because (they were) future, and now [iam] they cease to be future, it is established, that they cease *to be foreknown*, not according to a reckoning of that which it is *to know*, but according to a reckoning of 'being placed before' [ratione praepositionis].

To that, therefore, which is objected concerning eternity, it must be said, that some name conveys *purely* an eternal, but some name conveys the eternal *by connoting* the temporal. This name "*God*" conveys purely an eternal, but this word "*to foreknow*" means an eternal by connoting a temporal. — According to this it must be noted, that certain (names) connote a temporal as a *being in act*. And, because such a temporal can *be* and can *cease*, for that reason such acts about God are said to have a start and a terminus: as for example if there be said: "God conserves this thing", "*to conserve*" means the (Divine)[7] Essence by connoting (in act) an effect; for that reason He beings [incipit] and ceases to conserve (the effect). Certain (names) connote a temporal, as a *non-being in act*, but a being in potency or going to be. And, since a temporal cannot *start* to be a non-being or to be a future (being), before it is, but can *cease to be a non-being*, when it begins to be a being, *that ceases to be future*, when it beings to be present: hence it is, that God's Foreknowledge in respect of a created (thing) is said "*to cease*", but never "*to begin*"; and It ceases by reason of a temporal, not ceasing, but beginning.[8]

From this, that (saying) of Richard (of St. Victor) is clear, because, when[9] God ceases to foreknow, there is not signified, that some being ceases, but only that something begins; and, in this manner, that (doubt) is clear.

---

[1] What the Seraphic Doctor teaches here concerning the election to grace, is valid also concerning the whole of predestination and contains those things which have been said more diffusely above in a. 1, q. 2.

[2] From codices L O and Y we have restored "*of grace*" [gratiae], which is wanting in the Vatican edition.

[3] Cf. above d. 34, Doubt 5, where the Seraphic Doctor says the same in these words: "There is fittingly said: « a woman of egregious form », but there is never [nihil] said: « a woman of form »."

[4] According to Bl. (now St.) Albertus (Magnus), Sent., Bk. II, d. 29, a. 2, this authority is taken from (St.) Augustine.

[5] In the text of Master (Peter), ch. 2 — On this and the following doubt, cf. (Bl.) Peter of Tarentaise and Richard of Middleton, here on the text.

[6] That which is cited, here, as Richard's saying, is not found word for word in his writings, but there can be gathered from them what Richard taught about the diverse manners of being, in On the Trinity, Bk. I, ch. 4 and ch. 6 ff..

[7] Supply, with edition 1: *Divine* [divinam], and, then, after *by connoting* [connotando], supply with the Vatican ed. and cod. cc, *in act* [in actu].

[8] Cf. above d. 38, a. 2. q. 2; d. 39, a. 1. q. 3.

[9] The Vatican ed. alone and edd. 4 & 5 add *it is said* [dicitur].

DISTINCTION XLII

CHAPTER I

On the Omnipotence of God, for what reason is He called "omnipotent", since we can (do) many (things), which He Himself cannot (do)?

Now, one must deal with the Omnipotence of God, where there occurs the first consideration, "In what manner is God truly said (to be) "omnipotent" ?": whether because He can (do) all (things), or only, because (He can do all) those which He wills. For that God can (do) all (things), is completely proven by very many authorities. For (St.) Augustine says in the book of Questions on the Old and New Law:[1] « All (things), indeed, God can (do), but He does not do except what befits His Truth and Justice ». The same (says) in the same: « God could make all (things) at once, but reason prohibited (this) », that is (His) Will (prohibited it). Indeed [nempe], he named (His) Will, there, the "reason", because God's Will is reasonable and most fair [aequissima]. Therefore, it must be said [fatendum], that God can (do) all (things).

CHAPTER II

In what manner is God said "to be able (to do)" all (things)?

But there is asked, "In what manner is it said that He can (do) all, since we can[2] (do) certain (things), which He Himself cannot (do)?" For He cannot walk, speak and (do things) of this kind, which are entirely alien to [a] the Nature of the Divinity, since (His) incorporeal and simple Substance can to no extent have these instruments. — To which I judge that it must be responded, that actions of this kind, namely, walking and speaking and (those) of this kind, are not alien to God's Power, but pertain to It. For though God cannot have actions of this kind in Himself; for He cannot walk and/or speak and (do things) of this kind, yet He can work these in creatures. For He causes, that a man walks and speaks, and (does things) of this kind. Therefore, not through these actions is anything detracted from the Divine Power, because the omnipotent God[3] can also do this.

But there are other certain (things), which God, to no extent, can do, such as sins; for He cannot lie, He cannot sin. But, not for this reason is God's Omnipotence[4] de-

tracted and/or derogated in anything, if it is said that He cannot sin, because this would not belong to power, but to infirmity. For if He could (do) this, He would not be omnipotent. Therefore, not to *impotence*, but to *power* must it be imputed, that He cannot (do) these (things). Wherefore, (St.) Augustine in the fifteenth book, ON THE TRINITY (says):[5] « The great », he says, « power of God is that He cannot lie ». For there are certain (things), which in some things are to be deputed to power, but in others least of all, and which in some are able to be praised, but in others are reprehensible. Therefore, God is not for that reason less powerful, because He cannot sin, since he who can do this is to no extent omnipotent.

There are also even certain other (things), which God cannot (do); whence it seems that He cannot do all (things). For He cannot die and/or fail. Wherefore, (St.) Augustine in (his) book on the Creed (says):[6] « The Omnipotent God cannot die, He cannot fail, He cannot become miserable, He cannot be conquered. Indeed [utique], far be it, that the Omnipotent can (do) these and (those) of this kind. For if He could be subjected to passions and defects of this kind, He would least of all be omnipotent ». And, hence, He is shown (to be) omnipotent, because these do not prevail to draw near [propinquare] to Him; yet He can work these in others.

CHAPTER III

That the Omnipotence of God is considered according to two (acts).

Therefore,[7] to (those) diligently considering (the matter) in this manner, His Omnipotence appears according to two (acts), namely, (according) to which *He does* all which He wills, and *He suffers* entirely nothing. According to each He is most truly preached as the Omnipotent God, because there is neither something, which prevails to bring Him to [ei inferre ad] suffer corruption, nor something to contribute [afferre] to working (His) impediment. And so it is manifest, that God can *suffer* entirely nothing and can *do* all except those alone, by which His dignity would be wounded and His excellence derogated, in which, however, He is not less omnipotent. For to be able to do this[8] would not be a '*being able*', but rather a '*not being able*'. Let no one, therefore, presume to say that God is impotent in anything, He who can (do) all, which to be able (to do) belongs to power; and, hence, He is truly said (to be) "omnipotent".

---

[1] QUESTIONS ON THE NEW TESTAMENT, q. 97; the following passage is mixed from ibid., and q. 106.

[2] Codices A C D and E have *when we can* [cum possumus] for *since we can* [cum possimus]. — This and the many other (arguments), which follow in this Distinction have been taken from (Peter) Abelard's, INTRODUCTION TO THEOLOGY, Bk. III, n. 4.

[3] In codex D and the editions, except editions 1 and 5, there is read *the Omnipotent* [omnipotens] for *the omnipotent God* [omnipotens Deus].

[4] Editions 1, 2, 3, 4, 5 and 6 read *is there a detraction and/or derogation of God's Omnipotence in anything* [omnipotentiae Dei in aliquo detrahitur vel derogatur] for *is God's Omnipotence detracted and/or derogated in anything* [omnipotentia Dei in aliquo detrahitur vel derogatur].

[5] Chapter 15, n. 24. — Below in the Vatican edition and the other

editions there is read *can to no extent (be) omnipotent* [omnipotens nullatenus possit] for *is to not extent omnipotent* [omnipotens nullatenus sit], breaking with the codices and editions 1 and 6 (edition 5 in the margin).

[6] TO CATECHUMENS, ch. 1, n. 2; according to the sense. — A little further below this, for *hence* [inde] the Vatican edition and editions 2, 4, 5, 6, and 8, together with codex D, have *for this reason* [ideo].

[7] The Vatican edition, together with the other editions, except edition 1, and codex B, has less congruously *Therefore, to (those) diligently considering this* [Hic ergo etc.] for *Therefore, to (those) diligently considering (this matter) in this manner* [Sic ergo etc.]

[8] Codices C D and E read *For to be able to do these* [Haec enim posse] in place of *For to be able to do this* [Hoc enim posse]. Then only the Vatican edition and editions 4 and 6, have *because He* [quia] for *He who* [qui].

However, it is handed down from certain authorities, that He is truly said (to be) "omnipotent" for this reason, because whatever He wills, He can (do). Whence (St.) Augustine in THE ENCHIRIDION (says):[1] « He is truthfully not called "omnipotent" on account of anything else, but (this), that whatever He wills, He can (do), nor is the effect of the Will of the Omnipotent impeded by the will of any creature ». The same in the book, ON SPIRIT AND LETTER (says): « God cannot do unjust (things), because He Himself is Most High Justice and Goodness. However, He is omnipotent, not because He can do all, but because He can effect, whatever He wills, thus that nothing prevails to resist His Will being fulfilled [quin compleatur], or in any manner to impede the Same ». (St.) John Chrysostom in a certain Homily ON THE EXPOSITION OF THE CREED[3] says: « God is said (to be) "omnipotent", because His "*being able*" cannot find a "*not being able*", with the Prophet saying:[4] *All whatsoever He willed, He did.* He is, therefore, omnipotent, so that the whole, which He wills, He can (do). Wherefore the Apostle (says): *His Will*, he says, *who can resist?* ». With these authorities it seems to be shown, that God is said (to be) "omnipotent" from this only, that He can (do) all, which He wills, not because He can (do) all.

But, to this, it can be said, that (St.) Augustine, where he says: "He is not said (to be) "omnipotent", because He can (do) all" etc., accepts "*all*" [omnia] so amply and generally, that it would also include the evils, which God neither wills nor can (do). Therefore, He did not deny, that He can (do) all which befits His "being able". Similarly, when he says: "He is truthfully not called "omnipotent" on account of anything else, but (this), that whatever He wills, He can (do)", he does not deny, that He can (do) even those which He does not will; but against those, who used to say, that God wills many (things), which He could not (do), he affirms, that He can (do) whatever He wills, and that from this He is truly said (to be) "omnipotent", not on account of anything else, except[5] because He can (do) whatever He wills. But beware, in what manner you understand "*He can (do) whatever He wills*", whether (it means) "whatever He wills that He *can (do)*", or "whatever He wills *to do*", or "whatever He wills *be done*". For, if you say, that He is called "omnipotent" for this reason, because He can (do) whatever He wills that He *can (do)*, therefore, even Peter[6] and/or any of the blessed Saints, can similarly be said (to be) "omnipotent", because *He can* (do) whatever

He wills that He *can (do)*, and *He can do* whatever *He wills to do*. For He does not will *to do*, except what He does, nor *that He can (do)*, except what He can; but He cannot *do* whatever He wants *done*. For if He wants something to be done through Himself, He can do that through Himself, and through Himself He does (it), just as He made Heaven and Earth through Himself, because He willed (it). But if He wills that it be done through a creature and He works through that (creature) — just as through men He makes homes and artificial (things)[7] of this kind — and God can indeed (do these) *of Himself* and *through Himself*, but a man and/or Angel, howsoever much he is blessed, is not powerful *of himself* and/or *through himself.*

But, perhaps you will say, (that) the Son of God cannot (act) *from Himself* [a se], nor the Holy Spirit, but the Father alone. For the Latter *can (act) from Himself*, who *is from Himself*; but the Son, because *He is* not *from Himself*, but from the Father, *cannot (act) from Himself*, but (does so) *from the Father*; and (that) the Holy Spirit (acts) from Each. — To which we say, that though the Son *cannot (act)* from Himself nor *work from Himself*, He can, however, also work *through Himself*; thus too the Holy Spirit. Wherefore, (St.) Hilary (of Poitiers) in the ninth book, ON THE TRINITY (says):[8] « The Nature », he says, « which you contradict, o heretic, is this Unity, that the Son so acts *through Himself*, that He does not act *from Himself*, and He so acts not *from Himself*, as to act *through Himself* ». Moreover, He is said to act and to be powerful "*through Himself*", because He has the same natural Power, which the Father also (has), by which[9] He is powerful and works; but because He has That from the Father, not from Himself, for that reason He is said to be able and to act *from the Father*, not *from Himself.* But a man and/or an Angel has a gratuitous power, by which he is powerful. For that reason God the Trinity is truly and properly said (to be) "omnipotent", because *through Himself*, that is by (His) natural power, He can (do) whatever He wills be done, and whatever He wills that He can (do). For He wills nothing to be done, which He cannot do *through Himself* and/or *through creatures*;[10] and He wills that He can (do) nothing, which He cannot do: and everything which He wills to be done, He wills that He can (do); but not everything which He wills that He can do, He also wills be done. For if He willed (it), (it) also would be done, because nothing can resist His Will.[11]

---

[1] Chapter 96, n. 24.

[2] Chapter 5, n. 31 and the last, according to the sense.

[3] Which is not found in the new edition of Chrysostom's works, but in the ancient edition (cf. above d. XI, ch. 2, p. 208, footnote 8), where it is in Homily 2.

[4] Ps. 113:11; the following passage is Rom. 9:19.

[5] Thus the codices and edition 1; the others editions either omit *except* [nisi] or put *than* [quam].

[6] The codices adjoin a *now* [nunc], edition 1 a *then* [tunc].

[7] Only the Vatican edition reads *handiworks* [artificia] for *artificial (things)* [artificialia]; edition 1 has *buildings of artifice* [aedificia artificialia]. Then, the codices omit *he is* [est] after *much* [beatus].

[8] Number 48; in which text the Vatican ed. and edd. 4, 5, 6, 8 & 9, with the codd., have (the indicative) *acts not from Himself, that* [a se agit, ut].

[9] The Vatican edition and edition 8, together with codex E, have *He who* [qui] for *by which He* [qua].

[10] The codices and the Vatican edition have *a creature* [creaturam]. Then, trusting in the codices and in edition 1, we have adjoined *and* [et] after the colon, and *also* [et] and the end of the sentence.

[11] In this Distinction and in Distinctions XLIII and XLIV Master (Peter) takes many (things) word for word and/or according to sense from Hugh of St. Victor's, SUMMA SENTENTIARUM, tr. I, ch. 14, and his ON THE SACRAMENTS, Bk. I, p. II, ch. 22. From these two works Master (Peter) has also, in the preceding questions, transcribed other (things) now and then.

COMMENTARY ON DISTINCTION XLII

On God's Power in comparison to the possibiles, which He can (do).

Now, one must deal with the Omnipotence of God.

THE DIVISION OF THE TEXT

Above, Master (Peter) dealt with the Divine *Knowledge*, here he deals with the (Divine) *Power*. And because it happens that the (Divine) Power is considered in a threefold manner, namely, as much as regards *the quiddity of (Its) possibles*, and as much as regards *(Its) quantity*, and as much as regards *(Its) manner of operating*; for this reason this part contains three parts or three Distinctions. In the first, Master (Peter) determines concerning the Power in comparison to the possibles, which It can (do). In the second, he determines concerning the Power as much as regards (Its) quantity, showing Its immensity, below in the Forty-Third Distinction: *However, certain ones, glorying in their own understanding* etc.. In the third, he determines concerning It as much as regards (Its) manner, there in the Forty-Fourth Distinction: *Now it remains to be discussed, whether God can make anything better* etc..

The first part, which contains the present Distinction, has four parts. In the *first* Master (Peter) shows, that God's Power is Omnipotence, because It is in respect of all possibles, which to be able (to do) belongs to power.[1] In the *second* he removes those possibles, which to be able (to do) does not belong to power, there in the second chapter:[2] *But there is asked, "In what manner is it said that He can (do) all"* etc.. In the *third* he posits signs,[3] which attest to the Divine Power, there (where he says): *Therefore, to (those) diligently considering (the matter) in this manner, His Omnipotence* etc.. In the *fourth* Master (Peter) teaches that one reduces the other reckonings of omnipotence to the aforesaid (reckoning),[4] there (where he says): *However, it is handed down from certain authorities, that He is truly said (to be) "omnipotent" for this reason* etc.. And there he first posits authorities, then he teaches how to expound them, and this (he does) there (where he says): *But to this it can be said, that (St.) Augustine* etc..

TREATMENT OF THE QUESTIONS

For an understanding of this Distinction four (questions) are asked.

First, there is asked, whether God can (work) something other than Himself.

Second, granted than He can, there is asked, whether He is able unto everything,* which is possible for another agent.

Third, whether the Divine Power extends Itself to every that, which is impossible for another agent.

Fourth, there is asked, whether something is said (to be) "possible" simply [possibile simpliciter], according to superior causes or the Divine Power [potentiam divinam], and/or according to inferior ones or a created power.

---

[1] For *which to be able (to do) belongs to power* [quae posse potentiae est], which reading we have restored from cod. I and ed. 1, very many codd. have *which it is possible* [quae possibile est], a few others, with the Vatican ed., have *which it is possible to be* [quae possibile est esse]. The reading, restored by us, is not only commended by this, that it is, considered in itself, better, but also because the expression *which to be able (to do) belongs to power* both recurs in the following (sentences) and is had in the very text of Master (Peter).°

[2] The Vatican edition omits *in the second chapter* [secundo capitulo].

[3] The Vatican edition has *reasons* [rationes].

[4] Understand: *the aforesaid reckoning, which Master Peter established* [rationem, quam Magister statuerat]. — In place of *the aforesaid* [praedicatam], the Vatican edition has *the aforesaid two* [praedictas duas].

---

* *Trans. note*: Here the pithy Latin phrase, potest in omne, is rendered *is able unto everything*, rather than the other possible English translation, *is able in regard to everything*, because *to be able in regard to* speaks only of the relation and not the application of power, such as *being able unto* does. We shall see that in the second Question the Seraphic Doctor employs, in the arguments and his Response, the more simple construction *can (do) everything* [potest omne], which is more direct and less ambiguous.

° In this phrase *which to be able (to do) belongs to power*, the first word is a relative pronoun and the object of the two infinitives which follow; it is not a relative adjective referring to the first two infinitives which follow.

ARTICLE SOLE

On (the Divine) Power, in comparison to the possibles, which He can (do).

QUESTION I

Whether God can (work) anything other than himself?

Moreover, that God cannot (work) an other than Himself, is shown in this manner:

1. Every power, which acts upon (something) other than the substance, in which it is and/or of which it is, steps forth [egreditur] from that substance;[1] for power does not operate, except where it is. If, therefore, the Divine Substance operates through Its own Power upon anything other than Itself, Its Power begins to be [incipit esse] and/or comes to be [vel fieri] in another: therefore, It steps forth from the Substance. But every power, which steps forth, is elongated [elongatur] from (its) substance, and every such is distant [distat] from (its) substance; and every power distant from (its) substance is repugnant to simplicity: therefore, since this is impossible in God, it seems, that God does not act upon an 'other than Himself'.

2. Likewise, every power, whose work [opus] is upon another,[2] has a dependence from it. *Proof:* for a work, which passes into a subject matter, depends [pendet] in some manner out of it; but a power depends out of the same, out of which (its) act depends, because it is perfected through (its) act: therefore, if the Divine Power is upon another, It has a dependence.

3. Likewise, every power, which is unto something [in aliquid], which is not always conjoined to its own acting [suo actui],[3] has a need [indigentiam] — for it is not perfect, except when it acts, and it does not act, except when (its) object is present — therefore, when it is not always present, it is incomplete; but this is repugnant to the Divine Power: ergo etc..

4. Likewise, in God 'to be able' and 'to be' is the same;[4] but God is not other than Himself: therefore, He cannot (act) upon an other than Himself. *If you say*, that the (Divine) Power connotes, but the Essence (does) not; *on the contrary*: God can make something, which neither is nor was nor will be: therefore, It connotes nothing. *If you say*, that It connotes, what is in the Power; but God's Power is not other than God and what is in God: therefore, it also connotes nothing else.

BUT ON THE CONTRARY: 1. The good is diffusive of itself;[5] but the diffusion, according to which (it is) of this kind, is *unto another:* therefore, the good, according to which (it is) good, can (act) *upon another:* therefore, either according to *its own* power, or *another's.* If according to *another's:* therefore, it is not perfectly good, since it does not have a good act *through itself;* if through *its own* power: therefore, the good, according to which (it is) good, can (act) upon another; but God is most highly good: ergo etc..

2. Likewise, every perfection of a creature is in this, that it can produce an other than itself.[6] if, therefore, everything which belongs to perfection, is to be attributed to God, the power of producing another is to be attributed to God.

3. Likewise, if He can (produce) nothing other than Himself, therefore, He is before [praeest] nothing other than Himself, therefore, neither is anything beneath [subest] God: therefore, He is to be worshiped [est colendus] by none, He is to be adored by none, and nothing entirely is to be sought from Him; which is most unfitting [summum inconveniens], according to all.

4. Likewise, if He can (produce) nothing else, therefore, nothing is *for Him* [ad ipsum] nor *on account of Him* [propter ipsum]; but there is a goodness

---

[1] Cf. above d. 39, a. 1, q. 1, p. 686, footnote 4, where you will find the Aristotelian definition of a transient action. On the reason here adjoined by the Seraphic Doctor, see Aristotle, PHYSICS, Bk. VII, text 9 (ch. 2), where there is taught, that that, from which the beginning of the movement is, ought to be together with that which is moved. — A little below this from the more ancient manuscripts and edition 1, we have supplied *and every such is distant from (its) substance* [et omnis talis distat a substantia].

[2] That is, whose operation or action passes into something external. In this respect Aristotle, METAPHYSICS, Bk. V, text. 17, and Bk. IX, text 2 (Bk. IV, ch. 12, and Bk. VIII, ch. 1) defines an active power thus: the principle of a transmutation into another, according to which it is other.

[3] Understand: which is not always present to the power, or in a manner related to that which the power is not always in act. Cf. on this argument, Aristotle, METAPHYSICS, Bk. IX, text 13 ff. (Bk. VIII, ch. 8). — Next for *except when* [nisi cum] some codices, such as Z aa and bb, read *except when* [nisi quando].

[4] Aristotle, PHYSICS, Bk. III, text 32, (ch. 4): For 'to be able' dif-

fers nothing from 'to be' itself in perpetuity. — At the end of the argument after *is in God* [est in Deo] the Vatican edition alone adds *is God* [est Deus].

[5] This axiom seems to be formed from that which Dionysius (the Areopagite) proffers concerning the good in his ON THE CELESTIAL HIERARCHIES, ch. 4, § 1, and ON THE DIVINE NAMES, ch. 4, § 1 f. — A little further below this, for *through its own power* [per potentiam suam], which codex V and edition 1 have, the Vatican edition, together with very many codices, has less rightly *on account to its own power* [propter potentiam suam]; better codex Z which reads *according to its own power* [secundum potentiam suam].

[6] Cf. above d. 9, a. sole, q. 1, p. 180, footnote 5. — From this proposition it is understood, that the Seraphic Doctor rejected that system, which is called, "*Occasionalism*", which denies action to creatures, and concerning which Averroës had already said, in his Commentary on METAPHYSICS, Bk. IX, text 7 (Bk. VIII, ch. 3): This opinion is very foreign to the nature of man, and those who receive (an opinion) of this kind, do not have a brain naturally habilitated to the good. Cf. below d. 45, a. 2, q. 2, in reply to n. 1.

and order in things through their[1] relation to the Most High Good, from whom is every good: therefore, according to this no thing is good nor ordered in the universe; but this is most unfitting: therefore, it is necessary to posit, that He can (act) upon an other than Himself. The *first consequence* is manifest; for the ultimate resolution in *returning* regards [stat ad] that alone, in which is the first origin in *going forth*, as is manifest.

CONCLUSION

God can (work) another or upon another than Himself, but without any imperfection of distance, dependence and indigence.

I RESPOND: To understand this it must be noted, that "*being able (to work) another*" [posse aliud] or "*(being able) unto an other than oneself*" [in aliud a se], this is in a twofold manner: either unto another just as unto *a distinction* according to essence and (unto something) *remote* according to distance, just as one contrary acts upon another, because it is impossible, that two contraries be in the same subject; and in this manner "*being able unto another*" is through the egress of power from the substance, and for that reason there is an *elongation* and *distance* there. And, because it is elongated from its own substance, for that reason it depends from the substance, upon which it acts, and for that reason there is a *dependence* there; and because (there is) distance and dependence, for that reason (there is) *imperfection* and *indigence*. — In this manner, "*being able unto another*" does not befit God on account of the three, aforesaid conditions, just as has been shown,[3] because they are repugnant to the Divine Power, which (conditions) are *distance*, *dependence* and *indigence*.

In another manner, "*being able unto another*" is said just as unto (something) *divided* according to form and essence, yet not unto (something) *remote* according to any distance, because the Divine Essence, while it works (upon the other), is most interiorly in it. And, in this manner, it neither posits a distance nor a dependence nor an indigence. For since the Divine Essence is perfect according to every perfection, and Its Power is undivided according to an omnimodal indivision, It depends upon nothing else, It needs nothing else: therefore, in this manner it must be posited, that God is able *unto another than Himself* or (can work) *another than Himself*.

1. From these (what is) objected first is clear. For what it objects: the power, which is unto the other, steps forth from the one acting upon the one suffering; it must be said, that this is true, where the one acting upon the other is not in it according to truth; but where it is, there is entirely no necessity of (it) stepping forth.

2. To that which is objected, that the power, which is unto another, depends out of it; it must be said, that this is true of that, whose action is unto another as unto *one sustaining* (it); but the Divine Power does not need [indiget] another sustaining (It), which is clear, because It does not need a subject matter, but makes out of nothing [ex nihilo]. And the reason for this is, because since (His) Power is entirely undiffering both from (His) Essence and (from His) acting,[4] just as (His) Essence does not need (another) sustaining (It), so neither (does His) Power.

3. To that which is objected, that the power, which is unto another, has a need [indigentiam] of perfection; it must be said, that the power acting upon another is twofold: the certain one, which is *its own acting*, and thus, has nothing more, when it acts upon another, than when it does not act, and this is in no manner in need [indiget]; and such is the Divine Power on account of (Its) most high simplicity. The other is the power acting upon another through *an act different from itself*, and such has more, when it acts, that when it does not act, and such is, that which has an indigence in some manner, such as a created power (does). Not so is it concerning the Divine Power; and, for that reason, though it is unto another, which is not always present, yet, on account of this, it is neither indigent nor incomplete.

4. To the last (objection) it must be said, that power connotes the possible, and the possible is amplified regarding a being and regarding a non-being;[5] and just as the possible is amplified, so also the diversity of what is connoted. And, for that reason, not only is He said "*to be able unto another*", because He able unto another which *is*, but because He able unto another, which *can be*; but God cannot be other than Himself. For that reason that (objection) is clear.

SCHOLIUM

I. The Question is to be understood of (God's) active or executive power in the order regarding a transient act; that this is in God, is certain by faith. There is only the dispute among theologians, *whether* and *in what manner* according to our manner of understanding (God's) *Power* is to be distinguished from (His) *Intellect* and *Will*, and from the Divine *Nature* Itself. (Bl. John Duns) Scotus teaches, that the Divine Power out of the nature of the thing [ex natura rei] is not distinguished from the Will, since the latter is the immediate and effective cause of the divine works outside of God [extra Deum], outshining the Intellect as the directive principle.   St. Thomas, though he is not expounded in the same manner by his disciples, according to Gotti (I, tr. 4, q. 4, dubium 4) holds, that the attribute of omnipotence must be virtually [virtualiter] distinguished from the Divine Nature, but not from the boundary [a linea] of the Intellect and Will, and that it

---

[1] Namely that which belongs to *goodness* and *order*. For *their* [ipsorum] codex V has *their* [ipsarum], that is, *of the things*. — On this argument, cf. (St. Severinus) Boethius, ON THE SEVEN RULES, or "In what manner substances, in that which they are, are good" etc..

[2] Aristotle, TOPICS, Bk. II, ch. 3. (ch. 7.): For (it is) impossible, that contraries be together in the same (thing). Cf. also ON THE PREDICAMENTS, ch. "On *Opposites*". Hence if two contraries act, their action is placed such, that one expels the other from the subject, v. g. the heat coming forth from a fire expels the cold. — A little before this, for *one contrary* [unum contrarium] codd. R and V have *one of the contraries* [unum contrariorum].

[3] Cf. the first three opposed arguments.

[4] He wants to say this: (His) Power does not entirely differ from (His) Essence and Action. — Somewhat above this, for *unto one sustaining (it)* [in sustentans] many codices have *in one sustaining (it)* [in sustentante] and/or *in (those) sustained (by it)* [in sustentatis], in a depraved manner.

[5] The sense is: the possible does not only respect a being, but also a non-being. Wherefore the possible is also defined by some as: that which either is and/or which can be.

formally consists in the practical Intellect, to the extent that it is applied by the Will. (Peter) Aureolus, whom Suarez follows, thinks, that the Divine Nature Itself, as It is understood beforehand according to the divine attributes, is formally and immediately the operative Power. Others distinguish virtually the Divine Power both from the Nature and from the boundary of the Intellect and Will, which St. Bonaventure favors, below in d. 45, a. 2, q. 1, especially in reply to n. 2, and in a. 1, q. 2.

It must be noted, in regard to the solution to the reply to n. 3, that the Divine Power not only is always *in act*, but even is *Its own acts*, to the extent that *It remains within* [est immanens]. Hence, in respect of God, there cannot be applied the axiom of Aristotle, that any power is better than its own acts.

II. St. Bonaventure briefly and elegantly comprehends the whole doctrine concerning the Divine Power in his BREVILO-QUIUM, Bk. I, ch. 7. The conclusions themselves are established by the Faith and by reason. — On this question: Alexander of Hales, SUMMA, p. I. q. 20. m. 1. — (Bl. John Duns) Scotus, on this and the following question, DE RERUM PRINCIPIO, q. 2, a. 2, m. 8 ff.. — St. Thomas, here in q. 1, a. 1; SUMMA., I, q. 254, a. 1, 2 and 3; SUMMA CONTRA GENTILES, Bk. II, chs. 7, 8, 9 and 22. — Bl. (now St.) Albertus (Magnus), here in a. 1; SUMMA, p. I, tr. 19, q. 77, m. 1. — (Bl.) Peter of Tarentaise, here in q. 1, a. 1. — Richard of Middleton, here in q. 1. — Giles the Roman, here in the 1st princ., qq. 1 and 2. — Durandus (of Saint-Pourçain), here in q. 1. — (Bl.) Dionysius the Carthusian, here in q. 1.

QUESTION II

Whether God can (do) everything, which a created agent can (do)?

Second, there is asked, whether God is able unto everything else, unto which every created agent is able.

1. For he who says *"everything"* excepts nothing; but we do not say and believe only that God (is) powerful, but that God (is) omnipotent:[1] ergo etc..

2. Likewise, because God is *all knowing* [omnisciens], for that reason He knows all, whatsoever another knower [sciens] knows; for if anyone would know something, which God did not know, God would not be said (to be) "all knowing": for an equal reason He would not be said (to be) "all powerful", unless He could[2] (do) everything, which every other (agent) can (do).

3. Likewise, God is not said (to be) *"all willing"* [omnivolens], because He does not will all, which others will: therefore, for an equal reason, if He could (do) all which others can (do),[3] He would not be omnipotent.

4. Likewise, every *"being"* is from the first *"Being"*, therefore, every *"being able"* is from the first *"Being able"*: therefore, every power can (do) whatever it can (do) on account of the Divine Power; but « (that) on account of which each one (is), that (is) even more »:[4] ergo etc..

BUT ON THE CONTRARY: 1. Some creature, such as matter, can receive all *corporally*; some can receive all *spiritually*;[5] but God can receive

nothing: therefore, He cannot (do) everything which an other than Himself can (do). *If you say*, that (this) does not belong to power, but to impotence; *on the contrary*: no impotence is from God or from the Divine Power: therefore, according to this the power of matter or of a soul would not be from God.

2. Likewise, a man can suffer misery or endure punishment; (but) God cannot suffer: ergo etc. *If you say*, that the former belongs to impotence;[6] *on the contrary*: no work of virtue belongs to impotence; but to endure is the work of fortitude, which is most properly a virtue:[7] ergo etc.

3. Likewise, a man can sin, but God cannot; ergo etc.. Wherefore, if He can sin, He can be evil; which is unfitting. *If you say*, that 'being able (to do) this' does not belong to power; *on the contrary*: (St.) Augustine, ON THE CITY OF GOD, (says):[8] « Better is the nature, which can sin, than that which cannot sin »: therefore, 'being able to sin' pertains to the nobility and perfection of a nature, therefore, it does not mean an impotence.

4. Likewise, a man can *run* and *eat*, (but) God cannot do this: ergo etc.. *If you say*, that this belongs to impotence; *on the contrary*: every 'that' which means a positing (of something), is from a potency [potentia], which truly is a power [potentia]; but *"to run"* [currere] and *"to eat"* [comedere] do not mean privative

---

[1] The Apostles Creed (says). I believe in God the Father Almighty [Credo in Deum Patrem omnipotentem]. — For *but that God (is) omnipotent* [sed Deum omnipotentem] codex M read *but that He (is) also omnipotent* [sed etiam omnipotentem].

[2] Very many codices and edition 1 read *can* [possit].

[3] Cod. T with several others has less congruously *could (do)* [possent].

[4] Aristotle, POSTERIOR ANALYTICS, Bk. I, ch. 2.

[5] For which reason Aristotle also says, ON THE SOUL, Bk. III, text 37 (ch. 8), that the cognizing soul is in a certain manner all (things). (In regard to) what he wanted to mean by this sentence of his, see above d. 3, p. I, q. 1. On the power of matter to receive forms, see ibid., p. II, a. 1, q. 3, in reply to n. 4. — In this proposition, after the second *some* [aliqua] the Vatican ed., with many codices, interjects *power* [potentia], and with codd. P Q & X (K by a second hand) adds *such as a rational, created spirit* [ut spiritus rationalis creatus], and cod. O adds *such as a soul* [ut anima]. Not a few codd., with the Vatican ed., after *some* [aliqua] put *power* [potentia], but then omit *can* [potest]. Our reading is supported by codd. M V & X and ed. 1. A little below this, after *If you say, that* [Si dicas, quod] supply, with cod. K, *this* [hoc].

[6] For *belongs to impotence* [impotentiae] the Vatican edition, here and immediately after this, reads *is impossible* [est impossibile]; similarly in the following argument it has *is not possible* [non est possibile] for *does not belong to power* [non est potentiae] and, for *an impotence* [impotentiam], it has *"impossible"* [impossibile], which change of words the context and codices, together with edition 1, reprove.

[7] On fortitude and its acts, see Aristotle, ETHICS, Bk. III, ch. 6 ff..

[8] Book XII, ch. 1, n. 3, but not in the same words. To the words ON THE CITY OF GOD [de Civitate Dei] codices aa and bb adjoin *and/or* ON FREE WILL [sive de Libero arbitrio], in which book there is exhibited an extremely similarly testimony. For speaking of sinful souls, (St.) Augustine says there (Bk. III, ch. 5, n. 16): "since such are still better than those, which, since they have no rational and free judgement of will, they cannot sin." — Next, for *nobility* [nobilitatem], which word we have recalled from the better codices, such as K L N O P Q V Y and ff and edition 1, the Vatican edition has less well *goodness* [bonitatem], and not a few codices, together with editions 2 and 3, have faultily *will* [voluntatem].

acts, but positive ones:[1] therefore, they are from a power, inasmuch as it is powerful, not inasmuch as (it is) impotent: therefore, it is manifest that etc..

CONCLUSION

God can (do) everything which a created agent can (do), so long as "being able" does not mean an "impotence", yet thus, that through Himself and in Himself He can (do) what belongs to perfect power, but in another, what belongs to imperfect power, and to no extent, what belongs to an omnimodal imperfect power.

I **RESPOND:** It must be said, that, just as the Philosopher says in (his) FIRST PHILOSOPHY:[2] « There are certain (expressions), which mean a *power* as much as regards the manner of speaking, yet mean an *impotence* on the part of the thing, such as "*to be able to die*", (and) "*to be able to be corrupted*" ». On this account it must be understood, that there are certain (acts), which *to be able (to do)* belongs to power *simply* and to a perfect one, such as 'being able to understand', '(being able) to love' and '(being able) to work'. There are certain (acts), which *to be able (to do)* belongs to power, yet *to an imperfect one*, such as 'to run' and 'to walk'; for these acts mean together an action and passion or a defect in the agent.[3] Certain ones, which to be able (to do) simply belongs to *impotence*, such as privations, such as 'being able to sin', (and) 'being able to fail', speaking of these according to a reckoning of privation.

According to this it must be understood, that since God's Power is a most perfect power, God *through Himself* and *in Himself* can (do) those (acts), which belong to power simply, such as understanding and working. But those (acts), which belong to imperfect power, He can indeed (do) not *in Himself*, but *through Himself*: *through Himself* He can (do them) from that which belongs to perfection and power there; *in Himself* He cannot on account of that which belongs to the impotence and im-

perfection there, which do not occur in Him. But those, which belong simply to *impotence*, He cannot (do) *in Himself* nor can He (do them) *through Himself*. *In Himself* He cannot (do them), because imperfection does not occur in Him;[4] *through Himself* He cannot, because nothing is *from god*, which is not from God *through Himself* and immediately; but that which is a defect, cannot be *in God* nor *from God*, because God is not deficient in being nor in acting.

If one ask, therefore, whether God can (do) everything which another agent can (co); one must respond that (He can) not *simply*, but with the determination, that He can (do) all, the 'being able (to do) which' belongs to *power*; and *in Himself* He can (do) everything, which belongs to power simply;[5] *in another* He can (do) what belongs to imperfect power; and not *in Himself* nor *in another* (can He do), what belongs to an omnimodal impotence: and for this very (reason) He is said (to be) "*omnipotent*", because His Power is sufficient for all and deficient in none.

1. 2. 4. To that which is objected, that He cannot receive things nor the similitudes of things; is must be said regarding this and regarding all, concerning which it objects, that 'being able (to do) those' does not belong to *perfect power*. According to this, it must be understood, that there is a power entirely *sufficient* and *active*, such as the power of producing things; and there is a power *purely passive*, such as the power of receiving [sucipiendi]; and there is a *defective* power, such as the power of sinning; and there is a power *partly active, partly passive*, such as the power of walking; and there is a power *partly active* and *partly defective*, such as the power of receiving a punishment;[6] and a power *partly passive* and *partly defective*, such as the power of dying. — Therefore, it must be said, that God can (do) none [nihil] of these *in Himself*; for though they belong to some power, yet they derogate from the perfection of power. Nor is it similar concerning *knowledge*, because the known does not diminish from the reckoning of knowledge, just as the possible (does) from the reckoning of

---

[1] The Vatican edition, together with the other editions and very many codices, reads *acts of privation, but of positing* [actus privationis, sed positionis].

[2] METAPHYSICS, Bk. V, text 17 (Bk. IV, ch. 12), where the Philosopher, treating of power and impotence, distinguishes a twofold power, namely, the active and passive, to which twofold power there responds two manners of 'being able' [possibile], namely being able to act and being able to suffer or be changed. Of this second manner he says: But in the other (manner there is a 'being able'), if what is transmuted according to anything whatsoever, whether into worse or into better has a power (to effect such); for indeed what is corrupted seems to be a 'being able to be corrupted', otherwise it would not be corrupted, if it were not able; but now it has a certain disposition, cause and principle of the passion of this kind; for as often as on account of this that it has (it), so often on account of this, that which is deprived seems to be such ... but we say that it (is) a being equivocally; for which reason on account of this that it has a certain habit and principle it is a 'being able', and on account of this that it has a privation of this, if it is possible that it has a privation, (it is a 'not being able'). Cf. also METAPHYSICS, Bk. IX, text 2 ff. (Bk. VIII, ch. 1).

[3] Aristotle, ON THE SOUL, Bk. III, text 28, (ch. 7), assigning the difference between an act of physical movement and of the one sensing, says: « For (this) movement was the act of an imperfect (being); but simply the act, which is of a perfect (being), is (something) else ». Which words Averroës expounds thus: And (there is) a cause, on account of which to this (physical) movement there happens a transmutation and alteration, but (the knowing or cognizing of this) is not according to this, because

that movement, to which there accedes a transmutation, is a non-perfect action and a way to a complement, but (because of this, that) it is a perfect action, nay a complement. — It helps to cited what pertains to the following proposition, that of Aristotle, METAPHYSICS, Bk. IX, text. 19 (Bk. VIII, ch. 9): But it is necessary, that there be even in evils an end and an act worse in power; for indeed it is able (to do) both contraries .... Therefore, not whatever among these, which (are) from a beginning and which are perpetual, is evil or corrupt; for indeed corruption concerns evils.

[4] Here in the codices and also in the Vatican edition there is an error, which often occurs in manuscripts and is called an "homoioteleuton". For the proof of the first part of the disjunctive proposition, which precedes this, is missing, which proof we have supplied by adjoining from edition 1: *In Himself He cannot (do them), because imperfection does not occur* [In se non potest, quia imperfectio non cadit]. On account of the consonance of this with the preceding, these words were omitted by hasty or sleepy copyists.

[5] The Vatican edition, together with some codices, adds *and to a perfect (power)* [et perfectae]. — Master (Peter) teaches the same, here in ch. 2 of the text.

[6] Just as appears in him who inflicts a punishment on himself, for by acting thus he is wounded. « For punishment », as the Seraphic Doctor says in SENT., Bk. II, d. 41, a. 2. q. 3, « by a reckoning of punishment, names two (things), namely the wounding of nature and an instrument of the Divine Justice, the one as the material (element), the latter as the formal one. Wherefore a punishment is also an act of revenge [ultio] ... not whatsoever suffering ... but a wounding suffering, an afflicting suffering, a displeasing suffering ».

power,[1] because the known is not caused by knowledge, just as the possible (is) by power.

3. To that, however, which is said concerning the power of sinning, it must be understood, that if sinning means *the effect* with a deformity or an act, thus it not only means a defective power, but an active one by rea-

son of the substrate act, and in this manner it means a nobility; if (it is said) by reason of a *deformity*, thus it means simply a defect. Yet in whatsoever manner it be said, because it always concerns a defect, it in no manner convenes with God.

SCHOLIUM

I. The description of omnipotence (at the end of the body of the Response): "because His Power is sufficient for all and deficient in none", is explained in an outstanding manner in the BREVILOQUIUM, Bk. I, ch. 7. — The distinction between 'being able' *through oneself* and *in oneself* is taken from Alexander of Hales (SUMMA., p. I, q. 21, m. 1, a. 1). '*In Himself*' adds something upon that, which God can (do) '*through Himself*', namely that God Himself as the proximate principle effects the thing, v. g. creating, while '*through Himself*' He also causes those which He effects through other causes. — The somewhat obscure words at the end of the solution to nn. 1, 2 and 4, by which the question: "For what reason does God *know* all, both good and evil, but *cannot* (do) evil?", are explained by Richard of Middleton (here in a. 1. q. 2, in reply to n. 4): « Although '*to know the evil of a fault*' is a knowing, and '*to will that evil*' is a *willing*, yet '*to be able (to do) that evil*' is not a '*being able*'. For *knowing* looks back to the thing as much as to its "being" represented to the intellect ...

But *power* looks back to the object according to its real "being". And because evil under the reckoning by which (it is) evil is not something positive, but a defect of due good, for that reason '*being able (to do) the evil*', under the reckoning by which (it is) evil, is a '*being able to fail*'; but '*being able to fail*' is truly not a '*being able*' ». The sentence of St. Augustine (3rd opposed argument): "Better is the nature, which can sin" etc., is explained below in d. 44, Doubt 2. In regard to the whole solution to n. 2, cf. SENT., Bk. II, d. 34, a. 2, qq. 1, 2, and 3.

II. Alexander of Hales, SUMMA., p. I, q. 21, m. 1, a. 1. — St. Thomas, here in q. 2, a. 1; SUMMA. , I, q. 25, a. 3. — Bl. (now St.) Albertus (Magnus), here in a. 8. — (Bl.) Peter of Tarentaise, here in q. 2, a. 1 and 2. — Richard of Middleton, here in qq. 2 and 3. — Giles the Roman, here in 2nd princ., q. 1. — Durandus (of Saint-Pourçain), on this and the following question, here in q. 2. — (Bl.) Dionysius the Carthusian, here in q. 1.

QUESTION III

Whether God can (do) whatever are impossible for a created agent?

Third, there is asked, whether the Divine Power extents Itself to every that which is impossible for a created agent. And it seems that (it is) so.

For something is said[2] (to be) "impossible" on account of *the ordination of nature*, such as that from (being) blind one comes to be seeing; something (is said to be "impossible") on account of (its) *being past* [praeteritionem], such as that you were not, from which you were; third on account of *being opposed* [oppositionem], such as that the same be black and white. The first is impossible according to *nature*, the second, according to *time* or per accidens, the third can be said (to be) impossible according to *the discipline (of logic)*, because every knowledge supposes this principle, that opposites are at once not true of the same (subject).[3]

1. Therefore, that God can (do) every such impossible is shown in the first (chapter of the Gospel of St.) Luke (where there is written):[4] *No word shall be impossible with*

God: but he happens to say "*no*" [non omnia] in reference to this, a word: therefore, nothing such is impossible with God.

2. Likewise, in the third (chapter of St. Paul's Letter) to the Ephesians (there is written):[5] *But to Him, who can do more* [supra] *than we can understand*, therefore God can do more [plura], than our intellect can imagine [fingere]; but it can imagine every possible, which it can enunciate: therefore, God can also do that.

3. Likewise, (St.) Hilary (of Poitiers says):[6] « It belongs to perfect power that the nature of the one doing [facientis] can (do) that, which the speech of the one saying can signify ».

4. Likewise, (St.) Basil (the Great says):[7] "God can do more, than you can understand." — Therefore, through the *authorities* of the Canon (of Scripture) and of the Saints it seems, that God can (do) everything impossible.

---

[1] For 'to know whatsoever (is) knowable' is simply 'to know'; but 'to be able (to do) anything possible' either is simply impotence, and/or imperfect power, as has been said.

[2] Codex bb subjoines *to be* [esse].

[3] Cf. Aristotle, METAPHYSICS, Bk. IV, text 9 ff. (Bk. III, ch. 3). — Codex V adds *subject* [subiecto].

[4] Verse 37. — Next, the Vatican ed. omits the word *this* [hoc] before *a word* [verbo]; edition 1 reads *therefore, if he happens to say all these by "word"* [ergo si omnia haec verbo contingit dicere] instead of *but he happens to say "no" in reference to this, a word* [sed omnia contingit hoc verbo dicere].

[5] Verse 20, where the Vulgate reads: *But to Him, who is able to do all superabundantly, (more) than we ask or understand* [Ei autem, qui potens est omnia facere superabundanter, quam petimus aut intelligimus].

[6] ON THE TRINITY, Bk. V, n. 5.

[7] Whence this citation from (St.) Basil has been taken, we were

not able to discover. Frà Guglielmo de Marra in his unpublished COMPENDIUM (cf. above d. 35, a. sole, q. 1, p. 604, Scholium) directs the read to Basil's, HEXAÊMERON., Homily 6, n. 3, where in place of the words cited there are had these: « Nor will you say to me, that it cannot be caused, that these be separated from one another. For neither do I say, that it is possible for me and you (to effect) a separation of light from the body of the Sun, but those which can be divided in our thought, these I say can be separated by the Founder of nature, even according to the thing itself ». A similar sentence is found, also, in Homily 1, at the end: « And He who surpasses all thought by the multitude of His Power », and also in Homilies 2 and 10, and in (St.) Hilary (of Poitiers), ON THE TRINITY, Bk. III, n. 18: That you would believe that God can effect, (those) the effecting of which you cannot understand.

5. Likewise, it seems *by reason*, because that is more powerful, to which nothing is entirely impossible, than that to which something is impossible; but God is most powerful in a most high (degree): therefore, nothing is entirely impossible for Him.

6. Likewise, if something impossible is possible for God, either this is on account of a *privation*, or on account of a *positing*. If on account of a *privation*; on the contrary: no privation (is) greater than (that which belongs to) an entirely non-being [non-entis]; but God makes something[1] from nothing: therefore, not on account of a *privation*. If on account of a *positing*: therefore, it seems, that something is, which does not underlie the Divine Power and which does not obey It: therefore, God's Power has (something) resisting (It).

7. Likewise, it is shown *in particular*, that He can (do) the impossible according to *nature*, such as to make a bull-calf from a trunk of a tree [trunco].[2] Because a non-being is more distant from a being, than one being from another; but God makes a being from a non-being; therefore, He can make from one being another (being).

8. Likewise, that He can (do) the impossible according to *time*, seems, because that is impossible per accidens and[3] (is a "that") which posits no resistance, because it is not: therefore, if God can (do) the impossible per se and that which has even a resistance, since that is a greater impossible: therefore, He can (do) the impossible per accidens.

9. Likewise, that He can (do) the impossible according to *discipline*, seems, because the Creator is more distant from the creature, than one created being from another; but God could cause, that a creature be united to the Creator in the same Most Simply Hypostasis: therefore, much more strongly (He could cause), that opposites be together in the same, so that something be at once white and black. And this seems to have been done in Christ, because one and the same (Person) was eternal and temporal, passible and impassible, visible and invisible, and thus concerning the others.

10. Likewise, God caused a virgin to conceive, which is impossible according to *nature*, because the power of na-

ture in no manner regards this; and it is impossible[4] according to *the discipline (of logic)*, because (two) opposites (i. e. virginity and motherhood) are true together of the same; which is also more impossible than the impossible according to *accident*, namely, that a corrupted (woman) be whole or become a virgin; for giving-birth [partus] seems more incapable of being possible with [incompossibilis] virginity than carnal union [coitus] (is): ergo etc..

BUT ON THE CONTRARY: 1. That God cannot (do) the impossible according to *nature*, (St.) Augustine seems to say in the book, ON TRUE INNOCENCE.[5] « God », he says, « is so omnipotent, that He never uproots the established arraignments of His own Reason [ut nunquam rationis suae instituta evellat] ». Therefore, if anything impossible according to the institution of nature, it is simply impossible for God.

2. Likewise, it seems *by reason*, because God cannot work [facere] contrary to the order of *right reason*, as for example lie and (things) completely similar: therefore, He cannot work against the institution of *ordinate nature*: therefore, He cannot (do) the impossible according to nature.

3. Likewise, (it seems) that He cannot (do) the impossible per accidens. (For St.) Jerome (says):[6] « Though God can (do) all other (things), He cannot from a corrupted (woman) make a virgin », but it is established that this is not said, because [quod] He cannot repair enclosures [claustra], but because it is impossible that that, which has been corrupted, not have been corrupted: ergo etc..

4. Likewise, (St.) Augustine (say) in the twenty-sixth book, AGAINST FAUSTUS:[7] « This sentence, by which we say that (something) past was, God cannot make false ». And he gives a reason: « For if He would do this, this doing would be, such that those which are true, by this very (fact) that they are true, would be false, and thus (this) would be contrary to the truth ».

5. Likewise, it seems, that He cannot (do) the impossible according to *the discipline (of logic)*, namely, so that two opposites be together in the same: because just as opposites holds themselves to union, so (things) united to division; but God cannot cause, that two are three not be five, because (St.) Augustine says,[8] that (this) is true by a

---

[1] For *something* [aliquid] codex K has *a being* [ens].

[2] This example, (which is) very frequent in the books of the Scholastics, is ascribed to (St.) Anselm as author (cf. below q. 4, in the body of the Response), and according to Bl. (now St.) Albertus (Magnus), SUMMA., p. I, tr. 19, q. 76, ought to occur in (St.) Anselm's book, ON THE CONCEPTION OF THE VIRGIN. But it is not found in that book of his, and yet another example (ch. 11 in the recent edition) is exhibited there of the rib of Adam, from which Eve was formed, and of the formation of Adam from slime. The example of the trunk of the tree occurs already in Alan of Lille's, RULES OF THEOLOGY, rule 58.

[3] In codex T and not a few other codices, and also in the Vatican edition, there is lacking the *and* [et]. A little further below this, for *a greater* [maius] the Vatican edition, together with one or the other codex, has *more* [magis].

[4] On the authority of codex F (T by a second hand) we have substituted *it is impossible* [est impossibile], which the context demands, for the reading of the Vatican ed. *there is an impotence there* [est ibi impotentia].

[5] The sentence cited is found in Prosper of Aquitaine's, BOOK OF SENTENCES, excerpted from the works of (St.) Augustine, under n. 285. Cf. (St. Augustine's), ON A LITERAL EXPOSITION OF GENESIS, ch. 18, n. 29.

[6] Epistle 22, "To Eustochius", n. 5: Though God can (do) all, He cannot revive a virgin after (her) ruin. — For *Likewise* [Item] the Vatican edition alone reads *But on the contrary* [Sed contra].

[7] Chapter 4 f.: On which account, future (things) both cannot come to be, and have been made past; since it is not in God's

Will, that something is false by that, by which it is true. On which account all which truly are going to be, without doubt will come to be, but if they would not be made, they were not made: thus all those which truly are past, without doubt have passed away. And so anyone (who) says: "if God is omnipotent, let Him cause, that those which have been made, will have not been made," does not see that he says this: "if He is omnipotent, let Him cause, that those which are true, by that very (thing), by which they are true, be false". ... Therefore, (this) is not that, which we truly say has been, but it is true that it has been for this reason, because in our sentence it is true, not in that thing, which is not yet. The sentence, indeed, by which we say that something has been, is true for this reason, because that of which we say (it), presently is not. God cannot make this sentence false, because it is not contrary to the truth. — In the citation from (St.) Augustine, for *by which se say that (something) past was* [qua dicimu praeteritam fuisse], as is read in the original text, the Vatican edition, with edd. 2, 3, 4, 5 and 6, reads *which we say was past* [quam dicimus praeteritam fuisse], for which change of the text the vicious reading of the many codd., which exhibit *which we say was (something) past* [quam dicimus praeteritum fuisse], seems to have given occasion.

[8] ON FREE WILL, Bk. II, ch. 8, n. 21: « And whatever I touch with the sense of the body, just as I sense this sky and this earth and whatsoever other bodies (are) in them, so long as they are future, I know (them) not; but seven and three are ten, and (are such) not only now, but even always; nor were seven and three in any manner at any time not ten, nor will seven and three at any time not

truth, which does not begin and does not cease: therefore, for an equal reason He cannot cause, that two opposites be together.

6. Likewise, God cannot work against the truth of Justice. (For as is said) in the second chapter (of St. Paul's Letter) to Timothy:[1] *He remains faithful, He cannot deny Himself*, therefore, He cannot work against the order of Wisdom; but to confound opposites is to work against the order of Wisdom: ergo etc..

CONCLUSION

God can (do) every that, which is judged to be impossible for a created agent both on account to the limitation of (its) natural power, and on account of the limitation of our intelligence; but He cannot (do), what is impossible in itself, whether this is according to accident, or according to the discipline (of logic) or the order of Divine Wisdom.

I RESPOND: For an understanding of the aforesaid it must be noted, that we judge something (to be) impossible according to four causes.[2]

In one manner, through *the limitation of the power of nature* [naturalis potentiae], such as that a bull-calf be made from the trunk of a tree, and that a virgin give birth; for a woman without seed cannot conceive naturally. Likewise, the one being born [partus], with a closed womb [clausa porta], cannot go forth on account of (his) corpulence; similarly nature cannot immediately convert the trunk of tree into a bull-calf, since it has a limited power.

In a second manner, (something) is said (to be) "impossible" not on account of the limitation of power, but on account of *the limitation of our intelligence*, such as that two bodies be in the same place, and/or that the same body be in diverse (places), and/or that a greater body be in a lesser place, because in no manner can we grasp (such things), since our imagination always says the opposite. Wherefore, when God works in this manner in the Sacrament of the Altar, it is necessary, that reason be elevated against itself, so that it may believe [ratio contra se elevatur, ut credat].[3]

In a third manner, (something) is said (to be) "impossible" on account of *the privation of all existence* according to every comparison, that is, (according to the comparison) of a beginning, means and end [ultimi], such as that (what is) past not have been past. For every power, which is understood to cause something, looks back to a being either in the reckoning of a beginning, and/or of a terminus, and/or in each manner.[4] Whence from a *being* He can make a *non-being*, and vice versa, and from one (thing) another; but to make a *non-being* from a *non-being*, this belongs entirely to no power. Wherefore, although God concerning every created being can cause, that it not be, whether concerning a statement or concerning a thing; yet, concerning that which was and is not, to cause, that it was not, this is entirely impossible for God, because 'to cause this' is 'to cause nothing', just as will better presently appear.

In a fourth manner, (something) is said (to be) "impossible", according to the *illustration of Eternal Truth* and (according to) the order of Divine Wisdom, as for example [verbi gratia], 'that two opposites be in the same and according to the same', this, the Eternal Truth Itself, by this very (thing) that it is Truth, indicates and illustrates, that one is to judge (to be) impossible,[5] just as also this: 'that two and three not be five'.

Therefore, when it is argued, whether it is possible for God (to do) every impossible; it must be said concerning the impossible, which is impossible on account of a *limitation of (natural) power*, and/or[6] on account of *the limitation of (our) intelligence*, that it is possible for God, on account of this, that His Power is not limited, but infinite; and for that reason He can (act) above nature and intelligence, each of which is constrained. — Moreover, that impossible, which is impossible on account of the privation of *all existence*, and which[7] (is impossible) on account of *the illustration of Eternal Truth*, he cannot entirely (do). The first, indeed, He cannot (do), because *to be able (to do) that* is *to be able (to do) nothing*. The second He cannot (do), because that is *to be able (to act) in an inordinate manner* and to be able to (work) against the order of Wisdom. And since God is thus omnipotent, that He can (do) nothing, except that which befits [decet] His own Power and (which) does not disorder [deordinat] Wisdom: for that reason He cannot (do) these impossibles.

---

be ten ». (St.) Augustine says the same concerning truth itself, in SOLILOQUIES, Bk. I, ch. 15, n. 28 ff., and Bk. II, chs. 2 and 15.

[1] Verse 13. — Next after *therefore* [ergo] the Vatican edition omits faultily *not* [non].

[2] Codex Y and edition 1, for *according to four causes* [quatuor causis] have more clearly *from four causes* [quatuor de causis]; codex K has *according to four manners* [quatuor modis]. Then for *through the limitation* [per limitationem] edition 1 has *on account of the limitation* [propter limitationem].

[3] In SENT., Bk. III, d. 23, a. 1. q. 1, in reply to n. 4, the Seraphic Doctor distinguishes 'reason elevated upwards', enlightened by the light of Eternal Truth, and 'reason converted to inferiors and to sensible cognition'; and he teaches frequently that this latter judges, to be true what are false, and vice versa; and that illumined reason elevates itself against this by believing the Mysteries of the Faith. Cf. also above d. 19, p. I, Doubt 8. — For *against itself* [contra se] codices K P Q and ee have *above itself* [supra se].

[4] In other words: There is a threefold action, to which responds some effect, namely, *a simply productive (action)*, whose terminus simply is both a being and that by which something is produced from nothing; *a simply destructive (action)*, which in (its) beginning looks back to a being and is terminated at a non-being, or that by which an existing being is annihilated; and *an action, which*

mediates between each, inasmuch as it supposes the first as exercised, the second as possible, and this action looks back to a being and in (its) beginning and is terminated at a being, because through it one being is changed into another (being). The first and third action mean in themselves something positive, but the second something negative, namely, the subtraction of a positive action. The fourth action, which could be posited, namely that which both in (its) beginning and terminus and middle looks back to a non-being, is impossible, since no effect responds to it, and thus it would be no action. But such an action would be supposed, if God could cause (something) past, to not have been past.

[5] In the sermon "On the Gift of Understanding" (Bonelli's, SUPPLEMENTUM., tom. III, col. 476, n. 83) the Seraphic Doctor says: For (the spiritual Substance) in God is a mirror and a light: a mirror, inasmuch as It represents, and a light, inasmuch as *It indicates* (manifests). — For *indicates* [indicat] the Vatican edition, with several mss. and edition 1, has *judges* [iudicat], and, then, for *that one is to judge* [ut iudicet] the same Vatican edition, with not a few mss., has *that it is to be judged* [ut iudicetur], codex Y *that we are to judge* [ut iudicemus].

[6] Codices B and D and edition 1 have *and/or even* [vel etiam]. A little before this, for *it is argued* [argumentatur] codices P and Q have *it is argued* [arguitur], the Vatican edition has *it be asked* [quaeratur].

[7] The Vatican edition omits *which* [quod]; codex H adjoins here *is impossible* [est impossibile].

But someone will object, that that is false, namely, that the impossible per accidens be impossible on account of a privation of all existence. For a proposition concerning (something) past is true, and that truth is not founded upon nothing nor upon uncreated being, since it begins to be true, therefore, upon created being; and that has passed away: therefore, "(something) past" means "a being in some manner" [aliquo modo ens]; but every created being, howsoever much it has too little of being, it can loose it, if God wills (it): therefore, God can cause, that that which it was, was not. — And again, when I say, that this has passed away, either I say something, or nothing. If something: therefore, (there is) no response; but if I say nothing: therefore, it can be said,[1] that the chimera is past, and what (is) not past, which is nothing, has past away, which is manifestly false: therefore, it does not mean the privation of all existence. — Moreover, that[2] does not seem to subtract (it), from underlying* [quin subiaceat] the Divine Power. For "(something) future" does not mean "a being", and yet God can cause, that (something) future according to the truth never is going to be. — Similarly, the "not present" means nothing of entity; and God can cause, that that which is never present, be present at any time [unquam].[3] — Nor does it seem that it can still be evaded: for it can be asked, whether God can make of (something) past (something) present; and it is established, that in the other extreme there is posited a being: therefore, if (something) present has not passed away — and what is present has not passed away — He can cause concerning (something) past, that it not have passed away.

On account of these and (those) similar to these Gilbert of Porretain[4] had the opinion, that God has power [potest] over the impossible per accidens; for He can cause, that (which is) past never was. And those who follow him expound that (verse) of Blessed Jerome, that He cannot make a virgin from a corrupted (woman), that is, He does not show that He is able, since He has never done (it). And, similarly, that (verse) from (St.) Augustine, that God cannot make a sentence concerning the past false, is understood in this manner, saving the thing (signified).[5]

But, certainly, expositions of this kind are very strange [valde extraneae]. For, if (St.) Jerome says, that He cannot make of a corrupted (woman) a virgin, that is He does not show (that He can), similarly He cannot of a trunk make a bull-calf, since He does not show (that He can); therefore, (St. Jerome)[6] does not rightly say: « Though God can (do) all other things » etc.. — And, again, if the statement of (St.) Augustine is understood (to mean), that God cannot make that sentence false, with it supposed that it is past [supposito praeterito], similarly neither (can He make) a sentence concerning the future (false), while keeping its being future [salva futuritione]. — And, on this account, since the authorities of the great Doctors say this, that God, concerning that which was, cannot cause, that it was not; and (since) the intellect says the contrary in nothing; nor does the Faith moves or compel us to this: it must be said with the Saints, as more rationally and more securely, that God concerning that which was, cannot cause that it was not. — And I know not another reason for this at the present, except what has been aforesaid;[7] unless perchance it be said, that this is on account of an omnimodal indivision,[8] so that, just as He cannot unite opposites, remaining opposites, so neither (can) He divide a same by itself; and I say that what was for the time, in which it was, is united (to that time) in a omnimodal manner, and similarly that (what is) present (is united) in the time or instant, in which is it. Wherefore, this would be to divide the same by itself, namely, to cause what was not past (to be) past; and this is repugnant to the order of Divine Wisdom, just as to cause what is a triangle (to be what) is not also a figure; and this encloses in itself two (truths) opposed contradictorily.

Yet, the aforesaid reason is sufficiently fitting, if one understands (it) rightly. For, when there is said, that (something) past lacks existence, I do not say (that) on account of this, that when something is said to have been, nothing entirely is said, but on account of this, that it is true that something was, which at some time had "being", even if, of its "being", nothing entirely remains. Wherefore, if the whole (of) Caesar passed [cesserit] into nothing, it is (still) true, that Caesar was. And (St.) Anselm says this,[9] that if all created (things) pass entirely into nothing, it is (still) true, that the world was.

---

[1] The Vatican edition, together with codex cc, having changed the punctuation, reads thus: but if nothing: I say, that thus it can then be said [si autem nihil: dico, quod ita tunc potest dici].

[2] Namely that (something) past is not a being. — For Moreover [Praeterea], which we have restored from codex Z, very many codices, together with editions 2, 3, 4, 5 and 6, read And [Et], edition 1 has And for that reason [Et ideo]; the Vatican edition, together with codex cc, has And thus [Et ita], but faultily. For the following proposition does not contain a conclusion (drawn) from the preceding arguments. A little after this, codex X reads thus: For he does not say that a future (thing is) a present and/or existing being, and yet God etc. [Nam futuram non dicit praesens ens vel existens, et tamen etc.].

[3] The Vatican edition omits at any time [unquam], which we have supplied from codex T. For at any time [unquam] all the other codices and editions 1, 3 and 6, have faultily at no time [nunquam].

[4] Who in the exposition of chapter 4 of (St. Severinus) Boethius', ON THE TRINITY, speaks thus: For indeed each and every (being) is equally the subject of His Power, so that namely, just as whatsoever are not, are able to have been, and whatsoever are not and/or will not be, can be, so also whatsoever were, are able to not have been, and whatsoever are and/or will be, can not be.

[5] And/or, as is had in codex O, saving (it being) past [salvo praeterito].* For, just as it is impossible, that something be at once past and not past, so also it is impossible, that God can cause (something) past, while remaining past, to not have been past. But, yet, the

promoters of this opinion thought, that this possibility ceases, if (that which is) past is destroyed by God's Omnipotence. — A little before this for from (St.) Augustine [de Augustino] codex Y has of (St.) Augustine [Augustini].

[6] That is, (St.) Jerome, whose words you will find above in the 3rd arg. for the negative side. — A little before this, for that is He does not show [id est non ostendit] codd. P & Q have that is He has not shown [id est non ostenderit].

[7] Above, in the body of this Article, where there is expounded the third cause, on account of which we judge that something (is) impossible: In the third manner (something) is said (to be) "impossible" [Tertio modo dicitur impossibile etc.].

[8] That is on account of the omnimodal identity of the (thing as something) past, which, namely in virtue of that instant of past time was thus united (to the past), so that it could not be divided. — Next for He cannot unite [non potest unire] some codices, among which (is) also codex T (codex a by the primary hand), have less congruously there cannot be united [non possunt uniri], and a little further below this, for is united [est unitum] edition 1 reads is unique [est unicum].

[9] CUR DEUS HOMO, Bk. II, ch. 18: And just as when God makes something, after it has been made, it cannot presently not have been made, but it is always true that it has been made etc.. And in his DIALOGUE ON THE TRUTH, ch. 10, the same Doctor of the Church says of the past: And indeed about this there is truly said, that (something) past is something, because thus it is in a thing; and for that reason it is something past, because thus it is in the Most High Truth. Cf. also (St.) Augustine, SOLILOQUIES, Bk. II, ch. 2 and 15, and below in d. 46, q. 4, in reply to n. 3.

* Trans. note: Here by saving [salva] there is meant, 'with it still being true'.

On account of another reason, too, it can be said to lack existence, because it neither is[1] nor was ordered to the present. Wherefore the truth of a proposition concerning (something) *past* does not mean entirely nothing on the part of the thing, nor truly a being in act, but that which was and is not; and this indeed does not mean something created, which *is*, but which *was*. If, therefore, God is said to be able (to work) something upon this, so that [quod] it was not; either (He does this) *by resting*[2] or by working nothing, or *by doing something*, or *by destroying*. If *He rests* and does nothing, nevertheless on this account it has passed away and ceases to be; because, since is not, neither in act nor in potency, it neither needs one conserving (it) nor needs one producing (it). Not so is it concerning (something) *future*, because (something) future has been ordained to be, for that reason it needs one producing (it), and for that reason, if God did not will to make (something) future, it does not come to be, and thus will not be future.[3] — If, therefore, He can (do) anything, so that He causes, that that which was, to not have been; either this will be *by causing* or by *destroying* (something). But *to cause*, that it[4] was not, is to cause nothing, since "*to not have been*" does not mean a being: therefore, God by causing (this) causes nothing, which is an imperfection and the implication of a contradiction. — Similarly it is not something *to destroy*, since "*to have been*" does not mean some "*being*": therefore, if by destroying He does this,[5] by destroying He would destroy nothing, which is a similar unfitting (conclusion). Therefore, He cannot (do this) *by doing nothing*, nor *by causing* (nothing), nor *by destroying* (nothing): therefore, concerning (something) past, He cannot cause, that it was not (something) past.[6]

Therefore, the instances* are clear. For the truth of a proposition concerning (something) past is not necessarily founded upon something created, which *is*, but which *was*; and for that reason it remains, with everything created destroyed [interempto]. — It is also clear, that a preterition (i.e. a 'being past') does not mean entirely nothing, but means that something which was, also is not, unless perhaps the past means a temporal succession, which God certainly [utique] can

destroy; but ("preterition") is accepted in a broader sense here as a 'to have been'.[7] — The instance in regard to the future itself is also clear, because it is not similar. — The instance, that (something) past cannot come to be present, is (also) clear. Let it be, that this is understood,[8] nevertheless it is still understood *to have been*. — It is also clear, that God can destroy every proposition and every saying; but saving the proposition and its signification, He cannot falsify it, since this cannot be, unless He would change the thing signified; otherwise He would cause, that the statement, by that very (thing) by which it is true, be false, and this would be contrary to His Truth;[9] moreover He cannot change the thing (signified), and thus neither falsify the statement.

From these which have been said, the aforehad Response can be sufficiently confirmed [roborari].

1. 2. 3. 4. To that, therefore, which is objected, that He can (do) every sayable and thinkable [omne dicibile et cogitabile]; it must be said, this is understood of those only, which are said and thought according to a rightly understanding and rightly pronouncing reason [secundum rationem recte intelligentem et recte pronuntiantem]. For nothing reasonable can be said and/or thought, which God cannot do, and He can (do) even more.

5. To that which is objected, that that, to which all are possible, is more powerful; it must be said, that (this) is true of those, which to be able (to do) belongs to a noble power; for if one could (do) anything, which did not concern the nobility of power, as much as he could more do that, so much more is adversity and perversity powerful over him [in illum],[10] and thus he would be so much the less powerful.

6. To that which is objected: either on account of a privation etc.; it must be said, that (it is) on account of a privation of all *existence* in each extreme, and on account of a privation of *distinction*,[11] and on account of a *positing on the part of God*; because God's power looks back to something (which He can do)

---

[1] In not a few codices, and also in editions 3, 4 and 5, the words *neither is* [nec est] are wanting; in the Vatican edition there is added to these words *present* [praesens]. Next for *truly a being in act* [vere ens in actu] many codices, such as C F G I K L M O S V W etc., together with edition 1, read *truly a being and in act* [vere ens et actu]. Perhaps it is to be read as *truly a being in potency and act* [vere ens potentia et actu], which reading is insinuated by the reading of codex B: *truly a being in act and/or in potency* [vere ens in actu et in potentia]. Immediately after this for *that* [illud] the Vatican edition alone has *the other* [aliud].

[2] For the words *either (He does this) by resting* [aut quiescendo] the Vatican ed. reads well *that is either by resting* [hoc est aut quiescendo].

[3] For (something) future [futurum] is defined by the ancient Scholastics thus: "that which is ordered or determined in its causes to receive existence in a subsequent time." With this definition there convenes somewhat that, which is proposed by others in these words: "(something) future is that which now is not, but in a subsequent duration will be, such that the essence of (something) future conveys nothing other than a negation of existence for the now, and (an affirmation of) existence for the hereafter."

[4] Supply together with codex R and Y *(something) past* [praeteritum]. — A little further below this, for *is an imperfection* [est imperfectio] codd.s M and X have *belongs to imperfection* [est imperfectionis].

[5] Edition 1 has *He would do this* [faceret].

[6] Aristotle seems to have been of the same mind; for in ETHICS, Bk. VI, ch. 2, when praising Agatho he speaks thus: « On that account Agatho rightly said:

And indeed of this thing alone God Himself is deprived,
To be able to render (things) made, in the least manner unmade ».

Which words Averroës thus comments on: That which already was, is necessary, for this reason, that it is not possible, that it not be. And on this account it seemed to certain of the ancients, that either God is deprived

of power in this species of deeds alone, I mean to say, to cause that what already was has not been. Cf. also Aristotle, ON HEAVEN AND THE WORLD, Bk. I, text 138 (ch. 12).

[7] That preterition is by no means the same as this temporal succession, is easily understood from this, that, if we posit, that God had created only one creature, and that existing in one moment, it could be said, that this creature was, but it could not be said, that it is included in a temporal succession, since no other being anteceded or succeeded it. — At the beginning of this proposition for *preterition* [praeteritio] the Vatican edition reads *(something) past* [praeteritum].

[8] Namely, that (something) past comes to be present or to be reproduced in the present. — After *Let it be* [Esto] codex F subjoins *For* [enim], and the Vatican edition by adding *and* [et] and *now* [nunc] (which even the other codices have) reads *and let it be that this is now understood* [et esto quod nunc intelligatur hoc].

[9] The Vatican edition adds here: *by which He has that it is true* [a qua habet quod sit vera].

[10] The Vatican edition and codex cc here adjoin *according to (St.) Anselm* [secundum Anselmum], from whom these words truly seem to have been taken. For in the PROSLOGION, ch. 7, (St.) Anselm says thus: For he who can (do) these (lying, causing something true to be false etc.), can (do) what is not expedient for him and what he ought not (do): which as much as he can more (do), so much more is adversity and perversity powerful over him, and he the less (able to work) against them. Who therefore, can (act) thus, cannot do (so) by power, but by impotence.

[11] Codex Y (B in the margin) adds: *because what is past, is also entirely indistinct and indistinguishable* [quia quod praeteritum est, etiam est omnino indistinctum et indistinguibile]. At the end of the solution codex R and X before *to an ordered* [ordinatum] codices R and X repeat *as* [ut].

---

* *Trans. note*: An *instance* [instantia] in Scholastic terminology is an opposing or opposed example.

as *to an effected object*, and (His) Wisdom looks back (to it as) to an *ordered* (object).

7. To that which is objected, that He can (do) the impossible according to nature; it must be said, that that is true.

8. To that which is objected, that He can (do) the impossible per accidens, because it means no resistance; it must be said, that this is not on account of a resistance, but on account of an omnimodal non-existence, on account of which that '*being able*' is a '*being able (to do) nothing*'.

9. To[1] that which is objected concerning the Creator and the creature, it must be said, that every creature is material and possible in respect of God, and God is in every creature through the intimacy of (His) Substance; not thus (is) the opposed in respect of (its) opposed. — Therefore, what is objected, that they are more distant, is true as much as regards (their) natural difference, because they communicate in nothing, but it is not true as much as regards the existence of togetherness.

10. To that which is objected concerning that, which is 'the giving birth of a virgin'; it must be said, that it is impossible according to *nature*, but not impossible according to *(logical) opposition*, because '*to be a virgin*' and '*to give birth*' are not (logical) opposites,[2] similarly, neither (are) '*to be a virgin*' and '*to conceive*'; but they are judged opposites on account of the impotence of nature. But these are opposites: '*to be united carnally*' and '*to be a virgin*'; and, for that reason, that (objection) is clear.

1. To that which is objected, that He cannot (do) the impossible according to nature [impossibile secundum naturam] on account of (its) order; it must be said, that there is a *special* and *general* order of nature. The *special* order of nature can be transmuted and destroyed, because a thing can relapse into another difference, but the *general* (order can) not. Thus it must be said, that the *special* order is attained according to the power of a particular nature [naturae specialis], the *general* order according to the power of obedience, which is general;[3] against *this* order He does not work, but against *the other* (He does).

2. To that which is objected, that He cannot (work) against a dictate [dictamen] of right reason; it must be said, that it is true, insofar as "right reason" means, that one must not do evil, because to do this is to fail; but He does not fail in this manner by working against nature; and the reason for this will be clear below.[4]

SCHOLIUM

I. In the preceding Question the Seraphic Doctor has said, in what sense God can cause everything which is *possible* by created causes; here he inquires, whether He can (do) all which is *impossible* for a created agent. Moreover, since in the body of the Response there were cited four species of those which are judged by us (to be) impossible, it is entirely manifest, that the question ought to be solved in the affirmative in regard to the first and second species of impossibles. But there remains the question about the third and fourth species, and chiefly about the *third one* or about the impossible according to *time*. Wherefore he asks, whether God can cause, that a past thing not be past. For many, especially the Nominalists, strove to prove this by many sophistic reasons. On this point Brülifer says: « Gilbert of Porretain and William of Auxerre hold for the affirmative side ... and the doctors of the English University, namely Oxford, hold their opinion against the Parisians, wherefore Gregory of Rimini posits each opinion and their reasons ». Brülifer, however, together with the more principle Scholastics, disproves this opinion well. The chief arguments of Porretain are cited in the body of the Response.

Prescinding from this subtle question concerning the impossible per accidens, very many principles, useful to establish the sane doctrine of the possibility of miracles and to sole other questions, will be found in the Response and the solution of the arguments for the negative side.

II. Alexander of Hales, SUMMA., p. I, q. 21, m. 5, a. 2, 3 and 4. — (Bl. John Duns) Scotus, REPORTATIO., here in q. 2. — St. Thomas, here in q. 2, a. 2; SUMMA., I, q. 25, a. 3 and 4. — Bl. (now St.) Albertus (Magnus), here in a. 6. — (Bl.) Peter of Tarentaise, here in q. 2, a. 3. — Richard of Middleton, here in qq. 4, 5 and 6. — Giles the Roman, here in 2nd princ., q. 2. — (Bl.) Dionysius the Carthusian, here in qq. 1 and 2.

---

[1] In codex O the solution of this objection begins thus: *To the ninth (objection it must be said), that God has not conjoined human nature to the Divine (Nature), so that it would be the same nature, and/or that one Person would be God and man according to the same, but according to the one and the other. And thus there is no doubt, that He cannot conjoin contraries and also that He does not do this according to nature. To which there is objected concerning the Creator* etc. [Ad nonum (dicendum), quod Deus non coniunxit humanam naturam divinae, ita quod esset eadem natura, vel quod una persona secundum idem esset Deus et homo, sed secundum aliud et aliud. Et sic non est dubium, quin contraria coniungere possit et etiam natura hoc faciat. Ad illud obiicitur de Creatore etc.].

[2] In codex T there is here added, that which is also had in codex B in the margin: *but to have been deflowered or corrupted is opposed to being a virgin* [sed defloratum esse sive corruptam opponitur ad esse virginem]. A little above this, after *it must be said that* [dicendum quod] codex T inserts explicitly *it* [hoc].

[3] The obediential potential is the aptitude to elicit an act above the powers of the nature through divine virtue, or the aptitude of a creature to receive an act from God exceeding the powers of (its own) nature. It is called "*general*", because it looks back to the infinite Power and Will of God, which can elicit whatever is possible out of the creature. Cf. (St.) Augustine, ON THE LITERAL EXPOSITION OF GENESIS, Bk. IX, ch. 16, n. 29 ff., and AGAINST FAUSTUS, Bk. XXVI, ch. 3, and (St.) Bonaventure's COMMENTARIA, in the following Question.

[4] In the following Question. — A little before this, for *means* [dicit], codices K M P Q V and Z and edition 1 have *dictates* [dictat].

QUESTION IV

Whether the "simply possible" is said according to superior causes, or inferior ones?

Fourth and last, there is asked, whether *the "simply possible"* is said (to be) something according to *superior* causes, and/or according to *inferior* causes, that is, according to the Divine Power, or according to a created power. And it seems, that (it is) according to a created power or according to inferior causes.

1. For *potentiality* [potestas]¹ is from the same among things, from which *necessity* and *contingency* is simply; but *necessity* and *contingency* is attained in things not only according to superior causes, nay according to inferior, proximate and particular causes: therefore, also *potentiality*.

2. Likewise, just as anyone is said (to be) "*powerful*" from (his) active potentiality, so is (something)² said (to be) "*possible*" from (its) passive potentiality; but passive potentiality is first in that, in which there is first the power to *come to be*, and through that in others: therefore, since this is the material principle and a created cause, the "*possible*" simply (speaking) is said according to inferior causes.

3. Likewise, if (there is) a "*simply possible*", it would be said according to superior causes only, then, since *with God no word is impossible*,³ nothing would have to be judged impossible.

4. Likewise, if (it is said) according to superior causes, then since God can cause, that a blind man receive back (his) sight, it is possible that a blind man see; but if it would be possible that he see, *he could* see, and if he could, he would have the power of sight [potentiam visivam]; but this (is) false: ergo etc..

ON THE CONTRARY: 1. The "*possible*" is said denominatively from "power": therefore, the "*simply possible*" from "power" simply (speaking);⁴ but the power, which is power in a most high and simple manner, is the Divine Power, which is said according to superior causes: therefore, the "*simply possible*" is said according to superior causes.

2. Likewise, that the world be created and that the soul of the Antichrist be created and/or be, and (those) completely similar, are said to be "*simply possibles*"; and they are possible only according to superior causes: ergo etc..

3. Likewise, this is show, because if something follows after anything, if the antecedent is possible, the consequent (is) also; but with anything impossible demonstrated, such as that the trunk of a tree comes to be out of a bull-calf, it follows: 'It is possible, that God cause this':⁵ therefore this, namely, that the trunk of a tree come to be out of a bull-calf, is *simply possible*.

4. Likewise, everything true is possible, and everything which was true,⁶ can be true, and everything which can be true, is *simply possible*; and it is possible only according to superior causes: ergo etc..

CONCLUSION

The "simply possible" is sometimes said, prescinding from its causes, sometimes it is said according to both inferior and superior causes in comparison to the active power, to which it is referred, sometimes even to the passive one, so long as it does not belong to the obediential power.

I RESPOND: It must be said, that about this there were diverse manners of speaking.

For certain (authors) said, that the "*simply possible*" is accepted according to *both causes*, and they found themselves upon that (verse) in the first (chapter of St. Paul's) First (Letter) to the Corinthians:⁷ *Has God not made foolish the wisdom of this world?*, the Gloss (says): « He made (it) foolish, by declaring possible that which it judges impossible », because the "possible" means (something) common to each

---

¹ The term, potestas (i.e. "power"), can also be accepted in the passive sense (i. e. "ability"). Thus is it sometimes understood to be accepted in the ancient version of Aristotle, in which, v. g., METAPHYSICS, Bk. V, text 17 (Bk. IV, ch. 2) the word, potestas, occurs for the Greek, δύναμις; moreover, the Greek word, δύναμις, is employed by Aristotle in the active and passive sense. The Vatican edition here and in the following argument substitutes *possibility* [possibilitas] for *potentiality* [potestas]. — The reason, why there is a potentiality among things by the same, by which there is a necessity and contingency simply, can be sought form this, that the "necessary" is opposed to the "impossible", and the "possible" is confounded with the "contingent", concerning which see above d. 38, a. 2, q. 2, in the fundament. On the major proposition of the argument see above d. 38, a. 2, qq. 1 and 2.

² Supply, together with codices P and Q, *something* [aliquid]. — Next, for *there is first the power* [primo est potentia] codices K and V have *in which the first power is* [prima est potentia]. — On the reason touched upon in the conclusion ("since this is the material principle" etc.), cf. above d. 19, p. II, q. 3, in the fundament.

³ Luke 1:37.

⁴ Nor is what is simply such or first in any genus, the cause and measure of all [causa et mensura omnium] which belong to that genus,

as Aristotle would have it in METAPHYSICS, Bk. II, text 4, and Bk. X, text 2 ff. (in the shorter version, Bk. I, ch. 1, and Bk. IX, ch. 1).

⁵ The minor proposition, expressed a wider and more diffused sense, would sound thus: but with anything demonstrated (to be) impossible according to inferior causes, such as that a trunk of a tree comes to be out of a bull-calf, there nevertheless ought to be said, that God can do this, or that this is still possible. — On the major proposition of this argument, cf. above d. 38, a. 2, q. 2, 1st argument of the fundament. In this major proposition for *the antecedent is possible* [antecedens est possibile] codices A F G H I V W X and ee have *antecedent is impossible* [antecedens est impossibile] in a depraved manner, as is evident.

⁶ The sense is: what was true in the past can be true in the future, v. g. 'someone blind could see, therefore, the other blind man will be able to see'. — For *was* [erat] the Vatican edition alone has *will be* [erit].

⁷ Verse 20. — The words of the Gloss, which are cited here, are found neither in Walafrid (Strabo)'s nor in (Nicholas of) Lyra's collection of Glosses: but yet these words are had in Lyra's: « Which (the wisdom of this world) judges impossible, because it does not see (them) among the natures of things », and in (St.) Ambrose in his exposition of this passage (there are found) these (words): « For what

(cause). Yet, that does not seem to be able to stand fittingly, because[1] it is not admitted, that it is simply possible that, from (being) blind, one come to be seeing, nay, it is said (to be) "impossible": therefore, it would be at once [simul] possible and impossible, which is unfitting [inconveniens]. Yet, it is possible according to superior causes, because the Gloss does not say only, "*by declaring*", but it also says, "*by making (it) possible*": therefore, at first it was not possible. And, again, it says: *it has become foolish*, because worldly wisdom judged (it to be) so impossible, that it was possible to no one, and (, yet,) God declared that it is possible for Himself.

And, for that reason, there is another position, that according to which the sciences descend, so also the names of the sciences. and thus in natural philosophy the "*simply possible*" must be judged according to *inferior* causes. — Yet, this still does not seem (to be) a fitting position, because (St.) Anselm himself,[2] and (any) theologian, says, that it is impossible, that a bull-calf come to be from the trunk of a tree, and that the simply impossibles are possible for God.

On this account, it must be said in another manner, that the "*simply possible*" can mean the order of a substance[3] to that in respect of which it is, the order, I say, which *is*, and/or which *is going to be*, or a *present* and/or *future* power. If it means a *future* (power), then the sense is: "it is possible that a man run, that is, *that he have* the power to run." If it means a *present* power, then the sense is: "it is possible that the man is running, that is, the man *does have* the power to run"; and this twofold manner of speaking is accepted by the Philosopher,[4] who also expounds this in a twofold manner: « Every B happens to be A, that is everything which *is* B, and/or everything which *can be* B, happens to be A ».

But, insofar as it mean a power concerning (something) *future*, the "possible" can be accepted according to whatsoever causes, whether superior ones or inferior ones. And this is clear, because nothing other is then said, except that it will have the power for this; and by whomsoever it has (it), whether from God or from an Angel or from itself, it is true, that it will have the power. And, in this manner, it must be said, that it is possible to see, with it demonstrated that a blind man (is) to see, and that a virgin gives birth, and all other such (things), because to such there can be given power.

However, in another manner that which is "*possible*" means *actually* a power in the thing, which is signified to be ordered to another; and in this manner there is a general rule, that if in the thing, to which the simply possible is attributed,[5] is a power *simply*, then it is said (to be) a "*simply possible*"; but if (it is) a power secundum quid (i. e. a power according to something), then it is said (to be) a "possible secundum quid". For since the "possible" means the order of a power to an act or of something to anything by means of a power; for that reason the reckoning of speaking in regard to [in] that possible is taken from the power.

Moreover, the name of "power" [potentiae] is said in a twofold manner, namely, of *active* power, which is the principle of transmuting another, and of *passive* power, which is the principle of being transmuted by another.[6] And *active* power is found both in God and in a creature, and each is a power simply complete in respect of its own act. For *active* power, by that very (thing) that (it is) active, means a complete ordination to an act, as much as it concerns itself. However, *passive* power is found only in a creature. And, indeed, this power can be *proximate* [propinqua] to the act, and *remote* from the act; for that reason passive power is said *simply*, and secundum quid.[7] For a certain power is born to be reduced to an act by an *inferior* power, *with a superior (power) cooperating*, such as when it is with a *proximate disposition* [dispositione proprinqua], such as the power, which is in wood for ignition. A certain (power) is thus born to be reduced by a superior power in some manner *with a consonant inferior (power)*, such as the power of the impious for justification, and each is said (to be) a "*proximate (power)*". A certain (power) is thus distant from the act, which if it be reduced (to it), it cannot be reduced except by a superior power, and this, indeed, *with an entirely deficient* and/or *in no manner consonant*, active, inferior power, as for example that one be able to come to be living from (being) dead, and (that) from the trunk of a tree there come to be a bull-calf, and this is a power secundum quid.

(the wisdom of this age), considering God unmindful, judged impossible, has been declared possible ». The Seraphic Doctor has perhaps taken these words, cited under the name of the Gloss, out of Peter Lombard's COLLECTANEA, in which the words cited truly occur on the First Epistle to the Corinthians, with only the words *and making* [et faciendi] added after *by declaring* [declarando], which words even codex B exhibits in the margin, and which the Seraphic Doctor also cites a little below this, where he says: « because the Gloss does not say only "*by declaring*", but it also says "*by making (it) possible*" ». — In the citation from the Gloss, the Vatican edition falsely has *it (i. e. the world)* [ipse] for *it (i. e. the wisdom of the world)* [ipsa].

[1] For *because it* [quia], which we have put on the testimony of codices I P Q and T and edition 1, the other codices, together with editions 2 and 3, incongruously have *what* [quod]; the Vatican has better *since it* [cum] and then the subjunctive form of the verb *admitted* [admittatur]. Somewhat further below this, the same Vatican edition has *for* [nam] for *Yet* [Tamen].

[2] CUR DEUS HOMO., Bk. II, ch. 18: « Indeed, every necessity and impossibility, lies under God's will ». On the example cited, cf. above q. 3, p. 751, footnote 2. — After *(St.) Anselm himself* [ipse Anselmus] the Vatican edition interjects *and the Philosopher* [Philosophus].

[3] For *of a substance* [substantiae] the Vatican edition, together with codex cc, has faultily *of a power* [potentiae]. Our reading is supported by both the older codices and edition 1 and by the words of St. Bonaventure themselves, which are had somewhat below this in the body of this

Conclusion: "Therefore, that which is a "*possible*" can mean the order of a substance to *acting*" etc. [Potest ergo hoc quod est possibile dicere ordinem *substantiae* ad agere etc.]. — Next after *or* [sive] codex X repeats *it can mean* [potest dicere].

[4] PRIOR ANALYTICS, Bk. I, ch. 12: But since it happens that this is in that, there is an accepting (of it) in a twofold manner: for either in reference to that [cui] in which it is, or in reference to that in which the in-being itself happens (to be); for one of the two of these signify that concerning which B, there happens (to be) an A: either "concerning which there is said (to be) a B", or "concerning which it happens to be said (that there is a B)" etc.. — For *can be B* [potest esse B] in codices I and V there is read *happens to be B* [contingit esse B].

[5] Ed. 1 omits *simply* [simpliciter], which reading seems to be preferred. — A little further above this, for *which is signified* [quae significatur] the Vatican edition alone substitutes *by which it is indicated* [quo signatur], and a little below this after *or of something* [sive alicuius] the same Vatican edition, together with codex cc, faultily subjoins *or* [sive].

[6] The definition of power, both as active and passive, exhibited here, is insinuated by Aristotle, in METAPHYSICS, Bk. V, text 17, and Bk. IX, text 2 (Bk. IV, ch. 12, and Bk. VIII, ch. 1). The (Latin) gerund, transmutandi, in the first place, has an active meaning (i. e. *of transmuting*), in the second place, a passive meaning (i. e. *of being transmuted*).

[7] For *ignition* [ignitionem] the Vatican edition, together with codex cc, has *combustion* [combustionem], and a little after this for *such as the power of the impious* [ut potential impii] it substitutes *as for example of the impious* [ut puta impii].

From which it is clear, that *simply passive* power is attained according to superior and inferior causes. And because "secundum quid" is said through a defect in respect of the "*simply*", the *passive* power, which can be reduced to act solely according to superior causes, with the created, disposing and/or consonant, active power failing, is a power secundum quid and is said (to be) a power of "*obedience*". And concerning this (St.) Augustine says,[1] that « in the rib there was, not whence the woman would be made, but whence she could be made », namely a power of obedience. — Therefore, the "possible", which is said from a power, is not said *uniformly* nor is it said entirely *equivocally*, but *analogically* just as "healthy"; and for that reason its acceptation is determined through the adjoined (term).

Therefore, that which is a "*possible*" can mean the order of a substance to *acting*; and then it means an *active* power, and this is determined through the adjoined (term). For if it means the order of an uncreated Substance to an act, it means a power according to superior causes, such as if there is said: "That God creates a world and/or gives light [illuminare] to a blind man is possible." But if it means the order of a created substance (to an act),[2] it means an created, active power, such as if there is said: "It is possible that the Antichrist runs," and/or "It is possible that a blind man see", there is signified a power in the blind man; for that reason it is false simply.

Again,[3] it can mean the order of something to *becoming* [fieri], and this can be in a twofold manner: either *in comparison to something out of which*, or *without comparison*. If *in comparison to something out of which*, then it conveys a passive power according to *thing*. And if it be simply a passive power, such as that which is according to superior and inferior causes,[4] it is said (to be) "*simply* impossible". But if it be a passive power reducible only according to superior causes, it is only possible secundum quid; so that if there be said: "it is possible that a bull-calf come to be out of the trunk of a tree", it is simply to be denied,[5] unless there is added a contracting determination, such as if it be said (to be) "possible" by a power of obedience and/or "possible for God". — But, if it mean the order of something to becoming *without comparison to a principle out of which*, then it conveys a *passive* power according to a *manner*, but *active* according to *thing*; so that if there be said: "It is possible, that the soul of the Antichrist be created", and/or "It is possible, that a bull-calf come to be", this is to say, that someone can do (it); and for that reason without a determination it is possible either according to superior causes, or according to inferior

causes, because by reason of an active power it remains [salvatur] (possible)[6] in each manner [utrobique].

For, that which is "possible" can also mean an order and/or comparison of *a being to a 'to be'*, such as when there is said: "this can be, howsoever (it be) demonstrated"; and thus it means neither an *active* power nor a *passive* power determinately, neither according to superior causes nor according to inferior causes, wherefore it is said *simply*, in whatsoever[7] of these manners it be possible.

Therefore, only in one case is the "*possible* secundum quid" said according to superior causes, namely, when it means a passive power according to a *manner* and *thing*, such as when there is said: "From (being) blind one can come to be seeing", and "From the trunk of a tree a bull-calf can come to be", and "It is possible that a man come to be out of a donkey."

From these (considerations) all the objections to each side are clear: for the objections to the first side proceed from the "possible", according to which it means a passive power.

1. To that which is objected for the opposite, that the "possible" is said denominatively from a power; it must be said, that the "possible" can be said denominatively from an *active* and/or *passive* power; and because in God there is properly an *active* power, for that reason the "simply possible" is said,[8] according to which it is denominated by that, not according to which (it is denominated) by a *passive* (power).

2. To that which is objected concerning that, which it is "to create the world"; it must be said, that though it means a power through the manner of a *passion*, yet according to thing it means naught but *active* power, because before the creation of the world there is nothing except an *active* Power; and for that reason it is said simply according to superior causes.

3. To that which is objected, that it follows: 'if God can do (it), that a thing can come to be (it)'; it must be said, that it is true, according to which "*can*" means the same power through the manner of a *passion*, and this it does mean,[9] when it is said *simply*. But if it truly means a *passive* power, it does not follow, because that which is "*possible*" varies, as is clear, if there be said: "God can make of a blind man one who sees [videntem]": therefore, "a blind man can be one who sees", and/or "out of a blind man there can come to be one who sees." For the first ("can") meant an active power *simply* and the one afterwards a *passive* one; and for that reason it does not follow. Therefore, when there is said: "if the antecedent is possible, the consequent (is) also"; it must be understood according to *the same possibility* [eadem possibilitate].

4. To that, therefore, which is objected last, that every truth [verum] can be true, before it is: it must be

---

[1] On a Literal Exposition of Genesis, Bk. IX, chs. 16 and 17, nn. 30 and 31.

[2] Supply together with the Vatican edition *to an act* [ad actum]. — A little after, for *that the Antichrist run* [antichristum currere] codices T and T have faultily *that the Antichrist is* [esse Antichristum].

[3] After *again* [iterum] codex M and edition 1 interject rightly the "*possible*" [possibile] as the explicit subject.

[4] Or, as has been said above, which is born to be reduced to an act by an inferior power, with a superior one cooperating. — A little further above this, for *And if it be* [Et si sit] very many codices, together with editions 2, 3, 4, and 5 have falsely *And thus it comes to be* [Et sic fit].

[5] The Vatican edition alone, with changed punctuation, prefixes

and for that reason [et ideo] at the beginning of this clause. For *out of the trunk of a tree* [ex trunco] some codices, such as V and Z, together with edition 1, have *from the trunk of a tree* [de trunco].

[6] Supply: possible. — For *because* [quia] codex R has *and* [et], and then edition 1 reads *the reckoning of an active power remains in each* etc. [ratio potentiae activae etc.].

[7] Many codices, together with edition 1, read *whichsoever* [quicumque] for *in whatsoever ... it* [quocumque].

[8] In not a few codices and in editions 2, 3, 4, and 5, there is faultily omitted *is said* [dicitur], in place of which codex R has *is* [est].

[9] We have supplied *it does mean* [dicit] out of the manuscripts and editions 1, 2, and 3.

said, that it is true, and with it demonstrated that one is blind, that this saying[1] is true, is possible, because the "possible" is accepted there in respect of the true, and the saying "*that it is possible*", when it means an order to a '*to be*' [esse] and/or to a '*to be true*' [esse verum], means a power commonly regarding the active and passive, the superior and inferior. But then it does not follow *concerning the thing*: 'therefore, this one *can see*'; because (this term "*can*")[2] means an active created power, namely the power of sight. Nor does it follow: 'therefore, from a blind man there will be able to be

made a seer [videns]', according to which "*able*" posits a power in act in that one; because ("*can*" or "*able*")* means a *passive, disposed* power, nay there is a fallacy of the consequent there; because, since the "*possible*" is accepted in its generality, it has three causes of (its) truth: either because in the blind man there is a potentiality [potestas] to *see*, or a potentiality to *receive*, or because there is in another a potentiality to *give*; by reason of the latter[3] it has been said (to be) "possible", and it will come to be true at any time, just as is clear; and thus all the other objections are clear.

SCHOLIUM

I. The distinction between the "*simply* possible" [possibile simpliciter] and the "possible secundum quid" (i.e. the "possible according to something") is an ancient one. Moreover, the "possible" is not only considered absolutely *in itself*, to the extent that it is conceived according to the rules of logic as the "*not impossible*", but also in an order *to another*, such as its cause; and thus it means an order to some power, whether *active* or *passive*. It is manifest, that one and the same (thing) in comparison to one cause can be *possible* to one, but in comparison to another (cause be) *impossible* for another. Hence there arose the distinction between the "*simply* possible" and the "possible secundum quid", and also the question, "According to which *reckoning* or *comparison* to some power, created and/or uncreated, is something said (to be) *simply* possible, and/or possible secundum quid?" But St. Thomas cuts short this intricate question in his SUMMA, since he accepts the "*simply* possible" in the *absolute* sense. For he says there (I, q. 25, a. 3, in reply to n. 4): « The "absolute possible" is not said neither according to superior causes nor according to inferior ones, but according to itself. However, the "possible", which is said according to some power, is named a "possible" according to a proximate cause » etc.. — Moreover, the question under the form proposed by the ancient (Scholastics) pertains more to the manner of speaking.

(William) of Auxerre, as he is read in (Bl.) Dionysius the Carthusian's (Commentary), here in q. 3, reports three opinions. The *first* is, that only that is "simply possible", which can come to be according to inferior causes; the *second*, that (the "simply possible" is) everything and only that, which is possible for God; the *third*, that (the "simply possible" is) neither only according to superior causes, nor only according to inferior ones, but sometimes according to inferior causes, sometimes according to superior ones, according to the diverse adjoined (terms). Moreover, (William) of Auxerre himself prefers the second opinion, which Bl. (now St.) Albertus (Magnus) also seem to favor. Alexander of Hales (SUMMA., p. I. q. 21, m. 5, a. 1), having cited

these three opinions, adds and approves that one which is posited *here* in the second place. St. Bonaventure explains the third opinion, reported by (William) of Auxerre, in a most subtle manner and by employing many distinctions and he accurately determines that which each of the three opinions contains of the truth. So that his intricate doctrine may be sufficiently perceived, one must attend to that principle (placed before the midpoint of the body of the Response): « the "possible" means the order of a power to an act or of something to anything by means of a power; for that reason the reckoning of the speaking in regard to that possible is taken from the power ». Moreover, the author considers this *power* under various distinctions, the principles ones of which are these: first, power is either *future* and for that reason indeterminate, and/or *present* and determinate. According to this distinction he responds to the question through general conclusions. Again "*present* power" is distinguished into "*active*" and "*passive*" power, with other subdistinctions and conclusions, as is clear in the text. From which he concludes, that the "possible" is not always said univocally, but also *analogically*, and that its « acceptation is determined through the *adjoined* (term) ». For through this there is expressed either an order to *acting*, and/or to *becoming*, and/or to *being*. In this second part of the Response the principles and distinction posited in the first part are applied and determined more (clearly).

II. St. Thomas in his, COMMENTARY, here in q. 2, a. 3 convenes in very many distinctions and conclusions with St. Bonaventure. — The other resolve (the question) in a little different manner, so that there appears to be no notable difference, except in a manner of speaking.

Besides the authors (already) cited: (Bl. John Duns) Scotus, SENT., Bk. I, d. 43, q. sole, and REPORTATIO, ibid., q. sole. — Bl. Albertus, here in a. 9; SUMMA., p. I, tr. 19, q. 78, m. 1, 2 and 3. — (Bl.) Peter of Tarentaise, here in q. 2, a. 1. — Richard of Middleton, here in q. 7. — Giles the Roman, here in 2nd princ., q. 2. — (Bl.) Dionysius the Carthusian, here in q. 3.

DOUBTS ON THE TEXT OF THE MASTER

DOUBT I

In this part, are the doubts about (Master Peter's) text and first concerning this verse from (St.) Augustine. *God does not do except what befits His Truth and Justice.* For

it seems false, because in the Psalm[1] there is said: *The Mercy of the Lord (is) upon all His works*: therefore, he ought rather to have said, that He does not do, except what befits (His) *Mercy. And again*, what difference is there between (His) *Truth* and *Justice*?

---

[1] The Vatican edition, after its own manner, but not badly, adjoins "*he can see*" [iste potest videre]. A little below this, for *and the saying "that it is possible"* the same Vatican edition has *and it has been said that (it is) possible* [et dictum est quod possibile], codices ee and ff have *and the saying is possible* [et dictum est possibile], codices M R V X Z (T by a second hand) have *and thus the saying "that it is possible"*, edition 1 has *and just as it has been said, that it is possible* [et sicut dictum est, esse possibile].

[2] Understand: this term "*can*". — Then for *active* [activam] the Vatican edition, with codex cc, has *passive* [passivam]. Next, for *will be able to be made* [poterit], codex Y and ed. 1 have *can be made* [potest].

[3] Namely, because there is in another a potentiality to give.

[4] Psalm 144:9: *Sweet (is) the Lord to each and every, and His mercies (are) upon all His works* [Suavis Dominus universis, et eius super omnia opera eius].

I RESPOND: It must be said, that "*justice*" in one manner is the same as "*the demand of merits*" [exigentia meritorum], and, thus, is divided against "mercy"; in another manner it means the *co-fittingness of goodness* [condecentiam bonitatis], and in this manner it comprehends "mercy" and "justice" properly said. And thus does (St.) Augustine accept it in the aforesaid verse, and in this manner (God's Justice) differs from (God's) Truth according to the reckoning of speaking, though It is the same according to Thing. For (God's) *Truth* looks back to each thing according to itself; but (His) *Justice* looks back to one thing compared to another, according to which the one is gathered through due laws to the other.[1]

DOUBT II

Likewise, is asked concerning this which (St. Augustine) says: *God could make all (things) at once* [simul], *but reason prohibited (this).* For it seems that he speaks badly, because '*to be able to be prohibited*' belongs to impotence: therefore, if the Divine Power can be prohibited, It is impotent. — *Likewise*, that reason is either something *created*, or *uncreated*. If *created*: therefore, something other than God prohibited the Divine Virtue, therefore something can resist God. If *uncreated*: in what manner can it prohibit, since It is entire the Same? — *Moreover*, it does not seem that this (will) be prohibited, because in the eighteenth (chapter)[2] of Ecclesiasticus there is said: *He who lives forever* [in aeternum] *created all (things) at once.*

I RESPOND: It must be said, that here (God's) rational Will is called the "*reason*", and *reasonableness* in a will,[3] though it does not mean something as much as regards what is principally signified by the Divine Essence, yet it connotes another, namely *some congruity in the willed*, which indeed is not found in its opposite. Which is clear. If all were produced *at once* as much as regards a singular 'to be', no creature could cause anything, and there would not be a course of things[4] in the universe, which there is. Therefore, (God's) rational Will demanded this, that God not make all (things) at once, even though He could; wherefore "*prohibition*" is not accepted here for a repugnance, but for the constriction [arctatione] of power as much as regards (its) *act*, not as much as regards (its) *being able.* And this is a determination of indifference to this work, not to the opposite; and, thus, the objections are clear. For Ecclesiasticus understands (the matter) as much as regards the principal or prior parts, but (St.) Augustine speaks as much as regards individuals.[5]

DOUBT III

Likewise, is asked concerning the difference of those four (acts), which (St.) Augustine[6] removes from God, namely *to die* [mori], *to fail* [falli], *to be wretched* [miserum esse] and *to be conquered* [vinci].

I RESPOND: It must be said, that these mean the defects of man himself or of the soul in the body. Moreover, there is a fourfold *act* and a fourfold *power.* The first is vivificative [vivificativa], and its act is *to live*, and against this is the defect *to die.* The second is *cognitive*, the act of which is *to know* [nosse], and against this is *to fail.* The first is *affective*, and its act is *to will* or to love and to take delight in [delectari], and against this is *to be wretched.* The fourth is *operative*, and its act is *to act*, and against this is *to be conquered* and *to be overcome.* — And note, that from these which are said, the four genera of acts are removed from God, namely *the corporal* or instrumental[7] (acts), such as to run; *the culpable* acts, such as to sin, (and) to lie; *the passive* acts, such as to be conquered and to be overcome; *the defective* acts, such as to die and to fail, which have a power conjoined to a defect. And, hence, Master (Peter)[8] chooses the perfect reckoning of power, that can *do all (things)* and *suffer nothing.*

DOUBT IV

Likewise, is asked concerning that which (St.) Augustine says, because *he accepts "all" so amply, that he even would include evils.* For it seems that (Master Peter) says the false, because either *evil* is included by reason of a *substrate*, or by reason of a *deformity.* By reason of a *substrate* it is also included properly,[9] because an evil action, according to the reckoning of (its) substrate action [ratione actionis substratae], is by the Divine Power. If by reason of a *deformity*, since that is simply not a being, it does not seem able to be included.

I RESPOND: It must be said, that '*evil*' is accepted by reason of a deformity; and since "*all*" [omnia] distributes[10] there for "*possibility*", and the "*possible*" can be accepted generally, both from an active power and from a defective one, and, thus, it is accepted *amply* [amply], and it comprehends evil; and in this manner (St.) Augustine understands (it). In another manner, (it is accepted) as the "*possible*" is said from the power, which is a power according to thing and manner [secundum rem et modum], and then it is accepted *properly*, and then there is contained

---

[1] Cf. Alexander of Hales, SUMMA., p. I. q. 20, m. 5, in reply to n. 4; Bl. (now St.) Albertus (Magnus), here in a. 7.

[2] Verse 1. — Pro *(will) be prohibited* [prohibendum] the Vatican edition has *(has been) prohibited* [prohibitum].

[3] The Vatican edition, together with codex cc continues thus: *and this (reasonableness) of His, though it does not mean something else* [et ista quamvis non dicat aliquid aliud].

[4] For *a course of things* [rerum cursus] the Vatican edition, together with some codices, has *on this account a course* [propter hoc cursus], codices L O and Y read *, moreover, a course* [praeterea cursus], not a few other codices have *first a course* [primum cursus], codices F P and Q have *that course* [ille cursus]. We have taken our reading from codex R and edition 1. Cf. ITINERARIUM IN MENTIS DEUM, ch. 1.*

[5] Cf. SENT., Bk. II. d. 12, a. 1, q. 2, in reply to n. 2; Alexander of Hales, SUMMA., p. I. q. 20, m. 5, in reply to n. 5, and p. II, q. 44, m. 3; Bl. (now St.) Albertus (Magnus), here in a. 7; St. Thomas, (Bl.) Peter of Tarentaise, Richard of Middleton and Giles the Roman, here on the text.

[6] ON THE CREED FOR CATECHUMENS, Bk. I, ch. 1, n. 2. See the text of Master (Peter) here, in ch. 2. Cf. also (St. Augustine's), TO FAUSTUS, Bk. XXVI, ch. 5. — For *to be conquered* [vinci] many codices, together with the first editions, have *to lie* [mentiri], faultily.

[7] Codices X and V have *material* [materiales], which word even Alexander of Hales, SUMMA., p. I, q. 21, m. 1, a. 1, employs.

[8] Here in ch. 3. — Next for *that* [quod] the Vatican edition, together with codex cc, has *which* [quae]. — On this doubt, cf. also above q. 2; Alexander of Hales, SUMMA., p. I, q. 21, m. 1, a. 1; Bl. (now St.) Albertus (Magnus), here in a. 8; Richard of Middleton, here on the text.

[9] In the Vatican edition there are wanting the words *also ... properly* [etiam proprie], and, for *By reason* [Ratione], there is read *Not by reason* [Non ratione]. Even in the following proposition the Vatican edition substitutes *Not by reason* [Non ratione] for *If by reason* [Si ratione], and, then, after *of a deformity* [deformitatis], it inserts *because* [quia].

[10] Cf. above d. 4, a. sole, q. 2, Scholium, I, n. 2.

---

* *Trans. note*: The *course of things* is that consecution of things according to existence which results from the dependence of causality of those things who follow the initial act of creation.

there no evil, and in this manner it is accepted in common use, when we say *that God (is) omnipotent*. And thus it is clear, though it is not contained under a being, that it is not[1] similar concerning power.

DOUBT V

Likewise, is asked concerning this which (Master Peter) says, that *a man and/or an Angel has a gratuitous power, by which he is powerful*. For it seems that he speaks badly, because *generation* is a natural act, since one generates a similar in nature [similem in antura],[2] therefore, it is a natural power; but (it does) not (belong) to God, because God does not naturally produce a man: therefore, it belongs to man, therefore, a man has a natural power.

I RESPOND: It must be said, that the *"natural"*[naturale] is said in a twofold manner. In one manner, the "natural" means that which is had *by a nature* and *according to the consonance of nature*; and, in this manner, many creatures have natural powers. In another manner, a power is said (to be) "natural", which is in something through *its own nature* [per propriam naturam], thus, that it is not through another nature, neither giving nor conserving (the power); and in this manner the Divine Virtue alone is "natural", but every

other (power) has been given liberally by God, and is liberally conserved and assisted (by God), to act, and for that reason it is said (to be) "gratuitous".[3]

DOUBT VI

Likewise, is asked concerning this which (Master Peter) says, that *God the Trinity is truly and properly said (to be) "omnipotent"*. For it seems that he does not speak the truth, because He is not *properly* omniscient: therefore, neither omnipotent. — Likewise, in the last (chapter of the Gospel of St.) Matthew (there is said):[4] *There has been given unto Me every power in Heaven and on Earth*. And it seems (that it is said) of the others, because in the ninth (chapter of the Gospel of St.) Mark (there is written):[5] *If you can believe, all are possible for the one believing*.

I RESPOND: It must be said, that *omnipotence* belongs *properly* to God alone, because it means the infinite Power, which can be in no creature, neither in Christ nor in another according to human nature. And this will be clear better below in another place.[6] Wherefore if *"omnipotence"* be said of Christ, this is understood according to the communication of idioms. But if it be said of (those) believing, *the distribution* is *apt* [accomoda][7] only concerning (the working of) miracles. And, thus, that (Doubt) is clear.

DISTINCTION XLIII

CHAPTER I

An invective against those who say, that God can (do) nothing, but what He wills and does.

However, certain (authors), glorying in their own sense, have tried to constrain God's Power under a measure. For, when they say: "God is able up to this point [hucusque] and not more", what is this, other than to enclose and restrict His Power, which is infinite, to a measure? For they say: "For God can do [facere] other, than He does; and (He can) not make [facere] better that which He does [facit], nor omit something from those which He does." And they strive to fortify this first[1] opinion of theirs with seemingly true [verisimilibus] arguments and invented [commentitiis] causes and with even the testimonies of sacred authorities, saying: "God can cause [facere] naught, but that what is good and just come to be [fieri]. But there is no coming to be of the just and good from Him, except [nisi] that He cause (it). For, if 'that He cause the

just and good' is other, than He does [facit], therefore, He does not cause [facit] Himself to cause everything which is just and good. But who dares to say this?

They also add: "He cannot do [facit], except [nisi] what His Justice demands; but His Justice does not demand, that He do, except what He does: therefore, He cannot do, but [nisi] what He does. And the same Justice demands, that He does not do that, which He does not do; but He cannot work [facere] against His own Justice: therefore, He cannot do [facere] any of those, which He leaves off [dimitit] (doing)."

But, to these, we respond, opening the twofold understanding of the words and unrolling (those) involuted in them [ab eis involuta evolventes] thus: "God cannot do, but what is just and good", that is, (the proposition): "He cannot do, except that which, if He would do (it), would be good and just" is true; but He can do many (things), which are not good nor just, because they neither are not will be, nor come to be nor will come to be well, because they never will come to be.

Likewise, what has been proposed[2] second: "He cannot do, but what His own Justice demands; and He cannot do

---

[1] The Vatican edition, together with very many codices, reads *not, however,* [non tamen]. — On this doubt, cf. above q. 4, and (Bl.) Peter of Tarentaise, here on the text.

[2] Aristotle, ON THE SOUL, Bk. II, text 34 (c. 4): For the most natural work, which (is) among living (things) ... is to make another, such as oneself [quale ipsum].

[3] This doubt is solved, also, by Richard (of Middleton, in his own COMMENTARY), here on the text.

[4] Verse 18.

[5] Verse 22.

[6] SENT., Bk. III, d. 44, q. 3. q. 3.

[7] Concerning which, cf. above d. 39, Doubt 1, p. 517, footnote 3. — Cf. Alexander of Hales, SUMMA., p. I, q. 21, n. 1, a. 4; Bl. (now St.) Albertus (Magnus), here in a. 10; St. Thomas, SENT., Bk. I, d. 43, q. 1. a. 2.

NOTES ON THE BOOK OF SENTENCES
[1] Editions 2 and 5 have *depraved* [pravam] for *first* [primam]. Then the Vatican edition and the other editions, except ed. 1, have *they try* [conantur] for *they strive* [nituntur], with all the codices contradicting it.

[2] Only the Vatican edition and editions 4, 6 and 8 have *opposed* [oppositum]. Immediately after this codex C reads *demands, Him to do; and* [exigat, ut fiat; et] for *demands; and* [exigit; et].

that, which His own Justice demands, that He not do"; we say, because a verb of *demanding* [exactionis] is not congruously said of God, nor is it properly accepted. And in those expressions there is a twofold sense. For if you understand: "He cannot do, but what His own justice demands", that is, "but what His own just Will wills", you say the false. For the Justice of God is accepted as His Most Equitous Will [aequissima voluntas], in which manner (St.) Augustine[1] accepts (it), (when) expounding those words of the Lord, in Genesis, speaking to Lot: *I cannot do anything, until you enter in there*, he says: « He said that *He cannot* (do), that which without doubt He could (do) through (His) Power, but (which) He could not (do) through (His) Justice »; as if to say:[2] "He indeed could (do it); but He did not want to, and that Will was just." Therefore, if you understand through these words, "that He cannot do except that which, if He would do, it would convene with His Justice", you speak the truth. Similarly, distinguish this: "He cannot do what His Justice demands, that He not do", that is, "He cannot do that which He himself, who is the Most High Justice, does not want to do", (thus) it is false. But if you understand by these words, "that He cannot do that which cannot convene with His Justice", you speak the truth.

They also add, saying even other (things): "God cannot do but what He ought (to do); however, He ought not do but what He does. For if He ought to do others, therefore, He does not do everything which He ought; but if He does everything which He ought, He cannot do but what He ought: therefore, He cannot do but what He does." — Likewise, "either He ought to leave off (doing) what He leaves off, to do, or He ought not. If He ought not, He does not rightly leave off (doing); but if He ought to leave off doing: therefore, He ought not do. But if He ought not, and it is not fitting [decet] nor[3] necessary [oportet] that He do (them), therefore, He cannot do (them): therefore, He cannot do but what He does. Nor can he leave off (doing) that which He does, so as not to do it, because He ought to do that; and that which He ought to do, He cannot leave off (doing)." — But as it seems to be, this verb "*He ought*" has a poison. For it contains[4] a multiple and involuted understanding, nor does it properly befit [competit] God, who is not a debtor to us, except [nisi] perhaps on account of *a promise*, but we are debtors to Him on account of (what we have) *committed*. Moreover, to empty out (its) poison, distinguish the senses of the verb: "God cannot do but what He ought", that is, (in the sense of) "but what He wills", (then) it is false, for thus He Himself can be said *to owe something*, because *He wills it*. But, if there be said: "He cannot (do) but what He ought", that is, "He cannot (do) except that which, if He would do, would well convene with Him", (then) it is true.

They also add[5] saying: "He can do or leave off (doing) nothing, except for the best and reasonable cause, though it has been hidden from us, according to which (cause) it is necessary [oportet] that He do and leave off (doing), what He does and/or leaves off (doing). For the reason is from within Him, by which He does these and leaves off (doing) those; which reason is eternal and remaining always, besides which He cannot do and/or leave off (doing) anything. Therefore, with that remaining, He cannot leave off (doing) what He does, nor do what He leaves off (doing), and thus He cannot do but what he does." — And to this

we respond, determining the ambiguity of the expression. For when there is said: "The reason and/or best cause is from within God, by which He does all which He does, and leaves off (doing) those which He does", it is indeed true, because in Him the Will is Most Equitous and Most Upright, by which He does and leaves off (doing) what He wills, *against* which He cannot work, and *besides which* [praeter eam] He cannot work. Nor at any rate would He work *against* It nor *besides* It, if He would leave off (doing) those which He does, and/or would do those which He leaves off (doing); but with the reason and cause remaining the same, He could do other (things) and leave off (doing) these. Therefore, though the reason is from within Him, by which He does some, leaves off (doing) others, yet He can according to the same reason both leave off (doing) what He does, and do what He leaves off (doing).

Moreover[6] they add: "There is a reason, that He does what He does and not other (things); and He cannot do, except (that) on account of which there is a reason that He does (it): and thus He cannot do but what He does. Likewise, there is a reason, that He leaves off (doing) what He leaves off (doing); and He cannot not leave off (doing that) on account of which there is a reason that He leave off (doing it): and thus He cannot not leave off (doing) what He leaves off (doing)." — And to this we say, that the expressions are ambiguous, and for that reason (they are) to be determined. For if, when there is said: "He cannot do, except (that) on account of which there is a reason that He do (it)", you understand, "that He cannot do, except those thing which are reasonable, and those which, if He would do (them), they would be reasonable", the sense is true. But if you understand, "that He cannot do other reasonable and good (things), except those which He wills and does", the understanding is a false one.

Likewise, they adjoin another, saying: "If God can do other than He does, He can therefore, do what He has not foreknown; and if He can do what He has not foreknown, He can work without foreknowledge, because everything, which He foreknew He (was) going to do, He does, nor does He do something which He did not foreknow. Which, if it is impossible that anything come to be apart from [praeter] His Foreknowledge, it is necessary that everything which has been foreknown, come to be: therefore, it is possible according to no reckoning, that there comes to be (something) other, than comes to be: therefore, there cannot come to be from God, but what comes to be." — But this question concerning (God's) Foreknowledge can easily be determined through those which have been said further above,[7] when the Foreknowledge was dealt with.

Moreover, to these those scrutinizers, who *failed scrutinizing scrutinies*, adjoined the testimonies of the Saints. For (St.) Augustine says in the book, ON THE CREED:[8] « This alone God cannot (do): what He does not will (to do) ». Through which it seems that He cannot do anything, but what He wills; but He does not will but what He does: and thus it seems that He cannot (do) but what He does. — But that most be understood thus: "this alone God cannot (do): what He does want, namely, Himself to be able (to do)." — He says the same in the seventh book of THE CONFESSIONS,[9] speaking to God: « Nor art That thought (to be) unwilling regarding anything, because Thy Will is not greater than (Thy) Power; moreover, It would be greater, if Thou Thyself would be greater than Thy very Self ». From this it seems, that God cannot (do) more, than He wills, just as He does not will more, that He can (do). For just as (His) Will is not greater than (His) Power, so

---

[1] AGAINST GAUDENTIUS, Bk. I, ch. 30, n. 35. — The passage of Sacred Scripture is Gen 19:22. The Vulgate reads: *Because I will be able to do nothing, until you will enter unto there* [Quia non potero facere quidquam, donec ingrediaris illuc].

[2] Thus edition 8; the other editions and all the codices omit *to say* [dicat]; only the Vatican edition reads *Which* [Quod].

[3] The Vatican edition and editions 4, 5, 6, 7, 8, and 9 have not so well *it is not* [non].

[4] Codices A B D E and edition 1 have *has* [tenet].

[5] Codices C D and E and edition 1 read *adjoin* [Adiiciunt] (which St. Bonaventure also has in his Division of the Text).

[6] The Vatican edition and editions 2, 3, 4, 5, 6 and 9 have *They also* [Ipsi etiam] for *Moreover, they* [Ipsi autem]. A little further below this, the Vatican edition and editions 2, 3, 4, 6, 7, 8 and 9 read *that He leaves off (doing) those which He leaves off (doing)* [dimittere quae dimittit] for *that He leaves off (doing) what He leaves off (doing)* [dimittere quod dimittit].

[7] In Distinctions XXXVIII and XXXIX.

[8] In (his) Sermon, TO CATECHUMENS, ch. 1, n. 2. In the preceding there is an allusion to Ps. 63:7, where the Vulgate and editions 2 and 9 have *scrutinizing by a scrutiny* [scrutantes scrutinio].

[9] Chapter 4, n. 6.

neither is (His) Power greater than (His) Will. And for that reason, just as He does not will more, than He can (do), so (He does not will) that He can do more than they say He wills. — But to this we say, that neither is the Will greater than the Power, nor the Power than the Will, because the Power and the Will are one and the same Thing, namely, God Himself, who would be greater than Himself, if the Will would be greater than the Power, and/or the Power than the Will. Nor is it denied by this authority, that God can (do) more than He wills, because more have been subjected to His Power than to (His) Will.

And, so, let us say, that God can do many[1] (things), which He does not will, and that He can leave off (doing) those which He does. Which, so that it may be more certainly and firmly held, let us show [afferamus] by the testimonies of Scripture, that God can do more, than He does. The Truth Himself, according to (the Gospel of St.) Matthew,[2] says: « *Or do you think, that I cannot ask My Father, and He will bring forth* [exhibebat] *for Me now more than twelve legions of Angels?* From which words there is patently hinted, that the Son could ask for what He did not ask for, and the Father bring forth what He did not bring forth. Therefore, Each could do, what He did not do. (St.) Augustine also in (his) ENCHIRIDION says:[3] "(His) Omnipotent Will can do many (things), which He does not will nor does: for It could cause, twelve legions of Angels to fight against those who seized Christ." Likewise, in the same (he says):[4] « Why among certain (men) *were deeds of power* [virtutes] not *worked, which if they had been worked*, those men *would have done* *penance*; and (why) were they worked among those who were not going to believe? Then, there would not lie hidden [non latebit], what now lies hidden. Nor, certainly [utique], was God unjustly unwilling that they be saved, since they could have be saved, if He willed (it).[5] Then shall there be seen in the most clear light of Wisdom what the faith of the pious holds (fast to now), before it is seen by (that) manifest cognition, (namely) how certain and immutable and most efficacious is God's Will, which can do many (things) and[6] (yet) does not will (to do so), but (which) wills nothing which It cannot (do) ». Likewise, in the book, ON NATURE AND GRACE (he says):[7] « The Lord raised up Lazarus in body. Is it to be said, that He could not raise up Judas in mind? Indeed He could, but He was unwilling ».[8]

By these authorities and many others there is openly taught, that God can do many (things), which He does not will (to do). Which also can be proven by reason. For God does not want to justify all men, and yet who doubts, that He can? Therefore, God can do (something) other, than He does, and yet, if He would do (something) else, He would not be different [alius]. And He can will (something) other, than He wills, and yet His Will can neither be other nor new nor mutable in any manner. For[9] even if He can will what He never has willed, yet He cannot will newly nor by a new Will, but only by (His) sempiternal Will. For He can *will* what He is able to have *willed* from eternity. For He has the power of willing both now and from eternity, what He, however, never wills now nor has willed from eternity.

COMMENTARY ON DISTINCTION XLIII

On the Divine Power in regard to (Its) immensity.

However, certain (authors), glorying in their own sense.

THE DIVISION OF THE TEXT

Above, Master (Peter) showed, *what* God is able (to do); in this part he intends to show, *how much* He is able. And, since certain ones limited God's Power, for that reason Master (Peter) intends to show the falsity of this opinion, and with the falsity of this position shown, God's Power is found[1] to be infinite. And this part has three parts.

In the *first*, he proposes or narrates their erroneous opinion. In the *second*, he dissolves their multiple reason, there (where he says): *And they strive to fortify this first opinion of theirs with seemingly*

---

[1] The Vatican edition, with very many editions, has *more* [plura].

[2] Chapter 26:53.

[3] Chapter 95, n. 24; and ON SPIRIT AND LETTER, chs. 1 and 35, from which passages those which follow have been taken according to (their) sense. You will find the same words in Abelard's, SIC ET NON, ch. 35 (Migne, PATROLOGIA LATINA, tome 178).

[4] ENCHIRIDION, loc. cit., but with many (things) omitted and transposed by Master (Peter). In the text there is a reference to Mt. 11:21: *Because if in Tyre and Sidon there can been done the deeds of power* [virtutes], *which have been done in your (towns), they would have at once done penance in cilice and ashes* [Quia si in Tyro et Sidone factae essent virtutes, quae factae sunt in vobis, olim in cilicio et cinere poenitentiam egissent].

[5] Besides the Vatican edition and ed. 4, the other edd. have *if they willed (it)* [si vellent]; the ed. of (St.) Augustine's (works) now reads *if they willed (it)* [si vellent], the others have *if He willed (it)* [si vellet]. Our codices have *if He willed (it)* [si vellet], but codices B & C, by a second hand in the margin, have *if they willed (it)* [si vellent]. Each reading can be understood in a good sense, wherefore we have changed nothing, especially since *if He willed (it)* [si vellet] is more fitting with the subject of the discourse.

[6] Codices A and C have *which it* [quod] for *and* [et].

[7] Chapter 7, n. 8. — The passage of Sacred Scripture, which is referred to, is John 11:43.

[8] Only edition 8 repeats: *And/or thus only: because the Lord raised up Lazarus, without doubt He could; but because He did not raise up Judas, is it to be said, that He could not? therefore He could, but He was unwilling* [Vel sic tantum: quia Dominus Lazarum suscitavit, sine dubio potuit; quia vero Judam non suscitavit, nunquid dicendum est, non potuit? potuit ergo, sed noluit]; which words the genuine text of (St.) Augustine exhibit.

[9] Thus the codices and edition 1; the Vatican edition, together with the other editions, has *Wherefore even if* [Quod etsi] in place of *For even if* [Etsi enim]. Then, for *He can* [possit] codex D has *He could* [posset]. Then all the codices omit *Will* [voluntate] after *only* [tantum].

NOTES ON ST. BONAVENTURE'S COMMENTARY

[1] Codex M reads *is revealed* [aperitur]. A little before this, codex V to the word *opinion* [opinionis] prefixes *position of (their)* [positionis]; for *of this opinion* [huius opinionis] codex X has *of this position* [huius positionis].

true arguments etc.. In the *third*, he concludes and confirms the assertion of the truth, which is in (its) position[1] the contrary of this opinion, there (where he says): *And so let us say, that God can do many (things)* etc.. The *first* and *last* part remaining undivided, the middle part is divided according to the number of the reasons, which he adduces. The first has been taken from the reckoning of the good and the just. And this he forms in two manners, and it is posited there (where he says): *"God cannot do, except what is just and good", that is* etc.. The second has been taken from the reckoning of the due, and this he posits there (where he says): *They also add, saying even*

other (things): "God cannot do etc.". The third has been taken from the reckoning of doing and dismissing, and this he forms in two manners, there (where he says): *They also add saying* etc. The fourth has been taken from the reckoning of God's Foreknowledge, and this is posited there (where he says): *Likewise, they adjoin another, saying* etc.. The fifth has been taken from the authority of (St.) Augustine and this from a twofold authority, and it is posited there (where he says): *Moreover, to these those scrutinizers* etc.. And in any of these parts Master (Peter) posits the objections first, however, he posits the solution second; and the parts are manifest.

TREATMENT OF THE QUESTIONS

For an understanding of the present Distinction one asks concerning the quantity or the infinity of the Divine Power. And, about, this four (questions) are asked.

First, there is asked, whether the Power of God is infinite.

Second, granted that It is, there is asked, whether the Divine Essence Itself is infinite, just as the Power.

Third, there is asked, whether God can produce an infinite work.

Fourth, whether the reason for operating is infinite.

The first Question looks back to (His) infinity in *being able* [in possendo], the second (to His infinity) in *being*, the third (to His infinity) in *operating*, the fourth (to His infinity) in *the reason for (His) working*.

ARTICLE SOLE

On the infinity of the Divine Power.

QUESTION I

Whether God's Power, according to which (it is) of this kind, is infinite?

Therefore, first, there is asked, whether the Power of God is infinite; and that the Power itself, according to which (It is) of this kind, is infinite, is shown in this manner:

1. The "infinite" is said (to be) "that which has no terminus";[2] but the Divine Power, as much as regards (Its) '*being able*', does not have a terminus: ergo etc.. The *first* is manifest; the *second* is clear through (St. John) Chrysostom in a certain Homily:[3] « He is said (to be) "omnipotent", because His '*being able*' does not find a '*not being able*' »: therefore, if It always finds *that It is able*, there is always a further [ultra] accepting, by (those) accepting, of a quantity of power: therefore, (the Divine Power) is infinite.

2. Likewise, every active power, which is able unto infinite effects, is infinite in act; the Divine Power is of this kind: ergo etc.. *Proof of the first*: if

a power is purely in act, therefore, it has actually the whole (of its effects), which it can have: therefore, if it has actually the whole and nothing can accrue to it nor (can) anything be given[4] (it) anew [de novo], and (if) the power, as (something) powerful, extended itself to infinite (things): therefore, in act it has in itself an infinity. The *minor* is clear, because the Divine Power is never able unto so many effects, that it is not still able unto more: therefore, it is manifest, that It is infinite.

3. Likewise, every power, which is able unto an infinite act, if it is entirely in act, is simply infinite; but the Divine Virtue is of this kind: ergo etc.. The *major* is clear in this manner: just as a power holds itself to a power, so an act to an act; but an infinite act exceeds a finite one unto an infinite (degree), therefore, also an (infinite) power a (finite) power:

---

[1] For *in (its) position the contrary of* [contraria positione] the Vatican edition has *for the side contrary to* [contrariam partem].

·   [2] Cf. Aristotle, Physics, Bk. III, text 63 (ch. 6), and Metaphysics, Bk. XI, ch. 9 (Bk. X, ch. 10).

— [3] See the text of Master (Peter) in the preceding Distinction, ch. 3. — In the following proposition, that definition of the infinite is referred to, which is had in Aristotle, Physics, Bk. III, text 63 (ch. 6): Therefore, the in-

finite is that, of which, according to quantity, there is always an accepting of something more by those accepting [Infinitum igitur id est, cuius secundum quantitatem accipientibus semper aliquid accipere extra est].

[4] Trusting in very many codices, among which is also codex T, and supported by edition 1, we have substituted *(can) anything be given (it)* [aliquid dari] for *(can it) give anything* [aliquid dare], which the Vatican edition falsely exhibits.

therefore, if the power is entirely in act, it is infinite. The *minor* is clear, because God is said "to endure into infinity" [durare in infinitum] and He can conserve a creature into infinity: ergo etc..

4. Likewise, every power, which is able over extremes distant unto an infinite (degree), is infinite; but the Divine Power is of this kind, because It makes *something* from nothing, and between *something* and *nothing* there is an infinite distance: ergo etc..

5. Likewise, every power, which is entirely undiffering from the essence (of its subject), is infinite; but the Divine Power is of this kind: ergo etc.. *Proof of the first*: whensoever any two are entirely indistant, wheresoever one is, the remainder (is) also:[1] therefore, if a power is entirely undiffering from the essence (of its subject), wheresoever the power is, the essence (is) also. But where the essence is, there is the center of the power: therefore, wheresoever such a power can (act), it can (act) as in (its) center: therefore, since no power is limited in its center, but is more amply able (there), either the Divine Power can (do) nothing, or It can (do) as much as He wants, and in this manner unto infinity: therefore, as much as It is of Itself, that Power can work in infinite (acts).[2] But that Power is entirely undiffering and simple: therefore, in It [ibi] the breadth [latum] and intensity [intensum] is the same: therefore, if It is *extensively* infinite, (It is) also *intensively* (infinite): therefore, it is entirely infinite. And this is, that the Philosopher says in the book, ON CAUSES,[3] that « virtue as much as (it is) the more united, (is) so much the more infinite ». Therefore, since the Divine Power is most united, because it is entirely the same with Its Origin, It can (act) everywhere as in Its Origin: therefore, It never finds *that It is not able*.

ON THE CONTRARY: 1. Every that is finite, in which there is a finding of a *standing still*; but in the Divine Power there is a finding of a standing still, because there is an assigning of something, which It cannot (do), just as has been shown above,[4] such as corporal acts and deformed acts: ergo etc..

2. Likewise, what *is exceeded*[5] by anything is finite, because the infinite is in no manner exceeded; but

(God's) *Knowledge* exceeds (His) *power* in respect of knowables; for (His) Knowledge is of more than (His) Power, for *He knows* evils, and *cannot* (do them): ergo etc..

3. Likewise, we see among created powers, that *infinity* is from matter, but *finity* is from form:[6] therefore, since God's Power is entirely a form or formal, having entirely nothing of possibility, therefore, It is simply finite and in no manner infinite.

4. Likewise, among (those) contradictorily opposed there is an infinite distance; but the virtue of a creature reduces one finite to another, such as making one (who is) not running run, and yet (such a virtue) is finite: ergo.[7]

5. Likewise, I see that the soul has a power entirely undiffering from (its) essence, such as the power of vivifying the body; it also has a power for an infinite act, such as to endure or remain unto infinity; it has, nevertheless, a power for infinite acts;[8] and yet the power itself is finite in itself: therefore, it seems, for an equal reason, concerning the Divine Power, since the soul is an expressed image of God. Wherefore the aforesaid reason seem to be worth nothing.

CONCLUSION

The Divine Power is infinite in act and in habit.

I RESPOND: It must be said, that there is a positing of the Divine Power both entirely in *act* and in *habit* as infinite; just as has been proven[9] through (Its) effect *a posteriori*, because It has an effect infinite *in duration* and (effects) infinite *in apposition*, according to which It is compared as a pure act and as a whole cause. And for that reason It is[10] as One having in Itself a full and perfect actuality in respect of infinite (things); and it is necessary, since It has a whole (effect), that whenever [unquam] It is going to have (it), It also have it out of Itself [ex se], on which account, It Itself is infinite.

---

[1] The Vatican edition and codex cc to this clause *there* [ibi]. Next, codices F and S, with transposed words, read thus: *wheresoever the essence is, the power (is) also* [ubicumque est essential, et potentia]. — The conclusion, which is derived there, is supported by this axiom: "the principle of operating and of being is the same", or "to operate follows to be", concerning which, cf. above d. 3, p. II, a. 1. q. 3, p. 84, footnote 7.

[2] The Vatican edition, together with the other codices, has *unto infinity* [in infinitum].

[3] Proposition 47. — Next, following the reading of codices L O and X, we have substituted *most united* [unitissima] for *most infinite* [infinitissima], which the Vatican edition faultily exhibits, which word *most infinite* [infinitissima] does not response to the line of the argumentation.

[4] Distinction 42, q. 2.

[5] We have retained, together with the Vatican edition, *is exceeded* [exceditur], which is had in codex T, with not a few of the other codices dissenting, which (codices) put *has a 'being exceeding'* [habet excedi].

[6] Cf. Aristotle, PHYSICS, Bk. III, texts 63-66 (ch. 6), and METAPHYSICS, Bk. VII, text 40 (Bk. VI, ch. 11), from which book some things have already been cited above in d. 35, a. sole, q. 5, p. 612, footnote 7. — Next, for *of possibility* [possibilitatis] the Vatican edition has *of materiality* [materialitatis], and not a few codices have erroneously *of impossibility* [impossibilitatis]. — On this proposition, cf. (St. Severinus) Boethius, ON THE TRINITY, ch. 2, where it is taught that the Divine Substance is a form without matter.

[7] This objection is opposed to that which is said above in the 4th argument of the fundament; wherefore the conclusion will be this: "therefore, though God makes something from nothing, His Power will be finite." — A little before this, for *one finite* [unum finitum] the Vatican edition has only *one* [unum].

[8] For intellective power, because (it is) in itself incorruptible and perpetual, cannot elicit so many acts, that it cannot elicit more (co-categorically infinite or indefinite ones). — In codex O there is here added *just as is said in the third (book) ON THE SOUL* [sicut dicitur tertio de Anima], where in text 20 (ch. 5) immortality and perpetuity are also attributed to the intellective part of the soul. Then, codices V and X also at the beginning of this argument have *Likewise, it seems* [Item, videtur] for *Likewise, I see* [Item, video].

[9] Here in the 2nd and 4th arguments of the fundament. The expression, which occurs a little after this, *(effects) infinite in apposition* [infinitos (effectus) appositionis], is found in Aristotle, PHYSICS, Bk. III, text. 56 (ch. 6), where the Philosopher distinguishing the "infinite", speaks thus: « Therefore, the "infinite" itself is indeed said to be one thing according to potency, but another according to act. And there is indeed an "infinite" according to apposition, and also according to ablation ». Which words Averroës expounds thus: "That is, the infinite in power is found both in the addition of numbers and in the division of (the magnitudes) of measures ... not in act." Likewise, Averroës in his book, ON THE SUBSTANCE OF THE ORB distinguishes a twofold infinite power, namely the infinite *in duration* and the infinite *in strength* [in vigore]. Cf. also Alexander of Hales, SUMMA., p. I. q. 6, n. 1, in reply to n. 1.

[10] For *And for that reason It is* [Et ideo est] the Vatican edition, together with codex cc, reads *And the reason (is that It is)* [Et ratio], but the greater part of the codices and edition 1 have *And for that reason* [Et ideo], to which word we have added from codex M (T in the margin) *It is* [est]. For *It is as One having* [est habens] codices V and X read *It has* [habet]. A little below this, after *since It has a whole (effect)* [cum habeat] codices V X and Z insert *in Itself* [in se].

Another reason shows this as if *a priori*. On account of the most high indivision of (God's) Virtue with (His) Essence,[1] and on account of the most high unity of the Virtue Itself, wheresoever It is able, the whole (of It) is able, and as much in an extreme of the world as in the midst (of it), and as much as in (its) height as unto (its) breadth [in latus], and according to every measure of infinity.

Nor is there a completely similar reason in any creature neither as much as regards the *causality of the effect*, nor as much as regards the *production of the act*,[2] nor as much as regards the *unity* (of the power). Not as much as regards the *causality (of the effect)*, because no virtue of a creature in respect of an infinite *duration* is purely active, nay it is necessary that it be conserved through the Divine Influence. — Similarly, neither as much as regards the *production of the act*, whence it has a passive infinity even in receiving, and for that reason no (created power) is infinite *in act*, but only in *potency*. And because the infinite *in potency* depends out of the infinite *in act*, for that reason every infinity of a created duration and operation depends out of an infinite of uncreated Virtue. And this is what the Philosopher says in the book, ON CAUSES,[3] that « all infinite, dependent virtues are through the one First Infinite, which is the Virtue of virtues ». — Similarly, it is not similar concerning *simplicity* or *unity*. For the Divine Power is entirely *simply in Itself* and has an entirely *simple* Essence or *Substance*, (and) is entirely *undiffering* from That; and for that reason by an omnimodal union It is most united, and for that reason infinite. But of no creature, however so noble, is the power *entirely simple*, because every such power means some looking-back of dependence; nor is it founded in an *entirely simply substance*; nor is it entirely *undiffering*, because no creature is its own power, essentially speaking.[4] — And for that reason because every creature fails from the reckoning of most high *simplicity*, (it) also (fails from the reckoning) *of infinity* consequently [per consequens]. And in this manner it is clear, that *infinite is the Divine Power*,[5] and *the reckoning of (Its) infinity*.

And the response to the last reason, showing that the aforesaid reasons are not valid, is clear.

1. 2. To that, therefore, which is objected, that (the Divine Power) finds a *terminus*, and that It finds an *excess*; it must be said, that the Divine Power is infinite in respect of those which to be able (to do) is a '*to be able*';[6] in respect of others, which to be able (to do) belongs to *impotence*, it is neither finite nor infinite, because

it can (do) none of these. — For when it is said, that It finds a *terminus* and/or an *excess*; it must be said, that that it is false, because the *excess* and *terminus* of a thing is attained according to those to which the thing extends itself; and the Divine Power extends Itself only to good (things), and as much as regards such[7] (God's) Knowledge is never of more than (His) Power (is); nor, as much as regards such, does It find a terminus. And for that reason that (objection) is clear.

However, it can be said in another manner, that there is in a twofold manner a speaking of (God's) Power and Knowledge: either *in themselves*, or *through a comparison to (their) objects*. If *in itself*, thus one does not exceed the other, because whatever He knows, He can know, and whatever He can (do), He knows that He can do. And/or[8] *through a comparison to (it) object*, and in this manner there is a speaking (of these) in a twofold manner: either according to *form* or *appearance*, or according to *number*. If according to *number*, thus, since (His) Power is infinite, It is not exceeded by (His) Knowledge; but if according to *form*, thus, because (His) Power is in respect of goods only,[9] It is exceeded; yet from this it does not follow, that It is not infinite. — And there is (this) *example*: if one imagines two infinite lines, two are more than one, because one did not have an infinity according to number, but only according to length; and in this manner two are not greater and/or longer than one. Similarly, is it understood in the proposed. For (God's) Power is said (to be) "infinite" in respect of (Its) objects according to (their) *number*, but not according to (their) *quality*, because It is not able unto evil and/or privatory (acts). — And through this the first and the second (objection) is clear. For though It does find a terminus in respect of evil, yet not in respect of the good, and that terminus and/or excess works rather to (Its) infinity, because (such) is not a '*to be able*', but (rather) a '*not to be able*'; and for that reason, though it seems to give a terminus according to *the reckoning of understanding*, according to *the truth* it does not give (one), because that It cannot (work) evils, this is wholly on account of the immensity of (Its) virtue.

3. To that which is objected, that the infinite is a passion of material power; it must be said, that this is true of the infinite-through-a-privation-of-*completion* or (of the infinite-through-a-privation)-of-a-complete-'*to be*' [completi esse]; but it is not true of the infinite-through-a-privation-of-*limitation*. For the first is a infinite according to *passive* or *receptive power* [potentia], and, thus, in the first (manner)

---

[1] That is, on account of the most high identity of (His) Virtue and Essence. — A little before this, the Vatican edition, with codex cc, reads thus: *This is shown by another reason a priori. On account of the most high* etc. [Alia ratione ostenditur hoc a prior. Propter summam etc.].

[2] From codices V and X we have adjoined the words *nor as much as regards the production of the act* [nec quantum ad productionem actus], which, as it flows from the following, the Vatican falsely omits. Next, after *causality* [causalitatem] supply together with the Vatican edition and codex cc *of the effect* [effectus]. After a few (words), for *virtue of a creature* [virtus creaturae] coddices X and Z have *created virtue* [virtus creata].

[3] Proposition 16: « All virtues, for which there is no end, are dependent » etc.. Which proposition St. Thomas in his Commentary on this book expounds thus: Where it must be considered first, that there is said (to be) an "infinite power" of anything always existing ... inasmuch as, namely, we see, that those which can endure more, have a greater virtue of being. Wherefore those which can endure unto infinity, have as much as regards this an infinite power ... for that reason according to the intention of this author this first Infinite, from which all infinite virtues depend, is the first simply, wherefore It is God.

[4] Cf. above d. 3, p. II, a. 1, q. 3, chiefly in the solution of the objections, and in d. 8, p II, q. 2 throughout.

[5] The Vatican edition, with ed. 1, reads here *that the Divine Power is infinite, and that It alone is infinite and the reckoning of infinity* [quod divina potentia est infinita et quod sola est infinita et ratio infinitatis]., and then after *of infinity* [infinitatis] the Vatican ed. adds *is (Its) most high Simplicity* [est summa simplicitas].

[6] For *is a 'to be able'* [est posse] the Vatican edition reads *belongs to power* [est potentiae]. A little before this, for *a terminus* [terminum] codices L and O have *a standing-still* [statum].*

[7] For *such* [talia] the Vatican edition, with codex cc, has faultily *others* [alia]. At the beginning of this proposition in place of *For when* [Quando enim] edition 1 has *Therefore, when* [Quando ergo]. — Cf. Aristotle, METAPHYSICS, Bk. V, texts 21 and 22 (Bk. IV, chs. 16 and 17).

[8] For *And/or* [Vel] codex C has *If* [Si].

[9] The Vatican edition and codex cc here adjoin: *but (His) Knowledge (is) of goods and evils, for that reason* [scientia vero bonorum et malorum, ideo]. The a little further below this, for *one did not have an infinity* [habebat una infinitatem] the Vatican edition reads *they did not have one infinity* [habebant infinitatem].

---

* *Trans. note*: Here the original footnote has faultily *slatum* for *statum*.

it is in matter; the second is infinite *in act*, and for that reason it is truly and properly in Him alone, who[1] is only act and the pure and most perfect Act.

4. To that which is objected, that a creature is able over those which are distant in a most high manner; it must be said, that a *being* and a *non-being* are not said (to be) "most highly distant", because they are opposed contradictorily, but since they have nothing common neither as much as regards (their) *subject genus* nor as much as regards (their) *predicable genus*; but '*to rest*' and '*to move*', or '*to be moved*' and '*to not be moved*', (and) what is accepted for the same, have in each manner (something) common;[2] and thus there is no infinite distance, nor is it similar.

5. To that which is objected concerning the power to live,[3] it must be said, that "*to live*", in one manner means a con-sequent act, just as "*to move*" (does); and, thus it is from the soul by means of powers differing from the very essence (of it). In another manner, "*to live*" is said, according to which it is a *first act*, and it is from the essence of the soul as in the reckoning of a *form*, no in the reckoning of an *agent*; and on this account it is not considered to be there only in *working*,[4] just as whiteness whitens by its very self, so that it is not noted there nor is there an egress of something, as from an acting power. But we speak here both according to power as *acting* and as producing something, which[5] power, however so much it is the same, yet it means some inclination, and for that reason a dependence; and for that reason it deprives a *simplicity* and through this it deprives an *infinity*. But in God it is not so; and therefore, [ideo] that reason, rightly understood, has no instance.

SCHOLIUM

I. The definitions and various species of the infinite, which occur in this Distinction, have been for the most part taken from Aristotle, as can be seen in our notes; see also below, q. 2. — For an explanation of the terms this passage from Alexander of Hales (SUMMA., p. I, q. 6, n. 1) can be of use: « The "infinite" is said in a threefold manner, namely, *negatively, privatively, contrarily* or disparately. The "*infinite*" is said *negatively* through the denial of an end [finis], and in this manner the "infinite" is said (to be) "that which is not finished"; and in this manner the "infinite" is that which is not bound to be finished. The "infinite" *privatively* is that which is bound to be finished, yet is not finished. The "infinite" *contrarily* is that which has a contrary or disparate disposition regarding being finished. In the first manner the Divine Essence is infinite, because It has no end, but is finishing all, nor is It bound to be finished. Similarly, if the "infinite" be said *disparately*, thus It is still infinite, because It has a disparate disposition in respect of the simple; for we say that something (is) "infinite", which is unto so many, that it cannot be unto more » etc.. And ibid., in reply n. 1 (he says): « Though the "finite" is said through the positing of an end, the "infinite" through the removal of *an end*; but "end" is said *in a threefold manner*, and (so is) the "*finite*" and the "*infinite*". For the "*end*" is said (to be) a "terminus", and the "*finite*" and "*infinite*", according to which they are accepted from an "end", are congruent to a quantity alone; for they are taken according to the reckoning of a *terminus* in quantity. For because in a continuum there is no terminus of its *division*, we say that (it is) divisible ad infinitum [in infinitum] or *infinite according to division*. Similarly, because in a number there is no terminus in *adding*, we say, that it is *infinite according to addition*. Similarly, according to *place* the "finite" and "infinite" are said *according to duration*. — In another manner, an "*end*" is said (to be) the same as a "*perfection*"; nor is the "finite" and "infinite" said in regard to substance; and in this manner matter is said (to be) "infinite" according to itself, because it lacks perfection. — In a third manner, an "*end*" is said according to its own reckoning, by which it is, indeed, "that

for the sake of which each one (is)", and in this manner the "*finite*" is said from a boundary [a fine] through an order to an end [per ordinem ad finem], but the "infinite" through (its) being removed from an order [per deordinationem]; and in this manner the evil of a fault is said (to be) "infinite" ». Then the author distinguishes infinity according to a *dimensive* quantity and the other (infinity) according to *virtual* quantity, which alone can convene with God.

The "*infinity*", which is attributed to *matter*, St. Bonaventure, above in d. 35, a. 5, in reply to n. 4, names a "infinity *through defect*", to which there is opposed the "infinity *through excess*". St. Thomas (here in q. 2, a. 1; SUMMA., I, q. 7, a. 1) distinguishes in the same sense the "infinite on the part of *matter*", which befits a quantity, and the "infinite on the part of a *form*", not determined through matter", which has the reckoning of the perfect, wherefore it convenes with God. — On the *formal* concept of the infinite, which convenes with God, there is a controversy among the school of St. Thomas and (that of Bl. John Duns) Scotus, whether it consists in a *negation*, which however, is founded in the immense perfection of God, as the first School would have it, or rather in a *perfection positive* of every entity, as (Bl.) Scotus says. St. Bonaventure, here in q. 2, chiefly in reply to n. 6, favors (Bl.) Scotus (cf. what the former teaches above in d. 29, q. 1 concerning innascibility). Yet the Seraphic (Doctor) does not make the Scotistic distinction between "*radical* infinity", from which the Scotists infer the Simplicity of God, and "*formal* infinity"; but rather (here in 5th argument of the fundament) infers from the Divine Simplicity *a priori* (His) Infinite Power (concerning which, cf. above d. 37, p. I, a. 1, q. 1, in the body of the Response and in reply to n. 3, and d. 8, p. II, qq. 1 and 2).

II. That God (is) « according to Intellect and Will and every perfection, infinite » (Vatican I, Constitution *On the Faith*, ch. 1), reason itself also teaches. — The distinction (at the beginning of the body of the Response) between a power infinite *in act* and in *habit* is explained below in q. 4, in the body of the Response, and is accepted only according to our manner of understanding, since it is established, that all (acts) are in God through the manner of a *pure act*. — The 4th argument of the fundament is explained here in reply to n. 4, and below in q. 3, in reply to n. 4, and in SENT.,

---

[1] Very many codices, together with the six first editions, have incongruously *because He* [quia] for *who* [qui].

[2] For rest and movement are founded in the same real power of the subject, and for that reason they pertain also to the same predicament; cf. Aristotle, METAPHYSICS, Bk. IX, text 19 (Bk. VIII, ch. 9); but a being and a non-being are not founded in the same subject; cf. Aristotle, PHYSICS, Bk. IV, text 67 (ch. 8), where it is said, that nothing has no reckoning or proportion regarding a being. — After *(something) common* [commune] codices Y and bb adjoin: *namely, the subject itself of the movement or rest* [scilicet ipsum subiectum motus et quietis].

[3] The Vatican edition, together with codex cc, has *the power of vivifying* [potentia vivificandi] for *the power to live* [potentia vivendi]. Next, after *a consequent act* [actum consequentem] codices aa and bb add: *in another manner a first act. But according to which it means a consequent act* [alio modo actum primum. Sed secundum quod dicit actum consequentem], and, consequently after a

few (words) for *In another manner "to live"* is said [Alio modo dicitur vivere] they substitute *According to which it is a first act, it is* [Secundumq uod est actus primus, est]. This latter reading is also found in a good many other codices. — On the twofold signification of the verb "*to live*", cf. Aristotle, ON THE SOUL, Bk. II, text 5 f., and text 24 f. (chs. 1 and 2).

[4] The Vatican edition adjoins *but (also) in informing* [sed in informando].

[5] The word *which* [quae] is falsely omitted in very many codices and in edition 1; in codex T by another hand there is in place of this prefixed to the word *power* [potentia] the word *the first* [prima], namely the first of the two said manners of living. For *which* [quae] codex X has *because* [quia], but the Vatican edition, together with codex cc, reads only *but the power of the soul* [potential vero animae]. — What the difference is between the powers of the soul and the soul itself, see above d. 3, p. II, a. 1, q. 3.

Bk. II, d. 1, p. I, a. 2, q. 2. (Bl.) Scotus (SENT., Bk. IV, d. 1. q. 1), however, denies together with others, that there is an infinite distance between *something* and *nothing*).

III. Alexander of Hales, loc. cit.. — (Bl. John Duns) Scotus, on this and the following q., SENT., Bk. I, d. 2, qq. 1 and 2; REPORTATIO., Bk. I, d. 2. q. 3; QUODLIBETALS., q. 7. — St. Thomas,

here in q. 1, a. 1; SUMMA., I, q. 25, a. 2. — Bl. (now St.) Albertus (Magnus), here a. 1; SUMMA., p. I, tr. 19, q. 77, m. 3. — (Bl.) Peter of Tarentaise, here in q. 1, a. 2. — Richard of Middleton, here in q. 2. — Giles the Roman, here in 1st princ., q. 1. — Henry of Ghent, SUMMA., a. 45, q. 5. — Durandus (of Saint-Pourçain), here in q. 1. — (Bl.) Dionysius the Carthusian, here in q. 1. — (Gabriel) Biel, here in q. 1 at the end.

QUESTION II

Whether the Divine Essence is infinite?

Second, there is asked, whether the (Divine) *Essence* is infinite or (whether) the Divine Power is infinite as much as *regards (Its) 'being'*. And it seems, that it is so,

1. Because no power is more noble than (its) substance; but the Divine Power is infinite: therefore since (the Divine Power)[1] is not more noble nor greater than the (Divine) Substance, it is necessary, that the Substance be infinite.

2. Likewise, if any two — let one be allow to speak thus — are entirely the same, if one is infinite, the remainder is also; but (God's) *Substance* and *Power* are the Same, and (His) 'Being' and "*Being able*":[2] therefore since the Divine "*Being able*" is infinite, (His) 'Being' (is) also, and thus (His) *Essence* (is) too.

3. Likewise, whensoever any two so hold themselves, that one extends itself to nothing, to which the remainder does not extend itself equally, if one is infinite, the remainder (is) also; but the (Divine) Power extends Itself to entirely nothing, to which the (Divine) Essence does not extend Itself — God can never do as many as what His Substance can to be in, according to what is said in the eighth (chapter) of the third (book) of Kings:[3] *If the sky and the Heavens of the heavens* etc.. — ergo etc..

4. Likewise, than every finite something can be thought (to be) greater, namely the infinite itself; but the Divine Essence is so good and great, that nothing greater nor better can be thought,[4] otherwise It is not God: ergo etc..

5. Likewise, every finite good is better with another good than only through itself, because a finite added to a finite makes a greater: therefore, if the Divine Essence is finite, It will be a greater something with another, than only through Itself: therefore, it is not the most perfect nor the best; which one is entirely forbidden [nefas] to say.

6. Likewise, every finite good happens at some time to be equaled and rendered through the duplication of a finite, as is clear in a line — and I say this (under this condition): "if that which is doubled [duplatur], makes a greater": (for) this I say on account of a point[5] — if, therefore, the Divine Essence is finite according to nobility and goodness, if the goodness of a creature be doubled, by ascending at some time it will arrive at a goodness equal to the Divine Goodness; but it is false and impossible, that a creature be proportional to the Creator, and this (St.) Augustine says in the eighth (book), ON THE TRINITY:[6] therefore, also that, from which it follows, namely, that the Divine Essence is finite.

BUT ON THE CONTRARY: 1. « The finite and the infinite, as the Philosopher says,[7] are proper passions of quantity itself »; but the (Divine) Essence as an essence does not have a quantity of *mass*: therefore, if It is considered as in the abstraction (from a quantity) of *virtue* as an essence, the Divine Essence is neither finite nor infinite.

2. Likewise, every power, which can (cause) only one (effect), thus that (it can) not (cause) another, is a finite power: therefore, for an equal reason, every essence, which is only one (thing), such that (it is) nothing else, is a finite essence; but the Divine Essence is God and nothing else: ergo etc..

3. Likewise, every that which is finite to the Most High Truth, is simply finite — and this is clear, because the First Truth judges of each one, just as it is: it is also clear in the simile, such as "this is white and black and good to God, therefore, (it is) simply good" — but the Divine Essence is finite to the truth of the Divine Cognition, because God comprehends and knows [novit] It perfectly, and « what is known [scitur] », as (St.) Augustine[8] says, « is finished by the comprehension of the one knowing »: ergo etc..

---

[1] Supply, together with codex M, *the (Divine) Power* [potentia]. Then the same codex M after *greater* [maior] inserts *than* [quam] explicitly. — This argument is founded upon the axiom: 'to operate' follows 'to be' [operari sequitur esse].

[2] Understand these in reference to God. Cf. (St.) Augustine, ON THE TRINITY, Bks. VI and VII, ch. 1, ff..

[3] Verse 27, and 2 Paralipomenon 2:6. The first passage continues thus: *cannot grasp Thee, how much more this house, which I have built* [te capere non possunt, quanto magis domus haec, quam aedificavi]. — A little above this, codex Y prefixes *beczause* [quia] to *God can never* [nunquam Deus potest]; the Vatican edition adds *for* [enim] instead, and then *even (His) Substance* [etiam substantia] for *His Subtance* [eius substantia].

[4] (St. Severinus) Boethius, ON THE CONSOLATION OF PHILOSOPHY, Bk. III, prose 10, and (St.) Anselm, PROSLOGION., ch. 2, and also (his) book, AGAINST THE FOOLISH MAN, ch. 1 ff.. — Immediately after this, for *It is not God* [non est Deus] the Vatican edition has *It would not be God* [non esset Deus].

[5] For a point added to a point does not make it greater. Cf. above d. 37, p. II. a. 2, q. 2, p. 660, footnote 6. — A little before this, for *doubled* [duplatur] some codices have *duplicated* [duplicatur], others together with codex T have *doubled* [duplicetur] (in the subjunctive).

[6] Chapter 2, n. 3.

[7] PHYSICS, Bk. I, text 15 (ch. 2): « For the infinite is in a quantum ... for the reckoning of the infinite uses a quantum, but not substance nor quality ». Which words Averroës interprets thus: « For the infinite and the finite concern differences of quantity ». On the quantity of *mass* and *virtue*, cf. (St.) Augustine's book, ON THE QUANTITY OF THE SOUL, ch. 3, n. 4. — Before *of virtue* [virtutis], supply, together with edition 1, *from a quantity* [a quantitate]. In the Vatican edition, there is wanting *of mass* [molis], and in the place of *(from a quantity) of virtue* [virtutis] there is read *from a quantity* [a quantitate]. Then, after *as an essence* [ut essentia] codices V and X subjoin *is* [est].

[8] ON THE CITY OF GOD, Bk. XII, ch. 18.

4. Likewise, no infinite limits [finit] another, because nothing gives to another what it does not have:[1] therefore, if the Divine Essence is infinite, therefore, it limits nothing, therefore, It is the end of nothing; and if this: therefore, (It is) not at all [nihil] the Good.

5. Likewise, no infinite is comprehended by the Blessed, because otherwise they would not be blessed, unless they perfectly cognized God — for (their) appetite would always be born towards the more, and they would not be at rest, and thus would not be blessed — therefore, if it is comprehended, it is not infinite.

6. Likewise, no privation is more noble than a having: therefore, since the "*infinite*" means a privation, the "*finite*" means a having, and everything more noble must be attributed to God, it is clear that etc..

CONCLUSION

The Divine Essence is entirely infinite in act.

I RESPOND: To this certain (authors) wanted to say, that the Divine Essence under the reckoning of *essence* is finite, under the reckoning of *power* is infinite. For "the Essence" names God as (He is) *in Himself*, and thus He is finite, because (He is) perfect; (He is) also finite, because He is comprehended by the finite, as by the Blessed; and this they said on account of the Simplicity of the Essence, the whole of which they said is seen. But inasmuch as It is considered under the reckoning of *power*, thus It means a looking back to (Its) effects. And because there is no standing still there, because there is always something extra to accept,[2] they said, that under the reckoning of power It was infinite. — But that position was manifestly erroneous. For these two are not co-possible, 'that the (Divine) *Power* be infinite, with the *Substance*

existing as entirely finite', both because They are entirely the Same, and because the Substance is prior according to the reckoning of understanding, and because to whatever the Power extends Itself under the reckoning of power, the Essence (does) also (under the reckoning of essence), as has been shown.[3]

And, on this account, some said, that there is a *simply* infinite[4] and an infinite *to us*: and they wanted to say, that both the (Divine) Essence and Power is finite according to truth, because It is finite *to God*, who is the Truth; but yet each is infinite *to us*, because It exceeds us improportionally. Wherefore, « God is said (to be) "infinite", because He is neither comprehended by place nor by time nor by comprehension », as (St. John) Damascene says.[5] — But again this position of theirs cannot stand, since, just as has been proven above[6] concerning the (Divine) Power, that It does not have a *standing still* in being able, and again, It is entirely *in act*, and for that reason It is posited as truly infinite; so also can the (Divine) Essence be proven (to be such).

Therefore, it is necessary, that *It be* entirely *infinite in act*. And this must be conceded and it must be held as true, to this extend that it is more consonant with *the Faith*, which says that God (is) immense, and (is) more consonant with *the authorities of the Saints*, who all say that He (is) infinite, wherefore (St. John) Damascene[7] says, that God is « a certain, infinite sea of substance »; (it is) also more consonant with *the sentences of the masters (of theology)*, (it is) also more consonant with *reason*.

Therefore, for an understanding of the objections for the opposite it must be noted, that the "*infinite*" is said through an denial of an *end* [per abnegationem finis]. Therefore, the "infinite" can be said in a twofold manner, namely on the part of a *negation* and similarly on the part of an *end*.[8]

On the part of an *end*. for and "end" is said in a twofold manner, in one manner, as that which is a *complement*; and in this manner the "infinite" is said through a privation of a complement, and in this manner

---

[1] Aristotle, ELENCHAE, Bk. II, ch. 3 (ch. 22). — The last conclusion of this argument: *therefore, (It is) not at all the good* [ergo nihil bonum], plainly follows from the preceding, so long as this axiom is employed: 'the end and the good are, or are convertible as, the same', which axiom occurs very frequently in Aristotle, thus RHETORICS, Bk. I, ch. "On *the Good and the Useful*" (ch. 6); ETHICS, Bk. I, ch. 1; MAGNA MORALIA, Bk. I, ch. 2 f (ch. 1), METAPHYSICS, Bk. V, text 3 (Bk. IV, ch. 2). — Codex Y adjoins at the end of the argument: *but this (is) false: therefore, aslo that from which it follows* [sed hoc falsum: ergo et illud unde sequitur].

[2] A reference to the Aristotelian definition of the infinite, cited above in the preceding Question, p. 764, footnote 3.

[3] Here in the first three arguments of the fundament.

[4] The Vatican ed., with cod. cc, have *a simply finite* [finitum simpliciter]. In ed. 1 it reads thus: *And on this account some said, that (the Divine Essence) is not simply infinite, but (It is) infinite to us* [Et propter hoc dixerunt aliqui, quod non est infinitum simpliciter, sed infiinitum nobis].

[5] ON THE ORTHODOX FAITH, Bk. I, ch. 4. In the text cited, for *is said (to be) "infinite"* [infinitus dicitur] very many codices have *is infinite* [infinitus est]; some codices read instead *(is) infinite* [infinitus], omitting entirely anything else.

[6] In the preceding Question. — A little below this, for *in act* [actu] in the Vatican ed. there is had *an act* [actus], and then *truly* [vere] is omitted.

[7] ON THE ORTHODOX FAITH., Bk. I, ch. 9. — After the words *consonant with reason* [consonum rationi] there is had in codex M a long addition, which appears to have been composed from those which follow hereafter, with only a few things added. Therefore, the addition reads thus: "And/or for a better understanding of the aforesaid it must be noted, that in the question, in which there is a multiplicity of the name, it is first necessary according to the art (of logic) to distinguish, rather to assert and/or deny something. Therefore, it must be understood, that the "infinite" is said in a twofold manner, namely privatively and negatives. According to which it is said pri-

vatively, thus it deprives an act and leaves an aptitude, and in this manner there is said (to be) "infinite", that which is bound to be finished, yet is not finished, and in this manner it means [sonat in] an incompletion, such as matter is said (to be) "infinite"; but according to which it is said negatively, thus it simply removes an end or a finity. But this has in a twofold manner an understanding according to the twofold acceptation of "end": for and end is said (to be) a "terminus", (and) an end (is said to be) a "complement", and for that reason the "infinite" is said either through the denial of an end as a complement, and in this manner evil is said (to be) "infinite", and/or through the denial of an end as a terminus, and this can be in a twofold manner according to a twofold terminus: for there is a terminus according to a material quantity, and there is a terminus according to a spiritual quantity. The first is said (to be) a "quantity of mass" [quantitas molis], the second is said (to be) a "quantity of virtue" [quantitas virtutis]. Therefore, the "infinite" through a denial of a terminus about a quantity of mass always means some incompletion in some manner, either in act and/or in potency, because it means a recess from a simply quantity; for such a quantity cannot stand together with simplicity in the same (thing) and according to the same (consideration), and such an infinite never is in act, but only in potency, moreover, in act (it is) finite. However, the "infinite" through a denial of a terminus about the quantity of virtue does not mean some imperfection, but (rather) a most high perfection, because it is not repugnant to simplicity, nay it cannot be except in the Most Highly Simply; and in such a manner the authority of Scripture and the confession of the Faith posit infinity or immensity in God Himself, as the Most Simply One.

[8] The sense is: the "infinite" [infinitum], because it is a word composed out of a negative particle [in-] and the verb, *finished* [-finitum] can be considered in a twofold manner, both according to the negative particle, and according to the verb.

there is said (to be) an "infinite" in matter and in the genus of substance and in the other genera; and in this manner it does not occur in God, because He is most perfect. In another manner, an "end" is said (to be) a "*terminus*", just as the confines of a field [finis agri], and in this manner the "infinite" is said (to be) that which lacks a terminus and a standing still. — And this can be in a twofold manner according to *negation*, because it can be understood *privatively* and *negatively*: *privatively*, because it does not *have* a terminus, but yet *is bound* to have (one), on account of this that it has a limited 'being', and in this manner it means an *incompletion*, and is not in God. In another manner, *negatively*, as that which *does not have* a terminus nor *is bound* to have (one); and in this manner it is posited in God on account of (His) most high Immensity.[1]

1. To that, therefore, which is objected, that the 'infinite' is a passion of quantity; it must be said, that just as the name for *quantity* is extended to the quantity of *virtue*, similarly the name for *the infinite*. But the quantity of *virtue* is not only attained as much as regards the work, but also as much as regards the nobility of *value* [valoris]; and this is clear, because, as (St.) Augustine[2] says, « in spiritual (things) 'greater' and 'better' are the same ».

2. To that which is objected, that (the Divine Essence) is so one [unum], that It is not another; it must be said, that something can be compared to many in a twofold manner: either according to a comparison of *causality*, or according to a comparison of *identity*. To be compared to many under the reckoning of *causality* this befits the infinite, because (it is) infinite; but according to the reckoning of *identity*, (it does) not. Wherefore, because (the Divine Essence is) an Infinite (Being), for that reason It extends Itself to many,[3] but it does not follow, that It is many. Wherefore, if the (Divine) Essence and/or Power be compared according to the reckoning of *identity* to things, Neither is of many (things); wherefore neither the Divine Power is other powers, nor the (Divine) Essence other essences; if[4] according to the reckoning of *causality*, thus (the "infinite") convenes both

with the (Divine) Power and the (Divine) Essence. For, just as causing more convenes with the (Divine) Power, so being in more convenes with the (Divine) Essence.

3. To that which is objected, that (the Divine Essence) is (something) finite to the Most High Truth; it must be said, that this[5] is twofold: for either It is (something) finite to the Most High Truth, because *the Truth judges*, that It is finite, or because *It does not exceed Its comprehension*. In the first manner God is not finite to Himself, but infinite; for He truly knows, that He is infinite. In the second manner He is finite, because He does not exceed Himself, though He is infinite; and in this manner the argument is not valid, and there is a fallacy there <u>secundum quid</u> and *simply*: 'if It does not exceed an infinite: therefore It is (something) simply finite'.

4. To that which is objected, that the "infinite" does not finish; it must be said, that the "infinite" through a *privation of perfection* does not finish, but the "infinite" through a *negation of limitation* has a reckoning of being finished, because, when it most high, there is in it every standing-still: for in this the infinity is not repugnant to simplicity nor to a complement.

5. To that which is objected, that (the Divine Essence) is comprehended; it must be said, that It is not comprehended through *being included*, but It is comprehended through *perfect vision*, *dilection* and *holding*, and this on the part of the *one comprehending* and not (on the part of) the *one comprehended*; and for that reason, because (the one comprehending)[6] is perfected, he rests, even though he attains nothing further [ultra non].

6. What is objected last, has been solved; for it objects concerning the "infinite", according to which it is said *privatively*; but insofar as it is said of God, it does not mean a *privation* according to *thing*, but only as much as regards the *manner of signifying*; and a most high positing (of the "infinite" as 'unlimited by any constraint') does respond to this.[7] For nothing is said (to be) "immense", except what has a most high and most perfect actuality and (which) nothing constrains and determines. Wherefore even if (the "infinite") seems to be said *privatively* (of the Divine Essence), yet according to the truth *it excludes* every privation.

SCHOLIUM

I. The second opinion posited in the Response is more mildly censured by the Seraphic Doctor than the first, because the error, as is seen, can consist rather in a perverse manner of speaking, than in a depraved understanding (cf. in reply to nn. 3 and 4, and above in d. 35, q. 5, in reply to n. 1). — The solution

to n. 2 militates against pantheism. Alexander of Hales (SUMMA., p. I, q. 6, m. 1, in reply to n. 3) says in the same sense, « that something ought not to be said (to be) "finite", because *it is this and not (something) else*, but because *it is terminated at another*, and/or *is on account of another*, and/or because *it is perfected by another* ».

---

[1] On this twofold acceptation of the infinite, cf. Aristotle, PHYSICS, text 63 ff. (ch. 6), and METAPHYSICS, Bk. V, text 21 (Bk. IV. ch. 16). On the division between negation and privation, cf. Aristotle, ON THE PREDICAMENTS, ch. "On *Opposites*", and METAPHYSICS, Bk. IV, text 4 and also text 27 (Bk. III, ch. 2, and BK. IV, ch. 22). — A little further above this, for *that it has a limited 'being'* [quod habet esse limitatum] codex T has *that it means a limited 'being'* [quod dicit esse limitatum].

[2] ON THE TRINITY, Bk. VI, ch. 8, n. 9: (For) those which are great not in mass, that which it is 'to be better' is 'to be greater'. — The solution of the sentence is as follows: a quantity of virtue is not only attained in an effect or work in a manner related to an exterior magnitude, but also in a manner related to intrinsic nobility and essential strength; wherefore the Divine Essence, to which a quantity of virtue is befitting, because It is in a most noble manner, It will also be infinite.

[3] Breaking with the codices and even edition 1, the Vatican edition transforms *for that reason* [ideo] into *in God* [in Deo], and then after *to many* [ad multa] it proceeds thus: *because His Power and Essence are compared to many, yet from this it does not follow* etc. [quia potentia vel essentia eius comparatur ad multa, ex hoc tamen non sequitur etc.].

[4] For *if* [si] the Vatican edition, together with some manuscripts, has *but* [sed].

[5] Namely the proposition. — Somewhat below this for *In the second manner He is finite* [Secundo modo est finitus] very many codices faultily read *In the second manner He is infinite* [Secundo modo est infinitus]. Near the end of the solution before *It does not exceed* [non excedit] we have interjected *if* [si] on the authority of codices A R and T. — Cf. above d. 19, p. I. q. 1, in reply to n. 3.

[6] That is, because the one comprehending is completed and satiated. Cf. above d. 1, a. 3, q. 2, in reply to n. 2. — The Vatican edition, together with not a few codices, has *because the thing is perfected according to its own capacity, it rests, even though it does not attain to (anything) further* [quia perficitur res secundum suam capacitatem, quiescit, quamvis ultra non attingat]. Not a few other codices read thus: *because the thing is perfected, it rests, even though* etc. [quia perficitur res, quiescit, quamvis]. Our reading, which is more accurate, has been taken from codices B and D.

[7] For *positing (of the "infinite" as 'unlimited by any constraint')* the Vatican ed., with cod. cc, has *power* [potentia]. A little after this, for *Wherefore even if (the "infinite") seems* [unde etsi videatur] many codices read *Wherefore if (the "infinite") be said* [Unde si dicatur], incongruously.

St. Thomas (SUMMA., I, q. 7, a. 1, in reply to n. 3) solves the same objection from this principle, that God's 'Being' is *subsistent through Itself*, (and is) not received in another; and for that reason It is distinguished from all others, even though It is infinite.

II. Besides the (authors) cited: S. Thomas, SUMMA., I, q. 7, a. 1; SUMMA CONTRA GENTILES., I, c. 43. — Bl. (now St.) Albertus (Magnus), SENT., Bk. I, d. 2, a. 2. — (Bl.) Peter of Tarentaise, here in q. 1, a. 1. — Richard of Middleton, here in q. 1. — Henry of Ghent, SUMMA., a. 44, qq. 1 and 2.

QUESTION III

Whether the Divine Power is able unto an effect infinite in act?

Third, there is asked concerning the Divine Power, as much as *regards (Its) work*, whether, namely, the Divine Power is able unto an effect infinite in act. And that (it is) so, is shown in this manner:

1. Power holds itself proportionally to work, wherefore so great (a power) is able unto so great a work: therefore, a greater also unto a greater, and an infinite in act unto an infinite in act.

2. Likewise, every power, which works out of its whole self, if it is infinite, produces an infinite (effect), since it works out of its own whole virtue; but the Divine Power, since It is most simple, works by Its whole Self: therefore, it seems, that It produces an infinite effect. *If you say*, that this cannot be on account of the defect and limitation of the effect itself; *on the contrary*: without effect [frustra] is the power, which is not reduced to act; wherefore the Philosopher[1] also says, that without effect is the active power, to which there responds no passive (power): therefore, either the Divine Power is infinite without effect, or there responds to It an infinite effect and a infinite, passive power.

3. Likewise, every power can manifest itself, therefore, the Divine Power, since It is infinite, can manifest Its own infinity; but an infinite is not manifested except in an infinite effect: ergo etc.. *If you say*, that It is manifested in the production of the Son and the Holy Spirit; *then there is objected*, that the Holy Spirit has a infinite power: therefore, He can manifest Himself, but not in the production of an infinite Person: therefore, in the production of a creature.

4. Likewise, every possible (is) able to be posited in 'being'; but God can produces infinite (things): therefore, 'that infinite (things) be produced' is possible, therefore, (it is) able to be posited. But « with a possible posited in 'being', nothing unfitting happens [accidit] »:[2] therefore, with it posited, that God makes infinite (things), nothing unfitting happens.

But God can (make) every that which is not unfitting to be able (to make) and/or to make: therefore, God can cause, that there be infinite (things) in act.

5. Likewise, let every creatable be named "A"; then I ask: either A is finite, or infinite. If finite, and God cannot (make) but A: therefore, He cannot (make) but (things) finite: therefore, His Power is finite. If infinite, and God can make A: therefore, He can make some (things) infinite in act.

6. Likewise, « a continuum is divisible unto infinity »;[3] I ask, whether God can reduce the potency of a continuum to act. If He cannot: therefore, the potency of a continuum exceeds the Power of God; which is absurd, because then the Divine Power would be finite. If He can reduce that (potency) entirely to act; but this is not, except when (the continuum) has been in act divided into infinite parts: ergo etc..

BUT ON THE CONTRARY: 1. That (the Divine Power) is not able unto an effect infinite *in intension* [intensione],[4] it seems, because than an simply infinite there is nothing greater; therefore, if It produces an infinite effect, then, therefore, that than there is nothing greater: therefore, God is not greater. If, therefore, it belongs to the most high Nobility in God, that nothing can be equal to Him, (then) to produce such an effect is contrary to the Nobility of the Divine Power: ergo etc..

2. Likewise, everything which is infinite in act, is most highly simple. For if there is any composition, then there is a constriction [coarctatio] and limitation. Therefore, if God produces an infinite effect, that (effect) is most simple; but in a most simple the same is the essence, goodness and power: therefore, if the effect is infinite in power and goodness, therefore, (it is) a Most High Good, therefore, (it is) not good on account of another, therefore, (it is) not good on account of God: therefore, (it is) neither from God, because *each and every (things) has the Lord worked on account of Himself*;[5] and the same is the end, which (is) also the first

---

[1] These propositions: *without effect is the power, which is not reduced to act* [frusta est potentia, quae non reducitur ad actum], and: *without effect is the active power, to which there responds no passive (power)* [frustra est potentia activa, cui non respondet passiva] are founded upon the definitions, which Aristotle offers both for <u>frustra</u> and for *power* [potentia], active and passive. The Philosopher, PHYSICS, Bk. II, text 62 (ch. 6) teaches that that which is ordered to some end, which it does not obtain, is without effect [frustra] and vain. And in ON HEAVEN AND THE WORLD, text 32, (ch. 4), where he treats of bodies impeded in moving on another, which he teaches are without effect [frustra], he adjoins: « For we say that this footwear is without effect, which does not shod the foot [frustra enim calceamentum hoc dicimus, cuius non est calceatio] », but in the edition of Firmin.-Didot: « For we say that this sandal is without effect, which has no use [frustra enim calceamentum dicimus esse, cuius usus non est] ». Moreover, in regard to active and passive power, he defines these (propositions) thus in METAPHYSICS, Bk. V, text 17 (Bk. IV, ch. 12) and Bk. IX, text 2 (Bk. VIII, ch. 1), such that the definition of one includes the definition of the other. Cf. above d. 42, a. sole, q. 4, p. 757, footnote 6.

[2] Cf. above d. 38, a. 2, q. 1, p. 674, footnote 5. For *but with a possible posited* [sed possibili posito] the Vatican edition has faultily *but having posited that which is able to be posited* [sed ponibile posito]. In regard tot he first proposition of this argument we remind the reader of that verse of Aristotle, RHETORICS TO ALEXANDER, ch. 1: Possible are all (those), whichsoever can come to be [Possibilia sunt omnia, quaecumque fieri possunt].

[3] Aristotle, PHYSICS, Bk. III, text 1 and 69 (ch. 1 and 7), Bk. VI, text 15 (ch. 2), and ON HEAVEN AND THE WORLD, Bk. I, text 2. (St.) Augustine teaches the same ON A LITERAL EXPOSITION OF GENESIS, Bk. II, ch. 4, n. 8, and ON THE TRINITY, Bk. XI, chs. 10 and 17.

[4] Understand an effect of infinite perfection; wherefore the infinite in intension pertains to the infinite according to essence.

[5] Proverbs 16:4. — On the immediate subsequent proposition: *the same is the end* etc. [idem est finis], cf. Aristotle, METAPHYSICS, Bk. XII, text 37 (Bk. XI, ch. 7). — For *which (is) also the first principle* [quod et primum principium] codex V has *which (is) the first and the beginning* [quod est primum et principium].

principle: Therefore, if it is infinite, it is not from God: therefore, it is not an effect, and thus it is clear that etc..

3. Likewise, if God is able unto an effect infinite in act; I ask you, whether He is able unto another. If not: therefore, in acting He looses [amittit] power, and by acting He is debilitated in His Power. If, therefore, He is able unto another effect completely similar to that one, let it be that He causes (such); therefore, let (such) be posited. These two effects are completely similar in nature, therefore, they are in the same genus: therefore, if they are in the same genus,[1] then they have something more [in plus], in which *they convene*, and some (things) proper, through which *they differ*; therefore, they are exceeded by something, and constrained through something. But all such are finite: ergo etc..

4. Likewise, that It cannot cause (things) infinite in act, is shown, because there are not *more* infinites: therefore, if It would produce (things) infinite in act It could not produce more: therefore, God is[2] impotent. But nothing can make God impotent: ergo etc..

5. Likewise, where there is an actual infinity according to *number*, there is a deficiency of [deficit] a standing-still and order an distinction;[3] but the Divine Wisdom does not suffer, that God do anything without rule [sine modo] and measure: ergo etc..

CONCLUSION

The Divine Power can cause an (effect) infinite in potency, but to no extent infinite in act.

I RESPOND: It must be said, that there is a twofold infinite, namely in *act* and in *potency*.[4] The infinite in *potency*, God *can* cause and *does cause*; the infinite in *act*, He *cannot* cause nor *does cause*. I say, "He *cannot* cause", because it neither befits *Himself*, nor does it befit *the creature*.

It does not befit *Himself*: for since He is most highly good, He cannot cause but what is good, and thus He cannot[5] cause but that a thing (be) ordered to Himself. Therefore, since *order* presupposes *number*, and *number* presupposes *measure*, because none are ordered to another except *the numbered*, and none are numbered but *the limited*; for that reason, it was necessary, that God make all in *number, weight and measure*,[6] and He could not nor can He make in another manner, neither an infinite nor (things) infinite in act.

There is also the reason, that it in no manner befits a *creature*. For the 'infinite in *act*' is a pure act,

otherwise, if it had something of limitation and restraint [arctatione], it would be finite; but what is a pure act, is *its own 'to be'* through (its) essence, and nothing such accepts a 'to be' from another essence nor out of nothing. Therefore, if (it is) a creature, by the very (fact) that (it is) a creature, it is from another and out of nothing, (and) can in no manner be a pure act, (and) in no manner can it be infinite. — And, if one (creature) cannot be *infinite*, in no manner can there be infinite (creatures) according to *number*, because it is necessary, that those many be led back to some one creature; but that infinite (things) be led back to (one) finite, is impossible: therefore, it is clear that etc.. And that they are necessarily led back to some finite, is clear: because it is necessary to posit an ordination among creatures, not only to God, but even to one another.[7]

Therefore, the summary of the Response is, that *it is not fitting* [non decet] that God make a creature, which has no *order* and *measure*; and the reason (for this) is *on the part of the creature*, because it is necessary, that every creature be limited, by this, that (it is) out of nothing, and by this very (fact), that it has been composed.

1. To that, therefore, which is objected, that so great a power is able unto so great an effect or work; it must be said, that there is the work *being worked* and the work *worked*.[8] the work *being worked*, such a creating, the work *worked*, such as the creature. Therefore, it must be said, that the work *being worked* is infinite, just as the Creator Himself, but it is necessary tat the work *worked* be finite. Therefore, what is objected, that a work is proportioned to the power (which works it); if it be understood of the work *being worked* or of the action generally, it is true; but if it be understood of the work *worked*, it does not have truth, except when the caused and effect hold themselves through a univocation[9] and are of one genus; but this is not (the case) here.

2. To that which is objected, that God works out of (His) whole Power; it must be said, that a certain (agent) acting out of (its) whole power acts through (its) *nature*, and it acts only as much as it can, and only as much as it is; where there is a production of a similar. A certain (agent) acts through *deliberation* and *will*, and such does not act except according to order and as much as it wills: wherefore from the same power it makes (something) great and (something) small; and God acts in this manner. — To that which is objected, that the power, which is not reduced to act, is without effect; it is true concerning the power, which is completed[10] in an act; but the Divine Power is not completed through an act; and for that reason It is not without effect, even if It does not have a corresponding *passive*

---

[1] The Vatican edition omits the proposition *therefore if they are in the same genus (i. e. by a homoioteleuton)* [ergo si sunt in eodem genere], and then for *more* [in plus] (regarding the expression in plus, cf. above d. 19, p. I, a. sole, q. 4, p. 348, footnote 5) it substitutes *superior* [superius]. Somewhat further above this, for *If, therefore, He is able* [Si ergo potest] edition 1 has *If, however, He is able* [Si vero potest], and next after *completely similar to that* [consimilem illi] codex V has *effect* [effectui] for *one*.

[2] Codices V X & Y and edition 1 have *would be* [esset] for *is* [est].

[3] Cf. Aristotle, PHYSICS, Bk. III, text 41 (ch. 5).

[4] Aristotle, PHYSICS, Bk. III, text 56 (ch. 6).

[5] Codex T has *can neither* [nec potest] for *cannot* [non potest].

[6] Wisdom 11:21: But Thou has disposed all in measure and number and weight. — Cf. also above d. 19, p. II, q. 4, and d. 20, a. 2. q. 1.

[7] Cf. Aristotle, METAPHYSICS, Bk. XII, text 52 (Bk. XI, ch. 10). —

A little above this, the Vatican ed. with cod. cc omits *necessarily* [necessario], and, a little below this, in place of *Response* [responsionis] it exhibits *reckoning* [rationis].

[8] The expression *the work being worked* [opus operans] and *the work worked* [opus operatum] signify here the very action of the agent and the effect of the action, respectively.

[9] Or are *univocal*. For indeed a univocal cause is that which produces an effect similar in species to itself; to which there is opposed the equivocal cause. — A little above this the Vatican edition prefaces to the words *if it be understood of the work being worked* [si intelligatur de opere operante] the verb *I respond* [respondeo], and at the end of the solution for *of one genus* [unius generis] it has with codex cc *of the same genus* [eiusdem generis].

[10] Edition 1 adds *and perfected* [et perficitur]. Then for *in act* [in actu] the Vatican edition with codex cc, has *through an act* [per actum].

power. Yet, that proposition is understood not to have truth in the power, which is able (to cause things)[1] infinite, if it be understood that it is *entirely* reduced to act; yet it is reduced and can be reduced *according to part*; and for that reason it is not without effect.

3. To that which is objected, that the Divine Power, since It is infinite, ought to manifest Its own infinity in an infinite effect; it must be said, that God does manifest His own Infinity in an infinite *according to potency*, just as is clear, because, just as has been demonstrated above, (His) interminable duration manifests (His) infinite virtue. But in an infinite *according to act* (the Divine Infinity) cannot be manifested *simply*, because it is not fitting, but (It can be) *proportionally*, because a being exceeds a non-being unto an infinite (degree); and yet God makes a being out of nothing, among which there is an infinite distance.[3]

Wherefore, since the Divine Power is said (to be) "infinite" in a threefold manner: *by the eternity*[4] *of (Its) duration*, *by the immensity of (Its) Virtue* and *by the generality* or *numerosity* of (Its) *effects*; the *first* is manifested through the infinite in duration, which is a finite in act, (and) an infinite in potency; the *second* through a creation from nothing, where there is an infinite distance on account of the omnimodal improportion (of a being to a non-being): the *third* is manifested partly through a *positing*,[5] partly through a *privation*, because He worked so many and still is able unto more, and He did not work so many, that He is not still able unto more; yet this is manifested by another, twofold, manifest infinity. And, thus, it is clear, that it is not necessary, that there be an infinite (effect) in act.

Yet it can be said, just as has been touched upon,[6] that the Virtue of the Father is manifested in the production of the Word, and consequently the whole Divine Virtue, since the Virtue of the Son and the Holy Spirit is one, and They are equal in virtue.

4. To that which is objected concerning the possible, that it can be posited; it must be said, that there is a possible by *infinite* power, and a possible according to a *finite* power. The possible according to *finite* power can be posited, because (a finite power) can be entirely reduced to act;[7] but the possible according to *infinite* power cannot

be posited, because it is always in a (state of) '*being reduced*', and never in a (state of) '*having been reduced*'.

5. To that which is objected, that let every creatable be named "A"; let it be (that etc.).[8] Wherefore it asks, whether A be finite, and/or infinite; I say, that (it is) infinite, but it is not infinite in act, but in potency; and for that reason it does not follow, that if God can (cause) A, that He is able unto an infinite act. And if there be said: "Let it be posited, that God does cause A"; it must be said, that it is not able to be posited, for the aforesaid reason.

6. To that which is asked, whether (the Divine Power) can reduce the potency of a continuum to act; it must be said, that just as the potency in a continuum is a *passive*, infinite (potency) to division, so in God (there is) an *active* infinite (power). Wherefore, just as a continuum can *be divided* unto infinity, yet it is impossible, that *it be* totally *divided*, otherwise it would not be infinite; so it is possible that (there be) a *reducing of the (act of)* '*dividing unto infinity*' to act;[9] but, just as it is impossible, that the Divine Power be terminated, so it is impossible, that It exist [esse] at the end of the act of division [in termino divisionis]. Wherefore, God can *reduce* the potency of a continuum to act, because (the potency of a continuum) can exist [esse] in being reduced[10] and (can exist) always in being reduced, such that the potency never extends itself more than the Divine Action: but, yet, the continuum can never [exist] in a (state of) '*having been reduced (unto infinity)*', just as neither (can) God in a (state of) '*having reduced (it unto infinity)*'.

It must be conceded, therefore, that it is impossible, that there be anything infinite in act except God alone and His Power. And this is what Hugh of St. Victor[11] says: « Just as time does not equal God's Eternity, nor (any) place (His) Immensity; so neither (any) sense (His) Wisdom, nor (any) virtue (His) Goodness, nor (any) work (His) Power ». Wherefore when it is said, that God can cause (things) infinite, there is noted an infinity about *power*, not about *work*. Wherefore some distinguished this (proposition): "a continuum can be divided unto infinity", because that determination[12] can determine this verb "*can*", and/or this verb "*be divided*". Yet, in whatever manner it be distinguished, it must be always understood, that an actual infinity is proper to God alone.

---

[1] Codex A here interjects *unto (things)* [in], codd. L & O have instead *to be* [esse], the Vatican ed. with cod. cc has *to have (things)* [habere].*

[2] Here in q. 1.   [3] Cf. above q. 1, in reply to n. 4.

[4] For *eternity* [aeternitate], not a few codd. have *interminability* [interminabilitate]. A little before this, the Vatican ed. with cod. cc prefixes to the word *in a threefold manner* [tripliciter] the words *this is* [hoc est].

[5] For *a positing* [positionem] the Vatican edition, together with codex cc, has *power* [potentiam]. Next for *because He worked so many* [quia tot fecit] codices G K S T V X Y Z etc. have *because He works so many* [quia tot facit], and similarly for *and He did not work so many* [et non tot fecit] codex W has *and He does not work so many* [et non tot facit]. A little after for *yet this (truth)* [tamen hoc] codex Y has *yet this (infinity)* [tamen haec]. At the end of the proposition in place of the *manifested* [manifestata], which is read in the Vatican edition, we have placed, on the authority of codices A H T cc and ee *manifest* [manifesta].

[6] In the 3rd opposed argument.

[7] The Vatican edition has *(such a possible) can be entirely reduced to act* [quia omnino potest esse ad actum reductum] for *because (a finite power) can be entirely reduced to act* [quia omnino potest esse ad actum reducta]. Our reading, in favor of which many codices militate, is confirmed and explained by the reading of codex V: *because that power can be entirely reduced to act* [quia omnino potest illa potentia esse ad actum reducta].

[8] For *let it be that etc.*. *Wherefore* [esto. Quod] the Vatican edition reads *and what* [et quod], and, a little before this, for *is objected* [obicitur] it has *is posited* [ponitur].

[9] The sense is: Just as a continuum can be divined unto infinity according to potency, so the action of dividing, if it were to be exercised, will always exist in the dividing. — The Vatican edition, with a few codices in favor of it, reads thus: *to divide unto infinity is possible, to reduced to act impossible. And just as it is impossible* etc. [dividere in infinitum est possibile, ad actum reducere impossibile. Et sicut impossibile est etc.], a reading which is not false. — Cf. Aristotle, Physics, Bk. III, text 59 f. and 69 (ch. 6 f.).

[10] Accept in reducendo in the passive sense (i.e. as "in being reduced") and refer it to potentiam continui, so that the sense be: *because the potency of a continuum can exist in being reduced* [quia potentia continui potest esse in reduci]. — The words *and always in being reduced* [et semper in reducendo] are wanting in codex T.

[11] On the Sacraments, Bk. I, p. II, ch. 22, where in the original text *His* [eius] is added after (before in the English) *Wisdom* [sapientia]. A little before this for *that there be anything* [esse aliquid], which reading we have restored from codex X, the Vatican edition incongruously has *that there be anything* [quod sit aliquid] (since the remainder of the subordinate clause is in indirect discourse).

[12] That is: "unto infinity" [in infinitum]. — A little below this, after "*can*" [potest], codex Y adds well *and in this manner they used to conceded (it)* [et sic concedebant], and, then, after "*be divided*" [dividi] it equally well subjoins *and in this manner they used to deny (it)* [et sic negabant].

---

* *Trans. note*: Here the context requires the understanding, *to cause things infinite* [facere infinita], because, while St. Bonaventure has already denied the application of the proposition, "that the power, which is not reduced to act, is without effect" to God, whose Power alone is infinite simply speaking, he has not, yet, applied it to a created power which can cause infinite effects, such as the power to be divided ad infinitum, which passive power exists in things material, such as a continuum.

SCHOLIUM

I. Among all (authors) it is established, that there cannot be created an infinite according to *essence*. However, that the infinite in *some genus*, or according to a *quantity*, either *continuous* (e. g. a magnitude), and/ or *discrete* (e.g. number), whether according to an *intension*, or according to a *duration* can be created, the Nominalists wanted to defend as probable, with whom in regard to *duration* even certain (authors) of the school of St. Thomas and (Bl. John Duns) Scotus used to agree. — But St. Bonaventure, together with the more approved Scholastics, completely proves with many reasons the contrary sentence in an unconquerable manner. — The Response and (his) solutions to nn. 2, 3, 4, and 6 contain many things worthy of attention.

II. St. Thomas, SUMMA., I, q. 7, a. 3; DE VERITATE., q. 2, a. 10. — Bl. (now St.) Albertus (Magnus), on this and the following question, here in a. 2. — (Bl.) Peter of Tarentaise, here in q. 1, a. 3. — Richard of Middleton, here in qq. 4, 5 and 6. — Henry of Ghent, on this and the following question, here in SUMMA., a. 35, q. 5. — Durandus (of Saint-Pourçain), here in q. 2. — (Bl.) Dionysius the Carthusian, on this and the following question, here in q. 2. — (Gabriel) Biel, here i q. 1, at the end, and in d. 44, q. 1, at the end; SENT., Bk. II, d. 1, q. 3.

QUESTION IV

Whether the reason for the Divine Power extends itself to (things) infinite?

Fourth and last, there is asked concerning the infinity of the Divine Power as much as regards (Its) *reason for operating*, and there is asked, whether (Its) reason for operating[1] extends itself unto infinity. And that (it is) so, seems:

1. Because whatever God can (do), He can do reasonably; but He can (cause) infinite (things): therefore, He can reasonably (cause) infinite (things). And if this, therefore, the reason for the operating of His Power extends itself to (things) infinite.

2. Likewise, just as a *reason for knowing* holds itself to knowledge, so a *reason for producing* to power; but because the Divine Knowledge is infinite, for that reason It has in Itself infinite reasons for cognizing:[2] therefore since the Divine Power is infinite, It similarly has infinite reasons for producing.

3. Likewise, in God *the reason for operating* is not other than (His) Goodness and Wisdom; but (His) Goodness and Wisdom is infinite: therefore, (His) reason for operating[3] (is) too.

4. Likewise, in God *the reason for operating* is not other than God or the Divine Essence, whatever that reason be said (to be);[4] but the Divine Essence is infinite: therefore, (His) reason for operating (is) too.

ON THE CONTRARY: 1. (God's) Power extends Itself to works according to the exigency of (Its) reason — for It omits nothing concern those which (Its) reason (for operating) requires — if, therefore, (Its) *reason* (for operating) extends itself to (things) infinite, therefore, it seems, that the Divine Power produces (things) infinite, which is false.

2. Likewise, (Its) *reason for operating* is (Its) very Art and disposition; but (Its) disposition is not but of (things) infinite: therefore, (Its) reason for operating is not but of (things) finite.[5]

3. Likewise, (Its) *reason for operating* is the Divine Justice Itself, because *each and every way of the Lord (is) mercy and truth*;[6] but (His) Justice is not but of (things) finite: therefore, it seems that (Its) reason for operating (is) similarly.

4. Likewise, there is the objection [obiicitur] concerning (God's) Foreknowledge, which is similarly a reason for operating and is unto more than (God's) Power, because (It is) in respect of evils; and yet it is not in respect of (things) infinite. *If you say*, that (God's) *disposition* and/or *Foreknowledge* and/or *Justice* does not comprise the full reason, through which the Divine Power can operate;[7] *on the contrary*: if it does not comprise the whole (reason), therefore, the Divine Power can reasonably operate without these: therefore, it is possible, that God operate apart from disposition, apart from justice and apart from foreknowledge. But no such operates wisely nor uprightly: ergo etc.. Therefore, it remains, that it does comprise the whole reason.

CONCLUSION

In God the reason for operating in respect of the act, which is 'to be able', is accepted in regard to the habit and extends itself to (things) infinite; in respect of the act, which is 'to cause', it is accepted in regard to the act and is finite according to the Divine disposition.

I RESPOND: Just as Master (Peter) says in the text,[8] some wanted to say, the *reason* for the Divine Power is finite. And, on this account, they wanted to limit the Divine Power, both because It can do and/or leave off (doing) nothing but out of the best

---

[1] The Vatican edition in place of the words *and there is asked, whether (Its) reason for operating* [et quaeritur, utrum ratio operandi], which it suppressed, puts *whether it* [an]; codex cc *if it* [si].

[2] Cf. above d. 35, q. 5.

[3] Codex T has *for producing* [producendi].

[4] The Vatican edition, together with editions 4 and 5, has *means* [dicat] for *be said to be* [dicatur].

[5] Codex M has *but in respect of (things) finite* [nisi respectu finitorum]. — The Vatican edition puts this argument in the third position.

[6] Psalm 24:10.

[7] For (God's) disposition and Foreknowledge and Justice respect only *those which will be*, and they contain a reckoning [rationem] of these only, but not of those which *could* be, to which, however, the Divine Power extends Itself.

[8] Here in ch. 1. — A little after this, we have corrected, on the authority of the codices and editions 1, 2 and 3, the error of the Vatican edition, which exhibits *by reason* [ratione] for *the reason* [ratio].

reason, and because It can do nothing except as One foreknowing, nothing but in a just manner; and for that reason since these are of (things) finite, as for example of those which It does, they said, that the Divine Power cannot (work) others, than those which It works. — But this position is erroneous, just as Master (Peter) shows in the text, because it derogates the nobility of the Divine Power by limiting Its immensity; and it is said to have been (the opinion) of Master Peter Abelard [Baalardi].[1] Moreover, the reason for this foolish position was, because they did not know how to distinguish *the reason of a power* and *its acts*. For *the act* of a power is twofold: the one through the manner of a habit, namely '*to be able*', the other through the manner of an act, namely '*to operate*'.

Therefore, when it is asked, whether the reason of Divine Power is infinite; it must be said, that just as there is a twofold act, so[2] "reason" can be accepted in a twofold manner. For in respect of the act, which is '*to be able*', "reason" is accepted in regard to the habit [in habitu], that is, as the Divine Knowledge and the co-fittingness [condecentia] of the Divine Goodness; and this reason extends itself to (things) infinite, according to which manner the Power Itself (is) also in respect of the act, which is '*to be able*'. However, in respect of the act, which is '*to cause*', "reason" is accepted in regard to the act [in actu], namely, the Divine disposition or Foreknowledge and the demand of merits. For (God)[3] does nothing, except that which He disposes; He also pays back nothing, except according to which merits demand, when He pays back; He governs no thing nor rules in another manner, than His Nature or the Justice of (His) Nature [iustitia naturalis] demand.

And, according to this distinction, the response to the first question [primo quaesitum] and to the reasons brought forward (on its behalf), is clear: for certain ones proceed according to one way, certain ones according to the other.

3. 4. To that which is objected afterwards concerning *justice*, it must be said, that the (Divine) Justice, according to which it means the complete fittingness of the Divine Goodness and Possibility, thus is the *general reason*, which comprises the whole 'being able'; but inasmuch as It connotes a demand [exigentiam] on the part of merits, thus it does not comprise the whole '*being able*' nor the whole *acting*; however, inasmuch as It connotes the complete fittingness of the (Divine) Goodness in respect of anything of time in act,[4] thus it comprises *acting*, but not the '*being able*'. The (Divine) *disposition* and *Foreknowledge* similarly comprise the *acting*, but not the '*being able*'; but (the Divine Power's) *acting* is in respect of (things) finite, just as these are also (finite), but (Its) '*being able*' is in respect of (things) infinite.

Therefore, what it then objected, that God can operate reasonably without these; it must be said, that (this) is false and it does not follow from the former. For, though God can (do) more, than He wills, yet He cannot operate without a will; since He can *do* nothing, that He cannot will, thus (nothing which He cannot) both foreknow and dispose. For it is necessary, that the executing Power[5] be adequated to these, that is, to the (Divine) disposition and Will, but it is not necessary [non oportet] (that this) concern the Power, as powerful: for that reason it does not follow, that He can work without these.

SCHOLIUM

I. Abelard, together with others, indeed conceded, that the Divine Power *in Itself* and ad extra is infinite, but in regard to (Its) *reason* for operating ad extra (which is something which is within God) he wanted to limit the Divine Power. Against this error Master (Peter) disputes throughout this whole Distinction, and Alexander of Hales at length too in SUMMA., p. I, q. 21, m. 2, § 1 and 2. — Moved by other reasons, Wycliffe taught a worse error, namely, that God cannot do others, that which He does; with which very many philosophers, ancient and recent, nearly agree, who taught that God in (His) works ad extra does not act

freely, but acts out of the necessity of (His) Nature, blindly. Against these multiple errors the Response can be of the greatest utility. The whole force of the argumentation stands in the distinction of a "*reason* for operating" according to *first* and *second* act.

II. Alexander of Hales, loc. cit. — (Bl. John Duns) Scotus, SENT., Bk. I, d. 44, q. sole, and REPORTATIO. ere in q. 2, and d. 44, q. 1. — St. Thomas (in regard to the principles of the solution) SUMMA., I, q. 25, a. 5; SUMMA CONTRA GENTILES. Bk. II, chs. 26 and 27. — (Bl.) Peter of Tarentaise, here in q. 2, a. 3. — Richard of Middleton, here in q. 7. — Durandus (of Saint-Pourçain), here in q. 5. — (Gabriel) Biel, here in q. 1.

---

[1] Whose opinion is expressed in his INTRODUCTION TO THEOLOGY, Bk. III, n. 5. — Aristotle proffers a similar opinion in his METAPHYSICS, Bk. IX, text 5 (Bk. VIII, ch. 3): Moreover, there are certain ones, such as the Megarans (i.e. those of the school of Eucleides of Megara), who say, that (someone) is only able, when he acts, but when he does not act, that he is not able: as for example he who does not build, that he is not able to build, but when building (he is), since he builds.

[2] The Vatican edition with codex cc subjoins *too* [etiam], and, at the beginning of the next sentence, the Vatican ed. inserts *For* [enim], which particle the codd. and the six first edd. incongruously place after the accipitur (or in English before "*reason*"), which follows a little after this. — The expression which then occurs *the complete fittingness of the Divine Goodness* [divinae bonitatis condecentia] is to be understood as that which befits the Divine Goodness, considered precisely in Itself. The expression is taken from (St.) Anselm, PROSLOGION, ch. 10: However, when Thou doest spare the wicked, it is a just (act), not because of their merits, but because it is completely fitting to Thy Goodness [bonitati tuae condecens est].

[3] Edition 1 adjoins *God* [Deus], and then together with codex M (in the margin) for *He also ... nothing* [nihil etiam] it has *He also ... to no one* [nulli etiam]. In place of *He disposes* [disponit], which precedes the words *He also pays back* [nihil etiam], codex R has *He disposed* [disposuit]. Next, for *when He pays back* [quando retibuit] codex V and X have *when He pays back* [quod retribuat] (in the subjunctive). Immediately after this the Vatican edition inserts *because* [quia]. Then, the expression iustitia naturalis is not to be accepted in the moral sense, but only as a certain explicit circumlocution on behalf of *the Nature* [natura].

[4] That is of all those which come to be in time. — For *of time* [temporis] the Vatican edition has *of a work* [operis].

[5] Codices V and X read *the Power as One executing* [potentiam ut exsequentem]. A little before this, for *thus (nothing which He cannot) both foreknow and dispose* [sic et praescire et disponere] the Vatican edition, together with codex cc has *just as (He cannot) both foreknow and dispose (nothing)* [sicut et praescire et dispondere].

DOUBTS ON THE TEXT OF THE MASTER

DOUBT I

In this part are the doubts about (Master Peter's) text and first concerning the response of Master (Peter), by which he says: *But to these we respond, opening the twofold understanding of the words* etc.; from which comes, namely, the duplicity of this (proposition):[1] "God cannot do, except what is just" etc.: that this verb "*is*" can signify the justice, which *is*, and/or the justice, which *would be*, if God would cause (it). For this seems (to be) nothing, because if there be said: "It is just that this come to be", it is understood that it is just *now*. Similarly, in the proposed.

I RESPOND: It must be said, that Master (Peter)'s distinction is reasonable. Moreover, the reason for this multiplicity is, that this verb "*is*" can mean (something) present as *now*, and/or *simply*, and thus the justice, which *is now*, and/or which *would be*, if things were made.[2] Moreover, the multiplicity can be assigned from three (causes): *first* by reason of *the attribute*; for just as this verb "*runs*", said through itself, means a present (act) as *now*, but when there is added a determination, it can stand on behalf of a present (act) *simply*, as for example if there be said of a horse lying in a stable: "This horse runs well"; thus (the multiplicity) can be of this verb "*is*" by reason of that which is added, "*good and just*". *In another manner*, (the multiplicity) can be assigned on the part of the amplification [ampliationis][3] of this verb "*can*", because if the amplification of this verb "*can*" respects the whole saying, so that the implication falls under the amplification, thus it means (something) present as *now*; and according to this is accepted the twofold sense, which Master (Peter) assigns (to it). *In a third* manner, the reason can be assigned on the part

of that which is "*but*" [nisi], because it can be held *exceptively*, and/or *consecutively*.[4] If *exceptively*, then the act or (thing) excepted stands on behalf of (something) present as *now*, and the sense is: "God cannot (do), but what is just", that is, "God can (do) nothing besides that which is just". And/or it can be held *consecutively*; and then it is necessary, that this verb "*is*" be held *simply*, because the rule is, that the terms in the condition[5] are amplified regarding every tense; and then the sense is: God cannot (do), but what is just", that is "unless [nisi] it is just"; and thus it is amplified there regarding every tense. Yet, out of whichever cause the expression be accepted, it is truly manifold (in meaning).

DOUBT II

Likewise, is asked concerning this exposition by Master (Peter): «*... He could (do) through (His) Power, but (which) He could not (do) through (His) Justice*», because "*justice*" stands there for (His) Will. For it seems that he speaks badly, because God can do nothing, which He cannot will: therefore, if God's Justice is (His) Will, everything which He can simply (do), He can from (His) Justice, and <u>vice</u> <u>versa</u>. — *Likewise*, « with a possible posited in 'being', an impossible does not follow »:[6] if, therefore, God could through (His) Power overthrow or burn Lot; let it be posited. Then I ask: "Either this was just, or not?" If it is: "Therefore, He could (do it) through (His) Justice"; if not: "Therefore, He worked against (His) Justice, therefore, in an iniquitous manner"; which is entirely impossible.

I RESPOND: It must be said, that "*justice*" does not stand there for the Divine Will considered *simply* — for thus He could *will* what[7] He also could *do* —

---

[1] Namely: this proposition. For *of this* [huius] the Vatican edition has *of this kind of* [huiusmodi], which (edition) also, then, after *is just" etc.* [iustum est] interjects *If you say* [Si dicas]. Immediately after this, for *that* [quod] codd. V & X have *that* [quia], and next for *which would be* [quae esset] very many codd. with ed. 1, have *which He works* [quae efficit].

[2] Thus, also, Alexander of Hales, SUMMA, p. I, q. 21, m. 2, § 1, in reply to n. 1: To the first which says, that God cannot do, but what is good and just; it must be distinguished: this verb "*is*" can join an *indeterminate* present whether (something present) in *habit*, and/or (something) present as *now* or in act. In the first manner (the proposition) is true, and the sense is: "God cannot do, but what would be good and just, if He did (it)". In the second manner (the proposition) is false, and the sense is: "He cannot do, but what is good and just *now*". — A little further above this, for *that this verb* [quod hoc verbum] some codices, such as T and X, have *because this verb* [quia hoc verbum], and immediately after *if things were made* [si res fierent] in place of *Moreover, the multiplicity can be assigned* [Potest autem multiplicitas assignari] codices Y aa and bb have *Moreover, the reason for this multiplicity can be assigned* [Ratio autem huius multiplicitatis assignari], in place of which not a few other codices together with edition 1 have more briefly *It can be assigned* [Potest assignari]. After a few (words), by the word *of the attribute* [attributi] there is signified (the final part of the proposition): "*what is just*" [quod iustum est].

[3] On this subject Bl. (now St.) Albertus (Magnus), says here at the beginning of (his Commentary on this) Distinction: « For in this expression there is posited this verb "*can*", which has a force to amplify and it is posited about God as powerful, and that which

I say, "*is good and just to be done*" [iustum et bonum est fieri] falls under this verb "*can*", as (its) matter, in which the act of that power, which the verb "*is*" joins, is terminated: therefore, the expression (is) twofold, namely, it can be understood in regard to, that which first falls under the verb having the force to amplify (i. e. "can"), before it is restricted ... and then the word "*is*" [ly est] will not conjoin a present tense, but (something) confused responding to the power; and then (the proposition) is true under the sense, which Master (Peter) posits (it): "God cannot" etc.., that is, "He cannot do, but what would be good and just, if He did (it)". But if contrariwise the "good and just" is understood to be restricted first by the verb "*is*" to (some) present good and just (act), then the expression is false, because then it would follow, that God can do nothing, but what now is good and just to be done ». In nearly the same words St. Thomas, here on the text, solves this doubt. The same distinction recurs, below, in d. 44, a. 1. q. 4 at the end of the body of the Question. — For *the implication falls under* [implicatio cadat sub] edition 1 has *the implied (term) falls under* [implicatum cadat sub].

[4] Cf. the opuscle entitled: PARVORUM LOGICALIUM, ch. "On the Conjunction *Nisi*", (which work) is ascribed to Peter of Spain.

[5] For *in the condition* [in conditione] codex V has *in the conditional (proposition)* [in conditionali].

[6] Cf. above d. 38, a. 2, q. 1, p. 674, footnote 5. — On Lot, cf. Gen 19:12 ff.

[7] For *what* [quod] the Vatican edition has *that* [quia].

but it stands there for the Will *weighing merits* and the Will that pays back according to merits [voluntate retribuere merita]. And, since Lot had not merited to be submerged with those sinners, he could not be justly submerged, as much as it concerned the demand of merits. Nevertheless, however, God could do this, because He could elicit from this His own praise and Lot's utility, since it is not evil according to itself to truly[2] afflict the just man; for God can do this for his own good. — And through this the response to that which *it objects* is clear. For having posited, that this had been done, there is also posited, that it was just as much as regards *a co-fittingness* [condecentiam], though not as much as regards *merits*. For against the exigency of merits God can work and does work: according to the Gloss on the twentieth (chapter) of Jeremias:[2] « What I thought of doing for the sake of justice, I did not do on account of clemency ».

DOUBT III

Likewise, is asked concerning this which he says: *This verb "He ought" ... does it properly befit ... except perhaps on account of a promise*. For it seems that he speaks badly, because, just as he who ought (to act) out of a (something) *committed* (to him) is obliged, lest he incur ingratitude, so he who ought (to act) out of a promise, if he does not render (what is promised), incurs (the reputation of) falsehood: therefore, God truly has been obliged: therefore, He is both truly and properly a debtor.

I RESPOND: It must be said, that a debt out of (something) *committed* is properly a debt, because it goes before the will; for willing or not, one has been obliged[3] who accepts a benefice, if one is necessarily in need of the benefice. But a debt out of a *promise*, which belongs to a mere liberality, is a debt, which follows the largess of the one promising; and for that reason, according to the thing, it has more of the reckoning of a grace than of a debt; and in this manner God is a debtor, in the first manner (He is) not. For out of His own liberality *He promises*, so as to allure (us), but He receives nothing. Wherefore, He does not accept our acts of compliance [obsequia nostra] on account of (His own) indigence; for that reason *the reckoning of a debt*, according to which it means an obligation, does not properly occur in God. But, if we abuse the name, so that *"debt"* is understood in reference to [sonnet in] the complete fittingness of God's Goodness, in this manner it is received in God.[4]

DOUBT IV

Likewise, is asked concerning that which (Master Peter) says, that *with the reason ... remaining the same, He could do other (things) and leave off (doing) these*. For this seems to be false, because (St.) Augustine says,[5] that « man was established for one reason, the horse was established for another reason »: therefore, opposites comes to be for different reasons [alia et alia ratione]: therefore, with the reason remaining the same, He could not do the opposite.

I RESPOND: It must be said, that here Master (Peter) calls God's most equitous Will the "reason"; and just as has been said above,[6] that because God knows [novit] all (things), for that reason He can know [scire] opposites without an innovation of knowledge, so also concerning (His) Will too. Wherefore, (God's) *Will* is not understood *to be changed*, when God can will what He does not will, but (rather it is understood that) something *willed* is compared to It, with It remaining one and the same and immutable, but compared in another manner or regarding one and the other. And thus does Master (Peter) understand (it).[7]

DOUBT VI

Likewise, is asked concerning this which (Master Peter) says: *But this question concerning (God's) Foreknowledge can easily be determined through those which have been said further above*; through what further above is the saying determined? For it seems that an argument (is) necessary. For,[8] if God can work nothing, but that (which) He foreknows; and He does not foreknow, but what He does: ergo etc..

And, to this, it must be said, that God can foreknow more, than *He foreknows*, just as He can work more (than He works). Wherefore there is this kind of solution, that God's Foreknowledge can *be* of something, of which it is not, and thus God can do that; and (It can) *not be* of something, of which it is, and thus God can not do that; and never is it posited that He does something without (His) Foreknowledge. And it is manifest, that it is not necessary, that God foreknow what He foreknows; for if this were (so), then it would be impossible, that God do (something) else, than that which He does. And this is a manifest error.[9]

---

[1] For *truly* [vere] the Vatican edition, together with codex cc, has *lawfully* [iure].

[2] This citation, *on the twentieth (chapter) of Jeremias* [Ieremiae vigesimo], which is lacking in the Vatican edition, is found in the codices and in edition 1; but the Gloss, which is cited on this passage from St. Jerome, does not convene with the Gloss cited here by St. Bonaventure. For these are the words of the Gloss from (St.) Jerome: « He who is poor in spirit ... when he has obtained deliverance from the Lord, praises the Lord in spirit and glories, having himself been snatched from the hands of the worse men. But this is done not according to our merit, but by His grace, because He liberated the poor man nor does He regard the riches of overthrowing pride, but (rather) the humility of the liberated poor man ». Fr. Marra, in his own unpublished Commentary, would have the words cited by (St.) Bonaventure, as the words of the Gloss, be from the ordinary Gloss on Gen. 19:22; but they are not found there; yet in the same Gloss on Jonah 2:9 there is read: God, merciful by nature, was prepared, to save through clemency, those whom He cannot save through justice. — For what the word, <u>condecentia</u>, which occurs a little before this, signifies, see above q. 4, p.

775, footnote 2, and the following Doubt. — On this doubt, cf. Alexander of Hales, SUMMA, p. I, q. 21, m. 2, § 1; Bl. (now St.) Albertus (Magnus), here in a. 3; St. Thomas, here in q. 2, a. 2; (Bl.) Peter of Tarentaise and Richard of Middleton, there on the text.

[3] Edition 1 *is obliged* [obligatur].

[4] Cf. Alexander of Hales, SUMMA., p. I, q. 21, m. 2, § 1, in reply to n. 3; (Bl.) Peter (of Tarentaise) and Richard (of Middleton), here on the text.

[5] OF EIGHTY-THREE QUESTIONS, q. 46, n. 2. — At the end of the objection for *the opposite* [oppositum] the Vatican, together with a few codices, has *the opposite* [opposita] in the plural.

[6] Distinction 39, a. 2, q. 2; d. 40, a. 2, q. 1, in reply to n. 4; d. 41, a. 2, q. 2. — Next after *so also* [ita etiam] codex Y supplies well *it must be understood* [intelligendum est].

[7] Cf. below d. 44, a. 2, q. 1, and d. 45, a. 2, q. 1. Finally, cf. Alexander of Hales, SUMMA., p. I, q. 21, m. 2, § 2; and (Bl.) Peter of Tarentaise, here on the text, in which passage the two following Doubts are also solved.

[8] The Vatican edition, together with codex cc, has *therefore,* [ergo] for *For* [enim].

[9] Cf. above d. 4, and d. 39, a. 1, q. 3.

DOUBT VI

Likewise, is asked concerning this which (Christ) says: *Or do you think, that I cannot ask My Father* etc.. For it seems that that (has) not be well said, because either the Father *wanted* to grant (it), nor *not*. If *He wanted to*, and Christ *did not want to*: therefore They were discordant in will; but if *He was unwilling*, and Christ could ask: therefore, He could be discordant from the Father's Will, therefore, (He could) sin; which is openly against the truth.

I RESPOND: It must be said, that the Father was unwilling to grant (it), and Christ was unwilling to ask (for it); but Father could will (it), and Christ similarly (could) asked (for it), and thus They (could) not be discordant. Moreover, there would then be a discordance, if Christ could ask (for it), and the Father could not will (it). But in what manner God can will something, which He does not will, is had above.[1]

DOUBT VII

Likewise, is asked concerning this which (St. Augustine) says: *Is it to be said, that He could not raise up Judas in mind?* From this it seems, that God can save Judas (Iscariot): therefore, for an equal reason (He can) damn (St.) Peter. *On the contrary: He is just, and He cannot deny Himself:* therefore, (He can) neither work against justice. *If you say*, that He cannot (do) this: *on the contrary*. God could destroy all which He has made, which is (something) greater: therefore, much more strongly He can do this.

I RESPOND: Some distinguish here God's Power in a twofold manner, saying, that God can either from (His) *absolute* Power, and thus He can save Judas and damn (St.) Peter; or (that He can) from (His) *ordained* Power [potentia ordinata], and thus He cannot. — But this distinction does not seem to be fitting, because God can (do) nothing, which He cannot do ordinately [ordinate]. For *to be able to do (something) inordinately* is not a '*to be able*', just as '*to be able to sin*' and '*to be able to lie*'. Wherefore neither by (His) *absolute* nor (His) *ordinate* Power can He lie.[3]

Others say, in another manner, that He can *save* Judas, but not *damn* (St.) Peter, because *His mercy (is)*

upon all *His works*;[4] and *mercy is exalted over judgement*; and *to save Judas* would be (a work) of superabundant mercy, but *to damn (St.) Peter* would be (a work of) the greatest cruelty. — But yet, since God is most highly just and most highly merciful, just as He cannot work against (His) Mercy, so neither against (His) Justice.

For that reason others say in another manner, that God can (do) *neither*, and this does not derogate from His Power, because each would be an injustice and an inordinance [inordinatio], to recall him whom He finally damned, and who merited to be finally damned. Nor is it similar concerning (the Emperor) Trajan, because God so disposed (him) to do other special (works) for the honor of the Saints and His own (honor); and for that reason the death and damnation of Trajan, though it seemed final according to inferior causes, yet according to the Divine disposition and counsel it was otherwise.[5] — But yet who dares to say this, that God could not in this manner dispose of Judas, as He disposed of Trajan? and that He generally cannot do to all what He is proved to have done to one? And again, (St.) Augustine[6] says, that God could have given the Devil himself a good will.

And, on this account, it must be said, that, when it is asked, whether God could have saved Judas and damned (St.) Peter, it must be said, that either one is speaking *with their merits as they are* [salvis meritis], or *not as they are* [non salvis]. If *with their merits as they are*, thus I say, that He could not. For to say and ask this is the same, as if there would be asked, whether He could judge (them) unjustly; which indeed, without doubt, God cannot (do). But, if it be understood *with their merits not as they are*, thus without a doubt He could save Judas, by removing (his) sins and demerits by grace and by granting (him) merits. But to (St.) Peter He cannot grant evil merits; but yet, just as He liberally gave grace and nature, He can bear off each and only one of the two; and then Peter would be able to sin and God to eternally punish (him). For, just as God liberally[7] gave (St.) Peter a good will, so He also liberally *conserves* (it), and similarly also (his) *nature*. And, *in this manner*, the objections are clear.

---

[1] Here in Doubt 4, and in d. 40, a. 2, q. 1, in reply to n. 4.

[2] 2 Timothy 2:13.

[3] The Seraphic Doctor does not reprove the distinction between *absolute* and *ordained* power. For he makes this distinction in SENT., Bk. II, d. 7, p. I, a. 1. q. 1, in reply to n. 1; and in BREVILOQUIUM., p. I, ch. 7 he teaches: « It happens that "*ordained* power" is said in a threefold manner: either according to act, and/or according to aptitude on the part of the creature, and/or according to the aptitude on the part of the uncreated Virtue alone. What is possible for the (Divine) "Power", said in the first manner, is not only possible, but also actual. What (is such) in the second manner and not in the first, is simply possible, though not actual. But what (is such) in the third manner, and not in the first and/or second, is possible for God, but impossible for the creature. However, what is possible in none of the aforesaid manners, such as that which is directly repugnant to order according to primordial and eternal reasons and causes, is simply impossible ». The Seraphic Doctor in this passage impugns only the manner, in which this distinction was understood and applied by some, which can be gathered from the solution of this doubt, which next follows.

[4] Psalm 114:9, where the Vulgate has *acts of mercy* [miserationes] for *mercy* [misericordia]. The other citation is from James 2:13.

[5] In the Legend or LIFE OF ST. GREGORY, composed by John the Deacon (and had among the works of St. Gregory), there is narrated in Bk. II, ch. 44, that God, moved by the tears of St. Gregory, recalled the Emperor Trajan, (who had) been damned on account to of (his) idolatry, from Hell. On this, cf. our Prolegomena, p. LXIV, col. I.

[6] And/or which is taken rather from (St.) Fulgentius (of Ruspe)'s, ON THE FAITH TO PETER, ch. 3, nn. 32-34, which book used to be known under the name of (St.) Augustine. Cf. SENT., Bk. II, d. 7, p. I, a. 1, q, 1, where St. Bonaventure in solving the question: "Whether the effect and/or will of a demon can be rectified?", has recourse to the book cited. — A little above this, for *in this manner dispose* [hoc disponere], the Vatican edition, together with codex cc, has *by this disposition* [hac dispositione], and then to then read *of all* [de omnibus] to *to all* [omnibus].

[7] The Vatican edition omits the words *gave grace and nature, ... just as God liberally* [dedit gratiam ... liberaliter]. Somewhat above this, among the words *whether He could judge* [utrum posset iudicare], codices aa and bb interject the explicit subject *God* [Deus] for *He*. — The doubt treated here is also solved by Alexander of Hales, SUMMA, p. I. q. 21. m. 2, §1; Bl. (now St.) Albertus (Magnus), here in a. 3; St. Thomas, here in q. 2, a. 2, in reply to n. 5; (and) Richard (of Middleton), here in q. 7 and on the text.

DISTINCTION XLIV

CHAPTER I

Whether God can make something better, than He does,
and/or in another and/or better manner?

Now it remains to be discussed, whether God[1] can make something better, than He makes (it). For those scrutinizers (of this question) are accustomed to say, that those which God makes, He cannot make better, because if He could make (them better) and did not make (them such), He would be envious and not most highly good. And they strive to construe [astruere] this from a simile. For (St.) Augustine says in the book, OF EIGHTY-THREE QUESTIONS:[2] « God, since He could not generate Him, whom He begot, *better* than Himself — for nothing (is) better than God — ought to generate, Him as an *equal* (to Himself). For if He wanted to and could not, He is infirm; if He could and was unwilling, (He is) envious. From which it is concluded [conficitur], that He has generated an equal Son ». From the simile they want to say, that if God can make a thing better, than He makes (it), He is envious (for not having done so). — But the induction of this similitude is not valid, because He begot the Son from His own Substance; and for that reason, if He could beget an Equal and did not beget (Him), He would be envious. However, the other (things), which He does not make from His own Substance, He can make better.

However, here I demand that there be an response [responderi deposco] from them, why they say, that some thing or even the university of things, in which there has been expressed a greater consummation (of the good), cannot be better, than it is: whether for this reason, because it is most highly good, such that entirely no perfection of the good is lacking to it, or for this reason, because the greater good, which is lacking to it, it does not prevail to grasp? But, if it is thus said (to be) "most highly good", such that no perfection of the good is lacking to it, (then) a creature is already equated to the Creator. However, if it cannot be better for this reason, because the more ample good, which is lacking to it, it does not prevail to grasp; this very '*not being able*' already belongs to a defection (from the good), not to a consummation (in the good); and it can be better, if it becomes capable of a better good, which (greater good) He who made it is able (to work). Therefore, God can make a thing better, than He makes (it). Wherefore, (St.) Augustine on Genesis (says):[3] « God could make man such, that he could neither sin nor want (to sin); and if He would have made (him) such, who doubts, that he was better »? — From the aforesaid it is established, that God both can make (things) other, than He makes (them), and (can) make those which He makes, better than He makes (them).

After these, one must consider, whether He can make those, which He makes, *in another* and/or better *manner*, than He does make (them). If *the manner* of operation is referred to the *wisdom of the worker*, it cannot be other nor better.[4] for He cannot make something in another manner and/or better, than He makes (it), that is by another wisdom and/or by a greater wisdom; for He can make noth-

ing more wisely, than He makes (it). But if *the manner* is referred to the *thing itself*, which God makes, we say, that there can be another and better manner. And according to this it can be conceded, that those which he makes, He can make better and in another manner, than He does make (them), because He can offer to certain ones a better manner of existing, and to certain ones another (manner of existing). Wherefore, (St.) Augustine in the thirteenth book, ON THE TRINITY[5] says, that another manner of our liberation was possible to God, who can (do) all (things); but no other (manner) of healing our wretchedness was more convenient. Therefore, God can, of whose which He makes, make certain ones in another better manner, certain ones in an another, equally good manner, certain ones even in a less good (manner), than He does make (them); yet so that the manner be referred to the quality[6] of the creature, not to the Wisdom of the Creator.

CHAPTER II

Whether God can always (do) everything which He could (do)?

Moreover, it is customarily asked, whether God always can (do) everything which He once could (do). Which does not seem to certain ones who say: "God could become incarnate and He could die and rise again, and other (things) of this kind, which He now cannot (do). Therefore, He could (do), what He cannot now (do), and thus He had a power, which He does not now have. Wherefore it seems that His Power (is) diminished. — To which we say, that just as He always knows all, which He has at any time known, and always wills, what He has at any time willed, neither does He ever loose any knowledge, and/or change the Will, which He had: thus He always can (do) all, which He at one time could (do), nor is He ever deprived of any of His Power. Therefore, He has not been deprived of the power to become incarnate and/or to rise again, though He cannot now be incarnate and/or rise again. For just as He could once [olim] *be incarnate*, so also He is now able *to have been incarnate*, in which there is demonstrated a power for the same thing [eiusdem rei potentia]. For as He once knew, that He was going to rise again, and now knows, that He has risen again, nor is it that He once *knew* this by another knowledge, and now *knows* this (by another), but by entirely the same (knowledge); and just as He will once to rise again, and now that He has risen again, in which a will for one thing [unius rei voluntas] is expressed; so He could once *be born* and *rise again*, and now He[7] is able *to have been born* and *to have risen again*: and (His) power is for the same thing. For, if He could now *be born* and *rise again*, (His) '*being able*' would not be the same. For verbs for diverse times, pronounced in different tenses and adjoined to different adverbs, cause the same sense,[8] as speaking of *the now*, we say: "this one can *read* today", but *tomorrow* we say, "this one is able *to have read*, and/or could *read* yesterday", where there is also[9]

---

[1] The edd., except ed. 1, omit *God* [Deus], against the the codd.. A little after this, codd. A & B after *if He could make* [si posset] add *them better* [meliora]. Then, codd. A B D & E have *from a simile* [a simili] for *from a simile* [ex simili].

[2] Question 50 (cf. AGAINST MAXIMINUS, Bk. II; ch. 7). — The Vatican edition, together with very many editions and codices A C and E, omits the second *generate* [generare]; codex B and edition 1 have *He begot* [genuit] for *He ought to* [debuit].

[3] ON A LITERAL EXPOSITION OF GENESIS, Bk. XI, ch. 7, n. 9. — Immediately before this, the Vatican edition and the other editions, except edition 1, breaking with the codices, have the indicative *He makes* [facit] for *He makes* [faciat].

[4] The Vatican edition and the other editions, except edition 1, repeat *a manner* [modus], with the codices contradicting this.

[5] Chapter 10, n. 13, according to sense.

[6] The Vatican edition and the other editions add *of the work, that is* [operis, id est], breaking with the codices and edition 1.

[7] The Vatican edition, together with very many editions, adds explicitly *He* [ipse].

[8] On this opinion of Master (Peter), cf. (St. Bonaventure's) Commentary, here in a. 2, q. sole.

[9] The codices and editions 1 and 5 have *where* [ubi] for *where ... also* [ubique].

demonstrated a power for one thing. But if speaking of diverse times, we use verbs and adverbs of the same tense, saying *today*: "this one can read today", and saying *tomorrow*: "this one can read today"; we do not say, that He can (do) the same (act), but diverse (acts). Therefore, let us say, that God always can (do) whatever He at one time [semel] could (do), that is, that He has all that power, which He at one time had, and the power for that every thing, for which He had (it) at one time; but not that He always can do every that, which He at some time could do; indeed He is able to do or to have done what He could at one time (do). Similarly, whatever He willed, He also wills, that is, everything for which He has and now has a will; and for whatsoever thing He had a will, He also now has (one); yet He does not will that *there be* and/or *come to be* everything, which He at some time willed to be and/or to come to be, but He does will *that it was* and/or *was made*.

COMMENTARY ON DISTINCTION XLIV

On God's Power in comparison to the manner or quality of things.

Now it remains to be discussed, whether God can make something better etc.

THE DIVISION OF THE TEXT

Above,[1] Master (Peter) dealt with the (Divine) Power in comparison to the possible according to *substance* and *quantity*; here, he deals third with the (Divine) Power as much as regards *the manner* or *quality* of things. And this part has two parts. In the *first*, Master (Peter) deals with the (Divine) Power as much as regards the quality of possibles, of which indeed there is a greater and lesser goodness. *Second*, as much as regards the quality of the Power, which indeed is immutability, there (where he says): *Moreover, it is customarily asked, whether God* etc.

The *first* part has two (parts). In the first, he asks whether God could make a better world.[2] In the second, whether the things, which He makes, He can make in a better manner or in another manner, and this there (where he says): *After these one must consider* etc., where he deals as much as regards the manner.

Moreover, it is customarily asked, whether God etc.. This is the *second* part, where (Master Peter) asks concerning the immutability of the Divine Power, asking, whether God can (do) whatever He could (do), and this part has two (parts). In the first, he shows, that He cannot (do) whatever He could (do), and he does this by opposing (arguments).[3] However, in the second, He asserts the contrary in solving (them), there (where he says): *To which we say, that just as He always knows all* etc..

TREATMENT OF THE QUESTIONS

For an understanding of the present Distinction there is asked concerning the manner or quality of the Divine Power. And, about this, two (questions) are principally asked:

First, there is asked, whether God could make a better world.

Second there is asked concerning the immutability of the Divine Power, whether what God can (do) once [semel], He can (do) always.

About the first, four (questions) are asked.

First, there is asked, whether God could make a better world in regard to the substance of (its) integrating parts.

Second, whether He could make it better in regard to the properties of (its) integrating parts.

Third, there is asked, whether He could make a better world as much as regards the order of (its) parts.

Fourth, whether He could make a more ancient world.

---

[1] Distinction XLII and XLIII.

[2] The Vatican edition reads *whether God could make something better, than He makes (it)* [utrum Deus potuerit aliquid melius facere, quam facit].

[3] The Vatican reads thus: *In the first he asks, whether God always can (do) everything which He once could (do), and he opposes, that He cannot* [In prima quaerit, utrum Deus semper possit omne quod olim potuit, et opponit, quod non possit].

ARTICLE I

On the possibility of a better world.

QUESTION I

Whether God could have made the world better in regard to the substance of (its) integrating parts?

Moreover, that He could make a better world in regard to the *substance* of (its) integrating parts [partium integrantium], is shown in this manner:

1. The parts which make the world whole [integrantes mundum] are of a finite goodness both intensively and extensively; but than every finite something greater and better can be thought, but God can do more, than man can understand:[1] ergo etc.. *If you say*, that the world could not grasp [capere] more; this does not solve (it); because God causes (its) capacity: therefore He could grant (it) a greater capacity, since His Power is infinite.

2. Likewise, the supreme creature in the universe is finite, therefore, it is distant from God unto an infinite (degree); but in an infinite distance there is a positing of infinite grades: therefore, beyond the goodness of creatures there is an understanding of creatures having grades of goodness, and from these the world could be integrated: ergo etc..

3. Likewise, it is established, that God could make the world out of parts greater *in mass*, such as a more ample or wider sky and a wider earth: therefore, if He could make (it) greater *in mass*, for the same reason also greater *in virtue*: and if this, therefore, (He could make it) simply better.

4. Likewise, matter, according to its whole self [se totam] is capable of the most noble form, as is clears: therefore, if God could grant that the nature of matter could grasp (such), therefore, He could grant to the whole and to all the parts of matter a perfection of the most noble form, as for example (that) of a rational nature: therefore, He could make a world, which would be established out of rational substances alone. And if this, then the world would have all (its) parts according to better substances: ergo etc..

ON THE CONTRARY: 1. (St.) Augustine in the third book, ON FREE WILL (says):[2] « Whatever will have occurred to you in true reason [in vera ratione], know that God, as the Founder of all goods, has made; but He cannot (cause) not to be, what you think

by true reason. For neither can you think of anything better in a creature, which would escape the Craftsman of the creature ». Therefore no noble creature can be thought of, which does not concern the constitution of the world.

2. Likewise, (St.) Augustine (says) in the twelfth (book) of (his) CONFESSIONS:[3] « Two (things) has Thou made, Lord, one near Thee, the other near nothing », that is, the angelic creature and prime matter; but no greater ambit can be thought of than (that which stretches) from nearness to God toward nothing: therefore, a world could not be made, which would be born to embrace more natures of things: therefore, a better world could not be made as much as regards (its) capacity. But it is established, that that capacity is not vacuous as much as regards some grade (of goodness), otherwise the world would neither be perfect, nor could the universe be said to be perfect: therefore, neither could it be made to grasp more, nor another with a greater capacity [nec alius capacior].

3. Likewise, prime matter has been created in an omnimodal possibility and in perfect obedience in respect of the Creator:[4] therefore, if the capacity of matter itself is attained according to its own possibility and obedience, which it had regarding God, and it is created in a most high possibility and in a most high obedience, therefore, the world as much as regards (its) capacity could not be made better. Therefore, if God granted to each one, as much as it was capable, therefore, in no manner could it be made better.

4. Likewise, howsoever much a creature is made good, it is necessary that it be finite: therefore, it is necessary at some time to posit a standing still, such that the creature can in no manner be made better, derogating in nothing from the Divine Power; but by the reckoning by which there is a standing still [statur] in some species of creature, there is a standing still in the supreme species of spiritual creature: therefore, no creature and/or species can be made more noble that that. And, « if the best in a genus is better than the best in another (genus), and this simply (is) better than that »,[5] therefore, if the best in the universe is the best of every creature,

---

[1] Cf. above d. 42, q. 3, 4th argument for the affirmative.

[2] Chapter 5, n. 13. In the text of (St.) Augustine here very many propositions have been omitted; this is well illustrated below in the body of the Question, in these words: "that no more noble essence can reasonably (or as Augustine says, *by a true reason*) be thought to be in this world, which is not in it" [quod nulla essentia nobilior potest cogitari esse in hoc mundo rationabiliter, quae non sit ibi].

[3] Chapter 7, n. 7. — A little below this after *ambit* [ambitus] in codex Q (in the margin) there is added *and/or distance* [vel distantia].

[4] Or in both a perfect passive and a perfect obediential potency in regard to the Creator. — A little below this, for *could not* [non potuit] edition 1 has *could neither* [nec potuit].

[5] Aristotle, TOPICS, Bk. III, ch. 2, dealing with the things more able to be chosen [de eligibilioribus], says: « More amply, if this (is) simply better than that, the best of those in it (are) entirely better than that which is the best in the other of the two; so that if man (is) better than horse, even the best man (is) better than the best horse. And, if the best is better than the best, the

which can be a creature, that world is also simply so good, that a better than it cannot be made.

CONCLUSION

God could make another world better in regard to the substance of (its) parts, but this world (He could) only (make) better and greater according to (its) accidental (parts).

I RESPOND: It must be said, that an excess of substantial goodness in things can be attained in a twofold manner: either as much as regards the nobility and grades of *essences*, and in this manner there is said, that the species of man is better and more noble than the species of a donkey; or as much as regards (their) '*to be*', insofar as it concerns an *addition* or augment, just as it is said, that a mark[1] of gold is better than an ounce, not because it has a more noble form and/or essence, but because it has more of the substance of gold and through this (more) of the goodness and value (of gold).

Therefore, when it is asked, whether God could make a better world as much as regards the *substance* of (its) parts; if you understand (this) of an excess as much as regards the *first* manner, that the could would be established out of better and more noble essences, I say, that *the same* world, which now is, could not be made better, because it would not be this (world) of ours, but *another*, just as, if he who has been made a man, would have been made a donkey,[2] he would not be who he is. However, because His 'being able' has not been constricted nor limited, I do not see, for what reason He could not make a better world in this genus of being better [in hoc genere melioritatis].

But, if you understand (it) as much as regards the *second* manner, thus I say, that He could make better not only *another*, but even *this* (world), just as (He could) also (make it) greater. And if He had made (such), it would not be another; just as He could cause, that this boy would be as great as a giant, and have more of the substance and virtue (of a man), and yet would not be another, than he is.

Therefore, I concede the reasons proving, that God simply could have made *another* world better as much as regards the substance of (its) parts, and even *this* one according to the magnitude of (its) parts and virtues, yet not as much as regards a greater nobility of

essences. And this (St.) Augustine wants to say in the aforesaid authority ON FREE WILL,[3] that no more noble essence can reasonably be thought to be in this world, which is not in it [ibi]. For if you think, that there (can) be better parts, this is either according to *the whole*, or according to a *part*: if according to *the whole*, you think no longer of this world, but of another; if according to a *part*, then, therefore, you take away the order and perfection of this world: so that if you think, that God would have made the Moon as bright, as the Sun is, and/or the Earth just as the sky, you do not think reasonably, because you do away with [perimis] the universe. « For all would not be, if they were equal ».[4] And this is what (St.) Augustine says ON FREE WILL: « It is not true reason, but an envious infirmity, when you will have thought that something must be made better, wanting nothing else to be made now lower, as if, with the sky completed, you will be unwilling that the Earth be made, and where you would be thinking in an entirely iniquitous manner ».

And, in this manner, it is clear, that (what has) been objected last to the first side[5] is a sophistic one [sophisticum], in virtue of this that (it argues that) it befitted the universe, that matter, according to its whole self, would be perfected by a most noble form.

1. To that, therefore, which is objected to the contrary through authority of (St.) Augustine ON FREE WILL, the response is already clear, because he understand (this) of this world, and of a being better according to essence, as is clear from the text.[6]

2. To that which is objected, that there is a most high distance in the universe; it must be said, that "*near God*" [prope Deum] can be understood in a twofold manner, namely as much as regards an immediate *reception* and conversion unto God, or as much as regards a most high *imitation* and assimilation (to God). In the first manner the angelic nature is near God, simply speaking; but in the second manner (it is) not but in *comparison* (to Him), because it is more dissimilar than similar, and it is deficient in more than it expresses, nay it is distant by infinite grades;[7] and for that reason a greater nearness is thinkable by us and possible to God, though there is now no (such).

3. To that which is objected, that matter has been created in an omnimodal possibility; it must be said, in no creature does God complete the possibility of (its) obedience totally, because this is according to the omnimodal empire of the Creator, but He does complete (its) capacity and

---

former simply (is) better than the latter: so that if the best man (is) better than the best horse, a many simply (is) better than a horse simply ». Which words Averroës expounds thus: "because what is simply more outstanding than another thing, which is the first according to nobility in that genus, is more noble than the first according to nobility in the other genus, v. g., if a man is simply more noble than a horse, that which is first according to the nobility of men, is more outstanding according to nobility than a horse itself. And contrariwise, if the first according to nobility in this genus was more noble than the first of the other genus, the former genus is also more noble than the other genus. — For *in a genus* [in genere] the Vatican edition has *in one genus* [in uno genere].

[1] A "mark" [marca], as Du Cange explains in his GLOSSARIA MEDIAE ET INFIMAE LATINITATIS., is a weight, which weighs two-thirds of a royal pound, which merchants and ointment-makers and others use, and entirely all, who sell merchandise by weight ... Among us, therefore, a mark doubled makes a pound [librum], which is divided into 16 ounces; but an ounce

[uncia] is subdivided into 8 drachma and/or 24 scrupoli or denarii etc.. — A little before this, for *just as* [sicut] codex M has *as when* [ut cum], the Vatican edition has instead *thus* [sic].

[2] For *a donkey* [asinus] the Vatican edition and edition 1 have *an Angel* [Angelus], contraditing all the codices. A little above this, the Vatican edition, together with codex cc, omits *better and* [melioribus et], a a little below this to the word *better world* [mundum] it prefixes *another* [alium], supported by not a few codices.

[3] See here the 1st opposed argument.

[4] (St.) Augustine (of Hippo), in his book, OF EIGHTY-THREE QUESTIONS, q. 41. — The following text is had loc. cit., ch. 5, n. 13, where in the original the last word, *you would be thinking* [cogitares] is lacking.

[5] Namely in the fundament.

[6] Cited a little before this at the end of the body of the Question. — For *text* [textu] edition 1 has *context* [contextu].

[7] Cf. above d. 35, q. 1, in reply to n. 2.

possibility, as it is disposed through some[1] dispositions. And, in this manner, God completes matter, because He limited its capacity by due dispositions and he adjoined completive and perfective forms to these, such that He left nothing incomplete. Yet, who dares to say, that God could not more nobly dispose (it) and perfect (it) by more noble forms, according to the infinity of His Wisdom and Power? Therefore, what is said: "He gave to each one as much of goodness[2] as it was capable"; this is understood of (their) 'capacity', not insofar as it means a *distant* [longinquam] *possibility* and obedience in respect of the Creator, but, insofar as, with this, it means a *disposition* and exigency; and (thus) it is established [constans est] that God could make this one greater.

4. To that which is objected, that in creatures it is necessary that there be a standing still [necesse est stare]; it must be said, that just as a *number*

always has a standing still in act, yet never is there a granting of some standing still, beyond that which the Divine Power cannot extend Itself; so it must be understood in a *magnitude of mass* and *of goodness*, that,[3] however so much it be in a creature, there is always a standing still, because (it is) finite; and God acts well up to this point [hucusque], that He does not act more amply, but there is never, as I believe, a granting that He cannot (make the magnitude) more ample. And, for that reason, if He had made another world better than this one, there will still be a further asking, "For what reason did He not make (it) better, when He could?", and, by proceeding in the same manner, an even further (questioning), and for that reason such a question is irrational,[4] and a solution cannot be given except this, because He willed (it so), and He Himself knows the reason. But, yet, if He did not make (such a world), no one can prove, that [quia] this whole (world), which He has made, was a grace; nor (that) there was some exigency, according to the reckoning of which it could be posited that there was envy in Him.

SCHOLIUM

I. The Seraphic (Doctor) disputes on the perfection of the divine *works* (or *of the world*) under distinct questions more accurately than all the other ancient Scholastics. Moreover, since all creatures exhibit a certain whole, or, as they say, a certain organism, constituted from their integrating parts, (the Question) can respect both the goodness of the parts *in themselves* or the absolute (goodness), and their goodness *in regard to (their) order to an end* or (their) respective (goodness); which distinction is explained here in Doubt 2 and in Question 2. Questions 1 and 2 chiefly deal with (their) *absolute* goodness (which the Seraphic Doctor calls « simply better »); Question 3 with (their) goodness in the order *regarding (their) end*.

II. That a better world cannot be made on the part of the *efficient*, *exemplary* and *final* cause, nor on the part of the *manner* of acting, is manifest, and is proven by Alexander of Hales, SUMMA., p. I, q. 21, m. 3, and by St. Thomas., SUMMA., I, q. 25, a. 6, in reply to n. 1. But there is a doubt, whether a world itself, *considered in itself*, can be better; and this question according to the Seraphic Doctor (here in the body of the Response) can either be understood of this *same* world, and/or of *another possible* one, creatable by God. And again the word "*better*" can be understood in regard the essential and/or accidental perfection of the parts of the world. With these distinctions made, the system of

Optimism, which Leibniz, among others, defends, is destroyed with the common sentence. — Moreover, the 4th argument of the fundament is noted, by St. Bonaventure, as a sophistic one. — In the solution to n. 4 it is denied, that any creature can have an *ultimate* grade of perfection, such that there is in it a *standing still*, beyond which there can be no greater perfection. St. Thomas (loc. cit.) and others agree. (Bl. John Duns) Scotus (SENT., Bk. III, d. 13, q. 1), Durandus (of Saint-Pourçain) (here in q. 2, and in d. 43, q. 1), and as it seems, Henry of Ghent (QUODLIBETALS., 5, q. 22) think differently. For more on this matter, especially concerning the perfection of Christ and the Blessed Virgin Mary, see here Doubt 3, and above d. 17, p. II, q. 4.

III. Alexander of Hales, on this and the following questions, SUMMA., p. I, q. 21, m. 3, a. 1-7. — (Bl. John Duns) Scotus, on this and the following question, Report. here in q. 2. — St. Thomas, on this and the following questions, here in q. 1, a. 1, 2 and 3; SUMMA., I, q. 25, a. 6. — Bl. (now St.) Albertus (Magnus), on this and the following question, here in a. 2; SUMMA., p. I, tr. 19, q. 77, m. 3, a. 1, 2 and 3. — (Bl.) Peter of Tarentaise, here in the q. sole, a. 1. — Richard of Middleton, on this and the following questions, here in qq. 1, 4 and 5. — Giles the Roman, here in 1st princ., q. 1. — Durandus (of Saint-Pourçain), here in qq. 1 and 2. — (Bl.) Dionysius the Carthusian, on this and the following questions, here in qq. 1 and 2. — (Gabriel) Biel, on this and the following question, here in the q. sole.

QUESTION II

Whether the world could have been made better as much as regards the properties of (its) integrating parts?

Second, there is asked whether the world could be made better as much as regards *the properties* of (its) integrating parts. And that (it is) so, seems:

1. According to the thirtieth (chapter) of Isaias:[5] *The light of the Moon will be as the light of the Sun, and the light of the Sun as the light of seven days*; this

will be: therefore, it can be, therefore, God could found (it), and thus concerning the other bodies; and if this, (then) things would certainly [utique] be better: ergo etc..

2. Likewise, (St.) Augustine, ON A LITERAL EXPOSITION OF GENESIS, and Master (Peter, in the text,) adduces this authority:[6] « God could »,

---

[1] The Vatican edition, together with codex cc, has *other* [alias]. At the beginning of this solution the same Vatican edition adjoins *prime* [prima] to the word *matter* [materia], and somewhat below this, together with codex cc, has *those completive and perfective forms* [illas formas] for *completive and perfective forms to those* [illis formas].

[2] In the Vatican edition there is omitted *of goodness* [bonitatis]; in codex cc and in editions 2, 3, 4, 5 and 6 there is read *beatitude* [beatitudinem]; in the other codices there is not so well had *of beatitude* [beatitudinis], but in codex R there is had *of goodness* [bonitatis]. In the same codex R, a little above this, be-

fore the word *infinity* [infinitatem] there have been interjected the words *dignity and* [dignitatem et], and then to the verb *He gave* [dedit] several codices, such as K M N and V, prefix the subject explicitly *God* [Deus].

[3] For *that* [quod] the Vatican edition has *both* [et] and then *(there is) always also* [et semper] for *there is always* [est semper].

[4] Very many codices, such as A G I T and bb, together with edition 1, have *unreasonable* [irrationabilis].

[5] Verse 26. — Next, for *could* [potuit] the Vatican ed. has *can* [potest].

[6] Here in ch. 1.

he says, « make such a man, who would neither want to sin nor could (sin), and if He had made (him) such, who doubts, that he was better »: ergo etc..

3. Likewise, better is the property of incorruptibility and rest than of corruption and movement;[1] and all which God has made, He either make corruptible, or in some manner movable: therefore, He could make all (things) better.

4. Likewise, if creatures could not be made better, this was, either because *God* could not give more (of His Goodness), or because *creatures* could not grasp more. If because *God* could not give more amply, therefore, the Divine Power is limited; if because *creatures* could not grasp more amply; *on the contrary*: we see all the say long [tota die], that creatures ameliorate and deteriorate, with (their) substance and capacity remaining [salva]: ergo etc..

ON THE CONTRARY: 1. « It belongs to the best to bring forth [adducere] the best », just as Dionysius (the Areopagite) says;[2] but there cannot be a better than the best: therefore, if God, since He is the best, lead things (into existence) in the best manner, it is clear that etc..

2. Likewise, Plato[3] adds a reason: « Furthermore, because He is the best, however, every envy had been relegated from the best »; and for that reason He gave to each creature as much of goodness, as it could grasp. *If you say*, that the word of Plato is not valid, because envy is not in respect of an inferior; *on the contrary*: (St.) Augustine, ON A LITERAL EXPOSITION OF GENESIS (says):[4] « If He could not make good (things), (His) would be no power; if He could, but was unwilling, great would be (His) envying »: therefore, for an equal reason, if He could make (them) better and was unwilling, He would be envious.

3. Likewise, it seems *by reason*: because everything acting out of its whole substance[5] makes a thing in the best manner, in which it can be made, if nothing entirely impedes its power; but God is as One acting out of His whole Power in His every action, and His Power has no indigence nor resistance: therefore, whatever He makes, He makes so good, that it can in no manner be made better.

4. Likewise, this is true per se: « the good is diffusive of itself »,[6] therefore, the greater the good the greater (it is) diffusive, and the good in the greatest manner (is) diffusive in the greatest manner; but God is the Agent of the greatest goodness, therefore, He diffuses Himself in the greatest manner: therefore, it seems, that He makes each one in the best manner both as much as regards (its) substance and as much as regards (its) properties.

CONCLUSION

The transient *parts of this world in regard to (their) properties can be made better; likewise, the* permanent *parts, if they are considered absolutely, but not in relation to (their) end.*

I RESPOND: It must be said, that when one asks concerning the parts of the universe being better [de melioritate partium universi], one can ask as much as regards the twofold genus of (it) parts: either as much as regards (its) *permanent* parts, such as the intellectual, rational, celestial and elementary nature: or as much as regards (its) *transient* parts, such as this man and this horse.

If (one asked) as much as regards (their) *transient* parts, thus without distinction I concede, that they can be made better, as in more, as much as regards (their) properties, because they do not concern the substance of the universe, nor are they from God alone, but from God working together with a particular agent, which is impeded and deficient. — But, if we understand (the question) concerning the parts, which concern the *constitution and integrity* of the world and (which) are immediately from God, when one asks, whether they could be made better as much as regards (their) properties, a distinction must be made [distinguendum est]: because either you speak of them *absolutely*, or of them in relation *to (their) end*. If of them *absolutely*, it is clear, that they can have better conditions; if of them in relation *to one another* and/or *to (their) end*, they has the best properties; which is clear, because, just as (St.) Augustine[7] says: « God has indicated that men (are) better, if they freely served Him with zeal [liberaliter deservirent] ». Similarly, it was better, that all men would be out of one, and thus that they would have a living body [corpus animale]; and according to the exigency of this it was necessary, that other corporal creatures be disposed in movement and corruptibility.

From these the reasons brought forward for the first side are clear; for they proceed from the properties of things considered according to themselves.

1. To that, therefore, which is objected to the contrary from Dionysius (the Areopagite), it must be said, that that is understood concerning (their) *order*, just as will be presently (made) clear.[8]

2. To that which is objected from Plato, it must be said, that it does not have truth, unless it be understood *with the order* of the universe remaining [salvo], and this as much as regards (its) *essential* goodness, having considered (its) disposition in matter. Nor is his reckoning necessary, but only a persuasion in a *similar* (case): just as in a man, who can do good to another and

---

[1] Cf. Aristotle, PHYSICS, Bk. VIII, text 75 (ch. 9), and above on d. 37, p. II, a. 1, q. 3, p. 654, footnote 4.

[2] ON THE DIVINE NAMES., ch. 4, § 19.

[3] In the TIMAEUS (ed. Serrani, 1578; p. 29): ἀγαθὸς ἦν, ἀγαθῷ δὲ οὐδεὶς περὶ οὐδενὸς οὐδέποτε ἐγγίγνεται φθόνος. In English: Namely, He used to excel in goodness; but unto the good, nothing of any envy ever occurs [Bonitate videlicet praestabat; in bonum autem nulla de ulla unquam re cadit invidia].

[4] Book IV, ch. 16, n. 27, where the edition of (St.) Augustine's works has *but if He could and did not make (them)* [si autem posset nec faceret] for *if He could, but was unwilling* [si posset, sed nollet], and very many codices, together with edition 1 have *and was unwilling* [et nullet] for *but was unwilling* [sed nollet]. A little above this, codices K P Q V X and Y have *because envy is in respect of a superior, not of an inferior* [quia invidia est respectu superioris], some codices, together with edition 1, have *because inferior is in respect of an inferior* [quia invidia est respectu inferioris]. Cf. d. 20, Doubt 4.

[5] For *substance* [substantia] codex M, together with edition 1, has *power* [potentia], and conversely a little further below this, for *His whole Power* [ex tota sua potentia] codex X has *His whole substance* [substantia]; codex K has *He whole substance and power* [sua substantia et potentia].

[6] On this proposition of Dionysius (the Areopagite), cf. above d. 42, a. sole, q. 1, p. 746, footnote 5. — A little below this, for *in the best manner* [optime] the Vatican edition, together with codex cc, has *the best* [optumum].

[7] In his book, ON THE TRUE RELIGION., ch. 14, n. 27: For God has indicated that such servants are better, if they would serve Him freely. Cf. ON CHRISTIAN WARFARE., ch. 10, n. 11. — A little above this, many codices omits *and/or* [vel] before *to (their) end* [ad finem]. For this *and/or* [vel] codex T substitutes *or* [sive], codex F, together with edition 1, has *and* [et]; codex R and X omit both *and/or* [vel] and the antecedent *to one another* [ad invicem].

[8] In the following Question.

does not do (so), that he is judged (to do) this[1] from envy, and frequently he does leave off (doing good) on account of envy, and (in the man) who lacks envy and acts contrariwise [converso facit]; thus God worked, lacking envy; and in this manner the word of (St.) Augustine is understood.

3. To that which is objected, that the one acting out of (his) whole power produces in the best manner; it must be said, that a *certain* one acting out of (his) whole power acts according to an impetus, a *certain* one (acts) according to *art* and *wisdom*. And he who acts according to an *impetus* does as best as [quanto melius] he can; he who acts according to *art* and *wisdom* does as much

as he wills and as much as is fitting, while preserving order [salvo ordine], because « it belongs to the wise man to order ».[2] For that reason a certain (power) does good, a certain one better, a certain one best. And in this manner it is clear, that that (consequence) does not follow.

4. To that which is objected, that the Most High Good diffuses Itself most highly; it must be said, that this is true of natural diffusion, it is not true of voluntary (diffusion) or (diffusion) from a proposal (to have mercy).[3] In the first manner there is a diffusion in the production of the (Divine) Persons, in the second manner in the production of creatures.

SCHOLIUM

I. This Question is understood of the *accidental* properties of the parts of the world and, indeed, of *this* world, not of some *possible* world. — For an explanation of the sentence of Dionysius (the Areopagite) in the solution to n. 1, Alexander of Hales (SUMMA., p. I. q. 21, m. 3, a. 1, in reply to n. 3) says: « It must be said, that there is said (to be) a "*simply* best", and a "*best*" according to *genus* and according to *status* [status], and according to *order*. The *simply* Best is God; the best *according to genus* and *status*, such an in the genus of a creature and in the status of (its) condition, (is) Christ; the best *in order* and not simply, (is) the university of things. Therefore, "*it belongs to the*

best to lead to the best", this can be understood both as much as regards the *simply* best, such as in the procession of a Person, and as much as regards the best *in genus* and *status* of condition, such as in the production of Christ; and as much as regards the best *in an order*, such as in the production of the universe ».

II. See the authors cited in the Scholium here in Question 1, in addition to: (Bl.) Peter of Tarentaise, on this and the following question, here in the q. sole, a. 2. — Giles the Roman, on this and the following question, here in 1st princ., q. 2. — Durandus (of Saint-Pourçain), on this and the following question, here in q. 3.

QUESTION III

Whether God could have made the world better as much as regards the order of (its) parts?

Third, there is asked, whether God could have made the world better as much as regards the *order* of (its) parts. And that (He could) not, seems first *from authority*.

1. In the first (chapter) of Genesis:[4] *God saws all, which He had made, and they were very good*; the Gloss of (St.) Augustine (says): « Each (are) good in themselves, but best in the universe ». But nothing is better than the best: ergo etc..

2. Likewise, (St.) Augustine[5] says, « that, although another manner of our liberation was possible for God, none was more congruent for saving our wretchedness ». But just as God was the Most Wise Redeemer, so also the Most Wise Founder: therefore, if He redeemed

in a most ordinate manner, such that there could be no better nor more congruent manner, therefore, He holds Himself in making things in a similar manner: and, thus, it is clear that etc..

3. Likewise, if we consider the order of the elements in the world, it is established that they have been ordered optimally. Wherefore, it cannot be thought, that those four bodies are ordered better, whether according to (their) *qualities*, or according to *noble forms*, or according to *numeral proportions*, just as 8 and 27, which are two prime numbers of a solid quadrate [duo primi numeri solidi quadrati]:* are bound through two intermediaries, namely 12 and 18 [octodecim]:[6] ergo etc..

---

[1] The Vatican edition reads *that from this there is judged (to be)* envy [quod ex hoc iudicatur invidia] for *that he is judged (to do) this from* envy [quod hoc iudicatur invidia]. A little after this the same Vatican edition, together with codex cc, omits *thus God worked, lacking envy* [sic Deus careens invidia fecit].

[2] Cf. above d. 39, a. 1, q. 1, p. 685, footnote 1. On the division of agents into agents *according to an impetus* (impetus in the ancient version of the Greek is the word ορμή, as can be seen in the ancient editions of Aristotle and even in (St. John) Damascene, ON THE ORTHODOX FAITH, Bk. II,ch. 22, and signifies a manner of acting, proceeding out of a natural necessity) and agents *according to art*, see Aristotle, METAPHYSICS, Bk. I, ch. 1 (concerning which we have already remarked above in d. 35, a. sole, q. 1, p. 600, footnote 2), and ETHICS, Bk. VI, ch. 4, where the Philosopher, after having defined "art" as: « art is a certain, effective habit with a reason », says, « For neither is there art of those, which are and/or come to be out of necessity, nor of those which are *according to nature*; for in themselves these have a principle ». In what manner wisdom holds itself to art, see ibid., ch. 7. — A little above this, the Vatican edition twice has the neuter form for *a certain one* [quoddam] for the masculine *a certain one* [quidam] (and thus reads *its* for *his*), and then continues in the same sense reading *And the one which* [Et quod] for *And he who* [Et qui], and *the one which acts* [quod agit] for *he who acts* [qui agit] (and thus *it* for *he*).

[3] Cf. above d. 40, a. 3, q. 1. — A little before this for *of volun-*

tary (diffusion) [de voluntaria] the Vatican edition has *but of a voluntary (act)* [sed de voluntario], not a few codices and edition 1 have instead *but of a voluntary (diffusion)* [sed de voluntaria].

[4] Verse 31. — The Gloss cited next has been taken from (St.) Augustine, ON A LITERAL EXPOSITION OF GENESIS, Bk. III, ch. 24, n. 37, and in the original sounds like this: « And each [singula] are good in themselves, and in the universe very good ». Similarly, St. Augustine, speaking in his ENCHIRIDION, ch. 10, n. 3 (says): But yet (they are) good even singly; but together all (are) very good, because the admirable beauty of the university (of things) consists out of (them) all.

[5] ON THE TRINITY, Bk. XIII, ch. 10, n. 13. See the text of Master (Peter) here, in ch. 1. — In the cited text after *none* [nullus] the Vatican edition interjects *however* [tamen], and then for *saving* [salvandae] codices K P and Q, together with edition 1 and the edition of (St.) Augustine's works, have *healing* [sanandae], the Vatican edition as *raising* [levandae].

[6] Cf. (St.) Augustine, ON A LITERAL EXPOSITION OF GENESIS, Bk. IV, ch. 2, n. 3, and (St. Severinus) Boethius, ON ARITHMETICS, Bk. I, ch. 20, and here in the Scholium. — A little further above this, for *numeral* [numerales] not a few codices have faultily *numerable* [numerabilies]. Next for *of a solid quadrate* [solidi quadrati] the Vatican edition has *of a solid cube* [soildi cubi], codex O *of a solid cubic* [cubici]. The same codex O then reads *intermediary solid quadrates* [intermedios solidos quadratos] for *intermediaries* [intermedios].

---

* *Trans. note*: See, at the end of this Question, the Scholium, II, for an explanation of this term and argument.

4. Likewise, « it belongs to the wise man to order »:[1] therefore, (it belongs) to the most highly Wise to order most highly or optimally: therefore, God has ordered things so well, that in no manner could He order (them) better.

BUT ON THE CONTRARY: 1. That order is of a finite goodness: therefore, if God's Wisdom is infinite, and the infinite exceeds the finite, therefore, God knew how to order (them) in a better manner. But whatever God knew, He could (do): ergo etc..

2. Likewise, a more noble order, in which there occurs no inordinance [inordinatio], is better, than (that) in which it does occur;[2] but in the universe there occur many inordinacies and deformities: therefore, another order could be made better.

3. Likewise, what is nearer to (its) end is ordered better:[3] therefore, if all have been optimally ordered, all have been equally conjoined to (their) End: therefore, all participate in beatitude; which is absurd.

4. Likewise, the goodness of an order depends out of the goodness of (its) parts, just as (something) respective from (something) absolute; but things, according to absolute "being" are not the best: therefore, neither (is the goodness) in (their) order (the best).[4]

CONCLUSION

In regard to the order of the parts of the universe, the first and substantial parts have been optimally ordered, but the corruptible parts indeed could be absolutely ordered in a better manner, but not in relation to (their) End. In regard to (their) order to their End, with the order of the universe remaining (as it is), things have been optimally ordered.

I RESPOND: It must be said, that there is an order of parts *in the whole* [in toto], and there is an order of parts *unto (their) End*. The first order respects wisdom, the second order respects goodness. And those two orders have been so conjoined, that the one is conformed to the other, and the order of parts *in the universe* is on account of (their) ordination[5] *to (its) End*.

Therefore, if we speak of the order of parts *in the universe*, either this is as much as regards (its) *first and substantial* parts, and thus, without distinction, they have been ordered optimally, so that they could not be ordered in a better manner, because in them consists *the substantial order* and the immutable

beauty of the universe. And/or as much as regards (its) *corruptible and remote* parts, and this in a twofold manner: either *absolutely* and as (they are) *now*; and thus they could be ordered in a better manner and one day [aliquando][6] will have been ordered in a better manner; or *simply* and in relation *to (their) End*; and, thus, things have been ordered optimally in the universe, according to which it befits an order to an end.

Similarly, with the order of the universe remaining (as it is), things have been ordered optimally *unto (their) End*, because the universe is as the most beautiful song [carmen], which runs along [decurrit] according to the best consonances, with some parts succeeding others, thus that [quousque] things may be perfectly ordered unto (their) End.[7] Wherefore, just as in the production of things there is manifested a *power*, but in *comparison to* or in the order regarding non-being there is shown a *most high Power*, creating out of nothing: so the order of things in the universe *in itself* shows a Wisdom, and the order (of them) to (their) End a *Goodness*, but in the comparison of the one to the other there is shown a *most high Wisdom* and a *most high Goodness*, because nothing can de-order this order, just as will be more clear below.[8]

Therefore, the reason proving, that things have been ordered optimally, are to be conceded, because they respect each order.

1. To that which is objected, that (His) Wisdom is infinite; it must be said, that although (His) Wisdom is[9] infinite, yet things are not capable but of finite order; and that Most High Wisdom gives the highest [summum] order, which they can have.

2. To that which is objected, that an inordinance [inordinatio] does occur (in the universe)[10]; it must be said, that, if we consider these orders, that is, to *the End* and *in the universe*, thus they themselves comprise one another, wherefore there cannot be an inordinance there.

3. To that which is objected concerning nearness (to an end), it must be said, that this is true according to *their own* ordination,[11] but according to the *course of the universe* [decursum universi] it is necessary, that a thing be first far from (its) End, and afterwards approach (it).

4. To that which is objected, that order[12] depends from parts; it must be said, that jut as some *contingents* have in themselves an absolute, contingent '*being*',

---

[1] Cf. above d. 39, a. 1, q. 1, p. 685, footnote 1.

[2] For, as Aristotle says, TOPICS, Bk. III, ch. 4 (ch. 5): Those which are more unmingled with contraries are more such, as indeed (is something) more white, unmingled with black. — The codices and edition 1 put the 3rd argument in the 4th position.

[3] Aristotle, TOPICS, Bk. III, ch. 1: And of two (the better is), that which is nearer the end.

[4] Edition 1 reads *therefore, neither (have they) been ordered (in the best manner)* [ergo nec ordinatae] for *therefore neither (is the goodness) in (their) order (the best)* [ergo nec in ordine].

[5] Codex R has *(their) order* [ordinem] for *(their) ordination* [ordinationem]. Immediately after this, for *Therefore* [ergo] the Vatican edition, together with codex cc, has *Moreover* [autem].

[6] Namely, after the Final Judgement.

[7] (St.) Augustine, ON THE CITY OF GOD, Bk. XI, ch. 18: For neither would God create any of the Angels and/or of men, whom He would have foreknown was going to be evil, unless He equally knew, to which uses He would accommodate them, and thus (how) to honorably dignify [honestaret] the order of the ages as a most beautiful song out of certain quasi-antitheses ... Therefore, just as these contraries, opposed to contraries, render the beauty of speech, so by a certain eloquence not of words, but of

things contrary in opposition, is the beauty of the world [saeculum] composed. Cf. *ibid.*, ch. 22, and ON THE TRUE RELIGION, ch. 22, n. 42 f., and ch. 41, n. 77. — At the beginning of this proposition, the Vatican edition alone has *For simply* [Simpliciter enim] for *Similarly* [Similiter], which (edition) also somewhat below this, together with codex cc, has *in the order of non-being to being* [in ordine non-entis ad ens] for *in the order regarding non-being* [in ordine ad non-ens]. Next very many codices, together with the six first editions, omits *creating* [creans]. In place of this word *creating* [creans], codices K P Q T X and X put *because* [quia], and then one must supply *It produces* [producit].

[8] Distinction 46, qq. 3, 5, and 6; and d. 47, q. 3, and also SENT., Bk. II, d. 12, a. 1, q. 2, chiefly in reply to n. 4.

[9] Several codices, such as F H V and Z, with edition 1, read well *though ... be* [quamvis ... sit] for *although ... is* [quamvis ... est].

[10] Supply with the Vatican ed., *in the universe* [in universo]. A little further below, the codd. with the six first edd. omit *and* [et] before the same.

[11] In codex Y there is here added: *for when anyone shall be in glory, he will have been better ordered as much as regards his own ordination* [cum enim erit quis in gloria, melius ordinatus erit quantum ad propriam ordinationem]. In place of *their own ordination* [propriam ordinationem] edition 1 has *(their) first ordination* [primam ordinationem].

[12] The Vatican ed. has *the goodness of an order* [ordinis bonitas].

but a necessary *order*: so also must it be understood in the proposed, that, although it is not the best *in itself*, yet *it is ordered* in the best manner. And an example of this is patent in the parts of the body and in something artificial, in which there is consonance and harmony, such as in the cithara. For though the location [situs] of the eye is more noble than (that) of the foot, yet if we consider teach according to its office, both the eye and the foot have been optimally situated in the whole, such that neither the eye (is) better (situated) than the foot, nor <u>vice</u> <u>versa</u>.

And, thus, (St.) Augustine says ON (THE GOSPEL OF ST.) JOHN,[1] that just as an Angel (is situated) optimally in Heaven, so the maggot in the lowest (place), such as (it is) even on Earth. And similarly (an example) appears in the cithara: for all chords can be so proportioned, that if any is stretched [tendatur], to give it a better sound, the consonance (of all of them) will never remain. Similarly, sayings can be ordered to make a verse, such that from those sayings it is impossible that a better ordered verse be made; thus must it be understood in the proposed.

SCHOLIUM

I. For an understanding of the brilliant doctrine of this question one must attend to the many distinctions about *the order* of some thing. It does not deal with the *particular* order of anything, or (the order) « according to *their own* ordination », as is said in the solution to n. 3, but with *the universal order* of the parts of the world, which are ordered not only to their own acts and to their own perfection, but are also ordered, both to one another, because the more ignoble have been ordered as means to the more noble, and to the perfection *of the whole*, and to an *End superior* to the whole universe, such as is the salvation of the Elect and the Glory of God. The Scholastics accepted these distinctions chiefly from Aristotle (METAPHYSICS, Bk. XII, text 52). Cf. also below d. 47, q. 3, and chiefly St. Thomas, SUMMA., I, q. 65, a. 2.

II. In the 3rd argument of the fundament, where there is a discourse on the world of elements, there is supposed in accord with the then common sentence, that there are four elements, and that these have been ordered both according to four *qualities* (hot, cold, moist, dry), and according to many *noble forms*, and « according to *numeral* proportions ». These proportions of the elements, which respond to the numeral proportions, are rather

hinted at here with a few words, than explained. Wherefore besides that which has been said above in the Scholium of d. 2, q. 4, we note this these (words) from Brülifer. *Fire* and *earth*, as extremes are bound up amongst themselves through the two intermediary (elements): *air* and *water*; and they similarly have a proportion amongst themselves, and extreme (8 and 27) and intermediary (12 and 18) numbers: that is a *solid quadrate* number arises, when *the same* number is multiplied upon *itself*, such as $2 \times 2 \times 2 = 8$; and $3 \times 3 \times 3 = 27$; wherefore 8 and 27 are two prime, solid quadrate (cubic numbers). But, if some number is twice multiplied by *another* number, then there arises a *solid* (or cubic number), but not a *quadrate* (number), such as happens when $2 \times 2 \times 3 = 12$, and $2 \times 3 \times 3 = 18$. In this manner two intermediary numbers are produced between the first and second *solid quadrate*. Moreover, 8 and 12 have the same proportion, as 12 and 18, and 18 and 27. For $12 = 8 + 4$; $18 = 12 + 6$; and $27 = 18 + 9$. In a similar manner the qualities of the elements are distributed, so that fire is at once hot and dry; air, warm and moist, water, cold and most, earth, cold and dry.

(See) the authors (mentioned) in the Scholium to Question 1, in addition to Bl. (now St.) Albertus (Magnus), here in a. 3.

QUESTION IV

Whether God was able to make the world more ancient?

Fourth, there is asked, whether He could make the world more ancient. And that (it is) so, seems,

1. According to the last (chapter) of the Second (Letter) of (St.) Peter:[2] *A thousand years before God (are) as one day*. And in the Psalm: *A thousand years before Thy eyes (are) as the day of yesterday, which has passed away*: for an equal reason a hundred thousand years: therefore, if God could make the world before yesterday [ante diem hesternam], He could (do so) throughout the hundred thousand years before. And if this, it would be more ancient: ergo etc..

2. Likewise, the Divine Power and Operation does not dependent [dependet], neither upon matter nor upon time: therefore, by the reason by which

It is able in one instant, It is able in another; but by the reason by which (It is able) in a posterior (time), by the same reason in a prior one. Therefore, if this, the more world could be made more ancient: ergo etc..

3. Likewise, there was a Divine Essence and Power before the beginning of time; therefore, either It was potent to produce *before* (this), or *not*. If *not*: therefore, It was impotent; if *so*: therefore, It could make the world, before It did make (it).

4. Likewise, therefore, I ask, whether It could make (the world) *after* (this). If *yes*; but there is no greater reason [maior ratio] concerning an *after* than concerns a *before*: therefore, for an equal reason [pari ratione], It could make (it) *before* (It has). Or

---

[1] John. 1:3, tract 1, n. 13: Through whom the Angel was made, through whom the maggot was also made; but the Angel (was) worthy of Heaven, the maggot of the earth. He who created, He Himself disposed. If He had put the maggot in Heaven, you would reprehend (Him); if He willed that Angels be born from putrescent flesh, you would reprehend (Him) etc.. Cf. ON A LITERAL EXPOSITION OF GENESIS, Bk. III, ch. 24, and Bk. XI, ch. 8, n. 10, where there occurs the example of the *eye*; and ON THE TRUE RELIGION, ch. 22, n. 42 f., and, also, ON

THE NATURE OF THE GOOD, ch. 8, where he cites the example of *verse* or speech. — For *in the lowest, such as* [in imo, sicut] cod. R has *in slime or* [in limo sive], codd. V and ee have *in dirt* [in humo]. Next, for *be so proportioned* [ita proportionari] many codices have *so proportionally* [ita proportionaliter], a reading evidently mutilated, which codex R completes by adding *be stretched* [tendi], and codex T by adding *be ordered* [ordinari]; codices K and X complete it by adjoining *be* [esse].

[2] Verse 8. — The passage quoted next from the Psalms, is Ps. 89:4.

if It could not (do so) *before*, neither (could It) *after*, and thus it was necessary that (It did so) *then*: therefore, it seems, that It made the world then, as one compelled and not voluntary.

BUT ON THE CONTRARY: 1. Before the beginning of time there was nothing but eternity:[1] therefore, if (God) could make the world before the beginning of time, He could also make (it) in eternity; but what has "being" in eternity lacks a beginning, and nothing such can be created out of nothing: ergo etc..

2. Likewise, if He could make (it) *before*; *let it be posited (that He has)*. Similarly, therefore, I ask, "Whether (He could make it) *before* (this)?", and thus unto infinity; but the infinite on the part of a *before* is eternal: therefore, if He could make (it) unto an infinite before, He could also (make it) from eternity. If, therefore, He could not make the world eternal, because it would not have been made, neither[2] (could He make it) more ancient.

3. Likewise, it is necessary, that the world have a finite duration on the part of a *before*; but in every finite it is necessary that there be a standing still in something, beyond which there can come to be no progression [progressus]; but according to the reason by which there is a standing still in any finite instant, there is a standing still in that, in which the world has been founded: ergo etc..

4. Likewise, at the beginning of the whole of antiquity there cannot come to be and/or be thought (to be) something ancient; but time and/or the aevum, which begins with the world, is the principle of the whole of antiquity: therefore, than that[3] there can be nothing more ancient.

CONCLUSION

God could not make the world thus more ancient, to be from eternity, nor thus, to be without time; yet He could well make a time before this one and in that make a world.

I RESPOND: that when there is asked, whether God could make the world more ancient; it can be understood in a twofold manner: either[4] that He created it from eternity, though He produced (it) out of time, and then it would be more ancient; or, thus, that the world has endured for a longer time, yet, a finite one.

The *first* I believe (is) *simply impossible*, since it implies in itself a contradiction. For from this, that it is posited *to come to be*, it is posited to have a beginning. But from this, that it is posited (to be) *eternal*, it is posited to not

have a beginning. Wherefore, it is the same as asking, "Whether God could *before* the world cause,[5] that the world, having a beginning, would not have a beginning?"; and this includes each side of a contradiction.

Since as much as regards the *second* sense it seems (to be) impossible to *some*, because it implies in itself an opposition, since anteriority or antiquity start together with time. For in eternity there is no *before* and *after*, and time starts of necessity together with the world, just as being situated [situs] starts together with place, and place with the prime orb. Wherefore just as, if it would be asked, "Whether the prime orb could come to be higher?", there would be entirely[6] no question, nay it implies a contradiction, namely that there is a place outside of every place — and it comes from a false imagination, because it imagines, that the whole world is in local space, just as we imagines, that earth is surrounded about with water — similarly must it be understood in the proposed, that there is the implication of a contradiction; and it comes from a false imagination, because we imagine, that before the beginning of the world there was a duration of time, in which the would could come to be beforehand. Wherefore just as,[7] if it be asked, "Whether the whole world could come to be outside of the whole world, either above (it), and/or below (it)?", the question is a foolish one and implies opposites and comes out of a bad imagination: through this manner (of argument) they respond, if it be asked, whether the world could be made *before* and/or *more ancient*. Wherefore they say, that, if anything would have preceded, measuring "before" temporally, it could, certainly [utique] have been made;[8] similarly if there were a place outside (of the world), (the prime orb) could be made higher. — But there is a reason for this bad imagination of theirs: for when we imagine, that there was an eternity unto an infinite (degree) before time, we understand that as if (it were) an extended duration, in which there are diverse *nows*, in any of which time could have come to be. But this is entirely nothing, because eternity is a most simple *now*, in which there occurs entirely no diversity.[9] — Therefore, it must be conceded, that just as the reasons brought forward for this prove, that, just as He could not make the world in *another place*, because it is not in a place,[10] so neither *before*, because there is no antiquity but in it. — To that which is objected, that with God there is no force in any quantum of time [in aliquanto tempore], and that His Power is not dependent etc.; they say to all with one response, that though the Divine Virtue is constrained to nothing, yet,

---

[1] Cf. (St.) Augustine, ON THE CITY OF GOD, Bk. XI, chs. 5 and 6.

[2] The Vatican ed. prefixes *therefore* [ergo] to the word *neither* [nec].

[3] We have recalled the word *than that* [eo] from codex T, where it is indeed extant, written by a second, but ancient hand. For *than than* [eo] many codd. (even cod. T by a first hand) have *there also* [et] for *than that there* [eo], the Vatican has similarly *there also* [etiam]. The other codd., with ed. 1, having omitted *than that* [eo], substitute nothing else.

[4] The Vatican edition after *either* [aut] adds *thus* [ita].

[5] Codex R here reads *God could produce before the world?"*, which is, "Whether He could cause, etc [Deus potuerit ante mundum producere, quod est, utrum potuerit facere, etc.] for *God could before the world cause that etc.* [Deus potuerit ante mundum facere etc.]. A little further above this, for *I believe (is) simply impossible* [credo impossibile simpliciter] codex V has *is simply impossible for God* [est Deo impossibile simpliciter]. — You will find more regarding what pertains to this Question, in SENT., Bk. II, d. 1, p. I, a. 1, q. 2.

[6] For *entirely* [omnino] the codices, with the six first editions, have *in the world* [in mundo]. Next for *because it imagines* [quia imaginatur], the Vatican edition has *because we imagine* [quia imaginamur].

[7] In the Vatican edition and in not a few manuscripts there is lacking *just as* [sicut]. A little after this, for *is a foolish one* [stulta est] codex R has *would be a foolish one* [stulta esset].

[8] Codex R adds *and/or (be) more ancient* [vel antiquior]. In the following proposition, for *an extended duration* [durationem extensam] codices T W and cc have *extended in duration* [duratione extensam].

[9] Cf. (St.) Augustine, ON THE CITY OF GOD, Bk. XI, ch. 5 f., where the principles of this question are hinted at. — A little before this the Vatican edition and codex cc read *(something) most simple* [simplicissimum] for *a most simple now* [nunc simplicissimum]. A little before this, after *that, just as* [quod sicut] codex R inserts (as the explicit subject) *God* [Deus] for *He*, and then for *in another place* [in alio loco] codices I and O have *in any place* [in aliquo loco] and the Vatican edition has instead *in a higher place* [in loco; altiore].

[10] That is, it is not in a place which contains it. Cf. Aristotle, PHYSICS, Bk. IV, text 43 (ch. 5): That body is in a place, outside of which there is some other body, which contains it; but it is not in a place, outside of which there is no body.

It cannot make a *begun* without a beginning, nor [et ... non] a *temporal* without time, and it cannot make *the first temporal* except in *the beginning of time*, nor [et ... non] *the beginning of time* but in a *beginning of time*. For the opposite (of these) does not mean a power, but rather a contradiction and a repugnance. Yet neither is It constrained to make (the world) thus, because It could entirely not made (it). Wherefore just as it is foolish question, if one asks, whether He could[1] make the beginning of time before the beginning of time; similarly also (is) the aforesaid (question).

But since it seems hard to say, that God could not make the world more ancient, and that[2] He could not make another world, but only this one of ours; on this account *some* say, that, just as God could make the world more ample, so He could also make (it) more ancient without any distinction. — But yet that is not entirely similar, because God could make the sky more ample and more distant from the earth, with each nature remaining (as it is); but if God is understood to have caused, that this *now* of ours is more distant from the beginning of time, that *now* is understood to be another (now),[3] because even if the world is understood (to have) been made before, yet it would not be more ancient in respect of this *now* of ours, because it would only be as distant, as it is distant from the beginning; and thus it would not be more ancient.

And, for that reason, it is not to be simply denied nor simply conceded, just as neither is this: "God could make the world *higher*". For if you understand (the truth) of this *absolutely*, it is false, just as the first opinion says, and (it is) not intelligible, and (there is) an implication of a contradiction (in it). But if you understand (it) through *the concomitance of another place*, namely that God could make another world embracing this one of ours, in which[4] (this world) could have a higher and lower location [situs], it is true. Similarly, must it be judged concerning *antiquity*. — And, for that reason, if it be asked, "Whether God could make the world *beforehand*?", it must be distinguished just as even this (must be): "Whether God could make the world in *another place* and/or elsewhere?"; because the adverbial determina-

tion can fall *under the amplification* of the verb, and/or *outside of (it)*.[5] If *under the amplification* of the verb; then it is true, and the sense is, that God could make another place and in that place this whole world of ours. for He could make a hundred such worlds, and yet one embracing (them) all, and one in a higher place than another. Thus also in regard to [in] *time*, it must be understood, that God could make a time *before this one*, and in that make the world.

In another manner the adverbial determination can fall *outside the amplification* of the word [de ly][6] potest, and the sense is, that God can make this world of our in *another place*, which is outside of the world; and here[7] is the implication of the false, because there is no place but inside the world; and similarly must it be understood concerning *time*.

1. To that, therefore, which is objected, that before there was naught but eternity; it must be said that it is true; but yet God could cause, that there would be a time before (this one).

2. To that which is objected concerning the infinite *on the part of a before*, it must be said, that the infinite *on the part of a before* can be by adding [apponendo] either according to *act*, or according to *power*. In the first manner (such an infinite) means an eternity, in the second manner (it) least of all (means this), because "eternity" means an infinite in act.

3. To that which is objected, that it is necessary to posit a standing still (in some instant of time); it must be said, that it is true; but a standing still can belong to an infinite; and though in *power* there is no positing of a standing still, yet because an *act* is not consequent to the whole power, but is in some standing still (of an instant), for that reason (it is) in a finite standing still. But[8] why (it is) in this (instant) more than in another, the highest [summa] and most potent reason (for this) is the Will of the Maker [facientis].

4. To that which is objected, that antiquity began [coepit] with the world; it must be said, that (this) is true; bug God could cause, that (the world) would start beforehand; for that reason that reckoning is not valid. The reasons for the opposite are to be conceded; for they proceed according to the first way.

SCHOLIUM

I. Besides the principal question there is resolved briefly another question, namely, "Whether the world could be created *from eternity?*" If the words "*from eternity*" are not joined with the verb "*could*", but with the terms "*the world be created*", or, as is said here (in reply to n. 2.), by adding *the infinite on the part of the 'before'* not according to *power*, but according to *act*; then the Seraphic Doctor here and in SENT, Bk. II, d. 1, p. 1, a. 1. q. 2

entirely denies, that it is possible, that something be created from eternity. Richard of Middleton, Henry of Ghent and very many others, especially of our own age, agree. However others, together with St. Thomas and (Bl. John Duns) Scotus (who, however, holds this doubtfully), following the lead of Aristotle, judge that arguments taken from reason do not sufficiently prove this impossibility.

II. But regarding the question, "Whether the world, which is sup-

---

[1] Codex T, together with very many others, has *could* [potuit] in the indicative.

[2] Read quin here as *that ... not*. A little before this, for the indicative *could* [potuit] uithe Vatican edition has the subjunctive *could* [potuerit]. A little further below this, for *but only* [sed tantum] codex T, together with a good many other codices, has *and only* [et tantum], codex R has *but only* [nisi tantum], codices M T and ee *even before* [etiam ante].

[3] Or in other words: that which is numbered according to a certain distance from the actual beginning of the world in the present time, with the adjunct of a time on the part of a before, would not be the same. — Next for *because* [quia] codex R has *and* [et].

[4] Codex R here subjoins explicitly *this (world) of ours* [iste], and a little after this for *it is true* [est verum] it exhibits *in this manner it has*

truth [sic habet veritatem]. Very many codices, together with the six first editions, faultily omit *it is true* [est verum].

[5] Namely, outside of the amplification of the verb *could* [potuerit]. Cf. above d. 43, Doubt 1.

[6] In the ancient Gallic tongue, for the article "*le*", there was in use "*ly*" and/or "*li*". Thus de ly was used in place of τοῦ (to signify what we modern English speakers signify with encompassing quotation marks about a word or phrase).

[7] Codex T, together with very many others, has *this* [haec]. Next for *but inside* [nisi intra] codex O has *outside of* [extra].

[8] For *But* [Sed] the Vatican edition has *If it be asked* [Si quaeratur]. Next for *in a finite standing still* [in statu finito] codex O has *in some standing still in a finite instant* [in statu aliquot in instanti finito].

posed (to have) been created *not from eternity*, could be created *before* it was created in this order of Providence?", the first opinion responds negatively; and/or rather not a few affirm that the question itself is irrational in itself, indeed, because the question itself supposes the falsehood, that there is *time* before the start of the world. But that the *question* can be reasonably posited, is clear, if we posit the start of the measuring of the duration not in *the start of our world*, but in *this moment*, in which we live, if, that is, we ask, "Whether the duration of world from the present instant up until the start of the world can be greater?" The Seraphic Doctor responds rightly to this question with a distinction. For the *now* of the present

time, if it would be more distant from the beginning of time (and even *the first now*) would not be the *same now*, but *another*; because for the world, which is supposed before the course of our time, even *another time* would be ordained, and then it would also be *another world*, which God could have made. But if the *same* present *now* and the *same start* of time are supposed to be, then the creation of the world would fall *outside of time*, if there would be a real, more ancient world; which is impossible.

Treating of this question explicitly and in the same sense with the Seraphic (Doctor) are: (Bl.) Peter of Tarentaise, here in the q. sole, a. 4. — Bl. (now St.) Albertus (Magnus), here in a. 1. — Richard of Middleton, here in q. 3.

ARTICLE II

On the immutability of the Divine Power.

Consequently, as much as regards the second Article, there is asked concerning the immutability of the Divine Power, whether, namely, what It[1] can (do) once, It can (do) always.

QUESTION SOLE

Whether what God can (do) once, He can (do) always?

And that it is so, seems:

1. Because every power (of thing), which is the same as the essence (of that thing), has the same '*being able*' as (its) '*being*', and every that of which there is the same '*being able*' as '*being*',[2] if it has an immutable and eternal '*being*', it also has (an immutable and eternal) '*being able*'; but what God *is once* He is always, because His '*Being*' is immutable: therefore, also what *He can (do) once*, He can (do) always.

2. Likewise, every power, which is *infinite* and cannot not be infinite, always is in respect of equals,[3] because if it were in respect of a few, it would sometimes cease to be infinite and cease to be omnipotent; but the Divine Power always is infinite and omnipotent: therefore, nothing of the possible can accrue to it nor be withdrawn [descresit]: therefore, what It can (do) once, It can (do) always.

3. Likewise, every power, which is entirely sufficient and in no manner *dependent* upon a possible, can always (do) everything which it can (do),[4] if it remains in itself unchanged; but the Divine Power is of this kind, and it is not in Itself changed: ergo etc..

4. Likewise, whatever God could (do), He can still (do), if nothing of it has come to be;[5] but nothing can come to be from Him, which does not lie under the Divine Virtue: therefore, on account

of that having come to be [illud factum] there is not impeded, that He can still (work): therefore, He can (do) whatever He could (do).

BUT ON THE CONTRARY: 1. If God always can (do) whatever He once could (do); but He was able[6] to raise up Christ again [Christum resuscitare] from the dead and create the world: therefore, He can also now; which is a foolish (thing) to say.

2. Likewise, if He could always (do), whatever He can once (do); but He is able now to have created the world: therefore, from eternity He could have created (the world).

3. Likewise, if (He) also (can) always (do), whatever He can once (do); but before the world He was able to cause, that the world would not have been: therefore, He can also cause now, that the world would not have been.

4. Likewise, when there is said: "God can (do) this or can make this",[7] with it demonstrated (that He can), either *something* is connoted, or *nothing*. If *nothing*: therefore, it can equally truly be said, that God can (do) evil, as good. But if *something* is connoted, this is naught but a possibility *to be made*; but what has been made, the same itself does not have a possibility *to be made*: therefore God cannot make what has been made: and He could before: therefore, He cannot (do) whatever He could (do).

---

[1] The Vatican edition, and also cod. cc & ed. 1, add (as the explicit subject) *God* [Deus] for *It* (which is then understood also for the next *It*).

[2] Aristotle, PHYSICS, Bk. III, text 32 (ch. 4): For 'being able' differs nothing from 'being' itself in perpetuity.

[3] Or of infinites.

[4] For *it can (do)* [potest] codex Y, together with edition 1, has *it can (do) once* [semel potest]. Next, the Vatican edition to the word *of this kind* [huiusmodi] prefixes *always* [semper].

[5] The Vatican edition, having omitted the words *of it* [de eo], here not trusting in the older codices and edition 1 adjoins *which is not under His Virtue* [quod non subsit eius virtuti] and, a little after this, suppresses *from Him* [ab ipso].

[6] Codex V adds *once* [semel].

[7] The Vatican edition, together with edition 1, reads more briefly in this manner: *"God can do this", with it* etc. [Deus potest hoc facere, aliquot etc.].

CONCLUSION

Though the Divine Power in Itself is immutable, yet by reason of (anything) which It connotes, which was at any time possible and afterwards was made impossible, God cannot always (do), whatever He could (do).

I RESPOND: To this there is a twofold manner of responding, just as (there was) to the sophism concerning the (Divine) *Knowledge*.[1] For with it conceded, that the Divine Power according to the truth is entirely immutable, yet according to the position of the Nominalists they concede this: "He can (do) whatever He could (do)". And they respond to the illation: "but He could *raise up* [suscitare] Christ: therefore, He also can now"; they respond, that it ought not to be inferred under *that* time, but under *another*. "therefore, He is able *to have raised up* Christ", because this enunciable, adjoined to words of diverse tenses, is not[2] the same. For that reason they say, that the proposition is true, and if it is inferred in another manner, they assign the sin in the process (of referring it) according to a *figure of speech* or according to a (fallacy of) *accident*.

However, just as has been proven above,[3] this position does not have truth — though that position of their seems to have been probable, and Master (Peter) was of this position — because through this (manner of arguing) it did not solve (the question concerning knowledge); and again it does not solve (the question) in the proposed. First, because if God were to be said to be able (to do) whatever He could (do), because He is able *to have done* what[4] He could *do*; for an equal reason he who is now blind and the maimed can (do) whatever he could (do), because he is able *to have done* what he could *do*, and (the blind man) is now able *to have seen*, what he could *see*. *Moreover*, granting the opposite of this solution it happens that one still solves (it),[5] with a reckoning formed in this manner: 'He can (do) whatever He could (do); but He is able *to not have made* the world, before He made (it): therefore, even now He is able *to not have made* (it)': in place of that which is "*to not have made (it)*" there is not other granting of an equivalent. — Therefore, that response does not solve (it), most of all since Master (Peter) himself says in the text,[6] that God *cannot* do everything which *He could* at one time do, nor *does He want* to make and/or be and/or come to be what He at once time *willed* to make and/or be and/or come to be.

For that reason it must be said, just as has been said concerning *knowledge*,[7] that the Divine Knowledge, immutable in Itself, ceases [desinit]

to know some enunciable by reason of what it connotes, because the knowable ceases to be true, and the *knowledge* or *knowing* (of it) connotes *in one manner* a truth in the cognized. Similarly, it must be understood, that the Divine *Power* connotes *a possibility* in *the thing*, in respect of which It is said (to be); and such, I say, a possibility, which looks back to the acting Power under a reckoning of *power*, nor of *impotence*. Therefore, since it is thus, that many possibles come to be impossible per accidens,[8] and many possibles come to be beings and, then, are impossibles regarding a 'coming to be' — for to cause, that a *non-being* not be, is to cause nothing; similarly to make *what has been made* is to make nothing, and thus it is impossible that it comes to be — hence it is, that because God cannot (do) but the possible, which to be able (to do) belongs to power, that[9] with no change having been made in the Power, but with God existing equally powerful, something comes to be impossible for God on account of a change on the part of the thing. And this is to be conceded, that the Divine *Power* is *immutable*, and this to be denied: "whatever God *can (do) once, He can (do) always*".

1. 2. 3. To that, therefore, which is objected, that the Divine 'Being able' [divinum posse] is (the Divine) 'Being' [esse] and (is) *infinite* and *independent*; the whole (of which) concludes this, that (the Divine Power)[10] *Itself* is not changed; but nothing follows concerning *what It connotes*. Yet, it is true, that God's '*Being able*', in respect of what It connotes, is always infinite, because, let a finite be removed from an infinite, nevertheless it remains infinite: and, for that reason, though It does cease to be able to do something, yet, It can always (do things) infinite.

4. To that which is objected last — because the others are clear — from this, that the Divine Power dominates all which are; it must be said, that all are beneath Him; and yet it does not follow, that He can make what has been made; yet He can destroy that, but He cannot make (it), because by making (it) He makes *something*, or *nothing*. If *something*: therefore, there is *something* more now than before: therefore, He does not make what has been made. If *nothing*: therefore, by making (this) He makes nothing. Similarly, concerning that which *was*, to cause, that *it was not*, either he does this *by resting*, or by *operating*, or *by destroying*. Not *by resting*: for, if God causes (it to be) nothing, when it[11] has passed away, it is always (that which has) passed away. But, if He causes (the same) *by working*, since nothing comes to be from this — for that this

---

[1] See above d. 41, a. 2, q. 2, where the sentence of the Nominalists is expounded and refuted. — Cod. R reads *sophisms* [sophismata]. A little below this, cod. V to the words *He could (do) whatever He can (do)* [potest quidquid potuit] prefix as the explicit subject *God* [Deus], ed. 1 prefixes *that is* [scilicet].

[2] In the Vatican ed. alone there is wanting the *not* [non], and a little above this in the same and cod. cc there is put *and* [et] for *because* [quia].

[3] Distinction 41, a. 2. q. 2, where there is even had the reason, why there is a fallacy of a figure of speech here, namely, because it proceeds from an identity, in the manner of signifying, to an identity of thing. — You will find the sentence of Master (Peter) here in the text, in ch. 2. — A little below this, in the proposition *because through this (manner of arguing) it did not solve* [quia per hoc non solvit] (supply: in the question concerning knowledge [in quaestione de scientia]), we have restored the particle *not* [non] from cod. T, which reading as the true one is proven entirely from the context of the subsequent words, *and again it does not solve* [et iterum non solvit].

[4] For *what* [quod] codices F V W and others have *whatever* [quidquid]. Likewise, codex W a little below this, after *because he is able to have done* [quia potest fecisse], substitutes *whatever* [quidquid] for *what* [quod]. Then, after (before in the English) *is now able to have seen* [et potest nunc] codex Y subjoins *the blind man* [caecus].

[5] On this Aristotelian proposition, see above d. 4, Doubt 3, p. 104, footnote 11.

[6] Here in ch. 2.

[7] Above, in d. 41, a. 2. q. 2.

[8] Cf. above, d. 42. q. 3. — Next, after *come to be beings* [fiunt entia] codex P and Q adjoin *which when they are* [quae cum sunt]. Somewhat further above this, for *in the thing* [in re] the Vatican edition has *in Him* [in eo].

[9] The conjunction *that* [quod] is here repeated from the preceding expression *hence it is that* [hinc es quod]. Many codices, together with edition 1, for *that* [quod] faultily substitute *because* [quia], the Vatican edition has *and because* [et quia]. Next, after the words *on account of a change* [propter mutationem] codex K inserts *made* [factam].

[10] Supple with codex R *the Divine Power* [divina potentia].

[11] For *when it* [cum hoc] codex T has *yet that which* [tamen hoc quod] (which then requires the following *it* to be removed). Likewise, codex T, together with very many other codices and edition 1, a little after this, omits less well *by working* [operando].

past was not is not something — therefore, by causing (it) He causes nothing. But, if *by destroying* (what is past), since (what is) past, or what was, is not, He does nothing by destroying (it), and by destroying (it) He destroys nothing.[1] — Therefore, it must be conceded,

that He cannot (do) whatever He could (do), because there was, at one time, a possible which has been made impossible, not on account of the constriction [arctationem] of the Power, but on account of this, that (doing such) necessarily connotes a 'not being able' [impotentia]. And, in this manner, the objections are clear.

SCHOLIUM

This Question Master (Peter), here in ch. 2, does not sufficient solve. The same principles, which have been declared above in d. 41, a. 2, q. 2, are also employed by the Seraphic (Doctor) in determining this question. — The ancient doctors do not seem to disagree except somewhat in (their) manner of speaking.

Alexander of Hales., SUMMA., p. I, q. 21, m. 4. — St. Thomas, here in the q. sole, a. 4; SUMMA., I, q. 25, a. 4. — Bl. (now St.) Albertus (Magnus), here in a. 6; SUMMA., p. I, tr. 19, q. 77, m. 3, a. 1. — (Bl.) Peter of Tarentaise, here in the q. sole, a. 5 and 6. — Giles the Roman, here in 2nd princ., q. sole. — Durandus (of Saint-Pourçain), here in q. 4. — (Bl.) Dionysius the Carthusian, here in q. 3.

DOUBTS ON THE TEXT OF THE MASTER

DOUBT I

In this part are the doubts about (Master Peter's) text and first concerning this solution of Master (Peter's), by which he says, that *but the induction of this similitude is not valid, because He begot the Son from His own Substance.* For that response of his seems not be to be sufficient. For envy can[2] be attained in respect of (those) diverse in substance and nature, just as an Angel envies man: therefore, on this account envy is not excluded from God in respect of a creature.

I RESPOND: It must be said, that for *envy* these two concur, namely, a possibility [potestas][3] for equality and an *exigency* for the thing (to have been) done. For no one envies someone, unless because (that) someone is his peer [parificatur ei] and/or exceeds (him), and/or because he fears, that he not (his) peer. Likewise, a craftsman is not said (to be) "*envious*", except when he does not make a thing, according to which he is required [exigit], and is able. And on this account, because on the part of things there was no *exigency*, and again,[4] (since) they could *be (His) peer* in nothing; for that reason of whatsoever kind He would make them, envy is not proven conclusively [convincitur] to be in God, even if He had made no things. But in *the Son of God* there was a potency for equality and furthermore an exigency on this account, that He was of the Substance of the Father. Hence it is, that it is not similar, as Master (Peter) says; and his response is a good one. For he

posits *the antecedent* for *the consequent*, not because he wants to say, that envy is and/or can be solely in respect of a similar in nature; but, on account of the aforesaid reason, namely, of *exigency* and *equality*, which were in the generation of the Son, because He was of the Substance of the Father.[5]

DOUBT II

Likewise is asked concerning this which (St.) Augustine says, that *God could make man such, that he could neither sin nor want (to sin); and if He had made (him) such, who* doubts, *that he was better?* For the contrary seem to be said in the thirty-first (chapter) of Ecclesiasticus:[6] *He could transgress and he has not transgressed*, this is said in regard to [in tandem] "holy men" [sancti viri]. And (St.) Augustine says, ON A LITERAL EXPOSITION OF GENESIS,[7] that « God judged men better, if they freely served Him with zeal ». *And again*, in the book, ON THE CITY OF GOD he says, that « better is the substance, which can sin, than that which cannot ».

I RESPOND: It must be said, that "*better*" [melius] is said in a twofold manner: either *simply* [simpliciter], or in an *order to an end* [in ordine ad finem]. If we speak *simply*, better is the man confirm-

---

[1] Cf. above d. 42, q. 3. — Next, after *because* [quia] very many codices, such as F P Q and V, together with edition 1, interjects *something* [aliquid] for *it*, and then has *ultimately* [ultimo] for *necessarily* [necessario].

[2] Edition 1 reads *can well* [bene potest].

[3] The Vatican edition and not a few codices have *possibility* [possibilitas], concerning which, cf. above d. 42, a. sole, q. 4, p. 756, footnote 1.

[4] For *again, (since)* [iterum] the Vatican ed. has *because* [quia].

[5] Cf. above d. XX, chs. 2 and 3, and in (St. Bonaventure's) Commentary on the same, Doubt 4. Cf. also on this doubt here, Alexander of Hales, SUMMA., p. I, q. 21, m. 3, a. 1, in reply to n. 1, and Bl. (now St.)

Albertus (Magnus), here in a. 1.

[6] Verse 10. — Next, for *this is said* [hoc dicitur] the Vatican edition has *it says this* [hoc dicit].

[7] This sentence of (St.) Augustine is not found literally in his Commentary on Genesis, but, nevertheless, it can be construed from the work cited, Bk. VIII, ch. 12, n. 30 f., and Bk. XI, ch. 7, n. 9. It agrees more with what is said in ON THE TRUE RELIGION, ch. 14, n. 27, which we have already cited above, here in a. 1, q. 2, p. 784, footnote 7. On the text, cited from the book, ON THE CITY OF GOD, cf. above d. 42, a. sole, q. 2, p. 748, footnote 8.

ed in grace, than the one able to fall [potent labi]; if in (his) being ordered [ordinationem] *to an end*, which indeed consists in arriving (at it); thus it was better to make man in the liberty to sin; but yet the first is *simply* better, but the latter is better secundum quid. And for that reason the word of (St.) Augustine, *simply* speaking, has truth.

Moreover, what is said of the *just* man, is an *accidental* praise or (praise) as much as regards (his) accidental glory. For it is established, that Christ could not sin, and yet He was most glorious. Similarly, must be understood that word of (St.) Augustine on Genesis. But what is said, that better is the nature, which can sin, than that which cannot; it must be said, that "*to not be able to sin*" is from a twofold cause, either because one lacks *the will*, or *the vertibility* of will; and in the first manner (St.) Augustine understands (it), not in the second.[1]

Doubt III

Likewise, is asked concerning this which Master (Peter) says, that *God could make (things) better, than He made (them)*. For that seems not to have truth in all (things), and especially in Christ, whom He seems in no manner able to make better, through that which is said in the second (chapter of St Paul's Letter) to the Philippians:[2] *He gave Him the Name, which is above every name*: Likewise, in the third (chapter of the Gospel of St.) John (there is written):[3] *The Spirit was given to Him, not according to a measure*; therefore, in no manner could God give Christ more of the Spirit: therefore, He could not make Him better.

I Respond: It must be said, that Master (Peter) speaks of the universe and its parts; and since Christ is neither of the universe nor (is) a part of it, for that reason the verse has no place in Him.[4] Yet in regard to [in] Christ one still has (this) doubt. For if whatever the Humanity of Christ has, is finite, therefore, since God is able over every finite, He was more able [potuit maius]. And, *again*, Christ was made able to suffer and die [passibilis et mortalis], and He was able to be made immortal.

And, on this account, it must be said, that there is a speaking of Christ in a threefold manner, either as much as regards *the Union* [ad unionem], or as much as regards *the grace of the singular Person* [ad gratiam singularis personae], or as much as regards *the properties of (His) nature*. If as much as regards *the Union*, neither can God give more, nor[5] the creature receive

(more), because the grace of union on the part of the other extreme is of an infinite dignity, namely, that a man is God, though on the part of the Humanity whatever is there is finite: and thus there is posited no *limitation* on the part of *God*, nor an *infinite* capacity on the part of *the creature* except through the Union, namely, because a man is united to the Infinite Good, so that a man is God, who is the Infinite Good. — However, if we speak as much as regards *the grace of the singular Person*, thus I do concede, that God could give more, but the rational nature could not receive more amply; not because the capacity of the soul for grace is lessened through the conferral of grace, because it is neither lessened nor increased, but (rather) consummated and completed; and for that reason it is not possible for (something) more ample.[6] But if we speak as much as regards *the properties of the nature*, thus God both could give more of (His) Goodness, and the rational creature (could) receive (more), as much as regards those, namely, which are of the body — because He now has more, than when He was made — but (these properties) could not be made more congruent *to an end* and to our salvation.[7] For our salvation never would have been able to be repaired thus through an incorruptible and immortal substance, just as it has been repaired through His Death and Passion. Therefore, it is clear, in what manner Christ could be better, and in what manner (He could) not.[8]

Doubt IV

Likewise, is objected concerning the Blessed Virgin. For it seems, that She could not be made better, because (St.) Anselm (of Canterbury) says On the Virginal Conception:[9] « It was fitting, that the conception of that Man would come to be from the most pure Mother, than which purity there can be no greater understood under God »: therefore, it seems, that She could not be made better, and yet She was a part of the universe. *Likewise*, She has been exalted in grace above all the Choirs of the Angels: therefore, She has been wrought in a most high grace.

I Respond: It must be said, that there is a speaking of the Blessed Virgin as much as regards three conditions, that is, as much as regards *the grace of conception*, as much as regards *the grace of justification*, (and) as much as regards *nature*.[10] If as much as regards *the conception of offspring*, thus because She was the Mother of God, than Whom nothing more noble can be thought, and the Mother of the Most Noble Son, thus She has so great a dignity of goodness,

---

[1] More concerning this Doubt has been expounded above in q. 1 ff.. Cf. also Alexander of Hales, Summa., p. I, q. 21, m. 3, in reply to n. 4; Bl. (now St.) Albertus (Magnus), here in a. 5, and Richard of Middleton, here on the text.

[2] Verse 9. The Vulgate reads: *He granted* etc. [Donavit etc.].

[3] Verse 34. — Then, after *therefore* [ergo] the Vatican edition interjects *because* [quia]. Codex V places before *therefore* [ergo] an *if* [si].

[4] In the Vatican edition there is read: *for that reason it has no place in Him. But in regard to Christ* etc. [non habet locum in ipso. Verum etiam adhuc in Christo etc.]. For *in Christ* [in Christo] codex bb has *in Him* [in ipso].

[5] Codex V here repeats *can ... more* [potest plus].

[6] Cf. above d. 17, p. II, q. 4. — A little further above this, for *the rational nature* [rationalis natura] codices T and cc, together with the Vatican edition, have *a rational creature* [rationalis creatura], and then for *commsumated* [consumatur] codex I has *conserved* [conservatur].

[7] For *our salvation* [saluti nostrae] the Vatican edition alone reads *the salvation of (our) nature* [saluti naturae].

[8] The same solution to this doubt is given by Alexander of Hales, Summa., p. I. q. 21, m. 3, a. 5 f.; Bl. (now St.) Albertus (Magnus), here in a. 5; St. Thomas,

here in q. 1, a. 3, and in his Summa., I, q. 25, a. 6, in reply to n. 4; (Bl.) Peter of Tarentaise, here in a. 3; Giles the Roman, here in 1st princ, q. 3, and also (Bl.) Dionysius the Carthusian, here in q. 2.

[9] Chapter 18, where in the works of (St.) Anselm for *than which purity* [qua puritate] there is read: *namely it was fitting, that (He would come forth from) this purity, than which* [nempe decens erat, ut ea puritate qua].

[10] Very many codices, together with editions 2 and 3, faultily read *the nature of charity* [naturam caritatis] for *nature* [naturam]; the Vatican edition, together with edition 1, reads *the nature of the body* [naturam corporis], with which addition the notion of the word *nature* [natura] is exceedingly restricted. Our reading, which concerns *nature* simply, is supported by codices P and Q. This reading is also confirmed by the words, which are employed a little below this to expound those three conditions, mentioned here; which words are: *If as much as regards natural (goods), She had the best* [Si quantum ad naturalia, optima etc.], and which are extant in all the codices and also in editions 1, 2 and 3. A little further above this, for *as much as regards the grace of conception* [quantum ad gratiam conceptionis] edition 1 reads *as much as regards the conception of offspring* [quantum ad conceptionem prolis].

that no woman could grasp (one) more amply. For, if all creatures, howsoever much they ascended in grades of nobility, were to be present, all would owe reverence [deberent reverentiam] to the Mother of God. — But, if we speak as much as regards *the grace of justification*, She had as much, as a pure human or rational creature, which has been made in this manner,[1] could receive. — If as much as regards *natural (goods)*, She had the best, according to which it was suitable [competens] to (Her) end; yet, simply, She could receive,

and God give, better (goods). — And, thus, it is clear, that in nothing created does this word of Master (Peter) have an instance: "that God could make better, those which He made." It is also clear, that in some He has completed and fulfilled the capacity of grace; but in *Christ* (He has done this) through every standard of measure, in His *Mother*,[2] according to what a pure, rational creature in the *feminine in sex* is capable [capit], as much as regards those which pertain to the body, and (according to the same) in *a human soul*, as much as regards those which belong to grace.

DISTINCTION XLIV

CHAPTER I

On God's Will, which is God's Essence, and on Its signs.

Now, something must be said concerning God's Will in proportion to [pro] the imbecility of our understanding [sensus]. It must be known, therefore, that "*the Will*" or "*willing*" is said of God according to essence. For, it is not one (thing) for Him *to will* and another *to be*, but (each is) entirely the same. And just as it is the same for Him *to be good* as *to be God*, so (it is) the same for Him *to be willing* as *to be God*. For the Will, by which He is always willing, is not an affection [affectus] and/or a movement, which does not prevail to occur in God, but the Divine Ousia,* by which He is willing, is God,[1] and (is) of this kind.

CHAPTER II

That though for God it is the same to will as to be, yet God cannot be said to be all which He wills.

And though it be the same for God *to will* as *to be*, yet it must not be said, that God *is all (those things)* which He wills. Which certain ones, not thinking [sentientes] rightly of God's Will, objects to us, saying: "If it is the same for God *to will* as *to be*, therefore, when we say, that God wills all which He makes, we say, that He *is all* which He makes; otherwise the same is not signified there by that verb,[2] as is signified by this verb "*to be*", when it is said of God. And if it is thus, (then) "*to will*" is not always said of God according to essence. If, however, it is sometimes not said according to essence, in what manner, therefore, is it said of God? For ("to

will")[3] is never said relatively." — To which we say, that though it is thoroughly the same for God *to be* as *to know*, yet just as He neither is said "*to know all*", so also can He (neither) be said "*to be all*".

CHAPTER III

On the understanding of these expressions: "God knows, and/or God Wills", "God knows all and/or wills something".

And, wheresoever God is said "*to know*" and/or "*(to be) knowing*", and[4] "*to will*" and/or "*(to be) willing*", these are said of Him according to essence. For, when there is said: "God knows and/or God wills", or "God is knowing and/or willing", the Divine Essence is predicated and God is enunciated to be. But, when there is added "*all*" and/or "*something*" and/or "*somethings*", and there is said: "God knows all, and/or wills something and/or somethings"; the Divine Essence is indeed predicated, not simply and absolutely, but so that all may be shown (to have been)[5] subjected to the Knowledge, which He Himself is, and to the Will, which the very same (Knowledge) is, something and/or somethings are said to have been subjected, so that the sense becomes such: "God knows all", that is, "God is (He), to whose Knowledge, which is His Essence, all have been subjected". Similarly: "God wills these and/or those", that is, "God is (He), to whose Will, which He Himself is, these or those have been subjected". Therefore, God is said "*(to be) willing*" or "*to will*" according to essence, the Will of Whom is the sempiternal and immutable Essence — though those, which have been subject to It, vary and are transient [transeant] — Which cannot be unjust nor evil, because It is God.

---

[1] That is, as a pure creature. — In the Vatican edition, with changed punctuation, there is read thus: *which has been made, could thus receive* [quae facta est, sic recipere potuit], but then the words *which has been made* [quae facta est] are superfluous. The same a little after this, again with changed punctuation and having interjected the word *body*, reads thus: *If as much as regards the body: She has the best natural (goods)* [Si quantum ad corpus: naturalia optima habuit], breaking with all the codices and editions 1, 2 and 3, as we have already mentioned in the preceding footnote.

[2] The Vatican edition omits *His* [eius], in place of which many codices faultily have *for in* [in enim] for *in His* [in eius]. A little further above this, for *It is also clear, that in* [Patet etiam, quod in] the Vatican edition has *It is clear that for* [Patet quod].

NOTES ON THE BOOK OF SENTENCES

[1] Thus codices A C and E and edition 1; the Vatican edition and the other editions omit *is* [est]; codex D reads *is, both God and* [est, et Deus et]; codex B has *is, both is God, and* [est, et Deus est, et].

[2] Codex C adds "*to will*" [velle].

[3] Supply: "*to will*" [velle], or with editions 2 and 3 (the noun) "*will*" [voluntas].

[4] The Vatican edition, together with very many editions, has *either* [vel]. Then codices A C and E and editions 1, 4 and 5 have *of God* [de Deo] for *of Him* [de eo].

[5] Codices B C and D add *to have been* [esse]. Immediately before (in the English, after) this, edition 1 has *It Itself (i. e. the Divine Essence) is* [ipsa est] for *He Himself is* [ipse est].

---

* *Trans. note*: That is, the very Divine *Being*, the term in Greek for which, ουσια, St. Bonaventure transliterates here with the Latin, ousia.

CHAPTER IV

That God's most highly Good Will is the Cause of all which
naturally are, the cause of Which is not to be sought, because It
is the First and Most High Cause of all.

And, so, this most highly Good Will is the Cause of
all which naturally come to be and/or (have been) made or
are going to be, which no cause comes before, because It is
eternal. And for that reason no cause for It is to be sought.
For he who seeks Its cause, seeks something greater than
It, though nothing is greater than it. Wherefore, (St.) Augustine in the book, OF EIGHTY-THREE QUESTIONS (says):[1]
« He who seeks, for what reason God willed to make the
world, seeks the cause of God's Will. But every efficient
cause is greater than that which it effects. But nothing is
greater than God's Will. Therefore, Its cause is not to be
sought ». The same (says) in the book, ON GENESIS
AGAINST THE MANICHEANS:[2] « If any have said: "Why did
it please God to make Heaven and Earth?", it must be responded to them: "Those who desire to know [nosse]
God's Will, seek to know [scire] the causes of God's Will,[3]
though God's Will Itself is the Cause of all which are". For
if the Will has a cause, it is something, which antecedes
God's Will, which is a nefarious (thing) to believe. Therefore, he who says: "For what reason did God make Heaven
and Earth? it must be responded to him: "Because He
willed[4] (it)". For God's Will is the cause of Heaven and
Earth, and for that reason God's Will is greater than
Heaven and Earth. Moreover, he who says: "For what reason did He will to make Heaven and Earth?" seeks something greater, than God's Will is; but nothing greater can
be found. Therefore, let human temerity tread completely
upon itself [compescat se], and that which is not, let it not
seek, lest that which is, it not find ». — Behold here there
is openly insinuated by authorities, that there is no cause
of God's Will, and for that reason one is not to be sought.

« Therefore, God's Will », as (St.) Augustine says in
the third book, ON THE TRINITY,[5] « is the First and Most
High Cause of all species and motions. For nothing comes
to be, which does not step forth from the interior and intelligible inner-court [aula] of the Most High Emperor ».
« For, where is there not worked that which the Wisdom
of the Omnipotent God wills? Which *reaches thoroughly*
from end unto end strongly, and disposes all (things) sweetly »,[6]
« and does not only do those which do not admit of admiration from (their) continual customariness [persever-
antia consuetudinis] », « but even those which on account
of (their) rarity and an unusual event seem to be wonderful,
such as are the failings of the lights (of Heaven) and the
movements of the Earth and monstrous births of living
things and (those) similar to these, none [nihil] of which
comes to be without[7] God's Will, nor [sed ... non] appears
to very many. And, for that reason, it pleased the vanity of
philosophers to grant even these to other causes, since they
could not entirely see the Cause superior to all others,

that is the Will of God. And so non but God's Will is the
First Cause of health, sickness, rewards and punishments,
graces and retributions ». Therefore, It is the sole (Cause),
from which has arisen whatever is, and It Itself has not
arisen, but (is) eternal.

CHAPTER V

In what manners is God's "will" accepted.

Here, it must not be overlooked by us, that Sacred
Scripture is accustomed to speak of God's Will in various manners; and yet God's Will is not diverse, but there
is a diverse expression of the Will, because it accepts diverse (things) under the name of "will". For God's *Will*
is truly and properly said to be (That) which is in Him
and is His Essence; and This is one, nor does It receive
a multiplicity nor a mutability, which cannot be unfulfilled, concerning Which the Prophet says:[8] *All (things)*
whichsoever He has willed, the Lord has made. And the
Apostle (says): *His Will, who resists (It)?.* And in another
place: *So that you may show, that God's Will is good and*
well-pleasing and perfect. And this Will is rightly named
God's "good pleasure" or "disposition".

CHAPTER VI

That (God's) preception, prohibition, permission, counsel, (and)
operation are sometimes understood by the name of "will".

However, sometimes under a certain figure of
speech [dicendi] that which is not His Will according to
a property is called the "will" of God, such a (God's)
preception [praeceptio], *prohibition, counsel,* and also *per-*
mission and *operation.* And, for that reason, Scripture
sometimes pronounces (these) in the plural God's
"*wills*". Wherefore the Prophet (says):[9] *Great (are) the*
works of the Lord, exquisite in all His wills [in omnes vol-
untates eius]. Since there is naught but *one* Will of God,
which is Himself, yet it says in the plural "*wills*", because
God's "will" is accepted in various manners on behalf
of diverse (things), as has been said. For thus the same
Prophet, on account of (experiencing) many effects of
(God's) Mercy and Justice, says in the plural:[10] *The mer-*
cies of the Lord shall I sing in eternity. And in another
place: *The justices of the Lord (are) upright, gladdening*
hearts, yet though in God there is *one* Mercy, *one* Justice,
and the Same[11] is (His) Mercy which (is His) Justice,
namely the Divine Ousia.

Moreover, for this reason (God's) *preception* and *pro-*
hibition and even (His) *counsel,* though they are three, yet
each one of them is said (to be) God's "will", because
these are *the signs* of the Divine Will; according to which
standard of measure both *the signs* of (God's) anger [ira]
are said (to be His) "anger", and *the signs* of (His) dilection are named (His) "dilection"; and God is said

---

[1] Question 28.

[2] Book I, ch. 2, n. 1.

[3] The codices and editions, except the Vatican edition and edition
8, have *the causes and the Will of God* [causas et voluntatem Dei], and
immediately after this have *wherefore* [quod] for *though* [cum].

[4] The Vatican edition and editions 3, 4, 7, 8 and 9 read *wills* [vult].

[5] Chapter 4, n. 9; but the original has: ... of all *corporal* species
and motions. For nothing comes to be visibly and sensibly, which is not
from the interior, invisible and intelligible inner-court of the Most High
Emperor commanded or permitted (cod. D has: does not ... Emperor step
forth either with Him permitting it and/or causing it) according to (His)
ineffable Justice. — The following passage is ibid., ch. 1, n. 6, the third
is ibid., ch. 2, n. 7, and the fourth is ibid., ch. 3, n. 8, and ch. 4, n. 9.

[6] Wisdom 8:1.

[7] Codices A B C and E and edition 1 have *but by* [nisi] for
without [sine]. A little below this, only the Vatican edition, together
with the original, has *it was licit for* [licuit] in place of *it pleased*
[placuit], and finally codices A and D and all the editions, except edition 1, have *to attribute* [attribuere] for *to grant* [tribuere], but breaking with the original.

[8] Psalm 113:11; the passages, which follow, are Romans 9:19 and
Romans 12:2.

[9] Psalm 110:2.*

[10] Psalm 88:2; the other passage is Ps. 18:9.

[11] The Vatican edition and the other editions omit *and the Same*
[eademque],°, breaking with the codices and edition 1.

---

* *Tran. notes*: In regard to little before this: '*to precept*' is to command by establishing a principle of conduct. Even though in English *pre-*
ception no longer retains the meaning of the verb, but is employed a technical term regarding legacies in Roman Law, *preception* will be used for prae-
ceptio in this English translation, as signifying the same as *prohibition* does in regard to '*to prohibit*', that is an act of the verb.

° Here the original note evidently erred in having *and the One* [et una] for *and the Same* [eademque], since the former is nowhere found it the
critical text; the latter being placed here in the footnote from the critical text, to correct the footnote.

(to have been) "*angered*" [iratus], and yet there is no anger in Him: but yet *the signs*, which come to the fore [foris fiunt], by which He is shown (to be) angered, are named His "anger". And it is a figure of speech, according to which what is said is not false, but the true, which is said, is overshadowed [obumbratur] under the cloud of a trope [sub tropi nubilo]. And, according to these tropes, there are said (to be) diverse "wills" of God, because those which are said through a trope (to be) God's "will" are diverse.

On behalf of God's precept and, even, counsel, "will" can be accepted, as in this (verse):[1] *Thy Will be done, on Earth as it is in Heaven*. And in another place: *He who does the Will of My Father, who is in Heaven, he is My brother and sisters and mother*. And many (things) are done against this "will". Wherefore, (St.) Augustine (says) in the book, ON SPIRIT AND LETTER:[2] « The infidels », he says, « work against God's Will, when they do not believe His Gospel ».

CHAPTER VII

That God wills that, by all, there be done those which He precepts, and/or that not be done those which He prohibits.

And, if those three are said to be God's "will", for this reason, because they belong to the Divine Will, yet it must not be understood, that God wills that every that, which *He has precepted*, be done, and/or which *He has prohibited*, not be done. For He precepted Abraham to immolate (his) son, yet He did not will (it); nor for that reason did He precept, so that it would be done, but so that Abraham's faith would be proven.[3] And in the Gospel He precepted the healed man, lest he speak of his own (healing); but he preached (it) everywhere, understanding, that God had not prohibited (it) for this reason, that He willed that His own work not be preached, but so that He would give a form for turning away human praise from (Christ) the Man.

God's *permission* [permissio] and *operation* [operatio] are also called God's "will", in the manner that (St.) Augustine accepts (them) in (his) ENCHIRIDION,[4] saying: « Nothing comes to be, unless the Omnipotent wills (it) to come to be, either *by allowing*, that it comes to be, and/or *by Himself causing* (it). Nor must it be doubted, that God causes in a good manner even by allowing to come to be, whichsoever come to be in an evil manner. For He does not allow this except by a just judgement, and indeed everything which is just is good ». — Behold here you manifestly have,[5] that God's Will is named His *operation* and/or *permission*, when he says, that nothing comes to be, unless the Omnipotent wills it to come to be, where he includes both all good and evil (things), which come to be. And for that reason he openly distinguishes, in what manner he said that God willed, lest there would be understood that He wills good and evil (things) for the same reason, subjoining *either by allowing, it to come to be* — this he says as much as regards evil (things) — *and or by Himself causing (it)* — this (he says) as much as regards good (things). For He allows evil (things) to come to be, but does not cause (them); however, He does cause good (things). And for that reason he said, that He *wills*, because He, both, as One willing,[6] allows evil (things) and, as One willing, works good ones; and because of this (His) *permission* and *operation* are said (to be) God's "will".

Therefore, five were posited above, which are said according to a trope (to be) God's "will", because they are *signs* of the Divine Will, Which is one and immutable, namely God's Good Pleasure [Dei beneplacitum]. And, for that reason, the reader must distinguish diligently, where[7] Scripture reminds (us) of God's "will", in accord with the manner it must [oporteat] be accepted, whether, that is, on behalf of God's *Good Pleasure*, or on behalf of any of *the signs* for this. For great discretion is to be employed in the recognition [cognitione] of the Divine Will, because both God's *Good Pleasure* is His Will, and *the sign* of His *Good Pleasure* is said (to be) His "will". But His *Good Pleasure* is eternal, however, *the sign* of His *Good Pleasure* is not; and His *Good Pleasure* is consonant with the effects of things, and the very effects of things are not discordant from It. For everything which He wills to come to be by (His) *Good Pleasure*, come to be, and everything which He does not will to come to be, never comes to be. But no,t thus, does it concern *the signs*, because God *precepted* to many those which they do not, and *prohibits* those which they do not beware of, and *counsels* those which they do not fulfill.[8]

---

[1] Matthew 6:10; the following passage is Mt. 12:10. The Vulgate reads: *For whosoever has done* etc. [Quicumque enim fecerit etc.].

[2] Chapter 33, n. 58.

[3] A reference to Gen. 22:2 ff., and then to Mk. 1:14.

[4] Chapters 95 and 96, n. 24; in which text the Vatican edition, together with the other editions, except ed. 1, have *these except* [haec nisi] for *this except* [hoc nisi], contradicting the codd. and even the original.

[5] The Vatican ed. with very many edd. has *we ... have* [habemus].

[6] Only the Vatican edition has *One unwilling* [nolens], but faultily, and, then, with edition 1 and codices A and C, it omits *and* [et] after *allows* [sinit].

[7] Codices B and D have *wheresoever* [ubicumque]. A little after this the Vatican edition, together with very many editions, omits *that is* [scilicet].

[8] In (his) Tract on the Divine Will, Peter Lombard has taken very many of the propositions which he expresses word for word, others, however, according to (their) sense, from two opuscula of Hugh of St. Victor: SUMMA SENTENTIARUM, tr. I, ch. 13, and DE SACRAMENTIS, Bk. I, p. IV, ch. 2 ff. We have already observed on many occasions, that Master (Peter) has converted to his own use not a few (words) of Hugh, Abelard and perhaps even other authors, who composed Books of Sentences before him.

COMMENTARY ON DISTINCTION XLV

On (God's) Will according to Its own quiddity.

Now, something must be said concerning God's Will etc..

THE DIVISION OF THE TEXT

Above,[1] Master (Peter) dealt with (God's) *Knowledge* and *Power*, here he does deals third with (His) *Will*. And this part has three parts. In the first he deals with the Will according to Its quiddity. In the second according to Its fulfillment [impletionem] in respect of work, that is, in what manner It is fulfilled, below in the Forty-Sixth Distinction: *Here there arises a question: for it has been said* etc.. In the third, he determines, in what manner our will is conformed to the Divine (Will), and this in the Forty-Eighth Distinction: *It also must be known, that sometimes the will of the man willing* etc..

The first part has three parts. In the *first*, (Master Peter) shows, that God's Will is the Divine Essence Itself; in the *second*, that It is the cause of all, there (where he says): *And so this most highly Good Will is the Cause of all* etc.; in the *third* he shows, that the "will" of God is said in a multiple manner, there (where he says): *Here it must not be overlooked by us,* etc..

The *first* part has two (parts). In the first, he shows, that '*to will*' is in God '*to be*', and (that) the *Will* is the *Essence*.

In the second, he solves a doubt, there (where he says): *And though it be the same for God to will as to be* etc..

The *second* part similarly has two (parts). In the first he shows, that the Divine Will is the *First* Cause. In the second he shows, that It is *the most general cause*, there (where he says): « *Therefore, God's Will* », as (St.) Augustine says etc..

Here it must not be overlooked etc.. This is the *third* part, in which (Master Peter) deals with the multiplicity of that name, and this is not a multiplicity of equivocation, but of analogy; and there are in this part three subparts. In the first, he posits the principal manner of accepting concerning [circa] this name, which is "will" [voluntas], that, namely, it is accepted on behalf of (God's) Will of *good pleasure* [beneplaciti]. In the second, he posits the principle manners, namely[2] the tropological ones, according to which (a term) is accepted as a *sign* of (the Divine) Will [pro signo voluntatis], and this he does in this (verse): *However, sometimes under a certain figure of speech* etc.. In the third, he briefly summarizes the predetermined, there (where he says): *Therefore, five were posited above, which are said according to a trope* etc..

TREATMENT OF THE QUESTIONS

For an understanding of the present Distinction three (questions) are principally asked.

First, there is asked concerning the Divine Will, as much as regards (its) quiddity.

Second, as much as regards (Its) causality.

Third, as much as regards (Its) reckoning of being signified.

As much as regards the first, two (questions) are asked.

First, there is asked, whether in God there is a positing of a will.

Second, whether there is a saying of Him as "omnivolent" (i.e. all willing), just as He is said (to be) "omnipotent".

---

[1] In Distinctions XXXV-XLI on (God's) Knowledge, in Distinctions XLII ff., on (God's) Power.

[2] For *namely* [scilicet] the Vatican edition, together with edition 1 and not a few manuscripts, has *but* [sed].

ARTICLE I

On the Divine Will, as much as regards (Its) quiddity.

QUESTION I

Whether in God there is the positing of a will?

Moreover, that in God there is no positing of a will, is shown *by authority* and *reason*.

1. First in this manner: (St.) Augustine in (his) book, ON FREE WILL (says):[1] « The will is a rational movement, presiding over sense and appetite »; but in God there is no movement nor sense nor appetite: therefore, neither a will.

2. Likewise, (St.) Augustine (says) in (his) book, ON THE TWO SOULS:[2] « The will is a movement of the spirit [animi] to pursue and/or flee something »; but in God there is no positing of *flight* nor of *pursuit*: therefore, neither of a will.

3. Likewise, *by reason*:[3] because the will is in us, most of all, a vertible power, wherefore the other powers are not able unto evil, but the will alone is, from which there is sin; but in God there is entirely no vertibility toward evil: ergo etc..

4. Likewise, the will, by this very (thing) that it is a will, is for opposites, (and) by this very (thing) that (it is) for opposites, it is contingent and variable; but in God there occurs no contingency nor variety: ergo etc.. *Proof of the first.* The will, by this very (thing) that (it is) a will, is a rational power [potestas rationalis]; but « rational powers are for opposites », just as the Philosopher[4] says: ergo etc.. *Similarly,* by this very (thing), by which it is a will, it is free [libera]; and if this, (then) it has not been determined to one (thing), because then it would not have liberty, just as the neither (do) the natural powers [potentiae naturales]: therefore, it is for opposites, and thus variable.

BUT ON THE CONTRARY: 1. In the first (chapter of his Letter) to the Ephesians,[5] the Apostle (Paul) says: *According to the counsel of His Will*. And again in the same place: *According to the proposal of His Will*; and the whole of Scripture is full of this name for the Will, as it is in God: ergo etc..

2. Likewise, the Philosopher in the twelfth (book of his METAPHYSICS)[6] concludes, that « the Will is the action of God Himself ».

3. Likewise, it seems *by reason*, because the will is that, within which there resides the highest *power* [summa potestas][7] among created (things): therefore, if the will of itself means a power, because it presides over all in the kingdom of the soul, and nothing can command [imperare] it; but God is most potent [potentissimus], and everything which belongs to potency [potentiae], is to be attributed to Him: ergo etc..

4. Likewise, the will is (that), in which consists the highest pleasure [voluptas] or felicity — « for blessed is he who has everything which he wills »;[8] wherefore nothings is delighted except one having a will and/or something similar to a will — but God is most happy [felicissimus], in Whom there is every felicity and jocundity: ergo etc..

5. Likewise, the will is that, within which resides *justice* and *equity* — for justice is not other than a rectitude of will;[9] wherefore (those) not having a will are not capable [capabilia] of justice — but God is most just according to every understanding: therefore, He has a Will.

6. Likewise, the will is the force [vis], according to which

---

[1] The definition proposed here seems to have been formed from those which St. Augustine, ON FREE WILL, Bk. I, chs. 8-11, nn. 18-21, and Bk. III, ch. 1, nn. 1-4 proffers concerning the acts of reason and will which rule all the other movements of the spirit. In codex T by a second hand in place of the book, ON FREE WILL, there is cited the book, ON GRACE AND FREE WILL, in which, nevertheless, there is only taught (ch. 3, n. 5), that it belongs to man to resist concupiscence. In the same codex T (in the margin) a little before the word *First* [Primo] there is placed *By authority* [Auctoritate].

[2] Chapter 10, n. 14: The will is a movement of the spirit, with nothing driving (it), for either not losing and/or obtaining something.

[3] The Vatican edition and not a few codices subjoin *it seems* [videtur]. On the argument itself, cf. (St.) Anselm, ON THE VIRGINAL CONCEPTION, ch. 3 f..

[4] METAPHYSICS, Bk. IX, text 3 f., and text 10 (Bk. VIII, chs. 1 and 5). That the will is a rational power, Aristotle teaches ON THE SOUL, Bk. III, texts 42 and 50 (chs. 9 and 10). — In the text cited, in place of *for opposites* [ad opposita] the Vatican edition, together with codex cc, has *for the opposite* [ad oppositum]. Next, for *by this very (thing), by which* [eo ipso quo] codices H K X bb and ee have *by this very (thing), that* [eo ipso quod]. At the end of the argument, for *and thus* [et ita] the Vatican edition has *and, therefore,* [et igitur].

[5] Verse 11. — The following text is had ibid., v. 5.

[6] That is: METAPHYSICS, Bk. XII, text 39 (Bk. XI, ch. 7): Ἐπεὶ καὶ ἡδονὴ

ἡ ἐνέργεια τούτου, i. e. according to the Arabic-Latin version: "For (His) pleasure is His action", namely, the First Principle's [Voluptas enim est actio ipsius, scil. primi principii]. — The Seraphic Doctor here substitutes *will* [voluntas] for *pleasure* [voluptas], which is not done falsely, because there is (in a spiritual being) no pleasure without a will. Cf. also what he says in the 4th argument, and what he teaches above in d. 1, a. 2, q. 1, concerning delectation and enjoyment.

[7] Cf. (St.) Augustine, ON A LITERAL EXPOSITION OF GENESIS, Bk. VIII, ch. 6, n. 12. — (St.) Anselm says ON THE VIRGINAL CONCEPTION, ch. 4, that what follows *because it presides over all* etc. pertains to the reason: God subjected us and the power, which is in us, to a will, so that at its command [imperium] we cannot not move ourselves nor do what it wants, nay it moves us as its instruments ... The Lady, which God gave us, we can neither not obey, nor ought we etc. — Near the end of the argument for *belongs to potency* [potentiae est], which we have restores from codices F H K T and edition 1, the Vatican has *is possible* [possibile].

[8] (St.) Augustine, ON THE TRINITY, Bk. XIII, ch. 5, n. 8: Therefore, one is not blessed, unless he both has all which he wills and wills nothing evilly. Cf. ON THE BLESSED LIFE, n. 10 ff.. — On the following proposition, cf. above d. 1, Doubt 8.

[9] (St.) Anselm in his DIALOGUE ON THE TRUTH, ch. 12, defines justice in this manner: Therefore, justice is the rectitude of the will observed [servata] for its own sake.

there is attained the highest *liberality* — for every liberality comes out of a love [amore],[1] but it is established, that love is an act of the will — moreover, in God there is a positing of a most high Liberality: therefore, also Love and Will.

CONCLUSION

There is a Will in God more properly and in a more complete manner than in us, and without any imperfections.

I RESPOND: It must be said, that in God there is the positing of a *will*, just as the four aforesaid reasons show, on account of the four conditions, namely, *of power, of pleasure, of equity* and *of liberality*, which are about a will; and in God *more properly* and in a more complete manner than in us.

For the will in *us* is through (its) difference from (our) *substance* and (its) *acting* and through (its) distance *from (its) end*;[2] but in *God* (the Will is) through the omnimodal indifference of these, namely, *substance, virtue, acting* and *end*. And, because in us it is through (its) difference from substance and from acting, for that reason (our will is) as *one presiding over* the others and (is) *variable* according to (its) diverse acts. For, on account of[3] (its) difference from (our) *substance*, in which the other powers [potentiae] can be rooted, *it presides over* the other powers, such as sense and appetite. On account of (its) difference *from (its) acting*, there is a *variability* (in it) according to the alternation of (it) affections. But in God (there is) neither; for that reason (the Divine Will)

neither rules inferior powers (in God), nor has a 'being varied' [variari] according to various affections. And, for that reason,[4] because in us it is through (its) distance *from (its) end*, hence it is that it is *indigent*, and for that reason there is in it a *flight* and an *appetite*, and in it there also occurs *sadness*; and there occurs *malice* [malitia], because it can turn aside [obliquari] from (its) end, since it is not conjoined to it. But, in God, (the Divine Will) is entirely *conjoined to (Its) End*, for that reason It has neither *flight* nor *appetite*, nor *sadness* nor *malice*, but (rather) an omnimodal gladness [laetitiam] and justice.

1. 2. 3. And thus the response to the first three (objections) is clear, because though those conditions: *appetite, flight, malice* or *vertibility*, are conditions of a created will, yet they have been entirely separated [semotae sunt] from the Divine Will.

4. To that which is objected, that (a will) is contingent, and variable; it must be said, that there is a contingency *in an act* and/or *in an effect*. If we speak of a contingency *in an effect*, (this) is not only in our effect, but even in many (effects), which are from God. For God works many (things), which He was able to not work, with no repugnance [nullo repugnante]. But, if we speak of contingency *in an act*, by which the will *leaves off* willing and *starts* to will something now,[5] now it wills *something*, now it wills *the opposite*; this occurs in a human will, because between a human will and (its) act there is a difference; wherefore it is neither always in one act, nor in a uniform act. But the Divine Will on account of Its identity with (Its) act cannot entirely be varied, nor does It have in Itself any contingency; and for that reason all the (things) sought are clear.

SCHOLIUM

I. Articles I and II treat here of the Will in the proper sense; Article III of the Will (as Its) *signs*; concerning *liberty*, which befits the Divine Will in (Its) works ad extra, not a few (words) are said in the Tract on free will in SENT., Bk. II, d. 25, especially, p. I, q. 1, and p. II, qq. 1 and 2. — In what manner God's liberty can be posited together with His immutability, is a most difficult question, in which very many theologians have labored to clarify; cf. above d. 8, p. I, a. 2, qq. 1 and 2, d. 35, q. 2, in reply to n. 3; d. 43, Doubt 4; d. 39, Doubt 5; d. 47, qq. 1 and 2.

The doctors agree in the conclusions; yet, there are some,

who posit that *pursuit* and *flight* can in some manner be transferred to God.

II. Alexander of Hales, SUMMA., p. I, q. 34. m. 1 and 2. — (Bl. John Duns) Scotus, REPORTATIO., here in qq. 1 and 2. — St. Thomas, here in q. 1, a. 1; SUMMA., I, q. 19, a. 1; SUMMA CONTRA GENTILES., Bk. I, chs. 72 and 73. — Bl. (now St.) Albertus (Magnus), here in a. 1 and 2; SUMMA., p. I, tr. 20, q. 79, m. 1. — (Bl.) Peter of Tarentaise, here in q. 1, a. 1 and 2. — Richard of Middleton, here in a. 1, q. 1. — Giles the Roman, here in 1st princ., q. 1. — Henry of Ghent, SUMMA., a. 45, q. 1. — Durandus (of Saint-Pourçain), here in q. 1. — (Bl.) Dionysius the Carthusian, on this and the following question, here in q. 1.

---

[1] Cf. above d. 10, a. 1, q. 1 f..

[2] Or it differs from the substance of the soul and from the act of willing and is distant from its end. — On the difference of the will from the substance of the soul and from the act of willing, cf. above d. 3, p. II, a. 1, q. 3, and d. 8, p. II, q. 2; on the distance of the will from its end, cf. above d. 1, a. 3, qq. 1 and 2.

[3] Codex V before *On account of* [propter] repeats *As one presiding* [praesidens], beginning the new proposition thus: *As one presiding: on account of* etc. [Praesidens: propter]. A little further below this, for *there is a variability (in it) according to the alternation* [est variabilitas secundum alternationem] the Vatican edition has *it is variable according to the alteration* [est variabilis secundum alterationem].

[4] The Vatican edition omits *for that reason* [ideo], in place of which cod. R has *again* [iterum]. The reading received by us is less

smooth, but is confirmed by nearly all the codices. A little further below this, for *malice, because it can* [malitiam, quia potest] codex M has *a malice, by which it can* [malitiam, qua potest].

[5] The Vatican edition, together with codex cc, reads thus: *in an act, that the will now wills something, not leaves off willing something* [in actu, quod voluntas modo vult aliquid, modo desinit aliquid velle], which reading we have emended from codex T, as demanded here by the context. The other codices support our reading only in part; thus codices K and R, together with edition 1, omit the second *something* [aliquid]. Not a few codices falsely add *to be* [esse] after *something* [aliquid]. A little further below this, for *because between* [quia inter] very many codices, together with editions 2, and 3, faultily read *for which reason between* [quare inter], and at the end of the solution edition 1 has *the objections* [obiecta] for *the (things) sought* [quaesta].

QUESTION II

Whether God is said (to be) "omnivolent", just as (He is said to be) "omniscient" and "omnipotent"?

Second, with it supposed that in God there is a positing of a will, there is asked, whether there is a positing of Him[1] as omnivolent, so that He be said from (His) Will (to be) "*omnivolent*" (i. e. all willing), just as from (His) Power and Knowledge (He is said to be) "omnipotent" and "omniscient". And that (it is) so, seems:

1. Because God is not said (to be) "omnipotent", by this, that He can (do) all, but because He can (do) everything, which befits [decet] His Power[2] — for He cannot (do) evils — but similarly God wills everything which befits His Will to will: therefore, He ought to be said (to be) "*omnivolent*", just as (He is said to be) "omnipotent".

2. Likewise, just as God's *cognitive* (power) holds itself to the true, so (His) *affective* (power) or Will to the good;[3] but (His) cognitive (power) or Intelligence embraces every truth [verum] — wherefore he who would said, that God is ignorant of any truth, would narrow [arctaret] and derogates from His Intelligence — therefore, for an equal reason, since (His) Intelligence is not broader nor more perfect than (His) Will, (His) Will will be in respect of every good: therefore, just as He is said (to be) "*omniscient*", because He knows every truth, so "*omnivolent*", because He wills every good.

3. Likewise, just as God is said (to be) *the Truth of every truth* [verum omnis veri], from Whom, that is, every truth has truth [veritatem], so He is *the Good of every good* [bonum omnis boni], from Whom every good has goodness [bonitatem];[4] but God in seeing His own Truth, because It is the Reason for all, cognizes all: therefore, similarly, by loving [diligendo] His own Goodness loves every good. But everything which He loves, He wills: therefore, He wills every good, just as He also cognizes every truth [verum], and thus etc..

4. Likewise, a *good* will is that which extends itself to *many* goods: therefore, *a better (will)* to *more (goods)*, and *the best one* to all, therefore, *an Infinite one* to *infinite* (goods): therefore just as (God's) *Power* and *Knowledge* extend themselves to (things) all and infinite, so also (His) *Will*: therefore, according to the reckoning by which, He is said (to

be) "*omnipotent*" and "*omniscient*", by an equal reckoning He ought to be said (to be) "*omnivolent*".

ON THE CONTRARY: 1. In the Psalm (there is written).[5] *All whichsoever He willed, He has done*, therefore, He wills nothing, but what He does; but He can do more, and He cannot (do anything) but as One willing: therefore, He can will more. But, if God could know more, He would not be omniscient: ergo etc..

2. Likewise, if man knew something, which God did not know, He would not be the all knowing [omnisciens] God: therefore, since man wills something, which God does not will, as for example to commit theft [facere furtum], therefore, God is not all willing [omnivolens].

3. Likewise, if '*to be able (to do) an evil*' were a '*being able*', God would not be omnipotent, because He cannot (do) evils: therefore, since '*to will evil*' is *a willing*, and God does not will evils, God is not *omnivolent*. *Proof of the minor.* And evil (deed) is not evil, except because (it is) voluntary, because, according to (St.) Augustine,[6] « a sin to this extent is a voluntary » etc., therefore, the reckoning of a will is retained [salvatur] in an evil (deed), similarly also the act of the will in willing an evil (deed): ergo etc..

4. Likewise, '*to will an evil*' either is a *willing* [nolle], or it is a *not-willing* [nolle]. If a *willing*, I have (obtained) the proposed (conclusion); if a *not-willing*; but 'to not will an evil' is a good: therefore, '*to will an evil*'[7] is a good: therefore, if God wills every good, God wills an evil, which is false. Therefore, it remains, that '*to will an evil*' is a *willing*; and God does not will an evil: therefore, God is not *omnivolent*. — But that argument is a sophistic one, because it could similarly be objected concerning the (Divine) Power. — And for that reason there is asked, whence is this, that '*to will an evil*' is a *willing*, but '*to be able (to do) evil*' belongs not to power, but to impotence.

In accord with this, one asks concerning the comparison of *power*, *wisdom* and *will* to their objects, according to (their) ambit.

---

[1] The Vatican edition has *of It* (i.e. the Will) [ipsam], and then *and thus (whether)* [et ita] for *so that* [ut ita].

[2] See the words of (St.) Anselm cited above in d. 42, a. sole, q. 3, p. 754, footnote 10. — Next, codex T, with one or the other codex, omits *His* [eius] at *His Will* [voluntatem eius].

[3] For just as *the true* is the object of the intellect, so the good is the object of the will. Hence, even Aristotle, RHETORICS, Bk. I, ch. 25 (ch. 10) defines the will in this manner: Moreover, the will (is) a seeking after [appetitio] the good with reason; for no one wills, but what he thought is good. — Immediately after this, the Vatican edition with ed. 1 reads *(His) cognitive or intellective (power)* [cognitiva sive intellectiva] for *(His) cognitive (power) or Intelligence* [cognitiva sive intelligentia]. Then, the Vatican ed. with cod. cc omits *would narrow and* [arctaret et].

[4] On the first part of this proposition, cf. (St.) Augustine, SOLILO-QUIES, Bk. I, ch. 1, n. 2, and ON THE TRUE RELIGION, ch. 36, n. 66; and also (St.) Anselm, DIALOGUE ON THE TRUTH, ch. 10s and 13; on the second part see (St.) Augustine, ON THE TRINITY, Bk. VIII, ch. 3, n. 4, and (St. Severinus) Boethius, ON THE SEVEN RULES, or "In what manner substances, in that which they are, are good". — Next for *seeing* [videndo], which we have placed on the authority of codices P and Q (T in the margin) and even of edition 1, very many codices have *saying* [dicendo]; the Vatican edition, together with codex cc, has *cognizing* [cognoscendo].

Then edition 1 omits the particle *in* [in] before *seeing* [videndo], which reading would be preferable, if the codices did not withstand it.

[5] Psalm 113:11.

[6] In (his) book, ON THE TRUE RELIGION, ch. 14, v. 27, and in (his) RETRACTATIONS, Bk. I, ch. 43, n. 5: But now (I say) that a sin is a voluntary evil to this extent, that it is in no manner a sin, if it is not voluntary.

[7] In codex Z there is here interjected: *since it is the same as 'to not will' hypothetically* [cum sit idem quod nolle per hypothesim]. After a few (words) for *God wills an evil* [Deus vult malum] the Vatican edition, together with codex cc, has *God wills every evil* [Deus vult omne malum]. — Note, that the Seraphic Doctor, a little below this, calls this argument a "*sophistic one*" [sophisticum], and justly, because the first consequence: *therefore, 'to will an evil' is good* [ergo velle malum est bonum], as a proposition, is in itself false, and the sayings, "*to will an evil*" [velle malum] and "*to not will an evil*" [nolle malum] are not the same. That it is sophistic, is proven also from this reckoning, because, as the Seraphic Doctor rightly adjoins, *it could similarly be objected concerning the (Divine) Power* [similiter posset obiici de potentia]: for it could be similarly proven, that God either is not omnipotent, and/or can (do) evil, because 'to be able (to do) evil' either is a 'being able' or (is) not: ergo etc..

CONCLUSION

*It is simply denied, that God is said (to be) "omnivolent",
just as He is rightly said (to be) "omniscient" and
"omnipotent".*

I RESPOND: It must be said, that when it is asked,
"Whether God is *omnivolent?*", that expression can
cause a twofold understanding from this, that that,
which is *"omni-"*, can cause a distribution *simply* and/or
as *now.*[1] If it causes a distribution *simply* as much as regards act and habit, then one is said (to be) "omnivolent", because he wills every willable [volibile]; if as
now, one is said (to be) "omnivolent", because he wills
every *willed* [volitum].

In each sense it has a falsehood (in regard to God's
Will),[2] and in each sense it has truth in regard to [in]
(God's) *Power* and in regard to (God's) *Knowledge*. And
for that reason it is simply conceded, that God is *omniscient* and *omnipotent*, and it is simply denied, that He
is *omnivolent*.

The understanding of and reason for this is clear.
For if we accept (the matter) *simply*, (then) "God knows
every knowable and can (do) every possible, and does not
will every willable"; because the Divine Will conveys an
actual cause, but the Power abstracts from the reckoning
of actuality and posits the[3] *reckoning of a cause*, but the
Knowledge abstracts from the reckoning of *each*. Therefore, because God is not the *actual* Cause of all which He
can cause and/or will, just as *He does not* cause every willable, so *He does* not *will* (every willable). However, because *the Power* abstracts from the reckoning of *actuality*,
for that reason It is said not only in respect of (things) to
be done in act, but even in respect of (things) able [possi-
bilium] to be done by God. However, because *the Knowledge* abstracts from the reckoning of *each*, hence it is, that
the Knowledge is not only in respect of (things) to be
done, but even in respect of (things) possible, not only for
God, but even for others, such as [utpote] possible evils.
Therefore, this is the reason, because the act of *knowledge*,
such as 'to know', is through the manner of a *habit*; similarly too (the act)[4] of *power* (is) through the manner of *a
habit*, such as 'to be able'; *the will* (is) through the manner
of *an act*, such as 'to will'. For that reason, the (Divine)
Knowledge is of all knowables, the (Divine) Power (is) of
all possibles, which belong to power, but the (Divine) Will
is not of all willables. And, for that reason, God cannot
know and/or *be able (to do)* more, yet He can *will* more.

Similarly, if we accept the matter[5] as *now* in respect of a
foreseen thing and in respect of one *done* and *willed; the (Divine)*

Knowledge is in respect of every thing, in which the reckoning of knowledge is conserved [salvatur], and *the (Divine) Power* (is) in respect of every thing, in which the
reckoning of power is conserved; but *the (Divine) Will* is
not in respect of every thing, in which the reckoning of
a will is conserved. For *the Knowledge* is in respect of all
(things) future and present and past, good and evil, because in these [ibi] the reckoning of knowledge and of
nobility is conserved; because '*to know evil*' is a knowing,
and '*to know evil*' belongs to nobility.[6] Similarly, *the Power*
is in respect of all goods, in which there is alone conserved the reckoning of power. For '*to be able (to do) evil*'
is not a '*being able*'. Wherefore, '*to be able (to do) evil*' not
only derogates from *the perfection* of a power, but also
from *the power* itself, because '*to be able to fail*' is not a
'being able'; and for that reason (God is) still omnipotent.[7] However, *the Will* is in respect of goods alone, not
in respect of evils. And though in willing an evil the *dignity* of the will is not conserved, yet *the reckoning of willing* is conserved, because '*to will an evil*' is a willing. And
hence it is, that God is not said (to be) "omnivolent", because He does not will evil, but yet He is said (to be)
"omnipotent", even though He cannot (do) evil.

If *it be asked:*[8] "For what reason is the reckoning of
power not conserved in respect of evil, just as the reckoning of will (is)?", it must be said, that "*power*" means,
that very thing [id] which it means, through a manner
of *habit* and of *positing* (a perfection),[9] speaking of active
power; whence, when it is in respect of a privation, it is
no longer a power, but a defect of power; but "*will*"
means, that very thing which it means, through the
manner of a certain *indifference* and *complacency*. Therefore, because in evil the reckoning of consent [consen-
sus] and complacency is conserved, just as also in the
respect of good; for that reason '*to will evil*' is a willing,
but '*to be able (to do) evil*' is not a 'being able'.

1. To that which is objected, that God wills everything which befits (His Power); it must be said, that that
is not the reason, for which He is said (to be) "omnipotent",[10] but that which was assigned beforehand (is),
namely, because He can (do) everything which to be
able (to do) belongs to power.

2. To that which is objected, that the cognitive
(power) embraces every truth, and the affective (power)
every good; it must be said, that the latter embraces in
one manner, the former in another. For *the cognitive
(power)* embraces actually[11] by cognizing everything
which is true and which can be; but *the affective (power)*,
because its act is in the reckoning of an act, embraces
and wills the good alone, which is and/or shall be. *Again,*

---

[1] On the distributive sign, omne, see above d. 4, a. sole, q. 2, Scholium
I, n. 2. A distribution *simply* through this sign, omni-, comprehends both
what is such in act, and what is such in habit or what can be such; but a distribution as *now* comprehends only what is such in act. — A little before,
for *understanding* [intellectum] ed. 1 has *understainding* [intelligentiae].

[2] Supply together with edition 1 *in regard to God's will* [in vol-
untate]. The Vatican edition, together with codex cc, proceeds thus: *and
becasue in each ... and in regard to (God's) Knowledge, for that reason
it is simply* etc. [et quia in utroque ... et in scientia, ideo simplicter etc.].

[3] The Vatican edition and edition 1 adjoins *habitual*, with the
codices not supporting this. A little before this, for *and does not will* [et
non vult] the Vatican edition has *but does not will* [sed non vult].

[4] Supply with codex M *the act* [actus]. Next for *the will* [volun-
tas] the Vatican ed. with codex cc, has *(that) of the will* [voluntatis]

[5] For *the matter* [rem] the Vatican edition alone has *"omni-"*
[omne], and then has *foreknown* [praescitae] for *foreseen* [praevisae].
The words *in respect of every thing* [respectu omnis rei], which are next
had after *and the (Divine) Power (is)* [et potentia], we have recalled from
codices M X (T in the margin) and edition 1.

[6] Cf. above d. 39, a. 1, q. 2. — A little before this, for *and of nobility* [et nobilitatis] many codices have less congruously *and nobility* [et
nobilitatis].

[7] Understand: though He cannot do evils. Cf. above d. 42, q. 2.
— The Vatican edition reads *(God) is still said (to be) "omnipotent"*
[adhuc dicitur omnipotens].

[8] Codex R has *If, therefore, it be asked* [Si igitur quaratur].

[9] That is, it always in itself includes and respects something or being which is positive and good. Next, for *in respect of
a privation* [respectu privationis] codex R has *a cause of a privation* [causa privationis], and then for *indifference* [indifferen-
tiae] the Vatican edition, together with editions 4 and 5, has
adherence [adhaerentiae].

[10] Namely, "because He can (do) everything which befits His
Power", as is said in the objection.

[11] The Vatican edition alone has *habitually* [habitualiter]. Next,
for *because its act* [quia actus eius] codex R has *because its effect* [quia
effectus eius]. That each word signifies the same, is manifest below at the
end of the Question.

the act of the cognitive (power) embraces the whole truth, because nothing is known but the true[1] — for 'to know the false' is not a knowing — but an act of the will does not embrace the good entirely — for 'to will the opposite of the good' is a willing — and hence it is, that God by knowing every truth is said (to be) "omniscient", but not so by willing every good (is He said to be) "omnivolent".

3. To that which is objected, that God by cognizing Himself, who is the Truth Itself, cognizes every truth: ergo etc.; it must be said, that (this) is true, but in another manner: because by cognizing Himself[2] He is the *Exemplary* Cause, and the Exemplary Cause not only of (things) future, but even of (things) able to be done by God. But by loving Himself as the Good He is the *Actual* Cause, as will be clear;[3] and for that reason it does not follow, that He wills but the good, which will be and/or (which) He will do, and on account of this He cannot be said (to be) "omnivolent". Yet, there is another reason for this, as will be clear in (Master Peter's) text.[4]

4. To that which is objected concerning the will, that that which extends itself to more is better; it must be said, that the will is a rational act; wherefore the will is not said (to be) "better", because (it is) *simply* for more, but because (it is) *reasonably* for more. And since right reason dictates, that creatures come to be in a definite number, because an infinite number does not suit [competit][5] things; for that reason the best and most perfect Will wills good things to be in some number, but yet finite: and from this it does not follow, that the Will is of (things) infinite and/or of all possibles, nor even of all. — Yet, it can be said, that that, if it has truth anywhere, has it only there, where a will receives something from the willed; but God's Will receives nothing, and for that reason It is not better by willing three goods rather than one, and a thousand rather than three; and for that reason that reckoning is not valid in the proposed.

From these that, which is accustomed to be asked: "Whether *the (Divine) Will* and *Power* and *Wisdom* are equal?", is clear. For it must be said, that there is a speaking of these as much as regards (Their) *affecting* or *acting*, and as much as regards (Their) *effect*, and as much as regards (their) *object*.[6] If as much as regards (Their) *act*; thus there is among Them [ibi] an omnimodal equality and circumincession; as it clear, because whatever God knows and can (do), He wills to know and to be able (to do), and <u>vice</u> <u>versa</u>. If as much as regards (Their) *effect*; thus They are still equal, because God effects nothing except through (His) Power, Wisdom and Will. If as much as regards (Their) *object* or that which They connote [connotatum], They are[7] unequal: for *the (Divine) Knowledge* in this manner is in more, and *the Power* (is) in less, and *the Will* (is) in less. For *the known* is good and evil; *the possible* is only good, but (both) future and not future; but *the willed* is the good and future only.

SCHOLIUM

I. The Question is to be understood of (God's) *efficacious* Will, or (of the Will) to the extent that « it conveys *an actual cause* » (here in the body of the Response). For the Will is distinguished by the Seraphic Doctor (here in Doubt 2), as it means a *complacency*, and as it means a *cause*. Of the former he teaches: « Insofar as It means a *complacency*, I believe that it can well be said, that (God) *by willing Himself wills all*, because all are pleasing to Him, which are from Him and to Him ». By this love of complacency God loves even possible creatures, as is explicitly taught in SENT., Bk. III, d. 32, q. 1, in reply to n. 1. Therefore, certain (authors) entirely erred, who, with Fr. Bartolomeo Mastri de Moldola, O.F.M. Conv. (1602-1673), argued from this Question of ours, that St. Bonaventure denied, that God loves possible creatures. But, if under "*all*" we comprehend even *evil*, that proposition is to be understood thus, that in the complacency of a good there is implied that the opposite is *displeasing* [implicetur displicentia oppositi] (cf. here in a. 3, q. 2). — One must speak in another manner of (God's) *efficacious* Will, since God by willing Himself does not efficaciously will all possible goods. This it can be clear, in the other sense that the Seraphic (Doctor) and Alexander of Hales (SUMMA., p. I, q. 34, m. 2, in reply to the last) deny this proposition: "God, by willing Himself, wills all"; wherefore in this the Doctors do not contradict themselves. Otherwise, it is commonly taught, that the *primary, adequate* and *motive* object of the divine Will is the Divine Goodness Itself, but *the secondary* (object) is creatures, to the extent that they participate in the Divine Goodness (cf. Doubt 3, and above d. 1, Doubt 12). — At the end of the argument, there are posited two incidental questions; the first is solved at the end of the body of the Response, the second after the solution of objections.

II. Alexander of Hales, SUMMA., p. I, q. 34, m. 3, q. 21, m. 1, a. 2, collateral question. — St. Thomas, SUMMA CONTRA GENTILES., Bk. I, chs. 76 and 81; and in regard to the principle SUMMA., I, q. 19, a. 2 and 3. — Bl. (now St.) Albertus (Magnus), here in a. 5. — (Bl.) Peter of Tarentaise, here in q. 1, a. 3. — Richard of Middleton, here in a. 1, q. 5. — (Bl.) Dionysius the Carthusian, here in q. 1.

---

[1] Cf. above p. d. 39, a. 1, q. 3, p. 690, footnote 2.

[2] The Vatican edition adds *as true* [verum], codices T and X add *as cognized or true* [cognitum sive verum]. A little before this, codd. P & Q read *but in one and another manner* [sed aliter et aliter] for *but in another manner* [sed aliter]. A little further below this, the Vatican ed. prefixes to the words *the Exemplary Cause* [futurorum] the words *He is* [est].

[3] Here in a. 2, q. 1, where there is expounded, that the Divine Goodness is the reason of causing both in the reckoning of an *effective cause* and in the reckoning of a *final cause*.

[4] Below in d. XLVI, ch. 3 ff., where there is assigned this reason, that God cannot will evil; which reason the Seraphic Doctor also adduces here in the body of the Question. — For *will be clear* [patebit] the Vatican edition has *is clear* [patet].

[5] Concerning which, see above d. 43, q. 3. — A little after this, for *but yet* [sed tamen] edition 1 has *but only* [sed tantum].

[6] The Vatican ed. with codd. aa & bb omits *affecting or* [affectum sive], but codices aa and bb preface to *as much as regards (Their) act* [quantum ad actum] another new member alongside: *(Their) substance and/or quasi subject* [substantiam vel quasi subiectum], and, then, after *as much as regards (Their) object* [quandum ad obiectum] they proceed thus: *If in the first manner, thus they are entirely the same. If as much as regards (Their) act* etc. [Si primo modo, sic sunt omnino idem. Si quantum ad actum etc.]. The expression *circumincession*, which follows next, signifies here nothing other, than that that where one of these acts is present, there the other will also be.

[7] For *They are* [sunt] very many codices have *then (They are)* [tunc]. — On the incidental question here solved, cf. Alexander of Hales, SUMMA., p. I, q. 20, m. 4 and 5, and q. 34, m. 3, and Hugo of St. Victor's libellus, « On God's Power and Will, which be greater? », in which there occurs the same distinction as much as regards *affecting, effecting* and *respecting* (the object).

ARTICLE II

On God's Will, as much as regards (Its) causality.

As much as regards the second Article there is the question concerning the Divine Will, namely, as much as regards (Its) causality. And, about this, two (questions) are asked.

First, there is asked in general, whether God's Will is the Cause of things.

Second, whether It is (their) First and Immediate Cause.

QUESTION I

Whether God's Will is the cause of things in general?

And, that It is the Cause (of things in general), is shown in this manner:

1. (St.) Hilary (of Poitiers says) in (his) book, ON SYNODS: « To all creatures the (Divine) Will conferred [attulit] substance, but to the Son It gave the Nature ».

2. Likewise, (St.) Augustine (says) in (his) book, AGAINST THE MANICHEANS: « One must respond to those, who desire to know the Will of God, that the Will of God is the very Cause of all which are ».

3. Likewise, it seems *by reason.* because God is the Cause of things; but of every thing, of which God is the Cause, He is through (His) Knowledge, Power and Will: therefore, either He is the Cause, because (He is) *powerful*, or because (He is) *knowing*, or because (He is) *willing*. Not because (He is) *powerful*, because He can (do) many (things), which He does not do; similarly neither because (He is) *knowing*: therefore, because (He is) *willing*, for that reason He makes (all things). But « a cause is (that), of which there follows another "being" »:[3] ergo etc..

4. Likewise, God is the Cause of created things: therefore, either through *nature*, or through *will*, or through *chance* and *fortune*.[4] Not through *change* and *fortune*, because such are causes according to an imperfect reckoning; not through *nature*, because thus a similar is produced out of a similar: therefore, it remains that (God is the Cause of created things), through will: ergo etc..

ON THE CONTRARY: 1. If God's Will is the Cause (of all things in general), either (It is such) by reason of *what It principally signifies* [ratione principalis significati], or by reason of *what It connotes* [ratione connotati]. If[5] by reason of *what It principally signifies*: therefore, since

(God's) Wisdom, Power, Will and Essence signify the Same, for the same reason They ought to be said (to be) "the Cause". If by reason of *what It connotes*, I ask, "What is that?" There is not granting that (It connotes anything) but *an effect*; but *an effect* is consequent to the reckoning of a cause, and not the other way around: therefore not by reason of what It connotes. And *again*, if It connotes an effect: therefore, in no manner can there be said: "God wills Himself to be", since about Himself It effects entirely nothing, which is false.

2. Likewise, either (God's) Will is the Cause through *a property*, or through *an appropriation*. If through *a property*, then, therefore, (God's) Wisdom and Power are not causes. If through *an appropriation*, therefore, either because there is in the Will a reckoning of causality through (the consideration of what is) *prior*, or because (there is such) *more immediately*. Not because (there is something) *prior*, for (God's) Power and Wisdom antecede the Will according to the reckoning of understanding. Neither because (there is such a reckoning) *more immediately*, because Hugh (of St. Victor)[6] says that « God moves through (His) Will, disposes through (His) Wisdom, and executes through (His) Power »: therefore, (His) Knowledge and Power have a more immediate comparison to (His) work than (does His) Will: ergo etc..

3. Likewise, either (the Divine Will) is the Cause (of all things in general) on account of (Its) *virtue* of acting, or on account of (Its) *manner* (of acting). Not on account of (Its) *virtue*,[7] because "*will*" does not mean virtue, but "*power*" does. If on account of (Its) *manner of acting*: on the contrary: the manner of acting through the manner of nature is more noble: therefore, the (Divine) Nature is rather the Cause (of all things). *Proof*: that agent is more virtuous, which

---

[1] Number 58. You will find the original text above in d. 6, a. sole, q. 2, p. 127, footnote 2.

[2] ON GENESIS AGAINST THE MANICHEANS, Bk. I, ch. 2, n. 4. See the text of Master (Peter) here, in ch. 4.

[3] Cf. above d. 5, Doubt 3, p. 120, footnote 7.

[4] Cf. Aristotle, PHYSICS, Bk. II, text 49 (ch. 5), where he treats of (those) acting through nature and will. We have cited the text itself above in d. 2, a. sole, q. 4, p. 56, footnote 6. Cf. also PHYSICS, Bk. II, text 50 ff., where he deals with chance and fortune, which are imperfect causes or (causes) per accidens and in this they differ among themselves, wherefore fortune properly has a place in free causes, but chance in natural ones. Cf. also METAPHYSICS, Bk. VII, text 22 ff. (Bk. VI, ch. 7), and Bk. XII, text 13 ff. (Bk. XI, ch. 3) where these four causes, by which something comes to be, are adduced as one together.

[5] Codex T has *But if* [Sed si].

[6] ON THE SACRAMENTS, Bk. I, p. II, ch. 6, where dealing with these three perfecta and all perfecting (Causes), he says: And these three were the (Divine) Power, Wisdom, (and) Will; and these three concur to one effect, not is anything acquitted [absolvitur], unless these be at hand. The Will moves, the Knowledge disposes, the Power works. — In the passage from Hugh (of St. Victor), the Vatican edition, together with codex cc, falsely cites the author as (St.) Augustine [Augustinus], and, a little after this, for *comparison* [comparationem] it substitutes *cooperation* [cooperationem].

[7] After *virtue* [virtutem] the Vatican edition repeats *of acting* [agendi], and, a little below this, after *through the manner of nature* [per modum naturae] codex bb reads *is better and more noble: therefore* etc. [melius est et nobilior: ergo etc.].

is more sufficient and produces a more noble effect; but nature is more sufficient in acting and needs fewer (things) and produces a more noble effect than art or a voluntary agent:[1] ergo etc.. — Likewise, that (It is) not as much as regards *the manner* (of acting), seems, because an agent, which gives to the one produced completely similar, natural properties, acts through the manner of nature; but God gives to His own effects a unity, truth and goodness; nor can He make (anything) without these, and those are the natural properties of the Divine Substance: therefore, God acts through the manner of nature, not of will.

4. Likewise, everything acting voluntarily is an agent by preconceiving; but God does not act by preconceiving, just as Dionysius (the Areopagite) says, ON THE DIVINE NAMES,[2] because, just as the Sun illumines not by preconceiving, so God creates not by preconceiving: ergo etc..

CONCLUSION

The reckoning of causality is attributed to God under the reckoning of the Will, not so under other reckonings.

I RESPOND: For an understanding of the aforesaid it must be noted, that although the Divine Essence is one most simple Thing [quid], yet « It is an infinite sea of substance ».[3] And, for that reason, all which are found in us through diversity, all, I say, are found in God in a more noble manner through an omnimodal identity, yet nevertheless according to an omnimodal perfection and truth. Wherefore, just as in us *wisdom*, *power* and *will* is truly a being and the cause of the things, which are from us; so they are too in God, but yet they are one [unum]. And, although they be one,[4] because our intellect cannot comprehend the infinity of that Substance nor express (It) through one word;

for that reason we understand God in manner manners and express (Him) with diverse names; and according to which we understand (Him) through those manners, we enunciate more (Divine Names), so that we attributed to God something through one manner, which (we do) not according to another, and indeed truly, because all (names) have in God a true existence.[5] And for that reason since in one manner we understand God, when we say *that God (is) good*, in another, when we say *that God (is) eternal*; we concede, that He diffuses Himself, because He is *good*, not because (He is) *eternal*; for this is a property of *goodness*, not of *duration*. Hence it is, that when we understand, that there is truly a Will in God, and the property of a will is to produce those which go forth (from it) through the manner of liberality, (we understand) that we are saying, that God, inasmuch as He is *a will*, is the Cause of things.

Moreover, the reason, for which causality is attributed to the Will, is this, because the reckoning of causing is the *goodness* both in the reckoning of the *effective* (principle) and in the reckoning of the *end*. For « the good is said (to be) diffusive (of itself) », « and the good is (that) *on account of which all (are)* ».[6] Moreover, an *effective (principle)* is not made effective in an effect except *on account of an end*. Therefore, that, which means the conjunction of an effective principle with an end, is the reason for the causing in the effect; but a will is an act, according to which the good is reflected upon the good or goodness: therefore, a will unites an effective (principle) with an end. And hence it is, that a will is the reason working the causing in the effect; and for that reason we attribute to God the reckoning of causality under the reckoning of the Will, not so under other reckonings.

And this is gathered from the words of Dionysius in the fourth (book), ON THE DIVINE NAMES,[7] where he says, that « all (things) desire [appetunt] (that) Goodness as (their) *containment* [continentiam] and as (their) *beginning* and as (their) *end*: as the *beginning*, from which they are; as *the containment*, through which they are saved; as *the end*, unto which they tend ». Wherefore, « the Divine Love is a certain eternal

---

[1] Aristotle, ETHICS, Bk. II, ch. 6: But virtue is more exact and better than every art, according to which measure nature (is) too.

[2] Chapter 4, § 1. The words of Dionysius (the Areopagite) according to the version of Scotus Erigena are these: For even, just as indeed (is the understanding) which (is) according to us, the Sun is not thinking nor fore-choosing, but by its "being" illumines all which are sharing in its light according to their own reckoning of power; so also the Best above the Sun, as above (Its) obscure image, sends in an excellent manner the rays of (Its) whole Goodness above the principal example of Its Subsistence to all existing (things). — On the major proposition, cf. Aristotle, ETHICS, Bk. III, ch. 1 ff., and above in d. 40, a. 3, q. 1, p. 714, footnote 3.

[3] On this saying of (St. John) Damascene, cf. above d. 43, a. sole, q. 2, p. 769, footnote 7. — On the manner, in which God eminently contains the all the perfections of creatures, see Dionysius, ON THE DIVINE NAMES, ch. 5, § 3-10, and (St.) Anselm, MONOLOGION., chs. 15-18.

[4] The Vatican edition and codex cc omit *Although they be one* [quamvis unum sint]. After *they be one* [unum sint] codices Q and R insert *yet* [tamen], which particle codex Y inserts before *Although* [quamvis]. A little above this, the codices, together with edition 1, read *just as it is in us* [sicut in nobis est] for *just as in us* [sicut in nobis].

[5] Cf. above d. 22, q. 2 ff.. — Here codex Z reads *all are true and in God have a true existence* [omnia sunt vera et in Deo habent veram existentiam] for *all (names) have in God a true existence* [omnia in Deo habent veram existentiam]. A little below this after *we concede* [concedimus] the Vatican edition, together with codex cc, omits the explicit *He* [eum], and then edition 1 for *when we understand* [cum intelligimus] exhibits *since we understand* [cum intelligamus].

[6] These two texts are from Dionysius, the first of which has been taken

according to sense from (his) book, ON THE CELESTIAL HIERARCHIES, ch. 4, and from (his) book, ON THE DIVINE NAMES, ch. 4. The other text has been contracted from these words, which are had in (his) book, ON THE DIVINE NAMES, ch. 4, § 31: The beginning and the end will be the good. For on account of the good all, and whatsoever (are) contrary, (are). For indeed we even do the latter, desiring the good; for no one looking back to evil does what he does. Cf. above also Aristotle, METAPHYSICS, Bk. V, text 3, and Bk. XII, text 54 ff. (Bk. IV, ch. 2, and Bk. XI, ch. 19), MAGNA MORALIA, Bk. I, ch. 2 (ch. 1), and EUDEMEAN ETHICS, Bk. I, ch. 5 (ch. 8). — A little further below this, for *reason for the causing* [ratio causandi] many codices and edition 1 have *reason for the creating* [ratio creandi] and after a few (words) they have similarly *working the creating* [creare faciens] for *working the causing* [causare faciens].

[7] Chapter 4, § 4: « And all desire that (Goodness) as (their) beginning, as (their) containment, (and) as (their) end, and It is the Best, as the sayings say, out of Which all subsist and are as (things) adduced out of a most perfect cause, and in Which all have been constituted as guarded and comprehended in an omnipotent decree [consulto], and unto Which all are converted as each one unto its own height [summitatem], and all desire It ». The following text is had ibid., § 14: The Divine Love [amor] is shown differently, just as a certain, eternal cycle (κύκλος), through the Best, out of the Best and in the Best and unto the Best, circulating according to an ineffable course [inenarrabili conversione] both in the same and through the very same, and always going forward, remaining and revolved. — For *eternal cycle* [cyclus aeternus] edition 1 has *eternal circle* [circulus aeternus], but the other editions and all the codices have *eternal act* [actus aeternus]. But that reason seems to be an error of copyists.

cycle, out of the Best, through the Best and unto the Best ». From which there is gathered, that the Will means the conjunction of a Principle with an End, and for that reason the Cause in (God's Acting, when He wills to do (something); so that (His) actuality in causing is referred to the Will, not for the instant, in which He has a will, but in that (instant) in which He wills to make (something). Just as I will to hear Mass tomorrow, and (my) will[1] will cause me to be in act tomorrow in respect of the willed; in His own manner there is (a will) in God.

1. To that which is asked: "Whether the reckoning of causality convenes with the Will on account of what It connotes, and/or on account of the thing It signifies?"; I say, that neither on account of the *thing* signified only, nor on account of *what It connotes*, but on account of the thing signified *in this manner*, because the Divine Essence is signified as a will, to which manner of signifying there responds truth. Whence[2] just as, when we say, a stone is assimilated to God inasmuch as (it is) a *being*, an animal inasmuch as (it is) *living*, and a man inasmuch as (he is) *intelligent*, in truth [revera] essence, intelligence and life are the same in God, yet[3] the very same is given to be understood in another manner, not on account of the connotation, but on account of the infinity of the same Substance, in which all noble properties are one [unum]. Yet, they cannot be signified except through diverse (names).

2. To that which is objected, whether (the Divine Will) is the Cause through a property, or through an appropriation; I say, that simply speaking It is *most properly* the Cause. However, by comparing the Will to *the Knowledge* and *the Power*, It is said (to be) "the Cause" through *an appropriation*; and this, because the Will Itself signifies God as an *actual* cause. Wherefore in the Will there is found first the reckoning of *actuality*, not of causality.[4] For the (Divine) Power and Knowledge, even if they have the reckoning of a habitual cause, yet, not

of an actual one except through the Will. Wherefore the Will works a disposition from the Knowledge, or causes that the Knowledge be disposing, and the Power (to be) executing; for that reason *He disposes*, because He wills, and for that reason *He causes*, because He wills. And thus that (objection) is clear.

3. To that which is asked: "For what reason is the Will said (to be) "the Cause", whether on account of (Its) acting virtue,[5] and/or on account of (Its) manner of acting?"; I say, that (It is such) on account of *each* — for to God *to will* is *to be able* — yet, more principally by reason of (Its) *manner of acting*. For the production of a diverse in form and nature out of the liberality alone of the agent pertains to one acting through a will. — What *is objected*, that the manner of a natural agent is more noble; it is true, where the will is not omnipotent; but if art could do everything which it willed, it would not act less nobly[6] than nature. — Yet, it can be said, that the manner of producing of a nature befits [competit] a Person in respect of a Person, but not of the Divine Essence in respect of creatures, because they cannot convene in form.

To that which is objected, that God produces a similar according to properties; it must be said, that a nature produces a similar in special properties, if its is a *particular* agent; and/or if it is a *universal* agent, it produces necessarily, not out of its own liberality; but God (produces) in neither manner.

4. To that which is objected, that God is not a preconceiving agent; it must be said, that this is true concerning the aforethought [praecogitatione],[7] which precedes a will, but it is not true of aforethought in respect of a work. And, in the first manner, Dionysius speaks; but he himself opposes (the application of this principle to God) in the second manner.

SCHOLIUM

I. In the brilliant solution of this Question there is *first* proven in general, that God's *Will* is the Cause of things, and there is destroyed the worst error, which was widespread [late grassatur] in ancient and modern times and is common to all Pantheists, that, namely, God in (his) works ad extra acts through the necessity of the Nature. — *Second* there are brought forward profound reason, why *the (Divine) Will*, rather than *the Knowledge* and *the Power*, is said (to be) "the Cause of things", or why It « holds Itself more immediately to the three » (here in a. 3, q. 1, in reply to n. 1), which reason are found in the 3rd fundament, in the body (of the Response) and in the solution to n. 2. — Though not a few of the School of St. Thomas think, that the (Divine) Intellect through (Its) *command* [imperium] and *practical judgement* [iudicium practicum] concurs more immediately for

the production of things than does the Will; yet the sentence of St. Bonaventure is held as the more common one. — *Third* there is optimally explained that distinction between the Divine attributes, which is called by other either a *virtual* (distinction), or a *fundamental* (distinction), or (a distinction) *according to the reckoning of reasoning* [rationis ratiocinatae].

II. Alexander of Hales, SUMMA., p. I, q. 35, m. 2 and 1. — (Bl. John duns) Scotus, DE RERUM PRINCIPIO, q. 4, a. 2. — St. Thomas, on this and the following question, here in q. 1, a. 2 and 3; SUMMA., I, q. 19, a. 4. — Bl. (now St.) Albertus (Magnus), here in a. 4; SUMMA., p. I, tr. 20, q. 79, m. 2. — (Bl.) Peter of Tarentaise, here in q. 2, a. 1. — Richard of Middleton, here in a. 2, q. 1. — Giles the Roman, here in 2nd princ., q. 1. — Henry of Ghent, SUMMA., a. 36, q. 4. — Durandus (of Saint-Pourçain), here in q. 1. — (Bl.) Dionysius the Carthusian, on this and the following question, here in q. 2.

---

[1] Codices K P and Q, together with edition 1, read *and this will* [et haec voluntas]. A little further above this, for *in causing* [in causando] very many codices again, with edition 1, have *in creating* [in creando].

[2] *That from which* it either super-abounds, and/or exceeds something, *is*, for example, *in a similar manner.*

[3] For *yet* [tamen] the Vatican edition, together with codex cc, has *when* [cum]. Next, for *is given* [datur] very many codices, together with edition 1, have incongruously *are given* [dantur], codices K and Z have *give* [dant].

[4] In the Vatican edition there are missing the words *not of causality* [non causalitatis], which (words) rightly

respect the word *first* [primo]. A little further above this, for *and this, because* [et hoc, quia] codex R has *but through this, that* [sed per hoc quod]. At the end of the solution, the Vatican edition omits *and for that reason He causes, because He wills* [et ideo facit, quia vult].

[5] For *acting virtue* [virtutem agentem] the Vatican edition has *virtue of acting* [virtutem agendi].

[6] The Vatican edition, together with very many manuscripts, has less well *nobly* [noblius] for *nobly* [nobiliter], which codex Y exhibits. Next for *Yet it can* [Potest tamen] codex Z has *Yet it could* [Posset tamen].

[7] The Vatican edition has *preconception* [praeconceptione] for *aforethought* [praecogitatione].

QUESTION II

Whether God's Will is the First and Immediate Cause (of things)?

Second, there is asked, whether the Divine Will is the *First* and *Immediate* Cause (of all things). And that (It is) so, seems:

1. Through (St.) Augustine in the third (book) ON THE TRINITY:[1] « God's Will is the First and Most High Cause of all species and motions ».

2. Likewise, every cause, the first and proper act of which is the production of a thing, is a first and immediate cause; but the Divine Will is of this kind: ergo etc.. *Proof of the middle*: On that (verse) of the Psalm:[2] *Just (is) the Lord in all His ways*, the Gloss (says): « For God that is *to will* what (is) *to make*, because out of His Will things have (their) 'to be' ».

3. Likewise, it seems *by reason*. because every cause is first and immediate, prior to which there is no other;[3] but the Divine Will is a cause, prior to which there is no other, since It is the Same as God: therefore, the (His) Will is the First and Immediate Cause.

4. Likewise, every cause is first and immediate, which is unto a whole effect through its own action; but everything which comes to be, is from God, and nothing can be worked without Him, since it cannot be conserved in 'being' (through itself or without God);[4] and God cooperates with the whole (effect) and unto the whole (effect): ergo etc..

5. Likewise, everyone who cognizes a thing most certainly and nobly, cognizes through a proximate and immediate cause, but the one cognizing and seeing God cognizes things in Him most certainly and most nobly as in prior causes, as (St.) Augustine[5] says: therefore, in God there is a proximate and immediate cause; but (this is) naught but the Will, ergo etc..

6. Likewise, what is attributed to God, ought to be attributed to Him on the confines of all nobility [in fine totius nobilitatis]:[6] if, therefore, the reckoning of causality convenes with Him, the most noble causality ought to be attributed to Him. But this is the reckoning of a first and immediate cause: ergo etc..

ON THE CONTRARY: 1. Of one (thing) there is one immediate cause: therefore, if God is the Immediate Cause of all, it has no other cause than God; and if this, every operation ceases, and thus power ceases, and also goodness ceases, and all others are inactive [otiosa].[7]

2. Likewise, if the Divine Will is the proximate and immediate cause of all; but with a proximate and immediate cause posited, there is posited the effect:[8] therefore, since the Divine Will was from eternity, all other (things) are eternal.

3. Likewise, everything which has a proximate and immediate and necessary cause, is demonstrable:[9] therefore, if the Divine Will is the First and Immediate Cause of all, all are demonstrable.

4. Likewise, with the proximate and immediate cause cognized, there is no further seeking (of a cause):[10] therefore, with it known, that God wills something, he labors foolishly [stulte laborat] who seeks another cause. But of every good, which comes to be, we know that God is the Cause: therefore, there is none further to be sought. Therefore, there perishes and are vain the doctrinal sciences, nay all the sciences.

CONCLUSION

The (Divine) Will is the Immediate Cause of things, since It is the First Cause, the most universal and the most actual.

I RESPOND: For an understanding of this[11] it must be noted, that, since there is among *creatures* the finding of a *universal* and *particular* cause, the universal cause flows

---

[1] Chapter 4, n. 9. In the original text after *of all* [omnium] there is adjoined *corporal* [corporalium].

[2] Psalm 144:17. The Gloss, taken from Cassiodorus, is had in (Nicholas) of Lyra, in which in place of *For God* [Deo] there is read *With Him* [Apud illum].

[3] Aristotle, POSTERIOR ANALYTICS, Bk. I, ch. 2, dealing with the first and immediate principles of demonstration, says: For I say that "first" and "principle" (are) the same. But the principle of a demonstration (is) an immediate proposition. Moreover, an immediate (proposition) is (that), prior to which there is no other. — In the conclusion codices P and Q read *His Will* [voluntas eius] for *the Will* [voluntas].

[4] Understand: *through itself or without God* [per se sive sine Deo]. Cf. above d. 8, p. I, a. 2, q. 2, and d. 37, p. I, a. 1, q. 1. — On this simultaneous concursus of God with creatures in regard to an effect, cf. (St.) Augustine, ON A LITERAL EXPOSITION OF GENESIS, Bk. V, ch. 20, n. 40 ff.. Aristotle, EUDEMEAN ETHICS, Bk. VIII, ch. 18 (ch. 14) says: According to that measure which God is in the universe, all other (things) are alternatively in Him [edition of Firmin-Didot reads: so also (is He) in the soul]: for all are moved are moved by the Divine Power [numine] existing within us.

[5] ON A LITERAL EXPOSITION OF GENESIS, Bk. II, ch. 8, n. 17 ff., ibid., Bk. V, ch. 14, n. 32 ff., and ON THE CITY OF GOD, Bk. XI, ch. 29. — On the major proposition, cf. Aristotle, POSTERIOR ANALYTICS, Bk. I, ch. 2.

[6] This manner of speaking occurs already in Averroës, METAPHYSICS, Bk. XII, text 39, where the author attributes to God a *life on the confines of nobility*, i. e. to the greatest extent [summopere].

[7] Cf. above d. 42, a. sole, q. 1, p. 746, footnote 6.

[8] Cf. above d. 5, a. 2, q. 2, p. 118, footnote 2, and Avicenna, METAPHYSICS, Bk. IV, ch. 1.

[9] According to Aristotle, POSTERIOR ANALYTICS, Bk. I, chs. 2 and 24 (ch. 30), a demonstration ought to be established from first, true, immediate, prior, more known, and necessary principles and causes of the conclusion.

[10] Averroës expounding the words of Aristotle, PHYSICS, Bk. II, text 38 (ch. 3), « But it is necessary [oportet] to seek always the highest cause of each (thing) », says: It is necessary to intend principally concerning causes the ultimate cause in *the question*, not the ultimate one in 'being', and that is the proximate cause; for the ultimate one in 'being' is the remote cause, v. g. when anyone asks: "For what reason does any man build?" and it will be said, "Because he is a builder", and when there is said: "And for what reason is he a builder?", there will be said, "Because he has the art of building"; and here the seeking ends. Cf. also Aristotle, METAPHYSICS, Bk. VIII, text 12 (Bk. VI, ch. 4). — A little further below this, for *which comes to be* [quod fit] the Vatican edition has *in this manner* [sic].

[11] Codex R adds *question* [quaestionis].

in one manner more into the effect than the particular, in another manner less. For as much as regards *interiority* [intimitatem] the universal cause, because it is prior,[1] inflows more, but as much as regards *actuality* and as much as regards those which are *proper* to the thing, it inflows less. And the reason for this is, because a *created* universal cause does not have an omnimodal actuality nor a perfect power; and for that reason it cannot arrive ad the special form except <u>per accidens</u>, such as through a form of a particular agent, which is not from it.[2]

But *the Divine* Will is the First and Most Universal and Most Actual Cause; and for that reason It is able unto the whole effect and unto the whole substance of the thing even without the support [adminiculo] of the other cause; nor can any cause (do) anything and/or a little without It. And for that reason it is necessary, that It be the Immediate Cause in every action and thing. — And the reasons for this are to be conceded.

Regarding the objections unto the contrary, it must be understood, that since God is the Immediate Cause of all, yet He is *the Whole* Cause of certain (things), such as of those which are created; but of certain (things) He is a cause *together with some particular cause*, such as of those which are by nature and by a particular will.[3] And indeed this cause concurs not on account of the indigence of the Divine Will, but on account of (its) most high *Liberality*, which not only grants things to be, but (also) an operation and diffusion, and on account of *the order* and *connection* of each and every (thing) to one another. Nor does the one cause derogate from the other, but the whole effect is from the created cause, and the whole (is likewise) from the uncreated Will.

1. And thus the response to the first objection is clear: for it objects concerning an immediate cause in respect of another created cause, because there are not two created, immediate causes in the same genus of cause.

2. To that which is objected, that with an immediate cause posited etc.; it must be said, that there is a positing of a cause in a twofold manner, either in 'being', and/or in *operating*. And with a cause posited, there is not posited an effect[4] in act, unless (the cause) is posited in working; and it was not thus from eternity, but in time, in which It disposed and willed from eternity to produce the thing.

3. To that which is objected, that all would be demonstrable; it must be said, that it is true, if that cause is proper and determined to such effects.

4. To that which is asked, that another cause ought not be sought; it must be said, that if God's Will and disposition would be fully cognized in itself, no one would ever desire to know another cause; thus he would fully cognize (all) in (their) primordial causes. But yet because the Divine Will is not cognized, nor excludes in (Its) acting the operation of a created cause, It also does not exclude (it) either [nec] in being cognized;[5] and for that reason it is good and very useful to be trained [exerceri] in the consideration of created causes, so that in some manner we may come semi-fully unto the cognition of that Supreme Cause, which is the End of all cognition.

SCHOLIUM

I. God is called "the *First* Cause", because He precedes both in perfection and eternity all secondary causes; but He is not called "*the First*" in the sense, that in (His) concursus with the action of a secondary cause God acts beforehand *in time*. These are conceded by all. But there is a dispute concerning the question, whether in this concursus He ought to be conceived as the First Cause, as One acting beforehand *according to nature* or *by moving beforehand*. — The Seraphic Doctor (above d. 8, p. I, a. 2, q. 1, in reply to n. 1) calls that an "immediate cause", « between which and the effect there falls no other intermediary, causing substance ». By others there is distinguished a twofold *immediacy* [immediatio], namely (that) *of the supposit*, and (that) *of a virtue*. An immediate cause according to the immediacy of *virtue* works by its own virtue, not moved by another cause; which (manner of cause) does not convene with an instrumental cause, which works by means of the virtue of another. Moreover, the immediacy *of a supposit* is understood, when between the cause itself and the effect there is no other intermediary supposit. It is clear that one immediacy can be without the other. For in writing the pen is a *mediated* agent, because it is moved *by the virtue of another*, but according to the reckoning of a *supposit* it itself does attain to an immediate effect. On the contrary the one writing is in respect of the effect an immediate cause by reason of (his) *virtue*, but a mediated (cause) according to the reckoning of a *supposit*. Nevertheless, each immediacy is often conjoined, such as the water of a bath has an immediacy, both of virtue and supposit, in cooling (the body).

II. That God in (His) actions <u>ad extra</u>, of which He is *the sole* Cause, such as in creation, is the immediate Agent according to the reckoning of *supposit* and of *virtue*, is manifest (cf. Response, before the end). That the Seraphic Doctor (solution to n. 1) seems to teach the same twofold immediacy even in regard to (God's) *concursus* with the actions of secondary causes, as Frs. Petrus Trigosus de Catalayud, O.F.M. Cap., (SUMMA., q. 13, a. 4, dubium 4) and Bartolomeo de' Barbieri da Castelvetro, O.F.M. Cap., 1615-1697 A.D., (CURSUS THEOLOGICUS, tome I, disputation 6, q. 6) rightly note. For the Saint says, that *the same* effect can be immediately from an uncreated Cause and a created one, but not from *two created causes*. Nevertheless, there can well be the immediacy of *virtue* alone even in two created causes in respect of the same effect; but not an immediacy in each sense.

III. In regard to God's general concursus with the actions of secondary causes, there were two opinions, extreme and opposed to one another. The first opinion bore off from created things every, truly active and causative virtue; which error, already formulated beforehand by certain ancient philosophers, other later ones wished to defend under the name of *Occasionalism*. This absurd opinion is disproved by St. Bonaventure, SENT., Bk. II, d. 7, p. II, a. 2, q. 1, and elsewhere. — In opposition, Durandus (of Saint-Pourçain) (SENT., Bk. II, d. 1, q. 5; d. 37, q, 1) denies, that God immediately in every action of a creature acts together, to which opinion some both before the age of St. Bonaventure and

---

[1] The Vatican edition has *more potent* [potius] for *prior* [prius]. — Cf. above d. 37, p. I, a. sole, q. 2, p. 471, footnote 3.

[2] Namely a created, universal cause. Cf. above d. 40, Doubt 7. — The older codices, together with edition 1, have *it (i. e. the agent)* [ipso], faultily.

[3] See above d. 38, a. 1, q. 1, in the body (of the Response). — The Vatican edition, together with codex cc, reads *by a particular nature* [a natura particulari] for *by nature and by a particular will* [a natura et a voluntate particulari], and somewhat below this after reads *from the infinite, uncreated Will* [a voluntate infinita increata].

[4] The Vatican edition and codex cc, having inserted after *And with a cause posited* [Et posita causa] the words *in 'being'* [in esse], omits *an effect* [effecuts] (reading *it* for *there* before this). At the end of the solution, for *the thing* [rem] the more ancient codd. with edition 1, have *then* [tunc], codex X has *(the thing which) it then produced* [tunc produxit].

[5] The Vatican edition, having omitted *either* [nec] before *in being cognized* [cognoscendo], here adjoins *the cognition of human reason* [cognitionem rationis humanae] (and thus omits the prior understood *it* and reads *being cognized* as *cognizing*). A little further above this, for *to know another cause* [scire aliam causam] not a few codices have *to know any cause* [scire aliquam causam].

even afterwards adhered. On this question St. Bonaventure, SENT., Bk. II, d. 37, a. 1, q. 1, says: « About this question the positions of great men were to such extent diverse and to such an extent reasonable, that even Master (Peter) did not dare to define, which of them contains more truth. Nevertheless, because doubts are lead through much discussion to be manifested, it is now commonly held, that that opinion is more true, which says, that every action, whether the substrate for a sin or nor, according to this that it is an action, is from God. Nor (is it) undeservedly (held), because it is necessary to posit this, if one weights the eminence of the Divine Power and the indigence of the created power » etc.; which is established there and in a. 2, qq. 1 and 2, Doubt 2, and SENT., Bk. II, d. 14, p. I, a. 3, q. 1; d. 28, a. 2. q. 3, and elsewhere with various reasons. Alexander of Hales, SUMMA, p. II, q. 94, m. 3, a. 6, § 3; St. Thomas, SUMMA., I, q. 105, a. 3, 4, and 5; SUMMA CONTRA GENTILES, Bk. III, chs. 66, 67, and 70; (Bl. John Duns) Scotus, SENT., Bk. II, d. 37, q. 2 (for other passages see:

Fr. Girolamo da Montefortino, O.F.M., 1662-1738 A.D., SCOTI SUMMA., tome II, p. I, q. 105, a. 3, 4, and 5); and other others most commonly agree. On the opinion, which Durandus (of Saint-Pourçain) follows, Bl. (now St.) Albertus Magnus (SENT., Bk. II, d. 35, a. 7) says: « It has nearly yielded the court and is reputed by many moderns as heretical ». There were not lacking in later ages, those who with Suarez censured the same opinion as erroneous and/or proximate to heresy. — Nevertheless, about *the manner* of the Divine concursus, especially whether it is previous, or simultaneous, there is an open debate among Catholic Schools, concerning which more (will be said) elsewhere.

IV. Alexander of Hales, SUMMA., p. I, q. 35, m. 2, § 1. — St. Thomas, locis citt. here and in the preceding question. — Bl. (now St.) Albertus (Magnus), here in a. 8; SUMMA., p. I, tr. 20, q. 79, m. 2, a. 1, partic. 3. — (Bl.) Peter of Tarentaise, here in q. 2, q. 2. — Richard of Middleton, here in a. 2, q. 2. — Durandus (of Saint-Pourçain), here in q. 2. — (Bl.) Dionysius the Carthusian, here in q. 2. — (Gabriel) Biel, here in the q. sole.

ARTICLE III

On the Divine Will, as much as regards the reckoning of signifying.

Consequently, as much as regards the third Article there is asked concerning the Divine Will, as much as regards (Its) reckoning of being signified, and about this two (questions) are principally asked.

First, there is asked concerning the fittingness of that division of will into the will of good pleasure [voluntatem beneplaciti] and the will of a sign [voluntatem signi].

Second, there is asked concerning the number and sufficiency of the signs of the Divine Will.

QUESTION I

Whether the Divine Will is conveniently divided into the will of a sign and (the Will) of good pleasure'?

And, that the first division is not fitting, seems:

1. Because just as the (Divine) Will is in respect of things, so also the (Divine) Power and Knowledge; but the (Divine) Knowledge is not distinguished through the knowledge of truth and the knowledge of sign, similarly neither the Power: therefore neither the Will. *If you say*, that those do not have signs; *on the contrary*: just as creatures are the signs of the Will, so also do they hint at the (Divine) Knowledge out of their own *order*, and out of their own *magnitude* demonstrate the (Divine) Power: therefore if a sign leads thoroughly unto the one,[1] it is clear that etc..

2. Likewise, if it happens that the Divine Will is signified, (It is thus) either through *natural* signs, or through *voluntary* signs:[2] not through *natural* (signs), because *preception* and *prohibition* are not from the (Divine) Nature, but from the Will: not through *voluntary* (signs), because a voluntary sign is that which signifies out of an institution; but *preception* and *prohibition* signify out of an institution not the Will, but that which is precepted: ergo etc..

3. Likewise, the thing signified does not communicate its own name to the sign — wherefore, though the circle (above the door of a shop) is a sign of wine, it is not wine — therefore, though *precep-*

tion and *prohibition* etc. are *signs* of the Divine Will, yet they ought not to be said (to be) "wills": therefore, the Will ought not be divided into a will of a sign and a will of good pleasure.

4. Likewise, *preception* and *prohibition* and (signs) of this kind, either are signs according to the reckoning of the *act*, or according to the reckoning of (their) *object* or connoted (effect). If according to the reckoning of the *act*; but the act is the same as the Divine Will and God — because when I say: "God precepts", it is said of God, and thus it predicates the Divine Essence — therefore, according to this the same (thing) would be a sign of itself. Or according to the reckoning of (their) *effect*, and then, since *preception* and *prohibition* connote no effect, and *counsel* neither, there will be entirely no sign; and thus they seem in no manner (to be) signs.

BUT ON THE CONTRARY: 1. Scripture says, *that there are many "wills" of God*;[3] but it is established, that there is one Will of Good Pleasure: therefore, if there are *more*, it is necessary, that it stand for another will than (that) of the Good Pleasure. But there is no Will of God except *the Good Pleasure*, and/or *the sign* of It: ergo etc..

2. Likewise, it happens that we cognize God's Will;

---

[1] Cf. above d. 16, a. 1, q. 2, p. 282, footnote 2.
[2] On this division of signs into natural and voluntary, cf. above d. 16, a. 1, q. 2, p. 282, footnote 6.

[3] Cf. the text of Master (Peter) here, in ch. 5 ff.. — At the end of the argument, the Vatican edition has *except of the good pleasure* [nisi beneplaciti] for *except the Good Pleasure* [nisi beneplacitum].

but we cannot cognize It through Itself: it is necessary, therefore, that we cognize (It) through signs. But according to which we cognize (It), thus do we name (It): therefore, we ought not only say that the Will of Good Pleasure is a will, but also that *the sign of (It is)*.

3. Likewise, anyone's (act of) *precepting* is rightly said (to be) the will of that one, therefore, also God's (act of) *precepting*; but (this will) is not a causing[1] will, because *the (act of) precepting* is, even if nothing is done: therefore it is a "will" as (something) signifying (It).

CONCLUSION

By authority and reason it is proven, that the Will of Good Pleasure and (the will) of a sign are to be distinguished.

I RESPOND: Regarding this one must understand, that both *reason* and *authority* compel us to distinguish the Will of God into the will of a sign and the Will of Good Pleasure. *Authority*, indeed: because the Apostle says in the fourth (chapter of his) First (Letter) to the Thessalonians:[2] *This is the Will of God, your sanctification*; but that has not been said through (the manner of) *essence*, therefore, either through (the manner of) *a cause*, and/or through (the manner of) *a signification*; but not through (the manner of) a *cause*, therefore, through (the manner of) a *signification*. — Likewise, *reason* dictates (it), because we are accustomed according to the common use of speech [usu loquendi] to name (our) *precept* "our will".

On this account it must be understood, that just as *the intellect* is not absurdly said (to be) the intellective force and the understanding itself, so *the will* is said (to be) the very force for willing and the willing itself. And because God's Will is made known to us through the willing as through the visible sign, and « a sign is that which causes one to come unto another, while it offers itself to the senses [sensui] »;[3] hence it is, that we divide God's Will into the Will of *Good Pleasure* and into the will of a *sign*.

1. To that which is objected concerning the (Divine) Knowledge and Power, it must be said, that the Will Itself holds Itself more immediately to things, and since It has not been determined in regard to [in] indifferent future (things), for that reason It needs certain *signs*.[4] And on this account, since we ought to conform ourselves to Him, it is necessary [oportet] that we know It. But the Divine *Knowledge* is in respect of all, similarly the *Power* also, and *moreover* it is necessary that we conform ourselves to neither; for that reason there is not said (to be) a "*knowledge*" and/or "*power*" of a sign, just as there is said (to be) a "will".

2. To that which is objected, whether they are natural signs, and/or voluntary ones; it must be said, that a sign is a *being* and is a *sign*; therefore, it can be said (to be) "*natural*" inasmuch as (it is) a *being*, and/or inasmuch as (it is) a *sign*. Therefore, the signs of the Will, inasmuch as (they are) beings, are *voluntary*, because (they are) from the Will, but are *natural* inasmuch as (they are) signs,[5] because they signify naturally, just as effects naturally signify (their) cause.

3. From this the following (objection) is clear, because a thing does not communicate (its) name to a *given* sign, yet it does communicate (it) to a *natural* sign,[6] as is clear: for urine is said (to be) "healthy", because it is a sign of health; for it is a sign, which is caused naturally. Yet, this is not generally true, nor according to the propriety of speech, but according to a trope of speaking, just as Master (Peter) touches upon in the text.[7] And the reason for the transferring (of terms) is the similitude found [comperta] among the sign, which naturally signifies,* and the signified.

4. To that which is objected: "By a reckoning of which are they signs?", it must be said, that by a reckoning of the act caused[8] through the comparison to *the object*. For *the object* causes the Will to be made known, such as It is under the act of precepting and prohibiting and (acts) of this kind. Wherefore that which is precepted, is a sign of the Will, inasmuch as it is precepted.

SCHOLIUM

The distinction of "will" into a will of *good pleasure* and (a will) *of a sign* is founded in Sacred Scripture and (is) received by all the doctors; though by a few later Scholastics, such as Francis of Mayrone (c. 1280-1328 A. D.), the will of a sign is reduced to an act of good pleasure, but an inefficacious one, which (thesis) is most commonly reproved.

Alexander of Hales, on this & the next q., SUMMA., p. I, q. 36, m. 1. — St. Thomas, here in q. 1, a. 4; SUMMA., I, q. 19, a. 11. — Bl. (now St.) Albertus, here in a. 9; on this and the following question, SUMMA., p. I, tr. 20, q. 80. — (Bl.) Peter of Tarentaise, here in q. 3, a. 1. — Giles the Roman, on this and the following question, here in 3rd. princ.; q. 1. — Durandus, on this and the following question, here in q. 3. — (Bl.) Dionysius the Carthusian, on this and the following question, here in q. 3. — (Gabriel) Biel, on this and the following question, SENT., Bk. I, d. 46, q. 1.

---

[1] Many codices and editions 2, 3, 4, 5 and 6 have *the creating Will* [voluntas creans] for *a causing will* [voluntas causans].

[2] Verse 3. — A little before this, the Vatican edition alone omits *the Will of God into* [voluntatem Dei in]. A little below this, after *not through (the manner of) a cause* [non autem per causam] codex Q (in the margin) adjoins *because it does not sanctify all* [quia non omnes sanctificat].

[3] The words are (those) of (St.) Augustine, which are cited in (their) entirety above in d. 16, a. sole, q. 2, p. 282, footnote 2. — You will find more on what is taught here in (St.) Anselm's book, ON WILL, ch. 5 ff.. — A little before this very many codices and editions after *through the visible* [per visibilem] omits *sign* [signum], which the Vatican edition, together with edition 1, rightly supply.

[4] Here he means to say: since the (Divine) Will in regard to things, which can be and/or not be, and which can be in this and/or another manner, can determine this and/or that, for this reason It cannot be cognized <u>per se</u> with certainty by us, hence so that we may know, that the (Divine) Will has determined, it is necessary that It be manifested by certain signs. — For *and since it has not been determined* [et cum non sit determinata] the Vatican edition, with one or the other codex and edition 1, has *and yet not thus in a determinate manner* (ed. 1 has *thus determined*) [et tamen non sic determinate

(ed. 1 determinata)]. After a few (words), the same Vatican edition, together with edition 1, has *And moreover* [Et praeterea] for *And on this account* [Et propterea], and then with very many codd. and edd., it has faultily *it would be necessary* [oporteret] for *it is necessary* [oportet], which reading we have restored from codex T and edition 1.

[5] In codex X here is here added: *An example from the nods of men, which are natural, and through these we cognize (their) wills* [Exemplum de nutibus hominum, qui sunt naturales, et per ipsos cognoscimus voluntates].

[6] That is, because (it is) not an arbitrary sign, but only a natural sign, it is named with the same name, by which the thing is named. — The Vatican edition, with cod. cc, omits *(its) name* [nomen], and twice in place of *things do not communicate (their) ... they do communicate ...* [res ... communicant ... communicant] for *a thing does not ... communicate ... it does communicate* [res ... communicat ... communicat]. Codex Q (in the margin) after *a given sign* [signo dato] adds *that is an instituted one* [id est instituto].

[7] Here in ch. 6. — Then for *And the reason for ... is the similitude found* [Et ratio] very many codd. & editions 2, 3, 4, 5 and 6 have *And by the reckoning of ... a similitude has been found* [Et ratione], viciously.

[8] From codex Y we have restored *caused* [causati], in place of which very many codd. with the edd. have *created* [creati]. From the context it appears, that the reading taken from cod. Y is the true one. At the end of the solution, the Vatican ed. has *It precepts* [praecipit] for *it is precepted* [praecipitur].

* *Trans. note*: Here it seems that the original text omits the comma, less well.

QUESTION II

On the number and sufficiency of the signs of the Divine Will.

Second, there is asked concerning the number and sufficiency of the signs of the Divine Will.

And Master (Peter)[1] posits five signs, which are contained in this verse:

He precepts and prohibits, permits, counsels, fulfills.

And it seems, that there ought to be posited *fewer* (signs).

1. Since *"sign"* and *"signed"* are said correlatively, and if one of (two) opposed (terms) is said in a multiple manner, the remainder (is) also, but if one is not said in a multiple manner, neither (is) the remainder, through the logic [artem] of the TOPICS;[2] but the Will of God is one [una] and holding Itself in one manner: therefore, It ought to have only one sign.

2. Likewise, either these signs are distinguished by reason of (their) *manner of signifying*, or by reason of *the thing*.[3] If by reason of *the signifying thing*, therefore, there ought to be as many signs, as (there are) things, because every thing is a sign of the Divine Will, as of a cause. If by reason of (their) *manner of signifying*; but a *preception* and *prohibition* signify the Divine Will in the same manner: therefore, they are one sign.

3. Likewise, the Will of God, just as will be clear below,[4] is not in respect of evil, therefore, no sign of It ought to be accepted through a comparison to evil: therefore, since a *permission* and *prohibition* are in respect of an evil, they are not signs of the Divine Will.

That there are *more* (signs), seems:

4. Because, to any good there responds an evil ex opposito,* nay to one good (there are) many evils:[5] therefore, as many and/or more signs ought to be accepted on the part of the evil, just as on the part of a good. Therefore, since on the part of the good there are three (signs): it is clear that etc..

5. Likewise, just as to (an act of) *fulfilling* [impletioni] there responds a *permission* [permissio], so also (an act of) *restraining* [cohibitio],[6] nay much more strongly and moreso ex opposito: therefore, it seems, that there are more signs.

6. Likewise, just as to (an act of) *precepting* there is opposed (an act of) *prohibiting*, so to a *counsel*, (an act of) *dissuading* [dissuasio]: therefore it seems, that there are more (signs).

CONCLUSION

The number and sufficiency of the five signs of the Divine Will are explained.

I RESPOND: It must be said, that the number of signs is accustomed to be accepted in *one* manner thus. For the Divine Will, properly speaking, is of *(things) present* and *future*; but It either is not of (things) *past*, or[7] not in a manner other than of *(things) present*. — According to this it must be noted, that if It is in respect of (something) *present*, either that is *good*, or and thus (there is God's act of) *fulfilling*; or *evil*, and thus (there is His) *permission*. If in respect of (something) *future*, this (is) in a threefold manner: either (something) *evil*, and thus (there is God's) *prohibition*; or *a good of supererogation*, and thus (there is a Divine) *counsel*. Moreover, a good of supererogation does not have an opposed evil, for that reason *counsel* does not have an opposed sign.

In *another* manner, they can be distinguished thus: the Divine Will, just as will be clear below,[8] wills something *simply*, (and) wills something *conditionally* or as much as (it is) in itself; and in each manner it happens that It is signified. Therefore, the absolute Will can be compared to something either through a manner of *complacency*, or through a manner of *displeasure*. If through a manner of *displeasure*, that (something) in no manner comes to be; and thus it happens that this is not signified nor known by any exterior sign. If through a manner of *complacency*, either because *that which comes to be* is pleasing, and thus (there is God's act of) *fulfilling*; or because *something*[9] *out of it* is pleasing, and thus (there is God's) *permission*: and thus we have two signs. Again, the Divine Will can be signified as *antecedent* or *conditional*, and this in a twofold manner: either through a manner of *complacency*, such that (what is) opposed is displeasing, and thus (there is God's) *preception*; or through a manner of *displeasure*, and thus (there is God's) *prohibition*; or through a manner of *complacency*, yet, such that (what is) *opposed is not displeasing*, and thus (there is God's) *counsel*. However, through a manner of *displeasure*,[10] such that (what is) opposed is not pleasing,

---

[1] Here in ch. 6.

[2] Aristotle, TOPICS, Bk. I, ch. 13.

[3] The Vatican edition, together with codex cc, adjoins *signified* [significatae], which word it substitutes also immediately after this for *signifying* [significantis] (*of the thing signified* for *of the signifying thing*), but falsely, because *the Thing signified* here is the very Will of God.

[4] Distinction 46, q. 2.

[5] Similarly, Aristotle, ETHICS, Bk. II, ch. 6: « We can sin in many manners; for evil is of an infinite (number), as the Pythagoreans used to conjecture, but the good (is) of a finite (number) ». And Dionysius (the Areopagite), ON THE DIVINE NAMES, ch. 4, § 31 (says): Of the best (τῶν ἀγαθῶν) (there is) one cause, to the best, evil (is) the contrary, of evil (there are) many causes.

[6] The Vatican edition, together with codex cc, has *a prohibition* [prohibitio] for *(an act of) restraining* [cohibitio], but in the

solution of the objection the Vatican edition also reads *(an act of) restraining* [cohibitio].

[7] The Vatican edition, having suppressed the words *It either is not ..., or not* [aut non est, aut non], reads thus *however, of (things) past it is not in a manner other than* etc. [praeteritorum autem alio modo non est quam etc.]. For *or not in a manner other* [aut non alio modo] very many codices, together with edition 1, have *or in a manner other* [aut alio modo], having omitted *not* [non], which we have restored from codex T.

[8] Distinction 46, q. 1. — Immediately after this, for *wills something simply, (and) wills something* [aliquid vult simpliciter, aliquid vult] the Vatican ed. has *either wills simply, or wills* [aut vult simpliciter, aut vult].

[9] The Vatican edition, together with codex cc, has *(something) else* [aliud] for *something* [aliquid].

[10] Ed. 1 reads: *However, through a manner neither of pleasure nor of displeasure* [Per modum vero nec placentiae nec displicentiae].

---

* *Trans. note*: Here ex opposito is used as a shorthand for *out of the very nature of the logical relation of the terms themselves, as in an argument ab oppositis*, for which see the translator's footnote, above on p. 100.

(such) is not possible to be found. — And, according to this, the number and sufficiency (of the signs of God's Will) and the solution of the objections is clear.

1. For what is objected, that the Will of the Good Pleasure is not multiple; it must be said, that this is true as much as regards (Its) Substance; yet as much as regards those which it connotes [connotata] It is multiple, as has been seen. For the *absolute* Will connotes an effect, the *established* Will [voluntas conditionata] connotes the natural ordination of the thing to the outcome, just as (is the natural ordination of) all (things) to salvation.[1]

2. To that which is asked, whether[2] (these signs are distinguished) by reason of (their) manner of signifying etc.; it must be said, that (they are distinguished) by reason of (their) *manner of signifying*. For there is one manner of signifying the Will as *One detesting*, which a *prohibition* does; another manner as *One approving*, which a *preception* does.

3. To that which is objected, that the (Divine) Will is not in respect of evil; it must be said, that through the manner of *approbation* It is not in respect of an *evil*, but (in respect of a good)[3] *elicited out of evil*; however, through the manner of *one detesting* It is in respect of *an evil in itself.*

4. To that which is objected, that to any good there responds an evil <u>ex opposito</u>; it must be said, that it is true; yet to the good of *supererogation* there can be opposed an *evil* and a *non-evil*. For inasmuch as (it is a good) of *supererogation*, (what is) *less good* is opposed (to it); but inasmuch as (it is) *a good*, an *evil* (is opposed to it); but not the other (i. e. the non-evil), and the former (of these two, i.e. *an evil*), indeed, is opposed[4] to the good of a precept; and, for that reason, it falls under prohibition.

5. To that which is objected concerning *(an act of) restraining* [cohibitio], it must be said, that that impedes an effect, and on account of that it deprives the reckoning of signifying, as has been seen.

6. To that which is objected, that to a *counsel* there is opposed *(an act of) dissuading*; it must be said, that, just as an opinion is one of (two) contraries, because it is the accepting [acceptio] of one side with dread [formidine] for the other,[5] so a counsel, because it does not accept the other side in a determined manner, comprehends a *recommendation* [suasionem] and a *dissuasion* [dissuasionem]. For he who recommends counsels, and he who dissuades similarly counsels something.

SCHOLIUM

In assigning five signs of the Divine Will the ancient masters agree, but they do not hold to the same way, in manifesting the sufficiency and congruence of these signs. Alexander of Hales deals with these opinions diffusely, in the passage cited in q. 1; and on the signs themselves, <u>ibid.</u>, in qq. 37, 38, and 39.

Besides those already cited in Question 1: (Bl. John Duns) Scotus, SENT., Bk. I, d. 47, q. sole. — St. Thomas, here in q. 1, a. 4; SUMMA., I, q. 19, a. 12. — Bl. (now St.) Albertus (Magnus), here in a. 11. — (Bl.) Peter of Tarentaise, here in q. 3, a. 2 and 3. — Richard of Middleton, here in a. 3, q. 12.

DOUBTS ON THE TEXT OF THE MASTER

DOUBT I

In this part are the doubts about (Master Peter's) text and, first, concerning this, which Master (Peter) says, that *"will" is never said relatively*. For (this) seems false, because just as *"creator"* is said regarding a creature, and *"foreknowledge"* regarding a foreknown, so *"to will"* is said regarding a *willed*; but, above, it has been had in the Thirty-Fifth Distinction,[6] that these are said relatively: therefore, also *"to will"*.

I RESPOND: It must be said, that Master (Peter) accepts

"to be spoken relatively" here, insofar as a relative manner of speaking is distinguished from the manner of speaking according to substance, and this is *the personal one*, and thus it is accepted here.[7] Moreover, he himself objects concerning the relation in respect of a *creature*, which is as much as regards a manner of understanding, nor is it distinguished from the manner of speaking according to substance. — And/or it can be said, that Master (Peter) speaks according to the general understanding of the name, because *"to will"* is not only in respect of (something) created, as *"to foreknow"* and *"to create"* (are), but also in respect of God.[8]

---

[1] Cf. below d. 46, q. 1. — In the Vatican edition and codex cc there are wanting the words *connotes an effect, the established Will* [connotat effectum, voluntas conditionata].

[2] Supply, together with the Vatican edition, *are distinguished* [distinguantur]. Next, after *by reason of (their) manner* [ratione modi] in very many codd. and ed. 1 there is missing *of signifying* [significandi].

[3] Supply, together with codex O (Q in the margin), *a good* [boni], and/or together with codex V *in respect of a good* [respectu boni].

[4] For *and the former, indeed, is opposed* [et illud quidem opponitur] the Vatican edition has *than that which is opposed* [quam illud quod opponitur], which, also a little above this, together with not a few manuscripts, omits *for* [enim], in place of which codex O exhibits *it is* [est].

[5] Thus also Aristotle, POSTERIOR ANALYTICS, Bk. I, ch. 26 (ch. 33), says, that an opinion is by its nature something uncertain (ἀβέβαιον). — Next, after *in a determined manner* [determinate] the Vatican edition adds faultily *because* [quia].

[6] In Doubt 4.

[7] Cf. above, d. 22, q. 4. — At the beginning of the solution, the Vatican edition, together with a few manuscripts, omits (the verb) *to be spoken* [dici].

[8] You will also find the solution of this doubt in (the Commentaries of Bl.) Peter of Tarentaise and Richard of Middleton, here on the text (of this Distinction).

DOUBT II

Likewise, is asked concerning this which (Master Peter) says: *"God knows all", that is, "God is (He), to whose Knowledge, which is His Essence, all have been subjected".* For he seems to speak badly, because similarly *to the Divine Will* all have been subjected, because none resist His Will:[1] therefore, God wills all; which is not conceded.

Likewise, I, therefore, ask: "Since all knowables have been subjected to the Divine Knowledge and Essence, and similarly (all things) willed [volita]: for what reason do we not say, that God by willing Himself wills the others, just as by knowing Himself He knows others?" Which if you *concede* (this), then all others would be eternal. *If you say*, that it is not similar; (then) one asks: "Why not?" and it seems that it is similar, because, just as an act of the Divine Will is not deflected outside of God, and thus by knowing Himself He knows all, so it seems also concerning the (Divine) Will.

I RESPOND: It must be said, that they are not said (to have been) *"subjected to the Divine Knowledge"*, because they are *inferior*, but they are said (to have been) *"subjected"*, *in respect* of which there is an act of the Divine Cognition; and these, indeed, are all cognizable; and for that reason He knows [novit] all. Similarly, *they have been subjected to the (Divine) Will*,[2] and these are not all willables, for that reason that (doubt) is clear.

What is asked, "Whether by willing Himself He wills all?"; it must be said, that in one manner *"to will"* means a *complacency*, in another manner it means a *cause*. And insofar as it means a *complacency*, I believe that it can well be said, that by willing Himself He wills all, because all are pleasing to Him, which are *from Him* and *to Him*. However, insofar as it means *the progress of an effect* from Him, though the act does not step forth [egrediatur] outside, yet things do step forth, and for that reason it means a looking back to the outside.[3] Wherefore just as (this) is not conceded: "By being able (unto) Himself He is able (unto) all", so also in the proposed.

DOUBT III

Likewise, is asked concerning this which (St. Augustine) says: *For what reason did God make Heaven and Earth? It must be responded to him: "Because He willed (it)".* For the response seems to be a bad one, because then it seems easy to determine all (things); it seems also, that God's Will has no reason. *But on the contrary*: on that (verse) in the first (chapter of St. Paul's Letter) to the Ephesians:[4] *According to the counsel of*

His Will, the Gloss (says): « God's Will is on account of a reason [ex ratione] »: therefore, there is a seeking of a reason (for God's Will).

I RESPOND: It must be said, that our will, since it is excited by the willed, has both a cause and a reason, both as much as *regards itself* and as much as *regards the willed*, most of all when it wills something, which is for the sake of an end; but God's Will, the Act of which is Himself,[5] because It is not excited by any reason *other than Itself*, cannot have a cause as much as *regards Itself*. However, sometimes *the willed* has a cause *other* than the Will,[6] sometimes the Will *alone*, as in the creation of the world. The Will has a *reason*, but *not a cause*, because It is not irrational. Whence It does not have a reason as (something) *diverse* from Itself, but *the same*[7] *according to thing* [idem re]; and for that reason the Will of God cannot be irrational; and on this account in the Acts, which are totally from It, it is sufficient to know It itself, nor is it necessary [nec oportet] to seek further another reason. And, thus, that (doubt) is clear.[8]

DOUBT IV

Likewise, is asked concerning this which (St. Augustine) also says, that *God's Will is the Cause of all species and motions*. For it seems that he speaks badly, because then, since the Will of God is as one acting through an intention, it seems, that nothing comes to be by chance and fortune.

I RESPOND: It must be said, that God, though He is the Cause of all, yet is not the whole cause, but (is) Himself (such) together with created causes. On this account it must be noted, that an *effect* has (its) 'being compared' to the *Supreme* Cause, which is God, and thus nothing comes forth by chance and fortune; it also has (its) 'being compared' to a will or created cause, which is a nature and/or an intelligence, and thus, since many (things) come forth besides the intention, many come to be by chance and fortune.

DOUBT V

Likewise is asked concerning this which (St. Augustine) says, *that nothing comes to be, which does not step forth from the interior ... inner-court of the Most High Emperor.* For (this) seems false, because sins come to be, and they do not step forth from Him.

I RESPOND: It must be said, that the Master does not take

---

[1] Romans 9:19: *For His Will, who resists (It)?* [Voluntatis enim eius quis resistit?].

[2] Thus very many codices with edition 1. The Vatican ed., having a little before this put *have been* [sunt] for *are said (to have been)* [dicuntur], here interjects *in respect of which there is an act of divine unwillingness* [respectu quorum est actus divinae nolitionis], which addition even codd. B H and bb exhibit, except that they substitute *of the Divine Will* [divinae voluntatis] for *of divine unwillingness* [divinae nolitionis].

[3] For *it means a looking back to the outside* [dicit respectum extra] very many codd. with edd. 2, 3, 4, 5 & 6, have *an exemplar means a looking back* [dicit respectum exemplar]. A little before this, for *progress* [progressum] edition 1 has *egress* [egressum], and, then, with many codd. it has *from It (i.e. the Divine Will)* [ab ipsa] for *from Him* [ab ipso]. Next, after *step forth* [egrediatur] the Vatican ed. with cod. cc, omits *outside* [extra], and, a little further below this, for *is not conceded* [non conceditur] codex cc with edd. 2, 3, 4, 5 & 6, has *does not follow* [non sequitur].

[4] Verse 11. — The interlinear Gloss in (Nicholas) of Lyra: That is, according to (His) Will, which is on account of a reason [Id est secundum voluntatem, quae est ex ratione]. — At the end of the objection, supply together with edition 1 *for God's Will* [voluntatis Dei].

[5] The Vatican ed., breaking with the codd. & ed. 1, here adds *most*

of all when He wills Himself [maxime cum vult se], and next, together with a few manuscripts, prefaces to the word *have* [causam] the word *however* [tamen]. Somewhat above this, the same Vatican edition, after *cause and reason* [causam et rationem], interjects *from it (i. e. the willed)* [ab eo].

[6] The Vatican edition alone here adjoins *and then in respect of that it has a reason and a cause* [et tunc respectu eius habet rationem et causam], and then at the end of the sentence it inserts *and then* [et tunc].

[7] After *the same* [idem] codices L and O subjoin *as Itself* [sibi], and then codex O reads *the Will of God alone* [sola voluntas Dei] for *the Will of God* [voluntas Dei].

[8] What the Seraphic Doctor proffers here to solve the Doubt plainly agrees with that which he taught above in d. 41, a. 1, q. 2 concerning the cause and reason for predestination. — In agreement with the Seraphic Doctor's solution are Alexander of Hales, SUMMA., p. I. q. 35, m. 3; (Bl. John Duns) Scotus, DE RERUM PRINCIPIO., q. 4, a. 2, n. 20; Bl. (now St.) Albertus (Magnus), here in a. 7; St. Thomas, SUMMA, I, q. 19, a. 5; (Bl.) Peter of Tarentaise, here in q. 2, a. 3, and in the exposition of the text, and Richard of Middleton, here in a. 2, q. 4, and on the text.

up this quote, in the same manner as it is had in (St. Augustine's) original.[1] For there it is said, that *there it is not ordered, nor permitted*, and thus the objection has no place. Yet, nevertheless, it can be said, that Master (Peter) restricts its distribution to the things, which are by some nature. — *And/or* it must be said, that he amplifies the verb for "stepping forth" [egrediendi] to *doing* [facere] and *permitting* [permittere].

DOUBT VI

Likewise, is asked concerning this which (St. Augustine) says, that *monstrous births of living things and the movements of the Earth and (those) similar to these come to be by God's Will*. For it seems that he says the false, because "*monster*" means some disorder [deordinationem] in a nature: therefore, it is not from the Supreme Cause.

I RESPOND: It seems that it must be said according to some, that "*monster*" means some *disorder* in a nature, and (that) it also means some *substance*.[2] That *substance* has a positive cause, which is God, but that *inordinancy* does not have a positive cause, but (is rather) a privation; and this is, as very frequently happens [ut plurimum], an improportion of the virtue of the one acting to the matter: for either the matter *is superabundant*, or *deficient* according to the proportion of the heat of the one working and the virtue. And (St.) Augustine speaks of monsters as much as regards this, that they have a substrate.

Yet, it could be said in another manner, that monsters are also from God *as One punishing*, since[3] they are punishments; and in this manner they have a reckoning of *order*. For though God does not work against the order *unto the end*, yet He frequently does work against *the customary course* of nature, either for *vengeance*, and/or for *mercy*.[4]

DOUBT VII

Likewise, is asked concerning this which (St. Augustine) says: *It pleased the vanity of philosophers to grant even these to other causes*. For it seems, that he does not say this rightly [bene], because philosophers attributed (them) truly to other causes: therefore, in this they were not vain, as for example (when they taught that) the Moon is eclipsed, for this reason, that the Earth is interposed (between it and the Sun).

I RESPOND: It must be said, that they are not said (to be) "vain" *for this reason*, that they granted (them) to others, but because they so granted (them) to others, that they did not, however, refer (them) to the chief Cause. And for that reason *they grew vain* [evenuerunt],[5] because they did not come to the First and Chief Cause, which alone is a cause simply and simply (is) the most general (of them).

DOUBT VIII

Likewise is asked concerning this which (Master Peter) says: *The Divine Will does not receive into Itself a multiplicity*. For (this) seems false, because there are many *ideas*, for this reason, that (they are) of many ideated (things): therefore, similarly (there are) many *wills*, because (they are) of many willed (things).

I RESPOND: It must be said, that it is not similar, just as is clear in the Question concerning ideas:[6] because "*will*" means, what holds itself more on the part of *the one willing* both according to "*being*" and according to the *reckoning of speaking*, and for that reason *according to thing* and *reckoning* there is one Will of the Good Pleasure; but "*idea*" according to the *reckoning of speaking* holds itself more on the part of *the ideated*, because it means its similitude. And "*cognition*" according to the reckoning of understanding and speaking means a movement in *us* according to *thing*, from things to the soul, but in *God* according to the *reckoning of understanding*; but "*will*" (does) not. For that reason, according to this twofold reckoning, (a multiplicity) is conceded concerning *ideas*, not concerning a *will*.[7]

DOUBT IX

Likewise, is asked concerning this which (Master Peter) says, that *the (Divine) Will does not receive a mutability*. For (this) seems false, because God now wills something to be, which afterwards He will not will (it)[8] to be: therefore, it seems, that *He leaves off* willing and similarly (that) *He starts* (to will): therefore, the Divine Will seems to be changed.

I RESPOND: It must be said, that in expressions of this kind there is only a change in respect of *(what is) connoted*, which is compared to the Divine Will, by a reckoning of which there is posited a *start* and *stop* [inception et desitio] in those acts, which connote something concerning the present. For if there be said: "God wills, that this is going to be", He has willed (it) from eternity: but yet He was not the cause in *act* or actually causing (the thing), except when He willed to cause (it), that is for that instant, in which the act of (His) Will[9] is joined *to the work*, but not *to that subject being willed* [ipso subiecto volenti]. And thus it is clear, in what manner He be an actual cause in time, with no change wrought in It, because *He has* continuously *willed* (it), and thus was in act; but He was not *causing in act* except for the time, for which He willed, such that no *will* started about God, but the *effect* alone started.[10]

DOUBT X

Likewise, is asked concerning this which is said: *And God is said (to have been) "angered"* [iratus]; *but there is no anger in Him*. For it seems that

---

[1] See above Master Peter's d. XLV, ch. 4, p. 795, footnote 5. — A little further below this, for *Master (Peter)* [Magister] the Vatican edition has *the matter* [materia].

[2] For *some substance* [substantiam aliquam] not a few codices have *a substance from matter* [substantiam a materia], faultily.

[3] For *since* [quoniam] the Vatican ed. with cod. cc, has *when* [quando].

[4] On this doubt, cf. Alexander of Hales, SUMMA, p. II. q. 16, m. 3; (Bl.) Peter of Tarentaise, here on the text, where the following two Doubts are solves; Richard of Middleton, here on the text, in which passage the solution of the following Doubt is exhibited.

[5] Romans 1:21: *But they grew vain in their thoughts* [Sed evanuerunt in cogitationibus suis]. — On this doubt, cf. St. Thomas and Giles the Roman, here on the text.

[6] Distinction 35, q. 1. — A little after this, for *on the part of the one willing* [ex parte volentis] the more ancient codices, together with edition 1, have *on the part of a will* [ex parte voluntatis].

[7] On the twofold movement, namely from things to the soul and from the soul to things, cf. above d. 32, a. 2, q. 2, p. 562, footnote 10. — On this doubt, cf. Bl. (now St.) Albertus (Magnus), (in his Commentary), here, in a. 9.

[8] The Vatican edition, together with some manuscripts, reads *He does not will* [non vult] for *He will not will* [non volet].

[9] For *the act of (His) Will* [actus voluntatis] many codices have less well *the voluntary act* [actus voluntarius].

[10] On this doubt, cf. Bl. (now St.) Albertus (Magnus), here in a. 10, and Richard of Middleton, here on the text.

he speaks badly, because in God there is a *rational* and *concupiscible* force: therefore, for an equal reason there is to be posited in God an *irascible* one: therefore, just as there is truly in Him the act of the cognitive (power) and of love [amoris], so properly the act of fury.

I RESPOND: It must be said, that the "*irascible*" in some manner sounds unto imperfection from the reckoning of its name; and for that reason some say, that it is in no manner received in God except *transumptively*. — Yet, since *the acts* of this kind of force in us are *to glory* and *to dominate*, and these are in God; for what reason is this force not similarly in God?

And it must be said, on this account, that in God there is truly a force for *glorying* and *dominating*, which is the Divine Substance Itself. Yet because *anger*[1] has a conjoined passion from the reckoning of its name, for that reason it is not received in God nor (is) an *irascible* (power), nor *anger*, except transumptively and in the expression of a trope [in sermone tropico]. And it must be

noted, that God has the *signs* of anger, not which signify anger in Him, but which signify anger in us and truly (do so), when they are in us.

DOUBT XI

Likewise, is asked concerning this which (Master Peter) says, that *He precepted Abraham to immolate (his) son, yet He did not will (it)*; therefore, according to this, it seems, that the precepting was a false sign.

I RESPOND: It must be said, that the Will of God willed that the faith and devotion of Abraham *be manifested*[2] in preparation for (his) obeying; and this God willed, and this the *sign* conveyed and truly; but yet according to the estimation of Abraham it conveyed more, and through that more, which Abraham understood, the Lord *proved* his faith, so that there was in the sign neither a *falsehood*, nor in Abraham a *deception*, but a *proof* [probatio].[3]

DISTINCTION XLVI

CHAPTER I

That the Will of God, which He Himself is, can be cancelled in nothing.

Here, there arises a question. For it has been said in the above (sentences)[1] and completely fortified by authorities, that the Will of God, which He Himself is, and (which) is called His "Good Pleasure", cannot be cancelled, because by that Will *whatsoever He has willed, He has done in Heaven and on Earth*: Which, according to the testimony of the Apostle, *nothing resists*. « Therefore, it is asked, in what manner is what the Apostles says of the Lord:[2] *Who wills that all men to come to be saved*, is to be accepted. For since not all come to be saved, but more are damned, it seems, that there is at any rate not done, what God wills to be done, namely, with a human will impeding the Will of God. The Lord also, compelling the impious city in the Gospel, says: *How often I willed to gather thy children together, just as the hen gathers her chicks under (her) wings, and thou wouldst not!* Thus these are[3] said, as if God's Will has been overcome by the will of men, and (as if) as One most infirm in not willing (to oppose those) impeding (Him), the Most Powerful One could not do, what He wanted. Where is, therefore, that omnipotence, by which, ac-

cording to the Prophet, *all whatsoever He has willed, He has done in Heaven and on Earth*? And in what manner, *does nothing*, according to the Apostle, *resist His Will*, if He willed to gather the children of Jerusalem, and did not do (it) »?[4] For these seem to obviate very much the aforesaid.

CHAPTER II

In what manner is this to be understood: "I willed to gather thy children together, and thou wouldst not", and this: "He who wills all men to come to be saved"?

But, let us hear the solution; and let us see first, in what manner is that, which the Lord says, to be accepted. « For that has not been said out of this sense », as (St.) Augustine says in (his) ENCHIRIDION,[5] solving the aforesaid question, « as if the Lord willed to gather the children of Jerusalem, and what He willed was not done, because she was unwilling; but rather she indeed was unwilling that her children be gathered by Him, yet with her unwilling, He did gather all her sons whom He willed (to gather); because (it is) not (that) in Heaven and on Earth He has done certain (things which) He has willed, but certain (others) which He willed He has also not done, but *all*

---

[1] For *anger* [ira] very many codices with the first editions have *thus it* [ita]. Next, for *it is not received in God nor (is) an irascible (power)* [non recipitur in Deo nec irascibilis] the Vatican edition has *an irascible force is not received in God* [non recipitur in Deo vis irascibilis]. — On the question, whether in God there is to be received an irascible force, cf. above d. 10, a. 1, q. 2, in reply to n. 4, and ibid., Scholium, II.

[2] The Vatican edition, together with codex cc, has *willed to manifest the faith and devotion of Abraham* [volebat fidem et devotionem Abrahae manifestare] for *willed that the faith and devotion of Abraham be manifested* [volebat fidem et devotionem Abrahae manifestari].

[3] Cf. on this doubt Alexander of Hales, SUMMA., p. I. q. 37, m. 1; Bl. (now St.) Albertus (Magnus), here in a. 13, and Richard of Middleton, here in a. 2, q. 2.

NOTES ON THE BOOK OF SENTENCES

[1] In Distinction XLV. — The Vatican edition and very many edi-

tions, a little below this, having added *which* [quae], thus have: *which is called His "Good Pleasure"* [et quae beneplacitum eius vocatur] for *and (which) is called His "Good Pleasure"* [vocaturque beneplacitum eius]. — The following passages from Sacred Scripture are Ps. 113:11, and Rom. 9:19.

[2] 1 Timothy 2:4. The following passage is Mt. 23:37.

[3] The Vatican edition and editions 4, 5, 6 and 9 add *also* [etiam]; edition 8 reads *For thus these are* [Ita enim haec] for *Thus these are* [Ita haec]; the codices and the other editions read as above.

[4] The preceding have been excerpted from (St.) Augustine's ENCHIRIDION, ch. 97, n. 24.

[5] Loc. cit.. In which text the Vatican edition, together with the other editions, except edition 1, has *to gather together* [congregare] for *to gather* [colligere], and a little below this has *that one* [illa] for *she* [ipsa], contradicting the codices.

whatsoever He has willed, He has done », so that the sense is: *How often I have willed to gather thy children together, and thou wouldst not!* that is, "However, many I have gathered together by My ever efficacious Will, I have done (so), with thee unwilling". — Behold, it has been posited in an evident (manner), that[1] those words of the Lord are not repugnant to (those) above.

Now it remains for one to see, in what manner too the aforementioned words of the Apostle do not contradict the aforesaid, who speaking of God says: *(Who) wills all men to come to be saved.* By the occasion of which words many have deviated[2] from the truth, saying, that God wills that many (things) come to be, which do not come to be. But one must not understand, that that has been said according to this reckoning, as if God willed that some be saved, and they be not saved. « For who is so impious, as to say, that God cannot convert the evil wills of men, which (wills) He wills, and when He wills and where He wills, unto the good? It is certainly [utique] not true that in the Psalm there is said: *Whatsoever He has willed, He has done,* if He willed some (things) and did not do (them), and what is more unworthy, (that) He did not do (them) for this reason, since, the will of man impeded, that there would come to be, what the Omnipotent willed ».[3] And for that reason « when we hear and read in the Sacred Letters, that He wills that all men come to be saved, though it is certain for us, that not all men come to be saved,[4] yet we ought not derogate anything from the most Omnipotent Will of God, but understand thus what has been written: *He wills that all men come to be saved,* as if there were said, that no man comes to be saved, except him whom He has willed to come to be;[5] not that there is no one of men, except him whom He willed to be saved, but that none comes to be saved, except him whom He willed to be saved; and for that reason He must be asked [rogandus], to will (it), because it is necessary that it comes to be, if He wills it ». « For the Omnipotent is not to be believed to have willed anything to be done, which has not been done ». « This (verse) is also understood in the same manner:[6] *(Who) illumines every man coming into this world,* not because there is no one among men [nullus hominum], who is not illumined, but because none are illumined except by Him. That (verse) can also be understood in another manner, yet so long as we are not coerced [cogamur] to believe, that the Omnipotent has willed that something be done, and it has not been done, Who — if[7] *He has done,* without any ambiguities, *all whatsoever He has willed,* in Heaven and on Earth, just as the Truth chants — has not, in a word, willed to do whatsoever He has not done ». — From these there is openly shown, that God by that Will, which He Himself is, does not will anything to be done, which is not done, nor not to be done, which is done.

Chapter III

Whether evils come to be with God willing and/or unwilling?

And, for that reason, since it is established, that all goods, which come to be, come to be by His Will, which if He will be unwilling that they come to be, would to no extent come to be; rightly it is customarily asked: whether all evils too, that is sins, which come to be, come to be by God's Will, or come to be with Him unwilling. — On this diverse (men), thinking variously,[8] are found to contradict themselves. For some say, that God wills that there are and/or come to be evils, yet does not will evils. But others, that He neither wills evils to be nor to come to be. Yet, in this the latter and former agree, that each say, that God does not will evils. But each strive to fortify their own assertion with reasons and authorities.

For those who say, that God wills that there are and/or come to be evils, lessen their own intention[9] in these manners. For if, they say, He would will evils not to be and/or not to come to be, they would in no manner be and/or come to be, because, if He wills them not to be and/or not to come to be, and cannot effect this, namely, that they not be and/or not come to be, (then) something resists His Will and Power, and He is not omnipotent, because He cannot (do) everything which He wills, but is impotent, just as we are too, who do not prevail (to do) what we will and when (we will it). But because He is omnipotent and (is) in no manner impotent, it is certain, that evils cannot come to be and/or be, unless with Him willing (it). For in what manner, with Him unwilling and not willing [invito eo et nolente] (it), could an evil come to be from something, when it has been written: *His Will, who resists (It)?*. Above, (St.) Augustine[10] also has said: « Because it is necessary that it come to be, if He has willed (it) ». But He wills that evils come to be, or not come to be. If He wills (them) not to come to be, they do not come to be; but they do come to be: therefore, He wills (them) to come to be. — *Likewise,* it is good that evils are and/or come to be, otherwise the One most highly Good would not permit them to come to be. Wherefore, (St.) Augustine says in (his) ENCHIRIDION: « Though those, which are evil, inasmuch as they are evil, are not good, yet it is good not only that (there are) goods, but even (that) there are evils. For this were good, that there are evil evils, it would in no manner be allowed by the Omnipotent Good, for Whom, far from doubt, not allowing to be what He does not will is as easy, as causing what He wills. If we do not believe this,[11] our confession, by which we confess to believe in "the Father Almighty", is imperiled ». — Behold, here you openly, have that it is good that there are evils, but of every good God is the author, who wills, that everything which is, is good. Therefore, since it is good that evils come to be and/or are, therefore, He also wills that evils come to be and/or are. — These and also other reasons and authorities of this kind they use, who say, that God wills that evils are and/or come to be.[12]

Those, on the other hand, who say, that by the Will of God evils do not come to be and/or are not, respond thus to the aforementioned inductions, saying, that God neither wills evils to come to be, nor wills (them) not to come to be, and/or is unwilling that (they) come to be, but only does not will (them) to come to be. For, if He willed them to come to be and/or to be, He would certainly [utique] cause that they come to be and/or are, and thus He would be the an author of evils; however He is not an author of evils, as the authorities of the Saints protest: therefore, not by His Will do evils come to be. *Likewise,* if He were unwilling that evils come to be and/or willed (them) not to come to be, and yet they did come to be, He would not

---

[1] The codices and edition 1 have *that* [quia] for *that* [quod].

[2] Cf. d. XLV. — A little before this, the Vatican edition, together with a few editions, has *as if God wills* [Deus velit], editions 2, 2, 7 and 8 have *as if God would will* [Deus vellet] for *as if God willed* [Deus voluerit].

[3] The preceding have been taken from (St.) Augustine, ENCHIRIDION, partly from ch. 98, n. 25, partly from ch. 95, n. 24; but those which follow from ch. 103, n. 27.

[4] The words: *though it is certain ... to be saved* [are omitted in editions 1, 2, 3, 4, 5, 7, and 9].

[5] The Vatican edition and the other editions add *saved* [salvum], contradicting the original, edition 1 and the codices, except codex C.

[6] John 1:9.

[7] Thus rightly edd. 1 & 8, with the original; cod. C with edd. 2, 3,

[cont.] 4, 5, 7 & 9 have *just as* [sicut] for *if* [si]; codices A B and E and edition 1 *or* [sive] for the same; the Vatican ed. with codex D, lacks any particle.

[8] Thus in codices A B D and E and edition 1; in the Vatican edition and the other editions *various (things)* [varia].

[9] Codices A and D have *his assertion* [suam ... assertionem] for *his intention* [suam ... intentionem].* A little below this, codices A B and D omits *not* before *come to be, (then)* [fiant].

[10] ENCHIRIDION., ch. 103, n. 27; and what follows is ch. 96, n. 24.

[11] Thus the original, codices A B C and E, and edition 1, in the other editions there is read *these* [haec] for *this* [hoc]. Below before *He also wills* [et mala vult] codd. A B D & E and ed. 1 omit *therefore* [ergo].

[12] Codex B here adds: (St.) Gregory on Genesis (even though it is from his MORALS, Bk. VI, ch. 18, n. 33): « God propitiously concedes some, as One angered permits others, and what He permits He so toler-

---

* *Trans. note*: Here *intention* is used in the sense of *intended meaning*

be omnipotent, since His Will would be impeded by the effect of a human will. And for that reason they do not concede, that God wills evils to come to be, lest He be understood (to be) an author of evils; nor do they concede, that He wills evils not to come to be and/or (that) He is unwilling that (they) come to be, lest He seem to be impotent; but they say only, that He does not will evils to come to be, so that He may be shown (to be) not an author, but a permitter of evils. Whence, even the Evangelist, where he shows, that God is the Author of all goods, saying:[1] *All were made through Him*, consequently denies that He is an author of evils, saying: *And without Him nothing, that is* sin, *is made*. He did not say, "through Him it was made", and/or "with Him unwilling and not willing", but only "without Him", that is "without His Will", because sin does not come to be by His Will. Therefore, not with God *willing* and/or *not being unwilling*, but *with (Him) not willing* evils come to be, because it is not subject [subest] to God's Will, that an evil *come to be* and/or *not come to be*, but (only) that *He allow it to come to be*, because it is good that He allow evils to come to be; and certainly [utique] as One willing He allows (it), not as One willing *evils*, but as One willing *to allow*,[2] that they come to be; because neither are *evils* good, nor is it good *that they come to be* and/or *are*.

CHAPTER IV

In what manner is this (saying) of (St.) Augustine to be understood: "It is good that evils come to be".

However, what (St.) Augustine[3] says: "It is good that evils come to be", and "evils would not be allowed by the Omnipotent Good to come to be, unless it were good, that they be"; they assert has been said for this reason, because out of the evils, which come to be, God elicits goods, and that He Himself would not permit them to come to be, unless He worked something of good[4] from them. Wherefore, (St.) Augustine in the same book, the ENCHIRIDION,[5] openly indicating, that such is the understanding of the aforesaid words, says: « The Omnipotent God, to whom belongs the highest power over things [rerum est summa potestas], since He is most highly good, would in no manner allow, that anything of evil be in His own works, unless He were always to such an extent [usque adeo] omnipotent and good, that He even worked well from evil ». Likewise, in the same (he says): « God judged that (it was) better to work goods from evils than to permit no evils ». And so out of this sense it has been said and is true, that it is good that evils come to be, because out of the evils, which come to be, there accedes a goodness, that is a utility, for the good, *who according to (His) proposal (to have mercy) have been called (to be) Saints*.[6] For to such, as the Apostle says, *all (things) cooperate unto the good*, even evils, because (the evils) which stand in the way [obsunt] of others doing (them), benefit [prosunt] these (Saints). Whence there is even sometimes written in Scripture, that evil is named "good", as (St.) Jerome says on (the Gospel of St.) Mark:[7] "The evil of Judas, was good, that is, for us". Nor, if it is good for this one and/or

that one [illi vel illi], does it follow from this, that it is simply good. For (speaking) properly and simply the good is, that which in itself and to the one doing (it) is good.

CHAPTER V

On the multiple acceptation of the "good".

For there is something, which *in itself* and *for whom it is done* is good, but is not good *to the one doing (it)*, such as when one comes to the aid of a poor man, but not for God's sake. And there is something good *in itself* and *to the one doing (it)* and to him *to whom it is done*, such as when the Truth is preached for God's sake to the one believing (It). Wherefore the Apostles (says):[8] *to God we are a good fragrance* [odor], *to some the fragrance of life, to others the odor* [odor] *of death*. Moreover, there is another, which is also not good *in itself* and hurts and damns *the one doing (it)*, unless he repent, such as an evil (deed), (which) however, prevails *for something*. For as (St.) Augustine says in the ENCHIRIDION:[9] « By the most highly and equally and immutably Good Trinity all have been created neither most highly nor equally nor immutably good; but yet each (are) good. But one and all [universa] together (are) very good, because out of (them) all consists the admirable beauty of the university (of things); in which even that which is said (to be) "evil", well ordered and placed in its own place, commends more eminently (those which are) good, so that they are more pleasing and more worthy of praise, while they are compared to (those which are) evil ».

CHAPTER VI

That evils have value for the university (of things).

Hence, it is clear, that out of the evils, which come to be, some good comes forth, so long as (the things which are) good are more pleasing and stand forth as more praiseworthy. Even to those doing (them), out of the evil (deeds), which they do, there sometimes come forth good (things), if *according to (His) proposal they have been called (to be) Saints*. « For to such », as (St.) Augustine says in the book, ON CORRECTION AND GRACE,[10] « God always [usque] cooperates with all unto the good to such an extent, that, if any of them deviate and fall away [exorbitant], He even causes that this very (thing) profits [proficere] them unto the good, because they return more humble and more learned », as (St.) Peter. « Even those evils, which the faithful piously endure [perferunt] from the iniquitous », as (St.) Augustine says in the book, ON THE TRINITY,[11] « at least benefit them either to blot out sins, and/or to exercise and prove (their) justice, and/or to demonstrate the misery of this life ». And, for that reason, even

---

ates, that He turns (them) unto the use of His counsel. Wherefore, (in a wonderful manner) it comes to be, that what come to be or is done by the Will of God, is not contrary to the Will of God: because while evils done are turned unto a good use, those which are repugnant to His counsel also militate for His counsel. Hence also through the Psalmist (Ps. 110:2) there is said: Great the works of the Lord, exquisite in all His wills ». We have supplied some words from the edition of (St.) Gregory's works.

[1] Jonn 1:3.

[2] Thus the codices and editions 2, 3, and 7; in the other editions there is added not well *allows* [sinit].

[3] ENCHIRIDION., ch. 96, n. 24.

[4] All the codices and editions 1, 2, and 3 have *well* [bene] for *of good* [boni], which (differing) reading seems to have been taken from the words of (St.) Augustine following below, in which passage, however, *something* [aliquid] is missing.

[5] Chapter 11, n. 3. The following passage is ch. 27, n. 8.

[6] Romans 8:28. — A little above this, the Vatican ed. with several edd. has *"it is good that evils come to be"* [bonum est etc.] for *that it is good that evils come to be* [bonum esse etc], and immediately after this edd. 1 & 6 have *humility* [humilitas] for *a utility* [utilitas].

[7] Chapter 14: « Many, such as Judas, will do good; but it does not entirely profit them ». The commentary on this passage is not Jerome's.

[8] 2 Corinthians 2:15,16.   [9] Chapters 10-11, n. 3.

[10] Chapter 9, n. 24. — A little above this, for *there ... comes forth good (things)* [bona proveniunt] codd. A C & D and ed. 1 have *there ... comes good (things)* [bona veniunt], codex B has *there ... comes forth good (things)* [bona eveniunt]. — In regard to St. Peter, cf. Lk 22:61-62.

[11] Bk. XIII, ch. 16, n. 20. In which text codd. B C D & E and ed. 1 have *for demanded sins* [ad demanda peccata] for *to blot out sins* [ad delenda peccata]; the original reads *to emend sins* [ad emendanda peccata]. In regard to Job, cf. chs. 19, 21 and 42; in regard to St. Paul, cf. 2 Cor. 12:7. — Near the end, before *profited* [profecit], the codd. omit *well* [bene].

Job felt the Hand of God, and the Apostle, the goad of Satan; and each profited well, because he bore the evil well.

If anyone, therefore, diligently attends to (those things) which have been written, it is easy for him to perceive, that out of evils good (things) do come forth, and (that) from this reckoning it has been said, that it is good that evils *come to be* and/or *are*, not because an evil is good, and/or because it is good that an evil come to be. For it is not good that an evil come to be from someone, because it is not good, that anyone *work* evil. For if this were good, in a word, the God, who is the Author of every good, would be its author. Wherefore if God is its author, therefore, with Him as author man does evil,[1] and thus with Him as author man comes to be worse [deterior]. And, if with Him as author man comes to be worse, then with Him willing man comes to be worse. For it is the same to say that something comes to be "*with God as author*", as "*with God willing*"; but with God as author man does not come to be worse: therefore, neither with God willing, as (St.) Augustine in the book, OF EIGHTY-THREE QUESTIONS,[2] openly argues [astruit] a minori, saying thus: « By no wise man as author does a man come to be worse; for so great is that fault, that it cannot befall [cadere in] a wise man. But God is more outstanding [praestantior] than every wise man: for God's Will is much more outstanding than (that) of a wise man. Moreover, when there is said "*with Him as author*", there is said "*with Him willing*". Therefore, (that) by which a man is worse, is a vice of the[3] will. Which vice, if it is far away [longe abest] from God's Will, as reason teaches, one must seek, from whom it is ». — Behold, here (St.) Augustine openly says, that with God as author and/or willing man does not come to be worse, but (rather he does so) by a vice of his own will. Therefore, it is not with God as author, that an evil comes to be from someone, and thus with God willing evils do not come to be.

CHAPTER VII

That the cause, that man is worse, is not in God.

Then, the same (St.) Augustine[4] seeking, what is the cause, that man is worse, asserts that it is not in God, in the same book, saying thus: « The cause, that man is worse, either is in *him*, or in *another*, or in *nothing*. If in *nothing*, (then) there is no cause; if in *another*, either in *God*, or in any *other*[5] man, or in *that* which is neither God nor man. But (it is) not in *God*; for God is only the cause of good (things): therefore, either it is in man, or in that which (is) neither God nor man, or in nothing ».[6] — From these it is openly shown, that it is

not good, that man is worse, because God, who is only the cause of good (things), is not the cause of that thing. And if it is not good, that man comes to be worse, therefore, it is not good, that evil be done by him: therefore, God does not will, that evil be done by him.

Likewise, it is also shown in another manner, that with God as author, that is with (Him) willing, evils do not come to be, because He is not a cause *of tending to 'not-being'* [tendendi ad non-esse]. For *to tend* to '*not-being*' is evil. Moreover, He Himself is not an author of evil; but he who works evil tends to *not-being*: therefore, it is not with God as author, that anyone works evil. Therefore, it is not good, that anyone works evil, because God is only an author of good. Moreover, (St.) Augustine openly explains this in the same book,[7] saying thus: « He who is the Author of all which are, and to whose Goodness it pertains, that everything, which is, be, is the Cause only of the good. Wherefore [Quocirca] He is not an author of evil, and for that reason He is the Most High Good, from Whom there is in none a lacking [deficere] of the good; and evil is a lacking (of the good): therefore, He is not a cause of the lacking (of the good), that is of a tending to '*not-being*', Who, as I say, is the Cause of being [essendi causa]; because He is the Author of all which are, which inasmuch as they are, are good ». — Behold, you openly have, that to fail from God [deficere a Deo], who is the Most High Good, is evil: therefore, it is evil to work evils: therefore, not with God as author and/or willing do evils come to be.

It has already been sufficiently shown, that with God as author evils do not come to be. Yet certain (authors) proceeding [incedentes] *sophistically*, and for that reason *hateful to God*,[8] strive to prove, that it is from God as author, that evils come to be, in this manner: 'That evils come to be, is true; moreover, every truth [verum], which is, is from the Truth [veritate], which is God: therefore, it is from God, that evils come to be'. Moreover, that every truth is from God, they confirm by the authority of (St.) Augustine in (his) book of OF EIGHTY-THREE QUESTIONS,[9] saying thus: « That every truth (is) from the Truth, is true, but the Truth (is) God: therefore, every truth has God (as its) author ». But it is true, that evils come to be and/or are: therefore, with God as author it is, that there are and/or come to be evils.

To which it is easy for us to respond; but unworthy of a response seems that which they say: « For, indeed, every truth is from God », as (St.) Augustine says, with whom (St.) Ambrose[10] is consonant, who treating of that verse of the Apostle: *No one can say: "The Lord Jesus", except in the Holy Spirit*, says, that « every truth, by whomsoever it is said, is from the Holy Spirit ». And, thus, since it is true, that evils

---

[1] Thus the codices and edition 1; the Vatican edition and the other editions have *evils* [mala].

[2] Question 3, with not a few things omitted by Master (Peter).

[3] Contrary to the original and editions 1 and 6, there is added in the Vatican edition and the other editions, not well *human* [humanae], as is clear from the following proposition. A little below this after *Behold* [aperte dicit] very many editions omit *here* [hic].

[4] Ibid., q. 4. — A little below this after *asserts* [in Deo] the Vatican edition, together with a few editions, adds explicitly *it* [eam].

[5] The codices and edition 1 read *some* [aliquo], the original reads *any other* [aliquo alio].

[6] Thus the editions, except the Vatican, and all the codices. The words of (St.) Augustine have been contracted. For in the original after *for God is only the cause of good (things)* [bonorum Deus tantum causa est], there is had: « Therefore, if in a man, either *by force*, or *by persuasion*. But in no manner *by force*, lest he be stronger [valentior] than God. If indeed God made man so optimally, that if he wanted to remain the best, he would be impeded by nothing resisting. However, *by the persuasion* of another man, if we concede that man is depraved, again it will have to be asked, by whom was the persuader himself depraved. For the persuader of such can-

not not be depraved. It remains (therefore, that) I do not know what, that which is neither God nor man, (is); but yet this, whatever it is, either *was borne upon (him) by force* or *persuaded* (him). Concerning *force* it is responded as above; but concerning *persuasion* whatever it is, because persuasion does not move the unwilling, the cause of his depravation returns to the will of the same man, whether with someone or with no one persuading (him), he was depraved ». But the Vatican ed. reads thus more briefly: *if, therefore, it is in man, either (it is) by force or by persuasion, but (it is) in neither manner: neither is it even in that, which neither God, nor man: and from these* [si ergo in homine est, aut vi aut suasione, sed neutro modo: neque etiam in eo est, quod neque Deus, neque homo sit: et ex his].

[7] Question 21; but much changed and transposed by Master (Peter).

[8] A reference to Ecclesiasticus 37:23: *Who speaks sophistically, is hateful* [Qui sophistice loquitur, odibilis est].

[9] Question 1. The final words in the original are: *therefore, it has God as (its) author, as thus the soul (does)* [Deum igitur habet auctorem, ut sic anima].

[10] 1 Cor. 12:3: *For whatever truth is said by whomsoever, is said by the Holy Spirit* [Quidquid enim verum a quocumque dicitur, a sancto dicitur Spiritu.]

come to be, this truth, which is said by that expression, namely "evils come to be", is from God; but from this it does not follow, that from God it is, that evils come to be. For, if this were said, God would be understood to be the Author of evils. Which is shown (to be) manifestly false from a simile: 'God prohibits theft to be done, but "that theft is done" is true: therefore, He prohibits a truth'. A non sequitur.

Therefore, leaving this and the other inane (arguments) of this kind, (and) favoring the saner side of the aforementioned question, which is more fully approved by the testimonies of the Saints, let us say, that God does not *will that evils come to be*, yet neither *does He will that they not come to be*, nor *is He unwilling that they come to be*. For[1] everything which He wills *to come to be*, comes to be, and everything which He wills *not to come to be*, does not come to be. But many come to be, which He does not will to come to be, such as all evils.

COMMENTARY ON DISTINCTION XLVI

On the fulfillment of the Divine Will.

Here, there arises a question. For it has been said in the above etc..

THE DIVISION OF THE TEXT

This is the second part of the entire Tract on the (Divine) Will, in which (part) Master (Peter) deals with the fulfilling of the Divine Will. And this part has two parts. In the first, having supposed from the preceding, that God's Will of Good Pleasure is always fulfilled, he removes the doubts.[1] In the second, he explains the truth, below in the next Distinction (where he says): *Indeed, the Will of God is always efficacious.*

The first part has two parts. In the *first*, Master (Peter) removes a doubt (which arises) through the comparison to goods; in the *second*, (he removes another which arises) through a comparison to evils, there (where he says): *And for that reason since it is established, that all goods, which come to be* etc.. The *first* part has two parts. In the first, Master (Peter) objects. In the second, he solves (the doubt), there (where he says): *But let us hear the solution.*

And for that reason since it is established etc. This is the *second* part, in which Master (Peter) inquires, whether the Will of God is fulfilled in respect of evils; and for this reason he inquires, whether God wills that evils come to be. And, since there were two opinions here, one of which was, that God wills that evils come to be — and this opinion is false — the other opinion is, that God does not will that evils come to be — and this opinion is true — for that reason this part[2] has two parts. In the first, Master (Peter) opposes the false side. In the second, he opposes the true side, there (where he says): *If anyone, therefore, diligently attends* etc.. The first part has two (parts). In the first, he adduces reason for

the defense of the false opinion. In the second part, he posits the solutions, which they, who are of the contrary position, assign, and this (he does) there (where he says): *Those, on the other hand, who say, that by the Will of God evils do not come to be* etc.. And each of the parts has two (parts). For in opposing he brings forward two reasons,[3] one of which is supported by reason, the other by authority; and the part, in which he solves (the doubt), is divided according to this, because there are posited the two responses in accord with the two objections.

If anyone, therefore, diligently attends etc.. This is that part, in which Master (Peter) strives to build up [astruendam] the true side; and this part has two (parts). In the first, he induces true reasons;[4] in the second, he dissolves a certain sophistic reason, and this he does there (where he says): *It has already been sufficiently shown* etc.. The first part has three parts according to the three reasons, which he brings forward. The first has been taken from this, that it is the same that (something) come to be with God as author, and with God willing, and (this) is posited there (where he says): *If anyone, therefore, diligently attends* etc.. The second has been taken from this, that the cause, by which evil comes to be, and by which man is made worse, is the same, and (this) is posited there (where he says): *Then the same (St.) Augustine seeking* etc.. The third has been taken from this,[5] that evil causes (a thing) to tend to *not-to-be* [non-esse], and (this) is posited there (where he says): *Likewise, it is also shown in another manner, that with God as author* etc..

---

[1] The Vatican edition and the other editions have faultily *Therefore* [ergo], contradicting the codices and edition 1.

NOTES ON THE COMMENTARY

[1] The Vatican edition, a little before this, having omitted the word *God's* [Dei], and then before *he removes* [removet] having interjected *here* [hic], after *the doubts* [dubitationes] adjoins *which arise from this supposition* [quae ex hac suppositione oriuntur].

[2] In the Vatican edition here there is a very notable omission: the words from *and for this reason* [et ratione huius] up to *for that reason this part* [ideo haec pars] inclusively.

[3] The Vatican ed. has *objections* [obiectiones] for *reasons* [rationes], and, next, *two reasons* [duae rationes] for *two responses* [duae responsiones].

[4] The Vatican ed. has *responses* [responsiones] for *reasons* [rationes].

[5] The Vatican edition reads *for this* [ad hoc]. Near the end of the exposition (on the next page) for *this side* [hanc partem] codex Z has *this position* [hanc positionem].

Similarly, the second part, in which he dissolves the sophistic reason, has there (parts). In the first, he posits it, there (where he says): *It has already been sufficiently shown* etc.. In the second, he dissolves (it), there (where he says): *To which it is easy for us to respond* etc.. In the

third, he returns to the assertion of the truth, saying, that this side [hanc partem] is the true one, that God does not will that evils come to be, there (where he says): *Therefore, leaving this and the other* etc..

TREATMENT OF THE QUESTIONS

For the evidence of those which Master (Peter) determines in the present Distinction, six (things) are asked.

First, there is asked, whether God wills that all men come to be saved by the Will of (His) Good Pleasure.

Second, there is asked, whether God wills that evils come to be [fieri].

Third, whether it is good that evils come to be.

Fourth, whether it is true that evils come to be.

Fifth, whether evils are ordained by God.

Sixth and last, whether evils increase the adornment in the universe [decorem in universo].

ARTICLE SOLE

On God's Will in respect of the salvation of all, and in respect of the wicked.

QUESTION I

Whether God wills that all men come to be saved by the Will of (His) Good Pleasure?

Moreover, that God wills that all men come to be saved by the Will of (His) Good Pleasure, is shown in this manner:

1. In the second (chapter of St. Paul's) First (Letter) to Timothy (there is written):[1] *He wills that all men come to be saved*; but it is established, that this has not been said of the will of *a sign*, because (it is a sign) neither of a precept nor of the fulfilling (of God's Will) nor of (that) of any other — for this does not fall under a precept — therefore, it is established that it has been said of the Will of (His) *Good Pleasure*.

2. Likewise, (St. John) Damascene (says):[2] « It is necessary to know, that God wills *antecedently*, that all men come to be saved, and take possession [potiri fortuna] of His own kingdom; for God has not formed [plasmavit] us for punishment »: therefore, since (His) *antecedent* Will is the Will of (His) Good Pleasure, which is of the good (things), which are irrefragably good, by the Will of (His) Good Pleasure He wills that all men come to be saved or be saved [salvos fieri sive salvari].

3. Likewise, everyone having *charity* wills that all men come to be saved, howsoever much a small measure of love [modicam dilectionem][3] he has. Therefore, since God has a Most High Love and Charity, it seems, that He Himself wills that all men come to be saved.

4. Likewise, just as the Philosopher[4] would have it, The First (Being) holds Himself in one manner to all (things) or to all (men), therefore, as much as He is of Himself, He uniformly loves [diligit] all (men): therefore, if He wills to save some, (He) also (wills to save) all; and/or if He does not will (such) of some, for an equal reason (He will it) concerning none.

1. **AGAINST** this *first* is the instance, which Master (Peter) adduces in the text:[5] 'if He wills that all men come to be saved, and (that) more of all are damned, than saved, therefore, His Will is frustrated and cancelled'; which is openly contrary to the truth.

2. Likewise, all whom God wills to be saved, *He elects* to salvation [eligit ad salutem] — for God's "election" does not mean other than (His) "choosing to save" [dilectionem ad salvandum] — therefore, if He wills that all come to be saved, all have been elected. *On the contrary*, in the twenty-second (chapter of the Gospel of St.) Matthew (there is written):[6] *Many have been called, but few elected.*

3. Likewise, in (God's) *predestination* there are not but these two, namely, (God's) *precognition* and (His) *Will to save*, by reason of which God is said to predestine. For while He proposes to give grace and to prepare glory, He is said to predestine: therefore, since God's precognition is common

---

[1] Verse 4.

[2] ON THE ORTHODOX FAITH, Bk. II, ch. 29. See the original text above d. 41, a. 1, q. 1, p. 728, footnote 2. — Near the end of the argument. the Vatican edition reads thus: *by the Will of (His) Good Pleasure He wills (it), therefore, He wills that all men* etc. [vult voluntate beneplaciti, vult ergo omnes etc].

[3] The Vatican edition and cod. cc adjoin *and charity* [et caritatem].

[4] Understand the author of the BOOK OF CAUSES, whose words have already been cited above in d. 37, p. I, a. 3, q. 2, p. 646, foot-

note 1. Cf. also proposition 20, in which there is taught, that the First Cause by standing still in Its own Unity rules all (things). — The Vatican edition, after *First* [primum], adjoins *Being, namely God* [ens, scilicet Deus].

[5] Here in ch. 1. — Next for *come to be saved* [salvos fieri] the Vatican edition, together with codex cc, reads *be saved* [salvari].

[6] Verse 14. — On the minor proposition, which precedes, cf. above d. 40, a. 3, q. 1 f..

[7] See above d. 40, a. 1, q. 1, in reply to n. 5, and ibid., q. 2.

to all, if (His) Will of salvation is in respect of all, therefore, all have been predestined. But all the predestined shall be saved: therefore, all shall be saved; which is contrary to the Faith [quod est contra fidem]. *If you say* to me, that there is a twofold Will, *the absolute* and *the conditional*, and (that) God by (His) absolute Will only wills to save *those whom He has foreknown to be made conform to the Image of His Son*,[1] and those He has predestined, but by (His) conditional Will He wills that all (come to be saved), if they themselves will (it); *then it is objected*, that (His) conditional Will does not seem to convene with God, because this Will is semi-full, but God, whatever He wills, He wills fully. And, *again*, whatever He does, He does fully. And, *again*, this conditioned Will either is the Will of (His) *Good Pleasure*, or the will of *a sign*. If *of a sign*, then (it is) nothing regarding the proposed, because by the will for a sign He does not will that all men come to be saved. If (it is) the Will of (His) *Good Pleasure*; but This is and is said in only one manner and It is always fulfilled: therefore, all men are saved. And, *moreover*, this conditioned Will, by which it is said, that 'He wills (that all come to be saved), if they themselves will (it)', cannot have a place among the little ones [in parvulis], who die: therefore, this distinction still does not solve (the question).

4. Likewise, when it is, thus, said: "He wills this one to be saved" [vult hunc salvari], with anyone demonstrated (to be saved), either that which it is 'to will' connotes *something*, or *nothing*. If *nothing*: therefore, for an equal reason it can be said of a stone, that God wants to save it. If *something*, not but salvation: therefore, it follows, 'if He wills to save this one, that that one will be saved', in whatsoever manner "*to will*" be accepted. *If you say*, that it connotes a possibility and ordinability to salvation; *then it is objected*, that it can be said of anything ordainable to anything, that God wills (such); but any cleric is able to be ordained to the episcopate, and any soldier to the royal dignity: therefore, God wills, that all clerics be bishops, and that all soldiers be kings; which is not conceded.

CONCLUSION

God wills, that all by the Will of (His) Good Pleasure come to be saved, which can be understood either with (St.) Augustine of (His) consequent Will, or with (St. John) Damascene of (His) antecedent Will.

I RESPOND: It must be said, that since the Apostle says, that God wills this, namely, *that all men come to be saved*, on this account [quod] we hold that it is necessary to concede, that God *wills* (it). And, since it cannot be expounded of the will of a *sign*, we hold that it is necessary to expound it of the Will of (His) *Good Pleasure*. But, since not all are saved, and the Will of God is never frustrated, for that reason it is necessary, that the force (of its meaning) comes to be in *the manner of distributing*, and/or in the *manner of willing*.[2]

And the egregious Doctor, (St.) Augustine, gives [facit] a twofold force (to the expression) in *the manner of distributing* in (his) ENCHIRIDION:[3] *in one manner*, that the distribution be an *apt* one [accommoda], just as this is: "Every man is afraid in the sea", (which) according to the common manner of speaking is understood (to mean): "He who is in the sea (is afraid)". Similarly, (St.) Augustine[4] gives an example [exemplificat], if there be said: « 'That master teaches all the boys of that city', because, that is, he teaches all who are learning [addiscunt]. For none is taught except through him ». Similarly, « 'God wills that all men come to be saved', because none is saved, unless God wills (it), and for that reason He must be entreated [orandus est], to will (it) ».[5] — He also renders the force (of the meaning) *in another manner* in a distribution according to the common manner of distinguishing, since (the distribution) can be made on behalf of *each of the genera*, and in this manner (i.e. "He wills every single one of men to come to be saved") it is false, and the Apostle does not understand (it) thus; and/or on behalf of *the genera of each*, and in this manner (it is) true, because from every nation [gente] He willed and does will that some be saved, both from the Greeks and the Latins, and from those placed over (others) and those placed beneath (others) [prelatis et subditis], and from every nation; and for that reason the Apostle says,[6] that He is to be entreated on behalf of all. This is the response of (St.) Augustine, upon which Master (Peter) leans; and

---

[1] Romans 8:29. — Next after *all* [omnes] in codex V there is added *come to be saved* [salvos fieri], in codex W there is added *men (come to be saved)*.

[2] Or in other words: for that reason it is necessary, that either we accept the distributive sign "*all*" [omnes] by distinguishing (it) in a congruous sense, and/or that we distinguish the verb "*wills*" [vult], insofar as, that is, it can signify either the antecedent or the consequent Will.

[3] Chapter 103, n. 27. See it here in the text of Master (Peter), ch. 2. — A little after this for *apt* [accommoda] the Vatican edition has *accommodated* [accommodata]. On apt distribution, cf. above d. 29, Doubt 1, p. 517, footnote 3.

[4] In his book, ON NATURE AND GRACE AGAINST PELAGIUS, ch. 41, n. 48: « And thus "*all*" has been said, lest anyone believe in any other manner besides this one that they can come to be saved. For just as, with one master of letters constituted in a city, we most rightly say: "this one teaches all (their) letters here"; not because all the citizens are learning (their) letters, but because no one learns (them), except him whom he will have taught: thus no one is justified, except him whom Christ will have justified ». The same example is had in his unfinished work AGAINST JULIAN, Bk. II; sent. 444 in these words:

Just as we say of a master of letters, if he is the only one in a city: "this one teaches all (their) letters here"; not because all learn, but because no one (learns) but from him.

[5] (St.) Augustine, ENCHIRIDION, ch. 103, n. 27, where even those which follow here are found according to their sense. (St.) Augustine makes the same distinction, as here, in his unfinished work AGAINST JULIAN, Bk. IV, sent. 124: In what manner does God have mercy upon all, when some Scripture says: *Thou does not have mercy upon all who work iniquity* (Ps. 58:6), except because there are thus also among those upon whom He does not have mercy, "all" men, as "*all the genera* of" men, just as has been said: *You tithe every herb* (Lk. 11:42), i. e. every genus of herb? — A little below this after (before in the English) *can be made* [potest fieri] supply together with codices M Z ff and edition *distribution*; for *can be made* [potest fieri] codex H has *can distribute* [potest distribuere]; the Vatican edition reads thus: *according to every many of distributing, which (distribution) can come to be* etc. [secundum omnem modum distribuendi, quae potest fieri pro etc.]

[6] 1 Timothy 2:1 f.. — See the sentence here in the text of Master (Peter), in ch. 2.

it is necessary to solve (the matter) in this manner and/or in that, having supposed that *"to will"* means there the willing of God, according to which He is said to will by (His) quiet pleasure [placito quietato] or by (His) absolute Will, of which it is true to say: *All whichsoever He has willed, He has done.*[1]

But (St. John) Damascene[2] puts [facit] the force (of the meaning) in the *manner of willing*. For he distinguishes in God an *antecedent* Will and a *consequent* Will. And the *antecedent* Will is the Will in respect of that, for the sake of which God makes man, and It is irrefragably of the good. But the *consequent* Will is the Will, not which follows merits, but which wills some (things) according to the Foreknowledge of merits. The *first* one, namely the antecedent, is said by the masters (of theology to be) the *conditional* Will or the Will, by which God wills, as much as is Himself. But the *second* one, namely, the consequent, is said (to be) *the absolute* (Will). Moreover, the difference between this Will and that One is not according to a diversity of *affection* or of a manner of willing, which is *in God*, but according to the reckoning of *connoting* and *understanding*. — For insofar as God is said "to will the salvation of all", as much as it is in Himself *antecedently*, there is connoted in all men an ordinability[3] to salvation, both on the part of the nature given (to man), and on the part of the grace offered. For God gave a *nature*, according to which (men) could cognize Him and seek the One cognized and find the One sought and cleave to [inhaerere] the One found, and through this obtain salvation. Similarly, He offered *grace*, while He sent and offered the Son, the Price of which (grace) sufficed for the salvation of all. He also granted and showed the *Laws* and commandments of salvation. *He Himself* is also at hand for all seeking (Him) and *He is near to all invoking Him.*[4] Therefore, 'to will *antecedently* to save a man' is 'to cause (him to be) ordered to salvation' and 'to not be remiss that the one being willed [volenti] arrives (there)'. But 'to will *consequently* or absolutely to save (a man)' is 'to will to give *salvation* to him, whom He foreknows (is) going to arrive at salvation through His own

assistance and grace', and connotes *the outcome of salvation* [salutis eventum]. And, in this manner, there is no saying, that God wills that all men come to be saved.

With this response the masters (of theology) are more consonant, even though each is good. According to this, therefore, it must be responded, that God wills that all men come to be saved, as much as it is in Himself or by (His) *antecedent* Will, but not by (His) *absolute* or *consequent* Will.

1. 2. 3. 4. And, because the former (Will) does not connote the outcome of the effect, for that reason it is not impeded in this, that not all are saved. — The response to that which it objects concerning *predestination* or *election* is also clear, because in those is enclosed the absolute Will, not only the antecedent (Will). — The response to the last (objection) concerning (what is) connoted is also clear.

To that, however, which *is objected*, that a *conditioned* will does not occur in God; it must be said, that there is not posited in God a willingness [velleitas] as much as regards a defect[5] of fullness of the Will nor on account of diverse manners of willing, but on account of another comparison in connoting, and in this manner that (objection) is clear.

1. 2. However, to the reasons for the opposite, that God wills that all men come to be saved; it can be responded to the first two, that they conclude the truth and truly.

3. But to that which is objected concerning the charity of men, it must be said, that it is not similar, because we do not know the future merits of men in a final manner; and if anyone would know, that any had been foreknown, even though, as much as it is in him, (by charity) he would be obliged [deberet] to will that they be saved, yet not by (his) absolute will. But these (things) will be clear in a better manner below.[6]

4. To that which is objected, that God holds Himself in one manner to all; it must be said, that that word of the Philosopher has (its) place as much as regards (God's) governance [gubernationem] of things, not as much as regards their production; and/or as much as regards natural (things), not as much as regards gratuitous ones.

SCHOLIUM

I. Master (Peter) in this Distinction labors not a little, to sustain, that the Divine Will *never* comes to be cancelled, neither if *It wills* good, nor if *It does not will* evil. First of all he strives to explain the words of the Apostle (1 Tim 2:4): *Who wills that all men come to be saved* etc. [Qui omnes homines vult salvos fieri etc.]. Wherefore, there occurs this question, "Whether God truly wills the salvation of *all* men?"; with which there have been intimately connected two other questions: "Whether Christ died on behalf of all men?", and "Whether God confers and/or at least offers to all men the means

[media] sufficient for salvation?" — It has been noted, that Cornelius Jansen, following in the footsteps of (John) Calvin, responds *negatively* to these three questions for the state of fallen nature; likewise, that (Pope) Innocent X, in his Constitution, CUM OCCASIONE, May 31, 1653 A.D., damned the proposition of Jansen (which said): « It is semi-pelagian to say, that Christ died or poured out (His) Blood for entirely all men ». Cf. also among the proposition of Paschasius Quesnell, damned by (Pope) Clement XI in his Constitution UNIGENITUS, Sept. 8, 1713 A. D., propositions 30 and

---

[1] Psalm 113:11.

[2] ON THE ORTHODOX FAITH, Bk. II; ch. 29. See the words themselves of (St. John) Damascene above in d. 41, a. 1, q. 1, p. 728, footnote 2.

[3] For *ordinability* [ordinabilitas], which reading codices P Q and T (H in the margin) exhibit, the Vatican edition reads *ordered* [in omnibus ordinatis], having omitted *men an* [hominibus], which is extant in all the codices. Next after *For God gave* [Dedit enim] the same Vatican edition inserts *them* [eis], and then for *Him* [ipsum], which is incongru-

ously omitted by very many codices and edition 1, it substitutes *Him* [eum], in place of which codex T (by a second hand) has *God* [Deum]; there was first written in codex T *Him* [ipsum].

[4] Psalm 114:18.

[5] For a *defect* [defectum] many codices, together with the six first editions, have *an effect* [effectum]; codex T militates for *a defect* [defectum]. Immediately before this for *willingness* [velleitas] codices A I and W have *will* [voluntas].

[6] Distinction 48, a. 2, qq. 1 and 2, and Doubt 1.

32. — Against these errors St. Bonaventure taught, that Christ died for all, SENT., Bk. III, d. 20, q. 4, in the body of the Response and in reply to n. 1; SENT., Bk. IV, d. 4, p. I, a. 1. q. 3, in reply to n. 3; — likewise, that God offers sufficient assistances in diverse manners to all, SENT., Bk. II, d. 28, a. 1. q. 3, in reply to n. 1, and a. 2, q. 1, in reply to n. 1. — In regard to the little ones, dying without baptism, cf. SENT., Bk. II, d. 32, a. 3. q. 2, in reply to n. 6.

II. In regard to the exposition of that testimony of the Apostle: *Who wills that all men come to be saved*, it must be noted, that since the Pelagians and Semi-Pelagians abused this saying to confirm their own errors, St. Augustine thought out many interpretations, which understand the term *"all"* with a *restriction*, and the term *"wills"* in the sense of the *consequent* Will (that is the Will *absolute* and *efficacious* in respect of salvation). Thus Master (Peter) also interprets this passage, and St. Bonaventure and the other ancient masters report these expositions as good and probable; but they seem to prefer the other, plainer one of St. John Damascene, proposed here, as (Bl. John Duns) Scotus explicitly says (here in the q. sole, n. 3): « Yet it can be much better expounded of the *antecedent* Will ». St. Augustine himself (ON SPIRIT AND LETTER, ch. 33, and ON THE CATECHESIS OF THE UNLETTERED, ch. 26) sufficiently indicates an exposition according to the antecedent Will. In our age it is commonly taught, that the Divine Will of saving all pertains to the *antecedent* Will, but predestination and reprobation to the *consequent* Will.

III. About this distinction of an *antecedent* and *consequent* Will diverse sentences and been defended. In Alexander of Hales (SUMMA., p. I. q. 36, m. 2) there is posited in the first place the opinion, that the antecedent Will to save all is not the Will of *the Good Pleasure*, but the will of a *sign*; which sentence pleased even not a few, later theologians, but which is reproved by Alexander, St. Bonaventure, St. Thomas (DE VERITATE., q. 23, a. 3, SENT., Bk. I, d. 47, q. 1. a. 2) and others commonly. — Omitting the other obsolete explanations of this distinction, it is now commonly taught, that the *antecedent* Will in God attains the object *in itself*, abstracted [praecisis] from (its) circumstances, but the *consequent* (Will attains) the object *clothed with all (its) circumstances* (see St. Thomas's explanation, SUMMA, I, q. 19, a. 1, in reply to n. 1). In the final determination of these circumstances, theologians depart into diverse sentences. Those who defend a predestination after foreseen merits, think, that the prevision of the consent of the human will precedes God's consequent Will. But the opposite sentence of the Thomists would have it, that each Will, both the *antecedent* and the *consequent*, antecedes the prevision of merits, and that the *antecedent* Will prepares assistances and means sufficient for all, but the *consequent* (Will prepares) only efficacious assistances for the elect (Gotti, I, tr. 8, dubium 4, § 2).

IV. Let it suffice for us to put on display [in conspectu ponere] what St. Bonaventure teaches concerning this distinction here and below in d. 47, a. 1. These convene very much with those, which St. Thomas has in his Commentary on the Sentences (here in the q. sole, a. 1).

1. This distinction is attained not on the part of the Divine *Will* Itself, but on the part of *the willed*. « Moreover, the difference between this Will and that One is not according to a diversity of *affection* or of a manner of willing, which is *in God*, but according to the reckoning of *connoting* and *understanding* » (here in the Response). St. Thomas (loc. cit., in the Resp.) says: « This happens not from any diversity of the Divine *Will*, but on account of the diverse conditions of the willed *itself* ».

2. In the *antecedent* Will « there is connoted the ordinability[3] of all men to salvation, both on the part of the nature given (to man), and on the part of the grace offered » (St. Bonaventure, *ibid.*). St. Thomas says (ibid.): « The *effect* of this Will (i. e. the antecedent) is the very order of nature unto the end of salvation and (the things), commonly proposed to all, promoting [promoventia] unto the End, (things) both natural and gratuitous, just as (are) the natural powers and the precepts of the Law, and (things) of this kind ».

3. Wherefore the *antecedent* Will is not a pure willingness [velleitas], but in regard the its own *proper* effect (namely, the *ordinability* to and the means sufficient for salvation) It is always efficacious. This is explicitly taught (below in d. 47, q. 1, in the body of the Response): « Wherefore the (antecedent) Will is not cancelled, because It has a proper effect ».

4. The *consequent* Will connotes « the *outcome of salvation* » (here in the body of the Response); and just as « it connotes an *effect*, thus it connotes *the existence of a particular cause* », and « it connotes the concurrence of a created cause » (d. 47. q. 1, in reply to n. 2). St. Thomas (ibid.) notes in the consequent Will this circumstance, that a man « is willing and preparing himself for his own salvation, and/or is also repugnant or acting contrarily ».

5. In the *consequent* Will there is implied *the Foreknowledge of salvation*, because it is « a willing to give salvation to him, whom He foreknows (is) going to arrive at salvation through His own assistance and grace » (here in the body of the Response). « For He never would will (that this one is saved), unless He equally foreknew, that he was going to be saved » (d. 47, q. 1).

6. There is also implied in the same *consequent* Will *the Foreknowledge of good works*. « Moreover, the consequent Will is the Will, not which follows merits, but which wills some (things) according to the Foreknowledge of merits » (here in the body of the Resp.). « The Will of God according to (Its) convening with the (Divine) Foreknowledge wills those (things) which It wills » (d. 47, q. 1, in reply to n. 4). Similarly, St. Thomas (loc. cit. at the end of the body of the Resp.) says: « It is said (to be) the "consequent Will", for this, that It presupposes the Foreknowledge of works, not as the cause of the *Will*, but as the quasi *reason for the willed* ». Concerning the Foreknowledge of merits, to the extent that it can be a *motive reason* for the Will, we have observed, above in d. 41, a. 1,* qq. 1 and 2, that St. Bonaventure speaks in a little different manner than St Thomas.

V. Alexander of Hales, SUMMA., p. I, q. 36, m. 2, in reply to n. 1. — (Bl. John Duns) Scotus, here in the q. sole, in reply to n. 1. — St. Thomas, locc. citt. — Bl. (now St.) Albertus (Magnus), here in a. 1; d. 40, a. 8; SUMMA ., p. I, tr. 20, q. 79, m. 3, a. 2, incidental question. — (Bl.) Peter of Tarentaise, here in q. 1, a. 1. — Richard of Middleton, here in q. 1. — Giles the Roman, here in 1st. princ., q. sole. — Durandus (of Saint-Pourçain), here in q. 1. — (Bl.) Dionysius the Carthusian, partly in q. 1.

QUESTION II

Whether God wills that evils come to be?

Second, there is asked, whether God wills that evils come to be. And that (it is) so, is shown:

1. Through (St.) Anselm (of Canterbury):[1] "God does not will", he says, "that what is impossible come to be": therefore, through *the consequence from the con-* *verse manner* [per consequentiam e converso], that which is possible to come to be, God wills: but it is possible that evil come to be: therefore, that evil come to be is willable by God.

2. Likewise, every just (man) wills everything which be-

---

[1] This sentence seems to have been taken and been formed from CUR DEUS HOMO, Bk. II, ch. 18: « For nothing is necessary or impossible, except because He Himself wills (it) thus; for either that He wills or does not will something on account of necessity or impossibility, is alien from the truth ». In which text the proposition of (St.) Anselm cited here by the Seraphic Doctor is necessarily supposed, because the impossibility of things is demonstrated to impose no necessity or coercion [coactionem] upon God's Will. — The words *through the consequence from the converse (manner)* [per consequentiam e converso] or *from the contrary (manner)*, as had in edition 1 and also below in the solution of this objection, occur in Aristotle, TOPICS, Bk. II, ch. 3 (ch. 8). And it must be noted, that this consequence is comprehended under a *consequence of opposites*, which (consequence) differs generally in this from a *simple conse-*

longs to justice; but « every punishment is just »,[1] as (St.) Augustine says, and every evil (is) a punishment: therefore, every evil, which comes to be, has been willed by God to come to be. That every evil is a punishment, is clear through (St.) Augustine in the first (book) of (his) CONFESSIONS: « Thou has commanded, Lord », he says, « and so it is, that every inordinate spirit is a punishment to itself ».

3. Likewise, with two opposed proposals, among which there is no middle ground [medium], it is necessary, that one of the two be known by God: therefore, for an equal reason it is necessary, that one of the two be willed (by God). But with one demonstrated (to be) a sinner, "that this one sins", (and) "that this one does not sin" are opposites: therefore, God wills one of the two. But whichever God wills, that one comes to be: therefore, if He wills this one not to sin, this one does not sin, which is contrary to the hypothesis:[2] therefore, He wills that this one sins. But this is evil: therefore, that evil come to be is (something) willed by God.

4. Likewise, every (being) willing something by a counseled and deliberate will wills[3] that, without which the former cannot be — for even though someone wills to be an abbot, but not a monk, yet, if he deliberatively wills to be an abbot, he equally wills to be a monk — but God wills some good, which can never be without evil, such as that His Saints be proved and that His Son suffer: ergo etc..

ON THE CONTRARY: 1. Nothing is by anyone willed and/or willable, which entirely displeases and is odious to him; but in the twelfth (chapter)[4] of Ecclesiasticus there is said: *The Most High holds sinners in hatred*; but not but by reason of (their) sin or evil: therefore, He hates evil much more: therefore, He does not will it to come to be.

2. Likewise, (St.) Augustine in the book, OF EIGHTY-THREE QUESTIONS, (says):[5] « The same comes to be with God willing and with God as author »; but evil does not come to be with God as (its) author: therefore, evil does not come to be with God willing (it). The *first* he himself supposes, *the second* he proves, because « by no wise man does a man come to be worse »: therefore, much more strongly neither with God.

3. Likewise, it seems *by reason*: because every will either *is denominated* by the willed, or *denominates* the willed.[6] Therefore, if God wills an evil, either (His) will is "*evil*", or if (His) Will is good, the willed is "*good*": therefore, either nothing is evil, or God is evil, if He wills evil to come to be. But each (is) false: ergo etc..

4. Likewise, everyone willing an evil wills under the reckoning of (something) appearing (to be) good,[7] therefore, everyone willing an evil is deceived: therefore, if God wills that evils come to be, God is deceived: which is impossible.

5. Likewise, everyone who wills something, which he cannot (do), is wretched; but God cannot (work) evil, just as has been proven above:[8] therefore, if He wills it, He is wretched. But this is impossible: ergo etc..

CONCLUSION

Evil is neither willable by God, nor does God will that it be done by others.

I RESPOND: It must be said, just as the last reasons prove, that evil is not *willable by God*, the "evil", I say, (which is) of fault, because every will is inordinate, which is pleased by that evil; and this all concede.

Yet, some wanted to say, that God wills that evil *come to be*, though He Himself is not its cause, but another (is), with God willing (it so). And indeed they used to say that God willed this not by reason of Himself, by reason of that, which He elicits from it. — But this is contrary to (St.) Augustine, just as Master (Peter) has shown in the text,[9] who disproves this opinion. For that reason, neither is to be conceded, but, if it is read anywhere, it is to be expounded.

1. To that, therefore, which is objected to the contrary, that God does not will what is impossible to come to be; it must be said, that "*not willing*" [non velle] is said in a twofold manner, either *negatively*, or *privatively*. If *negatively* (i. e. "not to will"), that is not true, nor does (St.) Anselm understand (it) thus. If *privatively*, then the one saying is "*He is unwilling*" [non vult], and it is the third person (singular) of that (verb),

---

quence, which is among those, one of which follows the other and vice versa. And this consequence is twofold: a consequence *in the same manner* (ἐπὶ ταὐτά), and *from the contrary manner* (ἀνάπαλιν) — in a direct manner and in an inverse order — insofar as it is either inferred in the same order of opposite terms, and/or not in the same order, but in an inverse order. A consequence *in the same manner* is found only in convertibles, v. g. 'if it is a man, he is risible; but it is not a man: therefore, it is not risible'. An example of a consequence *from the contrary manner* (is): 'if it is a man, it is an animal; but it is not an animal: therefore, neither is it a man'. To speak briefly: a consequence *in the same manner* is, when from the first premise there is inferred the opposite of the predicate from the opposite of the subject; a consequence *from the contrary manner*, when from the first premise there is inferred the opposite of the subject from the opposite of the predicate. Concerning the consequence *from the contrary manner* Aristotle, loc. cit., and also St. Bonaventure below in the solution to this objection, teach, that they are valid in contradictories, but not in contraries, at least not in all (contraries).

[1] RETRACTATIONS, Bk. I, ch. 26, and ON FREE WILL, Bk. III, ch. 18, n. 51. — The text next cited from the first book of the Confessions is had there in ch. 12, n. 19, where in the edition of the Works of St. Augustine after *is* [poena] there is added *its own* [sua] for *a*. In the text cited, for *inordinate spirit* [inordinatus animus] the codices, together with edition 1, have *inordinate movement* [motus inordinatus]. In the major proposition of this argument, for *which belongs to justice* [quod iustitiae est] the Vatican edit ion has *which is just* [quod iustum est].

[2] For *hypothesis* [hypothesim] the Vatican edition has *position* [positionem].

[3] After *wills* [vult] the Vatican edition, together with one or the other codex, subjoins *every* [omne], and at the end of the argument, together with many codices and edition 1, it prefaces the word *also* [et] to the word *suffer* [Filium].

[4] Verse 3.

[5] Question 3. Cf. the text of Master (Peter) here, in ch. 6.

[6] The object of the will or the willed is the good; hence the will is either denominated by the willed *as good*, inasmuch as, that is, it wills something, which is in itself good, thus it is in respect of a created will; or it itself denominates the willed, inasmuch as, that is, the goodness of the will grants goodness to the object (of the will); thus it is in respect of the Divine Will.

[7] Cf. above d. 45, a. 2, q. 1, p. 804, footnote 6. On the subsequent proposition, cf. Aristotle, ETHICS, Bk. III, chs. 1 and 5, where there is taught, that every evil is unknown [irgnorantem]. Dionysius (the Areopagite), ON THE DIVINE NAMES, ch. 4, § 32 shows, that evil is per accidens, since it comes to be on account of a good. « On which account, what (is) not good, we judge (to be) good », i. e. we are deceived. — Next, for *evils* [mala] codex T has *evil* [malum].

[8] Distinction 42, q. 2. In regard to the major proposition of the argument, we cite the saying of (St.) Augustine, ON A BLESSED LIFE, n. 11: Therefore, everyone, I say, who does not have what he wills, is he wretched? All think so [Placuit omnibus]. Cf. also above d. 45, a. 1. q. 1, p. 798, footnote 8.

[9] Here in ch. 1.

which is "*I am unwilling*" [nolo]; and in this manner God is said "to be unwilling", because *He absolutely wills* that it not come to be. But in this manner there is no saying, that God is unwilling that evils come to be; and in this manner it has no *consequence from the contrary*, because it does not hold in contraries, but in contradictories.[1]

2. To that which is objected, that anyone just wills justice etc; it must be said, that anything is said (to be) "just" in a twofold manner, that is, *in itself* and *out of an order*. What is just *in itself*, according to that which it is, has been willed by God. But what is just *on account of (its) order* [ex ordine][2] has been willed by God, according to which (it has) been ordered; and evil has not been willed, according to which (it is) *evil*, but according to which *it punishes*, and thus according to which (it has) *been ordered*, and thus, according to that which *it is*, it has not been willed.

3. To that which is objected, that with two op-posed proposals, it is necessary that (God) know one of the two, therefore, it is necessary that He will one of the two; it must be said, that speaking of the Will of (His) *Good Pleasure* it is not similar. For (His) *Knowledge* is in respect of all which come to be, but *the Will of (His) Good Pleasure* is not but in respect of those which are from Him.[3]

4. To that which is objected, that he who wills something, wills everything adjoined to it; it must be said, that "*to will something*" [velle aliq-uid] is in a twofold manner: either by an *antecedent* will, or by a *consequent* will. What someone wills by an *antecedent* will, he wills everything necessarily adjoined to it. But what he wills by a *consequent* will, he can also will without (what is) adjoined (to it). For good can be elicited out of evil, which would not be elicited, unless that *evil deed* was dis-pleasing and *the good elicited* completely pleasing to him who knew how [novit] to elicit (it). — Yet, one can respond through *interemption*,[4] that the one willing, by a counseled will, wills something, yet he does not will that which is con-sequent; just as someone wills that someone rises up [surg-ere], but yet he does not will that he has killed.

Yet, it can be said in another manner and better, that "*to will something without another*" is in a twofold manner: either 'to will this and not to will the other', because the one is pleasing and the other is displeasing; and in this manner it is possible among[5] those which have been inseparably conjoined. In another manner, "*to will something without another*" is to say "*to will*, that something is without that*"; and in this manner 'to will something without the inseparably adjoined' is to will the impossible. In the first manner, it does not follow, that one wills that, even though (it cannot) not without that. For the sense is, not 'without *that being*', but, how-ever, 'without *that willed*'. And there is a sensible ex-ample: for I will that someone, who kills, rises up; thus that I do not will, that he has killed; yet I do will, that he rises up, so that he does not kill.

SCHOLIUM

I. Evil considered in itself is dealt with chiefly (by St. Bonaventure) in SENT., Bk. II, dd. 34 and 35; BREVILOQUIUM, p. III, ch. 1; and in his SERMON ON THE SOWER, nn. 42.46 (Bonelli's, SUPPLEMENT, tome I, col. 410 ff.). — Though there is a threefold evil, namely, *of nature*, *of fault* and *of punishment*, here the evil *of fault* is dealt with, and indeed of that *formally*. — And it must be noted, that "*to will evil*" can be understood either thus, that the evil itself is an *immediate* object of the will, so that it is in him who wills *to do* evil, and/or thus, that the evil *is done by another*. In each sense God does not will evil; but in respect of the second sense there were not lacking those, who were of the opinion, that God wills that evil is done by oth-ers, since it *de facto* is done. Among these is Hugo of St. Vic-tor, who in ON THE SACRAMENTS, Bk. I, p. 4, ch. 14, indeed, at the beginning says: « By such a question we are constrained and lead into ambiguity, so that we do not easily dare to affirm this or that something, either that God precepted that there be done what He does not want, and/or has permitted what He does not want done ». But at the end of the said sentence he affirms: « And for that reason a pious mind refutes this, not because what is said is not well said, but because what is said well is not understood well ». The same teaches similar (things) in (his) SUMMA SENTENTIARUM, ch. 13. This false sentence is refuted under the guidance of Master Peter (here in chs. 3 and 4) by St. Bonaventure and the other Scholastics. The error of Hugo con-sisted in this, that he did not sufficiently distinguish these three: "*God hates* sin"; this is said truly and formally of God; "*God does not will that sins be done*"; this "*not willing*" is not properly in God, because otherwise no sins could be done, wherefore God neither wills that sins *be done*, nor wills that they *not be done*; but the third is true: "God *permits* sins to be done". — In regard to the solution to n. 4 and the distinction between a fault *in itself* and a fault *ordered* (to something else), cf. above d. 40, a. 4, q. 2; d. 46, q. 5, and SENT., Bk. II, d. 36, a. 1. q. 1.

II. Alexander of Hales, SUMMA., p. I, q. 40, m. 1. — (Bl. John Duns) Scotus, REPORTATIO., Bk. I, d. 47, q. 1. — St. Thomas, here in q. 1, a. 4; SUMMA., I, q. 19, a. 9; SUMMA CONTRA GENTILES., Bk. I, ch. 95. — Bl. (now St.) Albertus (Magnus), here in a. 4; SUMMA., p. I, tr. 20, q. 80, m. 2, a. 3, partic. 1. — (Bl.) Peter of Tarentaise, here in q. 1, a. 2. — Richard of Mid-dleton, here in q. 2. — Giles the Roman, here in 2nd princ., q. 2. — Durandus (of Saint-Pourçain), here in q. 2.

---

[1] The sense (of this argument) is: "not willing" [non velle] *negatively* is "not having *the volition*"; "not willing" *privatively* (in the contrary sense) is "having an *unwilling-ness*" [habere nolitionem]. Which in other words can be ex-pressed thus: "not willing", taken *negatively*, means a negation of the will, not a will of negation; but "not will-ing", accepted *privatively*, means the will of a negation, not a negation of a will. Taken in the first sense that saying of (St.) Anselm (of Canterbury) is not true, because many (things) can come to be, the 'to be' or 'to come to be' of which God positively does not will, and thus there is said: "Without Him nothing, i.e. sin, has been done"; but it is true, if "*He is unwilling*" [non vult] is accepted in the sec-ond sense, and then the sense of this saying of his is: "it is impossible, that what God wills, is not and/or does not come to be". But, yet, in this manner there is not said, that God is unwilling that evils come to be; nor does a consequence hold from *not being willing that they come to be* to *willing that they come to be*; because between these two there is a middle position, namely, "not willing that they come to be", taken negatively. In the midst of the argument, for *then "He is unwilling" is one saying, and it is the third person* [tunc non vult est una dic-tio, et est tertia persona] the Vatican ed. has *then "He is unwilling" is one saying, and it is the third person* [tunc non velle est una dictio, et est tertia persona].

[2] Codex G and W read thus: *on account of (its) order and (has been) willed by God, is willed according to* etc. [ex ordine et volitum a Deo, est volitum secundum etc.]. A little further below this, for *it pun-ishes* [punit] codex R has *(it is) punitive* [punitivum].*

[3] Understand: *from God* [Deo]. — Codex R has *from It (i. e. the Will of His Good Pleasure)* [ipsa]. A little before this, for *come to be* [fiunt] codices S and V have *are* [sunt].*

[4] Cf. above in d. 3, p. II, a. 1, q. 3, p. 87, footnote 4. — Next, in the Vatican ed. is missing *that which* [quod] before *is consequent* [consequitur].

[5] The Vatican edition reads *for those* [his] for *among those* [in his], and then omits *to say* [dicere].°

---

* *Trans. notes*: In the critical edition above, the sign for footnote 2 is in the third position and that for footnote 3 is in the second, though the notes correspond to the text; since this appears to be a typesetter's error, the signs have been reversed, and the contents of both notes transposed.

° Which change requires the quotes "", signifying verbal statements to be changed to ' ', signifying notional statements.

QUESTION III

Whether it is good that evils come to be?

Third, there is asked, whether it is good that evils come to be. And that (it is) so, is shown in this manner:

1. That which is expedient for the one working for salvation, is good; but evil is of this kind — wherefore on that (verse) in the eighth (chapter of St. Paul's Letter) to the Romans:[1] *For those loving God all (things) cooperate unto the good*, the Gloss (says): « even chance itself »; and (St.) Augustine in the fourteenth (book), ON THE CITY (OF GOD), in the thirteenth chapter, says: « I dare to say, that for the proud it is useful to fall into some open and manifest sin, so that from this they may be displeasing to themselves, who have been ruined already by being pleasing to themselves » — therefore, 'that evil comes to be' [malum fieri] is good and useful to the one working for salvation: ergo etc..

2. Likewise, what is good for God and for the university (of things) is good simply, because the common good is preferred to the private good; but 'that evil come to be' is good for the university (of things): ergo etc.. (St. Severinus) Boethius in (his) book, ON THE CONSOLATION (OF PHILOSOPHY says):[2] « The Divine Force alone is (That), for which whatever (are) evil are good ». And (St.) Augustine in (his) book of CONFESSIONS (says): « Thou to whom (there is) nothing entirely evil, but neither for each and every one of Thy creatures [universae creaturae tuae], because there is nothing outside of Thee, which corrupts the order, which Thou has imposed ». therefore, if it is good for the university (of things) that evil comes to be, it is clear that etc..

3. Likewise, « whose use is good, it itself (is) also good »;[3] but the use of evil deeds is good: ergo etc.. The *minor* is clear through (St.) Augustine in the eleventh (book) ON THE CITY (OF GOD): « For neither would God have foreknown the wicked to be, if for an equal reason He did not foreknow, for which uses of the good He would accommodate them ».

4. Likewise, « everything which is just, is good » [omne quod iustum est, bonum est];[4] but 'that evils come to be' is just, because it is a punishment for a preceding sin, just as (St.) Gregory (the Great) would have it: therefore, it is good that evil come to be.

ON THE CONTRARY: 1. 'That evil comes to be' is 'that an evil be produced in 'being' [in esse]': therefore, if it is good that an evil come to be, the production of evil is good. But there is a rule in the art of the TOPICS,[5] « Whose generation or production is good, it itself (is) also good » [Cuius generatio vel productio bona est, ipsum quoque bonum]: therefore, if the production of evil is good, evil is good.

2. Likewise, 'that evil come to be' is the same as 'that good is deprived or corrupted': therefore, if it is good that evil come to be, the corruption of the good is good. But there is a rule: « Whose corruption (is) good, (is) itself also evil » [Cuius corruptio bona, ipsum quoque malum]: therefore, 'if the corruption of the good is good, the good is evil', which is absurd.

3. Likewise, of two convertibles, if one is good, the remainder (is) also;[6] but 'that an evil be done [malum fieri]' and 'that one do an evil [malum facere]' are convertibles: therefore, if 'that an evil be done' is good, 'that one do an evil' is also good. But for a good no one is to be punished: therefore, no one doing evils is to be punished.

4. Likewise, « if an opposite (is) in a opposite, (then) the proposed (is) also in the proposed » [si oppositum in opposito, et propositum in proposito];[7] therefore, if it is good *that evil come to be*: therefore, it is evil *that good come to be*. But it is absurd, that it be evil to do good: therefore, also the first.

5. Likewise, if it is good that evil come to be: therefore, either *in itself*, or because *there comes forth out of it*, or is consequent (to it), a good. Not *in itself*, it is established. If, therefore, because *a good comes forth from it*, he who says: *Let us do evils, so that good (things) may come forth*,[8] speaks well: therefore the Apostle badly reprehended (him).

---

[1] Verse 28. — See the entire Gloss from St. Augustine in the text of Master (Peter, here at the beginning of ch. 6. For *even chance itself* [etiam ipse casus] not a few codices unduly have *even according to a reckoning, chance itself* [etiam ratione ipse casus]. The text from (St.) Augustine, then cited differs little from the text exhibited in the edition of St. Augustine's Works. For there for *to fall* [incidere] there is had *to fall down* [cadere], for *so that from this* [ut inde] only the particle *whence* [unde], for *have been ruined* [corruerunt] the verb *had fallen* [ceciderant].

[2] Book IV, prose 6, where in the original text there is had *evils are also* [quoque mala sunt] for *whatever (are) evil are* [quaeque mala sunt]. The text cited from (St.) Augustine's book of CONFESSIONS, is had in Bk. VII, ch. 13, n. 19, and in its entirety sounds thus: And where there is entirely no evil, not only for Thyself, but neither for each and every one of Thy creatures, because outside of (Thee) there is nothing which breaks and corrupts the order, which Thou has imposed upon it [posuisti]. — To the name *(St. Severinus) Boethius* [Boethius] the Vatican edition prefaces *That it is good, says* [Quod sit bonum, dicit]. Similarly, codices P and Q preface *That it is good for God* [Quod sit bonum Deo], and then to the name *(St.) Augustine* [Augustinus] they prefix *that it is good for each* [quod sit bonum utrique].

[3] (St. Severinus) Boethius, ON THE TOPICAL DIFFERENCES, Bk. II. Cf. above d. 1, a. 1, q. 1, p. 31, footnote 1. — In the text of (St.) Augustine (ON THE CITY OF GOD, Bk. XI, ch. 18), which is next cited and (which) has been quoted in full above d. 44, a. 1, q. 3, p. 786, footnote 7, the Vatican edition after *God have* [Deus] interjects *created those whom He had* [illod crearet quos] and then reads *to be wicked* for *the wicked to be*.

[4] (St.) Augustine, ENCHIRIDION, ch. 96, n. 24. (Pope St.) Gregory, in his MORALS ON THE BOOK OF JOB, Bk. XXV, ch. 9, n. 22 says: Indeed, every sin, which is not washed away by a swift repenting, either is a sin and the cause of sin, or a sin and the punishment for sin.

[5] Aristotle, TOPICS, Bk. II, ch. 3 (ch. 9): For those the generations of which are good, are themselves good; and if they themselves are good, (their) generations (are) also good; but if (their) generations (are) evil, they themselves (are) also evil. But in corruptions (it is) the other way around: for if (their) corruptions (are) good, they themselves (are) evil; but if (their) corruptions (are) evil, they themselves are good. For the same reason both in effective and corruptive (causes): for those of which the effective (cause is) good, (are) themselves good; but those of which the corruptive (cause is) good, (are) themselves evil. Cf. also TOPICS, Bk. III, ch. 4 (ch. 6). The Rule concerning corruptions recurs in the following argument.

[6] Cf. Aristotle, TOPICS, Bk. II, ch. 1. — The Vatican edition reads *concerning* [de] for *of two* [de duobus].

[7] Cf. Aristotle., TOPICS, Bk. II, ch. 4, where to confirm the proposed axiom this example is offered: « So that if blindness (be) a certain insensibility (or privation of sight), sight (will be) a sense ». The axiom cited in other words can be expressed thus: if to any subject there convenes any predicate, (then) to the term, which is opposed to this subject, there will also convene the predicate opposed to the prior predicate.

[8] Romans 3:8.

CONCLUSION

'That evils come to be' is good according to no Covenant, but it can be the occasion of good, to the extent that it is ordained by God unto a good.

I RESPOND: For an understanding of the aforesaid it must be noted, that among works there is a saying that this (is) good and/or useful or conducive [conferens], which leads unto a good end or is a way to (something) good. But something is said "*to lead to a good*" in a threefold manner, namely, through the manner of a *cause*, and/or through the manner of *chance*, and/or through the manner of an *occasion*. And these three differ. For a *cause* leads through itself thus unto that,[1] about which it is posited, that it is *one producing* and *intending*. But chance deprives *intention*, but not *operation*, juts as is clear in one digging, who finds a treasure apart from (his) intention. Moreover, an *occasion* deprives *each*. For it does not mean a *producing principle*, but rather means something, which affects a principle, to *effect* (something):[2] just as someone, on account of a word heard, strikes another; the word heard was *the occasion*, not the (thing) effecting the percussion nor (something) cooperating with the one effecting (the blow), but (is) in a certain manner the one affecting (him).

And this occasion is in two manners. For there is a *certain* (occasion), which in a certain manner has the reckoning of an *active (cause)*, because in a certain manner it excites the efficient (cause), just as an evil example (excites others) to sin. *And/or*[3] (a certain occasion) which has a reckoning of a *passive (cause)*, so that it takes (its) reckoning from something of another, just as someone from the evil of another excites himself to do good.

According to this it must be understood, that "evil" means two (things), namely, a *privation* and *an ordainable nature*; and by reason of (its) *wickedness* [malitiae] it is compared to the good, which is elicited, just as an passive occasion; by reason of the *good*, which underlies (it, it is compared to the same), just as a in-some-manner *active* occasion, on account of which an evil is said (to be) an "occasion of good".

Therefore, though some (evil) may lead unto the good in these three manners, it has[4] a difference in leading in this manner. For anything can lead something to another either *out of itself* and/or through something of itself; and then it has the reckoning of a *cause through itself*. Or it can lead *through another*, to which, however, it is not ordered; but that (other) is ordered[5] to *a third*, taken as an occasion from it; and in this manner it has the reckoning of an *occasion*. Or it leads *with another*, to which, however, it is not ordered, nor (is) that (other ordered) to *the third*, but both together (are ordered to the third); and in this manner it has the reckoning of *chance*, which is out of the concourse of causes.

Therefore, from this it is clear, that that which leads through the manner of a *cause*, has *in itself* the reckoning of being ordered unto the end; and for that reason in it there is a goodness, and for that reason it is rightly denominated as "good". However, what leads through the manner of an *occasion*, has *within itself* no reckoning of being ordered unto the end, for that reason neither a goodness; and on account of this it cannot be denominated "good" through itself, except with the addition of that, *through which* it is ordered, in which, that is, the reckoning of being ordered and of goodness consists, and *about which* the goodness is posited.

Therefore, since *evil* does not lead to the good *out of itself*, but through that, which is elicited from it by the wise God, absolutely speaking, it is not good that evil comes to be; nay all completely similar (propositions) are to be denied, because (in them) a goodness is noted to be posited about evil itself. — But if there is added the good, which *is elicited*, and/or *the one eliciting (it)*; in this manner expressions of this kind are to be conceded: "it is good that evil come to be, for him who knows how to order (it) unto the good"; similarly: "it is good that evil comes to be, so that the elect may be proven".

1. 2. From this, therefore, the first two reckonings are clear; for they proceed with a determination, just as is clear in the authorities themselves.

3. To that which is objected third: whose use (is) good etc.; it must be said, that there is a twofold use of a thing: the one, to which the thing is ordered *from itself*, and of such it is true, just as is clear concerning the horse, which is for riding; the other use, which is *sometimes* and ex post facto: and this one can be good from the goodness of *the one using, not of the usable*, because a good user uses evils in a good manner. And of such a use there is no true rule; moreover, of such (St.) Augustine is speaking.

4. To that which is objected: what is just is good etc.; it must be said, that the "*just*" is said in a twofold manner: in one manner (it is) the justly ordered through the justice, which is *in itself*, and everything which is thus just, is good, since it has justice within itself; and/or it is *(something) declarative* of justice, and in this manner evil can show forth (justice).[6] For just as evil can *disposed* to the retribution of justice, so also (it can) *show (it) forth*. And in this manner it means the ordination of the justice *in the other*; nor does it follow, that it is good, because the "just" conveys the reckoning of order more. Yet, nevertheless, that argument [sermo] is not proper, by which there is said: "It is *just*, that *he who is among sordid (things), grows sordid*",[7] nay it is understood in a valid manner per accidens, because it is just, that one be abandoned by God, and to this follows, that one grows sordid still: wherefore it is understood per accidens.

---

[1] For *thus unto that* [ita in illud] very many codices, together with the first six editions, have *about that* [circa illud]; codex T alone exhibits *thus that* [ita illud], which reading we have received into the text as the saner and the true one, with the addition of the preposition *unto* [in], which the verb *leads* [ducit] requires. Then, on the authority of codices F P Q ee ff etc. and also edition 1, we have substituted *that it is* [quod sit] for *that it is* [quod est], in place of which codex X has *because it is* [quod est].

[2] For *affects the principle, to effect (something)* [principium afficit, ut efficiat] not a few codd. with ed. 1, have *effects and/or may effect the principle* [efficit vel efficiat]. A little further below this, for *the one effecting (the blow)* [efficienti] ed. 1 has *the one striking (the blow)* [percutienti].

[3] For *And/or (a certain occasion)* [Vel] codex M (Q in the margin) has *A certain (occasion)* [Quaedam], codex T has *There is also a certain (occasion)* [Quaedam etiam est]. Next, for *it takes* [sumit] codex cc, edition 1 and the Vatican edition have *it assumes* [assumit].

[4] Very many codices, together with edition 1, have less well *they (i. e. the three manners) have* [habent] for *it has* [habet]. A little below this, after *either out of itself* [aut ex se], to avoid confusion, on account of the other *or* [aut], which is had in the Vatican edition and also in many of the codices, we have placed with edition 1 (the following) *and/or* [vel].

[5] The Vatican edition, together with codex cc, reads *it orders* [ordinat] for *is ordered* [ordinatur], and somewhat below this *within itself* [intra se] for *in itself* [in se].

[6] Supply together with codex Y *justice* [iustitiam].

[7] Apocalypse 22:11. In expounding this text, the interlinear Gloss and (St.) Bede (the Venerable) recur to *the just* judgement of God. — After *grows sordid* [sordescat], codex Y, together with the Vulgate, adjoins *still* [adhuc].

SCHOLIUM

I. Of great moment is this Question, subtly discussed by the ancient masters, both to defend the honor of Divine Providence, and to understand rightly the axiom of Christian Ethics as unshaken, which, namely, "that it is never licit to do evils, so that good may come of it". The opinion of Master Peter cited (here in ch. 4), which simply concedes, that it is good that evil comes to be, was that of Hugo of St. Victor (ON THE SACRAMENTS, Bk. I, p. IV, ch. 13); but it is refuted by Master (Peter), with the approval of St. Bonaventure, St. Thomas and others, commonly.

II. For an understanding of the Response it must be noted, that in the Question the term "*good*" is not understood for *the honest* good, nor for *the delectable* good, but for *the useful* good, which leads as a medium to the end or as a *way* to the good. But *the useful* good can lead unto the end in a threefold manner, either *through itself* [per se], and then it is said (to be) "*the cause*", and/or *through an accident* [per accidens], and then in a twofold manner: either through the manner of a *cause*, in which *the end* is not intended, but yet the operation pertains even to the *effect* itself, though not intended (as is clear in the one digging, who by chance draws forth into the light a treasure), and/or through the manner of an *occasion*, in which the effect is neither intended nor produced (as when a tyrant by slaying a martyr neither *intends* nor *produces* his *crown* of glory). These are explained in other words in the *first* distinction of the Response. — In the *second* distinction, however, an *occasion* is again distinguished in a twofold manner according to a reckoning of *active* and *passive* (being); which must be understood, not as if *evil* has some action about the good itself, but about *the efficient* (cause) of the good, which (cause) the evil action, by some proportionality and causality, either excites to do good, and/or rather excites on its own part without some causality to (do something) contrary. In this second distinction there is properly posited the fundament of (the Seraphic Doctor's) subtle and brilliant solution, which consists in this,

that *the formal* (character or privation) of the sin is for God the *passive* occasion for working the good opposed to the evil; but the *material* (character) of the sin, because it has a nature *ordainable* to the good, though « it has *within itself* no reckoning of being ordered unto the end », can be lead through *another*, namely God, to the good. Thus the Crucifixion of Christ was ordained by God to produce enormous goods, and became the occasion of the good through a to-some-extent active manner. Here is the sense of the words, that evil « by reason of (its) wickedness is compared to the good, which is elicited, just as a passive occasion; by reason of the good, which underlies (it, it is compared to the same), just as an in-some-manner active occasion », but not in the reckoning of a *cause* (« out of itself and/or through something of itself »), but (in the reckoning) of an *occasion* (« through another »).

III. With these (distinctions) supposed, the solution to n. 3 is also easily understood, both that it is *never* and *to no extent* good, *to do* evil, even though it can be good, through the ordination of God, *that evil be done*. On this manner Alexander of Hales (SUMMA, p. I, q. 40, m. 2, in reply to n. 4): « In no manner is it to be conceded (that): "it is good *to do* evil"; for the reckoning (of this expression) is not similar in the *active* and *passive* (voice). For when there is said: "it is good *to do* evil", there is noted an *active* power. But the *active* power of an evil (action) is not good; but the *passive* power regarding this, that *it be ordained* (to the good, is good); for evil is *ordainable to the good* » (cf. below q. 5).

IV. Alexander of Hales, SUMMA., p. I, q. 40, m. 2. — S. Thomas, here in q. 1, a. 2; SUMMA. , I, q. 19, a. 9. — Bl. (now St.) Albertus (Magnus), here in a. 2; SUMMA., p. I, tr. 20, q. 80, m. 2, a. 3, partic. 2 and 3. — (Bl.) Peter of Tarentaise, here in q. 1, a. 3, and q. 2, a. 1 and 2. — Richard of Middleton , here in q. 6. — Giles the Roman, here in 2nd princ., q. 1. — (Bl.) Dionysius the Carthusian, here in q. 2.

QUESTION IV

Whether it is true that evils come to be?

Fourth, there is asked, whether it is true that evils come to be. And it seems, that (it is) so:

1. « Because, of any (saying, either) the affirmation and/or negation (is) true » [de quolibet affirmatio vel negatio vera];[1] but this is false, "no evils come to be"; therefore, the opposite is simply true, namely, "that evils come to be"

2. Likewise, « truth is the adequation of thing and intellect »:[2] therefore, as often as a man understands, just as is in the thing, both the understanding and the understood has truth. But he who understands that evils come to be, understands truly: therefore, if he truly understands, (what has been) understood is true: therefore, 'that evils come to be', is true.

3. Likewise, the truth of a proposition asserts the truth

in the saying — wherefore, if Socrates runs, 'that Socrates runs' is true — therefore, if evil comes to be, 'that evil come to be' is true: but evil does come to be, (that) is established: ergo etc..

4. Likewise, the truth of the one speaking [dicentis] posits the truth in the saying; but God, who is not mendacious, says that evils come to be, in the ninth (chapter of the Gospel of St.) Matthew:[3] *Why do you think evils in your hearts?* therefore, it is true, that evils are thought; for an equal reason it is true, that they come to be.

ON THE CONTRARY: 1. The true and the good are convertible; but that evils come to be, is not good, as has been proved above:[4] therefore, that evils come to be, is not true. *If perchance you say*, that (that saying) is true of an non-complex truth; it is shown

---

[1] On this proposition, which is from Aristotle, cf. above d. 4, a. sole, q. 1, p. 97, footnote 97. — After this, the Vatican ed.r with cod. cc, reads *Because both the affirmation and/or negation of anything together (is) true of nothing* [Quia de quolibet affirmatio vel negatio vera de nullo ambo simul].

[2] See above d. 40, a. 2, q. 1, p. 707, footnote 5. — A little further below this, for *both the understanding and the understood* [et intellectus et intellectum] edition 1, and codex T by a second hand, have *both the one understanding and the one understood* [et intelligens et intellectum], the Vatican edition reads *he has the truth and (his) intellect (has) the understood* [veritatem habet et intellectus intellectum].

[3] Verse 4.

[4] Here in ch. 3. — The major proposition is founded in this, that the

true and the good are really the same with being; concerning which, cf. above d. 1, a. 1, q. 2, p. 32, footnote 2, and d.8, p. I, a. 1. q. 1, p. 150, footnote 13. Next, after *If perchance you say, that* [Si forte dicas, quod] understand *that saying* [illud dictum], that is, "the true and the good are convertible". — Then, for *non-complex* [incomplexi] very many codices, together with the first six editions, have *complex* [complexi], with the other codices, such as O S and T, and the understanding of the argument, opposing this. Cf. also d. 8, p. I. a. 1. q. 1, 1st opposed argument, where a similar objection is brought forward, and also its Scholium, in which there is expounded, what is a complex truth, and what (is) a non-complex truth.

(to be true) of every truth, because every truth is a certain entity; and everything which participates in the reckoning of a being, participates in the reckoning of the good: ergo etc..

2. Likewise, every truth is from the Prime Truth, therefore, every true (word) from the First True (Word): therefore, if it is true that evil comes to be, 'that evil comes to be' is from God; but this has been disproved above:[1] ergo etc.. *If you say*, that that is true of the truth of a thing, non (of the truth) of a sign; this is nothing, because, just as things are from God, so also signs; and (St.) Ambrose says, that « every true (word) is from the Holy Spirit, by whomsoever it be said »; therefore, he speaks of truth in speech, and thus of the truth of a complexion or of a sign.

3. Likewise, every truth of a sign or of a complexion has (its) cause and rise from the truth of a non-complexion,[2] therefore, the truth of this: *"that this is stolen"* [istum furari], has (its) rise from the truth of theft; but "theft" does not mean a true action, nay a defective one: therefore for an equal reason, "that this is stolen" is not simply true. *If you say*, that the truth of a complexion is threefold, namely (the truth) of *positing*, of *privation* and of *negation*,[3] the first is caused by the truth of the thing, but the second and the third are not caused; *on the contrary*: the Philosopher[4] says generally, « that from this, that a thing is and/or is not, a statement [oratio] is said (to be) true and/or false »: therefore, this is true everywhere.

4. Likewise, everything which is true of the present, was from eternity true of the future:[5] therefore, if this evil is now true, it was from eternity true. But nothing was eternally true, unless it was God and/or in God as in a cause: therefore, if it was true that evil was going to be and it was not God, it was in God as in a cause, therefore, (it is) from God; but this is false: ergo etc..

CONCLUSION

'That evils come to be' is simply true.

I RESPOND: It must be said, that it is to be conceded without distinction, that it is true that evils come to be. For it is truly enunciated and truly understood. For a true saying of a complex (statement) respects the composition, just as the Philosopher[6] says, because truth and falsity consist about a composition; and for that reason it means the truth of a *sign*. But a *sign* is true, when it signified, that a thing holds itself, just as it does hold itself; for then it is said to be adequated (to the thing). And for that reason, since it holds itself in the thing thus, just as the sign expresses (it), simply speaking it is true that evils come to be.

1. To that which is objected, that the true and the good are convertible; it must be said, that (that) is true about *the same (thing)*. Wherefore, if a *thing* is true, it is good, and if a *sign* is true, it is good; but yet it does not follow, that if a *sign* is true, that *the signed* or *the thing* is good. And for that reason there is a *fallacy of the accident* here: "every truth is good, but 'that this is stolen' is true: therefore, 'that this is stolen' is good", from the variation of the extremity of the minor. For *"true"* is predicated of that saying by reason of the *composition*, since it is a modal saying, but *"good"* by reason of the *attribution*; and Master (Peter) gives this contrary example [instantiam facit] in the text.[7] There is a similar manner of arguing here: "I hear the Angels chant; but 'that the Angels are chanting' is true: therefore, I hear a truth". There is a completely similar manner of arguing in this reckoning:[8] 'every true (statement) is from God; it is true that this is stolen: ergo etc.'; and for that reason it must be similarly solved.

---

[1] Here in q. 2. — On this argument, cf. here the text of Master (Peter), ch. 7, where there is also had the text of (St.) Ambrose (or rather of Ambrosiaster, as they say), which is cited next.

[2] Cf. Aristotle, ON INTERPRETATION, Bk. I, ch. 1 ff., where there is taught, that since voices are notes or signs of concepts and concepts (are) the signs of things, for that reason the truth is found *inchoatively* both in the concepts and in the voices, but *completively* in enunciation. Cf. above d. 41, a. 2, q. 1, p. 737, footnote 8, and d. 40, a. 2, q. 1, p. 707, footnote 5, and also that (verse) of (St.) Anselm, DIALOGUE ON THE TRUTH, ch. 2: The truth of a true (saying) is in the true (saying) itself; but the thing enunciated is not in the true enunciation, whence not its truth, but the cause of its truth is to be said. — For *from the truth of a non-complexion* [a veritate incomplexionis] the Vatican ed. has *from the truth of a thing* [a veritate rei], and immediately after this the same Vatican edition omits *of this* [huius], which we have restored from codd. F K M Z ee & ff and ed. 1.

[3] According to Aristotle, ON INTERPRETATION, Bk. II, and PRIOR ANALYTICS, Bk. I, last chapter, four species of propositions are distinguished: the affirmative, negative, privative and infinite, the last two of which hold themselves in a similar manner, v. g. "He is an unjust man", and "He is not a just man", as (St. Severinus) Boethius says on this passage (in his first edition).

[4] ON THE PREDICAMENTS, ch. "On *Substance*"; cf. d. 40, a. 2. q. 1, p. 707, footnote 5.

[5] The Vatican edition, having omitted the words *of the future* [de futuro], proceeds thus: *therefore, if 'that evil is' is now, it is true* [ergo si malum esse modo est, est verum], contradicting the codices, some of which read less clearly thus: *therefore if evil is in this manner true* [ergo si malum est hoc modo verum],

others, such as codices F P and Q, exhibit our reading. Near the end of the argument after *as in a cause* [ut in causa] the Vatican edition, together with codex cc, omits *therefore* [ergo].

[6] ON INTERPRETATION, Bk. I, ch. 1: For about a composition and a division there is a true and false (saying). Cf. also ON THE SOUL, Bk. III, text 21 ff. (ch. 6.).

[7] Chapter 7. — We have already expounded above in d. 38, a. 2, q. 1, p. 674, footnote 2, what is a modular saying or proposition, and in d. 38, a. 2. q. 2, p. 678, footnote 1, we have also cited the four species of modal propositions. To these four Aristotle, in ON INTERPRETATION, Bk. II, ch. 3 (ch. 12) adds this fifth, namely *the true* and *the not-true*, which manner, as (St. Severinus) Boethius says on this passage (in his first edition), « is valid for the demonstration of all the manners »; but, as St. Thomas says, Aristotle does not cite this fifth species or this fifth manner in the first enumeration of manners, but does so here for this reason, so that this manner may be understood not to modify the copula of the proposition. The sense of the solution is: when there is said: "it is true that evil comes to be", this is understood of the truth of the proposition or of the saying, not of the truth of the attribution of the thing; for in the evil, inasmuch as it is evil, there is no truth or entity, but (there is) in this saying: "that evil comes to be"; and for that reason, when there is inferred: "therefore, that evil comes to be, is good", one sins by proceeding from the truth of the saying to the truth of a thing.

[8] Or argument. — For *in this reckoning: 'every ... ergo etc.'* [ratione] the Vatican edition, together with codex cc, has *in this statement: 'every ... ergo etc.'* [oratione].

3. To that which is objected, that the truth of a sign is from the truth of the thing; it must be said, that it is false. For then a sign is true, when it signifies that a thing, which is not, is not; and that it does not have truth, when that (thing) does not have (it). For just as something imperfect is perfectly equated with another imperfect, so a defective thing can be fully signified. Wherefore the Philosopher did not say: « From this, that a thing *is* such [est tantum] », but: "(that a thing) *is*, and/or *is not*". And the sense is: "from this, that a thing *is*, the statement, which signifies that it *is*, is true, and from this (the statement), which signifies that, that which it *is not*, is, is false"; it must be understood the other way around in the thing, which *is not*.[1] Wherefore though theft is a *being* secundum quid, yet the statement, which signifies that something is stolen, is *true simply*. Yet, it is true, that every complex truth is founded upon something; but it is not necessary [non oportet], that (it be founded) upon *a thing understood*, but (rather) upon *one understanding*, in whom the statement has (its) 'to be'. And thus that (objection) is clear.

Yet, it could be said, that it is founded upon a *being* secundum quid by reason of the deformity; and yet it is *simply true*[2] on account of the adequation, which is simply.

However, note, that concerning the fundament of the truth of the proposition diverse (authors) think in diverse manners.

For *some* distinguish, just as has been touched upon,[3] a threefold truth of the statement, namely, of the *positing*, as when there is said: "Caesar is a man"; of *privation*, as when there is said: "Caesar is a dead man"; of *negation*, as when there is said: "Caesar is not". They say that the first is founded upon a *being simply* [ens simpliciter], the second upon a *being* secundum quid, and they say that the third is not founded upon *something*, because such a statement posits nothing. — But yet that does not seem to suffice, because, when there is said: "this statement is true", "true" predicates some condition of a being: therefore, it is necessary that it be founded upon something, which is.

And, for that reason, *others* say, that it is founded upon *the principles* of Caesar. — But this does not suffice, because, let it be that Caesar has been entirely corrupted, both according to matter and according to form, yet this is still true: "Caesar was" or "Caesar is not".

And, for that reason, *others* say, that it is founded upon an *understanding*. — But that still does not seem sufficient: because, let it be, that no one actually understands (it), yet that statement, written on a wall: "Caesar was", is true.[4]

For that reason it must be said, that since the truth of the statement is *the truth of the sign*, and *the truth of the sign* does not mean an *absolute* quality — just as neither (does) the necessity of a consequence — but a *respective* (quality), just as the sign (does);[5] since it happens that everything, which happens to signify, signifies *truly*, and also *falsely*: just as for the reckoning of signifying it is not necessary [non oportet] that the thing be a being, but (rather than it be) cognizable, so neither for the reckoning of a true signification. And since everything which the intellect grasps, either is a being, and/or it grasps or imagines through a comparison to a being;[6] for that reason every signification and truth of a signifying statement either is founded *simply* upon a being, such as if there be said: "Peter is", and/or (is founded) *in an order regarding being* [in ordine ad ens]. Wherefore a proposition concerning (something) past is founded upon the order of that to (something) present; similarly a proposition concerning (something) future, such as a negative proposition, as if there be said: "It is not Caesar"; for there is some being, which is not Caesar; and in this manner concerning the others; similarly if there be said: "The chimera is not a unicorn [hirocervus]".

4. To that which is objected last, that 'that wickedness is going to be' is true from eternity; it must be said, that for this, that something be true, it is not necessary [non oportet], that it be in God as in a cause, but it suffices, that it be in God's Foreknowledge, which is not but of the true. Moreover, for this, that something be in God's Foreknowledge, it suffices, that it, and/or its cause, and/or its opposite, be in God as in a cause, just as has been said above[7] concerning God's Cognition.

---

[1] Cf. (St.) Anselm, DIALOGUE ON THE TRUTH, ch. 2. — The for *it must be understood the other way around in the thing, which is not* [e contrario intelligendum in re, quae non est] the Vatican edition reads thus: *that (thing) which is not ... : and from this (that statement), which signifies that, that which is not, is, is true: and from this (that statement), which signifies that that, which is, is not, is false* [ipsam: et ab eo quod non est, est vera, quae significat non esse: et ab eo quod est, est falsa, quae significat eam non esse]. For the words *which signify that ..., is,* [quae significat esse], which words precede the words first cited in this note, nearly all the codices (except T), together with edition 1, have faultily *which signify that ..., is not* [quae significant non esse]. Next, for *theft is a being* [furtum sit ens] cod. V has *theft is a non-being* [furtum sit non-ens].

[2] Edition 1 reads *it (i.e. the statement) is simply true* [vera est simpliciter] for *it is simply true* [verum est simpliciter].

[3] Here in the 3rd opposed argument.

[4] The sense is: if no one understood this proposition, then certainly in regard to this proposition there will be no formal truth, since formal truth consists in the cognizing intellect; but yet, if this proposition were written, then in that there would be the truth of a sign, that is, the rectitude of signification, not indeed in act, but only in potency.

[5] He wants to say: Just as *the necessity of a consequence* does not mean something absolutely of the thing itself, but (something) convening (in a respective manner) from the supposition (cf. above d. 38, a. 2, q. 1), so *the truth of a sign* does not mean some property, which convenes absolutely and always with the sign, but which thus convenes with it, that it can also not convene with it. Cf. (St) Anselm, DIALOGUE ON THE TRUTH, ch. 2, where the holy Doctor shows that the truth of the enunciation is not the statement itself, nor its signification, nor anything of those which are in the definition of the enunciation, because if this were so, it would always be true; but (is) something convening with that (enunciation) itself in a manner related to the thing, which it signifies; which is then had, when the proposition signifies the thing rightly, or as it ought. — At the beginning of this proposition, after *it must be said, that* [dicendum quod] the Vatican edition omits *since* [cum], and then a little below after *to signify* [significare], together with codex cc, it adjoins *something* [quid]; then the same Vatican edition, having placed a period after *falsely* [falso], prefixes to the word *just as* [sicut] the word *And* [Et], and after a few (words) for *a being* [entem] it substitutes *existing* [existentem].

[6] Cf. above d. 25, Doubt 3. — Next, for *signification and truth* [significatio et veritas] codex Y has *signification, which is the truth* [significatio, quae est veritas].

[7] Distinction 36, a. 3, q. 1, and d. 38, a. 1. q. 1.

SCHOLIUM

I. This question has already been touched upon by Master Peter (here in ch. 7, near the end) to destroy a certain sophistic argument. In the Response, there are supposed many (things) about the definition and distinction of truth, concerning which, see above d. 8, p. I, a. 1. q. 1, and its Scholium. St. Bonaventure responds affirmatively to the Question and without a distinction, while Richard of Middleton (here in q. 5) distinguishes *evil* according to *formal* (evil) and *material* (evil), and only in regard to *material* (evil) concedes an affirmative response; which distinction seems to be present here a little regarding the proposed, as is apparent from the solution to n. 3. — In the solution to n. 3, there is also resolved the question concerning *the fundament of the truth*. Having cited the four opinions, the Seraphic Doctor adheres to the last. — In the solution to n. 4, a question, of great interested in that age, is dealt with, (namely), in what manner can any truth, especially in respect of an evil, be from eternity. All the approved doctors teach, that no truth is eternal, except to the extent that it is in God. The contrary sentence is the seventh article condemned by « the University of the Masters of Paris in the time of Bishop William and Odo the Chancellor » (see SENT, Bk. II, d. 23, a. 2. q. 3, at the end). Alexander of Hales proves this at length, in his SUMMA., p. I, q. 15, m. 6 and 7 (cf. St. Thomas, SUMMA, I, q. 16, a. 7; Bl. (now St.) Albertus Magnus, SUMMA., p. I. tr. 6. q. 25, m. 2, a. 3).

II. Treating of the principal Question are: (Bl.) Peter of Tarentaise, here in q. 1, a. 1. — Richard of Middleton, here in q. 5. — (Bl.) Dionysius the Carthusian, here in q. 2.

QUESTION V

Whether evil is ordainable* by God's Will?

Fifth, there is asked, whether evil is ordainable by God's Will. And that (it is) so, seems:

1. Because on that (verse) of the Psalm:[1] *O Lord, My God, in Thee have I hoped*, the Gloss (says): « He who sees, that the merits of souls are thus ordered by God, so that the beauty of the university (of things) is violated in no part, praises God in all (things) », distinguishing, that the one, such as each and every good, God made and ordered, the other, such as evil, He did not make, but did order.

2. Likewise, (St.) Augustine (says) in (his) ENCHIRIDION:[2] « Evil, well ordered and put in its own place, more eminently commends the good ».

3. Likewise, it seems *by reason*, because every merit[3] is ordered to a reward or to retribution; but an evil (deed) merits punishment, just as good one (merits) glory: therefore, since the good of grace is ordainable, for an equal reason the evil of fault (is ordainable).

4. Likewise, (those) sinning are ordained unto [in] torments; but « (that) on account of which each one (is), that (is) even more »;[4] but the wicked are not ordained unto punishments except on account of evil (deeds): therefore an evil (deed) is much more ordainable.

5. Likewise, everything which increases the adornment of [decorum in] an ordered thing, has been ordered; but evil increases the adornment of the universe, which has been ordered: ergo etc. *Proof of the minor.* (St.) Augustine in the eleventh (book) ON THE CITY OF GOD (says):[5] « Just as a picture is more beautiful with the color black put in its own place, so the university of things is beautiful on account of sinners ».

ON THE CONTRARY: 1. (St.) Augustine (says): « Evil is a privation of a standard of measure, of beauty [speciei] and of order »;[6] but no privation participates in that of which it is a privation: therefore, if evil, by this that (it is) evil, deprives an order, (then) evil does not happen to be ordered.

2. Likewise, what is not, is not ordainable, for order presupposes "being"; but « evil, in this that (it is) evil, is nothing »:[7] therefore, it is not ordainable.

3. Likewise, everything ordainable is a possible for the one ordering; but evil is not possible for God, because God cannot work evil: therefore, it is not ordainable by God.

4. Likewise, if evil is ordainable, either by an order of parts *unto a whole*, or *unto an end*. Not in the *first* manner,

---

[1] Psalm 7:2. — In the Gloss, which is taken from (St.) Augustine's, ENARRATIONS on this Psalm, v. 18, n. 19, after *by God, so that* [a Deo, ut] there are lacking these words, which are had in the original text: *while His own are granted to each* [dum sua cuique tribuuntur]. The words, which then follow, *distinguishing, that the one* etc. [distinguens, Deum etc.] exhibit a summary of those (things) which (St.) Augustine teaches more at length, <u>loc. cit.</u>, where among other (things) he says: « For God said: *Let there be light, and light was made*. He did not say: "Let there be darkness, and darkness was made"; and yet He did order them. And for that reason there is said: *God divided between light and darkness, and God called the light, "day", and the darkness He called "night"*. This distinction (is) of Him: The one He made and ordered, but the other He did not make, but yet He still ordered it. However, sins are already signified by darkness, and in the Prophet there is found » etc..

[2] Chapter 11, n. 3. — In the text cited, the Vatican edition, together with some manuscripts, has *more evidently* [evidentius] for *more eminently* [eminentius].

[3] "Merit" here is taken in the broader sense, thus to include also demerit. — A little below this after *therefore* [ergo], the Vatican edition, together with some editions, and not a few codices, subjoins *too* [et].

[4] Aristotle, POSTERIOR ANALYTICS, Bk. I, ch. 2.

[5] Chapter 23, n. 1. The text exhibited here plainly does not convene with the text in the edition of the Works of St. Augustine, which is such: « Just as a picture, with the color black, placed in its own place: so the university of thing, if anyone can intuit (it), is also beautiful with sinners ». Just as the edition of the Works of St. Augustine, so also the greater part of the codices and editions read *placed* [posita] (in reference to the picture) for *placed* [posito] (in reference to the color black).

[6] In his book, ON THE NATURE OF THE GOOD, ch. 4: (Evil) is nothing other than the corruption either of the natural standard of measure, and/or of (natural) beauty and/or of the (natural) order.

[7] Dionysius (the Areopagite), ON THE DIVINE NAMES, ch. 4, § 20. (St.) Augustine, ON THE GOSPEL OF ST. JOHN, tract I, 1:3, under n. 13 says: Indeed, sin did not come to be through itself, and it is manifest, that because sin is nothing, men, when they sin, come to be nothing. Cf. (St.) Anselm (of Canterbury), ON THE DOWNFALL OF THE DEVIL, ch. 10 f..

---

* *Trans. note*: Here for the sake of a smoother English, *ordainable* is used to render the Latin <u>ordinabile</u>, rather than *able to be ordered* or the more unsuitable *orderable*, since *to order* in English can be confused with *to command*. Hence, throughout, *to ordain* and *to order* is used in the same sense: to put or establish in an order to something else.

because evil is a part of nothing; if in the *second* manner: therefore, since something is good out of an order *unto an end* [ex ordine in finem], then an evil would come to be a good.[1]

CONCLUSION

Evil is ordainable by God according to the order of justice, not as susceptive of order in itself, but as dispositive *and* ostensive *of this order.*

I RESPOND: For an understanding of the aforesaid it must be noted, that[2] — according to the standard of measure that anything is said to be "healthy" [sanum] in a threefold manner: either *subjectively*, such as an animal is said (to be) "healthy"; or *dispositively*, such as a drink is said (to be) "healthy"; or *ostensively*, such as urine (is said to be) "healthy" — so something is said to be "ordered"[3] in a threefold manner: either as *susceptive* of order, or as *dispositive* (of it), or as *ostensive* (of it).

As (something) *susceptive*, nothing is ordainable, except that which is a being and some nature; and thus evil is not ordainable except <u>per accidens</u>, that is through the substrate good.

As (something) *dispositive*, evil is ordainable, but not as a *positing* disposition, but as a *depriving* one. For there is a twofold order, namely, of *nature* and of *justice*. The order of *nature* has been instituted, the order of *justice* has been acquired.[4] But evil deprives the order of special nature and by depriving that it runs against [incurrit in] the order of justice, because it offends (it); wherefore the reason for (its) being ordained, as a disposition in the order of justice, is *merit*, and/or *demerit*.

As (something) *ostensive*, evil is ordainable and ordered, because it manifests the order of the good through the opposite, « for opposites placed alongside one another shine forth more ».[5]

Therefore, the reasons proving, that evil has been ordered, proceed according to the order of *justice* and according to *disposition* and *manifestation* [ostensionem].

1. To that, however, which is objected, that evil is the privation of order; it must be said, that it is true, (that it is a privation of order)[6] *of a particular nature*, but it is not true, insofar as "*order*" means the disposition of *universal Providence*, of which (St. Severinus) Boethius says:[7] « (That) order comprises all, by which it comes to be, that if anyone departs from the reckoning of order assigned to him, it is necessary, that he fall back into another difference ». An example (of this) is posited in a circumference encircling a center.

2. To that which is objected: 'to have been ordered' presupposes "being"; it must be said, that it is true in that which is ordered *through itself* and *in itself*, but evil is not ordered *through itself* nor *in itself*, and for that reason it is not necessary [non oportet], that it be, but it is sufficient, that there be another, in which the evil is substantified [substantificatur]; and this is a good, as Dionysius says.[8]

3. To that which is objected, that the ordainable is a possible for the one ordering; it must be said, that '*to be possible*' or 'to be subject to the Divine Power' is in a twofold manner: either to the *producing* Power, or to the *providing* (Power); and though evil is not subject to the Divine *production*, yet, it is subject to the (Divine) *provision*.

4. To that which is objected, "By which ordination is it ordainable?"; it must be said, that (it is ordainable) by (its) ordination to *the end*; but this is only <u>ex post facto</u>.[9] And for that reason it does not follow, that an evil is good, but that there follows from it a good. — Yet, it can be said, that though evil is not a part, yet that in which it is, is a part and holds the place and order of a part.

---

[1] Cf. Dionysius (the Areopagite), ON THE DIVINE NAMES, ch. 4, § 20 ff., where it is proved, that evil, inasmuch as (it is) evil, is useful for nothing and neither exists in things nor is ordered.

[2] From codices V Z ff and edition 1 we have added *that* [quod], in place of which the other codices have less congruously *since* [quoniam].

[3] The Vatican edition reads "*ordainable*" [ordinabile].

[4] Cf. (St.) Augustine, ON ORDER, Bk. I, ch. 7, n. 17, ff., and ON THE NATURE OF THE GOOD, ch. 37. In ON MUSIC, Bk. VI, ch. 11, n. 30 (St.) Augustine hints at this fourfold division of order with the expressions "*to enact a law*" [legem agere] and "*to be conducted according to a law*" [lege agi], and in the same book, ch. 14, n. 46, in these words (says): "For it is one (thing) to have an order; another to be held by an order". — After a few (words), for *because it offends (it)* [quia offendit] very many codices, together with editions 2, 3, 4, 5 and 6, have *because it shows (it) forth* [quia ostendit], and then for *in the order of justice* [in ordine iustitiae] very many codices have *in the order (of justice)* [in ordine].

[5] Cf. above d. 38, a. sole, p. 495, footnote 1. — A little before this, in place of *for* [enim] the Vatican edition, together with codex cc, has *moreover* [autem].

[6] One must supply: *that it is a privation of order* [quod est privatio ordinis].

[7] ON THE CONSOLATION OF PHILOSOPHY, Bk. IV, prose 6, where in the edition of the Works of (St Severinus) Boethius there is read: For a certain order comprises all, so that what has departed from (its) assigned reckoning of order, though it (falls back) into another (order), yet it falls back into an order, lest anything be licit to temerity in the Kingdom of (Divine) Providence. — The example next mentioned is well employed to illustrate the sentence of (St.) Boethius. For just as a circumference so encircles a center, that the center neither exceeds the circumference, nor the circumference relinquishes the center; so the divine order, as a circumference, so encircles man, that man can least of all flee from it, since, if he flees from one part of the circumference (from the order of mercy), he immediately approaches the other (the order of justice). Cf. St. Anselm (of Canterbury), CUR DEUS HOMO, Bk. I, ch. 15.

[8] Trusting in codices F M P Q Z ff etc. and also edition 1, we have substituted *Dionysius (the Areopagite)* [Dionysio] for *(St. Severinus) Boethius* [Boethio], to whom the Vatican edition attributes the cited sentence. Besides the cited codices even Bl. (now St.) Albertus Magnus, (SUMMA, p. I, tr. 6, q. 29, m. 2, at the end) and other Scholastics attributed this sentence to the name of Dionysius, who in his book, ON THE DIVINE NAMES, ch. 4, § 20, says (according to the version of Scotus Erigena): « A good also substantiates (οὐσιοῖ) its own privation by its entire participation ». Alexander of Hales, SUMMA, p. II. q. 94, m. 5, a. 1, renders this text of Dionysius in these words: The good makes itself sustain [sustentificat] its own privation. On this solution, cf. SENT., Bk. II, d. 34, a. 2. q. 2 and q. 3, where many (things) pertaining to this are treated and the same objection is also solved.

[9] For *ex post facto* edition 1 has *from a supposition* [ex suppositione]. Then, for *there follows from it* [ex ipso sequitur] codices Y and cc have *there may follow from it* [ex ipso sequatur], and, after a few (words), codex Y to the words *is not a part* [non sit pars] adds *of the universe* [universi].

SCHOLIUM

I. Alexander of Hales (SUMMA., p. I. q. 38, m. 3, a. 1) rightly teaches, that a *good* is ordainable according to its four causes, namely, (its) final, material, formal and efficient (cause), or by a reckoning of that *for which* it is, *in which* it is, *according to which* it is, and by a reckoning of that *which* is *out of it*; but that an *evil* is not ordainable except by a reckoning of that *in which* it is, namely, in a good, and *for which* it is, namely the contrary good, elicited by God. — This is proven subtly and with many employed distinctions by the Seraphic (Doctor). — It is to be noted, in the solution

to n. 4, namely, that an evil is not ordained to an and to a means [medium], which *through itself* and *before it has been wrought* has been willed and ordained by God. The contrary opinion is false, as has been explained above, in q. 3.

II. Alexander of Hales, loc. cit.. — St. Thomas, SENT., Bk. I, d. 39, q. 2, a. 2, in reply to n. 5; SUMMA., I, q. 22, a. 2, in reply to n. 2. — Bl. (now St.) Albertus (Magnus), SENT., Bk. I, d. 47, a. 2. — (Bl.) Pete of Tarentaise, here in q. 2, a. 4. — Richard of Middleton, here in q. 7. — (Bl.) Dionysius the Carthusian, on this and the following q., here in q. 3.

QUESTION VI

Whether evil concerns the complement of the universe?

Sixth and last, there is asked, whether evil concerns the complement of the universe. And that (it is) so, seems:

1. According to the thirty-third (chapter) of Ecclesiasticus:[1] *Against evil is the good, and against death life, and thus look upon all the works of the Most High.* If, therefore, an opposition of this kind pertains to the adornment [decorem] and complement of the universe: therefore, also evil.

2. Likewise, (St.) Augustine ON THE CITY OF GOD,[2] speaking of evils, for which reason they are allowed by God, says, that God honored the universe as if with certain antitheses; and he exemplified (this) in *speech* and in *pictures*: in *speech*, just as the Apostle uses, in the sixth (chapter) of the Second (Letter) to the Corinthians:[3] *Through glory and ignobility.* And in *pictures* similarly: for just as « a white picture, with the color black placed in its own place, is beautiful; so the universe with evils »: therefore, evil, according to this, decorates the universe. But every such concerns the complement of the universe: ergo etc.

3. Likewise, it seems *by reason*, because just as *evil* is a privation of the good, so *silence* is the privation of the voice, and *sleep* (the privation) of wakefulness [vigiliae]; but for the perfection and adornment of *speech* it is necessary, that there be interposed silence, and for the perfect and adornment of *an animal* it is necessary, that sleep sometimes be interposed among the times of wakefulness [vigiliis]: therefore, for the per-

fect adornment of the universe it is necessary, that evils be interposed among goods.[4]

4. Likewise, the universe has been founded to manifest God [ad Dei manifestationem]; but in God's works there is most of all manifested (His) Mercy and Truth;[5] but if there were no evil, neither (the Divine) Mercy nor the (Divine) Truth would be as perfectly manifested, as It is manifested in eternal punishment, forgiveness and redemption of sinners: therefore, the universe would not be complete.

ON THE CONTRARY: 1. In the first (chapter) of Genesis (there is written):[6] *God saw all which He has made, and they were very good*, and it is established, (that) He had not made (them) evil: therefore, apart from evils all (things) in the universe were very good. But the universe would not be very good, if perfection was missing from it: therefore, since evil was missing from it, it seems, that evil does not concern its perfection.

2. Likewise, (St.) Augustine in the third (book) ON FREE WILL,[7] speaking of the perfection of the universe, says: « Whatever will have occurred to you (to be) better according to a true reckoning, know that the Worker of all has done (it) ». Therefore, if He did not make the world with evils, but without evils, therefore, the world without evils was more perfect than with evils: therefore, evil does not concern the perfection of the universe.

3. Likewise, it seems *by reason*, because « whiter

---

[1] Verse 15. In the Vulgate in this passage there is added after *life* [vita] *thus too against the just man the sinner* [sic et contra virum iustum peccator].

[2] Book XI, ch. 18. See the very words of (St.) Augustine above, d. 44, a. 1, q. 3, p. 786, footnote 7.

[3] Verse 7. — The text, which is next cited, is from (St.) Augustine, ON THE CITY OF GOD, Bk. XI, ch. 23, n. 1, concerning which, cf. above q. 5, p. 830, footnote 5. Even in this passage, as above, for there is the same reading of *placed* [posito] in regard to the color black, rather than *placed* [posita], in regard to the picture, as very many codd. and the first edd. have; for *beautiful* [pulcra] cod. T has *more beautiful* [pulcrior].

[4] (St.) Augustine, ON THE NATURE OF THE GOOD, ch. 16: For if we by restraining (our) voice decently interpose silence in (our) speaking, how much more does He decently cause certain privations of things as the perfect Craftsman of all things) Cf. ON GENESIS ACCORDING TO THE LETTER, UNFINISHED,

ch. 5, n. 25; ON THE NATURE OF THE GOOD, ch. 8, and the book, AGAINST SECUNDINUS THE MANICHEE, ch. 15, and also ON MUSIC, Bk. III, ch. 8, n. 17 ff.. On the other similitude, namely, that of sleep, cf. Aristotle, ON SLEEP AND WAKEFULNESS, where even in ch. 1 there is had this definition of sleep: Sleep seems (to be) a certain privation of wakefulness.

[5] Psalm 24:10: *Each and every way of the Lord (is) mercy and truth* [Universae viae Domini misericordia et veritas].

[6] Verse 31. — Next after *therefore* [constat: ergo] the Vatican edition inserts *(it is established) that* [quod], and a little further below this, the same Vatican edition, together with codex cc, exhibits *the perfect* [perfectum] for *perfection* [perfectio].

[7] Chapter 5, n. 13. Cf. above d. 44, a. 1. q. 1, 1st opposed argument, and in the body of the Question.

(is) that which is more thoroughly unmixed [impermixtius] with black »,[1] therefore, more beautify and better (is) that which is more thoroughly unmixed with evil; but if in the world there were no evil, then the universe would be *more thoroughly unmixed* with evils, therefore, *better*, therefore, *more perfect*: therefore, the ordination of evil does not concern the complement of the universe.

4. Likewise, « the good and the beautiful (are) the same »,[2] just as Dionysius (the Areopagite) says, therefore, that which is the privation of the good is the privation of the beautiful; but evil is the privation of the good: therefore, it is the privation of the beautiful, therefore, evil disfigures [deturpat]. But what disfigures and befouls [foedat] does not pertain to beauty or adornment: therefore, neither (does) evil or the ordination of evil.

CONCLUSION

Evil, neither per se nor per accidens, works for the substantial adornment and/or complement of the universe; but it does work for (its) accidental (adornment) per accidens, and, indeed, in a threefold manner.

I RESPOND: Regarding this it must be noted, that about this diverse (authors) thought diverse (things).

For *some* said, that there is a speaking of evil, as it is in the *power of the one working* (it), and as it is *in the work* or in the deed. If we speak, as it is in the *power of the one working* (it), thus they wanted to say, that '*to be able to do evil*' concerned the perfection of the university (of things), because a creature had [debebat] to be made, which could sin and could abstain (from sin), for this that the universe would be perfected, just as is said in the third (book) ON FREE WILL.[3] If we speak of evil, as it is in the *deed's 'being'* [in facto esse], thus they say, that it in no manner pertains to the complement of the universe, neither *through itself* nor per accidens. — But since the authorities say the contrary, that out of the ordination of evil to the good there results a certain adornment, just as (St.) Augustine[4] expressly says, it is necessary [oportet] to speak in another manner.

For that reason *others* say, that a certain adornment of the university (of things) is *substantial* or as much as regards '*being*', a certain one (is) *accidental* or as much as regards *well 'being'* [bene esse]. As much as regards the *first*, evils are not (things) causing [facientia][5] adornment, neither *through themselves* nor per accidens; but as much regards any *accidental adornment* evils well ordered do cause (adornment), not because (they are) *evil*, but because (they are) *ordered*, and thus per accidens, just as they are ordered per accidens. And excluding that

adornment, the universe would still be decorous and perfect, even though it would not have this adornment.

Evils work for this adornment, not by reason of *themselves*, but by reason of *the subject*, which is ordained in punishment for the manifestation of the Divine Justice; and/or by reason of (their) *opposite*,[6] the adornment of which becomes more clear from the presence of evil, just as « opposites, placed along side themselves, shine forth more », just as is commonly said; and/or by reason of *the good elicited*. For many goods did[7] God work and have been worked, which had they not been worked, sin would have not been given an occasion, just as those which were done for our reparation [gesta sunt in nostra reparatione]. Yet, without all these the universe would have been complete.

However, if there is asked, "Whether (the universe) would be more beautiful then, than it is now?", one can respond, that (such a universe and this one of ours) hold themselves just as *one exceeding* and *one exceeded*:[8] just as two faces, in one of which there is no stain, in the other there is some scar well situated, which seems to make the face charming [venustare]. — And, if you proceed further (to ask): "Which adornment is more exceeding?" it can be said *without prejudice*, that the adornment, which is now, (is). And the reason for this is, because the Divine Force, eliciting good from evil, is more powerful [praepotens] than evil; and for that reason the good, which It elicits from it, prevails over the good, which the evil corrupted. And, for that reason the universe now is worth more, than it would have been worth then; in which there is now at present [nunc modo] commended the Wisdom of the Creator. Wherefore, (Pope St.) Gregory (the Great says) in the blessing of the Paschal Candle:[9] « O blessed fault, which has merited to have such a Redeemer ». And there is an *example* (of this) from the repaired reliquary [scypho sano], which is broken and bound back together with silver and/or gold wire, because it is better afterwards than before, not by reason of being broken, but by reason of being rebound.

And, if you ask of me: "Would it not be of greater value [melius valeret],[10] if all were blessed, than if certain ones (were) blessed and certain ones wretched?", it must be said, that, just as I believe, if man had stood firm [stetisset], more would not have arrived at the supernal Jerusalem, than thus are going to arrive. Wherefore, the wicked are (numbered) out of a quasi abundant (quantity) nor are they (numbered) in the computation (of the elect).

And thus it must be conceded, that the ordination of evil works for the *accidental* complement (of the universe); just as the reasons brought forward for the first side prove; but regarding the *substantial* complement or adornment (it works) for nothing, neither per se nor per accidens, just as the latter reasons show.

---

[1] Aristotle, TOPICS, Bk. III, ch. 4, (ch. 5). — A little further below this, for *then the universe would be thoroughly more unmixed* [tunc universum esset malis impermixtius] the Vatican edition has *nor would the universe be thoroughly mixed with evils* [nec universum esset malis permixtum].

[2] ON THE DIVINE NAMES, ch. 4, § 7. In the text of Dionysius, after *the beautiful* [idem] the codices, such as Y Z and cc, adjoin *are* [sunt], the Vatican edition adjoins *is* [est]. Then after *therefore, evil disfigures* [ergo malum deturpat] codex I adjoins *and befouls* [et foedat].

[3] Chapter 5, n. 12 ff., and ch. 9, n. 27, ff..

[4] ON FREE WILL, Bk. III, ch. 9, n. 27. Cf. also ON THE CITY OF GOD, Bk. XI, chs. 18 and 23, from which some of the things cited in the 2nd argument for the negative side have been taken.

[5] The Vatican edition reads thus: *evils do not work for the adornment (of the universe)* [mala non faciunt ad decorem]. For *(things) causing* [facientia] very many codices and the six first editions have *to cause* [facienda], faultily. A little below this after *but because (they are)* [sed quia] the Vatican edition, together with codex cc, interjects *well* [bene].

[6] Namely, the good. — Immediately after this for *the adornment of which* [cuius decor] the Vatican edition alone as *because (its) adornment* [quia], and, a little before this, the same Vatican edition has *ordered unto punishment* [in poenam] for *ordained in punishment* [in poena]. On the axiom cited next, cf. above d. 28, a. sole, p. 495, footnote 1.

[7] Codex T (by a second hand) has *does* [facit].

[8] The sense is: the universe without evils would exceed this universe on one side, but would be exceeded on the other side or in the comparison of goodness, as is here explained. — A little before this, the Vatican edition, with all the other edd. and very many mss., with changed punctuation, reads *than now, thus one can respond* [quam nunc, sic responderi potest].

[9] In the MISSALE ROMANUM, on Holy Saturday, in the Paschal Praeconium: *Exsultet*.

[10] For *of greater value* [melius valeret] the Vatican edition, with some of the codices, has *better* [melius esset]; several codices, together with edition 1, have incongruously *Would they not be of greater value* [valerent]. A little further below this, for *than thus* [quam sic] codex O has *than now* [quam nunc].

3. Nevertheless, what is objected for the first side through the simile in privations; it must be said, that it is not similar, because those privations[1] are not something subtracting or bearing off [adimentes nec auferentes] something of the good and/or beautiful; yet, evil does bear (them) off. For that reason, that (objection) is clear.

4. To that which is objected, that (God's) Mercy and Justice would not be manifested; it must be said, that, though they would not be manifested in *act*, yet, they would be man-ifested in their *origin*. For he who cognizes God in Himself see in that Eternal Exemplar, that *it befits* God to work mercy and justice equally and *He can* (do these) — though (he would) not (see this) entirely. Yet, nevertheless (His) *Mercy* would be shown in supererogation, and (His) *justice* in retribution, though not so clearly, as (He) now (does) in the work (of His Hands).[2]

SCHOLIUM

I. Though it has been very often said, that evil is ordainable by God unto a good, it is now asked, whether among the goods elicited by God out of evil there can be posited even *the adornment and complement of the universe*. This question is resolved in general, and then there are enumerated in particular the three goods, for which evil in the universe is ordained by God. Moreover, certain (things) are explicated more below in d. 47, q. 3. — Through the manner of a corollary, two adjoined questions are proposed and solved, as is clear in the text.

The question in respect of *the possibility* of evil, to the extent that this (possibility) is founded in a created free will, and the question concerning evil, as it is done and or has been done *in act* differ. That creatures created with the *potency* for evil concern the perfection of the universe, is the open doctrine of St. Augustine (see d. 47, q. 3, in the body of the Response) and is commonly admitted. The matter is otherwise in respect of *and evil done in act*. Yet the opinion, that the latter *in no manner*, nor indeed <u>per accidens</u>, pertain to the complement of the universe, is disproven with the common sentence. — On the question, whether the Word would have become incarnate, if Adam had not sinned, cf. SENT., Bk. III, d. 1, a. 2, q. 2.

In regard to the *first* adjoined question, cf. Alexander of Hales, SUMMA., p. I, q. 18, m. 10, a. 2 and 3; St. Thomas, SENT, Bk. I, d. 44, q. 2, in reply to n. 5; Bl. (now St.) Albertus (Magnus), SUMMA., p. I. tr. 6, q. 47, m. 5, 2nd incidental q.. — In regard to the *second* question we note, that St. Bonaventure seems to suppose, that none were reprobate, having supposed that Adam did not sin (cf. above d. 40, a. 3, q. 1, in reply to n. 3); and only problematically (« as I believe ») does he respond to the doubt, whether in this hypothesis *more* would have been predestined.

II. Alexander of Hales, <u>loc</u>. <u>cit</u>. — St. Thomas, SENT., Bk. I, d. 39, q. 2, a. 2, in reply to n. 5; SUMMA., I, q. 22, a. 2, in reply to n. 2. — Bl. (now St.) Albertus (Magnus), SENT., Bk. I, d. 47, a. 2. — (Bl.) Peter of Tarentaise, here in q. 2, a. 4. — Richard of Middleton, here in q. 7. — (Bl.) Dionysius the Carthusian, on this and the following question, here in q. 3.

DOUBTS ON THE TEXT OF THE MASTER

DOUBT I

In this part are the doubts about (Master Peter's) text and, first, concerning that word of (St.) Augustine: *unless He were always to such an extent omnipotent and good, that He even worked well from evil* [de malo]. For he seems to speak in an undue manner, because wickedness is a privation: therefore, it is not the matter of a good. *If you say*, that it is accepted by reason of the substrate, namely, "of evil", that is, "of that (man) who is evil He makes a good (man)"; *on the contrary*: this is nothing other than to destroy evil: therefore, from this there is not had, that God ought[3] *to allow evil (deeds)*, since it belongs to Him *to destroy (evil) deeds*.

I RESPOND: It must be said, that <u>de</u> there is not a causal nor a *material*, but an *occasional* (term), as if to say: "from [de] evil He works good", because after an evil He works a good,[4] with the *occasion* taken from the evil. But it objects, as if that which is <u>de</u> was held *causally* or *materially* (i.e. "of" or "out of evil").

DOUBT II

Likewise, is asked concerning this which (St. Augustine) says: *that which (is said to be) "evil", well ordered and placed in its own place* etc.. for he seems to speak badly, because of that which *is not*, there is no '*being placed*' [locari].[5] *If you say*, that it has a place by reason of (its) substrate; *on the contrary*: the place due and fitting for a rational

---

[1] That is, silence and sleep. — In the Vatican edition and codex cc, there are wanting the words it is not similar, because [non est simile quia].

2 To the extent, that is, that God rewards beyond condign (merit), and the justice of retribution is itself founded upon mercy, since, God indeed does not crown but His own gifts and beyond what is condign. — The Vatican edition omits in the work (of His hands) [in opere] and, a little before this, for and He can (work these) — though (he does) not (see this) entirely [et possit, licet non omnino], it exhibits and what He can (work), though not as clearly and as (He) now (does) in work [et quid possit, licet non ita clare et nunc in opere]. Very many codices prefix to the particle though [licet] an and [et].

[3] For ought to allow [debeat sinere] the Vatican edition reads has an allowing of [habeat sinere].

[4] The words because after an evil he works a good [quia post malum facit bonum] are lacking in the Vatican ed. and in cod. cc. A little before this, to the word occasional [occasionale] codices M and ff adjoin ordainable (ed. 1 has ordinal). — More on this doubt is had above in qq. 3, 5, and 6, and also in (Bl.) Peter of Tarentaise and Richard of Middleton, here on the text.

[5] Cf. above in d. 36, a. 1. q. 1, p. 620, footnote 5. — For of that which is not, there is no 'being placed' [quod non est non est locari] codices W and Z have that which is not, is not able to be placed [quod non est non est locabile], codex bb has that which is not, is not locally [quod non est non est localiter].

nature is glory: therefore, evil is placed in glory.

I RESPOND: It must be said, that when I say *"Hell"* [infernum] or *"the place of punishment"* [locum poenalem], I speak of two (things): both *part of the universe*, and *a state of vileness* [vilitatem]. Inasmuch as it is a *place*, it is due to a substrate nature; but inasmuch as it is *vile*, it is due to the deformity of fault: and thus evil has a *place* and a *vile one*, but a *place* by reason of the substrate, however, *a vile (place)* by reason of the deformity (of sin).[1]

DOUBT III

Likewise, is asked concerning this which (St. Augustine) says: *If any of them deviate and fall away* [exorbitant], *He will even cause that this very (thing) profits them unto the good*: therefore, it seems, that evils profit or cooperate (unto the good):[2] *On the contrary*. It belongs to evil to corrupt the good: therefore, in no manner is it that they cooperate or profit unto the good.

I RESPOND: It must be said, that anything can *profit* or *cooperate unto the good* of someone in a threefold manner, namely *by helping*, as grace cooperates with free will and/or the other way around; and/or *by exciting*, as poverty and misery, which excite or prod [pungunt] and impel one to the love of God, just as (Pope St.) Gregory (the Great) says;[3] and/or even *by withstanding* [obsistendo], just as hot water is more strongly frozen, because, while it resists, the action of the contrary (force) is invigorated. And in this manner it is said to cooperate, either because it causes man to be more excited to the good, and/or more because, while it stands in the way, and man prevails, the virtue of grace is invigorated and grows fervent [fervescit].[4]

DOUBT IV

Likewise, is asked concerning this which (Master Peter) says, that *(St.) Augustine argues a minori*. For he seems to say the false, because a topic from the minor [locus a minori] is not destructive, but positive;[5] but that argument (of St. Augustine) is destructive: "a wise man cannot make a man worse, therefore, neither (can) God": therefore, it is not (an argument) a minori.

I RESPOND: It must be said, that in truth that topic is not a minori, properly speaking, but a maiori; because in that (argument) *a lesser* thing[6] is not said (to be) lesser, but that which seems to be less in (it is said to be unable). Moreover, it seems rather, that a man can do evil than (that) God (can); but a wise man cannot: therefore, neither (can) God; and thus the argument is from a greater [a maiori]. — But, nevertheless, it can be said, that it is a minori; but it is reduced to an affirmative reason in this manner: it seems to be less, that the impossibility of doing evil is in a man than in God; but a wise man, remaining wise, is impotent *in regard to the lesser* according to making[7] someone worse: therefore, much more strongly (is) God (incapable of this).

DOUBT V

Likewise, is asked concerning this which (St. Augustine) says, that *fault cannot befall a wise man*. For this seems (to be) false, because, just as *wisdom* holds itself to ignorance, so *virtue* to fault: therefore, by permutation [permutatim], just as *virtue* (holds itself) to ignorance, so *wisdom* to fault. But virtue stands together with ignorance: therefore, wisdom stands together with fault.

I RESPOND: It must be said, that *"wisdom"* [sapientia] in one manner means a *true* cognition; in another manner it means a *true and most noble* cognition, because (it is had) through the highest causes; in a third manner it means a *true, noble* and *sapid* (i. e. savory); in a fourth manner *"wisdom"* does not mean a cognition other than *the Divine religion* or cult, according to which it is said, that *piety itself is wisdom* or theosebia; and this consists, as (St.) Augustine[8] says, in faith, hope and charity, and in this manner it encloses in itself virtue, and thus it is opposed to fault. And, in this manner, the response is clear.

DOUBT VI

Likewise is asked concerning this which (St. Augustine) says, that *God is not the cause of a tending to 'not-being'* [non-esse]. For he seems to say the false, because in the Canticle of Deuteronomy[9] there is

---

[1] Both this doubt and the one following are also solved by (Bl.) Peter of Tarentaise and Richard of Middleton, here on the text.

[2] Supply together with codices L and O *unto the good* [in bonum].

[3] MORALS ON THE BOOK OF JOB, Bk. XXVI, ch. 14, n. 24. — A little above this, the Vatican edition reads *'that anything profit and/or cooperate unto the good of someone' can be in a threefold manner* [proficere sive cooperari in bonum aliquid alicui potest tripliciter] for *that anything can profit or cooperate unto the good of someone in a threefold manner* [proficere sive cooperari in bonum aliquid alicui potest esse tripliciter].

[4] On this doubt, cf. Alexander of Hales, SUMMA., p. I, q. 38, m. 3, a. 2.

[5] It is useful here to cite what Peter of Spain says, in his SUMMULA, tract "On the Topical Syllogism", in regard to the expression *"a topic from the lesser"* [locus a minori]: « The greater, as it is taken here, is what is placed higher than something in power and virtue; the lesser is that which is also placed beneath. A *topic from the greater* [locus a maiori] is a habitude of the greater to the lesser, and is always a destructive (method of argument), such as 'A king cannot take the castle by storm, therefore, neither (can) a soldier'. The topic [locus] (is argued) *from the greater* [a maiori]. The maxim (for this is): "If that which the greater seems to be in, it is not in, (then) neither that, which the lesser seems to be in, it will be in". A *topic from the lesser* is a habitude of a lesser to a greater, and it is always constructive (method of argument), such as: 'a soldier can take the castle by storm, therefore, a king (can) too'. The topic (is argued) *from the lesser*. The maxim (for this is): "If that which the lesser seems to be in, is in, (then) also that which the greater seems to be in, will be in" ». Nearly the whole of this has been taken from (St. Severinus) Boethius, ON THE DIFFERENCES OF THE TOPICS, near the middle.*

[6] For *thing* [res] the Vatican edition, together with codex cc has *there is not said (to be) a lesser (being) or lesser (thing)* [non dicitur minus vel minor] for *a lesser thing is not said (to be) lesser* [non dicitur minus res minor].

[7] The Vatican edition has *is impotent to make* [est impotens ad faciendum] for *is impotent in regard to the lesser according to making* [est impotens in minus a faciendo]. — On this doubt, cf. St. Thomas and (Bl.) Peter of Tarentaise, here on the text.

[8] ENCHIRIDION, ch. 2 f.: « Moreover, the wisdom of a man is (his) piety. You have this in the book of Saint Job (Job 28:28), for in that there is read, that Wisdom Herself said to men: *Behold piety is wisdom* (The Vulgate reads: *Behold the fear of the Lord is wisdom itself*; the Septuagint reads: *Behold the worship of God is wisdom*.) But if you ask, which piety She spoke of in this passage, you will find more distinctly in the Greek, θεοσέβειαν, that it is the worship of God [cultus Dei] ... Here if I will respond, you are going to say that God, in a word, is to be worshipped by faith, hope, (and) charity ». etc.. The same say in the book, ON SPIRIT AND LETTER, ch. 11, n. 18, and ON THE TRINITY, Bk. XII, ch. 14, n. 22, and Bk. XIV, ch. 1, n. 1, ff., where diverse understandings are touched upon, which regard the word *"wisdom"* in the preceding, and (where) there is also insinuated, in what (manner) wisdom differs from knowledge; concerning which, cf. Aristotle, METAPHYSICS, Bk. I, ch. 1-4, and ETHICS, Bk. VI, ch. 2-8. — This doubt is also solved by St. Thomas, here on the text.

[9] Deuteronomy 32:39. — A little below this (on the next page) for *the corruption of tending* [corruptio tendendi] codex O has well enough *a corruption tending* [corruptio tendens].

---

* *Trans. note*: Cf. Aristotle, TOPICS, Bk. I, ch. 1, for the use of the term locus (topic) for a method or form of argumentation.

said: *I will slay, and I will bring to life* [vivere faciam]; *I will strike, and I shall heal*: therefore, it seems, that, since death is the corruption of tending to *not-being* [corruptio tendendi ad non-esse], God is a cause of this.

I **Respond**: It must be said, that '*not-being*' is not named here through the privation of whatever kind of '*being*' [esse], but of that which (St. Severinus) Boethius[1] defines, saying: « '*Being*' [esse] is that which retains order and serves nature ». And God does not reduce (one) according to *that*; but he objects concerning *the 'being' of a nature* [de esse naturali].

And/or it can be said, that he is speaking here according to the institution of nature, according to which it is said: *God did not make death*.[2] — However, what is said, that He *slays*, this is according to the punishment of justice; yet this will be spoken of better in the Second (Book).[3]

Doubt VII

Likewise, is asked concerning this which (St. Augustine) says, that *evil is a tending to not-being*. For he seems to speak badly, because if it tends to *non-being*, either this is said as much as regards *the 'being' of nature*, or *of grace*. If *of nature*: therefore, evil corrupts nature, which is contrary to Dionysius,[4] who says, that « evil corrupts nothing of (those) existing, in that which (is their) essence and/or nature ». But if it be understood as much as regards *the 'being' of grace*, this similarly seems (to be) false, because after the first fault there remains no gratuitous 'being' according to anything of itself, because it is totally expelled through a mortal (sin): therefore[5] fault does not tend to *not-being*, but it is already in (its) terminus.*

I **Respond**: It must be said, that in a just and good man there is the considering of three (things). For since he has a nature ordered through grace, there is the considering[6] of *the 'being' of the nature*, and *the ordinability* (of the nature) to *grace*, which is according to the common name is said (to be) an "ability" [habilitas], and *the order of grace* or the ordination of grace. Evil, therefore, speaking <u>per se</u>, corrupts the very ordinability, and from this distances (a man) from grace and causes

(him) to tend to *not-being*. And because the ability is never entirely taken away, so long as the nature remains [salva natura], and the nature is not corrupted; evil always causes (one) to tend to *not-being*, so that one is never in a terminus.[7]

Doubt VIII

Likewise, is asked concerning this which (St.) Ambrose says: *A truth* [verum], *by whomsoever it be said, is from the Holy Spirit*. For he seems to speak badly, because, if this is true, therefore, since a detractor frequently[8] by detracting speaks a truth, it seems, that he speaks from the Holy Spirit. *Similarly*, a devil says many true (things). *Similarly*, on that verse: *No one says: "The Lord Jesus", except in the Holy Spirit*,[9] there is an objection. For many sinners say this all the day long. — *Likewise*, "truth" [veritas] is appropriated to the Son: therefore, (St.) Ambrose ought to have rather said, that every truth [omne verum] is from the Son.

I **Respond**: It must be said, that *something* is said (to be) by the Holy Spirit enlightening [illustrante] *the intellect* and moving *the affection*; and that is true and good, because it is said (to be) something "true" out of charity. Likewise, there is *something* from the Holy Spirit moving *the affection*, but not enlightening the intellect; just as the Apostle[10] said, that he was going to go to the Spanish [ad Hispanos]. He said the false, but yet in saying (it) he merited, because charity moved him to say this. *Something* has been said (to be) by the Holy Spirit enlightening *the intellect*, but not rectifying the affection; and that can be evil, and yet it is the saying of (something) true. Therefore, the perfect includes each; and it is said *by the Holy Spirit* and *in the Holy Spirit*, and thus the Apostle understands (it); but (St.) Ambrose speaks in a larger (sense).

And, in this manner, that which is objected, that "truth" is appropriated to the Son, is clear: for it is responded, that "interpretation" is appropriated to the Holy Spirit. — And/or it must be said, that this is not said as an appropriated (name), and/or if (it is) an appropriated (name),[11] this is (now said of the Holy Spirit) according to reckoning of a gift.

---

[1] On the Consolation of Philosophy, Bk. IV, prose 2. — A little further below this, for *And God does not reduce (one) according to that* [Et ad illud Deus non deducit] codices aa and bb read: *And regarding that 'being', which is opposed to the former 'being', God does not reduce (one)* [Et ad illud esse, quod huic esse opponitur, Deus non deducit].°

[2] Wisdom 1:13.

[3] Sent., Bk. II, d. 36, a. 3, qq. 1 and 2. — The solution of this doubt is had also in Bl. (now St.) Albertus (Magnus), Summa., p. I, tr. 20, q. 80, m. 2, a. 3, part 1; and in St. Thomas, (Bl.) Peter of Tarentaise, Richard of Middleton and Giles of Rome, here on the text.

[4] In (his) book, On the Divine Names, ch. 4, § 23, where according to the version of Scotus Erigena there is thus read: And this entirely is not entirely evil; but neither is something of (things) existing corrupted, according to what (is their) essence and/or nature.

[5] The Vatican ed. with cod. cc, has *grace is totally expelled through a mortal (sin): therefore, it* [totaliter per mortale expellitur gratia: ergo] for *it is totally expelled through a mortal (sin): therefore, fault* [totaliter per mortale expellitur: culpa ergo]; cod. A reads the same as the Vatican but end with *a mortal (sin), therefore, fault* [gratia, culpa ergo]. Next, for *already* [iam] the Vatican ed. has *also* [etiam].

[6] In the Vatican edition and codex cc there is omitted this proposition: *For since he has a nature etc.* [Cum enim habeat etc.] and then for *to grace* [ad gratiam] there is had *and the grace* [et gratiam].

[7] This is explained more at length in Sent., Bk. II, d. 34, a. 2. q. 2, in the body of the Response. Cf. also Alexander of Hales, Summa, p. I, q. 19, m. 5; Bl. (now St.) Albertus (Magnus), here in a. 10; and by St. Thomas, (Bl.) Peter of Tarentaise, (and) Giles of Rome, here on the text.

[8] The Vatican edition and codex cc (in accord with the Thomistic definition of detraction) omit *frequently* [frequenter].

[9] 1 Corinthians 12:3.

[10] Romans 25:28. — A little above this for *because it is said (to be) something "true" out of charity* [quia dicitur verum aliquid ex caritate] the Vatican edition, beginning a new proposition, *And something is said (to be) true out of charity* [Et aliquid dicitur verum ex caritate], and then, having omitted the words *Likewise, there is something* [Item, est aliquid], it immediately connect the following words *from the Holy Spirit* etc. [a Spiritu sancto etc.] with the preceding ones. The words *Likewise, there is something* [Item, est aliquid], which we have restored from codices F and T, are also missing in very many manuscripts, and above for *because it is said* [quia dicitur] some codices, such as H and Y, have *it is sometimes said* [aliquando dicitur], to which codex cc subjoins *for* [enim], and a after a few (words) has *to will and say this* [velle hoc et dicere] for *to say this* [hoc dicere].

[11] The Vatican edition prefixes to the word *an appropriated (name)* [appropriatum] the word *just as* [sicut], and, in the preceding proposition, omits *for* [enim]. For *and/or if (it is) an appropriated (name), this is* [vel si appropriatum, hoc est] codices P and Q have *and/or if it is appropriated, this is now* etc. [vel si appropriator, hoc modo est etc.]. — On this doubt, cf. Alexander of Hales, Summa, p. I, q. 15, m. 9; Bl. (now St.) Albertus (Magnus), here in a. 19, and d. 2, a. 5; St. Thomas, Sent., Bk. II, d. 28, a. 1, a. 5; and (Bl.) Peter of Tarentaise, here on the text.

---

* *Trans. notes*: Here, *its terminus* refers to the destruction of grace, caused by mortal sin, in which terminus grace no longer exists, but fault remains and comes into being, since the fault and the destruction are simultaneous.

° The former '*being*' here is the 'to be' of a thing, its act of existence; "that being" here is the '*being*' of a nature, which is termed the "nature" or "essence" of a thing.

DISTINCTION XLVII

CHAPTER I

*That the Will of God concerning a man is fulfilled,
whithersoever he turns himself.*

Indeed, the Will of God is always efficacious, so
that everything which It wills, comes to be, and nothing
comes to be, which It does not will; which is always fulfilled concerning a man, whithersoever he turns himself. For nothing, as (St.) Augustine[1] says, constituted
in free will overcomes the Will of God; even if it works
against His Will, yet against His Will, which He Himself is, nothing must be thought to be so done, as if *He
wills* (it) to be done, and it is not done; and/or *He does
not will* (it) to be done, and it is done. For that Will, as
(St.) Augustine says in (his) ENCHIRIDION,[2] is always fulfilled either *concerning* us [de nobis], or *by* us [a nobis].
Concerning us It is fulfilled, but yet we do not fulfill It,
when we sin. *By* us It is fulfilled, when we do good; for,
we do (it) for this reason, because we know that it is
pleasing to God. Thus too, concerning a man, God always fulfils His Will, because man does nothing, concerning which God does not work that he will (it). For
God does not will, that any man sin. But if he has
sinned, He wills to spare the penitent, so that he may
live, but to punish the one persevering in sins, so that
the contumacious may not evade the power of Justice.
Just as He has prepared some from eternity for punishment, so He has prepared others for glory. « And these
are *the great works of the Lord, exquisite in all His wills*,[3] and
so wisely exquisite, that though the angelic and human
creature had sinned, that is, had done not what He, but
what he had willed, He even fulfilled, through the same
will of the creature, by which there was done, what the
Creator did not will, what He did will: as One most
highly Good, using well even evils for the damnation
of those, whom He justly predestined to punishment,
and for the salvation of those, whom He kindly predestined to grace.[4] For, as much as it concerns *the former*,
they did what God did not want; but as much as regards *God's Omnipotence*, they in no manner prevailed
to do it. Indeed in this very (thing), that they worked
against His will, His Will was done concerning them.
For, indeed, on this account *great (are) the works of the
Lord, exquisite in alls His wills*, so that in a wonderful
and ineffable manner there did not come to be *apart
from* [praeter] His Will what was even done *against*
His will; because it would not have been done, if He
had not allowed (it), nor did He allow (it) at any rate
as One unwilling, but as One willing, nor would as

One good would He have allowed that it be done in an
evil manner, if as One omnipotent He could not also
work well of evil ».[5] — With these words there is evidently demonstrated, that God's Eternal Will is always
fulfilled concerning a man, even if the man works *against*
God's will. But there must be diligently attended to, in
what manner there is said in the above (sentences), that
something is done *against* the will of God, which is not,
however, done *apart from* It; and in what manner this
must be understood: "As much as regards themselves,
they did what God did not will; but as much as regards
God's Omnipotence, they in no manner prevailed to do
it". For these (words) seem to withstand the (words)
above,[6] where it was said: "*Nothing resists His Will*".

Indeed, as we have said above,[7] the "will" of God
is accepted in diverse manners, which diversity in the
aforesaid words, if it be diligently noted, nothing of
contradiction is found therein. For where he says, that
there is not done *apart* from His Will even that which is
done *against* His will, he accepted "will" in a dissimilar
manner, and he willed that there be understood by the
aforesaid words not *that Will*, which God is and (which)
is sempiternal, but as *the signs* of It , that is a *prohibition*
or *preception* and a *permission*.

CHAPTER II

*In what sense certain (things) are said to be done "against"
the Will of God.*

For many (things) are done *against* [contra] God's
precept and/or *prohibition*, which, yet, are not done *apart
from* [praeter] His *permission*. For indeed by His *permission* all evils come to be, which, however, come to be
apart from His Will. Just as (St.) Augustine says on that
passage of the Psalm:[8] *That my mouth may not speak the
works of men.* For he says that the works of men (are)
those which are evil, « which are done apart from God's
Will », which He Himself is, but not apart from His *permission*, which He Himself is not. Yet, that is named
"God's *will*", because God as One willing allows that
evils to be done. They are done both against His *preception* and/or *prohibition*, but not against His *Will*,
which He Himself is, unless they are said "to be done
against" It, because they are done *apart from* It. Indeed *against* It nothing is so done, such that *He wills*
(it) to be done,[9] and it is not done. Which (St.) Augustine evidently noted there, where he says: "For as
much as it concerns *the former*, they did what God did
not want; but as much as regards *God's Omnipotence*,

---

[1] ENCHIRIDION, ch. 95: according to its sense.

[2] The words of (St.) Augustine are in the quote which next follows.

[3] Psalm 110:2.

[4] Codices A B and C and editions 1 and 6 (5 in the margin) have
glory [gloriam].

[5] ENCHIRIDION, ch. 100, n. 26. For *well* [bene] codices B and E
have *good* [bonum], and editions 2, 3, 4, 5, 7, and 9 have *good well*
[bonum bene].

[6] Distinction XLVI.

[7] Distinction XLV, ch. 6. — A little above this, codices A B and
D have *he accepts* [accipit] for *he accepted* [accipit].

[8] ENARRATIONS ON THE PSALMS, Ps. 16: 4. After the quote, the
Vatican edition adds *in the sense* [in sensu].

[9] Thus the codices and edition 1, in the other editions there is read
after this *which is also not done* [quod et non fiat] for *and it is not done*
[et non fiat].

they in no manner prevailed to do it"; as if he said, "they worked against God's *precept*, which is named "(His) will", but they did not work against God's *Omnipotent Will*, because this they did not prevail (to do), that they did prevail (to do); and thus through this, that they worked against God's will, that is (His) precept, there was done concerning them His Will, that is, there was fulfilled His Sempiternal Will, by Which He willed to damn them. Wherefore, (St.) Gregory (the Great says) on Job:[1] « Many accomplish [peragunt] the Will of God, which they strive to change [unde mutare contendunt], and they comply [obsequntur] with His counsel as ones resisting (it); because they serve [militat] It by a disposition of that, which results through human study ». — Here, there is openly shown, that while the wicked resist God's counsel and precept, which are named "the will of God", they do that, by which His Will, Which He Himself is, is fulfilled, which is called (His) "*disposition*" and/or "*Good Pleasure*". « For », as (St.) Augustine says in (his) ENCHIRIDION,[2] « however, many be the wills of Angels and/or of men, of the good and/or of the wicked, (be they) either of (those) willing that which (is) God, and/or (something) other than God; the Will of the Omnipotent is always unconquered, Which can never be evil, Which also, while It imposes [irrogat] (the penalties of) evils, is just, and That which is (indeed) just, is not evil. Therefore, the Omnipotent God, whether through mercy He is merciful to whom He wills, or through judgement hardens whom He wills, neither does anything iniquitously, nor does anything except as One willing, and does all whatsoever He wills ».

CHAPTER III

For what reason God precepted to all to do good and avoid evil, but does not will that this be fulfilled by all.

From the aforesaid it is clear, that the Will of God, which He Himself is, is always *unconquered* and is in nothing *cancelled*, but is through all (things) *fulfilled*. However, His *counsel* and also (His) *preception* or *prohibition* are not fulfilled by all, to whom they have been proposed and given. For that reason neither did He *precept* to all (to do) good and/or *prohibit* (them to do) evil and/or *counsel* (them to do) the best, to the extent that [quod] He wanted the good (things) which He precepted, to be done by all, and/or the evils which He prohibited, to be avoided — for, if He wanted, they certainly [utique] would also have been done, because in nothing can His Will be overcome and/or impeded by man — but to show His Justice to men, and so that the wicked would be inexcusable; finally, that the good would out of obedience be allotted glory, the wicked out of disobedience punishment, just as He prepared for each from eternity. Therefore, by this (Will), He willed that there be done and/or avoided by certain ones, but not by all, those (things) which He precepted and/or prohibited *to all*, and He precepted certain ones *personally* both in the Old and New Law, (to do) those (things) which He did not will to be done by those whom He precepted, such as Abraham concerning the immolation[3] of (his) son, and in the Gospel after having cured certain ones, those whom He precepted, not to speak of it.

COMMENTARY ON DISTINCTION XLVII

On God's Will in regard to (Its) efficacy.

Indeed, the Will of God is always efficacious.

THE DIVISION OF THE TEXT

Above, Master (Peter) removed the doubts, out of which the Will[1] of God seemed sometimes to be impeded. Here, he determines the truth, showing that the Will of God is always efficacious and is never impeded. And this part has four parts.

In the *first*, he shows by the authority of (St.) Augustine, that the Will of God is always efficacious and is never impeded. But, in the *second*, so that this would not be understood of the will of a *sign*, he distinguishes "will", to show, that this has been said of the Will of (His) *Good Pleasure*, there (where he says): *Indeed, as we have said above* etc.. In the *third*, Master (Peter) shows, that (that which is) against a certain will of a *sign* cannot[2] be done, there (where he says): *For many (things) are done against God's precept* etc.. But in the *fourth*, he briefly summarizes the predetermined, and this there (where he says): *From the aforesaid it is clear, that the Will of God, which He Himself is* etc..

---

[1] MORALS ON THE BOOK OF JOB, Bk. VI, ch. 18, n. 29. The codices and editions, except editions 7 and 8, cite: *(St.) Gregory (says), ON GENESIS* [Gregorius super Genesim]. Moreover, the text has been changed not a little by Master (Peter).

[2] Chapter 102, n. 26. In which text the Vatican edition alone, together with the original, has *(those) willing* [volentes] for *of (those) willing* [volentium].

[3] See distinction XLV, ch. 7, footnote 3.

NOTES ON THE COMMENTARY

[1] Very many codices, together with edition 1, read *out of which it seemed that the Will of God sometimes is impeded* [ex quibus voluntatem Dei aliquando impediri] for *out of which the Will of God seemed sometimes to be impeded* [ex quibus voluntas Dei aliquanto impediri].

[2] For *cannot be done* [non potest fieri] the Vatican edition reads *can well be done* [bene potest fieri], breaking with the codd. and even with ed. 1. Next, after *But in the fourth* [In quarta] several codd. adjoin *part* [parte].

TREATMENT OF THE QUESTIONS

For an understanding of those things which are said in this part, four (things) are asked.

First, there is asked, whether the Will of (God's) Good Pleasure can be impeded.

Second, whether anyone can work against the will of a sign.

Third, whether God ought to permit evils.

Fourth and last, whether God can precept (that) evils (be done).

ARTICLE SOLE

On the efficacy of the Divine Will.

QUESTION I

Whether Will of God's Good Pleasure can be impeded?

And, that the Will of (His) Good Pleasure cannot be impeded, is shown first by authority:

1. According to the last (chapter) of Genesis:[1] *Can we resist God's Will?* As if to say: "No."

2. Likewise, in the ninth (chapter of St. Paul's Letter) to the Romans (there is written):[2] *His Will, who resists (It)?*

3. Likewise, on that (verse) of the First (Letter of St. Paul) to Timothy:[3] *Who wills that all men come to be saved*, the Gloss (reads): « He is to be asked, to will (that), which, if He wills (it), is necessary to come to be ».

4. Likewise, on that (verse) of the Psalm: *Just (is) the Lord in all of His works*, the Gloss (reads):[4] « With God, 'to will' is that, which 'to do' (is) »; but He cannot be impeded so that He does not will, because He freely wills what He wills: therefore, (His Will) cannot be impeded, so that It not be done.

5. Likewise, every will, which can be impeded, can be overcome; but the Divine Will cannot be overcome, since It is supreme: therefore, the Divine Will cannot be impeded.[5]

6. Likewise, every cause, which is impeded from the prosecution of its effect, either is deficient or is changed; but the Divine Will is neither deficient nor is changed nor can it be deficient nor (can it) be changed: ergo etc..

7. Likewise, more noble is the agent and more noble the cause, which cannot be impeded, than that which can; but the Divine Will is the Most High and Supreme Cause of all, as has been demonstrated above:[6] ergo etc.

ON THE CONTRARY: 1. Every cause, the effect of which comes forth [evenit] contingently, can be impeded — for it cannot (be impeded), then the effect necessarily comes forth — but the Divine Will is of this kind, because it is of many contingents — otherwise either nothing would be contingent, which is contrary to the liberty of judgement [arbitrii libertatem] and to counsel and to chance, or God would not be its cause, each of which is absurd — ergo etc..

2. Likewise, every cause, which is completed [expletur] through any agent, if it is completed,[7] can be impeded through that failing [deficientem], if that can fail — this proposition is self evident [haec propositio est per se nota] — but the Divine Will is of this kind — for God wills that many (things) come to be through created causes, which He does not make without them, such as the generating of a man, of a donkey, and of (things) similar; similarly of those which are from our work; and these can fail — therefore, the Divine Will can be impeded.

3. Likewise, every cause, the virtue of which extends itself to the contrary of (its) will, can will (something) other, that it wills;[8] but the Divine Essence is of this kind — for God wills something, such as to damn this one, the opposite of which

---

[1] Verse 19.   [2] Verse 19.

[3] Verse 4. — The entire text of the ordinary Gloss cited here is this: He is to be asked, to will (it), because it is necessary that it comes to be, if He has willed (it).

[4] Psalm 114:17: *Just (is) the Lord in all His ways, and holy in all His works* [Iustus Dominus in omnibus viis suis, et sanctus in omnibus operibus suis]. — For *With God* [Apud Deum] in the edition of the Gloss there is read *With Him* [Apud illum].

[5] Cf. the text of Master (Peter), here in chs. 1 and 2. (St.) Augustine, ON GENESIS AGAINST THE MANICHEANS, Bk. II, ch. 29, n. 44, says: Whose Will overcomes all, on no side senses (itself) unwilling (to do) anything.

[6] Distinction 45, a. 2, qq. 1 and 2.

[7] In the Vatican ed. there is wanting *if it is completed* [si expletur].

[8] Aristotle, METAPHYSICS, Bk. IX, text 3 (Bk. VIII, ch. 2), distinguishes the powers, *which with reason are* from *irrationals* and then adds: And those (powers), indeed, which (are) all with reason, the same are of contraries; but the irrational (powers), (are) one of one, such as heat (is the power) alone of making warm itself; but the power of healing (is) of infirmity and health. — The Vatican ed. distorts this proposition in this manner: *Every cause, the virtue of which extends itself to a contrary, can by (its) will will* etc. [Omnis causa ... ad contrarium, voluntate potest etc.]. The same Vatican ed. with cod. cc, somewhat below this (on the next page) after *if this (is so)* [si hoc] interjects *therefore* [ergo].

He is able (to do); this is certain, otherwise He would not be omnipotent — therefore, He can do the opposite of that which He wills. But every possible (is) able to be posited; therefore, let it be posited, that God does the opposite of that which He willed; if this (is so), the Will of God is in vain and (has been) impeded: ergo etc..

4. Likewise, a (created) will[1] wills something, which God wills it to will; therefore, either it can will the contrary, or it cannot. If it can: therefore, the Divine Will can be impeded; if it cannot: therefore, it is necessary that its liberty be restricted [arctari].

CONCLUSION

God's consequent Will cannot be overcome nor cancelled nor impeded; but (His) antecedent (Will) can be impeded, but not overcome nor cancelled; yet the necessity, by which (His) consequent Will connotes an outcome, is a necessity of consequence, not (a necessity) of the consequent.

I **RESPOND**: For an understanding of the aforesaid it must be noted, that according to (St.) John Damascene[2] the Will of (God's) Good Pleasure is twofold, namely the *antecedent* and the *consequent*: the antecedent or *conditional* (Will), by which He wills as much as is in Him, the salvation of all, and the *absolute* (Will), by which He determinately wills something, which He knows certitudinally to come forth.

It must be understood, therefore, that it is not possible that any Will of God *be overcome*; it is not possible that any (Will of God) *be cancelled*; yet it is *possible* that some (Will), such as the antecedent (Will), *not be fulfilled*; it is *necessary* that some, such as the consequent (Will), *be fulfilled*, and it is *impossible* that it be impeded.

It is not possible, I say, that any *is overcome*. For if a man does not do what God wills, as much as is in Himself, or according to (His) *antecedent* (Will), God causes concerning him, that he wills according to (His) *consequent* (Will); and thus (His Will) is always fulfilled either *concerning* the man and/or *by the man*, and in this manner It is never conquered and/or overcome.[3]

It is also not possible, that the Will of God *be cancelled*. For something is said (to have been) "cancelled" [cassum], so long as it is deprived of (its) *proper* effect, for which it is;[4] moreover, no Will is deprived of the effect, for which It is properly. For what is said,

that God wills, "*that all men come to be saved*, as much as is in Him," this "will" does not connote *salvation*, nor properly is it for the effect of salvation, but connotes *the ordination* of a nature or a nature ordainable to salvation. Wherefore to say: "God wills that this one come to be saved, as much as is in Him", is nothing more than (to say):[5] "It pleased God to give to this one a nature, through which he could arrive at salvation, and that God was prepared to help, such that salvation is not lacking on account of a defection on God's part". Wherefore It *is* not *cancelled*, because It has (its) proper effect. Moreover, concerning (His) *absolute* Will it is plain, that It cannot be cancelled, because It posits all Its own effect and never with It remaining unfulfilled.

And, so, since it is true, that the Will of God can in no manner *be overcome* nor *be cancelled*, yet *it is necessary that the absolute* Will *be fulfilled, but that the conditional* (Will be fulfilled) *least of all*.

But one must attend, that there is a necessity of *the consequent* and a necessity of *consequence*, just as has been said above[6] concerning (God's) *Foreknowledge*, because It does not have a necessity of the *consequent*, but (It does have a necessity) of *consequence*, because it necessarily *infers*, and follows: 'God foreknows this, therefore, this will be'; but yet He does not *necessarily* foreknow (it), because in the Act of foreknowing there is frequently noted a contingent effect. — This must it be understood in the *Will*, that the *absolute* Will of God connotes the outcome of a thing; and for that reason there is a necessity of *consequence* There, but not (a necessity) of *the consequent*, because It does not change the outcome of the thing, nay God wills, that the contingent consequent come forth.[7] Wherefore just as (God's) Foreknowledge, because It necessarily infers an effect, cannot fail, so neither (His) *absolute* Will, because It necessarily infers, (and) cannot *be impeded*, nay it is necessary that It be fulfilled. However, it is not necessary that (God's) *conditioned* Will be entirely fulfilled, neither by a necessity of *the consequent* nor by a necessity of *consequence*, because It does not connote *the outcome* of the thing, but connotes that which is *ordainable to an outcome*, as has been said before.[8] Wherefore it well follows: 'He wills that this one be saved by (His) *absolute* Will: therefore, this one shall be saved'; for He would never will, but (what) He would equally foreknow, (namely) that he is to be saved. However, concerning (God's) *conditioned* Will, as has been seen,[9] it does not follow.

---

[1] Supply, together with codices P and Q, *created* [creata], and/or *man's* [hominis], which codex B exhibits in the margin; codex V to the word *will* [voluntas] faultily adds *of God* [Dei].

[2] ON THE ORTHODOX FAITH, Bk. II, ch. 29. The words of (St. John) Damascene themselves have already been quoted in d. 41, a. 1, q. 1, p. 728, footnote 2. — Next, after *namely the antecedent and the consequent* [scilicet antecedens et consequens] the older codices and edition 1, faultily, do not repeat *the antecedent*, which we adjoin as required by the context; the Vatican edition also omits this word, *the antecedent* [antecedens], together with the preceding words *and the consequent* [et consequens], but then after *the absolute* [et absoluta] it puts *or consequent* [sive consequens], and thus the reading of the Vatican edition is not to be blamed. Cf. above d. 46, q. 1, in the body (of the Response).

[3] Cf. here the text of Master (Peter), where are had those quotes which have been taken from (St.) Augustine, which are referred to here.

[4] Cf. above d. 43, a. sole, q. 3, p. 771, footnote 2, where we have cited a definition from Aristotle which is similar to this one. — Immediately after this instead of reading *no Will* [nulla] it reads *of no effect* [nullo]; cod. O reads *no Will of God* [nulla Dei].

[5] After *than (to say)* [quam] codex H (T by a second hand) subjoins *this* [hoc], codex W adds *namely* [scilicet], codices A G I V and ff subjoin *that is* [id est]. — On the doctrine proposed here, cf. above d. 46, q. 1, and (St.) Augustine, ON SPIRIT AND LETTER, ch. 33, n. 37 f..

[6] Distinction 38, a. 2. q. 1. — A little before this, the Vatican edition omits *a necessity of the consequent and* [necessitas consequentis et], and a little below this after *concerning (God's) Foreknowledge* [de praescientia] the particle *because* [quia].

[7] Edition 1 read *the consequent comes forth contingently* [eveniat consequens contingenter] for *the contingent consequent comes forth* [eveniat consequens contingens]. After a few (words), for *so neither* [sic nec]. In truth, *neither* [nec] would be rightly omitted, but it is extant in all the codices.

[8] Distinction 46, q. 1. — The Vatican edition begins this proposition thus: *However, it is not necessary that (God's) antecedent and/or conditioned Will be fulfilled* etc. [Voluntatem autem antecedentem vel conditionatam non est necesse impleri etc], and the for *It does not connote the outcome* [connotat eventum] it exhibits *It does not connote the effect* [connotat effectum].

[9] A little before this, and above in d. 46, q. 1. — After a few (words, on the next page,) the Vatican ed. omits the words *in Itself* [in se].

If, therefore, it be objected, that the Will of God is necessary in Itself, and necessarily infers an effect, therefore, It posits an omnimodal necessity [omnimodam ... necessitatem] about it; it must be said, that although it is necessary, that God wills and that His Will be in act, yet Its comparison is to a future contingent, and for that reason the effect comes forth contingently.

1. To that, therefore, which is objected, that (the Divine Will) can be impeded, since It is a contingent cause; it must be said, just as has been touched upon,[1] that, though there is a comparison of the Divine Will to a future contingent, yet the *comparison* of the Divine Will to *a willed* and *the coming forth of the willed* are necessarily concomitant to themselves, just as one contingent (is to) another; and for that reason It cannot be impeded. For a cause is then impeded, when, with its comparison and ordination to the effect remaining, the effect does not come forth. Therefore, what is proposed: "every cause, the effect of which is contingent, can be impeded"; is a false proposition and has an instance, if the effect is necessarily concomitant and consequent to the cause; and this is the instance in the proposed.

2. To that which is objected, that (the Divine Will) can be impeded on account of a defect of a cooperating cause; it must be said, that just as the Divine Will or the Divine Willing [divinum velle] connotes an effect, so It connotes the existence of a particular cause. For when there is said: "God wills that this one be saved", the sense is not, that He wills (this) in regard to every outcome,[2] but that He wills that this one be saved, and He wills that this one will (to be saved). Wherefore, just as the Divine Will connotes that this effect

comes forth, and for that reason the effect necessarily follows after It, so It connotes that a created cause concurs (to this). And, for this reason it necessarily follows, if God wills that this one be saved, that he also wills (it); and thus (the cooperating cause) never fails, just as neither (does) the effect, and thus It is never impeded.

3. To that which is objected, that God can (do) the opposite of that which He wills; it must be said, that the Divine Will does not restrict [arctat] the (Divine) Power in *being able* [possendo], wherefore He can (do) more, than He wills; yet It does restrict the Power in *acting* — for the Power never does [agit] anything, except what It wills — and it is impossible, that (God's) Action superexceed (His) Will. Wherefore He can do [facere] nothing, except what He can will.[3] — When, therefore, it is said, that (God) can do the contrary of His own Will; it can be understood in a twofold manner: either with the Will *moving* to the contrary, and in this manner there is noted a repugnance of the Will to the Power, and this is impossible; or with the Will *not moving*, and in this manner there is noted not impediment nor repugnance, but the Will, which can thus (do) this, can freely (do) that, which is its opposite. For He wills this thus, that He can will its opposite without being Himself changed [absque sui mutatione], just as has been said above[4] concerning (His) Foreknowledge. And the reason for this is, because by one and the same (act) He wills whatsoever He wills.

4. To the last (objection) it must be said, that the Will of God according to (Its) convening with the (Divine) Foreknowledge wills those which It wills. Wherefore, just as the Foreknowledge encompasses [ambit] the whole (Divine) *Willing*, *Being Able* and *Acting*, and none (of These) can fail without subtracting [non subtrahendo] the contingency of the thing coming forth; so also must it be understood in the proposed.

SCHOLIUM

I. By this Question there are confirmed and explained those (things) which have been said above in d. 46, q. 1, concerning (God's) antecedent and consequent *Will*, and in d. 38, a. 2, q. 1, and in d. 40, a. 1. qq. 1 and 2, concerning *the contingency* of things, which is nether taken away by God's Foreknowledge nor by predestination. — Here, there is to be noted the difference between *being overcome* [superari], *being cancelled* [cassari], (and) *not being fulfilled* [non impleri], as is well explained by the Seraphic (Doctor); likewise in the solution to n. 2 a doctrine of great moment, that in the consequent Will there is connoted not only the effect of salvation, but also the efficiency of the second cause (cf. St. Thomas, here in q. 1, a. 2, in reply to n. 3; Summa., I, q. 19, a. 6, in reply to n. 3; Richard of Middleton, here in q. 1, in reply to n. 3). — In regard to the solution to n. 3, cf. above d.

38, a. 2, q. 3, where a similar difficulty in regard to the Divine Foreknowledge is discussed.

II. Alexander of Hales, Summa., p. I, q. 36, m. 2, and q. 40, m. 4. — (Bl. John Duns) Scotus, in each version, Sent., Bk. I, d. 46, q. sole. — St. Thomas, here in q. 1, a. 1; Summa. , I, q. 19, a. 6. — Bl. (now St.) Albertus (Magnus), here in a. 1, and d. 46, a. 1; Summa ., p. I, tr. 20, q. 79, m. 2, a. 2. — (Bl.) Peter of Tarentaise, here in q. sole, a. 1 and 2. — Richard of Middleton, here in q. 1. — Giles the Roman, here in 1st princ., q. sole. — Durandus (of Saint-Pourçain), on this and the following question, here in q. 1. — (Bl.) Dionysius the Carthusian, Sent., Bk. I, d. 46, q. 1. — (Gabriel) Biel, on this and the following question, Sent., Bk. I, d. 46, qq. 1 and 2.

---

[1] Here, in the body (of the Question). — The words immediately following, *that, though there is a comparison of the Divine Will to a future contingent, yet* [quod, quamvis comparatio divinae voluntatis sit ad futurum contingens, tamen] the Vatican edition suppresses, placing in their place, the word *since* [cum], and then for *just as one contingent (is to) another* [sicut unum contingens aliud] it substitutes *just as one is contingent, so also the other* [sicut unum est contingens, ita et aliud]. At the end of the proposition for *does not come forth* [non evenit] codices F G K S T V Y cc ee and ff and edition 1 read *will not come forth* [non eveniet]. — The words, which are had in the middle of this proposition: *are necessarily concomitant to themselves* [se necesssario concomitantur], respect a necessity of *consequence*, not of *the consequent*, with which the contingency of the effect stands.

[2] That is by prescinding from every condition. — A little further above this, for *the existence of a particular cause* [existentiam causae particularis] the Vatican ed. alone reads *the efficiency of a particular cause* [efficientiam causae particularis], codd.s L & O have *the coexistence of a particular cause* [coexistentiam causae particularis]. A little further below this, for *and He wills* [et vult] cod. O has *that is, He wills* [id est vult]; not a few codd. with edd. 2, 3, 4, 5 & 6 have only *(and) He wills* [vult].

[3] Cf. above d. 45, a. 1. q. 2, at the end.

[4] Distinction 38, a. 2, q. 2. — A little further above this, for *but the Will, which can thus (do) this, can freely (do) that, which is its opposite* [sed voluntas libere potest, quae ita potest hoc, quod eius oppositum] the Vatican edition, together with one or the other codex, reads *but that that the Will can freely (do this), because it thus can (do) that, which is its opposite* [sed quod voluntas libere potest, quia ita potest hoc, quod eius oppositum].

QUESTION II

Whether anyone can work against the will of a sign?

Second, there is asked, whether anyone can work against the will of a *sign*. And that (he can)not, seems:

1. Because *the sign* and *the signed* ought to be conformed: therefore, what is done against one is done against the other [reliquum]: therefore, if one cannot (work) against the signed, neither against the sign. Otherwise if the signed cannot be worked against, and the sign (can be worked) against, then the sign is false. For if the sign leads unto the signed,[1] it signifies, that what is done against the signed, is done against itself.

2. Likewise, the least among all signs is a *permission*, since it is in respect of an evil, to which God's Good Pleasure is least of all ordered: therefore, if it accedes least of all to the Will of the Good Pleasure, if (something) cannot be done against a *permission*, much less (can something be done) against the other (signs). But (something) cannot be done against a *permission*, just as Master (Peter) says in the text[2] and (St.) Augustine, ON THE CITY (OF GOD), in the twentieth (chapter): « Just as no one of men rightly acts, unless helped by the Divine assistance; so no one of men and demons acts iniquitously, unless he be permitted by the same Divine and most just judgement ».

3. Likewise, more powerful is the will, which cannot be resisted neither in *thing*[3] nor in *sign*, than the one which can at least in a *sign*, even if not in *thing*; but God is most powerful: therefore, it seems, that neither His *Will* nor a *sign* of (His) Will can be resisted, and thus etc..

ON THE CONTRARY: 1. Among all the signs of a will a *preception* or a command [imperium] seems to be the most powerful; but (something) can be done and is done all day long against the Divine *command* [mandatum]: therefore, against *all the others*.

2. Likewise, it seems that (one can work) in particular [specialiter] against a *permission*, because a permission is not but of the evil of fault; but the evil of fault is not evil, unless it be done voluntarily, and if it is done voluntarily, it is able not to be done: therefore, with God permitting that someone work in an evil manner, he can not do (this): therefore, he can work against a *permission*.

3. Likewise, on that (verse) of the Psalm:[4] *He led them forth with silver and gold*, the Gloss says, that the same was precepted and permitted, namely, the carrying-off of the vessels [asportatio vasorum]: therefore, since (this) could be done against the precept, for an equal reason also against the permission and against the other (signs) per consequens: therefore, against every will of a sign.

CONCLUSION

Against three signs of the Divine Will something can be done, but against two nothing, which is proved by a twofold reason.

I RESPOND: It must be said, that (something) can be done against *some* sign of the Divine Will, against *some* (something can)not.

And the reason for this is twofold, out of the twofold manner of distinguishing the signs. For certain (signs) are in respect of (something) *present*, such as a *fulfillment* [impletio] and a *permission*; certain ones in respect of (something) *future*, such as a *preception* and a *counsel* and a *prohibition*. And since *concerning the present* it is impossible that what be done in the present not be done — since « everything which is, when it is, it is necessary that it is »[5] — for that reason in respect of the signs concerning *the present* there can be no resistance; because if there is a resistance, they are already non present. However, because (things) *future* and/or to be done can not be done; for that reason as much as regards the three following signs there can be a resistance.

The other reason is taken according to the other manner of distinguishing (the signs): because certain ones are signs of the *absolute* Divine Will, certain ones of *the conditioned* (Divine Will). I say, therefore, that because[6] (something) cannot be done against *the absolute Will*, it can also not be done against *the signs* of the absolute Will, as for example a *fulfillment and a permission*. However, because (something) can be done against *the antecedent* or conditioned Will, because a man can divert (himself) from the order, for which [ad quem] he has been founded out of his institution:[7] hence it is, that (something) can be done against the will of a sign, which signifies That, namely against a *prohibition*, a *preception* and a *counsel*.

1. To that, therefore, which is first objected, that (something) can be done against *no* (sign of the Divine Will); the solution is clear, that (the signs of the Divine Will) are not false (signs).[8]

---

[1] See above d. 16, a. sole, q. 2, p. 282, footnote 2. — Somewhat further above this, after *the other* [reliquum] the Vatican edition, together with a number of codices, has *and* [et] for *therefore* [ergo]. Then after *Otherwise if* [Alioquin si] several codices and edition 1 faultily omit *-not* [non], and, next, for *and the sign* [et contra] the Vatican edition has *but the sign* [sed contra].

[2] Here in ch. 2. — The passage, next cited from THE CITY OF GOD, is ch. 1, n. 2, where in the original text for *Just as* [Sicut] there is had *Though* [quamvis] and, having omitted *so* [sic], there is twice read *acts* [agat] in the subjunctive.

[3] For *thing* [re] the Vatican ed. with codex cc, has *Itself* [se].

[4] Psalm 104:37. — The ordinary Gloss is cited here only according to (its) sense, not word for word.

[5] We have exhibited this entire proposition of Aristotle above in d. 38, a. 2, q. 1, p. 674, footnote 3. In the proposition itself, cited here, for *everything* [omne] editions 1, 2 and 3, together with the original text have *to be* [esse]. After a few (words), for *if there is a resistance* [si sit resistentia] the Vatican edition, together with some codices, has *if there comes to be a resistance* [si fit resistentia].

[6] For *because* [quia] codex Z has *just as* [sicut].

[7] The Vatican edition, together with codex cc, has *constitution* [constitutione]. — On the antecedent and consequent Will, cf. the preceding question and d. 36, q. 1.

[8] Supply together with codex T *signs* [signa]. For *that (the signs of the Divine Will) are not false (signs)* [quod non sunt falsa] there is read in the Vatican edition *that it is not false* [quod non est falsum].

2. To that which is objected, that a permission is the least (of all the signs); it must be said, that a greater or lesser signification does nothing for this, but the effects quality of being present [praesentialitas], and/or even, because it signifies the absolute Will, which[1] connotes something absolutely.

3. To that which is objected, that that is more powerful [potentius], against the sign of which (something) cannot be done; it must be said, that (this)[2] is true, when a will wills entirely, that nothing be done, except what shows that it wills; but the Divine Will is not such, nay It wills, that each one have his own liberty and do what he does will. Wherefore, even the power of working against the Divine Will is from the Divine Will, and, for that reason, it would not be more powerful on this account. Wherefore one must distinguish, that 'to be able to work' against sign of the will of anyone is either against (his) will, and, thus, attests to (his) impotence; or that 'being able' is from (his) will, to which the sign belongs, and, thus, does not attest to an impotence, but rather to potency [potentiae].

1. To that which is objected, that (something can be done) against all (the signs), because (something) can be done against a preception, which is the greatest sign; (the objection) must be solved through interemption, (demonstrating) that it is not the greatest sign. Moreover, this does nothing

for the proposed, but the quality of being present in the effect and the absoluteness [absolutio] in the signed (do).[3]

2. To that which is objected, that (something) is done against a *permission*, because a sinner can sin not; it must be said, that God is not said "to permit to sin", except him who actually sins, while he is sinning, and then it is impossible, that he not sin.

3. To that which is objected last, that the same was there a *precept* and a *permission*; it must be said, that "*permission*" is accepted in many manners in Scripture. In the first manner a "permission" is said (to be) a "*not restraining*" [non cohibere], just as the Lord permits evils, because He does not restrain (them); and in this manner the sign of the Divine Will has been distinguished against a *precept*.[4] In another manner, (it means) *to not punish temporally*; and in this manner a bill of divorce [libellus repudii] is said "to be permitted", in the nineteenth (chapter of the Gospel of St.) Matthew:[5] *Moses permitted (it) for your hardness (of heart)*. In the third manner, (it means), *to not prohibit*, as the Psalm (says):[6] *Be angry and do not sin*, (where) the Gloss (says): « He permits what is of necessity », that is, He does not prohibit (it). In the fourth manner "to permit" is "*to indulge the less good*", (as is said) on that (verse) in the seventh (chapter of St. Paul's) First (Letter) to the Corinthians:[7] *But this I say according to indulgence* etc., (where) the Gloss (says): "He permits (it)".

SCHOLIUM

To be noted is the distinction between "*working against the Will of God*" and "*working apart from the will of God*", as St. Bonaventure observes here in Doubt 2. In the former there is *an absolute act of a will concerning the opposite*, but in the latter there is no such act, neither concerning the one willed nor concerning the opposite. Alexander of Hales (SUMMA., p. I, q. 40, m. 4, in reply to n. 1), and St. Thomas (here in q. 1, a. 2) agree.

The (other) authors (discussing this are): Alexander of Hales, SUMMA., p. I, q. 40, m. 4. — St. Thom as, here in q. 1, a. 2. — Bl. (now St.) Albertus (Magnus), here in a. 3. — (Bl.) Peter of Tarentaise, here in the q. sole, a. 4. — Richard of Middleton, here in q. 2. — Giles the Roman, here in 2nd princ., q. 1. — (Bl.) Dionysius the Carthusian, SENT., Bk. I, d. 46, q. 3, near the end.

QUESTION III

Whether God ought to permit evils?

Third, there is asked, whether God ought to permit evils. And it seems, that (it is) so.

1. On the twelfth (chapter of the Book) of Job:[8] *The tabernacles of plunderers abound* etc., (Pope St.) Gregory (the Great says): « The Omnipotent God, what He prohibits to be done, it is just, that He allow be done ».

2. Likewise, God ought to conserve the order,

which He instituted; but when God created man, He gave him a free will [liberam voluntatem]; but (his) will is said (to be) "free", by this, that he can freely (do) whatever he wills: therefore, if he wills (to do) evil, he is able unto an evil: therefore, since He ought not take away from man the power, which He gave (him), He ought to permit him to sin.[9]

---

[1] The Vatican edition, together with codex cc, has *by which* [qua].

[2] In codices P and Q (T in the margin) and edition 1 there is added *this* [hoc]. A little below this, after *Wherefore* [Unde] the Vatican edition, together with codex cc, omits *even* [et].

[3] Or, as was said above in the solution to n. 2, because it signifies the absolute Will, which connotes something absolutely. — For *the signed* [signato] the Vatican edition has *the signified* [significato], which edition, also a little further above this, after *the greatest sign* [maximum signum], with the support of a few codices, adds *because a fulfillment is greater* [quia impletio maius est]. — On a solution *through interemption*, cf. above d. 3, p. I, a. 1, q. 3, p. 87, footnote 4.

[4] For a precept respects good (deeds), but evil ones are as if permitted by God, not precepted; and thus in this sense the same work cannot be precepted and permitted together; but yet it can be, if "permission"

is taken on one of the following manners. — A little further above this, for *restraining* [cohibere] not a few codices have *preventing* [prohibere].

[5] Verse 8.

[6] Psalm 4:5. The ordinary Gloss on the verse is: Therefore, what belongs to custom, he permits. — In the codices and edition 1 there are missing the words *that is* [id est].

[7] Verse 6. — See the Gloss in (Nicolas) of Lyra.

[8] Verse 6. — The saying of (St.) Gregory is had in his book, MORALS ON THE BOOK OF JOB, Bk. XI, ch. 2, n. 3, in which saying the Vatican edition reads *does not prohibit* [non prohibit].

[9] Here let there be cited, what (St.) Augustine says ON THE CITY OF GOD, Bk. VII, ch. 30: And so in this manner He administers all which He has created, so that He allows them to exercise their own (powers) and enact (their own) movements.

3. Likewise, evil is frequently the occasion of a greater good, that[1] would not be done, if the evil had not preceded (it), as is clear in the Passion of Christ; but it is fitting [decet] that God do and permit that which is the way to the better: therefore, since He cannot do evil, He ought at least to permit (it).

4. Likewise, God does all for the sake of His own praise; but in evils there is manifested the praise of the Divine Justice and Mercy: therefore, if He ought not work against the amplification [ampliationem] of His own praise, He ought not impede, that evils be done: ergo etc..

ON THE CONTRARY: 1. On the first (chapter of St. Paul's Letter) to the Romans:[2] *Not only those who doe such (things) are worthy of death, but those who consent (to them)*, the Gloss (says): « To remain silent is to consent, when you can put (the matter) in clear light [arguere] »: therefore, since God can correct and impede evil, if He permits (it) and remains silent, He consents; but those who consent, are worthy of death: ergo etc..

2. Likewise, (St.) Augustine (says) in the nineteenth (book), ON THE CITY OF GOD, chapter sixteen: « To the office of the innocent pertains not only that he infer evil upon no one, but even that he restrain (others) from sin »: therefore, if God does not restrain (sinners), when He can, God is not innocent.

3. Likewise, it seems *by reason*: because all our virtues ought to have (their) exemplar in God; but in us there is the virtue of zeal: therefore, (it is) also in God. But zeal, as much as it can, obviates sin:[3] therefore, if God has zeal, as much as He can, He obviates (sin): ergo etc..

4. Likewise, *each and every way of the Lord (is) mercy and truth*:[4] if, therefore, He permits the just (man) to sin, either (this) belongs to *mercy* or *to justice*. Not *to mercy*, it is established; nor *to justice*, because the just (man) does not merit to fall: ergo etc..

CONCLUSION

God in a most ordinate manner permits that evils come to be, both for the sake of order in the universe, and for the sake of (its) order unto the end, whether this is the ultimate (order), which is the Divine Glory, or the intermediate one, which is the salvation of the Elect.

I RESPOND: It must be said, that God does permit that evils come to be, and this in a most ordinate manner [ordinatissime].

For there is a twofold order of things: one *in the universe*, the other *unto the end*; and each requires [exigit], that God permit that evils come to be.

The order *in the universe* indeed requires (this), because for the perfection of the university (of things) was necessary, that a creature be made free in judgement [arbitrio liberam] and able [potentem] to sin; but the administration of the university (of things) is, such that « God so administers the things (He has) founded, that He allows them to set in motion [agere] their own movements », just as (St.) Augustine says in the seventh (book), ON THE CITY OF GOD.[6] For that reason, since He ought to have given the power of sinning and He ought to have ruled, with the order of what He had founded remaining [salvo ordine suae conditionis]; if (man) wanted to sin, He ought to have *conserved* (him): and thus He ought to permit sins.

The order *to the end*[7] requires this, because one happens to find a twofold end in the universe: one is *the salvation of the Elect*, the other (is) *the Divine Praise*. — Since, therefore, the permission of evils renders *the Elect more glorious* through (their) *occasion*, and God does not care, whether through a cause, and/or through an occasion the glory of the Elect is increased; for this reason God rightly permits (evils). Wherefore, (St.) Augustine in the eleventh (book), ON THE CITY OF GOD[8] says, « that He would make none, whom He foreknew (to be) evil, unless He equally knew, for which uses of the good He would accommodate (him) ». And for that reason he says[9] concerning the fall of the world, that He permitted more to be wicked, because if they were few they would not dare to exercise the good. — The Divine *Praise* also requires this, because by the occasion of an evil there is most highly manifested the Divine *Mercy* in the Elect, in the donation of the Only-Begotten Son on behalf of the wicked, according to the time.[10] There is also most highly manifested the *Justice* of God in the eternal punishment of the reprobate. Wherefore, (St.) Augustine (says) in the twenty-first (book), ON THE CITY OF GOD:[11] « If all remained in punishment, in none would there appear the grace of the Merciful Redeemer [misericordis redimentis]. Again, if all were transferred to the Light, in none would there appear the severity of the (Divine) Vengeance ».

1. To that, therefore, which is objected, that to permit is to consent; it must be said, that 'to permit evil' is in a twofold manner: either by not *restraining the hand*[12] *and/or spirit (of a sinner)* neither in deed nor in retribution, and in this manner it is to consent; and/or by not *restraining (his) hand*, but yet *by punishing the transgressor* and by putting (the matter) continually in a clear light, and in this manner one does not consent; and in this manner God permits (evils), and does not consent.

---

[1] For *that* [quod] the Vatican edition with codex cc has *but it* [sed], and at the end of the argument *only* [solum] for *at least* [saltem].

[2] Verse 32, where the Vulgate reads: *Those who do such (things) are worthy of death, and not only those who do them, but even those who consent to those doing (them)*. — In the Gloss next cited the Vatican edition substitutes *to do* [facere] for *to remain silent* [tacere], contradicting (Nicolas of) Lyra and also breaking with codices P Q and T, in the authority of which we have restored *to remain silent* [tacere]; but yet with the Vatican edition, and not a few codices, and even with the original text consenting, we have restored *you can* [possis] for *one can* [possit].

[3] Cf. above (St. Bonaventure's Commentary on Master Peter's Prologue), p. 23, footnote 9. — For *can, obviates* [potest, obviat] the Vatican edition has *can obviate* [potest obviare].

[4] Psalm 24, 10.

[5] Cf. above d. 44, a. 1. q. 3, in the body (of the Response).

[6] Chapter 30; cf. previous page, footnote 9. — Next in codex T to the word *rule* [regere] there has been adjoined by a second hand the word *man* [hominem].

[7] Codex T subjoins *also* [etiam]. Then for *one happens to find* [contingit reperire] the Vatican edition has *there happens to be found* [contingit reperiri].

[8] Chapter 18; cf. above d. 44, a. 1, q. 3, p. 786, footnote 7. In the cited text for *uses of the good* [bonorum usibus] not a few codices have *uses of the blessed* [beatorum usibus].

[9] Sermon 15, (Ps. 25:8), ch. 9, n. 9: Nor do I want you to say to me: "At least if it were necessary for the sake of our exercise, that there were evils, few would be the wicked, and many would be the good. You do not attend, that if there were few, they would not harm the many? At any rate consider, o prudent man, that if the good were many, and the wicked were few, the few wicked would not dare to harm the many good. If they did not dare, the would not exercise (the good in virtue). — Codices V and X read: *he says in the book*, ON THE FALL OF THE WORLD [dicit in libro de Lapsu mundi].

[10] A reference to Rom. 5:6: *Such as why did Christ ... according to the time, die on behalf of the impious?* [Ut quid enim Christus ... secundum tempus pro impiis mortuus est?].

[11] Chapter 12; cf. above d. 41, a. 1, q. 2, p. 733, footnote 9, and also his ENCHIRIDION, ch. 99, n. 25.

[12] Very many codices, together with edition 1 here, and many more codices even in the second member of the distinction, have *the evil* [malum] for *he hand* [manum].

2. To that which is objected, that 'to restrain' pertains to the innocent; it must be said, that that is understood of restraining [cohibitione] as much as regards 'putting (the matter) in a clear light' [ad arguitionem] and punishing [punitionem], not as much as regard the compelling [coactionem] of a will.

3. To that which is objected, that zeal obviates sin; it must be said, that it is true, with the right of justice remaining [salvo iure iustitiae]; and justice, insofar as it is the order of the universe, requires this, that God permit, a man to go [ire][1] according to the command [imperium] of his own will.

4. To that which is objected last, the response is clear; because to permit someone to sin is a work of justice, not, I say, of the justice, which is the requirement for merits [exigentia meritorum], but (of justice which is) the co-fittingness [condecentia] of Divine Wisdom and Goodness.[2]

SCHOLIUM

I. Regarding more on this question, see above d. 46, qq. 2-6, and d. 44, a. 1, qq. 1-3, and in Alexander of Hales', SUMMA., p. I, q. 38 throughout, where more questions on this matter are solved. — On the twofold order of things, namely in *the universe* and regarding *the end*, cf. above d. 44, a. 1, q. 3; and on the distinction of (its) twofold end, namely (its) *ultimate* and principal end (the praise of God) and « *the end under the end* » (the salvation of the Elect), cf. SENT., Bk. II, d. 15, a. 2, q. 1, and d. 38, a. 1. q. 3.

II. Here is touched upon a question, which is popularly debated on both sides, concerning reprobation, whether the permission of sin is in God a *positive* act, and/or *the negation* of a positive act. The patrons of the first sentence cite Alexander of Hales, SUMMA., p. I, q. 36, m. 1, and St. Thomas, SUMMA, I, q. 23, a. 3, and Bartolomeo dei Barberii (CURSUS THEOLOGICUS., tom. I, d. 6, q. 11) even cites St. Bonaventure (here and in Doubt 3), whose words however, seem to us ambiguous. (Bl. John) Scotus (here in the q. sole), though he judges each sentence probable, prefers, however, the sentence, that in God permission is a negation of a positive act, but together with a positive act in a reflected manner.

III. The authors (treating of this question are): Alexander of Hales, SUMMA., p. I. q, 18, m. 10, a. 1, q. 38, m. 1 and 2. — (Bl.. John Duns) Scotus, here in q. 2. — Bl. (now St.) Albertus (Magnus), SENT., Bk. I, d. 46, a. 9. — (Bl.) Peter of Tarentaise, SENT., Bk. I, d. 46, q. 1, a. 3. — Richard of Middleton, here in q. 3, and in d. 46, q. 3. — Giles the Roman, here in 2nd princ., q. 2.

QUESTION IV

Whether God can precept evils?

Fourth and last, there is asked, whether God can precept evils. And it seems, that (it is) so.

1. Because He precepts in the first (chapter) of Osee,[3] *to take a prostitute as a wife*, and (St.) Bernard (of Clairvaux) expounds (this) according to the letter. *Which if you say*, that it must not be understood according to the letter; *it is* then *objected*: because He not only precepts (him) to take a wife, but even to make (for himself) sons of fornication; which if (his) wife were legitimate, they would not be sons of fornication.

2. Likewise, in the twelfth (chapter) of Exodus[4] He precepts the sons of Israel to steal [facere furtum]; but theft [furtum] is evil and against the law of nature: ergo etc.. *If you say*, that it is not evil according to itself, and for that reason can be well done; *it is objected*: because He precepts Abraham to slay (his) innocent son and one whom he knew (to be) innocent, according to the twenty-second (chapter) of Genesis;[5] and this is an evil according to itself [malum secundum se]: therefore, it seems, that God can precept evil.

3. Likewise, it seems *by reason*: because God is above every law: therefore, in every commandment He can grant a dispensation [dispensare]: therefore, He can precept the contraries of all precepts and prohibitions.

4. Likewise, a *non-being* [non-ens] is more distant from a being [ente] than *evil* (is) from good; but God, by the command [imperio] alone of (His) Will, makes a being out of a *non-being*: therefore, by the command alone of (His) Will He works [facit] good out of evil: therefore, He can precept evils, as it seems.

ON THE CONTRARY: 1. A (divine) *precept* is a sign of the Divine* Will: therefore, either it is a false sign, when it signifies, that God wills what He precepts,[6] or God wills that. But, if God wills an evil, He is evil; if He does not will (it), and precepts it, He is false; and each is impossible with God: ergo etc.

2. Likewise, no one obeying a divine precept ought to be punished: therefore, if God can precept an evil, evil can be done with impunity [impune]. But that evil remain un-

---

[1] In the Vatican edition there is lacking *to go* [ire].

[2] Cf. above d. 43, a. sole, q. 4, p. 775, footnote 2.

[3] Verse 2: *God, take as thy wife a woman of fornications and make for thyself sons of fornications* [Vade, sume tibi uxorem fornicationum et fac tibi filios fornicationum]. St. Bernard's exposition on this passage is had in his book, ON PRECEPT AND DISPENSATION, ch. 3, n. 6, where the holy Doctor, of the theft done by the sons of Israel in Egypt, which is mentioned in the following argument, says: « The one (deed) of whose, what would it be reputed but a field heavy with theft [grave furti fascinus]? the other, what but the turpitude of a disgraceful action [flagitii], if each deed,

the authority of the One commanding had not excused »? According to (St.) Augustine, AGAINST FAUSTUS, Bk. XXII, ch. 89, those words in Osee signify the calling of the gentiles to the Faith, and even that deed of theft is explained by the same holy Doctor ibid., ch. 41, in a mystical manner. — Near the end of the argument, for *sons of fornication* [filios fornicationis] the Vatican edition, together with codex cc, has *sons of a fornicator* [filios fornicarios].

[4] Verse 36.

[5] Verse 2.

[6] The Vatican edition, together with codex cc, here and a little afterwards, has *precepted* [praecepit].

---

* *Trans. note*: In the original Latin text, there is found here a comma, which seems to have been faultily inserted into the text; I have removed it, in the English translation, as required by the context and the flow of the argument, and as the syntax seems to require.

punished is contrary to the Divine Justice: therefore, God can work against Himself, therefore be His own adversary [sibi adversari]. But this is impossible: ergo etc..

3. Likewise, God precepts that evils are not done: if, therefore, He precepts that (they) be done, He precepts two opposites;[1] but that two opposites be done is impossible: therefore, God precepts the impossible. But to no such precept are we obliged: therefore, we are able to not obey God; which is absurd. *And again*, everyone precepting the impossible is foolish, and/or impious: therefore, God would be foolish, and/or impious, each of which is impossible. And, for that reason, (St.) Jerome[2] says: "He who says that God has precepted the impossible, let him be accursed [anathema sit]."

CONCLUSION

God can to no extent precept an evil, which remains under the reckoning of evil, and for that reason (He can) never (precept) that (act) which is evil according to itself; yet that (act) which is evil in itself, He can precept and by precepting cause a good.

I RESPOND: It must be said, that when it is asked, whether God can precept an evil (act), this can be understood in a twofold manner: either an evil (act) *remaining evil*, or thus, that by precepting (it) *He works the good*. The first is simply impossible; but the second is in some manner possible, though not entirely.

For there is something evil *in itself*, something evil *according to itself*. The (act) evil *in itself* can be well done; the (act) evil *according to itself* can in no manner be well[3] done, nay to understand that it is well done, is to understand, that the same is evil and good. Therefore, it can be said, that God can precept the (act) evil *in itself*, but not the (act) evil *according to itself*; because He can precept nothing, which is not good, after it has been precepted; and that is evil *in itself*, but not *according to itself*; for that reason He can precept the former and not the other.

And, hence there has (its) rise, that which (St.) Bernard says in the book, ON DISPENSATION AND PRECEPT,[4] that God can dispense in the precepts of *the second* tablet and not (in those) of *the first*. And the reason for this is, because in the precepts of the *second* tablet, as much as concerns the reckoning of a precept, there is touched upon or precepted the ordination *regarding (one's) neighbor*, and there is prohibited a deordination regarding the same. Moreover, a deordination in respect of (one's) neighbor, unless it be a deordination in respect of God, is (an act) evil *in itself* [malum in se]; but if in respect of God, it is (an act) evil *according to itself* [malum secundum se]: just as to know (a woman) not one's own is (an act) evil *in itself*, but to

know another's, or not one's own, out of passion [ex libidine] is (an act) evil *according to itself*. But God, in the precepts of *the second* tablet, dispenses [dispensat] and can dispense, and against those He can precept, for the aforesaid reason. Nor does it follow from this, that He precepts contraries, because a special commandment absolves from a common one, just as a special privilege (does).[5]

But in the precepts of *the first* tablet God cannot dispense, because their opposites are evil *according to themselves*; for the precepts themselves mean an ordination to God or unto the End from their own reckoning, and their opposites a deordination. And, for that reason, if He precepted the contrary, He would precept (something) against Himself; and but He cannot work against Himself. And, if He precepted these — since these are evil *according to themselves*, thus that they can in no manner be well done — God would either will an evil (act), which is unfitting; or an evil (act) would be done with impunity, or the same (act) would be good and evil, each of which is simply unfitting.

And for that reason there are to be conceded the reasons proving, that God cannot precept every[6] evil, as for example an evil (act) remaining evil, and this is evil *according to itself*. — Yet, the last reason concerning this, that He precepts[7] an evil, is not valid, and it has already been solved.

1. To that, therefore, which is objected concerning Osee, it must be said, that that (act) was evil *in itself*, namely to know (a woman) not one's own, and by the Divine precept it was made good for him. But according to which "fornication" means a libidinous act and (means) "to know some (woman) out of passion [ex libidine]", this the Lord never precepted.

2. To that which is objected concerning the authority from Exodus, what He precepted theft to the sons of Israel; it must be said, that that similarly He did precept, inasmuch as it, namely, accepting another's property [rem], was (an act) evil *in itself*; and this He could do, because, since He is the Lord of all, He could transfer the dominion (of the thing). But He never precepted, that they do this out of passion [ex libidine]; for that is an evil (act) *according to itself*.

To that which is objected concerning that which He precepted Abraham concerning Isaac; it must be said, that that was not (an act) evil *according to itself*, because Isaac, though he was not liable [reus] to the death being inflicted upon him by a man, yet, by reason of original sin he was liable [reus] of being put to a temporal death by God, for which (death) he had a necessity; and, for that reason, God had the authority, and, thus, de jure, could commit that (authority) to Abraham in the matter [ex causa]. — Yet, some want to say, that He die not precept (him) *to slay*, but to *offer*. But, against this is the Gloss,

---

[1] Codex V reads *two contradictorily opposed (acts)* [duo contradictorie opposita] for *two opposites* [duo opposita]. Immediately before this, the Vatican ed. with cod. cc has thrice *precepted* [praecepit] for *precepts* [praecipit].

[2] THE EXPLANATION OF THE CREED TO POPE DAMASUS (which opuscule, even if it is had among the words of St. Jerome, belongs to another author, namely Pelagius, as they say): We also execrate their blasphemy, they who say, that it is impossible that anything be precepted a man by God. Cf. also his Commentary on Mt. 6:44. — Note, that the Seraphic Doctor reproves this argument at the end of the body of the Question.

[3] For *well done* [bene], which occurs thrice in this proposition, codices L and O have thrice *made good* [bonum].

[4] Chapter 3, n. 6 f., where it is found in regard to its sense. Cf. above on the previous page, footnote 3.

[5] Edition 1 adds *derogates a general one* [derogat generali] for *(does)*.

[6] In the Vatican edition and codex cc there is wanting *every* [omne].

[7] Edition 1 has *precepted* [praecepit].

and the text,[1] because there is said, that *he carried fire and a short sword*.

3. To that which is objected, that He is able over every given law [super omnem legem datam]; it must be said, that it is true, that He is able, because He can *impose*, but He cannot *destroy* (a law which He has) already given [positam]. For, since some commandments mean an ordination to Him, just as He cannot work against His own Justice, so neither (can He) precept (anything) against them.

4. To that which is objected, that of a non-being [non-ente] He can make a being [ens]; it must be said, that it is true, that He can do (this), but this He cannot make, that something be at once [simul][2] a *being* and a *non-being*; and, because a *non-being* does not have a necessity regarding this, that it be a *non-being*, for that reason it can be made a *being*. But there are some evil (acts), which, if they are, are of necessity evil, such as to lie and to hate God. And, for that reason, it is not similar, because, if He made these to be good, He would cause, that the same was at once good and evil.

SCHOLIUM

I. It is manifest, that God cannot precept an evil (act), to the extent that it remains evil. There can only be asked, whether God in matter prohibited by His own precept can take away *the reckoning of evil* through a certain dispensation. — The distinction between (an act) evil *in itself* [malum in se] and (an act) evil *according to itself* [malum secundum se], supported by Alexander of Hales (SUMMA, p. I, q. 37, m. 2 and 3) and St. Thomas (here in q. 1, a. 4), St. Bonaventure explains by reducing it to a twofold order of things, namely, (that) in the universe and (that) regarding the ultimate end (cf. here the preceding question). A deordination against the first order, which is of one thing to another, is (an act) evil *in itself*, and prohibited by the precepts of the second tablet; but (an act) evil *according to itself*, is against the second order, in which there is also the reckoning of the first order.

II. The distinction of the Decalogue into precepts of the first and second tablet, thus that the first three precepts are attributed to the first tablet, but the other seven to the second, is, according to the Seraphic Doctor (SENT., Bk. III, c. 37, a. 2. q. 3), to be understood according to the mystical sense, but not (according to) the literal or historical one, since (as Josephus would have it), on each tablet were written five precepts.

That God can dispense in the precepts of the second tablet, is approved even by St. Thomas in (his) COMMENTARY (here in q. 1, a. 4). Yet, this must be understood with that restriction, which is hinted at by the Seraphic (Doctor) here in reply to nn. 1 and 2. Which restriction, if it is attended to, can be reconciled in its doctrine with the words of St. Thomas in (his) *Summa* (I, II, q. 100, a. 8), where it is said that even in regard to the precepts of the second tablet, that « they are entirely indispensable ». But these words are to be understood with (that) further explication, which is posited there in reply to n. 3. (Bl. John Duns) Scotus teaches nearly the same thing (SENT., III, d. 37, q. sole), though he opines, that not all the precepts of the second table strictly concern natural right [de iure naturali], and per consequens, that they are dispensable. — The deeds of Osee and Abraham (concerning which see here Doubt 5) and the despoiling of the Egyptians are explained in the same manner by Alexander (of Hales) and by St. Thomas, locis. citt..

III. Besides (those) mentioned: Bl. (now St.) Albertus (Magnus), SENT., Bk. I, d. 46, a. 9; SUMMA ., p. I, tr. 20, q. 80, a. 3, part. 1. — (Bl.) Peter of Tarentaise, here in the q. sole, a. 6. — Richard of Middleton, here in q. 4. — Giles the Roman here in 2nd princ., q. 3. — Durandus (of Saint-Pourçain), here in q. 4. — (Bl.) Dionysius the Carthusian, here in the q. sole. — (Gabriel) Biel, here in the q. sole.

DOUBTS ON THE TEXT OF THE MASTER

DOUBT I

In this part are the doubts about (Master Peter's) text and, first, concerning that word of (St.) Augustine: *For the damnation of those, whom He justly predestined to punishment*. For he seems to speak improperly, because above in the Fortieth Distinction[3] it is said, that *predestination* concerns salutary goods. — *Likewise*, (St. John) Damascene (says):[4] « Not do punish (us) has God formed [plasmavit] us »: therefore, he speaks badly. — In accord with this *there is asked*, since God is most highly just, just as (He is) most highly merciful: "For what reason is it said (to be) proper to God *to have mercy*, rather than *to condemn or punish*?"

I RESPOND: It must be said, that (St. John) Damascene distinguishes the Will of God into the *antecedent* and *consequent* (Will). There can be, therefore, a preparation as much as regards *each*; and thus there is a preparation of goods, and in this manner there is a preparation *simply* and a predestination *properly* said. In another manner "preparation" is accepted *broadly*, according to whichsoever Will; and in this manner it is of evils and it is a preparation *broadly* (speaking). Moreover, Master (Peter) and (St. John) Damascene above[5] have accepted ("preparation") *properly*, but (St.) Augustine accepts (it) *commonly*; and in this manner the solution of the contrary (assertion) is clear.

To that which *is asked* concerning the work of the (Divine) Mercy, it must be said, that it is more[6] proper to God *to have mercy* [misereri],

---

[1] Genesis 22:6: *He, on the other hand, was carrying in his hands fire and a short sword* [Ipse vero portabat in manibus ignem et gladium]. — The ordinary Gloss, ibid., on v. 5 says: With an undoubting spirit he was willing to slay his son [Indubitanti animo mactare filium volebat].

[2] In the Vatican edition and codex cc there is missing *at once* [simul].

[3] At the beginning.

[4] ON THE ORTHODOX FAITH, Bk. II, ch. 29. Cf. above d. 41, a. 1. q. 1, p. 728, footnote 2, in which passage and in d. 46, q. 1 you will also find, what is the antecedent and the consequent Will.

[5] Locis. citt., in the previous two footnotes. — At the verb *have accepted* [acceperunt], in place of which the Vatican edition has *accept* [accipiunt], understand: *"preparation"* [praeparationem]. A little after this, the Vatican edition omits *of the contrary (assertion)* [contrarii].

[6] For *more* [magis] the Vatican edition and not a few codices have *for this reason* [ideo], many other codices, together with editions 2 and 3 have *though* [quamvis] (which in English must be placed after *that*); but the word *more* [magis], which is had in codex H (T in the margin) and in edition 1, responds more to the context. — On this doubt, cf. Alexander of Hales, SUMMA., p. I, q. 40. m. 4, at the end; St. Thomas, (Bl.) Peter of Tarentaise and Richard of Middleton, here on the text.

because for the work of mercy there is not required but the Benignity of God; but for this, that He works the severity of justice, there is presupposed our iniquity: and for that reason the former is more appropriated to God Himself than the latter.

DOUBT II

Likewise, is asked concerning this which Master (Peter) says, that *evils come to be apart from* [praeter] *God's Will, but not apart from (His) permission.* For he seems to speak badly, because since a *permission* is a sign of the Divine Will, if (things) are done apart from (His) *Will*, therefore also apart from (His) *permission.*[1] *Likewise*, there is asked, "What is the difference between (something) being done *"apart from"* the (Divine) Will and *"against"* (It)?"; and it seems that (there is) none, because in the twelfth (chapter of the Gospel of St.) Matthew (there is written):[2] *He who is not with Me, is against Me.*

I RESPOND: It must be said, that that (something) is done *"apart from"* (God's) Will, this is, because the Will of God is not in *this being done*, nor in *its opposite*; and thus *apart from* the Will is done that which is not done according to [secundum] nor against [contra] (God's) Will, and between these is a medium. Moreover, the Lord in Matthew understands concerning the precepts, those (things) which he who neglects (them) is made an enemy of God. — What, therefore, *is objected*, that a (Divine) *permission* is a sign of the Will of the Good Pleasure; it must be said, that it is not a sign, that God wills that which *is permitted*, but that He wills that which *is elicited* out of it. And, in this manner, that (objection) is clear.[3]

DOUBT III

Likewise, is asked concerning this which (Master Peter) says: *But not apart from His permission, which He Himself is not.* According to this it seems, that God is not (His) *permission. On the contrary*: God is His own action: therefore, God is His own permission, since a permission is an action of God. *If you say*, that this has been said by reason of what it *connotes*; *then it is objected*, that the Will of God similarly connotes something about the willed.

I RESPOND: It can be said, that Master (Peter) speaks according to the opinion of those, who say, that the names of the six genera do not predicate anything *of* [de] God and/or *in* God, but *by* [in] God. But this opinion has been disproved above.[4] — And for that reason it can be said, that Master (Peter) speaks of a permission by reason of its own connoted, which it conveys according to the reckoning of its name. And if you *object* concerning the Will, that It connotes; it must be said, that (this)[5] is true on account of the adjunct, but it does not thus concern the principal signification of the name.

DOUBT IV

Likewise, is asked concerning this which (Master Peter) says: *Neither for that reason did He precept good (deeds) for this, that He willed that there be done by all the good (deeds), which He precepted.* For he seems to say the false, because a *precept* of God is a sign of the Will of God, just as our precept is a sign of our will; but an upright man never precepts anything to anyone, except what he wills to be done:[6] therefore, much more strongly neither (does) God Himself.

I RESPOND: It must be said, that (St.) Augustine and Master (Peter) following (St.) Augustine, when they speak of the "Will of *the Good Pleasure*", always accept for 'the Will, which God absolutely wills something to come forth'; and concerning this (acceptation), that which he says, is not doubtful. But furthermore the masters (of theology), according to (St. John) Damascene, distinguish the Will as *antecedent*[7] or as much as It is in Itself, and a sign of this (Will) is a *precept*; and (St.) Augustine is not speaking of this, nor (is) Master (Peter).

DOUBT V

Likewise, is asked concerning this which (Master Peter) says, that and *He precepted certain ones ... both in the Old and New Law, (to do) those (things) which He did not will to be done by those whom He precepted.* For he seems to speak badly, because a *precept* is a sign of the Divine Will: therefore, if He precepted what He did not want, it seems, that He deceived those, to whom He precepted (it). *Likewise*, it seems that he says the false, that *He did not will* the immolation of Isaac, because Abraham willed it: therefore, he did not conform[8] his own will to the Divine (Will): therefore, he did not merit, as it seems. *Likewise*, for what reason did Abraham prepare himself to obey, but the one cured in the Gospel (did) not?[9]

I RESPOND: It must be said, that the Lord precepted[10] certain (things) to *be done*, such as the moral precepts, certain ones to *prove*, that is (to) shown that one (is) proven, certain (ones) to *instruct* [ad erudiendum]; and two examples of these are touched upon in the text.[11] In (what was) precepted to Abraham, therefore, there is signified, not that God wants immolation, but that He wants Abraham *to will* (it), and for that reason, when he willed (it), he conformed himself to Himself.[12] In the precept, however, which He gave [facit] to the one cured, He signified, that He wants the contemning of praise [contemptum laudis]; and for that reason Abraham is to be praised in (his) willingness for obedience [in voluntate obedientiae], and the one cured in this, that he did not remain silent.

---

[1] In very many manuscripts and edition 1, there is read in inverse order, viciously: *if (things) are done apart from (His) permission, therefore, also apart from (His) Will.*

[2] Verse 30.   [3] Cf. above qq. 2 and 3.

[4] Distinction 35, Doubt 4, where this opinion is explained more verbosely. — A little below this, in place of *by reason of its own connoted* [ratione sui connotati] codex T with several others, and edition 1 read *by reason of what it connotes* [ratione connotati], and then after *connoted* [connotati] codex Y adjoins *that is, an evil (act)* [scilicet mali].

[5] Codex V reads *that this is true* [quod hoc verum est]. — This doubt is also solved by St. Thomas, (Bl.) Peter of Tarentaise and Richard of Middleton, here on the text.

[6] The codd. with ed. 1 have incongruously *to do* [facere] for *to be done* [fieri]. A little before this, for *upright* [rectus] cod. Y has *just* [iustus].

[7] The Vatican edition reads thus: *but, furthermore, (St.) John Damascene distinguishes the Will into the antecedent (Will)* [sed ulterius Ioannes Damascenus distinguit voluntatem etiam in antecedentem]. The same Vati-

can edition a little before this has *and concerning this* [et de hac] for *and concerning this (acceptation)* [et de hac]. — Cf. above q. 1, and also (Bl.) Peter of Tarentaise and Richard of Middleton, here on the text.

[8] Genesis 22:2 ff.

[9] Mark 1:40 ff., where there is narrated, that the leper, who had been cleansed by the Lord, preached and spread abroad that he had been healed, neglecting the Lord's prohibition.

[10] Not a few codices, together with edition 1, have *precepts* [praecipit].

[11] Chapter 3, namely the example which Abraham offered, and that which the cleansed leper offered. — For *are touched upon* [tanguntur] codices V and W have *are posited* [ponuntur].

[12] For *to Himself* [sibi] the Vatican edition has *to Him* [illi]. — On this doubt, cf. above q. 1; Alexander of Hales, SUMMA., p. I, q. 37, m. 1; Bl. (now St.) Albertus (Magnus), SUMMA., p. I, tr. 20, q. 80, m. 2, a. 1; St. Thomas, (Bl.) Peter of Tarentaise and Richard of Middleton, here on the text, and Durandus (of Saint-Pourçain), here in q. 3.

DISTINCTION XLVIII

CHAPTER I

*That man sometimes, with good will, wills (something)
other than God (wills), and, with bad (will, sometimes wills)
the same which God (wills).*

It must also be known, that sometimes the will of
the man willing the same (thing), which God wills to
be done, is evil; and sometimes the will of the man willing (something) other than (what) God (wills) is good.
For that the will of a man be good, it is necessary to attend to, *what* is congruent for him to will and *for what
end*. For there is so great a difference [tantum interest]
between the Will of God and the will of man, that in
certain (things) it is congruent for God to will one
(thing), for man another. Wherefore, (St.) Augustine in
(his) ENCHIRIDION[1] says: « Sometimes a man wills
something with good will, which God does not will
with good will in a much more ample and much more
certain manner — for His Will can never be evil — such
as [tanquam] if a good son wills that (his) father live,
whom God with good will wills to die. And, again, it
can come to be, that a man with bad will [mala vol-
untate] wills that, which God wills with good (will),
such as [velut] if an evil son wills that (his) father die,
(and) God also wills this. Namely, the former wills
what God does not will, but the latter does will that
which God also wills; and yet the piety of the former
is more consonant with God's good will, even though
(it is) of one willing (something) else, than the impiety
of the latter willing the same (thing). For there is
much difference between [multum interest], what is
congruent for a man to will, what (is congruent) for
God (to will),[2] and to which end anyone refers his own
will, so that it be approved and/or disapproved ». For
one can will a good, which is not congruent for him to
will, and one can will a good, which is congruent, but
not refer (it) to an upright end [ad finem rectum]; and
for that reason it is not a good will.

CHAPTER II

That God's Will is fulfilled through the evil wills of men.[3]

This, too, must not be overlooked, that sometimes
God's Good Will is fulfilled through man's evil will,
such as was done in the Crucifixion of Christ, whom
God with good will willed to die; but the Jews [Iudaei]
with an impious will crucified Him. And certain Jews
with bad will willed, what God willed with good will,
namely, that Christ would suffer and die; but they
also willed something else, which God did not will,
namely to slay the Christ, which was an evil action
and a sin. The *act*, indeed, of the Jews God did not will,

but *the Passion* of Christ He did will, just as Christ says
in the Psalm[4] to the Father: *Thou hast known My sitting*,
« that is, "Thou hast willed and hast approved My Passion »; for it pleased Thee". And so the whole Trinity
willed, that Christ would suffer, and yet did not will,
that the Jews would slay (Him); because (the whole
Trinity) willed Christ's punishment, but did not will the
Jews' fault, nor yet (God) was unwilling; for if (the
Most Holy Trinity) were unwilling, neither would
(Christ's Death) have been.[5]

But to this there is opposed thus: 'If God willed,
that Christ would suffer, He certainly [utique] willed,
that He would and/or would not suffer by the Jews. If
He willed, that He would not suffer by the Jews, since
He did suffer, there was done therefore [itaque], what
God willed not to be done. But, if He did will, that He
suffer by the Jews, therefore, He willed, that He be slain
by the Jews: and so He willed, that the Jews slay Him'.
— Responding to which, we say, that it simply must be
conceded, that God willed, that Christ suffer and die,
because His Passion was a good and the Cause of our
salvation. But, when there is said: "He willed, that He
suffer and/or be slain by the Jews"; this must be distinguished. For, if it is understood thus: "He willed, that
He sustain the passion or crucifixion brought on by the
Jews", the sense is true; if, however, it is understood
thus: "He willed, that the Jews slain Him", it is false.
For God did not will the action of the Jews, which was
evil, but He did will the good Passion; and this Will was
fulfilled through the evil wills of the Jews. Wherefore,
(St.) Augustine in (his) ENCHIRIDION (says):[6] « God certainly [utique] fulfills certain of His own Wills through
the evil wills of wicked men, just as through the malevolent Jews, with the good will of the Father, Christ was
slain on our behalf; which was so great a good, that the
Apostle Peter, when he was unwilling that that be done,
was called [diceretur] a *"satan"* [satanas] by Him who
was slain ». — Behold, you manifestly have, that it was
a great good, that Christ was slain; and because Peter
did not want this good, he was for that reason rebuked.

CHAPTER III

*Whether it pleased holy men, that Christ
would suffer and die?*

From which there is solved the question, by
which there is customarily asked, whether it ought to
have pleased holy men, that Christ would suffer
and/or be slain. For it ought to have been pleasing to
them, having seen our redemption, but not having
seen His[7] torment [intuitu ipius cruciatus]. Therefore,
they willed and vehemently desired, that Christ die
for the sake of man's liberation and the fulfillment

---

[1] Chapter 101, n. 26. — The Vatican edition, together with several editions, omits *says* [inquit].

[2] The Vatican edition, with a few editions, adds *to will* [velle].

[3] In codex E and edition 1 Distinction XLVIII begins here.

[4] Psalm 138:2, and (St.) Augustine, ENARRATIONS on this Psalm,
n. 4. — Even those which precede this have been gathered, according

to sense, from (St.) Augustine, ENCHIRIDION., ch. 101, n. 26.

[5] Codex D reads *neither would He have done it* [nec fecisset],
Codices A and B have *(Christ's Death) would not have been* [non fuisset]
for *neither would (Christ's Death) have been* [nec fuisset].

[6] Chapter 101, n. 26. — At the end there is a reference to Mt. 16:23.

[7] The codices read *His* [eius] for *His* [ipsius].

of the Divine Will; but they did not will (this) with de-light[1] in His affliction [delectatione ipsius afflictionis]. Therefore, concerning the same (thing), they were glad and were sad, but because of one (thing) they rejoiced and on account of the other they grieved. Therefore, they willed, that Christ die for man's redemption, and yet concerning His Death their hearts were moved variously from diverse causes.

CHAPTER IV

Whether we ought to will the sufferings of the Saints.

If, however, there is asked, whether one must think in the same manner concerning the passions and martyrdoms of the Saints; we say, that there is some difference between the passion of the Head and of the members. For indeed Christ's Passion is the Cause of our salvation, wherefore [quod] the passion of any Saint is not. For we have been redeemed by the passion of no one but of Christ. Indeed they do not profit those who have suffered, but their sufferings (do profit) the other faithful; but yet they are not our redemption: for this [hoc] His Passion alone could (obtain), He who is God and man. Therefore, His Passion the pious mind of believers willed and chose to be done, just as they believed (it was) going to be;[2] but the passions of the Saints we can will and not will, and each with a good will,

if we propose upright ends for ourselves. For he, whom (St.) Paul's passion pleased to this end [eo fine], because through doing and preparing for this [per hoc auctum et paratum] he determined [cernebat] his reward, seems to have had good will, which was congruent to his will, by which *he desired to be dissolved and to be with Christ.*[3] But he who willed, that he turn away from suffering and flee from the hands of the iniquitous, according to the compassion of (his) piety, also had good will. Wherefore, (St.) Augustine in (his) ENCHIRIDION (says):[4] « The wills of the pious faithful appeared good, who were unwilling, that the Apostle Paul go off [pergere] to Jerusalem, lest he suffer there the evils, which Agabus, the prophet, had foretold. And yet God willed the former to suffer this for announcing the Faith of Christ, exercising (thereby) Christ's martyr; nor did he himself fulfill his own good will through the good wills of the Christians, but through the evil ones of the Jews; and to him there rather pertained those who did not will what he willed, than those willing, through whom there was done, what he willed, because that very (thing) they did with an evil will, which God willed with a good will ».[5] Thus was it also done in the Passion of Christ. For what God willed, this same (thing did) Judas (Iscariot), the Jew [Iudaeus] and the Devil (also will), but they with an evil will, but God with a good will, namely, that Christ die. But, yet, they willed the act, which God did not will.

HERE ENDS THE FIRST BOOK;[6] HERE BEGINS THE SECOND.

COMMENTARY ON DISTINCTION XLVIII

On the conformity of our will to the Divine Will.

It must also be known, that sometimes the will of the man willing etc..

THE DIVISION OF THE TEXT

This is the third part, in which Master (Peter) deals with the conformity of our will to the Divine Will. And this part is divided into four parts.

In the *first*, Master (Peter) shows, that, for the conformity of our will and the Divine (Will), a conformity in the (act) willed is not sufficient. In the *second*, he shows, that a conformity in operation or in the work worked [in opere operato] does not suffice, there (where he says): *This, too, must not be overlooked* etc.. In the

third, Master (Peter) solves from this a certain question on the side [a latere], whether, namely, the Saints ought to will the Passion of Christ, there (where he says): *From which there is solved the question, by which there is customarily asked* etc. In the *fourth* and last, however, Master (Peter) moves a question according to this and determines (it), there (where he says): *If, however, there is asked, whether one must think in the same manner* etc.; where he shows, that one must judge in a dissimilarly manner concerning the passions of the Saints and (that) of Christ Himself.

---

[1] Codex D reads *the sorrow of* [dolorem], codex C *(this) with love of* [dilectione], codex E *the choice of* [dilectionem] for *(this) with delight in* [dilectatione].

[2] Thus the codices; the Vatican edition, together with the other editions, has *(it, i. e. the deed, was) going to be* [futurum] for *(it, i.e the Passion, was) going to be* [futuram].

[3] Philippians 1:23. — Immediately before this, the Vatican edition and edition 1 have *because* [quia] for *by which* [qua].

[4] Loc. cit.. — A reference to that deed, which is narrated in Acts. 21:10 ff.

[5] Thus the codd. & edd., except the Vatican, which with the original reads thus: *because that very (thing) did they, indeed, do, but He with a*

good (will) through them, but they with an evil will [quia id ipsum quidem, sed ipse per eos bona, illi autem mala voluntate fecerunt]. — Immediately after this the Vatican edition and editions 4, 8 and 9, omitting *Judas (Iscariot)* [Iudas], have *the Jews* [Iudaei], the others omit *the Jew* [Iudaeus].

[6] Thus cod. B; codd. A C & E have: *Here finishes the First Book on the Mystery of the Trinity: Here begins the Second on the Creation and Formation of corporal things and many* [which *many* is lacking in codex A] *other (things) pertaining to these* [Hic finitur primus liber de mysterio Trinitatis: incipit liber secundus de rerum creatione et formatione corporalium et aliis pluribus eis pertinentibus]. In cod. D and in the editions this rubric is exhibited in a slightly different manner.

TREATMENT OF THE QUESTIONS

For an understanding of the present Distinction there is asked concerning the conformity of our will to the Will of God. And about this two (questions) are principally asked.

First, there is asked concerning the conformity, as much as regards (its) quiddity.

Second, there is asked concerning (its) obligation.[1]

About the first Article, two (questions) are asked.

First, there is asked, whether it is possible, that our will be conformed to the Divine Will.

Second, whether the conformity of our will to the Divine (Will) makes our will just.

ARTICLE I

On the conformity of our will, in regard to (its) quiddity.

QUESTION I

Whether it is possible, that our will be conformed to the Divine Will?

Moreover, that it is not possible, that our will be conformed to the Divine (Will), is shown in this manner:

1. According to the fifty-fifth (chapter) of Isaias:[2] *Just as the heavens are exalted above the earth, so are My ways exalted above your ways, and My thoughts above your thoughts.* But just as it is among ways and thoughts, so also among wills: therefore, if sky and earth do not have a conformity, nay a difformity [difformitatem], it seems similarly, that neither (do) our will and the Divine Will (have a conformity). *If you say*, that the quote [auctoritas] is understood and speaks concerning the wicked; *on the contrary*: on that (verse) of the Psalm:[3] *Exalt you just*, the Gloss (says): « As much as God is distant form man, so much is the Will of God distant from the will of man »: ergo etc..

2. Likewise, of (things) infinitely distant there is no conformity;[4] but God and man are distant unto an infinite (degree), since one is finite and the other infinite: therefore, there is no conformity of wills (among them).

3. Likewise, if our will is conformed to the Divine (Will), therefore, either *according to its very self* [se ipsa], or in a *third* (something). If in a *third*: therefore, the Divine Will and the human convene in something com-

mon; and if this, therefore, they have something more simple than themselves;[5] which is unfitting, most of all in regard to [in] the Divine Will. It remains, therefore, that if it is conform, that it is conformed *according to its very self*: therefore, the will itself is the conformity. But a conformity cannot be difform: therefore, our will cannot be discordant from the Divine (Will), which (thesis) is manifestly false.

4. Likewise, if our will is conform to the Divine (Will), either in this it convenes *essentially*, or *through participation*. If *essentially*, the same (result) returns as before;[6] if *through participation*, I ask concerning that, through whose participation the will is conform, whether it be conform. If *not*, it cannot conform; if *so*, then either *essentially*, or *participatively*: therefore either there will be an *infinite regression* [abire in infinitum], and/or a standing still in some *created* (being), which is conform to God through *essence*, and/or the will is conformed to God through (something) *uncreated*. But there is no *infinite regression*, nor is it posited, that *God* is the conformity of the human will to God: therefore, something *created* is *essentially* conform. But what is

---

[1] That is, (one's) obligation (to be conformed in will to the Divine Will).

[2] Verse 9. — A little below this, for *difformity* [difformitatem] the Vatican edition, together with very many manuscripts, has incongruously *deformity* [deformitatem]; ed. 1 omits *nay a difformity* [immo difformitatem].

[3] Psalm 32:1. — The gloss cited is taken from (St.) Augustine, ENARRATIONS ON THE PSALMS, on the said Psalm, n. 2.

[4] The reason (for this) is, because a conformity is according to some convening and approximation. Cf. Aristotle, PHYSICS, Bk. VII, text 24 ff. (ch. 4). In regard to the minor proposition on must refer to that (saying) of Aristotle, ON HEAVEN AND THE WORLD, texts 52 and 64 (chs. 6 and 7): Of (things) finite to the infinite there is no proportion.

[5] Namely that common (being), in which they convene. Cf. Aristotle, POSTERIOR ANALYTICS, Bk. I, ch. 20 (ch. 24), where it is taught that a universal is more simple than particulars. — A little after this, for *difform* [difformis] the Vatican ed. with cod. cc, has *a difformity* [difformitas].

[6] That is, that our will cannot be discordant from the Divine Will; which is manifestly false, as was said in the preceding argument. — A little below this, after *whether it be conform* [utrum si conforme] the Vatican edition adds *and/or not* [vel non]. Then for *or participatively* [aut participative] codex T, together with very many other codices, has *or by participation* [aut participatione]. In the last proposition of the argument, the Vatican edition and codex cc, after the second *convenes* [convenit] repeats *with it* [cum illo].

essentially conform to something, convenes essentially with it, and what convenes essentially, is of the same essence: ergo etc..

ON THE CONTRARY: 1. According to the sixth (chapter) of the First (Letter of St. Paul) to the Corinthians:[1] *He who cleaves to God is one spirit* (with Him); but he is not one spirit through a unity of *nature*: therefore, he is not one through a conformity of *will*.

2. Likewise, in the twelfth (chapter of the Gospel of St.) Matthew (there is written):[2] *Everyone who does the will of My Father, who is in Heaven, he is My brother and sister* etc; but it is not true, that he is (His) brother through nearness of blood [per propinquitatem sanguinis]: therefore, he is a brother through a conformity of will and love [dilectionis].

3. Likewise, it happens that whatsoever wills will *the same* (thing) and will *opposites*, it happens that (these) *are conformed* and *difformed* [difformari] or made contrary [contrariari], but the Divine Will and the human (will) are of this kind: this is clear,[3] ergo etc..

4. Likewise, it happens that whichsoever wills are ordered to one another through a perfect mutual self-protection [perfectam praesidentiam] and obedience, it happens that (these) are conformed to one another; but it happens that the human will is subjected to and obeys the Divine (will) through all (things):[4] ergo etc..

CONCLUSION

A human will can be conformed to the Divine Will through a similar habitude to the act, to the object and to the end.

I RESPOND: It must be said, that '*that something be conformed to anything*' happens in a twofold manner: either as much as regards a *similitude*, or as much as regards a *habitude*.

As much as regards *similitude*, it happens in a threefold manner: either when any two participate in a *third*, in which they are assimilated, such as a swan and snow (are assimilated) in[5] whiteness; or when any two so hold themselves, that one *is* the similitude *of the other*, such as a species or a likeness [idolum] of color is assimilated or conformed to the color; or when anything *participates* in a similitude, such as a mirror [speculum] and/or eye is assimilated and/or conformed to a body, placed in its way [obiecto].

In the first manner, it is not possible, that any creature be conformed to God. In the second manner, some creature

is conformed to God, as for example grace, which is said (to be) God's similitude, and/or glory, which is deiformity [deiformitas]. In the third manner there is assimilated and conformed the soul, which has grace and glory. On this conformity nothing (will be said) for the present.

In another manner it happens that something is conformed to something according to a *completely similar habitude* [consimilem habitudinem] or comparison, which can be said (to be) a "*proportion*", when it is of things of the same genus, and a "*proportionality*", when it is of (things) of diverse genera or of (things) not communicating, to make a distinction in the word [ut fiat vis in verbo].[6] Yet broadly speaking each can be said (to be) a "*proportion*"; and this posits nothing common, because it is through a comparison of *two (things) to two (things)*, and it can be and is between (things) most highly distant.

And according to this our will can be conformed to the Divine (Will), namely through a similar habitude *to an act*, such as, just as God wills what He wills, liberally and charitably [caritative], so also a man; and through a similar[7] comparison *to an object*, such as that which God wills, the man wills; and *for the same end*, for which God wills (it), the man wills (it). This whole is possible to be, and the whole is possible not to be; and for that reason it is possible, that our will be conformed to and difformed from the Divine (Will). — And the reasons for this are to be conceded.

1. 2. To that, therefore, which is objected, that God is distant from man, and the human will from the Divine (Will) unto an infinite (degree); the response is already clear, because this does not impede a conformity of *comparison*, even though it does impede [licet impediat] a conformity of *equality* and *univocation*.

3. To that which is objected, whether (the human will) is conformed according to its very self and/or in a third; it must be said, that (it is) not (conformed) according to its very self,[8] unless we speak of a *distant* [longinqua] conformity, which is attained in the *image*. But if we speak of a *proximate* [propinqua] conformity, which consists in a *similitude*, thus it is not conformed according to its very self, but by means of grace, which is not as a third (something) participating in each [ab utroque participatum], but (which) is as *the similitude of one* and *the property of the other*. Wherefore grace is a similitude essentially; however, it is not necessary [non oportet], that they convene[9] essentially *in a third*, because the similitude convenes by its very self with That of which it is the similitude; and in this both [ambo] objections are clear.

---

[1] Verse 17. The Vulgate reads: *But he who cleaves to the Lord is one spirit* [Qui autem adhaeret Domino unus spiritus est].

[2] Verse 50. The Vulgate reads: *For whosoever has done the Will of My Father, who is in Heaven, He is My brother and sister* [Quicumque enim fecerit voluntatem Patris mei, qui est in caelis, ille meus frater et soror].

[3] Cf. (St.) Augustine, ENARRATIONS, 2, on Psalm 31, n. 26.

[4] Cf. (St.) Augustine, ENARRATIONS, on Psalm 44:7, n. 17; and ON A LITERAL EXPOSITION OF GENESIS, Bk. VIII, ch. 23, n. 44.

[5] With the Vatican edition we retain the *in* [in], even if this particle is wanting in very many codices. Codex X, which also omits *in* [in], and exhibits (*participate in*) *whiteness* [albedinem] for (*are assimilated*) *in whiteness* [in albedine], which reading Marra follows in his unpublished Commentary. The example cited in the second member of the distinction: *such as a species or likeness of a color is assimilated or conformed to the color* [ut species coloris sive idolum assimilatur colori sive conformatur], is exhibited mutilated in divers manners in the codd.. Several codd. read thus: *such as a species of color or is conformed* [ut species coloris sive conformatur]; cod. Y, besides having omitted *or is conformed* [sive conformatur], reads thus: *such as a species of color* [ut species coloris]; codex R has: *such as a species of color is conformed to itself* [ut species coloris sibi conformatur]; cod. F read more clearly: *such as a species of color is conformed to the color itself* [ut species coloris ipsi colori conformatur]; finally, ed. 1 and the Vatican ed. have: *such as a species of color or an idol are assimilated or*

conformed to Jove [ut species coloris sive idolum assimilatur sive conformatur Iovi]. Our reading is supported by the authority of codices H K M T V and editions 2 and 3. For the meaning of <u>idolum</u>, see above d. 37, p. II, a. 2, q. 3, p. 663, footnote 5. In the third member of the disjunction after *in a similitude* [similitudinem] codices F H P and Q adjoin *of another* [alterius].

[6] (St. Severinus) Boethius, ON ARITHMETIC, Bk. II, ch. 10: *Proportionality* is the similar habitude of two and/or more proportions, even if they have not been constituted by the same quantities and differences. But *the difference* among the numbers is a quantity. A *proportion* is a certain habitude of two terms regarding one another and in a certain manner quasi containing (both). — For *proportionality* [proportionalitas] the Vatican ed. with a few codd. has *proportionability* [proportionabilitas].

[7] Very many codices, such as H M P and Q, together with edition 1, have *completely similar* [consimilem], which word codices P and Q also employ a little above this before the word *habitude* [habitudinem] in place of *similar* [similem].

[8] The Vatican edition with codex cc, here and a little before this, has *in its very self* [in se ipsa] for *according to its very self* [se ipsa].

[9] Very many codices, together with the Vatican edition and edition 1, have *it convenes* [conveniat], faultily. A little further above this, for *but (which) is as* [sed est sicut] very many codices, together with editions 2 and 3, have *but (which) also (is) as* [sed etiam sicut].

Similarly, if we speak of a conformity as much as regards a *habitude*, we will say, that the (human) will is not conformed according to its very self, but through a *comparison to the other*, which, however, neither concerns the Essence of the Divine Will, nor of the human, nor (is) as a third (something) participating in each. And thus that (objection) is clear.

4. To that which is asked last, whether (a human will) is conformed through essence, or through participation; it must be said, that neither in the former manner, nor in the second manner, but it is conformed through a proportion or through a completely similar habitude. And, in this manner, that (objection) is clear.

SCHOLIUM

I. Above (in d. 31, p. II, a. 2, q. 2), a threefold conformity was distinguished: in *nature*, in *will*, (and) in *operation* or in the acts of the will. The Question (here) concerns conformity in *the free acts* (of the will) or in willing and not willing, and indeed not according to the *natural* entity (of the will), but (rather) *the moral* (entity of the same). — One must attend to the multiple distinctions posited in the body of the Question. The two members of the first and principal division (the conformity according to *similitude* and *habitude*) are in need of no explanation. The three members of the first subdivision are founded in the threefold similitude, which can be either in one form of the same species (v. g. in whiteness), and/or in (its) *imitation* and representation (as in a statue), and/or in a reckoning of *exemplarity*. This third member differs from the second, because in the second the statue *itself* is conform to the original, but in the third member, according to the example employed, neither the eye nor a mirror *is* something conform, but rather *contains* through participation the exemplar. — The second subdivision coincides with the common distinction of analogy in the analogy of *attribution* (or of proportion) and (the analogy) of *proportionality*.

On the analogy of *attribution* see above d. 45, q. 5, where *health* is distinguished in a threefold manner; the analogy of *proportionality* is dealt with above in d. 1, a. 3. q. 1, in reply to n. 1, and in the Scholium, and in d. 7, q. 4, in the Scholium. — Moreover, St. Bonaventure teaches, that a conformity of will is attained only according to a *habitude* et through a comparison to the other. Yet to the extent that the will is informed *by grace*, there is also a conformity according to *similitude*, as is taught in the solution to n. 3. — A conformity of habitude according to *act* and according to *end* is popularly called a conformity in *the manner of willing*; moreover, a conformity according to *object* is said (to be) a conformity in *the (thing) willed*.

II. Alexander of Hales, SUMMA., p. I, q. 41, m. 1. — St. Thomas., here in q. 1, a. 1; SUMMA. , I, II, q. 19, a. 9 and 10. — Bl. (now St.) Albertus (Magnus), here in a. 1; on this and the following questions, SUMMA., p. I, tr. 20, q. 80, m. 3. — (Bl.) Peter of Tarentaise, here in q. 1, a. 1. — Richard of Middleton, here in a. 1, q. 1. — Giles the Roman, here in 1st princ., q. 1. — Durandus (of Saint-Pourçain), on this and the following question, here in q. 1. — (Bl.) Dionysius the Carthusian, on this and the following questions, here in q. 1. — Biel, on this and the following questions, here in the q. sole.

QUESTION II

Whether the conformity of our will to the Divine (Will) makes it just?

Second, there is asked, whether the conformity of our will to the Divine (Will) makes it just. And it seems, that (it is) so:

1. Because on that (verse) of the Psalm:[1] *Complete praise befits the upright*, the Gloss (says): « The upright are those who direct their heart according to the Will of God, which is upright ».

2. Likewise, in the sixth (chapter of St. Paul's) Second (Letter) to the Corinthians (there is written):[2] *What participation of justice (is there) with iniquity? or what society of the light (is there) for darkness?* as if to say: "none". If, therefore, the Divine Will be Justice and Light, if a human will be iniquitous, it cannot be conform (with It): therefore, if it is conform, it is necessary that it be just.

3. Likewise, 'to be *conformed* to a rule of justice' is nothing other than 'to be *justified*'; but the Divine Will is the Rule of Justice, because It cannot be turned aside [obliquari] to anything iniquitous: therefore, 'to be conformed to the Divine Will' is 'to be justified'.[3]

4. Likewise, our *intellect* cannot be conformed to the Divine (Intellect), if it is not made true: therefore, neither can our *affection* [affectus] be conformed to the Divine (Affection), if its is not made just; for just as truth is the rectitude of the intellect, so justice is the rectitude of the affection.[4]

ON THE CONTRARY: 1. Master (Peter) says,[5] and it is a saying [verbum] of (St.) Augustine, that « the good Will of God is fulfilled through the evil wills of men »; but the one effect does not proceed from the one cause through another, unless those causes are conformed to one another: therefore, it happens that a evil will is conformed to the Divine (Will).

---

[1] Psalm 32:1. — The Gloss, which is cited next, has been taken from (St.) Augustine, ENARRATIONS ON THE PSALMS. 2, on the said Psalm, n. 2.

[2] Verse 14. The Vulgate reads: *For what participation* etc. [Quae enim participatio iustitiae cum iniquitate? aut quae societas luci ad tenebras?]. — A little after this, for *if a human will* [si humana] for *and a human will* [et humana].

[3] On this argument, cf. (St.) Augustine, ENARRATIONS, on Ps. 93:15, under n. 18 f.

[4] Cf. (St.) Anselm, DIALOGUE ON THE TRUTH, ch. 12, where justice is defined as « the rectitude of the will observed [servata] for its own sake »; and DI-

ALOGUE ON FREE WILL, ch. 8, where the holy Doctor says: « but no will is just, except that which wills what Gods that it wills »; and also in (his) book, ON THE CONCORDANCE OF GOD'S FOREKNOWLEDGE WITH FREE WILL, q. 1, ch. 6, where there is read: But since it is established that the justice, by which anyone is just, is the rectitude of the will, which I spoke about; which rectitude is then only in someone, when he himself wills what God wills that he wills.

[5] Here in ch. 2, where you will also find the entire verse of (St.) Augustine, cited next.

2. Likewise, a conformity of wills consists in willing and not willing the same (thing); but a impious (man) can will and not will what God wills and does not will, as (St.) Augustine[1] posits the example of the depraved son, who wills that (his) father die, which God also wills: therefore, conformity does not make the will just.

3. Likewise, although the Will of God is blessed, yet a will conform to That is not on this account blessed: therefore, for an equal reason, though It be just, not on account of this is a will conform (to It) just.

4. Likewise, if a conformity makes the will just, when (God)[2] wills to vindicate a man, who suffers injury, if the latter who suffers injury, wills to vindicate himself, he wills (this) justly: therefore, it is just to exact vengeance [exigere vindicatam]. *If you say*, that God wills to vindicate a man, but does not will, that a man vindicate himself; this does not solve (the matter), because it would then at least be licit for a man to desire [appetere], that God vindicate him.

CONCLUSION

The conformity of our will to the Divine (Will) both according to act and according to willed makes it just; however, a conformity alone in the willed (does) not.

I RESPOND: It must be said, that the conformity of our will to the Divine (Will) is attained according to a *proportion*, just as has been said.[3] There is, however, a twofold proportion of the will, namely, regarding the *act* and regarding the *willed*. A similar proportion regarding the *act* consists in this,

that, just as God wills, what He wills, out of charity and liberally or *justly* and *for a right end*, so also does the man will (this). A similar proportion regarding the *object*[4] is, that what God wills, a man also wills.

A conformity, therefore, can be attained according to *this twofold* similitude[5] and comparison; and in this manner it is sufficient and makes the will just. Again, it can be attained solely according to *the second*, as for example the willed; and in this manner it is deficient, since it lacks a similar habitude, and this does not suffice for justice.

Concerning the first conformity, the first reasons proceed, concerning the second, (those) second.

3. To that, however, which is objected third, that a conformity does not make the soul blessed, therefore neither just; it must be said, that "*beatitude*" means a consummated justice. Wherefore more is required for this, that a will be made blessed, than that it be made just; and for that reason it does not follow, that if it does not make (it) blessed, that it does not make it just. Yet, just as the *sufficient* conformity, which is in the willed and according to the reckoning of willing [ratione volendi], makes the will just, so the *superexcellent* conformity makes it just. But the former is superexcellent, when in all (things) it is conformed to the Divine (Will) and (when) in no part is it difform, nor in anything, even in the least [saltem in modico].[6]

4. To that which is objected last, the response is already clear; because the one desiring vengeance does not conform himself to God in *the manner of* or in the reason for *willing* [in ratione volendi]. For God, as a just judge, wills this from the zeal for justice; but he who desires avenging punishment [ultionem] for himself or for his injury, wills (this), as most (do), from a lust for vengeance [libidine vindictae]. But if some one desires (this) solely from the zeal for justice, just as God (does), and out of charity, then I would say, that he has a just will.

SCHOLIUM

I. For a greater elucidation (of the aforesaid) there can serve the words of Alexander of Hales (SUMMA., p. I, q. 41, m. 2): « A conformation can be attained according to four genera of causes, that is, in willing *what* God wills, in willing *as* He wills, in willing what *we know* Him to will, in willing *for what* He wills (it). The first is a *material* conformity, the second a *formal* one, the third is in the reckoning of an *efficient cause*, the fourth in the reckoning of an *end*. It must be said, therefore, that if these four concur, there is a *perfect* conformity or conformation. But a *sufficient* conformity is attained in the two, that is, that a man will *just as*

God wills, and *on account of which* He wills. But (there is) an *imperfect* conformation, when a man wills what He wills, and/or what he knows that God wills ». — St. Thomas employs the same distinction according to the four genera of causes, here in q. 1, a. 2.

II. Alexander of Hales, SUMMA., p. I, q. 41, m. 2. — (Bl. John Duns) Scotus, in each version (of his Commentary), here in the q. sole. — St. Thomas, SUMMA., I, II, q. 19, a. 9. — Bl. (now St.) Albertus (Magnus), here in a. 2. — (Bl.) Peter of Tarentaise, here in q. 2, a. 2, quaestiunc. 3. — Richard of Middleton, here in a. 1, q. 2. — Giles the Roman, here in 1st princ., q. 2.

---

[1] ENCHIRIDION., ch. 101, n. 26. See the text of Master (Peter) here in ch. 1. — On the major proposition, cf. Aristotle, ETHICS, Bk. IX, ch. 6, where he deals with the concord of friends; and also Cicero, ON FRIENDSHIP, ch. 6, concerning which, see below, a. 2, q. 2, argument 3.

[2] Supply together with codex T (by a second hand) *God* [Deus].

[3] In the preceding Question.

[4] For *the object* [obiectum] the Vatican ed. has *the willed* [volitum]; cod. R adjoins to *the object* [obiectum] *and the willed* [et volitum].

[5] Very many codices, such as H K V X (M and T in the margin) and edition 1 have *habitude* [habitudinem].

[6] Cf. (St.) Augustine, ON THE BLESSED LIFE, nn. 17-36, and ON THE TRINITY, Bk. XIII, ch. 5-9.

ARTICLE II

On the conformity of our will, as much as regards (its) obligation.

Consequently, as much as regards the second Article, there is the question concerning the obligation of [quaeritur de tentione ad] conformity to the Divine Will. And, about this, two (questions) are asked.

First, there is asked, whether we are bound to conform our will to the Divine Will in *the reason for willing*, [in ratione volendi], so that what we will, we will out of charity.

Second, whether we are bound to conform (our will) in *the (thing) willed* [in volito].

QUESTION I

Whether we are bound to conform our will to the Divine Will in the reason for willing?

Moreover, it seems, that we are bound in *the reason for willing*:

1. Because we are bound, to do, what we do, justly. Wherefore in the sixteenth (chapter) of Deuteronomy (there is written):[1] *Justly execute what is just*; but naught is done justly, except that which a man does according to a conformity of will as much as regards the reason for willing, so that he wills out of charity (what he wills): ergo etc.

2. Likewise, were are bound to love [diligere] God with our whole heart [ex toto corde], because this is precepted in the sixth (chapter) of Deuteronomy,[2] and the Lord repeats the same in the twenty-second (chapter of the Gospel of St.) Matthew; but this cannot be done except out of charity: therefore, we are bound to a conformity in the reason (for willing) or in the form of willing.

3. Likewise, we are bound to obey God truthfully; but one does not obey God truthfully, except (him) who does (this) by that will, which God accepts. But this is the will informed by charity: ergo etc.

4. Likewise, « (that) on account of which each one (is), that (is) even more »;[3] but on account of the conformity of will in the reason for willing we are obliged [obligamur] to a conformity in the *willed*, because *the end of the precept is charity*, as the Apostle says in the first (chapter of his) First (Letter) to Timothy:[4] therefore, much more strongly are we obliged to conformity in *the reason for willing*, to will, what we will, out of charity.

ON THE CONTRARY: 1. God wills and precepts that parents be honored;[5] let it be that the opportunity offers itself, and (that) someone honor (his) father out of natural piety, not out of charity, it is established that he does not sin; and he does not conform his own will except in *the willed*: therefore, he is not bound to *the reason for willing*.

2. Likewise, if we are bound to conform our will to the Divine (Will) in *the reason for willing*, just as in *the willed*, therefore, as often as we will something not out of charity, there is a lack of that [deficit illud] to which we are bound: therefore, we sin in every (such)[6] act: therefore, no act is indifferent.

3. Likewise, if we are bound to conform (our will) in *the reason for willing*, therefore, since a man [vir], as a sinner, has a will continually failing from God in this, because he does not have charity: therefore, he continually in every instant sins.

4. Likewise, no one can conform his own will to the Divine (Will) in *the reason for willing*, unless he has charity; but it is not in our power to have charity:[7] therefore, a man is bound to the impossible. *If you say*, that he can do (this), (and) with that done [quo facto] he will have charity, because he can dispose himself to charity; *it is objected* concerning the obstinate, and concerning him who actually is in sin: so long as he sins and is in that act, he cannot conform himself: therefore, he is not bound. Wherefore if he is not bound, and the others are bound, he obtains [reportat] an advantage [commodum] from (his) wickedness; wherefore if this is not fitting, therefore, none are bound.

CONCLUSION

Our will is bound to be conformed to the Divine Will in the reckoning of willing and indeed, to the extent that it is a negative precept, always and at all times, but to the extent that it is affirmative, not at all times, but according to time and place.

I RESPOND: It must be said, that we are bound to conform our will to the Divine Will in *the reason*

---

[1] Verse 20, where the Vulgate has *pursue* [persequeris] for *execute* [exsequeris].

[2] Verse 5: *Thou shalt love the Lord thy God with thy whole heart, and with thy whole soul, and with thy whole strength* [Diliges Dominum Deum tuum ex toto corde tuo, et ex tota anima tua, et ex tota fortitudine tua]. The other passage, which is cited from (the Gospel of St.) Matthew, is ibid., 22:37.

[3] Aristotle, POSTERIOR ANALYTICS, Bk. I, ch. 1.

[4] Verse 5.

[5] Deut. 5:16. — Next, for *and (that) someone* [et aliquis] the Vatican edition, together with codex cc, has *that someone* [quod aliquis].

[6] The Vatican edition after *in every* [in omni] interjects, not incongruously, *such* [tali]; codex O after *act* [actu] adjoins *and/or we merit* [vel meremur].

[7] For charity itself is not from us, but from God through the Holy Spirit, who pours it fourth in our hearts (Rom. 5:5). Cf. (St.) Augustine, ON GRACE AND FREE WILL, ch. 18, n. 37 ff.. — A little below this, after *he can do* [potest facere] the Vatican edition, without the authority of the codices and edition 1, adjoins *what is in him* [quod in se est] for *(this)*.

for willing, so that if we will something, we will (it) out of charity;[1] and this is clear, because we are bound to love Him out of charity.

Moreover, one must attend, that this is an obligation through the manner of an *affirmative precept*. For the obligation of an *affirmative* and a *negative* precept differ; for a *negative (precept)*[2] obliges always and at all times [ad semper]; but an *affirmative one* obliges only *always*, but not *at all times*, but according to place and time [pro loco et tempore]; and just as it does not oblige *at all times*, so neither regarding *every act* of the will, nor regarding *every precept*, but then solely, when we are bound to go forth unto an act of charity.

Wherefore it must be noted, that we are thus bound to this, that (we are) *never* (bound) to the contrary: as to will, what God wills, out of lust or passion [ex libidine].[3] We are also bound to this according to *place and time*, if we have charity; but if we do not have (charity), we are not bound to this, but to the equivalent, because we are bound to do what it is in us, to have; and similarly[4] we are bound to this according to place and time. From these (considerations) the response to the objections are clear.

1. 2. 3. For what is objected, that someone honors, without sin, (his) parents even out of natural piety; it must be said, that it is true; and from this it follows, that he is not bound in *every act* to conform (his will to the Divine Will in the reason for willing);[5] but it does not follow, that he is not bound. And through this the following is clear, which objects concerning *the generality of acts*. There is also clear the other, which objects concerning *the generality of time*.

4. To that which is objected last, that it is not in our power to have charity; it must be said, that it is in the[6] power of those having charity, and it is in the non-proximate, but *dispositive*, power of those not having (charity). For anyone can do (this), (and) with that done he has charity; and for that reason, if he does not do (it), it is imputed to him, nor is he excused through impossibility, because there is no impossibility, where power from another comes to one's aid [succurrit], and does not fail, except on account of our negligence.[7]

To that which is objected concerning *the obstinate* (man), it must be said, that no one is so [adeo] obstinate, that he cannot do what is in him, and that he cannot return to (his) heart;[8] and for that reason he is bound just as the others (are), though not in every instant [pro quilibet instanti], but according to *place and time*.

But if you *ask*, what is the *(proper) place and time*; the anointing (of the Holy Spirit)[9] will teach (you) better than the art (of theology); yet, when the Lord visits him with an interior allocution and/or in exterior preaching and/or in any such manner, in which there is an opportunity of returning to (one's) heart; if he then neglects (to do this), he falls into contempt and the sin of omission.

SCHOLIUM

I. That all are bound *always* and *at all times* [pro semper] to conform themselves to the Divine Will, speaking of a conformity in *habit*, is entirely established. But this Question concerns a conformation *in act*. — That a *negative* precept obliges always and at all times [ad semper], is taught most commonly, together with Alexander of Hales (SUMMA., p. I, q. 41, m. 3). But there remains the question in regard to an *affirmative* precept, in which question there is implied the celebrated controversy regarding which and how often is the obligation to elicit an act of charity. The Jansenists, and not a few patrons, among catholic (theologians), of (their) more rigid ethics, used to urge exceedingly the said obligation. On this, cf. St. Bonaventure, SENT., Bk. III, d. 27. a. 2. qq. 5 and 6.

II. St. Thomas, here in q. 1, a. 2; SUMMA. , I, II, q. 19, a. 10. — Bl. (now St.) Albertus (Magnus), here in a. 2 and 6. — (Bl.) Peter of Tarentaise, here in q. 1, a. 2; q. 2, a. 1. — Richard of Middleton, here in a. 2, q. 2. — Giles the Roman, here in 2nd princ., q. 1. — Durandus (of Saint-Pourçain), on this and the following question, here in q. 2.

---

[1] For *so that, if we will something, we will (it) out of charity* [ut si velimus aliquid, velimus ex caritate] very many codices, together with edition 1, and the Vatican edition, have *so that, namely, we will it out of charity* [ut scilicet velimus ex caritate], which reading we have corrected from codices R T Z and aa, supported in part also by codices A and S, which also, for the *namely* [scilicet], which is read in the Vatican edition, exhibit *if* [si], even if they then omit after the first *we will* [velimus], the *something, we will* [aliquid, velimus].

[2] The Vatican edition reads *(the obligation) of a negative (precept)* [negativi] for *a negative (precept)* [negativum], and then by reason of the same construction, *(the obligation) of an affirmative one* [affirmativi] for *an affirmative one* [affirmativum].

[3] The sense is: we are thus bound to this, namely, that if we will something, we will (it) out of charity, that it is never licit for us to will something by a contrary act of the will, that is, in an evil or libidinous manner. — For *out of lust or passion* [ex libidine] the Vatican edition has *out of liberality* [liberalitate], codex V and edition 1 have *out of charity* [ex caritate]. Codex K to the words *out of lust or passion* [ex libidine] prefaces the word *not* [non], codex Z the words *not to will* [non velle]. A little before this for *as to will* [sicut velle] codex O has *namely to will* [scilicet velle].*

[4] For *similarly* [similiter] edition has *simply* [simpliciter].

[5] Understand: his will to the Divine (Will) in the reason for willing. The Vatican edition alone here adjoins *proximate* [propinqua], and a little below this in place of *For anyone can do (this)* [Potest enim quilibet facere] it has *For he can (do) something* [Potest enim aliquid].

[6] Cf. above d. 40, a. 4, q. 2, p. 720, footnote 5. Cf. also (St.) Anselm, ON THE DOWNFALL OF THE DEVIL, ch. 3 ff., DIALOGUE ON FREE WILL, ch. 3, ff., and ON THE CONCORD OF GOD'S FOREKNOWLEDGE WITH FREE WILL, q. 3.

[7] A reference to Isaias 46:8: *Return, o prevaricators, to (your) heart* [Redite praevaricatores ad cor].° — A little before this, for *that he cannot do* [qui non posit facere] the Vatican edition has *that he cannot do* [quod non potest facere].

[8] 1 John 2:20: *But you have the anointing from the Holy One and you know all (things).* [Sed vos unctionem habetis a Sancto et nostis omnia] And ibid., v. 27: *And let the anointing, which you have received from Him, remain in you. And (it is) not necessary that you have anyone to teach you; but just as His anointing teaches you concerning all, and (this saying) is true, and it is not a lie. And just as He has told you, remain in Him* [Et vos unctionem quam acceptistis ab eo, maneat in vobis. Et non necese habetis, ut aliquis doceat vos; sed sicut unctio eius docet vos de omnibus, et verum est, et non est mendacium. Et sicut docuit vos, manete in eo.]

---

* *Trans. notes*: Here I have rendered ex libidine as *out of lust or passion* so as to encompass the two distinct meanings of the Latin, which two are necessary to understand the disparate possible objects of such an evil act.

° That is, examine your conscience, and recover charity by a perfect act of contrition, which was the only means in the Old Testament to regain charity, and which means is possible to all men by grace, when confession is not possible and God's Mercy for the individual has not been exhausted by abuse and presumption.

QUESTION II

Whether we are bound to conform our will to the Divine Will in the willed?

Second, there is asked, whether we are bound to conform òur will to the Divine Will in the *willed* [in volito]. And that (it is) so, seems:

1. According to the twelfth (chapter of the Gospel of St.) Matthew:[1] *He who is not with Me, is against Me*: therefore, if one is not consonant with God in the willed, one is against God: therefore, if we are bound not to be contrary to God, we are bound to will what God wills.

2. Likewise, on that (verse) of the Psalm:[2] *There did not cleave to me a depraved heart*, the Gloss (says): « A depraved and distorted heart has he who does not will that which God wills »; but we are bound to avoid depravity of heart: therefore, we are bound to will what God wills.

3. Likewise, (Marcus) Tullius (Cicero),[3] defining friendship [amicitiam], says, that "friendship" is 'to will the same' and 'to not-will the same' in honest things; but we are bound to keep friendship with God: therefore, also to will the same in honest (things). But God does not will but (what is) just and honest: therefore, we ought to conform our will to His in all (things).

4. Likewise, every *understanding*, which discords from the First Truth or in cognition,[4] is false: therefore, every *affection* is iniquitous, which does not concord with the Divine Will in the willed: ergo etc.

5. Likewise, we are bound to will what God precepts, therefore, either because *He precepts* (it), or because *He wills* (it). Not because *He precepts* (it), because those who had been cleansed, to whom there was given the precept by the Lord concerning keeping silent,[5] did not sin in revealing (the miracle), because they cognized by divine inspiration, that God did not want that which He precepted: therefore, we are bound to a precept, because we are bound to *the (Divine) Will*: therefore, we are bound to will what God wills.

6. Likewise, we are bound to believe not only what God precepts (us) to believe, but even that everything He says is true: therefore, a simili,* we are bound to will not only what God precepts (us) to will, but[6] everything which God indicates that He wills as (something) good: therefore, we are bound to will everything which we know God wills.

ON THE CONTRARY: 1. (St.) Augustine (says) in (his) ENCHIRIDION:[7] Sometimes a man wills with good will what God does not will.

2. Likewise, holy men [viri santi] frequently will opposite (things), just as the Apostle willed to be bound unto Jerusalem, and (his) disciples did not will (it), according to the twenty-first (chapter) of Acts;[8] but it is established, that God willed something of them: therefore, it is licit to will (something) contrary to the Divine Will, meritoriously: ergo etc..

3. Likewise, if we are bound to conform (our will) in the (thing) willed; therefore, since in (things) indifferent there is not for us a determined Divine Will, whosoever wills something indifferent determinately, commits himself to a distinction [discrimini] (from the Divine Will): therefore, he sins mortally, which is absurd. *If you say*, that he is bound, when he knows God's Will; *on the contrary*: knowledge [scientia] does not induce a new sin nor an obligation [tentionem], but only aggravates the sin: therefore, on account of knowledge no one is bound, just as neither (is one who is) ignorant.

4. Likewise, Jeremias grieved over the destruction of Jerusalem, in Lamentations [in Threnis]; Christ wept over Jerusalem, according to the nineteenth (chapter of the Gospel of St.) Luke;[9] the Blessed Virgin and the Apostles (wept) over the Passion of Christ. If they wept and grieved, and grief [dolor] concerns those things, which befall us unwilling: therefore, they did not want (these things). And it is established, that all these merited, and knew, that God willed the contrary: therefore, licitly and meritoriously we can will (something) contrary to the Divine Will, even where It is known.

5. Likewise, howsoever much my superior wills

---

[1] Verse 30. — Next for *therefore if one is not* [ergo si non] edition 1 has *therefore, he who is not* [ergo qui non].

[2] Psalm 100:3-4. — The Gloss in (Nicolas) of Lyra reads: *A heart depraved and distorted* [Cor pravum etc.] for *A depraved and distorted heart* [Pravum cor etc.]. Which (heart) is had by he who does not will all which God wills.

[3] In his book, ON FRIENDSHIP, ch. 6 says thus: « Moreover, friendship is nothing other but a most high consensus [consensio] of all divine and human things with benevolence and charity »; then in the following (sentences), having expounded the ends and laws of true friendship, the first of which is this: « that we seek honest (things) from (our) friends, (and) that we do honest (things) for the sake of (our) friends, so that, when the morals of (our) friends have been emended, there may be among them such a great community of all things, of counsels, (and) of wills without any exception ». Thus Tullius Cicero, with whose exposition of friendship the definition proposed here as the former's certainly convenes, if one regards its sense. But in regard to its words, it seems to be more congruent with that of (Gaius) Sallustius Crispus (86-36 B.C.), who in the book, whose title is, BELLUM CATILINIAE, ch. 20, defines "friendship" thus: "For to will and not will the same, this, at last, is first friendship." — A little further below this, the Vatican edition, breaking with the codices and even with edition 1, after *therefore, also to will the same* [ergo et idem velle] repeats *therefore, to will the same* [ergo idem velle].

[4] The Vatican edition reads *in the cognized* [in cognito] for *in cognition* [cognitione], codex cc has *in cognition in the cognized* [cognitione in cognito]. On this argument cf. above a. 1, q. 2, page 853, footnote 4.

[5] Mark 1:44. — The Vatican edition, together with codex cc, has thrice in this argument *precepted* [praecepit] for *precepts* [praecipit], and near the end of the argument it omits *to a precept, because we are bound to the (Divine) Will: therefore, we are bound* [ad praeceptum, quia tenemur ad voluntatem: ergo tenemur].

[6] Codex H subjoins *also* [etiam]; then the Vatican edition, together with codex cc, omits *God* [Deus].

[7] Chapter 101, n. 26.° See here the text of Master (Peter), ch. 1.

[8] Verses 12-14. — Next, for *willed* [volebat] very many codices, such as A G H S T V ee and ff have *did not will* [nolebat].

[9] Verse 41. — The definition for <u>dolor</u>, which is next proposed, is hinted at by (St.) Augustine, ON THE CITY OF GOD, Bk. XIV, ch. 15, n. 2, with these words: « But a pain of the flesh [dolor carnis] is only an offense to the soul on account of the flesh and a certain dissent from its suffering; just as the grief of the soul [animae dolor], which is named "sadness" [tristitia], is a dissent from those things, which befall us unwilling ». It is also hinted at by Nemesius, the Bishop of Emesa (in Syria, and sometime Governor of Cappadocia), in his book, ON THE NATURE OF MAN, ch. 17 in these words: « For cupidity, while it follows after what one wills, causes pleasure; on the contrary, while it does not follow after (it), (it causes) grief ». Codices T V and Z, having omitted the particle *If* [Si] after *Christ* [Christi], join the words *they wept and grieved* [flebant and dolebat] with the preceding. At the end of the argument for *to the Divine Will* [divinae voluntati] codices A T Z and cc and edition 1 read *to the Divine Will* [divinae voluntatis].

---

* *Trans. notes*: See translator's footnote above, on p. 180.

° This quotation from St. Augustine is a conflation of what Mas-
ter Peter quotes in his Distinction, chapter 1, from the first and third sentences cited therein, from the Saint.

something, I am not bound to will it, unless he precepts me, even if I know that he wills (it): therefore, for an equal reason, howsoever much God wills something, I am not bound to will it, howsoever much it is made known to me, unless God precepts me.

6. Likewise, what God counsels,[1] He wills, and we know that He wills (it), yet we are not bound to will (it), even though it pleases Him much, even more than a precept (does): therefore, we are not bound to will everything which we know God wills.

CONCLUSION

Our will is not bound to be conformed to the Divine Will in whatsoever willed, but only in every that which makes known to us that God wills (it) by (His) absolute Will, and/or in that in which there substantially consists the order of salvation.

I RESPOND: To this some say, that *we are* not *bound* to conform our will to the Divine Will in everything which God wills — but this belongs to *perfection* and to supererogation, and this will be in (our heavenly) Fatherland — but we are only bound to that, which He wills us to will. Moreover, they say, that God wills us to will only what *He precepts*, and does not will what *He prohibits*. For these (precepts) are *the signs*, though which He sufficiently indicates to us His will, by which[2] He wills us to will something. In other willeds, whether they are made known (to us) or not, it is licit to will the contrary without sin. And through this they solve (the Question) for each side. Wherefore they say, that it is licit for us to will somethings properly, because it is not decent to will (their) opposites, such as concerns[3] the destruction of our nation [gentis nostrae], and the calamities of the just, and (things) completely similar. Even if God lets rain (such things) and/or disposes (that such) rain, I can seek and will the opposite. — But though that way is easier, yet because (St.) Augustine[4] says, that he is impious, to whom the Divine Providence is not pleasing, it not only seems, that a man is bound to will God's commands, but even, that we are bound to will God's works. *And again*, in what manner is our will not recalcitrant to the Divine Will, when God wills something, and we entirely will the contrary? It seems entirely repugnant to Him. *And again*, the aforesaid gloss seems to say, that a man, who does not will what God wills, has a depraved heart; it does not say, that

God wills that he will, and/or that God precepts (him).

On account of this it must be said in another manner, that truly [revera] we are not bound to will everything which God wills, but only what *He wills* and *makes known*, nor even *every that* (which He wills). — For this reason it must be noted, that God shows that He wills something *absolutely* and as much as is *in Him*, such as the good (works), which He does. And these we are bound to will simply and by an absolute will, as much as is in us.

He shows that He wills something by an *absolute* will, but that He wills *the opposite*, as much as is in Him, such as the evils, which He inflicts. And these we are bound to will by an absolute and deliberative will; yet the opposite we can will by a will of *pity* [voluntate pietatis], as Hugo (of St. Victor) says.[5] Wherefore, just as God is not delighted in our punishments, but says rather: *Alas, alas, I am consoled over my enemies*, according to the first (chapter) of Isaias;[6] so also (are) we. Wherefore Hugo distinguishes in us a threefold will, namely, (that) of *reason*, of *pity* and of *the flesh*, and in Christ a fourfold one, extending the name for a will. Whence he says in the book, ON THE WILLS OF CHRIST, speaking of Christ: « The will of the Deity through justice dictated the sentence; the will of reason through obedience approved the truth; the will of pity through compassion sighed in the evil (of another);[7] the will of the flesh through suffering murmured in His own evil ». And for that reason by a will of *reason* we ought to will even the evil of punishment, which we know that God wills; but by the will of *pity* we can (do this) conditionally, or as much as is in us, if it is pleasing to God,[8] that we not will (it). For even God Himself, as much as is in Him, does not will (it), as has been said before.

God shows that He wills something, as much as is in Him, about which there *substantially* consists the *order* of salvation, such as are those (acts) which He precepts to be done, and precepts not to be done; and these we are bound to will.[9]

God shows that He wills something, as much as is in Him, about which there consists the *expediting* of (our) salvation, such as those (deeds) which He counsels. And to such He does not oblige (all men) nor wills to oblige (them): for He wills that some be saved in this manner, (and) that others go by a broader way.

From these (considerations), therefore, it is clear, that we are bound generally to will to conform our will (to the Divine Will),[10] not in every willed, but in every that which makes (It) known (to us) in the three, aforesaid

---

[1] The Vatican ed. reads *has counseled* [consulit] for *counsels* [consulit].

[2] Very many codices have *because* [quia], and not a few, such as V and X, have *when* [quando], for *by which* [qua].

[3] For *concerns* [est de] the Vatican edition, together with codex cc, has *is clear concerning* [patet de].

[4] ENARRATIONS, 2, on Ps. 31:11, under n. 25, and, ON ORDER, Bk. I, ch. 1, n. 1. — A little before this, for *I can* [possum] cod. A has *we can* [possumus].

[5] In his book, ON THE FOUR WILLS IN CHRIST: On that account the will of pity is called "the will of the humanity", because it belongs to a man to be moved by pity... But in this life, where we can neither know nor foreknow the sentence of the same Divine Justice, we can will even certain (things), which are not just according to It, without injustice, because this alone pertains to us, that were we do not know, what may rather please God, we may most ably choose that, which is concordant with pity.

[6] Verse 24. — On the difference of a will in us and in Christ, next cited from Hugo, this is read a the beginning of the book by the same

author, ON THE FOUR WILLS IN CHRIST: Moreover, the human will is considered in a threefold manner: according to reason, according to pity, (and) according to the flesh. therefore in Christ there was a will of the Divinity and a will of reason and a will of pity and a will of the flesh. The will of the Divinity dictated through justice ... the will of pity longed through compassion in the evil *of another* etc..*

[7] Supply: *of another* [alieno], as is read in the original text.

[8] Codex T has *it would be pleasing* [placeret] for *it is pleasing* [placet].

[9] Codices V and X, a little before this, after *precepts not to be done* [praecipit non fieri] add *and/or prohibits that one wills it* [praecipit non fieri vel prohibet illud nolle]. The Vatican edition before the same repeats *which* [quae].

[10] Supply together with codex K *to the Divine Will* [voluntati divinae]. A little before this, codices T and X omit *to will* [velle]; the Vatican edition after *to will* [velle] inserts *and* [et], and a little below this after *three* [tribus] adds *first* [primis].

---

* Trans. note: Here Hugo speaks, here, of the diverse motives or signs of the Divine and human will in Christ, not of the two wills, the Divine and human, according to nature, and thus <u>voluntas</u> is rendered *will* not *Will* in the first instance, in each passage, that is in reference to the Divine Will.

manners, otherwise (our) friendship (with Him) would be broken; and concerning such a willed run the reasons and authorities. For we are bound in a (Divine) precept to conform[1] ourselves for this reason, that He wills, that we will what He precepts; and (when) we know this. And I am bound to be conformed to my superior, in that, which I know that he expressly wills me to will; but in a superior I know naught but (what he makes known) through a command [mandatum], but in God I know through other signs, as has been said before.[2]

4. To that, therefore, which is objected, that an understanding, which is not false, can discord in nothing etc.; it must be said, that it is not similar concerning *the good* and *the true*. For the "*true*" is said *absolutely*, but the "*good*" in *relation to an end*. And because two opposites are not together,[3] for that reason true understandings cannot be discordant. But the "good" is said in *relation to an end*. And since willed opposites can be ordained to the same end, for that reason they can be good together, and the affections in respect of these (can) be upright. For that reason it is not necessary that (our will) be conformed (with the Divine Will) in every willed, because we can, in a holy manner, will the opposite, because (we can do so) in a manner ordained unto (our) End;[4] but the opposite of that, which *God wills* that we will, we cannot ordain unto (our) End, because God does not accept that.

To that which is objected in the Contrary, that we are not bound to every willed; it must be said, that it is true, because (we are bound) neither to a willed, because (it is) a *willed*, nor because (it is) a *known*, but because (it has) *been known* to have been *willed* by God,[5] so that *we* will it. — Yet, it can be said in another manner, that we are bound, because (it is) *absolutely* willed, but *we are excused* through ignorance, most of all where due diligence [debita diligentia] is employed, such as (when) someone is obliged, not to know (a woman) not his own. Wherefore concerning an obligation inducing a fault, that which it says is false, that *knowledge* does not induce a new obligation. For, just as *ignorance* of the deed [ignorantia facti] excuses entirely [a toto], so *knowledge*, concerning [per] (a deed) opposed with the Divine Will,[6] causes someone to be obliged, so that in no manner is he able unto the contrary, without fault. And thus (it is) in the proposed; and thus is that (objection) clear.

4. To that which is objected concerning Christ and the Blessed Virgin and others suffering with (Them) [aliis compatientibus], it must be said, just as has been said, that by an absolute will they willed what God willed; yet, by a conditioned will or by a will of pity they ought to have willed the contrary; and by this will they merited, since this[7] does not belong to *nature* only, but also *to reason*.

SCHOLIUM

I. Besides the two sentences posited in the Response, Alexander of Hales (SUMMA., p. I, q. 41, m. 5) mentions another in these words: « Some said, that there is a *rational* will and/or appetite and (one) of the *sensuality*; therefore, by the will of *reason* we are bound to will, what we know God wills, not by the will of the sensuality. Therefore, the Blessed Virgin and the Apostles willed the Passion of Christ by the will of *reason*, not (by that) of *the sensuality*, but they did grieve from the latter [de ea] ». Richard of Middleton reports the same opinion (here in a. 2, q. 1), in these words, that « by a deliberative will we are bound to will absolutely, and all things considered [omnibus pensatis], whatever we know God wills by (His) absolute Will, all things considered, yet so long as it is congruent for us to will it ». Yet this sentence is not approved by Richard; and whatever of the truth that sentence has is explained by St. Bonaventure here in the

reply to the last objection, and chiefly in Doubt 4.

On the same passages the Seraphic (Doctor) speaks in a most pious manner of the will of the Blessed Virgin Mary in the Passion of the Lord Jesus Christ; he, together with the common sentence, asserts, that She merited by suffering with (Him). This saying is contrary to (William) of Auxerre, who at least in regard to the Apostles explicitly denied this, according to his words, cited by (Bl.) Dionysius the Carthusian, because, that is, « that will of the sensuality was neither meritorious ».

II. Alexander of Hales, SUMMA., p. I, q. 41, m. 4, 5, and 6. — St. Thomas, here in q. 1, a. 4; SUMMA. , I, II, q. 19, a. 10. — Bl. (now St.) Albertus (Magnus), here in a. 2, 6, and 7. — (Bl.) Peter of Tarentaise, here in q. 2, a. 2, and q. 3, a. 1. — Richard of Middleton, here in a. 2, q. 1. — Giles the Roman, here in 2nd princ., q. 2.

---

[1] In the codices and edition 1 there is lacking *ourselves* [nos], which certainly, together with the Vatican edition, is to be supplied, or one must substitute *to be conformed* [conformari] for *to conform* [conformare]. Perhaps in the original text there was read *to be conformed* [conformari] for *to conform ourselves* [nos conformare], which by the carelessness of the copyists had been transmuted from the passive for the verb into the active, namely *to conform* [conformare] . Immediately before this the Vatican edition, to the word *precept* [praecepto], adjoins *Divine* [divino].

[2] Here in the body of the Question, and above in d. 45, a. 3, qq. 1 and 2.

[3] Cf. Aristotle, ON INTERPRETATION, Bk. II, ch. 4 (ch. 14), and PHYSICS, Bk. IV, text 125 (ch. 13). — On that which *the good* means in relation to the end, cf. above d. 43, a. sole, q. 2, p. 769, footnote 1.

[4] The Vatican edition, together with one or another codex, has *because (we can) order (it) unto (our) End* [quia ordinare in finem] for *because (we can do so) in a manner ordained unto (our) End* [quia ordinate in finem]. Next, for *ordain* [ordinare] not a few codices have *(will) in a manner ordained* [ordinate].

[5] And/or in other words: but because we know, that something has been willed by God. — For *(it has) been known to have been willed* [scitum esse volitum] cod. T has *the known has been willed* [scitum est volitum].

[6] The Vatican ed. with cod. cc, reads *so knowledge, through an opposite manner, when the Divine Will causes* etc. [ita scientia per oppositum, cum divina voluntas facit etc.] for *so knowledge, concerning (a deed) opposed with the Divine Will, causes* etc. [ita scientia per oppositum cum divine voluntati facit etc.]. Next, for *And thus (it is) in the proposed* [Et sic in proposito] cod. V with ed. 1 has *And thus it is in the proposed* [Et sic est in proposito].

[7] The Vatican edition has *it* [hoc] for *this (will)* [haec], which edition also then, with edd. 2, 3, 4, 5 & 6, after *to reason* [rationis] adds this proposition: *Moreover chiefly with this will did the Most Blessed Mother and Virgin, Mary, merit in the Passion of Christ (Her) Son, with Whom when suffering, as much as the fragility of the womanly sex was able to endure, She suffered* [Praecipue autem hac voluntate merebatur in Christi filii passione beatissima Mater et virgo Maria, cui patienti, quantum sexus mulierbris fragilitas sustinere poterat, compatiebatur], to which words it then annexes those which are had below near the end of the last Doubt: *Yet in no manner is it to be doubted* etc. [Nullo tamen modo est dubitandum].

DOUBTS ON THE TEXT OF THE MASTER

DOUBT I

In this part, there are the doubts about (Master Peter's) text and first concerning that which (St.) Augustine says: *For there is much difference between, what is congruent for God to will, what (is congruent) for a man (to will).* Therefore, from this it seems, that a man can licitly will something knowing, that[1] God wills the contrary. Therefore, let it be posited per impossibile, that to someone his own damnation is revealed; it is established, that God wills that this one be damned by (His) absolute Will. Therefore, either this one *is bound to will* (this), or (he is) *not*; and/or — whatever concerns (his) being bound (to this) — what is *more perfect* to will, whether *to will* to be damned, and/or (to) *not* (will to be damned)? If *he wills* to be damned: therefore, he wills to be separated from God; this[2] an upright will can never desire [appetere]. If *he does not will* to be damned: therefore, he does not perfectly conform himself: therefore, the opposite will is more perfect.

I RESPOND: It must be said, that it is impossible, that to anyone there be revealed his own damnation; and with the impossible posited, it is not to be wondered, if the impossible follows.[3] — Yet, if you ask, what is more perfect?, I respond, that in eternal damnation there are two (things), namely *the infliction of punishment* and an eternal *separation* from God. The eternal *separation* from God, I believe in no manner that any soul ought rightly to will, nay (he ought) always to will the contrary; but *the punishment*, if it has been revealed to him, he ought to will. And this is clear, because any just (man) ought to will concerning himself and concerning another, that everyone sinning unto the end [finaliter] be eternally punished: therefore, if there is posited a preexisting[4] cognition concerning himself, in a certitudinal manner, I believe, that as long as a good will perdures in him [durat ei], that he will will this.

But, if you ask concerning him, who sins, whether he ought to will that grace be subtracted from himself; because[5] it seems that (it is) so, since God wills (this), and he knows that it is just; it must be said to this, that 'that grace be subtracted from anyone' can be regarded under a threefold condition, either *simply*, or *for a time* [ad tempus]. And, for a time, (it can be regarded) in a yet twofold manner: either *in itself*, and/or insofar as it has the reckoning of a *punishment*. In this (third) manner,[6] God wills to subtract (grace), and in this manner the one sinning ought to will, that God punishes him. — Wherefore, there is a general rule, that in all (the things), which we know God wills *absolutely*, we are bound to will (the same) by an absolute will; yet it is licit for us to will the contrary by a conditioned will, or as much as is in us, because this befits [decet] us; and on this account (St.) Augustine[7] says: *For there is much difference* etc..

DOUBT II

Likewise, is asked concerning this which Master (Peter) says, that *the action of the Jews was evil.* For it seems that he says the false, because the action of the Jews was the cause of (His) Passion; but if the immediate cause (was) evil, the effect (is) also: therefore, if (their) action was evil, the Passion (of Christ is) also.

I RESPOND: It must be said, that this is true of an action and passion in the *same* genus of goodness, according to which one is the cause of the other. It must be said, therefore, that the action of the Jews was the cause of (Christ's) Passion in the genus of *(its) nature*, and in that genus, just as (their) action was evil, so also (His) passion; but (their action) was not the cause in the same genus of *morals* [moris], nay Christ's good intention (was),[8] which directed (His) voluntary passion unto a good end; (it was) contrariwise in the action of the Jews, not having an upright

---

[1] For *that* [quod] the Vatican edition has *of which* [cuius]. A little before this for *Therefore, from this* [Ergo ex hoc] edition 1 has *But from this* [Ex hoc autem].

[2] Codex Z has *but this* [sed hoc].

[3] Aristotle, ON HEAVEN AND THE WORLD, Bk. I, text 119 (ch. 12): Moreover, the impossible accedes out of the impossible. — At the beginning of this solution after the words *I respond: It must be said* [Respondeo: Dicendum] codex Z inserts these: *that there is a twofold will: by approving, and in this manner one is bound to will his own damnation, but by desiring (one is bound) not at all, because God has infixed this appetite in the soul, namely, (that) for beatitude, thus that no one can desire the contrary, because in this manner one would desire God more than oneself; and this cannot (be done) apart from grace, which makes one desire always the good. But this is impossible, because to will to be separated from God (is) also (to will) that one appreciate nothing; wherefore it must be said* [quod duplex est voluntas: approbando, et sic tenetur velle suam damnationem, appetendo autem nequaquam, quia Deus infixit istum appetitum in anima, scilicet beatitudinis, ita quod nullus potest appetere contrarium, quia sic diligeret Deum plus quam se; et hoc non potest absque gratia, quae facit semper appetere bonum. Hoc autem est impossibile, quia velle separari a Deo et ipsum nihil appretiare; unde dicendum].

[4] Very many codices, together with edition 1, have faultily *pre-requiring* [praeexigens]. Next for *about himself* [circa se] the Vatican edition, together with codex cc, has *about himself* [iuxta se].

[5] For *because it* [quia] the Vatican edition has *it also* [et], which edition also a little below this, after *that it is just* [hoc esse iustum], having placed a period, begins a new sentence proceeding thus: *I respond: It must be said* [Respondeo: Dicendum]. — Very many codices, together with edition 1, have incongruously *and it must be said to this* [et dicendum ad hoc].

[6] For *In this (third) manner* [Hoc modo] codex Z has more clearly *In (this) third manner* [Tertio modo]; codex T (in the margin) repeats the preceding words thus: *Insofar as it has the reckoning of a punishment, in this manner* [Prout habet rationem poenae, hoc modo] for *In this (third) manner* [Hoc modo].*

[7] ENCHIRIDION, ch. 101, n. 26. See here the text of Master (Peter), ch. 1, at the end. — This doubt is also solved by Alexander of Hales, SUMMA., p. I, q. 41, m. 5, in reply to n. 5; by Bl. (now St.) Albertus (Magnus), here in a. 5, in reply to the last objection; by St. Thomas, here in a. 4, in reply to n. 2; by (Bl.) Peter of Tarentaise, here in q. 3, a. 2; (and) by Richard of Middleton, here in a. 2, q. 1, in reply to n. 1.

[8] Understand: *was* [fuit]. — Next, we have restored *which* [quae], which word the Vatican edition had suppressed, by not supplying *was* [fuit]. For *which* [quae] codex O has *because it* [quia]. A little further below this, for *(it was) contrariwise in the action* [econtra in actione] nearly all the codices, together with edition 1 have *(it was) contrariwise with the action* [econtra actione], faultily.

---

* *Trans. note*: The third manner is *the subtraction of grace for a time, as a punishment.*

end: and for that reason in the genus of morals (their) *action* was evil and displeasing to God, and (His) *Passion* (was) good and pleasing to God. And in this manner the whole (doubt) is clear.[1]

DOUBT III

Likewise, is asked concerning this which (Master Peter) says, that *(God) willed that Christ suffer and die* etc.. For he seems to speak badly, because *to slay Christ* was *to do evil*: therefore, *that Christ be slain*, was *that evil be done*: if, therefore, God willed that Christ suffer, God willed that evil be done; which has been denied above.[2]

I **RESPOND**: It must be said, that *to slay Christ* was evil through the comparison to (its) Subject. When, therefore, "*passion*" is accepted, either it is accepted[3] *simply* in comparison to *the One suffering* [ad patientem] or to *the One enduring the punishment* [ad sustinentem], and thus it is simply good; or in comparison to *the one bringing (it) upon* [ad inferentem], and thus in that respect it is judged evil, because wickedness of morals respects the intention rather [potius] than the act. And in the first manner the sense is: "It is good that *Christ suffer* by the Jews", that is, "It is good, that Christ endure the punishment, which the Jews brought upon (Him)". In the second manner the sense is: "It is good, *that Christ suffer* by the Jews", that is, "It is good that the Passion of Christ be brought on by the Jews"; and in this manner it is false, because *the bringing on* of the Passion was naught but evil, but *(His) suffering* [sufferentia] was naught but good; and in this manner Master (Peter) distinguishes (it).[4]

DOUBT IV

Likewise, is asked concerning this which (St. Augustine) says: *This was so great a good, that the Apostle Peter, who was unwilling that it be done, was called a "satan" by Him who was slain*. According to this, it seems, that whosoever grieves and is saddened about the Passion of Christ, is to be rebuked [redarguendus]: therefore, the Most Blessed Virgin sinned, when She grieved, just as is said in the second (chapter of the Gospel of St.) Luke:[5] *Thy very own soul a sword shall pierce*. Similarly, the Apostles sinned. The Apostle in the second (chapter of his) Second (Letter) to Timothy also speaks a falsehood:[6] *If we suffer with (Him), we shall also reign with (Him)*.

I **RESPOND**: It must be said, that '*to grieve over someone*'[dolere de aliquo] is in a twofold manner: either thus that the one grieving wills by an *absolute* will of *reason* the contrary of that, over which he grieves; and in this manner it was licit to no one to grieve over the Passion of Christ, and, (St.) Peter, because he willed the contrary by a will of reason, was rebuked.[7] In another manner '*to grieve over someone*' is 'to be born to the contrary by a will of *pity*, yet, nevertheless, to will *this*[8] by an *absolute* will'; in this manner it is good to grieve with Christ and to be affected piously about Him, and in this manner holy men [viri sancti] are affected, who give great thanks to God for the Passion of Christ; but yet are moved piously in the consideration of (His) sorrows [dolorum]. Thus also the most pious soul of the Blessed Virgin, as much as She could endure (it), suffered together with Her most beloved Son, as He suffered [patienti].[9] Yet in no manner is it to be doubted, that Her virile spirit and most constant reason also willed that (Her) Only-Begotten be handed over[10] for the salvation of the human race, since as a Mother She was conform with the Father through all (things). And in this wonderful manner there ought to be praised and loved, what was pleasing to Her, that Her own Only-Begotten was offered for the salvation of the human race. And so much even did She suffer with (Him), that, if it could happen, all the torments which (Her) Son bore throughout (His Passion), She Herself would endure[11] much more willingly [multo libentius]. Therefore, She was truly strong and pious, equally sweet and severe, sparing [parca] with Herself, but most generous [largissima] to us. Therefore, She is to be chiefly loved and venerated after the Most High Trinity and Her Most Blessed Offspring, Our Lord Jesus Christ, from the telling [enarrando] of Whose Mystery of Divinity all other tongues fail, because *He is the consummation of sermons*.[12] *To Him, therefore, who can do all (things) superabundantly, (more) than we ask or understand, according to the virtue, which is at work in us, to Him (be) the glory, in the Church and in Christ Jesus unto all the generations of the Age of ages. Amen.*

HERE ENDS THE FIRST BOOK

---

[1] The Vatican edition and editions 2, 3, 4, 5 and 6, put this Doubt in the third position. — Cf. on this doubt, St. Thomas, (Bl.) Peter of Tarentaise, Richard of Middleton and Giles the Roman, here in the text.

[2] In Distinction 46, q. 2.

[3] After *is accepted simply* [simpliciter accipitur] the Vatican edition and codex cc subjoin *or* [aut]; but faultily, since, just as appears from the subjoined, in this proposition not three, but only two members are distinguished.

[4] This doubt is also solved by (Bl.) Peter of Tarentaise and Richard of Middleton, here on the text.

[5] Verse 35. — A little before this, for *is to be rebuked* [est redarguendus] the Vatican edition has *would have to be rebuked* [esset redarguendus], and then it has *Mother* [mater] for *Virgin* [Virgo].

[6] Verse 12. — In this text, the Vulgate and the Vatican edition have *we will endure* [sustinebimus] for *we suffer with (Him)* [compatimur].

[7] Mt 16:23: *Who having turned said to Peter: Get behind Me, satan, it is a scandal for Me; because you know not the things which are of God, but the things which (are) of men* [Qui conversus dixit Petro: Vade post me, satana, scandalum est mihi; quia non sapis ea quae Dei sunt, sed ea quae hominum]. — At the beginning of this proposition, for *is in a twofold manner* [est dupliciter] not a few codices, such as H and I have *is said in a twofold manner* [dicitur dupliciter].

[8] Understand: that Christ suffer.

[9] The Vatican edition, together with codex cc, having omitted the word *piously* [pie] above, exhibits the final part of the proposition in this manner, with the support of edd. 2, 3, 4, 5 & 6: *just as even the most benign Virgin Mary was moved in the Passion of Her Son* [sicut et benignissima Virgo Maria in Filii sui mota est passione]. The (words) which follow have been transferred by the Vatican edition to the end of q. 2, a. 2 above, as we have already mentioned above on p. 859, in footnote 7.

[10] The Vatican edition reads *willed also to hand over Her Son* [vel-let etiam tradere filium suum].

[11] The Vatican ed. has *would have endured* [sustinuisset], and a little before this *had been able to happen* [potuisset] for *could happen* [posset].

[12] Ecclesiasticus 43:29: *But the consummation of sermons is He in all* [Consummatio autem sermonum ipse est in omnibus]. — The following words *To Him, therefore, who can* etc. [Ei igitur, qui potest etc.] are from To Him, therefore, who can [Ei igitur quo potest] there is read in the Vatican edition *But to Him, who is able* [Ei autem, qui potens est]; for *superabundantly, (more)* [superabundantius] the Vatican edition has *more superabundantly,* [superabundantly]. — On this doubt, cf. above a. 2, q. 2; Alexander of Hales, SUMMA., p. I, q. 41, m. 5, in reply to n. 1; Bl. (now St.) Albertus (Magnus), here in a. 5, St. Thomas, (Bl.) Peter of Tarentaise and Giles the Roman, here on the text; (and) Richard of Middleton, here in a. 3. q. 1.

INDEX OF QUESTIONS

FOR ST. BONAVENTURE'S COMMENTARIES

ON THE FIRST BOOK OF SENTENCES

OF MASTER PETER LOMBARD

THE FIRST BOOK OF SENTENCES

ON THE ONE AND TRIUNE GOD

Glory to the Father, and to the Son, and to the Holy Spirit,

as it was in the beginning, is now, and will be forever,

and unto the Ages of ages. Amen !